REPRESENTATIVE AMERICAN PLAYS

From 1767 to the Present Day

EDITED WITH INTRODUCTIONS AND NOTES

BY

ARTHUR HOBSON QUINN

Author of *A History of the American Drama; American Fiction; Edgar Allan Poe.*

SEVENTH EDITION, REVISED AND ENLARGED

New York

APPLETON-CENTURY-CROFTS, INC.

636-22

Library of Congress Card Number: 53-5089

PRINTED IN THE UNITED STATES OF AMERICA
E 72453

TO

H. McK. Q.

But for whose eyes and whose heart
this book had never existed.

PREFACE TO THE FIFTH EDITION

The preparation of a new edition has led to several notable additions and substitutions of plays. Foremost among these is the publication for the first time in any form of *Margaret Fleming,* by James A. Herne. The only manuscript of this play, one of the landmarks in the development of American realism, was destroyed by fire in 1909, but it has been recreated from memory by Mrs. Herne, who acted Margaret Fleming and who has generously permitted the editor to have the honor of being the first to make the drama available to students of our stage. In order to keep the volume truly representative, two contemporary plays of distinction, *The Silver Cord,* by Mr. Sidney Howard, and *Paris Bound,* by Mr. Philip Barry, have been added. Another important change has been the substitution of *The Girl with the Green Eyes,* one of the best plays of Clyde Fitch, for *Her Great Match,* which is of less significance. When the first edition was issued, in 1917, the publishers of the Memorial Edition of Clyde Fitch would not permit the reprinting of any play included in that collection. This prohibition has now been removed, with certain limitations, so that it is possible to represent Fitch at the height of his achievement. These additions have made it necessary to omit, with regret, *The Triumph at Plattsburg,* by Richard Penn Smith, and *Leonora,* by Julia Ward Howe, which, while of historical importance, have proved to be least practicable for detailed study.

When this book was published in 1917, it was the first attempt to include in one collection a series of plays which illustrated the development of our native drama from its beginning to the present day. No other branch of our native literature has been so inaccessible. The work of the elder playwrights is still preserved largely in rare editions or in manuscript, and even that of the newer generation has frequently remained unpublished through considerations of a nature which fortunately obtain less and less, as the real significance of our drama is becoming better appreciated. Fortunately, conditions are improving radically, so that today practically every play of importance is published as soon as it is produced. Several collections of plays, in addition, have followed the publication of this one, so that the body of American drama available for study is becoming rapidly more adequate.

In selecting the plays for this anthology, the first consideration, obviously, was that they should have been written by native Americans. The only exception to this principle of selection has been made in the case of Dion Boucicault, who is so significant a force in our dramatic history that his inclusion seemed necessary. At the outset also, it was determined that no play should be selected which had not had actual stage representation by a professional company. The closet drama is interesting in its place, but its significance is slight compared to that of the acted play. This consideration, for example, determined the exclusion of the satiric plays of the Revolution, as there is no certain evidence that they were performed even by amateurs. Preference has been given to the plays dealing with native themes, twenty-one of the twenty-eight plays being laid in this country, while in one of the others American characters appear. Care has been taken also to include, so far as possible, the principal types of play into which our drama has run, so that if the book is used in connection with a course of lectures upon the American Drama, the material will be at hand to illustrate its development. The comparison of the plays with a background of war—*André, Shenandoah, Secret Service,* and *Sun-Up*—or of the social comedies—*The Contrast, Fashion, The Girl with the Green Eyes, The New York Idea,* and *Paris Bound*—will be found most interesting, while a contrast between *The Prince of Parthia* and *Francesca da Rimini* will illustrate the growth in the field of romantic tragedy where our earlier drama scored so many triumphs. No play, however, has been chosen simply for its interest as a type; all have had to justify themselves on the score of their intrinsic excellence, and the difficulty has been to choose among the wealth of material.

Before each play, a brief introduction explains its significance and gives a biographical sketch of the author, together with necessary information concerning his plays. No pains have been spared to make these introductions accurate, and the editor has fortunately had at his disposal not only the usual histories of the theatre, but also manuscript sources such as the Bird and Boker Papers and the Diary of William Wood, the Manager of the Chestnut Street Theatre in Philadelphia, as well as the printed sources that are included in the Clothier Collection of American Plays in the Library of the University of Pennsylvania. In the cases of the modern plays, the information has been checked in nearly every case by the playwrights themselves. In each of the introductions a selected bibliography has been given. It has seemed unnecessary to cumber these with long lists of magazine articles of a fugitive character, but it is hoped that the references given will be found helpful. A general bibliography of books relating to the American Drama has been placed at the end of the volume. Here again, the publication of the new edition has made it possible to bring up to date the references to the work of living playwrights, either by added notes or, where necessary, by a complete rewriting of the introductions. Revivals of the older plays, which are becoming more frequent, have also been noted.

In each introduction the source of the text is given. Where it was possible to obtain acting versions of the older texts, the differences between these and the reading versions have been indicated. In general, where emendations have been made, they have been included in square brackets. The spelling has followed that of the original text, and the stage directions have been reprinted in the older plays as originally given. Several of the modern plays have been revised by the authors and their wishes have naturally been followed both as to text and stage directions. Some slight alterations have been made even here for the sake of uniformity; and where the preparation of the text has fallen upon the editor alone, he has tried to present the stage directions in a readable form, according to modern standards of technique.

Many friends have helped in the preparation of this volume. Of primary importance was the establishment, through the generosity of Mr. Morris L. Clothier, of the Library of American Plays which bears his name. The continued interest of its donor in the collection, and the establishment of the fund by the editor's classmates for the purchase of books in this field, have been of a degree of service that is difficult to measure. Special acknowledgments are made in the separate introductions to those who have aided in the cases of individual plays. Valuable suggestions concerning the sources of the older plays were made by my colleagues, Professor J. P. W. Crawford and Professor Arthur C. Howland, and here, too, should be acknowledged the generous help in collation of texts and preparation of bibliography rendered in the original publication by Dr. John L. Haney, Dr. A. C. Baugh, Dr. F. A. Laurie, Dr. Clement Foust, and, in this last revision, by my daughter. The greatest help of all, however, came from her to whom this book is dedicated and for whose service there can be no adequate acknowledgment.

Note to Sixth Edition.

In order to keep this volume truly "representative" of the best American playwriting, the editor has added *Winterset*, by Maxwell Anderson, whose permanent significance in the history of American drama is now secure.

The volume has been completely revised, all introductions dealing with active playwrights have been brought up to date, and revivals and publication of earlier plays have been noted. The Bibliography has also been revised and the most important works in the field of American drama since 1930 have been added.

Note to Seventh Edition.

In making additions, the choice of *Command Decision*, by W. W. Haines, the best of the plays dealing with the Second World War was obvious. The introduction of the words to *South Pacific*, by Oscar Hammerstein, II and Joshua Logan, is a recognition of a new form of musical play in which the book and lyrics are literature.

The same revisions have been made as in the preparation of the Sixth Edition.

The Bibliographies have been revised so as to include works published since 1938. Dr. Edgar L. Potts has been good enough to read the proof of this edition.

A. H. Q.

University of Pennsylvania, 1953

CONTENTS

THE PRINCE OF PARTHIA

A TRAGEDY

BY

Thomas Godfrey

THE PRINCE OF PARTHIA

The Prince of Parthia is the first play written by an American to be performed in America by a professional company of actors. It was written by Thomas Godfrey, born December 4, 1736, in Philadelphia, the son of Thomas Godfrey, the inventor of the sea-quadrant. According to his biographer he was educated at "an English School" in that city. He was also a pupil of William Smith, Provost of the College of Philadelphia, and had as companions, Benjamin West, and Francis Hopkinson, the first original poet-composer in the colonies. Having been released from his indentures to a watch maker, he became in 1758 a lieutenant in the Pennsylvania militia for the expedition against Fort Duquesne. The next year he accepted a position as a factor in North Carolina where he stayed for three years and where he brought to completion *The Prince of Parthia.* Godfrey had probably seen the American Company act in Philadelphia in 1754 when, owing to the opposition to the theatre, the actors had been forced to play in a warehouse belonging to William Plumsted, one of the Trustees of the College, on Water Street. Being a pupil of William Smith, Godfrey had almost certainly attended the benefit which the American Company gave for the Charity School of the College, June 19, 1754. He may have offered the play to David Douglass, the Manager of the reorganized American Company, as early as 1759, but it was not acted until after Godfrey's death. He died August 3, 1763, in North Carolina, and *The Prince of Parthia,* together with his other poems, was published in 1765 by his friend, Nathaniel Evans, with an account of Godfrey. The play was produced on April 24, 1767, according to the following advertisement which appeared in No. 1272 of *The Pennsylvania Journal and the Weekly Advertiser,* Thursday, April 23, 1767.

BY AUTHORITY.
Never Performed Before.
By the AMERICAN COMPANY,
At the NEW THEATRE, in *Southwark,*
on FRIDAY, the *Twenty-fourth of April,* will be
presented, A TRAGEDY written by the late ingenious
Mr. *Thomas Godfrey,* of this city, called the
PRINCE of PARTHIA
The PRINCIPAL CHARACTERS by MR. HALLAM,
MR. DOUGLASS, MR. WALL, MR. MORRIS,
MR. ALLYN, MR. TOMLINSON, MR. BROAD-

BELT, MR. GREVILLE, MRS. DOUGLASS,
MRS. MORRIS, MISS WAINWRIGHT, *and*
MISS CHEER
To which will be added, *A Ballad Opera,* called
The CONTRIVANCES.
To begin exactly at *Seven* o'clock. *Vivant Rex & Regina.*

Seilhamer, in his *History of the American Theatre,* suggests a probable cast, based on the advertisement, which he curiously attributes to the *Pennsylvania Chronicle,* in which it does not appear. Considering the relative importance of the actors in the American Company, it is likely that this cast is correct, and it is given here, with an indication that is only problematical. A similar advertisement but without the actors' names appeared in *The Pennsylvania Gazette* of the same date.

The Prince of Parthia was revived by the Zelosophic Society of the University of Pennsylvania on March 26, 1915, at the New Century Drawing Room, Philadelphia, and proved to be an actable play, though the absence of any comedy element was noticeable. The play shows clearly the influence of *Hamlet, Julius Cæsar, Macbeth, Romeo and Juliet,* and also of Beaumont's *Maid's Tragedy,* but the blank verse is flexible and dignified and the correspondence of Godfrey proves that he conceived it with the purpose of actual stage representation and not merely as a closet play.

For an account of Godfrey see *Juvenile Poems on Various Subjects, with The Prince of Parthia,* by Nathaniel Evans, Philadelphia, 1765, and for criticism of the play, see Moses Coit Tyler, *A History of American Literature during the Colonial Time,* 2 vols., New York, 1878, Vol. 2, pp. 244-251, and George O. Seilhamer, *History of the American Theatre,* 3 vols., Philadelphia, 1888, Vol. 1, Chap. 18.

The Prince of Parthia is now reprinted, for the first time, from the original edition of 1765.

NOTE TO SECOND EDITION.

Shortly after the appearance of the first edition, a very interesting reprint of *The Prince of Parthia* was edited by Archibald Henderson, Boston, 1917. Mr. Henderson has reproduced the costumes worn by the members of the Zelosophic Society at the revival in 1915, has investigated the sources of the play in Parthian history and has written attractively of the life in Philadelphia and in Wilmington, North Carolina, that surrounded Godfrey.

JUVENILE POEMS

ON

VARIOUS SUBJECTS.

WITH THE

PRINCE OF PARTHIA,

A

T R A G E D Y.

BY THE LATE

Mr. *THOMAS GODFREY*, Junr.

of PHILADELPHIA.

To which is prefixed,

Some ACCOUNT of the *AUTHOR* and his *WRITINGS*.

Poeta nascitur non fit. HOR.

PHILADELPHIA,
Printed by HENRY MILLER, in Second-Street.
M DCC LXV.

DRAMATIS PERSONAE

MEN

Artabanus, King of Parthia.................................[Mr. Douglass]

Arsaces, } his Sons ....[Mr. Hallam]

Vardanes, } his Sons.....................................[Mr. Tomlinson]

Gotarzes, } his Sons ....[Mr. Wall]

Barzaphernes, Lieutenant-General, under Arsaces.............[Mr. Allyn]

Lysias, } Officers at Court. ....[Mr. Broadbelt]

Phraates, } Officers at Court. ....[Mr. Greville]

Bethas, a Noble Captive...[Mr. Morris]

WOMEN

Thermusa, the Queen.....................................[Mrs. Douglass]

Evanthe, belov'd by Arsaces.......................................[Miss Cheer]

Cleone, her Confidante...................................[Miss Wainwright]

Edessa, Attendant on the Queen..............................[Mrs. Morris]

Guards and Attendants

Scene, Ctesiphon

THE PRINCE OF PARTHIA

A TRAGEDY

ACT FIRST.

SCENE 1. *The Temple of the Sun.*

GOTARZES *and* PHRAATES.

GOTARZES. He comes, *Arsaces* comes, my gallant Brother
(Like shining Mars in all the pomp of conquest)
Triumphant enters now our joyful gates;
Bright Victory waits on his glitt'ring car,
And shows her fav'rite to the wond'ring croud;
While Fame exulting sounds the happy name
To realms remote, and bids the world admire.
Oh! 't is a glorious day:—let none presume
T' indulge the tear, or wear the gloom of sorrow;
This day shall shine in Ages yet to come,
And grace the PARTHIAN story.

PHRAATES. Glad *Ctes'phon* [1]
Pours forth her numbers, like a rolling deluge,
To meet the blooming Hero; all the ways,
On either side, as far as sight can stretch,
Are lin'd with crouds, and on the lofty walls
Innumerable multitudes are rang'd.
On ev'ry countenance impatience sate
With roving eye, before the train appear'd.
But when they saw the Darling of the Fates,
They rent the air with loud repeated shouts;
The Mother show'd him to her infant Son,
And taught his lisping tongue to name *Arsaces:*
E'en aged Sires, whose sounds are scarcely heard,
By feeble strength supported, tost their caps,
And gave their murmur to the gen'ral voice.

GOTARZES. The spacious streets, which lead up to the Temple,
Are strew'd with flow'rs; each, with frantic joy,
His garland forms, and throws it in the way.
What pleasure, *Phraates,* must swell his bosom,
To see the prostrate nation all around him,
And know he 's made them happy! to hear them
Tease the Gods, to show'r their blessings on him!
Happy *Arsaces!* fain I 'd imitate
Thy matchless worth, and be a shining joy!

PHRAATES. Hark! what a shout was that which pierc'd the skies!
It seem'd as tho' all Nature's beings join'd,
To hail thy glorious Brother.

GOTARZES. Happy *Parthia!*
Now proud *Arabia* dreads her destin'd chains,
While shame and rout disperses all her sons.
Barzaphernes pursues the fugitives,
The few whom fav'ring Night redeem'd from slaughter;
Swiftly they fled, for fear had wing'd their speed,
And made them bless the shade which saf'ty gave.

PHRAATES. What a bright hope is ours, when those dread pow'rs
Who rule yon heav'n, and guide the mov'ments here,
Shall call your royal Father to their joys:
In blest *Arsaces* ev'ry virtue meets;
He 's gen'rous, brave, and wise, and good,
Has skill to act, and noble fortitude
To face bold danger, in the battle firm,
And dauntless as a Lion fronts his foe.
Yet is he sway'd by ev'ry tender passion,
Forgiving mercy, gentleness and love;
Which speak the Hero friend of humankind.

GOTARZES. And let me speak, for 't is to him I owe

[1] Ctesiphon, a large village on the left bank of the Tigris.

That here I stand, and breathe the common air,
And 't is my pride to tell it to the world.
One luckless day as in the eager chace
My Courser wildly bore me from the rest,
A monst'rous Leopard from a bosky fen
Rush'd forth, and foaming lash'd the ground,
And fiercely ey'd me as his destin'd quarry.
My jav'lin swift I threw, but o'er his head
It erring pass'd, and harmless in the air
Spent all its force; my falchin [1] then I seiz'd,
Advancing to attack my ireful foe,
When furiously the savage sprung upon me,
And tore me to the ground; my treach'rous blade
Above my hand snap'd short, and left me quite
Defenceless to his rage; *Arsaces* then,
Hearing the din, flew like some pitying pow'r,
And quickly freed me from the Monster's paws,
Drenching his bright lance in his spotted breast.

PHRAATES. How diff'rent he from arrogant *Vardanes?*
That haughty Prince eyes with a stern contempt
All other Mortals, and with lofty mien
He treads the earth as tho' he were a God.
Nay, I believe that his ambitious soul,
Had it but pow'r to its licentious wishes,
Would dare dispute with Jove the rule of heav'n;
Like a Titanian son with giant insolence,
Match with the Gods, and wage immortal war,
'Til their red wrath should hurl him headlong down,
E'en to destruction's lowest pit of horror.

GOTARZES. Methinks he wears not that becoming joy
Which on this bright occasion gilds the court;
His brow 's contracted with a gloomy frown,
Pensive he stalks along, and seems a prey
To pining discontent.

PHRAATES. *Arsaces* he dislikes,
For standing 'twixt him, and the hope or Empire;
While Envy, like a rav'nous Vulture tears
His canker'd heart, to see your Brother's triumph.

GOTARZES. And yet *Vardanes* owes that hated Brother
As much as I; 't was summer last, as we
Were bathing in *Euphrates'* flood, *Vardanes*
Proud of strength would seek the further shore;
But ere he the mid-stream gain'd, a poignant pain
Shot thro' his well-strung nerves, contracting all,
And the stiff joints refus'd their wonted aid.
Loudly he cry'd for help, *Arsaces* heard,
And thro' the swelling waves he rush'd to save
His drowning Brother, and gave him life,
And for the boon the Ingrate pays him hate.

PHRAATES. There 's something in the wind, for I' ve observ'd
Of late he much frequents the Queen's apartment,
And fain would court her favour, wild is she
To gain revenge for fell *Vonones'* death,
And firm resolves the ruin of *Arsaces.*
Because that fill'd with filial piety,
To save his Royal Sire, he struck the bold
Presumptuous Traitor dead; nor heeds she
The hand which gave her Liberty, nay rais'd her
Again to Royalty.

GOTARZES. Ingratitude,
Thou hell-born fiend, how horrid is thy form!
The Gods sure let thee loose to scourge mankind,
And save them from an endless waste of thunder.

PHRAATES. Yet I 've beheld this now so haughty Queen,
Bent with distress, and e'en by pride forsook,
When following thy Sire's triumphant car,
Her tears and ravings mov'd the senseless herd,
And pity blest their more than savage breasts,
With the short pleasure of a moment's softness.
Thy Father, conquer'd by her charms, (for what

[1] Falchion, a broad curved convex-edged sword.

Can charm like mourning beauty) soon struck off
Her chains, and rais'd her to his bed and throne.
Adorn'd the brows of her aspiring Son,
The fierce *Vonones,* with the regal crown
Of rich *Armenia,* once the happy rule
Of *Tisaphernes,* her deceased Lord.

GOTARZES. And he in wasteful war return'd his thanks,
Refus'd the homage he had sworn to pay,
And spread Destruction ev'rywhere around,
'Til from *Arsaces'* hand he met the fate
His crimes deserv'd.

PHRAATES. As yet your princely Brother
Has 'scap'd *Thermusa's* rage, for still residing
In peaceful times, within his Province, ne'er
Has fortune blest her with a sight of him,
On whom she 'd wreck her vengeance.

GOTARZES. She has won
By spells, I think, so much on my fond father,
That he is guided by her will alone.
She rules the realm, her pleasure is a law,
All offices and favours are bestow'd,
As she directs.

PHRAATES. But see, the Prince, *Vardanes,*
Proud *Lysias* with him, he whose soul is harsh
With jarring discord. Nought but madding rage,
And ruffian-like revenge his breast can know,
Indeed to gain a point he 'll condescend
To mask the native rancour of his heart,
And smooth his venom'd tongue with flattery.
Assiduous now he courts *Vardanes'* friendship,
See, how he seems to answer all his gloom,
And give him frown for frown.

GOTARZES. Let us retire,
And shun them now; I know not what it means,
But chilling horror shivers o'er my limbs,
When *Lysias* I behold.—

SCENE 2.

VARDANES *and* LYSIAS.

(*Shout.*)

LYSIAS. That shout proclaims
Arsaces' near approach.

VARDANES. Peace, prithee peace,
Wilt thou still shock me with that hated sound,
And grate harsh discord in my offended ear?
If thou art fond of echoing the name,
Join with the servile croud, and hail his triumph.

LYSIAS. I hail him? By our glorious shining God,
I 'd sooner lose my speech, and all my days
In silence rest, conversing with my thoughts,
Than hail *Arsaces.*

VARDANES. Yet, again his name,
Sure there is magic in it, PARTHIA 's drunk
And giddy with the joy; the houses' tops
With gaping spectators are throng'd, nay wild
They climb such precipices that the eye
Is dazzl'd with their daring; ev'ry wretch
Who long has been immur'd, nor dar'd enjoy
The common benefits of sun and air,
Creeps from his lurking place; e'en feeble age,
Long to the sickly couch confin'd, stalks forth,
And with infectious breath assails the Gods.
O! curse the name, the idol of their joy.

LYSIAS. And what 's that name, that thus they should disturb
The ambient air, and weary gracious heav'n
With ceaseless bellowings? *Vardanes* sounds
With equal harmony, and suits as well
The loud repeated shouts of noisy joy.
Can he bid Chaos Nature's rule dissolve,
Can he deprive mankind of light and day,
And turn the Seasons from their destin'd course?
Say, can he do all this, and be a God?
If not, what is his matchless merit? What dares he,
Vardanes dares not? Blush not, noble prince,
For praise is merit's due, and I will give it;
E'en mid the croud which waits thy Brother's smile,
I 'd loud proclaim the merit of *Vardanes.*

VARDANES. Forbear this warmth, your friendship urges far.

Yet know your love shall e'er retain a place
In my remembrance. There is something here— (*Pointing to his breast.*)
Another time and I will give thee all;
But now, no more.—

LYSIAS. You may command my service,
I'm happy to obey. Of late your Brother
Delights in hind'ring my advancement,
And ev'ry boaster's rais'd above my merit,
Barzaphernes alone commands his ear,
His oracle in all.

VARDANES. I hate *Arsaces*,
Tho' he's my Mother's son, and churchmen say
There's something sacred in the name of Brother.
My soul endures him not, and he's the bane
Of all my hopes of greatness. Like the sun
He rules the day, and like the night's pale Queen,
My fainter beams are lost when he appears.
And this because he came into the world,
A moon or two before me: What's the diff'rence,
That he alone should shine in Empire's seat?
I am not apt to trumpet forth my praise,
Or highly name myself, but this I'll speak,
To him in ought, I'm not the least inferior.
Ambition, glorious fever! mark of Kings,
Gave me immortal thirst and rule of Empire.
Why lag'd my tardy soul, why droop'd the wing,
Nor forward springing, shot before his speed
To seize the prize?—'T was Empire—Oh! 't was Empire—

LYSIAS. Yet, I must think that of superior mould
Your soul was form'd, fit for a heav'nly state,
And left reluctant its sublime abode,
And painfully obey'd the dread command,
When Jove's controuling fate forc'd it below.
His soul was earthly, and it downward mov'd,
Swift as to the center of attraction.

VARDANES. It might be so— But I've another cause
To hate this Brother, ev'ry way my rival;
In love as well as glory he's above me;
I dote on fair *Evanthe*, but the charmer
Disdains my ardent suit, like a miser
He treasures up her beauties to himself:
Thus is he form'd to give me torture ever.—
But hark, they've reach'd the Temple,
Didst thou observe the croud, their eagerness,
Each put the next aside to catch a look,
Himself was elbow'd out?— Curse, curse their zeal—

LYSIAS. Stupid folly!

VARDANES. I'll tell thee, *Lysias*,
This many-headed monster multitude,
Unsteady is as giddy fortune's wheel,
As woman fickle, varying as the wind;
To day they this way course, the next they veer,
And shift another point, the next another.

LYSIAS. Curiosity's another name for man,
The blazing meteor streaming thro' the air
Commands our wonder, and admiring eyes,
With eager gaze we trace the lucent path,
'Til spent at length it shrinks to native nothing.
While the bright stars which ever steady glow,
Unheeded shine, and bless the world below.

SCENE 3.

QUEEN *and* EDESSA.

QUEEN. Oh! give me way, the haughty victor comes,
Surrounded by adoring multitudes;
On swelling tides of praise to heav'n they raise him;
To deck their idol, they rob the glorious beings
Of their splendor.

EDESSA. My royal Lady,
Chace hence these passions.

QUEEN. Peace, forever peace,
Have I not cause to hate this homicide?
'T was by his curséd hand *Vonones* fell,
Yet fell not as became his gallant spirit,
Not by the warlike arm of chief renown'd,
But by a youth, ye Gods, a beardless stripling,

Stab'd by his dastard falchin from behind;
For well I know he fear'd to meet *Vonones,*
As princely warriors meet with open daring,
But shrunk amidst his guards, and gave him death,
When faint with wounds, and weary with the fight.

EDESSA. With anguish I have heard his hapless fate,
And mourn'd in silence for the gallant Prince.

QUEEN. Soft is thy nature, but alas! *Edessa,*
Thy heart 's a stranger to a mother's sorrows,
To see the pride of all her wishes blasted;
Thy fancy cannot paint the storm of grief,
Despair and anguish, which my breast has known.
Oh! shower, ye Gods, your torments on *Arsaces,*
Curs'd be the morn which dawned upon his birth.

EDESSA. Yet, I intreat—

QUEEN. Away! for I will curse—
O may he never know a father's fondness,
Or know it to his sorrow, may his hopes
Of joy be cut like mine, and his short life
Be one continu'd tempest: if he lives,
Let him be curs'd with jealousy and fear,
And vext with anguish of neglecting scorn;
May tort'ring hope present the flowing cup,
Then hasty snatch it from his eager thirst,
And when he dies base treach'ry be the means.

EDESSA. Oh! calm your spirits.

QUEEN. Yes, I 'll now be calm,
Calm as the sea when the rude waves are laid,
And nothing but a gentle swell remains;
My curse is heard, and I shall have revenge:
There 's something here which tells me 't will be so,
And peace resumes her empire o'er my breast.
Vardanes is the Minister of Vengeance;
Fir'd by ambition, he aspiring seeks
T' adorn his brows with *Parthia's* diadem;
I 've fann'd the fire, and wrought him up to fury,
Envy shall urge him forward still to dare,
And discord be the prelude to destruction,
Then this detested race shall feel my hate.

EDESSA. And doth thy hatred then extend so far,
That innocent and guilty all alike
Must feel thy dreadful vengeance?

QUEEN. Ah! *Edessa,*
Thou dost not know e'en half my mighty wrongs,
But in thy bosom I will pour my sorrows.

EDESSA. With secrecy I ever have repaid
Your confidence.

QUEEN. I know thou hast, then hear,
The changeling King who oft has kneel'd before me,
And own'd no other pow'r, now treats me
With ill dissembl'd love mix'd with disdain,
A newer beauty rules his faithless heart,
Which only in variety is blest;
Oft have I heard him, when wrapt up in sleep,
And wanton fancy rais'd the mimic scene,
Call with unusual fondness on *Evanthe,*
While I have lain neglected by his side,
Except sometimes in a mistaken rapture
He 'd clasp me to his bosom.

EDESSA. Oh! Madam,
Let not corroding jealousy usurp
Your Royal breast, unnumber'd ills attend
The wretch who entertains that fatal guest.

QUEEN. Think not that I 'll pursue its wand'ring fires,
No more I 'll know perplexing doubts and fears,
And erring trace suspicion's endless maze,
For, ah! I doubt no more.

EDESSA. Their shouts approach.

QUEEN. Lead me, *Edessa,* to some peaceful gloom,
Some silent shade far from the walks of men,
There shall the hop'd revenge my thoughts employ,
And sooth my sorrows with the coming joy.

SCENE 4.

EVANTHE *and* CLEONE.

EVANTHE. No, I 'll not meet him now, for love delights

In the soft pleasures of the secret shade,
And shuns the noise and tumult of the croud.
How tedious are the hours which bring him
To my fond panting heart! for oh! to those
Who live in expectation of the bliss,
Time slowly creeps, and ev'ry tardy minute
Seems mocking of their wishes. Say, *Cleone,*
For you beheld the triumph, midst his pomp,
Did he not seem to curse the empty show,
The pageant greatness, enemy to love,
Which held him from *Evanthe?* haste, to tell me,
And feed my greedy ear with the fond tale—
Yet, hold—for I shall weary you with questions,
And ne'er be satisfied— Beware, *Cleone,*
And guard your heart from Love's delusive sweets.

CLEONE. Is Love an ill, that thus you caution me
To shun his pow'r?

EVANTHE. The Tyrant, my *Cleone,*
Despotic rules, and fetters all our thoughts.
Oh! wouldst thou love, then bid adieu to peace,
Then fears will come, and jealousies intrude,
Ravage your bosom, and disturb your quiet,
E'en pleasure to excess will be a pain.
Once I was free, then my exulting heart
Was like a bird that hops from spray to spray,
And all was innocence and mirth; but, lo!
The Fowler came, and by his arts decoy'd,
And soon the Wanton cag'd. Twice fifteen times
Has *Cynthia* dipt her horns in beams of light,
Twice fifteen times has wasted all her brightness,
Since first I knew to love; 't was on that day
When curs'd *Vonones* fell upon the plain,
The lovely Victor doubly conquer'd me.

CLEONE. Forgive my boldness, Madam, if I ask
What chance first gave you to *Vonones'* pow'r?
Curiosity thou know'st is of our sex.

EVANTHE. That is a talk will wake me to new sorrows,
Yet thou attend, and I will tell thee all.
Arabia gave me birth. my father held
Great Offices at Court, and was reputed
Brave, wise and loyal, by his Prince belov'd.
Oft has he led his conqu'ring troops, and forc'd
From frowning victory her awful honours.
In infancy I was his only treasure,
On me he wasted all his store of fondness.
Oh! I could tell thee of his wond'rous goodness,
His more than father's love and tenderness.
But thou wouldst jeer, and say the tale was trifling;
So did he dote upon me, for in childhood
My infant charms, and artless innocence
Blest his fond age, and won on ev'ry heart.
But, oh! from this sprung ev'ry future ill,
This fatal beauty was the source of all.

CLEONE. 'T is often so, for beauty is a flow'r
That tempts the hand to pluck it.

EVANTHE. Full three times
Has scorching summer fled from cold winter's
Ruthless blasts, as oft again has spring
In sprightly youth drest nature in her beauties,
Since bathing in *Niphates'*[1] silver stream,
Attended only by one fav'rite maid;
As we were sporting on the wanton waves,
Swift from the wood a troop of horsemen rush'd,
Rudely they seiz'd, and bore me trembling off,
In vain *Edessa* with her shrieks assail'd
The heav'ns, for heav'n was deaf to both our pray'rs.
The wretch whose insolent embrace confin'd me,
(Like thunder bursting on the guilty soul)
With curs'd *Vonones'* voice pour'd in my ears
A hateful tale of love; for he it seems
Had seen me at Arabia's royal court,
And took those means to force me to his arms.

[1] The Tigris.

CLEONE. Perhaps you may gain something from the Captives
Of your lost Parents.

EVANTHE. This I mean to try,
Soon as the night hides Nature in her darkness,
Veil'd in the gloom we 'll steal into their prison.
But, oh! perhaps e'en now my aged Sire
May 'mongst the slain lie weltring on the field,
Pierc'd like a riddle through with num'rous wounds,
While parting life is quiv'ring on his lips,
He may perhaps be calling on his *Evanthe.*
Yes, ye great Pow'rs who boast the name of mercy,
Ye have deny'd me to his latest moments,
To all the offices of filial duty,
To bind his wounds, and wash them with my tears,
Is this, is this your mercy?

CLEONE. Blame not heav'n,
For heav'n is just and kind; dear Lady, drive
These black ideas from your gentle breast;
Fancy delights to torture the distress'd,
And fill the gloomy scene with shadowy ills,
Summon your reason, and you'll soon have comfort.

EVANTHE. Dost thou name comfort to me, my *Cleone,*
Thou who know'st all my sorrows? plead no more,
'T is reason tells me I am doubly wretched.

CLEONE. But hark, the music strikes, the rites begin,
And, see, the doors are op'ning.

EVANTHE. Let 's retire;
My heart is now too full to meet him here,
Fly swift, ye hours, till in his arms I 'm prest,
And each intruding care is hush'd to rest.

SCENE 5. *The Scene draws and discovers, in the inner Part of the Temple, a large Image of the Sun, with an Altar before it. Around Priests and Attendants.*

KING, ARSACES, VARDANES, GOTARZES, PHRAATES, LYSIAS, *with* BETHAS *in chains.*

HYMN.

Parent of Light, to thee belong
Our grateful tributary songs;
Each thankful voice to thee shall rise,
And chearful pierce the azure skies;
While in thy praise all earth combines,
And Echo in the Chorus joins.

All the gay pride of blooming May,
The Lily fair and blushing Rose,
To thee their early honours pay,
And all their heav'nly sweets disclose.
The feather'd Choir on ev'ry tree
To hail thy glorious dawn repair,
While the sweet sons of harmony
With Hallelujahs fill the air.

'Tis thou hast brac'd the Hero's arm,
And giv'n the Love of praise to warm
His bosom, as he onward flies,
And for his Country bravely dies.
Thine 's victory, and from thee springs
Ambition's fire, which glows in Kings.

KING. (*Coming forward.*) Thus, to the Gods our tributary songs,
And now, oh! let me welcome once again
My blooming victor to his Father's arms;
And let me thank thee for our safety: PARTHIA
Shall thank thee too, and give her grateful praise
To her Deliverer.

OMNES. All hail! *Arsaces!*

KING. Thanks to my loyal friends.

VARDANES. (*Aside.*)
Curse, curse the sound,
E'en Echo gives it back with int'rest,
The joyful gales swell with the pleasing theme,
And waft it far away to distant hills.
O that my breath was poison, then indeed
I'd hail him like the rest, but blast him too.

ARSACES. My Royal Sire, these honours are unmerited,
Beneath your prosp'rous auspices I fought,
Bright vict'ry to your banners joyful flew,
And favour'd for the Sire the happy son.
But lenity should grace the victor's laurels,
Then, here, my gracious Father—

KING. Ha! 't is *Bethas!*
Know'st thou, vain wretch, what fate attends on those
Who dare oppose the pow'r of mighty Kings,

Whom heav'n delights to favour? sure some God
Who sought to punish you for impious deeds,
'T was urg'd you forward to insult our arms,
And brave us at our Royal City's gates.

BETHAS. At honour's call, and at my King's command,
Tho' it were even with my single arm, again
I 'd brave the multitude, which, like a deluge,
O'erwhelm'd my gallant handful; yea wou'd meet
Undaunted, all the fury of the torrent.
'T is honour is the guide of all my actions,
The ruling star by which I steer thro' life,
And shun the shelves of infamy and vice.

KING. It was the thirst of gain which drew you on;
'T is thus that Av'rice always cloaks its views,
Th' ambition of your Prince you gladly snatch'd
As opportunity to fill your coffers.
It was the plunder of our palaces,
And of our wealthy cities, fill'd your dreams,
And urg'd you on your way; but you have met
The due reward of your audacity.
Now shake your chains, shake and delight your ears
With the soft music of your golden fetters.

BETHAS. True, I am fall'n, but glorious was my fall,
The day was brav'ly fought, we did our best,
But victory 's of heav'n. Look o'er yon field,
See if thou findest one *Arabian* back
Disfigur'd with dishonourable wounds.
No, here, deep on their bosoms, are engrav'd
The marks of honour! 't was thro' here their souls
Flew to their blissful seats. Oh! why did I
Survive the fatal day? To be this slave,
To be the gaze and sport of vulgar crouds,
Thus, like a shackl'd tyger, stalk my round,
And grimly low'r upon the shouting herd.
Ye Gods!—

KING. Away with him to instant death.

ARSACES. Hear me, my Lord, O, not on this bright day,
Let not this day of joy blush with his blood.
Nor count his steady loyalty a crime,
But give him life, *Arsaces* humbly asks it,
And may you e'er be serv'd with honest hearts.

KING. Well, be it so; hence, bear him to his dungeon;
Lysias, we here commit him to thy charge.

BETHAS. Welcome my dungeon, but more welcome death.
Trust not too much, vain Monarch, to your pow'r,
Know fortune places all her choicest gifts
On ticklish heights, they shake with ev'ry breeze,
And oft some rude wind hurls them to the ground.
Jove's thunder strikes the lofty palaces,
While the low cottage, in humility,
Securely stands, and sees the mighty ruin.
What King can boast, to morrow as to day,
Thus, happy will I reign? The rising sun
May view him seated on a splendid throne,
And, setting, see him shake the servile chain. (*Exit guarded.*)

SCENE 6.

KING, ARSACES, VARDANES, GOTARZES, PHRAATES.

GOTARZES. Thus let me hail thee from the croud distinct,
For in the exulting voice of gen'ral joy
My fainter sounds were lost, believe me, Brother,
My soul dilates with joy to see thee thus.

ARSACES. Thus let me thank thee in this fond embrace.

VARDANES. The next will be my turn, Gods, I had rather
Be circl'd in a venom'd serpent's fold.

GOTARZES. O, my lov'd Brother, 't is my humble boon,
That, when the war next calls you to the field,
I may attend you in the rage of battle.

By imitating thy heroic deeds,
Perhaps, I may rise to some little worth,
Beneath thy care I'll try my feeble wings,
Till taught by thee to soar to nobler heights.

KING. Why that's my boy, thy spirit speaks thy birth,
No more I'll turn thee from the road to glory,
To rust in slothfulness, with lazy Gownsmen.

GOTARZES. Thanks, to my Sire, I'm now completely blest.

ARSACES. But, I've another Brother, where's *Vardanes?*

KING. Ha! what, methinks, he lurks behind the croud,
And wears a gloom which suits not with the time.

VARDANES. Doubt not my Love, tho' I lack eloquence,
To dress my sentiments and catch the ear,
Tho' plain my manners, and my language rude,
My honest heart disdains to wear disguise.
Then think not I am slothful in the race,
Or, that my Brother springs before my Love.

ARSACES. Far be suspicion from me.

VARDANES. So, 't is done,
Thanks to dissembling, all is well again.

KING. Now let us, forward, to the Temple go,
And let, with cheerful wine, the goblets flow;
Let blink-ey'd Jollity his aid afford,
To crown our triumph, round the festive board:
But, let the wretch, whose soul can know a care,
Far from our joys, to some lone shade repair,
In secrecy, there let him e'er remain,
Brood o'er his gloom, and still increase his pain.

END OF THE FIRST ACT.

ACT SECOND.

SCENE 1. *A Prison.*

LYSIAS, *alone.*

The Sun set frowning, and refreshing Eve
Lost all its sweets, obscur'd in double gloom.
This night shall sleep be stranger to these eyes,
Peace dwells not here, and slumber flies the shock;
My spirits, like the elements, are war[r]ing,
And mock the tempest with a kindred rage—
I, who can joy in nothing, but revenge,
Know not those boasted ties of Love and Friendship;
Vardanes I regard, but as he gives me
Some hopes of vengeance on the Prince *Arsaces*—
But, ha! he comes, wak'd by the angry storm,
'T is to my wish, thus would I form designs,
Horror should breed beneath the veil of horror,
And darkness aid conspiracies— He's here—

SCENE 2.

VARDANES *and* LYSIAS.

LYSIAS. Welcome, my noble Prince.

VARDANES. Thanks, gentle friend;
Heav'ns! what a night is this!

LYSIAS. 'T is filled with terror;
Some dread event beneath this horror lurks,
Ordain'd by fate's irrevocable doom;
Perhaps *Arsaces'* fall—and angry heav'n
Speaks it, in thunder, to the trembling world.

VARDANES. Terror indeed! it seems as sick'ning Nature
Had giv'n her order up to gen'ral ruin;
The Heav'ns appear as one continu'd flame,
Earth with her terror shakes, dim night retires,
And the red lightning gives a dreadful day,
While in the thunder's voice each sound is lost;
Fear sinks the panting heart in ev'ry bosom,
E'en the pale dead, affrighted at the horror,
As tho' unsafe, start from their marble gaols,
And howling thro' the streets are seeking shelter.

LYSIAS. I saw a flash stream thro' the angry clouds,

And bend its course to where a stately pine
Behind the garden stood, quickly it seiz'd,
And wrapt it in a fiery fold, the trunk
Was shiver'd into atoms, and the branches
Off were lopt, and wildly scatter'd round.

VARDANES. Why rage the elements, they are not curs'd
Like me? *Evanthe* frowns not angry on them,
The wind may play upon her beauteous bosom
Nor fear her chiding, light can bless her sense,
And in the floating mirror she beholds
Those beauties which can fetter all mankind.
Earth gives her joy, she plucks the fragrant rose,
Pleas'd takes its sweets, and gazes on its bloom.

LYSIAS. My Lord, forget her, tear her from your breast.
Who, like the *Phœnix,* gazes on the sun,
And strives to soar up to the glorious blaze,
Should never leave Ambition's brightest object,
To turn, and view the beauties of a flow'r.

VARDANES. O, *Lysias,* chide no more, for, I have done.
Yes, I 'll forget this proud disdainful beauty;
Hence with vain love— Ambition, now, alone,
Shall guide my actions, since mankind delights
To give me pain, I 'll study mischief too,
And shake the earth, e'en like this raging tempest.

LYSIAS. A night like this, so dreadful to behold,
Since my remembrance's birth, I never saw.

VARDANES. E'en such a night, dreadful as this, they say,
My teeming Mother gave me to the world.
Whence by those sages who, in knowledge rich,
Can pry into futurity, and tell
What distant ages will produce of wonder,
My days were deem'd to be a hurricane;
My early life prov'd their prediction false;
Beneath a sky serene my voyage began,
But, to this long uninterrupted calm,
Storms shall succeed.

LYSIAS. Then haste, to raise the tempest;
My soul disdains this one eternal round,
Where each succeeding day is like the former.
Trust me, my noble Prince, here is a heart
Steady and firm to all your purposes,
And here 's a hand that knows to execute
Whate'er designs thy daring breast can form,
Nor ever shake with fear.

VARDANES. And I will use it,
Come to my bosom, let me place thee here,
How happy am I clasping so much virtue!
Now, by the light, it is my firm belief,
One mighty soul in common swells our bosoms,
Such sameness can't be match'd in diff'rent beings.

LYSIAS. Your confidence, my Lord, much honours me,
And when I act unworthy of your love
May I be hooted from Society,
As tho' disgraceful to the human kind,
And driv'n to herd among the savage race.

VARDANES. Believe me, *Lysias,* I do not know
A single thought which tends toward suspicion,
For well I know thy worth, when I affront it,
By the least doubt, may I be ever curs'd
With faithless friends, and by his dagger fall
Whom my deluded wishes most would favour.

LYSIAS. Then let 's no longer trifle time away,
I 'm all impatience till I see thy brows
Bright in the glories of a diadem;
My soul is fill'd with anguish when I think
That by weak Princes worn, 't is thus disgrac'd.
Haste, mount the throne, and, like the morning Sun,
Chace with your piercing beams those mists away,
Which dim the glory of the *Parthian* state:
Each honest heart desires it, numbers there are
Ready to join you, and support your cause,

Against th' opposing faction.

VARDANES. Sure some God,
Bid you thus call me to my dawning honours,
And joyful I obey the pleasing summons.
Now by the pow'rs of heav'n, of earth and hell,
Most solemnly I swear, I will not know,
That quietude which I was wont to know,
'Til I have climb'd the height of all my wishes,
Or fell, from glory, to the silent grave.

LYSIAS. Nobly resolv'd, and spoken like *Vardanes,*
There shone my Prince in his superior lustre.

VARDANES. But, then, *Arsaces,* he 's a fatal bar—
O! could I brush this busy insect from me,
Which envious strives to rob me of my bloom,
Then might I, like some fragrant op'ning flow'r,
Spread all my beauties in the face of day.
Ye Gods! why did ye give me such a soul,
(A soul, which ev'ry way is form'd for Empire)
And damn me with a younger Brother's right?
The diadem should set as well on mine,
As on the brows of any lordly He;
Nor is this hand weak to enforce command.
And shall I steal into my grave, and give
My name up to oblivion, to be thrown
Among the common rubbish of the times?
No: Perish first, this happy hated Brother.

LYSIAS. I always wear a dagger for your service,
I need not speak the rest—
When humbly I intreated of your Brother
T' attend him as Lieutenant in this war,
Frowning contempt, he haughtily reply'd,
He entertain'd not Traitors in his service.
True, I betray'd *Orodes,* but with cause,
He struck me, like a sorry abject slave,
And still withheld from giving what he 'd promis'd.
Fear not *Arsaces,* believe me, he shall
Soon his Quietus have— But, see, he comes,—
What can this mean? Why at this lonely hour.
And unattended?— Ha! 't is opportune—
I 'll in, and stab him now I heed not what
The danger is, so I but have revenge,
Then heap perdition on me.

VARDANES. Hold, awhile—
'T would be better could we undermine him,
And make him fall by *Artabanus'* doom.

LYSIAS. Well, be it so—

VARDANES. But let us now retire,
We must not be observ'd together here.

SCENE 3.

ARSACES, *alone.*

'T is here that hapless *Bethas* is confin'd;
He who, but yesterday, like angry Jove,
When punishing the crimes of guilty men,
Spread death and desolation all around,
While PARTHIA trembl'd at his name; is now
Unfriended and forlorn, and counts the hours,
Wrapt in the gloomy horrors of a gaol.—
How dark, and hidden, are the turns of fate!
His rigid fortune moves me to compassion.
O! 't is a heav'nly virtue when the heart
Can feel the sorrows of another's bosom,
It dignifies the man: The stupid wretch
Who knows not this sensation, is an image,
And wants the feeling to make up a life—
I 'll in, and give my aid to sooth his sorrows.

SCENE 4.

VARDANES *and* LYSIAS.

LYSIAS. Let us observe with care, something we, yet,
May gather, to give to us the vantage;
No matter what 's the intent.

VARDANES. How easy 't is
To cheat this busy, tattling, censuring world!
For fame still names our actions, good or bad,
As introduc'd by chance, which ofttimes throws

Wrong lights on objects; vice she dresses up
In the bright form, and goodliness, of virtue,
While virtue languishes, and pines neglected,
Rob[b]'d of her lustre— But, let 's forward, *Lysias*—
Thou know'st each turn in this thy dreary rule,
Then lead me to some secret stand, from whence,
Unnotic'd, all their actions we may view.

LYSIAS. Here, take your stand behind—
See, *Bethas* comes.

(*They retire.*)

SCENE 5.

BETHAS, *alone.*

To think on Death, in gloomy solitude,
In dungeons and in chains, when expectation
Join'd with serious thought describe him to us,
His height'n'd terrors strike upon the soul
With awful dread; imagination rais'd
To frenzy, plunges in a sea of horror,
And tastes the pains, the agonies of dying—
Ha! who is this, perhaps he bears my fate?
It must be so, but, why this privacy?

SCENE 6.

ARSACES *and* BETHAS.

ARSACES. Health to the noble *Bethas,* health and joy!

BETHAS. A steady harden'd villain, one experienc'd
In his employment; ha! where 's thy dagger?
It cannot give me fear; I 'm ready, see,
My op'ning bosom tempts the friendly steel.
Fain would I cast this tiresome being off,
Like an old garment worn to wretchedness.
Here, strike for I 'm prepar'd.

ARSACES. Oh! view me better,
Say, do I wear the gloomy ruffian's frown?

BETHAS. Ha! 't is the gallant Prince, the brave *Arsaces,*
And *Bethas'* Conqueror.

ARSACES. And *Bethas'* friend,
A name I 'm proud to wear.

BETHAS. Away—away—
Mock with your jester to divert the court,
Fit Scene for sportive joys and frolic mirth;
Thinkst thou I lack that manly constancy
Which braves misfortune, and remains unshaken?
Are these, are these the emblems of thy friendship,
These rankling chains, say, does it gall like these?
No, let me taste the bitterness of sorrow,
For I am reconcil'd to wretchedness.
The Gods have empty'd all their mighty store,
Of hoarded Ills, upon my whiten'd age;
Now death—but, oh! I court coy death in vain,
Like a cold maid, he scorns my fond complaining.
'T is thou, insulting Prince, 't is thou hast dragg'd
My soul, just rising, down again to earth,
And clogg'd her wings with dull mortality,
A hateful bondage! Why—

ARSACES. A moment hear me—

BETHAS. Why dost thou, like an angry vengeful ghost,
Glide hither to disturb this peaceful gloom?
What, dost thou envy me my miseries,
My chains and flinty pavement, where I oft
In sleep behold the image of the death I wish,
Forget my sorrows and heart-breaking anguish?
These horrors I would undisturb'd enjoy,
Attended only by my silent thoughts;
Is it to see the wretch that you have made,
To view the ruins of unhappy *Bethas,*
And triumph in my grief? Is it for this
You penetrate my dark joyless prison?

ARSACES. Oh! do not injure me by such suspicions.
Unknown to me are cruel scoffs and jests;
My breast can feel compassion's tenderness,
The warrior's warmth, the soothing joys of friendship.

When adverse bold battalions shook the earth,
And horror triumph'd on the hostile field,
I sought you with a glorious enmity,
And arm'd my brow with the stern frown of war.
But now the angry trumpet wakes no more
The youthful champion to the lust for blood.
Retiring rage gives place to softer passions,
And gen'rous warriors know no longer hate,
The name of foe is lost, and thus I ask
Your friendship.

BETHAS. Ah! why dost thou mock me thus?

ARSACES. Let the base coward, he who ever shrinks,
And trembles, at the slight name of danger,
Taunt, and revile, with bitter gibes, the wretched;
The brave are ever[1] to distress a friend.
Tho' my dear country, (spoil'd by wasteful war,
Her harvests blazing, desolate her towns,
And baleful ruin shew'd her hag[g]ard face)
Call'd out on me to save her from her foes,
And I obey'd, yet to your gallant prowess,
And unmatch'd deeds, I admiration gave.
But now my country knows the sweets of safety,
Freed from her fears; sure now I may indulge
My just esteem for your superior virtue.

BETHAS. Yes, I must think you what you would be thought,
For honest minds are easy of belief,
And always judge of others by themselves,
But often are deceiv'd; yet *Parthia* breeds not
Virtue much like thine, the barb'rous clime teems
With nought else but villains vers'd in ill.

ARSACES. Dissimulation never mark'd my looks,
Nor flatt'ring deceit e'er taught my tongue,
The tale of falsehood, to disguise my thoughts:
To Virtue, and, her fair companion, Truth,
I 've ever bow'd, their holy precepts kept,
And scann'd by them the actions of my life.
Suspicion surely ne'er disturbs the brave,
They never know the fears of doubting thoughts;
But free, as are the altars of the Gods,
From ev'ry hand receive the sacrifice.

[1] The text is obscure here. The meaning is "The brave are always a friend to distress"

SCENE 7.

ARSACES, BETHAS, EVANTHE, *and* CLEONE.

EVANTHE. Heav'ns! what a gloom hangs round this dreadful place,
Fit habitation for the guilty mind!
Oh! if such terrors wait the innocent,
Which tread these vaults, what must the impious feel,
Who 've all their crimes to stare them in the face?

BETHAS. Immortal Gods! is this reality?
Or meer[1] illusion? am I blest at last,
Or is it to torment me that you 've rais'd
This semblance of *Evanthe* to my eyes?
It is! it is! 't is she!—

ARSACES. Ha!—what means this?—
She faints! she faints! life has forsook its seat,
Pale Death usurps its place—*Evanthe*, Oh!
Awake to life!— Love and *Arsaces* call!—

BETHAS. Off—give her to my arms, my warm embrace
Shall melt Death's icy chains.

CLEONE. She lives! she lives!—
See, on her cheeks the rosy glow returns.

ARSACES. O joy! O joy! her op'ning eyes, again,
Break, like the morning sun, a better day.

BETHAS. *Evanthe!*—

EVANTHE. Oh! my Father!—

ARSACES. Ha!—her Father!

BETHAS. Heav'n thou art kind at last, and this indeed
Is recompense for all the ills I 've past;
For all the sorrows which my heart has known,
Each wakeful night, and ev'ry day of anguish.
This, this has sweet'n'd all my bitter cup,
And gave me once again to taste of joy,
Joy which has long been stranger to this bosom.

[1] Mere.

Hence—hence disgrace—off, ignominy off—
But one embrace—I ask but one embrace,
And 't is deny'd.

EVANTHE. O, yes, around thy neck
I 'll fold my longing arms, thy softer fetters,
Thus press thee to my happy breast, and kiss
Away those tears that stain thy aged cheeks.

BETHAS. Oh! 't is too much! it is too much! ye Gods!
Life 's at her utmost stretch, and bursting near
With heart-swoln ecstasy; now let me die.

ARSACES. What marble heart
Could see this scene unmov'd, nor give a tear?
My eyes grow dim, and sympathetic passion
Falls like a gushing torrent on my bosom.

EVANTHE. O! happy me, this place, which lately seem'd
So fill'd with horror, now is pleasure's circle.
Here will I fix my seat; my pleasing task
Shall be to cherish thy remaining life.
All night I 'll keep a vigil o'er thy slumbers,
And on my breast repose thee, mark thy dreams,
And when thou wak'st invent some pleasing tale,
Or with my songs the tedious hours beguile.

BETHAS. Still let me gaze, still let me gaze upon thee,
Let me strain ev'ry nerve with ravishment,
And all my life be center'd in my vision,
To see thee thus, to hear thy angel voice,
It is, indeed, a luxury of pleasure!—
Speak, speak again, for oh! 't is heav'n to hear thee!
Celestial sweetness dwells on ev'ry accent;—
Lull me to rest, and sooth my raging joy,
Joy which distracts me with unruly transports.
Now, by thy dear departed Mother's shade,
Thou brightest pattern of all excellence,
Thou who in prattling infancy hast blest me,
I wou'd not give this one transporting moment,
This fullness of delight. for all—but. ah!
'T is vile, Ambition, Glory, all is vile,
To the soft sweets of love and tenderness.

EVANTHE. Now let me speak, my throbbing heart is full,
I 'll tell thee all,—alas! I have forgot—
'T 'as slipt me in the tumult of my joy.
And yet I thought that I had much to say.

BETHAS. Oh! I have curs'd my birth, indeed, I have
Blasphem'd the Gods, with unbecoming passion,
Arraign'd their Justice, and defy'd their pow'r,
In bitterness, because they had deny'd
Thee to support the weakness of my age.
But now no more I 'll rail and rave at fate,
All its decrees are just, complaints are impious.
Whate'er short-sighted mortals feel, springs from
Their blindness in the ways of Providence;
Sufficient wisdom 't is for man to know
That the great Ruler is e'er wise and good.

ARSACES. Ye figur'd stones!
Ye senseless, lifeless images of men,
Who never gave a tear to others' woe,
Whose bosoms never glow'd for others' good,
O weary heav'n with your repeated pray'rs,
And strive to melt the angry pow'rs to pity,
That ye may truly live.

EVANTHE. Oh! how my heart
Beats in my breast, and shakes my trembling frame!
I sink beneath this sudden flood of joy,
Too mighty for my spirits.

ARSACES. My *Evanthe,*
Thus in my arms I catch thy falling beauties,
Chear thee; and kiss thee back to life again:
Thus to my bosom I could ever hold thee,
And find new pleasure.

EVANTHE. O! my lov'd *Arsaces,*
Forgive me that I saw thee not before,
Indeed my soul was busily employ'd,
Nor left a single thought at liberty.
But thou, I know, art gentleness and love.
Now I am doubly paid for all my sorrows,
For all my fears for thee.

ARSACES. Then, fear no more:
Give to guilty wretches painful terrors:

Whose keen remembrance raises horrid forms,
Shapes that in spite of nature shock their souls
With dreadful anguish; but thy gentle bosom,
Where innocence beams light and gayety,
Can never know a fear, now shining joy
Shall gild the pleasing scene.

EVANTHE. Alas! this joy
I fear is like a sudden flame shot from
Th' expiring taper, darkness will ensue,
And double night I dread enclose us round.
Anxiety does yet disturb my breast,
And frightful apprehension shakes my soul.

BETHAS. How shall I thank you, ye bright glorious beings!
Shall I in humble adoration bow,
Or fill the earth with your resounding praise?
No, this I leave to noisy hypocrites,
A Mortal's tongue disgraces such a theme;
But heav'n delights where silent gratitude
Mounts each aspiring thought to its bright throne,
Nor leaves to language aught; words may indeed
From man to man their sev'ral wants express,
Heav'n asks the purer incense of the heart.

ARSACES. I'll to the King, ere he retires to rest,
Nor will I leave him 'til I've gain'd your freedom;
His love will surely not deny me this.

SCENE 8.

VARDANES *and* LYSIAS (*come forward*).

LYSIAS. 'T was a moving scene, e'en my rough nature
Was nighly melted.

VARDANES. Hence coward pity—
What is joy to them, to me is torture.
Now am I rack'd with pains that far exceed
Those agonies, which fabling Priests relate,
The damn'd endure: The shock of hopeless Love,
Unblest with any views to sooth ambition,
Rob me of all my reas'ning faculties.
Arsaces gains *Evanthe,* fills the throne,
While I am doom'd to foul obscurity,
To pine and grieve neglected.

LYSIAS. My noble Prince,
Would it not be a master-piece, indeed,
To make this very bliss their greatest ill,
And damn them in the very folds of joy?

VARDANES. This I will try, and stretch my utmost art,
Unknown is yet the means— We'll think on that—
Success may follow if you'll lend your aid.

LYSIAS. The storm still rages— I must to the King,
And know what further orders ere he sleeps:
Soon I'll return, and speak my mind more fully.

VARDANES. Haste, *Lysias,* haste, to aid me with thy council;
For without thee, all my designs will prove
Like night and chaos, darkness and confusion;
But to thy word shall light and order spring.—
Let coward Schoolmen talk of Virtue's rules,
And preach the vain Philosophy of fools;
Court eager their obscurity, afraid
To taste a joy, and in some gloomy shade
Dream o'er their lives, while in a mournful strain
They sing of happiness they never gain.
But form'd for nobler purposes I come,
To gain a crown, or else a glorious tomb.

END OF THE SECOND ACT.

ACT THIRD.

SCENE 1. *The Palace.*

QUEEN *and* EDESSA.

QUEEN. Talk not of sleep to me, the God of Rest
Disdains to visit where disorder reigns;
Not beds of down, nor music's softest strains,
Can charm him when 't is anarchy within.
He flies with eager haste the mind disturb'd,
And sheds his blessings where the soul 's in peace.

EDESSA. Yet, hear me, Madam!

QUEEN. Hence, away, *Edessa,*
For thou know'st not the pangs of jealousy.
Say, has he not forsook my bed, and left me
Like a lone widow mourning to the night?
This, with the injury his son has done me,
If I forgive, may heav'n in anger show'r
Its torments on me— Ha! is n't that the King?

EDESSA. It is your Royal Lord, great *Artabanus.*

QUEEN. Leave me, for I would meet him here alone,
Something is lab'ring in my breast—

SCENE 2.

KING *and* QUEEN.

KING. This leads
To fair *Evanthe's* chamber— Ha! the Queen.

QUEEN. Why dost thou start? so starts the guilty wretch,
When, by some watchful eye, prevented from
His dark designs.

KING. Prevented! how, what mean'st thou?

QUEEN. Art thou then so dull? cannot thy heart,
Thy changeling heart, explain my meaning to thee,
Or must upbraiding 'wake thy apprehension?
Ah! faithless, tell me, have I lost those charms
Which thou so oft hast sworn could warm old age,
And tempt the frozen hermit from his cell,
To visit once again our gayer world?
This, thou hast sworn, perfidious as thou art,
A thousand times; as often hast thou sworn
Eternal constancy, and endless love,
Yet ev'ry time was perjur'd.

KING. Sure, 't is frenzy.

QUEEN. Indeed, 't is frenzy, 't is the height of madness,
For I have wander'd long in sweet delusion.
At length the pleasing Phantom chang'd its form,
And left me in a wilderness of woe.

KING. Prithee, no more, dismiss those jealous heats;
Love must decay, and soon disgust arise,
Where endless jarrings and upbraidings damp
The gentle flame, which warms the lover's breast.

QUEEN. Oh! grant me patience heav'n! and dost thou think
By these reproaches to disguise thy guilt?
No, 't is in vain, thy art 's too thin to hide it.

KING. Curse on the marriage chain!—the clog, a wife,
Who still will force and pall us with the joy,
Tho' pow'r is wanting, and the will is cloy'd,
Still urge the debt when Nothing 's left to pay.

QUEEN. Ha! dost thou own thy crime, nor feel the glow
Of conscious shame?

KING. Why should I blush, if heav'n
Has made me as I am, and gave me passions?
Blest only in variety, then blame
The Gods, who form'd my nature thus, not me.

QUEEN. Oh! Traitor! Villain!

KING. Hence—away—
No more I 'll wage a woman's war with words. (*Exit.*)

QUEEN. Down, down ye rising passions, give me ease,
Or break my heart, for I must yet be calm—
But, yet, revenge, our Sex's joy, is mine;
By all the Gods! he lives not till the morn.
Who slights my love, shall sink beneath my hate.

SCENE 3.

QUEEN *and* VARDANES.

VARDANES. What, raging to the tempest?

QUEEN. Away!—away!—
Yes, I will rage—a tempest 's here within,
Above the trifling of the noisy elements.
Blow[,] ye loud winds, burst with your violence,
For ye but barely imitate the storm
That wildly rages in my tortur'd breast—
The King—the King—

VARDANES. Ha! what?—the King?

QUEEN. *Evanthe!*—

VARDANES. You talk like riddles, still obscure and short,
Give me some cue to guide me thro' this maze.
QUEEN. Ye pitying pow'rs!—oh! for a poison, some
Curs'd deadly draught, that I might blast her beauties,
And rob her eyes of all their fatal lustre.
VARDANES. What, blast her charms?—dare not to think of it—
Shocking impiety;—the num'rous systems
Which gay creation spreads, bright blazing suns,
With all th' attendant planets circling round,
Are not worth half the radiance of her eyes.
She 's heav'n's peculiar care, good spir'ts hover
Round, a shining band, to guard her beauties.
QUEEN. Be they watchful then; for should remissness
Taint the guard, I 'll snatch the opportunity,
And hurl her to destruction.
VARDANES. Dread *Thermusa,*
Say, what has rous'd this tumult in thy soul?
Why dost thou rage with unabating fury,
Wild as the winds, loud as the troubl'd sea?
QUEEN. Yes, I will tell thee—*Evanthe*—curse her—
With charms— Would that my curses had the pow'r
To kill, destroy, and blast where e'er I hate,
Then would I curse, still curse, till death should seize
The dying accents on my falt'ring tongue,
So should this world, and the false changeling man
Be buried in one universal ruin.
VARDANES. Still err'st thou from the purpose.
QUEEN. Ha! 't is so—
Yes, I will tell thee—for I know[,] fond fool,
Deluded wretch, thou dotest on *Evanthe*—
Be that thy greatest curse, be curs'd like me,
With jealousy and rage, for know, the King,
Thy father, is thy rival.

SCENE 4.

VARDANES, *alone.*

Ha! my rival!
How knew she that?—yet stay—she 's gone—my rival,
What then? he is *Arsaces'* rival too.
Ha!—this may aid and ripen my designs—
Could I but fire the King with jealousy,
And then accuse my Brother of Intrigues
Against the state—ha!—join'd with *Bethas,* and
Confed'rate with th' Arabians—'t is most likely
That jealousy would urge him to belief.
I 'll sink my claim until some fitter time,
'Til opportunity smiles on my purpose.
Lysias already has receiv'd the mandate
For *Bethas'* freedom: Let them still proceed,
This harmony shall change to discord soon.
Fortune methinks of late grows wond'rous kind,
She scarcely leaves me to employ myself.

SCENE 5.

KING, ARSACES, VARDANES.

KING. But where 's *Evanthe?* Where 's the lovely Maid?
ARSACES. On the cold pavement, by her aged Sire,
The dear companion of his solitude,
She sits, nor can persuasion make her rise;
But in the wild extravagance of joy
She weeps, then smiles, like April's sun, thro' show'rs.
While with strain'd eyes he gazes on her face,
And cries, in ecstasy, "Ye gracious pow'rs!
"It is too much, it is too much to bear!"
Then clasps her to his breast, while down his cheeks
Large drops each other trace, and mix with hers.
KING. Thy tale is moving, for my eyes o'erflow—
How slow does *Lysias* with *Evanthe* creep!
So moves old time when bringing us to bliss.
Now war shall cease, no more of war I 'll have,

Death knows satiety, and pale destruction
Turns loathing from his food, thus forc'd on him.
The trifling dust, the cause of all this ruin,
The trade of death shall urge no more.—

SCENE 6.

KING, ARSACES, VARDANES, EVANTHE, LYSIAS.

KING. *Evanthe!*—
See pleasure's goddess deigns to dignify
The happy scene, and make our bliss complete.
So *Venus*, from her heav'nly seat, descends
To bless the gay *Cythera* with her presence;
A thousand smiling graces wait the goddess,
A thousand little loves are flutt'ring round,
And joy is mingl'd with the beauteous train.

EVANTHE. O! Royal Sir, thus lowly to the ground
I bend, in humble gratitude, accept
My thanks, for this thy goodness, words are vile
T' express the image of my lively thought,
And speak the grateful fulness of my heart.
All I can say, is that I now am happy,
And that thy giving hand has made me blest.

KING. O! rise, *Evanthe*, rise, this lowly posture
Suits not with charms like thine, they should command,
And ev'ry heart exult in thy behests;—
But, where 's thy aged Sire?

EVANTHE. This sudden turn
Of fortune has so wrought upon his frame,
His limbs could not support him to thy presence.

ARSACES. This, this is truly great, this is the Hero,
Like heav'n, to scatter blessings 'mong mankind,
And e'er delight in making others happy.
Cold is the praise which waits the victor's triumph,
(Who thro' a sea of blood has rush'd to glory),
To the o'erflowings of a grateful heart,
By obligations conquer'd: Yet, extend
Thy bounty unto me. (*Kneels.*)

KING. Ha! rise, *Arsaces.*

ARSACES. Not till you grant my boon.

KING. Speak, and 't is thine—
Wide thro' our kingdom let thy eager wishes
Search for some jewel worthy of thy seeing;
Something that 's fit to show the donor's bounty,
And by the glorious sun, our worship'd God,
Thou shalt not have denial; e'en my crown
Shall gild thy brows with shining beams of Empire.
With pleasure I 'll resign to thee my honours,
I long for calm retirement's softer joys.

ARSACES. Long may you wear it, grant it bounteous heav'n,
And happiness attend it; 't is my pray'r
That daily rises with the early sweets
Of nature's incense, and the lark's loud strain.
'T is not the unruly transport of ambition
That urges my desires to ask your crown;
Let the vain wretch, who prides in gay dominion,
Who thinks not of the great ones' weighty cares,
Enjoy his lofty wish, wide spreading rule.
The treasure which I ask, put in the scale,
Would over-balance all that Kings can boast,
Empire and diadems.

KING. Away, that thought—
Name it, haste—speak.

ARSACES. For all the dang'rous toil,
Thirst, hunger, marches long that I 've endur'd,
For all the blood I 've in thy service spent,
Reward me with *Evanthe.*

KING. Ha! what said'st thou?—

VARDANES. (*Aside.*) The King is mov'd, and angry bites his lip—
Thro' my benighted soul all-chearing hope
Beams, like an orient sun, reviving joy.

ARSACES. The stern *Vonones* ne'er could boast a merit

But loving her.
KING. Ah! curse the hated name—
Yes, I remember when the fell ruffian
Directed all his fury at my life;
Then sent, by pitying heav'n, t' assert the right
Of injur'd Majesty, thou, *Arsaces,*
Taught him the duty he ne'er knew before,
And laid the Traitor dead.
ARSACES. My Royal Sire!
LYSIAS. My Liege, the Prince still kneels.
KING. Ha!—rebel, off—
(*Strikes him.*)
What, *Lysias,* did I strike thee? forgive my rage—
The name of curs'd *Vonones* fires my blood,
And gives me up to wrath.—
LYSIAS. I am your slave,
Sway'd by your pleasure—when I forget it,
May this keen dagger, which I mean to hide,
Deep in his bosom, pierce my vitals thro'. (*Aside.*)
KING. Did'st thou not name *Evanthe?*
ARSACES. I did, my Lord!
And, say, whom should I name but her, in whom
My soul has center'd all her happiness?
Nor can'st thou blame me, view her wond'rous charms,
She 's all perfection; bounteous heav'n has form'd her
To be the joy, and wonder of mankind;
But language is too vile to speak her beauties.
Here ev'ry pow'r of glowing fancy 's lost:
Rose blush secure, ye lilies still enjoy
Your silver whiteness, I 'll not rob your charms
To deck the bright comparison; for here
It sure must fail.
KING. He 's wanton in her praise—
(*Aside.*)
I tell thee, Prince, hadst thou as many tongues,
As days have wasted since creation's birth,
They were too few to tell the mighty theme.
EVANTHE. I 'm lost! I 'm lost! (*Aside.*)
ARSACES. Then I 'll be dumb for ever.
KING. O rash and fatal oath! is there no way,
No winding path to shun this precipice,
But must I fall and dash my hopes to atoms?
In vain I strive, thought but perplexes me,
Yet shews no hold to bear me up—now, hold
My heart awhile—she 's thine—'t is done.
ARSACES. In deep
Prostration, I thank my Royal Father.
KING. A sudden pain shoots thro' my trembling breast—
Lend me thy arm, *Vardanes*—cruel pow'rs!

SCENE 7.

ARSACES *and* EVANTHE.

EVANTHE. (*After a pause.*) E'er since the dawn of my unhappy life
Joy never shone serenely on my soul;
Still something interven'd to cloud my day.
Tell me, ye pow'rs, unfold the hidden crime
For which I 'm doom'd to this eternal woe,
Thus still to number o'er my hours with tears?
The Gods are just, I know, nor are decrees
In hurry shuffl'd out, but where the bolt
Takes its direction justice points the mark.
Yet still in vain I search within my breast,
I find no sins are there to shudder at—
Nought but the common frailties of our natures.
Arsaces,—Oh!—
ARSACES. Ha! why that look of anguish?
Why didst thou name me with that sound of sorrow?
Ah! say, why stream those gushing tears so fast
From their bright fountain? Sparkling joy should now
Be lighten'd in thine eye, and pleasure glow
Upon thy rosy cheek;—ye sorrows hence—
'T is love shall triumph now.
EVANTHE. Oh! (*Sighs.*)
ARSACES. What means that sigh?
Tell me why heaves thy breast with such emotion?
Some dreadful thought is lab'ring for a vent,

Haste, give it loose, ere strengthen'd by confinement
It wrecks thy frame, and tears its snowy prison.
Is sorrow then so pleasing that you hoard it
With as much love, as misers do their gold?
Give me my share of sorrows.

EVANTHE. Ah! too soon
You 'll know what I would hide.

ARSACES. Be it from thee—
The dreadful tale, when told by thee, shall please;
Haste, to produce it with its native terrors,
My steady soul shall still remain unshaken;
For who when bless'd with beauties like to thine
Would e'er permit a sorrow to intrude?
Far hence in darksome shades does sorrow dwell,
Where hapless wretches thro' the awful gloom,
Echo their woes, and sighing to the winds,
Augment with tears the gently murm'ring stream;
But ne'er disturbs such happiness as mine.

EVANTHE. Oh! 't is not all thy boasted happiness,
Can save thee from disquietude and care;
Then build not too securely on these joys,
For envious sorrow soon will undermine,
And let the goodly structure fall to ruin.

ARSACES. I charge thee, by our mutual vows, *Evanthe,*
Tell me, nor longer keep me in suspense:
Give me to know the utmost rage of fate.

EVANTHE. Then know—impossible!—

ARSACES. Ha! dost thou fear
To shock me?—

EVANTHE. Know, thy Father—loves *Evanthe.*—

ARSACES. Loves thee?

EVANTHE. Yea, e'en to distraction loves me.
Oft at my feet he 's told the moving tale,
And woo'd me with the ardency of youth.
I pitied him indeed, but that was all,
Thou would'st have pitied too.

ARSACES. I fear 't is true;
A thousand crouding circumstances speak it.
Ye cruel Gods! I 've wreck'd a Father's peace,
Oh! bitter thought!

EVANTHE. Didst thou observe, *Arsaces,*
How reluctant he gave me to thy arms?

ARSACES. Yes, I observ'd that when he gave thee up,
It seem'd as tho' he gave his precious life,
And who 'd forego the heav'n of thy love?
To rest on thy soft swelling breast, and in
Sweet slumbers sooth each sharp intruding care?
Oh! it were bliss, such as immortals taste,
To press thy ruby lips distilling sweets,
Or circl'd in thy snowy arms to snatch
A joy, that Gods—

EVANTHE. Come, then, my much-lov'd Prince,
Let 's seek the shelter of some kind retreat.
Happy Arabia opens wide her arms,
There may we find some friendly solitude,
Far from the noise and hurry of the Court.
Ambitious views shall never blast our joys,
Or tyrant Fathers triumph o'er our wills:
There may we live like the first happy pair
Cloth'd in primeval innocence secure.
Our food untainted by luxurious arts,
Plain, simple, as our lives, shall not destroy
The health it should sustain; while the clear brook
Affords the cooling draught our thirsts to quench.
There, hand in hand, we 'll trace the citron grove,
While with the songsters' round I join my voice,
To hush thy cares and calm thy ruffl'd soul:
Or, on some flow'ry bank reclin'd, my strains
Shall captivate the natives of the stream,
While on its crystal lap ourselves we view.

ARSACES. I see before us a wide sea of sorrows,
Th' angry waves roll forward to o'erwhelm us,
Black clouds arise, and the wind whistles loud.
But yet, oh! could I save thee from the wreck,
Thou beauteous casket, where my joys are stor'd,

Let the storm rage with double violence,
Smiling I 'd view its wide extended horrors.

EVANTHE. 'T is not enough that we do know the ill,
Say, shall we calmly see the tempest rise,
And seek no shelter from th' inclement sky,
But bid it rage?—

ARSACES. Ha! will he force thee from me?
What, tear thee from my fond and bleeding heart?
And must I lose thee ever? dreadful word!
Never to gaze upon thy beauties more?
Never to taste the sweetness of thy lips?
Never to know the joys of mutual love?
Never!—Oh! let me lose the pow'r of thinking,
For thought is near allied to desperation.
Why, cruel Sire—why did you give me life,
And load it with a weight of wretchedness?
Take back my being, or relieve my sorrows—
Ha! art thou not *Evanthe?*— Art thou not
The lovely Maid, who bless'd the fond *Arsaces?*— (*Raving.*)

EVANTHE. O, my lov'd Lord, recall your scatter'd spir'ts,
Alas! I fear your senses are unsettl'd.

ARSACES. Yes, I would leave this dull and heavy sense.
Let me grow mad; perhaps, I then may gain
Some joy, by kind imagination form'd,
Beyond reality.— O! my *Evanthe!*
Why was I curs'd with empire? born to rule?—
Would I had been some humble Peasant's son,
And thou some Shepherd's daughter on the plain;
My throne some hillock, and my flock my subjects,
My crook my sceptre, and my faithful dog
My only guard; nor curs'd with dreams of greatness.
At early dawn I 'd hail the coming day,
And join the lark the rival of his lay;
At sultry noon to some kind shade repair,
Thus joyful pass the hours, my only care,
To guard my flock, and please the yielding Fair.

SCENE 8.

KING.—VARDANES, *behind the Scene.*

KING. I will not think, to think is torment— Ha !
See, how they twine! ye furies cut their hold.
Now their hot blood beats loud to love's alarms;
Sigh presses sigh, while from their sparkling eyes
Flashes desire— Oh! ye bright heav'nly beings,
Who pitying bend to suppliant Lovers' pray'rs,
And aid them in extremity, assist me!

VARDANES. Thus for the Trojan, mourn'd the Queen of Carthage;
So, on the shore she raving stood, and saw
His navy leave her hospitable shore.
In vain she curs'd the wind which fill'd their sails,
And bore the emblem of its change away.
(*Comes forward.*)

KING. *Vardanes*—ha!—come here, I know thou lov'st me.

VARDANES. I do[,] my Lord; but, say, what busy villain
Durst e'er approach your ear, with coz'ning tales,
And urge you to a doubt?

KING. None, none[,] believe me.
I 'll ne'er oppress thy love with fearful doubt—
A little nigher—let me lean upon thee—
And thou be my support—for now I mean
T' unbosom to thee free without restraint:
Search all the deep recesses of my soul,
And open ev'ry darling thought before thee,
Which long I 've secreted with jealous care.
Pray, mark me well.

VARDANES. I will, my Royal Sire.

KING. On *Anna* thus reclin'd the love-sick Dido;
Thus to her cheek laid hers with gentle pressure,
And wet her sister with a pearly show'r,
Which fell from her sad eyes, then told her tale,
While gentle *Anna* gave a pitying tear,
And own'd 't was moving—thou canst pity too,

I know thy nature tender and engaging.
VARDANES. Tell me, my gracious Lord, what moves you thus?
Why is your breast distracted with these tumults?
Teach me some method how to sooth your sorrows,
And give your heart its former peace and joy;
Instruct, thy lov'd, *Vardanes.*—
KING. Yes, I 'll tell thee;
But listen with attention while I speak;
And yet I know 't will shock thy gentle soul,
And horror o'er thee 'll spread his palsy hand.
O, my lov'd Son! thou fondness of my age!
Thou art the prop of my declining years,
In thee alone I find a Father's joy,
Of all my offspring: But *Arsaces*—
VARDANES. Ha!
My Brother!—
KING. Ay—why dost start?—thy Brother
Pursues me with his hate: and, while warm life
Rolls the red current thro' my veins, delights
To see me tortur'd; with an easy smile
He meets my suff'rings, and derides my pain.
VARDANES. Oh!
KING. What means that hollow groan?—*Vardanes,* speak,
Death's image sits upon thy pallid cheek,
While thy low voice sounds as when murmurs run
Thro' lengthen'd vaults—
VARDANES. O! my foreboding thoughts, (*Aside.*)
'T was this disturb'd my rest; when sleep at night
Lock'd me in slumbers; in my dreams I saw
My Brother's crime—yet, death!—it cannot be—
KING. Ha!—what was that?—
VARDANES. O! my dread Lord, some Villain
Bred up in lies, and train'd in treach'ry,
Has injur'd you by vile reports, to stain
My Princely Brother's honour.
KING. Thou know'st more,
Thy looks confess what thou in vain wouldst hide—
And hast thou then conspir'd against me too,
And sworn concealment to your practices?—
Thy guilt—
VARDANES. Ha! guilt!—what guilt?—
KING. Nay, start not so—
I' ll know your purposes, spite of thy art.
VARDANES. O! ye Great Gods! and is it come to this?—
My Royal Father[,] call your reason home,
Drive these loud passions hence, that thus deform you.
My Brother— Ah! what shall I say?—My Brother
Sure loves you as he ought.
KING. Ha! as he ought?—
Hell blister thy evasive tongue—I 'll know it—
I will; I 'll search thy breast, thus will I open
A passage to your secrets—yet resolv'd—
Yet steady in your horrid villany—
'T is fit that I from whom such monsters sprung
No more should burthen earth— Ye Parricides!—
Here plant your daggers in this hated bosom—
Here rive my heart, and end at once my sorrows,
I gave thee being, that 's the mighty crime.
VARDANES. I can no more—here let me bow in anguish—
Think not that I e'er join'd in his designs.
Because I have conceal'd my knowledge of them;
I meant, by pow'rful reason's friendly aid,
To turn him from destruction's dreadful path,
And bring him to a sense of what he ow'd
To you as King and Father.
KING. Say on—I 'll hear.
VARDANES. He views thy sacred life with envious hate,
And 't is a bar to his ambitious hopes.
On the bright throne of Empire his plum'd wishes
Seat him, while on his proud aspiring brows
He feels the pleasing weight of Royalty.
But when he wakes from these his airy dreams,
(Delusions form'd by the deceiver hope,
To raise him to the glorious height of greatness)
Then hurl him from proud Empire to subjection.

Wild wrath will quickly swell his haughty breast,
Soon as he finds 't is but a shadowy blessing.—
'T was fav'ring accident discover'd to me
All that I know; this Evening as I stood
Alone, retir'd, in the still gallery,
That leads up to th' apartment of my Brother,
T' indulge my melancholy thoughts,—
KING. Proceed—
VARDANES. A wretch approach'd with wary step, his eye
Spoke half his tale, denoting villany.
In hollow murmurs thus he question'd me.
Was I the Prince?— I answer'd to content him—
Then in his hand he held this paper forth.
"Take this," says he, "this *Bethas* greets thee with,
"Keep but your word our plot will meet success."
I snatch'd it with more rashness than discretion,
Which taught him his mistake. In haste he drew,
And aim'd his dagger at my breast, but paid
His life, a forfeit, for his bold presuming.
KING. O Villain! Villain!
VARDANES. Here, read this, my Lord—
I read it, and cold horror froze my blood,
And shook me like an ague.
KING. Ha!—what 's this?—
"Doubt not Arabia's aid, set me but free,
"I'll easy pass on the old cred'lous King,
"For fair *Evanthe's* Father."— Thus to atoms—
(*Tears the paper into pieces.*)
Oh! could I tear these cursed traitors thus.
VARDANES. Curses avail you nothing, he has pow'r,
And may abuse it to your prejudice.
KING. I am resolv'd—
VARDANES. Tho' Pris'ner in his camp,
Yet, *Bethas* was attended like a Prince,
As tho' he still commanded the Arabians.
'T is true, when they approach'd the royal city,
He threw them into chains to blind our eyes,
A shallow artifice—
KING. That is a Truth.
VARDANES. And, yet, he is your Son.
KING. Ah! that indeed—
VARDANES. Why that still heightens his impiety,
To rush to empire thro' his Father's blood,
And, in return of life, to give him death.
KING. Oh! I am all on fire, yes, I must tear
These folds of venom from me.
VARDANES. Sure 't was *Lysias*
That cross'd the passage now.
KING. 'T is to my wish.
I 'll in, and give him orders to arrest
My traitor Son and *Bethas*.— Now, *Vardanes,*
Indulge thy Father in this one request—
Seize, with some horse, *Evanthe,* and bear her
To your command— Oh! I'll own my weakness—
I love with fondness mortal never knew—
Not Jove himself, when he forsook his heav'n,
And in a brutal shape disgrac'd the God,
E'er lov'd like me.
VARDANES. I will obey you, Sir.

SCENE 9.

VARDANES, *alone.*

I 'll seize her, but I 'll keep her for myself,
It were a sin to give her to his age—
To twine the blooming garland of the spring
Around the sapless trunks of wither'd oaks—
The night, methinks, grows ruder than it was,
Thus should it be, thus nature should be shock'd,
And Prodigies, affrighting all mankind,
Foretell the dreadful business I intend.
The earth should gape, and swallow cities up,
Shake from their haughty heights aspiring tow'rs,
And level mountains with the vales below;
The Sun amaz'd should frown in dark eclipse,
And light retire to its unclouded heav'n;
While darkness, bursting from her deep recess,
Should wrap all nature in eternal night.—
Ambition, glorious fever of the mind,
'T is that which raises us above mankind;
The shining mark which bounteous heav'n has gave,
From vulgar souls distinguishing the brave.

END OF THE THIRD ACT.

ACT FOURTH.

SCENE 1. *A Prison.*

GOTARZES *and* PHRAATES.

PHRAATES. Oh! fly my Prince, for safety dwells not here,
Hence let me urge thy flight with eager haste.
Last night thy Father sigh'd his soul to bliss,
Base murther'd—
GOTARZES. Murther'd? ye Gods!—
PHRAATES. Alas! 't is true.
Stabb'd in his slumber by a traitor's hand;
I scarce can speak it—horror choaks my words—
Lysias it was who did the damned deed,
Urg'd by the bloody Queen, and his curs'd rage,
Because the King, thy Sire, in angry mood,
Once struck him on his foul dishonest cheek.
Suspicion gave me fears of this, when first
I heard, the Prince, *Arsaces,* was imprison'd,
By fell *Vardanes'* wiles.
GOTARZES. Oh! horror! horror!
Hither I came to share my Brother's sorrows,
To mingle tears, and give him sigh for sigh;
But this is double, double weight of woe.
PHRAATES. 'T is held as yet a secret from the world.
Frighted by hideous dreams I shook off sleep,
And as I mus'd the garden walks along,
Thro' the deep gloom, close in a neighb'ring walk,
Vardanes with proud *Lysias* I beheld,
Still eager in discourse they saw not me,
For yet the early dawn had not appear'd;
I sought a secret stand, where hid from view,
I heard stern *Lysias,* hail the Prince *Vardanes*
As Parthia's dreaded Lord— "'T is done," he cry'd,
"'T is done, and *Artabanus* is no more.
"The blow he gave me is repay'd in blood;
"Now shall the morn behold two rising suns:
"*Vardanes,* thou, our better light, shalt bring
"Bright day and joy to ev'ry heart."
GOTARZES. Why slept
Your vengeance, oh! ye righteous Gods?
PHRAATES. Then told
A tale, so fill'd with bloody circumstance,
Of this damn'd deed, that stiffen'd me with horror.
Vardanes seem'd to blame the hasty act,
As rash, and unadvis'd, by passion urg'd,
Which never yields to cool reflection's place.
But, being done, resolv'd it secret, least
The multitude should take it in their wise
Authority to pry into his death.
Arsaces was, by assassination,
Doom'd to fall. Your name was mention'd also—
But hurried by my fears away, I left
The rest unheard—
GOTARZES. What can be done?— Reflection, why wilt thou
Forsake us, when distress is at our heels?
Phraates, help me, aid me with thy council.
PHRAATES. Then stay not here, fly to *Barzaphernes,*
His conqu'ring troops are at a trivial distance;
Soon will you reach the camp; he lov'd your Brother,
And your Father with affection serv'd; haste
Your flight, whilst yet I have the city-guard,
For *Lysias,* I expect, takes my command.
I to the camp dispatch'd a trusty slave,
Before the morn had spread her blushing veil.
Away, you'll meet the Gen'ral on the road,
On such a cause as this he'll not delay.
GOTARZES. I thank your love—

SCENE 2.

PHRAATES, *alone.*

I'll wait behind, my stay
May aid the cause; dissembling I must learn,
Necessity shall teach me how to vary
My features to the looks of him I serve.
I'll thrust myself disguis'd among the croud.

And fill their ears with murmurs of the deed:
Whisper all is not well, blow up the sparks
Of discord, and it soon will flame to rage.

SCENE 3.

QUEEN *and* LYSIAS.

QUEEN. Haste, and show me to the Prince *Arsaces,*
Delay not, see the signet of *Vardanes.*
LYSIAS. Royal *Thermusa,* why this eagerness?
This tumult of the soul?—what means this dagger?
Ha!— I suspect—
QUEEN. Hold—for I 'll tell thee, *Lysias.*
'T is—oh! I scarce can speak the mighty joy—
I shall be greatly blest in dear revenge,
'T is vengeance on *Arsaces*—yes, this hand
Shall urge the shining poniard to his heart,
And give him death—yea, give the ruffian death;
So shall I smile on his keen agonies.
LYSIAS. Ha! I am robb'd of all my hopes of vengeance,
Shall I then calmly stand with all my wrongs,
And see another bear away revenge?
QUEEN. For what can *Lysias* ask revenge, to bar
His Queen of hers?
LYSIAS. Was I not scorn'd, and spurn'd,
With haughty insolence? Like a base coward
Refus'd whate'er I ask'd, and call'd a boaster?
My honour sullied, with opprobrious words,
Which can no more its former brightness know,
'Til, with his blood, I 've wash'd the stains away.
Say, shall I then not seek for glorious vengeance?
QUEEN. And what is this, to the sad Mother's griefs,
Her hope cut off, rais'd up with pain and care?
Hadst thou e'er supported the lov'd Prattler?
Hadst thou, like me, hung o'er his infancy,
Wasting in wakeful mood the tedious night,
And watch'd his sickly couch, far mov'd from rest,
Waiting his health's return?—Ah! hadst thou known
The parent's fondness, rapture, toil and sorrow,
The joy his actions gave, and the fond wish
Of something yet to come, to bless my age,
And lead me down with pleasure to the grave,
Thou wouldst not thus talk lightly of my wrongs.
But I delay—
LYSIAS. To thee I then submit.
Be sure to wreck [1] a double vengeance on him;
If that thou knowest a part in all his body,
Where pain can most be felt, strike, strike him there—
And let him know the utmost height of anguish.
It is a joy to think that he shall fall,
Tho' 't is another hand which gives the blow.

SCENE 4

ARSACES *and* BETHAS.

ARSACES. Why should I linger out my joyless days,
When length of hope is length of misery?
Hope is a coz'ner, and beguiles our cares,
Cheats us with empty shews of happiness,
Swift fleeting joys which mock the faint embrace;
We wade thro' ills pursuing of the meteor,
Yet are distanc'd still.
BETHAS. Ah! talk not of hope—
Hope fled when bright *Astræa* spurn'd this earth,
And sought her seat among the shining Gods;
Despair, proud tyrant, ravages my breast,
And makes all desolation.
ARSACES. How can I
Behold those rev'rent sorrows, see those cheeks
Moist with the dew which falls from thy sad eyes,

[1] Wreak.

Nor imitate distraction's frantic tricks,
And chace cold lifeless reason from her throne?
I am the fatal cause of all this sorrow,
The spring of ills,—to know me is unhappiness;—
And mis'ry, like a hateful plague, pursues
My wearied steps, and blasts the springing verdure.

BETHAS. No;—It is I that am the source of all,
It is my fortune sinks you to this trouble;
Before you shower'd your gentle pity on me,
You shone the pride of this admiring world.—
Evanthe springs from me, whose fatal charms
Produces all this ruin.—Hear me heav'n!
If to another love she ever yields,
And stains her soul with spotted falsehood's crime,
If e'en in expectation tastes a bliss,
Nor joins *Arsaces* with it, I will wreck
My vengeance on her, so that she shall be
A dread example to all future times.

ARSACES. Oh! curse her not, nor threaten her with anger,
She is all gentleness, yet firm to truth,
And blest with ev'ry pleasing virtue, free
From levity, her sexes[1] character.
She scorns to chace the turning of the wind;
Varying from point to point.

BETHAS. I love her, ye Gods!
I need not speak the greatness of my love,
Each look which straining draws my soul to hers
Denotes unmeasur'd fondness; but mis'ry,
Like a fretful peevish child, can scarce tell
What it would wish, or aim at.

ARSACES. Immortals, hear!
Thus do I bow my soul in humble pray'r—
Thou, King of beings, in whose breath is fate,
Show'r on *Evanthe* all thy choicest blessings,
And bless her with excess of happiness;
If yet, there is one bliss reserv'd in store,
And written to my name, oh! give it her,
And give me all her sorrows in return.

BETHAS. 'Rise, 'rise my Prince, this goodness o'erwhelms me,

[1] Sex's.

She 's too unworthy of so great a passion.

ARSACES. I know not what it means, I 'm not as usual,
Ill-boding cares, and restless fears oppress me,
And horrid dreams disturb, and fright, my slumbers;
But yesternight, 't is dreadful to relate,
E'en now I tremble at my waking thoughts,
Methought, I stood alone upon the shore,
And, at my feet, there roll'd a sea of blood,
High wrought, and 'midst the waves, appear'd my Father,
Struggling for life; above him was *Vardanes,*
Pois'd in the air, he seem'd to rule the storm,
And, now and then, would push my Father down,
And for a space he 'd sink beneath the waves,
And then, all gory, rise to open view,
His voice in broken accents reach'd my ear,
And bade me save him from the bloody stream;
Thro' the red billows eagerly I rush'd,
But sudden woke, benum'd with chilling fear.

BETHAS. Most horrible indeed!—but let it pass,
'T is but the offspring of a mind disturb'd,
For sorrow leaves impressions on the fancy,
Which shew most fearful to us lock'd in sleep.

ARSACES. *Thermusa!* ha!—what can be her design?
She bears this way, and carries in her looks
An eagerness importing violence.
Retire—for I would meet her rage alone.

SCENE 5.

ARSACES *and* QUEEN.

ARSACES. What means the proud *Thermusa* by this visit,
Stoops heav'n-born pity to a breast like thine?
Pity adorns th' virtuous, but n'er dwells
Where hate, revenge, and rage distract the soul.

Sure, it is hate that hither urg'd thy steps,
To view misfortune with an eye of triumph.
I know thou lov'st me not, for I have dar'd
To cross thy purposes, and, bold in censure,
Spoke of thy actions as they merited.
Besides, this hand 't was slew the curs'd *Vonones.*

QUEEN. And darst thou[,] insolent[,] to name *Vonones?*
To heap perdition on thy guilty soul?
There needs not this to urge me to revenge—
But let me view this wonder of mankind,
Whose breath can set the bustling world in arms.
I see no dreadful terrors in his eye,
Nor gathers chilly fears around my heart,
Nor strains my gazing eye with admiration,
And, tho' a woman, I can strike the blow.

ARSACES. Why gaze you on me thus? why hesitate?
Am I to die?

QUEEN. Thou art—this dagger shall
Dissolve thy life, thy fleeting ghost I'll send
To wait *Vonones* in the shades below.

ARSACES. And even there I'll triumph over him.

QUEEN. O, thou vile homicide! thy fatal hand
Has robb'd me of all joy; *Vonones,* to
Thy *Manes* [1] this proud sacrifice I give.
That hand which sever'd the friendship of thy
Soul and body, shall never draw again
Imbitt'ring tears from sorr'wing mother's eyes.
This, with the many tears I've shed, receive— (*Offers to stab him.*)
Ha!—I'd strike; what holds my hand? 't is n't pity.

ARSACES. Nay, do not mock me, with the shew of death,
And yet deny the blessing; I have met
Your taunts with equal taunts, in hopes to urge
The blow with swift revenge; but since that fails,
I'll woo thee to compliance, teach my tongue
Persuasion's winning arts, to gain thy soul;

1 Shades.

I'll praise thy clemency, in dying accents
Bless thee for this, thy charitable deed.
Oh! do not stand; see, how my bosom heaves
To meet the stroke; in pity let me die,
'T is all the happiness I now can know.

QUEEN. How sweet the eloquence of dying men!
Hence Poets feign'd the music of the Swan,
When death upon her lays his icy hand,
She melts away in melancholy strains.

ARSACES. Play not thus cruel with my poor request,
But take my loving Father's thanks, and mine.

QUEEN. Thy Father cannot thank me now.

ARSACES. He will,
Believe me, e'en whilst dissolv'd in ecstacy
On fond *Evanthe's* bosom, he will pause,
One moment from his joys, to bless the deed.

QUEEN. What means this tumult in my breast? from whence
Proceeds this sudden change? my heart beats high,
And soft compassion makes me less than woman:
I'll search no more for what I fear to know.

ARSACES. Why drops the dagger from thy trembling hand?
Oh! yet be kind—

QUEEN. No: now I'd have thee live,
Since it is happiness to die: 'T is pain
That I would give thee, thus I bid thee live;
Yes, I would have thee a whole age a dying,
And smile to see thy ling'ring agonies.
All day I'd watch thee, mark each heighten'd pang,
While springing joy should swell my panting bosom;
This I would have— But should this dagger give
Thy soul the liberty it fondly wishes,
'T would soar aloft, and mock my faint revenge.

ARSACES. This mildness shews most foul, thy anger lovely.
Think that 't was I who blasted thy fond hope,
Vonones now lies number'd with the dead,
And all your joys are buried in his grave;
My hand untimely pluck'd the precious flow'r,

Before its shining beauties were display'd.

QUEEN. O Woman! Woman! where 's thy resolution?
Where 's thy revenge? Where 's all thy hopes of vengeance?
Giv'n to the winds— Ha! is it pity?—No—
I fear it wears another softer name.
I'll think no more, but rush to my revenge,
In spite of foolish fear, or woman's softness;
Be steady now my soul to thy resolves.
Yes, thou shalt die, thus, on thy breast, I write
Thy instant doom—ha!—ye Gods!
(*Queen starts, as in great fright, at hearing something.*)

ARSACES. Why this pause?
Why dost thou idly stand like imag'd vengeance,
With harmless terrors threatning on thy brow,
With lifted arm, yet canst not strike the blow?

QUEEN. It surely was the Echo to my fears,
The whistling wind, perhaps, which mimick'd voice;
But thrice methought it loudly cry'd, "forbear."
Imagination hence—I 'll heed thee not—
(*Ghost of Artabanus rises.*)
Save me—oh!—save me—ye eternal pow'rs!—
See!—see it comes, surrounded with dread terrors—
Hence—hence! nor blast me with that horrid sight—
Throw off that shape, and search th' infernal rounds
For horrid forms, there 's none can shock like thine.

GHOST. No; I will ever wear this form, thus e'er
Appear before thee; glare upon thee thus,
'Til desperation, join'd to thy damn'd crime,
Shall wind thee to the utmost height of frenzy.
In vain you grasp the dagger in your hand,
In vain you dress your brows in angry frowns,
In vain you raise your threatning arm in air,
Secure, *Arsaces* triumphs o'er your rage.
Guarded by fate, from thy accurs'd revenge,
Thou canst not touch his life; the Gods have giv'n
A softness to thy more than savage soul
Before unknown, to aid their grand designs.
Fate yet is lab'ring with some great event,
But what must follow I 'm forbid to broach—
Think, think of me, I sink to rise again,
To play in blood before thy aking sight,
And shock thy guilty soul with hell-born horrors—
Think, think of *Artabanus!* and despair—
(*Sinks.*)

QUEEN. Think of thee, and despair?—yes, I 'll despair—
Yet stay,—oh! stay, thou messenger of fate!
Tell me— Ha! 't is gone— and left me wretched—

ARSACES. Your eyes seem fix'd upon some dreadful object,
Horror and anguish cloath your whiten'd face,
And your frame shakes with terror; I hear you speak
As seeming earnest in discourse, yet hear
No second voice.

QUEEN. What! saw'st thou nothing?

ARSACES. Nothing.

QUEEN. Nor hear'd?—

ARSACES. Nor hear'd.

QUEEN. Amazing spectacle!—
Cold moist'ning dews distil from ev'ry pore,
I tremble like to palsied age— Ye Gods!
Would I could leave this loath'd detested being!—
Oh! all my brain 's on fire— I rave! I rave!— (*Ghost rises again.*)
Ha! it comes again—see, it glides along—
See, see, what streams of blood flow from its wounds!
A crimson torrent— Shield me, oh! shield me, heav'n.—

ARSACES. Great, and righteous Gods!—

QUEEN. Ah! frown not on me—
Why dost thou shake thy horrid locks at me?
Can I give immortality?—'t is gone—
(*Ghost sinks.*)
It flies me, see, ah!—stop it, stop it, haste—

ARSACES. Oh, piteous sight!—

QUEEN. Hist! prithee hist!—oh death!
I 'm all on fire—now freezing bolts of ice

Dart thro' my breast— Oh! burst ye cords of life—
Ha! who are ye?— Why do ye stare upon me?—
Oh!—defend me, from these bick'ring Furies!

ARSACES. Alas! her sense is lost, distressful Queen!

QUEEN. Help me, thou King of Gods! oh! help me! help!
See! they envir'n me round—*Vonones* too,
The foremost leading on the dreadful troop—
But there, *Vardanes* beck'ns me to shun
Their hellish rage—I come, I come!
Ah! they pursue me, with a scourge of fire.— (*Runs out distracted.*)

SCENE 6.

ARSACES, *alone.*

Oh!—horror!—on the ground she breathless lies,
Silent, in death's cold sleep; the wall besmear'd
With brains and gore the marks of her despair.
O guilt! how dreadful dost thou ever shew!
How lovely are the charms of innocence!
How beauteous tho' in sorrows and distress!—
Ha!—what noise?—
(*Clashing of swords.*)

SCENE 7.

ARSACES, BARZAPHERNES *and* GOTARZES.

BARZAPHERNES. At length we've forc'd our entrance—
O my lov'd Prince! to see thee thus, indeed,
Melts e'en me to a woman's softness; see
My eyes o'erflow— Are these the ornaments
For Royal hands? rude manacles! oh shameful!
Is this thy room of state, this gloomy gaol?
Without attendance, and thy bed the pavement?
But, ah! how diff'rent was our parting last!
When flush'd with vict'ry, reeking from the slaughter,
You saw Arabia's Sons scour o'er the plain
In shameful flight, before your conqu'ring sword;
Then shone you like the God of battle.

ARSACES. Welcome!—
Welcome, my loyal friends! *Barzaphernes!*
My good old soldier, to my bosom thus!
Gotarzes, my lov'd Brother! now I'm happy.—
But, say, my soldier, why these threatning arms?
Why am I thus releas'd by force? my Father,
I should have said the King, had he relented,
He'd not have us'd this method to enlarge [1] me.
Alas! I fear, too forward in your love,
You'll brand me with the rebel's hated name.

BARZAPHERNES. I am by nature blunt—the soldier's manner.
Unus'd to the soft arts practis'd at courts.
Nor can I move the passions, or disguise
The sorr'wing tale to mitigate the smart.
Then seek it not: I would sound the alarm,
Loud as the trumpet's clangour, in your ears;
Nor will I hail you, as our Parthia's King,
'Till you've full reveng'd your Father's murther.

ARSACES. Murther?—good heav'n!

BARZAPHERNES. The tale requires some time;
And opportunity must not be lost;
Your traitor Brother, who usurps your rights,
Must, 'ere his faction gathers to a head,
Have from his brows his new-born honours torn.

ARSACES. What, dost thou say, murther'd by *Vardanes?*
Impious parricide!—detested villain!—
Give me a sword, and onward to the charge,
Stop gushing tears, for I will weep in blood,
And sorrow with the groans of dying men.—
Revenge! revenge!—oh!—all my soul's on fire!

[1] Free.

GOTARZES. 'T was not *Vardanes* struck the fatal blow,
Though, great in pow'r usurp'd, he dares support
The actor, vengeful *Lysias;* to his breast
He clasps, with grateful joy, the bloody villain;
Who soon meant, with ruffian wiles, to cut
You from the earth, and also me.

ARSACES. Just heav'ns!—
But, gentle Brother, how didst thou elude
The vigilant, suspicious, tyrant's craft[?]

GOTARZES. *Phraates,* by an accident, obtain'd
The knowledge of the deed, and warn'd by him
I bent my flight toward the camp, to seek
Protection and revenge; but scarce I 'd left
The city when I o'ertook the Gen'ral.

BARZAPHERNES. 'Ere the sun 'rose I gain'd th' intelligence:
The soldiers when they heard the dreadful tale,
First stood aghast, and motionless with horror.
Then suddenly, inspir'd with noble rage,
Tore up their ensigns, calling on their leaders
To march them to the city instantly.
I, with some trusty few, with speed came forward,
To raise our friends within, and gain your freedom.
Nor hazard longer, by delays, your safety.
Already faithful *Phraates* has gain'd
A num'rous party of the citizens;
With these we mean t' attack the Royal Palace,
Crush the bold tyrant with surprize, while sunk
In false security; and vengeance wreck,
'Ere that he thinks the impious crime be known.

ARSACES. O! parent being, Ruler of yon heav'n!
Who bade creation spring to order, hear me.
What ever sins are laid upon my soul,
Now let them not prove heavy on this day,
To sink my arm, or violate my cause.
The sacred rights of Kings, my Country's wrongs,
The punishment of fierce impiety,
And a lov'd Father's death, call forth my sword.—

Now on; I feel all calm within my breast,
And ev'ry busy doubt is hush'd to rest;
Smile heav'n propitious on my virtuous cause,
Nor aid the wretch who dares disdain your laws.

END OF THE FOURTH ACT.

ACT FIFTH.

SCENE 1. *The Palace. The curtain rises, slowly, to soft music, and discovers* EVANTHE *sleeping on a sofa; after the music ceases,* VARDANES *enters.*

VARDANES. Now shining Empire standing at the goal,
Beck'ns me forward to increase my speed;
But, yet, *Arsaces* lives, bane to my hopes,
Lysias I 'll urge to ease me of his life,
Then give the villain up to punishment.
The shew of justice gains the changeling croud.
Besides, I ne'er will harbour in my bosom
Such serpents, ever ready with their stings—
But now one hour for love and fair *Evanthe*—
Hence with ambition's cares—see, where reclin'd,
In slumbers all her sorrows are dismiss'd,
Sleep seems to heighten ev'ry beauteous feature,
And adds peculiar softness to each grace.
She weeps—in dreams some lively sorrow pains her—
I 'll take one kiss—oh! what a balmy sweetness!
Give me another—and another still—
For ever thus I 'd dwell upon her lips.
Be still my heart, and calm unruly transports.—
Wake her, with music, from this mimic death. (*Music sounds.*)

Song.

Tell me, Phillis, tell me why,
You appear so wond'rous coy,
When that glow, and sparkling eye,
Speak you want to taste the joy?
Prithee give this fooling o'er,
Nor torment your lover more.

While youth is warm within our veins,
And nature tempts us to be gay,
Give to pleasure loose the reins,
Love and youth fly swift away.
Youth in pleasure should be spent,
Age will come, we 'll then repent.

EVANTHE. (*Waking.*) I come ye lovely shades—Ha! am I here?
Still in the tyrant's palace? Ye bright pow'rs!
Are all my blessings then but vis'onary?
Methought I was arriv'd on that blest shore
Where happy souls for ever dwell, crown'd with
Immortal bliss; *Arsaces* led me through
The flow'ry groves, while all around me gleam'd
Thousand and thousand shades, who welcom'd me
With pleasing songs of joy—*Vardanes*, ha!—

VARDANES. Why beams the angry lightning of thine eye
Against thy sighing slave? Is love a crime?
Oh! if to dote, with such excess of passion
As rises e'en to mad extravagance
Is criminal, I then am so, indeed.

EVANTHE. Away! vile man!—

VARDANES. If to pursue thee e'er
With all the humblest offices of love,
If ne'er to know one single thought that does
Not bear thy bright idea, merits scorn—

EVANTHE. Hence from my sight—nor let me, thus, pollute
Mine eyes, with looking on a wretch like thee,
Thou cause of all my ills; I sicken at
Thy loathsome presence—

VARDANES. 'T is not always thus,
Nor dost thou ever meet the sounds of love
With rage and fierce disdain: *Arsaces*, soon,
Could smooth thy brow, and melt thy icy breast.

EVANTHE. Ha! does it gall thee? Yes, he could, he could;
Oh! when he speaks, such sweetness dwells upon
His accents, all my soul dissolves to love,
And warm desire; such truth and beauty join'd!
His looks are soft and kind, such gentleness
Such virtue swells his bosom! in his eye
Sits majesty, commanding ev'ry heart.
Strait as the pine, the pride of all the grove,
More blooming than the spring, and sweeter far,
Than asphodels or roses infant sweets.
Oh! I could dwell forever on his praise,
Yet think eternity was scarce enough
To tell the mighty theme; here in my breast
His image dwells, but one dear thought of him,
When fancy paints his Person to my eye,
As he was wont in tenderness dissolv'd,
Sighing his vows, or kneeling at my feet,
Wipes off all mem'ry of my wretchedness.

VARDANES. I know this brav'ry is affected, yet
It gives me joy, to think my rival only
Can in imagination taste thy beauties.
Let him,—'t will ease him in his solitude,
And gild the horrors of his prison-house,
Till death shall—

EVANTHE. Ha! what was that? till death —ye Gods!
Ah, now I feel distress's tort'ring pang—
Thou canst not villain—darst not think his death—
O mis'ry!—

VARDANES. Naught but your kindness saves him,
Yet bless me, with your love, and he is safe;
But the same frown which kills my growing hopes,
Gives him to death.

EVANTHE. O horror, I could die
Ten thousand times to save the lov'd *Arsaces*.
Teach me the means, ye pow'rs, how to save him!
Then lead me to what ever is my fate.

VARDANES. Not only shall he die, but to thy view
I'll bring the scene, those eyes that take delight
In cruelty, shall have enough of death.
E'en here, before thy sight, he shall expire,
Not sudden, but by ling'ring torments; all
That mischief can invent shall be practis'd
To give him pain; to lengthen out his woe
I'll search around the realm for skillful men,
To find new tortures.

EVANTHE. Oh! wrack not thus my soul!

VARDANES. The sex o'erflows with various humours, he
Who catches not their smiles the very moment,
Will lose the blessing—I'll improve this softness.— (*Aside to her.*)

—Heav'n never made thy beauties to destroy,
They were to bless, and not to blast mankind;
Pity should dwell within thy lovely breast,
That sacred temple ne'er was form'd for hate
A habitation; but a residence
For love and gaiety.

EVANTHE. Oh! heav'ns!

VARDANES. That sigh,
Proclaims your kind consent to save *Arsaces.* (*Laying hold of her.*)

EVANTHE. Ha! villain, off—unhand me—hence—

VARDANES. In vain is opportunity to those, who spend
An idle courtship on the fair, they well
Deserve their fate, if they 're disdain'd: —her charms
To rush upon, and conquer opposition,
Gains the Fair one's praise; an active lover
Suits, who lies[1] aside the coxcomb's empty whine,
And forces her to bliss.

EVANTHE. Ah! hear me, hear me,
Thus kneeling, with my tears, I do implore thee:
Think on my innocence, nor force a joy
Which will ever fill thy soul with anguish.
Seek not to load my ills with infamy,
Let me not be a mark for bitter scorn,
To bear proud virtue's taunts and mocking jeers,
And like a flow'r, of all its sweetness robb'd,
Be trod to earth, neglected and disdain'd,
And spurn'd by ev'ry vulgar saucy foot.

VARDANES. Speak, speak forever—music 's in thy voice,
Still attentive will I listen to thee,
Be hush'd as night, charm'd with the magic sound.

EVANTHE. Oh! teach me, heav'n, soft moving eloquence,
To bend his stubborn soul to gentleness.—
Where is thy virtue? Where thy princely lustre?
Ah! wilt thou meanly stoop to do a wrong,
And stain thy honour with so foul a blot?
Thou who shouldst be a guard to innocence,
Leave force to brutes—for pleasure is not found

1 Lays.

Where still the soul 's averse; horror and guilt,
Distraction, desperation chace her hence.
Some happier gentle Fair one you may find,
Whose yielding heart may bend to meet your flame,
In mutual love soft joys alone are found;
When souls are drawn by secret sympathy,
And virtue does on virtue smile.

VARDANES. No more—
Her heav'nly tongue will charm me from th' intent.—
Hence coward softness, force shall make me blest.

EVANTHE. Assist me, ye bless't pow'rs!—oh! strike, ye Gods!
Strike me, with thunder dead, this moment, e'er
I suffer violation—

VARDANES. 'T is in vain,
The idle pray'rs by fancy'd grief put up,
Are blown by active winds regardless by,
Nor ever reach the heav'ns.

SCENE 2.

EVANTHE, VARDANES, *and* LYSIAS.

LYSIAS. Arm, arm, my Lord!—

VARDANES. Damnation! why this interruption now?—

LYSIAS. Oh! arm! my noble Prince, the foe 's upon us.
Arsaces, by *Barzaphernes* releas'd,
Join'd with the citizens, assaults the Palace,
And swears revenge for *Artabanus'* death.

VARDANES. Ha! what? revenge for *Artabanus'* death?—
'T is the curse of Princes that their counsels,
Which should be kept like holy mysteries,
Can never rest in silent secrecy.
Fond of employ, some cursed tattling tongue
Will still divulge them.

LYSIAS. Sure some fiend from hell,
In mischief eminent, to cross our views,
Has giv'n th' intelligence, for man could not.

EVANTHE. Oh! ever blest event!— All-gracious heav'n!
This beam of joy revives me.

Scene 3.

Vardanes, Evanthe, Lysias, *to them, an* Officer.

Officer. Haste! my Lord!
Or all will soon be lost; tho' thrice repuls'd
By your e'erfaithful guards, they still return
With double fury.
Vardanes. Hence, then, idle love—
Come forth, my trusty sword—curs'd misfortune!—
Had I but one short hour, without reluctance,
I 'd meet them, tho' they brib'd the pow'rs of hell,
To place their furies in the van: Yea, rush
To meet this dreadful Brother 'midst the war—
Haste to the combat— Now a crown or death—
The wretch who dares to give an inch of ground
Till I retire, shall meet the death he shun'd.
Away—away! delays are dang'rous now—

Scene 4.

Evanthe, *alone.*

Now heav'n be partial to *Arsaces'* cause,
Nor leave to giddy chance when virtue strives;
Let victory sit on his warlike helm,
For justice draws his sword: be thou his aid,
And let the opposer's arm sink with the weight
Of his most impious crimes—be still my heart,
For all that thou canst aid him with is pray'r.
Oh! that I had the strength of thousands in me!
Or that my voice could wake the sons of men
To join, and crush the tyrant!—

Scene 5.

Evanthe *and* Cleone.

Evanthe. My *Cleone*—
Welcome thou partner of my joys and sorrows.
Cleone. Oh! yonder terror triumphs uncontroul'd,
And glutton death seems never satisfy'd.
Each soft sensation lost in thoughtless rage,
And breast to breast, oppos'd in furious war,
The fiery Chiefs receive the vengeful steel.
O'er lifeless heaps of men the soldiers climb
Still eager for the combat, while the ground
Made slipp'ry by the gushing streams of gore
Is treach'rous to their feet.— Oh! horrid sight!—
Too much for me to stand, my life was chill'd,
As from the turret I beheld the fight,
It forc'd me to retire.
Evanthe. What of *Arsaces?*
Cleone. I saw him active in the battle, now,
Like light'ning, piercing thro' the thickest foe,
Then scorning to disgrace his sword in low
Plebeian blood—loud for *Vardanes* call'd—
To meet him singly, and decide the war.
Evanthe. Save him, ye Gods!—oh! all my soul is fear—
Fly, fly *Cleone,* to the tow'r again,
See how fate turns the ballance; and pursue
Arsaces with thine eye; mark ev'ry blow,
Observe if some bold villain dares to urge
His sword presumptuous at my Hero's breast.
Haste, my *Cleone,* haste, to ease my fears.

Scene 6.

Evanthe, *alone.*

Ah!—what a cruel torment is suspense!
My anxious soul is torn 'twixt love and fear,
Scarce can I please me with one fancied bliss
Which kind imagination forms, but reason,
Proud, surly reason, snatches the vain joy,
And gives me up again to sad distress.

Yet I can die, and should *Arsaces* fall
This fatal draught shall ease me of my sorrows.

SCENE 7.

CLEONE, *alone.*

Oh! horror! horror! horror!—cruel Gods!—
I saw him fall—I did—pierc'd thro' with wounds—
Curs'd! curs'd *Vardanes!*—hear'd the gen'ral cry,
Which burst, as tho' all nature had dissolv'd.
Hark! how they shout! the noise seems coming this way.

SCENE 8.

ARSACES, GOTARZES, BARZAPHERNES *and* OFFICERS, *with* VARDANES *and* LYSIAS, *prisoners.*

ARSACES. Thanks to the ruling pow'rs who blest our arms,
Prepare the sacrifices to the Gods,
And grateful songs of tributary praise.—
Gotarzes, fly, my Brother, find *Evanthe,*
And bring the lovely mourner to my arms.

GOTARZES. Yes, I'll obey you, with a willing speed. (*Exit* GOTARZES.)

ARSACES. Thou, *Lysias,* from yon tow'rs aspiring height
Be hurl'd to death, thy impious hands are stain'd
With royal blood— Let the traitor's body
Be giv'n to hungry dogs.

LYSIAS. Welcome grim death!—
I 've fed thy maw with Kings, and lack no more
Revenge— Now, do thy duty, Officer.

OFFICER. Yea, and would lead all traitors gladly thus,—
The boon of their deserts.

SCENE 9.

ARSACES, VARDANES, BARZAPHERNES.

ARSACES. But for *Vardanes,*
The Brother's name forgot—

VARDANES. You need no more,
I know the rest— Ah! death is near, my wounds
Permit me not to live—my breath grows short,
Curs'd be *Phraates* arm which stop'd my sword,
Ere it had reach'd thy proud exulting heart.
But the wretch paid dear for his presuming;
A just reward.—

ARSACES. He sinks, yet bear him up—

VARDANES. Curs'd be the multitude which o'erpow'r'd me,
And beat me to the ground, cover'd with wounds—
But, oh! 't is done! my ebbing life is done—
I feel death's hand upon me— Yet, I die
Just as I wish, and daring for a crown,
Life without rule is my disdain; I scorn
To swell a haughty Brother's sneaking train,
To wait upon his ear with flatt'ring tales,
And court his smiles; come, death, in thy cold arms,
Let me forget Ambition's mighty toil,
And shun the triumphs of a hated Brother—
O! bear me off— Let not his eyes enjoy
My agonies— My sight grows dim with death. (*They bear him off.*)

SCENE THE LAST.

ARSACES, GOTARZES, BARZAPHERNES, *and* EVANTHE *supported.*

EVANTHE. Lead me, oh! lead me, to my lov'd *Arsaces,*
Where is he?—

ARSACES. Ha! what 's this? Just heav'ns! —my fears—

EVANTHE. *Arsaces,* oh! thus circl'd in thy arms,
I die without a pang.

ARSACES. Ha! die?—why stare ye,
Ye lifeless ghosts? Have none of ye a tongue
To tell me I 'm undone?

GOTARZES. Soon, my Brother,
Too soon, you 'll know it by the sad effects;
And if my grief will yet permit my tongue
To do its office, thou shalt hear the tale.
Cleone, from the turret, view'd the battle

And on *Phraates* fix'd her erring sight,
Thy brave unhappy friend she took for thee,
By his garb deceiv'd, which like to thine he wore.
Still with her eye she follow'd him, where-e'er
He pierc'd the foe, and to *Vardanes* sword
She saw him fall a hapless victim, then,
In agonies of grief, flew to *Evanthe,*
And told the dreadful tale—the fatal bowl
I saw—

ARSACES. Be dumb, nor ever give again
Fear to the heart, with thy ill-boding voice.

EVANTHE. Here, I 'll rest, till death, on thy lov'd bosom,
Here let me sigh my— Oh! the poison works—

ARSACES. Oh! horror!—

EVANTHE. Cease—this sorrow pains me more
Than all the wringing agonies of death,
The dreadful parting of the soul from this,
Its wedded clay— Ah! there—that pang shot thro'
My throbbing heart—

ARSACES. Save her, ye Gods!—oh! save her!
And I will bribe ye with clouds of incense;
Such num'rous sacrifices, that your altars
Shall even sink beneath the mighty load.

EVANTHE. When I am dead, dissolv'd to native dust,
Yet let me live in thy dear mem'ry—
One tear will not be much to give *Evanthe.*

ARSACES. My eyes shall e'er two running fountains be,
And wet thy urn with everflowing tears,
Joy ne'er again within my breast shall find
A residence— Oh! speak, once more—

EVANTHE. Life 's just out—
My Father— Oh! protect his honour'd age,
And give him shelter from the storms of fate,
He 's long been fortune's sport— Support me— Ah!—
I can no more—my glass is spent—farewell—
Forever—*Arsaces!*—oh! (*Dies.*)

ARSACES. Stay, oh! stay,
Or take me with thee—dead! she 's cold and dead!
Her eyes are clos'd, and all my joys are flown—
Now burst ye elements, from your restraint,
Let order cease, and chaos be again.
Break! break tough heart!—oh! torture —life dissolve—
Why stand ye idle? Have I not one friend
To kindly free me from this pain? One blow,
One friendly blow would give me ease.

BARZAPHERNES. The Gods
Forefend!— Pardon me, Royal Sir, if I
Dare, seemingly disloyal, seize your sword,
Despair may urge you far—

ARSACES. Ha! traitors! rebels!—
Hoary rev'rend Villain! what, disarm me?
Give me my sword—what, stand ye by, and see
Your Prince insulted? Are ye rebels all?—

BARZAPHERNES. Be calm, my gracious Lord!

GOTARZES. Oh! my lov'd Brother!

ARSACES. *Gotarzes* too! all! all! conspir'd against me?
Still, are ye all resolv'd that I must live,
And feel the momentary pangs of death?—
Ha!—this, shall make a passage for my soul—
(*Snatches* BARZAPHERNES' *sword.*)
Out, out vile cares, from your distress'd abode— (*Stabs himself.*)

BARZAPHERNES. Oh! ye eternal Gods!

GOTARZES. Distraction! heav'ns!
I shall run mad—

ARSACES. Ah! 't is in vain to grieve—
The steel has done its part, and I 'm at rest.—
Gotarzes wear my crown, and be thou blest,
Cherish *Barzaphernes,* my trusty chief—
I faint, oh! lay me by *Evanthe's* side—
Still wedded in our deaths--*Bethas*—

BARZAPHERNES. Despair,
My Lord, has broke his heart, I saw him stretch'd,
Along the flinty pavement, in his gaol—
Cold, lifeless—

ARSACES. He 's happy then—had he heard
This tale, he'd— Ah! *Evanthe* chides my soul,

For ling'ring here so long—another pang
And all the world, adieu—oh! adieu!—
(*Dies.*)

GOTARZES. Oh!—
Fix me, heav'n, immoveable, a statue,
And free me from o'erwhelming tides of grief.

BARZAPHERNES. Oh! my lov'd Prince, I soon shall follow thee;
Thy laurel'd glories[,] whither are they fled?—
Would I had died before this fatal day!—
Triumphant garlands pride my soul no more,
No more the lofty voice of war can charm—
And why then am I here? Thus then—
(*Offers to stab himself.*)

GOTARZES. Ah! hold,
Nor rashly urge the blow—think of me, and
Live— My heart is wrung with streaming anguish,
Tore with the smarting pangs of woe, yet, will I
Dare to live, and stem misfortune's billows.
Live then, and be the guardian of my youth,
And lead me on thro' virtue's rugged path.

BARZAPHERNES. O, glorious youth, thy words have rous'd the
Drooping genius of my soul; thus, let me
Clasp thee, in my aged arms; yes, I will live—
Live, to support thee in thy kingly rights,
And when thou 'rt firmly fix'd, my task 's perform'd,
My honourable task— Then I 'll retire,
Petition gracious heav'n to bless my work,
And in the silent grave forget my cares.

GOTARZES. Now, to the Temple, let us onward move,
And strive t' appease the angry pow'rs above.
Fate yet may have some ills reserv'd in store,
Continu'd curses, to torment us more.
Tho', in their district, Monarchs rule alone,
Jove sways the mighty Monarch on his throne:
Nor can the shining honours which they wear,
Purchase one joy, or save them from one care.

FINIS

THE CONTRAST

BY

Royall Tyler

THE CONTRAST

The Contrast is the second play written by an American, to be produced in America by a professional company. It is our first comedy, and while its central theme is the contrast between native worth and affectation of foreign manners it is of especial significance as introducing to our stage in the character of "Jonathan" the shrewd, yet uncultivated type of New England farmer which has since become known as the "Stage Yankee." The example of *The Contrast* in introducing a Yankee character was soon followed. In 1792, *The Yorker's Stratagem, or Banana's Wedding,* by J. Robinson, was based upon the attempt of the hero "Amant" to win the hand of the heroine by pretending to be a simple Yankee merchant. In 1807 Barker introduced the character of "Nathan Yank" in his comedy, *Tears and Smiles.* The first Yankee character, however, which permanently held the stage was that of "Jonathan Ploughboy" in Samuel Woodworth's play of *The Forest Rose, or American Farmers.* It was a kind of opera, originally produced at the Chatham Theatre, New York, October 6, 1825. The characters are all conventional but that of "Jonathan" which had some flavor of reality. This play was produced in London and as far west as California. The character of "Jonathan" was acted at first by Alexander Simpson and later by Henry Placide, G. H. Hill and J. S. Silsbee. The success of *The Forest Rose* doubtless encouraged others, for we find J. H. Hackett, the actor, first telling Yankee stories in plays of another character and then modifying Colman's *Who Wants a Guinea?* to introduce the character of "Solomon Swap" and under the title of *Jonathan in England* producing the play in England with success. Among the other well known Yankee plays were *Yankee Land* (1834) introducing "Lot Sap Sago" and *The Vermont Wool Dealer,* (1840), whose hero was called "Deuteronomy Dutiful." Both of these plays were written by C. A. Logan. Joseph S. Jones, a prolific playwright, created the character of "Jedediah Homebred" in *The Green Mountain Boy* (1833) and "Solon Shingle" in *The People's Lawyer* (1839). These Yankee plays are most interesting on account of their historical value. As we read them now they seem trivial and conventional and the Yankee characters are introduced into the midst of surroundings with which they have usually little to do. Their farcical character, however, made them definite and their homeliness of expression gave them an appearance of reality which probably won them their popularity. They point forward, of course, to a time when James A. Herne and others produced more significant work in the same field.

The author of *The Contrast,* Royall Tyler, was born in Boston, July 18, 1757. He graduated from Harvard College and, after studying law, became aide-de-camp to General Benjamin Lincoln during the Revolution and later during Shays's Rebellion. Coming to New York City on a mission connected with Shays's Rebellion, he became interested in the theatre and wrote *The Contrast,* which was performed at the John Street Theatre, April 16, 1787, by the American Company, under Hallam and Henry. The principal part, that of "Jonathan," was played by Thomas Wignell. It was repeated several times in New York and was played in Baltimore (1787–8), in Philadelphia (1790) and in Boston. It was revived on June 6, 7, and 8, 1912, in connection with a Pageant given at Brattleboro, Vermont.

Tyler wrote a farce, *May Day in Town or New York in an Uproar,* which was performed at the John Street Theatre on May 19, 1787. He then returned to Boston, where he wrote in 1797, *A Georgia Spec or Land in the Moon,* which dealt with the rage for speculating in Georgia lands of the Yazoo Purchase. It was first played in Boston and later in New York at the John Street Theatre, December 20, 1797. According to Dunlap's manuscript Diary, *A Georgia Spec,* which he calls *A Good Spec,* was repeated February 12, 1798. Miss Helen Tyler Brown, great-granddaughter of Tyler, possesses manuscripts of four plays, *The Island of Barrataria, The Origin of the Feast of Purim, Joseph and His Brethren* and *The Judgment of Solomon.* Probably none of these was performed. Tyler also wrote a romance, *The Algerine Captive* (1797) but devoted himself definitely to the profession of law, becoming Chief Justice of the Supreme Court of Vermont in 1807. He died in August, 1826.

Tyler gave the copyright of *The Contrast* to Thomas Wignell and the latter published it in Philadelphia in 1790, with an introduction in which he states that "it was written by one who never critically studied the rules of the drama, and indeed had seen but few of the exhibitions of the stage; it was undertaken and finished in the course of three weeks." It was reprinted by the Dunlap Society in 1887 with an introduction by Thomas J. McKee. The other plays of Tyler are not now available.

The present edition is based upon a copy of the edition of 1790, which belonged to William B. Wood, the Philadelphia Manager.

NOTE TO SECOND EDITION.

On January 16 and 18, 1917, *The Contrast* was played under the auspices of the American Drama Committee of the Philadelphia Drama League at the Broad Street Theatre in connection with the celebration of the American Drama Year. The cast was drawn from the "Plays and Players" of Philadelphia, and the production revealed the truly remarkable qualities of the play, which was staged under the direction of Mrs. Otis Skinner.

THE
CONTRAST,
A
COMEDY;
IN FIVE ACTS:

WRITTEN BY A
CITIZEN OF THE *UNITED STATES*;

Performed with Applauſe at the Theatres in NEW-YORK,
PHILADELPHIA, and MARYLAND;

AND PUBLISHED *(under an Aſſignment of the Copy-Right)* BY
THOMAS WIGNELL.

Primus ego in patriam
Aonio——deduxi vertice Muſas.
VIRGIL.

(Imitated.)

Firſt on our ſhores I try THALIA's powers,
And bid the *laughing*, *uſeful* Maid be ours.

PHILADELPHIA:
FROM THE PRESS OF *PRICHARD & HALL*, IN MARKET STREET,
BETWEEN SECOND AND FRONT STREETS.
M. DCC. XC.

PROLOGUE

Written by a Young Gentleman of New-York, and Spoken by Mr. Wignell

Exult each patriot heart!—this night is shewn
A piece, which we may fairly call our own;
Where the proud titles of "My Lord! Your Grace!"
To humble Mr. and plain Sir give place.
Our Author pictures not from foreign climes
The fashions, or the follies of the times;
But has confin'd the subject of his work
To the gay scenes—the circles of New-York.
On native themes his Muse displays her pow'rs;
If ours the faults, the virtues too are ours.
Why should our thoughts to distant countries roam,
When each refinement may be found at home?
Who travels now to ape the rich or great,
To deck an equipage and roll in state;
To court the graces, or to dance with ease,
Or by hypocrisy to strive to please?
Our free-born ancestors such arts despis'd;
Genuine sincerity alone they priz'd;
Their minds, with honest emulation fir'd,
To solid good—not ornament—aspir'd;
Or, if ambition rous'd a bolder flame,
Stern virtue throve, where indolence was shame.

But modern youths, with imitative sense,
Deem taste in dress the proof of excellence;
And spurn the meanness of your homespun arts,
Since homespun habits would obscure their parts;
Whilst all, which aims at splendour and parade,
Must come from Europe, and be ready made.
Strange! we should thus our native worth disclaim,
And check the progress of our rising fame.
Yet onc, whilst imitation bears the sway,
Aspires to nobler heights, and points the way,
Be rous'd, my friends! his bold example view;
Let your own Bards be proud to copy you!
Should rigid critics reprobate our play,
At least the patriotic heart will say,
"Glorious our fall, since in a noble cause.
"The bold attempt alone demands applause."
Still may the wisdom of the Comic Muse
Exalt your merits, or your faults accuse.

But think not, 't is her aim to be severe;—
We all are mortals, and as mortals err.
If candour pleases, we are truly blest;
Vice trembles, when compell'd to stand confess'd.
Let not light Censure on your faults, offend,
Which aims not to expose them, but amend.
Thus does our Author to your candour trust;
Conscious, the free are generous, as just.

CHARACTERS

	New York	Maryland
COL. MANLY	Mr. Henry	Mr. Hallam
DIMPLE	Mr. Hallam	Mr. Harper
VANROUGH	Mr. Morris	Mr. Morris
JESSAMY	Mr. Harper	Mr. Biddle
JONATHAN	Mr. Wignell	Mr. Wignell
CHARLOTTE	Mrs. Morris	Mrs. Morris
MARIA	Mrs. Harper	Mrs. Harper
LETITIA	Mrs. Kenna	Mrs. Williamson
JENNY	Miss Tuke	Miss W. Tuke

Servants

Scene, New York

N. B. The lines marked with inverted commas, "thus" are omitted in the representation.

[For the sake of uniformity in this collection, the portions omitted in representation are enclosed in brackets of this character <>.]

THE CONTRAST

ACT FIRST.

SCENE 1. *An Apartment at* CHARLOTTE'S.

CHARLOTTE *and* LETITIA *discovered.*

LETITIA. And so, Charlotte, you really think the pocket-hoop unbecoming.

CHARLOTTE. No, I don't say so: It may be very becoming to saunter round the house of a rainy day; to visit my grand-mamma, or go to Quakers' meeting: but to swim in a minuet, with the eyes of fifty well-dressed beaux upon me, to trip it in the Mall, or walk on the battery, give me the luxurious, jaunty, flowing, bell-hoop. It would have delighted you to have seen me the last evening, my charming girl! I was dangling o'er the battery with Billy Dimple; a knot of young fellows were upon the platform; as I passed them I faultered with one of the most bewitching false steps you ever saw, and then recovered myself with such a pretty confusion, flirting my hoop to discover a jet black shoe and brilliant buckle. Gad! how my little heart thrilled to hear the confused raptures of—*"Demme, Jack, what a delicate foot!" "Ha! General, what a well-turn'd—"*

LETITIA. Fie! fie! Charlotte, (*stopping her mouth*) I protest you are quite a libertine.

CHARLOTTE. Why, my dear little prude, are we not all such libertines? Do you think, when I sat tortured two hours under the hands of my friseur, and an hour more at my toilet, that I had any thoughts of my aunt Susan, or my cousin Betsey? though they are both allowed to be critical judges of dress.

LETITIA. Why, who should we dress to please, but those who are judges of its merit?

CHARLOTTE. Why a creature who does not know *Buffon* from *Souflee*—Man!—my Letitia—Man! for whom we dress, walk, dance, talk, lisp, languish, and smile. Does not the grave Spectator assure us, that even our much bepraised diffidence, modesty, and blushes, are all directed to make ourselves good wives and mothers as fast as we can. Why, I 'll undertake with one flirt of this hoop to bring more beaux to my feet in one week, than the grave Maria, and her sentimental circle, can do, by sighing sentiment till their hairs are grey.

LETITIA. Well, I won't argue with you; you always out talk me; let us change the subject. I hear that Mr. Dimple and Maria are soon to be married.

CHARLOTTE. You hear true. I was consulted in the choice of the wedding clothes. She is to be married in a delicate white sattin, and has a monstrous pretty brocaded lutestring for the second day. It would have done you good to have seen with what an affected indifference the dear sentimentalist <turned over a thousand pretty things, just as if her heart did not palpitate with her approaching happiness, and at last made her choice, and> arranged her dress with such apathy, as if she did not know that plain white sattin, and a simple blond lace, would shew her clear skin, and dark hair, to the greatest advantage.

LETITIA. But they say her indifference to dress, and even to the gentleman himself, is not entirely affected.

CHARLOTTE. How?

LETITIA. It is whispered, that if Maria gives her hand to Mr. Dimple, it will be without her heart.

CHARLOTTE. Though the giving the heart is one of the last of all laughable considerations in the marriage of a girl of spirit, yet I should like to hear what antiquated notions the dear little piece of old fashioned prudery has got in her head.

LETITIA. Why you know that old Mr. John-Richard-Robert-Jacob-Isaac-Abraham-Cornelius Van Dumpling, Billy Dimple's father, (for he has thought fit to soften his name, as well as manners, during his English tour) was the most intimate friend of Maria's father. The old folks, about a year before Mr. Van Dumpling's death, proposed this match: the young folks were accordingly introduced, and told they must love one another. Billy was then a good natured, decent, dressing young fellow, with a little dash of the coxcomb, such as our young fellows of fortune usually have. At this time, I really believe she thought she loved him; and had they then been married, I doubt not, they might have jogged on, to the end of the chapter, a good kind of a sing-song lack-a-daysaical life, as other honest married folks do.

CHARLOTTE. Why did they not then marry?

LETITIA. Upon the death of his father, Billy went to England to see the world, and rub off a little of the patroon rust. During his absence, Maria like a good girl, to keep herself constant to her *nown true-love,* avoided company, and betook herself, for her amusement, to her books, and her dear Billy's letters. But, alas! how many ways has the mischievous demon of inconstancy of stealing into a woman's heart! Her love was destroyed by the very means she took to support it.

CHARLOTTE. How?—Oh! I have it—some likely young beau found the way to her study.

LETITIA. Be patient, Charlotte—your head so runs upon beaux.— Why she read Sir Charles Grandison, Clarissa Harlow, Shenstone, and the Sentimental Journey; and between whiles, as I said, Billy's letters. But as her taste improved, her love declined. The contrast was so striking betwixt the good sense of her books, and the flimsiness of her love-letters, that she discovered she had unthinkingly engaged her hand without her heart; and then the whole transaction managed by the old folks, now appeared so unsentimental, and looked so like bargaining for a bale of goods, that she found she ought to have rejected, according to every rule of romance, even the man of her choice, if imposed upon her in that manner—Clary Harlow would have scorned such a match.

CHARLOTTE. Well, how was it on Mr. Dimple's return? Did he meet a more favourable reception than his letters?

LETITIA. Much the same. She spoke of him with respect abroad, and with contempt in her closet. She watched his conduct and conversation, and found that he had by travelling acquired the wickedness of Lovelace without his wit, and the politeness of Sir Charles Grandison without his generosity. The ruddy youth who washed his face at the cistern every morning, and swore and looked eternal love and constancy, was now metamorphosed into a flippant, palid, polite beau, who devotes the morning to his toilet, reads a few pages of Chesterfield's letters, and then minces out, to put the infamous principles in practice upon every woman he meets.

CHARLOTTE. But, if she is so apt at conjuring up these sentimental bugbears, why does she not discard him at once?

LETITIA. Why, she thinks her word too sacred to be trifled with. Besides, her father, who has a great respect for the memory of his deceased friend, is ever telling her how he shall renew his years in their union, and repeating the dying injunctions of old Van Dumpling.

CHARLOTTE. A mighty pretty story! And so you would make me believe, that the sensible Maria would give up Dumpling manor, and the all-accomplished Dimple as a husband, for the absurd, ridiculous reason, forsooth, because she despises and abhors him. Just as if a lady could not be privileged to spend a man's fortune, ride in his carriage, be called after his name, and call him her *nown dear lovee* when she wants money, without loving and respecting the great he-creature. Oh! my dear girl, you are a monstrous prude.

LETITIA. I don't say what I would do; I only intimate how I suppose she wishes to act.

CHARLOTTE. No, no, no! A fig for sentiment. If she breaks, or wishes to break, with Mr. Dimple, depend upon it, she has some other man in her eye. A woman rarely discards one lover, until she is sure of another.— Letitia little thinks what a clue I have to Dimple's conduct. The generous man submits to render himself disgusting to Maria, in order that she may leave him at liberty to address me. I must change the subject. (*Aside, and rings a bell.*)

(*Enter* SERVANT.)

Frank, order the horses to.— Talking of marriage—did you hear that Sally Bloomsbury is going to be married next week to Mr. Indigo, the rich Carolinian?

LETITIA. Sally Bloomsbury married!—Why, she is not yet in her teens.

CHARLOTTE. I do not know how that is, but, you may depend upon it, 't is a done affair. I have it from the best authority. There is my aunt Wyerley's Hannah (you know Hannah—though a black, she is a wench that was never caught in a lie in her life); now Hannah has a brother who courts Sarah, Mrs. Catgut the milliner's girl, and she told Hannah's brother, and Hannah, who, as I said before, is a girl of undoubted veracity, told it directly to me, that Mrs. Catgut was making a new cap for Miss Bloomsbury, which, as it was very dressy, it is very probable is designed for a wedding cap: now, as she is to be married, who can it be to, but to Mr. Indigo? Why, there is no other gentleman that visits at her papa's.

LETITIA. Say not a word more, Charlotte. Your intelligence is so direct and well grounded, it is almost a pity that it is not a piece of scandal.

CHARLOTTE. Oh! I am the pink of prudence. Though I cannot charge myself with ever having discredited a tea-party by my silence, yet I take care never to report any thing of my acquaintance, especially if it is to their credit,—*discredit,* I mean—until I have searched to the bottom of it. It is true, there is infinite pleasure in this charitable pursuit. Oh! how delicious to go and condole with the friends of some backsliding sister, or to retire with some old dowager or maiden aunt of the family, who love scandal so well, that they cannot forbear gratifying their appetite at the expence of the reputation of their nearest relations! And then to return full fraught with a rich collection of circumstances, to retail to the next circle of our acquaintance under the strongest injunctions of secrecy,—ha, ha, ha!—interlarding the melancholy tale with so many doleful shakes of the head, and more doleful, "Ah! who would have thought it! so amiable, so prudent a young lady, as we all thought her, what a monstrous pity! well, I have nothing to charge myself with; I acted the part of a friend, I warned her of the principles of that rake, I told her what would be the consequence; I told her so, I told her so."—Ha, ha, ha!

LETITIA. Ha, ha, ha! Well, but Charlotte, you don't tell me what you think of Miss Bloomsbury's match.

CHARLOTTE. Think! why I think it is probable she cried for a plaything, and they have given her a husband. Well, well, well, the puling chit shall not be deprived of her plaything: 't is only exchanging London dolls for American babies— Apropos, of babies, have you heard what Mrs. Affable's high-flying notions of delicacy have come to?

LETITIA. Who, she that was Miss Lovely?

CHARLOTTE. The same; she married Bob Affable of Schenectady. Don't you remember?

(*Enter* SERVANT.)

SERVANT. Madam, the carriage is ready.

LETITIA. Shall we go to the stores first, or visiting?

CHARLOTTE. I should think it rather too early to visit; especially Mrs. Prim: you know she is so particular.

LETITIA. Well, but what of Mrs. Affable?

CHARLOTTE. Oh, I'll tell you as we go; come, come, let us hasten. I hear Mrs. Catgut has some of the prettiest caps arrived, you ever saw. I shall die if I have not the first sight of them. (*Exeunt.*)

SCENE 2. *A Room in* VAN ROUGH'S *House.* MARIA *sitting disconsolate at a Table, with Books, etc.*

Song.

I

The sun sets in night, and the stars shun the day;
But glory remains when their lights fade away!
Begin, ye tormentors! your threats are in vain,
For the son of Alknomook shall never complain.

II

Remember the arrows he shot from his bow;
Remember your chiefs by his hatchet laid low:
Why so slow?—do you wait till I shrink from the pain?
No—the son of Alknomook will never complain.

III

Remember the wood where in ambush we lay;
And the scalps which we bore from your nation away:
Now the flame rises fast, you exult in my pain;
But the son of Alknomook can never complain.

IV

I go to the land where my father is gone;
His ghost shall rejoice in the fame of his son:

Death comes like a friend, he relieves me
from pain;
And thy son, Oh Alknomook! has scorn'd
to complain.

There is something in this song which ever calls forth my affections. The manly virtue of courage, that fortitude which steels the heart against the keenest misfortunes, which interweaves the laurel of glory amidst the instruments of torture and death, displays something so noble, so exalted, that in despite of the prejudices of education, I cannot but admire it, even in a savage. The prepossession which our sex is supposed to entertain for the character of a soldier, is, I know, a standing piece of raillery among the wits. A cockade, a lapell'd coat, and a feather, they will tell you, are irresistible by a female heart. Let it be so.— Who is it that considers the helpless situation of our sex, that does not see we each moment stand in need of a protector, and that a brave one too. <Formed of the more delicate materials of nature, endowed only with the softer passions, incapable, from our ignorance of the world, to guard against the wiles of mankind, our security for happiness often depends upon their generosity and courage:— Alas! how little of the former do we find.> How inconsistent! that man should be leagued to destroy that honour, upon which, solely rests his respect and esteem. Ten thousand temptations allure us, ten thousand passions betray us; yet the smallest deviation from the path of rectitude is followed by the contempt and insult of man, and the more remorseless pity of woman: years of penitence and tears cannot wash away the stain, nor a life of virtue obliterate its remembrance. <Reputation is the life of woman; yet courage to protect it, is masculine and disgusting; and the only safe asylum a woman of delicacy can find, is in the arms of a man of honour. How naturally then, should we love the brave, and the generous; how gratefully should we bless the arm raised for our protection, when nerv'd by virtue, and directed by honour!> Heaven grant that the man with whom I may be connected—may be connected!— Whither has my imagination transported me—whither does it now lead me?— Am I not indissolubly engaged <by every obligation of honour, which my own consent, and my father's approbation can give,> to a man who can never share my affections, and whom a few days hence, it will be criminal for me to disapprove—to disapprove! would to heaven that were all—to despise. For, can the most frivolous manners, actuated by the most depraved heart, meet, or merit, anything but contempt from every woman of delicacy and sentiment?

(VAN ROUGH, *without.* Mary!)

Ha, my father's voice— Sir!—

(*Enter* VAN ROUGH.)

VAN ROUGH. What, Mary, always singing doleful ditties, and moping over these plaguy books.

MARIA. I hope, Sir, that it is not criminal to improve my mind with books; or to divert my melancholy with singing at my leisure hours.

VAN ROUGH. Why, I don't know that, child; I don't know that. They us'd to say when I was a young man, that if a woman knew how to make a pudding, and to keep herself out of fire and water, she knew enough for a wife. Now, what good have these books done you? have they not made you melancholy? as you call it. Pray, what right has a girl of your age to be in the dumps? hav n't you every thing your heart can wish; an't you going to be married to a young man of great fortune; an't you going to have the quit-rent of twenty miles square?

MARIA. One hundredth part of the land, and a lease for life of the heart of a man I could love, would satisfy me.

VAN ROUGH. Pho, pho, pho! child; nonsense, downright nonsense, child. This comes of your reading your story-books; your Charles Grandisons, your Sentimental Journals, and your Robinson Crusoes, and such other trumpery. No, no, no! child, it is money makes the mare go; keep your eye upon the main chance, Mary.

MARIA. Marriage, Sir, is, indeed, a very serious affair.

VAN ROUGH. You are right, child; you are right. I am sure I found it so to my cost.

MARIA. I mean, Sir, that as marriage is a portion for life, and so intimately involves our happiness, we cannot be too considerate in the choice of our companion.

VAN ROUGH. Right, child; very right. A young woman should be very sober when she is making her choice, but when she has once made it, as you have done, I don't see why she should not be as merry as a grig; I am sure she has reason enough to be so— Solomon says, that "there is a time to laugh, and a time to weep"; now a time for a young woman to laugh is when she has made sure of a good rich husband. Now a time to cry, according to you, Mary, is when she is making choice of him: but, I should think, that a young woman's time to cry was, when she despaired of *getting* one.— Why, there was your mother now; to be sure when I popp'd the question to her, she did look a little silly; but when she had once looked down on her apron-strings, as all modest young women us'd to do, and drawled out ye-s, she was as brisk and as merry as a bee.

MARIA. My honoured mother, Sir, had no motive to melancholy; she married the man of her choice.

VAN ROUGH. The man of her choice! And pray, Mary, an't you going to marry the man of your choice—what trumpery notion is this?— It is these vile books (*throwing them away*). I'd have you to know, Mary, if you won't make young Van Dumpling the man of *your* choice, you shall marry him as the man of *my* choice.

MARIA. You terrify me, Sir. Indeed, Sir, I am all submission. My will is yours.

VAN ROUGH. Why, that is the way your mother us'd to talk. "My will is yours, my dear Mr. Van Rough, my will is yours": but she took special care to have her own way though for all that.

MARIA. Do not reflect upon my mother's memory, Sir—

VAN ROUGH. Why not, Mary, why not? She kept me from speaking my mind all her *life,* and do you think she shall hen-peck me now she is *dead* too? Come, come; don't go to sniveling: be a good girl, and mind the main chance. I'll see you well settled in the world.

MARIA. I do not doubt your love, Sir; and it is my duty to obey you.— I will endeavor to make my duty and inclination go hand in hand.

VAN ROUGH. Well, well, Mary; do you be a good girl, mind the main chance, and never mind inclination.— Why, do you know that I have been down in the cellar this very morning to examine a pipe of Madeira which I purchased the week you were born, and mean to tap on your wedding day.— That pipe cost me fifty pounds sterling. It was well worth sixty pounds; but I over-reached Ben Bulkhead, the supercargo: I'll tell you the whole story. You must know that—

(*Enter* SERVANT.)

SERVANT. Sir, Mr. Transfer, the broker, is below. (*Exit.*)

VAN ROUGH. Well, Mary, I must go.— Remember, and be a good girl, and mind the main chance. (*Exit.*)

MARIA. (*Alone.*) How deplorable is my situation! How distressing for a daughter to find her heart militating with her filial duty! I know my father loves me tenderly, why then do I reluctantly obey him? <Heaven knows! with what reluctance I should oppose the will of a parent, or set an example of filial disobedience>; at a parent's command I could wed aukwardness and deformity. <Were the heart of my husband good, I would so magnify his good qualities with the eye of conjugal affection, that the defects of his person and manners should be lost in the emanation of his virtues.> At a father's command, I could embrace poverty. Were the poor man my husband, I would learn resignation to my lot; I would enliven our frugal meal with good humour, and chase away misfortune from our cottage with a smile. At a father's command, I could almost submit, to what every female heart knows to be the most mortifying, to marry a weak man, and blush at my husband's folly in every company I visited.— But to marry a depraved wretch, whose only virtue is a polished exterior; <who is actuated by the unmanly ambition of conquering the defenceless; whose heart, insensible to the emotions of patriotism, dilates at the plaudits of every unthinking girl>: whose laurels are the sighs and tears of the miserable victims of his specious behaviour.— Can he, who has no regard for the peace and happiness of other families, ever have a due regard for the peace and happiness of his own? Would to heaven that my father were not so hasty in his temper! Surely, if I were to state my reasons for declining this match, he would not compel me to marry a man—whom, though my lips may solemnly promise to honour, I find my heart must ever despise. (*Exit.*)

END OF THE FIRST ACT.

ACT SECOND.

Scene 1.

(*Enter* Charlotte *and* Letitia.)

Charlotte. (*At entering.*) Betty, take those things out of the carriage and carry them to my chamber; see that you don't tumble them.— My dear, I protest, I think it was the homeliest of the whole. I declare I was almost tempted to return and change it.

Letitia. Why would you take it?

Charlotte. <Did n't Mrs. Catgut say it was the most fashionable?

Letitia. But, my dear, it will never sit becomingly on you.

Charlotte. I know that; but did not you hear Mrs. Catgut say it was fashionable?

Letitia. Did you see that sweet airy cap with the white sprig?

Charlotte. Yes, and I longed to take it; but,> my dear, what could I do?— Did not Mrs. Catgut say it was the most fashionable; and if I had not taken it, was not that aukward gawky, Sally Slender, ready to purchase it immediately?

<Letitia. Did you observe how she tumbled over the things at the next shop, and then went off without purchasing any thing, nor even thanking the poor man for his trouble?— But of all the aukward creatures, did you see Miss Blouze, endeavouring to thrust her unmerciful arm into those small kid gloves?

Charlotte. Ha, ha, ha, ha!>

Letitia. Then did you take notice, with what an affected warmth of friendship she and Miss Wasp met? when all their acquaintances know how much pleasure they take in abusing each other in every company?

Charlotte. Lud! Letitia, is that so extraordinary? Why, my dear, I hope you are not going to turn sentimentalist.— Scandal, you know, is but amusing ourselves with the faults, foibles, follies and reputations of our friends;—indeed, I don't know why we should have friends, if we are not at liberty to make use of them. But no person is so ignorant of the world as to suppose, because I amuse myself with a lady's faults, that I am obliged to quarrel with her person, every time we meet; believe me, my dear, we should have very few acquaintances at that rate.

(Servant *enters and delivers a letter to* Charlotte, *and Exit.*)

Charlotte. You'll excuse me, my dear. (*Opens and reads to herself.*)

Letitia. Oh, quite excusable.

Charlotte. As I hope to be married, my brother Henry is in the city.

Letitia. What, your brother, Colonel Manly?

Charlotte. Yes, my dear; the only brother I have in the world.

Letitia. Was he never in this city?

Charlotte. Never nearer than Harlem Heights, where he lay with his regiment.

Letitia. What sort of a being is this brother of yours? If he is as chatty, as pretty, as sprightly as you, half the belles in the city will be pulling caps for him.

Charlotte. My brother is the very counterpart and reverse of me: I am gay, he is grave; I am airy, he is solid; I am ever selecting the most pleasing objects for my laughter, he has a tear for every pitiful one. And thus, whilst he is plucking the briars and thorns from the path of the unfortunate, I am strewing my own path with roses.

Letitia. My sweet friend, not quite so poetical, and little more particular.

Charlotte. Hands off, Letitia. I feel the rage of simile upon me; I can't talk to you in any other way. My brother has a heart replete with the noblest sentiments, but then, it is like—it is like—Oh! you provoking girl, you have deranged all my ideas—it is like—Oh! I have it—his heart is like an old maiden lady's band-box; it contains many costly things, arranged with the most scrupulous nicety, yet the misfortune is, that they are too delicate, costly, and antiquated, for common use.

Letitia. By what I can pick out of your flowery description, your brother is no beau.

Charlotte. No, indeed; he makes no pretension to the character. He'd ride, or rather fly, an hundred miles to relieve a distressed object, or to do a gallant act in the service of his country: but, should you drop your fan or bouquet in his presence, it is ten to one that some beau at the farther end of the room would have the honour of presenting it to you, before he had observed that it fell. I 'll tell you one of his antiquated, anti-gallant notions.— He said once in my presence, in a room full of company—would you believe it—in a large circle of ladies, that the best evidence a gentleman could give a young lady of his respect and affection, was, to endeavour in a friendly manner to rectify her foibles. I protest I was crimson to the eyes, upon reflecting that I was known as his sister.

LETITIA. Insupportable creature! tell a lady of her faults! If he is so grave, I fear I have no chance of captivating him.

CHARLOTTE. <His conversation is like a rich old fashioned brocade, it will stand alone; every sentence is a sentiment. Now you may judge what a time I had with him, in my twelve months' visit to my father. He read me such lectures, out of pure brotherly affection, against the extremes of fashion, dress, flirting, and coquetry, and all the other dear things which he knows I doat upon, that, I protest, his conversation made me as melancholy as if I had been at church; and heaven knows, though I never prayed to go there but on one occasion, yet I would have exchanged his conversation for a psalm and a sermon. Church is rather melancholy, to be sure; but then I can ogle the beaux, and be regaled with "here endeth the first lesson"; but his brotherly *here,* you would think had no end.> You captivate him! Why, my dear, he would as soon fall in love with a box of Italian flowers. There is Maria now, if she were not engaged, she might do something.— Oh! how I should like to see that pair of pensorosos together, looking as grave as two sailors' wives of a stormy night, with a flow of sentiment meandering through their conversation like purling streams in modern poetry.

LETITIA. Oh! my dear fanciful—

CHARLOTTE. Hush! I hear some person coming through the entry.

(*Enter* SERVANT.)

SERVANT. Madam, there 's a gentleman below who calls himself Colonel Manly; do you chuse to be at home?

CHARLOTTE. Shew him in. (*Exit* SERVANT.) Now for a sober face.

(*Enter* COLONEL MANLY.)

MANLY. My dear Charlotte, I am happy that I once more enfold you within the arms of fraternal affection. I know you are going to ask (amiable impatience!) how our parents do,—the venerable pair transmit you their blessing by me—they totter on the verge of a well-spent life, and wish only to see their children settled in the world, to depart in peace.

CHARLOTTE. I am very happy to hear that they are well. (*Coolly.*) Brother, will you give me leave to introduce you to our uncle's ward, one of my most intimate friends.

MANLY. (*Saluting* LETITIA.) I ought to regard your friends as my own.

CHARLOTTE. Come, Letitia, do give us a little dash of your vivacity; my brother is so sentimental, and so grave, that I protest he 'll give us the vapours.

MANLY. Though sentiment and gravity, I know, are banished the polite world, yet, I hoped, they might find some countenance in the meeting of such near connections as brother and sister.

CHARLOTTE. Positively, brother, if you go one step further in this strain, you will set me crying, and that, you know, would spoil my eyes; and then I should never get the husband which our good papa and mamma have so kindly wished me—never be established in the world.

MANLY. Forgive me, my sister—I am no enemy to mirth; I love your sprightliness; and I hope it will one day enliven the hours of some worthy man; but when I mention the respectable authors of my existence,—the cherishers and protectors of my helpless infancy, whose hearts glow with such fondness and attachment, that they would willingly lay down their lives for my welfare, you will excuse me, if I am so unfashionable as to speak of them with some degree of respect and reverence.

CHARLOTTE. Well, well, brother; if you won't be gay, we 'll not differ; I will be as grave as you wish. (*Affects gravity.*) And so, brother, you have come to the city to exchange some of your commutation notes for a little pleasure.

MANLY. Indeed, you are mistaken; my errand is not of amusement, but business; and as I neither drink nor game, my expences will be so trivial, I shall have no occasion to sell my notes.

CHARLOTTE. Then you won't have occasion to do a very good thing. Why, there was the Vermont General—he came down some time since, sold all his musty notes at one stroke, and then laid the cash out in trinkets for his dear Fanny. I want a dozen pretty things myself; have you got the notes with you?

Manly. I shall be ever willing to contribute as far as it is in my power, to adorn, or in any way to please my sister; yet, I hope, I shall never be obliged for this, to sell my notes. I may be romantic, but I preserve them as a sacred deposit. Their full amount is justly due to me, but as embarrassments, the natural consequences of a long war, disable my country from supporting its credit, I shall wait with patience until it is rich enough to discharge them. If that is not in my day, they shall be transmitted as an honourable certificate to posterity, that I have humbly imitated our illustrious Washington, in having exposed my health and life in the service of my country, without reaping any other reward than the glory of conquering in so arduous a contest.

Charlotte. Well said heroics. Why, my dear Henry, you have such a lofty way of saying things, that I protest I almost tremble at the thought of introducing you to the polite circles in the city. The belles would think you were a player run mad, with your head filled with old scraps of tragedy: and, as to the beaux, they might admire, because they would not understand you.— But, however, I must, I believe, venture to introduce you to two or three ladies of my acquaintance.

Letitia. And that will make him acquainted with thirty or forty beaux.

Charlotte. Oh! brother, you don't know what a fund of happiness you have in store.

Manly. I fear, sister, I have not refinement sufficient to enjoy it.

Charlotte. Oh! you cannot fail being pleased.

Letitia. Our ladies are so delicate and dressy.

Charlotte. And our beaux so dressy and delicate.

Letitia. Our ladies chat and flirt so agreeably.

Charlotte. And our beaux simper and bow so gracefully.

Letitia. With their hair so trim and neat.

Charlotte. And their faces so soft and sleek.

Letitia. Their buckles so tonish and bright.

Charlotte. And their hands so slender and white.

Letitia. I vow, Charlotte, we are quite poetical.

Charlotte. And then, brother, the faces of the beaux are of such a lily white hue! None of that horrid robustness of constitution, that vulgar corn-fed glow of health, which can only serve to alarm an unmarried lady with apprehensions, and prove a melancholy memento to a married one, that she can never hope for the happiness of being a widow. I will say this to the credit of our city beaux, that such is the delicacy of their complexion, dress, and address, that, even had I no reliance upon the honour of the dear Adonises, I would trust myself in any possible situation with them, without the least apprehensions of rudeness.

Manly. Sister Charlotte!

Charlotte. Now, now, now brother (*interrupting him*), now don't go to spoil my mirth with a dash of your gravity; I am so glad to see you, I am in tip-top spirits. Oh! that you could be with us at a little snug party. There is Billy Simper, Jack Chassé, and Colonel Van Titter, Miss Promonade, and the two Miss Tambours, sometimes make a party, with some other ladies, in a side-box at the play. Everything is conducted with such decorum,—first we bow round to the company in general, then to each one in particular, then we have so many inquiries after each other's health, and we are so happy to meet each other, and it is so many ages since we last had that pleasure, <and, if a married lady is in company, we have such a sweet dissertation upon her son Bobby's chin-cough> then the curtain rises, then our sensibility is all awake, and then by the mere force of apprehension, we torture some harmless expression into a double meaning, which the poor author never dreamt of, and then we have recourse to our fans, and then we blush, and then the gentlemen jog one another, peep under the fan, and make the prettiest remarks; and then we giggle and they simper, and they giggle and we simper, and then the curtain drops, and then for nuts and oranges, and then we bow, and it 's pray Ma'am take it, and pray Sir keep it, and oh! not for the world, Sir: and then the curtain rises again, and then we blush, and giggle, and simper, and bow, all over again. Oh! the sentimental charms of a side-box conversation! (*All laugh.*)

MANLY. Well, sister, I join heartily with you in the laugh; for, in my opinion, it is as justifiable to laugh at folly, as it is reprehensible to ridicule misfortune.

CHARLOTTE. Well, but brother, positively, I can't introduce you in these clothes: why, your coat looks as if it were calculated for the vulgar purpose of keeping yourself comfortable.

MANLY. This coat was my regimental coat in the late war. The public tumults of our state have induced me to buckle on the sword in support of that government which I once fought to establish. I can only say, sister, that there was a time when this coat was respectable, and some people even thought that those men who had endured so many winter campaigns in the service of their country, without bread, clothing, or pay, at least deserved that the poverty of their appearance should not be ridiculed.

CHARLOTTE. We agree in opinion entirely, brother, though it would not have done for me to have said it: it is the coat makes the man respectable. In the time of the war, when we were almost frightened to death, why, your coat was respectable, that is, fashionable; now another kind of coat is fashionable, that is, respectable. And pray direct the taylor to make yours the height of the fashion.

MANLY. Though it is of little consequence to me of what shape my coat is, yet, as to the height of the fashion, there you will please to excuse me, sister. You know my sentiments on that subject. I have often lamented the advantage which the French have over us in that particular. In Paris, the fashions have their dawnings, their routine and declensions, and depend as much upon the caprice of the day as in other countries; but there every lady assumes a right to deviate from the general *ton*, as far as will be of advantage to her own appearance. In America, the cry is, what is the fashion? and we follow it, indiscriminately, because it is so.

CHARLOTTE. Therefore it is, that when large hoops are in fashion, we often see many a plump girl lost in the immensity of a hoop petticoat, whose want of height and *em-bon-point* would never have been remarked in any other dress. When the high head-dress is the mode, how then do we see a lofty cushion, with a profusion of gauze, feathers, and ribband, supported by a face no bigger than an apple; whilst a broad full-faced lady, who really would have appeared tolerably handsome in a large head-dress, looks with her smart chapeau as masculine as a soldier.

MANLY. But remember, my dear sister, and I wish all my fair country-women would recollect, that the only excuse a young lady can have for going extravagantly into a fashion, is, because it makes her look extravagantly handsome.— Ladies, I must wish you a good morning.

CHARLOTTE. But, brother, you are going to make home with us.

MANLY. Indeed, I cannot. I have seen my uncle, and explained that matter.

CHARLOTTE. Come and dine with us, then. We have a family dinner about half past four o'clock.

MANLY. I am engaged to dine with the Spanish ambassador. I was introduced to him by an old brother officer; and instead of freezing me with a cold card of compliment to dine with him ten days hence, he, with the true old Castilian frankness, in a friendly manner, asked me to dine with him to-day—an honour I could not refuse. Sister, adieu— Madam, your most obedient— (*Exit.*)

CHARLOTTE. I will wait upon you to the door, brother; I have something particular to say to you. (*Exit.*)

LETITIA (*alone*). What a pair!— She the pink of flirtation, he the essence of everything that is *outré* and gloomy.— I think I have completely deceived Charlotte by my manner of speaking of Mr. Dimple; she 's too much the friend of Maria to be confided in. He is certainly rendering himself disagreeable to Maria, in order to break with her and proffer his hand to me. This is what the delicate fellow hinted in our last conversation. (*Exit.*)

SCENE 2. *The Mall.*

(*Enter* JESSAMY.)

Positively this Mall is a very pretty place. I hope the city won't ruin it by repairs. To be sure, it won't do to speak of in the same day with Ranelagh or Vauxhall; however, it 's a fine place for a young fellow to display his person to advantage. Indeed, nothing is lost here; the girls have taste, and I am very happy to find they have adopted the elegant

London fashion of looking back, after a genteel fellow like me has passed them. Ah! who comes here? This, by his aukwardness, must be the Yankee colonel's servant. I 'll accost him.

(*Enter* JONATHAN.)

Votre très—humble serviteur, Monsieur. I understand Colonel Manly, the Yankee officer, has the honour of your services.

JONATHAN. Sir!—

JESSAMY. I say, Sir, I understand that Colonel Manly has the honour of having you for a servant.

JONATHAN. Servant! Sir, do you take me for a neger,—I am Colonel Manly's waiter.

JESSAMY. A true Yankee distinction, egad, without a difference. Why, Sir, do you not perform all the offices of a servant? Do you not even blacken his boots?

JONATHAN. Yes; I do grease them a bit sometimes; but I am a true blue son of liberty, for all that. Father said I should come as Colonel Manly's waiter to see the world, and all that; but no man shall master me: my father has as good a farm as the colonel.

JESSAMY. Well, Sir, we will not quarrel about terms upon the eve of an acquaintance, from which I promise myself so much satisfaction,—therefore sans ceremonie—

JONATHAN. What?—

JESSAMY. I say, I am extremely happy to see Colonel Manly's waiter.

JONATHAN. Well, and I vow, too, I am pretty considerably glad to see you—but what the dogs need of all this outlandish lingo? Who may you be, Sir, if I may be so bold?

JESSAMY. I have the honour to be Mr. Dimple's servant, or, if you please, waiter. We lodge under the same roof, and should be glad of the honour of your acquaintance.

JONATHAN. You a waiter! By the living jingo, you look so topping, I took you for one of the agents to Congress.

JESSAMY. The brute has discernment notwithstanding his appearance.— Give me leave to say I wonder then at your familiarity.

JONATHAN. Why, as to the matter of that, Mr.—pray, what 's your name?

JESSAMY. Jessamy, at your service.

JONATHAN. Why, I swear we don't make any great matter of distinction in our state, between quality and other folks.

JESSAMY. This is, indeed, a levelling principle. I hope, Mr. Jonathan, you have not taken part with the insurgents.

JONATHAN. Why, since General Shays has sneaked off, and given us the bag to hold, I don't care to give my opinion; but you 'll promise not to tell—put your ear this way—you won't tell?— I vow, I did think the sturgeons were right.

JESSAMY. I thought, Mr. Jonathan, you Massachusetts men always argued with a gun in your hand.— Why did n't you join them?

JONATHAN. Why, the colonel is one of those folks called the Shin—shin—dang it all, I can't speak them lignum vitæ words—you know who I mean—there is a company of them—they wear a China goose at their button-hole—a kind of gilt thing.— Now the colonel told father and brother,—you must know there are, let me see—there is Elnathan, Silas, and Barnabas, Tabitha—no, no, she 's a she—tarnation, now I have it—there 's Elnathan, Silas, Barnabas, Jonathan, that 's I —seven of us, six went into the wars, and I staid at home to take care of mother. Colonel said that it was a burning shame for the true blue Bunker-hill sons of liberty, who had fought Governor Hutchinson, Lord North, and the Devil, to have any hand in kicking up a cursed dust against a government, which we had every mother's son of us a hand in making.

JESSAMY. Bravo!— Well, have you been abroad in the city since your arrival? What have you seen that is curious and entertaining?

JONATHAN. Oh! I have seen a power of fine sights. I went to see two marblestone men and a leaden horse, that stands out in doors in all weathers; and when I came where they was, one had got no head, and t' other wer 'nt there. They said as how the leaden man was a damn'd tory, and that he took wit in his anger and rode off in the time of the troubles.

JESSAMY. But this was not the end of your excursion.

JONATHAN. Oh, no; I went to a place they call Holy Ground. Now I counted this was a place where folks go to meeting; so I put my hymn-book in my pocket, and walked softly and grave as a minister; and when I came there, the dogs a bit of a meeting-house could I see. At last I spied a young gentlewoman standing by one of the seats, which they have here at the doors—I took her to be the deacon's daughter, and she looked so kind, and so obliging, that I thought I would go and ask her the way to lecture, and would you think it—she called me dear, and sweeting, and honey, just as if we were married; by the living jingo, I had a month's mind to buss her.

JESSAMY. Well, but how did it end?

JONATHAN. Why, as I was standing talking with her, a parcel of sailor men and boys got round me, the snarl headed curs fell a-kicking and cursing of me at such a tarnal rate, that, I vow, I was glad to take to my heels and split home, right off, tail on end like a stream of chalk.

JESSAMY. Why, my dear friend, you are not acquainted with the city; that girl you saw was a— (*Whispers.*)

JONATHAN. Mercy on my soul! was that young woman a harlot!— Well, if this is New York Holy Ground, what must the Holy-day Ground be!

JESSAMY. Well, you should not judge of the city too rashly. We have a number of elegant fine girls here, that make a man's leisure hours pass very agreeably. I would esteem it an honour to announce you to some of them.— Gad! that announce is a select word; I wonder where I picked it up.

JONATHAN. I don't want to know them.

JESSAMY. Come, come, my dear friend, I see that I must assume the honour of being the director of your amusements. Nature has give us passions, and youth and opportunity stimulate to gratify them. It is no shame, my dear Blueskin, for a man to amuse himself with a little gallantry.

JONATHAN. Girl huntry! I don't altogether understand. I never played at that game. I know how to play hunt the squirrel, but I can't play anything with the girls; I am as good as married.

JESSAMY. Vulgar, horrid brute! Married, and above a hundred miles from his wife, and think that an objection to his making love to every woman he meets! He never can have read, no, he never can have been in a room with a volume of the divine Chesterfield.— So you are married?

JONATHAN. No, I don't say so; I said I was as good as married, a kind of promise.

JESSAMY. As good as married!—

JONATHAN. Why, yes; there's Tabitha Wymen, the deacon's daughter, at home, she and I have been courting a great while, and folks say as how we are to be married; and so I broke a piece of money with her when we parted, and she promised not to spark it with Solomon Dyer while I am gone. You would n't have me false to my true love, would you?

JESSAMY. May be you have another reason for constancy; possibly the young lady has a fortune? Ha! Mr. Jonathan, the solid charms; the chains of love are never so binding as when the links are made of gold.

JONATHAN. Why, as to fortune, I must needs say her father is pretty dumb rich; he went representative for our town last year. He will give her—let me see—four times seven is—seven times four—nought and carry one;—he will give her twenty acres of land—somewhat rocky though—a bible, and a cow.

JESSAMY. Twenty acres of rock, a bible, and a cow! Why, my dear Mr. Jonathan, we have servant maids, or, as you would more elegantly express it, wait'resses, in this city, who collect more in one year from their mistresses' cast clothes.

JONATHAN. You don't say so!—

JESSAMY. Yes, and I'll introduce you to one of them. There is a little lump of flesh and delicacy that lives at next door, wait'ress to Miss Maria; we often see her on the stoop.

JONATHAN. But are you sure she would be courted by me?

JESSAMY. Never doubt it; remember a faint heart never—blisters on my tongue—I was going to be guilty of a vile proverb; flat against the authority of Chesterfield.— I say there can be no doubt, that the brilliancy of your merit will secure you a favourable reception.

JONATHAN. Well, but what must I say to her?

JESSAMY. Say to her! why, my dear friend, though I admire your profound knowledge on every other subject, yet, you will pardon my saying, that your want of opportunity has made the female heart escape the poignancy of your penetration. Say to her!— Why, when a man goes a-courting, and hopes for success, he must begin with doing, and not saying.

JONATHAN. Well, what must I do?

JESSAMY. Why, when you are introduced you must make five or six elegant bows.

JONATHAN. Six elegant bows! I understand that; six, you say? Well—

JESSAMY. Then you must press and kiss her hand; then press and kiss, and so on to her lips and cheeks; then talk as much as you can about hearts, darts, flames, nectar and ambrosia—the more incoherent the better.

JONATHAN. Well, but suppose she should be angry with I?

JESSAMY. Why, if she should pretend—please to observe, Mr. Jonathan—if she should pretend to be offended, you must— But I'll tell you how my master acted in such a case: He was seated by a young lady of eighteen upon a sopha, plucking with a wanton hand the blooming sweets of youth and beauty. When the lady thought it necessary to check his ardour, she called up a frown upon her lovely face, so irresistably alluring, that it would have warmed the frozen bosom of age: remember, said she, putting her delicate arm upon his, remember your character and my honour. My master instantly dropped upon his knees, with eyes swimming with love, cheeks glowing with desire, and in the gentlest modulation of voice, he said— My dear Caroline, in a few months our hands will be indissolubly united at the altar; our hearts I feel are already so—the favours you now grant as evidence of your affection, are favours indeed; yet when the ceremony is once past, what will now be received with rapture, will then be attributed to duty.

JONATHAN. Well, and what was the consequence?

JESSAMY. The consequence!— Ah! forgive me, my dear friend, but you New England gentlemen have such a laudable curiosity of seeing the bottom of every thing;—why, to be honest, I confess I saw the blooming cherub of a consequence smiling in its angelic mother's arms, about ten months afterwards.

JONATHAN. Well, if I follow all your plans, make them six bows, and all that; shall I have such little cherubim consequences?

JESSAMY. Undoubtedly.— What are you musing upon?

JONATHAN. You say you'll certainly make me acquainted?— Why, I was thinking then how I should contrive to pass this broken piece of silver—won't it buy a sugar-dram?

JESSAMY. What is that, the love-token from the deacon's daughter?— You come on bravely. But I must hasten to my master. Adieu, my dear friend.

JONATHAN. Stay, Mr. Jessamy—must I buss her when I am introduced to her?

JESSAMY. I told you, you must kiss her.

JONATHAN. Well, but must I buss her?

JESSAMY. Why, kiss and buss, and buss and kiss, is all one.

JONATHAN. Oh! my dear friend, though you have a profound knowledge of all, a pugnancy[1] of tribulation, you don't know everything. (*Exit.*)

JESSAMY (*alone*). Well, certainly I improve; my master could not have insinuated himself with more address into the heart of a man he despised.— Now will this blundering dog sicken Jenny with his nauseous pawings, until she flies into my arms for very ease. How sweet will the contrast be, between the blundering Jonathan, and the courtly and accomplished Jessamy!

END OF THE SECOND ACT.

ACT THIRD.

SCENE 1. DIMPLE'S *Room.*

DIMPLE *discovered at a Toilet, Reading.*

"Women have in general but one object, which is their beauty." Very true, my lord; positively very true. "Nature has hardly formed a woman ugly enough to be insensible to flattery upon her person." Extremely just, my lord; every day's delightful experience confirms this. "If her face is so shocking, that she must, in some degree, be conscious of it, her figure and air, she thinks, make ample amends for it." The sallow Miss Wan is a proof of this.— Upon my telling the distasteful wretch, the other day, that her countenance spoke the pensive language of sentiment, and that Lady Wortley Montague declared, that if the ladies were arrayed in the garb of innocence, the face would be the last part which would be admired as Monsieur Milton expresses it, she grin'd horribly a ghastly smile. "If her figure is deformed, she thinks her face counterbalances it."

(*Enter* JESSAMY *with letters.*)

[1] There is an obsolete word "pugnancy" meaning "opposition" but this is probably an attempt to imitate Jessamy's "poignancy." See p. 61.

DIMPLE. Where got you these, Jessamy?

JESSAMY. Sir, the English packet is arrived.

(DIMPLE *opens and reads a letter enclosing notes.*)

"Sir,

"I have drawn bills on you in favour of Messrs. Van Cash and Co. as per margin. I have taken up your note to Col. Piquet, and discharged your debts to my Lord Lurcher and Sir Harry Rook. I herewith enclose you copies of the bills, which I have no doubt will be immediately honoured. On failure, I shall empower some lawyer in your country to recover the amounts.

"I am, Sir,

"Your most humble servant,

"JOHN HAZARD."

Now, did not my lord expressly say, that it was unbecoming a well-bred man to be in a passion, I confess I should be ruffled. (*Reads.*) "There is no accident so unfortunate, which a wise man may not turn to his advantage; nor any accident so fortunate, which a fool will not turn to his disadvantage." True, my lord: but how advantage can be derived from this, I can't see. Chesterfield himself, who made, however, the worst practice of the most excellent precepts, was never in so embarrassing a situation. I love the person of Charlotte, and it is necessary I should command the fortune of Letitia. As to Maria!—I doubt not by my *sang-froid* behavior I shall compel her to decline the match; but the blame must not fall upon me. A prudent man, as my lord says, should take all the credit of a good action to himself, and throw the discredit of a bad one upon others. I must break with Maria, marry Letitia, and as for Charlotte—why, Charlotte must be a companion to my wife.— Here, Jessamy!

(*Enter* JESSAMY.)

(DIMPLE *folds and seals two letters.*)

DIMPLE. Here, Jessamy, take this letter to my love. (*Gives one.*)

JESSAMY. To which of your honour's loves?— Oh! (*reading*) to Miss Letitia, your honour's rich love.

DIMPLE. And this (*delivers another*) to Miss Charlotte Manly. See that you deliver them privately.

JESSAMY. Yes, your honour. (*Going.*)

DIMPLE. Jessamy, who are these strange lodgers that came to the house last night?

JESSAMY. Why, the master is a Yankee colonel; I have not seen much of him; but the man is the most unpolished animal your honour ever disgraced your eyes by looking upon. I have had one of the most *outré* conversations with him!— He really has a most prodigious effect upon my risibility.

DIMPLE. I ought, according to every rule of Chesterfield, to wait on him and insinuate myself into his good graces.— Jessamy, wait on the colonel with my compliments, and if he is disengaged, I will do myself the honour of paying him my respects.— Some ignorant unpolished boor—

(JESSAMY *goes off and returns.*)

JESSAMY. Sir, the colonel is gone out, and Jonathan, his servant, says that he is gone to stretch his legs upon the Mall— Stretch his legs! what an indelicacy of diction!

DIMPLE. Very well. Reach me my hat and sword. I'll accost him there, in my way to Letitia's, as by accident; pretend to be struck with his person and address, and endeavour to steal into his confidence. Jessamy, I have no business for you at present. (*Exit.*)

JESSAMY. (*Taking up the book.*) My master and I obtain our knowledge from the same source;—though, gad! I think myself much the prettier fellow of the two. (*Surveying himself in the glass.*) That was a brilliant thought, to insinuate that I folded my master's letters for him; the folding is so neat, that it does honour to the operator. I once intended to have insinuated that I wrote his letters too; but that was before I saw them; it won't do now; no honour there, positively.— "Nothing looks more vulgar (*reading affectedly*), ordinary, and illiberal, than ugly, uneven, and ragged nails; the ends of which should be kept even and clean, not tipped with black, and cut in small segments of circles"— Segments of circles! surely my lord did not consider that he wrote for the beaux. Segments of circles! what a crabbed term! Now I dare answer, that my master, with all his learning, does not know that this means, according to the present mode, to let the nails grow long, and then cut them off even at top. (*Laughing without.*) Ha! that's Jenny's titter. I protest I despair of ever teaching that girl to laugh; she has something so execrably natural in her laugh, that I declare it absolutely discomposes my nerves. How came she into our house!—(*Calls.*) Jenny!

(*Enter* JENNY.)

JESSAMY. Prythee, Jenny, don't spoil your fine face with laughing.

JENNY. Why, must n't I laugh, Mr. Jessamy?

JESSAMY. You may smile; but, as my lord says, nothing can authorise a laugh.

JENNY. Well, but I can't help laughing—Have you seen him. Mr. Jessamy? Ha, ha, ha!

JESSAMY. Seen whom?—

JENNY. Why, Jonathan, the New-England colonel's servant. Do you know he was at the play last night, and the stupid creature don't know where he has been. He would not go to a play for the world; he thinks it was a show, as he calls it.

JESSAMY. As ignorant and unpolished as he is, do you know, Miss Jenny, that I propose to introduce him to the honour of your acquaintance.

JENNY. Introduce him to me! for what?

JESSAMY. Why, my lovely girl, that you may take him under your protection, as Madam Rambouilliet did young Stanhope; that you may, by your plastic hand, mould this uncouth cub into a gentleman. He is to make love to you.

JENNY. Make love to me!—

JESSAMY. Yes, Mistress Jenny, make love to you; and, I doubt not, when he shall become domesticated in your kitchen, that this boor, under your auspices, will soon become *un aimable petit Jonathan.*

JENNY. I must say, Mr. Jessamy, if he copies after me, he will be vastly monstrously polite.

JESSAMY. Stay here one moment, and I will call him.—Jonathan!—Mr. Jonathan!— (*Calls.*)

JONATHAN. (*Within.*) Holla! there.—(*Enters.*) You promise to stand by me—six bows you say. (*Bows.*)

JESSAMY. Mrs. Jenny, I have the honour of presenting Mr. Jonathan, Colonel Manly's waiter, to you. I am extremely happy that I have it in my power to make two worthy people acquainted with each other's merit.

JENNY. So, Mr. Jonathan, I hear you were at the play last night.

JONATHAN. At the play! why, did you think I went to the devil's drawing-room!

JENNY. The devil's drawing-room!

JONATHAN. Yes; why an't cards and dice the devil's device; and the play-house the shop where the devil hangs out the vanities of the world, upon the tenterhooks of temptation. I believe you have not heard how they were acting the old boy one night, and the wicked one came among them sure enough; and went right off in a storm, and carried one quarter of the play-house with him. Oh! no, no, no! you won't catch me at a play-house, I warrant you.

JENNY. Well, Mr. Jonathan, though I don't scruple your veracity, I have some reasons for believing you were there; pray, where were you about six o'clock?

JONATHAN. Why, I went to see one Mr. Morrison, the *hocus pocus* man; they said as how he could eat a case knife.

JENNY. Well, and how did you find the place?

JONATHAN. As I was going about here and there, to and again, to find it, I saw a great croud of folks going into a long entry, that had lantherns over the door; so I asked a man, whether that was not the place where they played *hocus pocus?* He was a very civil kind man, though he did speak like the Hessians; he lifted up his eyes and said—"they play *hocus pocus* tricks enough there, Got knows, mine friend."

JENNY. Well—

JONATHAN. So I went right in, and they shewed me away clean up to the garret, just like a meeting-house gallery. And so I saw a power of topping folks, all sitting round in little cabbins, <just like father's corn-cribs;>—and then there was such a squeaking with the fiddles, and such a tarnal blaze with the lights, my head was near turned. At last the people that sat near me set up such a hissing—hiss—like so many mad cats; and then they went thump, thump, thump, just like our Peleg threshing wheat, and stampt away, just like the nation; and called out for one Mr. Langolee,—I suppose he helps act<s> the tricks.

JENNY. Well, and what did you do all this time?

JONATHAN. Gor, I—I liked the fun, and so I thumpt away, and hiss'd as lustily as the best of 'em. One sailor-looking man that sat by me, seeing me stamp, and knowing I was a cute fellow, because I could make a roaring noise, clapt me on the shoulder and said, you are a d——d hearty cock, smite my timbers! I told him so I was, but I thought he need not swear so, and make use of such naughty words.

JESSAMY. The savage!—Well, and did you see the man with his tricks?

JONATHAN. Why, I vow, as I was looking out for him, they lifted up a great green cloth, and let us look right into the next neighbour's house. Have you a good many houses in New York made so in that 'ere way?

JENNY. Not many: but did you see the family?

JONATHAN. Yes, swamp it; I see'd the family.

JENNY. Well, and how did you like them?

JONATHAN. Why, I vow they were pretty much like other families;—there was a poor, good natured, curse of a husband, and a sad rantipole of a wife.

JENNY. But did you see no other folks?

JONATHAN. Yes. There was one youngster, they called him Mr. Joseph; he talked as sober and as pious as a minister; but like some ministers that I know, he was a sly tike in his heart for all that: He was going to ask a young woman to spark it with him, and—the Lord have mercy on my soul!—she was another man's wife.

JESSAMY. The Wabash!

JENNY. And did you see any more folks?

JONATHAN. Why they came on as thick as mustard. For my part, I thought the house was haunted. There was a soldier fellow, who talked about his row de dow dow, and courted a young woman: but of all the cute folk I saw, I liked one little fellow—

JENNY. Aye! who was he?

JONATHAN. Why, he had red hair, and a little round plump face like mine, only not altogether so handsome. His name was Darby:—that was his baptizing name, his other name I forgot. Oh! it was, Wig—Wag—Wag-all, Darby Wag-all;—pray, do you know him?—I should like to take a sling with him, or a drap of cyder with a pepper-pod in it, to make it warm and comfortable.

JENNY. I can't say I have that pleasure.

JONATHAN. I wish you did, he is a cute fellow. But there was one thing I did n't like in that Mr. Darby; and that was, he was afraid of some of them 'ere shooting irons, such as your troopers wear on training days. Now, I 'm a true born Yankee American son of liberty, and I never was afraid of a gun yet in all my life.

JENNY. Well, Mr. Jonathan, you were certainly at the play-house.

JONATHAN. I at the play-house!—Why did n't I see the play then?

JENNY. Why, the people you saw were players.

JONATHAN. Mercy on my soul! did I see the wicked players?—Mayhap that 'ere Darby that I liked so, was the old serpent himself, and had his cloven foot in his pocket. Why, I vow, now I come to think on 't, the candles seemed to burn blue, and I am sure where I sat it smelt tarnally of brimstone.

JESSAMY. Well, Mr. Jonathan, from your account, which I confess is very accurate, you must have been at the play-house.

JONATHAN. Why, I vow I began to smell a rat. When I came away, I went to the man for my money again: you want your money, says he; yes, says I; for what, says he; why, says I, no man shall jocky me out of my money; I paid my money to see sights, and the dogs a bit of a sight have I seen, unless you call listening to people's private business a sight. Why, says he, it is the School for Scandalization.—The School for Scandalization!—Oh, ho! no wonder you New York folks are so cute at it, when you go to school to learn it: and so I jogged off.

JESSAMY. My dear Jenny, my master's business drags me from you; would to heaven I knew no other servitude than to your charms.

JONATHAN. Well, but don't go; you won't leave me so.—

JESSAMY. Excuse me.—Remember the cash. (*Aside to him, and—Exit.*)

JENNY. Mr. Jonathan, won't you please to sit down. Mr. Jessamy tells me you wanted to have some conversation with me.

(*Having brought forward two chairs, they sit.*)

JONATHAN. Ma'am!—

JENNY. Sir!—

JONATHAN. Ma'am!—

JENNY. Pray, how do you like the city, Sir?

JONATHAN. Ma'am!—

JENNY. I say, Sir, how do you like New York?

JONATHAN. Ma'am!—

JENNY. The stupid creature! but I must pass some little time with him, if it is only to endeavour to learn, whether it was his master that made such an abrupt entrance into our house, and my young mistress's heart, this morning. (*Aside.*) As you don't seem to like to talk, Mr. Jonathan—do you sing?

JONATHAN. Gor, I—I am glad she asked that, for I forgot what Mr. Jessamy bid me say, and I dare as well be hanged as act what he bid me do, I 'm so ashamed. (*Aside.*) Yes, Ma'am, I can sing—I can sing Mear, Old Hundred, and Bangor.

JENNY. Oh! I don't mean psalm tunes. Have you no little song to please the ladies; such as Roslin Castle, or the Maid of the Mill?

JONATHAN. Why, all my tunes go to meeting tunes, save one, and I count you won't altogether like that 'ere.

JENNY. What is it called?

JONATHAN. I am sure you have heard folks talk about it, it is called Yankee Doodle.

JENNY. Oh! it is the tune I am fond of; and, if I know anything of my mistress, she would be glad to dance to it. Pray, sing?

JONATHAN. (*Sings.*)

Father and I went up to camp,
Along with Captain Goodwin;
And there we saw the men and boys,
As thick as hasty pudding.
Yankee Doodle do, etc.

And there we saw a swamping gun,
Big as log of maple,
On a little deuced cart,
A load for father's cattle.
Yankee Doodle do, etc.

And every time they fired it off,
It took a horn of powder,
It made a noise—like father's gun,
Only a nation louder.
Yankee Doodle do, etc.

There was a man in our town,
His name was——

No, no, that won't do. Now, if I was with Tabitha Wymen and Jemima Cawley, down at father Chase's, I should n't mind singing this all out before them—you would be affronted if I was to sing that, though that 's a lucky thought; if you should be affronted, I have something dang'd cute, which Jessamy told me to say to you.

JENNY. Is that all! I assure you I like it of all things.

JONATHAN. No, no; I can sing more, some other time, when you and I are better acquainted, I 'll sing the whole of it—no, no—that 's a fib—I can't sing but a hundred and ninety verses: our Tabitha at home can sing it all.— (*Sings.*)

Marblehead 's a rocky place,
And Cape-Cod is sandy;
Charleston is burnt down,
Boston is the dandy.
Yankee Doodle do, etc.

I vow, my own town song has put me into such topping spirits, that I believe I 'll begin to do a little, as Jessamy says we must when we go a courting—(*Runs and kisses her.*) Burning rivers! cooling flames! red hot roses! pig-nuts! hasty-pudding and ambrosia!

JENNY. What means this freedom! you insulting wretch. (*Strikes him.*)

JONATHAN. Are you affronted?

JENNY. Affronted! with what looks shall I express my anger?

JONATHAN. Looks! why, as to the matter of looks, you look as cross as a witch.

JENNY. Have you no feeling for the delicacy of my sex?

JONATHAN. Feeling! Gor, I—I feel the delicacy of your sex pretty smartly (*rubbing his cheek*), though, I vow, I thought when you city ladies courted and married, and all that, you put feeling out of the question. But I want to know whether you are really affronted, or only pretend to be so? 'Cause, if you are certainly right down affronted, I am at the end of my tether;—Jessamy did n't tell me what to say to you.

JENNY. Pretend to be affronted!

JONATHAN. Aye, aye, if you only pretend, you shall hear how I 'll go to work to make cherubim consequences. (*Runs up to her.*)

JENNY. Begone, you brute!

JONATHAN. That looks like mad; but I won't lose my speech. My dearest Jenny—your name is Jenny, I think? My dearest Jenny, though I have the highest esteem for the sweet favours you have just now granted me—Gor, that 's a fib though, but Jessamy says it is not wicked to tell lies to the women. (*Aside.*) I say, though I have the highest esteem for the favours you have just now granted me, yet, you will consider, that as soon as the dissolvable knot is tied, they will no longer be favours, but only matters of duty, and matters of course.

JENNY. Marry you! you audacious monster! get out of my sight, or rather let me fly from you. (*Exit hastily.*)

JONATHAN. Gor! she's gone off in a swinging passion, before I had time to think of consequences. If this is the way with your city ladies, give me the twenty acres of rock, the bible, the cow, and Tabitha, and a little peaceable bundling.

SCENE 2. *The Mall.*

(*Enter* MANLY.)

It must be so, Montague! and it is not all the tribe of Mandevilles shall convince me, that a nation, to become great, must first become dissipated. Luxury is surely the bane of a nation: Luxury! which enervates both soul and body, by opening a thousand new sources of enjoyment, opens, also, a thousand new sources of contention and want: Luxury! which renders a people weak at home, and accessible to bribery, corruption, and force from abroad. When the Grecian states knew no other tools than the axe and the saw, the Grecians were a great, a free, and a happy people. The kings of Greece devoted their lives to the service of their country, and her senators knew no other superiority over their fellow-citizens than a glorious pre-eminence in danger and virtue. They exhibited to the world a noble spectacle,—a number of independent states united by a similarity of language, sentiment, manners, common interest, and common consent, in one grand mutual league of protection.—And, thus united, long might they have continued the cherishers of arts and sciences, the protectors of the oppressed, the scourge of tyrants, and the safe asylum of liberty: But when foreign gold, and still more pernicious, foreign luxury, had crept among them, they sapped the vitals of their virtue. The virtues of their ancestors were only found in their writings. Envy and suspicion, the vices of little minds, possessed them. The various states engendered jealousies of each other; and, more unfortunately, growing jealous of their great federal council, the Amphictyons, they forgot that their common safety had existed, and would exist, in giving them an honourable extensive prerogative. The common good was lost in the pursuit of private interest; and that people, who, by uniting, might have stood against the world in arms, by dividing, crumbled into ruin;—their name is now only known in the page of the historian, and what they once were, is all we have left to admire. Oh! that America! Oh! that my country, would in this her day, learn the things which belong to her peace!

(*Enter* DIMPLE.)

DIMPLE. You are Colonel Manly, I presume?

MANLY. At your service, Sir.

DIMPLE. My name is Dimple, Sir. I have the honour to be a lodger in the same house with you, and hearing you were in the Mall, came hither to take the liberty of joining you.

MANLY. You are very obliging, Sir.

DIMPLE. As I understand you are a stranger here, Sir, I have taken the liberty to introduce myself to your acquaintance, as possibly I may have it in my power to point out some things in this city worthy your notice.

MANLY. An attention to strangers is worthy a liberal mind, and must ever be gratefully received. But to a soldier, who has no fixed abode, such attentions are particularly pleasing.

DIMPLE. Sir, there is no character so respectable as that of a soldier. And, indeed, when we reflect how much we owe to those brave men who have suffered so much in the service of their country, and secured to us those inestimable blessings that we now enjoy, our liberty and independence, they demand every attention which gratitude can pay. For my own part, I never meet an officer, but I embrace him as my friend, nor a private in distress, but I insensibly extend my charity to him.—I have hit the Bum[p]kin off very tolerably. (*Aside.*)

MANLY. Give me your hand, Sir! I do not proffer this hand to everybody; but you steal into my heart. I hope I am as insensible to flattery as most men; but I declare (it may be my weak side), that I never hear the name of soldier mentioned with respect, but I experience a thrill of pleasure, which I never feel on any other occasion.

DIMPLE. Will you give me leave, my dear colonel, to confer an obligation on myself, by shewing you some civilities during your stay here, and giving a similar opportunity to some of my friends?

MANLY. Sir, I thank you; but I believe my stay in this city will be very short.

DIMPLE. I can introduce you to some men of excellent sense, in whose company you will esteem yourself happy; and, by way of amusement, to some fine girls, who will listen to your soft things with pleasure.

MANLY. Sir, I should be proud of the honour of being acquainted with those gentlemen;—but, as for the ladies, I don't understand you.

DIMPLE. Why, Sir, I need not tell you, that when a young gentleman is alone with a young lady, he must say some soft things to her fair cheek—indeed the lady will expect it. To be sure, there is not much pleasure, when a man of the world and a finished coquet meet, who perfectly know each other; but how delicious is it to excite the emotions of joy, hope, expectation, and delight, in the bosom of a lovely girl, who believes every tittle of what you say to be serious.

MANLY. Serious, Sir! In my opinion, the man, who, under pretensions of marriage, can plant thorns in the bosom of an innocent, unsuspecting girl, is more detestable than a common robber, in the same proportion, as private violence is more despicable than open force, and money of less value than happiness.

DIMPLE. How he awes me by the superiority of his sentiments. (*Aside.*) As you say, Sir, a gentleman should be cautious how he mentions marriage.

MANLY. Cautious, Sir! <No person more approves of an intercourse between the sexes than I do. Female conversation softens our manners, whilst our discourse, from the superiority of our literary advantages, improves their minds. But, in our young country, where there is no such thing as gallantry, when a gentleman speaks of love to a lady, whether he mentions marriage, or not, she ought to conclude, either that he meant to insult her, or, that his intentions are the most serious and honourable.> How mean, how cruel, is it, by a thousand tender assiduities, to win the affections of an amiable girl, and though you leave her virtue unspotted, to betray her into the appearance of so many tender partialities, that every man of delicacy would suppress his inclination towards her, by supposing her heart engaged! Can any man, for the trivial gratification of his leisure hours, affect the happiness of a whole life! His not having spoken of marriage, may add to his perfidy, but can be no excuse for his conduct.

DIMPLE. Sir, I admire your sentiments;—they are mine. The light observations that fell from me, were only a principle of the tongue; they came not from the heart—my practice has ever disapproved these principles.

MANLY. I believe you, Sir. I should with reluctance suppose that those pernicious sentiments could find admittance into the heart of a gentleman.

DIMPLE. I am now, Sir, going to visit a family, where, if you please, I will have the honour of introducing you. Mr. Manly's ward, Miss Letitia, is a young lady of immense fortune; and his niece, Miss Charlotte Manly, is a young lady of great sprightliness and beauty.

MANLY. That gentleman, Sir, is my uncle, and Miss Manly my sister.

DIMPLE. The devil she is! (*Aside.*) Miss Manly your sister, Sir? I rejoice to hear it, and feel a double pleasure in being known to you.—Plague on him! I wish he was at Boston again with all my soul. (*Aside.*)

MANLY. Come, Sir, will you go?

DIMPLE. I will follow you in a moment, Sir. (*Exit* MANLY.) Plague on it! this is unlucky. A fighting brother is a cursed appendage to a fine girl. Egad! I just stopped in time; had he not discovered himself, in two minutes more I should have told him how well I was with his sister.—Indeed, I cannot see the satisfaction of an intrigue, if one can't have the pleasure of communicating it to our friends. (*Exit.*)

END OF THE THIRD ACT.

ACT FOURTH.

SCENE 1. CHARLOTTE'S *Apartment.*

(CHARLOTTE *leading in* MARIA.)

CHARLOTTE. This is so kind, my sweet friend, to come to see me at this moment.

I declare, if I were going to be married in a few days, as you are, I should scarce have found time to visit my friends.

MARIA. Do you think then that there is an impropriety in it?—How should you dispose of your time?

CHARLOTTE. Why, I should be shut up in my chamber; and my head would so run upon—upon—upon the solemn ceremony that I was to pass through—I declare it would take me above two hours merely to learn that little monosyllable—*Yes.* Ah! my dear, your sentimental imagination does not conceive what that little tiny word implies.

MARIA. Spare me your raillery, my sweet friend; I should love your agreeable vivacity at any other time.

CHARLOTTE. Why this is the very time to amuse you. You grieve me to see you look so unhappy.

MARIA. Have I not reason to look so?

<CHARLOTTE. What new grief distresses you?

MARIA. Oh! how sweet it is, when the heart is borne down with misfortune, to recline and repose on the bosom of friendship! Heaven knows, that, although it is improper for a young lady to praise a gentleman, yet I have ever concealed Mr. Dimple's foibles, and spoke of him as of one whose reputation I expected would be linked with mine: but his late conduct towards me, has turned my coolness into contempt. He behaves as if he meant to insult and disgust me; whilst my father, in the last conversation on the subject of our marriage, spoke of it as a matter which laid near his heart, and in which he would not bear contradiction.

CHARLOTTE. This works well: oh! the generous Dimple. I'll endeavour to excite her to discharge him. (*Aside.*) But, my dear friend, your happiness depends on yourself:—Why don't you discard him? Though the match has been of long standing, I would not be forced to make myself miserable: no parent in the world should oblige me to marry the man I did not like.

MARIA. Oh! my dear, you never lived with your parents, and do not know what influence a father's frowns have upon a daughter's heart. Besides, what have I to allege against Mr. Dimple, to justify myself to the world? He carries himself so smoothly, that every one would impute the blame to me, and call me capricious.

CHARLOTTE. And call her capricious! Did ever such an objection start into the heart of woman? For my part, I wish I had fifty lovers to discard, for no other reason, than because I did not fancy them.> My dear Maria, you will forgive me; I know your candour and confidence in me; but I have at times, I confess, been led to suppose, that some other gentleman was the cause of your aversion to Mr. Dimple.

MARIA. No, my sweet friend, you may be assured, that though I have seen many gentlemen I could prefer to Mr. Dimple, yet I never saw one that I thought I could give my hand to, until this morning.

CHARLOTTE. This morning!

MARIA. Yes;—one of the strangest accidents in the world. The odious Dimple, after disgusting me with his conversation, had just left me, when a gentleman, who, it seems, boards in the same house with him, saw him coming out of our door, and the houses looking very much alike, he came into our house instead of his lodgings; nor did he discover his mistake until he got into the parlour, where I was: he then bowed so gracefully; made such a genteel apology, and looked so manly and noble!—

CHARLOTTE. I see some folks, though it is so great an impropriety, can praise a gentleman, when he happens to be the man of their fancy. (*Aside.*)

MARIA. I don't know how it was,—I hope he did not think me indelicate—but I asked him, I believe, to sit down, or pointed to a chair. He sat down, and instead of having recourse to observations upon the weather, or hackneyed criticisms upon the theatre, he entered readily into a conversation worthy a man of sense to speak, and a lady of delicacy and sentiment to hear. He was not strictly handsome, but he spoke the language of sentiment, and his eyes looked tenderness and honour.

CHARLOTTE. Oh! (*eagerly*) you sentimental grave girls, when your hearts are once touched, beat us rattles a bar's length. And so, you are quite in love with this he-angel?

MARIA. In love with him! How can you rattle so, Charlotte? am I not going to be miserable? (*Sighs.*) In love with a gentleman I never saw but one hour in my life, and don't know his name!—No: I only wished that the man I shall marry, may look, and talk, and act, just like him. Besides, my dear, he is a married man.

CHARLOTTE. Why, that was good natured. —He told you so, I suppose, in mere charity, to prevent your falling in love with him?

MARIA. He did n't tell me so (*peevishly*); he looked as if he was married.

CHARLOTTE. How, my dear, did he look sheepish?

MARIA. I am sure he has a susceptible heart, and the ladies of his acquaintance must be very stupid not to—

CHARLOTTE. Hush! I hear some person coming.

<(*Enter* LETITIA.)

LETITIA. My dear Maria, I am happy to see you. Lud! what a pity it is that you have purchased your wedding clothes.

MARIA. I think so. (*Sighing.*)

LETITIA. Why, my dear, there is the sweetest parcel of silks come over you ever saw. Nancy Brilliant has a full suit come; she sent over her measure, and it fits her to a hair; it is immensely dressy, and made for a court-hoop. I thought they said the large hoops were going out of fashion.

CHARLOTTE. Did you see the hat?—Is it a fact, that the deep laces round the border is still the fashion?>

DIMPLE. (*Within.*) Upon my honour, Sir!

MARIA. Ha! Dimple's voice! My dear, I must take leave of you. There are some things necessary to be done at our house.—Can't I go through the other room?

(*Enter* DIMPLE *and* MANLY.)

DIMPLE. Ladies, your most obedient.

CHARLOTTE. Miss Van Rough, shall I present my brother Henry to you? Colonel Manly, Maria,—Miss Van Rough, brother.

MARIA. Her brother! (*Turns and sees* MANLY.) Oh! my heart! The very gentleman I have been praising.

MANLY. The same amiable girl I saw this morning!

CHARLOTTE. Why, you look as if you were acquainted.

MANLY. I unintentionally intruded into this lady's presence this morning, for which she was so good as to promise me her forgiveness.

CHARLOTTE. Oh! ho! is that the case! Have these two penserosos been together? Were they Henry's eyes that looked so tenderly? (*Aside.*) And so you promised to pardon him? and could you be so good natured?—have you really forgiven him? I beg you would do it for my sake. (*Whispering loud to* MARIA.) But, my dear, as you are in such haste, it would be cruel to detain you: I can show you the way through the other room.

MARIA. Spare me, my sprightly friend.

MANLY. The lady does not, I hope, intend to deprive us of the pleasure of her company so soon.

CHARLOTTE. She has only a mantua-maker who waits for her at home. But, as I am to give my opinion of the dress, I think she cannot go yet. We were talking of the fashions when you came in; but I suppose the subject must be changed to something of more importance now.—Mr. Dimple, will you favour us with an account of the public entertainments?

DIMPLE. Why, really, Miss Manly, you could not have asked me a question more *mal-apropos*. For my part, I must confess, that to a man who has travelled, there is nothing that is worthy the name of amusement to be found in this city.

CHARLOTTE. Except visiting the ladies.

DIMPLE. Pardon me, Madam; that is the avocation of a man of taste. But, for amusement, I positively know of nothing that can be called so, unless you dignify with that title the hopping once a fortnight to the sound of two or three squeaking fiddles, and the clattering of the old tavern windows, or sitting to see the miserable mummers, whom you call actors, murder comedy, and make a farce of tragedy.

MANLY. Do you never attend the theatre, Sir?

DIMPLE. I was tortured there once.

CHARLOTTE. Pray, Mr. Dimple, was it a tragedy or a comedy?

DIMPLE. Faith, Madam, I cannot tell; for I sat with my back to the stage all the time, admiring a much better actress than any there;—a lady who played the fine woman to perfection;—though, by the laugh of the horrid creatures around me, I suppose it was comedy. Yet, on second thoughts, it might be some hero in a tragedy, dying so comically as to set the whole house in an uproar.—Colonel, I presume you have been in Europe?

MANLY. Indeed, Sir, I was never ten leagues from the continent.

DIMPLE. Believe me, Colonel, you have an immense pleasure to come; and when you shall have seen the brilliant exhibitions of Europe, you will learn to despise the amusements of this country as much as I do.

MANLY. Therefore I do not wish to see them; for I can never esteem that knowledge valuable, which tends to give me a distaste for my native country.

DIMPLE. Well, Colonel, though you have not travelled, you have read.

MANLY. I have, a little: and by it have discovered that there is a laudable partiality, which ignorant, untravelled men entertain for everything that belongs to their native country. I call it laudable; —it injures no one; adds to their own happiness; and, when extended, becomes the noble principle of patriotism. Travelled gentlemen rise superior, in their own opinion, to this: but, if the contempt which they contract for their country is the most valuable acquisition of their travels, I am far from thinking that their time and money are well spent.

MARIA. What noble sentiments!

CHARLOTTE. Let my brother set out from where he will in the fields of conversation, he is sure to end his tour in the temple of gravity.

MANLY. Forgive me, my sister. I love my country; it has its foibles undoubtedly;—some foreigners will with pleasure remark them—but such remarks fall very ungracefully from the lips of her citizens.

DIMPLE. You are perfectly in the right, Colonel—America has her faults.

MANLY. Yes, Sir; and we, her children, should blush for them in private, and endeavour, as individuals, to reform them. But, if our country has its errors in common with other countries, I am proud to say America, I mean the United States, have displayed virtues and achievements which modern nations may admire, but of which they have seldom set us the example.

CHARLOTTE. But, brother, we must introduce you to some of our gay folks, and let you see the city, such as it is. Mr. Dimple is known to almost every family in town;—he will doubtless take a pleasure in introducing you.

DIMPLE. I shall esteem every service I can render your brother an honour.

MANLY. I fear the business I am upon will take up all my time, and my family will be anxious to hear from me.

MARIA. His family! But what is it to me that he is married! (*Aside.*) Pray, how did you leave your lady, Sir?

CHARLOTTE. My brother is not married (*observing her anxiety*); it is only an odd way he has of expressing himself. —Pray, brother, is this business, which you make your continual excuse, a secret?

MANLY. No, sister: I came hither to solicit the honourable Congress that a number of my brave old soldiers may be put upon the pension-list, who were, at first, not judged to be so materially wounded as to need the public assistance. —My sister says true: (*To* MARIA.) I call my late soldiers my family.—Those who were not in the field in the late glorious contest, and those who were, have their respective merits; but, I confess, my old brother-soldiers are dearer to me than the former description. Friendships made in adversity are lasting; our countrymen may forget us; but that is no reason why we should forget one another. But I must leave you; my time of engagement approaches.

CHARLOTTE. Well, but brother, if you will go, will you please to conduct my fair friend home? You live in the same street;—I was to have gone with her myself— (*Aside.*) A lucky thought.

MARIA. I am obliged to your sister, Sir, and was just intending to go. (*Going.*)

MANLY. I shall attend her with pleasure.

(*Exit with* MARIA, *followed by* DIMPLE *and* CHARLOTTE.)

MARIA. Now, pray don't betray me to your brother.

CHARLOTTE. (*Just as she sees him make a motion to take his leave.*) One word with you, brother, if you please.

(*Follows them out.*)

(*Manent* DIMPLE *and* LETITIA.)

DIMPLE. You received the billet I sent you, I presume?

LETITIA. Hush!—Yes.

DIMPLE. When shall I pay my respects to you?

LETITIA. At eight I shall be unengaged.

(*Re-enter* CHARLOTTE.)

DIMPLE. Did my lovely angel receive my billet? (*To* CHARLOTTE.)

CHARLOTTE. Yes.

DIMPLE. What hour shall I expect with impatience?

CHARLOTTE. At eight I shall be at home, unengaged.

DIMPLE. Unfortunate! I have a horrid engagement of business at that hour.—Can't you finish your visit earlier, and let six be the happy hour?

CHARLOTTE. You know your influence over me.> (*Exeunt severally.*)

SCENE 2. VAN ROUGH'S *House.*
(VAN ROUGH, *alone.*)

It cannot possibly be true! The son of my old friend can't have acted so unadvisedly. Seventeen thousand pounds! in bills!—Mr. Transfer must have been mistaken. He always appeared so prudent, and talked so well upon money-matters, and even assured me that he intended to change his dress for a suit of clothes which would not cost so much, and look more substantial, as soon as he married. No, no, no! it can't be; it cannot be.—But, however, I must look out sharp. I did not care what his principles or his actions were, so long as he minded the main chance. Seventeen thousand pounds!—If he had lost it in trade, why the best men may have ill-luck; but to game it away, as Transfer says—why, at this rate, his whole estate may go in one night, and, what is ten times worse, mine into the bargain. No, no; Mary is right. Leave women to look out in these matters; for all they look as if they did n't know a journal from a ledger, when their interest is concerned, they know what 's what; they mind the main chance as well as the best of us.—I wonder Mary did not tell me she knew of his spending his money so foolishly. Seventeen thousand pounds! Why, if my daughter was standing up to be married, I would forbid the banns, if I found it was to a man who did not mind the main chance.—Hush! I hear somebody coming. 'T is Mary's voice: a man with her too! I should n't be surprized if this should be the other string to her bow.—Aye, aye, let them alone; women understand the main chance.—Though, i' faith, I 'll listen a little. (*Retires into a closet.*)

(MANLY *leading in* MARIA.)

MANLY. I hope you will excuse my speaking upon so important a subject, so abruptly; but the moment I entered your room, you struck me as the lady whom I had long loved in imagination, and never hoped to see.

MARIA. Indeed, Sir, I have been led to hear more upon this subject than I ought.

MANLY. Do you then disapprove my suit, Madam, or the abruptness of my introducing it? If the latter, my peculiar situation, being obliged to leave the city in a few days, will, I hope, be my excuse; if the former, I will retire: for I am sure I would not give a moment's inquietude to her, whom I could devote my life to please. I am not so indelicate as to seek your immediate approbation; permit me only to be near you, and by a thousand tender assiduities to endeavour to excite a grateful return.

MARIA. I have a father, whom I would die to make happy—he will disapprove—

MANLY. Do you think me so ungenerous as to seek a place in your esteem without his consent? You must—you ever ought to consider that man as unworthy of you, who seeks an interest in your heart, contrary to a father's approbation. A young lady should reflect, that the loss of a lover may be supplied, but nothing can compensate for the loss of a parent's affection. Yet, why do you suppose your father would disapprove? In our country, the affections are not sacrificed to riches, or family aggrandizement:—should you approve, my family is decent, and my rank honourable.

MARIA. You distress me, Sir.

MANLY. Then I will sincerely beg your excuse for obtruding so disagreeable a subject and retire. (*Going.*)

MARIA. Stay, Sir! your generosity and good opinion of me deserve a return; but why must I declare what, for these few hours, I have scarce suffered myself to think?—I am—

MANLY. What?—

MARIA. Engaged, Sir;—and, in a few days, to be married to the gentleman you saw at your sister's.

MANLY. Engaged to be married! And have I been basely invading the rights of another? Why have you permitted this?—Is this the return for the partiality I declared for you?

MARIA. You distress me, Sir. What

would you have me say? You are too generous to wish the truth: ought I to say that I dared not suffer myself to think of my engagement, and that I am going to give my hand without my heart? —Would you have me confess a partiality for you? If so, your triumph is complete; and can be only more so, when days of misery, with the man I cannot love, will make me think of him whom I could prefer.

MANLY. (*After a pause.*) We are both unhappy; but it is your duty to obey your parent,—mine to obey my honour. Let us, therefore, both follow the path of rectitude; and of this we may be assured, that if we are not happy, we shall, at least, deserve to be so. Adieu! I dare not trust myself longer with you.

(*Exeunt severally.*)

END OF THE FOURTH ACT.

ACT FIFTH.

SCENE 1. DIMPLE'S *Lodgings.*

JESSAMY *meeting* JONATHAN.

JESSAMY. Well, Mr. Jonathan, what success with the fair?

JONATHAN. Why, such a tarnal cross tike you never saw!—You would have counted she had lived upon crab-apples and vinegar for a fortnight. But what the rattle makes you look so tarnation glum?

JESSAMY. I was thinking, Mr. Jonathan, what could be the reason of her carrying herself so coolly to you.

JONATHAN. Coolly, do you call it? Why, I vow, she was fire-hot angry: may be it was because I buss'd her.

JESSAMY. No, no, Mr. Jonathan; there must be some other cause: I never yet knew a lady angry at being kissed.

JONATHAN. Well, if it is not the young woman's bashfulness, I vow I can't conceive why she shou'd n't like me.

JESSAMY. May be it is because you have not the Graces, Mr. Jonathan.

JONATHAN. Grace! Why, does the young woman expect I must be converted before I court her?

JESSAMY. I mean graces of person; for instance, my lord tells us that we must cut off our nails even at top, in small segments of circles;—though you won't understand that—In the next place, you must regulate your laugh.

JONATHAN. Maple-log seize it! don't I laugh natural?

JESSAMY. That 's the very fault, Mr. Jonathan. Besides, you absolutely misplace it. I was told by a friend of mine that you laughed outright at the play the other night, when you ought only to have tittered.

JONATHAN. Gor! I—what does one go to see fun for if they can't laugh?

JESSAMY. You may laugh;—but you must laugh by rule.

JONATHAN. Swamp it—laugh by rule! Well, I should like that tarnally.

JESSAMY. Why you know, Mr. Jonathan, that to dance, a lady to play with her fan, or a gentleman with his cane, and all other natural motions, are regulated by art. My master has composed an immensely pretty gamut, by which any lady, or gentleman, with a few years' close application, may learn to laugh as gracefully as if they were born and bred to it.

JONATHAN. Mercy on my soul! A gamut for laughing—just like fa, la, sol?

JESSAMY. Yes. It comprises every possible display of jocularity, from an *affettuoso* smile to a *piano* titter, or full chorus *fortissimo* ha, ha, ha! My master employs his leisure-hours in marking out the plays, like a cathedral chanting-book, that the ignorant may know where to laugh; and that pit, box, and gallery may keep time together, and not have a snigger in one part of the house, a broad grin in the other, and a d——d grum look in the third. How delightful to see the audience all smile together, then look on their books, then twist their mouths into an agreeable simper, then altogether shake the house with a general ha, ha, ha! loud as a full chorus of Handel's, at an Abbey-commemoration.

JONATHAN. Ha, ha, ha! that 's dang'd cute, I swear.

JESSAMY. The gentlemen, you see, will laugh the tenor; the ladies will play the counter-tenor; the beaux will squeak the treble; and our jolly friends in the gallery a thorough bass, ho, ho, ho!

JONATHAN. Well, can't you let me see that gamut?

JESSAMY. Oh! yes, Mr. Jonathan; here it is. (*Takes out a book.*) Oh! no, this is only a titter with its variations. Ah, here it is. (*Takes out another.*) Now you must know, Mr. Jonathan, this is a piece written by Ben Jonson, which I have set to my master's gamut. The places where you must smile, look grave, or laugh outright, are marked below the line. Now look over me.—"There was a certain man"—now you must smile.

JONATHAN. Well, read it again; I warrant I 'll mind my eye.

JESSAMY. "There was a certain man, who had a sad scolding wife,"—now you must laugh.

JONATHAN. Tarnation! That 's no laughing matter, though.

JESSAMY. "And she lay sick a-dying;"—now you must titter.

JONATHAN. What, snigger when the good woman 's a-dying! Gor, I—

JESSAMY. Yes; the notes say you must—"And she asked her husband leave to make a will,"—now you must begin to look grave;—"and her husband said"—

JONATHAN. Ay, what did her husband say?—Something dang'd cute, I reckon.

JESSAMY. "And her husband said, you have had your will all your life time, and would you have it after you are dead too?"

JONATHAN. Ho, ho, ho! There the old man was even with her; he was up to the notch—ha, ha, ha!

JESSAMY. But, Mr. Jonathan, you must not laugh so. Why, you ought to have tittered *piano*, and you have laughed *fortissimo*. Look here; you see these marks, A. B. C. and so on; these are the references to the other part of the book. Let us turn to it, and you will see the directions how to manage the muscles. This (*turns over*) was note D you blundered at.—"You must purse the mouth into a smile, then titter, discovering the lower part of the three front upper teeth."

JONATHAN. How! read it again.

JESSAMY. "There was a certain man"—very well!—"who had a sad scolding wife,"—why don't you laugh?

JONATHAN. Now, that scolding wife sticks in my gizzard so pluckily, that I can't laugh for the blood and nowns of me. Let me look grave here, and I 'll laugh your belly full where the old creature 's a-dying.—

JESSAMY. "And she asked her husband"—(*Bell rings.*) My master's bell! he 's returned, I fear—Here, Mr. Jonathan, take this gamut; and, I make no doubt but with a few years' close application you may be able to smile gracefully.

(*Exeunt severally.*)

SCENE 2. CHARLOTTE'S *Apartment.*

(*Enter* MANLY.)

MANLY. What, no one at home? How unfortunate to meet the only lady my heart was ever moved by, to find her engaged to another, and confessing her partiality for me! Yet engaged to a man, who, by her intimation, and his libertine conversation with me, I fear, does not merit her. Aye! there 's the sting; for, were I assured that Maria was happy, my heart is not so selfish, but that it would dilate in knowing it, even though it were with another.—But to know she is unhappy!—I must drive these thoughts from me. Charlotte has some books; and this is what I believe she calls her little library.

(*Enters a closet.*)

(*Enter* DIMPLE *leading* LETITIA.)

LETITIA. And will you pretend to say, now, Mr. Dimple, that you propose to break with Maria? Are not the banns published? Are not the clothes purchased? Are not the friends invited? In short, is it not a done affair?

DIMPLE. Believe me, my dear Letitia, I would not marry her.

LETITIA. Why have you not broke with her before this, as you all along deluded me by saying you would?

DIMPLE. Because I was in hopes she would ere this have broke with me.

LETITIA. You could not expect it.

DIMPLE. Nay, but be calm a moment; 't was from my regard to you that I did not discard her.

LETITIA. Regard to me!

DIMPLE. Yes; I have done everything in my power to break with her, but the foolish girl is so fond of me, that nothing can accomplish it. Besides, how can I offer her my hand, when my heart is indissolubly engaged to you?—

LETITIA. There may be reason in this; but why so attentive to Miss Manly?

DIMPLE. Attentive to Miss Manly! For heaven's sake, if you have no better opinion of my constancy, pay not so ill a compliment to my taste.

<LETITIA. Did I not see you whisper her to-day?

DIMPLE. Possibly I might—but something of so very trifling a nature, that I have already forgot what it was.

LETITIA. I believe, she has not forgot it.

DIMPLE. My dear creature,> how can you for a moment suppose I should have any serious thoughts of that trifling, gay, flighty coquette, that disagreeable—

(*Enter* CHARLOTTE.)

DIMPLE. My dear Miss Manly, I rejoice to see you; there is a charm in your conversation that always marks your entrance into company as fortunate.

LETITIA. Where have you been, my dear?

CHARLOTTE. Why, I have been about to twenty shops, turning over pretty things, and so have left twenty visits unpaid. I wish you would step into the carriage and whisk round, make my apology, and leave my cards where our friends are not at home; that you know will serve as a visit. Come, do go.

LETITIA. So anxious to get me out! but I 'll watch you. (*Aside.*) Oh! yes, I 'll go; I want a little exercise.—Positively (DIMPLE *offering to accompany her*), Mr. Dimple, you shall not go, why, half my visits are cake and caudle visits; it won't do, you know, for you to go.—

(*Exit, but returns to the door in the back scene and listens.*)

DIMPLE. This attachment of your brother to Maria is fortunate.

CHARLOTTE. How did you come to the knowledge of it?

DIMPLE. I read it in their eyes.

CHARLOTTE. And I had it from her mouth. It would have amused you to have seen her! She that thought it so great an impropriety to praise a gentleman, that she could not bring out one word in your favour, found a redundancy to praise him.

DIMPLE. I have done everything in my power to assist his passion there: your delicacy, my dearest girl, would be shocked at half the instances of neglect and misbehaviour.

CHARLOTTE. I don't know how I should bear neglect; but Mr. Dimple must misbehave himself, indeed, to forfeit my good opinion.

DIMPLE. Your good opinion, my angel, is the pride and pleasure of my heart; and if the most respectful tenderness for you and an utter indifference for all your sex besides, can make me worthy of your esteem, I shall richly merit it.

CHARLOTTE. All my sex besides, Mr. Dimple—you forgot your tête-à-tête with Letitia.

DIMPLE. How can you, my lovely angel, cast a thought on that insipid, wry-mouthed, ugly creature!

CHARLOTTE. But her fortune may have charms?

DIMPLE. Not to a heart like mine. The man who has been blessed with the good opinion of my Charlotte, must despise the allurements of fortune.

CHARLOTTE. I am satisfied.

DIMPLE. Let us think no more on the odious subject, but devote the present hour to happiness.

CHARLOTTE. Can I be happy, when I see the man I prefer going to be married to another?

DIMPLE. Have I not already satisfied my charming angel that I can never think of marrying the puling Maria. But, even if it were so, could that be any bar to our happiness; for, as the poet sings—

"Love, free as air, at sight of human ties,
"Spreads his light wings, and in a moment flies."

Come then, my charming angel! why delay our bliss! The present moment is ours; the next is in the hand of fate.

(*Kissing her.*)

CHARLOTTE. Begone, Sir! By your delusions you had almost lulled my honour asleep.

DIMPLE. Let me lull the demon to sleep again with kisses.

(*He struggles with her; she screams.*)

(*Enter* MANLY.)

MANLY. Turn, villain! and defend yourself.—

(*Draws.* VAN ROUGH *enters and beats down their swords.*)

VAN ROUGH. Is the devil in you? are you going to murder one another?

(*Holding* DIMPLE.)

DIMPLE. Hold him, hold him,—I can command my passion.

(*Enter* JONATHAN.)

JONATHAN. What the rattle ails you? Is the old one in you? Let the colonel alone, can't you? I feel chock full of fight,—do you want to kill the colonel?—

MANLY. Be still, Jonathan; the gentleman does not want to hurt me.

JONATHAN. Gor! I—I wish he did; I'd shew him Yankee boys play, pretty quick—Don't you see you have frightened the young woman into the *hystrikes?*

VAN ROUGH. Pray, some of you explain this; what has been the occasion of all this racket?

MANLY. That gentleman can explain it to you; it will be a very diverting story for an intended father-in-law to hear.

VAN ROUGH. How was this matter, Mr. Van Dumpling?

DIMPLE. Sir,—upon my honour—all I know is, that I was talking to this young lady, and this gentleman broke in on us, in a very extraordinary manner.

VAN ROUGH. Why, all this is nothing to the purpose: can you explain it, Miss? (*To* CHARLOTTE.)

(*Enter* LETITIA *through the back scene.*)

LETITIA. I can explain it to that gentleman's confusion. Though long betrothed to your daughter (*to* VAN ROUGH), yet allured by my fortune, it seems (with shame do I speak it), he has privately paid his addresses to me. I was drawn in to listen to him by his assuring me that the match was made by his father without his consent, and that he proposed to break with Maria, whether he married me or not. But whatever were his intentions respecting your daughter, Sir, even to me he was false; for he has repeated the same story, with some cruel reflections upon my person, to Miss Manly.

JONATHAN. What a tarnal curse!

LETITIA. Nor is this all, Miss Manly. When he was with me this very morning, he made the same ungenerous reflections upon the weakness of your mind as he has so recently done upon the defects of my person.

JONATHAN. What a tarnal curse and damn too!

DIMPLE. Ha! since I have lost Letitia, I believe I had as good make it up with Maria—Mr. Van Rough, at present I cannot enter into particulars; but, I believe I can explain everything to your satisfaction in private.

VAN ROUGH. There is another matter, Mr. Van Dumpling, which I would have you explain:—pray, Sir, have Messrs. Van Cash and Co. presented you those bills for acceptance?

DIMPLE. The deuce! Has he heard of those bills! Nay, then, all's up with Maria, too; but an affair of this sort can never prejudice me among the ladies; they will rather long to know what the dear creature possesses to make him so agreeable. (*Aside.*) Sir, you'll hear from me. (*To* MANLY.)

MANLY. And you from me, Sir.—

DIMPLE. Sir, you wear a sword.—

MANLY. Yes, Sir:—This sword was presented to me by that brave Gallic hero, the Marquis De La Fayette. I have drawn it in the service of my country, and in private life, on the only occasion where a man is justified in drawing his sword, in defence of a lady's honour. I have fought too many battles in the service of my country to dread the imputation of cowardice.—Death from a man of honour would be a glory you do not merit; you shall live to bear the insult of man, and the contempt of that sex, whose general smiles afforded you all your happiness.

DIMPLE. You won't meet me, Sir?—Then I'll post you for a coward.

MANLY. I'll venture that, Sir.—The reputation of my life does not depend upon the breath of a Mr. Dimple. I would have you to know, however, Sir, that I have a cane to chastise the insolence of a scoundrel, and a sword and the good laws of my country, to protect me from the attempts of an assassin.—

DIMPLE. Mighty well! Very fine, indeed! —ladies and gentlemen, I take my leave, and you will please to observe, in the case of my deportment, the contrast between a gentleman, who has read Chesterfield and received the polish of Europe, and an unpolished, untravelled American. (*Exit.*)

(*Enter* MARIA.)

MARIA. Is he indeed gone?—

LETITIA. I hope never to return.

VAN ROUGH. I am glad I heard of those bills; though it's plaguy unlucky: I hoped to see Mary married before I died.

MANLY. Will you permit a gentleman, Sir, to offer himself as a suitor to your daughter? Though a stranger to you, he is not altogether so to her, or unknown in this city. You may find a son-in-law of more fortune, but you can never meet with one who is richer in love for her, or respect for you.

VAN ROUGH. Why, Mary, you have not let this gentleman make love to you without my leave?

MANLY. I did not say, Sir—

MARIA. Say, Sir!—I—the gentleman, to be sure, met me accidentally.

VAN ROUGH. Ha, ha, ha! Mark me, Mary; young folks think old folks to be fools; but old folks know young folks to be fools.—Why, I knew all about this affair:—This was only a cunning way I had to bring it about—Hark ye! I was in the closet when you and he were at our house. (*Turns to the company.*) I heard that little baggage say she loved her old father, and would die to make him happy! Oh! how I loved the little baggage!—And you talked very prudently, young man. I have inquired into your character, and find you to be a man of punctuality and mind the main chance. And so, as you love Mary, and Mary loves you, you shall have my consent immediately to be married. I'll settle my fortune on you, and go and live with you the remainder of my life.

MANLY. Sir, I hope—

VAN ROUGH. Come, come, no fine speeches; mind the main chance, young man, and you and I shall always agree.

LETITIA. I sincerely wish you joy (*advancing to* MARIA); and hope your pardon for my conduct.

MARIA. I thank you for your congratulations, and hope we shall at once forget the wretch who has given us so much disquiet, and the trouble that he has occasioned.

CHARLOTTE. And I, my dear Maria,—how shall I look up to you for forgiveness? I, who, in the practice of the meanest arts, have violated the most sacred rights of friendship? I can never forgive myself, or hope charity from the world, but I confess I have much to hope from such a brother; and I am happy that I may soon say, such a sister.—

MARIA. My dear, you distress me; you have all my love.

MANLY. And mine.

CHARLOTTE. If repentance can entitle me to forgiveness, I have already much merit; for I despise the littleness of my past conduct. I now find, that the heart of any worthy man cannot be gained by invidious attacks upon the rights and characters of others;—by countenancing the addresses of a thousand;—or that the finest assemblage of features, the greatest taste in dress, the genteelest address, or the most brilliant wit, cannot eventually secure a coquette from contempt and ridicule.

MANLY. And I have learned that probity, virtue, honour, though they should not have received the polish of Europe, will secure to an honest American the good graces of his fair countrywoman, and, I hope, the applause of THE PUBLIC.

THE END.

ANDRÉ

BY

William Dunlap

ANDRÉ

André represents the tragedy of American history. It was not the first historical tragedy, but its predecessors were either school pieces like Brackenridge's *Battle of Bunker Hill* or else, like John Burk's dramatization of the same conflict, were of little worth.

William Dunlap was born February 19, 1766, at Perth Amboy, New Jersey. He grew up with a fondness for the theatre, and saw many of the productions of the British soldiers in New York City during the Revolution. From 1784 to 1787, he spent in England and there saw the best actors of that period. Returning to New York, he was inspired by the success of *The Contrast* to write plays. His first play to be performed, *The Father or American Shandyism,* was played by the American Company at the John Street Theatre, New York, September 7, 1789, and was a comedy of manners. His career as a playwright, which lasted until 1828, his activity as the manager of the American Company from 1796 to 1805, and his invaluable *History of the American Theatre,* make him the most important figure in our early dramatic history. He was connected with the theatre again from 1806 to 1812, but his most important work was done before 1805. He became Assistant Paymaster General of New York State from 1813 to 1816. Dunlap died in 1839.

Dunlap wrote or adapted more than sixty plays. Of the various fields in which he worked, the most significant were first, his plays based on native material, and second, his adaptations from the German and from the French. To the first group belong beside *The Father, Darby's Return,* played November 24, 1789, and printed in 1789, interesting on account of its association with Washington; *André; The Glory of Columbia;* and *Yankee Chronology,* an account of the fight between the *Constitution* and the *Guerrière,* played September 9, 1812, three weeks after the battle, and printed in the same year. His last play, *A Trip to Niagara,* performed November 28, 1828, and printed in 1830, was upon a native theme.

The Stranger, his first adaptation from the German of Kotzebue, was played December 10, 1798. It was made from an English version, but its success encouraged him to study German, and he adapted at least thirteen plays of Kotzebue, the best being *False Shame, or the American Orphan in Germany,* a domestic comedy played December 11, 1799, and printed in 1800; *The Virgin of the Sun,* a play laid in Peru, performed March 12, 1800, and printed the same year, and *Fraternal Discord,* a domestic drama, played October 24, 1800, and printed in 1809. He also adapted *Abaellino the Great Bandit,* from the German of Zchokke, performed February 11, 1801, and printed in 1802, while from a French source he produced *The Voice of Nature,* played February 4, 1803, and published in the same year.

One of the best of his plays, printed in 1807 as *Leicester* and played April 24, 1794, as *The Fatal Deception,* is a verse tragedy laid in Elizabethan England.

André was performed at the Park Theatre, New York, March 30, 1798. It was received, Dunlap tells us, with warm applause, until Cooper, who acted "Bland," in pleading for André's life, tore the American cockade from his casque and threw it from him. The incident was hissed, but the play proceeded and a change in the lines was made on the second night, which removed the cause of the trouble. The new lines have been inserted in their proper places in this edition.

On July 4, 1803, Dunlap produced a version of *André,* much changed, called *The Glory of Columbia.* The first Act deals with André's capture, and the last Act occurs at Yorktown. Washington is introduced with his officers and then André's captors come in and there is a general glorification of the American arms. *André* was more of a unit than *The Glory of Columbia* and the dramatic action was more intelligible. *The Glory of Columbia,* however, was printed in 1817 and held the stage as late as 1847.

Dunlap's plays must be read usually in the early editions, difficult now to obtain. The proposed Collected Edition in ten volumes seems to have been carried only to three; Vol. I, Philadelphia, 1806 and Vols. 2 and 3, New York, 1816.

Darby's Return has been reprinted in an appendix to *Washington and the Theatre,* by Paul Leicester Ford, Dunlap Society Reprint. New York, 1899. *André* was reprinted by the Dunlap Society with a very interesting introduction by Brander Matthews, New York, 1887. *The Father* was reprinted by the Dunlap Society with an introduction by T. J. McKee, New York, 1887. Dunlap's *History of the American Theatre,* New York, 1832, or in better form, London, 1833, should be consulted for his life and for a description of his plays. For a complete bibliography of his plays prepared by the present editor, see the *Cambridge History of American Literature* (Vol. I, pp. 496-499).

The present text is based on the edition of 1798. With the permission of the editor of the Dunlap Society Reprint, Professor Brander Matthews, that text has also been used in the preparation of this volume.

Note to Revised Edition.

A scholarly biography, *William Dunlap, a Study of His Life and Works,* by Oral S. Coad, was published in 1917. A complete Bibliography is included.

ANDRÉ;

A *TRAGEDY*, IN FIVE ACTS:

AS PERFORMED BY THE OLD AMERICAN COMPANY,
NEW-YORK, MARCH 30, 1798.

TO WHICH ARE ADDED

AUTHENTIC DOCUMENTS

RESPECTING

MAJOR ANDRÉ;

CONSISTING OF

LETTERS TO MISS SEWARD,

THE

COW CHACE,

PROCEEDINGS OF THE COURT MARTIAL, &c.

COPY RIGHT SECURED.

NEW-YORK:
Printed by T. & J. SWORDS, No. 99 Pearl-ſtreet.
—1798.—

PROLOGUE

Spoken by Mr. Martin.

A Native Bard, a native scene displays,
And claims your candour for his daring lays:
Daring, so soon, in mimic scenes to shew,
What each remembers as a real woe.
Who has forgot when gallant André died?
A name by Fate to Sorrow's self allied.
Who has forgot, when o'er the untimely bier,
Contending armies paus'd, to drop a tear.

Our Poet builds upon a fact to-night;
Yet claims, in building, every Poet's right;
To choose, embellish, lop, or add, or blend,
Fiction with truth, as best may suit his end;
Which, he avows, is pleasure to impart,
And move the passions but to mend the heart.

O, may no party spirit blast his views,
Or turn to ill the meanings of the Muse;
She sings of wrongs long past, Men as they were,
To instruct, without reproach, the Men that are;
Then judge the Story by the genius shown,
And praise, or damn it, for its worth alone.

CHARACTERS

GENERAL, dress, American staff uniform, blue, faced with buff, large gold epaulets, cocked hat, with the black and white cockade, indicating the union with France, buff waistcoat and breeches, boots .... Mr. Hallam

M'DONALD, a man of forty years of age, uniform nearly the same as the first .... Mr. Tyler

SEWARD, a man of thirty years of age, staff uniform .... Mr. Martin

ANDRÉ, a man of twenty-nine years of age, full British uniform after the first scene .... Mr. Hodgkinson

BLAND, a youthful but military figure, in the uniform of a Captain of horse—dress, a short blue coat, faced with red, and trimmed with gold lace, two small epaulets, a white waistcoat, leather breeches, boots and spurs; over the coat, crossing the chest from the right shoulder, a broad buff belt, to which is suspended a manageable hussar sword; a horseman's helmet on the head, decorated as usual, and the union cockade affixed .... Mr. Cooper

MELVILLE, a man of middle age, and grave deportment; his dress a Captain's uniform when on duty; a blue coat with red facings, gold epaulet, white waistcoat and breeches, boots and cocked hat, with the union cockade .... Mr. Williamson

BRITISH OFFICER .... Mr. Hogg

AMERICAN OFFICER .... Mr. Miller

CHILDREN .... Master Stockwell and Miss Hogg

AMERICAN SERGEANT .... Mr. Seymour

AMERICAN OFFICERS AND SOLDIERS, &c.

MRS. BLAND .... Mrs. Melmoth

HONORA .... Mrs. Johnson

Scene, the Village of Tappan, Encampment, and adjoining country. Time, ten hours.

ANDRE

ACT FIRST.

SCENE 1. *A Wood seen by star-light; an Encampment at a distance appearing between the trees.*

(*Enter* MELVILLE.)

MELVILLE. The solemn hour, "when night and morning meet,"
Mysterious time, to superstition dear,
And superstition's guides, now passes by;
Deathlike in solitude. The sentinels,
In drowsy tones, from post to post send on
The signal of the passing hour. "All 's well,"
Sounds through the camp. Alas, all is not well;
Else, why stand I, a man, the friend of man,
At midnight's depth, deck'd in this murderous guise,
The habiliment of death, the badge of dire
Necessitous coercion. 'T is not well.
—In vain the enlighten'd friends of suffering man
Point out, of war, the folly, guilt, and madness.
Still, age succeeds to age, and war to war;
And man, the murderer, marshals out in hosts
In all the gaiety of festive pomp,
To spread around him death and desolation.
How long! how long!—
—Methinks I hear the tread of feet this way.
My meditating mood may work me woe.
(*Draws.*)
Stand, whoso'er thou art. Answer. Who 's there?

(*Enter* BLAND.)

BLAND. A friend.
MELVILLE. Advance and give the countersign.
BLAND. Hudson.
MELVILLE. What, Bland!
BLAND. Melville, my friend, you *here*?
MELVILLE. And *well*, my brave young friend. But why do you,
At this dead hour of night, approach the camp
On foot, and thus alone?
BLAND. I have but now
Dismounted, and from yon sequester'd cot,
Whose lonely taper through the crannied wall
Sheds its faint beams and twinkles midst the trees,
Have I, adventurous, grop'd my darksome way.
My servant and my horses, spent with toil,
There wait till morn.
MELVILLE. Why waited not yourself?
BLAND. Anxious to know the truth of those reports
Which, from the many mouths of busy fame,
Still, as I pass'd, struck varying on my ear,
Each making th' other void. Nor does delay
The color of my hasteful business suit.
I bring dispatches for our great Commander;
And hasted hither with design to wait
His rising, or awake him with the sun.
MELVILLE. You will not need the last, for the blest sun
Ne'er rises on his slumbers; by the dawn
We see him mounted gaily in the field,
Or find him wrapt in meditation deep,
Planning the welfare of our war-worn land.
BLAND. Prosper, kind Heaven, and recompense his cares.
MELVILLE. You 're from the South, if I presume aright?
BLAND. I am; and, Melville, I am fraught with news.
The South teems with events—convulsing ones.
The Briton, there, plays at no mimic war;

With gallant face he moves, and gallantly is met.
Brave spirits, rous'd by glory, throng our camp;
The hardy hunter, skill'd to fell the deer,
Or start the sluggish bear from covert rude;
And not a clown that comes, but from his youth
Is trained to pour from far the leaden death,
To climb the steep, to struggle with the stream,
To labor firmly under scorching skies,
And bear, unshrinking, winter's roughest blast.
This, and that heaven-inspir'd enthusiasm
Which ever animates the patriot's breast,
Shall far outweigh the lack of discipline.

MELVILLE. Justice is ours; what shall prevail against her?

BLAND. But as I pass'd along, many strange tales
And monstrous rumors have my ears assail'd:
That Arnold had prov'd false; but he was ta'en
And hung, or to be hung—I know not what.
Another told that all our army, with their
Much-lov'd Chief, sold and betray'd, were captur'd.
But as I nearer drew, at yonder cot
'T was said that Arnold, traitor like, had fled;
And that a Briton, tried and prov'd a spy,
Was, on this day, as such, to suffer death.

MELVILLE. As you drew near, plain truth advanced to meet you.
'T is even as you heard, my brave young friend.
Never had people on a single throw
More interest at stake; when he who held
For us the die prov'd false and play'd us foul.
But for a circumstance of that nice kind,
Of cause so microscopic that the tongues
Of inattentive men call it the effect
Of chance, we must have lost the glorious game.

BLAND. Blest, blest be heaven! whatever was the cause!

MELVILLE. The blow ere this had fallen that would have bruis'd
The tender plant which we have striven to rear,
Crush'd to the dust, no more to bless this soil.

BLAND. What warded off the blow?

MELVILLE. The brave young man, who this day dies, was seiz'd
Within our bounds, in rustic garb disguis'd.
He offer'd bribes to tempt the band that seiz'd him;
But the rough farmer, for his country arm'd,
That soil defending which his ploughshare turn'd,
Those laws his father chose and he approv'd,
Cannot, as mercenary soldiers may,
Be brib'd to sell the public weal for gold.

BLAND. 'T is well. Just Heaven! O grant that thus may fall
All those who seek to bring this land to woe,
All those, who, or by open force, or dark
And secret machinations, seek to shake
The Tree of Liberty, or stop its growth,
In any soil where thou hast pleased to plant it.

MELVILLE. Yet not a heart but pities and would save him;
For all confirm that he is brave and virtuous;
Known, but till now, the darling child of Honor.

BLAND. (*Contemptuously.*) And how is call'd this—honorable spy?

MELVILLE. André 's his name.

BLAND. (*Much agitated.*) André!

MELVILLE. Aye! Major André.

BLAND. André!—O no, my friend, you 're sure deceiv'd—
I 'll pawn my life, my ever sacred fame,
My General's favor, or a soldier's honor,
That gallant André never yet put on
The guise of falsehood. O, it cannot be!

MELVILLE. How might I be deceiv'd? I 've heard him, seen him,
And what I tell, I tell from well-prov'd knowledge;
No second tale-bearer who heard the news.

BLAND. Pardon me, Melville. O, that well-known name,
So link'd with circumstances infamous!
My friend must pardon me. Thou wilt not blame
When I shall tell what cause I have to love him;

What cause to think him nothing more the pupil
Of Honor stern, than sweet Humanity.
Rememberest thou, when cover'd o'er with wounds
And left upon the field, I fell the prey
Of Britain? To a loathsome prisonship
Confin'd, soon had I sunk, victim of death,
A death of aggravated miseries;
But, by benevolence urg'd, this best of men,
This gallant youth, then favor'd, high in power,
Sought out the pit obscene of foul disease,
Where I and many a suffering soldier lay,
And, like an angel, seeking good for man,
Restor'd us light and partial liberty.
Me he mark'd out his own. He nurst and cur'd,
He lov'd and made his friend. I liv'd by him,
And in my heart he liv'd, till, when exchang'd,
Duty and honor call'd me from my friend.
Judge how my heart is tortur'd.—Gracious Heaven,
Thus, thus to meet him on the brink of death—
A death so infamous. Heav'n grant my prayer. (*Kneels.*)
That I may save him, O inspire my heart
With thoughts, my tongue with words that move to pity. (*Rises.*)
Quick, Melville, show me where my André lies.

MELVILLE. Good wishes go with you.

BLAND. I'll save my friend. (*Exeunt.*)

SCENE, *the Encampment by star-light.*

(*Enter the* GENERAL, M'DONALD, *and* SEWARD.)

GENERAL. 'T is well. Each sentinel upon his post
Stands firm, and meets me at the bayonet's point;
While in his tent the weary soldier lies,
The sweet reward of wholesome toil enjoying;
Resting secure as erst within his cot
He careless slept, his rural labor o'er;
Ere Britons dar'd to violate those laws,
Those boasted laws by which themselves are govern'd,
And strove to make their fellow-subjects slaves.

SEWARD. They know to whom they owe their present safety.

GENERAL. I hope they know that to themselves they owe it;
To that good discipline which they observe,
The discipline of men to order train'd
Who know its value, and in whom 't is virtue;
To that prompt hardihood with which they meet
Or toil or danger, poverty or death.
Mankind who know not whence that spirit springs,
Which holds at bay all Britain's boasted power,
Gaze on their deeds astonish'd. See the youth
Start from his plough and straightway play the hero;
Unmurmuring bear such toils as veterans shun;
Rest all content upon the dampsome earth;
Follow undaunted to the deathful charge;
Or, when occasion asks, lead to the breach,
Fearless of all the unusual din of war,
His former peaceful mates. O patriotism!
Thou wondrous principle of godlike action.
Wherever liberty is found, there reigns
The love of country. Now the self-same spirit
Which fill'd the breast of great Leonidas
Swells in the hearts of thousands on these plains,
Thousands who never heard the hero's tale.
'T is this alone which saves thee, O my country!
And, till that spirit flies these western shores,
No power on earth shall crush thee.

SEWARD. 'T is wondrous!
The men of other climes from this shall see
How easy 't is to shake oppression off;
How all-resistless is a union'd people;
And hence, from our success (which, by my soul,
I feel as much secur'd as though our foes

Were now within their floating prisons hous'd,
And their proud prows all pointing to the east),
Shall other nations break their galling fetters,
And re-assume the dignity of man.

M'DONALD. Are other nations in that happy state,
That, having broke Coercion's iron yoke,
They can submit to Order's gentle voice,
And walk on earth self-ruled? I much do fear it.
As to ourselves, in truth, I nothing see,
In all the wondrous deeds which we perform,
But plain effects from causes full as plain.
Rises not man forever 'gainst oppression?
It is the law of life; he can't avoid it.
But when the love of property unites
With sense of injuries past and dread of future,
Is it then wonderful that he should brave
A lesser evil to avoid a greater?

GENERAL. (*Sportively.*) 'T is hard, quite hard, we may not please ourselves,
By our great deeds ascribing to our virtue.

SEWARD. M'Donald never spares to lash our pride.

M'DONALD. In truth I know of naught to make you proud.
I think there's none within the camp that draws
With better will his sword than does M'Donald.
I have a home to guard. My son is—butcher'd—

SEWARD. Hast thou no nobler motives for thy arms
Than love of property and thirst for vengeance?

M'DONALD. Yes, my good Seward, and yet nothing wondrous.
I love this country for the sake of man.
My parents, and I thank them, cross'd the seas,
And made me native of fair Nature's world,
With room to grow and thrive in. I have thriven;
And feel my mind unshackled, free, expanding,
Grasping with ken unbounded mighty thoughts,
At which, if chance my mother had, good dame,
In Scotia, our revered parent soil,
Given me to see the day, I should have shrunk
Affrighted. Now, I see in this new world
A resting spot for man, if he can stand
Firm in his place, while Europe howls around him,
And all unsettled as the thoughts of vice,
Each nation in its turn threats him with feeble malice.
One trial, now, we prove; and I have met it.

GENERAL. And met it like a man, my brave M'Donald.

M'DONALD. I hope so; and I hope my every act
Has been the offspring of deliberate judgment;
Yet feeling seconds reason's cool resolves.
O! I could hate, if I did not more pity
These bands of mercenary Europeans,
So wanting in the common sense of nature,
As, without shame, to sell themselves for pelf
To aid the cause of darkness; murder man—
Without inquiry murder, and yet call
Their trade the trade of honor—high-soul'd honor—
Yet honor shall accord in act with falsehood.
O! that proud man should e'er descend to play
The tempter's part, and lure men to their ruin!
Deceit and honor badly pair together.

SEWARD. You have much shew of reason; yet, methinks
What you suggest of one, whom fickle Fortune,
In her changeling mood, hath hurl'd, unpitying,
From her topmost height to lowest misery,
Tastes not of charity. André, I mean.

M'DONALD. I mean him, too; sunk by misdeed, not fortune.
Fortune and chance, O, most convenient words!
Man runs the wild career of blind ambition,
Plunges in vice, takes falsehood for his buoy,
And when he feels the waves of ruin o'er him,
Curses, "in good set terms," poor Lady Fortune.

GENERAL. (*Sportively to* SEWARD.) His mood is all untoward; let us leave him.
Tho' he may think that he is bound to rail,
We are not bound to hear him. (*To* M'DONALD.) Grant you that?
M'DONALD. O, freely, freely! You I never rail on.
GENERAL. No thanks for that; you 've courtesy for office.
M'DONALD. You slander me.
GENERAL. Slander that would not wound.
Worthy M'Donald, though it suits full well
The virtuous man to frown on all misdeeds,
Yet ever keep in mind that man is frail;
His tide of passion struggling still with Reason's
Fair and favorable gale, and adverse
Driving his unstable Bark upon the
Rocks of error. Should he sink thus shipwreck'd,
Sure, it is not Virtue's voice that triumphs
In his ruin. I must seek rest. Adieu!
(*Exeunt* GENERAL *and* SEWARD.)
M'DONALD. Both good and great thou art; first among men;
By nature, or by early habit, grac'd
With that blest quality which gives due force
To every faculty, and keeps the mind
In healthful equipoise, ready for action;
Invaluable temperance—by all
To be acquired, yet scarcely known to any. (*Exit.*)

END OF THE FIRST ACT.

ACT SECOND.

SCENE, *a Prison.* ANDRÉ *discovered, in a pensive posture, sitting at a table; a book by him and candles; his dress neglected, his hair dishevelled; he rises and comes forward.*

ANDRÉ. Kind Heaven be thank'd for that I stand alone
In this sad hour of life's brief pilgrimage!
Single in misery; no one else involving,
In grief, in shame, and ruin. 'T is my comfort.
Thou, my thrice honor'd sire, in peace went'st down
Unto the tomb, nor knew to blush, nor knew
A pang for me. And thou, revered matron,
Could'st bless thy child, and yield thy breath in peace!
No wife shall weep, no child lament my loss.
Thus may I consolation find in what
Was once my woe. I little thought to joy
In not possessing, as I erst possest,
Thy love, Honora! André's death, perhaps,
May cause a cloud pass o'er thy lovely face;
The pearly tear may steal from either eye;
For thou mayest feel a transient pang, nor wrong
A husband's rights: more than a transient pang
O mayest thou never feel! The morn draws nigh
To light me to my shame. Frail nature shrinks—
And *is* death then so fearful? I have brav'd
Him, fearless, in the field, and steel'd my breast
Against his thousand horrors; but his cool,
His sure approach, requires a fortitude
Which naught but conscious rectitude can give.
(*Retires, and sits leaning.*)

(*Enter* BLAND, *unperceived by* ANDRÉ.)

BLAND. And is that André? O, how changed! Alas!
Where is that martial fire, that generous warmth,
Which glow'd his manly countenance throughout,
And gave to every look, to every act,
The tone of high chivalrous animation?
André, my friend, look up!
ANDRÉ. Who calls *me* friend?
BLAND. Young Arthur Bland.
ANDRÉ. (*Rising.*) That name sounds like a friend's. (*With emotion.*)
I have inquired for thee—wish'd much to see thee—
I prythee take no note of these fool's tears—
My heart was full—and seeing thee—
BLAND. (*Embracing him.*) O André!
I have but now arrived from the South—

Nor heard—till now—of this—I cannot speak.
Is this a place?—O, thus to find my friend!

ANDRÉ. Still dost thou call me friend? I, who dared act
Against my reason, my declared opinion;
Against my conscience and a soldier's fame?
Oft in the generous heat of glowing youth,
Oft have I said how fully I despis'd
All bribery base, all treacherous tricks in war:
Rather my blood should bathe these hostile shores,
And have it said, "he died a gallant soldier,"
Than with my country's gold encourage treason,
And thereby purchase gratitude and fame.

BLAND. Still mayest thou say it, for thy heart 's the same.

ANDRÉ. Still is my heart the same, still may I say it;
But now my deeds will rise against my words;
And should I dare to talk of honest truth,
Frank undissembling probity and faith,
Memory would crimson o'er my burning cheek,
And actions retrospected choak the tale.
Still is my heart the same. But there has past
A day, an hour, which ne'er can be recall'd.
Unhappy man! Tho' all thy life pass pure;
Mark'd by benevolence thy every deed;
The out-spread map, which shows the way thou 'st trod,
Without one devious track or doubtful line;
It all avails thee naught, if in one hour,
One hapless hour, thy feet are led astray;—
Thy happy deeds all blotted from remembrance;
Cancel'd the record of thy former good.
Is it not hard, my friend? Is 't not unjust?

BLAND. Not every record cancel'd.—O, there are hearts
Where Virtue's image, when 't is once engraved,
Can never know erasure.

ANDRÉ. Generous Bland!
(*Takes his hand.*)
The hour draws nigh which ends my life's sad story.
I should be firm—

BLAND. By heaven, thou shalt not die!
Thou dost not sure deserve it. Betray'd, perhaps—
Condemn'd without due circumstance made known?
Thou didst not mean to tempt our officers?
Betray our yeoman soldiers to destruction?
Silent! Nay, then 't was from a duteous wish
To serve the cause thou wast in honor bound.—

ANDRÉ. Kind is my Bland, who to his generous heart
Still finds excuses for his erring friend.
Attentive hear and judge me.—
Pleas'd with the honors daily shower'd upon me,
I glow'd with martial heat my name to raise
Above the vulgar herd, who live to die,
And die to be forgotten. Thus I stood,
When avarice or ambition Arnold tempted,
His country, fame, and honor to betray,
Linking his name to infamy eternal.
In confidence it was to me propos'd
To plan with him the means which should ensure
Thy country's downfall. Nothing then I saw
But confidential favor in the service,
My country's glory, and my mounting fame;
Forgot my former purity of thought,
And high-ton'd honor's scruples disregarded.

BLAND. It was thy duty so to serve thy country.

ANDRÉ. Nay, nay; be cautious ever to admit
That duty can beget dissimulation.
On ground, unoccupied by either part,
Neutral esteem'd, I landed, and was met.
But ere my conference was with Arnold clos'd,
The day began to dawn; I then was told
That till the night I must my safety seek
In close concealment. Within your posts convey'd,
I found myself involved in unthought dangers.
Night came. I sought the vessel which had borne
Me to the fatal spot; but she was gone.

Retreat that way cut off, again I sought
Concealment with the traitors of your army.
Arnold now granted passes, and I doff'd
My martial garb, and put on curs'd disguise.
Thus in a peasant's form I pass'd your posts;
And when, as I conceiv'd, my danger o'er,
Was stopt and seiz'd by some returning scouts.
So did ambition lead me, step by step,
To treat with traitors, and encourage treason;
And then, bewilder'd in the guilty scene,
To quit my martial designating badges,
Deny my name, and sink into the spy.

BLAND. Thou didst no more than was a soldier's duty,
To serve the part on which he drew his sword.
Thou shalt not die for this. Straight will I fly—
I surely shall prevail—

ANDRÉ. It is in vain.
All has been tried. Each friendly argument—

BLAND. All has not yet been tried. The powerful voice
Of friendship in thy cause has not been heard.
My General favors *me*, and loves my father—
My gallant father! would that he were here!
But he, perhaps, now wants an André's care,
To cheer his hours—perhaps now languishes
Amidst those horrors whence thou sav'd'st his son.
The present moment claims my thought. André,
I fly to save thee!

ANDRÉ. Bland, it is in vain.
But, hold—there is a service thou may'st do me.

BLAND. Speak it.

ANDRÉ. O, think, and as a soldier think,
How I must die—the *manner* of my death—
Like the base ruffian, or the midnight thief,
Ta'en in the act of stealing from the poor,
To be turn'd off the felon's—murderer's cart,
A mid-air spectacle to gaping clowns;—
To run a short, an envied course of glory,
And end it on a gibbet.—

BLAND. Damnation!

ANDRÉ. Such is my doom. O, have the manner changed,
And of mere death I'll think not. Dost thou think—?
Perhaps thou canst gain *that—?*

BLAND. (*Almost in a phrenzy.*) Thou shalt not die.

ANDRÉ. Let me, O, let me die a soldier's death,
While friendly clouds of smoke shroud from all eyes
My last convulsive pangs, and I'm content.

BLAND. (*With increasing emotion.*) Thou shalt not die! Curse on the laws of war!
If worth like thine must thus be sacrificed
To policy so cruel and unjust,
I will forswear my country and her service;
I'll hie me to the Briton, and with fire,
And sword, and every instrument of death
Or devastation, join in the work of war!
What! shall worth weigh for nought? I will avenge thee!

ANDRÉ. Hold, hold, my friend; thy country's woes are full.
What! wouldst thou make me cause another traitor?
No more of this; and, if I die, believe me,
Thy country for my death incurs no blame.
Restrain thy ardor—but ceaselessly entreat
That André may at least die as he lived,
A soldier.

BLAND. By heaven thou shalt not die!

(BLAND *rushes off;* ANDRÉ *looks after him with an expression of love and gratitude, then retires up the stage. Scene closes.*)

SCENE, *the* GENERAL'S *Quarters.*

(*Enter* M'DONALD *and* SEWARD, *in conversation.*)

M'DONALD. (*Coming forward.*) Three thousand miles the Atlantic wave rolls on,

Which bathed Columbia's shores, ere, on the strand
Of Europe, or of Africa, their continents,
Or sea-girt isles, it chafes.

SEWARD. O, would to heaven
That in midway between these sever'd worlds
Rose barriers, all impassable to man,
Cutting off intercourse, till either side
Had lost all memory of the other!

M'DONALD. What spur now goads thy warm imagination?

SEWARD. Then might, perhaps, one land on earth be found,
Free from th' extremes of poverty and riches;
Where ne'er a scepter'd tyrant should be known,
Or tyrant lordling, curses of creation;—
Where the faint shrieks of woe-exhausted age,
Raving, in feeble madness, o'er the corse
Of a polluted daughter, stained by lust
Of viand-pampered luxury, might ne'er be heard;
Where the blasted form of much abused
Beauty, by villany seduced, by knowledge
All unguarded, might ne'er be viewed, flitting
Obscene, 'tween lamp and lamp, i' th' midnight street
Of all-defiling city; where the child—

M'DONALD. Hold! Shroud thy raven imagination.
Torture not me with images so curst!

SEWARD. Soon shall our foes, inglorious, fly these shores.
Peace shall again return. Then Europe's ports
Shall pour a herd upon us, far more fell
Than those, her mercenary sons, who now
Threaten our sore chastisement.

M'DONALD. Prophet of ill,
From Europe shall enriching commerce flow,
And many an ill attendant; but from thence
Shall likewise flow blest science. Europe's knowledge,
By sharp experience bought, we should appropriate;
Striving thus to leap from that simplicity,
With ignorance curst, to that simplicity,
By knowledge blest; unknown the gulf between.

SEWARD. Mere theoretic dreaming.

M'DONALD. Blest wisdom
Seems, from out the chaos of the social world,
Where good and ill in strange commixture float,
To rise, by strong necessity impell'd;
Starting, like Love divine, from womb of Night,
Illuming all, to order all reducing;
And showing by its bright and noontide blaze
That happiness alone proceeds from justice.

SEWARD. Dreams, dreams! Man can know naught but ill on earth.

M'DONALD. I'll to my bed, for I have watch'd all night;
And may my sleep give pleasing repetition
Of these my waking dreams! Virtue's incentives. (*Exit.*)

SEWARD. Folly's chimeras rather: guides to error.

(*Enter* BLAND, *preceded by a Sergeant.*)

SERGEANT. Pacquets for the General. (*Exit.*)

BLAND. Seward, my friend!

SEWARD. Captain, I'm glad to see the hue of health
Sit on a visage from the sallow south.

BLAND. The lustihood of youth hath yet defied
The parching sun, and chilling dew of even.
The General—Seward—?

SEWARD. I will lead you to him.

BLAND. Seward, I must make bold. Leave us together,
When occasion offers. 'T will be friendly.

SEWARD. I will not cross your purpose. (*Exeunt.*)

SCENE, *a Chamber.*

(*Enter* MRS. BLAND.)

MRS. BLAND. Yes, ever be this day a festival
In my domestic calendar. This morn
Will see my husband free. Even now, perhaps,
Ere yet Aurora flies the eastern hills,
Shunning the sultry sun, my Bland embarks.
Already, on the Hudson's dancing wave,
He chides the sluggish rowers, or supplicates

For gales propitious; that his eager arms
May clasp his wife, may bless his little ones.
O, how the tide of joy makes my heart bound,
Glowing with high and ardent expectation!

(*Enter two* CHILDREN.)

FIRST CHILD. Here we are, Mamma, up, and dress'd already.

MRS. BLAND. And why were ye so early?

FIRST CHILD. Why, did not you tell us that Papa was to be home to-day?

MRS. BLAND. I said, perhaps.

SECOND CHILD. (*Disappointed.*) Perhaps!

FIRST CHILD. I don't like perhaps's.

SECOND CHILD. No, nor I neither; nor "may-be-so's."

MRS. BLAND. We make not certainties, my pretty loves;
I do not like "perhaps's" more than you do.

SECOND CHILD. O, don't say so, Mama! for I 'm sure I hardly ever ask you anything but you answer me with "may be so,"—"perhaps,"—or "very likely." "Mamma, shall I go to the camp to-morrow, and see the General?" "May be so, my dear." Hang "may be so," say I!

MRS. BLAND. Well said, Sir Pertness!

FIRST CHILD. But I am sure, Mama, you said, that, to-day, Papa would have his liberty.

MRS. BLAND. So your dear father, by his letters, told me.

SECOND CHILD. Why, then, *I am sure* he will be here to-day. When he can come *to us,* I 'm sure he will not stay among those strange Englishmen and Hessians. I often wish'd that I had wings to fly, for then I would soon be with him.

MRS. BLAND. Dear boy!

(*Enter* SERVANT, *and gives a letter to* MRS. BLAND.)

SERVANT. An express, Madam, from New York to Head-quarters, in passing, delivered this.

SECOND CHILD. Papa 's coming home to-day, John.

(*Exeunt* SERVANT *and* CHILDREN.)

MRS. BLAND. What fears assail me! O, I did not want
A letter now!
(*She reads in great agitation, exclaiming, while her eyes are fixed on the paper.*)
My husband! doomed to die!
Retaliation!
(*She looks forward with wildness, consternation, and horror.*)
To die, if André dies! *He* dies to-day!
My husband to be murdered! And to-day!
To-day, if André dies! Retaliation!
O curst contrivance! Madness relieve me!
Burst, burst, my brain! Yet—André is not dead;
My husband lives. (*Looks at the letter.*) "One man has power."
I fly to save the father of my children!
(*Rushes out.*)

END OF THE SECOND ACT.

ACT THIRD.

SCENE, *the* GENERAL'S *quarters. The* GENERAL *and* BLAND *come forward.*

GENERAL. (*Papers in his hand.*) Captain, you are noted here with honorable
Praises. Depend upon that countenance
From me, which you have prov'd yourself so richly
Meriting. Both for your father's virtues
And your own, your country owes you honor—
The sole return the poor can make for service.

BLAND. If from my country ought I 've merited,
Or gain'd the approbation of her champion,
At any other time I should not dare,
Presumptuously, to show my sense of it;
But now my tongue, all shameless, dares to name
The boon, the precious recompense, I wish,
Which, granted, pays all service, past or future,
O'erpays the utmost I can e'er achieve.

GENERAL. Brief, my young friend, briefly, your purpose.

BLAND. If I have done my duty as a soldier;
If I have brav'd all dangers for my country;
If my brave father has deserved aught;
Call all to mind—and cancel all—but grant
My one request—mine, and humanity's.

General. Be less profuse of words, and name your wish;
If fit, its fitness is the best assurance
That not in vain you sue; but, if unjust,
Thy merits, nor the merits of thy race,
Cannot its nature alter, nor my mind,
From its determined opposition change.

Bland. You hold the fate of my most lov'd of friends;
As gallant soldier as e'er fac'd a foe,
Bless'd with each polish'd gift of social life,
And every virtue of humanity.
To me, a savior from the pit of death,
To me, and many more, my countrymen.
Oh, could my words pourtray him what he is!
Bring to your mind the blessings of his deeds,
While thro' the fever-heated, loathsome holds
Of floating hulks, dungeons obscene, where ne'er
The dewy breeze of morn, or evening's coolness,
Breath'd on our parching skins, he pass'd along,
Diffusing blessings; still his power exerting,
To alleviate the woes which ruthless war,
Perhaps thro' dire necessity, heap'd on us;
Surely the scene would move you to forget
His late intent—(tho' only serving then
As duty prompted)—and turn the rigor
Of War's iron law from him, the best of men,
Meant only for the worst.

General. Captain, no more.

Bland. If André lives, the prisoner finds a friend;
Else helpless and forlorn—
All men will bless the act, and bless thee for it.

General. Think'st thou thy country would not curse the man
Who, by a clemency ill-tim'd, ill-judg'd,
Encourag'd treason? That *pride* encourag'd,
Which, by denying us the rights of nations,
Hath caus'd those ills which thou hast now pourtray'd?
Our prisoners, brave and generous peasantry,
As rebels have been treated, not as men.
'T is mine, brave yeomen, to assert your rights;
'T is mine to teach the foe, that, though array'd
In rude simplicity, ye yet are men,
And rank among the foremost. Oft their scouts,
The very refuse of the English arms,
Unquestion'd, have our countrymen consign'd
To death, when captur'd, mocking their agonies.

Bland. Curse them! (*Checking himself.*) Yet, let not censure fall on André.
O, there are Englishmen as brave, as good,
As ever land on earth might call its own;
And gallant André is among the best!

General. Since they have hurl'd war on us, we must show
That by the laws of war we will abide;
And have the power to bring their acts for trial
To that tribunal, eminent 'mongst men,
Erected by the policy of nations,
To stem the flood of ills, which else fell war
Would pour, uncheck'd, upon the sickening world,
Sweeping away all trace of civil life.

Bland. To pardon him would not encourage ill.
His case is singular; his station high;
His qualities admir'd; his virtues lov'd.

General. No more, my good young friend: it is in vain.
The men entrusted with thy country's rights
Have weigh'd, attentive, every circumstance.
An individual's virtue is by them
As highly prized as it can be by thee.
I know the virtues of this man and love them.
But the destiny of millions, millions
Yet unborn, depends upon the rigor
Of this moment. The haughty Briton laughs
To scorn our armies and our councils. Mercy,
Humanity, call loudly, that we make
Our now despised power be felt, vindictive.
Millions demand the death of this young man.
My injur'd country, he his forfeit life
Must yield, to shield thy lacerated breast
From torture. (*To* Bland.) Thy merits are not overlook'd.
Promotion shall immediately attend thee.

Bland. (*With contemptuous irony.*) Par-

don me, sir, I never shall deserve it.
(*With increasing heat.*) The country that forgets to reverence virtue;
That makes no difference 'twixt the sordid wretch
Who, for reward, risks treason's penalty,
And him unfortunate, whose duteous service
Is, by mere accident, so chang'd in form
As to assume guilt's semblance, I serve not:
Scorn to serve. I have a soldier's honor,
But 't is in union with a freeman's judgment,
And when I act, both prompt. Thus from my helm
I tear what once I proudly thought, the badge
Of virtuous fellowship. (*Tears the cockade from his helmet.*) My sword I keep. (*Puts on his helmet.*)
Would, André, thou hadst never put thine off.
Then hadst thou through oppo ers' hearts made way
To liberty, or bravely pierc'd thine own!
(*Exit.*)

GENERAL. Rash, headstrong, maddening boy!
Had not this action past without a witness,
Duty would ask that thou shouldst rue thy folly—
But, for the motive, be the deed forgotten. (*Exit.*)

SCENE, *a Village. At a distance some tents. In front muskets, drums, and other indications of soldiers' quarters.*

(*Enter* MRS. BLAND *and* CHILDREN, *attended by* MELVILLE.)

MELVILLE. The General's doors to you are ever open.
But why, my worthy friend, this agitation?
Our colonel, your husband—

MRS. BLAND. (*In tears, gives him the letter.*) Read, Melville.

FIRST CHILD. Do not cry, Mama, for I'm sure if Papa said he would come home to-day, he will come yet; for he always does what he says he will.

MRS. BLAND. He cannot come, dear love; they will not let him.

SECOND CHILD. Why, then, they told him lies. O, fye upon them!

MELVILLE. (*Returning the letter.*) Fear nothing, Madam, 't is an empty threat:
A trick of policy. They dare not do it.

MRS. BLAND. Alas, alas! what dares not power to do?
What art of reasoning, or what magic words,
Can still the storm of fears these lines have raised?
The wife's, the mother's fears? Ye innocents,
Unconscious on the brink of what a perilous
Precipice ye stand, unknowing that today
Ye are cast down the gulph, poor babes, ye weep
From sympathy. Children of sorrow, nurst,
Nurtur'd, 'midst camps and arms; unknowing man,
But as man's fell destroyer; must ye now,
To crown your piteous fate, be fatherless?
O, lead me, lead me to him! Let me kneel,
Let these, my children, kneel, till André, pardon'd,
Ensures to me a husband, them a father.

MELVILLE. Madam, duty forbids further attendance.
I am on guard to-day. But see your son;
To him I leave your guidance. Good wishes
Prosper you. (*Exit* MELVILLE.)

(*Enter* BLAND.)

MRS. BLAND. My Arthur, O my Arthur!

BLAND. My mother! (*Embracing her.*)

MRS. BLAND. My son, I have been wishing
For you—
(*Bursts into tears, unable to proceed.*)

BLAND. But whence this grief, these tears, my mother?
Why are these little cheeks bedew'd with sorrow?
(*He kisses the children, who exclaim, Brother, brother!*)
Have I done aught to cause a mother's sadness?

MRS. BLAND. No, my brave boy! I oft have fear'd, but never
Sorrow'd for thee.

BLAND. High praise! Then bless me, Madam;

For I have pass'd through many a bustling scene
Since I have seen a father or a mother.

MRS. BLAND. Bless thee, my boy! O, bless him, bless him, Heaven!
Render him worthy to support these babes,
So soon, perhaps, all fatherless—dependant.

BLAND. What mean'st thou, Madam? Why these tears?

MRS. BLAND. Thy father—

BLAND. A prisoner of war—I long have known it—
But made so without blemish to his honor,
And soon exchang'd, returns unto his friends,
To guard these little ones, and point and lead
To virtue and to glory.

MRS. BLAND. Never, never!
His life, a sacrifice to André's manes,[1]
Must soon be offer'd. Even now, endungeon'd,
Like a vile felon on the earth he lies,
His death expecting. André's execution
Gives signal for the murder of thy father—
André now dies!

BLAND. (*Despairingly.*) My father and my friend!

MRS. BLAND. There is but one on earth can save my husband—
But one can pardon André.

BLAND. Haste, my mother!
Thou wilt prevail. Take with thee in each hand
An unoffending child of him thou weep'st.
Save—save them both! This way—haste—lean on me. (*Exeunt.*)

SCENE, *the* GENERAL'S *Quarters.*

(*Enter the* GENERAL *and* M'DONALD.)

GENERAL. *Here* have I intimation from the foe,
That still they deem the spy we have condemn'd,
Merely a captive; by the laws of arms
From death protected; and retaliation,
As they term it, threaten, if we our purpose hold.
Bland is the victim they have singled out,
Hoping his threaten'd death will André save.

[1] Shade.

M'DONALD. If I were Bland I boldly might advise
My General how to act. Free, and in safety,
I will now suppose my counsel needless.

(*Enter an* AMERICAN OFFICER.)

OFFICER. Another flag hath from the foe arrived,
And craves admittance.

GENERAL. Conduct it hither.
(*Exit* OFFICER.)
Let us, unwearied hear, unbias'd judge,
Whate'er against our martial court's decision,
Our enemies can bring.

(*Enter* BRITISH OFFICER, *conducted by the* AMERICAN OFFICER.)

GENERAL. You are welcome, sir.
What further says Sir Henry?

BRITISH OFFICER. This from him.
He calls on you to think what weighty woes
You now are busy bringing on your country.
He bids me say, that if your sentence reach
The prisoner's life (prisoner of arms he deems him,
And no spy) on him alone it falls not.
He bids me loud proclaim it, and declare,
If this brave officer, by cruel mockery
Of war's stern law, and justice' feign'd pretence,
Be murder'd; the sequel of our strife, bloody,
Unsparing and remorseless, you will make.
Think of the many captives in our power.
Already one is mark'd; for André mark'd;—
And when his death, unparallel'd in war,
The signal gives, then Colonel Bland must die.

GENERAL. 'T is well, sir; bear this message in return.
Sir Henry Clinton knows the laws of arms:
He is a soldier, and, I think, a brave one.
The prisoners he retains he must account for.
Perhaps the reckoning 's near. I, likewise, am
A soldier; entrusted by my country.
What I shall judge most for that country's good,

That shall I do. When doubtful, I consult
My country's friends; never her enemies.
In André's case there are no doubts; 't is clear:
Sir Henry Clinton knows it.

BRITISH OFFICER. Weigh consequences.

GENERAL. In strict regard to consequence I act;
And much should doubt to call that action right,
Howe'er specious, whose apparent end
Was misery to man. That brave officer
Whose death you threaten, for himself drew not
His sword—his country's wrongs arous'd his mind;
Her good alone his aim; and if his fall
Can further fire that country to resistance,
He will, with smiles, yield up his glorious life,
And count his death a gain; and tho' Columbians
Will lament his fall, they will lament in blood.

(GENERAL *walks up the stage.*)

M'DONALD. Hear this, hear this, mankind!

BRITISH OFFICER. Thus am I answered?

(*Enter a* SERGEANT *with a letter.*)

SERGEANT. Express from Colonel Bland.
(*Delivers it and exit.*)

GENERAL. With your permission.
(*Opens it.*)

BRITISH OFFICER. Your pleasure, sir. It may my mission further.

M'DONALD. O Bland, my countryman, surely I know thee!

GENERAL. 'T is short; I will put form aside, and read it.
(*Reads.*) "Excuse me, my Commander, for having a moment doubted your virtue; but you love me. If you waver, let this confirm you. My wife and children, to you and my country. Do *your* duty."
Report this to your General.

BRITISH OFFICER. I shall, sir.
(*Bows, and exit with* AMERICAN OFFICER.)

GENERAL. O Bland, my countryman!
(*Exit, with emotion.*)

M'DONALD. Triumph of virtue!
Like him and thee, still be Americans.
Then, tho' all-powerful Europe league against us,
And pour in arms her legions on our shores;
Who is so dull would doubt their shameful flight?
Who doubt our safety, and our glorious triumph?

SCENE, *the Prison.*

(*Enter* BLAND.)

BLAND. Lingering, I come to crush the bud of hope
My breath has, flattering, to existence warmed.
Hard is the task to friendship! hard to say
To the lov'd object, there remains no hope,
No consolation for thee; thou *must* die
The worst of deaths, no circumstance abated.

(*Enter* ANDRÉ, *in his uniform and dress'd.*)

ANDRÉ. Is there that state on earth which friendship cannot cheer?

BLAND. Little *I* bring to cheer thee, André.

ANDRÉ. I understand. 'T is well. 'T will soon be past.
Yet, 't was not much I asked. A soldier's death,
A trifling change of form.

BLAND. Of that I spoke not.
By vehemence of passion hurried on,
I pleaded for thy precious life alone;
The which denied, my indignation barr'd
All further parley. But strong solicitation
Now is urg'd to gain the wish'd-for favor.

ANDRÉ. What is 't o'clock?

BLAND. 'T is past the stroke of nine.

ANDRÉ. Why, then, 't is almost o'er. But to be hung—
Is there no way to escape that infamy?
What then *is* infamy?—no matter—no matter.

BLAND. Our General hath received another flag.

ANDRÉ. Soliciting for me?

BLAND. On thy behalf.

ANDRÉ. I have been ever favor'd.

BLAND. Threat'nings, now;
No more solicitations. Harsh, indeed,
The import of the message; harsh, indeed.

ANDRÉ. I am sorry for it. Would that I were dead.

And all was well with those I leave behind.
BLAND. Such a threat! Is it not enough, just Heaven,
That I must lose this man? Yet there was left
One for my soul to rest on. But, to know
That the same blow deprives them both of life—
ANDRÉ. What mean'st thou, Bland? Surely my General
Threats not retaliation. In vengeance
Dooms not some better man to die for me?
BLAND. The best of men.
ANDRÉ. Thou hast a father, captive—I dare not ask—
BLAND. That father dies for thee.
ANDRÉ. Gracious Heaven, how woes are heap'd upon me!
What! cannot one, so trifling in life's scene,
Fall, without drawing such a ponderous ruin?
Leave me, my friend, awhile—I yet have life—
A little space of life—let me exert it
To prevent injustice.—From death to save
Thy father, thee to save from utter desolation.
BLAND. What mean'st thou, André?
ANDRÉ. Seek thou the messenger
Who brought this threat. I will my last entreaty
Send by him. My General, sure, will grant it.
BLAND. To the last thyself! (*Exit.*)
ANDRÉ. If, at this moment,
When the pangs of death already touch me,
Firmly my mind against injustice strives,
And the last impulse to my vital powers
Is given by anxious wishes to redeem
My fellow-men from pain; surely my end,
Howe'er accomplish'd, is not infamous.
(*Exit.*)

END OF THE THIRD ACT.

ACT FOURTH.

SCENE, *the Encampment.*

(*Enter* M'DONALD *and* BLAND.)

BLAND. It doth in truth appear, that as a—spy—
Detested word!—brave André must be view'd.
His sentence he confesses strictly just.
Yet sure, a deed of mercy from *thy* hand,
Could never lead to ill. By such an act,
The stern and blood-stain'd brow of War
Would be disarm'd of half its gorgon horrors;
More humanized customs be induced;
And all the race of civilized man
Yet sure, a deed of mercy, from *thy* suit;
'T will well become thy character and station.
M'DONALD. Trust me, young friend, I am alone the judge
Of what becomes my character and station;
And having judg'd that this young Briton's death,
Even 'though attended by thy father's murder,
Is necessary, in these times accurs'd,
When every thought of man is ting'd with blood,
I will not stir my finger to redeem them.
Nay, much I wonder, Bland, having so oft
The reasons for this necessary rigor
Enforced upon thee, thou wilt still persist
In vain solicitations. Imitate
Thy father!
BLAND. My father knew not André.
I know his value; owe to him my life;
And gratitude, that first, that best of virtues,—
Without the which man sinks beneath the brute,—
Binds me in ties indissoluble to him.
M'DONALD. That man-created virtue blinds thy reason.
Man owes to man all love; when exercised,
He does no more than duty. Gratitude,
That selfish rule of action, which commands
That we our preference make of men,
Not for their worth, but that they did *us* service,
Misleading reason, casting in the way
Of justice stumbling-blocks, cannot be virtue.
BLAND. Detested sophistry! 'T was André sav'd me.
M'DONALD. He sav'd thy life, and thou art grateful for it.

How self intrudes, delusive, on man's thoughts.
He sav'd thy life, yet strove to damn thy country;
Doom'd millions to the haughty Briton's yoke;
The best and foremost in the cause of virtue
To death, by sword, by prison, or the halter;
His sacrifice now stands the only bar
Between the wanton cruelties of war
And our much-suffering soldiers; yet when weigh'd
With gratitude, for that he sav'd *thy* life,
These things prove gossamer, and balance air;—
Perversion monstrous of man's moral sense!

BLAND. Rather perversion monstrous of all good
Is thy accurs'd, detestable opinion.
Cold-blooded reasoners, such as thee, would blast
All warm affection; asunder sever
Every social tie of humanized man.
Curst be thy sophisms, cunningly contriv'd
The callous coldness of thy heart to cover,
And screen thee from the brave man's detestation!

M'DONALD. Boy, boy!

BLAND. Thou knowest that André 's not a spy.

M'DONALD. I know him one. Thou hast acknowledg'd it.

BLAND. Thou liest!

M'DONALD. Shame on thy ruffian tongue! How passion
Mars thee! I pity thee. Thou canst not harm,
By words intemperate, a virtuous man.
I pity thee; for passion sometimes sways
My older frame, through former uncheck'd habit;
But when I see the havoc which it makes
In others, I can shun the snare accurst,
And nothing feel but pity.

BLAND. (*Indignantly.*) Pity me! (*Approaches him, and speaks in an under voice.*)
Thou canst be cool, yet, trust me, *passion* sways thee.
Fear does not warm the blood, yet 't is a *passion.*
Hast thou no feeling? I have call'd thee liar!

M'DONALD. If thou could'st make me one, I then might grieve.

BLAND. Thy coolness goes to freezing; thou 'rt a coward!

M'DONALD. Thou knowest thou tell'st a falsehood.

BLAND. Thou shalt know
None with impunity speaks thus of me.
That to rouse thy courage! (*Touches him gently with his open hand, in crossing him.* M'DONALD *looks at him unmoved.*) Dost thou not yet feel?

M'DONALD. For *thee* I feel. And, tho' another's acts
Cast no dishonor on the worthy man,
I still feel for thy father. Yet, remember,
I may not, haply, ever be thus guarded;
I may not always the distinction make,
However just, between the blow intended
To provoke, and one that 's meant to injure.

BLAND. Hast thou no sense of honor?

M'DONALD. Truly, yes:
For I am honor's votary. Honor, with me,
Is worth; 't is truth; 't is virtue; 't is a thing
So high preëminent, that a boy's breath,
Or brute's, or madman's blow can never reach it.
My honor is so much, so truly mine,
That none hath power to wound it, save myself.

BLAND. I will proclaim thee through the camp a coward.

M'DONALD. Think better of it. Proclaim not thine own shame.

BLAND. I 'll brand thee,—damnation!
(*Exit.*)

M'DONALD. O passion, passion!
A man who values fame far more than life;
A brave young man; in many things a good;
Utters vile falsehoods; adds injury to insult;
Striving with blood to seal such foul injustice;
And all from impulse of unbridled feeling. (*Pause.*)
Here comes the mother of this headstrong boy,
Severely rack'd. What shall allay her torture?
For common consolation, *here,* is insult.

(*Enter* MRS. BLAND *and* CHILDREN.)

MRS. BLAND. O my good friend!
M'DONALD. (*Taking her hand.*)
I know thy cause of sorrow.
Art thou now from our Commander?
MRS. BLAND. (*Drying her tears and assuming dignity.*) I am.
But vain is my entreaty. All unmov'd
He hears my words, he sees my desperate sorrow.
Fain would I blame his conduct,—but I cannot.
Strictly examin'd, with intent to mark
The error which so fatal proves to *me,*
My scrutiny but ends in admiration.
Thus when the prophet from the hills of Moab,
Look'd down upon the chosen race of Heaven,
With fell intent to curse, ere yet he spake,
Truth all resistless, emanation bright
From great Adonai, fill'd his froward mind,
And chang'd the curses of his heart to blessings.
M'DONALD. Thou payest high praise to virtue. Whither now?
MRS. BLAND. I still must hover round this spot until
My doom is known.
M'DONALD. Then to my quarters, lady;
There shall my mate give comfort and refreshment:
One of your sex can best your sorrows soothe. (*Exeunt.*)

SCENE, *the prison.*

(*Enter* BLAND.)

BLAND. Where'er I look, cold desolation meets me.
My father—André—and self-condemnation.
Why seek I André now? Am *I* a man
To soothe the sorrows of a suffering friend?
The weather-cock of passion! fool inebriate!
Who could with ruffian hand strive to provoke
Hoar wisdom to intemperance! who could lie!
Aye, swagger, lie, and brag!—Liar! Damnation!
O, let me steal away and hide my head,
Nor view a man, condemned to harshest death.
Whose words and actions, when by mine compar'd,
Show white as innocence and bright as truth.
I now would shun him, but that his shorten'd
Thread of life gives me no line to play with.
He comes with smiles, and all the air of triumph,
While *I* am sinking with remorse and shame;
Yet *he* is doom'd to death, and *I* am free.

(*Enter* ANDRÉ.)

ANDRÉ. Welcome, my Bland! Cheerly, a welcome hither!
I feel assurance that my last request
Will not be slighted. Safely thy father
Shall return to thee. (*Holding out a paper.*) See what employment
For a dying man. Take thou these verses;
And, after my decease, send them to her
Whose name is woven in them; whose image
Hath controul'd my destiny. Such tokens
Are rather out of date. Fashions
There are in love as in all else; they change
As variously. A gallant knight, erewhile,
Of Cœur de Lion's day, would, dying, send
His heart home to its mistress; degenerate
Soldier, I send but some blotted paper.
BLAND. If 't would not damp thy present cheerfulness,
I would require the meaning of thy words.
I ne'er till now did hear of André's mistress.
ANDRÉ. Mine is a story of that common kind,
So often told, with scanty variation,
That the pall'd ear loaths the repeated tale.
Each young romancer chuses for his theme
The woes of youthful hearts, by the cold hand
Of frosty age, arm'd with parental power,
Asunder torn. But I long since have ceas'd
To mourn; well satisfied that she I love,

Happy in holy union with another,
Shares not my wayward fortunes. Nor would I
Now these tokens send, remembrance to awaken,
But that I know her happy; and the happy
Can think on misery and share it not.

BLAND. (*Agitated.*)
Some one approaches.

ANDRÉ. Why, 't is near the time!
But tell me, Bland, say,—is the manner chang'd?

BLAND. I hope it, but I yet have no assurance.

ANDRÉ. Well, well!

HONORA. (*Without.*) I must see him.

ANDRÉ. Whose voice was that?
My senses!—Do I dream? (*Leans on* BLAND.)

(*Enter* HONORA.)

HONORA. Where is he?

ANDRÉ. 'T is she!
(*Starts from* BLAND *and advances towards* HONORA; *she rushes into his arms.*)

HONORA. It is enough! He lives, and *I* shall save him.
(*She faints in the arms of* ANDRÉ.)

ANDRÉ. She sinks—assist me, Bland! O, save her, save her!
(*Places her in a chair and looks tenderly on her.*)
Yet, why should she awake from that sweet sleep?
Why should she ope her eyes—(*wildly*) —to see me hung!
What does she here? Stand off—(*tenderly*)—and let her die.
How pale she looks! How worn that tender frame!—
She has known sorrow! Who could injure her?

BLAND. She revives—André—soft, bend her forward.
(ANDRÉ *kneels and supports her.*)

HONORA. André!—

ANDRÉ. Lov'd excellence!

HONORA. Yes, it is André!
(*Rises and looks at him.*)
No more deceived by visionary forms,
By him supported—(*Leans on him.*)

ANDRÉ. Why is this?
Thou dost look pale, Honora—sick and wan—
Languid thy fainting limbs—

HONORA. All will be well.
But was it kind to leave me as thou did'st?
So rashly to desert thy vow-link'd wife?

ANDRÉ. When made another's both by vows and laws—

HONORA. (*Quitting his support.*) What meanest thou?

ANDRÉ. Did'st thou not marry him?

HONORA. Marry!

ANDRÉ. Did'st thou not give thy hand away
From me?

HONORA. O, never, never.

ANDRÉ. Not married?

HONORA. To none but thee, and but in will to thee.

ANDRÉ. O blind, blind wretch!—Thy father told me—

HONORA. Thou wast deceived. They hurried me away,
Spreading false rumors to remove thy love—
(*Tenderly.*) Thou did'st too soon believe them.

ANDRÉ. Thy father—
How could I but believe Honora's father?
And he did tell me so. I reverenc'd age,
Yet knew age was not virtue. I believed
His snowy locks, and yet they did deceive me!
I have destroy'd myself and thee!—Alas,
Ill-fated maid, why did'st thou not forget me?
Hast thou rude seas and hostile shores explor'd
For this? To see my death? Witness my shame?

HONORA. I come to bless thee, André, and shall do it.
I bear such offers from thy kind Commander
As must prevail to save thee. Thus the daughter
May repair the ills her cruel sire inflicted.
My father, dying, gave me cause to think
That arts were us'd to drive thee from thy home;
But what those arts I knew not. An heiress left,
Of years mature, with power and liberty,
I straight resolv'd to seek thee o'er the seas.
A long-known friend, who came to join her lord,

Yielded protection and lov'd fellowship.—
Indeed, when I did hear of thy estate,
It almost kill'd me;—I was weak before—

ANDRÉ. 'T is I have murder'd thee!

HONORA. All shall be well.
Thy General heard of me, and instant form'd
The plan of this my visit. I am strong,
Compar'd with what I was. Hope strengthens me;
Nay, even solicitude supports me now;
And when thou shalt be safe, *thou* wilt support me.

ANDRÉ. Support thee!—O Heaven! What!—and *must* I die?
Die!—and leave her *thus*—suffering—unprotected!

(*Enter* MELVILLE *and* GUARD.)

MELVILLE. I am sorry that my duty should require
Service, at which my heart revolts; but, sir,
Our soldiers wait in arms. All is prepar'd—

HONORA. To death! Impossible! Has my delay,
Then, murder'd him? A momentary respite—

MELVILLE. Lady, I have no power.

BLAND. Melville, my friend,
This lady bears dispatches of high import,
Touching this business;—should they arrive too late—

HONORA. For pity's sake, and heaven's, conduct me to him;
And wait the issue of our conference.
O, 't would be murder of the blackest dye,
Sin execrable, not to break thy orders—
Inhuman, thou art not.

MELVILLE. Lady, thou say'st true;
For rather would I lose my rank in arms,
And stand cashier'd for lack of discipline,
Than gain 'mongst military men all praise,
Wanting the touch of sweet humanity.

HONORA. Thou grantest my request?

MELVILLE. Lady, I do.
Retire! (*Soldiers go out.*)

BLAND. I know not what excuse, to martial men,
Thou canst advance for this; but to thy heart
Thou wilt need none, good Melville.

ANDRÉ. O Honora!

HONORA. Cheer up, I feel assur'd. Hope wings my flight,
To bring thee tidings of much joy to come.

(*Exit* HONORA, *with* BLAND *and* MELVILLE.)

ANDRÉ. Eternal blessings on thee, matchless woman!—
If Death now comes, he finds the veriest coward
That e'er he dealt withal. I cannot think
Of dying. Void of fortitude, each thought
Clings to the world—the world that holds Honora! (*Exit.*)

END OF THE FOURTH ACT.

ACT FIFTH.

SCENE, *the Encampment.*

(*Enter* BLAND.)

BLAND. Suspence—uncertainty—man's bane and solace!
How racking now to me! My mother comes.
Forgive me, O my father, if in this war,
This wasting conflict of my 'wildering passions,
Memory of thee holds here a second place!
M'Donald comes with her. I would not meet him;
Yet I *will* do it. Summon up some courage—
Confess my fault, and gain, if not his love,
At least the approbation of *my* judgment.

(*Enter* MRS. BLAND *and* CHILDREN, *with* M'DONALD.)

BLAND. Say, Madam, is there no change of counsel,
Or new determination?

MRS. BLAND. *Nought new*, my son.
The tale of misery is told unheard.
The widow's and the orphans' sighs
Fly up, unnoted by the eye of man,
And mingle, undistinguish'd, with the winds.
My friend (*to* M'DONALD), attend thy duties. I must away.

SECOND CHILD. You need not cry, Mama, the General will do it, I am sure, for I saw him cry. He turn'd away his head from *you*, but I saw it.

MRS. BLAND. Poor thing! Come, let us home and weep. Alas!
I can no more, for war hath made men rocks.
(*Exeunt* MRS. BLAND *and* CHILDREN.)

BLAND. Colonel, I used thee ill this morning.

M'DONALD. No!
Thyself thou used'st most vilely, I remember.

BLAND. Myself sustained the injury, most true;
But the intent of what I said and did
Was ill to thee alone; I'm sorry for it.
See'st thou these blushes? They proceed from warmth
As honest as the heart of man e'er felt;
But not with shame unmingled, while I force
This tongue, debased, to own it slander'd thee,
And utter'd—I could curse it—utter'd falsehood.
Howe'er misled by passion, still my mind
Retains that sense of honest rectitude
Which makes the memory of an evil deed
A troublesome companion. I was wrong.

M'DONALD. Why, now, this glads me; for thou *now* art right.
O, may thy tongue, henceforward, utter naught
But Truth's sweet precepts, in fair Virtue's cause!
Give me thy hand. (*Takes his hand.*)
Ne'er may it grasp a sword
But in defence of justice.

BLAND. Yet, erewhile,
A few short hours scarce past, when this vile hand
Attempted on *thee* insult; and was raised
Against thy honor; ready to be raised
Against thy life. If this my deep remorse—

M'DONALD. No more, no more! 'T is past. Remember it
But as thou would'st the action of another,
By thy enlighten'd judgment much condemn'd;
And serving as a beacon in the storms
Thy passions yet may raise. Remorse is vice;
Guard thee against its influence debasing.
Say to thyself: "I *am* not what I *was;*
I am not *now* the instrument of vice;
I'm changed; I am a man; Virtue's firm friend;
Sever'd forever from my former self;
No link, but in remembrance salutary."

<BLAND.[1] How all men tower above me!

M'DONALD. Nay, not so.

[1] The lines marked < > were omitted after the first night and the following were inserted. (See Introduction.)

BLAND. Noble M'Donald, truth and honor's champion!
Yet think not strange that my intemperance wrong'd thee:
Good as thou art! for, would'st thou, can'st thou, think it?
My tongue unbridled, hath the same offence,
With action violent, and boisterous tone,
Hurl'd on that glorious man, whose pious labors
Shield from every ill his grateful country.
That man, whom friends to adoration love,
And enemies revere. Yes, M'Donald,
Even in the presence of the first of men
Did I abjure the service of my country,
And reft my helmet of that glorious badge
Which graces even the brow of Washington.
How shall I see him more?

M'DONALD. Alive himself to every generous impulse,
He hath excused the impetuous warmth of youth,
In expectation that thy fiery soul,
Chasten'd by time and reason, will receive
The stamp indelible of godlike virtue.
To me, in trust, he gave this badge disclaim'd,
With power, when thou should'st see thy wrongful error,
From him, to reinstate it in thy helm,
And thee in his high favor.
(*Gives the cockade.*)

BLAND. (*Takes the cockade and replaces it.*) Shall I speak my thoughts of thee and him?
No! let my actions henceforth show what thou
And he have made me. Ne'er shall my helmet
Lack again its proudest, noblest ornament,
Until my country knows the rest of peace,
Or Bland the peace of death. (*Exit.*)

Above what once thou wast, some few do rise;
None above what thou art.
BLAND. It shall be so.
M'DONALD. It is so.
BLAND. Then to prove it.
For I must yet a trial undergo,
That will require a consciousness of virtue. (*Exit.*)
M'DONALD. O, what a temper doth in man reside!
How capable of yet unthought perfection! (*Exit.*)

SCENE, *the General's quarters.*

(*Enter* GENERAL *and* SEWARD.)

GENERAL. Ask her, my friend, to send by thee her pacquets. (*Exit* SEWARD.)
O, what keen struggles must I undergo!
Unbless'd estate! to have the power to pardon;
The court's stern sentence to remit;—give life;—
Feel the strong wish to use such blessed power;
Yet know that circumstances strong as fate
Forbid to obey the impulse. O, I feel
That man should never shed the blood of man!

(*Enter* SEWARD.)

SEWARD. Naught can the lovely suitor satisfy,
But conference with thee, and much I fear
Refusal would cause madness.
GENERAL. Yet to admit,
To hear, be tortur'd, and refuse at last—
SEWARD. Sure never man such spectacle of sorrow.
Saw before. Motionless the rough-hewn soldiers
Silent view her, or walk aside and weep.
GENERAL. (*After a pause.*) Admit her. (SEWARD *goes out.*) O, for the art, the precious art,
To reconcile the sufferer to his sorrows!
(HONORA *rushes in, and throws herself wildly on her knees before him; he endeavors to raise her.*)
HONORA. Nay, nay, here is my place, or here, or lower,
Unless thou grant'st his life. All forms away!
Thus will I clasp thy knees, thus cling to thee—
I am his wife—'t is I have ruin'd him—
O, save him! Give him to me! Let us cross
The mighty seas, far, far—ne'er to offend again—
(*The* GENERAL *turns away, and hides his eyes with his hand.*)

(*Enter* SEWARD *and an* OFFICER.)

GENERAL. Seward, support her; my heart is torn in twain.
(HONORA, *as if exhausted, suffers herself to be raised, and leans on* SEWARD.)
OFFICER. This moment, sir, a messenger arrived
With well confirm'd and mournful information,
That gallant Hastings, by the lawless scouts
Of Britain taken, after cruel mockery
With show of trial and of condemnation,
On the next tree was hung.
HONORA. (*Wildly.*) O, it is false.
GENERAL. Why, why, my country, did I hesitate? (*Exit.*)
(HONORA *sinks, faints, and is borne off by* SEWARD *and* OFFICER.)

SCENE, *the Prison.*

(ANDRÉ *meeting* BLAND.)

ANDRÉ. How speeds Honora? (*Pause.*) Art thou silent, Bland?
Why, then, I know my task. The mind of man,
If not by vice debas'd, debilitated,
Or by disease of body quite unton'd,
Hath o'er its thoughts a power—energy divine.
Of fortitude the source and every virtue—
A godlike power, which e'en o'er circumstance
Its sov'reignty exerts. Now from my thoughts,
Honora! Yet she is left alone—expos'd—
BLAND. O, André, spurn me, strike me to the earth;
For what a wretch am I in André's mind,
That he can think he leaves his love alone,
And I retaining life!
ANDRÉ. Forgive me, Bland.

My thoughts glanc'd not on thee. Imagination
Pictur'd only, then, her orphan state, helpless;
Her weak and grief-exhausted frame. Alas!
This blow will kill her.

BLAND. (*Kneeling.*) Here, do I myself
Devote, my fortune consecrate, to thee,
To thy remembrance, and Honora's service.

ANDRÉ. Enough! Let me not see her more—nor think of her—
Farewell, farewell, sweet image! Now for death.

BLAND. Yet that thou should'st the felon's fate fulfil—
Damnation! My blood boils. Indignation
Makes the current of my life course wildly
Through its round and maddens each emotion.

ANDRÉ. Come, come, it matters not.

BLAND. I do remember,
When a boy at school, in our allotted tasks,
We, by our puny acts, strove to pourtray
The giant thoughts of Otway. I was Pierre.
O, thou art Pierre's reality—a soldier,
On whose manly brow sits fortitude enamor'd;
A Mars, abhorring vice, yet doom'd to die
A death of infamy; thy corse expos'd
To vulgar gaze—halter'd—distorted--oh—
(*Pauses, and then adds in a low hollow voice:*)
Pierre had a friend to save him from such shame—
And so hast thou.

ANDRÉ. No more, as thou dost love me.

BLAND. I have a sword, and arm, that never fail'd me.

ANDRÉ. Bland, such an act would justly thee involve,
And leave that helpless one thou sworest to guard
Expos'd to every ill. O, think not of it!

BLAND. If thou wilt not my aid—take it thyself.
(*Draws and offers his sword.*)

ANDRÉ. No, men will say that cowardice did urge me.
In my mind's weakness, I did wish to shun
That mode of death which error represented
Infamous: now let me rise superior;
And with a fortitude too true to start
From mere appearances, show your country
That she, in me, destroys a man who might
Have liv'd to virtue.

BLAND. (*Sheathing his sword.*) I will not think more of it;
I was again the sport of erring passion.

ANDRÉ. Go thou and guide Honora from this spot.

HONORA. (*Entering.*) Who shall oppose his wife? I will have way!
They, cruel, would have kept me from thee, André.
Say, am I not thy wife? Wilt thou deny me?
Indeed I am not dress'd in bridal trim.
But I have travelled far:—rough was the road—
Rugged and rough—that must excuse my dress.
(*Seeing* ANDRÉ'S *distress.*) Thou art not glad to see me.

ANDRÉ. Break my heart!

HONORA. Indeed, I feel not much in spirits. I wept but now.

(*Enter* MELVILLE *and* GUARD.)

BLAND. (*To* MELVILLE.) Say nothing.

ANDRÉ. I am ready.

HONORA. (*Seeing the* GUARD.) Are *they* here?
Here again—the *same*—but they shall not harm me.
I am with *thee,* my André—I am safe—
And *thou* art safe with me. Is it not so? (*Clinging to him.*)

(*Enter* MRS. BLAND.)

MRS. BLAND. Where is this lovely victim?

BLAND. Thanks, my mother.

MRS. BLAND. M'Donald sent me hither. My woes are past.
Thy father, by the foe released, already
Is in safety. This be forgotten now;
And every thought be turn'd to this sad scene.
Come, lady, home with me.

HONORA. Go home with thee?
Art thou my André's mother? We will home
And rest, for thou art weary—very weary. (*Leans on* MRS. BLAND.)
(ANDRÉ *retires to the* GUARD, *and goes off with them, looking on her to the*

last, and with an action of extreme tenderness takes leave of her. MELVILLE *and* BLAND *accompany him.*)

HONORA. Now we will go. Come, love! Where is he?
All gone!—I do remember—I awake—
They have him. Murder! Help! O, save him! save him!

(HONORA *attempts to follow, but falls.* MRS. BLAND *kneels to assist her. Scene closes.*)

SCENE, *the Encampment.*

(*Procession to the execution of* ANDRÉ. *First enter Pioneers—Detachment of Infantry—Military Band of Music—Infantry. The Music having passed off, enter* ANDRÉ *between* MELVILLE *and* AMERICAN OFFICER; *they sorrowful, he cheerfully conversing as he passes over the stage.*)

ANDRÉ. It may in me be merely prejudice,
The effect of young opinion deep engraved
Upon the tender mind by care parental;
But I must think your country has mistook
Her interests. Believe me, but for this I should
Not willingly have drawn a sword against her.

(*They bow their heads in silence.*)

Opinion must, nay, ought to sway our actions;
Therefore—

(*Having crossed the stage, he goes out as still conversing with them. Another detachment of Infantry, with muffled and craped drums, closes the procession; as soon as they are off—*

SCENE.

draws and discovers the distant view of the encampment.)

(*Procession enters in same order as before, proceeds up the stage, and goes off the opposite side.*)

(*Enter* M'DONALD, *leading* BLAND, *who looks wildly back.*)

BLAND. I dare not *thee* resist. Yet why, O why
Thus hurry me away?—

M'DONALD. Would'st thou behold—

BLAND. O, name it not!

M'DONALD. Or would'st thou, by thy looks
And gestures wild, o'erthrow that manly calmness
Which, or assumed or felt, so well becomes thy friend?

BLAND. What means that cannon's sound?

M'DONALD. (*After a pause.*) Signal of death
Appointed. André, thy friend, is now no more.

BLAND. Farewell, farewell, brave spirit! O! let my countrymen,
Henceforward when the cruelties of war
Arise in their remembrance; when their ready
Speech would pour forth torrents in their foe's dispraise,
Think on this act accurst, and lock complaint in silence.

(BLAND *throws himself on the earth.*)

M'DONALD. Such are the dictates of the heart, not head.
O, may the children of Columbia still
Be taught by every teacher of mankind,
Each circumstance of calculative gain,
Or wounded pride, which prompted our oppressors;
May every child be taught to lisp the tale;
And may, in times to come, no foreign force,
No European influence, tempt to misstate,
Or awe the tongue of eloquence to silence.
Still may our children's children deep abhor
The motives, doubly deep detest the actors;
Ever remembering that the race who plann'd,
Who acquiesced, or did the deeds abhor'd,
Has pass'd from off the earth; and, in its stead,
Stand men who challenge love or detestation
But from their proper, individual deeds
Never let memory of the sire's offence
Descend upon the son.

CURTAIN DROPS.

SUPERSTITION

BY

James Nelson Barker

SUPERSTITION

Superstition is one of the earliest plays based upon Colonial history. Five years before Cooper used the theme of the regicides in *The Wept of Wish-ton-Wish* and eleven years before Hawthorne published *The Gray Champion*, Barker had placed on the stage the dramatic story of the old Puritan issuing from his solitude to lead the villagers to victory against the Indians. This theme is interwoven with that of the intolerance of the Puritans and their persecution for witchcraft.

James Nelson Barker was born in Philadelphia, June 17, 1784. He had a public career of some distinction, as he became captain of an artillery regiment during the War of 1812, was elected Mayor of Philadelphia in 1819, was Collector of the Port from 1829 to 1838, and from 1838 to his death was Comptroller of the United States Treasury. He died in Washington, D. C., March 9, 1858.

Barker represents the play based upon a native theme. After a tentative effort, based on Cervantes, called *The Spanish Rover*, and a masque, *America*, neither printed nor performed, he wrote a comedy of American life, *Tears and Smiles*, acted March 4, 1807, at the Chestnut Street Theatre, and printed in Philadelphia in 1808. At the first Joseph Jefferson's suggestion, he put in the character of "Nathan Yank," thus forming a link between the character of "Jonathan" in *The Contrast* and the later "Jonathan Ploughboy" in *The Forest Rose* of Woodworth. *The Embargo or What News?* was acted on March 16, 1808, at the Chestnut Street Theatre. It supported the policy of the Embargo Act.

The Indian Princess or La Belle Sauvage, the earliest play on the Pocahontas story, was performed at the Chestnut Street Theatre, Philadelphia, April 6, 1808. Durang gives an interesting account of the commotion caused by the persecution of Webster the singer which prevented the piece from being heard. It was an opera for which the music was written by Bray, and it was acted afterwards in other places and printed in 1808. *Marmion, or The Battle of Flodden Field*, a dramatization of Scott's poem, was acted first in New York, at the Park Theatre, April 13, 1812. William Wood, the Manager of the Chestnut Street Theatre, says that it was announced in Philadelphia as by Thomas Morton, the English playwright, in order to avoid the neglect usually accorded to native playwrights, and that after running several nights with success, the author's name was announced, when the audiences fell off. Durang, however, in his *History of the Philadelphia Stage*, says "it lost none of its attraction after the mask was removed'' and the statement of receipts in Wood's Diary shows no falling off of importance. It was printed in 1816. Barker's play, *The Armourer's Escape or Three Years at Nootka Sound,* which was acted at the Chestnut Street Theatre, March 21, 1817, had a peculiar interest since John Jewitt, armorer of the ship *Boston,* on whose adventures the play was based, acted the leading part himself. *How to Try a Lover,* a comedy, printed in 1817, was performed as *The Court of Love,* March 26, 1836, at the Arch St. Theatre, Philadelphia. It is easily one of the best of Barker's plays.

Superstition was first acted at the Chestnut Street Theatre, Philadelphia, March 12, 1824. Wood tells us it was acted ''with deserved applause.'' F. C. Wemyss, who acted ''George Egerton,'' speaks in his *Twenty-six Years of the Life of an Actor and Manager* of the success of the play, and states that Wood did not put the play on oftener because Mrs. Duff in the character of ''Mary'' outshone Mrs. Wood in ''Isabella.'' ''I have been surprised,'' he adds, ''that no manager ever rescued so good a play from oblivion.''

Barker's plays are now hard to obtain. *Marmion* was reprinted, with *Superstition,* in 1826, in the ''Acting American Theatre'' of Lopez and Wemyss. An account of Barker's plays, written by himself, is to be found in Dunlap's *History of the American Theatre,* Vol. 2, pp. 308–316.

Note to Fourth Edition.

Superstition was revived on March 5, 1927, by the Laboratory Players of Columbia University, under the auspices of the Institute of Arts and Sciences, with gratifying results. It drew one of the largest audiences ever recorded at the University Theatre and has been repeated. The performances made clear how appealing the parts of Isabella, Mary, Charles, and the ''Unknown'' may be made to a modern audience, and how the character of Ravensworth, the concrete representation of Superstition, dominates the play.

Note to Fifth Edition.

An authoritative biography of Barker has been published under the title of *James Nelson Barker,* by Paul H. Musser, through the University of Pennsylvania Press (1929). This includes a reprint of the comedy *Tears and Smiles. The Indian Princess* is now available in Volume I of *Representative Plays by American Dramatists,* edited by Montrose J. Moses.

LOPEZ AND WEMYSS' EDITION.

THE

ACTING AMERICAN THEATRE.

THE TRAGEDY OF

SUPERSTITION,

BY

JAMES N. BARKER, ESQ.

AUTHOR OF MARMION A TRAGEDY, &C.

WITH A PORTRAIT OF

MRS. DUFF,

IN THE CHARACTER OF

MARY.

The Plays carefully corrected from the Prompt books of the *PHILADELPHIA THEATRE.*

By M. Lopez, Prompter.

PUBLISHED BY A. R. POOLE, CHESNUT STREET,

FOR THE PROPRIETORS.

And to be had of all the principal booksellers in the

UNITED STATES.

Price to non-subscribers, Fifty cents

DRAMATIS PERSONAE

Philadelphia.

Performed (First time) March 12, 1824.

Sir Reginald Egerton	Mr. Warren
George Egerton	Mr. Wemyss
Ravensworth	Mr. Darley
Walford	Mr. Wheatly
Charles	Mr. Wood
The Unknown	Mr. Duff
Judge	Mr. Greene
First Villager	Mr. Hathwell
Second Villager	Mr. Jones
Messenger	Mr. Bignall
First Officer	Mr. Johnston
Second Officer	Mr. Murray
Edward	Mr. Parker
Boy	Master H. Mestayer
Second Judge	Mr. Mestayer
Officer	Mr. J. Mestayer

Villagers, Indians, Sups.

Isabella	Mrs. Wood
Mary	Mrs. Duff
Alice	Mrs. Durang
Lucy	Mrs. Greene

Female Villagers..............Mrs. Mestayer, Bignall, Murray, Misses Parker, Hathwells, Mestayers.

Scene in New England, about the year 1675.

Time, a little more than Twenty-four hours.

SUPERSTITION

ACT FIRST.

SCENE 1. *A Village at a little distance. In front, on the left of the Stage, the cottage of* RAVENSWORTH; *a handsome rustic building. A large mansion, on an eminence nearer the Village, on the right.*

(*Enter from the Cottage,* MARY *and* ALICE.)

MARY. Nay, come away, dear Alice, every moment
Of your brief visit must be wholly mine;
Let 's leave our fathers to their grave discourse
Of witch and wizard, ere we laugh outright.

ALICE. It is a subject that the country round
Deems a most solemn one.

MARY. True: but to me,
'T is not the less absurd on that account.

ALICE. This levity 's misplac'd: your father claims
Your love and reverence—

MARY. And I do revere him,
And love him dearly, Alice; do I not?
How often have I striven to melt his sternness;
And, when my heart was sick of its own cares,
Lock'd up my selfish sorrows from his view,
And tried, by every filial endearment,
To win his smiles. E'en when his brow was darkest;
I 've brav'd its terrors; hung upon his neck,
And spoken of my mother: O how sweet
It were methought, even to weep with him.

ALICE. You 're an enthusiast, Mary. Ah, beware,
Lest this impetuous current of your feeling
Urge you, one day, against the perilous rock.

MARY. I 'm young, and youth is ardent, and should be
Cheerful, and full of bright and sunny thoughts;
I would be if I dared. You, too, are young,
Yet may be happy; for you have a parent
Who, tho' he guide you safely down the stream,
Does not, like angry pilots, chide, e'en louder
Than the loud storm.

ALICE. His high and holy office
May haply give to your good father's manner,
A grave solemnity, perhaps, a harshness—

MARY. And why a harshness? Sure, ah sure, Religion
Descends not like the vulture in its wrath;
But rather like the mild and gentle dove,
Emblem of peace and harbinger of joy,
Love in its eye and healing on its wing;
With pure and snowy plumage, downy soft,
To nestle in the bosom of its votaries.

ALICE. I cannot argue; I 'm content to follow
Where e'er our fathers lead. For you, I fear
You 've learn'd too much from this mysterious stranger.

MARY. O Alice, join not you with the slanderous crowd,
Against a noble lady, whom you know not.
For me, be satisfied I never more
Perhaps, shall see her: I 've obeyed my father;
And must, tho' it should break my heart: tho' Charles—

(*Pauses and crosses.*)

ALICE. And what of Charles?

MARY. Her son—

ALICE. I know: her son,
And what of him?

MARY. This very day, 't is said,
He will be here—

ALICE. Expell'd, they say, from college.

MARY. Disgrac'd— 'T is false: Charles cannot be disgrac'd;
If envy, persecution, drive him thence,

They but disgrace themselves, and not poor Charles.
ALICE. Mary?
MARY. Yes; take my secret; take it quickly,
Or it will burst my heart.
ALICE. Nay, but be calm.
MARY. You shall know all—surely you'll pity, Alice,
And perhaps, pardon me. Three years ago
When Charles's mother first came here to live;
From England, was it not—the village then
Had scarce begun to hate her, for as yet
She had not lavish'd charities abroad,
To purchase up ingratitude and envy.
Being her nearest neighbour, (my dear mother
Was then alive,) there rose at once between us
That intercourse which neighbourhood compels
At times, e'en with the most reserved. The lady,
I know not why, unless out of her goodness,
Graced me with her regard, and when my mother
Died, she took the desolate child to her bosom.
ALICE. 'T was kindly done.
MARY. O she was goodness all,
Her words, so sweet and soothing; as she spoke,
Alice, methought I saw my sainted mother
Lean o'er the bright edge of a silvery cloud
And smile upon her happy orphan girl,—
And there was Charles, so busy still around me,
Exhausting all his boyish gallantries,
With brotherly affection.—
ALICE. Charles, still Charles?
MARY. Can I forget it!—
ALICE. Nay, go on.
MARY. The winter
Soon pass'd away, and then the spring came on
With all its flowers, and still the earliest blossom
Was cull'd for me. O, we were then so happy—
I always lov'd the spring. Young nature then
Came to me like a play-mate. Ere the snows
Had left the hills, I've often wander'd forth,
And, all impatient for the verdure, clear'd
A patch of infant green; or even turn'd
With mighty effort, some recumbent stone,
To find the fresh grass under it.
ALICE. This is childish.
MARY. I was a child, then,—would I were e'en now,
As then I was—my life, I fear, will prove
A wintry waste with no green spot to cheer it;
ALICE. More visionary still.
MARY. Well, to my story:—
My father took me home, I think it was
About the time you came into the village,
Fell superstition now had spread around.
Reports—I scarce know what they meant—arose
Concerning Isabella; and my father
Made gloomier by my mother's death, and yielding
His strong mind to the doctrine of the times,
Grew daily still more stern, until at length,
At peril of his curse, he bade me never
To hold communion with that family.
ALICE. And you obeyed?
MARY. All that I could, I did.
But O the tales they tell—the horrid stories—
Her very virtues they distort to crimes.
And for poor Charles, his manliness and spirit,
The gayety of youth and innocence,
In him are vices. Could I help defending,
Knowing them as I did:—all others hating,
Could I help loving!—
ALICE. Loving, Mary?
MARY. Ay; most deeply, strongly loving Charles and his mother.
ALICE. But sure you have not seen this Charles?
MARY. Not often.—
Nay, frown not, friend, for how could I avoid it,
When chance insisted on an interview?
ALICE. Have ye met lately?
MARY. Yes.
ALICE. What pass'd between you?

MARY. A plight of faith: A vow to live or die,
Each for the other.

ALICE. Lost, lost girl.

MARY. Why, ay,
It may be so; if so, 't is Heaven's will.
You have my secret, Alice.

(*Enter from the House,* RAVENSWORTH *and* WALFORD.)

ALICE. Peace; our fathers.
(*They retire into house.*)

RAV. No, Walford, no: I have no charity
For what you term the weakness of our nature.
The soul should rise above it. It was this
That made the fathers of this land prevail,
When man and the elements opposed, and win
Their heritage from the heathen.

WALF. True; the times
Impos'd a virtue, almost superhuman.
But surely, the necessity is pass'd
For trampling on our nature.

RAV. We have grown
Luke-warm in zeal, degenerate in spirit;—
I would root out with an unsparing hand,
The weeds that choke the soil;—pride and rank luxury
Spring up around us;—alien sectaries,
Spite of the whip and axe, infest our limits;
Bold infidelity, dark sorcery—

WALF. Nay,
Nay, Ravensworth—

RAV. I tell thee, Walford, yea:
The powers of darkness are at work among us.
Not distant we have seen the fagot blaze,
And soon the stake may ask its victim here.

WALF. What victim point you at?

RAV. Turn your eye—thither
Upon yon haughty mansion—you have heard?—

WALF. Much idle rumour.

RAV. Do you deem it so.
Whence then, and who is this imperious dame,
That holds herself above her fellow creatures,
And scorns our church's discipline: her means—
Her business here?

WALF. The ignorant and envious
May find, in her superior intellect—
E'en in her ample wealth and proud reserve
Food for their hate, and therefore their suspicion;
But for us, Ravensworth—

RAV. No more, ere long,
These questions must be answer'd.

WALF. Be it so;
I shall be ready in all lawful ways
To seek the truth.

RAV. 'T is well, we soon may need you.
What public tidings hear you?

WALF. That King Philip
Our savage foe, after his late defeat,
Has gained his rocky hold, where he now lies,
With scarce a fragment of his former force.

RAV. Where are our troops?

WALF. They watch the enemy.

RAV. They should have followed up their victory,
To the extermination of the heathen.—
Has there aught chanc'd in the village?

WALF. There have arrived
Two persons from the court of Charles.

RAV. More vanity!
What do they here?

WALF. The elder, it is said,
Brings letters to the government.
(*Crosses.*)

RAV. Charles Stuart,
Is growing much concern'd about the people
His family have scourg'd, hunted and driven
From shed and shelter in their native land.
We needs must thank that most paternal care,
That, when the expos'd infant climbs to manhood
Comes for the first time, then, to claim his service.

WALF. You broach a startling topic—
But the day wears—
Fare thee well, Ravensworth.

RAV. Farewell, farewell.
(*Exit* WALFORD.)
Timid, weak-minded man.

(*Enter* MARY, *from House.*)

Come hither, daughter.

MARY. Father! (*Running to him.*)

RAV. What mean these tears?

MARY. I cannot check them.

RAV. They do displease me, tears can only flow

From frailty or from folly, dry them straight,
And listen to me. I have heard, the son
Of this strange woman is returning home,
And will again pollute our neighbourhood;
Remember my command, and shun his presence
As you would shun the adder. If report
Err not, his course of boyhood has been run
Without one gleam of virtue to redeem
The darkness of his vices.

MARY. I'll obey—
To the utmost of my power.— But, my dear father,
May not report err sometimes? You were wont
To instruct me never to withhold the truth;
And fearlessly to speak in their defence,
Whom I could vindicate from calumny;
That to protect the innocent, the absent—

RAV. How's this! the innocent—and calumny?
And whence do you presume to throw discredit
On general report.— What can you know?

MARY. Not much perhaps, of late: while I remain'd
At his mother's—he was in his boyhood then;
I knew him well; and there's one incident
Much dwelt on to his prejudice, that I
Was witness to—if you would bid me tell it.

RAV. O, by all means, come, your romance.

MARY. 'T is truth.
It was a wintry day, the snow was deep,
And the chill rain had fallen and was frozen,
That all the surface was a glittering crust.—
We were all gather'd in the lady's hall,
That overlook'd the lawn; a poor stray fawn
Came limping toward us. It had lost, perhaps,
Its dam, and chas'd by cruel hunters, came
To seek a refuge with us. Every bound
The forlorn creature made, its little feet
Broke through the crust, and we could mark that one
Of its delicate limbs was broken. A rude boy
Follow'd it fast, as it would seem, to kill it;
I could not choose but wish its life were sav'd,
And at the word Charles ran and took it up,
And gave it to me, and I cherish'd it
And bound its broken limb up; and it liv'd,
And seem'd to thank me for my care of it.

RAV. But was this all? Was not the village lad assailed and beaten?

MARY. He was rude and churlish,
And would have forc'd the animal from Charles.
And tho' 't was on his mother's grounds, Charles proffer'd him
The price of the fawn. But nothing would content him,
And he struck Charles; he was a larger boy,
But did not prove the stronger—so he went
And made the village all believe his story,
That Charles had robb'd and beaten him, for Charles
Had none to speak for him.

RAV. No more of this—
And never let me hear the name you've utter'd
Pass from your lips again. It is enough
I know this youth for a lewd libertine;
The woman, for a scoffer at things sacred,
At me, and at my functions—and perhaps,
Given to practices, that yet may need
A dreadful expiation. Get you gone,
And on your knees petition that you may not
Deserve my malediction.

MARY. I obey.

(*Exit* MARY, *into cottage, followed by* RAVENSWORTH.)

(*Enter* GEORGE EGERTON, *followed by* SIR REGINALD, *both in shooting dresses.*)

GEORGE. By Heaven a lovely creature!

SIR R. Softly, George,
Is this the game you point at? Have a care,
You're not in London now, where our gay monarch
Sets such a fine example, in these matters.
They'll have no poaching here, that I can tell you,

Among their wives and daughters. These same roundheads,
That crop their hair so short—a plague upon 'em—
Will cut your ears as close, if you're caught meddling.

GEORGE. Why what a heathen region have we come to.
What a deuce, uncle, did you bring me here for?
To shoot at bears and panthers; pleasant sport;
No women: zounds; I'll back to court again—
No women!

SIR R. None: the old they burn for witches,
The young they keep clos'd up, (like flies in amber)
In adamantine ice.—

GEORGE. They should be hang'd
For treason against nature. Let the old ones
Freeze, 'tis their charter; but youth should have fire.

SIR R. They've good laws here for gallants—t' other day
They put a man i' the stocks because he kiss'd
His wife o' Sunday.

GEORGE. They were in the right.
Kiss his own wife! it is a work-day business;
Play-days and holy-days are made for lovers.

SIR R. To lay hands on a maid here's present death.

GEORGE. It might be so in London, and no lives lost:
The law were a dead letter there—

SIR R. And widows
May not be spoken to, under the pain
Of fine and pillory.

GEORGE. Uncle, let's embark,
Tho' for the north pole; this clime is too cold—
Or to some catholic country, where a man
May have flesh sometimes: here 't is always lent.

SIR R. No: you must stay, your stomach must endure it.

GEORGE. I' faith, dear uncle, being a cavalier,
A gentleman of honour and of breeding,
I marvel much you could come hither; but
The greater wonder is, you'd have me with you,
Knowing my humour.

SIR R. Troth, my gentle nephew,
Knowing your humour, I could do no better
Than take you from the sphere of Charles's court;
From Rochester, and his dissolute companions,
To cool your blood here in the wilderness.

GEORGE. Well! there may come a time.

SIR R. As for my voyage,
Perhaps it was a royal jest; or haply
My clothes had grown too rusty for the court,
Or Charles was tired of the old cavalier,
Who had fought some battles for him, and consum'd
Some certain paltry acres—all he had—
And having left no vacant place at court,
He sent me here Ambassador.

GEORGE. But uncle,
Is that your character?

SIR R. Much the same thing,
In Christian countries, nephew; I'm a spy.

GEORGE. The devil!

SIR R. Yes; we read in ancient history,
Of Kings and Emperors, who have kept the men
Who help'd them to the Throne, (by simply putting
Their fathers out o' the way)—about their persons,
As their prime friends. But Charles, being advis'd
That this was in bad taste, and took place only
In semi-barbarous courts, finds it decorous
To grow a little angry with the persons
That kill'd his father. And being told, besides,
That his most loving and beloved subjects
This side the water—who, by the way, he never
Thought of before—had given food and shelter
To certain of the regicides, he sends me
To—

GEORGE. Well, Sir?

SIR R. Nothing. Come, 't is growing late.
We must regain our cottage. In the morning,
We leave the village.

GEORGE. 'Gad, with all my soul—
And so to England?

SIR R. Not so fast, good Springal,
We must have patience yet. Come, let's begone.

GEORGE. I'll see her in the morning, tho' they hang me.
(*Exeunt*, GEORGE *looking back.*)

END OF ACT ONE.

ACT SECOND.

SCENE 1. *A Forest. In the background an insulated caverned rock. Night. The* UNKNOWN *enters by a bridge formed of the trunk of a tree, which is let down from the rock.* (*His dress is of Skins: his general appearance, wild—but his air and manner dignified. He is armed.*)

UNK. Yes: it is near the dawn—the dawn! when man
Again shall greet his fellow man, and nature,
Through all her living kingdom shall rejoice.
I only of the human race, condemn'd
To shun my species, and in caves of night
Shut out the common day. Ye glorious stars,
I gaze on you—I look on you, ye Heavens,
With an unblenching eye. You read the heart,
And you can judge the act. If I was wrong;
If innocent blood rest on me—here I stand
To pay the dreadful forfeiture,—let fall
In drops of fire your red-hot vengeance on me.
Am I a murderer? Is the mark of Cain
Imprinted on my front!—I would not murmur—
But as I am but man, forgive it Heaven.
Torn from the beings that I fondly lov'd.—
For nineteen years an outlaw and a wanderer—
Proscribed and hunted like the ravening wolf;—
A price set on my felon head—A felon!
Am I so, Heaven! Did these wounds, receiv'd
In thy holy cause, stream with a felon's blood,
Was it a felon's courage nerved my arm,
A felon's zeal that burn'd within my heart?
Yet this I could endure—but when I think
Of thee, my child—my daughter—Ha! a step!
Perhaps a beast of prey! I fear not that,
The panther is my co-mate and my brother;
Man only is mine enemy—He comes.
(*Retires into cave.*)

(*Enter* CHARLES, *in a neat hunting dress of green, cap, etc., a short sword, or couteau-de-chasse slung, and a gun in his hand.*)

CHARLES. Each step I take but plunges me the deeper
In this wild labyrinth.— Here's a pretty scene
For those whose love o' the picturesque, could make them
Forget their bed and supper. My poor mother
Will be so disappointed—and, dear Mary,
Will not your hopes, too, rise with the lark: I'll on,
But whither? May I not be straying further:
I must needs make my couch e'en here.—What's this?
A bridge; and further on, methinks, a cavern,
'T will serve— But hold—perhaps I shall disturb
Some wild beast in his lair. Tut! 't is some hunter
Has made his cabin here—I'll try.
(*Going to cavern.*)

UNK. Pass not.
(*Enters from cave.*)

CHARLES. You speak commandingly.

UNK. And may, when strangers
Intrude upon my privacy. That cave
Is mine, my castle.

CHARLES. It must be confess'd
You play the Castellain right courteously.

UNK. No trifling, boy. Are you a spy?—What are you?

CHARLES. My answer's here.
(*Levelling his gun.*)

UNK. Tut, overweening child,
Level thy weapon at the timid deer
That fears thy puny skill. The wither'd leaf
Stirr'd by the falling nut, or passing breeze,
Startles as much as does thy idle menace.

CHARLES. To prove it is not idle—

UNK. Hold, rash boy;
If but this tube is rais'd, thou perish'st.

For years, as many as thou tell'st of life,
I 've wielded it.

CHARLES. I 've had some practice, too.

UNK. Do you provoke your fate!— But hold; no, no—
Though 't were my sole security, no blood.
He spoke of his mother too; I 'll not deprive
The mother of her child— Hear me, bold youth.
'T is meet that I should know so much of thee,
As to be well assur'd thou com'st not hither,
At this dark hour, for evil purpose—tell me—
I do not now command, but I request thee—
Wherefore this visit?

CHARLES. Now, sir, that your question
Is one a gentleman may give reply to,
I 'll frankly tell you. I 've a mother lives,
I trust, in the next town. A short time since
I left her, for the second time, for college,
To make a second trial for the honours,
I think, with due humility, I 'd merited.
Their worships as before play'd with my patience,
Till I grew tired of it, and told them so,
In good round terms. Glad of the fit excuse,
They just discover'd then, I was too wild
For their strait limits, and so they expell'd me.

UNK. You speak but lightly of a circumstance
That an ingenuous and aspiring youth,
And, such you seem, might well think serious.

CHARLES. I cannot be a hypocrite, and deem
The acts of solemn folly serious.
When I shall cease to scorn malevolence
And learn to reverence cant and superstition,
Then, not till then, I 'll weep at my expulsion.

UNK. But to your tale.

CHARLES. 'T is told: I turn'd my back
On my grave censors; seized my hunter's arms,
And struck in to the wilderness for home;
Which by the forest route I hoped to reach
Ere the light closed to-day. I was deceived.
Night came upon me; yet, I travell'd on,
For by a civil horseman that pass'd by
I had sent letters bidding them expect me.
Briefly, when I had fairly lost myself
I met a hunter, whose bark cabin stands
A few miles hence. He put me in the track,
And pointed out a certain star to steer by;
But passing clouds, and intervening boughs,
And perhaps thoughts of home, and those at home,
Marr'd my astronomy. I lost my star,
And then I lost my path, and then myself.
And so, through swamp and thicket, brake and bramble,
I 've scrambled on thus far—and, there 's my story.

UNK. Your way was perilous— Did you meet nothing?

CHARLES. Not much. Sometimes a snake I trod on coil'd
Around my leg, but I soon shook him off;
A howl at times approach'd—and as I pass'd,
The brake stirr'd near me with some living thing
Beside myself—but this was all.

UNK. 'T was wrong,
Rashly to tempt these dangers. If your air
Deceive me not, you are of foreign birth.

CHARLES. Not four years since, we left our native England.

UNK. England!

CHARLES. But why 's a mystery. We 're not known
Nor understood here; we 're of another world.

UNK. Your name?

CHARLES. 'T is Charles Fitzroy.

UNK. Fitzroy! Your mother's?

CHARLES. You 're somewhat curious; Isabella.

UNK. Ha!

CHARLES. What is it moves you?

UNK. Isabella, say you?

CHARLES. This strong emotion—

UNK. It is nothing, nothing.—
Or—is it strange that I should feel emotion
At the sad tale you tell?

CHARLES. Sad tale!

UNK. I wander.—
I 've been a solitary man so long

That—'T is no matter.— What dost think me, youth?

CHARLES. A hunter who loves freedom and the forest;
Who 'd rather kill his venison in the wood
Than toil for it in the town. Am I not right?

UNK. 'T is true—I am—a hunter—

CHARLES. But a strange one.—
But come, sir, will you put me on my way?

UNK. Will you not rather enter my poor cave
And take its shelter till the morning breaks?
'T will not be long.

CHARLES. I cannot lose a moment
In selfish rest, while those who love me suffer.

UNK. Give me your hand then. I 'm your friend.

CHARLES. I thank you.
'T is the first cordial grasp I've had from man.

UNK. Poor youth! But hold—Give me your solemn promise
To keep this meeting secret.

CHARLES. I hate secrets;
Lovers alone should have them.

UNK. There are reasons:—
I cannot now disclose them—solemn reasons—
I do implore you—

CHARLES. Sir, be satisfied;
I 'll not reveal it.

UNK. Nor allude to it,
However press'd—Nor give the darkest hint
That such a man as I exist!

CHARLES. I promise.

UNK. I'm satisfied. Your words are from the heart.
Fidelity and truth sit on your brow.
The blush of morn begins to tinge the east;
You are not far from home; you 'll soon embrace
Your mother, Charles. Come, this way lies the path. (*Exeunt.*)

SCENE 2. *An open Wood near the cottage of* RAVENSWORTH. *Early dawn.*

(*Enter* GEORGE EGERTON.)

GEORGE. Poor uncle! little does your vision dream,
(Being abed) what ramble I 'm upon.
A hopeful enterprize, this of my uncle's—
To tame me in a wild wood. Ay, and then
His bug-bear stories of the laws—confound 'em,
Last night they spoil'd the sweetest vision for me;
Methought I saw this beauteous puritan,
The parson's daughter; well, I woo'd and won—
A thing of course—But going to embrace her,
I hugg'd—my pillow, think you? no; a pillory!
Well: I'm resolved in spite of dream and omen,
To see her, if I can, before we go.
I 've three hours, good; and three hours may do much.—
By Vulcan, the intruding and lame God,
My uncle limping this way! Gout confound him.
A royal oak! Bend your umbrageous branches,
And saving me, be twice immortalized.
(*Conceals himself in a tree.*)

(*Enter* SIR REGINALD.)

SIR R. S 'blood! the young rebel, what a march he 's led me!
Tortur'd too, all the route, like a poor prisoner
By my own natural enemy the gout.
The worst of 't is I cannot find the rascal,
I 've been around the house. And I 'd ha' sworn
That was his mark. If I but catch him—Hey!

(*Enter* MARY.)

A pretty girl—I 'faith, a pretty girl!
I 'll speak to her, I will; there 's no one near—
Hem! Save you lady—

MARY. (*Who is anxiously looking another way.*) Would you aught with me, sir!

SIR R. Aught? Yes, egad: a very pretty girl—
My dear, I—that is—

GEORGE. So, so, my grave uncle.—

SIR R. I meant to say—'t is somewhat early, child,
For youth like yours—She 's beautiful by gad:—

To leave your downy slumbers—
GEORGE. Poetry!
MARY. It is my custom, sir—But age like yours
May suffer from the chill air of the morning.
GEORGE. A brave girl, faith:
MARY. (*Aside.*) 'T is one of those strange persons,
My father spoke of—would that he would go.
SIR R. Why, as you say, my dear,—that is—in fact—
GEORGE. Nay, charge again, brave cavalier.
SIR R. In truth then,
My errand here so early, was to seek
A runagate nephew.
GEORGE. Meaning me.—
SIR R. A rascal!
Pray, lady, have you met him?
MARY. Sir, I know not
The person you enquire for.
SIR R. I'll describe him.
GEORGE. Now for a flattering portrait.
SIR R. (*Aside.*) I'll disgust her
Lest he, perchance, should meet her—He's a fellow
Of an indifferent person, which his tailor
Cannot make handsome; yet he thinks himself
The only true Adonis. He has language
If you can understand it. When he speaks,
'T is in a lisp or oath. His gait's between
A swagger and a dance. His grin's from France,
His leer from Cyprus. He's a Turk in morals,
And is of that religion no man knows of:
In fine, he's as ridiculous as dangerous—
A mongrel thing; a slip of the coxcomb, madam,
Grafted upon the rake.
MARY. Sir, you describe
A monster.
SIR R. You have hit it: that is he,
Should he approach you shun him.
MARY. Sir, I shall.
GEORGE. Here's a kind uncle: but I'll be reveng'd.
(SIR REGINALD *bows and exit.*)
MARY. He should have come last night: yet here's the morning,
And yet he comes not. He cannot have pass'd me.
Is it because this is his homeward path
That I am loitering here? I fear it is—
O, I am most imprudent—most forgetful—
I fear most sinful.
GEORGE. (*Descending, and comes down the stage on the left.*)
Now he's out of sight.
And now for the encounter—Madam, your slave.
Nay start not; I am not the monster, lady,
That gouty person pictur'd. Did you know him
But half so well as I, you'd not believe him,
Or did you but know me, but half so well
As I would have you, and you would believe him
To be the most transcendant of romancers.
Bunyan's book, madam, is true history,
To that he speaks. He was a soldier once,
But was cashier'd for lying. Mandeville,
The greatest liar of antiquity,
May be hereafter quoted as authentic,
When he's believ'd—And I'm his nephew, too!
A pleasant jest: he kept the wild beasts, madam,
In London, till they turn'd him off for stealing
The lion's supper—Yet a single moment.
MARY. What would you, sir?
GEORGE. You see, before you, lady,
The most unfortunate young fellow breathing,
Banish'd to this strange country for the crime
Of being too susceptible—and sentenc'd
To die a lingering death upon the rack,
Unless your smile reprieve him.
MARY. This is strange:
I do not understand you.
GEORGE. If my words
Lack meaning, lady, look into my eyes,
And thro' them to my heart, and see enshrin'd
Your worshipp'd image there—
MARY. Most wonderful,
What language is 't you speak, sir?
GEORGE. Ma'am: what language?
English, I think. The pretty simpleton!
Bred in the woods, to her a metaphor
Is Heathen Greek. Madam, those foolish figures
Are all the mode at court; and mean, my dear.

In simple phrase—
MARY. I pray, sir, let me pass—
GEORGE. Not yet, my child—
MARY. Sure 't is a madman.
GEORGE. True,
And therefore treat me soothingly and kindly,
For of all madmen, your mad lover 's maddest.
Do you not fear me?
MARY. No.
GEORGE. Why, then you love me.
Come; I have seen such clouds before; they tell
Of coming sunshine—nay, you must not go.—
I will be monstrous kind to thee, and love thee
Most constantly—
MARY. Release me.
GEORGE. Ay, and take thee
To England, child, and make thee there, my dear,
The envy of thy sex.
MARY. If you 're a gentleman—
GEORGE. The conscious grove would blush its green leaves red,
Should I give back.
MARY. Do you not fear the laws?
GEORGE. Nor law, nor gospel now—Come, come, 't is folly—
MARY. O Heav'n: help, help!

(*Enter* CHARLES, *and comes down to centre.*)

CHARLES. Ruffian, unhand the lady!
GEORGE. So peremptory, boy?
CHARLES. Do you delay?
(*Throws him off.*)
GEORGE. Curse on my haste: I have forgot my sword.
MARY. O Charles!
CHARLES. My dearest Mary; my belov'd!
(MARY *retires up.*)
GEORGE. Hum; is it so? But s'death! I must n't bear it.
Hark ye, Sir.
CHARLES. Well, Sir.
GEORGE. I shall find a time.—
CHARLES. Best make it.
GEORGE. When?
CHARLES. Two hours hence, in the grove
East of the village.
GEORGE. I shall meet you there.
But look ye, sir, be punctual: I've engagements.
CHARLES. I shall not fail you.
GEORGE. 'Gad, a pretty fellow.
I 'll pink him first, and then I 'll patronize him. (*Exit.*)
MARY. O Charles! what pass'd between you? surely, surely
You will not honour him with further notice.
CHARLES. Speak not of him—he is not worth a thought—
We can employ our time to better purpose.
Tell me, have yet the calumnies against me,
Found shelter here?
MARY. You know they have not, Charles.
But I have much to tell you—We must part!
Heav'n! is not that my father? Oh, it is!
He comes this way; but has not yet descried us—
Ah! fly, fly quickly!
CHARLES. Fly?
MARY. Yes, if you wish
That we should ever meet—
CHARLES. But shall we meet!
MARY. That way—behind the trees—O quickly, quickly!
(CHARLES *goes up.*)
CHARLES. (*From the Grove.*) But tell me, Mary, will you walk this way
In the evening?
MARY. It is impossible; my father
Forbids my walks—
CHARLES. Why then, one place remains—
One only—I will visit you to-night—
You do not answer—Shall I?
MARY. O begone!
(*Exit* CHARLES, *behind the trees.*)
Did I consent? I fear he 'll think I did.
My father comes—should he have seen us part!
Am I the guilty creature that I feel?
He 's here—I cannot look him in the face.

(*Enter* RAVENSWORTH, *looks at* MARY *sternly for some time.*)

RAV. 'T is well; that air of shame becomes you well,
Is this your duty? Did I not forbid
These lonely walks? But get you home; anon,
I 'll talk with you.
MARY. (*As she goes out.*)
He did not see him!
RAV. Home.
(*Exeunt.*)

SCENE 3. *An Apartment at* ISABELLA'S.

(*Enter* ISABELLA, *meeting* LUCY.)

ISA. Speak; is he yet in sight?
LUCY. No, madam.
ISA. Go,
O! go again, good Lucy, and be swift
When he appears. (*Exit* LUCY.) My poor, poor boy! my Charles—
To be thus treated, and thy gentle heart
So full of kindness to all living creatures:
To have thy aspirations after fame,
Thus rudely scorn'd, thy youthful hopes thus blighted!
But he deserves it not; there's comfort yet,
And he may rise above it.—Not yet come.
He promis'd, and he would not break his word,
And to his mother, without serious cause
The way is full of peril, and I know
His temper shuns not danger. Gracious Heav'n!
If I should lose him—him, the only being—

(*Enter* LUCY, *hastily.*)

Now, Lucy, quick!
LUCY. Madam, he is in sight;
And flying up the avenue.
ISA. Thank Heaven!

(*Enter* CHARLES.)

CHARLES. Mother!
ISA. My son. (*Falls into his arms.*)
CHARLES. My ever dearest mother!
ISA. O Charles, how could you thus delay your coming?
The night was pass'd in watch.
CHARLES. I grieve to know it
I was benighted in the forest, mother,
And lost my way.
ISA. Alas! thou art spent with toil.
CHARLES. Not much.
ISA. Poor Charles: And so they have expelled thee—
Expell'd!
CHARLES. Nay, pry'thee let us forget it.
ISA. Wretches!
I could have borne all else—but to disgrace thee—
To spurn thee from them—thee! I could endure
The daily persecutions that assail me
With patience and with firmness—But I have thee.
Come, let us in: you need rest and refreshment.
You shall not leave me soon again, my son—
I am a child without you.
CHARLES. (*Aside.*) My poor mother.
ISA. But let us in—
CHARLES. I'll follow you, my mother.
I will but give an order. (*Exit* ISABELLA.)
Edward.

(*Enter* EDWARD.)

EDW. Sir.
CHARLES. Go, get my rapier ready, wrap it close,
And some hour hence, not later, choose a time,
And speed with it to the wood, east of the village,
There wait my coming.
EDW. Yes, sir.
CHARLES. But be sure
That no one see it.
EDW. I'll be careful, sir.
(*Exit* EDWARD.)

(*Enter* ISABELLA.)

ISA. Fye, sir; is this your breeding? must I wait?
CHARLES. Forgive me, madam, I am ready now. (*Exeunt.*)

END OF ACT TWO.

ACT THIRD.

SCENE 1. *An open Wood.*

(*Enter* CHARLES, *followed by* EDWARD.)

CHARLES. Give me the sword; remain at the edge of the wood;
If any one approach, haste to inform me.
(*Exit* EDWARD.)
I am here first, 't is well. My mother thinks
It is a softer interview I seek;
And while she cautioned me, her sad smile seem'd
To sanction what she fear'd. My dear, kind mother.
And should I fall—well: it would be my fate.
We are but barques upon the sea of life,
And when the storm is up, we greet the port,

Or meet the rock, as destiny determines,
Spite of our feeble efforts. Mary, too!
These thoughts are not in season. Here 's my man.

(*Enter* GEORGE EGERTON, *hastily.*)

Well met, sir.

GEORGE. Sir, I kiss your hands. I' faith,
I 've had a race to get here. My wise uncle
Hung round me like a bride in the first month—
Or rather like a wife in the second year,
When jealousy commences.—Come on, sir.

CHARLES. Best breathe awhile; I have the advantage of you.

GEORGE. You will not keep it long. My greater skill
Will give me still the odds.

CHARLES. It may be so,
Yet you may be deceived. My masters flatter'd
Or I, too, have some science.

GEORGE. I 'm glad of it;
For you 're a pretty fellow, and deserve
To fall with credit. Come, sir, to your guard.
We shall be interrupted.

CHARLES. Better so,
Than that we fight unfairly. You pant still, sir.

GEORGE. You are a soul of honour, and, were 't possible—
But no; the person of an Egerton
Must never be profan'd. Come, Sir, *en garde.*

CHARLES. If you will have it so.

GEORGE. I will.

CHARLES. Come on then.

(*They fight.* GEORGE *is wounded.*)

GEORGE. I 'm pink'd egad; who would have thought it? S' death!
I 'm out of practice.

CHARLES. Here, Sir, on this bank.
Your head against this tree—Your wound 's not deep
I hope. How feel you now?

GEORGE. I' faith, but faintly.

(*Enter* EDWARD.)

EDW. There is a gentleman approaching, Sir.

GEORGE. It is my uncle, like a keen old sportsman,
In at the death. Pry'thee begone, my friend,
'T were well you were not known.

CHARLES. This handkerchief—
So, press it close—I 'll haste to send you aid.—
But for the lady's fame, and your own honour,
The cause of this our meeting is a secret.

GEORGE. It shall be so: I thank you. But away!

(*Exeunt* CHARLES *and* EDWARD.)

That 's a fine lad. But where i' the devil's name,
Learn'd he to fence? I wonder, now I think on 't,
Who 'll write my epitaph. My uncle can't,
He has no genius. I would do 't myself,
Had I an amanuensis: let me see—
Hic jacet— (*Faints.*)

(*Enter* SIR REGINALD.)

SIR R. Gracious Heav'n, what is this!
My nephew bleeding, dead! no, he but faints,
With loss of blood. Soft, he revives; why, nephew—
My poor mad George, how fares it?

GEORGE. How d' ye, uncle?
Is 't day or night? Faith my eyes twinkle strangely.

SIR R. Cheerly, George, cheerly, we 'll do well enough,—
What shall I do?—But how came this about?
Was 't fairly done?

GEORGE. According to the rules.
Should I die, uncle, and my adversary
E'er be discover'd, testify for him—
He kill'd me like a gentleman and Christian.

SIR R. A duel! ah, George, George. But zounds! do the roundheads
Fight duels too! a pretty school I 've chosen
To teach you prudence in! will no one come!

(*Enter* TWO MEN, *with a Bier.*)

Ah, you are welcome, set it down, so, so.

GEORGE. A pretty ominous conveyance, this.

SIR R. I pry'thee hold thy peace, and get thee in.

GEORGE. A grain of opium now, were worth a jewel,
Uncle, I 'll never fight again without it.

SIR R. Be quiet, George—you waste your strength. So, so.

(*The men take him up and are about moving.*)

GEORGE. Head foremost if you please, my worthy friends;
'T is but fair play—heels first perhaps, to-morrow.
(*The men carry him a few paces.*)
Halt, if it please ye, gentlemen, one moment.
Two hobbles more and I 'm defunct.—Pray, general,
Drill those recruits to the step. In camp, now, uncle,
It were a pleasure to be carried out.
SIR R. Wilt hold thy peace then?
GEORGE. Yes.—The left foot, uncle—
SIR R. Now, gentlemen, at the word "march" lift up
The left foot each of you, and so move on.
GEORGE. Right, uncle.
SIR R. Hold your tongue. March!
GEORGE. Ay; so, so.
(*Exeunt.*)

SCENE 2. *The Village.*

(*Enter* CHARLES *and* EDWARD.)

CHARLES. Can it be true! the savages so near?
EDW. It is so said.
CHARLES. Edward, do you return,
And see the unfortunate gentleman I wounded
Placed in security. I 'll hasten home.
(*Exit* EDWARD.)
My first care is my mother—then for Mary! (*Exit* CHARLES.)

(*Enter* WALFORD, *meeting* ALICE.)

WALF. Whence this alarm?
ALICE. O father, we are lost.
A hunter has come in nigh dead with speed,
With tidings that the savages are coming.
WALF. How near?
ALICE. Alas! a few miles from the village.
WALF. Is 't possible! can they have thus eluded
Our watchful troops! we must prepare—O welcome!

(*Enter* RAVENSWORTH.)

Heard you the fearful tidings, Ravensworth?
RAV. I have, and will you now believe, our sins
Bring these afflictions on us? We have murderers
Lurking among us.
WALF. How!
RAV. This moment pass'd me.
The relative of the Knight, Sir Reginald;
Dying, or dead.
WALF. Whose was the act?
RAV. Whose was 't?
The act of him, whose every act is crime.
The son of this dark woman.
WALF. How is it known?
RAV. His sword and handkerchief stain'd both with blood,
And mark'd with his vile name, were found in the wood.
He has not been one day yet in the village,
And lo! these visitations. On the instant
He must be dealt with.
WALF. First for our defence—
What do you counsel?
RAV. Prayer and sacrifice.
WALF. 'T is too late now, we must take other means.

(*The* VILLAGERS *enter, exhibiting signs of wild affright.*)

WALF. Hark ye, my friend, have messengers been sent
To warn the scatter'd settlers round?
1ST VILLA. They have.
WALF. Why rings not the alarum bell!
1ST VILLA. I know not,
Unless the exposed position of the church—
WALF. Go, some of you and do it.—Hasten, friends,
Seize every man his arms.
(*Exeunt* VILLAGERS.)
RAV. Behold where comes
In all her pride, one of the moving causes
Of all this horror—mark with what an air,
How tranquil and compos'd she looks around
Upon the growing evil—safe, 'midst the fury
Of her own tempest.
(*As he speaks; Enter* ISABELLA; *the women shrink from her in fear.* ALICE *gazes upon her with interest;* RAVENSWORTH *fixes his eyes sternly upon her. She remains unmoved.*)
WALF. Ravensworth, forbear
Is this a time.—
(*Enter* 2D VILLAGER.)

Now, friend, what news have you?
2D VILLA. They have begun to issue from the wood.—

(*Enter* SIR REGINALD.)

SIR R. What is this I hear? the savages approaching!
Now plague upon this gout!—But I've an arm left
That yet can wield a sword.
WALF. Your nephew, Sir,
May need your care. You 're strange to our wild warfare.
SIR R. True; I'd forgot poor George. They 'll cut thro' me
Before they get a hair of him. (*Retires.*)

(*Re-enter* 1ST VILLAGER.)

WALF. How now?
1ST VILLA. We 've rallied at the church; but want a leader.
WALF. You shall not want one longer.
ALICE. O, my father!
WALF. Heav'n bless you, my dear daughter. Follow me.

(*Exit* WALFORD, *followed by* VILLAGERS. *Distant yell. The alarm bell rings, a few distant and straggling shots heard. Houses at a distance beginning to blaze;—a pause of the bell.*)

RAV. Now, where 's your son?
ISA. Gone, Sir, to save your daughter.
RAV. My daughter! I'd forgot.—Is she not here.

(*Runs wildly around. Bell rings. The shots are nearer and more frequent. The blaze increases.*)

RAV. My daughter! where, O where 's my daughter!

(*Enter* CHARLES, *bearing* MARY.)

CHARLES. There, Sir.

(RAVENSWORTH *receives her, and for a moment yields to his paternal feeling. But instantly withdraws from* CHARLES *with a scowl.* CHARLES, *after affectionately recognizing his mother, rushes out.* ALICE *joins* MARY; *who is prevented from addressing* ISABELLA, *by her father's frown.* ISABELLA *maintains her dignity and composure. Alarm continues, shouts, yells, etc.*)

(*The* VILLAGERS *enter in disorder, followed by* CHARLES *and* WALFORD.)

CHARLES. One effort more.
WALF. It is impossible,
Panic has seiz'd them all and we must perish.

(*The bell has ceased. A dreadful yell. The* VILLAGERS *turn and are about to fly in despair, when*
Enter the UNKNOWN.)

UNK. Turn back for shame—as ye are men, turn back!
As ye are husbands, fathers, turn, and save
From death and violation those ye love.—
If this not move you, as ye are Christian men
And do believe in God, tempt not his wrath
By doubting thus his providence. Behold
I am sent to save you.
OMNES. Save us, save us.
WALF. Say,
What shall we do; we 're ready to obey thee.
UNK. Front then and bear yourselves like men—'T is well.
The savage sees us rally; and the pause
His caution grants, secures us the advantage.

(*He passes rapidly along the line, dividing them into three bodies. Then addresses* WALFORD *and* CHARLES.)

This band be yours—this yours—Quick, lead them forth,
And each by a rapid circuit, turn the foe
By either flank. This will I lead myself
Against his front—holding him thus in check
Until I hear the horn sound your arrival—
Then while perplex'd he hesitates between us,
Rush to the onset all—close on the heathen,
And shower destruction on him—haste away.

(*Exeunt* UNKNOWN, WALFORD *and* CHARLES, *leading their bands.*)

ISA. How awful is this pause, that but precedes
The shock that may o'erwhelm us. God, to thee,
The mother turns. Not for myself,
Not for my sinful self—but for my son—
My innocent son I plead. Cut him not off
In the blossom of his days.
RAV. Mark, if the hag

Mutter not, even now, her incantations.
(*A few scattering shot heard.*)
The fronts have met, and from the forest coverts,
Exchange their cautious fire.
(*A bugle sounds, answered by another from a different quarter. Shouts, Yells, a general and continued discharge of musketry. Shouts and bugles.*)

RAV. The crisis has arrived—the fire has ceased,
And now the closer work of death commences.
Ascend yon tree, and say what thou observest.
(*To a boy, who ascends the tree.*)

BOY. I see them now. The Indians stand dismay'd.
We're pouring now upon them from the forest,
From every side.—Now, now the Indians turn—
They meet they close they're strug gling man to man.
Sword, knife and tomahawk are glancing.

ISA. Heaven!
Protect, protect my Charles!

ALICE. Save my dear father. (*Shout.*)

RAV. What shout is that? Hear ye the savage yell?

BOY. No, no, 't was ours,—we've conquer'd—and they come,
Dragging their prisoners with them. Here's my father.

(*Enter* 1ST VILLAGER *shouting "Victory," meets and caresses the boy.*)

(*General Shout, Bugles. Enter* WALFORD, CHARLES, VILLAGERS, *with* INDIAN PRISONERS. *They arrange themselves on each side; the Indians in the background.* CHARLES *flies to his mother, who sinks on her knees in his embrace.* ALICE *joins her father, various groups formed.* MARY *manifests much interest for* CHARLES, *who regards her tenderly.* RAVENSWORTH *preserves his suspicious and reserved demeanour.*)

(*Enter the* UNKNOWN. *He passes down the centre. All gaze on him with awe, and stretch forth their hands towards him, bending their bodies.*)

UNK. No; not to me this homage—not to man
Is your this day's deliverance owing. There—
To heaven address your gratitude. To God
Stretch forth your hands and raise your swimming eyes.
Before Jehovah bend your bodies down,
And from your humble hearts pour out the flood
Of Thankfulness. It was his care that watch'd
His eye that saw; his arm that smote the heathen—
His be the praise and glory.
(*All bend in adoration. The* UNKNOWN *casts a glance at* ISABELLA, *and exclaims as he goes out,*)
Yes; 't is she. (*Exit* UNKNOWN.)
(*After a short pause, they raise their heads and look around anxiously for the* UNKNOWN.)
(*Enter* SIR REGINALD.)

WALF. Has this thing been? Where is he? did he pass you?

SIR R. Who?

WALF. Our mysterious leader—

SIR R. I saw him not.

WALF. Was't an earthly being?

ALICE. O my father!
It was not mortal.

CHARLES. In the fight his arm,
Like the fierce lightning wither'd where it fell.

SIR R. You speak of wonders!

RAV. Woman, what think you—
Was it an angel—or a fiend?

WALF. What mean you?
(ISABELLA *turns from him proudly.* CHARLES *represses his anger on exchanging glances with* MARY.)

RAV. You'll know anon. Walford, you bleed. (*Crosses to* WALFORD.)

WALF. A trifle.

RAV. *He* does not bleed—

WALF. I think not; yet he dar'd
The thickest of the fight.

RAV. Can you not see?
Do you but mark?

WALF. Your meaning is most dark.

RAV. The murkiest night must fly before the day;
Illusion, strong as Hell must yield to Truth.
You understand me not—No matter—come—
Let these vile heathens be securely plac'd
To await their certain death—then to the temple—

There, to the Throne of Mercy to present
Our sacrifice of prayer and of thanksgiving.
(*Exeunt* CHARLES, ISABELLA, *and others.*)

END OF ACT THREE.

ACT FOURTH.

SCENE 1.[1] *Before the house of* RAVENSWORTH.

(*Enter* RAVENSWORTH *from the house, meeting* WALFORD.)

RAV. You come in happy time; I would have sought you
Walford, my soul is sick, even to death,
To look upon the miseries, our sins
Bring down upon us. But I am resolv'd;—
This day's events at length have steel'd my heart
Against the accursed cause; who must not longer
Pollute, unquestion'd thus, our wholesome air.
WALF. You know the cause then?
RAV. Who can know this woman,
This Isabella, and be ignorant!
But she must answer it—the time is come;
She and her son must answer for their deeds.
And since my letters to the government
Have fail'd to bring their aid—ourselves, my friend,
Must call them to the judgment seat.
WALF. Not so;
Your efforts have been crown'd with sad success.
Commissioners have even now arriv'd.—
I came to let you know it.
RAV. Thanks, my friend,
You make me happy.
WALF. Happy, Ravensworth!
RAV. And should I not rejoice that guilt like theirs
Should cease to spread its poison thro' the land?
WALF. Where shall we find the evidence of guilt?
RAV. The trial shall produce it, doubt it not;
Meantime, methinks the general belief
In their dark crimes; the universal horror
Inspir'd e'en by their presence—as if nature
Shudder'd instinctively at what was monstrous,
And hostile to its laws, were, of themselves,
A ground to rest the charge on.
WALF. Ah, my friend,
If reason in a mind like yours, so form'd,
So fortified by knowledge, can bow down
Before the popular breath, what shall protect
From the all-with'ring blasts of superstition
The unthinking crowd, in whom credulity,
Is ever the first born of ignorance?
RAV. Walford, what meanest thou by superstition!
Is there in our religion aught forbidding
Belief in sorcery! Look thro' this land,
Or turn thine eyes abroad—are not the men
Most eminent for piety and knowledge—
The shining lights of a benighted age,
Are they not, too, believers?
WALF. There have been,
In every age, among the learn'd, divines,
Statesmen, philosophers, astronomers,
Who have upheld with much ability,
The errors they believ'd in. Abstract points
In science, may be safely tolerated,
Altho' erroneous—But there may be doctrines,
So fatal in their influence, that, until
Their truth is manifest, 't were well not cast them,
With lavish hand, among the multitude.
RAV. And is not sorcery manifest as day?
Have not our senses testified unto it?
WALF. We have heard infant witnesses aver it,
And seen them while they seem'd to suffer it;
We have heard wretches in despair confess it,
And have seen helpless creatures perish for it;
And yet—
RAV. What yet?
WALF. O Ravensworth! these things
Have happened: on a day of gloom and terror,
When but to doubt was danger, to deny, death;
When childish petulance, e'en idiocy,

[1] This scene was omitted in the representation.

Were gravely listened to, when mere suspicion,
Could, with a hint destroy, and coward malice,
With whispers, reach'd at life; when frenzy's flame,
Like fire in tow, ran thro' the minds of men,
Fann'd by the breath of those in highest places,
E'en from the bench, yea, from the sacred desk.

RAV. Hold, Walford, I have held thee as my friend,
For many years, beware—

WALF. I know thy power
Over the multitude, but fear it not.
I have discharged my duty, fare thee well.

RAV. Stay, Walford, thou art honest, but mistaken,
We will dispute no more. But tell me, friend,
Have the commissioners enquired for me?

WALF. They have. Before they enter on their duties,
They 'd have thy counsel.

RAV. They shall have it straight,
I 'll go to them at once. 'T is almost night—
There is no hour to lose, I pray thee, Walford,
As I may haply, be detain'd abroad,
Let thy good Alice stay here with my daughter
Till my return.

WALF. Most willingly. I 'll haste,
And bring her hither.

RAV. Nay, we 'll go together.
(*Exeunt.*)

SCENE 2. *An Apartment at* ISABELLA'S.

(*Enter* ISABELLA *and* CHARLES.)

ISA. Ungrateful people!

CHARLES. Had they not presum'd
To cloud your clear name with their viperous breath,
I could forgive them. 'T was not for the herd
I drew my sword.

ISA. Unthankful wretches; what!
Upon the very act that saved their lives,
To found a charge that might endanger thine!

CHARLES. 'T is even so: I am in league, it seems.
With fiends, so say their worships; and the stranger,
Is no less, than the prince of fiends himself.
Nothing is too ridiculous for those
Whom bigotry has brutaliz'd, I laugh
At their most monstrous folly.

ISA. But such folly,
When it infects the crowd, is dangerous.
Already we 've had proof what dreadful acts
Their madness may commit, and each new day
The frenzy spreads. We are suspected too—
Then your imprudent duel—O my son,
We must remove from hence.

CHARLES. Remove, from hence?

ISA. Yes; ere the monsters catch us in the toils
They are preparing.

CHARLES. Mother, you were wont
To bear a mind whose firmness could resist
Your sex's common weaknesses!

ISA. I know not
How it is, Charles, but dark and sad forebodings
Hang o'er my subdued spirit; and I tremble
E'en for thy life.

CHARLES. Banish those thoughts, my mother.

ISA. I try, but cannot.—Yes; we will hence; my son.
Tho' on the verge, perhaps, of that discovery
The hope of which has held me here so long,
We will begone to-morrow.

CHARLES. So soon, mother?

ISA. You do not wish it. Charles, a mother's eye
Can penetrate the heart. The gentle Mary—
She will be left behind—is it not so?
But this is boyish, you are yet too young
To entertain such fantasies—and then
You know her father—sadder still my son;
Well, we 'll not cross the ocean—we 'll but seek
The nearest spot that is inhabited
By rational beings. And besides, your youth
Will wear a year or two. How say you. Charles,
Are you contented?

CHARLES. You 're the best of mothers.

And were my heart strings fasten'd to the spot,
I'd with you, tho' they sunder'd. But you spoke
A moment since, of some discovery
You were near making: what discovery?

ISA. It was an inadvertence—

CHARLES. Must I never
Hope to enjoy your confidence?

ISA. Not now—
Another time, my son.

CHARLES. Another time—
'T is ever thus you put my questions by.
Rather forbid me e'er again to ask
Of what so much concerns me, and I promise
However hard the task, I will obey you.
I trust you have ne'er found me disobedient!

ISA. You have been all a mother's heart could wish.
You ask but what you have a right to ask,
And I have always purposed a fit time—
When that your age were ripe enough—

CHARLES. Well, mother,
Has not that time arrived?

ISA. Your age, dear Charles,
Has scarce reach'd manhood yet. 'T is true, your courage,
Your conduct amidst danger—manly virtues,—
Are well approv'd. Your judgment too—so much,
A mother may believe and say—is far
Beyond the years you count. But there 's a quality;
A virtue it may be, which is the growth
Only of minds well disciplin'd; which looks
On human actions with a liberal eye.
That knows the weakness of the human heart,
Because it feels it; and will not condemn
In others, what itself is conscious of—
That will not with the tyrant prejudice,
Without allowance or extenuation,
Yea, without hearing pass its dreadful sentence.

CHARLES. And am I such a one? [1] thanks to my nature,
Which I feel is not quite so vile. My breeding,
Which has been liberal. Nay thanks to those
Who daily here exhibit its deformity,
I scorn this monster prejudice.

ISA. And yet—
Should you—I could not live if you should hate me.

CHARLES. Hate you, my mother? Had not all your actions
Been, as I've seen them, noble; all your precepts
As I have ever found them, full of goodness,
Could I recall the tenderness you've shewn
Towards me, and cease to love you.—Never, never!
All crimes however great. dwindle to atoms
Near filial ingratitude; the heart
That is that monster's throne, ne'er knew a virtue.

ISA. Ah! how shall I commence!—What would you know.

CHARLES. Why you left England? Why in this wilderness,
Amidst a race that scorn, that shun and loathe us,
You linger out existence? Chiefly, mother;
Who is my father? (*Taking her hand.*)

ISA. Ah! (*Turning away.*)

CHARLES. In our own England,
At school, among my frank and laughing mates,
When they have put this question, it was done
In merry mood, and I could bear it—well—
Although I could not answer it; but here,
O mother—to these cold and selfish beings,
Their smooth tongues dipp'd in bitterness, their eyes
Scowling suspicion—what can I reply?

ISA. Poor boy, poor boy! Well, Charles, the time is come
And if my spirits fail not—you shall know all.
Your father—but I cannot, no, I cannot
Commence my story there.—I was left, Charles,
Without a parent's care, just at that age
That needs it most. I had ne'er known my mother,
And was scarce fifteen when my father's fate
Forc'd him to abandon child and home and country;

[1] This passage is confused. It should probably read: Thanks to my nature,
Which I feel is not so vile, and to my breeding
Which has been liberal, nay, thanks to those
Who daily here exhibit its deformity,
I scorn this monster prejudice.

For he had been a patriot, as he deemed it,
Or, as his destiny decreed, a traitor.—
He fled to this new world.
CHARLES. Does he yet live?
ISA. Alas! I know not, rumours came to England
That he survived. It was to find my father,
And on my knees implore his benediction;—
Haply, should he forgive, to minister
Unto his age's comfort—I came hither.
CHARLES. 'T is strange, if living, he should seek concealment,
After the general amnesty.
ISA. O! Charles;
He was excepted in that act of mercy;
He had done that, the king might never pardon.
CHARLES. Unhappy man!
ISA. Most true.—But let me haste
To close my dark recital. I was plac'd
In charge of a kinsman a perfidious villain
Whose avarice sold, betray'd me.—O my son,
It is not fit thy ears should hear the tale,
And from my lips. I wept, implor'd, resisted—
Riches and pleasure tempted me in vain
Coupled with shame. But hellish craft at length
Triumph'd over credulous vanity—The altar
Was made the scene of sacrilegious mockery,
The holy vestments of the priest, became
A profane masking habit—
CHARLES. Power of Justice!
Could you behold this and forbear to strike!
ISA. The illusion vanish'd, and I fled, I fled
In horror and in madness.
CHARLES. Dreadful, dreadful!
ISA. It was thy birth that sav'd me from destruction—
I had thee to live for, and I liv'd; deep hid
In solitude, under an assum'd name,
Thou wer't rear'd, Charles, amidst thy mother's tears.
CHARLES. An assum'd name—in solitude—Shame, shame!
Why not unmask the villain to the world,
And boldly challenge what was yours?
ISA. His rank—
CHARLES. No rank should shield injustice. Quick, inform me
Who was the wretch? Give me the villain's name.
ISA. He was thy father, Charles.
CHARLES. In the sight of Heaven
I here disclaim and curse—
ISA. Forbear, forbear—
Or curse me too—
CHARLES. His name, his name—
ISA. You will destroy me!
(*She falls into his arms.*)
CHARLES. What have I done? I will be calm—forgive me.

(*Enter* LUCY.)

LUCY. A person from the village, madam, asks
To be admitted to your presence.
ISA. How!
Does he declare his business?
LUCY. He declines it,
Until he see yourself.
ISA. Admit him, Lucy.

(*Exit* LUCY.)

CHARLES. Madam, you tremble still, let me support you.
ISA. No; I must learn to overcome this weakness.

(*Enter* MESSENGER.)

Now, Sir, I'm she you ask for—to your business.
MESS. My business is with both. You, Isabella
And Charles, surnam'd Fitzroy, are cited both,
By a commission of the government,
To attend them at their session on the morrow
At nine in the morning.
CHARLES. And to what purpose?
MESS. That
You'll learn from them, farewell.

(*Exit* MESSENGER.)

CHARLES. Why farewell, gravity.
ISA. What can this mean?
CHARLES. They do not know themselves.
ISA. I fear I've been too tardy.
CHARLES. Nay, 't is nothing.
To question us, perhaps, upon our means,
And pack us from the parish, nothing more.
But, madam, you were interrupted, ere
I learn'd the name—
ISA. Not at this moment, Charles.
CHARLES. Well then, enough of sorrow for to-day—
I will return anon, and laugh with you

At the absurdities of these strange people.
At supper we'll discuss our plans for the future.
We may be happy yet.—

ISA. But whither go you?

CHARLES. I ought to visit him I wounded, madam,
And perhaps I may gather in the village,
Something that may concern us—and perhaps—

ISA. Well do not be long absent; it is night.

CHARLES. I will not, madam: I shall soon return.

(*Exit* CHARLES.)

ISA. He does not feel the danger, his frank spirit,
His careless youth, disdains it. We must fly.—

(*Enter* LUCY.)

Bid Edward, with all speed, prepare the horses,
Then follow to my chamber. We must prepare
In all haste, for a journey—

LUCY. Madam, a journey—
To-night?

ISA. To-night: it is most necessary. So, bid Edward
Be secret.

LUCY. He is here.

EDW. (*Within.*) You cannot pass.

(*Enter* EDWARD.)

ISA. What noise is this?

EDW. Madam, in spite of me
They press into your presence.

ISA. We are lost!

(*Enter several* OFFICERS.)

1ST. OFFICER. For that we do we have sufficient warrant.

ISA. What means this rudeness?

1ST OFFICER. Answer; where's your son?

ISA. He is not in the house.

1ST OFFICER. (*To attendants who go out.*) Go you, make search.

ISA. Again I ask, what is your business here?

1ST OFFICER. Read (*hands her a paper*).

ISA. Gracious Heav'n! Is this the charge against us!
But why this second visit! we are cited
To answer in the morning.

1ST OFFICER. But the judges
Have chang'd their mind. Your chamber is your prison
'Til you are sent for. We'll attend you thither.

ISA. But one word with my servant—

1ST OFFICER. Not one word;
It is forbidden, come—

ISA. My son, my son! (*She exchanges significant looks with* LUCY, *and Exit guarded.*)

LUCY. I understand (*going.*)

2ND OFFICER. And so do we—our duty.
You are not to stir hence, nor hold discourse
One with another. Lead them in—away.
(*Officers lead off* LUCY, *and* EDWARD.)

SCENE 3. *Before the house of* RAVENSWORTH

(*Enter* MARY *from house.*)

He does not come. I do not wish it, sure—
At least I ought not. But has he forgotten?—
That is impossible.—Perhaps he fears—
O no! Charles never fears—should he not come—
I ought to hope he could not—ah! a figure,
Stealing between the trees—should it be he:
But may it not be a stranger! ah, let me fly:

(*Exit, into the house.*)

(*Enter* CHARLES *cautiously.*)

'T was she, her white robe, emblem of her innocence,
Dispels the darkness of the libertine night,
And all around her's purity and brightness.
She is alone. As I pass'd thro' the village
I learn'd her father was in council there.—
She is alone and unprotected quite—
She loves me and confides in me—be that,
Tho' passion mount to madness, her protection.
The door is fasten'd, right; a common guest
Comes by a common passage—there are posterns
And wickets for the lover. Let me try.

(*Exit behind the house.*)

SCENE 4. *A chamber; a window in the flat; a light burning near the window.*

MARY *discovered, a book in her hand.*

I cannot read,—my thoughts are all confusion,
If it be he, will he not think the light
Was plac'd designedly. I will remove it.
(*Goes towards the window, starts on* CHARLES *appearing at it.*)

CHARLES. Be not alarm'd, my Mary: it is I.
MARY. O Charles, how could you?—
CHARLES. How could I refrain
When that the beacon light so fairly blaz'd
From steering to this haven?
MARY. There! I fear'd
You would presume to think—
CHARLES. But I think nothing—
Presume, know nothing, but that thou, my Mary,
Art the divinest creature on the earth
And I the happiest—O my best, my dearest,
That thou might'st live forever near this heart;
And why not there forever! What prevents it,
What can—what shall? My beauteous, my beloved.
MARY. No more;
This warmth alarms me—hear me, Charles—
I've given to thee my heart and maiden vow,
O, be content—and—leave me—
CHARLES. Leave thee, Love?
MARY. Before you teach me to despise myself;
Ere you yourself despise me.
CHARLES. Have I, Mary,
Have I deserv'd that from thee? Lo, I'm calm—
And gaze upon thee as the pilgrim looks
Upon the shrine he kneels at; the pure stars
Look not on angels with a holier light.
MARY. I do believe you, Charles—but O this meeting,
So rash, so—
CHARLES. 'T was presumptuous in me, Mary,
I do confess it.
MARY. Still you mistake me, Charles,
I do not say, I did not wish you here—
Yet I must wish you gone. It is so wrong—
I am so much to blame—
CHARLES. I will not stay,
To give you pain.
MARY. But do not go in anger—
CHARLES. Anger! at you!
MARY. A happier time will come—
Each moment now is full of peril, Charles;
My father may return, and should he find you!—
CHARLES. One word and I will leave you. You will hear,
To-morrow, that we've left this place for ever.
MARY. How, Charles?
CHARLES. My mother has resolv'd to fly
The persecutions that surround her here
And we depart to-morrow—if we may—
For we're already cited—
MARY. Heav'ns! for what?
CHARLES. It can be nothing surely. But, dear Mary,
Tho' absent, ah remember there is one
Who lives for you alone.
MARY. Charles, can you doubt it?
CHARLES. And should there, Mary, should there come an hour
Propitious to our loves; secure and safe—
Suspicion dead, her eye, nor ear to mark us—
And should the lover that adores you, Mary,
Appear at that blest hour, with certain means
To bear you far from cruelty and slav'ry,
To love and happiness?—
MARY. No more, no more—
CHARLES. Would you consent?
MARY. O tempt me not to sin—
'T would break my father's heart—
CHARLES. Give me your promise.

(*Enter* RAVENSWORTH, WALFORD, ALICE.)

MARY. (*Observing her father.*) Unhand me, oh unhand me—Father, father!
(*Faints in* CHARLES' *arms.*)
RAV. Thy father's here to save thee, hapless girl,
And hurl confusion on thy base betrayer.
CHARLES. (*Attending only to* MARY.) She's dead, she's dead!
RAV. Haste, tear her from his arms
Ere the pollution of his touch destroy her.

(ALICE *and* WALFORD *convey* MARY *out.*)

CHARLES. And have I killed her! (*gazing after her.*)
RAV. Wretch, and do you mourn
Over the clay, that would have kill'd the soul?

(*Re-enter* WALFORD.)

WALF. She has reviv'd, and calls for thee, my friend.
CHARLES. She lives, she lives! Then I defy my fate.
RAV. Outcast from Heav'n, thy doom is near at hand.
Walford, we'll strait convey him to the church,
Where by this time the judges have assembled,
To try his sinful mother.
CHARLES. How? my mother!
And have ye laid your sacrilegious hands
Upon my mother?
RAV. Silence wretched youth.
I will but see my daughter—meantime Walford,
Guard well your prisoner.
CHARLES. Guard me! heartless father,
That feelest not the ties of blood and nature—
Think you, at such an hour, I'd quit my mother?

(*Exeunt* RAVENSWORTH, CHARLES *and* WALFORD.)

END OF ACT FOUR.

ACT FIVE.

SCENE 1. *A Wood.* (*Stage dark.*)

(*Enter the* UNKNOWN.)

At length, unseen by human eye, I've gain'd
Her neighbourhood. The village lies before me;
And on the right rises the eminence
On which she dwells—She dwells! who dwells? O heart
Hold till thou art assur'd. Such were the features,
The stately form of her, whose cherish'd image,
Time spares my widow'd heart, fresh and unchang'd.—
I must be satisfied.— The night has fallen
Murky and thick; and in the western Heavens,
The last of day was shrouded in the folds
Of gathering clouds, from whose dark confines come,
At intervals, faint flashes, and the voice
Of muttering thunder: there will be a storm.
How is it that I feel, as never yet
I felt before, the threatening elements;
My courage is bow'd down and cowers, as though
The lowering canopy would fall in streams
Of death and desolation. Dark portents,
Hence! There's a Heaven beyond the tempest's scope,
Above the clouds of death. Wing your flight thither,
Thoughts—hopes, desires; there is your resting place. (*Exit.*)

SCENE 2. *The interior of the Church.* (*Arranged as a Hall of Justice.*) *Passages lead to doors on each side of the desk. The Judges seated at the desk.* CHARLES *stands on the left, near the Judges.* ISABELLA *nearer the front; on the same side* RAVENSWORTH, WALFORD, MARY, *and* ALICE; *on the opposite side, Villagers, Officers, etc.*

JUDGE. Ye have heard the charge—but ere ye answer to it
Bethink ye well. Confession may do much
To save you from the penalty; or mitigate
Your punishment. Denial must deprive you
Of every hope of mercy.—Answer then—
And first, you, madam.
ISA. Sorcery! Gracious Heaven!
Is it necessary, in this age of light,
And before men and Christians, I should deny
A charge so monstrous!
JUDGE. Answer to the question.
ISA. We are not guilty then; so aid us Heaven!
JUDGE. Speak for yourself alone. Will you disclose
Who—what ye are?
ISA. I am a gentlewoman—
More I cannot disclose.
JUDGE. Say, wherefore, madam,
You came among us?
ISA. Sir, I came to seek
A father.
JUDGE. Who is he?
ISA. I dare not name him.

RAV. Mark you, how she prevaricates?
JUDGE. What evidence
Have you against this woman?
RAV. Ye all remember
The terror and despair that fill'd each bosom
When the red comet, signal of Heaven's wrath,
Shook its portentous fires above our heads.
Ye all have seen, and most of ye have felt
The afflictions which this groaning land is vex'd with—
Our smiling fields wither'd by blight and blast,
The fruitful earth parch'd into eddying dust,—
On our fair coast the strewings of wreck'd commerce;
In town and city, fire and pestilence,
And famine, walking their destroying rounds—
Our peaceful villages, the scene of slaughter,
Echoing the savage yell, and frenzied shriek
Of maid and matron, or the piercing wail
Of widows and of orphans—
JUDGE. We deplore
The evils you recite; but what avails
Their repetition here; and how do they
Affect the cause in question?
RAV. Shall we forget
That worldly pride and irreligious lightness,
Are the provoking sins, which our grave synod
Have urg'd us to root out? Turn then to her,
Swelling with earth-born vanity, to her
Who scorns religion, and its meek professors;
And, to this hour—until compell'd, ne'er stood
Within these holy walls.
JUDGE. Yet this is nothing,
Touching the charge against her—you must be
Less vague and general. Produce your proofs.
RAV. There are two witnesses at hand; her servants—
Who have confess'd she had prepared to fly
This very night—a proof most clear and potent
Of conscious guilt. But why refer to this!
Each one that hears me is a witness of it,
It is the village horror. Call, at random,
One from the crowd, and mark if he will dare
To doubt the thing I speak of.
JUDGE. 'T must not be,
Nor can we listen further.
ISA. I beseech you
Let him proceed; let him endeavour still,
To excite the passions of his auditors;
It will but shew how weak he deems his proof
Who lays such stress on prejudice. I fear not,
But I can answer all his accusations.—
If I intended flight—need I remind you
Of what your fathers—what yourselves have done?
It was not conscious guilt bade them or you
Escape from that, was felt was persecution—
If I have thought the manner of my worship
A matter between Heaven and my conscience,
How can ye blame me, who in caves and rocks
Shunning the church, offer'd your secret prayers?
Or does my state offend? Habit and taste
May make some difference, and humble things
Seem great to those more humble; yet I have used
My little wealth in benefits. Your saints
Climb'd to high places—Cromwell to the highest—
As the sun seeks the eminence from which
He can diffuse his beams most bounteously.
RAV. The subtle power she serves does not withhold
The aid of sophistry.
ISA. I pray my judges
To shield me from the malice of this man,
And bring me to the trial. I will meet it,
As it concerns myself with firm indifference;
But as it touches him whom I exist in,
With hope that my acquittal shall dissolve
The fetters of my son.
RAV. (*Aside.*) That must not be.
JUDGE. Bring forth your proofs, and let the cause proceed.

RAV. Perhaps it is the weakness of the father
Prompts the suggestion—But I have bethought me,
It were most fit this youth should first be dealt with,
'Gainst whom there are a host of witnesses
Ready to testify—unless his actions,
Obvious and known, are proof enough—his life
Which is a course of crime and profligacy,
Ending, with contemplated rape and murder.
ISA. What do I hear?
JUDGE. How say you? rape and murder!
RAV. The victim of his bloody purpose lingers
Upon the verge of death—Here are the proofs
That point out the assassin! (*Showing the sword and handkerchief, which are held by a* VILLAGER *who is standing near him.*) For the violence—
Myself, my daughter here—
MARY. O father, father!
JUDGE. These things are terrible. But you forget,
They are not now the charge.
RAV. What matters it,
Whether by hellish arts of sorcery
He wrought upon the maiden,—or with force
Attempted violation—Let him answer—
Denying one, he but admits the other.
JUDGE. Bid him stand forth. We wait your answer, youth.
CHARLES. You wait in vain—I shall not plead.
JUDGE. Not plead!
RAV. (*Aside.*) This is beyond my hopes.
ISA. O Charles, my son!
JUDGE. What do you mean?
CHARLES. Simply, sir, that I will not
Place myself on my trial here.
JUDGE. Your reason?
Do you question then the justice of the court?
RAV. He does, no doubt he does.
CHARLES. However strong
Might be the ground for question—'t is not that
Determines me to silence.
JUDGE. If you hope
To purchase safety by this contumacy;
'T is fit you be aware that clinging there,
You may pull ruin on your head.
CHARLES. I know
The danger I incur, but dare to meet it.
ISA. O Charles, reflect—
CHARLES. Mother my soul is fixed;
They shall not call yon maiden to the bar.
Tremble not, weep not, pure and timid soul,
They shall not question thee.
RAV. Hence with thy spells—
Take thine eyes off my child, ere her weak frame
Yield to the charm she shakes with—hence I say!
(MARY *attempts to speak, but is prevented by her Father.*)
JUDGE. Prisoner, attend: at once inform the court
Of all you know concerning the strange being,
Who, like a supernatural visitant,
Appear'd this day among us. What connexion
Subsists between you?
CHARLES. None. I know him not.
RAV. And yet this morning, ere the dawn had broken,
They were both seen together in the forest,
Holding mysterious converse. Here 's a witness
Who will avouch the fact; and that the stranger
With the first day-beam, vanished from his sight.
ISA. (*Aside.*) He never told me this. Can he have met him?
JUDGE. Look on these things. They are mark'd with your name,
And stain'd with blood. They were found near the spot
Where a poor wretch lay bleeding. Can you explain it?
CHARLES. They are mine—I do confess it. I encounter'd
A person near that spot, and wounded him
In honourable duel. Nothing more
Can I explain.
MARY. (*Struggling.*) O father, let me speak.
RAV. Silence! Now answer me, and let the powers
Of darkness, that sustain you in your pride,
Yield and abandon you unto your fate.
Did you not robber like, this night break in
My unguarded house, and there, with ruffian force
Attempt the honour of this maiden?

ISA. Heaven!
RAV. D' ye hesitate! you dare not answer nay.
For here are witnesses to your confusion,
Who saw you clasp her in your vile embrace,
And heard her shrieks for help. Nay, here 's the maiden,
Who will herself aver it.
MARY. Father, father!
RAV. Come forth, my child.
(*Attempting to lead her forward.*)
CHARLES. Forbear! it shall not need.
RAV. Do you confess?
CHARLES. What e'er you will.
ISA. 'T is past.
(MARY *faints in the arms of* ALICE.)
RAV. Hear ye this, Judges! People, hear ye this? (*Storm commences.*)
And why do we delay! His doom were death,
Disdaining as he has to make his plea
To the charge of sorcery. Now, his full confession,
Which ye have heard, dooms him a second time.
(*Storm increases; Thunder and Lightning.*)
Then why do ye delay? The angry Heavens—
Hark, how they chide in thunder! Mark their lightnings.
(*The storm rages; the Judges rise; all is confusion; the people and two officers gather around* CHARLES; *officers seize him.*)
ISA. Save him! O Heaven! As ye are men, have mercy!
RAV. No; not beneath this roof: among the tombs,
Under the fury of the madden'd sky;
Fit time and place!
CHARLES. (*As they are dragging him out.*) Mary; my mother! Mary!
ISA. My son!
(*Leans nearly fainting in* LUCY'S *arms.*)
MARY. (*Reviving.*) Who calls me? Ah! What would ye do?
He 's innocent—he 's my betroth'd—my husband!
He came with my consent—he 's innocent!
RAV. Listen not to her; 't is his hellish magic
Speaks in her voice—away!
MARY. O Charles, my Charles!—
(*She faints.*)

(*They bear* CHARLES *out. The storm continues.*)
RAV. It is accomplish'd.

(*Enter the* UNKNOWN.)

UNK. What? what is accomplish'd?
RAV. Who 'rt thou that ask'st?
UNK. Nay, answer me. They tell
Of dreadful deeds ye are performing here.—
How 's this! Has death been here among you?
RAV. Yes,
Whatever thou may 'st be, death has been here
Guided by Heaven's vengeance.
UNK. Who is this?
'T is she, 't is she! Dost know me, Isabella?
ISA. Is it not—?
UNK. 'T is thy father.
ISA. Father, father!
Have I then found thee! But my son! my son!
UNK. Unhappy child, be calm—I know thy story,
And do forgive and bless thee.
ISA. Thanks, my father.—
(*Struggling to speak.*)
But—
UNK. What means this?
ISA. O, for a moment's strength—
Haste—haste—they murder him—my son—
UNK. Thy son,
O, where?
ISA. There—there—O Heaven! it is too late!
(*They enter with a Bier, carrying* CHARLES. *The* UNKNOWN *leads* ISABELLA *slowly towards it.*)

(*Enter* SIR REGINALD.)

SIR R. O fatal tardiness! and yet I came
The instant that I learned it. Bloody monsters!
How will ye answer this? Behold these papers,
They 're from the king! They bid me seek a lady,
Nam'd Isabella, whom he espoused in secret
And her son Charles Fitzroy—And is it thus—

(*Enter* GEORGE EGERTON, *pale and weak.*)

O George, look there!
GEORGE. O, brave, unhappy youth!

My generous foe, my honourable conqueror!

MARY. (*Reviving.*) Nay, ye shall not detain me—I will go,
And tell them all. Before I could not speak
My father held me here fast by the throat.
Why will you hold me? they will murder him—
Unless I speak for him. He spoke for me—
He sav'd my honour! Ah! what's here? O Heaven!
'T is he—is he asleep?—No, it is not he.—
I'd think 't were he, but that his eyes are swoll'n
Out of their sockets—and his face is black
With settled blood.—It is a murder'd man
You've brought me to—and not my Charles—my Charles!
He was so young and lovely.—Soft, soft, soft!
Now I remember.—They have made you look so,
To fright me from your love. It will not do—
I know you well enough—I know those lips
Tho' I have never touch'd them. There, love, there,
It is our nuptial kiss. They shall not cheat us—
Hark in thine ear, how we will laugh at them.

(*Leans her head down on the body, as if whispering.*)

SIR R. Alas! poor maniac.

(ISABELLA *who, supported by her father, had been bending over the body in mute despair, is now sinking.*)

UNK. Daughter—Isabella—

ISA. Father— (*Looking up in his face.*)

UNK. You will not leave me, Isabella?

ISA. I would remain to comfort you, my father,
But there's a tightness here.—For nineteen years
He was my only stay on earth—my good,
My duteous son. Ere I found thee, my father,
The cord was snapp'd—Forgive me—

(ISABELLA *falls, and is received in the arms of* LUCY.)

UNK. Bless thee, child—
I will not linger long behind thee.

(*Storm subsides.*)

SIR R. Sir,
If you're that lady's father, I have here
A pardon for you from the king.

UNK. I thank him;
But it is now too late.—She's gone.—The world
Has nothing left for me—deep in the wilderness,
I'll seek a grave, unknown, unseen by man.—

WALF. How fares your hapless friend?

ALICE. Her cold cheek rests
Against his cheek—not colder—

WALF. Place your hand
Upon her heart: is there no beating there?

ALICE. There is no beating there—She's dead!

RAV. Dead, dead!—

(RAVENSWORTH, *who thro' this scene, had shewn the signs of stern and settled despair, occasionally casting his eyes upon his daughter, or raising them to Heaven, but withdrawing them again in utter hopelessness, now sinks groaning into the arms of* WALFORD. ISABELLA *is on her knees, on the upper side of the bier, leaning on* LUCY. *The* UNKNOWN, *with his hands clasp'd, bends over his daughter.* ALICE *is kneeling at the side of her friend.* SIR REGINALD *and* GEORGE EGERTON *stand near the head of the bier.* LUCY *and* EDWARD *behind their mistress. The back ground filled up by the* JUDGES, VILLAGERS, *etc. The* CURTAIN *falls amidst a burst of the Storm, accompanied by* THUNDER *and* LIGHTNING.)

CHARLES THE SECOND

BY

John Howard Payne

CHARLES THE SECOND

Charles the Second illustrates the Comedy of Manners and represents the influence of the French stage upon ours. It is the brightest and the most finished of Payne's comedies.

John Howard Payne was born in New York City, June 9, 1791. He was brought up in Boston, and was carefully educated under the direction of his father, the head of a school. By the age of thirteen he had decided to go upon the stage and was sent into a mercantile house in New York City by his parents to cure him of the desire. He found time, however, to publish the *Thespian Mirror,* from December 28, 1805, to May 31, 1806, which contained dramatic criticism of a fair character. He also wrote his first play, *Julia or The Wanderer,* performed at the Park Theatre on February 7, 1806, and printed in the same year. He seems to have been a charming as well as a precocious youth, and through the interest of friends, especially John E. Seaman, he was sent to Union College, where he remained from July, 1806, to November, 1808, as a private pupil preparing to enter the Sophomore Class, under President Nott's instruction. Owing to a misunderstanding with his patron but also prompted by his continued desire to act, Payne made his début on February 24, 1809, as "Young Norval" in Home's play of *Douglas,* at the old Park Theatre in New York. He acted also in Baltimore, Philadelphia, Washington and other cities in 1809 and in 1811 and 1812. He had not been, however, as successful as he desired and in 1813 he welcomed an opportunity to go abroad for a year's study and travel. He did not return to this country till 1832, when his activities among the Indians and later his consulship at Tunis from 1842 to 1845 lie outside of our special interest. He died April 9, 1852, at Tunis.

Payne wrote or adapted over sixty plays. Much of his work consisted in translation from the French drama of his own time, or in the adaptation of English plays. His historical tragedy of *Brutus,* for example, played first at Drury Lane, London, December 3, 1818, is, according to his own statement, a compound of seven earlier plays on the same theme.

In domestic tragedy, his play of *Richelieu or the Broken Heart* is of considerable merit, although it is not original, being based on *La Jeunesse de Richelieu,* of Alexandre Duval. It was played first at Drury Lane, February, 1826, and was performed frequently in this country as *The Bankrupt's Wife.* In comedy, *Charles II* is representative. Payne wrote most frequently, however, a form of melodrama, such as *Thérèse, or the Orphan of Geneva,* produced first at Drury Lane, February 2, 1821. Forrest frequently acted "Carwin" in this play. *Clari, or the Maid of Milan,* an opera, derives its interest chiefly from the fact that it contains the song of "Home, Sweet Home." It was first played at Covent Garden, May 8, 1823, and at the Park Theatre, New York, November 12, 1823.

Charles the Second or The Merry Monarch was first played at the Theatre Royal, Covent Garden, London, May 27, 1824. It was acted at the Park Theatre, New York, October 25, 1824.

The comedy is of especial interest on account of Washington Irving's joint authorship in it. Irving collaborated more than once with Payne but insisted on his share being concealed. In *The Life and Letters of Washington Irving* by Pierre Irving (1883), an account is given of Irving's sending the manuscript to Payne, in November, 1823, after having revised it and added to it some new ideas. The idea of "Captain Copp" constantly trying to sing a song, and never being able to complete it, was conceived by Irving to meet the English taste for broad fun. In the introduction by Payne in the edition of 1824 he refers to the literary friend to whom he is "indebted for invaluable touches."

The work of both authors had as a model, a French play, *La Jeunesse de Henri V,* by Alexandre Duval (1760–1838), one of the leading dramatists of France at the time. Duval's play, performed at the Théâtre-Français, June 9, 1806, which was one of his most successful efforts, was in its turn based on another, *Charles II en un certain lieu,* by Mercier, and, according to Duval, even this was based on an earlier English play. Duval was forced by the censor to change his hero from Charles II to Henry V of England, with consequent anachronisms. Payne restored the rightful king to his own, but took the main plot from Duval and even the names of the principal characters are the same, with the exception of that of the heroine, who is "Betty" in the original. The dialogue at times follows the original though never slavishly and at times it differs radically, especially in the first and last Acts.

John Howard Payne, Dramatist, Poet, Actor and Author of "Home Sweet Home!" by Gabriel Harrison, revised ed. Philadelphia, 1885, is the standard life of Payne. *The Early Life of John Howard Payne,* by W. T. Hanson, Boston, 1913, is valuable for the first period of Payne's life. His important plays have frequently been reprinted. *Charles II, Brutus, Thérèse, Love in Humble Life, Peter Smink, The Two Galley Slaves, Mrs. Smith, or the Wife and the Widow, 'T was I, or the Truth a Lie,* can still be obtained in the Samuel French series. For a complete Bibliography by the present editor, see the *Cambridge History of American Literature. La Jeunesse de Henri V* can be found in *Œuvres Complètes d'Alexandre Duval,* Paris, 1822, Vol. 6.

The present edition of *Charles II* is a reprint of the rare London edition of 1824, which differs from the American reprints and is a better text.

CHARLES THE SECOND;

OR,

THE MERRY MONARCH.

A COMEDY,

IN THREE ACTS,

(WITH SOME SONGS):

FIRST PERFORMED AT THE THEATRE ROYAL, COVENT GARDEN,
ON THURSDAY EVENING, MAY 27, 1824.

BY

JOHN HOWARD PAYNE,

Author of Brutus, Clari, Therese, Accusation, Adeline, Ali Pacha, The Two Galley Slaves, Love in Humble Life, Mrs. Smith, and various other Pieces.

LONDON:

PRINTED FOR

LONGMAN, HURST, REES, ORME, BROWN, AND GREEN,

PATERNOSTER-ROW.

1824.

CHARACTERS

King Charles II..Mr. C. Kemble

Rochester..Mr. Jones

Edward (a page).......................................Mr. Duruset

Captain Copp..Mr. Fawcett

Two pages. Servants.

Lady Clara..Mrs. Faucit

Mary (adopted daughter of Copp)................Miss M. Tree

CHARLES THE SECOND

ACT FIRST.

SCENE 1. *The Royal Palace.*

(*Enter* ROCHESTER *and* LADY CLARA.)

LADY C. Yes, my lord, her majesty will have it, that you are the chief cause of the king's irregularities.

ROCH. Oh, I'll warrant it: and of his not loving her, too—is it not so?

LADY C. I did not say that; but, in truth, my lord, your continual jests on the married state—

ROCH. Heaven bless it!

LADY C. Your continual ridicule of married men—

ROCH. Heaven help them!

LADY C. Your licentious example, and still more licentious poetry—

ROCH. What's coming next?

LADY C. All these, I say, make you the most dangerous of men.

ROCH. Dangerous! My dear Lady Clara, you make me vain.

LADY C. It is well known that you are the king's prime companion in all his excesses.

ROCH. What, is my loyalty to be made my reproach? Must I not stand by my monarch in all his moods? Would you have me weep, when my sovereign laughs? Would you have me whine, when my sovereign calls for a jolly song? No, no, my lady, that might have done in the days of Praise-God-Barebones and the Roundheads; but times are altered.—We have a merry monarch to reign over us—A merry monarch makes a merry court—so God save the jovial king, and send him boon companions!

LADY C. (*Laughing.*) I see it is in vain to reason with you.

ROCH. Then give over the attempt.—Let us talk of something of a nearer and a dearer interest—of your merits and my most ardent flame.

LADY C. Ah, me! I fear, like many other of your flames, it will but end in smoke.—You talk of being desperately in love,—what proof have you ever given?

ROCH. What proof? Am I not ready to give the greatest proof a man can offer—to lay down this sweet bachelor life, and commit matrimony for your sake?

LADY C. Well, this last, I must say, coming from a Rochester, is a most convincing proof. I have heard *you* out, listen now to *me.* (ROCHESTER *bows.*) I will propose a bargain.—If, by your ascendancy over the king, you can disgust him with these nocturnal rambles, and bring him back to reason—

ROCH. Your ladyship forgets one of my talents.

LADY. C. Which is it?

ROCH. That of getting myself banished two or three times a year.

LADY C. And if the woman you profess to love should offer to *partake* your exile?—

ROCH. I am a lost man—I surrender.—That last shot reached my heart.

LADY C. (*Sighing.*) Ah, my lord—if that heart were only worth your head!—Well, is it agreed?

ROCH. It is your will—I undertake the sacrifice—but, madam, bear in mind my recompense.

LADY C. You may hope for everything. Adieu, my lord.—I now begin to believe in your passion, since you are willing to make a sacrifice to it, even of your follies.

(*Exit.*)

ROCH. (*Alone.*) A pretty task I have undertaken, truly! I—Rochester—become reformer! And, then, the convert I have to work upon! Charles, who glories in all kinds of rambling frolics!—True, he has had none but pleasant adventures as yet.—If I should trick him into some ridiculous dilemma?—My whole life has been a tissue of follies, and I am called a man of wit. I am now to attempt a rational act, and I shall be called a madman!—Well, be it so—matrimony will be sure to bring me to my senses.

(*Enter* EDWARD, *languidly.*)

ROCH. Ah! here comes my young protégé—How downcast he seems! How now, Edward, what's the matter with you, boy?

EDW. (*Sighing.*) Nothing, my lord.

ROCH. Good heaven, what a sigh to heave up nothing with! Tell me the truth this instant. Hast thou dared to fall in love?

EDW. I hope, my lord, there is no barm in indulging an honest attachment.

ROCH. An honest attachment! A young half-fledged page about court, who has hardly tried his wings in the sunshine of beauty, to talk of an honest attachment. Why, thou silly boy, is this the fruit of all the lessons I have given thee?

EDW. Did not your lordship tell me, that one of the first duties of a page was to be zealous in his devotion to the fair?

ROCH. Yes; but I told thee to skim over the surface of beauty, just dipping your wings, like a swallow, not plumping in like a goose—I told you to hover from flower to flower like a butterfly, not to bury yourself in one like a bee. An honest attachment!—What a plebeian phrase!—There 's a wife and seven children in the very sound of it.

EDW. My lord, I know your talent for putting things in a whimsical light, but, could you see the object of mv passion—

ROCH. Nay, a truce with all description.—But who, pray, is the object of this honest attachment?

EDW. (*Embarrassed.*) My lord!

ROCH. One of the maids of honour, I 'll be bound, who has privately been petting you with sweetmeats, and lending you love-tales.

EDW. No, my lord.

ROCH. Some veteran belle about court, too well known to the veteran beaux, and anxious to take in a new comer.

EDW. No such thing, my lord.

ROCH. Pray, then, give me some clue. What is the name of your beauty?

EDW. Her name, my lord, is Mary.

ROCH. Mary! a very pretty, posy-like name—And what sequestered spot may the gentle Mary embellish with her presence?

EDW. She lives at the Tav— Nay, my lord, promise not to laugh.

ROCH. Far be it from me to laugh in so serious a matter. Come, the residence of this fair one?

EDW. Why, then, my lord, she inhabits the tavern of the Grand Admiral, in Wapping.

ROCH. Usquebaugh and tobacco! the tavern of the Grand Admiral!—Ha! ha! ha!—An honest attachment for some pretty bar-maid!

EDW. No, my lord, no bar-maid, I assure you. Her uncle keeps the tavern.

ROCH. (*With mock gravity.*) Oh, I ask pardon, then she is heiress apparent to the tap-room, and you no doubt look forward to rise in the state through the dignities of drawer, tapster, and head-waiter, until you succeed to the fair hand of the niece, and the copper nose of the uncle, and rule with spigot in hand over the fair realms of Wapping. You, who I flattered myself would have made the torment and delight of all the pretty women at court!—*you* to be so completely gulled at the very outset,—the dupe of a green girl, and some old rogue of a publican!

EDW. Indeed, indeed, my lord, you do the uncle injustice. He is a perfectly honest, upright man—an old captain of a cruiser.

ROCH. Worse and worse! Some old buccaneer, tired of playing the part of a monster at sea, has turned shark on shore. And do you dare to appear in such a house with the dress of a royal page?

EDW. Oh! I have taken care to avoid that. I have introduced myself into the house as a music-master.

ROCH. And your musical name, gentle sir?

EDW. Georgini, at your service.

ROCH. Ha! ha! ha! very soft and Italianish—I 'll warrant this heroine bar-maid will turn out some unknown princess, carried off by the old buccaneer landlord, in one of his cruisings.

EDW. Your lordship is joking; but, really, at times, I think she is not what she seems.

ROCH. Ha! ha! ha! I could have sworn it. But silence—I hear his majesty dismount. Run to where your duty calls—we 'll take another opportunity to discuss the merits of this Wapping Princess.

EDW. (*Goes out, muttering.*) There 's many a true thing said in jest. I am certain her birth is above her condition.

(*Exit.*)

ROCH. I must see this paragon of bar-maids—She must be devilish pretty! The case admits of no delay—I 'll see her this very evening. Hold! Why not fulfil my promise to Lady Clara at the same time? It is decided:—I 'll give his majesty my first lesson in morals this very night. But, he comes.

(*Enter* CHARLES.)

CHAS. Good day, my lord!—What, musing! I never see thee with that air of grave cogitation, but I am sure there is some mischief devising.

ROCH. On the contrary, I am vehemently tempted to reform.

CHAS. Reform! ha! ha! ha! why, man, no one will credit thy conversion! Is not thy name a by-word? Do not mothers frighten their daughters with it, as formerly with that of Belzebub? Is not thy appearance in a neighborhood a signal for all the worthy burghers to bar their windows and put their womankind under lock and key?—Art thou not, in melancholy truth, the most notorious scapegrace in the kingdom?

ROCH. Heaven forefend that in anything I should take precedence of your majesty.

CHAS. But what proof do you give of your conversion?

ROCH. The most solemn—I am going to be married.

CHAS. Married! And who, pray, is the lady you have an idea of rendering miserable?

ROCH. The Lady Clara.

CHAS. The Lady Clara! The brilliant, the discreet, the virtuous Lady Clara! She marry Rochester! ha! ha! ha!

ROCH. Ah, my liege, heaven has given her a superabundance of virtues.—She will be able to make a very virtuous man of me with her superfluity.

CHAS. Well, when thou art married, I will undertake to write thy epithalamium.

ROCH. Then your majesty may at once invoke the Muses. All is settled. (*With great gravity.*) As soon as the rites are solemnized, I shall quit the court, and its mundane pleasures, and retire with my lovely bride to my castle at Rochester, under permission of my creditors, the faithful garrison of that fortress.

CHAS. What! is your castle again in pledge?

ROCH. No, my liege, not again. It has never, to my knowledge, been exactly out of keeping. A castle requires a custodian.

CHAS. Ah, Rochester! Rochester! Thou art an extravagant dog. I see I shall be called on to pay these usurers at last.

ROCH. Your majesty is ever bounteous. I should not have dared to solicit, and certainly shall not presume to decline.

CHAS. Ha! ha! Thou art an arrant juggler, and hast an admirable knack of extracting a gift out of an empty hand. But, to business,—where shall we pass the night?

ROCH. (*Assuming a serious air.*) I must beg your majesty to excuse me this evening—I have an engagement of a grave and important nature.

CHAS. Grave and important! Thou liest, Rochester, or thine eyes speak false—and whither does this grave engagement take thee?

ROCH. To the tavern of the Grand Admiral in Wapping!

CHAS. I thought it was some such haunt. And the object of this business?

ROCH. A young girl, beautiful as an angel, and virtuous as a dragon—about whom there hangs a mystery that I must investigate.

CHAS. A mysterious beauty! It is a case for royal scrutiny—I will investigate it myself.

ROCH. But, my liege—

CHAS. No buts. Provide disguises. We will go together. (*With mock gravity.*) I like to study human nature in all its varieties, and there is no school equal to a tavern. There 's something of philosophy in this—one often gets a useful lesson in the course of a frolic.

ROCH. (*Aside.*) It shall go hard but your majesty shall have one to-night. (*Aloud.*) Ah, how few, except myself, give your majesty credit for your philosophy! And yet, by many, I am considered the partaker of your majesty's excesses.

CHAS. Partaker! what a calumny! you are the promoter of them.

ROCH. The world will judge me in this instance with even more severity than your majesty has done, should any disagreeable adventure be the result.

CHAS. Psha! I take the consequences on myself. Provide two seamen's dresses, a purse well filled, and arrange everything for nine precisely. Till then, farewell. (*Exit.*)

ROCH. I will attend your majesty. So! the plot is in train. I'll off to Lady Clara, and report progress. Let me see. This night the lesson. To-morrow my disgrace. Within eight days my marriage, and then, at my leisure, to repent and reform. (*Exit.*)

END OF ACT THE FIRST.

ACT TWO.

SCENE 1. *Outside of Copp's Tavern, the Grand Admiral. A view of the Thames and Wapping.*

(*Enter* MARY *from the House.*)

(VOICES, *within.*) Wine! wine! house!—waiter!—more wine, ho! Huzza! huzza! huzza!

MARY. What a noise those sailors make in the bar-room—nothing but singing, and laughing, and shouting—I should like to take a peep at them—but no—my uncle forbids me to show myself in the public rooms—he scarcely lets me be seen by the guests—he brings me up more like a young lady than the niece of a tavern keeper—(*walks about restless*). Heigho! what a tiresome long day! what shall I do with myself? what can be the matter with me? I wonder what can keep Mr. Georgini away? For three days he has not been here to give me a lesson—no matter—(*pettishly*)—I don't care—I shall forget all my singing, that's certain—he was just teaching me such a pretty song, too—all about love—I'll try it—(*attempts to sing*)—no, I can't—it's all out of my head—well, so much the better! I suppose he is teaching it to some fine lady scholar—let him, I don't care—I don't believe he'll find her so apt a scholar.

Song.

Oh! not when other eyes may read
My heart upon my cheek,
Oh! not when other ears can hear
Dare I of love to speak—
But when the stars rise from the sea,
Oh then I think of thee, dear love!
Oh then I think of thee.

When o'er the olives of the dell
The silent moonlight falls,
And when upon the rose, the dew
Hangs scented coronals,
And buds close on the chestnut tree,
Oh then I think of thee, dear love!
Oh then I think of thee.

(*Enter* COPP.)

COPP. What, Mary, my little blossom, what cheer? what cheer? Keep close, my little heart—why do you stir out of port? Here be cruisers abroad.

MARY. Who are those people, uncle, that make such a noise?

COPP. Two hearty blades—mad roysters—oons how they drink. I was obliged to part company, old cruiser as I am, or they would soon have had me on my beam ends.

MARY. Are they sailors, uncle?

COPP. To be sure they are: who else would fling about money as they do, and treat a whole bar-room? The tallest in particular is a very devil. Hollo, Captain Copp, cries he every minute, another bottle to treat my brother tars.

MARY. By their swaggering about so, they must be very rich.

COPP. Pho, child, 't isn't the deepest laden ships that make the most rolling.

MARY. But they spend their money so freely.

COPP. A sure sign that it's running out. The longest cable must come to an end. He that pays out fastest, will soonest be brought up with a round turn.

MARY. To what ship do they belong?

COPP. That's more than I can say. Suppose they're a couple of man of war's men just paid off, who think they've a Spanish mine in each pocket—(*shout of laughter from within*). Ah, the jolly tars! I was just the same at their age.

MARY. I should like to have a look at them.

COPP. Avast, there—what, trust thee in the way of two such rovers? No, no, I recollect too well what it was to get on shore after a long voyage. The first glimpse of a petticoat—whew! up boarding pikes and grappling irons!—(*Recollecting himself.*) Ahem—no, no, child, mustn't venture in these latitudes.

MARY. Ah, my good uncle, you are always so careful of me.

COPP. And why not? What else have I in the whole world to care for, or to care for me? Thou art all that's left to me out of the family fleet—a poor slight little pinnace. I've seen the rest, one after another, go down; it shall go hard but I'll convoy thee safe into port.

MARY. I fear I give you a great deal of trouble, my dear uncle.

COPP. Thou 'rt the very best lass in the whole kingdom, and I love thee as I loved my poor brother; that's because you're his very image. To be sure, you haven't his jolly nose, and your little mouth is but a fool to his. But then, there are his eyes, and his smile, and the good humoured cut of his face—(*sigh-

ing)—poor Philip! What! I'm going again, like the other night—(*wiping his eyes*). Psha! let's change the subject, because, d'ye see, sensibility and all that, it does me no good—none—so let's talk of something else. What makes thee so silent of late, my girl? I've not heard a song from thee these three days!

MARY. It's three days since I've seen my music-master.

COPP. Well, and can't you sing without him?

MARY. Without him I can't sing well.

COPP. And what's become of him?

MARY (*pettishly*). I can't tell, it's very tiresome. If he did not mean to come again, he might have said so.

COPP. Oddsfish, neglect thee—neglect his duty!—I'll break him on the spot. Thou shalt have another master, my girl.

MARY (*eagerly*). Oh, no, on no account; I dare say he is not well, some accident has happened. Besides, there is no other teacher in town equal to him, he sings with such feeling.

COPP. Ah! girl, if I had my old messmate, Jack Rattlin, here, he'd teach thee to sing. He had a voice—faith it would make all the bottles dance, and glasses jingle on the table!—Talk of feeling! Why, when Jack would sit of an evening on the capstan when on watch, and sing about sweethearts and wives, and jolly tars, and true lover's knots, and the roaring seas, and all that; smite my timbers, but it was enough to melt the heart of a grampus. Poor Jack, he taught me the only song I ever knew, it's a main good one though—

(*Sings a Stave.*)

In the time of the Rump,
As old Admiral Trump,
With his broom swept the chops of the Channel:
And his crew of Tenbreeches,
Those Dutch sons of ——

MARY (*putting her hand on his mouth*). Oh, uncle, uncle, don't sing that horrible rough song.

COPP. Rough? that's the beauty of it. It rouses one up, pipes all hands to quarters like a boatswain's call. Go in, Mary, but go in at the other door; don't go near the bar: go up to your own room, my dear, and your music-master will come to you presently, never fear.

(*Exit* MARY.)

VOICE, *within.* Hollo—house! waiter! Captain Copp! another bottle, my hearty fellow.

COPP. There they go again! I can't stand it any longer. I am an old cruiser, and can't hear an engagement without longing to be in the midst of it. Avast, though (*stopping short*), these lads are spending too much money. Have a care, friend Copp, don't sink the sailor in the publican; don't let a free-hearted tar ruin himself in thy house—no, no, faith. If they want more wine they shall have it; but they shall drink as messmates, not as guests. So have at you, boys; it's my turn to treat now.—

(*Exit* COPP.)

SCENE 2. *A Room in Copp's House.*

(*Enter* MARY.)

MARY. How provoking this absence of Mr. Georgini! It would be serving him right to let my uncle discharge him: but then I should like just to learn that song he is teaching me—hark!—How my heart beats! Hark! I'll wager it's Georgini—I have a gift of knowing people before I see them—my heart whispers me—

(*Enter* EDWARD, *as* GEORGINI.)

MARY. So, sir, you are come at last, are you? I had supposed you did not intend to come any more, and was about to look out for another teacher.

EDW. Pardon me for my absence—you have no idea what I have suffered.

MARY (*with anxiety*). Suffered!—Have you been ill, then?

EDW. Very ill—

MARY. Indeed! and what was your complaint?

EDW. (*smiling*). The not seeing you.

MARY (*half piqued, half pleased*). Mighty fine, sir; it is a complaint that you might have cured in a moment.—I have been angry, sir—very angry at your neglect—don't smile, sir—I won't be laughed at—

EDW. Laugh at you!—Can you suspect me of such a thing?—I do but smile from the pleasure of seeing you again—nothing but circumstances that I could not control caused my absence.

MARY (*softening*). Well, it's very provoking to be interrupted in one's lessons just in the middle of a new song—I'll warrant you 've been teaching it all over town.

EDW. Indeed, I teach it to no one but yourself—for no one else can do it such justice.

MARY (*smiling*). Nay, now you are flattering—have you brought it with you?

EDW. Here it is—if you please, we will sing it at once.

MARY. Yes—but—but—don't look so steadily at me while I sing—it puts me out; and then—and then—I don't know what I 'm singing.

EDW. What!—have you fear of me, then?

MARY. Oh! yes; I fear that I may not please you.

EDW. (*apart*). Amiable innocence! for the world would I not betray thee.

Duetto.

Love one day essayed to gain
 Entrance into Beauty's bower,
Many a toil, and many a chain,
 Guarded round the precious flower.
But Love laid aside his bow,
 Veiled his wing, hid his dart,
Entered more than Beauty's bower,
 Entered also Beauty's heart.
Hence was the sweet lesson learnt,
 Fond hearts never should despair,
Kept with truth, and led by hope,
 What is there Love may not dare?

(*Enter* COPP, *a little gay, singing.*)

"In the time of the Rump," &c.

Aha! master crotchet and quaver, so you 've come at last, have you? What the deuce did you stay away for, and let my little girl get out of tune?

EDW. Oh! I have explained all, sir, and made my peace.

COPP. Ah, she 's a forgiving little baggage, and amazing fond of music—why, she 's always on the lookout for you an hour before the time.

MARY. Never mind, uncle. Are your strange companions here still?

COPP. Here still? ay, and likely to stay here—ha! ha! ha!—no getting rid of them—they 're a couple of devils, of right down merry devils, ha! ha! ha!—They 've flustered me a little, i' faith.

EDW. You seem to have a great deal of company in the house, sir; I 'll take my leave.

COPP. You shall take no such thing—you shall take tea with us, my little semibreve, and we 'll have a lesson of music too. Oddsfish! you shall give me a lesson—I am confoundedly out of practice. and can't turn my old song for the life of me. (*Begins.*) "In the time of the Rump"—

MARY. Never mind the song now, uncle, we must have tea first, and Mr. Georgini will help me make it.

COPP. Ay, faith, and we 'll add a bowl of punch and a flask of old Madeira to make a set out—my two messmates in the other room are to be of the party.

MARY. What, those wild sailors who have been keeping the house in an uproar?

COPP. To be sure—they 're good lads, though they have a little of the devil in them.—They asked to clink the cup with me, and you know I can't well refuse, by trade, to clink the cup with any one. In troth, they had put me in such rare good humour—ha! ha! ha!—that I could not refuse them for the life of me.

MARY. But they are such a couple of harebrains—

COPP. Oh! don't be afraid—they are rough, but good-natured—sailor-like: besides, am not I always within hail? One of them, I see, is heaving in sight already. Come with me, my girl, and help to prepare the punch and get the tea—*you*, my king of crotchets, will stay and receive our guests—make yourself at home.—(*Sings as he goes,*) "In the time of the Rump"—

(*Exeunt* COPP *and* MARY.)

EDW. Here 's a transformation! from a court page behold me master of ceremonies at a Wapping tavern! (*starts*). Good heaven! whom have we here? The Earl of Rochester in that rude garb!

(*Enter* ROCHESTER.)

ROCH. The shouts of those jolly fellows began to turn my brain—his majesty is in fine humour to get into a scrape; and if he does, to make his difficulties more perplexing, I have secured his purse, so that he cannot bribe his way out of them—Hey! Edward?

EDW. (*confused*). My lord Rochester—

ROCH. Silence, you rogue! I am no lord here, no Rochester. I am a seaman—my name Tom Taffrel. The king, my messmate, is Jack Mizen.

EDW. The king with you!—(*aside*). I see it all—he 's after Mary—ah! I am lost.

ROCH. Don't be alarmed, friend Georgini;

none but the most innocent motives have brought us here—

EDW. Innocent motives bring you and the king, at night, to a tavern in Wapping, where there is a beautiful girl? Ah! my lord, my lord—

ROCH. Nay, to convince you that you have nothing to fear, I permit you to remain with us—(*aside*) He may assist my scheme—(*aloud*) You must play off your character of music-master upon the king.

EDW. Impossible! His majesty will recognise my features.

ROCH. Psha! you have not been a page a month; he probably has not seen your face three times. But take care how you act; the least indiscretion on your part—

EDW. Ah! my lord, I am too much interested in keeping the secret.

ROCH. That is not all. In whatever situation the king may find himself, whatever chagrin he may suffer, I forbid you to assist him in the slightest manner. You are to see in him only the sailor, Jack Mizen.

EDW. Should his majesty chance to incur any danger, my lord, I can never be passive. In such case, I have but one course.

ROCH. There *can* be no danger—I shall myself watch over his safety.

EDW. That decides me—I think I apprehend the object, and will obey your lordship.

ROCH. The king approaches—Silence! let each resume his part.

(*Enter* CHARLES.)

CHAS. Well, messmate, shall we soon see this marvellous beauty?

EDW. (*apart*). So—this is his majesty's innocent motive!

ROCH. Peace, friend Jack, here's one of her admirers—her music-master—

CHAS. Ah! you teach the young lady music, do you? (*looking earnestly at him*). Zounds! how like he is to the page you gave me lately.

EDW. (*apart*). Ah! my face strikes him.

ROCH. Hum—I can't say I see much resemblance. He is taller than Edward, and older, and the expression of his countenance is not the same.

CHAS. No, no, not altogether, but there is a something—

ROCH. Why, to tell the truth, the page had a wild fellow for a father—and, your majesty knows, likenesses are stamped at random about the world sometimes.

CHAS. (*laughing*). I understand—duplicate impressions—like enough.

(*Enter* MARY *and* SERVANT *with Tea.*)

MARY (*to* SERVANT). Set the table in this room.

CHAS. (*to* ROCHESTER). By heaven, she's a divinity!

EDW. (*low to* ROCHESTER). What does he say?

ROCH. (*to* EDW.). That your divinity is a devilish fine girl.

CHAS. (*to* ROCHESTER). Amuse this confounded singing-master. I wish to have a duo with his mistress.—He'll only mar music.

ROCH. (*to* EDWARD, *with an air of great business*). My good Mr. Georgini, I have something particular to say to you—(*drawing him to a corner*). His majesty (*suppressing a laugh*) fancies that you are uncomfortable, and requests me to amuse you.

EDW. Yes, that he may have Mary all to himself— (*Drawing near her.*)

ROCH. (*drawing him back*). Come, don't be childish. What, you pretend to follow my lessons, and want complaisance! (CHARLES *has been making advances to* MARY, *who appears at first a little shy.*)

CHAS. Do let me assist you, my pretty lass.

MARY. Don't trouble yourself, sir; Mr. Georgini is to help me make tea.

EDW. (*breaking from* ROCHESTER). I am here, madam—what can I do to help you?

CHAS. (*puts the kettle, as if accidentally, against his hand. Dryly*). Take care, young man, you may scald your fingers.

ROCH. (*drawing* EDWARD *back, and speaking low*). Why, what a plague, boy, are you doing?

(CHARLES *continues to assist* MARY, *mingling little gallantries, and blundering in attempts to assist.*)

EDW. (*aside, and struggling with* ROCHESTER). I shall go mad!

MARY. Oh, dear sir, you're so kind, you quite put me out—(*laughing*)—hey!—you have taken my hand instead of the teapot. I will not say you are awkward, sir, but really, you have the oddest manner of assisting—nay—let go my hand, I beg.

CHAS. By Heaven, it is a beautiful one!

MARY. Nay, nay—pray, sir—(*withdrawing her hand with smiling confusion*).

(*Apart.*) Upon my word, I don't see any thing so very rude in these people.

EDW. (*endeavoring to get away from* ROCHESTER). Let me go, I entreat you; I can stand this no longer.

ROCH. (*holding him, and suppressing a laugh*). Psha! man, if you think to marry, or rise at court, you must learn to be deaf and blind upon occasion.

CHAS. (*in rather an under-tone to* MARY). And how is it possible so pretty a lass should not be married?

MARY. Married—bless me! I never thought of such a thing.

CHAS. No? never? and yet surrounded by lovers.

MARY. Lovers! I have n't one, sir.

CHAS. Indeed! and what is that young man, fidgeting yonder?

MARY. He?—he is my singing-master, sir.

CHAS. And he sings to some purpose, I 'll warrant.

MARY. Delightfully.

CHAS. And gives you a love-song now and then?

MARY. Oh, often, often.

CHAS. I thought so—he has it in his countenance.

EDW. (*to* ROCH.). You *must* let me go—you see I am wanted.

ROCH. Upon my word, they are getting on amazingly well without you.

CHAS. (*to* MARY). And so you are fond of music, my pretty lass?

MARY. Oh, I love it of all things.

CHAS. A pretty hand to beat time with (*taking her hand*).

MARY. Sir—(*withdrawing it*).

CHAS. And as pretty a little mouth to warble a love-song. I warrant, there come none but sweet notes from these lips. (*Offers to kiss her.*)

MARY (*resisting*). Sir, give over—let me go, sir.—Mr. Georgini—help, help!

(EDWARD *bursts from* ROCHESTER, *who is laughing. At this moment*

Enter COPP.)

COPP. Avast there, messmate! what the devil, yard arm and yard arm with my niece!

(CHARLES *desists, a little confused*—EDWARD *approaches* MARY.)

MARY (*flurried*). I am glad you are come, uncle—this rude stranger—

COPP (*taking her arm under his*). Thunder and lightning—what! insult Captain Copp's niece in his own house! Fire and furies!

CHAS. (*pretending to be a little gay*). I insult your niece, messmate? Since when has an honest tar's kissing a pretty girl been considered an insult? As to the young woman, if she takes offence at a piece of sailor civility, why, I ask pardon, that 's all.

COPP (*softened*). Oh, as to a piece of civility, d 'ye see, that alters the case; but, guns and blunderbusses! if any one should dare—

ROCH. Come, come, uncle Copp, what a plague! you were a youngster once, and a frolicsome one, I 'll warrant. I see it in your eye—what—didst ever think it a crime to kiss a pretty girl in a civil way.

COPP. No, no, in a civil way, no, certainly; I can make allowance when a lad and a lass, and a bottle, come pretty near each other—odds fish—you say right, at your age, I was a rattler myself.—Come, Mary, no harm done. Come, lads, take your seats—(*They seat themselves.* EDWARD *attempts to place himself by* MARY.—CHARLES *interferes, and takes the place.*) Come, my girl, pour out the tea—I 'll fill out the punch, and we 'll have a time of it, i 'faith—Come, I 'll give you a jolly song to begin with—(*Sings.*)

In the time of the Rump,
As old Admiral Trump—

MARY (*apart*). That odious song!—come, uncle, never mind the song, take a cup of tea—(*offering one*).

COPP. What, drown my song and myself in warm water? ha! ha! no, faith—not while there 's a drop in the punch bowl.

(MARY *helps* EDWARD *and* ROCHESTER, *omitting* CHARLES.)

CHAS. (*low to* MARY). Am I then excluded?

MARY (*looking down*). I thought punch would be more to your liking, sir.

CHAS. Then punch be it—Come, clink with me, neighbour Copp—clink with me, my boy.

COPP. Oh! I 'm not proud, I 'll clink with anybody—that 's to say, mind ye, when the liquor is good, and there 's a good fellow in the case.

CHAS. (*rising*). Well, here goes—To the health of Mary, the fair maid of Wapping.

COPP. With all my heart, here 's to her health—the darling child—Oh! messmate, there you touch a soft corner of my heart—did you but know how I love this little girl. Psha! I 'm a foolish old fellow, and when I have got punch, and sensibility, and all that on board—Come, let 's talk of something else.

MARY. My dear uncle—

CHAS. I don't wonder at your loving her, I can't help feeling a kind of admiration for her myself—(*offering to take her hand*).

COPP. Softly, shipmate, no grappling—admire at a distance as much as you please, but hands off. Come, my lads, a merry song—I love to sing when I drink. (*Sings.*)

In the time of the Rump,
As old Admiral Trump—

MARY. Not that song, my dear uncle—I entreat—

COPP. Ah, I recollect—ha! ha! my poor song; ha! ha!—well, well, since you don't like me to sing, sing it for me yourself, Mary.

CHAS. Ay, a song from the charming Mary (*significantly*), I dare say your master has some pretty love-song for you.

EDW. Oh, yes—I have brought one of the latest in vogue—one by the most fashionable poet of the day—the Earl of Rochester.

COPP. Rochester? fire and fury—roast Rochester! a rascally rogue!—the devil take Rochester, and his song, too!

CHAS. Bravo! Captain Copp—another broadside, old boy.

ROCH. Why, what the deuce, neighbor—has your powder magazine taken fire? Why, what has Rochester done to you, to occasion such a terrible explosion?

COPP. What 's that to you? What have you to do with my family secrets? Rochester! His very name makes my blood boil—

MARY. My dear uncle, be calm. You promised never to speak on this subject.

ROCH. Why, what connexion can there be between you and Rochester?

COPP. No matter, he has been put to the proof, that 's enough. (*To* MARY.) Don't be uneasy—I 'll say no more about it, my girl. You know me—when I say mum, that 's enough.

CHAS. This affair seems curious—I must have an explanation. (*With an air of authority.*) It is my pleasure—

COPP. Your pleasure, quotha—and who the devil are you? You 're a pleasant blade. (*Sturdily.*) But it 's not my pleasure, messmate, look ye.

CHAS. (*Recollecting himself.*) I mean to say, that I feel a deep interest in your welfare.

COPP (*gruffly*). Thank ye, thank 'e,—but I am not used to such warm friends on such short acquaintance. (*Apart.*) I wonder is it myself, or my niece, this chap has fallen in love with at first sight?

CHAS. (*apart to* ROCHESTER). I am curious to know what charge they have against you.

ROCH. (*apart to* CHARLES). And so am I, and I 'll make this old buccaneer speak plain, before we leave him.

CHAS. You have misunderstood me, friend Copp. I am no defender of Rochester. I know him to be a sad fellow.

COPP. As destitute of feeling as a stockfish.

EDW. He is a great genius, however.

COPP. He is an evil genius, I know.

EDW. He has a very clear head—

COPP. But a very black heart.

ROCH. This Rochester is a sad lightheaded fellow, that 's notorious; but will you have the goodness, my blunt Captain Copp, to mention one heartless act of his?

COPP (*loudly*). Ay, that I will. Is it not a burning shame—

MARY. My dear uncle, you forget your promise.

COPP. Let me alone, girl, let me alone—you 've nothing to fear; I have you under convoy.

ROCH. Out with it, what is his crime?

COPP. Crime! Is it not a burning shame, I say, to disclaim his own niece—to keep from her every stiver of her little fortune, and leave her to pass her days in a tavern, when she has a right to inhabit a palace?

EDW. (*eagerly*). What do I hear?

ROCH. What, and is this young woman the niece? How can that be?

COPP. Simply enough. Her father, Philip Copland, married a sister of Lord Rochester.

ROCH. (*apart*). Philip Copland is indeed the name.

CHAS. This is most singular. And this Philip Copland was your brother?

COPP. Ay, but worth a dozen of me—a steady man, an able officer, an ornament of the regular navy. I was always a wild dog, and never took to learning—

ran away from school—shipped myself on board a privateer. In time I became captain, and returned from my last cruise just in time to receive poor Philip's last breath—his sand was almost run out. "Brother," said he, "I feel that my cruising is over; but there 's my little girl. Take care of her for my sake, and never bother the Rochesters again."—"Brother," said I, "it 's a bargain; tip us your fist on it, and die in peace, like a good Christian." He grasped my hand, and gave it a gentle squeeze. I would have shook his, but it grew cold in mine, and poor Philip was no more!

(*With great feeling.*)

MARY. My dear uncle—(*laying her hand on his shoulder*).

COPP (*rousing himself*). But the girl was left, the girl was left (*embracing her*); and (*taking her arm under his*)—and I 'll keep my word to my poor brother, and take care of *her* as long as I have breath in my body.

CHAS. Well, brother Tom, what do *you* think of all this?

ROCH. It touches me to the soul.

CHAS. And so you took home the child?

MARY. Oh! yes: and my uncle's bounty and kindness have taken care of his poor girl ever since.

COPP. Oh! you should have seen what a little thing it was,—a little chubby-faced thing of four years old, no higher than a handspike. Now she 's a grown girl.

CHAS. And you have given her a good education, it appears?

COPP. And why not? What tho' *I 'm* a dunce, that 's no reason that Mary Copland should be a fool. Her father was a man of parts.

CHAS. And you have given up your voyages for her?

COPP. To be sure. Could I have a child running after me about deck? I sold my ship, and bought this tavern, where I receive none but good fellows, who drink, and smoke, and talk to me of voyages and battles all day long.

CHAS. But ambition might have induced you—

COPP. Ambition! you don't know me; my only ambition is to marry my niece to some honest citizen, and give her a dower of one thousand pounds, with as much more when old Captain Copp takes his long nap.

ROCH. (*apart*). Generous fellow! (*Aloud.*) Let me advise you to apply to the Earl of Rochester.

EDW. Oh! yes, *he* will provide *an honorable match* for your niece.

MARY (*piqued*). Much obliged, Mr. Georgini, but nobody asked your advice.

COPP. Apply to him!—no—no—I 'll have nothing to do with the Rochesters.

CHAS. But why not apply to the king himself?

COPP. Oddsfish! they say he is not much better—he 's a wild devil—a great friend of Rochester—and birds of a feather, you know—

CHAS. (*apart*). Now comes my turn.

ROCH. True enough, Captain Copp; they say he is a rover—rambles about at night—frolics in taverns.

COPP. Well, let him cruise, so he does not cruise into my waters. He 's a desperate rogue among the petticoats, they say—well, I like a merry heart, wherever it beats.—Charley has some good points, and if I could but give him a piece of my mind—

CHAS. What would it be, friend Copp?

COPP. To keep more in port, anchor himself at home, and turn that fellow, Rochester, adrift—there might then be some hopes of him.—But, come, 't is getting late—now, friends, it 's time to turn out, and turn in—these are late hours for the Grand Admiral—come, a parting cup. (*To* MARY.) See that the fires are out, my girl, and all hands ready for bed.

MARY. I will, but no more drinking, uncle.

COPP. Well, well—no more—only one parting cup.

MARY. Only one—recollect, you have promised—no more. (*Exit* MARY.)

COPP. Only this last drop.—Come, my lads, this farewell cup, and then you must push your boats.

ROCH. Now to execute my plan. (*Making signs that the king will pay.*) Hist, Captain Copp!

(*Whispers while* CHARLES *is drinking.*)

COPP. Ay, ay, all right.

ROCH. (*low to* EDWARD). Follow me quietly—I 've something to say to you. (*Apart, and chuckling as he goes out.*) Now, brother Jack, I think you 'll soon find yourself among the breakers!

(*Exit, followed by* EDWARD.)

COPP. Now, messmate, let 's square accounts,—(*handing a paper*) here 's a note of your expenses—you see I charge nothing for the last two bottles—nor for the tea-table—that 's my treat.

CHAS. (*looking over the paper*). Um! wine—punch—wine—punch—total five pounds ten—a mere trifle!

COPP. Do you call that a trifle?—Gad, messmate, you must have made good prizes in your last cruise—or you 've high wages, mayhap.

CHAS. (*laughing*). Ay, ay, I 'm pretty well paid—Here, Tom Taffrel, pay Copp's bill, and let 's be off.—(*Looking round.*) Hey—where is he?

COPP. Oh! he went off in a great hurry—he said he had to be aboard ship, but that you would pay the bill.

CHAS. With all my heart. (*Apart.*) It 's odd that he should leave me alone—my raillery has galled him.—Poor Rochester, (*laughing,*) how ill some people take a joke! (*feeling in his pockets*). Five pounds ten, you say?

COPP. Just so—five pounds ten.

CHAS. (*searching in all his pockets*). Well! this is the oddest thing—I am certain I had my purse.

COPP. (*apart*). My neighbour seems rather in a quandary.

CHAS. (*feeling more eagerly*). Some one has picked my pocket.

COPP. Avast there, friend—none but honest people frequent the Grand Admiral. —(*Apart.*) I begin to suspect this spark, who spends so freely, is without a stiver in his pocket.

CHAS. All I know, is, that one of these honest people must have taken my purse.

COPP. Come, come, messmate—I am too old a cruiser to be taken in by so shallow a manœuvre—I understand all this—your companion makes sail—you pretend to have been robbed—it 's all a cursed privateering trick—clear as day.

CHAS. Friend Copp—if you will wait till to-morrow, I 'll pay you double the sum.

COPP. Double the sum!!—thunder and lightning! what do you take me for?—Look ye, neighbour, to an honest tar in distress, my house and purse are open—to a jolly tar who wants a caper, and has no coin at hand, drink to-day and pay to-morrow is the word—but to a sharking land lubber, that hoists the colours of a gallant cruiser, to play off the tricks of a pirate, old Copp will show him his match any day.

CHAS. A land lubber?

COPP. Ay, a land lubber.—D 'ye think I can't see through you, and your shallow sailor phrases.—Who the devil are you?—none of the captains know you—what ship do you belong to?

CHAS. What ship? why, to—to—(*apart*) what the deuce shall I say?

COPP. A pretty sailor, truly—not know the name of his ship—a downright swindler—a barefaced impudent swindler—comes into my house, kicks up a bobbery, puts every thing in an uproar—treats all the guests—touzles my niece—and then wants to make off without paying.

CHAS. (*apart*). How shall I get out of this cursed scrape?—Oh, happy thought, my watch—(*aloud*) hearkee, Captain Copp—if I have n't money, may be this will do as well—what say you to my watch as pledge?

COPP (*taking the watch*). Let me see it—um—large diamonds. (*Shaking his head.*)

CHAS. (*gayly*). Well—that 's worth your five pounds ten—hey?

COPP. Um—I don't know that:—if the diamonds are *false*, it is not worth so much—if *real*, none but a great lord could own it—(*turning quick to him*),—how did you come by this watch?

CHAS. It 's my own.

COPP. Your own! A common sailor own a watch set with large diamonds! I 'll tell you what, messmate, it 's my opinion as how you stole this watch.

CHAS. Stole it? Give back my watch, fellow, or I 'll—

COPP. Softly, my lad, keep cool, or I 'll have you laid by the heels in a twinkling.

CHAS. (*apart*). What a bull-dog! Well, sir, what do you intend to do?

COPP. Lock you up here for the present, and have you lodged in limbo immediately.

CHAS. Will you not listen to reason?

COPP (*going*). Yes, through the key-hole! (*From the door.*) You shall have news of me presently, my fine fellow. (*Exit.*)

CHAS. Was ever monarch in such a predicament?—a prisoner in a tavern—to be presently dragged through the streets as a culprit—and to-morrow sung in lampoons, and stuck up in caricatures all through the city—What is to be done? This Copp seems a man of probity, suppose I avow myself to him? Um! will he credit me, and will he keep the matter secret? This sturdy veteran may be an old cruiser under the Commonwealth: if so, what have I not to apprehend? Alone—unarmed, at midnight (*shaking his head*). Charles! Charles! wilt thou never learn wisdom? Yes; let me but get out of *this* scrape, and I renounce these rambling humours for ever. (*A noise of unlocking the door.*) Hark! some one comes.

(*Enter* EDWARD *and* MARY. *Several Servants quaintly dressed, and armed, appear at the door.*)

MARY. Place yourselves outside and guard the passages.

CHAS. They are placing sentinels.

EDW. (*apart*). The earl has given me my lesson: no flinching.

MARY. I am afraid to go near him. I wish my uncle had not set us this task.—(MARY *is armed with an old cutlass,* EDWARD *with a long rusty pistol or carbine.*)

EDW. Be not afraid, I am here to defend you.

CHAS. (*advancing*). What! my pretty Mary in arms?

MARY. Ah, don't come near me! What a ferocious ruffian it is!

CHAS. (*gallantly*). Was that delicate hand made to grasp so rude a weapon?

EDW. (*low to* MARY). Don't let him touch your hand, or you are lost.

MARY (*drawing back*). He does not look so very ferocious, neither. Fie, sir, fie! what, steal the jewels of the crown?

CHAS. Is it, then, known already?

MARY. Yes, indeed, all is known. My uncle took the watch to our neighbour, the jeweller, who knew it instantly. It belongs to his royal majesty himself.

CHAS. Confusion!

EDW. (*low to* MARY). You hear he confesses.—(*Aloud.*) Well, Captain Copp will be here presently with the magistrate. Here will be a fine piece of work. All Wapping is already in an uproar.

CHAS. (*eagerly*). My friends, it is of the highest importance that I should escape before they come.

MARY. I have not a doubt of it. Oh! you culprit!

CHAS. (*with insinuation*). And would Mary, the pretty Mary, see me dragged to prison? I won't believe it. That sweet face bespeaks a gentle heart.

MARY. Poor creature! I can't but pity him.

CHAS. (*with gallantry*). I never saw a pretty woman yet, that would not help a poor fellow in distress—(*apart*) *She* yields. But I need other bribes for my gentleman—I have it—my ring. (*Aloud.*) Assist me to escape, and take this ring as a pledge of what I will do. It is of great value.

MARY. What a beautiful diamond ring! How it sparkles! Don't touch it, Georgini, it 's a stolen ring.

EDW. And for that very reason I take it. We can return both together to the right owner.

MARY (*apart to* EDWARD). He certainly has something genteel in his air. This unfortunate man may, perhaps, belong to decent people.

CHAS. I do indeed; my family is considered very respectable. Ah, bless that sweet face! I knew a hard heart could not belong to it.

EDW. (*apart*). Egad, I must get him off, or he 'll win his pretty jailor, culprit as she thinks him.

MARY (*taking* EDWARD *apart*). How penitent he seems, and his countenance is rather amiable too! What will they do with him?

EDW. (*carelessly*). Hum—why, they 'll hang him, of course.

MARY. Heavens! will they touch his life? oh, horrible! and so good looking a man! I would not have his death upon my mind for the whole world (*earnestly*).

CHAS. (*Who has been traversing the apartment uneasily, and eyeing them occasionally.*) Will this consultation never end! I dread the arrival of the officers.

MARY (*aloud*). Let us assist him to escape!

CHAS. Thanks, my generous girl: there 's nothing like a petticoat in time of trouble.

EDW. How shall we get him off? The door is guarded.

CHAS. Ay, but the window.

EDW. (*eagerly*). No, not the window, you may hurt yourself.

CHAS. (*surprised*). You are very considerate, my friend.

MARY. Oh! it is not very high, and opens into a lane that leads to the river.

CHAS. (*opening the window*). Psha! it 's nothing; with your assistance, I shall be on the ground in an instant.

MARY. It is, perhaps, very wrong in me to let you escape; but I beg you to listen to a word of advice.

CHAS. Oh, yes, I hear you.

MARY. It is on condition that you change your course of life.

CHAS. Yes, yes, I 'll change it, I warrant you.

MARY. And not drink, nor rove about this way at night.
CHAS. Not for the world.
MARY. And steal no more, for it will bring you to a shameful end.
CHAS. (*getting out of the window, assisted by* MARY). An excellent sermon! But I must *steal*—one kiss to impress it on my memory!
EDW. Did he steal a kiss, Mary?
MARY. Oh, yes, he did indeed.
EDW. Stop thief! stop thief!
CHAS. (*descending outside*). Tell uncle Copp to put it in the bill!
EDW. I hear them coming. (*Looks out of the window.*) He 's safe down—he 's off —(*apart*)—now I 'm easy.
MARY. But what shall we say to my uncle?
EDW. I 'll manage that; only say as I say, and fear nothing. (COPP *heard outside the door.*)
COPP. This way—this way.
EDW. Stop thief! stop thief! (*To* MARY.) Cry out as I do.
MARY (*feebly*). Stop the thief! stop the thief! I can't.

(*Enter* COPP, *with a double-barrelled gun, followed by two Servants.*)

COPP. Hollo—what the devil 's to pay here?
EDW. The culprit has jumped out of the window.
MARY. Oh, yes, out of the window!
COPP. Thunder and lightning! why did n't you stop him?
EDW. *I* was too far off. The young lady attempted, but he kissed her, and leaped out like a greyhound.
COPP. Fire and furies!—kissed her?
MARY. Yes, uncle, but he did n't hurt me.
EDW. And he said you might put it in the bill.
COPP. Guns and blunderbusses! this is running up an account with a vengeance (*looking out of the window*). I see something in the offing; we may overhaul him yet. Come along, all hands to the chase! Get to your room, Mary, there 's no knowing what might happen if this pirate should fall foul of you again. Come along—away with you all—divide at the street door—scour the three passages—I 'll show him what it is to come in the way of an old cruiser!—(*Bustle*—COPP *fires off his gun out of the window after* CHARLES. *Curtain falls.*)

END OF ACT SECOND.

ACT THIRD.

SCENE. *The Royal Palace.*

(*Enter* EDWARD, *in his habit, as a Page.*)

EDW. I 've had a hard scramble of it, to get here, and dress in time. The king must arrive presently, though my light heels have given me a good start of him. Hark! a noise in the king's private staircase—Softly, then, softly, (*seats himself in an arm-chair at the door of the king's chamber, and pretends to sleep*).

(*Enter* CHARLES, *his dress in disorder.*)

CHAS. Confound the city! what a journey it is!
EDW. (*aside*). Especially to foot passengers.
CHAS. I began to think I should never find the palace. (*Sitting down.*) Phew! I shall not forget this night in a hurry. Forced to escape like a thief,—to risk my neck from a window,—hunted about the streets by that old buccaneer and his crew! Egad! I fancy I can hear old Copp's voice, even now, like a huntsman giving the view-halloo, as I doubled about the mazes of Wapping.
EDW. (*Aside, and suppressing a laugh.*) A royal hunt, truly!
CHAS. Well, thank fortune, I am safe home at last, and seen by nobody but my confidential valet.
EDW. (*Aside.*) And the most discreet of pages.
CHAS. (*Seeing* EDWARD.) So, the page already in waiting. Deuce take him! he is exactly in the door-way of my chamber. So, so! Lady Clara coming! Oh, then, all 's over!

(*Enter* LADY CLARA, *goes to* EDWARD.)

LADY C. What! asleep at this hour, Edward?
EDW. I beg your pardon, my lady—I am waiting his majesty's rising.
LADY C. You will come, and let the queen know when the king is visible (*perceives* CHARLES). Heavens! your majesty in this dress?
CHAS. (*affecting an unembarrassed air*). What! it amuses you, ha! ha! My regular morning dress, I assure you. I have taken a whim for gardening lately, and, every morning, by day-light, I am on the terrace, planting, transplanting, and

training. Oh! you should see how busy I am, particularly among the roses.

LADY C. I have no doubt your majesty has an eye for every fresh one that blows.—But, how quiet you have been in these pursuits!

CHAS. One does not want all the world to know of one's caprices. But what has procured me the pleasure of seeing your ladyship so early?

LADY C. The queen, sire, knowing how deeply you were immersed in affairs of state, last night, sent me to enquire how your majesty had slept.

CHAS. Very restless—very restless—I tumbled and tossed about sadly.

LADY C. Ah! why does not your majesty take more care of yourself? You devote yourself too much to your people. This night-work will be too much for you.

CHAS. Why, yes, if it were often as severe as last night.

LADY C. Indeed, your majesty must give up these midnight labours to your ministers.

CHAS. (*apart*). To my ministers, ha! ha! Egad! I should like to see old Clarendon and Ormond hob or nobbing with uncle Copp, struggling for kisses with Mary, and scouring the lanes of Wapping at full speed.—(*aloud*). Well, my Lady Clara, have you anything further to communicate?

LADY C. Might I presume, I have a favour to request of your majesty. An author, in whose cause I take a warm interest, has offended a person high in power, and is threatened with a prosecution.

CHAS. The blockhead! let him write against me only, and they'll never trouble him.

LADY C. His pardon depends upon your majesty—would you but deign to sign it!

CHAS. (*Apart.*) Sinner that I am, it would but ill become me to be severe.—(*Aloud.*) Lady Clara, you look amazingly well this morning—I can refuse you nothing.—(*Signs the paper.*) And now, to make my toilette—(*aside*)—Safe at last! she suspects nothing.

LADY C. (*smiling*). He thinks he has deceived me.—Oh, these men, these men! how they will impose upon us easy, simple, *knowing* women!

(*Exeunt* LADY CLARA *and* EDWARD.)

(*Enter* COPP *and* MARY.)

COPP. Oddsfish! I never knew such a piece of work to get into a house before. If that good-looking gentlewoman had not seen us from the window, and taken our part, hang me, if I don't think they would have turn'd us adrift.

MARY. What beautiful rooms!

COPP. Gingerbread finery! I would not change the bar-room of the Grand Admiral for the best of them. But what a bother to give a watch back to the right owner! Why, there's no finding the king in his own house.—Now, for my part, I always stand on the threshold, and if any one comes, there's my hand.—Tip us your bone, says I, and make yourself welcome.—That's what I call acting like a king of good fellows.

MARY. Oh, uncle, I have always heard say, that the king is very kind and affable; and, I dare say, when you hand him back his watch, he will behave with generosity.

COPP. Generosity! Why, dost think, girl, I'd take a reward? No, no!—They say Charley's not overstocked with the shiners.—I want none of them. To be sure, he may do the civil thing—he may ask us to stay, and take pot-luck, perhaps.

MARY. Pot-luck, uncle!

COPP. Ay, in a friendly way, d'ye see? And I don't care if I did, if it were only to see how royalty messed. But, where the deuce is the king to be found? Oh! yonder is a fine gimcrack young gentleman, who, perhaps, can tell us—I'll hail him. Yo-ho! messmate!

(*Exit, hallooing after* EDWARD.)

MARY. What a beautiful place this is! But, without content, grandeur is not to be envied. The humble and the good, may be as happy in a cottage as a palace.

Recitative—MARY.

Thrice beautiful! Alas! that here
Should ever come a frown or tear;
But not beneath the gilded dome
Hath happiness its only home.

Not in the pictured halls,
Not amid marble walls
Will young Love dwell.

Love's home's the heart alone,
That heart, too, all his own,
Else, Love, farewell!

(*Enter* COPP, *pulling in* EDWARD, *who tries to hide his face.*)

COPP. Come along, young man—don't be so bashful—you need n't mind us.

EDW. (*aside*). Let me put on a steady

face—(*aloud*)—You come to speak to his majesty?

MARY. Yes, Sir, we come—(*apart*)—Dear uncle, those features—how my heart beats!—Did you ever see such a resemblance, uncle?

COPP (*looking at* EDWARD). Oddsfish! he is like, indeed!—But it can't be him!

MARY. I like Mr. Georgini's face better—it is more animated.

COPP. Don't talk to me of that Georgini. Didst not tell me, he took a ring of that land-pirate?—and, then, to disappear so suddenly.—Fire and fury! if I catch him—

EDW. No swearing in the king's palace.

COPP. Well, well, true; no swearing. But, thunder and lightning! what keeps the king so long?

EDW. I think I hear him. Step into that apartment—a lady will introduce you.

COPP. Ah! the same that I saw at the window;—very well. But, I say, Mister, don't keep me waiting. Just hint to the king, that I've no time to lose. Tell him, there's a launch at Wapping to-day —busy times at the Grand Admiral.

MARY. Let us retire, uncle. I dare say we shall be sent for in good time.

COPP. Very well, very well. But, do think of the Grand Admiral—all aback for want of me. If the king loses his watch again, the devil take me—Oh! I forgot—I must n't swear in the king's palace. (*Exeunt* COPP *and* MARY.)

EDW. This will be a whimsical court presentation, truly! His majesty's perplexities are not yet over.

(*Enter* CHARLES *in his riding dress.*)

CHAS. Has Rochester appeared?

EDW. Not yet, Sire.

CHAS. (*apart*). What could be his motive for the cruel trick he played me?

EDW. Your majesty asked for Lord Rochester; here he comes with Lady Clara.

CHAS. Pish! Lady Clara is one too many here. I shall not be able to explain myself before her. No matter—he shall not escape me.

(*Enter* ROCHESTER *and* LADY CLARA.)

ROCH. May I venture to ask, if your majesty has passed a comfortable night?

CHAS. Indifferent, my lord—(*low, to him*)—Traitor!

LADY C. (*smiling*). I understood his lordship had assisted your majesty in your labours.

ROCH. Not throughout, my lady. An accident obliged me to leave his majesty in rather a moment of perplexity.

CHAS. (*angrily*). Yes, his lordship left the whole weight of—business—upon my shoulders.

ROCH. I doubt not your majesty got through with your usual address.

CHAS. (*apart*). Perfidious varlet! (*Aloud.*) My lord, you will please to present yourself in my study at two o'clock. I have something particular to say to you.

ROCH. Deign to dispense with my attendance, sire. I quit London in a few moments for my estate, as I mentioned yesterday. I am a great offender.—It is time to exile myself from court, and turn hermit.

CHAS. (*harshly*). I approve the project; but will take the liberty of choosing your hermitage myself.

ROCH. (*low to* LADY CLARA). The king is furious against me.

LADY C. Courage, my lord—all will end well.

COPP (*shouting outside*). What the devil is the meaning of this? Am I to be kept here all day?

CHAS. What uproar is that?

LADY C. Oh! two persons, whom I met this morning, seeking to speak with his majesty, on some personal concern. As I know him to be so accessible to the people, I undertook to present them.

CHAS. Just now it is impossible.

LADY C. I am very sorry, especially on the young girl's account.

CHAS. A young girl, did you say?

LADY C. Beautiful as an angel!

CHAS. Oh! since you take such interest in her, Lady Clara—(*to* EDWARD,)—Show them in.

(*Enter* COPP *and* MARY.)

EDW. (*preceding them*). Come in—his majesty consents to hear you.

COPP. I'm taken all aback—my courage begins to fail me.

MARY. What have you to fear, my dear uncle?

(*Keeps her eyes modestly cast down.*)

COPP. Fear! it is n't fear, look ye. But, somehow, I never fell in with a king before in all my cruisings.

CHAS. (*Apart.*) Copp and his niece! here's a pretty rencontre.

(*Summoning up dignity.*)

COPP. Well, I suppose I must begin.—Oddsfish! I had it all settled in my head, and now, the deuce a word can I muster up.

MARY. Come, uncle, courage! I never saw you so cast down before.

COPP. Well, then, what I have to say is this—Mr. King.—(*Low.*) Hey, Mary, what is it I had to say?

CHAS. What is your name, my good friend?

COPP. Copp, at your service; that is to say, Coppland, or Captain Copp, as they call me. And here's Mary, my niece, who, though I say it, is one of the best girls—

(*While talking, he looks down and fumbles with his cap.*)

MARY. But, that's not the point, uncle.

COPP. Eh! true, very true, always keep to the point, like a good helmsman. First and foremost, then, you must know, my lord—when I say my lord, I mean your majesty.

CHAS. (*Apart.*) Egad, he's as much puzzled as I was, to give an account of myself.

COPP. (*Still looking down.*) In finis—primo to begin—you must know, then, that I command, that is to say, I keep the Grand Admiral, as honest a tavern as your majesty would wish to set your foot in—none but good company ever frequent it, excepting when a rogue or so drops in, in disguise—last night, for instance, a couple of gallows knaves, saving your majesty's presence—Ah! if I could only lay eyes on them again—I should know 'em, wherever I saw 'em—one in particular had a confounded hanging look—a man about the height of—(*Eyeing* ROCHESTER, *stops short.*) Mary! Mary! if there is n't one of the very rogues!

MARY. My dear uncle, hush, for heaven's sake! (*Apart.*) That wine is still in his head.

CHAS. (*Apart.*) Rochester's face seems to puzzle him.

COPP. I'll say no more; for the more I look—(*Low to Mary.*) hang me, if it is n't himself.

MARY. Hush, I entreat you—I will speak for you—(*Takes his place, her eyes still modestly cast down.*) My uncle has thought it his duty to inform your majesty, that two strangers came to his house last night, and after calling for a great deal of wine, were unable to pay, and went off, leaving a valuable watch in pledge, which has proved to belong to your majesty. (ROCHESTER *and* LADY CLARA *in bye play express great delight at the manner of* MARY.)

COPP. (*Apart, rubbing his hands.*) Oh! bless her! she talks like a book.

MARY. My uncle being an honest man, has brought the watch to your majesty.

COPP. Yes, by St. George, and here it is. The sharpers, to be sure, have run off with five pounds ten of my money, but that's neither here nor there—I don't say that, because I expect you to pay it, you know.—In short, without more palaver, (*Crossing, and giving it.*) here's the watch—(*Glancing at the King, stops short, and gives a long whistle.*) whew! (*Treads softly back.*)—(*Low to* MARY.) Smite my timbers! if it be n't the other rogue!

MARY. What ails you, uncle? surely, you are losing your senses to speak thus of his majesty!

COPP. (*Low to her.*) Majesty, or no majesty, I'll put my hand in the fire on 't he's the other.

CHAS. The watch is certainly mine.

LADY C. Your majesty's?

(*Smiling significantly at* ROCHESTER.)

ROCH. (*Affecting astonishment.*) Your majesty's watch?

[CHAS. Even so; and I might have lost it, but for this man's honesty. I shall be more on my guard in future.

(*Looking sternly at* ROCHESTER.)

MARY. (*Looking at* CHARLES *and* ROCHESTER.) The voice and the face are astonishingly alike. But it is impossible.]

COPP (*Rapping his forehead.*) I have it—I see how it is.—(*Low to* MARY.) We've made a pretty kettle of fish of it. The king, you know, is said to cruise under false colours.

MARY. Mercy on me! what will become of us?

COPP. (*To* MARY.) Let me alone—it's one of the king's mad frolics—but never you mind—I'll get *you* off—(*Aloud.*) Your majesty will not be angry with my little fool of a niece. The two strangers might be very worthy people—many a man has a gallows look, and is an honest fellow for all that.—The truth is, they were a brace of merry wags.—Besides, if I had known for certain, I would n't for the world—ha! ha!—because, d'ye see—honour bright—mum! (*Turning to*

MARY.) Come, I think I've got you pretty well out of the scrape, hey?

CHAS. Captain Copp, I am aware of all that passed at your house.

COPP. Ah! your majesty knows, that he who cracks a joke must not complain if he should chance to pinch his fingers.

CHAS. True, Captain. But was there not question of one Rochester?

COPP. Why, craving your majesty's pardon, I did let slip some hard truths about him.

ROCH. And do you know him of whom you spoke so bluntly?

COPP. Not I, thank heaven! But I only said, what everybody says—and what everybody says, you know, must be true.

CHAS. Spoken like an oracle—and did not you say, that this pretty lass was his niece?

COPP. Ay, as to that matter, I'll stick to that, proof in hand. Make a reverence, Mary, and no thanks to Rochester for the relationship.

CHAS. I will take care that he shall make a suitable provision for his niece, or provide her an honourable husband.

ROCH. I can assure your majesty, you only anticipated his intentions.

COPP. Avast there!—I don't give up my girl.

ROCH. But you will choose a match suited to her noble family.

COPP. I'll choose for her an honest man; but no ranticumscout companion to suit that Earl of Rochester you talk of.—(*Chuckling and winking.*) To tell the truth between friends, and all in confidence, I had a match in my eye, a young music master.—Nay, don't blush, girl—I know there was a sneaking kindness in the case.

CHAS. I oppose that match. That young man received a ring last night, but has not had the honesty, like Captain Copp, to seek the owner.

(MARY *involuntarily springs forward to defend* EDWARD *against the charge, which* LADY CLARA *and* ROCHESTER *observe and smile at.*)

EDW. (*Advancing.*) He only waited a suitable moment to return it to your majesty. (*Kneels and presents it.*)

CHAS. How! Edward!—The resemblance is no longer a wonder.

COPP. What, little crotchet and quaver! Aha! ha! ha! there's witchcraft in all this.

MARY. Oh, heavens! Georgini a gentleman! But my heart knew it.

CHAS. It is in vain, Lady Clara, to attempt concealment. Behold the heroes of the adventure.

LADY C. Pardon me, sire, I knew it all along—I was in the plot.

CHAS. How?

LADY C. Her majesty, the queen, was at the head of it. If the earl be guilty, it is we who induced him, and should undergo the punishment.

CHAS. I understand the whole. But the treachery of this earl I cannot forgive. He shall not obtain my pardon.

LADY C. (*Producing a paper.*) It is already obtained. Your majesty, ever merciful, has signed it.

CHAS. What! he, too, is the author for whom you have interested yourself.—Ha! ha! ha! fairly taken in at all points. Rochester, thou hast conquered.

(ROCHESTER *kneels.*)

COPP. (*Passionately.*) Thunder and lightning! this man Rochester!—come along, girl, come along!

MARY. What, can he be that hard-hearted man? He does not look so cruel, uncle.

COPP. (*Taking her under his arm.*) Come along, girl, come along.

ROCH. One moment, Captain Copp. (COPP *stops, and looks fiercely at him.*) It is true, I am Rochester—a sad fellow, no doubt, since all the world says so—but there is one grievous sin which I will not take to my conscience, for it is against beauty. I am not the Rochester who disclaimed this lovely girl—he was my predecessor, and is dead.

COPP. (*Sternly.*) Dead!—gone to his long reckoning.—(*Pauses.*) May Heaven deal kindlier with him than he did with this orphan child!

MARY. That's my own uncle!

CHAS. I have pardoned you, Rochester; but my eyes are opened to the follies which I have too frequently partaken. From this night I abjure them.

ROCH. And I, my liege, (*Bowing to* LADY CLARA) will mortify myself with matrimony, and hope to reform into a very rational and submissive husband. (*Taking* LADY CLARA'S *hand.*)

CHAS. There yet remains a party to be disposed of. What say you, Captain Copp?—What say you, my Lord of Rochester? Must we not find a husband for our niece?

COPP. Fair and softly, your majesty—

craving your majesty's pardon, I can't give up my right over my little girl. This lord is an uncle—I can't gainsay it; but he 's a new-found uncle.—I have bred her, and fed her, and been her uncle all her life, have n't I, Mary?

MARY. Oh, sir, you have been a father to me!

COPP. My good little girl—my darling girl. —Take thee away from thy own uncle? Pshaw! Ha! ha! I shall grow silly and soft again! Ha! ha!

CHAS. You are right, captain—you alone ought to dispose of her. But I hope to propose a match that shall please all parties.—What think you of my page—the music-master, who brought back the ring? I shall present him with a commission in my own regiment.

EDW. Oh! so much goodness!

COPP. Your majesty has fathomed my own wishes.

ROCH. And mine.

EDW. And mine.

(*Approaching* MARY.)

MARY. And—(*Extending her hand.*)—and mine.

COPP. So, here we are, all safe in port, after last night's squall. Oddsfish! I feel so merry!—my girl 's provided for—I have nothing now to care for—I 'll keep open house at the Grand Admiral—I 'll set all my liquor a-tap—I 'll drown all Wapping in wine and strong beer—I 'll have an illumination—I 'll make a bonfire of the Grand Admiral—I 'll give up business for the rest of my life—I 'll sing "In the time of the Rump"—

(MARY *runs down and stops him.*)

CHAS. Captain Copp, I am your debtor—five pounds ten?—accept this watch as a mark of my esteem. The ring I reserve for the lovely Mary. (*Putting it on her finger.*) And now, (*Beckoning all the characters to the front with an air of mystery.*) let me particularly enjoin on all present, the most profound secresy in regard to our whimsical adventures at Wapping.

COPP. (*Clapping his finger to his lips.*) Honour bright!—Mum!

POCAHONTAS

OR

THE SETTLERS OF VIRGINIA

BY

George Washington Parke Custis

POCAHONTAS

Pocahontas or the Settlers of Virginia represents the plays on Indian themes and also the drama written in the South. The first Indian play to be written by an American was the tragedy of *Ponteach or The Savages of America,* by Major Robert Rogers (1766). This was not acted. There were many Indian dramas in the first half of the nineteenth century—the earliest by an American to be performed being Barker's *Indian Princess,* (1808). It began the series of the Pocahontas plays, the theme being used by Custis in 1830 in the play now reprinted, by the Englishman, Robert Dale Owen, in his *Pocahontas,* acted February 8, 1838, at the Park Theatre, New York, in which Charlotte Cushman played "Rolfe," and by Mrs. Charlotte Barnes Conner in her *Forest Princess,* played in Philadelphia, February 16, 1848. Finally the motive ran to satire in John Brougham's burlesque of *Pocahontas or the Gentle Savage,* produced at Wallack's Theatre, New York, on December 24, 1855. Custis's drama is especially significant in a comparative study of the Pocahontas plays. Its author is deserving of recognition, if for nothing else, for his self-restraint in not endowing Pocahontas with the ability to speak blank verse. But his dramatic instinct showed itself most definitely in his handling of the theme. The trouble with the Pocahontas plays in general is that the most dramatic incident, the saving of Smith's life, comes too early in the play. The other playwrights in their endeavor to follow history have sacrificed dramatic effectiveness. Custis, with cheerful courage, took liberties with actual facts in order to put the striking event in the last Act.

Perhaps the most significant of the Indian plays in general was *Metamora or the Last of the Wampanoags,* written for Edwin Forrest by John A. Stone, and produced at the Park Theatre, New York, December 15, 1829. Forrest played in this for many years. *Metamora* exists in two manuscripts, one with Act IV missing, at the Utah University, and one containing the part of Metamora only, at the Forrest Home, Philadelphia. These were edited by E. H. Page, for *America's Lost Plays,* Vol. XIV (Princeton, 1941). Besides the Pocahontas series, the most important Indian play that has survived seems to have been Dr. Bird's *Oralloossa* (1832), laid in Peru. Very few of the forty Indian plays of which record has been made, have come down to us. They were popular between 1830 and 1850, but their picture of the Indian was not a true one.

George Washington Parke Custis was born at Mount Airy, Maryland, April

30, 1781. He was the son of John Parke Custis, the stepson of Washington, whose early death, of camp fever incurred in the Yorktown campaign, brought his two younger children under the direct charge of President and Mrs. Washington at Mount Vernon. Here young Custis grew up and here he lived till Mrs. Washington's death, when he built his house at Arlington, opposite Washington City. He was appointed a cornet of horse in the army of the United States in 1799 but did not see active service at that time, although he afterwards became a volunteer during the War of 1812. After his marriage to Mary Lee Fitzhugh in 1804 he lived on his large estate and devoted himself to the care of it. He was a writer of prose and verse and a speaker of ability, but with the instincts of the Southern landed proprietor he published comparatively little. After the visit of Lafayette to this country in 1824, he wrote his entertaining *Conversations with Lafayette,* and in 1826 he began in the *United States Gazette* his recollections of the private life of Washington which were continued in *The National Intelligencer* and which were published by his daughter in 1861. He died October 10, 1857.

His first play, *The Indian Prophecy,* was performed in Philadelphia at the Chestnut Street Theatre, July 4, 1827. According to the title page of the printed play, it was performed also in Baltimore and Washington. The same authority describes it as "A National Drama in two Acts founded upon a most interesting and romantic occurrence in the life of General Washington." In 1770, while on a surveying expedition to the Kanawha region in Virginia, Washington was visited by an Indian chief who told him that he had been the leader of the Indians at Braddock's defeat and that although their best marksmen had levelled their pieces at Washington they had been prevented from killing him by a higher power. The chief went on to prophesy that Washington would never die in battle but would live to be the chief and founder of a mighty empire. This incident, which is given in Custis's *Recollections,* became the climax of the play which is otherwise but a series of conversations between Woodford, a captain of rangers, Maiona, his wife, and their Indian protegée, Manetta, daughter of the chief Menawa, who delivers the prophecy. The play was published in Georgetown in 1828 as "By the author of the Recollections."

Pocahontas or the Settlers of Virginia, was played first at the Walnut Street Theatre, Philadelphia, January 16, 1830, and was performed for twelve nights, among them Washington's Birthday. Elaborate preparations were made for the production of the play, the theatre being closed from January 11th to January 16th. Durang states that it was received with great applause. On December 28, 1830, John Barnes produced it for his benefit at the Park Theatre, New York, playing "Hugo." It is probable, therefore, that *The Forest Princess,* written afterward by his daughter, Charlotte Barnes Conner, was inspired by

Custis's play, since she undoubtedly witnessed the performance, in which her mother took the part of "Pocahontas." The play was published in Philadelphia in 1830. That it was played again seems certain, for the Clothier Collection includes a prompt copy belonging to John Sefton, the manager of Niblo's Theatre, in New York, and of the Walnut Street Theatre, Philadelphia, under E. A. Marshall. In this copy the parts of "Hugo," "Mowbray," "Namoutac" and "Mantea" are omitted and the play is much cut.

On May 16, 1830, Custis's play of *The Railroad,* a national drama, was performed at the Walnut Street Theatre, Philadelphia. Durang, in his account, tells us that a locomotive steam carriage was introduced in the last act, which whistled as it went out! It moved off the stage to the music of the "Carrolton March," composed for the occasion by Mr. Clifton of Baltimore.

At the request of the manager of the Baltimore Theatre, Custis wrote a play called *North Point or Baltimore Defended,* in celebration of the battle of North Point, on whose anniversary, September 12, 1833, it was produced. It was completed according to the author in nine hours and was "a two-act piece with two songs and a finale." His *Eighth of January* was played January 8, 1834, at the Park Theatre, New York. He seems also to have written an Indian play, *The Pawnee Chief,* but accurate information concerning this is wanting. An account of Custis is given in *Recollections and Private Memoirs of Washington, by his Adopted Son, George Washington Parke Custis, with a Memoir of the Author by his Daughter* [Mary Custis Lee], Philadelphia, 1861. The original source of *Pocahontas* was Captain John Smith's *Generall Historie of Virginia, New England and the Summer Isles* (1624), as Smith's earlier *True Relation* (1608) does not mention the salvation of Smith by Pocahontas. For accounts of the productions of the plays, see Charles Durang, *History of the Philadelphia Stage,* Series 2, Chapters 51 and 53, and Joseph N. Ireland, *Records of the New York Stage,* Vol. I, p. 644 and Vol. II. p. 77.

POCAHONTAS;

OR,

THE SETTLERS OF VIRGINIA,

A NATIONAL DRAMA,

IN THREE ACTS.

Performed at the Walnut Street Theatre, Philadelphia, twelve nights, with great success.

WRITTEN BY

GEORGE WASHINGTON CUSTIS, ESQ.

Of Arlington House, Author of the Rail Road, Pawnee Chief, &c. &c.

PHILADELPHIA EDITION.
C. ALEXANDER, PR.
:::::::
1830

PREFACE

The national story upon which the play of POCAHONTAS is founded, was a tempting one for a dramatist, and more could not have been made of it than has been done in the present instance. Mr. WASHINGTON CUSTIS, in this production, has fully proved his capability as an author. The plot keeps up a lively interest; its gradual development, judging from the effect the piece produces on representation, is at once natural, and decidedly dramatic; and, no doubt, when supported by good actors, it will always be received with the same success that characterized its representation at the Walnut Street Theatre. This drama was peculiarly fortunate in being produced by that celebrated melodramatic director, the late Mr. S. Chapman. Had the piece been his own he could not have displayed a greater desire to render it effective; and his personation of Captain Smith will long be the theme of unqualified praise. The part of Matacoran was excellently played by Mr. CLARKE; Mr. BALL, a very young actor, showed considerable promise in Master Rolfe, and Messrs. PORTER and GREENE, in their respective parts of Powhatan and Hugo, were very successful; the heroine, Pocahontas, found an able representative in Mrs. GREENE. Indeed, few pieces have been more successful than this drama, and Mr. WASHINGTON CUSTIS has done the stage considerable service, by showing the resources for dramatic materials in the annals of American history; and we anticipate with pleasure his future productions, whether historical or otherwise.

DRAMATIS PERSONAE

ENGLISH

Captain Smith	Mr. S. Chapman
Lieutenant Percy	Mr. Allen
Master Rolfe	Mr. Ball
Master West	Mr. Thompson
Barclay	Mr. Waldegrave
Hugo De Redmond	Mr. Greene
Mowbray	Mr. Bloom

INDIANS

Powhatan	Mr. Porter
Matacoran	Mr. Clarke
Selictaz	Mr. James
Namoutac	Mr. Garson
Princess Pocahontas	Mrs. Greene
Omaya	Mrs. Hathwell
Mantea	Mrs. Slater

POCAHONTAS

ACT FIRST.

SCENE 1. *The banks of James' River. View of the river—two ships and a sloop at anchor in the distance—on one side of the stage a hut—composed of mats and reeds; on the other rocks and cliffs. Indians on the cliffs gazing at the shipping, and making signs to each other.*

(*Enter* MATACORAN *and* SELICTAZ, *as from the chase;* MATACORAN *with a light hunting spear in his hand,* SELICTAZ *carrying his bow and game—down rocks.*)

SELICTAZ. There, my prince, behold the great canoes. Have I not told thee truly?

MATACORAN. They are call'd barques, and bear the adventurous English in search of their darling gold, the god they worship! Away to Weorocomoco, and report this coming to the king. I will follow quickly on thy track. Fly with thy utmost speed—away.— (*Exit* SELICTAZ.) Barclay! English! come forth. (*Striking with his spear against the hut.*)

(*Enter* BARCLAY.)

BARCLAY. Give you good morrow, Prince. So early return'd from the chase; yet, by your game, it would seem you have not drawn an idle bow.

MATACORAN. Tell me, Englishman, are those the barques of thy country; or those wild rovers of which I have heard thee speak, who, acknowledged by no country, are consider'd enemies by all?

BARCLAY. (*Aside, with ecstasy.*) 'T is the flag of England. Prince, those are the barques so long expected with succours for the colony.— (*Aside.*) Alas! they have come too late.

MATACORAN. Why do they remain at rest? why not approach the shore?

BARCLAY. They await some signal of recognition from those they expect to find here. I have bethought me of the old pennon under which I sail'd when first leaving my native land to seek adventures in the New World. From amid the wreck of our misfortunes, I have preserv'd the flag with the fondness of an old man's treasure. An' it please you, Prince, I will ascend the cliff, and waving the well-known signal of friendship, they of the ships will answer with their ordnance, and presently prepare to land.

MATACORAN. Do as thou hast propos'd, and with the least delay. (BARCLAY *enters the hut, then returns bearing a flag, ascends the cliff and waves it. A gun is fired from the ship;* MATACORAN *starts, Indians utter cries, and fly from the cliffs in great terror.*) 'T is well; and now, Englishman, hear me. The strangers, no doubt, will question thee as to the fate of thy comrades; beware of thy speech in reply, lest they become alarm'd at thy tale. Speak of the great King's virtues and clemency; how he sav'd thy life, that thou might teach his people the arts of the white man; and hath given thee lands and wives; and how his favours have made thee forget that ever thou wert a native of countries beyond the sea.

BARCLAY. Since I have taken service with the great King, I have not much to complain of; but all his favours, and his kingdom in the bargain, can never make me forget Old England, the land of my birth and affections; and tho' far distant from her, she is ever present to my sleeping and waking thoughts, while my heart, at sight of those vessels, yearns for the embrace of my countrymen. Surely, Prince Matacoran, the brave in war, the just in peace, the favourite of his king, the friend of his country, must admire that patriotic feeling in another, which he himself possesses in no ordinary degree. 'T is one of the first of the virtues, and one of the last that will abandon the generous bosom.

MATACORAN. You 're right;—but if you English so love your own country, why cross the wide sea to deprive the poor Indian of his rude and savage forests? But see, the smaller barques approach laden with the strangers; hear me—look well to thyself. I must on to Weorocomoco, and report to the king. Be assur'd of his favour, if thou prove faithful—but, if false, beware of his anger, for it is terrible.

BARCLAY. That, Prince, we can only judge of by imagination. No victims having ever surviv'd, so as to be able to speak feelingly on that subject.

MATACORAN. Look well to thyself, thou knowest Matacoran, and by this time thou should'st know how to value his friendship and protection; and see, the spear of Matacoran is sharp.

(*Exit* MATACORAN.)

BARCLAY. Yes, and unsparing as 't is keen. They come, my countrymen come; I will retire, and observe them from a distance. (*Exit* BARCLAY *into the hut.*)

(*Boats arrive with* SMITH, PERCY, ROLFE, WEST, *and Soldiers. Trumpet sounds*—SMITH *draws his sword and leaps ashore. Banner of* SMITH *borne by* PERCY.—*Three Turks' heads on a field; motto—Vincere est Vivere, Accordamus.*)

SMITH. God save the King! Lieutenant, advance my banner—and now plant it deep, where nor force, nor fraud, shall ever root it out again. This goodly land, which the brave Raleigh nam'd from the virgin Queen, we will possess for her successor, the royal James; whom God preserve, and grant a long and prosperous reign over these fair realms. Welcome, comrades, welcome to Virginia.

PERCY. A right fair and goodly land it seemeth, but sadly deficient of inhabitants. We have only seen some fishers in light canoes, which at approach of our barques, and discharge of our ordnance, skimm'd like dolphins o'er the waves, and soon vanish'd from our sight.

ROLFE. It was surely no savage hand which hung the English pennon from the cliffs. Here seems to be a dwelling, and tho' rude, is yet of better structure than the Indian native wigwam.—What ho! there! within!

(*Enter* BARCLAY.)

BARCLAY. Save ye, noble sirs.

SMITH. Thy tongue is English, but the freshness of health so mark'd in the natives of Albion's salubrious isle, is marvellously chang'd in thy complexion, which is as tawney as a Morisco's. How fares the world with thee, comrade! wert thou of Weymouth's or of Grenville's crews?

BARCLAY. Thou see'st, Sir Cavalier, the solitary remnant of all the English, whom ambition and avarice have sent at various times to settle and to perish in this inhospitable land. Mine is a tale of sorrow.

SMITH. Let it be a short one, then; for we have come not to mourn over past misfortunes, but to prevent future ones. To your tale.

BARCLAY. Soon after the departure of the ships, the colonists, divided amongst themselves, threw off all rule, and instead of fortifying the tower, and cultivating the soil, began to oppress and plunder the natives, who, in return, waylaid and slew them. The wily Powhatan, profiting by our disunions and the weak state to which sickness had reduced us, surpris'd and laid waste the settlement, ere a second harvest had ripen'd for our use. I was alone preserv'd by the influence of the powerful Prince Matacoran, the general and chief counsellor to the King.

SMITH. Thy tale is as sombre as thy visage. But come, thy condition shall be mended; thou shalt take service under thine own liege lord, our gracious master. Thou canst materially aid us in our enterprise here, and the reward of thy fidelity shall be lands and privileges in this colony, which, trust me, profiting by the experience of those who have gone before us, we shall know how to conquer, aye, and to hold too; or, if thou would'st rather seek thy guerdon in thy native land, thou shalt be recommended in our despatches to the royal James.

BARCLAY. My allegiance is due to my rightful sovereign, whom I will well and truly serve. But, Sir Cavalier, I am now old, and my long sojourn from my native land would make me a stranger and friendless there, while I have here much consideration from the grandees of the savage court. My children, altho' the offspring of an aboriginal mother, are dear to me, and so may it please your gracious pleasure, I would prefer to end my days in Virginia.

SMITH. Be it so, I understand thee. Be secret and thou wilt be safe. Go gain us what intelligence thou canst.

(*Exit* BARCLAY.)

WEST. I do not much like this renegado.

SMITH. By my faith, Master West, but we are of the condition of the host, who having but one flaggon for the use of all his guests, must serve peer, and peasant alike; now be our thirst for intelligence ever so great, we must drink from this renegado, our only cup.

PERCY. The ruthless hand of Powhatan has indeed so lopp'd the branches from the colonial tree, as to have left only this wasted and wither'd stump. But let Esperance, the motto of the Percy, bear us out at every need.

ROLFE. From the tale of this renegade countryman of ours, I opine that in the King Powhatan we shall meet with a savage of no ordinary sort; an' he possess as much courage, as 't is said he hath craft, he may prove to us a troublesome customer.

SMITH. For my part, having held warfare with wild Tartar and Hern, the savages of the Old World, I care not how soon I break a lance with his savage majesty of the New. But come, my masters, let 's to our muster, and prepare our array for the morrow's pageant. 'T is fitting that we appear in our best harness, and that in its best burnish too, that we may strike upon the minds of the natives here, fair impressions of our might and grandeur. I pray of you, worthy sirs, that ye appear in all your braveries, for ye well know that first impressions are strongest, whether in love or warfare. Allons! we will pitch our camp and array our forces, and to-morrow on to the savage court, where we will invest his heathen majesty with the crown and mantle sent to him by the Lord's anointed; then demand, in behalf of our gracious sovereign, dominion in and over the countries from the mountains to the sea, and if denied us—why then—*Dieu et mon Droit*—for God and our right. (*Exeunt omnes.*)

SCENE 2. *The interior of the hut of* BARCLAY.—MANTEA *mending a net.*

(*Enter* POCAHONTAS *and* OMAYA, *with baskets of shells.*)

POCAHONTAS. The blessings of this fair morning upon you, Mantea, and good father Barclay. Do you know, that while with Omaya, gathering shells upon the beach, we heard a noise of thunder, and looking out upon the wide sea, we beheld those great canoes which bear the English, from one of which a white cloud arose; it seem'd as tho, it contain'd the spirit of sound, it floated awhile majestically in the air, and then disolv'd away; and while we gaz'd upon a spectacle so new and imposing, came to land the lesser canoes fill'd with the gallant strangers. Oh, 't was a rare sight to behold the chiefs as they leap'd on shore, deck'd in all their braveries; their shining arms, their lofty carriage, and air of command, made them seem like beings from a higher world, sent here to amaze us with their glory.

MANTEA. The English, my princess, have indeed arriv'd, and Barclay has gone to join his countrymen, while I have been so lost in fear and wonder, as to remain without the power even to look abroad. Whether this coming may prove of ill or good to Virginia we shall soon determine. I fear we shall have sad times again.

POCAHONTAS. Come good, come ill, Pocahontas will be the friend of the English. I know not how it is, but my attachments became fix'd upon the strangers the first moment I beheld them. Barclay has told me much of his native isle, and I have listen'd to his tale with all the admiration of a young untutor'd mind. But now I can well believe all that I have heard of that fair land, when I see that it doth produce such noble creatures.

MANTEA. Lady, beware how you make known your fondness for these strangers. Recollect you not, that your hand is destin'd to reward Prince Matacoran for his exploits against the English in the late wars? Powhatan so wills it.

POCAHONTAS. Matacoran is the sworn enemy of the whites, and implacable in his hatred; but sooner shall the sun cease to shine, and the waters to flow, than Pocahontas be the wife of Matacoran.

MANTEA. This powerful prince is the general and chief counsellor to the king, and first in his favor and affection, renown'd in war, and wise in council.

POCAHONTAS. Matacoran is brave, yet he lacks the best attribute of courage—mercy. Since the light of the Christian doctrine has shone on my before benighted soul, I have learn'd that mercy is one of the attributes of the divinity I now adore. To good father Barclay I owe the knowledge which I have acquir'd of the only true God, whose worship I in secret perform; and rather than be the bride of that fierce and vindictive prince, I would fly to the depths of the forests, and take up my abode with the panther.

(*Enter* BARCLAY *and* NAMOUTAC.)

BARCLAY. My princess—let me say my own good child, this poor hut is always made cheerful and happy by thy presence. Know you my companion?

OMAYA. Ah! it is, it is indeed Namoutac.

POCAHONTAS. Thy love hath made thee sharp-sighted, girl; thou hast the 'vantage of me.

BARCLAY. 'T is indeed Namoutac, tho' scarcely to be recognized as the wild Indian boy who used to climb like a squirrel for birds' nests, and dive in the rivers for shells. Namoutac can tell you much of his travels, and of the English who have just landed in Virginia.

OMAYA. Tell me, Namoutac, whether the English maidens wear their plumes as high as we do, and whether in painting they use most, the red or the yellow.

NAMOUTAC. Indeed, girl, I believe the English dames carry their heads to the full as lofty as ye do here, and they have quite as much red on their cheeks, tho' the yellow is not admired.

BARCLAY. Cannot you tell the princess somewhat of your adventures?

NAMOUTAC. Were I to live to the age of Powhatan, I could not relate a thousandth part of the wonders I have seen, or the persons I have met with in that world of itself. Agreeably to the orders of my king, I commenc'd notching a stick for every person I met, but soon threw it away in despair, as all the sticks in Virginia would not suffice to notch down the numbers in yon mighty realm.

OMAYA. Indeed, Namoutac, I do not think your travels abroad have much improv'd your taste in dress; I think you look'd far handsomer when you were formerly plum'd and painted among the young warriors in attendance on the king.

POCAHONTAS. Do tell me truly, Indian, what effects have your travels abroad had upon your attachments to your native country?

NAMOUTAC. In good truth, lady, I can say, all which I have seen has impress'd me with the most exalted ideas of the power and grandeur of a people, who are as gods are to men. Still amid all the splendours of the courts of Europe, I have never forgot my native land, but long'd to re-visit even its poverty and nothingness; while amid the pomp and pageantry of England, I sighed for the sports of our rude forests, and the wild, free life of an Indian. I wish'd to be away from the restraints of civiliz'd society, to throw off the cumbrous dress which fetter'd my limbs, and re-assume my primitive nakedness and liberty; to enjoy the hunt and the dance, and again to become a son of Virginia.

POCAHONTAS. How call you the chiefs of the English lately arrived?

NAMOUTAC. The leader is Smith, a renown'd chieftain in the three quarters of the world; his lieutenant, Master Percy, kinsman to the great Werowance Northumberland, whose territory alone could produce more bowmen than the whole kingdom of Powhatan; then Master West, related to the noble Lord de la War; then Master Rolfe, of gentle blood, with others of lesser note. I must to the king. How my heart will throb as I revisit Weorocomoco and its well-remember'd scenes, where the earliest and happiest days of my life have been pass'd.

OMAYA. And so you have not forgot the Weorocomoco and the merry dances we us'd to have there. I long to see you dress'd and painted as becomes you; for really, Namoutac, in these clothes you are hardly tolerable.

NAMOUTAC. The sun shines for the last time upon Namoutac the English. Its morning beams will cheer him while roaming in his native forests, seeking the favourite haunts of his youth, dress'd in the garb of his country, his limbs will again become vigorous and elastic, he will be as swift as the deer of the hills, his heart will be as light as the feathers of his plume; such will soon be Namoutac the Indian. Namoutac the English, will be no more. (*Exit* NAMOUTAC.)

BARCLAY. Behold the force of early habits, as exemplified in this young native. Princess, the strangers are bound to your father's court, and soon as the presents are landed, will invest Powhatan with the regalia sent by the English monarch. It will be an imposing spectacle.

POCAHONTAS. But I must hasten to Weorocomoco, to prepare fitting entertainments for such noble guests. Omaya, we will take the near way path.

OMAYA. We shall soon overtake Namoutac, and then we will fly by him to shew our speed, while in his clumsy clothes he will come toiling after us.

POCAHONTAS. Adieu, Mantea—adieu, good father Barclay—soon will I be here again; for I am no where so happy as under this hospitable roof.

(*Exit* POCAHONTAS *and* OMAYA.)

BARCLAY. Come, Mantea, you may now gaze on the ships without fear of the English. This way; be not alarm'd.

(*Exeunt both.*)

SCENE 3. *A wood.*

(*Enter* ROLFE.)

ROLFE. I am completely lost amid the mazes of this interminable wood. My companions, intent on the pursuit of game, have left me to indulge in the contemplation of the sublime and beautiful, which is every where to be found in the wild and picturesque scenery of these interesting regions. What a vast and splendid park this savage king possesses here; how insignificant appear our European pleasure grounds, where a few trees have been planted and train'd by the hand of art, when compar'd with these noble forests, planted by the hand of nature. Our pieces of water, too, as they are called, where a few small fishes are fed and fatten'd, to those magnificent rivers, which, rising in the mountains, traverse the country for some hundred miles, then rush with indescribable grandeur to the sea. And the contrast holds equally good with regard to animals; in the European parks a herd of tame stags lie lazily about the keeper's lodge; in the forests of Virginia, the wild buck arouses him from his leafy lair, flashes his bright eye indignant on his pursuers, and then bounds gracefully away over these interminable lawns. Verily, things are on a great scale in this New World. I will rest me awhile on this shady bank, till our hunter's horn announces the conclusion of the chase.

(*Reclines on a bank.*)

(*Enter* POCAHONTAS *and* OMAYA.)

OMAYA. Why, lady, you tire; Namoutac cannot be far before us.

POCAHONTAS. Indeed, girl, I am not much us'd to racing of late; I would fain take breath awhile. Hereabouts is the shady bank and the old oak at which we us'd to rest; we will stop but for a moment, and then resume our chase of Namoutac. Come—ah! 't is occupied, and by a stranger. (*Discovers* ROLFE.)

ROLFE. (*Coming forward.*) But will be most cheerfully relinquished, maidens, to your better use. 'T is a pleasant seat, and invites the weary to comfort and repose; I pray you rest from your fatigue.

POCAHONTAS. Thanks, courteous stranger; altho' our journey has been somewhat rapid, we have but little need of rest.

ROLFE. The duties of a Cavalier to your sex are the same whether in the Old World or the New; I therefore pray ye accept my service. Say whither do ye roam thro' these extensive forests? Seek ye your friends, or is it in the mere wantonness of health and spirits attendant on the gay morning of life, that ye have come abroad to gather flowers in this wild garden of nature?

POCAHONTAS. We go, Sir Cavalier, to Weorocomoco, the abode of Powhatan, the sovereign of these countries; where, if report speaks truth, we may soon expect the English.

ROLFE. I am greatly mistaken, if I am not addressing the Princess Pocahontas, the favourite daughter of the king, and the friend of Barclay.

POCAHONTAS. Such is my name and character.

ROLFE. Again I tender my duteous service; and tho' I should be but a bad guide in the forest, yet I may afford ye protection on your way.

POCAHONTAS. The paths are well known to us whose feet so often traverse them, and ere the shadows of the trees are much more aslant, we shall reach the abode of Powhatan. Adieu, courteous stranger, at Weorocomoco we shall meet again.

(*Exeunt* POCAHONTAS *and* OMAYA.)

ROLFE. What gone! why they have flitted away like the nimble fawns which start from the thicket to avoid the hunter's aim. And see, they now hold on their light and rapid course, and are now hidden by the luxuriant foliage. How full of grace and courtesy is this princess—savage, should I say. By my faith, and such be the damsels of the savage court, we shall need all the advantages of our civilization when we appear before them. (*Horn sounds.*) Aha! 't is our wild gallants; they have at length stricken the deer, and now blow a mort. Here they are.

(*Enter* PERCY *and* WEST.)

PERCY. Well, Master Rolfe, still given to meditation! but if our eyes have not deceiv'd us, thou art not solitary in thy musings—surely we saw something of the female form glide swiftly away, as tho' alarmed at our coming. Perhaps some sylvan deity of these shades, who pitying thy forlorn and solitary state, came to amuse thee, and to sing wood notes wild, as a cure for thy melancholy.

WEST. Or rather say the driads of this wood, who finding him absorb'd in dreamy musings on his absent love, came to console the hapless swain, and try if the tawny maidens of Virginia could not make him forget the fair dames of Europe. What say you, Master Rolfe?

ROLFE. Why, my merry masters, I say that ye are bad woodsmen, and have shot wide of your mark; an' ye draw no better bow at the stag, your arrow had as well remain'd in its quiver.

PERCY. We'll guess no more, Master Rolfe, but are all attention to your story.

ROLFE. Well, you must know, that while resting on this bank, and listening for echoes from your horn, came tripping by no less a personage than the Princess Pocahontas, and a light-footed damsel, her hand-maiden, and after a few words of fair and courteous speech, they vanish'd like fairies from a moon beam.

PERCY. And so, Sir Knight of the Wood, a fair princess has form'd thy adventure; but, if I mistake not, thou wilt yet have to win by sword and lance, and not by soft and gentle dalliance of words. Our valiant captain doubts the sincerity of the friendship with which we are to be receiv'd, and bids us all look to our arms. Now his experience of Turk, Tartar, and Hun, will make him keep a wary eye upon the proceedings of his savage majesty here, and at all events be prepar'd for the worst.

WEST. Master Rolfe looks grave. My broider'd doublet to a carman's frock but he is in love with this dark princess.

PERCY. A match, I say, between Master Rolfe, and the tawney daughter of Virginia.

WEST. Agreed, agreed.

ROLFE. My meeting with the damsel was purely accidental; still let me say, that tho' of dark complexion, she is well favour'd both in form and feature, of admir'd carriage, courteous and discreet in discourse.

WEST. Excellently well describ'd. A match, a match, I say: but hark'ee, Master Rolfe, an' ye succeed your father-in-law Pohawtan, who they say is well-stricken in years, and become king of these realms, I pray ye make me, your old camarado, your master of the horse.

ROLFE. Well, my merry masters, here's a hand to each of you, and right royally I swear, to grant all your wishes, and a thousand largesses beside, so soon as I wed the princess, succeed Powhatan, and become sovereign lord of these realms. The day I mount the throne of Pawmunkee, thou, Master West, shalt mount the horse of state, thou Master Percy, the viceregal seat in the government of the gold mountains; while our valiant captain, as commander of the forces, will march to the conquest of the Monecans, and tribes far westward toward the setting sun. Now, my bon camarados and merry wags, having dispos'd of the gifts of royalty, I become plain Master Rolfe again, and propose that we burnish our harness for the morning's pageant, as it is fitting we appear in proper knightly array where a princess is to be won. Lieutenant, we wait thy leading.

PERCY. Nay, my liege, we thy humble squires, know better our places than to precede the heir presumptive to a throne.

ROLFE. What! at your waggeries again—well, ye shall be pleasur'd. Allons, my noble vassals, allons. (*Exeunt omnes.*)

ACT SECOND.

SCENE 1. *The palace of Powhatan at Werocomoco.* POWHATAN *seated on a throne which is covered with bear skins.* POWHATAN *wearing a coronet of feathers, and a robe of skins, a spear in his hand; on his right the Princess, on his left,* OMAYA, *with fans of feathers, double rows of guards with spears, bows and arrows.*

(*Enter* MATACORAN.)

MATACORAN. The English have arriv'd, is it the great King's pleasure the strangers be brought before him?

POWHATAN. Bring they the presents?

MATACORAN. They do, great King.

POWHATAN. And their guns?

MATACORAN. They have weighty guns in their boats, such as ten of the strongest of our warriors could not lift.

POWHATAN. I like not their guns.

MATACORAN. They say these great pieces are brought to give salvos of welcome at thy coronation, such as is due at the coronation of a king.

POWHATAN. Well, be it so, introduce the strangers to my greatness.

(*Flourish of trumpets. Soldiers marching. Drums and trumpets. Banner of* SMITH *borne by* ROLFE. SMITH, *uncovered, bearing a scroll.* PERCY *bearing a coronet.* WEST, *the mantle. Soldiers.*)

POWHATAN. English, ye are welcome to the dominions of Powhatan—welcome.

SMITH. Great King, I will display, and read my credentials, which are under the sign manual of my sovereign, and the great seal of England. (*Reads.*) "To the high and mighty Powhatan, sovereign of Pawmunkee. These. We, James, by the grace of God, of Great Britain, France, and Ireland, King; Defender of the faith; greet thee well, and by these presents we do command our trusty and well beloved cavalier and captain, Smith, that he do invest thee with a crown, which we have sent as a token of our love; and to acknowledge thee by right and title as holding the realm of Virginia in vassalage of us, and our heirs, forever. And we do further command our right trusty and well-beloved cousin, Percy of Northumberland, that he do invest thee with the scarlet mantle as a badge of thy royalty, to be worn as such by thee, and thine heirs, forever. Sign manual and great seal of England."

(SMITH *and* PERCY, *bearing coronet and mantle, invest* POWHATAN *with them.*)

SMITH. In the name of the most puissant James, I crown thee King. (*Flourish.*)

PERCY. And I thus invest thee with the mantle of royalty. Hail to the King. (*Flourish.*)

SMITH. God save the great Powhatan, King of Pawmunkee. (*Flourish.*)

(*Flourish of drums and trumpets. Cannon fired without—at the firing the Indians exhibit great terror.* POWHATAN *leaves his throne.* SMITH *re-seats him.*)

SMITH. Our shew of gratulation hath alarm'd your highness; it is now over, dismiss thy terrors. These ceremonies were commanded by my royal Master, as due to the coronation of so great a King as thou. I pray your highness, that ye will be pleas'd to visit us at James' Town and inspect the presents.

POWHATAN. If your king has sent me presents, I also am a king; this is my land, you must come to me, not I to you. Yet, Captain Smith, many do inform me that your coming hither is to invade my people, and possess my country. We fear your arms, now lay them aside, for they are useless in times of peace.

SMITH. Great King, thou art falsely inform'd; we came not only to be friendly with thee, but to aid thee with our arms in thy wars with the Monecans.

POWHATAN. It suiteth not with my greatness to have foreign aid in my wars, Captain Smith; I am old, and have seen the death of my people for three generations. I know the difference between peace and war better than any one in my country. I am old, and soon must die. This tale, that thou art come to destroy my country with thy arms, troubleth me, and affrighteth my people. What can ye gain by war, when we can fly to the woods, whereby ye must perish for want of food. Think ye that Powhatan is so simple as not to know that it is better to eat good meat, laugh, and receive presents from you, than to live in the woods, eat acorns, and be hunted by you, that if a twig break every one cryeth, there cometh Captain Smith! thus ending my miserable life, and leaving my pleasures to you. Be assur'd of our love, and come not with guns and swords, as if to invade your foes.

SMITH. King!—our arms are a part of our apparel; had we intended to do you a harm, what has there been to prevent us? View kindly as friends those who would be terrible to thee as foes.

POWHATAN. Well, Captain Smith, ye are a great Werowance;[1] we will be kind to thee, and accept thy presents. But come, my favourite daughter hath entertainment for thee in a dance. Come, the dance, I say, the dance.

(SMITH, PERCY, ROLFE, *and* WEST *are placed on stools in the centre of the stage. Suddenly come dancing in from each side Indian girls with*

1 Ruler.

bows and arrows, then youths with spears; they present the weapons as if to slay them, retire, and bring in pine branches, which they hold over the English in form of a canopy. The English rise, the dancers form in two lines, the King, having POCAHONTAS *and* OMAYA *on each side of him, leads the way, the English follow, the Indians holding the pine branches over the train. Exeunt all but* MATACORAN, *who, during these ceremonies, stands apart, his arms folded, and looking sternly on. He comes forward.*)

MATACORAN. And lick we feet which soon will trample us in the dust, fold we to our bosoms those serpents which will soon entangle us in their coils, and then sting us to the death. Why this idle pageantry of crowning him a king, who is a king already! The coming of these pallid strangers bodes no good. Matacoran despises their friendship and disdains their gifts; and swears, by the heroic fame of his fathers, eternal enmity to the invader, and devoted fidelity to his king and country. (*Exit* MATACORAN.)

SCENE 2. *Interior of* BARCLAY'S *hut.*

(*Enter* MANTEA *and* ROLFE.)

MANTEA. Be seated, good sir; rest thee awhile, and such hospitality as this poor hut can afford, shall ever be at the service of Barclay's countrymen.

ROLFE. Thank thee, good dame. I left thy husband but a little while ago. I came to expedite the landing of the stores and presents.—Who have we here?

(*Enter* POCAHONTAS *and* OMAYA.)

POCAHONTAS. Mother, I have hasten'd to tell thee how we receiv'd the noble strangers. (*Sees* ROLFE.) Ha! the handsome Cavalier!

ROLFE. Lady, you have made the English for ever your debtors, by the kind and flattering manner in which you receiv'd them. Of a truth, we were all most happy and content while at Weorocomoco.

POCAHONTAS. Our means were small compar'd to the quality of our guests; yet, such as they were, most freely offer'd, and we hope most pleasingly receiv'd.

ROLFE. May we not hope, lady, that thou wilt not always bury thy rare qualities in these wilds; thou should'st to England, where many will approve thy visit, and thou find much to admire.

OMAYA. Oh do, dear lady; we shall be so delighted. Namoutac has told us of the royal court, and of the great ladies there, who are of such circumference that they could not enter the door of our king's palace, and so laden with braveries that pages are employ'd to carry them.

POCAHONTAS. I fear that a Virginian female would be but a poor personage where there is so much show and grandeur.

ROLFE. Pardon me, lady, thy worth and dignity will not be obscur'd, even by the state and splendour of the English court; the one is the genuine adornment of nature, the other the mere effect of art. An' ye will go, I could hope to be your squire; and trust me, lady, the kindness which you have shewn to my countrymen will be remember'd to thee in England.

OMAYA. Oh do, dear lady, go; and we will carry with us our best plumes, and good store of red paint; and when my lady is deck'd in her armlets and blue beads, she will appear as royally as the best of them.

POCAHONTAS. Good girl, thy warm imagination foresees many pleasures in the far country, while thy long and faithful attachment to me, makes it sure, that if I go abroad, thou shalt accompany me.

OMAYA. Thank 'ee, thank 'ee, dear lady; and when we come back, I shall take care to show Namoutac what it is to have travell'd—I shall indeed.

(*Enter an* INDIAN, *with fruit.*)

INDIAN. Barclay bade me give this fruit to an English Cavalier I should find here. He begs you will look to its seed immediately; it hath a rare seed, and ye 'll find it worthy of your notice.

ROLFE. (*Opens the fruit and discovers a billet.*) Aha! something in the wind. (*Aside.*) Indian, I find indeed it is a most pleasant fruit, and of a winning flavour; tell Barclay the seed will be well car'd for.—Away. (*Exit* INDIAN.)

ROLFE. (*Reads.*) "A panther lurks near the great oak, and will molest the gentle doe an' there be no lion to guard her on her way."—How 's this, the princess menac'd; treachery abroad! her safety be my care. Lady, it behooves thee to return to Weorocomoco without delay, but as a panther has been seen near the great oak, I will guard thee on thy way in safety to thy father's palace.

POCAHONTAS. Nay, good Sir Cavalier, we will not intrude so much upon thy courtesy. We have often tarried at the great oak, sometimes to enjoy the shade of its spreading branches, sometimes to shelter in its ample hollow from the summer shower, yet have we never seen beast other than the pretty deer that graze in the forest, or the nimble squirrel, leaping from tree to tree, chattering to its mates.

ROLFE. Not only duty and honour, but a warmer impulse, bids me be thy protector. I long to prove my sincerity: let 's away—an' the panther spring, I will defend my charge, aye, to the very death.

(*Exeunt* POCAHONTAS, OMAYA, *and* ROLFE.)

MANTEA. The good Spirit guard them in safety. Here comes my husband, he seems in haste, and much disorder'd.

(*Enter* BARCLAY.)

BARCLAY. Where is the princess and the Cavalier?

MANTEA. Gone, and the cavalier gone with her.

BARCLAY. Heaven be prais'd, then all is well. Hear me, Mantea—I have just discover'd a horrible conspiracy to surprise and murder my countrymen; and the Indians knowing the attachment of the princess to the English, have caus'd Namoutac to lie in ambush at the oak, to seize the amiable girl and bear her off, till the conspiracy is completed. Happily my billet has been read and understood, and the brave Cavalier will, I trust, defeat the plan, and protect the dear child from harm. Be secret on your life.

MANTEA. Return ye to Weorocomoco to give the alarm to the English?

BARCLAY. I dare not leave this place; the Prince Matacoran has order'd me to remain here in charge of the presents; altho' no one would steal them, for they consist of a grindstone, of which the Indians know not the use, and two demi-culverins, which twenty could not carry away. I have had no means of communication with my countrymen but by the billet—Heaven send them a safe deliverance.

MANTEA. I think I have discover'd that the princess and cavalier are not indifferent to each other.

BARCLAY. 'T is well; but let women alone, whether savage or civiliz'd, for finding out the secrets of her sex. Hear me, Mantea, be silent, be secret, if it is in the nature of a woman to keep a secret; your life, your husband's life, your children's lives depend upon your prudence in the matter of this conspiracy. Come, take up the nets, and let 's to our fishing; we must appear as if nothing had happen'd a little while—and then—

(*Exeunt* MANTEA *and* BARCLAY.)

SCENE 3. *A wood, within which is a temple of matting and poles—an image of the Okee, or God—a* PRIEST *prostrate before it.*

POWHATAN. Now, priest—what says Okee; is he propitious?

PRIEST. Great king, the god will indulge thy prayer, but demands a heavy sacrifice.

POWHATAN. Well, fifteen youths, I suppose, will content the Okee.

PRIEST. Fifteen, my king! Okee demands an hundred.

POWHATAN. Enormous! Why at that rate, I shall soon have none to offer; my kingdom will be depopulated. Go, try if he will not be content with fifty.

PRIEST. I dare not provoke the god; he will not be question'd a second time.

POWHATAN. An hundred! I never gave more than fifty in all my wars.

PRIEST. Thy wars were with Monecans—the English are not Monecans.

POWHATAN. If I give an hundred youths to the sacrifice, what am I promis'd, priest?

PRIEST. The entire discomfiture of all thy enemies.

POWHATAN. But their guns—?

PRIEST. Will become harmless as blunted arrows—their lightnings may flash, their thunders roll, but they will be no more than the rumbling and glare from the summer cloud, where no bolt descends to shiver the pine.

POWHATAN. Ensure me the head of Captain Smith, and the hundred is granted. Go, select the youths, array them in their white vestments, our affairs admit of no delay.

PRIEST. All thy enemies shall be in thy power—so the god has promis'd.

(*Exit* PRIEST.)

POWHATAN. But a little while, and these proud invaders will share the fate of their countrymen. They have brought me a crown, 't were better to have been an hoe or a hatchet. They ask the lands from the mountains to the sea; but will they be content with part, when their object is to take the whole? This Smith is a warrior; his air and manner is that of command—and then their dreadful fire arms. My daughter, too, favours these English; but I have sent Namoutac with a party, to seize and bear her to a distance, till my scheme has taken effect. I 'll to the prince and hold deep counsel; and, ere another moon, I trust that my land will be rid of these formidable invaders. (*Exit* POWHATAN.)

SCENE 4. *A wood. The great Oak in the centre—a hollow in its side.*

(*Enter* ROLFE.)

ROLFE. I have preceded my charge that I may reconnoitre the enemy, and see if the coast be clear. This is the spot alluded to in Barclay's billet. What a giant of the forest is here! Centuries have witness'd its growth, centuries have witness'd its prime, and centuries will elapse ere its final decay,—within its vast hollow, a cavalier, arm'd cap-a-pie, with lance in rest, might caracole a steed, and yet touch not the sides. But hark! I hear footsteps approaching; I will take 'vantage of the cover this mighty tree affords, and form my ambuscade.

(*Enters the tree.*)

(NAMOUTAC *and Indians come through the wood.*)

NAMOUTAC. Hide ye in the adjoining thickets, and when ye shall hear my whoop, rush forth, seize the princess and Omaya, and bear them to the canoes, which shall convey them to Pawmunkee. —Down, down, they are coming.

(*Indians hide.*)

(*Enter* POCAHONTAS *and* OMAYA.)

POCAHONTAS. Here is the great oak.

OMAYA. And nothing seems to disturb the stillness of the scene. save the birds, which sing in joyous melody. and the playful squirrel, which pursues his gambols amid the limbs of this aged father of the forest. All is peace, and sure no cruel animal lurks hereabout to destroy two such harmless beings as we are.

(*Whoop heard.* NAMOUTAC *and Indians rush forth to seize* POCAHONTAS *and* OMAYA—*at the same moment* ROLFE *comes from the tree, fires a pistol, Indians run off screaming.*)

NAMOUTAC. Aha! Sir Cavalier, is it thou? why you have really spoil'd a pleasant frolic.

ROLFE. Villain! confess thy treachery, or you die. (*Presents a pistol.*)

NAMOUTAC. A love affair, Master Rolfe, nothing more. I wish'd to surprise the damsels, and bear off Omaya, after the manner of love affairs, of which I have heard report in thy country; nothing more, Master Rolfe—nothing more.

ROLFE. Rascal, in my country where love affairs are conducted by treachery and outrage to the female parties, they end in the death of the traitors. Now you have play'd your part in this love affair, I shall play mine by shooting you thro' the head. (*Presenting pistol.*)

OMAYA. Oh, good Sir Cavalier, do spare poor Namoutac; his travels have turn'd his brain—he would not have behav'd so when he was only an Indian.

ROLFE. Begone, fellow! and when you next propose to alarm an innocent female, beware lest you find an English cavalier for her protector. (*Exit* NAMOUTAC.) Thy guileless heart, my princess, knows not yet of the ways of treachery and deceit. This alarming affair happily ended, let us proceed.

POCAHONTAS. Whatever may have been the intention of those who surpris'd us, thy gallant deliverance claims our gratitude and regard.

ROLFE. A regard, dear lady, which I hope will be mutually increased on our further acquaintance. Yet speak not so favourably of a service which every cavalier is bound to render to thy sex. Come, let 's on with our journey; and the gentle fawn of Virginia need fear no panther when the lion of England doth guard her on her way. (*Exeunt.*)

SCENE 5. *Wood. Distant view of Weorocomoco.*

(*Enter* MATACORAN *and* SELICTAZ.)

MATACORAN. Go, Selictaz, to all the tribes friendly to Powhatan, bid them muster their warriors and repair to Weorocomoco; promise them much bounty at the hands of the king, and great rewards in the spoils of the English.

SELICTAZ. I go, my prince, but opine they will come in but tardily, the tribes do so much fear the arms of the English.

MATACORAN. Bid them not fear those noisy weapons; the thunder rolls not always, and in its pauses our arrows will enter our enemies' bosoms, and our spears strike home. Tempt their avarice, Selictaz, by saying much of the riches of the strangers; say the king will relieve his people from the burthens lately impos'd —say every thing to induce the distant tribes to give their aid in driving these accurs'd English into the sea.

SELICTAZ. You shall be obey'd; and I hope to return with many of these fierce and hardy warriors.

MATACORAN. Yet stay, thou can'st not well be spar'd; we shall have need of thee in a daring enterprize that will be this night attempted. Go, send Yaamayden; teach him as I have taught thee; and say further, that Matacoran will lead in the war, and uphold the fame and manhood of the Indian.—Go. (*Exit* SELICTAZ.)

(*Enter* INDIAN.)

INDIAN. The king awaits thee near the ancient tomb.

MATACORAN. I come. (*Exit* INDIAN.) All now is prepar'd, an' if Powhatan do not shrink from the trial our success is certain; and from the fate of Smith and his comrades these pallid adventurers will learn in future better to respect the courage and ability of the Indian, than with a few score of followers to expect to overcome and conquer a country inhabited by thousands of warlike men. The accepted moment is at hand, and ere another sun shall rise to cheer with its beams the too confident English, the spear of Matacoran will have drank deeply of their blood, or Matacoran be gather'd to his fathers, to enjoy the happiness reserv'd for the brave.

(*Exit* MATACORAN.)

SCENE 6. *A wood—on one side of the stage the ruins of a tomb, in large letters thereon, "Madoc, 1170."*

(*Enter* POCAHONTAS.)

POCAHONTAS. 'T is superstitious awe gives privacy to this tomb, erected by the first conquerors of this country, and suppos'd to contain the ashes of Madoc, their chief. What could have caus'd Namoutac to lie in wait with arm'd men to surprise us in the wood, when but for the brave Cavalier, what might not have been our fate? All is not well.—Ah! here comes the king and with him Matacoran; they are in deep conference, and seek this secluded spot to hold their councils. Could I but learn the subject of their debate, it might throw much light upon late events. Time was, I should have fear'd to enter this sepulchre, but since the light of true faith dispell'd the first darkness of my mind, this solemn place with all its wild tales has no terrors for me. The prince being engag'd in this conference bodes no good to my English. I will retire into the tomb, and may learn that which will enable me to protect him who so late protected me.

(POCAHONTAS *goes into the tomb.*)

(*Enter* POWHATAN *and* MATACORAN.)

POWHATAN. To-night say'st thou? and the plan so well arrang'd that the English cannot escape? I have order'd the sacrifice of an hundred youths to the god; Okee would not for less ensure me the destruction of my enemies, the possession of their riches, and the heads of their chiefs.

MATACORAN. 'T is well to sacrifice to the gods; but, believe me, king, the gods of the English are as much superior to our gods, as their guns are superior to our bows and arrows. But if we cannot succeed by open force, we must resort to stratagem. Hear my plan. The feasts of the coronation being over, the English will return to the vicinity of their ships. I have selected for their guide Selictaz, who will conduct them to the old ruinous hunting lodge on the banks of the river; there supplied with good victuals, they will feast and carouse, for not like we do the English prepare for war, by fasting and hardihood; they are a people who have much regard for the belly and after eating they will sleep; then, my king, we will approach and pin them to the soil they so greedily covet.

POWHATAN. A good plan; but keep they no watch to alarm the sleepers of danger?

MATACORAN. Barclay has told me, that English warriors guard their camp by a charm'd word, which, if spoken by a foe.

makes that foe a friend. Now Selictaz is directed to obtain that charm'd word, which is always given out when the guard is set. That obtain'd, we proceed secure to the work of death.

POWHATAN. Brave and wise Matacoran, success to thee; and the English once destroy'd, name thy reward; a still greater Werowance shalt thou be, and rule over the countries conquer'd from the Monecans.[1] Bring me the head of Captain Smith, and thou shalt be second only to the king.

MATACORAN. Since first I enter'd the ranks of men, I have been in the service of my country; how faithfully, how daringly I have serv'd her, the renown of thy arms, O king! will best declare. Yet of all the spoils of war, what hath been the share of Matacoran? None—for Matacoran fought not for wealth, but for glory and Pocahontas. Now he must fight for glory and his country.

POWHATAN. Nay, my prince, be of good heart, the girl is young and knows not thy worth. Drive out the English from my shores, and the choicest of my gifts and my beloved daughter, shall be thy reward.—I swear it.

MATACORAN. No—as an unwilling bride I would not receive even Pocahontas to my arms. She has seen the strangers, and no longer looks upon an Indian warrior with favour or regard. 'T is no matter—Matacoran must have done with love. Glory and his country must return and possess his soul. Talk not of reward, king; thou hast often seen me return from the combat cover'd with mine own and my enemy's blood—say, did Matacoran ever ask reward? Tho' he hath added country to thy kingdom, and led many captives to thy feet, one boon alone he crav'd, and 't was her whose image nerv'd his arm in battle, and sooth'd the agonies of his many wounds—her who inspir'd the generous passion which bloom'd in his boyhood, and ripen'd in the man.

POWHATAN. Your long and constant attachment deserves the possession of its object. Pocahontas shall be thine.—Again I swear it.

MATACORAN. While I now bid adieu to a hopeless passion, the remembrance of once happy days clings in fondest twinings around my heart, and soothes me, as the mild radiance of twilight continues to shed its comforts on nature after the departure of the brighter sun. In my gay morning of life I sought renown in all the manly games, that my brow might receive the wreath from the hand of Pocahontas. How oft have I launched my light canoe, when the angry waves had driven our boldest fishers to the land, and drenched with the spray, have gain'd the distant shore to procure rare shells for the armlets of her I lov'd. How oft have I plung'd into the depths of the forests, and pierc'd with my arrows the bird of many dyes, that with its beauteous feathers I might plume the coronet of Pocahontas. Aye, I have dar'd death in an hundred battles, that, when returning victorious, Pocahontas might hail me with honour to the brave.

POWHATAN. My good and gallant prince, I swear my daughter shall—

MATACORAN. Enough, enough—'t is the expiring struggle of love. Now Matacoran breathes alone of war, and pants for the combat. The bowmen await their chief. Adieu, my king—Matacoran will deliver his country from her invaders, or soon exist only in his fame.

(*Exit* MATACORAN.)

POWHATAN. How brave and noble is this prince! and then that silly girl of mine to reject his love, and place her affections upon these pale-fac'd strangers. But Namoutac has by this time remov'd her afar, till the English are destroy'd, and Matacoran returns victorious to claim her as his bride. This night, this eventful night, Powhatan, old king, thou hast need of all thy craft and energy, or soon thy white head will no longer wear the crown so lately plac'd upon it. The sun which rises to-morrow will either behold thee a victorious king, or a humbled prisoner. (*Exit* POWHATAN.)

(POCAHONTAS *comes from the tomb.*)

POCAHONTAS. What have I heard! treachery and massacre against those whom they so lately receiv'd with every shew of hospitality and kindness. And Matacoran—he the brave and noble—and the reward of his achievement to be the hand of Pocahontas. No, chieftain, no. When Pocahontas rewards courage it must be unmix'd with treachery. Namoutac's conduct is explain'd. What is to be done? Can I fly to the English whom Selictaz leads on to sacrifice? The

1 Monacan, a nation to the west of Powhatan.

bands of Matacoran beset the path on every side; the river is the only hope. (*A flash of lightning.*) Ha! a storm is brewing, and how will these little hands, us'd only to guide the canoe in sportive race on a smooth and glassy surface, wage its struggling way, when raging billows uprear their foamy crests? Brave English, gallant, courteous Rolfe. (*Thunder.*) Night comes on apace—Oh, night of horror! (*Clasps her hands and looks up to heaven as if in prayer.*) Thank thee, good Spirit; I feel thy holy influence on my heart. English Rolfe, I will save thee, or Pocahontas be no more.

(*Rushes out.*)

SCENE 7. *A hunting lodge composed of mats and poles. View of the river.*

(*Enter* SELICTAZ, *leading the English. Indians following with baskets on their heads.*)

SELICTAZ. Rest ye here, my noble captain, and your good companions. The king, most careful of thy persons, commends thee to this rude lodge as a shelter against the falling dews, and the storm that seems fast gathering; and of his gracious bounty has sent ye good store of victual.

SMITH. The king is most royal in his bounty, and most ample in his stores.

SELICTAZ. The king desires that ye will not spare the victual, but feast and be merry. (*Aside.*) 'T will be thy last feast.

SMITH. On your return, present our humble duty to his highness; and had we a flask of good Rhenish here, in troth we would drink a deep carouse to his highness's health, and that of his daughter, our esteem'd good friend.

SELICTAZ. Had ye not better lay aside your armour? Sure it will hinder your rest.

SMITH. The English soldier is so us'd to his iron panoply that it seems as light to him as thy thin harness is to thee. Lieutenant, prepare for the night.

PERCY. The watch-word, an' so please ye, and we 'll set the guard.

(SELICTAZ *gives attention.*)

SMITH. What ye like; suppose thine own fair mistress.

ROLFE. What say ye to the Princess Pocahontas, our well approv'd friend?

SMITH. The princess then, with all my heart.

WEST. Aha! Master Rolfe, remember the wood—thou hast an arrow in thy heart—deep, deep, I say.

PERCY. This charm'd word will protect us in our rest, but disturb the sleep of our bon camarado.

WEST. Of a truth, she is the friend of the English.

SMITH. Be that the watch-word—Pocahontas, the friend of the English.

(SELICTAZ *retires satisfied.*)

PERCY. So please ye, any further orders?

SMITH. None. And now to rest, each in his soldier's cloak, his shield his pillow, and embracing his arms as he would soft and yielding beauty. Gentle sirs, good rest to ye, and many sweet dreamings of your lady loves; while wrapped up in my roquelaire, I will think awhile; till lull'd by the measur'd pacing of the guard, and the wild plaintive notes Virginia night birds sing, I too shall slumber. The guardian spirits which watch o'er the soldier's rude couch, keep ye all in their holy keeping. Give ye good night—good night.

(*Slow music—curtain falls.*)

ACT THIRD.

SCENE 1. *The hunting lodge as before. Night. Thunder and lightning. The river appears agitated. English asleep. Soldier on guard. Pocahontas is seen in a canoe struggling with the waves; she lands, and approaches the guard; a paddle in her hand.*)

SOLDIER. Who comes there? Stand.

POCAHONTAS. Oh, for breath (*leaning on her paddle*). I fear that I shall expire ere I can save them.

SOLDIER. What, ho! I say, the watch-word, or I fire. (*Presenting his piece.*)

POCAHONTAS. 'T is Pocahontas comes—Pocahontas, the friend of the English.

SOLDIER. Right—Pass.

POCAHONTAS. What, are they so still, and death so near? English, arouse ye, or ye die.

SMITH. (*Starting up.*) Who calls? Is it day-dawn already? Ah, my mistress, what can have brought thee abroad, and the elements so rude and angry? Surely thou has held some revelry to-night, and supposing that we poor soldiers are but illy content, have tripp'd down with thy light-footed damsels, and will again surprise us with a masquerade. But that my beard is grizzled, and my face marvellously ill-favour'd by scars of foreign service, I might hope this visit was made to me, and receive thee as my lady love.

POCAHONTAS. A more fearful fate awaits thee;—even now, Matacoran at the head of seven hundred bowmen, all chosen from my father's guard, comes to surprise and slay thee. Arm, arm; I pray thee arm, and away.

SMITH. To arms there, ho! (*English spring up, arm, and are mustered by Percy.*) By my faith tho', mistress, it would be but of ill savour to the fame of English cavaliers, were they to fly from the foe, leaving thee a distrest damsel behind. What say ye, Master Percy, could we expect favour from our dames were such ill fame to befall us?

PERCY. Let the enemy come, we will bide their brunt. The Percy fears no odds.

ROLFE. We are but eighteen in all; but then our men-at-arms are all veteran soldiers bred in battle, and for our captain, a braver heart never throbb'd against a corslet.

SMITH. Thank ye, my stout and worthy gentlemen. We will give this prince a right soldierly welcome—first a volley of hail shot, and then on him with sword and target.

POCAHONTAS. Nay, nay, your courage will not avail ye, the darkness will mar the superiority of your arms, while from every side will fly the poison'd arrows. Can Pocahontas ask a boon, which the English will deny?

SMITH. After thy generous service, lady, thy boon is granted ere 't is ask'd.

POCAHONTAS. Then fly! O! fly, my English, ere 't is too late. Fly, I beseech ye.

SMITH. Thou hast prevail'd. But thou must bear us company; within our steely circle we will place our protectress, and the harm that reaches her must first destroy us.

POCAHONTAS. No, I must return; should the king learn that I have preserv'd thee, not even his belov'd daughter will escape his wrath. Pocahontas gone, who will befriend the English?

SMITH. Lady, thy nobleness wins all our hearts. Grant me, I pray ye, a single feather of thy plume. (*She gives a feather.*) This will I wear on my helm.—Aye, and when the chivalry of Europe hold tournament in honour of their dames, I, thine own true knight, will appear in the lists, proclaim the Princess Pocahontas the most peerless of her sex, and shiver a lance in honour of the flower of Virginia. (*Exeunt all the English.*)

POCAHONTAS. Now all is well—yet how the wind roars among the lofty pines, the heaving surge beats heavily on the shore, while the blazing sky serves to light Matacoran on his way. I must launch my little barque, and as it tosses amid the foam and fury of the waves, feel sure that good and guardian Spirit, which urg'd me to the rescue of my fellow creatures, will not forsake me amid the dangers of the storm. (*Pocahontas re-embarks, and is seen at first struggling with the waves.—Exit.*)

(MATACORAN, SELICTAZ, *and Indians enter. They rush to the spot where a lamp burns, and where* SMITH *was sleeping.*)

MATACORAN. Now, soldiers, strike, and spare not; strike for your country—Hah, escap'd! (*Turning to* SELICITAZ.) Villain! thou hast deceiv'd me, and thou shalt die. Where are the English?

SELICITAZ. Dread chief, an' I play ye false, let my bosom receive your spear. I left them buried in sleep, what hath alarm'd them I know not. Some spirit, my Prince, some spirit has come to their aid, and marr'd thy purpose.

MATACORAN. Be it a good or evil spirit, I defy its power. Let 's on, the day is dawning—we dare do by courage what we have fail'd in by surprise. On, I say.

(*As they are going off, they meet Indians with* HUGO DE REDMOND *prisoner. Indians carrying his musket, shield, and sword.*)

MATACORAN. Stop—who have we here?

INDIAN. Prince, we found this old warrior lost in the mazes of the forest. We have disarm'd and brought him here to abide thy pleasure.

MATACORAN. Who art thou? How cam'st thou away from thy companions?

HUGO. So please ye, Sir Savage, I am Hugo de Redmond, an old man-at-arms in the service of King James. My limbs are stiff, I had sat me down to await the day dawn, when these painted devils sprang upon me, and master'd my arms; an' my match had not gone out, they would not have found me an easy conquest.

MATACORAN. Where is thy leader and his warriors?

HUGO. Not far off.

MATACORAN. What are the numbers of the English warriors?

HUGO. Including the soldiers in the barques, about three-score.

MATACORAN. Ha! not more?

HUGO. An' I be not greatly mistaken, you 'll find 'em enough.

MATACORAN. Do not deceive me; we Indians have strange tortures for our prisoners; we stick them full of splinters from the oily pine, and then light them into flame, and dance round, singing their funeral songs.

HUGO. Sure, an' the devil's own dance it must be. Well, old Hugo has stood fire in the four quarters of the Old World, and it matters little if he die by fire in the New. I was born in a camp, cradled in a buckler, and these white locks and batter'd arms, are proofs of my long and faithful service. I am thy prisoner, Sir Savage, do with me as you list.

MATACORAN. I like thy boldness. An' I give ye liberty what will ye do?

HUGO. Rejoin my banner with all speed.

MATACORAN. And then—

HUGO. Fight the enemies of my king and country.

MATACORAN. I like thee, old Warrior. Thou shalt return to thy chief, and tell him that Matacoran admires his valour, and bids him to the combat.

HUGO. On my life an' he 'll not baulk ye in your bidding.

MATACORAN. Thy sword and shield I keep in pledge, which thou may'st redeem in battle; take thy other arms, a brave soldier should never be unarm'd. Thou'rt free—Go.

HUGO. Thank 'ee, Sir Savage. Here 's my hand, in an hour hence it will seek thy life in battle. Hugo hopes to redeem his arms where the combat thickens. Farewell, noble, generous enemy, farewell. *(Exit* HUGO.*)*

MATACORAN. Soldiers! the hour is come. Be not alarm'd at their noisy arms; grapple with the foe, and his thunder will cease. We exceed them in numbers, of twenty to one—shame if they overcome us. They have great store of riches, win but the battle, and take all my share; this trusty blade will be all my spoil. On, comrades, on—the spirits of thy fathers, thy king, country, all, will behold thy battle. On to victory! 'T is Matacoran leads the way. *(Exeunt cheering.)*

SCENE 2. *Woody country. View of James River. Reports of musketry. Indians fly in terror across the stage.*

(Enter MATACORAN *and* SELICTAZ.*)*

MATACORAN. Fly, Selictaz, to the rear, and bid the guards receive these cowards on their spear points, and turn them back upon the English. *(Exit* SELICTAZ.*)* Now to my chosen guard, and form them on the river bank. The rout continues! Stop, cowards! Ah, those dreadful arms. Stop—'t is your general calls you. *(Exit* MATACORAN.*)*

(Enter SMITH, PERCY, ROLFE, WEST, *and Soldiers.)*

SMITH. Well done for the onset; spare your shot, and press them, brave comrades, with sword and target. Be my banner, like the eagle of Virginia, soaring above our battle, nor let it rest from its majestic flight, till it perches in triumph on the palace of Powhatan. On, I say! let my war cry be Victory and Virginia! *(Exeunt.)*

SCENE 3. *A Wood. Alarms. Reports of musketry.*

(Enter SMITH, *pressed by many Indians.* SMITH *with an Indian tied to his left arm, uses him as a buckler; he throws the Indian from him dead.* SMITH *is forced over the bank, and appears as fighting in the water. The Indians overpower, and bear him off in their arms.)*

(Enter MATACORAN.*)*

MATACORAN. There, now, stand firm: and if their armour should resist your arrows it will not repel a spear when thrust by the vigour of a brave man's arm. See, your prince advances first to meet the foe. Indians, place your trust in the spear, in courage, and Matacoran. *(Discharge of musketry heard, two Indians fall dead, the rest fly in disorder, uttering loud cries.)* All is lost. Oh! cowards, your general's curse, the curse of your king and country attend your flight.

What remains now to face the foe, nought but despair and Matacoran.

(*English enter and attack* Matacoran, *who defends himself bravely—he is beaten down on one knee.* Hugo *enters and covers him with his buckler.*)

Hugo. Spare, comrades, spare the prince; 't is your father Hugo commands ye. (*English desist.* Matacoran *rises.*) Brave, generous chief, the fortune of war is against thee, but thy courage demands esteem from thy enemies.

Matacoran. I have fought to the last, courted death, and hop'd to fall with my falling country.

Hugo. Prince, I now claim my old arms, and am happy that the act of their redemption has been in saving the life of a gallant enemy.

Matacoran. (*Giving up sword and buckler.*) There! in my hands they have been unfortunate, but not dishonour'd.

Hugo. When I was thy prisoner, thou said'st that a brave man should never be without arms, restor'd to me a part of mine; I admir'd thy courtesy then, and now offer thee in return a sword just flesh'd in this its maiden battle. Look, Prince, when old Hugo's wars are ended, and his last peace made, it will remind thee that honour and generosity could dwell in the bosom of so humble a being as a poor English man-at-arms.

Matacoran. Good old warrior, I accept thy gift, tho' it comes too late; for Matacoran has fought the last of his country's battles. Thy countrymen I can never love; but honour bids me say, they have about them much to admire. Lead on, lead your prisoner to your chief.

(*Exeunt all.*)

Scene 4. *Interior of* Barclay's *hut.*

(*Enter* Barclay—*meeting* Mantea.)

Mantea. Hath the thunder ceas'd—how fares the English?

Barclay. It still echoes among the pines. Three wounded English are just brought down to be embark'd—they report that our leader, the valiant Smith, is taken and carried to Weorocomoco. It seems impossible to believe it.

Mantea. Oh! sad, sad day for us all.

Barclay. Do not so soon despond—tho' a leader be slain, English soldiers are not long without another. The brave Percy may by this time have restor'd the day. The daring valour of Smith led him too far in pursuit of the flying enemy, when slipping from a bank into the river, he was overpower'd by numbers, and the hero, before whom hundreds had fled, was taken and carried captive to Powhatan. (*Knocking at the door.*) Be still, on your life. Who 's there? (*Without.*) Mowbray!

(*Barclay opens the door.*)

(*Enter* Mowbray.)

Barclay. My dear friend and countryman, what news, what news?

Mowbray. Good.—Victory to the English, thanks to the gallant Percy.

Barclay. And our leader—but I can see by thy looks—taken, Smith taken?

Mowbray. 'T is even so. His chivalric courage bore him head-long on the foe, when tired with slaying them, accident threw him into the water, where the weight of his armour, and the numbers who press'd upon him, render'd resistance vain, and he was borne off on the shoulders of the Indians.

Barclay. I trust the captain made his peace with God before the battle, for Powhatan allows his prisoners no time for prayer; and ere this the gallant soul of Smith is join'd to the souls of those made perfect in another and a better world.

Mowbray. Let 's still indulge a hope. Percy, Rolfe, and West, learning the fate of their leader, furiously charg'd the Indians sword in hand, routed, and pursued them towards the savage capital. Amid the rout <e> and carnage, one Indian, Prince Matacoran, was unappall'd; he fought like a lion, disdaining to fly, till old Hugo de Redmond, the father of our men, rush'd to the rescue, cover'd the chief with his buckler, bidding the soldiers spare so gallant an enemy. By this act of generosity calling forth shouts of admiration from our ranks.

Barclay. And the Prince—the brave, the stern Matacoran?

Mowbray. Despoil'd of his arms, he is led in chains, an hostage for the safety of the valiant Smith: ere this our troops have reach'd the savage capital, the soldiers rending the air with cries for their ador'd commander.

Barclay. Come, Mantea, let 's on to Weorocomoco. An' our leader lives, Virginia is ours.

MOWBRAY. Aye, Virginia will be ours—Victory and Virginia! (*Exeunt.*)

SCENE 5. *The palace of* POWHATAN. *Guards, etc.*

(*Enter* POWHATAN, *meeting* POCAHONTAS *and* OMAYA.)

POWHATAN. A strange tale this I hear of Namoutac and the Cavalier in the great tree. Namoutac is a fool, and deserv'd to be shot for his idle frolic. But, girl, something of greater moment claims attention. How comes it that ye continue to refuse the Prince as thy husband, the pride of my kingdom, the favourite of its king?

POCAHONTAS. I love not Matacoran, my affections are plac'd on another.

POWHATAN. Hear me, girl! the Prince is now engaged in combat with the English, whom he expects to destroy or drive from Virginia. An' he perform either of which good services thou shalt be his reward—aye, the bride of Matacoran.

POCAHONTAS. An' the Prince conquer the English, he will find better reward in their spoils, than in me, an unloving wife.

POWHATAN. He asks not reward, nay, refuses even thy ungrateful self; but I have sworn, yea, solemnly sworn, thou shalt be his, so prepare yourself to obey my will.

(*Enter* SELICTAZ, *in great haste.*)

POWHATAN. Ha! what news, Selictaz? what of the Prince? how goes the battle? speak, if thou canst gather as much breath. An' thy news be great as thy haste, 't will be worth relating.

SELICTAZ. Great King! Smith! the leader Smith.— (*Panting.*)

POWHATAN. Well—Smith is not near Werocomoco, I hope!

SELICTAZ. Aye, great King, very near.

POWHATAN. (*Alarmed.*) Guards there! say quickly thy say—

SELICTAZ. Smith is a prisoner, and will be here anon.

POWHATAN. Ha! prisoner! Smith a prisoner! and alive! Smith a prisoner!

SELICTAZ. 'T is even so—Smith is thy prisoner, and alive.

POWHATAN. Far beyond my hopes, thanks to the gods, and the brave Matacoran. Aha! girl, what say'st thou now to thy darling English, thy valiant Smith? Aha! wilt thou not now be the bride of Matacoran, the victorious Matacoran?

POCAHONTAS. Never! tho' he were victor of the world.

POWHATAN. Oh! joy, joy; say, Selictaz, how long before the remaining English are brought captives to my feet.

SELICTAZ. That, King, is a very doubtful matter; for tho' the leader is taken, the battle doth not abate. In truth, my King, there seemeth to be many Smiths in the field; they fight as tho' they were all Smiths.

POWHATAN. How fares the Prince?

SELICTAZ. I left him at his wonted place, the thickest of the battle. (*A yell.*) But hark, I hear the Indians who bear the captive Smith on their shoulders to make the greater haste to thy presence. Shall I usher them in?

POWHATAN. Wait yet a moment, while I ascend my throne, and put on the crown and mantle, that I may receive the prisoner in the royalty of his own making. Come, girl, take thy place at my side—take thy place, I say.

POCAHONTAS. Excuse me, father, I'm not us'd to such sights. I am not well.

POWHATAN. Thou wilt be well when the English are destroy'd. Take thy place.

(POCAHONTAS *and* OMAYA *take their places on the throne.* POWHATAN *ascends and seats himself on the throne.*)

POWHATAN. Now bring the captive to my feet. Take with thee my guard, Selictaz, lest he may escape.

(SELICTAZ *and guard go out and return with* SMITH, *his clothes stained and in disorder, his plumes broken. Indians bearing his arms.*)

POWHATAN. Thou 'rt welcome, Captain Smith, tho' thou now com'st with not quite so gallant a train as when thou last did deign to visit my poor house.

SMITH. My train will be here anon.

POWHATAN. Aye, as captives like thyself.

SMITH. No! but as conquerors, to plant my banner in victory on the throne where thou now sittest.

POWHATAN. How! and their leader taken?

SMITH. That 's no matter, the Percy does battle in my stead; and were he to fall, I would say, as old King Hal said of the Percy who fell at Chevy Chase, good he was, but thank God I 've many as good as he.

POWHATAN. Captain Smith, the king admires thy boldness. What would'st thou give for thy ransom? No doubt all the rich lading of thy barques; but then, Captain Smith, I would not set thee at liberty; for my people would fear thee, tho' thou wert in chains.

SMITH. Not a rusty nail would I give for ransom. I tell thee again, old fool, 't is not thee but we are the conquerors in this fray—that my banner, borne on the wings of victory, will soon be planted on thy throne—my war cry be heard in thy palace, and the royal James be sovereign of Virginia.

POWHATAN. Bold man, thou speak'st as tho' thou wert king, and I a captive.

SMITH. Accident overcame me; give me again but my sword and buckler, and see with what ease I 'll cut my way thro' thy guards—aye, and with their king to command them.

POWHATAN. 'T is too much—thou shalt die, and that forthwith.

SMITH. 'T is well.

POWHATAN. Yet the king is merciful—is there aught thou would wish to say ere the blow fall? (*A noise of musketry at a distance.*) Hah! thy moments are few. Executioners, bring forth the stone of sacrifice; and hark'ee, see that ye provide your heaviest clubs; and their heads be as hard as their hearts, ye will need your heaviest weapons.

(*Executioners bring in the stone, and poise their clubs, as if prepared for sacrifice.*)

POCAHONTAS. Oh! father! shew mercy to the brave unfortunate.

OMAYA. Spare, oh! King, the noble prisoner!

POWHATAN. Silence both.

POCAHONTAS. Delay, father, only till thou canst hear more of the battle—spare, spare the gallant Smith, thy daughter, thy favourite 't is who implores thee.

POWHATAN. Hah! thy tone is chang'd. The prisoner shall die, and that anon.

POCAHONTAS. Only till one other messenger arrives. Mercy, mercy.

POWHATAN. Guards! take these silly girls away.

(*Guards remove* POCAHONTAS *and* OMAYA *to the rear of the throne—guarding them there.*)

POWHATAN. Captain Smith, if you have aught to say, be brief, for thine hour is come.

SMITH. Thanks for thy savage courtesy. Hear me. When the blow is struck, and Smith ceases to live, but in his fame, do with my senseless corse as thou listeth; thou wilt find upon it many scars of honourable service. It matters not, whether it shall gorge the maws of thy cannibals, or be urn'd in marble, to await the slower progress of the worm. My heart preserve; give it my lieutenant, to be by him embalm'd and convey'd to England. That England, for whose glory it did so truly beat in life, will give it place amid the cemeteries of her illustrious dead.

POWHATAN. It shall be done, the king is merciful.

SMITH. Plant my banner on my grave, the three Turks' heads, the cognizance of my achievement on the plains of Transylvania, that when the chivalry of Europe shall hereafter pass that way, they may lower pennon and lance in memory of Smith.

POWHATAN. The king admires thy warlike fame; that too shall be done.

SMITH. Give my gold chain to thy admirable daughter; it was given me by Charitza, the most peerless lady of the Old World, and I now bestow it on Pocahontas, the most peerless of the New. I have done, proceed in thy bloody work. (*Noise of musketry nearer than before.*) Ah, 't is the glorious sounds of war, which for the last time I hear. Brave Percy, good lieutenant, spare thy shot, and on them with sword and target. See my pennon, how gaily it flies above the smoke—look on it, my veterans, and it will remind you of your lost commander. Hah! they fly! now, Percy, press them home. Give them not time to rally—well done. Now, comrades, shout my war cry in their despairing ears—Victory and Virginia! aye, victory and Virginia.

(SMITH, *exhausted, sinks into the arms of the Indians, who bind him, and lay his head on the stone of sacrifice.*)

SELICTAZ. (*Hastily, and in affright.*) From the height, O king, I beheld our army flying before the English like unto a herd of frighten'd deer, while the smoke from the enemy's guns can plainly be perceiv'd as it curls amongst the tops of the loftiest pines.

POWHATAN. Take with thee my chosen guard, and fly to the succour of the Prince—quick, away.

(*Exeunt* SELICTAZ *and guards.*)

POWHATAN. Executioners, I shall wave my fan of feathers thrice, and then cry strike. When you hear that word, let fall your weapons and with all thy force. Now attend—once, twice—

(*Waves the fan of feathers,* POCAHONTAS *breaks from her guard, and rushes to the feet of the king.*)

POCAHONTAS. King—father, if ever thy poor child found favour in thy sight, spare, O spare the noble prisoner; 't is Pocahontas, thy darling, who entreats thee—her, whom from infancy thou hast cherished in thy bosom. Spare, spare; here will I embrace thy feet, till thou shalt forget the king, and once again be the father.

POWHATAN. Away, girl—away.

(*Noise of musketry still nearer.*)

POCAHONTAS. Hark! hear you not those dreadful arms; think that ere long thou may have to ask that mercy thou now deny'st—Spare.

POWHATAN. Hah, impossible—attend there, thrice. (*Waves the fan.*) The word alone remains—attend.

(*Executioners raise their clubs.*)

POCAHONTAS. (*Rising with dignity.*) Attend, but first to me. Cruel king, the ties of blood which bound me to thee are dissever'd, as have been long those of thy sanguinary religion; for know that I have abjur'd thy senseless gods, and now worship the Supreme Being, the true Manitou, and the Father of the Universe; 't is his Almighty hand that sustains me, 't is his divine spirit that breathes in my soul, and prompts Pocahontas to a deed which future ages will admire.

(*She rushes down from the throne, throws herself on the body of* SMITH, *raises her arms, and calls to the executioners to "Strike"; they drop their weapons.* POWHATAN *descends, raises up and embraces his daughter.*)

POWHATAN. I am subdued, unbind the prisoner. My child, my child.

(SMITH *is unbound, and kneels to the Princess. Reports of musketry close at hand.* PERCY, ROLFE, WEST, *and soldiers enter, sword in hand, driving* INDIANS *before them.* PERCY *mounts the throne and plants the banner there.*)

PERCY. Victory—victory and Virginia. God save King James, Sovereign of Virginia.

(*Drums and trumpets. Soldiers shout.* PERCY, WEST, *and* ROLFE *embrace* SMITH. MATACORAN *is brought in, in chains, guarded.*)

PERCY. Thanks to God, we have arriv'd in time to the rescue of our noble commander.

SMITH. Nay, dear and valued friends, you must be content with victory. My rescue is due to her before whom I kneel in admiration and gratitude. (*Kneels.*)

PERCY. Thanks, noble mistress, thanks for the life of our belov'd Captain. An' we had not knowledge of thy excelling worth before this, thou would'st now amaze us with thy virtues. (*Kneels.*)

WEST. Honour thanks thee, England will thank thee, while Virginians to remotest ages will venerate thy fame, and genius hand thee over to immortality. (*Kneels.*)

ROLFE. And love thanks thee. (*Kneels.*)

HUGO. An old soldier's thanks for preserving the life of a rever'd comander. (*Kneels.*)

MOWBRAY. In behalf of all the veterans, who have grown grey under the command of Smith, thanks, noble lady, thanks.—Long live the flower of Virginia. (*Shouts.*)

SMITH. And now let me place my gold chain, the symbol of the preux chevalier, and which I bequeath'd to this lady at my death, around the neck of her who hath preserv'd my life.

PERCY. And bind two in thy golden shackle, the good and gallant Master Rolfe, and thou wilt unite the hands of those whose hearts have long since been united.

SMITH. Aha! Master Rolfe, do ye plead guilty to the charge?

ROLFE. Aye, and glory in the guilt.

SMITH. What sayeth the lady?

POCAHONTAS. She will most cheerfully submit to wear the chain which binds her to the honour'd master of her fate, even tho' the chain were of iron instead of gold.

SMITH. May every happiness attend this union of virtue and honour.

ALL. Amen, amen.

PERCY. So please ye, the prisoner.

(*Enter* MATACORAN, *guarded.*)

SMITH. Aye, true, unbind him; the brave honour the brave alike in misfortune and prosperity.

HUGO. So please ye to favour your veteran Hugo, let this grateful task be mine. When I was a prisoner, this chief releas'd me, and gave me a chance to redeem mine arms, and now old Hugo performs the most pleasing duty of all his long and arduous services—to relieve a fallen enemy.

(*Takes off* MATACORAN'S *chains.*)

SMITH. Chief, our wars are ended; thy noble bearing claims all our esteem. Thou hast fought for thy country—we for ours. Let 's in future be friends, and join in friendship those hands, which lately wielded the weapons of enmity. Matacoran shall be of power and influence in the country which he hath so gallantly defended, and shall hold of the royal James posts of honour and trust in the newly acquired colony of Virginia.

MATACORAN. Hear me, chief. Know that Matacoran scorns thy friendship, and hates all thy kind. The fortune of war is on thy side; thy gods are as much greater than the gods of the Indian, as thine arms are greater than his. But altho' thy gods and thine arms have prevail'd, say did not Matacoran fight bravely in the last of his country's battles? and when his comrades fled, singly did he face the thunders of his foe. Now that he can no longer combat the invaders he will retire before them, even to where tradition says, there rolls a western wave. There, on the utmost verge of the land which the Manitou gave to his fathers, when grown old by time, and his strength decay'd, Matacoran will erect his tumulus, crawl into it and die. But when in a long distant day, posterity shall ask where rests that brave, who disdaining alliance with the usurpers of his country, nobly dar'd to be wild and free, the finger of renown will point to the grave of Matacoran.

(MATACORAN *rushes out.*)

SMITH. Brave, wild, and unconquerable spirit, go whither thou wilt, the esteem of the English goes with thee.

POWHATAN. Captain Smith, after what hath pass'd thou might well distrust my friendship for the future. But experience makes even an Indian wise. We cannot resist thee as enemies, therefore, it becomes us to be thy friends. In the name of Virginia, I pledge friendship to the English, so long as grass grows and water runs.

SMITH. And dost consent to the union of thine admirable daughter with worthy Master Rolfe?

POWHATAN. Aye, and let their union be a pledge of the future union between England and Virginia.

(*Enter* BARCLAY, MANTEA *and* NAMOUTAC.)

POWHATAN. And mine be the privilege of giving away the bride. And may the fruits of this union of virtue and honour be a long line of descendants, inheriting those principles, gifted with rare talents, and the most exalted patriotism. Now it only remains for us to say, that looking thro' a long vista of futurity, to the time when these wild regions shall become the ancient and honour'd part of a great and glorious American Empire, may we hope that when the tales of early days are told from the nursery, the library, or the stage, that kindly will be received the national story of POCAHONTAS, OR THE SETTLEMENT OF VIRGINIA.

CURTAIN FALLS.

THE BROKER OF BOGOTA

BY

Robert Montgomery Bird

The Broker of Bogota is printed for the first time, from the original manuscript presented to the Library of the University of Pennsylvania by Mr. Robert Montgomery Bird.

THE BROKER OF BOGOTA

The Broker of Bogota represents the romantic verse tragedy, written under the inspiration of Edwin Forrest. It represents also the interest in the Spanish colonies in America, in which its author, Robert Montgomery Bird, laid so many of the scenes of his plays and novels. Bird was born February 5, 1806, in New Castle, Delaware. After completing his school life at Germantown Academy, near Philadelphia, he entered the Medical School of the University of Pennsylvania, graduating on April 6, 1827. Although he started practice and at a later time (1841–3) was a member of the Faculty of the Pennsylvania Medical College in Philadelphia, medicine was never the main interest in his life. While still attending the University he was writing plays, and completed in 1827 two romantic tragedies, *The Cowled Lover* and *Caridorf*, and two comedies, *A City Looking Glass* (1828) and *News of the Night,* both dealing with life in Philadelphia. None of these was acted.

Pelopidas or The Fall of the Polemarchs, a tragedy laid in Thebes, was finished in 1830 and was accepted by Edwin Forrest. It was, however, not played by him, probably since it did not provide an opportunity for Mr. Forrest properly to exhibit his talent. Instead *The Gladiator,* which was based on the revolt of Spartacus against the tyranny of Rome, was substituted and was played for the first time in New York City, September 26, 1831, at the Park Theatre, and for the first time in Philadelphia at the Arch Street Theatre, October 24, 1831. *The Gladiator* has been produced by Edwin Forrest, John McCullough, Robert Downing and other actors, hundreds of times since that day. Of Dr. Bird's other successful plays, the first, *Oralloossa,* was produced for the first time at the Arch Street Theatre, Philadelphia, October 10, 1832, and was a tragedy founded on the Spanish Conquest of Peru. It was successful, running at its initial presentation for five nights against the strong counter-attraction of the Kembles at the Chestnut Street Theatre, but it never had the wide popularity of *The Gladiator.*

The Broker of Bogota was put on at the Bowery Theatre in New York, February 12, 1834, and was played by Forrest at least thirty years. Among the Bird manuscripts is a letter from Forrest to Dr. Bird, dated February 12, 1834, in which he says: "I have just left the theatre—your tragedy was performed and crowned with entire success. *The Broker of Bogota* will live when our vile trunks are rotten." Certainly in the character of "Febro," with his middle-class mind, lifted into tragedy by his passionate love for his children and his betrayal by his oldest and best loved son, Bird drew one of the most living portraits in our dramatic history. The clever entanglement of "Febro" largely by circumstances and the climax of the fourth act in which "Juana" denounces "Ramon," must have been effective on the stage.

Bird abandoned his dramatic work at the height of success. Discouraged by his financial dealings with Forrest, which brought the author a total of five thousand dollars, while the actor made a fortune out of *The Gladiator* alone, and prevented from publishing his plays, partly by the copyright laws and partly by Forrest's opposition, he turned to fiction and produced several novels, *Calavar* (1834), *The Infidel* (1835), both dealing with Cortez's expedition, and *Nick of the Woods* (1837), a story of Indian life in Kentucky, which was put on the stage by Louisa Medina and was widely popular. *The Infidel* was dramatized by Benjamin H. Brewster, and played in Philadelphia in 1835. Dr. Bird travelled extensively in this country and visited England in 1834, then after some excursions into politics settled in Philadelphia as editor and part proprietor of the *North American* and died January 23, 1854.

None of his plays has been published. The present editor was fortunate enough to find *The Broker of Bogota* and *Oralloossa* in manuscript at the Forrest Home at Holmesburg, Pennsylvania, but it remained for Mr. Clement Foust, of the English Department of the University of Pennsylvania, to discover a complete collection of the manuscripts of Dr. Bird in the possession of the latter's grandson, Mr. Robert M. Bird, who has generously presented them to the Library of the University of Pennsylvania. Mr. Foust has in preparation a life of Dr. Bird, a critical edition of *The Gladiator* and the other important plays, and a selection from among the many interesting letters to and from Dr. Bird contained in his correspondence with other writers. Among the most interesting of these is a letter from Dr. Bird's son, Rev. Frederick M. Bird, requesting permission from Forrest, who apparently held the copyrights, to publish his father's plays and, in answer, Forrest's curt refusal. Each of the plays exists in several forms and the present text of *The Broker of Bogota* has been prepared by Mr. Foust after a comparative study of the manuscripts. Through his courtesy the editor is able to reproduce it here.

The text is based primarily upon the complete manuscript copy, made by Mrs. Bird, the wife of the dramatist. This has been collated with the two autograph copies, neither of which is complete, and the resultant text represents, in Mr. Foust's judgment, the reading the dramatist preferred. This text was then compared with the acting version, at the Forrest Home. Additions from this acting version are indicated by square brackets while words, lines, or scenes omitted in stage production are enclosed in brackets of this form <>.

For discussions of Bird's plays, see James Rees, *The Dramatic Authors of*

America, Philadelphia, 1845, and his *Life of Edwin Forrest,* Philadelphia, [1874]; W. R. Alger, *Life of Edwin Forrest,* Philadelphia, 1877; Lawrence Barrett, *Edwin Forrest,* Boston, 1882, who gives (p. 51) the cast of *The Gladiator* at Drury Lane, October 17, 1836; Charles Durang, *History of the Philadelphia Stage,* Third Series, Chaps. 16, 25; F. C. Wemyss, *Twenty-six Years of the Life of an Actor Manager,* New York, 1847, Vol. 2, p. 239; E. P. Oberholtzer, *Literary History of Philadelphia,* Philadelphia, 1907.

Note to Second Edition.

In 1919, Dr. Clement Foust published the *Life and Dramatic Works of Robert Montgomery Bird,* containing a reprint of *The Broker of Bogota,* and printing for the first time *The Gladiator, Pelopidas* and *Oralloossa.*

On May 21, 1920, the Zelosophic Society of the University of Pennsylvania reproduced *The Broker of Bogota* at the Bellevue-Stratford Ball Room, Philadelphia, under the direction of Mrs. William Merriman Price. The production revealed clearly the great appeal of the play from the point of view of dramatic structure, and the fine quality of the blank verse was apparent. As had been expected, the characters of "Febro" played by Kirk Heselbarth, of the Class of '21, and of "Juana" played by Elizabeth Canning of the Class of '20, were the most appealing, and it was interesting to see that in a play written for Edwin Forrest, the most effective scene (Act IV, Scene 4) was one in which he was not on the stage.

Note to Fifth Edition.

Bird's skill as a writer of comedy was revealed when *News of the Night* was played for the first time on any stage by the Columbia Laboratory Players at the McMillan Theatre in New York, on November 2, 1929. This early play, while farcical, proved to be bright in dialogue and rapid in movement. It deals with the deception of a miserly guardian by his two nieces, well-contrasted characters, and his capture by his housekeeper, one of the most vivid of the parts.

Note to Sixth Edition.

The City Looking Glass was edited by A. H. Quinn for *The Colophon,* New York, 1933, with a biographical introduction. The play was produced for the first time by the Zelosophic Society of the University of Pennsylvania, at Irvine Hall, January 20, 1933. The production established its significance as one of the earliest plays dealing with the seamy side of life in America. *The Cowled Lover, Caridorf, 'Twas All for the Best,* and *News of the Night* have been edited by Edward H. O'Neill for the American Play Text Series and will be published in the near future.

CHARACTERS

[Bowery Theatre, New York City, February 12, 1834.]

Marques De Palmera, Viceroy of New Granada................Mr. H. Gale

Fernando, his son..Mr. G. Jones

Baptista Febro, the broker..............................Mr. E. Forrest

Ramon, his sons..Mr. Ingersoll

Francisco, his sons......................................Mr. Connor

Mendoza, a merchant, father of Juana.....................Mr. Farren

Antonio De Cabarero, a profligate, friend of Ramon........Mr. H. Wallack

Pablo, an inn keeper.....................................Mr. McClure

Silvano, servant of Febro..................................

Leonor, daughter of Febro ....Mrs. Flynn

Juana, daughter of Mendoza..............................Mrs. McClure

Gentlemen of the Court, Citizens, Alguazils.

Scene, Santa Fé De Bogota.

THE BROKER OF BOGOTA

ACT FIRST.

SCENE 1. *The Street near* FEBRO'S *house.*

(*Enter* MENDOZA *and* RAMON.)

MENDOZA. You have your answer. Come no more near my house: I'll have no disobedient, disinherited sons there. <Come no more near to me.>

RAM. Señor Mendoza, you make my unhappiness my crime and condemn me for my misfortune.

MEN. Truly, I have so learned to criminate misfortune ever since I found that, when one grief springs from ill fate, twenty come from our own faults. I have never known a young man sink in the world, without finding he had overburdened himself with follies.

RAM. If you will listen to me, I will show you how much you wrong me.

MEN. Wrong you? I wrong you not: you are your own wronger. <I should be glad to be rid of you.>

RAM. You treat me with much shame, señor; but, for your daughter's sake, I forgive you.

MEN. So would I that your father did you for my daughter's sake; for then might I think of you for a son. But now, you must pardon me—Think no more of that.

RAM. Señor Mendoza, I have your promise to wed Juana.

MEN. I made that promise when you were your father's heir; and I break it, now that you are your father's outcast. I will have no discarded son for my child's husband, believe that.

RAM. My father will restore me to his favor.

MEN. When he does that, I will perhaps take thee to mine,—not before. <Fare thee well, señor.>

RAM. Señor Mendoza, it is said you will marry Juana <to another?

MEN. And if I do, señor, who is to gainsay me?>

RAM. To Marco, the young merchant of Quito?

MEN. Content thee, señor Ramon, Marco is neither discarded nor poor, nor ill spoken of; and will be a good husband for a good man's daughter. <Farewell—Come to me no more.>

RAM. By heaven, it shall not be!

MEN. Oho! it shall not be! You are the King of Castile, señor <Ramon!> You will have fathers marry their children to men of your choosing!

RAM. Señor, you will break my heart. It is enough to lose my father, my family—all—yet you will rob me of my betrothed wife.

MEN. Betrothed to Baptista Febro's heir, not to Ramon the penniless and houseless. <You are scurrilous.> I will talk with you no more. Farewell—and come no more near me: my daughter is not for you. (*Exit.*)

RAM. Misery follow thee, thou false old churl,
And age's torments! till they rack as sore
As the fresh pangs and agonies of youth.
Perhaps his daughter is not much averse:
Yet many an oath, with many a sigh, of old,
Breathed she for truth and loving constancy.

(*Enter* CABARERO.)

CAB. Hola, Ramon! brother Sorrowful! Señor Will-o'-the-wisp! are you there? I have been seeking <for> you.

RAM. I should think then thou hadst some execution upon me; for who else now seek me but my creditors?

CAB. Why, thy true friends, thy true friends (for am not I a host?), thy true friends, Cabarero. Come now, hast thou been petitioning thy father?

RAM. I tell thee, I had better ask an alms of the cutthroat on the highway, than of my father.

CAB. <An alms!> Oh, thou art the smallest-souled pretty fellow in all Granada here. Why dost thou talk of an alms? Art thou not thy father's eldest son?

Ram. Had I been the youngest, I should have been the happier.

Cab. Yea, thou shouldst have been a counter of beads, a beggar of blessings, a winner of the elder brother's portion. Pish! thy brother Francisco is a rogue; he has ousted thee from thine inheritance.

Ram. If any one have done that, thou art the man. I am ruined, Cabarero, and thou art my destroyer.

<Cab. Now, I think thou art repenting of thy sins; but thou goest about it the wrong way.>

Ram. Look, Cabarero, there is my father's roof. There is no swallow twittering under its eaves, that has a merrier heart or a gayer song, than were mine once, when I was a boy under it.

Cab. Ay, faith, and that wast because thou wert a boy, a silly boy. Now wert thou a man, a discreet and reasonable man, thou wouldst be even as merry as before. <Thou dost not think thou wert born to be always in a grin?>

Ram. I was the eye of my mother, the heart of—<my father>; my sister loved me; my brother—<ay, and my brother.> —ay, they all loved me; and there was no one that did not smile on me, from the priest at the confessional to the beggar at the door. By St. James, I had many friends then; and I deserved their favor, for I was of good fame and uncorrupted.

Cab. I see thou art a man whose head is likely to be as empty as his pockets. 'Slife! uncorrupted? <Thy nose uncorrupted!> Bad luck is the lot of the best.

Ram. Antonio, I say, thou hast destroyed me. Until I knew thee, I abhorred shame, and <it is true> my hand was as stainless as an infant's.

Cab. It was thy father's scurvy covetousousness that put thee on to showing thy spirit.

Ram. Thou didst delude me. By the heaven which has deserted me, I did not think this hand could rob!

Cab. Pho, thou art mad! Remember thou art in the street.

Ram. That is the word, Antonio.—I robbed him—robbed him like a base thief: and then I became the outcast.

Cab. And then thou becam'st a fool! Thou didst but take <what was> a part of thine inheritance.

Ram. <And> yet he forgave me that!

Cab. He did not hang thee, for that would have brought shame on his house. [Forgave thee!] He forced thee to be foolish, and then discarded thee—turned thee off like a sick servant—abandoned thee.

Ram. <I think he should not have done that. Had he forgiven me that!

Cab. Forgive! Nay, he forgave old Miguel the mule-driver a debt that would have kept thee in bread for a year; and yet it was evident to all that Miguel cheated him. But to forgive his own flesh and blood is another matter.

Ram. He forgave Miguel because he besought his pardon: I have not yet besought him. Dost thou remember the holy history of the prodigal?> Perhaps if I humble myself to him, he will forgive me.

Cab. If thou art of that mind, thou may'st see, o' the instant, how he will spurn thee. Look, he is here, with thy sister, and—Pho! thou tremblest!—'T is Mendoza, father of thy fair Juana.

(Febro, *with* Leonor *and* Mendoza, *crosses the stage.*)

Ram. He has discarded me too, and Juana is given to another. How can I entreat him? See, he will not look upon me!

Leon. Father, will you not speak? It is my brother Ramon.

Feb. The carrion vulture with him.—Get thee in.
I would I had no sons—What? in, I say!

(*Exit* Leonor *into the house.*)

Señor Mendoza, what you have said is well:
I must needs own the contract was too rash—
We are both agreed it shall not bind us more.
I hear young Marco is a worthy man:
Give him your daughter and heaven bless the match.
Will you enter, señor?

Men. I thank your favor, no.
This thing despatched, I will to other business.
Good evening, señor.

Feb. You will be happy, friend—
Take no wild hothead boy to be your son:
Look to his friends: If Marco have but one
Loves mirth more than integrity, discard him.
These gadflies are our curses—Fare you well.

(*Exeunt* Mendoza *and* Febro, *the latter into the house.*)

CAB. Oh! o' my conscience, a loving father!

RAM. He gave me no encouragement to speak to him. Had he but looked upon me kindly, that look would have cast me at his feet.

CAB. What, at his feet? Not if he were twenty times your father. <'Slid, at his feet! Why> he would have spurned thee. Didst thou hear? He has absolved Mendoza from the match,—robbed thee of Juana,—nay, and absolutely counselled the merchant to marry her to your rival. A loving and merciful father! He ruins thee every way. Were he mine own father, I would—

RAM. What wouldst thou do? Thou wouldst not kill him?

CAB. By mine honor, no. I hold any bodily harm done to one's parent altogether inexpiable. But I would not forgive him.

RAM. I will not!

CAB. Why, that was said like a man.

RAM. He forgives not me, he pardons not a folly, and how shall I forgive a cruelty? For a single weakness, he punishes me with all degradation and misery; expels me from his house; looks not on me in the street; leagues with those who wrong me; leaves me penniless and perishing; and even persuades another to break faith with me, and give my betrothed to a stranger: And how shall I forgive him?

CAB. Why, thou shalt not.

RAM. I will not. I am even a desperate man; and so I will yield me up to the wrath of desperation. Art thou my true friend?

CAB. Else may I have no better hope than purgatory.

RAM. We will kill the merchant of Quito.

CAB. No, the saints forbid! no murder. He hath not money enough with him.

RAM. Why, thou dost not think I will slay him for money?

CAB. And for what else should you be so bloody-minded? Thou art not mad enough to cut his throat because he loves thy mistress?

RAM. Thou knowest, if he live, he will marry her.

CAB. Oh! she detests him, and loves you.

RAM. Yet will she wed none her father mislikes; and her father likes not me.

CAB. Wherefore? Because you have lost your father's favor? No. Because you are called a wild fellow, and hate chapels? No. Because you are no longer the hopeful heir to Baptista Febro, the rich broker? Ay: there lies his disgust, thence comes his indignation. Now were you the veriest rogue in Bogota, he would love you well, so you had but money.

RAM. Why do you tell me that? I know he is mercenary; nothing will win his heart but money, a curse on it! I would I were rich for Juana's sake; but for myself, I care not for gold—It has been the ruin of me.

CAB. Thou speakest like an innocent goose. Money, <sirrah!> 't is the essence of all comfort and virtue. Thou carest not for gold! Give me gold, and I will show thee the picture of philosophy, the credential of excellence, the corner-stone of greatness. It is wisdom and reputation—the world's religion, mankind's conscience; and what is man without it? Pah! 'T is as impossible honesty should dwell easily in an empty pocket, as good humor in a hollow stomach, or wit in a full one. Didst thou ever see integrity revered in an old coat, or unworthiness scorned in a new? <Thou carest not for gold!> 'Slife, it made my blood boil to hear you say so.

RAM. Well, after all, as money or murder must rid me of my rival, tell me how one can be more easily come at than the other.

CAB. Why, you rogue, there is our silver mine! We have been hunting it long; we must needs be near the vein.

RAM. That stratagem is growing stale. I sware but this morning to an old friend, of whom I desired to borrow money that we had discovered the tomb of Bochica the Indian emperor, which was doubtless as full of gold as the Inca's grave in Peru; but the knave laughed at me, <and said if I found no gold in it, I should have plenty brass.>

CAB. The rascal! and he lent thee no money?

RAM. Not a real.

CAB. There is no gratitude among friends. <Do thy good offices to strangers; and courtesy will teach them the grace of thankfulness. Canst thou cheat nobody?

RAM. Cheat, Antonio?

CAB. Pho! be not in a passion. All 's honest that fetches money.> We must have gold, or Juana is lost.

RAM. Ay— Set me to what roguery you will, so it may regain her.

CAB. The tomb of Bochica, the Indian emperor! I know not by what hallucination it happens, but I never hear thee mention that, without thinking of the vaults of thy father.

RAM. Hah!

CAB. Now, were he not thy father, couldst thou not have the heart to rob him?

RAM. Rob him!

CAB. That is, as long as he oppresses thee so tyrannically. Faith, I would even steal mine own share.

RAM. Thou dost not seriously advise me to be such a villain?

CAB. No, good faith—I? I was jesting. But I will tell thee what thou shalt do. Thou shalt ask him for money.

RAM. And have him spurn me again?

CAB. Tell him thou art in danger of a prison.

RAM. I will go near him no more. No more begging! The prison first.

CAB. <Why, we must have money. I am sorry to tell thee, some evil rogues have disparaged us among the free gamesters, and they will be free with us no more.> Pablo the innkeeper is wrathful with thee, and says he must have money for thy food and lodging.

RAM. The villain! He has had my last dollar.

CAB. He is not so merciful as thy father; but he has harboured thee long. Hearken—I will go to thy father.

RAM. Thou!

CAB. And entreat him for thee very piteously.

RAM. <He will fill thy pockets with curses.

CAB. Why, then I will cheat him.

RAM. Cheat him?

CAB. Oh, thou dost not care?>

RAM. You may rob him, if you will: I care not.

CAB. I will cheat him with good security, and will fetch thee the money. <But I must not give thee too much hope: he will think I borrow it for thee, and will refuse me. But> do thou in the meanwhile endeavor to speak with Juana. Marco must not have her.

RAM. Not if any new dye upon my soul can preserve her. <Do what you will, or can; and if you fail, we will consider another way to amend our fortunes.>

CAB. All the men of Bogota are our enemies—How many of them have money in thy father's hands?

RAM. Why more than I can tell thee. But what has that to do with their enmity?

CAB. So much that if one were to break Baptista's vaults, we should have much feeding of grudges.

RAM. Say no more of this.

CAB. Look, here comes thy friend Mendoza again!

RAM. Where? Nay, thou art mistaken: 't is another, and a greater than Mendoza, and one not more our friend. Seest thou nothing beyond that muffled cloak? It is the Viceroy.

CAB. The Viceroy! I warrant me, he is spying over us. What does he in disguise? and near thy father's house?

RAM. Perhaps I could tell thee. But let us be gone. He hardens my father against me.—Let him not see us.

(*Exeunt.*)

SCENE 2. *A room in* FEBRO'S *house.*

(*Enter* FEBRO *and* LEONOR.)

FEB. Come hither, Leonora. What, my girl,
That stranger youth I bade thee see no more,
Dost thou still speak with him?

LEON. Alack, dear father,
I hope you are not angry.

<FEB. Is it so?
Comes he still near thee?

LEON. Oh, I am sure indeed,
I never gave him countenance.>

FEB. I charged thee
Give him such scorn, if still he followed thee,
As should have driven him from thee: for, indeed,
These trashbrained idlers, that do follow thee,
Sighing in chapel, staring in the street,
And strumming silly lovesongs at thy window,
They are but things of naught,—base, lazy rogues,
That hunt for rich men's daughters for their prey,
And now they haunt thy steps the more, because
The broker, weak old Febro, that must die,
In natural course of age, ere many years,
Hath but two heirs to share his hoards.

LEON. Dear father,
Will you not then forgive my brother Ramon?
I know he is very sorry he e'er grieved you;
And on his heart your wrath must needs be heavy.

FEB. If thou believ'st so, then, in time, beware
It fall not upon thine. <In sooth, I think,
Thou art leagued with him to vex me.—> O ye saints!
Punish these villains that seduce men's sons,
Making them villains; and with vengeance follow
The knaves that teach our daughters disobedience.

LEON. Dear father, none shall teach me that.

FEB. They shall not,
When thou seest no more rogue Rolandos.

LEON. Father,
Indeed, I think, he is honest.

FEB. Nay, a knave!
He doth not come to me, but ever shuns me.
He hath no friends; no man in Bogota
Hath made acquaintance with him: he flies all
Like a scared thief, save only thee alone,
<And comes to thee like one, cloaked, almost masked,
As when he followed thee from the carnival.
Now were my Ramon what in youth he was,
He should be thy protector, and soon drive me
This wasp away.

LEON. If he return again,>
I'll bid him come no more;—I will indeed,
Till he has talked with you, and satisfied you.

FEB. Why there's my girl! Let him but come to me;
I'll tell him that I mean thee for another.

LEON. Another, father! I do not wish to marry.

FEB. Thus silly maids will talk! Why, thou poor finch,
A gentleman hath asked thee for his wife,—
Rich, I assure thee, virtuous, honorable,
And a hidalgo.

LEON. And so is Roland, too.

FEB. Speak'st thou of Roland? Thou wilt anger me.
He a hidalgo! By my faith, I think,
Some heathenish villain, that with magic arts
Hath wound about thy spirits. He I meant,
Is Baltasar, son of Don Lucas Moron.
Dost thou name him and Roland in a breath?
I' faith, thou stirr'st me,—

(*Enter* SILVANO.)

What would'st thou, Silvano?

SILV. A customer to your worship.

FEB. It is a holiday.
I will no business do today.

SILV. Your favor
Must pardon me. It is his Excellency.

FEB. His Excellency! oh thou foolish knave.
To leave him waiting!—

(*Enter* PALMERA.)

Please, your noble highness,
Pardon my silly fellow.

PALM. Good Baptista,
Forget my state,— it is too cumbersome.
I am even your humble suitor and poor friend.—
My pretty Leonor! Now, by my life,
Which like a desert river, flows away,
I would some green and flourishing plant like thee
Had rooted by my current: then indeed
I should have seen the surges of my age
Dash with a sweet contented music on,
Nor thought their course was sterile.

FEB. A silly maid.
Your highness is too good.—Go, Leonora.
(*Exeunt* LEONORA <*and* SILVANO.>)
<A silly maid! and yet, or I do dream,
Loving and true. And yet—But that's no matter.—
I am at your highness' bidding.>

PALM. Sit down, Baptista.—
Oh, then, I must be viceroy and command you.—
I have much to say to thee.

FEB. I am sorry your grace
Did not command me to the palace.

PALM. No.
Perhaps I have a reason I could tell you.
Febro, you have my confidence, and know,
What were a wonder unto other men,
How one can sit upon a viceroy's chair,
Yet heap no wealth about him.

FEB. Please your highness,

Your predecessors on Granada's throne,
Ne'er found a lack of gain; and, sooth to say,
I do remember when no mine could yield,
Though by a thousand Indians daily wrought,
So rich a revenue as the rod of state
In one man's hands, were but that man the viceroy.

PALM. Such was its wealth, and such may be again,
To him with heart to use it. But for myself,
I cannot stoop to use those under means,
That fill the purse of office; and I would gnaw
Sooner my food from off my barren trappings,
Than gild them vilely with the fruits of fraud,
Sales, bribes, exactions, and monopolies,
The rich dishonor of prerogative.
<I will this kingdom leave with no man's curse,
And no man's scorn; and to mine own land bear
Even the poor burden that I brought with me,
An honest pride and pure integrity.
'T is from this thought that I make use of thee,
Out of that lean estate I have, to win
Such gain as my necessities require,
And such as though my state must keep it secret,
I have no shame to grasp at.

FEB. Would indeed
This principle should come with your successor.>

PALM. I have some gold, which I would have you place
Even at what profitable trade you can,
But not in peril; for indeed it is
After some worthless antique lands in Spain,
The only portion I can give my son,
But now arrived in Bogota.

FEB. Your highness
Shall faithfully be served.

PALM. I doubt not that.
Soon as you will, some trusty messenger
Send to the court, and he shall bear the gold.

FEB. My son shall be despatched.

PALM. Your son, Baptista!

FEB. My son Francisco,—I dare assure your highness,
A trusty youth, and most unequalled son.

PALM. In sooth, I thought you meant his elder brother.

FEB. Francisco, please your grace,—an excellent boy,
<Mine only hope and comfort,—a dutiful son.>
It is a holiday, and the youths have left
Their prisoned warehouses, and look for mirth
In the gay squares and streets,—all but Francisco.
He nooks him at his desk, and still pores o'er
The weary mysteries of accounts, as though
Wisdom, as well as wealth, were writ among them.

PALM. A commendable zeal. But tell me, Febro,—
This should have been the elder brother's office.
Pardon me, Febro; but beshrew my heart,
I speak to thee in friendship, when I meddle
In family affairs. You are too harsh:
Indeed it is the towntalk, your severity
To your discarded son.

FEB. It is the towntalk!
The town will disobedience teach to children,
Then censure fathers, who do punish them.
This is the course, and justice of the town!

PALM. But still, men say, the penance you inflict
Is all too heavy for his boyish follies.

FEB. Follies! No doubt, they told your excellency
He idled at his task, sometimes made blunders,
Played truant oft, and sometimes laughed at chapel—
Such follies!

PALM. No, I must needs own, for truth,
They were of darker color,—running forth
With youths disorderly and riotous,
Unto the tavern and the gaming-house.

FEB. Riotous friends!
Drinking, and gambling! Sir, these are such follies
In youth, as fraud and robbery in men;
And he who clouds his dawn of life with such
Shall have a fouller tempest for its close.

PALM. And yet these are such ills as gentleness

Might best reprove; and, for those after crimes,
Surely your son has not plunged into them?

FEB. I do not say it! There is no man dare say it.—
I say, my Ramon is a foolish boy.
Your highness cannot say I e'er accused him
Of aught but folly.

PALM. The more unwise your anger,
Which may compel him into crime. Baptista,
He is the only one of your three children
Whose weakness vexes you.

FEB. I'll not say that.

PALM. What, Febro? And the paragon, Francisco?

FEB. He never gave me pain.

PALM. And Leonor?
My pretty Leonor?

FEB. The world's best daughter!

PALM. O foolish man, that art not yet content,
When heaven that crowns thee with two perfect joys,
Dashes a little gall upon the third!
<Wilt thou be harsher than all other sires,
Because thou art happier? Oh, believe me Febro,
There is no father but must much forgive;
There is no father but must much lament;>
And I, that have but one child to mine age,
And him would have an angel in my love,
Even see him tainted with the spots of youth,
And envy thee that hast such bliss with thine.

FEB. Sir, I have heard the young Fernando bore him
Like a most just and virtuous gentleman.

PALM. And yet, though but few days in Bogota,
His heart is tangled in a low intrigue,
A base amour. But shall I drive him from me?
I will not ape thy cruelty, but bid thee
Follow mine own mild counsels, which will give thee
Thy son again, a loving penitent.

FEB. Sir, I would have him feel in sharp extreme
The bitter issues of his degradation.
'T is need he feel them.

PALM. They oppress him now:
I saw him sad and moody near thy house,
Humbled to earth.

FEB. Ay! but with Cabarero!
The villain that seduced him into folly,
And still cajoles him on. He has his choice,—
That caitiff, or his father—He has his choice!

PALM. Well, well, think better of him. He loves the man,
Who seems to be his fast unflinching friend.
Think of my counsel.

FEB. At your highness' feet!
Francisco shall attend you to the palace,—
What, boy! Francisco!

PALM. I prythee, keep thy house.
I will not have thee follow to the doors.

FEB. Your excellency's slave.

(*Exeunt.*)

SCENE 3. *The street at* FEBRO'S *door.*

(*Enter* SILVANO *and* FERNANDO.)

SILV. I do wonder at your presumption, señor Rolando.

FERN. And I do wonder at thine honesty. If thou wilt not for money, oh then for love bear my message to the fair Leonor.

SILV. To peep from the window, and see how prettily thou wilt kiss thy hand to her! Art thou really a hidalgo?

FERN. I am really a hidalgo, a Spanish hidalgo.

SILV. And your worship does really love my mistress?

FERN. My worship does most devoutly adore your divine mistress.

SILV. And if you gain her good will, you will make her your worship's wife?

FERN. If I gain her good will, I will fly straightway to the altar; <If not, I will e'en betake me to the halter.>

SILV. Why, if thou wert an honest gentleman, thou would'st demand her of her father. He would be glad to have a hidalgo for a son.

FERN. Oh, thou art a silly fellow. I am a poor hidalgo, which is naught to a rich commoner.

SILV. Señor Rolando, I like thy face indifferent well; but I think thou art some rogue, and no noble.

FERN. If thou wilt be as loving as I am noble, hear my petition, and beseech my young divinity to look from the window.

SILV. Who knows? Why, señor Febro is within.

FERN. How shall he hear the silver voice of his daughter, when his ears are filled with the golden jingle of his coffers?

SILV. Well, stay a moment till his excellency goes.

FERN. His excellency! What excellency?

SILV. Why, his excellency the Viceroy. <He is a great friend of my master.>

FERN. Oh! fire and furies! the Viceroy! Now, I remember me, I have to meet a friend in the great square.

SILV. Stay, señor Hidalgo, here comes his excellency. Señor, you are a rogue! God be with you! (*Exit* FERNANDO.) Well, thou art a mysterious, good-for-nothing, agreeable rascal, I warrant me; and somehow, I begin to love thee. But thou hast a wholesome dread of great men.

(*Enter, from house,* PALMERA, FEBRO, *and* FRANCISCO. LEONOR *appears at the door.*)

FEB. Heaven keep your excellence a thousand years!
Thou hast thy charge, Francisco.—Heaven save your highness!
(*Exeunt* PALMERA *and* FRANCISCO.)
Silvano, hast thou heard more things of Ramon?

SILV. Please your worship, I heard he was last night at Mateo's gambling house.

FEB. The wretched boy!

SILV. And, please your worship, he hurt one with his dagger for calling him a cheat.

FEB. A cheat! Would he had never been born!

SILV. But then, it was a slander; or how should he have stabbed a man for telling the truth?

FEB. Ay, slander, Silvano! He could not cheat.

SILV. <And the gambler's boy that told me, he is a most notorious liar.

FEB. I cannot but believe it was a lie.>

SILV. And then, if he had cheated, he should have had money; whereas, they say, he is in great poverty; and Pablo the innkeeper threatens to put him in prison.

FEB. In prison! I have been too harsh.

SILV. <But that, I think, is only to make your worship pay his debts; for Pablo is reckoned to be a rascal.

FEB. Will Ramon agree to this roguery? I will not pay a real.>

SILV. Please your worship, I have heard no more of his doings.

FEB. Well, I did love him well,—but that 's no matter.
My Rachel loved him too, as her first born;
And, for a boy, he was the lovingest one
Mine eyes ere looked upon. <Get in, Leonora.
Why wilt thou stand at doors, to be gazed on
By these young bawbling wantons of the town?
They 'll smirk at thee, and wink, and kiss their hands:
I know them very well,—such gewgaw brains,
And hearts of rotten stone, and trash and lies—
Wilt thou not hear me? What? (*Exit* LEONORA.) By all the saints,
She is the very apple of mine eye.
She does not love this fellow:—the whim of girls,
To have well-favored youths a-wooing them.—>
I know that rogue—is it not Cabarero?
Oh, the base villain! had he been but hanged
Six years agone, or ere he looked upon
My foolish boy!—Well, will he speak with me?

(*Enter* CABARERO.)

Come, let us in.

CAB. Hola, you money-vender!
You reverend old blood-grater of the poor!
Tarry, I 'll speak with you.

FEB. Now all the saints
Give me a little patience.

CAB. Come, how stand
Your vaults and money bags? Still filling, filling,
Like the horseleech's paunch, and crying "More!"?
I 'll be thy customer. What rate today?
Not cent per cent, with tenth of gross for premium?
Be reasonable, and I 'll deal with thee.
These are hard times, faith.

FEB. I will not be angry,
Why should I with a rascal? Señor, base fellow,
You may go hang or drown—I 'll give you naught.

CAB. No, by mine honor, no, you will not *give* me,
Else should the devil grow weary of the earth.
And leave 't to angels. Give me indeed! When pesos
Change to perditions, ducats to damnation,
Then will I look for gifts. But how now, señor?
'Slid, I believe you are angry!—What 's the news?
How fares my little soul, fair Leonor?
Upon my faith, she 's an exceeding girl:
What portion will you give her? Sometimes I
Do think of marriage; and hidalgo blood
Has often stooped to gutters.

FEB. Which is to say,
Your honor might be bribed to marry her?

CAB. Noble 's a noble dower; and so I say,
Verily so, if well thou portion'st her.

FEB. Then shalt thou hear it—When she weds a man
Like thee, her portion shall be cords and ratsbane,
Curses and misery! Oh, thou bold bad man,
How canst thou look me in the face, nor think
Of ruin'd Ramon?

CAB. I do think of him,
And wonder at the rage that ruins him.

FEB. Sirrah!

CAB. Why, how you fume? I come to you
To borrow money—good faith, a thousand ducats—
At highest rates of interest, with surety
Of good sufficient names, to be repaid
Out of my new discovered silver mine.—
I say, good names.

FEB. Were they angelical,
Thou shouldst not have a doit to hang thyself.

CAB. Harkee, old sir—I meant a part thereof
To feed thy starving Ramon.

FEB. Knave, thou liest!
It is to tempt him on to further shame.
To deeper ruin!

CAB. Thou art angry,—I forgive thee.
But know, unless thou send'st him money straight,
He will be lodged in prison. Ope thy heart;
Send him some gold.

FEB. Art thou his friend?

CAB. His best.

FEB. <Thou lovest my Ramon—ay, and thou lovest gold:>
I 'll teach thee how to serve him as a friend,
And how to win thee money.

CAB. Speak that *how*.

FEB. Leave Bogota forever; swear me that:
Get thee from hence to Spain; and I will give thee
A thousand ducats.

CAB. Faith, now you speak in jest!

FEB. I say, I 'll give them to thee, nay, and more,
Swear me but that, and keep thine oath.

CAB. A thousand?
A thousand ducats to leave Bogota?
No, not for five!

FEB. Wilt thou not go for five?

CAB. Art thou in earnest?

FEB. So may the saints befriend me;
Get thee to Spain; leave Ramon unto me,
And thou shalt have five thousand ducats.

CAB. 'Slid!
I take thy offer. Give me the gold.

FEB. Soft, soft:
I 'll have thine oath before a notary;
Find thee conveyance unto Carthegena;
Pay thee a portion when thou art embarked,
And count the rest, in yearly sums, to thee,
Only in Spain.

CAB. Five thousand on the nail,
Paid here in Bogota; to which e'en add
A thousand yearly to be paid in Spain,
During my term of life.

FEB. O grasping villain!
Thou wouldst have all, and yet wilt go with none.
If thou wilt more, there 's money in my vaults;
Break them, and rob me!

CAB. Oh! dost thou invite me?

FEB. Rob me, thou knave, that I may have thy life!
Do me that crime, and hang!

CAB. Most antique churl,
Thou shalt be sorry for this fantasy.
Thou hast no gold for Ramon?

FEB. Hence, begone!
And a deep curse go with thee, a father's curse!
Get thee to fraud and crime, to theft and murder.
Become notorious to thyself, and sleep,

Dreaming of gibbets, to wake up to racks;
Rob other sires of other sons; bring wo
On other houses; till the general curse
Heaped like a mountain o'er thy head, reach heaven,
And wall thee in its fiery hell forever!
Hence, monster, hence! (*Exeunt.*)

END OF ACT ONE.

ACT SECOND.

SCENE 1. *A street near* MENDOZA'S *house.*

(*Enter* RAMON *and* PABLO.)

PAB. I am a poor man, señor Ramon: I must have money.

RAM. Wert thou as penniless as a beggar, still couldst thou have nothing of me; for I am poorer.

PAB. Thy father is the richest man in Bogota. He should pay for thy food.

RAM. Get thee to him, and tell him so. Look, thou insatiate rogue, I have signed and countersigned all thy villainous obligations; I have owned me here thy debtor, and confessed thou canst justly hale me to prison. <What more can I do? If thou canst use these to any honest purposes, or dishonest either, I care not. Get thee to my father. If he will give thee money, I am content; if not, 't is but a word to the alguazil, and thou shalt have so much satisfaction as my incarcerated misery can give thee.>

PAB. Thou knowest I should be loath to be so unfriendly.

RAM. I know, thou art as much a cormorant as the rest <and as rapacious for my lean and impoverished body as ever thou wert in my days of fatness.> Get thee away: I have one honest friend left, whom I would not willingly have to see me in thy company.

PAB. Why, I hope thou art not ashamed of me?

RAM. No, I am now ashamed of nothing. The grace in me that would have once blushed at unworthiness, is gone; and I have nothing left for contempt but myself—myself. Go, get money, if thou canst; it is thy only hope; thy stay will only rob me of my last. Go, I prythee.

PAB. Well, God be with you. If I can cheat your father, you shall have some of the gain. (*Exit.*)

RAM. Thus doth severity still goad me on
Into a hateful villainy; and chains me
<Whate'er my sighs for better liberty>
To fellowship with rogues more vile than I.
Thou drivest me, father, to this noose of shame;
And wilt not bate thy wrath, till I am dead.—

(*Enter* JUANA.)

I looked for thee, Juana! for I knew
Though all else had deserted me, thou couldst not.

JUAN. Ramon, I have few words to speak to thee;
And even with these, I lay upon my soul
The sin of disobedience.

RAM. Ay, indeed!
You will obey your sire!

JUAN. What else should I?
I am his only child; in whom, in sooth,
Heaven would not pardon an unfilial act.

RAM. Speak boldly; leave me, like the rest, and fear not;
Say, Marco is a rich and honored man,
And Ramon lost to wealth and reputation:
There 's none but will commend thee.

JUAN. Say not that:
Thou know'st, I never loved thee for thy wealth;
For, sooth, I liked thee best when that was gone;
With thy hard father's heart: and, for thy name,
These evil tales destruction speaks of thee,
But spur me on to be thy advocate.
I never gave them faith.—

RAM. Lies! that are ever
Writ, by contempt, upon the poor man's brow,
But puffed, by flattery, from all jewelled fronts.
But yesterday men found the rich man's son
Worthy and honorable, without stain;
Today they find the fallen outcast's face
Charged with the sinful leprosy of years—
An hour for transformation!

JUAN. They will find thee
Stainless again, when thou art fortunate.
Hark to me, Ramon: there are not many days,
Ere I am lost to thee. Unless thou find
Before they pass, some happy road to wealth,

Fortune will come too late to purchase me.
Get gold, and win my father's heart again
Ere he do marry me to Marco.

RAM. Heaven
Smite his false, churlish heart!

JUAN. Curse not my father:
Do that which shall appease him.

RAM. Marry thee?
He had not thought it without thine own consent!

JUAN. How thou dost wound me, Ramon! O bright saints,
It was but now, as, at my lattice sitting,
I looked down on the gardens of our sires,
Which, in their days of friendship, our blest childhood,
Did make one common paradise.—I thought
Even of the thousand hours there, hand in hand,
We had roamed among the blossoms. All this time
My father was beseeching me for Marco.
I saw no Marco, at the lemon-tree;
It was not Marco, from the chirimoya,
Had stolen the fragrant buds to crown me with;
It was not he had caught the humming bird,
To keep him radiant in my memory;
I saw naught there but Ramon, and my heart
Even while I wept, was hardened to my father;
And with that sin, and with those tears, I won
A last grace for thee—still a week of trial;
A week wherein if fortune smile upon thee
The rites with Marco shall not be enforced.

RAM. And how shall fortune smile again?

JUAN. <I'll teach thee:
Give o'er all thought of mines; they will delude thee
On to a golden madness, but no wealth.

RAM. What else remains?>

JUAN Thy father,
<Ramon, thy father.>

RAM. My tyrant! my destroyer!

JUAN. Speak not thus,—
Though harsh and most unjust, thy father, Ramon!

RAM. Wed Marco! Now by heaven, not even for thee
Will I be spurned again.

JUAN. Ramon, not spurned.

RAM. Thou dost not know what wrong my sire has done me.
This wreck thou seest of what I was, this shred
Of my rent happiness, this squalid relic
Of a once fair and ample reputation,
This misery of heart and character—
'T is what my father makes me! No, thou knowst not
The depth of wrong he has done me.

JUAN. Still remember
What e'er thy suffering, that his wrath, first springing
From the base slanders of thine enemies,
Thine own rough pride still kindles. Nay, my Ramon—
I know his nature; and, though much incensed,
His heart is yearning to forgive thee,

RAM. Ay!
I have found it so!

JUAN. Thou didst not personally
Sue to him. Go thyself, go—send no more
Thy friend to him. I like not Cabarero;
I fear he is not the true friend you believe him.
Go to him, Ramon, and beseech his pardon.
Think, if thou gain'st him, thou gain'st me.

RAM. Well, well—
This day already did I go before him.
He frowned and passed me by; and, as to mad me
With the extreme of most vindictive wrath,
Did while I stood hard by, advise thy father
To marry thee to Marco.

JUAN. <Then heaven help me,
There is no hope!

RAM. Perhaps I'll find a mine.>

JUAN. Alas, once more, once more beseech him, Ramon.
Seek him alone, humble thyself before him.
I will beseech him too. It cannot be,
He has learned to hate thee. I will aid thy suit.
Once more, once more, or I am lost forever.

RAM. Well, well, I'll think of it.—But wed not Marco.

JUAN. Not till the week be o'er; but after that
I have sworn to do my father's bidding.

'T was by that oath, I gained this week for thee.

(*Enter* MENDOZA.)

Alack, I am torn from thee!

MEN. What, silly girl!
Get thee to house. Thou wilt not win this puppet
By wooing her i' the street. One last word, Señor,
A week hence is my daughter's wedding day.

(*Exit* MENDOZA, *with* JUANA.)

RAM. If I do go to him, he will not hear me—
A week?—Nay, though with tears I should conjure him
Ere he have brought a smile upon his face,
New words of new misdeeds will turn its light
Into a fiercer flame: he must needs find
Fresh stains of degradation—I will not go.
If he have thought to pardon me at all,
I 'll know't by Cabarero.

(*Enter* CABARERO.)

RAM. What, Antonio?
What said my father?

CAB. Your father? Humph!—Is Febro your father? I think we have all along made a mistake. What said he? I am afraid it will not comfort thee to hear. We will not talk it in the street; thou wilt relish it better over a cup of wine.

RAM. He has rejected my suit?

CAB. Wilt thou hear how? Let us begone to Pablo's; for, I swear to thee, rage and despair are making me very thirsty.

RAM. He will give me no relief?

CAB. Wilt thou search my pockets? I offered him good security. It is true, the names were not so honestly written; but he asked not to see them.—Not a penny, not a penny; not even to save thee from perdition.—Pho, how thou sighest! Come, shall we go to drink? Humph! —if thou knewest how foolish 't is to be melancholy.—Now have I been thinking, a quarter of a minute, how much thy silly face looks like an epitaph—a morsel of silent lamentation over thy dead and buried hopes. Well, thou art content to give up Juana?

RAM. Because Febro, the broker, loves me not!—I will call him father no more.—He would neither lend to you, who could give him the securities of law; nor to me, who have some of the claims of nature?

CAB. Not a penny. 'Sfuries, had you but seen how he reviled me like a dog! And the more I begged him in thy name, the more wrathfully did he abuse me. *Lend thee money?* said he; *I will lend thee the pangs of purgatory: Lend thee money! I will lend thee the whipping post.* Thou knowst he was thy father, otherwise I had pulled him by the beard. *Send me then comfort to thy afflicted and perishing son,* quoth I, with a moderate supplicatory air. *I will see him jailed, doomed and hanged first,* said he.

RAM. He did not say this?

CAB. Oh, not in such brief measures, to be sure: but that was the end of a ten minutes' malediction.

RAM. <Why then good luck to him and no more begging. Whose throat shall we cut? Money must be had.

CAB. Thy father has most shamefully treated thee, that 's certain.>

RAM. I will forget it when he has driven me to the grave, not sooner. Money must be had—and within a week. Men have been guilty of parricide. <Money, money! Have you no money?

CAB. Here is a handful [of] shabby pistareens, if thou art famishing. Let us go and drink a toast to Marco's fair wife.>

RAM. Shall we hang, drown, rob, or commit murder? I will now do any villainy thou canst recommend me.

CAB. Most unnaturally wronged, and unnaturally abandoned. This should excuse any vengeance. Thou must do thyself right. And thy milkfaced brother shall have thine inheritance! Thou must right thyself—

RAM. Before the week end; or I am in prison, and Juana married.

CAB. I could teach thee a way. Come let us begone. 'Sblood! are there no scavengers?—What have we here? By the mass, a key! Now might this belong to a rich man's door, and—

RAM. Hah!

CAB. Why what is the matter with thee? Is it gold? a basilisk?

RAM. The lost key of my father's vault!

CAB. Ho, have the saints forgot thee? Why, here is vengeance! wealth! Juana! —It is not thy father's key?

RAM. I have handled it a thousand times! 'T was lost a month ago.

CAB. Ha, ha! thy father bade me rob him! Give me the key. Look—thou art poor, miserable; this will make thee happy. Did destiny put it under thy foot for nothing?—Hark 'ee—this is the true mine! Come, Juana is waiting for thee! A little wine will put thee out of this stare,— and this will help thee to thine inheritance. (*Exeunt.*)

<SCENE 2. *The street before* FEBRO'S *door.*

(*Enter* LEONOR *and* FERNANDO.)

FERN. Trust me, sweet Leonor, I have good cause
To hide me from thy father.
LEON. It is no cause
Of a good man, that makes him shun the good.
FERN. The best, that have infirmities, are worst
Under their proper passions; and the foible,
Which, in thy sire, to other men, seems harmless,
May make him, in mine eyes, detestable.
LEON. What is 't that makes you say so? If indeed,
As I will not believe, thou lovest me,
My sire should seem an angel in thine eyes.
FERN. And so he should, did I not know, in his,
My own poor image would be devilish.
LEON. Well, I care not. You will be sorry soon,
When I am wedded to another.
FERN. Wedded!
You do but tell me this to mock my heart.
Then laugh me out of sorrow.
LEON. No indeed:
'T was but this morning that my father said,
I should be married to Don Baltasar.
And I do think, because you will not do
As love would still have taught you, for my sake,
It will be best to marry Baltasar.
FERN. To marry Baltasar! You cannot think
To be so false. What, wed? and Baltasar?
LEON. He asks my father for me.
FERN. So would I;
But that I know, the answer to my prayer
Would be, the curse to look on thee no more.
LEON. Not if thou beest an honest gentleman.
FERN. Honest I know not, for this love might seem
To my stern father, subtle and deceitful;
But so far honest, I would rather give
These limbs up, to be torn by wild horses,
Than ever do thee wrong. Sweet Leonor,
Know, if I seek thy sire, he will demand me
My father's name; whereat I needs must speak
Such hateful syllables, as will turn his heart
As by a fiendish magic, into coals;
And if he do not kill me (as, indeed
The sudden pang of rage may urge him to)
At least, he 'll drive me from thy face forever.
I am the son of his worst enemy.
LEON. Alas, he has no enemies. I ne'er heard him
Speak of an enemy.
FERN. The fiercest rage
Hides, like the wolf, from daylight; the rough vulture
Asleep upon his perch, doth seem as harmless
As the poor innocent dove that 's nested by.
And Febro, brooding o'er a secret hate,
May veil his anger with a face of peace.
Why should he speak of enemies to thee?
LEON. Art thou indeed his enemy?
FERN. No, not I.
I did forget the rage my father taught me
Soon as I looked on thee.—Wed Baltasar?
LEON. I will not marry Baltasar.
FERN. But lo,
Thy sire will have thee forced.
LEON. What shall I do?
Some maids would be so silly, they would fly
If much persuaded.
FERN. If thou look'st upon me
Howe'er my fearful thoughts may start at folly
I will persuade thee.
LEON. Not unless he force me!
He 'll ne'er forgive me.
FERN. O thou simple sweet,
If thy sire foam, mine own will anger more.
But we 'll forget them.
LEON. Come to me again,
And then perhaps I will—And if I do,
My father will be so lonely. But then indeed

He will forgive my brother: and, with my brother,
He will be happy! yes, indeed, more happy
Than with poor me.

FERN. Thou dost persuade thyself;
And, in thy arguments, I am resolved.
We will fly.

LEON. Not till he force me!

FERN. Shall I wait?
Till thou art married? Get thyself prepared:
And see thou have not store of bags and boxes,
As will o'erload a caravan of mules—
Tonight I'll come for thee.

LEON. No, not so soon.
Get thee away. There comes my brother Francisco!—
But come to me again,—yes, come again!
(Exeunt.)>

<SCENE 3. *A room in* FEBRO'S *house.*

(Enter FEBRO *and* SILVANO, *with books.)*

FEB. That money lent to Tomas Catalan,—
Four thousand marks,—is it not due today?
I' faith, 't was yesterday. Where is Francisco?
Doth he so slur my books? Why this way was
With Ramon, when he 'gan to change and fall,—
Four thousand marks—Threatened with prison too!—
A good, safe man.—His mother ne'er dreamed this,—
Threatened with prison—penniless—forsook.
Why then perhaps the penance is too sore;
His excellency says it is too heavy:
He is a good man, and a wise man too.
And it may be, if I deny him more,
Necessity may force him to such guilt,
As will his ancient follies make seem virtues.
Poverty has an angel's voice, to plead
Excuse of sin.—The town doth talk of me,
They call me overharsh; and Cabarero
Says, it is I myself that ruin him.
He'll lose his bride too. Think'st thou not, Silvano,
I might to Pablo's go, and no man see me?

SILV. To Pablo's, señor?

FEB. No, let him come to me. I will do naught to make men stare at me.

SILV. The saints forbid!—I think he has not his mind.
Rob him! and go to Pablo's! or have Pablo,
That low, base, scurvy rascal, come to him!

FEB. Say he be jailed, the lesson then is ended;
The foul familiar parts from him; and he
Repents him in his bonds. But that disgrace
May break his heart: I have known men die of shame.
For that, to lofty spirits, is such an air
As kills the lusty miner in the rift;
A breath is fatal.

SILV. Talk you of killing, master?

FEB. O foolish fellow, why dost thou stare at me?
Methinks Francisco tarries overlong.

SILV. He comes, sir.

(Enter FRANCISCO, *bearing gold.)*

FEB. Get thee hence—look to the door.
Thy duty. *(Exit* SILVANO.)

FRAN. Father, I have brought the gold:
An excellent sum too. Shall I to the vaults?

FEB. Look, boy, where are thy wits? I find me here
Four thousand marks that yesterday were due,
And not yet rendered.

FRAN. From Tomas Catalan?
Father, I saw him yesterday indeed,
And he desired me fetch it home today.

FEB. Why that was well. But wherefore spoke you not?
Will you do all and with no word from me?

FRAN. Father, I told you, and you did consent.

FEB. Did I so, boy? Ay, now I recollect me,—
This plague o' the heart doth dull the wit. 'T was well.
And Joseph Lucas, have you heard of him?
Is 't true his mine is flooded?

FRAN. Deluged, father.
Utterly lost.

FEB. And he hath nothing left
To pay me back that mine (I think I am mad
To lend such sum to any mortal man)
That mine of pesos I did lend to him?

FRAN. No, nothing, father; he is wholly ruined.
FEB. I shall be ruined too! Why 't was a fortune
For any man, a rich and princely fortune:
I slaved out years to win it. I shall be ruined.
I may live to see you brought to want.
FRAN. No, father.
Lose twice as much, enough remains for us.
FEB. You will have enough with Ramon's portion!
FRAN. >Father,
Forgive my brother, give my portion to him.—
I will live happy in a monastery,
To know he is content and you with him.
FEB. Thou art my loving boy!—Get thee to Catalan;
Bring me that money; and when thou hast marked it,
And also that his excellency gave thee,
Store me both in the vault.
FRAN. Shall I not have
The masons to wall up the garden door?
The match-key, father, of the outer door,—
Some rogue may find it.
FEB. It is about the house;
I did myself mislay it; and I will find it,
Soon as these troubles vex my mind no more.
But ne'ertheless, we 'll wall the door to-morrow.
Get thee away; be swift; and after that
Make haste to mark the coin and store it safely.
FRAN. Father?
FEB. What wilt thou?
FRAN. Father, when I am come
To Catalan's door, I shall be nigh to Pablo's.
FEB. Ay!
FRAN. If I might but speak then with my brother—
FEB. Get thee to Catalan; speak to none but Catalan;
And think of none but Catalan. Or indeed,
If thou must think of Ramon, let thy dreams
Bring thee instruction, and inform thy heart
What is the end of disobedience—sorrow,
Abasement, shame, neglect, abandonment.
Think of thy brother, but be far from him.> (*Exeunt.*)

SCENE 4. *The street before* FEBRO'S *house.*

(*Enter* MENDOZA *and* SILVANO.)

MEN. It is very strange.

SILV. He grieves, sir, much for his son; and I think that sorrow is e'en setting him crazy.

MEN. He talked with that debauched fellow, Cabarero?

SILV. Ay, señor; with the decayed and disreputable hidalgo, Cabarero—about Spain, and Carthagena, and a ship, and five thousand ducats. Señor, would a wise man invite another to rob him?

MEN. To rob him?

SILV. He said, there was money in his vaults. He might have told him, he could break in from the garden, and the cellar. To be sure he said he would hang him, when it should come to be discovered.

MEN. I have seen in him no sign of dotage, nor of madness; but this savors of both.

SILV. And what should make him think of Pablo? He asked me, might he not go to Pablo, and no one see him!

MEN. This is still as strange; for Pablo is notoriously suspected to be a rogue.

SILV. He talked of killing too; <and with poisons as deadly as the foul air of a mine.> Now had he thought of killing Pablo, I should not esteem him so mad: but to think of going to Pablo! That is most lunatic-like.

MEN. He shall not need that; for, see, here comes the knave Pablo to him.

(*Enter* PABLO.)

PAB. God save your worship, Señor Mendoza. Good e'en, honest Silvano. Is your master at home?

SILV. Why if he be at home, what is that to you?

PAB. So much that I must even beg of your friendship to be admitted to speak with him.

SILV. <To be dinged over the head with an old ledger, or a bundle of ingots? Why thou graceless, besotted vagabond! what puts it into thy mind to think he would lend thee anything?

PAB. Why if I have good security, why not? I am as honest a man as another,

I care not who knows it. I have business with Señor Febro, your master; and you were best tell him so, for it concerns him to know.

Men. If thou wert not beyond the belief of an honest man, thy impudence would utterly ruin the fame of an honest man.> How canst thou have the folly to think that Febro will speak with thee? Pr'ythee get thee gone, ere he come out and do thee some violence.

Pab. Who knows? I am here on mine own business; and I will have the law of any one that hinders me.

Silv. If thou wilt have the law, it must come to thee in shape of a halter. Go, you rogue, get you gone.—Law! were there any law in Bogota, thou shouldst have been the first chapter of its execution.

Pab. I will not go till I see Señor Febro; and if you cease not reviling me, you rascal crumb-eater! you door-hinge! you cloak-thumper! you hook for an old hat! I 'll beat your bones into brickdust. You rascal! You will have me in a passion? You will deny me to see your master? You will call me scurvy names?—

Men. Out, sirrah! will you brawl before Febro's door? See, your insolence has drawn him forth, and now you will answer it.

(*Enter* Febro.)

Silv. Ay, now look, you rascal; now you will be talked to.

Pab. Good, your worship, Señor Febro! I have a message from your son.

Feb. From Ramon?

Pab. From Ramon, señor; and this noisy, idle, lick-mouthed platter-monger—

Silv. Please, your worship, I said you would speak with no such base fellow.

Feb. You were overforward, sirrah!

Men. What, Febro! it is not creditable to notice such a man.

Feb. Good friend, you shall pardon me—I will be mine own adviser. Señor Mendoza, you are welcome. If you fear the taint of his presence, you can walk by.

Men. (*Apart to Silvano.*) We will observe this interview from a distance.

(*Exit, with* Silvano.)

Feb. Now, sirrah, what message sends Ramon by such a messenger?

Pab. I hope your favor will pardon me—I have harbored the young señor long.

Feb. Speak the message, and no more. He sends thee to me for money?

Pab. Hoping your excellent mercy will pity his misery, which is greater than he can bear, and my poverty, which enforces me to pray your goodness for some relief.

Feb. Why, what care I for thy poverty?

Pab. My friendship for the young man has brought me into great necessity; and here he acknowledges, unless I am paid, I may justly throw him into prison. But I hope your worship will not compel me.

Feb. <A thousand ducats! Thou art a lying knave: where got'st thou a thousand ducats to lend him?

Pab. O, there is much of that that was the cost of his food and lodging; and then for the rest, I borrowed it, to help him open his mine. But 't was opened without profit, the money was swallowed, my creditor is enraged; and now the end is this—I must send Señor Ramon to prison, or go myself which he here confesses, and prays your bounty to protect us both.

Feb. And hast thou the impudence to suppose I will give thee a penny to save thee from this fate?

Pab. No, señor, but I think you will do this much to save Ramon—whereby I shall be saved myself.>

Feb. Do as thou wilt; thou shalt have no money. Put him in prison—I am content. He shall have nothing to keep him from the fangs of thee and thy companions, whom he has chosen his friends.

Pab. Truly, sir, misfortune is no elector of friendships, as, by mine honesty, I know full well. I am myself forced by my necessities to love men I hate; and surely, I think, Señor Ramon would not, unless obliged by his misfortunes willingly consort with men of my degree.

<Feb. Dost thou speak this in honesty and humility? or is it a lure to deceive me?

Pab. Oh, sir, I have known better days; and therefore do I pity Señor Ramon, because I see him treading the same path of folly, which led me into my present baseness.

Feb. I have mistaken thee!>

Pab. I have counselled him, too, against his gambling and his drinking; for, besides that I saw how such courses would utterly ruin him, I had no hopes of ever being paid for the cost of supplying him.

FEB. Oh, then, if thy interest run the same way with thy humanity, I have much reason to believe thee honest.

PAB. Truly, it is a sad sight to see a young man led astray by evil companions—a young man, and good.

FEB. Young, and once good!

PAB. I cautioned him that Cabarero was a most dangerous companion; it was no honor to be friends with such a hidalgo.

FEB. Thou didst!

PAB. In faith, I told him, Don Antonio had been the ruin of every young man he had sworn love to; and he might see what good had come of his friendship, when he looked on his own wretchedness.

FEB. <Is it possible I have wronged thee so much?> Thou didst tell him this? Well, what said he?

PAB. He wept, and said, his father's severity had left him no other choice—

FEB. Ah!

PAB. And swore if thou wouldst forgive him, he would never more speak with Cabarero. But, he knew, thou wouldst not.

FEB. Tell me the truth, Pablo, and thou shalt not be sorry. Did Ramon say this? What! never more speak with Cabarero.

PAB. I were but an infidel to belie him—he said this, with many tears—

FEB. With tears?

PAB. Crying, in his despair, it was no matter, thou hadst forsaken him and the sooner his ruin was accomplished, the better; thou wouldst have no more shame, when he was in his grave.

FEB. In his grave? Is he reduced to this despair?

PAB. Despair indeed! All last night while Cabarero was drinking, he did nothing but kiss an old rosary, that he wears round his neck, with a devout passion <that nothing but great misery could breed up in a young man.>

FEB. That rosary did I give him, in his youth.
It is enough—he is not all depraved.
Pablo! mine own eyes shall be witness
Of his contrition; and haply, if I find
What thou hast spoken is to them confirmed,
Thou shalt have all that he does rightly owe thee,
And more, to mark my favor.

PAB. Please your worship, 't is very true—A thousand ducats, señor.

FEB. Till I am satisfied thou shalt have nothing.
Tonight, I 'll come to thee, and suddenly
Appear before him; <when, indeed, if sorrow
Be working at his heart, it needs must out
Into a bursting penitence.>

PAB. God bless your worship.
I 'll have Antonio set aside.

FEB. That villain!
I have had sinful dreams, and sometimes, almost
Have thought to buy some rogue to take his life.
<I fear me, Ramon cannot be my Ramon,
While Cabarero lives to tempt him.>

PAB. O, your worship,
There are men, who for a recompense would put him
Out of the way—Perhaps a thousand ducats—
At most two thousand—yes, in faith, two thousand,
With some few charges to escape the law,
Might have him cared for.

FEB. Nay, leave him to heaven:
I 'll buy no Ramon at the price of blood.
<After the nightfall, I will come to thee.>
Be sure thou dost not speak of mine intent—
<Thou shalt have nothing else: speak not a word.>
Expect me—Now, away.

PAB. Alack, your worship
Will give me no relief? Some little money
To buy the boy a supper—we are very wretched!

FEB. What, wanting food? O, heaven, my strictness runs
Into a wicked, barbarous cruelty!
Here 's gold—Buy food; but say not whence it comes.
I 'll bear enough to free him from thy hands,
After the vespers—Mark me, after vespers.
<Away now, thou shalt see me after vespers!> (*Exeunt.*)

END OF ACT SECOND.

ACT THIRD.

SCENE 1. *A room in* PABLO'S *Inn.*

(*Enter* CABARERO *and* PABLO.)

CAB. After the vespers? he will come himself? Every way, this is extravagant good fortune. He will bring gold too? Better still! That gold, were he an angel, shall witness him out of heaven. He shall call me rogue and cur, and such vile names, and not be remembered? he shall gibe me when I offer to ennoble his dowdy daughter? Oh, I have often dreamed how he should repent him!

PAB. Come, 'slife, this will be too improbable, and dangerous.

CAB. He would hire thee to assassinate me too?

PAB. Ay, never believe me else: he offered me two thousand ducats to slay thee. But I told him thou wert my true friend and I would not kill thee for so little.

CAB. A rope for a dagger! a gibbet for a ditch! Oh, I see him, as in a picture, with the priest at his side, the hangman at his neck, and the multitude hooting him to the scaffold, and all the while, I am rattling his dollars in my pocket!

PAB. <I tell thee, I like not this plan. Here are two others:—First—we will take Ramon into our counsel, reconcile him with his father and use him for our banker.

CAB. Hang him, no: his milk and water cowardice will keep us beggars. If his father forgive him, he will repent and forsake us.

PAB. Why, then—as the old man will bring a thousand ducats with him—we may help him to a ditch, and so make sure of that: for otherwise, he will see I am cheating him, and give me nothing.

CAB. No killing!—except by the laws. Every way, I assure thee, this plan is the best. It is easiest, it veils us from suspicion, and it makes us most profit. If we are in danger, it is our only safety.>

PAB. Well, I understand all—But if the viceroy should hang me?

CAB. Thou art the king's witness, thy life is secure; 't is but a week in prison, and thou comest out purified with a pardon.

PAB. A week in prison! Before the week is over, they may sift out the truth and give me to Satan.

CAB. Why, then, we will bribe thee out of the jailer's hands, though it should cost a thousand pesos.

PAB. That 's too much! I will get a man out for half that.

CAB. Wouldst thou be economical with thine own neck? Thy share shall not be the less, whatsoever be the cost.

PAB. The story will be too incredible.

CAB. Is not Ramon a good witness? Who shall resist his testimony?

PAB. But will he appear?

CAB. As surely as thou shalt; for he has that baseness of cowardice, he will sell the lives of all his friends, to save the worthlessness of his own.

PAB. I must have a full third.

CAB. A full half! Methinks that were but scurvy generosity to share our gains with this whining, unnatural rogue, who is but the cipher of the triumvirate!

PAB. I think so too! <'T is but honest to cheat him who cheats his father.>

CAB. Remember that every coin carries the private mark of the broker; wherefore we must bury it till the hue and cry be over, and then melt it into ingots, as if it came from a mine. Harkee!—we will bury it in two portions, in one a thousand pesos or so; *this* shalt thou show the officers. But the other thou must swear was hidden from thee.

PAB. <I warrant me; but if you deceive me, I will impeach you, by St. Geronimo, I will!

CAB. Fear not; I can do nothing without thee. We will to Spain together.

PAB. With all my heart, and without Ramon?

CAB. Oh, he will marry Mendoza's daughter; and in the rapture of his matrimony, what will be the loss of a little money to him?>

PAB. Well, I am agreed: I long for the vesper bell. But remember, I say, Cabarero, no roguery!

CAB. Not a little, I tell thee: we will rob and cheat like honest gentlemen and friends, <and enjoy our good fortune together.> Come, I left Ramon at the bottle, and now he will be brave enough to lead to the vaults of darkness, or—his father. (*Exeunt.*)

SCENE 2. *A room in* FEBRO'S *house.*

(*Enter* LEONOR *and* FERNANDO.)

LEON. Pray you, begone; I did not promise you;
And if my father hear you, oh, dear saints,
I shall have no more peace to stay with him.

FERN. Wilt thou then stay and marry Baltasar?

Now, wert thou half as wise as other maids,
Thou wouldst not fright at this brave opportunity.
But chain me on the instant. Silly love!
Though I am mad enough to fly tonight,
Tomorrow may my father's strength prevail,
And bond me to another.

LEON. Indeed, indeed!
And is there fear your sire will be so cruel?

FERN. Nay, very certain. The anger of your father
Is but a matchlight, kindling on the instant,
And, on the instant, with a sigh put out;
But my sire's rage will be a conflagration.
<Lit in a mine, and roaring on forever.
Oh, I could tell the stories of my sire,
And of myself, if so I durst, would make thee
Instant and resolute. For know, thou doubter,
Whate'er his worth, my father loves me well:
And know I not how long I might have courage
To act the sin will lose me all that love,
And gain me all that fury.> Wherefore, quick!
While our fates smile on us, let us begone.

LEON. In sooth, 't is wrong.

FERN. Why, here 's a delicate bundle
Might grace the shoulder of a soldier's spouse,
As sister to a knapsack.

LEON. Alack, for pity!
'T will break my father's heart.

FERN. <It shall be mended.
Now, with my life> I'll warrant his forgiveness:
Would I could hope my father's! A rogue am I.—
Thou know'st not at how rich a cost I buy thee.
Come, do not weep: I swear, this flight will bring thee
Nothing but happiness. 'T is I alone
Will feel the punishment.

LEON. And wilt thou feel it?
I am determined then I will not fly,—
Thus to bring trouble to thee.

FERN. <Why, here 's a wind,
Fooling the compass! and yet so sweet and pleasant,
Breathing the gentle odors of true love,
That I'll forgive it. Fear not thou for me;>
Whate'er of state and men's consideration,
Whate'er of hope, or what of certainty,
To rise to greatness, I give up for thee,
<I give up with good will—at first, with fear
And strong reluctance, but, at this good hour
With joy and pride;> for now I know that fate
May hide more happiness in a lowly cot,
Than e'er the thrones in great men's palaces.
<So to a cot we 'll hie us, in some nook
Of a delicious valley, where the mountains,
Walling us in with azure, up to heaven,
Shut out all things but heaven.>

LEON. O, heaven be with me!
I fear to fly. Come thou some other time:
Let me think more of this. Come back tomorrow—
Let me think more; and, as I think, once more
Look on my father's face.

FERN. A thousand times,
After tonight, for he will soon forgive thee.
Nay, look not back.

LEON. Ah! hark! we are discovered!—
Another time—He is stirring in the vault!

FERN. Pause not, the door is open.

LEON. It is too late:
I hear my brother's step! Away, Rolando!

FERN. This comes of trembling!

LEON. Tomorrow night—

FERN. Tomorrow!
Farewell, and dream of me. (*Exit.*)

LEON. He 'll see the bundle!—

(*Enter* JUANA.)

My friend and Ramon's love! She saw Rolando!

JUAN. Why, Leonor, does no one watch the door?
This might invite a robbery.

LEON. Odd's heart, a robbery!

JUAN. And how you tremble!

LEON. I am not afeard!
My father is in the vaults; and so I am not
Afeard of him or any other man.

JUAN. Afeard of him! Oh! you are much confused.

Afraid of *him!* Why, sure it was no rogue,
Although, good sooth, he muffled up his face,
As he brushed by me—Tell me, Leonor—
I thought 't was Ramon!

LEON. And perhaps it was—

JUAN. Was it indeed! and did he see his father?
And will his father pardon him?—Oh, for pity!
How could it be so, when so timorously
He stole away, and stole away from me?
<Why shouldst thou hide it from me?>

LEON. Did you see anybody?
Why Ramon was not here.

JUAN. Who could it be?
Sure you are not ignorant, some man—some stranger,
Cloaked to the eyes, was stealing through the house?
Indeed you should call your father.

LEON. He would be angry—
Frightened, I mean—

JUAN. Oho! a bundle nicely tied
In a fair Eastern kerchief! and a man
Stealing away! and then these thousand blushes,
And contradictions!—

LEON. Oh, my dear Juana!
You 'll not betray me!

JUAN. Shall I laugh at thee?
I will not frown; I am not one of those
That step between true hearts, and break them—Go;
Think what thou doest, before thou art resolved;
Think what thou doest, before thou leavest thy father;
Think of him well; think of thy brothers too;
Think of thy lover, is he good and worthy;
<Think of thyself, thy maiden reputation—>
Think of *thyself;* then, if thy heart confirms thee,
Follow the guidance of thy love, and go,
<With heaven to comfort thee—*I* will not stay thee.
I would have no heart suffer, save my own.>
But be not rash, be not precipitate:
Methinks your flight would break your father's heart.

LEON. I will not leave him, for I know indeed,
(Heaven pardon me that e'er I should forget it!)
He is wo enough for Ramon.

JUAN. Is he indeed?
If that be so, then have I happier hopes
To charm his anger into loving pardon.
I came to be his suitor.

LEON. Shall I call him?
And yet I fear to have you pray him now.
He has been vexed a thousand times today.
And was a little strange and irritable.
These crosses move him deeper than of old—
Tomorrow will be better.

JUAN. Think not so.
The happiness, almost the life of Ramon
Rests on a speedy pardon.

LEON. He is in the vault
About some project. If you 'll wait awhile,
Francisco will come back, and call him forth—
Nay, there 's my brother!

(*Enter* MENDOZA *and* SILVANO.)

MEN. I tell thee, good Silvano,
It is impossible.

SILV. Ask my mistress else.

JUAN. Father!

LEON. What is the señor's will?

MEN. By heaven!
There 's roguery afoot! Where is your father?
There are knaves a-robbing him.
(*Exit* SILVANO.)

LEON. Good sir, for pity,
What do you mean? My father, these two hours,
Has been i' the vaults.

MEN. I say it cannot be:
There are ruffians in the garden: by this hand,
I saw a lantern twice flash through the trees,
Heard voices murmuring and—

(*Re-enter* SILVANO.)

SILV. The vault is locked:
Heaven guard him well, my master is not there!
I 'll to the garden. (*Exit.*)

LEON. He did not come out!
Perhaps they have murdered him!

MEN. What, help! ho, help!
Here 's villainy! foul, bloody villainy!

(*Enter* FRANCISCO.)

O, wretched boy, your father's vaults are robbed,
And he perhaps is murdered!
(*Exit* FRANCISCO.)

LEON. Give him help:
He is old and feeble.

JUAN. <Do not be dismayed.>

(*Re-enter* SILVANO, *bearing a cloak.*)

SILV. Thieves! thieves! we are robbed! the garden gate is open,
The cellar wall broke through, the vault exposed.

(*Re-enter* FRANCISCO.)

This found I hanging on a cactus bush;
This morn I noted it on Pablo's back.
I know the robber!

FRAN. Run thou for alguazils,
And follow me to Pablo's—Sister, fear not:
The door is locked, my father is not there—
It is no murder, but a robbery.
Señor Mendoza, will you go with me,
Or tarry here, and break this to my father?

MEN. Nay, I will go with you—Stay with the girl. (To JUANA.)
O my life, the strangest marvel! Robbed by Pablo!
We must be quick—A most strange villainy! (*Exeunt.*)

SCENE 3. *A room in* PABLO'S *Inn.*

(*Enter* PABLO, RAMON, *and* CABARERO *each bearing a bag of coin.*)

CAB. Victoria! Thou art revenged, enriched and beatified; the mine is found, and Juana is thine own! We will melt these dollars into ingots, show them to Mendoza, and, tomorrow, thou wilt be in paradise.

RAM. In hell, I think; for what devil is blacker than I? But he forced me to it!

CAB. Ay, he forced thee to it.

RAM. We are followed too; I hear the hue and cry! Let us escape—Do you not hear?

CAB. I hear the beating of thy silly heart. Why what a cowardly poor-spirited knave hath vile liquor made thee!—Pablo, thou art the king of cheats—Wine, and a crucible, and a roaring hot fire—I tell thee, thou art mad! All is safe.

RAM. Hark, hark, Antonio!

CAB. 'T is the rumbling of a cart. Fy upon thy white gizzard! Wilt thou never make a rascal of spirit?
(*A knocking.*)

RAM. }
PAB. } Hark!

RAM. We are lost! we are lost!

CAB. (*To* PABLO.) Down with thee to the door, and be wise.

(*Exit* PABLO [CABARERO *hides the gold*].)

RAM. We are undone!

CAB. I will stab thee, if thou goest on with this clamor.

RAM. Antonio!

CAB. Art thou not now a rascal? and why shouldst thou not have the wit and courage of a rascal? Put on a face of iron, and harden thy nerves into the same metal.—This is a friend—Lo, he comes to spy on thee!

(*Re-enter* PADLO, *conducting* FEDRO [FEBRO *bearing a bag of coin.*])

He can never forgive thee *now,* remember that.—Good even, Señor Febro, you are very welcome.

FEB. Away, bad man! I'll have no words with thee.
My office here is full of love and peace.
And hath no part in thee, except to steal
A victim from thee. Hark thee, Ramon, boy;
Thou once wert good, and dutiful and loving—
Loving, I say, and then, besides, thou wert
The first life of thy mother. What thou wert
To mine own old affections, I'll not speak.
Thou hast acted many follies; yet, because
<Of mine own weakness, and because I know>
They have weighed thee down with heavy misery,
I am willing to forgive them.

RAM. Hah!

FEB. <Forgive them!>
One thing alone—and if thy heart yet holds
A grain of love, it will not start at that;
<One thing alone will bear thee back again
Into my house—perhaps my heart too.> Bid

Farewell unto this man, who loves thee not;
Know him no more; and here am I to free thee
From his bad thraldom—Look, I have gold with me.
(*Displaying a bag.*)
Enough to ransom thee.

RAM. What, gold!

FEB. I heard
How far thy miseries had carried thee.

RAM. What gold? hah! gold for me?

FEB. Thou seest! enough
Perhaps o' the present, to discharge thy debts.
And make thee good and happy once again.

RAM. Ha! ha!
Thou couldst relent then? Why thou art gone mad—
Thou bring'st me money! It is too late.

<CAB. (*Apart to* RAMON.) Well said!
Thou art a man. He waited his pleasure. What has he made thee?>

FEB. Ramon, my son!

RAM. Oho! thy son!
Why what a father had that son? a father
Who, while forgiveness would have wrought the son
Into a holy penitent, gave him wrath,
And turned him to perdition—*What a father!*
To do this mischief to his child; and when
He saw his child i' the gulf of hell, to taunt him
With words of pardon!

CAB. Bravo! a proper spirit!
Thou seest, old man! thou wouldst not hearken to me.
Oho, I begged you; but you called me rogue—
Villain, and rogue.—

FEB. Ramon, thou knowst not what thou sayest. Perhaps
I was too hard with thee; but I repent me,
Wilt thou have pardon? love and pardon?

RAM. Yea;
Curses for pardon, and a knife for love!
I am not thy son; the thing that was thy Ramon
Is perished! lost, forever lost! no atom
That once was his, left breathing,—all destroyed,
And made the elements of fiends—Oh, hence!
Away! old maniac, hence!

FEB. Do I live
And listen to my boy?

PAB. Hark!

VOICES WITHIN. Thieves!

FEB. O, heaven,
Thou judgest sorely! Is it so indeed?
Would I had died or ere I heard these words,
These worse than death! Well, God be with thee, Ramon:
Thou hast killed thy father.

VOICES. Thieves! thieves! thieves!

(*Enter* FRANCISCO, SILVANO, MENDOZA, *with Alguazils. As they enter,* CABARERO *seizes upon* FEBRO.)

CAB. Stand fast!
Old rogue, dost think to 'scape! The laws will have thee.
The laws, I say, hah!

FRAN. Father!

CAB. Off, thou cub!
Touch not the rogue. Your prisoner, officers!
Febro, the robber of Febro!

FRAN. Villain and fiend!
(*He is held.*)

FEB. What is the matter, son? Will no man drag
This fellow from me?

CAB. Your prisoner, officers!
A felon knave.

FRAN. O, father! father!—Brother!
Why don't you speak? Why don't you kill the villain?

CAB. (*Apart to* RAMON.) Away with thee! (*Exit* RAMON.)
Your prisoner, officers!
Whom I do here accuse, with witnesses
More perfect than myself, of robbery
And fraud upon his trust. And here you have
In his own hands, part of his felony;
And, there i' the corner, more of his vile crime.

FEB. Thou raving ruffian!

MEN. What, Antonio?
Chargest thou Febro with self-robbery?

FEB. Why, who is robbed?

FRAN. O, father!

CAB. It shall be proved.

PAB. I claim the royal mercy.

MEN. Shake off this stare,
Art thou insane? They do accuse thee, Febro,
Of robbing thine own vaults.

FEBRO. Do I not dream?

MEN. <Thy doors are broke.

FEB. I am ruined!

CAB. Hark! he owns it!
It shall be proved before his excellency,
Perfectly proved, with witnesses enough.
Here 's Pablo, his accomplice, has confessed.>
FRAN. O, father!
FEB. Robbed?
CAB. <Take him before the viceroy—
FEB. I 'll have the villain for ten thousand ducats:
I 'll have it proclaimed.
FRAN. O, father!
FEB. Robbed?
CAB. Away?>
—He apes amaze. Carry him to the viceroy.
It shall be proved before his excellency.
[ALL. Away! Away! Away!]
(*Exeunt* [*Omnes.* FEBRO *in the hands of the Alguazil*].)

END OF ACT THIRD.

ACT FOURTH.

SCENE 1. *A room in the vice-regal palace.*

(*Enter the Viceroy, attended.*)

PALM. They are insane that say 't—the broker robbed!
And Febro turned a rogue! Now surely madness
May sweep o'er nations like a pestilence,
And folly, like a corporal epidemic,
Fever the minds of all. What is 't but madness,
Could fill the city with this riotous cry,
Febro is robbed. Febro hath done a fraud?
<I know the man—sure of all men most honest,
And—I did think—most cautious. Yet it may be,
As my fear whispers me, he has been robbed,
And those—I know, I feel, how that may be—
Those who have suffered in his losses, raise,
From grief and rage, the cry of villainy—>
What! do they bring their fury to the palace?
1ST OFFICER. Even so, your excellency; they have dragged
The broker to the gates, and cry for justice.
PALM. Justice for all! Set them before us straight,
That he who needs it most, this poor old man,
May be protected from the accusers' rage,
And they be taught how foolishly they wrong him.

(*Enter* CABARERO, RAMON, MENDOZA, FRANCISCO, *with officers bringing* FEBRO *and* PABLO. CABARERO, *and some others, crying Justice! justice!*)

PALM. What now, ye violent and thoughtless men,
What crime you are committing, know you not,
Thus, with rude hands, dishonoring the body,
And, with rude tongues, the name and reputation,
Of a most honest worthy citizen?
CAB. Your excellency is deceived; this man
Is a most subtle and confirmed rogue,
<As will be witnessed to your excellency.
PALM. What, Febro! dost thou hear? What means this charge?
Why do I find thee thus?>
FRAN. Oh, noble viceroy,
Punish these men, that, with such slanderous hate,
Destroy my father.
CAB. The prisoner, please your highness,
Has been discovered in a knavish fraud.
PALM. Hold thy peace, yet.—What, Febro!
FEB. I will speak—
Thou rogue, I 'll have thee howl! Ay, by my troth,
And every man of them. Are they all crazed?
<Oh, I am glad to see your excellency—
These rogues! these rogues! O, but that I have lost
My faculties in wonder, I could speak
Till they were struck with shame. What is the matter?>
Their cry is, I am robbed. I know not that;
<Pray you discharge me, let me see to it.
I cannot think 't; and yet it may be so.
I may be robbed (heaven pity mine old age!)

And many wronged with me—But 't is not *that*.>
What do they mean? I pray, your highness, mark them.
They charge me with dishonest practices.
Dishonest practices! If there be law,
I will have vengeance on them.

PALM. So thou shalt,
To the extreme of justice—Good Mendoza—
Thou art the calmest here; speak what thou knowst
Of this same robbery. *Is there* a robbery?
<Hath any man been spoiled of property?>
Have Febro's chests been broken?

MEN. Please, your highness,
'T is even too true; and true it is (I say it
With shame and sorrow, and with much amazement)
There are particulars of damning moment,
That show connivance where one would not think it.

FEB. By heaven! 't is false! Who is there could connive
Of all my house? Will any say 't was I?
<Ay, they do say it; they do charge it on me!>
Pray, good your excellency, search this well;
<Pray you, be quick, and let me know it all.
There is some plot against me; I am robbed.
Well, is not that enough? I am then ruined—
If robbed, why ruined; for, of all still left,
There 's not enough to cover o'er that loss,
That will bring many into need. Search well;>
Find me the rogues, and give me back my gold;
I can with that pay all, and more than all.

PALM. Febro, I pity thee.—this looks not well—
Say'st thou, connivance? <In some hour of madness,
Spirits of virtue have themselves forgot,
And, in one deed, turned villains.>
Speak, Mendoza,
Utter the charge, if charge thou hast to make;
<Tell me thy tale, if any wrong thou know'st;>
And, in my quality of arbiter,
I will forget who is the man accused,
And judge him as a stranger.

FEB. Let him speak;
I do defy him; let him speak; let all.
All men, my foemen and my friends alike,
I do defy to speak a wrong of me!

<MEN. Until today, I dreamed no wrong of Febro;
Nor, please your highness, could I dream it now,
But that I think he has not his proper mind.

FEB. Why that may be; you keep me still bewildered,
Knowing myself all ruined, but not how;
Traduced, maligned, but wherefore ignorant.
Despatch, Mendoza, for I have no fear.
You will be sorry to have thought this wrong.
Not in my mind! In sooth, you do distract me.>

MEN. Please, your excellency,
Pablo, the innkeeper, here throws himself
On the king's mercy; and, himself avowing
Accomplice in the act, Baptista charges
To have been his leader.

FRAN. Oh, your noble highness,
This is an open villainy. That Pablo
Is a notorious rogue, <a thief and liar,>
Not to be hearkened to by honest men.

PALM. Silence, Francisco; be not over-rash;
Thy father shall have justice.

MEN. Noble sir,
What the youth says of Pablo is most true;
No honest man should hearken to his speech;
Yet Febro spoke with him, and I myself
Witnessed the conference.

FEB. Why, so I did;
I spoke with him.

PALM. Peace, Febro, Heaven be with thee!
<This is a cloud that gathers to a storm!>
He spoke with Pablo?

MEN. Yes, and gave him money.

His man Silvano there stood at my side,
And watched him with me. <At my words of wonder,
(For truth 't was wonderful to see the broker
In earnest speech with such a man as Pablo)
Silvano> [and] told me how, short time before,
Febro demanded, if he might not steal
To Pablo unobserved; and did assure me
He feared his master was not in his mind;
Wherefore, in proof, he told me how, before,
Febro had talked with señor Cabarero,
Inviting him to robbery and flight,
And such wild things as surely proved him mad.

CAB. Put me on oath, and let me swear this true.

FEB. Why this *is* true.

FRAN. O, father! father!

PALM. Febro!

FEB. I say 't is true; where is the need to swear it?

PALM. Febro, be wise;—I pity thee.

FEB. I never
Thought to conceal it. Without fear, I own it;
I talked with Cabarero, and did urge him
To rob me.—

CAB. He confesses!

FRAN. Pray you, stop him:
He knows not what he says—O, father!

FEB. Boy,
Did I e'er teach thee then to lie?—I own it;
I bade him rob me, <at the evil urgings
Of my bad fancy;> for I hoped that act
Might bring him to the scaffold; and I thought,
If he were dead, Ramon, my outcast Ramon,
Might be mine own again.

CAB. Now by my faith,
That Ramon, whom he seems to love so well,
He kept in want and misery, and knew it.
For Ramon I besought him, he denied me.
He owns the urging—ay, he urged me sore.
I will not say with what rich tempting offers.
In sooth, I thought him mad; for wherefore should he,
In his old age, invent so wild a fraud?
'T is true, he had had losses—and perhaps
These same had turned his brains; wherefore I hope
Your excellency will be merciful.
Sure he was mad; though subtle and discreet
In the vile plan he showed me.

FEB. O, thou villain!
I am sorry I did spare thee. For a little
I could have bought thy life.—Your highness
Hears him!

CAB. Your highness hears him! Pablo will confess
He would have bought him to assassinate me.
It was not safe for him to have me live;
But nevertheless I bring not that against him.

FEB. It is not true; and Pablo knows I told him,
We would this bad man leave to heaven.

PALM. Still Pablo!
And wilt thou still, unhappy, Febro, darken
Thy hope by such admissions? What, indeed!
Hold speech with Pablo? and on such black subjects?
Talk with a wretch about another's murder?

FEB. I talked with Pablo; will your highness blame me?
It was of Ramon, and his miseries;
I gave him money too—it was for Ramon!
I sought his house, but it was still for Ramon!

CAB. And Ramon should have been his accessory!
(*Apart to Ramon.*) Peace, <on thy life!> There is good proof of this;
Wilt not your excellency list to Pablo?
The bark was ready on the river; seek it;
It waits for Febro—Pablo can speak all.

PALM. He shall be heard. Speak thou again, Mendoza.
I am amazed and shocked. What know'st thou more,
To make this madness yet more probable?

MEN. My terrace roof o'erlooks Baptista's garden.
I sat above, to breathe the vesper air;
And twice or thrice, I marked a glimmering lamp

Among the shrubs, and, in the end, a light
Flashing as from an open door, where was
No door, save one ne'er opened. <This thing moved me;
And giving all my faculties to watch,
Forthwith I heard low murmurs as of voices,
And, once or twice, the crashing of men's feet
Along the pebbled alleys.> Straight I ran
To give the alarm. Febro was in the vault,
And all the evening had been; so I learned
From his affrighted daughter, who was sure
(And so Silvano) he had not passed out.
Judge my surprise to find the door well locked,
And Febro vanished! how, but through the door
That opened on the garden? and with what,
Save the rich treasures which were there no more?

FRAN. Alas, the key that oped that garden door,
Was lost a month ago; and my poor father
Tomorrow would have walled it up.

PALM. Tomorrow?
For a whole month he left his vaults exposed?
This—Leave the substance of confiding men
To a month's accidents and knaveries!—
This looks but darkly. Speak; what more, Mendoza?

MEN. Some wild words dropped from mine own daughter's lips:
She had abruptly visited the house,
And stumbled on a man close muffled up,
Who brushed by her, and fled; and, in addition,
Found Leonor confounded and perturbed,
Her mantle in her hand, and at her side
A bundle, seemingly prepared for flight.—

FEB. My daughter! If thou beest a man and father,
Discharge me straight, and let me save my child.
That slave Rolando! O, I see it now;
He is the rogue! 't is he has broke my vaults,
And steals my girl away!—Let me begone.
My Leonor!—I'll give you up my life,
If you seek that; but let me save my child!

PALM. Stay. My heart bleeds for thee. I cannot free thee.
This charge is heavy, and most like to truth.

FEB. You have no heart!—Francisco, you are free;
You have not robbed, nobody calls *you* rogue—
Get thee to home, and to thy sister.

FRAN. Father!

FEB. Save me thy sister, or I'll live to curse thee!— (*Exit* FRANCISCO.)
I thought your excellency was a man!
You gave me friendship too.

PALM. I did, Baptista,
And will—disprove this fearful charge.

FEB. My child!
You keep me here, to set me mad with charges
That make me seem a rogue; and all the while
Dishonor seeks my child—A step might save her!

MEN. Let him be satisfied; his girl is safe;
I left Juana with her.

FEB. Heaven reward thee!
I will forgive thee all thou hast said against me.
She has not fled! How could I think she would?
Fly from me in my wretchedness! and with
The man that robbed me!

CAB. Is not this well carried?—
(*Apart to* RAMON.) Hold up thy head
—Thou seest how fortune helps us.

PALM. Hast thou still more, Mendoza?

MEN. Silvano here
Picked up the cloak of Pablo.

PAB. I am guilty,
I lost it in the garden.

MEN. But little more
Have I to say, but, haply, that most fatal.
With officers, we followed to the inn;
And there, in the hands of Cabarero, stood
Unhappy Febro.

FEB. Ay, most miserable!
<Ramon, why didst thou say those things to me?
I think they have turned my brain!

MEN. Wretched Baptista;>

With still, even in his frightened grasp, a bag
Of the same coin that had that moment vanished.
FEB. I took it there—Why look ye thus upon me?
I bore it with me to redeem my son.
CAB. Ay, sooth, with three bags more! (*Apart to* RAMON.) Think of Juana!
<This thing is for a time.> Señor Mendoza
Will say he found them: faith, 't was Pablo brought them.
I can attest how this was all discovered.
PALM. Mendoza, is this true?
MEN. Indeed most true;
Here is the gold.
PALM. What fiend possessed thee, Febro?
FEB. Well, do you judge it true? How got it there?
I do not know; I took but one bag with me,
To save my boy.
PALM. Whom didst thou counsel with?
Alas, all weighs against thee. Hadst thou spoke
But to thy daughter, or thy man, of this.
FEB. I spoke with none: and wherefore should I speak?
Will Pablo charge me? Pablo did deceive me;
He told me lies of Ramon.
CAB. There again!
He told some truths—he told where they had hid
Their ruffian spoils.
FEB. He did! and are they found?
All will be well again! Confess all, Pablo,
Where didst thou hide the gold?
PALM. <Now, but that I
Here see the wanderings of a dotish man,
I should pronounce this folly innocence.
Febro, attend: thy star is darkening fast;
And the old trunk, whose wealthy branches hid
The secret rot that hollowed at its heart,
Is trembling in the tempest: lo, the bolt
Comes to the earth, and hisses at thy front
A moment, ere it fells thee.> Speak no more,
If not more wisely—Thou, Mendoza, art,
In all thou hast said, confirmed?
MEN. I am.
PALM. And thou, Antonio, on thy hopes of heaven,
Speak'st but the truth?
CAB. I do. <(*Apart to* RAMON.) Shudder no more.—>
And Pablo will swear all as I have said.
If they do find the gold he swore they buried,
'T will show his truth.
MEN. They have already found it;
Yet a small part alone—some thousand ducats.
PALM. Thou swear'st this, Pablo?
PAB. Yes, your highness, yes:
I hope for mercy!
PALM. Tell mine officers
Where lie the greater profits of thy crime.
PAB. I know no more; I left the bags with Febro,
And him i' the garden, that I might straight bury
Mine own share in the place whereof I told them.
As for the rest, good faith, I know no more;
Febro had charge of that.
FEB. Now, were heaven just,
Thou shouldst die with this slander in thy throat,
Monster of falsehood! Has it come to this?
Is 't true? is 't possible? a man like me,
Old,—in the twilight of my years, and looking
Into the dusky midnight of my grave,—
An old man that has lived a life, whereon
No man hath found a stain <Oh! you are mad,
To think this thing of me.> A fraud? a fraud!
What! *I* commit it? with these gray hairs too?
And without aim,—save to enrich this rogue,
That swears away my life?
PALM. Aimless, indeed,
Unnatural, and most incredible;
And therefore easily disproved, hadst thou
One proof beyond its wonder. <Give me proof;
Discredit not this knave, I know him well;
But show thou wert not with him,—or for what;
And hadst no gold with thee—or wherefore hadst it;
Or do what will be better for thy soul,—

Rouse from this dotish fit that has transformed thee,>
Repent, confess, deliver up the spoils
<Of thy unhallowed avarice; and, in memory
Of thy once stainless fame (no more unsullied)>
And in regard of years that should be reverend,
In pity and in peace, we will discharge thee.

FEB. I do repent me—of my miseries;
I do confess—that I am wronged and lost,
Robbed, and traduced, and by collusion slain,
Trapped by false witnesses, and by an unjust judge
Unrighteously condemned.

PALM. Say'st thou, Baptista!
'An unjust judge?' 'unrighteously condemned?'
What say the witnesses? thy friend, Mendoza?
Will he traduce thee? What Antonio here?
Does he gain aught to harm thee? What this Pablo?
Who prates his own life into jeopardy?
And what—By heaven, I would have spared thee that!—
What says thy son?

FEB. My son! my Ramon! Ay, let Ramon speak.—
Hah! what! does Ramon charge me?

PALM. Hear'st thou, Ramon?

CAB. <(*Apart to* RAMON.) Wilt thou be ruined?>

FEB. Ramon?

PALM. Dost thou see!
Horror hath made him dumb. Had he a word
To aid thy misery, he had spoken it.

FEB. Dost thou accuse me, boy? I do defy thee!
What! swear against thy father? Ope thy lips;
<Speak what thou canst. Oh, now I have been mad!—>
Thou know'st full well for what I sought thee out.
Why art thou silent? <Lo, a word of thine
Would clear up all; speak thou that word. Accuse me?
My son accuse me?> By the curse, not yet
Uttered nor thought of—by the father's curse,
That wilt convert thy bosom to a hell,
Ne'er to be quenched by penitence and prayers,
Speak, and speak truly.

PALM. Stand aside.

FEB. Ha, ha!
One word clears all; and he will speak it. Hark!
(RAMON, *endeavoring to speak, falls into a swoon.*)
My son! my son! oh, you have killed my Ramon!

PALM. 'T is thou hast done it. <What! though thou wert so cruel,
Though thou hadst driven him from thy roof and love,
He could not speak the word that should destroy thee.>
Bear him away; his silence speaks enough,
I will not force him to unlock his lips,
In the unnatural charge.
(RAMON *is led out.*)
Art thou content?
All speaks thy guilt. Confess; repair thy fault;
Disgorge thy spoils.

FEB. Do with me what you will,
You have robbed and ruined me among you all,
<What care I now how soon you take my life?>
You make me out a felon, and have turned,—
Heaven plague you all—have turned my children 'gainst me.

PALM. Obstinate still? Confess, and take our mercy.

FEB. The mercy of oppressors! Heaven confound you!
I know why you condemn me, ay, full well:
<I could have paid you all—I have claims yet;>
You kill me for your losses.—When you will:
The grave is quiet, and Heaven will yet avenge me.

PALM. Amazed and sorrowing, we pronounce thee guilty
Of a most mad, most base, and wicked fraud,
For which our laws of Spain demand thy life.
Yet, in respect of thy augmented years,
We spare thee that. Depart; live and repent thee.
What property still openly is thine

We seize for benefit of the many wronged.
We give thee life, but judge thee ignominious.
And to remain in ward of officers,
In thine own house, till all be satisfied.

FEB. Why you were better take my life at once;
<You leave me naught to feed me! and> the air
You grant me leave to breathe, is but the poison
Of a corrupted reputation. Kill me;
What matters it? Your mercy is a name
For a new rack, wherewith you will torment me—
The rack of shame and pitiless degradation.
A rogue!—a felon!—

(FEBRO *is led out.*)

PALM. <Poor wretch! I'll think of thee;
I have a dream—and though all seem to speak thee
Dotard and knave, it shows me other things
But hide them yet.

CAB. May it please your excellency,
Permit me to depart, and look to Ramon,
A very unhappy man.

PALM. Away!

(*Exit* CABARERO.)

PALM Thou, Pablo,
We do adjudge to prison, to resolve
More fitly of thy fate.

PAB. I claim the royal pardon.

PALM. I'll find if thou hast won it.

(PABLO *is led out.*)

Look to it, officers: this man, Antonio
Watch strictly; have him ever in your eyes;
Give him no passage from the gates. For Pablo,
Fright him with words of death, and find what secrets
May drop from terror. Watch me Ramon too.
I have strange fancies,—but these hints will serve you.
Mendoza, have thine eye upon Baptista;
What misery may come to him thou know'st;
Let him not want, nor let his children suffer.
What cost soever thou art at to help them,
I will requite thee; look to them tonight;
Tomorrow come to me again; I have
A thought to hold discourse on—but not now.>

(*Exeunt.*)

<SCENE 2. *The street before the Palace.*

(*Enter* CABARERO *and* RAMON.)

RAM. The Viceroy has given him his life? Well, I am glad of that.—Else should I have confessed all. His freedom too!

CAB. Ay, I tell thee,—his life and freedom,—all which is contrary to law.—Such a fraud is a matter for hanging.

RAM. And thou thought'st, when thou persuadest me to witness against him, that he should die!

CAB. By my faith, no:—I knew his life was in no danger. I told thee the viceroy was too much his friend.

RAM. He will come to want, Antonio! We will send him money.

CAB. 'Slife, this is superfluous—and full of risk.

RAM. I tell thee, he shall have money and relief, though it bring me to the gallows.

CAB. Wilt thou be wise?

RAM. He was coming to me with pardon! With money to relieve me! and with that money did I witness him to destruction.

CAB. Foh! thou said'st not a word.

RAM. Hah! that's true: no man can accuse me—I said nothing against him.—But my silence—my silence damned him, and it damns me. There is no fiend like to me. Witness against my father! Kill my father!—Cain killed his brother, and his forehead was marked with the finger of God.—I—I—What is justice? *I* have no mark, who have killed my father!

CAB. Faith, not a jot—there is no mark about thee.—

RAM. Thou liest,—it is *here,*—my soul is sealed with horror—black, black,—the leprosy of an Ethiop—the gangrene of a demon—all darkness—darkness—of horror.

CAB. Why, thou madman, wilt thou betray thyself? Think of Juana.

RAM. Have I not bought her, even with my soul's perdition? How shall I look her in the face?

CAB. Hark'ee! I am tired of thy whining. If thou wilt be a man, I am thy friend still;—if thou wilt endanger thyself, and me too, by thy puling, boyish fright, I will leave thee to manage thine own affairs.—By my faith, I will.

RAM. Desert me not, or I have lost Juana. —Give me thy advice; I will follow thy bidding.

CAB. Let us depart.—Thy father is coming.—They are turning him from the palace.

RAM. Horror!—I cannot look on him. Away! away!— (*Exeunt.*)>

<SCENE 3. *A room in* FEBRO'S *house.*

(*Enter* FRANCISCO *and* LEONOR.)

FRAN. Ask me not a word, not now,—not now,—I will tell thee anon.—Our father is alive, I tell thee,—alive and well:—Is not that enough? It will break her heart,—Is not that enough? At the palace, I tell thee, sister.

LEON. I am glad of that.—He is safe with the Viceroy. And the robbers, Francisco?

FRAN. Yes, yes!—heaven will discover them.—The robbers! the robbers! Sister, you have done wrong to entertain a lover in secret. My father accuses him of the robbery.

LEON. Him! brother! Rolando! what, Rolando! Oh, he was with me. He is a gentleman. My father does him a great wrong.—

FRAN. It may be so. Heaven protect thee.—Receive him no more. Tarry here; I will to the vault a moment,—I will be near thee. (*Exit* FRANCISCO.)

(*Enter* FERNANDO.)

LEON. Oh, Rolando, Rolando, my brother, my father—

FERN. Peace, Leonor, I overheard thy brother.—Dost thou think me a robber?

LEON. What, *thou?* You must forgive my poor father.—This robbery has perplexed him sorely. But what disturbs thee? Thou art very pale, Rolando!

FERN. Listen: this moment is the last I can look upon thee—

LEON. Rolando!

FERN. If thou wilt fly with me, I will give up my father—my hopes—my station—everything, for thee; if thou wilt not, I can never look upon thee more.

LEON. You are jesting with me, Rolando! Oh, I can never leave my father.

FERN. Heaven bless thee, Farewell.

LEON. Rolando!

FERN. We must forget one another—I could tell thee a reason—but thou wilt hear it from others.

LEON. O, my father! my father!

FERN. I will love thee better, and forever —Thou shalt be happier too. Thou fliest from misery. (*Exeunt.*)

(*Re-enter* FRANCISCO, *with a Rosary.*)

FRAN. This is enough to sear mine eyes
forever,
And turn my heart to ashes.—Wretched
brother!
Thrice wretched father! Leonor, ho!
Leonor!
Sister! Sister! Gone! oh, vanished!—
Heaven,
Thou art awroth with us! What, sister! sister! (*Exit.*)>

SCENE 4. *The street before* MENDOZA'S *house.*

(*Enter* JUANA *and* RAMON.)

JUAN. Prosperity,—wealth,—happiness!—
They come too late.
Oh, Ramon, Ramon! talk'st thou thus to
me?
Witness against thy father! say no more
Of happy fortune; but disprove this tale,
That racks my heart with horror.—
Happy indeed!
Thou art awroth with us! What, disprove it:
Witness against thy father! Didst thou,
Ramon!
Say *no*, and make me happy.

RAM. They deceived thee—
I spake no word against him,—not a
word,
No man can charge me that.

JUAN. No, not a word!—
They charge not that. But thou wert
there against him!
Thy presence was enough!

RAM. Reproach no more:
I chose not to be with his enemies—
They dragged me with them. Speak of
this no more.

JUAN. Of this forever, till thou clear up
all!
Ramon, thou know'st me not.—Be thou
the man

My heart has pictured thee, oppressed but worthy,
Sore tempted, but with yet a noble spirit,
That thrones its nakedness on a rock of honor;
And poor and wretched though thou be, deserted,
Contemned and hated—nay, by all men cursed—
Still do I rest thy friend and advocate—
Thy more than friend, thy loving wife forever!

RAM. I am what thou behold'st—thy long betrothed,
Once faith-preserved, and ever faithful Ramon—
One and the same.

JUAN. Ah, no, no more the same—
Thy father, Ramon!—

RAM. Who, for thy love, have borne
Sorrow and wrath, and dreamed they were not ills,
Locked hands with shame, and deemed me undefiled,
Councilled with villainy, and thought it virtue,
Because it pointed out a path to thee.

JUAN. A word
And I have done with thee.—Then for what fate
Heaven has in store, the altar or the grave—
I shall not care.—This do they charge thee, Ramon—
Thy father was accused by noted knaves—
His son—no, no—his son did *not* accuse him;
But when adjured—(thou tremblest!) When adjured
By the poor father, yea, besought, to speak
Against the charge which he did know was false,
Condemned his father with accusing looks—
With a dumb lip assented, and with that silence
Sealed him to shame and death!

RAM. What could I more?
I did all this for thee.

JUAN. For me! for me!
Thou might'st have stabbed thy brother in the dark,
Bartered thy sister for a villain's gold,
Done anything unnatural and base,
And told me, 't was for me! for me! for me!

RAM. Thou art unjust.—In this is grief enough,
Without thy keen reproaches.—What could I more?
I held my peace.—Wouldst thou have had me charge him?

JUAN. Didst thou then *know* him guilty? Speak me that.
Upon thy soul's eternal welfare speak,
Speak me the truth.—What, dost thou know him guilty?
Know him a felon?

RAM. This is then thy fear:—
Thou scorn'st the felon's son?

JUAN. Hah! if I do?
What, trap him to 't?—Wo 's me!

RAM. Juana, time will show
Who is the guilty wretch—

JUAN. Oh, Time will show!
Give it not up to time! By all the grief
That stains thy sire's gray hairs—by all the pure
And solemn magic round thy mother's grave,
I charge thee speak the truth.—Thou dost not think
Thy father 's guilty?

RAM. Nay, Juana!

JUAN. Speak,
Or never speak me more.—Tremble not—speak—
Thou dost not think him guilty?—

RAM. No,—no,—

JUAN. Wretch!—
Thy lips were dumb, and thou didst know him innocent!
You heard him slandered, and stood silent by!
You saw him perish, and held back the truth
That would have saved him!

RAM. Is it come to this?
Is this the guerdon to reward my love?

JUAN. Love! Did I love thee! What, this spirit, that, in
A case of flesh, was all of adamant—
A disguised devil! *Is* it come to this?
Thou say'st that well.—For now I know thee well,
And hate thee—yes, abhor thee!

RAM. Still unjust,
Thou kill'st me for my faith.

JUAN. Now do I know
They spoke the truth, who called thee base and vile—
This fiendish act is warranty enough
For any depth of lowness.—Oh, how fallen

Thou art now, Ramon! A year, a month ago!—
But that no more.—I could have died for thee,
Hadst thou held fast to thine integrity—
Now, though it break my heart, I cast thee from me
Forever, forever—I 'll never see thee more.

RAM. Thou mak'st me mad.—The wrongs that I have done
I did for thee.—I had no other hope,
No other way to win thee. Dost thou leave me?—
Then I am lost,—and nothing left with me
But the sharp goadings of a vain repentance.
False hearted maid! 't is thou hast led me on
Into this gulf of crime: What but a hope
To win thee, could have made me what I am
A thief and parricide!

JUAN. Oh, heaven, that opest
Mine eyes upon this horror, still support me—
A thief! a thief!

RAM. I said not that.

JUAN. A demon
Blacker than all! Confess thy crime and die.
Confess, for all shall know thee!—O, away,
And perish in the desert,—I denounce thee—
What ho, my father—ho!

RAM. Juana!

JUAN. Father!
Justice! there shall be justice done to all,—
Justice, I tell thee, monster, though I die—
Justice, ho, father!

(*Enter* MENDOZA—RAMON *flies.*)

MEN. What 's the matter, girl?
That wretched Ramon!—

JUAN. To the palace, father—
Quick, lead me to the Viceroy.

MEN. Art thou raving?

JUAN. Oh, father, I 've a story for his highness,
Will make all rave.—And let me speak it now,
While I have strength.

MEN. Come in, compose thyself—
<Thou art disturbed, and know'st not what thou say'st,
The palace, indeed—Thou art fitter for thy couch—
So wan and ghastly.—>

JUAN. The palace, father, the palace!
(*He leads her in.*)

END OF ACT FOURTH.

ACT FIFTH.

SCENE 1. *A room in* FEBRO'S *house.*

(*Enter* SILVANO *and* FEBRO.)

FEB. A rogue! a felon! convicted and condemned!
No wretch upon the street more given to scorn—
No mine-slave, fretting under blows and lashes,
Held to more shame.—Robbed, and for reparation
Despoiled of all—even of my children's bread—
And a good honest name too.—Well, indeed,
Heaven looks upon the sparrow's unfledged brood,
When murderers kill the dam—And Ramon too!
Well, I 've two children yet;—<where is Francisco?
And Leonor? my children?> It is true,
Their sire brings shame upon them—But I think
They will not turn upon me—Dost thou hear me?
Where is Francisco?

SIL. Oh, alas, dear master,
The house is empty.

FEB. Ah!

SIL. The doors all open—
No living creatures present but ourselves.

FEB. <My children, I tell thee!

SIL. Master!>

FEB. O, blest heaven,
Strike me to death, for I am desperate—
My children leave me:—Turn my heart to earth,
Ere I do curse them!

SIL. I think, I hope
My mistress now is with Mendoza's daughter.

FEB. Why, so she is! I should have thought of that—

I dare be sworn she is—Francisco too—
Where should he be, but with his sister?
—Go—
Fetch them to me. And tell them not to fear
I'll weigh upon them long—this wrong will end
Ere many days, and then men will forget
To charge them with the shame of their dead father.

SILV. Francisco, sir!

(*Enter* FRANCISCO.)

FEB. My daughter, boy,—my Leonor!
Where did you leave your sister?

FRAN. <O, dear father,
You'll curse me when I tell you!

FEB. Fled, boy, fled!—
Ha! ha! eloped!—dishonored!

FRAN. Father, dear father!

FEB. Drugged to the bottom!—No gall and venom now,
But I must drink them! With a villain fled!
From shame to deeper shame—And in mine hour
Of misery too! Oh, curse her! curse her!

FRAN. Father—
Be not so rash—she may be yet recovered—

FEB. I gave her to thy charge!>

FRAN. Oh, dear my father,
I left her but an instant—but an instant
Looked through the vault—and in that instant she
Was stolen away—Father, I followed her—
Saw her, at distance, with the ravisher—
He bore her to the palace.

FEB. To the palace!
A ruffian of the guard—a Spanish ruffian
Shall steal my child, and have the Court's protection—
I'll have her back though the proud viceroy's self
Should bar against me with his villains all—

FRAN. Father, I followed to the door—the guards
Denied me entrance, though I prayed it of them—
Struck me back with their staves, and with rude voices
Taunted and menaced me.

FEB. Why back again!
Thou wert the felon's son—that was the reason
They jeered thee with thine infamy—
Thou seest!
'T is infamy to bear the name of Febro.
Struck thee back with their staves! because thou sought'st
To save thy sister! They shall strike me too—
The blows that bruise the body are not much,
When that the heart is crushed—Come thou with me—
A felon though I be, I will have entrance—
Though infamous and lost, I will have justice. (*Exeunt.*)

SCENE 2. *A room in the palace.*

(PALMERA *and others discovered.*)

PALM. Frighted with death, and will not make confession?
I know not why—all circumstances bring
New confirmation of the broker's guilt,
And yet, within my breast, some gentle spirit
Whispers me doubt, and plays the advocate.
That Pablo leave not yet—Hark to me, officer;
Carry him to the rack, but harm him not—
<Place him before the engine, let his fancy
Work on its terrors, till it paints his joints
Crackling and sundering, his sinews bursting,
His strong bones crashing in the ordeal—
Nay, for an instant bind him to the wheel,>
Make him believe that ye will torture him,—
(Yet torture not, ye shall not harm a hair—)
Thus far put on the executioner,
<And, in his terror, if no words of guilt
Burst from his lips, my conscience doubts no more,
And the poor mad old man is lost forever.> (*Exit* OFFICER.)

FEBRO. (*Within.*) I will have entrance! Villains, stand aside!
I'll see the Viceroy, and I'll have my daughter!

PALM. What now! the broker! At this midnight hour,
Madding before the palace!

(*Re-enter* OFFICER.)

OFF. Please, your excellency,
Febro is struggling with the guards for entrance,
He will not be driven back,—he calls your highness,
And raves about his daughter.
PALM. He is distracted:—
Let him come in—Poor wretch, I pity him.

(*Enter* FEBRO, FRANCISCO, *and* SILVANO.)

<What now, old man? What is the matter with thee?>
FEB. You bar your doors against me, and you put
Armed rogues therein to thrust me back with staves,
And keep my daughter from me.
PALM. What would you, Febro?
My doors are shut against the ignominious.
FEB. Ay, ignominious! But I'll have my child—
<I'll have my daughter; fetch her to me straight,>
Were you a crowned king, I'll have her!
PALM. Now
What fiend hath seized thee, Febro? If thy child
Have fled from thee, heaven pity thy gray hairs,
Why shouldst thou seek her here?
FEB. Why, she is here!
Your rogue has stolen her; you know that well—
And you protect him. <Oh, heaven visit you
With pangs and misery>. Give me back my child—
Give me my daughter, and I will forgive you
The other mischiefs you have done me.
PALM. Alas,
'T is madness fills thee with this fantasy:
<How should thy child be here!
FEB. Will you not yield her?>
I do beseech you, give me back my child—
My loving Leonor! Oh, now, for pity, (*He kneels.*)
Be just to me. Look on me, noble sir,
You have broke my heart, but give me back my daughter.

PALM. Rise up, thou old and miserable man,
I pity thee, but know not of thy child.
FEB. (*Arising.*) I do demand her; keep her, if you dare!
What if I be a miserable man,
A gray, old, broken, miserable man,
A most dishonest and convicted felon,
Ashes upon my head, and, in my heart,
Anguish that 's measureless—a man despised,
Stained, shunned, shut out from all men's sympathies?
I have my rights, and, though so friendless, seek them;
I have my rights, and, though so poor, will speak them;
<I have my rights, and, though so weak, will have them.>
I ask my child, and, by my life, I'll have her.
I say I'll have her.—Some ruffian of your guard
Ravished her from me, while you kept me here—
Rolando—
PALM. Again art thou deceived,
I have no villains in my keeping, Febro,
And know,—of all my household, there is none
So named Rolando.
FEB. 'T is a false name, then,
The wretch is here—he has my daughter too—
Francisco followed him, and saw him enter,
My daughter with him.
PALM. Say'st thou this, Francisco?
FRAN. I do, my lord; I followed him, and saw him
Pass, with my sister, through the private gate—
PALM. What ho, my guard!—the axeman with his block!
Let every man o' the court appear before me.
Thou shalt have justice, Febro, on the head
Of him that wrongs thee.

(ALL *come in.*)

If thou know'st the man,
Point me him out among this multitude,
Dishonored though thou be, by all the saints,
There is no man so noble, that shall wrong thee,
And pay no reckoning to thy miseries.

FEB. Hah! no, no, thou art *not* Rolando—No—
Dost thou not see him, boy? <Is he not here?
Mine eyes are dimming.> Let the villain speak,
If he will straightway give me up my child,
I will forgive him;—yea—and will pursue
This thing no further.
FRAN. Rolando is not here.
PALM. Thou seest, thou wert mistaken, boy.
FRAN. Your highness, no—
I saw them well, Rolando and my sister—
She turned her face, when I did call to her;
Rolando dragged her on.—
PALM. Are all men here?
This moves me much. Search thou the palace o'er. (*To an* OFFICER.)
Every man's lodge, even to mine own apartments.
Let no man stay thee. (*Exit* OFFICER.)
Hath any of the guard
Fled from the palace? The ruffian shall be found;
I'll search the city for him.

(*Enter* FERNANDO.)

FEB. Hah!
FRAN. Rolando!
FEB. Ha! ha! the rogue! the villain! I have him fast!
Give up my child!
PALM. How! Febro!
FEB. This is the man!
PALM. <My son! my son! Down from my seat of pomp,
Into the earth of shame; I am as miserable,
As wretched now as Febro. Dost thou charge *him?*
What him, Baptista?> This is my son, Fernando!
FEB. Thy son? Thy son shall ruin my poor girl,
And break my heart! Oh, wretch, where is my daughter?
<Thou didst delude her from me! Ruined, ruined!
Howl thou in hell for this! yes, howl, forever!>
Thou hast stolen the dearest daughter of the earth,
And given her up to shame; oh, heaven distract thee,
Make thy heart mad, but not thy brain, that thou
May'st rot within, and have a sense of it!
<FERN. Oh, saints, avert this curse, so undeserved.
Most rash old man.>
PALM. Didst thou ensnare the girl?
<Oh, wretched boy!>
FERN. Dear father! Father, pardon! (*Kneeling.*)
FEB. You hear him? He confesses. <O bitter wretch!>
PALM. Stand up before me as a criminal,
What—to his chambers! Bring the maiden forth,
Old man, thou shalt have justice, though the gift
Leave me all childless.
(*Some officers go out.*)
FERN. Father!
PALM. Peace, false wretch—
Thy judge—no more thy father. (*A noise.*) More woes to mad us!
(*Cries of "Febro is innocent!"*)
What cry is this?
(RAMON *and* CABARERO *are brought in, and* JUANA *and* MENDOZA.)
JUAN. Justice, your excellency!
Justice for Febro! Villains have entrapped him!
False witnesses have sworn his life away,
And there thou seest the falsest!
FEB. <Oh, the villain!
Give me my daughter, and then judge the rogues.>
PALM. Speak, maiden, speak—if heaven have left me now
One satisfaction greater than the grave,
'T will be to right this wronged man. Which is he
Thou call'st the falsest witness?
JUAN. Look—'t is Ramon—
FEB. Ramon, my son!
JUAN. He did confess to me,
He knew his father innocent.
FEB. Oho, you hear!
I knew my boy would right me.
(*Going toward* RAMON.)
JUAN. Hence, stand back,
Touch not corruption—look on him no more.
I do denounce him to your excellency,
As one conspiring 'gainst his father's life.
PALM. Oh, most unnatural—
FEB. Hearken not to her—
My Ramon ne'er conspired against me.
JUAN. Hear me.

He was my betrothed spouse, and well I loved him:—
I give him up to justice, and accuse him,
Even on his own admission, that he is—
I live to say 't—a false witness and a robber!
<Palm. Can this be so?>
Feb. Oh, thou unnatural girl!
Hearken no more, your highness—she belies him.—

(*Re-enter* 1st Officer.)

Ramon is wronged, and very innocent.
1st Off. Please, your excellency,
Pablo, in terror of the rack, confesses,—
Feb. Pablo 's the rogue and robber.
1st Off. He confesses
Himself participant in the robbery—
Cab. He lies, base knave!
1st Off. And charges, with his oath,
This man, Antonio, and the broker's son
Ramon, to be his principals.
Palm. Just heaven!
And I have wronged thee, Febro?
Feb. Pablo 's a rogue!
<What, Ramon? Ramon rob me? Ramon, my son!>
I warn your highness, Pablo is a rogue,
Not to be trusted.
Cab. An atrocious rogue—
A rogue foresworn—and moved to this invention
By terror of the wheel.
Fran. Brother, confess—
Ram. Away—
Fran. Confess, and save thy father's life—
Repair the wrongs which thou hast done him.
Feb. Sirrah,
What dost thou mean?
Fran. What, not a word? Oh, heaven,
Look down with pity on my father now!
Oh, now, your highness, spare my brother's life,
For he is guilty of the robbery.
<Cab. Hark to the cub!—next he accuses me.>
Feb. Why, thou base boy, dost thou accuse thy brother?
Thy brother, wretch?
Fran. Father, I do; forgive me.
Feb. I curse thee, devil!
Fran. Oh, curse me not, my father—
I charge him to save *thee*—Hear me, my father—
Thou know'st this rosary—
Feb. 'T is Ramon's—ay—
It was his mother's, and to keep her ever
Before his eyes—his pure and holy mother—
With mine own hands I hung it round his neck,
To be the talisman of his memory.
Fran. Father, this found I in the vault.
Feb. The vault!
Ramon! my son! My Ramon!—
Ram. Guilty! guilty!
Give me to death—for I have killed my father!
I am the robber and the parricide—
The doomed and lost—the lost—oh, lost forever! (*Rushes out.*)
Palm. Secure young Ramon:—This vile Antonio too—
This devil-born destroyer of men's sons:
I 'll make him an example. Look to them—
Have them in waiting.

(Cabarero *is taken out.* Mendoza *goes with them.*)

Fy, how now, Baptista?
We have done thee wrong?
Feb. Well, boy, we will go home—
Confess and pray—Call Leonor!
Fran. Oh, father!
Palm. His wits are fled—oh, fate, these thunderpeals
So flashing through the heart, have done their work,
And the mind's temple tumbles into ruin.
Arouse thee, Febro! Thy wealth shall be restored—
Lucas, the miner, hath his pit recovered,
And pays thee back a golden recompense.
Fran. He thinks no more of that.
Palm. Thy daughter, Febro!
Feb. I 'll have you moan for this!
Palm. Thou shalt have justice.

(Leonor *is brought in.*)

Behold thy daughter! Thou shalt have justice full.
Feb. My child! my child!
Leon. Dear father! (*Kneels.*)
Feb. O man of stone!
Was I not wo enough, but you must steal
My seraph from me?
Palm. Name thou his punishment.
If it be death, the knave shall die.
Fern. (*Kneeling.*) Forgive me!
I could not speak while Febro seemed a felon;
Punish me now, since he is innocent.
I stole thy daughter, but I wronged her not;
Sire, I deceived thee, but I am no villain—

Revoke thy curse; and, father, bless my wife!
FEB. Is it even so? thy wife?
PALM. Naught else is left
For reparation—I the rites acknowledge
And as my daughter here do welcome her.
FEB. Thy wife! thy honored wife!—You do receive her?
Why, now we shall be happy—Heaven be thanked!
Ha, ha! a noble husband for my daughter!
<A virtuous, honorable gentleman!>
I'll make thee rich! She's worthy of a king.—
Happy! happy! (*A cry.*)
(*Re-enter* MENDOZA, *with an officer.*)
MEN. Alas, your highness, Ramon—
FEB. Hah, Ramon!—Oh, thy white and quivering lips
Speak a new horror!
MEN. Pitying his grief,
And agony of mind, we led him forth
On the balcony, where, confessing straight
In what dark corner he had hid the gold,
O' the sudden, with a shriek of desperation,
He flung him from the height—and—
PALM. Heaven!
MEN. So perished.
[FEB. God, God, God!] (FEBRO *falls.*)
<PALM. What, Febro? Hast this last blow cracked thy heart?
There comes no sin without its sequent wo;—
No folly but begets its punishment;
And heaven, that strikes the malefactor down,
Even with the greater culprits smites the less—
The rigid sire and disobedient son.>

TORTESA THE USURER

BY

Nathaniel Parker Willis

TORTESA THE USURER

Tortesa the Usurer is a representative of the romantic comedy in verse. While not nearly so frequently written as the verse tragedy, this form of play had some notable examples, such as Boker's *Betrothal.* The author of *Tortesa,* Nathaniel Parker Willis, was born in Portland, Maine, January 20, 1806, of Puritan ancestry. He was educated at the Boston Latin School and graduated from Yale College in 1827. While in college he wrote verse, much of it of a religious character, which represented a phase of his development out of which he later passed entirely. In 1831 he went to New York City and with George R. Morris and Theodore S. Fay published the *New York Mirror.* The next five years he spent in Europe and the East, meeting everywhere interesting people and reflecting his experiences in letters to the *Mirror* which were published in his *Pencillings by the Way* (1835). After his return to this country in 1836 he spent some time in Washington and lived for five years at Glenmary, a spot near the head-waters of the Susquehanna River, where he wrote his *Letters from Under a Bridge* (1839), probably the best of his prose work, and it was during this most significant period of Willis's life that his plays were written. Financial necessity compelled him to return to New York, however. In 1843 he became editor of the *New Mirror* and in 1846 of the *Home Journal.* The last years of his life were spent in a heroic effort to keep the *Journal* going, despite the draw-back of ill health. One of the most appealing phases of our literary history reflects his generosity toward the other writers of the time, especially toward Poe. His defense of Poe which he published in the *Home Journal* as an answer to Griswold's attack, is a fine example of true sympathy and understanding combined with rare delicacy of expression. Willis died January 20, 1867.

His first play, *Bianca Visconti,* was written in competition for a prize offered by Josephine Clifton for the best play suited to her talents. It was first played at the Park Theatre, New York, August 25, 1837, and was performed afterward in Boston and Philadelphia. It was played as late as May, 1852, by Miss M. Davenport in Philadelphia. It is a verse tragedy, laid in Milan in the fourteenth century, and is based on the history of the real Francesco Sforza who married the natural daughter of Philip Visconti and later became Duke of Milan. In the same year, November 29, 1837, Miss Clifton produced a comedy by Willis, called *The Kentucky Heiress,* which was not successful.

Tortesa the Usurer was written for James W. Wallack, who produced it at the National Theatre in New York, April 8, 1839, playing "Tortesa." It was very successful and was considered by Wallack to contain one of his best parts. When after the burning of the National Theatre in 1839 the elder Wallack returned for a time to England, he produced *Tortesa* at the Surrey Theatre, London, in August, 1839. He afterward played "Tortesa" frequently, and the first professional appearance of Lester Wallack, his son, was in the character of "Angelo" when he supported his father in this English tour. In this country the play was acted as far south as Mobile, Alabama, where E. S. Connor played "Angelo" in 1845, the part he had acted with Wallack in 1839.

In character delineation, in the use of practical stage devices, and in the manner in which the playwright has, without making the language stilted, placed such excellent poetry in the mouths of the characters, *Tortesa the Usurer* is noteworthy. The influence of *Romeo and Juliet* and of *The Winter's Tale* is probably sufficiently evident. The direct source of the play goes back to the Florentine story of Genevra degli Amieri, who was married to Francesco Agolanti while in love with Antonio Rondinelli, and who apparently died and was buried. Coming to life during the night she escaped from the vault and was refused admittance by her husband, her father and her uncle, all of whom thought she was a spirit. She then went to Antonio's house and was tenderly and considerately treated by him. They were afterwards married, the former marriage being annulled. The story, which suggested merely the main outlines of one incident in the play, is to be found in the story of *La Sepolta Viva,* by Domenico Maria Manni, translated by Thomas Roscoe in his *Italian Novelists,* London, 1825, vol. 4. Eugene Scribe wrote an opera on the theme with the title of *Guido et Genevra ou La Peste de Florence,* played and published in 1838. This is so different from Willis's play that it is unlikely that he used it as a source, unless he took the idea of Genevra rising from the tomb from it instead of from the Italian. Scribe made Guido a sculptor, but his art plays no part in the play as in Angelo's case. Shelley also used the theme in his fragment, *Genevra.*

Tortesa the Usurer and *Bianca Visconti* were published in 1839 in New York and also in London. They are now hard to obtain. For references to the plays, see Ireland, *Records of the New York Stage,* Vol. 2, p. 283; Lester Wallack, *Memories of Fifty Years,* New York, 1889, p. 35. For the Life of Willis, see Henry H. Beers, *Nathaniel Parker Willis,* American Men of Letters Series, Boston, 1885, and for an interesting criticism of *Tortesa,* see Poe's articles in Burton's *Gentleman's Magazine,* August, 1839, later expanded and incorporated in a discussion of *The American Drama,* in the *American Whig Review,* August, 1845. They are to be found in vol. 10, p. 27, and vol. 13, p. 33, of the Virginia edition of Poe's works.

TORTESA THE USURER.

A Play.

BY N. P. WILLIS.

NEW-YORK:
PUBLISHED BY SAMUEL COLMAN,
No. 8 Astor House,
BROADWAY
1839.

DRAMATIS PERSONAE

[National Theatre, New York City, April 8, 1839.]

DUKE OF FLORENCE.......................................Mr. Rogers

COUNT FALCONE.......................................Mr. T. Matthews

TORTESA,—a usurer.......................................Mr. Wallack

ANGELO,—a young painter.......................................Mr. Conner

TOMASO,—his servant.......................................Mr. Lambert

ISABELLA DE FALCONE.......................................Miss Monier

ZIPPA,—a Glover's daughter.......................................Mrs. W. Sefton

Other characters—a Counsellor, a page, the Count's Secretary, a Tradesman, a Monk, Lords, Ladies, Officer, Soldiers, etc.

TORTESA THE USURER

ACT FIRST.

SCENE 1. (*A drawing-room in* TORTESA'S *house.* SERVANT *discovered reading the bill of a tradesman, who is in attendance.*)

SERVANT (*reading*). "Silk hose, doublet of white satin, twelve shirts of lawn." He 'll not pay it to-day, good mercer!

TRADESMAN. How, master Gaspar? When I was assured of the gold on delivery? If it be a *credit* account, look you, there must be a new bill. The charge is for ready money.

SERVANT. Tut—tut—man, you know not whom you serve. My master is as likely to overpay you if you are civil, as to keep you a year out of your money if you push him when he is cross'd.

TRADESMAN. Why, this is the humor of a spendthrift, not the careful way of a usurer.

SERVANT. Usurer! humph. Well, it may be he is—to the rich! But the heart of the Signor Tortesa, let me tell you, is like the bird's wing—the dark side is turned upwards. To those who look up to him he shows neither spot nor stain. Hark! I hear his wheels in the court. Step to the ante-room—for he has that on his hands to-day which may make him impatient. Quick! Give way! I 'll bring you to him if I can find a time.

TORTESA (*speaking without*). What ho! Gaspar!

SERVANT. Signor!

TORTESA. My keys! Bring me my keys!

(*Enter* TORTESA, *followed by* COUNT FALCONE.)

Come in, Count.

FALCONE. You 're well lodged.

TORTESA. The Duke waits for you
To get to horse. So, briefly, there 's the deed!
You have your lands back, and your daughter 's mine—
So ran the *bargain!*

FALCONE (*coldly*). She 's *betroth'd*, Sir, to you!

TORTESA. Not a half hour since, and you hold the parchment!
A free transaction, see you!—for you 're *paid*,
And I 'm but *promised!*

FALCONE (*aside*). (What a slave is this,
To give my daughter to! My daughter? Psha!
I 'll think but of my lands, my precious *lands!*)
Sir, the Duke sets forth—

TORTESA. Use no ceremony!
Yet stay! A word! Our nuptials follow quick
On your return?

FALCONE. That hour, if it so please you!

TORTESA. And what 's the bargain if her humor change?

FALCONE. The lands are yours again—'t is understood so.

TORTESA. Yet, still a word! You leave her with her maids.
I have a right in her by this betrothal.
Seal your door up till you come back again!
I 'd have no foplings tampering with my wife!
None of your painted jackdaws from the court,
Sneering and pitying her! My lord Falcone!
Shall she be private?

FALCONE (*aside*). (Patience! for my lands!)
You shall control my door, sir, and my daughter!
Farewell now! (*Exit* FALCONE.)

TORTESA. Oh, omnipotence of money!
Ha! ha! Why, there 's the haughtiest nobleman
That walks in Florence. *He!*—whom I have bearded—
Checked—made conditions to—shut up his daughter—
And all with *money!* They should pull down churches
And worship it! Had I been *poor*, that man
Would see me rot ere give his hand to me.
I—as I stand here—dress'd thus—looking thus—
The same in all—save money in my purse—

He would have scorn'd to let me come so near
That I could breathe on him! Yet, that were little—
For pride sometimes outdoes humility,
And your great man will please to be familiar,
To show how he can stoop. But halt you there!
He *has* a jewel that you may not name!
His *wife's* above you! You're no company
For his most noble *daughter!* You are brave—
'T is nothing! comely—nothing! honorable—
You are a phœnix of all human virtues—
But, while your blood's mean, there's a frozen bar
Betwixt you and a *lady,* that will melt—
Not with religion—scarcely with the grave—
But like a mist, with *money!*

(*Enter a* SERVANT.)

SERVANT. Please you, sir!
A tradesman waits to see you!

TORTESA. Let him in!
(*Exit* SERVANT.)
What need have I of forty generations
To build my name up? I have bought with money
The fairest daughter of their haughtiest line!
Bought her! Falcone's daughter for so much!
No wooing in't! Ha! ha! I harp'd on that
Till my lord winced! "My bargain!" still "my *bargain.*"
Nought of my *bride!* Ha! ha! 'T was excellent!

(*Enter* TRADESMAN.)

What's thy demand?

TRADESMAN. Ten ducats, please your lordship!

TORTESA. Out on "your lordship!" There are *twelve* for ten!
Does a lord pay like that? Learn some name sweeter
To my ears than "Your lordship!" I'm no lord!
Give me thy quittance! Now, begone! Who waits?

SERVANT. The Glover's daughter, please you, sir!

(*Enter* ZIPPA.)

TORTESA. Come in,
My pretty neighbor! What! my bridal gloves!
Are they brought home?

ZIPPA. The signor pays so well,
He's well served.

TORTESA. Um! why, pertinently answered!
And yet, my pretty one, the words were sweeter
In any mouth than yours!

ZIPPA. That's easy true!

TORTESA. I would 't were liking that had spurr'd your service—
Not *money,* Zippa, sweet!
(*She presents her parcel to him, with a meaning air.*)

ZIPPA. Your bridal gloves, sir!

TORTESA (*aside*). (What a fair shrew it is!) My gloves are paid for!
And will be thrown aside when worn a little.

ZIPPA. What then, sir!

TORTESA. Why, the bride is paid for, too!
And may be thrown aside, when worn a little!

ZIPPA. You mock me now!

TORTESA. You know Falcone's palace,
And lands, here, by Fiesole? I bought them
For so much money of his creditors,
And gave them to him, in a plain, round bargain,
For his proud daughter! What think you of that?

ZIPPA. What else but that you loved her!

TORTESA. As I love
The thing I give my money for—no more!

ZIPPA. You *mean* to love her?

TORTESA. 'T was not in the bargain!

ZIPPA. Why, what a monster do you make yourself!
Have you no heart?

TORTESA. A loving one, for you!
Nay, never frown! I marry this lord's daughter
To please a *devil* that inhabits me!
But there's an *angel* in me—not so strong—
And this last loves you!

ZIPPA. Thanks for your weak angel!
I'd sooner 't were the devil!

TORTESA. Both were yours!
But for the burning fever that I have
To pluck at their proud blood.

ZIPPA. Why, this poor lady
Cannot have harm'd you!

TORTESA. Forty thousand times!
She's noble-born—there's one wrong in her cradle!

She 's proud—why, that makes every pulse an insult—
Sixty a minute! She 's profuse in smiles
On those who are, to *me,* as stars to glow-worms—
So I 'm disparaged! I have pass'd her by,
Summer and winter, and she ne'er looked on me!
Her youth has been one tissue of contempt!
Her lovers, and her tutors, and her heart,
Taught her to scorn the low-born—*that am I!*
Would you have more?

ZIPPA. Why, this is moon-struck madness.

TORTESA. I 'd have her *mine,* for all this—jewell'd, perfumed—
Just as they 've worshipped her at court—my slave!
They 've mewed her breath up in their silken beds—
Blanch'd her with baths—fed her on delicate food—
Guarded the unsunn'd dew upon her skin—
For some *lord's* pleasure! If I could not get her,
There 's a contempt in that, would make my forehead
Hot in my grave!

ZIPPA. (*Aside.*) (Now Heaven forbid *my* fingers
Should make your bridal gloves!) Forgive me, Signor!
I 'll take these back, so please you!
(*Takes up the parcel again.*)

TORTESA. (*Not listening to her.*) But for this—
This devil at my heart, thou should'st have wedded
The richest commoner in Florence, Zippa!
Tell me thou wouldst!

ZIPPA. (*Aside.*) (Stay! stay! A thought! If I
Could *feign* to love him, and so work on him
To put this match off, and at last to break it—
'T is possible—and so befriend this lady,
Whom, from my soul, I pity! Nay, I will!)
Signor Tortesa!

TORTESA. You 've been dreaming now,
How you would brave it in your lady-gear;
Was 't not so?

ZIPPA. No.

TORTESA. What then?

ZIPPA. I *had* a thought,
If I dare speak it.

TORTESA. Nay, nay, speak it out!

ZIPPA. I had forgot your riches, and I thought
How lost you were!

TORTESA. How *lost?*

ZIPPA. Your qualities,
Which far outweigh your treasure, thrown away
On one who does not love you!

TORTESA. Thrown away?

ZIPPA. Is it not so to have a gallant shape,
And no eye to be proud on 't—to be full
Of all that makes men dangerous to women,
And marry where you 're scorn'd?

TORTESA. There 's reason there!

ZIPPA. You 're wise in meaner riches! You have gold,
'T is out at interest!—lands, palaces,
They bring in rent. The gifts of nature only,
Worth to you, Signor, more than all your gold,
Lie profitless and idle. Your fine stature—

TORTESA. Why—so, so!

ZIPPA. Speaking eyes—

TORTESA. Ay—passable!

ZIPPA. Your voice, uncommon musical—

TORTESA. Nay, *there,*
I think you may be honest!

ZIPPA. And your look,
In all points lofty, like a gentleman!
(*Aside.*) (That last must choke him!)

TORTESA. You 've a judgment, Zippa,
That makes me wonder at you! We are both
Above our breeding—I have often thought so—
And lov'd you—but to-day so more than ever,
That my revenge must have drunk up my life,
To still sweep over it. But when I think
Upon that proud lord and his scornful daughter—
I say not you 're forgot—*myself am lost*—
And love and memory with me! I must go
And visit her! I 'll see you to the door—
Come, Zippa, come!

ZIPPA. (*Aside.*) (I, too, will visit her!

You 're a brave Signor, but against two women
You 'll find your wits all wanted!)

TORTESA. Come away!
I must look on my bargain! my good bargain!
Ha! ha! my *bargain!* (*Exeunt.*)

SCENE 2. (*The Painter's Studio.* ANGELO *painting.* TOMASO *in the foreground, arranging a meagre repast.*)

TOMASO. A thrice-pick'd bone, a stale crust, and—excellent water! Will you to breakfast, Master Angelo?

ANGELO. Look on this touch, good Tomaso, if it be not life itself—(*Draws him before his easel.*) Now, what think'st thou?

TOMASO. Um—fair! fair enough!

ANGELO. No more?

TOMASO. Till it mend my breakfast, I will never praise it! Fill me up that *outline,* Master Angelo! (*Takes up the naked bone.*) *Color* me that water! To what end dost thou dabble there?

ANGELO. I am weary of telling thee to what end. Have patience, Tomaso!

TOMASO. (*Coaxingly.*) Would'st thou but paint the goldsmith a sign, now, in good fair letters!

ANGELO. Have I no genius for the art, think'st thou?

TOMASO. *Thou?* ha! ha!

ANGELO. By thy laughing, thou wouldst say *no!*

TOMASO. Thou a genius! Look! Master Angelo! Have I not seen thee every day since thou wert no bigger than thy pencil?

ANGELO. And if thou hast?

TOMASO. Do I not know thee from crown to heel? Dost thou not come in at that door as I do?—sit down in that chair as I do?—eat, drink, and sleep, as I do? Dost thou not call me Tomaso, and I thee Angelo?

ANGELO. Well?

TOMASO. Then how canst thou have genius? Are there no marks? Would I clap thee on the back, and say good morrow? Nay, look thee! would I stand here telling thee in my wisdom what thou art, if thou wert a genius? Go to, Master Angelo! I love thee well, but thou art comprehensible!

ANGELO. But think'st thou never of my works, Tomaso?

TOMASO. *Thy* works! Do I not grind thy paints? Do I not see thee take up thy palette, place thy foot thus, and dab here, dab there? I tell thee thou hast never done stroke yet, I could not take the same brush and do after thee. Thy works, truly!

ANGELO. How think'st thou would Donatello paint, if he were here?

TOMASO. Donatello! I will endeavor to show thee! (*Takes the palette and brush with a mysterious air.*) The picture should be there! His pencil (*Throws down* ANGELO'S *pencil, and seizes a broom.*) his pencil should be as long as this broom! He should raise it thus—with his eyes rolling thus—and with his body thrown back thus!

ANGELO. What then?

TOMASO. Then he should see something in the air—a sort of a hm-ha-r-r-rrrr-(you understand.) And he first strides off here and looks at it—then he strides off there and looks at it—then he looks at his long brush—then he makes a dab! dash! flash! (*Makes three strokes across* ANGELO'S *picture.*)

ANGELO. Villain, my picture! Tomaso! (*Seizes his sword.*) With thy accursed broom thou hast spoiled a picture Donatello could ne'er have painted! Say thy prayers, for, by the Virgin!—

TOMASO. Murder! murder! help! Oh, my good master! Oh, my kind master!

ANGELO. Wilt say thy prayers, or die a sinner? Quick! or thou 'rt dead ere 't is thought on!

TOMASO. Help! help! mercy! oh mercy!

(*Enter the* DUKE *hastily, followed by* FALCONE *and attendants.*)

DUKE. Who calls so loudly? What! drawn swords at mid-day?
Disarm him! Now, what mad-cap youth art thou? (*To* ANGELO.)
To fright this peaceful artist from his toil?
Rise up, sir! (*To* TOMASO.)

ANGELO. (*Aside.*) (Could my luckless star have brought
The Duke here at no other time!)

DUKE. (*Looking round on the pictures.*) Why, here 's
Matter worth stumbling on! By Jove, a picture
Of admirable work! Look here, Falcone!
Did'st think there was a hand unknown in Florence
Could lay on color with a skill like this?

TOMASO. (*Aside to* ANGELO.) Did'st thou hear that?
(DUKE *and* FALCONE *admire the pictures in dumb show.*)
ANGELO. (*Aside to* TOMASO.) (The palette 's on thy thumb—
Swear 't is thy work!)
TOMASO. Mine, master?
ANGELO. Seest thou not
The shadow of my fault will fall upon it
While I stand here a culprit? The Duke loves thee
As one whom he has chanc'd to serve at need,
And kindness mends the light upon a picture,
I know that well!
FALCONE. (*To* TOMASO.) The Duke would know your name, Sir!
TOMASO. (*As* ANGELO *pulls him by the sleeve.*) Tom— Angelo, my lord!
DUKE. (*To* FALCONE.) We 've fallen here
Upon a treasure!
FALCONE. 'T was a lucky chance
That led you in, my lord?
DUKE. I blush to think
That I might ne'er have found such excellence
But for a chance cry, thus! Yet now 't is found
I 'll cherish it, believe me.
FALCONE. 'T is a duty
Your Grace is never slow to.
DUKE. I 've a thought—
If you 'll consent to it?
FALCONE. Before 't is spoken,
My gracious liege!
DUKE. You know how well my duchess
Loves your fair daughter. Not as maid of honor
Lost to our service, but as parting child,
We grieve to lose her.
FALCONE. My good lord!
DUKE. Nay, nay—
She is betroth'd now, and you needs must wed her!
My thought was, to surprise my grieving duchess
With a resemblance of your daughter, done
By this rare hand, here. 'T is a thought well found,
You 'll say it is!
FALCONE. (*Hesitating.*) Your Grace is bound away
On a brief journey. Were 't not best put off
Till our return?
DUKE. (*Laughing.*) I see you fear to let
The sun shine on your rose-bud till she bloom
Fairly in wedlock. But this painter, see you,
Is an old man, of a poor, timid bearing,
And may be trusted to look close upon her.
Come, come! I 'll have my way! Good Angelo, (*To* TOMASO.)
A pen and ink! And you, my lord Falcone!
Write a brief missive to your gentle daughter
T' admit him privately.
FALCONE. I will. Duke.
(*Writes.*)
ANGELO. (*Aside.*) (Now
Shall I go back or forwards? If he writes
Admit this Angelo, why, I am he,
And that rare phœnix, hidden from the world,
Sits to my burning pencil. She 's a beauty
Without a parallel, they say in Florence.
Her picture 'll be remembered! Let the Duke
Rend me with horses, it shall ne'er be said
I dared not pluck at Fortune!)
TOMASO. (*Aside to* ANGELO.) Signor!
ANGELO. (Hush!
Betray me, and I 'll kill thee!)
DUKE. Angelo!
ANGELO. (*Aside to* TOMASO.) Speak, or thou diest!
TOMASO. (*To the* DUKE.) My lord!
DUKE. Thou hast grown old
In the attainment of an excellence
Well worth thy time and study. The clear touch,
Won only by the patient toil of years,
Is on your fair works yonder.
TOMASO. (*Astonished.*) Those, my lord?
DUKE. I shame I never saw them until now,
But here 's a new beginning. Take this missive
From Count Falcone to his peerless daughter.
I 'd have a picture of her for my palace.
Paint me her beauty as I know you can,
And as you do it well, my favor to you
Shall make up for the past.
TOMASO. (*As* ANGELO *pulls his sleeve.*) Your Grace is kind!

DUKE. For this rude youth, name you his punishment! (*Turns to* ANGELO.)
His sword was drawn upon an unarm'd man.
He shall be fined, or, as you please, imprisoned.
Speak!

TOMASO. If your Grace would bid him pay—

DUKE. What sum?

TOMASO. Some twenty flasks of wine, my gracious liege,
If it so please you. 'T is a thriftless servant
I keep for love I bore to his dead father.
But all his faults are nothing to a thirst
That sucks my cellar dry!

DUKE. He 's well let off!
Write out a bond to pay of your first gains
The twenty flasks!

ANGELO. Most willingly, my liege. (*Writes.*)

DUKE. (*To* TOMASO.) Are you content?

TOMASO. Your Grace, I am!

DUKE. Come then!
Once more to horse! Nay, nay, man, look not black!
Unless your daughter were a wine-flask, trust me
There 's no fear of the painter!

FALCONE. So I think,
And you shall rule me. 'T is the roughest shell
Hides the good pearl. Adieu, Sir! (*To* TOMASO.)

(*Exeunt* DUKE *and* FALCONE. ANGELO *seizes the missive from* TOMASO, *and strides up and down the stage, reading it exultingly. After looking at him a moment,* TOMASO *does the same with the bond for the twenty flasks.*)

ANGELO. Give the letter!
Oh, here is golden opportunity—
The ladder at my foot, the prize above,
And angels beckoning upwards. I will paint
A picture now, that in the eyes of men
Shall live like loving daylight. They shall cease
To praise it for the constant glory of it.
There 's not a stone built in the palace wall
But shall let thro' the light of it, and Florence
Shall be a place of pilgrimage for ever
To see the work of low-born Angelo.
Oh, that the world were made without a night,
That I could toil while in my fingers play
This dexterous lightning, wasted so in sleep.
I 'll out, and muse how I shall paint this beauty,
So, wile the night away. (*Exit.*)

TOMASO. (*Coming forward with his bond.*) Prejudice aside, that is a pleasant-looking piece of paper! (*Holds it off, and regards it with a pleased air.*) Your bond *to pay*, now, is an ill-visaged rascal—you would know him across a church—nay—with the wind fair, *smell* him a good league! But this has, in some sort, a smile. It is not like other paper. It reads mellifluously. Your name is in the right end of it for music. Let me dwell upon it! (*Unfolds it, and reads.*) "I, Tomaso, promise to pay"—stay! "I, Tomaso,—I, Tomaso, promise to pay to Angelo, my master, twenty flasks of wine!" (*Rubs his eyes, and turns the note over and over.*) There 's a damnable twist in it that spoils all. "I, Tomaso," —why, that's *I*. And "I promise to pay"—Now, I promise no such thing! (*Turns it upside down, and after trying in vain to alter the reading, tears it in two.*) There are some men that cannot write ten words in their own language without a blunder. Out, filthy scraps. If the Glover's daughter have not compassion upon me, I die of thirst! I'll seek her out! A pest on ignorance!
(*Pulls his hat sulkily over his eyes, and walks off.*)

SCENE 3. *An Apartment in the* FALCONE *Palace.*

(ANGELO *discovered listening.*)

ANGELO. Did I hear footsteps? (*He listens.*) Fancy plays me tricks
In my impatience for this lovely wonder!
That window 's to the north. The light falls cool.
I 'll set my easel here, and sketch her—Stay!
How shall I do that? Is she proud or sweet?
Will she sit silent, or converse and smile?
Will she be vexed or pleased to have a stranger
Pry through her beauty for the soul that 's in it?

Nay, then I hear a footstep—she is here!
(*Enter* ISABELLA, *reading her father's missive.*)

ISABELLA. "The Duke would have your picture for the duchess
Done by this rude man, Angelo! Receive him
With modest privacy, and let your kindness
Be measured by his merit, not his garb."

ANGELO. Fair lady!

ISABELLA. Who speaks?

ANGELO. Angelo!

ISABELLA. You 've come, Sir,
To paint a dull face, trust me!

ANGELO. (*Aside.*) (Beautiful,
Beyond all dreaming!)

ISABELLA. I 've no smiles to show you,
Not ev'n a mock one! Shall I sit?

ANGELO. No, lady!
I 'll steal your beauty while you move, as well!
So you but breathe, the air still brings to me
That which outdoes all pencilling.

ISABELLA. (*Walking apart.*) His voice
Is not a rude one. What a fate is mine,
When ev'n the chance words on a poor youth's tongue,
Contrasted with the voice which I should love,
Seems rich and musical!

ANGELO. (*To himself, as he draws.*) How like a swan,
Drooping his small head to a lily-cup,
She curves that neck of pliant ivory!
I 'll paint her thus!

ISABELLA. (*Aside.*) Forgetful where he is,
He thinks aloud. This is, perhaps, the rudeness
My father fear'd might anger me.

ANGELO. What color
Can match the clear red of those glorious lips?
Say it were possible to trace the arches,
Shaped like the drawn bow of the god of love—
How tint them, after?

ISABELLA. Still, he thinks not of me,
But murmurs to his picture. 'T were sweet praise,
Were it a lover whispering it. I 'll listen,
As I walk, still.

ANGELO. They say, a cloudy veil
Hangs ever at the crystal-gate of heaven,
To bar the issue of its blinding glory.
So droop those silken lashes to an eye
Mortal could never paint!

ISABELLA. There 's flattery,
Would draw down angels!

ANGELO. Now, what alchymy
Can mock the rose and lily of her cheek!
I must look closer on 't! (*Advancing.*)
Fair lady, please you,
I 'll venture to your side.

ISABELLA. Sir!

ANGELO. (*Examining her cheek.*) There 's a mixture
Of white and red here, that defeats my skill.
If you 'll forgive me, I 'll observe an instant,
How the bright blood and the transparent pearl
Melt to each other!

ISABELLA. (*Receding from him.*) You 're too free, Sir!

ANGELO. (*With surprise.*) Madam!

ISABELLA. (*Aside.*) And yet, I think not so. He must look on it,
To paint it well.

ANGELO. Lady! the daylight 's precious!
Pray you, turn to me! In my study, here,
I 've tried to fancy how that ivory shoulder
Leads the white light off from your arching neck,
But cannot, for the envious sleeve that hides it.
Please you, displace it!
(*Raises his hand to the sleeve.*)

ISABELLA. Sir, you are too bold!

ANGELO. Pardon me, lady! Nature's masterpiece
Should be beyond your hiding, or my praise!
Were you less marvellous, I were too bold;
But there 's a pure divinity in beauty,
Which the true eye of art looks on with reverence,
Though, like the angels, it were all unclad!
You have no right to hide it!

ISABELLA. How? No right?

ANGELO. 'T is the religion of our art, fair madam!
That, by oft looking on the type divine
In which we first were moulded, men remember
The heav'n they 're born to! You 've an errand here,
To show how look the angels. But, as Vestals
Cherish the sacred fire, yet let the priest

Light his lamp at it for a thousand altars,
So is your beauty unassoiled, though I
Ravish a copy for the shut-out world!

ISABELLA. (*Aside.*) Here is the wooing that should win a maid!
Bold, yet respectful—free, yet full of honor!
I never saw a youth with gentler eyes;
I never heard a voice that pleased me more;
Let me look on him?

(*Enter* TORTESA, *unperceived.*)

ANGELO. In a form like yours,
All parts are perfect, madam! yet, unseen,
Impossible to fancy. With your leave
I 'll see your hand unglov'd.

ISABELLA. (*Removing her glove.*) I have no heart
To keep it from you, signor! There it is!

ANGELO. (*Taking it in his own.*) Oh, God! how beautiful thy works may be!
Inimitably perfect! Let me look
Close on the tracery of these azure veins!
With what a delicate and fragile thread
They weave their subtle mesh beneath the skin,
And meet, all blushing, in these rosy nails!
How soft the texture of these tapering fingers!
How exquisite the wrist! How perfect all! (TORTESA *rushes forward.*)

TORTESA. Now have I heard enough! Why, what are you,
To palm the hand of my betrothed bride
With this licentious freedom? (ANGELO *turns composedly to his work.*) And you, madam!
With a first troth scarce cold upon your lips--
Is this your chastity?

ISABELLA. My father's roof
Is over me! I 'm not your wife!

TORTESA. Bought! paid for!
The wedding toward—have I no right in you?
Your father, at my wish, bade you be private;
Is this obedience?

ISABELLA. Count Falcone's will
Has, to his daughter, ever been a law;
This, in prosperity—and now, when chance
Frowns on his broken fortunes, I were dead
To love and pity, were not soul and body
Spent for his smallest need! I did consent
To wed his ruthless creditor for this!
I would have sprung into the sea, the grave,
As questionless and soon! My *troth* is yours!
But I 'm not wedded yet, and till I am,
The hallowed honor that protects a maid
Is round me, like a circle of bright fire!
A savage would not cross it—nor shall you!
I 'm mistress of my presence. Leave me, Sir!

TORTESA. There 's a possession of some lordly acres
Sold to Falcone for that lily hand!
The deed 's delivered, and the hand 's my own!
I 'll see that no man looks on 't.

ISABELLA. Shall a lady
Bid you begone twice?

TORTESA. Twenty times, if 't please you!

(*She looks at* ANGELO, *who continues tranquilly painting.*)

ISABELLA. Does he not wear a sword? Is he a coward,
That he can hear this man heap insult on me,
And ne'er fall on him?

TORTESA. Lady! to your chamber!
I have a touch to give this picture, here,
But want no model for 't. Come, come.

(*Offers to take her by the arm.*)

ISABELLA. Stand back!
Now, will he see this wretch lay hands on me,
And never speak? He cannot be a coward!
No, no! some other reason—not a coward!
I could not love a coward!

TORTESA. If you will,
Stay where you 're better miss'd—'t is at your pleasure;
I 'll hew your kisses from the saucy lips
Of this bold painter—look on 't, if you will!
And first, to mar his picture!

(*He strikes at the canvas, when* ANGELO *suddenly draws, attacks, and disarms him.*)

ANGELO. Hold! What wouldst thou?
Fool! madman! dog! What wouldst thou with my picture?
Speak!—But thy life would not bring back a ray

Of precious daylight, and I cannot waste
it!
Begone! begone! (*Throws* TORTESA'S *sword from the window, and returns to his picture.*) I'll back to paradise!
'T was this touch that he marr'd! So! fair again!

TORTESA. (*Going out.*) I'll find you, Sir, when I'm in cooler blood!
And, madam, *you!* or Count Falcone *for* you,
Shall rue this scorn! (*Exit.*)

ISABELLA. (*Looking at* ANGELO.) Lost in his work once more!
I shall be jealous of my very picture!
Yet one who can forget his passions so—
Peril his life, and, losing scarce a breath,
Turn to his high, ambitious toil again—
Must have a heart for whose belated waking
Queens might keep vigil!

ANGELO. Twilight falls, fair lady!
I must give o'er! Pray heaven, the downy wing
Of its most loving angel guard your beauty!
Good night!

ISABELLA. Good night!
(*She looks after him a moment, and then walks thoughtfully off the stage.*)

END OF THE FIRST ACT.

ACT SECOND.

SCENE 1. (TOMASO *discovered sitting at his supper, with a bottle of water before him.*)

TOMASO. Water! (*Sips a little with a grimace.*) I think, since the world was drowned in it, it has tasted of sinners. The pious throat refuses it. Other habits grow pleasant with use—but the drinking of water lessens the liking of it. Now, why should not some rivers run wine? There are varieties in the *eatables*—will any wise man tell me why there should be but one *drinkable* in nature—and that water? My mind's made up—it's the curse of transgression. (*A rap at the door.*) Come in!

(*Enter* ZIPPA, *with a basket and bottle.*)

ZIPPA. Good even, Tomaso!

TOMASO. Zippa! I had a presentiment—

ZIPPA. What! of my coming?

TOMASO. No—of thy bottle! Look! I was stinting myself in water to leave room!

ZIPPA. The reason is superfluous. There would be room in thee for wine, if thou wert drowned in the sea.

TOMASO. God forbid!

ZIPPA. What—that thou shouldst be drowned?

TOMASO. No—but that being drowned, I should have room for wine.

ZIPPA. Why, now?—why?

TOMASO. If I had room for wine, I should want it—and to want wine in the bottom of the sea, were a plague of Sodom.

ZIPPA. Where's Angelo?

TOMASO. What's in thy bottle? Show! Show!

ZIPPA. Tell me where he is—what he has done since yesterday—what thought on—what said—how he has looked, and if he still loves me; and when thou art thirsty with truth-telling—(dry work for such a liar as thou art,)—thou shalt learn what is in my bottle!

TOMASO. Nay—learning be hanged!

ZIPPA. So says the fool!

TOMASO. Speak advisedly! Was not Adam blest till he knew good and evil?

ZIPPA. Right for once.

TOMASO. Then he lost Paradise by too much learning.

ZIPPA. Ha! ha! Hadst thou been consulted, we should still be there!

TOMASO. Snug! I would have had my inheritance in a small vineyard!

ZIPPA. Tell me what I ask of thee.

TOMASO. Thou shalt have a piece of news for a cup of wine—pay and take—till thy bottle be dry!

ZIPPA. Come on, then! and if thou must lie, let it be flattery. That's soonest forgiven.

TOMASO. And last forgotten! Pour out! (*She pours a cup full, and gives him.*) The Duke was here yesterday.—

ZIPPA. Lie the first!

TOMASO. And made much of my master's pictures.

ZIPPA. Nay—that would have made two good lies. Thou 'rt prodigal of stuff!

TOMASO. Pay two glasses, then, and square the reckoning!

ZIPPA. Come! Lie the third!

TOMASO. What wilt thou wager it's a lie, that Angelo is painting a court lady for the duchess?

ZIPPA. Oh, Lord! Take the bottle! They say there's truth in wine—but as truth is impossible to thee, drink thyself, at least, down to probabilities!

TOMASO. Look you there! When was virtue encouraged? Here have I been telling God's truth, and it goes for a lie. Hang virtue! Produce thy cold chicken, and I'll tell thee a lie for the wings and two for the side-bones and breast. (*Offers to take the chicken.*)

ZIPPA. Stay! stay! It's for thy master, thou glutton!

TOMASO. Who's ill a-bed, and forbid meat. (ANGELO *enters.*) I would have told thee so before, but feared to grieve thee. (She *would* have a lie!)

ZIPPA. (*Starting up.*) Ill! Angelo ill! Is he *very* ill, good Tomaso?

TOMASO. Very! (*Seizes the chicken, as* ANGELO *claps him on the shoulder.*)

ANGELO. Will thy tricks never end?

TOMASO. Ehem! ehem! (*Thrusts the chicken into his pocket.*)

ANGELO. How art thou, Zippa?

ZIPPA. Well, dear Angelo! (*Giving him her hand.*) And thou wert not ill, indeed?

ANGELO. Never better, by the test of a true hand! I have done work to-day, I trust will be remembered!

ZIPPA. Is it true it's a fair lady?

ANGELO. A lady with a face so angelical, Zippa, that—

ZIPPA. That thou didst forget mine?

ANGELO. In truth, I forgot there was such a thing as a world, and so forgot all in it. I was in heaven!

TOMASO. (*Aside, as he picks the leg of the chicken.*) (Prosperity is excellent whitewash, and her love is an old score!)

ZIPPA. (*Bitterly.*) I am glad thou wert pleased, Angelo!—very glad!

TOMASO. (*Aside.*) (Glad as an eel to be fried.)

ZIPPA. (*Aside.*) ("In Heaven," was he! If I pay him not that, may my brains rot! By what right, loving me, is he "in Heaven" with another?)

TOMASO. (*Aside.*) (No more wine and cold chicken from that quarter!)

ZIPPA. (*Aside.*) (Tortesa loves me, and my false game may be played true. If he wed not Falcone's daughter, he will wed me, and so I am revenged on this fickle Angelo! I have the heart to do it!)

ANGELO. What dost thou muse on, Zippa?

ZIPPA. On one I love better than thee, Signor!

ANGELO. What, angry? (*Seizes his pencil.*) Hold there till I sketch thee! By Jove, thou 'rt not half so pretty when thou 'rt pleased!

ZIPPA. Adieu, Signor! your mockery will have an end! (*Goes out with an angry air.*)

ANGELO. What! gone? Nay, I'll come with thee, if thou 'rt in earnest! What whim's this? (*Takes up his hat.*) Ho, Zippa! (*Follows in pursuit.*)

TOMASO. (*Pulls the chicken from his pocket.*) Come forth, last of the chickens! She will ne'er forgive him, and so ends the succession of cold fowl! One glass to its memory, and then to bed! (*Drinks, and takes up the candle.*) A woman is generally unsafe—but a jealous one spoils all confidence in drink.

(*Exit, muttering.*)

SCENE 2. (*An Apartment in the Falcone Palace. Enter* SERVANT, *shewing in* ZIPPA.)

SERVANT. Wait here, if 't please you!

ZIPPA. Thanks! (*Exit* SERVANT.)
My heart misgives me!
'T is a bold errand I am come upon—
And I a stranger to her! Yet, perchance
She needs a friend—the proudest do sometimes—
And mean ones may be welcome. Look! she comes!

ISABELLA. You wished to speak with me?

ZIPPA. I *did*—but now
My memory is crept into my eyes;
I cannot think for gazing on your beauty!
Pardon me, lady!

ISABELLA. You're too fair yourself
To find my face a wonder. Speak! Who are you?

ZIPPA. Zippa, the Glover's daughter, and your friend!

ISABELLA. My friend?

ZIPPA. I said so. You're a noble lady
And I a low-born maid—yet I have come
To offer you my friendship.

ISABELLA. This seems strange!

ZIPPA. I'll make it less so, if you'll give me leave.

ISABELLA. You'll please me!

ZIPPA. Briefly—for the time is precious
To me as well as you—I have a lover,

A true one, as I think, who yet finds boldness
To seek your hand in marriage.
ISABELLA. How? We're rivals!
ZIPPA. Tortesa loves me, and for that I'd wed him.
Yet I'm not sure I love him more than you—
And you must hate him.
ISABELLA. So far freely spoken—
What was your thought in coming to me now?
ZIPPA. To mar your match with him, and so make mine!
ISABELLA. Why, free again! Yet, as you love him not
'T is strange you seek to wed him!
ZIPPA. Oh, no, madam!
Woman loves once unthinkingly. The heart
Is born with her first love, and, new to joy,
Breathes to the first wind its delicious sweetness,
But gets none back! So comes its bitter wisdom!
When next we think of love, *'t is who loves us!*
I said Tortesa loved me!
ISABELLA. You shall have him
With all my heart! See—I'm your friend already!
And friends are equals. So approach, and tell me,
What was this first love like, that you discourse
So prettily upon?
ZIPPA. (*Aside.*) (Dear Angelo!
'T will be a happiness to talk of him!)
I loved a youth, kind madam! far beneath
The notice of your eyes, unknown and poor.
ISABELLA. A handsome youth?
ZIPPA. Indeed, I thought him so!
But you would not. I loved him out of pity;
No one cared for him.
ISABELLA. Was he so forlorn?
ZIPPA. He was our neighbor, and I knew his toil
Was almost profitless; and 't was a pleasure
To fill my basket from our wasteful table,
And steal, at eve, to sup with him.
ISABELLA. (*Smiling.*) Why, that
Was charity, indeed! He loved you for it—
Was 't not so?
ZIPPA. He was like a brother to me—
The kindest brother sister ever had.
I built my hopes upon his gentleness:
He had no other quality to love.
Th' ambitious change—so do the fiery-hearted:
The lowly are more constant.
ISABELLA. And yet, he
Was, after all, a false one?
ZIPPA. Nay, dear lady!
I'll check my story there! 'T would end in anger,
Perhaps in tears. If I am not too bold,
Tell me, in turn, of all your worshippers—
Was there ne'er one that pleased you?
ISABELLA. (*Aside.*) (Now could I
Prate to this humble maid, of Angelo,
Till matins rang again!) My gentle Zippa!
I have found all men prompt to talk of love,
Save only one. I will confess to you,
For that one could I die! Yet, so unlike
Your faithless lover must I draw his picture,
That you will wonder how such opposites
Could both be loved of women.
ZIPPA. Was he fair,
Or brown?
ISABELLA. In truth, I marked not his complexion.
ZIPPA. Tall?
ISABELLA. That I know not.
ZIPPA. Well—robust, or slight?
ISABELLA. I cannot tell, indeed! I heard him speak—
Looked in his eyes, and saw him calm and angered—
And see him now, in fancy, standing there—
Yet know not limb or feature!
ZIPPA. You but saw
A shadow, lady!
ISABELLA. Nay—I saw a *soul!*
His eyes were light with it. The forehead lay
Above their fires in calm tranquillity,
As the sky sleeps o'er thunder-clouds. His look
Was mixed of these—earnest, and yet subdued—
Gentle, yet passionate—sometimes half god-like
In its command, then mild and sweet again,
Like a stern angel taught humility!
Oh! when he spoke, my heart stole out to him!

There was a spirit-echo in his voice—
A sound of thought—of under-playing music—
As if, before it ceased in human ears,
The echo was caught up in fairy-land!

ZIPPA. Was he a courtier, madam?

ISABELLA. He's as lowly
In birth and fortunes, as your false one, Zippa!
Yet rich in genius, and of that ambition,
That he'll outlast nobility with fame.
Have you seen such a man?

ZIPPA. Alas! sweet lady!
My life is humble, and such wondrous men
Are far above *my* knowing. I could wish
To *see* one ere I died!

ISABELLA. You *shall*, believe me!
But while we talk of lovers, we forget
In how brief time you are to win a husband.
Come to my chamber, Zippa, and I'll see
How with your little net you'll snare a bird
Fierce as this rude Tortesa!

ZIPPA. We will find
A way, dear lady, if we die for it!

ISABELLA. Shall we? Come with me, then! (*Exeunt.*)

SCENE 3. (*An apartment in the Falcone Palace.* TORTESA *alone waiting the return of the Count.*)

TORTESA. (*Musing.*) There are some luxuries too rich for purchase.
Your *soul*, 't is said, will buy them, of the devil—
Money's too poor! What would I not give, now,
That I could *scorn* what I can hate and ruin!
Scorn is the priceless luxury! In heaven,
The angels *pity*. They are blest to do so;
For, pitying, they look down. We do 't by *scorn!*
There lies the privilege of noble birth!—
The jewel of that bloated toad is *scorn!*
You may take all else from him. You—being mean—
May get his palaces—may wed his daughter—
Sleep in his bed—have all his peacock menials
Watching your least glance, as they did "my lord's";
And, well-possess'd thus, you may pass him by
On his own horse; and while the vulgar crowd
Gape at your trappings, and scarce look on him—
He, in his rags, and starving for a crust—
You'll feel his *scorn*, through twenty coats of mail,
Hot as a sun-stroke! Yet there's something for us!
Th' archangel fiend, when driven forth from heaven,
Put on the serpent, and found sweet revenge
Trailing his slime through Eden! So will I!

(*Enter* FALCONE, *booted and spurred.*)

FALCONE. Good morrow, signor.

TORTESA. Well-arrived, my lord!
How sped your riding?

FALCONE. Fairly! Has my daughter
Left you alone?

TORTESA. She knows that I am here.
Nay—she'll come presently! A word in private,
Since we're alone, my lord!

FALCONE. I listen, signor!

TORTESA. Your honor, as I think, outweighs a bond?

FALCONE. 'T was never questioned.

TORTESA. On your simple word,
And such more weight as hangs upon the troth
Of a capricious woman, I gave up
A deed of lands to you.

FALCONE. You did.

TORTESA. To be
Forfeit, and mine again—the match not made?

FALCONE. How if *you* marr'd it?

TORTESA. *I?* I'm not a boy!
What I would yesterday, I will to-day!
I'm not a lover—

FALCONE. How? So near your bridal,
And not a lover? Shame, sir!

TORTESA. My lord count,
You take me for a fool!

FALCONE. Is 't like a fool
To love a high-born lady, and your bride?

TORTESA. Yes; a thrice-sodden fool—if it were I!
I'm not a mate for her—you know I am not!
You know that, in her heart, your haughty daughter
Scorns me—ineffably!

FALCONE. You seek occasion
To slight her, signor?

TORTESA. No! I 'll marry her
If all the pride that cast down Lucifer
Lie in her bridal-ring! But, mark me still!
I 'm not one of your humble citizens,
To bring my money-bags and make you rich—
That, when we walk together, I may take
Your shadow for my own! These limbs are clay—
Poor, common clay, my lord! And she that weds me,
Comes down to my estate.

FALCONE. By this you mean not
To shut her from her friends?

TORTESA. You 'll see your daughter
By coming to my house—not else! D' ye think
I 'll have a carriage to convey my wife
Where she will hear me laughed at?—buy fine horses
To prance a measure to the mocking jeers
Of fools that ride with her? Nay—keep a table
Where I 'm the skeleton that mars the feast?
No, no—no, no!

FALCONE. (*Aside.*) (With half the provocation,
I would, ere now, have struck an emperor!
But baser pangs make this endurable.
I 'm poor—so patience!) What was it beside
You would have said to me?

TORTESA. But this: Your daughter
Has, in your absence, covered me with scorn!
We 'll not talk of it—if the match goes on,
I care not to remember it! (*Aside.*) (*She* shall—
And bitterly!)

FALCONE. (*Aside.*) (My poor, poor Isabella!
The task was too much!)

TORTESA. There 's a cost of feeling—
You may not think it much—*I* reckon it
A thousand pounds per day—in playing thus
The suitor to a lady cramm'd with pride!
I 've writ you out a bond to pay me for it!
See here!—to pay me for my shame and pains,
If I should lose your daughter for a wife,
A thousand pounds per day—dog cheap at that!
Sign it, my lord, or give me back my deeds,
And *traffic* cease between us!

FALCONE. Is this earnest,
Or are you mad or trifling? Do I not
Give you my daughter with an open hand?
Are you betroth'd, or no?

(*Enter a* SERVANT.)

Who 's this?

SERVANT. A page
Sent from the Duke.

FALCONE. Admit him!

(*Enter* PAGE, *with a letter.*)

PAGE. For my lord,
The Count Falcone.

TORTESA. (*Aside.*) (In a moment more
I would have made a bond of such assurance
Her father on his knees should bid me take her.
(*Looking at* FALCONE, *who smiles as he reads.*)
What glads him now?)

FALCONE. You shall not have the bond!

TORTESA. No? (*Aside.*) (Here 's a change! What hint from Duke or devil
Stirs him to this?) My lord, 't were best the bridal
Took place upon the instant. Is your daughter
Ready within?

FALCONE. You 'll never wed my daughter!

(*Enter* ISABELLA.)

TORTESA. My lord!

FALCONE. She 's fitlier mated! Here she comes!
My lofty Isabella! My fair child!
How dost thou, sweet?

ISABELLA. (*Embracing him.*) Come home, and I not know it!
Art well? I see thou art! Hast ridden hard?
My dear, dear father!

FALCONE. Give me breath to tell thee
Some better news, my lov'd one!

ISABELLA. Nay, the joy
To see you back again 's enough for now.
There can be no news better, and for this
Let 's keep a holiday twixt this and sunset!
Shut up your letter, and come see my flowers,

And hear my birds sing, will you?

FALCONE. Look, my darling,
Upon this first! (*Holds up the letter.*)

ISABELLA. No! you shall tell me all
You and the Duke did—where you slept, where ate,
Whether you dream'd of me—and, now I think on 't,
Found you no wild-flowers as you cross'd the mountains?

FALCONE. My own bright child! (*Looks fondly upon her.*)

TORTESA. (*Aside.*) ('T will mar your joy, my lord!
To see the Glover's daughter in your palace,
And your proud daughter houseless!)

FALCONE. (*To* ISABELLA.) You'll not hear
The news I have for you?

TORTESA. (*Advancing.*) Before you tell it,
I'll take my own again!

ISABELLA. (*Aside.*) (Tortesa here!)
(*Curtseys.*)
I crave your pardon, sir; I saw you not!
(Oh, hateful monster!) (*Aside.*)

FALCONE. Listen to my news,
Signor Tortesa! It concerns you, trust me!

ISABELLA. (*Aside.*) (More of this hateful marriage!)

TORTESA. Tell it briefly,
My time is precious!

FALCONE. Sir, I'll sum it up
In twenty words. The Duke has information,
By what means yet I know not, that my need
Spurs me to marry an unwilling daughter.
He bars the match!—redeems my lands and palace,
And has enrich'd the young Count Julian,
For whom he bids me keep my daughter's hand!
Kind, royal master! (*Reads the note to himself.*)

ISABELLA. (*Aside.*) (Never.)

TORTESA. (*Aside, with suppressed rage.*)
('T is a lie!
He 's mad, or plays some trick to gain the time—
Or there 's a woman hatching deviltry!
We'll see.) (*Looks at* ISABELLA.)

ISABELLA. (*Aside.*) (I'll die first! Sold and taken back,
Then thrust upon a husband paid to take me!
To save my father I have weigh'd myself,
Heart, hand, and honor, against so much land!
I—Isabella! I 'm not hawk nor hound,
And, if I change my master, I will choose him!

TORTESA. (*Aside.*) She seems not over-pleased!

PAGE. Your pardon, Count!
I wait your answer to the Duke!

FALCONE. My daughter
Shall give it you herself. What sweet phrase have you,
Grateful and eloquent, to bear your thanks?
Speak, Isabella!

ISABELLA. (*Aside.*) (There 's but one way left!
Courage, poor heart, and think on Angelo!)
(*Advances suddenly to* TORTESA.)
Signor Tortesa!

TORTESA. Madam!

ISABELLA. There 's my hand!
Is 't yours, or no?

TORTESA. There *was* a troth between us!

ISABELLA. Is 't broke?

TORTESA. *I* have not broke it!

ISABELLA. Then why stand you
Mute as a statue, when 't is struck asunder
Without our wish or knowledge? Would you be
Half so indifferent had you lost a horse?
Am I worth having?

TORTESA. Is my life worth having?

ISABELLA. Then are you robb'd! Look to it!

FALCONE. Is she mad?

TORTESA. You'll marry me?

ISABELLA. I will!

FALCONE. By heaven you shall not!
What, shall my daughter wed a leprosy—
A bloated money-canker? Leave her hand!
Stand from him, Isabella!

ISABELLA. Sir! you gave me
This "leper" for a husband, three days gone;
I did not ask my heart if I could love him!
I took him with the meekness of a child,
Trusting my father! I was shut up for him—
Forc'd to receive no other company—
My wedding-clothes made, and the match proclaim'd
Through Florence!

FALCONE. Do you love him?—tell me quickly!
ISABELLA. You never ask'd me that when I was bid
To wed him!
FALCONE. I am dumb!
TORTESA. Ha! ha! well put!
At him again, 'Bel! Well! I've had misgivings
That there was food in me for ladies' liking.
I've been too modest!
ISABELLA (*aside*). (Monster of disgust!)
FALCONE. My daughter! I would speak with you in private!
Signor! you'll pardon me.
ISABELLA. Go you, dear father!
I'll follow straight. (*Exit* FALCONE.)
TORTESA (*aside*). (She loiters for a kiss!
They're all alike! The same trick woos them all!)
Come to me, 'Bel!
ISABELLA (*coldly*). Tomorrow at this hour
You'll find the priest here, and the bridesmaids waiting.
Till then, adieu! (*Exit.*)
TORTESA. Hola! what, gone? Why, Bella!
Sweetheart! I say! So! She would coy it with me!
Well, well, to-morrow! 'T is not long, and kisses
Pay interest by seconds! There's a leg!
As she stood there, the calf shewed handsomely.
Faith, 't is a shapely one! I wonder now,
Which of my points she finds most admirable!
Something I never thought on, like as not.
We do not see ourselves as others see us.
'T would not surprise me now, if 't were my beard—
My forehead! I've a hand indifferent white!
Nay, I've been told my waist was neatly turn'd.
We *do not* see ourselves as others see us!
How goes the hour? I'll home and fit my hose
To tie trim for the morrow. (*Going out.*) Hem! the door's
Lofty. I like that! I will have mine raised.
Your low door makes one stoop! (*Exit.*)

END OF THE SECOND ACT.

ACT THIRD.

SCENE 1.

(ANGELO *discovered in his studio, painting upon the picture of* ISABELLA.)

ANGELO. My soul is drunk with gazing on this face.
I reel and faint with it. In what sweet world
Have I traced all its lineaments before?
I know them. Like a troop of long-lost friends,
My pencil wakes them with its eager touch,
And they spring up, rejoicing. Oh, I'll gem
The heaven of Fame with my irradiate pictures,
Like kindling planets—but this glorious one
Shall be their herald, like the evening star,
First-lit, and lending of its fire to all.
The day fades—but the lamp burns on within me.
My bosom has no dark, no sleep, no change
To dream or calm oblivion. I work on
When my hand stops. The light tints fade. Good night,
Fair image of the fairest thing on earth,
Bright Isabella!
(*Leans on the rod with which he guides his hand, and remains looking at his picture.*)

(*Enter* TOMASO, *with two bags of money.*)

TOMASO. For the most excellent painter, Angelo, two hundred ducats! The genius of my master flashes upon me. The duke's greeting and two hundred ducats! If I should not have died in my blindness but for this eye-water, may I be hanged. (*Looks at* ANGELO.) He is studying his picture. What an air there is about him—lofty, unlike the vulgar! Two hundred ducats! (*Observes* ANGELO'S *hat on the table.*) It strikes me now that I can see genius in that hat. It is not like a common hat. Not like a bought hat. The rim turns to the crown with an intelligence. (*Weighs the ducats in his hand.*) Good heavy ducats. What it is to refresh the vision! I have looked round, ere now, in this very chamber, and fancied that the furniture expressed a melancholy dulness. When he hath talked to me of his pictures, I have seen the chairs smile. Nay, as if shamed to listen, the very table has looked foolish. Now, all about me expresseth a choice peculiarity—as you would say, how like a genius to have such chairs! What a painter-like table! Two hundred ducats!

ANGELO. What hast thou for supper?

TOMASO. Two hundred ducats, my great master.

ANGELO (*absently*). A cup of wine! Wine, Tomaso! (*Sits down.*)

TOMASO. (So would the great Donatello have sat upon his chair! His legs thus! His hand falling thus!) (*Aloud.*) There is nought in the cellar but stale beer, my illustrious master! (Now, it strikes me that his shadow is unlike another man's—of a *pink* tinge, somehow—yet that may be fancy.)

ANGELO. Hast thou no money? Get wine, I say!

TOMASO. I saw the duke in the market-place, who called me Angelo (we shall rue that trick yet), and with a gracious smile asked me if thou hadst paid the twenty flasks.

ANGELO (*not listening*). Is there no wine?

TOMASO. I said to his grace, no! Pray mark the sequel: In pity of my thirst, the duke sends me two—ahem! *one* hundred ducats. Here they are!

ANGELO. Didst thou say the wine was on the lees?

TOMASO. With these *fifty* ducats we shall buy nothing but wine. (He will be rich with fifty.)

ANGELO. What saidst thou?

TOMASO. I spoke of *twenty* ducats sent thee by the duke. Wilt thou finger them ere one is spent?

ANGELO. I asked thee for wine—I am parched.

TOMASO. Of these *ten* ducats, think'st thou we might spend one for a flask of better quality?

ANGELO. Lend me a ducat, if thou hast one, and buy wine presently. Go!

TOMASO. I'll lend it thee, willingly, my illustrious master. It is my last, but as much mine as thine.

ANGELO. Go! Go!

TOMASO. Yet wait! There's a scrap of news. Falcone's daughter marries Tortesa, the usurer. To-morrow is the bridal.

ANGELO. How?

TOMASO. I learned it in the market-place! There will be rare doings!

ANGELO. Dog! Villain! Thou hast lied! Thou dar'st not say it!

TOMASO. Hey! Art thou mad? Nay—borrow thy ducat where thou canst! I'll spend that's my own. Adieu, master!

(*Exit* TOMASO, *and enter* TORTESA *with a complacent smile.*)

ANGELO. Ha!—well arrived!

(*Draws his sword.*)

TORTESA. Good eve, good Signor Painter.

ANGELO. You struck me yesterday.

TORTESA. I harmed your picture—
For which I'm truly sorry—but not you!

ANGELO. Myself! myself! My picture is myself!
What are my bones that rot? Is this my hand?—
Is this my eye?

TORTESA. I think so.

ANGELO. No, I say!
The hand and eye of Angelo are there!
There—there—(*Points to his pictures.*)—immortal! Wound me in the flesh,
I will forgive you upon fair excuse.
'T is the earth round me—'t is my shell—my house;
But in my picture lie my brain and heart—
My soul—my fancy. For a blow at these
There's no cold reparation. Draw, and quickly!
I'm in the mood to fight it to the death.
Stand on your guard!

TORTESA. I will not fight with you.

ANGELO. Coward!

TORTESA. I'm deaf.

ANGELO. Feel then!

(TORTESA *catches the blow as he strikes him, and coldly flings back his hand.*)

TORTESA. Nay, strike me not!
I'll call the guard, and cry out like a woman.

ANGELO (*turning from him contemptuously*). What scent of dog's meat brought me such a cur!
It is a whip I want, and not a sword.

TORTESA (*folding his arms*). I have a use for life so far above
The stake you quarrel for, that you may choose
Your words to please yourself. They'll please me, too.
Yet you're in luck. I killed a man on Monday
For spitting on my *shadow.* Thursday's sun
Will dry the insult, though it light on *me!*

ANGELO. Oh, subtle coward!

TORTESA. I am what you will,
So I 'm alive to marry on the morrow!
'T is well, by Jupiter! Shall you have power
With half a breath to pluck from me a wife!
Shall I, against a life as poor as yours—
Mine being precious as the keys of Heaven—
Set all upon a throw, and no odds neither?
I know what honor is as well as you!
I know the weight and measure of an insult—
What it is worth to take or fling it back.
I have the hand to fight if I 've a mind;
And I 've a heart to shut my sunshine in,
And lock it from the scowling of the world,
Though all mankind cry "Coward!"

ANGELO. Mouthing braggart!

TORTESA. I came to see my bride, my Isabella!
Show me her picture!
(*Advances to look for it.*)

ANGELO. Do but look upon 't,
By heaven's fair light, I 'll kill you!
(*Draws.*)

TORTESA. Soft, she 's mine!
She loves me! and with that to make life precious,
I have the nerve to beat back Hercules,
If you were he!

ANGELO (*attacking him*). Out! Out! thou shameless liar!

TORTESA (*retreating on the defence*). Thy blows and words fall pointless! Nay, thou 'rt mad!
But I 'll not harm thee for her picture's sake!

ANGELO. Liar! she hates thee!
(*Beats him off the stage and returns, closing the door violently.*)
So! once more alone!
(*Takes* ISABELLA'S *picture from the easel, and replaces it with* ZIPPA'S.)
Back to the wall, deceitful loveliness!
And come forth, Zippa, fair in honest truth!
I 'll make *thee* beautiful!
(*Takes his pencil and palette to paint. A knock is heard.*)
Who knocks? Come in!

(*Enter* ISABELLA, *disguised as a monk.*)

ISABELLA. Good morrow, signor!

ANGELO (*turning sharply to the monk*).
There 's a face, old monk,
Might stir your blood—ha! You shall tell me, now,
Which of these heavenly features hides the soul!
There *is* one! I have worked upon the picture
Till *my* brain 's thick—I cannot see like you.
Where is 't?

ISABELLA (*aside*). (A picture of the Glover's daughter!
What does he, painting *her!*) Is 't for its *beauty*
You paint that face, sir?

ANGELO. Yes—th' immortal beauty!
Look here! What see you in that face? The skin—

ISABELLA. Brown as a vintage-girl's!

ANGELO. The mouth—

ISABELLA. A good one
To eat and drink withal!

ANGELO. The eye is—

ISABELLA. Grey!
You 'll buy a hundred like it for a penny!

ANGELO. A hundred eyes?

ISABELLA. No. Hazel-nuts!

ANGELO. The forehead—
How find you that?

ISABELLA. Why, made to match the rest!
I 'll cut as good a face out of an apple—
For all that 's fair in it!

ANGELO. Oh, heaven, how dim
Were God's most blessed image did all eyes
Look on 't like thine! Is 't by the red and white—
Is 't by the grain and tincture of the skin—
Is 't by the hair's gloss, or the forehead's arching,
You know the bright inhabitant? I tell thee
The spark of their divinity in some
Lights up an *inward* face—so radiant,
The outward lineaments are like a veil
Floating before the sanctuary—forgot
In glimpses of the glory streaming through!

ISABELLA (*mournfully*). Is Zippa's face so radiant?

ANGELO. Look upon it!
You see thro' all the countenance she 's *true!*

ISABELLA. True to *you*, signor!

ANGELO. To herself, old man!
Yet *once*, to *me*, too! (*Dejectedly.*)

ISABELLA (*aside*). (Once to him! Can Zippa
Have dared to love a man like Angelo!

I think she dare not. Yet if he, indeed,
Were the inconstant lover that she told of—
The youth who was "her neighbor!")
Please you, signor!
Was that fair maid your neighbor?

ANGELO. Ay—the best!
A loving sister were not half so kind!
I never supp'd without her company.
Yet she was modest as an unsunn'd lily,
And bounteous as the constant perfume of it.

ISABELLA (*aside*). ('T was he, indeed!
Oh! what a fair outside
Has falsehood there! Yet stay! If it were *I*
Who made him false to her? Alas, for honor,
I must forgive him—tho' my lips are weary
With telling Zippa how I thought him perjured!
I cannot trust her more—I'll plot alone!)

(*Turns, and takes her own picture from the wall.*)

ISABELLA. What picture's this, turned to the wall, good signor?

ANGELO. A painted lie!

ISABELLA. A lie!—nay—pardon me!
I spoke in haste. Methought 't was like a lady
I'd somewhere seen!—a lady—Isabella!
But she was true!

ANGELO. Then 't is not she I've drawn.
For that's a likeness of as false a face
As ever devil did his mischief under.

ISABELLA. And yet methinks 't is done most lovingly!
You must have thought it fair to dwell so on it.

ANGELO. Your convent has the picture of a saint
Tempted, while praying, by the shape of woman.
The painter knew that woman was the devil,
Yet drew her like an angel!

ISABELLA (*aside*). (It is true
He praised my beauty as a painter may—
No more—in words. He praised me as he drew—
Feature by feature. But who calls the lip
To answer for a perjured oath in love?
How should love breathe—how not die, choked for utterance,
If *words* were all. He loved me with his eyes.
He breathed it. Upon every word he spoke
Hung an unuttered worship that his tongue
Would spend a life to make articulate.
Did he not take my hand into his own?
And, as his heart sprang o'er that bridge of veins,
Did he not call to mine to pass him on it—
Each to the other's bosom! I have sworn
To love him—wed him—die with him—and yet
He never *heard* me—but he *knows* it well,
And, in his heart holds me to answer for it.
I'll try once more to find this anger out.
If it be jealousy—why—then, indeed,
He'll call me black, and I'll forgive it him!
For then my errand's done, and I'll away
To play the cheat out that shall make him mine.)

(*Turns to* ANGELO.) Fair signor, by your leave, I've heard it said
That in the beauty of a human face
The God of Nature never writ a lie.

ANGELO. 'T is likely true!

ISABELLA. That howsoe'er the features
Seem fair at first, a blemish on the soul
Has its betraying speck that warns you of it.

ANGELO. It should be so, indeed!

ISABELLA. Nay—here's a face
Will show at once if it be true or no.
At the first glance 't is fair!

ANGELO. Most heavenly fair!

ISABELLA. Yet, in the lip, methinks, there lurks a shadow—
Something—I know not what—but in it lies
The devil you spoke of!

ANGELO. Ay—but 't is not there!
Not in her lip! Oh, no! Look elsewhere for it.
'T is passionately bright—but lip more pure
Ne'er passed unchallenged through the gate of heaven.
Believe me, 't is not there!

ISABELLA. How falls the light?
I see a gleam not quite angelical
About the eye. Maybe the light falls wrong—

ANGELO (*drawing her to another position*).
Stand here! D'ye see it now?

ISABELLA. 'T is just so here!

ANGELO (*sweeps the air with his brush*).

There 's some curst cobweb hanging from the wall
That blurs your sight. Now, look again!

ISABELLA. I see it
Just as before.

ANGELO. What! still? You 've turn'd an eyelash
Under the lid. Try how it feels with winking.
Is 't clear?

ISABELLA. 'T was never clearer!

ANGELO. Then, old man!
You 'd best betake you to your prayers apace!
For you 've a failing sight, death's sure forerunner—
And cannot pray long. Why, that eye 's a star,
Sky-lit as Hesperus, and burns as clear.
If you e'er marked the zenith at high noon,
Or midnight, when the blue lifts up to God—
Her eye 's of that far darkness!

ISABELLA (*smiling aside*). Stay—'t is gone!
A blur was on my sight, which, passing from it,
I see as you do. Yes—the eye is clear.
The forehead only, now I see so well,
Has in its arch a mark infallible
Of a false heart beneath it.

ANGELO. Show it to me!

ISABELLA. Between the eyebrows there!

ANGELO. I see a tablet
Whereon the Saviour's finger might have writ
The new commandment. When I painted it
I plucked a just-blown lotus from the shade,
And shamed the white leaf till it seemed a spot—
The brow was so much fairer! Go! old man,
Thy sight fails fast. Go! Go!

ISABELLA. The nostril 's small—
Is 't not?

ANGELO. No!

ISABELLA. Then the cheek 's awry so near it,
It makes it seem so!

ANGELO. Out! thou cavilling fool!
Thou 'rt one of those whose own deformity
Makes all thou seest look monstrous. Go and pray
For a clear sight, and read thy missal with it.
Thou art a priest, and livest by the altar,
Yet dost thou recognize God's imprest seal,
Set on that glorious beauty!

ISABELLA (*aside*). (Oh, he loves me!
Loves me as genius loves—ransacking earth
And ruffling the forbidden flowers of heaven
To make celestial incense of his praise.
High-thoughted Angelo! He loves me well!
With what a gush of all my soul I thank him—
But he 's to win yet, and the time is precious.)
(*To* ANGELO.) Signor, I take my leave.

ANGELO. Good day, old man!
And, if thou com'st again, bring new eyes with thee,
Or thou wilt find scant welcome.

ISABELLA. You shall like
These same eyes well enough when next I come! (*Exit.*)

ANGELO. A crabbed monk! (*Turns the picture to the wall again.*) I'll hide this fatal picture
From sight once more, for till he made me look on 't
I did not know my weakness. Once more, Zippa,
I'll dwell on thy dear face, and with my pencil
Make thee more fair than life, and try to love thee! (*A knock.*)
Come in!

(*Enter* ZIPPA.)

ZIPPA. Good day, Signor Angelo!

ANGELO. Why, Zippa! is 't thou? is 't thou, indeed!

ZIPPA. Myself, dear Angelo!

ANGELO. Art well?

ZIPPA. Ay!

ANGELO. Hast been well?

ZIPPA. Ay!

ANGELO. Then why, for three long days, hast thou not been near me?

ZIPPA. Ask thyself, Signor Angelo!

ANGELO. I have—a hundred times since I saw thee.

ZIPPA. And there was no answer?

ANGELO. None!

ZIPPA. Then shouldst thou have ask'd the picture on thy easel!

ANGELO. Nay—I understand thee not.

ZIPPA. Did I not find thee feasting thy eyes upon it?

ANGELO. True—thou didst.

ZIPPA. And art thou not enamoured of it —wilt tell me truly?

ANGELO (*smiling*). 'T is a fair face!

ZIPPA. Oh, unkind Angelo!

ANGELO. Look on 't! and, seeing its beauty, if thou dost not forgive me, I will never touch pencil to it more.

ZIPPA. I 'll neither look on 't, nor forgive thee. But if thou wilt love the picture of another better than mine, thou shalt paint a new one! (*As she rushes up to dash it from the easel,* ANGELO *catches her arm, and points to the picture. She looks at it, and, seeing her own portrait, turns and falls on his bosom.*) *My* picture! and I thought thee so false! Dear, dear Angelo! I could be grieved to have wronged thee, if joy would give me time. But thou 'lt forgive me?

ANGELO. Willingly! Willingly!

ZIPPA. And thou lovest me indeed, indeed! Nay, answer not! I will never doubt thee more! Dear Angelo! Yet— (*Suddenly turns from* ANGELO *with a troubled air.*)

ANGELO. What ails thee now? (ZIPPA *takes a rich veil from under her cloak, throws it over her head, and looks on the ground in embarrass'd silence.*) Dost thou stand there for a picture of Silence?

ZIPPA. Alas! dear Angelo! When I said I forgave and lov'd thee, I forgot that I was to be married to-morrow!

ANGELO. Married! to whom?

ZIPPA. Tortesa, the usurer!

ANGELO. Tortesa, saidst thou?

ZIPPA. Think not ill of me, dear Angelo, till I have told thee all! This rich usurer, as thou knowest, would for *ambition* marry Isabelle de Falcone.

ANGELO. He would, I know.

ZIPPA. But for *love,* he would marry your poor Zippa.

ANGELO. *Know* you that?

ZIPPA. He told me so the day you anger'd me with the praises of the court lady you were painting. What was her name, Angelo?

ANGELO (*composedly*). I—I 'll tell thee presently! Go on!

ZIPPA. Well—jealous of this unknown lady, I vow'd, if it broke my heart, to wed Tortesa. He had told me Isabella scorn'd him. I flew to her palace. She heard me, pitied me, agreed to plot with me that I might wed the usurer, and then told me in confidence that there was a poor youth whom she loved and would fain marry.

ANGELO (*in breathless anxiety*). Heard you his name?

ZIPPA. No! But as I was to wed the richer and she the poorer, she took my poor veil, and gave me her rich one. Now canst thou read the riddle?

ANGELO (*aside*). (A "poor youth!" What if it is I? She "loves and will wed him!" Oh! if it were I!)

ZIPPA. Nay, dear Angelo! be not so angry! I do not love him! Nay—thou knowst I do not!

ANGELO (*aside*). (It may be—nay—it must! But I will know! If not, I may as well die of that as of this jealous madness.) (*Prepares to go out.*)

ZIPPA. Angelo! where go you? Forgive me, dear Angelo! I swear to thee I love him not!

ANGELO. I 'll know who that poor youth is, or suspense will kill me!

(*Goes out hastily, without a look at* ZIPPA. *She stands silent and amazed for a moment.*)

ZIPPA. Why cares he to know who that poor youth is? "Suspense will kill him?" Stay! a light breaks on me! If Isabella were the Court lady whom he painted! If it were Angelo whom she loved! He is a poor youth!—The picture! The picture will tell all!

(*Hurriedly turns round several pictures turned to the wall, and last of all,* ISABELLA'S. *Looks at it an instant, and exclaims*)

Isabella!

(*She drops on her knees, overcome with grief, and the scene closes.*)

SCENE 2. *A Lady's dressing-room in the Falcone Palace.* ISABELLA *discovered with two phials.*

ISABELLA. Here is a draught will still the breath so nearly,
The keenest-eyed will think the sleeper dead,—
And *this* kills quite. Lie ready, trusty friends,
Close by my bridal veil! I thought to baffle
My ruffian bridegroom by an easier cheat;
But Zippa 's dangerous, and if I fail
In *mocking* death, why *death indeed* be welcome!

(*Enter* ZIPPA *angrily.*)

ZIPPA. Madam!

ISABELLA. You come rudely!
ZIPPA. If I offend you more, I still have cause—
Yet as the "friend" to whom you gave a husband,
(So kind you were!) I *might* come unannounced!
ISABELLA. What is this anger?
ZIPPA. I'm not angry, madam!
Oh, no! I'm patient!
ISABELLA. What's your errand, then?
ZIPPA. To give you back your costly bridal veil
And take my mean one.
ISABELLA. 'T was *your* wish to change.
'T was *you* that plotted we should wed together—
You in my place, and I in yours—was't not?
ZIPPA. Oh, heaven! you're calm! Had *you* no plotting, too?
You're noble born, and so your face is marble—
I'm poor, and if my heart aches, 't will show through.
You've robb'd me, madam!
IABELLA. I?
ZIPPA. Of gold—of jewels!—
Gold that would stretch the fancy but to dream of,
And gems like stars!
ISABELLA. You're mad!
ZIPPA. His love was worth them!
Oh, what had you to do with Angelo?
ISABELLA. Nay—came you not to wed Tortesa freely?
What should *you* do with Angelo?
ZIPPA. You mock me!
You are a woman, though your brow's a rock,
And know what love is. In a ring of fire
The tortured scorpion stings himself, to die—
But love will turn upon itself, and grow
Of its own fang immortal!
ISABELLA. Still, you left him
To wed another?
ZIPPA. 'T is for that he's mine!
What makes a right in any thing, but pain?
The diver's agony beneath the sea
Makes the pearl his—pain gets the miser's gold—
The noble's coronet, won first in battle,
Is his by bleeding for't—and Angelo
Is ten times mine because I gave him up—
Crushing my heart to do so!
ISABELLA. Now you plead
Against yourself. Say it would kill *me* quite,
If you should wed him? Mine's the greater pain,
And so the fairer title!
ZIPPA (*falling on her knees*). I implore you
Love him no more! Upon my knees I do!
He's not like you! Look on your snow-white arms!
They're form'd to press a noble to your breast—
Not Angelo! He's poor—and fit for mine!
You would not lift a beggar to your lips!—
You would not lean from your proud palace-stairs
To pluck away a heart from a poor girl
Who has no more on earth!
ISABELLA. I will not answer!
ZIPPA. Think what it is! Love is to you like music—
Pastime! You think on't when the dance is o'er—
When there's no revel—when your hair's unbound,
And its bright jewels with the daylight pale—
You want a lover to press on the hours
That lag till night again! But I—
ISABELLA. Stop there!
I love him better than you've soul to dream of!
ZIPPA (*rising*). 'T is false! How can you? He's to you a lamp
That shines amid a thousand just as bright!
What's one amid your crowd of worshippers?
The glow-worm's bright—but oh! 't is wanton murder
To raise him to the giddy air you breathe,
And leave his mate in darkness!
ISABELLA. Say the worm
Soar from the earth on his own wing—what then?
ZIPPA. Fair reasons cannot stay the heart from breaking.
You've stol'n my life, and you can give it back!
Will you—for heaven's sweet pity?
ISABELLA. Leave my presence!
(*Aside.*) (I pity her—but on this fatal love
Hangs my life, too.) What right have such as you

To look with eyes of love on Angelo?
ZIPPA. What right?
ISABELLA. I say so. Where's the miracle
Has made you fit to climb into the sky—
A moth—and look with love upon a star!
ZIPPA (*mournfully*). I'm lowly born, alas!
ISABELLA. Your *soul's* low born!
Forget your anger and come near me, Zippa,
For e'er[1] I'm done you'll wonder! Have you ever,
When Angelo was silent, mark'd his eye—
How, of a sudden, as 't were touch'd with fire,
There glows unnatural light beneath the lid?
ZIPPA. I have—I've thought it strange!
ISABELLA. Have you walk'd with him
When he has turn'd his head, as if to list
To music in the air—but you heard none—
And presently a smile stole through his lips,
And some low words, inaudible to you,
Fell from him brokenly.
ZIPPA. Ay—many times!
ISABELLA. Tell me once more! Hast never heard him speak
With voice unlike his own—so melancholy,
And yet so sweet a voice, that, were it only
The inarticulate moaning of a bird,
The very tone of it had made you weep?
ZIPPA. 'T is strangely true, indeed!
ISABELLA. Oh, heaven! You say so—
Yet never dreamt it was a spirit of light
Familiar with you!
ZIPPA. How?
ISABELLA. Why, there are seraphs
Who walk this common world, and want, as we do—
Here, in our streets—all seraph, save in wings—
The look, the speech, the forehead like a god—
And he the brightest!
ZIPPA (*incredulously*). Nay—I've known him long!
ISABELLA. Why, listen! There are worlds, thou doubting fool!
Farther to flee to than the stars in heaven,
Which Angelo can walk as we do this—
And does—while you look on him!
ZIPPA. Angelo!

1 Ere.

ISABELLA. He's never at your side one constant minute
Without a thousand messengers from thence!
(O block! to live with him, and never dream on 't!)
He plucks the sun's rays open like a thread,
And knows what stains the rose and not the lily—
He never sees a flower but he can tell
Its errand on the earth—(they all have errands—
You knew not that, oh dulness!) He sees shapes
Flush'd with immortal beauty in the clouds—
(You've seen him mock a thousand on his canvas,
And never wonder'd!) Yet you talk of love!
What love you?
ZIPPA. Angelo—and not a dream!
Take you the dream and give me Angelo!
You may talk of him till my brain is giddy—
But, oh, you cannot praise him out of reach
Of my true heart.—He's here, as low as I!—
Shall he not wed a woman, flesh and blood?
ISABELLA. See here! There was a small, earth-creeping mole,
Born by the low nest of an unfledged lark.
They lived an April youth amid the grass—
The soft mole happy, and the lark no less,
And thought the bent sky leaned upon the flowers.
By early May the fledgling got his wings;
And, eager for the light, one breezy dawn,
Sprang from his nest, and buoyantly away,
Fled forth to meet the morning. Newly born
Seem'd the young lark, as in another world
Of light, and song, and creatures like himself,
He soar'd and dropp'd, and sang unto the sun,
And pitied every thing that had not wings—
But most the mole, that wanted even eyes
To see the light he floated in!

ZIPPA. Yet still
She watch'd his nest, and fed him when he came—
Would it were Angelo and I indeed!

ISABELLA. Nay, mark! The bird grew lonely in the sky.
There was no echo at the height he flew!
And when the mist lay heavy on his wings
His song broke, and his flights were brief and low—
And the dull mole, that should have sorrowed with him,
Joy'd that he sang at last where she could hear!

ZIPPA. Why, happy mole again!

ISABELLA. Not long!—for soon
He found a mate that loved him *for his wings!*
One who with feebler flight, but eyes still on him,
Caught up his dropp'd song in the middle air,
And, with the echo, cheered him to the sun!

ZIPPA (*aside*). (I see! I see! His *soul* was never mine!
I was the blind mole of her hateful story!
No, no! he never loved me! True, we ate,
And laugh'd, and danced together—but no love—
He never told his thought when he was sad!
His folly and his idleness were mine—
No more! The rest was lock'd up in his soul!
I feel my heart grow black!) Fair madam, thank you!
You've told me news! (She shall not have him neither,
If there's a plot in hate to keep him from her!
I must have room to think, and air to breathe—
I choke here!) Madam, the blind mole takes leave!

ISABELLA. Farewell! (*Exit* ZIPPA.)
(*Takes the phial from the table.*)
And now, come forth, sweet comforter!
I'll to my chamber with this drowsy poison,
And from my sleep I wake up Angelo's,
Or wake no more! (*Exit.*)

END OF THE THIRD ACT.

ACT FOURTH.

SCENE 1. (*A sumptuous Drawing-room in the Falcone Palace. Guests assembled for the bridal. Lords and ladies promenading, and a band of musicians in a gallery at the side of the stage.*)

1ST LORD. Are we before the hour? or does the bridegroom
Affect this tardiness?

2ND LORD. We're bid at twelve.

1ST LORD. 'T is now past one. At least we should have music
To wile the time. (*To the musicians.*) Strike up, good fellows!

2ND LORD. Why,
A man who's only drest on holidays
Makes a long toilet. Now, I'll warrant he
Has vex'd his tailor since the break of day
Hoping to look a gentleman. D'ye know him?

1ST LORD. I've never had occasion!

2ND LORD. Poor Falcone!
He'd give the best bleed in his veins, I think,
To say as much!

1ST LORD. How's this! I see no stir
Among the instruments. Will they not play?

2ND LORD. Not they! I ask'd before you, and they're bid
To strike up when they hear Tortesa's horses
Prance thro' the gateway—not a note till then! (*Music plays.*)

1ST LORD. He comes!

(*Enter* TORTESA, *dressed over-richly.*)

TORTESA. Good day, my lords!

1ST LORD. Good day!

2ND LORD. The sky
Smiles on you, Signor! 'T is a happy omen
They say, to wed in sunshine.

TORTESA. Why, I think
The sun is not displeased that I should wed.

1ST LORD. We're happy, Sir, to have you one of us.

TORTESA. What have I been *till now!* I was a man
Before I saw your faces! Where's the change?
Have I a tail since? Am I grown a monkey?

(LORDS *whisper together, and walk from him.*)
Oh, for a mint to coin the world again
And melt the mark of gentlemen from clowns!
It puts me out of patience! Here 's a fellow
That, by much rubbing against better men,
Has, like a penny in a Jew's close pocket,
Stolen the color of a worthier coin,
And thinks he rings like sterling courtesy!
Yet look! he cannot phrase you a good morrow,
Or say he 's sad, or glad, at any thing,
But close beneath it, rank as verdigrease,
Lies an insulting rudeness! He was *"happy"*
That I should now be one of them. *Now!* Now!
As if, *till now,* I 'd been a dunghill grub,
And was but just turn'd butterfly!

(*A* LADY *advances.*)

LADY. Fair Sir,
I must take leave to say, were you my brother,
You 've made the choice that would have pleas'd me best!
Your bride 's as good as fair.

TORTESA. I thank you, Madam!
To be *your* friend, she should be—good and fair!
(*The* LADY *turns, and walks up the stage.*)
How like a drop of oil upon the sea
Falls the apt word of woman! So! her "brother"!
Why, there could be no contumely there!
I might, for all I *look,* have been her brother,
Else her first thought had never coupled us.
I 'll pluck some self-contentment out of that!

(*Enter suddenly the* COUNT'S SECRETARY.)

How now!

SECRETARY. I 'm sent, Sir, with unwelcome tidings.

TORTESA. Deliver them the quicker!

SECRETARY. I shall be
Too sudden at the slowest.

TORTESA. Pshaw! what is 't?
I 'm not a girl! Out with your news at once!
Are my ships lost?

SECRETARY. (*Hesitatingly.*) The lady Isabella—

TORTESA. What? run away!

SECRETARY. Alas, good Sir! she 's dead!

TORTESA. Bah! just as dead as I! Why, thou dull blockhead!
Cannot a lady faint, but there must be
A trumpeter like thee to make a tale on 't?

SECRETARY. Pardon me, Signor, but—

TORTESA. Who sent you hither?

SECRETARY. My lord the Count.

TORTESA. (*Turning quickly aside.*) He put it in the bond,
That if by any humor of my own,
Or accident that *sprang not from himself,*
Or from his daughter's will, the match were marr'd,
His tenure stood intact. If she *were* dead—
I don't believe she is—but if she were,
By one of those strange chances that do happen—
If she were dead, I say, the silly fish
That swims with safety among hungry sharks
To run upon the pin-hook of a boy,
Might teach me wisdom. (*The* SECRETARY *comes forward, narrating eagerly to the company.*) Now, what says this jackdaw?

SECRETARY. She had refused to let her bridesmaids in—

LADY. And died alone?

SECRETARY. A trusty serving maid
Was with her, and none else. She dropp'd away,
The girl said, in a kind of weary sleep.

1ST LORD. Was no one told of it?

SECRETARY. The girl watch'd by her,
And thought she slept still; till, the music sounding,
She shook her by the sleeve, but got no answer;
And so the truth broke on her!

TORTESA. (*Aside.*) (Oh, indeed!
The plot is something shallow!)

2ND LORD. Might we go
And see her as she lies?

SECRETARY. The holy father
Who should have married her, has check'd all comers,
And staying for no shroud but bridal dress,
He bears her presently to lie in state
In the Falcone chapel.

TORTESA. (*Aside.*) (Worse and worse—
They take me for a fool!)

1st Lord. But why such haste?
Secretary. I know not.
All. Let us to the chapel!
Tortesa. (*Drawing his sword, and stepping between them and the door.*) Hold!
Let no one try to pass!
1st Lord. What mean you, Sir!
Tortesa. To keep you here till you have got your story
Pat to the tongue—the truth on 't, and no more!
Lady. Have you a doubt the bride is dead, good Signor?
Tortesa. A palace, see you, has a tricky air!
When I am told a tradesman's daughter 's dead,
I know the coffin holds an honest corse,
Sped, in sad earnest, to eternity.
But were I stranger in the streets to-day,
And heard that an ambitious usurer,
With lands and money having bought a lady
High-born and fair, she died before the bridal,
I would lay odds with him that told me of it
She 'd rise again—before the resurrection.
So stand back all! If I'm to fill today
The pricking ears of Florence with a lie,
The bridal guests shall tell the tale so truly,
And mournfully, from eyesight of the corse,
That ev'n the shrewdest listener shall believe,
And I myself have no misgiving of it.
Look! where they come! (*Door opens to funeral music, and the body of* Isabella *is borne in, preceded by a* Monk, *and followed by* Falcone *and mourners.* Tortesa *confronts the* Monk.) What 's this you bear away?
Monk. Follow the funeral, but stay it not.
Tortesa. If thereon lie the lady Isabella,
I ask to see her face before she pass!
Monk. Stand from the way, my son, it cannot be!
Tortesa. What right have you to take me for a stone?
See what you do! I stand a bridegroom here.
A moment since the joyous music playing
Which promised me a fair and blushing bride.
The flowers are fragrant, and the guests made welcome;
And while my heart beats at the opening door,
And eagerly I look to see her come,—
There enters in her stead a covered corse!
And when I ask to look upon her face—
One look, before my bride is gone for ever,—
You find it in your hearts to say me nay!—
Shame! Shame!
Falcone. (*Fiercely.*) Lead on!
Tortesa. My lord, by covenant—
By contract writ and seal'd—by value rendered—
By her own promise—nay, by all, save taking,
This body 's mine! I 'll have it set down here
And wait my pleasure! See it done, my lord,
Or I will, for you!
Monk. (*To the bearers.*) Set the body down!
Tortesa. (*Takes the veil from the face.*)
Come hither all! Nay, father, look not black!
If o'er the azure temper of this blade
There come no mist, when laid upon her lips,
I 'll do a penance for irreverence,
And fill your sack with penitential gold!
Look well! (*Puts his sword blade to* Isabella's *lips, and after watching it with intense interest a moment, drops on his knees beside the bier.*)
She 's dead indeed! Lead on!
(*The procession starts again to funereal music, and* Tortesa *follows last.*)

Scene 2. *A Street in Florence. The funereal music dying away in the distance.*

(*Enter* Zippa, *straining her eyes to look after it.*)

Zippa. 'T is Angelo that follows close behind,
Laying his forehead almost on her bier!
His heart goes with her to the grave!
Oh, Heaven!
Will not Tortesa pluck out of his hand
The tassel of that pall? (*She hears a footstep.*) Stay, stay, he 's here!
(*Enter* Tortesa, *musing.* Zippa *stands aside.*)

TORTESA. I 've learned to-day a lord may be a Jew,
I 've learned to-day that grief may kill a lady;
Which touches me the most I cannot say,
For I could fight Falcone for my loss
Or weep, with all my soul, for Isabella.
(ZIPPA *touches him on the shoulder.*)
ZIPPA. How is 't the Signor follows not his bride?
TORTESA. I did—but with their melancholy step
I fell to musing, and so dropp'd behind—
But here 's a sight I have not seen to-day!
(*Takes her hand smilingly.*)
ZIPPA. What 's that?
TORTESA. A friendly face, my honest Zippa!
Art well? What errand brings thee forth?
ZIPPA. None, Signor!
But passing by the funeral, I stopped,
Wondering to see the bridegroom lag behind,
And give his sacred station next the cross
To an obtrusive stranger.
TORTESA. Which is he?
ZIPPA. (*Points after* ANGELO.) Look there!
TORTESA. His face is buried in his cloak.
Who is 't?
ZIPPA. Not *know* him? Had I half the cause
That *you* have, to see through that mumming cloak,
The shadow of it would speak out his name!
TORTESA. What mean you?
ZIPPA. Angelo! What right has he
To weep in public at her funeral?
TORTESA. The painter?
ZIPPA. Ay—the peasant Angelo!
Was 't not enough to dare to love her living,
But he must fling the insult of his tears
Betwixt her corse and you? Are you not mov'd?
Will you not go and pluck him from your place?
TORTESA. No, Zippa! for my spirits are more apt
To grief than anger. I 've in this half hour
Remember'd much I should have thought on sooner,—
For, had I known her heart was capable
Of breaking for the love of one so low,
I would have done as much to make her his
As I have done, in hate, to make her mine.
She lov'd him, Zippa. (*Walks back in thought.*)
ZIPPA. (*Aside.*) (Oh, to find a way
To pluck that fatal beauty from his eyes!
'T is twilight, and the lamp is lit above her,
And Angelo will watch the night out there,
Gazing with passionate worship on her face.
But no! he shall not!)
TORTESA. (*Advancing.*) Come! what busy thought
Vexes your brain now?
ZIPPA. Were your pride as quick
As other men's to see an insult, Signor!
I had been spared the telling of my thought.
TORTESA. You put it sharply!
ZIPPA. Listen! you are willing
That there should follow, in your place of mourner,
A youth, who, by the passion of his grief
Shews to the world he 's more bereaved than you!
TORTESA. Humph! well!
ZIPPA. Still follows he without rebuke;
And in the chapel where she lies to-night,
Her features bared to the funereal lamp,
He 'll, like a mourning bridegroom, keep his vigil,
As if all Florence knew she was his own.
TORTESA. Nay, nay! he may keep vigil if he will!
The door is never lock'd upon the dead
Till bell and mass consign them to the tomb;
And custom gives the privilege to all
To enter in and pray—and so may he.
ZIPPA. Then learn a secret which I fain had spared
My lips the telling. Question me not how,
But I have chanced to learn, that Angelo,
To-night, will *steal the body from its bier!*
TORTESA. To-night! What! Angelo! Nay, nay, good Zippa!
If he 's enamoured of the corse, 't is there—
And he may watch it till its shape decay,
And holy church will call it piety.
But he who steals from consecrated ground,

Dies, by the law of Florence. There 's no end
To answer in 't.

ZIPPA. You know not, Angelo!
You think not with what wild, delirious passion
A painter thirsts to tear the veil from beauty.
He painted Isabella as a maid,
Coy as a lily turning from the sun.
Now she is dead, and, like a star that flew
Flashing and hiding thro' some fleecy rack,
But suddenly sits still in cloudless heavens,
She slumbers fearless in his steadfast gaze,
Peerless and unforbidding. O! to him
She is no more your bride! A statue fairer
Than ever rose enchanted from the stone,
Lies in that dim-lit chapel, clad like life.
Are you too slow to take my meaning yet?
He cannot loose the silken boddice *there!*
He cannot, *there* upon the marble breast
Shower the dark locks from the golden comb!

TORTESA. Hold!

ZIPPA. Are you mov'd? Has he no *end* to compass
In stealing her away from holy ground?
Will you not lock your bride up from his touch?

TORTESA. No more! no more! I thought not of all this!
Perchance it is not true. But twilight falls,
And I will home to doff this bridal gear,
And, after, set a guard upon the corse.
We 'll walk together. Come!

ZIPPA. (*Aside.*) (He shall not see her!)
(*Exeunt.*)

SCENE 3. (*A Street in front of the Falcone Palace. Night. Enter* ISABELLA *in her white bridal dress. She falters to her father's door, and drops exhausted.*)

ISABELLA. My brain swims round! I 'll rest a little here!
The night 's cold, chilly cold. Would I could reach
The house of Angelo! Alas! I thought
He would have kept *one* night of vigil near me,
Thinking me dead. Bear up, good heart! Alas!
I faint! Where am I? (*Looks around.*) 'T is my father's door.
My undirected feet have brought me home—
And I must in, or die! (*Knocks with a painful effort.*) So ends my dream!

FALCONE. (*From above.*) Who 's that would enter to a mourning house?

ISABELLA. Your daughter!

FALCONE. Ha! what voice is that I hear?

ISABELLA. Poor Isabella's.

FALCONE. Art thou come to tell me,
That with unnatural heart I killed my daughter?
Just Heaven! thy retribution follows fast!
But, oh, if holy and unnumbered masses
Can give thee rest, perturb'd and restless spirit!
Haunt thou a weeping penitent no more!
Depart! I 'll in, and pass the night in prayer!
So shalt thou rest! Depart!
(*He closes the window, and* ISABELLA *drops with her forehead to the marble stair.*)

(*Enter* TOMASO, *with a bottle in his hand.*)

TOMASO. It 's like the day after the deluge. Few stirring and nobody dry. I 've been since twilight looking for somebody that would drink. Not a beggar athirst in all Florence! I thought that, with a bottle in my hand, I should be scented like a wild boar. I expected drunkards would have come up out of the ground—like worms in a shower. When was *I* ever so difficult to find by a moist friend? Two hundred ducats in good wine and no companion! I 'll look me up a dry dog. I 'll teach him to tipple, and give up the fellowship of mankind!

ISABELLA. (*Faintly.*) Signor!

TOMASO. Hey! What!

ISABELLA. Help, Signor!

TOMASO. A woman! Ehem! (*Approaching her.*) Would you take something to drink by any chance? (*Offers her the bottle.*) No? Perhaps you don't like to drink out of the bottle.

ISABELLA. I perish of cold!

TOMASO. Stay! Here 's a cloak! My master 's out for the night, and you shall home with me. Come! Perhaps when you get warmer, you 'd like to drink a little. The wine 's good! (*Assists her in *rising.*) By St. Genevieve, a soft hand! Come! I 'll bring you where there 's fire and a clean flagon.

ISABELLA. To any shelter, Signor!

TOMASO. Shelter! nay, a good house, and two hundred ducats in ripe wine. Steady, now! (This shall pass for a good action! If my master smell a rat, I 'll face him out the woman 's honest!) This way, now! Softly! That 's well stepp'd! Come!

(*Goes out, assisting her to walk.*)

END OF THE FOURTH ACT.

ACT FIFTH.

SCENE 1. (ANGELO'S *Studio. A full-length picture, in a large frame, stands on the floor against an easel, placed nearly in the centre of the room. Two curtains, so arranged as to cover the picture when drawn together.* ANGELO *stands in an imploring attitude near the picture, his pencil and palette in his hands, appealing to* ISABELLA, *who is partly turned from him in an attitude of refusal. The back wall of the room such as to form a natural ground for a picture.*)

ANGELO. Hear me, sweet!

ISABELLA. No, we 'll keep a holiday,
And waste the hours in love, and idleness.
You shall not paint to-day, dear Angelo!

ANGELO. But listen!

ISABELLA. Nay, I 'm jealous of my picture;
For all you give to that is stol'n from me.
I like not half a look that turns away
Without an answer from the eyes it met!
I care not you should see my lips' bright color
Yet wait not for the breath that floats between!

ANGELO. Wilt listen?

ISABELLA. Listen? Yes! a thousand years!
But there 's a pencil in those restless fingers,
Which you 've a trick of touching to your lips—
And while you talk, my hand would do as well!
And if it 's the same tale you told before
Of *certain vigils* you forgot to keep,
Look deep into my eyes till it is done—
For, like the children's Lady-in-the-well,
I only hark because you 're looking in!
Will you talk thus to me?

ANGELO. Come night I will!
But close upon thy voice, sweet Isabella!
A boding whisper sinks into mine ear
Which tells of sudden parting! If 't is false,—
We shall have still a lifetime for our love,
But if 't is true, oh, think that, in my picture,
Will lie the footprint of an angel gone!
Let me but make it clearer!

ISABELLA. Now, by heaven!
I think thou lov'st the picture, and not me!
So different am I, that, did I think
To lose thee presently, by death or parting,
For thy least word, or look, or slightest motion—
Nay, for so little breath as makes a sigh
I would not take, to have it pass untreasured,
The empire of a star!

(*While she was uttering this reproach,* ANGELO *has looked at her with delight, and touched his portrait with a few rapid strokes.*)

ANGELO. My picture 's done!

(*Throws his pencil to the ground.*)

Break, oh enchanted pencil! thou wilt never
On earth again, do miracles so fair!
Oh, Isabella! as the dusky ore
Waits for the lightning's flash to turn to gold—
As the dull vapor waits for Hesperus,
Then falls in dew-drops, and reflects a star—
So waited I that fire upon thy lips,
To make my master-piece complete in beauty!

ISABELLA. This is ambition when I look'd for love,
The fancy flattering where the heart should murmur.
I think you have no heart!

ANGELO. Your feet are on it!
The heart is ever lowly with the fortunes,
Tho' the proud mind sits level with a king!
I gave you long ago both heart and soul,
But only one has dared to speak to you!
Yet, if astonishment will cure the dumb,
Give it a kiss—

ISABELLA. (*Smiling.*) Lo! Where it speaks at last!

(*A loud knock is heard.*)

Hark, Angelo!

(*He flies to the window, and looks out.*)
ANGELO. Tortesa with a guard!
Alas! that warning voice! They 've traced thee hither!
Lost! Lost!
ISABELLA. (*Hastily drawing the curtain, and disappearing behind it.*) No!
No! defend thy picture only,
And all is well yet!
ANGELO. Thee and it with life!
(*Draws his sword, and stands before the curtains in an attitude of defiance.*)

(*Enter* TORTESA, *with officers and guard.*)

What is your errand?
TORTESA. I 'm afraid, a sad one!
For, by your drawn sword and defying air,
Your conscious thought foretells it.
ANGELO. Why,—a blow—
(You took one, Signor, when you last were here—
If you 've forgot it, well!)—but, commonly,
The giver of a blow needs have his sword
Promptly in hand. You 'll pardon me!
TORTESA. I do!
For, if my fears are just, good Signor painter!
You 've not a life to spare upon a quarrel!
In brief, the corse of a most noble lady
Was stol'n last night from holy sanctuary.
I have a warrant here to search your house;
And, should the body not be found therein,
I 'm bid to see the picture of the lady—
Whereon, (pray mark me!) if I find a trace
Of charms fresh copied, more than may beseem
The modest beauty of a living maid,
I may arrest you on such evidence
For instant trial!
ANGELO. Search my house and welcome!
But, for my picture, tho' a moment's glance
Upon its pure and hallowed loveliness
Would give the lie to your foul thought of me,
It is the unseen virgin of my brain!
And as th' inviolate person of a maid
Is sacred ev'n in the presence of the law,
My picture is my own—to bare or cover!
Look on it at your peril!
TORTESA. (*To the guard.*) Take his sword.
(*The guards attack and disarm him.*)
ANGELO. Coward and villain!
(TORTESA *parts the curtains with his sword, and* ANGELO *starts amazed to see* ISABELLA, *with her hands crossed on her breast, and her eyes fixed on the ground, standing motionless in the frame which had contained his picture. The tableau deceives* TORTESA, *who steps back to contemplate what he supposes to be the portrait of his bride.*)
TORTESA. Admirable work!
'T is Isabella's self! Why, this is wondrous!
The brow, the lip, the countenance—how true!
I would have sworn that gloss upon the hair,
That shadow from the lash, were nature's own—
Impossible to copy! (*Looks at it a moment in silence.*) Yet methinks
The color on the cheek is something faint!
ANGELO. (*Hurriedly.*) Step this way farther!
TORTESA. (*Changing his position.*) Ay—'t is better here!
The hand is not as white as Isabella's—
But painted to the life! If there 's a feature
That I would touch again, the lip, to me,
Seems wanting in a certain scornfulness
Native to her! It scarcely marr'd her beauty.
Perhaps 't is well slurr'd over in a picture!
Yet stay! I see it, now I look again!
How excellently well! (*Guards return from searching the house.*) What! found you nothing?
SOLDIER. (*Holding up* ISABELLA'S *veil.*) This bridal veil—no more.
ANGELO. (*Despairingly.*) Oh! luckless star!
TORTESA. Signor! you 'll trust me when I say I 'm sorry
With all my soul! This veil, I know it well—
Was o'er the face of that unhappy lady
When laid in sanctuary. You are silent!
Perhaps you scorn to satisfy me here!
I trust you can—in your extremity!
But I must bring you to the Duke! Lead on!
ANGELO. An instant!
TORTESA. (*Courteously.*) At your pleasure!

ANGELO. (*To* ISABELLA, *as he passes close to her.*) I conjure you,
By all our love, stir not!

ISABELLA. (*Still motionless.*) Farewell!

(TORTESA *motions for* ANGELO *to precede him with the guard, looks once more at the picture, and with a gesture expressive of admiration, follows. As the door closes,* ISABELLA *steps from the frame.*)

ISABELLA. I'll follow
Close on thy steps, beloved Angelo!
And find a way to bring thee home again!
My heart is light, and hope speaks cheerily!
And lo! bright augury!—a friar's hood
For my disguise! Was ever omen fairer!
Thanks! my propitious star!

(*Envelopes herself in the hood, and goes out hastily.*)

SCENE 2. (*A Street. Enter* TOMASO, *with his hat crushed and pulled sulkily over his eyes, his clothes dirty on one side, and other marks of having slept in the street. Enter* ZIPPA *from the other side, meeting him.*)

ZIPPA. Tomaso! Is 't thou? Where's Angelo?

TOMASO. It is I, and I don't know!

ZIPPA. Did he come home last night?

TOMASO. *"Did* he come home!" Look *there!* (*Pulls off his hat, and shews his dirty side.*)

ZIPPA. Then thou hast slept in the street!

TOMASO. Ay!

ZIPPA. And what has that to do with the coming home of Angelo?

TOMASO. What had thy father to do with thy having such a nose as his? (ZIPPA *holds up a ducat to him.*) What! gave thy mother a ducat?—cheap as dirt!

ZIPPA. Blockhead, no! I'll give thee the ducat if thou wilt tell me, straight on, what thou know'st of Angelo!

TOMASO. I will—and thou shalt see how charity is rewarded.

ZIPPA. Begin!—begin!

TOMASO. Last night, having pray'd later than usual at vespers—

ZIPPA. Ehem!

TOMASO. I was coming home in a pious frame of mind—

ZIPPA. —And a bottle in thy pocket.

TOMASO. No!—in my hand. What should I stumble over—

ZIPPA. —But a stone.

TOMASO. A woman!

ZIPPA. Fie! what's this you're going to tell me?

TOMASO. She was dying with cold. Full of Christian charity—

ZIPPA. —And new wine.

TOMASO. *Old* wine, Zippa! The wine was old!

ZIPPA. Well!

TOMASO. I took her home.

ZIPPA. Shame!—at thy years?

TOMASO. And Angelo being out for the night—

ZIPPA. There! there! you may skip the particulars.

TOMASO. I say my own bed being in the garret—

ZIPPA. Well, well!

TOMASO. I put her into Angelo's.

ZIPPA. Oh, unspeakable impudence! Didst thou do that?

TOMASO. I had just left her to make a wine posset, (for she was well nigh dead,) when in popped my master,—finds her there—asks no questions,—kicks me into the street, and locks the door! *There's* the reward of virtue!

ZIPPA. Did he not turn out the woman, too?

TOMASO. Not as I remember.

ZIPPA. Oh, worse and worse! And thou hast not seen him since?

TOMASO. I found me a soft stone, said my prayers, and went to sleep.

ZIPPA. And hast thou not seen him to-day?

TOMASO. Partly, I have!

ZIPPA. Where? Tell me quickly!

TOMASO. Give me the ducat.

ZIPPA. (*Gives it him.*) Quick! say on!

TOMASO. I have a loose recollection, that, lying on that stone, Angelo called me by name. Looking up, I saw two Angelos, and two Tortesas, and soldiers with two spears each. (*He figures in the air with his finger as if trying to remember.*)

ZIPPA. (*Aside.*) (Ha! he is apprehended for the murder of Isabella! Say that my evidence might save his life! Not unless he love me!) Which way went he, Tomaso? (TOMASO *points.*) This way? (Then has he gone to be tried before the Duke.) Come with me, Tomaso! Come.

TOMASO. Where?

ZIPPA. To the Duke's palace! Come! (*Takes his arm.*)

TOMASO. To the Duke's palace? There'll be kicking of heels in the ante-chamber! —Dry work! I'll spend thy ducat as we go along. Shall it be old wine, or new? (*Exeunt.*)

SCENE 3. (*Hall of Judgment in the Ducal Palace. The* DUKE *upon a raised throne on the left.* FALCONE *near his chair, and* ANGELO *on the opposite side of the stage with a guard.* ISABELLA *behind the guard disguised as a monk.* TORTESA *stands near the centre of the stage, and* ZIPPA *and* TOMASO *in the left corner, listening eagerly. Counsellors at a table, and crowd of spectators at the sides and rear.*)

DUKE. Are there more witnesses?
COUNSELLOR. No more, my liege!
DUKE. None for the prisoner?
COUNSELLOR. He makes no defence
Beyond a firm denial.
FALCONE. Is there wanting
Another proof, my liege, that he is guilty?
DUKE. I fear he stands in deadly peril, Count.
(*To the* COUNSELLOR.)
Sum up the evidence. (*He reads.*)
COUNSELLOR. 'T is proved, my liege,
That for no honest or sufficient end,
The pris'ner practised on your noble Grace
And Count Falcone a contriv'd deceit,
Whereby he gain'd admittance to the lady.
(TOMASO *exhibits signs of alarm.*)
DUKE. Most true!
COUNSELLOR. That, till the eve before her death.
He had continual access to the palace;
And, having grown enamoured of the bride,
Essay'd by plots that never were matured,
And quarrels often forced on her betrothed,
To stay the bridal. That, against the will
Of her most noble father and the Duke,
The bride was resolute to keep her troth;
And so, preparing for the ceremony,
Upon her bridal morning was found dead.
'T is proved again—that, while she lay in state,
The guard, at several periods of the night,
Did force the pris'ner from the chapel door;
And when the corse was stol'n from sanctuary
All search was vain, till, in the pris'ner's hands
Was found the veil that shrouded her. To these
And lighter proofs of sacrilege and murder
The prisoner has opposed his firm denial—
No more!
DUKE. Does no one speak in his behalf?
TORTESA. My liege! so far as turns the evidence
Upon the prisoner's quarrels with myself,
I'm free to say that they had such occasion
As any day may rise 't wixt men of honor.
As one of those aggriev'd by his offences,
You'll wonder I'm a suitor for his pardon—
But so I am! Besides that there is room
To hope him innocent, your Grace's realm
Holds not so wondrous and so rare a painter!
If he has killed the lady Isabella,
'T is some amends that in his glorious picture
She's made immortal! If he stole her corse,
He can return, for that disfigured dust,
An Isabella fresh in changeless beauty!
Were it not well to pardon him, my Lord?
ISABELLA. (*Aside.*) Oh, brave Tortesa!
DUKE. You have pleaded kindly
And eloquently, Signor! but the law
Can recognize no gift as plea for pardon.
For his rare picture he will have his fame;
But if the Isabella he has painted
Find not a voice to tell his innocence,
He dies at sunset!
ISABELLA. (*Despairingly.*) He is dead to *me!*
Yet he shall live!
(*She drops the cowl from her shoulders, and with her arms folded, walks slowly to the feet of the* DUKE.)
FALCONE. (*Rushing forward.*) My daughter!
ANGELO. (*With a gesture of agony.*) Lost!
TORTESA. Alive!
ZIPPA. (*Energetically.*) Tortesa'll have her
(ISABELLA *retires to the back of the stage with her father, and kneels to him, imploring in dumb show; the* DUKE *and others watching.*)
TORTESA. (*Aside.*) So! all's right again?

Now for my lands, or Isabella?—Stay!
'T is a brave girl, by Heaven! (*Reflects a moment.*) A sleeping draught,
And so to Angelo! Her love for *me*
A counterfeit to take suspicion off!
It was well done! I feel my heart warm to her! (*Reflects again.*)
Where could he hide her from our search to-day?
(*Looks round at* ISABELLA.)
No? Yet the dress is like! It *was* the picture!
Herself—and *not* a picture! Now, by Heaven,
A girl like that should be the wife of Cæsar!
(*Presses his hand upon his heart.*)
I've a new feeling here!
(FALCONE *comes forward, followed by* ISABELLA *with gestures of supplication.*)

FALCONE. I will not hear you!
My liege, I pray you keep the prisoner
In durance till my daughter's fairly wed.
He has contriv'd against our peace and honor.
And howsoe'er this marvel be made clear,
She stands betroth'd, if he is in the mind,
To the brave Signor, yonder!

DUKE. This were well—
What says Tortesa?

TORTESA. If my liege permit,
I will address my answer to this lady.
(*Turns to* ISABELLA.)
For reasons which I need not give you now,
Fair Isabella! I became your suitor.
My motives were unworthy you and me—
Yet I was true—I never said I lov'd you!
Your father sold you me for lands and money—
(Pardon me, Duke! And you, fair Isabella!
You will—ere I am done!) I push'd my suit!
The bridal day came on, and clos'd in mourning;
For the fair bride it dawn'd upon was dead.
I had my shame and losses to remember—
But in my heart sat sorrow uppermost,
And pity—for I thought your heart was broken.
(ISABELLA *begins to discover interest in his story, and* ANGELO *watches her with jealous eagerness.*)
I see you here again! You are my bride!
Your father holds me to my bargain for you!
The lights are burning on the nuptial altar—
The bridal chamber and the feast, all ready!
What stays the marriage now?—*my new-born love!*
That nuptial feast were fruit from Paradise—
I cannot touch it till *you* bid me welcome!
That nuptial chamber were the lap of Heaven—
I cannot enter till *you* call me in!
(*Takes a ring from his bosom.*)
Here is the golden ring you should have worn.
Tell me to give it to my rival there—
I'll break my heart to do so!
(*Holds it toward* ANGELO.)

ISABELLA. (*Looking at her father.*) Would I might!

TORTESA. You shall, if 't please you!

FALCONE. I command thee, never!
My liege, permit me to take home my daughter!
And, Signor, you—if you would keep your troth—
To-morrow come, and end this halting bridal!
Home! Isabella!
(*Takes his daughter's hand.*)

TORTESA. (*Taking it from him.*) Stay! she is not yours!
My gracious liege, there is a law in Florence,
That if a father, for no guilt or shame,
Disown, and shut his door upon his daughter,
She is the child of him who succors her;
Who, by the shelter of a single night,
Becomes endowed with the authority
Lost by the other. Is 't not so?

DUKE. So runs
The law of Florence, and I see your drift—
For, look my lord! (*To* FALCONE.) if that dread apparition
You saw last night, was this your living daughter,
You stand within the peril of that law.

FALCONE. My liege!

ISABELLA. (*Looking admiringly at* TORTESA.) Oh, noble Signor!

TORTESA. (*To* ISABELLA.) Was 't well done?
Shall I give Angelo the ring?
(*As she is about to take it from him,*

TOMASO *steps in behind. and pulls* ISABELLA *by the sleeve.*)

TOMASO. Stay there!
What wilt thou do for dowry? I 'm thy father?
But—save some flasks of wine—

ISABELLA. (*Sorrowfully.*) Would I were richer
For thy sake, Angelo!

(TORTESA *looks at her an instant, and then steps to the table and writes.*)

ANGELO. (*Coming forward with an effort.*) Look, Isabella!
I stand between thee and a life of sunshine.
Thou wert both rich and honor'd, *but for me!*
That thou *couldst* wed me, beggar as I am,
Is bliss to think on—but see how I rob thee!
I have a loving heart—but am a beggar!
There is a loving heart—(*Points to* TORTESA.) With wealth and honor!

(TORTESA *steps between them, and hands a paper to* ANGELO.)

TORTESA. (*To* ISABELLA.) Say thou wilt wed the poorer?

ISABELLA. (*Offers her hands to* ANGELO.) So I will!

TORTESA. Then am I blest, for he 's as rich as I—
Yet, in his genius, has one jewel more!

ISABELLA. What say'st thou?

(ANGELO *reads earnestly.*)

TORTESA. In a mortal quarrel, lady!
'T is thought ill-luck to have the better sword;
For the good angels, who look sorrowing on,
In heavenly pity take the weaker side!

ISABELLA What is it, Angelo?

ANGELO. A deed to *me*
Of the Falcone palaces and lands,
And all the moneys forfeit by your father!—
By Heaven, I 'll not be mock'd!

TORTESA. The deed is yours—
What mockery in that?

ISABELLA. (*Tenderly to* TORTESA.) It is not kind
To make refusal of your love a pain!

TORTESA. I would 't would *kill* you to refuse me, lady!
So should the blood plead for me at your heart!
Shall I give up the ring?

(*Offers it.*)

ISABELLA. (*Hesitatingly.*) Let me look on it!

TORTESA. (*Withdrawing it.*) A moment yet! You 'll give it ere you think!
Oh, is it fair that Angelo had *days*,
To tell his love, and I have not *one hour?*
How know you that I cannot love as well?

ISABELLA. 'T is possible!

TORTESA. Ah! thanks!

ISABELLA. But I have given
My heart to him!

TORTESA. You gave your *troth* to me!
If, of these two gifts you must take back one,
Rob not the poorer! Shall I keep the ring?

(ISABELLA *looks down.*)

ANGELO. She hesitates! I 've waited here too long!

(*Tears the deed in two.*)

Perish your gift, and farewell, Isabella!

ISABELLA. (*Advancing a step with clasp'd hands.*) You 'll kill me, Angelo! Come back!

TORTESA. (*Seizing him by the hand as he hesitates, and flinging him back with a strong effort.*) He shall!

ANGELO. Stand from my path! Or, if you care to try
Some other weapon than a glozing tongue,
Follow me forth where we may find the room!

TORTESA. You shall not go.

ANGELO. (*Draws.*) Have at thee then!

(*Attacks* TORTESA, *who disarms him, and holds his sword-point to his breast.* DUKE *and others come forward.*)

TORTESA. The bar
'Twixt me and heaven, boy! is the life I hold
Now at my mercy! Take it, Isabella!
And with it the poor gift he threw away!
I 'll write a new deed ere you 've time to marry,
So take your troth back with your bridal ring,
And thus I join you!

(*Takes* ISABELLA'S *hand, but* ANGELO *refuses his.*)

ANGELO. (*Proudly.*) Never! But for me,
The hand you hold were joyfully your own!
Shall I receive a life and fortune from you,
Yet stand 'twixt you and *that?*

ISABELLA. (*Turning from* ANGELO.) Thou dost not love me!

TORTESA. Believe it not! He does! An instant more
I 'll brush this new-spun cobweb from his eyes. (*Crosses to* ZIPPA.)
Fair Zippa! in this cross'd and tangled world
Few wed the one they could have lov'd the best,
And fewer still wed well for happiness!
We each have lost to-day what best we love.
But as the drops that mingled in the sky,
Are torn apart in the tempestuous sea,
Yet with a new drop tremble into one,
We two, if you 're content, may swim together!
What say you?

ZIPPA. (*Giving her hand.*) I have thought on it before,
When I believed you cold and treacherous.
'T is easy when I know you kind and noble.

TORTESA. To-morrow, then, we 'll wed; and now, fair Signor,
(*To* ANGELO.)
Take you her hand, nor fear to rob Tortesa!
(*Turns to the* DUKE.)
Shall it be so, my liege?

DUKE. You please me well.
And if you 'll join your marriage feasts together
I 'll play my part, and give the brides away!

TORTESA. Not so, my liege! I could not see her *wed him.*
To *give her to him* has been all I could;
For I have sought her with the dearest pulses
That quicken in my heart, my *love and scorn.*
She 's taught me that the high-born may be true.
I thank her for it—but, too close on that
Follow'd the love, whose lightning flash of honor
Brightens; but straight is dark again! My liege,
The poor who leap up to the stars for duty
Must drop to earth again! and here, if 't please you,
I take my feet forever from your palace,
And, match'd as best beseems me, say farewell.
(*Takes* ZIPPA'S *hand, and the curtain drops.*)

THE END.

FASHION

BY

Anna Cora Mowatt Ritchie

FASHION

Fashion, while not our first dramatic social satire, for that honor belongs to *The Contrast,* is of special interest as inspiring a series of plays dealing with the follies of those who aspire to secure an assured position without being aware of social values. The best of this later series is *Nature's Nobleman,* by Henry O. Pardey, (1851), for Mrs. Bateman's *Self,* (1856), E. G. Wilkins' *Young New York,* (1856), and Cornelius Mathews' *False Pretences, or Both Sides of Good Society* (1856) are merely caricature.

Anna Cora Ogden, the author of *Fashion,* was born in Bordeaux, France, in 1819, the daughter of Samuel G. Ogden, of New York, who was tried and acquitted for complicity in the Miranda expedition to liberate South America. She was interested in the stage from childhood, taking the part of a judge in a French version of *Othello* when she was five years of age. At fourteen she had put on an English translation of Voltaire's *Alzire* at her home in Flatbush. She married James Mowatt, a barrister in New York, when she was fifteen. At sixteen she published her first literary venture, a poetical romance, *Pelayo or the Cavern of Covadonga.* Being threatened with tuberculosis of the lungs, she took a sea voyage and went to London and to Hamburg, and later to Paris, where she saw Rachel act, and where she wrote *Gulzara or the Persian Star,* a play in six acts which was acted afterwards at her home in Flatbush by her sisters, and on two other occasions, at least. It was published in the *New World* in 1840. Mr. Mowatt lost his fortune and Mrs. Mowatt began to give public readings with considerable success. Notwithstanding her constant struggle against ill health, she wrote copiously for the leading magazines, sometimes contributing several articles under different names to the same journal. Her novel of *The Fortune Hunter* (1842), had quite a wide sale and was translated into German. Her other novel, *Evelyn,* a domestic story, was published after her début, in 1845.

Fashion was produced first at the Park Theatre, New York, March 24, 1845. An interesting account of its production is given in her *Autobiography.* It ran for three weeks and was withdrawn only owing to engagements of stars at the Park Theatre. It was played in Philadelphia at the Walnut Street Theatre while the New York engagement was on. The success of the play and also her financial necessities induced her to go on the stage and she made her début at the Park Theatre as "Pauline" in the *Lady of Lyons,* on June 13, 1845. Her modest accounts of her stage beginning show that she made a success from the first and she toured the country, going as far south as New Orleans. She played "Gertrude" in *Fashion* for the first time in Philadelphia apparently and repeated it in other places several times but the part was not a favorite one with her.

During the summer of 1847 she wrote *Armand, the Child of the People*, intending the name part for E. L. Davenport, her leading man, and the part of "Blanche" for herself. It was produced at the Park Theatre, September 27, 1847, with success and "Blanche" became one of her leading characters. It is a comedy melodrama, laid in the time of Louis XV, partly in blank verse. Mrs. Mowatt appeared at the Theatre Royal, Manchester, December 7, 1847, as "Pauline" and made so favorable an impression that she and Davenport were engaged to take Macready's place at the Theatre Royal, Marylebone, London, when the latter came to America. During this engagement she put on *Armand*, January 18, 1849, when it ran twenty-one consecutive nights. *Fashion* was played at the Royal Olympic Theatre, where she and Mr. Davenport were playing, on January 9, 1850, and ran for two weeks. In January, 1851, she went to Dublin and was given a wonderful reception. Mr. Mowatt died in 1851 and she returned to America on July 9th of that year. She continued her stage career under the discouragement of ill health and accident until 1854, when, after a long illness, she retired. Her last performance was on June 3, 1854, at Niblo's Garden, in the character of "Pauline," in which she had made her début. It was made the occasion for a great testimonial to her. In 1854 she published her *Autobiography*, a fascinating account of her experiences from childhood to that time. She married William F. Ritchie, of the *Richmond Enquirer*, June 7, 1854.

Her later publications include a number of works of fiction, the most important of which is *Mimic Life, or Before and Behind the Curtain*, (1855), a series of stories dealing with life on the stage in which her own experiences are to a certain extent reflected. After 1861 she lived mostly abroad and died in London, July 28, 1870.

For an interesting contemporary criticism see Edgar A. Poe, *The New Comedy by Mrs. Mowatt, Broadway Journal*, March 29, 1845, and *Mrs. Mowatt's Comedy, Broadway Journal*, April 5, 1845, reprinted in the Virginia Edition of Poe's Works, Vol. 12, pp. 112–121 and 124–129. His criticisms of her acting may be found in Vol. 12, pp. 184–192, also reprinted from the *Broadway Journal*, of July 19 and 26, 1845.

Fashion was published in London in 1850, and was reprinted, with *Armand*, in Boston, in 1855. The present edition is based upon a collation of these two texts, which differ very slightly.

The play was revived at the Provincetown Theatre, New York, Feb. 3, 1924, and after moving successively to the Greenwich Village and Cort Theatres, ran for 235 consecutive performances, until August 30.

FASHION;

OR,

LIFE IN NEW YORK.

A Comedy,

IN FIVE ACTS.

BY

ANNA CORA MOWATT,

AUTHOR OF "ARMAND," "EVELYN," "THE FORTUNE HUNTER."
ETC., ETC.

" Howe'er it be—it seems to me
'Tis only noble to be good ;
Kind hearts are more than coronets,
And simple faith than Norman blood."
TENNYSON.

LONDON:

W. NEWBERY, 6, KING STREET, HOLBORN

1850.

CAST OF CHARACTERS

	Park Theatre, New York, 1845	Royal Olympic Theatre, London 1850
ADAM TRUEMAN................	Mr. Chippendale	Mr. E. Davenport
COUNT JOLIMAITRE, a fashionable European Importation.........	Mr. Crisp	Mr. A. Wigan
COLONEL HOWARD, an officer in the United States Army........	Mr. Dyott	Mr. Belton
MR. TIFFANY, a New York Merchant	Mr. Barry	Mr. J. Johnstone
T. TENNYSON TWINKLE, a modern Poet	Mr. DeWalden	Mr. Kinloch
AUGUSTUS FOGG, a drawing room appendage	Mr. J. Howard	Mr. J. Howard
SNOBSON, a rare species of confidential clerk.................	Mr. Fisher	Mr. H. Scharf
ZEKE, a colored servant..........	Mr. Skerrett	Mr. J. Herbert
MRS. TIFFANY, a lady who imagines herself fashionable........	Mrs. Barry	Mrs. H. Marston
PRUDENCE, a maiden lady of a certain age..................	Mrs. Knight	Mrs. Parker
MILLINETTE, a French lady's maid	Mrs. Dyott	Mrs. A. Wigan
GERTRUDE, a governess...........	Miss Ellis	Miss F. Vining
SERAPHINA TIFFANY, a belle......	Miss Horn	Miss Gougenheim

FASHION

ACT FIRST.

SCENE 1. *A splendid Drawing Room in the House of* MRS. TIFFANY. *Open folding doors, discovering a Conservatory. On either side glass windows down to the ground. Doors on right and left. Mirror, couches, ottomans, a table with albums, beside it an arm chair.* MILLINETTE *dusting furniture.* ZEKE *in a dashing livery, scarlet coat.*

ZEKE. Dere 's a coat to take de eyes ob all Broadway! Ah! Missy, it am de fixin's dat make de natural *born* gemman. A libery for ever! Dere 's a pair ob insuppressibles to 'stonish de colored population.

MILLINETTE. Oh, *oui,* Monsieur Zeke. (*Very politely.*) I not *comprend* one word he say! (*Aside.*)

ZEKE. I tell 'ee what, Missy, I 'm 'stordinary glad to find dis a bery 'spectabul like situation! Now, as you 've made de acquaintance ob dis here family, and dere you 've had a supernumerary advantage ob me—seeing dat I only receibed my appointment dis morning. What I wants to know is your publicated opinion, privately expressed, ob de domestic circle.

MIL. You mean vat *espèce,* vat kind of personnes are Monsieur and Madame Tiffany? Ah! Monsieur is not de same ting as Madame,—not at all.

ZEKE. Well, I s'pose he ain't altogether.

MIL. Monsieur is man of business,—Madame is lady of fashion. Monsieur make de money,—Madame spend it. Monsieur nobody at all,—Madame everybody altogether. Ah! Monsieur Zeke, de money is all dat is *necessaire* in dis country to make one lady of fashion. Oh! it is quite anoder ting in *la belle France!*

ZEKE. A bery lucifer explanation. Well, now we 've disposed ob de heads ob de family, who come next?

MIL. First, dere is Mademoiselle Seraphina Tiffany. Mademoiselle is not at all one proper *personne.* Mademoiselle Seraphina is one coquette. Dat is not de mode in *la belle France;* de ladies, dere, never learn *la coquetrie* until dey do get one husband.

ZEKE. I tell 'ee what, Missy, I disreprobate dat proceeding altogeder!

MIL. Vait! I have not tell you all *la famille* yet. Dere is Ma'mselle Prudence —Madame's sister, one very *bizarre* personne. Den dere is Ma'mselle Gertrude, but she not anybody at all; she only teach Mademoiselle Seraphina *la musique.*

ZEKE. Well now, Missy, what 's your own special defunctions?

MIL. I not understand, Monsieur Zeke.

ZEKE. Den I 'll amplify. What 's de nature ob your exclusive services?

MIL. *Ah, oui! je comprend.* I am Madame's *femme de chambre*—her lady's maid, Monsieur Zeke. I teach Madame *les modes de Paris,* and Madame set de fashion for all New York. You see, Monsieur Zeke, dat it is me, *moi-même,* dat do lead de fashion for all de American *beau monde!*

ZEKE. Yah! yah! yah! I hab de idea by de heel. Well now, p'raps you can 'lustrify my officials?

MIL. Vat you will have to do? Oh! much tings, much tings. You vait on de table,—you tend de door,—you clean de boots,—you run de errands,—you drive de carriage,—you rub de horses,—you take care of de flowers,—you carry de water,—you help cook de dinner,—you wash de dishes,—and den you always remember to do everyting I tell you to!

ZEKE. Wheugh, am dat *all?*

MIL. All I can tink of now. To-day is Madame's day of reception, and all her grand friends do make her one *petite* visit. You mind run fast ven de bell do ring.

ZEKE. Run? If it was n't for dese superfluminous trimmings, I tell 'ee what, Missy, I 'd run—

MRS. TIFFANY. (*Outside.*) Millinette!

MIL. Here comes Madame! You better go, Monsieur Zeke.

ZEKE. Look ahea, Massa Zeke, does n't dis open rich! (*Aside.*) (*Exit* ZEKE.)

(*Enter* MRS. TIFFANY, *dressed in the most extravagant height of fashion.*)

MRS. TIF. Is everything in order, Millinette? Ah! very elegant, very elegant, indeed! There is a *jenny-says-quoi* look about this furniture,—an air of fashion and gentility perfectly bewitching. Is there not, Millinette?

MIL. Oh, *oui,* Madame!

MRS. TIF. But where is Miss Seraphina? It is twelve o'clock; our visitors will be pouring in, and she has not made her appearance. But I hear that nothing is more fashionable than to keep people waiting.—None but vulgar persons pay any attention to punctuality. Is it not so, Millinette?

MIL. Quite *comme il faut.*—Great personnes always do make little personnes wait, Madame.

MRS. TIF. This mode of receiving visitors only upon one specified day of the week is a most convenient custom! It saves the trouble of keeping the house continually in order and of being always dressed. I flatter myself that *I* was the first to introduce it amongst the New York *ee-light.* You are quite sure that it is strictly a Parisian mode, Millinette?

MIL. Oh, *oui,* Madame; entirely *mode de Paris.*

MRS. TIF. This girl is worth her weight in gold. (*Aside.*) Millinette, how do you say *arm-chair* in French?

MIL. *Fauteuil,* Madame.

MRS. TIF. *Fo-tool!* That has a foreign —an out-of-the-wayish sound that is perfectly charming—and so genteel! There is something about our American words decidedly vulgar. *Fowtool!* how refined. *Fowtool! Arm-chair!* what a difference!

MIL. Madame have one charmante pronunciation. *Fowtool* (*mimicking aside*) charmante, Madame!

MRS. TIF. Do you think so, Millinette? Well, I believe I have. But a woman of refinement and of fashion can always accommodate herself to everything foreign! And a week's study of that invaluable work—*"French without a Master,"* has made me quite at home in the court language of Europe! But where is the new valet? I 'm rather sorry that he is black, but to obtain a white American for a domestic is almost impossible; and they call this a free country! What did you say was the name of this new servant, Millinette?

MIL. He do say his name is Monsieur Zeke.

MRS. TIF. Ezekiel, I suppose. Zeke! Dear me, such a vulgar name will compromise the dignity of the whole family. Can you not suggest something more aristocratic, Millinette? Something *French!*

MIL. *Oh, oui,* Madame; *Adolph* is one very fine name.

MRS. TIF. A-dolph! Charming! Ring the bell, Millinette! (MILLINETTE *rings the bell.*) I will change his name immediately, besides giving him a few directions.

(*Enter* ZEKE. MRS. TIFFANY *addresses him with great dignity.*)

Your name, I hear, is *Ezekiel.*—I consider it too plebeian an appellation to be uttered in my presence. In future you are called A-dolph. Don't reply,—never interrupt me when I am speaking. A-dolph, as my guests arrive, I desire that you will inquire the name of every person, and then announce it in a loud, clear tone. That is the fashion in Paris.

(MILLINETTE *retires up the stage.*)

ZEKE. Consider de office discharged, Missus. (*Speaking very loudly.*)

MRS. TIF. Silence! Your business is to obey and not to talk.

ZEKE. I 'm dumb, Missus!

MRS. TIF. (*Pointing up stage.*) A-dolph, place that *fowtool* behind me.

ZEKE. (*Looking about him.*) I hab n't got dat far in de dictionary yet. No matter, a genus gets his learning by nature.

(*Takes up the table and places it behind* MRS. TIFFANY, *then expresses in dumb show great satisfaction.* MRS. TIFFANY, *as she goes to sit, discovers the mistake.*)

MRS. TIF. You dolt! Where have you lived not to know that *fow-tool* is the French for *arm-chair?* What ignorance! Leave the room this instant.

(MRS. TIFFANY *draws forward an arm-chair and sits.* MILLINETTE *comes forward suppressing her merriment at* ZEKE'S *mistake and removes the table.*)

ZEKE. Dem 's de defects ob not having a libery education. (*Exit.*)

(PRUDENCE *peeps in.*)

PRU. I wonder if any of the fine folks have come yet. Not a soul,—I knew they had n't. There 's Betsy all alone. (*Walks in.*) Sister Betsy!

MRS. TIF. Prudence! how many times have I desired you to call me *Elizabeth?* *Betsy* is the height of vulgarity.

PRU. Oh! I forgot. Dear me, how spruce we do look here, to be sure,—everything in first rate style now, Betsy. (MRS. T. *looks at her angrily.*) *Elizabeth,* I mean. Who would have thought, when you and I were sitting behind that little mahogany-colored counter, in Canal Street, making up flashy hats and caps—

MRS. TIF. Prudence, *what do* you mean? Millinette, leave the room.

MIL. *Oui,* Madame.

(MILLINETTE *pretends to arrange the books upon a side table, but lingers to listen.*)

PRU. But I always predicted it,—I always told you so, Betsy,—I always said you were destined to rise above your station!

MRS. TIF. Prudence! Prudence! have I not told you that—

PRU. No, Betsy, it was *I* that told *you,* when we used to buy our silks and ribbons of Mr. Antony Tiffany—*"talking Tony,"* you know we used to call him, and when you always put on the finest bonnet in our shop to go to his,—and when you staid so long smiling and chattering with him, I always told you that *something* would grow out of it—and didn't it?

MRS. TIF. Millinette, send Seraphina here instantly. Leave the room.

MIL. *Oui,* Madame. So dis Americaine ladi of fashion vas one *milliner?* Oh, vat a fine country for *les marchandes des modes!* I shall send for all my relation by de next packet! (*Aside.*)

(*Exit* MILLINETTE.)

MRS. TIF. Prudence! never let me hear you mention this subject again. Forget what we *have* been, it is enough to remember that we *are* of the *upper ten thousand!*

(PRUDENCE *goes up and sits down.*)

(*Enter* SERAPHINA, *very extravagantly dressed.*)

MRS. TIF. How bewitchingly you look, my dear! Does Millinette say that that head dress is strictly Parisian?

SERAPHINA. Oh, yes, Mamma, all the rage! They call it a *lady's tarpaulin,* and it is the exact pattern of one worn by the Princess Clementina at the last court ball.

MRS. TIF. Now, Seraphina, my dear, don't be too particular in your attentions to gentlemen not eligible. There is Count Jolimaitre, decidedly the most fashionable foreigner in town,—and so refined,—so much accustomed to associate with the first nobility in his own country that he can hardly tolerate the vulgarity of Americans in general. You may devote yourself to him. Mrs. Proudacre is dying to become acquainted with him. By the by, if she or her daughters should happen to drop in, be sure you don't introduce them to the Count. It is not the fashion in Paris to introduce—Millinette told me so.

(*Enter* ZEKE.)

ZEKE. (*In a very loud voice.*) Mister T. Tennyson Twinkle!

MRS. TIF. Show him up. (*Exit* ZEKE.)

PRU. I must be running away! (*Going.*)

MRS. TIF. Mr. T. Tennyson Twinkle—a very literary young man and a sweet poet! It is all the rage to patronize poets! Quick, Seraphina, hand me that magazine.—Mr. Twinkle writes for it.

(SERAPHINA *hands the magazine,* MRS. TIFFANY *seats herself in an armchair and opens the book.*)

PRU. (*Returning.*) There 's Betsy trying to make out that reading without her spectacles.

(*Takes a pair of spectacles out of her pocket and hands them to* MRS. TIFFANY.)

There, Betsy, I knew you were going to ask for them. Ah! they 're a blessing when one is growing old!

MRS. TIF. What do you mean, Prudence? A woman of fashion *never* grows old! Age is always out of fashion.

PRU. Oh, dear! what a delightful thing it is to be fashionable.

(*Exit* PRUDENCE. MRS. TIFFANY *resumes her seat.*)

(*Enter* TWINKLE. *He salutes* SERAPHINA.)

TWIN. Fair Seraphina! the sun itself grows dim,
Unless you aid his light and shine on him!

SERA. Ah! Mr. Twinkle, there is no such thing as answering you.

TWIN. (*Looks around and perceives* MRS. TIFFANY.) The "New Monthly Vernal

Galaxy." Reading my verses by all that 's charming! Sensible woman! I won't interrupt her. (*Aside.*)

MRS. TIF. (*Rising and coming forward.*) Ah! Mr. Twinkle, is that you? I was perfectly *abimé* at the perusal of your very *distingué* verses.

TWIN. I am overwhelmed, Madam. Permit me. (*Taking the magazine.*) Yes, they do read tolerably. And you must take into consideration, ladies, the rapidity with which they were written. Four minutes and a half by the stop watch! The true test of a poet is the *velocity* with which he composes. Really they do look very prettily, and they read tolerably—*quite* tolerably—*very* tolerably,—especially the first verse. (*Reads.*) "To Seraphina T——."

SERA. Oh! Mr. Twinkle!

TWIN. (*Reads.*) "Around my heart"—

MRS. TIF. How touching! Really, Mr. Twinkle, quite tender!

TWIN. (*Recommencing.*) "Around my heart"—

MRS. TIF. Oh, I must tell you, Mr. Twinkle! I heard the other day that poets were the aristocrats of literature. That 's one reason I like them, for I do dote on all aristocracy!

TWIN. Oh, Madam, how flattering! Now pray lend me your ears! (*Reads.*) "Around my heart thou weavest"—

SERA. That is such a *sweet* commencement, Mr. Twinkle!

TWIN. (*Aside.*) I wish she would n't interrupt me! (*Reads.*) "Around my heart thou weavest a spell"—

MRS. TIF. Beautiful! But excuse me one moment, while I say a word to Seraphina! Don't be too affable, my dear! Poets are very ornamental appendages to the drawing room, but they are always as poor as their own verses. They don't make eligible husbands! (*Aside to* SERAPHINA.)

TWIN. Confound their interruptions! (*Aside.*) My dear Madam, unless you pay the utmost attention you cannot catch the ideas. Are you ready? Well, now you shall hear it to the end! (*Reads.*)
"Around my heart thou weavest a spell
"Whose"—

(*Enter* ZEKE.)

ZEKE. Mister Augustus Fogg! A bery misty lookin young gemman? (*Aside.*)

MRS. TIF. Show him up, Adolph! (*Exit* ZEKE.)

TWIN. This is too much!

SERA. Exquisite verses, Mr. Twinkle,—exquisite!

TWIN. Ah, lovely Seraphina! your smile of approval transports me to the summit of Olympus.

SERA. Then I must frown, for I would not send you so far away.

TWIN. Enchantress! It 's all over with her. (*Aside.*)

(*Retire up and converse.*)

MRS. TIF. Mr. Fogg belongs to one of our oldest families,—to be sure he is the most difficult person in the world to entertain, for he never takes the trouble to talk, and never notices anything or anybody,—but then I hear that nothing is considered so vulgar as to betray any emotion, or to attempt to render oneself agreeable!

(*Enter* MR. FOGG, *fashionably attired but in very dark clothes.*)

FOGG. (*Bowing stiffly.*) Mrs. Tiffany, your most obedient. Miss Seraphina, yours. How d' ye do, Twinkle?

MRS. TIF. Mr. Fogg, how do you do? Fine weather,—delightful, is n't it?

FOGG. I am indifferent to weather, Madam.

MRS. TIF. Been to the opera, Mr. Fogg? I hear that the *bow monde* make their *debutt* there every evening.

FOGG. I consider operas a bore, Madam.

SERA. (*Advancing.*) You must hear Mr. Twinkle's verses, Mr. Fogg!

FOGG. I am indifferent to verses, Miss Seraphina.

SERA. But Mr. Twinkle's verses are addressed to me!

TWIN. Now pay attention, Fogg! (*Reads*)—
"Around my heart thou weavest a spell
"Whose magic I"—

(*Enter* ZEKE.)

ZEKE. Mister—No, he say he ain't no Mister—

TWIN. "Around my heart thou weavest a spell
"Whose magic I can never tell!"

MRS. TIF. Speak in a loud, clear tone, A-dolph!

TWIN. This is terrible!

ZEKE. Mister Count Jolly-made-her!

MRS. TIF. Count Jolimaitre! Good gracious! Zeke, Zeke—A-dolph I mean.—

Dear me, what a mistake! (*Aside.*) Set that chair out of the way,—put that table back. Seraphina, my dear, are you all in order? Dear me! dear me! Your dress is so tumbled! (*Arranges her dress.*) What are you grinning at? (*To* ZEKE.) Beg the Count to *honor* us by walking up! (*Exit* ZEKE.)

Seraphina, my dear (*aside to her*), remember now what I told you about the Count. He is a man of the highest,—good gracious! I am so flurried; and nothing is so ungenteel as agitation! what will the Count think! Mr. Twinkle, pray stand out of the way! Seraphina, my dear, place yourself on my right! Mr. Fogg, the conservatory—beautiful flowers,—pray amuse yourself in the conservatory.

FOGG. I am indifferent to flowers, Madam.

MRS. TIF. Dear me! the man stands right in the way,—just where the Count must make his *entray!* (*Aside.*) Mr. Fogg, pray—

(*Enter* COUNT JOLIMAITRE, *very dashingly dressed, wears a moustache.*)

MRS. TIF. Oh, Count, this unexpected honor—

SERA. Count, this inexpressible pleasure—

COUNT. Beg you won't mention it, Madam! Miss Seraphina, your most devoted! (*Crosses.*)

MRS. TIF. What condescension! (*Aside.*) Count, may I take the liberty to introduce—Good gracious! I forgot. (*Aside.*) Count, I was about to remark that we never introduce in America. All our fashions are foreign, Count.

(TWINKLE, *who has stepped forward to be introduced, shows great indignation.*)

COUNT. Excuse me, Madam, our fashions have grown antediluvian before you Americans discover their existence. You are lamentably behind the age—lamentably! 'Pon my honor, a foreigner of refinement finds great difficulty in existing in this provincial atmosphere.

MRS. TIF. How dreadful, Count! I am very much concerned. If there is anything which I can do, Count—

SERA. Or I, Count, to render your situation less deplorable—

COUNT. Ah! I find but one redeeming charm in America—the superlative loveliness of the feminine portion of creation,—and the wealth of their obliging papas. (*Aside.*)

MRS. TIF. How flattering! Ah! Count, I am afraid you will turn the head of my simple girl here. She is a perfect child of nature, Count.

COUNT. Very possibly, for though you American women are quite charming, yet, demme, there 's a deal of native rust to rub off!

MRS. TIF. *Rust?* Good gracious, Count! where do you find any rust? (*Looking about the room.*)

COUNT. How very unsophisticated!

MRS. TIF. Count, I am so much ashamed,—pray excuse me! Although a lady of large fortune, and one, Count, who can boast of the highest connections, I blush to confess that I have never travelled,—while you, Count, I presume are at home in all the courts of Europe.

COUNT. *Courts?* Eh? Oh, yes, Madam, very true. I believe I am pretty well known in some of the courts of Europe—*police courts.* (*Aside, crossing.*) In a word, Madam, I had seen enough of civilized life—wanted to refresh myself by a sight of barbarous countries and customs—had my choice between the Sandwich Islands and New York—chose New York!

MRS. TIF. How complimentary to our country! And, Count, I have no doubt you speak every conceivable language? You talk English like a native.

COUNT. Eh, what? Like a native? Oh, ah, demme, yes, I am something of an Englishman. Passed one year and eight months with the Duke of Wellington, six months with Lord Brougham, two and a half with Count d'Orsay—knew them all more intimately than their best friends—no heroes to me—had n't a secret from me, I assure you,—*especially of the toilet.* (*Aside.*)

MRS. TIF. Think of that, my dear! Lord Wellington and Duke Broom! (*Aside to* SERAPHINA.)

SERA. And only think of Count d'Orsay, Mamma! (*Aside to* MRS. TIFFANY.) I am so wild to see Count d'Orsay!

COUNT. Oh! a mere man milliner. Very little refinement out of Paris! Why, at the very last dinner given at Lord—Lord Knowswho, would you believe it, Madam, there was an individual present who wore a *black* cravat and took *soup twice!*

MRS. TIF. How shocking! the sight of him

would have spoilt my appetite! Think what a great man he must be, my dear, to despise lords and counts in that way. (*Aside to* SERAPHINA.) I must leave them together. (*Aside.*) Mr. Twinkle, your arm. I have some really very *foreign exotics* to show you.

TWIN. I fly at your command. I wish all her exotics were blooming in their native soil! (*Aside, and glancing at the* COUNT.)

MRS. TIF. Mr. Fogg, will you accompany us? My conservatory is well worthy a visit. It cost an immense sum of money.

FOGG. I am indifferent to conservatories, Madam; flowers are such a bore!

MRS. TIF. I shall take no refusal. Conservatories are all the rage,—I could not exist without mine! Let me show you, —let me show you.

(*Places her arm through* MR. FOGG'S, *without his consent. Exeunt* MRS. TIFFANY, FOGG, *and* TWINKLE *into the conservatory, where they are seen walking about.*)

SERA. America, then, has no charms for you, Count?

COUNT. Excuse me,—some exceptions. I find you, for instance, particularly charming! Can't say I admire your country. Ah! if you had ever breathed the exhilarating air of Paris, ate creams at Tortoni's, dined at the Café Royale, or if you had lived in London—felt at home at St. James's, and every afternoon driven a couple of Lords and a Duchess through Hyde Park, you would find America—where you have no kings, queens, lords, nor ladies—insupportable!

SERA. Not while there was a Count in it?

(*Enter* ZEKE, *very indignant.*)

ZEKE. Where 's de Missus?

(*Enter* MRS. TIFFANY, FOGG, *and* TWINKLE, *from the conservatory.*)

MRS. TIF. Whom do you come to announce, A-dolph?

ZEKE. He said he would n't trust me—no, not eben wid so much as his name; so I would n't trust him up stairs, den he ups wid *his stick* and I *cuts mine.*

MRS. TIF. Some of Mr. Tiffany's vulgar acquaintances. I shall die with shame. (*Aside.*) A-dolph, inform him that I am *not at home.* (*Exit* ZEKE.) My nerves are so shattered, I am ready to sink. Mr. Twinkle, that *fow tool,* if you please!

TWIN. What? What do you wish, Madam?

MRS. TIF. The ignorance of these Americans! (*Aside.*) Count, may I trouble you? That *fow tool,* if you please!

COUNT. She 's not talking English, nor French, but I suppose it 's American. (*Aside.*)

TRUE. (*Outside.*) Not at home!

ZEKE. No, Sar—Missus say she 's not at home.

TRUE. Out of the way, you grinning nigger!

(*Enter* ADAM TRUEMAN, *dressed as a farmer, a stout cane in his hand, his boots covered with dust.* ZEKE *jumps out of his way as he enters.*)

(*Exit* ZEKE.)

TRUE. Where 's this woman that 's not *at home* in her own house? May I be shot! if I wonder at it! I should n't think she 'd ever feel *at home* in such a showbox as this! (*Looking round.*)

MRS. TIF. What a plebeian looking old farmer! I wonder who he is? (*Aside.*) Sir—(*advancing very agitatedly*) what do you mean, Sir, by this *ow*dacious conduct? How dare you intrude yourself into my parlor? Do you know who I am, Sir? (*With great dignity.*) You are in the presence of Mrs. Tiffany, Sir!

TRUE. Antony's wife, eh? Well now, I might have guessed that—ha! ha! ha! for I see you make it a point to carry half your husband's shop upon your back! No matter; that 's being a good helpmate—for he carried the whole of it once in a pack on his own shoulders—now you bear a share!

MRS. TIF. How dare you, you impertinent, *ow*dacious, ignorant old man! It 's all an invention. You 're talking of somebody else. What will the Count think! (*Aside.*)

TRUE. Why, I thought folks had better manners in the city! This is a civil welcome for your husband's old friend, and after my coming all the way from Catteraugus to see you and yours! First a grinning nigger tricked out in scarlet regimentals—

MRS. TIF. Let me tell you, Sir, that liveries are all the fashion!

TRUE. The fashion, are they? To make men wear the *badge of servitude* in a free land,—that 's the fashion, is it? Hurrah, for republican simplicity! I will venture to say now, that you have your coat of arms too!

MRS. TIF. Certainly, Sir; you can see it on the panels of my *voyture.*

TRUE. Oh! no need of that. I know what your escutcheon must be! A band-box *rampant* with a bonnet *couchant,* and a peddlar's pack *passant!* Ha, ha, ha! that shows both houses united!

MRS. TIF. Sir! you are most profoundly ignorant,—what do you mean by this insolence, Sir? How shall I get rid of him? (*Aside.*)

TRUE. (*Looking at* SERAPHINA.) I hope that is not Gertrude! (*Aside.*)

MRS. TIF. Sir, I'd have you know that—Seraphina, my child, walk with the gentlemen into the conservatory.

(*Exeunt* SERAPHINA, TWINKLE, FOGG *into conservatory.*)

Count Jolimaitre, pray make due allowances for the errors of this rustic! I do assure you, Count— (*Whispers to him.*)

TRUE. Count! She calls that critter with a shoe brush over his mouth, Count! To look at him, I should have thought he was a tailor's walking advertisement! (*Aside.*)

COUNT. (*Addressing* TRUEMAN *whom he has been inspecting through his eye-glass.*) Where did you say you belonged, my friend? Dug out of the ruins of Pompeii, eh?

TRUE. I belong to a land in which I rejoice to find that you are a foreigner.

COUNT. What a barbarian! He doesn't see the honor I'm doing his country! Pray, Madam, is it one of the aboriginal inhabitants of the soil? To what tribe of Indians does he belong—the Pawnee or Choctaw? Does he carry a tomahawk?

TRUE. Something quite as useful,—do you see that? (*Shaking his stick.*)

(COUNT *runs behind* MRS. TIFFANY.)

MRS. TIF. Oh, dear! I shall faint! Millinette! (*Approaching.*) Millinette!

(*Enter* MILLINETTE, *without advancing into the room.*)

MILLI. *Oui,* Madame.

MRS. TIF. A glass of water!

(*Exit* MILLINETTE.)

Sir, (*crossing to* TRUEMAN) I am shocked at your plebeian conduct! Tis is a gentleman of the highest standing, Sir! He is a *Count,* Sir!

(*Enter* MILLINETTE, *bearing a salver with a glass of water. In advancing towards* MRS. TIFFANY, *she passes in front of the* COUNT, *starts and screams. The* COUNT, *after a start of surprise, regains his composure, plays with his eye glass, and looks perfectly unconcerned.*)

MRS. TIF. What is the matter? What *is* the matter?

MILLI. Noting, noting,—only— (*Looks at* COUNT *and turns away her eyes again.*) only—noting at all!

TRUE. Don't be afraid, girl! Why, did you never see a live Count before? He's tame,—I dare say your mistress there leads him about by the ears.

MRS. TIF. This is too much! Millinette, send for Mr. Tiffany instantly!

(*Crosses to* MILLINETTE, *who is going.*)

MILLI. He just come in, Madame!

TRUE. My old friend! Where is he? Take me to him,—I long to have one more hearty shake of the hand!

MRS. TIF. (*Crosses to him.*) Count, honor me by joining my daughter in the conservatory, I will return immediately.

(COUNT *bows and walks towards conservatory,* MRS. TIFFANY *following part of the way and then returning to* TRUEMAN.)

TRUE. What a Jezebel! These women always play the very devil with a man, and yet I don't believe such a damaged bale of goods as *that* (*looking at* MRS. TIFFANY) has smothered the heart of little Antony!

MRS. TIF. This way, Sir, sal vous plait.

(*Exit with great dignity.*)

TRUE. *Sal vous plait.* Ha, ha, ha! We'll see what Fashion has done for him. (*Exit.*)

END OF ACT FIRST.

ACT SECOND.

SCENE 1. *Inner apartment of* MR. TIFFANY'S *Counting House.* MR. TIFFANY, *seated at a desk looking over papers.* MR. SNOBSON, *on a high stool at another desk, with a pen behind his ear.*

SNOBSON. (*Rising, advances to the front of the stage, regards* TIFFANY *and shrugs his shoulders.*) How the old boy frets and fumes over those papers, to be sure! He's working himself into a perfect fever—ex-actly,—therefore *bleeding's* the prescription! So here goes!

(*Aside.*) Mr. Tiffany, a word with you, if you please, Sir?

TIF. (*Sitting still.*) Speak on, Mr. Snobson, I attend.

SNOB. What I have to say, Sir, is a matter of the first importance to the credit of the concern—the *credit* of the concern, Mr. Tiffany!

TIF. Proceed, Mr. Snobson.

SNOB. Sir, you 've a handsome house—fine carriage—nigger in livery—feed on the fat of the land—everything first rate—

TIF. Well, Sir?

SNOB. My salary, Mr. Tiffany!

TIF. It has been raised three times within the last year.

SNOB. Still it is insufficient for the necessities of an honest man,— mark me, an *honest* man, Mr. Tiffany.

TIF. (*Crossing.*) What a weapon he has made of that word! (*Aside.*) Enough—another hundred shall be added. Does that content you?

SNOB. There is one other subject, which I have before mentioned, Mr. Tiffany,—your daughter,—what 's the reason you can't let the folks at home know at once that I 'm to be *the man?*

TIF. Villain! And must the only seal upon this scoundrel's lips be placed there by the hand of my daughter? (*Aside.*) Well, Sir, it shall be as you desire.

SNOB. And Mrs. Tiffany shall be informed of your resolution?

TIF. Yes.

SNOB. Enough said! That 's the ticket! The CREDIT *of the concern 's safe,* Sir!

(*Returns to his seat.*)

TIF. How low have I bowed to this insolent rascal! To rise himself he mounts upon my shoulders, and unless I can shake him off he must crush me! (*Aside.*)

(*Enter* TRUEMAN.)

TRUE. Here I am, Antony, man! I told you I 'd pay you a visit in your money-making quarters. (*Looks around.*) But it looks as dismal here as a cell in the States' prison!

TIF. (*Forcing a laugh.*) Ha, ha, ha! States' prison! You are so facetious! Ha, ha, ha!

TRUE. Well, for the life of me I can't see anything so amusing in that! I I should think the States' prison plaguy uncomfortable lodgings. And you laugh, man, as though you fancied yourself there already.

TIF. Ha, ha, ha!

TRUE. (*Imitating him.*) Ha, ha, ha! What on earth do you mean by that ill-sounding laugh, that has nothing of a laugh about it! This *fashion*-worship has made heathens and hypocrites of you all! *Deception* is your household God! A man laughs as if he were crying, and cries as if he were laughing in his sleeve. Everything is something else from what it seems to be. I have lived in your house only three days, and I 've heard more lies than were ever invented during a Presidential election! First your fine lady of a wife sends me word that she 's not at home—I walk up stairs, and she takes good care that *I* shall not be *at home*—wants to turn me out of doors. Then *you* come in—take your old friend by the hand—whisper, the deuce knows what, in your wife's ear, and the tables are turned in a tangent! Madam curtsies—says she 's enchanted to see me—and orders her grinning nigger to show me a room.

TIF. We were exceedingly happy to welcome you as our guest!

TRUE. Happy? *You* happy? Ah, Antony! Antony! that hatchet face of yours, and those criss-cross furrows tell quite another story! It 's many a long day since you were *happy* at anything! You look as if you 'd melted down your flesh into dollars, and mortgaged your soul in the bargain! Your warm heart has grown cold over your ledger—your light spirits heavy with calculation! You have traded away your youth—your hopes—your tastes, for wealth! and now you *have* the wealth you coveted, what does it profit you? Pleasure it cannot buy; for you have lost your *capacity* for enjoyment—Ease it will not bring; for the love of gain is never satisfied! It has made your counting-house a penitentiary, and your home a fashionable *museum* where there is no niche for you! You have spent so much time *ciphering* in the one, that you find yourself at last a very *cipher* in the other! See me, man! seventy-two last August!—strong as a hickory and every whit as sound!

TIF. I take the greatest pleasure in remarking your superiority, Sir.

TRUE. Bah! no man takes pleasure in remarking the superiority of another! Why the deuce, can't you speak the truth, man? But it's not the *fashion* I suppose! I have not seen one frank, open face since—no, no, I can't say that either, though lying *is* catching! There's that girl, Gertrude, who is trying to teach your daughter music—but Gertrude was bred in the country!

TIF. A good girl; my wife and daughter find her very useful.

TRUE. Useful? Well, I must say you have queer notions of *use!*—But come, cheer up, man! I'd rather see one of your old smiles, than know you'd realized another thousand! I hear you are making money on the true, American, high pressure system—better go slow and sure—the more steam, the greater danger of the boiler's bursting! All sound, I hope? Nothing rotten at the core?

TIF. Oh, sound—quite sound!

TRUE. Well, that's pleasant—though I must say you don't look very pleasant about it!

TIF. My good friend, although I am solvent, I may say, perfectly solvent—yet you—the fact is, you can be of some assistance to me!

TRUE. That's the *fact* is it? I'm glad we've hit upon one *fact* at last! Well—

(SNOBSON, *who during this conversation has been employed in writing, but stops occasionally to listen, now gives vent to a dry chuckling laugh.*)

TRUE. Hey? What's that? Another of those deuced ill-sounding, city laughs! (*Sees Snobson.*) Who's that perched up on the stool of repentance—eh, Antony?

SNOB. The old boy has missed his text there—*that's* the stool of repentance! (*Aside and looking at* TIFFANY'S *seat.*)

TIF. One of my clerks—my confidential clerk!

TRUE. Confidential? Why he looks for all the world like a spy—the most inquisitorial, hang-dog face—ugh! the sight of it makes my blood run cold! Come, (*crosses*) let us talk over matters where this critter can't give us the benefit of his opinion! Antony, the next time you choose a confidential clerk, take one that carries his credentials in his face—those in his pocket are not worth much without!

(*Exeunt* TRUEMAN *and* TIFFANY.)

SNOB. (*Jumping from his stool and advancing.*) The old prig has got the tin, or Tiff would never be so civil! All right—Tiff will work every shiner into the concern—all the better for me! Now I'll go and make love to Seraphina. The old woman need n't try to knock me down with any of her French lingo! Six months from to-day if I ain't driving my two footmen tandem, down Broadway—and as fashionable as Mrs. Tiffany herself, then I ain't the trump I thought I was! that's all. (*Looks at his watch.*) Bless me! eleven o'clock and I have n't had my julep yet! Snobson, I'm ashamed of you! (*Exit.*)

SCENE 2. *The interior of a beautiful conservatory; walk through the centre; stands of flower pots in bloom; a couple of rustic seats.* GERTRUDE, *attired in white, with a white rose in her hair; watering the flowers.* COLONEL HOWARD *regarding her.*

HOW. I am afraid you lead a sad life here, Miss Gertrude?

GER. (*Turning round gaily.*) What! amongst the flowers?

(*Continues her occupation.*)

HOW. No, amongst the thistles, with which Mrs. Tiffany surrounds you; the tempests, which her temper raises!

GER. They never harm me. Flowers and herbs are excellent tutors. I learn prudence from the reed, and bend until the storm has swept over me!

HOW. Admirable philosophy! But still this frigid atmosphere of fashion must be uncongenial to you? Accustomed to the pleasant companionship of your kind friends in Geneva, surely you must regret this cold exchange?

GER. Do you think so? Can you suppose that I could possibly prefer a ramble in the woods to a promenade in Broadway? A wreath of scented wild flowers to a bouquet of these sickly exotics? The odour of new-mown hay to the heated air of this crowded conservatory? Or can you imagine that I could enjoy the quiet conversation of my Geneva friends, more than the edifying chit-chat of a fashionable drawing room? But I see you think me totally destitute of taste?

HOW. You have a merry spirit to jest thus at your grievances!

GER. I have my *mania,*—as some wise person declares that all mankind have,—and mine is a love of independence! In Geneva, my wants were supplied by two kind old maiden ladies, upon whom I know not that I have any claim. I had abilities, and desired to use them. I came here at my own request; for here I am no longer *dependent! Voila tout,* as Mrs. Tiffany would say.

How. Believe me, I appreciate the confidence you repose in me!

Ger. Confidence! Truly, Colonel Howard, the *confidence* is entirely on your part, in supposing that I confide that which I have no reason to conceal! I think I informed you that Mrs. Tiffany only received visitors on her reception day—she is therefore not prepared to see you. Zeke—Oh! I beg his pardon—Adolph, made some mistake in admitting you.

How. Nay, Gertrude, it was not Mrs. Tiffany, nor Miss Tiffany, whom I came to see; it—it was—

Ger. The conservatory perhaps? I will leave you to examine the flowers at leisure! (*Crosses.*)

How. Gertrude—listen to me. If I only dared to give utterance to what is hovering upon my lips! (*Aside.*) Gertrude!

Ger. Colonel Howard!

How. Gertrude, I must—must—

Ger. Yes, indeed you *must*, must leave me! I think I hear somebody coming—Mrs. Tiffany would not be well pleased to find you here—pray, pray leave me—that door will lead you into the street.

(*Hurries him out through door; takes up her watering pot, and commences watering flowers, tying up branches, &c.*)

What a strange being is man! Why should he hesitate to say—nay, why should I prevent his saying, what I would most delight to hear? Truly man *is* strange—but woman is quite as incomprehensible!

(*Walks about gathering flowers.*)

(*Enter* Count Jolimaitre.)

Count. There she is—the bewitching little creature! Mrs. Tiffany and her daughter are out of ear-shot. I caught a glimpse of their feathers floating down Broadway, not ten minutes ago. Just the opportunity I have been looking for! Now for an engagement with this captivating little piece of prudery! 'Pon honor, I am almost afraid she will not resist a *Count* long enough to give value to the conquest. (*Approaching her.*) *Ma belle petite,* were you gathering roses for me?

Ger. (*Starts on first perceiving him, but instantly regains her self-possession.*) The roses here, Sir, are carefully guarded with thorns—if you have the right to gather, pluck for yourself!

Count. Sharp as ever, little Gertrude! But now that we are alone, throw off this frigidity, and be at your ease.

Ger. Permit me to *be alone,* Sir, that I *may* be at my ease!

Count. Very good, *ma belle,* well said! (*Applauding her with his hands.*) Never yield too soon, even to a *title!* But as the old girl may find her way back before long, we may as well come to particulars at once. I love you; but that you know already. (*Rubbing his eye-glass unconcernedly with his handkerchief.*) Before long I shall make Mademoiselle Seraphina my wife, and, of course, you shall remain in the family!

Ger. (*Indignantly.*) Sir—

Count. 'Pon my honor you shall! In France we arrange these little matters without difficulty!

Ger. But I am an *American!* Your conduct proves that you are not one!

(*Going, crosses.*)

Count. (*Preventing her.*) Don't run away, my immaculate *petite Americaine!* Demme, you 've quite overlooked my condescension—the difference of our stations—you a species of upper servant—an orphan—no friends.

(*Enter* Trueman *unperceived.*)

Ger. And therefore more entitled to the respect and protection of every *true gentleman!* Had you been one, you would not have insulted me!

Count. My charming little orator, patriotism and declamation become you particularly! (*Approaches her.*) I feel quite tempted to taste—

True. (*Thrusting him aside.*) An American hickory-switch! (*Strikes him.*) Well, how do you like it?

Count. Old matter-of-fact! (*Aside.*) Sir, how dare you?

True. My stick has answered that question!

Ger. Oh! now I am quite safe!

True. Safe! not a bit safer than before! All women would be safe, if they knew how virtue became them! As for you, Mr. Count, what have you to say for yourself? Come, speak out!

Count. Sir,—aw—aw—you don't understand these matters!

TRUE. That 's a fact! Not having had *your* experience, I don't believe I *do* understand them!

COUNT. A piece of pleasantry—a mere joke—

TRUE. A joke was it? I'll show you a joke worth two of that! I'll teach you the way we natives joke with a puppy who don't respect an honest woman! (*Seizing him.*)

COUNT. Oh! oh! demme—you old ruffian! let me go. What do you mean?

TRUE. Oh! a piece of pleasantry—a mere joke—very pleasant is n't it?

(*Attempts to strike him again;* COUNT *struggles with him. Enter* MRS. TIFFANY *hastily, in her bonnet and shawl.*)

MRS. TIF. What IS the matter? I am perfectly *abimé* with terror. Mr. Trueman, what has happened?

TRUE. Oh! we have been *joking!*

MRS. TIF. (*To* COUNT, *who is re-arranging his dress.*) My dear Count, I did not expect to find you here—how kind of you!

TRUE. Your *dear* Count has been showing his *kindness* in a very *foreign* manner. Too *foreign* I think, he found it to be relished by an *unfashionable native!* What do you think of a puppy, who insults an innocent girl all in the way of *kindness?* This Count of yours —this importation of—

COUNT. My dear Madam, demme, permit me to explain. It would be unbecoming —demme—particular unbecoming of you —aw—aw—to pay any attention to this ignorant person. (*Crosses to* TRUEMAN.) Anything that he says concerning a man of my standing—aw—the truth is, Madam—

TRUE. Let us have the truth by all means, —if it is only for the novelty's sake!

COUNT. (*Turning his back to* TRUEMAN.) You see, Madam, hoping to obtain a few moments' private conversation with Miss Seraphina—with *Miss Seraphina* I say and—aw—and knowing her passion for flowers, I found my way to your very tasteful and *recherché* conservatory. (*Looks about him approvingly.*) *Very* beautifully arranged—does you great credit, madam! Here I encountered this young person. She was inclined to be talkative; and I indulged her with—with a—aw—demme—a few *common places!* What passed between us was mere *harmless badinage*—on *my* part. You, madam, you—so conversant with our European manners you are aware that when a man of fashion—that is, when a woman—a man is bound—amongst noblemen, you know—

MRS. TIF. I comprehend you perfectly—*parfittement,* my dear Count.

COUNT. 'Pon my honor, that 's very obliging of her. (*Aside.*)

MRS. TIF. I am shocked at the plebeian forwardness of this conceited girl!

TRUE. (*Walking up to* COUNT.) Did you ever keep a reckoning of the lies you tell in an hour?

MRS. TIF. Mr. Trueman, I blush for you! (*Crosses to* TRUEMAN.)

TRUE. Don't do that—you have no blushes to spare!

MRS. TIF. It is a man of rank whom you are addressing, Sir!

TRUE. A rank villain, Mrs. Antony Tiffany! A *rich one* he would be, had he as much *gold* as *brass!*

MRS. TIF. Pray pardon him, Count; he knows nothing of *how ton!*

COUNT. Demme, he 's beneath my notice. I tell you what, old fellow—(TRUEMAN *raises his stick as* COUNT *approaches, the latter starts back*) the sight of him discomposes me—aw—I feel quite uncomfortable—aw—let us join your charming daughter? I can't do you the honor to shoot you, Sir—(*to* TRUEMAN) you are beneath me—a nobleman can't fight a commoner! Good bye, old Truepenny! I—aw—I 'm insensible to your insolence!

(*Exeunt* COUNT *and* MRS. TIFFANY.)

TRUE. You won't be insensible to a cow hide in spite of your nobility! The next time he practises any of his foreign fashions on you, Gertrude, you 'll see how I 'll wake up his sensibilities!

GER. I do not know what I should have done without you, sir.

TRUE. Yes, you do—you know that you would have done well enough! Never tell a lie, girl! not even for the sake of pleasing an old man! When you open your lips let your heart speak. Never tell a lie! Let your face be the looking-glass of your soul—your heart its clock —while your tongue rings the hours! But the glass must be clear, the clock true, and then there 's no fear but the tongue will do its duty in a woman's head!

GER. You are very good, Sir!

TRUE. That 's as it may be!—How my

heart warms towards her! (*Aside.*) Gertrude, I hear that you have no mother?

GER. Ah! no, Sir; I wish I had.

TRUE. So do I! Heaven knows, so do I! (*Aside, and with emotion.*) And you have no father, Gertrude?

GER. No, Sir—I often wish I had!

TRUE. (*Hurriedly.*) Don't do that, girl! don't do that! Wish you had a mother—but never wish that you had a father again! Perhaps the one you had did not deserve such a child!

(*Enter* PRUDENCE.)

PRU. Seraphina is looking for you, Gertrude.

GER. I will go to her. (*Crosses.*) Mr. Trueman, you will not permit me to thank you, but you cannot prevent my gratitude! (*Exit.*)

TRUE. (*Looking after her.*) If falsehood harbours there, I 'll give up searching after truth!

(*Crosses, retires up the stage musingly, and commences examining the flowers.*)

PRU. What a nice old man he is to be sure! I wish he would say something! (*Aside.*)

(*Crosses, walks after him, turning when he turns—after a pause,*)

Don't mind *me*, Mr. Trueman!

TRUE. Mind you? Oh! no, don't be afraid (*crosses.*)—I was n't minding you. Nobody seems to mind you much!

(*Continues walking and examining the flowers*—PRUDENCE *follows.*)

PRU. Very pretty flowers, ain't they? Gertrude takes care of them.

TRUE. Gertrude? So I hear—(*advancing*) I suppose you can tell me now who this Gertrude—

PRU. Who she 's in love with? I *knew* you were going to say that! I 'll tell you all about it! Gertrude, she 's in love with—Mr. Twinkle! and he 's in love with her. And Seraphina she 's in love with Count Jolly—what-d' ye-call-it: but Count Jolly don't take to her at all—but Colonel Howard—he 's the man—he 's desperate about her!

TRUE. Why you feminine newspaper! Howard in love with that quintessence of affectation! Howard—the only, frank, straightforward fellow that I 've met since—I 'll tell him my mind on the subject! And Gertrude hunting for happiness in a rhyming dictionary! The girl 's a greater fool than I took her for! (*Crosses.*)

PRU. So she is—you see I know all about them!

TRUE. I see you do! You 've a wonderful knowledge—wonderful—of *other people's concerns!* It may do here, but take my word for it, in the county of Catteraugus you 'd get the name of a great *busy-body*. But perhaps you know that too?

PRU. Oh! I always know what 's coming. I feel it beforehand all over me. I knew something was going to happen the day you came here—and what 's more I can always tell a married man from a single—I felt right off that you were a bachelor!

TRUE. Felt right off I was a bachelor did you? you were sure of it—sure?—quite sure? (*Prudence assents delightedly.*) Then you felt wrong!—a bachelor and a widower are not the same thing!

PRU. Oh! but it all comes to the same thing—a widower 's as good as a bachelor any day! And besides I knew that you were a farmer *right off*.

TRUE. On the spot, eh? I suppose you saw cabbages and green peas growing out of my hat?

PRU. No, I did n't—but I knew all about you. And I knew—(*looking down and fidgeting with her apron*) I knew you were for getting married soon! For last night I dream't I saw your funeral going along the streets, and the mourners all dressed in white. And a funeral is a sure sign of a wedding, you know! (*Nudging him with her elbow.*)

TRUE. (*Imitating her voice.*) Well I can't say that I *know* any such thing! you know! (*Nudging her back.*)

PRU. Oh! it does, and there 's no getting over it! For my part, I like farmers—and I know all about setting hens and turkeys, and feeding chickens, and laying eggs, and all that sort of thing!

TRUE. May I be shot! if mistress newspaper is not putting in an advertisement for herself! This is your city mode of courting I suppose, ha, ha, ha! (*Aside.*)

PRU. I 've been west, a little; but I never was in the county of Catteraugus, myself.

TRUE. Oh! you were not? And you have taken a particular fancy to go there, eh?

PRU. Perhaps I should n't object—

TRUE. Oh!—ah!—so I suppose. Now

pay attention to what I am going to say, for it is a matter of great importance to yourself.

PRU. Now it 's coming—I know what he 's going to say! (*Aside.*)

TRUE. The next time you want to tie a man for life to your apron-strings, pick out one that don't come from the county of Catteraugus—for greenhorns are scarce in those parts, and modest women plenty! (*Exit.*)

PRU. Now who 'd have thought he was going to say that! But I won't give him up yet—I won't give him up. (*Exit.*)

END OF ACT SECOND.

ACT THIRD.

SCENE 1. MRS. TIFFANY'S *Parlor. Enter* MRS. TIFFANY, *followed by* MR. TIFFANY.

TIF. Your extravagance will ruin me, Mrs. Tiffany!

MRS. TIF. And your stinginess will ruin me, Mr. Tiffany! It is totally and *toot a fate* impossible to convince you of the necessity of *keeping up appearances.* There is a certain display which every woman of fashion is forced to make!

TIF. And pray who made *you* a woman of fashion?

MRS. TIF. What a vulgar question! All women of fashion, Mr. Tiffany—

TIF. In this land are *self-constituted,* like you, Madam—and *fashion* is the cloak for more sins than charity ever covered! It was for *fashion's* sake that you insisted upon my purchasing this expensive house—it was for *fashion's* sake that you ran me in debt at every exorbitant upholsterer's and extravagant furniture warehouse in the city—it was for *fashion's* sake that you built that ruinous conservatory—hired more servants than they have persons to wait upon—and dressed your footman like a harlequin!

MRS. TIF. Mr. Tiffany, you are thoroughly plebeian, and insufferably *American,* in your grovelling ideas! And, pray, what was the occasion of these very *mal-ap-pro-pos* remarks? Merely because I requested a paltry fifty dollars to purchase a new style of head-dress—a *bijou* of an article just introduced in France.

TIF. Time was, Mrs. Tiffany, when you manufactured your own French head-dresses—took off their first gloss at the public balls, and then sold them to your shortest-sighted customers. And all you knew about France, or French either, was what you spelt out at the bottom of your fashion plates—but now you have grown so fashionable, forsooth, that you have forgotten how to speak your mother tongue!

MRS. TIF. Mr. Tiffany, Mr. Tiffany! Nothing is more positively vulgarian—more *unaristocratic* than any allusion to the past!

TIF. Why I thought, my dear, that *aristocrats* lived principally upon the past—and traded in the market of fashion with the bones of their ancestors for capital?

MRS. TIF. Mr. Tiffany, such vulgar remarks are only suitable to the counting house, in my drawing room you should—

TIF. Vary my sentiments with my locality, as you change your *manners* with your *dress!*

MRS. TIF. Mr. Tiffany, I desire that you will purchase Count d'Orsay's "Science of Etiquette," and learn how to conduct yourself—especially before you appear at the grand ball, which I shall give on Friday!

TIF. Confound your balls, Madam; they make *footballs* of my money, while you dance away all that I am worth! A pretty time to give a ball when you know that I am on the very brink of bankruptcy!

MRS. TIF. So much the greater reason that nobody should suspect your circumstances, or you would lose your credit at once. Just at this crisis a ball is absolutely *necessary* to save your reputation! There is Mrs. Adolphus Dashaway—she gave the most splendid fête of the season—and I hear on very good authority that her husband has not paid his baker's bill in three months. Then there was Mrs. Honeywood—

TIF. Gave a ball the night before her husband shot himself—perhaps you wish to drive me to follow his example? (*Crosses.*)

MRS. TIF. Good gracious! Mr. Tiffany, how you talk! I beg you won't mention anything of the kind. I consider black the most unbecoming color. I 'm sure I 've done all that I could to gratify you. There is that vulgar old torment, Trueman, who gives one the lie fifty times a day—have n't I been very civil to him?

TIF. Civil to his *wealth*, Mrs. Tiffany! I told you that he was a rich, old farmer —the early friend of my father—my own benefactor—and that I had reason to think he might assist me in my present embarrassments. Your civility was *bought*—and like most of your *own* purchases has yet to be *paid* for. (*Crosses.*)

MRS. TIF. And will be, no doubt! The condescension of a woman of fashion should command any price. Mr. Trueman is insupportably indecorous—he has insulted Count Jolimaitre in the most outrageous manner. If the Count was not so deeply interested—so *abimé* with Seraphina, I am sure he would never honor us by his visits again!

TIF. So much the better—he shall never marry my daughter!—I am resolved on that. Why, Madam, I am told there is in Paris a regular matrimonial stock company, who fit out indigent dandies for this market. How do I know but this fellow is one of its creatures, and that he has come here to increase its dividends by marrying a fortune?

MRS. TIF. Nonsense, Mr. Tiffany. The Count, the most fashionable young man in all New York—the intimate friend of all the dukes and lords in Europe—not marry my daughter? Not permit Seraphina to become a Countess? Mr. Tiffany, you are out of your senses!

TIF. That would not be very wonderful, considering how many years I have been united to you, my dear. Modern physicians pronounce lunacy infectious!

MRS. TIF. Mr. Tiffany, he is a man of fashion—

TIF. Fashion makes fools, but cannot *feed* them. By the bye, I have a request, —since you are bent upon ruining me by this ball, and there is no help for it, —I desire that you will send an invitation to my confidential clerk, Mr. Snobson.

MRS. TIF. Mr. Snobson! Was there ever such an *you-nick* demand! Mr. Snobson would cut a pretty figure amongst my fashionable friends! I shall do no such thing, Mr. Tiffany.

TIF. Then, Madam, the ball shall not take place. Have I not told you that I am in the power of this man? That there are circumstances which it is happy for you that you do not know—which you cannot comprehend,—but which render it essential that you should be civil to Mr. Snobson? Not you merely, but Seraphina also? He is a more appropriate match for her than your foreign favorite.

MR. TIF. A match for Seraphina, indeed! (*Crosses.*) Mr. Tiffany, you are determined to make a *fow pas.*

TIF. Mr. Snobson intends calling this morning. (*Crosses.*)

MRS. TIF. But, Mr. Tiffany, this is not reception day—my drawing-rooms are in the most terrible disorder—

TIF. Mr. Snobson is not particular—he must be admitted.

(*Enter* ZEKE.)

ZEKE. Mr. Snobson.

(*Enter* SNOBSON, *exit* ZEKE.)

SNOBSON. How dye do, Marm? (*Crosses.*) How are you? Mr. Tiffany, your most!—

MRS. TIF. (*Formally.*) *Bung jure. Comment vow portè vow, Monsur Snobson?*

SNOB. Oh, to be sure—very good of you—fine day.

MRS. TIF. (*Pointing to a chair with great dignity.*) *Sassoyez vow,* Monsur Snobson.

SNOB. I wonder what she 's driving at? I ain't up to the fashionable lingo yet! (*Aside.*) Eh? what? Speak a little louder, Marm?

MRS. TIF. What ignorance! (*Aside.*)

TIF. I presume Mrs. Tiffany means that you are to take a seat.

SNOB. Ex-actly—very obliging of her—so I will. (*Sits.*) No ceremony amongst friends, you know—and likely to be nearer—you understand? *O. K.*, all correct. How *is* Seraphina?

MRS. TIF. Miss Tiffany is not visible this morning. (*Retires up.*)

SNOB. Not visible? (*Jumping up.*) I suppose that 's the English for can't see her? Mr. Tiffany, Sir—(*walking up to him*) what am I to understand by this *de-fal-ca-tion,* Sir? I expected your word to be as good as your bond—beg pardon, Sir—I mean *better*—considerably better—no humbug about it, Sir.

TIF. Have patience, Mr. Snobson. (*Rings bell.*)

(*Enter* ZEKE.)

Zeke, desire my daughter to come here.

MRS. TIF. (*Coming down.*) Adolph—I say, Adolph—

(ZEKE *straightens himself and assumes*

foppish airs, as he turns to MRS. TIFFANY.)

TIF. Zeke.

ZEKE. Don't know any such nigga, Boss.

TIF. Do as I bid you instantly, or off with your livery and quit the house!

ZEKE. Wheugh! I 'se all dismission! (*Exit.*)

MRS. TIF. A-dolph, A-dolph! (*Calling after him.*)

SNOB. I brought the old boy to his bearings, did n't I though! Pull that string, and he is sure to work right. (*Aside.*) Don't make any stranger of me, Marm—I 'm quite at home. If you 've got any odd jobs about the house to do up, I sha'n't miss you. I 'll amuse myself with Seraphina when she comes—we 'll get along very cosily by ourselves.

MRS. TIF. Permit me to inform you, Mr. Snobson, that a French mother never leaves her daughter alone with a young man—she knows your sex too well for that!

SNOB. Very *dis*-obliging of her—but as we 're none French—

MRS. TIF. You have yet to learn, Mr. Snobson, that the American *ee-light*—the aristocracy—the *how-ton*—as a matter of conscience, scrupulously follow the foreign fashions.

SNOB. Not when they are foreign to their interests, Marm—for instance—(*enter* SERAPHINA). There you are at last, eh, Miss? How d' ye do? Ma said you were n't visible. Managed to get a peep at her, eh, Mr. Tiffany?

SERA. I heard you were here, Mr. Snobson, and came without even arranging my toilette; you will excuse my negligence?

SNOB. Of everything but *me*, Miss.

SERA. I shall never have to ask your pardon for *that*, Mr. Snobson.

MRS. TIF. Seraphina—child—really—

(*As she is approaching* SERAPHINA, MR. TIFFANY *plants himself in front of his wife.*)

TIF. Walk this way, Madam, if you please. To see that she fancies the surly fellow takes a weight from my heart. (*Aside.*)

MRS. TIF. Mr. Tiffany, it is highly improper and not at all *distingué* to leave a young girl—

(*Enter* ZEKE.)

ZEKE. Mr. Count Jolly-made-her!

MRS. TIF. Good gracious! The Count—Oh, dear!—Seraphina, run and change your dress,—no there 's not time! A-dolph, admit him. (*Exit* ZEKE.) Mr. Snobson, get out of the way, will you? Mr. Tiffany, what are you doing at home at this hour?

(*Enter* COUNT JOLIMAITRE, *ushered by* ZEKE.)

ZEKE. Dat 's de genuine article ob a gemman. (*Aside.*) (*Exit.*)

MRS. TIF. My dear Count, I am overjoyed at the very sight of you.

COUNT. Flattered myself you 'd be glad to see me, Madam—knew it was not your *jour de reception.*

MRS. TIF. But for you, Count, all days—

COUNT. I thought so. Ah, Miss Tiffany, on my honor, you 're looking beautiful. (*Crosses.*)

SERA. Count, flattery from you—

SNOB. What? Eh? What 's that you say?

SERA. Nothing but what etiquette requires. (*Aside to him.*)

COUNT. (*Regarding* MR. TIFFANY *through his eye glass.*) Your worthy Papa, I believe? Sir, your most obedient.

(MR. TIFFANY *bows coldly;* COUNT *regards* SNOBSON *through his glass, shrugs his shoulders and turns away.*)

SNOB. (*To* MRS. TIFFANY.) Introduce me, will you? I never knew a Count in all my life—what a strange-looking animal!

MRS. TIF. Mr. Snobson, it is not the fashion to introduce in France!

SNOB. But, Marm, we 're in America. (MRS. T. *crosses to* COUNT.) The woman thinks she 's somewhere else than where she is—she wants to make an *alibi?* (*Aside.*)

MRS. TIF. I hope that we shall have the pleasure of seeing you on Friday evening, Count?

COUNT. Really, madam, my invitations—my engagements—so numerous—I can hardly answer for myself: and you Americans take offence so easily—

MRS. TIF. But, Count, everybody expects you at our ball—you are the principal attraction—

SERA. Count, you *must* come!

COUNT. Since you insist—aw—aw—there 's no resisting you, Miss Tiffany.

MRS. TIF. I am so thankful. How can I repay your condescension! (COUNT *and* SERAPHINA *converse.*) Mr. Snobson, will you walk this way?—I have *such* a cactus in full bloom—remarkable flower! Mr. Tiffany, pray come here—I have something particular to say.

TIF. Then speak out, my dear—I thought it was highly improper just now to leave a girl with a young man? (*Aside to her.*)

MRS. TIF. Oh, but the Count—that is different!

TIF. I suppose you mean to say there 's nothing of *the man* about him?

(*Enter* MILLINETTE *with a scarf in her hand.*)

MIL. Adolph tell me he vas here. (*Aside.*) Pardon, Madame, I bring dis scarf for Mademoiselle.

MRS. TIF. Very well, Millinette; you know best what is proper for her to wear.

(MR. *and* MRS. TIFFANY *and* SNOBSON *retire up; she engages the attention of both gentlemen.*)

(MILLINETTE *crosses towards* SERAPHINA, *gives the* COUNT *a threatening look, and commences arranging the scarf over* SERAPHINA'S *shoulders.*)

MIL. Mademoiselle, *permettez-moi. Perfide!* (*Aside to* COUNT.) If Mademoiselle vil stand *tranquille* one *petit moment.* (*Turns* SERAPHINA'S *back to the* COUNT, *and pretends to arrange the scarf.*) I must speak vid you to-day, or I tell all—you find me at de foot of de stair ven you go. *Prends garde!* (*Aside to* COUNT.)

SERA. What is that you say, Millinette?

MIL. Dis scarf make you so very beautiful, Mademoiselle—*Je vous salue, mes dames.* (*Curtsies.*) (*Exit.*)

COUNT. Not a moment to lose! (*Aside.*) Miss Tiffany, I have an unpleasant—a particularly unpleasant piece of intelligence—you see, I have just received a letter from my friend—the—aw—the Earl of Airshire; the truth is, the Earl's daughter—beg you won't mention it—has distinguished me by a tender *penchant.*

SERA. I understand—and they wish you to return and marry the young lady; but surely you will not leave us, Count?

COUNT. If *you* bid me stay—I should n't have the conscience—I could n't *afford* to tear myself away. I 'm sure that 's honest. (*Aside.*)

SERA. Oh, Count!

COUNT. Say but one word—say that you should n't mind being made a Countess—and I 'll break with the Earl to-morrow.

SERA. Count, this surprise—but don't think of leaving the country, Count—we could not pass the time without you! I—yes—yes, Count—I do consent!

COUNT. I thought she would! (*Aside, while he embraces her.*) Enchanted, rapture, bliss, ecstacy, and all that sort of thing—words can't express it, but you understand. But it must be kept a secret—postively it *must!* If the rumour of our engagement were whispered abroad—the Earl's daughter—the delicacy of my situation, aw—you comprehend? It is even possible that our nuptials, my charming Miss Tiffany, *our nuptials* must take place in private!

SERA. Oh, that is quite impossible!

COUNT. It 's the latest fashion abroad—the very latest. Ah, I knew that would determine you. Can I depend on your secrecy?

SERA. Oh, yes! Believe me.

SNOB. (*Coming forward in spite of* MRS. TIFFANY'S *efforts to detain him.*) Why, Seraphina, hav[e] n't you a word to throw to a dog?

TIF. I should n't think she had after wasting so many upon a puppy. (*Aside.*)

(*Enter* ZEKE, *wearing a three-cornered hat.*)

ZEKE. Missus, de bran new carriage am below.

MRS. TIF. Show it up,—I mean, Very well, A-dolph. (*Exit* ZEKE.) Count, my daughter and I are about to take an airing in our new *voyture,*—will you honor us with your company?

COUNT. Madam, I—I have a most *pressing* engagement. A letter to write to the *Earl of Airshire*—who is at present residing in the *Isle of Skye.* I must bid you good morning.

MRS. TIF. Good morning, Count. (*Exit* COUNT.)

SNOB. *I 'm* quite at leisure, (*crosses to* MRS. T.) Marm. Books balanced—ledger closed—nothing to do all the afternoon,—I 'm for you.

MRS. TIF. (*Without noticing him.*) Come, Seraphina, come!

(*As they are going* SNOBSON *follows them.*)

SNOB. But, Marm—I was saying, Marm, I am quite at leisure—not a thing to do; have I, Mr. Tiffany?

MRS. TIF. Seraphina, child—your red

shawl—remember—Mr. Snobson, *bon swear!*

(*Exit, leading* SERAPHINA.)

SNOB. Swear! Mr. Tiffany, Sir, am I to be fobbed off with a *bon swear?* D—n it, I will swear!

TIF. Have patience, Mr. Snobson, if you will accompany me to the counting house—

SNOB. Don't count too much on me, Sir. I'll make up no more accounts until these are settled! I'll run down and jump into the carriage in spite of her *bon swear.* (*Exit.*)

TIF. You'll jump into a hornet's nest, if you do! Mr. Snobson, Mr. Snobson! (*Exit after him.*)

SCENE 2. *Housekeeper's room.*

(*Enter* MILLINETTE.)

MIL. I have set dat bête, Adolph, to vatch for him. He say he would come back so soon as Madame's voiture drive from de door. If he not come—but he vill—he vill—he *bien etourdi,* but he have *bon cœur.*

(*Enter* COUNT.)

COUNT. Ah! Millinette, my dear, you see what a good-natured dog I am to fly at your bidding—

MIL. Fly? Ah! *trompeur!* Vat for you fly from Paris? Vat for you leave me—and I love you so much? Ven you sick—you almost die—did I not stay by you—take care of you—and you have no else friend? Vat for you leave Paris?

COUNT. Never allude to disagreeable subjects, *mon enfant!* I was forced by uncontrollable circumstances to fly to the land of liberty—

MIL. Vat you do vid all de money I give you? The last sou I had—did I not give you?

COUNT. I dare say you did, ma petite—wish you'd been better supplied! (*Aside.*) Don't ask any questions here—can't explain now—the next time we meet—

MIL. But, ah! ven shall ve meet—ven? You not deceive me, not any more.

COUNT. Deceive you! I'd rather deceive myself—I wish I could! I'd persuade myself you were once more washing linen in the Seine! (*Aside.*)

MIL. I vil tell you ven ve shall meet—On Friday night Madame give one grand ball—you come *sans doute*—den ven de supper is served—de Americans tink of noting else ven de supper come—den you steal out of de room, and you find me here—and you give me one grand *explanation!*

(*Enter* GERTRUDE, *unperceived.*)

COUNT. Friday night—while supper is serving—*parole d'honneur* I will be here—I will explain every thing—my sudden departure from Paris—my—demme, my countship—every thing! Now let me go—if any of the family should discover us—

GER. (*Who during the last speech has gradually advanced.*) They might discover more than you think it advisable for them to know!

COUNT. The devil!

MIL. *Mon Dieu!* Mademoiselle Gertrude!

COUNT. (*Recovering himself.*) My dear Miss Gertrude, let me explain—aw—aw—nothing is more natural than the situation in which you find me—

GER. I am inclined to believe that, Sir.

COUNT. Now—'pon my honor, that's not fair. Here is Millinette will bear witness to what I am about to say—

GER. Oh, I have not the slightest doubt of that, Sir.

COUNT. You see, Millinette happened to be lady's-maid in the family of—of—the Duchess Chateau D'Espagne—and I chanced to be a particular friend of the Duchess—*very particular* I assure you! Of course I saw Millinette, and she, demme, she saw me! Did n't you, Millinette?

MIL. Oh! *oui*—Mademoiselle, I knew him ver vell.

COUNT. Well, it is a remarkable fact that—being in correspondence with this very Duchess—at this very time—

GER. That is sufficient, Sir—I am already so well acquainted with your extraordinary talents for improvisation, that I will not further tax your invention—

MIL. Ah! Mademoiselle Gertrude do not betray us—have pity!

COUNT. (*Assuming an air of dignity.*) Silence, Millinette! My word has been doubted—the word of a nobleman! I will inform my friend, Mrs. Tiffany, of this young person's audacity. (*Going.*)

GER. His own weapons alone can foil this villain! (*Aside.*) Sir—Sir—Count! (*At the last word the* COUNT *turns.*)

Perhaps, Sir, the least said about this matter the better!

COUNT. (*Delightedly.*) The least said? We won't say anything at all. She's coming round—could n't resist me. (*Aside.*) Charming Gertrude—

MIL. *Quoi?* Vat that you say?

COUNT. My sweet, adorable Millinette, hold your tongue, will you? (*Aside to her.*)

MIL. (*Aloud.*) No, I vill not! If you do look so from out your eyes at her again, I vill tell all!

COUNT. Oh, I never could manage two women at once,—jealousy makes the dear creatures so spiteful. The only valor is in flight! (*Aside.*) Miss Gertrude, I wish you good morning. Millinette, *mon enfant,* adieu. (*Exit.*)

MIL. But I have one word more to say. Stop, Stop! (*Exit after him.*)

GER. (*Musingly.*) Friday night, while supper is serving, he is to meet Millinette here and explain—what? This man is an impostor! His insulting me—his familiarity with Millinette—his whole conduct—prove it. If I tell Mrs. Tiffany this she will disbelieve me, and one word may place this so-called Count on his guard. To convince Seraphina would be equally difficult, and her rashness and infatuation may render her miserable for life. No—she shall be saved! I must devise some plan for opening their eyes. Truly, if I *cannot* invent one, I shall be the first woman who was ever at a loss for a stratagem—especially to punish a villain or to shield a friend. (*Exit.*)

END OF ACT THIRD.

ACT FOURTH.

SCENE 1. *Ball room splendidly illuminated. A curtain hung at the further end.* MR. *and* MRS. TIFFANY, SERAPHINA, GERTRUDE, FOGG, TWINKLE, COUNT, SNOBSON, COLONEL HOWARD, *a number of guests—some seated, some standing. As the curtain rises, a cotillion is danced;* GERTRUDE *dancing with* HOWARD, SERAPHINA *with* COUNT.

COUNT. (*Advancing with* SERAPHINA *to the front of the stage.*) To-morrow then —to-morrow—I may salute you as my bride—demme, my Countess!

(*Enter* ZEKE, *with refreshments.*)

SERA. Yes, to-morrow.

(*As the* COUNT *is about to reply,* SNOBSON *thrusts himself in front of* SERAPHINA.)

SNOB. You said you'd dance with me, Miss—now take my fin, and we'll walk about and see what's going on.

(COUNT *raises his eye-glass, regards* SNOBSON, *and leads* SERAPHINA *away;* SNOBSON *follows, endeavoring to attract her attention, but encountering* ZEKE, *bearing a waiter of refreshments; stops him, helps himself, and puts some in his pockets.*)

Here's the treat! get my to-morrow's luncheon out of Tiff.

(*Enter* TRUEMAN, *yawning and rubbing his eyes.*)

TRUE. What a nap I've had, to be sure! (*Looks at his watch.*) Eleven o'clock, as I'm alive! Just the time when country folks are comfortably *turned in,* and here your grand *turn-out* has hardly begun yet. (*To* TIFFANY, *who approaches.*)

GER. (*Advancing.*) I was just coming to look for you, Mr. Trueman. I began to fancy that you were paying a visit to dream-land.

TRUE. So I was, child—so I was—and I saw a face—like yours—but brighter!—even brighter. (*To* TIFFANY.) There's a smile for you, man! It makes one feel that the world has something worth living for in it yet! Do you remember a smile like that, Antony? Ah! I see you don't—but I do—I do! (*Much moved.*)

HOW. (*Advancing.*) Good evening, Mr. Trueman. (*Offers his hand.*)

TRUE. That's right, man; give me your whole hand! When a man offers me the tips of his fingers, I know at once there's nothing in him worth seeking beyond his fingers ends.

(TRUEMAN *and* HOWARD, GERTRUDE *and* TIFFANY *converse.*)

MRS. TIF. (*Advancing.*) I'm in such a fidget lest that vulgar old fellow should disgrace us by some of his plebeian remarks! What it is to give a ball, when one is forced to invite vulgar people!

(MRS. TIFFANY *advances towards* TRUEMAN; SERAPHINA *stands conversing flippantly with the gentlemen who surround her; amongst them is* TWINKLE, *who having taken a magazine from his pocket, is reading to her, much to the undisguised annoyance of* SNOBSON.)

Dear me, Mr. Trueman, you are very late—quite in the fashion, I declare!

TRUE. Fashion! And pray what is *fashion,* madam? An agreement between certain persons to live without using their souls! to substitute etiquette for virtue—decorum for purity—manners for morals! to affect a shame for the works of their Creator! and expend all their rapture upon the works of their tailors and dressmakers!

MRS. TIF. You have the most *ow-tray* ideas, Mr. Trueman—quite rustic, and deplorably *American!* But pray walk this way.

(MRS. TIFFANY *and* TRUEMAN *go up.*)

COUNT. (*Advancing to* GERTRUDE, HOWARD *a short distance behind her.*) Miss Gertrude—no opportunity of speaking to you before—in demand you know!

GER. I have no choice, I must be civil to him. (*Aside.*) What were you remarking, Sir?

COUNT. Miss Gertrude—charming Ger—aw—aw—I never found it so difficult to speak to a woman before. (*Aside.*)

GER. Yes, a very charming ball—many beautiful faces here.

COUNT. Only one!—aw—aw—one—the fact is—

(*Talks to her in dumb show.*)

HOW. What could old Trueman have meant by saying she fancied that puppy of a Count—that paste jewel thrust upon the little finger of society.

COUNT. Miss Gertrude—aw—'pon my honor—you don't understand—really—aw—aw—will you dance the polka with me?

(GERTRUDE *bows and gives him her hand; he leads her to the set forming;* HOWARD *remains looking after them.*)

HOW. Going to dance with him too! A few days ago she would hardly bow to him civilly—could old Trueman have had reasons for what he said? (*Retires up.*)

(*Dance, the polka;* SERAPHINA, *after having distributed her bouquet, vinaigrette and fan amongst the gentlemen, dances with* SNOBSON.)

PRU. (*Peeping in as dance concludes.*) I don't like dancing on Friday; something strange is always sure to happen! I'll be on the look out.

(*Remains peeping and concealing herself when any of the company approach.*)

GER. (*Advancing hastily.*) They are preparing the supper—now if I can only dispose of Millinette while I unmask this insolent pretender! (*Exit.*)

PRU. (*Peeping.*) What 's that she said? It 's coming!

(*Re-enter* GERTRUDE, *bearing a small basket filled with bouquets; approaches* MRS. TIFFANY; *they walk to the front of the stage.*)

GER. Excuse me, Madam—I believe this is just the hour at which you ordered supper?

MRS. TIF. Well, what 's that to you! So you 've been dancing with the Count—how dare you dance with a nobleman—*you?*

GER. I will answer that question half an hour hence. At present I have something to propose, which I think will gratify you and please your guests. I have heard that at the most elegant balls in Paris, it is customary—

MRS. TIF. What? what?

GER. To station a servant at the door with a basket of flowers. A bouquet is then presented to every lady as she passes in—I prepared this basket a short time ago. As the company walk in to supper, might not the flowers be distributed to advantage?

MRS. TIF. How *distingué!* You are a good creature, Gertrude—there, run and hand the *bokettes* to them yourself! You shall have the whole credit of the thing.

GER. Caught in my own net! (*Aside.*) But, Madam, *I* know so little of fashions—Millinette, being French herself, will do it with so much more grace. I am sure Millinette—

MRS. TIF. So am I. She will do it a thousand times better than you—there go call her.

GER. (*Giving basket.*) But, Madam, pray order Millinette not to leave her station till supper is ended—as the company pass out of the supper room she may find that some of the ladies have been overlooked.

MRS. TIF. That is true very thoughtful of you, Gertrude. (*Exit* GERTRUDE.) What a *recherché* idea!

(*Enter* MILLINETTE.)

Here, Millinette, take this basket. Place yourself there, and distribute these *bo-*

kettes as the company pass in to supper; but remember not to stir from the spot until supper is over. It is a French fashion you know, Millinette. I am so delighted to be the first to introduce it—it will be all the rage in the *bow-monde!*

MIL. Mon Dieu! dis vill ruin all! (*Aside.*) Madame, Madame, let me tell you, Madame, dat in France, in Paris, it is de custom to present *les* bouquets ven every body first come—long before de supper. Dis vould be *outré! barbare!* not at all la mode! Ven dey do come in—dat is de fashion in Paris!

MRS. TIF. Dear me! Millinette, what is the difference? besides I'd have you to know that Americans always improve upon French fashions! here, take the basket, and let me see that you do it in the most *you-nick* and genteel manner.

(MILLINETTE *poutingly takes the basket and retires up stage.* A MARCH. *Curtain hung at the further end of the room is drawn back, and discloses a room, in the centre of which stands a supper table, beautifully decorated and illuminated; the company promenade two by two into the supper room;* MILLINETTE *presents bouquets as they pass;* COUNT *leads* MRS. TIFFANY.)

TRUE. (*Encountering* FOGG, *who is hurrying alone to the supper room.*) Mr. Fogg, never mind the supper, man! Ha, ha, ha! Of course you are indifferent to suppers!

FOGG. Indifferent! suppers—oh, ah—no, Sir—suppers? no—no—I'm not indifferent to suppers!

(*Hurries away towards table.*)

TRUE. Ha, ha, ha! Here's a new discovery I've made in the fashionable world! Fashion don't permit the critters to have *heads* or *hearts,* but it allows them stomachs! (*To* TIFFANY, *who advances.*) So it's not fashionable to *feel,* but it's fashionable to *feed,* eh, Antony? ha, ha, ha!

(TRUEMAN *and* TIFFANY *retire towards supper room. Enter* GERTRUDE, *followed by* ZEKE.)

GER. Zeke, go to the supper room instantly,—whisper to Count Jolimaitre that all is ready, and that he must keep his appointment without delay,—then watch him, and as he passes out of the room, place yourself in front of Millinette in such a manner, that the Count cannot see her nor she him. Be sure that they do not see each other—every thing depends upon that. (*Crosses.*)

ZEKE. Missey, consider dat business brought to a scientific conclusion.

(*Exit into supper room. Exit* GERTRUDE.)

PRU. (*Who has been listening.*) What can she want of the Count? I always suspected that Gertrude, because she is so merry and busy! Mr. Trueman thinks so much of her too—I'll tell him this! There's something wrong—but it all comes of giving a ball on a Friday! How astonished the dear old man will be when he finds out how much I know!

(*Advances timidly towards the supper room.*)

SCENE 2. *Housekeeper's room; dark stage; table, two chairs.*

(*Enter* GERTRUDE, *with a lighted candle in her hand.*)

GER. So far the scheme prospers! and yet this imprudence—if I fail? Fail! to lack courage in a difficulty, or ingenuity in a dilemma, are not woman's failings!

(*Enter* ZEKE, *with a napkin over his arm, and a bottle of champagne in his hand.*)

Well, Zeke—Adolph!

ZEKE. Dat's right, Missey; I feels just now as if dat was my legitimate title; dis here's de stuff to make a nigger feel like a gemman!

GER. But he is coming?

ZEKE. He's coming! (*Sound of a champagne cork heard.*) Do you hear dat, Missey? Don't it put you all in a froth, and make you feel as light as a cork? Dere's nothing like the *union brand,* to wake up de harmonies ob de heart.

(*Drinks from bottle.*)

GER. Remember to keep watch upon the outside—do not stir from the spot; when I call you, come in quickly with a light—now, will you be gone!

ZEKE. I'm off, Missey, like a champagne cork wid de strings cut. (*Exit.*)

GER. I think I hear the Count's step. (*Crosses, stage dark; she blows out candle.*) Now if I can but disguise my voice, and make the best of my French.

(*Enter* COUNT.)

COUNT. Millinette, where are you? How am I to see you in the dark?

GER. (*Imitating* MILLINETTE'S *voice in a whisper.*) Hush! *parle bas.*

COUNT. Come here and give me a kiss.

GER. Non—non—(*retreating alarmed,* COUNT *follows*) make haste, I must know all.

COUNT. You did not use to be so deuced particular.

ZEKE. (*Without.*) No admission, gemman! Box office closed, tickets stopped!

TRUE. (*Without.*) Out of my way; do you want me to try if your head is as hard as my stick?

GER. What shall I do? Ruined, ruined!

(*She stands with her hands clasped in speechless despair.*)

COUNT. Halloa! they are coming here, Millinette! Millinette, why don't you speak? Where can I hide myself? (*Running about stage, feeling for a door.*) Where are all your closets? If I could only get out—or get in somewhere; may I be smothered in a clothes' basket, if you ever catch me in such a scrape again! (*His hand accidentally touches the knob of a door opening into a closet.*) Fortune's favorite yet! I'm safe!

(*Gets into closet and closes door. Enter* PRUDENCE, TRUEMAN, MRS. TIFFANY, *and* COLONEL HOWARD, *followed by* ZEKE, *bearing a light; lights up.*)

PRU. Here they are, the Count and Gertrude! I told you so!

(*Stops in surprise on seeing only* GERTRUDE.)

TRUE. And you see what a lie you told!

MRS. TIF. Prudence, how dare you create this disturbance in my house? To suspect the Count too—a nobleman!

HOW. My sweet Gertrude, this foolish old woman would—

PRU. Oh! you need n't talk—I heard her make the appointment—I know he 's here—or he 's been here. I wonder if she has n't hid him away!

(*Runs peeping about the room.*)

TRUE. (*Following her angrily.*) You 're what I call a confounded—troublesome —meddling—old—prying—(*as he says the last word,* PRUDENCE *opens closet where the* COUNT *is concealed.*) Thunder and lightning!

PRU. I told you so!

(*They all stand aghast;* MRS. TIFFANY, *with her hands lifted in surprise and anger;* TRUEMAN, *clutching his stick;* HOWARD, *looking with an expression of bewildered horror from the* COUNT *to* GERTRUDE.)

MRS. TIF. (*Shaking her fist at* GERTRUDE.) You depraved little minx! this is the meaning of your dancing with the Count!

COUNT. (*Stepping from the closet and advancing.*) I don't know what to make of it! Millinette not here! Miss Gertrude—oh! I see— a disguise—the girl 's desperate about me—the way with them all. (*Aside.*)

TRUE. I 'm choking—I can't speak—Gertrude—no—no—it is some horrid mistake! (*Partly aside, changes his tone suddenly.*) The villain! I 'll hunt the truth out of him, if there 's any in—(*crosses, approaches* COUNT *threateningly*) do you see this stick? You made its first acquaintance a few days ago; it is time you were better known to each other.

(*As* TRUEMAN *attempts to seize him,* COUNT *escapes, and shields himself behind* MRS. TIFFANY, TRUEMAN *following.*)

COUNT. You ruffian! would you strike a woman?—Madam—my dear Madam—keep off that barbarous old man, and I will explain! Madam, with—aw—your natural *bon gout*—aw—your fashionable refinement—aw—your—aw—your knowledge of *foreign customs*—

MRS. TIF. Oh! Count, I hope it ain't a *foreign custom* for the nobility to shut themselves up in the dark with young women? We think such things *dreadful* in *America.*

COUNT. Demme—aw—hear what I have to say, Madam—I 'll satisfy all sides—I am perfectly innocent in this affair—'pon my honor I am! That young lady shall inform you that I am so herself!—can't help it, sorry for her. Old matter-of-fact won't be convinced any other way,—that club of his is so particularly unpleasant! (*Aside.*) Madam, I was summoned here *malgré moi,* and not knowing whom I was to meet—Miss Gertrude, favor the company by saying whether or not you directed—that—aw —aw—that colored individual to conduct me here?

GER. Sir, you well know—

COUNT. A simple yes or no will suffice.

MRS. TIF. Answer the Count's question instantly, Miss.

GER. I did—but—

COUNT. You hear, Madam—

TRUE. I won't believe it—I can't! Here, you nigger, stop rolling up your eyes, and let us know whether she told you to bring that critter here?

ZEKE. I 'se refuse to gib ebidence; dat 's de device ob de skilfullest counsels ob de day! Can't answer, Boss—neber git a word out ob dis child—Yah! yah! (*Exit.*)

GER. Mrs. Tiffany,—Mr. Trueman, if you will but have patience—

TRUE. Patience! Oh, Gertrude, you 've taken from an old man something better and dearer than his patience—the one bright hope of nineteen years of self-denial—of nineteen years of—

(*Throws himself upon a chair, his head leaning on table.*)

MRS. TIF. Get out of my house, you *owdacious*—you ruined—you *abîmé* young woman! You will corrupt all my family. Good gracious! don't touch me,—don't come near me. Never let me see your face after to-morrow. Pack. (*Goes up.*)

HOW. Gertrude, I have striven to find some excuse for you—to doubt—to disbelieve—but this is beyond all endurance! (*Exit.*)

(*Enter* MILLINETTE *in haste.*)

MIL. I could not come before— (*Stops in surprise at seeing the persons assembled.*) Mon Dieu! vat does dis mean?

COUNT. Hold your tongue, fool! You will ruin everything, I will explain to-morrow. (*Aside to her.*) Mrs. Tiffany—Madam—my dear Madam, let me conduct you back to the ball-room. (*She takes his arm.*) You see I am quite innocent in this matter; a man of my standing, you know,—aw, aw—you comprehend the whole affair.

(*Exit* COUNT *leading* MRS. TIFFANY.)

MIL. I will say to him von vord, I will! (*Exit.*)

GER. Mr. Trueman, I beseech you—I insist upon being heard,—I claim it as a right!

TRUE. Right? How dare you have the face, girl, to talk of rights? (*Comes down.*) You had more rights than you thought for, but you have forfeited them all! All right to love, respect, protection, and to not a little else that you don't dream of. Go, go! I'll start for Catteraugus to-morrow,—I 've seen enough of what fashion can do! (*Exit.*)

PRU. (*Wiping her eyes.*) Dear old man, how he takes on! I 'll go and console him! (*Exit.*)

GER. This is too much! How heavy a penalty has my imprudence cost me!—his esteem, and that of one dearer—my home—my— (*Burst of lively music from ball-room.*) They are dancing, and I—I should be weeping, if pride had not sealed up my tears.

(*She sinks into a chair. Band plays the polka behind till Curtain falls.*)

END OF ACT FOURTH.

ACT FIFTH.

SCENE 1. MRS. TIFFANY'S *Drawing Room—same Scene as Act First.* GERTRUDE *seated at a table, with her head leaning on her hand; in the other hand she holds a pen. A sheet of paper and an ink-stand before her.*

GER. How shall I write to them? What shall I say? Prevaricate I cannot—(*rises and comes forward*) and yet if I write the truth—simple souls! how can they comprehend the motives for my conduct? Nay—the truly pure see no imaginary evil in others! It is only vice, that reflecting its own image, suspects even the innocent. I have no time to lose—I must prepare them for my return. (*Resumes her seat and writes.*) What a true pleasure there is in daring to be frank! (*After writing a few lines more pauses.*) Not so frank either,—there is one name that I cannot mention. Ah! that he should suspect—should despise me. (*Writes.*)

(*Enter* TRUEMAN.)

TRUE. There she is! If this girl's soul had only been as fair as her face,—yet she dared to speak the truth,—I 'll not forget that! A woman who refuses to tell a lie has one spark of heaven in her still. (*Approaches her.*) Gertrude,

(GERTRUDE *starts and looks up.*)

what are you writing there? Plotting more mischief, eh, girl?

GER. I was writing a few lines to some friends in Geneva.

TRUE. The Wilsons, eh?

GER. (*Surprised, rising.*) Are you acquainted with them, Sir?

TRUE. I should n't wonder if I was. I

suppose you have taken good care not to mention the dark room—that foreign puppy in the closet—the pleasant surprise—and all that sort of thing, eh?

GER. I have no reason for concealment, Sir! for I have done nothing of which I am ashamed!

TRUE. Then I can't say much for your modesty.

GER. I should not wish you to say more than I deserve.

TRUE. There 's a bold minx! (*Aside.*)

GER. Since my affairs seem to have excited your interest—I will not say *curiosity,* perhaps you even feel a desire to inspect my correspondence? There, (*handing the letter*) I pride myself upon my good nature,—you may like to take advantage of it?

TRUE. With what an air she carries it off! (*Aside.*) Take advantage of it? So I will. (*Reads.*) What 's this? "French chambermaid—Count—impostor—infatuation—Seraphina—Millinette — disguised myself—expose him." Thunder and lightning! I see it all! Come and kiss me, girl! (GERTRUDE *evinces surprise.*) No, no—I forgot—it won't do to come to that yet! She 's a rare girl! I 'm out of my senses with joy! I don't know what to do with myself! Tol, de rol, de rol, de ra. (*Capers and sings.*)

GER. What a remarkable old man! (*Aside.*) Then you do me justice, Mr. Trueman?

TRUE. I say I don't! Justice? You 're above all dependence upon justice! Hurrah! I've found one true woman at last? *True?* (*Pauses thoughtfully.*) Humph! I did n't think of that flaw! Plotting and manœuvering—not much truth in that? An honest girl should be above stratagems!

GER. But my *motive,* Sir, was good.

TRUE. That 's not enough—your *actions* must be *good* as well as your *motives!* Why could you not tell the silly girl that man was an impostor?

GER. I did inform her of my suspicions —she ridiculed them; the plan I chose was an imprudent one, but I could not devise—

TRUE. I hate devising! Give me a woman with the *firmness* to be *frank!* But no matter—I had no right to look for an angel out of Paradise; and I am as happy—as happy as a Lord! that is, ten times happier than any Lord ever was! Tol, de rol, de rol! Oh! you—you—I 'll thrash every fellow that says a word against you!

GER. You will have plenty of employment then, Sir, for I do not know of one just now who would speak in my favor!

TRUE. Not *one,* eh? Why, where 's your dear Mr. Twinkle? I know all about it —can't say that I admire your choice of a husband! But there 's no accounting for a girl's taste.

GER. Mr. Twinkle! Indeed you are quite mistaken!

TRUE. No—really? Then you 're not taken with him, eh?

GER. Not even with his rhymes.

TRUE. Hang that old mother meddlemuch! What a fool she has made of me. And so you 're quite free, and I may choose a husband for you myself? Heart-whole, eh?

GER. I—I—I trust there is nothing *unsound* about my heart.

TRUE. There it is again. Don't prevaricate, girl! I tell you an *evasion* is a *lie in contemplation,* and I hate lying! Out with the truth! Is your heart *free* or not?

GER. Nay, Sir, since you *demand* an answer, permit *me* to demand by what right you ask the question?

(*Enter* HOWARD.)

Colonel Howard here!

TRUE. I 'm out again! What 's the Colonel to her? (*Retires up.*)

HOW. (*Crosses to her.*) I have come, Gertrude, to bid you farewell. To-morrow I resign my commission and leave this city, perhaps for ever. You, Gertrude, it is you who have exiled me! After last evening—

TRUE. (*Coming forward to* HOWARD.) What the plague have you got to say about last evening?

HOW. Mr. Trueman!

TRUE. What have you got to say about last evening? and what have you to say to that little girl at all? It 's Tiffany's precious daughter you 're in love with.

HOW. Miss Tiffany? Never! I never had the slightest pretension—

TRUE. That lying old woman! But I 'm glad of it! Oh! Ah! Um! (*Looking significantly at* GERTRUDE *and then at* HOWARD.) I see how it is. So you don't choose to marry Seraphina, eh? Well now, whom do you choose to marry? (*Glancing at* GERTRUDE.)

HOW. I shall not marry at all!

TRUE. You won't? (*Looking at them both again.*) Why you don't mean to say that you don't like—

(*Points with his thumb to* GERTRUDE.)

GER. Mr. Trueman, I may have been wrong to boast of my good nature, but do not presume too far upon it.

HOW. You like frankness, Mr. Trueman, therefore I will speak plainly. I have long cherished a dream from which I was last night rudely awakened.

TRUE. And that 's what you call speaking plainly? Well, I differ with you! But I can guess what you mean. Last night you suspected Gertrude there of—(*angrily*) of what no man shall ever suspect her again while I 'm above ground! You did her injustice,—it was a mistake! There, now that matter 's settled. Go, and ask her to forgive you,—she 's woman enough to do it! Go, go!

HOW. Mr. Trueman, you have forgotten to whom you dictate.

TRUE. Then you won't do it? you won't ask her pardon?

HOW. Most undoubtedly I will not—not at any man's bidding. I must first know—

TRUE. You won't do it? Then if I don't give you a lesson in politeness—

HOW. It will be because you find me your *tutor* in the same science. I am not a man to brook an insult, Mr. Trueman! but we 'll not quarrel in presence of the lady.

TRUE. Won't we? I don't know that—

GER. Pray, Mr. Trueman—Colonel Howward, pray desist, Mr. Trueman, for my sake! (*Taking hold of his arm to hold him back.*) Colonel Howard, if you will read this letter it will explain everything.

(*Hands letter to* HOWARD, *who reads.*)

TRUE. He don't deserve an explanation! Did n't I tell him that it was a mistake? Refuse to beg your pardon! I 'll teach him, I 'll teach him!

HOW. (*After reading.*) Gertrude, how have I wronged you!

TRUE. Oh, you 'll beg her pardon now? (*Between them.*)

HOW. Hers, Sir, and yours! Gertrude, I fear—

TRUE. You need n't,—she 'll forgive you. You don't know these women as well as I do,—they 're always ready to pardon; it 's their nature, and they can't help it. Come along, I left Antony and his wife in the dining room; we 'll go and find them. I 've a story of my own to tell! As for you, Colonel, you may follow. Come along. Come along!

(*Leads out* GERTRUDE, *followed by* HOWARD.)

(*Enter* MR. *and* MRS. TIFFANY, MR. TIFFANY *with a bundle of bills in his hand.*)

MRS. TIF. I beg you won't mention the subject again, Mr. Tiffany. Nothing is more plebeian than a discussion upon economy—nothing more *ungenteel* than looking over and fretting over one's bills!

TIF. Then I suppose, my dear, it is quite as ungenteel to *pay* one's bills?

MRS. TIF. Certainly! I hear the *ee-light* never condescend to do anything of the kind. The honor of their invaluable patronage is sufficient for the persons they employ!

TIF. *Patronage* then is a newly invented food upon which the working classes fatten? What convenient appetites poor people must have! Now listen to what I am going to say. As soon as my daughter marries Mr. Snobson—

(*Enter* PRUDENCE, *a three-cornered note in her hand.*)

PRU. Oh, dear! oh, dear! what shall we do! Such a misfortune! Such a disaster! Oh, dear! oh, hear!

MRS. TIF. Prudence, you are the most tiresome creature! What *is* the matter?

PRU. (*Pacing up and down the stage.*) Such a disgrace to the whole family! But I always expected it. Oh, dear! oh, dear!

MRS. TIF. (*Following her up and down the stage.*) What are you talking about, Prudence? Will you tell me what has happened?

PRU. (*Still pacing,* MRS. TIFFANY *following.*) Oh! I can't, I can't! You 'll feel so dreadfully! How could she do such a thing! But I expected nothing else! I never did, I never did!

MRS. TIF. (*Still following.*) Good gracious! what do you mean, Prudence? Tell me, will you tell me? I shall get into such a passion! What *is* the matter?

PRU. (*Still pacing.*) Oh, Betsy, Betsy! That your daughter should have come to that! Dear me, dear me!

TIF. Seraphina? Did you say Seraphina? What has happened to her? what has she done?

(*Following* PRUDENCE *up and down the stage on the opposite side from* MRS. TIFFANY.)

MRS. TIF. (*Still following.*) What *has* she done? what *has* she done?

PRU. Oh! something dreadful—dreadful—shocking!

TIF. (*Still following.*) Speak quickly and plainly—you torture me by this delay,—Prudence, be calm, and speak! What is it?

PRU. (*Stopping.*) Zeke just told me—he carried her travelling trunk himself—she gave him a whole dollar! Oh, my!

TIF. Her trunk? where? where?

PRU. Round the corner!

MRS. TIF. What did she want with her trunk? You are the most vexatious creature, Prudence! There is no bearing your ridiculous conduct!

PRU. Oh, you will have worse to bear—worse! Seraphina 's gone!

TIF. Gone! where?

PRU. Off!—eloped—eloped with the Count! Dear me, dear me! I always told you she would!

TIF. Then I am ruined!

(*Stands with his face buried in his hands.*)

MRS. TIF. Oh, what a ridiculous girl! And she might have had such a splendid wedding! What could have possessed her?

TIF. The devil himself possessed her, for she has ruined me past all redemption! Gone, Prudence, did you say gone? Are you *sure* they are gone?

PRU. Did n't I tell you so! Just look at this note—one might know by the very fold of it—

TIF. (*Snatching the note.*) Let me see it! (*Opens the note and reads.*) "My dear Ma,—When you receive this I shall be a *countess!* Is n't it a sweet title? The Count and I were forced to be married privately, for reasons which I will explain in my next. You must pacify Pa, and put him in a good humour before I come back, though now I 'm to be a countess I suppose I should n't care!" Undutiful huzzy! "We are going to make a little excursion and will be back in a week

"Your dutiful daughter Seraphina."

A man's curse is sure to spring up at his own hearth,—here is mine! The sole curb upon that villain gone, I am wholly in his power! Oh! the first downward step from honor—he who takes it cannot pause in his mad descent and is sure to be hurried on to ruin!

MRS. TIF. Why, Mr. Tiffany, how you do take on! And I dare say to elope was the most fashionable way after all!

(*Enter* TRUEMAN, *leading* GERTRUDE, *and followed by* HOWARD.)

TRUE. Where are all the folks? Here, Antony, you are the man I want. We 've been hunting for you all over the house. Why—what 's the matter? There 's a face for a thriving city merchant! Ah! Antony, you never wore such a hang-dog look as that when you trotted about the country with your pack upon your back! Your shoulders are no broader now—but they 've a heavier load to carry—that 's plain!

MRS. TIF. Mr. Trueman, such allusions are highly improper! What would my daughter, *the Countess*, say!

GER. The Countess? Oh! Madam!

MRS. TIF. Yes, the Countess! My daughter Seraphina, the Countess *dee* Jolimaitre! What have you to say to that? No wonder you are surprised after your *recherché, abimé* conduct! I have told you already, Miss Gertrude, that you were not a proper person to enjoy the inestimable advantages of my patronage. You are dismissed—do you understand? Discharged!

TRUE. Have you done? Very well, it 's my turn now. Antony, perhaps what I have to say don't concern you as much as some others—but I want you to listen to me. You remember, Antony, (*his tone becomes serious*), a blue-eyed, smiling girl—

TIF. Your daughter, Sir? I remember her well.

TRUE. None ever saw her to forget her! Give me your hand, man. There—that will do! Now let me go on. I never coveted wealth—yet twenty years ago I found myself the richest farmer in Catteraugus. This cursed money made my girl an object of speculation. Every idle fellow that wanted to feather his nest was sure to come courting Ruth. There was one—my heart misgave me the instant I laid eyes upon him—for he was a city chap, and not over fond of the truth. But Ruth—ah! she was too pure herself to look for guile! His fine words and his fair looks—the old story—she was taken with him—I said, "no"—but the girl liked her own way better than her old father's—girls always do! and one morning—the rascal robbed me—not of my money, he would have been welcome to that—but of the only treasure I cherished—my daughter!

TIF. But you forgave her!

TRUE. I did! I knew she would never forgive herself—that was punishment enough! The scoundrel thought he was marrying my gold with my daughter—he was mistaken! I took care that they should never want; but that was all. She loved him—what will not woman love? The villain broke her heart—mine was tougher, or it would n't have stood what it did. A year after they were married, he forsook her! She came back to her old home—her old father! It could n't last long—she pined—and pined—and—then—she died! Don't think me an old fool—though I am one—for grieving won't bring her back.

(*Bursts into tears.*)

TIF. It was a heavy loss!

TRUE. So heavy, that I should not have cared how soon I followed her, but for the child she left! As I pressed that child in my arms, I swore that my unlucky wealth should never curse it, as it had cursed its mother! It was all I had to love—but I sent it away—and the neighbors thought it was dead. The girl was brought up tenderly but humbly by my wife's relatives in Geneva. I had her taught true independence—she had hands—capacities—and should use them! Money should never buy her a husband! for I resolved not to claim her until she had made her choice, and found the man who was willing to take her for herself alone. She turned out a rare girl! and it 's time her old grandfather claimed her. Here he is to do it! And there stands Ruth's child! Old Adam's heiress! Gertrude, Gertrude!—my child!

(GERTRUDE *rushes into his arms.*)

PRU. (*After a pause.*) Do tell; I want to know! But I knew it! I always said Gertrude would turn out somebody, after all!

MRS. TIF. Dear me! Gertrude an heiress! My dear Gertrude, I always thought you a very charming girl—quite YOU-NICK—an heiress! I must give her a ball! I 'll introduce her into society myself—of course an heiress must make a sensation! (*Asidz.*)

HOW. I am too bewildered even to wish her joy. Ah! there will be plenty to do that now—but the gulf between us is wider than ever. (*Aside.*)

TRUE. Step forward, young man, and let us know what you are muttering about. I said I would never claim her until she had found the man who loved her for herself. I *have* claimed her—yet I never break my word—I think I *have* found that man! and here he is. (*Strikes* HOWARD *on the shoulder.*) Gertrude 's yours! There—never say a word, man—don't bore me with your thanks—you can cancel all obligations by making that child happy! There—take her!—Well, girl, and what do you say?

GER. That I rejoice too much at having found a parent for my first act to be one of disobedience!

(*Gives her hand to* HOWARD.)

TRUE. How very dutiful! and how disinterested!

(TIFFANY *retires up—and paces the stage, exhibiting great agitation.*)

PRU. (*To* TRUEMAN.) All the *single folks* are getting married!

TRUE. No they are not. You and I are single folks, and we 're not likely to get married.

MRS. TIF. My dear Mr. Trueman—my sweet Gertrude, when my daughter, the Countess, returns, she will be delighted to hear of this *deenooment!* I assure you that the Countess will be quite charmed!

GER. The Countess? Pray, Madam, where *is* Seraphina?

MRS. TIF. The Countess *dee* Jolimaitre, my dear, is at this moment on her way to—to Washington! Where after visiting all the fashionable curiosities of the day—including the President—she will return to grace her native city!

GER. I hope you are only jesting, Madam? Seraphina is not married?

MRS. TIF. Excuse me, my dear, my daughter had this morning the honor of being united to the Count *dee* Jolimaitre!

GER. Madam! He is an impostor!

MRS. TIF. Good gracious! Gertrude, how can you talk in that disrespectful way of a man of rank? An heiress, my dear, should have better manners! The Count—

(*Enter* MILLINETTE, *crying.*)

MIL. Oh! Madame! I will tell everyting—oh! dat monstre! He break my heart!

MRS. TIF. Millinette, what is the matter?

MIL. Oh! he promise to marry me—I love him much—and now Zeke say he run away vid Mademoiselle Seraphina!

MRS. TIF. What insolence! The girl is mad! Count Jolimaitre marry my *femmy de chamber!*

MIL. Oh! Madame, he is not one Count, not at all! Dat is only de title he go by in dis country. De foreigners always take de large title ven dey do come here. His name *à Paris* vas Gustave Treadmill. But he not one Frenchman at all, but he do live one long time *à Paris.* First he live vid Monsieur Vermicelle—dere he vas de head cook! Den he live vid Monsieur Tire-nez, de barber! After dat he live wid Monsieur le Comte Frippon-fin—and dere he vas le Comte's valet! Dere, now I tell everyting I feel one great deal better!

MRS. TIF. Oh! good gracious! I shall faint! Not a Count! What will everybody say? It's no such thing! I say he *is* a Count! One can see the foreign *jenny says quoi* in his face! Don't you think I can tell a Count when I see one? I say he *is* a Count!

(*Enter* SNOBSON, *his hat on—his hands thrust in his pocket—evidently a little intoxicated.*)

SNOB. I won't stand it! I say I won't!

TIF. (*Rushing up to him.*) Mr. Snobson, for heaven's sake— (*Aside.*)

SNOB. Keep off! I'm a hard customer to get the better of! You'll see if I don't come out strong!

TRUE. (*Quietly knocking off* SNOBSON'S *hat with his stick.*) Where are your manners, man?

SNOB. My business ain't with you, Catteraugus; you've waked up the wrong passenger!—Now the way I'll put it into Tiff will be a caution. I'll make him wince! That extra mint julep has put the true pluck in me. Now for it! (*Aside.*) Mr. Tiffany, Sir—you need n't think to come over me, Sir—you'll have to get up a little earlier in the morning before you do *that,* Sir! I'd like to know, Sir, how you came to assist your daughter in running away with that foreign loafer? It was a downright swindle, Sir. After the conversation I and you had on that subject she was n't your property, Sir.

TRUE. What, Antony, is that the way your city clerk bullies his boss?

SNOB. You're drunk, Catteraugus—don't expose your-self—you're drunk! Taken a little too much toddy, my old boy! Be quiet! I'll look after you, and they won't find it out. If you want to be busy, you may take care of my *hat*—I feel so deuced weak in the chest, I don't think I *could* pick it up myself.—Now to put the screws to Tiff. (*Aside.*) Mr. Tiffany, Sir—you have broken your word, as no virtuous individual—no honorable member—of—the—com—mu—ni—ty—

TIF. Have some pity, Mr. Snobson, I beseech you! I had nothing to do with my daughter's elopement! I will agree to anything you desire—your salary shall be doubled—trebled— (*Aside to him.*)

SNOB. (*Aloud.*) No you don't. No bribery and corruption.

TIF. I implore you to be silent. You shall become partner of the concern, if you please—only do not speak. You are not yourself at this moment. (*Aside to him.*)

SNOB. Ain't I, though? I feel *twice* myself. I feel like two Snobsons rolled into one, and I'm chock full of the spunk of a dozen! Now Mr. Tiffany, Sir—

TIF. I shall go distracted! Mr. Snobson, if you have one spark of manly feeling— (*Aside to him.*)

TRUE. Antony, why do you stand disputing with that drunken jackass? Where's your nigger? Let him kick the critter out, and be of use for once in his life.

SNOB. Better be quiet, Catteraugus. This ain't your hash, so keep your spoon out of the dish. Don't expose yourself, old boy.

TRUE. Turn him out, Antony!

SNOB. He dare n't do it! Ain't I up to him? Ain't he in my power? Can't I knock him into a cocked hat with a word? And now he's got my steam up—I *will* do it!

TIF. (*Beseechingly.*) Mr. Snobson—my friend—

SNOB. It's no go—steam's up—and I don't stand at anything!

TRUE. You won't *stand* here long unless you mend your manners—you're not the first man I've *upset* because he did n't know his place.

SNOB. I know where Tiff's place is, and that's in the *States' Prison!* It's bespoke already. He would have it! He would n't take pattern of me, and behave like a gentleman! He 's a *forger,* Sir! (TIFFANY *throws himself into a chair in an attitude of despair; the others stand transfixed with astonishment.*) He 's been forging Dick Anderson's endorsements of his notes these ten months. He 's got a couple in the bank that will send him to the wall anyhow—if he can't make a raise. I took them there myself! Now you know what he 's worth. I said I 'd expose him, and I have done it!

MRS. TIF. Get out of the house! You ugly, little, drunken brute, get out! It 's not true. Mr. Trueman, put him out; you have got a stick—put him out!

(*Enter* SERAPHINA, *in her bonnet and shawl—a parasol in her hand.*)

SERA. I hope Zeke has n't delivered my note.

(*Stops in surprise at seeing the persons assembled.*)

MRS. TIF. Oh, here is the Countess! (*Advances to embrace her.*)

TIF. (*Starting from his seat, and seizing* SERAPHINA *violently by the arm.*) Are —you—married?

SERA. Goodness, Pa, how you frighten me! No, I 'm not married, *quite.*

TIF. Thank heaven.

MRS. TIF. (*Drawing* SERAPHINA *aside.*) What 's the matter? Why did you come back?

SERA. The clergyman was n't at home—I came back for my jewels—the Count said nobility could n't get on without them.

TIF. I may be saved yet! Seraphina, my child, you will not see me disgraced—ruined! I have been a kind father to you—at least I have tried to be one—although your mother's extravagance made a *madman* of me! The Count is an impostor—you seemed to like him—(*pointing to* SNOBSON). Heaven forgive me! (*Aside.*) Marry *him* and save *me.* You, Mr. Trueman, you will be my friend in this hour of extreme need—you will advance the sum which I require—I pledge myself to return it. My wife—my child—who will support them were I—the thought makes me frantic! You will aid me? You had a child yourself.

TRUE. But I did not *sell* her—it was her own doings. Shame on you, Antony! Put a price on your own flesh and blood! Shame on such foul traffic!

TIF. Save me—I conjure you—for my father's sake.

TRUE. For your *father's* SON'S sake I will *not* aid you in becoming a greater villain than you are!

GER. Mr. Trueman—Father, I should say —save him—do not embitter our happiness by permitting this calamity to fall upon another—

TRUE. Enough—I did not need your voice, child. I am going to settle this matter my own way.

(*Goes up to* SNOBSON—*who has seated himself and fallen asleep—tilts him out of the chair.*)

SNOB. (*Waking up.*) Eh? Where 's the fire? Oh! it 's you, Catteraugus.

TRUE. If I comprehend aright, you have been for some time aware of your principal's forgeries?

(*As he says this, he beckons to* HOWARD, *who advances as witness.*)

SNOB. You 've hit the nail, Catteraugus! Old chap saw that I was up to him six months ago; left off throwing dust into my eyes—

TRUE. Oh, he did!

SNOB. Made no bones of forging Anderson's name at my elbow.

TRUE. Forged at your elbow? You saw him do it?

SNOB. I did.

TRUE. Repeatedly.

SNOB. Re—pea—ted—ly.

TRUE. Then you, Rattlesnake, if he goes to the States' Prison, you 'll take up your quarters there too. You are an accomplice, an *accessory!*

(TRUEMAN *walks away and seats himself,* HOWARD *rejoins* GERTRUDE. SNOBSON *stands for some time bewildered.*)

SNOB. The deuce, so I am! I never thought of that! I must make myself scarce. I 'll be off! Tif, I say, Tif! (*Going up to him and speaking confidentially*) that drunken old rip has got us in his power. Let 's give him the slip and be off. They want men of genius at the West,—we 're sure to get on! You—you can set up for a writing master, and teach copying *signatures;* and I—I 'll give lectures on *temperance!* You won't come, eh? Then I 'm off without you. Good bye, Catteraugus! Which is the way to California? (*Steals off.*)

TRUE. There 's one debt your city owes me. And now let us see what other nuisances we can abate. Antony, I 'm not given to preaching, therefore I shall not say much about what you have done. Your face speaks for itself,—the crime has brought its punishment along with it.

TIF. Indeed it has, Sir! In *one year* I have lived a *century* of misery.

TRUE. I believe you, and upon one condition I will assist you—

TIF. My friend—my first, ever kind friend,—only name it!

TRUE. You must sell your house and all these gew gaws, and bundle your wife and daughter off to the country. There let them learn economy, true independence, and home virtues, instead of foreign follies. As for yourself, continue your business—but let moderation, in future, be your counsellor, and let *honesty* be your confidential clerk.

TIF. Mr. Trueman, you have made existence once more precious to me! My wife and daughter shall quit the city tomorrow, and—

PRU. It 's all coming right! It 's all coming right! We 'll go to the county of Catteraugus.

(*Walking up to* TRUEMAN.)

TRUE. No, you won't,—I make that a stipulation, Antony; keep clear of Catteraugus. None of your fashionable examples there!

(JOLIMAITRE *appears in the Conservatory and peeps into the room unperceived.*)

COUNT. What can detain Seraphina? We ought to be off!

MIL. (*Turns round, perceives him, runs and forces him into the room.*) Here he is! Ah, Gustave, mon cher Gustave! I have you now and we never part no more. Don't frown, Gustave, don't frown—

TRUE. Come forward, Mr. Count! and for the edification of fashionable society confess that you 're an impostor.

COUNT. An impostor? Why, you abominable old—

TRUE. Oh, your feminine friend has told us all about it, the cook—the valet—barber and all that sort of thing. Come, confess, and something may be done for you.

COUNT. Well, then, I do confess I am no count; but really, ladies and gentlemen, I may recommend myself as the most capital cook.

MRS. TIF. Oh, Seraphina!

SERA. Oh, Ma!

(*They embrace and retire up.*)

TRUE. Promise me to call upon the whole circle of your fashionable acquaintances with your own advertisements and in your cook's attire, and I will set you up in business to-morrow. Better turn stomachs than turn heads!

MIL. But you will marry me?

COUNT. Give us your hand, Millinette! Sir, command me for the most delicate *paté*—the daintiest *croquette à la royale*—the most transcendent *omelette soufflée* that ever issued from a French pastry-cook's oven. I hope you will pardon my conduct, but I heard that in America, where you pay homage to titles while you profess to scorn them—where *Fashion* makes the basest coin current—where you have no kings, no princes, no *nobility*—

TRUE. Stop there! I object to your use of that word. When justice is found only among lawyers—health among physicians—and patriotism among politicians, *then* may you say that there is no *nobility* where there are no titles! But we *have* kings, princes, and nobles in abundance—of *Nature's stamp,* if not of *Fashion's,*—we have honest men, warm hearted and brave, and we have women—gentle, fair, and true, to whom no *title* could add *nobility.*

EPILOGUE.

PRU. I told you so! And now you hear and see.
I told you *Fashion* would the fashion be!
TRUE. Then both its point and moral I distrust.
COUNT. Sir, is that liberal?
HOW. Or is it just?
TRUE. The guilty have escaped!
TIF. Is, therefore, sin
Made charming? Ah! there 's punishment within!
Guilt ever carries his own scourge along.
GER. Virtue her own reward!
TRUE. You 're right, I 'm wrong.
MRS. TIF. How we have been deceived!
PRU. I told you so.
SERA. To lose at once a title and a beau!
COUNT. A count no more, I 'm no more of *account.*
TRUE. But to a nobler title you may mount,

And be in time—who knows?—an honest man!

COUNT. Eh, Millinette?

MIL. Oh, *oui*—I know you can!

GER. (*To audience.*) But ere we close the scene, a word with you,—
We charge you answer,—Is this picture true?
Some little mercy to our efforts show,
Then let the world your honest verdict know.
Here let it see portrayed its ruling passion,
And learn to prize at its just value—*Fashion.*

FRANCESCA DA RIMINI

BY

George Henry Boker

Reprinted from the original autograph manuscripts through the courtesy of Mrs. George Boker.

FRANCESCA DA RIMINI

Francesca da Rimini marks the climax of romantic tragedy in this country. It illustrates also the tendency to lay the scenes of romantic plays in Italy, Spain, or France; our playwrights feeling apparently that the removal of the scene of such plays from their native land was an essential. With Boker, however, the choice was based on broader lines and was justified by his real understanding of the characters and their story.

George Henry Boker was born in Philadelphia, October 6, 1823, coming from a well established family, and graduating from Princeton College in 1842. He studied law but never practised it, and after marriage and some foreign travel, devoted his entire attention to his literary work. His first publication, *The Lesson of Life and other Poems* (1848), consisted of lyric and ethical verse, and except for the sonnets gave no indication of his later ability. He next published *Calaynos,* his first play, in 1848. This was played without his permission being asked, by Samuel Phelps, at the Sadlers Wells Theatre in London on May 10, 1849, and was successful. It was first performed in this country by James E. Murdoch at the Walnut Street Theatre, Philadelphia, January 20, 1851, running for nine nights, and was several times played in Chicago, Albany, and Baltimore. E. L. Davenport appeared as "Calaynos" at the Walnut Street Theatre in April, 1855. In this first tragedy, Boker showed where his strength lay, that is in the representation of strong passion in verse. *Calaynos* is based on the dislike of the Spaniard for Moorish blood, and in a masterly way he represented the pride of race on both sides that resulted inevitably in disaster.

Anne Boleyn, his next play, was intended for the stage, but was not acted. It was published in 1850, and there are evidences that Charlotte Cushman was considering it, at one time. *The Betrothal* was first played at the Walnut Street Theatre, Philadelphia, on September 25, 1850, where it ran for ten nights, according to Durang, "with as brilliant success as ever greeted any production within the walls of the edifice." It was played in New York, November 18, 1850, and had two successful runs, and was put on in London in 1853. *The Betrothal* is a romantic comedy in verse, concerned with the rescue of Costanza di Tiburzzi from the proposed marriage to Marzio, a rich merchant, who has her father in his power. It is a distinct advance over *Calaynos* and *Anne Boleyn* in dramatic effectiveness.

The World a Mask, a prose comedy, with occasional passages in blank verse, was played for eight nights at the Walnut Street Theatre, Philadelphia, beginning April 21, 1851. The scene is laid in London in 1851 and the plot is one of intrigue with an accompaniment of social satire. It was never printed and exists to-day in manuscript. It is not one of Boker's strong plays.

The Widow's Marriage, written in 1852, was accepted by Marshall, the manager of the Walnut Street Theatre, but as he was unable to find a proper actress to take the leading part of "Lady Goldstraw," the play was not acted. It is a comedy, in blank verse, laid in England at the time of George II, the plot being concerned with a trick played upon a vain old widow by which she is cured of her foolishness.

Leonor de Guzman, his next play, was a tragedy based on Spanish history, of the time of Alphonso XII of Castile, whose mistress, Leonor, is the heroine. The hatred of Queen Maria for her rival and her revenge are the main motives of the play, which is a powerful one. It was first played at the Walnut Street Theatre on Monday, October 3, 1853, with Julia Dean as "Leonor." It was successful both in Philadelphia and New York, where it was put on at the Broadway Theatre, April 24, 1854.

Francesca da Rimini was played for the first time at the Broadway Theatre, New York, September 26, 1855, continuing till October 5th. E. L. Davenport acted "Lanciotto," Mme. Ponisi, "Francesca," and J. W. Lanergan, "Paolo." It was well received, but its great vogue came later when it was revived by Lawrence Barrett at Haverly's Theatre, Philadelphia, September 14, 1882, Mr. Barrett playing "Lanciotto," Mr. Otis Skinner, "Paolo," and Miss Marie Wainwright, "Francesca." Mr. Barrett played this part for several years. On August 22, 1901, Mr. Otis Skinner revived the play at the Grand Opera House, Chicago, Mr. Skinner playing "Lanciotto," Mr. Aubrey Boucicault playing "Paolo," and Miss Marcia Van Dresser, "Francesca." It was played throughout the winter during the season of 1901–02.

Of all American plays written before the Civil War *Francesca da Rimini* shows the most vitality. This has been due partly to the lofty conception of Lanciotto's character, the sympathetic interpretation of the medieval woman in Francesca, and the noble expression in a blank verse that has rarely been excelled in English. But in addition to these literary qualities, the strength of *Francesca da Rimini* lies in its qualities as an acting play. It has never been put on the stage as it is printed. The printed version represents Boker's best judgment of the form in which it should be read, but in 1853 an acting version was prepared by Boker, and in 1882 another version was made by Mr. Barrett. In preparing the present text, the printed version, checked by the original autograph manuscript, has been taken as the basis. In indicating how the play was actually performed, the acting version of 1853 has been taken as the standard. When in this version lines have been omitted, these have been indicated by brackets of this character <> and insertions are shown by square brackets

Certain changes in entire scenes have been indicated in the notes. To have indicated also all the changes made in the acting version of 1882 would have led to confusion, but some of the most important alterations have been mentioned in the notes. The acting version was corrected by Boker so that "Paolo" should be pronounced as two syllables. These corrections have been followed, but in those portions of the play which were omitted on the stage, Boker made no corrections. There are in consequence certain inconsistencies in the text so far as the pronunciation of this word is concerned but the editor has naturally left the lines as Boker wrote them.

The Bankrupt, the last of Boker's plays to be actually performed, was played at the Broadway Theatre on December 5, 1855. This is a prose melodrama, laid apparently in Philadelphia in 1850 and exists in an autograph manuscript, dated 1853. *Königsmark,* published in 1869 but written probably before 1857, is a closet play laid in Hanover in 1694. In 1885 and 1886, encouraged by the revival of *Francesca da Rimini,* Boker wrote two plays on the same theme, *Nydia* and *Glaucus.* They were written probably for Mr. Barrett, though they were never played, and are based on the *Last Days of Pompeii* of Bulwer. They are, however, entirely original in expression and contain some of the best verse that Boker wrote.

Boker's public career was a distinguished one. From 1871 to 1875 he was Minister to Turkey and from 1875 to 1878 Minister to Russia. He took an active part on the Union side during the war, his poetry, such as "The Black Regiment" and the "Dirge for a Soldier" being representative. He died in Philadelphia, January 2, 1890.

Boker's plays and poems were published in two volumes in 1856 and were reprinted in 1857, 1883, and 1891. This collected edition contains *Calaynos, Anne Boleyn, Leonor de Guzman, Francesca da Rimini, The Betrothal,* and *The Widow's Marriage. Köningsmark* was published in 1869 and *Francesca da Rimini* has been republished in a popular edition. The other plays exist in manuscript in the possession of Princeton University. Among these manuscripts are included biographical material and information concerning the plays on which this introduction is based. See *A History of the American Drama from the Beginning to the Civil War.* New York, 1923. Chapter XII.

Note to Fifth Edition.

An authoritative biography, *George Henry Boker, Poet and Patriot,* by Edward S. Bradley (Philadelphia, 1927), has been issued by the University of Pennsylvania Press. Dr. Bradley has also published for the first time *Nydia,* and *Sonnets, A Sequence on Profane Love* (University of Pennsylvania Press, 1929).

CASTS OF FRANCESCA DA RIMINI

	Broadway Theatre, New York, Sep. 26, 1855	Haverly's Theatre, Philadelphia, Sep. 14, 1882	Grand Opera House, Chicago, Aug. 26, 1901
MALATESTA, Lord of Rimini	Mr. David Whiting	Mr. Ben. C. Rogers	Mr. W. J. Constantine
GUIDO DA POLENTA, Lord of Ravenna	Mr. Canoll	Mr. F. C. Mosley	Mr. E. A. Eberle
LANCIOTTO, MALATESTA's son	Mr. E. L. Davenport	Mr. Lawrence Barrett	Mr. Otis Skinner
PAOLO, his brother	Mr. J. W. Lanergan	Mr. Otis Skinner	Mr. Aubrey Boucicault
PEPE, MALATESTA's jester	Mr. Charles Fisher	Mr. Louis James	Mr. William Norris
CARDINAL, friend to GUIDO	Mr. Hodges	Mr. Charles Rolfe	Mr. Frederick van Rensselar
RENE, a troubadour	Mr. Leon J. Vincent	Mr. Percy Winter	Mr. Fletcher Norton
FRANCESCA DA RIMINI, GUIDO's daughter	Mme. Ponisi	Miss Marie Wainwright	Miss Marcia Van Dresser
RITTA, her maid	Miss Josephine Manners	Miss Josie Batchelder	Miss Gertrude Norman

Lords, Ladies, Knights, Priests, Soldiers, Pages and Attendants.

Scene, Rimini, Ravenna, and the neighborhood.

Time, about 1300 A. D.

FRANCESCA DA RIMINI

ACT FIRST.

SCENE 1.[1] *Rimini. The Garden of the Palace.* PAOLO *and a number of noblemen are discovered, seated under an arbor, surrounded by* RENÉ *and other Troubadours, and attendants.*

PAOLO. I prithee, René, charm our ears again
With the same song you sang me yesterday.
Here are fresh listeners.
RENÉ. Really, my good lord,
My voice is out of joint. A grievous cold— (*Coughs.*)
PAOLO. A very grievous, but convenient cold,
Which always racks you when you would not sing.
RENÉ. O, no, my lord! Besides, I hoped to hear
My ditty warbled into fairer ears,
By your own lips; to better purpose, too.
(*The Noblemen all laugh.*)
FIRST NOBLEMAN. René has hit it. Music runs to waste
In ears like ours.
SECOND NOBLEMAN. Nay, nay; chaunt on, sweet Count.
PAOLO. (*Coughing.*) Alack! you hear, I've caught poor René's cough.
FIRST N. That would not be, if we wore petticoats. (*The others laugh.*)
PAOLO. O, fie!
FIRST N. So runs the scandal to our ears.
SECOND N. Confirmed by all our other senses, Count.
FIRST N. Witnessed by many a doleful sigh, poured out
By many a breaking heart in Rimini.
SECOND N. Poor girls!
FIRST N. (*Mimicking a lady.*) Sweet Count! sweet Count Paolo! O!
Plant early violets upon my grave!
Thus go a thousand voices to one tune.
(*The others laugh.*)
PAOLO. 'Ods mercy! gentlemen, you do me wrong.
FIRST N. And by how many hundred, more or less?
PAOLO. Ah! rogues, you'd shift your sins upon my shoulders.
SECOND N. You'd bear them stoutly.
FIRST N. It were vain to give
Drops to god Neptune. You're the sea of love
That swallows all things.
SECOND N. We the little fish
That meanly scull about within your depths.
PAOLO. Go on, go on! Talk yourselves fairly out.
(PEPE *laughs without.*)
But, hark! here comes the fool! Fit company
For this most noble company of wits!

(*Enter* PEPE, *laughing violently.*)

Why do you laugh?
PEPE. I'm laughing at the world.
It has laughed long enough at me; and so
I'll turn the tables. Ho! ho! ho! I've heard
A better joke of Uncle Malatesta's
Than any I e'er uttered. (*Laughing.*)
ALL. Tell it, fool.
PEPE. Why, do you know—upon my life, the best
And most original idea on earth:
A joke to put in practice, too. By Jove!
I'll bet my wit 'gainst the stupidity
Of the best gentlemen among you all,
You cannot guess it.
ALL. Tell us, tell us, fool.
PEPE. Guess it, guess it, fools.
PAOLO. Come, disclose, disclose!
PEPE. He has a match afoot.—
ALL. A match!
PEPE. A marriage.
ALL. Who?—who?
PEPE. A marriage in his family.
ALL. But, who?
PEPE. Ah! there's the point.
ALL. [Count] Paolo?
PEPE. No.
FIRST N. The others are well wived. Shall we turn Turks?

[1] In the acting version of 1853 the play begins with Act Second, Scene One, and there is a note in Boker's hand, directing that when Lanciotto is the prominent part, the whole of that scene is to be omitted, and the play is to begin as in the present reading version.

PEPE. Why, there 's the summit of his joke, good sirs.
By all the sacred symbols of my art—
By cap and bauble, by my tinkling bell—
He means to marry Lanciotto!
(*Laughs violently.*)

ALL. (*Laughing.*) Ho!—

PAOLO. Peace! peace! What tongue dare echo yon fool's laugh?
Nay, never raise your hands in wonderment;
I 'll strike the dearest friend among ye all
Beneath my feet, as if he were a slave,
Who dares insult my brother with a laugh![1]

<PEPE. By Jove! ye 're sad enough. Here 's mirth's quick cure!
Pretty Paolo has a heavy fist,
I warn you, sirs. Ho! ho! I trapped them all; (*Laughing.*)
Now I 'll go mar old Malatesta's message. (*Aside.*) (*Exit.*)

PAOLO. Shame on ye, sirs! I have mistaken you.
I thought I harboured better friends. Poor fops,
Who 've slept in down and satin all your years,
Within the circle Lanciotto charmed
Round Rimini with his most potent sword!—
Fellows whose brows would melt beneath a casque,
Whose hands would fray to grasp a brand's rough hilt,
Who ne'er launched more than braggart threats at foes!—
Girlish companions of luxurious girls!
Danglers round troubadours and wine-cups!—Men
Whose best parts are their clothes! bundles of silk,
Scented like summer! rag-men, nothing more!—
Creatures as generous as monkeys—brave
As hunted hares—courteous as grinning apes—
Grateful as serpents—useful as lap-dogs—
(*During this, the* NOBLEMEN *steal off.*)
By heaven, I am alone! So let me be.
Till Lanciotto fill the vacant room
Of these mean knaves, whose friendship is but breath. (*Exit.*)>

SCENE 2. *The Same. A Hall in the Castle.*

(*Enter* MALATESTA *and* LANCIOTTO.)

MALATESTA. Guido, ay, Guido of Ravenna, son—
Down on his knees, as full of abject prayers
For peace and mercy as a penitent.

LANCIOTTO. His old trick, father. While his wearied arm
Is raised in seeming prayer, it only rests.
Anon, he 'll deal you such a staggering blow,
With its recovered strength, as shall convert
You, and not him, into a penitent.

MAL. No, no; your last bout leveled him. He reeled,
Into Ravenna, from the battle-field,
Like a stripped drunkard, and there headlong fell—
<A mass of squalid misery, a thing
To draw the jeering urchins. I have this
From faithful spies. There 's not a hope remains
To break the shock of his great overthrow.>
I pity Guido.

LAN. 'S death! go comfort him!
I pity those who fought, and bled, and died,
Before the armies of this Ghibelin.
I pity those who halted home with wounds
Dealt by his hand. I pity widowed eyes
That he set running; maiden hearts that turn,
Sick with despair, from ranks thinned down by him;

---

1 In the acting versions, the following lines, in Boker's hand, are here substituted for the lines enclosed in brackets < >.

ALL. Pardon, my lord!

PAOLO. (*With a troubled air.*) Oh, pardon 's easily said.
But do you credit it?

RENÉ. Almost. The jests
Of impish Pepe seldom fail in truth.

PAOLO. Forgive me my hot temper, gentlemen,
I must seek Lanciotto. This strange news,
If true may bring a blessing or a curse!
Let us walk on. How fair the morning is!
(*Exit thoughtfully, the others following.*)

Mothers that shriek, as the last stragglers fling
Their feverish bodies by the fountain-side,
Dumb with mere thirst, and faintly point to him,
Answering the dame's quick questions. I have seen
Unburied bones, and skulls—that seemed to ask,
From their blank eye-holes, vengeance at my hand—
Shine in the moonlight on old battle-fields;
And even these—the happy dead, my lord—
I pity more than Guido of Ravenna!

MAL. What would you have?

LAN. I'd see Ravenna burn,
Flame into heaven, and scorch the flying clouds;
I'd choke her streets with ruined palaces;
I'd hear her women scream with fear and grief,
As I have heard the maids of Rimini.
All this I'd sprinkle with old Guido's blood,
And bless the baptism.

MAL. You are cruel.

LAN. Not I;
But these things ache within my fretting brain.
The sight I first beheld was from the arms
Of my wild nurse, her husband hacked to death
By the fierce edges of these Ghibelins.
One cut across the neck—I see it now,
Ay, and have mimicked it a thousand times,
Just as I saw it, on our enemies.—
Why, that cut seemed as if it meant to bleed
On till the judgement. My distracted nurse
Stooped down, and paddled in the running gore
With her poor fingers; then a prophetess,
Pale with the inspiration of the god,
She towered aloft, and with her dripping hand
Three times she signed me with the holy cross.
'T is all as plain as noon-day. Thus she spake,—
"May this spot stand till Guido's dearest blood
Be mingled with thy own!" The soldiers say,
In the close battle, when my wrath is up,
The dead man's blood flames on my vengeful brow
Like a red planet; and when war is o'er,
It shrinks into my brain, defiling all
My better nature with its slaughterous lusts.
Howe'er it be, it shaped my earliest thought,
And it will shape my last.

MAL. You moody churl!
You dismal knot of superstitious dreams!
<Do you not blush to empty such a head
Before a sober man? Why, son, the world
Has not given o'er its laughing humour yet,
That you should try it with such vagaries.—Poh!>
I'll get a wife to teach you common sense.

LAN. A wife for me! (*Laughing.*)

MAL. Ay, sir, a wife for you.
<You shall be married, to insure your wits.>

LAN. 'T is not your wont to mock me.

MAL. <How now, son!
I am not given to jesting.> I have chosen
The fairest wife in Italy for you.
<You won her bravely, as a soldier should:
And when you'd woo her, stretch your gauntlet out
And crush her fingers in its steely grip.>
If you will plead, I ween, she dare not say—
No, by your leave. <Should she refuse, howe'er,
With that same iron hand you shall go knock
Upon Ravenna's gates, till all the town
Ring with your courtship.> I have made her hand
The price and pledge of Guido's future peace.

LAN. All this is done!

MAL. Done, out of hand; and now
I wait a formal answer, nothing more.
<Guido dare not decline. No, by the saints,
He'd send Ravenna's virgins here in droves,
To buy a ten days' truce.

LAN. Sir, let me say,
You stretch paternal privilege too far,
To pledge my hand without my own consent.
Am I a portion of your household stuff,

That you should trade me off to Guido thus?>
Who is the lady I am bartered for?

MAL. Francesca, Guido's daughter.—Never frown;
It shall be so!

LAN. By heaven, it shall not be!
My blood shall never mingle with his race.

MAL. According to your nurse's prophecy,
Fate orders it.

LAN. Ha!

MAL. Now, then, I have struck
The chord that answers to your gloomy thoughts.
Bah! on your sibyl and her prophecy!
<Put Guido's blood aside, and yet, I say,
Marry you shall.

LAN. 'T is most distasteful, sir.>

MAL. Lanciotto, look ye! You brave gentlemen,
So fond of knocking out poor people's brains,
In time must come to have your own knocked out:
What, then, if you bequeath us no new hands,
To carry on your business, and our house
Die out for lack of princes?

LAN. Wed my brothers:
They 'll rear you sons, I 'll slay you enemies.
Paolo and [fair] Francesca! Note their names;
They chime together like sweet marriage-bells.
A proper match. 'T is said she 's beautiful;
And he is the delight of Rimini,—
The pride and conscious centre of all eyes,
The theme of poets, the ideal of art,
The earthly treasury of Heaven's best gifts!
I am a soldier; from my very birth,
Heaven cut me out for terror, not for love.
<I had such fancies once, but now—>

MAL. Pshaw! son,
<My faith is bound to Guido; and if you
Do not throw off your duty, and defy,
Through sickly scruples, my express commands,
You 'll yield at once.> No more: I 'll have it so! *(Exit.)*

LAN. Curses upon my destiny! What, I—
Ho! I have found my use at last—What. I. *(Laughing.)*
I, the great twisted monster of the wars,
The brawny cripple, the herculean dwarf,
The spur of panic, and the butt of scorn—
I be a bridegroom! Heaven, was I not cursed
More than enough, when thou didst fashion me
To be a type of ugliness,—a thing
By whose comparison all Rimini
Holds itself beautiful? Lo! here I stand,
A gnarléd, blighted trunk! There 's not a knave
So spindle-shanked, so wry-faced, so infirm,
Who looks at me, and smiles not on himself.
<And I have friends to pity me—great Heaven!
One has a favorite leg that he bewails,—
Another sees my hip with doleful plaints,—
A third is sorry o'er my huge swart arms,—
A fourth aspires to mount my very hump,
And thence harangue his weeping brotherhood!>
Pah! it is nauseous! Must I further bear
The sidelong shuddering glances of a wife?
The degradation of a showy love,
That over-acts, and proves the mummer's craft
Untouched by nature? And a fair wife, too!—
Francesca, whom the minstrels sing about!
<Though, by my side, what woman were not fair?
Circe looked well among her swine, no doubt;
Next me, she 'd pass for Venus. Ho! ho! ho! *(Laughing.)*
Would there were something merry in my laugh!>
Now, in the battle, if a Ghibelin
Cry, "Wry-hip! hunchback!" I can trample him
Under my stallion's hoofs; or haggle him
Into a monstrous likeness of myself:
But to be pitied,—to endure a sting
Thrust in by kindness, with a sort of smile!—
'S death! it is miserable!

(Enter PEPE.*)*

PEPE. My lord—

LAN. My fool!

PEPE. We'll change our titles when your bride's bells ring—
<Ha, cousin?
LAN. Even this poor fool has eyes,
To see the wretched plight in which I stand. (*Aside.*)
How, gossip, how?
PEPE. I, being the court-fool,
Am lord of fools by my prerogative.>
LAN. Who told you of my marriage?
PEPE. Rimini!
A frightful liar; but true for once, I fear.
The messenger from Guido has returned,
And the whole town is wailing over him.
Some pity you, and some the bride; but I,
Being more catholic, I pity both.
LAN. Still, pity, pity! (*Aside. Bells toll.*) Ha! whose knell is that?
PEPE. Lord Malatesta sent me to the tower,
To have the bells rung for your marriage-news.
How, he said not; so I, as I thought fit,
Told the deaf sexton to ring out a knell. (*Bells toll.*)
How do you like it?
LAN. Varlet, have you bones,
To risk their breaking? I have half a mind
To thrash you from your motley coat! (*Seizes him.*)
PEPE. Pardee!
Respect my coxcomb, cousin. Hark! ha, ha! (*Laughing.*)
(*Bells ring a joyful peal.*)
Some one has changed my music. Heaven defend!
How the bells jangle! Yonder gray-beard, now,
Rings a peal vilely. <He's more used to knells,
And sounds them grandly.> Only give him time,
And, I'll be sworn, he'll ring your knell out yet.
<LAN. Pepe, you are but half a fool.
PEPE. My lord,
I can return the compliment in full.
LAN. So, you are ready.
PEPE. Truth is always so.>
LAN. I shook you rudely; here's a florin. (*Offers money.*)
PEPE. No:
My wit is merchandise, but not my honour.
LAN. Your honour, sirrah!
PEPE. Why not? You great lords
Have something you call lordly honour; pray,
May not a fool have foolish honour too?
Cousin, you laid your hand upon my coat—
'T was the first sacrilege it ever knew—
And you shall pay it. Mark! I promise you.
LAN. (*Laughing.*) Ha, ha! you bluster well. Upon my life,
You have the tilt-yard jargon to a breath.
Pepe, if I should smite you on the cheek—
Thus, gossip, thus—(*Strikes him*) what would you then demand?
PEPE. Your life!
LAN. (*Laughing*). Ha, ha! there is the camp-style, too—
A very cut-throat air! How this shrewd fool
Makes the punctilio of honor show!
Change helmets into coxcombs, swords to baubles,
And what a figure is poor chivalry!
Thanks for your lesson, Pepe. (*Exit.*)
PEPE. Ere I'm done,
You'll curse as heartily, you limping beast!
<Ha! so we go—Lord Lanciotto, look! (*Walks about, mimicking him.*)
Here is a leg and camel-back, forsooth,
To match your honour and nobility!
You miscreated scarecrow, dare you shake,
Or strike in jest, a natural man like me?—
You curséd lump, you chaos of a man,
To buffet one whom Heaven pronounces good!> (*Bells ring.*)
There go the bells rejoicing over you:
I'll change them back to the old knell again.
You marry, faugh! Beget a race of elves;
Wed a she-crocodile, and keep within
The limits of your nature! Here we go,
Tripping along to meet our promised bride,
Like a rheumatic elephant!—ha, ha! (*Laughing.*)
(*Exit, mimicking* LANCIOTTO.)

SCENE 3.[1] *The Same. A Room in the Same.*

[1] There was no scene change in the acting version. There is a clash of arms indicated without and Lanciotto begins his speech

Was that a signal, made by heaven itself
To warn my soul against this coming marriage?

(*Enter* LANCIOTTO, *hastily.*)

LANCIOTTO. <Why do these prodigies environ me?
In ancient Rome, the words a fool might drop,
From the confusion of his vagrant thoughts,
Were held as omens, prophecies; and men
Who made earth tremble with majestic deeds,
Trembled themselves at fortune's lightest threat.>
I like it not. My father named this match
While I boiled over with vindictive wrath
Towards Guido and Ravenna. Straight my heart
Sank down like lead; a weakness seized on me,
A dismal gloom that I could not resist;
I lacked the power to take my stand, and say—
Bluntly, I will not! <Am I in the toils?
Has fate so weakened me, to work its end?
There seems a fascination in it, too,—
A morbid craving to pursue a thing
Whose issue may be fatal.> Would that I
Were in the wars again! These mental weeds
Grow on the surface of inactive peace.
I'm haunted by myself. Thought preys on thought.
My mind seems crowded in the hideous mould
That shaped my body. What a fool am I
To bear the burden of my wretched life,
To sweat and toil under the world's broad eye,
Climb into fame, and find myself—O, what?—
A most conspicuous monster! Crown my head,
Pile Cæsar's purple on me—and what then?
My hump shall shorten the imperial robe,
<My leg peep out beneath the scanty hem,
My broken hip shall twist the gown awry;>
And pomp, instead of dignifying me,
Shall be by me made quite ridiculous.
The faintest coward would not bear all this:
Prodigious courage must be mine, to live;
To die asks nothing but weak will,[1] <and I
Feel like a craven. Let me skulk away
Ere life o'ertask me.
(*Offers to stab himself.*)>

(*Enter* PAOLO.)

PAOLO. (*Seizing his hand.*) Brother! what is this?
Lanciotto, are you mad? Kind Heaven! look here—
Straight in my eyes. Now answer, do you know
How near you were to murder? Dare you bend
Your wicked hand against a heart I love?
Were it for you to mourn your wilful death,
With such a bitterness as would be ours,
The wish would ne'er have crossed you. <While we're bound
Life into life, a chain of loving hearts,
Were it not base in you, the middle link,
To snap, and scatter all?> Shame, brother, shame!
<I thought you better metal.>
LAN. [Nay, Paolo, you mistake,
I did but think upon Death's sweet relief;
I dare not practise it. But spare your words.]
I know the seasons of our human grief,
And can predict them without almanac.
A few sobs o'er the body, and a few
Over the coffin; then a sigh or two,
Whose windy passage dries the hanging tear;
Perchance, some wandering memories, some regrets;
Then a vast influx of consoling thoughts—
Based on the trials of the sadder days
Which the dead missed; and then a smiling face
Turned on to-morrow. Such is mortal grief.
It writes its histories within a span,
And never lives to read them.
PAOLO. Lanciotto,
I heard the bells of Rimini, just now,
Exulting o'er your coming marriage-day,

---

[1] In the acting version of 1853 these lines are inserted here.

(*Draws and gazes upon his dagger.*)
What floods
Of joy might enter through the wound thou'dst give
Had I but hardihood.

<While you conspire to teach them gloomier sounds.>
Why are you sad?

LAN. [Sad] Paolo, I am wretched;
Sad 's a faint word. But of my marriage-bells—
Heard you the knell that Pepe rang?

PAOLO. 'T was strange:
<A sullen antic of his crabbed wit.>

LAN. It was portentous. All dumb things find tongues
Against this marriage. As I passed the hall,
My armour glittered on the wall, and I
Paused by the harness, as before a friend
Whose well-known features slack our hurried gait;
Francesca's name was fresh upon my mind,
So I half-uttered it. Instant, my sword
Leaped from its scabbard, as with sudden life,
Plunged down and pierced into the oaken floor,
Shivering with fear! Lo! while I gazed upon it—
Doubting the nature of the accident—
Around the point appeared a spot of blood,
Oozing upon the floor, that spread and spread—
As I stood gasping by in speechless horror—
Ring beyond ring, until the odious tide
Crawled to my feet, and lapped them, like the tongues
Of angry serpents! <O, my God! I fled
At the first touch of the infernal stain!>
Go—you may see—go to the hall!

<PAOLO. Fie! man,
You have been ever played on in this sort
By your wild fancies. When your heart is high,
You make them playthings; but in lower moods,
They seem to sap the essence of your soul,
And drain your manhood to its poorest dregs.

LAN. Go look, go look!>

PAOLO. (*Goes to the door, and returns.*)
There sticks the sword, indeed,
Just as your tread detached it from its sheath;
Looking more like a blessed cross, I think,
Than a bad omen. As for blood—Ha, ha! (*Laughing.*)
It sets mine dancing. Pshaw! away with this!
Deck up your face with smiles. Go trim yourself
For the young bride. New velvet, gold, and gems,
Do wonders for us. Brother, come; I 'll be
Your tiring-man, for once.

LAN. Array this lump—
Paolo, hark! There are some human thoughts
Best left imprisoned in the aching heart,
Lest the freed malefactors should dispread
Infamous ruin with their liberty.
There 's not a man—the fairest of ye all—
Who is not fouler than he seems. This life
Is one unending struggle to conceal
Our baseness from our fellows. Here stands one
In vestal whiteness with a lecher's lust;—
There sits a judge, holding law's scales in hands
That itch to take the bribe he dare not touch;—
Here goes a priest with heavenward eyes, whose soul
Is Satan's council-chamber;—there a doctor,
With nature's secrets wrinkled round a brow
Guilty with conscious ignorance;—and here
A soldier rivals Hector's bloody deeds—
Out-does the devil in audacity—
With craven longings fluttering in a heart
That dares do aught but fly! Thus are we all
Mere slaves and alms-men to a scornful world,
That takes us at our seeming.

PAOLO. Say 't is true;
What do you drive at?

LAN. At myself, full tilt.
I, like the others, am not what I seem.
Men call me gentle, courteous, brave.—They lie!
I 'm harsh, rude, and a coward. Had I nerve
To cast my devils out upon the earth,
I 'd show this laughing planet what a hell
Of envy, malice, cruelty, and scorn,
It has forced back to canker in the heart
Of one poor cripple!

PAOLO. <Ha!> [Cripple!]
LAN. Ay, now 't is out!
A word I never breathed to man before.
Can you, who are a miracle of grace,
Feel what it is to be a wreck like me?
Paolo, look at me. Is there a line,
In my whole bulk of wretched contraries,
That nature in a nightmare ever used
Upon her shapes till now? Find me the man,
Or beast, or tree, or rock, or nameless thing,
So out of harmony with all things else,
And I 'll go raving with bare happiness,—
Ay, and I 'll marry Helena of Greece,
And swear I do her honor!
<PAOLO. Lanciotto,
I, who have known you from a stripling up,
Never observed, or, if I did, ne'er weighed
Your special difference from the rest of men.
You 're not Apollo—
LAN. No!
PAOLO. Nor yet are you
A second Pluto. Could I change with you—
My graces for your nobler qualities—
Your strength, your courage, your renown—by heaven,
We 'd e'en change persons, to the finest hair.
LAN. You should be flatterer to an emperor.
PAOLO. I am but just.> Let me beseech you, brother,
To look with greater favor on yourself;
<Nor suffer misty phantoms of your brain
To take the place of sound realities>
Go to Ravenna, wed your bride, and lull
Your cruel delusions in domestic peace.
<Ghosts fly a fireside: 't is their wont to stalk
Through empty houses, and through empty hearts.
I know Francesca will be proud of you.
Women admire you heroes. Rusty sages,
Pale poets, and scarred warriors, have been
Their idols ever; while we fair plump fools
Are elbowed to the wall, or only used
For vacant pastime.>
LAN. To Ravenna?—no!
In Rimini they know me; at Ravenna
I 'd be a new-come monster, and exposed
To curious wonder. <There will be parade
Of all the usual follies of the state;
Fellows with trumpets, tinselled coats, and wands,
Would strut before me, like vain mountebanks
Before their monkeys. Then, I should be stared
Out of my modesty;> and when they look,
How can I tell if 't is the bridegroom's face
Or hump that draws their eyes? I will not go.
To please you all, I 'll marry; but to please
The wonder-mongers of Ravenna—Ha!
[Dear] Paolo, now I have it. You shall go,
To bring Francesca; and you 'll speak of me,
Not as I ought to be, but as I am.
If she draw backward, give her rein; and say
That neither Guido nor herself shall feel
The weight of my displeasure. You may say,
I pity her—
PAOLO. For what?
LAN. For wedding me.
In sooth, she 'll need it. Say—
PAOLO. Nay, Lanciotto,
I 'll be a better orator in your behalf,
Without your promptings.
LAN. She is fair, 't is said;
And, [my] dear Paolo, if she please your eye,
And move your heart to anything like love,
Wed her yourself. The peace would stand as firm
By such a match.
PAOLO. (*Laughing.*) Ha! that is right: be gay!
Ply me with jokes! I 'd rather see you smile
Than see the sun shine.
LAN. I am serious,
I 'll find another wife, less beautiful,
More on my level, and—
PAOLO. An empress, brother,
Were honoured by your hand. You are by much
Too humble in your reckoning of yourself.
I can count virtues in you, to supply
Half Italy, if they were parcelled out.
Look up!

LAN. I cannot: Heaven has bent me down.
[But] to you, Paolo, I could look, however,
Were my hump made a mountain. Bless him, God!
Pour everlasting bounties on his head!
<Make Crœsus jealous of his treasury,
Achilles of his arms, Endymion
Of his fresh beauties,—though the coy one lay
Blushing beneath Diana's earliest kiss,
On grassy Latmos; and may every good,
Beyond man's sight, though in the ken of heaven,>
Round his fair fortune to a perfect end!
O, you have dried the sorrow of my eyes;
My heart is beating with a lighter pulse;
The air is musical; the total earth
Puts on new beauty, and within the arms
Of girdling ocean dreams her time away,
And visions bright to-morrows!

(*Enter* MALATESTA *and* PEPE.)

MALATESTA. Mount, to horse!
<PEPE. (*Aside.*) Good Lord! he 's smiling! What 's the matter now?
Has anybody broken a leg or back?
Has a more monstrous monster come to life?
Is hell burst open?—heaven burnt up? What, what
Can make yon eyesore grin?—I say, my lord,
What cow has calved?
PAOLO. Your mother, by the bleat.
PEPE. Right fairly answered—for a gentleman!
When did you take my trade up?
PAOLO. When your wit
Went begging, sirrah.
PEPE. Well again! My lord,
I think he 'll do.
MAL. For what?
PEPE. To take my place.
Once fools were rare, and then my office sped;
But now the world is overrun with them:
One gets one's fool in one's own family,
Without much searching.
MAL. Pepe, gently now.>
Lanciotto, you are waited for. The train
Has passed the gate, and halted there for you.
LAN. I go not to Ravenna.
MAL. Hey! why not?
PAOLO. For weighty reasons, father. Will you trust
Your greatest captain, hope of all the Guelfs,
With crafty Guido? Should the Ghibelins
Break faith, and shut Lanciotto in their walls—
Sure the temptation would be great enough—
What would you do?
MAL. I'd eat Ravenna up!
PEPE. Lord! what an appetite!
PAOLO. But Lanciotto
Would be a precious hostage.
MAL. True; you 're wise;
Guido 's a fox. Well, have it your own way.
What is your plan?
PAOLO. I go there in his place.
MAL. Good! I will send a letter with the news.
LAN. I thank you, brother.
(*Apart to* PAOLO.)
PEPE. Ha! ha! ha!—O! O! (*Laughing.*)
MAL. Pepe, what now?
PEPE. O! lord, O!—ho! ho! ho!
(*Laughing.*)
<PAOLO. Well, giggler?
PEPE. Hear my fable, uncle.
MAL. Ay.
PEPE. Once on a time, Vulcan sent Mercury
To fetch dame Venus from a romp in heaven.
Well, they were long in coming, as he thought;
And so the god of spits and gridirons
Railed like himself—the devil. But—now mark—
Here comes the moral. In a little while,
Vulcan grew proud, because he saw plain signs
That he should be a father; and so he
Strutted through hell, and pushed the devils by,
Like a magnifico of Venice. Ere long,
His heir was born; but then—ho! ho!—the brat
Had wings upon his heels, and thievish ways,
And a vile squint, like errant Mercury's,
Which honest Vulcan could not understand;—
Can you?>
PAOLO. 'S death! fool, I'll have you in the stocks.
Father, your fool exceeds his privilege.
PEPE. (*Apart to* PAOLO.) Keep your own bounds, <Paolo. In the stocks
I'd tell more fables than you 'd wish to hear.

And so ride forth.> But, cousin, don't forget
To take Lanciotto's picture to the bride.
Ask her to choose between it and yourself.
I'll count the moments, while she hesitates,
And not grow gray at it.
<PAOLO. Peace, varlet, peace!
PEPE. (*Apart to him.*) Ah, now I have it. There's an elephant
Upon the scutcheon; show her that, and say—
Here's Lanciotto in our heraldry!>
PAOLO. Here's for your counsel!
(*Strikes* PEPE, *who runs behind* MALATESTA.)
MAL. Son, son, have a care!
We who keep pets must bear their pecks sometimes.
Poor knave! Ha! ha! thou'rt growing villainous. (*Laugh and pats* PEPE.)
PEPE. Another blow! another life for that! (*Aside.*)
PAOLO. Farewell, Lanciotto. You are dull again.
LAN. Nature will rule.
MAL.. Come, come!
LAN. God speed you, brother!
I am too sad; my smiles all turn to sighs.
PAOLO. More cause to haste me on my happy work.
(*Exit with* MALATESTA.)
PEPE. I'm going, cousin.
LAN. Go.
PEPE. Pray, ask me where.
LAN. Where, then?
PEPE. To have my jewel carried home:
And, as I'm wise, the carrier shall be
A thief, a thief, by Jove! The fashion's new. (*Exit.*)
LAN. In truth, I am too gloomy and irrational.
[And] Paolo must be right. I always had
These moody hours and dark presentiments,
Without mischances following after them.
The camp is my abode. A neighing steed,
A fiery onset, and a stubborn fight,
Rouse my dull blood, and tire my body down
To quiet slumbers when the day is o'er,
And night above me spreads her spangled tent,
Lit by the dying cresset of the moon.
Ay, that is it; I'm homesick for the camp. (*Exit.*)

ACT SECOND.

SCENE 1. *Ravenna. A Room in* GUIDO'S *Palace.*

(*Enter* GUIDO *and a* CARDINAL.)

CARDINAL. I warn thee, Count.
GUIDO. I'll take the warning, father,
On one condition: show me but a way
For safe escape.
CAR. I cannot.
GUI. There's the point.
<We Ghibelins are fettered hand and foot.
There's not a florin in my treasury;
Not a lame soldier, I can lead to war;
Not one to man the walls. A present siege,
Pushed with the wonted heat of Lanciotto,
Would deal Ravenna such a mortal blow
As ages could not mend. Give me but time
To fill the drainéd arteries of the land.>
The Guelfs are masters, we their slaves; <and we
Were wiser to confess it, ere the lash
Teach it too sternly.> It is well <for you>
To say you love Francesca. So do I;
But neither you nor I have any voice
For or against this marriage.
CAR. 'T is too true.
GUI. Say we refuse: Why, then, before a week,
We'll hear Lanciotto rapping at our door,
With twenty hundred ruffians at his back.
What's to say then? My lord, we waste our breath.
<Let us look fortune in the face, and draw
Such comfort from the wanton as we may.>
CAR. And yet I fear—
GUI. You fear! and so do I.
I fear Lanciotto as a soldier, though,
More than a son-in-law.
CAR. But have you seen him?
GUI. Ay, ay, and felt him, too. I've seen him ride
The best battalions of my horse and foot

Down like mere stubble: I have seen his sword
Hollow a square of pikemen, with the ease
You'd scoop a melon out.

CAR. Report declares him
A prodigy of strength and ugliness.

GUI. Were he the devil—But why talk of this?—
Here comes Francesca.

<CAR. Ah, unhappy child!

GUI. Look you, my lord! you'll make the best of it;
You will not whimper.> Add your voice to mine,
Or woe to poor Ravenna!

(*Enter* FRANCESCA *and* RITTA.)

FRANCESCA. Ha! my lord—
And you, my father!—But do I intrude
Upon your counsels? How severe you look!
Shall I retire?

GUI. No, no.

<FRAN. You moody men
Seem leagued against me. As I passed the hall,
I met your solemn Dante, with huge strides
Pacing in measure to his stately verse.
The sweeping sleeves of his broad scarlet robe
Blew out behind, like wide-expanded wings,
And seemed to buoy him in his level flight.
Thinking to pass, without disturbing him,
I stole on tip-toe; but the poet paused,
Subsiding into man, and steadily
Bent on my face the lustre of his eyes.
Then, taking both my trembling hands in his—
You know how his God-troubled forehead awes—
He looked into my eyes, and shook his head,
As if he dared not speak of what he saw;
Then muttered, sighed, and slowly turned away
The weight of his intolerable brow.
When I glanced back, I saw him, as before,
Sailing adown the hall on out-spread wings.
Indeed, my lord, he should not do these things:
They strain the weakness of mortality
A jot too far. As for poor Ritta, she
Fled like a doe, the truant.

RITTA. Yes, forsooth:
There's something terrible about the man.
Ugh! if he touched me, I should turn to ice.> [1]
I wonder if Count Lanciotto looks—

GUI. Ritta, come here. (*Takes her apart.*)

RIT. My lord.

GUI. 'T was my command,
You should say nothing of Count Lanciotto.

RIT. Nothing, my lord.

GUI. You have said nothing, then?

RIT. Indeed, my lord.

GUI. 'T is well. Some years ago,
My daughter had a very silly maid,
Who told her sillier stories. So, one day,
This maiden whispered something I forbade—
In strictest confidence, for she was sly:
What happened, think you?

RIT. I know not, my lord.

GUI. I boiled her in a pot.

RIT. Good heaven! my lord.

GUI. She did not like it. I shall keep that pot
Ready for the next boiling.
(*Walks back to the others.*)

RIT. Saints above!
I wonder if he ate her! Boil me—me!
I'll roast or stew with pleasure; but to boil
Implies a want of tenderness,—or rather
A downright toughness—in the matter boiled,
That's slanderous to a maiden. What, boil me—
Boil me! O! mercy, how ridiculous!
(*Retires, laughing.*)

<(*Enter a* MESSENGER.)

MESSENGER. Letters, my lord, from great Prince Malatesta.
(*Presents them, and exit.*)

GUI. (*Aside.*) Hear him, ye gods!—"from great Prince Malatesta!"

---

1 In place of the above speech, the acting version continues Guido's speech as follows:

We spoke of you,
Francesca, your betrothed is on the way:
Perhaps, even now, he's riding toward Ravenna.
Count Lanciotto is not used to wait,
And looks to find you in your fairest trim.
I have his father's hand to this effect.

Greeting, no doubt, his little cousin Guido.
Well, well, just so we see-saw up and down. (*Reads.*)
"*Fearing our treachery,*"—by heaven, that 's blunt,
And Malatesta-like!—"*he will not send*
His son, Lanciotto, to Ravenna, but"—
But what?—a groom, a porter? or will he
Have his prey sent him in an iron cage?
By Jove, he shall not have her! O! no, no;
"*He sends his younger son, the Count Paolo,*
To fetch Francesca back to Rimini."
That 's well, if he had left his reasons out.
And, in a postscript—by the saints, 't is droll!—
" '*T would not be worth your lordship's while, to shut*
Paolo in a prison; for, my lord,
I 'll only pay his ransom in plain steel:
Besides, he 's not worth having." Is there one,
Save this ignoble offshoot of the Goths,
Who 'd write such garbage to a gentleman?
Take that, and read it.
(*Gives letter to* CARDINAL.)

CAR. I have done the most.
She seems suspicious.

GUI. Ritta's work.

CAR. Farewell! (*Exit.*)

FRAN. Father, you seem distempered.

GUI. No, my child,
I am but vexed. Your husband 's on the road,
Close to Ravenna. What 's the time of day?

FRAN. Past noon, my lord.

GUI. We must be stirring, then.>

FRAN. I do not like this marriage.

GUI. But I do.

FRAN. But I do not. Poh! to be given away,
Like a fine horse or falcon, to a man
Whose face I never saw!

RIT. That 's it, my lady.

GUI. Ritta, <run down, and see if my great pot
Boils to your liking.>

RIT. <(*Aside.*) O! that pot again!>
My lord, my heart betrays me; but you know
How true 't is to my lady (*Exit.*)

FRAN. What ails Ritta?

GUI. The ailing of your sex, a running tongue.
Francesca, 't is too late to beat retreat:
Old Malatesta has me—you, too, child—
Safe in his clutch. <If you are not content,
I must unclose Ravenna, and allow
His son to take you.> Poh, poh! have a soul
Equal with your estate. A prince's child
Cannot choose husbands. Her desires must aim,
Not at herself, but at the public good.
<Both as your prince and father, I command;
As subject and good daughter, you 'll obey.

FRAN. I knew that it must be my destiny,
Some day, to give my hand without my heart;
But—

GUI. But, and I will butt you back again!
When Guido da Polenta says to you,
Daughter, you must be married,—what were best?

FRAN. 'T were best Francesca, of the self-same name,
Made herself bridal-garments.
(*Laughing.*)

GUI. Right!

FRAN. My lord,>
Is Lanciotto handsome—ugly—fair—
Black—sallow—crabbed—kind—or what is he?

GUI. <You 'll know ere long. I could not alter him,
To please your taste.>

FRAN. You always put me off;
You never have a whisper in his praise.

GUI. The world reports it.—Count my soldiers' scars,
And you may sum Lanciotto's glories up.

FRAN. I shall be dutiful, to please you, father.
<If aught befall me through my blind submission,
Though I may suffer, you must bear the sin.
Beware, my lord, for your own peace of mind!>
My part has been obedience; and now
I play it over to complete my task;
And it shall be with smiles upon my lips,—
Heaven only knows with what a sinking heart! (*Exeunt.*)

SCENE 2. *The Same. Before the Gates of the City. The walls hung with banners and flowers, and crowded with citizens. At the side of the scene is a canopied dais, with chairs of state upon it. Music, bells, shouts, and other sounds of rejoicing, are occasionally heard.*

(*Enter* GUIDO, *the* CARDINAL, *Noblemen, Knights, Guards, with banners and arms.*)

GUIDO. My lord, I'll have it so. You talk in vain.
Paolo is a marvel in his way:
I've seen him often. If Francesca take
A fancy to his beauty, all the better;
For she may think that he and Lanciotto
Are like as blossoms of one parent branch.
<In truth, they are, so far as features go—
Heaven help the rest! Get her to Rimini,
By any means, and I shall be content.>
The fraud cannot last long; but long enough
To win her favor to the family.

<CARDINAL. 'T is a dull trick. Thou hast not dealt with her
Wisely nor kindly, and I dread the end
If, when this marriage was enjoined on thee,
Thou hadst informed Francesca of the truth,
And said, now, daughter, choose between
Thy peace and all Ravenna's; who that knows
The constant nature of her noble heart
Could doubt the issue? There'd have been some tears,
Some frightful fancies of her husband's looks;
And then she'd calmly walk up to her fate,
And bear it bravely. Afterwards, perchance,
Lanciotto might prove better than her fears,—
No one denies him many an excellence,—
And all go happily. But, as thou wouldst plot,
She'll be prepared to see a paragon,
And find a satyr. It is dangerous.
Treachery with enemies is bad enough,
With friends 't is fatal.

GUI. Has your lordship done?

CAR. Never, Count Guido, with so good a text.
Do not stand looking sideways at the truth;
Craft has become thy nature. Go to her.

GUI. I have not heart.

CAR. I have. (*Going.*)

GUI. Hold, Cardinal!
My plan is better. Get her off my hands,
And I care not.

CAR. What will she say of thee,
In Rimini, when she detects the cheat?

GUI. I'll stop my ears up.

CAR. Guido, thou art weak,
And lack the common fortitude of man.

GUI. And you abuse the license of your garb,
To lessen me. My lord, I do not dare
To move a finger in these marriage-rites.
Francesca is a sacrifice, I know,—
A limb delivered to the surgeon's knife,
To save our general health. A truce to this.
Paolo has the business in his hands:
Let him arrange it as he will; for I
Will give Count Malatesta no pretext
To recommence the war.

CAR. Farewell, my lord.
I'll neither help nor countenance a fraud.
You crafty men take comfort to yourselves,
Saying, deceit dies with discovery.
'T is false; each wicked action spawns a brood,
And lives in its succession. You, who shake
Man's moral nature into storm, should know
That the last wave which passes from your sight
Rolls in and breaks upon eternity!
(*Exit.*)

GUI. Why, that's a very grand and solemn thought:
I'll mention it to Dante. Gentlemen,>
What see they from the wall?

NOBLEMAN. The train, my lord.

GUI. Inform my daughter.

NOB. She is here, my lord.

(*Enter* FRANCESCA, RITTA, *Ladies and Attendants.*)

FRANCESCA. See, father, what a merry face I have,
And how my ladies glisten! I will try
To do my utmost, in my love for you
And the good people of Ravenna. Now,
As the first shock is over, I expect
To feel quite happy. I will wed the Count,

Be he whate'er he may. <I do not speak
In giddy recklessness. I've weighed it all,—
'Twixt hope and fear, knowledge and ignorance,—
And reasoned out my duty to your wish.
I have no yearnings towards another love:
So, if I show my husband a desire
To fill the place with which he honors me,
According to its duties, even he—
Were he less noble than Count Lanciotto—
Must smile upon my efforts, and reward
Good will with willing grace.> One pang remains.
Parting from home and kindred is a thing
None but the heartless, or the miserable,
Can do without a tear. This home of mine
Has filled my heart with two-fold happiness,
Taking and giving love abundantly.
Farewell, Ravenna! If I bless thee not,
'T is that thou seem'st too blessed; and 't were strange
In me to offer what thou 'st always given.

<GUI. (*Aside.*) This is too much! If she would rail a while
At me and fortune, it could be endured.>
(*Shouts and music within.*)

FRAN. Ha! there's the van just breaking through the wood!
Music! that 's well; a welcome forerunner.
Now, Ritta—here—come talk to me. Alas!
How my heart trembles! What a world to me
Lies 'neath the glitter of yon cavalcade!
Is that the Count?

RITTA. Upon the dapple-gray?

FRAN. Yes, yes.

RIT. No; that 's his—

GUI. (*Apart to her.*) Ritta!

RITT. Ay; that 's—that 's—

<GUI. Ritta, the pot! (*Apart to her.*)

RIT. O! but this lying chokes! (*Aside.*)>
Ay, that 's Count Somebody, from Rimini.

FRAN. I knew it was. Is that not glorious?

RIT. My lady, what?

FRAN. To see a cavalier
Sit on his steed with such familiar grace.

RIT. To see a man astraddle on a horse!
It don't seem much to me.

FRAN. Fie! stupid girl!
<But mark! the minstrels thronging round the Count!
Ah! that is more than gallant horsemanship.
The soul that feeds itself on poesy,
Is of a quality more fine and rare
Than Heaven allows the ruder multitude.
I tell you, Ritta, when you see a man
Beloved by poets, made the theme of song,
And chaunted down to ages, as a gift
Fit for the rich embalmment of their verse,
There 's more about him than the patron's gold.>
If that 's the gentleman my father chose,
He must have picked him out from all the world.
The Count alights. Why, what a noble grace
Runs through his slightest action! Are you sad?
You, too, my father? Have I given you cause?
I am content. If Lanciotto's mind
Bear any impress of his fair outside,
We shall not quarrel ere our marriage-day.
<Can I say more? My blushes speak for me:
Interpret them as modesty's excuse
For the short-comings of a maiden's speech.>

RIT. Alas! dear lady! (*Aside.*)

GUI. (*Aside.*) <'Sdeath! my plot has failed,
By overworking its design.> Come, come;
Get to your places. See, the Count draws nigh.

(GUIDO *and* FRANCESCA *seat themselves upon the dais, surrounded by* RITTA, *Ladies, Attendants, and Guards. Music, shouts, ringing of bells. Enter Men-at-arms, with banners; Pages bearing costly presents on cushions; then* PAOLO, *surrounded by Noblemen, Knights, Minstrels, and followed by other Men-at-arms. They range themselves opposite the dais.*)

GUI. Ravenna welcomes you, my lord, and I
Add my best greeting to the general voice.
This peaceful show of arms from Rimini
Is a new pleasure, stranger to our sense
Than if the East blew zephyrs, <or the balm
Of Summer loaded rough December's gales,
And turned his snows to roses.>

PAOLO. Noble sir,
We looked for welcome from your courtesy,
Not from your love, <but this unhoped for sight
Of smiling faces, and the gentle tone
In which you greet us, leave us naught to win
Within your hearts.> I need not ask, my lord,
Where bides the precious object of my search;
For I was sent to find the fairest maid
Ravenna boasts, among her many fair.
I might extend my travel many a league,
And yet return, to take her from your side.
I blush to bear so rich a treasure home,
As pledge and hostage of a sluggish peace;
For beauty such as hers was meant by Heaven
To spur our race to gallant enterprise,
And draw contending deities around
The dubious battles of a second Troy.

GUI. Sir Count, you please to lavish on my child
The high-strained courtesy of chivalry;
<Yet she has homely virtues that, I hope,
May take a deeper hold in Rimini,
After the fleeting beauty of her face
Is spoiled by time, or faded to the eye
By its familiar usage.

PAOLO. As a man
Who ever sees Heaven's purpose in its works,>
I must suppose so rare a tabernacle
Was framed for rarest virtues. Pardon me
<My public admiration. If my praise
Clash with propriety, and bare my words
To cooler judgment, 't is not that I wish
To win a flatterer's grudged recompense,
And gain by falsehood what I'd win through love.>
When I have brushed my travel from my garb,
I'll pay my court in more befitting style
(*Music. Exit with his train.*)

GUI. (*Advancing.*) Now, by the saints, Lanciotto's deputy
Stands in this business with a proper grace,
Stretching his lord's instructions till they crack.
<A zealous envoy! Not a word said he
Of Lanciotto—not a single word;
But stood there, staring in Francesca's face
With his devouring eyes.—By Jupiter,>
I but half like it!

FRAN. (*Advancing.*) Father?

GUI. Well, my child.

FRAN. How do you like—

GUI. The coxcomb! I've done well!

FRAN. No, no; Count Lanciotto?

GUI. Well enough.
But hang this fellow—hang your deputies!
I'll never woo by proxy.

FRAN. Deputies!
And woo by proxy!

GUI. Come to me anon.
I'll strip this cuckoo of his gallantry!
(*Exit with Guards.*)

FRAN. Ritta, my father has strange ways of late.

RIT. I wonder not.

FRAN. You wonder not?

RIT. No, lady:
<He is so used to playing double games,
That even you must come in for your share.
Plague on his boiling! I will out with it. (*Aside.*)>
Lady, the gentleman who passed the gates—

FRAN. Count Lanciotto? As I hope for grace,
A gallant gentleman! How well he spoke!
With what sincere and earnest courtesy
The rounded phrases glided from his lips!
He spoke in compliments that seemed like truth.
Methinks I'd listen through a summer's day,
To hear him woo.—And he must woo to me—
I'll have our privilege—he must woo a space,
Ere I'll be won, I promise.

RIT. But, my lady,
He'll woo you for another.

FRAN. He?—ha! ha! (*Laughing.*)
I should not think it from the prologue, Ritta.

RIT. Nor I.

FRAN. Nor any one.

RIT. 'T is not the Count—
'T is not Count Lanciotto.

FRAN. Gracious saints!
Have you gone crazy? Ritta, speak again,
Before I chide you.

RIT. 'T is the solemn truth.

That gentleman is [the] Count Paolo, lady,
Brother to Lanciotto, and no more
Like him than—than—
FRAN. Than what?
<RIT. Count Guido's pot,
For boiling waiting-maids, is like the bath
Of Venus on the arras.>
FRAN. [But] Are you mad,—
Quite mad, poor Ritta?
RIT. Yes; perhaps I am,
<Perhaps Lanciotto is a proper man—
Perhaps I lie—perhaps I speak the truth—
Perhaps I gabble like a fool. O! heavens,
That dreadful pot!>
FRAN. Dear Ritta!—
RIT. By the mass,
They shall not cozen you, <my gentle mistress!
If my lord Guido boiled me, do you think
I should be served up to the garrison,
By way of pottage? Surely they would not waste me.
FRAN. You are an idle talker. Pranks like these
Fit your companions. You forget yourself.
RIT. Not you, though, lady.> Boldly I repeat,
That he who looked so fair, and talked so sweet,
Who rode from Rimini upon a horse
Of dapple-gray, and walked through yonder gate,
Is not Count Lanciotto.
FRAN. This you mean?
RIT. I do, indeed!
FRAN. Then I am more abused—
More tricked, more trifled with, more played upon—
By him, my father, and by all of you,
Than anything, suspected of a heart,
Was ever yet!
RIT. [But] in Count Paolo, lady,
Perchance there was no meditated fraud.
FRAN. How, dare you plead for him?
RIT. I but suppose:
Though in your father—O! I dare not say.
FRAN. I dare. It was ill usage, gross abuse,
Treason to duty, meanness, craft—dishonour!
What if I'd thrown my heart before the feet
Of this sham husband! cast my love away
Upon a counterfeit! <I was prepared
To force affection upon any man
Called Lanciotto. Anything of silk,
Tinsel, and gewgaws, if he bore that name,
Might have received me for the asking. Yes,
I was inclined to venture more than half
In this base business—shame upon my thoughts!—
All for my father's peace and poor Ravenna's.
And this Paolo, with his cavalcade,
His minstrels, music, and his pretty airs,
His showy person, and his fulsome talk,
Almost made me contented with my lot.
O! what a fool> in faith, I merit it—
<Trapped by mere glitter! What an easy fool!>
Ha! ha! I'm glad it went no further, girl; (*Laughing.*)
I'm glad I kept my heart safe, after all.
There was my cunning. I have paid them back,
I warrant you! I'll marry Lanciotto;
<I'll seem to shuffle by this treachery. No!
I'll seek my father, put him face to face
With his own falsehood; and I'll stand between,
Awful as justice, meting out to him
Heaven's dreadful canons 'gainst his conscious guilt.
I'll marry Lanciotto. On my faith,
I would not live another wicked day
Here, in Ravenna, only for the fear
That I should take to lying, with the rest.>
Ha! ha! it makes me merry, when I think
How safe I kept this little heart of mine!
(*Laughing.*)
(*Exit, with Attendants.*)
<RIT. So, 't is all ended—all except my boiling,
And that will make a holiday for some.
Perhaps I'm selfish. Fagot, axe, and gallows,
They have their uses, after all. They give
The lookers-on a deal of harmless sport.
Though one may suffer, twenty hundred laugh;
And that's a point gained. I have seen a man—
Poor Dora's uncle—shake himself with glee,
At the bare thought of the ridiculous style
In which some villain died. "Dancing," quoth he,
"To the poor music of a single string!

Biting," quoth he, "after his head was off!
What use of that?" Or, "Shivering," quoth he,
"As from an ague, with his beard afire!"
And then he 'd roar until his ugly mouth
Split at the corners. But to see me boil—
O! that will be the queerest thing of all!
I wonder if they 'll put me in a bag,
Like a great suet-ball? I 'll go, and tell
Count Guido, on the instant. How he 'll laugh
To think his pot has got an occupant!
I wonder if he really takes delight
In such amusements? Nay, I have kept faith:
I only said the man was not Lanciotto;
No word of Lanciotto's ugliness.
I may escape the pot, for all. Pardee!
I wonder if they 'll put me in a bag!
(*Exit, laughing.*)>

SCENE 3. *The Same. A Room in* GUIDO'S *Palace.*

(*Enter* GUIDO *and* RITTA.)

<RITTA. There now, my lord, this is the whole of it:
I love my mistress more than I fear you.
If I could save her finger from the axe,
I 'd give my head to do it. So, my lord,
I am prepared to stew.

GUIDO. Boil, Ritta, boil.

RIT. No; I prefer to stew.

GUI. And I to boil.

RIT. 'T is very hard, my lord, I cannot choose
My way of cooking. I shall laugh, I vow,
In the grim headsman's face, when I remember
That I am dying for my lady's love.
I leave no one to shed a tear for me;
Father nor mother, kith nor kin, have I,
To say, "Poor Ritta!" o'er my lifeless clay.
They all have gone before me, and 't were well
If I could hurry after them.

GUI. Poor child! (*Aside.*)
But, baggage, said you aught of Lanciotto?

RIT. No, not a word; and he 's so ugly, too!

GUI. Is he so ugly?

RIT. Ugly! he is worse
Than Pilate on the hangings.

GUI. Hold your tongue
Here, and at Rimini, about the Count,
And you shall prosper.

RIT. Am I not to boil?

GUI. No, child. But be discreet at Rimini.
Old Malatesta is a dreadful man—
Far worse than I—he bakes his people, Ritta;
Lards them, like geese, and bakes them in an oven.

RIT. Fire is my fate, I see that.

GUI. Have a care
It do not follow you beyond this world.
Where is your mistress?

RIT. In her room, my lord.
After I told her of the Count Paolo,
She flew to have an interview with you;
But on the way—I know not why it was—
She darted to her chamber, and there stays
Weeping in silence. It would do you good—
More than a hundred sermons—just to see
A single tear, indeed it would, my lord.

GUI. Ha! you are saucy. I have humored you
Past prudence, malpert! Get you to your room! (*Exit* RITTA.)
More of my blood runs in yon damsel's veins
Than the world knows. Her mother to a shade;
The same high spirit, and strange martyr-wish
To sacrifice herself, body and soul,
For some loved end. All that she did for me;
And yet I loved her not. O! memory!
The darkest future has a ray of hope,
But thou art blacker than the sepulchre!
Thy horrid shapes lie round, like scattered bones,
Hopeless forever! I am sick at heart.
The past crowds on the present: as I sowed,
So am I reaping. Shadows from myself
Fall on the picture, as I trace anew
These rising spectres of my early life,
And add their gloom to what was dark before.
O! memory, memory! How my temples throb! (*Sits.*)

(*Enter* FRANCESCA, *hastily.*)

FRANCESCA. My lord, this outrage—(*He looks up.*) Father, are you ill?
You seem unhappy. Have I troubled you?
You heard how passionate and bad I was,
When Ritta told me of the Count Paolo.

Dear father, calm yourself; and let me ask
A child's forgiveness. 'T was undutiful
To doubt your wisdom. It is over now,
I only thought you might have trusted me
With any counsel.

GUI. (*Aside.*) Would I had!

FRAN. Ah! well,
I understand it all, and you were right.
Only the danger of it. Think, my lord,
If I had loved this man at the first sight:
We all have heard of such things. Think, again,
If I had loved him—as I then supposed
You wished me to—'t would have been very sad.
But no, dear sir, I kept my heart secure,
Nor will I loose it till you give the word.
I 'm wiser than you thought me, you perceive.
But when we saw him, face to face, together,
Surely you might have told me then.

GUI. Francesca,
My eyes are old—I did not clearly see—
Faith, it escaped my thoughts. Some other things
Came in my head. I was as ignorant
Of Count Paolo's coming as yourself.
The brothers are so like.

FRAN. Indeed?

GUI. Yes, yes,
One is the other's counterpart, in fact;
And even now it may not be—O! shame!
I lie by habit. (*Aside.*)>

FRAN. Then there is hope? [Ritta may be deceived.]
He may be Lanciotto, after all?
O! joy—

(*Enter a* SERVANT.)

SERVANT. The Count Paolo. (*Exit.*)

FRAN. [Ah.] Misery!
That name was not Lanciotto!

<GUI. Farewell, child.
I 'll leave you with the Count: he 'll make it plain.
It seems 't was Count Paolo. (*Going.*)

FRAN. Father!

GUI. Well.

FRAN. You knew it from the first! (*Exit* GUIDO.) Let me begone:
I could not look him in the face again
With the old faith. Besides, 't would anger him
To have a living witness of his fraud
Ever before him; and I could not trust—
Strive as I might—my happiness to him,
As once I did. I could not lay my hand
Upon his shoulder, and look up to him,
Saying, dear father, pilot me along
Past this dread rock, through yonder narrow strait.
Saints, no! The gold that gave my life away
Might, even then, be rattling in his purse,
Warm from the buyer's hand. Look on me, Heaven!
Him thou didst sanctify before my eyes,
Him thou didst charge, as thy great deputy,
With guardianship of a weak orphan girl,
Has fallen from grace, has paltered with his trust;
I have no mother to receive thy charge,—
O! take it on thyself; and when I err,
Through mortal blindness, Heaven, be thou my guide!>
Worse cannot fall me. Though my husband lack
A parent's tenderness, he yet may have
Faith, truth, and honour—the immortal bonds
That knit together honest hearts as one.
Let me away to Rimini. Alas!
It wrings my heart to have outlived the day
That I can leave my home with no regret! (*Weeps.*)

(*Enter* PAOLO.)

PAOLO. Pray, pardon me. (*Going.*)

FRAN. You are quite welcome, Count.
A foolish tear, a weakness, nothing more:
But present weeping clears our future sight.
They tell me you are love's commissioner,
A kind of broker in the trade of hearts:
Is it your usual business? or may I
Flatter myself, by claiming this essay
As your first effort?

PAOLO. Lady, I believed
My post, at starting, one of weight and trust;
When I beheld you, I concluded it
A charge of honor and high dignity.
I did not think to hear you underrate
Your own importance, by dishonouring me.

<FRAN. You are severe, my lord.

PAOLO. No, not severe;
Say candid, rather. I am somewhat hurt
By my reception. If I feel the wound,
'T is not because I suffer from the jest,
But that your lips should deal it.

FRAN. Compliments
Appear to be the staple of your speech.

You ravish one with courtesy, you pour
Fine words upon one, till the listening head
Is bowed with sweetness. Sir, your talk is drugged;
There 's secret poppy in your sugared phrase.
I 'll taste before I take it.
PAOLO. Gentle lady—
FRAN. I am not gentle, or I missed my aim.
I am no hawk to fly at every lure.
You courtly gentlemen draw one broad rule—
All girls are fools. It may be so, in truth,
Yet so I 'll not be treated.
PAOLO. Have you been?
If I implied such slander by my words,
They wrong my purpose. If I compliment,
'T is not from habit, but because I thought
Your face deserved my homage as its due.
When I have clearer insight, and you spread
Your inner nature o'er your lineaments,
Even that face may darken in the shades
Of my opinion. For mere loveliness
Needs inward light to keep it always bright.
All things look badly to unfriendly eyes.
I spoke my first impression; cooler thought
May work strange changes.
FRAN. Ah, Sir Count, at length
There 's matter in your words.
PAOLO. Unpleasant stuff,
To judge by your dark brows. I have essayed
Kindness and coldness, yet you are not pleased.
FRAN. How can I be?
PAOLO. How, lady?
FRAN. Ay, sir, how?>
Your brother—my good lord that is to be—
Stings me with his neglect; and in the place
He should have filled, he sends a go-between,
A common carrier of others' love;
How can the sender, or the person sent,
Please overmuch? Now, were I such as you,
I 'd be too proud to travel round the land
With other people's feelings in my heart;
Even to fill the void which you confess
By such employment.
PAOLO. Lady, 't is your wish
To nettle me, to break my breeding down,
And see what natural passions I have hidden
Behind the outworks of my etiquette.
I neither own nor feel the want of heart
With which you charge me. You are more than cruel;
<You rouse my nerves until they ache with life,
And then pour fire upon them. For myself
I would not speak, unless you had compelled.>
My task is odious to me. Since I came,
Heaven bear me witness how my traitor heart
Has fought against my duty; and how oft
I wished myself in Lanciotto's place,
Or him in mine.
FRAN. You riddle.
PAOLO. Do I? Well,
Let it remain unguessed.
<FRAN. You wished yourself
At Rimini, or Lanciotto here?
You may have reasons.
PAOLO. Well interpreted!
The Sphinx were simple in your skilful hands!
FRAN. It has become your turn to sneer.
PAOLO. But I
Have gall to feed my bitterness, while you
Jest in the wanton ease of happiness.
Stop! there is peril in our talk.
FRAN. As how?
PAOLO. 'T is dangerous to talk about one's self;
It panders selfishness.> My duty waits.
FRAN. My future lord's affairs? I quite forgot
Count Lanciotto.
PAOLO. I, too, shame upon me. (*Aside.*)
FRAN. Does he resemble you?
PAOLO. Pray, drop me, lady.
FRAN. Nay, answer me.
PAOLO. Somewhat—in feature.
FRAN. Ha!
Is he so fair?
PAOLO. No, darker. He was tanned
In long campaigns, and battles hotly fought,
While I lounged idly with the troubadours,
Under the shadow of his watchful sword.
FRAN. In person?
PAOLO. He is shorter, I believe,

But broader, stronger, more compactly knit.
FRAN. What of his mind?
PAOLO. Ah, now you strike the key!
A mind just fitted to his history,
An equal balance 'twixt desert and fame.
<No future chronicler shall say of him,
His fame outran his merit; or his merit
Halted behind some adverse circumstance,
And never won the glory it deserved.>
My love might weary you, if I rehearsed
The simple beauty of his character;
His grandeur and his gentleness of heart,
His warlike fire and peaceful love, his faith,
His courtesy, his truth. <I'll not deny
Some human weakness, to attract our love,
Harbors in him, as in the rest of us.
Sometimes against our city's enemies
He thunders in the distance, and devotes
Their homes to ruin. When the brand has fallen,
He ever follows with a healing rain,
And in his pity shoulders by revenge.
A thorough soldier, lady. He grasps crowns,
While I pick at the laurel.
FRAN. Stay, my lord!
I asked your brother's value, with no wish
To hear you underrate yourself. Your worth
May rise in passing through another's lips.>
Lanciotto is perfection, then?
PAOLO. To me:
Others may think my brother over-nice
Upon the point of honour; over-keen
To take offence where no offence is meant;
A thought too prodigal of human life,
Holding it naught when weighed against a wrong;
<Suspicious of the motives of his friends;
Distrustful of his own high excellence;
And with a certain gloom of temperament,
When thus disturbed, that makes him terrible
And rash in action. I have heard of this.
I never felt it. I distress you, lady?>
Perhaps I throw these points too much in shade,
By catching at an enemy's report.
But, then, Lanciotto said, "You'll speak of me,
Not as I ought to be, but as I am."
He loathes deceit.
FRAN. That's noble! Have you done?
I have observed a strange reserve, at times,
<An over-carefulness in choosing words,>
Both in my father and his nearest friends,
When speaking of your brother; as if they
Picked their way slowly o'er rocky ground,
<Fearing to stumble. Ritta, too, my maid,
When her tongue rattles on in full career,
Stops at your brother's name, and with a sigh
Settles herself to dismal silence. Count,>
These things have troubled me. From you I look
For perfect frankness. Is there naught withheld?
<PAOLO. (*Aside.*) O, base temptation! What if I betray
His crippled person—imitate his limp—
Laugh at his hip, his back, his sullen moods
Of childish superstition?—tread his heart
Under my feet, to climb into his place?—
Use his own warrant 'gainst himself; and say,
Because I loved her, and misjudged your jest,
Therefore I stole her? Why, a common thief
Would hang for just such thinking! Ha! ha! ha! (*Laughing.*)
I reckon on her love, as if I held
The counsels of her bosom. No, I swear
Francesca would despise so mean a deed.
Have I no honour either? Are my thoughts
All bound by her opinion?
FRAN. This is strange!
Is Lanciotto's name a spell to all?
I ask a simple question, and straight you
Start to one side, and mutter to yourself,
And laugh, and groan, and play the lunatic,
In such a style that you astound me more
Than all the others. It appears to me
I have been singled as a common dupe
By every one. What mystery is this

Surrounds Count Lanciotto? If there be
A single creature in the universe
Who has a right to know him as he is,
I am that one.

PAOLO. I grant it. You shall see,
<And shape your judgment by your own remark.>
All that my honour calls for I have said.

FRAN. <I am content. Unless I greatly err,
Heaven made your breast the seat of honest thoughts.>
You know, my lord, that, once at Rimini,
There can be no retreat for me. By you,
Here at Ravenna, in your brother's name,
I shall be solemnly betrothed. And now
I thus extend my maiden hand to you;
If you are conscious of no secret guilt,
Take it.

PAOLO. I do. (*Takes her hand.*)

FRAN. You tremble!

PAOLO. With the hand,
Not with the obligation.

FRAN. Farewell, Count!
T' were cruel to tax your stock of compliments,
That waste their sweets upon a trammelled heart;
Go fly your fancies at some freer game.
(*Exit.*)

PAOLO. O, heaven, if I have faltered and am weak,
'T is from my nature! Fancies, more accursed
Than haunt a murderer's bedside, throng my brain—
Temptations, such as mortal never bore
Since Satan whispered in the ear of Eve.
Sing in my ear—and all, all are accursed!
At heart I have betrayed my brother's trust,
Francesca's openly. Turn where I will.
As if enclosed within a mirrored hall,
I see a traitor. Now to stand erect,
Firm on my base of manly constancy;
Or, if I stagger, let me never quit
The homely path of duty, for the ways
That bloom and glitter with seductive sin! (*Exit.*)

[In the acting version of 1882, everybody was sent on and the act ended with Paolo taking Francesca's hand and speaking the words. "On to Rimini!"]

ACT THIRD.

SCENE I.[1] *Rimini. A room in the Castle.*
LANCIOTTO *discovered reading.*

LANCIOTTO. O! fie, philosophy! This Seneca
Revels in wealth, and whines about the poor!
Talks of starvation while his banquet waits,
And fancies that a two hours' appetite
Throws light on famine! Doubtless he can tell,
As he skips nimbly through his dancing-girls,
How sad it is to limp about the world
A sightless cripple! Let him feel the crutch
Wearing against his heart, and then I'd hear
This sage talk glibly; or provide a pad,
Stuffed with his soft philosophy, to ease
His aching shoulder. Pshaw; he never felt,
Or pain would choke his frothy utterance.
<'T is easy for the doctor to compound
His nauseous simples for a sick man's health;
But let him swallow them, for his disease,
Without wry faces. Ah! the tug is there.>
Show me philosophy in rags, in want,
Sick of a fever, with a back like mine,
Creeping to wisdom on these legs, and I
Will drink its comforts. Out! away with you!
There 's no such thing as real philosophy!
(*Throws down the book.*)

(*Enter* PEPE.)

Here is a sage who 'll teach a courtier
The laws of etiquette, a statesman rule,
A soldier discipline, a poet verse,
And each mechanic his distinctive trade;
Yet bring him to his motley, and how wide
He shoots from reason! We can understand
All business but our own, and thrust advice
In every gaping cranny of the world;
While habit shapes us to our own dull work,
And reason nods above his proper task.
Just so philosophy would rectify

[1] In the acting version of 1853 this scene placed in Act Second.

All things abroad, and be a jade at home.
<Pepe, what think you of the Emperor's aim
Towards Hungary?

PEPE. A most unwise design;
For mark, my lord—

LAN. Why, there! the fact cries out.
Here 's motley thinking for a diadem!—
Ay, and more wisely in his own regard.

PEPE. You flout me, cousin.

LAN. Have you aught that 's new?—
Some witty trifle, some absurd conceit?

PEPE. Troth, no.

LAN. Why not give up the Emperor,
And bend your wisdom on your duties, Pepe?

PEPE. Because the Emperor has more need of wisdom
Than the most barren fool of wit.

LAN. Well said!
Mere habit brings the fool back to his art.>
This jester is a rare philosopher.
Teach me philosophy, good fool.

PEPE. No need.
You 'll get a teacher when you take a wife.
If she do not instruct you in more arts
Than Aristotle ever thought upon,
The good old race of woman has declined
Into a sort of male stupidity.
<I had a sweetheart once, she lectured grandly;
No matter on what subject she might hit,
'T was all the same, she could talk and she would,
She had no silly modesty; she dashed
Straight in the teeth of any argument,
And talked you deaf, dumb, blind. Whatever struck
Upon her ear, by some machinery,
Set her tongue wagging. Thank the Lord, she died!—
Dropped in the middle of a fierce harangue,
Like a spent horse. It was an even thing,
Whether she talked herself or me to death.
The latest sign of life was in her tongue;
It wagged till sundown, like a serpent's tail,
Long after all the rest of her was cold.
Alas! poor Zippa!

LAN. Were you married, fool?

PEPE. Married! Have I the scars upon me? No;
I fell in love; and that was bad enough.
And far enough for a mere fool to go.
Married! why, marriage is love's purgatory,
Without a heaven beyond.

LAN. Fie, atheist!
Would you abolish marriage?

PEPE. Yes.

LAN. What?

PEPE. Yes

LAN. Depopulate the world?

PEPE. No fear of that.
I 'd have no families, no Malatesti,
Strutting about the land, with pedigrees
And claims bequeathed them by their ancestors;
No fellows vapouring of their royal blood;
No one to seize a whole inheritance,
And rob the other children of the earth.
By Jove, you should not know your fathers, even!
I 'd have you spring, like toadstools, from the soil—
Mere sons of women—nothing more nor less—
All base-born, and all equal. There, my lord,
There is a simple commonwealth for you!
In which aspiring merit takes the lead,
And birth goes begging.

LAN. It is so, in truth;
And by the simplest means I ever heard.

PEPE. Think of it, cousin. Tell it to your friends,
The statesmen, soldiers, and philosophers;
Noise it about the earth, and let it stir
The sluggish spirits of the multitudes.
Pursue the thought, scan it, from end to end,
Through all its latent possibilities.
It is a great seed dropped, I promise you,
And it must sprout. Thought never wholly dies;
It only wants a name—a hard Greek name—
Some few apostles, who may live on it—
A crowd of listeners, with the average dulness
That man possesses—and we organize;
Spread our new doctrine, like a general plague;
Talk of man's progress and development,
Wrongs of society, the march of mind,
The Devil, Doctor Faustus, and what not;
And, lo! this pretty world turns upside down,
All with a fool's idea!

LAN. By Jupiter,

You hit our modern teachers to a hair!
I knew this fool was a philosopher.
Pepe is right. Mechanic means advance;
Nature bows down to Science' haughty tread,
And turns the wheel of smutty artifice;
New governments arise, dilate, decay,
And foster creeds and churches to their tastes:
At each advance, we cry, "Behold, the end!"
Till some fresh wonder breaks upon the age.
But man, the moral creature, midst it all
Stands still unchanged; nor moves towards virtue more,
Nor comprehends the mysteries in himself,
More than when Plato taught academies,
Or Zeno thundered from his Attic porch.

PEPE. I know not that: I only want my scheme
Tried for a while. I am a politician,
A wrongs-of-man man. Hang philosophy!
Let metaphysics swallow, at a gulp,
Its last two syllables, and purge itself
Clean of its filthy humours! I am one
Ready for martyrdom, for stake and fire,
If I can make my great idea take root!
Zounds! cousin, if I had an audience,
I'd make you shudder at my eloquence!
I have an itching to reform the world.

LAN. Begin at home, then.

PEPE. Home is not my sphere;
Heaven picked me out to teach my fellow-men.
I am a very firebrand of truth—
A self-consuming, doomed, devoted brand—
That burns to ashes while I light the world!
I feel it in me. I am moved, inspired,
Stirred into utterance, by some mystic power
Of which I am the humble instrument.

LAN. A bad digestion, sage,—a bilious turn,
A gnawing stomach, or a pinching shoe.

PEPE. O! hear, but spare the scoffer! Spare the wretch
Who sneers at the anointed man of truth!
When we reached that, I and my followers
Would rend you limb from limb. There!—ha! ha! ha! *(Laughing.)*
Have I not caught the slang these fellows preach;
A grand, original idea, to back it;
And all the stock in trade of a reformer?

LAN. You have indeed; nor do I wonder, Pepe.
Fool as you are, I promise you success
In your new calling, if you'll set it up.
The thing is far too simple.>

(Trumpet sounds within.)

PEPE. Hist! my lord.

LAN. That calls me to myself.

PEPE. At that alarm,
All Rimini leaped up upon its feet.
Cousin, your bridal-train. You groan! 'Ods wounds!
Here is the bridegroom sorely malcontent—
The sole sad face in Rimini. Since morn,
A quiet man could hardly walk the streets,
For flowers and streamers. All the town is gay.
Perhaps 't is merry o'er your misery.

LAN. Perhaps; but that it knows not.

PEPE. Yes, it does:
It knows that when a man's about to wed,
He's ripe to laugh at. Cousin, tell me, now,
Why is [Count] Paolo on the way so long?
Ravenna's but eight leagues from Rimini—

LAN. That's just the measure of your tongue, good fool.
You trouble me. I've had enough of you—
Begone!

<PEPE. I'm going; but you see I limp.
Have pity on a cripple, gentle Count. *(Limps.)*

LAN. Pepe!

PEPE. A miracle, a miracle!
See, see, my lord, at Pepe's saintly name
The lame jog on.>

MALATESTA. *(Without.)* Come, Lanciotto!

LAN. Hark!
My father calls.

PEPE. If he were mine, I'd go—
That's a good boy! *(Pats LANCIOTTO'S back.)*

LAN. *(Starting.)* Hands off! you'll rue it else! *(Exit.)*

PEPE. *(Laughing.)* Ha! ha! I laid my hand upon his hump!
Heavens, how he squirmed! And what a wish I had
To cry, Ho! camel! leap upon his back,
And ride him to the devil! <So, we've had

A pleasant flitting round philosophy!
The Count and fool bumped heads, and struck ideas
Out by the contact! Quite a pleasant talk—
A friendly conversation, nothing more—
'Twixt nobleman and jester.> Ho! my bird,
I can toss lures as high as any man.
So, I amuse you with my harmless wit?
Pepe 's your friend now—you can trust in him—
An honest, simple fool! Just try it once,
You ugly, misbegotten clod of dirt!
Ay, but the hump—the touch upon the hump—
The start and wriggle—that was rare! Ha! ha! (*Exit, laughing.*)

SCENE 2.[1] *The Same. The Grand Square before the Castle. Soldiers on guard, with banners. Citizens, in holiday dresses, cross the scene. The houses are hung with trophies, banners, and garlands.*

(*Enter* MALATESTA, *with guards, attendants.*)

MALATESTA. Captain, take care the streets be not choked up
By the rude rabble. Send to Cæsar's bridge
A strong detachment of your men, and clear
The way before them. <See that nothing check
The bride's first entrance into Rimini.
Station your veterans in the front. Count Guido
Comes with his daughter, and his eyes are sharp.
Keep up a show of strength before him, sir;
And set some laborers to work upon
The broken bastion.> Make all things look bright;
As if we stood in eager readiness,
And high condition, to begin a war.
CAPTAIN. I will, my lord.
MAL. Keep Guido in your eye;
And if you see him looking over-long
On any weakness of our walls, just file
Your bulkiest fellows round him; <or get up
A scuffle with the people; anything—

[1] In both acting versions this scene begins the Third Act.

Even if you break a head or two—to draw
His vision off. But where our strength is great,
Take heed to make him see it.> You conceive?
CAPT. Trust me, my lord.
(*Exit with guards.*)

(*Enter* PEPE.)

PEPE. Room, room! A hall; a hall!
I pray you, good man, has the funeral passed?
MAL. Who is it asks?
PEPE. Pepe of Padua,
A learned doctor of uncivil law.
MAL. But how a funeral?
PEPE. You are weak of wit.
Francesca of Ravenna 's borne to church,
And never issues thence.
MAL. How, doctor, pray?
PEPE. Now, for a citizen of Rimini,
You 're sadly dull. Does she not issue thence
Fanny of Rimini? A glorious change,—
A kind of resurrection in the flesh!
<MAL. (*Laughing.*) Ha! ha! thou cunning villain! I was caught.
I own it, doctor.
PEPE. (*Aside.*) This old fool would laugh
To see me break a straw, because the bits
Were of unequal length. My character
Carries more dulness, in the guise of wit,
Than would suffice to break an ass's back.> (*Distant shouts and music.*)
Hark! here comes Jeptha's daughter, jogging on
With timbrels and with dances.
MAL. Jeptha's daughter!
How so?
PEPE. Her father's sacrifice.
MAL. (*Laughing.*) <Ho! ho!
You 'll burst my belt! O! you outrageous wretch.
To jest at Scripture!
PEPE. You outlandish heathen,
'T is not in Scripture!
MAL. Is it not?
PEPE. No more
Than you are in heaven. Mere Hebrew history.
She went up to the mountains, to bewail
The too-long keeping of her honesty.
There 's woman for you! there 's a character!
What man would ever think of such a thing?
Ah! we of Rimini have little cause

For such a sorrow. Would she 'd been my wife!
I 'll marry any woman in her case.
MAL. Why, Pepe?
PEPE. Why? because, in two months' time,
Along comes father Jeptha with his knife,
And there 's an end. Where is your sacrifice?
Where 's Isaac, Abraham? Build your altar up:
One pile will do for both.
MAL. That 's Scripture, sure.
PEPE. Then I 'm a ram, and you may slaughter me
In Isaac's stead.>
MAL. Here comes the vanguard. Where,
Where is that laggard?
PEPE. At the mirror, uncle,
Making himself look beautiful. He comes, (*Looking out.*)
Fresh as a bridegroom! Mark his doublet's fit
Across the shoulders, and his hose!—
By Jove, he nearly looks like any other man!
MAL. You 'd best not let him hear you. Sirrah, knave,
I have a mind to swinge you! (*Seizes his ear.*)
PEPE. <Loose my ear!
You 've got the wrong sow, swineherd!> You 're unjust.
Being his father, I was fool sufficient
To think you fashioned him to suit yourself,
By way of a variety. The thought
Was good enough, the practice damnable.
MAL. Hush! or I 'll clap you in the pillory.

<(*Enter* LANCIOTTO.)>

PEPE. (*Sings.*) Ho, ho, ho, ho!—old Time has wings—
We 're born, we mourn, we wed, we bed,
We have a devilish aching head;
So down we lie,
And die, and fry;
And there 's a merry end of things!
(*Music, within.*)
Here come Ravenna's eagles for a roost
In Rimini! The air is black with them.
When go they hence? Wherever yon bird builds,
The nest remains for ages. Have an eye,
Or Malatesta's elephant may feel
The eagle's talons.
LANCIOTTO.[1] You 're a raven, croaker.
PEPE. And you no white crow, to insure us luck.
MAL. There 's matter in his croak.
PEPE. There always is;
But men lack ears.
MAL. Then eyes must do our work.
<Old Guido shall be looked to. If his force
Appear too great, I 'll camp him out of town.
LAN. Father, you are a sorry host.
MAL. Well, well,
I 'm a good landlord, though.> I do not like
This flight of eagles more than Pepe. 'S death!
Guido was ever treacherous.
<LAN. My lord,
You mar my holiday by such a thought.
My holiday! Dear saints! it seems to me
That all of you are mocking me.>
PEPE. So—so—
Guido was ever treacherous?—so—so!
MAL. So—so! How so?
PEPE. What if this treachery
Run in the blood? We 'll tap a vein then—so!
MAL. Sew up your mouth, and mind your fooling, fool!
PEPE. Am I not fooling? Why, my lord, I thought
The fooling exquisite.
<LAN. (*Aside.*) This thoughtless knave
Hits near us sometimes with his random shafts.
Marriage for me! I cannot comprehend,
I cannot take it to my heart; the thing
Seems gross, absurd, ridiculous. Ah! well,
My father bears the folly of it all;
I 'm but an actor in his comedy.
My part is bad, but I must through with it. (*Retires.*)>
(*Shouts and music within.*)
PEPE. Look! here 's the whole parade! <Mark yonder knave—
The head one with the standard. Nature, nature!
Hadst thou a hand in such a botch-work? Why,
A forest of his legs would scarcely make
A bunch of fagots.> Mark old Guido, too!
He looks like Judas with his silver. Ho!
Here 's news from sweet Ravenna!

1 In the acting version Malatesta has this line as Lanciotto is not on the stage.

MAL. (*Laughing.*) Ha! ha! ha!
PEPE. Ah! now the bride!—that 's something—she is toothsome.
Look you, my lord—now, while the progress halts—
Cousin Paolo, has he got the dumps?
Mercy! to see him, one might almost think
'T was his own marriage. What a doleful face!
The boy is ill. He caught a fever, uncle,
Travelling across the marshes. Physic! physic!
<If he be really dying, get a doctor,
And cut the matter short. 'T were merciful.>
MAL. For heaven's sake, cease your clamor! I shall have
No face to meet them else. 'T is strange, for all:
What ails [poor] Paolo?
PEPE. Dying, by this hand!
MAL. Then I will hang you.
PEPE. Don't take up my craft.
Wit 's such a stranger in your brain that I
Scarce knew my lodger venturing from your mouth.
Now they come on again.
MAL. Stand back!
<PEPE. (*Looking round.*) The bridegroom?
He flies betimes, before the bride shows fight.
(*Walks back, looking for* LANCIOTTO.)>
(*Music, shouts, ringing of bells. Enter Men-at-arms, with banners,* GUIDO, *Cardinal, Knights, Attendants; then* PAOLO, *conducting* FRANCESCA, *followed by* RITTA, *Ladies, Pages, and other Men-at-Arms. They file around the stage, and halt.*)
MAL. Welcome to Rimini, Count Guido! Welcome.
And fair impressions of our poor abode,
To you, my daughter! You are well returned,
My [dear] son, Paolo! Let me bless you, son.
(PAOLO *approaches.*)
How many spears are in old Guido's train? (*Apart to* PAOLO.)
PAOLO. Some ten-score.
MAL. Footmen?
PAOLO. Double that.
MAL. 'T is well.
Again I bid you welcome! Make no show
Of useless ceremony with us. Friends
Have closer titles than the empty name.
<We have provided entertainment, Count,
For all your followers, in the midst of us.
We trust the veterans of Rimini
May prove your soldiers that our courtesy
Does not lag far behind their warlike zeal.>
Let us drop Guelf and Ghibelin henceforth,
Coupling the names of Rimini and Ravenna
As bridegroom's to his bride's.
GUIDO. Count Malatesta,
<I am no rhetorician, or my words
Might keep more even with the love I feel:>
Simply, I thank you. With an honest hand
I take the hand which you extend to me,
And hope our grasp may never lose its warmth.—
You marked the bastion by the waterside?
Weak as a bulrush.
(*Apart to a* KNIGHT.)
KNIGHT. Tottering weak, my lord.
GUI. Remember it; and when you 're private, sir,
Draw me a plan.
KNIGHT. I will, my lord.
GUI. How 's this?
I do not see my future son-in-law.
MAL. Lanciotto!
LAN. (*Advancing.*) I am here, my lord.[1]
FRANCESCA. (*Starting.*) O! heaven!
Is that my husband, [fair] Count Paolo? You,
You then, among the rest, have played me false!
He is— (*Apart to* PAOLO.)
PAOLO. My brother.
LAN. (*Aside.*) Ha! she turns from me.
<PEPE. (*Approaching* LANCIOTTO, *sings.*)
Around, around the lady turned,
She turned not to her lord;
She turned around to a gallant, gallant knight,
Who ate at his father's board.
A pretty ballad! all on one string though.
LAN. Pepe, go hence! (PEPE *retires.*)
(*Aside.*) I saw her start and pale,>
Turn[s] off with horror; as if she had seen—

[1] In the acting versions, Lanciotto comes on here for the first time in this act.

What?—simply me. For, am I not enough,
And something over, to make ladies quail,
Start, hide their faces, whisper to their friends,
Point at me—dare she?—and perform such tricks
As women will when monsters blast their sight?
O! saints above me, have I come so low?
<Yon damsel of Ravenna shall bewail
That start and shudder. I am mad, mad, mad!>
I must be patient. They have trifled with her:
Lied to her, lied! <There 's half the misery
Of this broad earth, all crowded in one word.
Lied, lied!—Who has not suffered from a lie?>
They 're all aghast—all looking at me, too.
Francesca 's whiter than the brow of fear:
<Paolo talks.—Brother, is that well meant?>
What if I draw my sword, and fight my way
Out of this cursed town? 'T would be relief.
<Has shame no hiding-place? I 've touched the depth
Of human infamy, and there I rest.>
By heaven, I'll brave this business out! Shall they
Say at Ravenna that Count Lanciotto,
Who 's driven their shivering squadrons to their homes,
Haggard with terror, turned before their eyes
And slunk away? They 'll look me from the field,
When we encounter next. Why should not I
Strut with my shapeless body, as old Guido
Struts with his shapeless heart? I 'll do it! (*Offers, but shrinks back.*)
'S death!
<Am I so false as to forswear myself?>
Lady Francesca! (*Approaches* FRANCESCA.)

FRAN. Sir—my lord—

LAN. Dear lady,
I have a share in your embarrassment,
And know the feelings that possess you now.

FRAN. O! you do not.

PAOLO. (*Advancing.*) My lady—

LAN. Gentle brother,
Leave this to me. (PAOLO *retires.*)

FRAN. Pray do not send him off.

LAN. 'T is fitter so.

FRAN. He comforts me.

LAN. Indeed?
Do you need comfort?

FRAN. No, no—pardon me!
But then—he is—you are—

LAN. Take breath, and speak.

FRAN. I am confused, 't is true. But, then, my lord,
You are a stranger to me; and [Count] Paolo
I 've known so long!

LAN. Since yesterday.

FRAN. Ah! well:
But the relationship between us two
Is of so close a nature, while the knowledge,
That each may have of each, so slender is
That the two jar. Besides, [Count] Paolo is
Nothing to me, while you are everything.
Can I not act? (*Aside.*)

LAN. I scarcely understand.
You say your knowledge of me, till to-day,
Was incomplete. Has naught been said of me
[Either] by Count Paolo or your father?

FRAN. Yes;
But nothing definite.

LAN. Perchance, no hint
As to my ways, my feelings, manners, or—
Or—or—as I was saying—ha! ha!—or— (*Laughing.*)
As to my person?

FRAN. Nothing, as to that.

LAN. To what?

FRAN. Your—person.

LAN. That 's the least of all. (*Turns aside.*)
Now, had I Guido of Ravenna's head
Under this heel, I 'd grind it into dust!
<False villain, to betray his simple child!
And thou, Paolo—not a whit behind—
Helping his craft with inconsiderate love!>
Lady Francesca, when my brother left,
I charged him, as he loved me, to conceal
Nothing from you that bore on me: and now
That you have seen me, and conversed with me,
If you object to anything in me,—
Go, I release you.

FRAN. But Ravenna's peace?
LAN. Shall not be periled.
GUI. (*Coming behind, whispers her.*) Trust him not, my child;
I know his ways; he 'd rather fight than wed.
'T is but a wish to have the war afoot.
Stand firm for poor Ravenna!
LAN. Well, my lady,
Shall we conclude a lasting peace between us
By truce or marriage rites?
GUI. (*Whispers her.*) The devil tempts thee:
Think of Ravenna, think of me!
LAN. My lord,
I see my father waits you.
(GUIDO *retires.*)
FRAN. Gentle sir,
You do me little honour in the choice.
LAN. My aim is justice.
FRAN. Would you cast me off?
LAN. Not for the world, if honestly obtained;
Not for the world would I obtain you falsely.
FRAN. The rites were half concluded ere we met.
LAN. Meeting, would you withdraw?
FRAN. No. Bitter word! (*Aside.*)
LAN. No! Are you dealing fairly?
FRAN. I have said.
LAN. O! rapture, rapture! Can it be that I—
Now I 'll speak plainly; for a choice like thine
Implies such love as woman never felt.
Love me! Then monsters beget miracles,
And Heaven provides where human means fall short.
Lady, I 'll worship thee! I 'll line thy path
With suppliant kings! Thy waiting-maids shall be
Unransomed princesses! Mankind shall bow
One neck to thee, as Persia's multitudes
Before the rising sun! From this small town,
This centre of my conquests, I will spread
An empire touching the extremes of earth!
I 'll raise once more the name of ancient Rome;
And what she swayed she shall reclaim again!
If I grow mad because you smile on me,
Think of the glory of thy love; and know
How hard it is, for such an one as I,
To gaze unshaken on divinity!
There 's no such love as mine alive in man.
From every corner of the frowning earth,
It has been crowded back into my heart.
Now, take it all! If that be not enough,
Ask, and thy wish shall be omnipotent!
Your hand. (*Takes her hand.*) It wavers.
FRAN. So does not my heart.
LAN. Bravo! Thou art every way a soldier's wife;
Thou shouldst have been a Cæsar's! Father, hark!
I blamed your judgment, only to perceive
The weakness of my own.
MAL. What means all this?
LAN. It means that this fair lady—though I gave
Release to her, and to Ravenna—placed
The liberal hand, which I restored to her,
Back in my own, of her own free good-will.
Is it not wonderful?
MAL. How so?
LAN. How so!
<PAOLO. Alas! 't is as I feared!
(*Aside.*)>
MAL. You 're humble?—How?
LAN. <Now shall I cry aloud to all the world.
Make my deformity my pride, and say,
Because she loves me, I may boast of it?
(*Aside.*)>
No matter, father, I am happy; you,
As the blessed cause, shall share my happiness.
Let us be moving. Revels, dashed with wine,
Shall multiply the joys of this sweet day!
There 's not a blessing in the cup of life
I have not tasted of within an hour!
<FRAN. (*Aside.*) Thus I begin the practice of deceit,
Taught by deceivers, at a fearful cost.
The bankrupt gambler has become the cheat,
And lives by arts that erewhile ruined me.
Where it will end, heaven knows; but I—
I have betrayed the noblest heart of all![1]>
LAN. Draw down thy dusky vapours, sullen night—
Refuse, ye stars, to shine upon the world—
Let everlasting blackness wrap the sun,

[1] Both acting versions omit this speech, which is essential to the tragedy.

And whisper terror to the universe!
We need ye not! we 'll blind ye, if ye dare
Peer with lack-lustre on our revelry!
I have at heart a passion, that would make
All nature blaze with recreated light!
(*Exeunt.*)

ACT FOURTH.

SCENE 1. *The Same. An Apartment in the Castle.*

(*Enter* LANCIOTTO.)

LANCIOTTO. It cannot be that I have duped myself,
That my desire has played into the hand
Of my belief; yet such a thing might be.
We palm more frauds upon our simple selves
Than knavery puts upon us. Could I trust
The open candor of an angel's brow,
I must believe Francesca's. But the tongue
Should consummate the proof upon the brow,
And give the truth its word. The fault lies there.
I 've tried her. Press her as I may to it,
She will not utter those three little words—
"I love thee." She will say, "I 'll marry you;—
I 'll be your duteous wife;—I 'll cheer your days;—
I 'll do whate'er I can." But at the point
Of present love, she ever shifts the ground,
Winds round the word, laughs, calls me "Infidel!—
How can I doubt?" So, on and on. But yet,
For all her dainty ways, she never says,
Frankly, I love thee. I am jealous—true!
Suspicious—true! distrustful of myself;—
She knows all that. <Ay, and she likewise knows,
A single waking of her morning breath
Would blow these vapours off. I would not take
The barren offer of a heartless hand,
If all the Indies cowered under it.>
Perhaps she loves another? No; she said,
"I love you, Count, as well as any man";
<And laughed, as if she thought that precious wit.
I turn her nonsense into argument,
And think I reason. Shall I give her up?
Rail at her heartlessness, and bid her go
Back to Ravenna? But she clings to me,
At the least hint of parting.> Ah! 't is sweet,
Sweeter than slumber to the lids of pain,
To fancy that a shadow of true love
May fall on this God-stricken mould of woe,
From so serene a nature. <Beautiful
Is the first vision of a desert brook,
Shining beneath its palmy garniture,
To one who travels on his easy way;
What is it to the blood-shot, aching eye
Of some poor wight who crawls with gory feet,
In famished madness, to its very brink;
And throws his sun-scorched limbs upon the cool
And humid margin of its shady strand,
To suck up life at every eager gasp?
Such seems Francesca to my thirsting soul;
Shall I turn off and die?>

(*Enter* PEPE.)

PEPE. Good-morning, cousin!
LAN. Good-morning to your foolish majesty!
PEPE. The same to your majestic foolery!
LAN. You compliment!
PEPE. I am a troubadour,
A ballad-monger of fine mongrel ballads,
And therefore running o'er with elegance.
Wilt hear my verse?
LAN. With patience?
PEPE. No, with rapture.
You must go mad—weep, rend your clothes, and roll
Over and over, like the ancient Greeks,
When listening to the Iliad.
LAN. Sing, then, sing!
And if you equal Homer in your song,
Why, roll I must, by sheer compulsion.
PEPE. Nay,
You lack the temper of the fine-eared Greek.
You will not roll; but that shall not disgrace
My gallant ballad, fallen on evil times.
(*Sings.*)

My father had a blue-black head,
  My uncle's head was reddish—maybe,
My mother's hair was noways red,
  Sing high ho! the pretty baby!

Mark the simplicity of that! 'T is called
"The Babe's Confession," spoken just before
His father strangled him.

LAN. Most marvellous!
You struggle with a legend worth your art.

PEPE. Now to the second stanza. Note the hint
I drop about the baby's parentage:
So delicately too! A maid might sing,
And never blush at it. <Girls love these songs
Of sugared wickedness. They 'll go miles about,
To say a foul thing in a cleanly way.
A decent immorality, my lord,
Is art's specific. Get the passions up,
But never wring the stomach.>

LAN. Triumphant art!
(PEPE *sings.*)

My father combed his blue-black head,
  My uncle combed his red head—maybe,
My mother combed my head, and said,
  Sing high ho! my red-haired baby.

LAN. Fie, fie! go comb your hair in private.

PEPE. What!
Will you not hear? Now comes the tragedy. (*Sings.*)

My father tore my red, red head,
  My uncle tore my father's—maybe,
My mother tore both till they bled—
  Sing high ho! your brother's baby!

LAN. Why, what a hair-rending!

PEPE. Thence wigs arose;
A striking epoch in man's history.
<But did you notice the concluding line,
Sung by the victim's mother? There 's a hit!

"Sing high ho! your brother's baby!"

Which brother's, pray you? That 's the mystery,
The adumbration of poetic art,
And there I leave it to perplex mankind.>
It has a moral, fathers should regard,—
A black-haired dog breeds not a red haired cur.
<Treasure this knowledge: you 're about to wive;
And no one knows what accident—

LAN. Peace, fool!>
So all this cunning thing was wound about,
To cast a jibe at my deformity?
(*Tears off* PEPE'S *cap.*)
There lies your cap, the emblem that protects
Your head from chastisement. Now, Pepe, hark!
Of late you 've taken to reviling me;
Under your motley, you have dared to jest
At God's inflictions. Let me tell you, fool,
No man e'er lived, to make a second jest
At me, before your time!

PEPE. Boo! Bloody-bones!
If you 're a coward—which I hardly think—
You 'll have me flogged, or put into a cell,
Or fed to wolves. If you are bold of heart,
You 'll let me run. Do not; I 'll work you harm!
I, Beppo Pepe, standing as a man,
Without my motley, tell you, in plain terms,
I 'll work you harm—I 'll do you mischief, man!

LAN. I, Lanciotto, Count of Rimini,
Will hang you, then. Put on your jingling cap;
You please my father. But remember, fool,
No jests at me!

PEPE. I will try earnest next.

LAN. And I the gallows.

PEPE. Well, cry quits, cry quits!
I 'll stretch your heart, and you my neck—quits, quits!

LAN. Go, fool! Your weakness bounds your malice.

PEPE. Yes.
So you all think, you savage gentlemen,
Until you feel my sting. Hang, hang away!
It is an airy, wholesome sort of death,
Much to my liking. When I hang, my friend,
You 'll be chief mourner, I can promise you.
Hang me! I 've quite a notion to be hung:
I 'll do my utmost to deserve it. Hang!
(*Exit.*)

LAN. I am bemocked on all sides. My sad state
Has given the licensed and unlicensed fool

Charter to challenge me at every turn.
The jester's laughing bauble blunts my sword,
His gibes cut deeper than its fearful edge;
And I, a man, a soldier, and a prince,
Before this motley patchwork of a man,
Stand all appalled, as if he were a glass
Wherein I saw my own deformity.
O Heaven! a tear—one little tear—to wash
This aching dryness of the heart away!

(*Enter* PAOLO.)

<PAOLO. What ails the fool? He passed me, muttering
The strangest garbage in the fiercest tone.
"Ha! ha!" cried he, "they made a fool of me—
A motley man, a slave; as if I felt
No stir in me of manly dignity!
Ha! ha! a fool—a painted plaything, toy—
For men to kick about this dirty world!
My world as well as theirs.—God's world, I trow!
I will get even with them yet—ha! ha!
In the democracy of death we 'll square.
I 'll crawl and lie beside a king's own son;
Kiss a young princess, dead lip to dead lip;
Pull the Pope's nose; and kick down Charlemagne,
Throne, crown, and all, where the old idiot sprawls,
Safe as he thinks, rotting in royal state!"
And then he laughed and gibbered, as if drunk
With some infernal ecstasy.

LAN. Poor fool!
That is the groundwork of his malice, then,—
His conscious difference from the rest of men?
I, of all men, should pity him the most.
Poor Pepe! I 'll be kinder. I have wronged
A feeling heart. Poor Pepe!>

PAOLO. [What, Lanciotto, art thou] Sad again!
Where has the rapture gone of yesterday?

LAN. Where are the leaves of summer? Where the snows
Of last year's Winter? Where the joys and griefs
That shut our eyes to yesternight's repose,
And woke not on the morrow? <Joys and griefs,
Huntsmen and hounds, ye follow us as game,
Poor panting outcasts of your forest-law!
Each cheers the others,—one with wild halloos,
And one with whines and howls.—A dreadful chase,
That only closes when horns sound *a mort!*

PAOLO. Thus ever up and down!> Arouse yourself,
Balance your mind more evenly, and hunt
For honey in the wormwood.

LAN. Or find gall
Hid in the hanging chalice of the rose:
Which think you better? If my mood offend,
We 'll turn to business, <to the empty cares
That make such pother in our feverish life.>
When at Ravenna, did you ever hear
Of any romance in Francesca's life?
A love-tilt, gallantry, or anything
That might have touched her heart?

PAOLO. Not lightly even.
I think her heart as virgin as her hand.

LAN. Then there is hope.

PAOLO. Of what?

LAN. Of winning her.

PAOLO. Grammercy! Lanciotto, are you sane?
You boasted yesterday—

LAN. And changed to-day.
Is that so strange? I always mend the fault
Of yesterday with wisdom of to-day.
She does not love me.

PAOLO. Pshaw! she marries you:
'T were proof enough for me.

LAN. Perhaps, she loves you.

PAOLO. Me, Lanciotto, me! For mercy's sake,
Blot out such thoughts—they madden me! What, love—
She love—yet marry you!

LAN. It moves you much.
'T was but a fleeting fancy, nothing more.

PAOLO. You have such wild conjectures!

LAN. Well, to me
They seem quite tame; they are my bed-fellows.
Think, to a modest woman, what must be
The loathsome kisses of an unloved man—
A gross, coarse ruffian!

PAOLO. O, good heavens, forbear! [1]
LAN. What shocks you so?
PAOLO. The picture which you draw,
Wronging yourself by horrid images.
LAN. Until she love me, till I know, beyond
The cavil of a doubt, that she is mine—
Wholly, past question—do you think that I
Could so afflict the woman whom I love?
PAOLO. You love her, Lanciotto!
LAN. Next to you,
Dearer than anything in nature's scope.
PAOLO. (*Aside.*) O! Heaven, that I must bear this! <Yes, and more,—
More torture than I dare to think upon,
Spreads out before me with the coming years,
And holds a record blotted with my tears,
As that which I must suffer!>
LAN. Come, Paolo, [come]
<Come> help me [to] woo. I need your guiding eye,
To signal me, if I should sail astray.
PAOLO. O! torture, torture! (*Aside.*)
LAN. You and I, perchance,
Joining our forces, may prevail at last.
They call love like a battle. As for me,
I 'm not a soldier equal to such wars,
Despite my arduous schooling. <Tutor me
In the best arts of amorous strategy.
I am quite raw, Paolo. Glances, sighs,
Sweets of the lip, and arrows of the eye,
Shrugs, cringes, compliments, are new to me;
And I shall handle them with little art.>
Will you instruct me?
PAOLO. <Conquer for yourself.
Two captains share one honour: keep it all.
What if I ask to share the spoils?
LAN. (*Laughing.*) Ha! ha!
I 'll trust you, brother.> Let us go to her:
Francesca is neglected while we jest.
I know not how it is, but your fair face,
And noble figure, always cheer me up,
More than your words; there 's healing in them, too,
For my worst griefs. Dear brother, let us in. (*Exeunt.*)

---

[1] The following lines in Boker's handwriting were substituted in the acting version of 1853 for the remainder of the scene, which had already been cut as indicated.

PAOLO.[1] Oh! good heaven, forbear!
But this is idle talk. (*Bells ring.*) Your marriage bells
Are pealing on the air. The guests attend.
Bestir you, if you are not yet attired
Quite to your liking.
LANCIOTTO. Does he mock me, too?
Nay, I more wrong myself in wronging him. (*Aside.*)

(*Enter* RENÉ, TROUBADOURS *and* NOBLEMEN.)

RENÉ. Bestir yourselves, good gentlemen. The church
Awaits your presence, Count Lanciotto, come!
Can you be slow to win so fair a prize?
1ST NOBLEMAN. Go fetch the bride, Count Paolo. This command
Your father bade me bear you.
PAOLO. Break, my heart!
Why stretch the torture through another day? (*Aside.*)
Come, brother, hasten! (*Exit.*)
LANCIOTTO. As you will. In sooth,
You all look joyous. Are you honest, then,
To urge this marriage? If I once say, no!
Not all the fathers that begot their kind
Since man was man can shake my uttered will.
1ST. NOBLEMAN. Think of the bride, my lord.
RENÉ. Oh! such a slight,
To hurl your *no* against her whispered *yes*.
LAN. So be it then, I have called in the world
To counsel with me, and you all approve
The love-sick yearnings of my heart. O God,
I trust I do no creature shaped by thee,
In thy own image—not in mine—a wrong
By mating with the fairest of them all!
Marriage! why, marriage is, like birth and death
The common lot of all. Then why should I,
Who never feared the sternest mood of man,
Fear woman at her tenderest? Gently, sirs:
Let us walk softly to the sacred church;
Mindful that other rites than marriages
Make it a portal opening into Heaven.
(*Exeunt.*)

Scene 2.[1] *The Same. A Chamber in the Same.* Francesca *and* Ritta *discovered at the bridal toilet.*

<Ritta. (*Sings.*)
Ring high, ring high! to earth and sky;
A lady goes a-wedding;
The people shout, the show draws out,
And smiles the bride is shedding.

No bell for you, ye ragged few;
A beggar goes a-wedding;
The people sneer, the thing 's so queer,
And tears the bride is shedding.

Ring low, ring low! dull bell of woe,
One tone will do for either;
The lady glad, and beggar sad,
Have both lain down together.

Francesca. A mournful ballad!
Rit. I scarce knew I sang.>
I 'm weary of this wreath. These orange-flowers
Will never be adjusted to my taste:
Strive as I will, they ever look awry.
<My fingers ache!
Fran. Not more than my poor head.
There, leave them so.
Rit. That 's better, yet not well.
Fran. They are but fading things, not worth your pains:
They 'll scarce outlive the marriage merriment.>
Ritta, these flowers are hypocrites; they show
An outside gayety, yet die within,
Minute by minute. You shall see them fall,
Black with decay, before the rites are o'er.
Rit. How beautiful you are!
Fran. Fie, flatterer!
White silk and laces, pearls and orange-flowers,
Would do as much for any one.
Rit. No, no!
You give them grace, they nothing give to you.
<Why, after all, you make the wreath look well;
But somewhat dingy, where it lies against
Your pulsing temple, sullen with disgrace.>
Ah! well, your Count should be the proudest man
That ever led a lady into church,
Were he a modern Alexander. Poh!
What are his trophies to a face like that?

[1] This scene was omitted in the 1882 version, and a portion of it put in Scene 1.

Fran. I seem to please you, Ritta.
Rit. Please yourself,
And you will please me better. You are sad:
I marked it ever since you saw the Count.
I fear the splendor of his victories,
And his sweet grace of manner—for, in faith,
His is the gentlest, grandest character,
Despite his—
Fran. Well?
Rit. Despite his—
Fran. Ritta, what?
Rit. Despite his difference from Count Paolo, [lady].—
(Francesca *staggers.*)
What is the matter? (*Supporting her.*)
Fran. Nothing; mere fatigue.
Hand me my kerchief. I am better now.
What were you saying?
Rit. <That I fear the Count
Has won your love.
Fran. Would that be cause for fear?
(*Laughing.*)
Rit. O! yes, indeed! Once—long ago—I was
Just fool enough to tangle up my heart
With one of these same men. 'T was terrible!
Morning or evening, waking or asleep,
I had no peace. Sighs, groans, and standing tears,
Counted my moments through the blessed day.
And then to this there was a dull, strange ache
Forever sleeping in my breast,—a numbing pain,
That would not for an instant be forgot.
O! but I loved him so, that very feeling
Became intolerable. And I believed
This false Giuseppe, too, for all the sneers,
The shrugs and glances, of my intimates.
They slandered me and him, yet I believed.
He was a noble, and his love to me
Was a reproach, a shame, yet I believed.
He wearied of me, tried to shake me off,
Grew cold and formal, yet I would not doubt.
O! lady, I was true! Nor till I saw
Giuseppe walk through the cathedral door
With Dora, the rich usurer's niece, upon
The very arm to which I clung so oft,
Did I so much as doubt him. Even then—
More is my shame—I made excuses for him.

"Just this or that had forced him to the course:
Perhaps, he loved me yet—a little yet.
His fortune, or his family, had driven
My poor Giuseppe thus against his heart.
The low are sorry judges for the great.
Yes, yes, Giuseppe loved me!" But at last
I did awake. It might have been with less:
There was no need of crushing me, to break
My silly dream up. In the street, it chanced,
Dora and he went by me, and he laughed—
A bold, bad laugh—right in my poor pale face,
And turned and whispered Dora, and she laughed.
Ah! then I saw it all. I've been awake,
Ever since then, I warrant you. And now
I only pray for him sometimes, when friends
Tell his base actions towards his hapless wife.
O! I am lying—I pray every night!
(*Weeps.*)

FRAN. Poor Ritta. (*Weeping.*)

RIT. No! blest Ritta! Thank kind heaven,
That kept me spotless when he tempted me,
And my weak heart was pleading with his tongue,
Pray, do not weep. You spoil your eyes for me.
But never love; oh! it is terrible!

FRAN. I'll strive against it.

RIT. Do: because, my lady,
Even a husband may be false, you know;
Ay, even to so sweet a wife as you.
Men have odd tastes. They'll surfeit on the charms
Of Cleopatra, and then turn aside
To woo her blackamoor. 'T is so, in faith;
Or Dora's uncle's gold had ne'er outbid
The boundless measure of a love like mine.
Think of it, lady, to weigh love with gold!
What could be meaner?

FRAN. Nothing, nothing, Ritta.
Though gold 's the standard measure of the world,
And seems to lighten everything beside.
Yet heap the other passions in the scale,
And balance them 'gainst that which gold outweighs—
Against this love—and you shall see how light
The most supreme of them are in the poise!
I speak by book and history; for love
Slights my high fortunes. Under cloth of state
The urchin cowers from pompous etiquette,
Waiving his function at the scowl of power,
And seeks the rustic cot to stretch his limbs
In homely freedom. I fulfill a doom.
We who are topmost on this heap of life
Are nearer to heaven's hand than you below;
And so are used, as ready instruments,
To work its purposes. Let envy hide
Her witless forehead at a prince's name,
And fix her hopes upon a clown's content.
You, happy lowly, know not what it is
To groan beneath the crowned yoke of state,
And bear the goadings of the sceptre. Ah!
Fate drives us onward in a narrow way,
Despite our boasted freedom.>

(*Enter* PAOLO, *with Pages bearing torches.*)

Gracious saints! [my lord]
What brought you here?

PAOLO. The bridegroom waits.

FRAN. He does?
Let him wait on forever! I'll not go!
O! dear [dear] Paolo—

PAOLO. Sister!

FRAN. It is well.
I have been troubled with a sleepless night.
My brain is wild. I know not what I say.
Pray, do not call me sister; it is cold.
<I never had a brother, and the name
Sounds harshly to me. When you speak to me,>
Call me Francesca.

PAOLO. You shall be obeyed.

FRAN. I would not be obeyed. I'd have you do it
Because—because you love me—as a sister—
And of your own good-will, not my command,
Would please me.—Do you understand?

PAOLO. Too well! (*Aside.*)
'T is a nice difference.

FRAN. Yet you understand?
Say that you do.
PAOLO. I do.
FRAN. That pleases me.
'T is flattering if our—friends appreciate
Our nicer feelings.
PAOLO. I await you, lady.
FRAN. Ritta, my gloves.—Ah, yes, I have them on;
Though I'm not quite prepared. Arrange my veil;
It folds too closely. That will do; retire.
(RITTA *retires.*)
[And] So, Count Paolo, you have come, hot haste,
To lead me to the church,—to have your share
In my undoing? And you came, in sooth,
Because they sent you? You are very tame!
And if they sent, was it for you to come?
PAOLO. Lady, I do not understand this scorn.
I came, as is my duty, to escort
My brother's bride to him. When next you're called,
I'll send a lackey.
<FRAN. I have angered you.
PAOLO. With reason: I would not appear to you
Low and contemptible.
FRAN. Why not to me?
PAOLO. Lady, I'll not be catechized.
FRAN. Ha! Count!
PAOLO. No! if you press me further, I will say
A word to madden you.—Stand still! You stray
Around the margin of a precipice.
I know what pleasure 't is to pluck the flowers
That hang above destruction, and to gaze
Into the dread abyss, to see such things
As may be safely seen. 'T is perilous:
The eye grows dizzy as we gaze below,
And a wild wish possesses us to spring
Into the vacant air. Beware, beware!
Lest this unholy fascination grow
Too strong to conquer!
FRAN. You talk wildly, Count;
There's not a gleam of sense in what you say;
I cannot hit your meaning.
PAOLO. Lady, come!>
FRAN. Count, you are cruel! (*Weeps.*)
PAOLO. O! no; I would be kind.
<But now, while reason over-rides my heart
And seeming anger plays its braggart part—>
In heaven's name, come!
FRAN. One word—one question more:
Is it your wish this marriage should proceed?
PAOLO. It is.
FRAN. Come on! You shall not take my hand:
I'll walk alone—now, and forever!
PAOLO. (*Taking her hand.*) Sister!
(*Exeunt* PAOLO *and* FRANCESCA, *with Pages.*)
<RITTA. O! misery, misery!—it is plain as day—
She loves Paolo! Why will those I love
Forever get themselves ensnared, and heaven
Forever call on me to succor them?
Here was the mystery, then—the sighs and tears,
The troubled slumbers, and the waking dreams!
And now she's walking through the chapel-door,
Her bridal robe above an aching heart,
Dressed up for sacrifice. 'T is terrible!
And yet she'll smile and do it. Smile, for years,
Until her heart breaks; and the nurses ask
The doctor of the cause. He'll answer too,
In hard thick Latin, and believe himself.
O! my dear mistress! Heaven, pray torture me!
Send back Giuseppe, let him ruin me,
And scorn me after; but, sweet heaven, spare her!
I'll follow her. O! what a world is this!
(*Exit.*)>

SCENE 3. *The Same. Interior of the Cathedral.* LANCIOTTO, FRANCESCA, PAOLO, MALATESTA, GUIDO, RITTA, PEPE, *Lords, Knights, Priests, Pages, a bridal-train of Ladies, Soldiers, Citizens, Attendants, discovered before the High Altar. Organ music. The rites being over, they advance.*

MALATESTA. By heaven—
PEPE. O! uncle, uncle, you're in church!
MAL. I'll break your head, knave!
PEPE. I claim sanctuary.
MAL. Why, bridegroom, will you never kiss the bride?
We all are mad to follow you.

PEPE. Yes, yes;
<Here was [Count] Paolo wetting his red lips
For the last minute. Kiss, and> give <him> [us] room.

MAL. You heaven-forsaken imp, be quiet now!

PEPE. Then there 'd be naught worth hearing.

MAL. Bridegroom, come!

PEPE. Lord! he don't like it! Hey!—I told you so—
He backs at the first step. Does he not know
His trouble 's just begun?

LANCIOTTO. Gentle Francesca,
Custom imposes somewhat on thy lips:
I 'll make my levy. (*Kisses her. The others follow.*) (*Aside.*) Ha! she shrank! I felt
Her body tremble, and her quivering lips
Seemed dying under mine! I heard a sigh,
Such as breaks hearts—O! no, a very groan;
And then she turned a sickly, miserable look
On pallid Paolo, and he shivered, too!
There is a mystery hangs around her,—ay,
[And] Paolo knows it, too.—By all the saints,
I 'll make him tell it, at the dagger's point!
Paolo!—here! [here!] I do adjure you, brother,
By the great love I bear you, to reveal
The secret of Francesca's grief.

PAOLO. I cannot.

LAN. She told you nothing?

PAOLO. Nothing.

LAN. Not a word?

PAOLO. Not one.

LAN. What heard you at Ravenna, then?

PAOLO. Nothing.

LAN. Here?

PAOLO. Nothing.

LAN. Not the slightest hint?—
Don't stammer, man! Speak quick! I am in haste.

PAOLO. Never.

LAN. What know you?

PAOLO. Nothing that concerns
Your happiness, Lanciotto. If I did,
Would I not tell unquestioned?

LAN. Would you not?
You ask a question for me: answer it.

PAOLO. I have.

LAN. You juggle, you turn deadly pale.
Fumble your dagger, stand with head half round,
Tapping your feet.—You dare not look at me!
By Satan! [now,] Count Paolo, let me say,
You look much like a full-convicted thief!

PAOLO. Brother!—

LAN. Pshaw! brother! You deceive me, sir:
You and that lady have a devil's league,
To keep a devil's secret. Is it thus
You deal with me? Now, by the light above,
I 'd give a dukedom for some fair pretext
To fly you all! She does not love me? Well,
I could bear that, and live away from her.
Love would be sweet, but want of it becomes
An early habit to such men as I.
But you—ah! there 's the sorrow—whom I loved
An infant in your cradle; you who grew
Up in my heart, with every inch you gained;
You whom I loved for every quality,
Good, bad, and common, in your natural stock;
Ay, for your very beauty! It is strange, you 'll say,
For such a crippled horror to do that,
Against the custom of his kind! O! yes,
I love, and you betray me!

PAOLO. Lanciotto,
This is sheer frenzy. Join your bride.

LAN. I 'll not!
What, go to her, to feel her very flesh
Crawl from my touch? to hear her sigh and moan,
As if God plagued her? Must I come to that?
<Must I endure your hellish mystery
With my own wife, and roll my eyes away
In sentimental bliss?> No, no! until
I go to her, with confident belief
In her integrity and candid love,
I 'll shun her as a leper.
(*Alarm-bells toll.*)

MAL. What is that?

(*Enter, hastily, a* MESSENGER *in disorder.*)

MESSENGER. My lord, the Ghibelins are up—

LAN. And I
Will put them down again! I thank thee, heaven,
For this unlooked-for aid! (*Aside.*)

[GUIDO. My lord, believe
I had no hand nor heart in this new trial.
MALATESTA. We do not doubt you.
GUIDO. Else I must depart.
MAL. Pray you remain. He longs to lead the war
Despite his protest.] Friend, what force have they? (*To* MESSENGER.)
LAN. It matters not,—nor yet the time, place, cause,
Of their rebellion. I would throttle it,
Were it a riot, or a drunken brawl!
MAL. Nay, son, your bride—
LAN. My bride will pardon me;
Bless me, perhaps, as I am going forth:—
Thank me, perhaps, if I should ne'er return. (*Aside.*)
A soldier's duty has no bridals in it.
PAOLO. Lanciotto, this is folly. Let me take
Your usual place of honour.
LAN. (*Laughing.*) Ha! ha! ha!
What! thou, a tilt-yard soldier, lead my troops!
My wife will ask it shortly. Not a word
Of opposition from the new-made bride?
Nay, she looks happier. O! accursed day,
That I was mated to an empty heart! (*Aside.*)
<MAL. But, son—
LAN. Well, father?
PEPE. Uncle, let him go.
He'll find it cooler on a battle-field
Than in his—
LAN. Hark! the fool speaks oracles.>
You, soldiers, who are used to follow me,
And front our charges, emulous to bear
The shock of battle on your forward arms,—
Why stand ye in amazement? Do your swords
Stick to their scabbards with inglorious rust?
Or has repose so weakened your big hearts,
That you can dream with trumpets at your ears?
Out with your steel! It shames me to behold
Such tardy welcome to my war-worn blade! (*Draws.*)
(*The Knights and Soldiers draw.*)
Ho! draw our forces out! Strike camp, sound drums,
And set us on our marches! As I live,
I pity the next foeman who relies
On me for mercy! Farewell! to you all—
To all alike—a soldier's short farewell! (*Going.*)
(PAOLO *stands before him.*)
Out of my way, thou juggler! (*Exit.*)
PAOLO. He is gone!

ACT FIFTH.

<SCENE 1.[1] *The Same. The Garden of the Castle.*

(*Enter* PEPE, *singing.*)

PEPE. 'T is jolly to walk in the shady greenwood
With a damsel by your side;
'T is jolly to walk from the chapel-door,
With the hand of your pretty bride;
'T is jolly to rest your weary head,
When life runs low and hope is fled,
On the heart where you confide:
'T is jolly, jolly, jolly, they say,
They say—but I never tried.

Nor shall I ever till they dress their girls
In motley suits, and pair us, to increase
The race of fools. 'T would be a noble thing,
A motley woman, had she wit enough
To bear the bell. But there's the misery:
You may make princes out of any stuff;
Fools come by nature. She'll make fifty kings—
Good, hearty tyrants, sound, cruel governors—
For one fine fool. There is Paolo, now,
A sweet-faced fellow with a wicked heart—
Talk of a flea, and you begin to scratch.
Lo! here he comes. And there's fierce crookback's bride
Walking beside him—O, how gingerly!
Take care, my love! that is the very pace
We trip to hell with. Hunchback is away—
That was a fair escape for you; but, then,
The devil's ever with us, and that's worse.
See, the Ravenna gigglet, Mistress Ritta,
And melancholy as a cow.—How's this?
I'll step aside, and watch you, pretty folks.
(*Hides behind the bushes.*)

(*Enter* PAOLO *and* FRANCESCA, *followed by*

[1] In the 1853 version, this entire scene was omitted. It was restored in the 1882 version.

RITTA. *He seats himself in an arbor, and reads.*)
FRANCESCA. Ritta.
RITTA. My lady.
FRAN. You look tired.
RIT. I'm not.
FRAN. Go to your chamber.
RIT. I would rather stay,
If it may please you. I require a walk
And the fresh atmosphere of breathing flowers,
To stir my blood. I am not very well.
FRAN. I knew it, child. Go to your chamber, dear.
Paolo has a book to read to me.
RIT. What, the romance? I should so love to hear!
I dote on poetry; and Count Paolo
Sweetens the Tuscan with his mellow voice.
I'm weary now, quite weary, and would rest.
FRAN. Just now you wished to walk.
RIT. Ah! did I so?
Walking, or resting, I would stay with you.
FRAN. The Count objects. He told me, yesterday,
That you were restless while he read to me;
And stirred your feet amid the grass, and sighed,
And yawned, until he almost paused.
RIT. Indeed
I will be quiet.
FRAN. But he will not read.
RIT. Let me go ask him.
(*Runs toward* PAOLO.)
FRAN. Stop! Come hither, Ritta.
(*She returns.*)
I saw your new embroidery in the hall,—
The needle in the midst of Argus' eyes;
It should be finished.
RIT. I will bring it here.—
O, no! my finger's sore; I cannot work.
FRAN. Go to your room.
RIT. Let me remain, I pray.
'T is better, lady; you may wish for me;
I know you will be sorry if I go.
FRAN. I shall not, girl. Do as I order you.
Will you be headstrong?
RIT. Do you wish it, then?
FRAN. Yes, Ritta.
RIT. Yet you made pretexts enough,
Before you ordered.
FRAN. You are insolent.
Will you remain against my will?
RIT. Yes, lady;
Rather than not remain.
FRAN. Ha! impudent!
RIT. You wrong me, gentle mistress.
Love like mine
Does not ask questions of propriety,
Nor stand on manners. I would do you good,
Even while you smote me; I would push you back,
With my last effort, from the crumbling edge
Of some high rock o'er which you toppled me.
FRAN. What do you mean?
RIT. I know.
FRAN. Know what?
RIT. Too much
Pray, do not ask me.
FRAN. Speak!
RIT. I know—dear lady,
Be not offended—
FRAN. Tell me, simpleton!
RIT. You know I worship you; you know I'd walk
Straight into ruin for a whim of yours;
You know —
FRAN. I know you act the fool. Talk sense!
RIT. I know Paolo loves you.
FRAN. Should he not?
He is my brother.
RIT. More than brother should.
FRAN. Ha! are you certain?
RIT. Yes, of more than that.
FRAN. Of more?
RIT. Yes, lady; for you love him, too.
I've said it! Fling me to the carrion crows,
Kill me by inches, boil me in the pot
Count Guido promised me,—but, O, beware!
Back, while you may! Make me the sufferer,
But save yourself!
FRAN. Now, are you not ashamed
To look me in the face with that bold brow?
I am amazed!
RIT. I am a woman, lady;
I too have been in love; I know its ways,
Its arts, and its deceits. Your frowning face,
And seeming indignation, do not cheat.
Your heart is in my hand.
PAOLO. (*Calls.*) Francesca!
FRAN. Hence,
Thou wanton-hearted minion! hence, I say!—
And never look me in the face again!—

Hence, thou insulting slave!
RIT. (*Clinging to her.*) O lady, lady—
FRAN. Begone. (*Throws her off.*)
RIT. I have no friends—no one to love—
O, spare me!
FRAN. Hence!
RIT. Was it for this I loved—
Cared for you more than my own happiness—
Ever at heart your slave—without a wish
For greater recompense than your stray smiles?
PAOLO. (*Calls.*) Francesca!
FRAN. Hurry!
RIT. I am gone. Alas!
God bless you, lady! God take care of you,
When I am far away! Alas, alas!
(*Exit weeping.*)
FRAN. Poor girl!—but were she all the world to me,
And held my future in her tender grasp,
I 'd cast her off, without a second thought,
To savage death, for dear Paolo's sake!
Paolo, hither! Now he comes to me;
I feel his presence, though I see him not,
Stealing upon me like the fervid glow
Of morning sunshine. Now he comes too near—
He touches me—O heaven!
PAOLO. Our poem waits.
I have been reading while you talked with Ritta.
How did you get her off?
FRAN. By some device.
She will not come again.
PAOLO. I hate the girl:
She seems to stand between me and the light.
And now for the romance. Where left we off?
FRAN. Where Lancelot and Queen Guenevra strayed
Along the forest, in the youth of May.
You marked the figure of the birds that sang
Their melancholy farewell to the sun—
Rich in his loss, their sorrow glorified—
Like gentle mourners o'er a great man's grave.
Was it not there? No, no; 't was where they sat
Down on the bank, by one impulsive wish
That neither uttered.
PAOLO. (*Turning over the book.*) Here it is. (*Reads.*)
"So sat
Guenevra and Sir Lancelot"—'T were well
To follow them in that.
(*They sit upon a bank.*)
FRAN. I listen: read.
Nay, do not; I can wait, if you desire.
PAOLO. My dagger frets me; let me take it off. (*Rises.*)
In thoughts of love, we'll lay our weapons by.
(*Lays aside his dagger, and sits again.*)
Draw closer: I am weak in voice to-day.
(*Reads.*)
"So sat Guenevra and Sir Lancelot,
Under the blaze of the descending sun,
But all his cloudy splendors were forgot.
Each bore a thought, the only secret one,
Which each had hidden from the other's heart,
That with sweet mystery well-nigh overrun.
Anon, Sir Lancelot, with gentle start,
Put by the ripples of her golden hair,
Gazing upon her with his lips apart.
He marvelled human thing could be so fair;
Essayed to speak; but, in the very deed,
His words expired of self-betrayed despair.
Little she helped him, at his direst need,
Roving her eyes o'er hill, and wood, and sky,
Peering intently at the meanest weed;
Ay, doing aught but look in Lancelot's eye.
Then, with the small pique of her velvet shoe,
Uprooted she each herb that blossomed nigh;
Or strange wild figures in the dust she drew;
Until she felt Sir Lancelot's arm around
Her waist, upon her cheek his breath like dew.
While through his fingers timidly he wound
Her shining locks; and, haply, when he brushed
Her ivory skin, Guenevra nearly swound:
For where he touched, the quivering surface blushed,
Firing her blood with most contagious heat,
Till brow, cheek, neck, and bosom, all were flushed.
Each heart was listening to the other beat.
As twin-born lilies on one golden stalk,

Drooping with Summer, in warm languor meet,
So met their faces. Down the forest walk
Sir Lancelot looked—he looked east, west, north, south—
No soul was nigh, his dearest wish to balk:
She smiled; he kissed her full upon the mouth." (*Kisses* FRANCESCA.)
I 'll read no more!
(*Starts up, dashing down the book.*)

FRAN. Paolo!

PAOLO. I am mad!
The torture of unnumbered hours is o'er,
The straining cord has broken, and my heart
Riots in free delirium! O, heaven!
I struggled with it, but it mastered me!
I fought against it, but it beat me down!
I prayed, I wept, but heaven was deaf to me;
And every tear rolled backward on my heart,
To blight and poison!

FRAN. And dost thou regret?

PAOLO. The love? No, no! I'd dare it all again,
Its direst agonies and meanest fears,
For that one kiss. Away with fond remorse!
Here, on the brink of ruin, we two stand;
Lock hands with me, and brave the fearful plunge!
Thou canst not name a terror so profound
That I will look or falter from. Be bold!
I know thy love—I knew it long ago—
Trembled and fled from it. But now I clasp
The peril to my breast, and ask of thee
A kindred desperation.

FRAN. (*Throwing herself into his arms.*) Take me all,—
Body and soul. The women of our clime
Do never give away but half a heart:
I have not part to give, part to withhold,
In selfish safety. When I saw thee first,
Riding alone amid a thousand men,
Sole in the lustre of thy majesty,
And Guido da Polenta said to me,
"Daughter, behold thy husband!" with a bound
My heart went forth to meet thee. He deceived,
He lied to me—ah! that's the aptest word—
And I believed. Shall I not turn again,
And meet him, craft with craft? Paolo, love,
Thou 'rt dull—thou 'rt dying like a feeble fire
Before the sunshine. Was it but a blaze,
A flash of glory, and a long, long night?

PAOLO. No, darling, no! You could not bend me back;
My course is onward; but my heart is sick
With coming fears.

FRAN. Away with them! Must I
Teach thee to love? and reinform the ear
Of thy spent passion with some sorcery
To raise the chilly dead?

PAOLO. Thy lips have not
A sorcery to rouse me as this spell.
(*Kisses her.*)

FRAN. I give thy kisses back to thee again:
And, like a spendthrift, only ask of thee
To take while I can give.

PAOLO. Give, give forever!
Have we not touched the height of human bliss?
And if the sharp rebound may hurl us back
Among the prostrate, did we not soar once?—
Taste heavenly nectar, banquet with the gods
On high Olympus? If they cast us, now,
Amid the furies, shall we not go down
With rich ambrosia clinging to our lips,
And richer memories settled in our hearts?
Francesca.

FRAN. Love?

PAOLO. The sun is sinking low
Upon the ashes of his fading pyre,
And gray possesses the eternal blue;
The evening star is stealing after him,
Fixed, like a beacon, on the prow of night;
The world is shutting up its heavy eye
Upon the stir and bustle of to-day;—
On what shall it awake?

FRAN. On love that gives
Joy at all seasons, changes night to day,
Makes sorrow smile, plucks out the barbéd dart
Of moaning anguish, pours celestial balm
In all the gaping wounds of earth, and lulls
The nervous fancies of unsheltered fear
Into a slumber sweet as infancy's!
On love that laughs at the impending sword,
And puts aside the shield of caution: cries,

To all its enemies, "Come, strike me now!—
Now, while I hold my kingdom, while my crown
Of amaranth and myrtle is yet green,
Undimmed, unwithered; for I cannot tell
That I shall e'er be happier!" Dear Paolo,
Would you lapse down from misery to death,
Tottering through sorrow and infirmity?
Or would you perish at a single blow,
Cut off amid your wildest revelry,
Falling among the wine-cups and the flowers,
And tasting Bacchus when your drowsy sense
First gazed around eternity? Come, love!
The present whispers joy to us; we'll hear
The voiceless future when its turn arrives.

PAOLO. Thou art a siren. Sing, forever sing;
Hearing thy voice, I cannot tell what fate
Thou hast provided when the song is o'er;—
But I will venture it.

FRAN. In, in, my love!
(*Exeunt.*)

(PEPE *steals from behind the bushes.*)

PEPE. O, brother Lanciotto!—O, my stars!—
If this thing lasts, I simply shall go mad!
(*Laughs, and rolls on the ground.*)
O Lord! to think my pretty lady puss
Has tricks like this, and we ne'er know of it!
I tell you, Lanciotto, you and I
Must have a patent for our foolery!
"She smiled; he kissed her full upon the mouth!"—
There's the beginning; where's the end of it?
O poesy! debauch thee only once,
And thou'rt the greatest wanton in the world!
O cousin Lanciotto—ho, ho, ho!
(*Laughing.*)
Can a man die of laughter? Here we sat;
Mistress Francesca so demure and calm;
Paolo grand, poetical, sublime!—
Eh! what is this? Paolo's dagger? good!
Here is more proof, sweet cousin broken-back.
"In thoughts of love, we'll lay our weapons by!"
(*Mimicking* PAOLO.)
That's very pretty! Here's its counterpart:
In thoughts of hate, we'll pick them up again! (*Takes the dagger.*)
Now for my soldier, now for crook-backed Mars!
Ere long all Rimini will be ablaze.
He'll kill me? Yes: what then? That's nothing new,
Except to me: I'll bear for custom's sake.
More blood will follow; like the royal sun,
I shall go down in purple. Fools for luck;
The proverb holds like iron. I must run,
Ere laughter smother me.—O, ho, ho, ho!
(*Exit, laughing.*)>

SCENE 2. *A camp among the Hills. Before* LANCIOTTO'S *tent.*

(*Enter, from the tent,* LANCIOTTO.)

LANCIOTTO. The camp is strangely quiet. Not a sound
Breaks nature's high solemnity. <The sun
Repeats again his every-day decline;
Yet all the world looks sadly after him,
As if the customary sight were new.
Yon moody sentinel goes slowly by,
Through the thick mists of evening, with his spear
Trailed at a funeral hold. Long shadows creep
From thing beyond the furthest range of sight,
Up to my very feet. These mystic shades
Are of the earth; the light that causes them,
And teaches us the quick comparison,
Is all from heaven. Ah! restless man might crawl
With patience through his shadowy destiny,
If he were senseless to the higher light
Towards which his soul aspires.> How grand and vast
Is yonder show of heavenly pageantry!
How mean and narrow is the earthly stand
From which we gaze on it! <Magnificent,
O God, art thou amid the sunsets! Ah.>

What heart in Rimini is softened now,
Towards my defects, by this grand spectacle?
Perchance, [dear] Paolo now forgives the wrong
Of my hot spleen. Perchance, Francesca now
Wishes me back, and turns a tenderer eye
On my poor person and ill-mannered ways;
Fashions excuses for me, schools her heart
Through duty into love, and ponders o'er
The sacred meaning in the name of wife.
Dreams, dreams! Poor fools, we squander love away
On thankless borrowers; when bankrupt quite,
We sit and wonder of their honesty.
Love, take a lesson from the usurer,
And never lend but on security.
<Captain!

(*Enter a* CAPTAIN.)

CAPTAIN. My lord.
LAN. They worsted us to-day.
CAPT. Not much, my lord.
LAN. With little loss, indeed.
Their strength is in position. Mark you, sir.
(*Draws on the ground with his sword.*)
Here is the pass; it opens towards the plain,
With gradual widening, like a lady's fan.
The hills protect their flanks on either hand;
And, as you see, we cannot show more front
Than their advance may give us. Then, the rocks
Are sorry footing for our horse. Just here,
Close in against the left-hand hills, I marked
A strip of wood, extending down the gorge:
Behind that wood dispose your force ere dawn.
I shall begin the onset, then give ground,
And draw them out; while you, behind the wood,
Must steal along, until their flank and rear
Oppose your column. Then set up a shout,
Burst from the wood, and drive them on our spears.
They have no outpost in the wood, I know;
'T is too far from their centre. On the morrow,
When they are flushed with seeming victory,
And think my whole division in full rout,
They will not pause to scrutinize the wood;
So you may enter boldly. We will use
The heart to-day's repulse has given to them,
For our advantage. Do you understand?
CAPT. Clearly, my lord.
LAN. If they discover you,
Before you gain your point, wheel, and retreat
Upon my rear. If your attack should fail
To strike them with a panic, and they turn
In too great numbers on your small command,
Scatter your soldiers through the wood:
Let each seek safety for himself.
CAPT. I see>
LAN. [What, Marco! ho! (*To* PAGE *who enters.*)]
Have Pluto shod; he cast a shoe to-day:
Let it be done at once. My helmet, too,
Is worn about the lacing; look to that.
<Where is my armorer?
CAPT. At his forge.
LAN. Your charge
Must be at sunrise—just at sunrise, sir—
Neither before nor after. You must march
At moonset, then, to gain the point ere dawn.
That is enough.
CAPT. Good-even! (*Going.*)
LAN. Stay, stay, stay!>
My sword-hilt feels uneasy in my grasp;
(*Gives his sword.*)
Have it repaired; and grind the point.
<Strike hard!
I'll teach these Ghibelins a lesson.
(*Loud laughter within.*)
What is that clamor? Ha!>

(*Enter hastily* PEPE, *tattered and travel-stained.*)

PEPE. News from Rimini!
(*Falls exhausted.*)
LAN. Is that you, Pepe? <Captain, a good-night! (*Exit* CAPTAIN.)>
I never saw you in such straits before.
Wit without words!
PEPE. That 's better than—O!—O!—
(*Panting.*)
Words without wit.

LAN. (*Laughing.*) You'll die a jester, Pepe.
PEPE. If so, I'll leave the needy all my wit.
You, you shall have it, cousin.—O! O! O!
(*Panting.*)
Those devils in the hills, the Ghibelins,
Ran me almost to death. My lord—ha! ha!
(*Laughing.*)
It all comes back to me—O! Lord 'a mercy—
The garden, and the lady, and the Count!
Not to forget the poetry—ho! ho!
(*Laughing.*)
O! cousin Lanciotto, such a wife,
And such a brother! Hear me, ere I burst!
LAN. You're pleasant, Pepe!
PEPE. Am I?—Ho! ho! ho!
(*Laughing.*)
You ought to be; your wife's a—
LAN. What?
PEPE. A lady—
A lady, I suppose, like all the rest.
I am not in their secrets. Such a fellow
As [fine] Count Paolo is your man for that.
I'll tell you something, if you'll swear a bit.
LAN. Swear what?
PEPE. First, swear to listen till the end.—
O! you may rave, curse, howl, and tear your hair;
But you must listen.
LAN. For your jest's sake? Well.
PEPE. You swear?
LAN. I do.
PEPE. Next, swear to know the truth.
LAN. The truth of a fool's story!
PEPE. You mistake.
Now, look you, cousin! You have often marked—
I know, for I have seen—strange glances pass
Between [Count] Paolo and your lady wife.—
LAN. Ha! Pepe!
PEPE. Now I touch you to the quick.
I know the reason of those glances.
LAN. Ha!
Speak! or I'll throttle you!
(*Seizes him.*)
PEPE. Your way is odd.
Let go my <gullet> [throat then] and I'll talk you deaf.
Swear my last oath: only to know the truth.
LAN. But that may trouble me.
PEPE. Your honour lies—
Your precious honour, cousin Chivalry—
Lies bleeding with a terrible great gash,
Without its knowledge. Swear!
LAN. My honour? Speak!
PEPE. You swear?
LAN. I swear. Your news is ill, perchance?
PEPE. Ill! would I bring it else? Am I inclined
To run ten leagues with happy news for you?
O, Lord, that's jolly!
LAN. You infernal imp,
Out with your story, ere I strangle you!
PEPE. Then take a fast hold on your two great oaths,
To steady tottering manhood, and attend.
Last eve, about this hour, I took a stroll
Into the garden.—Are you listening, cousin?
LAN. I am all ears.
PEPE. Why, so an ass might say.
LAN. Will you be serious?
PEPE. Wait a while, and we
Will both be graver than a church-yard. Well,
Down the long walk, towards me, came your wife,
With [the] Count Paolo walking at her side.
It was a pretty sight, and so I stepped
Into the bushes. Ritta came with them;
And lady Fanny had a grievous time
To get her off. That made me curious.
Anon, the pair sat down upon a bank,
To read a poem;—the tenderest romance,
All about Lancelot and Queen Guenevra.
The Count read well—I'll say that much for him—
Only he stuck too closely to the text,
Got too much wrapped up in the poesy,
And played Sir Lancelot's actions, out and out,
On Queen Francesca. Nor in royal parts
Was she so backward. When he struck the line—
"She smiled; he kissed her full upon the mouth;"
Your lady smiled, and, by the saints above,
Count Paolo carried out the sentiment!
Can I not move you?
LAN. With such trash as this?
And so you ran ten leagues to tell a lie?—
Run home again.
PEPE. I am not ready yet.
After the kiss, up springs our amorous Count,
Flings Queen Guenevra and Sir Lancelot

Straight to the devil; growls and snaps his teeth,
Laughs, weeps, howls, dances; talks about his love,
His madness, suffering, and the Lord knows what,
Bullying the lady like a thief. But she,
All this hot time, looked cool and mischievous;
<Gave him his halter to the very end,>
And when he calmed a little, up she steps
And takes him by the hand. You should have seen
How tame the furious fellow was at once!
How he came down, snivelled, and cowed to her,
And fell to kissing her again! It was
A perfect female triumph! Such a scene
A man might pass through life and never see.
More sentiment then followed,—buckets full
Of washy words, not worth my memory.
But all the while she wound his Countship up,
Closer and closer; till at last—tu!—wit!—
She scoops him up, and off she carries him,
Fish for her table! <Follow, if you can;
My fancy fails me.> All this time you smile!

LAN. You should have been a poet, not a fool.

PEPE. I might be both.

LAN. You made no record, then?
Must this fine story die for want of ink?
Left you no trace in writing?

PEPE. None.

LAN. Alas!
Then you have told it? 'T is but stale, my boy;
I 'm second hearer.

PEPE. You are first, in faith.

LAN. In truth?

PEPE. In sadness. You have got it fresh.
<I had no time; I itched to reach your ear.>
Now go to Rimini, and see yourself.
You 'll find them in the garden. Lovers are
Like walking ghosts, they always haunt the spot
Of their misdeeds.

LAN. But have I heard you out?
You told me all?

PEPE. All; I have nothing left.

LAN. Why, you brain-stricken idiot, to trust
Your story and your body in my grasp!
(*Seizes him.*)

PEPE. Unhand me, cousin!

LAN. When I drop you, Pepe,
You 'll be at rest.

PEPE. I will betray you—O!

LAN. Not till the judgment day.
(*They struggle.*)

PEPE. (*Drawing* PAOLO'S *dagger.*) Take that!

LAN. (*Wresting the dagger from him.*) Well meant,
But poorly done! Here 's my return.
(*Stabs him.*)

PEPE. O! beast! (*Falls.*)
This I expected; it is naught—Ha! ha!
(*Laughing.*)
I 'll go to sleep; but you—what you will bear!
Hunchback, come here!

<LAN. Fie! say your prayers.>

PEPE. Hark, hark!
[Your brother] <Paolo> hired me, swine, to murder you.

LAN. That is a lie; you never cared for gold.

PEPE. He did, I say! I 'll swear it, by heaven!
Do you believe me?

LAN. No!

PEPE. You lie! you lie!
Look at the dagger, cousin—Ugh!—good-night! (*Dies.*)

LAN. O! horrible! It was a gift of mine—
He never laid it by. Speak, speak, fool, speak! (*Shakes the body.*)
How didst thou get it?—speak! Thou 'rt warm—not dead—
Thou hast a tongue—O! speak! Come, come, a jest—
Another jest from those thin mocking lips!
Call me a cripple—hunchback—what thou wilt;
But speak to me! He cannot. Now, by heaven,
I 'll stir this business till I find the truth!
Am I a fool? It is a silly lie,
Coined by yon villain with his last base breath.
What ho! without there!

(*Enter* CAPTAIN *and Soldiers.*)

CAPTAIN. Did you call, my lord?

LAN. Did Heaven thunder? Are you deaf, you louts?

Saddle my horse! <What are you staring at?
Is it your first look at a dead man? Well,
Then look your fill. Saddle my horse, I say!>
Black Pluto—stir! Bear that assassin hence.
Chop him to pieces, if he move. My horse!

<CAPT. My lord, he 's shoeing.

LAN. Did I ask for shoes?
I want my horse. Run, fellow, run! Unbarbed—
My lightest harness on his back. Fly, fly! *(Exit a Soldier.)*
(The others pick up the body.)
Ask him, I pray you, if he did not lie!

CAPT. The man is dead, my lord.

LAN. *(Laughing.)* Then do not ask him!>
(Exeunt Soldiers with the body.)
By Jupiter, I shall go mad, I think!
(Walks about.)

CAPT. Something disturbs him. Do you mark the spot
Of purple on his brow?
(Apart to a Soldier.)

SOLDIER. Then blood must flow.

LAN. Boy, boy! *(Enter a* PAGE.) My cloak and riding-staff. Quick, quick!
How you all lag! *(Exit* PAGE.) I ride to Rimini.
Skirmish to-morrow. Wait till my return—
I shall be back at sundown. You shall see
What slaughter is then!

CAPT. Ho! turn out a guard!—

LAN. I wish no guard; I ride alone.

[1] <*(Re-enter* PAGE, *with a cloak and staff.)*

(Taking them.) Well done!
Thou art a pretty boy.—And now my horse!

(Enter a SOLDIER.)

SOLDIER. Pluto is saddled—

LAN. 'T is a damned black lie!

SOL. Indeed, my lord—

LAN. O! comrade, pardon me:
I talk at random. What, Paolo, too,—
A boy whom I have trotted on my knee!
Poh! I abuse myself by such a thought.
Francesca may not love me, may love him—
Indeed she ought; but when an angel comes
To play the wanton on this filthy earth,
Then I'll believe her guilty. Look you, sir!
Am I quite calm?

CAPT. Quite calm, my lord.

LAN. You see
No trace of passion on my face?—No sign
Of ugly humours, doubts, or fears, or aught
That may disfigure God's intelligence?
I have a grievous charge against you, sir,
That may involve your life; and if you doubt
The candour of my judgment, choose your time:

---

[1] In the acting version of 1853, the following speech of Lanciotto occupies the rest of the scene.

(Lanciotto continues)
I wish no guard, I ride alone. My Paolo—
A boy whom I have trotted on my knee;
And young Francesca with her angel face!—
Ah, but I saw the signals of your eyes
Made and returned. Now, if there be one grain
Of solid truth in all this hideous lie,
I cannot answer for the work thou 'lt do
(To the dagger.)
Thou edged and pointed instrument of wrath
Laid in my hand by Justice! Glorious race
Of iron men, and women far too proud
To be unchaste, ye whisper in my ear
The vengeance due to your dishonored son!
Let me embrace it, lest your scornful hiss,
Drive your degraded offspring from your tombs,
And cast him on a dunghill! Must I lash
My broken spirit into flame with dreams?
No, no! O mighty ancestry, your words,
Erewhile a whisper, tear the vault of heaven,
With thunder upon thunder. Blood, blood, blood!
Ye shout, and I re-echo it! To horse!—
O, give me wings, not feet, to make my way;
That like a famished eagle scenting blood,
I may swoop down on sleeping Rimini!
(Exeunt omnes.)

Shall I arraign you now?
CAPT. Now, if you please.
I'll trust my cause to you and innocence
At any time. I am not conscious—
LAN. Pshaw!
I try myself, not you. And I am calm—
That is your verdict—and dispassionate?
CAPT. So far as I can judge.
LAN. 'T is well, 't is well!
Then I will ride to Rimini. Good-night!
(*Exit.*)
(*The others look after him, amazedly, and exeunt.*)>

SCENE 3. *Rimini. The Garden of the Castle.*

(*Enter* PAOLO *and* FRANCESCA.)

FRANCESCA. Thou hast resolved
PAOLO. I've sworn it.
FRAN. Ah, you men
Can talk of love and duty in a breath;
Love while you like, forget when you are tired,
And salve your falsehood with some wholesome saw;
But we, poor women, when we give our hearts,
Give all, lose all, and never ask it back.
PAOLO. What couldst thou ask for that I have not given?
With love I gave thee manly probity,
Innocence, honor, self-respect, and peace.
Lanciotto will return, and how shall I—
O! shame, to think of it!—how shall I look
My brother in the face? take his frank hand?
Return his tender glances? I should blaze
With guilty blushes.
FRAN. Thou canst forsake me, then,
To spare thyself a little bashful pain?
[But] Paolo, dost thou know what 't is for me,
<A woman—nay, a dame of highest rank—
To lose my purity? to walk a path
Whose slightest slip may fill my ear with sounds
That hiss me out to infamy and death?>
Have I no secret pangs, no self-respect,
No husband's look to bear? <O! worse than these,
I must endure his loathsome touch; be kind
When he would dally with his wife, and smile
To see him play thy part. Pah! sickening thought!
From that thou art exempt.> Thou shalt not go!
Thou dost not love me!
PAOLO. Love thee! Standing here,
With countless miseries upon my head,
I say, my love for thee grows day by day.
It palters with my conscience, blurs my thoughts
Of duty, and confuses my ideas
Of right and wrong. Ere long, it will persuade
My shaking manhood that all this is just.
FRAN. Let it! I'll blazon it to all the world,
Ere I will lose thee. <Nay, if I had choice,
Between our love and my lost innocence,
I tell thee calmly, I would dare again
The deed which we have done.> O! thou art cruel
To fly me, like a coward, for thine ease.
<When thou art gone, thou 'lt flatter thy weak heart
With hopes and speculations; and thou 'lt swear
I suffer naught, because thou dost not see.>
I will not live to bear it.
PAOLO. Die,—'t were best;
'T is the last desperate comfort of our sin.
<FRAN. I'll kill myself!
PAOLO. And so would I, with joy;
But crime has made a craven of me. O!
For some good cause to perish in! Something
A man might die for, looking in God's face;
Not slinking out of life with guilt like mine
Piled on the shoulders of a suicide!>
FRAN. Where wilt thou go?
PAOLO. I care not; anywhere
Out of this Rimini. The very things
That made the pleasures of my innocence
Have turned against me. There is not a tree,
Nor house, nor church, nor monument, whose face
Took hold upon my thoughts, that does not frown
Balefully on me. <From their marble tombs

My ancestors scowl at me; and the night
Thickens to hear their hisses. I would pray,
But heaven jeers at it.> Turn where'er I will,
A curse pursues me. [Ay, thy very face
Is black with curses.]
FRAN. Heavens! O, say not so!
I never cursed thee, love; <I never moved
My little finger, ere I looked to thee
For my instruction.>
PAOLO. But thy gentleness
Seems to reproach me; and, instead of joy,
It whispers horror!
FRAN. Cease! cease!
PAOLO. I must go.
<FRAN. And I must follow. All that I call life
Is bound in thee. I could endure for thee
More agonies than thou canst catalogue—
For thy sake, love—bearing the ill for thee!
With thee, the devils could not so contrive
That I would blench or falter from my love!
Without thee, heaven were torture!
PAOLO. I must go. (*Going.*)>
FRAN. O! no[, no,]—Paolo—dearest!—
(*Clinging to him.*)
PAOLO. Loose thy hold!
'T is for thy sake, and Lanciotto's; I
Am as a cipher in the reckoning.
I have resolved. Thou canst but stretch the time.
Keep me to-day, and I will fly to-morrow—
Steal from thee like a thief.
(*Struggles with her.*)
FRAN. [Ah,] Paolo—love—
<Indeed, you hurt me!—Do not use me thus!>
Kill me, but do not leave me. I will laugh—
A long, gay, ringing laugh—if thou wilt draw
Thy pitying sword, and stab me to the heart!

(*Enter* LANCIOTTO *behind.*)

Nay, then, one kiss!
LANCIOTTO. (*Advancing between them.*)
Take it: 't will be the last.
PAOLO. Lo! Heaven is just!
<FRAN. The last! so be it.
(*Kisses* PAOLO.)
LAN. Ha!
Dare you these tricks before my very face?
FRAN. Why not? I 've kissed him in the sight of heaven;
Are you above it?
PAOLO. Peace, Francesca, peace!>
LAN. [Count] Paolo—why, thou sad and downcast man,
Look up! I have some words to speak with thee.
Thou art not guilty?
PAOLO. Yes, I am. But she
Has been betrayed; so she is innocent.
Her father tampered with her. I—
FRAN. 'T is false!
The guilt is mine. <Paolo> [your brother] was entrapped
By love and cunning. [by my—] <I am shrewder far
Than you suspect.>
PAOLO. Lanciotto, <shut thy ears;>
She would deceive thee.
LAN. Silence, both of you!
Is guilt so talkative in its defence?
Then, let me make you judge and advocate
In your own cause. You are not guilty?
PAOLO. Yes.
LAN. Deny it—but a word—say no. Lie, lie!
And I'll believe.
PAOLO. I dare not.
LAN. Lady, you?
FRAN. If I might speak for him—
LAN. It cannot be:
Speak for yourself. Do you deny your guilt?
FRAN. No! I assert it; but—
LAN. In heaven's name, hold!
Will neither of you answer no to me?
A nod, a hint, a sign, for your escape.
Bethink you, life is centered in this thing.
Speak! I will credit either. No reply?
What does your crime deserve?
PAOLO. Death.
FRAN. Death to both.
LAN. Well said! You speak the law of Italy;
And by the dagger you designed for me,
In Pepe's hand,—your bravo?
PAOLO. It is false!
If you received my dagger from his hand,
He stole it.
LAN. There, sweet heaven, I knew! And now
You will deny the rest? You see, my friends,
How easy of belief I have become!—
How easy 't were to cheat me!

Paolo. No; enough!
I will not load my groaning spirit more;
A lie would crush it.[1]

<Lan. Brother, once you gave
Life to this wretched piece of workmanship,
When my own hand resolved its overthrow.
Revoke the gift.
(*Offers to stab himself.*)

Paolo. (*Preventing him.*) Hold, homicide!

Lan. But think,
You and Francesca may live happily,
After my death, as only lovers can.

Paolo. Live happily, after a deed like this!>[2]

Lan. Now, look ye! there is not one hour of life
Among us three. [Count]Paolo, you are armed—
You have a sword, I but a dagger: see!
I mean to kill you.

<Fran. (*Whispers* Paolo.) Give thy sword to me.

Paolo. Away! thou 'rt frantic!> I will never lift
This wicked hand against thee.

Lan. Coward, slave!
Art thou so faint? Does Malatesta's blood
Run in thy puny veins? Take that!
(*Strikes him.*)

Paolo. And more:
Thou canst not offer more than I will bear.

<Lan. Oh, Paolo, what a craven has thy guilt
Transformed thee to! Why,> I have seen the time
When thou 'dst have struck at heaven for such a thing!
Art thou afraid?

Paolo. I am.

Lan. O! infamy!
Can man sink lower? I will wake thee, though:—
Thou shalt not die a coward. See! look here!
(*Stabs* Francesca.)

Fran. O!—O!— (*Falls.*)

Paolo. Remorseless man, dare you do this,
And hope to live? Die, murderer!
(*Draws, rushes at him, but pauses.*)

Lan. Strike, strike!
Ere thy heart fail.

Paolo. I cannot.
(*Throws away his sword.*)

Lan. Dost thou see
Yon bloated spider—hideous as myself—
Climbing aloft, to reach that wavering twig?
When he has touched it, one of us must die.
Here is the dagger.—Look at me, I say!

---

[1] The speech of Lanciotto given below is substituted in Boker's handwriting in the acting version of 1853 for the lines omitted (as far as 2).

[Lanciotto. Then this nameless deed,—
At which our nature cannot even blush,
So pale is she with horror—is confessed?
Alas! Francesca, whom I loved at sight!
(*Turns to her.*)
Why, woman, what harm did I do to thee—
What else but love thee—when I saw thee come,
Like a descending angel bearing peace
Into my lonely life? Wouldst thou convert
My very virtues into crime? Make love
Do murder, tempted by thy loveliness?
Fool that I was to credit thee! Thy lies,
Fair-faced deluder, in the sight of Heaven,
Make thee more monstrous than this blighted trunk!
Speak! Is the devil that inspires thee dumb?
Cast out thy devil! Speak, speak, for your lives!
She cannot! (*Turns to* Paolo.) Paolo, is there aught to say,—
In thy boy's voice, as thou hast often hung
With silken arms about my armed neck,
In days, oh! not forgotten, let me trust?
Brother, my brother, it must be that I
Am ill, bewildered, in a nightmare,—Speak!
Say but a word, and wake me to myself!
He too is speechless! Yet there sails the moon;
And this is earth beneath me; and there stands
A misty shape that one time was my wife;
And there a shade that personates the man
Whom I loved most of men; and only I
Ah! only I am changed so horribly!
For if I be not mad, I am in a hell
To which sin's vision were a paradise!
(*A pause, during which he looks from one to the other.*)]

Keep your eyes from that woman! Look, think, choose!—
Turn here to me: thou shalt not look at her!> [1]
PAOLO. O, heaven!
LAN. 'T is done!
PAOLO. (*Struggling with him.*) O! Lanciotto, hold!
Hold, for thy sake. Thou wilt repent this deed.
LAN. I know it.
<FRAN. (*Rising.*) Help!—O! murder! —help, help, help!>
(*She totters towards them, and falls.*)
[MALATESTA. (*Without.*) Help! this way,—this way—help! help! help!]
LAN. Our honour, boy!
(*Stabs* PAOLO, *he falls.*)
<FRAN. Paolo!
PAOLO. Hark! she calls.
I pray thee, brother, help me to her side.
(LANCIOTTO *helps him to* FRANCESCA.)
LAN. Why, there!
PAOLO. God bless thee!>
LAN. Have I not done well?
What were the honor of the Malatesti,
With such a living slander fixed to it?
<Cripple! that 's something—cuckold! that is damned!
You blame me?
PAOLO. No.
LAN. You, lady?
FRAN. No, my lord.
LAN. May God forgive you!> We are even now:
Your blood has cleared my honour, and our name
Shines to the world as ever.
<PAOLO. O!—O!—
FRAN. Love,
Art suffering?
PAOLO. But for thee.
FRAN. Here, rest thy head
Upon my bosom. Fie upon my blood!
It stains thy ringlets. Ha! he dies! Kind saints,
I was first struck, why cannot I die first?
Paolo, wake!—God's mercy! wilt thou go
Alone—without me? Prithee, strike again!
Nay, I am better—love—now—O!
(*Dies.*)
LAN. (*Sinks upon his knees.*) Great heaven!>
MALATESTA. (*Without.*) This way, I heard the cries.

(*Enter with* GUIDO, *and Attendants.*)

GUIDO. O! horrible!
MAL. O! bloody spectacle! Where is thy brother?
LAN. So Cain was asked. <Come here, old men! You shrink
From two dead bodies and a pool of blood—
You soldiers, too! Come here!
(*Drags* MALATESTA *and* GUIDO *forward.*)
MAL. O!—O!—
LAN. You groan!
What must I do, then?> Father, here it is,—
The blood of Guido mingled with our own,
As my old nurse predicted. And the spot
Of her infernal baptism burns my brain
Till reason shudders! <Down, upon your knees!
Ay, shake them harder, and perchance they 'll wake.
Keep still! Kneel, kneel! You fear them? I shall prowl
About these bodies till the day of doom.
MAL. What hast thou done?
GUI. Francesca!—O! my child!
LAN. Can howling make this sight more terrible?
Peace! You disturb the angels up in heaven,
While they are hiding from this ugly earth.
Be satisfied with what you see. You two
Began this tragedy, I finished it.
Here, by these bodies, let us reckon up
Our crimes together.> Why, how still they lie!
A moment since, they walked, and talked, and kissed!
Defied me to my face, dishonored me!

---

[1] In the 1853 version the following lines were substituted for the above speech.

[Dost thou see
Yon dusky cloud that slowly steals along;
Like a shrewd thief upon a traveller,
To blot the glory of the jocund moon?
When it has dimmed the lustre of her edge,
She 'll shrink behind it to avoid the sight
She else might see on this disfigured earth,
When it has crossed her, one of us, who now
Is touched to wonder by her radiance
Shall gaze upon her with an altered face—
As pale, and cold and vacant as her own.]

They had the power to do it then; but now,
Poor souls, who'll shield them in eternity?
Father, the honor of our house is safe;
<I have the secret. I will to the wars,
And do more murders, to eclipse this one.
Back to the battles; there I breathe in peace;
And I will take a soldier's honour back.—
Honour! what's that to me now? Ha! ha! ha! (*Laughing.*)
A great thing, father! I am very ill.>
I killed thy son for honour: thou mayst chide.
O God! I cannot cheat myself with words!
I loved him more than honour—more than life—
This man, [my] Paolo—this stark, bleeding corpse!
[1] Here let me rest, till God awake us all!
(*Falls on* PAOLO'S *body.*)

[1] In the 1853 version, the last line is
Here let me rest, till all together wake!

THE OCTOROON

OR

LIFE IN LOUISIANA

BY

Dion Boucicault

THE OCTOROON

The Octoroon is a play of singular interest. Dealing with the slavery question in 1859, it represented so truly the actual conditions in Louisiana that it won the sympathy of Northerners and Southerners alike. It represents also the genius of Boucicault in its maturity.

Dion Boucicault was born in Dublin, Ireland, upon either December 26, 1820, or December 20, 1822, though the evidence seems to point to the earlier date. He was educated at private school, at London University, and at a collegiate school at Brentford, and after having been apprenticed to a civil engineer, he broke away from that calling and devoted himself to the stage. His first appearance on the stage seems to have occurred in the spring of 1837, and in the same year he probably wrote his first play, *A Lover by Proxy,* which was not accepted by Charles Mathews, the manager of Covent Garden Theatre. Mathews did, however, accept his next play, the comedy of *London Assurance,* played March 4, 1841, which proved to be a great success and which has been revived as late as 1913.

According to his latest biographer, Boucicault wrote or adapted one hundred and twenty-four plays. We are concerned most with those he wrote upon American soil. Having married Miss Agnes Robertson, to be so long associated with leading rôles in his plays, he came to New York in 1853. He may be said to have soon dominated the American stage. His significant works during the periods of his American residence, 1853 to 1860, and again from 1872 to his death, fall into several groups. From the point of view of American drama, such plays as *The Octoroon,* and *The Poor of New York* (1857), an adaptation of *Les Pauvres de Paris,* of Brisebar and Nus, to conditions of the panic of 1857, are most interesting. Interesting also is his share of *Rip Van Winkle,* although this was not first produced in this country, but was first played in London on September 4, 1865.

The second group includes the Irish plays. The earliest of these, *The Colleen Bawn,* was performed first at Laura Keene's Theatre, New York, March 29, 1860. It was founded on Gerald Griffin's novel, *The Collegians,* which had first been dramatized by J. E. Wilks in London in 1831. Later in 1842 a version by Louisa Medina was played in New York. Boucicault painted the Irish character truly and sympathetically and followed his first success with many others, the best of which were *Arrah Na Pogue* (1864), *The O'Dowd* (1873) and *The Shaughraun* (1874).

Another group would include his dramatization of the greater English novels;

among them, *Dot,* a version of *The Cricket on the Hearth* (1859), *Smike,* founded on *Nicholas Nickleby* (1859) and *The Trial of Effie Deans* (1860), based on *The Heart of Midlothian.* Other well-known plays which had distinct successes were *Jessie Brown or the Relief of Lucknow,* acted first at Wallack's Theatre, February 22, 1858, and *Led Astray,* an adaptation from Octave Feuillet's *La Tentation,* performed first at the Union Square Theatre, New York, December 8, 1873, which Boucicault wrote while in California.

The Octoroon was first performed at the Winter Garden, New York, December 5, 1859, Boucicault playing "Wahnotee," the Indian, and Mrs. Boucicault "Zoe," and after the play had run a week, Boucicault and his wife withdrew on account of a quarrel with the management and the play was continued without them until January 21, 1860. *The Octoroon* was advertised widely and it was a daring attempt to place upon the stage material of such an inflammable character. The skill with which Boucicault balanced the abstract belief in the wrong of slavery with the concrete sympathy for Southern characters, satisfied audiences everywhere.

The Octoroon was based on a novel by Mayne Reid, *The Quadroon,* which had been published in New York in 1856, dramatized in London and played at the City of London Theatre. Boucicault, however, borrowed only the outlines of the plot. In the novel an Englishman under the name of Edward Rutherford saves a beautiful Creole, Eugénie Besançon, from drowning through the explosion of the river steamboat, and falls in love with her quadroon slave, Aurore. Through the dishonesty of her trustee, the Creole, Gayarre, Eugénie loses her estate which is to be sold. Eugénie loves Rutherford and, in male disguise, aids him in obtaining funds with which he trys to buy Aurore at the slave auction but fails. After kidnapping Aurore he is about to be lynched when he is saved by the sheriff, and at the ensuing trial it turns out that Gayarre has embezzled funds belonging to Eugénie and that Aurore has been freed by her former master. Rutherford and Aurore marry.

It will be seen that the theme of the contrast between North and South is lacking in the novel, that the only characters that have any prototypes, such as "George Peyton," "Dora Sunnyside," "Zoe," and "McClosky," are entirely different in the play, and that characters like "Salem Scudder," "Wahnotee," and "Old Pete" are creations of Boucicault. The very change of title shows Boucicault's sense of the picturesque. It is interesting to note that when *The Octoroon* was played in London, "Zoe" did not die, for a happy ending seemed possible to an English audience. The device of the accidental photographing of the murder of "Paul" is found in *The Filibuster,* an English novel by Albany Fonblanque (1859).

The following plays produced in America may be obtained in the reprints of Samuel French or of the Dramatic Publishing Company of Chicago:

To Parents and Guardians, Andy Blake, Jessie Brown, Grimaldi or the Life of an Actress, The Queen of Spades, The Phantom, The Poor of New York, The Pope of Rome, Pauvrette, The Octoroon, The Colleen Bawn, The O'Dowd, Led Astray, The Shaughraun.

Among the plays written in England, *London Assurance* (1841), *Old Heads and Young Hearts* (1844), *Arrah na Pogue* (1864), may be read as illustrating his earlier and later period.

For biography see *The Career of Dion Boucicault* by Townsend Walsh, Series 3, Vol. I, of the Dunlap Society Publications, New York, 1915, to which the present editor acknowledges his indebtedness. Interesting accounts of individual plays are to be found in *Plays of the Present*, by Clapp and Edgett, Series 2, Extra Vol. of the Dunlap Society Publications, New York, 1902. For the relation of *The Quadroon* with the play, see the novel itself, *The Quadroon, or a Lover's Adventures in Louisiana,* New York, 1856, and *Mayne Reid, a Memoir of His Life,* by Elizabeth Reid, London, 1887, pp. 215–217.

The present text is a reprint of the privately printed edition.

Note to Seventh Edition.

A new biography of Boucicault, by Julius Tolson, based on research in England will soon be published. Dr. Tolson has permitted Allardyce Nicoll and F. T. Cloak, editors of the Boucicault Volume in *America's Lost Plays* Series, to print *Louis XI,* for the first time. *Forbidden Fruit, Dot, Flying Scud, Robert Emmet,* and *Presumptive Evidence* are also printed for the first time.

THE ORIGINAL CAST OF CHARACTERS

At the Winter Garden, New York, December 5, 1859.

George Peyton .... Mr. A. H. Davenport
Salem Scudder .... Mr. Joseph Jefferson
Mr. Sunnyside .... Mr. George Holland
Jacob M'Closky .... Mr. T. B. Johnston
Wahnotee .... Mr. Dion Boucicault
Lafouche .... Mr. J. H. Stoddart
Captain Ratts .... Mr. Harry Pearson
Colonel Pointdexter
Jules Thibodeaux
Judge Caillou
Jackson
Old Pete .... Mr. George Jamieson
Paul (a boy slave) .... Miss Ione Burke
Solon

Mrs. Peyton .... Mrs. W. R. Blake
Zoe .... Miss Agnes Robertson
Dora Sunnyside .... Mrs. J. H. Allen
Grace
Minnie
Dido

THE OCTOROON

ACT FIRST.

The scene opens on a view of the Plantation Terrebonne, in Louisiana. A branch of the Mississippi is seen winding through the Estate. A low built, but extensive Planter's Dwelling, surrounded with a veranda, and raised a few feet from the ground, occupies the left side. On the right stand a table and chairs. GRACE *is discovered sitting at breakfast-table with the negro children.*

(SOLON *enters, from the house.*)

SOLON. Yah! you bomn'ble fry—git out—a gen'leman can't pass for you.

GRACE. (*Seizing a fly whisk.*) Hee!—ha git out!

(*She drives the children away: in escaping they tumble against* SOLON, *who falls with the tray; the children steal the bananas and rolls that fall about.*)

(*Enter* PETE, *who is lame; he carries a mop and pail.*)

PETE. Hey! laws a massey! why, clar out! drop dat banana! I'll murder this yer crowd.

(*He chases children about; they leap over railing at back.*) (*Exit* SOLON.)

Dem little niggers is a judgment upon dis generation.

(*Enter* GEORGE, *from the house.*)

GEORGE. What's the matter, Pete?

PETE. It's dem black trash, Mas'r George; dis ere property wants claring; dem's getting too numerous round: when I gets time I'll kill some on 'em, sure!

GEORGE. They don't seem to be scared by the threat.

PETE. Stop, you varmin! stop till I get enough of you in one place!

GEORGE. Were they all born on this estate?

PETE. Guess they nebber was born—dem tings! what, dem?—get away! Born here—dem darkies? What, on Terrebonne! Don't b'lieve it, Mas'r George; dem black tings never was born at all; dey swarmed one mornin' on a sassafras tree in the swamp; I cotched 'em; dey ain't no 'count. Don't believe dey'll turn out niggers when dey're growed; dey'll come out sunthin' else.

GRACE. Yes, Mas'r George, dey was born here; and old Pete is fonder on 'em dan he is of his fiddle on a Sunday.

PETE. What? dem tings—dem?—get away. (*Makes blow at the children.*) Born here! dem darkies! What, on Terrebonne? Don't b'lieve it, Mas'r George,—no. One morning dey swarmed on a sassafras tree in de swamp, and I cotched 'em all in a sieve,—dat's how dey come on top of dis yearth—git out, you,—ya, ya! (*Laughs.*) (*Exit* GRACE.)

(*Enter* MRS. PEYTON, *from the house.*)

MRS. P. So, Pete, you are spoiling those children as usual!

PETE. Dat's right, missus! gib it to ole Pete! he's allers in for it. Git away dere! Ya! if dey ain't all lighted, like coons, on dat snake fence, just out of shot. Look dar! Ya, ya! Dem debils. Ya!

MRS. P. Pete, do you hear?

PETE. Git down dar! I'm arter you! (*Hobbles off.*)

MRS. P. You are out early this morning, George.

GEORGE. I was up before daylight. We got the horses saddled, and galloped down the shell road over the Piney Patch; then coasting the Bayou Lake, we crossed the long swamps, by Paul's Path, and so came home again.

MRS. P. (*Laughing.*) You seem already familiar with the names of every spot on the estate.

(*Enter* PETE, *who arranges breakfast.*)

GEORGE. Just one month ago I quitted Paris. I left that siren city as I would have left a beloved woman.

MRS. P. No wonder! I dare say you left at least a dozen beloved women there, at the same time.

GEORGE. I feel that I departed amid universal and sincere regret. I left my loves and my creditors equally inconsolable.

Mrs. P. George, you are incorrigible. Ah! you remind me so much of your uncle, the judge.

George. Bless his dear old handwriting, it 's all I ever saw of him. For ten years his letters came every quarter-day, with a remittance and a word of advice in his formal cavalier style; and then a joke in the postcript, that upset the dignity of the foregoing. Aunt, when he died, two years ago, I read over those letters of his, and if I did n't cry like a baby—

Mrs. P. No, George; say you wept like a man. And so you really kept those foolish letters?

George. Yes; I kept the letters, and squandered the money.

Mrs. P. (*Embracing him.*) Ah! why were you not my son—you are so like my dear husband.

(*Enter* Salem Scudder.)

Scud. Ain't he! Yes—when I saw him and Miss Zoe galloping through the green sugar crop, and doing ten dollars' worth of damage at every stride, says I, how like his old uncle he do make the dirt fly.

George. O, aunt! what a bright, gay creature she is!

Scud. What, Zoe! Guess that you did n't leave anything female in Europe that can lift an eyelash beside that gal. When she goes along, she just leaves a streak of love behind her. It 's a good drink to see her come into the cotton fields—the niggers get fresh on the sight of her. If she ain't worth her weight in sunshine you may take one of my fingers off, and choose which you like.

Mrs. P. She need not keep us waiting breakfast, though. Pete, tell Miss Zoe that we are waiting.

Pete. Yes, missus. Why, Minnie, why don't you run when you hear, you lazy crittur? (*Minnie runs off.*) Dat 's de laziest nigger on dis yere property. (*Sitting down.*) Don't do nuffin.

Mrs. P. My dear George, you are left in your uncle's will heir to this estate.

George. Subject to your life interest and an annuity to Zoe, is it not so?

Mrs. P. I fear that the property is so involved that the strictest economy will scarcely recover it. My dear husband never kept any accounts, and we scarcely know in what condition the estate really is.

Scud. Yes, we do, ma'am; it 's in a darned bad condition. Ten years ago the judge took as overseer a bit of Connecticut hardware called M'Closky. The judge did n't understand accounts—the overseer did. For a year or two all went fine. The judge drew money like Bourbon whisky from a barrel, and never turned off the tap. But out it flew, free for everybody or anybody to beg, borrow, or steal. So it went, till one day the judge found the tap would n't run. He looked in to see what stopped it, and pulled out a big mortgage. "Sign that," says the overseer; "it 's only a formality." "All right," says the judge, and away went a thousand acres; so at the end of eight years, Jacob M'Closky, Esquire, finds himself proprietor of the richest half of Terrebonne—

George. But the other half is free.

Scud. No, it ain't; because, just then, what does the judge do, but hire another overseer—a Yankee—a Yankee named Salem Scudder.

Mrs. P. O, no, it was—

Scud. Hold on, now! I 'm going to straighten this account clear out. What was this here Scudder? Well, he lived in New York by sittin' with his heels up in front of French's Hotel, and inventin'—

George. Inventing what?

Scud. Improvements—anything, from a stay-lace to a fire-engine. Well, he cut that for the photographing line. He and his apparatus arrived here, took the judge's likeness and his fancy, who made him overseer right off. Well, sir, what does this Scudder do but introduces his inventions and improvements on this estate. His new cotton gins broke down, the steam sugar-mills burst up, until he finished off with his folly what Mr. M'Closky with his knavery began.

Mrs. P. O, Salem! how can you say so? Have n't you worked like a horse?

Scud. No, ma'am, I worked like an ass—an honest one, and that 's all. Now, Mr. George, between the two overseers, you and that good old lady have come to the ground; that is the state of things, just as near as I can fix it.

(Zoe *sings without.*)

George. 'T is Zoe.

Scud. O, I have not spoiled that anyhow. I can't introduce any darned improvement there. Ain't that a cure for old age; it kinder lifts the heart up, don't it?

MRS. P. Poor child! what will become of her when I am gone? If you have n't spoiled her, I fear I have. She has had the education of a lady.

GEORGE. I have remarked that she is treated by the neighbors with a kind of familiar condescension that annoyed me.

SCUD. Don't you know that she is the natural daughter of the judge, your uncle, and that old lady thar just adored anything her husband cared for; and this girl, that another woman would 'a' hated, she loves as if she 'd been her own child.

GEORGE. Aunt, I am prouder and happier to be your nephew and heir to the ruins of Terrebonne, than I would have been to have had half Louisiana without you.

(*Enter* ZOE, *from the house.*)

ZOE. Am I late? Ah! Mr. Scudder, good morning.

SCUD. Thank 'ye. I 'm from fair to middlin', like a bamboo cane, much the same all the year round.

ZOE. No; like a sugar cane; so dry outside, one would never think there was so much sweetness within.

SCUD. Look here: I can't stand that gal! if I stop here, I shall hug her right off. (*He sees* PETE, *who has set his pail down up stage, and goes to sleep on it.*) If that old nigger ain't asleep, I 'm blamed. Hillo!

(*He kicks pail from under* PETE, *and lets him down. Exit.*)

PETE. Hi! Debbel 's in de pail! Whar 's breakfass?

(*Enter* SOLON *and* DIDO *with coffee-pot and dishes.*)

DIDO. Bless'ee, Missey Zoe, here it be. Dere 's a dish of penpans—jess taste, Mas'r George—and here 's fried bananas; smell 'em do, sa glosh.

PETE. Hole yer tongue, Dido. Whar 's de coffee? (*He pours it out.*) If it don't stain de cup, your wicked ole life 's in danger, sure! dat right! black as nigger; clar as ice. You may drink dat, Mas'r George. (*Looks off.*) Yah! here 's Mas'r Sunnyside, and Missey Dora, jist drove up. Some of you niggers run and hole de hosses; and take dis, Dido. (*He gives her coffee-pot to hold, and hobbles off, followed by* SOLON *and* DIDO.)

(*Enter* SUNNYSIDE *and* DORA.)

SUNNY. Good day, ma'am. (*He shakes hands with George.*) I see we are just in time for breakfast. (*He sits.*)

DORA. O, none for me; I never eat. (*She sits.*)

GEORGE. (*Aside.*) They do not notice Zoe.—(*Aloud.*) You don't see Zoe, Mr. Sunnyside.

SUNNY. Ah! Zoe, girl; are you there?

DORA. Take my shawl, Zoe. (ZOE *helps her.*) What a good creature she is.

SUNNY. I dare say, now, that in Europe you have never met any lady more beautiful in person, or more polished in manners, than that girl.

GEORGE. You are right, sir; though I shrank from expressing that opinion in her presence, so bluntly.

SUNNY. Why so?

GEORGE. It may be considered offensive.

SUNNY. (*Astonished.*) What? I say, Zoe, do you hear that?

DORA. Mr. Peyton is joking.

MRS. P. My nephew is not acquainted with our customs in Louisiana, but he will soon understand.

GEORGE. Never, aunt! I shall never understand how to wound the feelings of any lady; and, if that is the custom here, I shall never acquire it.

DORA. Zoe, my dear, what does he mean?

ZOE. I don't know.

GEORGE. Excuse me, I 'll light a cigar. (*He goes up.*)

DORA. (*Aside to* ZOE.) Is n't he sweet! O, dear, Zoe, is he in love with anybody?

ZOE. How can I tell?

DORA. Ask him, I want to know; don't say I told you to inquire, but find out. Minnie, fan me, it is so nice—and his clothes are French, ain't they?

ZOE. I think so; shall I ask him that too?

DORA. No, dear. I wish he would make love to me. When he speaks to one he does it so easy, so gentle; it is n't barroom style; love lined with drinks, sighs tinged with tobacco—and they say all the women in Paris were in love with him, which I feel *I* shall be. Stop fanning me; what nice boots he wears.

SUNNY. (*To* MRS. PEYTON.) Yes, ma'am, I hold a mortgage over Terrebonne; mine 's a ninth, and pretty near covers all the property, except the slaves. I believe Mr. M'Closky has a bill of sale on them. O, here he is.

(*Enter* M'CLOSKY.)

SUNNY. Good morning, Mr. M'Closky.

M'CLOSKY. Good morning, Mr. Sunnyside; Miss Dora, your servant.

DORA. (*Seated.*) Fan me, Minnie.—(*Aside.*) I don't like that man.

M'CLOSKY. (*Aside.*) Insolent as usual.—(*Aloud.*) You begged me to call this morning. I hope I 'm not intruding.

MRS. P. My nephew, Mr. Peyton.

M'CLOSKY. O, how d' ye do, sir? (*He offers his hand,* GEORGE *bows coldly.*) (*Aside.*) A puppy—if he brings any of his European airs here we 'll fix him.—(*Aloud.*) Zoe, tell Pete to give my mare a feed, will ye?

GEORGE. (*Angrily.*) Sir!

M'CLOSKY. Hillo! did I tread on ye?

MRS. P. What is the matter with George?

ZOE. (*She takes fan from* MINNIE.) Go, Minnie, tell Pete; run! (*Exit* MINNIE.)

MRS. P. Grace, attend to Mr. M'Closky.

M'CLOSKY. A julep, gal, that 's my breakfast, and a bit of cheese.

GEORGE. (*Aside to* MRS. PEYTON.) How can you ask that vulgar ruffian to your table!

MRS. P. Hospitality in Europe is a courtesy; here, it is an obligation. We tender food to a stranger, not because he is a gentleman, but because he is hungry.

GEORGE. Aunt, I will take my rifle down to the Atchafalaya. Paul has promised me a bear and a deer or two. I see my little Nimrod yonder, with his Indian companion. Excuse me, ladies. Ho! Paul! (*He enters house.*)

PAUL. (*Outside.*) I'ss, Mas'r George.

(*Enter* PAUL *with the Indian.*)

SUNNY. It 's a shame to allow that young cub to run over the swamps and woods, hunting and fishing his life away instead of hoeing cane.

MRS. P. The child was a favorite of the judge, who encouraged his gambols. I could n't bear to see him put to work.

GEORGE. (*Returning with rifle.*) Come, Paul, are you ready?

PAUL. I'ss, Mas'r George. O, golly! ain't that a pooty gun.

M'CLOSKY. See here, you imp; if I catch you, and your redskin yonder, gunning in my swamps, I 'll give you rats, mind. Them vagabonds, when the game 's about, shoot my pigs.

(*Exit* GEORGE *into house.*)

PAUL. You gib me rattan, Mas'r Clostry, but I guess you take a berry long stick to Wahnotee. Ugh, he make bacon of you.

M'CLOSKY. Make bacon of me, you young whelp! Do you mean that I 'm a pig? Hold on a bit.

(*He seizes whip, and holds* PAUL.)

ZOE. O, sir! don't, pray, don't.

M'CLOSKY. (*Slowly lowering his whip.*) Darn you, redskin, I 'll pay you off some day, both of ye.

(*He returns to table and drinks.*)

SUNNY. That Indian is a nuisance. Why don't he return to his nation out West?

M'CLOSKY. He 's too fond of thieving and whiskey.

ZOE. No; Wahnotee is a gentle, honest creature, and remains here because he loves that boy with the tenderness of a woman. When Paul was taken down with the swamp fever the Indian sat outside the hut, and neither ate, slept, nor spoke for five days, till the child could recognize and call him to his bedside. He who can love so well is honest—don't speak ill of poor Wahnotee.

MRS. P. Wahnotee, will you go back to your people?

WAHNOTEE. Sleugh.

PAUL. He don't understand; he speaks a mash-up of Indian and Mexican. Wahnotee Patira na sepau assa wigiran?

WAHNOTEE. Weal Omenee.

PAUL. Says he 'll go if I 'll go with him. He calls me Omenee, the Pigeon, and Miss Zoe is Ninemoosha, the Sweetheart.

WAHNOTEE. (*Pointing to* ZOE.) Ninemoosha.

ZOE. No, Wahnotee, we can't spare Paul.

PAUL. If Omenee remain, Wahnotee will die in Terrebonne.

(*During the dialogue,* WAHNOTEE *has taken* GEORGE'S *gun.*)

(*Enter* GEORGE.)

GEORGE. Now I 'm ready.

(GEORGE *tries to regain his gun;* WAHNOTEE *refuses to give it up;* PAUL *quietly takes it from him and remonstrates with him.*)

DORA. Zoe, he 's going; I want him to stay and make love to me; that 's what I came for to-day.

MRS. P. George, I can't spare Paul for an hour or two; he must run over to the landing; the steamer from New Orleans passed up the river last night, and if there 's a mail they have thrown it ashore.

SUNNY. I saw the mail-bags lying in the shed this morning.

MRS. P. I expect an important letter from Liverpool; away with you, Paul; bring the mail-bags here.

PAUL. I 'm 'most afraid to take Wahnotee to the shed, there 's rum there.

WAHNOTEE. Rum!

PAUL. Come, then, but if I catch you drinkin', O, laws a mussey, you 'll get snakes! I 'll gib it you! now mind. (*Exit with Indian.*)

GEORGE. Come, Miss Dora, let me offer you my arm.

DORA. Mr. George, I am afraid, if all we hear is true, you have led a dreadful life in Europe.

GEORGE. That 's a challenge to begin a description of my feminine adventures.

DORA. You have been in love, then?

GEORGE. Two hundred and forty-nine times! Let me relate you the worst cases.

DORA. No! no!

GEORGE. I 'll put the naughty parts in French.

DORA. I won't hear a word! O, you horrible man! go on.

(*Exit* GEORGE *and* DORA *to the house.*)

M'CLOSKY. Now, ma'am, I 'd like a little business, if agreeable. I bring you news; your banker, old Lafouche, of New Orleans, is dead; the executors are winding up his affairs, and have foreclosed on all overdue mortgages, so Terrebonne is for sale. Here 's the *Picayune* (*Producing paper*) with the advertisement.

ZOE. Terrebonne for sale!

MRS. P. Terrebonne for sale, and you, sir, will doubtless become its purchaser.

M'CLOSKY. Well, ma'am, I s'pose there 's no law agin my bidding for it. The more bidders, the better for you. You 'll take care, I guess, it don't go too cheap.

MRS. P. O, sir, I don't value the place for its price, but for the many happy days I 've spent here; that landscape, flat and uninteresting though it may be, is full of charm for me; those poor people, born around me, growing up about my heart, have bounded my view of life; and now to lose that homely scene, lose their black, ungainly faces! O, sir, perhaps you should be as old as I am, to feel as I do, when my past life is torn away from me.

M'CLOSKY. I 'd be darned glad if somebody would tear my past life away from *me.* Sorry I can't help you, but the fact is, you 're in such an all-fired mess that you could n't be pulled out without a derrick.

MRS. P. Yes, there is a hope left yet, and I cling to it. The house of Mason Brothers, of Liverpool, failed some twenty years ago in my husband's debt.

M'CLOSKY. They owed him over fifty thousand dollars.

MRS. P. I cannot find the entry in my husband's accounts; but you, Mr. M'Closky, can doubtless detect it. Zoe, bring here the judge's old desk; it is in the library. (*Exit* ZOE *to the house.*)

M'CLOSKY. You don't expect to recover any of this old debt, do you?

MRS. P. Yes; the firm has recovered itself, and I received a notice two months ago that some settlement might be anticipated.

SUNNY. Why, with principal and interest this debt has been more than doubled in twenty years.

MRS. P. But it may be years yet before it will be paid off, if ever.

SUNNY. If there 's a chance of it, there 's not a planter round here who would n't lend you the whole cash, to keep your name and blood amongst us. Come, cheer up, old friend.

MRS. P. Ah! Sunnyside, how good you are; so like my poor Peyton.

(*Exit* MRS. PEYTON *and* SUNNYSIDE *to the house.*)

M'CLOSKY. Curse their old families—they cut me—a bilious, conceited, thin lot of dried up aristocracy. I hate 'em. Just because my grandfather was n't some broken-down Virginia transplant, or a stingy old Creole, I ain't fit to sit down to the same meat with them. It makes my blood so hot I feel my heart hiss. I 'll sweep these Peytons from this section of the country. Their presence keeps alive the reproach against me that I ruined them. Yet, if this money should come! Bah! There 's no chance of it. Then, if they go, they 'll take Zoe—she 'll follow them. Darn that girl; she makes me quiver when I think of her; she 's took me for all I 'm worth. (*Enter* ZOE *from house, with the desk.*) O, here, do you know what the annuity the old judge left you is worth to-day? Not a picayune.

ZOE. It 's surely worth the love that dictated it; here are the papers and accounts. (*Putting the desk on the table.*)

M'CLOSKY. Stop, Zoe; come here! How would you like to rule the house of the richest planter on Atchafalaya—eh? or say the word, and I 'll buy this old barrack, and you shall be mistress of Terrebonne.

ZOE. O, sir, do not speak so to me!

M'CLOSKY. Why not! look here, these Peytons are bust; cut 'em; I am rich, jine me; I 'll set you up grand, and we 'll give these first families here our dust, until you 'll see their white skins shrivel up with hate and rage; what d' ye say?

ZOE. Let me pass! O, pray, let me go!

M'CLOSKY. What, you won't, won't ye? If young George Peyton was to make you the same offer, you 'd jump at it pretty darned quick, I guess. Come, Zoe, don't be a fool; I 'd marry you if I could, but you know I can't; so just say what you want. Here, then, I 'll put back these Peytons in Terrebonne, and they shall know you done it; yes, they 'll have you to thank for saving them from ruin.

ZOE. Do you think they would live here on such terms?

M'CLOSKY. Why not? We 'll hire out our slaves, and live on their wages.

ZOE. But I 'm not a slave.

M'CLOSKY. No; if you were I 'd buy you, if you cost all I 'm worth.

ZOE. Let me pass!

M'CLOSKY. Stop.

(*Enter* SCUDDER.)

SCUD. Let her pass.

M'CLOSKY. Eh?

SCUD. Let her pass!

(*He takes out his knife. Exit* ZOE *to house.*)

M'CLOSKY. Is that you, Mr. Overseer? (*He examines paper.*)

SCUD. Yes, I 'm here, somewhere, interferin'.

M'CLOSKY. (*Sitting.*) A pretty mess you 've got this estate in—

SCUD. Yes—me and Co.—we done it; but, as you were senior partner in the concern, I reckon you got the big lick.

M'CLOSKY. What d' ye mean?

SCUD. Let me proceed by illustration. (*Sits.*) Look thar! (*Points with his knife off.*) D' ye see that tree?—it 's called a live oak, and is a native here; beside it grows a creeper; year after year that creeper twines its long arms round and round the tree—sucking the earth dry all about its roots—living on its life—overrunning its branches, until at last the live oak withers and dies out. Do you know what the niggers round here call that sight? they call it the Yankee hugging the Creole.

M'CLOSKY. Mr. Scudder, I 've listened to a great many of your insinuations, and now I 'd like to come to an understanding what they mean. If you want a quarrel—

SCUD. No, I 'm the skurriest crittur at a fight you ever see; my legs have been too well brought up to stand and see my body abused; I take good care of myself, I can tell you.

M'CLOSKY. Because I heard that you had traduced my character.

SCUD. Traduced! Whoever said so lied. I always said you were the darndest thief that ever escaped a white jail to misrepresent the North to the South.

M'CLOSKY. (*He raises hand to back of his neck.*) What!

SCUD. Take your hand down—take it down. (M'CLOSKY *lowers his hand.*) Whenever I gets into company like yours, I always start with the advantage on my side.

M'CLOSKY. What d 'ye mean?

SCUD. I mean that before you could draw that bowie-knife, you wear down your back, I 'd cut you into shingles. Keep quiet, and let 's talk sense. You wanted to come to an understanding, and I 'm coming thar as quick as I can. Now, Jacob M'Closky, you despise me because you think I 'm a fool; I despise you because I know you to be a knave. Between us we 've ruined these Peytons; you fired the judge, and I finished off the widow. Now, I feel bad about my share in the business. I 'd give half the balance of my life to wipe out my part of the work. Many a night I 've laid awake and thought how to pull them through, till I 've cried like a child over the sum I could n't do; and you know how darned hard 't is to make a Yankee cry.

M'CLOSKY. Well, what 's that to me?

SCUD. Hold on, Jacob, I 'm coming to that—I tell ye, I 'm such a fool—I can't bear the feeling, it keeps at me like a skin complaint, and if this family is sold up—

M'CLOSKY. What then?

SCUD. (*Rising.*) I'd cut my throat—or yours—yours I'd prefer.

M'CLOSKY. Would you now? why don't you do it?

SCUD. 'Cos I's skeered to try! I never killed a man in my life—and civilization is so strong in me I guess I could n't do it—I'd like to, though!

M'CLOSKY. And all for the sake of that old woman and that young puppy—eh? No other cause to hate—to envy me—to be jealous of me—eh?

SCUD. Jealous? what for?

M'CLOSKY. Ask the color in your face: d' ye think I can't read you, like a book? With your New England hypocrisy, you would persuade yourself that it was this family alone you cared for; it ain't—you know it ain't—'t is the "Octoroon"; and you love her as I do; and you hate me because I'm your rival—that's where the tears come from, Salem Scudder, if you ever shed any—that's where the shoe pinches.

SCUD. Wal, I do like the gal; she's a—

M'CLOSKY. She's in love with young Peyton; it made me curse whar it made you cry, as it does now; I see the tears on your cheeks now.

SCUD. Look at 'em, Jacob, for they are honest water from the well of truth. I ain't ashamed of it—I do love the gal; but I ain't jealous of you, because I believe the only sincere feeling about you is your love for Zoe, and it does your heart good to have her image thar; but I believe you put it thar to spile. By fair means I don't think you can get her, and don't you try foul with her, 'cause if you do, Jacob, civilization be darned, I'm on you like a painter, and when I'm drawed out I'm pizin.

(*Exit* SCUDDER *to house.*)

M'CLOSKY. Fair or foul, I'll have her—take that home with you! (*He opens desk.*) What's here—judgments? yes, plenty of 'em; bill of costs; account with Citizens' Bank—what's this? "Judgment, $40,000, 'Thibodeaux against Peyton,'"—surely, that is the judgment under which this estate is now advertised for sale—(*He takes up paper and examines it*) yes, "Thibodeaux against Peyton, 1838." Hold on! whew! this is worth taking to—in this desk the judge used to keep one paper I want—this should be it. (*Reads.*) "The free papers of my daughter Zoe, registered February 4th, 1841." Why, judge, was n't you lawyer enough to know that while a judgment stood against you it was a lien on your slaves? Zoe is your child by a quadroon slave, and you did n't free her; blood! if this is so, she's mine! this old Liverpool debt—that may cross me—if it only arrive too late—if it don't come by this mail—Hold on! this letter the old lady expects—that's it; let me only head off that letter, and Terrebonne will be sold before they can recover it. That boy and the Indian have gone down to the landing for the post-bags; they'll idle on the way as usual; my mare will take me across the swamp, and before they can reach the shed, I'll have purified them bags—ne'er a letter shall show this mail. Ha, ha!—(*Calls.*) Pete, you old turkey-buzzard, saddle my mare. Then, if I sink every dollar I'm worth in her purchase, I'll own that Octoroon.

ACT SECOND.

The Wharf with goods, boxes, and bales scattered about—a camera on a stand; DORA *being photographed by* SCUDDER, *who is arranging photographic apparatus,* GEORGE *and* PAUL *looking on at back.*

SCUD. Just turn your face a leetle this way—fix your—let's see—look here.

DORA. So?

SCUD. That's right. (*Putting his head under the darkening apron.*) It's such a long time since I did this sort of thing, and this old machine has got so dirty and stiff, I'm afraid it won't operate. That's about right. Now don't stir.

PAUL. Ugh! she looks as though she war gwine to have a tooth drawed!

SCUD. I've got four plates ready, in case we miss the first shot. One of them is prepared with a self-developing liquid that I've invented. I hope it will turn out better than most of my notions. Now fix yourself. Are you ready?

DORA. Ready!

SCUD. Fire!—one, two, three.

(SCUDDER *takes out watch.*)

PAUL. Now it's cooking; laws mussey! I feel it all inside, as if I was at a lottery.

SCUD. So! (*Throws down apron.*) That's

enough. (*Withdrawing slide, turns and sees* PAUL.) What! what are you doing there, you young varmint! Ain't you took them bags to the house yet?

PAUL. Now, it ain't no use trying to get mad, Mas'r Scudder. I'm gwine! I only come back to find Wahnotee; whar is dat ign'ant Ingiun?

SCUD. You'll find him scenting round the rum store, hitched up by the nose. (*Exit into the room.*)

PAUL. (*Calling at the door.*) Say, Mas'r Scudder, take me in dat telescope?

SCUD. (*Inside the room.*) Get out, you cub! clar out!

PAUL. You got four of dem dishes ready. Gosh, would n't I like to hab myself took! What's de charge, Mas'r Scudder? (*He runs off.*)

(*Enter* SCUDDER, *from the room.*)

SCUD. Job had none of them critters on his plantation, else he'd never ha' stood through so many chapters. Well, that has come out clear, ain't it? (*Showing the plate.*)

DORA. O, beautiful! Look, Mr. Peyton.

GEORGE. (*Looking.*) Yes, very fine!

SCUD. The apparatus can't mistake. When I travelled round with this machine, the homely folks used to sing out, "Hillo, mister, this ain't like me!" "Ma'am," says I, "the apparatus can't mistake." "But, mister, that ain't my nose." "Ma'am, your nose drawed it. The machine can't err—you may mistake your phiz but the apparatus don't." "But, sir, it ain't agreeable." "No, ma'am, the truth seldom is."

(*Enter* PETE, *puffing.*)

PETE. Mas'r Scudder! Mas'r Scudder!

SCUD. Hillo! what are you blowing about like a steamboat with one wheel for?

PETE. *You* blow, Mas'r Scudder, when I tole you: dere's a man from Noo Aleens just arriv'd at de house, and he's stuck up two papers on de gates: "For sale—dis yer property," and a heap of oder tings—an he seen missus, and arter he shown some papers she burst out crying—I yelled; den de corious of little niggers dey set up, den de hull plantation children—de live stock reared up and created a purpiration of lamentation as did de ole heart good to har.

DORA. What's the matter?

SCUD. He's come.

PETE. Dass it—I saw 'm!

SCUD. The sheriff from New Orleans has taken possession—Terrebonne is in the hands of the law.

(*Enter* ZOE.)

ZOE. O, Mr. Scudder! Dora! Mr. Peyton! come home—there are strangers in the house.

DORA. Stay, Mr. Peyton: Zoe, a word! (*She leads her forward—aside.*) Zoe, the more I see of George Peyton the better I like him; but he is too modest—that is a very impertinent virtue in a man.

ZOE. I'm no judge, dear.

DORA. Of course not, you little fool; no one ever made love to you, and you can't understand; I mean, that George knows I am an heiress; my fortune would release this estate from debt.

ZOE. O, I see!

DORA. If he would only propose to marry me I would accept him, but he don't know that, and he will go on fooling, in his slow European way, until it is too late.

ZOE. What's to be done?

DORA. You tell him.

ZOE. What? that he is n't to go on fooling in his slow—

DORA. No, you goose! twit him on his silence and abstraction—I'm sure it's plain enough, for he has not spoken two words to me all the day; then joke round the subject, and at last speak out.

SCUD. Pete, as you came here, did you pass Paul and the Indian with the letter-bags?

PETE. No, sar; but dem vagabonds neber take the 'specable straight road, dey goes by de swamp. (*Exit up the path.*)

SCUD. Come, sir!

DORA. (*To* ZOE.) Now's your time.—(*Aloud.*) Mr. Scudder, take us with you—Mr. Peyton is so slow, there's no getting him on.

(*Exit* DORA *and* SCUDDER.)

ZOE. They are gone!—(*Glancing at* GEORGE.) Poor fellow, he has lost all.

GEORGE. Poor child! how sad she looks now she has no resource.

ZOE. How shall I ask him to stay?

GEORGE. Zoe, will you remain here? I wish to speak to you.

ZOE. (*Aside.*) Well, that saves trouble.

GEORGE. By our ruin you lose all.

ZOE. O, I'm nothing; think of yourself.

GEORGE. I can think of nothing but the image that remains face to face with me; so beautiful, so simple, so confiding, that I dare not express the feelings that have grown up so rapidly in my heart.

ZOE. (*Aside.*) He means Dora.

GEORGE. If I dared to speak!

ZOE. That 's just what you must do, and do it at once, or it will be too late.

GEORGE. Has my love been divined?

ZOE. It has been more than suspected.

GEORGE. Zoe, listen to me, then. I shall see this estate pass from me without a sigh, for it possesses no charm for me; the wealth I covet is the love of those around me—eyes that are rich in fond looks, lips that breathe endearing words; the only estate I value is the heart of one true woman, and the slaves I 'd have are her thoughts.

ZOE. George, George, your words take away my breath!

GEORGE. The world, Zoe, the free struggle of minds and hands is before me; the education bestowed on me by my dear uncle is a noble heritage which no sheriff can seize; with that I can build up a fortune, spread a roof over the heads I love, and place before them the food I have earned; I will work—

ZOE. Work! I thought none but colored people worked.

GEORGE. Work, Zoe, is the salt that gives savor to life.

ZOE. Dora said you were slow; if she could hear you now—

GEORGE. Zoe, you are young; your mirror must have told you that you are beautiful. Is your heart free?

ZOE. Free? of course it is!

GEORGE. We have known each other but a few days, but to me those days have been worth all the rest of my life. Zoe, you have suspected the feeling that now commands an utterance—you have seen that I love you.

ZOE. Me! you love *me?*

GEORGE. As my wife,—the sharer of my hopes, my ambitions, and my sorrows; under the shelter of your love I could watch the storms of fortune pass unheeded by.

ZOE. *My* love! *My* love? George, you know not what you say! *I* the sharer of your sorrows—your wife! Do you know what I am?

GEORGE. Your birth—I know it. Has not my dear aunt forgotten it—she who had the most right to remember it? You are illegitimate, but love knows no prejudice.

ZOE. (*Aside.*) Alas! he does not know, he does not know! and will despise me, spurn me, loathe me, when he learns who, what, he has so loved.—(*Aloud.*) George, O, forgive me! Yes, I love you—I did not know it until your words showed me what has been in my heart; each of them awoke a new sense, and now I know how unhappy—how very unhappy I am.

GEORGE. Zoe, what have I said to wound you?

ZOE. Nothing; but you must learn what I thought you already knew. George, you cannot marry me; the laws forbid it!

GEORGE. Forbid it?

ZOE. There is a gulf between us, as wide as your love, as deep as my despair; but, O, tell me, say you will pity me! that you will not throw me from you like a poisoned thing!

GEORGE. Zoe, explain yourself—your language fills me with shapeless fears.

ZOE. And what shall I say? I—my mother was—no, no—not her! Why should I refer the blame to her? George, do you see that hand you hold? look at these fingers; do you see the nails are of a bluish tinge?

GEORGE. Yes, near the quick there is a faint blue mark.

ZOE. Look in my eyes; is not the same color in the white?

GEORGE. It is their beauty.

ZOE. Could you see the roots of my hair you would see the same dark, fatal mark. Do you know what that is?

GEORGE. No.

ZOE. That is the ineffaceable curse of Cain. Of the blood that feeds my heart, one drop in eight is black—bright red as the rest may be, that one drop poisons all the flood; those seven bright drops give me love like yours—hope like yours—ambition like yours—life hung with passions like dew-drops on the morning flowers; but the one black drop gives me despair, for I 'm an unclean thing—forbidden by the laws—I 'm an Octoroon!

GEORGE. Zoe, I love you none the less; this knowledge brings no revolt to my heart, and I can overcome the obstacle.

ZOE. But *I* cannot.

GEORGE. We can leave this country, and go far away where none can know.

ZOE. And your mother, she who from infancy treated me with such fondness, she who, as you said, has most reason to spurn me, can she forget what I am? Will she gladly see you wedded to the child of her husband's slave? No! she would revolt from it, as all but you would; and if I consented to hear the cries of my heart, if I did not crush out my infant love, what would she say to the poor girl on whom she had bestowed so much? No, no!

GEORGE. Zoe, must we immolate our lives on her prejudice?

ZOE. Yes, for I'd rather be black than ungrateful! Ah, George, our race has at least one virtue—it knows how to suffer!

GEORGE. Each word you utter makes my love sink deeper into my heart.

ZOE. And I remained here to induce you to offer that heart to Dora!

GEORGE. If you bid me do so I will obey you—

ZOE. No, no! if you cannot be mine, O, let me not blush when I think of you.

GEORGE. Dearest Zoe!

(*Exit* GEORGE *and* ZOE.)

(*As they exit,* M'CLOSKY *rises from behind a rock and looks after them.*)

M'CLOSKY. She loves him! I felt it—and how she can love! (*Advances.*) That one black drop of blood burns in her veins and lights up her heart like a foggy sun. O, how I lapped up her words, like a thirsty bloodhound! I'll have her, if it costs me my life! Yonder the boy still lurks with those mail-bags; the devil still keeps him here to tempt me, darn his yellow skin! I arrived just too late, he had grabbed the prize as I came up. Hillo! he's coming this way, fighting with his Injiun.

(*Conceals himself.*)

(*Enter* PAUL, *wrestling with* WAHNOTEE.)

PAUL. It ain't no use now: you got to gib it up!

WAHNO. Ugh!

PAUL. It won't do! You got dat bottle of rum hid under your blanket—gib it up now, you—. Yar! (*Wrenching it from him.*) You nasty, lying Injiun! It's no use you putting on airs; I ain't gwine to sit up wid you all night and you drunk. Hillo! war's de crowd gone? And dar's de 'paratus—O, gosh, if I could take a likeness ob dis child! Uh—uh, let's have a peep. (*Looking through camera.*) O, golly! yar, you Wahnotee! you stan' dar, I see you. Ta demine usti-

(*He looks at* WAHNOTEE *through the camera;* WAHNOTEE *springs back with an expression of alarm.*)

WAHNO. No tue Wahnotee.

PAUL. Ha, ha! he tinks it's a gun. You ign'ant Injiun, it can't hurt you! Stop, here's dem dishes—plates—dat's what he call 'em, all fix: I see Mas'r Scudder do it often—tink I can take likeness—stay dere, Wahnotee.

WAHNO. No, carabine tue.

PAUL. I must operate and take my own likeness too—how debbel I do dat? Can't be ober dar an' here too—I ain't twins. Ugh! ach! 'Top; you look, you Wahnotee; you see dis rag, eh? Well when I say go, den lift dis rag like dis, see! den run to dat pine tree up dar (*Points*) and back ag'in, and den pull down de rag so, d' ye see?

WAHNO. Hugh!

PAUL. Den you hab glass ob rum.

WAHNO. Rum!

PAUL. Dat wakes him up. Coute, Wahnotee in omenee dit go Wahnotee, poina la fa, comb a pine tree, la revieut sala, la fa.

WAHNO. Fire-water!

PAUL. Yes, den a glass ob fire-water; now den. (*Throwing mail-bags down and sitting on them.*) Pret, now den go.

(WAHNOTEE *raises the apron and runs off.* PAUL *sits for his picture*—M'CLOSKY *appears.*)

M'CLOSKY. Where are they? Ah, yonder goes the Indian!

PAUL. De time he gone just 'bout enough to cook dat dish plate.

M'CLOSKY. Yonder is the boy—now is my time! What's he doing; is he asleep? (*Advancing.*) He is sitting on my prize! darn his carcass! I'll clear him off there—he'll never know what stunned him.

(*He takes Indian's tomahawk and steals to* PAUL.)

PAUL. Dam dat Injiun! is dat him creeping dar? I dare n't move fear to spile myself.

(M'CLOSKY *strikes him on the head—he falls dead.*)

M'CLOSKY. Hooraw; the bags are mine—now for it!—(*Opening the mail-bags.*) What's here? Sunnyside, Pointdexter, Jackson, Peyton; here it is—the Liverpool postmark, sure enough!—(*Opening letter—reads.*) "Madam, we are instructed by the firm of Mason and Co., to inform you that a dividend of forty per cent. is payable on the 1st proximo, this amount in consideration of position, they send herewith, and you will find enclosed by draft to your order, on the Bank of Louisiana, which please acknowledge—the balance will be paid in full, with interest, in three, six, and nine months—your drafts on Mason Brothers at those dates will be accepted by La Palisse and Compagnie, N. O., so that you may command immediate use of the whole amount at once, if required. Yours, etc., James Brown." What a find! this infernal letter would have saved all. (*During the reading of letter he remains nearly motionless under the focus of the camera.*) But now I guess it will arrive too late—these darned U. S. mails are to blame. The Injiun! he must not see me. (*Exit rapidly.*)

(WAHNOTEE *runs on, and pulls down the apron. He sees* PAUL, *lying on the ground and speaks to him, thinking that he is shamming sleep. He gesticulates and jabbers to him and moves him with his feet, then kneels down to rouse him. To his horror he finds him dead. Expressing great grief he raises his eyes and they fall upon the camera. Rising with a savage growl, he seizes the tomahawk and smashes the camera to pieces. Going to* PAUL *he expresses in pantomime grief, sorrow, and fondness, and takes him in his arms to carry him away.*)

ACT THIRD

(*A Room in* MRS. PEYTON'S *house showing the entrance on which an auction bill is pasted.* SOLON *and* GRACE *are there.*)

PETE. (*Outside.*) Dis way—dis way.

(*Enter* PETE, POINTDEXTER, JACKSON, LAFOUCHE *and* CAILLOU.)

PETE. Dis way, gen'l'men; now, Solon—Grace—dey 's hot and tirsty—sangaree, brandy, rum.

JACKSON. Well, what d 'ye say, Lafouche—d 'ye smile?

(*Enter* THIBODEAUX *and* SUNNYSIDE.)

THIBO. I hope we don't intrude on the family.

PETE. You see dat hole in dar, sar? I was raised on dis yar plantation—nebber see no door in it—always open, sar, for stranger to walk in.

SUNNY. And for substance to walk out.

(*Enter* RATTS.)

RATTS. Fine southern style that, eh!

LAFOUCHE. (*Reading the bill.*) "A fine, well-built old family mansion, replete with every comfort."

RATTS. There 's one name on the list of slaves scratched, I see.

LAFOUCHE. Yes; No. 49, Paul, a quadroon boy, aged thirteen.

SUNNY. He 's missing.

POINT. Run away, I suppose.

PETE. (*Indignantly.*) No, sar; nigger nebber cut stick on Terrebonne; dat boy 's dead, sure.

RATTS. What, Picayune Paul, as we called him, that used to come aboard my boat?—poor little darkey, I hope not; many a picayune he picked up for his dance and nigger songs, and he supplied our table with fish and game from the Bayous.

PETE. Nebber supply no more, sar—nebber dance again. Mas'r Ratts, you hard him sing about de place where de good niggers go, de last time.

RATTS. Well!

PETE. Well, he gone dar hisself; why I tink so—'cause we missed Paul for some days, but nebber tout nothin' till one night dat Injiun Wahnotee suddenly stood right dar 'mongst us—was in his war paint, and mighty cold and grave—he sit down by de fire. "Whar 's Paul?" I say—he smoke and smoke, but nebber look out ob de fire; well knowing dem critters, I wait a long time—den he say, "Wahnotee great chief;" den I say nothing—smoke anoder time—last, rising to go, he turn round at door, and say berry low—O, like a woman's voice he say, "Omenee Pangeuk,"—dat is, Paul is dead—nebber see him since.

RATTS. That red-skin killed him.

SUNNY. So we believe; and so mad are the folks around, if they catch the red-skin they 'll lynch him sure.

RATTS. Lynch him! Darn his copper carcass, I 've got a set of Irish deck-hands aboard that just loved that child; and after I tell them this, let them get a sight of the red-skin, I believe they would eat him, tomahawk and all. Poor little Paul!

THIBO. What was he worth?

RATTS. Well, near on five hundred dollars.

PETE. (*Scandalized.*) What, sar! You p'tend to be sorry for Paul, and prize him like dat! Five hundred dollars! (*To* THIBODEAUX.) Tousand dollars, Massa Thibodeau.

(*Enter* SCUDDER.)

SCUD. Gentlemen, the sale takes place at three. Good morning, Colonel. It 's near that now, and there 's still the sugar-houses to be inspected. Good day, Mr. Thibodeaux—shall we drive down that way? Mr. Lafouche, why, how do you do, sir? you 're looking well.

LAFOUCHE. Sorry I can't return the compliment.

RATTS. Salem 's looking a kinder hollowed out.

SCUD. What, Mr. Ratts, are you going to invest in swamps?

RATTS. No; I want a nigger.

SCUD. Hush.

PETE. Eh! wass dat?

SCUD. Mr. Sunnyside, I can't do this job of showin' round the folks; my stomach goes agin it. I want Pete here a minute.

SUNNY. I 'll accompany them certainly.

SCUD. (*Eagerly.*) Will ye? Thank ye; thank ye.

SUNNY. We must excuse Scudder, friends. I 'll see you round the estate.

(*Enter* GEORGE *and* MRS. PEYTON.)

LAFOUCHE. Good morning, Mrs. Peyton. (*All salute.*)

SUNNY. This way, gentlemen.

RATTS. (*Aside to Sunnyside.*) I say, I 'd like to say summit soft to the old woman; perhaps it would n't go well, would it?

THIBO. No; leave it alone.

RATTS. Darn it, when I see a woman in trouble, I feel like selling the skin off my back.

(*Exit* THIBODEAUX, SUNNYSIDE, RATTS, POINTDEXTER, GRACE, JACKSON, LAFOUCHE, CAILLOU, SOLON.)

SCUD. (*Aside to Pete.*) Go outside there; listen to what you hear, then go down to the quarters and tell the boys, for I can't do it. O, get out.

PETE. He said "I want a nigger." Laws, mussey! What am goin' to cum ob us! (*Exit slowly, as if trying to conceal himself.*)

GEORGE. My dear aunt, why do you not move from this painful scene? Go with Dora to Sunnyside.

MRS. P. No, George; your uncle said to me with his dying breath, "Nellie, never leave Terrebonne," and I never *will* leave it, till the law compels me.

SCUD. Mr. George, I 'm going to say somethin' that has been chokin' me for some time. I know you 'll excuse it. Thar 's Miss Dora—that girl 's in love with you; yes, sir, her eyes are startin' out of her head with it: now her fortune would redeem a good part of this estate.

MRS. P. Why, George, I never suspected this!

GEORGE. I did, aunt, I confess, but—

MRS. P. And you hesitated from motives of delicacy?

SCUD. No, ma'am; here 's the plan of it. Mr. George is in love with Zoe.

GEORGE. Scudder!

MRS. P. George!

SCUD. Hold on, now! things have got so jammed in on top of us, we ain't got time to put kid gloves on to handle them. He loves Zoe, and has found out that she loves him. (*Sighing.*) Well, that 's all right; but as he can't marry her, and as Miss Dora would jump at him—

MRS. P. Why did n't you mention this before?

SCUD. Why, because *I* love Zoe, too, and I could n't take that young feller from her; and she 's jist living on the sight of him, as I saw her do; and they so happy in spite of this yer misery around them, and they reproachin' themselves with not feeling as they ought. I 've seen it, I tell you; and darn it, ma'am, can't you see that 's what 's been a hollowing me out so—I beg your pardon.

MRS. P. O, George,—my son, let me call you,—I do not speak for my own sake, nor for the loss of the estate, but for the poor people here: they will be sold, divided, and taken away—they have been born here. Heaven has denied me children; so all the strings of my heart have grown around and amongst them, like the fibres and roots of an old tree in its native earth. O, let all go, but save them! With them around us, if we have not wealth, we shall at least have the home that they alone can make—

GEORGE. My dear mother—Mr. Scudder—you teach me what I ought to do; if Miss Sunnyside will accept me as I am, Terrebonne shall be saved: I will sell myself, but the slaves shall be protected.

MRS. P. *Sell* yourself, George! Is not Dora worth any man's—

SCUD. Don't say that, ma'am; don't say that to a man that loves another gal. He 's going to do an heroic act; don't spile it.

MRS. P. But Zoe is only an Octoroon.

SCUD. She 's won this race agin the white, anyhow; it 's too late now to start her pedigree. (*As* DORA *enters.*) Come, Mrs. Peyton, take my arm. Hush! here 's the other one: she 's a little too thoroughbred—too much of the greyhound; but the heart 's there, I believe.

(*Exeunt* SCUDDER *and* MRS. PEYTON.)

DORA. Poor Mrs. Peyton.

GEORGE. Miss Sunnyside, permit me a word: a feeling of delicacy has suspended upon my lips an avowal, which—

DORA. (*Aside.*) O, dear, has he suddenly come to his senses?

(*Enter* ZOE, *stopping at back.*)

GEORGE. In a word, I have seen and admired you!

DORA. (*Aside.*) He has a strange way of showing it. European, I suppose.

GEORGE. If you would pardon the abruptness of the question, I would ask you, Do you think the sincere devotion of my life to make yours happy would succeed?

DORA. (*Aside.*) Well, he has the oddest way of making love.

GEORGE. You are silent?

DORA. Mr. Peyton, I presume you have hesitated to make this avowal because you feared, in the present condition of affairs here, your object might be misconstrued, and that your attention was rather to my fortune than myself. (*A pause.*) Why don't he speak?—I mean, you feared I might not give you credit for sincere and pure feelings. Well, you wrong me. I don't think you capable of anything else but—

GEORGE. No, I hesitated because an attachment I had formed before I had the pleasure of seeing you had not altogether died out.

DORA. (*Smiling.*) Some of those sirens of Paris, I presume. (*Pausing.*) I shall endeavor not to be jealous of the past; perhaps I have no right to be. (*Pausing.*) But now that vagrant love is—eh, faded—is it not? Why don't you speak, sir?

GEORGE. Because, Miss Sunnyside, I have not learned to lie.

DORA. Good gracious—who wants you to?

GEORGE. I do, but I can't do it. No, the love I speak of is not such as you suppose,—it is a passion that has grown up here since I arrived; but it is a hopeless, mad, wild feeling, that must perish.

DORA. Here! since you arrived! Impossible: you have seen no one; whom can you mean?

ZOE. (*Advancing.*) Me.

GEORGE. Zoe!

DORA. You!

ZOE. Forgive him, Dora; for he knew no better until I told him. Dora, you are right. He is incapable of any but sincere and pure feelings—so are you. He loves me—what of that? You know you can't be jealous of a poor creature like me. If he caught the fever, were stung by a snake, or possessed of any other poisonous or unclean thing, you could pity, tend, love him through it, and for your gentle care he would love you in return. Well, is he not thus afflicted now? I am his love—he loves an Octoroon.

GEORGE. O, Zoe, you break my heart!

DORA. At college they said I was a fool—I must be. At New Orleans, they said, "She 's pretty, very pretty, but no brains." I 'm afraid they must be right; I can't understand a word of all this.

ZOE. Dear Dora, try to understand it with your heart. You love George; you love him dearly; I know it; and you deserve to be loved by him. He will love you—he must. His love for me will pass away—it shall. You heard him say it was hopeless. O, forgive him and me!

DORA. (*Weeping.*) O, why did he speak to me at all then? You 've made me cry, then, and I hate you both!

(*Exit through room.*)

(*Enter* MRS. PEYTON *and* SCUDDER, M'CLOSKY *and* POINTDEXTER.)

M'CLOSKY. I 'm sorry to intrude, but the business I came upon will excuse me.

MRS. PEY. Here is my nephew, sir.

ZOE. Perhaps I had better go.

M'CLOSKY. Wal, as it consarns you, perhaps you better had.

SCUD. Consarns Zoe?

M'CLOSKY. I don't know; she may as well hear the hull of it. Go on, Colonel—Colonel Pointdexter, ma'am—the mortgagee, auctioneer, and general agent.

POINT. Pardon me, madam, but do you know these papers?

(*He hands the papers to* MRS. PEYTON.)

MRS. PEY. (*Taking them.*) Yes, sir; they were the free papers of the girl Zoe; but they were in my husband's secretary. How came they in your possession?

M'CLOSKY. I—I found them.

GEORGE. And you purloined them?

M'CLOSKY. Hold on, you 'll see. Go on, Colonel.

POINT. The list of your slaves is incomplete—it wants one.

SCUD. The boy Paul—we know it.

POINT. No, sir, you have omitted the Octoroon girl, Zoe.

MRS. PEY. } Zoe
ZOE. } Me!

POINT. At the time the judge executed those free papers to his infant slave, a judgment stood recorded against him; while that was on record he had no right to make away with his property. That judgment still exists: under it and others this estate is sold to-day. Those free papers ain't worth the sand that 's on 'em.

MRS. PEY. Zoe a slave! It is impossible!

POINT. It is certain, madam: the judge was negligent, and doubtless forgot this small formality.

SCUD. But the creditors will not claim the gal?

M'CLOSKY. Excuse me; one of the principal mortgagees has made the demand. (*Exeunt* M'CLOSKY *and* POINTDEXTER.)

SCUD. Hold on yere, George Peyton; you sit down there. You 're trembling so, you 'll fall down directly. This blow has staggered me some.

MRS. PEY. O, Zoe, my child! don't think too hard of your poor father.

ZOE. I shall do so if you weep. See, I 'm calm.

SCUD. Calm as a tombstone, and with about as much life. I see it in your face.

GEORGE. It cannot be! It shall not be!

SCUD. Hold your tongue—it must. Be calm—darn the things; the proceeds of this sale won't cover the debts of the estate. Consarn those Liverpool English fellers, why could n't they send something by the last mail? Even a letter, promising something—such is the feeling round amongst the planters. Darn me, if I could n't raise thirty thousand on the envelope alone, and ten thousand more on the postmark.

GEORGE. Zoe, they shall not take you from us while I live.

SCUD. Don't be a fool; they 'd kill you, and then take her, just as soon as—stop: old Sunnyside, he 'll buy her; that 'll save her.

ZOE. No, it won't; we have confessed to Dora that we love each other. How can she then ask her father to free me?

SCUD. What in thunder made you do that?

ZOE. Because it was the truth, and I had rather be a slave with a free soul, than remain free with a slavish, deceitful heart. My father gives me freedom—at least he thought so. May Heaven bless him for the thought, bless him for the happiness he spread around my life. You say the proceeds of the sale will not cover his debts. Let me be sold then, that I may free his name. I give him back the liberty he bestowed upon me; for I can never repay him the love he bore his poor Octoroon child, on whose breast his last sigh was drawn, into whose eyes he looked with the last gaze of affection.

MRS. PEY. O, my husband! I thank Heaven you have not lived to see this day.

ZOE. George, leave me! I would be alone a little while.

GEORGE. Zoe!

(*Turning away overpowered.*)

ZOE. Do not weep, George. Dear George, you now see what a miserable thing I am.

GEORGE. Zoe!

SCUD. I wish they could sell *me!* I brought half this ruin on this family, with my all-fired improvements. I deserve to be a nigger this day—I feel like one, inside. (*Exit* SCUDDER.)

ZOE. Go now, George—leave me—take her with you. (*Exit* MRS. PEYTON *and* GEORGE.) A slave! a slave! Is this a dream—for my brain reels with the blow? He said so. What! then I shall be sold!—sold! and my master—O! (*She falls on her knees, with her face in her hands.*) No—no master but one. George—George—hush—they come! save me! No, (*Looks off.*) 't is Pete and the servants—they come this way. (*Enters the inner room.*)

(*Enter* PETE, GRACE, MINNIE, SOLON, DIDO, *and all Niggers.*)

PETE. Cum yer now—stand round, 'cause

I've got to talk to you darkies—keep dem chil'n quiet—don't make no noise, de missus up dar har us.

SOLON. Go on, Pete.

PETE. Gen'l'men, my colored frens and ladies, dar's mighty bad news gone round. Dis yer prop'ty to be sold—old Terrebonne—whar we all been raised, is gwine—dey's gwine to tak it away—can't stop here nohow.

OMNES. O-o!—O-o!

PETE. Hold quiet, you trash o' niggers! tink anybody wants you to cry? Who's you to set up screeching?—be quiet! But dis ain't all. Now, my cullud brethren, gird up your lines, and listen—hold on yer bref—it's a comin'. We tought dat de niggers would belong to de ole missus, and if she lost Terrebonne, we must live dere allers, and we would hire out, and bring our wages to ole Missus Peyton.

OMNES. Ya! ya! Well—

PETE. Hush! I tell ye, 't ain't so—we can't do it—we've got to be sold—

OMNES. Sold!

PETE. Will you hush? she will har you. Yes! I listen dar jess now—dar was ole lady cryin'—Mas'r George—ah! you seen dem big tears in his eyes. O, Mas'r Scudder, he did n't cry zackly; both ob his eyes and cheek look like de bad Bayou in low season—so dry dat I cry for him. (*Raising his voice.*) Den say de missus, "'T ain't for de land I keer, but for dem poor niggers—dey'll be sold—dat wot stagger me." "No," say Mas'r George, "I'd rather sell myself fuss; but dey shan't suffer, nohow,—I see 'em dam fuss."

OMNES. O, bless 'um! Bless Mas'r George.

PETE. Hole yer tongues. Yes, for you, for me, for dem little ones, dem folks cried. Now, den, if Grace dere wid her chil'n were all sold, she'll begin screechin' like a cat. She did n't mind how kind old judge was to her; and Solon, too, he'll holler, and break de ole lady's heart.

GRACE. No, Pete; no, I won't. I'll bear it.

PETE. I don't tink you will any more, but dis here will; 'cause de family spile Dido, dey has. She nebber was worth much a' dat nigger.

DIDO. How dar you say dat, you black nigger, you? I fetch as much as any odder cook in Louisiana.

PETE. What's the use of your takin' it kind, and comfortin' de missus' heart, if Minnie dere, and Louise, and Marie, and Julie is to spile it?

MINNIE. We won't, Pete; we won't.

PETE. (*To the men.*) Dar, do ye hear dat, ye mis'able darkies; dem gals is worth a boat load of kinder men dem is. Cum, for de pride of de family, let every darky look his best for the judge's sake—dat ole man so good to us, and dat ole woman—so dem strangers from New Orleans shall say, Dem's happy darkies, dem's a fine set of niggers; every one say when he's sold, "Lor' bless dis yer family I'm gwine out of, and send me as good a home."

OMNES. We'll do it, Pete; we'll do it.

PETE. Hush! hark! I tell ye dar's somebody in dar. Who is it?

GRACE. It's Missy Zoe. See! see!

PETE. Come along; she har what we say, and she's cryin' for us. None o' ye ign'rant niggers could cry for yerselves like dat. Come here quite: now quite.

(*Exeunt* PETE *and all the Negroes, slowly.*)

(*Enter* ZOE *who is supposed to have overheard the last scene.*)

ZOE. O! must I learn from these poor wretches how much I owe, and how I ought to pay the debt? Have I slept upon the benefits I received, and never saw, never felt, never knew that I was forgetful and ungrateful? O, my father! my dear, dear father! forgive your poor child. You made her life too happy, and now these tears will flow. Let me hide them till I teach my heart. O, my—my heart!

(*Exit, with a low, wailing, suffocating cry.*)

(*Enter* M'CLOSKY, LAFOUCHE, JACKSON, SUNNYSIDE *and* POINTDEXTER.)

POINT. *Looking at his watch.*) Come, the hour is past. I think we may begin business. Where is Mr. Scudder?

JACKSON. I want to get to Ophelensis to-night.

(*Enter* DORA.)

DORA. Father, come here.

SUNNY. Why, Dora, what's the matter? Your eyes are red.

DORA. Are they? thank you. I don't

care, they were blue this morning, but it don't signify now.

SUNNY. My darling! who has been teasing you?

DORA. Never mind. I want you to buy Terrebonne.

SUNNY. Buy Terrebonne! What for?

DORA. No matter—buy it!

SUNNY. It will cost me all I'm worth. This is folly, Dora.

DORA. Is my plantation at Comptableau worth this?

SUNNY. Nearly—perhaps.

DORA. Sell it, then, and buy this.

SUNNY. Are you mad, my love?

DORA. Do you want *me* to stop here and *bid* for it?

SUNNY. Good gracious, no!

DORA. Then I'll do it if you don't.

SUNNY. I will! I will! But for Heaven's sake go—here comes the crowd. (*Exit* DORA.) What on earth does that child mean or want?

(*Enter* SCUDDER, GEORGE, RATTS, CAILLOU, PETE, GRACE, MINNIE, *and all the Negroes. A large table is in the center of the background.* POINTDEXTER *mounts the table with his hammer, his clerk sitting at his feet. The Negro mounts the table from behind. The rest sit down.*)

POINT. Now, gentlemen, we shall proceed to business. It ain't necessary for me to dilate, describe or enumerate; Terrebonne is known to you as one of the richest bits of sile in Louisiana, and its condition reflects credit on them as had to keep it. I'll trouble you for that piece of baccy, Judge—thank you—so, gentlemen, as life is short, we'll start right off. The first lot on here is the estate in block, with its sugar-houses, stock, machines, implements, good dwelling-houses and furniture. If there is no bid for the estate and stuff, we'll sell it in smaller lots. Come, Mr. Thibodeaux, a man has a chance once in his life—here's yours.

THIB. Go on. What's the reserve bid?

POINT. The first mortgagee bids forty thousand dollars.

THIB. Forty-five thousand.

SUNNY. Fifty thousand.

POINT. When you have done joking, gentlemen, you'll say one hundred and twenty thousand. It carried that easy on mortgage.

LAFOUCHE. Then why don't you buy it yourself, Colonel?

POINT. I'm waiting on your fifty thousand bid.

CAILLOU. Eighty thousand.

POINT. Don't be afraid: it ain't going for that, Judge.

SUNNY. Ninety thousand.

POINT. We're getting on.

THIB. One hundred—

POINT. One hundred thousand bid for this mag—

CAILLOU. One hundred and ten thousand—

POINT. Good again—one hundred and—

SUNNY. Twenty.

POINT. And twenty thousand bid. Squire Sunnyside is going to sell this at fifty thousand advance to-morrow. (*Looking round.*) Where's that man from Mobile that wanted to give one hundred and eighty thousand?

THIB. I guess he ain't left home yet, Colonel.

POINT. I shall knock it down to the Squire—going—gone—for one hundred and twenty thousand dollars. (*Raising hammer.*) Judge, you can raise the hull on mortgage—going for half its value. (*Knocking on the table.*) Squire Sunnyside, you've got a pretty bit o' land, Squire. Hillo, darkey, hand me a smash dar.

SUNNY. I got more than I can work now.

POINT. Then buy the hands along with the property. Now, gentlemen, I'm proud to submit to you the finest lot of field hands and house servants that was ever offered for competition: they speak for themselves, and do credit to their owners. (*Reading.*) "No. 1, Solon, a guest boy, and a good waiter."

PETE. That's my son—buy him, Mas'r Ratts; he's sure to sarve you well.

POINT. Hold your tongue!

RATTS. Let the old darkey alone—eight hundred for that boy.

CALLIOU. Nine.

RATTS. A thousand.

SOLON. Thank you, Mas'r Ratts: I die for you, sar; hold up for me, sar.

RATTS. Look here, the boy knows and likes me, Judge; let him come my way?

CALLIOU. Go on—I'm dumb.

POINT. One thousand bid. He's yours, Captain Ratts, Magnolia steamer. (SOLON *goes and stands behind* RATTS.) "No. 2, the yellow girl, Grace, with two children—Saul, aged four, and Victoria, five." (*They get on table.*)

SCUD. That's Solon's wife and children, Judge.

GRACE. (*To* RATTS.) Buy me, Mas'r Ratts, do buy me, sar?

RATTS. What in thunder should I do with you and those devils on board my boat?

GRACE. Wash, sar—cook, sar—anyting.

RATTS. Eight hundred agin, then—I 'll go it.

JACKSON. Nine.

RATTS. I 'm broke, Solon—I can't stop the Judge.

THIB. What 's the matter, Ratts? I 'll lend you all you want. Go it, if you 're a mind to.

RATTS. Eleven.

JACKSON. Twelve.

SUNNY. O, O!

SCUD. (*To Jackson.*) Judge, my friend. The Judge is a little deaf. Hello! (*Speaking in his ear-trumpet.*) This gal and them children belong to that boy Solon there. You 're bidding to separate them, Judge.

JACKSON. The devil I am! (*Rising.*) I 'll take back my bid, Colonel.

POINT. All right, Judge; I thought there was a mistake. I must keep you, Captain, to the eleven hundred.

RATTS. Go it.

POINT. Eleven hundred—going—going—sold! "No. 3, Pete, a house servant."

PETE. Dat 's me—yer, I 'm comin'—stand around dar. (*Tumbles upon the table.*)

POINT. Aged seventy-two.

PETE. What 's dat? A mistake, sar—forty-six.

POINT. Lame.

PETE. But don't mount to nuffin—kin work cannel. Come, Judge, pick up. Now 's your time, sar.

JACKSON. One hundred dollars.

PETE. What, sar? me! for me—look ye here! (*He dances.*)

GEORGE. Five hundred.

PETE. Mas'r George—ah, no, sar—don't buy me—keep your money for some udder dat is to be sold. I ain't no 'count, sar.

POINT. Five hundred bid—it 's a good price. He 's yours, Mr. George Peyton. (*Pete goes down.*) "No. 4, the Octoroon girl, Zoe."

(*Enter* ZOE, *very pale, and stands on table.* M'CLOSKY *who hitherto has taken no interest in the sale, now turns his chair.*)

SUNNY. (*Rising.*) Gentlemen, we are all acquainted with the circumstances of this girl's position, and I feel sure that no one here will oppose the family who desires to redeem the child of our esteemed and noble friend, the late Judge Peyton.

OMNES. Hear! bravo! hear!

POINT. While the proceeds of this sale promises to realize less than the debts upon it, it is my duty to prevent any collusion for the depreciation of the property.

RATTS. Darn ye! You 're a man as well as an auctioneer, ain't ye?

POINT. What is offered for this slave?

SUNNY. One thousand dollars.

M'CLOSKY. Two thousand.

SUNNY. Three thousand.

M'CLOSKY. Five thousand.

GEORGE. Demon!

SUNNY. I bid seven thousand, which is the last dollar this family possesses.

M'CLOSKY. Eight.

THIBO. Nine.

OMNES. Bravo!

M'CLOSKY. Ten. It 's no use, Squire.

SCUD. Jacob M'Closky, you shan't have that girl. Now, take care what you do. Twelve thousand.

M'CLOSKY. Shan't I! Fifteen thousand. Beat that any of ye.

POINT. Fifteen thousand bid for the Octoroon.

(*Enter* DORA.)

DORA. Twenty thousand.

OMNES. Bravo!

M'CLOSKY. Twenty-five thousand.

OMNES. (*Groan.*) O! O!

GEORGE. Yelping hound—take that.

(*He rushes on* M'CLOSKY. M'CLOSKY *draws his knife.*)

SCUD. (*Darting between them.*) Hold on, George Peyton—stand back. This is your own house; we are under your uncle's roof; recollect yourself. And, strangers, ain't we forgetting there 's a lady present? (*The knives disappear.*) If we can't behave like Christians, let 's try and act like gentlemen. Go on, Colonel.

LAFOUCHE. He did n't ought to bid against a lady.

M'CLOSKY. O, that 's it, is it? Then I 'd like to hire a lady to go to auction and buy my hands.

POINT. Gentlemen, I believe none of us have two feelings about the conduct of that man; but he has the law on his side—we may regret, but we must respect it. Mr. M'Closky has bid twenty-five thousand dollars for the Octoroon. Is there any other bid? For the first time, twenty-five thousand—last time! (*Brings hammer down.*) To Jacob M'Closky, the Octoroon girl, Zoe, twenty-five thousand dollars.

ACT FOURTH.

SCENE. *The Wharf. The Steamer "Magnolia," alongside, a bluff rock.* RATTS *discovered, superintending the loading of ship.*

(*Enter* LAFOUCHE *and* JACKSON.)

JACKSON. How long before we start, captain?

RATTS. Just as soon as we put this cotton on board.

(*Enter* PETE, *with a lantern, and* SCUDDER, *with note book.*)

SCUD. One hundred and forty-nine bales. Can you take any more?

RATTS. Not a bale. I've got engaged eight hundred bales at the next landing, and one hundred hogsheads of sugar at Patten's Slide—that'll take my guards under—hurry up thar.

VOICE. (*Outside.*) Wood's aboard.

RATTS. All aboard then.

(*Enter* M'CLOSKY.)

SCUD. Sign that receipt, captain, and save me going up to the clerk.

M'CLOSKY. See here—there's a small freight of turpentine in the fore hold there, and one of the barrels leaks; a spark from your engines might set the ship on fire, and you'll go with it.

RATTS. You be darned! Go and try it, if you've a mind to.

LAFOUCHE. Captain, you've loaded up here until the boat is sunk so deep in the mud she won't float.

RATTS. (*Calling off.*) Wood up thar, you Pollo—hang on to the safety valve—guess she'll crawl off on her paddles. (*Shouts heard.*)

JACKSON. What's the matter?

(*Enter* SOLON.)

SOLON. We got him!

SCUD. Who?

SOLON. The Injiun!

SCUD. Wahnotee? Where is he? D'ye call running away from a fellow catching him?

RATTS. Here he comes.

OMNES. Where? Where?

(*Enter* WAHNOTEE. *They are all about to rush on him.*)

SCUD. Hold on! stan' round thar! no violence—the critter don't know what we mean.

JACKSON. Let him answer for the boy then.

M'CLOSKY. Down with him—lynch him.

OMNES. Lynch him! (*Exit* LAFOUCHE.)

SCUD. Stan' back, I say! I'll nip the first that lays a finger on him. Pete, speak to the red-skin.

PETE. Whar's Paul, Wahnotee? What's come ob de child?

WAHNOTEE. Paul wunce—Paul pangeuk.

PETE. Pangeuk—dead!

WAHNOTEE. Mort!

M'CLOSKY. And you killed him?

(*They approach him.*)

SCUD. Hold on!

PETE. Um, Paul reste?

WAHNOTEE. Hugh vieu. (*Goes.*) Paul reste ci!

SCUD. Here, stay! (*Examining the ground.*) The earth has been stirred here lately.

WAHNOTEE. Weenee Paul.

(*He points down, and shows by pantomime how he buried* PAUL.)

SCUD. The Injun means that he buried him there! Stop! here's a bit of leather (*Drawing out the mail-bags.*) The mail-bags that were lost! (*Sees the tomahawk in* WAHNOTEE'S *belt—draws it out and examines it.*) Look! here are marks of blood—look thar, red-skin, what's that?

WAHNOTEE. Paul!

(*Makes a sign that* PAUL *was killed by a blow on the head.*)

M'CLOSKY. He confesses it; the Indian got drunk, quarrelled with him, and killed him.

(*Re-enter* LAFOUCHE, *with smashed apparatus.*)

LAFOUCHE. Here are evidences of the crime; this rum-bottle half emptied—this photographic apparatus smashed—and there are marks of blood and footsteps around the shed.

M'CLOSKY. What more d'ye want—ain't that proof enough? Lynch him!

OMNES. Lynch him! Lynch him!

SCUD. Stan' back, boys! He's an Injiun—fair play.

JACKSON. Try him, then—try him on the spot of his crime.

OMNES. Try him! Try him!

LAFOUCHE. Don't let him escape!

RATTS. I'll see to that. (*Drawing revolver.*) If he stirs, I'll put a bullet through his skull, mighty quick.

M'CLOSKY. Come, form a court then, choose a jury—we'll fix this varmin.

(*Enter* THIBODEAUX *and* CAILLOU.)

THIBO. What's the matter?

LAFOUCHE. We've caught this murdering Injiun, and are going to try him.

(WAHNOTEE *sits, rolled in blanket.*)

PETE. Poor little Paul—poor little nigger!

SCUD. This business goes agin me, Ratts—'t ain't right.

LAFOUCHE. We're ready; the jury's impanelled—go ahead—who'll be accuser?

RATTS. M'Closky.

M'CLOSKY. Me?

RATTS. Yes; you was the first to hail Judge Lynch.

M'CLOSKY. Well, what's the use of argument whar guilt sticks out so plain; the boy and Injiun were alone when last seen.

SCUD. Who says that?

M'CLOSKY. Everybody—that is, I heard so.

SCUD. Say what you know—not what you heard.

M'CLOSKY. I know then that the boy was killed with that tomahawk—the redskin owns it—the signs of violence are all round the shed—this apparatus smashed—ain't it plain that in a drunken fit he slew the boy, and when sober concealed the body yonder?

OMNES. That's it—that's it.

RATTS. Who defends the Injiun?

SCUD. I will; for it is agin my natur' to b'lieve him guilty; and if he be, this ain't the place, nor you the authority to try him. How are we sure the boy is dead at all? There are no witnesses but a rum bottle and an old machine. Is it on such evidence you'd hang a human being?

RATTS. His own confession.

SCUD. I appeal against your usurped authority. This lynch law is a wild and lawless proceeding. Here's a pictur' for a civilized community to afford; yonder, a poor, ignorant savage, and round him a circle of hearts, white with revenge and hate, thirsting for his blood: you call yourselves judges—you ain't—you're a jury of executioners. It is such scenes as these that bring disgrace upon our Western life.

M'CLOSKY. Evidence! Evidence! Give us evidence. We've had talk enough; now for proof.

OMNES. Yes, yes! Proof, proof!

SCUD. Where am I to get it? The proof is here, in my heart.

PETE. (*Who has been looking about the camera.*) 'Top, sar! 'Top a bit! O, laws-a-mussey, see dis! here's a pictur' I found stickin' in that yar telescope machine, sar! look, sar!

SCUD. A photographic plate. (PETE *holds his lantern up.*) What's this, eh? two forms! The child—'t is he! dead—and above him—Ah! ah! Jacob M'Closky, 't was you murdered that boy!

M'CLOSKY. Me?

SCUD. You! You slew him with that tomahawk; and as you stood over his body with the letter in your hand, you thought that no witness saw the deed, that no eye was on you—but there was, Jacob M'Closky, there was. The eye of the Eternal was on you—the blessed sun in heaven, that, looking down, struck upon this plate the image of the deed. Here you are, in the very attitude of your crime!

M'CLOSKY. 'T is false!

SCUD. 'T is true! the apparatus can't lie. Look there, jurymen. (*Showing plate to jury.*) Look there. O, you wanted evidence—you called for proof—Heaven has answered and convicted you.

M'CLOSKY. What court of law would receive such evidence? (*Going.*)

RATTS. Stop! *this* would! You called it yourself; you wanted to make us murder that Injiun; and since we've got our hands in for justice, we'll try it on *you.* What say ye? shall we have one law for the red-skin and another for the white?

OMNES. Try him! Try him!

RATTS. Who'll be accuser?

SCUD. I will! Fellow-citizens, you are convened and assembled here under a higher power than the law. What's the law? When the ship's abroad on the ocean, when the army is before the enemy, where in thunder's the law? It is in the hearts of brave men, who can tell right from wrong, and from whom justice can't be bought. So it is here, in the wilds of the West, where our hatred of crime is measured by the speed of our executions—where necessity is law!

I say, then, air you honest men? air you true? Put your hands on your naked breasts, and let every man as don't feel a real American heart there, bustin' up with freedom, truth, and right, let that man step out—that 's the oath I put to ye—and then say, Darn ye, go it!

OMNES. Go on! Go on!

SCUD. No! I won't go on; that man 's down. I won't strike him, even with words. Jacob, your accuser is that picter of the crime—let that speak—defend yourself.

M'CLOSKY. (*Drawing knife.*) I will, quicker than lightning.

RATTS. Seize him, then! (*They rush on* M'CLOSKY, *and disarm him.*) He can fight though he 's a painter: claws all over.

SCUD. Stop! Search him, we may find more evidence.

M'CLOSKY. Would you rob me first, and murder me afterwards?

RATTS. (*Searching him.*) That 's his programme—here 's a pocket-book.

SCUD. (*Opening it.*) What 's here? Letters! Hello! To "Mrs. Peyton, Terrebonne, Louisiana, United States." Liverpool postmark. Ho! I 've got hold of the tail of a rat—come out. (*Reading.*) What 's this? A draft for eighty-five thousand dollars, and credit on Palisse and Co., of New Orleans, for the balance. Hi! the rat 's out. You killed the boy to steal this letter from the mail-bags—you stole this letter, that the money should not arrive in time to save the Octoroon; had it done so, the lien on the estate would have ceased, and Zoe be free.

OMNES. Lynch him! Lynch him! Down with him!

SCUD. Silence in the court: stand back, let the gentlemen of the jury retire, consult, and return their verdict.

RATTS. I 'm responsible for the crittur—go on.

PETE. (*To* WAHNOTEE.) See, Injiun; look dar, (*Showing him the plate.*) see dat innocent; look, dar 's de murderer of poor Paul.

WAHNOTEE. Ugh! (*Examining the plate.*)

PETE. Ya! as he? Closky tue Paul—kill de child with your tomahawk dar: 't was n't you, no—ole Pete allus say so. Poor Injiun lub our little Paul.

(WAHNOTEE *rises and looks at* M'CLOSKY—*he is in his war paint and fully armed.*)

SCUD. What say ye, gentlemen? Is the prisoner guilty, or is he not guilty?

OMNES. Guilty!

SCUD. And what is to be his punishment?

OMNES. Death! (*All advance.*)

WAHNOTEE. (*Crosses to* M'CLOSKY.) Ugh!

SCUD. No, Injiun; we deal out justice here, not revenge. 'T ain't you he has injured, 't is the white man, whose laws he has offended.

RATTS. Away with him—put him down the aft hatch, till we rig his funeral.

M'CLOSKY. Fifty against one! O! if I had you one by one alone in the swamp, I 'd rip ye all.

(*He is borne off in boat struggling.*)

SCUD. Now, then, to business.

PETE. (*Re-enters from boat.*) O, law, sir, dat debil Closky, he tore hisself from de gen'lam, knock me down, take my light, and trows it on de turpentine barrels, and de shed 's all afire!

(*Fire seen.*)

JACKSON. (*Re-entering.*) We are catching fire forward: quick, cut free from the shore.

RATTS. All hands aboard there—cut the starn ropes—give her headway!

ALL. Ay, ay!

(*Cry of "Fire" heard—Engine bells heard—steam whistle noise.*)

RATTS. Cut all away, for'ard—overboard with every bale afire.

(*The Steamer moves off with the fire still blazing.*)

(M'CLOSKY *re-enters, swimming.*)

M'CLOSKY. Ha! have I fixed ye? Burn! burn! that 's right. You thought you had cornered me, did ye? As I swam down, I thought I heard something in the water, as if pursuing me—one of them darned alligators, I suppose—they swarm hereabout—may they crunch every limb of ye. (*Exit.*)

(WAHNOTEE *is seen swimming. He finds trail and follows* M'CLOSKY. *The Steamer floats on at back, burning.*)

ACT FIFTH.

SCENE 1. *Negroes' Quarters.*

(*Enter* ZOE.)

ZOE. It wants an hour yet to daylight—here is Pete's hut—(*Knocks.*) He sleeps—no: I see a light.

DIDO. (*Enters from hut.*) Who dat?

ZOE. Hush, aunty! 'T is I—Zoe.

DIDO. Missey Zoe? Why you out in de swamp dis time ob night; you catch de fever sure—you is all wet.

ZOE. Where 's Pete?

DIDO. He gone down to de landing last night wid Mas'r Scudder; not come back since—kint make it out.

ZOE. Aunty, there is sickness up at the house; I have been up all night beside one who suffers, and I remembered that when I had the fever you gave me a drink, a bitter drink, that made me sleep —do you remember it?

DIDO. Did n't I? Dem doctors ain't no 'count; dey don't know nuffin.

ZOE. No; but you, aunty, you are wise—you know every plant, don't you, and what it is good for?

DIDO. Dat you drink is fust rate for red fever. Is de folks' head bad?

ZOE. Very bad, aunty; and the heart aches worse, so they can get no rest.

DIDO. Hold on a bit, I get you de bottle. (*Exit.*)

ZOE. In a few hours that man, my master, will come for me: he has paid my price, and he only consented to let me remain here this one night, because Mrs. Peyton promised to give me up to him to-day.

DIDO. (*Re-enters with phial.*) Here 't is —now you give one timble-full—dat 's nuff.

ZOE. All there is there would kill one, would n't it?

DIDO. Guess it kill a dozen—nebber try.

ZOE. It 's not a painful death, aunty, is it? You told me it produced a long, long sleep.

DIDO. Why you tremble so? Why you speak so wild? What you 's gwine to do, missey?

ZOE. Give me the drink.

DIDO. No. Who dat sick at de house?

ZOE. Give it to me.

DIDO. No. You want to hurt yourself. O, Miss Zoe, why you ask old Dido for dis pizen?

ZOE. Listen to me. I love one who is here, and he loves me—George. I sat outside his door all night—I heard his sighs—his agony—torn from him by my coming fate; and he said, "I 'd rather see her dead than his!"

DIDO. Dead!

ZOE. He said so—then I rose up, and stole from the house, and ran down to the bayou: but its cold, black, silent stream terrified me—drowning must be so horrible a death. I could not do it. Then, as I knelt there, weeping for courage, a snake rattled beside me. I shrunk from it and fled. Death was there beside me, and I dared not take it. O! I 'm afraid to die; yet I am more afraid to live.

DIDO. Die!

ZOE. So I came here to you; to you, my own dear nurse; to you, who so often hushed me to sleep when I was a child; who dried my eyes and put your little Zoe to rest. Ah! give me the rest that no master but One can disturb—the sleep from which I shall awake free! You can protect me from that man—do let me die without pain.

DIDO. No, no—life is good for young ting like you.

ZOE. O! good, good nurse: you will, you will.

DIDO. No—g' way.

ZOE. Then I shall never leave Terrebonne —the drink, nurse; the drink; that I may never leave my home—my dear, dear home. You will not give me to that man? Your own Zoe, that loves you, aunty, so much, so much. (*She gets the phial.*) Ah! I have it.

DIDO. No, missey. O! no—don't.

ZOE. Hush! (*Runs off.*)

DIDO. Here, Solon, Minnie, Grace.

(*They enter.*)

ALL. Was de matter?

DIDO. Miss Zoe got de pizen. (*Exit.*)

ALL. O! O! (*Exeunt.*)

SCENE 2. *In a Cane-brake Bayou, on a bank, with a canoe near by,* M'CLOSKY *is seen asleep.*)

M'CLOSKY. Burn, burn! blaze away! How the flames crack. I 'm not guilty; would ye murder me? Cut, cut the rope—I choke—choke!—Ah! (*Waking.*) Hello! where am I? Why, I was dreaming—curse it! I can never sleep now without dreaming. Hush! I thought I heard the sound of a paddle in the water. All night, as I fled through the cane-brake, I heard footsteps behind me. I lost them in the cedar swamp—again they haunted my path down the bayou, moving as I moved, resting when I rested —hush! there again!—no; it was only the wind over the canes. The sun is rising. I must launch my dug-out, and put for the bay, and in a few hours I shall be safe from pursuit on board of one of the coasting schooners that run from Galveston to Matagorda. In a little time this darned business will blow over, and I can show again. Hark! there 's that noise again! If it was the ghost of that murdered boy haunting me! Well—I did n't mean to kill him, did I? Well, then, what has my all-cowardly heart got to skeer me so for?

(*He gets in canoe and rows off.* WAHNOTEE *appears in another canoe. He gets out and finds trail and paddles off after* M'CLOSKY.)

SCENE 3. *A cedar Swamp.*

(*Enter* SCUDDER *and* PETE.)

SCUD. Come on, Pete, we shan't reach the house before midday.

PETE. Nebber mind, sa, we bring good news—it won't spile for de keeping.

SCUD. Ten miles we 've had to walk, because some blamed varmin onhitched our dug-out. I left it last night all safe.

PETE. P'r'aps it floated away itself.

SCUD. No; the hitching line was cut with a knife.

PETE. Say, Mas'r Scudder, s'pose we go in round by de quarters and raise de darkies, den dey cum long wid us, and we 'proach dat ole house like Gin'ral Jackson when he took London out dar.

SCUD. Hello, Pete, I never heard of that affair.

PETE. I tell you, sa—hush!

SCUD. What?

PETE. Was dat?—a cry out dar in the swamp—dar again!

SCUD. So it is. Something forcing its way through the undergrowth—it comes this way—it 's either a bear or a runaway nigger.

(*He draws a pistol.* M'CLOSKY *rushes on, and falls at* SCUDDER'S *feet.*)

SCUD. Stand off—what are ye?

PETE. Mas'r Clusky.

M'CLOSKY. Save me—save me! I can go no farther. I heard voices.

SCUD. Who 's after you?

M'CLOSKY. I don't know, but I feel it 's death! In some form, human, or wild beast, or ghost, it has tracked me through the night. I fled; it followed. Hark! there it comes—it comes—don't you hear a footstep on the dry leaves!

SCUD. Your crime has driven you mad.

M'CLOSKY. D 'ye hear it—nearer—nearer—ah!

(WAHNOTEE *rushes on, and attacks* M'CLOSKY.)

SCUD. The Injuin! by thunder.

PETE. You 'se a dead man, Mas'r Clusky—you got to b'lieve dat.

M'CLOSKY. No—no. If I must die, give me up to the law; but save me from the tomahawk. You are a white man; you 'll not leave one of your own blood to be butchered by the red-skin?

SCUD. Hold on now, Jacob; we 've got to figure on that—let us look straight at the thing. Here we are on the selvage of civilization. It ain't our side, I believe, rightly; but Nature has said that where the white man sets his foot, the red man and the black man shall up sticks and stand around. But what do we pay for that possession? In cash? No—in kind—that is, in protection, forbearance, gentleness, in all them goods that show the critters the difference between the Christian and the savage. Now, what have you done to show them the distinction? for, darn me, if I can find out.

M'CLOSKY. For what I have done, let me be tried.

SCUD. You have been tried—honestly tried and convicted. Providence has chosen your executioner. I shan't interfere.

PETE. O, no; Mas'r Scudder, don't leave Mas'r Closky like dat—don't, sa—'t ain't what good Christian should do.

SCUD. D' ye hear that, Jacob? This old nigger, the grandfather of the boy you murdered, speaks for you—don't that go through you? D' ye feel it? Go on, Pete, you 've waked up the Christian here, and the old hoss responds. (*He throws bowie-knife to* M'CLOSKY.) Take that, and defend yourself.

(*Exeunt* SCUDDER *and* PETE. WAHNOTEE *faces him. They fight.* M'CLOSKY *runs off,* WAHNOTEE *follows him.—Screams outside.*)

SCENE 4. *Parlor at Terrebonne.*

(*Enter* ZOE.)

ZOE. My home, my home! I must see you no more. Those little flowers can live, but I cannot. To-morrow they 'll bloom the same—all will be here as now, and I shall be cold. O! my life, my happy life, why has it been so bright?

(*Enter* MRS. PEYTON *and* DORA.)

DORA. Zoe, where have you been?
MRS. P. We felt quite uneasy about you.
ZOE. I 've been to the negro quarters. I suppose I shall go before long, and I wished to visit all the places, once again, to see the poor people.
MRS. P. Zoe, dear, I 'm glad to see you more calm this morning.
DORA. But how pale she looks, and she trembles so.
ZOE. Do I? (*Enter* GEORGE.) Ah! he is here.
DORA. George, here she is.
ZOE. I have come to say good-by, sir; two hard words—so hard, they might break many a heart; might n't they?
GEORGE. O, Zoe! can you smile at this moment?
ZOE. You see how easily I have become reconciled to my fate—so it will be with you. You will not forget poor Zoe! but her image will pass away like a little cloud that obscured your happiness a while—you will love each other; you are both too good not to join your hearts. Brightness will return amongst you. Dora, I once made you weep; those were the only tears I caused anybody. Will you forgive me?
DORA. Forgive you—(*Kisses her.*)
ZOE. I feel you do, George.
GEORGE. Zoe, you are pale. Zoe!—she faints!
ZOE. No; a weakness, that 's all—a little water. (DORA *gets some water.*) I have a restorative here—will you pour it in the glass? (DORA *attempts to take it.*) No; not you—George. (GEORGE *pours the contents of the phial into glass.*) Now, give it to me. George, dear George, do you love me?
GEORGE. Do you doubt it, Zoe?
ZOE. No! (*She drinks.*)
DORA. Zoe, if all I possess would buy your freedom, I would gladly give it.
ZOE. I am free! I had but one Master on earth, and he has given me my freedom!
DORA. Alas! but the deed that freed you was not lawful.
ZOE. Not lawful—no—but I am going to where there is no law—where there is only justice.
GEORGE. Zoe, you are suffering—your lips are white—your cheeks are flushed.
ZOE. I must be going—it is late. Farewell, Dora. (*Retiring.*)
PETE. (*Outside.*) Whar 's Missus—whar 's Mas'r George?
GEORGE. They come.

(*Enter* SCUDDER.)

SCUD. Stand around and let me pass—room thar! I feel so big with joy, creation ain't wide enough to hold me. Mrs. Peyton, George Peyton, Terrebonne is yours. It was that rascal M'Closky—but he got rats, I swow—he killed the boy, Paul, to rob this letter from the mail-bags—the letter from Liverpool you know—he sot fire to the shed—that was how the steamboat got burned up.
MRS. P. What d' ye mean?
SCUD. Read—read that.
(*He gives letter to them.*)
GEORGE. Explain yourself.

(*Enter* SUNNYSIDE.)

SUNNY. Is it true?
SCUD. Every word of it, Squire. Here, you tell it, since you know it. If I was to try, I 'd bust.
MRS. P. Read, George. Terrebonne is yours.

(*Enter* PETE, DIDO, SOLON, MINNIE, *and* GRACE.)

PETE. Whar is she—whar is Miss Zoe?
SCUD. What 's the matter?
PETE. Don't ax me. Whar 's de gal? I say.
SCUD. Here she is—Zoe!—water—she faints.
PETE. No—no. 'T ain't no faint—she 's a dying, sa: she got pizon from old Dido here, this mornin'.
GEORGE. Zoe!
SCUD. Zoe! is this true?—no, it ain't—darn it, say it ain't. Look here, you 're free, you know; nary a master to hurt you now: you will stop here as long as you 're a mind to, only don't look so.
DORA. Her eyes have changed color.
PETE. Dat 's what her soul 's gwine to do. It 's going up dar, whar dere 's no line atween folks.
GEORGE. She revives.
ZOE. (*On the sofa.*) George—where—where—
GEORGE. O, Zoe! what have you done?
ZOE. Last night I overheard you weeping

in your room, and you said, "I 'd rather see her dead than so!"

GEORGE. Have I then prompted you to this?

ZOE. No; but I loved you so, I could not bear my fate; and then I stood between your heart and hers. When I am dead she will not be jealous of your love for me, no laws will stand between us. Lift me; so—(GEORGE *raises her head*)—let me look at you, that your face may be the last I see of this world. O! George, you may, without a blush, confess your love for the Octoroon.

(*She dies.* GEORGE *lowers her head gently and kneels beside her.*)

RIP VAN WINKLE

AS PLAYED BY

Joseph Jefferson

Reprinted by special permission of the heirs of Mr. Joseph Jefferson and of Dodd, Mead and Company.

RIP VAN WINKLE

Rip Van Winkle is a growth. The first attempts to dramatize Irving's story began about ten years after its publication in 1819. On May 26, 1828, a play by that name was produced on the Albany stage by Thomas Flynn, written by an anonymous native of that town. Durang tells us that in October, 1829, a new drama founded on Washington Irving's tale was produced for the first time in Philadelphia. He further states that it was by John Kerr, an actor to whom he refers as "Old Mr. Kerr" and that it had a long run of success. Kerr was an English actor, who came to this country in 1827, with his two children, a boy and girl. They were all members of the troupe brought by Francis C. Wemyss for the Chestnut Street Theatre. This version was printed in Philadelphia without date, and gives the cast at the Walnut Street Theatre and at Tottenham Street Theatre in London. In Philadelphia, W. Chapman and later Hackett played "Rip" and J. Jefferson, "Knickerbocker." This may have been the first Joseph Jefferson as he was still acting that season, or it may have been John Jefferson, his son. The cast in London includes Master Kerr as "Gustaffe" and Miss Kerr as "Lowenna," and the date of their arrival in Philadelphia naturally indicates that this version had an earlier performance in London which, indeed, seems to have been the case. Hackett also acted in a version prepared by W. Bayle Bernard, and the second Joseph Jefferson had a version also. Charles Burke, half brother to the third Joseph Jefferson, revised Kerr's version and acted "Rip" in it, at the Arch Street Theatre in Philadelphia in 1850. Mr. Jefferson himself acted in this version, taking the part of "Seth Slough," the landlord of the inn. While there are certain changes, notably in expression, Burke's version is much like Kerr's. Mr. Jefferson tells us that the idea of acting "Rip" came to him in the year 1859 when reading the life of Irving and he proceeded first to work up his costume and then with some aid from the older versions to produce a play in three acts which was acted in Washington. The play was disappointing, although the character was there. In 1865 Mr. Jefferson requested Dion Boucicault to revise the play, which he did and this composite drama was produced at the Adelphi Theatre in London September 4, 1865.

This was a three-act version, and Mr. Jefferson later changed it to four acts by dividing the first act into two. A comparison between the versions of Kerr and Burke and that given in this volume will show many changes in the structure of the plot. In the first place the plot is simpler and the ending is more natural. The pathetic scene at the end of the second act in which Gretchen turns Rip out of doors is not found in the earlier versions. In these there is a contract of marriage between Rip's daughter and Herman; in the Jefferson version this becomes an acknowledgment that he makes to Derrick that he is to give him all his property in exchange for sixteen pounds Derrick has given him. The love story between Knickerbocker and Alice is eliminated and Knickerbocker's election to Congress with the consequent political interest is omitted. The changes in the plot, however, are not so significant as the changes in character drawing and in language. Mr. Jefferson says in his introduction to the play:

"From the moment Rip meets the spirits of Hendrick Hudson and his crew, I felt that the colloquial speech and lazy and commonplace actions of Rip should cease. After he meets the elves, in the third act, the play drifts from realism into idealism and becomes poetical. After this it is a fairy tale, and the prosaic elements of the character should be eliminated, and because Rip is a fairy he neither laughs nor eats in the fourth act." Another idea of Mr. Jefferson's was to arrange that in his interview with the dwarfs no voice but Rip's was to be heard, thus imparting a more lonely and desolate character to the scene.

While the supernatural interest is, therefore, made more definite there is a growth also in the depth of the human interest. Fewer characters are introduced, and consequently there is more time to develop the relations of Rip, his wife and his daughter. The language owes little to the earlier version—outside of a few phrases in the last act, when Rip enters the village, the speeches are practically all different. How much of this difference is due to Boucicault it is of course now impossible to say, but since Mr. Jefferson undoubtedly made changes from time to time it is safe to assume that by the time the play was printed in 1895 it was mostly his own. The text of the play as given by him was first published in that year by Dodd, Mead and Company, sumptuously illustrated, with an introduction by Mr. Jefferson. Through the courtesy of the Jefferson family, especially Mrs. Joseph Jefferson and Mr. Frank Jefferson, and of Dodd, Mead and Company, the editor is able to reproduce this text.

The version by John Kerr, *Rip Van Winkle or The Demons of the Catskill Mountains! A National Drama,* Philadelphia, n. d. is hard to obtain. The version by Charles Burke, *Rip Van Winkle, a Legend of the Catskills,* was published by Samuel French as No. CLXXIV, of their "Standard Drama."

Joseph Jefferson was a member of the fourth generation of a family of actors who have borne prominent parts in theatrical history. Thomas Jefferson (1728?–1807) his great-grandfather, an English actor, was the first of the line, and his son, the first Joseph Jefferson (1774–1832), came to this country in 1795, and after a short season in Boston, acted in New York until 1803. He then became the leading comedian at the Chestnut Street Theatre in Philadelphia, and on the stage of this city he remained for twenty-seven years. His son, the second Joseph Jefferson (1804–1842), was also a comedian, though of lesser ability than his father or his son. The third Joseph Jefferson, the son of the second Joseph and the producer of the present play, was born in Philadelphia, February 20, 1829, and was on the stage from early childhood. During his early years, his family moved from place to place, and in 1849 he came to New York, acting at Chanfrau's New National Theatre. After several ventures and a trip to Europe in 1856 he joined Laura Keene's Company in New York. Here he became famous for his performance of "Asa Trenchard" in *Our American Cousin,* in 1857, the play afterwards known as *Lord Dundreary.* In 1861 he sailed for Australia and spent four years there, going to London in 1865, and acting "Rip Van Winkle" as above described. He returned to America in 1866 and played the revised version of "Rip" at the Olympic Theatre on September 3d. Though he acted other parts, notably, "Caleb Plummer," "Bob Acres," "Asa Trenchard," and "Dr. Pangloss," he became so definitely associated with his most famous part, that to most theatre-goers he is thought of as the impersonator of Rip Van Winkle. In 1875 he made a second English tour. Mr. Jefferson was twice married, first in 1850 to Miss Margaret C. Lockyer, a member of the company at the National Theatre, New York, who died in 1861. In 1867 he married Miss Sarah Warren, who survives him. Mr. Jefferson continued acting until less than a year before his death, which occurred on April 23, 1905, at Palm Beach, Florida.

For biography of Mr. Jefferson, see *The Autobiography of Joseph Jefferson,* New York, 1890; William Winter, *The Jeffersons,* Boston, 1881; M. J. Moses, *Famous Actor Families in America,* New York, 1906. For the development of the play, see H. S. Phelps, *Players of a Century,* Albany, 1880; C. Durang, *History of the Philadelphia Stage,* Second Series, Chap. 48.

Note to Third Edition.

For a detailed account of the development of *Rip van Winkle,* see the editor's *History of the American Drama from the Beginning to the Civil War,* New York, 1923, pp. 325–332.

PERSONS OF THE PLAY

RIP VAN WINKLE

DERRICK VON BEEKMAN

NICHOLAS VEDDER

HENDRICK

COCKLES

SETH SLOUGH

JACOB STEIN

GRETCHEN

MEENIE

KÄTCHEN

DEMONS AND VILLAGERS

RIP VAN WINKLE

ACT I.

SCENE 1. *The village of Falling Waters, set amid familiar and unmistakable Hudson River scenery, with the shining river itself and the noble heights of the Kaatskills visible in the distance. In the foreground, to the left of the stage, is a country inn bearing the sign of George III. In the wall of the inn, a window closed by a solid wooden shutter. To the right of the stage, an old cottage with a door opening into the interior; before the cottage stands a bench holding a wash-tub, with a washboard, soap and clothes in the tub. In the centre of the stage, a table and chairs, and on the table a stone pitcher and two tin cups.*

As the curtain rises, GRETCHEN *is discovered washing, and little* MEENIE *sitting near by on a low stool. The sound of a chorus and laughter comes from the inn.*

GRETCHEN. Shouting and drinking day and night. (*Laughter is heard from the inn.*) Hark how they crow over their cups while their wives are working at home, and their children are starving.

(*Enter* DERRICK *from the inn with a green bag, followed by* NICK VEDDER. DERRICK *places his green bag on the table.*)

DERRICK. Not a day, not an hour. If the last two quarters' rent be not paid by this time tomorrow, out you go!

NICK. Oh, come, Derrick, you won't do it. Let us have a glass, and talk the matter over; good liquor opens the heart. Here, Hendrick! Hendrick!

(*Enter* HENDRICK.)

HENDRICK. Yes, father.

DERRICK. So that is your brat?

NICK. Yes, that is my boy.

DERRICK. Then the best I can wish him is that he won't take after his father, and become a vagabond and a penniless outcast.

NICK. Those are hard words to hear in the presence of my child.

HENDRICK. Then why don't you knock him down, father?

GRETCHEN. I'll tell you why—

DERRICK. Gretchen!

GRETCHEN. (*Wiping her arms and coming to front of tub.*) It is because your father is in that man's power. And what's the use of getting a man down, if you don't trample on him?

NICK. Oh, that is the way of the world.

GRETCHEN. (*To* HENDRICK.) Go in, boy. I want to speak to your father, and my words may not be fit for you to hear. Yonder is my little girl; go and play with her.

(HENDRICK *and* MEENIE *exeunt into the cottage.*)

GRETCHEN. Now, Derrick, Vedder is right; you won't turn him out of his house yonder.

DERRICK. And why not? Don't he owe me a year's rent?

GRETCHEN. And what do you owe him? Shall I sum up your accounts for you? Ten years ago, this was a quiet village, and belonged mostly to my husband, Rip Van Winkle, a foolish, idle fellow. That house yonder has since been his ruin. Yes; bit by bit, he has parted with all he had, to fill the mouths of sots and boon companions, gathered around him in yonder house. And you, Derrick—you supplied him with the money to waste in riot and drink. Acre by acre, you've sucked in his land to swell your store. Yonder miserable cabin is the only shelter we have left; but that is mine. Had it been his, he would have sold it you, Derrick, long ago, and wasted its price in riot.

(VEDDER, *who has been enjoying* DERRICK'S *discomfiture during this speech, is unable to control himself, and at the end of the speech, bursts into a loud laugh.*)

GRETCHEN. Aye, and you too, Nick Vedder; you have ruined my husband between you.

NICK. Oh, come, Mrs. Van Winkle, you're too hard. I could n't refuse Rip's money in the way of business; I had my rent to pay.

GRETCHEN. And shall I tell you why you can't pay it? it is because you have given Rip credit, and he has ended by drinking you out of house and home. Your window-shutter is not wide enough to hold the score against him; it is full of chalk. Deny it if you can.

NICK. I do deny it. There now!

GRETCHEN. Then why do you keep that shutter closed? I 'll show you why. (*Goes to inn, opens shutter, holds it open, pointing at* RIP'S *score.*) That 's why, Nick Vedder, you 're a good man in the main, if there is such a thing. (DERRICK *laughs.*) Aye, and I doubt it. (*Turning on him.*) But you are the pest of this village; and the hand of every woman in it ought to help pull down that drunkard's nest of yours, stone by stone.

NICK. Come, Dame Van Winkle, you 're too hard entire; now a man must have his odd time, and he 's none the worse for being a jolly dog.

GRETCHEN. No, none the worse. He sings a good song; he tells a good story—oh, he 's a glorious fellow! Did you ever see the wife of a jolly dog? Well, she lives in a kennel. Did you ever see the children of a jolly dog? They are the street curs, and their home is the gutter.

(*Goes up to the wash-tub, and takes revenge on the clothing she scrubs.*)

NICK. (*Getting up and approaching* GRETCHEN *timidly.*) I tell you what it is, Dame Van Winkle, I don't know what your home may be, but judging from the rows I hear over there, and the damaged appearance of Rip's face after having escaped your clutches—(GRETCHEN *looks up angrily;* NICK *retreats a few paces hastily*)—I should say that a gutter was a luxurious abode compared with it, and a kennel a peaceful retreat.

(*Exit hurriedly, laughing, to the inn.* GRETCHEN *looks up angrily, and throws the cloth she has been wringing after him, then resumes washing.* DERRICK *laughs at* VEDDER'S *exit, walks up to* GRETCHEN, *and puts one foot on the bench.*)

DERRICK. Is it true, Gretchen? Are you truly miserable with Rip?

GRETCHEN. Ain't you pleased to hear it? Come then and warm your heart at my sorrow. Ten years ago I might have had you, Derrick. But I despised you for your miserly ways, and threw myself away on a vagabond.

DERRICK. You and I shared him between us. I took his estate, and you took his person. Now, I 've improved my half. What have you done with yours?

GRETCHEN. I can't say that I have prospered with it. I 've tried every means to reclaim him, but he is as obstinate and perverse as a Dutch pig. But the worst in him—and what I can't stand—is his good-humour. It drives me frantic when, night after night, he comes home drunk and helplessly good-humoured! Oh, I can't stand that!

DERRICK. Where is he now?

GRETCHEN. We had a tiff yesterday, and he started. He has been out all night. Only wait until he comes back! The longer he stops out, the worse it will be for him.

DERRICK. Gretchen, you 've made a great mistake, but there is time enough to repair it. You are comely still, thrifty, and that hard sort of grain that I most admire in woman. (*Looks cautiously around. Leans on tub.*) Why not start Rip for ever, and share my fortune?

GRETCHEN. Oh, no, Derrick; you 've got my husband in your clutches, but you can't get them around me. If Rip would only mend his ways, he would see how much I love him; but no woman could love you, Derrick; for woman is not a domestic animal, glad to serve and fawn upon a man for the food and shelter she can get; and that is all she would ever get from you, Derrick.

(*Piling the clothes on the washboard, and shouldering it.*)

DERRICK. The time may come when you 'll change your tune.

GRETCHEN. Not while Rip lives, bad as he is. (*Exit into cottage.*)

DERRICK. Then I 'll wait until you 've killed him. Her spirit is not broken yet. But patience, Derrick, patience; in another month I 'll have my claws on all that remains of Rip's property—yonder cottage and grounds; then I 'll try you again, my lady.

(*Enter* COCKLES, *with papers in his hand, running towards the inn.*)

DERRICK. How now, you imp? What brings you here so full of a hurry? Some mischief 's in your head, or your heels would not be so busy.

COCKLES. I 've brought a letter for you from my employer. There it is.

DERRICK. (*Examining letter.*) Why, the seal is broken!

COCKLES. Yes, I read it as I came along.

DERRICK. Now I apprenticed this vagabond to my lawyer, and this is his gratitude.

COCKLES. Don't waste your breath, Nunky, for you 'll want it; for when you read that, if it don't take you short in the wind, I 'll admire you.

DERRICK. (*Reads.*) "You must obtain from Rip Van Winkle a proper conveyance of the lands he has sold to you. The papers he has signed are in fact nothing but mortgages on his estate. If you foreclose, you must sell the property, which has lately much advanced in value; and it would sell for enough to pay off your loan, and all your improvements would enure to the benefit of Rip Van Winkle."

COCKLES. There, now, see what you 've been doing of!—wasting your money and my expectations on another chap's property. Do you want to leave me a beggar?

DERRICK. (*Reads.*) "I enclose a deed for him to sign that will make him safe."

COCKLES. Of course he 'll sign it; he won't wait to be asked—he 'll be in such a hurry.

DERRICK. All my savings—all my money—sunk in improving this village!

COCKLES. Yes, instead of physicking Rip, as you thought, you 've been coddling him all the while.

DERRICK. All these houses I 've built are on another man's land. What shall I do?

COCKLES. Pull them down again; pull them down.

DERRICK. Ass!—dolt that I have been!

COCKLES. Calling yourself names won't mend it, Nunky.

DERRICK. The imp is right. Rip must be made to sign this paper. But how—how?

COCKLES. How? How? How 's a big word sometimes, ain't it, Nunky?

DERRICK. Rip would not do it if he knew what he was about. But he can't read—nor write, for the matter of that. But he can make his cross, and I can cajole him.

COCKLES. Look sharp, Nunky. The man that 's looking round for a fool and picks up Rip Van Winkle, will let him drop again very quick.

DERRICK. He is poor; I 'll show him a handful of money. He 's a drunkard; I 'll give him a stomachful of liquor. Go in, boy, and leave me to work this; and let this be a lesson to you hereafter; beware of the fatal effects of poverty and drink.

COCKLES. Yes,—and parting with my money on bad security.

(*Exit. Laughter outside.*)

DERRICK. Here he comes now, surrounded by all the dogs and children in the district. They cling around him like flies around a lump of sugar.

RIP *enters, running and skipping, carrying one small child pickaback, and surrounded by a swarm of others hanging on the skirts of his coat. He is laughing like a child himself, and his merry blue eyes twinkle with delight. He is dressed in an old deerskin coat, a pair of breeches which had once been red, now tattered, patched, and frayed, leather gaiters and shoes equally dilapidated, a shapeless felt hat with a bit of the brim hanging loose—the whole stained and weather-worn to an almost uniform clay-colour, except for the bright blue of his jean shirt and the scarlet of his long wisp of a necktie. One of the boys carries his gun.*)

RIP. (*Taking his gun from the boy.*) There, run along mit you; run along.

DERRICK. (*The children scamper off.*) The vagabond looks like the father of the village.

RIP. (*Who has stood laughing and watching the children, suddenly calls after them.*) Hey! You let my dog Schneider alone there; you hear that, Sock der Jacob der bist eine for donner spits poo—yah—

DERRICK. Why, what 's the matter, Rip?

RIP. (*Coming down and shaking hands with* DERRICK.) Oh, how you was, Derrick? how you was?

DERRICK. You seem in trouble.

RIP. Oh, yah; you know them fellers. Vell, I tole you such a funny thing. (*Laughing.*) Just now, as me and Schneider was comin' along through the willage—Schneider 's my dawg; I don't know whether you know him? (RIP *always speaks of Schneider as if he were a person, and one in whom his hearer took as profound an interest as he does himself.*) Well, them fellers went and tied a tin kettle mit Schneider's tail, and how he did run then, mit the kettle banging about. Well, I did n't hi him comin'. He run betwixt me and my legs, an' spilt me an' all them children in the mud;—yah, that 's a fact.

(RIP *leans his gun against the cottage.*)

DERRICK. (*Aside.*) Now 's my time. (*Aloud.*) Vedder! Vedder! (VEDDER *appears at the door of the inn.*) Bring us a bottle of liquor. Bring us your best, and be quick.

NICK. What 's in the wind now? The devil 's to pay when Derrick stands treat!

(*Exit. Re-enters, with bottle and cups in left hand. Hands bottle to* DERRICK. RIP *lounges forward, and perches on the corner of the table.*)

DERRICK. (*Rising and approaching* RIP.) Come, Rip, what do you say to a glass?

RIP. (*Takes a cup and holds it to be filled.*) Oh, yah; now what do I generally say to a glass? I say it 's a fine thing—when there 's plenty in it. (Ve gates! Ve gates!) (*Shakes hands with* NICK.) And then I says more to what 's in it than I do to the glass. Now you would n't believe it—that 's the first one I 've had today.

DERRICK. How so?

RIP. (*Dryly.*) Because I could n't get it before, I suppose.

DERRICK. Then let me fill him up for you.

RIP. No, that is enough for the first one.

NICK. Come, Rip, a bumper for the first one.

RIP. That is enough for the first one.

DERRICK. Come, Rip, let me fill him up for you.

RIP. (*With ludicrous decision and dignity.*) I believe I know how much to drink. When I says a thing, I mean it.

DERRICK. Oh, well—

(*Turns aside, and starts to fill his own cup.*)

RIP. All right; come along. (*Holding out his glass, and laughing at his own inconsistency.*) Here 's your good health and your families', and may they live long and prosper!

(*They all drink. At the end,* NICK *smacks his lips and exclaims "Ah!"* DERRICK *repeats the same and* RIP *repeats after* DERRICK.)

RIP. (*To* NICK, *sadly.*) Ah, you may well go "Ah!" and smack your chops over that. You don't give me such schnapps [1] when I come. Derrick, my score is too big now. (*Jerking his head towards the shutter, he notices for the first time that it is open.*) What you go and open that window for?—That 's fine schnapps, Nick. Where you got that?

NICK. That 's high Dutch, Rip—high Dutch, and ten years in bottle. Why, I had that in the very day of your wedding. We broached the keg under yonder shed. Don't you recollect?

RIP. Is that the same?

NICK. Yes.

RIP. I thought I knowed that licker. You had it ten years ago? (*Laughing suddenly.*) I would not have kept it so long. But stop, mein freund; that 's more than ten years ago.

NICK. No, it ain't.

RIP. It 's the same day I got married?

NICK. Yes.

RIP. Well, I know by that. You think I forgot the day I got married? Oh, no, my friend; I remember that day long as I live.

(*Serious for a moment. Takes off his hat, and puts it on the table.*)

DERRICK. Ah! Rip, I remember Gretchen then, ten years ago.—Zounds, how I envied you!

RIP. (*Looking up, surprised.*) Did you? (*Winks at* NICK. *Then, suddenly remembering.*) So did I. You did n't know what was comin', Derrick.

DERRICK. She was a beauty.

RIP. What, Gretchen?—Yes, she was. She was a pretty girl. My! My! Yah, we was a fine couple altogether. Well, come along.

(*Holding out his cup to* DERRICK, *who fills it from the bottle.*)

NICK. Yes, come along.

(*Takes water pitcher from the table, and starts to fill up* RIP'S *cup.* RIP *stops him.*)

RIP. (*Who has been lounging against the table, sits on it, and puts his feet on the chair.*) Stop! I come along mitout that, Nick Vedder. (*Sententiously.*) Good licker and water is like man and wife.

DERRICK and NICK. How 's that, Rip?

RIP. (*Laughing.*) They don't agree together. I always like my licker single. Well, here 's your good health, and your families', and may they live long and prosper!

(*They all drink.*)

1 Whiskey.

NICK. That 's right, Rip; drink away, and drown your sorrow.

RIP. (*Drolly.*) Yes; but she won't drown. My wife is my sorrow, and you cannick drown her. She tried it once, but could n't do it.

DERRICK and NICK. Why, how so?

RIP. (*Puts down his cup and clasps his knee, still perched on the corner of the table.*) Did n't you know that Gretchen like to got drown?

DERRICK and NICK. No.

RIP. (*Puts hat on.*) That 's the funniest thing of the whole of it. It 's the same day I got married; she was comin' across the river there in the ferry-boat to get married mit me—

DERRICK and NICK. Yes.

RIP. Well, the boat she was comin' in got upsetted.

DERRICK and NICK. Ah!

RIP. Well, but she was n't in it.

DERRICK and NICK. Oh!

RIP. (*Explaining quite seriously.*) No, that 's what I say; if she had been in the boat what got upsetted, maybe she might have got drowned. (*More and more reflective.*) I don't know how it was she got left somehow or other. Women is always behind that way—always.

DERRICK. But surely, Rip, you would have risked your life to save such a glorious creature as she was.

RIP. (*Incredulously.*) You mean I would yump in and pull Gretchen out?

DERRICK. Yes.

RIP. Oh, would I? (*Suddenly remembering.*) Oh, you mean then—yes, I believe I would then. (*With simple conviction.*) But it would be more my duty now than it was then.

DERRICK. How so?

RIP. (*Quite seriously.*) Why, you see when a feller gets married a good many years mit his wife, he gets very much attached to her.

NICK. (*Pompously.*) Ah, he does indeed.

RIP. (*Winks at* DERRICK, *and points at* NICK *with his thumb.*) But if Mrs. Van Winkle was a-drowning in the water now, an' she says to me, "Rip, come an' save your wife!" I would say, "Mrs. Van Winkle, I will yust go home and think about it." Oh, no, Derrick, if ever Gretchen tumbles in the water, she 's got to swim now, you mind that.

DERRICK. She was here just now, anxiously expecting you home.

RIP. I know she 's keeping it hot for me.

NICK. What, your dinner, Rip?

RIP. No, the broomstick.

(*Exit* NICK *into house, laughing.*)

RIP. (*Confidentially.*) Derrick, whenever I come back from the mountains, I always stick the game-bag in the window and creep in behind.

DERRICK. (*Seating himself on the table by the side of* RIP.) Have you anything now?

RIP. (*Dropping into the chair* DERRICK *has just left. Leaning back, and putting hands behind his head.*) What for game? No, not a tail, I believe, not a feather.

(*With humorous indifference.*)

DERRICK. (*Touching* RIP *on the shoulder and shaking a bag of money.*) Rip, suppose you were to hang this bagful of money inside, don't you think it would soothe her down, eh?

RIP. (*Sitting up.*) For me, is that?

DERRICK. Yes.

RIP. (*With a shrewd glance.*) Ain't you yokin' mit me?

DERRICK. No, Rip, I 've prospered with the lands you 've sold me, and I 'll let you have a loan on easy terms. I 'll take no interest.

RIP. (*Getting up and walking forward, with decision.*) No, I 'm afraid I might pay you again some day, Derrick.

DERRICK. And so you shall, Rip, pay me when you please. (*Puts the bag in* RIP'S *hands, and forces his fingers over it, turns, and goes to the table, speaking as he goes.*) Say in twenty years—twenty years from this day. Ah, where shall we be then?

RIP. (*Quizzically, and half to himself.*) I don't know about myself; but I think I can guess where you 'll be about that time.

(*Takes chair and sits down.*)

DERRICK. Well, Rip, I 'll just step into the inn and draw out a little acknowledgment.

RIP. (*Who has been sitting, leaning forward with his elbows on his knees, softly chinking the bag of money in his hand, looks up suddenly.*) 'Knowledgment—for what is that?

DERRICK. Yes, for you to put your cross to.

RIP. (*Indifferently.*) All right; bring it along.

DERRICK. No fear of Gretchen now, eh, Rip?

RIP. (*Plunged in thought.*) Oh, no.

DERRICK. You feel quite comfortable now, don't you, Rip? (*Exit to inn.*)

RIP. Oh, yah! (*Suddenly becoming serious and much mystified at* DERRICK'S *conduct.*) Well, I don't know about that Derrick! Derrick! (*Holding up the bag and chinking it.*) It don't chink like good money neither. It rattles like a snake in a hole. (*Grimly.*)

GRETCHEN. (*Inside the cottage.*) Out with that lazy, idle cur! I won't have him here. Out, I say!

RIP. I 'm glad I 'm not in there now. I believe that 's Schneider what she 's lickin'; he won't have any backbone left in him. (*Sadly.*) I would rather she would lick me than the dog; I 'm more used to it than he is. (*Gets up, and looks in at the window.*) There she is at the wash-tub. (*Admiring her energy, almost envying it.*) What a hard-workin' woman that is! Well, somebody must do it, I suppose. (*With the air of a profound moral reflection.*) She 's comin' here now; she 's got some broomstick mit her, too.

(RIP *snatches up his gun and slinks off around the corner of the house.*)

(*Enter* GRETCHEN *with broomstick, followed by* HENDRICK *and* MEENIE, *carrying clothes-basket.*)

GRETCHEN. Come along, children. Now, you take the washing down to Dame Van Sloe's, then call at the butcher's and tell him that my husband has not got back yet, so I will have to go down myself to the marsh, and drive up the bull we have sold to him. Tell him the beast shall be in his stable in half an hour; so let him have the money ready to pay me for it. (*During this,* RIP *has crept in and sat on the bench by the side of the tub behind* GRETCHEN.) Ah, it is the last head of cattle we have left. Houses, lands, beasts, everything gone —everything except a drunken beast who nobody would buy or accept as a gift. Rip! Rip! wait until I get you home! (*Threatening an imaginary* RIP *with broomstick. With a comical grimace,* RIP *tiptoes back behind the house.*) Come, children, to work, to work! (*Exit.*)

(*Re-enter* RIP, *cautiously.*)

RIP. (*Laughing to himself.*) She gone to look after the bull. She better not try the broomstick on him; he won't stand it.

(*Drops into the chair, with his back to the audience.*)

HENDRICK. Oh, Meenie, there 's your father.

RIP. (*Holds out his arms, and* MEENIE *runs into them. Taking her in his arms, and embracing her with great tenderness.*) Ah, little gorl, was you glad to see your father come home?

MEENIE. Oh, yes!

RIP. (*Holding her close.*) I don't believe it, was you? Come here. (*Getting up and leading her to the chair by the side of the table.*) Let me look at you; I don't see you for such a long time; come here. I don't deserve to have a thing like that belong to me. (*Takes his hat off as if in reverence.*) You 're too good for a drunken, lazy feller like me, that 's a fact.

(*Bites his underlip, looks up, and brushes away a tear.*)

MEENIE. (*Kneeling by him.*) Oh, no, you are a good papa!

RIP. No, I was n't: no good father would go and rob his child; that 's what I 've done. Why, don't you know, Meenie, all the houses and lands in the village was mine—they would all have been yours when you grew up? Where they gone now? I gone drunk 'em up, that 's where they gone. Hendrick, you just take warnin' by that; that 's what licker do; see that? (*Holds up the skirt of coat.*) Bring a man to hunger and rags. Is there any more in that cup over there? Give it to me. (*Drinks.*)

(RIP *makes this confession with a childlike simplicity. The tears come, and he brushes them away once or twice. When he asks for the cup, at the end, it seems but the natural conclusion of his speech.*)

HENDRICK. (*Hands him cup.*) Don't cry, Rip; Meenie does not want your money, for when I 'm a big man I shall work for her, and she shall have all I get.

MEENIE. Yes, and I 'll have Hendrick too.

RIP. (*Greatly amused.*) You 'll have Hendrick, too. (*With mock gravity.*) Well, is this all settled?

HENDRICK. Yes, Meenie and me have made it all up.

RIP. I did n't know, I only thought you might speak to me about it, but if it 's all settled, Meenie, then git married mit him. (*Laughing silently, and suddenly.*) You goin' to marry my daughter? well, now, that 's very kind of you. Marry one another? (*The children nod.* RIP, *with immense seriousness.*) Well, here 's your good health, and your family, may they live long and prosper. (*To* HENDRICK.) What you goin' to do when you get married, and grow up and so? (*Leans forward.*)

HENDRICK. I 'm not going to stop here with father; oh, no, that won't do. I 'm going with Uncle Hans in his big ship to the North Pole, to catch whales.

RIP. Goin' to cotch wahales mit the North Pole? That 's a long while away from here.

HENDRICK. Yes, but uncle will give me ten shillings a month, and I will tell him to pay it all to Meenie.

RIP. There! He 's goin' to pay it all to you; that 's a good boy, that 's a good boy.

MEENIE. Yes, and I 'll give it all to you to keep for us.

RIP. (*With one of his little explosive laughs.*) I would n't do that, my darlin'; maybe if you give it to me, you don't get it back again. Hendrick! (*Suddenly earnest.*) You shall marry Meenie when you grow up, but you must n't drink.

HENDRICK. (*Slapping* RIP *on the knee.*) I 'll never touch a drop.

RIP. (*Quite seriously.*) You won't, nor me either; shake hands upon it. Now we swore off together. (*With a change of tone.*) I said so so many times, and never kept my word once, never. (*Drinks.*)

HENDRICK. I 've said so once, and I 'll keep mine.

DERRICK. (*Outside.*) Well, bring it along with you.

RIP. Here comes Derrick; he don't like some children; run along mit you. (*Exit children with basket.*)

(*Enter* DERRICK *from inn with document.*)

DERRICK. There, Rip, is the little acknowledgment. (*Handing it to him.*)

RIP. 'Knowledgment. (*Putting on hat.*) For what is that?

DERRICK. That is to say I loaned you the money.

RIP. (*Lounging back in his chair.*) I don't want that; I would lose it if I had it. (*Fills his cup from the bottle.*) I don't want it. (*Blandly.*)

DERRICK. Don't you? But I do.

RIP. (*With simple surprise.*) For what?

DERRICK. Why, for you to put your cross to. Why, bless me, I 've forgotten my pen and ink.

(*Enter* COCKLES.)

But luckily here comes my nephew with it. (*Aside.*) And in time to witness the signature.

RIP. Say, Derrick, have you been writing all that paper full in the little time you been in the house there?

(*Turns the paper about curiously. Pours out more schnapps.*)

DERRICK. Yes, every word of it.

RIP. Have you? Well, just read it out loud to me. (*With an air of great simplicity.*)

DERRICK. (*Aside.*) Does he suspect? (*Aloud.*) Why, Rip, this is the first time you ever wanted anything more than the money.

RIP. (*Clasping his hands behind his head with an air of lordly indifference.*) Yes, I know; but I got nothing to do now. I 'm a little curious about that, somehow.

COCKLES. (*Aside to* DERRICK.) The fish has taken the ground bait, but he 's curious about the hook.

DERRICK. (*Aside.*) I dare not read a word of it.

COCKLES. (*Aside.*) Nunkey 's stuck.

DERRICK. Well, Rip, I suppose you don't want to hear the formalities.

RIP. The what?

DERRICK. The preliminaries.

RIP. (*Indolently.*) I 'll take it all—Bill, Claws, and Feathers.

(*Leans forward and rests his head on his hand, and looks at the ground.*)

DERRICK. "Know all men by these presents, that I, Rip Van Winkle, in consideration of the sum of sixteen pounds received by me from Derrick Von Beekman"—(*Looks around at* COCKLES; *they wink knowingly at each other. Continues as if reading. Watching* RIP.)—"Do promise and undertake to pay the same in twenty years from date." (RIP *looks up; as he does so,* DERRICK *drops his eyes on document, then looks as if he had just finished reading.*) There, now are you satisfied?

RIP. (*Takes the document. In childlike surprise.*) Well, well, and does it take all that pen and ink to say such a little thing like that?

DERRICK. Why, of course it does.

COCKLES. (*Aside to* DERRICK.) Oh, the fool! he swallows it whole, hook and all.

RIP. (*Spreading the paper on the table.*) Where goes my cross, Derrick?

DERRICK. (*Pointing.*) There, you see I 've left a nice little white corner for you.

RIP. (*Folds up paper in a leisurely manner and puts it in game-bag.*) W-e-l-l, I 'll yust think about it.

(*Looks up at* DERRICK *innocently.*)

DERRICK. Think about it? Why, what 's the matter, Rip, is n't the money correct?

RIP. Oh, yes, I got the money all right. (*Chuckling.*) Oh! you mean about signing it. (*Rising. At a loss for a moment.*) Stop, yesterday was Friday, was n't it?

DERRICK. So it was.

RIP. (*With an air of conviction.*) Well, I never do nothing like that the day after Friday, Derrick.

(RIP *walks away towards his cottage.*)

DERRICK. (*Aside.*) The idiot! what can that signify? But I must not arouse his suspicions by pressing him. (*Aloud.*) You are right, Rip; sign it when you please; but I say, Rip, now that you 're in funds, won't you help your old friend Nick Vedder, who owes me a year's rent?

RIP. (*Coming back to the table.*) Oh, yah, I will wipe off my schore, and stand treat to the whole willage.

DERRICK. Run, boy, and tell all the neighbours that Rip stands treat.

RIP. (*Leans on back of chair.*) An', Cockles, tell them we 'll have a dance.

COCKLES. A dance! (*Runs off.*)

DERRICK. And I 'll order the good cheer for you. (*Exit.*)

RIP. So do! so do! (*Cogitating dubiously.*) I don't understand it.

(*Re-enter* HENDRICK *with the basket over his head, followed by* MEENIE.)

Oh, you 've come back?

HENDRICK. Yes, we 've left the clothes.

RIP. Meenie, you take in the basket. (*Exit* MEENIE *with the basket into the cottage.* HENDRICK *is following.*) Hendrick, come here. (HENDRICK *kneels between* RIP'S *knees.*) So you are going to marry my daughter? (HENDRICK *nods.*) So, so. That 's very kind of yer. (*Abruptly.*) Why you don't been to school today, you go to school some times, don't you?

HENDRICK. Yes, when father can spare me.

RIP. What do you learn mit that school, —pretty much something? (*Laughing at his mistake.*) I mean, everything?

HENDRICK. Yes; reading, writing and arithmetic.

RIP. Reading, and what?

HENDRICK. And writing, and arithmetic.

RIP. (*Puzzled.*) Writing and what?

HENDRICK. Arithmetic.

RIP. (*More puzzled.*) What meticks is that?

HENDRICK. Arithmetic.

RIP. (*With profound astonishment and patting* HENDRICK'S *head.*) I don't see how the little mind can stand it all. Can you read?

HENDRICK. Oh, yes!

RIP. (*With a serious affectation of incredulity.*) I don't believe it; now, I 'm just goin' to see if you can read. If you can't read, I won't let you marry my daughter. No, sir. (*Very drolly.*) I won't have nobody in my family what can't read. (*Taking out the paper that* DERRICK *has given him.*) Can you read ritmatics like that?

HENDRICK. Yes, that 's writing.

RIP. (*Nonplussed.*) Oh! I thought it was reading.

HENDRICK. It 's reading and writing, too.

RIP. What, both together. (*Suspiciously looking at the paper.*) Oh, yes; I did n't see that before; go long with it.

HENDRICK. (*Reads.*) "Know all men by these presents"—

RIP. (*Pleased, leaning back in his chair.*) Yah! that 's right, what a wonderful thing der readin' is; why you can read it pretty nigh as good as Derrick, yes you do; go long.

HENDRICK. "That I, Rip Van Winkle"—

RIP. (*Taking off his hat, and holding it with his hands behind his head.*) Yah, that 's right; you read it yust as well as Derrick; go long.

HENDRICK. "In consideration of the sum of sixteen pounds received do hereby sell and convey to Derrick Von Beekman all my estate, houses, lands whatsoever"— (*Hat drops.*)

RIP. (*Almost fiercely.*) What are you

readin', some ritmatics what ain't down there: where you got that?

(*Looking sharply at* HENDRICK.)

HENDRICK. (*Pointing.*) There. Houses! Lands, whatsoever.

RIP. (*Looking not at the paper but at* HENDRICK *very earnestly, as if turning over in his mind whether the boy has read it correctly. Then satisfied of the deception* DERRICK *has practiced upon him and struck by the humour of the way in which he has discovered it, he laughs exultantly and looks towards the inn-door through which* DERRICK *disappeared a short time before.*) Yes, so it is. Go long mit the rest.

(*He leans forward, and puts his ear close to* HENDRICK, *so as not to miss a word.*)

HENDRICK. "Whereof he now holds possession by mortgaged deeds, from time to time executed by me."

RIP. (*Takes paper, and looks towards the inn fiercely exultant.*) You read it better than Derrick, my boy, much better. (*After a moment's pause, recollects himself. Kindly to* HENDRICK.) That will do, run along mit you.

(*Exit* HENDRICK.)

RIP. Aha, my friend, Derrick! I guess you got some snakes in the grass. Now keep sober, Rip; I don't touch another drop so long what I live; I swore off now, that 's a fixed fact.

(*Enter* DERRICK, VEDDER, STEIN, *and villagers.*)

DERRICK. Come, Rip, we 'll have a rouse.

RIP. (*Seriously; half fiercely still.*) Here, Nick Vedder, here is the gelt; wipe off my score, and drink away. I don't join you; I swore off.

NICK. Why, Rip, you 're king of the feast.

RIP. (*Absently, still intent on* DERRICK.) Am I dat?

OMNES. Swore off? What for?

RIP. I don't touch another drop.

JACOB STEIN. (*Coming down towards* RIP *with cup.*) Come, Rip, take a glass.

RIP. (*Turning on him, almost angry.*) Jacob Stein, you hear what I said?

STEIN. Yes.

RIP. (*Firmly.*) Well, when I said a thing, I mean it.

(*Leans back in his chair with his hands behind his head.*)

STEIN. Oh, very well.

(*Turns away;* NICK *comes down and holds cup under* RIP'S *nose.* RIP *looks to see if they are watching him. He can resist no longer, and takes the cup.*)

RIP. (*Laughing.*) Well, I won't count this one. Here 's your good health and your families', may they all live long and prosper.

DERRICK. Here come the fiddlers and the girls.

(*Enter girls.*)

(RIP *walks over and closes the shutter which has held his score, then returns and seats himself on a low stool, and keeps time to the music as the villagers dance. Finally, the rhythm fires his blood. He jumps to his feet, snatches one of the girls away from her partner, and whirls into the dance. After a round or two, he lets go of her, and pirouettes two or three times by himself. Once more he catches her in his arms, and is in the act of embracing her, when he perceives* GRETCHEN *over her shoulder. He drops the girl, who falls on her knees at* GRETCHEN'S *feet. There is a general laugh at his discomfiture, in which he joins half-heartedly. As the curtain descends,* RIP *is seen pointing at the girl as if seeking, like a modern Adam, to put the blame on her.*)

ACT SECOND.

SCENE 1. *The dimly lighted kitchen of* RIP'S *cottage. The door and window are at the back. It is night, and through the window a furious storm can be seen raging, with thunder, lightning, and rain. A fire smoulders on the hearth, to the right, and a candle gutters on the table in the centre; a couple of chairs, a low stool, and a little cupboard, meagrely provided with cups and plates, complete the furniture of the room. Between the door and the window a clothes-horse, with a few garments hanging on it, forms a screen. To the left is a small door leading to the other rooms of the cottage.*

(*As the curtain rises,* MEENIE *is seen sitting by the window, and* GRETCHEN *en-*

ters, takes off cloak, and throws a broomstick on the table.)

GRETCHEN. Meenie! Has your father come yet?

MEENIE. No, mother.

GRETCHEN. So much the better for him. Never let him show his face in these doors again—never!

MEENIE. Oh, mother, don't be so hard on him.

GRETCHEN. I 'm not hard; how dare you say so. (MEENIE *approaches her.*) There, child, that father of yours is enough to spoil the temper of an angel. I went down to the marsh to drive up the bull. I don't know what Rip has been doing to the beast; he was howling and tearing about. I barely escaped with my life. (*A crash outside.*) What noise is that?

MEENIE. That 's only Schneider, father's dog.

GRETCHEN. (*Picking up broomstick.*) Then I 'll Schneider him. I won't have him here. (*Exit through the door leading to the rest of the cottage.*) Out, you idle, vagabond cur; out, I say!

MEENIE. (*Following her to the door, and crying.*) Oh, don't, don't hurt the poor thing!

(*Re-enter* GRETCHEN.)

GRETCHEN. He jumped out of the window before I could catch him. He 's just like his master. Now, what are you crying for?

MEENIE. Because my poor father is out in all this rain. (*A peal of thunder is heard.*) Hark, how it thunders!

GRETCHEN. Serve him right—do him good. Is the supper ready?

MEENIE. Yes, mother; it is there by the fireside. (*Pointing to the soup-bowl by the fire.*) Shall I lay the table?

GRETCHEN. Yes. (*Again it thunders.*) It 's a dreadful night; I wonder where Rip is?

MEENIE. (*Bringing the cups and platters from the sideboard, together with a loaf of bread.*) Shall I lay the table for two, mother, or for three?

GRETCHEN. For two, girl; he gets no supper here tonight. (*Another peal of thunder.*) Mercy, how the storm rages! the fool, to stop out in such a downpour. I hope he 's found shelter. I must look out the old suit I washed and mended for him last week, and put them by the fire to air. The idiot, to stop out in such a down-pour! I 'll have him sick on my hands next; that 's all I want to complete my misery. (*She fetches clothes from the horse and hangs them on the back of the chair in front of the fire.*) He knows what I am suffering now, and that 's what keeps him out. (*Lightning.*) Mercy, what a flash that was! The wretch will be starved with the cold! Meenie!

MEENIE. Yes, mother.

GRETCHEN. You may lay the table for three. (*There is a knock at the outer door.*) There he is now!

(*Enter* HENDRICK, *who shakes rain from his hat.*)

Where 's Rip? Is he not at your father's?

HENDRICK. No; I thought he was here.

GRETCHEN. He 's gone back to the mountain. He 's done it on purpose to spite me.

HENDRICK. (*Going to the fire.*) Shall I run after him, and bring him home? I know the road. We 've often climbed it together.

GRETCHEN. No; I drove Rip from his house, and it 's for me to bring him back again.

MEENIE. (*Still arranging the supper table.*) But, mother—(*She pauses, with embarrassment.*) If he hears your voice behind him, he will only run away the faster.

GRETCHEN. Well, I can't help it; I can't rest under cover, while he is out in the storm. I shall feel better when I 'm outside sharing the storm with him. Sit down, and take your suppers. I 'll take my cloak along with me.

(*Exit.* MEENIE *has seated herself by the window.* HENDRICK *carries stool to the centre of the stage, in front of the table.*)

HENDRICK. Meenie! Meenie!

MEENIE. Eh?

(HENDRICK *beckons to her. She runs to him. He stops her suddenly, then puts the stool down with great deliberation, and sits on it, while* MEENIE *kneels beside him.*)

HENDRICK. (*In a very solemn tone.*) I hope your father ain't gone to the mountains tonight, Meenie?

MEENIE. (*In distress.*) Oh, dear! he will die of the cold there.

HENDRICK. (*Suddenly.*) Sh! (MEENIE

starts.) It ain't for that. (*Mysteriously.*) I 've just heard old Clausen, over at father's, saying, that on this very night, every twenty years, the ghosts—

MEENIE. (*Catching his wrist.*) The what?

HENDRICK. (*In an awed tone.*) The ghosts of Hendrick Hudson, and his pirate crew, visit the Kaatskills above here.

(*The two children look around, frightened.*)

MEENIE. Oh, dear! did he say so?

HENDRICK. Sh! (*Again they look around, frightened.*) Yes; and the spirits have been seen there smoking, drinking, and playing at tenpins.

MEENIE. Oh, how dreadful!

HENDRICK. Sh! (*He goes cautiously to the chimney, and looks up, while* MEENIE *looks under the table; then he returns to the stool, speaking as he comes.*) Yes; and every time that Hendrick Hudson lights his pipe there 's a flash of lightning. (*Lightning and* MEENIE *gives a gasp of fear.*) And when he rolls the balls along, there is a peal of thunder. (*Loud rumbles of thunder.* MEENIE *screams and throws herself into* HENDRICK'S *arms.*) Don't be frightened, Meenie; I 'm here.

(*In a frightened tone, but with a manly effort to be courageous.*)

(*Re-enter* GRETCHEN *with her cloak.*)

GRETCHEN. Here, stop that! (*The children separate quickly.* HENDRICK *looks up at the ceiling and whistles, with an attempt at unconsciousness, and* MEENIE *assumes an innocent and unconcerned expression.*) Now, don't you be filling that child's head with nonsense, but remain quietly here until I return. Hush, what noise is that? There is someone outside the window.

(*She steps behind the clothes-horse.* RIP *appears at the window, which he opens, and leans against the frame.*)

RIP. Meenie!

MEENIE and HENDRICK. (*Trying to make him perceive* GRETCHEN, *by a gesture in her direction.*) Sh!

(RIP *turns, and looks around outside to see what they mean, then, discovering nothing, drops his hat in at the window, and calls again, cautiously.*)

RIP. Meenie!

MEENIE and HENDRICK. (*With the same warning gesture.*) Sh!

(GRETCHEN *shakes her fist at the children, who assume an air of innocence.*)

RIP. What 's the matter? Meenie, has the wild-cat come home? (RIP *reaches in after his hat.* GRETCHEN *catches him by his hair, and holds his head down.*) Och, my darlin', don't do that, eh!

HENDRICK and MEENIE. (*Who run towards* GRETCHEN.) Don't, mother! don't, mother! don't!

RIP. (*Imitating their tone.*) Don't, mother, don't! Don't you hear the children? Let go my head, won't you? (*Getting angry.*)

GRETCHEN. No; not a hair.

RIP. (*Bantering.*) Hold on to it then, what do I care?

HENDRICK and MEENIE. (*Catching* GRETCHEN'S *dress.*) Don't, mother! Don't, mother! Don't!

(GRETCHEN *lets go of* RIP, *and turns upon them. They escape, and disappear through the door to the left.*)

RIP. (*Getting in through the window, and coming forward, apparently drunk, but jolly; and his resentment for the treatment he has just received is half humorous.*) For what you do dat, hey? You must want a bald-headed husband, I reckon!

(GRETCHEN *picks up chair, and bangs it down;* RIP *imitates her with the stool. She sits down angrily, and slaps the table.* RIP *throws down his felt hat with a great show of violence, and it makes no noise, then seats himself on the stool.*)

GRETCHEN. Now, then!

RIP. Now, den; I don't like it den, neider.

(*When* RIP *is drunk, his dialect grows more pronounced.*)

GRETCHEN. Who did you call a wildcat?

RIP. (*With a sudden little tipsy laugh, and confused.*) A wildcat—dat 's when I come in at the window?

GRETCHEN. Yes; that 's when you came in the window.

RIP. (*Rising, and with a tone of finality.*) Yes; that 's the time I said it.

GRETCHEN. Yes; and that 's the time I heard it.

RIP. (*With drunken assurance.*) That 's all right; I was afraid you would n't hear it.

GRETCHEN. Now who did you mean by that wildcat?

RIP. (*Confused.*) Who did I mean? Now, let me see.

GRETCHEN. Yes; who did you mean?

RIP. How do I know who-oo I mean? (*With a sudden inspiration.*) Maybe it 's the dog Schneider, I call that.

GRETCHEN. (*Incredulously.*) The dog Schneider; that 's not likely.

RIP. (*Argumentatively.*) Of course it is likely; he's my dog. I'll call him a wildcat much as I please.

(*Conclusively. He sits down in the chair on which his clothes are warming, in front of the fire.*)

GRETCHEN. And then, there 's your disgraceful conduct this morning. What have you got to say to that?

RIP. How do I know what I got to say to that, when I don't know what I do-a, do-a? (*Hiccoughs.*)

GRETCHEN. Don't know what you do-a-oo! Hugging and kissing the girls before my face; you thought I would n't see you.

RIP. (*Boldly.*) I knowed you would—I knowed you would; because, because—(*Losing the thread of his discourse.*) Oh-h, don' you bodder me.

(*He turns and leans his head against the back of the chair.*)

GRETCHEN. You knew I was there?

RIP. (*Laughing.*) I thought I saw you.

GRETCHEN. I saw you myself, dancing with the girl.

RIP. You saw the girl dancin' mit me. (GRETCHEN *remembers* RIP'S *clothes, and goes over to see if he is wet, and pushes him towards the center of the stage.* RIP *mistakes her intention.*) You want to pull some more hair out of my head?

GRETCHEN. Why, the monster! He is n't wet a bit! He 's as dry as if he 'd been aired!

RIP. Of course I'm dry. (*Laughing.*) I'm always dry—always dry.

GRETCHEN. (*Examines game-bag, and pulls out a flask, which she holds under* RIP'S *nose.*) Why, what 's here? Why, it 's a bottle—a bottle!

RIP. (*Leaning against the table.*) Yes; it 's a bottle. (*Laughs.*) You think I don't know a bottle when I see it?

GRETCHEN. That 's pretty game for your game-bag, ain't it?

RIP. (*Assuming an innocent air.*) Somebody must have put it there.

GRETCHEN. (*Putting the flask in her pocket.*) Then, you don't get it again.

RIP. (*With a show of anger.*) Now mind if I don't get it again—well—all there is about it—(*Breaking down.*) I don't want it. I have had enough.

(*With a droll air of conviction.*)

GRETCHEN. I'm glad you know when you 've had enough.

RIP. (*Still leaning against the table.*) That 's the way mit me. I 'm glad I know when I got enough—(*Laughs.*) An' I'm glad when I 've got enough, too. Give me the bottle; I want to put it in the game-bag.

GRETCHEN. For what?

RIP. (*Lounging off the table, and coming forward and leaning his arms on* GRETCHEN'S *shoulders.*) So that I can't drink it. Here 's the whole business—(*He slides his hand down to* GRETCHEN'S *pocket and tries to find the bottle while he talks to her.*) Here 's the whole business about it. What is the use of anybody—well—wash the use of anybody, anyhow—well—oh—(*Missing the pocket.*) What you talkin' 'bout (*Suddenly his hand slips in her pocket, and he begins to pull the bottle out, with great satisfaction.*) Now, now I can tell you all 'bout it.

GRETCHEN. (*Discovering his tactics, and pushing him away.*) Pshaw!

RIP. If you don't give me the bottle, I just break up everything in the house.

GRETCHEN. If you dare!

RIP. If I dare! Have n't I done it two or three times before? I just throw everything right out of the window.

(RIP *throws the plates and cups on the floor and overturns a chair, and seats himself on the table.* GRETCHEN *picks them up again.*)

GRETCHEN. Don't Rip; don't do that! Now stop, Rip, stop! (GRETCHEN *bangs down a chair by the table and seats herself.*) Now, then, perhaps you will be kind enough to tell where you 've been for the last two days. Where have you been? Do you hear?

RIP. Where I 've been? Well, it 's not my bottle, anyhow. I borrowed that bottle from another feller. You want to know where I been?

GRETCHEN. Yes; and I will know.

RIP. (*Good-humouredly.*) Let 's see. Last night I stopped out all night.

GRETCHEN. But why?

RIP. Why? You mean the reason of it?

GRETCHEN. Yes, the reason.

RIP. (*Inconsequently.*) The reason is why? Don't bother me.

GRETCHEN. (*Emphasizing each word with a bang on the table.*) Why—did—you—stop—out—all—night?

RIP. (*Imitating her tone.*) Because—I—want—to—get—up—early—in—the—morning. (*Hiccough.*) Come don't get so mad mit a feller. Why, I've been fillin' my game-bag mit game.

(RIP *gets down off the table, and* GRETCHEN *comes towards him and feels his game-bag.*)

GRETCHEN. Your game-bag is full of game, is n't it?

RIP. (*Taking her hand and holding it away from her pocket.*) That? Why, that would n't hold it. (*Finding his way into* GRETCHEN'S *pocket.*) Now I can tell you all about it. You know last night I stopped out all night—

GRETCHEN. Yes; and let me catch you again. (*He is pulling the bottle out, when* GRETCHEN *catches him, and slaps his hand.*) You paltry thief!

RIP. Oh, you ain't got no confidence in me. Now what do you think was the first thing I saw in the morning?

(*Dragging a chair to the front of the stage.*)

GRETCHEN. I don't know. What?

RIP. (*Seating himself.*) A rabbit.

GRETCHEN. (*Pleased.*) I like a rabbit. I like it in a stew.

RIP. (*Looking at her, amused.*) I guess you like everything in a stew—everything what's a rabbit I mean. Well, there was a rabbit a-feedin' mit the grass,—you know they always come out early in der mornin' and feed mit the grass?

GRETCHEN. Never mind the grass. Go on.

RIP. Don't get so patient; you wait till you get the rabbit. (*Humorously.*) Well, I crawl up—

GRETCHEN. Yes, yes!

RIP. (*Becoming interested in his own powers of invention.*) An' his little tail was a-stickin' up so—

(*With a gesture of his forefinger.*)

GRETCHEN. (*Impatiently.*) Never mind his tail. Go on.

RIP. (*Remonstrating at her interruption.*) The more fatter the rabbit, the more whiter is his tail—

GRETCHEN. Well, well, go on.

RIP. (*Taking aim.*) Well, I haul up—

GRETCHEN. Yes, yes!

RIP. And his ears was a-stickin' up so—

(*Making the two ears with his two forefingers.*)

GRETCHEN. Never mind his ears. Go on.

RIP. I pull the trigger.

GRETCHEN. (*Eagerly.*) Bang went the gun, and—

RIP. (*Seriously.*) And the rabbit run away.

GRETCHEN. (*Angrily.*) And so you shot nothing?

RIP. How will I shot him when he run away? (*He laughs at her disappointment.*) There, don't get so mad mit a feller. Now I'm going to tell you what I did shot; that's what I did n't shot. You know that old forty-acre field of ours?

GRETCHEN. (*Scornfully.*) Ours! Ours, did you say?

RIP. (*Shamefacedly.*) You know the one I mean well enough. It used to be ours.

GRETCHEN. (*Regretfully.*) Yes; it used, indeed!

RIP. It ain't ours now, is it?

GRETCHEN. (*Sighing.*) No, indeed, it is not.

RIP. No? Den I won't bodder about it. Better let somebody bodder about that field what belongs to it. Well, in that field there's a pond; and what do you think I see in that pond?

GRETCHEN. I don't know. Ducks?

RIP. Ducks! More an' a thousand.

GRETCHEN. (*Walking to where broomstick is.*) More than a thousand ducks?

RIP. I haul up again—

GRETCHEN. (*Picking up broomstick.*) Yes, and so will I. And if you miss fire this time—

(*She holds it threateningly over* RIP'S *shoulder.*)

RIP. (*Looking at it askance out of the corner of his eye, then putting up his hand and pushing it aside.*) You will scare the ducks mit that. Well, I take better aim this time as I did before. I pull the trigger, and—bang!

GRETCHEN. How many down?

RIP. (*Indifferently.*) One.

GRETCHEN. (*Indignantly.*) What! only one duck out of a thousand?

RIP. Who said one duck?

GRETCHEN. You did!

RIP. (*Getting up and leaning on the back of the chair.*) I did n't say anything of the kind.

GRETCHEN. You said "one."

RIP. Ah! *One.* But I shot more as one duck.

GRETCHEN. Did you?

RIP. (*Crosses over, and sits on the low stool, laughing silently.*) I shot our old bull. (GRETCHEN *flings down the broomstick, and throws herself into the chair at the right of the table, in dumb rage.*) I did n't kill him. I just sting him, you know. Well, then the bull come right after me; and I come right away from him. O, Gretchen, how you would laugh if you could see that—(*With a vain appeal to her sense of humor.*) the bull was a-comin', and I was a-goin'. Well, he chased me across the field. I tried to climb over the fence so fast what I could,—(*Doubles up with his silent laugh.*) an' the bull come up an' save me the trouble of that. Well, then, I rolled over on the other side.

GRETCHEN. (*With disgust.*) And then you went fast asleep for the rest of the day.

RIP. That 's a fact. That 's a fact.

GRETCHEN. (*Bursting into tears, and burying her head in her arms on the table.*) O, Rip, you 'll break my heart! You will.

RIP. Now she 's gone crying mit herself! Don't cry, Gretchen, don't cry. My d-a-r-l-i-n,' don't cry.

GRETCHEN. (*Angrily.*) I will cry.

RIP. Cry 'way as much as you like. What do I care? All the better soon as a woman gets cryin'; den all the danger 's over. (RIP *goes to* GRETCHEN, *leans over, and puts his arm around her.*) Gretchen, don't cry; my angel, don't. (*He succeeds in getting his hand into her pocket, and steals the bottle.*) Don't cry, my daarlin'. (*Humorously.*) Gretchen, won't you give me a little drop out of that bottle what you took away from me?

(*He sits on the table, just behind her, and takes a drink from the bottle.*)

GRETCHEN. Here 's a man drunk, and asking for more.

RIP. I was n't. I swore off. (*Coaxingly.*) You give me a little drop an' I won't count it.

GRETCHEN. (*Sharply.*) No!

RIP. (*Drinking again.*) Well, den, here 's your good health, an' your family, and may they live long and prosper!

(*Puts bottle in his bag.*)

GRETCHEN. You unfeeling brute. Your wife 's starving. And, Rip, your child 's in rags.

RIP. (*Holding up his coat, and heaving a sigh of resignation.*) Well, I 'm the same way; you know dat.

GRETCHEN. (*Sitting up, and looking appealingly at* RIP.) Oh, Rip, if you would only treat me kindly!

RIP. (*Putting his arms around her.*) Well, den, I will. I 'm going to treat you kind. I 'll treat you kind.

GRETCHEN. Why, it would add ten years to my life.

RIP. (*Over her shoulder, and after a pause.*) That 's a great inducement; it is, my darlin'. I know I treat you too bad, an' you deserve to be a widow.

GRETCHEN. (*Getting up, and putting her arms on* RIP'S *shoulder.*) Oh, Rip, if you would only reform!

RIP. Well, den, I will. I won't touch another drop so long as I live.

GRETCHEN. Can I trust you?

RIP. You must n't suspect me.

GRETCHEN. (*Embracing him.*) There, then, I will trust you. (*She takes the candle and goes to fetch the children.*) Here, Hendrick, Meenie? Children, where are you?

(*Exit through the door on the left.*)

RIP. (*Seats himself in the chair to the right of the table, and takes out flask.*) Well, it 's too bad; but it 's all a woman's fault anyway. When a man gets drinkin' and that, they ought to let him alone. So soon as they scold him, he goes off like a sky-rocket.

(*Re-enter* GRETCHEN *and the children.*)

GRETCHEN. (*Seeing the flask in* RIP'S *hand.*) I thought as much.

RIP. (*Unconscious of her presence.*) How I did smooth her down! I must drink her good health. Gretchen, here 's your good health. (*About to drink.*)

GRETCHEN. (*Snatching the bottle, and using it to gesticulate with.*) Oh, you paltry thief!

RIP. (*Concerned for the schnapps.*) What you doin'? You 'll spill the licker out of the bottle. (*He puts in the cork.*)

GRETCHEN. (*Examining the flask.*) Why, the monster, he 's emptied the bottle!

RIP. That 's a fac'. That 's a fac'.

GRETCHEN. (*Throwing down the flask.*) Then that is the last drop you drink under my roof!

RIP. What! What!

(MEENIE *approaches her father on tiptoe, and kneels beside him.*)

GRETCHEN. Out, you drunkard! Out, you sot! You disgrace to your wife and to your child! This house is mine.

RIP. (*Dazed, and a little sobered.*) Yours! Yours!

GRETCHEN. (*Raising her voice above the storm, which seems to rage more fiercely outside.*) Yes, mine, mine! Had it been yours to sell, it would have gone along with the rest of your land. Out then, I say— (*Pushing open the door.*) for you have no longer any share in me or mine. (*A peal of thunder.*)

MEENIE. (*Running over, and kneeling by* GRETCHEN.) Oh, mother, hark at the storm!

GRETCHEN. (*Pushing her aside.*) Begone, man, can't you speak? Are you struck dumb? You sleep no more under my roof.

RIP. (*Who has not moved, even his arm remaining outstretched, as it was when* MEENIE *slipped from his side, murmurs in a bewildered, incredulous way.*) Why, Gretchen, are you goin' to turn me out like a dog? (GRETCHEN *points to the door.* RIP *rises and leans against the table with a groan. His conscience speaks.*) Well, maybe you are right. (*His voice breaks, and with a despairing gesture.*) I have got no home. I will go. But mind, Gretchen, after what you say to me tonight, I can never darken your door again—never— (*Going towards the door.*) I will go.

HENDRICK. (*Running up to* RIP.) Not into the storm, Rip. Hark, how it thunders!

RIP. (*Putting his arm around him.*) Yah, my boy; but not as bad to me as the storm in my home. I will go. (*At the door by this time.*)

MEENIE. (*Catching* RIP'S *coat.*) No, father, don't go!

RIP. (*Bending over her tenderly, and holding her close to him.*) My child! Bless you, my child, bless you!

(MEENIE *faints.* RIP *gives a sobbing sigh.*)

GRETCHEN. (*Relenting.*) No, Rip—I—

RIP. (*Waving her off.*) No, you have drive me from your house. You have opened the door for me to go. You may never open it for me to come back. (*Leaning against the doorpost, overcome by his emotion. His eyes rest on* MEENIE, *who lies at his feet.*) You say I have no share in this house. (*Points to* MEENIE *in profound despair.*) Well, see, then, I wipe the disgrace from your door.

(*He staggers out into the storm.*)

GRETCHEN. No, Rip! Husband, come back!

(GRETCHEN *faints, and the curtain falls.*)

ACT THIRD.

SCENE 1. *A steep and rocky clove in the Kaatskill Mountains, down which rushes a torrent, swollen by the storm. Overhead, the hemlocks stretch their melancholy boughs. It is night.*

(RIP *enters, almost at a run, with his head down, and his coat-collar turned up, beating his way against the storm. With the hunter's instinct, he protects the priming of his gun with the skirt of his jacket. Having reached a comparatively level spot, he pauses for breath, and turns to see what has become of his dog.*)

RIP. (*Whistling to the dog.*) Schneider! Schneider! What 's the matter with Schneider? Something must have scared that dog. There he goes head over heels down the hill. Well, here I am again—another night in the mountains! Heigho! these old trees begin to know me, I reckon. (*Taking off his hat.*) How are you, old fellows? Well, I like the trees, they keep me from the wind and the rain, and they never blow me up; and when I lay me down on the broad of my back, they seem to bow their heads to me, an' say: Go to sleep, Rip, go to sleep. (*Lightning.*) My, what a flash that was! Old Hendrick Hudson 's lighting his pipe in the mountains tonight; now, we 'll hear him roll the big balls along. (*Thunder.* RIP *looks back over the path he has come and whistles again for his dog.*) Well, I—no—Schneider! No; whatever it is, it 's on two legs. Why, what a funny thing is that a comin' up the hill? I thought nobody but me ever come nigh this place.

(*Enter a strange dwarfish figure, clad all in gray like a Dutch seaman of the seventeenth century, in short-skirted doublet, hose, and high-crowned hat drawn over his eyes. From beneath the latter his long gray beard streams down till it almost touches the ground. He carries a keg on his shoulder. He advances slowly towards* RIP, *and, by his gesture, begs* RIP *to set the keg down for him.* RIP *does so, and the dwarf seats himself upon it.*)

RIP. (*With good-humoured sarcasm.*) Sit down, and make yourself comfortable. (*A long pause and silence.*) What? What 's the matter? Ain't ye goin' to speak to a feller? I don't want to speak to you, then. Who you think you was, that I want to speak to you, any more than you want to speak to me; you hear what I say? (RIP *pokes the dwarf in the ribs, who turns, and looks up.* RIP *retreats hastily.*) Donner an' Blitzen! What for a man is das? I have been walking over these mountains ever since I was a boy, an' I never saw a queer looking codger like that before. He must be an old sea-snake, I reckon.

(*The dwarf approaches* RIP, *and motions* RIP *to help him up the mountain with the keg.*)

RIP. Well, why don't you say so, den? You mean you would like me to help you up with that keg? (*The dwarf nods in the affirmative.*) Well, sir, I don't do it. (*The dwarf holds up his hands in supplication.*) No, there 's no good you speakin' like that. I never seed you before, did I? (*The dwarf shakes his head,* RIP, *with great decision, walking away, and leaning against a tree.*) I don't want to see you again, needer. What have you got in that keg, schnapps? (*The dwarf nods.*) I don't believe you. (*The dwarf nods more affirmatively.*) Is it good schnapps? (*The dwarf again insists.*) Well, I 'll help you. Go 'long; pick up my gun, there, and I follow you mit that keg on my shoulder. I 'll follow you, old broadchops.

(*As* RIP *shoulders the keg, a furious blast whirls up the valley, and seems to carry him and his demon companion before it. The rain that follows blots out the landscape. For a few moments, all is darkness. Gradually, the topmost peak of the Kaatskill Mountains becomes visible, far above the storm. Stretching below, the country lies spread out like a map. A feeble and watery moonlight shows us a weird group, gathered upon the peak,—Hendrick Hudson, and his ghostly crew. In the foreground, one of them poises a ball, about to bowl it, while the others lean forward in attitudes of watchful expectancy. Silently he pitches it; and, after a momentary pause, a long and rumbling peal of thunder reverberates among the valleys below. At this moment, the demon, carrying* RIP'S *gun, appears over the crest of the peak in the background, and* RIP *toils after with the keg on his shoulder. Arrived at the summit, he drops the keg on his knee, and gasps for breath.*)

RIP. (*Glancing out over the landscape.*) I say, old gentleman, I never was so high up in the mountains before. Look down into the valley there; it seems more as a mile. I— (*Turning to speak to his companion, and perceiving another of the crew.*) You 're another feller! (*The second demon nods assent.*) You 're that other chap's brother? (*The demon again assents.* RIP *carries the keg a little further, and comes face to face with a third.*) You 're another brother? (*The third demon nods assent.* RIP *takes another step, and perceives* HENDRICK HUDSON *in the centre, surrounded by many demons.*) You 're his old gran'father? (HUDSON *nods.* RIP *puts down the keg in perplexity, not untinged with alarm.*) Donner and Blitzen! here 's the whole family; I 'm a dead man to a certainty.

(*The demons extend their arms to* HUDSON, *as if inquiring what they should do. He points to* RIP, *they do the same.*)

RIP. My, my, I suppose they 're speakin' about me! (*Looking at his gun, which the first demon has deposited on the ground, and which lies within his reach.*) No good shootin' at 'em; family 's too big for one gun.

(HENDRICK HUDSON *advances, and seats himself on the keg facing* RIP. *The demons slowly surround the two.*)

RIP. (*Looking about him with growing apprehension.*) My, my, I don't like that kind of people at all! No, sir! I don't like any sech kind. I like that old gran'father worse than any of them. (*With a sheepish attempt to be genial, and appear at his ease.*) How you was, old gentleman? I did n't mean to intrude on you, did I? (HUDSON *shakes his head.*) What? (*No reply.*) I'll tell you how it was; I met one of your gran'children, I don't know which is the one— (*Glancing around.*) They 're all so much alike. Well— (*Embarrassed and looking at one demon.*) That 's the same kind of a one. Any way, this one, he axed me to help him up the mountain mit dat keg. Well, he was an old feller, an' I thought I would help him. (*Pauses, troubled by their silence.*) Was I right to help him? HUDSON *nods.*) I say, was I right to help him? (HUDSON *nods again.*) If he was here, he would yust tell you the same thing any way, because— (*Suddenly perceiving the demon he had met below.*) Why, dat 's the one, ain't it? (*The demon nods.*) Yes; dat is the one, dat 's the same kind of a one dat I met. Was I right to come? (HUDSON *nods approval.*) I did n't want to come here, anyhow; no, sir, I did n't want to come to any such kind of a place. (*After a pause, seeing that no one has anything to say.*) I guess I better go away from it. (RIP *picks up his gun, and is about to return by the way he came; but the demons raise their hands threateningly, and stop him. He puts his gun down again.*) I did n't want to come here, anyhow— (*Grumbling to himself, then pulling himself together with an effort, and facing* HUDSON.) Well, old gentleman, if you mean to do me any harm, just speak it right out— (*Then with a little laugh.*) Oh! I will die game— (*Glancing around for a means of escape, and half to himself.*) If I can't run away.

(HUDSON *extends a cup to* RIP, *as if inviting him to drink.*)

RIP. (*Doubtfully.*) You want me to drink mit you? (HUDSON *nods.* RIP *approaches him cautiously, unable to resist the temptation of a drink.*) Well, I swore off drinkin'; but as this is the first time I see you, I won't count this one— (*He takes the cup.* HUDSON *holds up another cup.* RIP *is reassured, and his old geniality returns.*) You drink mit me? We drink mit one another? HUDSON *nods affirmatively.* RIP *feels at home under these familiar circumstances, and becomes familiar and colloquial again.*) What 's the matter mit you, old gentleman, anyhow? You go and make so (*Imitating the demon*) mit your head every time; was you deaf? (HUDSON *shakes his head.*) Oh, nein. (*Laughing at his error.*) If you was deaf, you would n't hear what I was sayin'. Was you dumb? (HUDSON *nods yes.*) So? You was dumb? (HUDSON *nods again.*) Has all of your family the same complaint? (HUDSON *nods.*) All the boys dumb, hey? All the boys dumb. (*All the demons nod. Then, suddenly, as if struck with an idea.*) Have you got any girls? (HUDSON *shakes his head.*) Don't you? Such a big family, and all boys?

(HUDSON *nods.*)

RIP. (*With profound regret.*) That 's a pity; my, that 's a pity. Oh, my, if you had some dumb girls, what wives they would make— (*Brightening up.*) Well, old gentleman, here 's your good health, and all your family—(*Turning, and waving to them.*)—may they live long and prosper.

(RIP *drinks. As he does so, all the demons lean forward, watching the effect of the liquor.* RIP *puts his hand to his head. The empty cup falls to the ground.*)

RIP. (*In an awed and ecstatic voice.*) What for licker is that! (*As he turns, half reeling, he sees* HUDSON *holding out to him another cup. He snatches it with almost frantic eagerness.*) Give me another one! (*He empties it at a draught. A long pause follows during which the effect of the liquor upon* RIP *becomes apparent; the light in his eyes fades, his exhilaration dies out, and he loses his grasp on the reality of his surroundings. Finally, he clasps his head with both hands, and cries in a muffled, terrified voice.*) Oh, my, my head was so light, and now, it 's heavy as lead! (*He reels, and falls heavily to the ground. A long pause. The demons begin to disappear.* RIP *becomes dimly conscious of this, and raises himself on his elbow.*) Are you goin' to leave me, boys? Are you goin' to leave me all alone? Don't leave me; don't go away. (*With a last effort.*) I will drink your good health, and your family's—

(*He falls back heavily, asleep*)

CURTAIN.

ACT FOURTH.

SCENE 1. *As the curtain rises, the same high peaks of the Kaatskills, and the far-stretching valley below, are disclosed in the gray light of dawn.*

RIP *is still lying on the ground, as in the last act, but he is no longer the* RIP *we knew. His hair and beard are long and white, bleached by the storms that have rolled over his head during the twenty years he has been asleep.*

As he stirs and slowly rises to a half-sitting posture, we see that his former picturesque rags have become so dilapidated that it is a matter of marvel how they hold together. They have lost all traces of color, and have assumed the neutral tints of the moss and lichens that cover the rocks.

His voice, when he first speaks, betrays even more distinctly than his appearance the lapse of time. Instead of the full round tones of manhood, he speaks in the high treble of feeble old age. His very hands have grown old and weather-beaten.

RIP. (*Staring vacantly around.*) I wonder where I was. On top of the Kaatskill Mountains as sure as a gun! Won't my wife give it to me for stopping out all night? I must get up and get home with myself. (*Trying to rise.*) Oh, I feel very bad! Vat is the matter with my elbow? (*In trying to rub it, the other one gives him such a twinge that he cries out.*) Oh! the other elbow is more badder than the other one. I must have cotched the rheumatix a-sleepin' mit the wet grass. (*He rises with great difficulty.*) Och! I never had such rheumatix like that. (*He feels himself all over, and then stands for a moment pondering, and bewildered by a strange memory.*) I was n't sleeping all the time, needer. I know I met a queer kind of a man, and we got drinkin' and I guess I got pretty drunk. Well, I must pick up my gun, and get home mit myself. (*After several painful attempts, he succeeds in picking up his gun, which drops all to pieces as he lifts it.* RIP *looks at it in amazement.*) My gun must have cotched the rheumatix too. Now, that 's too bad. Them fellows have gone and stole my good gun, and leave me this rusty old barrel. (RIP *begins slowly to climb over the peak towards the path by which he had ascended, his memory seeming to act automatically. When he reaches the highest point, where he can look out over the valley, he stops in surprise.*) Why, is that the village of Falling Waters that I see? Why, the place is more than twice the size it was last night. I— (*He sinks down.*) I don't know whether I am dreaming, or sleeping, or waking. (*Then pulling himself together with a great effort, and calling up the image of his wife to act as whip and spur to his waning powers, he says, with humorous conviction, as he gets up painfully, again:—*) I go home to my wife. She 'll let me know whether I 'm asleep or awake or not. (*Almost unable to proceed.*) I don't know if I will ever get home, my k-nees are so stiff. My backbone, it 's broke already.

(*As the curtain falls,* RIP *stands leaning on the barrel of his gun as on a staff, with one hand raised, looking out over the valley.*)

SCENE 2. *A comfortable-looking room in* DERRICK'S *house. As the curtain rises,* MEENIE *and* GRETCHEN *enter.* MEENIE *is a tall young woman of twenty-six, and* GRETCHEN *is a matronly figure with white hair. They are well dressed, and have every appearance of physical and material prosperity.*

GRETCHEN. I am sent to you by your father, Meenie.

MEENIE. Oh, don't call him so; he is not my father! He is your husband, mother; but I owe him no love. And his cruel treatment of you—

GRETCHEN. Hush, child! Oh, if he heard you, he would make me pay for every disrespectful word you utter.

MEENIE. Yes; he would beat you, starve and degrade you. You are not his wife, mother, but his menial.

GRETCHEN. My spirit is broken, Meenie. I cannot resent it. Nay, I deserve it; for as Derrick now treats me, so I treated your poor father when he was alive.

MEENIE. You, mother? You, so gentle? You, who are weakness and patience itself?

GRETCHEN. Yes; because for fifteen years I have been Derrick's wife. But it was my temper, my cruelty, that drove your father from our home twenty years ago.

You were too young then to remember him.

MEENIE. No, mother, I recollect dear father taking me on his knee, and saying to Hendrick that I should be his wife; and I promised I would.

GRETCHEN. Poor Rip! Poor, good-natured, kind creature that he was! How gently he bore with me; and I drove him like a dog from his home. I hunted him into the mountains, where he perished of hunger or cold, or a prey to some wild beast.

MEENIE. Don't cry, mother!

(*Enter* DERRICK, *now grown old and bent over his cane, and infinitely more disagreeable than before. He, too, has thriven, and is dressed in a handsome full suit of black silk.*)

DERRICK. Snivelling again, eh? Teaching that girl of yours to be an obstinate hypocrite?

MEENIE. Oh, sir, she

DERRICK. Hold your tongue, Miss. Speak when you're spoken to. I'll have you both to understand that there's but one master here. Well, mistress, have you told her my wishes; and is she prepared to obey them?

GRETCHEN. Indeed, sir, I was trying to—

DERRICK. Beating about the bush, prevaricating, and sneaking, as you usually do.

MEENIE. If you have made her your slave, you must expect her to cringe.

DERRICK. (*Approaching her threateningly.*) What's that?

GRETCHEN. Meenie! Meenie! For Heaven's sake, do not anger him!

DERRICK. (*Raising his cane.*) She had better not.

MEENIE. (*Defiantly.*) Take care how you raise your hand to me, for I'll keep a strict account of it. And when Hendrick comes back from sea, he'll make you smart for it, I promise you.

DERRICK. Is the girl mad?

MEENIE. He thrashed your nephew once for being insolent to me. Go and ask him how Hendrick pays my debts; and then when you speak to me you'll mind your stops.

DERRICK. (*To* GRETCHEN.) Oh, you shall pay for this!

GRETCHEN. No, Derrick, indeed, indeed I have not urged her to this! O, Meenie, do not speak so to him; for my sake forbear!

MEENIE. For your sake, yes, dear mother. I forgot that he could revenge himself on you.

DERRICK. As for your sailor lover, Hendrick Vedder, I've got news of him at last. His ship, the *Mayflower,* was lost three years ago, off Cape Horn.

MEENIE. No, no. Not lost?

DERRICK. If you doubt it, there's the *Shipping Gazette,* in on my office table. You can satisfy yourself that your sailor bully has gone to the bottom.

GRETCHEN. Oh, sir, do not convey the news to her so cruelly.

DERRICK. That's it. Because I don't sneak and trick and lie about it, I'm cruel. The man's dead, has been dead and gone these two years or more. The time of mourning is over. Am I going to be nice about it this time of day?

MEENIE. Then all my hope is gone, gone forever!

DERRICK. So much the better for you Hendrick's whole fortune was invested in that ship. So there's an end of him and your expectations. Now you are free, and a beggar. My nephew has a fancy for you. He will have a share of my business now, and my money when —when I die.

GRETCHEN. Do not ask her to decide now!

DERRICK. Why not? If she expects to make a better bargain by holding off, she's mistaken.

GRETCHEN. How can you expect her to think of a husband at this moment?

DERRICK. Don't I tell you the other one is dead these two years?

GRETCHEN. (*Leading* MEENIE *away.*) Come, my child. Leave her to me, sir; I will try and persuade her.

DERRICK. Take care that you do; for if she don't consent to accept my offer, she shall pack bag and baggage out of this house. Aye, this very day! Not a penny, not a stitch of clothes but what she has on her back, shall she have! Oh, I've had to deal with obstinate women before now, and I've taken them down before I've done with them. You know who I mean? Do you know who I mean? Stop. *Answer me! Do you know who I mean?*

GRETCHEN. (*Submissively.*) Yes, sir.

DERRICK. Then why did n't you say so before? Sulky, I suppose. There, you may be off. (*Exeunt.*)

SCENE 3. *The village of Falling Waters, which has grown to be a smart and flourishing town, but whose chief features remain unchanged.*

To the left, as of yore, is the inn, bearing scarcely any mark of the lapse of time, save that the sign of George III has been replaced by a portrait of George Washington. To the right, where RIP'S *cottage used to stand, nothing remains, however, but the blackened and crumbling ruins of a chimney. A table and chairs stand in front of the inn porch.*

Into this familiar scene RIP *makes his entrance, but not as before,—in glee, with children clinging about him. Faint, weak, and weary, he stumbles along, followed by a jeering, hooting mob of villagers; while the children hide from him in fear, behind their elders. His eyes look dazed and uncomprehending, and he catches at the back of a chair as if in need of physical as well as mental support.*

KATCHEN. (*As* RIP *enters.*) Why, what queer looking creature is this, that all the boys are playing—

SETH. Why, he looks as though he 's been dead for fifty years, and dug up again!

RIP. My friends, *Kanst du Deutsch sprechen?*

FIRST VILLAGER. I say, old fellow, you ain't seen anything of an old butter-tub with no kiver[1] on, no place about here, have you?

RIP. (*Bewildered, but with simplicity.*) What is that? I don't know who that is.

SECOND VILLAGER. I say, old man, who 's your barber?

(*The crowd laughs, and goes off repeating, "Who's your barber?" Some of the children remain to stare at* RIP; *but when he holds out his hand to them, they, too, run off frightened.*)

RIP. Who 's my barber; what dey mean by dat? (*Noticing his beard.*) Why is that on me? I did n't see that before. My beard and hair is so long and white. Gretchen won't know me with that, when she gets me home. (*Looking towards the cottage.*) Why, the home 's gone away!

(RIP *becomes more and more puzzled like a man in a dream who sees unfamiliar things amid familiar surroundings, and cannot make out what has happened; and as in a dream a man preserves his individuality, so* RIP *stumbles along through his bewilderment, exhibiting flashes of his old humour, wit, and native shrewdness. But with all this he never laughs.*)

SETH. I say, old man, had n't you better go home and get shaved?

RIP. (*Looking about for the voice.*) What?

SETH. Here, this way. Had n't you better go home and get shaved?

RIP. My wife will shave me when she gets me home. Is this the village of "Falling Waters" where we was?

SETH. Yes.

RIP. (*Still more puzzled, not knowing his face.*) Do you live here?

SETH. Well, rather. I was born here.

RIP. (*Reflectively.*) Then you live here?

SETH. Well, rather; of course I do.

RIP. (*Feeling that he has hold of something certain.*) Do you know where I live?

SETH. No; but I should say you belong to Noah's Ark.

RIP. (*Putting his hand to his ear.*) That I belong mit vas?

SETH. Noah's Ark.

RIP. (*Very much hurt.*) Why will you say such thing like that? (*Then, with a flash of humour, and drawing his beard slowly through his fingers.*) Well, look like it, don't I? (*Beginning all over again to feel for his clue.*) My friend, did you never hear of a man in this place whose name was Rip Van Winkle?

SETH. Rip Van Winkle, the laziest, drunken vagabond in the country?

RIP. (*Somewhat taken aback by this description, but obliged to concur in it.*) Yah, that is the one; there is no mistaking him, eh?

SETH. I know all about him.

RIP. (*Hopefully.*) Do you?

SETH. Yes.

RIP. (*Quite eagerly.*) Well, if you know all about him; well, what has become of him?

SETH. What has become of him? Why, bless your soul, he 's been dead these twenty years!

RIP. (*Looking at* SETH.) Then I am dead, I suppose. So Rip Van Winkle was dead, eh?

SETH. Yes; and buried.

RIP. (*Humorously.*) I 'm sorry for that; for he was a good fellow, so he was.

[1] Cover.

SETH. (*Aside.*) There appears to be something queer about this old chap; I wonder who he is. (*Rising and taking chair over to* RIP.) There, old gentleman, be seated.

RIP. (*Seating himself with great difficulty, assisted by* SETH.) Oh, thank you; every time I move a new way, I get another pain. My friend, where is the house what you live in?

SETH. (*Pointing at inn.*) There.

RIP. Did you live there yesterday?

SETH. Well, rather.

RIP. No, it is Nick Vedder what live in that house. Where is Nick Vedder?

SETH. Does he? Then I wish he 'd pay the rent for it. Why, Nick Vedder has been dead these fifteen years.

RIP. Did you know Jacob Stein, what was with him?

SETH. No; but I 've heard of him. He was one of the same sort as Rip and Nick.

RIP. Yes, them fellows was all pretty much alike.

SETH. Well, he went off the hooks a short time after Rip.

RIP. Where has he gone?

SETH. Off the hooks.

RIP. What is that, when they go off the hooks?

SETH. Why, he died.

RIP. (*With an air of hopelessness.*) Is there anybody alive here at all? (*Then, with a sudden revulsion of feeling, convinced of the impossibility of what he hears.*) That man is drunk what talks to me.

SETH. Ah, they were a jolly set, I reckon.

RIP. Oh, they was. I knowed them all.

SETH. Did you?

RIP. Yes, I know Jacob Stein, and Nick Vedder, and Rip Van Winkle, and the whole of them. (*A new idea strikes him, and he beckons to* SETH, *whom he asks, very earnestly.*) Oh, my friend, come and see here. Did you know Schneider?

SETH. Schneider! Schneider! No, I never heard of him.

RIP. (*Simply.*) He was a dog. I thought you might know him. Well, if dat is so, what has become of my child Meenie, and my wife Gretchen? Are they gone, too? (*Turning to look at the ruins of the house.*) Yah, even the house is dead.

SETH. Poor, old chap! He seems quite cast down at the loss of his friends. I 'll step in and get a drop of something to cheer him up. (*Exit.*)

RIP. (*Puzzling it out with himself.*) I can't make it out how it all was; because if this here is me, what is here now, and Rip Van Winkle is dead, then who am I? That is what I would like to know. Yesterday, everybody was here; and now they was all gone. (*Very forlorn.*)

(*Re-enter* SETH, *followed by the villagers.*)

SETH. (*Offering* RIP *the cup.*) There, old gent, there 's a drop of something to cheer you up.

RIP. (*Shaking hands with* SETH *and* KATCHEN.) Oh, thank you. I—I—I swore off; but this is the first time what I see you. I won't count this one. (*His voice breaks.*) My friend, you have been very kind to me. Here is your good health, and your family's, and may they all live long and prosper!

SETH. I say, wife, ain't he a curiosity fit for a show?

RIP. (*Aside.*) That gives me courage to ask these people anodder question. (*He begins with difficulty.*) My friend, I don't know whether you knowed it or not, but there was a child of Rip,—Meenie her name was.

SETH. Oh, yes; that 's all right.

RIP. (*With great emotion, leaning forward.*) She is not gone? She is not dead? No, no!

SETH. No; she is alive.

RIP. (*Sinking back with relief.*) Meenie is alive. It 's all right now,—all right now.

SETH. She 's the prettiest girl in the village.

RIP. I know dat.

SETH. But if she wastes her time waiting on Hendrick Vedder, she 'll be a middle-aged woman before long.

RIP. (*Incredulously.*) She 's a little child, only six years old.

SETH. Six-and-twenty, you mean.

RIP. (*Thinking they are making fun of him.*) She 's a little child no bigger than that. Don't bodder me; I don't like that.

SETH. Why, she 's as big as her mother.

RIP. (*Very much surprised that* SETH *knows* GRETCHEN.) What, Gretchen?

SETH. Yes, Gretchen.

RIP. Is n't Gretchen dead?

SETH. No. She 's alive.

RIP. (*With mixed emotions.*) Gretchen is alive, eh! Gretchen 's alive!

SETH. Yes; and married again.

RIP. (*Fiercely.*) How would she do such a thing like that?

SETH. Why, easy enough. After Rip died, she was a widow, was n't she?

RIP. Oh, yes. I forgot about Rip's being dead. Well, and then?

SETH. Well, then Derrick made love to her.

RIP. (*Surprised, and almost amused.*) What for Derrick? Not Derrick Von Beekman?

SETH. Yes, Derrick Von Beekman.

RIP. (*Still more interested.*) Well, and then?

SETH. Well, then her affairs went bad; and at last she married him.

RIP. (*Turning it over in his mind.*) Has Derrick married Gretchen?

SETH. Yes.

RIP. (*With a flash of his old humour, but still with no laughter.*) Well, I did n't think he would come to any good; I never did. So she cotched Derrick, eh? Poor Derrick!

SETH. Yes.

RIP. Well, here 's their good health, and their family's, and may they all live long and prosper! (*Drinks.*)

SETH. Now, old gent, had n't you better be going home, wherever that is?

RIP. (*With conviction.*) Where my home was? Here 's where it is.

SETH. What, here in this village? Now do you think we 're going to keep all the half-witted strays that choose to come along here? No; be off with you. Why, it 's a shame that those you belong to should allow such an old tramp as you to float around here.

VILLAGERS. (*Roughly, and trying to push him along.*) Yes; away with him!

RIP. (*Frightened, and pleading with them.*) Are you going to drive me away into the hills again?

FIRST VILLAGER. Yes; away with him! He 's an old tramp.

(*Enter* HENDRICK, *with stick and bundle, followed by some of the women of the village.*)

VILLAGERS. Away with him!

HENDRICK. (*Throwing down bundle.*) Avast there, mates. Where are you towing that old hulk to? What, you won't? (*Pushing crowd aside, and going forward.*) Where are you towing that old hulk to?

SETH. Who are you?

HENDRICK. I 'm a man, every inch of me; and if you doubt it, I 'll undertake to remove the suspicions from any two of you in five minutes. Ain't you ashamed of yourselves? Don't you see the poor old creature has but half his wits?

SETH. Well, this is no asylum for worn out idiots.

VILLAGERS. (*Coming forward.*) No, it ain't!

HENDRICK. Ain't it?

OMNES. No, it ain't.

HENDRICK. Then I 'll make it a hospital for broken heads if you stand there much longer. Clear the decks, you lubberly swabs! (*Drives them aside. Turns to* RIP, *who stands bewildered.*) What is the cause of all this?

RIP. (*Helplessly.*) I don't know, do you?

HENDRICK. (*To villagers.*) Do any of you know him?

FIRST VILLAGER. No; he appears to be a stranger.

HENDRICK. (*To* RIP.) You seem bewildered. Can I help you?

RIP. (*Feebly.*) Just tell me where I live.

HENDRICK. And don't you know?

RIP. No; I don't.

HENDRICK. Why, what 's your name?

RIP. (*Almost childishly.*) I don't know; but I believe I know vat it used to be. My name, it used to be Rip Van Winkle.

VILLAGERS. (*In astonishment.*) Rip Van Winkle?

HENDRICK. Rip Van Winkle? Impossible!

RIP. (*Pathetically feeble, and old.*) Well, I would n't swear to it myself. I tell you how it was: Last night, I don't know about the time, I went away up into the mountains, and while I was there I met a queer kind o' man, and we got drinkin'; and I guess I got pretty drunk. And then I went to sleep; and when I woke up this morning, I was dead. (*All laugh.*)

HENDRICK. Poor old fellow; he 's crazy. Rip Van Winkle has been dead these twenty years. I knew him when I was a child.

RIP. (*Clutching at a faint hope.*) You don't know me?

HENDRICK. No; nor anybody else here, it seems.

(*The villagers, finding that there is to be no amusement for them, straggle off to their occupations.*)

SETH. (*As he goes into the inn.*) Why, wife, he 's as cracked as our old teapot.

RIP. (*With simple pathos.*) Are we so soon forgot when we are gone? No one remembers Rip Van Winkle.

HENDRICK. Come, cheer up, my old hearty, and you shall share my breakfast. (*Assists* RIP *to sit at the table.* RIP *has fallen into a dream again. To* KATCHEN.) Bring us enough for three, and of your best.

KATCHEN. That I will. (*Exit into inn.*)

HENDRICK. So here I am, home again. And yonder 's the very spot where, five years ago, I parted from Meenie.

RIP. (*Roused by the name.*) What, Meenie Van Winkle?

HENDRICK. And she promised to remain true to Hendrick Vedder.

RIP. Oh, yah; that was Nick Vedder's son.

HENDRICK. (*Turning to* RIP.) That 's me.

RIP. (*Resentfully.*) That was you! You think I 'm a fool? He 's a little child, no bigger than that,—the one I mean.

HENDRICK. How mad he is!

(*Enter* KATCHEN *from inn with tray, on which is laid a breakfast. She puts it on table, and exits into inn.*)

There, that 's right. Stow your old locker full while I take a cruise around yonder house, where, five years ago, I left the dearest bit of human nature that was ever put together. I 'll be back directly. Who comes here? It 's surely Derrick and his wife. Egad, I 'm in luck; for now the old birds are out, Meenie will surely be alone. I 'll take advantage of the coast being clear, and steer into harbour alongside. (*Exit.*)

(*Enter* DERRICK, *followed by* GRETCHEN.)

DERRICK. So you have come to that conclusion, have you?

GRETCHEN. I cannot accept this sacrifice.

RIP. (*Starting from his reverie, and turning to look at her.*) Why, that is Gretchen's voice. (*As he recognizes her, and sees how aged she is.*) My, my! Is that my wife?

DERRICK. Oh, you can't accept! Won't you kindly allow me a word on the subject?

RIP. (*Aside, humorously.*) No, indeed, she will not. Now, my friend, you are going to cotch it.

GRETCHEN. There is a limit even to my patience. Don't drive me to it.

RIP. (*Aside, drolly.*) Take care, my friend; take care.

DERRICK. Look you, woman; Meenie has consented to marry my nephew. She has pledged her word to do so on condition that I settle an annuity on you.

GRETCHEN. I won't allow my child to break her heart.

DERRICK. You won't allow? Dare to raise your voice, dare but to speak except as I command you, you shall repent it to the last hour of your life.

RIP. (*Expectantly.*) Now she 'll knock him down, flat as a flounder.

DERRICK. (*Sneeringly.*) You won't allow? This is something new. Who are you; do you think you are dealing with your first husband?

GRETCHEN. Alas, no; I wish I was.

RIP. (*Lost in wonderment.*) My, my, if Rip was alive, he never would have believed it!

DERRICK. So you thought to get the upper hand of me, when you married me; did n't you?

GRETCHEN. I thought to get a home for my little girl—shelter, and food; want drove me to your door, and I married you for a meal's victuals for my sick child.

DERRICK. So you came to me as if I was a poor-house, eh? Then you can't complain of the treatment you received. You sacrificed yourself for Meenie, and the least she can do now, is to do the same for you. In an hour, the deeds will be ready. Now, just you take care that no insolent interference of yours spoils my plans; do you hear?

GRETCHEN. Yes, sir.

DERRICK. Why can't you be kind and affectionate to her, as I am to you. There, go and blubber over her; that 's your way. You are always pretending to be miserable.

GRETCHEN. Alas, no sir! I am always pretending to be happy.

DERRICK. Don't cry. I won't have it; come now, none of that. If you come home today with red eyes, and streaky cheeks, I 'll give you something to cry for; now you know what 's for supper. (*Exit.*)

RIP. (*Still amazed.*) Well, if I had n't seen it, I never would have believed it!

GRETCHEN. (*Absorbed in her grief.*) Oh, wretch that I am, I must consent, or that man will surely thrust her out of doors to starve, to beg, and to become—

(*Seeing* RIP.) Yes, to become a thing of rags and misery, like that poor soul.

RIP. She always drived the beggars away; I suppose I must go.

(*Getting up, and starting to go.*)

GRETCHEN. (*Taking penny from her pocket.*) Here, my poor man, take this. It is only a penny; but take it, and may God bless you, poor wanderer, so old, so helpless. Why do you come to this strange place, so far from home?

RIP. (*Keeping his face turned away from her.*) She don't know me; she don't know me!

GRETCHEN. Are you alone in the world?

RIP. (*Trying to bring himself to look directly at* GRETCHEN.) My wife asks me if I'm alone.

GRETCHEN. Come with me. How feeble he is; there, lean on me. Come to yonder house, and there you shall rest your limbs by the fire.

(GRETCHEN *takes his arm, and puts it in her own. As they move towards her house,* RIP *stops, and, with an effort, turns and looks her full in the face, with a penetrating gaze, as if imploring recognition, but there is none; and, sadly shaking his head, he shrinks into himself, and allows her to lead him tottering off.*)

SCENE 4. *The same room in* DERRICK'S *home as in Scene 2.*

(*Enter* DERRICK.)

DERRICK. I don't know what women were invented for, except to make a man's life miserable. I can get a useful, hard-working woman to keep my house clean, and order my dinner for me, for half that weak, snivelling creature costs me.

(*Enter* COCKLES.)

COCKLES. Well, uncle, what news; will she have me?

DERRICK. Leave it to me; she must, she shall.

COCKLES. If she holds out, what are we to do? It was all very well, you marrying Rip's widow, that choked off all inquiry into his affairs; but here's Meenie, Rip's heiress, who rightly owns all this property; if we don't secure her, we're not safe.

DERRICK. You've got rid of Hendrick Vedder; that's one obstacle removed.

COCKLES. I'm not so sure about that. His ship was wrecked on a lonely coast; but some of the crew may have, unfortunately, been saved.

DERRICK. If he turns up after you're married, what need you care?

COCKLES. I'd like nothing better; I'd like to see his face when he saw my arm around his sweetheart—my wife. But if he turns up before our marriage—

DERRICK. I must put the screw on somewhere.

COCKLES. I'll tell you, Meenie will do anything for her mother's sake. Now you are always threatening to turn her out, as she turned out Rip. That's the tender place. Meenie fears more for her mother, than she cares for herself.

DERRICK. Well, what am I to do?

COCKLES. Make Gretchen independent of you; settle the little fortune on her, that you are always talking about doing, but never keeping your word. The girl will sell herself to secure her mother's happiness.

DERRICK. And it would be a cheap riddance for me. I was just talking about it to Gretchen this morning. You shall have the girl; but I hope you are not going to marry her out of any weak feeling of love. You're not going to let her make a fool of you by and by?

COCKLES. I never cared for her until she was impudent to me, and got that sailor lover of hers to thrash me; and then I began to feel a hunger for her I never felt before.

DERRICK. That's just the way I felt for Gretchen.

COCKLES. 'T ain't revenge that I feel; it's enterprise. I want to overcome a difficulty.

DERRICK. (*Chuckling.*) And so you shall. Come, we'll put your scheme in train at once; and let this be a warning to you hereafter, never marry another man's widow.

COCKLES. No, uncle; I'll take a leaf out of your book, and let it be a warning to her.

(*Exeunt.*)

SCENE 5. *A plain sitting-room in* DERRICK'S *house. A table stands in the centre with several chairs around it. There are cups, a jug, and a workbasket on the table. As the curtain rises,* MEENIE *is discovered seated by the table.*

MEENIE. Why should I repine? Did my mother hesitate to sacrifice her life to make a home for me? No; these tears are ungrateful, selfish.

(*The door at the back opens.*)

(GRETCHEN *enters, leading* RIP, *who seems very feeble and a little wild.*)

GRETCHEN. Come in and rest a while.

RIP. This your house, your home?

GRETCHEN. Yes. Meenie, Meenie, bring him a chair.

RIP. (*Turning aside so as to shield his face from* MEENIE.) Is that your daughter?

GRETCHEN. That is my daughter.

RIP. (*Looking timidly at* MEENIE, *as* GRETCHEN *helps him into a chair.*) I thought you was a child.

GRETCHEN. (*Crossing to go into another room, and speaking to* MEENIE, *who starts to follow her.*) Stay with him until I get some food to fill his wallet. Don't be frightened, child, he is only a simple, half-witted creature whose misery has touched my heart.

(*Exit.* MEENIE *takes her workbasket and starts to follow.*)

RIP. (*Holding out his hand to detain her, and speaking with hardly suppressed excitement.*) One moment, my dear. Come here, and let me look at you. (*Pathetically.*) Are you afraid? I won't hurt you. I only want to look at you; that is all. Won't you come? (MEENIE *puts down her workbasket; and* RIP *is relieved of his great fear that she might leave him. His excitement increases as he goes on in his struggle to make her recognize him.*) Yes, I thought you would. Oh, yah, that is Meenie! But you are grown! (MEENIE *smiles.*) But see the smile and the eyes! That is just the same Meenie. You are a woman, Meenie. Do you remember something of your father?

(*He looks at her eagerly and anxiously, as if on her answer hung his reason and his life.*)

MEENIE. I do. I do. Oh, I wish he was here now!

RIP. (*Half rising in his chair, in his excitement.*) Yah? But he is n't? No? No?

MEENIE. No; he 's dead. I remember him so well. No one ever loved him as I did.

RIP. No; nobody ever loved me like my child.

MEENIE. Never shall I forget his dear, good face. Tell me—

RIP. (*Eagerly and expectantly.*) Yah?—

MEENIE. Did you know him?

RIP. (*Confused by her question, and afraid to answer.*) Well—I thought I did. But I— When I say that here, in the village, the people all laugh at me.

MEENIE. He is wandering.

(*She starts to go.*)

RIP. (*Making a great effort of will, and resolved to put the question of his identity to the test.*) Don't go away from me. I want you to look at me now, and tell me if you have ever seen me before.

MEENIE. (*Surprised.*) No.

RIP. (*Holding out his arms to her.*) Try, my darlin', won't you?

MEENIE. (*Frightened.*) What do you mean? Why do you gaze so earnestly and fondly on me?

RIP. (*Rising from his chair, in trembling excitement, and approaching her.*) I am afraid to tell you, my dear, because if you say it is not true, it may be it would break my heart. But, Meenie, either I dream, or I am mad; but I am your father.

MEENIE. My father!

RIP. Yes; but hear me, my dear, and then you will know. (*Trying to be logical and calm, but labouring under great excitement.*) This village here is the village of Falling Waters. Well, that was my home. I had here in this place my wife, Gretchen, and my child Meenie—little Meenie— (*A long pause, during which he strives to reassemble his ideas and memories more accurately.*) and my dog Schneider. That 's all the family what I 've got. Try and remember me, dear, won't you? (*Pleadingly.*) I don't know when it was— This night there was a storm; and my wife drived me from my house; and I went away—I don't remember any more till I come back here now. And see, I get back now, and my wife is gone, and my home is gone. My home is gone, and my child—my child looks in my face, and don't know who I am!

MEENIE. (*Rushing into his arms.*) I do! Father!

RIP. (*Sobbing.*) Ah, my child! Somebody knows me now! Somebody knows me now!

MEENIE. But can it be possible?

RIP. Oh, yah; it is so, Meenie! (*With a pathetic return of his uncertainty.*)

Don't say it is not, or you will kill me if you do.

MEENIE. No. One by one your features come back to my memory. Your voice recalls that of my dear father, too. I cannot doubt; yet it is so strange.

RIP. Yah, but it is me, Meenie; it is me.

MEENIE. I am bewildered. Surely mother will know you.

RIP. (*Smiling.*) No, I don't believe she 'll know me.

MEENIE. She can best prove your identity. I will call her.

RIP. No. You call the dog Schneider. He 'll know me better than my wife.

(*They retire to a sofa in the background, where* RIP *sits with his arm around* MEENIE.[1])

(*Enter* DERRICK, *with documents.*)

DERRICK. What old vagabond is this?

(MEENIE *starts to resent insult.*)

RIP. Don't you say a word.

DERRICK. Here, give him a cold potato, and let him go. (*To* GRETCHEN, *who has entered, followed by* COCKLES. GRETCHEN *seats herself in the chair at the right of the table.*) Come you here, mistress. Here are the papers for the young couple to sign.

COCKLES. (*Aside.*) And the sooner, the better. Hush, Uncle, Hendrick is here.

DERRICK. Young Vedder? Then we must look sharp. (*To* GRETCHEN.) Come, fetch that girl of yours to sign this deed.

GRETCHEN. Never shall she put her name to that paper with my consent. Never.

DERRICK. Dare you oppose me in my own house? Dare you preach disobedience under my roof?

GRETCHEN. I dare do anything when my child's life 's at stake. No, a thousand times, no! You shall not make of her what you have of me. Starvation and death are better than such a life as I lead.

DERRICK. (*Raising cane.*) Don't provoke me.

GRETCHEN. (*Kneeling.*) Beat me, starve me. You can only kill me. After all, I deserve it. (*Rising.*) But Meenie has given her promise to Hendrick Vedder, and she shall not break her word.

COCKLES. (*Seated at right of table.*) But Hendrick Vedder is dead.

(*The door is flung open, and* HENDRICK *enters.*)

HENDRICK. That 's a lie! He 's alive!

GRETCHEN and MEENIE. (*Rushing to him.*) Alive!

HENDRICK. (*To* MEENIE.) I 've heard all about it. They made you believe that I was dead. (*To* DERRICK.) Only wait till I get through here. (*Embracing* MEENIE.) What a pleasure I 've got to come! (*To* DERRICK.) And what a thrashing I 've brought back for you two swabs.

DERRICK. (*Angrily.*) Am I to be bullied under my own roof by a beggarly sailor? Quit my house all of you. (*Seizes* GRETCHEN, *and drags her away from the crowd.*) As for you, woman, this is your work, and I 'll make you pay for it.

GRETCHEN. Hendrick, save me from him. He will kill me.

HENDRICK. Stand off!

DERRICK. (*Raising cane.*) No; she is my wife, mine.

GRETCHEN. Heaven help me, I am!

(RIP *has risen from the sofa, and come forward, and leans against the centre of the table, with one hand in his game-bag. He is fully awake now, and has recovered all his old shrewdness.*)

RIP. Stop. I am not so sure about that. If that is so, then what has become of Rip Van Winkle?

COCKLES. He 's dead.

RIP. That 's another lie. He 's no more dead than Hendrick Vedder. Derrick Von Beekman, you say this house and land was yours?

DERRICK. Yes.

RIP. Where and what is the paper what you wanted Rip Van Winkle to sign when he was drunk, but sober enough not to do it? (*Taking an old paper out of game-bag, and turning to* HENDRICK.) Have you forgot how to read?

[1] In reply to a question why "Rip" should sit with his arm around "Meenie," during the next scene, when the other persons in the drama are still present, and are still ignorant of his identity, Mr. Jefferson said: "The other persons are occupied with their own affairs, and are not supposed to see this. It is natural that 'Rip' should embrace his daughter whom he has just found, but the others are not supposed to see this. It is like a side speech on a stage. I went to a Chinese theatre once, and after the Chinese lady got through with her song, they brought her a glass of gin; she turned her back to the audience, and drank it, as much as to say, 'That's not in the play.' We are dealing with the impossible all the time on the stage; and we have got to make it appear possible. Dramatically, things may often be right, when, realistically, they are wrong. What we do is often the result of averaging the thing, determining how far good taste will admit of an error, you see; like the discord in music, —not good in itself, but good in its place."

HENDRICK. No.

RIP. Then you read that.

(HENDRICK *takes the document from* RIP, *and looks it over.*)

DERRICK. What does this mad old vagabond mean to say?

RIP. I mean, that is my wife, Gretchen Van Winkle.

GRETCHEN. (*Rushing to* RIP.) Rip! Rip!

COCKLES. I say, uncle, are you going to stand that? That old impostor is going it under your nose in fine style.

DERRICK. I 'm dumb with rage. (*To the villagers, who have come crowding in.*) Out of my house, all of you! Begone, you old tramp!

HENDRICK. Stay where you are. (*To* DERRICK.) This house don't belong to you. Not an acre of land, not a brick in the town is yours. They have never ceased to belong to Rip Van Winkle; and this document proves it.

DERRICK. 'T is false. That paper is a forgery.

HENDRICK. Oh, no, it is not; for I read it to Rip twenty years ago.

RIP. Clever boy! Clever boy! Dat 's the reason I did n't sign it then, Derrick.

DERRICK. (*Approaching* HENDRICK.) And do you think I 'm fool enough to give up my property in this way?

HENDRICK. No. You 're fool enough to hang on to it, until we make you refund to Rip every shilling over and above the paltry sum you loaned him upon it. Now, if you are wise, you 'll take a hint. There 's the door. Go! And never let us see your face again.

RIP. Yah; give him a cold potato, and let him go.

(*Exit* DERRICK *in a great rage. All the villagers laugh at him.*) HENDRICK *follows him to the door.*)

COCKLES. (*Kneeling to* MEENIE.) O, Meenie! Meenie!

HENDRICK. (*Coming down, and taking him by the ear.*) I 'll Meenie you!

(*Takes him and pushes him out. All the villagers laugh.* MEENIE *gives* RIP *a chair.*)

GRETCHEN. (*Kneeling by the side of* RIP.) O, Rip! I drove you from your home; but do not desert me again. I 'll never speak an unkind word to you, and you shall never see a frown on my face. And Rip—

RIP. Yah.

GRETCHEN. You may stay out all night, if you like.

RIP. (*Leaning back in his chair.*) No, thank you. I had enough of that.

GRETCHEN. And, Rip, you can get tight as often as you please.

RIP. (*Taking bottle, and filling the cup from it.*) No; I don't touch another drop.

MEENIE. (*Kneeling by the other side of* RIP.) Oh, yes, you will, father. For see, here are all the neighbours come to welcome you home.

(GRETCHEN *offers* RIP *the cup.*)

RIP. (*With all his old kindliness and hospitality.*) Well, bring in all the children, and the neighbours, and the dogs, and— (*Seeing the cup which* GRETCHEN *is offering to him.*) I swore off, you know. Well, I won't count this one; for this will go down with a prayer. I will take my cup and pipe and tell my strange story to all my friends. Here is my child Meenie, and my wife Gretchen, and my boy Hendrick. I 'll drink all your good health, and I 'll drink your good health, and your families', and may they all live long and prosper!

CURTAIN.

HAZEL KIRKE

A PLAY IN FOUR ACTS

BY

Steele MacKaye

Published, 1916.

HAZEL KIRKE

Hazel Kirke represents the domestic drama of the late seventies, and the work of a singularly interesting pioneer in the dramatic and theatrical history of this country. (James) Steele MacKaye was born June 6, 1842, at Fort Porter, in Buffalo, New York. His father, Colonel James M. MacKaye, a prominent lawyer and art connoisseur, was an abolitionist and a friend of Garrison, Emerson, and Lincoln. As a lad, Steele MacKaye studied art first at Newport under William Hunt in 1858 and 1859 and later in Paris in the Ecole des Beaux Arts and under Gérome, Coûture, and others. The Civil War brought him back to this country and he served for eighteen months, in the Seventh Regiment of New York and then in Colonel Burney's regiment, where he had the rank of Major. Illness compelling his retirement, he went again to Paris, and here, while executing commissions as an expert buyer of paintings, he became interested in photo-sculpture and afterwards introduced it into this country. On his return to Paris in 1869 he met François Delsarte and became his disciple in his classes in expression. The war of 1870 broke up this occupation and he returned to America where by lecturing on the principles of Delsarte, he secured funds with which he aided his master who had been ruined by the war. His initial lecture given in Boston, March 21, 1871, marks an epoch in our theatrical history, since his gospel was that of quiet natural force in expression as opposed to the artificial, over-emphatic style of the day. To express these ideas further he appeared on the stage in New York at the St. James Theatre, January 8, 1872, in his adaptation of Washington Allston's novel *Monaldi,* in which Francis Durivage was his collaborator. His success was real in all but financial return, and worn out with his first efforts as a manager he returned to Paris, studying and acting in French at the Conservatoire, under Régnier, where he played "Hamlet" among other parts and then going to England, where he became acquainted with Charles Reade and Tom Taylor. Under the latter's management, he acted "Hamlet" from May 3, 1873, to August of the same year in London and the provinces. After that, except for occasional benefits he acted only in his own plays, his most important parts being "Dunstan Kirke," "Arthur Carringford" and "Aaron Rodney" in *Hazel Kirke,* "Paul Kauvar" and "Duroc" in *Paul Kauvar,* and "John Fleming" in *Won at Last.*

Steele MacKaye's work as a teacher was of great significance. He founded and conducted four schools of expression, the most important being the Lyceum Theatre School in New York which began in 1884. This school, through Mac

Kaye's association with the Frohmans and Mr. David Belasco, had a strong influence on the future of the stage, while his direct influence on his many pupils is hard properly to estimate. As an organizer and stage manager he had to his credit two theatres, numerous theatrical companies, and the Spectatorium at Chicago in 1893. He built the Madison Square Theatre and the Lyceum Theatre in New York, modeling the former on the Théâtre Français, and hoping to bring together a permanent company of artists. He planned also to pay properly the dramatists who were to write plays for his company. Yet, so careless was he in financial dealings, that his contract with the capitalists who controlled the theatre gave him but a salary of $5,000 yearly and he shared in none of the profits of *Hazel Kirke,* which amounted to $200,000 in two years. His final achievement as an organizer and director was the Spectatorium in Chicago in connection with the World's Fair in 1893, a great project which failed owing to the financial crisis of that summer. In this immense auditorium he was planning to produce *The World Finder,* a "Spectatorio" based on the Columbus story. He died February 25, 1894, having lived to see some of his ideas vindicated on a smaller scale in the production of a working model of the original plan, known as the Scenitorium, on February 5, 1894.

As a dramatist, Steele MacKaye represents the transition from the older theatrical tradition to the newer realism. His work was not by any means free from the older devices, but there is a decided advance in the naturalness of the characters and in the quietude of expression. His acted plays were as follows:

Monaldi, with Francis Durivage, first produced at the St. James Theatre, New York, January 8, 1872; *Marriage,* adapted from the French of Octave Feuillet's *Julie,* first produced at the St. James Theatre, New York, February 12, 1872; *Arkwright's Wife,* with Tom Taylor, first produced at the Theatre Royal, Leeds, England, July 7, 1873; *Rose Michel,* based on the French of Ernest Blum, produced for the first time at the Union Square Theatre, New York, November 23, 1875; *Queen and Woman,* with J. V. Pritchard, first produced at the Brooklyn Theatre, Brooklyn, New York, February 14, 1876; *Twins,* with A. C. Wheeler, produced for the first time at Wallack's Theatre, New York, April 12, 1876; *Won at Last,* produced at Wallack's Theatre, New York, December 10, 1877; *Through the Dark,* produced for the first time at the Fifth Avenue Theatre, New York, March 10, 1879; *An Iron Will,* produced for the first time at Low's Opera House, Providence, Rhode Island, October 27, 1879; its revision, *Hazel Kirke,* produced for the first time at the Madison Square Theatre, New York, February 4, 1880; *A Fool's Errand,* a dramatization of Judge Tourgee's novel, first produced at the Arch Street Theatre, Philadelphia, October 26, 1881; *Dakolar,* based on Georges Ohnet's *Le Maître de Forges,* first produced at the Lyceum Theatre, New York, April 6, 1885; *In Spite of All,* a play based on Sardou's *Andrea,* first produced at the Lyceum Theatre, New York, September 15, 1885; *Rienzi,* based on Bulwer Lytton's novel of the same name, first performed at Albaugh's Opera House, Washington, December 13, 1886; *The Drama of Civilization,* a pageant from W. F. Cody's "Wild West," first performed at the Madison Square Garden, New York, November 27, 1887; *Anarchy,* first performed at the Academy of Music, Buffalo, New York, May 30, 1887, and afterward revised as *Paul Kauvar,* at the Standard Theatre, New York, December 24, 1887; *A Noble Rogue,* first performed at the Chicago Opera House, Chicago, Illinois, July 3, 1888; *An Arrant Knave,* first produced at the Chicago Opera House, Chicago, Illinois, September 30, 1889; *Colonel Tom,* first produced at the Tremont Theatre, Boston, Mass., January 20, 1890; *Money Mad,* first produced at the Standard Theatre, New York, April 7, 1890 a revision of *Through the Dark* and *A Noble Rogue.*

Of these nineteen plays, none was an utter failure, nearly all were successes in their day, and three, *Hazel Kirke, Won at Last,* and *Paul Kauvar,* were played for years in stock. *Hazel Kirke* was written in the town of Dublin, New Hampshire, where Steele MacKaye spent the summers of 1878 and 1879. The heroine's name was suggested by the sprigs of hazel boughs nearby. It was first played under the title of *An Iron Will.* It had been the intention of its author to present it at the Madison Square Theatre, but owing to delay in the completion of that theatre it was first produced in Providence, Rhode Island, October 27, 1879, and taken on tour through Philadelphia, Baltimore, Washington, and other cities. On February 4, 1880, the play was put on at the Madison Square Theatre under the present name, and ran consecutively for about two years. It has continued on the stage for thirty years and in America has been acted at the same time by ten companies. It has been produced in England, Australia, Japan, Hawaii, and elsewhere. Its success has been due to its human quality, and to the fact that it appeals to the primary instincts. It was noteworthy in the absence of "the stage villain"—the incidents were developed naturally, and it points forward in our stage technique.

Hazel Kirke was privately printed in 1880 and has been reprinted by Samuel French. For permission to reprint the play, the editor is indebted to the courtesy of Mrs. Steele MacKaye who, with her son, Mr. Percy MacKaye, has carefully collated the two editions, and prepared a definitive text and furnished valuable biographical and critical information.

Note to Fourth Edition.

In *Epoch: The Life of Steele MacKaye,* 2 vols. (1927), Percy Mackaye has written an authoritative biography of Steele MacKaye, which is also a picture of the American theatre of his time.

The original cast of *Hazel Kirke,* as first produced at the Madison Square Theatre, New York City, February 4th, 1880

HAZEL KIRKE

A Comedy Drama in Four Acts, written expressly for this Theatre

by

STEELE MACKAYE

CAST OF CHARACTERS

HAZEL KIRKE...Miss Effie Ellsler
DOLLY DUTTON..Miss Gabrielle Du Sauld
EMILY CARRINGFORD [LADY TRAVERS]....................Mrs. Cecil Rush
MERCY KIRKE...Mrs. Thomas Whiffen
CLARA, a maid...Miss Annie Ellsler
ARTHUR CARRINGFORD [LORD TRAVERS]...............Mr. Eben Plympton
DUNSTAN KIRKE.......................................Mr. C. W. Couldock
AARON RODNEY..Mr. Dominick Murray
PITTACUS GREEN......................................Mr. Thomas Whiffen
METHUSELAH MIGGINS [called MET]...................Mr. Joseph Frankau
BARNEY O'FLYNN, a valet............................Mr. Edward Coleman
JOE, a miller...Mr. Fred P. Barton
DAN, a miller..Mr. George Grey
THOMAS, a servant..Mr. Henry Jones

Millers, Servants, etc.

ACT I.—Scene.—Exterior of Blackburn Mill.
ACT II.—Scene.—A boudoir in the villa of Fairy Grove.
ACT III.—Scene.—Kitchen of Blackburn Mill. Night.
ACT IV.—Scene.—Kitchen of Blackburn Mill. Morning.

100th performance, May 11, 1880.
300th performance November 29, 1880.
Withdrawn May 31, 1881, after 486 consecutive performances.

HAZEL KIRKE

ACT FIRST.

SCENE. *Exterior of* DUNSTAN KIRKE'S *mill. At right, exterior of house, opening into courtyard; at left, a large gateway. Walls to courtyard covered with vines; view of mill-wheel in background. Down right, a bench; down left, a rustic table and two chairs; a pile of empty bags up stage center; broom in porch; piano visible within. As curtain rises, Joe is discovered marking bags; miller boys cross behind the wall, with bags of grain on their shoulders.*

DUNSTAN. (*Inside.*) Now, then, Dan, you dolt—more bags! Be off, boys!

DAN. (*Appearing behind wall, to* JOE.) More bags—more bags for market.

JOE. Drat it. Give me time to mark 'em, can't ye?

DAN. Oh! I don't care how long ye take—but old man Kirke is gettin' into one of his tempers.

JOE. Oh! His tempers be hanged! I'm doin' my best—no man can do more. (MET. *is heard outside playing a pipe.*) There's that young ne'er-do-weel, Methusaleh Miggins, blowing that frightful pipe o' his again!

DAN. Aye, and he's always a-blowin' it. By the way, wherever did Maister Kirke find the creature?

JOE. He was left on Maister Kirke's hands by some help he had, who had the impudence to die, and leave this baby for maister to take care on. He growed up the mischievous booby ye see him—and nobody can do nothin' wi' him.

DAN. Except Mistress Hazel Kirke. She can manage him wi' a look.

DUNSTAN. (*Outside.*) Hi there! Are ye never coomin' wi' those bags?

DAN. There goes the miller. Hoorry, man! or we'll all be killed.

JOE. (*Handing bags to him.*) Here, take these and coom back for more.

DUNSTAN. (*Outside.*) Will ye bring those bags, ye lazy dolts?

DAN. (*Running off.*) Aye, aye—I'm coomin'. (*Exit.*)

(*Enter* MERCY.)

MERCY. (*Calls.*) Dolly! Dolly, child!

DOLLY. (*Inside.*) Aye, aye, aunt.

MERCY. Hoorry! Bring the bundles for market into the courtyard, lass.

(*Millers appear with bags on their shoulders.*)

DAN. (*Rushing in.*) Bags! More bags, Joe!

JOE. (*Handing bags.*) Here ye are, I'll bring the rest myself.

(*Takes up bags; passes through gateway behind wall, and disappears right.*)

MERCY. (*Impatiently.*) Dolly! Dolly, lass—what's keepin' ye?

DOLLY. (*Entering with bundles.*) Here I am, Aunt Mercy.

MERCY. Has thee got the homespun, lass?

DOLLY. Aye—here 't is, bundled and ready to go.

MERCY. That's a good child. Here, tie it up wi' the rest o' these.

DOLLY. (*Tying bundles.*) La, Aunt Mercy! Is Uncle Kirke going to take all these to market wi' him?

MERCY. Aye, girl—times be hard, and money must be had for Hazel's wedding-day.

DOLLY. Hazel's wedding day!

MERCY. Aye, child, that'll soon be now. Her father has decided that Hazel must marry Squire Rodney within three months.

DOLLY. Oh! How I hate that Squire Rodney!

MERCY. Hate him? What for, pray?

DOLLY. For stealing our Hazel away from her happiness.

MERCY. What dost mean, girl?

DOLLY. You're going to make Hazel marry Squire Rodney for gratitude, but it won't do, Aunt Mercy—Gratitude is not the stuff to make a happy marriage of.

MERCY. Peace, lass—peace!

DOLLY. La, Aunt Mercy! Thee'd say peace to the wicked one himself, if he were here.

MERCY. I think he be here indeed, Dolly—in thy temper.

DOLLY. Temper! Well, who has a better right to a temper:—my mother was thy husband's sister, and all the world knows that Dunstan Kirke has the worst temper in all Lancashire!

DUNSTAN (*Outside, in rage.*) Coom! Coom! off wi' ye—don't lollop around here all day! (*Millers cross as before, with bags, followed by* DUNSTAN.) Hoorry to market, and don't loaf, for I 'll be after ye wi' the young colt, as fast as ever I can.

(*He goes out after them behind the wall.*)

MERCY. Is everything here, Dolly?

DOLLY. Aye, all I had to get.

DUNSTAN. (*Outside, left.*) Here! here, I say! Stand round and make them things right. So—and—so and so—don't ye see?

DOLLY. Talk of tempers—listen to Uncle Kirke, raging like a maddened bull.

MET. (*Flying across.*) Hi! look out, he 's comin'! (*Exit.*)

DUNSTAN. (*Entering excitedly.*) Drat 'em! drat 'em, I say! They 're enough to make a divil o' a saint, so they are!

MERCY. (*Soothingly.*) There, there, dear heart, have patience, patience.

DUNSTAN. Patient! I am patient—patient as an angel.—Confound 'em. It 's taken me all day to get 'em off. (HAZEL *sings outside. As he listens,* DUNSTAN'S *anger passes away, and he sinks into a chair near the table.*) Ah! that does me good! that does me good! My Hazel 's a lass, bless her, to gladden a feyther's heart: as modest as a girl should be, and as fine-mannered and accomplished as any lady i' the land.

(*Enter* RODNEY, *left, with samples of grain.*)

MERCY. Yes, she 's well eddicated, now.

DUNSTAN. Thanks to Squire Rodney, God bless him. 'T was he got her the larnin'.

DOLLY. And he 'll be well paid for it too, when she 's his wife.

DUNSTAN. Weel, that 'll soon be now—that 'll soon be now.

(MERCY *and* DOLLY *go in the house.*)

RODNEY. (*Advancing.*) I 'm not so sure of that.

DUNSTAN. Ah! Maister Rodney, I do declare, here at last! An' what 's that ye 're not so sure on?

RODNEY. (*Sits at left of table.*) That Hazel will ever be my wife.

DUNSTAN. (*Seated at right.*) Not be thy wife! Why, man, what 's coom to thee, man, to say so strange a word? Did n't ye save me from ruin, and the whole mill from changin' hands, seven year ago, and did n't Hazel promise then to be your wife, and did n't ye send her off to school, that she might learn to be the lady o' Rodney Hall?

RODNEY. True, Dunstan, but she was only fourteen then, and I in my forties; but I forgot that when she came of age I 'd be fifty and growing old. There 's many a slip 'twixt the cup and the lip, ye know.

DUNSTAN. Why! whatever do ye mean, man?

RODNEY. Why, I mean accidents may happen, and a young girl's heart may change.

DUNSTAN. Oh! no, no!

RODNEY. Ever since you saved young Carringford from drowning, and brought him in here, I 've noticed a change in Hazel's manner to me. You don't look with my eyes, Dunstan, you don't see what I see.

DUNSTAN. And what dost see, sir?

RODNEY. I see a fine, handsome, brave young man lying ill and helpless; I see a lovely young girl waiting upon him, nursing him back to life; I see two young hearts looking at each other through young eyes; talking to each other with young tongues; touching each other with young hands, and—well, Dunstan, I know what this must come to soon.

DUNSTAN. Maister Rodney, there is a holy book, that my bairn reads to us every day. Dost think that she can ever forget that the book commands us to keep our faith?

RODNEY. Ah! Dunstan, when the heart speaks, all other voices are dumb.

DUNSTAN. (*Rising.*) A promise be a promise! (*Striking the table.*) If my child were to break her word, I 'd drive her out as I would a scorpion on my hearth. Everybody knows the metal I 'm made on. What I say, I 'll do. (*He strikes the table again.*) And I tell thee now, Aaron Rodney, that this day three months Hazel Kirke shall be thy wife.

HAZEL. (*Outside.*) Thanks, I 've found them—I 'll go myself.

RODNEY. (*Rising.*) Hush! That 's her voice, she 's coming! Not a word of my fears to her!

DUNSTAN. Oh! That 's all right.

HAZEL. (*Entering, porch, right, goes to* DUNSTAN.) Here, father, are some letters I want you to post. You won't forget?

DUNSTAN. Nothing that thee can ask, lass—not while thy face shines as bright wi' innocence as it does now! But look, child, there's Maister Rodney, child.

(*Enter* MERCY *and* DOLLY.)

HAZEL. Good-morning, Mr. Rodney. (*She gives her hand.*)

DUNSTAN. Nay, lass, don't mind us, give him a kiss—a good, hearty, honest girl's kiss.

HAZEL. (*Laughing.*) That's something I never refused him yet. (RODNEY *kisses her; she turns to* MERCY.) Now, mother, have you given father the list of things you want?

MERCY. Not yet, lass—sit down and write it for him.

(HAZEL *sits at table and writes.*)

DUNSTAN. (*To* RODNEY.) Well, now, what girl could have given a franker kiss than that?

RODNEY. Aye, Dunstan, 't was frank enough; 't was frank enough.

DUNSTAN. To be sure it was.

HAZEL. (*Going to* DUNSTAN.) Here, father, is the list of things for you to get.

DUNSTAN. A' reet, girl. Now, wife, where's the stuff for me to take to market?

(*All begin to load him with things.*)

DOLLY. Here's the rags and the hose.

MERCY. And here's the homespun.

RODNEY. And here are my samples of grain.

HAZEL. And here are my letters. Be sure you don't forget the list!

DUNSTAN. No, girl, I shan't forget anything. I am not the forgettin' kind. (*Going, stops and turns.*) Ah! I'm forgettin' one thing now, to ask after Maister Carringford. How is he this mornin', lass?

HAZEL. Better, I think.

DUNSTAN. Ah! he better be. He's been here more nor a month. He's a long time a-gettin' well.

HAZEL. But think how horribly he was hurt! (*Exit* RODNEY.)

DUNSTAN. Aye, but I've seen older bones sooner mended. It's time he were well and off to his work; this is no place for idle hands. Give him a hint, girl—and here, my darling, gi' me a partin' kiss. (*He kisses her.*) God be wi' ye, child, and keep ye always the blessin' that ye are. (*Exit.*)

HAZEL. (*Sitting.*) Ah! thank heaven! he cannot see the wickedness in my wretched, wretched heart.

JOE. (*Outside.*) Get out of this!

MET. (*Outside.*) Hi! Hold on! take that! (*A crash is heard.*)

HAZEL. (*Starting.*) What's that?

DOLLY. Oh! another row between Joe and Met.

HAZEL. Joe is always abusing poor Met. (*Cries are heard outside.*)

(MET *rushes in.*)

MET. (*Hiding behind* HAZEL.) Save me! save me!

(JOE *enters.*)

JOE. (*With a stick.*) Where is he? Let me get at him.

HAZEL. No, no, you shall not touch him.

JOE. (*In rage.*) I will, and no woman shall stop me!

MET. (*Squaring off.*) Come on, Joe! I'd rather fight than blow my pipe.

DOLLY. (*Laughing.*) Ha, ha! The boy has found a bit of pluck at last.

HAZEL. (*Soothingly.*) Let him alone. There, there, Joe, let him alone; no more of this—leave him to me, and I'll punish him for you.

MET. I'd rather be punished by you, missus, than petted by a' the rest.

HAZEL. Well, then, come with me.

MET. (*Suspiciously.*) Are ye goin' to Maister Carringford?

HAZEL. Why do you ask that?

MET. Because if ye are, I won't go.—I hate him!

HAZEL. Hate him? What for?

MET. Because you love him so.

HAZEL. (*Severely.*) How dare you say that?

MET. Because it's true.

HAZEL. (*With mock severity, extending her hand.*) Met, come with me this instant, sir.

MET. Where?

HAZEL. To pick some flowers.

MET. Oh! then I'll go, mistress—then I'll go. (*He takes her hand, turns at gate, bahs at* JOE, *and goes out with* HAZEL. JOE *starts after him.*)

DOLLY. (*Holding* JOE *back.*) Oh! never mind that fellow. Come, come, Joe—I want you to help me bring my things out here.—It's cooler working here than inside.

JOE. (*Going with her.*) All right, Miss

Dolly, show me the things you want. (*They go into the house.*)

(*Enter* BARNEY, *followed by* DAN.)

DAN. Here 's the house and this be the mill ye 're askin' after. (*Exit.*)

BARNEY. Thankee! thankee! So there 's the mill-dam, where my master was drowned about six weeks since.

DOLLY. (*Appears at the door with* JOE, *carrying table.*) Take care now, Joe—don't spill the potatoes.

BARNEY. (*Stepping aside.*) Some one coming; I 'll step aside and recognog the situation.

(DOLLY *and* JOE *place the table left.*)

DOLLY. There, now; that 's all I want of you. Go and look after Met.

JOE. (*Going.*) Look after Met? I 'd rather look after the fiend himself.

(*Exit.* BARNEY *comes forward and coughs.*)

DOLLY. (*Turns.*) Who 's this?

BARNEY. Only myself, Miss.

DOLLY. And who are you?

BARNEY. Barney O'Flynn—the lackey of my lord.

DOLLY. And who 's he?

BARNEY. One of your lodgers, I belave.

DOLLY. A lord lodging here! Ye 're wrong, man; this is no place for lords.

BARNEY. True enough, darlin', true enough, darlin'—but still my lord is here.

DOLLY. Will you give me the lie in my own house? Get out of this, ye unmannerly brute!

(*Raises broom and chases him.*)

BARNEY. Hould now! hould now! hould! sure, here 's his own direcshon in my own hand this minute. (*He shows a letter.*) Lord Travers, at Dunstan Kirke's mill, Blackburn, Lancashire—Is n't this Lancashire?

DOLLY. Yes.

BARNEY.. And is n't this the mill of Dunstan Kirke?

DOLLY. Yes.

(*She turns and slaps her broom at him.*)

BARNEY. Very well, thin, Lord Travers is here, just as sure as I 'm Barney O'Flynn, an' there 's the proof av it, a letter calling Master Arthur home to onst.

DOLLY. Arthur—Arthur Carringford!

BARNEY. Yes, of course, he 's Lord Travers, and my master.

DOLLY. Mr. Carringford a lord!

BARNEY. Of course he 's a lord—of course he 's a lord, and I 've been sent down from London to take him home, in a howl of a hurry too. Where is he?

DOLLY. There—(*pointing right*) in the house.

BARNEY. Oh! he is, is he? Now ain't you ashamed of yourself, and you were going to drive me out of this! (*Imitating her.*) "Will ye give me the lie in my own house?" Never mind, darlin', I forgive ye, I forgive—

DOLLY. (*Striking him with the broom.*) Get out o' this, ye fool! (*Exit* BARNEY, *with a howl into the house.*) Mr. Carringford a lord! And in love with Hazel too! Aye he is—I know he is—I can see it in his face every time he looks at her. Ah! if poor Hazel were only free, she might be Lady Travers, rich and grand! He has her heart already, aye, and except for Mr. Rodney, he 'd have her hand as well. (*Goes to table and begins to clean carrots.*) Ah! if I were Hazel, I know what I 'd do. I 'd marry the man I loved in spite of all the world. (GREEN *is heard singing outside "The King's Highway."*) Ah! who 's that fine young swell coming this way?

(GREEN *enters humming; sees her, stops, strikes an attitude, sings "My face is my fortune, sir, she said."* DOLLY *stares, amazed.*)

What sort of a creature is this?

(*Holding a carrot in her hand, she moves toward him.*)

GREEN. Stand where you are.
You 're the sweetest picture of surprise,
That ever yet has blessed my eyes!
Oh! 't is true, and by my soul I swear it!
(*Pointing to the wall.*) Will you permit me?

DOLLY. Permit ye what?

GREEN. To change the situation—thus. (*He leaps over the wall.*) Ha! ha!

DOLLY. Who are ye, sir?

GREEN. A hunter of heroes.

DOLLY. What brings you here?

GREEN. A tyrant called Curiosity.

DOLLY. La, the man is mad!

GREEN. No, I grieve to say I 'm not. I wish I were:—madmen are monsters, everything monstrous is fascinating, but I, alas! I 'm not fascinating, am I?

DOLLY. La, man! I don't know what ye are.

GREEN. You may not believe it, but I

once was born, a baby too! Oh! I tell you funny things have happened to me. At the early age of one minute, (DOLLY *starts*) I howled to see the world.

Luckily my father made
A handsome fortune in lemonade,
By aid of which aid, I am glad to say
I am enabled now to-day
To see the world and have my way;
That way, remark, is this:

(DOLLY, *slightly frightened, looks at* GREEN *in astonishment during this tirade.*)

GREEN. I go where I please, say what I please, and please where I can; do you understand?

DOLLY. Not a single word you say.

GREEN. That's just what I supposed. Then I will be plain with you: plain in fact; to be plain in feature is impossible. I was born—is that clear?

DOLLY. (*Keeps her eye on* GREEN, *wondering.*) Of course.

GREEN. And born queer.

DOLLY. That's clearer still.

GREEN.

That queerness born in me,
Now brings me here to thee—
For let me tell you here
That this is how I'm queer.

(DOLLY *starts back.*) A monster or a hero I adore; ordinary mortals I detest; they are too much like Pittacus Green.

DOLLY. And who is Pittacus Green?

GREEN. The humble and devoted slave now gazing in those lovely eyes. (*Seeing the carrot in her hand.*) Will you permit me to relieve you of the ponderous vegetable that cumbers these fair hands? Ah, yes! Thank you.

(*He takes it to the table.*)

DOLLY. And so you are Pittacus Green?

GREEN. That is my distinguished name: Pit-ta-cus Green, or, as I am called for short, Pitty Green, which is maddening! If it was Pitty Brown, Black, or Blue, but Pitty Green—it's so hanged appropriate. Of course everybody does pity Green. You may not believe it, but they say I'm cracked.

(*Very serious, he slowly crosses to right center.*)

DOLLY. (*Drawing back.*) I knew it.

GREEN. Don't be alarmed. It's lovely to be cracked!

DOLLY. Lovely to be cracked!

GREEN. Of course. Convince men that you are cracked, and they will let you do the oddest things. They'll smile instead of frown, and I, to gain a smile from lips like yours, again I'd play any game. Do you understand me now?

DOLLY. (*Laughing.*) I'd be a donkey if I didn't. I understand and like you, too, and (*frankly*) there's Dolly Dutton's hand to prove it.

GREEN. You may not believe it, but you're an angel! Dolly Dutton! So your name is Dolly Dutton? Delightful Dolly Dutton. D, D, D, indeed! You are an angel. (*Pointing to her hand.*) Will you permit me?

DOLLY. Anything that's honest.

(GREEN *attempts to kiss her hand. She snatches her hand away and he kisses his own hand.*)

GREEN. 'T is honest. Fair exchange is no robbery. Ah! I see! Consider me a beggar at your feet.

DOLLY. Now tell me truly—what it is that brings you here.

GREEN. As I said before, a monster or a hero I adore.

DOLLY. And do you expect to find a monster here?

GREEN. Yes, one in particular, Dunstan Kirke, the miller of Blackburn Mill. He is the monster that I mean, the rarest monster ever seen. A monster of goodness, who, during the last ten years, has saved from death by drowning at least forty souls, with their bodies attached to them.

DOLLY. And so you're here to see my surly old uncle, who saves other folks, perhaps, while he destroys his own daughter.

GREEN. Destroys his own daughter? Superb! Does he destroy her often? I mean is he taken so frequently? A charming old creature! Sit down. (*Politely bowing, showing chair.*) Make yourself at home; I do. Tell me all about him. (*He sits at the table.*)

DOLLY. (*Joining him at the table.*) Well, sir, you've heard of the many he's saved. Have you heard of the one he's sold?

GREEN. No! Someone sold? Delightful! Who was it?

DOLLY. The pride of this family, sir, my cousin, Hazel Kirke; she's the one that's sold.

GREEN. Oh! Is she? Indeed! poor

thing, I sympathize; I 've been sold myself. Who sold her?

DOLLY. Her own father, Dunstan Kirke, your hero!

GREEN. Dear me! Why did he do it?

DOLLY. Because he loves his old mill more than anything else in the world. Seven years ago the bank that held my uncle's savings broke, and the old man was about to lose the mill, when Aaron Rodney loaned him money without interest or security.

GREEN. He was a jolly old idiot! What was his little game?

DOLLY. When the mill was safe, Dunstan Kirke asked the 'Squire what he could do to prove his thankfulness.

GREEN. Oh! ho! I smell a rat.

DOLLY. "Sir," said the 'Squire, "you have a daughter whom I like; give me leave to send her off to school, have her taught, and then become my wife and the lady of Rodney Hall."

GREEN. Just so. That 's the rat I smelt. Ah! ha! precisely—Rodney goes to her, makes love to her, fills her mind with gaudy pictures, chromos, thromos, and tells her of the good his wealth will do for her and hers; and so she, a thoughtless child, makes a rash promise to an old scoundrel, which promise is sure to play the dev—Mephistopheles with them both.

DOLLY. Why, man, how did you know that?

GREEN. Quite simply; I guessed it. (*Rising slightly, he leans over the table.*)

DOLLY. Well, then, ye 're not so much of a fool as ye look.

GREEN. Bless you for those kind words! (*Drawing back.*) Tell me, what became of your cousin?

DOLLY. Seven years ago she was sent to school; six months ago she returned.

GREEN. Then she was awfully fond of old Rod, of course?

DOLLY. She 's proud and silent, sir, but I, who love her, read her heart, and I know that Aaron Rodney is not the man she loves.

GREEN. Egad! The situation inspires me! What would you say if I were to clear your Cousin Hazel of her bargain with the 'Squire?

DOLLY. (*Rises and goes toward the house.*) I 'd say ye were the best man that ever crossed the threshold of Blackburn Mill.

GREEN. (*Excited, follows her.*) That being the case, what would you give me to have it done?

DOLLY. Anything I 've got.

GREEN. Even your heart?

DOLLY. La, man! I have n't got any.

GREEN. Have n't you? Well, then, would you give this fashionable substitute?

DOLLY. Oh, yes, if ye 'd care to take it. (*Sticking out a dirty hand.*)

GREEN. (*Taking it.*) H'm! It 's a little mouldy, misty, mildewy, millery, the soil of honest labor, I mean. Yes, this is romance, and I 'm the Roman. I 'll be your best man; I 'll outwit old Rod or die.

DOLLY. But how, man? How?

GREEN. You may not believe it, but I once had a mother; funny things have happened to me. That mother, she never could wind a yarn without making a snarl, and I could never undo the snarl without telling a yarn.

DOLLY. What of that?

GREEN. I have great faith in the power of a yarn to undo a snarl. Now there 's a snarl in this family; give me the leave to tell yarns enough, and I 'll guarantee to undo the snarl. Ha! ha! ha! Why, bless me, it 's perfectly delightful! (*He paces up and down,* DOLLY *following him.*) I 'm tempted to play a new rôle, turn dramatist in real life! We 've only to manage a little to make the play what we please. There 's the stern father, Dunstan Kirke; the heavy villain, old Rod; the pretty victim, Hazel Kirke; the scheming cousin, that 's you; the good-natured idiotic busy-body,—

DOLLY. That 's you; and why do you stop?

GREEN. Confound it, there 's something lacking! We 'll imagine here 's our Andromeda chained to a rock, and about to be devoured by a dragoon—no, a dragon:—wanted, the hero, Perseus, to deliver her. Where shall we get a hero? As Byron says: "I want a hero; an uncommon want, when every month sends forth a new one."—that 's Don Juan. Egad! I have it! We 'll advertise. (ARTHUR *whistles outside.*) Hello! How 's this? Who 's that?

DOLLY. Only one of my uncle's patients.

GREEN. Who is he?

(*Enter* ARTHUR.)

DOLLY. Here he comes; find out for yourself.

GREEN. Fate, I thank thee! The conquering hero comes. (*He goes right.*)

ARTHUR. Ah, Miss Dolly! Have you seen my dog?

DOLLY. Perhaps he 's with Hazel. She went off with Met a little while ago. Shall I find her for you?

ARTHUR. You 're very kind; if it is n't too much trouble. I should be glad of a little of Miss Hazel's company, if she 's at leisure. You know I must soon leave this dear old place.

(*He sits at the table.*)

DOLLY. I 'll try to find her, sir.

(*Exit left center.*)

GREEN. (*Looks at* ARTHUR *and starts.*) Ye great gods of war!

ARTHUR. (*Noticing him for the first time.*) Ha! What idiot is this?

GREEN. It is, it is! By the bolts of Jove, it is!

ARTHUR. (*Coolly.*) Indeed! Is it?—what is?

GREEN. You is—am—you are—Either I 'm a cow, or this is Lord Travers!

ARTHUR. (*Rising angrily.*) Who is Lord Travers?

GREEN. You is—am—are. Look at me sharp. Don't you remember P. G.? Have you forgotten our tiger hunt in India? Ah! there was a monster worth meeting: he met you and treed you too. Can't you recall your old comrade of the jungle, Pittacus, the mouse that freed you, the lion? Why, it was the proudest shot of my life!

ARTHUR. (*Extending his hand.*) On my word! Is it possible—you here?

GREEN. Of course I am! (*Wringing* ARTHUR's *hand.*) And, bless my soul, how glad I am to see you.

ARTHUR. Hold on, stop; do you know what you are doing?

GREEN. What am I doing?

ARTHUR. The arm you are torturing is only half mended.

GREEN. Gracious! What do you mean?

ARTHUR. That this is a broken arm but slightly convalescent.

GREEN. (*Seizing a carrot from the table.*) Travers, I 'm a brute! Take that indigestible vegetable and crack my skull!

(*He offers the carrot.*)

ARTHUR. (*Sitting again.*) Thanks, dear boy, it 's cracked enough already.

GREEN. Yes, precisely; I see your vengeance is complete. (GREEN *keeps the carrot and seats himself.*)

ARTHUR. Now tell me how you found me out?

GREEN. Oh! Quite naturally! By accident, the usual way. How did you get here?

ARTHUR. Came to Lancashire to escape the tiresome nonsense of town life; went shooting with my dog, attempted to cross the stream by a tree that lay over it, just above the dam there. (*Points.*)

GREEN. The what?

ARTHUR. The dam.

GREEN. Oh! dam!

ARTHUR. Slipped like a fool, fell, broke my arm in falling and sank unconscious into the water.

GREEN. (*Breaking the carrot in two.*) Merciful powers!

ARTHUR. My dog sprang in and held me above the surface; Kirke, the miller, caught sight of us, and jumped in; pulled me out and lodged me here, where I 've had the best of care for six weeks.

GREEN. (*Holds up each half of the carrot, to represent the sold and the saved, and at end of his speech, places the small half on top of the other and holds it upright.*) Great fortune! I see it all. It 's the saved and the sold, side by side, beneath the same roof; she is the sold, and you are now the saved. Two hearts with but a single stock. Travers, my dear boy, you may not believe it, but there 's more than accident in this arrangement.

ARTHUR. Undoubtedly, but your exclamations are somewhat obscure.

GREEN. Look here, old man, let 's get to business. Time flies. I helped you when you were in a carrot—no, no—I mean a stew, a pickle; and now you must help me.

ARTHUR. With pleasure! How can I do it?

GREEN. By falling desperately in love.

ARTHUR. (*Laughing.*) Oh! Falling in love! Why, that 's your business; you were always falling in love.

GREEN. Of course, why not? "I love to live, and I live to love." As the poet says, "Come live with me and be my love."

ARTHUR. Eccentric dog! You always manage to make logic and delight agree.

GREEN. Ah! Travers, I 've met my fate at last!

ARTHUR. Nonsense! You were always meeting your fate. Who is it this time?

GREEN. Dolly Dutton, the miller's niece.

ARTHUR. You 'll find her rather a lively fate. I fancy.

GREEN. Precisely! I know I shall, that 's the way I like 'em. She 's a perfect monster.

ARTHUR. Monster?

GREEN. Yes, a monster of beauty and goodness; but come, I say again, will you do me a favor and fall in love?

ARTHUR. Certainly, with whom?

GREEN. With a friend of mine. Will you do it?

ARTHUR. Certainly. I find there 's nothing easier than to fall; I 've tried one element, I 've no fear to try another. With whom must I fall in love?

GREEN. An angel in a fix; Hazel Kirke, the miller's daughter.

ARTHUR. (*Sternly.*) Stop, sir; I shall not tolerate nonsense that touches her good name. Understand this at once.

GREEN. (*Staring.*) Capital! I 'm more than satisfied! I 'm ecstatic. You 're in love with her already.

ARTHUR. (*Rising angrily.*) Sir! (HAZEL *sings outside.* GREEN *crosses to right center.* ARTHUR *goes to the gate, starts, returns slowly and seats himself. At the end of the song he goes to* GREEN.) Green, Miss Kirke is coming. I 'm known here simply as Arthur Carringford; you must not betray my title; it would only raise a barrier between me and the golden hearts to whom I owe so much.

GREEN. (*Taking his hand.*) Travers, I honor your sentiments, and will respect your wish.

DOLLY. (*Appearing at gate.*) Here she is, Mr. Carringford.

(*Enter* HAZEL, *with a basket of flowers, followed by* MET.)

HAZEL. (*At gate, to* MET.) Now, Met, go to Mother Weedbury's cottage and cut some wood for the poor thing, and stop there till I come. I will be there to help her with the children this afternoon.

MET. All right, Missus, I 'll go; but mind it 's for you, not for the old woman. (*Exit.*)

HAZEL. Good-morning, Mr. Carringford.

ARTHUR. Good-morning, Miss Hazel, I 'm glad to have a glimpse of you at last.

MET. (*Appearing in gate.*) Hi! Missus, I say, may I go by the big woods?

HAZEL. No, Met, take the straight path.

GREEN. And follow your nose. (*Exit* MET.) I 'm afraid you 've given him a terrible task; if he follows his nose he will have a long journey before he gets to the end of it. Still, a brute with a long nose generally has some scents about him, ha, ha, ha! Do you see? you may not believe it, but that 's a joke. (HAZEL *notices him with surprise.*) Oh! Excuse me! (GREEN *speaks aside to* ARTHUR.) Travers, don't you see what an idiot I am making of myself? Have mercy! Why don't you present me to the lady?

ARTHUR. Miss Kirke, permit me to present a very dear old friend, Mr. Pittacus Green.

HAZEL. (*Extending her hand.*) He 's doubly welcome, as your friend, and for his own frank face.

GREEN. (*Clasping her hand.*) Ah! Miss Kirke, I 'm a very old-fashioned young fool. Will you permit me? (*Kisses her hand.*) I am your slave. (*Aside.*) Pittacus, there 's no use, you 're an assassin from this hour; the one dear purpose of your life is to get Squire Rodney cremated without delay.

(*Enter* RODNEY *by the gate. He watches* HAZEL.)

HAZEL. Let me share my treasures. (*She places a flower in* GREEN'S *coat.*) There, what do you say to that?

GREEN. I say nothing, nothing! I am dumb with delight. (*Aside.*) Decidedly, old Rod is a doomed man.

(PITTACUS *goes toward the wall and sees* RODNEY *appear in the gateway.*)

HAZEL. (*To* ARTHUR, *embarrassed.*) Will you accept a flower?

ARTHUR. (*Taking it.*) Thanks. (*He withdraws a little.*)

RODNEY. (*Coming forward.*) Hazel, now ye 've served the others, can't ye think o' me a little?

HAZEL. (*Starting; then with composure.*) I beg your pardon. I did not see you, Mr. Rodney; you are welcome to what remains.

(*She hands him the basket.*)

RODNEY. (*Taking out leaves.*) Emblem of my hopes, nothing but leaves; dead and withered leaves!

(*He puts the basket on the table, and goes out through the gate.*)

GREEN. (*Looking after him.*) As Dr. Hamlet says, that 's nux vomica for the gentleman.

ARTHUR. (*Coming down, right, speaks to* GREEN.) Let us go, we 're in the way. —Miss Hazel, if you 'll permit me, I 'll take my friend to my room for a talk of old times.

HAZEL. Sorry to lose you.

(ARTHUR *goes out.*)

GREEN. My dear Miss Kirke, you may not believe it, but, by the justice of Jove, we 'll meet again.

(HAZEL *goes out through the gate.* GREEN *sings "We shall meet again," and goes towards the porch.*)

DOLLY. (*Barring his passage.*) Stop! stop! stop!

GREEN. (*Ending his song with a trill.*) I must finish in the right key.

DOLLY. Well, now, look here; you promised me to free my cousin Hazel from her bargain with the Squire. When are you going to begin?

GREEN. The very next time I meet old Ram Rod. He was here just now. If there 's a timid bone in his body, I 'll make him come to terms, and he 'll die a bachelor, just as sure as—you 're the prettiest girl that ever blest my eyes.

DOLLY. La, Mr. Green, you 're too full of sweet words, I 'm thinking.

GREEN. Dear me, if my words were only as sweet as your face, I 'd put 'em on the market and bust up the sugar trade, I would.

DOLLY. Hoity toity, man! (*Going.*) Keep your promise, Master Green, an' I 'll keep mine.

(*She goes out through the porch.*)

GREEN. (*Looking after her, at door.*) Pittacus, you may not believe it, but the day that girl was born was the brightest in all the year! Oh, love! love! love! Romeo and Juliet! Oh, roses! Nightingales! balconies, rope ladders, and various things attached to the passion of love! At last, poor Pitty, you have a work to do. And what a work! To save two young and loving hearts from misery and a monster! (*Turns and sees* RODNEY *coming.*) Stars of the summer night, far in yon azure height! The monster!

(*Enter* RODNEY, *by gate.*)

Why, you 're the very man I want to see.

RODNEY. Well, sir, I 'm here and easily seen.

GREEN. (*At right of table.*) You 'll permit me? (*He shows a chair.* RODNEY *drops into the chair at left of table.*) First, then, let me inform you that

I 'm Captain Green, of Her Majesty's marine.
But I 'm not so verdant as my name may seem!
I know a wronged man when I see him, sir, and permit me to assure you, sir, that you are one.

(*He sits at right of table.*)

RODNEY. Indeed, sir, how am I wronged?

GREEN. As Shakespeare, a poet, says: "She who steals my heart steals trash: 't was mine, 't is hers, and hath been slave to thousands; but she who filches from me my purse, robs me of that which much enriches her, and leaves me poor indeed." (RODNEY *laughs.*) Do you see the point?

RODNEY. No, it 's a little dull.

GREEN. Then I 'll sharpen it. A certain rich Squire saves a certain poor father from ruin, and spends a little fortune in having the daughter taught to become his wife—that is the taking of the purse.

RODNEY. Well?

GREEN. Before the wedding 's had, and the purse is paid for, a good-for-nothing young fellow tumbles into a ditch, is fished out by the father, nursed by the daughter, and that is the stealing of the heart—do you understand?

RODNEY. I think I do.

GREEN. Do you see the danger?

RODNEY. Not yet.

GREEN. Why, it 's as plain as your face, ha, ha, ha, ha! You see, women are curious creatures. You may not believe it, but the silly fools prefer hearts to pennies; youth and beauty they like better than age and ugliness. Do you see now?

RODNEY. (*Rises.*) Thanks to your extreme politeness, I should think I might.

(*He crosses to gate.*)

GREEN. Squire, there 's but one way out of this: Threaten to fight the fellow, challenge him and frighten him away. Do you take?

RODNEY. (*At gate.*) I do.

GREEN. Spoken like a man. When shall the fight begin?

(DOLLY *enters, watching them from the porch.*)

RODNEY. Without delay.

(DOLLY *draws back in door, right.*)

GREEN. You 're a hero, sir, a man of nerve; I 'm proud to know you. Count on me, count on me, sir, to fix things right. (*He offers his hand.* RODNEY *does not take it, but lifts his hat and goes out.*) Still, Squire, I 'm exceedingly proud to know you. (*With delight.*) Splendissimus! Gloria et victoria!

DOLLY. (*In disgust, coming forward.*) So, sir, you be mighty thick with Maister Rodney now!

GREEN. Exactly; but my thickness is the thinnest thickness that ever was thicked; do you understand that?

DOLLY. My heart, man! Ye daze me dumb with your talk.

GREEN. My dear, the snarl is settled. He's the easiest ass to manage I ever met. Before another day, he'll challenge Carringford and go in haste (*Pointing downward.*)—to heaven.

DOLLY. (*In astonishment.*) To heaven!

GREEN. Then, Miss Dolly, your cousin will be free, and you'll be bound, yes, bound, to keep your promise: your heart, your hand, or both.

DOLLY. You'll get my hand over your head if you don't mind.

GREEN. Delightful! I'd like that—let me show you how. (*Taking her hand, he lifts it over his head.*) There, over my head, so. (*Putting it round his neck, he kisses her.*)—And so!

DOLLY. (*Flinging him off.*) How dare you, sir?

GREEN. Now I've done my part, it is your turn. (DOLLY *pretends to strike him.*) Oh, no, not that!

MERCY. (*Outside.*) All right, Mr. Rodney, I'll tell Dunstan what ye say.

GREEN. Whose honey-laden organ is that?

DOLLY. That's Hazel's mother.

GREEN. Dear me! Hazel had a mother?

DOLLY. Why, of course, she has her now.

GREEN. Oh! I see, funny things happen to others as well as me! Well, then, now, seriously your part is to see her mother, and tell her you know that Rodney is not the man that Hazel loves.

DOLLY. I'd never dare do that.

GREEN. What! would you desert me now? upon the verge of great success? No! Courage! Speak! and your cousin will be blest.

(*Enter* MERCY *at door.*)

Ah! Here she comes! I'll leave her to the tender mercies of your tongue. (*He goes to the table for his hat.*) Madame, will you permit me? (He *takes the hat, going.*) I'll humbly take my leaf. (*Takes a leaf from the basket. At door.*) Madame, in the words of the immortal bard, Avon, if all the world were in the right, you and I would never be in the wrong. This was sometime a paradox, but now—(*Sings, "When the bloom is on the rye."*) you may not believe it, it's true, it's true!

(*Exit through the porch, putting on his hat.*)

MERCY. Dolly, who be that?

DOLLY. A man named Pitty Green.

MERCY. Pitty Green! An odd name, an' he seems queer a bit, here! (*Points to her forehead.*)

DOLLY. That's all right, Aunt, so long as he's sound here. (*Points to her heart.*)

MERCY. Aye, that's true, Dolly, that's true.

DOLLY. Aunt Mercy!

MERCY. Well, Dolly?

DOLLY. Did ye mark the look in Hazel's face this morning, when her father told her Mr. Carringford had been here long enough?

MERCY. What sort o' look, girl?

DOLLY. A pale, frightened, suffering look, Aunt; she's in love with Mr. Carringford, as sure as I'm a living woman.

MERCY. (*Starting.*) My heart, child! does thee really mean what thee says?

DOLLY. Indeed I do.

(*Enter* HAZEL.)

But hush! Here she comes.

HAZEL. Mother dear, be sure to let me know when father returns. You won't forget? Don't forget it, please.

MERCY. Where's thee goin', child?

HAZEL. I'm going to take my drawing lesson from Mr. Carringford.

MERCY. Thee can wait a bit. I've a word to say to thee. Dolly, thee'll find work in the house.

DOLLY. All right, aunt. (*Exit.*)

MERCY. (*Sitting left.*) Hazel, child, come here and kneel at my feet as thee did when a little one, and I taught thee to pray. (HAZEL *kneels beside her.*) My child, many i' this world may say they love thee, but none'll ever do it as I do. Thee may have loads o' friends and lovers too, but thee can never have but one mother. Well, child, can't thee trust her?

HAZEL. Trust her? Have I ever distrusted her?

MERCY. Aye, thee's distrustin' her now—there's that in thy heart she ought to know.

HAZEL. (*Embarrassed.*) Why, mother, what do you mean?

MERCY. Oh! Thee knows well eno' what I mean; I've been foolish, child, and blind. I forgot the dangers o' youthful blood, and I felt too sure o' thy promise to be Aaron Rodney's wife. But my eyes are open now; I 've discovered thy secret, lass; and I must speak to thee.

HAZEL. (*In anguish.*) Oh! mother, spare me—spare me—it is too late! It is too late!

(*Buries her face in* MERCY'S *lap.*)

MERCY. (*In horror, rising.*) Too late! what does thee mean, child? Speak! Lift up thy head and look me i' the face.

(HAZEL *looks her in the face.*)

HAZEL. Mother!

MERCY. (*Relieved.*) Ah! it 's a' reet, thee can look me i' the eye still, like an honest lass. But oh! I see it all now. That Maister Carringford be a bad man —a bad man.

HAZEL. (*Indignantly.*) Mother!

MERCY. There 's no use, Hazel—I know all thee 'd say for him! But thy feyther saved his life, and cherished him in his house, and this is his gratitude, to make love to thee—the plighted wife o' another man.

HAZEL. No, mother, you wrong him! He has never spoken a word of love to me in his life.

MERCY. An' has thee been won then wi'-out wooing?

HAZEL. Oh! how can I tell? All that I know is that day by day his voice has grown sweeter, his words wiser, his very presence more precious. I did not realize how empty my life would be without him, till now the time has come for him to go. It seems as if the shadow of death were upon my heart—it has grown so dull and heavy—so dull and heavy!

MERCY. Does thee say he has never told thee that he loves thee?

HAZEL. Never! And yet I know he does. When my back is turned I can feel his eyes upon me.—I saw them once by accident in the glass. I knew all then, for I saw in them my own misery—my own love.

(*She goes to* MERCY'S *arms.*)

MERCY. My poor child! But we must do the right, if it kills us. There 's but one remedy for this, the short and sharp one.

(*Starts to go.*)

HAZEL. Where are you going, mother?

MERCY. He must leave this house at once.

(*Going.*)

HAZEL. (*Stops her.*) No, it is not for you to send him away; that is my duty. It will be less of insult to him, and less of agony to me.

MERCY. Thee has not the strength to do it.

HAZEL. I will find it! Send him here to me, and I promise you I will tell him we must part at once.

MERCY. (*Speaks as she goes.*) Aye, it 's better so. Perhaps thee 'll fret less if thee send him away. Thee shall have it thy way, Hazel, child. (HAZEL *comes to her and she kisses her.*) Courage, lass, be strong i' the battle today, and thee 'll be rich i' the triumph tomorrow.

(*She goes out through the porch.*)

HAZEL. What am I going to do? Drive away the happiness that heaven sends me? Insult the man I honor most—and all for what? To keep the rash promise of a silly, thoughtless girl, and so break two harmless loving hearts! (*She crosses to the table, and sits at right.*) Oh! I must not think of it or I shall rebel.

(*Enter* ARTHUR.)

ARTHUR. (*Coming to the table.*) Why, Hazel, what 's the matter? (*She rises coldly. He checks himself.*) Pardon me, Miss Kirke, I have just learned that you wished to speak to me.

HAZEL. (*With emotion, looks about the room.*) Mr. Carringford, I have sent for you to say what may sound strangely from me—but you must leave this place at once.

ARTHUR. Leave this—? May I know why?

HAZEL. No, not from my lips.

ARTHUR. Do you wish me to go?

HAZEL. (*With nervous vehemence.*) Yes, yes, go quickly!

(RODNEY *enters, unseen by them.*)

ARTHUR. (*After a pause; sadly.*) Yes, you are right—I will go—I was going. (*Extending his hand.*) Bid me good-bye. (*She turns her face away; extends her hand. He takes it, kisses it tenderly. She falls sobbing in the chair; he leans over her.*) Hazel! You must have mercy upon me, and let me speak.

HAZEL. No, I beseech you, leave me—leave me without a word.

(ARTHUR *turns to go.*)

RODNEY. (*Coming forward.*) Stay, Mr. Carringford, one word with me. I know. (ARTHUR *stares;* HAZEL *turns in consternation;* RODNEY *controls his emotion.*) I know that you love Hazel, and that she loves you. (HAZEL *draws back.*) Have no fear, Hazel, child, I 'm not the man to rail at ye. (HAZEL *looks at him.*) I shall only—

(*He pauses, staggers.*)

HAZEL. (*Rushing to him.*) Oh! Mr. Rodney!

RODNEY. Nay, it 's nothing, lass—it 's nothing! I 'm a bit dazed—that 's all.

(*He sinks into chair, hiding his face in his hands.*)

HAZEL. (*Kneeling.*) Oh! Mr. Rodney, forgive us—forgive us! He did not know, for I was resolved to do my duty to you.

(*She bows her head on his knees.*)

RODNEY. Nay, nay, now—no more o' that! There 's misery enough i' this world without an old thing like me making more of it. Don't weep, child, don't weep. Every tear you shed falls like hot lead on my heart. There, there, child, cheer up, cheer up, and we 'll see what 's best to be done.

HAZEL. You do not hate me, then?

RODNEY. Hate ye? Aaron Rodney will never live to see the day he can hate ye. No, lass, I love ye still, God help me; love ye too well to ask anything save your own happiness. I only fear for what your father may do; you know how headstrong he is, and how wildly he rages at things he thinks are wrong.

HAZEL. I cannot help the past, but I can be brave for the future. I can do my duty, keep my promise—

RODNEY. And become my wife? No, child, no. (*He walks away.*) I would not ask it of ye. But this is a bad affair, Hazel. A bad affair. I did not know how far things had gone, or I would not have done what I have done.

ARTHUR. What have you done?

RODNEY. I have written to your mother, Mr. Carringford, begging her to call you away from this place at once. I know the pride of your race, sir, and I know too well your mother will never consent to your marriage with this child, and I warn ye, if ye seek to dishonor her—there is no living power will prevent me from murdering you.

ARTHUR. And I should deserve something worse if I could be false to her.

RODNEY. (*Taking his hand.*) I believe ye, lad, I believe ye, and I 'll not stand in your way.

HAZEL. Oh! Mr. Rodney, my noble friend!

RODNEY. Aye, lass, only thy friend now, but stanch till death. (*Holding* HAZEL'S *hand.*) Mr. Carringford, this child has been bound up in my heart ever since, as a little one, I held her on my knee. Well, sir, for the sake of her happiness, I 'll cancel my prior claim to her hand in your favor, but you must promise me to love and cherish her so long as life shall last.

ARTHUR. I promise.

(*He approaches them.*)

RODNEY. Give me your hand. As far as it lies in my power, I here bestow upon you a treasure that I would have sacrificed life itself to obtain. Take her, sir, take her, and for her sake may heaven be with you both.

(*He extends his left hand to* ARTHUR, *and is joining their hands, when* DUNSTAN *is heard outside; instantly they separate.*)

DUNSTAN. (*Outside.*) There, there! No matter yet, let the horses stand till I 've taken in these things.

RODNEY. Your father 's back, Hazel. Not a word to him of what has passed between us. I must speak with him myself first, but I cannot do it now; I 've not the strength to meet him yet. I 'll go this way. (*In the porch he turns, extending his arms. She goes to him; he kisses her forehead.*) Have no fear, child! I 'll do what I can to soften him, and so God bless you, my darling, God bless you. (*He goes out.*)

ARTHUR. (*Taking her hand.*) This is the bitterest and sweetest moment of my life.

(*Enter* DUNSTAN *with bundles. They separate.*)

DUNSTAN. Ah! lass, and here 's thy bundles. I got thy things, but left the rest for Farmer Kennedy to bring along.

HAZEL. Thanks, father, but how quickly you 've returned.

DUNSTAN. Aye, lass, there was a letter at post, so I hurried home. They said it was for me. Here, lass, read it for me.—Let me hear what it says. (*He hands her the letter; she opens it and starts.*) Well, lass, and what says the letter? (HAZEL *becomes faint; he assists her to a chair.*) My heart, child, what be the matter? There, sit down, sit down. What 's the trouble: is it bad news? Out with it. Who 's it from? Let 's hear.

HAZEL. It is signed, "Emily Carringford."

(ARTHUR *starts.*)

DUNSTAN. (*Looking at him.*) What ha' she got to say to me? Read it, lass, what does she say?

HAZEL. (*Aside.*) There 's no use, I shall be forced to read it. "Dunstan Kirke: Dear Sir, I have been startled by learning of my son's presence in your home, and deeply pained by hearing of his conduct with your child—."

DUNSTAN. Eh? What be that? What be that?

HAZEL. "I have besought him to return to me instantly. If he refuses, I call on you to add the force of your commands to my prayers."

DUNSTAN. Aye, aye, it 's getting clearer, it 's getting clearer. Go on, child, what more does she say?

HAZEL. "I cannot describe my indignation at the thought of my son's love for—" (*She breaks down.*)

DUNSTAN. (*Sternly.*) Stop there, lass. That 's enough!—Ye need read no more! (*To* ARTHUR.) Mr. Carringford, I 've only gotten one child in all the world, and God knows I love her better than my life. Well, sir, I 'd rather bury her wi' my own hands than have her faithless to her word. Now, ye know she be the plighted wife o' Aaron Rodney. Well, then, are ye a serpent I 've cherished in my breast to bite me and mine? Have ye dared to think o' making love to Hazel Kirke?

ARTHUR. Fate threw me helpless at her feet; 't was her hands nursed me back to life. Well, sir, I confess what I could not wish to help—I learned to love her!

DUNSTAN. Hazel, thee hears what he says, and thee knows the duty of an honest girl. Bid him begone at once.

HAZEL. No, father, I cannot.

DUNSTAN. (*Astounded.*) What 's that thee says?

HAZEL. If he must go, I—should go, for I, too, am guilty.

DUNSTAN. What! My child avows dishonor?

HAZEL. Father, hear me!

DUNSTAN. Hear thee! No, no; I 've heard too much already. (*Advancing.*) I could take thy shameless heart out.

(HAZEL, *with a cry of fear, draws back into* ARTHUR'S *arms.*)

ARTHUR. (*Shielding her.*) Stand back, sir, stand back!

(*Enter* DOLLY *and* MERCY *from the house. Millers appear behind the wall and in the gateway.*)

DUNSTAN. What! In that man's arms? Before my very eyes? Out on thee, thou foul disgrace! Hear thy father's curse!

MERCY. (*In anguish.*) No, no; she is thy child, thine only child!

DUNSTAN. Begone! Thou misbegotten bairn, begone. I cast thee out adrift, adrift forever from thy feyther's love, and may my eyes no more behold thee.

HAZEL. (*Extending her arms toward* MERCY *with a cry.*) Mother! Mother!

DUNSTAN. (*Waving her back.*) Stand back; she 's lost to thee forever!

(HAZEL *recoils into* ARTHUR'S *arms; he leans over her.*)

ACT SECOND.

SCENE. *Interior of villa at Fairy Grove; a room bright with sunlight. On table at left are cigarettes and matches, also a bell; water and glass are on stand at right.*

At rise of curtain, CLARA, *a servant, is discovered dusting the room. Outside a pipe is heard playing.*

CLARA. (*Looking off.*) There 's that worthless boy blowing his pipe again, instead of minding the garden. Why did Mr. Carringford ever bring the ninny here?

(*Enter* MET. *with pipe, dressed as a gardener, and carrying flowers.*)

MET. Hi! I say, Mistress Clara, where 's the missus?

CLARA. What do you want of her?

MET. Here 's some flowers I 've been picking for her. Where is she, I say?

CLARA. She 's about here somewhere, crying, I suppose.

MET. Cryin'? What do you mean?

CLARA. For the last three days she seems to be awfully put out about something.

MET. My heart! what be the matter wi' her?

CLARA. Oh! She 's so lonely, I suppose. She goes nowhere, sees nobody, and for a week her husband has been away. I never knew him to stay so long from her before. I 'm afraid there 's something wrong here, Met. What can it be?

MET. How should I know?

CLARA. You knew the missus before she came here, did n't you?

MET. What makes ye think that?

CLARA. Because she brought you here.

MET. No, she did n't bring me here; I followed her; and I 'd follow her to the end of the earth if she 'd let me.

CLARA. (*Sitting down.*) Let me see. That was just one year ago. Where did she come from?

MET. That 's her business, not yours.

CLARA. Who was she before Mr. Carringford married her?

MET. A lady, every inch of her, and too good for him.

CLARA. Why too good for him?

MET. Now, look ye here, lass, why is it that he brings no one here to see her? Why is it his mother and none of his folks don't never come near here at all?

CLARA. I don't know.

MET. Why, of course not. Ye don't know nothing, you don't. (*Looking out of the window right.*) There she be on the shore o' the park lake. I 'll take her the flowers.

CLARA. (*Rises.*) Hold on, Met., tell me first—

MET. I 'll tell ye nothin', and that 's more than ye desarve. (*Exit.*)

CLARA. There 's a secret somewhere about this house; I can smell it in the air, and that boy knows what it is, but he 's as close as the grave, and as devoted to my mistress as a miser to his gold. (*Stops suddenly at window and looks out.*) Well, I declare, what sort of a man is this coming up the path? How he mutters and shakes his head as though he were crazy. What can he want here? I must call Barney to get rid of him.

(*She goes right.*)

(*Enter* RODNEY, *left.*)

RODNEY. Young woman, one moment, please.

CLARA. (*Turning.*) Well, sir, what is it?

RODNEY. Is this place called Fairy Grove?

CLARA. Yes, sir; this is Fairy Grove.

RODNEY. (*Looking round, dubiously.*) So this is where he has hidden her!

CLARA. There he goes, muttering and shaking his head.

RODNEY. So she 's here, surrounded by luxury and never dreaming of her shame —never dreaming of her shame. (*Growing excited.*) I have found you at last, Arthur Carringford, and you shall right the wrong you 've done her, or I shall have your life—your life!

CLARA. (*Approaching him.*) Good man, what do you want here?

RODNEY. (*Turning to her.*) Is your mistress in?

CLARA. You mean Mrs. Carringford?

RODNEY. (*Intensely.*) Is she called that here?

CLARA. Is who called what, sir?

RODNEY. Your mistress, is she in?

CLARA. Certainly. Do you want to see her?

RODNEY. (*Startled.*) No, no; it would only frighten her. But you know she is not—No, no, not for the world! It would sadden her to see me. What am I saying? What am I saying?

CLARA. (*Aside.*) I must get Barney here at once.

(*She runs to door at right.*)

RODNEY. (*Turns and sees her going.*) Stop! Come back! (*Clara returns.*) Don't go till ye tell me—

CLARA. Tell you what, sir?

RODNEY. Does he treat her well? Is she happy here?

CLARA. (*Astonished.*) I don't know.— What do you mean, sir?

RODNEY. If he made her unhappy, I 'd tear his heart out.

CLARA. (*Terrified, screams, and runs right, calling:*) Barney! Barney!

(RODNEY *follows and brings her back.*)

RODNEY. Hush! Be quiet! or you 'll bring her here. If you make a noise she 'll come. Don't fear. I mean no harm. I 'll go now. I only want to be sure I 've found the right place. What 's your name?

CLARA. Clara, sir.

RODNEY. Clara!—a goodly name and you have a kind face. I 'll trust you with a message. Tell Hazel for me—I mean your mistress—tell her not to grieve. Tell her heaven has her in its blessed keeping. Tell her that I 'm near at hand to guard her life, to enforce her rights; tell her this, please, from me.

CLARA. Who are you, sir?

RODNEY. I 'm Mr.— (*Checks himself.*) A friend, that 's all, a friend! She must not know my name; you won't tell her that, will you?

CLARA. I don't know it, sir.

RODNEY. True, that 's good; take this.

(*Handing her money.*)

CLARA. What is it?

RODNEY. Gold. Money.

CLARA. I—I—don't want it, sir—would n't take it for the world!

RODNEY. Yes, take it, to pay for the service I want of you. (*Taking her hand.*) Watch him, see how he treats her. (*Going.*) Now to return to this man's mother; bring her here and learn her decision at once. (*At door.*) You are to tell me all when we meet again.

(*He goes out at left.*)

CLARA. (*Looking after him.*) Meet again! Not if I see you first! The man 's as crazy as a loon!

(*Looks at the money.*)

(*Enter, right,* BARNEY, *singing.*)

BARNEY. Is that you, darlin'? What 's that ye 're lookin' at?

CLARA. Gold, I think. I can hardly believe it 's real though.

BARNEY. (*Snatching, examines the money.*) Faith! that 's pure gold, sure enough, the genuine article, like yourself, heaven bless you. Ah! Clara, this is the sovereign of the world, but you, you 're the sovereign of my heart.

(*Turns away.*)

CLARA. Ah! ha! Barney, no nonsense, give me my money.

BARNEY. (*Comes back.*) And how do I know it 's yours?

CLARA. Did n't you snatch it out of my hand just now?

BARNEY. Sure, that don't prove it 's yours.

CLARA. Come, come now, give me my money.

BARNEY. Where did ye get it?

CLARA. From a crazy creature who was here just now.

BARNEY. Crazy, was he?

CLARA. Yes.

BARNEY. Of course he was crazy, or he would n't have given it to you. I 'll go and find that lunatic and restore his fortune. (*Going.*)

CLARA. (*Following him.*) Barney O'Flynn, will you give me that sovereign?

BARNEY. How can I give what is n't my own, dear?

CLARA. Do you mean to keep it yourself?

BARNEY. Keep it! No, indeed, I mane to exchange it.

CLARA. For what, Barney?

BARNEY. For the sweetest thing a man could drame of, wan of your kisses, my darlin'.

(*She screams, flings him off, and goes out right, as* ARTHUR *enters left with overcoat on arm, smoking a cigarette.*)

ARTHUR. Well, Barney!

BARNEY. (*Starting.*) Mealy murther! Master, ye frightened me; sure, sir, I 'm glad ye 're back again.

ARTHUR. (*Tossing his overcoat to* BARNEY.) Where 's my wife?

BARNEY. Your wife, sir?

ARTHUR. Certainly, my wife.

BARNEY. (*With a cough.*) Oh! yes, certainly, she 's in the garden, I belave.

ARTHUR. (*Sitting at the table.*) Let her know that I 've arrived.

BARNEY. All right, sir. (*Going, he looks back.*) He 's in one of his quare moods again. He 's getting tired of this already. I knew it! I knew it! I knew it! He 'll end it soon—they always do. Ah! there 's nothing like a Scotch marriage on the wrong side of the line to save the trouble of a divorce and chate the lawyers. (*Exit.*)

ARTHUR. (*Taking out a letter, reads.*) "My dear Travers, your mother is in a very dangerous condition. To-day she arose for the first time in six months, laboring under some great excitement that is giving her temporary strength; she asks the most searching questions concerning you. She grows more impatient every day for your marriage with Lady Maud." (*Folding the letter.*) Strange; very strange; I hoped for good news. Ah! will this never end? Shall I never be able to show the world the noble woman who is my wife?

(*He falls in a reverie.*)

(HAZEL *runs in. Seeing him, she creeps up behind and puts her hands over his eyes. He exclaims gladly:*)

Hazel! Hazel!

HAZEL. Ah! you are back at last, my darling.

ARTHUR. (*Embracing her.*) Apparently.

HAZEL. Oh! I 'm so glad, so glad; I 've been almost dead with loneliness.

ARTHUR. Have you really missed me then so much?

HAZEL. More than you will ever know or care, I fear.

ARTHUR. Oh! I love to have you miss me.

HAZEL. Of course you do; you would n't love me if you did n't.

ARTHUR. And you 're not tired yet of these iron bonds of matrimony?

HAZEL. I call them golden bonds.

ARTHUR. And so they are, so they are, darling. May they always hold us heart to heart.

HAZEL. (*Saddens.*) Heigh ho! (*Rises.*)

ARTHUR. Heigh ho? (*Amazed.*) Well, well, what does this mean?

HAZEL. Oh! Only a silly thought. I 'm superstitious; too much happiness is dangerous, sometimes, you know, that 's all.

ARTHUR. (*Taking her hand.*) Little woman, do you know I 'm not blind—there 's something troubles you. What is it?

HAZEL. (*Imitating him.*) Big man, do you know I 'm not blind, and there 's something troubles you? What it is?

ARTHUR. Come, come, dear, I 'm in earnest.

HAZEL. (*Sobered.*) And so am I, dear. For the last few weeks, whenever you 've been at home, you 've been so silent and moody. Oh, Arthur, can't you trust me with your sorrow as well as with your joy? Come, dear, tell me what troubles you, darling?

ARTHUR. Business, that 's all. But you, Hazel, you have no such excuse for sadness.

HAZEL. I, sad? (*Laughing, she rises.*) Why, I 'm the gayest creature in the world.

ARTHUR. (*Holds her hands.*) You try to be before me, but when you 've supposed me absent, I 've seen you in tears. Have I not done all that I could to make you happy?

(*He puts his arms about her.*)

HAZEL. (*Ardently.*) Oh, indeed you have!

ARTHUR. Then why have I failed?

HAZEL. Failed! You have not failed! You have made me too happy. My happiness startles me sometimes, I so little deserve it. I confess at moments I am haunted.

ARTHUR. Haunted by what, dear?

HAZEL. (*Going to the couch at right.*) I hardly know—a vague, uncertain dread. This past year has been so strange, the way we met, our secret marriage in Scotland—

ARTHUR. Yes, but you know why our marriage had to be so secret.

HAZEL. Yes, because your proud mother had set her heart upon another marriage for you.

ARTHUR. My mother has been determined to make me the husband of Maud Wetherby; she has been very ill for years. To have acknowledged my marriage with you would surely have been to kill her. So I was forced to have our marriage take place in the way that offered least risk of discovery by her.

HAZEL. Oh! my darling, I do hate this hiding! It gives our marriage the color of a crime. How much longer must it last?

ARTHUR. I have been hoping every day that my mother would grow strong enough to learn the news that you are my precious little wife, but I am disappointed; she is no better.—I even fear she is growing worse.

HAZEL. Your mother deceived! My father broken-hearted! Oh! it is horrible! (*She moves away.*)

ARTHUR. (*Angrily.*) What a fool I 've been! (*He paces the floor.*)

HAZEL. (*In dismay.*) What do you mean?

ARTHUR. I 've been stupid enough to fancy that my love—my devotion—might suffice to make you forget—to make you happy!

HAZEL. (*Going to him.*) And so they do, dear. I was wrong to confess these foolish fears to you. Say you forgive me?

ARTHUR. (*Embracing her.*) Forgive you? No, little woman, it is for you to forgive!

HAZEL. Forgive what, dear?

ARTHUR. (*Gravely.*) Forgive me that I have not rendered you the open honor that was due you as my wife.

(*He turns his head away.*)

HAZEL. How strangely you say that! What can you mean?

ARTHUR. No matter now, dear. (*Affecting gaiety, he crosses to left of table.*) Away with gloomy thoughts; all 's well that ends well! Where are my cigarettes, Hazel? No objection to my smoking, dear?

HAZEL. Oh, no. On the contrary, I 'll light one for you.

ARTHUR. Thanks, that will be delightful. Equal to the task?

HAZEL. (*Gaily taking a cigarette from the table.*) Don't burn me! Take care! (*He lights match, while she draws on the cigarette, lights it, and hands it to him with a cough.*) There, take the horrid thing! (*She goes away.*)

ARTHUR. (*Smoking, he follows her and

puts his arm around her.) Horrid thing! Why, I declare, it 's the most delicious cigarette I ever smoked in my life. Thanks, little woman, may all our sorrows end like this, in smoke and a kiss. (*He kisses her.*)

(*Enter* GREEN, *at center, a sun umbrella over his head, and laden with sporting traps. He coughs.*)

I declare,—it 's our dear old Pitty.

(HAZEL *and* ARTHUR *separate.*)

GREEN. 'T is true, 't is Pitty, and pity 't is, 't is true! You may not believe it, but these things are a bore, and this has two bores.

(*He holds up a double-barrelled gun.*)

HAZEL. (*Laughing, goes to* GREEN.) Talk of matrimonial misery and bandboxes! What are they to the awful doom of a bachelor devoted to sport?

GREEN. Oh! I say, don't make sport of a man in mortal agony. Come to the rescue, take the umbrageous curio. (*Handing* HAZEL *his umbrella.*) The idea! billing and cooing still, a year after marriage, too. It 's an outrage on society.

ARTHUR. (*Having unloaded him.*) So it is, Green! Now, tell us to what do we owe your sudden advent here?

GREEN. To the same old lady, Dame Rumor, the despot of my life.

HAZEL. (*Laughing.*) Ah! What monstrous thing has she reported here?

GREEN. Monstrous bliss! The fame of your fishes, the taste of your game, the sound of your kisses is wafted on the breath of rumor to the uttermost end of an envious world. So here am I, with all my senses, wild to see, hear, smell, taste, and touch. I 'll begin with touch. Give me your fists, ye pair of blissful curiosities! (*Taking them by the hands, he points to her hand.*) Will you permit me? (*She laughs. He kisses her hand.*) Won't you share your monstrosities with me?

HAZEL. (*With laughter.*) All we can.

GREEN. All but the kisses, I suppose.

ARTHUR. I don't see how we can reserve much else.

HAZEL. (*Sitting down.*) But what are you going to give us for letting you into our paradise?

GREEN. For you I have some news, and for that mortal I have a sermon.

ARTHUR. Well, let it be a galloping sermon, then. I 'll go and order the horses at once. (*Strikes the bell on table.*)

GREEN. Capital!

HAZEL. Sermon or ride?

GREEN. Capital, my dear, referred to his going.

ARTHUR. I 'm off. Beware, I have my eye upon you.

GREEN. Keep your ear off, that 's all we ask.

(*Enter* BARNEY, *right.*)

ARTHUR. (*Pointing to the tackle.*) Pick up those things and follow me.

(*Exit, left.*)

BARNEY. (*Taking the things.*) I will, sir; I will, sir; I will, sir. Bad luck to the game; they 've got divil the chance now. (*Exit.*)

HAZEL. Now for your news!

GREEN. I 'm just from Blackburn Mill.

HAZEL. And you have letters for me?

GREEN. No, not yet. Your father declares that the first who writes you shall leave his house.

HAZEL. (*Sadly.*) Is he still so angry with me, then?

GREEN. Angry with you? That 's putting it mild. I call him the pig-headedest old hard-heart I ever knew. He won't let them breathe your name.

HAZEL. How did you learn this?

GREEN. Dolly told me.

HAZEL. (*Puzzled.*) Dolly, is that what you call her?

GREEN. Oh, yes, if a person's name is Dolly, no harm to call her so, is there? Oh! I forgot, you don't know, do you?

HAZEL. Know what?

GREEN. Why, about Dolly. She 's done for!

HAZEL. Done for?

GREEN. Yes, going to make a fool of herself.

HAZEL. How?

GREEN. By becoming the better half of P. Green. Pity, is n't it?

HAZEL. (*Amazed.*) Do you mean to say you 're going to marry my cousin?

GREEN. Oh. no! She 's going to marry me.

HAZEL. Oh, I am so glad!

(*Offers her hand in congratulation.*)

GREEN. You may not believe it, but so am I. Will you permit me?

(*He kisses her hand.*)

HAZEL. (*Sitting on the couch.*) Now sit right down here by me, and tell me all about it.

GREEN. (*Sitting.*) Oh! it was just like Dolly herself, short and sweet. After you left Lancashire, the doors of the old mill were sternly closed, especially against me. But it did n't matter, you see. I always have an object in life, so I suddenly became interested in dams—mill-dams. There was one near the mill: there always is a dam attached to a mill. I used to visit that dam and sketch that dam—the sight of anything damned was a relief to me. Weeks passed, but the door of the old mill remained closed. Fever ensued; I got dam on the brain and went muttering damn, damn, all day. However, nothing could dampen the ardor of my disease. At last the crisis appeared, Dolly appeared, and took Pitty, Yes, she relieved my delirium, and to ensure a curse, consented to become a ma -dam.

HAZEL. (*Laughing.*) You dear, silly old thing. So you 're going to become my cousin.

GREEN. Bless me, so I am. I did n't think of that! (*Takes her hand.*) Will you *now* permit me?

(*He kisses her hand.*)

(ARTHUR *enters at left.*)

ARTHUR. (*Approaching them.*) Hallo there! I say! I say!

GREEN. (*Coolly.*) So do I—I say. I not only say, but I do, don't I? Will you permit me? (*He kisses* HAZEL'S *hand again.*) I say, cousinship is good. A duty I owe to society, cousinship, my boy, cousinship.

(*He kisses* HAZEL, *then rises and walks away.*)

ARTHUR. (*To* HAZEL.) What does the rascal mean?

HAZEL. Something wonderful. He means—

GREEN. Hush! Quietly; his nerves are weak. Have you ordered the horses?

ARTHUR. Yes, but—

GREEN. Stop! but me no buts, but say I make peace. Hazel, my dear, go and get ready to ride and leave this reprobate to the tender mercies of the family prime minister, your cousin Pit.

HAZEL. (*Laughing as she goes.*) Oh! very well. Don't forget the sermon.

(*Exit, right.*)

ARTHUR. Now, sir, please explain!

(*He slaps* GREEN *on the back.*)

GREEN. *I* explain? Why, sir, I 've travelled three hundred miles to make you explain.

ARTHUR. Explain what?

GREEN. (*Handing to* ARTHUR *a slip of newspaper.*) That, sir.

ARTHUR. (*Reading.*) "Another important engagement in high life announced—that of Lord Travers to Lady Maud Wetherby."

GREEN. Yes, sir; that, sir, is a cutting from the *Morning Post*—a most respectable paper, and very reliable authority.

ARTHUR. (*Laughing.*) Evidently.

GREEN. (*Solemnly.*) Well, what are you laughing at? I don't see anything to laugh at.

ARTHUR. Don't you? Then suppose you look in the glass.

GREEN. Come, come, sir, this is a most serious matter.

ARTHUR. Clearly, a most solemn affair; almost as awful as the paragraph about you a few weeks since.

GREEN. About me?

ARTHUR. Something like this: "We understand that, after long and serious consideration, the Hon. P. Green has decided to become—a bachelor!" What do you think of that?

GREEN. I think it is a lie.

ARTHUR. That 's what I think of this.

(*He tears the newspaper cutting and throws it in the waste basket.*)

GREEN. There 's no analogy in the cases, sir. How can I become a bachelor since I am one?

ARTHUR. How can I marry since I am married?

GREEN. But confound it, sir, you 're not married!

(ARTHUR *turns on* GREEN.)

ARTHUR. If I 'm not married, then you must be an old maid.

GREEN. Eh? What? I don't see that! Do you dare to say that in consequence of your villainy my sex is to suffer? No, sir, it 's your manhood, not mine, that 's at stake!

ARTHUR. Are you mad?

GREEN. Yes, sir, I am, blind mad. Who would n't be under the circumstances?

ARTHUR. (*Irritated.*) Under what circumstances?

GREEN. Why, sir, you commit a crime, and when I am about to implore you not to commit another, you impeach my sex, sir. You actually impeach my sex.

ARTHUR. By Jove! You are insane!

GREEN. Insane! I wish I could say as much for you. Insanity is the only excuse for such exasperating, outrageous, scoundrelly conduct as yours.

ARTHUR. Good heavens, Green! Are you really serious?

GREEN. Serious? I should think so. I'm as serious as an avalanche, an earthquake and a volcano boiled down into one.

ARTHUR. What a frightful row about nothing!

GREEN. Nothing? Is it nothing to deceive an honest girl into believing she's a married woman when she is n't? Is it nothing to marry one woman and swear to love and honor her, when you love, if you don't honor, another? Is it nothing to betray where you are trusted most? Is it nothing to be a smooth, cool, calculating villain, and sit there and look as innocent and serene as an angel?

ARTHUR. My dear boy, of whom are you talking?

GREEN. (*Staggered.*) Oh! this is wicked, Travers. It's pure malignant cruelty. Have n't I always been a loyal friend?

ARTHUR. Of course you have.

GREEN. (*Sitting down.*) Then why could n't you have trusted me?

ARTHUR. I've never distrusted you.

GREEN. Oh, yes, you have; you dealt with me in a beastly mean manner! You've made me an unconscious accomplice in a piece of business I despise.

ARTHUR. There you go again. I vow it's enough to irritate a saint. Can't you tell me plainly what in the world you mean?

GREEN. What! do you mean to say on your honor you don't understand?

ARTHUR. I mean to say that your gabble for the last half-hour has been Patagonian gibberish to me.

(*He moves about the room.*)

GREEN. Patty—Gibb—Gabby? Can it be possible!

ARTHUR. Can what be possible?

GREEN. Can it be possible that you don't understand your own situation?

ARTHUR. What is my situation?

GREEN. Travers, you're either the most accomplished hypocrite or the biggest fool in the world. Take your choice.

ARTHUR. Enough of this—come to the point. What do you mean?

GREEN. As I said before, that's precisely what I've travelled three hundred miles to make you tell me. What is it you mean? (*Rises.*)

ARTHUR. (*Disgusted.*) Ah! if this is one of your peculiar jokes, it's in very bad taste. (*Going.*) I'll leave you to find the fun of it yourself.

GREEN. (*Astonished.*) A joke! The idea! It's no use, that floors me! (*Running after* ARTHUR, *brings him back.*) Here, Travers, come back, there must be some mistake! I give in; you've turned the tables on me. I'll explain myself.

ARTHUR. Well, begin.

GREEN. (*Hesitating.*) Confound it—

ARTHUR. What's the matter now?

GREEN. I don't know how to begin—it's such an awful business. You see I've been sneaking about the old mill lately, and a rumor reached me there that just covered me with goose flesh.

ARTHUR. Whoever suspected you of any other covering?

GREEN. Yes, I see my name is—oh! hang my name—let's get to the point. It seems Squire Rodney has been looking into your affairs, and, by Jove! he swears you've deceived Hazel Kirke!

ARTHUR. Deceived her? How?

GREEN. He says that your marriage to her was a pretence, a farce, a lie.

ARTHUR. And you, my friend, have believed him?

GREEN. How could I help it? The whole thing is so circumstantial! He declares that he has positive proof that you went towards Scotland with the pretence of marrying Hazel by Scottish law, but that you cunningly stopped on the border, and went through the flimsy Scotch ceremony upon English ground.

ARTHUR. It's an infamous slander!

GREEN. Can you prove that?

ARTHUR. I'll soon convince you.

(*He strikes the bell.*)

GREEN. How?

ARTHUR. By the testimony of a witness to my marriage—Barney.

GREEN. Barney! He's the very one that Rodney named as your accomplice.

(*Enter* BARNEY.)

ARTHUR. Absurd! Barney, I want—

GREEN. Hold on! (*Stopping* ARTHUR, *he speaks to him aside.*) I'll question him. We want to get at the truth, you know, and these chaps easily slip into a lie.

ARTHUR. I don't understand.

GREEN. You will presently. Barney, your master called you because the time has come for us to settle a certain matter, and we wish to be sure everything is all right, you know.

BARNEY. All right, sir. Faith, sir, I'm at your service.

GREEN. Well, then, my good Barney, tell

us frankly, are you quite sure that the place where Lord Travers went through the ceremony of marriage with Miss Kirke was not in Scotland?

ARTHUR. (*Starting.*) I protest—

GREEN. As you 're an honest man, keep quiet. Answer my question, Barney.

BARNEY. I will, sir, when my master bids me.

(GREEN *looks in astonishment at* ARTHUR.)

ARTHUR. (*Aside, astonished.*) What a strange thing for him to say!

GREEN. Shall he answer my question?

ARTHUR. (*Looks at him in suspicion.*) Certainly; Barney, speak freely.

BARNEY. (*To* GREEN.) Well, then. sir, your question be a mighty quare one.

GREEN. Ah! In what respect?

BARNEY. Do ye think I 'd betray my master?

GREEN. Oh! of course not.

BARNEY. I was brought up in the service of the gentry, sir, all my life. Do you be after taking me for a fool?

(*He turns to* ARTHUR.)

GREEN. No, I never judge a man by his looks.

BARNEY. Looks is it? Well, I know how to look after my master's interests, sir, and that 's look enough for me; so of course I took good care to have such a marriage as he wanted come off in the wrong place.

(ARTHUR *starts. He faces* BARNEY, *leaning against the table.*)

GREEN. (*Looking at* ARTHUR.) What place was that?

BARNEY. Faith! the wrong place for a Scotch marriage is the English side of the Scottish line.

ARTHUR. (*Going to him appalled.*) Do you mean to say that the inn you took us to was on the border, but not in Scotland?

BARNEY. (*Astonished.*) Of course I do, sir.

ARTHUR. (*Frenzied.*) You miserable, dastardly villain, I could brain you!

(*He grasps him by the throat.*)

BARNEY. Sure, sir, I only followed your own orders.

ARTHUR. (*Amazed.*) Followed my orders?

BARNEY. To the letther, sir. Did n't you come to me all of a suddint one night, at the old tavern in Blackburn, and did n't you say, "Barney, I want to get married to onst secretly, in Scotland"?

ARTHUR. I did, you rascal.

BARNEY. Did n't ye tell me to take ye to the borders?

ARTHUR. Well?

BARNEY. Well, sir, and so I did. To the borders of matrimony, as I thought ye intended.

ARTHUR. (*Shaking him.*) Idiot! Scoundrel! Wretch! (GREEN *interferes, saying "Travers! Travers!" and frees* BARNEY. *In agony,* ARTHUR *turns away.*) Hazel dishonored—deceived, and by me—by me! Oh! It is horrible! horrible!

(*He rushes again at* BARNEY.)

GREEN. (*Interposing.*) There 's something better to be done now.

ARTHUR. Yes, you are right. We will go find a curate—and I will marry her at once. (*To* BARNEY.) Imbecile! I 'm about to take measures partially to amend the outrage that you have committed. Let us have no more mistakes—tell my wi— (*Pauses; then with ardor.*) Yes, before heaven and my own heart, she is my wife! Tell my wife that I have been called away, but will return soon. And, understand, not a word of this to anyone.

BARNEY. Not for the world.

ARTHUR. (*To* GREEN.) Come, let us hurry; every instant now is torture till Hazel is my wife.

(*They both hasten out.*)

BARNEY. Faith, thin, I can't make this out for the life o' me! He 's lost his head as well as his heart entirely, and to a peasant's child, too. Eh! Who 's this old party coming up the walk? It 's Squire Rodney. That bodes no good to this house! O, murther! Who 's that behind him? If it is n't Lady Travers herself! The powers purtect us—she 's found us out! Oh, dear! oh, dear! may the powers purtect us! what shall we do, at all at all! Whist! She 's here.

(*Enter* RODNEY, *followed by* LADY TRAVERS, *old, very ill, leaning on the arm of a footman in livery.*)

RODNEY. This is the place, my lady, and this is the man.

LADY TRAVERS. Barney, is that you?

BARNEY. Yes, your ladyship, I belave it is (*Aside.*) I 'm not quite sure.

LADY T. I thought you were abroad with my son.

BARNEY. Yes, ma'am, I 'm with your son, and sure I fale abroad too—leastways, I don't fale at home.

LADY T. (*Faintly.*) A chair! (RODNEY *helps her to a chair.*) Water! (BARNEY *gives her a glass of water. She drinks it, handing back the glass.*) Is my son here?

(RODNEY *withdraws a little.*)

BARNEY. No, my lady.

LADY T. (*Aside.*) So much the better! (*Aloud.*) Is the lady of the house in?

BARNEY. Is it Lady Travers ye mane, my lady?

LADY T. (*Sternly.*) It is not Lady Travers that I mean.

BARNEY. (*Aside.*) She knows all! (*Aloud.*) She is in, my Lady.

LADY T. Inform her that a lady would speak with her on important business.

BARNEY. (*Going.*) I will, my lady.

LADY T. Stay—not a word of who it is.

BARNEY. Oh! not for the world, my lady.

LADY T. And, Barney—

BARNEY. Yes, my lady?

LADY T. When I strike twice on this bell come here instantly. Do you understand?

BARNEY. I do, very well, my lady.

LADY T. You may go.

BARNEY. Thank you, my lady. (*Aside, going.*) Faith! I wish I were anywhere out of this. (*Exit.*)

LADY T. Thomas, return to the carriage and wait till I send for you. (*Servant bows and goes out.*) Mr. Rodney, I deem it best I should see this girl alone.

RODNEY. Yes, madam, you are right. 'T is best I should go! But, oh! madam, have pity upon her; break all gently; let your woman's heart feel for a woman's wrongs!

LADY T. It does, for wrongs of which he little dreams.

RODNEY. I have been merciful to you, madam; you must be merciful to her.

LADY T. How have you been merciful to me?

RODNEY. How? Madam, when I first learned the truth, I started out to find your son, to take his life for wronging her. Yes—

LADY T. Ah!

RODNEY. Yes, but I thought of you, his mother, and I said, "I will spare him for her sake, for she will force him to do his duty."

LADY T. And so she will!

RODNEY. I knew it, my lady! I knew it!

LADY T. (*Aside.*) A duty more imperative than to this low-born girl.

RODNEY. Believing this, I sought you out and told you all, for, believe me, madam, I never should have brought you here to put this child to shame, except it were to save her from that shame itself.

LADY T. And so you 're sure her marriage to my son—

RODNEY. Alas! my lady, it was none at all —none at all!

LADY T. (*Aside.*) Thank heaven for that! (*Aloud.*) You may go and wait for me at the inn.

RODNEY. I will, my lady. Oh, madam, I will pray heaven to bless you for this day's noble work! (*Exit.*)

LADY T. His blessings are worse than any curse! Why is this girl so long in coming? This suspense is sapping all my strength.

(*Enter* HAZEL.)

Ah! She 's here.

HAZEL. (*Coming forward in wonder.*) You wished to see me, madam?

LADY T. I did. Please be seated near me. (HAZEL *goes for a chair.* LADY TRAVERS *speaks aside.*) The old story, the fatal power of a handsome face!

HAZEL. (*Aside, as she is getting the chair.*) What a strange commanding tone! I wonder who she is?

(*Returning, she sits near* LADY TRAVERS, *who speaks after a pause.*)

LADY T. I am Lady Travers. (HAZEL *starts.*) You need not fear me; I have not come to curse, but to beg.

HAZEL. To beg of me? But why, madam, why?

LADY T. Because in your hands lies the honor of an old and noble family. I see shining in your eyes the womanhood that has so bewitched my son. And see, to that womanhood, I kneel to beg, implore a fearful sacrifice from you. (*She kneels.*)

HAZEL. (*Helping her back to the chair.*) Oh, madam, you shall not kneel! You shall not kneel! (*Aside.*) What can she mean? (*Aloud.*) Madam, ask any sacrifice I can make in honor, and I will gladly make it for your son.

LADY T. Alas! You do not know what you promise. Listen! My husband had a ward whose fortune he wrongfully used and lost. Upon his dying bed he confessed this to me, and made me promise to hide his shame, by marrying our only son to this ward.

HAZEL. Well, madam?

LADY T. I promised, and I have lived since but to keep my word and save our honor.

HAZEL. Oh, madam! How terrible!

LADY T. My son never knew why I was so determined to make this match, but he, to humor me, promised to marry Lady Maud! Suddenly I heard he was living here with you; with grief and shame I gathered strength enough to drag myself here, to implore you to save us all.

HAZEL. Oh, what can I do? What can I do?

LADY T. Be heroic for his sake; fly from him, and save him from disgrace!

HAZEL. From disgrace?

LADY T. Yes, within a month Lady Maud will come of age, and demand a settlement of her estate. Nothing but her marriage to my son can save him from ruin and shame.

HAZEL. Oh, how horrible! My punishment begins. I, who should prove his blessing, am his curse! Beggary, humiliation and shame stare him in the face, and all—all because of me!

LADY T. Then leave him—fly from him at once.

HAZEL. And never see him in this world again? No, no, you ask more than I have strength to do—besides, what use is that? I am his wife, his wretched, wretched wife!

LADY T. What if you were not his wife?

HAZEL. Ah! Then perhaps heaven would give me the courage to fly for his sake.

LADY T. (*Rising.*) It will, heroic girl, for he is free.—You are not his wife!

HAZEL. (*Turns, stunned.*) Not his wife?

LADY T. As he has deceived me by loving you, so he has betrayed you by a pretended marriage.

HAZEL. He! Arthur? Betrayed me? 'T is false! I'll not believe it! Give me the proofs! The proofs!

LADY T. (*Sways, gasps.*) Ah! Have mercy or I shall die!

HAZEL. (*Throwing herself at her feet.*) Oh, madam! forgive me. I will be wise, calm, patient, only take back the cruel words that disgrace the man I love. Tell me that Arthur is not false, and I will leave him, bear disgrace or death, only so that he may be free from every stain.

LADY T. Poor child! (*Strikes the bell twice.*) Would that I could spare you this blow! But there is at stake a thing of greater value than your happiness or my life—the good name of an old and honorable race.

(*Enter* BARNEY.)

This man will tell you I speak the truth, when I say you are not the wife of Arthur Carringford.

(HAZEL *rises,* BARNEY *starts.*)

HAZEL. This man? Why, he was witness of my marriage.

LADY T. A Scotch marriage upon English ground, and so, illegal, worthless, void.

HAZEL. (*To* BARNEY.) Can this be true?

BARNEY. Heaven forgive us, miss, but it is.

HAZEL. True? This, then, is what he meant when he said he had not done his duty to me as a wife. He, Arthur, my brave, gentle Arthur, has deceived me. betrayed me, and I trusted him as though he were a god. Oh, my heart is breaking.

(*She sobs.*)

LADY T. (*Rising, goes and puts her arms about her.*) Courage, child, courage.

HAZEL. (*Breaking from her.*) Courage for what? To face the agony of love deceived here in my own heart? To face the taunting finger of a cruel world pointing at my shame? No, never! He shall right my wrong. He shall make me an honorable wife, or—I will—

LADY T. (*Staggering.*) Stop! Child, stop! Or you will add my murder to his other crimes!

(*She clutches her chair for support.*)

HAZEL. Murder? No, forgive me, I have done wrong enough. I see it all! It is my father's curse, my father's curse! Oh, God! (*Taking off her jewels, she puts them on the table.*) Madam! you have asked me to fly for his sake, the sake of the man who has so degraded me. Here is my answer. I accepted these as tokens of love, given to an honored wife. I scorn them now. He shall have all—all! (*About to take off her wedding-ring, she stops.*) No, not this. My marriage ring! (*Kisses it.*) This I have bought with a wife's love, a woman's perdition! This I will keep! (*Going.*) The rest I leave forever.—I go to cover up his infamy with my shame—and may heaven forgive you all!

(*Exit.* LADY TRAVERS *staggers and falls back rigid in her chair.*)

ACT THIRD.

SCENE. *Evening; kitchen at Blackburn Mill; door lit by glow of fire; clothes horse with towels on it before the fire; at right, clock and cupboard, in which are pipe, matches, tobacco, food, and dishes; a lighted candle on the table, centre.* MERCY *and* DOLLY *are discovered at the table, which is between two chairs. They are ironing; the room is dim; the clock is striking.*

MERCY. Eight o'clock! It 's time for evening prayers. Dolly, go to the mill, and call Joe and Dan.

DOLLY. All right, aunt.

(Exit, right.)

MERCY. Now to put awa' the linen. (*She does so in drawers at right, and returns to the table. Outside a pipe is heard playing.* MERCY *starts.*) What 's that? (*She listens, the pipe stops.*) Strange! Met used to play that tune, and it sounds like Met's pipe, too. What can it mean? Has he left Hazel? Aye, perhaps he 's coom to see me, with news of her. (*Opens the door and calls.*) Met, Met! Is that you? Met, Met! Is it you?

(MET. *enters, pale, ragged, haggard.*)

Coom in, lad, coom in and tell us the news! What 's the word? Speak, lad, speak.

MET. I want her—where is she?

MERCY. Who?

MET. Hazel—I want her—I 've tramped four hundred miles to find her.

MERCY. My heart, lad! What are ye sayin'?

MET. I must see Hazel—she 's here.

MERCY. Hazel! Hazel! Here? No, she 's not here. (MET *staggers to a chair.*) Mercy on us, what 's coom to thee, lad?

MET. Not here? Where can she be, where can she be?

MERCY. Wi' her hoosband, I suppose.

MET. No, no, she left him a month ago.

MERCY. Left him! Why?

MET. I don't know—I don't know!

MERCY. Where did she go?

MET. (*Who is seated.*) Why, I thought she 'd coom here, so I followed her on foot, but (*rising*) I 'll go back again; I 'll walk till I die, but I 'll find her.

MERCY. Ah, what are you saying, Met?

MET. (*At the door, turns back to* MERCY.) I 'm sayin' there 's something wrong; that man's mother came to the house; she was found dead there and Hazel gone.

MERCY. Great heavens, Met! You frighten me!

MET. Hazel is somewhere, wandering now, as I have been for a month, ill, cold, starving, perhaps, as I am! But I 'll go to her; I must. I will find her.

MERCY. Stop, an' I 'll go with you, lad.

MET. (*Takes her hands.*) Oh, mistress, heaven will bless you for that word.

MERCY. But you must wait till after prayers; Dunstan would miss me if I went off now; he 'd ask questions, and oh, Met, he must not know—he 's been very ill—this news would kill him.

MET. Then, mistress, you go to the master. I 'll run down to Squire Rodney's house; if I can find him, he 'll help me.

(Goes to the door.)

MERCY. (*Following him.*) Aye, so he will, lad. Go, then, go quickly; I will meet you at his house within an hour.

MET. Never fear, missus, we 'll find her now for sure. (*Exit.*)

MERCY. So we will—so we will. Now to get ready to find her.

(MERCY *crosses to door at left.*)

(DOLLY *enters, followed by* JOE *and* DAN.)

DOLLY. We 're all here now, Aunt Mercy.

MERCY. Aye, aye, all but the one who ought to be here the most.

DOLLY. (*Taking up a lighted candle.*) What do you mean, aunt?

MERCY. I cannot tell thee now; tomorrow, perhaps. Coom, coom, child, coom.

(*She hurries within, left. The others follow her, closing the door. The room is left in darkness. There is a pause, then a knock on the outer door. The knocking is repeated; the door opens;* GREEN *appears, looks around, then beckons outside.*)

(ARTHUR *enters.*)

ARTHUR. Well?

GREEN. Not a soul in sight; quiet as the grave.

ARTHUR. Look yonder, she may be inside. (GREEN *opens the door at left, draws back and removes his hat.*) Well?

GREEN. They are at prayers.

ARTHUR. (*Removing his own hat.*) And Hazel?

GREEN. She is not among them.

ARTHUR. (*Sits in chair at right of table.*) Oh, shall I never find her? Never see her precious face again?

(*A psalm is sung outside, they listen reverently.*)

GREEN. Their prayers are over now; they 'll soon be here, and when they come, we 'll ask them if they have heard anything of your—of her.

ARTHUR. And if she has not been here, what are we to do?

GREEN. (*Sits at left.*) Well, you may not believe it, but I'll be hanged if I know.

ARTHUR. I have searched for her everywhere without discovering a trace. My last hope has been to find her here. If we fail now, I shall believe the worst.

GREEN. And what is that?

ARTHUR. That she has taken her own life—murdered by me! (*Rising.*) Oh, the thought will drive me mad!

(GREEN, *rising, follows him, pacifying, and pats him on the shoulder.*)

GREEN. (*Starting.*) They'll soon be here!

ARTHUR. What of it?

GREEN. We forget—they'll recognize you!

ARTHUR. What if they do?

GREEN. The old miller hates you! If he knows where Hazel is, you are the one man in the world he'll keep her hidden from.

ARTHUR. What's to be done?

GREEN. You must leave me till Dolly comes. Once I set her tongue at work, we'll soon know all. Go, wait outside till I've had a chance to make her talk.

ARTHUR. (*Going.*) You'll find me at the old seat near the lock. The moment you get news—

GREEN. I'll fly like lightning to tell you.

ARTHUR. (*In the doorway.*) If I do not find her this time, I shall despair—despair— (*Exit.*)

GREEN. (*At door.*) Poor fellow, he's broken-hearted, and I feel as if I've no more backbone than a caterpillar!

DOLLY. (*Inside.*) All right, aunt, I'm going.

GREEN. Dolly's voice! She's coming, she'll see me! The shock might shake her. I'll spare her feelings for a while.

(*Leaves glove on the table and hides behind the clothes horse.*)

(*Enter* DOLLY *with basket and candle, lighting up the room. She is followed by* JOE *and* DAN.)

JOE and DAN. Good-night!

DOLLY. Don't forget to tell Squire Rodney that Uncle Kirke wants to see him here to-night.

DAN. Very good, Miss Dolly, I'll tell the Squire myself.

(*Exit right, followed by* JOE.)

DOLLY. (*Going to the table, sees glove.*) Dear me! What's this?—a glove! Whose glove? A man's! (*Smells; sternly.*) Pittacus! (*Turns glove.*) As sure as I'm a woman! So he's been here, he's been here and gone away without a word! (GREEN *looks out, unseen by* DOLLY.) Oh, that's just like the heartless brute.—Six weeks since he left me, promising to go and see Hazel and send me news of her; not a word since then. (*Tearfully.*) Oh, these men! these men! Why are they ever made? I can't see the use o' the faithless things. (GREEN *comes up behind her. She continues snappishly.*) Oh, don't I wish I had him here now, how I'd make his ears burn and his head ache! (GREEN *dodges behind the clothes horse.*) How I'd warm the brass of his cheeks for him! (*She slaps the glove across her hand, then puts it in her apron pocket. Beginning to take clothes from the horse, she slams them into the basket. While she does so,* GREEN *dodges behind clothes that remain, comically trying to conceal himself.*) The base deceitful hypocrite! (*Slams a towel in the basket*) pretending he could n't live a day without me! (*Same.*) And then leaving me here—(*Same*) for weeks and weeks (*Same*) with a breaking heart! (GREEN *snatches off the last towel.*) Mercy! Who's that? (*Recoiling to chair at right of table, she tips it over and falls. There, as she stares up at* GREEN, *he peers over at her.*) What! So you're there, Mr. Green?

(*Rising, she picks up the chair.*)

GREEN. No, Dolly, I'm not there, I'm here. I was there, Dolly, but I've just moved.—Dolly, I'm not Green now, I'm blue, truly blue, to see you so severe. (*Kneeling near* DOLLY.) Dolly, oh, Dolly, pity Blue!

DOLLY. (*Sternly.*) What are you doing here, sir?

GREEN. Kneeling, I believe. You may not believe me, 't is not an kneesy thing for me to do. (*Rises, rubbing his knees.*) Ha, ha! d' ye see?

DOLLY. Yes, I see a donkey.

(*She turns away.*)

GREEN. (*Following and embracing her very lovingly, sings to the air of "Comin' thro' the rye":*)

If a donkey see a donkey
Need a donkey sigh?
And if a donkey kiss a donkey
Need a donkey cry?

(*Kisses her.*)

DOLLY. Don't! don't touch me, sir!

(*She crosses left, and moves basket to the floor.*)

GREEN. "Sir" to me? That's queer.

DOLLY. Queer? I should think it was, queer.

(*She busies herself about the room, paying no attention to him, while she moves the clothes horse and basket.*)

GREEN. Dolly, Dolly, I say!

DOLLY. Who cares what you say?

GREEN. But, Dolly, I want—

DOLLY. Who cares what you want?

GREEN. But really, my darling—

DOLLY. Don't dare to darling me after—after what's happened.

GREEN. What's happened?

DOLLY. Oh, you know well enough.

(*She sits in chair at left of table, and slaps the glove on the table.*)

GREEN. Don't jag my glove about in that manner! (*Aside.*) Oh, I see, Hazel's been here, and told Dolly everything, and she thinks I've been an accomplice in this infernal business! (*Aloud.*) Don't, Dolly, don't!

DOLLY. Don't what, sir?

GREEN. Suspect me; I'm not the man who did it.

DOLLY. (*Excited, amazed.*) You're not the man who did it?

GREEN. I am not that man.

DOLLY. (*Aside.*) Not the man, who deserted me all these weeks? He is not the man, and he says this to my face! (*Rises, exploding.*) Oh, you brazen rogue!

GREEN. It wasn't me who did it—it was Barney, Barney O'Flynn.

DOLLY. Barney O'Flynn, who's she?

GREEN. He isn't a she, she's a he.

DOLLY. What are you talking about?

GREEN. Barney O'Flynn.

DOLLY. What of her?

GREEN. Hang it—he isn't a her—she's a him!

DOLLY. (*Tartly.*) What is she?

GREEN. Look here, I say Barney's a man—male, masculine, first person singular, of the Irish gender—do you understand?

DOLLY. (*Arms akimbo.*) Oh—so you pretend it's a man that's kept you away all this time, do you?

(*She sits at right of table.*)

GREEN. (*Sitting at left.*) Yes, and the most unmitigated ass of a man I ever saw. Dolly, if Hazel told you—that I was to blame—

DOLLY. (*Leaning over the table.*) Hazel tell me? How could she tell me anything?

GREEN. (*Puzzled.*) Eh?

DOLLY. I haven't seen her blessed face for over a year—and never will see it again, I'm afraid.

GREEN. (*Astonished.*) Hasn't Hazel been here? Has she be—

DOLLY. Here?

GREEN. (*Stammering.*) Don't you know?—No, she don't!

DOLLY. Know what?

GREEN. (*Stuttering.*) I—I mean that she must be—I that—n-nothing.

DOLLY. What do you mean by all this talk?

GREEN. N-nothing, except—that is—I only mean—to—to—hang it—I don't know what I'm talking about.

DOLLY. (*Fiercely.*) Pittacus—you're deceiving me! Something's happened; don't deny it.

GREEN. I don't—yes—I don't—no—I do.

DOLLY. Where's Hazel?

GREEN. Bless me—that's—that's what I wanted you to tell me.

DOLLY. Then you don't know where she is?

GREEN. No, ding it—I wish I did.

DOLLY. Haven't you seen her, then?

GREEN. Oh, yes, that is, no—not since—I say I saw, I saw that I see, saw—oh, what am I see-sawing about? I say that I see, that I saw that I see—

DOLLY. Not since when?

GREEN. Well, since the deluge, if you will have it—since she ran away.

DOLLY. Ran away—from whom?

GREEN. From her—that is—(*Looking at her, then dropping his eyes as he says*) Lord Travers.

DOLLY. From her husband, you mean?

GREEN. Y-yes, I suppose I do.

DOLLY. Suppose you do? Don't you know he's her husband?

GREEN. (*Utterly broken, rises.*) I don't—don't know anything. I only know that life's a nuisance—and it's a swindle that ever I was born.

DOLLY. (*Kneeling to him, as he sits again.*) Pittacus, Pittacus! You're hiding something—what's come to Hazel? Why has she run away—why do you talk to me so strangely?

GREEN. Dolly, my darling, hang it! Don't look so miserable—and I'll try to tell you all—you see—

DUNSTAN. (*Inside, calling.*) Dolly, Dolly, child!

DOLLY. (*Starting.*) That's her father—

he 's wanting me—hurry—tell me quickly.

GREEN. No, no, not now! He 'll come and hear me, and he must never know. I must run, dear.—Meet me outside near the old tree, where we used to talk so much. The moon is shining! I 'll tell you all.

(*Rising, he starts to go.*)

DOLLY. All right, I 'll go to you the moment I get away from my uncle.

DUNSTAN. (*Inside.*) Dolly, child, are you never coomin'?

DOLLY. Yes, uncle, I 'm coming.

GREEN. (*Detaining her.*) Why don't the old bear come here to you?

DOLLY. Why, poor dear heart! He 's blind.

GREEN. Blind!

DOLLY. Yes, just after you went away, he got news of some kind that made him awfully ill. For days he was out of his mind, raving about Hazel; and when the fever went away, it left him blind.

DUNSTAN. (*Appearing in the doorway, very old and broken.*) Why, Dolly, child, what keeps thee so long, when thee hears me call?

(DOLLY *runs to him.*)

DOLLY. Here I be. (*Leading him to chair.*) I had work to finish here, uncle.

DUNSTAN. (*Sitting.*) Bring me my pipe, child.—I have much thinkin' to do to-night, an' nothin' helps me to think like my pipe.

DOLLY. All right, uncle dear, I 'll bring it to ye. (*She goes to* GREEN, *sees him out of the door, where he points outside, seeming to ask her if she 'll meet him. She motions "Yes." He kisses her loudly and goes out.*)

DUNSTAN. What be that?

DOLLY. (*Getting his pipe.*) What 's what, uncle?

DUNSTAN. That noise.

DOLLY. What noise, uncle?

DUNSTAN. 'T were a noise that sounded like a kiss, girl.

DOLLY. (*Filling his pipe.*) Oh, it must have been the—the—sputtering of the fire.

DUNSTAN. The only fire I ever heard spooter like that be the fire o' love, lass.—Who 's been here?

DOLLY. When, uncle?

DUNSTAN. Just now.

DOLLY. Here 's your pipe, uncle;—will I light it for you?

(*Striking a match.*)

DUNSTAN. Aye, lass, do. (*As she lights his pipe.*) I wish thee could only light my eyes as easy as thee lights the pipe.

DOLLY. Oh, uncle, don't talk like that. I can't abide it.

(DOLLY *puts her arm round* DUNSTAN'S *neck, and places her cheek against his head.*)

DUNSTAN. There, there, child, I 'm a weak old fool to bother thee with my burdens. Go, find thy Aunt Mercy; she be above stairs; tell her I must see her, and then get to bed.

DOLLY. All right, uncle. (*Going.*) I 'll not go to bed this night till I 've got news of Hazel. (*Exit.*)

(HAZEL *appears outside, looking through the window. Opening the casement, pale and ragged, she sees* DUNSTAN, *and pauses.*)

DUNSTAN. (*Laying down his pipe, with a sigh.*) There 's no use, even the pipe can't comfort me to-night. I moost tell my poor wife a' now. It 's hard, bitter hard, to leave the auld mill—a pauper, too—but it moost be done. Better starvation, death, anything, than more debt to Squire Rodney. Oh, that child o' mine, my only bairn, why should she have been her feyther's curse? Oh, my old heart is heavy to-night! would that I were dead, would that I were dead! (*He sobs.* HAZEL *moans and drops her head on the sill.* DUNSTAN *starts up.*) Hark, what 's that? Who 's there? Some one at the window. Who is it? Is there any one there? That 's strange.

(*He feels his way toward the window.*)

(*Enter* MERCY.)

MERCY. What art doin' there, Dunstan?

DUNSTAN. I could ha' sworn, wife, that I heard some one at the window.

MERCY. (*Starting.*) Some one at the window?

DUNSTAN. Aye, I heard a noise like a moan, and then, when I cried out, it seemed as though the window were closed quick and sharp like.

MERCY. (*Aside.*) My darling child, I know it is! I know it is! I can feel it here. What if it were Hazel? Yes, it is my child, she may be there, longin' to return! (*She takes* DUNSTAN *to his chair.*) Come, Dunstan, sit down, and let me speak to thee. Perhaps I can make thee understand the noise at the window.

(HAZEL *appears as before.*)

DUNSTAN. (*Sitting.*) What dost think it were, wife?

MERCY. Dost know what day this be, sweetheart?

DUNSTAN. Thursday, I believe.

MERCY. Yes, Thursday, the 10th day of October.

DUNSTAN. Ah! Ah-a-a-h!

MERCY. This day, two and twenty year ago, our Hazel were born.

DUNSTAN. Hist, wife, hist! Don't 'mind me o' that now.

MERCY. Oh, feyther, dear, why not? why not? That were a sweet day to us, then.

DUNSTAN. Aye, but it be a bitter day to us now.

MERCY. Feyther, what if thy child were at thy door now, longin' to coom back to the old house?

DUNSTAN. I'd bid her begone.

MERCY. Oh, Dunstan!

DUNSTAN. I'd point at these sightless eyes an' say, "This be thy work." I'd point at thee, and say, "Look at thy mother (*The wind sounds outside.*) a beggar wi' thy feyther in the street; thy work, too."

MERCY. What dost mean, Dunstan?

DUNSTAN. I mean, Mercy, wife, that the end be coom. I owe everything we gotten in the world to Squire Rodney—an' debt to him I can bear no longer now. I've sent for him to coom this very night and take possession o' the mill—and to-morrow thee and I an' Dolly moost wander out beggars, but beggars no longer to the man our flesh and blood has wronged.

MERCY. Oh, Dunstan, can thee never forgive?

DUNSTAN. Never! (*The wind sounds.*) Strangers she chose; to strangers let her look, for she be dead to us forever! (HAZEL, *with moan of despair, disappears, leaving the window open.* DUNSTAN *starts.*) Hark—that moan again!

MERCY. (*Going to the window.*) Aye and see—the window's open! Oh, Dunstan, what if it be our child, our Hazel!

DUNSTAN. Hoot, woman, it were the wind! (*It sounds again.*) There's a storm coomin' up. Maister Rodney 'ull not be here to-night. Better lock up the mill. Close the window, wife, and bolt the door, then get thee to bed. (MERCY *goes to the window and looks out.* DUNSTAN *feels his way to the door.*) Mercy, I'll go once more over the old mill I've loved so long and these hands have tended so well. Good-night, wife! Good-night, wife! Good-night!

MERCY. Good-night, Dunstan, and may the angels be wi' you, this last night i' the old mill.—An' my child may be out in the night—homeless and hungry!—No, no; I'll go for Maister Rodney. He will save Hazel, an' he's able to break the iron o' her feyther's will.

(*Exit, weeping.*)

(HAZEL *appears at the window; slowly opening the door, she steals wearily in, and shivers over the fire.*)

HAZEL. Oh, how cold I am! But no fire will ever warm me again. (*Looking about her.*) And this is home, the home that I have lost, the home I have cursed! My father's chair! How often have I sat here upon his lap, my arms about his neck, and heard him sing his dear old songs! How often have I knelt here at my mother's feet and prayed as I can never pray again! (*She sinks on her knees by the chair.*) As I never can pray again! Oh, father, father! Heaven has heard your curse.

(*With a sob, she buries her face in chair.* DUNSTAN *appears, right. He gropes across the room, places his hand on the back of the chair at which she kneels;* HAZEL *draws back with a groan. He starts.*)

DUNSTAN. What be that? (*The wind sounds.*) Nothing but the sobbing of the storm. Ah, it does me good to hear it. It sounds like the voice of my own heart. Dear old mill, my eyes will never, never more behold thee, and my hands have felt thy timbers for the last, last time. (HAZEL *follows him across the room, removes a chair from his path, kisses the lapel of his coat.*) But God's will be done! God's will be done.

(*He gropes his way to the door left, lifts his hands in prayer, and passes out.* HAZEL *goes back and bows her head on the arm of the chair.*)

(RODNEY *enters. His coat is closely buttoned up.*)

RODNEY. A fearful night! Dunstan has sent for me. What for, I cannot imagine. Perhaps he has word of Hazel. I wonder—Is that you, Dolly—asleep? (HAZEL *starts and looks up.* RODNEY, *recognizing her, draws back, then kneels at her feet.*) Here? Back again? Oh, Hazel, my angel, my poor sufferin' saint—bless ye for coming back! You've brought life, salvation, joy once more to the old mill!

HAZEL. (*Rises and starts to go, right.*) Oh, Mr. Rodney, don't kneel to me, don't speak to me! Let me go, let me go, and carry the misery and shame I bring, away from here, forever!

RODNEY. (*Stopping her.*) Let you go now? Never! You bring misery and shame here? No, no, girl, that 's not true, that 's not true!

HAZEL. Oh, but you do not know!

RODNEY. Yes, child, I know all. I know that a villain wronged ye, but the friend's heart, the mother's arms, the father's home all are open to ye now.

HAZEL. Mr. Rodney, you don't know what you say. My father but now, a moment ago, declared he would never own me in this world again. To-morrow he leaves this dear old mill, driven by my broken promise, by my shame.

RODNEY. What, quit the mill, girl? No, that shall never be.

HAZEL. Ah, sir, who can prevent it now?

RODNEY. You, girl, you.

HAZEL. I? Impossible! He would never accept a service from me, now.

RODNEY. Yes, girl, one service, one that would pay his debt to me a thousand-fold.

HAZEL. What service is that?

RODNEY. Keep the old promise; become my wife.

HAZEL. (*Amazed.*) Oh, Mr. Rodney, and would you marry me, now?

RODNEY. Yes, and be the proudest man on earth to call you wife.

HAZEL. (*Turns from him.*) Oh, sir!—I—

RODNEY. (*Takes her hand.*) I know all ye'd say, child: your heart has been another's—you could never give me a wife's love. Why, Hazel, dear, I do not ask it. If you will but marry me, it 's only as a beloved daughter I will hold ye, a daughter I shall have the right to cherish and to guard.

HAZEL. (*Leaving him.*) Oh, what shall I do, what shall I do?

RODNEY. Be brave, girl; marry me, save your father—bless your mother—bring happiness to us all once more; speak—promise you 'll do this.

HAZEL. Yes, on one condition.

RODNEY. And what is that, child?

HAZEL. (*Utterly heart-broken.*) Call my father—he is blind—he cannot see me. If he consents to let me pay his debt to you, you shall have my hand, and I will be your wife.

RODNEY. (*Kissing her hand.*) Noble girl! Heaven will reward ye for this resolution. I 'll call your father instantly. Wait here.—You 'll see—all will yet be well.

(*Exit, left. The wind sounds.*)

HAZEL. Another promise I have made this noble man. This time I 'll keep my word in spite of my own miserable heart.

(*Enter* RODNEY *and* DUNSTAN *together.*)

DUNSTAN. Why, Maister Rodney, is that you, sir? How did ye get in? The door was bolted.

(HAZEL *places a chair for* DUNSTAN.)

RODNEY. Some good angel must have drawn the bolt, then; but enough of that. You sent for me. I was delayed. I am here at last. Tell me, what 's the good word to-night, Dunstan?

DUNSTAN. (*Sitting.*) Maister Rodney, you 've been a good friend to us. For eight long years I 've been in debt to ye—a debt I thought my child would pay, but —well, when she broke her faith and left us, I strove hard to make the old mill earn enough to pay the money that I owed ye. Fever laid hold on me and left me blind; all hope of work for me is over now. And I have but one way to pay my debt, and that is to gi' ye up the mill.

RODNEY. (*Leaning over* DUNSTAN'S *chair.*) And do ye think I 'll take it?

DUNSTAN. Yes, for I shall leave it. I owe ye too much a'ready; I an' mine have wronged ye every way. I 'll do penance for my child as a beggar in the street.

RODNEY. No, no, Dunstan. Let Hazel do penance for herself; let all be as it was; let her pay your debt by marrying me.

DUNSTAN. She, marry you?

RODNEY. Aye, why not? you know she 's free.

(HAZEL *gradually sinks down in front of* DUNSTAN.)

DUNSTAN. Free of what? Of stains o' shame?

RODNEY. Come, come, sir, no more o' that.

DUNSTAN. No, no, sir, she can never pay debt o' mine.

RODNEY. Dunstan, will you hear me—

DUNSTAN. No, no, not one word! (HAZEL *kneels before him.*) If she were now before my very face, kneeling at my feet, prayin' for my consent to marry ye, I 'd tell her nay, never! I 'd tell her she had wronged ye bad enough wi'out seeking to make ye the hoosband of a dishonored creetur like herself.

(*The wind moans.* HAZEL *falls to the ground.*)

RODNEY. (*Raising her.*) Silence, hard-hearted man! Silence, for fear the curse of heaven may fall upon your iron will, and break its strength forever.

(*He places* HAZEL *in chair.*)

DUNSTAN. Mr. Rodney, I only do my duty, sir, to you and my own pride.

RODNEY. So you 'll not consent to have her marry me?

DUNSTAN. Never!

RODNEY. Very well, then, I'll do all I can to induce her to marry me without your consent.

DUNSTAN. A'reet, sir, a'reet! Good-night, Maister Rodney; if you have no objection, I 'll see ye out now and bolt the door.

(*He rises and starts for the door.*)

RODNEY. (*Intercepts and leads him left.*) Not yet; go call Mercy and bid her come here.

DUNSTAN. Mercy? What do ye want o' her?

RODNEY. Good advice, that you can neither give nor take.

DUNSTAN. A'reet, sir. I'll tell Mercy that you want to speak to her, but mind this—Mercy has given her word not to set eyes upon her child wi'out my consent. I warn ye she 'll not lie; no, not even to please you, Maister Rodney, and so good-night. Good-night, Maister Rodney, good-night. (*Exit.*)

RODNEY. (*Going to* HAZEL, *who sits dazed in chair.*) Oh, heart of iron! Hazel, don't mind that now. All the world knows that a mother's love—Hazel, Hazel, dear! (*He touches her. She starts as if in dream.*) Hazel! Hazel, child, in heaven's name speak to me!

HAZEL. (*Rising.*) Mr. Rodney, do you love me still?

RODNEY. More than life—or all the world —but as a father, Hazel, dear, a father, and no other way.

HAZEL. If you love me, leave me—let me alone tonight; tomorrow will settle all for the best, I hope.

RODNEY. Must I leave you, then?

HAZEL. If you care for my happiness.

RODNEY. But we 'll meet again?

HAZEL. I hope so—(*He kisses her hand. She murmurs aside*) in heaven.

RODNEY. Then, good-night, my darling; your mother 's coming; you can rest on her heart and be at peace. Good-night, Hazel! May pitying angels guard and bless you. (*Exit, right.*)

HAZEL. All is over; I know the worst now, and I know what I must do. I 'll go, and there in the water that has brought so much misery to this home, I 'll drown my sorrows and my sins. (*Going.*) Good-bye, old home—farewell, sweet memories, fond hopes—farewell, mother, father, life—life—life!

(*She goes out. The wind moans louder. After a pause,* DUNSTAN *speaks outside.*)

DUNSTAN. Mercy, Mercy, where be ye?

(*Entering.*)

Why don't ye answer me? Mercy has gone, Maister Rodney; where can she be? Oh, why don't ye answer? No one here, the house deserted! What can it mean? —Maister Rodney, Maister Rodney!

MET. (*Outside.*) Help! help! She 's drowning! Drowning! Hazel 's drowning! I saw her jump in—it 's Hazel, Hazel! (*Rushing across at back.*) Hurry, help, help!

DUNSTAN. (*In horror.*) Hazel, drowning! Dying! Here, before my face? No, no, I 'll save her! Ah, heaven! I cannot! I am blind! (*Falling on his knees.*) Oh, God! this is thy punishment! I was blind when I drove her out —and now, when I could save her—I cannot see—I cannot see—I cannot see!

(*He falls to the ground.*)

ACT FOURTH.

SCENE. *Same as Act Third; morning; the fire is out, the table cleared, a jug of water and a mug on the table.* DOLLY *discovered asleep in a chair, near the table, head in arms.*

(*Enter* GREEN, *smoking a cigarette, and singing a line of "Molly Bawn."*)

GREEN. (*Calls gently.*) Doll! Dolly! Dolly don't answer; Dolly 's in heaven now. Sleep is a delightful don't-care-a-ducat sort of state, and yet who would sleep always? Not I—nor shall she. How lovely she looks—yes, a veritable sleeping beauty; but her time has come— the prince is here, and will wake her with a kiss. Will you permit me? Of course she will. (*He kisses her.* DOLLY *makes motion as though brushing away a fly.*) She takes me for a fly—I'll fly it again. (*He kisses her.*) She's the kind of a fish that won't rise at a fly. Fire in the shape of a kiss is a failure—we'll try what smoke will do.

(*He puffs smoke in her face.*)

DOLLY. (*Awakes with a sneeze.*) Pah!—smoke! Where's the fire?

GREEN. (*Leans against the table.*) Here—here—in my breast—consuming my heart for you.

DOLLY. (*Going to him.*) Oh, Pittacus, I'm so glad you've come! I have so much to tell you! Such queer things have happened.

GREEN. Strange! Let's hear it. I adore queer things—that's why I adore you.

(*Embraces her.*)

DOLLY. No nonsense now; listen, and explain if you can.

GREEN. I can explain everything—except the power a woman has to make a donkey of a man.

DOLLY. No nonsense now. Last night, after I returned from my meeting with you—when you told me all about my poor dear Hazel— (*She wipes her eyes.*)

GREEN. Well?

DOLLY. I found Uncle Dunstan lying here—unconscious—on the floor. I was terribly frightened—called for help—there was no one in the house—even Aunt Mercy had disappeared—gone off to Squire Rodney's house, to meet that crazy creature, Met.

GREEN. What did you do?

DOLLY. You won't believe me when I tell you.

GREEN. I dare say I won't, but tell me to fill in the time.

DOLLY. Well, sir, I dragged that big man into the other room and laid him on the lounge myself! There!

GREEN. The tale is a tough one, but—(*Takes her hand and arm; she throws up her arm; he feels her muscle.*) you may not now believe it—but I believe it now.

DOLLY. Aunt Mercy came in soon after; we worked for hours until we brought him to. We've been up with him all night long, for ever since he came to consciousness, he's been out of his head.

GREEN. Out of his head! What an unpleasant position for the rest of his body! Oh, I see, you mean out of his mind; that's nothing, when you're used to it as I am.

DOLLY. You are?

GREEN. Yes, and it's all your fault.

DOLLY. What do ye mean?

GREEN. It's very queer, but I have always noticed that, if you ever remarked it, it is a peculiar physiological fact, while a man may lose his mind without its affecting his heart—he can rarely have an affection of the heart, without running the risk of losing his mind. (*Embracing her.*) Now, I say, darling, did you ever feel as if you were losing your mind?

DOLLY. Never!

GREEN. That's because you've no mind to lose.

DOLLY. (*Pushing him off.*) Not on your account, sir.

(MERCY *appears left.*)

Hush—my aunt—

(GREEN *draws away, right.*)

MERCY. (*Looking back as she comes.*) At last he seems to be asleep. (*Turns and sees* GREEN.) What, you here, Mr. Green?

GREEN. (*Embarrassed.*) Well, madam—you may not believe it—but I rather think I am.

MERCY. And Hazel—my child—have you any news of her?

GREEN. (*Confused.*) Well, you see—that is— (*Aside to* DOLLY.) Does she know the truth?

DOLLY. Nothing from me.

MERCY. Well, sir—can't you answer me?

GREEN. Yes, of course—that is, I could if you—I—we—only knew what you meant.

MERCY. Ah, sir! Something terrible has happened.—I feel it in my heart—but I'm so dazed with grief, I can't quite make it out. Last night Met appeared; told me Hazel had left her husband and could not be found. I promised to join Met at Aaron Rodney's house. I went there late last night; neither Met nor Maister Rodney was there. I hurried home and found my husband dangerously ill. What happened while I was gone I cannot say, but I think Hazel must have come and—

GREEN and DOLLY. (*Together, eagerly.*) Well—well?

MERCY. I fear he heard her—had a fit of rage—drove her out again, and was struck down by the power of his passion.

GREEN. Impossible! If Hazel had been here she would not have gone without a word to you.

MERCY. It's hard to think it, and yet I cannot tell—I cannot tell.

(*Enter* RODNEY.)

Ah, thank heaven! Maister Rodney, have you seen Hazel?

RODNEY. Certainly—here.

ALL. Here?

RODNEY. Last night. We were to meet again this morning.

MERCY. Where?

RODNEY. Here.

MERCY. Then she is coming!

RODNEY. Coming? Has she gone?

MERCY. We do not know.

GREEN. (*Starting.*) Good heavens! I have an idea.

DOLLY. What is it?

GREEN. I see it all.—She s' gone with her husband.

MERCY. Her husband!

GREEN. He came down here to look for her; when I returned to our lodgings last night he was not there. I did n't mind it, for ever since she left him he 's had a fashion of wandering out at night till very late.

RODNEY. Well—well—go on.

GREEN. When I awoke this morning, he was not in his room.

DUNSTAN. (*Inside; calling.*) Water, water!

MERCY. Hark—'t is Dunstan.

DUNSTAN. (*Appearing in doorway, followed by* JOE.) Water, water, water!

RODNEY. What does this mean?

MERCY. He 's raving again.

DUNSTAN. Water—quick, quick—I 'm burning up! I'm burning up! (DOLLY *gives him water.*) This is the lake that burneth forever—remorse, remorse, remorse! (DOLLY *holds the glass for* DUNSTAN; *about to drink, he pauses; then puts the glass from him.*) Water—no, no—take it away—'t was water killed her.

RODNEY. What 's that he says?

DUNSTAN. Hark, I hear that cry again! Oh, God—save her—save her—she 's drowning, drowning!

ALL. Drowning?

DUNSTAN. Hush—not so loud—see how sweetly she is sleeping.

MERCY. (*With a cry.*) Ah! my child is drowned, drowned.

(*She falls on* RODNEY'S *breast.*)

RODNEY. No, no—it cannot be.

(*He supports* MERCY *to a chair near the fireplace.*)

DUNSTAN. Hush, not so loud, you 'll wake her! Yes, she was drowned! I did it—I held her till she died—I could n't help it. Something forced me on. What was it? What was it? This hard, hard, hard heart of mine!

RODNEY. Horrible! Horrible!

(DOLLY *sobs.*)

DUNSTAN. See, see! there she goes to the mill—she beckons me! Quite right, lass; quite right, lass. Yes, yes—I 'm cooming, cooming, cooming! (*He starts toward the right;* JOE *leads him.*) Yes, take me to the mill, take me to the mill! The noise there will drown the awful voices here, here, here!

(*Striking his forehead, he goes out with* JOE.)

RODNEY. (*Aside.*) And this is the bitter end of all! No, no; there's something still to do. (*To* GREEN.) There is a duty here for you and for me.—Let us go.

MERCY. (*Starting up.*) Where are ye going?

RODNEY. To search for Hazel—there!

(*He points off. Outside* MET'S *pipe plays merrily. All start and listen.*)

MERCY. Hark! 'T is Met, 't is Met! and he has news of her.

(*She hastens to the door.*)

(MET. *rushes in.*)

ALL. Hazel—where 's Hazel?

MET. She 's saved!

ALL. Saved?

MET. Yes, by her husband.

ALL. Her husband?

MERCY. Where is she, lad? Where is she?

MET. Coming here with him. God bless him! God bless him!

GREEN. How did he save her?

MET. Last night, when she fell in the river —I called for help and jumped in. The river was runnin' strong, and when I caught her in my arms, she was unconscious. I was growin' faint and beginnin' to despair—when I saw a man standin' on the bank. I shouted; he heard, and plunged in—

ALL. Go on, brave boy—go on!

MET. It was Hazel's husband—and, ah—it 's a stout heart, and a strong arm he has. He landed us both near Farmer Woodford's house. There he took Hazel, and there he nursed her back to life—as she had nursed him a year before.

MERCY. Thank heaven—thank heaven!

(*She weeps for joy.*)

(HAZEL *appears at right, followed by* ARTHUR.)

HAZEL. (*Holding out her arms.*) Mother! Mother!

ALL. Hazel!

MERCY. (*Embracing her.*) My child—precious child!

(*All gather round them with delight,* MET. *dancing ecstatically.*)

GREEN. Ah—will you permit me?

(*He kisses* HAZEL'S *hand.*)

RODNEY. (*To* ARTHUR.) You 've won her now, sir, and I can't help believing you mean to right her wrongs.

ARTHUR. Ah, sir, how can I right such wrongs as hers?

RODNEY. By making her indeed your wife.

ARTHUR. (*Handing him a letter.*) My answer to that is this. (RODNEY *takes the letter and goes to the window.*) Oh, Green, this is a happy day, but I thank heaven my mother never lived to see it.

GREEN. Why do you say that?

ARTHUR. I told you of the shame that was overhanging our house?

GREEN. You did.

ARTHUR. Well, I ordered my solicitor to settle my estate, and satisfy every claim of Lady Maud's against my father, if it took the last penny I had in the world. He observed my orders, and there remains to me now—nothing.

GREEN. Nothing?

ARTHUR. Nothing but my own hands; my own brains, and the endless wealth of my love for her. (*He points at* HAZEL.)

GREEN. (*Grasping his hand.*) Travers, I congratulate you. You 're above a lord now—you 're every inch a man.

RODNEY. (*Coming forward.*) Ah, my friends! Can this be possible? Here is indeed cause for rejoicing. From this letter I gather that the inn at which the ceremony was performed was not on the English, but on the Scottish side of the border; therefore your marriage with Hazel was a legal one after all, and it seems that Barney, the scoundrel, was the only one to blame.

(*He embraces* HAZEL.)

GREEN. Oh, no, don't blame Barney, but blame the world that educated him. We ought to be satisfied that he did not put it on the Irish side of the border.

DUNSTAN. (*Inside.*) Save her! Do ye hear me? Save her!

HAZEL. Hark! What 's that?

DUNSTAN. (*Inside.*) Where is she? Where is she?

MERCY. Oh, Hazel, it is your father.

HAZEL. He will not drive me out again?

MERCY. No, no; he shall not; he cannot do it now.

DUNSTAN. (*Appearing at the door, followed by* JOE *and* DAN.) Let me get at her, let me get at her! Fools, stand back—give her air—air!

HAZEL. Heaven help me! he 's mad, mad! What shall we do, what shall we do?

RODNEY. Sing the song you used to sing to him so long ago—it may calm his wretched soul and soothe his brain.

(HAZEL *sings.*)

DUNSTAN. (*Stands listening.*) Her voice—from heaven—singing to me the old song! No, it 's gone; I hear her shriek for help—it 's Hazel! She 's drowning—let me out of this! Where 's the door? Bring me a light—a light!

(HAZEL *takes his hand.*)

MERCY. (*Comes to them.*) Have patience, poor heart, have patience.

DUNSTAN. (*Mistaking* HAZEL *for* MERCY.) Who be that, Mercy,—thee?

MERCY. Aye, Dunstan, I be here at thy side.

DUNSTAN. I 'm glad thee 's coom—but why did n't thee bring a light? I 'm so weary o' this darkness.

(ARTHUR *brings a chair.*)

MERCY. Patience, dear heart, the light will coom—the light will coom.

DUNSTAN. Aye, Mercy, wife, thee always brings the light to my heart, my faithful, loving wife.

(ARTHUR *and* HAZEL *place* DUNSTAN *in the chair.* HAZEL *returns to* MERCY.)

MERCY. No, no, Dunstan, don't say that, for I have a sin to confess to thee.

DUNSTAN. (*Sitting.*) Thee—a sin to confess to me? I 'll not believe it.

MERCY. It 's true, Dunstan; I 've broken my promise to thee.

DUNSTAN. Broken thy promise?

MERCY. I 've seen our child—wi'out thy consent.

DUNSTAN. (*Starting up.*) Seen Hazel! Yes, yes, I know—I know—thee 's seen her poor dead face—thee 's not seen her. No, she 's there—above—praying to God to forgive me—forgive me—forgive me.

MERCY. No, Dunstan, no, it 's not her body alone I 've seen, but her soul too, shining in her eyes, wi' living love for thee—her feyther.

DUNSTAN. (*Rising.*) Then she 's alive—saved!

MERCY. (*Goes to* DUNSTAN; HAZEL *kneels before him.* ARTHUR *stands behind him.*) Aye, Dunstan, by her hoosband. The man who took her from thee has brought her back to thy old arms.

DUNSTAN. Where is she? Where is she?

MERCY. Stretch forth thy hands and feel her face.

DUNSTAN. (*Feeling her face.*) Who 's this?

HAZEL. Thy child—thine only child.

DUNSTAN. (*With a cry falls back in the chair, dragging her upon his breast.*) Hazel, Hazel, coom to my heart! My child, my child!

RODNEY. At last, Dunstan, the iron of thy will has melted in the fire of a father's love.

DOLLY. (*Embraces* GREEN.) Oh, Pittacus, my happiness is perfect now!

GREEN. You may not believe it, but so is mine—No, stop—not quite.

(*He steps forward, speaking to the audience.*)

Will you permit me?—Thank you.—'T was our way,
From earliest time, of winding up a play;
A kindly custom,—actors know its worth,
Peace after pain, and after sadness, mirth.
You 've seen tonight a conscientious man
Offend his soul as only conscience can;
You 've seen the sufferings that he caused and felt
Ere yet his iron will was forced to melt;
You guess the lesson we would fain instill,
That human heart is more than human will.
You 've dropped your tears, perhaps,—pray let me now beguile
Your friendly faces of one parting smile.
You 've seen me drifting through this troubled scene
And turning everything—well—turning one thing, (*taking* DOLLY'S *hand*) Green.
'T is nature's general and her favorite tint,
And therefore—well—I merely drop the hint—
Green though I am, I 've brought these lovers through,
And what I 've done for them I 'll do for you.
Don't brood on care—the trouble that you make
Is always hard to bear, and harder still to shake;
Smile on the world—the trouble that is sent
In patience take it as your punishment.
He wins who laughs—he does n't care a rap, he,
And so, like Pittacus, he 's always happy.

SHENANDOAH

BY

Bronson Howard

Reprinted from the privately printed edition, by permission of the Society of American Dramatists and Composers, from a copy furnished by Samuel French.

SHENANDOAH

Shenandoah represents the Civil War play. It also represents the work of the playwright who illustrates in his career the development of modern American drama. Bronson Crocker Howard was born in Detroit, Michigan, October 7, 1842, the son of Charles Howard, a merchant of Detroit, who was at one time Mayor of the city. After being educated at the local schools in Detroit, he prepared for Yale College, but did not enter, owing to eye trouble. He began newspaper work in Detroit, and wrote plays. The first of these to be performed was a dramatization of an episode in *Les Miserables* under the title of *Fantine,* which was played in Detroit in 1864. In 1865 Mr. Howard came to New York and after he had had the usual struggles to obtain a hearing, Augustin Daly put on *Saratoga* at the Fifth Avenue Theatre, December 21, 1870. The play was a great success, running one hundred and one nights. It is a comedy, bordering on farce, reflecting the manners of 1870 and concerned with the adventures of Bob Sackett, who is engaged to be married to four girls at once. It was adapted for the English stage by Frank Marshall and produced by Sir Charles (then Mr.) Wyndham under the title of *Brighton* at the Court Theatre, London, May 25, 1874. Later Mr. Wyndham played it in Germany in a German translation.

Diamonds, a comedy, produced in New York September 26, 1872, and *Moorcroft or The Double Wedding,* a comedy, played in New York, October 17, 1874, and partly suggested by a short story by John Hay, were not so significant as *The Banker's Daughter,* produced first at Hooley's Theatre, Chicago, September 4, 1873, as *Lillian's Last Love,* and under its final title at the Union Square Theatre, New York, September 30, 1878. This play, based on the theme of a woman's self-sacrifice for her father's sake, through which she marries a man she does not love, still holds the stage. An interesting account of the building of this play is given in Mr. Howard's *The Autobiography of a Play.*

Next came in rapid succession, *Old Love Letters,* a charming one-act play, based on the return of a package of letters between two former lovers, which was played at the Park Theatre, New York, August 31, 1878; *Hurricanes,* a comedy produced first in Chicago at Hooley's Theatre, May 27, 1878, and later in England under the title *Truth; Wives,* a comedy adapted from Molière's *Ecole des Femmes* and *Ecole des Maris,* played at Daly's Theatre, New York, October 18, 1879, and *Fun in a Green Room,* a comedy played at Booth's Theatre, New York, April 10, 1882. His next most significant play was *Young Mrs. Winthrop,* a study of the estrangement of a husband and wife through circumstances and their reconciliation through their child. It was first played at the Madison Square

Theatre, New York, October 9, 1882. A very successful comedy, *One of Our Girls,* the scene of which is laid in France, was first played at the Lyceum Theatre, New York, November 10, 1885. *Met by Chance,* a romantic play, performed at the Lyceum Theatre, New York, January 11, 1887, was not a success, but on September 26 of the same year *The Henrietta* began its career at the Union Square Theatre. This is a dramatization of the motives that move Wall Street and in it Mr. William H. Crane and Mr. Stuart Robson achieved one of the great successes of their joint careers. It was revived by Mr. Crane in 1913 after revision by Winchell Smith. *Baron Rudolf,* played originally in 1881, was revived in New York, October 25, 1887. *Shenandoah* came in 1888 and *Aristocracy,* a comedy in which social types, both national and international, are contrasted was put on first at Palmer's Theatre, New York, November 14, 1892. *Peter Stuyvesant,* an historical comedy, written in collaboration with Mr. Brander Matthews, and played at Wallack's Theatre, New York, October 2, 1899, was the last play of Mr. Howard's to be performed. *Knave and Queen* and *Kate,* the latter a clever international play, have not been performed. Mr. Howard died at Avon, New Jersey, August 4, 1908.

Shenandoah, which he wrote at the height of his career, was first put on at the Boston Museum on November 19, 1888. It was based upon an earlier work which Mr. Howard had produced in Louisville, Kentucky, about twenty years before and at its first tryout in Boston it was not a success. After revision, however, it was brought out at the Star Theatre, New York, September 9, 1889, and ran in New York, during the entire season. It has proved to be the most popular of Mr. Howard's plays.

Saratoga (1870), and *Young Mrs. Winthrop* (1882), have been published by Samuel French. *Kate* was published in 1906 by Harper and Brothers. *The Henrietta* has been published in England by French, but in this country has been only privately printed. The same is true of *Old Love Letters, The Banker's Daughter, Shenandoah* and *Aristocracy.* The present text of *Shenandoah* is based on the privately printed edition prepared by Mr. Howard. It was furnished the editor by Samuel French through the courtesy of the Society of American Dramatists and Composers.

For biography of Mr. Howard, see the volume *In Memoriam—Bronson Howard,* published by the American Dramatists Club, New York, 1910. This contains a biography by H. P. Mawson, an appreciation by Brander Matthews, *The Autobiography of a Play* by Bronson Howard and a list of the plays with the original casts. *The Autobiography of a Play* has been reprinted with an introduction by Augustus Thomas in the *Publications of the Dramatic Museum of Columbia University,* New York, 1915. See also *Plays of the Present,* ed. by J. B. Clapp and E. F. Edgett, New York, 1902, and *A History of the American Drama from the Civil War to the Present Day,* by A. H. Quinn, New York, 1936, Vol. I, pp. 39-65.

Of especial interest is the article on Bronson Howard in William Archer's *English Dramatists of Today* (1882), in which Mr. Archer, while pointing out Mr. Howard's merits, accuses him of vulgarity for certain expressions in *Saratoga,* which are not included in the play, and which were therefore, most probably inserted by the English adaptor.

[FROM PREFACE TO SHENANDOAH]

In ACT I, just before the opening of the war, HAVERHILL is a Colonel in the Regular Army. KERCHIVAL WEST and ROBERT ELLINGHAM are Lieutenants in his regiment, having been classmates at West Point.

ACT I

CHARLESTON HARBOR IN 1861. AFTER THE BALL

The citizens of Charleston knew almost the exact hour at which the attack on Fort Sumter would begin, and they gathered in the gray twilight of the morning to view the bombardment as a spectacle.—*Nicolay, Campaigns of the Civil War, Vol. I.*

"I shall open fire in one hour."—*Beauregard's last message to Major Anderson. Sent at* 3:20 *A. M., April* 12, 1861.

ACTS II AND III

The Union Army, under General Sheridan, and the Confederate Army, under General Early, were encamped facing each other about twenty miles south of Winchester, on Cedar Creek. * * * Gen. Sheridan was called to Washington. Soon after he left, a startling despatch was taken by our own Signal Officers from the Confederate Signal Station on Three Top Mountain.—*Pond, Camp. Civ. War, Vol. XI.*

On the morning of Oct. 19th, the Union Army was taken completely by surprise. Thoburn's position was swept in an instant. Gordon burst suddenly upon the left flank. The men who escaped capture streamed through the camps along the road to Winchester.—*Pond, supra.*

Far away in the rear was heard cheer after cheer.—*Three years in the Sixth Corps.*

ACT IV

WASHINGTON, 1865. RESIDENCE OF GENERAL BUCKTHORN

I feel that we are on the eve of a new era, when there is to be great harmony between the Federal and Confederate.—*Gen. Grant's Memoirs.*

CASTS OF SHENANDOAH

		Original Cast Boston Museum, Nov. 19, 1888	First New York Production Star Theatre, N.Y., September 9, 1889
General Haverhill	Officers of Sheridan's Cavalry	Thomas L. Coleman	Wilton Lackaye
Colonel Kerchival West		John B. Mason	Henry Miller
Captain Heartsease		Henry M. Pitt	Morton Selton
Lieutenant Frank Bedloe		Edgar L. Davenport	G. W. Bailey
Major-General Francis Buckthorn, Commander of the 19th Army Corps		C. Leslie Allen	Harry Harwood
Sergeant Barket		George W. Wilson	James O. Barrows
Colonel Robert Ellingham, 10th Virginia		Charles J. Bell	Lucius Henderson
Captain Thornton, Secret Service, C. S. A.		Willis Granger	John E. Kellerd
Mrs. Constance Haverhill		Annie M. Clarke	Dorothy Dorr
Gertrude Ellingham		Viola Allen	Viola Allen
Madeline West		Helen Dayne	Nanette Comstock
Jenny Buckthorn		Miriam O'Leary	Effie Shannon
Mrs. Edith Haverhill		Grace Atwell	Alice B. Haines
Hardwick, Surgeon		George Blake	W. L. Dennison
Captain Lockwood, U. S. Signal Corps		Herbert Potter	C. C. Brandt
Lieutenant of Signal Corps			Harry Thorn
Lieutenant of Infantry			George Maxwell
Corporal Dunn		James Nolan	W. J. Cummings
Benson		Charles S. Abbe	William Barnes
Old Margery		Kate Ryan	Mrs. Haslam
Janette		Miss Harding	Esther Drew
Wilkins		Henry MacDonna	

SHENANDOAH

ACT FIRST.

CHARLESTON HARBOR IN 1861. "AFTER THE BALL."

SCENE. *The Interior of a Southern Residence on the shore of Charleston Harbor. Large double doors at the rear of the stage are open. A large, wide window, with low sill, extends down the right side of the stage. A veranda is seen through the doors and the window. There is a wide opening on the left with a corridor beyond. The furniture and appointments are quaint and old-fashioned, but the general tone of the walls and upholstery is that of the old Colonial period in its more ornamental and decorative phase, as shown in the early days of Charleston. Old candlesticks and candelabra, with lighted candles nearly burned down, light the room, and in addition the moon-light streams in. Beyond the central doors and the window there is a lawn, with Southern foliage, extending down to the shores of the harbor; a part of the bay lies in the distance, with low-lying land beyond. The lights of Charleston are seen over the water along the shore. The gray twilight of early morning gradually steals over the scene as the Act progresses. As the curtain rises,* KERCHIVAL WEST *is sitting in a chair, his feet extended and his head thrown back, a handkerchief over his face.* ROBERT ELLINGHAM *strolls in on the veranda, beyond the window, smoking. He looks to the right, starts and moves to the window; leans against the upper side of the window and looks across.*

ELLINGHAM. Kerchival!

KERCHIVAL. (*Under the handkerchief.*) Eh? H'm!

ELLING. Can you sleep at a time like this? My own nerves are on fire.

KER. Fire? Oh—yes—I remember. Any more fire-works, Bob?

ELLING. A signal rocket from one of the batteries, now and then. (*He goes up beyond the window.* KERCHIVAL *arouses himself, taking the handkerchief from his eyes.*)

KER. What a preposterous hour to be up. The ball was over an hour ago, all the guests are gone, and it's nearly four o'clock. (*Looking at his watch.*) Exactly ten minutes of four. (*He takes out a cigar.*) Our Southern friends assure us that General Beauregard is to open fire on Fort Sumter this morning. I don't believe it. (*Lighting the cigar and rising, he looks out through the window.*) There lies the old fort—solemn and grim as ever, and the flag-staff stands above it, like a warning finger. If they do fire upon it (*shutting his teeth for a moment and looking down at the cigar in his hand*) the echo of that first shot will be heard above their graves, and Heaven knows how many of our own, also; but the flag will still float!—over the graves of both sides.

(ELLINGHAM *enters from the central door and approaches him.*)

Are you Southerners all mad, Robert?

ELLING. Are you Northerners all blind? (KERCHIVAL *sits down.*) We Virginians would prevent a war if we could. But your people in the North do not believe that one is coming. You do not understand the determined frenzy of my fellow Southerners. Look! (*Pointing toward the rear of the stage.*) Do you see the lights of the city, over the water? The inhabitants of Charleston are gathering, even now, in the gray, morning twilight, to witness the long-promised bombardment of Fort Sumter. It is to be a gala day for them. They have talked and dreamed of nothing else for weeks. The preparations have become a part of their social life—of their amusement—their gayeties. This very night at the ball—here—in the house of my own relatives—what was their talk? What were the jests they laughed at? Sumter! War! Ladies were betting bonbons that the United States would not dare to fire a shot in return, and pinning ribbons on the breasts of their "heroes." There was a signal rocket from one of the forts, and the young men who were dancing here left their partners standing on the floor to return to the batteries—as if it were the night before another Waterloo. The ladies themselves hurried away to watch the "spectacle" from their own verandas. You won't see the truth! I tell you, Kerchival, a war between the North and South is inevitable!

KER. And if it does come, you Virginians will join the rest.

ELLING. Our State will be the battle ground, I fear. But every loyal son of Virginia will follow her flag. It is our religion!

KER. My State is New York. If New York should go against the old flag, New York might go to the devil. That is my religion.

ELLING. So differently have we been taught what the word "patriotism" means!

KER. You and I are officers of the same regiment of the United States Regular Army, Robert; we were classmates at West Point, and we have fought side by side on the plains. You saved my scalp once; I'd have to wear a wig, now, if you had n't. I say, old boy, are we to be enemies?

ELLING. (*Laying his hand over his shoulder.*) My dear old comrade, whatever else comes, our friendship shall be unbroken!

KER. Bob! (*Looking up at him.*) I only hope that we shall never meet in battle!

ELLING. In battle? The idea is horrible!

KER. (*Rising and crossing to him.*) My dear old comrade, one of us will be wrong in this great fight, but we shall both be honest in it. (*He gives his hand;* ELLINGHAM *grasps it warmly, then turns away.*)

ELLING. Colonel Haverill is watching the forts, also; he has been as sad to-night as we have. Next to leaving you, my greatest regret is that I must resign from his regiment.

KER. You are his favorite officer.

ELLING. Naturally, perhaps; he was my guardian.

(*Enter* HAVERILL *from the rear. He walks down, stopping in the center of the stage.*)

HAVERILL. Kerchival! I secured the necessary passports to the North yesterday afternoon; this one is yours; I brought it down for you early in the evening. (KERCH. *takes the paper and goes to the window.*) I am ordered direct to Washington at once, and shall start with Mrs. Haverill this forenoon. You will report to Captain Lyon, of the 2d Regiment, in St. Louis. Robert! I have hoped for peace to the last, but it is hoping against hope. I feel certain, now, that the fatal blow will be struck this morning. Our old regiment is already broken up, and you, also, will now resign, I suppose, like nearly all your fellow Southerners in the Service.

ELLING. You know how sorry I am to leave your command, Colonel!

HAVER. I served under your father in Mexico; he left me, at his death, the guardian of you and your sister, Gertrude. Even since you became of age, I have felt that I stood in his place. But you must be your sister's only guardian now. Your father fell in battle, fighting for our common country, but you—

ELLING. He would have done as I shall do, had he lived. He was a Virginian!

HAVER. I am glad, Robert, that he was never called upon to decide between two flags. He never knew but one, and we fought under it together. (*Exit.*)

ELLING. Kerchival! Something occurred in this house to-night which—which I should n't mention under ordinary circumstances, but I—I feel that it may require my further attention, and you, perhaps, can be of service to me. Mrs. Haverill, the wife of the Colonel—

KER. Fainted away in her room.

ELLING. You know?

KER. I was one of the actors in the little drama.

ELLING. Indeed!

KER. About half-past nine this evening, while the ladies were dressing for the ball, I was going upstairs; I heard a quick, sharp cry, sprang forward, found myself at an open door. Mrs. Haverill lay on the floor inside, as if she had just reached the door to cry for help, when she fell. After doing all the unnecessary and useless things I could think of, I rushed out of the room to tell your sister, Gertrude, and my own sister, Madeline, to go and take care of the lady. Within less than twenty minutes afterwards, I saw Mrs. Haverill sail into the drawing-room, a thing of beauty, and with the glow of perfect health on her cheek. It was an immense relief to me when I saw her. Up to that time I had a vague idea that I had committed a murder.

ELLING. Murder!

KER. M—m. A guilty conscience. Every man, of course, does exactly the wrong thing when a woman faints. When I rushed out of Mrs. Haverill's room, I left my handkerchief soaked with water upon her face. I must ask her for it, it 's a silk one. Luckily, the girls got there in time to take it off; she would n't have come to if they had n't. It never occurred to me that she 'd need to breathe in my absence. That 's all I know about the matter. What troubles you? I suppose every woman has a right to faint whenever she chooses. The scream that I heard was so sharp, quick and intense that—

ELLING. That the cause must have been a serious one.

KER. Yes! So I thought. It must have been a mouse.

ELLING. Mr. Edward Thornton has occupied the next room to that of Mrs. Haverill to-night.

KER. (*Quickly.*) What do you mean?

ELLING. During the past month or more he has been pressing, not to say insolent, in his attentions to Mrs. Haverill.

KER. I 've noticed that myself.

ELLING. And he is an utterly unscrupulous man; it is no fault of mine that he was asked to be a guest at this house to-night. He came to Charleston, some years ago, from the North, but if there are any vices and passions peculiarly strong in the South, he has carried them all to the extreme. In one of the many scandals connected with Edward Thornton's name, it was more than whispered that he entered a lady's room unexpectedly at night. But, as he killed the lady's husband in a duel a few days afterwards, the scandal dropped.

KER. Of course; the gentleman received ample satisfaction as an outraged husband, and Mr. Thornton apologized, I suppose, to his widow.

ELLING. He has repeated the adventure.

KER. Do—you—think—that?

ELLING. I was smoking on the lawn, and glanced up at the window; my eyes may have deceived me, and I must move cautiously in the matter; but it could n't have been imagination; the shadow of Edward Thornton's face and head appeared upon the curtain.

KER. Whew! The devil!

ELLING. Just at that moment I, too, heard the stifled scream.

(*Enter* EDWARD THORNTON.)

THORNTON. Gentlemen!

ELLING. Your name was just on my tongue, Mr. Thornton.

THORNTON. I thought I heard it, but you are welcome to it. Miss Gertrude has asked me to ride over to Mrs. Pinckney's with her, to learn if there is any further news from the batteries. I am very glad the time to attack Fort Sumter has come at last!

ELLING. I do not share your pleasure.

THORNTON. You are a Southern gentleman.

ELLING. And you are a Northern "gentleman."

THORNTON. A Southerner by choice; I shall join the cause.

ELLING. We native Southerners will defend our own rights, sir; you may leave them in our keeping. It is my wish, Mr. Thornton, that you do not accompany my sister.

THORNTON. Indeed!

ELLING. Her groom, alone, will be sufficient

THORNTON. As you please, sir. Kindly offer my excuses to Miss Gertrude. You and I can chat over the subject later in the day, when we are alone. (*Moving up the stage.*)

ELLING. By all means, and another subject, also, perhaps.

THORNTON. I shall be entirely at your service. (*Exit to the veranda.*)

ELLING. Kerchival, I shall learn the whole truth, if possible, to-day. If it is what I suspect—what I almost know—I will settle with him myself. He has insulted our Colonel's wife and outraged the hospitality of my friends. (*Walking to the right.*)

KER. (*Walking to the left.*) I think it ought to be my quarrel. I'm sure I 'm mixed up in it enough.

MADELINE. (*Without, calling.*) Kerchival!

ELLING. Madeline. (*Aside, starting,* KERCHIVAL *looks across at him sharply.*)

KER. (*Aside.*) I distinctly saw Bob give a start when he heard Madeline. Now, what can there be about my sister's voice to make a man jump like that?

GERT. (*Without.*) Brother Robert!

KER. Gertrude! (*Aside, starting,* ELLINGHAM *looks at him sharply.*) How the tones of a woman's voice thrill through a man's soul!

(*Enter* MADELINE.)

MADELINE. Oh, Kerchival—here you are.

(*Enter* GERTRUDE, *from the apartment, in a riding habit, with a whip.*)

GERT. Robert, dear! (*Coming down to* ROBERT; *they converse in dumb show.*)

MADELINE. Where are your field glasses? I've been rummaging all through your clothes, and swords, and sashes, and things. I've turned everything in your room upside down.

KER. Have you?

MADELINE. I can't find your glasses anywhere. I want to look at the forts. Another rocket went up just now. (*Runs up the stage and stands on the piazza looking off.*)

KER. A sister has all the privileges of a wife to upset a man's things, without her legal obligation to put them straight again. (*Glances at* GERTRUDE.) I wish Bob's sister had the same privileges in my room that my own has.

GERT. Mr. Thornton is n't going with me, you say?

ELLING. He requested me to offer you his apologies.

KER. May *I* accompany you? (ELLINGHAM *turns to the window on the right.*)

GERT. My groom, old Pete, will be with me, of course; there 's no particular need of anyone else. But you may go along, if you like. I've got my hands full of sugar plums for Jack. Dear old Jack—he always has his share when we have company. I'm going over to Mrs. Pinckney's to see if she 's had any more news from General Beauregard; her son is on the General's staff.

MADELINE. (*Looking off to the right.*) There 's another rocket from Fort Johnson; and it is answered from Fort Moultrie. Ah! (*Angrily.*) General Beauregard is a bad, wicked man! (*Coming down.*)

GERT. Oh! Madeline! You are a bad, wicked Northern girl to say such a thing.

MAD. I *am* a Northern girl.

GERT. And I am a Southern girl. (*They face each other.*)

KER. (*Dropping into a chair.*) The war has begun.

(ELLINGHAM *has turned from the window; he strolls across the stage, watching the girls.*)

GERT. General Beauregard is a patriot.

MAD. He is a Rebel.

GERT. So am I.

MAD. Gertrude!—You—you—

GERT. Madeline!—You—

MAD. I—I—

GERT. I—

BOTH. O—O-h! (*Bursting into tears and rushing into each other's arms, sobbing, then suddenly kissing each other vigorously.*)

KER. I say, Bob, if the North and South do fight, that will be the end of it.

GERT. I've got something to say to you, Madeline, dear. (*Confidentially and turning with her arms about her waist. The girls sit down talking earnestly.*)

ELLING. Kerchival, old boy! There 's—there 's something I'd like to say to you before we part to-day.

KER. I'd like a word with you, also!

MAD. You don't really mean that, Gertrude—with me?

ELLING. I'm in love with your sister, Madeline.

KER. The devil you are!

ELLING. I never suspected such a thing until last night.

GERT. Robert was in love with you six weeks ago. (MADELINE *kisses her.*)

KER. *I've* made a discovery, too, Bob.

MAD. *I've* got something to say to *you*, Gertrude.

KER. I'm in love with *your* sister.

ELLING. (*Astonished.*) You are?

MAD. Kerchival has been in love with you for the last three months. (GERTRUDE *offers her lips—they kiss.*)

KER. I fell in love with her the day before yesterday. (*The two gentlemen grasp each other's hands warmly.*)

ELLING. We understand each other, Kerchival. (*He turns up the stage and stops at the door.*) Miss Madeline, you said just now that you wished to watch the forts. Would you like to walk down to the shore?

MAD. Yes! (*Rising and going up to him. He takes one of her hands in his own and looks at her earnestly.*)

ELLING. This will be the last day that we shall be together, for the present. But we shall meet again—sometime—if we both live.

MAD. If we both live! You mean—if *you*

live. You must go into this dreadful war, if it comes.

ELLING. Yes, Madeline, I must. Come let us watch for our fate.

(*Exeunt to the veranda.*)

KER. (*Aside.*) I must leave Charleston to-day. (*He sighs.*) Does she love me?

GER. I am ready to start, Mr. West, when you are.

KER. Oh! Of course, I forgot. (*Rising.*) I shall be delighted to ride at your side.

GERT. At my side! (*Rising.*) There is n't a horse in America that can keep by the side of my Jack, when I give him his head, and I'm sure to do it. You may follow us. But you can hardly ride in that costume; while you are changing it, I'll give Jack his bonbons. (*Turning to the window.*) There he is, bless him! Pawing the ground, and impatient for me to be on his back. Let him come, Pete. (*Holding up bonbons at window.*) I love you.

KER. Eh? (*Turning suddenly.*)

GERT. (*Looking at him.*) What?

KER. You were saying—

GERT. Jack! (*Looking out. The head of a large black horse appears through the window.*) You dear old fellow. (*She feeds him with bonbons.*) Jack has been my boy ever since he was a little colt. I brought you up, did n't I, Jack? He's the truest, and kindest, and best of friends; I would n't be parted from him for the world, and I'm the only woman he'll allow to be near him.

KER. (*Earnestly.*) You are the only woman, Miss Gertrude, that I—

GERT. Dear Jack!

KER. (*Aside.*) Jack embarrasses me. He's a third party.

GERT. There! That will do for the present, Jack. Now go along with Pete! If you are a very good boy, and don't let Lieutenant Kerchival West come within a quarter of a mile of me, after the first three minutes, you shall have some more sugar plums when we get to Mrs. Pinckney's. (*An old negro leads the horse away.* GERTRUDE *looks around at* KERCHIVAL.) You have n't gone to dress, yet; we shall be late. Mrs. Pinckney asked a party of friends to witness the bombardment this morning, and breakfast together on the piazza while they are looking at it. We can remain and join them, if you like.

KER. I hope they won't wait for breakfast until the bombardment begins.

GERT. I'll bet you an embroidered cigar-case, Lieutenant, against a box of gloves that it will begin in less than an hour.

KER. Done! You will lose the bet. But you shall have the gloves; and one of the hands that go inside them shall be— (*Taking one of her hands; she withdraws it.*)

GERT. My own—until some one wins it. You don't believe that General Beauregard will open fire on Fort Sumter this morning?

KER. No; I don't.

GERT. Everything is ready.

KER. It's so much easier to get everything ready to do a thing than it is to do it. I have been ready a dozen times, this very night, to say to you, Miss Gertrude, that I—that I— (*Pauses.*)

GERT. (*Looking down and tapping her skirt with her whip.*) Well?

KER. But I did n't.

GERT. (*Glancing up at him suddenly.*) I dare say, General Beauregard has more nerve than you have.

KER. It is easy enough to set the batteries around Charleston Harbor, but the man who fires the first shot at a woman—

GERT. Woman!

KER. At the American flag—must have nerves of steel.

GERT. You Northern men are so slow, to—

KER. I have been slow; but I assure you, Miss Gertrude, that my heart—

GERT. What subject are we on now?

KER. You were complaining because I was too slow.

GERT. I was doing nothing of the kind, sir!—let me finish, please. You Northern men are so slow, to believe that our Southern heroes—Northern *men* and Southern *heroes*—you recognize the distinction I make—you won't believe that they will keep their promises. They have sworn to attack Fort Sumter this morning, and—they—will do it. This "American Flag" you talk of is no longer our flag: it is foreign to us!—It is the flag of an enemy!

KER. (*Tenderly and earnestly.*) Am I your enemy?

GERT. You have told me that you will return to the North, and take the field.

KER. Yes, I will. (*Decisively.*)

GERT. You will be fighting against my friends, against my own brother, against me. We *shall* be enemies.

KER. (*Firmly.*) Even that, Gertrude—(*She looks around at him, he looks squarely into her eyes as he proceeds*)—if you will have it so. If my country needs my services, I shall not refuse them, though it makes us enemies! (*She wavers a moment, under strong emotion, and turns away; sinks upon the seat, her elbow on the back of it, and her tightly-clenched fist against her cheek, looking away from him.*)

GERT. I will have it so! I am a Southern woman!

KER. We have more at stake between us, this morning, than a cigar-case and a box of gloves. (*Turning up the stage.*)

(*Enter* MRS. HAVERILL *from apartment.*)

MRS. H. Mr. West! I 've been looking for you. I have a favor to ask.

KER. Of me?—with pleasure.

MRS. H. But I am sorry to have interrupted you and Gertrude. (*As she passes down* KERCHIVAL *moves up the stage.* GERTRUDE *rises.*) (*Apart.*) There are tears in your eyes, Gertrude, dear!

GERT. (*Apart.*) They have no right there.

MRS. H. (*Apart.*) I 'm afraid I know what has happened. A quarrel! and you are to part with each other so soon. Do not let a girl's coquetry trifle with her heart until it is too late. You remember the confession you made to me last night?

GERT. (*Apart.*) Constance! (*Starting.*) That is my secret; more a secret now than ever.

MRS. H. (*Apart.*) Yes, dear; but you do love him. (GERTRUDE *moves up the stage.*)

GERT. You need not ride over with me, Mr. West.

KER. I can be ready in one moment.

GERT. I choose to go alone! Old Pete will be with me; and Jack, himself, is a charming companion.

KER. If you prefer Jack's company to mine—

GERT. I do. (*Exit on the veranda.*)

KER. Damn Jack! But you will let me assist you to mount. (*Exit after her.*)

MRS. H. We leave for the North before noon, but every hour seems a month. If my husband should learn what happened in my room to-night, he would kill that man. What encouragement could I have given him? Innocence is never on its guard—but, (*drawing up*) the last I remember before I fell unconscious, he was crouching before me like a whipped cur! (*She starts as she looks out of the window.*) There is Mr. Thornton, now—Ah! (*Angrily.*) No—I must control my own indignation. I must keep him and Colonel Haverill from meeting before we leave Charleston. Edward Thornton would shoot my husband down without remorse. But poor Frank! I must not forget him, in my own trouble. I have but little time left to care for his welfare.

(*Re-enter* KERCHIVAL.)

KER. You said I could do you a favor, Mrs. Haverill?

MRS. H. Yes, I wanted to speak with you about General Haverill's son, Frank. I should like you to carry a message to Charleston for me as soon as it is light. It is a sad errand. You know too well the great misfortune that has fallen upon my husband in New York.

KER. His only son has brought disgrace upon his family name, and tarnished the reputation of a proud soldier. Colonel Haverill's fellow officers sympathize with him most deeply.

MRS. H. And poor young Frank! I could hardly have loved the boy more if he had been my own son. If he had not himself confessed the crime against the bank, I could not have believed him guilty. He has escaped from arrest. He is in the City of Charleston. I am the only one in all the world he could turn to. He was only a lad of fourteen when his father and I were married, six years ago; and the boy has loved me from the first. His father is stern and bitter now in his humiliation. This note from Frank was handed to me while the company were here last evening. I want you to find him and arrange for me to meet him, if you can do it with safety. I shall give you a letter for him.

KER. I 'll get ready at once; and I will do all I can for the boy.

MRS. H. And—Mr. West! Gertrude and Madeline have told me that—that—I was under obligations to you last evening.

KER. Don't mention it. I merely ran for them, and I—I 'm very glad you did n't choke—before they reached you. I trust you are quite well now?

MRS. H. I am entirely recovered, thank you. And I will ask another favor of you, for we are old friends. I desire very much that General Haverill should not know that—that any accident occurred to me to-night—or that my health has not been perfect.

KER. Certainly, madam!

MRS. H. It would render him anxious without cause.

KER. (*Aside.*) It looks as if Robert was right; she does n't want the two men to meet.

(*Enter* HAVERILL, *a white silk handkerchief in his hand.*)

HAVER. Constance, my dear, I 've been all over the place looking for you. I thought you were in your room. But—by the way, Kerchival, this is your handkerchief; your initials are on it.

(KERCHIVAL *turns and stares at him a second.* MRS. HAVERILL *starts slightly and turns front.* HAVERILL *glances quickly from one to the other, then extends his hands toward* KERCHIVAL, *with the handkerchief.* KERCHIVAL *moves to him and takes it.* MRS. HAVERILL *drops into the chair.*)

KER. Thank you. (*He walks up and exits with a quick glance back.* HAVERILL *looks at* MRS. HAVERILL, *who sits nervously, looking away. He then glances up after* KERCHIVAL. *A cloud comes over his face and he stands a second in thought. Then, with a movement as if brushing away a passing suspicion, he smiles pleasantly and approaches* MRS. H.; *leaning over her.*)

HAVER. My fair Desdemona! (*Smiling.*) I found Cassio's handkerchief in your room. Have you a kiss for me? (*She looks up, he raises her chin with a finger and kisses her.*) That 's the way I shall smother you.

MRS. H. (*Rising and dropping her head upon his breast.*) Husband!

HAVER. But what is this they have been telling me?

MRS. H. What have they said to you?

HAVER. There was something wrong with you in the early part of the evening; you are trembling and excited, my girl!

MRS. H. It was nothing, John; I—I—was ill, for a few moments, but I am well now.

HAVER. You said nothing about it to me.

MRS. H. Do not give it another thought.

HAVER. Was there anything besides your health involved in the affair? There was. (*Aside.*) How came this handkerchief in her room?

MRS. H. My husband! I do not want to say anything more—at—at present—about what happened to-night. There has never been a shadow between us—will you not trust me?

HAVER. Shadow! You stand in a bright light of your own, my wife; it shines upon my whole life—there can be no shadow there. Tell me as much or as little as you like, and in your own time. I am sure you will conceal nothing from me that I ought to know. I trust my honor and my happiness to you, absolutely.

MRS. H. They will both be safe, John, in my keeping. But there is something else that I wish to speak with you about; something very near to your heart—your son!

HAVER. My son!

MRS. H. He is in Charleston.

HAVER. And not—in prison? To me he is nowhere. I am childless.

MRS. H. I hope to see him to-day; may I not take him some kind word from you?

HAVER. My lawyers in New York had instructions to provide him with whatever he needed.

MRS. H. They have done so, and he wants for nothing; he asks for nothing, except that I will seek out the poor young wife—only a girl herself—whom he is obliged to desert, in New York.

HAVER. His marriage was a piece of reckless folly, but I forgave him that.

MRS. H. I am sure that it was only after another was dependent on him that the debts of a mere spendthrift were changed to fraud—and crime.

HAVER. You may tell him that I will provide for her.

MRS. H. And may I take him no warmer message from his father?

HAVER. I am an officer of the United States Army. The name which my son bears came to me from men who had borne it with honor, and I transmitted it to him without a blot. He has disgraced it, by his own confession.

MRS. H. *I* cannot forget the poor mother who died when he was born; her whose place I have tried to fill, to both Frank and to you. I never saw her, and she is sleeping in the old graveyard at home. But I am doing what she would do to-day, if she were living. No pride—no disgrace—could have turned her face from him. The care and the love of her son has been to me the most sacred duty which one woman can assume for another.

HAVER. You have fulfilled that duty, Constance. Go to my son! I would go with you, but he is a man now; he could not look into my eyes, and I could not trust myself. But I will send him something which a man will understand. Frank loves you as if you were his own mother; and I—I would like him to—to think tenderly of me, also. He will do it when he looks at this picture. (*Taking a miniature from his pocket.*)

MRS. H. Of me!

HAVER. I have never been without it one hour, before, since we were married. He will recognize it as the one that I have carried through every campaign, in every scene of danger on the Plains; the one that has always been with me. He is a fugitive from justice. At times, when despair might overcome him, this may give him nerve to meet his future life manfully. It has often nerved me, when I might have failed without it. Give it to him, and tell him that I send it. (*Giving her the miniature.*) I could not send a kinder message, and he will understand it. (*Turning, he stands a moment in thought.* THORNTON *appears at the window looking at them quietly, over his shoulder, a cigar in his hand.* MRS. HAVERILL *sees him, and starts with a suppressed breath, then looks at* HAVERILL, *who moves away. He speaks aside.*) My son! My son! We shall never meet again! (*Exit.*)

(MRS. H. *looks after him earnestly, then turns and looks at* THORNTON, *drawing up to her full height.* THORNTON *moves up the stage, beyond the window.*)

MRS. H. Will he dare to speak to me again?

(*Enter* THORNTON; *he comes down the stage quietly. He has thrown away the cigar.*)

THORN. Mrs. Haverill! I wish to offer you an apology.

MRS. H. I have not asked for one, sir!

THORN. Do you mean by that, that you will not accept one?

MRS. H. (*Aside.*) What can I say? (*Aloud.*) Oh, Mr. Thornton!—for my husband's sake, I—

THORN. Ah! You are afraid that your husband may become involved in an unpleasant affair. Your solicitude for his safety, madame, makes me feel that my offense to-night was indeed unpardonable. No gentleman can excuse himself for making such a mistake as I have made. I had supposed that it was Lieutenant Kerchival West, who—

MRS. H. What do you mean, sir?

THORN. But if it is your husband that stands between us—

MRS. H. Let me say this, sir: whatever I may fear for my husband, he fears nothing for himself.

THORN. He knows? (*Looking at her, keenly.*)

(*Enter* KERCHIVAL WEST, *now in riding suit.*)

(*He stops, looking at them.*)

You are silent. Your husband does know what occurred to-night; that relieves my conscience. (*Lightly.*) Colonel Haverill and I can now settle it between us.

MRS. H. No, Mr. Thornton! My husband knows nothing, and, I beg of you, do not let this horrible affair go further. (*Sees* KERCHIVAL.)

KER. Pardon me. (*Stepping forward.*) I hope I am not interrupting you. (*Aside.*) It *was* Thornton. (*Aloud.*) You said you would have a letter for me to carry, Mrs. Haverill.

MRS. H. Yes, I—I will go up and write it at once. (*As she leaves she stops and looks back. Aside.*) I wonder how much he overheard.

KER. (*Quietly.*) I suppose eight o'clock will be time enough for me to go?

MRS. H. Oh, yes! (*glancing at him a moment*) —quite. (*Exit.*)

KER. (*Quietly.*) Mr. Thornton! you are a scoundrel! Do I make myself plain?

THORN. You make the fact that you desire to pick a quarrel with me quite plain, sir; but I choose my own quarrels and my own enemies.

KER. Colonel Haverill is my commander, and he is beloved by every officer in the regiment.

THORN. On what authority, may I ask, do you—

KER. The honor of Colonel Haverill's wife is under our protection.

THORN. Under your protection? You have a better claim than that, perhaps, to act as her champion. Lieutenant Kerchival West is Mrs. Haverill's favorite officer in the regiment.

KER. (*Approaching him.*) You dare to suggest that I—

THORN. If I accept your challenge, I shall do so not because you are her protector, but my rival.

KER. Bah! (*Striking him sharply on the cheek with his glove. The two men stand facing each other a moment.*) Is it my quarrel now?

THORN. I think you are entitled to my attention, sir.

KER. My time here is limited.

THORN. We need not delay. The Bayou La Forge is convenient to this place.

KER. I'll meet you there, with a friend, at once.

THORN. It will be light enough to see the sights of our weapons in about one hour.

(*They bow to each other, and* THORNTON *goes out.*)

KER. I've got ahead of Bob.

GERT. (*Without.*) Whoa! Jack! Old boy! Steady, now—that's a good fellow.

KER. She has returned. I *must* know whether Gertrude Ellingham loves me—before Thornton and I meet. He is a good shot.

GERT. (*Without, calling.*) O—h! Pete! You may take Jack to the stable. Ha—ha—ha! (*She appears at window; to* KERCHIVAL.) Old Pete, on the bay horse, has been doing his best to keep up with us; but Jack and I have led him such a race! Ha—ha—ha—ha! (*Disappearing beyond the window.*)

KER. Does she love me?

GERT. (*Entering at the rear and coming down.*) I have the very latest news from the headquarters of the Confederate Army in South Carolina. At twenty minutes after three this morning General Beauregard sent this message to Major Anderson in Fort Sumter: "I shall open fire in one hour!" The time is up!—and he will keep his word! (*Turning and looking out of the window.* KERCHIVAL *moves across to her.*)

KER. Gertrude! I must speak to you; we may never meet again; but I must know the truth. I love you. (*Seizing her hand.*) Do you love me? (*She looks around at him as if about to speak; hesitates.*) Answer me! (*She looks down with a coquettish smile, tapping her skirt with her riding whip.*) Well? (*A distant report of a cannon, and low rumbling reverberations over the harbor.* GERTRUDE *turns suddenly, looking out.* KERCHIVAL *draws up, also looking off.*)

GERT. A low—bright—line of fire—in the sky! It is a shell. (*A second's pause; she starts slightly*). It has burst upon the fort. (*Looks over her shoulder at* KERCHIVAL, *drawing up to her full height.*) Now!—do you believe that we Southerners are in deadly earnest?

KER. We Northerners are in deadly earnest, too. I have received my answer. (*He crosses quickly and then turns.*) We are—enemies! (*They look at each other for a moment.*)

(*Exit* KERCHIVAL.)

GERT. Kerchival! (*Moving quickly half across stage, looking after him eagerly; then stops.*) Enemies! (*She drops into the chair sobbing bitterly. Another distant report, and low, long reverberations as the curtain descends.*)

ACT SECOND.

The scene is the exterior of the Ellingham Homestead in the Shenandoah Valley. Three Top Mountain is seen in the distance. A corner of the house, with the projecting end of the veranda is seen on the left. A low wall extends from the veranda across the stage to the center, then with a turn to the right it is continued off the stage. There is a wide opening in the wall at the center, with a low. heavy stone post, with flat top, on each side. Beyond the wall and the opening, a road runs across the stage. At the back of this road there is an elevation of rock and turf. This slopes up to the rear, is level on the top about twelve feet, then slopes down to the road, and also out behind the wood, which is seen at the right. The level part in the centre rises to about four feet above the stage. Beyond this elevation in the distance is a broad valley, with Three Top Mountain rising on the right. The foliage is appropriate to Northern Virginia. Rustic seats and table are on the right. There is a low rock near the stone post. When curtain rises it is sunset. As the act proceeds this fades into twilight and then brightens into moonlight. At the rise of the curtain a trumpet signal is heard, very distant. GERTRUDE *and* MADELINE *are standing on the elevation.* GERTRUDE *is shading her eyes with her hand and looking off to the left.* MADELINE *stands a little below her, on the incline, resting her arm about* GERTRUDE'S *waist, also looking off.*

GERT. It is a regiment of Union Cavalry The Federal troops now have their lines three miles beyond us, and only a month ago the Confederate Army was north of Winchester. One army or the other has been marching up and down the Shenandoah Valley for three years. I wonder what the next change will be. We in Virginia have had more than our share of the war. (*Looking off.*)

MAD. You have, indeed, Gertrude. (*Walking down to a seat.*) And we at home in Washington have pitied you so much. But everybody says that there will be peace in the valley after this. (*Dropping into the seat.*)

GERT. Peace! (*Coming down.*) That word means something very different to us poor Southerners from what it means to you.

MAD. I know, dear; and we in the North know how you have suffered, too. We were very glad when General Buckthorn was appointed to the command of the Nineteenth Army Corps, so that Jenny could get permission for herself and me to come and visit you.

GERT. The old General will do anything for Jenny, I suppose.

MAD. Yes. (*Laughing.*) We say in Washington that Jenny is in command of the Nineteenth Army Corps herself.

GERT. I was never more astonished or delighted in my life than when you and Jenny Buckthorn rode up, this morning, with a guard from Winchester; and Madeline, dear, I—I only wish that my brother Robert could be here, too. Do you remember in Charleston, darling—that morning—when I told you that—that Robert loved you?

MAD. He—(*looking down*)—he told me so himself only a little while afterwards, and while we were standing there, on the shore of the bay—the—the shot was fired which compelled him to enter this awful war—and me to return to my home in the North.

GERT. I was watching for that shot, too. (*Turning.*)

MAD. Yes—(*rising*)—you and brother Kerchival—

GERT. We won't talk about that, my dear. We were speaking of Robert. As I told you this morning, I have not heard from him since the battle of Winchester, a month ago. Oh, Madeline! the many, many long weeks, like these, we have suffered, after some terrible battle in which he has been engaged. I do not know, now. whether he is living or dead.

MAD. The whole war has been one long suspense to me. (*Dropping her face into her hands.*)

GERT. My dear sister! (*Placing her arm about her waist and moving to the left.*) You are a Northern girl, and I am a Rebel—but we are sisters. (*They mount the veranda and pass out. An old countryman comes in. He stops and glances back, raises a broken portion of the capstone of the post, and places a letter under it.* GERTRUDE *has stepped back on the veranda and is watching him. He raises his head sharply, looking at her and bringing his finger to his lips. He drops his head again, as with age, and goes out.* GERTRUDE *moves down to the stage and up to the road, looks to the right and left, raises the broken stone, glancing back as she does so, then takes the letter and moves down.*) Robert is alive! It is his handwriting! (*She tears open the wrapper.*) Only a line from him! and this—a dispatch—and also a letter to me! Why, it is from Mrs. Haverill—from Washington—with a United States postmark. (*She reads from a scrap of paper.*) "The enclosed dispatch must be in the hands of Captain Edward Thornton before eight o'clock tonight. We have signaled to him from Three Top Mountain, and he is waiting for it at the bend in Oak Run. Our trusty scout at the Old Forge will carry it if you will put it in his hands." The scout is not there, now; I will carry it to Captain Thornton myself. I—I have n't my own dear horse to depend on now; Jack knew every foot of the way through the woods about here; he could have carried a dispatch himself. I can't bear to think of Jack; it 's two years since he was captured by the enemy—and if he is still living—I—I suppose he is carrying one of their officers No! Jack would n't fight on that side. He was a Rebel—as I am. He was one of the Black Horse Cavalry—his eyes always flashed towards the North. Poor Jack! my pet. (*Brushing her eyes.*) But this is no time for tears. I must do the best I can with the gray horse. Captain Thornton shall have the dispatch. (*She reads from note.*) "I also inclose a letter for you. I found it in a United States mail-bag which we captured from the enemy." Oh—that 's the way Mrs. Haverill's letter came—Ha—ha—ha—by way of the Rebel army! (*Opens it;*

reads.) "My Darling Gertrude: When Colonel Kerchival West was in Washington last week, on his way from Chattanooga, to serve under Sheridan in the Shenandoah Valley, he called upon me. It was the first time I had seen him since the opening of the war. I am certain that he still loves you, dear." (*She kisses the letter eagerly, then draws up.*) It is quite immaterial to me whether Kerchival West still loves me or not. (*Reads.*) "I have kept your secret, my darling."—Ah! My secret!—"but I was sorely tempted to betray the confidence you reposed in me at Charleston. If Kerchival West had heard you say, as I did, when your face was hidden in my bosom, that night, that you loved him with your whole heart—"—Oh! I could bite my tongue out now for making that confession— (*She looks down at letter with a smile.*) "I am certain that he still loves you." (*A Trumpet Signal. She kisses the letter repeatedly. The Signal is repeated louder than at first. She starts, listening.*)

(JENNY BUCKTHORN *runs in, on the veranda.*)

JEN. Do you hear, Gertrude, they are going to pass this very house. (*A Military band is playing "John Brown" in the distance. A chorus of soldiers is heard.*) I've been watching them through my glass; it is Colonel Kerchival West's regiment.

GERT. (*Eagerly, then coldly.*) Colonel West's! It is perfectly indifferent to me whose regiment it is.

JEN. Oh! Of course. (*Coming down.*) It is equally indifferent to me; Captain Heartsease is in command of the first troop. (*Trumpet Signal sounds.*) Column right! (*She runs up to the road. Looking off to the left.*) They are coming up the hill.

GERT. At my very door! And Kerchival West in command! I will not stand here and see them pass. The dispatch for Captain Thornton! I will carry it to him as soon as they are gone. (*Exit up the veranda, the band and chorus increasing in volume.*)

JEN. Cavalry! That 's the branch of the service I was born in; I was in a fort at the time—on the Plains. Sergeant Barket always said that my first baby squall was a command to the garrison; if any officer or soldier, from my father down, failed to obey my orders, I court-martialed him on the spot. I'll make 'em pass in review. (*Jumping up on the rustic seat.*) Yes! (*Looking off to the left.*) There 's Captain Heartsease himself, at the head of the first troop. Draw sabre! (*With parasol.*) Present! (*Imitating the action. The band and chorus are now full and loud; she swings the parasol in time. A trumpet Signal. Band and chorus suddenly cease.*) Halt! Why, they are stopping here. (*Trumpet Signal sounds.*) Dismount! I—I wonder if they are going to—I do believe—(*Looking eagerly. Trumpet Signal.*) Assembly of Guard Details! As sure as fate, they are going into camp here. We girls will have a jolly time. (*Jumping down.*) Ha—ha—ha—ha! Let me see. How shall I receive Captain Heartsease? He deserves a court-martial, for he stole my lace handkerchief—at Mrs. Grayson's reception—in Washington. He was called away by orders to the West that very night, and we have n't met since. (*Sighs.*) He 's been in lots of battles since then; I suppose he 's forgotten all about the handkerchief. We girls, at home, don't forget such things. We are n't in battles. All we do is to—to scrape lint and flirt with other officers.

(*Enter* CAPTAIN HEARTSEASE, *followed by* COLONEL ROBERT ELLINGHAM, *then stops at the gate.*)

HEART. This way, Colonel Ellingham. (*They enter. As they come down* HEARTSEASE *stops suddenly, looking at* JENNY, *and puts up his glasses.*) Miss Buckthorn!

JEN. Captain Heartsease!

HEART. (*Very quietly and with perfect composure.*) I am thunderstruck. The unexpected sight of you has thrown me into a fever of excitement.

JEN. Has it? (*Aside.*) If he gets so excited as that in battle it must be awful. (*Aloud.*) Colonel Ellingham!

ELLING. Miss Buckthorn! You are visiting my sister? I am what may be called a visitor—by force—myself.

JEN. Oh! You 're a prisoner!

ELLING. I ventured too far within the Union lines to-night, and they have picked me up. But Major Wilson has kindly accepted my parole, and I shall make the best of it.

JEN. Is Major Wilson in command of the regiment?

HEART. Yes. Colonel West is to join us at this point, during the evening.

ELLING. I am very glad you are here, Miss Buckthorn, with Gertrude.

JEN. Somebody here will be delighted to see you, Colonel.

ELLING. My sister can hardly be pleased to see me as a prisoner.

JEN. Not your sister. (*Passing him and crossing to the veranda. She turns and beckons to him. She motions with her thumb, over her shoulder. He goes up the steps of the veranda and turns.*)

ELLING. What do you mean?

JEN. I mean this—(*Reaching up her face, he leans down, placing his ear near her lips*)—somebody else's sister! When she first sees you, be near enough to catch her.

ELLING. I understand you! Madeline! (*Exit on veranda.* JENNY *runs up steps after him, then stops and looks back at* HEARTSEASE *over the railing.* HEARTSEASE *takes a lace handkerchief from his pocket.*)

JEN. I do believe that 's my handkerchief.

(*A guard of Sentries marches in and across the stage in the road. The Corporal in command orders halt and a sentry to post, then marches the guard out. The sentry stands with his back to the audience, afterwards moving out and in, appearing and disappearing during the Act.*)

HEART. Miss Buckthorn! I owe you an apology. After I left your side, the last time we met, I found your handkerchief in my possession. I assure you, it was an accident.

JEN. (*Aside, pouting.*) I thought he *intended* to steal it. (*Aloud.*) That was more than a year ago. (*Then brightly.*) Do you always carry it with you?

HEART. Always; there. (*Indicating his left breast pocket.*)

JEN. Next to his heart!

HEART. Shall I return it to you?

JEN. Oh, if a lace handkerchief can be of any use to you, Captain, during the hardships of a campaign—you—you may keep that one. You soldiers have so few comforts—and it 's real lace.

HEART. Thank you. (*Returning the handkerchief to his pocket.*) Miss Buckthorn, your father is in command of the Nineteenth Army Corps. He does n't like me.

JEN. I know it.

HEART. But you are in command of him.

JEN. Yes; I always have been.

HEART. If ever you decide to assume command of any other man, I—I trust you will give *me* your orders.

JEN. (*Aside, starting back.*) If that was intended for a proposal, it 's the queerest-shaped one I ever heard of. (*Aloud.*) Do you mean, Captain, that—that you—I must command myself now. (*Shouldering her parasol.*) 'Bout—face! March! (*Turning squarely around, marching up and out, on the veranda.*)

HEART. I have been placed on waiting orders. (*Stepping up the stage and looking after her; then very quietly and without emotion.*) I am in an agony of suspense. The sight of that girl always arouses the strongest emotions of my nature.

(*Enter* COLONEL KERCHIVAL WEST, *looking at the paper in his hand. The sentinel, in the road, comes to a salute.*)

Colonel West!

KER. Captain!

HEART. You have rejoined the regiment sooner than we expected.

KER. (*Looking at the paper.*) Yes; General Haverill is to meet me here at seven o'clock. Major Wilson tells me that some of your company captured Colonel Robert Ellingham, of the Tenth Virginia.

HEART. He is here under parole.

KER. And this is the old Ellingham homestead. (*Aside.*) Gertrude herself is here, I suppose; almost a prisoner to me, like her brother; and my troops surround their home. She must, indeed, feel that I am her enemy now. Ah, well, war is war. (*Aloud.*) By the bye, Heartsease, a young Lieutenant, Frank Bedloe, has joined our troop?

HEART. Yes; an excellent young officer.

KER. I sent for him as I came through the camp. Lieutenant Frank "Bedloe" is the son of General Haverill.

HEART. Indeed! Under an assumed name!

KER. He was supposed to have been killed in New Orleans more than a year ago; but he was taken prisoner instead.

HEART. He is here.

KER. I should never have known him; with his full beard and bronzed face. His face was as smooth as a boy's when I last met him in Charleston.

(*Enter* LIEUTENANT FRANK BEDLOE; *he stops, saluting.*)

FRANK. You wished me to report to you, Colonel?

KER. You have been assigned to the regiment during my absence.

FRANK. Yes, sir.

(KERCHIVAL *moves to him and grasps his hand; looks into his eyes a moment before speaking.*)

KER. Frank Haverill.

FRANK. You—you know me, sir?

KER. I saw Mrs. Haverill while I was passing through Washington on Saturday. She told me that you had escaped from prison in Richmond, and had reentered the service. She did not know then that you had been assigned to my regiment. I received a letter from her, in Winchester, this morning, informing me of the fact, and asking for my good offices in your behalf. But here is the letter. (*Taking a letter from wallet and giving it to him.*) It is for you rather than for me. I shall do everything I can for you, my dear fellow.

FRANK. Thank you, sir. (*He opens the letter, dropping the envelope upon the table.*) Kind, thoughtful and gentle to my faults, as ever—(*Looking at the letter*)—and always thinking of my welfare. My poor little wife, too, is under her protection. Gentlemen, I beg of you not to reveal my secret to my father.

KER. General Haverill shall know nothing from us, my boy, you have my word for that.

HEART. Nothing.

KER. And he cannot possibly recognize you. What with your full beard, and thinking as he does, that you are—

FRANK. That I am dead. I am dead to him. It would have been better if I had died. Nothing but my death—not even that—can wipe out the disgrace which I brought upon his name.

HEART. General Haverill has arrived.

(*Enter* GENERAL HAVERILL, *with a Staff Officer.*)

FRANK. (*Moving down.*) My father!

HAVER. (*After exchanging salutes with the three officers, he turns to the Staff Officer, giving him a paper and brief instructions in dumb show. The Officer goes out over the incline. Another Staff Officer enters, salutes and hands him a paper, then stands up.*) Ah! The men are ready. (*Looking at the paper, then to* KERCHIVAL.) Colonel! I have a very important matter to arrange with you; there is not a moment to be lost. I will ask Captain Heartsease to remain. (FRANK *salutes and starts up the stage;* HAVERILL *looks at him, starting slightly; raises his hand to detain him.*) One moment; your name!

HEART. Lieutenant Bedloe, General, of my own troop, and one of our best officers.

(HAVERILL *steps to* FRANK, *looking into his face a moment.*)

HAVER. Pardon me! (*He steps down the stage.* FRANK *moves away from him, then stops and looks back at him.* HAVERILL *stands up a moment in thought, covers his face with one hand, then draws up.*) Colonel West! We have a most dangerous piece of work for a young officer—(FRANK *starts joyfully*)—to lead a party of men, whom I have already selected. I cannot *order* an officer to undertake anything so nearly hopeless; he must be a volunteer.

FRANK. Oh, sir, General! Let me be their leader.

HAVER. I thought you had passed on.

FRANK. Do not refuse me, sir. (HAVERILL *looks at him a moment.* HEARTSEASE *and* KERCHIVAL *exchange glances.*)

HAVER. You are the man we need, my young friend. You shall go. Listen! We wish to secure a key to the cipher dispatches, which the enemy are now sending from their signal station on Three Top Mountain. There is another Confederate Signal Station in the valley, just beyond Buckton's Ford. (*Pointing to the left.*) Your duty will be this: First, to get inside the enemy's line; then to follow a path through the woods, with one of our scouts as your guide; attack the Station suddenly, and secure their code, if possible. I have this moment received word that the scout and the men are at the fort, now, awaiting their leader. Major McCandless, of my staff, will take you to the place. (*Indicating the Staff Officer.* FRANK *exchanges salutes with him.*) My young friend! I do not conceal from you the dangerous nature of the work on which I am sending you. If—if you do not return, I—I will write, myself, to your friends. (*Taking out a note book.*) Have you a father living?

FRANK. My—father—is—is—he is—

HAVER. I understand you. A mother? Or—

KER. I have the address of Lieutenant Bedloe's friends, General.

HAVER. I will ask you to give it to me, if

necessary. (*He extends his hand.*) Good-bye, my lad. (FRANK *moves to him.* HAVERILL *grasps his hand, warmly.*) Keep a brave heart and come back to us.

(FRANK *moves up the stage. Exit Staff Officer.*)

FRANK. He is my father still. (*Exit.*)

HAVER. My dead boy's face! (*Dropping his face into both hands.*)

HEART. (*Apart to* KERCHIVAL.) He shall not go alone. (*Aloud.*) General! Will you kindly give me leave of absence from the command?

HAVER. Leave of absence! To an officer in active service—and in the presence of the enemy?

KER. (*Taking his hand. Apart.*) God bless you, old fellow! Look after the boy.

HAV. A—h— (*With a sudden thought, turns.*) I think I understand you, Captain Heartsease. Yes; you may have leave of absence.

HEART. Thank you. (*He salutes.* HAVERILL *and* KERCHIVAL *salute. Exit* HEARTSEASE.)

KER. Have you any further orders for me, General?

HAVER. I wish you to understand the great importance of the duty to which I have just assigned this young officer. General Sheridan started for Washington this noon, by way of Front Royal. Since his departure, we have had reason to believe that the enemy are about to move, and we must be able to read their signal dispatches, if possible. (*Sitting down.*) I have ordered Captain Lockwood, of our own Signal Corps to report to you here, with officers and men. (*He takes up the empty envelope on table, unconsciously, as he speaks, tapping it on the table.*) If Lieutenant Bedloe succeeds in getting the key to the enemy's cipher, we can signal from this point—(*pointing to the elevation*)—to our station at Front Royal. Men and horses are waiting there now, to carry forward a message, if necessary, to General Sheridan himself. (*He starts suddenly, looking at the envelope in his hand; reads address. Aside.*) "Colonel Kerchival West"—in my wife's handwriting!

KER. I'll attend to your orders.

HAVER. Postmarked at Washington, yesterday. (*Reads.*) "Private and confidential." (*Aloud.*) Colonel West! I found a paragraph, to-day, in a paper published in Richmond, taken from a prisoner. I will read it to you. (*He takes a newspaper slip from his wallet and reads.*) "From the *Charleston Mercury.* Captain Edward Thornton, of the Confederate Secret Service, has been assigned to duty in the Shenandoah Valley. Our gallant Captain still bears upon his face the mark of his meeting, in 1861, with Lieutenant, now Colonel Kerchival West, who is also to serve in the valley, with Sheridan's Army. Another meeting between these two men would be one of the strange coincidences of the war, as they were at one time, if not indeed at present, interested in the same beautiful woman." (*Rises.*) I will ask you to read the last few lines, yourself. (*Crossing, he hands* KERCHIVAL *the slip.*)

KER. (*Reading.*) "The scandal connected with the lovely wife of a Northern officer, at the opening of the war, was overshadowed, of course, by the attack on Fort Sumter; but many Charlestonians will remember it. The lady in defense of whose good name Captain Thornton fought the duel"—he defended her good name!—"is the wife of General Haverill, who will be Colonel West's immediate commander." (*He pauses a moment, then hands back the slip.*) General! I struck Mr. Thornton, after a personal quarrel.

HAVER. And the cause of the blow? There is much more in this than I have ever known of. I need hardly say that I do not accept the statement of this scandalous paragraph as correct. I will ask you to tell me the whole story, frankly, as man to man.

KER. (*After a moment's thought.*) I will tell you—all—frankly, General.

(*Enters* SERGEANT BARKET.)

BARKET. Colonel Wist? Adjutant Rollins wishes to report—a prisoner—just captured.

HAVER. We will meet again later, to-night when the camp is at rest. We are both soldiers, and have duties before us, at once. For the present, Colonel, be on the alert; we must watch the enemy. (*He moves up the stage.* BARKET *salutes.* HAVERILL *stops and looks at envelope in his hands, reading.*) "Private and confidential." (*Exit.*)

KER. Sergeant Barket! Lieutenant Bedloe has crossed the enemy's line, at Buckton's Ford, with a party of men. I wish you to ride to the ford yourself, and remain there, with your horse in readiness and fresh. As soon as any survivor of the party returns, ride back with the first news at full speed.

BARKET. Yes, sir. (*Starting.*)

KER. You say a prisoner has been captured? Is it a spy?

BARKET. Worse—a petticoat.

KER. A female prisoner! (*Dropping into the seat.*)

BARKET. I towld the byes your honor would n't thank us fer the catchin' of her. The worst of it is she 's a lady; and what 's worse still, it 's a purty one.

KER. Tell Major Wilson, for me, to let her take the oath, and everything else she wants. The Government of the United States will send her an apology and a new bonnet.

BARKET. The young lady is to take the oath, is it? She says she 'll see us damned first.

KER. A lady, Barket?

BARKET. Well! she did n't use thim exact words. That 's the way I understand her emphasis. Ivery time she looks at me, I feel like getting under a boom-proof. She was dashing through the woods on a gray horse, sur; and we had the divil's own chase. But we came up wid her, at last, down by the bend in Oak Run. Just at that moment we saw the figure of a Confederate officer, disappearing among the trays on the ither side.

KER. A—h!

BARKET. Two of us rayturned wid the girl; and the rist wint after the officer. Nothing has been heard of thim yet.

KER. Have you found any dispatches on the prisoner?

BARKET. Well!—yer honor, I 'm a bachelor, meself; and I 'm not familiar with the taypography of the sex. We byes are in mortal terror for fear somebody might order us to go on an exploring expedition.

KER. Tell them to send the prisoner here, Barket, and hurry to Buckton's Ford yourself, at once.

BARKET. As fast as me horse can carry me, sir, and it 's a good one. (*Exit.*)

KER. I 'd rather deal with half the Confederate army than with one woman, but I must question her. They captured her down by the Bend in Oak Run. (*Taking out the map, and looking at it.*) I see. She had just met, or was about to meet, a Confederate officer at that point. It is evident that she was either taking him a dispatch or was there to receive one. Oak Run. (CORPORAL DUNN *and two soldiers enter, with* GERTRUDE *as a prisoner. They stop,* KERCHIVAL *sits, studying the map.* GERTRUDE *glances at him and marches down with her head erect; she stops, with her back to him.*)

CORP. DUNN. The prisoner, Colonel West!

KER. Ah! Very well, Corporal; you can go. (*Rising; he motions the guard to retire.* CORP. DUNN *gives the necessary orders and exit with guard.*) Be seated, madam. (GERTRUDE *draws up, folding her arms and planting her foot, spitefully.* KERCHIVAL *shrugs his shoulders. Aside.*) I wish they 'd capture a tigress for me, or some other female animal that I know how to manage better than I do a woman. (*Aloud.*) I am very sorry, madam; but, of course, my duty as a military officer is paramount to all other considerations. You have been captured within the lines of this army, and under circumstances which lead me to think that you have important dispatches upon your person. I trust that you will give me whatever you have, at once. I shall be exceedingly sorry if you compel me to adopt the extreme—and the very disagreeable course—for both of us—of having—you—I—I hesitate even to use the word, madame—but military law is absolute—having you—

GERT. Searched! If you dare, Colonel West! (*Turning to him suddenly and drawing up to her full height.*)

KER. Gertrude Ellingham! (*Springs across to her, with his arms extended.*) My dear Gertrude!

GERT. (*Turning her back upon him.*) Not "dear Gertrude" to you, sir!

KER. Not?—Oh! I forgot.

GERT. (*Coldly.*) I am your prisoner.

KER. Yes. (*Drawing up firmly, with a change of manner.*) We will return to the painful realities of war. I am very sorry that you have placed yourself in a position like this, and, believe me, Gertrude—(*With growing tenderness.*)—I am still more sorry to be in such a position myself. (*Resting one hand on her arm, and his other arm about her waist.*)

GERT. (*After looking down at his hands.*) You don't like the position? (*He starts back, drawing up with dignity.*) Is that the paramount duty of a military officer?

KER. You will please hand me whatever

dispatches or other papers may be in your possession.

GERT. (*Looking away.*) You will *force* me, I suppose. I am a woman; you have the power. Order in the guard! A Corporal and two men—you 'd better make it a dozen—I am dangerous! Call the whole regiment to arms! Beat the long roll! I won't give up, if all the armies of the United States surround me.

(*Enter* GENERAL BUCKTHORN.)

KER. General Buckthorn! (*Saluting.*)

BUCK. Colonel West.

GERT. (*Aside.*) Jenny's father! (BUCKTHORN *glances at* GERTRUDE, *who still stands looking away. He moves down to* KERCHIVAL.)

BUCK. (*Apart, gruffly.*) I was passing with my staff, and I was informed that you had captured a woman bearing dispatches to the enemy. Is this the one?

KER. Yes, General.

BUCK. Ah! (*Turning, he looks at her.*)

GERT. I wonder if he will recognize me. He has n't seen me since I was a little girl. (*She turns toward him.*)

BUCK. (*Turning to* KERCHIVAL *and punching him in the ribs.*) Fine young woman!—(*He turns and bows to her very gallantly, removing his hat. She bows deeply in return*) A-h-e-m! (*Suddenly pulling himself up to a stern, military air; then gruffly to* KERCHIVAL, *extending his hand.*) Let me see the dispatches.

KER. She declines positively to give them up.

BUCK. Oh! Does she? (*Walks up the stage thoughtfully, and turns.*) My dear young lady! I trust you will give us no further trouble. Kindly let us have those dispatches.

GERT. (*Looking away.*) I have no dispatches, and I would not give them to you if I had.

BUCK. What! You defy my authority? Colonel West, I command you! Search the prisoner!

(GERTRUDE *turns suddenly towards* KERCHIVAL, *facing him defiantly. He looks across at her, aghast. A moment's pause.*)

KER. General Buckthorn—I decline to obey that order.

BUCK. You—you decline to obey my order! (*Moves down to him fiercely.*)

KER. (*Apart.*) General! It is the woman I love.

BUCK. (*Apart.*) Is it? Damn you, sir! I would n't have an officer in my army corps who *would* obey me, under such circumstances. I 'll have to look for those dispatches myself.

KER. (*Facing him, angrily.*) If you dare, General Buckthorn!

BUCK. (*Apart.*) Blast your eyes! I 'd kick you out of the army if you 'd *let* me search her; but it 's my military duty to swear at you. (*To* GERTRUDE.) Colonel West has sacrificed his life to protect you.

GERT. His life!

BUCK. I shall have him shot for insubordination to his commander, immediately. (*Gives* KERCHIVAL *a huge wink, and turns up stage.*)

GERT. Oh, sir! General! I have told you the truth. I have no dispatches. Believe me, sir, I have n't so much as a piece of paper about me, except—

BUCK. Except? (*Turning sharply.*)

GERT. Only a letter. Here it is. (*Taking letter from the bosom of her dress.*) Upon my soul, it is all I have. Truly, it is.

BUCK. (*Taking the letter.*) Colonel West, you 're reprieved. (*Winks at* KERCHIVAL, *who turns away, laughing.* BUCKTHORN *reads letter.*) "Washington"—Ho—ho! From within our own lines—"Colonel Kerchival West"—

KER. Eh?

GERT. Please, General!—Don't read it aloud.

BUCK. Very well! I won't.

KER. (*Aside.*) I wonder what it has to do with me.

BUCK. (*Reading. Aside.*) "If Kerchival West had heard you say, as I did—m—m—that you loved him with your whole heart—" (*He glances up at* GERTRUDE, *who drops her head, coyly.*) This is a very important military document. (*Turns to the last page.*) "Signed, Constance Haverill." (*Turns to front page.*) "My dear Gertrude!" Is this Miss Gertrude Ellingham?

GERT. Yes, General.

BUCK. I sent my daughter, Jenny, to your house, with an escort, this morning.

GERT. She is here.

BUCK. (*Tapping her under the chin.*) You 're an arrant little Rebel, my dear; but I like you immensely. (*Draws up suddenly, with an Ahem!, then turns to* KERCHIVAL.) Colonel West, I leave this dangerous young woman in your charge. (KERCHIVAL *approaches.*) If she disobeys you in any way, or attempts to escape—read that letter! (*Giving him the letter.*)

GERT. Oh! General!

BUCK. But not till then.

KER. (*Tenderly, taking her hand.*) My—prisoner!

GERT. (*Aside.*) I could scratch my own eyes out—or his, either—rather than have him read that letter.

(*Enter* CORPORAL DUNN, *with a guard of four soldiers and* CAPTAIN EDWARD THORNTON *as a prisoner.*)

KER. Edward Thornton!

GERT. They have taken him, also! He has the dispatch!

DUNN. The Confederate Officer, Colonel, who was pursued by our troops at Oak Run, after they captured the young lady.

BUCK. The little witch has been communicating with the enemy!

KER. (*To* GERTRUDE.) You will give me your parole of honor until we next meet?

GERT. Yes. (*Aside.*) That letter! I *am* his prisoner. (*She walks up the steps, looking back at Captain Thornton, and then leaves the stage.*)

KER. We will probably find the dispatches we have been looking for now, General.

BUCK. Prisoner! You will hand us what papers you may have.

THORN. I will hand you nothing.

BUCK. Colonel!

(KERCHIVAL *motions to* THORNTON, *who looks at him sullenly.*)

KER. Corporal Dunn!—search the prisoner. (DUNN *steps to* THORNTON, *taking him by the shoulder and turning him rather roughly so that* THORNTON'S *back is to the audience.* DUNN *throws open his coat, takes the paper from his breast, hands it to* KERCHIVAL, *who gives it to* BUCKTHORN.) Proceed with the search.

(DUNN *continues the search.* BUCKTHORN *drops upon the seat, lights a match and looks at the paper.*)

BUCK. (*Reading.*) "General Rosser will rejoin General Early with all the cavalry in his command, at—" This is important.

(*Continues to read with matches. The* CORPORAL *hands a packet to* KERCHIVAL. *He removes the covering.*)

KER. (*Starting.*) A portrait of Mrs. Haverill! (*He touches* CORPORAL DUNN *on the shoulder quickly and motions him to retire.* DUNN *falls back to the guard.* KERCHIVAL *speaks apart to* THORNTON, *who has turned front.*) How did this portrait come into your possession?

THORN. That is my affair, not yours!

BUCK. Anything else, Colonel?

KER. (*Placing the miniature in his pocket.*) Nothing!

THORN. (*Apart, over* KERCHIVAL'S *shoulder.*) A time will come, perhaps, when I can avenge the insult of this search, and also this scar. (*Pointing to a scar on his face.*) Your aim was better than mine in Charleston, but we shall meet again; give me back that picture.

KER. Corporal! Take your prisoner!

THORN. Ah!

(*He springs viciously at* KERCHIVAL; CORPORAL DUNN *springs forward, seizes* THORNTON *and throws him back to the Guard.* KERCHIVAL *walks to the right,* DUNN *stands with his carbine levelled at* THORNTON, *looks at* KERCHIVAL, *who quietly motions him out.* CORPORAL DUNN *gives the orders to the men and marches out, with* THORNTON.)

BUCK. Ah! (*Still reading with matches.*) Colonel! (*Rising.*) The enemy has a new movement on foot, and General Sheridan has left the army! Listen! (*Reads from dispatches with matches.*) "Watch for a signal from Three Top Mountain to-night."

KER. We hope to be able to read that signal ourselves.

BUCK. Yes, I know. Be on your guard. I will speak with General Haverill, and then ride over to General Wright's headquarters. Keep us informed.

KER. I will, General.

(*Saluting.* BUCKTHORN *salutes and exit.*)

KER. "Watch for a signal from Three Top Mountain to-night." (*Looking up at Mountain.*) We shall be helpless to read it unless Lieutenant Bedloe is successful. I only hope the poor boy is not lying dead, already, in those dark woods beyond the ford. (*He turns down, taking the miniature from his pocket.*) How came Edward Thornton to have this portrait of Mrs. Haverill in his possession?

(GERTRUDE *runs in on the veranda.*)

GERT. Oh, Colonel West! He 's here! (*Looks back.*) They are coming this way with him.

KER. Him! Who?

GERT. Jack.

KER. Jack!

GERT. My own horse!

KER. Ah, I remember! He and I were acquainted in Charleston.

GERT. Two troopers are passing through the camp with him.

KER. He is not in your possession?

GERT. He was captured at the battle of Fair Oaks, but I recognized him the moment I saw him; and I am sure he knew me, too, when I went up to him. He whinnied and looked so happy. You are in command here— (*Running down.*) —you will compel them to give him up to me?

KER. If he is in my command, your pet shall be returned to you. I 'll give one of my own horses to the Government as a substitute, if necessary.

GERT. Oh, thank you, my dear Kerchival! (*Going to him; he takes her hand, looking into her eyes.*) I—I could almost—

KER. Can you almost confess, at last, Gertrude, that you—love me? (*Tenderly; she draws back, hanging her head, but leaving her hand in his.*) Have I been wrong? I felt that that confession was hovering on your tongue when we were separated in Charleston. Have I seen that confession in your eyes since we met again to-day—even among the angry flashes which they have shot out at me? During all this terrible war—in the camp and the trench—in the battle—I have dreamed of a meeting like this. You are still silent?

(*Her hand is still in his. She is looking down. A smile steals over her face, and she raises her eyes to his, taking his hand in both her own.*)

GERT. Kerchival! I— (*Enter* BENSON. *She looks around over her shoulder.* KERCHIVAL *looks up. A trooper leading a large black horse, now caparisoned in military saddle, bridle, follows* BENSON *across; another trooper follows.*) *Jack!*

(*She runs up the stage, meeting the horse.* KERCHIVAL *turns.*)

KER. Confound Jack! That infernal horse was always in my way!

GERT. (*With her arm about her horse's neck.*) My darling old fellow! Is he not beautiful, Kerchival? They have taken good care of him. How soft his coat is!

KER. Benson, explain this!

BENSON. I was instructed to show this horse and his leader through the lines, sir.

KER. What are your orders, my man? (*Moving up, the trooper hands him a paper. He moves down a few steps, reading it.*)

GERT. You are to be mine again, Jack, mine! (*Resting her cheek against the horse's head and patting it.*) The Colonel has promised it to me.

KER. Ah! (*With a start, as he reads the paper.* GERTRUDE *raises her head and looks at him.*) This is General Sheridan's horse, on his way to Winchester, for the use of the General when he returns from Washington.

GERT. General Sheridan's horse? He is mine!

KER. I have no authority to detain him. He must go on.

GERT. I have hold of Jack's bridle, and you may order your men to take out their sabres and cut my hand off.

KER. (*He approaches her and gently takes her hand as it holds the bridle.*) I would rather have my own hand cut off, Gertrude, than bring tears to your eyes, but there is no alternative! (GERTRUDE *releases the bridle and turns front, brushing her eyes, her hand still held in his, his back to the audience. He returns the order and motions troopers out; they move out, with the horse.* KERCHIVAL *turns to move.* GERTRUDE *starts after the horse; he turns quickly to check her.*) You forget—that—you are my prisoner.

GERT. I *will* go!

KER. General Buckthorn left me special instructions—(*taking out the wallet and letter*)—in case you declined to obey my orders—

GERT. Oh, Colonel! Please don't read that letter. (*She stands near him, dropping her head. He glances up at her from the letter. She glances up at him and drops her eyes again.*) I will obey you.

KER. (*Aside.*) What the deuce can there be in that letter?

GERT. Colonel West! Your men made me a prisoner this afternoon; to-night you have robbed me, by your own orders, of —of—Jack is only a pet, but I love him; and my brother is also a captive in your hands. When we separated in Charleston you said that we were enemies. What is there lacking to make those words true to-day? You *are* my enemy! A few moments ago you asked me to make a confession to you. You can judge for yourself whether it is likely to be a confession of—love—or of hatred!

KER. Hatred!

GERT. (*Facing him.*) Listen to my confession, sir! From the bottom of my heart—

KER. Stop!

GERT. I will not stop!

KER. I command you.

GERT. Indeed! (*He throws open the wallet in his hand and raises the letter.*) Ah! (*She turns away; turns again, as if to speak. He half opens the letter. She stamps her foot and walks up steps of the veranda. Here she turns again.*) I tell you, I— (*He opens the letter. She turns, and exits with a spiteful step.*)

KER. I wonder if that document orders me to cut her head off! (*Returning it to wallet and pocket.*) Was ever lover in such a position? I am obliged to cross the woman I love at every step.

(*Enter* CORPORAL DUNN, *very hurriedly.*)

DUNN. A message from Adjutant Rollins, sir! The prisoner, Capt. Thornton, dashed away from the special guard which was placed over him, and he has escaped. He had a knife concealed, and two of the Guard are badly wounded. Adjutant Rollins thinks the prisoner is still within the lines of the camp—in one of the houses or the stables.

KER. Tell Major Wilson to place the remainder of the Guard under arrest, and to take every possible means to recapture the prisoner. (CORP. DUNN *salutes, and exit.*) So! Thornton has jumped his guard, and he is armed. I wonder if he is trying to get away, or to find me. From what I know of the man, he does n't much care which he succeeds in doing. That scar which I gave him in Charleston is deeper in his heart than it is in his face. (*A signal light suddenly appears on Three Top Mountain. The "Call."*) Ah! —the enemy's signal!

(*Enter* CAPTAIN LOCKWOOD, *followed by the* LIEUTENANT OF SIGNAL CORPS.)

Captain Lockwood! You are here! Are your signalmen with you?

LOCK. Yes, Colonel; and one of my Lieutenants.

(*The* LIEUTENANT *is looking up at the signal with his glass.* CAPTAIN LOCKWOOD *does the same.*)

(HAVERILL *enters, followed by two staff officers.*)

HAVER. (*As he enters.*) Can you make anything of it, Captain?

LOCKWOOD. Nothing, General! Our services are quite useless unless Lieutenant Bedloe returns with the key to their signals.

HAVER. A—h! We shall fail. It is time he had returned, if successful.

SENTINEL. (*Without.*) Halt! Who goes there? (KERCHIVAL *runs up the stage and half way up the incline, looking off.*) Halt! (*A shot is heard without.*)

BARKET. (*Without.*) Och!—Ye murtherin spalpeen!

KER. Sentinel! Let him pass; it is Sergeant Barket.

SENTINEL. (*Without.*) Pass on.

KER. He did n't give the countersign. News from Lieutenant Bedloe, General!

BARKET. (*Hurrying in, up the slope.*) Colonel Wist, our brave byes wiped out the enemy, and here 's the papers.

KER. Ah! (*Taking the papers.—Then to* LOCKWOOD.) Is that the key?

LOCK. Yes. Lieutenant!

(LIEUTENANT *hurries up to the elevation, looking through his glass.* LOCKWOOD *opens the book.*)

HAVER. What of Lieutenant Bedloe, Sergeant?

BARKET. Sayreously wounded, and in the hands of the inimy!

HAVER. (*Sighing.*) A—h.

BARKET. (*Coming down the stone steps.*) It is reported that Captain Heartsease was shot dead at his side.

KER. Heartsease dead!

LIEUT. OF SIGNAL CORPS. (*Reading Signals.*) Twelve—Twenty-two—Eleven.

BARKET. Begorra! I forgot the Sintinil entirely, but he did n't forget me. (*Holding his left arm.*)

HAVER. Colonel West! We must make every possible sacrifice for the immediate exchange of Lieutenant Bedloe, if he is still living. It is due to him. Colonel Robert Ellingham is a prisoner in this camp; offer him his own exchange for young Bedloe.

KER. He will accept, of course. I will ride to the front with him myself, General, and show him through the lines.

HAVER. At once! (KERCHIVAL *crosses front and exit on the veranda.*) Can you follow the dispatch, Captain?

LOCK. Perfectly; everything is here.

HAVER. Well!

LIEUT. OF SIGNAL CORPS. Eleven—Twenty-two—One—Twelve.

LOCK. (*From the book.*) "General Longstreet is coming with—"

HAVER. Longstreet!

LIEUT. OF SIGNAL CORPS. One—Twenty-one.

LOCK. "With eighteen thousand men."

HAVER. Longstreet and his corps!

LIEUT. OF SIGNAL CORPS. Two—Eleven—Twenty-two.

LOCK. "Sheridan is away!"

HAVER. They have discovered his absence!

LIEUT. OF SIGNAL CORPS. Two—Twenty-two—Eleven—One—Twelve—One.

LOCK. "We will crush the Union Army before he can return."

HAVER. Signal that dispatch from here to our Station at Front Royal. Tell them to send it after General Sheridan—and ride for their lives. (LOCKWOOD *hurries out.*) Major Burton! We will ride to General Wright's headquarters at once—our horses!

(*The noise of a struggle is heard without.*)

BARKET. What the devil is the row out there?

(*Exit, also one of the Staff Officers.*)

HAVER. (*Looking off to the left.*) What is this! Colonel West wounded!

(*Enter* KERCHIVAL WEST, *his coat thrown open, with* ELLINGHAM, BARKET *assisting.*)

ELLING. Steady, Kerchival, old boy! You should have let us carry you.

KER. Nonsense, old fellow! It's a mere touch with the point of the knife. I—I'm faint—with the loss of a little blood—that's all. Bob!—I—

(*He reels suddenly and is caught by* ELLINGHAM *as he sinks to the ground, insensible.*)

ELLING. Kerchival. (*Kneeling at his side.*)

HAVER. Go for the Surgeon! (*To the Staff Officer, who goes out quickly on veranda.*) How did this happen?

(*Enter* CORPORAL DUNN *and Guard, with* THORNTON. *He is in his shirt sleeves and disheveled, his arms folded. They march down.*)

Captain Thornton!

ELLING. We were leaving the house together; a hunted animal sprang suddenly across our path, like a panther. (*Looking over his shoulder.*) There it stands. Kerchival!—my brother!

CORP. DUNN. We had just brought this prisoner to bay, but I'm afraid we were too late.

HAVER. This is assassination, sir, not war. If you have killed him—

THORN. Do what you like with me; we need waste no words. I had an old account to settle, and I have paid my debt.

ELLING. General Haverill! I took these from his breast when he first fell.

(*Handing up wallet and miniature to* HAVERILL. HAVERILL *starts as he looks at the miniature.* THORNTON *watches him.*)

HAVER. (*Aside.*) My wife's portrait!

THORN. If I have killed him—your honor will be buried in the same grave.

HAVER. Her picture on his breast! She gave it to him—not to my son!

(*Dropping into the seat.* CAPT. LOCKWOOD *enters with a Signalman, who has a burning torch on a long pole; he hurries up the elevation.* CAPT. LOCKWOOD *stands below, facing him. Almost simultaneously with the entrance of the Signalman,* GERTRUDE *runs in on veranda.*)

GERT. They are calling for a surgeon! Who is it? Brother!—you are safe. Ah! (*Uttering a scream, as she sees* KERCHIVAL, *and falling on her knees at his side.*) Kerchival! Forget those last bitter words I said to you. Can't you hear my confession? I do love you. Can't you hear me? I love you!

(*The Signalman is swinging the torch as the curtain descends,* LOCKWOOD *looking out to the right.*)

ACT THIRD.

The scene is the same as in the Second Act. It is now bright daylight, with sunshine flecking the foreground and bathing the distant valley and mountains. As the curtain rises JENNY BUCKTHORN *is sitting on the low stone post, in the center of the stage, looking toward the left. She imitates a Trumpet Signal on her closed fists.*

JENNY. What a magnificent line! Guides-posts! Every man and every horse is eager for the next command. There comes the flag! (*As the scene progresses trumpet signals are heard without and she follows their various meanings in her speech.*) To the standard! The regiment is going to the front. Oh! I do wish I could go with it. I always do, the moment I hear the trumpets. Boots and Saddles! Mount! I wish I was in command of the regiment. It was born in me. Fours right! There they go! Look at those horses' ears! Forward. (*A military band is heard without, playing "The Battle Cry of Freedom."* JENNY *takes the attitude of holding a bridle and trotting.*) Rappity—plap—plap—plap, etc. (*She imitates the motions of a soldier on horseback, stepping down to the rock at side of post; thence to the ground and about the stage, with the various curvettings of a spirited horse. A chorus of soldiers is heard without, with the band. The music becomes more and more distant.* JENNY *gradually stops as the music is dying away, and stands, listening. As it dies entirely away, she suddenly starts to an enthusiastic attitude.*) Ah! If I were only a man! The enemy! On Third Battalion, left, front, into line, march! Draw sabres! Charge! (*Imitates a trumpet signal. As she finishes, she rises to her full height, with both arms raised, and trembling with enthusiasm.*) Ah! (*She suddenly drops her arms and changes to an attitude and expression of disappointment—pouting.*) And the first time Old Margery took me to Father, in her arms, she had to tell him I was a girl. Father was as much disgusted as I was. But he'd never admit it; he says I'm as good a soldier as any of 'em—just as I am.

(*Enter* BARKET, *on the veranda, his arm in a sling.*)

BARKET. Miss Jenny!

JENNY. Barket! The regiment has marched away to the front, and we girls are left here, with just you and a corporal's guard to look after us.

BARKET. I've been watching the byes mesilf. (*Coming down.*) If a little military sugar-plum like you, Miss Jenny, objects to not goin' wid 'em, what do you think of an ould piece of hard tack like me? I can't join the regiment till I've taken you and Miss Madeline back to Winchester, by your father's orders. But it is n't the first time I've escorted you, Miss Jenny. Many a time, when you was a baby, on the Plains, I commanded a special guard to accompany ye's from one fort to anither, and we gave the command in a whisper, so as not to wake ye's up.

JENNY. I told you to tell Father that I'd let him know when Madeline and I were ready to go.

BARKET. I tould him that I'd as soon move a train of army mules.

JENNY. I suppose we must start for home again to-day?

BARKET. Yes, Miss Jenny, in charge of an ould Sargeant wid his arm in a sling and a couple of convalescent throopers. This department of the United States Army will move to the rear in half an hour.

JENNY. Madeline and I only came yesterday morning.

BARKET. Whin your father got ye's a pass to the front, we all thought the fightin' in the Shenandoey Valley was over. It looks now as if it was just beginning. This is no place for women, now. Miss Gertrude Ellingham ought to go wid us, but she won't.

JENNY. Barket! Captain Heartsease left the regiment yesterday, and he has n't rejoined it; he is n't with them, now, at the head of his company. Where is he?

BARKET. I can't say where he is, Miss Jenny. (*Aside.*) Lyin' unburied in the woods, where he was shot, I'm afraid.

JENNY. When Captain Heartsease does rejoin the regiment, Barket, please say to him for me, that—that I—I may have some orders for him, when we next meet. (*Exit, on veranda.*)

BARKET. Whin they nixt mate. They tell us there is no such thing as marriage in Hiven. If Miss Jenny and Captain Heartsease mate there, they'll invint somethin' that's mighty like it. While I was lyin' wounded in General Buckthorn's house at Washington, last summer, and ould Margery was taking care of me, Margery tould me, confidentially, that they was in love wid aitch ither; and I think she was about right. I've often seen Captain Heartsease take a sly look at a little lace handkerchief, just before we wint into battle. (*Looking off the stage.*) Here's General Buckthorn himself. He and I must make it as aisy as we can for Miss Jenny's poor heart.

(*Enter* GENERAL BUCKTHORN.)

BUCK. Sergeant Barket! You have n't started with those girls yet?

BARKET. They're to go in half an hour, sir.

BUCK. Be sure they do go. Is General Haverill here?

BARKET. Yes, sur; in the house with some of his staff, and the Surgeon.

BUCK. Ah! The Surgeon. How is Colonel West, this morning, after the wound he received last night?

BARKET. He says, himself, that he's as well as iver he was; but the Colonel and Surgeon don't agray on that subject. The dochter says he must n't lave his room for a month. The knife wint dape; and there's somethin' wrong inside of him. But the Colonel, bein' on the outside himsilf, can't see it. He's as cross as a bear, baycause they would n't let him go to the front this morning, at the head of his regiment. I happened to raymark that the Chaplain was prayin' for his raycovery. The Colonel said he'd court-martial him if he did n't stop that—quick; there's more important things for the Chaplain to pray for in his official capacity. Just at that moment the trumpets sounded, "Boots and Saddles." I had to dodge one of his boots, and the Surgeon had a narrow escape from the ither one. It was lucky for us both his saddle was n't in the room.

BUCK. That looks encouraging. I think Kerchival will get on.

BARKET. Might I say a word to you, sur, about Miss Jenny?

BUCK. Certainly, Barket. You and old Margery and myself have been a sort of triangular mother, so to speak, to the little girl since her own poor mother left her to our care, when she was only a baby, in the old fort on the Plains. (*He unconsciously rests his arm over* BARKET'S *shoulder, familiarly, and then suddenly draws up.*) Ahem! (*Gruffly.*) What is it? Proceed.

BARKET. Her mother's bosom would have been the softest place for her poor little head to rest upon, now, sur.

BUCK. (*Touching his eyes.*) Well!

BARKET. Ould Margery tould me in Washington that Miss Jenny and Captain Heartsease were in love wid aitch ither.

BUCK. (*Starting.*) In love!

BARKET. I approved of the match.

BUCK. What the devil!

(BARKET *salutes quickly and starts up stage and out.* BUCKTHORN *moves up after him, and stops at the post.* BARKET *stops in the road.*)

BARKET. So did ould Margery.

BUCK. (*Angrily.*) March! (BARKET *salutes suddenly and marches off.*) Heartsease! That young jackanapes! A mere fop; he'll never make a soldier. My girl in love with—bah! I don't believe it; she's too good a soldier, herself.

(*Enter* HAVERILL, *on the veranda.*)

Ah, Haverill!

HAVER. General Buckthorn! Have you heard anything of General Sheridan since I sent that dispatch to him last evening?

BUCK. He received it at midnight and sent back word that he considers it a ruse of the enemy. General Wright agrees with him. The reconnoissance yesterday showed no hostile force, on our right, and Crook reports that Early is retreating up the valley. But General Sheridan may, perhaps, give up his journey to Washington, and he has ordered some changes in our line, to be executed this afternoon at four o'clock. I rode over to give you your instructions in person. You may order General McCuen to go into camp on the right of Meadow Brook, with the second division.

(HAVERILL *is writing in his note-book.*)

(*Enter* JENNY, *on the veranda.*)

JENNY. Oh, Father! I've so glad you've come. I've got something to say to you.

(*Running down and jumping into his arms, kissing him. He turns with her, and sets her down, squarely on her feet and straight before him.*)

BUCK. And I've got something to say to you—about Captain Heartsease.

JENNY. Oh! That's just what I wanted to talk about.

BUCK. Fall in! Front face! (*She jumps into military position, turning towards him.*) What's this I hear from Sergeant Barket? He says you've been falling in love.

JENNY. I have. (*Saluting.*)

BUCK. Young woman! Listen to my orders. Fall out! (*Turns sharply and marches to* HAVERILL.) Order the Third Brigade of Cavalry, under Colonel Lowell, to occupy the left of the pike.

JENNY. Father! (*Running to him and seizing the tail of his coat.*) Father, dear!

BUCK. Close in Colonel Powell on the extreme left—(*slapping his coat-tails out of* JENNY'S *hands, without looking around*)—and hold Custer on the second line, at Old Forge Road. That is all at present. (*Turning to* JENNY.) Goodbye, my darling! (*Kisses her.*) Remember your orders! You little pet! (*Chuckling, as he taps her chin; draws up suddenly and turns to* HAVERILL.) General! I bid you good-day.

HAVER. Good-day, General Buckthorn.

(*They salute with great dignity.* BUCKTHORN *starts up stage;* JENNY *springs after him, seizing his coattails.*)

JENNY. But I want to talk with you, Father; I can't fall out. I—I—have n't finished yet.

(*Clinging to his coat, as* BUCKTHORN *marches out rapidly, in the road, holding back with all her might.*)

HAVER. It may have been a ruse of the enemy, but I hope that General Sheridan has turned back from Washington. (*Looking at his note-book.*) We are to make changes in our line at four o'clock this afternoon. (*Returning the book to his pocket, he stands in thought.*) The Surgeon tells me that Kerchival West will get on well enough if he remains quiet; otherwise not. He shall not die by the hand of a common assassin; he has no right to die like that. My wife gave my own picture of herself to him—not to my son—and she looked so like an angel when she took it from my hand! They were both false to me, and they have been true to each other. I will save his life for myself.

(*Enter* GERTRUDE, *on the veranda.*)

GERT. General Haverill! (*Anxiously, coming down.*) Colonel West persists in disobeying the injunctions of the Surgeon. He is preparing to join his regiment at the front. Give him your orders to remain here. Compel him to be prudent!

HAVER. (*Quickly.*) The honor of death at the front is not in reserve for him.

GERT. Eh? What did you say, General?

HAVER. Gertrude! I wish to speak to you, as your father's old friend; and I was once your guardian. Your father was my senior officer in the Mexican War. Without his care I should have been left dead in a foreign land. He, himself, afterwards fell fighting for the old flag.

GERT. The old flag. (*Aside.*) My father died for it, and he—(*looking toward the left*)—is suffering for it—the old flag!

HAVER. I can now return the kindness your father did to me, by protecting his daughter from something that may be worse than death.

GERT. What do you mean?

HAVER. Last night I saw you kneeling at the side of Kerchival West; you spoke to him with all the tender passion of a Southern woman. You said you loved him. But you spoke into ears that could not hear you. Has he ever heard those words from your lips? Have you ever confessed your love to him before?

GERT. Never. Why do you ask?

HAVER. Do not repeat those words. Keep your heart to yourself, my girl.

GERT. General! Why do you say this to me? And at such a moment—when his life—

HAVER. His life! (*Turning sharply.*) It belongs to me!

GERT. Oh!

KER. Sergeant! (*Without. He steps into the road, looking back.* HAVERILL *comes down.*) See that my horse is ready at once. General! (*Saluting.*) Are there any orders for my regiment beyond those given to Major Wilson, in my absence, this morning? I am about to ride on after the troops and reassume my command.

HAVER. (*Quietly.*) It is my wish, Colonel, that you remain here under the care of the Surgeon.

KER. My wound is a mere trifle. This may be a critical moment in the campaign, and I cannot rest here. I must be with my own men.

HAVER. (*Quietly.*) I beg to repeat the wish I have already expressed.

(KERCHIVAL *walks to him, and speaks apart, almost under his breath, but very earnest in tone.*)

KER. I have had no opportunity, yet, to explain certain matters, as you requested me to do yesterday; but whatever there may be between us, you are now interfering with my duty and my privilege as a soldier; and it is my right to be at the head of my regiment.

HAVER. (*Quietly.*) It is my positive order that you do not reassume your command.

KER. General Haverill, I protest against this—

HAVER. (*Quietly.*) You are under arrest, sir.

KER. Arrest!

GERT. Ah!

(KERCHIVAL *unclasps his belt and offers his sword to* HAVERILL.)

HAVER. (*Quietly.*) Keep your sword; I have no desire to humiliate you; but hold yourself subject to further orders from me.

KER. My regiment at the front!—and I under arrest! (*Exit.*)

HAVER. Gertrude! If your heart refuses to be silent—if you feel that you must confess your love to that man—first tell him what I have said to you, and refer him to me for an explanation. (*Exit.*)

GERT. What can he mean? He would save me from something worse than death, he said. "His life—It belongs to me!" What can he mean? Kerchival told me that he loved me—it seems many years since that morning in Charleston—and when we met again, yesterday, he said that he had never ceased to love me. I will not believe that he has told me a falsehood. I have given him my love, my whole soul and my faith. (*Drawing up to her full height.*) My perfect faith!

(JENNY *runs in, to the road, and up the slope. She looks down the hill, then toward the left and enters.*)

JENNY. A flag of truce, Gertrude. And a party of Confederate soldiers, with an escort, coming up the hill. They are carrying someone; he is wounded.

(*Enter, up the slope, a Lieutenant of Infantry with an escort of Union Soldiers, their arms at right shoulder, and a party of Confederate Soldiers bearing a rustic stretcher.* LIEUTENANT FRANK BEDLOE *lies on the stretcher.* MAJOR HARDWICK, *a Confederate Surgeon, walks at his side.* MADELINE *appears at the veranda, watching them.* GERTRUDE *stands with her back to the audience. The Lieutenant gives orders in a low tone, and the front escort moves toward the right, in the road. The Confederate bearers and the Surgeon pass through the gate. The rear escort moves on in the road, under the Lieutenant's orders. The bearers halt in the front of the stage; on a sign from the Surgeon, they leave the stretcher on the ground, stepping back.*)

MAJ. HARD. Is General Haverill here?

GERT. Yes; what can we do, sir?

MAD. The General is just about mounting with his staff, to ride away. Shall I go for him, sir?

MAJ. Say to him, please, that Colonel Robert Ellingham, of the Tenth Virginia, sends his respects and sympathy. He instructed me to bring this young officer to this point, in exchange for himself, as agreed upon between them last evening. (*Exit* MADELINE.)

JENNY. Is he unconscious or sleeping, sir?

MAJ. Hovering between life and death. I thought he would bear the removal better. He is waking. Here, my lad! (*Placing his canteen to the lips of* FRANK, *who moves, reviving.*) We have reached the end of our journey.

FRANK. My father!

MAJ. He is thinking of his home.

(FRANK *rises on one arm, assisted by the Surgeon.*)

FRANK. I have obeyed General Haverill's orders, and I have a report to make.

GERT. We have already sent for him. (*Stepping to him.*) He will be here in a moment.

FRANK. (*Looking into her face, brightly.*) Is not this—Miss—Gertrude Ellingham?

GERT. You know me? You have seen me before?

FRANK. Long ago! Long ago! You know the wife of General Haverill?

GERT. I have no dearer friend in the world.

FRANK. She will give a message for me to the dearest friend *I* have in the world. My little wife! I must not waste even the moment we are waiting. Doctor! My note-book! (*Trying to get it from his coat. The Surgeon takes it out. A torn and blood-stained lace handkerchief also falls out.* GERTRUDE *kneels at his side.*) Ah! I—I—have a message from another—(*holding up the handkerchief*)—from Captain Heartsease. (JENNY *makes a quick start towards him.*) He lay at my side in the hospital, when they brought me away; he had only strength enough to put this in my hand, and he spoke a woman's name; but I—I—forget what it is. The red spots upon it are the only message he sent.

(GERTRUDE *takes the handkerchief and looks back at* JENNY, *extending her hand.* JENNY *moves to her, takes the handkerchief and turns back, looking down on it. She drops her face into her hands and goes out sobbing, on the veranda.*)

(*Enter* MADELINE *on the veranda.*)

MAD. General Haverill is coming. I was just in time. He was already on his horse.

FRANK. Ah! He is coming. (*Then suddenly.*) Write! Write! (GERTRUDE *writes in the note-book as he dictates.*) "To—my wife—Edith:—Tell our little son, when he is old enough to know—how his father died; not how he lived. And tell her who filled my own mother's place so lovingly—she is your mother, too—that my father's portrait of her, which she gave to me in Charleston, helped me to be a better man!" And—Oh! I must not forget this—"It was taken away from me while I was a prisoner in Richmond, and it is in the possession of Captain Edward Thornton, of the Confederate Secret Service. But her face is still beside your own in my heart. My best—warmest, last—love—to you, darling." I will sign it.

(GERTRUDE *holds the book, and he signs it, then sinks back very quietly, supported by the Surgeon.* GERTRUDE *rises and walks away.*)

MAD. General Haverill is here.

(*The Surgeon lays the fold of the blanket over* FRANK'S *face and rises.*)

GERT. Doctor!

MAJ. He is dead.

(MADELINE, *on the veranda, turns and looks away. The Lieutenant orders the guard, "Present Arms."*)

(*Enter* HAVERILL, *on the veranda. He salutes the guard as he passes. The Lieutenant orders, "Carry Arms."* HAVERILL *comes down.*)

HAVER. I am too late?

MAJ. I'm sorry, General. His one eager thought as we came was to reach here in time to see you.

(HAVERILL *moves to the bier, looks down at it, then folds back the blanket from the face. He starts slightly as he first sees it.*)

HAVER. Brave boy! I hoped once to have a son like you. I shall be in your father's place to-day, at your grave. (*He replaces the blanket and steps back.*) We will carry him to his comrades in the front. He shall have a soldier's burial, in sight of the mountain-top beneath which he sacrificed his young life; that shall be his monument.

MAJ. Pardon me, General. We Virginians are your enemies, but you cannot honor this young soldier more than we do. Will you allow my men the privilege of carrying him to his grave?

(HAVERILL *inclines his head. The Surgeon motions to the Confederate Soldiers, who step to the bier and raise it gently.*)

HAVER. Lieutenant!

(*The Lieutenant orders the guard "Left Face." The Confederate bearers move through the gate, preceded by* LIEUTENANT HARDWICK. HAVERILL *draws his sword. reverses it, and moves up behind the bier with bowed head. The Lieutenant orders "Forward March," and the cortège disappears. While the girls are still watching it, the heavy sound of distant artillery is heard, with booming reverberations among the hills and in the valley.*)

MAD. What is that sound, Gertrude?

GERT. Listen!

(*Another and more prolonged distant sound, with long reverberations.*)

MAD. Again! Gertrude!

(GERTRUDE *raises her hand to command silence; listens. Distant cannon again.*)

GERT. It is the opening of a battle.

MAD. Ah! (*Running down stage. The sounds are heard again, prolonged.*)

GERT. How often have I heard that sound! (*Coming down.*) This is war, Madeline! You are face to face with it now.

MAD. And Robert is there! He may be in the thickest of the danger—at this very moment.

GERT. Yes. Let our prayers go up for him; mine do, with all a sister's heart.

(KERCHIVAL *enters on veranda, without coat or vest, his sash about his waist, looking back as he comes in.*)

Kerchival!

KER. Go on! Go on! Keep the battle to yourselves. I'm out of it. (*The distant cannon and reverberations are rising in volume.*)

MAD. I pray for Robert Ellingham—and for the *cause* in which he risks his life! (KERCHIVAL *looks at her, suddenly; also* GERTRUDE.) Heaven forgive me if I am wrong, but I am praying for the enemies of my country. His people are my people, his enemies are my enemies. Heaven defend him and his, in this awful hour.

KER. Madeline! My sister!

MAD. Oh, Kerchival! (*Turning and dropping her face on his breast.*) I cannot help it—I cannot help it!

KER. My poor girl! Every woman's heart, the world over, belongs not to any country or any flag, but to her husband—and her lover. Pray for the man you love, sister—it would be treason not to. (*Passes her before him to the left of the stage. Looks across to* GERTRUDE.) Am

I right? (GERTRUDE *drops her head.* MADELINE *moves up veranda and out.*) Is what I have said to Madeline true?

GERT. Yes! (*Looks up.*) Kerchival!

KER. Gertrude! (*Hurries across to her, clasps her in his arms. He suddenly staggers and brings his hand to his breast.*)

GERT. Your wound!

(*Supporting him as he reels and sinks into seat.*)

KER. Wound! I have no wound! You do love me! (*Seizing her hand.*)

GERT. Let me call the Surgeon, Kerchival.

KER. You can be of more service to me than he can. (*Detaining her. Very heavy sounds of the battle; she starts, listening.*) Never mind that! It's only a battle. You love me!

GERT. Be quiet, Kerchival, dear. I do love you. I told you so, when you lay bleeding here, last night. But you could not hear me. (*At his side, resting her arm about him, stroking his head.*) I said that same thing to—to—another, more than three years ago. It is in that letter that General Buckthorn gave you. (KERCHIVAL *starts.*) No—no—you must be very quiet, or I will not say another word. If you obey me, I will repeat that part of the letter, every word; I know it by heart, for I read it a dozen times. The letter is from Mrs. Haverill.

KER. (*Quietly.*) Go on.

GERT. "I have kept your secret, my darling, but I was sorely tempted to betray the confidence you reposed in me at Charleston. If Kerchival West—(*she retires backward from him as she proceeds*) —had heard you say, as I did, when your face was hidden in my bosom, that night, that you loved him with your whole heart—"

KER. Ah!

(*Starting to his feet. He sinks back. She springs to support him.*)

GERT. I will go for help.

KER. Do not leave me at such a moment as this. You have brought me a new life. (*Bringing her to her knees before him and looking down at her.*) Heaven is just opening before me. (*His hands drop suddenly and his head falls back.*)

GERT. Ah! Kerchival! You are dying!

(*Musketry. A sudden sharp burst of musketry, mingled with the roar of artillery near by.* KERCHIVAL *starts, seizing* GERTRUDE'S *arm and holding her away, still on her knees. He looks eagerly toward the left.*)

KER. The enemy is close upon us!

(BARKET *runs in, up the slope.*)

BARKET. Colonel Wist! The devils have sprung out of the ground. They're pouring over our lift flank like Noah's own flood. The Union Army has started back for Winchester, on its way to the North Pole; our own regiment, Colonel, is coming over the hill in full retrate.

KER. My own regiment! (*Starting up.*) Get my horse, Barket. (*Turns.*) Gertrude, my life! (*Embraces* GERTRUDE.)

BARKET. Your horse is it? I'm wid ye! There's a row at Finnegan's ball, and we're in it. (*Springs to the road, and runs out.*)

KER. (*Turns away. Stops.*) I am under arrest.

(*The retreat begins. Fugitives begin to straggle across the stage from the left.*)

GERT. You must not go, Kerchival; it will kill you.

KER. Arrest be damned! (*Starts up toward the center, raising his arms above his head with clenched fist, and rising to full height.*) Stand out of my way, you cowards!

(*They cower away from him as he rushes out among them. The stream of fugitives passing across the stage swells in volume.* GERTRUDE *runs through them and up to the elevation, turning.*)

GERT. Men! Are you soldiers? Turn back! There is a leader for you! Turn back! Fight for your flag—and mine!—the flag my father died for! Turn back! (*She looks out toward the left and then turns toward the front.*) He has been marked for death already, and I—I can only pray. (*Dropping to her knees.*)

(*The stream of fugitives continues, now over the elevation also. Rough and torn uniforms, bandaged arms and legs; some limping and supported by others, some dragging their muskets after them, others without muskets, others using them as crutches. There is a variety of uniforms, both cavalry and infantry; flags are draggled on the ground, the rattle of near musketry and roar of cannon continue; two or three wounded fugitives drop down beside the hedge.* BENSON *staggers in and drops upon a rock near the post. Artillerists, rough, torn and wounded, drag and force a field-piece across.* CORPORAL DUNN, *wounded, staggers to the top of elevation. There is a lull in the sounds of the battle. Distant cheers are heard without.*)

DUNN. Listen, fellows! Stop! Listen! Sheridan! General Sheridan is coming! (*Cheers from those on stage.* GERTRUDE *rises quickly. The wounded soldiers rise, looking over the hedge. All on stage stop, looking eagerly toward the left. The cheers without come nearer, with shouts of "Sheridan! Sheridan!"*) The horse is down; he is worn out.

GERT. No! He is up again! He is on my Jack! Now, for your life, Jack, and for me! You've never failed me yet. (*The cheers without now swell to full volume and are taken up by those on the stage. The horse sweeps by with General Sheridan.*) Jack! Jack!! Jack!!!

(*Waving her arms as he passes. She throws up her arms and falls backward, caught by* DUNN. *The stream of men is reversed and surges across the stage to the left, in the road and on the elevation, with shouts, and throwing up of hats. The field-piece is forced up the slope with a few bold, rough movements; the artillerists are loading it, and the stream of returning fugitives is still surging by in the road as the curtain falls.*)

ACT FOURTH.

A living room in the residence of GENERAL BUCKTHORN *in Washington. There is a fireplace slanting upward from the left toward the center of the stage. On the right toward the center there is a small alcove. On the left there is an opening to the hall with a stair-case beyond. There is a door on the right and a wide opening with portières leads on the left toward another room. There is an upright piano toward the front of the stage on the right and an armchair and low stool stand before the fireplace. A small table is set for tea. It is afternoon;* MRS. HAVERILL, *in an armchair, is resting her face upon her hand, and looking into the fire.* EDITH *is on a low stool at her side, sewing a child's garment.*

EDITH. It seems hardly possible that the war is over, and that General Lee has really surrendered. There is music in the streets nearly all the time, now, and everybody looks so cheerful and bright. (*Distant fife and drums are heard playing "Johnnie Comes Marching Home."* EDITH *springs up and runs up to window, looking out.*) More troops returning! The old tattered battle-flag is waving in the wind, and people are running after them so merrily. Every day, now, seems like a holiday. The war is over. All the women ought to feel very happy, whose—whose husbands are—coming back to them.

MRS. H. Yes, Edith; those women whose—husbands are coming back to them. (*Still looking into the fire.*)

EDITH. Oh! (*Dropping upon the stool, her head upon the arm of the chair.*)

MRS. H. (*Resting her arm over her.*) My poor, little darling! *Your* husband will not come back.

EDITH. Frank's last message has never reached me.

MRS. H. No; but you have one sweet thought always with you. Madeline West heard part of it, as Gertrude wrote it down. His last thought was a loving one, of you.

EDITH. Madeline says that he was thinking of you, too. He knew that you were taking such loving care of his little one, and of me. You have always done that, since you first came back from Charleston, and found me alone in New York.

MRS. H. I found a dear, sweet little daughter. (*Stroking her head.*) Heaven sent you, darling! You have been a blessing to me. I hardly know how I should have got through the past few months at all without you at my side.

EDITH. What is your own trouble, dear? I have found you in tears so often; and since last October, after the battle of Cedar Creek, you—you have never shown me a letter from—from my—Frank's father. General Haverill arrived in Washington yesterday, but has not been here yet. Is it because I am here? He has never seen me, and I fear that he has never forgiven Frank for marrying me.

MRS. H. Nonsense, my child; he did think the marriage was imprudent, but he told me to do everything I could for you. If General Haverill has not been to see either of us, since his arrival in Washington, it is nothing that you need to worry your dear little head about. How are you getting on with your son's wardrobe?

EDITH. Oh! Splendidly! Frankie is n't a baby any longer; he 's a man, now, and he has to wear a man's clothes. (*Holding up a little pair of trousers, with maternal pride.*) He 's rather young to be dressed like a man, but I want Frank to grow up as soon as possible. I long to have him old enough to understand me when I repeat to him the words in which General Haverill told the whole world how his father died! (*Rising.*) And yet, even in his official report to the Government, he only honored him as Lieutenant Bedloe. He has never forgiven his son for the disgrace he brought upon his name.

MRS. H. I know him so well—(*rising*)—the unyielding pride, that conquers even the deep tenderness of his nature. He can be silent, though his own heart is breaking. (*Aside.*) He can be silent, too, though *my* heart is breaking. (*Dropping her face in her hand.*)

EDITH. *Mother!* (*Putting her arm about her.*)

(*Enter* JANNETTE.)

JAN. A letter for you, Madam.

MRS. H. (*Taking note. Aside.*) He has answered me. (*She opens and reads the letter, and inclines her head to* JANNETTE, *who goes out to the hall. Aloud.*) General Haverill will be here this afternoon, Edith. (*Exit.*)

EDITH. There is something that she cannot confide to me, or to anyone. General Haverill returned to Washington yesterday, and he has not been here yet. He will be here to-day. I always tremble when I think of meeting him.

(GENERAL BUCKTHORN *appears in the hall.*)

BUCK. Come right in; this way, Barket. Ah, Edith!

BARKET. (*Entering.*) As I was saying, sur—just after the battle of Sayder Creek began—

BUCK. (*To* EDITH.) More good news! The war is, indeed, over now!

BARKET. Whin Colonel Wist rode to the front to mate his raytrating rigiment—

BUCK. General Johnston has surrendered his army, also; and that, of course, does end the war.

EDITH. I 'm very glad that all the fighting is over.

BUCK. So am I; but my occupation, and old Barket's, too, is gone. Always at work on new clothes for our little soldier?

EDITH. He 's growing so, I can hardly make them fast enough for him. But this is the time for his afternoon nap. I must go now, to see if he is sleeping soundly.

BUCK. Our dear little mother! (*Tapping her chin.*) I always claim the privilege of my white hair, you know. (*She puts up her lips; he kisses her. She goes out.*) The sweetest young widow I ever saw! (BARKET *coughs.* BUCKTHORN *turns sharply;* BARKET *salutes.*) Well! What the devil are you thinking about now?

BARKET. The ould time, sur. Yer honor used to claim the same privilege for brown hair.

BUCK. You old rascal! What a memory you have! You were telling me for the hundredth time about the battle of Cedar Creek; go on. I can never hear it often enough. Kerchival West was a favorite of mine, poor fellow!

BARKET. Just afther the battle of Sayder Creek began, when the Colonel rode to the front to mate his raytrating rigiment—

BUCK. I 'll tell Old Margery to bring in tea for both of us, Barket.

BARKET. For both of us, sur?

BUCK. Yes; and later in the evening we 'll have something else, together. This is a great day for all of us. I'm not your commander to-day, but your old comrade in arms—(*Laying his arm over* BARKET'S *shoulder*)—and I 'm glad I don't have to pull myself up now every time I forget my dignity. Ah! you and I will be laid away before long, but we 'll be together again in the next world, won't we, Barket?

BARKET. Wid yer honor's permission. (*Saluting.*)

BUCK. Ha—ha—ha! (*Laughing.*) If we do meet there, I 'm certain you 'll salute me as your superior officer. There 's old Margery, now. (*Looking toward the door and calling.*) Margery! Tea for two!

MARGERY. (*Without.*) The tay be waiting for ye, sur; and it be boilin' over wid impatience.

BUCK. Bring up a chair, Barket. (*Sitting down in the arm-chair.*)

BARKET. (*Having placed table and drawing up a chair.*) Do you know, Gineral, I don't fale quite aisy in my moind. I 'm not quite sure that Margery will let us take our tay together.

(*Sits down, doubtfully.*)

BUCK. I had n't thought of that. I— (*Glancing to the right.*)—I hope she will, Barket. But, of course, if she won't—she 's been commander-in-chief of my household ever since Jenny was a baby.

BARKET. At Fort Duncan, in Texas.

BUCK. You and Old Margery never got along very well in those days; but I thought you had made it all up; she nursed you through your wound, last summer, and after the battle of Cedar Creek, also.

BARKET. Yis, sur, bliss her kind heart, she 's been like a wife to me; and that 's the trouble. A man's wife is such an angel when he 's ill that he dreads to get well; good health is a misfortune to him. Auld Margery and I have had anither misunderstanding.

BUCK. I 'll do the best I can for both of us, Barket. You were telling me about the battle of—

BARKET. Just afther the battle of Sayder Creek began, whin Colonel Wist rode to the front to mate his raytrating rigiment—

(*Enter* OLD MARGERY, *with a tea-tray. She stops abruptly, looking at* BARKET. *He squirms in his chair.* BUCKTHORN *rises and stands with his back to the mantel.* OLD MARGERY *moves to the table, arranges things on it, glances at* BARKET, *then at* BUCKTHORN, *who looks up at the ceiling, rubbing his chin.* OLD MARGERY *takes up one of the cups, with saucer.*)

OLD MARG. I misunderstood yer order, sur. I see there 's no one here but yerself. (*Going.*)

BUCK. Ah, Margery! (*She stops.*) Barket tells me that there has been a slight misunderstanding between you and him.

OLD MARG. Day before yisterday, the ould Hibernian dhrone had the kitchen upside down, to show anither old milithary vagabone loike himself how the battle of Sayder Creek was fought. He knocked the crame pitcher into the basket of clane clothes, and overturned some raspberry jam and the flat-irons into a pan of fresh eggs. There *has* been a misunderstanding betwane us.

BUCK. I see there has. I suppose Barket was showing his friend how Colonel Kerchival West rode forward to meet his regiment, when he was already wounded dangerously.

OLD MARG. Bliss the poor, dear young man! He and I was always good frinds, though he was something of a devil in the kitchen himself, whin he got there. (*Wiping her eye with one corner of her apron.*) And bliss the young Southern lady that was in love wid him, too. (*Changing the cup and wiping the other eye with the corner of her apron.*) Nothing was iver heard of ayther of thim after that battle was over, to this very day.

BUCK. Barket was at Kerchival's side when he rode to the front. (OLD MARGERY *hesitates a moment, then moves to the table, sets down the cup and marches out.* BUCKTHORN *sits in the arm-chair again, pouring tea.*) I could always find some way to get Old Margery to do what I wanted her to do.

BARKET. You 're a great man, Gineral; we 'd niver have conquered the South widout such men.

BUCK. Now go on, Barket; you were interrupted.

BARKET. Just afther the battle of Sayder Creek began, whin—

(*Enter* JANNETTE, *with a card, which she hands to* BUCKTHORN.)

BUCK. (*Reading card.*) Robert Ellingham! (*Rises.*) I will go to him. (*To* JANNETTE.) Go upstairs and tell Miss Madeline to come down.

JANNETTE. Yes, sir. (*Going.*)

BUCK. And, Jannette, simply say there is a caller; don't tell her who is here. (*Exit* JANNETTE. BUCKTHORN *follows her out to the hall.*) Ellingham! My dear fellow!

(*Extending his hand and disappearing.*)

BARKET. Colonel Ellingham and Miss Madeline—lovers! That 's the kind o' volunteers the country nades now!

(*Enter* BUCKTHORN *and* ELLINGHAM.)

BUCK. (*As he enters.*) We 've been fighting four years to keep you out of Washington, Colonel, but we are delighted to see you within the lines, now.

ELLING. I am glad, indeed, General, to have so warm a welcome. But can you tell me anything about my sister, Gertrude?

BUCK. About your sister? Why, can't you tell us? And have you heard nothing of Kerchival West on your side of the line?

ELLING. All I can tell you is this: As soon as possible after our surrender at Appomattox, I made my way to the Shenandoah Valley. Our home there is utterly deserted. I have hurried down to Washington in the hopes that I might learn something of you. There is no human being about the old homestead; it is like a haunted house—empty, and dark, and solitary. You do not even know where Gertrude is?

BUCK. We only know that Kerchival was not found among the dead of his own regiment at Cedar Creek, though he fell among them during the fight. The three girls searched the field for him, but he was not there. As darkness came on, and they were returning to the house, Gertrude suddenly seized the bridle of a stray horse, sprang upon its back and rode away to the South, into the woods at the foot of Three Top Mountain. The other two girls watched for her in vain. She did not return, and we have heard nothing from her since.

ELLING. Poor girl! I understand what was in her thoughts, and she was right. We captured fourteen hundred prisoners that day, although we were defeated, and Kerchival must have been among them. Gertrude rode away, alone, in the darkness, to find him. I shall return to the South at once and learn where she now is.

(JANNETTE *has re-entered, down the stairs.*)

JANNETTE. Miss Madeline will be down in a moment. (*Exit in hall.*)

BARKET. (*Aside.*) That name wint through his chist like a rifle ball.

BUCK. Will you step into the drawing-room, Colonel? I will see Madeline myself, first. She does not even know that you are living.

ELLING. I hardly dared ask for her. Is she well?

BUCK. Yes; and happy—or soon will be.

ELLING. Peace, at last!

(*Exit to the apartment.* BUCKTHORN *closes the portières.*)

BUCK. I ought to prepare Madeline a little, Barket; you must help me.

BARKET. Yis, sur, I will.

(*Enter* MADELINE, *down the stairs.*)

MADELINE. Uncle! Jannette said you wished to see me; there is a visitor here. Who is it?

BARKET. Colonel Robert Ellingham.

MAD. Ah! (*Staggering.*)

BUCK. (*Supporting her.*) You infernal idiot! I'll put you in the guard-house!

BARKET. You wanted me to help ye, Gineral.

MAD. Robert is alive—and here?

(*Rising from his arms, she moves to the portières, holds them aside, peeping in; gives a joyful start, tosses aside the portières and runs through.*)

BUCK. Barket! There 's nothing but that curtain between us and Heaven.

BARKET. I don't like stayin' out o' Hiven, myself, sur. Gineral! I'll kiss Ould Margery—if I die for it! (*Exit.*)

BUCK. Kiss Old Margery! I'll give him a soldier's funeral.

(*Enter* JENNY *from hall, demurely.*)

Ah! Jenny, my dear! I have news for you. Colonel Robert Ellingham is in the drawing-room.

JENNY. Oh! I am delighted. (*Starting.*)

BUCK. A-h-e-m!

JEN. Oh!—exactly. I see. I have some news for *you,* papa. Captain Heartsease has arrived in Washington.

BUCK. Oh! My dear! I have often confessed to you how utterly mistaken I was about that young man. He is a soldier—as good a soldier as you are. I'll ask him to the house.

JEN. (*Demurely.*) He is here now.

BUCK. Now?

JEN. He 's been here an hour; in the library.

BUCK. Why! Barket and I were in the library fifteen minutes ago.

JEN. Yes, sir. We were in the bay-window; the curtains were closed.

BUCK. Oh! exactly; I see. You may tell him he has my full consent.

JEN. He has n't asked for it.

BUCK. Has n't he? And you 've been in the bay-window an hour? Well, my darling—I was considered one of the best Indian fighters in the old army, but it took me four years to propose to your mother. I'll go and see the Captain. (*Exit.*)

JEN. I wonder if it will take Captain Heartsease four years to propose to me. Before he left Washington, nearly two years ago, he told everybody in the circle of my acquaintance, except me, that he was in love with me. I 'll be an old lady in caps before our engagement commences. Poor, dear mother! The idea of a girl's waiting four years for a chance to say, "Yes." It 's been on the tip of my tongue so often, I 'm afraid it 'll pop out, at last, before he pops the question.

(*Enter* BUCKTHORN *and* HEARTSEASE *from the hall.*)

BUCK. Walk right in, Captain; this is the family room. You must make yourself quite at home here.

HEARTSEASE. Thank you.

(*Walking down toward the right.*)

BUCK. My dear! (*Apart to* JENNY.) The very first thing he said to me, after our greeting, was that he loved my daughter.

JEN. Now he 's told my father!

BUCK. He 's on fire!

JEN. Is he? (*Looking at* HEARTSEASE, *who stands quietly stroking his mustache.*) Why does n't he tell *me?*

BUCK. You may have to help him a little; your mother assisted me. When you and Jenny finish your chat, Captain—(*Lighting a cigar at the mantel*)—you must join me in the smoking room.

HEART. I shall be delighted. By the way, General—I have been in such a fever of excitement since I arrived at this house—

JEN. (*Aside.*) Fever? Chills!

HEART. That I forgot it entirely. I have omitted a very important and a very sad commission. I have brought with me the note-book of Lieutenant Frank Bedloe—otherwise Haverill—in which Miss Gertrude Ellingham wrote down his last message to his young wife.

JEN. Have you seen Gertrude?

BUCK. (*Taking the book.*) How did this note-book come into your possession?

HEART. Miss Ellingham visited the prison in North Carolina where I was detained. She was going from hospital to hospital, from prison to prison, and from burial-place to burial-place, to find Colonel Kerchival West, if living—or some record of his death.

BUCK. Another Evangeline! Searching for her lover through the wilderness of this great war!

HEART. I was about to be exchanged at the time, and she requested me to bring this to her friends in Washington. She had not intended to carry it away with her. I was not exchanged, as we then expected, but I afterwards escaped from prison to General Sherman's Army.

BUCK. I will carry this long-delayed message to the widowed young mother.

(*Exit.*)

JEN. I remember so well, when poor Lieutenant Haverill took out the note-book and asked Gertrude to write for him. He—he brought me a message at the same time.

(*Their eyes meet. He puts up his glasses. She turns away, touching her eyes.*)

HEART. I—I remember the circumstances you probably allude to; that is—when he left my side—I—I gave him my—I mean your—lace handkerchief.

JEN. It is sacred to me!

HEART. Y-e-s—I would say—is it?

JEN. (*Wiping her eyes.*) It was stained with the life-blood of a hero!

HEART. I must apologize to you for its condition. I had n't any chance to have it washed and ironed.

JEN. (*Looking around at him, suddenly; then, aside.*) What could any girl do with a lover like that?

(*Turning up the stage.*)

HEART. (*Aside.*) She seems to remember that incident so tenderly! My blood boils!

JEN. Did n't you long to see your—your friends at home—when you were in prison, Captain?

HEART. Yes—especially—I longed especially, Miss Buckthorn, to see—

JEN. *Yes!—to see—*

HEART. But there were lots of jolly fellows in the prison.

(JENNY *turns away.*)

HEART. We had a dramatic society, and a glee club, and an orchestra. I was one of the orchestra. I had a banjo, with one string; I played one tune on it, that I used to play on the piano, with one finger. But, Miss Buckthorn, I am a prisoner again, to-night—your prisoner.

JEN. (*Aside.*) At last!

HEART. I 'll show you how that tune went.

(*Turns to the piano and sits.*)

JEN. (*Aside.*) Father said I 'd have to help him, but I don't see an opening.

(HEARTSEASE *plays part of an air with one finger and strikes two or three wrong notes.*)

HEART. There are two notes down there, somewhere, that I never could get right. The fellows in prison used to dance while I played—(*Playing*)—that is, the lame ones did; those that were n't lame could n't keep the time.

JEN. You must have been in great danger, Captain, when you escaped from prison.

HEART. Y-e-s. I was badly frightened several times. One night I came face to face, on the road, with a Confederate Officer. It was Captain Thornton.

JEN. Oh! What did you do?

HEART. I killed him. (*Very quietly, and trying the tune again at once. Enter* JANNETTE, *from the hall; she glances into the room and goes up the stairs.*) I used to skip those two notes on the banjo. It 's very nice for a soldier to come home from the war, and meet those—I mean the one particular person—that he—you see, when a soldier loves a woman, as—as—

JEN. (*Aside.*) As he loves me.

(*Approaches him.*)

HEART. As soldiers often do—(*Plays; she turns away, petulantly; he plays the tune through correctly.*) That 's it!

JEN. (*Aside.*) I 'm not going to be made love to by piece-meal, like this, any longer. (*Aloud.*) Captain Heartsease! Have you anything in particular to say to me? (*He looks up.*)

HEART. Y-e-s. (*Rising.*)

JEN. Say it! You told my father, and all my friends, that you were in love with me. Whom are you going to tell next?

HEART. I *am* in love with you.

JEN. It was my turn.

HEART. (*Going near to her.*) Do you love me?

JEN. (*Laying her head quietly on his breast.*) I must take time to consider.

HEART. (*Quietly.*) I assume that this means "Yes."

JEN. It isn 't the way a girl says "No."

HEART. My darling!

JEN. Why! His heart is beating as fast as mine is!

HEART. (*Quietly.*) I am frantic with joy. (*He kisses her. She hides her face on his breast. Enter* MRS. HAVERILL, *down-stairs, followed by* JANNETTE. MRS. HAVERILL *stops suddenly.* JANNETTE *stands in the doorway.* HEARTSEASE *inclines his head to her, quietly looking at her over* JENNY.) I am delighted to see you, after so long an absence; I trust that we shall meet more frequently hereafter.

JEN. (*Looking at him*). Eh?

HEART. (*Looking down at her.*) I think, perhaps, it might be as well for us to repair to another apartment, and continue our interview, there!

JEN. (*Dropping her head on his breast again.*) This room is very comfortable.

MRS. H. Jenny, dear!

(JENNY *starts up; looks from* MRS. HAVERILL *to* HEARTSEASE.)

JEN. Constance! I—'Bout face! March!

(*She turns and goes out.*)

MRS. H. I am glad to see you again, Captain, and happy as well as safe.

HEART. Thank you, Madam. I am happy. If you will excuse me, I will join—my father—in the smoking-room.

(MRS. HAVERILL *inclines her head, and* HEARTSEASE *walks out.*)

MRS. H. Jannette! You may ask General Haverill to come into this room. (*Exit* JANNETTE. MRS. HAVERILL *walks down the stage, reading a note.*) "I have hesitated to come to you personally, as I have hesitated to write to you. If I have been silent, it is because I could not bring my hand to write what was in my mind and in my heart. I do not know that I can trust my tongue to speak it, but I will come."

(*Enter* HAVERILL, *from the hall; he stops.*)

HAVER. Constance!

MRS. H. My husband! May I call you husband? After all these months of separation, with your life in almost daily peril, and my life—what? Only a weary longing for one loving word—and you are silent.

HAVER. May I call you wife? I do not wish to speak that word except with reverence. You have asked me to come to you. I am here. I will be plain, direct and brief. Where is the portrait of yourself, which I gave you, in Charleston, for my son?

MRS. H. Your son is dead, sir; and my portrait lies upon his breast, in the grave. (HAVERILL *takes the miniature from his pocket and holds it towards her in his extended hand. She starts back.*) He gave it to you? And you ask me where it is?

HAVER. It might have lain in the grave of Kerchival West!

MRS. H. Ah!

HAVER. Not in my son's. I found it upon *his* breast. (*She turns front, dazed.*) Well! I am listening! It was not I that sought this interview, madam; and if you prefer to remain silent, I will go. You know, now, why I have been silent so long.

Mrs. H. My only witnesses to the truth are both dead. I shall remain silent. (*Turning towards him.*) We stand before each other, living, but not so happy as they. We are parted, forever. Even if you should accept my unsupported word—if I could so far forget my pride as to give it to you—suspicion would still hang between us. I remain silent.

(Haverill *looks at her, earnestly, for a moment, then approaches her.*)

Haver. I cannot look into your eyes and not see truth and loyalty there. Constance!

Mrs. H. No, John! (*Checking him.*) I will not accept your blind faith! (*Moving.*)

Haver. (*Looking down at the picture in his hand.*) My faith is blind; blind as my love! I do not wish to see!

(*Enter* Edith. *She stops and looks at* Haverill. *He raises his head and looks at her.*)

Edith. This is General Haverill? (*Dropping her eyes.*) I am Edith, sir.

Haver. (*Gently.*) My son's wife. (*Kisses her forehead.*) You shall take the place he once filled in my heart. His crime and his disgrace are buried in a distant grave.

Edith. And you have not forgiven him, even yet?

Mrs. H. Is there no atonement for poor Frank's sin—not even his death? Can you only bury the wrong and forget the good?

Haver. The good?

Mrs. H. Your own words to the Government, as his commander!

Haver. What do you mean?

Mrs. H. "The victory of Cedar Creek would have been impossible without the sacrifice of this young officer."

Haver. My own words, yes—but—

Edith. "His name must take its place forever, in the roll of names which his countrymen honor."

Haver. Lieutenant Bedloe!

Mrs. H. Haverill! You did not know?

Haver. My—son.

Edith. You did not receive mother's letter?—after his death?

Haver. My son! (*Sinking upon a chair.*) I left him alone in his grave, unknown; but my tears fell for him then, as they do now. He died before I reached him.

Edith. Father! (*Laying her hand gently on his shoulder.*) You shall see Frank's face again. His little son is lying asleep upstairs; and when he wakes up, Frank's own eyes will look into yours. I have just received his last message. I will read it to you. (*She opens the note-book and reads.*) "Tell our little son how his father died, not how he lived. And tell her who filled my own mother's place so lovingly." (*She looks at* Mrs. Haverill, *moves to her and hides her face in her bosom.*) My mother!

Mrs. H. Edith—my child! Frank loved us both.

Edith. (*Reading.*) "Father's portrait of her, which she gave to me in Charleston —(Haverill *starts*)—helped me to be a better man."

Haver. (*Rising to his feet.*) Constance!

Edith. (*Reading.*) "It was taken from me in Richmond, and it is in the possession of Captain Edward Thornton."

Haver. One moment! Stop! Let me think! (Edith *looks at him.*) Thornton was a prisoner—and to Kerchival West. A dispatch had been found upon him—he was searched! (*He moves to her and takes both her hands in his own, bowing his head over them.*) My head is bowed in shame.

Mrs. H. Speak to me, John, as you used to speak! Tell me you still love me!

Haver. The—the words will come—but they are—choking me—now. (*He presses her hand to his lips.*)

Mrs. H. We will think no more of the past, except of what was bright in it. Frank's memory, and our own love, will be with us always.

(*Enter* Buckthorn, *followed by* Heartsease.)

Buck. Haverill! You are back from the war, too. It begins to look like peace in earnest.

Haver. Yes. Peace and home.

(*Shaking hands with him.* Mrs. Haverill *joins* Edith.)

(*Enter* Barket.)

Barket. Gineral! (Buckthorn *moves to him.* Haverill *joins* Mrs. Haverill *and* Edith. Barket *speaks apart, twisting one side of his face.*) I kissed her!

Buck. Have you sent for a surgeon?

Barket. I felt as if the inimy had surprised us agin, and Sheridan was sixty miles away.

HAVER. This is old Sergeant Barket. (BARKET *salutes.*) You were the last man of us all that saw Colonel West.

BARKET. Just afther the battle of Sayder Creek began—whin Colonel Wist rode to the front to mate his retrayting rigiment—the byes formed in line, at sight of him, to raysist the victorious inimy. It was just at the brow of a hill—about there, sur—(*pointing with his cane*) and—here! (*He takes the tray from the table and sets it on the carpet, then lays the slices of bread in a row.*) That be the rigiment. (*All are interested.* MADELINE *and* ELLINGHAM *enter, and look on.* BARKET *arranges the two cups and saucers in a row.*) That be the inimy's batthery, sur.

(*Enter* MARGERY. *She goes to the table, then looks around, sharply at* BARKET.)

OLD MARG. Ye ould Hibernian dhrone! What are yez doin' wid the china on the floor? You 'll break it all!

BUCK. Ah—Margery! Barket is telling us where he last saw Colonel Kerchival West.

OLD MARG. The young Colonel! The taycups and saucers be's the inimy's batthery? Yez may smash 'em, if ye loike!

BUCK. Go on, Barket.

(JENNY *and* HEARTSEASE *have entered, as* BARKET *proceeds, the whole party lean forward, intensely interested.* GERTRUDE *enters in the hall, looks in, beckons as if to some one without, and* KERCHIVAL *follows. They move to the center of the stage, back of the rest and listen unseen.*)

BARKET. Just as the rigiment was rayformed in line, and Colonel Wist was out in front—widout any coat or hat, and wid only a shtick in his hand—we heard cheers in the rear. Gineral Sheridan was coming! One word to the men—and we swept over the batthery like a whirlwind! (*Slashing his cane through the cups and saucers.*)

OLD MARG. Hoo-roo!

BARKET. The attack on the lift flank was checked. But when we shtopped to take breath, Colonel Wist was n't wid us. (GERTRUDE *turns lovingly to* KERCHIVAL. *He places his arm about her.*) Heaven knows where he is now. Afther the battle was over, poor Miss Gertrude wint off by hersilf into the wilderness to find him.

KER. My wife! You saved my life, at last. (*Embracing her.*)

BARKET. They 'll niver come together in this world. I saw Miss Gertrude, myself, ride away into the woods and disappear behind a school-house on the battle-field, over there.

GERT. No, Barket—(*All start and look*)—it was the little church; we were married there this morning!

MARGARET FLEMING

BY

James A. Herne

REVISED AND EDITED, 1929, BY
MRS. JAMES A. HERNE

MARGARET FLEMING

Margaret Fleming represents the realistic play of American life, dealing with a great moral problem sincerely and fearlessly. It is the best play of James A. Herne, who is rightly considered to be a pioneer in the struggle for natural expression both in the drama and in the theatre. In the words of William Dean Howells, it was "an epoch-making play."

James A. Herne was born at Cohoes, New York, February 1, 1839. He first acted in 1859 in Troy, New York, in *Uncle Tom's Cabin;* then, after two seasons' experience, he joined the company at the Holliday Street Theatre in Baltimore. In 1866 he married the actress Helen Western, and after their separation became the leading man for her sister, Lucille Western, and in her company made his first visit to California. Later he returned to San Francisco as stage manager at Maguire's New Theatre, and adapted novels like *Oliver Twist* and *Charles O'Malley,* producing also his own version of *Rip Van Winkle.* In his article, "Art for Truth's Sake in the Drama" (*Arena*, February, 1897), he tells us how the influence of Dickens and Boucicault made him prefer the characters which revealed their human quality most easily and naturally. It was at the Baldwin Theatre, where in 1876 he became stage manager and leading character actor, that he was associated with David Belasco in the adapting of earlier plays. Here, too, he met Katharine Corcoran, a young pupil of Julia Melville, an actress well known at that period, and gave her her first professional opportunity. In 1878 they were married and Mrs. Herne joined the Baldwin Theatre Stock Company. From that time she was his inspiration. For her he wrote his most important plays, while scenes and characters were often suggested to him by her. In June, 1879, Herne and Belasco adapted *Camilla's Husband,* by Watts Phillips, under the name of *Marriage by Moonlight,* with radical changes, and on September 9, 1879, their joint effort, *Chums,* was produced at the Baldwin Theatre. It was based on an earlier English play, *The Mariner's Compass,* by H. J. Leslie, but was entirely rewritten, and the melodramatic climax of Leslie's play was replaced by a quiet and effective ending. The theme is that of a man of middle age, Terry Dennison, who has brought up two orphans, a boy and girl, who love each other but who give up their own happiness for his sake. He in turn, when he realizes the situation, leaves for a long voyage, and after several years returns to find them married and to die contented. *Chums* was rechristened *Hearts of Oak* and became one of the most popular plays of its time, Herne acting Terry Dennison, and Mrs. Herne, Chrystal, the young wife. *The Minute Men of 1774–1775,* produced at the Chestnut Street Theatre, Philadelphia, April 6, 1886, dealt with the opening of the Revolution, and while it provided a good part, Dorothy Foxglove, for Mrs. Herne, is not so important as the later plays. *Drifting Apart,* called originally *Mary, the Fishermen's Child,* first performed at the People's Theatre, New York, May 7, 1888, was laid in Gloucester, Massachusetts, among the seafaring folk. Its most striking feature, apart from the reality of its characters, was the introduction of a dream in Acts III and IV, in which the tragedy of poverty caused by drink was powerfully portrayed, and the play was then resumed in Act V. This was an early use of such a stage device, probably too early for the audiences, for the play was not a great success, although it ran on tour for 250 performances.

Nothing daunted by this comparative failure, Herne wrote *Margaret Fleming.* It was first tried out at Lynn, Massachusetts, for three performances beginning July 4, 1890. In this production Herne acted Philip Fleming, and Mrs. Herne, Margaret Fleming. The play was too daring in its realism for the managers of 1890, who prevented Herne from securing theatres in New York or Boston, so he was forced to rent Chickering Hall, a small auditorium in Boston, where the play was produced May 4, 1891, and ran for three weeks. Herne acted Joe Fletcher in this production. It was really the first "Little Theatre" in America, and Howells, Hamlin Garland, Mary Wilkins, and other leaders of the realistic movement in the novel, made it a notable occasion and welcomed Herne into their fellowship. He became recognized by the discriminating as a conscious artist, but the play was too far ahead of its time for popular approval. It was played at Chickering Hall, again, in October, 1891; in New York City on December 9, 1891, at Palmer's Theatre; was revived in 1892 in Chicago, at McVicker's Theatre, in the revised form here printed, and was played at Miner's Fifth Avenue Theatre in New York, April 9, 1894. In 1907 it was given at the New Theatre in Chicago, with Chrystal Herne as Margaret, and in 1915 it was again played, with Julie Herne in the title rôle. In its first form, there was an interval of five years between Act III and Act IV, during which Maria had stolen Lucy out of revenge for her sister's disgrace and death. There were scenes on Boston Common and in a shop; and the final scene took place in a police station, where Philip and Margaret had gone to find Lucy, and where they parted, Margaret refusing to forgive him. Mrs. Herne is confident that the revised version of the play is an improvement, for it is more unified, and proceeds more logically. She realizes that unhappiness is not necessarily artistic, unless it is inevitable, and that, given the character of Margaret and the personality of Philip, they would probably be reconciled. The only manuscripts of *Margaret Fleming* were burned in the fire which destroyed Herne Oaks, in 1909, but Mrs. Herne has recreated the play from her memory. This was rendered possible not only through her acting of Margaret, but also because she had taken an active part in the original creation of the play.

After a romantic play, *My Colleen,* Herne wrote *Shore Acres,* a domestic drama based upon his study of the people at Frenchman's Bay, on the Maine coast, near Bar Harbor. In this he created a very lovable character, Uncle Nat Berry, acted by himself, who rises into the quiet nobility of self-sacrifice. The ending of this play, in which Uncle Nat closes the house and, without a word, conveys by his expressive acting the sense of the ending of an episode, was far ahead of its time. Produced at McVicker's Theatre, Chicago, May 17, 1892, it anticipates the famous ending of *The Cherry Orchard,* for example, by twelve years. The ease and comfort which the great success of *Shore Acres* brought Herne gave him the opportunity to write his drama of the Civil War, *Griffith Davenport.* It was based upon a novel, *An Unofficial Patriot,* by Helen H. Gardener, but the characters and scenes were radically changed. Griffith Davenport is a circuit-rider in Virginia, and the scenes are laid in Virginia and Washington. The climax occurs when Davenport, who is a Union man and an abolitionist, is asked by Lincoln to lead the Federal troops through his native State. It was highly praised by the best critical judgment at the time of its production at the Lafayette Square Theatre in Washington, January 16, 1899, but it was not successful. The manuscript was destroyed and, curiously enough, it was only through the keen interest of William Archer in the play, which led him to request a copy of it, that the fourth Act, found after his death among his papers, has been preserved. Herne's last play, *Sag Harbor,* named after the village on Long Island, near his home, started as a rewriting of *Hearts of Oak,* but such vital changes were made in it that it became a distinct play. The central character is no longer the husband, but is the middle-aged Captain Marble, a guardian angel of the neighborhood, played by Herne. There is an advance in character drawing over *Hearts of Oak,* and much more modern technique. *Sag Harbor* opened at the Park Theatre, Boston, October 24, 1899. It was a substantial success, but during its run Herne broke down and returned to his home in New York, where he died of pleuro-pneumonia, June 2, 1901.

Hearts of Oak, Shore Acres, and *Sag Harbor* were published by Samuel French in one volume in 1928, under the title of *Shore Acres and Other Plays,* edited by Mrs. James A. Herne, with a biographical account of Herne by his daughter, Julie A. Herne. *Margaret Fleming* is here published for the first time, from a text furnished by the courtesy of Mrs. Herne, who has revised the play especially for this edition. *Marriage by Moonlight* (later called *Hap-hazard*), *The Minute Men of 1774–75, Mary, the Fishermen's Child* (later called *Drifting Apart*), are in manuscript in the possession of Mrs. Herne, who has kindly presented copies to the Clothier Collection of American Plays at the University of Pennsylvania. A copy of Act IV of *Griffith Davenport* is in the same collection.

For Herne's theories of the drama, see his articles in the *Arena,* "Old Stock Days in the Theatre," Vol. VI (Sept., 1892), 401–416, and "Art for Truth's Sake in the Drama," Vol. XVII (Feb., 1897), 361–370. For contemporary criticism, see John Corbin, "Drama," *Harper's Weekly,* Vol. XLIII (Feb. 11 and March 4, 1899), 139; 213; B. O. Flower, "Mask or Mirror," *Arena,* Vol. VIII (Aug., 1893), 304–313; Hamlin Garland, "Mr. and Mrs. Herne," *Arena,* Vol. IV (Oct., 1891), 543–560; and "On the Road with James A. Herne," *Century Magazine,* Vol. LXXXVIII N. S. (Aug., 1914), 574–581; "An Appreciation: James A. Herne, Actor, Dramatist and Man," articles by Hamlin Garland, J. J. Enneking, and B. O. Flower, *Arena,* Vol. XXVI (Sept., 1901), 282–291; Norman Hapgood, *The Stage in America,* pp. 61–69; W. D. Howells, Editor's Study, *Harper's Magazine,* Vol. LXXXIII (Aug., 1891), 478–479; Marco Tiempo, "James A. Herne in Griffith Davenport," *Arena,* Vol. XXII (Sept., 1899), 375–382. For detailed criticism of the plays, see the editor's *History of the American Drama from the Civil War to the Present Day,* Vol. I, Chapter VI.

Note to Sixth Edition.

Margaret Fleming was revived on November 17th and 18th, 1930, by Plays and Players at their playhouse in Philadelphia. This performance showed clearly how modern the play is in characterization and motive, and how apparent are its acting qualities.

Within an Inch of His Life, Herne's adaptation of Gaboriau's *La Corde au Cou, The Minute Men of 1774–75, Drifting Apart,* and Act IV of *The Reverend Griffith Davenport,* edited by A. H. Quinn, were published in *America's Lost Play* Series.

Note to Seventh Edition.

An authoritative biography of Herne is in preparation by Miss Julie Herne. She has recently discovered Act III of *Griffith Davenport,* which was published in *American Literature,* Vol. XXIV (1952).

CAST OF CHARACTERS *

PHILIP FLEMING, *mill owner.*
DOCTOR LARKIN
JOE FLETCHER
MR. FOSTER, *manager of the mill.*
WILLIAMS, *foreman.*
BOBBY, *office boy.*
CHARLIE BURTON
MARGARET FLEMING, *wife of Philip Fleming.*
MARIA BINDLEY, *a nurse.*
MRS. BURTON
HANNAH, *the cook.*
JANE, *a maid.*

ACT I

SCENE 1—Philip Fleming's private office at the mill.
SCENE 2—The living-room in Margaret's home.

ACT II

The living-room in Margaret's home.

ACT III

A room in Mrs. Burton's cottage.

ACT IV

The living-room in Margaret's home.

The action takes place in Canton, Mass., in 1890.

* The play in its earliest form contained several characters not in the revised version, which in its turn includes two not in the first version. To give all the actors in the various versions would therefore lead to confusion. Mrs. Herne acted Margaret in all the productions of 1890, 1891, 1892 and 1894. Mr. Herne acted in 1890, in May, 1891, and in 1892, but not in the Boston production in October, 1891, or in the New York production of 1894.

MARGARET FLEMING

ACT FIRST.

SCENE I. *It is a morning in Spring in* PHILIP FLEMING'S *private office at the mill. Bright sunlight floods the room at first. Later it becomes cloudy until at the end of the act, rain is falling fitfully. The room is handsomely furnished. There is a table in the center at the back between two windows. Above the table and attached to the wall is a cabinet with a mirror in the door. In the right corner is an umbrella-stand and hat-rack beside a door leading to the street. There are two windows below the door. A little to the right of the center of the room is an armchair, and in the same position on the left is a flat-top office desk, with a chair on either side. Behind it on the left is a door leading to the mill. There is a bunch of flowers on the desk, and two silver frames holding pictures of* MARGARET *and* LUCY. *There are also pictures on the wall, including one of the mill and one of* PHILIP'S *father as a young man.*

As the curtain rises, BOBBY *enters from the left with a desk-basket of mail, which he places on the desk. He rearranges the chairs slightly. As he is about to go out a key is heard in the door on the right.* BOBBY *pauses expectantly.* PHILIP FLEMING, *carrying an umbrella and a rain-coat, enters from the street door on the right. He is a well dressed, prosperous, happy-looking man about thirty-five. He hangs up his hat and coat, and places his umbrella in the stand. Then he glances carelessly into the hat-rack mirror and runs his hand lightly over his hair.*

PHILIP. (*In a friendly manner.*) Good morning, Bobby.

BOBBY. (*Grinning appreciatively.*) Good morning, sir.

(PHILIP *goes to his desk and, shifting one or two articles out of his way, begins the duties of the day.*)

PHILIP. Did you get wet this morning in that big shower?

BOBBY. Yes, sir, a little, but I'm all right now.

(PHILIP *glances rapidly through the letters and with an eager manner selects two large envelopes, opens one, glances through a document it contains and places it in his inside coat-pocket with a satisfied smile.*)

PHILIP. (*Chatting, as he continues his work.*) Still doing the four mile sprint?

BOBBY. Yes, sir. Oh, I like it, sir—when it don't rain.

(PHILIP *opens other letters rapidly, glancing with a quick, comprehensive eye through each before placing it in the growing heap on the desk.*)

PHILIP. How about the bicycle?

BOBBY. Well, sir, Mr. Foster says he thinks he'll be able to recommend me for a raise pretty soon, if I keep up my record.

PHILIP. (*Looking at him quizzically.*) A raise, Bobby?

BOBBY. Yes, Mr. Fleming, and my mother says I can save all I get and I guess I'll have a bicycle pretty soon then.

PHILIP. How long have you been here?

BOBBY. Six months the day after tomorrow.

PHILIP. (*Smiling kindly.*) I guess I'll have to talk to Foster, myself.

BOBBY. Oh, thank you, Mr. Fleming.

(PHILIP *opens a letter which appears to disturb him. He pauses over it with a worried frown.*)

PHILIP. Ask Mr. Foster to come here at once, please. (*As* BOBBY *starts to go.*) And tell Williams I want to see him.

BOBBY. Yes, sir. (*He goes out the door on the left. There is a moment's pause, and then* FOSTER *enters from the same door. He is a bright, active young man about twenty-eight or thirty.*)

PHILIP. Good morning, Foster.

FOSTER. Good morning, Mr. Fleming.

PHILIP. Here's a letter from the receiver for Reed and Vorst. He wants to know if we'll accept an immediate settlement of forty percent.

FOSTER. (*Becoming serious.*) Gee, Mr. Fleming, I don't see how we can. I was depending on at least fifty percent to carry us through the summer. It's always a dull season, you know, and—

PHILIP. Why, we have more orders now than we had this time last year.

FOSTER. Yes, I know, sir. But, I was going to speak to you. The Cotton Exchange Bank doesn't want to renew those notes.

PHILIP. Doesn't, eh? Well, then, we'll have to accept Reed and Vorst's offer.

FOSTER. I think it would be a mistake just now, sir. If we hold out they've got big assets.

PHILIP. Can't be helped. I'm hard-pressed. We're short of ready money.

FOSTER. I don't understand it. We've had a better winter than we've had for years.

PHILIP. (*Smiling.*) That last little flier I took wasn't as successful as the former ones.

FOSTER. You've been too lenient with the retailers.

PHILIP. "Live and let live" 's my motto.

FOSTER. I'd hate to see anything happen to the mill.

PHILIP. Nothing's going to happen. Let me do the worrying. Our credit's good. I'll raise the money tomorrow.

FOSTER. I hope so, sir. Anything else?

PHILIP. (*Giving him the letters.*) Wire the answers to these right away. That's all.

FOSTER. All right, sir. (*He goes out.*)

(PHILIP *takes up a large sheet of paper which contains a report from one of the departments of the mill. He scans it closely and makes some calculations upon a sheet of paper.* WILLIAMS *enters.*)

PHILIP. (*Looking up.*) Good morning, Williams.

(WILLIAMS *is quite an old man, but has the attitude of one who knows his business and can do things. He stands with bent shoulders and arms hanging limp. He is chewing tobacco, and speaks with a quick, sharp, New England accent.*)

WILLIAMS. Good morning, Mr. Fleming.

PHILIP. (*Holding the report in his hand.*) Williams, a short time ago you told me that the main supply belt in the finishing room was only repaired a few times during the last six months. I find here from your report that it has broken down about twice a week since last January. How long does it take to make a repair?

WILLIAMS. Oh, sometimes about ten minutes—other times again, twenty minutes. We have done it in five minutes.

PHILIP. There are about one hundred and ten operators in that room?

WILLIAMS. One hundred and seven.

PHILIP. Why, you should have reported this condition the first week it arose. Poor economy, Williams. (*He makes a few, rapid calculations upon the back of a report.*) Twelve hundred dollars lost time. (*He shakes his head.*) We could have bought a new belt a year ago and saved money in the bargain.

WILLIAMS. I told Mr. Baker several times, sir, in the beginning and he didn't seem to think anything of it.

PHILIP. Well, report all such details to me in the future. (*He writes a few lines rapidly and rings the bell.* BOBBY *enters briskly.*) Tell Mr. Foster to get those firms over long distance, and whichever one can make the quickest delivery to place orders there—see?

BOBBY. Yes, sir. (*He has a soiled card in his hand, which he offers to* PHILIP *with a grin.*) A man outside told me to hand you his visiting card.

WILLIAMS. Is that all, sir?

PHILIP. Yes. (*He smiles as he reads the card.*) Joe Fletcher! Tell him to come in. (*He resumes work at his desk.* WILLIAMS *goes out.*)

BOBBY. Yes, sir. (*He follows* WILLIAMS.)

(*After a moment* JOE FLETCHER *enters. He is a man of middle age, well made but heavy and slouching in manner. He has a keen, shrewd eye in a weak and dissipated face, which is made attractive, nevertheless, by a genial and ingratiating smile. He is wearing a shabby linen coat called a "duster," which hangs, crushed and limp, from his neck to his ankles. Strung from his left shoulder is a cord hung with sponges of various sizes. Several lengths of chamois are dangling with the sponges across his breast and back, draping his right hip and leg. In one hand he has a weather beaten satchel. He carries by a leather thong a heavy stone hanging from a cracked plate. There are two holes in the rim of the plate through one of which runs the thong by which it is carried. The other, the big stone, is fastened to it with a piece of chain. He carries it unconscious of its weight. There is a pervading sense of intimacy between the man and his equipment, and from his battered hat to his spreading shoes the stains of the road, like a varnish, bind them together in a mellow fellowship.*)

PHILIP. Hello, Joe. (*He looks at him with humorous curiosity.*)

JOE. (*Light-heartedly.*) How d'do, Mr. Fleming. (*His voice is broken and husky. He gives a little, dry cough now and then in an ineffectual attempt to clear it. He crosses to the corner of the table, and shows by his step that his feet are sore and swollen.*)

PHILIP. What are you doing now, Joe?

JOE. (*Indicating his effects. While he talks he places the stone against a corner of the table on the floor, and puts the valise on the edge of the table.*) Traveling merchant; agent for Brummell's Giant Cement; professional corn doctor—soft and hard corns—calluses—bunions removed instantly, ingrowing nails treated 'thout pain or loss of blood—*or* money refunded. Didn't ye read m'card? (*He coughs.*)

PHILIP. (*Laughing.*) Well, not all of it, Joe.

JOE. (*Reminiscently.*) Inventor of Dr. Fletcher's famous cough mixture, warranted to cure coughs colds, hoarseness and loss o' voice. An infallible remedy fur all chronic conditions of the *pull-mon*-ary organs. (*He coughs again.*) When not too fur gone. (*He takes a labelled bottle, containing a brown mixture from his inside pocket, shakes it and holds it up proudly before* PHILIP.) Kin I sell ye a bottle? (*He smiles ingratiatingly.*)

PHILIP. (*Smiling but shaking his head.*) No, Joe, I guess not today.

JOE. (*Opening the satchel insinuatingly.*) Mebbe a few boxes o' corn salve? It's great. (PHILIP *shakes his head.*) Would ye like to consider a box o' cement?

PHILIP. (*Still smiling.*) No, but I'll take one of those big sponges.

JOE. I thought I could sell ye something. (*He unhooks a large sponge and lays it upon the desk.* PHILIP *hands him a bill. He takes it carelessly, looks at it, shakes his head regretfully and puts it into his pocket. Then he feels in his other pocket and taps his vest pockets.*) Gosh, I'm sorry, but I ain't got a bit of change.

PHILIP. Oh, never mind the change, Joe. (*He laughs indulgently.*)

JOE. (*Regretfully.*) Well, I'd feel better if *I hed* the change. (JOE *has been standing to the left of the desk.*) Kin I set down fur a minnit, Mr. Fleming? M'feet gets so tired.

PHILIP. Yes, Joe, sit down.

JOE. I got pretty wet a while ago in that shower. My, but it did come down.

PHILIP. (*Warmly.*) Perhaps you'd like a hot drink? (*He indicates with a nod of the head, the cabinet back of* JOE, *as the latter is about to sit down.* JOE *shows a lively interest.*)

JOE. (*Glancing at* PHILIP *with a shy twinkle in his eye.*) Oh, kin I, Mr. Fleming? Thank ye. (*He shuffles over to the cabinet, opens the door and gloats over the vision of joy which greets him. He selects a bottle.*)

PHILIP. Hold on, Joe. Wait for some hot water.

JOE. (*Hastily.*) No, thank ye. I'm afraid I'd be like the Irishman in the dream.

PHILIP. What was that, Joe?

JOE. (*As he pours out a generous portion.*) Well, the Irishman was dreaming that he went to see the priest, and the priest asked him to have a drink. "I will, thank ye kindly," says Pat. "Is it hot or cold. ye'll have it?" says the priest? "Hot, if ye plaze, yer Riverence," says Pat, and while they were waiting fur the hot water, Pat wakes up. "Bad luck to me," says he, "why didn't I take it cold?" (*He drains the glass, smacks his lips and chuckles.*) My, but that's good stuff! Mr. Fleming, are ye as fond of it yourself as ye used to be?

PHILIP. (*Smiling and shaking his head.*) No, Joe. I've got through with all that foolishness. I've sowed my wild oats.

JOE. (*Chuckling as he sits in the chair.*) You must have got a pretty slick crop out o' yourn.

PHILIP. Every man gets a pretty full crop of those, Joe, before he gets through.

JOE. Ye've turned over a new leaf, eh?

PHILIP. Yes—married.

JOE. Married?

PHILIP. Yes, and got a baby.

JOE. Thet so! Did ye marry out'n the mill?

PHILIP. Oh, no. She was a Miss Thorp, of Niagara. (*He hands the picture of the child to* JOE.)

JOE. (*Showing interest immediately, and gazing at the picture, while gradually a gentle responsive smile plays over his features. He says, admiringly.*) By George! that's a great baby! (*He gives a chuckling laugh at it.*) Boy?

PHILIP. (*Proudly.*) No. Girl!

JOE. Thet so! Should a thought you'd a wanted a boy. (*With sly significance, and chuckling at his own joke.*) Ye've hed so many girls.

PHILIP. (*He laughs lightly.*) Tut, tut, Joe, no more of that for me. (*He hands him the frame containing* MARGARET'S *picture.*) My wife.

JOE. (*His expression becoming grave as the sweetness and dignity of the face touches him. He takes a long breath.*) My, but that's a fine face. Gee, if she's as good as that, you're a lucky man, Mr. Fleming.

PHILIP. Yes, Joe, I've got more than I deserve, I guess. (*He becomes serious for the first time and a shadow flits over his face. He sighs.*)

JOE. (*Sympathetically.*) Oh, I understand just how you feel. I'm married m'self. (*He sits down facing the audience, his hands clasped, his thumbs gently rolling over each other. A far-away tender look comes into his eyes.*)

PHILIP. (*Surprised.*) Married? (JOE *nods his head.*) Where's your wife?

JOE. Left me. (*He gives a sigh of self pity.*)

PHILIP. (*Touched.*) Left you! (*He shakes his head compassionately, then the thought comes to him.*) If my wife left me I'd kill myself.

JOE. (*Philosophically.*) Oh, no, no, ye wouldn't. You'd get over it, just as I did. (*He sighs.*)

PHILIP. How did it happen? What did you do?

JOE. (*Innocently.*) Not a durn thing! She was a nice, German woman, too. She kept a gent's furnishing store down in South Boston, and I married her.

PHILIP. (*Recovering himself and speaking gaily.*) Oh, Joe. (*He shakes his head in mock reproval.*) You married her for her money, eh? (*He laughs at him.*)

JOE (*Ingenuously.*) No, I didn't, honest. I thought I might get a whack at the till once in a while, but I didn't.

PHILIP. (*Quizzing him.*) Why not, Joe?

JOE. She fixed me up a pack and sent me out on the road to sell goods, and when I got back, she was gone. There was a new sign on the store, "Isaac Litchenstein, Ladies and Gents' Drygoods." (*He draws a big sigh.*)

PHILIP. And you've never seen her since?

JOE. (*Shaking his head sadly.*) No, siree, never!

PHILIP. (*Serious again, impressed by* JOE.) That's pretty tough, Joe.

(BOBBY *enters.*)

BOBBY. Doctor Larkin would like to see you, sir.

JOE. (*Gathering himself and his merchandise together.*) Well, I guess I'll get out and drum up a few sales. Much obliged to you, Mr. Fleming.

PHILIP. Oh, stop at the house, Joe. Mrs. Fleming might want something. It's the old place on Linden Street.

JOE. Got a dog?

PHILIP. Yes.

JOE. That settles it.

PHILIP. Only a pug, Joe.

JOE. Oh, a snorer. I'll sell him a bottle of cough mixture. (*As* DR. LARKIN *enters.*) Hello, Doc! How are you? Raining?

(JOE *goes to the door on the right, crossing the* DOCTOR *who is walking toward* PHILIP *on the left.*)

DOCTOR. (*Looking at him, mystified.*) Good morning, sir. No, it's not raining. (JOE *goes out.* DR. LARKIN *is a tall, gaunt man who looks older than he is, with quite a stoop in his shoulders. He has dark brown hair and a beard, streaked with grey, and soft, kind blue eyes. He carries the medicine satchel of a homeopathic physician. His manner is usually distant and cold but extremely quiet and gentle. In the opening of this scene he is perturbed and irritated, later he becomes stern and authoritative.*)

PHILIP. Good morning, Doctor Larkin.

DOCTOR. (*Turning to* PHILIP.) Who is that fellow? (*He looks after* JOE *as he goes out.*)

PHILIP. Don't you remember him? That's Joe Fletcher. (PHILIP *is standing to the right of the desk, and* DOCTOR LARKIN *at the left center of the stage.*)

DOCTOR. Is that Joe Fletcher? Why he used to be quite a decent sort of fellow. Wasn't he a foreman here in your father's time?

PHILIP. Yes, he was one of the best men in the mill.

DOCTOR. (*Shaking his head.*) He is a sad example of what liquor and immorality will bring a man to. He has indulged his appetites until he has no real moral nature left.

PHILIP. (*Lightly.*) Oh, I don't think Joe ever had much "moral nature."

(*The sunlight leaves the room. It is growing cloudy outside.*)

DOCTOR. Every man has a moral nature. In this case it is love of drink that has destroyed it. There are some men who are moral lepers, even lacking the weakness of the tippler as an excuse.

PHILIP. Have you been to the house, doctor? About midnight Margaret thought little Lucy had a fever. She was going to call you up—but—

DOCTOR. (*Abruptly.*) She would not have found me in at midnight.

PHILIP. Ah, is that so? Someone very ill? (*The telephone rings.*) Excuse me, doctor. Hello. Oh, is that you, Margaret? How is Lucy now? Good! I knew she'd be all right. Yes, of course. Do—bring her. (*To the* DOCTOR.) She's bringing baby to the 'phone. Hello, Lucy. Many happy returns of the day. Good-bye. Yes, I'll be home at twelve sharp. Apple pie? Yes, of course, I like it. That is, *your* apple pie. (*He leaves the phone with a joyous air.*) This is baby's birthday, you know, doctor.

DOCTOR. I've just left a baby (*He speaks bitterly, looking at* PHILIP *significantly.*) that should never have had a birthday.

PHILIP. (*Without noticing the* DOCTOR'S *manner, he goes to the cabinet and, taking a box of cigars, offers the box to the* DOCTOR.) Why, Doctor, you're morbid today. Take a cigar, it will quiet your nerves.

(*The rain begins to fall, beating heavily against the windows.*)

DOCTOR. No, thank you. (*With a subtle shade of repugnance in his tone.*) I'll smoke one of my own.

(PHILIP *smiles indulgently, goes to the desk, sits in the chair to the left of it, lights a cigar, leans back luxuriously, with his hands in his pockets, and one leg over the other, and tips back the legs of the chair.*)

PHILIP. (*Carelessly.*) What's the matter, doctor? You used to respect my cigars.

DOCTOR. (*Hotly.*) I used to respect you.

PHILIP. (*Rather surprised but laughing good-naturedly.*) Well, doctor, and don't you now? (*He is bantering him.*)

DOCTOR. (*Quietly but sternly.*) No, I don't.

PHILIP. (*Smoking placidly.*) Good Lord—why?

DOCTOR. (*His satchel resting upon his knees, his hands clasping the metal top, he leans over a trifle and, looking impressively into* PHILIP'S *face, says, in a low, calm voice.*) At two o'clock last night Lena Schmidt gave birth to a child.

PHILIP. (*Becoming livid with amazement and fear, and staring blankly before him, the cigar dropping from his parted lips.*) In God's name, how did they come to send for you?

DOCTOR. Doctor Taylor—he called me in consultation. He was frightened after the girl had been in labor thirty-six hours.

PHILIP. (*Murmuring to himself.*) Thirty-six hours! Good God! (*There is a pause, then he partly recovers himself.*) I suppose she told you?

DOCTOR. She told me nothing. It was a lucky thing for you that I was there. The girl was delirious.

PHILIP. Delirious! Well, I've done all I could for her, doctor.

DOCTOR. Have you? (*His tone is full of scorn.*)

PHILIP. She's had all the money she wanted.

DOCTOR. Has she? (*He speaks in the same tone.*)

PHILIP. I tried to get her away months ago, but she wouldn't do it. She was as stubborn as a mule.

DOCTOR. Strange she should want to remain near the father of her child, isn't it?

PHILIP. If she'd done as I told her to, this thing would never have happened.

DOCTOR. You'd have forced some poor devil to run the risk of state's prison. By God, you're worse than I thought you were.

PHILIP. Why, doctor, you must think I'm—

DOCTOR. I don't think anything about it. I know just what brutes such men as you are.

PHILIP. Well, I'm not wholly to blame. You don't know the whole story, doctor.

DOCTOR. I don't want to know it. The *girl's* not to blame. She's a product of her environment. Under present social conditions, she'd probably have gone wrong anyhow. But you! God Almighty! If we can't look for decency in men like you—representative men,—where in God's name are we to look for it, I'd like to know?

PHILIP. If my wife hears of this, my home will be ruined.

DOCTOR. (*Scornfully.*) Your home! Your home! It is just such damn scoundrels as you that make and destroy homes.

PHILIP. Oh, come now, doctor, aren't you a little severe?

DOCTOR. Severe! Severe! Why, do you realize, if this thing should become known, it will stir up a stench that will offend the moral sense of every man, woman and child in this community?

PHILIP. Well, after all, I'm no worse than other men. Why, I haven't seen the girl for months.

DOCTOR. Haven't you? Well, then suppose you go and see her now.

PHILIP. (*He springs to his feet.*) I'll do nothing of the sort.

DOCTOR. Yes, you will. She shan't lie there and die like a dog.

PHILIP. (*He walks around the room greatly perturbed.*) I tell you I'll not go!

DOCTOR. Yes, you will.

PHILIP. (*He comes over to the* DOCTOR *and looks down upon him.*) What'll you do if I don't?

DOCTOR. I don't know, but you'd best go and see that girl.

PHILIP. (*He turns away.*) Well, what do you want me to say to her?

DOCTOR. Lie to her as you have before. Tell her you love her.

PHILIP. I never lied to her. I never told her I loved her.

DOCTOR. Faugh!

PHILIP. I tell you I never did!

DOCTOR. (*Rising from his chair.*) You'd better get Mrs. Fleming away from here until this thing blows over. When I think of a high-minded, splendid little woman like her married to a man like you—ugh! (*The* DOCTOR *goes out quickly.*)

(PHILIP, *left alone, walks about like an old man, seems dazed for a moment, then goes mechanically to the telephone.*)

PHILIP. Lindon, 3721. Margaret. (*He speaks in a broken, hushed voice.*) Margaret! Yes, it's I, Philip. Yes! Well, I'm tired. No, I can't come home now. I will not be home to luncheon. I have a business engagement. No, I cannot break it off. It's too important. Eh? Why, with a man from Boston. Yes, certainly, I will, just as soon as I can get away. Yes, dear —I will—good-bye. (*Just before he finishes,* FOSTER *enters.*) Hello, Foster.

FOSTER. (*Consulting a memorandum.*) I couldn't get the Harry Smith Company, New York, until noon, sir. They say that the belting can be shipped by fast express at once. The Boston people want ten cents a square foot more than they ask, but we can save that in time and express rates.

PHILIP. When would the New York shipment get here?

FOSTER. At the earliest, tomorrow afternoon.

PHILIP. White and Cross can ship at once, you say?

FOSTER. Yes, sir.

PHILIP. Well, give them the order. Their stuff is better, anyhow. Have a covered wagon at the station for the four-ten train. Keep enough men over time tonight to put it up.

FOSTER. Yes, sir, the sooner it's done, the better.

PHILIP. Yes, Williams is getting old. He's not the best man for that finishing room. Put him where you can keep an eye on him. He's all right. I have an appointment and will not be in the office again today. Get the interest on those notes off.

FOSTER. Yes, I've attended to that already. Anything else?

PHILIP. No.

FOSTER. All right, sir. Good morning.

(PHILIP *who has braced himself for this, relaxes again. The rain continues. He goes about the room, lights a cigar, puts on a rain-coat, looks at his watch, buttons his coat, all the while sunk in deep thought. He takes his umbrella and hat and goes out quietly, shutting the door so that the click of the latch is heard, as the curtain falls.*)

SCENE 2. *The scene is the living-room in* MARGARET'S *home. At the back large glass doors open on to a spacious porch with a garden beyond. There is a fire-place with logs burning, in the corner on the left, and beside it a French window opening on the garden. Below it is a door leading to another room. There is another door on the right going to the main part of the house. There is a table in the center, a baby grand piano on the lower right, and a baby carriage close by the doors at the back. The room is furnished in exquisite taste showing in its distinct character the grace and individuality of a well-bred woman.*

MARGARET *is seated in a low rocking-chair near the fire with the baby in her lap. A large bath towel is spread across her knees. She is exquisitely dressed in an evening gown.*

MARIA BINDLEY, *the nurse-maid, is dressed in a black dress, cap and apron. She is a middle-aged German woman, dark in complexion, and of medium build and height. She speaks with a not too pronounced German accent. She is gathering up the baby's garments which are scattered about* MARGARET'S *feet. She is furtively weeping and makes an occasional effort to overcome her emotion.* MARGARET *is putting the last touches to the baby's night toilet. She is laugh-*

ing and murmuring mother talk to her. A shaded lamp is burning on the table to the right. The effect of the light is subdued. The glare of the fire is the high note, making a soft radiance about MARGARET *and the child.* MARIA *is in the shadow, except as she flits into the light whenever she moves near* MARGARET. *The sound of the rain beating against the windows, is heard now and then.*

MARGARET. (*In a low, laughing tone.*) No—no—*no!* You little beggar. You've had your supper! (*She fastens the last two or three buttons of her dress.*) No more! Time to go to sleep now! No use staying awake any longer for naughty father. Two, whole, hours—late! No, he doesn't care a bit about you; not a bit! (*She shakes her head.*) No, nor me either. Never mind, darling, we'll punish him well for this. Yes, we will. Perhaps we'll leave *him* some day, and then we'll see how he likes being left alone. Naughty, bad father—isn't he? *Yes he is!* Staying away all day! Never mind, ladybird—hush, go to sleep now—Mother loves her! Go to sleep—close your eyes. (*This is all said in a cooing, soothing voice. She begins to sing a lullaby.*) Go—to—sleep—blossom—go to sl—

(MARIA *comes close to* MARGARET *and picks up two little socks. As she rises, she sniffs in an effort to suppress her tears. This attracts* MARGARET'S *attention, and immediately she is all commiseration.*)

MARGARET. Don't cry, Maria—please don't—it distresses me to see you cry.

MARIA. (*Smiling a little at* MARGARET'S *sympathy. As she talks, she smooths the socks and folds them.*) I cannot help it, Mrs. Fleming—I am an unhappy woman. I try not to cry, but I cannot keep back de tears. (*She puts the socks in the basket on the table.*) I have had an unhappy life—my fadder vas a brute. (*She picks up the dress and shakes it.*) My first husband, Ralph Bindley, vas a goot, honest man. (*She puts the dress in the basket.*) Und my second husband vas dot tramp vot vas here dis morning. Vat I have told you aboudt already. (*She gathers together the other garments.*) Und now my sister—my little Lena—is dying.

MARGARET. (*In dismay.*) Dying! Why, you didn't tell me *that,* Maria!

MARIA. Vell, she is not dying yust this very moment, but the doctor says she vill never leave dot bed alive. My sweet little Lena! My lovely little sister. I have nursed her, Mrs. Fleming, yust like you nurse your baby now.

MARGARET. (*Holding the child to her breast.*) What did you say her name was?

MARIA. (*Working mechanically and putting the things neatly away.*) Lena,—Lena Schmidt. She does not go by my name—she goes by my fadder's name.

MARGARET. And, you say, she ran away from you?

MARIA. Ya—I tried to find her every place. I hunted high und low, but she does not come, und von day I meet an olt friend on Vashington Street, Chris Anderson, und Chris, he tell me that two or three weeks before he see her by the public gartens. Und she vas valking by the arm of a fine, handsome gentleman—und she look smiling and happy, und Chris, he says dot he knows *dot* gentleman—*dot* he vas a rich man vot lives down in Canton where Chris vonce worked when he comes to dis country first.

MARGARET. And didn't you ask the man's name?

MARIA. Ach, I forget. Und Chris go back to de olt country, und I never find out. Und den I tink maybe she is married to dot man—und she is ashamed of me and dot miserable husband of mine. I say to myself, "I vill go and see—und find oudt if she is happy." Den I vill go far away, where she vill never see me again. Und I come here to Canton, und at last I find her—und Ach Gott! She is going to be a mutter—und she is no man's vife! (*She has been weeping silently but has continued to work, only pausing at some point in her story that moved her.*)

MARGARET. (*Deeply touched.*) Did she tell you the man's name?

MARIA. Ach! No! You could not drag dot oudt of her mit red-hot irons. She says she loves dis man, und she vill make him no trouble. But, by Gott, I vill find dot man oudt, und I vill choke it from his troat. (*She is beside herself with vindictive passion.*)

MARGARET. (*Terrified at her ferocity and crushing her child to her breast.*) Oh, Maria—don't—please don't! You frighten me!

MARIA. (*At once all humility.*) Excuse me, Mrs. Fleming. I did not mean to do dot.

MARGARET. (*Kindly.*) You need not remain any longer. I can manage baby myself. You had best go to your sister at once.

If I can be of any help to you, please tell me, won't you?

MARIA. Ya, Mrs. Fleming, I tank you. Und if she is vorse maybe I stay all night.

MARGARET. Yes, certainly. You need not come back tonight.

MARIA. (*Very softly and humbly.*) I am much obliged to you, Mrs. Fleming.

MARGARET. (*As* MARIA *is going.*) Oh! You had best take my rain-coat.

MARIA. Ah, you are very goot, Mrs. Fleming. (*She has finished her work and is going but hesitates a moment and turns back.*) If you please, don't tell Mr. Fleming about me und my poor sister!

MARGARET. (*Slightly annoyed.*) Decidedly not! Why should I tell such things to him?

MARIA. Vell—men don't have sympathy mit peoples like us. He is a fine gentleman, und if he knowed about *her*—he might not like to have *me* by his vife und child. He might tink *I* vas as badt as she was. Good night, Mrs. Fleming.

MARGARET. Good night, Maria. No need to hurry back in the morning. (*There is a wistful sympathy in her face. As her eyes rest upon the door through which* MARIA *has passed, she is lost in thought. Presently a door slams, then she is all alert with expectation. There is a moment's pause, she listens then quickly puts the child in the baby carriage and runs to the door.*) Is that you, Philip?

JANE. (*Outside.*) No, ma'am, it is not Mr. Fleming. It was only the post man.

(MARGARET *turns away with a sigh of disappointment, goes to the French window and peers out at the rain. The* MAID *enters with several letters, leaves them on the table and goes out.* MARGARET *turns from the window, brushes the tears away impatiently, and drifts purposelessly across the room toward the right, her hands clasped behind her back. Finding herself at the piano she listlessly sits before it and plays a plaintive air, softly. Then suddenly she dashes into a prelude to a gay love song. As she sings half through a stanza, the song gradually loses spirit. Her hands grow heavy over the keys, her voice breaks, and the words come slow and faltering. She ends by breaking into tears, with her head lowered and her fingers resting idly upon the keys. The child attracts her and she goes quickly to her. She laughs through her tears into the wide-open eyes, and begins scolding her for not going to sleep. Soft endearing notes come and go in her voice. A tender joy takes possession of her spirit. She takes the child in her arms.*)

MARGARET. Well, my lady, wide awake! Come, come, no more nonsense, now! No. Go to sleep! Late hours—will—certainly spoil—your beauty. Yes! Close up your eyes—quick! Come! There, that's nice. She's a sweet, good child! (*She hums.*) Go—to—sleep! (*She sways slowly from right to left, then swinging with a rhythmic step with the lullaby, she lilts softly.*) Blow, blow, Blossom go—into the world below—I am the west wind wild and strong—blossoms must go when they hear my song. (*She puts out the lamp, leaving the room in the warm glare of the firelight.*) Go, little blossom, go—into the world below. Rain, rain, rain is here. Blossoms must learn to weep. (*She reaches the French window. As she turns* PHILIP *is seen through the filmy curtains. He enters unnoticed.*) I am the east wind, bleak and cold, poor little blossoms their petals must fold. Weep, little blossoms, weep, into your cradles creep. (*She is unconscious of* PHILIP'S *presence. His rain-coat and hat are dripping wet. He is pale and weary, his manner is listless and abstracted and he looks as though he had been wandering about in the rain for hours. He drifts into the room.* MARGARET *turns around and takes a step, her eyes upon the child, then her lullaby grows indistinct as she notices that the baby is asleep. Another step takes her into* PHILIP'S *arms. She gives a cry of alarm.*)

MARGARET. . . Oh, Philip! You frightened me! Why did you do that?

PHILIP. Why are you in the dark, Margaret? (*He goes toward her as if to take her in his arms.*) Dearest!

MARGARET. (*Drawing back from him with a shade of petulance.*) You're all wet. Don't come near baby. She was wakeful. I've put her to sleep. Where have you been all day?

PHILIP. Didn't I tell you over the 'phone I had an engagement?

MARGARET. (*As she flits swiftly into the room on the left.*) Did it take you all day to keep it? (*She remains in the room long enough to put the child in the crib and then returns.*)

PHILIP. Yes. A lot of things came up—that I didn't expect. I've been detained. (*He is still standing where she left him.*)

MARGARET. (*Turning up the lamp.*) Why, dear, look! Your umbrella is dripping all over the floor.

PHILIP. (*Noticing the little puddle of water.*) Oh, how stupid of me! (*He hurries out the door on the right, removes his hat and rain-coat, leaves the umbrella, and returns quickly.*)

(MARGARET, *meanwhile has mopped up the water. Then she turns on the lamp on the table to the right.*)

MARGARET. (*Reproachfully.*) We've been awfully lonesome here all day, baby and I!

PHILIP. (*By the fire.*) Forgive me, sweetheart. I've had a very hard day.

MARGARET. Did you forget it was Lucy's birthday?

PHILIP. (*Smiling gravely.*) No, I didn't forget. You have both been in my mind the whole day.

MARGARET. (*Glowing with love and a welcome that she refused to give until now.*) Oh, Philip! (*She throws herself in his arms.*) It's good to get you back. So good! (*After a moment she rings the bell. The* MAID *answers.*) Jane, I wish you would serve dinner in here.

JANE. Yes, Mrs. Fleming.

PHILIP. (*Drawing her close to him again.*) Dear little wife! (*As though a long time had passed since he parted from her.*)

JANE. (*Coming in with a tray containing food and silver, and going to the center table.*) Shall I lay the table here, Mrs. Fleming?

MARGARET. No—here—cosy—by the fire. (JANE *dresses the table deftly and without bustle. She goes away and returns with the dinner.*) You need not return, Jane. I'll ring if we need you.

JANE. Very well, Mrs. Fleming. (*She goes off.*)

PHILIP. (*Sitting to the right of the table, and taking a large envelope from his pocket, he withdraws a bank book and hands it to* MARGARET, *who is about to sit down on the left.*) Here, Margaret—I want you to look over that.

MARGARET. (*Taking the book and reading the cover.*) Margaret Fleming in account with Boston Providence Savings Bank. (*She opens the book and reads.*) "By deposit, May 3, 1890, $5,000." Five thousand dollars! Oh, Philip!

PHILIP. (*Smiling complacently.*) There's something else.

MARGARET. Yes? (PHILIP *nods his head, and hands her a large envelope which he has taken from his pocket. She looks at it and reads.*) "Margaret Fleming, guardian for Lucy Fleming." (*She takes a document from the envelope.*) A certificate for $20,000 worth of United States bonds, maturing 1930. Why, Philip! How wonderful. But, can you afford it? (*He smiles and nods his head, and then begins to serve the dinner.* MARGARET, *in childish joy, rushes to the door of the room where the child is.*) Oh, baby! Lucy! You are rich, rich! (*She stops and peeps in.*) Oh, my, I must not wake her. *The little heiress!* (*She sits at the table and begins to serve.*)

PHILIP. (*Handing her another envelope. Tenderly.*) For you Margaret!

MARGARET. (*Taking it and becoming breathless as she reads it.*) It's a deed for this house and all the land! Ah, Philip, how generous you are, and this is what has kept you away all day! And I was cross with you. (*Tears come to her eyes.*) Forgive me, dear, please do. (*She goes to him and kneels by his side.*) But, why do you do all this? What need? What necessity for me to have a deed of property from you?

PHILIP. Well, things have not been going just our way at the mill. The new tariff laws may help some, but I doubt it. At all events, before anything serious—

MARGARET. (*A little awed.*) Serious?

PHILIP. Well, you never can be sure. At any rate, in times of stress a business man should protect his family.

MARGARET. Is there danger—of—trouble?

PHILIP. No! I hope not. I think I'll be able to tide it over.

MARGARET. But, dear—you—this property, is worth a lot of money. Why not sell it? Wouldn't that be a great help? A resource in case—

PHILIP. Sell the home?

MARGARET. No, sell the house. The home is where we are. (*She rises and stands partly back of his chair with her arms about his neck.*) Where *love is*—no matter *where,* just so long as we three are there together. A big house—a little house—of course, I do love this place, where you were born, and baby— (*Taking a long breath.*) It's very precious—but—(*She has moved back to the head of the table and now lays down the deed.*) I cannot take it, dear. It frightens me. It's too valuable—all this—land—no—let us guard it together and if bad times come, it will be—a fine thing to have—

PHILIP. (*Protesting.*) Now, my dear!

MARGARET. I don't want the responsibility. Suppose something happened to me. (*She sits at the table, on the left.*)

PHILIP. Ah—Margaret—

MARGARET. (*Laughing.*) Well—I just said "suppose."

PHILIP. (*Laughing.*) Well—*don't say it.* We'll think of nothing "suppose." *Nothing,* but bright—*beautiful* things.

MARGARET. Come, dear, eat. I should think you were famished. You've touched nothing yet.

PHILIP. I don't feel hungry. I'm tired—awfully tired.

MARGARET. No wonder, after all you've been through today. I'll make you a cup of tea. (*She rings the bell.* JANE *enters.*) Boiling water, Jane, please, and bring the tea things. (*While she is busy over the tea things she stops and looks at him quizzically.*) Who was that tramp you sent here this morning?

PHILIP. (*Innocently.*) What tramp?

MARGARET. Why, the one with the plate and the big stone—the cough medicine,—the sponges and *the voice.* (*She imitates* JOE.)

PHILIP. (*Laughing.*) Ah, he's not a tramp —that's Joe Fletcher.

MARGARET. Did you know that he was Maria's husband?

PHILIP. (*Amazed.*) What! Maria's husband? What did he say to her?

MARGARET. (*Smiling reminiscently.*) He didn't say much— *She* did all the talking.

PHILIP. What did *she* say?

MARGARET. I don't know. She spoke in German. I think, she was swearing at him. When I came she had him by the ears and was trying to pull his head off. Then she got him to the floor and threw him down the front steps. It was the funniest thing I ever saw. I couldn't help laughing, yet my heart ached for her.

PHILIP. Poor Joe! That's the second time she's thrown him out.

MARGARET. She never did that before?

PHILIP. He says she did.

MARGARET. Well, she didn't. He robbed her and left her.

PHILIP. What?

MARGARET. She went out on the road to sell goods and left him in charge of the shop. When she came back he was gone and he had sold out the place to a secondhand dealer.

PHILIP. (*In wonderment.*) What a liar that fellow is!

MARGARET. Well, if he told you any other story—he certainly is. (*She notices a change in his face.*) Why, Philip! You look awfully white! Are you ill? Are you keeping anything from me? Oh, please tell me—do. Let me share your trouble. (*She goes to him, and puts her arms about his shoulders, with her face against his as she finishes the last line.*)

PHILIP. No—no—dear heart—nothing! There's nothing more to tell. I'm very tired.

MARGARET. Oh, how selfish of me. You should have gone to bed the moment you came.

PHILIP. I'll be all right in the morning. I must have caught a chill. (*He shudders.*) My blood seems to be congealed.

MARGARET. (*Alarmed.*) Oh, my dear—my poor boy! It was a dreadful thing you did. (*He starts guiltily.*) Going about in the rain all day. (*She goes swiftly into the room on the left and returns with a handsome dressing gown and slippers.* PHILIP *has gone over to the fire.*) I must give you some aconite. A hot drink—and a mustard foot bath. (*She fusses over him, helps him to get into his dressing gown, and warms his slippers by the fire.*)

PHILIP. I don't think I need anything, dear, but a hot drink, perhaps, and a night's rest. I'll be all right in the morning. I think I'll take a little brandy.

MARGARET. (*Quickly.*) I'll get it for you, dear. Keep by the fire. (*She rushes out the door on the right, and returns quickly with a silver tray holding a cut-glass decanter of brandy and a glass. She pours out some and holds up the glass.*) Is that enough?

PHILIP. Plenty—thank you! (*He drinks it, while* MARGARET *replaces the tray on the small table at the back.*)

MARGARET. Now, dear, I'll look after that mustard bath.

PHILIP. (*Protesting.*) Oh, Margaret, please don't bother. I really don't need it.

MARGARET. (*Laughing at him.*) Yes, you do. (*She shakes her finger threateningly at him.*) You might just as well make up your mind that you've got to have it.

PHILIP. (*Smiling resignedly.*) All right— *"boss."*

MARGARET. (*Laughing at him as she starts to go.*) You know, Philip, dear, you gave me the strangest feeling when you stood there—the rain dripping from you—you didn't look a bit like yourself. (*She gives an apologetic laugh.*) You gave me a dreadful fright. Just like a spirit! A lost spirit. (*She laughs again.*) Now, wasn't that silly of me? (*She runs off to the right, still laughing.*)

(PHILIP *sits in the fire light looking sadly after her, as the curtain falls.*)

ACT SECOND

The scene is the same as the Second Scene of the First Act. The large doors at the back are open showing a luxuriant garden in brilliant sunshine. The baby is in her carriage by the garden door. MARGARET, *in a dainty house dress, is seated in a low chair in the center of the room, mending one of the baby's dresses.* DR. LARKIN, *sitting at the table on the left with his back turned to her, is folding little packages of medicine.* MARGARET *looks happy and contented as she chats with him.*

DOCTOR. You say you have no pain in the eyes?

MARGARET. No pain at all . . . only, once in awhile there is . . . a . . . sort of a dimness.

DOCTOR. Yes, a dimness.

MARGARET. As if my eyes were tired.

DOCTOR. Yes!

MARGARET. When I read too long, or . . .

DOCTOR. (*Turning about and looking at her.*) Do you know what would be a good thing for you to do?

MARGARET. What, doctor?

DOCTOR. Wear glasses.

MARGARET. Why, doctor, aren't you dreadful! (*She laughs at him.*) Why, I'd look a sight.

DOCTOR. Well, it would be a good idea, all the same. You should wear glasses when you are reading or sewing, at least.

MARGARET. (*Laughing gaily at him.*) Well, I'll do nothing of the sort. Time enough for me to wear glasses, years and years from now.

DOCTOR. (*Smiling indulgently.*) It would be a good thing to do now. How is "Topsy" this morning?

MARGARET. (*Glancing proudly in the direction of the baby.*) Oh, she's blooming.

DOCTOR. Mrs. Fleming, any time you want to sell that baby, Mrs. Larkin and I will give you ten thousand dollars for her.

MARGARET. (*Laughing and beaming with pride.*) Yes . . . doctor . . . *when* we *want* to sell her. How is Mrs. Larkin?

DOCTOR. She's doing very nicely. I'm going to try to get her up to the mountains this summer. (*He finishes the packages.*) There . . . take one of these powders three times a day. Rest your eyes as much as possible. Don't let anything fret or worry you, and keep out-doors all you can. (*He closes the bag after putting a couple of bottles and a small medicine case in it.*)

MARGARET. Oh, doctor, aren't you going to leave something for Philip?

DOCTOR. (*Giving a dry, little grunt.*) Hum! I forgot about him. (*Standing by the table, he takes a small case from his satchel removes two large bottles of pellets from it, fills two phials from them and makes a number upon the cork of each with a fountain pen.*) You say he was pretty wet when he came home last night?

MARGARET. Yes, and tired out. He had a very hard day, I think. I never saw him so completely fagged. It seemed to me he had been tramping in the rain for hours. I gave him a good scolding too, I tell you. I doctored him up as well as I could and put him to bed. (*Smiling contentedly.*) He's as bright as a lark this morning, but all the same, I insisted upon his remaining home for a rest.

DOCTOR. You take good care of him, don't you? (*He beams upon her kindly.*)

MARGARET. (*Playfully.*) I've got to . . . he's all I have, and men like Philip are not picked up every day, now, I tell you.

DOCTOR. (*Drily.*) No, men like Philip Fleming are certainly not to be found easily.

MARGARET. I hope there's nothing wrong with him. I was worried last night. You know, he has been working awfully hard lately.

DOCTOR. (*Kindly.*) Now, don't fret about imaginary ills. He's probably a little over-worked. It might be a good idea to have him go away for a week or two.

MARGARET. (*Entering into the suggestion.*) Yes . . . a little trip somewhere would help him a lot, I'm sure.

DOCTOR. (*Holding up his finger.*) But, you must go with him, though.

(MARGARET, *by this time, is standing up, with the baby's dress tucked under her arm. She takes stitches as she talks.*)

MARGARET. (*Eagerly.*) Of course! I wouldn't let him go alone. Somebody might steal him from me. (*She smiles.*)

DOCTOR. (*Snapping the clasp of his satchel, vehemently murmurs under his breath.*) Hum! They'd bring him back mighty quick, I guess. (*He turns to her.*) Give him these. Tell him to take two alternately every hour.

MARGARET. (*Taking the phials, and nodding her head as if to remember.*) Two every hour—thank you.

(PHILIP *enters from the garden, gaily humming an air. He has a freshly plucked rose in his hand.*)

PHILIP. Good morning, doctor.

DOCTOR. (*Coldly.*) Good morning.

MARGARET. (*Noticing the rose, regretfully.*) Oh, Philip, you plucked that rose.

PHILIP. Yes, isn't it lovely? It's the first of the season. (*He smells it.*)

MARGARET. Yes, and I've been watching it. I wanted it to open yesterday for baby's birthday.

PHILIP. (*Playfully.*) It saved itself for today for baby's mother. (*He puts it on her breast.*)

MARGARET. (*Pleased.*) Well, I'd rather it had bloomed yesterday for her. Excuse me, doctor, I must run into the kitchen. We have a new cook and she needs watching.

PHILIP. (*Gaily.*) And she's a dandy. (*He breaks into a chant.*) Oh, I'm glad we've got a new cookie. I'm glad we've got a new cook. She's . . .

MARGARET. (*Laughing at him.*) Hush! Hush! Philip, stop—be quiet! (*She puts her hand over his mouth. He tries to sing through her fingers.*) She'll hear you. Oh, doctor, isn't he terrible? He's poking fun at her all the time, but she is funny, though. (*She runs off joyously to the right.*)

PHILIP. What a glorious morning, after yesterday.

DOCTOR. (*Eyeing him coldly.*) Yes—it is—you're in high feather this morning, eh?

PHILIP. (*Cheerily.*) Of course I am. What's the good in worrying over things you can't help?

DOCTOR. Have you seen . . . ?

PHILIP. (*Quickly.*) Yes. (*In a low voice.*) I've made arrangements for her to go away as soon as she is well enough.

DOCTOR. *Humph!*

PHILIP. It's a terrible mess. I'll admit I never realized what I was doing, but, I shall make things all right for this girl, and her child. (*He sits on the edge of the table to the left. The* DOCTOR *is standing to the right of him.*) Doctor I'm going to tell my wife this whole, miserable story.

DOCTOR. (*Aghast.*) What?

PHILIP. (*Hastily interrupting.*) Ah, not now—in the future. When we both have grown closer together. When I have shown her by an honest and decent life that I ought to be forgiven—when I feel sure of her faith and confidence—then I shall confess and ask her to forgive me.

DOCTOR. (*Shaking his head.*) That would be a mighty hazardous experiment. You would draw a woman's heart strings closer and closer about you—and then deliberately tear them asunder. Best keep silent forever.

PHILIP. There would be no hazard. I know Margaret—of course if she found me out now—I admit it—it would be a terrible thing, but—

DOCTOR. (*Abruptly.*) You'd better get Mrs. Fleming away from here for a few weeks.

PHILIP. (*Surprised.*) Away? (*He smiles confidently.*) What need?

DOCTOR. She is threatened with a serious affection of the eyes.

PHILIP. (*His smile fading away, then recovering quickly and laughing lightly.*) Aren't you trying to frighten me, doctor?

DOCTOR. (*Annoyed by his levity.*) I don't care anything about you, but, I tell you, your wife has a tendency to an affection of the eyes called glaucoma.

PHILIP. (*Interested.*) Glaucoma? Affection of the eyes? Why, Margaret has magnificent eyes.

DOCTOR. Yes, she has magnificent eyes, but, her child is the indirect cause of the development of an inherent weakness in them.

PHILIP. In what way?

DOCTOR. Conditions incident to motherhood. Shock. She is showing slight symptoms now that if aggravated would cause very serious consequences.

PHILIP. (*Puzzled.*) I do not understand.

DOCTOR. The eye—like other organs, has its own special secretion, which keeps it nourished and in a healthy state. The inflow and outflow of this secretion is equal. The physician sometimes comes across a patient of apparently sound physique, in whom he will find an abnormal condition of the eye where this natural function is through some inherent weakness, easily disturbed. When the patient is subject to illness, great physical or mental suffering—the too great emotion of a sudden joy or sorrow,—the stimulus of any one of these causes may produce in the eyes a super-abundant influx of this perfectly healthy fluid and the fine outflowing ducts cannot carry it off.

PHILIP. Yes. What then?

DOCTOR. The impact continues—until the result—is—

PHILIP. Yes? What is the result?

DOCTOR. Blindness.

PHILIP. (*Awed.*) Why—that is horrible—is there no remedy?

DOCTOR. Yes. A very delicate operation.

PHILIP. Always successful?

DOCTOR. If performed under proper conditions—yes.

PHILIP. And my wife is in danger of this? (*He walks up and down the room.*)

DOCTOR. There is no danger whatever to Mrs. Fleming, if the serenity of her life is not disturbed. There are slight, but nevertheless serious symptoms that must be remedied at once, with ordinary care. She will outgrow this weakness. Perhaps you will understand now, how necessary it is that she leave Canton for a few weeks.

PHILIP. (*Deeply impressed by the* DOCTOR'S *recital.*) Yes, I do. I will set about getting her away at once. I can leave the mill for a while in Foster's hands.

DOCTOR. Yes, he is an honest, capable fellow. Above all things, do not let Mrs. Fleming suspect that there is anything serious the matter. Keep her cheerful.

PHILIP. Ah, Margaret is the sunniest, happiest disposition—nothing troubles her.

DOCTOR. Well, you keep her so. (PHILIP *takes out his cigar case and offers it to the* DOCTOR. *The latter refuses laconically.*) Thank you, I have my own. (*He has taken a cigar from his vest pocket.* PHILIP *strikes a match and offers it to the doctor. At the same time, the* DOCTOR *is lighting his cigar with his own match, ignoring* PHILIP'S *attention.* PHILIP *shrugs his shoulders indulgently, lights his cigar and good-naturedly watches the* DOCTOR, *who takes up his satchel and leaves the room hastily with a curt.*) Good morning.

PHILIP. (*Genially.*) Good morning, Dr. Larkin. (*He sits in the armchair to the right and comfortably contemplates the convolutions of the cigar smoke.*)

(*The closing of the front door is heard.* JOE FLETCHER *appears at the French window, stealthily peering into the room. He sees* PHILIP *and coughs.*)

JOE. Hello, Mr. Fleming!

PHILIP. (*Looking up.*) Hello, Joe—come in.

JOE. (*In a whisper.*) Is it safe?

PHILIP. (*Laughing.*) Yes, I guess so.

JOE. (*Slouching inside.*) Where's Maria?

PHILIP. Gone out.

JOE. (*Relieved.*) Say, that was a damn mean trick you played on me yesterday.

PHILIP. What trick?

JOE. Sending me up here—you knew durn well she'd go fer me.

PHILIP. (*Laughing.*) I didn't know Maria was your wife, honest I didn't.

JOE. Oh, tell that to the marines. I want my sign. (*As* PHILIP *looks puzzled.*) The sample of giant's cement with the plate.

PHILIP. (*Remembering.*) Oh, yes. (*He chuckles to himself, goes to the door at the right and brings back the cracked plate with the big stone hung to it.* JOE *takes it and turns to go.*) Why did you lie to me yesterday?

JOE. I didn't lie to you.

PHILIP. You told me your wife ran away from you.

JOE. So she did.

PHILIP. *She* says you robbed her and left her.

JOE. She's a liar, and I'll tell it to her face.

PHILIP. (*Laughing.*) Come, Joe, you wouldn't dare.

JOE. She's a liar. I'm not afraid of her.

PHILIP. She made you run yesterday.

JOE. (*Holding up the sign.*) Didn't she have this? What chance has a fellow got when a woman has a *weapon* like this?

PHILIP. (*Laughing at him.*) And you were in the war.

JOE. Yes, and I was in the war! The Johnnies didn't fight with things like this.

PHILIP. (*Enjoying the situation.*) Come, Joe, I believe she'd make you run without that.

JOE. She's a liar. I can lick her. (*With conviction.*) I have licked her. (*He grows bolder.*) An' I'll lick her again.

PHILIP. (*Laughing heartily.*) Come, Joe, that'll do. The best way for you to lick 'er is there. (*He points to the decanter upon the side table.* JOE *gazes upon it tenderly and chuckles with unctuous satisfaction.*)

JOE. That's a great joke, Mr. Fleming. *Kin I?* (*He shuffles over to the decanter.*)

PHILIP. Yes, go ahead.

(JOE *pours the liquor into a glass.* MARIA *walks hastily in through the window and sees* PHILIP.)

MARIA. (*Diffidently.*) Excuse me, Mr. Fleming, I did not know you vas here. I always come in dot way mit de baby.

(JOE *is in the act of carrying the glass to his lips. He hears* MARIA'S *voice and stands terrified.* MARIA *sees him and becomes inflamed with indignation. She puts her hands on her hips and glares at him.*) Vell, you dom scoundrel!

JOE. (*Soothingly extending a hand to her.*) There now, Maria, keep cool. Don't lose your temper.

MARIA. (*Mocking him.*) Yah, don't lose my temper. Didn't I tell you never to darken dis house again? Du teufel aus Hölle! (*She makes a lunge at him. He dodges and hops on tip-toe from side to side in a zig-zag.*)

JOE. Just a minute, Maria! (*He gulps.*) I can—I can explain—the whole—thing. (*He makes a desperate bolt, but* MARIA *is on his heels. He stumbles and falls sprawling upon his hands and face, with his head to the front, in the center of the room. She swoops upon him, digs her hands into the loose folds of his coat between the shoulders and drags him to his feet. He limps with fright, puffing and spluttering, awkwardly helping himself and dropping the sign.*) Maria, for God's sake, don't! I ain't ever done anything to you.

MARIA. (*Dragging him toward the window.*) Ach, Gott! No, you have never done nutting to me.

JOE. I'll make it all right with you. Let me go. I want my sign! Ugh! (*She throws him through the French window. He stumbles and staggers out of sight.* MARIA *picks up the sign and flings it after him. All the time she is scolding and weeping with anger.*)

MARIA. Don't you dare come here no more to a decent house, you loafer. You can't explain nutting to me, you tief—you loafer— (*She sinks into the chair at the right of the table, leans her arms across the table, buries her face in them and sobs bitterly. All her fury has vanished and she is crushed and broken.*)

PHILIP. (*Laughing and calling after* JOE.) Joe, come back! Joe! (*He goes out through the window.*) Joe!

MARGARET. (*Rushing in and up to the garden door, afraid some harm has come to the child.*) What on earth is the matter? An earthquake?

MARIA. (*Sobbing.*) No. Mrs. Fleming. It vas dot miserable husband of me.

MARGARET. What?

MARIA. Yah, I yust came in now, und I find him dere drinking of Mr. Fleming's brandy.

MARGARET. Good gracious—what did you do, Maria?

MARIA. I skipped dot gutter mit him, I bet my life. (*She is still weeping.*)

MARGARET. (*A smile flickering about her lips.*) There, Maria, don't cry. Don't let him trouble you so. How is your sister?

MARIA. Vorse, Mrs. Fleming.

MARGARET. Worse. Oh, I'm so sorry.

MARIA. Yah. I don't tink she vill ever leave dot bed alive. My poor little Lena. Mrs. Fleming, I ask you—mebbe you vill come to see her. She talks about you all de time now.

MARGARET. (*Surprised.*) Talks about me? Why, how does she know me?

MARIA. Vell, she ask about you—a lot—und I tell her of you and your beautiful home und your little baby, und now she says she'd like yust once to look into your face.

MARGARET. (*Hesitating a moment.*) Well, I'll go. If I only could do anything for her, poor girl.

MARIA. Yah, she is a poor girl, Mrs. Fleming. Mebbe she vill tell you the name of dis man vot—

MARGARET. (*With repugnance.*) Oh, no, no! I don't want to know the brute, or his name.

MARIA. (*Vindictively.*) Oh, Gott! If I vould know it—

MARGARET. (*Breaking in upon her, kindly.*) But, I'll go to see her.

MARIA. Tank you, Mrs. Fleming. You are a goodt lady.

MARGARET. Where did you say she lives?

MARIA. (*Still quietly weeping.*) Forty-two Millbrook St. By Mrs. Burton's cottage.

MARGARET. Very well. (PHILIP'S *voice is heard outside, laughing.*) Oh, there's Mr. Fleming. Come, Maria, don't let him see you crying. Come, go to the kitchen and tell Hannah— (*She has urged* MARIA *to her feet and is pressing her toward the door.*)

MARIA. Is dot new girl come?

MARGARET. Yes.

MARIA. Hannah is her name?

MARGARET. (*Pressing her.*) Yes, tell her to

make you a nice cup of tea, and then you'd best go back to your sister.

MARIA. Tank you, Mrs. Fleming. I don't want no tea. Mebbe she needs me. I go right back to her. You'll come sure, Mrs. Fleming?

MARGARET. (*Putting her through the door on the right as* PHILIP *comes in through the window on the left.*) Yes, I'll come in a little while.

PHILIP. Oh, Margaret, I wish you'd been here. (*He begins to laugh.*) Such a circus. The funniest thing I ever saw.

MARGARET. Yes, Maria told me. Poor thing. I'm sorry for her. (PHILIP *laughs. She goes to her work basket which is on the center table, and takes out the two phials.* PHILIP *crosses to the right and* MARGARET *goes to him.*) Here, dear—some medicine Dr. Larkin left for you.

PHILIP. (*Pushing her hand away gently.*) Oh, I don't want any medicine. There's nothing the matter with me. (*He begins to chuckle again.*) If you could—

MARGARET. (*Shaking him by the lapels of his jacket.*) Yes, there is a great deal the matter with you. (*She looks at him seriously and he becomes serious.*) Doctor says you're all run down. You've got to have a rest. Here, now, take two of these pellets, alternating every hour. (*He takes the phials and puts them in his vest pocket.*) Take some now!

PHILIP. Oh! Now? Must I?

MARGARET. (*Shaking him.*) Yes, this minute. (*He takes two pellets and pretends to choke. She shakes him again.*) Look at your watch. Note the time.

PHILIP. Yes'm.

MARGARET. Well, in an hour, take two from the other phial.

PHILIP. Yes'm. (*He lights a fresh cigar, and* MARGARET *gives a cry of reproval.*)

MARGARET. Philip! What are you doing? (*She rushes at him and takes the cigar from him.*) Don't you know you mustn't smoke when you are taking medicine.

PHILIP. Why not?

MARGARET. It'll kill the effect of it. You may smoke in a hour.

PHILIP. I've got to take more medicine in an hour?

MARGARET. Well, I guess you'll have to give up smoking.

PHILIP. What!

MARGARET. Until you're well.

PHILIP. But, I'm well now.

MARGARET. (*Going through the door on the left.*) *Until you have stopped taking those pellets!*

PHILIP. All right. I'll forget them.

MARGARET. Philip!

PHILIP. (*Going to the baby in the garden doorway.*) The cigars! What are you doing?

MARGARET. Changing my gown. I'm going out.

PHILIP. Where are you going?

MARGARET. Oh, just a little errand.

PHILIP. Well, hurry back.

MARGARET. Yes, I won't be long. (*She gives a little scream.*) Oh!

PHILIP. What's the matter?

MARGARET. Nothing. Stuck a pin into my finger, that's all.

PHILIP. My! You gave me a shock. (*He puts his hand to his heart playfully.*)

MARGARET. (*Laughing.*) Sorry. Did you see my gloves?

PHILIP. Yes.

MARGARET. Where?

PHILIP. On your hands, of course.

MARGARET. Now, don't be silly!

PHILIP. (*Playing with the baby.*) Margaret, you know, baby's eyes are changing.

MARGARET. No.

PHILIP. Yes. They're growing like yours.

MARGARET. Nonsense. She has your eyes.

PHILIP. (*Eyeing the baby critically.*) No, they're exactly like yours. She's got my nose though.

MARGARET. (*Giving a little cry of protest.*) Oh, Philip—don't say that.

PHILIP. Why?

MARGARET. It would be terrible if she had your nose. Just imagine my dainty Lucy with a great big nose like yours.

PHILIP. (*Feeling his nose.*) Why, I think I have a very nice nose.

MARGARET. (*Coming in, laughing.*) Oh, yes, it's a good enough nose—as noses go—but— (*She touches the bell.*)

PHILIP. (*Noticing her gown.*) Your new suit?

MARGARET. (*Gaily.*) Yes. Like it?

PHILIP. It's a dandy. Turn around. (*She dances over to him and twirls about playfully.*) Wait, there's a thread. (*He picks it off her skirt.*)

(JANE *enters.*)

MARGARET. Jane, please tell Hannah to come here.

JANE. Yes, ma'am. (*She goes.*)

(PHILIP *begins to chuckle.*)

MARGARET. Now, Philip, I implore you to keep still. Please don't get me laughing while I'm talking to her.

PHILIP. (*Indignantly.*) I'm not going to say anything.

(HANNAH *appears. She is very large, stout and dignified.*)

MARGARET. (*Hurriedly, in haste to be off.*) Hannah! I'm going out and I shall not be able to look after the baking of the bread. When the loaves have raised almost to the top of the pans put them in the oven.

HANNAH. (*Who has been studying admiringly* MARGARET'S *costume.*) Yes, Ma'am. I does always put the bread in when it's almost up to the top in the pans.

MARGARET. And bake them just one hour.

HANNAH. Ah! Yes, ma'am. I always bakes 'em an hour.

(PHILIP *smothers a laugh in a cough.* MARGARET *stares at him.*)

MARGARET. And, have luncheon on at half past twelve, please.

HANNAH. Yes, I always has the lunch on at half past twelve, sharp.

MARGARET. (*Who has been putting on her gloves.*) Thank you, Hannah, that's all. Well, I'm off. (*To* PHILIP.) Good-bye, dear. (*She starts off hastily.*)

HANNAH. Good-bye, ma'am. (*She goes out.*)

MARGARET. (*Pausing to look at* PHILIP *as he plays with the baby in the carriage.*) Oh, how dear you both look there together.

PHILIP. (*Looking at his watch.*) You'd best hurry if you want to get back at *half past twelve sharp.* (*He imitates* HANNAH.)

MARGARET. (*Rapturously gazing at them.*) Oh, if I could paint, what a picture I would make of you two!

PHILIP. Are you going?

MARGARET. Yes, I'm going. (*She notices* PHILIP *giving the baby his watch, and giving a little scream of alarm, she rushes at him.*) Philip, what are you doing?

PHILIP. That's all right. She won't hurt it.

MARGARET. Suppose she'd swallow it.

PHILIP. Well!

MARGARET. (*Mocking him.*) Well! There, put it in your pocket. And have some sense. (*She picks up the rattle and the big rubber ball and puts them in his hands.*) There, you can play with these. (*They both laugh with the fun of it all.*)

PHILIP. Oh! Go on Margaret, and hurry home.

MARGARET. (*Kissing him and the baby.*) All right. Won't be long. Don't forget your medicine, and please don't smoke when my back is turned.) (*She dances out through the French window, overflowing with fun and animation. This scene must be played rapidly, with a gay, light touch.*)

ACT THIRD

The scene is a neat, plainly furnished sitting-room in MRS. BURTON'S *cottage. The walls are covered with old-fashioned wall paper of a faded green color. Sunlight streams in through two windows at the back. In one there is a small table holding a few pots of geraniums, and in the second, a hanging basket of ivy. A few straggling vines creep about the window-frame. There are doors at the left center, down left and on the right. In the center of the room stands a table with a chair to the right of it, and a few haircloth chairs are here and there. A sofa stands against the left wall below the door, and there is a low rocking-chair on the left.*

The room is empty and after a moment the stillness is broken by the wail of an infant. The hushed notes of a woman's voice are heard from the open door on the left, soothing the child. A low knock is heard at the door to the right. The door opens slowly and DOCTOR LARKIN *enters.* MRS. BURTON *emerges from the room on the left with a tiny baby wrapped in a soft white shawl in her arms. She is a motherly woman, large and placid, with a benign immobility of countenance. She speaks with a New England drawl.*

MRS. BURTON. Good morning, doctor. I didn't hear ye knock.

DOCTOR. How is your patient this morning?

MRS. BURTON. Why, ain't yer seen Dr. Taylor? Didn't he tell ye?

DOCTOR. No. She's—?

MRS. BURTON. (*Nodding her head.*) Yes.

DOCTOR. When did it happen?

MRS. BURTON. About an hour ago. She seemed brighter this morning. After her sister went out she slept for a while. When I came in the room she opened her eyes and asked me for a pencil and paper. I brought 'em to her and she writ for quite a spell. Then she lay back on the pillow. I asked her if she wouldn't take a little nourishment. She smiled and shook her head. Then she gave a long sigh—an'—an'—that was all there was to it.

DOCTOR. How's the child?

MRS. BURTON. Poor little critter— (*She looks down at it.*) I can't do nothing for it. I've tried everything. It ought to have mother's milk—that's all there is to it. Be quiet, you poor little motherless critter.

DOCTOR. It would be better for it if it had gone with her.

MRS. BURTON. Why, doctor, ain't ye awful?

DOCTOR. Why, what chance has that child got in this world? I'll send you something for it. (*He turns to go.*)

MRS. BURTON. Don't ye want to see her?

DOCTOR. No! What good can I be to her now, poor devil?

(CHARLEY BURTON, *a sturdy lad of ten breaks boisterously into the room from the door on the right, carrying a baseball and bat.*)

CHARLEY. Ma! Ma! Here's a woman wants to see Mrs. Bindley.

MRS. BURTON. (*Reprimanding him.*) Lady! And take your hat off.

(DR. LARKIN *and* MRS. BURTON *look expectantly toward the door.* MARGARET *enters slowly, her eyes bent upon her glove which she is unfastening.* DR. LARKIN *is dumbfounded at the sight of her. She takes a few steps toward him and looks up.*)

MARGARET. (*Pleasantly surprised at seeing him.*) Why, doctor! I didn't know that you were on this case.

DOCTOR. (*Confused.*) I'm not. Dr. Taylor—he—called me in consultation. But, what in the name of all that's wonderful brings you here?

MARGARET. Maria!

DOCTOR. What Maria? Not—

MARGARET. Yes, our Maria—this sick girl is her sister. (*She removes her hat and places it with her gloves on the table.*)

DOCTOR. (*In consternation.*) Her sister! Then you know?

MARGARET. I know that there is a poor sick girl here who wants—

DOCTOR. (*Going to her, brusquely.*) Mrs. Fleming, you'd best not remain here—the girl is dead. Go home.

MARGARET. (*Pityingly.*) Dead? Poor thing!

DOCTOR. Yes. Does your husband know you are here?

MARGARET. (*Shaking her head.*) Oh, no!

DOCTOR. Come, you must go home! (*He almost pushes her out of the room in his urgency.*)

MARGARET. (*Resisting him gently.*) Ah, no, doctor. Now that I am here, let me stay. I can be of some help, I know.

DOCTOR. No, you can be of no use. Everything has been done.

MARGARET. Well, I'll just say a word to Maria. Where is she?

DOCTOR. I don't know—I don't know anything about Maria.

MRS. BURTON. She's in there. (*She nods toward the door on the left.*)

(*The* DOCTOR *has crowded* MARGARET *almost through the door in his eagerness to have her out of the house. She is reluctantly yielding to him, when* MRS. BURTON'S *voice arrests her. She turns quickly and, looking over the* DOCTOR'S *shoulder, notices the child in* MRS. BURTON'S *arms. She impulsively brushes the* DOCTOR *aside and goes toward her, her face beaming with tender sympathy.*)

MARGARET. Oh, is this the baby?

MRS. BURTON. Yes'm.

MARGARET. (*Going close to her on tip-toes and gazing with maternal solicitude down upon the child.*) Poor little baby! What a dear mite of a thing it is.

MRS. BURTON. Yes'm.

MARGARET. (*Impulsively.*) Doctor, we must take care of this baby.

DOCTOR. (*Impatiently.*) You've got a baby of your *own,* Mrs. Fleming.

MARGARET. Yes, and that's why I pity this one. I suppose, I always did love babies, anyhow. They are such wonderful, mysterious little things, aren't they?

MRS. BURTON. Yes'm.

DOCTOR. (*Spurred by a growing sense of catastrophe.*) Mrs. Fleming, there is danger to your child in your remaining here.

MARGARET. (*Alarmed.*) Oh, doctor!

DOCTOR. I hated to tell you this before—but—there is contagion in this atmosphere.

MARGARET. (*Hastily taking her hat from the table.*) Doctor, why didn't you— (*She is hurrying away when she is checked by a poignant moan. She turns a frightened face and sees* MARIA *coming from the room on the left with a letter in her hand.* MARIA'S *face is distorted by grief.*)

MARIA. Ah, Mrs. Burton, I have found out who dot man is. He is— (*She sees* MARGARET *and smiles bitterly upon her.*) So, —you have come, Mrs. Fleming?

MARGARET. (*Making a movement of sympathy.*) Maria!

MARIA. Vell, you may go back again. You can do nutting for her now. She is dead. (*Perversely.*) But, ven you do go, you vill take dot baby back mit you. He shall now have two babies instead of one.

MARGARET. (*Smiling.*) What do you mean, Maria? Who shall have two babies?

MARIA. (*Fiercely.*) Philip Fleming—dot's who.

(MARGARET *stares at her, only comprehending half what* MARIA *means.* DR. LARKIN *goes quickly to her.*)

DOCTOR. Come away, Mrs. Fleming—the woman is crazy. (*He tries to draw her away.*)

MARIA. (*Contemptuously.*) No, I ain't crazy! (*She shakes the letter at* MARGARET.) You read dot letter and see if I vas crazy!

(MARGARET, *in a dazed way, reaches for the letter, and tries to read it, turning it different ways.*)

MARGARET. I cannot make it out. (*She hands it to the doctor, and says helplessly.*) Read it—to me—doctor—please.

DOCTOR. (*Beside himself and snatching the letter.*) No, nor shall you. (*He makes a motion to tear the letter.*)

MARIA. (*Threateningly.*) Don't you tear dot letter, doctor.

MARGARET. (*Putting her hand out gently.*) You must not destroy that letter, doctor. Give it back to me. (DR. LARKIN *returns the letter reluctantly.* MARGARET *attempts to read it, fails, becomes impatient, and hands it to* MARIA, *helplessly.*) You read it to me, Maria.

(MARIA, *whose passion has subsided, takes the letter in an awed manner and begins to read it. The* DOCTOR *is in a daze.* MARGARET *sinks into the chair to the right of the table. She has recovered her calm poise, but does not seem to be at all the same* MARGARET.)

MARIA. (*Reading in a simple, unaffected manner.*)

Canton, June 10,

DEAR MR. FLEMING:

You was good to come to see me, and I thank you. I will not trouble you no more. I am sorry for what has happened. I know you never loved me and I never asked you to, but I loved you. It was all my fault. I will never trouble you no more. You can do what you like with the baby. I do not care. Do not be afraid, I shall never tell. They tried to get me to but I never shall. Nobody will ever know. No more at present, from your obedient servant,

LENA SCHMIDT.

MARGARET. (*Turning to the* DOCTOR, *who is standing close to her chair.*) Did you know—anything of this—doctor?

DOCTOR. (*Evasively.*) Well—I knew—something of it—but, this girl may be lying. Such as she is—will say anything sometimes.

MARIA. (*Fiercely.*) Don't you say dot, doctor. She would not tell nutting to hurt him, not to save her soul.

DOCTOR. (*With finality.*) Well, now that you know the worst, come away from here—come home.

MARIA. (*Bitterly.*) Oh! Ya! She can go home. She have alvays got a home und a husband und fine clothes, because she is his vife, but my poor sister don't have any of dese tings, because she is only de poor mistress. But, by Gott, she shall not go home unless she takes dot baby back mit her.

DOCTOR. She shall do nothing of the sort.

MARIA. Vell, den, I vill take it, und fling it in his face.

MARGARET. (*Calmly, and rising from the chair.*) You shall not go near him. You shall not say—one word to him!

MARIA. Von't I? Who is going to stop me? I vould yust like to know dot?

MARGARET. (*Quite calmly.*) I am!

MARIA. (*Mockingly.*) You—you vill take his part, because you are his vife! (*Fiercely.*) Vell! (*She draws a pistol from her dress pocket.*) Do you see dot gun? Vell, I buy dot gun, und I swore dot ven I find out dot man I vill have his life. Und, if you try to stop me, I vill lay you stiff und cold beside her.

MARGARET. (*Calmly, pityingly, holding out her hand as though to quiet her.*) Maria! Stop! How dare you talk like that to me? Give me that pistol. (MARIA, *awed by* MARGARET'S *spirit, meekly hands her the weapon.*) You think—I—am happy—because I am his wife? Why, you poor fool, that girl (*She points to the door on the left*) never in all her life suffered one thousandth part what I have suffered in these past five minutes. Do you dare to compare her to me? I have not uttered one word of reproach, even against her, and yet she has done me a wrong, that not all the death-bed letters that were ever written can undo. I wonder what I have ever done to deserve this! (*She loses control of herself and sinks sobbing, into the chair, her arms upon the table, and her head dropping upon them.*)

DOCTOR. (*Overcome by the situation, throws*

his arms about her and tries to draw her to her feet.) For God's sake, Mrs. Fleming, let me take you out of this hell.

MARGARET. (*Gently resisting him.*) Ah, doctor, you cannot take *this hell* out of my breast. (*Suddenly her manner changes. She says with quick decision.*) Maria, get me a sheet of writing paper. Doctor, give me a pencil.

(DR. LARKIN *puts his hand into his vest pocket.* MARIA, *who seems dazed, looks helplessly about as though the paper might be within reach. Then suddenly thinking of the letter in her hand, she tears off the blank half of it and quickly lays it on the table before* MARGARET.)

DOCTOR. (*Giving her the pencil.*) What are you going to do?

MARGARET. Send—for *him!*

DOCTOR. No—not here!

MARGARET. Yes—here— (*She writes nervously, mumbling what she writes.*) "Philip: I am waiting for you, here. That *girl* is *dead.*" (*She folds the letter.*) Where's that boy?

(MARIA *and* MRS. BURTON *both make a movement in search of* CHARLEY.)

MARIA. Charley! (*She goes to the door at the back and calls again in a hushed voice.*) Charley! (CHARLEY *enters. She whispers to him that the lady wants him.*) You, go quick! (CHARLEY *goes to* MARGARET.)

MARGARET. (*In tense nervousness.*) Charley, do you know Mr. Fleming?

CHARLEY. Yes'm.

MARGARET. Do you know where he lives?

CHARLEY. Yes'm—on Canton Street.

MARGARET. Yes—go there—don't ring the bell—go through the garden—you will find him there, playing with the baby. Give him this.

CHARLEY. Any answer?

MARGARET. (*At nervous tension.*) No! Go quick! Quick! (*She springs to her feet.*) Now, doctor—I want you to leave me!

DOCTOR. Mrs. Fleming, for God's sake don't see him here.

MARGARET. Yes, here—and—alone! Please go. (*The* DOCTOR *does not respond.*) I don't want you or any other living being to hear what passes between him and me, and, (*She points to the room*) *that dead girl.* Please go!

DOCTOR. Mrs. Fleming, as your physician, I order you to leave this place at once.

MARGARET. No, doctor—I must see him, *here.*

DOCTOR. (*With gentle persuasion.*) Mrs. Fleming, you have no right to do this. Think of your child.

MARGARET. (*Remembering.*) My baby! My poor, little innocent baby! Oh, I wish to God that she were dead. (*She is beside herself and not realizing what she says. She crosses to the left.*)

DOCTOR. (*Following her.*) Mrs. Fleming, in God's name, calm yourself! I have tried to keep it from you, but, I am forced to tell you— (*He is so deeply moved that he is almost incoherent.*) If you continue in this way, dear lady, you are exposing yourself to a terrible affliction—this—trouble—with your eyes. You are threatened with—if you keep up this strain—a sudden blindness may fall upon you.

MARGARET. (*Appalled.*) Blind! Blind! (*She speaks in a low terrified voice.*) Oh, no doctor, not *that*—not *now*—not until after I've seen him.

DOCTOR. Not only that, but if you keep up this strain much longer, it may cost you your life.

MARGARET. I don't care—what happens to me, only, let me *see* him, and then, the sooner it all comes the better. (*She crosses to the left with the* DOCTOR *following her.*)

DOCTOR. (*Growing desperate, and throwing his arms about her.*) Mrs. Fleming, you must leave this place! Come home.

MARGARET. No. Doctor, please leave me alone. (*She draws herself from him.*) I tell you I've got to see him here. (*Then with a sweet intimacy, she goes to him.*) A woman has a strange feeling for the physician who brings her child into the world—I love you—I have always obeyed your orders, haven't I? (*She speaks brokenly.*)

DOCTOR. (*Quietly.*) Always.

MARGARET. Then, let me be the doctor now, and I order you to leave this house at once.

DOCTOR. (*Hopelessly.*) You are determined to do this thing?

MARGARET. (*With finality.*) Yes.

DOCTOR. Very well then—good-bye. (*He holds out his hand, which she takes mechanically. He holds her hand warmly for a moment. She clings to him as though afraid to let him go, then slowly draws away.*)

MARGARET. Good-bye!

(*The* DOCTOR *leaves the room quickly.* MARGARET *takes a step after him until she touches the left side of the table in the center. She stands there gazing into space, the calmness of death upon her face. The sunlight streaming through the window falls upon her.* MRS. BURTON *is sitting in a rocking-chair in the corner of the room.* MARIA *is sitting on the sofa at the left, weeping silently, with clasped hands, her arms lying in her lap, her body bent. She makes a plaintive moan before she speaks.*)

MARIA. Ah—Mrs. Fleming, you must not do dis ting. Vat vas I—vot was she, I'd like to know—dot ve should make dis trouble for you? You come here, like an angel to help us, und I have stung you like a snake in dot grass. (*She goes to* MARGARET *and falls upon her knees beside her.*) Oh, Mrs. Fleming, on my knees I ask you to forgive me.

(MARGARET *stands immobile at the table, her right hand resting upon its edge—her left hand partly against her cheek. She is lost in spiritual contemplation of the torment she is suffering. She shows impatience at the sound of* MARIA'S *voice as though loath to be disturbed. She replies wearily.*)

MARGARET. I have nothing to forgive. Get up, Maria. You have done nothing to me—go away!

MARIA. (*In a paroxysm of contrition.*) Oh, I beg, Mrs. Fleming, dot you vill take dot gun and blow my brains out.

MARGARET. Don't go on like that, Maria! (MARIA'S *weeping irritates her.*) Get up! Please go away. Go away! I say.

(MARIA *slinks away quietly into the back room.* MARGARET *takes a long, sobbing breath, which ends in a sigh. She stares into space and a blank look comes into her face as though she were gazing at things beyond her comprehension. Presently the silence is broken by a low wail from the infant. It half arouses her.*)

MARGARET. What is the matter with that child? (*Her voice seems remote. Her expression remains fixed.*) Why don't you keep it quiet?

MRS. BURTON. (*In a hushed voice.*) It's hungry.

MARGARET. (*In the same mood, but her voice is a little querulous.*) Well, then, why don't you feed it?

MRS. BURTON. I can't get nothing fit for it. I've tried everything I could think of, but it's no use. (*She gets up and places the child upon the sofa to the left.*) There, be still, you poor little critter, an' I'll see what I ken get fer ye. (*As she goes to the door at the back,* MARGARET *speaks wearily.*)

MARGARET. Bring a lamp—it's getting dark here. (*She is still in the same attitude by the table. There is a silence, then the child's wail arouses her. She half turns her head in its direction—and tries to quiet it.*) Hush—child—hush— (*Then she reaches out her hand as if to pat it.*) There—there—poor little thing. Don't fret—it's no use to fret, child—be quiet now—there—there, now. (*She turns and slowly gropes her way to the sofa, sits on the edge of it, and feels for the child and gently pats it. She murmurs softly.*) Hush—baby—go to sleep.

(*There is a silence while a soft flood of sunshine plays about her. A pitying half smile flits across her face. She utters a faint sigh and again drifts away into that inner consciousness where she evidently finds peace. Again the child is restless—it arouses her and, hopeless of comforting it, she takes it in her arms. After a moment, she rises to her feet and stumbles toward the table. She knocks against the low chair. At the same moment,* PHILIP FLEMING *dashes breathlessly into the room through the door on the right. He pauses in horror as* MARGARET *raises her head, her eyes wide open, staring into his—her face calm and remote. She hushes the child softly, and sits in the low chair.* PHILIP *stands in dumb amazement watching her. The child begins to fret her again. She seems hopeless of comforting it. Then scarcely conscious of what she is doing, suddenly with an impatient, swift movement she unbuttons her dress to give nourishment to the child, when the picture fades away into darkness.*)

ACT FOURTH

The scene is the same as the Second Act. The doors and window leading into the garden are open.

MARIA *is seated close to the open door, sewing. She occasionally looks into the garden as if guarding something. She is neatly dressed, fresh and orderly looking. Her manner is subdued. A bell rings and a closing door is heard. Then* DR. LARKIN *enters.* MARIA *goes to meet him and scans his face anxiously.*

MARIA. Goot morning, doctor.

DOCTOR. Good morning. Well! Any news?

MARIA. (*Losing interest and shaking her head sadly.*) No, doctor. No vord from him yet. It is seven days now—I hoped —mebbe you might have some.

DOCTOR. No—nothing. How is Mrs. Fleming?

(MARIA *sits down to the left of the center of the room and the doctor to the right.*)

MARIA. Yust the same as yesterday, und the day before, und all the udder days. Ach, so bright, und so cheerful, but I tink all the same she is breaking her heart. Ach, ven I look into her sad eyes—vot cannot see me—I am ashamed to hold my head up. (*She brushes away the tears.*)

DOCTOR. Does she talk about him at all?

MARIA. No, she never speaks his name.

DOCTOR. How is the child?

MARIA. (*Brightening.*) She is fine. Dot little tooth came trough dis morning und she don't fret no more now.

DOCTOR. And, the *other* one?

MARIA. (*Indifferently.*) Oh, he's all right. I put him beside Lucy in her crib dis morning und she laughs and pulls at him und plays mit him yust like he vas a little kitten. Dis is no place for him, doctor. Ven Mr. Fleming comes home he vill fix tings, und I vill take him away by myself—vere she no more can be troubled mit him.

DOCTOR. Things will come out all right. You'd best keep quiet. Have nothing whatever to say in this matter.

MARIA. Ya. I make enough trouble already mit my tongue. You bet I keep it shut in my head now. Shall I call Mrs. Fleming? She is in the garden.

DOCTOR. She's there a great deal now, isn't she?

MIRIA. Ya, she is always dere by the blossoms, und the babies. (*She goes to the door and says in slow, deferential voice.*) Mrs. Fleming, Doctor Larkin is here.

MARGARET. (*Outside.*) Yes, I'll come. (*She slowly emerges from the garden into the doorway, her arms filled with flowers. She is daintily dressed and there is a subtle dignity and reserve about her. She smiles cheerily.*) Good morning, doctor. Maria, there are some daffodils out by the yellow bed. Bring them, please. (*She slowly enters the room.*)

(*The* DOCTOR *goes to her and gently leads her to the table on the right where she puts the flowers, after carefully locating a place to lay them.*)

DOCTOR. Well, well, where did you get such a lot of roses? I couldn't gather so many in a month from my scrubby bushes. The bugs eat 'em all up.

MARGARET. Why don't you spray them? (MARIA *brings a large loose bunch of daffodils.*) Bring some jars, Maria.

DOCTOR. I did spray them.

MARGARET. When?

DOCTOR. When I saw the rose bugs.

MARGARET. (*Smiling.*) That's a fine time to spray bushes. Don't you know that the time to prevent trouble is to look ahead? From potatoes to roses, spray before anything happens—*then* nothing *will* happen.

DOCTOR. (*Laughing.*) Yes, of course, I know, but I forgot to do it until I saw two big, yellow bugs in the heart of every rose and all the foliage chewed up.

MARGARET. There's no use in it now. You are just wasting time. Start early next year before the leaves open.

DOCTOR. (*Admiringly.*) What a brave, cheery little woman you are.

MARGARET. What's the use in being anything else? I don't see any good in living in this world, unless you can live right.

DOCTOR. And this world needs just such women as you.

MARGARET. What does the world know or care about me?

(*The bell rings and the door opens and shuts.*)

DOCTOR. Very little, but it's got to feel your influence. (*He pats her hand.*)

(*The* MAID *enters.*)

MAID. Mr. Foster wishes to see you for a moment, Mrs. Fleming.

MARGARET. Tell him to come in. (*The* MAID *goes out. In a moment* FOSTER *enters, flurried and embarrassed.*) Good morning, Mr. Foster. (*She holds out her hands to him.*) Anything wrong at the mill?

FOSTER. Good morning, Mrs. Fleming. Oh, no—not at all, not at all. How do you do, doctor? (*He shakes hands with the* DOCTOR *with unusual warmth.*)

DOCTOR. (*Somewhat surprised and looking at him quizzically.*) Hello, Foster.

MARGARET. Will you sit down, Mr. Foster?

FOSTER. Thank you—yes, I will. What beautiful flowers. Mother says you have the loveliest garden in Canton.

MARGARET. (*Pleased.*) That's awfully nice of her. I had a delightful visit with her yesterday.

FOSTER. (*Nervously.*) Yes, she told me so.

MARGARET. We sat in the garden. What a sweet, happy soul she is.

FOSTER. (*Fussing with his hat and getting up and moving his chair close to the* DOCTOR's.) Yes. Mother always sees the bright side of the worst things.

MARGARET. She's very proud of you.

FOSTER. (*Laughing foolishly.*) Oh, yes, she is happy over anything I do. (*He looks at* MARGARET *furtively, then at the doctor. He evidently has something to say. Suddenly in a tense whisper he speaks to the doctor.*) Mr. Fleming has come back.

DOCTOR. Hush! Where is he? At the mill?

FOSTER. No. Here—outside.

DOCTOR. How does he look?

FOSTER. He's a wreck. He wants to see her.

DOCTOR. Well, tell her—I'll go— (He *rises.*)

FOSTER. No! (*He grabs him by the coat.*) For God's sake don't go. You tell her—you're her doctor.

(MARGARET *who has been busy with the flowers, becomes suddenly interested.*)

MARGARET. What are you two whispering about?

FOSTER. (*Laughing nervously.*) Oh, just a little advice, that's all. (*He goes to* MARGARET.) I'll say good morning, Mrs. Fleming. Glad to see you—er—looking—ah—so well. (*He shakes hands and rushes out.*)

(MARGARET *stands a little mystified. The* DOCTOR *approaches her gently.*)

DOCTOR. (*Very tenderly.*) Mrs. Fleming—I have something to say to you.

MARGARET. (*Standing tense and with ominous conviction.*) Philip is dead!

DOCTOR. No. He is not dead.

MARGARET. Where is he?

DOCTOR. *Outside.*

MARGARET. Why doesn't he come in?

DOCTOR. He's ashamed—afraid.

MARGARET. This is his home. Why should he be afraid to enter it? I will go to him. (*She starts toward the door, and then staggers. The* DOCTOR *puts an arm around her.*)

DOCTOR. There now. Keep up your courage. Don't forget, everything depends upon you.

MARGARET. (*Brokenly.*) I'm brave, doctor. I—perhaps it's best for you to tell him to come here.

DOCTOR. (*Patting her on the shoulder.*) Remember, you are very precious to us all. We cannot afford to lose *you.*

(MARGARET *stands by the table, calm and tense.* PHILIP *comes in from the right, carrying his cap in his hands. He looks weary and broken. He crosses behind* MARGARET *to the center of the stage and standing humbly before her, murmurs her name softly.*)

PHILIP. Margaret!

MARGARET. Well, Philip. (*After a slight pause.*) You have come back.

PHILIP. (*Humbly.*) Yes.

MARGARET. (*Gently.*) Why did you go away?

PHILIP. (*Overwhelmed with shame.*) I couldn't face you. I wanted to get away somewhere, and hide forever. (*He looks sharply at her.*) Can't you see me, Margaret?

MARGARET. (*Shaking her head.*) No!

PHILIP. (*Awed.*) You are blind! Oh!

(MARGARET *sits down in a chair by the table.* PHILIP *remains standing.*)

MARGARET. Don't mind. I shall be cured. Doctor Norton sees me every day. He will operate as soon as he finds me normal.

PHILIP. You have been suffering?

MARGARET. Oh, no. (*After a pause.*) Philip, do you think that was right? To run away and hide?

PHILIP. I did not consider whether it was right or wrong. (*He speaks bitterly.*) I did not know the meaning of those words. I never have.

MARGARET. Oh, you are a man—people will soon forget.

PHILIP. (*Fiercely.*) I do not care about others. It is you, Margaret—will you ever forget? Will you ever forgive?

MARGARET. (*Shaking her head and smiling sadly.*) There is nothing to forgive. And, I want to forget.

PHILIP. (*Bewildered by her magnanimity,*

but full of hope.) Then you will let me come back to you? You will help me to be a better—a wiser man?

MARGARET. (*Smiling gently.*) Yes, Philip.

(*A quick joy takes hold of* PHILIP. *He makes a warm movement to go to her, then checks himself, and approaches her slowly while speaking, overcome by the wonder and beauty of her kindness.*)

PHILIP. All my life, Margaret, I will make amends for what I have done. I will atone for my ignorance— Oh, my wife—my dear, dear wife. (*He hangs over her tenderly, not daring to touch her.*)

(*At the word "wife"* MARGARET *rises, shrinking from him as though some dead thing was near her. A look of agony flits across her face.*)

MARGARET. No! Philip, not that! No! (*She puts out her hands to ward him off.*)

PHILIP. (*Beseechingly.*) Margaret!

MARGARET. (*Her face poignant with suppressed emotion, she confesses, brokenly.*) The wife-heart has gone out of me.

PHILIP. Don't—don't say that, Margaret.

MARGARET. I must. Ah, Philip, how I worshipped you. You were my idol. Is it my fault that you lie broken at my feet?

PHILIP. (*With urgency.*) You say you want to forget—that you forgive! Will you—?

MARGARET. Can't you understand? It is not a question of forgetting, or of forgiving— (*For an instant she is at a loss how to convince him.*) Can't you understand? Philip! (*Then suddenly.*) Suppose—I—had been unfaithful to you?

PHILIP. (*With a cry of repugnance.*) Oh, Margaret!

MARGARET. (*Brokenly.*) There! You see! You are a man, and you have your ideals of—the—sanctity—of—the thing you love. Well, I am a woman—and perhaps—I, too, have the same ideals. I don't know. But, I, too, cry "pollution." (*She is deeply moved.*)

PHILIP. (*Abashed.*) I did not know. I never realized before, the iniquity—of my—behavior. Oh, if I only had my life to live over again. Men, as a rule, do not consider others when urged on by their desires. How you must hate me.

MARGARET. No, I don't—I love you—I pity you.

PHILIP. Dear, not now—but in the future—some time—away in the future—perhaps, the old Margaret—

MARGARET. Ah, Philip, the old Margaret is dead. The truth killed her.

PHILIP. Then—there is no hope for me? (*There is a dignity and a growing manliness in his demeanor as the scene progresses.*)

MARGARET. (*Warmly.*) Yes. Every hope.

PHILIP. Well, what do you want me to do? Shall I go away?

MARGARET. No. Your place is here. You cannot shirk your responsibilities now.

PHILIP. I do not want to shirk my responsibilities, Margaret. I want to do whatever you think is best.

MARGARET. Very well. It is best for us both to remain here, and take up the old life together. It will be a little hard for you, but you are a man—you will soon live it down.

PHILIP. Yes—I *will* live it down.

MARGARET. Go to the mill tomorrow morning and take up your work again, as though this thing had never happened.

PHILIP. Yes. All right. I'll do that.

MARGARET. Mr. Foster, you know, you have an unusually capable man there?

PHILIP. Yes, I appreciate Foster. He's a nice chap, too.

MARGARET. He has carried through a very critical week at the mill.

PHILIP. Don't worry, Margaret, everything will be all right there now. I will put my whole heart and soul into the work.

MARGARET. Then, you must do something for your child.

PHILIP. Yes, our dear child.

MARGARET. No, not our child—not Lucy. Your son.

PHILIP. My son?

MARGARET. Yes.

PHILIP. Where is he?

MARGARET. Here.

PHILIP. (*Resentfully.*) Who brought him here?

MARGARET. I did.

PHILIP. (*Amazed.*) You brought that child here?

MARGARET. Yes, where else should he go?

PHILIP. You have done that?

MARGARET. What other thing was there for me to do? Surely if he was good enough to bring into the world, he is good enough to find a shelter under your roof.

PHILIP. (*Moved by her magnanimity.*) I never dreamed that you would do that, Margaret.

MARGARET. Well, he is here. Now, what are you going to do with him?

PHILIP. (*Helplessly.*) What can I do?

MARGARET. Give him a name, educate him. Try to make atonement for the wrong you did his mother. You must teach him never to be ashamed of her, to love her memory—motherhood is a divine thing—remember that, Philip, no matter when, or how. You can do fine things for this unfortunate child.

PHILIP. (*Contemptuously.*) Fine things for him! I am not fit to guide a young life. A fine thing I have made of my own.

MARGARET. There is no use now lamenting what was done yesterday. That's finished. Tomorrow? What are you going to do with that?

PHILIP. There does not seem any "tomorrow" worth while for me. The past—

MARGARET. The past is dead. We must face the living future. Now, Philip, there are big things ahead for you, if you will only look for them. They certainly will not *come* to *you*. I will help you—we will fight this together.

PHILIP. Forgive me, please. I'll not talk like that any more.

MARGARET. Of course, there will be a lot of talk—mean talk—but they will get tired of that in the end. Where have you been all this time?

PHILIP. In Boston.

MARGARET. What have you been doing?

PHILIP. Nothing—I've been—in the hospital.

MARGARET. (*Stretching out her arms to him with an infinite tenderness.*) Ah, Philip, you have been ill?

PHILIP. No!

MARGARET. What was it. (*He is silent.*) Please tell me.

PHILIP. (*Rather reluctantly reciting his story.*) I was walking across the bridge over the Charles river one night—I was sick of myself—the whole world—I believed I should never see your face again. The water looked so quiet, it fascinated me. I just dropped into it and went down. It seemed like going to sleep. Then I woke up and I was in a narrow bed in a big room.

MARGARET. (*Breathless.*) The hospital?

PHILIP. Yes.

MARGARET. Oh, that was a cruel thing to do. Were they kind to you there?

PHILIP. Yes. There was an old nurse there—she was sharp. She told me not to be a fool, but to go back to my wife. She said—"If she's any good, she will forgive you." (*He smiles whimsically.*) Margaret, some day I am going to earn your respect, and then—I know, I shall be able to win you back to me all over again.

MARGARET. (*Smiling sadly.*) I don't know. That would be a wonderful thing. (*She weeps silently.*) A very wonderful thing. (*Then suddenly she springs to her feet.*) Ah, dreams! Philip! Dreams! And we must get to work.

(PHILIP *is inspired by her manner, and there is a quickening of his spirit, a response to her in the new vibration in his voice.*)

PHILIP. Work! Yes—I'll not wait until tomorrow. I'll go to the mill now.

MARGARET. That's fine. Do it.

PHILIP. Yes, I'll take a bath and get into some fresh clothing first.

MARGARET. Do. You must look pretty shabby knocking about for a week without a home.

PHILIP. Oh, I'll be all right. I'd like to see Lucy. (*He looks about.*) Where is she?

(MARGARET *is at the table occupied with the flowers.*)

MARGARET. They are both out there. (*She indicates with a turn of her head.*) In the garden.

(PHILIP *goes quickly to the door opening upon the garden and gazes out eagerly.* MARGARET, *at the table, pauses in her work, gives a long sigh of relief and contentment. Her eyes look into the darkness and a serene joy illuminates her face. The picture slowly fades out as* PHILIP *steps buoyantly into the garden.*)

THE END OF THE PLAY

SECRET SERVICE

A DRAMA OF "THE SOUTHERN CONFEDERACY"

IN FOUR ACTS

BY

William Gillette

SECRET SERVICE

Secret Service represents another phase of the Civil War from that portrayed in *Shenandoah.* It is also the most representative play of its author. William Gillette was born at Hartford, Connecticut, July 24, 1855, the son of Francis Gillette, at one time Senator of the United States. At the beginning of his stage career, he took special courses at Harvard and Boston Universities and the Massachusetts Institute of Technology, and as early as 1875, acted in *Across the Continent* at New Orleans. His first professional appearance was at the Globe Theatre, Boston, as "Guzman" in *Faint Heart Never Won Fair Lady,* September 15, 1875. After a number of stage successes, he produced his first play *The Professor* at the Madison Square Theatre, New York, June 1, 1881, in which he played "Professor Hopkins," and at the same theatre, on October 29, 1881, his play *Esmeralda,* founded on a story of Mrs. Francis Hodgson Burnett, was first performed. On September 29, 1884, he appeared at the Comedy Theatre, New York, in *Digby's Secretary,* adapted by him from Von Moser's *Der Bibliothekar.* The same night, Mr. A. M. Palmer brought out Mr. Charles Hawtrey's version of the same play, called *The Private Secretary* and a contest ensued. As Mr. Gillette had made the proper arrangements with the German playwright, while Mr. Hawtrey had not, a compromise resulted in his continuing his version, somewhat modified, under Mr. Palmer's management, under the title of *The Private Secretary.*

His first Civil War play, *Held by the Enemy,* was produced at the Criterion Theatre, Brooklyn on February 22, 1886, being the first successful play written upon the Civil War. It was afterwards produced at the Madison Square Theatre, New York City, in August, 1886. The play is laid in the South, and has as its main interest the love of a Southern girl for a Northern soldier. It was acted at the Princess Theatre, London, April 2, 1887. *A Legal Wreck,* a play dealing with the life in a sea coast town in New England, was first played at the Madison Square Theatre, New York, August 14, 1888. *All the Comforts of Home,* an amusing farce comedy, adapted from the German, was produced at the Boston Museum, March 3, 1890, and next came *Mr. Wilkinson's Widows,* a similar type of play, depicting the complications consequent upon a man marrying two women, supposedly on the same day. Its first New York production was at Proctor's Theatre, March 30, 1891. *Too Much Johnson,* his next important play, a clever farce, was first produced in Holyoke, Massachusetts, October 25, 1894, and was put on at the Standard Theatre, New York City, November 26, 1894.

For this play he borrowed from *La Plantation Thomasin,* by Maurice Ordonneau, the idea of the trip to a tropical island, but the main plot and the central characters were original. After a successful career in this country, Mr. Gillette appeared as "Augustus Billings" in this play in London, at the Garrick Theatre, April 18, 1898. In the meantime he had produced *Secret Service,* and a very successful farce comedy, *Because She Loved Him So,* from the French play, *Jalouse,* of Bisson and Leclerq, played first in New Haven, October 28, 1898. After a "tryout" at Wilkes-Barre and Buffalo, *Sherlock Holmes* was first put on in New York City at the Garrick Theatre, November 6, 1899, and after touring this country, Mr. Gillette began a long run in the title rôle at the Lyceum Theatre in London, on September 9, 1901. He next appeared in a one-act play, *The Painful Predicament of Sherlock Holmes,* on March 23, 1905, at the Metropolitan Opera House, New York City, and on September 13, 1905, at the Duke of York's Theatre in London, he played for the first time the character of "Dr. Carrington" in his comedy of *Clarice.* Returning to this country he toured in *Clarice* and then appeared at the Criterion Theatre, New York, October 19, 1908, in the character of "Maurice Brachard" in *Samson,* adapted by him from the French of Henri Bernstein. His last play, *Electricity,* produced first at the Park Theatre, Boston, September 26, 1910, was an attempt to make use of modern electrical devices in a farcical situation but was not successful. Other plays of Mr. Gillette of less significance are *She* (1887), *Settled Out of Court* (1892), *Ninety Days* (1893), *The Red Owl* (1907), *Ticey, or That Little Affair of Boyd's* (1908), *The Robber* (1909), *Among Thieves* (1909). Mr. Gillette has continued his career on the stage, taking part in the all-star revival of *Diplomacy* in 1914–15 and appearing in his own plays in 1915–16.

Secret Service was first performed at the Broad Street Theatre, Philadelphia, as *The Secret Service,* May 13, 1895. It was at first only moderately successful, but when it was put on at the Garrick Theatre, New York, October 5, 1896, Mr. Gillette appearing in the character of "Lewis Dumont" for the first time, it was a pronounced success. The play ran until March 6, 1897, when it was taken to Boston and afterward on tour. On May 15, 1897, Mr. Gillette made his first appearance on the London stage at the Adelphi Theatre in this play, at the beginning of a run which lasted till August 4. The play was acted by English companies afterward and a French version by Pierre Decourcelle was played at the Théâtre de la Renaissance in Paris on October 2, 1897. During the season of 1915–16 *Secret Service* was revived with Mr. Gillette in the part of "Lewis Dumont." The exact number of performances up to the present day is 1791.

In *Secret Service,* Mr. Gillette carried to its highest point the conception of a cool, resourceful man of action. This same character appears in serious situations in *Held by the Enemy* and *Sherlock Holmes,* and in farcical situations in *All the Comforts of Home* and *Too Much Johnson.* It is the unifying quality in

Mr. Gillette's work, and the form of realism which he has contributed to the stage in America is distinctly important and distinctly American.

Esmeralda, Held by the Enemy, Too Much Johnson, and *Secret Service* have been published by Samuel French and *All the Comforts of Home* by Dick and Fitzgerald. *Electricity* appeared in *The Drama,* for December, 1913, and will be reprinted shortly by Samuel French. *A Legal Wreck* has been published in novel form. For a lecture by Mr. Gillette "On the Illusion of the First Time in Acting" see the publications of the Dramatic Museum of Columbia University, Series 2, Vol. 1, New York, 1915.

For biographical details see *Who's Who in the Theatre* (1912), and for information concerning the plays, *Plays of the Present,* by J. B. Clapp and E. F. Edgett, New York, 1902, to which the present editor acknowledges his indebtedness, as also to the courtesy of Mr. Francis E. Reid, of the Empire Theatre. The editor, however, is indebted in the largest measure to Mr. Gillette himself who has furnished him accurate information concerning the dates and circumstances of production of the plays, much of which has hitherto been unavailable in print.

For criticism see Norman Hapgood, *The Stage in America,* 1901, Chap. 3, pp. 61–79.

The text has been revised with the greatest care by Mr. Gillette, and the alterations have been so marked that this edition of *Secret Service* may almost be looked upon as a new creation. It represents, so far as is possible in print, the actual stage production as Mr. Gillette directs it. For this reason, although its form is different from that of the other plays in the volume, the editor has reprinted the manuscript exactly as Mr. Gillette prepared it, feeling sure that readers of the book will be interested in seeing the interpretation of his own work by a dramatist who is also an actor and stage director.

For permission to use the text the editor is indebted to Mr. Gillette and to Samuel French.

Note to Sixth Edition.

In *The Dream Maker,* produced at the Empire Theatre, New York, November 21, 1921, Mr. Gillette created out of a short story by Howard E. Merton, a play whose leading character was that of Dr. Paul Clement, who to save the daughter of the woman he had loved, baffles a set of blackmailers in his own resourceful way. *Winnie and the Wolves,* based on short stories by Bertram Akey, was produced at the Lyric Theatre, Philadelphia, May 21, 1923. Mr. Gillette did not act in this play, which had as its heroine the daughter of a man who has been defrauded by certain people upon whom she becomes revenged.

William Gillette died April 29, 1937. His last appearance was in a revival of Austin Strong's *Three Wise Fools* in 1936.

AN EVENING IN RICHMOND DURING THE WAR OF THE REBELLION AT A TIME WHEN THE NORTHERN FORCES WERE ENTRENCHED BEFORE THE CITY AND ENDEAVORING BY ALL POSSIBLE MEANS TO BREAK DOWN THE DEFENSES AND CAPTURE THE CONFEDERATE CAPITAL.

* * *

ACT I	DRAWING-ROOM AT GEN. VARNEY'S HOUSE FRANKLIN STREET	EIGHT O'CLOCK
ACT II	THE SAME PLACE	NINE O'CLOCK
ACT III	TELEGRAPH OFFICE WAR DEPARTMENT	TEN O'CLOCK
ACT IV	DRAWING-ROOM AT THE VARNEY HOUSE AGAIN	ELEVEN O'CLOCK

* * *

WHILE NO SPECIAL EFFORT HAS BEEN MADE IN THE DIRECTION OF HISTORICAL ACCURACY THE MANAGEMENT TAKES THE LIBERTY OF REMINDING THE PUBLIC THAT THE CITY OF RICHMOND AT THE TIME SET FORTH IN "SECRET SERVICE" WAS IN A STATE OF THE UTMOST EXCITEMENT AND CONFUSION. WOUNDED AND DYING WERE BEING BROUGHT IN FROM THE DEFENSES BY THE CAR-LOAD. CHURCHES, LIBRARIES AND PUBLIC BUILDINGS WERE CONVERTED INTO HOSPITALS. OWING TO THE SCARCITY OF SURGEONS AND MEDICAL ATTENDANTS WOMEN AND EVEN YOUNG GIRLS ASSISTED AT THE DRESSING OF WOUNDS AND NURSED THE SUFFERERS DAY AND NIGHT. OTHER WOMEN WERE OCCUPIED SEWING COARSE AND HEAVY SAND BAGS FOR THE STRENGTHENING OF THE FORTIFICATIONS. STRICT MILITARY DISCIPLINE WAS IMPOSSIBLE. COURTS MARTIAL IF HELD AT ALL WERE COMPOSED OF ANY AVAILABLE MATERIAL, EVEN PRIVATE CITIZENS SERVING IF NECESSARY. TROOPS WERE BEING HURRIED IN FROM THE SOUTH AND NO CAREFUL SCRUTINY WAS ATTEMPTED. THIS MADE IT POSSIBLE FOR MANY NORTHERN SECRET SERVICE MEN TO ENTER THE CITY AND REMAIN THERE IN VARIOUS DISGUISES. IN THE MIDST OF THIS TROUBLE A BRAVE ATTEMPT AT GAYETY WAS KEPT UP—CHIEFLY BY THE YOUNG PEOPLE—IN A DESPERATE ENDEAVOR TO DISTRACT THEIR MINDS FROM THE TERRIBLE SITUATION. THERE WERE DANCES AND "STARVATION PARTIES" SO CALLED BECAUSE OF THE NECESSARILY LIMITED FARE PROVIDED, AND THE BOOMING OF THE GREAT SIEGE GUNS OFTEN SOUNDED ABOVE THE STRAINS OF A DREAMY WALTZ OR THE LIVELY BEAT OF A POLKA.

CAST OF CHARACTERS

Garrick Theatre, New York, October 5, 1896.

GENERAL NELSON RANDOLPH, commanding in Richmond..Mr. Joseph Brennan
MRS. GENERAL VARNEY, wife of a Confederate officer of high
rank ....Miss Ida Waterman
EDITH VARNEY, her daughter............................Miss Amy Busby
WILFRED VARNEY, her youngest son....................Mr. Walter Thomas
CAROLINE MITFORD, from across the street................Miss Odette Tyler
LEWIS DUMONT, United States Secret Service—known in Richmond
as Captain Thorne.............................Mr. William Gillette
HENRY DUMONT, United States Secret Service—LEWIS DUMONT'S
brother ....Mr. M. L. Alsop
MR. BENTON ARRELSFORD, Confederate Secret Service.....Mr. Campbell Gollan
MISS KITTRIDGE, sewing for the hospitals..............Miss Meta Brittain
MARTHA, negro house servant............................Miss Alice Leigh
JONAS, negro house servant..............................Mr. H. D. James
LIEUT. MAXWELL, President's detail..................Mr. Francis Neilson
LIEUT. FORAY, first operator military telegraph lines.....Mr. William B. Smith
LIEUT. ALLISON, second operator military telegraph lines....Mr. Louis Duval
LIEUT. TYREE, artillery
LIEUT. ENSING, artillery.
SERGEANT WILSON..Mr. I. N. Drew
SERGEANT ELLINGTON...................................Mr. Henry Wilton
CORPORAL MATSON......................................Mr. H. A. Morey
CAVALRY ORDERLY
ARTILLERY ORDERLY
HOSPITAL MESSENGER
FIRST WAR DEPT. MESSENGER
SECOND WAR DEPT. MESSENGER
THIRD WAR DEPT. MESSENGER
FOURTH WAR DEPT. MESSENGER
TELEGRAPH OFFICE MESSENGER A
TELEGRAPH OFFICE MESSENGER B
EDDINGER

SECRET SERVICE

ACT I

The SCENE *is a drawing-room in* GENERAL VARNEY'S *House on Franklin Street in Richmond.*

EIGHT O'CLOCK.

A richly furnished room.—Southern characteristics.

Fireplace on the left side. A wide door or arch up L. or L. C. set diagonally, open to a front hall. The portières on this door or arch draw, completely closing the opening. A stairway is seen through this door or arch, in the hall, at the back, ascending from a landing a few steps high back of the center of the opening, and rising off to the left. Entrance to the front hall—which communicates with other parts of the house, or via front door to the street, is off L. below stairs. Entrance to the dining-room and kitchen off R. below stairs. Both of these openings are back of the wide door or arch up L. C.[1] *A wide door up C. opens to a back parlor which is being used for women who come there to sew and work for hospitals. In elaborate production, when the doors are opened, these women are seen in the room at the back, seated at tables working. Two double French windows on the right side, one up stage set oblique, and one down, both opening to a wide veranda. There is shrubbery beyond the veranda and vines on the balustrade and the posts of the veranda—which must be in the line of sight for the whole house outside the upper of these two windows. Both these windows are "French," extending down to the floor, and opening and closing on hinges. They also have curtains or draperies which can easily be drawn to cover them. Below the window down R. a writing desk and a chair. Between these windows stand a pedestal and a vase of flowers to be knocked over by* THORNE *in* ACT IV. *A chair near the pedestal. A chair and a cabinet R. of C. door against wall. Table up C. or trifle L. of C., on which is a lamp and vase of flowers. Couch down R. C. Small table and two chairs L. C. Chair each side of the fireplace at the left. Hall seat in the hall. Pedestal and statue on the landing in the hall. Dark or nearly dark outside the windows R. with moonlight effect. The lights are on in the hall outside the door up left and in the room up center but are not glaring. The light in the room itself is full on but is shaded so that it gives a subdued effect. No fire is in the fireplace. The portières on both windows closed at the rise. Windows are closed at the rise.*

[*At the rise of the curtain low distant boom of cannonading rolls in the distance and quiets down—then is heard again.*]

[MISS KITTRIDGE, *one of the women who are sewing for the hospitals, enters C. D. and comes down C. a little. She stops, listens to the sound of cannon with some anxiety,—and crosses to the window up R. and looks out. Flashes on her face. She turns and goes down toward the table at the left. She gathers up the pieces of cloth and linen rags that are on the table. Looks toward the window again. Then she takes the cloth off at the door up C., closing it carefully after her.*]

[*Sound of a heavy door closing outside up Left.*]

[*Enter at the door up L. C. from L.* WILFRED VARNEY, *a boy of about sixteen—impetuous—Southern—black-eyed—dark hair. He is fairly well dressed, but in a suit that has evidently been worn for some time, and of a dark shade. He comes rapidly into the room, looking about. Goes to the door which he opens a little way and looks off. Closes it, goes to window up R. Throws open the portières and windows and looks anxiously off. Red flashes on backing. Distant boom and low thunder of cannon.*]

[*Enter* MARTHA, *an old negro servant, through the door at the foot of the stairs.* WILFRED, *turning, sees her, and crosses toward her.*]

[1] Entrances and exits marked "Up L. C. to L." and "Up L. C. to R." indicate to front hall, or to door to dining room and back of house, respectively; and "Up L. C. from L." and "Up L. C. from R." indicate coming from front hall or from dining room, respectively.

WILFRED. Where's Mother?

MARTHA. She's up staars with Mars Howard sah.

WILFRED. I've got to see 'er!

MARTHA. Mars Howard he's putty bad dis ebenin'—I dunno's she'd want to leave 'im—I'll go up an' see what she says.

[*Exit door up L. and up the stairway.*]

[WILFRED, *left alone, moves restlessly about, especially when low rumble of distant cannon is heard. Effect of passing artillery in the street outside.—On hearing it he hurries to the window and looks out, continuing to do so while the sounds of the passing guns, horses and men are heard. While he is at the window R.,* MRS. VARNEY *enters, coming down the stairway and on at door U. L. C. She is quiet, pale, with white or nearly white hair and a rather young face. Her dress is black and though rich, is plain. Not in the least "dressy" or fashionable.—In manner she is calm and self-possessed. She stops and looks at* WILFRED *a moment.—He turns and sees her.—*MARTHA *follows her down the stairway and exits door at foot of the stairway.*]

WILFRED. [*Goes toward* MRS. VARNEY.] Howard is n't worse is he?

MRS. VARNEY. [*Meeting* WILFRED *near* C.] I'm afraid so.

WILFRED. Anything I can do?

MRS. VARNEY. [*Shakes head*] No—no.—We can only wait—and hope. [WILFRED *walks away a little as if he could not quite say the thing on his mind*] I'm thankful there's a lull in the cannonading. Do they know why it stopped? [*Boom of cannon—a low distant rumble*]

WILFRED. [R. C.] It has n't stopped altogether—don't you hear?

MRS. VARNEY. [C.] Yes, but compared to what it was yesterday—you know it shook the house. Howard suffered dreadfully! [WILFRED *suddenly faces her*]

WILFRED. So did I, Mother! [*Slight pause*] [*Low boom of cannon*]

MRS. VARNEY. You!

WILFRED. When I hear those guns and know the fighting's on, it makes me——

MRS. VARNEY. [*Goes toward table* L. C. *Interrupting quickly*] Yes yes—we all suffered—we all suffered dear! [*Sits* R. *of table* L. C.]

WILFRED. Mother—you may not like it but you must listen—[*Going toward her*] —you must let me tell you how——

MRS. VARNEY. Wilfred! [*He stops speaking.—She takes his hand in hers tenderly.—A brief pause*] I know.

WILFRED. [*Low pleading voice*] But it's true Mother! I can't stay back here any longer! It's worse than being shot to pieces! I can't do it! [MRS. VARNEY *looks steadily into* WILFRED'S *face but says nothing. Soon she turns away a little as if she felt tears coming into her eyes*] Why don't you speak?

MRS. VARNEY. [*Turning to him. A faint attempt to smile*] I don't know what to say.

WILFRED. Say you won't mind if I go down there and help 'em!

MRS. VARNEY. It would n't be true!

WILFRED. I can't stay here!

MRS. VARNEY. You're so young!

WILFRED. No younger than Tom Kittridge—no younger than Ell Stuart—nor cousin Stephen—nor hundreds of the fellows fighting down there!— See Mother—they've called for all over eighteen—that was weeks ago! The seventeen call may be out any minute—the next one after that takes me! Do I want to stay back here till they *order* me out! I should think not! [*Walks about to* C. *Stops and speaks to* MRS. VARNEY] If I was hit with a shell an' *had* to stay it would be different! But I can't stand this—I can't do it Mother!

MRS. VARNEY. [*Rising and going to him*] I'll write to your Father.

WILFRED. Why that'll take forever! You don't know where his Division is—they change 'em every day! I can't wait for you to write.

MRS. VARNEY. [*Speaks finally*] I could n't let you go without his consent! You must be patient! [WILFRED *starts slowly across toward door* L. *with head lowered in disappointment,—but not ill-naturedly.* MRS. VARNEY *looks yearningly after him a moment as he moves away, then goes toward him*] Wilfred! [WILFRED *turns and meets her and she holds him and smooths his hair a little with her hand*] Don't feel bad that you have to stay here with your mother a little longer!

WILFRED. Aw—no——it is n't that!

MRS. VARNEY. Darling boy—I know it!

You want to fight for your country—and I'm proud of you! I want my sons to do their duty! But with your father commanding a brigade at the front and one boy lying wounded—perhaps mortally— [*Pause.*—MRS. VARNEY *turns and moves away a few steps toward* R.]

WILFRED. [*After pause—goes to her*] You will write to Father to-night—won't you?

MRS. VARNEY. Yes—yes! I'll write to him. [*Door bell is heard ringing in distant part of the house.*—WILFRED *and* MRS. VARNEY *both listen.*—MARTHA *enters up* L. C. *from* R. *and crosses outside door up* L. C. *on her way to the front door, going off up* L. *to* L.—*Heavy sound of door off up* L.—*In a moment she returns up* L. *from* L. *and stands in the wide doorway up* L. C.]

MARTHA. Hit's one o' de men fum de hossiple ma'am. [WILFRED *hurries to door up* L. *and exits to* L. *to see the messenger*]

MRS. VARNEY. We've just sent all the bandages we have Martha.

MARTHA. He says dey's all used up, an' two more trains juss come in crowded full o' wounded sojers—an' mos' all of 'em drefful bad!

MRS. VARNEY. Is Miss Kittridge here yet?

MARTHA. Yass'm, she's yeah.

MRS. VARNEY. Ask her if they've got enough to send. Even if it's only a little let them have it. What they need most is bandages.

MARTHA. [*Crossing toward door up* C.] Yaas'm. [*Exits door up* C.—MRS. VARNEY *goes toward the door up* L. C. *Stops near the door and speaks a word to* MESSENGER *who is waiting at front door outside to* L. *to attract his attention—then beckons him*]

MRS. VARNEY. Oh— [*Beckoning*] Come in please! [*She moves toward* C.—MESSENGER *appears at the door up* L. C. *from* L. *He is a crippled soldier in battered Confederate uniform. His left arm is in a sling*] What hospital did you come from?

MESSENGER. [*Remains up near door up* L. C.] The Winder ma'am.

MRS. VARNEY. Have you been to St. Paul's? You know the ladies are working there to-night.

MESSENGER. Yes—but they hain't a-workin' for the hospitals, ma'am—they're a-making of sandbags for the fortifications.

MRS. VARNEY. I do hope we can give you something.

MESSENGER. Yes ma'am. [MISS KITTRIDGE *enters at door up* C. *bringing a small bundle of lint, etc.*—MRS. VARNEY *moves down and soon seats herself on couch down* R. C.]

MISS KITTRIDGE. This is all there is now. [*She hands the package to the* MESSENGER] If you'll come back in an hour we'll have more. [MESSENGER *takes package and exits at door up* L. C. *to* L.—*Sound of heavy door closing outside up* L.] We're all going to stay to-night, Mrs. Varney. There's so many more wounded come in it won't do to stop now.

MRS. VARNEY. [*On couch*] No no—we must n't stop.

MISS KITTRIDGE. [*Near* C.] Is—is your son—is there any change?

MRS. VARNEY. I'm afraid the fever's increasing.

MISS KITTRIDGE. Has the Surgeon seen him this evening?

MRS. VARNEY. No—oh no! [*Shaking her head*] We could n't ask him to come twice—with so many waiting for him at the hospital.

MISS KITTRIDGE. But they could n't refuse *you* Mrs. Varney!—There's that man going right back to the hospital! I'll call him and send word that—[*Starting toward the door up* L.]

MRS. VARNEY. [*Rises*] No no—I can't let you!

[MISS KITTRIDGE *stops and turns to* MRS. VARNEY *in surprise*]

MISS KITTRIDGE. Not for—your own son?

MRS. VARNEY. Think how many own sons must be neglected to visit mine twice!

[*Sound of door outside up* L.—*Enter* EDITH VARNEY *at door up* L. C. *from* L.—*a light quick entrance—coming from outside—hat in hand as if taking it off as she comes in*]

MRS. VARNEY. [*Meeting* EDITH] Edith dear! How late you are! You must be tired to death!

EDITH. Oh no I'm not!—Besides, I have n't been at the hospital *all* day. Good-bye Miss Kittridge—I want to tell Mama something.

MISS KITTRIDGE. O dear! [*Turning up*] I'll get out of hearing right quick! [*Goes out at door up* C.]

EDITH. [*Up to door lightly and calling after* MISS KITTRIDGE] I hope you don't mind!

MISS KITTRIDGE. [*As she exits up* C.]

Mercy no—I should think not! [EDITH *closes the door and goes to* MRS. VARNEY *taking her down stage to chair* R. *of table* L. C.—MRS. VARNEY *sits in chair and* EDITH *on stool close to her on her* L., *in front of the table*]

EDITH. Mama—what do you think? What *do* you think?

MRS. VARNEY. What is it dear?

EDITH. I've been to see the President!

MRS. VARNEY. Mr. Davis!

EDITH. Um hm! [*Assent*] An' I asked him for an appointment for Captain Thorne on the War Department Telegraph Service—an' he gave it to me—a Special Commission Mama—appointing him to duty here in Richmond—a very important position—so now he won't have to be sent back to the front—an' it'll be doing his duty just the same!

MRS. VARNEY. But Edith—you don't——

EDITH. Yes it will, Mama! The President told me they needed a man who understood telegraphing and who was of high enough rank to take charge of the Service! And you know Cap'n Thorne is an expert! Since he's been here in Richmond he's helped 'em in the telegraph office over an' over again—Lieutenant Foray told me so! [MRS. VARNEY *slowly rises and moves away toward* C.—*After a slight pause*] Now Mama, you're going to scold an' behave dreadfully—an' you must n't—because it's all fixed—an' there's no trouble—an' the commission 'll be sent over here in a few minutes—just as soon as it can be made out! An' the next time he comes I'm to hand it to him myself! [*Turns* L. *and moves away a little beyond the table* L. C.]

MRS. VARNEY. [*Moves back toward table* L. C.] He's coming this evening.

EDITH. [*Turns quickly at down* L. *and looks at* MRS. VARNEY *an instant before speaking—then in low voice*] How do you know?

MRS. VARNEY. [*Moving toward table* L. C.] This note came half an hour ago. [*Reaching toward the note to get it for* EDITH.—EDITH *however sees the note instantly, and impulsively snatches it and goes toward* R. *with it*]

EDITH. Has it been here—all this time? [*Takes note from the already opened envelope as she pauses near* C. *and eagerly glances at it*]

MRS. VARNEY. [*After a moment*] You see what he says—this 'll be his last call.—He's got his orders to leave. [*Sits* R. *of table* L. C.]

EDITH. [*Sitting on couch* R. C.] Why it's too ridiculous! Just as if the Commission from the President would n't supersede everything! It puts him at the head of the Telegraph Service! He'll be in the command of the Department!—He says—[*Glancing at note*] "good-by call" does he! All the better—it'll be that much more of a surprise. [*Rising and going toward* MRS. VARNEY] Now Mama, don't you breathe—I want to tell him myself!

MRS. VARNEY. But Edith dear—I don't quite approve of your going to the President about this.

EDITH. [*Changing from light manner to earnestness*] But listen, Mama—I could n't go to the War Department people—Mr. Arrelsford's there in one of the offices—and ever since I refused him you know how he's treated me!—[*Slight deprecatory motion from* MISS VARNEY] If I'd applied for the appointment there he'd have had it refused—and he'd have got them to order Cap'n Thorne away right off—I know he would—and—[*Stands motionless as she thinks of it*] That's where his orders to go came from!

MRS. VARNEY. But my dear——

EDITH. It is, Mama! [*Slight pause*] Is n't it lucky I got that commission today! [*Emphasis on "Is n't."—Crossing down* R.—*at* R. C. *near lounge*] [*Door bell rings in distant part of the house.*—JONAS *appears above door up* L. C. *from* R. *and goes off* L. *to front door.*—MRS. VARNEY *moves up stage a little waiting to see who it is.*—EDITH *listening.*—*Heavy sound of door closing outside up* L.—JONAS *enters at the door up* L. C. *from* L.]

JONAS. [*Coming down* R. *of* MRS. VARNEY] It's a officer, ma'am. He says he's fum de President—an'—[*Hands a card to* MRS. VARNEY] he's got ter see Miss Edith pussonully.

EDITH. [*Going up* C. *a little.*—*Low voice*] It's come, Mama!

MRS. VARNEY. [*Rises and goes up* C.] Ask the gentleman in. [JONAS *exits at door up* L. C. *to* L.—MRS. VARNEY *gives* EDITH *the card*]

EDITH. [*After a glance at the card*] Oh yes!

MRS. VARNEY. [*Low voice*] Do you know who it is?

EDITH. [*Low voice*] No! But he 's from the President so it must be the Commission!

[*Enter* JONAS *at door up* L. C. *from* L. *He comes on a little way, bowing someone in*]

[*Enter* LIEUT. MAXWELL *at door up* L. C. *from* L.—*He is a very dashing young officer, handsome, polite and dressed in a showy and perfectly fitting uniform.*—JONAS *exits at door up* L. C. *to* R.—MRS. VARNEY *advances a little*]

LIEUT. MAXWELL. Good evening. [*Bowing*] [MRS. VARNEY *bows slightly.*—*To* MRS. VARNEY] Have I the honah of addressing Miss Varney?

MRS. VARNEY. [C.] I am Mrs. Varney, sir. [*Emphasizing "Mrs." a little*]

LIEUT. MAXWELL. [L. C.—*Bowing to* MRS. VARNEY] Madam—I 'm very much afraid this looks like an intrusion on my part, but I come from the President and he desires me to see Miss Varney personally!

MRS. VARNEY. [*Inclining her head graciously*] Anyone from the President could not be otherwise than welcome.—This is my daughter. [*Indicating* EDITH *who is* R. C.]

(LIEUT. MAXWELL *bows to* EDITH *and she returns the salutation. He then walks across to her, taking a large brown envelope from his belt*]

LIEUT. MAXWELL. Miss Varney, the President directed me to deliver this into your hands—with his compliments. [*Handing the envelope to* EDITH] He is glad to be able to do this not only at your request, but as a special favor to your father, General Varney.

EDITH. [*Taking envelope*] Oh thank you!

MRS. VARNEY. Won't you be seated, Lieutenant?

EDITH. [*In front*] O yes—do! [*Holds envelope pressed very tight against her side*]

LIEUT. MAXWELL. Nothing would please me so much I assure you—but I 'm compelled to be back at the President's house right away—I 'm on duty this evening.—Would you mind writing me off a line or two Miss Varney—just to say you have the communication?

EDITH. Why certainly!—[*Takes a step or two toward desk at right*] You want a receipt—I—[*Stops hesitating—then turns and crosses toward door up* L.] I 'll go upstairs to my desk—it won't take a minute! [*Turns at door*] And—could I put in how much I thank the President for his kindness?

LIEUT. MAXWELL. [C.] I 'm very sure he 'd be more than pleased! [EDITH *exits at door up* L. C. *and hastens up the stairway*]

MRS. VARNEY. [*Moving forward slowly*] We have n't heard so much cannonading to-day, Lieutenant. Do they know what it means?

LIEUT. MAXWELL. [*Going forward with* MRS. VARNEY] I don't think they 're quite positive ma'am, but they can't help lookin' for a violent attack to follow.

MRS. VARNEY. I don't see why it should quiet down before an assault!

LIEUT. MAXWELL. [*Near* C.] It might be some signal, ma'am, or it might be they 're moving their batteries to open on a special point. They 're tryin' ev'ry way to break through our defenses—ev'ry way they know!

[*Door bell rings in distant part of house*]

MRS. VARNEY. It 's very discouraging! [*Seats herself* R. *of table* L. C.] We can't seem to drive them back this time!

LIEUT. MAXWELL. No ma'am, but we 're holding 'em where they are! They 're no nearer now than they were six weeks ago, an' they 'll never get in unless they do it by some scurvy trick—that 's where the danger lies! [*Heavy sound of door outside up* L.]

[*Enter* EDITH *coming lightly and quickly down the stairway up* L.]

EDITH. [*Entering at door up* L. C. *from stairway, with a note in her hand, and without the official envelope, which she has left in her room*] Is Lieutenant Maxwell—[*Seeing him down stage with* MRS. VARNEY *and going across toward him*] O yes!

[LIEUT. MAXWELL *moves up* R. C. *meeting* EDITH]

[JONAS *enters at door up* L. C. *from* L. *as* EDITH *reaches* C., *showing in* CAPTAIN THORNE]

JONAS. [*As he enters and stands back for* THORNE *to pass*] Will you jess kinely step dis way suh!

[MRS. VARNEY *rises and moves down in front of and then up* L. *of table.*—MAXWELL *meets* EDITH *up* R. C.]

EDITH. [*Meeting* MAXWELL *up* R. C.] I did n't know but you—[*She stops—hearing* JONAS *up* L.—*and quickly turns, looking off* L.] Oh!—Captain Thorne!

[*Enter* CAPTAIN THORNE *at door up* L. C. *from* L., *meeting and shaking hands with* EDITH *up* L. C.—THORNE *wears the uniform of a Confederate Captain of Artillery. It is somewhat worn and soiled.* LIEUT. MAXWELL *turned and moved up a little on* EDITH'S *entrance, remaining a little* R. *of* C.—JONAS *exits door up* L. C. *to* R.]

EDITH. [*Up* L. C.—*Giving* THORNE *her hand briefly*] We were expecting you!—Here 's Captain Thorne, mama!

[MRS. VARNEY *moves up* L. C. *meeting* THORNE *and shaking hands with him graciously.*—EDITH *turns away and goes to* LIEUT. MAXWELL *up* R. C.—THORNE *and* MRS. VARNEY *move up* C. *near small table and converse*]

EDITH. [R. C.] I was n't so very long writing it, was I Lieutenant? [*She hands* LIEUT. MAXWELL *the note*]

LIEUT. MAXWELL. [R. C.] I 've never seen a quicker piece of work, Miss Varney. [*Putting the note in belt or pocket*] When you want a clerkship ovah at the Government offices you must shorely let me know!

EDITH. [*Smilingly*] You 'd better not commit yourself—I might take you at your word!

LIEUT. MAXWELL. Nothing would please me so much I 'm sure! All you 've got to do is just to apply!

EDITH. Lots of the girls are doing it—they have to, to live! Are n't there a good many where you are?

LIEUT. MAXWELL. Well we don't have so many as they do over at the Treasury. I believe there are more ladies there than men!

MRS. VARNEY. [*Comes down a little*] Perhaps you gentlemen have met!—[*Glancing toward* LIEUT. MAXWELL *and back to* THORNE]

[THORNE *shakes head a little and takes a step forward* L. C. *facing* MAXWELL]

MRS. VARNEY. [*Introducing*] Cap'n Thorne—Lieutenant Maxwell.

THORNE. [*Slight inclination of head*] Lieutenant.

LIEUT. MAXWELL. [*Returning bow pleasantly*] I have n't had that pleasure—though I 've heard the Cap'n's name mentioned several times!

THORNE. Yes? [MRS. VARNEY *and* EDITH *are looking at* MAXWELL]

LIEUT. MAXWELL. [*As if it were rather amusing*] In fact, Cap'n, there 's a gentleman in one of our offices who seems mighty anxious to pick a fight with you!

[EDITH *is suddenly serious and a look of apprehension spreads over* MRS. VARNEY'S *face*]

THORNE. [*Easily*] Pick a fight! Really! Why what office is that, Lieutenant?

LIEUT. MAXWELL. [*Slightly annoyed*] The War Office, sir!

THORNE. Oh dear! I did n't suppose you had anybody in the *War* Office who wanted to fight!

LIEUT. MAXWELL. [*Almost angry*] An' why not, sir?

THORNE. [*Easily*] Well he 'd hardly be in an office would he—at a time like this?

LIEUT. MAXWELL. [*Trying to be light again*] I 'd better not tell him that, Cap'n—he 'd certainly insist on havin' you out!

THORNE. [*Moving down* L. C. *with* MRS. VARNEY] That would be too bad—to interfere with the gentleman's office hours! [THORNE *and* MRS. VARNEY *move down* L. C. *near table—in conversation*]

LIEUT. MAXWELL. [*To* EDITH] He does n't believe it Miss Varney,—but it 's certainly true, an' I dare say you know who the——

EDITH. [*Quickly interrupting* MAXWELL—*low voice*] Please don't Lieutenant!—I—[*An apprehensive glance toward* THORNE] I 'd rather not—[*With a slight catch of breath*]—talk about it!

LIEUT. MAXWELL. [*After short pause of surprise*] Yes, of course!—I did n't know there was any——

EDITH. [*Interrupting again, with attempt to turn it off*] Yes! [*A rather nervous effort to laugh lightly*]—You know there 's always the weather to fall back on!

LIEUT. MAXWELL. [*Picking it up easily*] Yes—an' mighty bad weather too—most of the time!

EDITH. [*Laughingly*] Yes—is n't it! [*They laugh a little and go on talking and laughing to themselves, moving toward* R. *upper window for a moment and soon move across toward door up* L. *as if* MAXWELL *were going*]

MRS. VARNEY. [*Back of table* L. C., R. *of* THORNE] From your note Captain

Thorne, I suppose you're leaving us soon. Your orders have come.

THORNE. [*Back of table* L.C.—L. *of* MRS. VARNEY] Yes—Mrs. Varney, they have. —I'm very much afraid this'll be my last call.

MRS. VARNEY. Is n't it rather sudden? It seems to me they ought to give you a little time.

THORNE. [*Slight smile*] We have to be ready for anything you know!

MRS. VARNEY. [*With a sigh*] Yes—I know!—It's been a great pleasure to have you drop in on us while you were here. We shall quite miss your visits.

THORNE. [*A slight formality in manner*] Thank you Mrs. Varney—I shall never forget what they've been to me.

[MAXWELL *is taking leave of* EDITH *up* C.]

EDITH. [*Up* C.] Lieutenant Maxwell is going, Mama!

MRS. VARNEY. So soon! Excuse me a moment, Captain! [*Goes hurriedly toward* MAXWELL.—THORNE *goes down* L. *of table* L.C. *near mantel*] I'm right sorry to have you hurry away, Lieutenant. We shall hope for the pleasure of seeing you again. [R. *of* MAXWELL]

LIEUT. MAXWELL. I shall certainly call, Mrs. Varney—if you'll allow me.—[*Crosses toward door*]—Cap'n! [*Saluting* THORNE *from near door up* L.]

THORNE. [*Turning from mantel. Half salute*] Lieutenant!

MAXWELL. Miss Varney! Mrs. Varney! [*Bowing to each. Exits door up* L. C. *to* L.—MRS. VARNEY *follows* MAXWELL *off at door up* L. C. *to* L. *speaking as she goes*]

MRS. VARNEY. [*As she goes off with* MAXWELL] Now remember Lieutenant, you're to come sometime when duty does n't call you away so soon!

[EDITH *turns and moves slowly to table up* C. *on* MAXWELL'S *exit*]

LIEUT. MAXWELL. [*Outside.—Voice getting more distant*] Trust me to attend to that, Mrs. Varney!

[*Sound of heavy door closing off up* L.]

THORNE. [*Moving toward* EDITH *who is up* C. *at small table*] Shall I see Mrs. Varney again?

EDITH. [*Getting a rose from vase on table up* C.] Oh yes—you'll see her again!

THORNE. [*At the little table up* L. C. *near* EDITH—*on her left*] I have n't long to stay.

EDITH. Oh—not long!

THORNE. No—I'm sorry to say.

EDITH. [*Moving slowly down* L. C.] Well —do you know—I think you have more time than you really think you have! It would be odd if it turned out that way—would n't it? [*Playing with the flower in her hand*]

THORNE. [*Who moves down* L. C *as* EDITH *does*] Yes—but it won't turn out that way.

EDITH. Yes—but you—[*She stops as* THORNE *is taking the rose from her hand —which she was holding up in an absent way as she talked.*—THORNE *at the same time holds the hand she had it in. She lets go of the rose and draws away her hand*]

[*Slight pause*]

EDITH. [*A little embarrassed*] You know —you can sit down if you want to! [*Indicating chair at* L. *of table*]

THORNE. [*Smiles a little*] Yes—I see. [*He has the rose*]

EDITH. [*Sits* R. *of table* L. C.] You'd better!—I have a great many things to say!

THORNE. Oh—you have!

EDITH. [*Nodding.—Her left hand is on the table*] Yes.

THORNE. I have only one.

EDITH. [*Looking up at him*] And—that is——?

THORNE. [*Leaning toward her over table, and covering her hand with his*] Good-bye.

EDITH. But I don't really think you'll have to say it!

THORNE. [*Earnestly—looking down into her eyes*] I know I will!

EDITH. [*Low voice—more serious*] Then it'll be because you want to!

THORNE. [*Quickly*] Oh no! It will be —because I must.

EDITH. [*Rising slowly and looking at him a little mischievously as she does so*] Oh—because you must! [THORNE *nods a little—saying "yes" with his lips.*—EDITH *walks toward* C. *thinking how to tell him.—He watches her.—She suddenly turns back and goes again to table* L. C.] You don't know some things I do! [*She sits in chair* R. *of table*]

THORNE. [*Laughing a little first*] I think that's more than likely Miss Varney! [*Moves to* L. *of table and seats himself in chair facing* EDITH] Would you mind telling me a few so I can somewhat approach you in that respect?

EDITH. [*Seriously*] I would n't mind

telling you one, and that is, it 's very wrong for you to think of leaving Richmond yet!

THORNE. Ah—but you don't——

EDITH. [*Breaking quickly in*] Oh yes I do!

THORNE. [*Looking up at her amused*] Well—what?

EDITH. Whatever you were going to say! Most likely it was that there 's something or other I don't know about!—But I know this—[*Looking away front—eyes lowered a little*] you were sent here only a few weeks ago to recover from a very bad wound—[THORNE *looks down and a little front quickly*]—and you have n't nearly had time for it yet!

THORNE. [*As if amused*] Ha ha—yes. [*Looking up at* EDITH *with usual expression*] I do look as if the next gentle breeze would blow me away, don't I?

EDITH. [*Turning to him earnestly—half rising*] No matter how you look, you ought not—Oh—[*Rising fully and turning away from him*] You 're just making fun of it like you always do! [*Goes up* C. *a little.—Turns to* THORNE *again a little up* C.] No matter! You can make all the fun you like, but the whole thing is settled and you are n't going away at all!

[THORNE *has risen with* EDITH *and stands near table* L. C. *watching her smilingly—his hat in left hand*]

THORNE. Oh—I 'm *not!*

EDITH. No—you 're *not!* Does n't that surprise you?

THORNE. Well rather! [*Puts hat on table and moves up near* EDITH *going back of table*] Now you 've gone into the prophesying business perhaps you would n't mind telling me what I am going to do?

EDITH. [*Up* C. *a little. Turning to him*] I would n't mind at all—an' it 's this—you see I 've been to the—[*Hesitates*] Now! I 'm almost afraid to tell you!

THORNE. [*Near* EDITH*—left of her*] Don't tell me Miss Varney—because it 's true that my orders have come—I 'm leaving tonight.

[EDITH *looks at* THORNE *an instant—then turns and goes* R. C. *and sits on couch. Turns and looks at him from there*]

EDITH. [*After looking at* THORNE *an instant*] Where—to the front?

THORNE. [*Moving easily across to the couch where* EDITH *sits*] Well—[*Little laugh*] you see we—[*Sits on couch* R. C. *near* EDITH] we can't always tell where orders will take us Miss Varney.

EDITH. But listen! Supposing there were other orders—from a higher authority—appointing you to duty here?

THORNE. [*Eyes lowered before him*] It would n't make any difference.

EDITH. [*Sudden alarm*] You don't—you don't mean you 'd go—in spite of them? [THORNE *raises his eyes to hers in slight surprise and looks at her an instant. Then he nods affirmatively*] But if it proved your first order was a mistake—and—[*In her earnestness she makes a little motion with her left hand within his reach*]

THORNE. [*Catching her hand and holding it close in both of his*] My first order is n't a mistake Miss Varney.—I—I don't suppose I shall ever see you—[*He stops suddenly—then rises quickly and moves up* R. C. *a little, standing faced up toward window*]

[*After watching* THORNE *until he is motionless* EDITH *rises and crosses up* C. *to* L. *of him*]

EDITH. [*Up* C.*—With a new apprehension*] Is it—is it something dangerous?

THORNE. [*Turning to* EDITH *and speaking lightly*] Well I hope so—enough to make it interesting!

EDITH. [*Low voice*] Don't be angry if I ask you again about your orders—I—Oh I must know!

THORNE. Why?

EDITH. Tell me!—Please tell me!

THORNE. I can't do that Miss Varney.

EDITH. You need n't! I know! [THORNE *very slight apprehensive glance to down* L. *but instantly back to her*] They 're sending you on some mission where death is almost certain! They 'll sacrifice your life because they know you are fearless and will do *anything!* There 's a chance for you to stay here in Richmond and be just as much use—and I 'm going to ask you to do this! It is n't *your* life alone—there are other lives to think of—that 's why I ask you!—It may not sound well—but—you see——

THORNE. [*Catching her hands passionately*] Ah my dear one—my dear—my darling—how can I——[*Suddenly stops. Recovers control of himself*] No! [*Head turned slightly away*] You shan't have this against me too!

EDITH. Oh no! No! I could never have

anything against you!—What do you mean?

THORNE. [*Holding her hands close*] I mean that I must go—my business is elsewhere—I ought never to have seen you or spoken to you—but I had to come to this house—and you were here—and now it's only you in the—[*Stops. Releases her hands. Turns blindly* R. *Then turns* L. *starting toward door up* L. C.] Your mother—I'll say good-bye to her!

EDITH. [*Stepping quickly in his way*] No!—You must listen! [THORNE *stops before her near* C.] They need you here in Richmond more than anywhere else—the President told me so himself!—Your orders are to stay! You are given a Special Commission on the War Department Telegraph service, and you——

THORNE. [*Quickly, decisively, but in subdued voice*] No no! I won't take it! I could n't take it Miss Varney!

EDITH. You'll do that much for me!

THORNE. [*Seizing her hands again*] It's for you that I'll do nothing of the kind! If you ever think of me again remember that I refused it!

EDITH. [*Breaking into* THORNE'S *last few words*] You can't refuse! It's the President's request—it's his order! [*Breaking away from him and going toward door up* L. C.] Please wait a minute! I left it upstairs and you'll see for yourself that——

THORNE. Don't get it Miss Varney! [*Following her*] I won't look at it!

EDITH. [*Stops and turns*] But I want you to see what it is! It puts you at the head of everything! You have entire control! When you see it I know you'll accept! Please wait! [EDITH *exits at door up* L. C. *and runs lightly up the stairway*]

THORNE. [*Following her up toward stairway*] Miss Varney—I can't——

EDITH. [*As she goes*] Oh yes you can!

[THORNE *stands looking up the stairway after* EDITH *for an instant. Then turns and hurries down to the table at* L. C. *and seizing his hat and the rose starts rapidly up towards door up* L. C. *as if to go.—As* THORNE *starts down for hat sound of heavy door closing outside up* L.]

[*Enter at door up* L. C. *from* L. CAROLINE MITFORD, *skipping in lightly, and crossing in front of* THORNE—*who has stepped up out of the way.—She is breathless from having run across the street.—Her dress is made of her great grandmother's wedding gown—as light and pretty as possible—with a touch of the old-fashioned in cut and pattern. She is very young and charming*]

CAROLINE. [*Comes quickly on to* C. *Stops abruptly*] Oh!—Cap'n Thorne!

THORNE. [*Saluting mechanically*] Miss Mitford! [*Turns and looks up the stairway again*]

CAROLINE. [*Saluting*] Yes of co'se—I forgot!—How lucky this is! You're just the very person I wanted to see! [*Going toward couch at* R. C.] I'll tell you all about it in just a minute! Goodness me! [*Sits on couch*] I'm all out o' breath—just runnin' ovah from our house! [*Devotes herself to breathing for a moment*]

THORNE. [*Going quickly down to* CAROLINE *at* R. C.] Miss Mitford—would you do something for me!

CAROLINE. Why of co'se I would!

THORNE. [*Rapidly*] Thank you very much!—Tell Miss Varney when she comes down—Just say good-night for me and tell her I've gone!

CAROLINE. [*Pretending astonishment*] Why I would n't do such a thing for the wide wide world! It would be a wicked dreadful lie—because you *won't* be gone!

THORNE. Well I'm sorry you look at it that way.—Good-night Miss Mitford! [*Turns to go*]

CAROLINE. [*Jumping to her feet and running round on his left between him and the door*] No no!—You don't seem to understand! I've got something to say to you!

THORNE. [*Hurriedly*] Yes—I understand that all right—but some other time! [*Trying to pass* CAROLINE]

CAROLINE. [*Detaining him*] No no no!—Wait! [THORNE *stops*] There is n't any other time! It's to-night!—We're going to have a Starvation Party!

THORNE. Good heavens—another of those things!

CAROLINE. Yes we are! It's goin' to be ovah at mah house this time! Now we'll expect you in half an hour. [*Her finger up to emphasize the time*]

THORNE. Thank you very much Miss Mitford, but I can't come! [*Indicating off* L.] I've got to be—

CAROLINE. [*Interrupting*] N—n—n—[*Until she quiets him*] Now that wouldn't do at all! You went to Mamie Jones's! Would you treat me like that?

THORNE. Mamie Jones—that was last week Thursday—[CAROLINE *trying to stop him with "now now—now!" etc.*] and her mother—[CAROLINE *louder with "now—now!"*—THORNE *raises his voice above the din*] Her mother——

[*As* CAROLINE *is still going on he gives it up and turns front in despair*]

CAROLINE. [*When quiet has come.—Very distinctly*] Now there isn't any use o' talkin'!

THORNE. Yes I see that!

CAROLINE. Didn't you promise to obey when I gave orders? Well these are orders!

THORNE. [*Turning to her for a last attempt*] Yes, but this time——

CAROLINE. This time is just the same as all the other times only *worse!* [*Turns away and goes to back of table* L. C. *and picks up something from table*]

[THORNE *turns and goes a little way toward up* R. C. *as if discouraged*]

CAROLINE. [*Without turning*] Besides that, she expects it.

[THORNE *turns and looks across at* CAROLINE]

THORNE. What did you say?

CAROLINE. [*At table* L. C.—*Smelling a flower daintily. Facing front*] I say she expects it—that's all!

THORNE. Who do you mean? [*Moves toward her to* C. *enquiringly*]

CAROLINE. [*Turns and looks at him*] Who?

THORNE. [*Assent*] Um hm!

CAROLINE. [*Innocently*] Who expects you?

THORNE. [*Assent again*] Ah ha!

CAROLINE. Why Edith of co'se! Who did you s'pose I was talkin' about all this time?

THORNE. You mean—you mean she expects me to—[*Slight motion of hand toward door up* L. C.]

CAROLINE. Why of co'se she does!—Just to take her ovah that's all!—Goodness me—you needn't *stay* if you don't want to! Now I'll go an' tell her you're waiting—that's what I'll do! [*Starts up toward door up* L. C.—*Stops and turns*] You won't go now? [*Emphasize "go"*]

THORNE. [*Hesitating*] Well—e—I—I—— If she expects it Miss Mitford [*Moving up toward* CAROLINE] I'll wait an' take her over—but I can't stay at your party a minute!

CAROLINE. I *thought* you'd come to your senses some time or other!—You don't seem to quite realize what you've got to do!—See here, Mr. Captain—[*Taking hold of the left sleeve of his coat and bringing him down* C. *a little way*] Was she most ready?

THORNE. Well—e—how do I—how—

CAROLINE. What dress did she have on?

THORNE. Dress?—Why I hardly——

CAROLINE. Oh you *men!* Why she's only got two!

THORNE. [*Relieved*] Yes—well then very likely this was one of them, Miss Mitford!

CAROLINE. [*Starting up toward door up* L. C.] Oh, no mattah—I'm going up anyhow! [THORNE *moves up* C. *as* CAROLINE *goes up* L. C.—CAROLINE *stops up* L. C. *near door and turns back to* THORNE] Cap'n Thorne—you can wait out there on the veranda! [*Pointing to window up* R.]

THORNE. [*Glances where she points—then to her*] Yes of course—but if I wait right here I can see her when she——

CAROLINE. [*Majestically*] Those are orders! [THORNE *looks at her an instant—then salutes and wheels about making complete military turn to* R. *and marches toward the window at up* R.—CAROLINE *is watching him admiringly. Speaks as* THORNE *reaches up* R. C.] It's cooler outside you know!

THORNE. [*Turning to her at up* R. C. *and standing in stiff military attitude*] Pardon me Miss Mitford—orders never have to be explained!

CAROLINE. That's right!—I take back the explanation! [*Taking one step to her* R. *as she gives an odd little salute*]

THORNE. [*With deferential salute in slight imitation of hers—but with step to his left*] That's right Miss Mitford—take it back! [*Turns and is reaching to pull aside curtains of window up* R. *with right hand*]

CAROLINE. And—oh yes—Cap'n!

[THORNE *turns to her again questioningly—right hand still holding curtain behind him*]

CAROLINE. [*A peremptory order*] Smoke!

[*For an instant* THORNE *does not understand. Then he sees it and relapses at once into easy manner, stepping forward a little and feeling with right hand in breast of coat front for cigar—turning somewhat to front*]

THORNE. [*As above*] Oh—ha ha—[*Smiling*] you mean one of those Nashville sto—

CAROLINE. Silence sir! [THORNE *looks at her quickly*] Orders never have to be explained!

THORNE. [*With salute*] Right again Miss Mitford—orders never have to be explained! [*Salutes, turns and goes off at window up* R.]

CAROLINE. [*Looks admiringly after* THORNE] He's splendid! If Wilfred was only like that! [*Moves down* C. *slowly, thinking it over*] But then—our engagement's broken off anyhow so what's the diff!—Only—if he was like that I'd—no! I don't think I would either! [*Shakes her head*] No!—Still —I must say it would make a heap of difference! An' then if he was like that——[*In same tone—seeing* MRS. VARNEY *close to her*] Why how dy do!

[MRS. VARNEY *has entered on earlier cue, at door up* L. C. *from* L., *and noticing* CAROLINE *has come down to her on her left*]

MRS. VARNEY. Why Caroline dear, what are you talking about all to yourself?

CAROLINE. [*Confused*] Oh—just—I was just saying you know—that—why I don't know—I don't really know what I was goin' to—e—Do you think it's goin' to rain?

MRS. VARNEY. Dear me, child—I have n't thought about it!—Why what have you got on? Is that a new dress?

CAROLINE. New *dress!* Well I should think it was—I mean *is!* These are my great grandmother's mother's weddin' clothes! Are n't they just the most beaufleist you ever saw! Just in the nick of time too! I was on my very last rags, an' I did n't know what to do—an' Mama gave me a key and told me to look in an old horsehair trunk in the attic—an' I did—and these were in it! [*Takes a dance step or two, holding skirt out*] Just in time for the Starvation party to-night! Ran ovah to show it to Edith—where is she?

MRS. VARNEY. She won't be over to-night, I'm afraid. [*Crosses to* R. C.]

CAROLINE. [C.] Oh yes she will!

MRS. VARNEY. But I've just come down dear!

CAROLINE. Yes but I'm just going *up* dear! [*Turns and runs off at door up* L. C. *and up the stairway, disappearing at the upper landing.*—MRS. VARNEY *alone a moment. After a little she moves forward in thought. Then turns to desk* R. *and prepares to write a letter. Suddenly* CAROLINE *races down the stairs again and runs lightly on at door up* L. C.—MRS. VARNEY *looks up surprised.*—CAROLINE *hurries across toward window up* R. *as if going out*] You see Caroline, it was no use!

CAROLINE. [*Turning*] No *use!* [*Comes down in front of couch near* MRS. VARNEY]

MRS. VARNEY. [*At desk* R.] Why you don't mean—in this short time——

CAROLINE. Goodness me! I did n't stop to argue with her—I just *told* her!

MRS. VARNEY. Told her what, child!

CAROLINE. Why—that Cap'n Thorne was waitin' for her out yere on the v'randah!

MRS. VARNEY. But she is n't going is she?

CAROLINE. Well, I would n't like to say for sure—[*Moving nearer* MRS. VARNEY *and in lower voice*] but you just watch which dress she has on when she comes down! Now I'll go out there an' tell him she'll be down in a minute—then the whole thing's finished up all round! [*Turns* L. *and goes around couch and up toward window up* R. *speaking as she goes*] I have more work getting people fixed up so they can come to my party than it would take to run a blockade into Savannah every fifteen minutes! [*She runs lightly off at window up* R.]

[MRS. VARNEY *looks after* CAROLINE *with a smile and then taking some paper and envelopes in her hand, rises and moves as if to go to door up* L.—*Enter* WILFRED *at door up* L. C. *from* L. *coming in as though he wished to avoid being seen, and looking off up the stairway as he enters. He carries a large bundle stuffed loosely under his coat, which is done up in a paper. He turns quickly seeing* MRS. VARNEY *and makes a very slight movement as if to better conceal the package he carries. Stands looking at her*]

MRS. VARNEY. What have you got there Wilfred?

WILFRED. Here?

MRS. VARNEY. Yes—under your coat.

WILFRED. Oh—this! [*Tapping the place where his coat protrudes*] Why it's only a—that is, it's one of the—e—Have you written that letter yet?

MRS. VARNEY. No dear, I've been too busy. But I'm going to do it right now.

[MRS. VARNEY *goes across to door up* L. C.—*Near the door she glances round a little anxiously at* WILFRED.—WILFRED *is looking at her.*—*Then she turns and exits at door up* L. C. *and goes up the stairway*]

[WILFRED *turns away after she has gone. Glances round room. Goes to table down* L. C. *and begins to undo the package cautiously. He has hardly more than loosened the paper when* CAROLINE *appears at window up* R.]

CAROLINE. [*Speaking off at window up* R.] Those are orders Cap'n—an' orders never have to be explained!

[WILFRED *hurriedly stuffs the loosened bundle inside his coat again*]

THORNE. [*Outside the window up* R.] Right you are Miss Mitford! I'll see that they're carried out!

[CAROLINE *enters through window up* R. *closing it after her, but does not close the portières.*—WILFRED *is about to start toward down* L.—CAROLINE *turning from window* R. *sees* WILFRED.—*Both stand an instant*]

CAROLINE. [*After the pause*] Good evening Mr. Varney! [*Emphasize "Mr. Varney"*]

WILFRED. [*Coldly*] Good evening Miss Mitford! [*Emphasize "Miss Mitford"*] [*Both now start rapidly toward door up* L. C., *but as it brings them toward each other they stop simultaneously up* L. *in order to avoid meeting in the doorway*]

CAROLINE. Excuse me—I'm in a *great* hurry!

WILFRED. That's plain enough! [*Looks at her*] Another party I reckon! [*"Party" with contemptuous emphasis*]

CAROLINE. You reckon perfectly correct—it *is* another party! [*Turns and moves slowly down toward* C.]

WILFRED. Dancing! [*Moves down* L. C.]

CAROLINE. Well—what of it! What's the matter with dancing I'd like to know!

WILFRED. [L. C.] Nothing's the matter with it—if you want to *do* it! [*Stands looking away to down* L.]

CAROLINE. Well I want to *do* it fast enough if that's all you mean! [*Turns away a little toward* R.]

WILFRED. [*An emphatic turn toward her*] But I must say it's a pretty way to carry on—with the sound of the cannon not six miles away!

[WILFRED *is dead in earnest not only in this scene but throughout the entire performance. To give the faintest idea that he thinks there is anything humorous about his lines or behavior would be inexcusable*]

CAROLINE. [*Turning back to him*] Well what do you want us to do—sit down and cry about it?—A heap o' good *that* would do now would n't it?

WILFRED. Oh—I have n't time to talk about it! [*Turns up as if to go*]

CAROLINE. Well it was you who started *out* to talk about it—I'm right sure *I* did n't!

[WILFRED *stops dead on* CAROLINE'S *speech, and after a quick glance to see that no one is near, goes down to her*]

WILFRED. You need n't try to fool me! I know well enough how you've been carrying on since our engagement was broken off! Half a dozen officers proposing to you—a dozen for all I know!

CAROLINE. What difference does it make? I have n't got to *marry* 'em have I?

WILFRED. [L. C.] Well—[*Twist of head*] it is n't very nice to go on like that I must say—proposals by the wholesale! [*Turning away*]

CAROLINE. [C.] Goodness gracious—what's the use of talking to me about it? *They're* the ones that propose—*I* don't!

WILFRED. [*Turning on her* L. C.] Well what do you let 'em *do* it for?

CAROLINE. [C.] How can I help it?

WILFRED. Ho! [*Sneer*] Any girl can help it!—You helped it with *me* all right!

CAROLINE. Well—[*An odd little glance to floor in front*] that was different!

WILFRED. And ever since you threw me ovah—

CAROLINE. [*Looking up at him indignantly*] Oh!—I *did n't* throw you ovah—you just *went* ovah! [*Turns away to* R. *a little*]

WILFRED. Well I went over because you walked off alone with Major Sillsby that night we were at Drury's Bluff an' encouraged him to propose—[CAROLINE *looks round in wrath*] Yes—[*Advancing to* C.] *encouraged* him!

CAROLINE. [R. C.] Of *co'se* I did! I did n't want 'im hangin' round forever did I? That's the on'y way to finish 'em off!

WILFRED. [C.] You want to finish too many of 'em off! Nearly every officer in the 17th Virginyah, I'll be sworn!

CAROLINE. Well what do you want me to do—string a placard round my neck saying "No proposals received here—apply at the office!" Would that make you feel any better?

WILFRED. [*Throwing it off with pretended carelessness*] Oh—it does n't make any difference to me what you do! [*Turns away*]

CAROLINE. Well if it does n't make any difference to you, it does n't even make as much as that to me! [*Turns and goes to couch at* R. C. *and sits on left end of it*]

WILFRED. [*Turning on her again*] Oh—it does n't! I think it *does* though!—You looked as if you enjoyed it pretty well while the 3rd Virginyah was in the city!

CAROLINE. [*Jumping to her feet*] Enjoyed it! I should think I did! I just love every one of 'em! They 're on their way to the front! They 're going to fight for us—an'—an' die for us—an' I *love* 'em! [*Turns front*]

WILFRED. Well why don't you accept one of 'em an' done with it!

CAROLINE. How do you know but what I 'm going to?

WILFRED. [*Goes toward her a little*] I suppose it 'll be one of those *smart* young fellows with a cavalry uniform!

CAROLINE. It 'll be *some* kind of a uniform—I can tell you that! It won't be anybody that stays here in Richmond—

WILFRED. [*Unable for a few seconds to say anything. Looks about room helplessly. Then speaks in low voice*] Now I see what it was! I had to stay in Richmond—an' so you—an' so——

CAROLINE. [*In front of couch* R. C.] Well—[*Looking down—playing with something with her foot*] that made a heap o' difference! [*Looks up.—Different tone*] Why I was the on'y girl on Franklin Street that did n't have a—a—[*Hesitates*]—someone she was engaged to at the front! The on'y one! Just *think* what it was to be out of it like that! [WILFRED *simply looks at her*] Why you 've no idea what I suffered! Besides, it 's our—it 's our *duty* to help all we can!

WILFRED. [*Looking up toward front*] Help! [*Thinking of the trousers under his coat*]

CAROLINE. Yes—help! There are n't many things we girls can do—I know that well enough! But Colonel Woodbridge—he 's one o' Morgan's men you know—well he told Mollie Pickens that the boys fight *twice* as well when they have a—a sweetheart at home! [WILFRED *glances quickly about as he thinks*]

WILFRED. He said *that* did he!

CAROLINE. Yes—an' if we can make 'em fight twice as well why we just ought to do it—that 's all! We girls can't do much but we can do *something!*

WILFRED. [*Short pause.—He makes an absent-minded motion of feeling of the package under his arm*] You 're in earnest are you?

CAROLINE. Earnest!

WILFRED. You really want to help—all you can!

CAROLINE. Well I should think I *did!*

WILFRED. Yes—but do you *now?*

CAROLINE. Of co'se—that 's what I say!

WILFRED. An' if I was—[*Glances around cautiously*]—if I was going to join the army—would you help *me?*

CAROLINE. [*Looking front and down.—Slight embarrassment*] Why of co'se I would—if it was anything I could do! [*Emphasize "do" slightly*]

WILFRED. [*Earnestly—quite near her*] Oh it 's something you can *do* all right!

CAROLINE. [R. C.—*Hardly daring to look up*] What is it?

WILFRED. [*Unrolling a pair of old gray army trousers taking them from under his coat so that they unfurl before her on cue*] Cut these off! [*Short pause.*—CAROLINE *looking at trousers.*—WILFRED *looking at her.* WILFRED *soon goes on very earnestly, holding trousers before his own legs to measure*] They 're about twice too long! All you got to do is to cut 'em off about there, an' sew up the ends so they won't ravel out!

CAROLINE. [R. C.—*The idea beginning to dawn on her*] Why they 're for the Army! [*Taking trousers and hugging them to her—legs hanging down*]

WILFRED. [C.] Sh!—Don't speak so loud for heaven's sake! [*A glance back as if afraid of being overheard*] I 've got a jacket here too! [*Shows her a small army coat*] Nearly a fit—came from the hospital—Johnny Seldon wore it—he won't want it any more you know——an' he was just about my size!

CAROLINE. [R. C.—*Low voice*] No—he won't want it any more. [*Stands thinking*]

WILFRED. [C.—*After a slight pause*] Well!—What is it!—I thought you said you wanted to help!

CAROLINE. [*Quickly*] Oh yes—I do! I do!

WILFRED. Well go on—what are you waiting for?

CAROLINE. [R. C. *near end of couch*] Yes! Yes! [*Hurriedly drops on knees on floor and takes hold, spreading trousers out exactly and patting them smooth*] This is the place is n't it? [*Pointing to near the knees*]

WILFRED. No—not up there—Here! [*Indicating about five inches from the bottom of the trouser leg*]

CAROLINE. Oh yes—I see! [*Hurriedly snatches pins from her dress. Puts one in mouth and one in place* WILFRED *indicates. All very rapid and earnest. Takes hold of other leg of trousers. Speaking as if pin in mouth. Innocently —and without looking up*] The other one just the same? [*A musical rise to voice at end of this.*—WILFRED *does not deign to reply.*—CAROLINE *hearing nothing looks up at him*] Oh yes, o' co'se! [*She quickly puts pin in other leg of trousers*]

[*From this time on* CAROLINE'S *demeanor toward* WILFRED *is entirely changed. It is because he is going to join the army*]

[CAROLINE *on floor with trousers and coat takes hold of the work with enthusiasm—very busy—pins—etc.—etc.*] Do you see any scissors around anywhere! [WILFRED *dashes about looking on tables, after throwing jacket on end of couch* R. C.] This won't never tear—[*Trying to tear off the trousers' leg*]—for all I can do!

WILFRED. [*First looking on table down* L. C. *and picking up the paper jacket was wrapped in. Getting a work-basket from table up* C. *and quickly bringing it*] There must be some in here! [*Hands the scissors out of the basket to* CAROLINE.—*As she reaches up from her position on the floor to take them, she looks in* WILFRED'S *face an instant—then quickly down to work again. Then she works with head down.*—WILFRED *leaves wrapping paper up stage out of the way*]

[*Brief pause.*—CAROLINE *working.*—WILFRED *standing near* C. *looking down at her*]

CAROLINE. [*On her knees* R. C. *near couch. Low voice—not looking up at him*] When are you goin' to wear 'em?

WILFRED. [*Rather gruffly*] When they 're cut off!

[CAROLINE *looks up at him. Thread or scissors in mouth*]

CAROLINE. You mean—you 're really——

WILFRED. Um hm! [*Assent*]

CAROLINE. But your mother——

WILFRED. She knows.

CAROLINE. Oh!

WILFRED. She 's going to write the General to-night.

CAROLINE. But how about if he won't let you?

WILFRED. [*With boyish determination—but keeping voice down*] I 'll go just the same!

CAROLINE. [*Suddenly jumps to her feet dropping everything on the floor and catches his hand*] Oh I 'm so glad! Why it makes another thing of it! When I said that about staying in Richmond I did n't know! Oh, I *do* want to help all I can!

WILFRED. [*Who has been regarding her burst of enthusiasm rather coldly*] You do!

CAROLINE. Indeed—indeed I do!

WILFRED. Then cut those off for Heaven's sake!

CAROLINE. Oh yes! [*She catches up trousers, jacket, etc., and sits quickly on lounge and excitedly paws them over*] Where shall I cut 'em?

WILFRED. The same place—I have n't grown any!

CAROLINE. Dear me—I don't know where it was!

WILFRED. You stuck some pins in!

CAROLINE. [*Finding pins*] Oh yes—here they are! [*Seizing the trousers and going to work, soon cutting off one of the legs*]

WILFRED. That 's it!

CAROLINE. When did you say she was going to write?

WILFRED. To-night.

CAROLINE. [*Looking up with distrust*] She does n't want you to go does she?

WILFRED. I don't reckon she does—very much!

CAROLINE. She 'll tell him not to let you!

WILFRED. [*Looks at her with wide open eyes*] No!

CAROLINE. That 's the way they always do!

WILFRED. The devil!

CAROLINE. I should think so!

WILFRED. What can I do?

CAROLINE. Write to him yourself!

WILFRED. Good idea!

CAROLINE. Then you can just tell him what you like!

WILFRED. I'll tell him I *can't* stay here!

CAROLINE. [*Excitedly rising—letting the jacket fall on floor at one side*] Tell him you're coming anyhow!

WILFRED. I will!

CAROLINE. Whether he says so or not!

WILFRED. Then he'll say so won't he?

CAROLINE. O' co'se he will—there ain't anythin' else to say!

WILFRED. I'll *do* it! [*Starts to go up* L. *Stops and goes back to* CAROLINE] Say —you're pretty good! [*Catching one of* CAROLINE'S *hands impulsively.*—CAROLINE *looks down at work on floor*] I'll go upstairs an' write it now! [*Starts toward door up* L. C.—CAROLINE *watches him.*—*He turns back and she looks quickly down again*] Finish those things as soon as you can an' leave 'em here—in the hall closet! [*Indicating outside* L.]

CAROLINE. [*Nodding her head*] Yes—I will.

WILFRED. An' don't let anyone see 'em whatever you do!

CAROLINE. [*Shaking her head*] No—I won't.

[WILFRED *hurries off at door up* L. C. *to* L.—CAROLINE *looks after him with expression of ecstasy—lapsing into dreaminess as she turns to front. Suddenly recollects with a start and a little "O" and slipping down on floor near couch she goes excitedly to work on the trousers, cutting at the other leg with violence and rapidity, getting it nearly cut through so that later it dangles by a few threads. Suddenly she stops work and listens. Then with great haste she gathers up all the things she can, leaving the jacket however where it fell, and jumps to her feet with them in her arms, hugging the confused bundle close against her and hastily tucking in portions that hang out so that* MRS. VARNEY *won't see what it is*]

[*Enter* MRS. VARNEY *door up* L. C. *coming down the stairway and into the room*]

MRS. VARNEY. Oh Caroline—you have n't gone yet!

CAROLINE. Not quite!—I mean not yet!—It does n't begin for an hour you know!

MRS. VARNEY. What does n't begin?

CAROLINE. The party!

MRS. VARNEY. Oh—then you have plenty of time! [*Turning as if to go up* C.]

CAROLINE. [*Hastening across toward door up* L. C. *with her arms full of things*] Yes—but I'll have to go now sure enough! [*Near* C. *she drops the scissors*]

MRS. VARNEY. [*Up* C.—*Turning*] You dropped your scissors dear!

CAROLINE. Oh! [*Coming back for them*] I—I thought I heard something! [*In picking them up she lets the cut-off end of a trouser leg fall but does not notice it and goes toward door up* L. C.]

MRS. VARNEY. [*Coming down* C.] What are you making, Caroline?

CAROLINE. [*Turning near door up* L. C.] Oh—I—I was just altering a dress—that's all! [*Turning to go*]

MRS. VARNEY. [*Stooping and picking up the piece of trouser leg*] Here Carrie!—you dropped a—a—[*Looks at it*]

CAROLINE. [*Hurrying to* MRS. VARNEY *and snatching the piece—stuffing it in with rest*] Oh yes!—Ha ha! [*Looks at* MRS. VARNEY *an instant. The other piece of the trouser leg is hanging by its shred in full sight*] That—that was one of the *sleeves!* [*Turns and hurries off at door up* L. C. *and exits to* R. *at door near foot of stairway*]

[MRS. VARNEY *after a moment turns and goes toward door up* C.—*Seeing something on the couch* R. C. *she stops and goes to pick it up. On coming to it she finds the little gray soldier's jacket left by* CAROLINE *in her hasty scramble. She stoops and picks it up and stands for a moment looking at it*]

[*After a brief pause the sound of hurried opening of front door outside left and tramp of heavy feet in the hall is heard*]

[MRS. VARNEY *looks up and across up left, letting the coat fall on the couch*]

[*Enter* MR. BENTON ARRELSFORD *at door up* L. C. *from* L.—*He is a tall fine looking Southern man of about thirty-five or forty, dressed in citizen's clothes—black frock coat, and of rather distinguished appearance. He is seen outside door up* L. C. *hurriedly placing a guard of Confederate soldiers at doors outside up left and also at foot of stairway.*—MRS. VARNEY, *much surprised, moves toward door up* L. C.—MR. ARRELSFORD *at the same time and as noiselessly as possible, hastens into the room*]

MRS. VARNEY. [*As he enters*] Mr. Arrelsford! [*Goes toward* C. *up a little*]

ARRELSFORD. [*Comes quickly across to*

MRS. VARNEY. *Speaks in a low voice and rapidly*] I was obliged to come in without ceremony Mrs. Varney. You 'll understand when I tell you what it is!

MRS. VARNEY. And those men—[*Motions toward guard outside door up* L. C.]

ARRELSFORD. [*Low voice*] They 're on guard at the doors out there!

MRS. VARNEY. [*Low voice*] On guard!—You mean that in this house you——

ARRELSFORD. I'm very much afraid Mrs. Varney, that we 've got to put you to a little inconvenience. [*Glances about cautiously.*—MRS. VARNEY *stands astonished*] Is there anybody in that room? [*Pointing to door up* C.]

MRS. VARNEY. Yes.

ARRELSFORD. Who?

MRS. VARNEY. There are quite a number of ladies there—sewing for the hospitals.

ARRELSFORD. Kindly come this way a little. [*Going down* L. C. *with* MRS. VARNEY] One of your servants has got himself into trouble, Mrs. Varney, an' we 're compelled to have him watched!

MRS. VARNEY. One of my servants!—Why what kind of trouble?

ARRELSFORD. [*Low voice*] Pretty serious ma'am—that 's the way it looks now!—You 've got an old white-haired niggah here——

MRS. VARNEY. You mean Jonas?

ARRELSFORD. I believe that 's his name!

MRS. VARNEY. You *suspect* him of something!

ARRELSFORD. [*Keeping voice down*] We don't suspect—we *know* what he 's done! [*Glances round before going on*] He 's been down in the Libby Prison under pretense of selling something to the Yankees we 've got in there, an' he now has on his person a written communication from one of those Yankees which he intends to deliver to another one that 's here in Richmond! [ARRELSFORD *goes around in front of table and up* L. *of it to near door up* L. C.]

[MRS. VARNEY *stands motionless a second. She soon recovers*]

MRS. VARNEY. Send for the man! [*Starting to move up stage and toward* L.] Let us see if there 's any truth in such a—

ARRELSFORD. [*Up* L. C. *near* R. *upper corner of table* L. C.—*Quickly stopping her*] No! Not yet! [*Glances quickly round at doors and windows—then speaks in lowered voice but with great intensity and clearness*] I 've got to get that paper! If he 's alarmed he 'll destroy it! I 've *got* to have it! It 's the clue to one o' their cursed plots! They 've been right close on this town for months—trying to make a break in our defenses and get in. This is some rascally game they 're at to weaken us from the inside! —Two weeks ago we got word from one of our agents over there in the Yankee lines telling us that two brothers—Lewis and Henry Dumont—have been under Secret Service orders to do some rascally piece of work here in Richmond. We had close descriptions of these two men but we 've never been able to lay our hands on 'em till last night!

MRS. VARNEY. [*Up* C. *and a little* L. *near* ARRELSFORD.—*Intense whisper*] You 've got them?

ARRELSFORD. [*Up* L. C.—*Low voice, but intense*] We 've got one o' them! An' it won't take long to run down the othah!

MRS. VARNEY. [*Low voice*] The one—the one you caught—was he here in Richmond?

ARRELSFORD. [*Low voice*] No—he was brought in last night with a lot o' men we captured making a raid.

MRS. VARNEY. You mean he was taken prisoner?

ARRELSFORD. [*Nods affirmatively.*—*Glances round*] Let himself be taken! That 's one of their tricks for getting through our lines when they want to bring a message or give some signal.

MRS. VARNEY. They—they actually get into Libby Prison?

ARRELSFORD. [*Low voice. Great intensity*] Yes! Damn them! [*This oath indistinctly between his teeth*] But we were on the lookout for this man an' we spotted him mighty quick! I gave orders not to search him or take away his clothes but to put him in with the others and keep the closest watch on him that was ever kept on a man! Here was one of the Dumont brothers an' we knew from his coming in that the othah must be here in the city waiting to hear from him, an' he 'd send him a message the first chance he got!

MRS. VARNEY. [*Low voice*] But Jonas! —How could he——

ARRELSFORD. [*Low and intense*] Easy enough!—Easy *enough!* He comes down to Libby to sell goubers to the prisoners —we let 'im pass in—he fools around awhile until he gets a chance to brush against this man Dumont—we 're watching, an' we see a bit of paper pass between 'em! The old nigger 's got that paper on 'im now ma'am, an' besides these men in heah I 've got a dozen more on the outside watching him through the windows! [*Turns and moves up, glancing off up* L. *with some anxiety*]

MRS. VARNEY. [*After slight pause turns and speaks in intense but subdued voice —almost whisper*] The man he gives it to! *He 's* the one we want!

ARRELSFORD. [*Approaching her quickly.— Low voice but intense*] Yes—but I can't wait long! If the niggah sees a man or hears a sound he 'll destroy it before we can jump in on 'im—an' I *must* have that paper! [*Strides quickly up,* MRS. VARNEY *following a step or two.— Speaking off up* L. *in low but sharp voice*] Corporal!

[*Enter* CORPORAL *at door up* L. C. *from* L.— *He salutes and stands in the large arched doorway*]

How is it now?

CORPORAL. [*Low voice*] All quiet sir!

[ARRELSFORD *and* MRS. VARNEY *face each other*]

ARRELSFORD. [*Low, intense*] It won't do to wait—I've *got* to get that paper! It 's the key to the game they 're trying to play an' we must have it!

MRS. VARNEY. [*Intense.—Half whisper*] No no—the man who 's going to play it! Get *him!*

ARRELSFORD. [*Low—intense*] That paper the nigger 's got might give us a clue! If not I 'll make him tell who it was *for*—damn it I 'll shoot it out of him! [*Turns to* CORPORAL] How quick can you get at him from that door! [*Pointing off up* L. C. *to door* R. *of stairway*]

CORPORAL. [*No salute. Low voice*] It 's through a hallway sir—and across the dining-room.

ARRELSFORD. [*Low voice*] Well, take two men and——

MRS. VARNEY. [*Interrupting—touching* ARRELSFORD *to stop him. Low voice*] Why not keep your men out of sight and let me send for him—here?

ARRELSFORD. [*After a second's thought. Low voice*] That 's better—we 'll get 'im in here! While you 're talking to him they can nab him from behind! [*Turns to* CORPORAL] You heard!

CORPORAL. [*Low voice*] Yes sir.

ARRELSFORD. [*Low voice*] Keep your men out of sight—get 'em back there in the hall—an' while we 're making him talk send a man down each side and pin him! Hold 'im stiff! He must n't destroy any paper he 's got! Look out for that!

[CORPORAL *salutes and exits with men door up* L. C. *and to* L.—*After exit of* CORPORAL *and* MEN, MRS. VARNEY *moves swiftly to* L. *side, and taking the bell-cord in her hand, turns toward* ARRELSFORD.—*Pause.— Both motionless for four seconds*]

MRS. VARNEY. [*After the motionless pause.—Low voice—but distinct*] *Now* Mr. Arrelsford?

ARRELSFORD. [*Low voice*] Yes.

[MRS. VARNEY *rings the bell.—Short pause.—Enter* MARTHA *at door up* L. C. *from* R. *She stands up* L. C. *below the doorway*]

MRS. VARNEY. [*Down* L. *near mantel*] Is there anyone I can send to the hospital Martha?

MARTHA. [*Up* L. C.] Luther 's out yere, mam.

MRS. VARNEY. Luther? [*Considers*] No —he 's too small. I don't want a boy.

MARTHA. Jonas is yere, mam—if you want him.

MRS. VARNEY. Oh, Jonas—yes! Tell him to come here right away.

MARTHA. Yaas 'm. [*Exits at door up* L. C. *to* R.]

[MRS. VARNEY *crosses back of table* L. C. *to* R. C. *and sits on couch.—* ARRELSFORD *waits up* C.]

[OLD JONAS *appears at the door up* L. C. *coming from* R.—*He is a thick-set grayhaired old negro.—He comes a few steps into the room*]

[MRS. VARNEY *looks at* JONAS *and he at her.—At first he is entirely unsuspecting, but in a moment, seeing* ARRELSFORD *standing up* C. *his eyes shift restlessly for an instant*]

MRS. VARNEY. [*On couch* R. C.] Jonas——

JONAS. [*Up* L. C.] Yes 'm.

MRS. VARNEY. Have you any idea why I sent for you?

JONAS. I heers you was wantin' to sen' to de hossiple ma'am.

[CORPORAL *and* MEN *enter very quietly up* L. C. *from* L. *and on to behind* JONAS]

MRS. VARNEY. Oh—then Martha told you?

[CORPORAL *motions to* MEN *and two instantly step forward—one on each side of* JONAS, *and stand there motionless*]

JONAS. Wall she did n't ezzackly say whut you—[*Sees man each side of him and stops in the midst of his speech. He does not start, but is frozen with terror. Expression of face scarcely changes. Soon he lowers his eyes and then begins stealthily to get his right hand toward his inside breast pocket*]

[CORPORAL *gives a sharp order.—The two* MEN *instantly seize* JONAS.—CORPORAL *quickly feels in his pockets.*—JONAS *struggles desperately but in an instant the* CORPORAL *has the paper which he hands—with a salute—to* ARRELSFORD.—MRS. VARNEY *has risen as* MEN *seized* JONAS]

ARRELSFORD. [R. *of* MEN *and* JONAS] See if there 's anything more! [ARRELSFORD *stands watching the search*]

[CORPORAL *quickly searches* JONAS—*feeling rapidly along body, arms, down each leg, etc.,* MEN *raising his arms above head, etc., for the purpose. Pushes fingers down into slippers—which are sufficiently loose for this.—After the search* MEN *release* JONAS *and stand guard one on each side of him*]

CORPORAL. [*Rises and comes to salute*] That 's all sir!

[ARRELSFORD *turns quickly away to lamp on table up* C. *opening the paper as he does so.*—MRS. VARNEY *watches him intently.*—ARRELSFORD *reads the paper quickly and at once wheels round on* JONAS *coming down* R. *of him*]

ARRELSFORD. [*Low voice—but sharp and telling*] Who was this for? [JONAS *stands silent*] If you don't tell it 's going to be mighty bad for you! [JONAS *stands silent*] [*After a pause* ARRELSFORD *turns to* MRS. VARNEY] I 'm right sorry ma'am but it looks like we 've got to shoot 'im! [*Eyeing* JONAS *a moment—then goes down* C.] Corporal! [*Motions* CORPORAL *to approach.*—CORPORAL *steps to* ARRELSFORD *on salute.*—*To* CORPORAL *in a low voice*] Take him outside and get it out of him! String him up till he talks! You understand! [CORPORAL *salutes and is about to turn*] Here! [CORPORAL *turns back to* ARRLESFORD *on salute.*—ARRELSFORD *glances toward the windows at* R. *and then to* L.] Go down on that side—back of the house! [*Indicating up* L.] And keep it quiet! Nobody must know of this! Not a soul!

[CORPORAL *salutes again and goes up to* MEN. *Gives a low-voiced order.*—MEN *turn on order and march* JONAS *off at door up* L. C. *and off* L. *All very quick with military precision. The* CORPORAL *goes with them.*—ARRELSFORD *stands watching exit of* JONAS *and* MEN *until they are gone and the sound of the closing of heavy front door is heard outside left. He then turns to* MRS. VARNEY.—ARRELSFORD *and* MRS. VARNEY *keep voices down to nearly a whisper in the coming scene—but speak with the utmost force and intensity*]

MRS. VARNEY. [*Indicating the paper in* ARRELSFORD'S *hand*] Was there anything in that—

ARRELSFORD. [*Near* MRS. VARNEY *on her* L.] We 've got the trick they want to play!

MRS. VARNEY. But not the *man*—not the man who is to *play* it?

ARRELSFORD. I did n't say that!

MRS. VARNEY. You mean there 's a clue—*to him?*

ARRELSFORD. I mean there 's a clue *to him!*

MRS. VARNEY. Will it answer? Do you know who it is? Do you——

ARRELSFORD. [*Interrupting*] As plain as if we had his name!

MRS. VARNEY. Thank God! [*Motionless an instant—then she extends her hand for the paper*] Let me see! [ARRELSFORD *momentary hesitation—then hands her the paper.—She looks at paper, then reads it aloud—not too easily*] "ATTACK TO-NIGHT—PLAN 3—USE TELEGRAPH."—[*Slight motion or sound from* ARRELSFORD *to quiet her, and a quick glance about.—After the glance about by* ARRELSFORD *she goes on in low voice*] What does it mean?

ARRELSFORD. [*Takes paper from her. Low voice but incisive*] They attack tonight!—The place where they strike is indicated by "Plan 3." [*Finger on the words on paper in his hand*]

MRS. VARNEY. Plan three?

ARRELSFORD. He knows what they mean by that!—It 's arranged beforehand!

MRS. VARNEY. And—the last—the last there! [*Excited motion toward the paper in* ARRELSFORD'S *hands*] "Use Telegraph"?—What does that——

ARRELSFORD. He 's to use our War Department Telegraph Lines to send some false order and weaken that position—the one they indicate by "Plan Three"—so they can break through and come down on the city!

MRS. VARNEY. Oh! [*A breathless exclamation of indignation.—A second's pause—then suddenly*] But the *man*—the man who is to do this—there 's nothing about *him!*

ARRELSFORD. There *is* something about him!

MRS. VARNEY. [*Rapidly—almost run together*] What? Where? I don't see it!

ARRELSFORD. "Use Telegraph"! [*A pause.—Both stand motionless regarding one another.—*ARRELSFORD *goes on after playing this pause to the limit*] We know every man on the Telegraph Service—and every man of them's true! But there 's some who want to get *on* that service that we don't know quite so well!

MRS. VARNEY. [*Indicating the paper*] He would be one—of course!

ARRELSFORD. There are n't so very many! [*These speeches given suggestively—with slight pause after each.—All very low voice and intense*] It is n't *every* man that 's an expert!—The niggah brought this paper to *your house,* Mrs. Varney!

MRS. VARNEY. My—[*Hesitates—beginning to realise*]—my house you say!

ARRELSFORD. For more than a month your daughter has been working to get an appointment for someone on the Telegraph Service—perhaps *she* could give us some idea—[*Stops in the midst of speech and stands looking at* MRS. VARNEY]

[*A moment's pause.—Suddenly* MRS. VARNEY *turns and hurries to window up* R. *and quickly pulls curtains together, turning and facing back to* ARRELSFORD *at same instant*]

ARRELSFORD. [*Almost whisper—but with utmost intensity*] IS HE THERE? [MRS. VARNEY *nods affirmatively. She then comes down toward* ARRELSFORD] Could he hear what we said?

MRS. VARNEY. [*Shakes head negatively. Almost whisper*] He 's at the further end! [*Comes back to* R. *of* ARRELSFORD.—ARRELSFORD *glances at windows* R. *nervously.—*MRS. VARNEY*—after a pause—in low voice*] You have a description you say!

ARRELSFORD. [*Nods affirmatively*] At the office.

MRS. VARNEY. Then this man—this Captain Thorne—

ARRELSFORD. [*Breaking in savagely but in low voice*] There *is* no Captain Thorne! This fellow you have in your house is Lewis Dumont!

[*Short pause*]

MRS. VARNEY. You mean—he came here to—

ARRELSFORD. [*With vindictive fury breaking through in spite of himself—yet voice subdued almost to a sharp whisper*] He came to this town—he came to this house—knowing your position and the influence of your name—for the sole purpose of getting some hold on our Department Telegraph Lines!—He 's corrupted your servants—he 's thick with the men in the telegraph office—what he has n't done God A'mighty knows! But Washington ain't the only place where there 's a Secret Service! We 've got one here in Richmond! Oh—[*A shake of his head*] two can play at that game—an' it 's my move now! [*Goes up* R. C. *a few steps*]

[*Enter* EDITH VARNEY *running rapidly down the stairway up left and in at door up* L. C.*—She wears a white dress and has in her hand the large official envelope which she took upstairs at the end of her first scene.—*ARRELSFORD *goes toward windows up* R.]

EDITH. [*As she runs down the stairway*] Mama! Mama!—Quick Mama! [MRS. VARNEY *hurries toward door up* L. C. *to meet her.—*ARRELSFORD *turns in surprise looking toward door up* L. C.—EDITH *meeting* MRS. VARNEY] Under my window—in the garden—they 're hurting someone frightfully—I 'm sure they are! Oh—come! [*Starting toward door to lead the way.—*MRS. VARNEY *stands looking at* EDITH.—EDITH *stops surprised that* MRS. VARNEY *does not follow*] If you are n't coming I 'll go myself! [*Turning to go*] It 's terrible!

MRS. VARNEY. Wait, Edith! [EDITH *stops up* L. C. *and turns back to* MRS. VARNEY.—MRS. VARNEY *goes to her and brings her a little way down* L. C.] I must tell you something—it will be a terrible shock I 'm afraid! [EDITH *moves down with* MRS. VARNEY.—ARRELSFORD *turns away a little—standing near* R. C. *watching window*] A man we trusted as a friend has shown himself a treacherous conspirator against us!

EDITH. [*After a slight pause.—Low voice*] Who? [*Pause.*—MRS. VARNEY *cannot bring herself to speak the name*] Who is it?

ARRELSFORD. [*Swinging round on her at* R. *—Low voice—suppressed vindictiveness*] It is the gentleman, Miss Varney, whose attentions you have been pleased to accept in the place of mine!

[*Short pause.*—EDITH *white and motionless looking at* ARRELSFORD. *Soon she turns her face appealing to her mother.*—MRS. VARNEY *nods slowly in affirmation*]

EDITH. [*Low voice*] Is it Mr. Arrelsford who makes this accusation?

ARRELSFORD. [*Breaking out hotly but keeping voice in suppressed voice*] Yes—since you wish to know! From the first I 've had my suspicions that this— [*He stops on seeing* EDITH'S *move toward the window up* R.]

[EDITH, *on cue "Yes" quickly thrusts envelope containing commission into belt or waist of her dress, and starts rapidly toward the window up* R. *crossing* MRS. VARNEY.—ARRELSFORD *breaks off in his speech and steps before her*]

ARRELSFORD [R. C.—*Low voice—speaking rapidly*] Where are you going?

EDITH. [C.—*Low voice*] For Captain Thorne.

ARRELSFORD. [*Low voice*] Not now!

EDITH. [*Turning with flashing indignation on* ARRELSFORD] Mr. Arrelsford, if this is something you 're afraid to say to him—don't you *dare* say it to me!

ARRELSFORD. [*Indignantly.—Low voice*] Miss Varney, if you——

MRS. VARNEY. [L. C.—*Interrupting quickly.—Low voice*] Edith—listen to me! [EDITH *turns quickly to* MRS. VARNEY] Mr. Arrelsford has good reasons for not meeting Captain Thorne just now!

EDITH. I should think he had! [*Quick turn back to* ARRELSFORD] The man who said that to his face would n't *live* to speak again!

MRS. VARNEY. My dear, you don't——

EDITH. [C.] Mama—this man has left his desk in the War Department so that he can have the pleasure of persecuting me! He 's never attempted anything in the active service before! And when I ask him to face the man he accuses he turns like a coward!

ARRELSFORD. [*Angrily, but keeping voice down*] Mrs. Varney, if she thinks—

EDITH. [*Low voice*] I think nothing! I *know* that a man of Captain Thorne's character is above suspicion!

ARRELSFORD [*Low voice*] His character! [*Sneeringly*] Where did he come from? —Who is he?

EDITH. [*Low voice*] Who are you?

ARRELSFORD. That 's not the question!

EDITH. [*Low voice*] Neither is it the question who *he* is! If it were I 'd answer it—the answer above all others—he 's a soldier who has fought and been wounded for his country!

ARRELSFORD. [*Low voice but incisive*] We 're not so sure of that!

EDITH. [*After a pause of indignation*] He brought us letters from General Stonewall Jackson and from—

ARRELSFORD. [*Quick and sharp*] Jackson was killed before his letter was presented!

EDITH. What does that signify if he wrote it?

ARRELSFORD Nothing—*if* he wrote it! [*Accent on "if" with vindictive fury*]

EDITH. Mr. Arrelsford—if you mean— [MRS. VARNEY *goes to* EDITH *putting her hand on* EDITH'S *arm*]

MRS. VARNEY. [*Low voice*] Listen Edith! They have proofs of a conspiracy on our Government Telegraph Lines. [ARRELSFORD *says "Sh" and goes to window up* R.—EDITH *turns from* ARRELSFORD *and looks before her, listening on mention of "Telegraph Lines."*—MRS. VARNEY *leads* EDITH *a little* L. *of* C.—ARRELSFORD *stands near window up* R.] A treacherous conspiracy on the War Department lines to the front. Two men in the Northern Secret Service have been sent here to carry it out. One is in Libby Prison. He 's just been brought in—and he allowed himself to be taken prisoner so as to get in here and bring a message to the other. Our old Jonas went there to-day—secretly took that message from him and brought it here! [EDITH *turns toward* MRS. VARNEY *sharply.*] Yes Edith—he brought it to this house! We 've just had Jonas in and found that paper on him!

[ARRELSFORD *quietly moves down* R. *looking off through curtains at windows down* R.]

EDITH. [*Rapidly — desperately — in low*

voice] But he has n't said it was for——

[*Heavy sound of front door closing outside* L.]

ARRELSFORD. [*Low voice but incisively*] Not yet—but he will! [EDITH *looks at* ARRELSFORD *not comprehending.—Enter* CORPORAL *at door up* L. C. *from* L.*—He stands on salute.—*LADIES *turn to him.—* EDITH *breathless with anxiety.—*MRS. VARNEY *calm but intent.—*ARRELSFORD *goes quickly across from* R. C. *to* CORPORAL *up* L. C. *Low voice*] Well—what does he say?

CORPORAL. [*Low voice*] Nothing!—He won't speak!

ARRELSFORD. [*Sharply, but voice subdued*] Won't speak! What have you done?

CORPORAL. Strung him up three times and——

ARRELSFORD. [*Enraged but keeping his voice down*] Well string him up again! If he won't speak shoot it out of him! Kill the dog! [*Comes blindly down* L.*—* CORPORAL *salutes and exits at door up* L. C. *to* L.*—*ARRELSFORD *turns to ladies coming down* L. *back of table*] We don't need the niggah's evidence—there 's enough without it! [*Takes his hat from table*]

EDITH. [*Up* C.*—Low voice*] There is nothing!

ARRELSFORD. [L. *of table* L. C.*—Low voice*] By twelve o'clock to-night you 'll have all the proof you want!

EDITH. [*Low voice*] There 's no proof at all!

ARRELSFORD. [*Low voice*] I 'll show it to you at the telegraph office! Do you dare go there with me?

EDITH. [*Low voice*] Dare! [*Moves toward him*] I *will* go with you!

ARRELSFORD. [*Low voice*] I 'll call for you in half an hour! [*Goes toward door up* L. C.]

EDITH. Wait! [ARRELSFORD *stops and turns to her up* L. C.] What are you going to do?

ARRELSFORD. [*Comes down back of table. —Low voice but incisive*] I 'm going to let him get this paper! When he looks at it he 'll know what they want him to do—and then we 'll see him try to do it!

EDITH. [L. C.] You 're going to spy on him—hound him like a criminal!

ARRELSFORD. I 'm going to prove what he *is!*

EDITH. Then prove it openly! Prove it at once! It 's a shame to let a suspicion like that rest on an honorable man! Let him come in here and—

ARRELSFORD [*Low voice*] Impossible! [*Goes down* L. *of table a little.*]

EDITH. [*Low voice*] Then do something else but do it now! [*Turning away goes up* C. *a little, speaks desperately*] We must know that he—that he 's innocent! We must know that! [*A thought. Turns to* ARRELSFORD] You say— [ARRELSFORD *makes a movement to go*] Wait! *Wait!* [ARRELSFORD *stops*] You say the man in Libby Prison is his brother—that 's what you said—his brother! Bring him here! Go to the prison and bring that man here!

ARRELSFORD. [L. *of table speaking across it. Subdued exclamation*] What!

EDITH. Let them meet! Bring them face to face! Then you can see whether——

ARRELSFORD. [*Low voice.—Speaks rapidly*] You mean—bring them together here?

EDITH. Yes! Here!—Anywhere! Wherever you please!

ARRELSFORD. As if the prisoner was trying to escape?

EDITH. Any way you like—but end it!

ARRELSFORD. When?

EDITH. Now! Now!—I won't have such a suspicion as that hanging over him!

ARRELSFORD. [*After instant's thought*] I 'm willing to try that!—Can you keep him here? [*With a motion toward windows* R.]

EDITH. [*Scarcely more than a movement of lips*] Yes.

ARRELSFORD. It won't be more than half an hour.—Be out there on the veranda.—When I tap on the glass bring him into this room and leave him alone! You understand—*alone!*

EDITH. [*Hardly more than a whisper*] Yes. [*Turns away toward front*]

ARRELSFORD. [*Goes rapidly toward door up* L. C.*—Stops and turns near door*] I rely on you Miss Varney to give him no hint or sign that we suspect—

MRS. VARNEY. [*Interrupting* ARRELSFORD *indignantly*] Mr. Arrelsford!

[EDITH *does not notice anything*]

[ARRELSFORD *stands an instant—then bows stiffly and exits at door up* L. C. *to* L.*—Sound of closing of heavy door outside* L. *shortly after his disappearance.—*EDITH *stands where she was as if stunned.—*MRS. VARNEY *remains* R. C. *looking after* ARRELSFORD*—then turns to* EDITH]

EDITH. [*After pause—not looking round—nearly whisper*] Mama! [*Reaches out her hand as if feeling for help or support.*—MRS. VARNEY *comes down to* EDITH *on her left and takes her hand*] Mama!

MRS. VARNEY. [*Low voice*] I'm here, Edith!

[*Pause.*—EDITH *thinking of something—her eyes wide open—staring vacantly before her*]

EDITH. [*Holding tight to* MRS. VARNEY'S *hand*] Do you think—do you think—that could be what he meant? [MRS. VARNEY *looking intently at* EDITH] The Commission I got for him—this afternoon—you know!

MRS. VARNEY. [*Low voice*] Yes—yes!

EDITH. The Commission—from the President—for the—for the Telegraph Service! He—he—refused to take it!

MRS. VARNEY. Refused!

EDITH. [*Nodding a little—hardly able to speak*] He said—he said it was for me that he could not!

MRS. VARNEY. [*Sudden deep emphasis*] It's true then!

EDITH. [*Turning quickly to* MRS VARNEY *and trying to stop her by putting her hand over her mouth. Speaking rapidly, breathlessly—yet not in loud voice*] No no! Don't say it!—Don't say it!

MRS. VARNEY. [*Putting* EDITH'S *hand away*] Yes!

EDITH. Oh no!

MRS. VARNEY. Infamous traitor! They ought to lash him through the streets of Richmond!

EDITH. [*Impulsively trying to stop* MRS. VARNEY] No Mama! No — no — no! [*She stops. A moment's pause. She realizes the truth. Speaks in almost a whisper*] Yes—yes—[*Fainter and fainter*] Yes—yes—[*Stops—pauses—stands erect—looks about—makes very slight motion asking* MRS. VARNEY *to leave her*]

[MRS. VARNEY *turns quietly and leaves the room going out at the door up* L. C. *and to* L.—EDITH *stands supporting herself without knowing that she does so—one hand on a table or back of chair.—Soon coming to herself she turns and goes toward the window up* R. *When near* C. *she hesitates, stands there a moment looking toward the window, then brushes her hand quickly across her eyes and takes the President's Commission from her waist or belt. She looks at it a moment, folds it slowly and puts it back again. Walks to the window, throws aside the curtains and pushes it open*]

[*Upon* EDITH *pushing open the window up* R. CAPTAIN THORNE *outside* R. *at some distance, makes sound with chair as though he rose and pushed or set it back, and the sound of his footsteps outside approaching the window briskly follows at once.*—EDITH *moves back away from the window and across to up* L. C. *near table, and stands there looking across at the window up* R. *for an instant, but soon turning away, so that she is not looking at* THORNE *as he enters.—After footsteps and after* EDITH *is motionless at up* L. C. CAPTAIN THORNE *walks easily and unsuspiciously into the room at window up* R., *glancing about as he does so—not seeing* EDITH *until he is a little way in. Upon seeing her he stops an instant where he is, and then goes directly across to her and is about to take her hand as he speaks*]

THORNE. [*Coming to* EDITH *up* L. C.] Miss Varney——

EDITH. [*Quickly snatching her hand away and shrinking backward to left a step or two.—Speaks rapidly—breathlessly—with almost a gasp*] No—don't touch me! [*A second's pause.—She recovers almost instantly*] Oh—it was you! [*Smiling as if at her own stupidity*] Why how perfectly absurd I am! [*Crossing in front of* THORNE *lightly and going to window at up* R.] I'm sure I ought to be ashamed of myself! [*Turns to him at* R.] Do come out a minute—on the veranda.—I want to talk to you about a whole lot o' things! There's half an hour yet before the party! [*Turning to go*] Isn't it a perfectly lovely evening! [*She exits at the window up* R. *with forced gaiety of manner, disappearing in the darkness*]

[THORNE *stands looking at* EDITH *when she first speaks. As she crosses* R. *he is looking down a little but looks slowly up toward front and turns a little after her crossing, looking at her as she stands for a moment in the window up* R. *After her exit he slowly turns toward front and his eyes glance about and down once as he weighs the chances*]

EDITH. [*After brief pause for above—*

calling gaily from outside up R. *not too near the window*] Oh, Cap'n Thorne! [*Emphasis on 'Oh'*]

[THORNE *turns quickly looking off* R. *again. Hesitates an instant. Makes up his mind. Walks rapidly to window up* R. *A very slight hesitation there—without stopping. Exits at window up* R.—*Ring as* THORNE *passes out at the window*]

[CURTAIN]

ACT II

SCENE:—*The same room.*

NINE O'CLOCK.

Furniture as in ACT I. *Electric calciums for strong moonlight outside both windows at* R. *Portières are closed at both windows.*

[MRS. VARNEY *discovered seated at desk down* R.—*She is not busy with anything but sits there to see that no one goes out to the veranda at* R.—*Sound of closing of door outside* L.—*Enter* MISS KITTRIDGE *at door up* L. C. *from* L.—*The door up* C. *stands ajar as if she had recently come out*]

MRS. VARNEY. Was it the same man?

MISS KITTRIDGE. [*Pausing up* C.] No—they sent another this time.

MRS. VARNEY. Did you have anything ready?

MISS KITTRIDGE. Oh yes—I gave him quite a lot. We've all been at the bandages—that's what they need most. [MRS. VARNEY *rises. Seems preoccupied. Goes across to up* L. *and looks off.*—MISS KITTRIDGE *watches her rather anxiously*] Did you want anything Mrs. Varney?

MRS. VARNEY. [*Turning at up* L.] No—I—nothing thank you. [MISS KITTRIDGE *is turning to go, but stops when* MRS. VARNEY *speaks again.*—MRS. VARNEY *goes nearer to* MISS KITTRIDGE] Perhaps it would be just as well if any of the ladies want to go, to let them out the other way—through the dining room I mean. We're expecting someone here on important business.

MISS KITTRIDGE. I'll see to it Mrs. Varney.

MRS. VARNEY. Thank you. [*Exit* MISS KITTRIDGE *at door up* C.—MRS. VARNEY *stands a moment, then goes down* L. *and rings bell. Crosses to* R. C., *going back of table* L. C. *Then goes slowly up* C. *waiting*] [*Enter* MARTHA *at door up* L. C. *from* R.] Did Miss Caroline go home?

MARTHA. [*Up* L. C. *near door*] No'm—she's been out yere in de kitchen fur a while.

MRS. VARNEY. In the kitchen!

MARTHA. Yaas'm.

MRS. VARNEY. What has she been doing?

MARTHA. She been mostly sewin' and behavin' mighty strange about sumfin a great deal o' de time. I bleeve she gittin' ready to go home now.

MRS. VARNEY. Ask her to come here a moment.

MARTHA. Yaas'm. [MARTHA *turns and exits up* L. C. *to* R.] [MRS. VARNEY *waits a little. Then goes forward* R. C. *a few steps*] [*Enter* CAROLINE *at door up* L. C. *from* R. *She comes into the room trying to look perfectly innocent*]

MRS. VARNEY. [R. C.] Caroline—[CAROLINE *goes down* C. *with* MRS. VARNEY. *She is expecting to hear something said about the sewing she has been doing*] Are you in a hurry to get home? Because if you can wait a few minutes while I go up stairs to Howard it will be a great help.

CAROLINE. [*Looking round in some doubt*] You want me to—just wait?

MRS. VARNEY. Yes.—You see I—[*Hesitates a little*]—I don't want anyone to go out on the veranda—just now.

CAROLINE. [*Doubtfully*] Oh.

MRS. VARNEY. Edith and—and—

CAROLINE. —And Captain Thorne——

(MRS. VARNEY *nods very slightly*]

CAROLINE. [*Suddenly comprehending*] Oh yes! [*Glances toward windows* R.] I know how *that* is!—I'll attend to it Mrs. Varney! [*Crosses to up* R. C.]

MRS. VARNEY. Yes—if you will—just while I'm upstairs—it won't be long! [*Goes to door up* L. C. *Turns at door*] Be careful won't you dear! [*Exit at door up* L. C. *and up the stairway*]

CAROLINE. [*Up* R. C.] Careful!—Well I should think so! As if I did n't know enough for that! [*Goes toward window up* R. *and pauses up* R. C. *Her face is radiant with the imagined romance of the situation. Goes to window up* R. *and peeps out slyly through curtains. After a moment she turns, an idea having occurred to her, and quickly rolls the couch up across before the window. Kneels on it with her back to the audience and tries to peep through curtains again.—Enter* WILFRED VARNEY *door up* L. C. *from* L.

coming in cautiously and as if he had been watching for an opportunity. He stops just within the door and looks back up stairway. He has on the trousers which CAROLINE *fixed for him in the previous act, and also the Army Jacket.—* CAROLINE *rises and turns from the couch up* R. *and sees* WILFRED.—*He turns to her.—She stands adoring him in his uniform*]

[*These clothes are not by any means new.—The trousers must be all right as to length though showing strange folds and awkwardness at bottom from being cut off and sewed by an amateur. But on no account must there be anything grotesque or laughable*]

CAROLINE. [*Up* R. *Subdued exclamation as she sees* WILFRED *in uniform*] Oh!

WILFRED. [L. C.—*Low voice—speaking across from door*] Mother is n't anywhere around is she?

CAROLINE. [*Coming out to up* C.] She she just went upstairs.

WILFRED. [*Down* L. C. *a little*] I'm not running away—but if she saw me with these things on she might feel funny.

CAROLINE. [*Half to herself*] She might not feel so very funny!

WILFRED. Well—[*Going over to desk down* R. *and taking papers and letters from pockets*]—you know how it is with a feller's mother. [CAROLINE *nods affirmatively from up* C.] [WILFRED *business of hurriedly finding letter among others—feeling in different pockets for it—so that he speaks without much thinking what he says*] Other people don't care—but mothers—well—they 're different.

CAROLINE. [C.—*Speaks absently*] Yes—other people don't care! [*Moves over toward up* L.—*The thought of* WILFRED *actually going gives her a slight sinking of the heart at which she herself is surprised*]

WILFRED. I've written that letter to the General!—Here it is—on'y I've got to end it off some way! [*Pulls a chair sideways to desk and half sits on it—intent on finishing the letter.—Business with pen, etc. and running hand into his hair impetuously*] I 'm not going to say "Your loving son" or any such rubbish as that! It would be an almighty let-down! I *love* him of course—*that 's* all right you know—but this is n't that kind of a letter! [*Pointing out writing on letter and speaking as if he supposed* CAROLINE *was at his shoulder*] I've been telling him—[*Looking round sees that* CAROLINE *is standing at a considerable distance up* L. C. *looking at him*]—What 's the matter?

CAROLINE. Nothing—! That is—I was only——

WILFRED. I thought you wanted to help!

CAROLINE. [*Quickly*] Oh yes—I do! I do! [*Goes down at once to* WILFRED *at desk*]

WILFRED. [*Looks in her face an instant.—A slight pause*] [CAROLINE *stammeringly asks*] The—the—[*Indicating his trousers by a little gesture*]—are they how you wanted 'em?

WILFRED. What?

CAROLINE. Those things. [*Pointing to trousers* WILFRED *is wearing*]

WILFRED. [*Glances at legs*] Oh—*they 're* all right!—Fine!—Now about this letter—tell me what you think! [*Turning to letter again*]

CAROLINE. Tell me what you said!

WILFRED. Want to hear it?

CAROLINE. I've got to have n't I? How could I help you if I did n't know what it was all about!

WILFRED. You 're pretty good! [*Looks at her briefly*] You *will* help me won't you? [*Catching hold of her* R. *hand as she stands near him on his* L.]

CAROLINE. O' co'se I will—[*After an instant's pause draws hand away from him*]—about the letter!

WILFRED. That 's what I mean!—It 's mighty important you know! Everything depends on it!

CAROLINE. Well I should *think* so! [CAROLINE *gets chair from up between windows and pulls it around near* WILFRED *on his left, and sits looking over the letter while he reads*]

WILFRED. I just gave it to him strong!

CAROLINE. That 's the *way* to give it to him!

WILFRED. You can't fool round with *him* much! He means business! But he 'll find out I mean business too!

CAROLINE. That 's right—everybody means business!—What did you say?

WILFRED. I said this!—[*Reads letter*] "General Ranson Varney—Commanding Division Army of Northern Virginia—Dear Papa! This is to notify you that I want you to let me come right now! If you don't I 'll come anyhow—that 's all! The seventeen call is almost out—

the sixteen comes next an' I 'm not going to wait for it! Do you think I 'm a damned coward? Tom Kittridge has gone! He was killed yesterday at Cold Harbor. Billy Fisher has gone. So has Cousin Stephen and he ain't sixteen. He lied about his age but I don't want to do that unless you make me. Answer this right now or not at all!"

CAROLINE. That 's *splendid!*

WILFRED. [*Surprised and delighted*] Do you think so?

CAROLINE. It 's just the thing!

WILFRED. But how 'm I going to end it?

CAROLINE. Why just end it!

WILFRED. How?

CAROLINE. Sign your name.

WILFRED. Nothing else?

CAROLINE. What else is there?

WILFRED. Just "Wilfred"?

CAROLINE. O' co'se!

WILFRED. [*Looks at her an instant then turns suddenly to desk and writes his name*] That 's the thing! [*Holds it up*] Will the rest of it do?

CAROLINE. Do! I should think so! [*Rising*] I wish he had it now! [*Goes toward* C.]

WILFRED. [*Rising*] So do I!—It might take two or three days! [*Moves toward* C.] I *can't* wait that long!—Why the Seventeen call might—[*Stops.—Thinks frowningly*]

CAROLINE. [*Suddenly turning at* C.] I 'll tell you what to do!—Telegraph! [WILFRED *looks at her—she at him.—After an instant he glances at the letter*]

WILFRED. [C. *at* R.] Whew! [*A whistle*] I have n't got money enough!

CAROLINE. [C. *at* L.] 'T won't take so very much!

WILFRED. Do you know what they 're charging now? Over seven dollars a word!

CAROLINE. Let 'em charge! We can cut it down so there 's only a few words an' it means just the same! [*They both go at the letter each holding it on his or her side*] You know the address won't cost a thing!

WILFRED. Won't it?

CAROLINE. No! They never do! There 's a heap o' money saved right now! We can use that to pay for the rest! [WILFRED *looks at her a little puzzled*] What comes next? [*Both look over the letter*]

WILFRED. [*Looks at letter*] "Dear Papa"—

CAROLINE. Leave that out! [*Both scratch at it with pens or pencils*]

WILFRED. I did n't care much for it anyway!

CAROLINE. He knew it before.

WILFRED. Of course he did!—I 'm glad it 's out!

CAROLINE. So 'm I!—What 's next? [*Reading*] "This-is-to-notify-you-that-I want-you-to-let-me-come-right-now." We might leave out that last "to."

WILFRED and CAROLINE. [*Reciting it off together experimentally to see how it reads without the "to"*] "I-want-you—let-me-come-right-now." [*After instant's thought both shake heads*]

WILFRED. [*Shaking head*] No!

CAROLINE. [*Shaking head*] No!

WILFRED. It does n't sound right.

CAROLINE. That 's only a little word anyhow!

WILFRED. So it is. What 's after that? [*Both eagerly look at letter*]

CAROLINE. Wait—here it is! [*Reads*] "If-you-don't — I 'll — come — anyhow—that 's—all." [*They consider*]

WILFRED. We might leave out "that 's all."

CAROLINE. [*Quickly*] No! Don't leave that out! It 's very important. It does n't seem so but it is! It shows—[*Hesitates*] well—it shows that 's all there is about it! That one thing might convince him!

WILFRED. We 've got to leave out something!

CAROLINE. Yes—but not that! Perhaps there 's something in the next! [*Reads*] "The-seventeen-call-is-almost-out"—That 's *got* to stay!

WILFRED. [*Reads*] "The-sixteen-comes-next."

CAROLINE. *That 's* got to stay!

WILFRED. [*Shaking head*] Yes!

CAROLINE. [*Taking it up*] "And-I 'm-not-going-to-wait-for-it!" [*Shaking her head without looking up*] No! No!

WILFRED. [*Shaking head*] No!

CAROLINE. We 'll find something in just a minute! [*Reading*] "Do-you-think-I 'm-a-damned-coward!" [*Both look up from the letter simultaneously and gaze at each other in silence for an instant*]

WILFRED. [*After the pause*] We might leave out the——

CAROLINE. [*Breaking in on him with almost a scream*] No! [*They again regard each other*]

WILFRED. [*After the pause*] That damn 's

going to cost us seven dollars and a half!

CAROLINE. It's *worth* it! Why it's the best thing you've got in the whole thing! Your papa's a general in the army! He'll *understand* that! What's next? I know there's something now.

WILFRED. [*Reads*] "Tom-Kittridge-has-gone. He-was-killed-yesterday-at-Cold-Harbor."

CAROLINE. [*Slight change in tone—a little lower*] Leave out that about his [*Very slight catch of breath*] about his being killed.

WILFRED. [*Looking at* CAROLINE] But he was!

CAROLINE. [*She is suddenly very quiet*] I know he was—but you haven't got to tell him the news have you?

WILFRED. That's so! [*They both cross off the words*]

CAROLINE. [*Becoming cheerful again*] How does it read now? [*They are both looking over the letter*]

WILFRED. It reads just the same—except that about Tom Kittridge.

CAROLINE. [*Looking at* WILFRED *astonished*] Just the same! After all this work!

[*They look at one another rather astounded, then suddenly turn to the letter again and study over it earnestly.—Sound of door bell in distant part of house.—Soon after* MARTHA *crosses outside up* L. C. *coming from door* R. *of stairway and disappearing outside up* L. C. *to* L.—*Sound of door off* L.—*A moment later she enters up* L. C. *from* L. *and goes up the stairway carrying a large envelope.*—WILFRED *and* CAROLINE *are so absorbed in work that they do not observe the bell or* MARTHA'S *movements*]

CAROLINE. [*Looking up from letter*] Everything else has *got* to stay!

WILFRED. Then we can't telegraph—it would take hundreds of dollars!

CAROLINE. [*With determination*] Yes we can! [WILFRED *looks at her.—She takes the letter*] I'll send it! [*Backing up a little toward door up* L. C.]

WILFRED. How can you—

CAROLINE. Never you mind!

WILFRED. [*Follows her up a little*] See here! [*Taking hold of the letter*] I'm not going to have you spending money!

CAROLINE. Ha—no danger! I haven't got any to spend!

WILFRED. [*Releases hold on letter*] Then what are you going to do?

CAROLINE. [*Turning up toward door up* L. C. *with letter*] Oh—I know! [*Turns toward* WILFRED] I reckon Douglass Stafford'll send it for me!

WILFRED. [*Quickly to her*] No he won't! [*They face each other.*—CAROLINE *surprised*]

CAROLINE. What's the reason he won't?

WILFRED. [*Slight pause*] If he wants to send it for *me* he can—but he won't send it for *you!*

CAROLINE. What do you care so long as he sends it?

WILFRED. [*Up* C.—*Looking at* CAROLINE—*slight change of tone*] Well—I care!—that's enough! [*They look at each other, then both lower eyes, looking in different directions*]

CAROLINE. [*Up* L. C.] Oh well—if you feel like that about it—! [*Turns away down* L. C.]

WILFRED. [*Up* C.—*Eyes lowered*] That's the way I feel! [*Pause.*—WILFRED *looks up at her—then moves down toward her*] You—you won't give up the idea of helping me because I feel like that—will you?

CAROLINE. [*Impulsively, with start and turn toward* WILFRED] Mercy no—I'll help you all I can—[WILFRED *impulsively takes her hand as if in gratitude and so quick that she draws it away and goes on with only a slight break*]—about the letter!

WILFRED. That's what I mean! [*They stand an instant,* CAROLINE *looking down,* WILFRED *at her*]

CAROLINE. [*Suddenly turning toward desk and crossing him to* R.] I'm going to see if we can't leave out something else! [*Sits at desk.*—WILFRED *goes down* R. *near her on her* L. *and stands looking over her, intent on the letter*]

[*Enter* MRS. VARNEY, *coming down the stairway and into the room at door up* L. C.—*She has an open letter in her hand. Also brings a belt and cap rolled up together. She pauses near the door and motions someone who is outside up* L. C. *to come in—then comes in a little way.*—MARTHA *follows her down and exits through door* R. *of stairway*]

[*Enter an orderly up* L. C. *from* L. *just from his horse after a long ride. Dusty, faded and bloody uniform; yellow stripes. Face sunburned and grim. He stands near the door up* L. C. *waiting, without effort to be precise or formal, but nevertheless being entirely soldierly.*—MRS. VARNEY *waits up* L. C. *until he enters*]

MRS. VARNEY. [*Turning to* WILFRED *and moving toward* C.] Wilfred! [WILFRED *and* CAROLINE *turn quickly. They both stare motionless for a moment*] Here 's a letter from your Father. He sent it by the orderly. [WILFRED *moves a step or two toward* MRS. VARNEY *and stands looking at her.*—CAROLINE *slowly rises with her eyes on* MRS. VARNEY.—MRS. VARNEY *speaks calmly but with the measured quietness of one who is controlling herself*] He tells me—[*She stops a little but it is only her voice that fails. Holds letter toward* WILFRED] You read it!

[WILFRED, *after a glance at* CAROLINE, *steps quickly to* MRS. VARNEY *and takes the letter. Reads it*—MRS. VARNEY *looking away a little as he does so.*—CAROLINE'S *eyes upon* WILFRED *as he reads.—The* ORDERLY *faced to* R. *on obliqued line of door.* —WILFRED *finishes very soon—only two or three seconds necessary. He glances at the* ORDERLY, *then hands the letter to his Mother as he steps across to him*]

WILFRED. [*Standing before the* ORDERLY] The General says I 'm going back with you!

ORDERLY. [*Saluting*] His orders sir!

WILFRED. When do we start?

ORDERLY. Soon as you can sir—I 'm waiting!

WILFRED We 'll make it right now! [WILFRED *turns and walks quickly to his Mother*] You won't mind, Mother?

[MRS. VARNEY *does not speak, but quietly strokes the hair back from his forehead with a trembling hand—and only once. She then hands him the belt and cap. Old and worn cap. Belt that has seen service*]

MRS. VARNEY. [*Low voice*] Your brother wanted you to take these—I told him you were going. [WILFRED *takes them. Puts on the belt at once*] He says he can get another belt—when he wants it. You 're to have his blanket too—I 'll get it. [*She crosses* WILFRED *and goes off at door up* L. C. *to* L., *going back of* ORDERLY]

[WILFRED *finishing adjusting the belt.* —CAROLINE *motionless down* R. *but now looking down at the floor—facing nearly front*]

WILFRED. [*Suppresses excitement*] Fits as if it was made for me! [*To orderly*] I 'll be with you in a jiffy! [WILFRED *goes to* CAROLINE] We won't have to send that now—[*indicating letter they have been working on*] will we? [WILFRED *stands on her* L.—CAROLINE *shakes her head a little without looking up—then slowly raises left hand in which she has the letter and holds it out to him, her eyes still on the floor.*—WILFRED *takes the letter mechanically and keeps it in his hand during the next few lines, tearing it up absent-mindedly*] You 're pretty good—to help me like you did! You can help me again if you—if you want to! [CAROLINE *raises her eyes and looks at him*] *I 'd* like to fight twice as well if— [*Hesitates.*—CAROLINE *looks at him an instant longer and then looks down without speaking*] Good-bye! [WILFRED *holds out his hand.*—CAROLINE *puts her hand in his without looking at him*] Perhaps you 'll write to me about —about helping me fight twice as well! I would n't mind if you telegraphed! That is—if you telegraphed that you would! [*Slight pause.* WILFRED *holding* CAROLINE'S *hand boyishly.*—CAROLINE *looking down.*—WILFRED *trying to say something but not finding the words. —Enter* MRS. VARNEY *at door up* L. C. *from* L.—WILFRED *hears her and turns—leaving* CAROLINE *and meeting his mother near* C.—*She brings an army blanket rolled up and tied.*—WILFRED *takes it and slings it over his shoulder*] Good-bye mother! [*He kisses her rather hurriedly.*—MRS. VARNEY *stands passive*] You won't mind, will you! [WILFRED *crosses at once to* ORDERLY] Ready sir! [*Saluting.*—ORDERLY *turns and marches off at door up left.*—WILFRED *follows the* ORDERLY.—*Brief pause*]

[*The opening and heavy closing of the door outside left is heard, and then it is still.*—MRS. VARNEY *is the first to move. She turns and walks slowly up a few steps, her back to the audience, but with no visible emotion. It is as if her eyes filled with tears and she turned away.—When* MRS. VARNEY *stops up* C. CAROLINE *moves a little, her eyes still down, walking slowly across toward the door up* L. C.—MRS. VARNEY *hears her and turns in time to speak just before she reaches the door up* L. C.]

MRS. VARNEY. Going, dear? [CAROLINE

nods her head a little without looking round] Oh yes! [*Speaks with a shade of forced cheerfulness*] Your party of course! You ought to be there! [CAROLINE *stops and speaks back into the room without looking at* MRS. VARNEY]

CAROLINE. [*Subdued voice. With a sad little shake of head*] There won't—there won't be any party to-night. [*Exit at door up* L. C. *to* L.]

MRS. VARNEY. [*After an instant's wait starts toward door up* L. C.] Caroline! Stop a moment! [*At door*] I don't want you to go home alone! [*She goes down* L. *and rings the bell*]

CAROLINE. [*Outside up* L.] Oh I don't mind!

[*Sounds of front door and heavy steps of men outside up left.*—MRS. VARNEY *goes up* L. C. *looking off, and then retires back a little to up* C.]

[*Enter* ARRELSFORD *and two soldiers at the door up* L. C. *from* L.—ARRELSFORD *motions men to stand at the door and goes quickly to* MRS. VARNEY *up* C.]

ARRELSFORD. [*Low voice*] Is he—? [*A motion toward window at* R.]

MRS. VARNEY. [*To* ARRELSFORD, *hardly above a whisper*] Yes!

[*Enter* CAROLINE *at door up* L. C. *from* L.]

CAROLINE. [*Up* L. C.] Oh Mrs. Varney—there's a heap o' soldiers out yere! You don't reckon anything's the mattah do you?

[*Enter* MARTHA *at door up* L. C. *from door* R. *of stairway.*—ARRELSFORD *goes back of* MRS. VARNEY *to* R.—*Looks through curtains of window down* R.]

MRS. VARNEY. [*Hastening to* CAROLINE] Sh!—No—there's nothing the matter! Martha, I want you to go home with Miss Mitford—at once! [*Urging* CAROLINE *off*] Good night dear! [*Kissing her*]

CAROLINE. [*Up* L. C.] Good night! [*Looks up in* MRS. VARNEY'S *face*] You don't reckon she could go with me to—[*Hesitates*] to somewhere else, do you?

MRS. VARNEY. [*Up* L. C., R. *of* CAROLINE] Why where do you want to go?

CAROLINE. Just to—just to the telegraph office!

[ARRELSFORD *turns sharply and looks at* CAROLINE *from window down* R.]

MRS. VARNEY. Now! At this time of night!

CAROLINE. I've *got* to! Oh, it's very important business!

[ARRELSFORD R. *watching* CAROLINE]

MRS. VARNEY. Of course, then, Martha must go with you! Good night!

CAROLINE. Good night! [*Exit* CAROLINE *and* MARTHA *at door up* L. C. *to* L.]

MRS. VARNEY. [*Calling off up* L. C. *to* L.] Martha, don't leave her an instant!

MARTHA. [*Outside* L. *or just going*] No'm—I'll take care!

[MARTHA *does not come into room for foregoing scene. She remains back of archway or opening up* L. C.—*Heavy sound of door outside up* L.]

ARRELSFORD. [*Going up* C. *quickly—low, sharp voice*] What is she going to do at the telegraph office?—What is it?

MRS. VARNEY. [*Going down* L. C. *a little. Low voice*] I've no idea! [*Accent on first syllable of "idea"*]

ARRELSFORD. [*Low voice*] Has she had any conversation with him? [*Motion toward* R.]

MRS. VARNEY. [*Low voice*] Why—they were talking together here—early this evening! But it is n't possible that Caroline could have any——

ARRELSFORD. [*Interrupting. Low voice*] *Anything* is possible! [*Goes over to* CORPORAL *at up* L. C. *quickly, passing back of* MRS. VARNEY.—MRS. VARNEY *moves to up* R. C. *as* ARRELSFORD *crosses at back*] Have Eddinger follow that girl! She's going to the telegraph office.—Don't let her get any despatch off until I see it! Make no mistake about that! [CORPORAL *exits with salute at door up* L. C. *to* L.—*Brief pause.*—ARRELSFORD *turns to* MRS. VARNEY] Are they both out there? [*Motioning toward veranda at* R]

MRS. VARNEY. [*Up* R. C.—*Low tone*] Yes!—Did you bring the man from Libby Prison?

ARRELSFORD. [L. *of her.*—*Low voice*] The guard's holding him out in the street. When she gets Thorne in here and leaves him alone I'll have them bring him up to that window [*Pointing to window up* R.] and then shove him into the room.

[CORPORAL *re-appears at the door up* L. C. *from* L. *and awaits further orders.*—ARRELSFORD *and* MRS. VARNEY *continue in low tones*]

MRS. VARNEY. [R. C.] Where shall I——

ARRELSFORD. Out there [*Pointing up* L. *and going toward door a little*] where you can get a view of this room!

MRS. VARNEY. But if he sees me——

ARRELSFORD. He won't if it's dark in the hall! [*Turns to* CORPORAL *and gives order in low distinct voice*] Shut off those lights out there! [*Indicating lights outside the door or archway up left.*—CORPORAL *exits up* L. C. *to* L.—*An instant later the lights outside up* L. *go off*] We can close these curtains can't we?

MRS. VARNEY. Yes. [ARRELSFORD *draws curtains or portières across at door or archway up* L. C.]

[CORPORAL *and* MEN *are out of sight behind the drawn curtains*]

ARRELSFORD. [*Turning front*] I don't want much light in here! [*Indicating drawing-room*]

[ARRELSFORD *goes to table up* C. *and turns down the lamp.*—MRS. VARNEY *turns down lamp on desk down* R.—*Stage in dim light*]

ARRELSFORD. [*Carefully moves couch away from window up* R. *and opens portières of window.*—*Almost in a whisper*] Now open those curtains!—Carefully!—Don't attract attention! [*Indicating window down* R.]

[MRS. VARNEY *very quietly draws back the curtains to window down* R.—*Moonlight on through window down* R. *covering as much of stage as possible. Moonlight also strong on backing up* R. *and also in across room from there*]

ARRELSFORD. [*Moving over to up* L. C.—*Speaking across to* MRS. VARNEY *after the lights are down*] Are those women in there yet? [*Indicating door up* C.]

MRS. VARNEY. Yes.

ARRELSFORD. Where's the key? [MRS. VARNEY *moves noiselessly to the door up* C.] Is it on this side?

[MRS. VARNEY *turns and nods affirmatively*]

ARRELSFORD. Lock the door!

[MRS. VARNEY *turns the key as noiselessly as possible.*—EDITH *suddenly appears at window up* R. *coming on quickly and closing the window after her.*—MRS. VARNEY *and* ARRELSFORD *both turn and stand looking at her.*

EDITH. [*Going down* R. C. *and stretching out left hand toward* MRS. VARNEY.—*Very low voice—but breathlessly*] Mama! [MRS. VARNEY *hurries forward with her* C.—EDITH *on her* R.—ARRELSFORD *remains up* L. C. *looking on*] I want to speak to you!

ARRELSFORD. [L. C.—*Low tone.*—*Stepping forward*] We can't wait!

EDITH. [C.] You must! [ARRELSFORD *moves back protestingly.*—EDITH *turns to* MRS. VARNEY.—*Almost a whisper*] I can't—I can't do it! Oh—let me go!

MRS. VARNEY. [C.—*Very low voice*] Edith! You were the one who——

EDITH. [*Almost a whisper*] I was sure then!

MRS. VARNEY. Has he confessed?

EDITH. [*Quickly*] No no! [*Glance toward* ARRELSFORD]

ARRELSFORD. [*Low voice—sharp*] Don't speak so loud!

MRS. VARNEY. [*Low voice*] What is it Edith—you *must* tell me!

EDITH. [*Almost a whisper*] Mama—he loves me! [*Breathless*]—Yes—and I—— Oh—let someone else do it!

MRS. VARNEY. You don't mean that you—

[ARRELSFORD *comes forward quickly* L. C.]

EDITH. [*Seeing* ARRELSFORD *approach and crossing* MRS. VARNEY *to him*] No no! Not now! Not now!

MRS. VARNEY. [C. R.—*Low voice*] More reason now than ever!

ARRELSFORD. [C. L.—*Low voice*] We *must* go on!

EDITH. [C.—*Turning desperately upon* ARRELSFORD.—*Low voice*] Why are *you* doing this?

ARRELSFORD. [*Low voice*] Because I please!

EDITH. [*Low voice—but with force*] You never pleased before! Hundreds of suspicious cases have come up—hundreds of men have been run down—but you preferred to sit at your desk in the War Department!

MRS. VARNEY. [*Low voice*] Edith!

ARRELSFORD. [*Low voice*] We won't discuss that now!

EDITH. [*Low voice*] No—we'll end it! I'll have nothing more to do with the affair!

ARRELSFORD. [*Low voice*] You won't!

MRS. VARNEY. [*Low voice*] Edith—!

EDITH. [*Low voice*] Nothing at all!—Nothing!—Nothing!

ARRELSFORD. [*Low voice but with vehemence*] At your own suggestion Miss Varney, I agreed to a plan by which we could criminate this friend of yours—or establish his innocence. At the critical moment—when everything's ready, you propose to withdraw—making it a failure and perhaps allowing him to escape altogether!

MRS. VARNEY. [*Low voice*] I can't allow you to do this Edith!

EDITH. [*Low voice—desperately*] He's there!—the man is there—at the further end of the veranda! What more do you want of me!

ARRELSFORD. [*Low voice. Sharp. Intense*] Call him into this room! If anyone else should do it he'd suspect—he'd be on his guard!

EDITH. [*After pause. Low voice*] Very well—I'll call him into this room. [*Turning away as if to do so*]

ARRELSFORD. [*Low voice*] One thing more! [EDITH *turns back to him*] I want him to have this paper! [*Holding out paper that was taken from* JONAS *in* ACT I] Tell him where it came from—tell him the old niggah got it from a prisoner in Libby!

EDITH. [*Quietly. Low voice*] Why am I to do this?

ARRELSFORD. [*Low but very strong*] Why not? If he's innocent where's the harm?—If not—if he's what I think he is—the message on that paper will send him to the telegraph office to-night and that's just where we want him!

EDITH. [*Low voice*] I never promised that!

ARRELSFORD. [*Hard sharp voice though subdued*] Do you still believe him innocent?

[*Pause.—*EDITH *slowly raises her head erect. Looks* ARRELSFORD *full in the face*]

EDITH. [*Almost whisper*] I still—believe him—innocent!

ARRELSFORD. Then why are you afraid to give him this? [*Indicating paper*]

[*Pause.—*EDITH *turns to* ARRELSFORD. *Stretches out her hand for the paper.—*ARRELSFORD *puts the paper in* EDITH'S *hand.—*ARRELSFORD *and* MRS. VARNEY *watch her.—She turns and moves up a few steps toward the window. Stops and stands listening up* L. C.*—Noise of chair being set back on veranda outside* R.]

EDITH. [*Low voice*] Captain Thorne's coming.

ARRELSFORD. [*Going to door up* L. C. *and holding curtains back*] This way Mrs. Varney!—Quick!—Quick! [ARRELSFORD *and* MRS. VARNEY *hasten off at the door up* L. *closing portières after them*]

[EDITH *moves across to down* L. C. *and stands near table.—Sound of* THORNE'S *footsteps on veranda outside windows* R.*—*EDITH *slowly turns toward the window up* R. *and stands looking at it with a fascinated dread.—*THORNE *opens the window up* R. *and enters at once, coming a few steps into the room. He stops and stands an instant looking at* EDITH *as she looks strangely at him. Then he goes to her*]

THORNE. [*Low voice—near* EDITH] Is anything the matter?

EDITH. [*Slightly shakes her head before speaking.—Nearly a whisper*] Oh no! [*Emphasize "no."—Stands looking up in his face*]

THORNE. [*Low voice*] You've been away a long time!

EDITH. [*Low voice*] Only a few minutes!

THORNE. [*Low voice*] Only a few years.

EDITH. [*Easier*] Oh—if that's a few years—[*Turning away front a little*] what a lot of time there is!

THORNE. [*Low voice*] There's only to-night!

EDITH. [*Turning to him. A breathless interrogation*] What!

THORNE. [*Taking her hands and drawing her into his arms*] There's only to-night and you in the world!—Oh—see what I've been doing! I came here determined not to tell you that I love you—I love you—I love you—and for the last half hour I've been telling you nothing else! Ah, my darling—there's only to-night and you!

EDITH. [*A breathless whisper*] No no—you must n't! [*A quick apprehensive glance around toward left and back*]—*not now!* [*Her head is turned a little away from him*]

[THORNE, *still holding her, is motionless an instant. Then he gives a lightning-quick glance about—to* R. *and up—and almost instantly his eyes are back to her. He slowly releases her and stands back a step*]

THORNE. [*Low voice*] Don't mind what I said Miss Varney—I must have forgotten myself. Believe me I came to make a friendly call and—and say good-bye. [*Bowing slightly*] Permit me to do so now. [*Turns up at once making turn to* L. *and walks toward door up* L. C.]

EDITH. [*Quickly across to* C. *as* THORNE *goes*] Oh!—Cap'n Thorne! [*This is timed to stop* THORNE *just before he reaches the closed portières of door up* L. C.*—*THORNE *turns up* L. C. *and looks at* EDITH.*—Calcium across from window*

R. *on him.—*EDITH *trying to be natural—but her lightness somewhat forced*] Before you go I—[*Slight quiver in her voice*]—I wanted to ask your advice about something! [*She stands near* C. *turned a little to front*]

[THORNE *looks at her motionless an instant. Then turns his head slowly toward the portières on his left. Turns back to* EDITH *at* C. *again and at once moves down to her on her* L.]

THORNE. [*As he comes down to* EDITH] Yes?

EDITH. What do you think—this means? [*Holds the piece of paper out toward* THORNE *but avoids looking in his face*]

THORNE. [L. *of* EDITH. *Stepping quickly to her and taking the paper easily*] Why, what is it? [*A half-glance at the paper as he takes it*]

EDITH. It's a—[*Hesitates slightly. Recovers at once and looks up at him brightly*] That's what I want you to tell me.

THORNE. [*Looking at the paper*] Oh—you don't know!

EDITH. [*Shaking her head slightly*] No. [*Stands waiting—eyes averted.—*THORNE *glances quickly at her an instant on peculiar tone of "no"*]

THORNE. [*Looking again at the paper*] A note from someone?

EDITH. It might be.

THORNE. [*Glancing about*] Well, it's pretty dark here! [*Sees the low-turned lamp on desk down* R. *and crosses to it*] If you'll excuse me I'll turn up this lamp a little—[*Comes to desk*] then we can see what it is. [*Turns up lamp.—Lights on foot* 1–2] There we are! [*Looks at paper, holding it down in light from lamp. Reads as if with much difficulty*] "Attack . . . . to-night" . . . . There's something about "Attack to-night"—[*Turns easily to* EDITH] Could you make out what it was?

[EDITH *shakes head negatively. Her lips move, but she cannot speak. She turns away*]

[THORNE *looks at her a second—then a slow turn of head (turning it to his* L.) *glancing up stage.—Then quickly turns to examine the paper again*] "Attack . . . . to-night . . . . plan . . . . three." [*Looks up to front as if considering. Repeats*] Plan three! [*Considering again.—Slight laugh*] Well—this thing must be a puzzle of some kind, Miss Varney. [*Turning to* EDITH]

EDITH. [*Slowly. Strained voice, as if forcing herself to speak*] It was taken from a Yankee prisoner!

THORNE. [*Instantly coming from former easy attitude into one showing interest and surprise. Looking at* EDITH] So!—Yankee prisoner eh? [*While speaking he is holding paper in right hand as if to look at it again when he finishes speaking to* EDITH]

EDITH. Yes—down in Libby!—He gave it to one of our servants—old Jonas!

THORNE. [*Turning quickly to paper*] Why here—this might be something—[*Looks again at the paper*] "Attack to-night—plan three—use Telegraph—" [*Second's pause. He looks up front*] Use telegraph! [*Turns quickly to* EDITH *and goes toward her*] This might be something important Miss Varney! Looks like a plot on our Department Telegraph Lines! Who did Jonas give it to?

EDITH. No one!

THORNE. No one!—Well—how—how—

EDITH. We took it away from him!

THORNE. Oh! [*An "Oh!" meaning "What a pity!"*] [*Starting at once as if to cross above* EDITH *to door up* L. C.] That was a mistake!

EDITH. [*Detaining him.—Speaks rapidly—almost a whisper*] What are you going to do?

THORNE. [*Strong. Determined*] Find that nigger and make him tell who this paper was for—he's the man we want! [*Crossing back of her—toward door up* L. C.]

EDITH. [*Turning quickly to him*] Cap'n Thorne—they've lied about you!

THORNE. [*Wheeling round like a flash up* L. C. *and coming down quickly to her*] Lied about me! What do you mean? [*Seizing her hands and looking in her face to get the answer there*]

EDITH. [*Quick—breathless—very low—almost whisper*] Don't be angry—I did n't think it would be like this!

THORNE. [*With great force*] Yes—but what have you done?

EDITH. [*Breaking loose from him and crossing to* L.] No!

THORNE. [*As she crosses before him—trying to detain her*] But I must know!

[*Sound of heavy door outside* L. *and of steps and voices in the hall—"Here! This way!" etc.*]

CORPORAL. [*Speaking outside door up* L. C.

to L.] This way! Look out on that side will you?

[THORNE *on hearing* CORPORAL *etc. backs away to* R. C. *keeping his eyes on door up* L. C. *and at same time snatching revolver from holster. Stands motionless down* L. C.*—eyes on door—revolver ready*]

EDITH. Oh! [*Going rapidly up* L.]—I don't want to be here! [*She exits door up* L. *and goes up stairs out of the way of the soldiers*]

[*Enter at once on exit of* EDITH, CORPORAL *with two men at door up* L. C. *from* L.*—They cross rapidly toward window up* R., CORPORAL *leading carrying a lighted lantern.*—THORNE, *seeing* CORPORAL, *at once breaks position and moves across towards up* C. *as men cross, watching* CORPORAL *who is up* R. C. *directing his men*]

CORPORAL. [*Near window up* R.] Out here! Look out now!

[*The men exit at window up* R.]

THORNE. [*Quick on* CORPORAL'S *speech so as to stop him at* R. C.] What is it Corporal? [*Putting revolver back into holster*]

[THORNE *stands up* C. *in light from window up* R. *facing* CORPORAL]

CORPORAL. [*Turning at up* R. C. *and saluting*] Prisoner sir—broke out o' Libby! We 're run him down the street—he turned in here somewhere! If he comes in that way [*Indicating the window down* R.] would you be good enough to let us know!

THORNE. Go on, Corporal! [*Starts across to window down* R.] I'll look out for this window!

[*Exit* CORPORAL *window up* R.]

[THORNE *strides rapidly to window down* R. *Pushes curtains back each side and stands within the window looking off. Right hand on revolver in holster. Left hand holding curtains back.—Moonlight on through window down* R. *across stage and also from window up* R.*—Dead pause for an instant.—Suddenly the two men who crossed with* CORPORAL *appear at window up* R. *holding* HENRY DUMONT. *With a sudden movement they force him on through the window into the room and disappear quickly outside off to* R.—DUMONT *stands an instant where he landed up* R. C.*—Looks back through window up* R., *not comprehending what is going on. He gives a quick glance about the room.* DUMONT *wears a worn and tattered uniform of a United States Cavalry private. He is pale as from lack of food—but not emaciated or ill.—Hold this Tableau:*—THORNE *standing motionless just within the window down* R. *his eyes sharply watching off to* R., *his hand on the butt of his revolver;*—DUMONT *up* R. C., *holding position he came to on being forced into the room, with enough light through window up* R. *to show the blue of his uniform.—After a second's pause* DUMONT *turns from the window and looks slowly about the room, taking in the various points like a caged animal, turning his head very slowly as he looks one way and another. Soon he moves a few steps down toward* C. *and pauses. Turns and makes out a doorway up* L. C. *and after a glance round, he walks rapidly toward it. Just before he reaches the door the blades of four bayonets come down into position between the drawn curtain or portières, barring his exit there.—Light from outside window* R. *to strike across on blades of bayonets.—Very slight steely click of bayonets striking together as they come down into position.*—DUMONT *stops instantly and stands motionless.*—THORNE *at window down* R. *turns sharply on click of bayonets looking into room, and advancing a few steps in as he does so, coming to a stand with right hand on chair that is near, and trying to see who it is on the opposite side of the room.—Bayonets withdrawn at once after they are shown.*—DUMONT *turns from the door and begins to move slowly down at* L. *along the wall. Just as he is coming around table down* L. *toward* C. *he sees* THORNE *and stops dead.—Both men motionless, their eyes upon each other.—Hold it several seconds.*—DUMONT *makes a start as if to escape through window up* R., *moving across toward it*]

THORNE. [*Quick and loud order as* DUMONT *starts toward window*] Halt!—You 're a prisoner!

[DUMONT, *after instant's hesitation on* THORNE'S *order, starts rapidly toward window up* R. *again.*—THORNE *heads him off, meeting him up* R. C. *and seizes him*]

THORNE. [*As he heads* DUMONT *off*] Halt! I say!

[DUMONT *grapples with* THORNE *and the two men struggle together, moving quickly down stage to* L. C., *very close to front—getting as far as possible from those who are watching them*]

THORNE. [*Loud voice, as they struggle down stage*] Here 's your man Corporal! What are you waiting for! Here 's your man I say!

DUMONT. [*When they are down as far as possible—holding* THORNE *motionless an instant and hissing out between his teeth, without pause or inflection on the words*] ATTACK TO-NIGHT—PLAN THREE—TELEGRAPH—DO YOU GET IT?

THORNE. [*Quick on it*] YES!

[*This dialogue in capitals shot at each other with great force and rapidity—and so low that people outside door up* L. *could not hear*]

DUMONT. [*Low voice—almost whisper*] They 're watching us! Shoot me in the leg!

THORNE. [*Holding* DUMONT *motionless*] No no! I can't do that!

DUMONT. You must!

[*They are struggling desperately—but with little movement*]

THORNE. [*Quick on it*] I can't shoot my own brother!

DUMONT. It 's the only way to throw 'em off the scent!

THORNE. Well I won't do it anyhow!

DUMONT. If you won't do it I will! Give me that gun! [*Pushing left arm out to get revolver*]

THORNE. [*Holding* DUMONT'S *arm back motionless*] No no Harry! You 'll hurt yourself!

DUMONT. [*Struggling to get revolver*] Let me have it!

[*They are now struggling in real desperation, moving quickly up* C. *as they do so, coming into light from windows at* R]

THORNE. [*Calling out as he struggles up* C. *with* DUMONT] Here 's your man Corporal! What 's the matter with you!

[DUMONT *gets hold of* THORNE'S *revolver and pulls it out of holster*]

THORNE. [*As* DUMONT *holds him up* C. *and is getting revolver*]—[*Loud—aspirated—sharp*] Look out Harry! You 'll hurt yourself! [*Gets his* R. *hand on revolver to hold it*] [DUMONT *manages with his* L. *hand to wrench* THORNE'S *hand loose from the revolver and hold it up while he seizes the weapon with his* R. *hand and pulls it out of the holster. At the same time he shoves* THORNE *off toward down* R.]

THORNE. [*As* DUMONT *throws him off* R.] Look out! [*As* DUMONT *throws* THORNE *off toward down* R. *he backs quickly—with same motion—up* C. *the revolver in his right hand.—Before* THORNE *can recover and turn at right* DUMONT *fires.—There is a quick sharp scream from ladies outside up* L. C. *behind portières.—*DUMONT *staggers down* C. *and falls, holding the revolver in his hand until he is down and then releasing it, so that it lies on the floor near him*]

THORNE. [*Back against chair at* R.*—which he was flung against*] Harry—you 've shot yourself! [*Instantly on this he dives for the revolver that* DUMONT *has dropped and gets it, coming up on same motion with it in right hand and stands in careless attitude just over* DUMONT'S *body to* R. *of it.—Men's voices heard outside up* L. *and outside windows* R. *and up* R.]

[*Instantly on* THORNE *stooping to snatch up revolver, enter at up* L. C. *through the portières* ARRELSFORD *and* MEN *followed by* EDITH, MRS. VARNEY *and* MISS KITTRIDGE, *and from windows up* R. *and* R. *the* CORPORAL *and* MEN.—ARRELSFORD *runs at once to table up* C. *and turns up the lamp.—Others stand on tableau—*MRS. VARNEY *and* EDITH *at left,* MISS KITTRIDGE *up* L. MEN *in doorway and up* R. C. *near window*]

[*Lights full on instantly on* ARRELSFORD *reaching the lamp*]

ARRELSFORD, MRS. VARNEY, EDITH, MISS KITTRIDGE, CORPORAL, MEN. [*As they enter*] Where is he!—What has he done!—He 's shot the man!—This way now! [*These different exclamations from the different characters and nearly together as they rush into the room, but quieting down at once as they see* THORNE *standing over* DUMONT]

THORNE. [*Instantly on people stopping quiet.—With easy swing of revolver crossing toward* C. *as he brings it up to put back into holster*] There 's your prisoner Corporal—look out for him! [*Stands at* R. C. *putting revolver back into holster*]

[CURTAIN]

ACT III

SCENES:—*The War Department Telegraph Office.*

TEN O'CLOCK

Plain and somewhat battered and grimy room on the second floor of a public building. Moldings and stucco-work broken and discolored. Stained and smoky walls. Large windows—the glass covered with grime and cobwebs. Plaster fallen or knocked from walls and ceiling in some places. All this from neglect —not from bombardment. The building was once a handsome one, but has been put to war purposes. Very large and high double doors up R. C. *obliqued. These doors open to a corridor showing plain corridor-backing of a public building. This door must lead off well to* R. *so that it shall not interfere with window showing street up* L. C. *Three wide French windows up* L. *and* L. C. *obliqued a little and opening down to floor, with balcony outside extending* R. *and* L. *and showing several massive white columns, bases at balcony and extending up out of sight as if for several stories above. Part of the building with columns shown in perspective, as if a wing. Backing of windows showing night view of city roofs and buildings as from height of second floor. Large disused fireplace with elaborate marble mantel in bad repair and very dirty on* R. *side behind telegraph tables. Door up* C. *opening to cupboard with shelves on which are battery jars and telegraph office truck of various kinds. Room lighted by gas on* R. *above* R. *telegraph table, several burners branching from a main pipe and all to turn on and off easily by means of one cock in main pipe, just above the telegraph table. Show evening through windows up* L.*—dark, with lights of buildings very faint and distant, keeping general effect outside window of darkness in order to avoid distracting attention from interior of room. Electric Calciums (moonlight) to throw on at windows up* L. C. *and* L. *on cues, and also to hold on the massive white columns and on the characters who go out on the balcony. Corridor outside door up* R. C. *not strongly illuminated. In the room itself fair light but not brilliant. Plain, solid table with telegraph instruments down* R. C. *Another plain plank table with instruments along wall at right side. Table down* R. C. *braced to look as if fastened securely to the floor. Also see that wire connections are properly made from all the instruments in the room to wires running up the wall on right side, thence across along ceiling to up* L. C. *and out through broken lights in half circle windows above the French windows at up* L. C. *This large bunch of wires leading out, in plain sight, is most important. Large office clock over mantel set at* 10 *o'clock at opening and to run during the Act.*

Two instruments, A. *and* D., *on table down* R. C.—A. *is at* R. *end of table and is the only one regularly used at that table,* D. *being for emergency. Two instruments,* B. *and* C. *on long table at* R. *against fireplace.* B. *is at lower end of table.* C. *at upper end. One chair at table down* R. C. *Two chairs at table* R. *One chair up* C. *No sound of cannonading in this Act.*

[*At opening there are two Operators at work, one at table down* R. C., *one at table on* R. *side. They are in old gray uniforms, but in shirt sleeves. Coats are hung up or thrown on chairs. Busy click-effect of instruments from an instant before curtain rises, and continues. After first continued clicking for a moment there are occasional pauses. Messengers* A. *and* B. *near door up* R. C. *Messenger No.* 3 *in front of door* C. *talking to messenger No.* 4. *Messenger No.* 2 *looking out of middle window over* L.]

SECOND OPERATOR. [LIEUT. ALLISON] [*At table* R.—*instrument* B.—*finishing writing a dispatch*] Ready here! [*Messenger* A. *steps quickly forward and takes dispatch*] Department! The Secretary must have it to-night! [MESSENGER *salutes and exits quickly at door up* R. C. *with dispatch.—Short pause.—Other* MESSENGERS *standing on attention*]

FIRST OPERATOR. [LIEUT. FORAY] [*At table down* R. C.—*instrument* A.] Ready here! [MESSENGER B.—*steps quickly down and takes dispatch from* FIRST OPERATOR] To the President—General Watson—marked private! [MESSENGER B. *salutes and exits quickly doors up* R. C.]

[*Business continues a short time as before.—Busy clicking of instruments. calls of sentries far below in the square.*—SECOND OPERATOR *at* R. *moves to another instrument when it begins to click and answers call*]

[FIRST MESSENGER *enters hurriedly at doors up* R. C. *and comes down* L. *of table* R. C. *with dispatch*]

FIRST MESSENGER. Major Bridgman!

FIRST OPERATOR. [*Looking up from work*] Bridgman! Where 's that?

SECOND MESSENGER. [*Glances at dispatch*] Longstreet's Corps.

FIRST OPERATOR. That 's yours Allison. [*Resumes work at instrument* A.]

[SECOND OPERATOR *holds out hand for dispatch.*—FIRST MESSENGER *crosses back of table* R. C. *gives it to him and exits at door up* R.—SECOND OPERATOR *sends message on instrument* B. —*Sound of band of music in distance increasing very gradually.*—MESSENGERS *go to windows up* L. C. *and look out but glance now and then at* OPERATORS]

SECOND MESSENGER. [*Opening* C. *window and looking out while music is coming on and still distant*] What 's that going up Main Street?

THIRD MESSENGER. [*Looks out*] Richmond Grays!

SECOND and FOURTH MESSENGERS. [*Together*] No!

[MESSENGERS *look out through middle window up* L.]

SECOND MESSENGER. That 's what they are, sure enough!

THIRD MESSENGER. They 're sending 'em down the river!

SECOND MESSENGER. Not to-night!

FOURTH MESSENGER. Seems like they was, though!

THIRD MESSENGER. I did n't reckon they 'd send the Grays out without there was something going on!

FOURTH MESSENGER. How do you know but what there is?

SECOND MESSENGER. To-night! Why good God! It 's as quiet as a tomb!

FOURTH MESSENGER. I reckon that 's what 's worrying 'em! It 's so damned unusual!

[*Sound of band gradually dies away. Before music is quite off,* FIRST OPERATOR *finishes a dispatch from instrument* A. *and calls*]

FIRST OPERATOR. Ready here! [THIRD MESSENGER *comes down to him to* L. *of table* R. C. *and takes dispatch*] Department—from General Lee—duplicate to the President!

[THIRD MESSENGER *salutes and exits quickly at doors up* R. C. *Business goes on.—Enter an* ORDERLY, *doors up* R. C. *Goes quickly down to* FIRST OPERATOR. SECOND *and* FOURTH MESSENGERS *stand talking near windows up* L. C.]

ORDERLY. [L. *of table* R. C. *salutes*] The Secretary would like to know if there 's anything from General Lee come in since nine o'clock this evening.

FIRST OPERATOR. Just sent one over an' a duplicate went out to the President.

ORDERLY. The President 's with the Cabinet yet—he did n't go home! They want an operator right quick over there to take down a cipher.

FIRST OPERATOR. [*Calling out to* SECOND OPERATOR] Got anything on, Charlie?

SECOND OPERATOR. Not right now!

FIRST OPERATOR. Well go over to the Department—they want to take down a cipher.

[SECOND OPERATOR *gets coat and exits doors up* R. C. *putting coat on as he goes, followed by the* ORDERLY *who came for him.—Business and click of instruments goes on.—Doors up* R. C. *are opened from the outside by a couple of young officers in showy and untarnished uniforms, who stand in most polite attitudes waiting for a lady to pass in.*—FIRST OPERATOR *very busy writing at table* R. C. *taking message from instrument* A.]

FIRST YOUNG OFFICER. Right this way, Miss Mitford!

SECOND YOUNG OFFICER. Allow me, Miss Mitford! *This* is the Department Telegraph office!

[*Enter at the doors up* R. C. CAROLINE MITFORD.—*The young officers follow her in.*—MARTHA *enters after the officers, and waits near door well up stage*]

CAROLINE. [*Coming down* C. *as she comes in. Speaks in rather subdued manner and without vivacity, as if her mind were upon what she came for*] Thank you!

FIRST YOUNG OFFICER. [*On her* L.] I'm

afraid you 've gone back on the Army, Miss Mitford!

[CAROLINE *looks at* FIRST YOUNG OFFICER]

CAROLINE. [C.] Gone where?

SECOND YOUNG OFFICER. [*On* CAROLINE'S R.] Seems like we ought to a' got a salute as you went by!

CAROLINE. Oh yes! [*Salutes in perfunctory and absent-minded manner and turns away glancing about room and moving down a step or two*] Good evening! [*Nodding to one of the* MESSENGERS *waiting up* L. C.]

SECOND MESSENGER. [*Touching cap and stepping quickly to* CAROLINE *to* L. *of* FIRST YOUNG OFFICER] Good evening, Miss Mitford! Could we do anything for you in the office to-night?

[FIRST MESSENGER *remains up near window*]

CAROLINE. I want to send a telegram!

[*The three officers stand looking at* CAROLINE *quieted for a moment by her serious tone*]

SECOND YOUNG OFFICER. I 'm afraid you 've been havin' bad news, Miss Mitford?

CAROLINE. [C.] No— [*Shaking her head*] No! I mean—not specially.

FIRST YOUNG OFFICER. [L. C.] Maybe some friend o' yours has gone down to the front!

CAROLINE. [*Beginning to be interested*] Well supposing he had—would you call that bad news?

FIRST YOUNG OFFICER. Well I did n't know as you 'd exactly like to——

CAROLINE. Then let me tell you—as you did n't know—that *all* my friends go down to the front!

SECOND YOUNG OFFICER. I hope not *all* Miss Mitford!

CAROLINE. Yes—all! If they did n't they would n't *be* my friends!

FIRST YOUNG OFFICER. But some of us are obliged to stay back here to take care of you.

CAROLINE. Well there 's altogether too many trying to take care of me! You 're all discharged! [*Goes across to down* L.]

[THIRD MESSENGER *enters doors up* R. C. *and joins* FOURTH MESSENGER *up* L. C. *near upper window.—Officers fall back a little, looking rather foolish but entirely good-natured*]

SECOND YOUNG OFFICER. [C.] Well—if we 're really discharged Miss Mitford, looks like we 'd have to go!

FIRST YOUNG OFFICER. [L. C.] Yes—but we 're mighty sorry to see you in such bad spirits Miss Mitford!

SECOND YOUNG OFFICER and SECOND MESSENGER. [L. C. *and* C.—*Murmuring nearly together*] Yes indeed we are, Miss Mitford!

CAROLINE. [*Turning on them at down* L.] Would you like to put me in real good spirits?

FIRST YOUNG OFFICER. Would we!

SECOND YOUNG OFFICER. You try us once!

SECOND MESSENGER. I reckon there ain't anything we 'd like bettah!

CAROLINE. [L.] Then I 'll tell you *just* how to do it! [*They listen eagerly*] Start out this very night and never stop till you get to where my friends are—lying in trenches and ditches and earthworks between us and the Yankee guns!

SECOND YOUNG OFFICER, FIRST YOUNG OFFICER, SECOND MESSENGER. [*Remonstrating*] But really, Miss—You don't mean—[*etc.*]

CAROLINE. Fight Yankees a few days and lie in ditches a few nights till those uniforms you 've got on look like they 'd been some *use* to somebody! If you 're so mighty anxious to do something for me, *that 's* what you can do! [*Turning away to* L.] It 's the only thing I want!

[*The* YOUNG OFFICERS *stand rather discouraged an instant*]

FIRST OPERATOR. [*Business*] Ready here! [THIRD MESSENGER *steps quickly down to* L. *of table* R. C.] Department! Commissary General's office! [THIRD MESSENGER *salutes, takes dispatch and exits doors up* R. C.—SECOND MESSENGER *returns to* FOURTH MESSENGER *during this, and stands with him near window up* L. C.]

[MESSENGER A. *enters quickly at doors up* R. C. *and comes down to* FIRST OPERATOR L. *of table* R. C. *handing him a dispatch and at once makes his exit again doors up* R. C.—FIRST *and* SECOND YOUNG OFFICERS *exit dejectedly at doors up* R. C. *after this* MESSENGER]

CAROLINE. [*Going across with determined air to* R. C. *near* FIRST OPERATOR *when she sees an opportunity*] Oh Lieutenant Foray! [*Accent on "Oh"*]

FIRST OPERATOR. [*Turns and rises quickly with half salute.*—CAROLINE *gives a little attempt at a military salute*] Beg your pardon Miss! [*Gets his coat which is on chair or table near at* R. *and hastily starts to put it on*] I did n't know——

CAROLINE. [*Up* C. *a little*] No no—don't! I don't mind. You see—I came on *business!*

FIRST OPERATOR. [*Puts on coat*] Want to send something out?

CAROLINE. Yes! That 's it.—I mean I *do.*

FIRST OPERATOR. [*Going to her, crossing back of table* R. C.] 'Fraid we can't do anything for you here! This is the War Department Miss.

CAROLINE. I know that—but it 's the on'y way to send, an' I—[*Sudden loud click of instrument* B. *on table* R.—FIRST OPERATOR *turns and listens*]

FIRST OPERATOR. [*Crossing back of table* R. C.] Excuse me a minute, won't you? [*Going to lower instrument on table* R. *and answering. Writing down message, etc.*]

CAROLINE. Yes—I will. [*A trifle disconcerted, stands uneasily near* C.] [*Speaks absently while she watches him*] I 'll—excuse you—of co'se.

FIRST OPERATOR. Ready here! [SECOND MESSENGER *down quickly to* L. *of* FIRST OPERATOR *at table* R.] Department! Quick as you can—they 're waiting for it! [SECOND MESSENGER *takes dispatch —salutes and exits at door up* R. FIRST OPERATOR *rises and crosses to* CAROLINE *who is up* C.—*To* CAROLINE] Now what was it you wanted us to do Miss?

CAROLINE. [C.] Just to [*Short gasp*] to send a telegram.

FIRST OPERATOR. [R. C.] I reckon it 's private business?

CAROLINE. [*Looking at him with wide open eyes*] Ye—yes! It 's—private!—Oh yes —I should *say* so!

FIRST OPERATOR. Then you 'll have to get an order from some one in the department. [*Goes to back of table* R. C. *and picks up papers*]

CAROLINE. That 's what I thought [*taking out a paper*] so I got it. [*Hands it to* OPERATOR]

FIRST OPERATOR. [*Glancing at paper*] Oh—Major Selwin!

CAROLINE. Yes—he—he 's one of my——

FIRST OPERATOR. It 's all right then! [*Instrument* B. *calls. Quickly picks up a small sheet of paper and a pen and places them on table* L. C. *near* CAROLINE *and pushes chair up with almost the same movement*] You can write it here Miss [*This is on upper side of telegraph table down* R. C.]

CAROLINE. Thank you. [*Sits at table—looks at small sheet of paper—picks out large sheet—smooths it out. She starts writing*]

[FIRST OPERATOR *returns to table at down* R. *and answers call and sits—writes hurriedly, taking down dispatch.*—CAROLINE *earnestly writing —pausing an instant to think once or twice and a nervous glance toward* FIRST OPERATOR.—FIRST OPERATOR *very busy.*—MARTHA *standing motionless up stage, waiting—her eyes fixed on the telegraph instruments.*— CAROLINE *bus. of start and drawing away suspiciously on loud click of instrument* A. *near her. Moves over to* L. *side of table, looking suspiciously at the instrument. Puts pen in mouth—gets ink on tongue—makes wry face. After writing she carefully folds up her despatch, and turns down a corner.*—FIRST OPERATOR *when nearly through, motions to* FOURTH MESSENGER *and speaks hurriedly*]

FIRST OPERATOR. [*Still writing*] Here! [FOURTH MESSENGER *comes down quickly* L. *of* FIRST OPERATOR *and business*] Department! Try to get it in before the President goes! [*Handing* FOURTH MESSENGER *dispatch.*—FOURTH MESSENGER *salutes and exits at doors up* R. C.— FIRST OPERATOR *rising, to* CAROLINE] Is that ready yet Miss?

CAROLINE. [*Rising, hesitating, getting* L. *of and a little above table* R. C.] Yes, but I—[*Finally starts to hand it up to him*] Of course you 've—[*Hesitates*] You 've got to *take* it!

FIRST OPERATOR. [*Near* CAROLINE *on her* R.—*A brief puzzled look at her*] Yes of course.

[*She hands him the dispatch.—He at once opens it*]

CAROLINE. [*Sharp scream*] Oh! [*Quickly seizes the paper out of his hand. They stand looking at one another a little* L. *of and above table* R. C.] Why I did n't tell you to *read* it!

FIRST OPERATOR. [*After look at her*] Well what did you want?

CAROLINE. I want you to *send* it!

FIRST OPERATOR. How am I going to send it if I don't read it?

CAROLINE. [*After looking at him in con-*

sternation] Do—you—mean—to—say——

FIRST OPERATOR. I 've got to spell out every word! Did n't you know that?

CAROLINE. [*Sadly, and shaking her head from side to side*] Oh—I must have—but I—[CAROLINE *pauses trying to think what to do*]—you see——

FIRST OPERATOR. Would there be any harm in my——

CAROLINE. [*Turning on him with sudden vehemence*] Why I would n't have you see it for worlds! My gracious! [*She soon opens the dispatch and looks at it*]

FIRST OPERATOR. [*Good-naturedly*] Is it as bad as all that!

CAROLINE. Bad! It is n't bad at all! On'y—I only don't want it to get out all over the town—that 's all!

FIRST OPERATOR. It won't ever get out from this office Miss. [CAROLINE *looks steadfastly at* FIRST OPERATOR] We would n't be allowed to mention anything outside!

CAROLINE. [*A doubtful look at him*] You would n't!

FIRST OPERATOR. No Miss. All sorts of private stuff goes through here.

CAROLINE. [*With new hope*] Does it?

FIRST OPERATOR. Every day! Now if that 's anything important——

CAROLINE. [*Impulsively*] O yes—it 's [*Recovering herself*]—it is!

FIRST OPERATOR. Then I reckon you 'd better trust it to me.

[CAROLINE *looks at* OPERATOR *a moment*]

CAROLINE. Ye—yes—I reckon I had! [*She hesitatingly hands him her telegram*]

[FIRST OPERATOR *takes the paper and at once turns to the table* R. *as if to send it on instrument* B.]

CAROLINE. [*Quickly*] Oh stop! [FIRST OPERATOR *turns and looks at her from table down* R.] Wait till I— [*Turns and goes up stage toward door hurriedly*] I don't want to be here—while you *spell out every word!* Oh no—I could n't *stand* that!

[FIRST OPERATOR *stands good-naturedly waiting.*—CAROLINE *takes hold of* MARTHA *to start out of door with her.—Enter* EDDINGER—*a private in a gray uniform—at doors up* R. C.—CAROLINE *and* MARTHA *stand back out of his way.—He glances at them and at once goes down to* FIRST OPERATOR *on his* L., *salutes and hands him a written order and crosses in front of table* R. C. *to* L. C., *wheels and stands at attention facing* R.—FIRST OPERATOR *looks at the order, glances at* EDDINGER, *then at* CAROLINE.—CAROLINE *and* MARTHA *move as if to go out at doors up* R. C.]

FIRST OPERATOR. Wait a minute please! [CAROLINE *and* MARTHA *stop and turn toward* FIRST OPERATOR] Are you Miss Mitford?

CAROLINE. Yes—I 'm Miss Mitford!

FIRST OPERATOR. I don't understand this! Here 's an order just come in to hold back any dispatch you give us.

CAROLINE. [*After looking speechless at* FIRST OPERATOR *a moment*] Hold back any—hold back—

FIRST OPERATOR. Yes Miss. And that ain't the worst of it!

CAROLINE. Wh—what else is there? [*Comes down* C. *a little way looking at* FIRST OPERATOR *with wide open eyes.*—MARTHA *remains up near door up* R.]

FIRST OPERATOR. [R.] This man has orders to take it back with him.

[*There is a slight pause*]

CAROLINE. [C.] [*Rather weakly*] Take it back with him? [*Brief pause—then suddenly with great animation*] Take what back with him?

FIRST OPERATOR. [*Near table down* R.] Your dispatch Miss. [CAROLINE *simply opens mouth and slowly draws in her breath*] There must be some mistake, but that 's what the order says.

CAROLINE. [*With unnatural calmness*] And where does it say to take it back to?

FIRST OPERATOR. [*Looks at the order*] The name is Arrelsford! [*Brief pause*]

CAROLINE. The order is for that man—[*Indicating* EDDINGER L. C.] to take my dispatch back to Mr. Arrelsford?

FIRST OPERATOR. Yes Miss.

CAROLINE. An' does it say in there what I 'm to be doin' in the meantime?

FIRST OPERATOR. [*Shakes head*] No Miss.

CAROLINE. That 's too bad!

FIRST OPERATOR. I 'm right sorry this has occurred Miss, and—

CAROLINE. Oh—there is n't any occasion yet for your feeling sorry—because it has n't occurred! And besides that it is n't goin' to occur! [*Becoming excited*] When it does you can go aroun' bein' sorry all you like! Have you got the faintest idea that I 'm goin' to let him take my telegram away with him and show it to that man! Do you suppose——

MARTHA. [*Coming forward a step from up* R. C. *near the door. Breaking in, in a voice like a siren*] No—*sir!* You ain't a goin' ter do it—you can be right sure you ain't!

FIRST OPERATOR. [R.] But what can I do Miss?

CAROLINE. [C.—*Advancing*] It's perfectly simple what you can do—you can either send it, or hand it back to me—that's what you can do!

MARTHA. [*Calling out from up* R. C.] Yes suh—that's the very best thing you can do! An' the sooner you do it the quicker it'll be done—I kin tell you that right now!

FIRST OPERATOR. But this man has come here with orders to——

CAROLINE. [*Going defiantly to* EDDINGER *and facing him*] Well this man can go straight back and report to Mr. Arrelsford that he was unable to carry out his orders! [*Defiant attitude toward* EDDINGER L. C.] That's what *he* can do!

MARTHA. [*From up* R. C.—*now thoroughly roused and coming to a sense of her responsibility*] Let 'im take it! Let 'im take it ef he wants to so pow'fle bad! Just let the other one there give it to 'im—an' then see 'im try an' git out through this do' with it! [*Standing solidly before door up* R. C. *with folded arms and ominously shaking head.* MARTHA *talks and mumbles on half to herself*] I want to see him go by! I'm just a' waitin' fur a sight o' him gittin' past dis do'! That's what I'm waitin' fur! [*Goes on talking half to herself, quieting down gradually*] I'd like to know what they s'pose it was I come aroun' yere for anyway—these men with their orders an' fussin' an'——

FIRST OPERATOR. [*When quiet is restored*] Miss Mitford, if I was to give this dispatch back to you now it would get me into a heap o' trouble.

CAROLINE. What kind of trouble?

FIRST OPERATOR. [R.] Might be prison—might be shot!

CAROLINE. You mean to say they might——

FIRST OPERATOR. Sure to do one or the other!

CAROLINE. Just for givin' me back my own writin'?

FIRST OPERATOR. That's all.

CAROLINE. [*After looking silently at* FIRST OPERATOR *a moment*] Then you'll have to keep it!

FIRST OPERATOR. [*After slight pause*] Thank you Miss Mitford!

CAROLINE. [*A sigh—reconciling herself to the situation*] Very well—that's understood! You don't give it back to me—an' you *can't* give it to him—so nobody's disobeying any orders at all! [*Turning up and getting a chair from up* C. *and bringing it forward*] And that's the way it stands! [*Banging chair down close to* EDDINGER *and directly between him and the* FIRST OPERATOR. *Then plumps herself down on the chair and facing* R., *looks entirely unconcerned*] I reckon I can stay here as long as he can! [*Half to herself*] I haven't got much to do!

FIRST OPERATOR. But Miss Mitford——

CAROLINE. Now there ain't any good o' talkin'! If you've got any telegraphin' to do you better do it. I won't disturb you!

[*Rapid steps heard in corridor outside up* R.—*Enter* MR. ARRELSFORD *doors up* R. C. *coming in hurriedly, somewhat flushed and excited. He looks hastily about, and goes at once down* R. C.]

ARRELSFORD. [R. C.] What's this! Didn't he get here in time?

FIRST OPERATOR. [R.] Are you Mr. Arrelsford?

ARRELSFORD. Yes. [*Sharp glance at* CAROLINE] Are you holding back a dispatch?

FIRST OPERATOR. Yes sir.

ARRELSFORD. Why didn't he bring it?

FIRST OPERATOR. Well—Miss Mitford—[*Hesitates. A motion toward* CAROLINE]

ARRELSFORD. [*Comprehending*] Oh! [*Crosses back of* CAROLINE *and* EDDINGER *to* L.] Eddinger! [EDDINGER *wheels to* L. *facing him*] Report back to Corporal Matson. Tell him to send a surgeon to General Varney's house on Franklin Street. He's to attend to a Yankee prisoner there who was shot—if he isn't dead by this time! [*Moves over to* L. *as* EDDINGER *goes up.*—CAROLINE *turns and looks at* ARRELSFORD *on hearing cue "prisoner," rising at same time and pushing chair back up* C.—EDDINGER *salutes and exits quickly up* R. C., *going back of* CAROLINE.—ARRELSFORD *turns and starts toward* FIRST OPERATOR] Let me see what that dispatch—

[FIRST OPERATOR *stands* R. *with* CAROLINE'S *dispatch in his hand.*—CAROLINE *steps quickly in front of* ARRELSFORD.—ARRELSFORD *stops in some surprise at* CAROLINE'S *sudden move*]

CAROLINE. [*Facing* ARRELSFORD] I expect you think you're going to get my telegram an' read it?

ARRELSFORD. [L. C.] I certainly intend to do so!

CAROLINE. [C.] Well there's a great big disappointment loomin' up right in front of you!

ARRELSFORD. [*With suspicion*] So! You've been trying to send out something you don't want us to see!

CAROLINE. What if I have?

ARRELSFORD. Just this! You won't send it—and I'll see it! [*About to pass* CAROLINE] This is a case where— [CAROLINE *steps in front of* ARRELSFORD *again so that he has to stop*]

CAROLINE. This is a case where you ain't goin' to read my private writin'— [*Stands looking at him with blazing eyes*]

ARRELSFORD. Lieutenant—I have an order here putting me in charge! Bring that dispatch to me!

[FIRST OPERATOR *about to move toward* ARRELSFORD *with the dispatch when* MARTHA *steps down in front of him with ponderous tread and stands facing him*]

MARTHA. [R. C.—*Facing* R. *to* FIRST OPERATOR] Mistah Lieutenant can stay juss about whar he is! [*Brief pause*]

ARRELSFORD. [L. C.—*To* FIRST OPERATOR] Is that Miss Mitford's dispatch in your hand?

FIRST OPERATOR. [R.] Yes sir!

ARRELSFORD. Read it! [CAROLINE *turns with a gasp of horror.*—MARTHA *turns in slow anger.*—FIRST OPERATOR *stands surprised for an instant*] Read it out!

CAROLINE. You shan't do such a thing! You have no right to read a private telegram—[etc.]

MARTHA. [*Speaking with* CAROLINE] No sah! He ain't no business to read her letters—none whatsomever! [etc.]

ARRELSFORD. [*Angrily*] Silence! [CAROLINE *and* MARTHA *stop talking*] If you interfere any further with the business of this office I'll have you both put under arrest! [*To* FIRST OPERATOR] Read that dispatch!

[CAROLINE *gasps breathless at* ARRELSFORD—*then turns and buries her face on* MARTHA'S *shoulder sobbing*]

FIRST OPERATOR. [*Reads with some difficulty*] "Forgive me—Wilfred—darling — please — forgive — me — and — I—will—help—you—all—I—can."

ARRELSFORD. That dispatch can't go! [*Turns and moves left a few steps*]

CAROLINE. [*Turning and facing* ARRELSFORD] That dispatch *can* go! An' that dispatch *will* go! [ARRELSFORD *turns and looks at* CAROLINE *from* L.—MARTHA *moves up on right side ready to exit, standing well up* C. *and turning toward* ARRELSFORD] I know someone whose orders even *you* are bound to respect and someone who'll come here with me an' see that you *do* it!

ARRELSFORD. [L.] I can show good and sufficient reasons for what I do!

CAROLINE. [C.] Well you'll have to show good and sufficienter reasons than you've shown to me—I can tell you *that* Mr. Arrelsford!

ARRELSFORD. I give my reasons to my *superiors* Miss Mitford!

CAROLINE. Then you'll have to go 'round givin' 'em to everybody in *Richmond*, Mr. Arrelsford! [*Saying which* CAROLINE *makes a deep courtesy and turns and sweeps out through doors up* R. C. *followed in the same spirit by* MARTHA *who turns at the door and also makes a profound courtesy to* ARRELSFORD, *going off haughtily*]

[FIRST OPERATOR *sits down at table* R. C. *and begins to write.*—ARRELSFORD *looks after* CAROLINE *an instant and then goes rapidly over to* FIRST OPERATOR]

ARRELSFORD. Let me see that dispatch!

FIRST OPERATOR. [*Slight doubt*] You said you had an order sir?

ARRELSFORD. [*Impatiently*] Yes—yes! [*Throws order down on telegraph table*] Don't waste time!

[FIRST OPERATOR *picks up order and looks closely at it being careful to show no haste*]

FIRST OPERATOR. Department order sir?

ARRELSFORD. [*Assenting shortly*] Yes—yes!

FIRST OPERATOR. I suppose you're Mr. Arrelsford all right?

ARRELSFORD. Of course!

FIRST OPERATOR. We have to be pretty careful here. [*Hands him* CAROLINE'S *telegram and goes on writing.*—ARRELS-

FORD *takes* CAROLINE'S *telegram eagerly and reads it. Thinks an instant*]

ARRELSFORD. [C.] Did she seem nervous or excited when she handed this in?

FIRST OPERATOR. She certainly did!

ARRELSFORD. Anxious not to have it seen?

FIRST OPERATOR. Anxious! I should say so! She did n't want *me* to see it!

ARRELSFORD. We 've got a case on here and she 's mixed up in it!

FIRST OPERATOR. But that dispatch is to young Varney—the General's son!

ARRELSFORD. So much the worse if he 's mixed up in it. The lying scoundrel has made dupes of all of them—and this Mitford girl too!

FIRST OPERATOR. Who 's that sir?

ARRELSFORD. Well—no matter now. You 'll know before long! It 's one of the ugliest affairs we ever had! I had them put me on it and I 've got it down pretty close! [*Going across to* L. C.] We 'll end it right here in this office inside of thirty minutes!

[*Enter a* PRIVATE *at doors up* R. C.—*He comes down at once to* ARRELSFORD]

ARRELSFORD. [L. C.—*To* PRIVATE] Well what is it?

PRIVATE. [L. C.—R. *of* ARRELSFORD] The lady 's here sir!

ARRELSFORD. Where is she?

PRIVATE. Waiting down below—at the front entrance.

ARRELSFORD. Did she come alone?

PRIVATE. Yes sir.

ARRELSFORD. Show her the way up. [PRIVATE *salutes and exits at door up* R. —ARRELSFORD *comes* C. *to* FIRST OPERATOR] I suppose you 've got a revolver there? [FIRST OPERATOR *brings up revolver in matter-of-fact way from shelf beneath table with left hand and lays it on table at his left without looking up at* ARRELSFORD—*and scarcely interrupting his writing*] I 'd rather handle this thing myself—but I might call on you. Be ready—that 's all!

FIRST OPERATOR. Yes sir.

ARRELSFORD. Obey any orders you get an' send out all dispatches unless I stop you.

FIRST OPERATOR. Very well sir. [*Soon puts revolver back on shelf beneath table*]

[*Doors up* R. C. *are opening by the* PRIVATE *last on, and* EDITH *is shown in.*—ARRELSFORD *meets her.*—*The* PRIVATE *exits at doors up* R. C.—EDITH *stops a little way down from doors and looks at* ARRELSFORD. *She is slightly breathless—not from exertion but owing to the situation*]

EDITH. I—I accepted your invitation Mr. Arrelsford!

ARRELSFORD. [*Up* C.] I 'm greatly obliged Miss Varney! As a matter of justice to me it was—

EDITH. [*Interrupting*] I did n't come here to oblige you! I came to see—I came to see that no more—[*A slight break before she can speak the word*] murders are committed in order to satisfy your singular curiosity. [*After brief pause; moves down* C.]

[ARRELSFORD *waits until* EDITH *is down* C. *and then goes down near her on her left*]

ARRELSFORD. [*Low voice*] Is the man dead?

EDITH. [*Turning and looking at* ARRELSFORD *steadily*] The man is dead.

[ARRELSFORD *stands a few seconds looking at* EDITH—*then turns front slowly. Turns to her again*]

ARRELSFORD. [*With cutting emphasis but low voice*] It 's a curious thing Miss Varney that a Yankee prisoner more or less should make so much difference to you! They 're dying down in Libby by the hundreds!

EDITH. At least they 're not killed in our houses—before our very eyes! [*Turns and moves up* C.]

[*Enter an* ORDERLY *who is a Special Agent of the War Department, at doors up* R. C. *He comes quickly in and crosses to* ARRELSFORD L. C. *Glances round toward* FIRST OPERATOR *and quickly back to* ARRELSFORD]

ARRELSFORD. [L. C.—*Low voice*] Where is he? Have you kept track of him?

ORDERLY. [L. C.—*Low voice*] He 's coming up Fourth Street sir!

ARRELSFORD. [*Low voice*] Where has he been?

ORDERLY. [*Low voice*] To his quarters on Cary Street. We got in the next room and watched him through a transom.

ARRELSFORD. [*Low voice*] What was he doing? What was it?

ORDERLY. [*Low voice*] Working at some papers or documents.

ARRELSFORD. [*Low voice*] Could you see them? Could you see what it was?

ORDERLY. [*Low voice*] Headings looked like orders from the War Department.

ARRELSFORD. [*Low voice*] He 's coming in here with forged orders!

ORDERLY. [*Low voice*] Yes sir.

ARRELSFORD. [*Low voice*] His game is to get control of these wires and then send out dispatches to the front that 'll take away a battery or division from some vital point!

ORDERLY. [*Low voice*] Looks like it sir.

ARRELSFORD. [*Low voice*] And that vital point is what the Yankees mean by "Plan Three!" That 's where they 'll hit us. [*Glances round quickly considering. Goes up* L. *to above line of middle window. Turns to* ORDERLY] Is there a guard in this building?

ORDERLY. [*Going up near* ARRELSFORD *on his* R.—*Low voice*] Not inside—there 's a guard in front and sentries around the barracks over in the square.

ARRELSFORD. [*Low voice*] They could hear me from this window, could n't they?

ORDERLY. [*Low voice*] The guard could hear you sir. [*A glance toward doors* R. C.] He must be nearly here by this time—you 'd better look out!

EDITH. [*Up* C.—*Low voice*] Where shall I go?

ARRELSFORD. [*Up* L.—*Low voice*] Outside here on the balcony—I 'll be with you!

EDITH. [*Low voice*] But—if he comes to the window! He may come here and look out!

ARRELSFORD. [*Low voice*] We 'll go along to the next window and step in there—out of sight. [*To* ORDERLY] See if the window of the Commissary-General's office is open.

[ORDERLY *crosses* ARRELSFORD *and steps quickly out of windows up* L. *through middle window, and goes off along balcony to* L. *He returns at once, re-entering through middle window*]

ORDERLY. The next window 's open sir.

ARRELSFORD. That 's all I want of you—report back to Corporal Matson. Tell him to get the body of that prisoner out of the Varney house—he knows where it 's to go!

ORDERLY. Very well sir! [*Salutes, crosses and exits doors up* R. C.]

ARRELSFORD. [*To* EDITH] This way please. [*Conducts* EDITH *out through middle window to the balcony up* L.—*She exits to* L.—ARRELSFORD *is closing the window to follow when he sees a* MESSENGER *enter at doors up* R. C., *and thereupon he stops just in the window keeping out of sight of* MESSENGER *behind window frame*]

[*Enter* FIRST MESSENGER *at doors up* R.C.—*He takes his position up stage waiting for messages as before.*—ARRELSFORD *eyes him sharply an instant—then comes into the room a step or two*]

ARRELSFORD. [*From near window up* L.] Where did you come from?

FIRST MESSENGER. [*Up* C.] War Department sir.

ARRELSFORD. Carrying dispatches?

FIRST MESSENGER. Yes sir.

ARRELSFORD. You know me don't you?

FIRST MESSENGER. I 've seen you at the office sir.

ARRELSFORD. I 'm here on Department business. All you 've got to do is to keep quiet about it! [*Exit* ARRELSFORD *at middle window up* L., *which he closes after him, and then disappears from view along balcony to* L.]

[*Enter* SECOND MESSENGER *at door up* R. C. —*He takes his place at up* L. C. *with* FIRST MESSENGER.—FIRST OPERATOR *busy at table* R. C.—*A moment's wait.*— *Enter* CAPTAIN THORNE *at doors up* R. C. *As he comes down he gives one quick glance about the room but almost instantly to front again, so that it would hardly be noticed. He wears cap and carries an order in his belt. Goes down at once to* L. *of table* R. C. *and faces* FIRST OPERATOR]

[FIRST OPERATOR *on seeing* THORNE *rises with off hand salute*]

THORNE. [*Saluting*] Lieutenant! [*Hands* FIRST OPERATOR *the order which he carried in his belt*]

[FIRST OPERATOR *takes the order, opens and looks at it*]

FIRST OPERATOR. Order from the Department. [*Moves* R. *a little looking closely at the order*]

THORNE. [*Motionless, facing to* R.] I believe so. [*A quick glance at doors up* R. C. *as* OPERATOR *is looking at the order*]

FIRST OPERATOR. They want me to take a cipher dispatch ovah to the President's house.

THORNE. [*Moving to take* FIRST OPERATOR'S *place at table—pulls chair back a little and tosses cap over on table* R.] Yes—I 'm ordered on here till you get back. [*Goes to place back of table* R. C.

and stands arranging things on the table]

FIRST OPERATOR. [*At table* R. *looking front*] That's an odd thing. They told me the President was down here with the Cabinet! He must have just now gone home I reckon.

THORNE. [*Standing at table* R. C. *and arranging papers, etc.*] Looks like it. If he is n't there you 'd better wait. [*Looking through a bunch of dispatches as he speaks*]

FIRST OPERATOR. [*Gets his cap from table* R. *and puts it on.—At table* R.] Yes—I'll wait! [*Pause*] You'll have to look out for Allison's wires, Cap'n—he was called ovah to the Department.

[THORNE *stops and eyes to front an instant on mention of* ALLISON]

THORNE. [*Easy manner again*] Ah ha—Allison.

FIRST OPERATOR. Yes.

THORNE. Be gone long? [THORNE *business of throwing used sheets in waste-basket and arranging a couple of large envelopes ready for quick use*]

FIRST OPERATOR. Well, you know how it is—they generally whip around quite a while before they make up their minds what they want to do. I don't expect they'll trouble you much! It's as quiet as a church down the river. [*Starting up toward doors up* R. C.]

THORNE. [*Seeing a cigar on the table near instrument*] See here—wait a minute—you 'd better not walk out and leave a—[FIRST OPERATOR *stops and turns back to* THORNE *coming* C. *a little*] O well—no matter—it's none of my business! [*Tapping with the end of a long envelope on table where the cigar is*] Still, if you want some good advice, that's a dangerous thing to do!

FIRST OPERATOR. [*Coming down nearer on* L.] Why what is it Cap'n?

THORNE. That!—[*Striking at cigar with envelope*] Leave a cigar lying around this office like that! [*Picks it up with* L. *hand and lights a match with* R.] Anybody might walk in here any minute and take it away! [*About to light cigar*] I can't watch your cigars all day—[*Lighting cigar*]

FIRST OPERATOR. [*Grinning*] Oh!—Help yourself Cap'n!

THORNE. [*Suddenly snatching cigar out of mouth with* L. *hand and looking at it*] What's the matter with it?—Oh well—I'll take a chance. [*Puts it in his mouth and resumes lighting*]

[FIRST OPERATOR *hesitates a moment, then goes nearer to* THORNE *on his* L., L. *of table* R. C.]

FIRST OPERATOR. [*Low voice*] Oh Cap'n—if there's any trouble around here you'll find a revolver under there. [*Indicating shelf under table.—*THORNE *stops lighting cigar an instant, letting match blaze in his hand—eyes motionless to front*]

THORNE. [*At once resuming nonchalance—finishing lighting cigar*] What about that? What makes you think—[*Pulling in to light cigar*] there's going to be trouble?

FIRST OPERATOR. Oh well, there might be!

THORNE. [*Tossing match away*] Been having a dream?

FIRST OPERATOR. Oh no—but you never can tell! [*Starts up toward doors up* R. C.]

THORNE. [*Cigar in mouth.—Going at papers again*] That's right! You never can tell. [*A thought*] But see here—hold on a minute! [*Reaching down and getting revolver from shelf and tossing it on table near* L. *end*] If you never can tell you'd better take that along with you. I've got one of my own. [*Rather sotto voce*] I can tell!

[*Click of instrument* A.—THORNE *answers on instrument* A. *at* R. *end of table* R. C. *and slides into chair*]

FIRST OPERATOR. Well, if you've got one here, I might as well. [*Takes revolver*] Look out for yourself Cap'n! [*Goes up.—Instrument* A. *begins clicking off a message.—*THORNE *sits at table* R. C. *listening and ready to take down what comes*]

THORNE. [*Listening to instrument at* R.] Same to you old man—and many happy returns of the day! [*Exit* FIRST OPERATOR *doors up* R. C.—THORNE *writes message and briefly addresses a long envelope.—Instrument* A. *stops receiving as* THORNE *addresses envelope.—*THORNE O. K.'s *dispatch and puts it in envelope which he quickly seals*] Ready here! [FIRST MESSENGER *down to* THORNE *and salutes* L. *of table* R. C.] Quartermaster-General. [*Handing dispatch to* MESSENGER]

FIRST MESSENGER. Not at his office sir!

THORNE. Find him—he's got to have it!

FIRST MESSENGER. Very well sir! [*Salutes and exits quickly up* R.]

[*Brief pause. Silence. No instruments clicking.—*THORNE *eyes front. After a moment he turns slowly* L.

looking to see if there is a MESSENGER *there. Sees there is one without looking entirely around.—A second's wait.—Instrument* C. *at upper end of table* R. *begins to click.—*THORNE *rises and going to instrument* C. *answers call—drops into chair* R.*—writes message—puts it in envelope—and* O. K.*'s call, etc.*]

THORNE. Ready here! [SECOND MESSENGER *goes quickly across to* L. *of table* R. C. *and salutes*] Secretary of the Treasury—marked private.—Take it to his house. [*Begins to read a dispatch he twitched off from a file*]

SECOND MESSENGER. He's down yere at the cabinet sir.

THORNE. Take it to his house and wait till he comes!

[SECOND MESSENGER *salutes and exits doors up* R. C. *closing them after him.—On the slam of doors after exit of* MESSENGER, THORNE *crushes dispatch in his right hand and throws it to floor—and wheels front—his eyes on the instrument down* R. C. *all one quick movement. Then he rises and with cat-like swiftness springs to the doors up* R. C. *and listens—opens one of the doors a little and looks off. He closes it quickly, turning and moving swiftly to* C., *and opens the door to cupboard up* C. *glancing in, then moves to the windows up* L. C. *Pushes the window up* L. *open a little and looks off to balcony, beginning at same time to unbuckle belt and unbutton coat. Turns and moves down toward the telegraph table* R. C. *at same time throwing belt over to* R. *above* R. *table, and taking off coat. Glances back up* L.*—looks to see that a document is in breast pocket of coat—letting audience see that it is there—and lays coat over back of chair above table* R. C. *with document in sight so that he can get it without delay. Takes revolver from right hip pocket and quickly but quietly lays it on the table* R. C. *just to right of instrument* A. *and then seizes key of that instrument and gives a certain call:* (—.... .. ..) *Waits. A glance rapidly to left. He is standing at table—cigar in mouth. Makes the call again:* (—.... .. ..) *Waits again. Gives the call third time:* (—.... .. ..) *Goes to lower end of table* R. *and half sits on it, folding arms, eyes on instrument, chewing cigar, with a glance or two up stage, but his eyes back quickly to instrument. Slides off table—takes cigar out of his mouth with* L. *hand and gives the call again with right:* (—.... .. ..) *Puts cigar in mouth again and turning and walking toward up* L. C. *looking about. Soon he carelessly throws some scraps of torn paper—which he took from* R. *pocket—off up stage. Just as he throws papers—facing to* L.*—the call is answered:* (—.... .. ..) THORNE *is back at the table* R. C. *in an instant and telegraphing rapidly—cigar in mouth.—When he has sent for about five seconds, steps are heard in corridor outside up* R.*—*THORNE *quickly strikes a match—which is close at hand to* R. *of instrument—and sinks into the chair, appearing to be lazily lighting his cigar as a* MESSENGER *comes in at door up* R. C.]

[FOURTH MESSENGER *enters as soon as he hears match strike, at doors up* R. C. *He goes down at once to* L. *of table* R. C. *with a dispatch, which he extends toward* THORNE *as he salutes*]

FOURTH MESSENGER. Secretary of War, Cap'n! Wants to go out right now! [THORNE *tosses away match, takes dispatch and opens it.* FOURTH MESSENGER *salutes, turns and starts up toward doors up* R. C.]

THORNE. Here! Here! What's all this! [*Looking at the dispatch.—*FOURTH MESSENGER *returns to* THORNE*—salutes*] Is that the Secretary's signature? [*Indicating a place on the dispatch which he holds in his hand*]

FOURTH MESSENGER. Yes sir—I saw him sign it.

[THORNE *looks closely at the signature. Turns it so as to get gas light from* R. *Turns and looks sharply at the* MESSENGER]

THORNE. [*Writing*] Saw him sign it did you?

FOURTH MESSENGER. Yes sir.

[THORNE *turns and laying dispatch on table begins to O. K. it*]

THORNE. [*Writing*] Got to be a little careful to-night!

FOURTH MESSENGER. I can swear to that

one sir. [*Salutes—turns and goes up and exits at doors up* R. C.]

[THORNE *listens—faced front—for exit of* MESSENGER, *the dispatch in his left hand. Instantly on slam of doors up* L. C. *he puts cigar down at end of table, rises, laying the dispatch down flat on table. Quickly folds and very dexterously and rapidly cuts off the lower part of the paper—which has the signature of the Secretary of War upon it—with a paper knife, and holds it between his teeth while he tears the rest of the order in pieces, which he is on the point of throwing into waste-basket at* L. *of table, when he stops and changes his mind, stuffing the torn-up dispatch into his* R. *hand trousers pocket. Picks up coat from back of chair and takes the document out of inside breast pocket. Opens it out on table and quickly pastes to it the piece of the real order bearing the signature, wipes quickly with handkerchief, puts handkerchief back into* R. *trousers pocket, picks up cigar which he laid down on table and puts it in mouth, at same time sitting and at once beginning to telegraph rapidly on instrument* A.—THORNE *intent, yet vigilant.—During business of* THORNE *pasting dispatch,* ARRELSFORD *appears outside windows up* L. *on balcony at side of columns. He motions off toward* L.—EDITH *comes into view there also.*—ARRELSFORD *points toward* THORNE, *calling her attention to what he is doing.—They stand at the window watching* THORNE—*the strong moonlight bringing them out sharply.—After a few seconds* ARRELSFORD *accidentally makes a slight noise with latch of window.—Instantly on this faint click of latch* THORNE *stops telegraphing and sits absolutely motionless—his eyes front.*—ARRELSFORD *and* EDITH *disappear instantly and noiselessly on balcony to* L.—*Dead silence.—After a motionless pause,* THORNE *begins to fumble among papers on the table with his left hand, soon after raising the dispatch or some other paper with that hand in such a way that it will screen his right hand and the telegraph instrument on the key of which it rests, from an observer on the left. While he appears to be scanning this paper or dispatch with the greatest attention, his right hand slowly slips off the telegraph key and toward his revolver which lies just to the right of the instrument. Reaching it, he very slowly moves it over the right edge of the table, and down against his right leg. He then begins to push things about on the table with his left hand as if looking for something, and soon rises as if not able to find it, and looks still more carefully, keeping the revolver close against his right leg, out of sight from windows up left. He looks about on table, glances over to table on right as if looking for what he wanted there, puts cigar down on table before him—after about to do so once and taking a final puff—and steps over to table at* R. *still looking for something and now—as he turns right—shifting revolver around in front of him. As he looks about among papers on table* R. *he raises* L. *hand carelessly to the cock of the gas bracket and suddenly shuts off light.—Stage dark.—Instantly on lights off,* THORNE *drops on one knee behind (that is to* R. *of) table* R. C.—*facing toward* L. *and revolver—with table for a rest—covering windows up* L.—*Light from windows up* L. *gauged to strike across to* THORNE *at table with revolver.—After holding it a short time, he begins slowly to edge up stage first seizing chair with his coat on it, and crouching behind it—then moving up from that crouched with revolver ready and eyes on windows up* L. *until within reach of doors up* L. C. *Reaching behind him—without taking eyes or revolver off windows up* L. *he finds big heavy bolt and suddenly slides it thus locking the doors on the inside. From doors up* R. C. THORNE *glides with a dash—throwing aside the chair in the way—at the door of cupboard up* C. *which opens down stage and hinges on its* L. *side. With motion of reaching it he has it open—if not already open —and pushes it along before him as he moves left toward window.—When moving slowly behind this door with his eyes and revolver on window, the telegraph instrument down* R. C. *suddenly gives two or three sharp clicks.—*THORNE *makes an instantaneous turn front covering the instrument with revolver. Seeing what it was he turns left again. Just as he gets door nearly wide open against wall at back he dashes at the upper window up left and bangs it open with his left hand covering all outside with revolver in his right. In an instant he sees that no one is there, and straightens up—looking. He makes a quick spring past first window stopping close behind the upright between first and second windows, and at same time banging these windows open and covering with revolver. Sees no one. Looks this way and that. Makes quick dash outside and covers over balustrade—as if someone might be below. In again quick. Looks about with one or two quick glances. Concludes he must have been mistaken, and starts down toward table* R. C. *Stops after going two or three steps and looks back. Turns and goes rapidly down to table. Picks up cigar with left hand. Puts revolver at right end of table with right hand, and gets a match with that hand. Stands an instant looking left. Strikes match and is about to relight cigar. Pause—eyes front. Match burning. Listening. Looks* L. *Lights cigar. As he is lighting cigar thinks of gas being out, and stepping to right, turns it on and lights it with match he used for cigar.—Lights full on.—*THORNE *turns quickly, looking left as lights on. Then steps at once—after glancing quickly about room—to telegraph table, puts down cigar near upper* R. *corner of table with* L. *hand and begins to telegraph with* L. *hand, facing front.—Sudden sharp report of revolver outside through lower window, up* L. *with crash of glass, and on it* ARRELSFORD *springs on at middle window* L. *with revolver in his hand.* THORNE *does not move on shot except quick recoil from instrument, leaning back a little, expression of pain an instant. His* L. *hand—with which he was telegraphing—is covered with blood. He stands motionless an instant. Eyes then down toward his own revolver. Slight pause. He makes a sudden plunge for it getting it in his* R. *hand. At same instant quick turn on* ARRELSFORD *but before he can raise the weapon* ARRELSFORD *covers him with revolver and* THORNE *stops where he is, holding position*]

ARRELSFORD. [L. C.—*Covering* THORNE] Drop it! [*Pause*] Drop that gun or you 're a dead man! Drop it I say! [*A moment's pause.—*THORNE *gradually recovers to erect position, looking easily front, and puts revolver on the table, picking up cigar with same hand and putting it casually into his mouth as if he thought he 'd have a smoke after all, instead of killing a man. He then gets handkerchief out of pocket with* R. *hand and gets hold of a corner of it not using his* L.*—*ARRELSFORD *advances a step or two, lowering revolver, but holding it ready*] Do you know why I did n't kill you like a dog just now?

THORNE. [*Low voice—as he twists handkerchief around his wounded hand*] Because you 're such a damn bad shot.

ARRELSFORD. Maybe you 'll change your mind about that!

THORNE. [*Speaks easily and pleasantly*] Well I hope so I 'm sure. It is n't pleasant to be riddled up this way you know!

ARRELSFORD. Next time you 'll be riddled somewhere else besides the hand! There 's only one reason why you 're not lying there now with a bullet through your head!

THORNE. Only one eh?

ARRELSFORD. Only one!

THORNE. [*Still fixing hand and sleeve*] Do I hear it?

ARRELSFORD. Simply because I gave my word of honor to someone outside there that I would n't kill you now!

[THORNE *on hearing "Someone outside there" turns and looks at* ARRELSFORD *with interest*]

THORNE. [*Taking cigar out of mouth and holding it in* R. *hand as he moves toward* ARRELSFORD] Ah! Then it is n't a pleasant little tête-à-tête between ourselves! You have someone with you! [*Stopping near* C. *coolly facing* ARRELSFORD]

ARRELSFORD. [*Sarcastically*] I *have* someone with me Captain Thorne! Someone who takes quite an interest in what you 're doing to-night!

THORNE. Quite an interest, eh! That 's

kind I'm sure. [*Knocking the ashes from his cigar with a finger of right hand*] Is the gentleman going to stay out there all alone on the cold balcony, or shall I have the pleasure [*Enter* EDITH *from balcony up* L. *through the upper window, where she stands supporting herself by the sides. She is looking toward* R. *as if intending to go, but not able for a moment, to move. Avoids looking at* THORNE] of inviting him in here and having a charming little three-handed— [*Glancing toward* L. *he sees* EDITH *and stops motionless with eyes toward left. After a moment he turns front and holds position*]

EDITH. [*Does not speak until after* THORNE *looks front.—Low voice*] I'll go, Mr. Arrelsford!

ARRELSFORD. Not yet Miss Varney!

EDITH. [*Coming blindly into the room a few steps as if to get across to the doors up* R. C.] I don't wish to stay—any longer! [*Moves toward* R.]

ARRELSFORD. [*Down* L. C.] One moment please! We need you!

EDITH. [*Stopping up* C.] For what?

ARRELSFORD. A witness.

EDITH. You can send for me. I'll be at home. [*About to start toward door*]

ARRELSFORD. [*Sharply*] I'll have to detain you till I turn him over to the guard —it won't take a moment! [*Steps to the middle window up* L. *still keeping an eye on* THORNE, *and calls off in loud voice*] Corporal o' the guard! Corporal o' the guard! Send up the guard will you?

[EDITH *shrinks back up* C. *not knowing what to do*]

VOICE. [*Outside* L. *in distance—as if down below in the street*] What's the matter up there! Who's calling the guard!

ARRELSFORD. [*At window*] Up here! Department Telegraph! Send 'em up quick!

VOICES. [*Outside* L. *in distance as before*] Corporal of the Guard Post Four! [*Repeated more distant*] Corporal of the Guard Post Four! [*Repeated again almost inaudible*] Corporal of the Guard Post Four! Fall in the guard! Fall in! [*These orders gruff—indistinct—distant. Give effect of quick gruff shouts of orders barely audible. If* VOICES *seem close at hand it will be disastrous*]

EDITH. [*Up* C.*—Turning suddenly upon* ARRELSFORD] I'm going Mr. Arrelsford—I don't *wish* to be a witness!

ARRELSFORD. [L. C.*—After an instant's look at* EDITH*—suspecting the reason for her refusal*] Whatever your *feelings* may be Miss Varney, we can't permit you to refuse!

EDITH. [*With determination*] I do refuse! If you won't take me down to the street I'll find the way out myself! [*Stops as she is turning to go, on hearing the* GUARD *outside*]

[*Sound of* GUARD *outside running through lower corridors. Tramp of men coming up stairway and along hallways outside up* R.—THORNE *holds position looking steadily front, cigar in right hand*]

ARRELSFORD. [*Loud voice to stop* EDITH] You can't get out—the guard is here! [*Steps down* L. C. *with revolver, his eyes on* THORNE]

[EDITH *stands an instant and then as the* GUARD *is heard nearer in the corridor outside up* R. *she moves up to window up* L. *and remains there until sound of* GUARD *breaking in the door. Then she makes her exit off to* L. *on balcony, disappearing so as to attract no attention*]

ARRELSFORD. [*Shouting across to* THORNE *above noise of* GUARD] I've got you about where I want you at last! [THORNE *motionless.—Sound of hurried tread of men outside up* R. *as if coming on double quick toward the doors on the bare floor of corridor*] You thought you was almighty smart—but you'll find we can match your tricks every time!

[*Sound of the* GUARD *coming outside up* R. *suddenly ceases close to the doors up* R. C.]

SERGEANT OF THE GUARD. [*Close outside door up* R.] What's the matter here! Let us in!

THORNE. [*Loud, incisive voice. Still facing front*] Break down the door Sergeant! Break it down! [*As he calls he begins to back up stage toward up* R.]

[*Officers and men outside at once begin to smash in the door with the butts of their muskets*]

ARRELSFORD. [L. C.*—Surprised*] What are you saying about it!

THORNE. [*Up* R. C.] You want 'im in here don't you!

[ARRELSFORD *moves up a little as* THORNE *does, and covers him with revolver*]

ARRELSFORD. [L. C.*—Through noise of smashing door*] Stand where you are!

[THORNE *has backed up* R. C. *until*

nearly between ARRELSFORD *and the door, so that the latter cannot fire on him without hitting others. But he must stand a trifle to right of line the men will take in rushing across to* ARRELSFORD]

THORNE. [*Up* R. C. *facing* ARRELSFORD] Smash in the door! What are you waiting for! Smash it in Sergeant! [*Keeps up this call till doors break down and men rush in.—Doors are quickly battered in and* SERGEANT *and men dash through and into the room.*—THORNE, *continuing without break from last speech, above all the noise, pointing to* ARRELSFORD *with* L. *hand*] Arrest that man! [SERGEANT OF THE GUARD *and six men spring forward past* THORNE *and seize* ARRELSFORD *before he can recover from his astonishment, throwing him backward to* L. *and nearly down in the first struggle, but pulling him to his feet and holding him fast.—As soon as quiet* THORNE *moves down* C.] He's got in here with a revolver and he's playing Hell with it!

ARRELSFORD. [L. C.] Sergeant—my orders are—

THORNE. [*At* C. *facing* ARRELSFORD] Damn your orders! You haven't got orders to shoot everybody you see in this office! [ARRELSFORD *makes a sudden effort to break loose*] Get his gun away—he'll hurt himself! [*Turns* R. *at once and goes to table* R. C. *putting his coat in better position on back of chair, and then getting things in shape on the table, at same time putting cigar back in mouth and smoking.*—SERGEANT *and men twist the revolver out of* ARRELSFORD'S *hands*]

ARRELSFORD. [L. C.—*Continuing to struggle and protest*] Listen to me! Arrest him! He's sending out a false——

SERGEANT OF THE GUARD. [L. C.] Now that'll do! [*Silencing* ARRELSFORD *roughly by hand across his mouth.—To* THORNE] What's it all about, Cap'n?

THORNE. [*Standing at table* R.C. *arranging things*] All about! I haven't got the slightest—[*Sudden snatch of cigar out of mouth with* R. *hand and then to* SERGEANT *as if remembering something*] He says he came out of some office! Sending out dispatches here he began letting off his gun at me. [*Turns back arranging things on table*] Crazy lunatic!

ARRELSFORD. [*Struggling to speak*] It's a lie! Let me speak—I'm from the—

SERGEANT OF THE GUARD. [*Quietly to avoid laugh*] Here! That'll do now! [*Silencing* ARRELSFORD. *To* THORNE] What shall we do with him?

THORNE. [*Tossing things into place on table with one hand*] I don't care a damn—get him out o' here—that's all I want!

SERGEANT OF THE GUARD. Much hurt Cap'n?

THORNE. [*Carelessly*] Oh no—did one hand up a little—I can get along with the other all right. [*Sits at table and begins telegraphing*]

ARRELSFORD. [*Struggling desperately*] Stop him! He's sending a—Wait! Ask Miss Varney! She saw him! Ask her! Ask Miss Varney! [*Speaks wildly—losing all control of himself*]

SERGEANT OF THE GUARD. [*Breaking in on* ARRELSFORD] Here! Fall in there! We'll get him out. [*The guard quickly falls in behind* ARRELSFORD, *who is still struggling*] Forward——

[*Enter an* OFFICER *striding in quickly at doors up* R.]

OFFICER. [*Loud voice—above the noise*] Halt! The General! [OFFICER *remains up stage standing* L. *of doors up* R.]

SERGEANT OF THE GUARD. [*To* MEN] Halt! [MEN *on motion from* SERGEANT *stand back, forming a double rank behind* ARRELSFORD, *two men holding him in front rank.—All facing to center.* SERGEANT *up* L. C.]

[*Enter* MAJOR GENERAL HARRISON RANDOLPH *striding in at doors up* R. C.—CAROLINE *comes to doors after the* GENERAL, *and stands just within, up* R. C.—ARRELSFORD *has been so astonished and indignant at his treatment that he can't find his voice at first.*—OFFICERS *salute as* GENERAL RANDOLPH *comes in.*—THORNE *goes on working instrument at table down* R. C. *cigar between his teeth. He has the dispatch with signature pasted on it, spread on table before him*]

GENERAL RANDOLPH. [*Comes down* C. *and stops*] What's all this about refusing to send Miss Mitford's telegram! Is it some of your work, Arrelsford?

ARRELSFORD. [*Breathless, violent, excited*] General!—They've arrested me!—A conspiracy!—A—[*Sees* THORNE *working at telegraph instrument*] Stop that man—for God's sake stop him before it's too late!

[CAROLINE *edging gradually up* R. C.

quietly slips out at doors up R. C. *Make this exit unnoticed if possible*]

GENERAL RANDOLPH. [C.] Stop him! What do you mean?

THORNE. [*Rising quickly with salute—timed to speak on cue*] He means me sir! He 's got an idea some dispatch I 'm sending out is a trick of the Yankees!

ARRELSFORD. [*Excitedly*] It 's a conspiracy. He 's an impostor—a—a——

THORNE. [*Subdued voice*] Why the man must have gone crazy General! [THORNE *stands facing* L. *motionless*]

ARRELSFORD. I came here on a case for——

GENERAL RANDOLPH. [*Sharply*] Wait!—I 'll get at this! [*To* SERGEANT—*without turning to him*] What was he doing?

SERGEANT OF THE GUARD. [*Up* L. C. *saluting*] He was firing on the Cap'n sir.

ARRELSFORD. He was sending out a false order to weaken our lines at Cemetery Hill and I—Ah! [*Suddenly recollecting*] Miss Varney! [*Looking excitedly about*] She was here—she saw it all!

GENERAL RANDOLPH. [*Gruffly*] Miss Varney!

ARRELSFORD. Yes sir!

GENERAL RANDOLPH. The General's daughter?

ARRELSFORD. [*Nodding affirmatively with excited eagerness*] Yes sir!

GENERAL RANDOLPH. What was she doing here?

ARRELSFORD. She came to see for herself whether he was guilty or not!

GENERAL RANDOLPH. Is this some personal matter of yours?

ARRELSFORD. He was a visitor at their house—I wanted her to know!

GENERAL RANDOLPH. Where is she now? Where is Miss Varney?

ARRELSFORD. [*Looking about excitedly*] She must be out there on the balcony! Send for her! Send for her!

GENERAL RANDOLPH. [*After looking at* ARRELSFORD *in silence for a few seconds*] Sergeant! [SERGEANT *steps down* L. *of* GENERAL RANDOLPH *and salutes*] Step out there on the balcony. Present my compliments to Miss Varney and ask her to come in!

[SERGEANT *salutes and steps quickly out on the balcony through middle window up* L. *Walks off along balcony disappearing at* L. *Re-appears walking back as far as balcony goes. Turns and re-enters room, coming down* L. C. *and saluting*]

SERGEANT OF THE GUARD. [*Saluting*] No one there sir!

[THORNE *turns quietly and opening instrument* A. *begins to send dispatch, picking up the forged order with* L. *hand as if sending from that copy and telegraphing with* R.]

ARRELSFORD. She must be there! She 's in the next office! The other window. Tell him to—[*Sees* THORNE *working at instrument* A.] Ah! [*Almost a scream*] Stop him! He 's sending it now!

GENERAL RANDOLPH. [*To* THORNE] One moment Cap'n! [THORNE *stops. Salutes. Drops dispatch in left hand to table.—Pause for an instant—all holding their positions.*—GENERAL RANDOLPH *after above pause—to* ARRELSFORD] What have *you* got to do with this?

ARRELSFORD. It 's a Department Case! They assigned it to me!

[THORNE *picks up the forged dispatch and examines it*]

GENERAL RANDOLPH. What 's a Department Case?

ARRELSFORD. The whole plot—to send the order—it 's the Yankee Secret Service! His brother brought in the signal to-night!

[GENERAL RANDOLPH *looks sharply at* ARRELSFORD]

THORNE. [*Very quiet and matter-of-fact*] This ought to go out sir—it 's very important.

GENERAL RANDOLPH. Go ahead with it!

[THORNE *salutes and quickly turns to instrument* A. *dropping dispatch on table and begins sending rapidly as he stands before the table, glancing at the dispatch as he does so as if sending from it*]

ARRELSFORD. [*Seeing what is going on*] No no! It 's a——

GENERAL RANDOLPH. Silence!

ARRELSFORD. [*Excitedly*] Do you know what he 's telling them!

GENERAL RANDOLPH. No!—Do you?

ARRELSFORD. Yes! If you 'll——

GENERAL RANDOLPH. [*To* THORNE] Wait! [THORNE *stops telegraphing, coming at once to salute, military position a step back from table facing front*] Where 's that dispatch? [THORNE *goes to* GENERAL RANDOLPH *and hands him the dispatch with salute, then back a step.*—GENERAL RANDOLPH *takes the dispatch. To* ARRELSFORD] What was it? What has he been telling them? [*Looks at dispatch in his hand*]

ARRELSFORD. [*Excitedly*] He began to give an order to withdraw Marston's Division from its present position!

GENERAL RANDOLPH. That is perfectly correct.

ARRELSFORD. Yes—by that dispatch—but that dispatch is a forgery! [THORNE *with a look of surprise turns sharply toward* ARRELSFORD] It's an order to withdraw a whole division from a vital point! A false order! He wrote it himself! [THORNE *stands as if astounded*]

GENERAL RANDOLPH. Why should he write it? If he wanted to send out a false order he could do it without setting it down on paper could n't he?

ARRELSFORD. Yes—but if any of the operators came back they 'd catch him doing it! With that order and the Secretary's signature he could go right on! He could even order one of *them* to send it!

GENERAL RANDOLPH. How did he get the Secretary's signature?

ARRELSFORD. He tore it off from a genuine dispatch!—Why General—look at that dispatch in your hand! The Secretary's signature is *pasted on!* I saw him do it!

THORNE. [R. C.] Why—they often come that way! [*Turns away toward front*]

ARRELSFORD. [L. C.] He 's a liar! They never do!

[THORNE *turns on "liar" and the two men glare at each other a moment*]

THORNE. [R. C.—*Recovering himself*] General, if you have any doubts about that dispatch send it back to the War Office and have it verified!

[ARRELSFORD *is so thunderstruck that he starts back a little unable to speak. Stands with his eyes riveted on* THORNE *until cue of telegraph click below*]

GENERAL RANDOLPH. [*Speaks slowly, his eyes on* THORNE] Quite a good idea! [*Brief pause*] Sergeant! [*Holding out the dispatch.*—SERGEANT OF THE GUARD *salutes and waits for orders*] Take this dispatch over to the Secretary's office and—[*Sudden loud click of telegraph instrument* A. *on table* R. C.—GENERAL RANDOLPH *stops—listening. To* THORNE] What 's that?

[ARRELSFORD *looking at the instrument.* THORNE *stands motionless excepting that he took his eyes off* ARRELSFORD *and looked across to down* L. *listening*]

THORNE. [*After slight wait*] Adjutant-General Chesney.

GENERAL RANDOLPH. From the front?

THORNE. Yes sir.

GENERAL RANDOLPH. What does he say?

[THORNE *turns and steps to the table and gives quick signal on instrument* A. *closing circuit to receive, and then stands erect listening—eyes toward front*]

THORNE. His compliments sir—[*Pause—Continued click of instrument*] He asks—[*Pause.—Continued click of instrument*] for the rest—[*Pause—continued click of instrument*] of that dispatch—[*Pause—continued click of instrument which then stops*] It 's of vital importance. [THORNE *stands motionless*]

GENERAL RANDOLPH. [*After very slight pause abruptly turns and hands the dispatch back to* THORNE] Let him have it! [THORNE *hurried salute, takes dispatch—sits at table and begins sending*]

ARRELSFORD. General—if you——

GENERAL RANDOLPH. [*Sharply to* ARRELSFORD] That 's enough! We 'll have you examined at headquarters! [*Hurried steps in corridor outside up* R. *and enter quickly at doors up* R. *the* FIRST OPERATOR. *He is breathless and excited*]

ARRELSFORD. [*Catching sight of* FIRST OPERATOR *as he comes in*] Ah! Thank God! There 's a witness! He was sent away on a forged order! Ask him! Ask him! [*Pause.*—FIRST OPERATOR *standing up stage* R. C. *looking at others surprised*—THORNE *telegraphing grimly and desperately*]

GENERAL RANDOLPH. [*After instant's pause during which click of instrument is heard*] Wait a moment, Cap'n!

[THORNE *stops telegraphing, sits motionless, hand on the key, eyes straight front.—An instant of dead silence.*—GENERAL RANDOLPH *moves up* C. *a little to speak to* FIRST OPERATOR]

GENERAL RANDOLPH. [*Up* C. *to* FIRST OPERATOR. *Gruffly*] Where did you come from?

FIRST OPERATOR. [*Up* R. C.—*Not understanding what is going on.—Salutes*] There was some mistake sir!

[ARRELSFORD *gives gasp of triumph quick on cue.—Brief pause of dead silence*]

GENERAL RANDOLPH. Mistake eh?—Who made it?

FIRST OPERATOR. I got an order to go to the President's house, and when I got there the President——!

THORNE. [*Rising at telegraph table, on cue "President's house"*] This delay will be disastrous sir! Permit me to go on—if there's any mistake we can rectify it afterwards! [*Turns to instrument and begins sending as he stands before it*]

ARRELSFORD. [*Cry of remonstrance*] No!

GENERAL RANDOLPH. [*Who has not given heed to* THORNE'S *speech—to* FIRST OPERATOR] Where did you get the order?

ARRELSFORD. He's at it again sir!

GENERAL RANDOLPH. [*Suddenly sees what* THORNE *is doing*] Halt there! [THORNE *stops telegraphing*] What are you doing! [*Stepping down* C.] I ordered you to wait!

THORNE. [*Turns* L. *to* GENERAL RANDOLPH] I was sent here to attend to the business of this office and that business is going on! [*Turning again as if to telegraph*]

GENERAL RANDOLPH. [*His temper rising*] It is not going on sir, until I'm ready for it!

THORNE. [*Turning back to the* GENERAL] My orders come from the War Department—not from you! This dispatch came in half an hour ago—they're calling for it—and it's my business to send it out! [*Turning at end of speech and seizing the key endeavors to rush off the rest of the dispatch*]

GENERAL RANDOLPH. Halt! [THORNE *goes on telegraphing.—To* SERGEANT OF THE GUARD] Sergeant! [SERGEANT *salutes*] Hold that machine there! [*Pointing at telegraph instrument.—* SERGEANT OF THE GUARD *and two men spring quickly across to right.* SERGEANT *rushes against* THORNE *with arm across his breast forcing him over to* R. *against chair and table on right—chair a little away from table to emphasize with crash as* THORNE *is flung against it—and holds him there.—The two men cross bayonets over instrument and stand motionless. All done quickly, business-like and with as little disturbance as possible.* GENERAL RANDOLPH *strides down* C. *and speaks across to* THORNE] I'll have you court-martialed for this!

THORNE. [*Breaking loose from* SERGEANT *and coming down* R.] You'll answer yourself sir, for delaying a dispatch of vital importance!

GENERAL RANDOLPH. [*Sharply*] Do you mean that!

THORNE. I mean that! And I demand that you let me proceed with the business of this office!

GENERAL RANDOLPH. By what authority do you send that dispatch?

THORNE. I refer you to the Department!

GENERAL RANDOLPH. Show me your order for taking charge of this office!

THORNE. I refer you to the Department! [*Stands motionless facing across to* L.]

[EDITH *appears at upper window up* L. *coming on from balcony left, and moves a little into room up* L. C.—SERGEANT OF THE GUARD *remains at* R. *above table when* THORNE *breaks away from him*]

GENERAL RANDOLPH. By God then I'll *go* to the Department! [*Swings round and strides up* C. *a little way*] Sergeant! [SERGEANT OF THE GUARD *salutes*] Leave your men on guard there and go over to the War Office—my compliments to the Secretary and will he be so good as to——

ARRELSFORD. [*Suddenly breaking out on seeing* EDITH *up* L. C.] Ah! General! [*Pointing to* EDITH] Another witness! Miss Varney! She was here! She saw it all!

[THORNE *on* ARRELSFORD'S *mention of another witness glances quickly up* L. *toward* EDITH, *and at once turns front and stands motionless, waiting.* —GENERAL RANDOLPH *turns left and sees* EDITH]

GENERAL RANDOLPH. [*Up* C. *on* R. *bluffly touching hat*] Miss Varney! [EDITH *comes forward a little* L. *of* C.] Do you know anything about this?

EDITH. [*Speaks in low voice*] About what sir?

GENERAL RANDOLPH. Mr. Arrelsford here claims that Captain Thorne is acting without authority in this office and that you can testify to that effect.

EDITH. [*Very quietly, in low voice*] Mr. Arrelsford is mistaken—he has the highest authority.

[ARRELSFORD *aghast.*—GENERAL RANDOLPH *surprised.*—THORNE *facing* L. *listening—motionless*]

GENERAL RANDOLPH. [*After an instant's pause*] What authority has he?

EDITH. [*Drawing the Commission used in Act I from her dress. While her voice is low and controlled it trembles slightly and she has to pause a little twice*] The authority—of the President—of the Confederate States of America! [*Handing the Commission to* GENERAL RANDOLPH.—GENERAL RANDOLPH *takes the Commission and at once opens and examines it.*—EDITH *stands a moment where she was, looking neither at* ARRELSFORD *nor* THORNE, *then slowly retires up and stands back of others out of the way*]

GENERAL RANDOLPH. [C.—*Looking at the Commission*] What's this! Major's Commission! Assigned to duty on the Signal Corps! In command of the Telegraph Department!

ARRELSFORD. [L. C.—*Breaking out*] That commission—let me explain how she——I beg you to——

GENERAL RANDOLPH. That'll do!—I suppose this is a forgery too?

ARRELSFORD. Let me tell you sir——

GENERAL RANDOLPH. You've told me enough! Sergeant—take him to headquarters!

SERGEANT OF THE GUARD. [*Quick salute*] Fall in there! [*Motioning men at instrument. Men at instrument hurry across to* L. *and fall into rank*] Forward march!

[SERGEANT *and* GUARD *quickly rush* ARRELSFORD *across to doors up* R. C. *and off—the* SERGEANT *shouting to him to keep quiet, and continuing to until out of hearing outside up* R.]

ARRELSFORD. [*Resisting and protesting as he is forced across and off at doors up* R. C. No!—For God's sake General—listen to me! It's the Yankee Secret Service! Never mind me, but don't let that dispatch go out! He's a damned Yankee Secret Agent! His brother brought in the signal to-night! [Etc.]

[*Sounds of footsteps of the* GUARD *and voices of* ARRELSFORD *and* SERGEANT *dying away down the corridor outside up* R.—*Short pause.*—THORNE *motionless through above looking front.*—GENERAL RANDOLPH, *who crossed to up* L. C. *on men forcing* ARRELSFORD *off, goes down* C. *and looks across at* THORNE]

GENERAL RANDOLPH. [*Gruffly*] Cap'n Thorne! [THORNE *comes to erect military position. Turns* L. *and goes to the* GENERAL *at* C. *saluting*] It's your own fault Cap'n! If you'd had the sense to mention this before we'd have been saved a damned lot o' trouble!—There's your Commission! [*Handing Commission to* THORNE.—THORNE *takes it saluting.*—GENERAL *turns to go*] I can't understand why they have to be so cursed shy about their Secret Service Orders! [*Goes up toward door up* R. C. *Stops and speaks to* FIRST OPERATOR *who is standing at* R. *of door*] Lieutenant! [FIRST OPERATOR *salutes*] Take your orders from Major Thorne. [*Turns and goes heavily off at doors up* R. C. *very much out of temper*] [*Note.*—GENERAL *must on no account emphasize "Major"*]

[FIRST OPERATOR *goes down* R. *and sits at telegraph table on extreme* R. *going to work on papers.—No noise.*—THORNE *stands facing* L., *Commission in his* R. *hand, until the* GENERAL *is off. Turns head slowly around to front and looks across to* R. *watching to see when the* GENERAL *is gone—at the same time crushing the Commission in his right hand. After exit of* GENERAL *he instantly glides to telegraph instrument* A. *and begins sending with* R. *hand still holding commission in it.*—EDITH *comes quickly down to* THORNE *on his left and very near him*]

EDITH. [*Speaks breathlessly in a half whisper*] Cap'n Thorne! [THORNE *stops telegraphing—hand still on key—but does not look at her.—She goes on in low voice, hurried—breathless*] That Commission—gives you authority—long enough to escape from Richmond!

THORNE. Escape! After all this! Impossible! [*Seizes key and begins to send*]

EDITH. Oh!—You would n't do it—*now!* [THORNE *instantly stops telegraphing and looks at her*]

EDITH. I brought it—*to save your life!* I did n't think you'd use it—*for anything else!* Oh—you would n't!

[THORNE *stands looking at her.—Sudden sharp call from instrument* A.—*He instantly turns back to it. His hand moves to grasp it—hovers uncertainly over it as he hesitates.*—EDITH *sees his hand at the key again—covers her face and moans, at the same time turning away* L. *She moves up to the doors up* R. C. *and goes out.*—THORNE *stands in a desperate struggle with himself as instrument* A. *is clicking off the same signal that he made when calling up the front. He almost seizes the key—then resists—and finally, with a bang of right fist on the table, turns and strides across to up* L. C.—*the Commission crushed in his* R. *hand*]

FIRST OPERATOR. [*Who has been listening to calls of instrument* A. *on table* R. C., *rising at* R. *as* THORNE *comes to a stand up* L. C.] They 're calling for that dispatch sir! What shall I do?

THORNE. [*Turning quickly*] Send it!

[FIRST OPERATOR *drops into seat at table* R. C. *and begins sending at same time spreading out the dispatch which he is sending from near left end of table*]

[THORNE *stands motionless an instant. As* OPERATOR *begins to send he turns round a little up to* R. *slowly and painfully,* R. *arm up across eyes in a struggle with himself. Suddenly he breaks away and dashes toward table* R. C.]

THORNE. No no—stop! [*Seizes the dispatch from the table in his* R. *hand which still has the Commission crumpled in it*] I can't do it! I can't do it! [FIRST OPERATOR *rises in surprise on* THORNE *seizing the dispatch, and stands facing him.*—THORNE *points at instrument unsteadily*] Revoke the order! It was a mistake!—I refuse to act under this Commission! [*Throwing the papers in his* R. *hand down on the floor—then turning away to* L. *and walking uncertainly up toward* L. C.—*turning there and after slight hesitation walking across to doors up* R. C.—*pausing an instant as he supports himself with hand on the upper door as it stands open—then exits unsteadily at doors up* R. C. *and passes out of sight down the corridor to* R.]

[CURTAIN]

ACT IV

ELEVEN O'CLOCK

[SCENE:—*Drawing room at* GENERAL VARNEY'S. *This is the same set as in Acts I and II.—The furniture is somewhat disordered as if left as it was after the disturbances at the close of the Second Act. —Couch up* R. *where* ARRELSFORD *put it end of Act II. Nothing is broken or upset. Half light in room. Lamps lighted but not strong on. See that portières on windows down* R. *are closed.—Thunder of distant cannonading and sounds of volleys of musketry and exploding shells on very strong at times during this act. Quivering and rather subdued flashes of light—(the artillery is some miles distant)—shown at windows* R. *on cues. Violent and hurried ringing of church bells in distant parts of the city—deep, low tones booming out like fire bells. Sounds of hurried passing in the street outside of bodies of soldiers—artillery—cavalry, etc. on cues, with many horse-hoof and rattling gun carriage and chain effects—shouting to horses—orders, bugle calls, etc.*]

[NOTE:—*This thunder of cannonading, shelling fortifications, musketry, flashes, etc., must be kept up during the act, coming in now and then where it will not interfere with dialogue, and so arranged that the idea of a desperate attack will not be lost. Possible places for this effect will be marked thus in the manuscript—* [XXX]

[*At rise of curtain, thunder of artillery and flashes of light now and then. Ringing of church and fire bells in distance*]

[CAROLINE *is discovered in window up* R. *shrinking back against curtains and looking out through the window in a terified way*]

[XXX]

[*Enter* MRS. VARNEY *coming hurriedly down the stairway from up* L. *and entering through door or arch up* L. C.]

MRS. VARNEY. Caroline! [CAROLINE *goes to her.—She takes* CAROLINE *forward a little*] Tell me what happened? She won't speak! Where has she been? Where was it?

CAROLINE. [*Frightened*] It was at the telegraph office!

MRS. VARNEY. What did she do? What happened there? Do try to tell!

[*Flashes—cannonading—bells, etc., kept up strong. Effect of passing artillery begins in the distance very faint*]

CAROLINE. Oh I *don't* know! How can I tell? I was afraid and ran out! [*Alarm bell very strong*] It 's the alarm bell, Mrs. Varney—to call out the reserves!—That 's to call out the reserves!

MRS. VARNEY. Yes—yes, I know it dear! [*A glance of anxiety toward windows right*] They 're making a terrible attack to-night. Lieutenant Maxwell was right! That quiet spell was the signal! [*Artillery effect louder*]

CAROLINE *crosses timidly to window up* R.]

CAROLINE [*Turning to* MRS. VARNEY *and speaking above the noise, which is not yet on full*] It 's another regiment of artillery goin' by! They 're sendin' 'em all over to Cemetery Hill! That 's where the fighting is! Cemetery Hill! [*Effect on loud*]

[CAROLINE *watches from window.—* MRS. VARNEY *crosses over left and rings bell.—As artillery effect dies away* MARTHA *enters door up* L. C. *from* R.]

MRS. VARNEY. [*To* MARTHA] Go up and stay with Miss Edith till I come. Don't leave her a moment Martha—not a moment!

MARTHA. No 'm—I won't. [*She turns and hastens off at door up* L. C. *and up the stairway*]

[*Alarm bell and cannon on strong*]

MRS. VARNEY. Do close the curtains Caroline! [*Moves toward up* C.]

[CAROLINE *closes the window curtains at right*]

CAROLINE. I 'm afraid they 're goin' to have a right bad time to-night! [*Going to* MRS. VARNEY]

MRS. VARNEY. Indeed I 'm afraid so!—Now try to think dear, who was at the telegraph office? Can't you tell me something?

CAROLINE. [*Shaking her head*] No—only —they arrested Mr. Arrelsford!

MRS. VARNEY. Mr. Arrelsford! Why you don't mean that he was—that he was actually arrested!

CAROLINE. Yes I do—an' I was glad of it!—An' General Randolph—he came—I went an' brought him there—an' Oh—he was in a frightful temper!

MRS. VARNEY. And Edith—now you can tell me—what did *she* do?

CAROLINE. I can't Mrs. Varney—I don't know! I just waited for her outside—an' when she came out she could n't speak—an' then we hurried home! That 's all I know Mrs. Varney—truly!

[*Loud ringing of door bell in another part of the house.*—CAROLINE *and* MRS. VARNEY *turn toward door up* L. C.—*Noise of heavy steps outside left and* ARRELSFORD *almost immediately strides into the room, followed by two privates, who stand at the door*]

[CAROLINE *steps back up stage a little as* ARRELSFORD *enters, and* MRS. VARNEY *faces him*]

[XXX]

ARRELSFORD. [L. C.—*Roughly*] Is your daughter in the house?

MRS. VARNEY. [*After a second's pause*] Certainly!

[XXX]

ARRELSFORD. I 'll see her if you please!

MRS. VARNEY. I don't know that she 'll care to receive you at present.

ARRELSFORD. What she cares to do at present is of small consequence! Shall I go up to her room with these men or will you have her come down here to me?

MRS. VARNEY. Neither one nor the other until I know your business.

[*Effect of passing cavalry and artillery*]

ARRELSFORD. [*Excitedly*] My business! You 'll know mighty quick! It 's a very simple matter Mrs. Varney! Got a few questions to ask!—Listen to that! [*Cannonading becomes heavy*] Now you know what "Attack To-night Plan Three" means! Now you know!

MRS. VARNEY. Is that—Is that the attack they meant!

ARRELSFORD. That 's the attack Madam! They 're breaking through our lines at Cemetery Hill! That was PLAN THREE! We 're rushing over the reserves but they may not get there in time!—Now if you please I 'll see Miss Varney!

[XXX]

[CAROLINE *has crossed at back to door up* L. C. *as if going out, but turns near door to hear what* ARRELSFORD *is saying*]

MRS. VARNEY. What has my daughter to do with this?

ARRELSFORD. Do with it! She did it!

MRS. VARNEY. [*Astonished*] What!

ARRELSFORD. Do you hear what I say—she did it!

[*Noise of passing Cavalry Officers going by singly*]

MRS. VARNEY. Impossible!

ARRELSFORD. Impossible or not as you choose!—We had him there—in his own trap—under arrest—*under arrest you understand*—when she brought in that Commission!

MRS. VARNEY. [*Horrified*] You don't mean she—

ARRELSFORD. I mean she put the game in his hands! He got the wires! His cursed dispatch went through! As soon as I got to headquarters they saw the trick! They rushed the guard back—the scoundrel had got away! But we 're after him hot, an' if she knows where he is—[*About to turn toward door up* L. C.] I 'll get it out of her!

[XXX]

MRS. VARNEY. You don't suppose my daughter would—

ARRELSFORD. I suppose anything!

MRS. VARNEY. I 'll not believe it!

ARRELSFORD. We can't stop for what you believe! [*Turns to go up* L. C.]

[*Alarm bells gradually cease*]

MRS. VARNEY. Let me speak to her!

[*Passing cavalry effect has died away by this time*]

ARRELSFORD. I 'll see her myself! [*Going up* L.]

[CAROLINE *has stepped quietly down so that as* ARRELSFORD *turns to go toward stairway she confronts him just within the door or arch up* L. C.]

CAROLINE. [*Up* L. C. *between* ARRELSFORD *and the door.*—*Almost on cue of his last speech*] Where is your order for this?

ARRELSFORD. [*Stopped by* CAROLINE *up* L. C.—*After an instant's surprise*] I 've got a word or two to say to you—after I 've been upstairs!

CAROLINE. Show me your order for *going* upstairs!

ARRELSFORD. Department business—I don't

require an order! [*Moves as if to pass her*]

CAROLINE. [*Stepping in his way again*] Oh, you 've made a great mistake about that! This is a private house! It is n't the telegraph office! If you want to go up any stairs or see anybody about anything you 'll have to bring an order! I don't know much—but I know *something*—an' that 's it! [*She turns and exits door up* L. C. *and runs up the stairway*]

[XXX *light*]

ARRELSFORD. [*Turns sharply to* MRS. VARNEY] Am I to understand Madam, that you—

[*Loud ringing of door bell in distant part of house, followed almost immediately by the sound of heavy door outside* L. *and tramp of many feet in the hallway*]

[*The sound of cavalry begins again*]

[ARRELSFORD *and* MRS. VARNEY *turn*]

[*Enter at door or arch up* L. C. *from* L. *a* SERGEANT *and four men. Men are halted up* L. OFFICER *advances to* MRS. VARNEY.—ARRELSFORD *steps back a little up* C.]

SERGEANT. [*Touching his cap roughly*] Are you the lady that lives here ma'am?

MRS. VARNEY. [R. C.] I am Mrs. Varney!

SERGEANT. [C.] I 've got an order to search the house! [*Showing* MRS. VARNEY *the order*]

ARRELSFORD. [*Coming quickly down* L. C.] Just in time!—I 'll go through the house if you please!

SERGEANT. [*Roughly*] You can't go through on this order—it was issued to me.

MRS. VARNEY. You were sent here to——

SERGEANT. Yes ma'am! Sorry to trouble you but we 'll have to be quick about it! If we don't get him here we 've got to follow down Franklin Street—he 's over this way somewhere! [*Turns* L. *about to give orders to men*]

MRS. VARNEY. Who? Who is it you——

SERGEANT. [*Turning hurriedly at* L. C.] Man named Thorne—Cap'n of Artillery—that 's what he went by! [*Turns to his men*] Here—this way! That room in there! [*Indicating room up* C.] Two of you outside! [*Pointing to windows*] Cut off those windows.

[*Two men run into room up* C. *and two off at windows* R. *as indicated, throwing open curtains and windows as they do so.*—MRS. VARNEY *stands aside* R. C.—SERGEANT *glances quickly round the room—pushing desk out and looking behind it, etc.—Keep cavalry effects on and flashes intermittently during this business.—Also occasional low thunder of distant artillery. Cavalry effects distant—as if going down a street several blocks away.—During bus.* ARRELSFORD *goes to door* L. *and gives an order to his men. Then he exits door left.—Men who came with* ARRELSFORD *exit after him*]

[*As the cannonading begins again, the two men who went off at door up* C. *to search, re-enter shoving the old negro* JONAS *roughly into the room.—He is torn and dirty and shows signs of rough handling.—They force him down* C. *a little way and he stands crouching*]

SERGEANT. [R. C.—*To men*] Where did you get that?

PRIVATE. [C.] Hiding in a closet sir.

SERGEANT. [*Going* C.—*To* JONAS] What are you doing in there? If you don't answer me we 'll kick the life out of you! [*Short pause.—To* MRS. VARNEY] Belongs to you I reckon?

MRS. VARNEY. [R. C.] Yes—but they want him for carrying a message——

SERGEANT. [*Interrupting*] Well if they want him they can come an' get him—we 're looking for someone else! [*Motions to men*] Throw him back in there! [*Men shove* JONAS *off at door up* C.—*Other men re-enter from windows at right*] Here—this room! Be quick now! Cover that door! [*Two men have quick business of searching down* R. *and* .L—*The other two men stand on guard door up* L. C.] Sorry to disturb you ma'am! [*Bell rings in distant part of house*]

MRS. VARNEY. Do what you please—I have nothing to conceal! [*Sound of heavy door outside up* L.]

[XXX]

[*Voice of* ORDERLY *calling outside up* L.]

ORDERLY. [*Outside up* L.] Here! Lend a hand will you!

[*Two men at door up left exit at left to help someone outside*] [*Enter the* ORDERLY *who took* WILFRED *away in Act II. coming on hurriedly at door up* L. C. *from* L.—*Stands just below door—a few steps into room. He is splashed with foam and mud from hard riding. He sees* SERGEANT *and salutes.*—SERGEANT *salutes* ORDERLY *and goes over, looking out of window up* R.—MRS. VARNEY *upon seeing the* ORDERLY *utters a low cry of alarm*]

ORDERLY. I 've brought back the boy ma'am!

MRS. VARNEY. [R. C.—*Starting forward*] Oh! What do you— What——

ORDERLY. We never got out there at all! The Yankees made a raid down at Mechanicsville not three miles out! The Home Guard was goin' by on the dead run to head 'em off, an' before I knew it he was in with 'em riding like mad! There was a bit of a skirmish an' he got a clip across the neck—nothing at all ma'am—he rode back all the way an'— [*Cavalry effects die away gradually*]

MRS. VARNEY. [*Moving toward* C.] Oh—Wilfred! He 's—he 's hurt!

ORDERLY. Nothing bad ma'am—don't upset yourself!

MRS. VARNEY. [*Starts toward the door*] Where did you—[*Stops on seeing* WILFRED] [*Enter* WILFRED *at door left supported by the two* MEN.—*He is pale and has a bandage about his neck.*—MRS. VARNEY, *after the slight pause on his entrance goes to him at once*]

MRS. VARNEY. [*Going to* WILFRED] Wilfred!

WILFRED. [*Weak voice—motioning* MRS. VARNEY *away*] It 's all right—it 's all right—you don't understand! [*Tries to free himself from the men who are supporting him*] What do you want to hold me like that for? [*Frees himself and walks toward* C. *a little unsteadily*]—You see—I can walk all right! [MRS. VARNEY *comes down anxiously on his right and holds him*] [WILFRED *turns and sees his mother and takes her hand with an effort to do it in as casual a manner as possible*] How-dy-do Mother!—Did n't expect me back so soon, did you?—Tell you how it was—[*Turns and sees* ORDERLY. *To* ORDERLY] Don't you go away now—I 'm going back with you—just wait till I rest up about a minute.—See here! They 're ringing the bells to call out the reserves! [*Starting weakly toward door* L.] That settles it—I 'll go right now!

[XXX]

MRS. VARNEY. [*Gently holding him back*] No no Wilfred—not now!

[NOTE: WILFRED *must get well over to* R. C. *when he speaks to* MRS. VARNEY, *and not move back to left more than a step or two, in order to be near the couch*]

[*The cannonading sounds more loudly*]

WILFRED. [*Weakly*] Not now! — You hear that—you hear those bells—and tell me—not now!—I—[*Sways a little*] I—[MRS. VARNEY *supports him tenderly*]

SERGEANT. [*Quick undertone to* MEN] Stand by there! [WILFRED *faints.*—MRS. VARNEY *supports him, but almost immediately the* TWO MEN *come to her assistance.*—SERGEANT *and* TWO MEN *push the couch forward down* R. C. *and they quickly lay him on it with his head on the right.*—MRS. VARNEY *goes to head of couch and holds* WILFRED'S *head as they lay him down*]

[*Cannonading and other effects gradually cease*]

SERGEANT. [*To one of the men*] Find some water will you? [*To* MRS. VARNEY] Put his head down ma'am—put his head down an' he 'll be all right in a minute.

[*A* PRIVATE *hurries off at door up* L. C. *to* R. *on order to get water.*—SERGEANT *gets chair from up* C. *and puts it back of couch.*—MRS. VARNEY *goes back of couch attending to* WILFRED.—PRIVATE *re-enters with basin of water and gives it to* MRS. VARNEY]

OFFICER. [*To* MEN] This way now!

[MEN *move quickly to door or arch up* L. C.—OFFICER *gives quick directions to* MEN *at door. All exit at door up* L. C.—*one or two going* R. *and* SERGEANT *with most of men going up the stairway.*—ORDERLY *is left standing* L. *a little below door, exactly as he was.*—MRS. VARNEY *kneeling back of* WILFRED *and bathing his head tenderly—using her handkerchief*]

ORDERLY. [*After brief pause*] If there ain't anything else ma'am, I 'd better report back.

MRS. VARNEY. Yes—don't wait!—The wound is dressed is n't it?

ORDERLY. Yes ma'am—I took him to the Winder Hospital—they said he 'd be on his feet in a day or two—he only wants to keep quiet a bit.

MRS. VARNEY. Tell the General just how it happened!

ORDERLY. [*Touching cap*] I sure will ma'am. [*He turns and hurries off at door up* L. C. *to* L.]

[*Short pause.*—MRS. VARNEY *gently bathing* WILFRED'S *head and wrists*] [*Sound of alarm bells dies away excepting that from a very distant one which continues to ring in muffled tones*] [CAROLINE *appears coming down the stairway up* L. *absent-mindedly, stopping when part way down because she sees someone on couch with* MRS. VARNEY *bathing his head. She looks more intently. Then suddenly starts and runs down the rest of the way and into the room at door up* L. C. *stopping dead when a little way in and looking across at what is going on.*—MRS. VARNEY *does not see her at first.*—CAROLINE *stands motionless—face very white.* —MRS. VARNEY *after a moment's pause sees* CAROLINE]

MRS. VARNEY. [*Rising quickly*] Caroline dear! [*Goes to* CAROLINE C.] It 's *nothing!* [*Holds* CAROLINE, *though the girl seems not to know it, her face expressionless and her eyes fixed on* WILFRED] He 's hardly hurt at all! There —there—don't *you* faint too, dear!

CAROLINE. [*Very low voice*] I'm not going to faint! [*Sees the handkerchief in* MRS. VARNEY'S *hand*] Let me—[*Takes the handkerchief and goes across, toward front of couch. Turns to* MRS. VARNEY]—I can take care of him—I don't need anybody here *at all!* [*Goes toward* WILFRED]

MRS. VARNEY. But Caroline——

CAROLINE. [*Still with a strange quiet.—Looks calmly at* MRS. VARNEY] Mrs. Varney—there 's a heap o' soldiers goin' round upstairs—lookin' in all the rooms. I reckon you 'd better go an' attend to 'em.

MRS. VARNEY. Upstairs! Why I did n't know they——

CAROLINE. Well they did.—I was keepin' 'em quiet as long as I could.

MRS. VARNEY. I—I must go up and see to it! [*Turns and moves up* L. C.—*Turns back*] You know what to do dear!

CAROLINE. Oh yes! [*Dropping down on the floor beside* WILFRED *in front of couch*]

MRS. VARNEY. Bathe his forehead—he is n't badly hurt!—I won't be long! [*Exit hurriedly door up* L. C. *closing the portières or curtains together after her*] [CAROLINE *on her knees close to* WILFRED, *tenderly bathing his forehead and smoothing his hair*] [WILFRED *soon begins to show signs of reviving*]

CAROLINE. [*Speaking to* WILFRED *in low tone as he revives.—Not a continued speech, but with pauses—*] Wilfred dear!—Wilfred! You 're not hurt much are you?—Oh no—you 're not! There there!—You 'll feel better in just a minute!—Yes—just a minute!

WILFRED [*Weakly.—Before he realizes what has happened*] Is there—are you—[*Looks round with wide open eyes*]

CAROLINE. Oh Wilfred—don't you know me?

WILFRED. [*Looks at her for a moment before speaking.—Voice weak—but clear and audible throughout this scene with* CAROLINE] What are you talking about? Of course I know you!—Say—what am I doing anyhow—taking a bath?

CAROLINE. No no!—You see Wilfred—you just fainted a little an'——

WILFRED. Fainted! [CAROLINE *nods*] *I fainted!* [*A weak attempt to rise. Begins to remember*] Oh—[*Sinks back weakly*]—Yes of course!—I was in a fight with the Yanks—an' got knocked—[*Begins to remember that he was wounded.—He thinks about it a moment, then looks strangely at* CAROLINE]

CAROLINE. [*After looking at* WILFRED *in silence*] Oh—what is it?

WILFRED. I'll tell you one thing right yere! I 'm not going to load you up with a cripple! Not much!

CAROLINE. Cripple!

WILFRED. I reckon I 've got an arm knocked off have n't I?

CAROLINE. [*Quickly*] No no! You have n't Wilfred! [*Shaking head emphatically*] They 're both on all right!

WILFRED. [*After thinking a moment. Weak voice*] Maybe I had a hand shot away?

CAROLINE. Oh no—not a single one!

WILFRED. Are my—are my ears on all right?

CAROLINE. [*Looks on both sides of his head*] Yes—they 're all right Wilfred—you need n't trouble about them a minute! [WILFRED *thinks a moment. Then turns his eyes slowly upon her*]

WILFRED. How many legs have I got left?

CAROLINE. [*Looks to see*] All of 'em—Every one!

[*Last alarm bell ceases*]

WILFRED. [*After pause*] Then—if there 's enough of me left to—to amount to anything—[*Looks in* CAROLINE'S *face a mo-*

ment] you 'll take charge of it just the same?—How about that?

CAROLINE. [*After pause*] That 's all right too! [CAROLINE *suddenly buries her face on his shoulder.*—WILFRED *gets hold of her hand and kisses it.*—CAROLINE *suddenly raises her head and looks at him*] I tried to send you a telegram—an' they would n't let me!

WILFRED. Did you? [CAROLINE *nods*] What did you say in it? [*Pause*] Tell me what you said!

CAROLINE. It was something nice! [*Looks away*]

WILFRED. It was, eh? [CAROLINE *nods with her head turned away from him.*—WILFRED *reaches up and turns her head toward him again*] You 're sure it was something nice!

CAROLINE. Well I would n't have gone to work an' telegraphed if it was something *bad* would I?

WILFRED. Well if it was good, why did n't you send it?

CAROLINE. Goodness gracious! How could I when they would n't let me!

WILFRED. Would n't let you!

CAROLINE. I should think *not!* [*Moves back a little for* WILFRED'S *business of getting up*] Oh they had a terrible time at the telegraph office!

WILFRED. Telegraph office. [*Tries to recollect*] Telegr—were you there when—[*Raising himself*]

[*Alarm bell begins to ring again in distant part of the town*]

[XXX]

[CAROLINE *moves back a little frightened—without getting up—watching him.*—WILFRED *suddenly tries to get up*] That was it!—They told me at the hospital! [*Attempts to rise*]

[*The cannonading becomes louder*]

CAROLINE. [*Rising*] Oh,—you must n't! [*She tries to prevent him from rising*]

WILFRED. [*Gets partly on his feet and pushes* CAROLINE *away with one hand, holding to the chair near the desk* R. *for support with the other*] He gets hold of our Department Telegraph—sends out a false order—weakens our defense at Cemetery Hill—an' they 're down on us in a minute! An' she gave it to him!—My sister Edith! She gave him the Commission that allowed him to do it!

CAROLINE. [L. *of* WILFRED] But you don't know how the——

WILFRED. [*Imperiously*] I know this—if the General was here he 'd see her! The General is n't here—I 'll attend to it!

[*Sounds of cannon*]

[WILFRED *begins to feel a dizziness and holds to the desk or chair near it for support.*—CAROLINE *starts toward him in alarm.*—*He braces himself erect again with an effort and motions her off.*—*She stops*]

WILFRED. [*Weakly but with clear voice, and commandingly*] Send her to me! [CAROLINE *stands almost frightened with her eyes upon him*]

[*Enter* MRS. VARNEY *coming down the stairway and in at door up* L. C.—CAROLINE *hurries toward her in a frightened way—with a glance back at* WILFRED]

CAROLINE. He wants to see Edith!

MRS. VARNEY. [*Going toward* WILFRED] Not now Wilfred—you 're too weak and ill!

[CAROLINE *remains up* C.]

WILFRED. [R.] Tell her to come here!

MRS. VARNEY. [L. *of* WILFRED] It won't do any good—she won't speak!

WILFRED. I don't *want* her to speak—I 'm going to speak to *her!*

MRS. VARNEY. Some other time!

WILFRED. [*Leaves the desk or chair that he held to and moves toward door up* L. C. *as if to pass his mother and* CAROLINE] Very well—if you won't send her to me—I 'll——

MRS. VARNEY. [*Stopping him*] There there! If you insist I 'll call her!

WILFRED. I insist!

[*Cannonading*]

MRS. VARNEY. [*Turns toward door and goes a few steps, crossing* CAROLINE. *Stops. Turns back to* CAROLINE] Stay with him dear!

WILFRED. [*Weak voice but commandingly*] No!—I 'll see her alone!

[MRS. VARNEY *looks at him an instant. Sees that he means what he says. Motions* CAROLINE *to come.*—CAROLINE *looks at* WILFRED *a moment, then turns and slowly goes to door up* L. *where* MRS. VARNEY *is waiting for her. Looks sadly back at* WILFRED *again, and then goes out with* MRS. VARNEY *at door up* L. C. *and up the stairway*]

[XXX]

[WILFRED *stands motionless an instant down* R. C. *as he was when the two ladies left the room.*—*Noise of approaching men—low shouts—steps on gravel, etc., outside up* R., *begins in distance.—On this* WILFRED *turns and moves up* C. *looking off to right. Then moves up into the doorway opening up* C. *but does not open the door*]

[XXX]

[*Alarm bell ceases.—Low sound of distant voices and the tramp of hurrying feet quickly growing louder and louder outside right.—When it is on strong,* THORNE *appears springing over balustrade of veranda above window up* R. *and instantly runs forward into the room backing close against right wall below window and holding curtain or hanging between him and the window as he does so. A stand with vase is thrown over with this movement and crashes down in front of lower window. He stands there panting—face pale—eyes hunted and desperate and revolver clutched in right hand held at ready. His left hand is bandaged roughly. He has no hat, or coat, hair is disheveled, shoes dusty, trousers and shirt torn and soiled. As the noise of his pursuers dies away he turns into the room and makes a rapid start across toward* L. *looking quickly about as if searching for someone*]

[WILFRED—*who has been watching him from up* C. *in the doorway—turns quickly down* C. *as* THORNE *crosses, coming right of him and seizing him by right arm and shoulder*]

WILFRED. [*Seizing hold of* THORNE'S *right arm and shoulder as* THORNE *crosses*] Halt! You're under arrest!

THORNE. [*With a quick glance back at* WILFRED] Wait a minute! [*Shaking loose from* WILFRED] Wait a minute an' I'll go with you! [*Going up* L. C. *looking this way and that*]

WILFRED. [*A step toward* THORNE *as if to follow*] Halt I say! You're my prisoner!

THORNE. [*Turning and going quickly to* WILFRED] All right—prisoner—anything you like! [*Pushing his revolver into* WILFRED'S *hands*] Here—take this! Shoot the life out of me—but let me see my brother first!

WILFRED. [*Taking the revolver*] Your brother!

THORNE. [*Nods—breathless*] One look in his face—one look—that's all I ask!

WILFRED. Where is he?

THORNE. [*Breathless*] I don't know! [*Quick glance about. Points toward the door up* C.] Maybe they took him in there! [*Striding up* C. *toward door as he speaks*]

WILFRED. [*Springing up between* THORNE *and the door and covering him with revolver*] What is he doing?

THORNE. [*Facing* WILFRED *half way up* C.] What!

WILFRED. [*Still covering* THORNE] What's he doing in there?

THORNE. Nothing! . . . He's dead!

[WILFRED *looks at* THORNE *a moment. Then begins to back slowly up to door up* C., *keeping eyes on* THORNE *and revolver ready but not aimed.—Opens door up* C. *Quick look into the room. Faces* THORNE *again*]

WILFRED. It's a lie!—There's no one there!—It's another trick of yours! [*Starts toward window up* R.—*half backing so that he can still cover* THORNE *with revolver*] Call in the Guard! Call the Guard! Captain Thorne is here in the house!

[WILFRED *exits at window* R. *calling the* GUARD. *His voice is heard outside* R. *growing fainter and fainter in the distance*]

[THORNE *stands an instant after* WILFRED *disappears—then springs to the door up* C. *Opens it and looks into the room, going part way off at the door. He glances this way and that within the room, then attitude of despair—left hand dropping from frame of door to his side as he comes to erect position—right hand retaining hold of knob of door*]

[*On* THORNE *standing erect* EDITH *enters through the portières of the door up* L. C.—*expecting to find* WILFRED. *She stands just within the doorway to the* L. *of it*]

[THORNE *turns and comes out of room up* C., *closing the door as he does so. Turning away from the door—right hand still on the knob—he sees* EDITH *and stops motionless facing her*]

[*A pause for an instant*]

THORNE. [*Going toward* EDITH *a step or two*] You would n't tell me would you! He was shot in this room—an hour ago—my brother Harry!—I'd like one look in his dead face before they send me the same way! Can't you tell me that much Miss Varney? Where is he? If you won't speak to me perhaps you'll make some sign so I'll know? It's my brother Miss Varney! [EDITH *looks in his face an instant motionless—then turns and moves slowly down* L. C. *and stands near the table there*]

[*As* EDITH *stops near table* L. C. THORNE *turns away and goes toward window up* R.—*Before he reaches it there is a sudden burst of shouts and yells outside up* R.—*short and savage.*—THORNE *stops up* R. C. *on the shouts and stands supporting himself a little by the upper wall or a door frame. He turns front with a grim smile—a flash from distant artillery action lighting his face for an instant from window* R.]

THORNE. Ha!—They're on the scent at last! [*Muttering it to himself*] They'll get me now—and then it won't take long to finish me off! [*Turns toward* EDITH] And as that'll be the last of me—[*Moves toward her*] As that'll be the last of me Miss Varney—[*Comes down* L. C. *near her*] maybe you'll listen to one thing! We can't all die a soldier's death—in the roar of battle—our friends around us—under the flag we love!—No—not all! Some of us have orders for another kind of work—desperate—dare-devil work—the hazardous schemes of the Secret Service. We fight our battles alone—no comrades to cheer us on—ten thousand to one against us—death at every turn! If we win we escape with our lives—if we lose—dragged out and butchered like dogs—no soldier's grave—not even a trench with the rest of the boys—alone—despised—forgotten! These were my orders Miss Varney—this is the death I die to-night—and I don't want you to think for one minute that I'm ashamed of it.

[*Sudden shouts and noise of many men running outside up* R. *and also outside up* L.—THORNE *swings round and walks up* C. *in usual nonchalant manner, and stands up* C. *waiting and faced a little to* R. *of front, leaning on side of door with outstretched right arm. He simply waits—his face utterly atonic—no attitude or expression of bravado martyrdom*]

[EDITH *moves to left and stands near mantel*]

[*The shouts and stamping of running feet grow quickly louder on both* R. *and* L. *gauged so that as* THORNE *stands motionless up* C. *squads of Confederate soldiers rush in from both windows* R. *and from door up* L. C. *from* L.—*those on right headed by the* SERGEANT *who searched the house early in this act, and those on left by* CORPORAL.—WILFRED VARNEY *with revolver still in his hand, enters at window down* R. *in lead of others, coming to* R. C. *and letting men pass him.—The men from both sides run savagely toward* THORNE *and stand each side of him with bayonets charged hoping for the order to run him through*]

SERGEANT. Halt! Halt! [*The* MEN *stand motionless*]

WILFRED. [R. C.—*To* SERGEANT] There's your man Sergeant—I hand him over to you!

SERGEANT. [*Up* R. C.—*Advancing to* THORNE *and putting hand roughly on his shoulder*] Prisoner!

[XXX]

[*Enter* ARRELSFORD *hurriedly at door up* L. C. *from* L.]

ARRELSFORD. [*Breaking through between men at* L.] Where is he? [*Sees* THORNE] Ah! We've got him have we! [*Stands* L. C. *looking at* THORNE]

SERGEANT. Young Varney here captured him sir!

[*Enter* MRS. VARNEY *door up* L. C. *from stairway. She goes down left side*]

ARRELSFORD. So!—Run down at last! [THORNE *pays no attention to* ARRELSFORD.—*He merely waits for the end of the disturbance*] Now you'll find out what it costs to play your little game with our Government Telegraph Lines! [*Turns to* SERGEANT] Don't waste any time! Take him down the street and shoot him full of lead!—Out with him! [*Turns and goes down* L. C.]

[*Low shouts of approval from men, and general movement as if to start, the* SERGEANT *at same time shoving* THORNE *a little to swing him around toward left*]

SERGEANT. [*With other shouts*] Come along here!

WILFRED. [*A step toward* C.—*Revolver still in hand. Speaking with all his force*] No! [*Men and officers stand *motionless*] Whatever he is—whatever he's done—he has a right to a trial! [THORNE *turns and looks at* WILFRED]

ARRELSFORD. [*Down* L. C.] General Tarleton said to me, "If you find him shoot him on sight!"

WILFRED. [*Down* R. C.] I don't *care* what General Tarleton said—I captured the man—he's in this house—and he's not going out without he's treated fair! [WILFRED *looks up toward* THORNE.—*Their eyes meet.—After an instant* THORNE *turns away up stage, resting left hand against* L. *side of door frame*]

ARRELSFORD. [*Suddenly. Angrily*] Well—let him have it!—We'll give him a drum-head, boys—but it'll be the quickest drum-head ever held on earth! [*To* SERGEANT] Stack muskets here an' run 'em in for the court!

SERGEANT. [*Stepping a little down* C. *and facing about—back to audience*] Fall in here! [MEN *break positions each side and run up stage, falling quickly into a double rank just above* SERGEANT.—THORNE *is up* C. *above this double rank*] Fall in the Prisoner! [MEN *separate* R. *and* L. *leaving space at* C.—THORNE *steps down into position and stands*] Stack—arms! [*Front rank men stack.—Rear rank men pass pieces forward.—Front rank men lay them on stacks.*—SERGEANT *turns right to* MRS. VARNEY *and touches cap*] Where shall we find a vacant room ma'am?

MRS. VARNEY. At the head of the stairs—there's none on this floor.

SERGEANT. [*Turning to men*] Escort—left face! [*Men left face*—THORNE *obeying the order with them*] Forward—march!—File left!

[SOLDIERS *with* THORNE *march rapidly out of the room at door up* L. C. *and disappear up the stairway outside up* L.—*The* SERGEANT *exits door up* L. C. *and up stairway after men*]

[ARRELSFORD *exits after men door up* L. C. *following them closely up the stairway and off to* L.—WILFRED *follows off at door up* L. C. *and up the stairway with some effort.*—MRS. VARNEY *exits at door up* L. C. *and off to left*]

[EDITH *turns and crosses slowly to window at right. Pauses a moment there, flashes of light from distant cannonading on her face. She stands in window right—partly hidden by curtains—looking off*]

[*The door up* C. *slowly opens a little way and the old negro* JONAS *looks cautiously through from outside. Soon he opens the door and comes in almost crawling, and looking fearfully this way and that. After a moment his eyes light on the stacks of muskets. He goes to the one up* L. C.—*Looks about fearfully—apprehensively. Hesitates an instant.—During his next movements—artillery and cavalry effects on strong. Cannon and musketry fire in distance—alarm bells on strong—begin as men go upstairs*]

[JONAS *makes up his mind. He drops down on knees by stack of muskets up* L. C.—*snaps the breech lock of one without moving it from the stack—gets out the cartridge, looks at it, bites it with his teeth and looks at it again. Bites again and makes motions of getting the ball off and putting it in his pocket. Puts cartridge back in the musket, snaps the lock shut, and moves on to the next. Repeats the movement of taking the cartridge out, but is much quicker, biting off the ball at once. Repeats more rapidly and quickly with another musket, crawling quickly round the stack. Moves over to stack at* R. C. *Make scene as rapid as the action will permit*]

[*As* JONAS *gets well to work on muskets* EDITH *turns at window up* R. *and sees him. She stands a moment motionless—then comes down on right, and stands looking at him without moving.*—JONAS, *who began after leaving stack* L. C. *at upper side of stack* R. C.—*has worked around down stage on the stack, and has come to the lower side.*—EDITH *stands near the desk at* R. *and drops a book upon it, after the last musket but one, to make* JONAS *look up.*—JONAS *looks up and sees* EDITH. *He stops*]

[*Effects of cannonading have gradually been dying down to a low distant rumble, and passing artillery and cavalry discontinued. Alarm bells in distance, however, are still heard*]

JONAS. [*After pause. Very low voice*] Dhey's a-goin' ter shoot 'im—shoot 'im down like a dog, Missy—an' I could n't b'ar to see 'em do dat! I would n't like to see 'im killed—I would n't like it noways! You won't say nuffin' 'bout dis—fer de sake of ole Jonas what was always so fond o' you—ebber sense ye was a little chile! [*He sees that* EDITH *does not appear angry, and goes on with his work of getting the bullet out of the last cartridge*] Ye see—I jiss take away dis yer—an' den dar won't be no harm to 'im what-some-ebber—less 'n day loads 'em up agin! [*Slowly hobbles to his feet as he speaks*] When dey shoots—an' he jiss draps down, dey 'll roll 'im over inter de gutter an' be off like dey was mad! Den I can be near by—an'— [*Suddenly thinks of something. A look of blank consternation comes over his face. He speaks in almost whisper*] How's he goin' ter know! Ef he don't drap down dey 'll shoot him agin—an' dey 'll hab bullets in 'em nex' time! [*Anxiously glances around an instant*] Dey 'll hab bullets in 'em next time! [*Looks about. Suddenly to* EDITH] *You* tell 'im! *You* tell him Missy—it 's de ony-est way! Tell 'im to drap down! [*Supplicatingly*] Do dis fur ole Jonas honey—do it fur me—an' I 'll be a slabe to ye ez long ez I lib! [*Slight pause.—Sudden yell outside up left from a dozen men shut inside a room on the floor above.*—JONAS *starts and turns. Half whisper*] Dey 's a-goin' ter kill 'im!

[*Noise of heavy tramp of feet outside up* L. *above—doors opening, etc.—An indistinct order or two before regular order heard.*—JONAS *goes limping hurriedly to door up* C.]

SERGEANT. [*Outside up* L.—*Above*] Fall in!—Right face!—Forward—March!

JONAS. [*At door up* C.] Oh—tell 'im Missy! Tell 'im to drap down for God's sake! [*Exit* JONAS *at door up* C. *carefully closing it after him*]

[*Cannonading stronger*]

[*After an instant's pause* EDITH *crosses to* L. C. *and stands waiting near the table there, her face quite expressionless*]

[XXX]

[WILFRED *enters from* L. *at top of stairway, comes down the stairs and into the room at door up* L. C.—*Enter* CAROLINE *at door up* L. C. *from* L. *as* WILFRED *goes down* C. *She hurries after him with an anxious glance up stairway and entering at door up* L. C.]

CAROLINE. [*Overtaking* WILFRED—*on his* L.—*Low voice*] What are they—going to do?

WILFRED. [C.] Shoot him!

CAROLINE. When?

WILFRED. Now.

CAROLINE. [*Low exclamation of pity*] Oh!

[WILFRED *goes* R. C. *below lounge.*—CAROLINE *follows and stands near him on his* L. *looking on as* SOLDIERS *and others enter*]

[*Enter, coming down stairway up left at back the* SERGEANT, *followed by escort of* SOLDIERS. *They enter room at door or archway up* L. C. *and turn* R. *marching to position they were formerly in above the stacks of muskets*]

[*Enter* ARRELSFORD *up* L. *from above following down the stairway after the escort of* MEN. *He comes in through door or arch up* L. C. *and goes across to up* R. C.—MRS. VARNEY *enters at door up* L. C. *from* L. *and goes down left side*]

SERGEANT. [*Who is at* C. *facing up*] Halt! [MEN *halt*] Left face! [MEN *face front*]

[THORNE *enters at top of stairway up* L. *and comes down unconcernedly and a trifle absently—for his thoughts of certain persons far away. He is followed by* CORPORAL *with his carbine.*—THORNE *comes into position at* L. *of front line of men.*—CORPORAL *stands at* L. *of* THORNE]

SERGEANT. [*After* THORNE *is in position at* L. *of* MEN] Take—arms! [MEN *at once take muskets. All very quick*] Carry—arms! [*Bus.*—MEN *stand in line waiting*] Fall in the Prisoner! [THORNE *walks in front of* MEN *to* C. *and falls into position*] Left—face! [THORNE *and* MEN *face to left on order*] Forward——

EDITH. Wait!—[*Motion of hand to stop them without looking round. She controls her voice with difficulty*] Who is the officer in command?

SERGEANT. [*Turning to* EDITH *and touching cap awkwardly*] I'm in command, Miss!

EDITH. I 'd like to—speak to the prisoner!

SERGEANT. Sorry Miss, but we have n't got *time!* [*Turns back to give order to* MEN]

EDITH. [*Sudden turn on him and hand out*] Oh—*Wait!* [SERGEANT *stops and turns slowly toward her again*] Only a word! [*Whispers it over to herself*] Only a word!

[SERGEANT *hesitates an instant—turns to* MEN *and steps up* L. C. *a little*]

SERGEANT. Right face! [MEN *face to front again on order.*—THORNE *obeying order with others*] Fall out the prisoner! [THORNE *moves forward one step out of rank and stands motionless*] Now Miss!

WILFRED. [R. C.—*Starting indignantly toward* C.] No!

[SERGEANT *turns in surprise*]

CAROLINE. [*Holding to* WILFRED *and speaking in a low voice*] Oh Wilfred—why can't she speak to him? She only wants to say good-bye!

[WILFRED *looks at* CAROLINE. *Then with gesture to* SERGEANT *indicates that he may go on, and turns away* R. *with* CAROLINE]

SERGEANT. [*Turning to* THORNE] The lady!

[THORNE *looking front as before. Then he turns slowly and looks at* SERGEANT.—SERGEANT *motions with his head indicating* EDITH.—THORNE *walks down to her, stopping close on her right, standing in military position, faced in same direction he walked, a little to* L. *of front*]

[ARRELSFORD *up* R. C. *looking at* EDITH *and* THORNE.—CAROLINE *with* WILFRED *down* R. C. *gives an occasional awed and frightened glance at* THORNE *and* EDITH.—*No movement after the* SERGEANT'S *order to "fall out the prisoner" and* THORNE'S *walk to* EDITH]

[EDITH, *after slight pause, speaks slowly, in almost a whisper and as if with an effort, but without apparent feeling, and without turning to* THORNE]

EDITH. [*Voice for* THORNE *alone to hear. Slowly. Distinctly. Without inflection. A slight occasional tremor. Pauses as indicated*] One of the servants—has taken the musket balls—out of the guns! If you care to fall on the ground when they fire—you may escape with your life!

THORNE. [*After motionless pause.—To* EDITH.—*Low voice*] Do you wish me to do this?

EDITH. [*Low voice—without turning*] It's nothing to me.

[THORNE, *with slight movement at the cue, turns slowly away.—Brief pause.—He turns toward* EDITH *again*]

THORNE. [*Very low voice*] Were you responsible in any way for—[EDITH *shakes her head slightly without looking at him.*—THORNE *turns and walks right to* C.—*Makes turn there and walks up* C. *and turns to* L. *facing the* SERGEANT *a little* R. *of* C. *and out of the way of bayonets in coming business*] Sergeant— [*As if making an ordinary military report*] You'd better take a look at your muskets—they've been tampered with.

SERGEANT. [*Snatching musket from man nearest him*] What the— [*Quickly snaps it open. Cartridge drops to floor.* SERGEANT *picks it up and looks at it*] Here!— [*Handing musket back to man.*—*Turns to squad and gives orders quickly as follows: Business on these orders very effective if carried out promptly and with precision*] Squad—ready! [MEN *come in one movement from "carry" to position for loading*] Draw—cartridge! [MEN *draw cartridges, the click and snap of locks and levers ringing out simultaneously along the line*] With ball cartridge—reload! [MEN *quickly reload. Same bus. of rapid click of locks and levers down the line*] Carry—arms! [MEN *come to carry on the instant. Motionless. Eyes front.—To* THORNE—*with off-hand salute*] Much obliged sir!

THORNE. [*Low voice. Off-hand—as if of no consequence*] That's all right. [*Stands facing* L. *waiting for order to fall in.*—WILFRED, *after* THORNE'S *warning to officer about muskets, watches him with open admiration*]

WILFRED. [*Suddenly walking up to* THORNE] I'd like to shake hands with you!

[THORNE *turns and looks at* WILFRED, *who is just below him a little to his right. A smile breaks gradually over his face*]

THORNE. [*Smiling*] Is this for yourself—or your father?

WILFRED. [*Earnestly*] For both of us sir! [*Putting out his hand a little way.*—THORNE *grasps his hand. They look into each other's faces a moment.*—WILFRED *turns away to down* R. C. *and goes up back of couch to* CAROLINE.—THORNE *looks after* WILFRED *to front an instant—then turns* L.] That's all, Sergeant!

SERGEANT. [*Lower voice than before*] Fall in the Prisoner! [THORNE *steps to place in the line and turns front*] Escort—left face! [MEN *and* THORNE *left face*] Forward ma—[*Sharp cry of "Halt! Halt!" outside up* L., *followed by bang of heavy door outside* L.]

SERGEANT. Halt! [MEN *stand motionless*

at left face. On seeing the ORDERLY *approaching—just before he is on*] Right face!

[MEN *and* THORNE *face to front*]

[*Enter quickly at door up* L. C. *from* L. *an* AID—*wearing Lieutenant's uniform.*—SERGEANT, *faced front up* L. C. *just forward of his men, salutes.*—AID *salutes*]

[XXX]

AID. [*Standing up* L. C.] General Randolph's compliments sir, and he's on the way with orders!

ARRELSFORD. [*Up* R. C.] What orders, Lieutenant?—Anything to do with this case?

AID. [*No salute to* ARRELSFORD] I don't know what the orders are, sir. He's been with the President.

ARRELSFORD. I sent word to the Department we'd got the man and were going to drum-head him on the spot.

[WILFRED *and* CAROLINE *move unobtrusively to the upper side of couch*]

AID. Then this must be the case sir. I believe the General wishes to be present.

ARRELSFORD. Impossible! We've held the court and I've sent the finding to the Secretary! The messenger is to get his approval and meet us at the corner of Copley Street.

AID. I have no further orders sir! [*Retires up with quick military movement and turns facing front. Stands motionless*]

[*The cannonading becomes louder*]
[*Sound of heavy door outside up* L. *and the tread of the* GENERAL *as he strides across the hall*]

SERGEANT. [*Low voice to* MEN] Present—arms! [MEN *present*]

[SERGEANT, ORDERLY, ETC., *on salute*]

[*Enter* GENERAL RANDOLPH *at door up* L. C. *from* L. *striding on hurriedly—returning salutes as he goes down* C. *glancing about*]

[LIEUT. FORAY, *the* FIRST TELEGRAPH OPERATOR, *follows* GENERAL RANDOLPH *in at door up* L. C. *from* L. *He stands waiting up* L. C. *near door, faced front, military position*]

SERGEANT. [*Low order to* MEN] Carry—arms! [MEN *come to carry again*]

GENERAL RANDOLPH. Ah Sergeant!—[*Going down and across to* R.] Got the prisoner in here have you?

SERGEANT. [*Saluting*] Just taking him out sir.

GENERAL RANDOLPH. [C.] Prison?

SERGEANT. No sir—to execute the sentence of the Court.

GENERAL RANDOLPH. Had his trial then?

ARRELSFORD. [*Stepping down* R. C. *with a salute*] All done according to regulations, sir—the finding has gone to the Secretary.

GENERAL RANDOLPH. [R. *to* ARRELSFORD] Found guilty I judge?

ARRELSFORD. Found guilty sir.—No time now for hanging—the court ordered him shot.

GENERAL RANDOLPH. What were the grounds for this?

ARRELSFORD. Conspiracy against our government and the success of our arms by sending a false and misleading dispatch containing forged orders.

GENERAL RANDOLPH. Court's been misinformed—that dispatch was never sent.

[EDITH *looks up with sudden breathless exclamation.*—WILFRED *turns with surprise.*—*Others are greatly astonished*]

ARRELSFORD. [*Coming down on right of* GENERAL] Why General—the dispatch—I saw him——

GENERAL RANDOLPH. I say the dispatch wasn't sent! I expected to arrive in time for the trial and brought Foray here to testify. [*Calls to* LIEUTENANT FORAY *without looking round*] Lieutenant!

[LIEUTENANT FORAY *comes quickly down* L. C. *facing* GENERAL RANDOLPH.—*Salutes*]

Did Captain Thorne send out any dispatches after we left you with him in the office an hour ago?

LIEUTENANT FORAY. No sir. I was just going to send one under his order, but he countermanded it.

GENERAL RANDOLPH. What were his words at the time?

LIEUTENANT FORAY. He said he refused to act under that commission.

[EDITH *turns toward* THORNE *and her eyes are upon him for a moment*]

GENERAL RANDOLPH. That will do, Lieutenant! [LIEUTENANT FORAY *salutes and retires up* L.] In addition we learn from General Chesney that no complete order was received over the wire—that Marston's Division was not withdrawn—that our position was not weakened in any way and the attack at that point has been repulsed. It's plain, therefore, that the Court has been acting under error. The President for this reason finds himself compelled to disapprove the finding and it is set aside.

ARRELSFORD. [*With great indignation*] General Randolph, this case was put in my hands and I——

GENERAL RANDOLPH. [*Interrupting bluffly, but without temper*] Well I take it out of your hands! Report back to the War Office with my compliments! [*Crossing to* R. C.]

[ARRELSFORD *turns and starts toward the door up* L. C. *but after proceeding a few steps stops and turns*]

ARRELSFORD. Had n't I better wait and see—

GENERAL RANDOLPH. No—don't wait to see anything. [ARRELSFORD *looks at* GENERAL RANDOLPH *an instant, then turns and after raising his hat to the ladies down left, walks with dignity out at door up* L. C. *and exits to* L.—*Sound of heavy door outside up* L. *closed with force.*—GENERAL RANDOLPH *in front of couch* R. C.] Sergeant! [SERGEANT *quickly down to* GENERAL RANDOLPH *on salute*] Hold your men back there. I 'll see the prisoner. [SERGEANT *salutes, turns, marches straight up from where he is to the left division of the escort so that he is a little to left of* THORNE, *and turns front*]

SERGEANT. Order—arms! [*Squad obeys with precision*] Parade—rest! [*Squad obeys order*] Fall out the Prisoner! [THORNE *steps forward one step out of the rank and stands*] The General! [THORNE *starts down* C. *to* GENERAL RANDOLPH.—*As* THORNE *steps forward on order—"The General"*—EDITH *moves quickly toward* C. *and intercepts him about two-thirds of the way down, on his left.*—THORNE *stopped by* EDITH *shows slight surprise for an instant, but quickly recovers and looks straight front*]

EDITH. [*To* THORNE *as she meets him.—Impulsively. Low voice*] Oh—why did n't you tell me!—I thought you sent it! I thought you—

GENERAL RANDOLPH. [*Surprised*] Miss Varney!

EDITH. [*Crossing* THORNE *to the* GENERAL] There 's nothing against him General Randolph!—He did n't send it so there 's nothing to try him for now!

GENERAL RANDOLPH. You 're very much mistaken Miss Varney. The fact of his being caught in our lines without his uniform is enough to swing him off in ten minutes.

[EDITH *moans a little, at same time moving back from* GENERAL *a step*]

GENERAL RANDOLPH. Cap'n Thorne—[THORNE *steps down and faces the* GENERAL] or whatever your name may be—the President is fully informed regarding the circumstances of your case, and I need n't say that we look on you as a cursed dangerous character! There is n't any doubt whatever that you 'd ought to be exterminated right now!—But considering the damned peculiarity of your behavior—and that you refused—*for some reason*—to send that dispatch when you might have done so, we 've decided to keep you out of mischief some other way. The Sergeant will turn you over to Major Whitfield sir! [SERGEANT *up* R. C. *salutes*] You 'll be held as a prisoner of war! [*Turns and goes* R. *a few steps*]

[EDITH *turns suddenly to* THORNE, *coming down before him as he faces* R.]

EDITH. [*Looking in his face.—Speaks in low voice*] Oh—that is n't nearly so bad!

[THORNE *holds her hand in his right*]

THORNE. No—?

EDITH. No!—Because—sometime—

THORNE. [*Low voice*] Ah—if it 's sometime, there 's nothing else in the world.

[*Slight pause.*—EDITH *sees* MRS. VARNEY *at* L. *and crosses to her,* THORNE *retaining her hand as she crosses—releasing it only when he has to*]

EDITH. Mamma, won't you speak to him?

[MRS. VARNEY *and* EDITH L. *talk quietly*]

WILFRED. [*Suddenly leaving* CAROLINE R. C., *striding down from behind couch to* THORNE, *and extending hand*] I'd like to shake hands with you!

THORNE. [*Turning to* WILFRED] What—again? [*Taking* WILFRED'S *hand*]

[WILFRED, *shaking hands with* THORNE *and crossing him to* L. *as he does so—back to audience, laughing and very jovial about it*]

CAROLINE. [*Coming quickly down on right of* THORNE] So would I! [*Holding out her hand*]

[THORNE *lets go* WILFRED'S *hand—now on his left—and takes* CAROLINE'S]

WILFRED. Don't you be afraid now—it 'll be all right! They 'll give you a parole and——

CAROLINE. [*Breaking in enthusiastically*] A parole! Goodness gracious—they 'll give you *hundreds* of 'em! [*Turning away with funny little comprehensive gesture of both hands*]

GENERAL RANDOLPH. [*Gruffly*] One moment if you please! [THORNE *turns at once, facing* GENERAL RANDOLPH *near* C. —CAROLINE *and* WILFRED *go up* R. C. *to above couch.*—EDITH *stands* L. C.—MRS. VARNEY *near table* L. C.] There 's only one reason on earth why the President has set aside a certain verdict of death. You held up that false order and made a turn in our favor. We expect you to make the turn complete and enter our service.

THORNE. [*After an instant's pause.—Quietly*] Why General—that 's impossible!

GENERAL RANDOLPH. You can give us your answer later!

THORNE. You have it now sir.

GENERAL RANDOLPH. You 'll very much regret that decision sir. It means you 'll be held a prisoner here and kept in close confinement until the Confederate Army marches into Washington!

THORNE. Why General, you 're making me a prisoner for life!

GENERAL RANDOLPH. Nothing of the kind sir! You 'll see it in another light before many days. And it would n't surprise me if Miss Varney had something to do with your change of views!

EDITH. [*Coming a little way toward* C.] You 're mistaken General Randolph--I think he 's perfectly right!

[THORNE *turns to* EDITH]

GENERAL RANDOLPH. [*Gruffly*] Oh you do eh! Very well—we 'll see what a little prison life will do. [*A sharp order*] Sergeant! [SERGEANT *comes down* R. C. *and salutes*] Report with the prisoner to Major Whitfield! [*Turns away to front*]

[SERGEANT *turns at once to* THORNE.—THORNE *and* EDITH *are looking into each other's eyes.*—THORNE *takes her hand and presses it against his breast*]

THORNE. [*Low voice to* EDITH] What is it—love and good-bye?

EDITH. [*Almost a whisper*] No no—only the first—and that one every day—every hour—every minute—until we meet again!

THORNE. Until we meet again!

SERGEANT. [R. C.] Fall in the Prisoner!

[THORNE *turns and walks up, quickly taking his place in the Squad.*—EDITH *follows him up a step or two as he goes, stopping a little* L. *of* C.]

SERGEANT. Attention! [*Squad comes to attention*] Carry—arms! [*Squad comes to carry*] Escort—left—face! [*Squad with* THORNE—*left face on the order*] Forward—march!

[*Escort with* THORNE *marches out at door up* L. C. *and off to* L.]

[CURTAIN]

MADAME BUTTERFLY

A TRAGEDY OF JAPAN

DRAMATIZED BY

David Belasco

From the Story by John Luther Long

Printed by permission of Mr. David Belasco and Mr. John Luther Long.

MADAME BUTTERFLY [1]

Madame Butterfly represents the spirit of romance which has never been entirely absent from our stage and which seems to be in process of revival. It represents also the dramatic ability of Mr. David Belasco working with the material furnished by the imagination of Mr. John Luther Long.

David Belasco was born in San Francisco, July 25, 1853. Even before he left school in the early seventies his mind was on the theatre, and during the next few years he was callboy, actor, stage manager, adaptor, and writer of plays. Mr. Belasco wrote or adapted thirty-nine plays during his career in California, beginning with *Jim Black or the Regulator's Revenge,* written when he was a mere boy, and including his share in *Marriage by Moonlight* and *Hearts of Oak,* in which he collaborated with James A. Herne. *La Belle Russe,* which he put on first at the Baldwin Theatre, San Francisco, of which he was stage manager, attracted the attention of Eastern managers and was produced by Lester Wallack at his theatre, May 8, 1882. Shortly afterward Mr. Belasco became stage manager of the Madison Square Theatre in New York where his play, *May Blossom,* was produced April 12, 1884. After assisting Bronson Howard in *Baron Rudolph* in 1887, he became associated with Henry C. DeMille in the writing of a number of plays, all well constructed and entertaining, if at times verging on the sentimental and melodramatic. Of these *The Wife* was produced November 1, 1887, *Lord Chumley,* in which Mr. E. H. Sothern starred, on August 21, 1888, and *The Charity Ball,* November 19, 1889, all at the Lyceum Theatre, and all associated with the sterling group of players then gathered together there. *Men and Women,* also with DeMille, was produced at Proctor's Theatre, October 21, 1890. His next significant play was *The Girl I Left Behind Me,* with Mr. Franklin Fyles, produced at the Empire Theatre, January 25, 1893, and having its initial performance at the Sadler's Wells Theatre, London, January 6, 1893. *The Heart of Maryland,* in which Mrs. Leslie Carter starred at the Herald Square Theatre on October 22, 1895, represents the emotional melodrama of a popular kind, and *DuBarry,* played at the National Theatre in Washington, December 12, 1901, the melodrama based on historical material.

The next period of his work, and probably the most artistic, was that in which he was associated with Mr. John Luther Long in the field of exotic romance. On March 5, 1900, at the Herald Square Theatre, Mr. Belasco produced his dramatization of Mr. Long's story of *Madame Butterfly,* in a combination bill with his farce of *Naughty Anthony,* originally performed on

[1] This Introduction has been entirely revised for the Fifth Edition.

bination bill with his farce of *Naughty Anthony,* originally performed in Washington, December 25, 1899. After a month's run in New York, *Madame Butterfly* was produced at the Duke of York's Theatre, London, April 28, 1900, and ran for over two months. During the next session, it was taken on tour through the United States. The play follows the language of the story almost entirely, but there are certain changes in the plot. In the book, Pinkerton does not return to the house, but leaves money with the consul for Madame Butterfly, which she refuses. The interview between her and Mrs. Pinkerton takes place in the consul's office; and Madame Butterfly lets her mother-love conquer and, after attempting suicide, decides to live. A grand opera, *Madama Butterfly,* composed by Giacomo Puccini, was first performed in New York in English translation, November 12, 1906. Its most significant production, however, was in the original Italian, in New York, February 11, 1907, with Geraldine Farrar as Cio-Cio-San, Louise Homer as Susuki, and Enrico Caruso as Pinkerton. Through the opera, based on the play, Madame Butterfly has become an international character.

Mr. Belasco and Mr. Long next collaborated in the writing of *The Darling of the Gods,* first produced at the New National Theatre, Washington, November 17, 1902. This is the romantic tragedy of a Japanese princess, played by Blanche Bates, in which the themes of love, loyalty, and patriotism were artistically blended. *Adrea,* a fine romantic tragedy laid in the fifth century A. D., was produced first at the Convention Hall in Washington, December 26, 1904. This was the last collaboration with Mr. Long.

The Girl of the Golden West, played first October 3, 1905, and *The Rose of the Rancho,* written with Mr. Richard Walton Tully, and played November 12, 1906, reflect Mr. Belasco's knowledge of the West. The supernatural romance was illustrated by *The Return of Peter Grimm,* played first in Boston, January 2, 1911. Among Mr. Belasco's other productions were *Sweet Kitty Bellairs* (1903); *A Grand Army Man,* with Miss Pauline Phelps and Miss Marion Short (1907); *Van Der Decken* (1915); several adaptations from the French, *Valerie,* from Sardou's *Fernande* (1886), *Miss Helyett* (1891), *Zaza* (1898), *The Lily* (1909), *The Secret* (1913), *Kiki* (1921), *The Comedian* (1923); and *Laugh, Clown, Laugh,* from the Italian of Fausto Martini (1923). On December 21, 1922, he presented Mr. David Warfield in a superb production of *The Merchant of Venice,* in which Mr. Belasco translated to a modern audience the beauty with which the Elizabethan imagination endowed the performances of Shakespeare. Mr. Belasco's contribution to the stage has been recognized by dinners tendered to him on March 20, 1921, by the Society of American Dramatists and Composers and on December 11, 1921, by the Society of Arts and Sciences, of New York. These occasions were made noteworthy by the tributes paid to him by representatives from every walk of life. In 1924 he was presented by the French Government with the decoration of "Chevalier de la Légion d'Honneur," in recognition of his services to the cause of France.

Mr. Belasco's career as a manager can only be alluded to here. He was a pioneer in the movement toward natural methods in the theatre. Since 1905 he has produced his plays at his own theatre, where he has set a standard for perfection of detail, especially for interesting effects of stage lighting. He was the first to do away with footlights, and the "bridge of light" used in *Peter Grimm* was unheralded and unseen, but the effect was true to nature.

Mr. John Luther Long was born in Hanover, Pennsylvania, January 1, 1861. He became a lawyer, engaging in practice in Philadelphia. In addition to the plays noted above, he dramatized *Dolce,* one of his own short stories, for Mrs. Fiske in 1906; wrote *Kassa,* a tragic drama, laid in Austria-Hungary, for Mrs. Carter in 1909 and *Crowns,* a highly imaginative poetic drama, produced at the Provincetown Theatre in November, 1922. He was also joint author with Edward Childs Carpenter of *The Dragon Fly* (1905). Mr. Long died in 1927. His story of *Madame Butterfly,* printed originally in the *Century Magazine* in 1897, has also been issued in book form.

Madame Butterfly was published for the first time in 1917 through the courtesy of Mr. Belasco and Mr. Long from a manuscript prepared especially for this collection. For information concerning the plays the editor is indebted to Mr. Belasco and to Mr. Thomas A. Curry of the Belasco Theatre. *May Blossom* was published by French (1882). *Six Plays: Madame Butterfly, Du Barry, The Darling of the Gods, Adrea, The Girl of the Golden West,* and *The Return of Peter Grimm,* with Introduction by Mr. Belasco and Notes by Montrose J. Moses, were published in one volume by Little, Brown and Company (1928). Of especial interest is also *The Theatre through the Stage Door,* by David Belasco, edited by L. V. De Foe (New York, 1919).

An authoritative *Life of David Belasco* in two volumes written by the late William Winter, was published in 1918. This is more accurate than *My Life Story,* the autobiography, begun in *Hearst's Magazine* in March, 1914, but not published in book form. For individual plays, *Plays of the Present,* by J. V. Clapp and E. F. Edgett, is useful. For detailed study of the plays, see *A History of the American Drama from the Civil War to the Present Day,* Revised Edition; two volumes in one (1936), Vol. I, Chap. 7, and for complete list of plays, Vol. II, pp. 321–326. This list is based upon the monograph, *Plays Produced under the Stage Direction of David Belasco,* privately printed (1925), and upon Mr. Winter's list, checked by other sources.

NOTE TO SIXTH EDITION.

David Belasco died May 15, 1931, in New York City.

THE ORIGINAL CAST OF CHARACTERS

Herald Square Theatre, New York, March 5, 1900.

CHO-CHO-SAN (MADAME BUTTERFLY) .... Miss Blanche Bates

SUZUKI, her servant .... Miss Marie Bates

MR. SHARPLESS, the American Consul .... Mr. Claude Gillingwater

LIEUTENANT B. F. PINKERTON, of the war ship *Connecticut*.. Mr. Frank Worthing

YAMADORI, a citizen of New York .... Mr. Albert Bruning

THE NAKODO, a marriage broker .... Mr. E. P. Wilks

KATE, PINKERTON'S wife .... Miss Katherine Black

"TROUBLE" .... Little Kittie

ATTENDANT .... Mr. William Lamp

ATTENDANT .... Mr. Westropp Saunders

NOTE: During the scene in which MADAME BUTTERFLY waits at the shoji for her lover, a night is supposed to pass and the story is resumed on the morning of the following day.

MADAME BUTTERFLY

The play takes place in Japan in MADAME BUTTERFLY'S *little house at the foot of Higashi Hill, facing the harbor. Everything in the room is Japanese save the American locks and bolts on the doors and windows and an American flag fastened to a tobacco jar. Cherry blossoms are abloom outside, and inside. A sword rack, a shrine on which lie a sword and a pair of men's slippers, a chest of drawers on top of which is a tray containing two red poppies, rouge, powder and hair ornaments, a stand for the tobacco jar and tea, are the only pieces of furniture in the room. As the curtain rises,* MADAME BUTTERFLY *is spraying the growing flowers with a small watering pot. She snips off two little bunches, lays them on a plate of rice which she sets reverently on the shrine, then kneels, putting her hands on the floor, her forehead on them.*

MADAME BUTTERFLY. Oh, Shaka! Hail! Hail! Also perceive! Look down! I have brought a sacrifice of flowers and new rice. Also, I am quite clean. I am shivering with cleanness. Therefore grant that Lef-ten-ant B. F. Pik-ker-ton may come back soon.

(*She rises, clasps her hands, comes down to a floor cushion, and sits, fanning herself.*)

SUZUKI. (*Entering with a low bow.*) Madame Butterfly's wish?

MADAME BUTTERFLY. Suzuki, inform me, if it please you, how much more nearer beggary we are today than yesterday?

SUZUKI. Aye. (*She takes some coins from a small box in her sleeve, and lays them in three piles on her palm, touching them as she speaks.*) Rin, yen, sen. . . .

MADAME BUTTERFLY. (*Reprovingly.*) Suzuki, how many time I tellin' you—no one shall speak anythin' but those Unite' State' languages in these Lef-ten-ant Pik-ker-ton's house? (*She pronounces his name with much difficulty.*) Once more—an' I put you outside shoji! . . . That 's one thin' aeverbody got recomlec' account it 's 'Merican house—his wife, his maid.

SUZUKI. (*Mouthing to herself, making no sound, counting on her fingers.*) Two dollar.

(*She drops the money into the box, giving it to* MADAME BUTTERFLY.)

MADAME BUTTERFLY. O, how we waste my husban's be-autiful moaneys! Tha 's shame! Mos' gone.

SUZUKI. This moaney hav' kep' us two year . . . Wha 's happen to us now, if he don' come back?

MADAME BUTTERFLY. (*Scoffing, putting the money in her sleeve.*) O, if he don' come back! . . . Course he come back! He 's gone so long accoun' he 's got business in those his large country. If he 's not come back to his house, why he sign Japanese lease for nine hundred and ninety nine year for me to live? Why he put 'Merican lock to bolt it door, to shut it window? Answer me those question.

SUZUKI. (*Doubtfully.*) I dunno.

MADAME BUTTERFLY. Of course you dunno! You don' know whichaever. Wael I goin' tell you: to keep out those which are out, and in, those which are in. Tha 's me.

(*She rises, goes to the window and looks out.*)

SUZUKI. But he don't writin' no ledder.

MADAME BUTTERFLY. 'Merican men don' naever write ledder—no time.

SUZUKI. (*Cynically.*) Aye . . . I don' naever know 'Merica navy man with Japanese wive come back.

MADAME BUTTERFLY. (*Impassively, her eyes narrowing.*) Speak concerning marriage once more, you die! (*She fans herself.* SUZUKI *salaams and backs quickly towards the door.* MADAME BUTTERFLY *claps her hands and* SUZUKI *pauses.*) Don' come back! Lef-ten-ant B. F. Pik-ker-ton don' come back! Ha! Me! I know w'en he comes back—he told me. W'en he goin' 'way, he say in tha's doors: "Madame Butterfly, I have had ver' nice times with my Japanese sweets heart, so now I goin' back to my own country and here's moaney—an' don' worry 'bout me—I come back w'en 'Robins nes' again!'" Ha-ha! Tha's w'en he come back—w'en robins nes' again.

(*She sways her head triumphantly from side to side, fanning herself.*)

SUZUKI. (*Not impressed.*) Yaes, I did n't like ways he said it—like those . . .

(*She imitates a flippant gesture of farewell.*)

MADAME BUTTERFLY. (*Laughing.*) Aha, that's 'Merican way sayin' good-bye to girl. Yaes, he come back w'en robins nes' again. Shu'h! Shu'h! (*She claps her hands with delight.* SUZUKI, *with a look of unbelief starts to go.*) Sa-ey! Why no "shu'h" on you face for? Such a fools! (*Looking towards the window.*) O look! Suzuki—a robins. The firs' these Spring! Go, see if he's stay for nes'.

SUZUKI. (*Looking.*) It *is* a robins, O Cho-Cho-San!

MADAME BUTTERFLY. (*Running to the window.*) O! O!

SUZUKI. But he's fly away.

MADAME BUTTERFLY. O! How they are slow this year! Sa-ey, see if you don' fin' one tha's more in-dus-trial an' domestics.

SUZUKI. (*Looking out.*) There are none yet.

MADAME BUTTERFLY. But soon they nes' now. Suzuki, w'en we see that ship comin' in—sa-ey—then we goin' put flowers aevery where, an' if it's night, we goin' hang up mos' one thousan' lanterns—eh-ha?

SUZUKI. No got moaney for thousan'.

MADAME BUTTERFLY. Wael, twenty, mebby; an' sa-ey, w'en we see him comin' quick up path—(*imitates*) so—so—so—(*lifts her kimono and strides in a masculine fashion*) to look for liddle wive—me—me jus' goin' hide behind shoji (*making two holes with her wet finger in the low paper shoji and peeking through*) an' watch an' make believe me gone 'way; leave liddle note—sayin': "Goon-bye, sayonara, Butterfly." . . . Now he come in. . . . (*Hides.*) Ah! An' then he get angery! An' he say all kinds of 'Merican languages—debbils—hells! But before he get too angery, me run out an' flew aroun' his neck! (*She illustrates with* SUZUKI, *who is carried away and embraces her with fervor.*) Sa-ey! *You* no flew roun' his neck—jus' me. (*They laugh in each other's arms.*) Then he'll sit down an' sing tha's liddle 'Merican song—O, how he'll laugh. . . . (*She sings as though not understanding a word of it.*)

"I call her the belle of Japan—of Japan
Her name it is O Cho-Cho-San, Cho-Cho-San!
Such tenderness lies in her soft almond eyes,
I tell you, she's just 'ichi ban.'"

(*Laughs.*) Then I'll dance like w'en I was Geisha girl.

(*She dances as* SHARPLESS, *the American consul, appears in the doorway, followed by the* NAKODO.)

NAKODO. This is the house, your Excellency.

SHARPLESS. (*Removing his clogs outside.*) You may wait.

(NAKODO *bows and* SHARPLESS *enters.*)

I beg pardon. . . .

(MADAME BUTTERFLY *still dancing, begins the song again.* SHARPLESS *goes to the door and knocks to attract her attention.*)

MADAME BUTTERFLY. Ah!

(SUZUKI, *bowing low, leaves the room.*)

SHARPLESS. This is Madame Cho-Cho-San?

MADAME BUTTERFLY. No, I am Mrs. Leften-ant B. F. Pik-ker-ton.

SHARPLESS. I see. . . . Pardon my interruption. . . . I am Mr. Sharpless, the American consul.

MADAME BUTTERFLY. (*Once more salaaming to the ground, drawing in her breath between her teeth to express pleasure.*) O, your honorable excellency, goon night,—no, not night yaet: aexcuse me, I'm liddle raddle',—I mean goon mornin', goon evenin'. Welcome to 'Merican house, mos' welcome to 'Merican girl! (*Pointing to herself. They both bow.*) Be seat. (SHARPLESS *sits on a cushion on the floor, and* MADAME BUTTERFLY *sits at a little distance. There is a slight pause.*) How are those health? You sleepin' good? How are that honorable ancestors—are they well? And those parens'? That grandmother—how are she?

SHARPLESS. Thanks. They're all doing well, I hope.

MADAME BUTTERFLY. (*She claps her hands;* SUZUKI *enters and puts the little stand between them and leaves the room.*) Accep' pipe, your excellency. O, I forgettin'—I have still of those large American cigarette.

(MADAME BUTTERFLY *gestures towards* PINKERTON'S *tobacco jar decorated with the flag of his country.*)

SHARPLESS. (*Accepting a cigarette while she fills her pipe.*) Thanks. I 'm on a little visit of inquiry, Madame Butterfly,—your name, I believe in our language. Lieutenant Pinkerton wrote to me to find out—

MADAME BUTTERFLY. (*Almost breathless.*) Ah, you have hear from him? He is well?

SHARPLESS. O, he 's all right.

MADAME BUTTERFLY. (*Relieved.*) Ah! Tha 's mak' me mos' bes' happy female woman in Japan—mebby in that whole worl'—w'at you thing?

SHARPLESS. Ha—ha! (*Puffing at the cigarette.*) Sawdust. Pinkerton must have left these!

MADAME BUTTERFLY. O! I so glad you came. . . . I goin' as' you a liddle question.

SHARPLESS. Well?

MADAME BUTTERFLY. You know 'bout birds in those your country?

SHARPLESS. Something.

MADAME BUTTERFLY. Tha 's what I thing —you know aeverything. Tha 's why your country sen' you here.

SHARPLESS. You flatter me.

MADAME BUTTERFLY. O, no, you got big head.

SHARPLESS. Pinkerton again—I can hear him!

MADAME BUTTERFLY. O, aexcuse me: I forgettin' my manners. I got liddle more raddle. (*She offers him her pipe which he gravely touches, returning it. She touches it again, then puts it down.*) Now, what you know 'bout jus' robins?

SHARPLESS. What?

MADAME BUTTERFLY. 'Bout when do they nes' again? Me, I thing it mus' be mor' early in Japan as in America, accoun' they nestin' here now.

SHARPLESS. O, at the same time I fancy.

MADAME BUTTERFLY. (*Disappointed.*) Yaes? . . . then they 's nestin' there. (*Then taking hope again.*) Sa-ey, I tell you—perhaps some time sooner, some time later, jus' how they feel like.

SHARPLESS. Possibly. Why do you ask?

MADAME BUTTERFLY. Because Lef-ten-ant B. F. Pik-ker-ton say he will come back to me w'en the robins nes' again.

SHARPLESS. (*To himself.*) Poor devil! One of his infernal jokes.

MADAME BUTTERFLY. (*Clapping her hands.*) Me, I thing it 's time. . . . I 've wait so long.

(SUZUKI *enters with a tea-pot.* MADAME BUTTERFLY *gives* SHARPLESS *a cup of tea.*)

NAKODO. (*Appearing at the door.*) Tea, most illustrious?

MADAME BUTTERFLY. Ah! Enter, Nakodo. Your presence lights up my entire house. (*She gives him a cup. Accepting it, he goes up to a cushion and sits.*) Tha 's bad man. W'en my husban 's gone 'way, he try for get me marry again.

NAKODO. The rich Yamadori. Madame Cho-Cho-San is very poor.

MADAME BUTTERFLY. (*Bowing politely.*) O, liddle ol' frien'; those are my business.

NAKODO. Rejected advice makes the heart sad.

MADAME BUTTERFLY. We-el, if those heart hurt you so much, you better not arrive here no more.

SHARPLESS. Madame Butterfly; may I ask—er—where are your people?

NAKODO. They have outcasted her!

MADAME BUTTERFLY. Sa-ey, tha 's foanny! My people make me marry when I don' want; now I am marry, they don' want. Before I marry Lef-ten-ant B. F. Pikker-ton, my honorable Father—(*she bows low*—NAKODO *bows*—SHARPLESS *bows*) die—he 's officer. These are his sword . . . (*pointing to an inscription*) 't is written. . . .

(*She holds out the sword that the inscription may be read.*)

NAKODO. (*Reading.*) "To die with honor, when one can no longer live with honor."

(*He bows, then turns and bows towards the shrine and goes back to his cushion where he sits.*)

MADAME BUTTERFLY. He 's kill' himself accoun' he soldier of Emporer an' defeat in battle. Then we get—O—ver' poor. Me? I go dance liddle. Also I thing if some rich man wish me, I gettin' marry for while, accoun' my grandmother, (*she bows respectfully*—NAKODO *bows*—SHARPLESS *politely nods*) don' got no food, no obi. Then ol' Nakodo, he say a (NAKODO *picks up his cushion and moves down to join in the conversation*) man 's jus' as' him for nice wive for three monse. Nakodo tell him he don' know none more nizer as me.

NAKODO. (*Salaaming.*) Nizer as you.

MADAME BUTTERFLY. (*Salaaming.*) Nizer as me.

SHARPLESS. (*Looking from one to the other.*) Could n't be nicer! . . .

(*He salaams profoundly—then all salaam.*)

MADAME BUTTERFLY. Then Nakodo say—

NAKODO. I say—I don' lig him account he 'Merica—jin.

MADAME BUTTERFLY. He also remark with me that he is barbarian an' beas'. But aeveryone say: "Yaes, take him—take him beas'—he 's got moaneys." So I say for jus' liddle while, perhaps I can stan'. So Nakodo bring him. . . .

NAKODO. . . . For look-at meeting.

MADAME BUTTERFLY. (*Laughing.*) Me? Well, I thing that day Lef-ten-ant B. F. Pik-ker-ton is jus' a god! Gold button—lace on his unicorn. At firs', I frightened—he hol' my hans' so close—like—(*she illustrates by giving both hands to* SHARPLESS) and kizz. Japanese girl no lig' kizz; but when Lef-tenant B. F. Pik-ker-ton kizz me, I like ver' much. . . . What 's use lie? It 's not inside of me. (*Noticing that her hands are still in* SHARPLESS'.) O, I beg your honorable pardon. (*She tucks her hands in her sleeves.*) So we 's gettin' marry and then his ship order away an' me—I am jus' waitin'—sometimes cryin', sometimes watchin', but always waitin'.

NAKODO. (*In the doorway—bowing with servility.*) My client, the prosperous Yamadori, approaches for the third time today.

MADAME BUTTERFLY. Now I have my liddle joke again. You watch, he comes all time to make smash with me.

SHARPLESS. Pinkerton's slang.

(YAMADORI *enters attended by two servants.* SHARPLESS *rises and bows ceremoniously.* MADAME BUTTERFLY *does not rise, but bends her head and fans herself coquettishly. The two servants squat.*)

YAMADORI. Mr. Sharpless: always a pleasure to meet you here or in New York.

SHARPLESS. Thanks, Mr. Yamadori.

MADAME BUTTERFLY. (*Coquettishly.*) You have somethin' nize say to me again today?

YAMADORI. Perseverance shall be the religion of my life until the capricious Butterfly deigns to believe me.

MADAME BUTTERFLY. You goin' tell me 'gain you kill yourself I don' make kizz with you?

YAMADORI. (*Very much embarrassed—looking at consul.*) O!

MADAME BUTTERFLY. You can speak—consul know—I been tellin' him 'bout your liddle foolishness.

YAMADORI. Such treatment, Mr. Sharpless, is one of the penalties we incur when madly in love with a charming woman.

MADAME BUTTERFLY. Tha 's ver' nize. Ha-ha!

(*Winks behind her fan at* SHARPLESS.)

SHARPLESS. Heavens! Pinkerton's very wink.

(MADAME BUTTERFLY *gives a cup of tea to* YAMADORI *who drinks it and rolls a cigarette.*)

YAMADORI. (*To* SHARPLESS.) I am in Japan for two months—a pleasure trip. Do you blame me?

(*Pointing to* MADAME BUTTERFLY.)

MADAME BUTTERFLY. Aevery time he come home, get 'nother woman: must have mor'en eight now.

YAMADORI. But I *married* them all. . . .

MADAME BUTTERFLY. O *he!* He jus' marry whenaever he thing 'bout it.

YAMADORI. You shall be different. I will bury *you* with my ancestors. (*To* SHARPLESS.) I offered her a thousand servants.

NAKODO. (*Stunned.*) Thousan'!

MADAME BUTTERFLY. Ha! (*Fans.*)

YAMADORI. And a palace to live in.

(*The* NAKODO *is overcome by such generosity.*)

MADAME BUTTERFLY. He!

YAMADORI. Everything her heart can wish.

MADAME BUTTERFLY. Ha! Ha!

YAMADORI. Is that not enough? (*She shakes her head.*) Then in the presence of this statesman of integrity, I will give you a solemn writing. (SHARPLESS *gives him a quizzical glance.*) Is *that* enough?

MADAME BUTTERFLY. Wha 's good of that to married womans?

(*Pointing to herself.*)

YAMADORI. According to the laws of Japan, when a woman is deserted, she is divorced. (MADAME BUTTERFLY *stops fanning and listens.*) Though I have travelled much abroad, I know the laws of my own country.

MADAME BUTTERFLY. An' I know laws of my *husban's* country.

YAMADORI. (*To* SHARPLESS.) She still fancies herself married to the young officer. If your excellency would explain. . . .

MADAME BUTTERFLY. (*To* SHARPLESS.) Sa-ey, when some one gettin' married in America, don' he stay marry?

SHARPLESS. Usually—yes.

MADAME BUTTERFLY. Well, tha 's all right. I 'm marry to Lef-ten-ant B. F. Pik-ker-ton.

YAMADORI. Yes, but a Japanese marriage!

SHARPLESS. Matrimony is a serious thing in America, not a temporary affair as it often is here.

MADAME BUTTERFLY. Yaes, an' you can't like 'Merican mans. Japanese got too many wive, eh?

SHARPLESS. (*Laughing.*) We are not allowed more than one at a time.

MADAME BUTTERFLY. Yaes, an' you can't divorce wive like here, by sayin': "walk it back to parent"—eh??

SHARPLESS. O, no.

MADAME BUTTERFLY. Tha 's right, aexactly. When I as' Lef-ten-ant B. F. Pik-ker-ton, he explain those law to me of gettin' divorce in those Unite' State'. He say no one can get aexcept he stan' up before Judge 2—3—4—7—year. Ver' tiresome. Firs' the man he got tell those Judge all he know 'bout womans; then womans, she got tell; then some lawyer quarrel with those Judge; the Judge get jury an' as' wha' they thing—an' if they don' know, they 'll all get put in jails. Tha 's all right! (*Folds hands.*)

YAMADORI. Your friend has told her everything she wanted him to tell her.

MADAME BUTTERFLY. (*Who has paid no attention.*) Tha 's ver' nize, too, that 'Merican God.

SHARPLESS. I beg your pardon?

MADAME BUTTERFLY. Once times, Lef-tenant B. F. Pik-ker-ton—

YAMADORI. (*Aside to* SHARPLESS.) Pinkerton again!

MADAME BUTTERFLY. He 's in great troubles, an' he said "God he'p me"; an' sunshine *came right out*—and God he did! Tha 's ver' quick—Japanese gods take more time. Aeverything quick in America. Ha—me—sometime I thing I pray large American God to get him back soon; but no use,—he don' know me where *I* live. (*Attracted by a sound.*) Wha 's that? . . . You hear?

SHARPLESS. No. (MADAME BUTTERFLY *runs to the window and listens; then takes up the glasses while* SHARPLESS *speaks in a low voice to* YAMADORI.) Lieutenant Pinkerton's ship was due yesterday. His young wife from America is waiting here to meet him. (*At the word "wife,"* YAMADORI *smiles—takes his fan from his sleeve and fans himself. The* NAKODO, *who is listening, is struck by an idea and departs in such haste that he tumbles over one of* YAMADORI'S *attendants who jabbers at him.*) I 'm devilish sorry for that girl.

YAMADORI. Then tell her the truth.

MADAME BUTTERFLY. Aexcuse me; but I always hearin' soun' like ship gun—ha—ha—tha 's naturels.

YAMADORI. (*Preparing to go.*) Good morning, Mr. Sharpless. (*Shaking hands. Turning to* MADAME BUTTERFLY.) I leave you today. Tomorrow the gods may prompt you to listen to me! (*He bows.*)

MADAME BUTTERFLY. (*Bowing.*) Mebby. (YAMADORI *and attendants go off, bowing. She turns to* SHARPLESS.) Mebby not. Sa-ey, somehow could n't you let that Lef-ten-ant B. F. Pik-ker-ton know they 's other all crazy 'bout me?

SHARPLESS. Madame Butterfly, sit down. (*While she, struck by his solemn manner, looks at him and obeys, he removes the tea-pot and sits on the stand, to the astonishment of* MADAME BUTTERFLY.) I am going to read you part of a letter I have received from Pinkerton.

(*He takes a letter from his pocket.*)

MADAME BUTTERFLY. O, jus' let me look at those ledder! (*She slips it under her kimono on her heart and with an indrawn breath, hands it back.*) Now read quick, you mos' bes' nize man in all the whole worl'.

SHARPLESS. (*Reads.*) "Find out about that little Jap girl. What has become of her? It might be awkward now. If little Butterfly still remembers me, perhaps you can help me out and make her understand. Let her down gently. You won't believe it, but for two weeks after I sailed, I was dotty in love with her."

(SHARPLESS *is amazed to see* MADAME BUTTERFLY *convulsed with silent joy.*)

MADAME BUTTERFLY. Oh, all the gods how it was sweet!

SHARPLESS. Why really—

MADAME BUTTERFLY. Tha 's what I 'm afraid: that he loave' me so much he 's goin' desert his country an' get in trouble with American eagle—what you thing? Oh, it 's more bedder I wait than those!

SHARPLESS. (*Folding the letter.*) No use—you can't understand. Madame Butterfly, suppose this waiting should never end; what would become of you?

MADAME BUTTERFLY. Me? I could dance, mebby, or—die?

SHARPLESS. Don't be foolish. I advise you to consider the rich Yamadori's offer.

MADAME BUTTERFLY. (*Astonished.*) *You* say those? You, 'Merican consul?—when you know that me, I am marry?

SHARPLESS. You heard Yamadori: it is not binding.

MADAME BUTTERFLY. Yamadori lies!

SHARPLESS. His offer is an unusual opportunity for a girl who—for any Japanese girl in your circumstances.

MADAME BUTTERFLY. (*Enraged—she claps her hands.*) Suzuki! The excellent gentleman—(*bowing sarcastically*) who have done us the honor to call—he wish to go hurriedly. His shoes—hasten them!

(SUZUKI, *who has entered carrying a jar, gets* SHARPLESS' *clogs and gives them to him—then passes off with her jar.*)

SHARPLESS. (*Holding the clogs awkwardly.*) I 'm really very sorry.

MADAME BUTTERFLY. No, no, don' be angery. But jus' now you tol' me—O, gods! You mean— (*Looks at him pitifully.*) I not Lef-ten-ant B. F. Pik-kerton's wive—Me?

SHARPLESS. Hardly.

MADAME BUTTERFLY. O, I— (*She sways slightly.* SHARPLESS *goes to her assistance, but she recovers and fans herself.*) Tha 's all right. I got liddle heart illness. I can't . . . I can't someways give up thingin' he 'll come back to me. You thing tha 's all over? All finish? (*Dropping her fan.* SHARPLESS *nods assent.*) Oh, no! Loave don' forget some thin's or wha 's use of loave? (*She claps her hands—beckoning off.*) Loave 's got remember . . . (*pointing*) some thin's!

(*A child enters.*)

SHARPLESS. A child. . . . Pinkerton's? . . .

MADAME BUTTERFLY. (*Showing a picture of* PINKERTON'S.) Look! Look! (*Holding it up beside the child's face.*) Tha 's jus' his face, same hair, same blue eye. . . .

SHARPLESS. Does Lieutenant Pinkerton know?

MADAME BUTTERFLY. No, he come after he goe. (*Looking at the child with pride.*) You thing fath-er naever comes back—tha 's what *you* thing? He do! You write him ledder; tell him 'bout one bes' mos' nize bebby aever seen. . . . Ha—ha! I bed all moaneys he goin' come mos' one million mile for see those chil'. Surely this is tie—bebby. Sa-ey, you did n' mean what you said 'bout me not bein' marry? You make liddle joke? (*Moved,* SHARPLESS *nods his head in assent, to the great relief of* MADAME BUTTERFLY.) Ha! (*She lays the baby's hand in* SHARPLESS'.) Shake hand consul 'Merican way.

SHARPLESS. (*Shaking hands with the child.*) Hm . . . hm . . . what 's your name?

MADAME BUTTERFLY. Trouble. Japanese bebby always change it name. I was thinkin' some day w'en he come back, change it to Joy.

SHARPLESS. Yes . . . yes . . . I 'll let him know.

(*Glad to escape, he takes an abrupt departure.*)

SUZUKI. (*In the distance, wailing.*) Ay . . . ay . . . ay . . .

MADAME BUTTERFLY. Tha 's wail . . .

SUZUKI. (*Nearer.*) O, Cho-Cho-San! (MADAME BUTTERFLY *goes to the door to meet* SUZUKI.) Cho-Cho-San!

MADAME BUTTERFLY. Speak!

SUZUKI. We are shamed through the town. The Nakodo—

NAKODO. (*Appearing.*) I but said the child—(*he points to the baby, whom* MADAME BUTTERFLY *instinctively shelters in her arms*) was a badge of shame to his father. In his country, there are homes for such unfortunates and they never rise above the stigma of their class. They are shunned and cursed from birth.

MADAME BUTTERFLY. (*Who has listened stolidly—now with a savage cry, pushing him away from her until he loses his balance and falls to the floor.*) You lie!

NAKODO. (*On the floor.*) But Yamadori—

MADAME BUTTERFLY. (*Touching her father's sword.*) Lies! Lies! Lies! Say again, I kill! Go . . . (*The* NAKODO *goes quickly.*) Bebby, he lies. . . . Yaes, it 's lie. . . . When your fath-er knows how they speak, he will take us 'way from bad people to his own country.

I am finish here. (*Taking the American flag from the tobacco jar and giving it to the child.*) Tha 's your country—your flag. Now wave like fath-er say w'en excite—wave like "hell!" (*Waves the child's hand.*) Ha'rh! Ha'rh! (*A ship's gun is heard.*) Ah! (MADAME BUTTERFLY *and* SUZUKI *start for the balcony.* MADAME BUTTERFLY *runs back for the child as the gun is heard again; then returning to the shoji, looks through the glasses.*) Look! Look! Warship! Wait . . . can't see name. . . .

SUZUKI. Let me—

MADAME BUTTERFLY. No! Ah! Name is "Con-nec-ti-cut"! His ship! He 's come back! He 's come back! (*Laughing, she embraces* SUZUKI—*then sinks to the floor.*) He 's come back! Those robins nes' again an' we did n' know! O, bebby, bebby—your fath-er come back! Your fath-er 's come back! O! O! (*Shaking a bough of cherry blossoms, which fall on them both.*) This is the bes' nize momen' since you was borned. Now your name 's Joy! Suzuki; the Moon Goddess sent that bebby straight from Bridge of Heaven to make me courage to wait so long.

SUZUKI. Ah, ship 's in. . . .

MADAME BUTTERFLY. (*Rising in great excitement.*) Hoarry, Suzuki, his room. (SUZUKI *pulls out a screen to form a little room.*) We mus' hoarry—(*Picking flowers from the pots and decorating the room*) like we got eagle's wings an' thousan' feets. His cigarettes. (*Setting the jar in the room.*) His slipper. (SUZUKI *gets them from the shrine.*) His chair, Suzuki—hustle! (SUZUKI *hastens off.* MADAME BUTTERFLY *shakes a cushion and drops it on the floor.*) His bed. (SUZUKI *enters with a steamer chair, which she places upside down.*) Now his room fixed! (SUZUKI *closes the shoji.* MADAME BUTTERFLY *adjusts the chair and sets the lanterns about the room.*) Bring me my wides' obi, kanzashi for my hair, poppies—mus' look ver' pretty!

SUZUKI. Rest is bes' beauty. He not come yet. Sleep liddle firs'. . . .

MADAME BUTTERFLY. No, no time. (*Taking up a small mirror and looking critically at herself.*) He mus' see me look mos' pretty ever. You thing I change since he went away—not so beauty? (SUZUKI *is silent.*) W'at? . . . I am! (*Brandishing the mirror.*) Say so!

SUZUKI. Perhaps you rest liddle, once more you get so pretty again.

MADAME BUTTERFLY. *Again?* . . .

SUZUKI. Trouble, tha 's make change. . . .

MADAME BUTTERFLY. Moach change. (*Still looking in the glass.*) No, I am no more pretty—an' he come soon. (*On her knees in front of* SUZUKI—*resting her forehead on the maid's feet.*) Ah, Suzuki, be kin' with me—make me pretty . . . don' say you can't—you moas'. An' tomorrow, the gods will. Ah, yes! You can—you can—you got to! Bring powder, comb, rouge, henna, fix it hair like on wedding day. (SUZUKI *brings the toilet articles and they sit on the floor.* SUZUKI *puts the poppies and pins in* MADAME BUTTERFLY'S *hair, and she, in turn, dresses the baby, enveloping him in an obi, so wide that it almost covers the child.*) Now, bebby, when you cry, he 'll sing you those liddle 'Merican song he sing me when I cry—song all 'Merican sing for bebby. (*Sitting with the baby in front of her, swaying it by the arms, she sings.*)

"Rog' a bye bebby,
Off in Japan,
You jus' a picture,
Off of a fan."

(SUZUKI *has found it very difficult to finish the toilet, but at last she accomplishes it.* MADAME BUTTERFLY *lifts the baby up, gives it a doll, then touches it with rouge and adds a final dash of rouge to her own face.*) Now for watch for pa-pa!

(*Putting the flag in the child's hand, she takes it up to the window and makes three holes in the shoji, one low down for the baby. As the three look through the shoji, they form the picture she has already described.*)

(*During the vigil, the night comes on.* SUZUKI *lights the floor lamps, the stars come out, the dawn breaks, the floor lights flicker out one by one, the birds begin to sing, and the day discovers* SUZUKI *and the baby fast asleep on the floor; but* MADAME BUTTERFLY *is awake, still watching, her face white and strained. She reaches out her hands and rouses* SUZUKI.)

SUZUKI. (*Starting to her feet, surprised*

and looking about the room.) He no come?

MADAME BUTTERFLY. No. . . .

SUZUKI. (*Pityingly.*) Oh!

MADAME BUTTERFLY. (*With an imperious gesture.*) No "Oh"! He will come. . . . Bring fresh flowers. (*She collects the lanterns as* SUZUKI *brings in fresh flowers.* MADAME BUTTERFLY *tears up the roses and throws their leaves in Pinkerton's room. Then pointing to the upper part of the house.*) Now I watch from liddle look out place. (*She picks up the child whose doll drops from its hand.* Have mos' bes' nize breakfas' ready w'en he come.

(*She leaves the room and* SUZUKI *goes to prepare the breakfast.*)

(*The stage is empty. Very faintly a strain of "I call her the Belle of Japan" is heard.* MADAME BUTTERFLY *is singing that she may not weep. A pause. Some one knocks on the door.* LIEUTENANT PINKERTON'S *voice calls outside the shoji.*)

LIEUTENANT PINKERTON. Madame Butterfly? Madame Butterfly? (*Coming into the room, he looks about.*) Butterfly?

SHARPLESS. (*Following him.*) They've seen the ship—these decorations were not here when I called.

MADAME BUTTERFLY. (*Singing to hush the baby.*)

"Rog'—a—bye, bebby,
Off in Japan,"

(LIEUTENANT PINKERTON *listens to the song coming from above.*)

"You jus' a picture,
Off of a fan."

LIEUTENANT PINKERTON. She is watching the ship. (*Noticing the screened off part of the room.*) My room . . . just as it used to look . . . my chair. (*Picking up the doll which the child has dropped.*) Poor kid! Poor little devil! . . . Sharpless, I thought when I left this house, the few tears, sobs, little polite regrets, would be over as I crossed the threshold. I started to come back for a minute, but I said to myself: "Don't do it; by this time she's ringing your gold pieces to make sure they're good." You know that class of Japanese girl and—

SHARPLESS. (*Seeing* NAKODO *who is at the shoji.*) Look here: I have something to settle with you! (NAKODO *comes in cautiously.*) Why did you seek out my friend's wife at the pier?

LIEUTENANT PINKERTON. Why did you tell her that story—the child and all? Answer me?

NAKODO. (*To* SHARPLESS.) Your Excellency, I but thought if trouble came between the two women, he would surely break with Cho-Cho-San, and then she would be glad to marry the rich Yamadori and I get big fee. (*Exit.*)

SHARPLESS. You'll never get it. (*To* PINKERTON.) She'll starve first.

LIEUTENANT PINKERTON. Sharpless, thank God, that's one thing I can do—money.

(*He takes out an envelope containing some money.*)

SHARPLESS. What did your wife say, Pinkerton?

LIEUTENANT PINKERTON. Well, it was rather rough on her,—only married four months. Sharpless, my Kate's an angel, —she offered to take the child . . . made me promise I'd speak of it to Butterfly.

MADAME BUTTERFLY. (*Calling from above.*) Suzuki?

SHARPLESS. She's coming.

(PINKERTON *instinctively draws behind the screen.*)

MADAME BUTTERFLY. (*Coming down the stairs with the sleeping baby on her back, calling.*) Suzuki? Come for bebby. (*Kissing the child.*) Nize liddle eye, pick out of blue sky, all shut up.

LIEUTENANT PINKERTON. (*Aside to* SHARPLESS, *his eyes fixed on the mother and child.*) I can't face it! I'm going. Give her the money.

SUZUKI. (*Entering, and seeing* PINKERTON *as he passes out of the door.*) Ah!

(SHARPLESS *gives her a warning gesture.*)

MADAME BUTTERFLY. (*Seeing* SUZUKI'S *astonished face.*) Wha'—? (*She puts the baby in* SUZUKI'S *arms.* SUZUKI *goes out quickly.* MADAME BUTTERFLY *sees the Consul.*) You! Oh! (*Joyously.*) You seen him?

SHARPLESS. Yes.

MADAME BUTTERFLY. An' you tole him?

SHARPLESS. Well . . .

MADAME BUTTERFLY. But you tole him . . . of bebby?

SHARPLESS. Yes.

MADAME BUTTERFLY. (*Wiping her dry lips.*) Yaes . . . tha's right. Tha's what I—as' you do . . . an'—an' what he *say?*

SHARPLESS. Well . . . (*Taking out the envelope, and giving her the money which she takes without looking at it.*) He said—er—he was crazy to see you and—(*Aside*) What the devil can I say! (*To her.*) You know he can't leave the ship just yet. (*Pointing to the package in her hand.*) That is in remembrance of the past. He wishes you to be always happy, to have the best of luck; he hopes to see you soon—and—

(*The lies die out on his lips.*)

MADAME BUTTERFLY. (*Bending and kissing his hand.*) All—all the gods in the heavens bless you!

(*Overcome, she staggers.* SHARPLESS *catches her, puts her into the chair—she leans against him—her face upraised, her eyes closed.*)

(KATE, *entering hurriedly.*)

KATE. Has Lieutenant Pinkerton gone? Has my husband been here?

(MADAME BUTTERFLY *hears and opens her eyes.*)

SHARPLESS. For God's sake—(*He looks at* MADAME BUTTERFLY *whose eyes are fixed on his with a look of despair.*) Come, we can overtake him.

KATE (*In a lower voice.*) Did he speak to her of the—

SHARPLESS. No.

KATE. Then I will ask. (*For the first time seeing* MADAME BUTTERFLY.) Is this—(SHARPLESS *nods and goes. There is a short pause, while the two women look at each other, then* MADAME BUTTERFLY, *still seated, slowly bows her head.*) Why, you poor little thing . . . who in the world could blame you or . . . call you responsible . . . you pretty little plaything.

(*Takes* MADAME BUTTERFLY *in her arms.*)

MADAME BUTTERFLY. (*Softly.*) No—playthin' . . . I am Mrs. Lef-ten-ant B. F.—No—no—now I am, only—Cho-Cho-San, but no playthin'. . . . (*She rises, then impassively.*) How long you been marry?

KATE. Four months. . . .

MADAME BUTTERFLY. (*Counting on her fingers.*) Oh . . . four.

KATE. Won't you let me do something for the child? Where is he? (MADAME BUTTERFLY *gestures toward the next room.* KATE, *seeing the child.*) Ah! The dear little thing! May I—

MADAME BUTTERFLY. No! Can look . . . no can touch. . . .

KATE. Let us think first of the child. For his own good . . . let me take him home to my country. . . . I will do all I would do for my own.

MADAME BUTTERFLY. (*Showing no emotion.*) He not know then—me—his mother?

KATE. It 's hard, very hard, I know; but would it not be better?

MADAME BUTTERFLY. (*Taking the money box from her sleeve, and giving the coins to* KATE.) Tha 's his . . . two dollar. All tha 's lef' of his moaneys. . . . I shall need no more. . . . (*She hands* KATE *the envelope which* SHARPLESS *has just given.*) I lig if you also say I sawry—no—no—*no*—glad—*glad!* I wish him that same happiness lig he wish for me . . . an' tell him . . . I shall be happy . . . mebby. Thang him . . . Mister B. F. Pik-ker-ton for also that kindness he have been unto me . . . an' permit me to thang *you,* augustness, for that same. . . . You—you mos' bes' lucky girl in these whole worl'. . . . Goon-night—

(*She stands stolidly with her eyes closed.*)

KATE. (*Wiping her eyes.*) But the child?

MADAME BUTTERFLY. Come back fifteen minute. . . . (*With closed eyes, she bows politely.*) Sayonara. (KATE *reluctantly goes.*) God he'p me, but no sun kin shine. (SUZUKI, *who has listened, sinks at* MADAME BUTTERFLY'S *feet.*) Don' cry, Suzuki, liddle maiden . . . accoun' I dizappoint, a liddle dizappoint'—don' cry. . . . (*Running her hand over* SUZUKI'S *head—as she kneels.*) Tha 's short while ago you as' me res'—sleep. . . . (*Wearily.*) Well—go way an' I will res' now. . . . I *wish* res'—sleep . . . long sleep . . . an' when you see me again, I pray you look whether I be not beautiful again . . . as a bride.

SUZUKI. (*Understanding, sobbing.*) No—no—no.

MADAME BUTTERFLY. So that I suffer no more—goon bye, liddle maiden. (SUZUKI *does not go.* MADAME BUTTERFLY *claps her hands, and sobbing,* SUZUKI *leaves the room.* MADAME BUTTERFLY *bolts the shoji, and the door, lights fresh incense before the shrine, takes down her father's sword and reads the inscription:*) "To die with honor . . . when one can no longer live with honor." . . .

(*She draws her finger across the blade, to test the sharpness of the sword, then picks up the hand glass, puts on more rouge, re-arranges the poppies in her hair, bows to the shrine, and is about to press the blade of the sword against her neck, when the door is opened and the child is pushed into the room by* SUZUKI, *who keeps out of sight.* MADAME BUTTERFLY *drops the sword and takes the baby in her arms. A knocking is heard but she pays no heed. She sets the child on a mat, puts the American flag in its hand, and picking up the sword, goes behind the screen that the child may not see what she is about to do. A short pause—the sword is heard to drop.* MADAME BUTTERFLY *reappears, her face deathly—a scarf about her neck to conceal the wound.* SUZUKI *opens the door, sees the face of her mistress—backs out of the room in horror.* MADAME BUTTERFLY *drops to her knees as she reaches the child, and clasps it to her. A hand is thrust through the shoji and the bolt is drawn.*)

(KATE *enters quickly urging the reluctant* PINKERTON *to follow her.*)

LIEUTENANT PINKERTON. (*Discerning what she has done.*) Oh! Cho-Cho-San!

(*He draws her to him with the baby pressed to her heart. She waves the child's hand which holds the flag —saying faintly.*)

MADAME BUTTERFLY. Too bad those robins did n' nes' again. (*She dies.*)

THE GIRL WITH THE GREEN EYES

BY

Clyde Fitch

THE GIRL WITH THE GREEN EYES

The Girl with the Green Eyes represents the drama of human character possessed by one absorbing vice, in this case jealousy. It stands also for social comedy and it is representative of the work of its author in his best period.

Clyde Fitch was born in Elmira, New York, May 2, 1865. His father was a captain in the United States Army during the Civil War. He attended the Holderness School, New Hampshire, graduated from Amherst College in 1886, and was already noteworthy in his college days for his interest in costume and rather luxurious accessories of life. He determined from the beginning to devote himself to the stage, and settled in New York, supporting himself by giving readings and tutoring while waiting for recognition. This came first when Richard Mansfield produced his *Beau Brummell* at the Madison Square Theatre, May 17, 1890. This picture of the Georgian dandy remains one of his most characteristic conceptions. Notwithstanding the success of this play and that of *Frédérick Lemaître* (1890), in which Henry Miller starred, Fitch had to wait and work hard before he attained a secure footing. He succeeded, however, in becoming probably the most prolific and the most successful of American playwrights. He was indefatigable in his exertions and produced in twenty years thirty-three original plays, besides twenty-two that were either adaptations from the French or German, revisions of other men's work, or dramatizations of novels. He lived surrounded by every luxury, and he made frequent trips to Europe, and died at Châlons-sur-Marne, September 4, 1909.

The early work of Clyde Fitch was tentative, but when he produced *The Climbers,* January 15, 1901, he entered upon a more definite period of workmanship, and showed himself a master in delineation of the actions and motives of people moving in social relations. This social consciousness had been in his work from the first, but *Beau Brummell* is not so significant, since it reflected the manners of an earlier day in England, and was a play of types rather than of real people. Fitch, however, did not limit himself to social satire; his greatest plays have in them a central idea, which unifies the drama and gives it body. In *The Stubbornness of Geraldine,* played after a tryout in New Haven, at the Garrick Theatre, New York, November 3, 1902, by Mary Mannering, the theme is the fidelity and trust of a woman for the man she loves.

In *The Girl with the Green Eyes,* produced with Clara Bloodgood in the leading rôle at the Savoy Theatre, New York, December 25, 1902, the central idea is that of jealousy and its terrible effects. Fitch was eight years in maturing his conception of "Jinny" Austin, who is one of his most vivid characters. Jinny inherits from her parents the fault of jealousy, but while their common possession of the vice has led them to mutual understanding, the very fact that John Austin is incapable of that weakness helps to bring about both contrast and conflict, the life of drama. The scene in the Vatican is characteristic of Fitch, for the emotions of the characters have to be concealed on account of the constant danger of interruption. The third act, in which the disclosure of Geoffrey **Tillman's** bigamy is made to Jinny by Ruth, is one of the very strongest scenes in modern drama. The English rights for the play were sold to Ellis Jeffreys in 1909, but the production was delayed until Fitch could make certain revisions, which his death prevented. In *The Truth,* tried out in Cleveland, Ohio, October 15, 1906, and later played in New York with Clara Bloodgood as Becky and in London in 1907 with Marie Tempest in the same part, there is a masterly study of the effects of lying on the part of a woman who is not inherently bad but who is incapable of resisting the temptation of the moment to prevaricate. In *The City,* produced after his death, on December 21, 1909, at the Lyric Theatre, New York City, there is a study of the effect upon people of coming to the city from a small town where they have been the principal family for many years. Even in a play that is more frankly melodrama, *The Woman in the Case* (1905), there is a well-conceived unity of action, since the theme turns upon the devotion of a wife to a husband who has been accused of murder, and upon her saving him by her association with a woman of doubtful reputation who holds the key to his release.

Fitch varied his social study with an international setting in *The Coronet of a Duchess* (1904) and in *Her Great Match* (1905), and he wrote several plays which had an historical interest. Of these *Nathan Hale,* played first in Chicago, January 31, 1898, and *Major André* (1903), were tragedies of the Revolution, and *Barbara Frietchie,* first put on in Philadelphia, October 10, 1899, was a tragedy of the Civil War, in which the atmosphere of Maryland during the war is well portrayed. His interest in a play representing a "period" is illustrated by *Captain Jinks of the Horse Marines* (1901), laid in New York City in the early seventies. Fitch succeeded quite well, too, in such a play as *Lovers' Lane* (1901), especially in his interpretation of a child's mind. In *The Girl and the Judge* (1901), laid in a Western town, he showed his ability in creating a situation, even if he did not develop it to the best advantage. The more important plays of Fitch are as follows: *Beau Brummell* (1890); *Frédérick Lemaître* (1890); *Betty's Finish* (1890); *Pamela's Prodigy* (1891); *A Modern Match* (1892); *The Masked Ball* (1892), from *Le Veglione* of Bisson and Carré; *The Social Swim* (1893), from Sardou's *La Maison Neuve*; *April Weather* (1893); *His Grace de Grammont* (1894); *Mistress Betty* (1895), produced ten years later as *The Toast of the Town*; *Bohemia* (1896), adapted from *La Vie de Bohème* by Barrière and Murger; *Nathan Hale* (1898); *The Moth and the Flame* (1898); *The Cowboy and the Lady* (1899); *Barbara Frietchie* (1899); *Captain Jinks of the Horse Marines* (1901); *The Climbers* (1901); *Lovers' Lane* (1901); *The Last of the Dandies* (1901); *The Way of the World* (1901); *The Girl and the Judge* (1901); *The Stubbornness of Geraldine* (1902); *The Girl with the Green Eyes* (1902); *Her Own Way* (1903); *Major André* (1903); *Glad of It* (1903); *The Coronet of a Duchess* (1904); *The Woman in the Case* (1905); *Her Great Match* (1905); *Wolfville* (1905), with Willis Steell, an adaptation of the novel by A. H. Lewis; *The Girl Who Has Everything* (1906); *The Truth* (1906); *The Straight Road* (1906); *Her Sister* (1907), with Cosmo Gordon Lennox; *A Happy Marriage* (1909); *The Bachelor* (1909); and *The City* (1909). This list includes all his original plays.

The following plays have been published: *Pamela's Prodigy* (Allen, 1893), *Nathan Hale* (R. H. Russell, 1899; rep. by W. H. Baker), * *Barbara Frietchie* (Life Publishing Co., 1900), * *Captain Jinks of the Horse Marines* (Doubleday, Page and Co., 1902); * *The Climbers* (1906); * *The Girl with the Green Eyes* (1905); * *The Stubbornness of Geraldine* (1906); * *The Truth* (1907); * *Her Own Way* (1907), by The Macmillan Company; * *Beau Brummell* (John Lane, 1908). Those starred can be obtained in the Samuel French reprints, and all of them except *Pamela's Prodigy,* and in addition *Lovers' Lane, The Woman in the Case,* and *The City,* have been republished in the Memorial Edition, edited by M. J. Moses and Virginia Gerson (Little, Brown and Company, 1915). *Her Great Match* appears only in earlier editions of this collection. Through the courtesy of Mrs. J. H. Edmonds and of the American Play Company, manuscript copies of the following plays have been deposited in the Library of the University of Pennsylvania: *Frédérick Lemaître, A Modern Match, The Social Swim, Bohemia, Glad of it, Wolfville, Her Sister, A Happy Marriage.* The manuscript of *The Bachelor* is in the Amherst College Library.

For a bibliography of Clyde Fitch, see *A Reading List of Clyde Fitch,* by John A. Lowe, *Bulletin of Bibliography,* Vol. 7, p. 30 (July, 1912). For biography, see *Clyde Fitch and His Letters,* by Montrose J. Moses and Virginia Gerson (Boston, 1924), and Archie Bell, *The Clyde Fitch I Knew* (New York, 1909). For criticism, see L. C. Strang, *Players and Plays of the Last Quarter Century* (Boston, 1902, Vol. 2), Chap. 6; W. P. Eaton, *At the New Theatre and Others* (1910), pp. 258–282; B. H. Clark, *The British and American Drama of Today* (New York, 1915); W. L. Phelps, *Essays on Modern Dramatists* (1921), pp. 142–178; A. H. Quinn, *A History of the American Drama from the Civil War to the Present Day* (1936), Vol. I, pp. 265–296 and Vol. II, pp. 345–349; and among many articles, Martin Bernbaum, "Clyde Fitch, an Appreciation," *Independent,* Vol. 67, pp. 123–131; Ada Patterson, "How a Rapid-Fire Dramatist Writes His Plays," *Theatre,* Vol. 7, pp. 14–16 (January, 1907)—practically a statement by Fitch himself of his methods.

CAST OF CHARACTERS

Savoy Theatre, New York, December 25, 1902.

"Jinny" Austin	Miss Clara Bloodgood
Mr. Tillman	Mr. Charles Abbott
Mrs. Tillman	Mrs. Harriet Otis Dellenbaugh
Geoffrey Tillman	Mr. John M. Albaugh, Jr.
Susie	Miss Edith Taliaferro
Miss Ruth Chester	Miss Lucille Flaven
Miss Grace Dane	Miss Mary Blyth
Miss Bell Westing	Miss Helena Otis
Miss Gertrude Wood	Miss Felice Morris
Maggie	Miss Lucile Watson
Housemaid	Miss Angela Keir
Butler	Mr. Gardner Jenkins
Footman	Mr. Walter Dickinson
John Austin	Mr. Robert Drouet
Mrs. Cullingham	Mrs. McKee Rankin
Peter Cullingham	Mr. Harry E. Asmus
Mrs. Lopp	Miss Ellen Rowland
Carrie	Miss Clara B. Hunter
A French Couple	Mr. Henry De Barry Miss Louise Delmar
A German Couple	Mr. J. R. Cooley Miss Elsa Ganett
A Guide	Mr. Frank Brownlee
A Driver	Mr. Lou W. Carter
A Group of Tourists	Miss Elizabeth French Miss Gertrude Bindley Miss Myrtle Lane

ACT I—The Tillmans' House, New York. The Wedding.
(Two months elapse.)

ACT II—The Vatican, Rome. The Honeymoon.
(Three weeks elapse.)

ACT III—The Austins' House, New York. Home.
(The night passes.)

ACT IV—The Same.
Scene I—Dawn of the Next Day.
Scene II—Early the Same Morning.

THE GIRL WITH THE GREEN EYES

ACT FIRST

A charming room in the TILLMANS' *house. The walls are white woodwork, framing in old tapestries of deep foliage design, with here and there a flaming flamingo; white furniture with old, green brocade cushions. The room is in the purest Louis XVI. The noon sunlight streams through a window on the Left. On the opposite side is a door to the hall. At back double doors open into a corridor which leads to the ballroom. At Left Centre are double doors to the front hall. A great, luxurious sofa is at the left, with chairs sociably near it, and on the other side of the room a table has chairs grouped about it. On floral small table are books and objets d'art, and everywhere there is a profusion of white roses and maidenhair fern.*

In the stage directions Left and Right mean Left and Right of actor, as he faces audience.

Three smart-looking SERVANTS *are peering through the crack of the folding door, their backs to the audience. The pretty, slender* MAID *is on a chair. The elderly* BUTLER *dignifiedly stands on the floor. The plump, overfed little* HOUSEMAID *is kneeling so as to see beneath the head of the* BUTLER.

HOUSEMAID. [*Gasping.*] Oh, ain't it a beautiful sight!

BUTLER. [*Pompously.*] Not to me who 'ave seen a lord married in Hengland.

MAGGIE. Oh, you make me sick, Mr. Potts, always talking of your English Aristocracy! I'm sure there never was no prettier wedding than this. Nor as pretty a bride as Miss Jinny.

BUTLER. [*Correcting her.*] Mrs. Haustin!

HOUSEMAID. She looks for all the world like one of them frosted angels on a Christmas card. My, I wish I could 'a' seen her go up the aisle with the organ going for all it was worth!

MAGGIE. It was a *beautiful* sight!

BUTLER. A good many 'appens to be 'aving the sense to be going now.

HOUSEMAID. Could you hear Miss Jinny say "I do," and make them other remarks?

MAGGIE. Yes, *plain,* though her voice was trembly like. But Mr. Austin he almost shouted! [*Laughing nervously in excitement.*]

BUTLER. 'E's glad to get 'er!

MAGGIE. *And her him!*

HOUSEMAID. Yes, that's what I likes about it. Did any one cry?

MAGGIE. Mrs. Tillman. Lots of people are going now.

HOUSEMAID. What elegant clothes! Oh, gosh!

BUTLER. [*Superciliously.*] Mrs. Cullingham don't seem in no 'urry; she's a common lot!

MAGGIE. I don't care, she's rich and Miss Jinny likes her; she just throws money around to any poor person or church or hospital that wants it, or *don't!* So she can't be so *very common* neither, Mr. Potts!

HOUSEMAID. Say, I catch on to something! Young Mr. Tillman's sweet on that there tall bridesmaid.

MAGGIE. [*Sharply.*] Who?

BUTLER. Miss Chester. I've seen there was something goin' hon between them whenever she's dined or lunched 'ere.

MAGGIE. [*Angry.*] 'Tain't true!

BUTLER. I'll bet my month's wages.

MAGGIE. I don't believe you!

BUTLER. Why, what's it to *you,* please?

MAGGIE. [*Saving herself.*] Nothing—

HOUSEMAID. Well, I guess it's truth enough. That's the second time I've seen him squeeze her hand when no one wasn't lookin'.

MAGGIE. Here, change places with me! [*Getting down from her chair.*] If you was a gentleman, Mr. Potts, you'd have given me *your place!* [*Witheringly.*]

BUTLER. If I was a *gentleman,* miss, I wouldn't be here; *I'd* be on the other side of the door. [*He moves the chairs away.*]

MAGGIE. [*To Housemaid.*] Honest, you saw something between them?

HOUSEMAID. Who?

MAGGIE. Him and her? Mr. Geoffrey and Miss Chester—

HOUSEMAID. *Cheese it!* they're coming this way! [*She and the* MAID *and the* BUTLER *vanish through the door Right.*]

[GEOFFREY *and* RUTH *enter through the double doors quickly at back.* GEOFFREY *is a young, good-looking man, but with a weak face. He is of course very smartly dressed.* RUTH *is a very serenely beautiful girl, rather noble in type, but unconscious and unpretending in manner. They close the doors quickly behind them.*]

GEOFFREY. We'll not be interrupted here, and I must have a few words with you before you go. [*He follows her to the sofa, where she sits, and leans over it, with his arm about her shoulder.*]

RUTH. Oh, Geof,—Geof, why weren't we married like this?

GEOFFREY. It couldn't be helped, darling!

RUTH. It isn't the big wedding I miss, oh, no, it's only it seemed sweeter in a church. Why did we have to steal off to Brooklyn, to that poor, strange little preacher in his stuffy back parlour, and behave as if we were doing something of which we were ashamed?

GEOFFREY. You love me, I love you,—isn't that the chief thing, dearest?

RUTH. But how much longer must we keep it secret?

GEOFFREY. Till I can straighten my affairs out. I can't explain it all to you; there are terrible debts,—one more than all the others,—a debt I made when I was in college.

RUTH. If I could only help you! I have a *little* money.

GEOFFREY. No, I love you too much; besides, this debt isn't *money,* and I hope to get rid of it somehow before long.

RUTH. Forgive me for worrying you. It is only that every one is so happy at this wedding except me,—dear Jinny brimming over with joy, as I would be,—and it's made me feel—a little—

GEOFFREY. [*Comes around the sofa and sits beside her.*] I know, dear, and it's made me feel what a brute I am! Oh, if you knew how I hate myself for all I've done, and for the pain and trouble I cause you now!

[MAGGIE, *her sharp features set tense, appears in the doorway on the left behind the curtains and listens.*]

RUTH. Never mind, we won't think of that any more.

GEOFFREY. I can never throw it off, not for a minute! I'm a worthless fellow and how can you love me—

RUTH. [*Interrupting him.*] I *do!* You are worth everything to me, and you will be worth much to the world yet!

GEOFFREY. I love you, Ruth—that's the one claim I can make to deserve you. But it's helped me to give up *all* the beastly pleasures I used to indulge in!

RUTH. [*Softly.*] Geof!

GEOFFREY. Which I used to think the only things worth living for, and which now, thanks to you, I loathe,—every one of them.

RUTH. I'm so glad! I've been some help, then.

GEOFFREY. If I'd only got you earlier, I'd have been a different man, Ruth!

RUTH. [*Smiling and taking his nervous hand in hers.*] Then I mightn't have fallen in love with you if you were a *different* man!

GEOFFREY. Dear girl! Anyway, this is the good news that I want to tell you—I hope now to have things settled in a couple of weeks.

RUTH. [*In glad relief.*] Geoffrey!

GEOFFREY. But—I mayn't be successful; it might be, Ruth—it might be, we would have to wait—for years—

RUTH. [*Quietly.*] I don't think I could bear that! It's not easy for me to lie and deceive as I've had to the last few months; I don't think I could keep it up.

[PETER CULLINGHAM *enters suddenly, from the ballroom, a pale young man, but, unlike* GEOFFREY, *hard and virile.*]

PETER. Oh, here you are! I say, are you two spoony? Just the way *I* feel! [*Laughing.*] I caught and hugged old Mrs. Parmby just now! I think it's sort of in the air at weddings, don't you?

GEOFFREY. [*Rising.*] I'm surprised to see you've left the refreshment table, Peter.

PETER. They sent me to find Miss Chester—they're going to cut the bridesmaids' cake, and if you two really are spoony, Miss Chester, you'd better not miss it—you might get the ring! [*They laugh as* PETER *takes out a bottle from which he takes a round, black tablet which he puts in his mouth.*]

RUTH. [*Also rising.*] I'd better go.

[PETER *is making frantic efforts to swallow the tablet*]

GEOFFREY. [*Noticing him.*] What's the matter with you?

PETER. O dear! I've eaten so many ices and fancy cakes, I've got awful indigestion, and I'm trying to swallow a charcoal tablet.

RUTH. Come with me and get a glass of water.

PETER. No, it's very bad to drink water with your meals; but I'll get a piece of bridesmaid's cake—that'll push it down!

[PETER *and* RUTH *go out through the double doors. The moment they are out of the room,* MAGGIE *comes from behind the curtain and goes straight up to* GEOFFREY. *He looks astonished and frightened.*]

GEOFFREY. What do you want? Have you been listening?

MAGGIE. So that's it, is it? You want to marry her when you can get rid of me.

GEOFFREY. [*With relief.*] What do you mean?

MAGGIE. Oh, I may not have heard everything, but I heard and saw enough to catch on that you're in love with Miss Chester.

GEOFFREY. Well?

MAGGIE. Well, you won't marry her—I'll never set you free.

GEOFFREY. Sh! [*Looking about and closing the doors.*]

MAGGIE. Oh, they're all in the dining room.

GEOFFREY. [*Angry.*] What do you want, anyway?

MAGGIE. [*She pleads a little.*] When I came here to your house and got a position, it was because I *loved* you, if you *had* treated me bad, and I hoped by seeing you again, and being near you, you might come back to me and everything be made straight!

GEOFFREY. Never! Never! It's impossible.

MAGGIE. [*Angry again.*] Oh, is it! Well, the dirty little money you give me now only holds my tongue quiet so long's you behave yourself and don't run after any other girls! But the minute you try to throw me down, I'll come out with the whole story.

GEOFFREY. I was drunk when I married you!

MAGGIE. More shame to you!

GEOFFREY. You're right. But I was only twenty—and you—led me on—

MAGGIE. [*Interrupting him.*] Me! led you on! *Me,* as decent and nice a girl as there was in New Haven if I do do housework, and that's my wedding ring and you put it there, and mother's got the certificate locked up good and safe in her box with my dead baby sister's hair and the silver plate off my father's coffin!

GEOFFREY. We mustn't talk here any more!

MAGGIE. You look out! If I wasn't so fond of your sister Miss Jinny, and if the old people weren't so good to me, I'd just show you right up *here—now!*

GEOFFREY. I'll *buy* you off if I can't divorce you!

MAGGIE. *You!* Poof!

[GIRLS' *voices are heard from the ballroom.*]

GEOFFREY. Look out—some one's coming!

MAGGIE. [*Going.*] You haven't got a red cent; my cheque's always one of your *father's!* [*She goes out Right.*]

GEOFFREY. Good God! what am I going to do—shoot myself, if I don't get out of this soon—I must get some air! [*He goes out Left.*]

[JINNY *opens the double doors, looks in, and then enters. She is an adorable little human being, pretty, highstrung, temperamental, full of certain feminine fascination that defies analysis, which is partly due to the few faults she possesses. She is, of course, dressed in the conventional wedding-dress, a tulle veil thrown over her face.*]

JINNY. Not a soul! Come on! [*She is followed in by the four* BRIDESMAIDS—*nice girls every one of them—and also, very slyly, by* SUSIE, *a very modern spoiled child, who sits unobserved out of the way at the back.*] Now, my dears, I wish to say good-by all by ourselves so I can make you a little speech! [*All laugh gently.*] In the first place I want to tell you that there's nothing like marriage! And you must every one of you try it! Really, I was never so happy in my life!

GRACE. Must we stand, or may we sit down?

JINNY. Oh, stand; it won't be long and you'll only crush your lovely frocks. In fact, I advise you not to lose any time sitting down again until you've got the happy day fixed!

RUTH. You know, Jinny darling, that there is no one so glad for your happiness as your four bridesmaids are—isn't that so, girls?

ALL. Yes!

[*And they all together embrace* JINNY,

saying, "Dear old Jinny," "Darling Jinny," "We'll miss you dreadfully," *etc., ad lib., till they get tearful.*]

JINNY. Good gracious, girls, we mustn't cry. I'll get red eyes, and Jack'll think what an awful difference just the marriage service makes in a woman.

[*The doors at the back open, and* AUSTIN *appears in the doorway.* AUSTIN *is a typical New Yorker in appearance, thirty-two years old, good-looking, manly, self-poised, and somewhat phlegmatic in temperament.*]

AUSTIN. Hello! May a mere man come in to this delectable tea party?

JINNY. *No,* Jack! But *wait*—by the door till I call you!

AUSTIN. [*Amused.*] Thank you! [*He goes out, closing the door.*]

GERTRUDE. We'll miss you so awfully, Jinny.

JINNY. Just what I say! Get a man to keep you company, and then you won't miss any one.

BELLE. Yes, but attractive men with lots of money don't come into the Grand Central Station by every train!

JINNY. [*Putting her arm about her.*] You want too much, my dear Belle! And you aren't watching the Grand Central Station either half so much as you are the steamer docks for a suitable person. Now don't be angry; you know you want a good big title, and you've got the money to pay, but, my dear Belle, it's those ideas of yours that have kept you single till—twenty-six!—now *that* you must confess was nice of me, to take off *three* years!

BELLE. [*Laughing.*] Jinny, you're horrid!

JINNY. No, I'm not! You know I'm *really* fond of you, or you wouldn't be my bridesmaid to-day; it's only that I want *your wedding* to be as happy as *mine*—that's all, and here's a little gift for you to remember your disagreeable but loving friend by! [*Giving her a small jewelry box.*]

BELLE. Thank you, Jinny! Thank you! [*A little moved.*]

GRACE. Mercy! I hope you're not going to take each one of us!

JINNY. I am, and come here, *you're* next!

GRACE. I'll swear I don't want to get married at all!

JINNY. Don't be silly, you *icicle!* Of course you don't; you freeze all the men away, so that you've no idea how nice and comfy they can be! My advice to you, Grace darling,—and I *love* you, or I wouldn't bother,—is to *thaw!* [*Laughs.*] I used to be awfully jealous of you—

GRACE. [*Interrupting.*] Oh!

JINNY. Yes, I was! You're lots prettier than I am.

GRACE. Jinny.

JINNY. You *are!* But I got over it because I soon saw you were so cold, there was no danger of any conflagration near you! Oh, I've watched your *eyes* often to see if any man had lighted the fires in them yet. And now I'm determined they shall be lighted. You're too *cold!* Thaw, dear,—not to *everybody,*—that would be like slushy weather, but don't keep yourself so continually so far below zero that you won't have time to strike—well—say eighty-five in *the shade,* when the right bit of masculine sunshine *does* come along! Here—with my best love! [*Giving her a small jewelry box.*]

[GRACE *kisses* JINNY.]

GERTRUDE. I am the next *victim,* I believe!

JINNY. All I've got to say to *you,* Miss, is, that if you don't decide pretty soon on *one* of the half dozen men you are flirting with *disgracefully* at present, they'll every one find you out and you'll have to go in for widowers.

GERTRUDE. [*Mockingly.*] Horrors!

JINNY. Oh, I don't know! I suppose a widower is sort of *broken in* and would be more likely to put up with your caprices! For the sake of your charm and wit and true heart underneath it all, you dear old girl you! [*Giving her a small jewel box.*]

GERTRUDE. Thank you, Jinny. I'm only afraid I will do the wrong thing with you away! You know you're always my ballast!

JINNY. Nonsense! Female ballast is no good; masculine ballast is the only kind that's safe if you want to make life's journey in a love balloon. [SHE *turns to* RUTH CHESTER.] Ruth—the trouble with you is, you're too sad lately, and show such a lack of interest. I should think you might be in love, only I haven't been able to find the man. Anyway, if you aren't in love, you must *pretend* an interest in things. Of course, men's affairs are awfully dull, but they don't like you to talk about them, so it's really very easy. All you have to do is listen, stare them straight in the eyes, think of whatever you like, and look pleased! It *does* flatter them, and they think *they* are *interesting*, and you *charming!* Wear this, and think of me, [*Giving her a box.*] and be happy! I *want* you to be *happy* —and I can see you aren't!

RUTH. [*Kissing her.*] Thank you, dear!

JINNY. There, that's all!—except—when I come home from abroad in October, if every one of you isn't engaged to be married, I'll wash my hands of you—

[*They all laugh.*]

[SUSIE, *sliding off her chair at back, comes forward.*]

SUSIE. Now, it's my turn! You can't chuck me!

JINNY. [*Trying not to laugh.*] Susie! where did you come from and *what do* you mean?

SUSIE. Oh, you give me a pain!—I went up the aisle with you to-day, too—what's the matter with telling me how to get married?

JINNY. I'll tell you this, your language is dreadful; where do you get all the boy's slang? You don't talk like a lady.

SUSIE. I'm not a lady. I'm a little girl!

JINNY. You *talk* much more like a common boy.

SUSIE. Well, I'd rather *be* a *boy!*

JINNY. Susie, I shall tell Aunt Laura her daughter needs looking after.

SUSIE. Oh, very well, cousin Jinny. If you're going to make trouble, why, forget it! [*Turns and goes out haughtily, Right.*]

JINNY. [*Going to the double doors, calls.*] Now you can come in, Jack.

[AUSTIN *enters.*]

AUSTIN. And now I've only time to say good-by. All your guests have gone except the Cullinghams, who are upstairs with your mother, looking at the presents.

GERTRUDE. Come! All hands around him!

[*The five* GIRLS *join hands, with* AUSTIN *in the centre.*]

BELLE. We don't care if every one else has gone or not, *we're* here yet!

AUSTIN. So I see! But I am ordered by my father-in-law—ahem! [*all laugh*]—to go to my room, or he thinks there will be danger of our losing our train.

ALL THE BRIDESMAIDS. [*Ad lib.*] Where are you going? Where are you going? We won't let you out till you tell us.

AUSTIN. I daren't—I'm afraid of my wife!

JINNY. Bravo, Jack!

GRACE. Very well, then, we'll let you out, on *one* condition, that you kiss us all in turn.

[*The* GIRLS *laugh.*]

JINNY. No! No! [*Breaking away.*] He shan't do any such thing!

[*They all laugh and break up the ring.*]

GERTRUDE. Dear me, isn't she jealous!

BELLE. Yes, it is evidently time we all went! Good-by, Jinny! [*Kissing her.*] A happy journey to *Washington!*

JINNY. No, it isn't!

[*General good-bys.* JINNY *begins with* RUTH *at one end, and* AUSTIN *at the other; he says good-by and shakes hands with each girl.*]

GERTRUDE. [*Kissing* JINNY.] Good-by, and a pleasant trip to *Niagara Falls!*

JINNY. Not a bit!

GRACE. [*Kissing* JINNY.] Good-by, I believe it's *Boston* or *Chicago!*

JINNY. *Neither!*

RUTH. Good-by, dear, and all the happiness in the world! [*Kisses her.*]

JINNY. Thank you. [*She turns and goes with the other three girls to the double doors at back, where they are heard talking.*]

RUTH. Mr. Austin?

AUSTIN. Yes? [*Joining her.*]

RUTH. [*Embarrassed.*] You like your new brother, *don't* you?

AUSTIN. Geoff? Most certainly I do, and Jinny adores him.

RUTH. I know, then, you'll be a good friend to him if he needs one.

AUSTIN. Surely I will.

RUTH. I think he does need one.

AUSTIN. Really—

[*The* GIRLS *are passing out through the doors.*]

BELLE. Come along, Ruth.

[THEY *pass out and* JINNY *stands in the doorway talking to them till they are out of hearing.*]

RUTH. Sh! Please don't tell any one, not even Jinny, what I've said! I may be betraying something I've no right to do, and don't tell *him* I've spoken to you.

AUSTIN. All right!

[JINNY *turns around in the doorway.*]

RUTH. Thank you—and good-by. [*Shaking his hand again.*]

[JINNY *notices that they shake hands twice. A queer little look comes into her face.*]

AUSTIN. Good-by.

RUTH. Have they gone?—Oh! [*Hurrying past* JINNY.] Good-by, dear. [*She goes out through the double doors.*]

JINNY. [*In a curious little voice.*] Good-by . . . [*She comes slowly down the room toward* AUSTIN, *and smiles at him quizzically.*] What are you two saying?

AUSTIN. Good-by!

JINNY. But you'd said it once to her already! Why did you have to say good-by *twice* to *Ruth?* Once was enough for all the other girls!

AUSTIN. [*Banteringly.*] The first time *I* said good-by to *her,* and the second time *she* said good-by to *me!*

JINNY. Do you know what I believe—*Ruth Chester's in love with you!*

AUSTIN. Oh, darling! [*Laughs.*]

JINNY. Yes, that explains the whole thing. No wonder she was *triste* to-day.

AUSTIN. [*Laughing.*] Jinny, sweetheart, don't get such an absurd notion into your head.

JINNY. [*Looks straight at him a moment, then speaks tenderly.*] No—no—I know it's not your fault. There was no other woman in this house for you to-day but *me, was* there?

AUSTIN. There was no other woman in the world for me since the first week I knew you. [*Taking her into his arms.*]

JINNY. This is good-by to *Jinny Tillman!* [*He kisses her.*] Jack, darling, do you think I could sit on your knee like a little child and put my arm around your neck and rest my head on your shoulder for just five seconds—I'm *so tired!*

[MRS. CULLINGHAM *opens the door.*]

MRS. CULLINGHAM. Oh! [*Shuts the door quickly and knocks.*]

[JINNY *and* AUSTIN *laugh.*]

JINNY. Yes, yes—come in!

[MRS. CULLINGHAM *enters. She is a handsome, whole-souled, florid woman; one of those creatures of inexhaustible vitality who make people of a nervous temperament tired almost on contact by sheer contrast. She is the kindest, best meaning creature in the world.*]

MRS. CULLINGHAM. Oh, do excuse me! I haven't any more tact!—and I hate to interrupt you, but I must say good-by. [*Calls.*] Peter!

PETER. Yes'm. [*Entering with a glass of water and a powder. He sits in the armchair at Right, and constantly looks at his watch.*]

AUSTIN. I'm much obliged to you, Mrs. Cullingham, for the interruption, as I was sent long ago to make myself ready for the train, if you'll excuse me!

MRS. CULLINGHAM. Certainly!

JINNY. Good-by! [*Taking his hand as he passes her.*]

AUSTIN. Good-by! [*He goes out Right.*]

MRS. CULLINGHAM. If it's time for *him,* it's certainly time for *you.* I won't keep you a minute!

JINNY. No, really we've plenty of time,—[*Both sit on sofa.*] Wasn't it a lovely wedding!

MRS. CULLINGHAM. I never saw a sweeter, my dear! And it was perfectly elegant! Simply great!

JINNY. And isn't Jack—

MRS. CULLINGHAM. He is! And so are you! In fact I've been telling your mother I don't know how to thank you both. You've asked me to-day to meet the swellest crowd I've ever been in where I was *invited,* and didn't have to buy tickets, and felt I had a right to say something besides "excuse me," and "I beg your pardon." Of course, I've sat next to them all before in restaurants and at concerts, but this time I felt like the real thing myself, and I shall never forget it! If you or your husband ever want any mining tips, come to me; what my husband don't know about mines isn't worth knowing!

JINNY. I'm as glad as I can be if you've had a good time, and you mustn't feel indebted to us. Ever since we met in Egypt that winter, mamma and I have always felt you were one of our best friends.

MRS. CULLINGHAM. Of course you know it isn't for *my own* sake I'm doing these stunts to get into Society. It's all for *my boy.* He's *got* to have the best—or the *worst,* however you look at it! [*Laughing.*] Anyway, I want him to have a chance at it, and it belongs to him through his father, for my first husband was a real swell! [*Looking at* PETER *lovingly.*]

[*At this moment,* PETER, *having again looked at his watch, tips up the powder on his tongue, and swallows it down with water.*]

MRS. CULLINGHAM. Poor darling! He suffers terribly from indigestion. That's an alkali powder he takes twenty minutes after eating. Peter, we must say good-by now.

PETER. [*Coming up.*] Good-by, Miss Jinny.

MRS. CULLINGHAM. *Mrs. Austin!*

JINNY. Oh, I'll always be "Miss Jinny" to Peter!

PETER. Thank you! We've had a great time at your wedding! *Bully food!* But I'm *feeling* it! [*He turns aside.*] Excuse me!

MRS. CULLINGHAM. I was just telling Mrs. Austin—[*Interrupted.*]

JINNY. "Jinny"—don't change.

MRS. CULLINGHAM. Thank you—[*Rises to go.*] I was just saying we won't forget in our social life, will we, Peter, that Miss Jinny gave us the biggest boost up we've had yet?

[JINNY *also rises.*]

PETER. Well, you know, mother, I don't think the game's worth the candle. It's begun to pall on me already.

MRS. CULLINGHAM. I really think he's going to be superior to it!

PETER. I only go now for your sake.

[MRS. TILLMAN, *coming from Right, speaks off stage.*]

MRS. TILLMAN. Jinny! Jinny!

JINNY. Mother!

[MRS. TILLMAN *enters.*]

JINNY. I ought to dress?

MRS. TILLMAN. [*To* MRS. CULLINGHAM.] She'll be late if she isn't careful.

JINNY. I'm going to. Is Maggie there?

MRS. TILLMAN. Yes, waiting!

JINNY. Good-by. [*Kisses* MRS. CULLINGHAM.] Good-by. [*Shakes* PETER'S *hand.*]

PETER. Many happy returns!

[JINNY *goes out Right.*]

MRS. TILLMAN. Come, I want to give you some of Jinny's flowers to take home with you. Would you like some?

MRS. CULLINGHAM. I should love them!

[*They go out through the doors at back.*]

[PETER *is suffering with indigestion. He takes a charcoal tablet, and* SUSIE *cautiously enters Right.*]

SUSIE. There you are! Have you got 'em?

PETER. No, I gave them back to you.

SUSIE. Then they're in there on the table—get 'em quick, the trunks are coming down now!

[PETER *goes out quickly at back, as the* BUTLER *and* MAN SERVANT *enter Right, carrying a large new trunk with a portmanteau on top of it.*]

SUSIE. Put them right over there for a minute. [*They put them down in the centre of the room, and the* FOOTMAN *goes out Right.*] And mind, you don't split on us, Thomas. Auntie Tillman knows all about it—it's just to be a nice little surprise for Cousin Jinny and my new uncle.

BUTLER. Very well, miss. [*He also goes out Right.*]

[*At the same time* PETER *reënters at back with a roll of papers and some broad white satin ribbon. The papers are about half a foot broad and two feet long, and on them is printed, "We are on our honeymoon."*]

PETER. [*With gay excitement.*] I've got 'em.

SUSIE. Get some water—there's sticky stuff on the back!

[PETER *gives her the papers and ribbons and goes out again at back.*]

SUSIE. Quick! [*Ties a big white bow on the portmanteau and on a trunk handle.*] If Auntie Tillman sees 'em, I'll bet she'll grab 'em off. She'll be as mad as *hops!*

[*The* BUTLER *and* FOOTMAN *reënter Right, and bring down an old steamer trunk and a gentleman's dressing-bag.*]

BUTLER. [*To the* FOOTMAN.] Go and see if the carriage is there!

FOOTMAN. Yes, sir. [*He goes out Left. As* PETER *reënters from the back, with the water.*]

SUSIE. Quick now! Quick!

[*They stick one label on the big steamer trunk facing the audience.*]

PETER. I say isn't that great!

[SUSIE *giggles aloud with delight. The* BUTLER, *standing at one side, smiles. They put another label on the other trunk.*]

SUSIE. [*Giggling.*] I heard them plan it,—they're taking one old trunk purposely so as people would not catch on they were just married! [*Giggles delightedly.*]

[*The* FOOTMAN *reënters with a driver, Left.*]

FOOTMAN. Yes, sir, it's here.

BUTLER. [*To the driver.*] You can take that first. [*Pointing to the steamer trunk.*]

[DRIVER *goes out Left with it on his shoulder, and the portmanteau.*]

BUTLER. Now, James, you're to go over with the luggage to Twenty-third Street Ferry and check the heavy baggage; you know where to.

FOOTMAN. Yes, sir.

SUSIE. [*Eagerly.*] Oh, *where to?*

BUTLER. I am hunder hoath not to tell, Miss.

SUSIE. O pish! [*Kneeling in the big arm-chair and watching proceedings from behind its back.*]

BUTLER. [*Continues to the* FOOTMAN.] And wait with the checks and Mr. Austin's dressing-bag—[*Showing it.*]—until they come.

FOOTMAN. Yes, sir.

PETER. And make haste, or, I say, somebody'll turn up and give our whole joke away!

[*The* DRIVER *reënters.*]

SUSIE. Yes, *do* hurry!

FOOTMAN. [*To the* DRIVER.] Come along.

[*They take the big trunk out Left.* BUTLER *follows with the dressing-bag.*]

MRS. CULLINGHAM. [*Calls from the room at back.*] Peter darling, are you there?

SUSIE. Phew! Just in time! [*Sliding down into a more correct position in the chair.*]

PETER. Yes, mother! [*Going to back.*]

MRS. CULLINGHAM. [*In the doorway, at back.*] Come, take these beautiful roses from Mrs. Tillman!

[MRS. CULLINGHAM *and* MRS. TILLMAN *enter.*]

MRS. TILLMAN. [*With her arms full of roses.*] Thomas will take them down.

PETER. No, I'd like to. Aren't they bully? [*He takes them.*]

MRS. CULLINGHAM. [*To* MRS. TILLMAN.] Good-by, and thank you again. I know you must want to go up to Jinny.

MRS. TILLMAN. Yes, she may need me to help her a little. Good-by. Good-by, Peter.

PETER. Good-by, ma'm.

[MRS. TILLMAN *goes out Right.*]

MRS. CULLINGHAM. Why, Susie, how do you do?

SUSIE. [*Glides out of the chair and stands before it.*] How do you do? [*Embarrassed.*]

MRS. CULLINGHAM. You're a good little girl, I hope?

SUSIE. I don't! I hate good little girls!

MRS. CULLINGHAM. O my! [*She goes out, laughing, Left.*]

[PETER, *coming to* SUSIE, *catches her in his arms and kisses her, much against her will.*]

SUSIE. [*Furious.*] Oh, you horrid, nasty thing, you! [*She strikes at him; he runs; she chases him from one side of the room to the other, around a sofa and table, and out Left, screaming as she chases him.*] I hate you! I hate you!

[MAGGIE *enters Right.*]

MAGGIE. Miss Susie, Mrs. Tillman wants to see you upstairs.

SUSIE. What for?

MAGGIE. I don't know, Miss.

SUSIE. Pshaw! have I got to go? All right! [*Going toward the door at Right.*]

[AUSTIN *enters, meeting* SUSIE.]

AUSTIN. Hello! Where are *you* going?

SUSIE. Oh, up to Auntie Tillman's room. Goodness knows what for; it's an awful bore! Want to come along?

AUSTIN. No, thank you; but if you see your Cousin Jinny, you might tell her I am down.

SUSIE. [*Hanging on to him.*] I say! Where are you and Cousin Jinny going to, anyway?

AUSTIN. [*Smiling.*] I don't know.

SUSIE. O my, what a fib! And that's a nice example to set a little girl! [*She goes out Right.*]

MAGGIE. [*Coming forward.*] I beg pardon, sir, but may I speak to you a minute?

AUSTIN. Certainly, Maggie, what is it?

MAGGIE. I've been trying for a chance to see you alone. I wouldn't bother you, sir—but it's only because I'm fond of Miss Jinny, and of Mr. and Mrs. Tillman, and they've all been so good to me; I know it would nearly kill 'em if they knew.

AUSTIN. Come, Maggie, knew what?

MAGGIE. Well, *one member* of this family ain't been good to me, sir. [*From this point her feelings begin to get the better of her and she speaks rapidly and hysterically.*] He's been bad, bad as he could, and somebody's got to talk to him, and I don't see who's a-goin' to do it but you. If he don't change, I'll not hold my tongue any longer. It's all I can do for their sakes to hold it now!

AUSTIN. Look here, what are you talking about? You don't mean Mr. Geoffrey?

MAGGIE. Yes, I do, sir; he's my husband.

AUSTIN. What!!

MAGGIE. We was married when he was at Yale, sir; I was in a shop there.

AUSTIN. But—! Well, after all, isn't this your and Geoffrey's affair? Why bring me in?

MAGGIE. Because he's making love to Miss Chester, and promising to marry *her* now, and if he don't stop—I'll make trouble!

AUSTIN. But if he's married to you, as you say—he can't marry—any one else.

MAGGIE. He's tried to make me believe our marriage ain't legal, because he was only twenty and he'd been drinking!

AUSTIN. What makes you think Mr. Geoffrey cares for—Miss Chester?

MAGGIE. I just heard and see him making love to her *here!*

AUSTIN. This is a pretty bad story, Maggie.

MAGGIE. Yes, sir, and the worst is, sir, I know I ain't good enough for him, and that's why I've kept still about it these three years, but I can't help loving him no matter how ugly he's treated me. [*Breaking down into tears.*] I just can't help it! I *love* him, sir, even if I'm only a servant girl, and I can't stand it thinking he's going to try and get rid of me for some one else! [*She sobs out loud.*]

AUSTIN. Sh!—Maggie. Sit down a minute, and control yourself. Somebody'll hear you, and besides they'll be coming down presently. I'll have a talk with Mr. Geoffrey when I come back— [*Interrupted as* GEOFFREY *enters Left. He doesn't see* MAGGIE, *who is collapsed in a corner of the sofa.*]

GEOFFREY. [*To* AUSTIN.] Ah! Thank goodness I've caught you; I had an awful headache and went out for a breath of air, and then I was afraid I might have missed you! I knew in that case Jinny would never forgive me, nor—I—myself—for that—matter— [*His voice grows less exuberant in the middle of his speech and finally at the end almost dies away, as he sees the expression in* AUSTIN'S *face and realizes that something is wrong somewhere. When he stops speaking,* MAGGIE *gives a gasping sob. He hears it, and starting, sees her.*]

GEOFFREY. Maggie!

AUSTIN. Geoffrey, is what this girl says true?

GEOFFREY. That I married her in New Haven? Yes.

MAGGIE. [*Rises.*] I'll go, please, I'd rather go.

AUSTIN. Yes, go, Maggie; it's better.

[MAGGIE *goes out Right.*]

GEOFFREY. [*As soon as she is out of the room.*] Promise me, Jack, you won't tell any one! It's awful, I know! For two years at college I went all to pieces and led a rotten life,—and one night, drunk, I married her, and it isn't so much her fault. I suppose she thought I loved her,—but this would break up the old lady and gentleman so, if they knew, I couldn't stand it! And Jinny, for God's sake, don't tell Jinny. *She respects me.* You won't tell her, will you?

AUSTIN. No. But Maggie says you want to marry some one else now.

GEOFFREY. [*With a change, in great shame.*] That's true, too. [*He sits in utter dejection on the sofa.*]

AUSTIN. How are you going to do it?

GEOFFREY. I must make money somehow and buy off Maggie.

AUSTIN. Yes, go out to Sioux Falls, get a divorce there on respectable grounds, and settle a sum of money on Maggie.

GEOFFREY. But I can't do that!

AUSTIN. Why not?

GEOFFREY. I can't do anything that would give publicity, and that divorce would.

AUSTIN. Any divorce would; you can't get rid of that.

GEOFFREY. I tell you I can't have publicity. Ruth—Miss Chester—would hear of it.

AUSTIN. Well, if she loves you, she'll forgive your wild oats, especially as every one sees now what a steady, straight fellow you've become.

GEOFFREY. It's Ruth! But I can't do that. No, Jack, you must help—you will, won't you? Oh, *do,* for Jinny's sake! Help me to persuade Maggie to keep silent for good, tear up that certificate of marriage. I was only twenty; it's hardly legal, and I'll settle a good sum— [*Interrupted.*]

AUSTIN. [*Going straight to him, puts his hand heavily on his shoulder.*] Good God, you're proposing bigamy! You've done enough; don't stoop to *crime!*

[*The two* MEN *face each other a moment.* GEOFFREY'S *head drops.*]

AUSTIN. Forget you ever said that; do what I tell you when Jinny and I have gone abroad, so she will be away from it a little, and if you want money, let me know.

[JINNY *enters Right, with nervous gaiety, covering an upheaving emotion which is very near the surface.*]

JINNY. Ready! And there *you* are, Geof. I've been sending all over the house after you! Good-by! [*Throwing her arms about him.*] Dear old Geof! Haven't we had good times together! Always, always from the youngest days I can remember—I don't believe there were ever a brother and sister so sympathetic; I know there was never a brother such a perfect darling as you were—I'll miss you, Geof! [*The tears come into her voice, anyway.*] I used to think I'd never marry at all if I couldn't marry *you,* and I *do* think *he* is the only man in the world who could have taken me away from home, so long as you were there! [*To* AUSTIN, *smiling.*] You aren't jealous?

AUSTIN. No!

JINNY. [*In jest.*] Isn't it awful! You can't *make* him jealous! I think it's a positive flaw in his character! Not like —*us,* is he?

GEOFFREY. Dear old girl—

JINNY. [*Whispers to him.*] And I've noticed how you've overcome certain things, dear Geof. I know it's been *hard,* and I'm proud of you.

GEOFFREY. Sh! Jinny, dear old sister! I'll miss *you!* By George, Jin, the house'll be awful without—but you—[*His voice grows husky.*]—just excuse me a minute! [*He is about to break down, and so hurries out Right.*]

JINNY. [*Sniffling.*] He was going to cry! Oh, Jack, you'll be a brother to Geoffrey, won't you? You know he's been awfully dissipated, and he's changed it all, all by himself! *If he should go wrong again* —I believe it would break my heart, I love him so!

AUSTIN. I'll do *more* for him, if he ever needs me, than if he were *my own* brother, because he's *yours!*

JINNY. [*Presses his hand and looks up at him lovingly and gratefully.*] Thank you. Wait here just a minute; I know he won't come back to say good-by. He's gone up to his room, I'm sure—I'll just surprise him with a hug and my hands over his eyes like we used to do years ago. [*She starts to go out Right, and meets* MR. *and* MRS. TILLMAN, *who enter.*]

TILLMAN. The carriage is here!

JINNY. I won't be a second—[*She goes out Right.*]

MRS. TILLMAN. Where has she gone?

AUSTIN. Up to her brother.

MRS. TILLMAN. Her father's been locked up in his study for three hours—he *says* thinking, but to *me* his eyes look very suspicious! [*Taking her husband's arm affectionately.*]

TILLMAN. [*Clears his throat.*] Nonsense!

MRS. TILLMAN. Well, *how many cigars did you smoke?*

TILLMAN. Eight.

MRS. TILLMAN. The amount of emotion that a man can soak out of himself with tobacco is wonderful! He uses it just like a sponge!

TILLMAN. Jack, the first thing I asked about you when I heard that—er—that things were getting this way was, does he smoke? A man who smokes has always that outlet. If things go wrong—go out and smoke a cigar, and when the cigar's *finished,* ten to one everything's got right, somehow! If you lose your temper, don't speak!—a cigar, and when it's finished, then speak! You'll find the temper all gone up in the smoke! A woman's happiness is safest with a man who smokes. [*He clears his throat, which is filling.*] God bless you, Jack, it *is* a wrench; our only girl, you know. She's been a great joy—ahem! [*He quickly gets out a cigar.*]

MRS. TILLMAN. [*Stopping him from smoking.*] No, no, dear, they're *going now!*

TILLMAN. Well, the best I can say is, I wish you as happy a married life as her mother and I have had.

MRS. TILLMAN. Thirty-five *dear* years! But now, George, let me say a word—you always have monopolized our new son—he'll be much fonder of you than *me!*

TILLMAN. Old lady!—Jealous!—

MRS. TILLMAN. Turn about is fair play—you're jealous still of Jinny and me. [*She pauses a moment.*] I think we'd better tell him!

TILLMAN. All right. The only rifts in our lute, Jack, have been little threads of jealousy that have snapped sometimes!

MRS. TILLMAN. Nothing ever serious—of course, but it's a fault that Jinny shares with us, and the *only fault* we've ever been able to find.

TILLMAN. We called her for years the girl with the green eyes. She goes it pretty *strong* sometimes!

AUSTIN. Oh, that's all right—I shall *like* it!

MRS. TILLMAN. You'll always bear with her, won't you, if she should ever get jealous of you?

AUSTIN. Of *me?* I'll never give *her* the chance.

MRS. TILLMAN. It isn't a question of chance; you just can't help it sometimes, can you, George?

TILLMAN. No, you can't.

MRS. TILLMAN. And so—

AUSTIN. Don't worry! Your daughter's

safe with me. I'm not the jealous sort myself and I love Jinny so completely, so calmly, and yet with my heart, and soul, and mind, and body, she'll never have a *chance* even to *try* to be jealous of *me!*

TILLMAN. Sh!

[JINNY *enters Right.*]

JINNY. I found poor Maggie up in my room crying! She says she can't bear to have me go away. I think she's sorry now she wouldn't come with me as maid —and I said good-by to cook and she sniffed!

[AUSTIN *looks at his watch.*]

AUSTIN. Oh! we ought to go!

MRS. TILLMAN. Good-by, darling! [*Kissing* JINNY *and embracing her a long time, while* AUSTIN *and* TILLMAN *shake hands warmly and say good-by.*]

JINNY. [*Going to her father.*] Good-by, father. Dear old father! [*With happy emotion.*]

[AUSTIN *meanwhile is shaking hands with* MRS. TILLMAN.]

JINNY. [*Returns to her mother.*] Darling—oh, how good you've always been to me! Oh, mummy darling, I *shall* miss you! You'll send me a letter to-morrow, won't you, or a telegram? Send a telegram—you've got the address!

MRS. TILLMAN. [*With tears in her eyes.*] Yes, it's written down!

JINNY. You can tell father, but no one else! [*Hugs and kisses her mother.*]

TILLMAN. Come, Susan! They'll lose their train!

[JINNY *again embraces her father.*]

ALL. Good-by! Good-by!

[JINNY, *starting to go with* AUSTIN, *suddenly leaves him and runs back again to her mother and throws herself in her arms. They embrace, in tears.*]

JINNY. Good-by, mother!

MRS. TILLMAN. Good-by, my darling!

TILLMAN. Come, come! they'll lose their train!

[JINNY *runs to* AUSTIN, *and with his arms about her, they hurry to the door Left. The* TILLMANS *go through the doors at back to window in the corridor.* JINNY *stops at the door and she and* AUSTIN *face each other a moment.*]

JINNY. [*Looking up at him.*] Oh, Jack! [*She throws her arms about his neck and buries her face on his shoulder.*]

AUSTIN. Jinny, Jinny dear, you're not sorry?

JINNY. [*Slowly raises her head and looks at him, smiling through her tears, and speaks in a voice full of tears and little sobs.*] Sorry? Oh, no! Oh, no! It hurts me to leave them, but I never was so *happy* in my life! [*He kisses her and they hurry out, with his arm about her.*]

MRS. TILLMAN. [*In the corridor, lifts the window.*] I hear the door—

TILLMAN. There they are!

[SUSIE *rushes across the stage with a bowl of rice in her arms and goes out Left.* MR. *and* MRS. TILLMAN *wave and say* "Good-by!" "Good-by!" "Good-by!" *They close the window in silence. The sound is heard as the window frame reaches the bottom. They turn and come slowly forward,* TILLMAN *wiping his eyes and* MRS. TILLMAN *biting her lips to keep the tears back. They come into the front room and stop, and for a second they look around the empty room.* TILLMAN *puts his hand in his pocket and takes out his cigar case.* MRS. TILLMAN, *turning, sees him; she goes to him swiftly and touches his arm, looking up at him through her tears. He turns to her and slowly takes her in his arms and holds her there close and kisses her tenderly on the cheek.* SUSIE *enters Left, with empty bowl, sobbing aloud, as*

THE CURTAIN FALLS

ACT SECOND

(*Two months later*)

The Vatican, Rome; The Tribune of the Apollo Belvedere; a semicircular room with dark red walls; in the centre is the large statue of Apollo. There are doorways at Right and Left. There is a bench on the right side of the room. A single LADY TOURIST *enters Right, takes a hasty glance, yawns, and looking down at her Baedeker, goes out Left.* A PAPAL GUARD *is seen passing outside in the court.* A FRENCHMAN *and his* WIFE (*with Baedekers*) *are seen approaching; they are heard talking volubly. They enter Left.*

BOTH. Ah!—

[*They stand a moment in silent admiration.*]

HE. [*Reading from Baedeker.*] Apollo Belvedere. [*He looks up.*] *C'est superbe!*

SHE. [*Beaming with admiration.*] *Magnifique! Voilà un homme!*

HE. *Quelle grace!*

SHE. *Quelle force!*

[*Both talk at once in great admiration and intense excitement for a few moments. Then he suddenly drops into his ordinary tone and manner.*]

HE. *Allons, allons nous!*

SHE. [*In the same tone.*] *Oui, j'ai faim!*

[*They go out Right.*]

[JINNY *and* AUSTIN *enter Left, he looking over his shoulder. They stand a moment just inside the doorway.*]

JINNY. What are you looking back so much for, Jackie?

AUSTIN. I thought I saw some one I know.

JINNY. Who?

AUSTIN. I didn't know who; it just seemed to be a familiar back.

JINNY. [*Playfully.*] Oh, come! I think the present works of art and your loving wife are quite enough for you to look at without hunting around for familiar backs!

AUSTIN. And Baedeker! [*Reading from Baedeker about the Apollo.*] Apollo Belvedere, found at the end of the fifteenth century, probably in a Roman villa—

JINNY. Of course, Apollo!

AUSTIN. Great, isn't it?

JINNY. Stunning! [*She turns and looks at him, smiling quizzically.*] *Still*—but I suppose I'm prejudiced!

AUSTIN. [*Obtuse.*] Still what?

JINNY. You dear old stupid! You know, Jack, you're deeply and *fundamentally* clever and brilliant, but you're not quite —*bright*—*not quick!* [*Laughing.*]

AUSTIN. Don't you think having *one* in the family quick as chain lightning is enough? What have I missed this time, Jinny? You don't mean you've found a family likeness in the statue over there? I don't want to be unappreciative, but it doesn't suggest your father to me in the least,—nor even Geoffrey.

JINNY. *Stupid!!* Of course it doesn't *suggest* anybody to me—I was only thinking I sympathized with Mrs. Perkins of Boston,—don't you know the old story about her?

AUSTIN. No, what was it?

JINNY. [*After a quick look around to see that they are alone.*] Well—Mrs. Perkins from Boston was personally conducted here once and shown this very statue, and she looked at it for a few moments, and then turned around and said, "Yes, it's all right, but give *me Perkins!*"

AUSTIN. Jinny! [*Laughing.*]

JINNY. Are you shocked? Come, I'm tired; let's sit down here and read my letters—there's one from Geof.

[*They sit on the bench at Right, and* JINNY *takes out a letter from* GEOFFREY.]

AUSTIN. I'll read ahead in Baedeker and you tell me if there's any news. [*He opens the Baedeker and reads, and she opens and reads the letter.*] Where is Geof's letter from?

JINNY. New York, of course; where else would it be?

AUSTIN. I had an idea he was going away.

JINNY. Geof! Where?

AUSTIN. West, a good way somewhere.

JINNY. But *why* would he go West?

AUSTIN. Oh, he had some business, I believe; I remember thinking it was a good idea when he told me. It was the day we were married—I was waiting for you to come downstairs.

JINNY. I think it's very funny Geof never said anything about it to *me.*

AUSTIN. My dear, what time had *you?* You were *getting married!!*

JINNY. I *was!* Thank heaven! I'm *so happy,* Jack! [*Snuggling up to him on the bench.*]

AUSTIN. [*Steals a little, quick hug with his arm about her waist.*] Bless you, darling, I don't think there was ever a man as happy as I am!

[*They start apart quickly as a* GERMAN COUPLE *enter Right, with a* YOUNG DAUGHTER, *who is munching a cake, and hanging, a tired and unwilling victim, to her mother's hand.*]

WOMAN. *Ach! schön! sehr schön!!*

MAN. *Grösses, nicht?*

WOMAN. *Yah!*

[*They stand admiring.*]

AUSTIN. By the way, when you answer your brother's letter, I wish you'd say I seemed surprised he was still in New York.

JINNY. [*Reading.*] Um—um—

MAN. [*Wiping his warm brow.*] *Wunderbau!*

WOMAN. *Yah!!*

[*They go out Left, talking.*]

JINNY. [*Looking up from her letter.*] Oh! what do you think?

AUSTIN. That you're the sweetest woman in the world.

JINNY. No, *darling,* I mean *who* do you think Geoffrey says is over here and in Italy?

AUSTIN. I haven't the most remote idea! So far as *I've* been able to observe there has been absolutely *no one* in Italy but *you and me.*

JINNY. If you keep on talking like that, I shall kiss you!

AUSTIN. What! before the tall, white gentleman? [*Motioning to Apollo.*] I am dumb.

JINNY. [*Very lovingly.*] Silly! Well! —Mrs. Cullingham and Peter are over here and have brought Ruth Chester!

AUSTIN. [*Speaking without thinking.*] Then it *was* her back.

JINNY. [*With the smallest sharpening of the look in her eye.*] When?

AUSTIN. That I saw just now.

JINNY. [*With the tiniest suggestion of a strain in her voice.*] You said you didn't know whom it reminded you of.

AUSTIN. Yes, I know, I didn't quite.

JINNY. But if you thought it was Ruth Chester, why not have said so?

AUSTIN. No reason, dear, I simply didn't think.

JINNY. Well—[*Sententiously.*]—*next time —think!*

AUSTIN. What else does Geoffrey say?

JINNY. Oh, nothing. The heat for two days was frightful—already they miss me more than he can say—[*Interrupted.*]

AUSTIN. I'll bet.

JINNY. Father smoked nineteen cigars a day the first week I was gone.

AUSTIN. *I* haven't *had* to smoke *any!*

JINNY. Mercy! don't boast!—and he thinks they will all soon go to Long Island for the summer.

AUSTIN. Doesn't he say a word nor a hint at his going West?

JINNY. No, he says he may go to Newport for August, and that's all. [*Putting away letter, and getting out others.*]

AUSTIN. Going to read all those?

JINNY. If you don't mind, while I rest. *Do* you mind?

AUSTIN. Of course not, but I think while you're reading I'll just take a little turn and see if I can't come across the Cullinghams. [*Rising.*]

JINNY. [*After the merest second's pause, and looking seriously at him.*] Why don't you?

AUSTIN. I'll bring them here if I find them—[*He goes out Right.*]

[JINNY *looks up where he went off and gazes, motionless, for a few moments. Then she throws off the mood and opens a letter. Two tired Americans enter Right, a girl and her mother,* MRS. LOPP *and* CARRIE.]

MRS. LOPP. What's this, Carrie?

CARRIE. [*Looking in her Baedeker.*] I don't know; I've sort of lost my place, somehow!

MRS. LOPP. Well, we must be in Room No. 3 or 4—ain't we?

CARRIE. [*Reads out.*] The big statue at the end of Room No. 3 is Diana the Huntress.

MRS. LOPP. This must be it, then,—Diana! Strong-looking woman, ain't she?

CARRIE. Yes, very nice. You know she was the goddess who wouldn't let the men see her bathe.

MRS. LOPP. Mercy, Carrie! and did all the other goddesses? I don't think much of their habits. I suppose this is the same person those Italians sell on the streets at home, and call the Bather.

[JINNY *is secretly very much amused, finally she speaks.*]

JINNY. Excuse me, but you are in one of the cabinets—and this is the Apollo Belvedere.

MRS. LOPP. Oh, thank you very much. I guess we've got mixed up with the rooms, —seems as if there's so many.

CARRIE. [*Triumphantly.*] There! I *thought* it was a man all the time!

MRS. LOPP. Well, what with so many of the statues only being piecemeal, as it were, and so many of the men having kinder women's hair, I declare it seems as if I don't know the ladies from the gentlemen half the time.

CARRIE. Did the rest of us go through here?

JINNY. I beg your pardon?

CARRIE. Thirty-four people with a gassy guide? We got so tired hearing him talk that we jes' sneaked off by ourselves, and now we're a little scared about getting home; we belong to the Cook's Gentlemen and Ladies.

JINNY. Oh, no, the others haven't passed through here; probably they have gone to see the pictures; you'd better go back and keep asking the attendants the way to the pictures till you get there.

MRS. LOPP. [*With rather subdued voice.*] Thank you! We've come to do Europe and the Holy Land in five weeks for $400—but I don't know, seems as if I'm getting awful tired—after jes' seven days.

CARRIE. [*Affectionately.*] Now, mommer, don't give up; it's because you haven't got over being seasick yet; that's all!

JINNY. [*Helplessly.*] Oh, yes, you'll find it much less tiring in a few days, I'm sure.

MRS. LOPP. Still Rome does seem a powerful way from *home!* How'll we ask for the pictures?

CARRIE. Why, mommer! "Tableaux!" "Tableaux!" I should think you'd 'a' learned that from our church entertainments! Good-by; thank you ever so much.

MRS. LOPP. You haven't lost *your party,* too, have you?

JINNY. [*Smiling.*] I hope not! He *promised* to come back!!

MRS. LOPP. Oh! pleased to have met you—Good-by!

[*They start off Left.*]

JINNY. No, not that way—back the way you came.

MRS. LOPP. Oh, thank you! [*She drops her black silk bag; out of it drop crackers, an account book, a thimble, a thread-and-needle case, a bottle of pepsin tablets, etc. They all stoop to pick the collection up.* JINNY *helping.*]

JINNY. [*Handing.*] I'm sure you'll want these!

MRS. LOPP. Yes, indeed; don't you find them coupon meals very dissatisfactory?

CARRIE. Thank you ever so much again. Come on, mommer!

[MRS. LOPP *and* CARRIE *go out Left.* JINNY *looks at her watch and goes back to her letter.*

[MRS. CULLINGHAM *enters Left.*]

MRS. CULLINGHAM. [*Screams.*] Jinny!

JINNY. [*Jumps up.*] Mrs. Cullingham! [*They embrace.*] Did Jack find you?

MRS. CULLINGHAM. No, we haven't seen him! Ruth and Peter are dawdling along, each on their own; I like to shoot through a gallery. There's no use spending so much time; when it's over you've mixed everything all up just the same!

JINNY. [*Laughing.*] Well, I've this minute read a letter from Geoffrey saying you were over here. And Jack, who thought he got a glimpse of you a little while ago, went straight off to try and find you.

MRS. CULLINGHAM. What fun it is to see you—and how *happy* you look!

JINNY. I couldn't *look* as happy as I *feel!*

MRS. CULLINGHAM. [*Glancing at the statue.*] Who's your friend? Nice gent, isn't he? [*Laughing.*]

JINNY. Mr. Apollo! Would you like to meet him?

MRS. CULLINGHAM. [*Hesitates.*] Er—no—I don't think! You must draw the line somewhere! He wouldn't do a thing to Corbett, would he?

JINNY. Who was Corbett?

MRS. CULLINGHAM. He was a prize fighter, and *is*—but that's another story— Do you mean to say you've never heard of him?

JINNY. Oh, the name sounds familiar. But this, you know, is Apollo.

MRS. CULLINGHAM. No, I don't know; was he a champion?

JINNY. No, he was a Greek god!

MRS. CULLINGHAM. Oh, was he? Well, I wouldn't have cared about being in the tailoring business in those days, would you? Let's sit down. [*They sit on bench Right.*] Of course you know we wouldn't accept a thing like that in Peoria, where I come from, as a gift! No, indeed! If the King of Italy sent it over to our Mayor, he'd return it C.O.D.

JINNY. Sounds like Boston and the Macmonnies Bacchante!

MRS. CULLINGHAM. Oh, my dear, *worse* than that! It reminds me of a man at home who kept an underclothing store in our principal street and had a plaster cast of this gent's brother, I should think, in his window to show a suit of Jaegers on,—you know, a "combination"! And our Town Committee of Thirteen for the moral improvement of Peoria made the man take it out of his window and hang the suit up empty!

JINNY. Poor man!

MRS. CULLINGHAM. You ought to see our Park!—you know we've got a perfectly beautiful park,—and all the *men* statues wear Prince Alberts, and stand like this—[*She poses with lifted arm at right angle to body.*]—as if they were saying, "This way out" or "To the monkey cage and zoo."

JINNY. [*Laughing.*] But the women statues?

MRS. CULLINGHAM. My dear! They only have heads and hands; all the rest's just clumps of drapery—we only have "Americans" and "Libertys," anyway. They apply the Chinese emigration law to all Venuses and *sich ladies!*

[*They both laugh.*]

JINNY. Where did you say Peter and Ruth were?

MRS. CULLINGHAM. Well, I left Peter—who isn't at all well; I hoped this trip would help his indigestion, but it seems to have made it worse!—I left him—er—in a room with a lot of *broken-up Venuses*—I thought it was all right; he was eating candy, and there wasn't a whole woman among 'em!

JINNY. [*Slight strain in her voice.*] How did you happen to bring over Ruth Chester?

MRS. CULLINGHAM. Well, you know I always liked her. She never snubbed me in her life—I don't think any one you've introduced me to has been quite so nice to Peter and me as Mrs. Chester and her daughter.

JINNY. O they *are* real people!

MRS. CULLINGHAM. Ruth is terribly depressed over something. She's thin as a rail and the family are worried. She says there's nothing worrying her, and the doctors can't find anything the matter with her,—so Mrs. Chester asked me if I wouldn't take her abroad. They thought the voyage and change might do her good, and I seem to have a more cheery influence over her than most people. So here we are! [*As* PETER *enters Left, eating.*] Here's Peter! How do you think the darling looks?

PETER. How do you do, Mrs. Austin?

JINNY. How do you do, Peter? [*They shake hands.*] I'm sorry to hear you are seedy, but you eat too many sweet things.

PETER. I'm not eating candy; it's soda mints! [*Showing a small bottle.*] I *am* bad to-day, mother.

MRS. CULLINGHAM. If you don't get better, we'll go to Carlsbad.

JINNY. How do you like Rome, Peter?

PETER. Oh, I don't know—too much Boston and not enough Chicago to make it a real lively town.

JINNY. [*Laughing.*] I think I'll go look for Jack and tell him you've turned up.

MRS. CULLINGHAM. Perhaps he's found Ruth.

JINNY. [*With a change in her voice.*] Yes, perhaps. [*She goes out Right.*]

PETER. [*Going to the doorway Right, calls after her.*] Ruth's in a room on your left, with rows of men's heads on shelves, Emperors and things,—but gee, such a *job lot!* [*Comes back and looks up at the statue.*]

MRS. CULLINGHAM. Isn't it beautiful, Peter?

PETER. No, it's *too big!*

MRS. CULLINGHAM. Still this one isn't broken!

PETER. That's a comfort! Yes, it has been mended, too! [*Examining.*] Oh, yes, it's only another of these second-hand statues. Say, you missed one whole one, the best I've seen yet! A Venus off in a fine little room, all mosaics and painted walls,—that's where I've been.

MRS. CULLINGHAM. Why, Peter Cullingham! *Alone?* What kind of a Venus?

PETER. Oh, beautiful! I forgot to take my medicine!

MRS. CULLINGHAM. Was she—er—*dressed,* darling?

PETER. We—you know—she *had* been, but she'd sort of pushed it a good way off!

MRS. CULLINGHAM. [*With a sigh.*] You know we *ought* to admire these things, Peter darling; that's partly what we've come to Europe for!

PETER. Oh pshaw! here comes a gang of tourists. Come on, let's skip!

MRS. CULLINGHAM. But Ruth and Mrs. Austin?

PETER. We didn't agree to wait, and we can all meet at our hotel.

[*A crowd of* TOURISTS, *let by a* GUIDE, *presses and crowds in the doorway. They drag their tired feet in a listless shuffle across the room and stand in a somewhat sheepish and stupid bunch at the statue. One or two of the younger women nudge each other and giggle. The* GUIDE *stands a little in advance of them. The* GUIDE *describes the statue, and while he is doing so* PETER *and* MRS. CULLINGHAM *go out Right. Most of the* TOURISTS *turn and watch them go instead of looking at the statue.*]

GUIDE. This is the Apollo Belvedere, discovered at the end of the fifteenth century, some say in a Roman villa or farmhouse near the Grotter Terratter. Very fine specimen both as marble and man. This statyer is calculated to make Sandow et cetery look like thirty cents. Height seven feet, weight—

A MAN TOURIST. How much?

A GIRL TOURIST. Was he married?

[*Titters from the group.*]

GUIDE. Give it up! Should judge he was. The god once held a bow in his left hand

and probably a laurel wreath in his right.

ANOTHER WOMAN TOURIST. A what?

GUIDE. A laurel wreath. You want to take a good look at this, as it is a very fine piece. Now come along, please—make haste; we must finish up this place before feeding! [*He leads the way out Right, and the* TOURISTS *follow, shuffling along, without speaking,* MRS. LOPP *and* CARRIE *lagging in the rear.*]

[AUSTIN *enters Left, followed by* RUTH.]

AUSTIN. This is where I left her with Apollo! [*Calls.*] Jinny! She seems to have gone! [*He looks behind the statue and out door, Right.*]

RUTH. Probably the Cullinghams, who were headed in this direction, found her, and they've all gone back for us; you see I walked all around the court first without going into the rooms, so I missed them, but found you.

AUSTIN. What shall we do? Sit down here and wait for them to come back, or shall I go in search?

RUTH. Oh, no, you might miss them, and then we'd all be lost! If you left Jinny here, she's sure to come back to meet you. [*She sits on the bench and* AUSTIN *stands behind her.*]

AUSTIN. I'm sorry to learn you've been ill.

RUTH. Oh! it's nothing.

AUSTIN. Ah, I'm afraid it's a good deal. Will you forgive me if I say I think I know what it is! [*She looks up startled. After a moment.*] You haven't forgotten the day of Jinny's and my wedding, when you told me Geoffrey Tillman needed a friend?

RUTH. I hoped *you'd* forgotten; I oughtn't to have told you; I *oughtn't* to have!

AUSTIN. Why not? I had a talk with Geoffrey, then, and he told me everything.

RUTH. He did! You are sure?

AUSTIN. Sure. [*He sits beside her.*]

RUTH. That he and I—

AUSTIN. Love each other.

RUTH. Oh, but that isn't all.

AUSTIN. I know the rest!

RUTH. He told you—about—about—

AUSTIN. The marriage?—Yes.

RUTH. Oh, I'm so glad, so glad! Now I can speak of it to some one, and some one who can advise me, and will help us.

AUSTIN. I have already advised him, but he doesn't seem to be taking my advice; it has worried me.

RUTH. When I left he was awfully depressed. He said he saw no prospect of being able to publish our marriage for years, maybe!

AUSTIN. *What* marriage? [*In astonishment.*]

RUTH. *Our* marriage, in Brooklyn! [*She notices his expression and is alarmed.*] You said he had told you!

AUSTIN. [*Recovering himself, and speaking at first with hesitation.*] Yes, but not the details, not—wait, I'm a little confused. [*Rising and walking a moment.*] Let's get it all quite clear now, that's the only way I can help you—both; I ought, of course, to have gone through it all with him, but there really wasn't time.

RUTH. I can't go on like this much longer. It's killing me to deceive mother; I *must* tell her soon!

AUSTIN. [*Quickly, stops walking.*] No. You mustn't, not yet, if I'm going to help you; you'll obey me, won't you?

RUTH. Yes, if you only will help us!

AUSTIN. You said you and Geoffrey Tillman were married where?

RUTH. In Brooklyn.

AUSTIN. When?

RUTH. A month before your wedding.

AUSTIN. [*To himself.*] It's impossible! [*Walking up and down.*]

RUTH. [*Smiling sadly.*] Oh, no! I remember the date only too well.

AUSTIN. I didn't mean that.

RUTH. I lied to my mother that day for the first time—at any rate, since I was a child—and I've been lying to her ever since.

AUSTIN. [*Probing her.*] But—but why were you married so secretly?

RUTH. We couldn't afford to marry and set up for ourselves. He expected then to be sent off at once to the Philippines, and—well, he didn't want to leave me behind, free; I'm afraid he's rather jealous—you must have found out by now that Jinny is. They all are! And *I* didn't want him to go so far off without my belonging to him either; *I'm* that jealous, too! [*Smiling.*] So—that's why!

AUSTIN. And this long period of secrecy since then—do you understand that?

RUTH. Hasn't he explained to you his debts? You know before he loved me he was very fast, but since—

AUSTIN. Yes, I know how he gave up every one of his old habits with a great deal of courage.

RUTH. *Nobody* knows what it cost him! How can you help us? Get him something to do to pay off his debts? Or can't you make him feel even if we do have to go on living at our different homes for a while, it is better to publish the the fact that we are married?—

AUSTIN. I shall go back at once to America if I can persuade Jinny!

RUTH. And I, too?

AUSTIN. No. You must stay abroad till I send word for you to come home. If I am going to help you, you will help me by doing exactly as I say, won't you?

RUTH. Yes.

AUSTIN. It's *very* important that you should *absolutely obey me!*

RUTH. *I will.*

[*A pause.*]

[JINNY, *unnoticed by either of them, appears in the doorway at Right.* AUSTIN *is walking up and down.* RUTH *is leaning her elbow on the back of the bench and burying her face in her hands.*]

AUSTIN. It's awful! My God, it's awful!

JINNY. [*In a strained, assumed nonchalant tone.*] *What is?*

RUTH. Jinny! [*Rising.*]

AUSTIN. I didn't hear you, Jinny!

JINNY. No, you both seemed so absorbed.

RUTH. [*Going to* JINNY.] I'm so glad to see you. [*Kisses her, but* JINNY *only gives her her cheek and that rather unwillingly; she is looking all the time at her husband.*]

JINNY. Thank you, I've just left the Cullinghams. They sent word to you they were going and would wait for you outside.

RUTH. Oh, then, I mustn't keep them waiting. We'll all meet at dinner to-night, won't we? Good-by—good-by. [*With a grateful look at* AUSTIN, *she goes out Right.*]

JINNY. [*Watches her go; then turns to* AUSTIN.] That wasn't true, what I told her—I haven't seen the Cullinghams, and I don't know where they are, and what's more, I don't care!

AUSTIN. What do you mean?

JINNY. [*Beginning by degrees to lose control of herself.*] What did *she* mean by *following you* to Rome?

AUSTIN. Jinny!

JINNY. Oh, don't try to deny it; that'll only make me suspect *you!*

AUSTIN. My dear girl, you don't know what you're saying!

JINNY. She's ill, they say at home! Yes, and they don't know what's the matter with her, do they? No! But I can tell them! She's in love with another woman's husband!

AUSTIN. [*Taking her hand.*] Hush! I won't allow you to say such things!

JINNY. [*With a disagreeable little laugh.*] Oh, won't you? *You'd* better be careful, —my eyes are opened!

AUSTIN. Yes, and much too wide.

JINNY. A half-blind person would have known there was something between you two. When I came into this room just now, it was in the air—it was in both your faces! [*She sits on the bench.*]

AUSTIN. You've worked yourself up to such a pitch you're not responsible for what you're saying!

JINNY. *I* not *responsible!* What was it you were saying was *so* "awful" when I came in here? "My God, so awful!" [*He doesn't answer.*]

[*Almost hysterical, she rises.*]

She had told you she loved you! She'd confessed she'd followed you over here!

AUSTIN. Absolutely false, *both* your suppositions!

JINNY. Oh, of course you'd protect her; you're a gentleman! But if *I thought* you *knew* she was coming over—

AUSTIN. Jinny! Jinny! How *can* you have such a thought?

JINNY. Well, why didn't you tell me when you thought you saw her a little while ago?

AUSTIN. Oh—

JINNY. Oh, it's very easy to say "Oh!" [*Imitating him.*] but *why didn't you?*

AUSTIN. I told you I didn't think who it was; I only thought something familiar flashed across my eyes. Jinny darling, this is sheer madness on your part, letting yourself go like this. It has no reason, it has no excuse! Ask your own heart, and your own mind, if in speaking to *me* as you have, you haven't done me at least an injustice and my love for you a *little* wrong.

JINNY. Well, I'm sure *she's* in love with you, anyway.

AUSTIN. No, she isn't! And it's disgraceful of you to say so! I know she isn't—

JINNY. How do you know she isn't?

AUSTIN. There's no question of it. I'm sure of it! You mustn't think, dear, that because *you* love me, everybody does—you idealize me! [*Smiling apologetically.*]

JINNY. Oh, you're so modest you don't see! But I do—on the steamer, in the hotels, everywhere we go, always, all the women admire you awfully! I see it!

AUSTIN. [*Laughing.*] What utter nonsense! [*Taking her into his arms.*] You've got something in your *eyes!*

JINNY. Only tears!

AUSTIN. No, something else,—something *green.*

JINNY. [*Laughs through her tears.*] Somebody's told you my old nickname!

AUSTIN. What?

JINNY. [*Laughs and is a little embarrassed.*] The girl with the green eyes.

AUSTIN. Ahem!—

JINNY. Well, I don't care if it is appropriate, I can't help it. [*Slipping from his arms.*]

AUSTIN. You must—or it will threaten our happiness if you let yourself be carried away by jealousy for no earthly reason outside of your dear, little imagination, as you have this time— [*Interrupted.*]

JINNY. You honestly don't think she cares for you?

AUSTIN. Not a bit!

JINNY. But what was it you were so serious about—what *is* between you?

AUSTIN. She is in a little trouble, and I happen to know about it.

JINNY. How?

AUSTIN. [*After a second's hesitation.*] That you mustn't ask me; it was not from her I knew of it.

JINNY. Truly?

AUSTIN. Truly.

JINNY. I don't care, she hadn't any business to go to you! I should think she'd have gone to a *woman* instead of a *man* for sympathy. She's got Mrs. Cullingham!

AUSTIN. She can't go to her, poor girl. Mrs. Cullingham knows nothing about it.

JINNY. Now don't you get too sympathetic *—that's very dangerous!*

AUSTIN. Look out, your imagination is peeping through the keyhole.

[*A moment's pause.*

JINNY. [*In a sympathetic tone, the jealousy gone.*] What is her trouble, Jack?

AUSTIN. That, dear, I can't tell you now; some day, perhaps, if you want me to, but not now. Only I give you my word of honor, it has nothing to do with you and me—does not touch our life! And I want you to tell me you believe me, and *trust* me, and won't let yourself be jealous again!

JINNY. I do believe you, and I do trust you, and I will *try* not to be jealous again!

AUSTIN. That's right.

JINNY. You know that book of De Maupassant's [*They move away together.*] I was reading in the train the other day, —about the young girl who killed herself with charcoal fumes when her lover deserted her?

AUSTIN. [*Half laughing.*] This is apropos of what, please? I have absolutely *no* sympathy with such people.

JINNY. In America that girl would have simply turned on the gas.

AUSTIN. You're getting morbid, Jinny!

JINNY. No, I'm not! but if ever—

AUSTIN. [*Interrupting—laughing it off.*] I shall install *electric light* as soon as we get home!

[*They both laugh.*]

JINNY. I'm sorry I was so disagreeable to Ruth, but I'll try to make up for it in every way I can. [*She sits on the bench and he leans over the back toward her.*]

AUSTIN. There's one other thing, Jinny, I'd like to speak of now. Would you mind giving up the Lakes and going home this week?

JINNY. Going *home*—at once?

AUSTIN. Yes—*Wall Street* is very uncertain. I'm worried,—I don't mind telling you,—and I want to see Geoffrey about his business.

JINNY. [*Half in earnest.*] Jack! You're not running away from *her,* are you?

AUSTIN. Jinny! *After all* we've said!

JINNY. No! I wasn't in earnest! I'm ready to go. I've seen the Lakes, and whether you are in Italy or in New York, so long as we are together, it's our honeymoon just the same.

AUSTIN. And may it last *all our lives!*

JINNY. Still, I don't mind owning up that leaving Ruth Chester behind here is rather pleasanter! [*She rises quickly with a sudden thought.*] *She* is not going back, too?

AUSTIN. Oh, no, not for a long time. They are over here indefinitely.

JINNY. I've been too horrid and nasty for words this morning, Jack—I'm so sorry.

AUSTIN. It's over and forgotten now.

JINNY. You *do* forgive me?

AUSTIN. Of course, dear; only I want to say this one thing to you: to suspect unjustly a *true* love is to insult that love!

JINNY. I didn't really suspect you.

AUSTIN. Of course I know you didn't! This is only by way of a grandfatherly warning! It is possible to insult a true love too often—and love can die—

JINNY. Sh! don't, please, say any more. You have forgiven me, haven't you?

AUSTIN. Yes!

JINNY. Then kiss me!

AUSTIN. [*Smiling.*] Here! My dear, some one will see us!

JINNY. No, only Apollo; see, there's no one else about—it's luncheon hour!

AUSTIN. But— [*Taking her hand.*]

JINNY. [*Pulling him.*] Come along, then, behind the statue. No one will see us there!

[*They are behind the statue a moment and then come around the other side.*]

JINNY. There! no one saw us, and I'm so *happy,* are you?

AUSTIN. *"So happy!"*

[JINNY *takes his arm and they go to the Left entrance. She stops and looks up at him.*]

JINNY. Are my eyes *green* now?

AUSTIN. Now they're *blue!*

JINNY. Hurrah! and I'm going, from now on, to be *so good,* you won't know me.

[*And hugging his arm tight they go out as—*]

THE CURTAIN FALLS

ACT THIRD

(*Three weeks later*)

The Austins' library; a warm, attractive room, with dark woodwork, and the walls hung in crimson brocade; Dutch marqueterie furniture; blue and white china on the mantel and tops of the book shelves; carbon photographs of pictures by Reynolds, Romney, and Gainsborough on the wall. There is a double window at the back. A door at Right leads to the hall, and another on the Left side of the room leads to JINNY'S *own room.* MRS. TILLMAN *sits at a pianola Right, playing "Tell me, Pretty Maiden"; she stops once in a while, showing that she is unaccustomed to the instrument.* JINNY *enters from Left, singing as her mother plays.*

JINNY. Darling mother! [*She puts her arms about her and kisses her.*]

[*They come away from the pianola together, to a big armchair.*]

MRS. TILLMAN. I really must get one of those sewing-machine pianos for your father. I believe even he could play it, and it would be lots of amusement for us.

JINNY. Jack adores it; I gave it to him for an anniversary present.

MRS. TILLMAN. What anniversary? [*Sitting in the chair.*]

JINNY. Day before yesterday. The eleventh Tuesday since our marriage. Have you been in town all day? I *am* glad to see you! [*She sits on the arm of the chair with her arm about her mother.*]

MRS. TILLMAN. Yes, and I told your father to meet me here and we'd take the six-thirty train from Long Island City.

JINNY. Jack and I are going to the theatre to-night.

MRS. TILLMAN. I thought they were all closed!

JINNY. Oh, no, there are several musical comedies on,—Jack's favorite form of amusement,—and I've bought the tickets myself for a sort of birthday party.

MRS. TILLMAN. Is it his birthday?

JINNY. No, that's only my excuse!

MRS. TILLMAN. [*Laughing.*] Had we dreamed you and Jack were coming home in June, your father and I wouldn't have gone into the country so early.

JINNY. We've been home two weeks and it hasn't been hot yet.

MRS. TILLMAN. And you're still ideally happy aren't you, darling?

JINNY. Yes— [*She rises and goes to a table near the centre of the room and looks at the titles of several books without realizing what they are.*]

MRS. TILLMAN. Why, Jinny,—what does that mean?

JINNY. Oh, it's all my horrid disposition!

MRS. TILLMAN. Been seeing green?

JINNY. Um! Um! Once in Rome, and on the steamer, and again since we've been back.

MRS. TILLMAN. Nothing serious?

JINNY. [*Hesitatingly, she turns and faces her mother.*] No—but the last time Jack was harder to bring around than before, and he looked at me for fully five minutes without a particle of love in his eyes, and they were almost—*dead* eyes!

MRS. TILLMAN. What was it all about?

JINNY. Ruth Chester, principally.

MRS. TILLMAN. Why Ruth?

JINNY. Well, the first real scene I made was in Rome in the Vatican. I was jealous of her; I can't explain it all to you—as a matter of fact, it hasn't been all explained to *me!* Something was troubling Ruth that Jack knew, and he said he'd help her.

MRS. TILLMAN. What?

JINNY. That's just it; Jack won't tell me. And the day we sailed from Naples a telegram came, and of course I opened it, and it said, "Trust me, I will do everything you say. Ruth."

MRS. TILLMAN. Why haven't you told me anything of all this before, dear?

JINNY. [*Going back to her mother.*] I was ashamed to! Somehow, in the end I always knew I was wrong and had hurt him—hurt him terribly, mother, the man I love better than everything else in the world! Yes, even better than you and father and Geoffrey—all together! [*In her mother's arms, crying a little.*]

MRS. TILLMAN. Oh, this curse of jealousy! I was in hopes he was so strong he would help you to overcome it.

JINNY. He does try hard, I can see sometimes; but he hasn't a spark of it in him, and he can't understand it, and I know I'm unreasonable, and before I know it I am saying things I don't know what, and some day he won't forgive them! I'm sure some day he won't!— [*Breaking down again. She rises and turns away.*]

MRS. TILLMAN. [*Rising and putting her arms about her.*] Come, dear! Now you're getting yourself all unstrung, and that won't do you any good; you've got to fight this battle out, I'm afraid, by yourself, trusting in the deep love of your husband to teach him forbearance. Your father's and my troubles were never very big because we *shared* the curse, so we knew how to sympathize with each other!

JINNY. What an awful thing it is!

MRS. TILLMAN. Yes, my dear child. Jealousy has no saving grace, and it only destroys what is always most precious to you. Jinny, don't let it destroy *your best* happiness!

JINNY. Mother, if it *should,* I'd kill myself!

MRS. TILLMAN. [*Shocked, but quite disbelieving her.*] My dear!

[MAGGIE *enters Right.*]

MAGGIE. Mr. Tillman is downstairs, madam.

MRS. TILLMAN. Tell him to come up.

MAGGIE. Yes, madam. [*She goes out Right.*]

JINNY. Don't tell father anything before me.

MRS. TILLMAN. I don't know that I shall tell him at all; he would only advise more cigars!

[TILLMAN *enters Right.* MRS. TILLMAN *sits on the sofa at Left.*]

TILLMAN. Are you here?

JINNY. [*Going to meet him.*] We are, father dear, and your presence *almost* completes us. [*Kisses him.*] I say *almost,* because Jack hasn't come up town yet, and Geoffrey's heartless enough to stay on fishing at Cape Cod!

TILLMAN. No, he isn't; he's back to-day. [*He sits in the armchair at Right.*]

JINNY. Oh, I do want to see him! [*Sitting near her father.*]

TILLMAN. He ought to have been in by now—I met him this morning. He was to lunch with Jack, and he's going to put up for a few days at the University.

JINNY. He must dine with us every night.

TILLMAN. Jinny!—[*Looking at her.*]—You look as if you've been crying!

[*The two* WOMEN *are embarrassed, and* JINNY *doesn't reply.*]

TILLMAN. [*Hurt.*] Oh, if you prefer to have secrets from your father, it's all right! *I don't begrudge* your mother her *first place* in your affections!

JINNY. Not at all, father; with you and mother there's no first place. She will tell you all about it on the way home! Please, mother.

MRS. TILLMAN. Very well, dear.

TILLMAN. A little "scrap" between you and Jack?

JINNY. Yes, but it's all over!

TILLMAN. Um!— [*Thinks a second, then taking out his cigar case, he empties it of cigars and hands them to* JINNY.] Give your husband these, please, when he comes in!

[JINNY *and her* MOTHER *exchange a smile.*]

JINNY. But, father, Jack's got boxes full—

TILLMAN. Never mind; give him those *from me, with my compliments!*

JINNY. [*Laughing.*] Very well!

TILLMAN. How are you and Maggie getting on?

JINNY. Splendidly.

MRS. TILLMAN. Such a nice girl!

JINNY. And wasn't it odd Jack was bitterly opposed to my taking her?

MRS. TILLMAN. My dear, if we hadn't lent her to you for these few weeks, you wouldn't have got anybody decent for so short a time.

TILLMAN. Why didn't Jack want her to come?

JINNY. I don't know, he just didn't want her; and then last week he talked with her in the library for three-quarters of an hour by my watch.

MRS. TILLMAN. Why?

JINNY. Oh, it seems *she* has troubles, too! All single young women with troubles, of no matter what class, seem to make a bee line for my husband, even if they have to cross the ocean!

TILLMAN. What do you mean?

JINNY. [*Half laughing.*] Oh, nothing, but it was about that talk with Maggie that we had our last quarrel.

[MAGGIE *enters Right.*]

MAGGIE. Mrs. Cullingham.

[*A second's dead silence, the announcement falling like a bombshell.*]

JINNY. [*Astounded.*] Who? [*She rises.*]

TILLMAN AND MRS. TILLMAN. *Who?*

MAGGIE. Mrs. Cullingham and her son, madam.

JINNY. They're in Europe.

MRS. TILLMAN. Are you sure you're not mistaken, Maggie?

MAGGIE. Oh, yes'm. Even if you *could* mistake Mrs. Cullingham, you couldn't mistake Mr. Peter!

JINNY. Ask them to please come up, Maggie.

MAGGIE. Yes'm. [*She goes out Right.*]

TILLMAN. Why, they only just sailed the other day, didn't they?

MRS. TILLMAN. Yes, and they were supposed to be gone all summer at least, for Ruth Chester's health! What in the world can they have come back for?

JINNY. [*With curious determination.*] *That* is what *I* intend to find out.

TILLMAN. [*Rising.*] We must be going, Susan; we've lost our train as it is.

MRS. TILLMAN. [*Rising.*] We can take the seven-two.

[MAGGIE *shows in* MRS. CULLINGHAM *and* PETER. PETER *shakes hand with* MRS. TILLMAN, *then with* JINNY, *and then with* MR. TILLMAN. MRS. CULLINGHAM *kisses* MRS. TILLMAN *and shakes hands with* MR. TILLMAN.]

MRS. CULLINGHAM. Jinny, you angel, aren't you surprised! [*Kissing her.*]

JINNY. Well, rather!

MRS. CULLINGHAM. Well, you aren't a bit more surprised than I am. [*A clock strikes six-thirty.*] There goes the half hour, Peter; you must take your powder.

PETER. I beg your pardon, mother; it's the tablet now.

MRS. CULLINGHAM. Excuse me, dear, I'm so dead tired. [*Sits on the sofa.*]

JINNY. [*To* PETER.] Will you have some water?

PETER. No, thank you, I've learned now to take them *au naturel,* and without much, if any, inconvenience! [*Takes his tablet with still a certain amount of difficulty, and sits Right.*]

MRS. TILLMAN. [*To* MRS. CULLINGHAM.] Did you have a bad voyage?

MRS. CULLINGHAM. No, perfectly beautiful!

PETER. [*Reproachfully, and with a final swallow.*] Oh, mother!

MRS. CULLINGHAM. Except, of course, for poor Peter; he gets worse every trip! He can eat *absolutely nothing*—that is *for long!* But it's the Custom House that's worn me out; I was there from twelve till four.

MRS. TILLMAN. But you wouldn't have had time to buy anything!

MRS. CULLINGHAM. Of course not! But I took plenty of new dresses for the entire summer; most of them hadn't been worn, and they were determined to make me pay duty.

JINNY. We had to pay awfully for things! I wanted to try and smuggle, but Jack wouldn't let me!

MR. TILLMAN. I'm afraid *we* must go!

[*All rise.*]

MRS. CULLINGHAM. What do you think the Inspector had the impudence to ask me finally,—if I wanted to bring the dresses in as theatrical properties!

[*They laugh.*]

MRS. TILLMAN. You must have some *gorgeous* frocks!

MRS. CULLINGHAM. Oh, there are some *paillettes!* But who do you suppose he took me for—Sarah Bernhardt!

TILLMAN. [*Looking at his watch.*] I don't wish to interrupt this vital political conversation, but, Susan, if you don't want to miss the seven-two train, too—!

MRS. TILLMAN. [*Rising.*] Oh, no, we mustn't do that. Good-by. [*To* MRS. CULLINGHAM, *shaking hands.*] It's nice to see you again, anyway. Is Ruth better?

MRS. CULLINGHAM. I'm sorry to say—I don't think she is—good-by. [*To* MR.

TILLMAN, *who says good-by. General good-bys.*]

MRS. TILLMAN. [*To* JINNY.] You want me to tell your father?

JINNY. Yes, it's better; it does make him jealous if he thinks I tell you things and keep secrets from him.

TILLMAN. Good-by, Peter.

MRS. TILLMAN. Good-by, Peter.

PETER. By-by.

[MR. *and* MRS. TILLMAN *quickly go out Right,* JINNY *going to the door with them.*]

JINNY. [*Coming back from doorway.*] Now do tell me what it means. I thought you were abroad indefinitely, or for the summer at least.

MRS. CULLINGHAM. So did I! I'm just as surprised to be here as you *seem to be!* [*They sit down near each other.*] Didn't you really know we were coming?

JINNY. No! How should I?

MRS. CULLINGHAM. I don't know—I thought— [*She hesitates, embarrassed. After a pause.*]

JINNY. What did you think?

MRS. CULLINGHAM. Nothing, except that you must know we were coming home.

JINNY. Why—that *I* must?

MRS. CULLINGHAM. You mustn't put me into a corner like that!

JINNY. How do you mean "corner"? How did you happen to come home like this?

MRS. CULLINGHAM. Ruth suddenly got a cable—she didn't tell me from whom—but she said she must go home at once.

JINNY. But her mother's never been better!

MRS. CULLINGHAM. [*Carelessly.*] The cable wasn't from her mother.

JINNY. Oh, then, you know who it was from? [*No answer.*] Oh, I see now why you thought I ought to know about it; the cable was from *Jack, wasn't it?*

MRS. CULLINGHAM. [*Relieved.*] Yes.

JINNY. Oh, it was!

MRS. CULLINGHAM. I looked at it when she was out of the room; of course, it was sort of by accident—[*Very much embarrassed.*]—that is, I just happened to see— O dear, there! You know what I mean; it was dreadful of me, but I couldn't help it.

JINNY. [*In a strained voice.*] Jack and Ruth are very good friends and he looks after some of her affairs. You know having no man in the family complicates things.

PETER. Oh! I say! [*Standing up, suddenly.*]

MRS. CULLINGHAM. What *is it,* dear?

PETER. I believe I haven't got my before-dinner tabs.

MRS. CULLINGHAM. Oh, look carefully!

PETER. [*He looks in his right-hand pocket, takes out a bottle.*] Soda mints! [*From his left-hand pocket a box.*] Alkali powders! [*From third pocket a bottle.*] Charcoal tablets! [*From fourth pocket another bottle.*] Dr. Man's Positive Cure! [*From fifth pocket a box.*] Bicarbonate soda!

MRS. CULLINGHAM. There's your other pocket!

PETER. That's my saccharine [*Showing bottle.*] and my lithia tabs. [*Showing another bottle.*] We'll have to go, mother; I've left them home!

MRS. CULLINGHAM. We must go, anyway, my dear. [*Rising.*]

[JINNY *also rises.*]

PETER. [*Suddenly claps his hand behind him and speaks joyfully.*] No, we needn't go after all; I forgot my hip pocket. Here they are! [*Bringing them out.*]

MRS. CULLINGHAM. We must go all the the same! [*To* JINNY.] Sometimes I think he takes too much medicine stuff!

JINNY. I should think so! Peter, you ought to diet.

PETER. I can't! I've tried, and I lose my appetite right away!

MRS. CULLINGHAM. Good-by, dear. How long will you be in town?

JINNY. I don't know—several weeks, I imagine. Jack came home on some business, you know, and I don't think it's settled yet. Good-by. [*To* PETER.]

PETER. Good-by. You know you mustn't drink water with your meals; that's the great thing. So I drink only champagne.

[*He goes out Right.*]

MRS. CULLINGHAM. [*Waits and speaks to* JINNY *with real feeling.*] I'm awfully ashamed of myself, and I hope I haven't made any trouble or fuss with my meddling. Don't let me!

JINNY. No, of course not. [*With a strained smile.*]

MRS. CULLINGHAM. I wish I could believe you.

JINNY. Well, *do.*

MRS. CULLINGHAM. Good-by. [*She goes out Right.*]

JINNY. Good-by. Where's that telegram that came for him a little while ago?

[*Going to the desk at Right, and finding the telegram.*] Of course it's from her, saying that she's arrived. That's the trouble with telegrams; the address doesn't give the handwriting away. She must have sent it from the dock! Couldn't even wait till she was home! [*She walks to the window and stands there a moment, then comes back, looking at her watch.*] Nearly seven already, and no sign of him, and we must dress and dine—huh! I think I might as well tear up my theatre tickets! [*She paces up and down the room, stopping now and then with each new thought that comes to her.*] I wonder if he went down there to meet her—he must have known the boat; if he cabled her to come back, she must have cabled an answer and what boat she'd take! But no other telegram has come for Jack here to my knowledge—oh! of course, what am I thinking of, she sent *that one* to *his office* to-day; she was afraid he might have left before this one could get there, so she risked it here. Good Heavens! why am I maudling on like this to myself out loud? It's really nothing—Jack will *explain* once more that he *can't* explain, but that Ruth has "troubles," and I'll believe him again! But I won't! He promised me she should stay over there! [*Looks at her watch again.*] He's there, with her! *Nothing ever* kept him half as late down town as this! What a little fool I am!

[GEOFFREY *enters suddenly Right.*]

JINNY. [*Cries out, joyfully.*] Geoffrey! [*And rushing to him, embraces him.*] You brute, you, not to come straight back to New York when you heard I was home! You dear old darling, you!

GEOFFREY. I couldn't, old girl; there were reasons—I don't have to tell you I wanted to.

JINNY. I don't know! Was there a pretty girl up there, Geof? I'm sure I shouldn't think her pretty if you were in love with her. I believe I shall be awfully jealous of your wife when you get one!

GEOFFREY. Rubbish! Hasn't Jack come back yet?

JINNY. "Come back" from where?

GEOFFREY. Brooklyn.

JINNY. Brooklyn! Why, he told me—what did he go there for?

GEOFFREY. [*Embarrassed.*] I don't know if you don't—

JINNY. You *do!!*

GEOFFREY. No—really—I—

JINNY. Oh, it's something to be concealed, then?

GEOFFREY. Hang it, Jinny! drop the subject. I thought he said he was going to Brooklyn; probably I was mistaken.

JINNY. [*Satirically.*] One is so apt to think just casually that every one's going to Brooklyn! [*Looks at her watch.*] Of course it's Brooklyn. [*Goes and looks at the telegram; turns.*] So you're going back on *me*, too, are you? You're going to *protect Jack* at *my* expense!

[AUSTIN *enters Right.*]

AUSTIN. [*Absorbed.*] Good evening, Jinny dear.

JINNY. It's after seven!

AUSTIN. [*Pleasantly.*] Is it? Have you been waiting long, Geoffrey?

GEOFFREY. No, I've only just now come in.

JINNY. It's *I* who have done the waiting!

AUSTIN. I'm sorry, but it couldn't be helped.

JINNY. You didn't tell me you were going to Brooklyn.

AUSTIN. [*After a quick, sharp look at Geoffrey, who shakes his head once emphatically.*] It must have escaped my mind.

JINNY. That's very likely! Going to Brooklyn's the sort of thing one talks about and dreads for days.

AUSTIN. Well, Jinny, that will bear postponement, and my conversation with Geoffrey won't; will you please leave us together here for a while?

JINNY. And what about the theatre?

AUSTIN. What theatre?

JINNY. Oh, you've *forgotten* entirely my little birthday party! Thanks!

AUSTIN. Oh, Jinny! I *did!* Forgive me! I'm awfully sorry! I've got a lot on my mind to-day. [*Tries to put his arms about her and kiss her. She pushes herself away from him, refusing to let him kiss her.*]

JINNY. Yes—I know you have—[*At door Left.*]—I'll leave you two to your confidences. You can trust Geof; he just now refused to betray you.

[AUSTIN *only looks at her fixedly, seriously. She looks back at him with bravado. Then she deliberately crosses the room, gets the cable, and recrosses with it and goes out Left.*]

AUSTIN. Poor Jinny! [*Turning to* GEOFFREY.] And that, too, lies largely on your already overcrowded shoulders.

GEOFFREY. [*Breaking down.*] I know! I know!

AUSTIN. [*Sitting in the corner of the sofa.*] Here, don't cry! You've got to be strong now, and you've no use nor time for crying. I've had another long interview with the Brooklyn minister.

GEOFFREY. Yes?—

AUSTIN. [*Drawing a chair near to him and sitting.*] Well, of course we both know that he's doing wrong to keep silent, but he will. He wishes I hadn't told him, because he thinks he'd never have noticed your divorce from Maggie when it was granted—nor remembered your name if he had seen it in the papers.

GEOFFREY. That's what I *told* you!

AUSTIN. *You* only argued that for fear I'd insist on *your* going to this minister yourself. But in the bottom of your heart you know it was a risk we couldn't afford to run. I've explained everything to him—how such a fine, sweet girl would suffer if he did expose you, and I gave him my word you would be remarried to Ruth at once after the divorce. Of course we both know it's wrong, but we both hope the end justifies the means that removes difficulty number two.

GEOFFREY. You're sure about Maggie?

AUSTIN. She's signed a paper; she realizes you'll never live with her, and—it's pathetic—she loves you—that girl, too—so much as to give you your freedom—Good Lord! what is it about you weak men that wins women so? What is it in *you* that has made two women love *you* to such a self-sacrificing extent?

GEOFFREY. [*Half tragic, half comic laugh.*] I give it up!

AUSTIN. [*Bitterly.*] So do I. Well, Maggie is to have six hundred dollars a year.

GEOFFREY. Where'll I get it?

AUSTIN. We'll talk about that when the time comes. [*He rises.*] *Now* the most important, the most painful, task of all must be done and *you* must do it. *Not I this time—you!*

GEOFFREY. [*Looking up, frightened.*] What?

AUSTIN. Ruth Chester landed this morning.

GEOFFREY. [*Starting up.*] Impossible! [*Rising.*]

AUSTIN. The moment Maggie signed my paper I cabled Miss Chester to return. You can't go out West and institute proceedings for divorce without her *knowing the whole truth from you* first! You don't want her to find it out from the newspapers, do you?

GEOFFREY. And you want *me* to tell her?

AUSTIN. *To-day.* And to-morrow you start west!

GEOFFREY. [*Facing* AUSTIN.] I *won't* tell her.

AUSTIN. [*Calmly.*] You've got to!

GEOFFREY. I'd rather shoot myself; do you understand me—I'd rather shoot myself!

AUSTIN. That's nothing! That would be decidedly the *easiest* course out of it, *and* the most *cowardly.*

GEOFFREY. She'll hate me! She'll loathe me! How could she help it at first! But just after a little, if I weren't there, the love she has for me might move her somehow or other—and by degrees perhaps—to forgive—

AUSTIN. I don't deny that you will have to go through a terrible degradation with her—but that is nothing compared with what you deserve. If *you* tell her, at least the humiliation is secret, locked there between you two, and no one else in the world can ever know what happens; *but* if you send some one else, and no matter who,—*any one* else but you *is* an outsider,—you ask her to make a spectacle of her humiliation, to let a third in as witness to the relations and emotions between you two! It's insulting her *again!* Don't you *see?*

[*A pause.*]

GEOFFREY. Yes, I see! My God! I *must* tell her myself.

AUSTIN. That's right, don't waver, make up your mind and do it— Come! [*Urging him up.*]

GEOFFREY. [*Hesitates a moment.*] And Jinny?

AUSTIN. Oh, she'll come round all right; she always does.

GEOFFREY. And she doesn't suspect?

AUSTIN. Not the slightest.

[*A pause*]

GEOFFREY. Need she?

AUSTIN. The worst? No, *never!*

GEOFFREY. [*He rises, with new encouragement.*] You'll give me your word?

AUSTIN. Yes. [*Shakes his hand.*] I know how much she loves you; *I* wouldn't have her know anything. It's made us some ugly scenes, but they soon pass, and when you are once out of your trouble for good, we'll have no excuse, I'm sure, for any more!

GEOFFREY. Then I shall go to bed to-night with the respect still of at least two women who are dear to me, my mother and Jinny, even if I lose the respect and love of the one woman who is dearer! Only think, Jack, how I've got to stand up there—never mind about myself—and make *her suffer tortures!* Good-by. God give me courage to do the heart-breaking thing I must do.

AUSTIN. I am sure the one hope you have of forgiveness is in your manliness of going to her as you are doing and telling her yourself *all* the truth!

GEOFFREY. And that, like everything else, I owe to you.

AUSTIN. No, to *Jinny!* Good luck!

[*He shakes* GEOFFREY's *hand and* GEOFFREY *goes out Right.*]

AUSTIN. [*Goes to the door Left, opens it, and calls to* JINNY, *in the next room.*] Jinny, Geoffrey's gone,—what are you doing?

JINNY. [*Answers in a very little staccato voice.*] Waiting till you should have the leisure to receive me!

AUSTIN. Come along! [*Leaves the doorway.*]

[JINNY *enters Left and stands in the doorway.*]

JINNY. [*With affected nonchalance.*] I didn't care to go downstairs for dinner, so I have had a tray up here. Maggie brought up something for you, too; would you like it now?

AUSTIN. [*Ignoring purposely her mood and manner.*] I shouldn't mind! I do feel a little hungry. [*He sits in the armchair.*]

JINNY. [*Speaks off through the doorway Left.*] Bring in the tray for Mr. Austin, Maggie.

MAGGIE. [*Off stage.*] Yes'm.

[JINNY *pulls forward a little tea table beside his chair. Her whole manner must be one of slow, dragging carelessness, like the calm before a storm. Her expression must be hard. She carries the telegram still unopened, and on top of it the theatre tickets torn into pieces.*]

[MAGGIE *brings in the tray, puts it on the table, and goes out Right. On the tray are chops, peas, some whiskey, a syphon, a roll, etc.*]

AUSTIN. [*Sits down quickly and with a show of eagerness.*] Ah! [*Begins to eat as if he were hungry and enjoyed it.*]

[JINNY *sits on the sofa at his Left, and looks at him,*—AUSTIN *is of course conscious of* JINNY'S *mood, but pretends not to notice it.*]

AUSTIN. [*After a silence during which he eats.*] I say I *am* hungry! And these chops *are* very good, aren't they? [*No answer.*] I'll tell you what it is, Jinny! Of course travelling is great sport and all the rest of it, but after all one does get tired of hotels, and to quote a somewhat familiar refrain, "There's no place like home." [*No answer.*] Have you a headache, Jinny?

JINNY. [*Very short.*] No.

AUSTIN. That's a good thing, and I hope you are not as disappointed as I am about the theatre.

JINNY. [*Half laughs.*] Humph!

AUSTIN. I'll celebrate *your* birthday to-morrow and take *you.*

JINNY. [*Quickly.*] *Why* did you go to Brooklyn?

AUSTIN. On the private business of some one else.

JINNY. [*With all her nerves tied tight.*] That's the best answer you will give me?

AUSTIN. My dear girl, it's the only answer I *can* give you.

JINNY. When you are through I have something for you!

AUSTIN. What?

JINNY. I'll give it to you when you have finished.

AUSTIN. I'm ready. [*He rises.* JINNY *rises too, and gives him the telegram with the torn tickets on top, and then rings the bell, at Right.*] What are these torn papers?

JINNY. Our theatre tickets! [*He looks at her.*]

AUSTIN. And when did this telegram come?

JINNY. This afternoon.

AUSTIN. Why didn't I get it when I came in?

JINNY. [*Bitingly.*] I kept it to have the *pleasure* of giving it to you myself; it's from Ruth Chester.

AUSTIN. How do you know?

JINNY. Oh, I haven't opened it! But I I know. When I held it in my hand it burnt my fingers! [MAGGIE *enters Right.*] Take away the tray, please, Maggie.

MAGGIE. Yes'm. [*She leaves the room with the tray.*]

[JINNY *replaces the small table care-*

lessly, almost roughly. AUSTIN *opens and reads the telegram; there is a second's pause.*]

JINNY. May I read it?

AUSTIN. [*After a moment's hesitation.*] Yes, if you wish. [*Not handing it to her.*]

JINNY. I *do!*

AUSTIN. [*Reaches over and hands her the telegram; he speaks quietly.*] When you behave like this it's impossible for me to feel the same toward you.

JINNY. And how do you think I feel when I read this? [*Reads it, satirically, bitterly.*] "Arrived safely; please let me see you before the day goes. Ruth." *"Ruth"* if you please!

AUSTIN. [*Standing over* JINNY.] I want you to be careful to-night. I want you to control yourself. I've been through a great deal to-day, and if you make me angry God knows what I mightn't say and *do!*

JINNY. And I've been through a great deal *for many a day now,* and I want the truth about this at last! It's all very well for you to spare her by not telling me what this *mysterious* trouble is about which you've been hoodwinking me ever since we were married, but *now* you've got to choose between sparing *her* and sparing *me!* [*She sits determinedly.*]

AUSTIN. Is this your answer to me when I beg you to be very careful to-night to control yourself?

JINNY. It's your turn to be careful! What did you marry me for if you were in love with Ruth?

AUSTIN. *Jinny!*

JINNY. [*A little frightened, to excuse herself.*] You gave me your word of honor she would stay abroad indefinitely.

AUSTIN. Nonsense! I said I understood she was going to stay some time—indefinitely.

JINNY. It's the same thing, and here she is back practically the moment we are!

AUSTIN. I can't control Miss Chester's movements—I couldn't foresee when she would come back. In Rome she told me she would stay on.

JINNY. [*Rising and facing him.*] Ah! that's what I wanted to see, if you really *would lie* to me!

AUSTIN. What do you mean?

JINNY. [*Beside herself.*] Liar! [*He only looks at her, with his face hard and set; she is insane with jealousy for the moment.*] *You sent* for Ruth to come back.

AUSTIN. *And* if *I did?*

JINNY. You tried to deceive me about it. And if you'll tell me a lie about one thing, you'll tell me a lie about another, and I don't believe one word of all your explanations about the intrigue between you and Ruth Chester!

AUSTIN. [*Taking her two hands.*] Sit down! [*She sits in the armchair, half forced by him.*]

JINNY. *Why* did you send for Ruth Chester to come back?

AUSTIN. I have told you before, I am trying to help Miss Chester.

JINNY. *"Ruth!"*

AUSTIN. I am trying to help her in a great and serious trouble.

JINNY. Why did you send for her to come back? What's the trouble?

AUSTIN. I've told you before I can't tell you.

JINNY. You daren't tell me, and you haven't even the face to tell another lie about it!

AUSTIN. If you say another word, I shall *hate* you! If you *won't* control *yourself,* I must make you, as well as keep my own sane balance. You have insulted my love for you to-night as you've never done before; you've struck at my own ideal of *you;* you've almost done, in a word, what I warned you you might do—*kill* the love I have for you!

JINNY. [*Frightened.*] Jack!

AUSTIN. I mean what I say!

JINNY. [*In tears.*] That—that you—you don't love me?

AUSTIN. That is not what I said, but I tell you now that since I first began to care for you, never have I loved you so little as I do to-night.

JINNY. [*With an effort at angry justification.*] And suppose I tell you it is your own fault, because you haven't treated me—

AUSTIN. [*Interrupting her.*] Like a *child,* instead of a *woman!*

JINNY. No, because you've kept part of yourself from me, and that part you've given—

AUSTIN. For God's sake, stop! [*A pause*—JINNY *is now thoroughly frightened; slowly she comes to her senses.*] Do you *want* a rupture for good between us? [*No answer.*] Can't you see what I tell you is true? That I can't bear any more to-night? That if you keep on you will rob *me* of every bit of love I have for you, just as you've already robbed me of the woman I thought you were?

JINNY. "Already!" No, no, Jack, don't say that. Oh, what have I done! [*She cries.*]

AUSTIN. You've done something very serious, and before you do more—[*Speaking hardly.*]—I think we'd better not stay in this evening; it would be wiser for both of us if we went out somewhere.

JINNY. No, I couldn't go out feeling this way! I've hurt you, hurt you terribly! Oh, why do I do it? Why can't I help myself?

AUSTIN. I think one more scene to-night would finish things for us. I *warn* you of that, Jinny—[*He goes to the desk and sits at it, looking blankly before him. She comes slowly, almost timidly, behind his chair.*]

JINNY. No, don't say it! don't say it! Try to forgive me—oh, Jack, I hate myself, and I'm so ashamed of myself! I know I've disappointed you awfully, awfully! You *did* idealize me; I knew it when you married me, but I told you then I wasn't worth your loving me, didn't I? I never pretended to be worthy of you. I always knew I wasn't.

AUSTIN. Hush!

JINNY. It's true! it's only too awfully true. But do you remember how you answered me then when I told you I wasn't worth your loving me?

AUSTIN. [*Coldly and without looking at her.*] No.

JINNY. You took me in your arms and held me so I couldn't have got away if I'd wanted to—which I didn't—and stopped the words on my lips with your *kisses.* [*Her throat fills. He makes no reply. She goes on very pathetically.*] *How I wish* you'd answer me that way now!

AUSTIN. Whose fault is it?

JINNY. Oh, mine! *mine!* I know it. *You* don't know it one-half so well as I! I love you better than anything in the world, love everything of you—the turn of your head, the blessed touch of your hand, the smallest word that comes from your dear lips—the thoughts that your forehead hides, but which my heart guesses when I'm sane! And yet, try as hard as I can, these mad fits take hold of me, and although I'd willingly *die* to save you *pain,* still *I, I* myself, hurt and wound you past all bearing! It doesn't make any difference that *I* suffer too! *I ought* to! I deserve to—you *don't!* Oh, no! I know I'm a disappointment and a failure! [*Her eyes fill up with tears and her voice breaks.*]

AUSTIN. [*He turns to her.*] No, Jinny, not so bad as that, only I thought you were *big*—and you're *so little,* oh, *so small!*

JINNY. Yes, it's true; I'm small—I'm *small!* Oh, I'd like to be big, too! I want to be noble and strong, but I'm not—I'm as weak as water—only it's *boiling* water! I want to be Brunhilde, and I'm only Frou Frou! Yes, I'm little; but I *love* you—*I love you!* [*She sinks on to a stool beside him. A moment's pause. With a trembling voice.*] You don't mind my sitting here?

AUSTIN. No—[*Very quietly, he places his arm about her neck, his hand on her shoulder. She quickly steals up her hand to take his, and leaning her head over it, kisses his hand. He draws it away and kisses her hair.*]

JINNY. [*Timidly, very softly.*] You forgive me?

AUSTIN. [*With a long sigh.*] Yes.

JINNY. [*Bursting into tears and burying her face upon his knees.*] Thank you—thank you—I know I don't deserve it—I don't deserve it—I don't deserve it!

AUSTIN. [*Softly.*] Sh!—

[JINNY. *half turns and looks up at him.*]

JINNY. [*Very, very quietly.*] You forgive me—but still—yes, I see it in your face, you don't love me the same. You look so tired, dear.

AUSTIN. [*Also very quietly.*] I am, Jinny.

JINNY. And—happy?

AUSTIN. I'm *not* quite happy.

JINNY. I wish I could make you so—make you love me the old way. You used to smile a little when you looked at me—Jack, you don't any more. But I mean to make you to-night, if I can, and to make you love me as much as ever you did.

AUSTIN. Good luck, dear.

JINNY. [*Brightening.*] What time is it?

AUSTIN. [*Looking at his watch.*] Nearly nine.

JINNY. I suppose it is too late for me to dress and for us to go to the theatre?

AUSTIN. Oh, yes,—and I'm too tired.

JINNY. [*Triumphantly.*] Well, then, you shall have your theatre at home! If Mahomet won't go to the mountain, the mountain must go to your lordship!

AUSTIN. I don't understand!

JINNY. Well, just wait—[*She blows her nose.*]—till I bathe my face and eyes a little; I feel rather bleary! [*Starting to go, she stops and turns.*] Good-by? [*Questioningly.*]

AUSTIN. [*Quietly.*] Good-by.

JINNY. [*Who wanted him to call her to him and kiss her.*] Oh, very well! but I'll *make* you smile yet and *kiss* me of your own accord to-night—you'll see! [*She goes out Left. She is heard singing in her room.* AUSTIN *goes to the desk and after a long sigh he begins to write.*]

AUSTIN. [*Writing.*] Dear Ruth. The satisfaction of the visit to Brooklyn prevents me from being disappointed at having missed your telegram till too late to go to your house to-night. My heart aches for the blow you must have this evening, but please God you will bear it bravely. The man who loves you is not bad, but he has been weak. However, I feel once he can shake off the burden of his present marriage, you will never have cause to complain of him again. And if your future happiness lies truly in his hands, it will be safe there.

JINNY. [*Calls from her room.*] Are you ready?

AUSTIN. Yes. [*He stops writing.*]

JINNY. In your orchestra chair?

AUSTIN. Yes.

JINNY. What will you have, tragedy or comedy?

AUSTIN. [*Smiling.*] Shall we begin with tragedy?

JINNY. All right.

AUSTIN. [*Continues to write.*] So far I have been able to keep Jinny in absolute ignorance, but I fear the blow must fall upon her soon, and I dread to think of what she, too, will suffer. Help me to keep it from her as long as we can, won't you?

[JINNY *comes back; she has changed her dress to a loose negligée gown, with a red turban on her head; she brings two sheets with her.*]

JINNY. Excuse me one minute while I set the stage! [*Moving toward each other the big armchair and the sofa, she covers them with the sheets.* AUSTIN *turns from his letter on the desk, to watch.*] Uncle Tom's Cabin, Act Four! [*She goes out only for a moment, and reënters, wearing a man's overcoat, with a pillow tied in the middle with a silk scarf, eyes, nose, and mouth made on it with a burnt match.*] Eliza crossing the ice! Come, honey darling! [*To the pillow.*] Mammy'll save you from de wicked white man! [*Jumping up on the sofa, and moving with the springs.*] *You* ought to do the bloodhounds for me, Jack! Excuse me, but you look the part! [AUSTIN *watches her, not unamused, but without smiling.*] Hold tight to Lize, honey, and don't be afeerd o' dat big black man over dah—dat's Uncle Tom. [*Crossing to the armchair.*] Don't be afeerd, honey; it's Lize dat's cuttin' de ice this time. [*She throws the pillow away and drags off the two sheets.*] Oh, I can see this is too serious for you! [*She starts singing a cakewalk and dances across the room until she reaches him, where she finishes.*]

AUSTIN. Very good, Jinny! I'm sure we couldn't have seen better at the theatre.

JINNY. Ah! You're getting yourself again!—Darling! Come!—Come!—come to the pianola and you shall have the sextette! It's in there ready; I heard mother struggling with it. You don't suppose she has designs upon the Casino, do you? Now—ready? [*He goes to the pianola and starts to play the sextette from "Florodora." She runs to the opposite side of the room and begins to sing and dance, crossing to* AUSTIN *as he plays.*]

AUSTIN. [*After a few moments.*] But I can't see you and play at the same time; I don't like it!

JINNY. [*Delighted.*] You *want to see me,* do you?

AUSTIN. Of course I do!

JINNY. Jack! [*Delighted.*] Well, then, turn round!

[JINNY, *hurrying the time of the song, turns it into a regular skirt dance. She dances delightfully and* AUSTIN *cannot resist her charm. His face lightens, he smiles, and love comes into his eyes.* JINNY *sees and dances and sings all the better till she reaches him.*]

AUSTIN. [*Rising, he takes her into his arms.*] You adorable Jinny!

JINNY. Ah, Jack! You're smiling again and—*you love me!* [*Clasping her arms about his neck.*]

AUSTIN. Yes! Is the theatre finished?

JINNY. No, only the first act. [*He sits in the big armchair,* JINNY *on his knee.*]

I'm *tired!* [*He kisses her. There is a pause. There is a knock on the door at Right.*] Oh, hang it! [*Knock repeated.*] *Don't* answer it! We haven't half made up yet!

AUSTIN. But we must answer it, dear.

JINNY. [*As she rises unwillingly.*] I don't see why—I should have let her knock till she went away.

AUSTIN. Come in!

[MAGGIE *enters with a letter.*]

JINNY. What is it, Maggie?

MAGGIE. A note from Miss Chester, ma'm, and she's downstairs herself waiting for an answer.

JINNY. For *me?* [*Taking the letter.*]

MAGGIE. No, ma'm; I think she said it was for *Mr.* Austin.

JINNY. *Oh!*—You may wait outside for the answer, Maggie.

MAGGIE. Yes, ma'm. [*She goes out.*]

JINNY. [*Slowly goes to* AUSTIN *and gives him the letter, lightly.*] I see now why you were so anxious to let Maggie in. Perhaps you were expecting this.

AUSTIN. Jinny! [*Holding her by the hand and trying to pull her over to him.*] Come, I'll give you a kiss for the letter.

JINNY. No, thank you, I don't want kisses that are given by you for letters from Ruth Chester. Yes! do kiss me! [*He kisses her.*] I *won't* be jealous! *I won't be!* [*Clinching her teeth.*] See, I'm not jealous a bit! Read your old letter!

[AUSTIN *opens the note and reads it. As he does so* JINNY *has passed on to the desk and sees* AUSTIN'S *unfinished letter to* RUTH, *which after a little hesitation she picks up and reads.* AUSTIN, *having read* RUTH'S *note, looks up thoughtfully a second, and then re-reads it.* JINNY *is furious over what she reads. As she finishes she gives a little cry from the very depths of her heart.*]

JINNY. Oh, *Jack!*

AUSTIN. What is it?

JINNY. Nothing! [*She sinks by the desk, crushing the letter in her hand. She looks over at him, and then down at the letter, and then back at him.*]

AUSTIN. Maggie!

JINNY. [*Rising suddenly. She speaks with a voice trembling with only half-contained emotion and passion.*] I told her to wait in the hall; may I read it? [*Holding out her hand for the letter.*]

AUSTIN. Now look here, Jinny,—I always let you read everything, don't I?

JINNY. [*Hiding his letter behind her back.*] Yes. [*Holding out her other hand.*] Give it to me!

AUSTIN. Now begin to show that you really are going to turn over a new leaf, and that your love is going to have perfect confidence, and don't ask to see this letter.

JINNY. But I *do* ask to see it!

AUSTIN. Then this time I must refuse you!

JINNY. What! is it even more compromising than *your* letter to her?

AUSTIN. What letter? [*Looking first on the desk, he looks across at her and sees it in her hand. He is angry, but also frightened for fear it has told her her brother's secret.*] And you've read it?

JINNY. It lay open on the desk there, and anyway the end justifies me!

AUSTIN. [*In an agony.*] What does it tell you? I forget what I wrote!

JINNY. It tells me that my jealousy all along has been right, that I've been a fool to let you blind me!

AUSTIN. [*With a great sigh of relief.*] Is that all?

JINNY. [*Beside herself.*] "Is that all!" Isn't that enough? Dear God, isn't that enough? That there's an understanding between you and Ruth to get rid of *me!*

AUSTIN. If it tells you that, the letter lies! Give it to me!

JINNY. No! *I'll* read it to you! [*Reads with bitter emphasis.*] "The satisfaction of the visit to Brooklyn prevents me from being disappointed at having missed your telegram till too late to go to your house to-night!" So—you and she went to Brooklyn, did you, and that's why you came back too late to go to the theatre with me? You *cheat!* [*She screams in her madness. A pause.*] Why don't you answer—why don't you say something?

AUSTIN. Because if I speak as I feel, I'm afraid of saying something I'll regret all my life!

JINNY. You don't deny, then?

AUSTIN. Yes! that is due to Ruth. Whatever you may feel about *me,* you have no *right* to *insult* her!

JINNY. Oh, *there's more to* the letter!

AUSTIN. Jinny, don't you see what you're doing?

JINNY. Yes, I'm getting at the truth at last! [*Reads.*] "My heart aches for the blow you must have this evening! The man who loves you—"

AUSTIN. You shan't read any more; you're

mad now! [*Tearing the letter away from her.*]

JINNY. I don't need the letter, the words are burning in here! [*Pressing her hands to her forehead.*] "The man who loves you isn't bad, only weak. However, I feel once we can shake off the burden of *this present marriage*"—oh! you—you *brute* to say that!—"you will never have cause to complain of him again! So far I have been able to keep Jinny in perfect ignorance, but I feel the blow must fall upon her now—" [*Interrupted.*]

AUSTIN. Shall I tell you *the truth?*

JINNY. You don't have to; I've found it out for myself!

AUSTIN. [*In weariness, in disgust, in utter hopelessness.*] No! what's the use. You've done it now—let it go! Let it all go—the whole thing! What's the use!—it's finished!—[*A knock on the door at Right.*] Come in!

[MAGGIE *enters and closes the door behind her.*]

MAGGIE. Please, sir, Miss Chester came upstairs and made me knock again to see if there was an answer and if you will see her now or not.

JINNY. [*Suddenly—aflame with her idea.*] Yes! Maggie, show her in!

AUSTIN. No, no! What do you want to do! I'll see Miss Chester to-morrow, Maggie.

[JINNY *has crossed to the door, Right.*]

JINNY. Ruth! Ruth!

RUTH. [*Off stage.*] Yes? May I come?

JINNY. *Do* come in! [*She recrosses room; she and* AUSTIN *face each other for a second.*]

AUSTIN. [*In a lowered voice.*] For God's sake, be careful!

[RUTH *enters Right.*]

RUTH. Jinny! [*Going to her quickly to embrace her.*]

[JINNY, *without speaking, draws away and stares at her with a look of hatred.* RUTH, *seeing it, stops short, and looks from* JINNY *to* AUSTIN *for explanation—she turns to* AUSTIN *and gives him her hand, which he takes, presses, and drops;* JINNY'S *shoulders contract at this moment;* RUTH *immediately turns again to* JINNY.]

RUTH. What is it, Jinny? [*To* AUSTIN.] Surely she doesn't blame *me* in any way.

JINNY. *Blame you!*

AUSTIN. She doesn't *know.*

JINNY. That's a lie! I know everything, Ruth! I know why you followed my husband to Rome, and why he sent for you to come back here. I know that you and he were in Brooklyn this afternoon, and that you only plan to get rid of me by some divorce, and by hook or crook to marry each other!

RUTH. No!—No!—

JINNY. Oh, you can lie, too, can you? I won't keep you waiting long! You've stolen my husband from me—take him. I won't *share* him with any woman! He's yours now, and I'll soon be out of your way!

AUSTIN. *Jinny!*

RUTH. [*To* AUSTIN.] She must be told the truth.

[AUSTIN *bows his head.*]

JINNY. Now you'll make up your story, will you? I tell you it's useless. If he wouldn't let me see your compromising letter, I've seen a letter from *him* to *you* to-night that gives the whole thing away.

RUTH. [*Very quietly.*] Your husband went to Brooklyn *without me,* as your *brother* will tell you, to see the clergyman who married me, or *thought* he *married* me to *Geoffrey Tillman* three months ago! [JINNY *looks up with a start.*] That marriage was *illegal* because your brother was already married, and Mr. Austin tried and did get the promise of silence this afternoon about the Brooklyn service, to prevent a charge of bigamy against your brother. The first marriage, which still holds good, was with—Maggie, your present servant—

[JINNY *stands immovable. There is a silence.*]

AUSTIN. Geoffrey is not at your house?

RUTH. No, he left when I came on here. As I wrote you in the note I sent upstairs, I was too stunned by what he told me to answer then, and I wanted a word of advice with you. [*She turns to* JINNY.] *I* knew what I thought was my *marriage* to your brother must be kept secret, but I could not learn why. This was my trouble, which, after your marriage, I selfishly laid on your husband's shoulders, thinking he might help me! [*No answer from* JINNY, *who stands as if struck dumb and into stone.*] Mr. Austin only learned the whole truth when we met that day in Rome. *I* did not learn till to-day that I was not honestly your brother's wife. I had to be told, because divorce proceedings are to be started at once to break—the other—marriage. [*No answer from* JINNY.] To spare me, and above all to spare you the knowledge of your brother's sin, your husband has kept Geoffrey's secret from you. You have *well* repaid him! [*She turns again to* AUSTIN.] Good-by—I feel to-night I couldn't marry Geoffrey again. He's tumbled so far off his pedestal he has fallen out of my heart. But still—we'll see; I've told him to come to-morrow. *Thank you* from the bottom of my heart—it's full of gratitude, even if it is broken! [*She goes out Right.*]

[JINNY *slowly turns, almost afraid to look at* AUSTIN. *He stands stern, with set face.*]

JINNY. [*In a low voice, ashamed to go near him.*] Can you forgive me? Can you—

AUSTIN. Ugh! [*Crossing room for his coat.*]

JINNY. I'm mad! You know I don't know what I do. But I *love you*—I love you! Forgive me!

AUSTIN. Never! [*Taking up his coat.*]

JINNY. Where are you going?

AUSTIN. Out of this house.

JINNY. If you leave me, I'll not bear it! I'll kill myself! I warn you!

AUSTIN. Bah!—Good-by! [*Going to the door Right.*]

JINNY. No! Where are you going?

AUSTIN. Out of this house *for good!* [*At the door he turns and looks at her.*]

JINNY. [*Echoes.*] For good?

AUSTIN. *For good!* [*He goes out, slamming the door behind him.*]

[JINNY *stands a moment motionless. She then cries faintly*—"Jack!" *She goes to the door and pushes it open, crying out again in loud, strong despair,* "Jack!" *There is a moment's pause. She cries out again weakly, heartbrokenly,* "Jack!"—*comes back into the room, and throwing herself down on the floor, her head resting on her arms in the armchair, she sobs hysterically, wildly,* "What have I done! Dear God, what have I done!" *as*

THE CURTAIN FALLS

ACT FOURTH

SCENE I

Dawn of the next day. At the rise of the curtain JINNY *is by the open window, whose curtains she has thrown aside. The sky is blood-red and streaked with gold the moment before sunrise.* JINNY *is worn and haggard, with hair dishevelled.*

JINNY. [*Turning and leaning against the window.*] Day at last! What a night—what a night—but now it's morning and he hasn't come back! He means it! And it's my own fault—it's my own fault! [*She shivers. She closes the window and comes away. After a momoment's pause she goes deliberately and looks at the several gas fixtures in the room. She then closes all the doors and locks them. She carefully draws down the shade and closes in the curtains of the window. She hesitates, then pulls aside the curtains and the shade, and takes a long, last look at the dawn. She closes it all in again. She gets* AUSTIN'S *picture from the desk and places it on the table near the centre of the room. She then goes to the gas bracket at the Right and turns on the gas. She lights it to see if the gas is all right; then blows it out. She then crosses to the other bracket and turns that on; she goes to the chandelier at centre, and, mounting a chair, turns on its three jets. She then sits down by the table with* AUSTIN'S *picture before her, and looking into its eyes, her elbows on the table, her head in her hands, she waits.*] Oh, Jack, my beloved! I couldn't help it—I never for one minute stopped loving you better than everything else in my life, but no more than I could stop loving you could I stop or help being jealous! Once the cruel idea has got hold of me it seems to *have* to work its way out! Everything gets red before me and I don't seem to know what I say or do! It's no excuse, I know. I've got no excuse, only I *love* you! You'll forgive me when I'm gone, won't you, Jack? You'll know I *loved* you!—loved you so I couldn't *live* without you!—loved you!—*loved* you! [*She kisses the photograph tenderly, adoringly, slowly, in tears.*] Loved—you—loved you!—loved—

[*Her head drops forward as*

THE CURTAIN FALLS

SCENE II

The same morning, three hours later. The curtain rises on the same scene in a dull. cold, early morning light. The lamp has burnt itself out. A tiny ray of sunlight steals through a slip between the curtains. JINNY *sits by the table, her arms spread over it and her head on her arms —she is perfectly still.* AUSTIN'S *picture is before her. There is a moment's silence. Voices are heard outside, approaching door, at Right. Gradually what they say is distinguished.*

MAGGIE. No, sir. She hasn't been to bed; I've been to her bedroom—that door's not unlocked.

TILLMAN. She's been here all night?

MAGGIE. Yes, sir. But twice in the night, sir, I came to the door and spoke to her and she wouldn't answer me—but I could hear her walking up and down and sometimes talking to herself.

TILLMAN. [*Calls softly.*] Jinny! [*Knocks softly.*] It's father! [*No answer.*] It looks as if she were asleep now.

AUSTIN. [*At a little distance.*] Father!

TILLMAN. I'm outside the library door.

AUSTIN. [*Nearer.*] I can't wait—have you seen her? Will she see me?

TILLMAN. She's locked herself in here. She's not been to her own room.

AUSTIN. Not been to bed at all! Poor Jinny—God forgive me.

TILLMAN. Maggie says she's walked the floor all night. [*He knocks on the door Right.*]

AUSTIN. [*Outside the door, Right, rather softly.*] Jinny! I'm so sorry! I can't say how sorry! I've thought it out through the night, and I think I understand things better. [*He waits a moment for an answer.*] Jinny, answer me! you shall be as jealous as you like, and I'll always explain and kiss away those doubts of yours, and I'll have no more secrets from you, dear. Not one! *Jinny!* [*As he calls there is a slight movement of one of* JINNY'S *arms. With a note of alarm.*] Father! I can't hear a sound of breathing! [*A moment's pause as they listen.*] She threatened—she threatened it several times! [*With great determination.*] We must get into this room—do you hear me —we must get in if we have to break the door down! [*They shake the door. He calls a little louder.*] Jinny, Jinny darling—do you hear me? [JINNY *makes a sort of feeble effort to lift her head, but fails.*] Jinny, for God's sake, answer me! I love you Jinny—*Jinny!* [*Very slowly* JINNY *lifts her head and, with difficulty, she hears as if in a dream; she is dazed, barely alive.*] She doesn't answer!

TILLMAN. See if the key is in the lock.

AUSTIN. No.

TILLMAN. Get the other keys, Maggie.

AUSTIN. *Father!* Gas! Don't you smell it?

TILLMAN. What!

AUSTIN. Gas, I tell you! O God! she's killed herself! Jinny! Jinny! [*Beating the door.*]

[JINNY *staggers up, she tries to call "Jack"—but the word only comes out in a half-articulate whisper! She tries again, but fails.*]

MAGGIE. Here's a key, sir.

[JINNY *tries to go to the door; She staggers a few steps and then falls.*]

[*They try one key—it does not unlock the door; they try another.*]

[JINNY *half raises herself and makes an effort to crawl, but is unable and sinks back upon the floor.*]

AUSTIN. Break the door in, father! We daren't waste any more time!

TILLMAN. No, this has done it!

[*They open the door and rush in. They stop aghast at* JINNY *and the oppressiveness of the gas in the room.*]

TILLMAN. Jinny!

AUSTIN. Quick—the window! [TILLMAN *tears aside the curtains and throws open the window. The sunshine of full morning pours in. He then rushes to the opposite gas burners and turns them off.*

AUSTIN. [*Kneeling quickly beside her.*] Jinny! *My wife!* My beloved! [*He takes her up in his arms and hurries to the window.*]

TILLMAN. Are we too late?

AUSTIN. I don't know. No! she's breathing—and see—see!—she knows me!—she knows me! [JINNY *smiles at him pathetically.*] Send Maggie for the doctor!

[TILLMAN *goes out Right.*]

AUSTIN. Jinny, forgive me! Forgive me! Forgive me! [*She slips her two arms up and joins them about his neck.* AUSTIN *kisses her.*] Father! We've saved her! Oh, thank God, we've saved her! [*Bringing her to big chair and putting her in it, he kneels at her feet.*]

JINNY. [*Whispers faintly.*] *Dear Jack!* You forgive *me*—all my beastly jealousy?

AUSTIN. There's one thing stronger even than jealousy, my Jinny. And that's LOVE! That's *LOVE!* [*He kisses her hands, and*

THE CURTAIN FALLS

THE NEW YORK IDEA

BY

Langdon Mitchell

THE NEW YORK IDEA

The New York Idea represents American social comedy at its best. It portrays impersonally and artistically the effects of our divorce laws upon a group of very human beings, indicating cleverly the restraining influence upon their actions exercised by their varying respect for the importance of social values. They are all, however, fully aware of these values.

Langdon Elwyn Mitchell was born in Philadelphia, February 17, 1862. He is the son of the late Dr. S. Weir Mitchell, the physician and novelist. He was educated at St. Paul's School, at Concord, New Hampshire, and after three years' study abroad, studied law at Harvard and Columbia Universities and was admitted to the New York Bar in 1886. He has been a poet and playwright since 1883, his earlier works appearing under the pen-name of John Philip Varley. His first published drama was *Sylvian,* a tragedy partly in verse, laid in Cordova in the seventeenth century, published in *Sylvian and Other Poems* (1885). His other poetical work appeared under the title of *Poems* (1894). *Love in the Backwoods* (1896) consisted of short stories and novelettes. In 1892 Mr. Mitchell married Miss Marion Lea, of Philadelphia, who created the part of "Vida Phillimore" in *The New York Idea.* The dramatization of his father's novel *The Adventures of François,* played by Henry E. Dixey, was not successful, but his play *Becky Sharp,* founded on Thackeray's *Vanity Fair,* and played by Mrs. Fiske at the Fifth Avenue Theatre, September 12, 1899, was a decided success for two years and was revived by Mrs. Fiske ten years later. So great indeed was the success of the play that another American version was played during 1900–1, until stopped by injunction, and two versions were given in England during the season of 1901.

The New York Idea was first produced by Mrs. Fiske at the Lyric Theatre, New York City, November 19, 1906, with the cast as given. It was a very successful play and has been revived, Miss Grace George playing it in repertory during the season of 1915–16.

Under the name of *Jonathans Tochter, The New York Idea* was translated into German and played at the Kammerspiel Theater, Berlin, under the direction of Max Reinhardt, October 7, 1916. The criticism in the Berlin newspapers, especially the *Vossische Zeitung,* indicated that from the critics' point of view, the comedy was a charming one, but that international complications prevented at first, an impartial judgment of the play. Since then, it has had considerable success and is now being translated into Danish, Swedish and Hungarian.

Mr. Mitchell wrote no plays for some years, but has recently resumed active work. On October 11, 1916, at Atlantic City, New Jersey, his dramatization of

Thackeray's *Pendennis* was placed on the stage with Mr. John Drew in the leading part of "Major Pendennis." After a satisfactory tryout, it was taken to New York City.

The New York Idea was published in 1908 by W. H. Baker and Company. It is here reprinted through the courtesy of Mr. Mitchell and the publishers. The editor is indebted to Mr. Mitchell for a careful revision of the text made especially for this volume.

For an interesting criticism of *Becky Sharp,* see William Winter, *The Wallet of Time,* New York, 1913, vol. 2, pp. 273–286, and, for a very appreciative analysis of *The New York Idea* see Mr. William Archer's notice of the play in *The London Tribune* of May 27, 1907, reprinted in the published play. See also for *Becky Sharp, Plays of the Present,* by J. B. Clapp and E. F. Edgett, New York, 1902, pp. 32–4.

Note to Fifth Edition.

In 1928 Mr. Mitchell became the first occupant of the Chair of Playwriting, founded by the Mask and Wig Club of the University of Pennsylvania and for two years conducted courses in practical playwriting at the University. In 1929 the Players' Club of New York City revived *Becky Sharp,* with distinguished success.

Note to Sixth Edition.

Langdon Mitchell died October 21, 1935. For detailed criticism, see *A History of the American Drama from the Civil War to the Present Day,* Revised Edition; two volumes in one. Appleton-Century-Crofts, Inc., 1936. Vol. 2, Chapter XV.

To Marion Lea

THE ORIGINAL CAST OF CHARACTERS

Lyric Theatre, New York City, November 19, 1906

Philip Phillimore	Mr. Charles Harbury
Mrs. Phillimore, his mother	Miss Ida Vernon
The Reverend Matthew Phillimore, his brother	Mr. Dudley Clinton
Grace Phillimore, his sister	Miss Emily Stevens
Miss Heneage, his aunt	Miss Blanche Weaver
William Sudley, his cousin	Mr. William B. Mack
Mrs. Vida Phillimore, his divorced wife	Miss Marion Lea
Brooks, her footman	Mr. George Harcourt
Benson, her maid	Miss Belle Bohn
Sir Wilfrid Cates-Darby	Mr. George Arliss
John Karslake	Mr. John Mason
Mrs. Cynthia Karslake, his divorced wife	Mrs. Fiske
Nogam, his valet	Mr. Dudley Digges
Tim Fiddler	Mr. Robert V. Ferguson
Thomas, the Phillimores' family servant	Mr. Richard Clarke

ACT I—Drawing-room in the Phillimore house, Washington Square. Wednesday afternoon, at five o'clock.

ACT II—Mrs. Vida Phillimore's Boudoir, Fifth Avenue. Thursday morning, at eleven.

ACT III—Same as Act I. Thursday evening, at ten.

ACT IV—John Karslake's House, Madison Avenue. Thursday, at midnight.

Scene—New York. Time—The Present

THE NEW YORK IDEA

ACT FIRST.

SCENE. *Living room in the house of* PHILIP PHILLIMORE. *Five o'clock of an afternoon of May. The general air and appearance of the room is that of an old-fashioned, decorous, comfortable interior. There are no electric lights and no electric bells. Two bell ropes as in old-fashioned houses. The room is in dark tones inclining to sombre and of old-fashioned elegance.*

(*The curtain rises, disclosing* MISS HENEAGE, MRS. PHILLIMORE *and* THOMAS. MISS HENEAGE *is a solidly built, narrow-minded woman in her sixties. She makes no effort to look younger than she is, and is expensively but quietly dressed, with heavy elegance. She commands her household and her family connection, and on the strength of a large and steady income feels that her opinion has its value.* MRS. PHILLIMORE *is a semi-professional invalid, refined and unintelligent. Her movements are weak and fatigued. Her voice is habitually plaintive and she is entirely a lady without a trace of being a woman of fashion.* THOMAS *is an easy-mannered, but entirely respectful family servant, un-English both in style and appearance. He has no deportment worthy of being so called, and takes an evident interest in the affairs of the family he serves.* MISS HENEAGE, *seated at the tea-table, faces the footlights.* MRS. PHILLIMORE *is seated at the left side of the table.* THOMAS *stands near by. The table is set for tea. There is a vase with flowers, a silver match-box, and a large old-fashioned tea urn on the table. The "Evening Post" is on the table.* MISS HENEAGE *and* MRS. PHILLIMORE *both have cups of tea.* MISS HENEAGE *sits up very straight, and pours tea for* GRACE, *who has just entered. She is a pretty and fashionably dressed girl of twenty. She speaks superciliously, coolly, and not too fast. She sits on the sofa, and does not lounge, wearing a gown suitable for spring visiting, hat, parasol, and gloves.*)

GRACE. (*As she crosses and sits down.*) I never in my life walked so far and found so few people at home. (*She pauses, taking off her gloves, and somewhat querulously continues.*) The fact is the nineteenth of May is ridiculously late to be in town.

MISS HENEAGE. Thomas, Mr. Phillimore's sherry?

THOMAS. The sherry, ma'am. (THOMAS *indicates a table where the decanter is set.*)

MISS HENEAGE. Mr. Phillimore's *Post?*

THOMAS. (*Pointing to the "Evening Post" on the tea-table.*) The *Post*, ma'am.

MISS HENEAGE. (*Indicates the cup.*) Miss Phillimore.

(THOMAS *takes a cup of tea to* GRACE. *There is silence while they all sip tea.* THOMAS *goes back, fills the sherry glass, remaining round and about the tea-table. They all drink tea during the following scene.*)

GRACE. The Dudleys were at home. They wished to know when my brother Philip was to be married, and where and how?

MISS HENEAGE. If the Dudleys were persons of breeding, they 'd not intrude their curiosity upon you.

GRACE. I *like* Lena Dudley.

MRS. PHILLIMORE. (*Speaks slowly and gently.*) Do I know Miss Dudley?

GRACE. She knows Philip. She expects an announcement of the wedding.

MRS. PHILLIMORE. I trust you told her that my son, my sister and myself are all of the opinion that those who have been divorced should remarry with modesty and without parade.

GRACE. I told the Dudleys Philip's wedding was here, to-morrow.

MISS HENEAGE. (*To* MRS. PHILLIMORE, *picking up a sheet of paper from the table.*) I have spent the afternoon, Mary, in arranging and listing the wedding gifts, and in writing out the announcements of the wedding. I think I have attained a proper form of announcement. (*She takes the sheet of note paper and gives it to* THOMAS.) Of course, the announcement Philip himself made was quite out of the question. (GRACE *smiles.*) However, there is mine.

(*She points to the paper.* THOMAS *gives the list to* MRS. PHILLIMORE *and moves away.*)

GRACE. I hope you'll send an announcement to the Dudleys.

MRS. PHILLIMORE. (*Reading plaintively, ready to make the best of things.*) "Mr. Philip Phillimore and Mrs. Cynthia Dean Karslake announce their marriage, May twentieth, at three o'clock, Nineteen A, Washington Square, New York." (*She replaces paper on* THOMAS'S *salver.*) It sounds very nice.

(THOMAS *hands the paper to* MISS HENEAGE.)

MISS HENEAGE. In my opinion it barely escapes sounding nasty. However, it is correct. The only remaining question is—to whom the announcement should not be sent. (*Exit* THOMAS.) I consider an announcement of the wedding of two divorced persons to be in the nature of an intimate communication. It not only announces the wedding—it also announces the divorce. (*She returns to her teacup.*) The person I shall ask counsel of is Cousin William Sudley. He promised to drop in this afternoon.

GRACE. Oh! We shall hear all about Cairo.

MRS. PHILLIMORE. William is judicious.

(*Re-enter* THOMAS.)

MISS HENEAGE. (*With finality.*) Cousin William will disapprove of the match unless a winter in Cairo has altered his moral tone.

THOMAS. (*Announces.*) Mr. Sudley.

(*Enter* WILLIAM SUDLEY, *a little oldish gentleman. He is and appears thoroughly insignificant. But his opinion of the place he occupies in the world is exalted. Though he is filled with self-importance, his manners, voice, presence are all those of a man of breeding.*)

MRS. PHILLIMORE *and* MISS HENEAGE. (*They rise and greet* SUDLEY; *a little tremulously.*) My dear William!

(*Exit* THOMAS.)

SUDLEY. (*He shakes hands with* MRS. PHILLIMORE, *soberly glad to see them.*) How d'ye do, Mary? A very warm May you're having, Sarah.

GRACE. (*She comes to him.*) Dear Cousin William!

MISS HENEAGE. Was n't it warm in Cairo when you left?

(*She will have the strict truth, or nothing; still, on account of* SUDLEY'S *impeccable respectability, she treats him with more than usual leniency*)

SUDLEY. (*Sitting down.*) We left Cairo six weeks ago, Grace, so I've had no news since you wrote in February that Philip was engaged. (*Pause.*) I need not to say I consider Philip's engagement excessively regrettable. He is a judge upon the Supreme Court bench with a divorced wife—and such a divorced wife!

GRACE. Oh, but Philip has succeeded in keeping everything as quiet as possible.

SUDLEY. (*Acidly.*) No, my dear! He has not succeeded in keeping his former wife as quiet as possible. We had not been in Cairo a week when who should turn up but Vida Phillimore. She went everywhere and did everything no woman should!

GRACE. (*Unfeignedly interested.*) Oh, what did she do?

SUDLEY. She "did" Cleopatra at the tableaux at Lord Errington's! She "did" Cleopatra, and she did it robed only in some diaphanous material of a nature so transparent that—in fact she appeared to be draped in moonshine. (MISS HENEAGE *indicates the presence of* GRACE. *She rises.*) That was only the beginning. As soon as she heard of Philip's engagement, she gave a dinner in honor of it! Only divorcées were asked! And she had a dummy—yes, my dear, a dummy—at the head of the table. He stood for Philip—that is he sat for Philip! (*He rises, and goes up to table.*)

MISS HENEAGE. (*Irritated and disgusted.*) Ah!

MRS. PHILLIMORE. (*With dismay and pain.*) Dear me!

MISS HENEAGE. (*Confident of the value of her opinion.*) I disapprove of Mrs. Phillimore.

SUDLEY. (*Taking cigarette.*) Of course you do, but has Philip taken to Egyptian cigarettes in order to celebrate my winter at Cairo?

GRACE. Those are Cynthia's.

SUDLEY. (*Thinking that no one is worth knowing whom he does not know.*) Who is "Cynthia"?

GRACE. Mrs. Karslake— She's staying here, Cousin William. She'll be down in a minute.

SUDLEY. (*Shocked.*) You don't mean to tell me—?—!

MISS HENEAGE. Yes, William, Cynthia is Mrs. Karslake—Mrs. Karslake has no

New York house. I disliked the publicity of a hotel in the circumstances, and accordingly when she became engaged to Philip, I invited her here.

SUDLEY. (*Suspicious and distrustful.*) And may I ask *who* Mrs. Karslake is?

MISS HENEAGE. (*With confidence.*) She was a Deane.

SUDLEY. (*Walking about the room, sorry to be obliged to concede good birth to any but his own blood.*) Oh, oh—well the Deanes are extremely nice people. (*Going to table.*) Was her father J. William Deane?

MISS HENEAGE. (*Nodding, still more secure.*) Yes.

SUDLEY. (*Giving in with difficulty.*) The family is an old one. J. William Deane's daughter? Surely he left a very considerable—

MISS HENEAGE. Oh, fifteen or twenty millions.

SUDLEY. (*Determined not to be dazzled.*) If I remember rightly she was brought up abroad.

MISS HENEAGE. In France and England—and I fancy brought up with a very gay set in very gay places. In fact she is what is called a "sporty" woman.

SUDLEY. (*Always ready to think the worst.*) We might put up with that. But you don't mean to tell me Philip has the—the—the—assurance to marry a woman who has been divorced by—

MISS HENEAGE. Not at all. Cynthia Karslake divorced her husband.

SUDLEY. (*Gloomily, since he has less fault to find than he expected.*) She divorced him! Ah! (*He sips his tea.*)

MISS HENEAGE. The suit went by default. And, my dear William, there are many palliating circumstances. Cynthia was married to Karslake only seven months. There are no—(*glancing at* GRACE) no hostages to Fortune! Ahem!

SUDLEY. (*Still unwilling to be pleased.*) Ah! What sort of a young woman is she?

GRACE. (*With the superiority of one who is not too popular.*) Men admire her.

MISS HENEAGE. She 's not conventional.

MRS. PHILLIMORE. (*Showing a faint sense of justice.*) I am bound to say she has behaved discreetly ever since she arrived in this house.

MISS HENEAGE. Yes, Mary—but I sometimes suspect that she exercises a degree of self-control—

SUDLEY. (*Glad to have something against some one.*) She claps on the lid, eh? And you think that perhaps some day she 'll boil over? Well, of course fifteen or twenty millions—but who 's Karslake?

GRACE. (*Very superciliously.*) He owns Cynthia K. She 's the famous mare.

MISS HENEAGE. He 's Henry Karslake's son.

SUDLEY. (*Beginning to make the best of it.*) Oh!—Henry!—Very respectable family. Although I remember his father served a term in the senate. And so the wedding is to be to-morrow?

MRS. PHILLIMORE. (*Assenting.*) To-morrow.

SUDLEY. (*Rising, his respectability to the front when he thinks of the ceremony.* GRACE *rises.*) To-morrow. Well, my dear Sarah, a respectable family with some means. We must accept her. But on the whole, I think it will be best for me not to see the young woman. My disapprobation would make itself apparent.

GRACE. (*Whispering to* SUDLEY.) Cynthia 's coming. (*He does n't hear.*)

(CYNTHIA *enters, absorbed in reading a newspaper. She is a young creature in her twenties, small and high-bred, full of the love of excitement and sport. Her manner is wide awake and keen and she is evidently in no fear of the opinion of others. Her dress is exceedingly elegant, but with the elegance of a woman whose chief interests lie in life out of doors. There is nothing horsey in her style, and her expression is youthful and ingenuous.*)

SUDLEY. (*Sententiously and determinedly epigrammatic.*) The uncouth modern young woman, eight feet high, with a skin like a rhinoceros and manners like a cave dweller—an habitué of the racetrack and the divorce court—

GRACE. (*Aside to* SUDLEY.) Cousin William!

SUDLEY. Eh, oh!

CYNTHIA. (*Coming down, reading, immersed, excited, trembling. She lowers the paper to catch the light.*) "Belmont favorite—six to one—Rockaway—Rosebud, and Flying Cloud. Slow track—raw wind—hm, hm, hm— At the half, Rockaway forged ahead, when Rosebud under the lash made a bold bid for victory—neck by neck—for a quarter—when Flying Cloud slipped by the pair and won on the post by a nose in one forty nine!" (*Speaking with the enthusiasm *of a sport.*) Oh, I wish I'd seen the dear thing do it. Oh, it's Mr. Sudley! You must think me very rude. How do you do, Mr. Sudley?

(*She goes to* SUDLEY.)

SUDLEY. (*Bowing without cordiality.*) Mrs. Karslake.

(*Pause;* CYNTHIA *feels he should say something. As he says nothing, she speaks again.*)

CYNTHIA. I hope Cairo was delightful? Did you have a smooth voyage?

SUDLEY. (*Pompously.*) You must permit me, Mrs. Karslake—

CYNTHIA. (*With good temper, somewhat embarrassed, and talking herself into ease.*) Oh, please don't welcome me to the family. All that formal part is over, if you don't mind. I'm one of the tribe now! You're coming to our wedding to-morrow?

SUDLEY. My dear Mrs. Karslake, I think it might be wiser—

CYNTHIA. (*Still with cordial good temper.*) Oh, but you must come! I mean to be a perfect wife to Philip and all his relations! That sounds rather miscellaneous, but you know what I mean.

SUDLEY. (*Very sententiously.*) I am afraid—

CYNTHIA. (*Gay and still covering her embarrassment.*) If you don't come, it'll look as if you were not standing by Philip when he's in trouble! You'll come, won't you—but of course you will.

SUDLEY. (*After a self-important pause.*) I will come, Mrs. Karslake. (*After a pause.*) Good-afternoon. (*In a tone of sorrow and light compassion.*) Good-bye, Mary. Good-afternoon, Sarah. (*Sighing.*) Grace, dear. (*To* MISS HENEAGE.) At what hour did you say the alimony commences?

MISS HENEAGE. (*Quickly and commandingly to cover his slip.*) The ceremony is at three P. M., William.

(SUDLEY *goes toward the door.*)

MRS. PHILLIMORE. (*With fatigued voice and manner as she rises.*) I am going to my room to rest awhile.

(MRS. PHILLIMORE *goes up.*)

MISS HENEAGE. (*To* SUDLEY.) Oh, William, one moment—I entirely forgot! I've a most important social question to ask you! (*She goes up slowly to the door with him.*) In regard to the announcements of the wedding—whom they shall be sent to and whom not. For instance—the Dudleys—

(*Exeunt* SUDLEY *and* MISS HENEAGE, *talking.*)

CYNTHIA. So that's Cousin William?

GRACE. Don't you like him?

CYNTHIA. (*Calmly sarcastic.*) Like him? I love him. He's so generous. He could n't have received me with more warmth if I'd been a mulatto.

(THOMAS *re-enters.* PHILLIMORE *enters.* PHILIP PHILLIMORE *is a self-centered, short-tempered, imperious member of the respectable fashionables of New York. He is well and solidly dressed and in manner and speech evidently a man of family. He is accustomed to being listened to in his home circle and from the bench, and it is practically impossible for him to believe that he can make a mistake.*)

GRACE. (*Outraged.*) Really you know— (CYNTHIA *crosses the stage and sits at the table.*) Philip!

(PHILIP *nods to* GRACE *absent-mindedly. He is in his working suit and looks tired. He comes down silently, crosses to tea-table, and bends over and kisses* CYNTHIA *on forehead. He goes to his chair, which* THOMAS *has moved to suit him. He sits, and sighs with satisfaction.*)

PHILIP. Ah, Grace! (*Exit* GRACE.) Well, my dear, I thought I should never extricate myself from the court room. You look very debonnair!

CYNTHIA. The tea's making. You'll have your glass of sherry?

PHILIP. (*The strain of the day has evidently been severe.*) Thanks! (*Taking it from* THOMAS; *sighing.*) Ah!

CYNTHIA. I can see it's been a tiring day with you.

PHILIP. (*As before.*) Hm!

(*He sips the tea.*)

CYNTHIA. Were the lawyers very long winded?

PHILIP. (*Almost too tired for speech.*) Prolix to the point of somnolence. It might be affirmed without inexactitude that the prolixity of counsel is the somnolence of the judiciary. I am fatigued, ah! (*A little suddenly, awaking to the fact that his orders have not been carried out to the letter.*) Thomas! My *Post* is not in its usual place!

CYNTHIA. It's here, Philip.

(THOMAS *gets it.*)

PHILIP. Thanks, my dear. (*Opening the "Post."*) Ah! This hour with you—is —is really the—the—(*absently*) the one vivid moment of the day. (*Reading.*) Hm—shocking attack by the president on vested interests. Hm—too bad—but it's to be expected. The people insisted on electing a desperado to the presidential office—they must take the hold-up that follows. (*Pause; he reads*) Hm! His English is lacking in idiom, his spelling in conservatism, his mind in balance, and his character in repose.

CYNTHIA. (*Amiable but not very sympathetic.*) You seem more fatigued than usual. Another glass of sherry, Philip?

PHILIP. Oh, I ought not to—

CYNTHIA. I think you seem a little more tired than usual.

PHILIP. Perhaps I am. (*She pours out sherry.* PHILIP *takes the glass.*) Ah, this hour is truly a grateful form of restful excitement. (*Pause.*) You, too, find it—eh? (*He looks at* CYNTHIA.)

CYNTHIA. (*With veiled sarcasm.*) Decidedly.

PHILIP Decidedly what, my dear?

CYNTHIA. (*As before.*) Restful.

PHILIP. Hm! Perhaps I need the calm more than you do. Over the case to-day I actually—eh—(*sipping*) slumbered. I heard myself do it. That's how I know. A dressmaker sued on seven counts. (*Reading newspaper.*) Really, the insanity of the United States Senate—you seem restless, my dear. Ah—um—have you seen the evening paper? I see there has been a lightning change in the style or size of hats which ladies—

(*He sweeps a descriptive motion with his hand, giving paper to* CYNTHIA, *then moves his glass, reads, and sips.*)

CYNTHIA. The lamp, Thomas.

(THOMAS *blows out the alcohol lamp on the tea-table with difficulty. He blows twice. Each time he moves* PHILIP *starts. He blows again.*)

PHILIP. (*Irritably.*) Confound it, Thomas! What are you puffing and blowing at—?

THOMAS. It's out, ma'am—yes, sir.

PHILIP. You're excessively noisy, Thomas!

THOMAS. (*In a fluster.*) Yes, sir—I am.

CYNTHIA. (*Soothing* THOMAS's *wounded feelings.*) We don't need you, Thomas.

THOMAS. Yes, ma'am.

PHILIP. Puffing and blowing and shaking and quaking like an automobile in an ecstasy! (*Exit* THOMAS.)

CYNTHIA. (*Not unsympathetically.*) Too bad, Philip! I hope my presence is n't too agitating?

PHILIP. Ah—it's just because I value this hour with you, Cynthia—this hour of tea and toast and tranquillity. It's quite as if we were married—happily married—already.

CYNTHIA. (*Admitting that married life is a blank, begins to look through paper.*) Yes, I feel as if we were married already.

PHILIP. (*Not recognizing her tone.*) Ah! It's the calm, you see.

CYNTHIA. (*As before.*) The calm? Yes—yes, it's—it's the calm.

PHILIP. (*Sighing.*) Yes, the calm—the Halcyon calm of—of second choice. Hm! (*He reads and turns over leaves of paper.* CYNTHIA *reads. Pause.*) After all, my dear—the feeling which I have for you—is—is—eh—the market is in a shocking condition of plethora! Hm—hm—and what are you reading?

CYNTHIA. (*Embarrassed.*) Oh, eh—well—I—eh—I'm just running over the sporting news.

PHILIP. Oh! (*He looks thoughtful.*)

CYNTHIA. (*Beginning to forget* PHILIP *and to remember more interesting matters.*) I fancied Hermes would come in an easy winner. He came in nowhere. Nonpareil was ridden by Henslow—he's a rotten bad rider. He gets nervous.

PHILIP. (*Reading still.*) Does he? Hm! I suppose you do retain an interest in horses and races. Hm—I trust some day the—ah—law will attract— Oh (*turning a page*), here's the report of my opinion in that dressmaker's case—Haggerty *vs.* Phillimore.

CYNTHIA. Was the case brought against you? (*Puzzled.*)

PHILIP. (*A little uncomfortable.*) Oh—no. The suit was brought by Haggerty, Miss Haggerty, a dressmaker, against the—in fact, my dear, against the former Mrs. Phillimore. (*Pause; he reads.*)

CYNTHIA. (*Curious about the matter.*) How did you decide it?

PHILIP. I was obliged to decide in Mrs. Phillimore's favor. Haggerty's plea was preposterous.

CYNTHIA. Did you—did you meet the—the—former—?

PHILIP. No.

CYNTHIA. I often see her at afternoon teas.

PHILIP. How did you recognize—

CYNTHIA. Why—(*opening paper*) because Mrs. Vida Phillimore's picture appears in every other issue of most of the evening papers. And I must confess I was curious. But, I'm sure you find it very painful to meet her again.

PHILIP. (*Slowly, considering.*) No,—would you find it so impossible to meet Mr.—

CYNTHIA. (*Much excited and aroused.*) Philip! Don't speak of him. He's nothing. He's a thing of the past. I never think of him. I forget him!

PHILIP. (*Somewhat sarcastic.*) That's extraordinarily original of you to forget him.

CYNTHIA. (*Gently, and wishing to drop the subject.*) We each of us have something to forget, Philip—and John Karslake is to me— Well, he's dead!

PHILIP. As a matter of fact, my dear, he *is* dead, or the next thing to it—for he's bankrupt. (*Pause.*)

CYNTHIA. Bankrupt? (*Excited and moved.*) Let's not speak of him. I mean never to see him or think about him or even hear of him!

(*He assents. She reads her paper. He sips his tea and reads his paper. She turns a page, starts and cries out.*)

PHILIP. God bless me!

CYNTHIA. It's a picture of—of—

PHILIP. John Karslake?

CYNTHIA. Picture of him, and one of me, and in the middle between us "Cynthia K!"

PHILIP. "Cynthia K"?

CYNTHIA. (*Excited.*) My pet riding mare! The best horse he has! She's an angel even in a photograph! Oh! (*Reading.*) "John Karslake drops a fortune at Saratoga."

(*Rises and goes up and down excitedly. PHILIP takes paper and reads.*)

PHILIP. (*Unconcerned, as the matter hardly touches him.*) Hem—ah—Advertises country place for sale—stables, famous mare "Cynthia K"—favorite riding mare of former Mrs. Karslake who is once again to enter the arena of matrimony with the well known and highly respected judge of—

CYNTHIA. (*Sensitive and much disturbed.*) Don't! Don't, Philip, please don't!

PHILIP. My dear Cynthia—take another paper—here's my *Post!* You'll find nothing disagreeable in the *Post.*

(CYNTHIA *takes the paper.*)

CYNTHIA (*After reading, sits near table.*) It's much worse in the *Post.* "John Karslake sells the former Mrs. Karslake's jewels—the famous necklace now at Tiffany's, and the sporty ex-husband sells his wife's portrait by Sargent"! Philip, I can't stand this.

(*She puts the paper on table.*)

PHILIP. Really, my dear, Mr. Karslake is bound to appear occasionally in print—or even you may have to meet him.

(*Enter* THOMAS.)

CYNTHIA. (*Determined and distressed.*) I won't meet him! I won't meet him. Every time I hear his name or "Cynthia K's" I'm so depressed.

THOMAS. (*Announcing with something like reluctance.*) Sir, Mr. Fiddler. Mr. Karslake's trainer.

(*Enter* FIDDLER.)

(*He is an English horse trainer, a wide-awake stocky well-groomed little cockney. He knows his own mind and sees life altogether through a stable door. Well-dressed for his station, and not young.*)

CYNTHIA. (*Excited and disturbed.*) Fiddler? Tim Fiddler? His coming is outrageous!

FIDDLER. A note for you, sir.

CYNTHIA. (*Impulsively.*) Oh, Fiddler—is that you?

FIDDLER. Yes'm!

CYNTHIA. (*In a half whisper, still speaking on impulse.*) How is she! Cynthia K? How's Planet II and the colt and Golden Rod? How's the whole stable? Are they well?

FIDDLER. No'm—we're all on the bum. (*Aside.*) Ever since you kicked us over!

CYNTHIA. (*Reproving him, though pleased.*) Fiddler!

FIDDLER. The horses is just simply gone to Egypt since you left, and so's the guv'nor.

CYNTHIA. (*Putting an end to* FIDDLER.) That will do, Fiddler.

FIDDLER. I'm waiting for an answer, sir.

CYNTHIA. What is it, Philip?

PHILIP. (*Uncomfortable.*) A mere matter of business. (*Aside to* FIDDLER.) The answer is, Mr. Karslake can come. The—the coast will be clear.

(*Exit* FIDDLER.)

CYNTHIA. (*Amazed; rising.*) You're not going to see him?

PHILIP. But Karslake, my dear, is an old acquaintance of mine. He argues cases before me. I will see that you do not have to meet him.

(CYNTHIA *crosses in excited dejection.*)

(*Enter* MATTHEW. *He is a high church clergyman to a highly fashionable congregation. His success is partly due to his social position and partly to his elegance of speech, but chiefly to his inherent amiability, which leaves the sinner in happy peace and smiles on the just and unjust alike.*)

MATTHEW. (*Most amiably.*) Ah, my dear brother!

PHILIP. Matthew. (*Meeting him.*)

MATTHEW. (*Nodding to* PHILIP.) Good afternoon, my dear Cynthia. How charming you look! (CYNTHIA *sits at the tea-table. To* CYNTHIA) Ah,—why were n't you in your pew yesterday? I preached a most original sermon.

(*He lays his hat and cane on the divan.*)

THOMAS. (*Aside to* PHILIP.) Sir, Mrs. Vida Phillimore's maid called you up on the telephone, and you 're to expect Mrs. Phillimore on a matter of business.

PHILIP. (*Astonished and disgusted.*) Here, impossible! (*To* CYNTHIA.) Excuse me, my dear!

(*Exit* PHILIP, *much embarrassed, followed by* THOMAS.)

MATTHEW. (*Coming down to chair, happily and pleasantly self-important.*) No, really, it was a wonderful sermon, my dear. My text was from Paul—"It is better to marry than to burn." It was a strictly logical sermon. I argued—that, as the grass withereth, and the flower fadeth,—there is nothing final in Nature; not even Death! And, as there is nothing final in Nature, not even Death;—so then if Death is not final—why should marriage be final? (*Gently.*) And so the necessity of—eh—divorce! You see? It was an exquisite sermon! All New York was there! And all New York went away happy! Even the sinners—if there were any! I don't often meet sinners—do you?

CYNTHIA. (*Indulgently, in spite of his folly, because he is kind.*) You 're such a dear, delightful Pagan! Here 's your tea!

MATTHEW. (*Sipping his tea.*) Why, my dear—you have a very sad expression!

CYNTHIA. (*A little bitterly.*) Why not?

MATTHEW. (*With sentimental sweetness.*) I feel as if I were of no use in the world when I see sadness on a young face. Only sinners should feel sad. You have committed no sin!

CYNTHIA. (*Impulsively.*) Yes, I have!

MATTHEW. Eh?

CYNTHIA. I committed the unpardonable sin—whe—when I married for love!

MATTHEW. One must not marry for anything else, my dear!

CYNTHIA. Why am I marrying your brother?

MATTHEW. I often wonder why? I wonder why you did n't choose to remain a free woman.

CYNTHIA. (*Going over the ground she has often argued with herself.*) I meant to; but a divorcée has no place in society. I felt horridly lonely! I wanted a friend. Philip was ideal as a friend—for months. Is n't it nice to bind a friend to you?

MATTHEW. Yes—yes!

(*He sets down the teacup.*)

CYNTHIA. (*Growing more and more excited and moved as she speaks.*) To marry a friend—to marry on prudent, sensible grounds—a man—like Philip? That 's what I should have done first, instead of rushing into marriage—because I had a wild, mad, sensitive, sympathetic—passion and pain and fury—of, I don't know what—that almost strangled me with happiness!

MATTHEW. (*Amiable and reminiscent.*) Ah—ah—in my youth—I,—I too!

CYNTHIA. (*Coming back to her manner of every day.*) And besides—the day Philip asked me I was in the dumps! And now—how about marrying only for love?

(*Re-enter* PHILIP.)

MATTHEW. Ah, my dear, love is not the only thing in the world!

PHILIP. (*Speaking as he enters.*) I got there too late, she 'd hung up.

CYNTHIA. Who, Philip?

PHILIP. Eh—a lady—eh—

(*Enter* THOMAS, *flurried, with card on salver.*)

THOMAS. A card for you, sir. Ahem—ahem—Mrs. Phillimore—that was, sir.

PHILIP. Eh?

THOMAS. She 's on the stairs, sir. (*He turns. Enter* VIDA. THOMAS *announces her as being the best way of meeting the difficulty.*) Mrs. Vida Phillimore!

(VIDA *comes in slowly, with the air of a spoiled beauty. She stops just inside the door and speaks in a very casual manner. Her voice is languorous and caressing. She is dressed in the excess of the French fashion and carries an outré parasol. She smiles and comes, undulating, to the middle of the stage. Exit* THOMAS.)

VIDA. How do you do, Philip. (*Pause.*) Don't tell me I'm a surprise! I had you called up on the 'phone and I sent up my card—and, besides, Philip dear, when you have the—the—habit of the house, as unfortunately I have, you can't treat yourself like a stranger in a strange land. At least, I can't—so here I am. My reason for coming was to ask you about that B. and O. stock we hold in common. (*To* MATTHEW, *condescendingly, the clergy being a class of unfortunates debarred by profession from the pleasures of the world.*) How do you do? (*Pause. She then goes to the real reason of her visit.*) Do be polite and present me to your wife-to-be.

PHILIP. (*Awkwardly.*) Cynthia—

CYNTHIA. (*Cheerfully, with dash, putting the table between her and* VIDA.) We're delighted to see you, Mrs. Phillimore. I need n't ask you to make yourself at home, but will you have a cup of tea?

(MATTHEW *sits near the little table.*)

VIDA. (*To* PHILIP.) My dear, she's not in the least what I expected. I heard she was a dove! She's a very dashing kind of a dove! (*To* CYNTHIA; *coming to tea-table.*) My dear, I'm paying you compliments. Five lumps and quantities of cream. I find single life very thinning. (*To* PHILIP, *very calm and ready to be agreeable to any man.*) And how well you're looking! It must be the absence of matrimonial cares—or is it a new angel in the house?

CYNTHIA. (*Outraged at* VIDA'S *intrusion, but polite though delicately sarcastic.*) It's most amusing to sit in your place. And how at home you must feel here in this house where you have made so much trouble—I mean tea. (*Rising.*) Do you know it would be in much better taste if you would take the place you're accustomed to?

VIDA. (*As calm as before.*) My dear, I'm an intruder only for a moment; I shan't give you a chance to score off me again! But I must thank you, dear Philip, for rendering that decision in my favor—

PHILIP. I assure you—

VIDA. (*Unable to resist a thrust at the close of this speech.*) Of course, you would like to have rendered it against me. It was your wonderful sense of justice, and that's why I'm so grateful—if not to you, to your Maker!

PHILIP. (*He feels that this is no place for his future wife. Rises quickly and irascibly. To* CYNTHIA.) Cynthia, I would prefer that you left us.

(MATTHEW *comes to the sofa and sits.*)

CYNTHIA. (*Determined not to leave the field first, remains seated.*) Certainly, Philip!

PHILIP. I expect another visitor who—

VIDA. (*With flattering insistence, to* CYNTHIA.) Oh, my dear—don't go! The truth is—I came to see you! I feel most cordially towards you—and really, you know, people in our position should meet on cordial terms.

CYNTHIA. (*Taking it with apparent calm, but pointing her remarks.*) Naturally. If people in our position could n't meet, New York society would soon come to an end.

(*Enter* THOMAS.)

VIDA. (*Calm, but getting her knife in too.*) Precisely. Society's no bigger than a band-box. Why, it's only a moment ago I saw Mr. Karslake walking—

CYNTHIA. Ah!

THOMAS. (*Announcing clearly. Every one changes place, in consternation, amusement or surprise.* CYNTHIA *moves to leave the stage, but stops for fear of attracting* KARSLAKE'S *attention.*) Mr. John Karslake!

(*Enter* KARSLAKE. *He is a powerful, generous personality, a man of affairs, breezy, gay and careless. He gives the impression of being game for any fate in store for him. His clothes indicate sporting propensities and his taste in waistcoats and ties is brilliant.* KARSLAKE *sees first* PHILIP *and then* MATTHEW. *Exit* THOMAS.)

PHILIP. How do you do?

JOHN. (*Very gay and no respecter of persons.*) Good-afternoon, Mr. Phillimore. Hello—here's the church. (*Crossing to* MATTHEW *and shaking hands. He slaps him on the back.*) I had n't the least idea—how are you? By George, your reverence, that was a racy sermon of yours on Divorce! What was your text? (*Seeing* VIDA, *and bowing very politely.*) Galatians 4:2: "The more the merrier," or "Who next?" (*Smiling.*) As the whale said after Jonah!

(CYNTHIA *makes a sudden movement, and turns her cup over.* JOHN *faces about quickly and they face each other.* JOHN *gives a frank start. A pause.*)

JOHN. (*Bowing; astounded, in a low voice.*) Mrs. Karslake— I was not aware of the pleasure in store for me. I understood you were in the country. (*Recovering, crosses to chair.*) Perhaps you'll be good enough to make me a cup of tea?—that is if the teapot wasn't lost in the scrimmage. (*Pause.* CYNTHIA, *determined to equal him in coolness, returns to the tea-tray.*) Mr. Phillimore, I came to get your signature in that matter of Cox *vs.* Keely.

PHILIP. I shall be at your service, but pray be seated.

(*He indicates a chair by tea-table.*)

JOHN. (*Sitting beyond but not far from the tea-table.*) And I also understood you to say you wanted a saddle horse.

PHILIP. You have a mare called—eh—"Cynthia K"?

JOHN. (*Promptly.*) Yes—she's not for sale.

PHILIP. Oh, but she's just the mare I had set my mind on.

JOHN. (*With a touch of humor.*) You want her for yourself?

PHILIP. (*A little flustered.*) I—eh—I sometimes ride.

JOHN. (*He is sure of himself now.*) She's rather lively for you, Judge. Mrs. Karslake used to ride her.

PHILIP. You don't care to sell her to me?

JOHN. She's a dangerous mare, Judge, and she's as delicate and changeable as a girl. I'd hate to leave her in your charge!

CYNTHIA. (*Eagerly, but in a low voice.*) Leave her in mine, Mr. Karslake!

JOHN. (*After slight pause.*) Mrs. Karslake knows all about a horse, but— (*Turning to* CYNTHIA.) Cynthia K's got rather tricky of late.

CYNTHIA. (*Haughtily.*) You mean to say you think she'd chuck me?

JOHN. (*With polite solicitude and still humorous. To* PHILIP.) I'd hate to have a mare of mine deprive you of a wife, Judge. (*Rising.*) She goes to Saratoga next week, C. W.

VIDA. (*Who has been sitting and talking to* MATTHEW *for lack of a better man, comes to talk to* KARSLAKE.) C. W.?

JOHN. (*Rising as she rises.*) Creditors willing.

VIDA. (*Crossing and sitting left of tea-table.*) I'm sure your creditors are willing.

JOHN. Oh, they're a breezy lot, my creditors. They're giving me a dinner this evening.

VIDA. (*More than usually anxious to please.*) I regret I'm not a breezy creditor, but I do think you owe it to me to let me see your Cynthia K! Can't you lead her around to my house?

JOHN. At what hour, Mrs. Phillimore?

VIDA. Say eleven? And you, too, might have a leading in my direction—771 Fifth Avenue.

(JOHN *bows.* CYNTHIA *hears and notes this.*)

CYNTHIA. Your cup of tea, Mr. Karslake.

JOHN. Thanks. (JOHN *gets tea and sips it.*) I beg your pardon—you have forgotten, Mrs. Karslake—very naturally, it has slipped from your memory, but I don't take sugar.

(CYNTHIA, *furious with him and herself. He hands cup back. She makes a second cup.*)

CYNTHIA. (*Cheerfully; in a rage.*) Sorry!

JOHN. (*Also apparently cheerful.*) Yes, gout. It gives me a twinge even to sit in the shadow of a sugar maple! First you riot, and then you diet!

VIDA. (*Calm and amused; aside to* MATTHEW.) My dear Matthew, he's a darling! But I feel as if we were all taking tea on the slope of a volcano!

(MATTHEW *sits.*)

PHILIP. It occurred to me, Mr. Karslake, you might be glad to find a purchaser for your portrait by Sargent?

JOHN. It's not *my* portrait. It's a portrait of Mrs. Karslake, and to tell you the truth—Sargent's a good fellow—I've made up my mind to keep it—to remember the artist by.

(CYNTHIA *is wounded by this.*)

PHILIP. Hm!

(CYNTHIA *hands second cup of tea to* JOHN.)

CYNTHIA. (*With careful politeness.*) Your cup of tea, Mr. Karslake.

JOHN. (*Rising and taking tea with courteous indifference.*) Thanks—sorry to trouble you.

(*He drinks the cup of tea standing by the tea-table.*)

PHILIP. (*To make conversation.*) You're selling your country place?

JOHN. If I was long of hair—I'd sell that.

CYNTHIA. (*Excited. Taken out of her-*

self by the news.) You're not really selling your stable?

JOHN. (*Finishing his tea, he places empty cup on tea-table and reseats himself.*) Every gelding I've got—seven foals and a donkey! I don't mean the owner.

CYNTHIA. (*Still interested and forgetting the discomfort of the situation.*) How did you ever manage to come such a cropper?

JOHN. Streak of blue luck!

CYNTHIA. (*Quickly.*) I don't see how it's possible—

JOHN. You would if you'd been there. You remember the head man? (*Sits.*) Bloke?

CYNTHIA. Of course!

JOHN. Well, his wife divorced him for beating her over the head with a bottle of Fowler's Solution, and it seemed to prey on his mind. He sold me—

CYNTHIA. (*Horrified.*) Sold a race?

JOHN. About ten races, I guess.

CYNTHIA. (*Incredulous.*) Just because he'd beaten his wife?

JOHN. No. Because she divorced him.

CYNTHIA. Well, I can't see why that should prey on his mind!

(*Suddenly remembers.*)

JOHN. Well, I have known men that it stroked the wrong way. But he cost me eighty thousand. And then Urbanity ran third in the thousand dollar stakes for two-year-olds at Belmont.

CYNTHIA. (*She throws this remark in.*) I never had faith in that horse.

JOHN. And, of course, it never rains monkeys but it pours gorillas! So when I was down at St. Louis on the fifth, I laid seven to three on Fraternity—

CYNTHIA. Crazy! Crazy!

JOHN. (*Ready to take the opposite view.*) I don't see it. With her record she ought to have romped it an easy winner.

CYNTHIA. (*Pure sport.*) She hasn't the stamina! Look at her barrel!

JOHN. Well, anyhow, Geranium finished me!

CYNTHIA. You didn't lay odds on Geranium!

JOHN. Why not? She's my own mare—

CYNTHIA. Oh!

JOHN. Streak o' bad luck—

CYNTHIA. (*Plainly anxious to say "I told you so."*) Streak of poor judgment! Do you remember the day you rode Billy at a six foot stone wall, and he stopped and you didn't, and there was a hornets' nest (MATTHEW *rises*) on the other side, and I remember you were hot just because I said you showed poor judgment? (*She laughs at the memory. A general movement of disapproval. She remembers the situation.*) I beg your pardon.

MATTHEW. (*Rising to meet* VIDA. *Hastily.*) It seems to me that horses are like the fourth gospel. Any conversation about them becomes animated almost beyond the limits of the urbane!

(VIDA, *disgusted by such plainness of speech, rises and goes to* PHILIP, *who waves her to a chair.*)

PHILIP. (*Formally.*) I regret that you have endured such reverses, Mr. Karslake. (JOHN *quietly bows.*)

CYNTHIA. (*Concealing her interest, she speaks casually.*) You haven't mentioned your new English horse—Pantomime. What did he do at St. Louis?

JOHN. (*Sitting.*) Fell away and ran fifth.

CYNTHIA. Too bad. Was he fully acclimated? Ah, well—

JOHN. We always differed—you remember—on the time needed—

MATTHEW. (*Coming to* CYNTHIA, *speaking to carry off the situation as well as to get a tip.*) Isn't there a—eh—a race to-morrow at Belmont Park?

JOHN. Yes. I'm going down in my auto.

CYNTHIA. (*Evidently wishing she might be going too.*) Oh!

MATTHEW. And what animal shall you prefer?

(*Covering his personal interest with amiable altruism.*)

JOHN. I'm backing Carmencita.

CYNTHIA. (*Gesture of despair.*) Carmencita! Carmencita!

(MATTHEW *goes to* VIDA.)

JOHN. You may remember we always differed on Carmencita.

CYNTHIA. (*Disgusted at* JOHN'S *dunderheadedness.*) But there's no room for difference. She's a wild, headstrong, dissatisfied, foolish little filly. The deuce couldn't ride her—she'd shy at her own shadow—"Carmencita." Oh, very well, then, I'll wager you—and I'll give you odds too—"Decorum" will come in first, and I'll lay three to one he'll beat Carmencita by five lengths! How's that for fair?

JOHN. (*Never forgetting the situation.*) Sorry I'm not flush enough to take you.

CYNTHIA. (*Impetuously.*) Philip, dear, you lend John enough for the wager.

MATTHEW. (*As nearly horrified as so soft a soul can be.*) Ahem! Really—

JOHN. It's a sporty idea, Mrs. Karslake, but perhaps in the circumstances—

CYNTHIA. (*Her mind on her wager.*) In what circumstances?

PHILIP. (*With a nervous laugh.*) It does seem to me there is a certain impropriety—

CYNTHIA. (*Remembering the conventions, which, for a moment, had actually escaped her.*) Oh, I forgot. When horses are in the air—

MATTHEW. (*Pouring oil on troubled waters. Crossing, he speaks to* VIDA *at back of armchair, where she sits.*) It's the fourth gospel, you see.

(*Enter* THOMAS *with a letter on a salver, which he hands to* PHILIP.

CYNTHIA. (*Meekly.*) You are quite right, Philip. The fact is, seeing Mr. Karslake again (*laying on her indifference with a trowel*) he seems to me as much a stranger as if I were meeting him for the first time.

MATTHEW. (*Aside to* VIDA.) We are indeed taking tea on the slope of a volcano.

VIDA. (*She is about to go, but thinks she will have a last word with* JOHN.) I'm sorry your fortunes are so depressed, Mr. Karslake.

PHILIP. (*Looking at the card that* THOMAS *has just brought in.*) Who in the world is Sir Wilfrid Cates-Darby?

(*General move.*)

JOHN. Oh—eh—Cates-Darby? (PHILIP *opens letter which* THOMAS *has brought with card.*) That's the English chap I bought Pantomime of.

PHILIP. (*To* THOMAS.) Show Sir Wilfrid Cates-Darby in.

(*Exit* THOMAS. *The prospect of an Englishman with a handle to his name changes* VIDA'S *plans and instead of leaving the house, she goes to the sofa, and sits there.*)

JOHN. He's a good fellow, Judge. Place near Epsom. Breeder. Over here to take a shy at our races.

(*Enter* THOMAS.)

THOMAS. (*Announcing.*) Sir Wilfrid Cates-Darby.

(*Enter* SIR WILFRID CATES-DARBY. *He is a high-bred, sporting Englishman. His manner, his dress and his diction are the perfection of English elegance. His movements are quick and graceful. He talks lightly and with ease. He is full of life and unsmiling good temper.*)

PHILIP. (*To* SIR WILFRID *and referring to the letter of introduction in his hand.*) I am Mr. Phillimore. I am grateful to Stanhope for giving me the opportunity of knowing you, Sir Wilfrid. I fear you find it warm?

SIR WILFRID. (*Delicately mopping his forehead.*) Ah, well—ah—warm, no—hot, yes! Deuced extraordinary climate yours, you know, Mr. Phillimore.

PHILIP. (*Conventional.*) Permit me to present you to—(*The unconventional situation pulls him up short. It takes him a moment to decide how to meet it. He makes up his mind to pretend that everything is as usual, and presents* CYNTHIA *first.*) Mrs. Karslake.

(SIR WILFRID *bows, surprised and doubtful.*)

CYNTHIA. How do you do?

PHILIP. And to Mrs. Phillimore. (VIDA *bows nonchalantly, but with a view to catching* SIR WILFRID'S *attention.* SIR WILFRID *bows, and looks from her to* PHILIP.) My brother—and Mr. Karslake you know.

SIR WILFRID. How do, my boy? (*Half aside, to* JOHN.) No idea you had such a charming little wife— What?— Eh?

(KARSLAKE *goes up to speak to* MATTHEW *and* PHILIP *in the further room.*)

CYNTHIA. You'll have a cup of tea, Sir Wilfrid?

SIR WILFRID. (*At table.*) Thanks, awfully. (*Very cheerfully.*) I'd no idea old John had a wife! The rascal never told me!

CYNTHIA. (*Pouring tea and facing the facts.*) I'm not Mr. Karslake's wife!

SIR WILFRID. Oh!— Eh?— I see—

(*Business of thinking it out.*)

VIDA. (*Who has been ready for some time to speak to him.*) Sir Wilfrid, I'm sure no one has asked you how you like our country?

SIR WILFRID. (*Going to* VIDA *and speaking, standing by her at sofa.*) Oh, well, as to climate and horses, I say nothing. But I like your American humor. I'm acquiring it for home purposes.

VIDA. (*Getting down to love as the basis of conversation.*) Aren't you going to acquire an American girl for home purposes?

SIR WILFRID. The more narrowly I look the agreeable project in the face, the more I like it. Ought n't to say that in the presence of your husband.

(*He casts a look at* PHILIP, *who has gone into the next room.*)

VIDA. (*Cheerful and unconstrained.*) He's not my husband!

SIR WILFRID. (*Completely confused.*) Oh—eh?—my brain must be boiled. You are—Mrs.—eh—ah—of course, now I see! I got the wrong names! I thought you were Mrs. Phillimore. (*He sits by her.*) And that nice girl Mrs. Karslake! You 're deucedly lucky to be Mrs. Karslake. John 's a prime sort. I say, have you and he got any kids? How many?

VIDA. (*Horrified at being suspected of maternity, but speaking very sweetly.*) He 's not my husband.

SIR WILFRID. (*His good spirits all gone, but determined to clear things up.*) Phew! Awfully hot in here! Who the deuce is John's wife?

VIDA. He has n't any.

SIR WILFRID. Who 's Phillimore's wife?

VIDA. He has n't any.

SIR WILFRID. Thanks, fearfully! (*To* MATTHEW, *whom he approaches; suspecting himself of having lost his wits.*) Would you excuse me, my dear and Reverend Sir—you 're a churchman and all that—would you mind straightening me out?

MATTHEW. (*Most gracious.*) Certainly, Sir Wilfrid. Is it a matter of doctrine?

SIR WILFRID. Oh, damme—beg your pardon,—no, it 's not words, it 's women.

MATTHEW. (*Ready to be outraged.*) Women!

SIR WILFRID. It 's divorce. Now, the lady on the sofa—

MATTHEW. *Was* my brother's wife; he divorced her—incompatibility—-Rhode Island. The lady at the tea-table *was* Mr. Karslake's wife; she divorced him—desertion—Sioux Falls. One moment—she is about to marry my brother.

SIR WILFRID. (*Cheerful again.*) I 'm out! Thought I never would be! Thanks!

(VIDA *laughs.*)

VIDA. (*Not a whit discountenanced and ready to please.*) Have you got me straightened out yet?

SIR WILFRID. Straight as a die! I say, you had lots of fun, did n't you? (*Going back to sofa.*) And so *she 's* Mrs. John Karslake?

VIDA. (*Calm, but secretly disappointed.*) Do you like her?

SIR WILFRID. My word!

VIDA. (*Fully expecting personal flattery.*) Eh?

SIR WILFRID. She 's a box o' ginger!

VIDA. You have n't seen many American women!

SIR WILFRID. Oh, have n't I?

VIDA. If you 'll pay me a visit to-morrow —at twelve, you shall meet a most charming young woman, who has seen you once, and who admires you—ah!

SIR WILFRID. I 'm there—what!

VIDA. Seven hundred and seventy-one Fifth Avenue.

SIR WILFRID. Seven seventy-one Fifth Avenue—at twelve.

VIDA. At twelve.

SIR WILFRID. Thanks! (*Indicating* CYNTHIA.) She 's a thoroughbred—you can see that with one eye shut. Twelve. (*Shaking hands.*) Awfully good of you to ask me. (*He joins* JOHN.) I say, my boy, your former 's an absolute certainty. (*To* CYNTHIA.) I hear you 're about to marry Mr. Phillimore, Mrs. Karslake?

(KARSLAKE *crosses to* VIDA; *they both go to sofa, where they sit.*)

CYNTHIA. To-morrow, 3 P. M., Sir Wilfrid.

SIR WILFRID. (*Much taken with* CYNTHIA, *he addresses her.*) Afraid I 've run into a sort of family party, eh? (*Indicating* VIDA.) The Past and the Future—awfully chic way you Americans have of asking your divorced husbands and wives to drop in, you know—celebrate a christenin', or the new bride, or—

CYNTHIA. Do you like your tea strong?

SIR WILFRID. Middlin'.

CYNTHIA. Sugar?

SIR WILFRID. One!

CYNTHIA. Lemon?

SIR WILFRID. Just torture a lemon over it. (*He makes a gesture as of twisting a lemon peel. She gives tea.*) Thanks! So you do it to-morrow at three?

CYNTHIA. At three, Sir Wilfrid.

SIR WILFRID. Sorry!

CYNTHIA. Why are you sorry?

SIR WILFRID. Hate to see a pretty woman married. Might marry her myself.

CYNTHIA. Oh, but I 'm sure you don't admire American women.

SIR WILFRID. Admire you, Mrs. Karslake—

CYNTHIA. Not enough to marry me, I hope.

SIR WILFRID. Marry you in a minute! Say the word. Marry you now—here.

CYNTHIA. You don't think you ought to know me a little before—

SIR WILFRID. Know you? Do know you.

(CYNTHIA *covers her hair with her handkerchief.*)

CYNTHIA. What color is my hair?

SIR WILFRID. Pshaw!

CYNTHIA. You see! You don't know whether I'm a chestnut or a strawberry roan! In the States we think a few months of friendship is quite necessary.

SIR WILFRID. Few months of moonshine! Never was a friend to a woman—thank God, in all my life.

CYNTHIA. Oh—oh, oh!

SIR WILFRID. Might as well talk about being a friend to a whiskey and soda.

CYNTHIA. A woman has a soul, Sir Wilfrid.

SIR WILFRID. Well, good whiskey is spirits—dozens o' souls!

CYNTHIA. You are so gross!

SIR WILFRID. (*Changing seat to above table.*) Gross? Not a bit! Friendship between the sexes is all fudge! I'm no friend to a rose in my garden. I don't call it friendship—eh—eh—a warm, starry night, moonbeams and ilex trees, "and a spirit who knows how" and all that—eh—(*Getting closer to her.*) You make me feel awfully poetical, you know—(PHILIP *comes down, glances nervously at* CYNTHIA *and* SIR WILFRID, *and walks up again.*) What's the matter? But, I say—poetry aside—do you, eh—(*Looking around to place* PHILIP.) Does he—y' know—is he—does he go to the head?

CYNTHIA. Sir Wilfrid, Mr. Phillimore is my sober second choice.

SIR WILFRID. Did you ever kiss him? I'll bet he fined you for contempt of court. Look here, Mrs. Karslake, if you're marryin' a man you don't care about—

CYNTHIA. (*Amused and excusing his audacity as a foreigner's eccentricity.*) Really!

SIR WILFRID. Well, I don't offer myself—

CYNTHIA. Oh!

SIR WILFRID. Not this instant—

CYNTHIA. Ah!

SIR WILFRID. But let me drop in to-morrow at ten.

CYNTHIA. What country and state of affairs do you think you have landed in?

SIR WILFRID. New York, by Jove! Been to school, too. New York is bounded on the North, South, East and West by the state of Divorce! Come, come, Mrs. Karslake, I like your country. You've no fear and no respect—no can't and lots of can. Here you all are, you see—your former husband, and your new husband's former wife—sounds like Ollendoff! Eh? So there you are, you see! But, jokin' apart—why do you marry him? Oh, well, marry him if you must! You can run around the corner and get a divorce afterwards—

CYNTHIA. I believe you think they throw one in with an ice-cream soda!

SIR WILFRID. (*Rising.*) Damme, my dear lady, a marriage in your country is no more than a—eh—eh—what do you call 'em? A "thank you, ma'am." That's what an American marriage is—a "thank you, ma'am." Bump—bump—you're over it and on to the next.

CYNTHIA. You're an odd fish! What? I believe I like you!

SIR WILFRID. 'Course you do! You'll see me when I call to-morrow—at ten? We'll run down to Belmont Park, eh?

CYNTHIA. Don't be absurd!

VIDA. (*She has finished her talk with* JOHN, *and breaks in on* SIR WILFRID, *who has hung about* CYNTHIA *too long to suit her.*) To-morrow at twelve, Sir Wilfrid!

SIR WILFRID. Twelve!

VIDA. (*Shaking hands with* JOHN.) Don't forget, Mr. Karslake—eleven o'clock to-morrow.

JOHN. (*Bowing assent.*) I won't!

VIDA. (*Coming to the middle of the stage and speaking to* CYNTHIA.) Oh, Mrs. Karslake, I've ordered Tiffany to send you something. It's a sugar bowl to sweeten the matrimonial lot! I suppose nothing would induce you to call?

CYNTHIA. (*Distantly and careless of offending.*) Thanks, no—that is, is "Cynthia K" really to be there at eleven? I'd give a gold mine to see her again.

VIDA. Do come!

CYNTHIA. If Mr. Karslake will accommodate me by his absence.

VIDA. Dear Mr. Karslake, you'll have to change your hour.

JOHN. Sorry, I'm not able to.

CYNTHIA. I can't come later for I'm to be married.

JOHN. It 's not as bad as that with me, but I am to be sold up—Sheriff, you know. Can't come later than eleven.

VIDA. (*To* CYNTHIA.) Any hour but eleven, dear.

CYNTHIA. (*Perfectly regardless of* VIDA, *and ready to vex* JOHN *if possible.*) Mrs. Phillimore, I shall call on you at eleven—to see Cynthia K. I thank you for the invitation. Good-afternoon.

VIDA. (*Aside to* JOHN, *crossing to speak quietly to him.*) It 's mere bravado; she won't come.

JOHN. You don't know her.

(*Pause. There is general embarrassment.* SIR WILFRID *plays with his eye-glass.* JOHN *is angry;* CYNTHIA *is triumphant;* MATTHEW *is embarrassed;* VIDA *is irritated;* PHILIP *is puzzled; everybody is at odds.*)

SIR WILFRID. (*For the first time being a witness to the pretty complications of divorce, he speaks to* MATTHEW.) Do you have it as warm as this ordinarily?

MATTHEW. (*For whom these moments are more than usually painful, and wiping his brow.*) It 's not so much the heat as the humidity.

JOHN. (*Looking at watch; he is glad to be off.*) I shall be late for my creditors' dinner.

SIR WILFRID. (*Coming down.*) Creditors' dinner.

JOHN. (*Reading note.*) Fifteen of my sporting creditors have arranged to give me a blow-out at Sherry's, and I 'm expected right away or sooner. And by the way, I was to bring my friends—if I had any. So now 's the time to stand by me! Mrs. Phillimore?

VIDA. Of course!

JOHN. (*Ready to embarrass* CYNTHIA, *if possible, and speaking as if he had quite forgotten their former relations.*) Mrs. Karslake—I beg your pardon. Judge? (PHILIP *declines.*) No? Sir Wilfrid?

SIR WILFRID. I 'm with you!

JOHN. (*To* MATTHEW.) Your Reverence?

MATTHEW. I regret—

SIR WILFRID. Is it the custom for creditors—

JOHN. Come on, Sir Wilfrid! (THOMAS *opens the door.*) Good-night, Judge—Your Reverence—

SIR WILFRID. Is it the custom—

JOHN. Hang the custom! Come on—I 'll show you a gang of creditors worth having!

(*Exit* SIR WILFRID *with* JOHN, *preceded by* VIDA. MATTHEW *crosses the stage, smiling, as if pleased, in a Christian way, with this display of generous gaiety. He looks at his watch.*)

MATTHEW. Good gracious! I had no idea the hour was so late. I 've been asked to a meeting with Maryland and Iowa, to talk over the divorce situation. (*Exit. His voice is heard off the stage.*) Good-afternoon! Good-afternoon!

(CYNTHIA *is evidently much excited. The outer door slams.* PHILIP *comes down the stage slowly.* CYNTHIA *stands, her eyes wide, her breathing rapid, until* PHILIP *speaks, when she seems suddenly to realize her position. There is a long pause.*)

PHILIP. (*With a superior air.*) I have seldom witnessed a more amazing cataclysm of jocundity! Of course, my dear, this has all been most disagreeable for you.

CYNTHIA. (*Excitedly.*) Yes, yes, yes!

PHILIP. I saw how much it shocked your delicacy.

CYNTHIA. (*Distressed and moved.*) Outrageous. (PHILIP *sits.*)

PHILIP. Do be seated, Cynthia. (*Taking up paper. Quietly.*) Very odd sort of an Englishman—that Cates-Darby!

CYNTHIA. Sir Wilfrid?—Oh, yes! (PHILIP *settles down to paper. To herself.*) Outrageous! I 've a great mind to go at eleven—just as I said I would!

PHILIP. Do sit down, Cynthia!

CYNTHIA. What? What?

PHILIP. You make me so nervous—

CYNTHIA. Sorry—sorry.

(*She sits down and seeing the paper, she takes it, looking at the picture of* JOHN KARSLAKE.)

PHILIP. (*Sighing with content.*) Ah! now that I see him, I don't wonder you could n't stand him. There 's a kind of —ah—spontaneous inebriety about him. He is incomprehensible! If I might with reverence cross question the Creator, I would say to him: "Sir, to what end or purpose did you create Mr. John Karslake?" I believe I should obtain no adequate answer! However (*sighing*) at last we have peace—and the *Post!* (PHILIP, *settling himself, reads paper;* CYNTHIA *looks at her paper, occasionally looking across at* PHILIP.) Forget the dust of the arena—the prolixity of counsel—the involuntary fatuity of things in general. (*Pause. He reads.*) Compose yourself!

(MISS HENEAGE, MRS. PHILLIMORE *and* GRACE *enter.*)

(CYNTHIA *sighs without letting her sigh be heard. She tries to compose herself. She glances at paper and then hearing* MISS HENEAGE, *starts slightly.* MISS HENEAGE *and* MRS. PHILLIMORE *stop at table.*)

MISS HENEAGE. (*She carries a sheet of paper.*) There, my dear Mary, is the announcement as I have now reworded it. I took William's suggestion. (MRS. PHILLIMORE *takes and casually reads it.*) I also put the case to him, and he was of the opinion that the announcement should be sent *only* to those people who are really *in* society.

(*She sits near table.* CYNTHIA *braces herself to bear the Phillimore conversation.*)

GRACE. I wish you'd make an exception of the Dudleys.

(CYNTHIA *rises and crosses to chair by the table.*)

MISS HENEAGE. And of course, that excludes the Oppenheims—the Vance-Browns.

MRS. PHILLIMORE. It's just as well to be exclusive.

GRACE. I do wish you'd make an exception of Lena Dudley.

MISS HENEAGE. We might, of course, include those new Girardos, and possibly—possibly the Paddingtons.

GRACE. I do wish you would take in Lena Dudley. (*They are now sitting.*)

MRS. PHILLIMORE. The mother Dudley is as common as a charwoman, and not nearly as clean.

PHILIP. (*Sighing, his own feelings as usual to the fore.*) Ah! I certainly am fatigued!

(CYNTHIA *begins to slowly crush the newspaper she has been reading with both hands, as if the effort of self-repression were too much for her.*)

MISS HENEAGE. (*Making the best of a gloomy future.*) We shall have to ask the Dudleys sooner or later to dine, Mary—because of the elder girl's marriage to that dissolute French Marquis.

MRS. PHILLIMORE. (*Plaintively.*) I don't like common people any more than I like common cats and of course in my time—

MISS HENEAGE. I think I shall include the Dudleys.

MRS. PHILLIMORE. You think you'll include the Dudleys?

MISS HENEAGE. Yes, I think I will include the Dudleys!

(*Here* CYNTHIA *gives up. Driven desperate by their chatter, she has slowly rolled her newspaper into a ball, and at this point tosses it violently to the floor and bursts into hysterical laughter.*)

MRS. PHILLIMORE. Why, my dear Cynthia—compose yourself.

PHILIP. (*Hastily.*) What is the matter, Cynthia? (*They speak together.*)

MISS HENEAGE. Why, Mrs. Karslake, what is the matter?

GRACE. (*She comes quickly forward, saying.*) Mrs. Karslake!

ACT SECOND.

SCENE. MRS. VIDA PHILLIMORE'S *boudoir. The room is furnished to please an empty-headed, pleasure-loving and fashionable woman. The furniture, the ornaments, what pictures there are, are all witness to taste up-to-date. Two French windows open on to a balcony, from which the trees of Central Park can be seen. There is a table between them; a mirror and a scent bottle upon it. A lady's writing table stands between two doors, nearer centre of stage. There is another door near an open fireplace, which is filled with potted plants and andirons, not in use. Over it is a tall mirror. On the mantelpiece are French clock, candelabra, and vases. On a line with the fireplace, a lounge, gay with silk pillows. A florist's box, large and long, filled with American Beauty roses is on a low table near the head of the lounge. Small tables and light chairs are here and there. At rise of the curtain* BENSON *is seen looking about her. She is a neat and pretty little English lady's maid in black silk and a thin apron. She comes down the stage still looking about her, and inspects the flower box; then goes to the door of* VIDA'S *room and speaks to her.*

BENSON. Yes, ma'am, the flowers have come.

(*She holds the door open.*)

(VIDA, *in a morning gown, enters, slowly. She is smoking a cigarette in as æsthetic a manner as she can, and is evidently turned out in her best style for conquest.*)

VIDA. (*Speaking with her back to the audience, always calm and, though civil, a little disdainful of her servant.*) Terribly garish light, Benson. Pull down the— (BENSON *obeys.*) Lower still—that will do. (*As she speaks, she goes about the room, giving the furniture a push here and there, arranging vases, etc.*) Men hate a clutter of chairs and tables. (*Stopping and taking up hand mirror, standing with back to audience.*) I really think I'm too pale for this light.

BENSON. (*Quickly, understanding what is implied.*) Yes, ma'am. (*Exit* BENSON. VIDA *sits at the table. Knock at the door.*) Come!

(*Enter* BROOKS.)

BROOKS. (*An ultra-English footman, in plush and calves.*) Any horders, m' lady?

VIDA. (*Incapable of remembering the last man, or of considering the new one.*) Oh,—of course! You're the new—

BROOKS. Footman, m' lady.

VIDA. (*As a matter of form.*) Your name?

BROOKS. Brooks, m' lady.

(*Reënter* BENSON *with rouge.*)

VIDA. (*Carefully giving instructions while she keeps her eyes on the glass and is rouged by* BENSON.) Brooks, I am at home to Mr. Karslake at eleven, not to any one else till twelve, when I expect Sir Wilfrid Cates-Darby.

(BROOKS *is inattentive, watching* BENSON.)

BROOKS. Yes, m' lady.

VIDA. (*Calm, but wearied by the ignorance of the lower classes.*) And I regret to inform you, Brooks, that in America there are no ladies, except salesladies!

BROOKS. (*Without a trace of comprehension.*) Yes, m' lady.

VIDA. I am at home to no one but the two names I have mentioned. (BROOKS *bows and goes out. She dabs on rouge while* BENSON *holds glass.*) Is the men's club room in order?

BENSON. Perfectly, ma'am.

VIDA. Whiskey and soda?

BENSON. Yes, ma'am, and the ticker's been mended. The British sporting papers arrived this morning.

VIDA. (*Looking at her watch which lies on the dressing table.*) My watch has stopped.

BENSON. (*Glancing at the French clock on the chimney-piece.*) Five to eleven, ma'am.

VIDA. (*Getting promptly to work.*) Hm, hm, I shall be caught. (*Rises.*) The box of roses, Benson! (BENSON *brings the box of roses, uncovers the flowers and places them at* VIDA'S *side.*) My gloves—the clippers, and the vase! (*Each of these things* BENSON *places in turn within* VIDA'S *range where she sits on the sofa. She has the long box of roses at her side on a small table, a vase of water on the floor by her side. She cuts the stems and places the roses in the vase. When she feels that she has reached a picturesque position, in which any onlooker would see in her a creature filled with the love of flowers and of her fellow man, she says:*) There!

(*The door opens and* BROOKS *enters;* VIDA *nods to* BENSON.)

BROOKS. (*Announcing stolidly.*) Sir John Karslake.

(*Enter* JOHN, *dressed in very nobby riding togs.*)

(*He comes in gaily and forcibly.* BENSON *gives way as he comes down. Exeunt* BROOKS *and* BENSON. JOHN *stops near the table.* VIDA, *from this point on, is busied with her roses.*)

VIDA. (*Languorously, but with a faint suggestion of humor.*) Is that really you, Sir John?

JOHN. (*Lively and far from being impressed by* VIDA.) I see now where we Americans are going to get our titles. Good-morning! You look as fresh as paint. (*He takes chair.*)

VIDA. (*Facing the insinuation with gentle pain.*) I hope you don't mean that? I never flattered myself for a moment you'd come. You're riding Cynthia K?

JOHN. (*Who has laid his gloves and riding crop on the table.*) Fiddler's going to lead her round here in ten minutes!

VIDA. Cigars and cigarettes! Scotch?

(*She indicates that he will find them on a small table up stage.*)

JOHN. Scotch!

(*Going up quickly to the table and helping himself to Scotch and seltzer.*)

VIDA. And now *do* tell me all about *her!*

(*Putting in her last roses; she keeps one rosebud in her hand, of a size suitable for a man's buttonhole.*)

JOHN. (*As he drinks.*) Oh, she 's an adorable creature—delicate, high-bred, sweet-tempered—

VIDA. (*Showing her claws for a moment.*) Sweet-tempered? Oh, you 're describing the horse! By "her," I meant—

JOHN. (*Irritated by the remembrance of his wife.*) Cynthia Karslake? I 'd rather talk about the last tornado.

(*Sits.*)

VIDA. (*Soothing the savage beast.*) There is only one thing I want to talk about, and that is, *you!* Why were you unhappy?

JOHN. (*Still cross.*) Why does a dollar last such a short time?

VIDA. (*With curiosity.*) Why did you part?

JOHN. Did you ever see a schooner towed by a tug? Well, I parted from Cynthia for the same reason that the hawser parts from the tug—I could n't stand the tug.

VIDA. (*Sympathizing.*) Ah! (*Pause.*)

JOHN. (*Still cross.*) Awful cheerful morning chat.

VIDA. (*Excusing her curiosity and coming back to love as the only subject for serious conversation.*) I must hear the story, for I 'm anxious to know why I 've taken such a fancy to you!

JOHN. (*Very nonchalantly.*) Why do *I* like you?

VIDA. (*Doing her best to charm.*) I won't tell you—it would flatter you too much.

JOHN. (*Not a bit impressed by* VIDA, *but as ready to flirt as another.*) Tell me!

VIDA. There 's a rose for you.

(*Giving him the one she has in her hand.*)

JOHN. (*Saying what is plainly expected of him.*) I want more than a rose—

VIDA. (*Putting this insinuation by.*) You refuse to tell me—?

JOHN. (*Once more reminded of* CYNTHIA, *speaks with sudden feeling.*) There 's nothing to tell. We met, we loved, we married, we parted; or at least we wrangled and jangled. (*Sighing.*) Ha! Why were n't we happy? Don't ask me, why! It may have been *partly* my fault!

VIDA. (*With tenderness.*) Never!

JOHN. (*His mind on* CYNTHIA.) But I believe it 's all in the way a girl 's brought up. Our girls are brought up to be ignorant of life—they 're ignorant of life. Life is a joke, and marriage is a picnic and a man is a shawl-strap—'Pon my soul, Cynthia Deane—no, I can't tell you!

(*During the following, he walks about in his irritation.*)

VIDA. (*Gently.*) Please tell me!

JOHN. Well, she was an heiress, an American heiress—and she 'd been taught to think marriage meant burnt almonds and moonshine and a yacht and three automobiles, and she thought—I don't know what she thought, but I tell you, Mrs. Phillimore, marriage is three parts love and seven parts forgiveness of sins.

VIDA. (*Flattering him as a matter of course.*) She never loved you.

JOHN. (*On whom she has made no impression at all.*) Yes, she did. For six or seven months there was not a shadow between us. It was perfect, and then one day she went off like a pistol-shot! I had a piece of law work and could n't take her to see Flashlight race the Maryland mare. The case meant a big fee, big Kudos, and in sails Cynthia, Flashlight mad! And will I put on my hat and take her? No—and bang she goes off like a stick o' dynamite—what did I marry her for?—and words—pretty high words, until she got mad, when she threw over a chair and said, oh, well,—marriage was a failure, or it was with me, so I said she 'd better try somebody else. She said she would, and marched out of the room.

VIDA. (*Gently sarcastic.*) But she came back!

JOHN. She came back, but not as you mean. She stood at the door and said, "Jack, I shall divorce you." Then she came over to my study table, dropped her wedding ring on my law papers, and went out. The door shut, I laughed; the front door slammed, I damned. (*Pause. He crosses to the window.*) She never came back.

(*He comes back to where* VIDA *sits. She catches his hands.*)

VIDA. (*Hoping for a contradiction.*) She 's broken your heart.

JOHN. Oh, no!

(*He crosses to the chair by the lounge.*)

VIDA. (*Encouraged, begins to play the game again.*) You 'll never love again!

JOHN. (*Speaking to her from the foot of her sofa.*) Try me! Try me! Ah, no, Mrs. Phillimore, I shall laugh, live, love and make money again! And let me tell you one thing—I 'm going to rap her one over the knuckles. She had a stick of a Connecticut lawyer, and he—well, to cut a legal story short, since Mrs. Karslake's been in Europe, I have been quietly testing the validity of the decree of divorce. Perhaps you don't understand?

VIDA. (*Letting her innate shrewdness appear.*) Oh, about a divorce, everything!

JOHN. I shall hear by this evening whether the divorce will stand or not.

VIDA. But it's to-day at three she marries—you won't let her commit bigamy?

JOHN. (*Shaking his head.*) I don't suppose I'd go as far as that. It may be the divorce will hold, but anyway I hope never to see her again.

(*He sits beside her facing up the stage as she faces down.*)

VIDA. Ah, my poor boy, she has broken your heart. (*Believing that this is her psychological moment, she lays her hand on his arm, but draws it back as soon as he attempts to take it.*) Now don't make love to me.

JOHN. (*Bold and amused, but never taken in.*) Why not?

VIDA. (*With immense gentleness.*) Because I like you too much! (*More gaily.*) I might give in, and take a notion to like you still more!

JOHN. Please do!

VIDA. (*With gush and determined to be womanly at all hazards.*) Jack, I believe you'd be a lovely lover!

JOHN. (*As before.*) Try me!

VIDA. (*Not hoping much from his tone.*) You charming, tempting, delightful fellow, I could love you without the least effort in the world,—but, no!

JOHN. (*Playing the game.*) Ah, well, now *seriously!* Between two people who have *suffered* and made their own mistakes—

VIDA. (*Playing the game too, but not playing it well.*) But you see, you don't *really* love me!

JOHN. (*Still ready to say what is expected.*) Cynthia—Vida, no man can sit beside you and look into your eyes without feeling—

VIDA. (*Speaking the truth as she sees it, seeing that her methods don't succeed.*) Oh! That's not love! That's simply—well, my dear Jack, it's beginning at the wrong end. And the truth is you hate Cynthia Karslake with such a whole-hearted hate, that you have n't a moment to think of any other woman.

JOHN. (*With sudden anger.*) I hate her!

VIDA. (*Very softly and most sweetly.*) Jack—Jack, I could be as foolish about you as—oh, as foolish as anything, my dear! And perhaps some day—perhaps some day you'll come to me and say, Vida, I am totally indifferent to Cynthia—and then—

JOHN. And then?

VIDA. (*The ideal woman in mind.*) Then, perhaps, you and I may join hands and stroll together into the Garden of Eden. It takes two to find the Garden of Eden, you know—and once we're on the inside, we'll lock the gate.

JOHN. (*Gaily, and seeing straight through her veneer.*) And lose the key under a rose-bush!

VIDA. (*Agreeing very softly.*) Under a rose-bush! (*Very soft knock.*) Come!

(JOHN *rises quickly.*)

(*Enter* BENSON *and* BROOKS.)

BROOKS. (*Stolid and announcing.*) My lady—Sir Wilf—

(BENSON *stops him with a sharp movement and turns toward* VIDA.)

BENSON. (*With intention.*) Your dressmaker, ma'am.

(BENSON *waves* BROOKS *to go. Exit* BROOKS, *very haughtily.*)

VIDA. (*Wonderingly.*) My dressmaker, Benson? (*With quick intelligence.*) Oh, of course, show her up. Mr. Karslake, you won't mind for a few minutes using my men's club room? Benson will show you! You'll find cigars and the ticker, sporting papers, whiskey; and, if you want anything special, just 'phone down to my "chef."

JOHN. (*Looking at his watch.*) How long?

VIDA. (*Very anxious to please.*) Half a cigar! Benson will call you.

JOHN. (*Practical.*) Don't make it too long. You see, there's my sheriff's sale on at twelve, and those races this afternoon. Fiddler will be here in ten minutes, remember!

(*Door opens.*)

VIDA. (*To* JOHN.) Run along! (*Exit* JOHN. VIDA *suddenly practical, and with a broad gesture to* BENSON.) Everything just as it was, Benson! (BENSON *whisks the roses out of the vase and replaces them in the box. She gives* VIDA *scissors and empty vases, and when* VIDA *finds herself in precisely the same position which preceded* JOHN'S *entrance, she says:*) There!

(*Enter* BROOKS, *as* VIDA *takes a rose from the basket.*)

BROOKS. (*Stolidly.*) Your ladyship's dressmaker! M 'lady!

(*Enter* SIR WILFRID *in morning suit with boutonnière.*)

VIDA. (*With tender surprise and busy with the roses.*) Is that really you, Sir Wilfrid! I never flattered myself for an instant that you 'd remember to come.

SIR WILFRID. (*Coming to her above end of sofa.*) Come? 'Course I come! Keen to come see you. By Jove, you know, you look as pink and white as a huntin' mornin'.

VIDA. (*Ready to make any man as happy as possible.*) You 'll smoke?

SIR WILFRID. Thanks! (*He watches her as she trims and arranges the flowers.*) Awfully long fingers you have! Wish I was a rose, or a ring, or a pair of shears! I say, d' you ever notice what a devil of a fellow I am for originality, what? (*Unlike* JOHN, *he is evidently impressed by her.*) You 've got a delicate little den up here! Not so much low livin' and high thinkin', as low lights and no thinkin' at all, I hope—eh?

(*By this time* VIDA *has filled a vase with roses and rises to sweep by him and if possible make another charming picture to his eyes.*)

VIDA. You don't mind my moving about?

SIR WILFRID. (*Impressed.*) Not if you don't mind my watchin'. (*He sits on the sofa.*) And sayin' how well you do it.

VIDA. It 's most original of you to come here this morning. I don't quite see why you did.

(*She places the roses here and there, as if to see their effect, and leaves them on a small table near the door through which her visitors entered.*)

SIR WILFRID. Admiration.

VIDA. (*Sauntering slowly toward the mirror as she speaks.*) Oh, I saw that you admired her! And of course, she did say she was coming here at eleven! But that was only bravado! She won't come, and besides, I 've given orders to admit no one!

SIR WILFRID. May I ask you—

(*He throws this in in the middle of her speech, which flows gently and steadily on.*)

VIDA. And indeed, if she came now, Mr. Karslake has gone, and her sole object in coming was to make him uncomfortable. (*She goes toward the table: stopping a half minute at the mirror to see that she looks as she wishes to look.*) Very dangerous symptom, too, that passionate desire to make one's former husband unhappy! But, I can't believe that your admiration for Cynthia Karslake is so warm that it led you to pay me this visit a half hour too early in the hope of seeing—

SIR WILFRID. (*Rising; most civil, but speaking his mind like a Briton.*) I say, would you mind stopping a moment! (*She smiles.*) I 'm not an American, you know; I was brought up not to interrupt. But you Americans, it 's different with you! If somebody did n't interrupt you, you 'd go on forever.

VIDA. (*She passes him to tantalize.*) My point is you come to see Cynthia—

SIR WILFRID. (*He believes she means it.*) I came hopin' to see—

VIDA. (*As before.*) Cynthia!

SIR WILFRID. (*Perfectly single-minded and entirely taken in.*) But I would have come even if I 'd known—

VIDA. (*Evading him while he follows.*) I don't believe it!

SIR WILFRID. (*As before.*) Give you my word I—

VIDA. (*The same.*) You 're here to see *her!* And of course—

SIR WILFRID. (*Determined to be heard because, after all, he 's a man.*) May I have the—eh—the floor? (VIDA *sits in a chair.*) I was jolly well bowled over with Mrs. Karslake, I admit that, and I hoped to see her here, but—

VIDA. (*Talking nonsense and knowing it.*) You had another object in coming. In fact, you came to see Cynthia, and you came to see me! What I really long to know, is why you wanted to see *me!* For, of course, Cynthia 's to be married at three! And, if she was n't she would n't have you!

SIR WILFRID. (*Not intending to wound; merely speaking the flat truth.*) Well, I mean to jolly well ask her.

VIDA. (*Indignant.*) To be your wife?

SIR WILFRID. Why not?

VIDA. (*As before.*) And you came here, to my house—in order to ask her—

SIR WILFRID. (*Truthful even on a subtle point.*) Oh, but that 's only my first reason for coming, you know.

VIDA. (*Concealing her hopes.*) Well, now I *am* curious—what is the second?

SIR WILFRID. (*Simply.*) Are you feelin' pretty robust?

VIDA. I don't know!

SIR WILFRID. (*Crossing to buffet.*) Will you have something, and then I 'll tell you!

VIDA. (*Gaily.*) Can't I support the news without—

SIR WILFRID. (*Trying to explain his state of mind, a thing he has never been able to do.*) Mrs. Phillimore, you see it 's this way. Whenever you 're lucky, you 're too lucky. Now, Mrs. Karslake is a nipper and no mistake, but as I told you, the very same evenin' and house where I saw her—

(*He attempts to take her hand.*)

VIDA. (*Gently rising and affecting a tender surprise.*) What!

SIR WILFRID. (*Rising with her.*) That 's it!—You 're over!

(*He suggests with his right hand the movement of a horse taking a hurdle.*)

VIDA. (*Very sweetly.*) You don't really mean—

SIR WILFRID. (*Carried away for the moment by so much true womanliness.*) I mean, I stayed awake for an hour last night, thinkin' about you.

VIDA. (*Speaking to be contradicted.*) But, you 've just told me—that Cynthia—

SIR WILFRID. (*Admitting the fact.*) Well, she did—she did bowl my wicket, but so did you—

VIDA. (*Taking him very gently to task.*) Don't you think there 's a limit to—

(*She sits.*)

SIR WILFRID. (*Roused by so much loveliness of soul.*) Now, see here, Mrs. Phillimore! You and I are not bottle babies, eh, are we? You 've been married and—I—I 've knocked about, and we both know there 's a lot of stuff talked about—eh, eh, well, you know:—the one and only—that a fellow can't be awfully well smashed by two at the same time, don't you know! All rubbish! You know it, and the proof of the puddin 's in the eatin', I am!

VIDA. (*As before.*) May I ask where I come in?

SIR WILFRID. Well, now, Mrs. Phillimore, I 'll be frank with you, Cynthia 's my favorite, but you 're runnin' her a close second in the popular esteem!

VIDA. (*Laughing, determined not to take offense.*) What a delightful, original, fantastic person you are!

SIR WILFRID. (*Frankly happy that he has explained everything so neatly.*) I knew you 'd take it that way!

VIDA. And what next, pray?

SIR WILFRID. Oh, just the usual,—eh,—thing,—the—eh—the same old question, don't you know. Will you have me if she don't?

VIDA. (*A shade piqued, but determined not to risk showing it.*) And you call that the same old usual question?

SIR WILFRID. Yes, I know, but—but will you? I sail in a week; we can take the same boat. And—eh—eh—my dear Mrs. —may n't I say Vida, I 'd like to see you at the head of my table.

VIDA. (*With velvet irony.*) With Cynthia at the foot?

SIR WILFRID. (*Practical, as before.*) Never mind Mrs. Karslake,—I admire her—she 's—but you have your own points! And you 're here, and so 'm I!—damme, I offer myself, and my affections. and I 'm no icicle, my dear, tell you that for a fact, and, and in fact what 's your answer!—(VIDA *sighs and shakes her head.*) Make it, yes! I say, you know, my dear Vida—

(*He catches her hands.*)

VIDA. (*She slips them from him.*) Unhand me, dear villain! And sit further away from your second choice! What can I say? I 'd rather have *you* for a lover than any man I know! You must be a lovely lover!

SIR WILFRID. I am!

(*He makes a second effort to catch her fingers.*)

VIDA. Will you kindly go further away and be good!

SIR WILFRID. (*Quite forgetting* CYNTHIA.) Look here, if you say yes, we 'll be married—

VIDA. In a month!

SIR WILFRID. Oh, no—this evening!

VIDA. (*Incapable of leaving a situation unadorned.*) This evening! And sail in the same boat with *you?* And shall we sail to the Garden of Eden and stroll into it and lock the gate on the inside and then lose the key—under a rose-bush?

SIR WILFRID. (*Pausing, and after consideration, saying.*) Yes; yes, I say—that 's too clever for me!

(*He draws nearer to her to bring the understanding to a crisis.*)

VIDA. (*A soft knock at the door.*) My maid—come!

SIR WILFRID. (*Swinging out of his chair and going to sofa.*) Eh?

(*Enter* BENSON.)

BENSON. (*To* VIDA.) The new footman, ma'am—he 's made a mistake. He 's told the lady you 're at home.

VIDA. What lady?

BENSON. Mrs. Karslake; and she 's on the stairs, ma'am.

VIDA. Show her in.

(SIR WILFRID *has been turning over the roses. On hearing this, he faces about with a long stemmed one in his hand. He uses it in the following scene to point his remarks.*)

SIR WILFRID. (*To* BENSON, *who stops.*) One moment! (*To* VIDA.) I say, eh—I 'd rather not see her!

VIDA. (*Very innocently.*) But you came here to see her.

SIR WILFRID. (*A little flustered.*) I 'd rather not. Eh,—I fancied I 'd find you and her together—but her—(*coming a step nearer*) findin' me with you looks so dooced intimate,—no one else, d 'ye see, I believe she 'd—draw conclusions—

BENSON. Pardon me, ma'am—but I hear Brooks coming!

SIR WILFRID. (*To* BENSON.) Hold the door!

VIDA. So you don't want her to know—?

SIR WILFRID. (*To* VIDA.) Be a good girl now—run me off somewhere!

VIDA. (*To* BENSON.) Show Sir Wilfrid the men's room.

(*Enter* BROOKS.)

SIR WILFRID. The men's room! Ah! Oh! Eh!

VIDA. (*Beckoning him to go at once.*) Sir Wil—

(*He hesitates, then as* BROOKS *comes on, he flings off with* BENSON.)

BROOKS. Lady Karslake, milady!

VIDA. Anything more inopportune! I never dreamed she 'd come—(*Enter* CYNTHIA, *veiled. She comes down quickly.*) My dear Cynthia, you don't mean to say— (*Languorously.*)

CYNTHIA. (*Rather short, and visibly agitated.*) Yes, I 've come.

VIDA. (*Polite, but not urgent.*) Do take off your veil.

CYNTHIA. (*Doing as* VIDA *asks.*) Is no one here?

VIDA. (*As before.*) Won't you sit down?

CYNTHIA. (*Agitated and suspicious.*) Thanks, no— That is, yes, thanks. Yes! You have n't answered my question?

(CYNTHIA *waves her hand through the smoke, looks at the smoke suspiciously, looks for the cigarette.*)

VIDA. (*Playing innocence in the first degree.*) My dear, what makes you imagine that any one 's here!

CYNTHIA. You 've been smoking.

VIDA. Oh, puffing away!

(CYNTHIA *sees the glasses on the table.*)

CYNTHIA. And drinking—a pair of drinks? (*She sees* JOHN'S *gloves on the table at her elbow.*) Do they fit you, dear? (VIDA *smiles;* CYNTHIA *picks up crop and looks at it and reads her own name.*) "Jack, from Cynthia."

VIDA. (*without taking the trouble to double for a mere woman.*) Yes, dear; it 's Mr. Karslake's crop, but I 'm happy to say he left me a few minutes ago.

CYNTHIA. He left the house? (VIDA *smiles.*) I wanted to see him.

VIDA. (*With a shade of insolence.*) To quarrel?

CYNTHIA. (*Frank and curt.*) I wanted to see him.

VIDA. (*Determined to put* CYNTHIA *in the wrong.*) And I sent him away because I did n't want you to repeat the scene of last night in my house.

CYNTHIA. (*Looks at* JOHN'S *riding crop and is silent.*) Well, I can't stay. I 'm to be married at three, and I had to play truant to get here!

(*Enter* BENSON.)

BENSON. (*To* VIDA.) There 's a person, ma'am, on the sidewalk.

VIDA. What person, Benson?

BENSON. A person, ma'am, with a horse.

CYNTHIA. (*Happily agitated.*) It 's Fiddler with Cynthia K.

(*She goes up rapidly and looks out back through the window.*)

VIDA. (*To* BENSON.) Tell the man I 'll be down in five minutes.

CYNTHIA. (*Looking down from the balcony with delight.*) Oh, there she is!

VIDA. (*Aside to* BENSON.) Go to the club room, Benson, and say to the two gentlemen I can't see them at present—I 'll send for them when—

BENSON. (*Listening.*) I hear some one coming.

VIDA. Quick!

(BENSON *leaves the door, which opens, and* JOHN *enters.* JOHN *comes in slowly, carelessly.* VIDA *whispers to* BENSON.)

BENSON. (*Crosses, goes close to* JOHN *and whispers.*) Beg par—

VIDA. (*Under her breath.*) Go back!

JOHN. (*Not understanding.*) I beg pardon!

VIDA. (*As before.*) Go back!

JOHN. (*The same.*) Can't! I 've a date! With the sheriff!

VIDA. (*A little cross.*) Please use your eyes.

JOHN. (*Laughing and flattering* VIDA.) I am using my eyes.

VIDA. (*Fretted.*) Don't you see there 's a lovely creature in the room?

JOHN. (*Again taking the loud upper-hand.*) Of course there is.

VIDA. Hush!

JOHN. (*Teasingly.*) But what I want to know is—

VIDA. Hush!

JOHN. (*Delighted at getting a rise.*)—is when we 're to stroll in the Garden of Eden—

VIDA. Hush!

JOHN. —and lose the key. (*To put a stop to this, she lightly tosses her handkerchief into his face.*) By George, talk about attar of roses!

CYNTHIA. (*Up at window, excited and moved at seeing her mare once more.*) Oh, she 's a darling! (*She turns.*) A perfect darling! (JOHN *starts; he sees* CYNTHIA *at the same instant that she sees him.*) Oh! I did n't know you were here. (*Pause; then with "take-it-or-leave-it" frankness.*) I came to see *you!*

(JOHN *looks extremely dark and angry;* VIDA *rises.*)

VIDA. (*To* CYNTHIA, *most gently, and seeing there 's nothing to be made of* JOHN.) Oh, pray feel at home, Cynthia, dear! (*Stands by door; to* JOHN.) When I 've a nice street frock on, I 'll ask you to present me to Cynthia K.

(*Exit* VIDA.)

CYNTHIA. (*Agitated and frank.*) Of course, I told you yesterday I was coming here.

JOHN. (*Irritated.*) And I was to deny myself the privilege of being here?

CYNTHIA. (*Curt and agitated.*) Yes.

JOHN. (*Ready to fight.*) And you guessed I would do that?

CYNTHIA. No.

JOHN. What?

CYNTHIA. (*Above table. She speaks with agitation, frankness and good will.*) Jack—I mean, Mr. Karslake,—no, I mean, Jack! I came because—well, you see, it 's my wedding day!—and—and—I—I—was rude to you last evening. I 'd like to apologize and make peace with you before I go—

JOHN. (*Determined to be disagreeable.*) Before you go to your last, long home!

CYNTHIA. I came to apologize.

JOHN. But you 'll remain to quarrel!

CYNTHIA. (*Still frank and kind.*) I will not quarrel. No!—and I 'm only here for a moment. I 'm to be married at three, and just look at the clock! Besides, I told Philip I was going to Louise's shop, and I did—on the way here; but, you see, if I stay too long he 'll telephone Louise and find I 'm not there, and he might guess I was here. So you see I 'm risking a scandal. And now, Jack, see here, I lay my hand on the table, I 'm here on the square, and,—what I want to say is, why—Jack, even if we have made a mess of our married life, let 's put by anger and pride. It 's all over now and can't be helped. So let 's be human, let 's be reasonable, and let 's be kind to each other! Won't you give me your hand? (JOHN *refuses.*) I wish you every happiness!

JOHN. (*Turning away, the past rankling.*) I had a client once, a murderer; he told me he murdered the man, and he told me, too, that he never felt so kindly to anybody as he did to that man after he 'd killed him!

CYNTHIA. Jack!

JOHN. (*Unforgiving.*) You murdered my happiness!

CYNTHIA. I won't recriminate!

JOHN. And now I must put by anger and pride! I do! But not self-respect, not a just indignation—not the facts and my clear memory of them!

CYNTHIA. Jack!

JOHN. No!

CYNTHIA. (*With growing emotion, and holding out her hand.*) I give you one more chance! Yes, I 'm determined to be generous. I forgive everything you ever did to me. I 'm ready to be friends. I wish you every happiness and every—every—horse in the world! I can't do more than that! (*She offers her hand again.*) You refuse?

JOHN. (*Moved, but surly.*) I like wildcats and I like Christians, but I don't like Christian wildcats! Now I'm close hauled, trot out your tornado! Let the Tiger loose! It's the tamer, the man in the cage that has to look lively and use the red hot crowbar! But by Jove, I'm out of the cage! I'm a mere spectator of the married circus!

(*He puffs vigorously.*)

CYNTHIA. Be a game sport then! Our marriage was a wager; you wagered you could live with me. You lost; you paid with a divorce; and now is the time to show your sporting blood. Come on, shake hands and part friends.

JOHN. Not in this world! Friends with you, no! I have a proper pride. I don't propose to put my pride in my pocket.

CYNTHIA. (*Jealous and plain spoken.*) Oh, I would n't ask you to put your pride in your pocket while Vida's handkerchief is there. (JOHN *looks angered.*) Pretty little bijou of a handkerchief! (CYNTHIA *takes handkerchief out.*) And she is charming, and divorced, and reasonably well made up.

JOHN. Oh, well, Vida is a woman. (*Toying with handkerchief.*) I'm a man, a handkerchief is a handkerchief, and as some old Aristotle or other said, whatever concerns a woman, concerns me!

CYNTHIA. (*Not oblivious of him, but in a low voice.*) Insufferable! Well, yes. (*She sits. She is too much wounded to make any further appeal.*) You're perfectly right. There's no possible harmony between divorced people! I withdraw my hand and all good feeling. No wonder I could n't stand you. Eh? However, that's pleasantly past! But at least, my dear Karslake, let us have some sort of beauty of behavior! If we cannot be decent, let us endeavor to be graceful. If we can't be moral, at least we can avoid being vulgar.

JOHN. Well—

CYNTHIA. If there's to be no more marriage in the world—

JOHN. (*Cynical.*) Oh, but that's not it; there's to be more and more and more!

CYNTHIA. (*With a touch of bitterness.*) Very well! I repeat then, if there's to be nothing but marriage and divorce, and remarriage, and redivorce, at least, at least, those who *are* divorced can avoid the vulgarity of meeting each other here, there, and everywhere!

JOHN. Oh, that's where you come out!

CYNTHIA. I thought so yesterday, and today I know it. It's an insufferable thing to a woman of any delicacy of feeling to find her husband—

JOHN. Ahem—former!

CYNTHIA. *Once* a husband always—

JOHN. (*Still cynical.*) Oh, no! Oh, dear, no.

CYNTHIA. To find her—to find the man she has once lived with—in the house of —making love to—to find you here! (JOHN *smiles and rises.*) You smile,—but I say, it should be a social axiom, no woman should have to meet her former husband.

JOHN. (*Cynical and cutting.*) Oh, I don't know; after I've served my term I don't mind meeting my jailor.

CYNTHIA. (JOHN *takes a chair near* CYNTHIA.) It's indecent—at the horse-show, the opera, at races and balls, to meet the man who once— It's not civilized! It's fantastic! It's half baked! Oh, I never should have come here! (*He sympathizes, and she grows irrational and furious.*) But it's entirely your fault!

JOHN. My fault?

CYNTHIA. (*Working herself into a rage.*) Of course. What business have you to be about—to be at large. To be at all!

JOHN. Gosh!

CYNTHIA. (*As before.*) To be where I am! Yes, it's just as horrible for you to turn up in my life as it would be for a dead person to insist on coming back to life and dinner and bridge!

JOHN. Horrid idea!

CYNTHIA. Yes, but it's *you* who behave just as if you were not dead, just as if I'd not spent a fortune on your funeral. You do; you prepare to bob up at afternoon teas,—and dinners—and embarrass me to death with your extinct personality!

JOHN. Well, of course we *were* married, but it did n't quite kill me.

CYNTHIA. (*Angry and plain spoken.*) You killed yourself for me—I divorced you. I buried you out of my life. If any human soul was ever dead, you are! And there's nothing I so hate as a gibbering ghost.

JOHN. Oh, I say!

CYNTHIA. (*With hot anger.*) Go gibber and squeak where gibbering and squeaking are the fashion!

JOHN. (*Laughing and pretending to a coldness he does not feel.*) And so, my dear child, I 'm to abate myself as a nuisance! Well, as far as seeing you is concerned, for my part it 's just like seeing a horse who 's chucked you once. The bruises are O. K., and you see him with a sort of easy curiosity. Of course, you know, he 'll jolly well chuck the next man!—Permit me! (JOHN *picks up gloves, handkerchief and parasol and gives her these as she drops them one by one in her agitation.*) There 's pleasure in the thought.

CYNTHIA. Oh!

JOHN. And now, may I ask you a very simple question? Mere curiosity on my part, but, why did you come here this morning?

CYNTHIA. I have already explained that to you.

JOHN. Not your real motive. Permit me!

CYNTHIA. Oh!

JOHN. But I believe I have guessed your real—permit me—your real motive!

CYNTHIA. Oh!

JOHN. (*With mock sympathy.*) Cynthia, I am sorry for you.

CYNTHIA. H'm?

JOHN. Of course we had a pretty lively case of the fever—the mutual attraction fever, and we *were* married a very short time. And I conclude that 's what 's the matter with *you!* You see, my dear, seven months of married life is too short a time to cure a bad case of the fancies.

CYNTHIA. (*In angry surprise.*) What?

JOHN. (*Calm and triumphant.*) That 's my diagnosis.

CYNTHIA. (*Slowly and gathering herself together.*) I don't think I understand.

JOHN. Oh, yes, you do; yes, you do.

CYNTHIA. (*With blazing eyes.*) What do you mean?

JOHN. Would you mind not breaking my crop! Thank you! I mean (*With polite impertinence.*) that ours was a case of premature divorce, and, ahem, you 're in love with me still.

(*He pauses.* CYNTHIA *has one moment of fury, then she realizes at what a disadvantage this places her. She makes an immense effort, recovers her calm, thinks hard for a moment more, and then, has suddenly an inspiration.*)

CYNTHIA. Jack, some day you 'll get the blind staggers from conceit. No, I 'm not in love with you, Mr. Karslake, but I should n't be at all surprised if she were. She 's just your sort, you know. She 's a man-eating shark, and you 'll be a toothsome mouthful. Oh, come now, Jack, what a silly you are! Oh, yes, you are, to get off a joke like that; me—in love with— (*She looks at him.*)

JOHN. Why are you here? (*She laughs and begins to play her game.*) Why are you here?

CYNTHIA. Guess! (*She laughs.*)

JOHN. Why are you—

CYNTHIA. (*Quickly.*) Why am I here! I 'll tell you. I 'm going to be married. I had a longing, an irresistible longing to see you make an ass of yourself just once more! It happened!

JOHN. (*Uncertain and discomfited.*) I know better!

CYNTHIA. But I came for a more serious purpose, too. I came, my dear fellow, to make an experiment on myself. I 've been with you thirty minutes; and— (*She sighs with content.*) It 's all right!

JOHN. What 's all right?

CYNTHIA. (*Calm and apparently at peace with the world.*) I 'm immune.

JOHN. Immune?

CYNTHIA. You 're not catching any more! Yes, you see, I said to myself, if I fly into a temper—

JOHN. You did!

CYNTHIA. If I fly into a temper when I see him, well that shows I 'm not yet so entirely convalescent that I can afford to have Jack Karslake at my house. If I remain calm I shall ask him to dinner.

JOHN. (*Routed.*) Ask me if you dare! (*He rises.*)

CYNTHIA. (*Getting the whip hand for good.*) Ask you to dinner? Oh, my dear fellow. (JOHN *rises.*) I 'm going to do much more than that. (*She rises.*) We must be friends, old man! We must meet, we must meet often, we must show New York the way the thing should be done, and, to show you I mean it—I want you to be my best man, and give me away when I 'm married this afternoon.

JOHN. (*Incredulous and impatient.*) You don't mean that! (*He puts back chair.*)

CYNTHIA. There you are! Always suspicious!

JOHN. You don't mean that!

CYNTHIA. (*Hiding her emotion under a sportswoman's manner.*) Don't I? I ask you, come! And come as you are! And I 'll lay my wedding gown to Cynthia K that you won't be there! If you 're there, you get the gown, and if you 're not, I get Cynthia K!—

JOHN. (*Determined not to be worsted.*) I take it!

CYNTHIA. Done! Now, then, we 'll see which of us two is the real sporting goods! Shake! (*They shake hands on it.*) Would you mind letting me have a plain soda? (JOHN *goes to the table, and, as he is rattled and does not regard what he is about, he fills the glass three-fourths full with whiskey. He comes to* CYNTHIA *and gives her this. She looks him in the eye with an air of triumph.*) Thanks. (*Maliciously, as* VIDA *enters.*) Your hand is a bit shaky. I think *you* need a little King William.

(JOHN *shrugs his shoulders, and as* VIDA *immediately speaks,* CYNTHIA *defers drinking.*)

VIDA. (*To* CYNTHIA.) My dear, I'm sorry to tell you your husband—I mean, my husband—I mean Philip—he 's asking for you over the 'phone. You must have said you were coming here. Of course, I told him you were not here, and hung up.

(*Enter* BENSON.)

BENSON. (*To* VIDA.) Ma'am, the new footman 's been talking with Mr. Phillimore on the wire. (VIDA *makes a gesture of regret.*) He told Mr. Phillimore that his lady was here, and if I can believe my ears, ma'am, he 's got Sir Wilfrid on the 'phone now!

(*Enter* SIR WILFRID.)

SIR WILFRID. (*Comes from room, perplexed and annoyed.*) I say y' know—extraordinary country; that old chap, Phillimore, he 's been damned impertinent over the wire! Says I 've run off with Mrs. Karslake—talks about "Louise"! Now who the dooce is Louise? He 's comin' round here, too—I said Mrs. Karslake was n't here—(*Seeing* CYNTHIA.) Hello! Good job! What a liar I am!

BENSON. (*To* VIDA.) Mr. Fiddler, ma'am, says the mare is gettin' very restive.

(JOHN *hears this and moves at once. Exit* BENSON.)

JOHN. (*To* VIDA.) If that mare 's restive, she 'll break out in a rash.

VIDA. (*To* JOHN.) Will you take me?

JOHN. Of course. (*They go to the door.*)

CYNTHIA. (*To* JOHN.) Tata, old man! Meet you at the altar! If I don't, the mare 's mine!

(SIR WILFRID *looks at her amazed.*)

VIDA. (*To* CYNTHIA.) Do the honors, dear, in my absence!

JOHN. Come along, come along, never mind them! A horse is a horse!

(*Exeunt* JOHN *and* VIDA, *gaily and in haste. At the same moment* CYNTHIA *drinks what she supposes to be her glass of plain soda. As it is whiskey straight, she is seized with astonishment and a fit of coughing.* SIR WILFRID *relieves her of the glass.*)

SIR WILFRID. (*Indicating contents of glass.*) I say, do you ordinarily take it as high up—as seven fingers and two thumbs?

CYNTHIA. (*Coughs.*) Jack poured it out. Just shows how groggy he was! And now, Sir Wilfrid—

(*She gets her things to go.*)

SIR WILFRID. Oh, you can't go!

(*Enter* BROOKS.)

CYNTHIA. I am to be married at three.

SIR WILFRID. Let him wait. (*Aside to* BROOKS, *whom he meets near the door.*) If Mr. Phillimore comes, bring his card up.

BROOKS. (*Going.*) Yes, Sir Wilfrid.

SIR WILFRID. (*To* BROOKS, *as before.*) To me! (*He tips him.*)

BROOKS. (*Bowing.*) To you, Sir Wilfrid.

(*Exit* BROOKS.)

SIR WILFRID. (*Returning to* CYNTHIA.) I 've got to have my innings, y' know! (*He looks at her more closely.*) I say, you 've been crying!—

CYNTHIA. King William!

SIR WILFRID. You *are* crying! Poor little gal!

CYNTHIA. (*Tears in her eyes.*) I feel all shaken and cold.

(*Enter* BROOKS, *with card.*)

SIR WILFRID. (*Astonished and sympathetic.*) Poor little gal.

CYNTHIA. (*As before.*) I did n't sleep a wink last night. (*With disgust.*) Oh, what is the matter with me?

SIR WILFRID. Why, it 's as plain as a pikestaff! You—(BROOKS *has brought salver to* SIR WILFRID. *A card lies upon it.* SIR WILFRID *takes it and says aside to* BROOKS.) Phillimore? (BROOKS *assents. Aloud to* CYNTHIA, *calmly deceitful.*) Who 's Waldorf Smith? (CYNTHIA *shakes her head. To* BROOKS, *returning card to salver.*) Tell the gentleman Mrs. Karslake is not here!

(*Exit* BROOKS.)

CYNTHIA. (*Aware that she has no business where she is.*) I thought it was Philip!

SIR WILFRID. (*Telling the truth as if it were a lie.*) So did I! (*With cheerful confidence.*) And now, Mrs. Karslake, I'll tell you why you're cryin'. (*He sits beside her.*) You're marryin' the wrong man! I'm sorry for you, but you're such a goose. Here you are, marryin' this legal luminary. What for? You don't know! He don't know! But I do! You pretend you're marryin' him because it's the sensible thing; not a bit of it. You're marryin' Mr. Phillimore because of all the other men you ever saw he's the least like Jack Karslake.

CYNTHIA. That's a very good reason.

SIR WILFRID. There's only one good reason for marrying, and that is because you'll die if you don't!

CYNTHIA. Oh, I've tried that!

SIR WILFRID. The Scripture says: "Try! try! again!" I tell you, there's nothing like a w'im!

CYNTHIA. What's that? W'im? Oh, you mean a *whim!* Do please try and say W*h*im!

SIR WILFRID. (*For the first time emphasizing his H in the word.*) Whim. You must have a w'im—w'im for the chappie you marry.

CYNTHIA. I had—for Jack.

SIR WILFRID. Your w'im was n't wimmy enough, my dear! if you'd had more of it, and tougher, it would ha' stood y' know! Now, I'm not proposin'!

CYNTHIA. (*Diverted at last from her own distress.*) I hope not!

SIR WILFRID. Oh, I will later! It's not time yet! As I was saying—

CYNTHIA. And pray, Sir Wilfrid, when will it be time?

SIR WILFRID. As soon as I see you have a w'im for me! (*Rising, he looks at his watch.*) And now, I'll tell you what we'll do! We've got just an hour to get there in, my motor's on the corner, and in fifty minutes we'll be at Belmont Park.

CYNTHIA. (*Her sporting blood fired.*) Belmont Park!

SIR WILFRID. We'll do the races, and dine at Martin's—

CYNTHIA. (*Tempted.*) Oh, if I only could! I can't! I've got to be married! You're awfully nice; I've almost got a "w'im" for you already.

SIR WILFRID. (*Delighted.*) There you are! I'll send a telegram!

(*She shakes her head. He sits and writes at the table.*)

CYNTHIA. No, no, no!

SIR WILFRID. (*Reads what he writes.*) "Off with Cates-Darby to races. Please postpone ceremony till seven-thirty."

CYNTHIA. Oh, no, it's impossible!

SIR WILFRID. (*Accustomed to have things go his way.*) No more than breathin'! You can't get a w'im for me, you know, unless we're together, so together we'll be!

(*Enter* JOHN KARSLAKE.)

And to-morrow you'll wake up with a jolly little w'im—(*Reads.*) "Postpone ceremony till seven-thirty." There. (*He puts on her cloak. Sees* JOHN.) Hello!

JOHN. (*Surly.*) Hello! Sorry to disturb you.

SIR. WILFRID. (*Cheerful as possible.*) Just the man! (*Giving him the telegraph form.*) Just step round and send it, my boy. Thanks! (JOHN *reads it.*)

CYNTHIA. No, no, I can't go!

SIR WILFRID. Cockety-coo-coo-can't. I say, you must!

CYNTHIA. (*Positively.*) *No!*

JOHN. (*Astounded.*) Do you mean you're going—

SIR WILFRID. (*Very gay.*) Off to the races, my boy!

JOHN. (*Angry and outraged.*) Mrs. Karslake can't go with you there!

(CYNTHIA *starts, amazed at his assumption of marital authority, and delighted that she will have an opportunity of outraging his sensibilities.*)

SIR WILFRID. Oho!

JOHN. An hour before her wedding!

SIR WILFRID. (*Gay and not angry.*) May I know if it's the custom—

JOHN. (*Jealous and disgusted.*) It's worse than eloping—

SIR WILFRID. Custom, y' know, for the husband, that was, to dictate—

JOHN. (*Thoroughly vexed.*) By George, there's a limit!

CYNTHIA. What? What? What? (*Gathers up her things.*) What did I hear you say?

SIR WILFRID. Ah!

JOHN. (*Angry.*) I say there's a limit—

CYNTHIA. (*More and more determined to arouse and excite* JOHN.) Oh, there 's a limit, is there?

JOHN. There is! I bar the way! It means reputation—it means—

CYNTHIA. (*Enjoying her opportunity.*) We shall see what it means!

SIR WILFRID. Aha!

JOHN. (*To* CYNTHIA.) I 'm here to protect your reputation—

SIR WILFRID. (*To* CYNTHIA.) We 've got to make haste, you know.

CYNTHIA. Now, I 'm ready—

JOHN. (*To* CYNTHIA.) Be sensible. You 're breaking off the match—

CYNTHIA. (*Excitedly.*) What 's that to you?

SIR WILFRID. It 's boots and saddles!

JOHN. (*He takes his stand between them and the door.*) No thoroughfare!

SIR WILFRID. Look here, my boy—!

CYNTHIA. (*Catching at the opportunity of putting* JOHN *in an impossible position.*) Wait a moment, Sir Wilfrid! Give me the wire! (*Facing him.*) Thanks! (*She takes the telegraph form from him and tears it up.*) There! Too rude to chuck him by wire! But you, Jack, you 've taken on yourself to look after my interests, so I 'll just ask you, old man, to run down to the Supreme Court and tell Philip—nicely, you know—I 'm off with Sir Wilfrid and where! Say I 'll be back by seven, if I 'm not later! And make it clear, Jack, I 'll marry him by eight-thirty or nine at the latest! And mind *you 're* there, dear! And now, Sir Wilfrid, we 're off.

JOHN. (*Staggered and furious, giving way as they pass him.*) I 'm not the man to—to carry—

CYNTHIA. (*Quick and dashing.*) Oh, yes, you are.

JOHN. —a message from you.

CYNTHIA. (*Triumphant.*) Oh, yes, you are; you 're just exactly the man!

(*Exeunt* CYNTHIA *and* SIR WILFRID.)

JOHN. Great miracles of Moses!

ACT THIRD.

SCENE.—*The same as that of Act First, but the room has been cleared of too much furniture, and arranged for a wedding ceremony. The curtain rises on* MRS. PHILLIMORE *reclining on the sofa,* MISS HENEAGE *is seated left of table,* SUDLEY *is seated at its right, while* GRACE *is on the sofa. There are cushions of flowers, alcove of flowers, flowers in vase, pink and white hangings, wedding bell of roses, calla lilies, orange blossoms, a ribbon of white stretched in front of an altar of flowers; two cushions for the couple to kneel on; two candelabra at each side of back of arch on pedestals. The curtain rises. There is a momentary silence, that the audience may take in these symbols of marriage. Every member of the Phillimore family is irritable, with suppressed irritation.*

SUDLEY. (*Impatiently.*) All very well, my dear Sarah. But you see the hour. Twenty to ten! We have been here since half-past two.

MISS HENEAGE. You had dinner?

SUDLEY. I did not come here at two to have dinner at eight, and be kept waiting until ten! And, my dear Sarah, when I ask where the bride is—

MISS HENEAGE. (*With forced composure.*) I have told you all I know. Mr. John Karslake came to the house at lunch time, spoke to Philip, and they left the house together.

GRACE. Where is Philip?

MRS. PHILLMORE. (*Feebly irritated.*) I don't wish to be censorious or to express an actual opinion, but I must say it 's a bold bride who keeps her future mother-in-law waiting for eight hours. However, I will not venture to—

(MRS. PHILLIMORE *reclines again and fades away into silence.*)

GRACE. (*Sharply and decisively.*) I do! I 'm sorry I went to the expense of a silver ice-pitcher.

(MRS. PHILLIMORE *sighs.* MISS HENEAGE *keeps her temper with an effort which is obvious.*)

(*Enter* THOMAS.)

SUDLEY. (*To* MRS. PHILLIMORE.) For my part, I don't believe Mrs. Karslake means to return here or to marry Philip at all!

THOMAS. (*To* MISS HENEAGE.) Two telegrams for you, ma'am! The choir boys have had their supper.

(*Slight movement from every one;* THOMAS *steps back.*)

SUDLEY. (*Rises.*) At last we shall know!

MISS HENEAGE. From the lady! Probably!

(MISS HENEAGE *opens telegram. She reads first one at a glance, laying it on salver again with a glance at*

SUDLEY. THOMAS *passes salver to* SUDLEY, *who takes telegram.*)

GRACE. There 's a toot now.

MRS. PHILLIMORE. (*Feebly confused.*) I don't wish to intrude, but really I can't imagine Philip marrying at midnight.

(*As* SUDLEY *reads,* MISS HENEAGE *opens the second telegram, but does not read it.*)

SUDLEY. (*Reads.*) "Accident, auto struck"—something! "Gasoline"—did something—illegible, ah! (*Reads.*) "Home by nine forty-five! Hold the church!"

(*General movement from all.*)

MISS HENEAGE. (*Profoundly shocked.*) "Hold the church!" William, she still means to marry Philip! and to-night, too!

SUDLEY. It 's from Belmont Park.

GRACE. (*Making a great discovery.*) She went to the races!

MISS HENEAGE. This is from Philip! (MISS HENEAGE *reads second telegram.*) "I arrive at ten o'clock. Have dinner ready." (MISS HENEAGE *motions to* THOMAS *to withdraw. Exit* THOMAS. MISS HENEAGE *looks at her watch.*) They are both due now. (*Movement.*) What 's to be done?

(*She rises.* SUDLEY *shrugs shoulders.*)

SUDLEY. (*Rising.*) After a young woman has spent her wedding day at the races? Why, I consider that she has broken the engagement,—and when she comes, tell her so.

MISS HENEAGE. I 'll telephone Matthew. The choir boys can go home—her maid can pack her belongings—and when the lady arrives—

(*Very distant toot of an auto-horn is heard coming nearer and nearer.* GRACE *flies up stage and looks out of door.* MRS. PHILLIMORE *does not know what to do, or where to go.* SUDLEY *moves about excitedly.* MISS HENEAGE *stands ready to make herself disagreeable.*)

GRACE. (*Speaking rapidly and with excitement.*) I hear a man's voice. Cates-Darby and brother Matthew.

(*Loud toot. Laughter and voices off back heard faintly.* GRACE *looks out of the door, and leaves it rapidly.*)

MISS HENEAGE. Outrageous!

SUDLEY. Disgraceful!

MRS. PHILLIMORE. (*Partly rising as voices and horn are heard.*) Shocking! I shall not take any part at all, in the—eh— (*She fades away.*)

MISS HENEAGE. (*Interrupting her.*) Don't trouble yourself.

(*Voices and laughter grow louder.* CYNTHIA'S *voice is heard.*)

(SIR WILFRID *appears at the back. He turns and waits for* CYNTHIA *and* MATTHEW. *He carries wraps. He speaks to* CYNTHIA, *who is still off of stage.* MATTHEW'S *voice is heard and* CYNTHIA'S. CYNTHIA *appears at back, followed by* MATTHEW. *As they appear,* CYNTHIA *speaks to* MATTHEW. SIR WILFRID *carries a newspaper and a parasol. The hat is the one she wore in Act Second. She is in get-up for auto. Goggles, veil, an exquisite duster in latest Paris style. All three come down rapidly. As she appears,* SUDLEY *and* MISS HENEAGE *exclaim, and there is a general movement.*)

SUDLEY. 'P on my word!

GRACE. Hah!

MISS HENEAGE. (*Rising with shocked propriety.*) Shocking!

(GRACE *remains standing above sofa.* SUDLEY *moves toward her.* MISS HENEAGE *sits down again.* MRS. PHILLIMORE *reclines on sofa.* CYNTHIA *begins to speak as soon as she appears and speaks fluently to the end.*)

CYNTHIA. No! I never was so surprised in my life, as when I strolled into the paddock and they gave me a rousing reception—old Jimmy Withers, Debt Gollup, Jack Deal, Monty Spiffles, the Governor and Buckeye. All of my old admirers! They simply fell on my neck, and, dear Matthew, what do you think I did? I turned on the water main! (*Movements and murmurs of disapprobation from the family.* MATTHEW *indicates a desire to go.*) Oh, but you can't go!

MATTHEW. I 'll return in no time!

CYNTHIA. I 'm all ready to be married. Are they ready? (MATTHEW *waves a pious, polite gesture of recognition to the family.*) I beg everybody's pardon! (*She takes off her wrap and puts it on the back of a chair.*) My goggles are so dusty, I can't see who 's who! (*To* SIR WILFRID.) Thanks! You *have* carried it well!

(*Takes parasol from* SIR WILFRID.)

SIR WILFRID. (*Aside to* CYNTHIA.) When may I—?

CYNTHIA. See you next Goodwood!

SIR WILFRID. (*Imperturbably.*) Oh, I 'm coming back!

(CYNTHIA *comes down.*)

CYNTHIA. Not a bit of use in coming back! I shall be married before you get here! Ta! Ta! Goodwood!

SIR WILFRID. (*As before.*) I 'm coming back.

(*He goes out quickly. More murmurs of disapprobation from family. Slight pause.*)

CYNTHIA. (*Beginning to take off her goggles, and coming down slowly.*) I do awfully apologize for being so late!

MISS HENEAGE. (*Importantly.*) Mrs. Karslake—

SUDLEY. (*Importantly.*) Ahem!

(CYNTHIA *lays down her goggles, and sees their severity.*)

CYNTHIA. Dear me! (*She surveys the flowers, and for a moment pauses.*) Oh, good heavens! Why, it looks like a smart funeral!

(MISS HENEAGE *moves; then speaks in a perfectly ordinary natural tone, but her expression is severe.* CYNTHIA *immediately realizes the state of affairs in its fullness.*)

MISS HENAGE. (*To* CYNTHIA.) After what has occurred, Mrs. Karslake—

(CYNTHIA *glances at table.*)

CYNTHIA. (*Sits at table, composed and good tempered.*) I see you got my wire —so you know where I have been.

MISS HENEAGE. To the race-course!

SUDLEY. With a rowdy Englishman.

(CYNTHIA *glances at* SUDLEY, *uncertain whether he means to be disagreeable, or whether he is only naturally so.*)

MISS HENEAGE. We concluded you desired to break the engagement!

CYNTHIA. (*Indifferently.*) No! No! Oh! No!

MISS HENEAGE. Do you intend, despite of our opinion of you—

CYNTHIA. The only opinion that would have any weight with me would be Mrs. Phillimore's.

(*She turns expectantly to* MRS. PHILLIMORE.)

MRS. PHILLIMORE. I am generally asleep at this hour, and accordingly I will not venture to express any—eh—any—actual opinion.

(*She fades away.* CYNTHIA *smiles.*)

MISS HENEAGE. (*Coldly.*) You smile. We simply inform you that as regards *us*, the alliance is not grateful.

CYNTHIA. (*Affecting gaiety and unconcern.*) And all this because the gasoline gave out.

SUDLEY. My patience has given out!

GRACE. So has mine. I 'm going.

(*Exit* GRACE.)

SUDLEY. (*Vexed beyond civility. To* CYNTHIA.) My dear young lady: You come here, to this sacred—eh—eh—spot —altar!—odoriferous of the paddock!—speaking of Spiffles and Buckeye,—having practically eloped!—having created a scandal, and disgraced our family!

CYNTHIA. (*As before.*) How does it disgrace you? Because I like to see a high-bred, clean, nervy, sweet little four-legged gee play the antelope over a hurdle!

MISS HENEAGE. Sister, it is high time that you—

(*Turns to* CYNTHIA.)

CYNTHIA. (*With quiet irony.*) Mrs. Phillimore is generally asleep at this hour, and accordingly she will not venture to express—

SUDLEY. (*Spluttering with irritation.*) Enough, madam—I *venture* to—to—to—to say, you are leading a fast life.

CYNTHIA. (*With powerful intention.*) Not in this house! For six heavy weeks have I been laid away in the grave, and I 've found it very slow indeed trying to keep pace with the dead!

SUDLEY. (*Despairingly.*) This comes of horses!

CYNTHIA. (*Indignant.*) Of what?

SUDLEY. C-c-caring for horses!

MISS HENEAGE. (*With sublime morality.*) What Mrs. Karslake cares for is—men.

CYNTHIA. (*Angry and gay.*) What would you have me care for? The Ornithorhyncus Paradoxus? or Pithacanthropus Erectus? Oh, I refuse to take you seriously.

(SUDLEY *begins to prepare to leave; he buttons himself into respectability and his coat.*)

SUDLEY. My dear madam, I take myself seriously—and madam, I—I retract what I have brought with me (*he feels in his waistcoat pocket*) as a graceful gift,—an Egyptian scarab—a—a—sacred beetle, which once ornamented the person of a—eh—mummy.

CYNTHIA. (*Getting even with him.*) It should never be absent from your pocket, Mr. Sudley.

(SUDLEY *walks away in a rage.*)

MISS HENEAGE. (*Rising. To* SUDLEY.) I 've a vast mind to withdraw my—

(CYNTHIA *moves.*)

CYNTHIA. (*Interrupts; maliciously.*) Your wedding present? The little bronze cat!

MISS HENEAGE. (*Moves, angrily.*) Oh!

(*Even* MRS. PHILLIMORE *comes momentarily to life, and expresses silent indignation.*)

SUDLEY. (*Loftily.*) Sarah, I 'm going.

(*Enter* PHILIP *at back with* GRACE. PHILIP *looks dusty and grim.* GRACE, *as they come in, speaks to him.* PHILIP *shakes his head. They pause up stage.*)

CYNTHIA. (*Emotionally.*) I shall go to my room! However, all I ask is that you repeat to Philip—

(*She comes suddenly on* PHILIP, *and speaks to him in a low tone.*)

SUDLEY. (*To* MISS HENEAGE, *determined to win.*) As I go out, I shall do myself the pleasure of calling a hansom for Mrs. Karslake—

(PHILIP *comes down two or three steps.*)

PHILIP. As you go out, Sudley, have a hansom called, and when it comes, get into it.

SUDLEY. (*Furious, and speaking to* PHILIP.) Eh,—eh,—my dear sir, I leave you to your fate.

(PHILIP *angrily points him the door.* SUDLEY *goes out.*)

MISS HENEAGE. (*With weight.*) Philip, you 've not heard—

PHILIP. (*Interrupts.*) Everything—from Grace! (CYNTHIA *goes to the table.*) My sister has repeated your words to me—and her own! I 've told her what I think of *her*.

(PHILIP *looks witheringly at* GRACE.)

GRACE. I shan't wait to hear any more.

(*Exit* GRACE, *indignantly.*)

PHILIP. Don't make it necessary for me to tell you what I think of you. (PHILIP *gives his arm to his mother.* MISS HENEAGE *goes towards the door.*) Mother, with your permission, I desire to be alone. I expect both you and Grace, Sarah, to be dressed and ready for the ceremony a half hour from now.

(*As* PHILIP *and* MRS. PHILLIMORE *are about to cross,* MISS HENEAGE *speaks.*)

MISS HENEAGE. I shall come or not as I see fit. And let me add, my dear nephew, that a fool at forty is a fool indeed.

(*Exit* MISS HENEAGE, *high and mighty, and much pleased with her quotation.*)

MRS. PHILLIMORE. (*Stupid and weary as usual, to* PHILIP, *as he leads her to the door.*) My dear son—I won't venture to express—

(CYNTHIA *goes to the table.*)

PHILIP. (*Soothing a silly mother.*) No, mother, don't! But I shall expect you, of course, at the ceremony. (*Exit* MRS. PHILLIMORE. PHILIP *takes the tone and assumes the attitude of the injured husband.*) It is proper for me to tell you that I followed you to Belmont. I am aware—I know with whom—in fact, *I know all!* (*Pauses. He indicates the whole censorious universe.*) And now let me assure you—I am the last man in the world to be jilted on the very eve of—of—everything with you. I won't be jilted. (CYNTHIA *is silent.*) You understand? I propose to marry you. I won't be made ridiculous.

CYNTHIA. (*Glancing at* PHILIP.) Philip, I did n't mean to make you—

PHILIP. Why, then, did you run off to Belmont Park with that fellow?

CYNTHIA. Philip, I—eh—

PHILIP. (*Sitting at the table.*) What motive? What reason? On our wedding day? Why did you do it?

CYNTHIA. I 'll tell you the truth. I was bored.

PHILIP. Bored? In my company?

(PHILIP, *in a gesture, gives up.*)

CYNTHIA. I was bored, and then—and besides, Sir Wilfrid asked me to go.

PHILIP. Exactly, and that was why you went. Cynthia, when you promised to marry me, you told me you had forever done with love. You agreed that marriage was the rational coming together of two people.

CYNTHIA. I know, I know!

PHILIP. Do you believe that now?

CYNTHIA. I don't know what I believe. My brain is in a whirl! But, Philip, I am beginning to be—I 'm afraid—yes, I am afraid that one can't just select a great and good man (*she indicates him*) and say: I will be happy with him.

PHILIP. (*With dignity.*) I don't see why not. You must assuredly do one or the other: You must either let your heart choose or your head select.

CYNTHIA. (*Gravely.*) No, there 's a third scheme; Sir Wilfrid explained the theory to me. A woman should marry whenever she has a whim for the man, and then leave the rest to the man. Do you see?

PHILIP. (*Furious.*) Do I see? Have I ever seen anything else? Marry for whim! That's the New York idea of marriage.

CYNTHIA. (*Giving a cynical opinion.*) New York ought to know.

PHILIP. Marry for whim and leave the rest to the divorce court! Marry for whim and leave the rest to the man. That was the former Mrs. Phillimore's idea. Only she spelled "whim" differently; she omitted the "w." (*He rises in his anger.*) And now you—*you* take up with this preposterous—(CYNTHIA *moves uneasily.*) But, nonsense! It's impossible! A woman of your mental calibre— No. Some obscure, primitive, female *feeling* is at work corrupting your better judgment! What is it you *feel?*

CYNTHIA. Philip, you never felt like a fool, did you?

PHILIP. No, never.

CYNTHIA. (*Politely.*) I thought not.

PHILIP. No, but whatever your feelings, I conclude you are ready to marry me.

CYNTHIA. (*Uneasy.*) Of course, I came back. I am here, am I not?

PHILIP. You are ready to marry me?

CYNTHIA. (*Twisting in the coils.*) But you haven't had your dinner.

PHILIP. Do I understand you refuse?

CYNTHIA. Couldn't we defer—?

PHILIP. You refuse?

CYNTHIA. (*A slight pause; trapped and seeing no way out.*) No, I said I'd marry you. I'm a woman of my word. I will.

PHILIP. (*Triumphant.*) Ah! Very good, then. Run to your room. (CYNTHIA *turns to* PHILIP.) Throw something over you. In a half hour I'll expect you here! And, Cynthia, my dear, remember! I cannot cuculate like a wood pigeon, but—I esteem you!

CYNTHIA. (*Hopelessly.*) I think I'll go, Philip.

PHILIP. I may not be fitted to play the love-bird, but—

CYNTHIA. (*As before.*) I think I'll go, Philip.

PHILIP. I'll expect you,—in half an hour.

CYNTHIA. (*With leaden despair.*) Yes.

PHILIP. And, Cynthia, don't think any more about that fellow, Cates-Darby.

CYNTHIA. (*Amazed and disgusted by his misapprehension.*) No.

(*Exit* CYNTHIA.)

(THOMAS *enters from the opposite door.*)

PHILIP. (*Not seeing* THOMAS *and clumsily defiant.*) And if I had that fellow, Cates-Darby, in the dock—!

THOMAS. Sir Wilfrid Cates-Darby.

PHILIP. Sir what—what—wh-who?

(*Enter* SIR WILFRID, *in evening dress.* PHILIP *looks* SIR WILFRID *in the face and speaks to* THOMAS.)

Tell Sir Wilfrid Cates-Darby I am not at home to him.

(THOMAS *embarrassed.*)

SIR WILFRID. (*Undaunted.*) My dear Lord Eldon—

PHILIP. (*Speaks to* THOMAS, *as before.*) Show the gentleman the door.

(*Pause.* SIR WILFRID *glances at door with a significant gesture.*)

SIR WILFRID. (*Goes to the door, examines it and returns to* PHILIP.) Eh,—I admire the door, my boy! Fine, old carved mahogany panel; but don't ask me to leave by it, for Mrs. Karslake made me promise I'd come, and that's why I'm here. (THOMAS *exits.*)

PHILIP. Sir, you are—impudent—!

SIR WILFRID. (*Interrupting.*) Ah, you put it all in a nutshell, don't you?

PHILIP. To show your face here, after practically eloping with my wife!

SIR WILFRID. (*Pretending ignorance.*) When were you married?

PHILIP. We're as good as married.

SIR WILFRID. Oh, pooh, pooh! You can't tell me that grace before soup is as good as a dinner! (*He takes cigar-case out.*)

PHILIP. Sir—I—demand—

SIR WILFRID. (*Calmly carrying the situation.*) Mrs. Karslake is *not* married. *That's* why I'm here. I am here for the same purpose *you* are; to ask Mrs. Karslake to be my wife.

PHILIP. Are you in your senses?

SIR WILFRID. (*Touching up his American cousin in his pet vanity.*) Come, come, Judge—you Americans have no sense of humor. (*He takes a small jewel-case from his pocket.*) There's my regards for the lady—and (*reasonably*), if I must go, I will. Of course, I would like to see her, but—if it isn't your American custom—

(*Enter* THOMAS.)

THOMAS. Mr. Karslake.

SIR WILFRID. Oh, well, I say; if he can come, I can!

(*Enter* JOHN KARSLAKE *in evening dress, carrying a large and very smart bride's bouquet which he hands to* PHILIP. PHILIP *takes it because he is n't up to dropping it, but gets it out of his hands as soon as he can.* PHILIP *is transfixed;* JOHN *comes to the front of the stage. Deep down he is feeling wounded and unhappy. But, as he knows his coming to the ceremony on whatever pretext is a social outrage, he carries it off by assuming an air of its being the most natural thing in the world. He controls the expression of his deeper emotion, but the pressure of this keeps his face grave, and he speaks with force.*)

JOHN. My compliments to the bride, Judge.

PHILIP. (*Angry.*) And you, too, have the effrontery?

SIR WILFRID. There you are!

JOHN. (*Pretending ease.*) Oh, call it friendship— (THOMAS *goes out.*)

PHILIP. (*Puts bouquet on table. Ironically.*) I suppose Mrs. Karslake—

JOHN. She wagered me I would n't give her away, and of course—

(*Throughout this scene* JOHN *hides the emotions he will not show behind a daring irony. He has* PHILIP *on his left, walking about in a fury;* SIR WILFRID *sits on the edge of the table, gay and undisturbed.*)

PHILIP. (*Taking a step toward* JOHN.) You will oblige me—both of you—by immediately leaving—

JOHN. (*Smiling and going to* PHILIP.) Oh, come, come, Judge—suppose I *am* here? Who has a better right to attend his wife's obsequies! Certainly, I come as a mourner—for *you!*

SIR WILFRID. I say, is it the custom?

JOHN. No, no—of course it 's not the custom, no. But we 'll make it the custom. After all,—what 's a divorced wife among friends?

PHILIP. Sir, your humor is strained!

JOHN. Humor,—Judge?

PHILIP. It is, sir, and I 'll not be bantered! Your both being here is—it is—gentlemen, there is a decorum which the stars in their courses do not violate.

JOHN. Now, Judge, never you mind what the stars do in their divorces! Get down to earth of the present day. Rufus Choate and Daniel Webster are dead. You must be modern. You must let peroration and poetry alone! Come along now. Why should n't I give the lady away?

SIR WILFRID. Hear! Hear! Oh, I beg your pardon!

JOHN. And why should n't we both be here? American marriage is a new thing. We 've got to strike the pace, and the only trouble is, Judge, that the judiciary have so messed the thing up that a man can't be sure he *is* married until he 's divorced. It 's a sort of marry-go-round, to be sure! But let it go at that! Here we all are, and we 're ready to marry my wife to you, and start her on her way to him!

PHILIP. (*Brought to a standstill.*) Good Lord! Sir, you cannot trifle with monogamy!

JOHN. Now, now, Judge, monogamy is just as extinct as knee-breeches. The new woman has a new idea, and the new idea is—well, it 's just the opposite of the old Mormon one. Their idea is one man, ten wives and a hundred children. Our idea is one woman, a hundred husbands and one child.

PHILIP. Sir, this is polyandry.

JOHN. Polyandry? A hundred to one it 's polyandry; and that 's it, Judge! Uncle Sam has established consecutive polyandry,—but there 's got to be an interval between husbands! The fact is, Judge, the modern American marriage is like a wire fence. The woman 's the wire—the posts are the husbands. (*He indicates himself, and then* SIR WILFRID *and* PHILIP.) One—two—three! And if you cast your eye over the future you can count them, post after post, up hill, down dale, all the way to Dakota!

PHILIP. All very amusing, sir, but the fact remains—

JOHN. (*Going to* PHILIP. PHILIP *moves away.*) Now, now, Judge, I like you. But you 're asleep; you 're living in the dark ages. You want to call up Central. "Hello, Central! Give me the present time, 1906, New York!"

SIR WILFRID. Of course you do, and—there you are!

PHILIP. (*Heavily.*) There I am not, sir! And—(*To* JOHN) as for Mr. Karslake's ill-timed jocosity,—sir, in the future—

SIR WILFRID. Oh, hang the future!

PHILIP. I begin to hope, Sir Wilfrid, that in the future I shall have the pleasure of hanging you! (*To* JOHN.) And as to you, sir, your insensate idea of giving away your own—your former—my—your—oh! Good Lord! This is a nightmare! (*He turns to go in despair.*)

(*Enter* MATTHEW, *who, seeing* PHILIP, *speaks as he comes in from door.*)

MATTHEW (*To* PHILIP.) My dear brother, Aunt Sarah Heneage refuses to give Mrs. Karslake away, unless you yourself,—eh—

PHILIP. (*As he exits.*) No more! I'll attend to the matter!

(*Exit. The choir boys are heard practicing in the next room.*)

MATTHEW. (*Mopping his brow.*) How do you both do? My aunt has made me very warm. (*He rings the bell.*) You hear our choir practicing—sweet angel boys! Hm! Hm! Some of the family will not be present. I am very fond of you, Mr. Karslake, and I think it admirably Christian of you to have waived your—eh—your—eh—that is, now that I look at it more narrowly, let me say, that in the excitement of pleasurable anticipation, I forgot, Karslake, that your presence might occasion remark—

(*Enter* THOMAS.)

Thomas! I left, in the hall, a small handbag or satchel containing my surplice.

THOMAS. Yes, sir. Ahem!

MATTHEW. You must really find the handbag at once.

(THOMAS *turns to go, when he stops startled.*)

THOMAS. Yes, sir. (*Announcing in consternation.*) Mrs. Vida Phillimore.

(*Enter* VIDA PHILLIMORE, *in full evening dress. She steps gently to* MATTHEW.)

MATTHEW. (*Always piously serene.*) Ah, my dear child! Now this is just as it should be! That is, eh—(*He comes to the front of the stage with her; she pointedly looks away from* SIR WILFRID.) That is, when I come to think of it—your presence might be deemed inauspicious.

VIDA. But, my dear Matthew,—I had to come. (*Aside to him.*) I have a reason for being here.

(THOMAS *enters.*)

MATTHEW. But, my dear child—

THOMAS. (*With sympathetic intention.*) Sir, Mr. Phillimore wishes to have your assistance, sir—with Miss Heneage *immediately!*

MATTHEW. Ah! (*To* VIDA.) One moment! I'll return. (*To* THOMAS.) Have you found the bag with my surplice?

(*He goes out with* THOMAS, *speaking.* SIR WILFRID *comes to* VIDA. JOHN *watches the door.*)

SIR WILFRID. (*To* VIDA.) You're just the person I most want to see!

VIDA. (*With affected iciness.*) Oh, no, Sir Wilfrid, Cynthia isn't here yet! (*Crossing to table.* JOHN *comes toward her and she speaks to him, with obvious sweetness.*) Jack, dear, I never was so ravished to see any one.

SIR WILFRID. (*Taken aback.*) By Jove!

VIDA. (*Very sweet.*) I knew I should find you here!

JOHN. (*Annoyed but civil.*) Now don't do that!

VIDA. (*As before.*) Jack!

(*They sit down.*)

JOHN. (*Civil but plain spoken.*) Don't do it!

VIDA. (*In a voice dripping with honey.*) Do what, Jack?

JOHN. Touch me with your voice! I have troubles enough of my own.

(*He sits not far from her, the table is between them.*)

VIDA. And I know *who* your troubles are! Cynthia!

(*From this moment* VIDA *gives up* JOHN *as an object of the chase and lets him into her other game.*)

JOHN. I hate her. I don't know why I came.

VIDA. You came, dear, because you couldn't stay away—you're in love with her.

JOHN. All right, Vida, what I feel may be *love*—but all I can say is, if I could get even with Cynthia Karslake—

VIDA. You can, dear—it's as easy as powdering one's face; all you have to do is to be too nice to me!

JOHN. (*Looks inquiringly at* VIDA.) Eh!

VIDA. Don't you realize she's jealous of you? Why did she come to my house this morning? She's jealous—and all you have to do—

JOHN. If I can make her wince, I'll make love to you till the Heavenly cows come home!

VIDA. Well, you see, my dear, if you make love to me it will (*she delicately indicates* SIR WILFRID) cut both ways at once!

JOHN. Eh,—what! Not Cates-Darby? (*Starting.*) Is that Cynthia?

VIDA. Now don't get rattled and forget to make love to me.

JOHN. I've got the jumps. (*Trying to accept her instructions.*) Vida, I adore you.

VIDA. Oh, you must be more convincing; that won't do at all.

JOHN. (*Listening.*) Is that she now?

(*Enter* MATTHEW, *who goes to the inner room.*)

VIDA. It's Matthew. And, Jack, dear, you'd best get the hang of it before Cynthia comes. You might tell me all about your divorce. That's a sympathetic subject. Were you able to undermine it?

JOHN. No. I've got a wire from my lawyer this morning. The divorce holds. She's a free woman. She can marry whom she likes. (*The organ is heard, very softly played.*) Is that Cynthia?

(*He rises quickly.*)

VIDA. It's the organ!

JOHN. (*Overwhelmingly excited.*) By George! I should never have come! I think I'll go.

(*He crosses to go to the door.*)

VIDA. (*She rises and follows him remonstratingly.*) When I need you?

JOHN. I can't stand it.

VIDA. Oh, but, Jack—

JOHN. Good-night!

VIDA. I feel quite ill. (*Seeing that she must play her last card to keep him, pretends to faintness; sways and falls into his arms.*) Oh!

JOHN. (*In a rage, but beaten.*) I believe you're putting up a fake.

(*The organ swells as* CYNTHIA *enters sweepingly, dressed in full evening dress for the wedding ceremony.* JOHN, *not knowing what to do, holds* VIDA *up as a horrid necessity.*)

CYNTHIA. (*Speaking as she comes on, to* MATTHEW.) Here I am. Ridiculous to make it a conventional thing, you know. Come in on the swell of the music, and all that, just as if I'd never been married before. Where's Philip?

(*She looks for* PHILIP *and sees* JOHN *with* VIDA *in his arms. She stops short.*)

JOHN. (*Uneasy and embarrassed.*) A glass of water! I beg your pardon, Mrs. Karslake— (*The organ plays on.*)

CYNTHIA. (*Ironical and calm.*) Vida!

JOHN. She has fainted.

CYNTHIA. (*As before.*) Fainted? (*Without pause.*) Dear, dear, dear, terrible! So she has. (SIR WILFRID *takes flowers from a vase and prepares to sprinkle* VIDA'S *forehead with the water it contains.*) No, no, not her forehead, Sir Wilfrid, her frock! Sprinkle her best Paquin! If it's a real faint, she will not come to!

VIDA. (*As her Paris importation is about to suffer comes to her senses.*) I almost fainted.

CYNTHIA. Almost!

VIDA. (*Using the stock phrase as a matter of course, and reviving rapidly.*) Where am I? (JOHN *glances at* CYNTHIA *sharply.*) Oh, the bride! I beg every one's pardon. Cynthia, at a crisis like this, I simply couldn't stay away from Philip!

CYNTHIA. Stay away from Philip?

(JOHN *and* CYNTHIA *exchange glances.*)

VIDA. Your arm, Jack; and lead me where there is air.

(JOHN *and* VIDA *go into the further room;* JOHN *stands left of her. The organ stops.* SIR WILFRID *comes down. He and* CYNTHIA *are practically alone on the stage.* JOHN *and* VIDA *are barely within sight. You first see him take her fan and give her air; then he picks up a book and reads from it to her.*)

SIR WILFRID. I've come back.

CYNTHIA. (*To* SIR WILFRID.) Asks for air and goes to the green-house. (CYNTHIA *crosses stage.* SIR WILFRID *offers her a seat.*) I know why you are here. It's that intoxicating little whim you suppose me to have for you. My regrets! But the whim's gone flat! Yes, yes, my gasoline days are over. I'm going to be garaged for good. However, I'm glad you're here; you take the edge off—

SIR WILFRID. Mr. Phillimore?

CYNTHIA. (*Sharply.*) No, Karslake. I'm just waiting to say the words

(*Enter* THOMAS.)

"love, honor and obey" to Phillimore—(*looks up back*) and *at* Karslake! (CYNTHIA *sees* THOMAS.) What is it? Mr. Phillimore?

THOMAS. Mr. Phillimore will be down in a few minutes, ma'am. He's very sorry, ma'am, (*lowers his voice and comes nearer* CYNTHIA, *mindful of the respectabilities*) but there's a button off his waistcoat.

CYNTHIA. (*Excited, with irony. Rising.*) Button off his waistcoat!

(*Exit* THOMAS.)

SIR WILFRID. (*Delightedly.*) Ah! So much the better for me. (CYNTHIA *looks up back.*) Now, then, never mind those two! (CYNTHIA *moves restlessly.*) Sit down.

CYNTHIA. I can't.

SIR WILFRID. You 're as nervous as—

CYNTHIA. Nervous! Of course I 'm nervous! So would you be nervous if you 'd had had a runaway and smash up, and you were going to try it again. (*Looking up back.* SIR WILFRID *is uneasy.*) And if some one does n't do away with those calla lilies—the odor makes me faint! (SIR WILFRID *moves.*) No, it 's not the lilies! It 's the orange blossoms!

SIR WILFRID. Orange blossoms.

CYNTHIA. The flowers that grow on the tree that hangs over the abyss. (SIR WILFRID *gets the vase of orange blossoms.*) They smell of six o'clock in the evening. When Philip 's fallen asleep, and the little boys are crying the winners outside, and I 'm crying inside, and dying inside and outside and everywhere.

(SIR WILFRID *comes down.*)

SIR WILFRID. Sorry to disappoint you. They 're artificial. (CYNTHIA *shrugs her shoulders.*) That 's it! They 're emblematic of artificial domesticity! And I 'm here to help you balk it. (*He sits;* CYNTHIA *half rises and looks toward* JOHN *and* VIDA.) Keep still now, I 've a lot to say to you. Stop looking—

CYNTHIA. Do you think I can listen to you make love to me when the man who —who—whom I most despise in all the world, is reading poetry to the woman who—who got me into the fix I 'm in!

SIR WILFRID. (*Leaning over the chair in which she sits.*) What do you want to look at 'em for? (CYNTHIA *moves.*) Let 'em be and listen to me! Sit down; for damme, I 'm determined.

(CYNTHIA *at the table.*)

CYNTHIA. (*Half to herself.*) I won't look at them! I won't think of them. Beasts!

(SIR WILFRID *interposes between her and her view of* JOHN.)

(*Enter* THOMAS.)

SIR WILFRID. Now, then— (*He sits.*)

CYNTHIA. Those two *here!* It 's just as if Adam and Eve should invite the snake to their golden wedding. (*She sees* THOMAS.) What is it, what 's the matter?

THOMAS. Mr. Phillimore's excuses, ma'am. In a very short time—

(THOMAS *exits.*)

SIR WILFRID. I 'm on to you! You hoped for more buttons!

CYNTHIA. I 'm dying of the heat; fan me. (SIR WILFRID *fans* CYNTHIA.)

SIR WILFRID. Heat! No! You 're dying because you 're ignorin' nature. Certainly you are! You 're marryin' Phillimore! (CYNTHIA *appears faint.*) Can't ignore nature, Mrs. Karslake. Yes, you are; you 're forcin' your feelin's. (CYNTHIA *glances at him.*) And what you want to do is to let yourself go a bit—up anchor and sit tight! I 'm no seaman, but that 's the idea! (CYNTHIA *moves and shakes her head.*) So just throw the reins on nature's neck, jump this fellow Phillimore and marry me!

(*He leans over to* CYNTHIA.)

CYNTHIA. (*Naturally, but with irritation.*) You propose to me here, at a moment like this? When I 'm on the last lap—just in sight of the goal—the gallows—the halter—the altar, I don't know what its name is! No, I won't have you! (*Looking toward* KARSLAKE *and* VIDA.) And I won't have you stand near me! I won't have you talking to me in a low tone! (*As before.*) Stand over there—stand where you are.

SIR WILFRID. I say—

CYNTHIA. I can hear you—I 'm listening!

SIR WILFRID. Well, don't look so hurried and worried. You 've got buttons and buttons of time. And now my offer. You have n't yet said you would—

CYNTHIA. Marry you? I don't even know you!

SIR WILFRID. (*Feeling sure of being accepted.*) Oh,—tell you all about myself. I 'm no duke in a pickle o' debts, d 'ye see? I can marry where I like. Some o' my countrymen are rotters, ye know. They 'd marry a monkey, if poppa-up-the-tree had a corner in cocoanuts! And they do marry some queer ones, y' know.

(CYNTHIA *looks up, exclaims and turns.*—SIR WILFRID *turns.*)

CYNTHIA. Do they?

SIR WILFRID. Oh, rather. That 's what 's giving your heiresses such a bad name lately. If a fellah 's in debt he can't pick and choose, and then he swears that American gals are awfully fine lookers, but they 're no good when it comes to continuin' the race! Fair dolls in the drawin'-room, but no good in the nursery.

CYNTHIA. (*Thinking of* JOHN *and* VIDA *and nothing else.*) I can see Vida in the nursery.

SIR WILFRID. You understand when you want a brood mare, you don't choose a Kentucky mule.

CYNTHIA. I think I see one.

SIR WILFRID. Well, that 's what they 're saying over there. They say your gals run to talk (*He plainly remembers* VIDA'S *volubility.*), and I have seen gals here that would chat life into a wooden Indian! That 's what you Americans call being clever.—All brains and no stuffin'! In fact, some of your American gals are the nicest boys I ever met.

CYNTHIA. So that 's what you think?

SIR WILFRID. Not a bit what *I* think—what my countrymen think!

CYNTHIA. Why are you telling me?

SIR WILFRID. Oh, just explaining my character. I 'm the sort that can pick and choose—and what I want is heart.

CYNTHIA. (*Always having* VIDA *and* JOHN *in mind.*) No more heart than a dragon-fly!

(*The organ begins to play softly.*)

SIR WILFRID. That 's it, dragon-fly. Cold as stone and never stops buzzing about and showin' off her colors. It 's that American dragon-fly girl that I 'm afraid of, because, d' ye see, I don't know what an American expects when he marries; yes, but you 're not listening!

CYNTHIA. I am listening. I am!

SIR WILFRID. (*Speaking directly to her.*) An Englishman, ye see, when he marries expects three things; love, obedience and five children.

CYNTHIA. Three things! I make it seven!

SIR WILFRID. Yes, my dear, but the point is, will you be mistress of Traynham?

CYNTHIA. (*Who has only half listened to him.*) No, Sir Wilfrid, thank you, I won't. (*She turns to see* JOHN *crossing the drawing-room at back, with* VIDA, *apparently absorbed in what she says.*) It 's outrageous!

SIR WILFRID. Eh? Why, you 're cryin'!

CYNTHIA. (*Almost sobbing.*) I am not.

SIR WILFRID. You 're not crying because you 're in love with me?

CYNTHIA. I 'm not crying—or if I am, I 'm crying because I love my country. It 's a disgrace to America—cast-off husbands and wives getting together in a parlor and playing tag under a palm-tree.

(JOHN *with intention and determined to stab* CYNTHIA, *kisses* VIDA'S *hand.*)

SIR WILFRID. Eh! Oh! I 'm damned! (*To* CYNTHIA.) What do you think that means?

CYNTHIA. I don't doubt it means a wedding here, at once—after mine!

(VIDA *and* JOHN *come down.*)

VIDA. (*Affecting an impossible intimacy to wound* CYNTHIA *and tantalize* SIR WILFRID.) Hush, Jack—I 'd much rather no one should know anything about it until it 's all over!

CYNTHIA. (*Starts and looks at* SIR WILFRID.) What did I tell you?

VIDA. (*To* CYNTHIA.) Oh, my dear, he 's asked me to champagne and lobster at *your* house—his house! Matthew is coming! (CYNTHIA *starts, but controls herself.*) And you 're to come, Sir Wilfrid. (VIDA *speaks, intending to convey the idea of a sudden marriage ceremony.*) Of course, my dear, I would like to wait for your wedding, but something rather—rather important to me is to take place, and I know you 'll excuse me. (*Organ stops.*)

SIR WILFRID. (*Piqued at being forgotten.*) All very neat, but you have n't given me a chance, even.

VIDA. Chance? You 're not serious?

SIR WILFRID. I am!

VIDA. (*Striking while the iron is hot.*) I 'll give you a minute to offer yourself.

SIR WILFRID. Eh?

VIDA. Sixty seconds from now.

SIR WILFRID. (*Uncertain.*) There 's such a thing as bein' silly.

VIDA. (*Calm and determined.*) Fifty seconds left.

SIR WILFRID. I take you—count fair. (*He hands her his watch and goes to where* CYNTHIA *stands.*) I say, Mrs. Karslake—

CYNTHIA. (*Overwhelmed with grief and emotion.*) They 're engaged; they 's going to be married to-night, over champagne and lobster at my house!

SIR WILFRID. Will you consider your—

CYNTHIA. (*Hastily, to get rid of him.*) No, no, no, no! Thank you, Sir Wilfrid, I will not.

SIR WILFRID. (*Calm and not to be laid low.*) Thanks awfully. (*Crosses to* VIDA. CYNTHIA *walks away.*) Mrs. Phillimore—

VIDA. (*She gives him back his watch.*) Too late! (*To* KARSLAKE.) Jack, dear, we must be off.

SIR WILFRID. (*Standing and making a general appeal for information.*) I say, is it the custom for American girls—that sixty seconds or too late? Look here! Not a bit too late. I 'll take you around to Jack Karslake's, and I 'm going to ask you the same old question again, you know. (*To* VIDA.) By Jove, you know in your country it 's the pace that kills.

(*Exeunt* SIR WILFRID *and* VIDA.)

JOHN. (*Gravely to* CYNTHIA, *who comes to the front of the stage.*) Good-night, Mrs. Karslake, I 'm going; I 'm sorry I came.

CYNTHIA. Sorry? Why are you sorry? (JOHN *looks at her; she winces a little.*) You 've got what you wanted. (*Pause.*) I would n't mind your marrying Vida—

JOHN. (*Gravely.*) Oh, would n't you?

CYNTHIA. But I don't think you showed good taste in engaging yourselves *here.*

JOHN. Of course, I should have preferred a garden of roses and plenty of twilight.

CYNTHIA. (*Rushing into speech.*) I 'll tell you what you *have* done—you 've thrown yourself away! A woman like that! No head, no heart! All languor and loose—loose frocks—she 's the typical, worst thing America can do! She 's the regular American marriage worm!

JOHN. I have known others—

CYNTHIA. (*Quickly.*) Not me. I 'm not a patch on that woman. Do you know anything about her life? Do you know the things she did to Philip? Kept him up every night of his life—forty days out of every thirty—and then, without his knowing it, put brandy in his coffee to make him lively at breakfast.

JOHN. (*Banteringly.*) I begin to think she is just the woman—

CYNTHIA. (*Unable to quiet her jealousy.*) She is *not* the woman for *you!* A man with your bad temper—your airs of authority—your assumption of—of—everything. What you need is a good, old-fashioned, bread poultice woman!

(CYNTHIA *comes to a full stop and faces* JOHN.)

JOHN. (*Sharply.*) Can't say I 've had any experience of the good old-fashioned bread poultice.

CYNTHIA. I don't care what you say! If you marry Vida Phillimore—you shan't do it. (*Tears of rage choking her.*) No, I liked your father and for *his* sake, I 'll see that his son does n't make a donkey of himself a second time.

JOHN. (*Too angry to be amused.*) Oh, I thought I was divorced. I begin to feel as if I had you on my hands still.

CYNTHIA. You have! You shall have! If you attempt to marry her, I 'll follow you—and I 'll find her—I 'll tell Vida—(*He turns to her.*) I will. I 'll tell Vida just what sort of a dance you led me.

JOHN. (*Quickly on her last word but speaking gravely.*) Indeed! Will you? And *why* do you care what happens to me?

CYNTHIA. (*Startled by his tone.*) I—I—ah—

JOHN. (*Insistently and with a faint hope.*) *Why* do you *care?*

CYNTHIA. I don't. Not in your sense—

JOHN. How dare you then pretend—

CYNTHIA. I don't pretend.

JOHN. (*Interrupting her; proud, serious and strong.*) How dare you look me in the face with the eyes that I once kissed, and pretend the least regard for me? (CYNTHIA *recoils and looks away. Her own feelings are revealed to her clearly for the first time.*) I begin to understand our American women now. Fireflies—and the fire they gleam with is so cold that a midge could n't warm his heart at it, let alone a man. You 're not of the same race as a man! You married me for nothing, divorced me for nothing, because you *are* nothing!

CYNTHIA. (*Wounded to the heart.*) Jack! What are you saying?

JOHN. (*With unrestrained emotion.*) What,—you feigning an interest in me, feigning a lie—and in five minutes—(*Gesture indicating altar.*) Oh, you 've taught me the trick of your sex—you 're the woman who 's not a woman!

CYNTHIA. (*Weakly.*) You 're saying terrible things to me.

JOHN. (*Low and with intensity.*) You have n't been divorced from me long enough to forget—what you should be ashamed to remember.

CYNTHIA. (*Unable to face him and pretending not to understand him.*) I don't know what you mean.

JOHN. (*More forcibly and with manly emotion.*) You 're not able to forget me! You know you 're not able to forget me; ask yourself if you are able to forget me, and when your heart, such as it is, answers "no," then—(*The organ is plainly heard.*) Well, then, prance gaily up to the altar and marry that, if you can!

(*He exits quickly.* CYNTHIA *crosses to arm-chair and sinks into it. She trembles as if she were overdone. Voices are heard speaking in the next room. Enter* MATTHEW *and* MISS HENEAGE. *Enter* PHILIP. CYNTHIA *is so sunk in the chair they do not see her.* MISS HENEAGE *goes up to sofa back and waits. They all are dressed for an evening reception and* PHILIP *in the traditional bridegroom's rig.*)

MATTHEW. (*As he enters.*) I am sure you will do your part, Sarah—in a spirit of Christian decorum. (*To* PHILIP.) It was impossible to find my surplice, Philip, but the more informal the better.

PHILIP. (*With pompous responsibility.*) Where's Cynthia?

(MATTHEW *gives glance around room.*)

MATTHEW. Ah, here's the choir! (*He goes to meet it. Choir boys come in very orderly; divide and take their places, an even number on each side of the altar of flowers.* MATTHEW *vaguely superintends.* PHILIP *gets in the way of the bell. Moves out of the way. Enter* THOMAS.) Thomas, I directed you—One moment, if you please.

(*He indicates table and chairs.* THOMAS *hastens to move the chairs and the table against the wall.* PHILIP *comes down.*)

PHILIP. (*Looking for her.*) Where's Cynthia?

(CYNTHIA *rises.* PHILIP *sees her when she moves and crosses toward her, but stops. The organ stops.*)

CYNTHIA. (*Faintly.*) Here I am.

(MATTHEW *comes down. The organ plays softly.*)

MATTHEW. (*Coming to* CYNTHIA.) Ah, my very dear Cynthia, I knew there was something. Let me tell you the words of the hymn I have chosen:

"Enduring love; sweet end of strife!
Oh, bless this happy man and wife!"

I'm afraid you feel—eh—eh!

CYNTHIA. (*Desperately calm.*) I feel awfully queer—I think I need a scotch.

(*The organ stops.* PHILIP *remains uneasily at a little distance.* MRS. PHILLIMORE *and* GRACE *enter back slowly, as cheerfully as if they were going to hear the funeral service read. They remain near the doorway.*)

MATTHEW. Really, my dear, in the pomp and vanity—I mean—ceremony of this—this unique occasion, there should be sufficient exhilaration.

CYNTHIA. (*As before.*) But there is n't! (*She sits.*)

MATTHEW. I don't think my Bishop would approve of—eh—anything *before!*

CYNTHIA. (*Too agitated to know how much she is moved.*) I feel very queer.

MATTHEW. (*Piously sure that everything is for the best.*) My dear child—

CYNTHIA. However, I suppose there's nothing for it—now—but—to—to—

MATTHEW. Courage!

CYNTHIA. (*Desperate and with sudden explosion.*) Oh, don't speak to me. I feel as if I'd been eating gunpowder, and the very first word of the wedding service would set it off!

MATTHEW. My dear, your indisposition is the voice of nature.

(CYNTHIA *speaks more rapidly and with growing excitement,* MATTHEW *going toward the choir boys.*)

CYNTHIA. Ah,—that's it—nature! (MATTHEW *shakes his head.*) I've a great mind to throw the reins on nature's neck.

PHILIP. Matthew!

(*He moves to take his stand for the ceremony.*)

MATTHEW. (*Looking at* PHILIP. *To* CYNTHIA.) Philip is ready.

(PHILIP *comes down. The organ plays the wedding march.*)

CYNTHIA. (*To herself, as if at bay.*) Ready? Ready? Ready?

MATTHEW. Cynthia, you will take Miss Heneage's arm. (MISS HENEAGE *comes down near table.*) Sarah! (MATTHEW *indicates to* MISS HENEAGE *where* CYNTHIA *is.* MISS HENEAGE *advances a step or two.* MATTHEW *goes up and speaks in a low voice to choir.*) Now please don't forget, my boys. When I raise my hands so, you begin, "Enduring love, sweet end of strife." (CYNTHIA *has risen. On the table is her long lace cloak. She stands by this table.* MATTHEW *assumes sacerdotal importance and takes his position inside the altar of flowers.*) Ahem! Philip! (*He indicates to* PHILIP *that he take his position.*) Sarah! (CYNTHIA *breathes fast, and supports herself on table.* MISS HENEAGE *goes toward her and stands for a moment looking at* CYNTHIA.) The ceremony will now begin.

(*The organ plays Mendelssohn's wedding march.* CYNTHIA *turns and faces* MISS HENEAGE. MISS HENEAGE *comes to* CYNTHIA *slowly, and extends her hand in her readiness to lead the bride to the altar.*)

MISS HENEAGE. Mrs. Karslake!

PHILIP. Ahem!

(MATTHEW *steps forward two or three steps.* CYNTHIA *stands turned to stone.*)

MATTHEW. My dear Cynthia. I request you—to take your place. (CYNTHIA *moves one or two steps across as if to go up to the altar. She takes* MISS HENEAGE'S *hand and slowly they walk toward* MATTHEW.) Your husband to be—is ready, the ring is in my pocket. I have only to ask you the—eh—necessary questions—and—eh—all will be blissfully over in a moment.

(*The organ is louder.*)

CYNTHIA. (*At this moment, just as she reaches* PHILIP, *she stops, faces round, looks him,* MATTHEW *and the rest in the face and cries out in despair.*) Thomas! Call a hansom! (THOMAS *exits and leaves door open.* MISS HENEAGE *crosses the stage.* MRS. PHILLIMORE *rises.* CYNTHIA *grasps her cloak on table.* PHILIP *turns and* CYNTHIA *comes forward and stops.*) I can't, Philip—I can't. (*Whistle of hansom is heard off; the organ stops.*) It is simply a case of throwing the reins on nature's neck—up anchor—and sit tight! (MATTHEW *crosses to* CYNTHIA.) Matthew, don't come near me! Yes, yes, I distrust you. It 's your business, and you 'd marry me if you could.

PHILIP. (*Watching her in dismay as she throws on her cloak.*) Where are you going?

CYNTHIA. I 'm going to Jack.

PHILIP. What for?

CYNTHIA. To stop his marrying Vida. I 'm blowing a hurricane inside, a horrible, happy hurricane! I know myself—I know what 's the matter with me. If I married you and Miss Heneage—what 's the use of talking about it—he must n't marry that woman. He shan't. (CYNTHIA *has now all her wraps on; goes up rapidly. To* PHILIP.) Sorry! So long! Good-night and see you later.

(CYNTHIA *goes to door rapidly;* MATTHEW, *in absolute amazement, throws up his arms.* PHILIP *is rigid.* MRS. PHILLIMORE *sinks into a chair.* MISS HENEAGE *is supercilious and unmoved.* GRACE *is the same. The choir, at* MATTHEW'S *gesture, mistakes it for the concerted signal, and bursts lustily into the Epithalamis.*

"Enduring love—sweet end of strife!
Oh, bless this happy man and wife!"

ACT FOURTH.

The scene is laid in JOHN KARSLAKE'S *study and smoking-room. There is a bay window on the right. A door on the right leads to stairs, and the front door of house, while a door at the back leads to the dining-room. A fireplace is on the left and a mantel. A bookcase contains law books and sporting books. A full-length portrait of* CYNTHIA *is on the wall. Nothing of this portrait is seen by the audience except the gilt frame and a space of canvas. A large table with writing materials is littered over with law books, sporting books, papers, pipes, crops, and a pair of spurs. A wedding ring lies on it. There are three very low easy-chairs. The general appearance of the room is extremely gay and garish in color. It has the easy confusion of a man's room. There is a small table on which is a woman's sewing-basket. The sewing-basket is open. A piece of rich fancy work lies on the table, as if a lady had just risen from sewing. On the corner are a lady's gloves. On a chair-back is a lady's hat. It is a half hour later than the close of Act Third. Curtains are drawn over the window. A lamp on the table is lighted. Electric lights about the room are also lighted. One chair is conspicuously standing on its head.*

(*Curtain rises on* NOGAM, *who busies himself at a table, at the back. The door at the back is half open.*)

SIR WILFRID. (*Coming in door.*) Eh—what did you say your name was?

NOGAM. Nogam, sir.

SIR WILFRID. Nogam? I 've been here thirty minutes. Where are the cigars? (NOGAM *motions to a small table near the entrance door where the cigars are.*) Thank you. Nogam, Mr. Karslake was to have followed us here, immediately.

(*He lights a cigar.*)

NOGAM. Mr. Karslake just now 'phoned from his club (SIR WILFRID *comes down the stage.*), and he 's on his way home, sir.

SIR WILFRID. Nogam, why is that chair upside down?

NOGAM. Our orders, sir.

VIDA. (*Speaking as she comes on.*) Oh, Wilfrid! (SIR WILFRID *turns.* VIDA *comes slowly down the stage.*) I can't be left longer alone with the lobster! He reminds me too much of Phillimore!

SIR WILFRID. Karslake 's coming; stopped at his club on the way! (*To* NOGAM.) You have n't heard anything of Mrs. Karslake—?

NOGAM. (*Surprised.*) No, sir!

SIR WILFRID. (*In an aside to* VIDA, *as they move to appear to be out of* NOGAM'S *hearing.*) Deucedly odd, ye know—for the Reverend Matthew declared she left Phillimore's house before *he* did,—and she told him she was coming here!

(NOGAM *evidently takes this in.*)

VIDA. Oh, she 'll turn up.

SIR WILFRID. Yes, but I don't see how the Reverend Phillimore had the time to get here and make us man and wife, don't y' know—

VIDA. Oh, Matthew had a fast horse and Cynthia a slow one—or she 's a woman and changed her mind! Perhaps she 's gone back and married Phillimore. And besides, dear, Matthew was n't in the house four minutes and a half; only just long enough to hoop the hoop. (*She twirls her new wedding ring gently about her finger.*) Was n't it lucky he had a ring in his pocket?

SIR WILFRID. Rather.

VIDA. And are you aware, dear, that Phillimore bought and intended it for Cynthia? Do come (*she goes up to the door through which she entered*), I 'm desperately hungry! Whenever I 'm married that 's the effect it has!

(VIDA *goes out.* SIR WILFRID *sees her through door, but stops to speak to* NOGAM.)

SIR WILFRID. We 'll give Mr. Karslake ten minutes, Nogam. If he does not come then, you might serve supper.

(*He follows* VIDA.)

NOGAM. (*To* SIR WILFRID.) Yes, sir.

(*Door opens.*)

(*Enter* FIDDLER.)

FIDDLER. (*Easy and business-like.*) Hello, Nogam, where 's the guv'nor? That mare 's off her oats, and I 've got to see him.

NOGAM. He 'll soon be here.

FIDDLER. Who was the parson I met leaving the house?

NOGAM. (*Whispering.*) Sir Wilfrid and Mrs. Phillimore have a date with the guv'nor in the dining-room, and the reverend gentleman—

(*He makes a gesture as of giving an ecclesiastical blessing.*)

FIDDLER. (*Amazed.*) He has n't spliced them? (NOGAM *assents.*) He has? They 're married? Never saw a parson could resist it!

NOGAM. Yes, but I 've got another piece of news for you. Who do you think the Rev. Phillimore expected to find *here?*

FIDDLER. (*Proud of having the knowledge.*) Mrs. Karslake? I saw her headed this way in a hansom with a balky horse only a minute ago. If she hoped to be in at the finish—

(FIDDLER *is about to set chair on its legs.*)

NOGAM. (*Quickly.*) Mr. Fiddler, sir, please to let it alone.

FIDDLER. (*Putting chair down in surprise.*) Does it live on its blooming head?

NOGAM. Don't you remember? *She* threw it on its head when she left here, and he won't have it up. Ah, that 's it—hat, sewing-basket and all,—the whole rig is to remain as it was when she handed him his knock-out. (*A bell rings outside.*)

FIDDLER. There 's the guv'nor—I hear him!

NOGAM. I 'll serve the supper. (*Taking letter from pocket and putting it on mantel.*) Mr. Fiddler, would you mind giving this to the guv'nor? It 's from his lawyer—his lawyer could n't find him and left it with me. He said it was very important. (*Bell rings again. Speaking off to* SIR WILFRID.) I 'm coming, sir!

(NOGAM *goes out, and shuts door. Enter* JOHN KARSLAKE. *He looks downhearted, his hat is pushed over his eyes. His hands are in his pockets. He enters slowly and heavily. He sees* FIDDLER, *who salutes, forgetting the letter.* JOHN *slowly sits in armchair at the study table.*)

JOHN. (*Speaking as he walks to his chair.*) Hello, Fiddler!

(*Pause.* JOHN *throws himself into a chair, keeping his hat on. Throws down his gloves, sighing.*)

FIDDLER. Came in to see you, sir, about Cynthia K.

JOHN. (*Drearily.*) Damn Cynthia K!—

FIDDLER. Could n't have a word with you?

JOHN. (*Grumpy.*) No!

FIDDLER. Yes, sir.

JOHN. Fiddler.

FIDDLER. Yes, sir.

JOHN. Mrs. Karslake—(FIDDLER *nods.*) You used to say she was our mascot?

FIDDLER. Yes, sir.

JOHN. Well, she 's just married herself to a—a sort of a man!

FIDDLER. Sorry to hear it, sir.

JOHN. Well, Fiddler, between you and me, we 're a pair of idiots.

FIDDLER. Yes, sir!

JOHN. And now it 's too late!

FIDDLER. Yes, sir—oh, beg your pardon, sir—your lawyer left a letter.

(JOHN *takes the letter; opens it and reads it, indifferently at first.*)

JOHN. (*As he opens letter.*) What 's he got to say, more than what his wire said? —Eh—(*as he reads, he is dumbfounded*) what?—Will explain.—Error in wording of telegram.—Call me up.—(*Turning to telephone quickly.*) The man can't mean that she 's still— Hello! Hello! (JOHN *listens.*)

FIDDLER. Would like to have a word with you, sir—

JOHN. Hello, Central!

FIDDLER. That mare—

JOHN. (*Looks at letter; speaks into 'phone.*) 33246a 38! Did you get it?

FIDDLER. That mare, sir, she 's got a touch of malaria—

JOHN. (*At the 'phone.*) Hello, Central—33246a—38!—Clayton Osgood—yes, yes, and say, Central—get a move on you!

FIDDLER. If you think well of it, sir, I 'll give her a tonic—

JOHN. (*Still at the 'phone.*) Hello! Yes —yes—Jack Karslake. Is that you, Clayton? Yes—yes—well—

FIDDLER. Or if you like, sir, I 'll give her—

JOHN. (*Turning on* FIDDLER.) Shut up! (*To 'phone.*) What was that? Not you —not you—a technical error? You mean to say that Mrs. Karslake is still— my— Hold the wire, Central—get off the wire! Get off the wire! Is that you, Clayton? Yes, yes—she and I are still— I got it! Good-bye!

(*He hangs up the receiver and falls back in the chair. For a moment he is overcome. He takes up the telephone book.*)

FIDDLER. All very well, Mr. Karslake, but I must know if I 'm to give her a—

JOHN. (*Turning over the leaves of the telephone book in hot haste.*) What 's Phillimore's number?

FIDDLER. If you 've no objections, I think I 'll give her a—

JOHN. (*As before.*) L—M—N—O—P— It 's too late! She 's married by this! Married!—and—my God—I—I am the cause. Phillimore—

FIDDLER. I 'll give her—

JOHN. Give her wheatina!—give her grape nuts—give her away! (FIDDLER *moves away.*) Only be quiet! Phillimore!

(*Enter* SIR WILFRID.)

SIR WILFRID. Hello! We 'd almost given you up!

JOHN. (*Still in his agitation unable to find* PHILLIMORE'S *number.*) Just a moment! I 'm trying to get Phillimore on the 'phone to—to tell Mrs. Karslake—

SIR WILFRID. No good, my boy—she 's on her way here! (JOHN *drops book and looks up dumbfounded.*) The Reverend Matthew was here, y' see—and he said—

JOHN. (*Rising, he turns.*) Mrs. Karslake is coming here? (SIR WILFRID *nods.*) To this house? Here?

SIR WILFRID. That 's right.

JOHN. Coming here? You 're sure? (SIR WILFRID *nods assent.*) Fiddler, I want you to stay here, and if Mrs. Karslake comes, don't fail to let me know! Now then, for Heaven's sake, what did Matthew say to you?

SIR WILFRID. Come along in and I 'll tell you.

JOHN. On your life now, Fiddler, don't fail to let me—

(*Exeunt* JOHN *and* SIR WILFRID.)

VIDA. (*Voice off.*) Ah, here you are!

FIDDLER. Phew!

(*There is a moment's pause, and* CYNTHIA *enters. She comes in very quietly, almost shyly, and as if she were uncertain of her welcome.*)

CYNTHIA. Fiddler! Where is he? Has he come? Is he here? Has he gone?

FIDDLER. (*Rattled.*) Nobody 's gone, ma'am, except the Reverend Matthew Phillimore.

CYNTHIA. Matthew? He 's been here and gone? (FIDDLER *nods assent.*) You don't mean I'm too late? He's married them already?

FIDDLER. Nogam says he married them!

CYNTHIA. He's married them! Married! Married before I could get here! (*Sitting in armchair.*) Married in less time than it takes to pray for rain! Oh, well, the church—the church is a regular quick marriage counter. (*Voices of* VIDA *and* JOHN *heard in light-hearted laughter.*) Oh!

FIDDLER. I'll tell Mr. Karslake—

CYNTHIA. (*Rising and going to the door through which* JOHN *left the stage; she turns the key in the lock and takes it out.*) No—I would n't see him for the world! (*She comes down with key to the work-table.*) If I'm too late, I'm too late! and that's the end of it! (*She lays key on table and remains standing near it.*) I've come, and now I'll go! (*Long pause.* CYNTHIA *looks about the room and changes her tone.*) Well, Fiddler, it's all a good deal as it used to be in my day.

FIDDLER. No, ma'am—everything changed, even the horses.

CYNTHIA. (*Absent-mindedly.*) Horses—how are the horses?

(*Throughout this scene she gives the idea that she is saying good-bye to her life with* JOHN.)

FIDDLER. Ah, when husband and wife splits, ma'am, it's the horses that suffer. Oh, yes, ma'am, we're all changed since you give us the go-by,—even the guv'nor.

CYNTHIA. How's he changed?

FIDDLER. Lost his sharp for horses, and ladies, ma'am—gives 'em both the boiled eye.

CYNTHIA. I can't say I see any change; there's my portrait—I suppose he sits and pulls faces at me.

FIDDLER. Yes, ma'am, I think I'd better tell him of your bein' here.

CYNTHIA. (*Gently but decidedly.*) No, Fiddler, no! (*She again looks about her.*) The room's in a terrible state of disorder. However, your new mistress will attend to that. (*Pause.*) Why, that's not her hat!

FIDDLER. Yours, ma'am.

CYNTHIA. Mine! (*She goes to the table to look at it.*) Is that my work-basket? (*Pause.*) My gloves? (FIDDLER *assents.*) And I suppose—(*She hurriedly goes to the writing-table.*) My—yes, there it is: my wedding ring!—just where I dropped it! Oh, oh, oh, he keeps it like this—hat, gloves, basket and ring, everything just as it was that crazy, mad day when I—(*Glances at* FIDDLER *and breaks off.*) But for Heaven's sake, Fiddler, set that chair on its feet!

FIDDLER. Against orders, ma'am.

CYNTHIA. Against orders?

FIDDLER. You kicked it over, ma'am, the day you left us.

CYNTHIA. No wonder he hates me with the chair in that state! He nurses his wrath to keep it warm. So, after all, Fiddler, everything *is* changed, and that chair is the proof of it. I suppose Cynthia K is the only thing in the world that cares a whinney whether I'm alive or dead. (*She breaks down and sobs.*) How is she, Fiddler?

FIDDLER. Off her oats, ma'am, this evening.

CYNTHIA. Off her oats! Well, she loves me, so I suppose she will die, or change, or—or something. Oh, she'll die, there's no doubt about that—she'll die. (FIDDLER, *who has been watching his chance, takes the key off the table while she is sobbing, tiptoes up the stage, unlocks the door and goes out. After he has done so,* CYNTHIA *rises and dries her eyes.*) There—I'm a fool—I must go—before—before—he—

(*As she speaks her last word* JOHN *comes on.*)

JOHN. Mrs. Karslake!

CYNTHIA. (*Confused.*) I—I—I just heard Cynthia K was ill—(JOHN *assents.* CYNTHIA *tries to put on a cheerful and indifferent manner.*) I—I ran round—I—and—and— (*Pausing, she turns and comes down.*) Well, I understand it's all over.

JOHN. (*Cheerfully.*) Yes, it's all over.

CYNTHIA. How is the bride?

JOHN. Oh, she's a wonder.

CYNTHIA. Indeed! Did she paw the ground like the war horse in the Bible? I'm sure when Vida sees a wedding ring she smells the battle afar off. As for you, my dear Karslake, I should have thought once bitten, twice shy! But, you know best.

(*Enter* VIDA.)

VIDA. Oh, Cynthia, I've just been through it again, and I feel as if I were eighteen. There's no use talking about it, my dear, with a woman it's never the second time! And how nice you were.

Jack,—he never even laughed at us! (*Enter* SIR WILFRID, *with hat and cane.* VIDA *kisses* JOHN.) That 's the wages of virtue!

SIR WILFRID. (*In time to see her kiss* JOHN.) I say, is it the custom? Every time she does that, my boy, you owe me a thousand pounds. (*Seeing* CYNTHIA, *who approaches them, he looks at her and* JOHN *in turn.*) Mrs. Karslake. (*To* JOHN.) And then you say it 's not an extraordinary country!

(CYNTHIA *is more and more puzzled.*)

VIDA. (*To* JOHN.) See you next Derby, Jack. (*Crossing to door. To* SIR WILFRID.) Come along, Wilfrid! We really ought to be going. (*To* CYNTHIA.) I hope, dear, you have n't married him! Phillimore 's a tomb! Good-bye, Cynthia—I 'm so happy! (*As she goes.*) Just think of the silly people, dear, that only have this sensation once in a lifetime!

(*Exit* VIDA. JOHN *follows* VIDA *off.*)

SIR WILFRID. (*To* CYNTHIA.) Good-bye, Mrs. Karslake. And I say, ye know, if you have married that dull old Phillimore fellah, why, when you 've divorced him, come over and stay at Traynham! I mean, of course, ye know, bring your new husband. There 'll be lots of horses to show you, and a whole covey of jolly little Cates-Darbys. Mind you come! (*With real delicacy of feeling and forgetting his wife.*) Never liked a woman as much in my life as I did you!

VIDA. (*Outside; calling him.*) Wilfrid, dear!

SIR WILFRID. (*Loyal to the woman who has caught him.*) —except the one that 's calling me!

(*Reënter* JOHN. SIR WILFRID *nods to him and goes off.* JOHN *shuts the door and crosses the stage. A pause.*)

CYNTHIA. So you 're not married?

JOHN. No. But I know that you imagined I was. (*Pause.*)

CYNTHIA. I suppose you think a woman has no right to divorce a man—and still continue to feel a keen interest in his affairs?

JOHN. Well, I 'm not so sure about that, but I don't quite see how—

CYNTHIA. A woman can be divorced—and still—(JOHN *assents; she hides her embarrassment.*) Well, my dear Karslake, you 've a long life before you, in which to learn how such a state of mind is possible! So I won't stop to explain. Will you be kind enough to get me a cab?

(*She moves to the door.*)

JOHN. Certainly. I was going to say I am not surprised at your feeling an interest in me. I 'm only astonished that, having actually married Phillimore, you come here—

CYNTHIA. (*Indignantly.*) I 'm not married to him! (*A pause.*)

JOHN. I left you on the brink—made me feel a little uncertain.

CYNTHIA. (*In a matter-of-course tone.*) I changed my mind—that 's all.

JOHN. (*Taking his tone from her.*) Of course. (*A pause.*) Are you going to marry him?

CYNTHIA. I don't know.

JOHN. Does he know you—

CYNTHIA. I told him I was coming here.

JOHN. Oh! He 'll turn up here, then—eh? (CYNTHIA *is silent.*) And you 'll go back with him, I suppose?

CYNTHIA. (*Talking at random.*) Oh—yes—I suppose so. I—I have n't thought much about it.

JOHN. (*Changing his tone.*) Well, sit down; do. Till he comes—talk it over. (*He places the armchair more comfortably for her.*) This is a more comfortable chair!

CYNTHIA. (*Shamefacedly.*) You never liked me to sit in that one!

JOHN. Oh, well—it 's different now. (CYNTHIA *crosses and sits down, near the upset chair. There is a long pause.* JOHN *crosses the stage.*) You don't mind if I smoke?

CYNTHIA. (*Shaking her head.*) No.

JOHN. (*He lights his pipe and sits on arm of chair.*) Of course, if you find my presence painful, I 'll—skiddoo.

(*He indicates the door.* CYNTHIA *shakes her head.* JOHN *smokes pipe and remains seated.*)

CYNTHIA. (*Suddenly and quickly.*) It 's just simply a fact, Karslake, and that 's all there is to it—if a woman has once been married—that is, the first man she marries—then—she may quarrel, she may hate him—she may despise him—but she 'll always be jealous of him with other women. Always!

(JOHN *takes this as if he were simply glad to have the information.*)

JOHN. Oh— Hm! ah—yes—yes. (*A pause.*)

CYNTHIA. You probably felt jealous of Phillimore.

JOHN. (*Reasonably, sweetly, and in doubt.*) N-o! I felt simply: Let him take his medicine. (*Apologetically.*)

CYNTHIA. Oh!

JOHN. I beg your pardon—I meant—

CYNTHIA. You meant what you said!

JOHN. (*Comes a step to her.*) Mrs. Karslake, I apologize—I won't do it again. But it 's too late for you to be out alone —Philip will be here in a moment—and of course, then—

CYNTHIA. It is n't what you *say*—it 's—it 's—it 's everything. It 's the entire situation. Suppose by any chance I don't marry Phillimore! And suppose I were seen at two or three in the morning leaving my former husband's house! It 's all wrong. I have no business to be here! I 'm going! You 're perfectly horrid to me, you know—and—the whole place—it 's so familiar, and so—so associated with—with—

JOHN. Discord and misery—I know—

CYNTHIA. Not at all with discord and misery! With harmony and happiness —with—with first love, and infinite hope —and—and—Jack Karslake,—if you don't set that chair on its legs, I think I 'll explode.

(JOHN *crosses the stage rapidly and sets chair on its legs. His tone changes.*)

JOHN. (*While setting chair on its legs.*) There! I beg your pardon.

CYNTHIA. (*Nervously.*) I believe I hear Philip. (*Rises.*)

JOHN. (*Going up to the window.*) N-o! That 's the policeman trying the front door! And now, see here, Mrs. Karslake,—you 're only here for a short minute, because you can't help yourself, but I want you to understand that I 'm not trying to be disagreeable—I don't want to revive all the old unhappy—

CYNTHIA. Very well, if you don't—give me my hat. (JOHN *does so.*) And my sewing! And my gloves, please! (*She indicates the several articles which lie on the small table.*) Thanks! (CYNTHIA *throws the lot into the fireplace, and returns to the place she has left near table.*) There! I feel better! And now—all I ask is—

JOHN. (*Laughs.*) My stars, what a pleasure it is!

CYNTHIA. What is?

JOHN. Seeing you in a whirlwind!

CYNTHIA. (*Wounded by his seeming indifference.*) Oh!

JOHN. No, but I mean, a real pleasure! Why not? Time 's passed since you and I were together—and—eh—

CYNTHIA. And you 've forgotten what a vile temper I had!

JOHN. (*Reflectively.*) Well, you did kick the stuffing out of the matrimonial buggy—

CYNTHIA. (*Pointedly but with good temper.*) It was n't a buggy; it was a break cart— (*She stands back of the armchair.*) It 's all very well to blame me! But when you married me, I 'd never had a bit in my mouth!

JOHN. Well, I guess I had a pretty hard hand. Do you remember the time you threw both your slippers out of the window?

CYNTHIA. Yes, and do you remember the time you took my fan from me by force?

JOHN. After you slapped my face with it!

CYNTHIA. Oh, oh! I hardly touched your face! And do you remember the day you held my wrists?

JOHN. You were going to bite me!

CYNTHIA. Jack! I never! I showed my teeth at you! And I said I would bite you!

JOHN. Cynthia, I never knew you to break your word! (*He laughs casually.*) And anyhow—they were awfully pretty teeth! (CYNTHIA, *though bolt upright, has ceased to seem pained.*) And I say —do you remember, Cyn—

(*He leans over the armchair to talk to her.*)

CYNTHIA. (*After a pause.*) You ought n't to call me "Cyn"—it 's not nice of you. It 's sort of cruel. I 'm not—Cyn to you now.

JOHN. Awfully sorry; did n't mean to be beastly, Cyn. (CYNTHIA *turns quickly.* JOHN *stamps his foot.*) Cynthia! Sorry. I 'll make it a commandment: thou shalt not Cyn!!

(CYNTHIA *laughs and wipes her eyes.*)

CYNTHIA. How can you, Jack? How can you?

JOHN. Well, hang it, my dear child, I—I 'm sorry, but you know I always got foolish with you. Your laugh 'd make a horse laugh. Why, don't you remember that morning in the park before breakfast—when you laughed so hard your horse ran away with you!

CYNTHIA. I do, I do! (*Both laugh. The door opens.*)

(NOGAM *enters.*)

But what was it started me laughing? (*Laughing, sits down and laughs again.*) That morning. Was n't it somebody we met? (*Laughs.*) Was n't it a man on a horse? (*Laughs.*)

JOHN. (*Laughing too.*) Of course! You did n't know him in those days! But I did! And he looked a sight in the saddle!

(NOGAM, *trying to catch their attention, comes to right of table.*)

CYNTHIA. Who was it?

JOHN. Phillimore!

CYNTHIA. He 's no laughing matter now. (*Sees* NOGAM.) Jack, he 's here!

JOHN. Eh? Oh, Nogam?

NOGAM. Mr. Phillimore, sir—

JOHN. In the house?

NOGAM. On the street in a hansom, sir—and he requests Mrs. Karslake—

JOHN. That 'll do, Nogam. (*Exit* NOGAM. *Pause.* JOHN *from near the window.* CYNTHIA *faces audience.*) Well, Cynthia?

(*He speaks almost gravely and with finality.*)

CYNTHIA. (*Trembling.*) Well?

JOHN. It 's the hour of decision; are you going to marry him? (*Pause.*) Speak up!

CYNTHIA. Jack,—I—I—

JOHN. There he is—you can join him. (*He points to the street.*)

CYNTHIA. Join Phillimore—and go home—with him—to his house, and Miss Henage and—

JOHN. The door 's open. (*He points to the door.*)

CYNTHIA. No, no! It 's mean of you to suggest it!

JOHN. You won't marry—

CYNTHIA. Phillimore—no; never. (*Runs to window.*) No; never, never, Jack.

JOHN. (*He calls out of the window, having opened it.*) It 's all right, Judge. You need n't wait.

(*Pause.* JOHN *comes down.* JOHN *bursts into laughter.* CYNTHIA *looks dazed. He closes door.*)

CYNTHIA. Jack! (JOHN *laughs.*) Yes, but I 'm here, Jack.

JOHN. Why not?

CYNTHIA. You 'll have to take me round to the Holland House!

JOHN. Of course, I will! But, I say Cynthia, there 's no hurry.

CYNTHIA. Why, I—I—can't stay here.

JOHN. No, of course you can't stay here. But you can have a bite, though. (CYNTHIA *shakes her head.* JOHN *places the small chair which was upset, next to table.*) Oh, I insist. Just look at yourself—you 're as pale as a sheet and—here, here. Sit right down. I insist! By George, you must do it!

(CYNTHIA *crosses to chair beside table and sits.*)

CYNTHIA. (*Faintly.*) I *am* hungry.

JOHN. Just wait a moment. (*Exit* JOHN.)

CYNTHIA. I don't want more than a nibble! (*Pause.*) I am sorry to give you so much trouble.

JOHN. No trouble at all. (*He can be heard off the stage, busied with glasses and a tray.*) A hansom of course, to take you round to your hotel? (*Speaking as he comes down.*)

CYNTHIA. (*To herself.*) I wonder how I ever dreamed I could marry that man.

JOHN. (*By table by this time.*) Can't imagine! There!

CYNTHIA. I am hungry. Don't forget the hansom.

(*She eats; he waits on her, setting this and that before her.*)

JOHN. (*Going to door; opens it and speaks off.*) Nogam, a hansom at once.

NOGAM. (*Off stage.*) Yes, sir.

JOHN. (*Back to above table; from here on he shows his feelings for her.*) How does it go?

CYNTHIA. (*Faintly.*) It goes all right. Thanks! (*Hardly eating at all.*)

JOHN. You always used to like anchovy. (CYNTHIA *nods and eats.*) Claret? (CYNTHIA *shakes her head.*) Oh, but you must!

CYNTHIA. (*Tremulously.*) Ever so little. (*He fills her glass and then his.*) Thanks!

JOHN. Here 's to old times. (*Raising glass.*)

CYNTHIA. (*Very tremulous.*) Please not!

JOHN. Well, here 's to your next husband.

CYNTHIA. (*Very tenderly.*) Don't!

JOHN. Oh, well, then, what shall the toast be?

CYNTHIA. I 'll tell you—(*pause*) you can drink to the relation I am to you!

JOHN. (*Laughing.*) Well—what relation are you?

CYNTHIA. I 'm your first wife once removed!

JOHN. (*Laughing, he drinks.*) I say, you 're feeling better.

CYNTHIA. Lots.

JOHN. (*Reminiscent.*) It's a good deal like those mornings after the races—is n't it?

CYNTHIA. (*Nodding.*) Yes. Is that the hansom? (*Half rises.*)

JOHN. (*Going up to the window.*) No.

CYNTHIA. (*Sitting again.*) What is that sound?

JOHN. Don't you remember?

CYNTHIA. No.

JOHN. That's the rumbling of the early milk wagons.

CYNTHIA. Oh, Jack.

JOHN. Do you recognize it now?

CYNTHIA. Do I? We used to hear that—just at the hour, did n't we—when we came back from awfully jolly late suppers and things!

JOHN. H'm!

CYNTHIA. It must be fearfully late. I must go.

(*She rises, crosses to chair, where she has left her cloak. She sees that* JOHN *will not help her and puts it on herself.*)

JOHN. Oh, don't go—why go?

CYNTHIA. (*Embarrassed and agitated.*) All good things come to an end, you know.

JOHN. They don't need to.

CYNTHIA. Oh, you don't mean that! And, you know, Jack, if I were caught—seen at this hour, leaving this house, you know—it's the most scandalous thing any one ever did my being here at all. Good-bye, Jack! (*Pause; almost in tears.*) I'd like to say, I—I—I—well, I shan't be bitter about you hereafter, and— (*Pause.*) Thank you awfully, old man, for the fodder and all that! (*She turns to go out.*)

JOHN. Mrs. Karslake—wait—

CYNTHIA. (*Stopping to hear.*) Well?

JOHN. (*Serious.*) I've rather an ugly bit of news for you.

CYNTHIA. Yes?

JOHN. I don't believe you know that I have been testing the validity of the decree of divorce which you procured.

CYNTHIA. Oh, have you?

JOHN. Yes; you know I felt pretty warmly about it.

CYNTHIA. Well?

JOHN. Well, I've been successful. (*Pause.*) The decree's been declared invalid. Understand?

CYNTHIA. (*Looking at him a moment; then speaking.*) Not—precisely.

JOHN. (*Pause.*) I'm awfully sorry—I'm awfully sorry, Cynthia, but, you're my wife still. (*Pause.*)

CYNTHIA. (*With rapture.*) Honor bright? (*She sinks into the armchair.*)

JOHN. (*Nodding, half laughingly.*) Crazy country, is n't it?

CYNTHIA. (*Nodding. Pause.*) Well, Jack—what's to be done?

JOHN. (*Gently.*) Whatever you say.

NOGAM. (*Quietly enters.*) Hansom, sir. (*Exits.* CYNTHIA *rises.*)

JOHN. Why don't you finish your supper? (CYNTHIA *hesitates.*)

CYNTHIA. The—the—hansom—

JOHN. Why go to the Holland? After all—you know, Cyn, you're at home here.

CYNTHIA. No, Jack, I'm not—I'm not at home here—unless—unless—

JOHN. Out with it!

CYNTHIA. (*Bursting into tears.*) Unless I—unless I'm at home in your heart, Jack!

JOHN. What do you think?

CYNTHIA. I don't believe you want me to stay.

JOHN. Don't you?

CYNTHIA. No, no, you hate me still. You never can forgive me. I know you can't. For I can never forgive myself. Never, Jack, never, never!

(*She sobs and he takes her in his arms.*)

JOHN. (*Very tenderly.*) Cyn! I love you! (*Strongly.*) And you've got to stay! And hereafter you can chuck chairs around till all's blue! Not a word now. (*He draws her gently to a chair.*)

CYNTHIA. (*Wiping her tears.*) Oh, Jack! Jack!

JOHN. I'm as hungry as a shark. We'll nibble together.

CYNTHIA. Well, all I can say is, I feel that of all the improprieties I ever committed this—this—

JOHN. This takes the claret, eh? Oh, Lord, how happy I am!

CYNTHIA. Now don't say that! You'll make me cry more.

(*She wipes her eyes.* JOHN *takes out the wedding ring from his pocket; he lifts a wine glass, drops the ring into it and offers her the glass.*)

JOHN. Cynthia!

CYNTHIA. (*Looking at it and wiping her eyes.*) What is it?

JOHN. Benedictine!

CYNTHIA. Why, you know I never take it.

JOHN. Take this one for my sake.

CYNTHIA. That 's not benedictine. (*With gentle curiosity.*) What is it?

JOHN. (*He slides the ring out of the glass and puts his arm about* CYNTHIA. *He slips the ring on to her finger and, as he kisses her hand, says.*) Your wedding ring!

THE WITCHING HOUR

BY

Augustus Thomas

THE WITCHING HOUR *

The Witching Hour represents the play that reflects a phase of modern interest, in this case telepathy. It also represents Mr. Thomas's work in the most significant period of his playwriting. Augustus Thomas was born in St. Louis, Missouri, January 8, 1857, the son of Dr. Elihu B. Thomas. His father was associated with the theatre, being director for a time of the St. Charles Theatre in New Orleans. Mr. Thomas tells us, that after his father returned to St. Louis in 1865, Dr. Thomas told him much concerning the actors with whom he had come in contact. Augustus Thomas was taken to the theatre early in his life and has grown up in its atmosphere. He was educated in the public schools of St. Louis, was a page in the Forty-first Congress and up to his twenty-second year was in the service of the freight department of various railroads, where, he tells us, he learned much about human nature. Later on, he became a special writer on newspapers in St. Louis, Kansas City, and New York, and was for a time editor and proprietor of the *Kansas City Mirror*.

He began to write plays when he was fourteen years old. By the time he was seventeen he had organized an amateur company which he took on circuit. It was at this time that such early efforts as *Alone* (1875), or *A Big Rise* (1882), his earliest plays known by name, were written. In 1883 he dramatized Mrs. Burnett's *Editha's Burglar,* and organized a professional company which he took around the country playing this and other plays. In 1889 a four-act play by the title of *The Burglar* became a success in New York and since then Mr. Thomas has devoted himself to playwriting. He was for a time the Art Director of the Charles Frohman interests. On August 1, 1922 he became the Executive Chairman of the Producing Managers' Association, and in that capacity he has taken a leading part in adjusting the difficulties between the actors and the producing managers. In November 1924 the French Government bestowed upon Mr. Thomas the decoration of "Chevalier de la Légion d'Honneur" in recognition of the valuable services he had rendered the cause of France.

Mr. Thomas produced sixty-five plays including one act plays and dramatizations or adaptations of other material. He stands in our drama for literary craftsmanship combined with practical knowledge of the stage and for a serious interest in the furtherance of dramatic progress. His work is not the result of accidental inspiration, but he has proceeded on a basis of logical deduction from observed facts to an establishment of fundamental principles in dramatic construction. His art is native, too; his first significant play, *Alabama,* produced

* This introduction has been entirely revised for the Fifth Edition.

April 1, 1891, at the Madison Square Theatre, New York, had as its theme the reunited country. *In Mizzoura* (1893) pictured in a less significant though amusing manner the customs of that State. *Arizona,* produced first, June 12, 1899, at Hamlin's Grand Opera House, Chicago, is a better play than any of the ones which preceded it, and Mr. Thomas may be said to have entered into his most significant period with this play. It was laid at the time of the Spanish-American War, but the war itself was of little significance. The play portrayed American life in its picturesque western form, not the "bad man" of fiction, but the actual life of the great ranches, with real characters in them. *Arizona* had a successful London production in 1902. Mr. Thomas produced next some charming comedies, either like *Oliver Goldsmith* (1899), an imaginative treatment of literary history, or like *The Earl of Pawtucket* (1903), or *Mrs. Leffingwell's Boots* (1905), clever treatments of modern life.

The Witching Hour, produced first at the Hackett Theatre, New York City, November 18, 1907, is probably Mr. Thomas's greatest play. It represents the next phase of his work, the study of modern modes of interest. One would call them "problems," except that the word suggests an element that is absent from Mr. Thomas's plays. The central theme of the play, the influence of human minds through the strength of suggestion, had been with Mr. Thomas for many years. Incidents that had proved to him the possibility of such suggestions had occurred in his early days when he was managing companies in the West, and he waited till the time was ripe and public interest was ready. In *As a Man Thinks,* he treated the relations of the modern American husband and wife, and put into dramatic form the real reason for the prevalence of the so-called double standard of morality. It is a sane and healthful play, for it not only deals with this question without morbidity or suggestiveness, but it also shows the futility of race antagonism and it calls attention to the permanent force of character, through the masterly portrait of "Dr. Seelig." In *The Copperhead* he painted a remarkable portrait of the middle-western town during the early days of the Civil War and also showed in dramatic form the influence of Lincoln upon a patriot who was willing to appear a Confederate spy in order more effectively to serve his country.

The following list of plays has been based upon that given by Mr. Thomas in *The Print of My Remembrance,* but certain additions and corrections have been made, after submission to the playwright himself. One-act plays are starred. Collaborations or dramatizations of other material are indicated by a dagger. *Alone* (1875), *The Big Rise* (1882), *Editha's Burglar* * † (1883), *A New Year's Call* * (1883), *A Man of the World* * (1883), *A Leaf from the Woods* * (1883), *A Studio Picture* * (1883), *Combustion* (1884), *The Burglar* (1889), *A Woman of the World* * (1890) *Reckless Temple* (1890), *After Thoughts* * (1890), *The Outside Man* (1890), *A Night's Frolic* (1891), *Alabama* (1891), *For Money* †

(1891), *Colonel Carter of Cartersville* † (1892), *The Holly Tree Inn* * † (1892), *Surrender* (1892), *In Mizzoura* (1893), *A Proper Impropriety* * (1893), *The Music Box* * (1894), *New Blood* (1894), *The Man Upstairs* * (1895), *The Capitol* (1895), *Chimmie Fadden* † (1896), *The Jucklins* † (1897), *The Hoosier Doctor* (1897), *The Meddler,* first played as *Don't Tell Her Husband* (1898), *Colonel George of Mount Vernon* (1898), *That Overcoat* * (1898), *The Bonnie Brier Bush* † (1898), *Arizona* (1899), *Oliver Goldsmith* (1899), *On the Quiet* (1901), *Champagne Charlie* (1901), *Colorado* (1901), *Soldiers of Fortune* (1902), *The Earl of Pawtucket* (1903), *The Other Girl* (1903), *Mrs. Leffingwell's Boots* (1905), *The Education of Mr. Pipp* † (1905), *The Embassy Ball* (1905), *De Lancey* (1905), *The Ranger* (1907), *The Member from Ozark* (1907), *The Witching Hour* (1907), *The Harvest Moon* (1909), *The Matinée Idol* (1909), *As a Man Thinks* (1911), *The Model* (1912), *Mere Man* (1912), *At Bay* † (1913) with George Scarborough, *The Three of Hearts* † (1913), *Indian Summer* (1913), *The Battle Cry* † (1914), *The Nightingale* (1914), *Rio Grande* (1916), *The Copperhead* (1918), *The Cricket of Palmy Days* (1919), *Speak of the Devil* (1920), *Tent of Pompey* * (1920), *Nemesis* (1921), *Still Waters* (1925).

Alabama and *Arizona* have been published by the Dramatic Publishing Company, *As a Man Thinks* by Duffield and in Baker's *Modern American Plays.* Samuel French has published *The Witching Hour, Oliver Goldsmith, The Harvest Moon, In Mizzoura, Mrs. Leffingwell's Boots, The Other Girl, The Earl of Pawtucket, The Copperhead, Colonel George of Mount Vernon* and *The Cricket of Palmy Days,* with accounts by Mr. Thomas of the genesis of the plays. These introductions contain valuable material for students of dramatic technique.

The Print of My Remembrance, published by Scribners in 1922, is a fascinating autobiography of Mr. Thomas, which will be of great value to students of the drama.

For a thorough analysis of Mr. Thomas's plays, see William Winter, *The Wallet of Time,* Vol. 2, pp. 529–557. See also W. P. Eaton, *The American Stage of Today* (1908), pp. 27–44, which contains an analysis of *The Witching Hour.* A criticism of the first performance appears in *The Theatre,* Vol. 8, p. 2, 1908.

The present text has been revised especially for this collection by Mr. Thomas, to whom the editor is indebted for permission to reprint it.

Note to Sixth Edition.

Augustus Thomas died August 12, 1934 at the Clarkstown Country Club, near Nyack, New York. A critical treatment of Mr. Thomas's work is to be found in the present editor's *History of the American Drama from the Civil War to the Present Day,* Revised Edition, two volumes in one, Appleton-Century-Crofts, Inc. (1936), Vol. 1, pp. 239–264, Vol. 2, pp. 395–398.

THE ORIGINAL CAST OF CHARACTERS

Hackett Theatre, New York City, November 18, 1907

In the order of their first appearance

Jo, a servant	Mr. S. E. Hines
Jack Brookfield, professional gambler	Mr. John Mason
Tom Denning	Mr. Freeman Barnes
Harvey, a servant	Mr. Thomas C. Jackson
Mrs. Alice Campbell, Jack's sister	Miss Ethel Winthrop
Mrs. Helen Whipple, Clay's mother	Mrs. Jeanne Eustace
Viola Campbell	Miss Adelaide Nowak
Clay Whipple	Mr. Morgan Coman
Frank Hardmuth	Mr. George Nash
Lew Ellinger	Mr. William Sampson
Justice Prentice	Mr. Russ Whytal
Justice Henderson	Mr. E. I. Walton
Colonel Bayley	Mr. Harry Hadfield
Mr. Emmett, a reporter	Mr. Fawnesgaines

THE WITCHING HOUR

ACT FIRST.

SCENE. *The library and card-room at* JACK BROOKFIELD'S, *Louisville.*

There is a large doorway in the center, at the back, which leads into a hallway, in which the banister of a stairway that descends to the street level is seen. A second and smaller doorway is near the front in the wall to the left of the stage. This doorway leads to the dining-room. The second plan of the left wall is occupied by a fireplace and mantel, surmounted by a marine painting. The fireplace is surrounded by a garde au feu *club seat.*

The rest of the left wall, as well as the rear wall on both sides of the center door and all of the right wall, is fitted with bookcases about five feet high, in which are books handsomely bound.

The walls above these bookcases are hung with heavy brocaded Genoese velvet of a deep maroon in color and loosely draped. The ceiling is of carved wood, gilded. On the wall velvet, at proper intervals, are paintings by celebrated modern artists. Some of these paintings are fitted with hooded electric lights. Such a fitting is above a noticeable Corot, which hangs to the right of the center door.

A dark-red rug of luxuriant thickness is on the floor. The furniture is simple, massive, and Colonial in type. It consists of a heavy sofa above the fireplace and running at right angles to the wall. A heavy table fitted with books is in the center; a smaller table for cards is at the stage, right. Chairs are at both tables.

Above the center door is a marble bust of Minerva, surmounted by a bronze raven, lacquered black, evidently illustrating Poe's poem. The Antommarchi deathmask of Napoleon in bronze hangs on the dark wood fireplace. A bronze mask of Beethoven is on one of the bookcases and on another is a bust of Dante. A bronze Sphinx is on another bookcase.

The room is lighted by a standing lamp at the back and by the glow from the fireplace. Over the table, center, is suspended an electric lamp in a large bronze shade. This lamp, while not lighted, is capable of being turned on by a push button, which depends from it.

On the table, center, is a large paper-cutter made of an ivory tusk.

Empty stage. After a pause there is a sound of laughter and dishes, left.

(*Enter* JO, *sleek negro of Pullman car variety, by stairway and center door. He goes to door, left, and pauses—laughter ceases.*)

JO. Massar Brookfield.

JACK. (*Outside, left.*) Well, Jo?

JO. Mr. Denning, sah.

JACK. Ask Mr. Denning to come up.

JO. Yes, sah.

(*Exit center. More talk and laughter, left.*)

(JACK *enters left. He walks to center on way toward main door. Pauses. Returns, left.*)

JACK. (*At door, left.*) Lew! I say—Lew—you ladies excuse Mr. Ellinger a moment?

HELEN, ALICE, VIOLA. (*Outside.*) Oh—yes. Certainly.

(*Enter* LEW ELLINGER, *from dining-room, left.*)

LEW. See me?

JACK. Tom Denning's here—he expects a game. My sister and Mrs. Whipple object to the pasteboards—so don't mention it before them.

LEW. (*Anxiously.*) Not a word—but, Tom—?

JACK. I'll attend to Tom.

LEW. Good.

(*Starts back to dining-room.*)

(*Enter* TOM DENNING, *right center; he is fat, indolent type.*)

TOM. Hello, Lew. (LEW *stops and turns.* JACK *motions him out and* LEW *goes.*)

What you got to-night? Young Rockefeller?

JACK. Some ladies—

TOM. (*Grinning.*) What—

JACK. (*Sternly.*) My sister and her daughter—and a lady friend of theirs.

TOM. (*Disappointed.*)—No game?

JACK. Not until they go.

TOM. (*Getting a peek off into dining-room.*) Oh—chafing-dish.

JACK. They 've been to the opera.—I had Harvey brew them some terrapin.

TOM. (*Complaining.*) My luck!

(*His hands hang limp.*)

JACK. No, I think there 's some left. (*Pause.*) I 'm going to take a long chance and introduce you, Tom, only don't say anything about poker before the ladies.

TOM. Thought you said your *sister*—

JACK. I did.

TOM. Well, she 's on, is n't she?

JACK. But she does n't like it—and my *niece*—my niece does n't like it.

(*Enter* HARVEY, *old negro servant, from dining-room, left.*)

HARVEY. I 've made some coffee, Mars Jack. You have it in the dining-room or heah, sah?

JACK. (*Going.*) I 'll ask the ladies.

TOM. How are you, Harvey?

HARVEY. (*Bowing.*) Mars Denning—

JACK. (*Who has paused at door, left.*) Got some terrapin for Mr. Denning, Harvey?

HARVEY. Yas, sah. (*To* TOM.) Yas, sah. (*Exit* JACK, *left.*)

TOM. They left some of the rum, too, I hope.

HARVEY. Could n't empty my ice-box in one evening, Mars Denning. (*Starts off. Pause.*) De ladies getting up.

(*Stands up stage in front of fire.* TOM *goes right. A pause.*)

(*Enter* JACK.)

JACK. The ladies will have their coffee in here, Harvey.

HARVEY. Yes, sir.

(*Enter* ALICE. *She is smartly gowned and is energetic.*)

JACK. Alice—this is my friend, Mr. Denning—my sister—Mrs. Campbell.

ALICE. Mr. Denning.

(*Enter* HELEN *and* VIOLA. HELEN *is thoroughly feminine in type, and is young-looking for the mother of a boy of twenty*—VIOLA *is an athletic Kentucky girl.*)

HELEN. I never take coffee even after dinner and at this hour—never!

(*Exit* HARVEY.)

JACK. Mrs. Whipple, may I present Mr. Denning?

HELEN. (*Bowing.*) Mr. Denning.

TOM. Good-evening!

JACK. My niece, Miss Viola Campbell.

TOM. How are you? (VIOLA *bows.*)

JACK. Mr. Denning 's just left the *foundry* and he 's very hungry.

TOM. And thirsty—

JACK. (*Pushing him toward dining-room.*) Yes, and thirsty. Uncle Harvey 's going to save his life.

TOM. Ha, ha! Excuse me! (*Exit.*)

ALICE. The foundry?

(*Sits right of table.*)

JACK. Never did a day's work in his life. That 's Tom Denning. (*Nods off.*)

VIOLA. (*On sofa at fireplace.*) Tom Denning 's the name of the big race-horse.

JACK. Yes—he 's *named after* the race-horse.

HELEN. (*On sofa, beside* VIOLA.) *What* does he do?

JACK. His father—father 's in the packing business—Kansas City; this fellow has four men *shoveling* money away from him so he can breathe.

(*Starts toward dining-room.*)

ALICE. (*In amused protest.*) Oh, Jack!

JACK. Yes—I 'm one of them—you 'll find cigarettes in that box.

ALICE. Jack! (*Rises.*)

JACK. (*Apologizing.*) Not *you,* Alice, but—

VIOLA. (*Protesting.*) Well, certainly not for *me,* Uncle Jack?

JACK. Of course, not you . . .

HELEN. Thank you, Mr. Brookfield!

ALICE. (*Joining* JACK.) My dear brother, you confuse the Kentucky ladies with some of your Eastern friends.

JACK. Careful, Alice. *Helen* lived in the East twenty years, remember.

HELEN. But even my *husband* did n't smoke.

JACK. No?

HELEN. *Never*—in his life—

JACK. In his *life?* Why make such a pessimistic distinction?

(HELEN *turns away right.*)

ALICE. Jack! (*After a look to* HELEN.) How can you say a thing like that?

JACK. *She's* the man's widow—*I've got* to say it if any one does.

(*Enter* HARVEY *with coffee.*)

Mr. Denning's got his tortoise, Uncle Harvey?

HARVEY. (*Offering tray to* HELEN.) He's got the same as we all had, Mars Jack. Yas, sah. (*Laughs.*)

HELEN. None, thank you.

(HARVEY *moves on.*)

JACK. I'll take it, Uncle Harvey. I think three or four of them'll help this head of mine.

ALICE. (*Taking coffee.*) Why don't you let Viola cure your headache?

VIOLA. (*Taking coffee.*) Yes, Uncle Jack.

JACK. No, the coffee'll fix it, I'm sure.

(*Exit* HARVEY.)

VIOLA. Sit here while you drink it.

JACK. No—no, Viola. It is n't enough for that. I'll conserve your mesmeric endowment for a real occasion.

(*Swallows coffee in one mouthful.*)

VIOLA. Goodness! Just to please me?

JACK. (*Shaking head.*) Don't want to spoil your awful stories.

(*Exit to dining-room.*)

HELEN. Is Viola a magnetic healer, too?

(*Sits right of table.*)

VIOLA. (*Taking a book, and returning to the sofa, carrying also a large ivory tusk paper-cutter.*) Oh, no.

ALICE. (*Sitting left of table.*) Yes—a remarkable one.

VIOLA. Only headaches, Mrs. Whipple. Those I *crush* out of my victims.

HELEN. I remember Jack used to have a wonderful ability that way as a young man.

VIOLA. He says only with the girls.

ALICE. We know better, don't we?

HELEN. Yes.

VIOLA. Well, for myself, I'd rather have Uncle Jack sit by me than any regular physician I ever saw.

HELEN. You mean if you were ill?

VIOLA. Of course.

ALICE. You must be very clear with Mrs. Whipple on that point, Viola, because she used to prefer your Uncle Jack to sit by her, even when she was n't ill.

HELEN. (*To* VIOLA.) But especially when ill, my dear. (*To* ALICE.) And has he quit it?

ALICE. Yes—you know Jack went into politics for a while.

HELEN. Did he?

ALICE *Local* politics—yes—something about the police did n't please him and then he quit all of his curative work.

HELEN. Why?

ALICE. Well, in politics, I believe there's something unpleasant about the word "heeler."

HELEN. Oh!

VIOLA. Entirely different spelling, however.

HELEN. Our English language is so elastic in that way.

ALICE. Yes, the papers joked about his magnetic touch. The word "touch" is used offensively also. So Jack dropped the whole business.

HELEN. And Viola inherits the ability?

ALICE. Well, if one can inherit ability from an uncle.

HELEN. From a family.

ALICE. That's even more generous, but Viola is like Jack in every way in which a girl may resemble a man. Horses and boats and every kind of personal risk—and—

VIOLA. (*Rises.*) I'm *proud* of it.

ALICE. And Jack spoils her.

VIOLA. Am I spoiled?

(*Goes to back of table.*)

ALICE. He could n't love her more if he were her father—

(*Enter* CLAY, *a boy of twenty.*)

CLAY. (*Pausing at door.*) May I come in?

VIOLA. Certainly.

CLAY. Is n't this a jolly room, mother?

HELEN. Beautiful.

CLAY. (*Waving hand above.*) And the sleeping apartments are what I take pride in. Private bath to every bedroom, reading-lamps just over the pillows—

VIOLA. Have n't you seen the house, Mrs. Whipple?

HELEN. Not above this floor.

ALICE. Would it interest you?

(*Rises and goes left.*)

HELEN. Very much.

ALICE. (*At door of dining-room.*) Jack—

JACK. (*Outside.*) Yes—

ALICE. (*To* HELEN.) Will I do as your guide?

HELEN. (*Rises.*) Oh, yes.

(*Enter* JACK.)

ALICE. I want to show Helen over the house.

JACK. Do.

ALICE. The rooms are empty?

JACK. Empty, of course.

ALICE. Don't be too indignant, they 're not always empty. (*To* HELEN.) In *Jack's* house one is liable to find a belated pilgrim in any room.

HELEN. (*Laughing.*) And a lady walking in unannounced would be something of a surprise, would n't she?

JACK. Well—two ladies would, certainly.

ALICE. Jack!

JACK. My dear sister—they *would*. Hard lines when the reputation of a man's house is n't respected by his own sister—ha!

(*Exit left, with mock indignation.*)

HELEN. (*Smiling.*) The same Jack.

ALICE. Intensified and confirmed! (*Pausing at door.*) Will you come, too, Viola?

VIOLA. No, thank you, mother.

(HELEN *looks at* ALICE. *She and* ALICE *go.*)

CLAY. What was Frank Hardmuth saying to you.

(*He indicates the dining-room.*)

VIOLA. When?

CLAY. At supper—and in the box at the theater, too?

VIOLA. Oh—Frank Hardmuth—nobody pays any attention to him.

CLAY. I thought *you* paid a great deal of attention to what he was saying.

VIOLA. In the same theater party a girl 's got to listen—or leave the box.

CLAY. Some persons listen to the opera.

VIOLA. I told him that was what I wanted to do.

CLAY. Was he making love to you, Viola?

VIOLA. I should n't call it that.

CLAY. Would anybody else have called it that if they 'd overheard it?

VIOLA. I don't think so.

CLAY. Won't you tell me what it was about?

VIOLA. I don't see why you ask.

CLAY. I asked because he seemed so much in earnest—and because *you* seemed so much in earnest.

VIOLA. Well?

CLAY. And Frank Hardmuth 's a fellow that 'll stand watching. (*Looks off left.*)

VIOLA. (*Smiling.*) He stood a good deal to-night.

CLAY. I mean that he 's a clever lawyer and would succeed in making a girl commit herself in some way to *him* before she knew it.

VIOLA. I think that depends more on the way the *girl* feels.

CLAY. Well—I don't want you to listen to Frank Hardmuth under the idea that he 's the only chance in Kentucky.

VIOLA. Why, Clay Whipple—

CLAY. You know very well *I 've* been courting you myself, Viola, don't you?

VIOLA. You have n't. You 've been coming round like a big boy.

CLAY. (*Follows right.*) Have I gone with any other girl—anywhere?

VIOLA. I don't know. (*Sits right.*)

CLAY. And I 've spoken to your Uncle Jack about it.

VIOLA. To Uncle Jack?

CLAY. Yes.

VIOLA. (*Rises.*) Nobody told you to speak to Uncle Jack.

CLAY. Mother did.

VIOLA. *Your* mother?

CLAY. Yes. Mother 's got regular old-fashioned ideas about boys and young ladies and she said, "if you think Viola *likes* you, the *honorable* thing to do is to speak to her guardian first."

VIOLA. Oh!—you *thought* that, did you?

CLAY. I certainly did.

VIOLA. I can't imagine why.

CLAY. I thought that because you 're Jack Brookfield's niece, and nobody of his blood would play a game that is n't fair.

VIOLA. I wish you would n't always throw that up to me. (*Goes to sofa.*) 'T is n't our fault if Uncle Jack 's a sporting man. (*Sits.*)

CLAY. (*Following.*) Why, Viola, I was praising him. I think your Uncle Jack the gamest man in Kentucky.

VIOLA. Nor that either. I don't criticize my Uncle Jack, but he 's a lot better man than just a fighter or a card-player. I love him for his big heart.

CLAY. So do I. If I 'd thought you cared I 'd have said you were too much like him at heart to let a fellow come a-courtin' if you meant to refuse him—and that was all that was in my mind when I asked about Frank Hardmuth—and I don't care what Hardmuth said either, if it was n't personal that way.

VIOLA. Frank Hardmuth 's nothing to me.

CLAY. And he won't be? (*Pause.*) Will he—? (*Pause.*) Say that. Because I 'm awfully in love with you.

VIOLA. Are you?

CLAY. You bet I am. Just Tom-fool heels over head in love with you.

VIOLA. You never said so.

CLAY. Mother said a boy in an architect's office had better wait till he was a partner—but I can't wait, Viola, if other fellows are pushing me too hard.

VIOLA. (*Rises.*) Uncle Jack says you *are* a regular architect if there ever was one.

CLAY. It 's what *you* think that makes the difference to me.

VIOLA. Well, I think—(*Pause*)—Uncle Jack certainly *knows.*

CLAY. And an architect 's just as good as a lawyer.

VIOLA. Every bit.

CLAY. Viola. (*Takes her in his arms.*)

VIOLA. Now—I don't *mind* tellin' you—he was speakin' for himself—Frank Hardmuth.

CLAY. By Jove—on this very night.

VIOLA. Yes.

CLAY. Seems like the Hand of Providence that I was here. Let 's sit down. (*They sit.*) You 've got confidence in me, have n't you?

VIOLA. Yes—I 've always said to mother—Clay Whipple 'll make his mark some day—I should say I *had* confidence in you.

CLAY. Huh. (*Laughs.*) Of course the *big* jobs *pay.* Things like insurance buildings—but my heart 's in domestic architecture—and if you don't laugh at me, I 'll *tell* you something.

VIOLA. Laugh at you—about your work and your ambition! Why, Clay!

CLAY. I do most of the domestic interiors for the firm already—and whenever I plan a second floor or a staircase I can see *you* plain as day walkin' through the rooms—or saying good-night over the banisters.

VIOLA. Really? (CLAY *nods.*) You mean in your mind?

CLAY. No, with my eyes. Domestic architecture 's the most poetic work a man can get into outside of *downright* poetry itself.

VIOLA. It must be if you can *see* it all that way.

CLAY. Every room—I can see your short sleeves as you put your hands on the banisters—and sometimes you push up your front hair with the back of your hand that way— (*Brushes his forehead.*)

VIOLA. Oh, this—(*Repeats the gesture.*)—all girls do that.

CLAY. But not just the same way as you do it. Yes, sir! I can see every little motion *you* make.

VIOLA. Whenever you care to think about me.

CLAY. Bless you, no—that 's the trouble of it.

VIOLA. What trouble?

CLAY. The pictures of you—don't come just when I *want* them to come—and they don't go when I want them to go—especially in the dark.

VIOLA. Why, how funny.

CLAY. Sometimes I 've had to light the gas in order to go to sleep.

VIOLA. Why, I never heard of anything like that.

CLAY. Well, it happens with me often. I designed this room for your Uncle Jack—but before I put a brush in my color-box I saw this very Genoese velvet and the picture frames in their places—and that Corot right there—I 've got kind of a superstition about that picture.

VIOLA. (*Rises.*) A superstition!
(*Regards the Corot.*)

CLAY. I said to Jack, have anything else you want on the other walls, but right there I want you to put a Corot that I 've seen at a dealer's in New York—and he did it.

VIOLA. Uncle Jack generally has his own way about pictures.

CLAY. I only mean that he approved my taste in the matter—but my idea of this house really started *with*—and grew around that canvas of Corot's.

VIOLA. Then it is n't always *me* that you see?

CLAY. Always you when I think about a real house, you bet—a house for *me*—and you 'll be there, won't you?
(*Takes her in his arms.*)

VIOLA. Will I?

CLAY. Yes—say, "I will."

VIOLA. I will.

(*Reënter* ALICE *and* HELEN.)

ALICE. (*Astonished.*) Viola!
(VIOLA *goes left.*)

CLAY. I 've asked her—mother.

ALICE. Helen, you knew?

HELEN. Yes.

CLAY. (*To* ALICE.) And I asked Jack, too.

ALICE. You mean—

CLAY. We 're engaged—if you say it 's all right.

ALICE. And you—Viola?

VIOLA. (*Nodding.*) Yes—

ALICE. (*Going to chair left of table.*) Well, if Jack 's been consulted and you *all* know of it—I should make a very hopeless minority.

CLAY. Why any minority?

ALICE. Only the necessary considerations. (*To* HELEN.) Clay's prospects—his youth.

VIOLA. Why, he designs most of the work for his firm now.

CLAY. That is, dwellings.

HELEN. I should advise waiting—myself—until Clay is in the firm—(*To* CLAY.) And I did advise delay in speaking to Viola herself.

CLAY. I 'd 'a' waited, mother, only Frank Hardmuth proposed to Viola *to-night!*

ALICE. To-night?

VIOLA. At the opera.

ALICE. (*To* HELEN.) One is n't safe anywhere.

CLAY. You would n't want *him!* So you do consent, don't you?

ALICE. I think your mother and I should talk it over.

CLAY. Well, it 's a thing a fellow does n't usually ask his mother to arrange, but— (*Pause.*)

VIOLA. You mean privately?

ALICE. Yes.

CLAY. We can go to the billiard room, I suppose?

VIOLA. Come on.

CLAY. (*At the center door with* VIOLA.) You know, mother—how I feel about it. (*Exit with* VIOLA.)

HELEN. I supposed you had guessed it. (*Sits right of table.*)

ALICE. I had—but when the moment arrives after all, it 's such a surprise that a mother can't act naturally.

HELEN. Clay is really very trustworthy for his years.

ALICE. There 's only one thing to discuss. I have n't mentioned it because—well, because I 've seen so little of you since it began and because the fault is in my own family.

HELEN. Fault?

ALICE. Yes—Jack's fault—(*Pause.*) Clay is playing.

HELEN. You mean—

ALICE. Here with Jack's friends.

HELEN. Clay gambling!

ALICE. (*Wincing.*) I don't quite get used to the word, though we 've had a lifetime of it—(*Sits left of table.*) gambling.

HELEN. I should n't have thought Jack would do that—with *my* boy.

ALICE. Jack has n't our feminine viewpoint, Helen—and, besides, Jack is calloused to it.

HELEN. You should have talked to Jack yourself.

ALICE. Talked to him? I did much more—that is, as much more as a sister dependent on a brother for support could do. You know Jack really *built* this place for me and Viola.

HELEN. I 'd thought so—yes.

ALICE. Viola is the very core of Jack's heart—well, we both left the house and went into our little apartment and are there now. A woman can't do much more than that and still take her living from a man, can she?

HELEN. No—

ALICE. And it hurt him—hurt him past any idea.

HELEN. You did that because my Clay was—was playing here?

ALICE. Not entirely Clay—everybody! (*Pause—a distant burst of laughter comes from the men in the dining-room.*) There is n't a better-hearted man nor an abler one in the State than Jack Brookfield, but I had my daughter to consider. There were two nights under our last city government when nothing but the influence of Frank Hardmuth kept the police from coming to this house and arresting everybody—think of it.

HELEN. Dreadful—

ALICE. Now, that 's something, Helen, that I would n't tell a soul but you. *Viola* does n't know it—but Jack's card-playing came between you and him years ago and you—*may* know it. (*Rises and looks toward dining-room.*) You may even have some influence with Jack.

HELEN. I—ah, no.

ALICE. Yes—this supper to-night was Jack's idea for you. The box at the opera for you.

HELEN. Why, Jack did n't even sit with us.

ALICE. Also—for you—Jack Brookfield is a more notable character in Louisville to-day than he was twenty-two years ago. His company would have made you the subject of unpleasant comment. That 's why he left us alone in the box.

HELEN. Is n't it a pity—a terrible pity! (*Laughter off left.* HELEN *rises.*)

(*Enter* HARDMUTH, JACK, DENNING, *and* LEW. HARDMUTH *is the aggressive prosecutor.*)

HARDMUTH. I tell the gentlemen we 've left the ladies to themselves long enough, Mrs. Campbell.

ALICE. *Quite* long enough, Mr. Hardmuth.
DENNING. Where 's the young lady? Jack's niece?
HELEN. In the billiard room, I believe.
DENNING. (*To* HELEN, *disappointed.*) Oh—Jack 's been telling us what a great girl she is.
HARDMUTH. Some of us knew that without being told.
DENNING. And she 's wonderfully like you —wonderfully.
HELEN. You compliment me—
JACK. Are you under the impression you 're speaking to Viola's mother?
DENNING. Ain't I?
JACK. This lady is Mrs. Whipple.
DENNING. Oh, Clay's mother? (HELEN *bows.*) Well, your boy, Mrs. Whipple, plays in the hardest luck of all the people I ever sat next to.
HELEN. You mean—
JACK. (*Interrupting and putting his arm about* DENNING.) You depreciate yourself, Tom. There 's no hard luck in merely sitting next to you.
DENNING. Ha, ha.
HELEN. (*To* ALICE.) I think Clay and I should be going.
JACK. (*Consulting his watch.*) Oh, no—only a little after twelve and no one ever goes to sleep here before two. (*To* DENNING.) I told you to keep still about card games.
DENNING. I meant unlucky at billiards. *They 're* all right, ain't they?
JACK. Oh— (*Walks away impatiently.*)
DENNING. Let 's go and see the young lady play billiards with Clay. (*To* ALICE.) I can see now your daughter resembles you.

(*Moves up with* ALICE *toward door.* LEW *follows.*)

JACK. Shall we join them?
HELEN. I'd like it.

(JACK *and* HELEN *start up.*)

HARDMUTH. Jack! Just a minute.
JACK. (*To* HELEN.) Excuse me—
DENNING. (*To* ALICE *as they go.*) No, Kansas City 's my *home*, but I don't live there. (*Exit with* ALICE.)
JACK. Be right in, Lew.

(*Exit* HELEN *with* LEW.)

Well, Frank—
HARDMUTH. I took advantage of your hospitality, old man, to-night.
JACK. Advantage?
HARDMUTH. Yes—I 've been talking to your niece.
JACK. Oh!
HARDMUTH. Proposed to her.
JACK. Yes?
HARDMUTH. Yes, Jack.

(*Enter* JO *at back, from downstairs.*)

JO. A gentleman called you on the telephone, sah.
JACK. (*Regarding watch.*) Who?
JO. Judge Brennus—name sounds like. Holdin' the wire, sah.
JACK. I don't know any Judge Brennus.
JO. Says you don't know him, sah, but he 's got to leave town in the mornin' and he 'd be very much obliged if you 'd see him to-night.
JACK. Did you tell him we were dark to-night?
JO. He did n't want no game. It 's about a picture—a picture *you 've* got.
JACK. A picture?
JO. He wants to look at it.

(JACK *looks at* HARDMUTH.)

HARDMUTH. It 's a blind.
JACK. (*Consulting watch.*) Well, this is a good night to work a blind on me. (*To* JO.) Tell the gentleman I 'll be up for half an hour.
JO. Yes, sah. (*Exit.*)
JACK. So you proposed to Viola?
HARDMUTH. Yes. How do you feel about that?
JACK. You know the story of the barkeeper asking the owner, "Is Grady good for a drink?"—"Has he had it?"—"He has."—"He is."
HARDMUTH. Just that way, eh? JACK *nods.*) Well—she has n't answered me.
JACK. (*Musing.*) Ha—
HARDMUTH. And under those conditions, how 's Grady's credit with you?
JACK. Well, Frank, on any *ordinary* proposition you 're aces with me. You know that.
HARDMUTH. (*Seated right of table.*) But for the girl?
JACK. It 's different.
HARDMUTH. Why?
JACK. She 's only nineteen—you know.
HARDMUTH. My sister married at *eighteen.*
JACK. I mean *you 're* thirty-five.
HARDMUTH. That 's not an unusual difference.
JACK. Not an impossible difference, but I think unusual—and rather unadvisable.
HARDMUTH. That 's what *you* think.
JACK. That 's what I think.
HARDMUTH. But suppose the lady is willing to give that handicap? (*Pause—*

JACK *shrugs his shoulders.*) What then?

JACK. Let's cross the bridge when we come to it.

HARDMUTH. You mean *you'd* still drag a little?

JACK. (*Pause.*) Do you think Viola likes you well enough to say yes?

HARDMUTH. Let's cross *that* bridge when we come to it.

JACK. We have come to that one, Frank. There's another man in the running and I think she likes him.

HARDMUTH. You mean young Whipple? (*Rises, goes to fireplace.*) Well, he took second money in the box party to-night —at the supper table, too. I'll agree to take care of him, if you're with *me*.

JACK. (*At table, center.*) I think *he's* your biggest opposition.

HARDMUTH. But you. Can I count on you in the show-down?

JACK. (*Pause. Sits right of table.*) If Viola did n't care enough for you, Frank. to accept you in spite of everything, I should n't try to influence her in your favor.

(*Enter* LEW, *center, from left.*)

LEW. I think a bum game of billiards is about as thin an entertainment for the outsiders as "Who's got the button?"

HARDMUTH. (*Meeting* LEW *up left center.*) I've got a little business, Lew, with Jack for a minute.

LEW. Well, I can sit in by the bottle, can't I? (*Moves towards dining-room.*)

JACK. Help yourself, Lew.

LEW. Such awful stage waits while they chalk their cues. (*Exit left.*)

HARDMUTH. But you would n't try to influence her against me.

JACK. (*Pause.*) She's about the closest thing to me there *is*—that niece of mine.

HARDMUTH. (*Pause.*) Well?

JACK. I'd protect her happiness to the limit of my ability.

HARDMUTH. If she likes me—or should come to like me—enough—her—happiness would be with *me*, would n't it? (*Sits again.*)

JACK. She might think so.

HARDMUTH. Well?

JACK. But she'd be mistaken. It would be a mistake, old chap.

HARDMUTH. I know twenty men—twelve to fifteen years older than their wives—all happy—wives happy, too.

JACK. 'T is n't just that.

HARDMUTH. What is it?

JACK. She's a fine girl—that niece of mine—not a blemish.

HARDMUTH. Well—

JACK. I want to see her get the best—the very best—in family—position—character—

HARDMUTH. Anything against the Hardmuths? (JACK *shakes head.*) I'm assistant district attorney—and next trip I'll be *the* district attorney.

JACK. I said character.

HARDMUTH. Character?

JACK. Yes.

HARDMUTH. You mean there's anything against my reputation?

JACK. No—I mean character pure and simple—I mean the moral side of you!

HARDMUTH. Well, by God!

JACK. You see, I'm keeping the *girl* in mind all the time.

HARDMUTH. *My morals!*

JACK. Let's say your moral fiber.

HARDMUTH. (*Rises.*) Well, for richness this beats anything I've struck. Jack Brookfield talking to me about my moral fiber! (*Goes toward fire.*)

JACK. You asked for it.

HARDMUTH. (*Returns aggressively.*) Yes —I did, and now I'm going to ask for the show-down. What do you mean by it?

JACK. (*With fateful repression.*) I mean —as long as you've called attention to the "richness" of Jack Brookfield talking to you on the subject—that Jack Brookfield is a professional gambler—people get from Jack Brookfield just what he promises—a square game. Do you admit that?

HARDMUTH. I admit that. Go on.

JACK. (*Rises, front of table.*) You're the assistant prosecuting attorney for the city of Louisville; the people *don't* get from you just what *you* promised—not by a jugful—

HARDMUTH. I'm the *assistant* prosecuting attorney, remember—I promised to assist in prosecution, not to institute it.

JACK. I expect technical defense, old man, but this was to be a show-down.

HARDMUTH. Let's have it—I ask for particulars.

JACK. Here's one. You play *here* in my house and you know it's against the law that you've sworn to support.

HARDMUTH. I'll support the law whenever it's invoked. Indict me and I'll plead guilty.

JACK. This evasion is what I mean by lack of moral fiber.

HARDMUTH. Perhaps we're a little shy somewhere on mental fiber.

JACK. You make me say it, do you, Frank? Your duty, at least, is to keep secret the information of your office; contrary to that duty you've betrayed the secrets of your office to warn me and other men of this city when their game was in danger from the police.

HARDMUTH. You *throw* that up to me?

JACK. (*Sits on left end of table.*) Throw nothing—you asked for it.

HARDMUTH. I stand by my friends.

JACK. Exactly—and you've taken an oath to stand by the people.

HARDMUTH. Do you know any sure politician that does n't stand by his friends?

JACK. Not one.

HARDMUTH. Well, there!

JACK. But I don't know any sure politician that I'd tell my niece to marry.

HARDMUTH. That's a little too fine-haired for me! (*Turns to fire.*)

JACK. I think it is.

HARDMUTH. (*Returns.*) I'll bet you a thousand dollars I'm the next prosecuting attorney of this city.

JACK. I'll take half of that if you can place it. I'll bet even money you're anything in politics that you go after for the next ten years.

HARDMUTH. Then I don't understand your kick.

JACK. But I'll give odds that the time'll come when you're way up there—full of honor and reputation and pride—that somebody'll drop to you, Frank, and flosh! *You* for the down and outs.

HARDMUTH. Rot!

JACK. It's the same in every game in the world—the crook either gets too gay or gets too slow, or both, and the "come on" sees him make the pass. I've been pallbearer for three of the slickest men that ever shuffled a deck in Kentucky—just a little *too* slick, that's all—and they've always got it when it was hardest for the family.

HARDMUTH. So that'll be my finish, will it?

JACK. Sure.

HARDMUTH. (*Going back of table.*) You like the moral fiber of this Whipple kid?

JACK. I don't know. (*Crosses to fireplace.*)

HARDMUTH. Weak as dishwater.

JACK. I don't think so.

HARDMUTH. I'll do him at any game you name.

JACK. He's only a boy—you should.

HARDMUTH. I'll do him at this game.

JACK. What game?

HARDMUTH. The girl! I thought I could count on you because—well, for the very tips you hold against me; but you're only her uncle, old man, after all. (*Swaggers down right.*)

JACK. That's all.

HARDMUTH. And if she says "yes"—

JACK. Frank! (*Comes to front of table. Pause. The men confront each other.*) Some day the truth'll come out—as to who murdered the governor-elect of this State.

HARDMUTH. Is there any doubt about that?

JACK. Is n't there?

HARDMUTH. The man who fired that shot's in jail.

JACK. I don't want my niece mixed up in it.

HARDMUTH. (*Angrily.*) What do you mean by that?

(*Enter* HELEN, *center. An awkward pause.*)

The young people still playing?

HELEN. Yes.

HARDMUTH. I'll look 'em over. (*Exit.*)

HELEN. Won't you come, too?

JACK. I'd rather stay here with you.

HELEN. That gentleman that called after supper—

JACK. Mr. Denning—

HELEN. Yes. He seems to take pleasure in annoying Clay—

JACK. (*Seriously.*) Yes—I know that side of Denning (*Goes to door of dining-room.*) Lew!

LEW. Yes.

JACK. I wish you'd go into the billiard room and look after Tom Denning.

LEW. (*Entering left.*) What's he doing? (JACK *turns to* HELEN.)

HELEN. (*To* JACK.) Commenting humorously—hiding the chalk and so on.

LEW. (*As he goes up.*) Lit up a little I suppose.

JACK. (*Nodding.*) Just "ride herd" [1] on him. (*Exit* LEW.)

HELEN. (*Going left to sofa.*) He does n't seem much of a gentleman, this Mr. Denning.

JACK. He was n't expected to-night.

[1] "Take care of," in the sense of a cowboy who rounds up the herd and keeps them out of mischief.

HELEN. Is he one of your "clients"?

JACK. (*Smiling.*) One of my *"clients"?*

HELEN. Clay meets him here?

JACK. Yes—*has* met him here.

HELEN. I did n't think you 'd do that—Jack—with *my* boy.

JACK. Do what?

HELEN. Gamble.

JACK. (*Smiling.*) It 's no gamble with your boy, Helen—sure thing. He has n't won a dollar!

HELEN. I 'm glad you 're able to smile over it.

JACK. Perhaps it would be more humorous to you if he 'd won.

HELEN. If he plays—I 'd rather see him win, of course.

JACK. (*Beside sofa.*) That 's what puts me in the *business*—winning. The thing that makes every gambler stick to it is winning occasionally. I 've never let your boy get up from the table a dollar to the good and because he *was* your boy.

HELEN. Why let him play at all?

JACK. He 'll play somewhere till he gets sick of it—or marries.

HELEN. Will marriage cure it?

JACK. It would have cured me—but you did n't see it that way.

HELEN. You made your choice.

JACK. I asked you to trust me—you wanted some ironclad pledge—well, my dear Helen—that was n't the best way to handle a fellow of spirit.

(*Goes front of table.*)

HELEN. So *you* chose the better way?

JACK. No choice—I stood pat—that 's all.

HELEN. And wasted your life.

JACK. (*Sitting on edge of table.*) That depends on how you look at it. You married a doctor who wore himself out in the Philadelphia hospitals. I 've had three meals a day—and this place—and —a pretty fat farm and a stable with some good blood in it—and—

HELEN. (*Coming to him.*) And every one of them. Jack, is a monument to the worst side of you.

JACK. (*Stands and takes her hands; he smiles.*) Prejudice, my dear Helen. You might say that, if I 'd earned these things in some respectable business combination that starved out all its little competitors—but I 've simply furnished a fairly expensive entertainment—to eminent citizens—looking for rest.

HELEN. I know all the arguments of your —profession—Jack, and I don't pretend to answer them any more than I answer the arguments of reckless women who claim that they are more commendable than their sisters who make loveless marriages.

JACK. (*Goes to chair, right.*) I 'm not flattered by the implied comparison—still—

HELEN. I only feel sure that anything which the majority of good people condemn is wrong. (*Sits left of table.*)

JACK. (*Sits right of table.*) I 'm sorry—

HELEN. I 'd be glad if you meant that—but you 're not sorry.

JACK. I *am* sorry—I 'm sorry not to have public respect—as long as you think it 's valuable.

HELEN. I amuse you—don't I?

JACK. (*Elbows on knees.*) Not a little bit—but you make me blue as the devil, if that 's any satisfaction.

HELEN. I 'd be glad to make you blue as the devil, Jack, if it meant discontent with what you 're doing—if it could make you do better.

JACK. I 'm a pretty old leopard to get nervous about my spots.

HELEN. Why are you blue?

JACK. You.

HELEN. In what way?

JACK. I had hoped that twenty years of charitable deeds had made you also charitable in your judgment.

HELEN. I hope it has.

JACK. Don't seem to ease up on my specialty.

HELEN. You called your conduct "wild oats" twenty years ago.

JACK. It was—but I found such an excellent market for my wild oats that I had to stay in that branch of the grain business. Besides, it has been partly your fault, you know.

(HELEN *plays with the ivory paper-knife, balancing it on the front edge of table.*)

HELEN. Mine?

JACK. Your throwing me over for my wild oats—put it up to me to prove that they were a better thing than you thought.

HELEN. Well—having demonstrated that—

JACK. Here we are—

HELEN. Yes—here we are.

JACK. Back in the old town. Don't you think it would be rather a pretty finish, Helen, if despite all my—my leopard's spots—and despite that—(*pause*)—that Philadelphia episode of yours—

HELEN. You call twenty years of marriage episodic?

JACK. I call any departure from the main story episodic.

HELEN. And the main story is—

JACK. You and I—

HELEN. Oh—

(*Paper-knife falls to floor*—JACK *rises and picks it up, stands in front of table left hand on* HELEN'S—*his right gesticulating with paper-knife.*)

JACK. Would n't it be a pretty finish if you took my hand and I could walk right up to the camera and say, "I told you so"—? You know I always felt that you were coming back.

HELEN. Oh, did you?

JACK. (*Playfully, and going right center.*) Had a candle burning in the window every night.

HELEN. You 're sure it was n't a red light?

JACK. (*Remonstrating.*) Dear Helen! have some poetry in your composition. Literally "red light" of course—but the real flame was here—(*hand on breast*)—a flickering hope that somewhere—somehow—somewhen I should be at rest—with the proud Helen that loved and—rode away.

HELEN. (*Almost accusingly.*) I—believe—you.

JACK. Of course you believe me.

HELEN. You had a way, Jack—when you were a boy at college, of making me write to you.

JACK. Had I? (*Goes back of table.*)

HELEN. You know you had—at nights—about this hour—I 'd find it impossible to sleep until I 'd got up and written to you—and two days later I 'd get from you a letter that had crossed mine on the road. I don't believe the word "telepathy" had been coined then—but I guessed something of the force—and all these years, I 've felt it—nagging! Nagging!

JACK. Nagging?

HELEN. Yes—I could not keep you out of my waking hours—out of my thought—but when I surrendered myself to sleep the *call* would come—and I think it was rather cowardly of you, really.

JACK. (*Back of table.*) I plead guilty to having thought of you, Helen—lots—and it was generally when I was alone—late—my—clients gone. This room—

"Whose lights are fled,
Whose garlands dead,
And all but he departed."

HELEN. And as you say—here we are.

JACK. Well, what of my offer? Shall we say to the world—"We told you so?" What of my picturesque finish?

HELEN. You know my ideas—you 've known them twenty-two years.

JACK. No modification?

HELEN. None!

JACK. I'll be willing to sell the tables. (*Points above to second floor.*) And—well—I don't think I could get interested in this bridge game that the real good people play—would you object to a gentleman's game of "draw" now and then?

HELEN. You called it a gentleman's game in those days.

JACK. No leeway at all?

HELEN. No compromise, Jack—no—

JACK. M—(*Pause.*) I trust you won't consider my seeming hesitation uncomplimentary?

HELEN. Not unprecedented, at least.

JACK. You see it opens up a new line of thought—and—

(*Passing his hand over forehead.*)

HELEN. (*Rising in sympathy.*) And you have a headache, too—it is n't kind I 'm sure.

(*Enter* JO.)

JACK. Oh, nothing—nothing. (*To* JO.) Well?

JO. That gentleman, sah, about the picture.

JACK. I'll see him. (*Exit* JO.)

HELEN. A caller?

JACK. Won't be a minute—don't go away, because I think we can settle this question to-night, you and I.

HELEN. Please don't put me in the light of waiting for an answer.

JACK. Dear Helen—we 're both past that—are n't we? If I can only be sure that I could be worthy of you. I 'm the one that 's waiting for an answer—from my own weak character and rotten irresolution.

(JACK *goes with* HELEN *to door, center, kisses her hand. She goes;* JACK *retains her hand as long as possible and when he lets it go, it falls limply to* HELEN'S *side as she disappears.*)

They say cards make a fellow superstitious. (*Pause.*) Well—I—guess they do—

(*Enter* Jo *and* Justice Prentice. Prentice *wears overcoat, carries cane and silk hat.*)

Jack. Judge de Brennus?

Prentice. (*After amused look at* Jo.) Justice Prentice. (*Exit* Jo.)

Jack. Oh, Justice Prentice! Good-evening!

Prentice. You are Mr. Brookfield?

Jack. Yes.

Prentice. I should n't have attempted so late a call but that a friend pointed you out to-night at the opera, Mr. Brookfield, and said that your habit was—well—

Jack. Not to retire immediately?

Prentice. Yes.

Jack. Will you be seated?

Prentice. I 'm only passing through the city. I called to see a Corot that I understand you bought from Knoedler.

Jack. That 's it.

Prentice. Oh—thank you. (*Starts.*) You don't object to my looking at it?

Jack. Not at all.

(*Touches button, light shows on picture.*)

Prentice. (*After regard.*) That 's it. (*Pause.*) I thought at one time that I would buy this picture.

Jack. You know it, then?

Prentice. Yes. (*Pause.*) Are you particularly attached to it, Mr. Brookfield?

Jack. (*Sitting.*) I think not irrevocably.

(*Takes pad of paper and figures mechanically.*)

Prentice. Oh. (*Pause, during which the* Justice *looks at the picture.*) Do I understand that is what you paid for it, or what you intend to ask me for it?

(Jack *starts.*)

Jack. What?

Prentice. Sixty-five hundred.

Jack. (*Astonished.*) I did n't speak the price, did I?

Prentice. Did n't you—oh. (*Pause.*) I could n't pay that amount.

Jack. (*Puzzled.*) That 's its price—however.

Prentice. I regret I did n't buy it from the dealer when I had my chance. (*Looks about at other pictures on back wall.*) I could n't have given it so beautiful a setting, Mr. Brookfield, nor such kindred—but it would not have been friendless—(*At fireplace.*) That 's a handsome marine.

Jack. Yes.

Prentice. Pretty idea I read recently in an essay of Dr. van Dyke's. His pictures were for him his windows by which he looked out from his study onto the world. (*Pause.*) Yes?

Jack. Quite so.

Prentice. (*Regarding a picture over dining-room door.*) M— Washington!

Jack. (*Again astonished.*) What?

Prentice. My home is Washington—I thought you asked me?

Jack. No, I did n't.

Prentice. I beg your pardon—

Jack. (*Front of table; aside.*) But I 'm damned if I was n't going to ask him.

Prentice. (*Viewing other pictures.*) And the phases of your world, Mr. Brookfield, have been very prettily multiplied.

Jack. Thank you—may I offer you a cigar? (*Opens box on table.*)

Prentice. Thank you, I won't smoke.

Jack. Or a glass of wine?

Prentice. Nothing. I 'll return to the hotel—first asking you again to excuse my untimely call.

Jack. I wish you 'd sit down awhile.

Prentice. But I did n't know until I 'd missed it from Knoedler's how large a part of my world—my dream world—I had been looking at through this frame. (*Regards the Corot again.*)

Jack. Well, if it 's a sentimental matter, Mr. Justice, we might talk it over.

Prentice. I must n't submit the sentimental side of it, Mr. Brookfield, and where I have so—so intruded.

Jack. That 's the big side of anything for me—the sentimental.

Prentice. I 'm sure of it—and I must n't take advantage of that knowledge.

Jack. You 're sure of it?

Prentice. Yes.

Jack. Is that my reputation?

Prentice. I don't know your reputation.

Jack. Then, how are you sure of it?

Prentice. (*Impressively.*) Oh—I see you—and—well, we have *met.*

Jack. Ah—

Prentice. Good-night. (*Going up.*)

Jack. One moment. (*Pause.*) You said your address was Washington?

Prentice. Yes.

Jack. You thought at the time I was about to ask you that question?

Prentice. I thought you had asked it.

Jack. And you thought a moment before I had said sixty-five hundred for the picture?

Prentice. Yes.

JACK. Do you often—pick answers that way?
PRENTICE. Well, I think we all do—at times.
JACK. We all do?
PRENTICE. Yes—but we speak the answers only as we get older and less attentive and mistake a person's thought for his spoken word.
JACK. A person's thought?
PRENTICE. Yes.
JACK. Do you mean you know what I think?
PRENTICE. (*Returning to table.*) I had n't meant to claim any monopoly of that power. It 's my opinion that every one reads the thoughts of others—that is, some of the thoughts.
JACK. Every one?
PRENTICE. Oh, yes.
JACK. That *I* do?
PRENTICE. (*Regarding him.*) I should say *you* more generally than the majority of men.
JACK. There was a woman said something like that to me not ten minutes ago.
PRENTICE. A woman would be apt to be conscious of it.
JACK. You really believe that—that stuff? (*Sits left of table.*)
PRENTICE. Oh, yes—and I 'm not a pioneer in the belief. The men who declare the stuff most stoutly are scientists who have given it most attention.
JACK. How do they prove it?
PRENTICE. They *don't* prove it—that is, not universally. Each man must do that for himself, Mr. Brookfield.
JACK. How—
PRENTICE. (*Pause. Smiles.*) Well, I 'll tell you all I know of it. (*Becoming serious.*) Every thought is active—that is, born of a desire—and travels from us—or it is born of the desire of some one else and comes to us. We send them out—or we take them in—that is all.
JACK. How do we know which we are doing?
PRENTICE. If we are idle and empty-headed, our brains are the playrooms for the thought of others—frequently rather bad. If we are active, whether benevolently or malevolently, our brains are workshops—*power-houses.* I was passively regarding the pictures; your active idea of the price—registered, that 's all—so did your wish to know where I was from.
JACK. You say *"our* brains"—do you still include mine?
PRENTICE. Yes.
JACK. You said mine more than the majority of men's.
PRENTICE. I think so.
JACK. Why has n't this whatever it is—effect—happened to me, then?
PRENTICE. It has.
JACK. (*Pause.*) Why did n't I know it?
PRENTICE. Vanity? Perhaps.
JACK. Vanity?
PRENTICE. Yes—often some—friend has broached some independent subject and you have said, "I was just about to speak of that myself."
JACK. Very often, but—
PRENTICE. Believing the idea was your own—your vanity shut out the probably proper solution—that it was his.
JACK. Well, how, then, does a man tell which of his thoughts are his own?
PRENTICE. It 's difficult. Most of his idle ones are not. When we drift we are with the current. To go against it or to make even an eddy of our own we must swim—Most everything less than that is hopeless.
JACK. (*Smiling.*) Well—I have n't been exactly helpless.
PRENTICE. No one would call you so, Mr. Brookfield. (*Going.*) You have a strong psychic—a strong hypnotic ability.
JACK. (*Smiling.*) You think so?
PRENTICE. I know it.
JACK. This business?
(*Makes slight pass after manner of the professional hypnotist.*)
PRENTICE. (*Smiling.*) That business for the beginner, yes—
JACK. You mean that I could hypnotize anybody?
PRENTICE. Many persons—yes—but I would n't do it if I were you—
JACK. Why not?
PRENTICE. Grave responsibility.
JACK. In what way?
PRENTICE. (*Pause. Smiles.*) I 'll send you a book about it—if I may.
JACK. Instructions?
PRENITCE. And cautions—yes—(*Goes up to picture again.*) If you tire of your Corot, I 'd be glad to hear from you.
JACK. Why could n't I save postage by just *thinking* another price?
PRENTICE. The laws on contracts have n't yet recognized that form of tender.

(*Enter* TOM, *center. He laughs and shows signs of drink.*)

TOM. I say, Jack—here 's the greatest joke you ever saw—(*Sees the* JUSTICE.) Oh, excuse me.

(*Enter* LEW, *following.*)

LEW. That won't do, Tom.—(*To* JACK.) Excuse me, Jack, but I had to get him out of there.

JACK. I 'll go downstairs with you, Mr. Justice. (*Exit with the* JUSTICE.)

TOM. Who 's that old bird?

LEW. You 'll offend Jack if you 're not careful, Tom. You 've got half a jag now.

TOM. J' ever see anything 's as funny as that? He don't like my scarf-pin—ha, ha—well I don't like it—but my valet put it on me and what 's difference—

(*Enter* HARDMUTH.)

HARDMUTH. What was that?

TOM. My scarf-pin!

HARDMUTH. Scarf-pin?

TOM. Yes—he pushed me away from him and I said what 's matter. He said I don't like your scarf-pin—ha, ha—I said don't? I don't like your face.

LEW. Very impolite with the ladies there.

HARDMUTH. Why should he criticize Tom's scarf-pin?

TOM. 'Zactly. I said I can change my scarf-pin—but I don't like your face.

(*Enter* CLAY *from dining-room, excitedly.*)

CLAY. Where 's Jack?

LEW. Saying good-night to some old gentleman below.

TOM. (*Interposing as* CLAY *starts up left center.*) And I don't like your face.

CLAY. That 's all right, Mr. Denning. (*Tries to pass.*) Excuse me.

TOM. (*With scarf-pin in hand.*) Excuse *me.* What 's the matter with that scarf-pin?

CLAY. It 's a cat's-eye and I don't like them, that 's all—I don't like to look at them.

LEW. Let him alone, Tom.

TOM. Damn 'f 'ee ain't scared of it, ha, ha!

(*Pushing pin in front of* CLAY'S *face.*)

CLAY. (*Greatly excited.*) Don't do that.

HARDMUTH. (*Sneering.*) 'T won't bite you, will it?

CLAY. (*Averts his face.*) Go away, I tell you.

TOM. (*Holds* CLAY *with left hand. Has pin in right.*) 'T will bite him—bow—wow—wow—

CLAY. Don't, I tell you—don't.

TOM. (*Still holding him.*) Bow—wow—wow—

LEW. Tom!

HARDMUTH. (*Laughing.*) Let them alone.

CLAY. Go away.

TOM. Bow—wow—

(*Enter* JACK.)

JACK. What 's the matter here?

TOM. (*Pursuing* CLAY.) Wow—

(CLAY *in frenzy swings the large ivory paper-knife from table, blindly strikes* TOM, *who falls.*)

JACK. Clay!

CLAY. (*Horrified.*) He pushed that horrible cat's-eye right against my face.

JACK. What cat's-eye?

HARDMUTH. (*Picks up the pin which* DENNING *has dropped.*) Only playing with him—a scarf-pin.

LEW. (*Kneeling by* DENNING.) He 's out, Jack.

(*Enter* JO.)

CLAY. I did n't mean to hurt him; really I did n't mean that.

HARDMUTH. (*Taking the paper-cutter from* CLAY.) The hell you did n't. You could kill a bull with that ivory tusk.

JACK. Put him on the window seat—give him some air.

(*Enter* ALICE, *left center.*)

ALICE. Jack, we 're going now—all of us.

(*Enter* HARVEY.)

JACK. (*Turning to* ALICE.) Wait a minute. (*To* JO.) Help Mr. Ellinger there.

(JO, LEW, *and* HARVEY *carry off* TOM *into the dining-room.*)

ALICE. What is it?

JACK. An accident—keep Helen and Viola out of these rooms.

ALICE. Had n't we better go? Clay is with us.

CLAY. I can't go just now, Mrs. Campbell—(*Looks off.*) I hope it is n't serious—I did n't mean to hurt him, really. (*Exit left.*)

ALICE. A quarrel?

(LEW *enters and waves hand, meaning "All over."*)

HARDMUTH. (*With paper-knife.*) A murder!

(*Enter* HELEN *and* VIOLA.)

VIOLA. What 's the matter?

(*Enter* CLAY.)

CLAY. (*In panic and up right center. To* HELEN.) Oh, mother, I 've killed him.

HELEN. (*Taking* CLAY *in her arms.*) Killed him—whom?

HARDMUTH. Tom Denning.

CLAY. But I never meant it—Jack; I just struck—struck wild.

HARDMUTH. With this.

HELEN. With that! Oh, my boy!

JACK. That will do! Everybody—Lew, telephone Dr. Monroe it 's an emergency case and to come in dressing-gown and slippers. (*Exit* LEW, *right center.*) Alice, I know you 're not afraid of a sick man—or—that sort of thing. Help me and Jo. (*Leads* ALICE, *left. She braces herself.*) Viola, you take Mrs. Whipple upstairs and wait there.

HARDMUTH. (*Starting up right.*) I 'll notify the police.

HELEN. Oh!

JACK. (*Interposing.*) *Stop!* You 'll stay just where you are!

HARDMUTH. You tryin' to hide this thing?

JACK. The doctor 'll tell us exactly what this thing is. And then the boy 'll have the credit himself *of notifying the police.*

ACT SECOND.

SCENE. *The library-living room of* JUSTICE PRENTICE, *Washington, D. C.*

The walls of this room are bookcases glassed quite to the ceiling, and filled with books mostly in sheepskin binding. This array is broken by a large bay window at the back, center, which is equipped with a window seat, and by two doors near the front of the stage, one on the right and one on the left.

At the left is also a fireplace with a log fire. In the upper left-hand corner of the room there is a buffet, fitted with glasses and decanters. A dark rug is on the floor.

The furniture of the room is dark oak in Gothic. It consists of a table and three chairs at the center, sofa and smaller table up right. The smaller table holds a lamp.

Over the buffet there is a small canvas by Rousseau showing a sunset.

JUSTICE PRENTICE *and* JUDGE HENDERSON *are playing chess.*

HENDERSON. Checkmate in three moves.

PRENTICE. I don't see that.

HENDERSON. Well, Knight to—

PRENTICE. Yes, yes, I see. Checkmate in three moves. That 's one game each. Shall we play another?

HENDERSON. Let us look at the enemy. (*Draws watch.*) By Jove! Quarter of twelve. I guess Mrs. Henderson will be expecting me soon. (*Pause.*) I 'll play a rubber with you, and its result shall decide your position on the Whipple case.

PRENTICE. Why, Mr. Justice, I 'm surprised at you. A United States Supreme Court decision—shaped by a game of chess. We 'll be down to the level of the intelligent jurymen soon—flipping pennies for the verdict.

HENDERSON. And a very good method in just such cases as this. Well, if you won't play—(*rises*)—I 'll have to go.

PRENTICE. (*Rises.*) Not without another toddy.

HENDERSON. Yes.

PRENTICE. (*At sideboard up left.*) Oh, no. Come, now, don't you like this liquor?

HENDERSON. Immensely. Where did you say you got it?

PRENTICE. Kentucky. One lump?

HENDERSON. Only one!

PRENTICE. My old home, sir,—and a bit of lemon?

HENDERSON. A piece of the peel—yes.

PRENTICE. They make it there.

HENDERSON. I 'll pour the water.

PRENTICE. There, there, don't drown me.

HENDERSON. My folks were Baptists, you see. What do you say it costs you?

PRENTICE. Fifty cents a gallon.

HENDERSON. What!! I think I 'll take water. (*Puts down glass.*)

PRENTICE. That 's what it cost me. Its value I don't know. An old friend sends it to me. Fifty cents for express.

HENDERSON. Oh!

PRENTICE. That 's different, is n't it?

HENDERSON. (*Recovers glass.*) Very!

PRENTICE. He makes it down there. Why, it 's in the same county in which this Whipple murder occurred.

HENDERSON. How about that point? We might as well admit it and remand the case.

PRENTICE. No. There 's no constitutional point involved.

HENDERSON. A man 's entitled to an open trial.

PRENTICE. Well, Whipple had it.

HENDERSON. No, he did n't. They would n't admit the public.

PRENTICE. Oh, come now; the court-room was crowded and the Judge refused admission to others—only when there was danger of the floor breaking.

HENDERSON. But, my dear Mr. Justice, that would have been all right to limit the attendance—

PRENTICE. Well, that 's all he did.

HENDERSON. Only he did it by having the sheriff issue tickets of admission. That placed the attendance entirely in the control of the prosecution and the defense is right in asking a rehearing.

PRENTICE. Oh, nonsense! Justice is a little too slow in my old State and I 'm impatient with technical delays. It is two years since they openly assassinated the governor-elect and the guilty man is still at large.

HENDERSON. Why should the killing of Scovill bear on this case!

PRENTICE. It bears on me. I 'm concerned for the fair fame of Kentucky.

HENDERSON. Well, if you won't, you won't and there 's an end of it.

(*Rings call bell.*)

PRENTICE. Have another?

HENDERSON. Not another drop.

(*Enter* SERVANT.)

Get my coat!

PRENTICE. A nightcap.

SERVANT. I beg pardon, sir.

PRENTICE. Speaking to the Justice.

(*Exit* SERVANT.)

HENDERSON. No, I must n't. Mrs. Henderson filed her protest against my coming home loaded and I 've got to be moderate.

PRENTICE. Well, if you won't, you won't.

HENDERSON. (*Front of table, picks up book.*) Hello! Reading the Scriptures in your old age?

PRENTICE. It does look like a Bible, does n't it? That 's a flexible binding I had put on a copy of Bret Harte. I admire him very much.

HENDERSON. I like some of his stuff.

PRENTICE. When I get home from the Capitol and you prosy lawyers, I 'm too tired to read Browning and those heavy guns, so I take Bret Harte—very clever, I think; I was reading before you came —(*takes book*)—"A Newport Romance." Do you know it?

HENDERSON. I don't think I do.

PRENTICE. It 's about an old house at Newport—that 's haunted—a young girl in the colonial days dies of a broken heart in this house, it seems. Her sweetheart sailed away and left her—and here 's the way Bret Harte tells of her coming back. (HENDERSON *sits.*) Oh, I 'm not going to read all of it to you—only one verse. (*Looks at book.—Pause.*) Oh, I forgot to tell you that when this chap left the girl he gave her a little bouquet—understand? That 's a piece of material evidence necessary to this summing up.

(HENDERSON *nods.* PRENTICE *reads.*)

"And ever since then when the clock strikes two,
She walks unbidden from room to room,
And the air is filled, that she passes through,
With a subtle, sad perfume.

The delicate odor of mignonette,
The ghost of a dead-and-gone bouquet,
Is all that tells of her story; yet
Could she think of a sweeter way?"

Is n't that charming, eh?

HENDERSON. A very pretty idea.

PRENTICE. Beautiful to have a perfume suggest her. I suppose it appeals to me especially because I used to know a girl who was foolishly fond of mignonette.

HENDERSON. Well, you don't believe in that stuff, do you?

PRENTICE. What stuff?

HENDERSON. That Bret Harte stuff—the dead coming back—ghosts and so forth?

PRENTICE. Yes, in one way I do. I find as I get older, Judge, that the things of memory become more real every day—every day. Why, there are companions of my boyhood that I have n't thought of for years—that seem to come about me—more tangibly, or as much so as they were in life.

HENDERSON. Well, how do you account for that? Spiritualism?

PRENTICE. Oh, no. It 's Time's perspective.

HENDERSON. Time's perspective?

PRENTICE. Yes. (*Pause.*) I 'll have to illustrate my meaning. (*Indicates a painting.*) Here 's a sunset by Rousseau. I bought it in Paris last summer. Do you see what an immense stretch of land there is in it?

HENDERSON. Yes.

PRENTICE. A bird's-eye view of that

would require a chart reaching to the ceiling. But see Rousseau's perspective. The horizon line is n't two inches from the base.

HENDERSON. Well?

PRENTICE. (*Returns to table.*) Well, my dear Judge, that is the magic in the perspective of Time. My boyhood's horizon is very near to my old eyes now. The dimmer they grow, the nearer it comes, until I think sometimes that when we are through with it all—we go out almost as we entered—little children.

HENDERSON. (*Pause.*) That 's a very beautiful painting, Judge—a Russell, you say?

PRENTICE. A Rousseau.

HENDERSON. Oh—

PRENTICE. Yes—cost me three thousand only, and a funny thing about it: the canvas just fitted into the top of my steamer trunk, and it came through the custom-house without a cent of duty. I completely forgot it.

HENDERSON. Your memory is n't so retentive, then, as it seems?

PRENTICE. Not on those commercial matters.

(*Enter* SERVANT *with coat. In crossing front of table to* HENDERSON, *the coat knocks a miniature from the table to the floor.*)

PRENTICE. You dropped your tobacco-box, I guess, Mr. Justice.

HENDERSON. (*Examines pocket.*) No.

SERVANT. (*Picks up miniature.*) It was this picture, sir.

PRENTICE. My gracious—my gracious! It might have been broken.

SERVANT. Oh, it often falls when I 'm dusting, sir.

PRENTICE. Oh, does it? Well, I 'll put it away. (*Exit* SERVANT.) An ivory miniature by Wimar. I prize it highly —old-fashioned portrait, see! Gold back.

HENDERSON. A beautiful face.

PRENTICE. (*Eagerly.*) Is n't it? Is n't it?

(*Looks over* HENDERSON'S *shoulder.*)

HENDERSON. Very. What a peculiar way of combing the hair—long, and over the ears.

PRENTICE. The only becoming way women ever wore their hair. I think the scrambly style they have now is disgraceful.

HENDERSON. Your mother?

PRENTICE. Dear, no, a young girl I used to know. Oh, don't smile, she 's been dead a *good* thirty years—married and had a large family.

HENDERSON. Very sweet—very sweet, indeed.

PRENTICE. Is n't it?

(*Enter* SERVANT.)

Well?

SERVANT. Card, sir.

PRENTICE. Gentleman here?

(*Takes card.*)

SERVANT. Yes, sir.

PRENTICE. I 'll see him. (*Exit* SERVANT.)

HENDERSON. Call?

PRENTICE. Yes. The man owns a picture that I 've been trying to buy—a Corot.

HENDERSON. Oh—another of these perspective fellows?

PRENTICE. Yes—his call does n't surprise me, for he 's been in my mind all day.

HENDERSON. Seems to be in a hurry for the money—coming at midnight.

PRENTICE. I set him the example besides, midnight is just the shank of the evening for Mr. Brookfield. He 's supposed to be a sporting man—ahem.

(*Enter* SERVANT *and* JACK. JACK *is paler and less physical than in first act.*)

PRENTICE. Good-evening.

JACK. You remember me, Mr. Justice?

PRENTICE. Perfectly, Mr. Brookfield—this is Justice Henderson.

HENDERSON. Mr. Brookfield.

JACK. Pleased to meet you, Mr. Justice. (*To* PRENTICE.) I hope I 'm not intruding.

HENDERSON. I 'm just going, Mr. Brookfield. (*To* PRENTICE.) To-morrow?

PRENTICE. To-morrow!

HENDERSON. (*At door, inquiringly.*) No constitutional point about it? Eh?

PRENTICE. None.

HENDERSON. Good-night.

PRENTICE. Good-night. (*To* JACK.) Have a chair.

JACK. Thank you.

(*Stands by chair left of table.*)

PRENTICE. (*Toward buffet.*) I 've some medicine here that comes directly from your city.

JACK. I don't think I will—if you 'll excuse me.

PRENTICE. Ah—(*Pause. Smiles.*) Well, have you brought the picture?

JACK. The picture is still in Louisville—I—I 'm in Washington with my niece.

PRENTICE. Yes?

JACK. And—a lady friend of hers. They 're very anxious to meet you, Mr. Justice.

PRENTICE. Ah. (*Pause.*) Well—I go to the Capitol at noon to-morrow and—

JACK. To-night!—They 're leaving the city to-morrow—as you were when I had the pleasure of receiving you.

PRENTICE. I remember.

JACK. (*With watch.*) They were to come after me in five minutes if I did n't return, and those five minutes, Mr. Justice, I hoped you would give to me.

PRENTICE. With pleasure.

(*Sits right of table.*)

JACK. (*Plunging at once into his subject.*) Those two books you sent me—

PRENTICE. Yes?

JACK. I want to thank you for them again —and to ask you how far you go—with the men that wrote them—especially the second one. Do you believe that book?

PRENTICE. Yes.

JACK. You do?

PRENTICE. I do. I know the man who wrote it—and I believe him.

JACK. Did he ever do any of his stunts for you—that he writes about?

PRENTICE. He did n't call them "stunts," but he has given me many demonstrations of his ability—and mine.

JACK. For example?

PRENTICE. For example? He asked me to think of him steadily at some unexpected time and to think of some definite thing. A few days later—this room—two o'clock in the morning—I concentrated my thoughts—I mentally pictured him going to his telephone and calling me.

JACK. And did he do it?

PRENTICE. No—(*pause*)—but he came here at my breakfast hour and told me that at two o'clock he had waked and risen from his bed—and walked to his 'phone in the hallway with an *impulse* to call me—and then had stopped—because he had no message to deliver and because he thought his imagination might be tricking him.

JACK. You had n't given him any tip, such as asking him how he 'd slept?

PRENTICE. None. Five nights after that I repeated the experiment.

JACK. Well?

PRENTICE. That time he called me.

JACK. What did he say?

PRENTICE. He said, "Old man, you ought to be in bed asleep and not disturbing honest citizens," which was quite true.

JACK. By Jove, it 's a devilish creepy business, is n't it?

PRENTICE. Yes.

JACK. And if it 's so—

PRENTICE. And it *is* so.

JACK. Pay a man to be careful what he thinks—eh?

PRENTICE. It will very well pay your type of man to do so.

JACK. I don't want to be possessed by any of these bughouse theories, but I 'll be blamed if a few things have n't happened to me, Mr. Justice, since you started me on this subject.

PRENTICE. Along this line?

JACK. Yes. (*Pause.*) And I 've tried the other side of it, too.

PRENTICE. What other side?

JACK. The mesmeric business. (*Pause. Makes passes.*) I can do it.

PRENTICE. Then I should say, Mr. Brookfield, that for you the obligation for clean and unselfish thinking was doubly imperative.

JACK. Within this last year I 've put people—well—practically asleep in a chair and I 've made them tell me what a boy was doing—a mile away—in a jail.

PRENTICE. I see no reason to call clairvoyance a "bughouse" theory.

JACK. I only know that I do it.

PRENTICE. Yes—you have the youth for it—the glorious strength. Does it make any demand on your vitality?

JACK. (*Passes hand over his eyes.*) I 've fancied that a headache to which I 'm subject is more frequent—that 's all.

PRENTICE. But you find the ability—the power—increases—don't you?

JACK. Yes—in the last month I 've put a man into a hypnotic sleep with half a dozen waves of the hand. (*Makes pass.*)

PRENTICE. Why any motion?

JACK. Fixed his attention, I suppose.

PRENTICE. (*Shaking head.*) Fixes your attention. When in your own mind your belief is sufficiently trained, you won't need this. (*Another slight pass.*)

JACK. I won't?

PRENTICE. No.

JACK. What 'll I do?

PRENTICE. Simply think. (*Pause.*) You have a headache, for example.

JACK. I have a headache for a fact.

(JACK *again passes hand over eyes and forehead.*)

PRENTICE. Well—some persons could cure it by rubbing your forehead.

JACK. I know that.

PRENTICE. Others could cure it by the passes of the hypnotist. Others by simply willing that it should—(*pause*)—*be cured.*

JACK. Well, that 's where I can't follow you—and your friend the author.

PRENTICE. You simply think your headache.

JACK. I know it aches.

PRENTICE. I think it does n't.

JACK. (*Astonished.*) What?

PRENTICE. I—think—it does n't.

JACK. (*Pause.*) Well, just this moment, it does n't, but—(*pause*)—is n't that—simply mental excitement—won't it come back?

PRENTICE. It won't come back to-day.

JACK. That 's some comfort. The blamed things have made it busy for me since I 've been studying this business.

PRENTICE. It is a two-edged sword—

JACK. You mean it 's bad for a man who tries it?

PRENTICE. I mean that it constantly opens to the investigator new mental heights, higher planes—and every man, Mr. Brookfield, is ill in some manner who lives habitually on a lower level—than the light he sees.

(*Enter* SERVANT.)

SERVANT. Two ladies, sir.

PRENTICE. Your friends?

JACK. I think so.

(PRENTICE *and* JACK *look at* SERVANT.)

SERVANT. Yes, sir.

PRENTICE. Ask them up.

(*Exit* SERVANT.)

JACK. Thank you.

PRENTICE. (*Rises.*) I 'll put away Judge Henderson's glass.

JACK. They 're Kentucky ladies, Mr. Justice.

PRENTICE. (*Indicating* JACK.) But I don't want any credit for a hospitality I have n't earned.

JACK. I see.

(*Enter* SERVANT *with* HELEN *and* VIOLA.)

JACK. My niece, Miss Campbell.

PRENTICE. Miss Campbell.

JACK. And—

HELEN. One moment, Jack, I prefer to introduce myself.

PRENTICE. Won't you be seated, ladies?

(*Exit* SERVANT. HELEN *sits right of table.* VIOLA *goes to the window-seat.* JACK *stands center.*)

HELEN. You are not a married man, Justice Prentice?

PRENTICE. I am not.

HELEN. But you have the reputation of being a very charitable one.

PRENTICE. (*Sits left of table.*) That 's pleasant to hear—what charity do you represent?

HELEN. None. I hardly know how to tell you my object.

PRENTICE. It 's a personal matter, is it?

JACK. (*Back of table.*) Yes, a very personal matter.

PRENTICE. Ah!

HELEN. I have here an autograph book—

PRENTICE. (*To* JACK.) I usually sign my autograph for those who wish it—at the—

HELEN. I did not come for an autograph, Justice Prentice, I have brought one.

PRENTICE. Well, I don't go in for that kind of thing very much. I have no collection—my taste runs more toward—

HELEN. The autograph I have brought is one of yours, written many years ago. It is signed to a letter. Will you look at it?

(*Opens autograph book and gives small folded and old lace handkerchief from book to* VIOLA, *who joins her.*)

PRENTICE. With pleasure. (*Takes book.*) Is this the letter? Ah—(*Reads.*) "June 15, 1860." Dear me, that 's a long time ago. (*Reads.*) "My dear Margaret: The matter passed satisfactorily—a mere scratch. Boland apologized.—Jim." What is this?

HELEN. A letter from you.

PRENTICE. And my dear Margaret—1860. Why, this letter—was it written to Margaret?

HELEN. To Margaret Price—

PRENTICE. Is it possible—well—well. (*Pause.*) I wonder if what we call coincidences are ever mere coincidences. Margaret Price. Her name was on my lips a moment ago.

JACK. Really, Mr. Justice?

PRENTICE. (*To* JACK.) Yes. Did you know Margaret Price?

JACK. Yes.

(*Looks at* HELEN—PRENTICE'S *gaze follows.*)

HELEN. She was my mother—

PRENTICE. Margaret Price was—

HELEN. Was my mother.

PRENTICE. Why, I was just speaking of her to Justice Henderson whom you saw go out. Her picture dropped from the table here. (*Gets it.*) This miniature! Margaret Price gave it to me herself. And you are her daughter?

HELEN. Yes, Justice Prentice.

PRENTICE. Yes, I can see the likeness. At twenty you must have looked very like this miniature.

(*Passes miniature to* HELEN.)

HELEN. (*As* JACK *and* VIOLA *look at miniature.*) I have photographs of myself that are very like this. (*To* PRENTICE.) And you were speaking of her just now?

PRENTICE. Not five minutes ago.—But be seated, please. (VIOLA *sits again at window.*) I'm very delighted to have you call.

HELEN. Even at such an hour?

PRENTICE. At any hour. Margaret Price was a very dear friend of mine; and to think, you're her daughter. And this letter 1860—what's this?

HELEN. Oh, don't touch that. It will break. It's only a dry spray of mignonette, pinned to the note when you sent it.

PRENTICE. (*Musingly.*) A spray of mignonette.

HELEN. My mother's favorite flower and perfume.

PRENTICE. I remember. Well, well, this is equally astonishing.

JACK. Do you remember the letter, Mr. Justice?

PRENTICE. Perfectly.

JACK. And the circumstances it alludes to?

PRENTICE. Yes. It was the work of a romantic boy. I—I was very fond of your mother, Mrs.— by the way, you have n't told me your name.

HELEN. Never mind that now. Let me be Margaret Price's daughter for the present.

PRENTICE. Very well. Oh, this was a little scratch of a duel—they 've gone out of fashion now, I'm thankful to say.

HELEN. Do you remember the cause of this one?

PRENTICE. Yes; Henry Boland had worried Margaret some way. She was frightened, I think, and fainted.

HELEN. And you struck him?

PRENTICE. Yes, and he challenged me.

HELEN. I've heard mother tell it. Do you remember what frightened her?

PRENTICE. I don't believe I do. Does the letter say?

HELEN. No. Try to think.

PRENTICE. Was it a snake or a toad?

HELEN. No—a jewel.

PRENTICE. A jewel? I remember now—a—a—cat's-eye. A cat's-eye jewel, was n't it?

HELEN. (*With excitement.*) Yes, yes, yes. (*Weeping.*)

PRENTICE. My dear madam, it seems to be a very emotional subject with you.

HELEN. It is. I've so hoped you would remember it. On the cars I was praying all the way you would remember it. And you do—you do.

PRENTICE. I do.

VIOLA. (*Comes to* HELEN.) Compose yourself, dear. Remember what depends on it.

PRENTICE. It is evidently something in which I can aid you.

HELEN. It is—and you will?

PRENTICE. There is nothing I would not do for a daughter of Margaret Price. You are in mourning, dear lady; is it for your mother?

HELEN. For my son.

PRENTICE. (*To* JACK.) How long has he been dead?

HELEN. He is not dead. Justice Prentice, my boy—the grandson of Margaret Price—is under a sentence of death.

PRENTICE. Sentence of death?

HELEN. Yes. I am the mother of Clay Whipple.

PRENTICE. (*Rises.*) But, madam—

HELEN. He is to die. I come—

PRENTICE. (*Retreats toward second door.*) Stop! You forget yourself. The case of Whipple is before the Supreme Court of the United States. I am a member of that body—I cannot listen to you.

HELEN. You must.

PRENTICE. You are prejudicing his chances. (*To* JACK.) You are making it *necessary* for me to rule against him. (*To* HELEN.) My dear madam, for the sake of your boy, do not do this. It is unlawful—without dignity or precedent. (*To* JACK.) If the lady were not the mother of the boy I should call your conduct base—

VIOLA. But she is his mother.

HELEN. (*Following.*) And Justice Prentice, I am the daughter of the woman you loved.

PRENTICE. I beg you to be silent.

JACK. Won't you hear us a moment?

PRENTICE. I cannot. I dare not—I must leave you. (*Going.*)

VIOLA. Why?

PRENTICE. I have explained—the matter is before the court. For me to hear you would be corrupt.

HELEN. I won't talk of the question before your court. That, our attorneys tell us, is a constitutional point.

PRENTICE. That is its attitude.

HELEN. I will not talk of that. I wish to speak of this letter.

JACK. You can listen to that, can't you, Mr. Justice?

PRENTICE. Do you hope for its influence indirectly?

HELEN. No; sit down, Justice Prentice, and compose yourself. I will talk calmly to you.

PRENTICE. My dear madam, my heart bleeds for you. (*To* JACK.) Her agony must be past judicial measurement.

JACK. Only God knows, sir!

(HELEN *sits at table;* VIOLA *stands by her side;* PRENTICE *sits by the fire;* JACK *remains standing.*)

HELEN. (*Pause.*) Justice Prentice.

PRENTICE. Mrs. Whipple.

HELEN. You remember this letter—you have recalled the duel. You remember—thank God—its cause?

PRENTICE. I do.

HELEN. You know that my mother's aversion to that jewel amounted almost to an insanity?

PRENTICE. I remember that.

HELEN. I inherited that aversion. When a child, the sight of one of them would throw me almost into convulsions.

PRENTICE. Is it possible?

HELEN. It is true. The physicians said I would outgrow the susceptibility, and in a measure I did so. But I discovered that Clay had inherited the fatal dislike from me.

JACK. You can understand that, Mr. Justice?

PRENTICE. Medical jurisprudence is full of such cases. Why should we deny them? Is nature faithful only in physical matters? You are like this portrait. Your voice *is* that of Margaret Price. Nature's behest should have also embraced some of the less apparent possessions, I think.

JACK. We urged all that at the trial, but they called it invention.

PRENTICE. Nothing seems more probable to me.

HELEN. Clay, my boy, had that dreadful and unreasonable fear of the jewel. I protected him as far as possible, but one night over a year ago, some men—companions—finding that the sight of this stone annoyed him, pressed it upon his attention. He did not know, Justice Prentice, he was not responsible. It was insanity, but he struck his tormentor and the blow resulted in the young man's death.

PRENTICE. Terrible—terrible!

HELEN. My poor boy is crushed with the awful deed. He is not a murderer. He was never that, but they have sentenced him, Justice Prentice—he—is to die. (*Rises impulsively.*)

JACK. (*Catching her.*) Now—now—my dear Helen, compose yourself.

VIOLA. (*Embracing her.*) You promised.

HELEN. Yes, yes, I will.

(VIOLA *leads* HELEN *aside.*)

PRENTICE. All this was ably presented to the trial court, you say?

JACK. By the best attorneys.

PRENTICE. And the verdict?

JACK. Still was guilty. But, Mr. Justice, the sentiment of the community has changed very much since then. We feel that a new trial would result differently.

HELEN. When our lawyers decided to go to the Supreme Court, I remembered some letters of yours in this old book. Can you imagine my joy when I found the letter was on the very point of this inherited trait on which we rested our defense?

JACK. We have ridden twenty-four hours to reach you. The train came in only at ten o'clock.

HELEN. You—you are not powerless to help me. What is an official duty to a mother's love? To the life of my boy?

PRENTICE. My dear, dear madam, that is not necessary—believe me. This letter comes very properly under the head of new evidence. (*To* JACK.) The defendant is entitled to a rehearing on that.

HELEN. Justice Prentice! Justice Prentice! (*Turns again to* VIOLA.)

VIOLA. There—there— (*Comforts* HELEN.)

PRENTICE. Of course that is n't before us, but when we remand the case on this constitutional point—

HELEN. Then you will—you will remand it?

PRENTICE. (*Prevaricating.*) Justice Henderson had convinced me on the point as you called. So I think there is no doubt of the decision.

HELEN. You can never know the light you let into my heart.

(VIOLA *returns the lace handkerchief to the book which* HELEN *opens for the purpose, closing it again on the handkerchief.*)

PRENTICE. What is that perfume? Have you one about you?

HELEN. Yes, on this handkerchief.

PRENTICE. What is it?

HELEN. Mignonette.

PRENTICE. Mignonette.

HELEN. A favorite perfume of mother's. This handkerchief of hers was in the book with the letter.

PRENTICE. Indeed.

HELEN. Oh, Justice Prentice, do you think I can save my boy?

PRENTICE. (*To* JACK.) On the rehearing I will take pleasure in testifying as to this hereditary aversion—and what I knew of its existence in Margaret Price.

JACK. May I tell the lawyers so?

PRENTICE. No. They will learn it in the court to-morrow. They can stand the suspense. I am speaking comfort to the mother's heart.

HELEN. Comfort. It is life!

PRENTICE. (*To* JACK.) Say nothing of this call, if you please. Nothing to any one.

JACK. We shall respect your instructions, Mr. Justice. My niece, who has been with Mrs. Whipple during this trouble, is the fiancée of the boy who is in jail.

PRENTICE. You have my sympathy, too, my dear.

VIOLA. Thank you.

(*Goes to* PRENTICE *and gives him her hand.*)

PRENTICE. And now good-night.

VIOLA. Good-night.

(*Goes to door where* JACK *joins her.*)

HELEN. Good-night, Justice Prentice. You must know my gratitude—words cannot tell it. (*Exit* VIOLA.)

PRENTICE. Would you do me a favor?

HELEN. Can you ask it?

(JACK *waits at the door.*)

PRENTICE. If that was the handkerchief of Margaret Price, I'd like to have it.

(*With a moment's effort at self-control,* HELEN *gives* PRENTICE *the handkerchief. She does not dare to speak, but turns to* JACK *who leads her out.* PRENTICE *goes to the table and takes up the miniature. A distant bell tolls two.*)

PRENTICE. Margaret Price. People will say that she has been in her grave thirty years, but I'll swear her spirit was in this room to-night and directed a decision of the Supreme Court of the United States.

(*Noticing the handkerchief which he holds he puts it to his lips.*)

"The delicate odor of mignonette,
The ghost of a dead-and-gone bouquet,
Is all that tells of her story; yet
Could she think of a sweeter way?"

ACT THIRD.

SCENE—*Same as Act First.* JACK *is sitting in the chair with his elbows on his knees, apparently in deep thought.*

(*Enter* HARVEY, *left.*)

HARVEY. Mars Jack.

JACK. Well, Uncle Harvey?

HARVEY. 'Scuse me, sah, when you wants to be alone, but I'se awful anxious myself. Is dey any word from the courthouse?

JACK. None, Uncle Harvey.

HARVEY. 'Cause Jo said Missus Campbell done come in, an' I thought she'd been to the trial, you know.

JACK. She has. You're not keeping anything from me, Uncle Harvey?

HARVEY. 'Deed, no, sah. Ah jes' like to ask you, Mars Jack, if I'd better have de cook fix sumpun' to eat—maybe de other ladies comin' too?

JACK. Yes, Uncle Harvey, but whether they'll want to eat or not'll depend on what word comes back with the jury.

HARVEY. Yes, sah. (*Exit left.*)

(*Enter* ALICE, *right center.*)

ALICE. (*In astonishment and reproach.*) Jack—

JACK. Well—

ALICE. Why are you here?

JACK. Well—I live here.

ALICE. But I thought you'd gone to Helen and Viola.

JACK. No.

ALICE. You should do so, Jack. Think of them alone when that jury returns—as it may at any moment—with its verdict.

JACK. The lawyers are there and Lew Ellinger is with them.
ALICE. But Helen—Helen needs you.
JACK. I may be useful here.
ALICE. How?
JACK. There 's one man on that jury that I think is a friend.
ALICE. One man?
JACK. Yes.
ALICE. Out of a jury of twelve.
JACK. One man can stop the other eleven from bringing in an adverse verdict—and this one is with us.
ALICE. Would your going to Helen and Viola in the court-house stop his being with us?
JACK. Perhaps not, but it would stop my being with him.
ALICE. What? (*Looks about.*) I don't understand you.
JACK. Justice Prentice told me that he could sit alone in his room and make another man get up and walk to the telephone and call him by simply thinking steadily of that other man.
ALICE. Superstitious people imagine anything.
JACK. Imagine much—yes—but this is n't imagination.
ALICE. It 's worse—Jack. I call it spiritualism.
JACK. Call it anything you like—spiritualism—or socialism—or rheumatism—it 's there. I know nothing about it scientifically, but I 've tried it on and it works, my dear Alice, it works.
ALICE. You 've tried it on?
JACK. Yes.
ALICE. With whom?
JACK. With you.
ALICE. I don't know it if you have.
JACK. That is one phase of its terrible subtlety.
ALICE. When did you try it on?
JACK. (*Inquiringly.*) That night, a month ago, when you rapped at my door at two o'clock in the morning and asked if I was ill in any way?
ALICE. I was simply nervous about you.
JACK. Call it "nervousness" if you wish to—but that was an experiment of mine—a simple experiment.
ALICE. Oh!
JACK. Two Sundays ago you went right up to the church door—hesitated, and turned home again.
ALICE. Lots of people do that.
JACK. I don't ask you to take stock in it, but that was another experiment of mine. The thing appeals to me. I can't help Helen by being at the court-house, but, as I 'm alive and my name 's Jack Brookfield, I do believe that my thought reaches that particular juryman.
ALICE. That 's lunacy, Jack, dear.
JACK. (*Rises and walks.*) Well, call it "lunacy." I don't insist on "rheumatism."
ALICE. Oh, Jack, the boy's life is in the balance. Bitter vindictive lawyers are prosecuting him, and I don't like my big strong brother, who used to meet men and all danger face to face, treating the situation with silly mind-cure methods—hidden alone in his rooms. I don't like it.
JACK. You can't acquit a boy of murder by having a strong brother thrash somebody in the court-rooms. If there was anything under the sun I could do with my physical strength, I 'd do it; but there is n't. Now, why not try this? Why not, if I believe I can influence a juryman by my thought,—why not try?
(ALICE *turns away.*)

(*Enter* JO, *right center.*)

JACK. Well?
JO. Mistah Hardmuth.
ALICE. (*Astonished.*) Frank Hardmuth?
JO. Yes.
JACK. Here 's one of the "bitter vindictive" men you want me to meet face to face. You stay here while I go and do it. (*Starts up.*)

(*Enter* HARDMUTH.)

HARDMUTH. Excuse me, but I can't wait in an anteroom.
JACK. That 'll do, Jo. (*Exit* JO.)
HARDMUTH. I want to see you alone.
JACK. (*To* ALICE.) Yes—
ALICE. (*Going.*) What do you think it is?
JACK. Nothing to worry over.
(*Conducts her to door. Exit* ALICE.)
HARDMUTH. (*Threateningly.*) Jack Brookfield.
JACK. Well? (*Confronts* HARDMUTH.)
HARDMUTH. I 've just seen Harvey Fisher—of the *Courier.*
JACK. Yes.
HARDMUTH. He says you 've hinted at something associating me with the shooting of Scovill.
JACK. Right.
HARDMUTH. What do you mean?
JACK. I mean, Frank Hardmuth, that you

shan't hound this boy to the gallows without reckoning with me and the things I know of you.

HARDMUTH. I'm doing my duty as a prosecuting attorney.

JACK. You are, and a great deal more—you're venting a personal hatred.

HARDMUTH. That hasn't anything to do with this insinuation you've handed to a newspaper man, an insinuation for which anybody ought to kill you.

JACK. I don't deal in "insinuations." It was a charge.

HARDMUTH. A statement?

JACK. A charge! You understand English—a specific and categorical charge.

HARDMUTH. That I knew Scovill was to be shot.

JACK. That you knew it? No. That you planned it and arranged and *procured* his assassination.

HARDMUTH. (*In low tone.*) If the newspapers print that, I'll kill you—damn you, I'll kill you.

JACK. I don't doubt your willingness. And they'll print it—if they haven't done so already—and if they don't print it, by God, I'll print it myself and *paste it on the fences.*

HARDMUTH. (*Weakening.*) What have I ever done to you, Jack Brookfield, except to be your friend?

JACK. You've been much too friendly. With this murder on your conscience, you proposed to take to yourself, as wife, my niece, dear to me as my life. As revenge for her refusal and mine, you've persecuted through two trials the boy she loved, and the son of the woman whose thought regulates the pulse of my heart, an innocent, unfortunate boy. In your ambition you've reached out to be the governor of this State, and an honored political party is seriously considering you for that office to-day.

HARDMUTH. That Scovill story's a lie—a political lie. I think you mean to be honest, Jack Brookfield, but somebody's strung you.

JACK. Wait! The man that's now hiding in Indiana—a fugitive from your feeble efforts at extradition—sat upstairs drunk and desperate—his last dollar on a case card. I pitied him. If a priest had been there he couldn't have purged his soul cleaner than poor Raynor gave it to me. If *he* put me on, am I strung?

HARDMUTH. (*Frightened.*) Yes, you are. I can't tell you why, because this jury is out and may come in any moment and I've got to be there, but I can square it. So help me God, I can square it.

JACK. You'll have to square it.

(*Enter* ALICE, *from the left, followed by* PRENTICE. *The Justice carries a folded newspaper.*)

ALICE. Jack. (*Indicates* PRENTICE.)

PRENTICE. Excuse me, I—

HARDMUTH. Oh—Justice Prentice.

JACK. Mr. Hardmuth—the State's attorney.

PRENTICE. I recognize Mr. Hardmuth. I didn't salute him because I resent his disrespectful treatment of myself during his cross-examination.

HARDMUTH. Entirely within my rights as a lawyer and—

PRENTICE. Entirely—and never within the opportunities of a gentleman.

HARDMUTH. Your side foresaw the powerful effect on a local jury of any testimony by a member of the Supreme Court, and my wish to break that—

PRENTICE. Was quite apparent, sir,—quite apparent,—but the testimony of every man is entitled to just such weight and consideration as that man's character commands. But it is not that disrespect which I resent. I am an old man—That I am unmarried—childless—without a son to inherit the vigor that time has reclaimed, is due to—a sentiment that you endeavored to ridicule, Mr. Hardmuth, a sentiment which would have been sacred in the hands of any true Kentuckian, which I am glad to hear you are not.

JACK. That's all.

HARDMUTH. Perhaps not. (*Exit.*)

PRENTICE. My dear Mr. Brookfield, that man certainly hasn't seen this newspaper?

JACK. No—but he knows it's coming.

PRENTICE. When I urged you as a citizen to tell anything you knew of the man, I hadn't expected a capital charge.

ALICE. What is it, Jack,—what have you said?

JACK. (*To* ALICE.) All in the headlines—read it. (*Gives* ALICE *the paper. To* PRENTICE.) That enough for your purpose, Justice Prentice?

PRENTICE. I never dreamed of an attack of that—that magnitude— Enough!

ALICE. Why—why did you do this, Jack?

JACK. Because I'm your big strong brother—and I had the information.

PRENTICE. It was necessary, Mrs. Campbell,—necessary.

ALICE. Why necessary?

JACK. My poor sister, you don't think. If that jury brings in a verdict of guilty—what then?

ALICE. What then? I don't know.

JACK. An appeal to the governor—for clemency.

ALICE. Well?

JACK. Then we delay things until a new governor comes in. But suppose that new governor is Hardmuth himself.

ALICE. How can the new governor be Hardmuth?

PRENTICE. Nothing can stop it if he gets the nomination, and the convention is in session at Frankfort to-day with Mr. Hardmuth's name in the lead.

JACK. (*Indicating paper.*) I 've served that notice on them and they won't dare nominate him. That is, I think they won't.

ALICE. But to charge him with murder?

PRENTICE. The only thing to consider there is,—have you your facts?

JACK. I have.

PRENTICE. Then it was a duty and you chose the psychological moment for its performance. "With what measure you mete—it shall be measured to you again." I have pity for the man whom that paper crushes, but I have greater pity for the boy he is trying to have hanged. (*Goes to* ALICE.) You know, Mrs. Campbell, that young Whipple is the grandson of an old friend of mine.

ALICE. Yes, Justice Prentice, I know that.

(*Enter* JO, *followed by* HELEN *and* VIOLA.)

JO. Mars Jack!

JACK. (*Turning.*) Yes?

HELEN. Oh, Jack!—

(*Comes down to* JACK. VIOLA *goes to* ALICE.)

JACK. What is it?

(*Catches and supports* HELEN.)

VIOLA. The jury returned and asked for instructions.

JACK. Well?

HELEN. There 's a recess of an hour.

VIOLA. The court wishes them locked up for the night, but the foreman said the jurymen were all anxious to get to their homes and he felt an agreement could be reached in an hour.

PRENTICE. Did he use exactly those words—"to their homes"?

VIOLA. "To their homes"—yes.

PRENTICE. (*Smiling at* JACK.) There you are.

HELEN. What, Jack?

JACK. What?

PRENTICE. Men with vengeance or severity in their hearts would hardly say they 're "anxious to get to their homes." They say, "the jury is anxious to get away," or "to finish its work."

HELEN. Oh, Justice Prentice, you pin hope upon such slight things.

PRENTICE. That is what hope is for, my dear Mrs. Whipple; the frail chances of this life.

VIOLA. And now, Uncle Jack, Mrs. Whipple ought to have a cup of tea and something to eat.

HELEN. Oh, I could n't—we must go back at once.

VIOLA. Well, I could—I—I must.

ALICE. Yes—you must—both of you.

(*Exit to dining-room.*)

VIOLA. (*Returning to* HELEN.) You don't think it 's heartless, do you?

HELEN. You dear child. (*Kisses her.*)

VIOLA. You come, too.

HELEN. (*Refusing.*) Please.

(*Exit* VIOLA. HELEN *sinks to sofa.*)

JACK. And now, courage, my dear HELEN; it 's almost over.

HELEN. At the other trial the jury delayed—just this way.

PRENTICE. Upon what point did the jury ask instruction?

HELEN. Degree.

PRENTICE. And the court?

HELEN. Oh, Jack, the Judge answered—guilty in the first degree, or not guilty.

PRENTICE. That all helps us.

HELEN. It does?

JACK. Who spoke for the jury?

HELEN. The foreman—and one other juryman asked a question.

JACK. Was it the man in the fourth chair—first row?

HELEN. (*Inquiringly.*) Yes—?

JACK. Ah.

HELEN. Why?

JACK. I think he 's a friend, that 's all.

HELEN. I should die, Jack, if it was n't for your courage. You won't get tired of it—will you—and forsake my poor boy—and me?

JACK. (*Encouragingly.*) What do you think?

HELEN. All our lawyers are kindness itself, but—but—you—Jack—you somehow—

(*Enter* VIOLA.)

VIOLA. Oh, Uncle Jack—here 's a note our lawyer asked me to give to you—I forgot it until this minute.

JACK. Thank you. (*Takes note.*)

VIOLA. Please try a cup of tea.

HELEN. No—no—Viola. (*Exit* VIOLA.) What is it, Jack? Are they afraid?

JACK. It 's not about the trial at all. (*Hands note to* PRENTICE.)

HELEN. Really?

JACK. Yes.

HELEN. But why don't you show it to us, then?

JACK. (PRENTICE *returns note.*) I will—if my keeping it gives you so much alarm as that. (*Turns on the large drop light and stands under it.*) Colonel Bayley says—"Dear Jack, I 've seen the paper; Hardmuth will shoot on sight."

HELEN. (*Quickly to* JACK'S *side.*) Oh, Jack, if anything should happen to you—

JACK. "Anything" is quite as likely to happen to Mr. Hardmuth.

HELEN. But not even that—my boy has killed a man—and—you—Jack—you—well, you just must n't let it happen, that 's all.

JACK. I must n't let it happen because—?

HELEN. Because—I—could n't bear it.

(JACK *lifts her hand to his face and kisses it.*)

(*Enter* ALICE.)

ALICE. What was the letter, Jack?

JACK. (*Hands letter to* ALICE *as he passes, leading* HELEN *to door.*) And, now I 'll agree to do the best I can for Mr. Hardmuth if you 'll take a cup of tea and a biscuit.

HELEN. There is n't time.

JACK. There 's plenty of time if the adjournment was for an hour.

ALICE. (*In alarm.*) Jack!

JACK. Eh—(*Turns to* ALICE.) Wait one minute. (*Goes on to door with* HELEN.) Go. (*Exit* HELEN.)

ALICE. (*As* JACK *returns.*) He threatens your life.

JACK. Not exactly. Simply Colonel Bayley's opinion that he will shoot on sight.

ALICE. (*Impatiently.*) Oh—

JACK. There is a difference, you know.

(*Enter* JO.)

JO. Mr. Ellinger, sah.

(*Enter* LEW.)

LEW. (*Briskly.*) Hello, Jack. (*Exit* JO.)

JACK. Well, Lew?

LEW. (*With newspaper.*) Why, that 's the damnedest thing—(*To* ALICE.) I beg your pardon.

ALICE. Don't, please,—some manly emphasis is a real comfort, Mr. Ellinger.

LEW. That charge of yours against Hardmuth is raisin' more h-h-high feeling than anything that ever happened.

JACK. I saw the paper.

LEW. You did n't see this—it 's an extra. (*Reads.*) "The charge read to the convention in night session at Frankfort—Bill Glover hits Jim Macey on the nose—De Voe of Carter County takes Jim's gun away from him. The delegation from Butler get down to their stomachs and crawl under the benches—some statesmen go through the windows. Convention takes a recess till morning. Local sheriff swearin' in deputies to keep peace in the barrooms." That 's all you 've done.

JACK. (*To* ALICE.) Good! (*To* PRENTICE.) Well, they can't nominate Mr. Hardmuth now.

LEW. (*To* ALICE.) I been hedgin'—I told the fellows I 'd bet Jack had n't said it.

JACK. Yes—I did say it.

LEW. In just those words—? (*Reads.*) "The poor fellow that crouched back of a window sill and shot Kentucky's governor deserves hanging less than the man whom he is shielding—the man who laid the plot of assassination, the present prosecuting attorney by appointment—Frank Allison Hardmuth." Did you say that?

JACK. Lew, that there might be no mistake—I wrote it.

(LEW *whistles;* JACK *takes the paper and scans it.*)

LEW. Is it straight?

JACK. Yes.

(*Pushes hanging button and turns off the large drop-light.*)

LEW. He *was* in the plot to kill the governor?

JACK. He organized it.

LEW. Well, what do you think of that? And now he 's runnin' for governor himself—a murderer?

JACK. Yes.

LEW. (*To* PRENTICE.) And for six months he 's been houndin' every fellow in Louisville that sat down to a game of cards. (JACK *nods.*) The damned rascal 's nearly put me in the poorhouse.

JACK. Poor old Lew!

LEW. (*To* PRENTICE.) Why, before I could get to that court-house to-day I had to take a pair of scissors that I used to cut coupons with and trim the whiskers off o' my shirt cuffs. (*To* JACK.) How long have you known this?

JACK. Ever since the fact.

PRENTICE. Mm—

LEW. Why do you spring it only now?

JACK. Because until now I lacked the character and the moral courage. I spring it now by the advice of Justice Prentice to reach that convention at Frankfort.

LEW. Well, you reached them.

PRENTICE. The convention was only a secondary consideration with me—my real object was this jury with whom Mr. Hardmuth seemed too powerful.

LEW. Reach the jury?

JACK. (*Enthusiastically.*) The jury? Why, of course,—the entire jury,—and I was hoping for one man—

LEW. Why, they don't see the papers—the jury won't get a line of this.

JACK. I think they will.

LEW. You got 'em fixed?

JACK. (*Indignantly.*) *Fixed?* No.

LEW. Then how will they see it?

PRENTICE. (*Firmly and slowly to* LEW, *who is half dazed.*) How many people in Louisville have already read that charge as you have read it?

LEW. Thirty thousand, maybe, but—

PRENTICE. And five hundred thousand in the little cities and the towns. Do you think, Mr. Ellinger, that all those minds can be at white heat over that knowledge and none of it reach the thought of those twelve men? Ah, no—

JACK. To half a million good Kentuckians to-night Frank Hardmuth is a repulsive thing—and that jury's faith in him—is dead.

LEW. (*Pause.*) Why, Jack, old man, you 're dippy.

(ALICE *turns away wearily, agreeing with* LEW.)

PRENTICE. Then, Mr. Ellinger, I am dippy, too. (ALICE *turns back.*)

LEW. You mean you think the jury gets the public opinion—without anybody tellin' them or their reading it.

PRENTICE. Yes. (*Pause.* LEW *looks stunned.*) In every widely discussed trial the defendant is tried not alone by his twelve peers, but by the entire community.

LEW. Why, blast it! The community goes by what the newspaper says!

PRENTICE. That is often the regrettable part of it—but the fact remains.

JACK. And that 's why you asked me to expose Frank Hardmuth?

PRENTICE. Yes.

LEW. Well, the public will think you did it because he closed your game.

JACK. Hardmuth did n't close my game.

LEW. Who did?

JACK. (*Pointing to* PRENTICE.) This man.

PRENTICE. (*To* JACK.) Thank you.

LEW. How the he—er—heaven's name did he close it?

JACK. He gave my self-respect a slap on the back and I stood up. (*Exit.*)

LEW. (*Thoroughly confused. Pause.*) Stung! (*Turns to* PRENTICE.) So you are responsible for these—these new ideas of Jack's?

PRENTICE. In a measure. Have the ideas apparently hurt Mr. Brookfield?

LEW. They 've put him out of business—that 's all.

PRENTICE. Which business?

LEW. Why, this house of his.

PRENTICE. I see. But his new ideas? Don't you like them, Mr. Ellinger?

LEW. I love Jack Brookfield—love him like a brother—but I don't want even a brother askin' me if I 'm sure I 've "thought it over" when I 'm startin' to take the halter off for a pleasant evenin'. Get my idea?

PRENTICE. I begin to.

LEW. In other words—I don't want to take my remorse first. It dampens fun. The other day a lady at the races said, "We 've missed you, Mr. Ellinger." And I said, "Have you?—Well I 'll be up this evening," and I 'm pressing her hand and hanging on to it till I 'm afraid I 'll get the carriage grease on my coat—feelin' only about thirty-two, you know, then I turn round and Jack has those sleepy lamps on me—and "bla"—

(*Turns and sinks on to sofa.*)

PRENTICE. And you don't go?

LEW. (*Bracing up.*) I *do* go—as a matter of self-respect—but I don't make a hit. I 'm thinking so much more about those morality ideas of Jack's than I am about the lady that it cramps my style and we never get past the weather, and "when did you last hear from So-and-so?" (*Rises.*) I want to reform all right. I believe in reform. But first I want to have the fun of fallin' and fallin' hard.

Jo. (*Distant and outside.*) 'Fore God, Mars Clay!

Clay. Jo, is my mother here?

Alice. (*Entering left.*) Why, that's Clay.

(*Voices off continue together and approach.*)

Lew. (*To* Prentice.) It's the boy.

Alice. His mother! (*Starts to call* Helen, *then falters in indecision.*) Oh!

(*The outside voices grow louder.*)

Prentice. Acquittal!

(*Enter* Clay, *followed by* Colonel Bayley, *his attorney.*)

Alice. Clay, Clay!

Clay. Oh, Mrs. Campbell.

(Alice *embraces him.*)

(*Enter* Jack, Helen, *and* Viola.)

Jack. (*Seeing* Clay *and speaking back to* Helen.) Yes.

Helen. (*As she enters.*) My boy!

Clay. Mother!

(*They embrace.* Clay *slips to his knee with his face hidden in* Helen's *lap, repeating her name.* Helen *standing sways and is caught by* Jack. Clay *noting this weakness rises and helps support her.*)

Jack. (*Rousing her.*) He's free, Helen, he's free.

Clay. Yes, mother, I'm free.

(Viola, *who has crossed back of* Clay *and* Helen, *weeps on shoulder of* Alice, *who comforts her.*)

Helen. My boy, my boy!

(Viola *looks at them.* Helen *sees* Viola *and turns* Clay *toward her.* Clay *takes* Viola *in his arms.*)

Clay. Viola, my brave sweetheart!

Viola. It's really over?

Clay. Yes.

Jack. It's a great victory, Colonel.

Bayley. Thank you.

Jack. If ever a lawyer made a good fight for a man's life, you did. Helen, Viola, you must want to shake this man's hand.

Viola. I could have thrown my arms around you when you made that speech.

Bayley. (*Laughing.*) Too many young fellows crowding into the profession as it is.

Helen. (*Taking his hand.*) Life must be sweet to a man who can do so much good as you do.

Bayley. I could n't stand it, you know, if it was n't that my ability works both ways.

(*Enter* Harvey, *left.*)

Harvey. Mars Clay.

Clay. Harvey! Why, dear old Harvey.

(*Half embraces* Harvey *and pats him affectionately.*)

Harvey. Yes, sah. Could—could you eat anything, Mars Clay?

Clay. Eat anything! Why, I'm starvin', Harvey.

Harvey. Ha, ha. Yes, sah.

(*Exit quickly.*)

Clay. But *you* with me, mother—and *Viola.*

Helen. My boy! Colonel!

(*Turns to* Bayley. *Exeunt* Clay, Viola, Helen, Bayley, *and* Alice *to dining-room.*)

Jack. (*Alone with* Prentice. *Picks up* Bayley's *letter; takes hold of push button over head.*) I shall never doubt you again.

Prentice. Mr. Brookfield, never doubt yourself.

(*Enter* Hardmuth. *He rushes down toward toward dining-room and turns back to* Jack *who is under the lamp with his hand on its button.*)

Hardmuth. You think you'll send me to the gallows, but, damn you, you go first yourself.

(*Thrusts a derringer against* Jack's *body.*)

Jack. Stop! (*The big light flashes on above* Hardmuth's *eyes. At* Jack's *"Stop,"* Prentice *inclines forward with eyes on* Hardmuth *so that there is a double battery of hypnotism on him. A pause.*) You can't shoot—that—gun. You can't pull the trigger. (*Pause.*) You can't even hold the gun. (*Pause. The derringer drops from* Hardmuth's *hand.*) Now, Frank, you can go.

Hardmuth. (*Recoiling slowly.*) I'd like to know—how in hell you did that—to me.

ACT FOURTH.

The scene is the same as in Act Third. All the lights are on, including the large electric light. Clay *and* Viola *seated on sofa near the fire-place.*

VIOLA. I must really say good-night and let you get some sleep.

CLAY. Not before Jack gets home. Our mothers have considerately left us alone together. They 'll just as considerately tell us when it 's time to part.

VIOLA. *My* mother said it was time half an hour ago.

CLAY. Wait till Jack comes in.

(*Enter* JO.)

JO. Mars Clay?

CLAY. Well, Jo?

JO. Dey 's another reporter to see you, sah?

VIOLA. Send him away—Mr. Whipple won't see any more reporters.

CLAY. (*Rises.*) Wait a minute—who is he? (JO *hands card.*) I 've got to see this one, Viola.

VIOLA. (*Complaining.*) Why "got to"?

CLAY. He 's a friend—I 'll see him, Jo.

JO. Yas, sah— (*Exit.*)

VIOLA. (*Rises.*) You 've said that all day —they 're all friends.

CLAY. Well, they are—but this boy especially. It was fine to see you and mother and Jack when I was in that jail —great—but you were there daytimes. This boy spent hours on the other side of the bars helping me pass the awful nights. I tell you—death-cells would be pretty nearly hell if it was n't for the police reporters—ministers ain't in it with 'em.

(*Enter* EMMETT, *a reporter.*)

EMMETT. Good-evening.

CLAY. How are you, Ned? You know Miss Campbell?

EMMETT. (*Bowing.*) Yes.

VIOLA. Good-evening.

CLAY. Have a chair.

EMMETT. Thank you. (*Defers to* VIOLA *who sits first on sofa. Pause.*) This is different. (*Looks around the room.*)

CLAY. Some.

EMMETT. Satisfied? The way we handled the story?

CLAY. Perfectly. You were just bully, old man.

EMMETT. (*To* VIOLA.) That artist of ours is only a kid—and they work him to death on the "Sunday"—so—(*Pause. To* CLAY.) You understand.

CLAY. Oh—I got used to the—pictures a year ago.

EMMETT. Certainly. (*Pause.*) Anything you want to say?

VIOLA. For the paper?

EMMETT. Yes.

CLAY. I think not.

(*Enter* HELEN *and* ALICE. EMMETT *rises.*)

HELEN. Clay, dear—(*Pause.*) Oh—

CLAY. You met my mother?

EMMETT. No—

CLAY. Mother—this is Mr. Emmett of whom I 've told you so often.

HELEN. Oh—the good reporter.

EMMETT. (*To* CLAY.) Gee! That 'd be a wonder if the gang heard it. (*Taking* HELEN'S *hand as she offers it.*) We got pretty well acquainted—yes, 'm.

CLAY. (*Introducing* ALICE.) Mrs. Campbell.

ALICE. Won't you sit down, Mr. Emmett?

EMMETT. Thank you. I guess we 've covered everything, but the chief wanted me to see your son (*turns to* CLAY) and see if you 'd do the paper a favor?

CLAY. If possible—gladly—

EMMETT. I don't like the assignment because—well for the very reason that it was handed to me—and that is because we 're more or less friendly.

(*Enter* JACK *in fur coat with cap and goggles in hand.*)

JACK. Well, it 's a wonderful night outside.

ALICE. You 're back early.

JACK. Purposely. (*To* EMMETT.) How are you?

EMMETT. (*Rising.*) Mr. Brookfield.

JACK. I thought you girls might like a little run in the moonlight before I put in the machine.

HELEN. Mr. Emmett has some message from his editor.

JACK. What is it?

EMMETT. There 's a warrant out for Hardmuth—you saw that?

VIOLA. Yes, we saw that. (*Goes to* JACK.)

JACK. To-night's paper—

EMMETT. If they get him and he comes to trial and all that, it 'll be the biggest trial Kentucky ever saw.

CLAY. Well?

EMMETT. Well—the paper wants you to agree to report it for them—the trial— there 'll be other papers after you, of course.

VIOLA. Oh, no—

EMMETT. Understand, Clay, I 'm not asking it. (*To* VIOLA.) I 'm here under orders just as I 'd be at a fire or a bread riot.

CLAY. (*Demurring.*) And—of course—you understand, don't you?

EMMETT. Perfectly—and I told the chief myself you would n't see it.

CLAY. Paper 's been too friendly for me to assume any—any—

JACK. Unnecessary dignity—

CLAY. Exactly—but—I just could n't, you see—

EMMETT. (*Going.*) Oh, leave it to me—I 'll let 'em down easy.

CLAY. Thank you.

EMMETT. You expect to be in Europe or—

CLAY. But I don't.

(JACK *removes fur coat, puts it on chair up right center.*)

VIOLA. We 're going to stay right here in Louisville—

CLAY. And work out my—my own future among the people who know me.

EMMETT. Of course—Europe 's just to stall off the chief—get him on to some other dope—

HELEN. (*Rising.*) But—

JACK. (*Interrupting.*) It 's all right.

HELEN. (*To* JACK.) I hate to begin with a falsehood.

EMMETT. Not your son—me—. Saw some copy on our telegraph desk, Mr. Brookfield, that 'd interest you.

JACK. Yes.

EMMETT. Or maybe you know of it? Frankfort—

JACK. No.

EMMETT. Some friend named you in the caucus.

JACK. What connection?

EMMETT. Governor.

VIOLA. (*To* EMMETT.) Uncle Jack?

EMMETT. Yes, 'm—that is, for the nomination.

JACK. It 's a joke.

EMMETT. Grows out of these Hardmuth charges, of course.

JACK. That 's all.

EMMETT. Good-night—(*Bows.*) Mrs. Whipple—ladies— (*Exit.*)

CLAY. (*Going to door with* EMMETT.) You 'll make that quite clear, won't you?

EMMETT. (*Outside.*) I 'll fix it.

CLAY. (*Returning.*) If it was n't for the notoriety of it, I 'd like to do that. (*Sits right of table.*)

HELEN. (*Reproachfully.*) My son!

JACK. Why would you like to do it?

CLAY. To get even. I 'd like to see Hardmuth suffer as he made me suffer. I 'd like to *watch* him suffer and write of it.

JACK. That 's a bad spirit to face the world with, my boy.

CLAY. I hate him. (*Goes to* VIOLA.)

JACK. Hatred is heavier freight for the shipper than it is for the consignee.

CLAY. I can't help it.

JACK. Yes, you can help it. Mr. Hardmuth should be of the utmost indifference to you. To hate him is weak.

VIOLA. Weak?

JACK. Yes, weak-minded. Hardmuth was in love with you at one time—he hated Clay. He said Clay was as weak as dishwater—(*to* CLAY)—and you were at that time. You 've had your lesson—profit by it. Its meaning was self-control. Begin now if you 're going to be the custodian of this girl's happiness.

HELEN. I 'm sure he means to, Jack.

JACK. You can carry your hatred of Hardmuth and let it embitter your whole life—or you can drop it—so—(*Drops a book on table.*) The power that any man or anything has to annoy us we give him or it by our interest. Some idiot told your great-grandmother that a jewel with different colored strata in it was "bad luck"—or a "hoodoo"—she believed it, and she nursed her faith that passed the lunacy on to your grandmother.

HELEN. Jack, don't talk of that, please.

JACK. I 'll skip one generation—but I 'd like to talk of it.

ALICE. (*Rising, comes to* HELEN.) Why talk of it?

JACK. It was only a notion, and an effort of will can banish it.

CLAY. It was more than a notion.

JACK. Tom Denning's scarf-pin which he dropped there (*indicates floor*) was an exhibit in your trial—Judge Bayley returned it to me to-day. (*Puts hand in pocket.*)

VIOLA. I wish you would n't, Uncle Jack. (*Turns away.*)

JACK. (*To* CLAY.) You don't mind, do you?

CLAY. I 'd rather not look at it—to-night.

JACK. You need n't look at it. I 'll hold it in my hand and you put your hands over mine.

ALICE. I really don't see the use in this experiment, Jack.

JACK. (*With* CLAY's *hand over his.*) That does n't annoy you, does it?

CLAY. I 'm controlling myself, sir—but I feel the influence of the thing all through and through me.

HELEN. Jack!

(VIOLA *turns away in protest.*)

JACK. Down your back, is n't it, and in the roots of your hair—tingling—?

CLAY. Yes.

HELEN. Why torture him?

JACK. Is it torture?

CLAY. (*With brave self-control.*) I shall be glad when it 's over.

JACK. (*Severely.*) What rot! That 's only my night-key—look at it. I have n't the scarf-pin about me.

CLAY. Why make me think it was the scarf-pin?

JACK. To prove to you that it 's only thinking—that 's all. Now, be a man—the cat's-eye itself is in that table drawer. Get it and show Viola that you 're not a neuropathic idiot. You 're a child of *the everlasting God* and nothing on the earth or under it can harm you in the slightest degree. (CLAY *opens drawer and takes pin.*) That 's the spirit—look at it—I 've made many a young horse do that to an umbrella. Now, give it to me. (*To* VIOLA.) You 're not afraid of it?

VIOLA. Why, of course I 'm not.

JACK. (*Putting pin on her breast.*) Now, if you want my niece, go up to that hoodoo like a man.

(CLAY *embraces* VIOLA.)

HELEN. Oh, Jack, do you think that will last?

JACK. Which—indifference to the hoodoo or partiality to my niece?

CLAY. They 'll both last.

JACK. Now, my boy, drop your hatred of Hardmuth as you drop your fear of the scarf-pin. Don't look back—your life 's ahead of you. Don't mount for the race over-weight.

(*Enter* JO.)

JO. Mr. Ellinger.

(*Enter* LEW.)

LEW. I don't intrude, do I?

JACK. Come in.

LEW. (*To* LADIES.) Good-evening, Ah, Clay. (*Shakes hands with* CLAY.) Glad to see you looking so well. Glad to see you in such good company. (*To* JACK, *briskly.*) I 've got him.

JACK. Got whom?

LEW. Hardmuth. (*To* LADIES.) Detectives been hunting him all day, you know.

HELEN. He 's caught, you say?

LEW. No—but I 've treed him—(*to* JACK) —and I thought I 'd just have a word with you before passing the tip. (*To* LADIES.) He 's nearly put me in the poorhouse with his raids and closing laws, and I see a chance to get even.

JACK. In what way?

LEW. They 've been after him nearly twenty-four hours—morning paper 's going to offer a reward for him, and I understand the State will also. If I had a little help I 'd hide him for a day or two and then surrender him for those rewards.

JACK. Where is Hardmuth?

(*Sits at table.*)

LEW. Hiding.

JACK. (*Writing a note.*) Naturally.

LEW. You remember Big George?

JACK. The darkey?

LEW. Yes—used to be on the door at Phil Kelly's?

JACK. Yes.

LEW. He 's there. In Big George's cottage—long story—Big George's wife—that is, she—well, his wife used to be pantry maid for Hardmuth's mother. When they raided Kelly's game, Big George pretended to turn State's evidence, but he really hates Hardmuth like a rattler—so it all comes back to me. You see, if I 'd win a couple of hundred at Kelly's I used to slip George a ten going out. Your luck always stays by you if you divide a little with a nigger or a humpback—and in Louisville it 's easier to find a nigger—so—

JACK. He 's there now?

LEW. Yes. He wants to get away. He 's got two guns and he 'll shoot before he gives up—so I 'd have to con him some way. George's wife is to open the door to Kelly's old signal, you remember—(*raps*)—one knock, then two, and then one.

JACK. Where is the cottage?

LEW. Number 7 Jackson Street—little dooryard—border of arbor-vitæ on the path.

JACK. One knock—then two—and then one— (*Rises with note written.*)

LEW. What you gonta do?

JACK. Send for him.

LEW. Who you gonta send?

JACK. That boy there.

CLAY. Me?

JACK. Yes.

HELEN. Oh, no—no.

JACK. And my niece.

VIOLA. What! To arrest a man?

JACK. (*To* CLAY.) My machine is at the door. Give Hardmuth this note. He 'll come with you quietly. Bring him here. We 'll decide what to do with him after that.

ALICE. I can't allow Viola on such an errand.

JACK. When the man she 's promised to marry is going into danger—

VIOLA. If Mr. Hardmuth will come for that note—why can't I deliver it?

JACK. You may—if Clay 'll let you.

CLAY. (*Quietly taking note as* JACK *offers it to* VIOLA.) I 'll hand it to him.

JACK. I hope so. (*Gives goggles and coat.*) Take these—remember—one rap, then two, then one.

CLAY. I understand—number seven—?

LEW. Jackson Street.

ALICE. I protest.

HELEN. So do I.

JACK. (*To* CLAY *and* VIOLA.) You 're both of age. I ask you to do it. If you give Hardmuth the goggles, nobody 'll recognize him and with a lady beside him you 'll get him safely here.

CLAY. Come. (*Exit with* VIOLA.)

LEW. (*Following to door.*) I ought to be in the party.

JACK. No—you stay here.

ALICE. That 's scandalous.

JACK. But none of us will start the scandal, will we?

HELEN. Clay knows nothing of that kind of work—a man with two guns—think of it.

JACK. After he 's walked barehanded up to a couple of guns a few times, he 'll quit fearing men that are armed only with a scarf-pin.

HELEN. (*Hysterically.*) It 's cruel to keep constantly referring to that—that —mistake of Clay's—I want to forget it.

JACK. (*Going to* HELEN. *Tenderly.*) The way to forget it, my dear Helen, is not to guard it as a sensitive spot in your memory, but to grasp it as the wise ones grasp a nettle—crush all its power to harm you in one courageous contact. We think things are calamities and trials and sorrows—only names. They are spiritual gymnastics and have an eternal value when once you front them and make them crouch at your feet. Say once for all to your soul and thereby to the world—"Yes, my boy killed a man—because I 'd brought him up a half-effeminate, hysterical weakling, but he 's been through the fire and I 've been through the fire, and we 're both the better for it."

HELEN. I can say that truthfully, but I don't want to make a policeman of him, just the same. (*Exit to dining-room.*)

ALICE. (*Following.*) Your treatment 's a little too heroic, Jack. (*Exit.*)

LEW. Think they 'll fetch him?

JACK. (*Sits left of table.*) Yes.

LEW. He 'll come, of course, if he does, under the idea that you 'll help him when he gets here.

JACK. Yes.

LEW. Pretty hard double-cross, but he deserves it. I 've got a note of fifteen thousand to meet to-morrow, or, damn it, I don't think I 'd fancy this man-hunting. I put up some Louisville-Nashville bonds for security, and the holder of the note 'll be only too anxious to pinch 'em.

JACK. You can't get your rewards in time for that.

LEW. I know—and that 's one reason I come to you, Jack. If you see I 'm in a fair way to get a reward—

JACK. I 'll lend you money, Lew.

LEW. Thank you. (JACK *takes check-book and writes.*) I thought you would. If I lose those bonds they 'll have me selling programs for a livin' at a grandstand. You see, I thought hatin' Hardmuth as you do, and your reputation bein' up through that stuff to the papers—

JACK. There. (*Gives check.*)

LEW. Thank you, old man. I 'll hand this back to you in a week.

JACK. (*Rises.*) You need n't.

LEW. What?

JACK. You need n't hand it back. It 's only fifteen thousand and you 've lost a hundred of them at poker in these rooms.

LEW. Never belly-ached, did I?

JACK. Never—but you don't owe me that fifteen.

LEW. Rot! I 'm no baby—square game, was n't it?

JACK. Perfectly.

LEW. And I 'll sit in a square game any time I get a chance.

JACK. I know, Lew, all about that.

LEW. I 'll play you for this fifteen right away. (*Displays check.*)

JACK. No. (*Walks aside.*)

LEW. Ain't had a game in three weeks —and, besides, I think my luck 's changin'? When Big George told me about

Hardmuth I took George's hand before I thought what I was doin'—and you know what shakin' hands with a nigger does just before any play.

JACK. (*Resisting* LEW's *plea.*) No, thank you, Lew.

LEW. My money 's good as anybody else's, ain't it?

JACK. Just as good, but—

LEW. It ain't a phoney check, is it? (*Examines check.*)

JACK. The check 's all right.

LEW. (*Taunting.*) Losing your nerves?

JACK. No (*pause*)—suppose you shuffle those and deal a hand. (*Indicates small table, right.*)

LEW. That 's like old times; what is it —stud-horse or draw? (*Sits at table.*)

JACK. (*Goes to fireplace.*) Draw if you say so.

LEW. I cut 'em?

JACK. You cut them.

LEW. (*Dealing two poker hands.*) Table stakes—check goes for a thousand.

JACK. That suits me.

LEW. (*Taking his own cards.*) Sit down.

JACK. (*At other side of room looking into fire.*) I don't need to sit down just yet.

LEW. As easy as that, am I?

JACK. Lew!

LEW. Yes?

JACK. (*Pause.*) Do you happen to have three queens?

(LEW *looks at* JACK, *then carefully at back of his own cards, then at the deck.*)

LEW. Well, I can't see it.

JACK. No use looking—they 're not marked.

LEW. Well, I shuffled 'm all right.

JACK. Yes.

LEW. And cut 'm? (JACK *nods.*) Could n't 'a' been a cold deck?

JACK. No.

LEW. Then, how did you know I had three queens?

JACK. I did n't know it. I just thought you had.

LEW. Can you do it again?

JACK. I don't know. Draw one card.

LEW. (*Drawing one card from deck.*) All right.

JACK. (*Pause.*) Is it the ace of hearts?

LEW. It is.

JACK. Mm—turns me into a rotter, does n't it?

(*Comes gloomily to the big table.*)

LEW. Can you do that every time?

JACK. I never tried it until to-night—that is, consciously. I 've always had luck and I thought it was because I took chances on a game—same as any player —but that don't look like it, does it?

LEW. Beats me.

JACK. And what a monster it makes of me —these years I 've been in the business.

LEW. You say you did n't know it before?

JACK. I did n't know it—no—but—some things have happened lately that have made me think it might be so; that jury yesterday—some facts I 've had from Justice Prentice. Telepathy of a very common kind—and I guess it 's used in a good many games, old man, we are n't on to.

LEW. Well—have you told anybody?

JACK. No.

LEW. (*Excitedly.*) Good! (*Rises and comes to* JACK.) Now, see here, Jack, if you can do that right along I know a game in Cincinnati where it 'd be like takin' candy from children.

JACK. Good God! you 're not suggesting that I keep it up?

LEW. Don't over-do it—no—(*Pause.*) Or you show me the trick and *I 'll* collect all right.

JACK. (*Slowly.*) Lew—(*Pause.*) Some of the fellows I 've won from in this house have gone over to the park and blown their heads off.

LEW. Some of the fellows anybody wins from in any house go somewhere and blow their heads off.

JACK. True— (*Pause.*)

LEW. Three queens—before the draw— well, you could 'a' had me all right—and you won't tell me how you do it?

JACK. I don't know how I do it; the thought just comes to my mind stronger than any other thought.

LEW. (*Reprovingly.*) God A'mighty gives you a mind like that and you won't go with me to Cincinnati.

(*Goes to card table; studies cards.*)

(*Enter* JO.)

JO. Justice Prentice, sah.

JACK. Ask him to step up here.

JO. Yes, sah. (*Exit.*)

JACK. (*Goes to door, left.*) Alice—Helen —Justice Prentice has called; I 'd like you to join us.

LEW. Can the old man call a hand like that, too?

JACK. I 'm sure he could.

LEW. And—are there others?

JACK. I believe there are a good many

others who unconsciously have the same ability.

LEW. Well, it's a God's blessin' there's a sucker born every minute. I'm a widow and an orphan 'longside o' that.

(*Throws cards in disgust onto table.*)

(*Enter* ALICE *and* HELEN.)

ALICE. Been losing, Mr. Ellinger?

LEW. Losing? I just saved fifteen thousand I was gonta throw 'way like sand in a rathole. I'm a babe eatin' spoon victuals and only gettin' half at that.

(*Enter* PRENTICE.)

JACK. Good-evening.

PRENTICE. Good-evening.

(*Shakes hands with* ALICE *and* HELEN.)

JACK. I stopped at your hotel, Mr. Justice, but you were out.

(*Enter* VIOLA.)

ALICE. (*Anxiously.*) Viola.

HELEN. Where's Clay?

VIOLA. Downstairs. Good-evening.

PRENTICE. Good-evening.

JACK. (*To others.*) Pardon. (*To* VIOLA.) Did the—gentleman come with you?

VIOLA. Yes.

(LEW *flutters and shows excitement.*)

JACK. Won't you ask Clay, my dear, to take him through the lower hall and into the dining-room until I'm at liberty?

VIOLA. Certainly. (*Exit.*)

PRENTICE. I am keeping you from other appointments?

JACK. Nothing that can't wait.

PRENTICE. I am leaving for Washington in the morning.

JACK. We'll all be at the train to see you off.

PRENTICE. That's good, because I should like to say good-bye to—to the young people—I can see them there—I shan't see you then, Mr. Ellinger—

(*Goes to* LEW, *who stands at card table.*)

LEW. Good-bye, Judge—you—you've given me more of a "turn over" than you know.

PRENTICE. Really?

LEW. I'd 'a' saved two hundred thousand dollars if I'd 'a' met you thirty years ago.

PRENTICE. Well, that's only about six thousand a year, is n't it?

LEW. That's so—and, damn it, I have lived.

(*Smiles—looks dreamily into the past.*)

PRENTICE. Good-night. (*Exit* PRENTICE.)

JACK. Good-night—good-night.

ALICE. Is that Hardmuth in there?

(*Points to dining-room.*)

JACK. Yes.

ALICE. I don't want to see him.

JACK. Very well, dear, I'll excuse you.

ALICE. (*Going.*) Come, Helen.

JACK. (*At door, left.*) Come in. (*To* HELEN, *who is going with* ALICE.) Helen! I'd like *you* to stay.

HELEN. Me?

JACK. Yes. (*Exit* ALICE.)

(*Enter* CLAY, HARDMUTH, *and* VIOLA. VIOLA *lays automobile coat on sofa.* HARDMUTH *bows to* HELEN. HELEN *bows.*)

JACK. Your mother has just left us, Viola. You'd better join her.

VIOLA. Very well.

JACK. (*Taking her hand as she passes him.*) And I want you to know—I appreciate very much, my dear, your going on this errand for me—you're the right stuff. (*Kisses her. Exit* VIOLA. *To* HARDMUTH.) You're trying to get away?

HARDMUTH. This your note?

JACK. Yes.

HARDMUTH. You say you'll help me out of the State?

JACK. I will.

HARDMUTH. When?

JACK. Whenever you're ready.

HARDMUTK. I'm ready now.

JACK. Then I'll help you now.

LEW. Now?

JACK. Yes.

HELEN. Does n't that render you liable in some way, Jack, to the law?

JACK. Yes—but I've been liable to the law in some way for the last twenty years. (*To* CLAY.) You go down and tell the chauffeur to leave the machine and walk home. I'm going to run it myself and I'll turn it in.

CLAY. Yes, sir. (*Exit.*)

HARDMUTH. You're going to run it yourself?

JACK. Yes.

HARDMUTH. Where to?

JACK. Across the river, if that's agreeable to you—or any place you name.

HARDMUTH. Is anybody—waiting for you—across the river?

JACK. No.

HARDMUTH. (*Again with note.*) This is all on the level?

JACK. Completely.

LEW. Why, I think you mean that.

JACK. I do.

LEW. (*Aggressively.*) But I 've got something to say, have n't I?

JACK. I hope not.

LEW. (*Quitting.*) If you 're in earnest, of course. But I don't see your game.

JACK. I 'm not fully convinced of Mr. Hardmuth's guilt.

LEW. Why, he 's running away?

(*Enter* CLAY.)

HARDMUTH. I know what a case they 'd make against me, but I 'm not guilty in any degree.

JACK. I want to do this thing for you, Frank—don't make it too difficult by any lying. When I said I was n't fully convinced of your guilt, my reservation was one you would n't understand. (*To* CLAY.) He gone?

CLAY. Yes.

JACK. My coat and goggles?

CLAY. Below in the reception-room.

JACK. Thank you. I wish now you 'd go to Viola and her mother and keep them wherever they are.

CLAY. All right. (*Exit.*)

JACK. (*To* HARDMUTH.) Hungry? (*Touches push button.*)

HARDMUTH. No, thank you.

JACK. Got money?

HARDMUTH. Yes.

(*Enter* JO.)

JACK. Jo, take Mr. Hardmuth below and lend him one of the fur coats. (*To* HARDMUTH.) I 'll join you immediately. (*Exit* HARDMUTH *with* JO.)

HELEN. What does it all mean, Jack?

JACK. Lew, I called that ace of hearts, did n't I?

LEW. And the three queens.

JACK. Because the three queens and the ace were in your mind.

LEW. I don't see any other explanation.

JACK. Suppose, instead of the cards there 'd been in your mind a well-developed plan of assassination—the picture of a murder—

LEW. Did you drop to him that way?

JACK. No. Raynor told me all I know of Hardmuth—but here 's the very *hell* of it. Long before Scovill was killed I thought he deserved killing and I thought it *could* be done just—as—it—was done.

HELEN. Jack!

JACK. I never breathed a word of it to a living soul, but Hardmuth planned it exactly as I dreamed it—and by God, a guilty thought is almost as criminal as a guilty deed. I 've always had a considerable influence over that poor devil that 's running away to-night, and I 'm not sure that before the Judge of both of us the guilt is n't mostly mine.

HELEN. That 's morbid, Jack, dear, perfectly morbid.

JACK. I hope it is—we 'll none of us ever know—in this life—but we can all of us— (*Pause.*)

LEW. What?

JACK. Live as if it were true. (*Change of manner to brisk command.*) I 'm going to help him over the line—the roads are watched, but the police won't suspect me and they won't suspect Lew—and all the less if there 's a lady with us—(*To* LEW.) Will you go?

LEW. The limit.

JACK. Get a heavy coat from Jo.

LEW. Yes. (*Exit.*)

JACK. (*Alone with* HELEN.) You know you said I used to be able to make you write to me when I was a boy at college?

HELEN. Yes.

JACK. And you were a thousand miles away—while this fellow—Hardmuth—was just at my elbow half the time.

HELEN. It can't help you to brood over it.

JACK. It can help me to know it, and make what amend I can. Will you go with me while I put this poor devil over the line?

HELEN. (*Taking* VIOLA'S *fur coat.*) Yes, I 'll go with you.

JACK. Helen, you stood by your boy in a fight for his life.

HELEN. Did n't you?

JACK. Will you stand by *me* while I make my fight?

HELEN. (*Giving her hand.*) You 've made your fight, Jack, and you 've won. (JACK *kisses her hand, which he reverently holds in both of his.*)

THE FAITH HEALER

BY

William Vaughn Moody

THE FAITH HEALER

The Faith Healer represents the drama of revolt, in which the protest of the individual is made against the controlling power of social law and custom. Only as long as the "Faith Healer" has confidence in himself does his power survive the ever-present disbelief of the world. This drama of revolt found its most powerful expression in the work of a group of dramatists to which Mr. Moody, Mr. George Cabot Lodge, and, to a certain extent, Mr. Percy MacKaye, belonged.

William Vaughn Moody was born at Spencer, Indiana, July 8, 1869, the son of Francis Burdette Moody, a steamboat captain, and Henrietta Stoy, to whom he pays such an exquisite tribute in "The Daguerreotype." He was brought up in the town of New Albany, Indiana, and after teaching in a neighboring school, came east to Riverside Academy, New York, where he also taught while preparing to enter Harvard College, from which he graduated in 1893. Having already completed his work for the bachelor's degree in 1892 he travelled in Europe for a year and then returning to the Graduate School at Harvard University he took his master's degree in 1894. After being a member of the Department of English at Harvard for a year, he became Instructor in English at the University of Chicago in 1895 and remained there, as Instructor and Assistant Professor, until 1903. Two European trips occurred during this period and Mr. Moody's poems, especially the lyrics and the verse plays, show the result of the experiences encountered in his wanderings. Notwithstanding his success as a teacher and lecturer, he gave up active work at the University of Chicago after 1902, retaining merely a nominal connection with the English department. He felt that his best work was to be done as a poet and to do that work well he must have freedom from academic drudgery. His *History of English Literature* written in collaboration with Robert M. Lovett, and the publications of which he was editor, served simply to provide him with the means to devote himself to poetry. Already he had become recognized through his poems on public affairs, such as the "Ode in Time of Hesitation," as one of the foremost of American poets, and though his first volume, published in 1902, contained only a small number of poems, this was due to his capacity for selection rather than to lack of inspiration.

Mr. Moody's early death, which occurred at Colorado Springs, October 17, 1910, cut short his career just as his work was reaching its best development. His lyrics are exquisite and at times magnificent in their phrasing. In the poems on public affairs he expresses true patriotism and concern for his country's fidelity to her ideals. In his love poetry he shows deep insight into the emotional phases of life. Besides the lyrics he had to his credit the verse dramas, and the prose plays with which his widest public notice came. *The Fire Bringer,* which celebrated the sacrifice of Prometheus in bringing fire to mankind; *The Masque of Judgment,* which had for its theme the conquest of all things by the serpent; and the incomplete fragment, *The Death of Eve,* were to have formed a trilogy in which the relations of God and man were to have been developed dramatically, according to the modern doctrine of revolt. The plays in verse show the influence of the Greek drama, and, as is the case with all Mr. Moody's work, the influence of Puritanism and the reaction against it. *The Fire Bringer* was written with the idea of actual stage production.

As early as 1898 Mr. Moody had begun to think of the theme of a faith healer as a fit subject for a play, which at first he planned to write in verse. He put aside this theme for a time, however, to write *The Great Divide,* which was performed first under the title of *The Sabine Woman* by Miss Margaret Anglin in Chicago, April, 1906. It was afterward played at the Princess Theatre, New York, in October, 1906, by Mr. Henry Miller and Miss Anglin and had a long run there and throughout the United States. In September, 1909, it was produced for a short run at the Adelphi Theatre in London. *The Great Divide* portrayed the conflict of the ideals of Puritanism, with its capacity of self-torture, and the freer conceptions of life prevalent in the West.

The Faith Healer was first played in St. Louis on March 15, 1909. It was put on at the Savoy Theatre, New York, January 19, 1910, and was played at Cambridge, Massachusetts, on January 24, 1910. It was not a popular success but it is a significant play. The situation is dramatic and the handling convincing, while the native quality of the play is apparent. The struggle which is the essential part of every drama occurs here between human love and the dedication to a purpose and is only incidentally associated with the religious type. The obvious means of ending the struggle would have been to have "The Healer" either renounce love for his dedicated purpose or renounce the purpose in favor of his love. Mr. Moody with a finer art shows in the play that love and work are not necessarily irreconcilable interests and that by substituting for the selfishness of a personal claim the more impersonal and unselfish type of love, the hero could make a resolution of his problem which included every aspect of a man's life.

The most convenient form in which to read Mr. Moody's work is in the complete edition, the *Poems and Plays of William Vaughn Moody,* in two volumes, published by the Houghton, Mifflin Company in 1912. This edition contains a study of Mr. Moody's work and a brief biography by Professor John M. Manly, to whom the present editor acknowledges his indebtedness. The separate publications of Mr. Moody include *The Masque of Judgment* (1900), *Poems* (1902),

The Fire Bringer (1904), *The Great Divide* (1909), and *The Faith Healer* (1909) and (1910). An interesting volume entitled *Some Letters of William Vaughn Moody,* edited by Daniel E. Mason, was published in 1913. For general criticism of Moody's work, see articles by N. O. Barr, *The Lyrist and Lyric Dramatist,* and by C. H. Caffin, *The Dramatist,* in *The Drama,* No. 2, May, 1911. For criticism of *The Faith Healer* see *The Nation,* vol. 88, pp. 175–76, Feb., 1909. *Hampton's Magazine,* Vol. 24, pp. 561–65, April, 1910. Criticism of *The Great Divide* is found in *The Nation,* Vol. 89, p. 387, October, 1909, and by B. R. Hertz in *The Forum,* vol. 43, pp. 90–92, Jan., 1910.

Mrs. Moody has kindly revised the text of the edition of 1912 for the present editor, who gratefully acknowledges her courtesy in obtaining for him the right to reprint the play and for valuable biographical information.

Note to Sixth Edition.

The Faith Healer was revived by Plays and Players of Philadelphia for three nights beginning Wednesday, December 18th, 1929. The revival was eminently successful, the acting qualities as well as the spiritual values of the play being apparent.

A singularly interesting series of letters by Moody to Mrs. Moody was edited by Percy MacKaye under the title of *Letters to Harriet,* Boston, 1935. See also *William Vaughn Moody, A Study,* by David D. Henry, Boston, 1934.

For a discussion of Moody's place at the head of the dramatic impulses of the Twentieth Century, see the present editor's *History of the American Drama from the Civil War to the Present Day,* Revised Edition, two volumes in one, Appleton-Century-Crofts, Inc. (1936), Vol. 2, pp. 1–17 and pp. 382–383.

Note to Seventh Edition.

See *A House in Chicago,* by Olivia H. Dunbar, University of Chicago Press (1947), for an interesting account of the group that centered in Mrs. Moody's home.

THE ORIGINAL CAST OF CHARACTERS

St. Louis, March 15, 1909

ULRICH MICHAELIS..Mr. Henry Miller
MATTHEW BEELER..Mr. William J. Butler
MARY BEELER, his wife..................................Miss Gertrude Berkeley
MARTHA BEELER, his sister.......................................Miss Lillian Dix
ANNIE BEELER, his daughter............................Miss Gladys Heulette
RHODA WILLIAMS, MRS. BEELER's niece......................Miss Thais Lawton
DR. GEORGE LITTLEFIELD.............................Mr. George Saule Spencer
REV. JOHN CULPEPPER..................................Mr. Henry Hanscombe
UNCLE ABE, an old negro..................................Mr. James Kirkwood
LAZARUS, an Indian boy..................................Mr. Henry B. Walthall
A YOUNG MOTHER WITH HER CHILD..................Miss Laura Hope Crews

Various sick people and others attendant upon them.

THE FAITH HEALER

ACT FIRST.

A large old-fashioned room in Matthew Beeler's *farm-house, near a small town in the Middle West. The room is used for dining and for general living purposes. It suggests, in architecture and furnishings, a past of considerable prosperity, which has now given place to more humble living. The house is, in fact, the ancestral home of* Mr. Beeler's *wife,* Mary, *born Beardsley, a family of the local farming aristocracy, now decayed. At the rear is a large double window, set in a broad alcove. To the right of the window is the entrance door, which opens upon the side yard, showing bushes, trees, and farm buildings.*

In the right wall of the room a door and covered stairway lead to the upper story. Farther forward is a wall cupboard, and a door leading into the kitchen. Opposite this cupboard. in the left-hand wall of the room, is a mantel-piece and grate; farther back a double door, leading to a hall. Off the hall open two bedrooms (not seen), one belonging to Mr. *and* Mrs. Beeler, *the other to* Rhoda Williams, *a niece of* Mrs. Beeler, *child of her dead sister.*

The room contains, among other articles of furniture, a dining table (with detachable leaves to reduce its bulk when not in use for eating purposes), an invalid's wheel-chair, a low sofa of generous size, and a book-shelf, upon which are arranged the scientific books which Mr. Beeler *takes a somewhat untutored but genuine delight in. Tacked upon the wall near by are portraits of scientific men, Darwin and Spencer conspicuous among them, cut from periodicals. Other pictures, including family daguerreotypes and photographs, are variously distributed about the walls. Over the mantel shelf hangs a large map of the United States and Mexico, faded and fly-specked.*

As the curtain rises, the room is dark, except for a dull fire in the grate. The ticking of the clock is heard; it strikes six. Martha Beeler, *a woman of forty-five, enters from the kitchen, carrying a lighted lamp. She wears a shawl over her shoulders, a print dress, and a kitchen apron. She places the lamp on the table, which is set for breakfast, and puts coal on the grate, which soon flames more brightly.*

She goes into the hall and is heard knocking and calling.

Martha. Rhody! Rhody! (Matthew Beeler, *a man of fifty, enters. He is not quite dressed, but finishes as he comes in.* Martha *follows him.*) Where 's that niece of yours got to now?

Beeler. She 's helping Mary dress.

Martha. What in time 's Mary gettin' up for? She 's only in the way till the work 's done.

Beeler. She 's restless.

Martha. (*Significantly.*) I should n't wonder. (*Pause.*) I hope you know *why* Mary did n't sleep.

Beeler. (*Evasively.*) She 's always been a light sleeper, since she got her stroke.

Martha. Look here, Mat Beeler! I 'm your born sister. Don't try to fool me! You know why your wife did n't sleep last night.

Beeler. Maybe I do, Sis. (*Points to the ceiling.*) Is he up yet?

Martha. Up! I don't believe he 's been abed. (*They listen, as to the tread of some one on the floor above.*) Back and forth, like a tiger in a cage!

Beeler. (*Shrugs.*) Queer customer.

Martha. Yes. (*Imitates him.*) "Queer customer," that 's you. But come to doin' anything about it!

Beeler. Give me time, Sis, give me time!

Martha. How much time do you want? He 's been in this house since Wednesday night, and this is Saturday morning.

Beeler. Well, he 's payin' his board, ain't he? (*At window, rolls up curtain.*) Goin' to have just such another day as yesterday. Never seen such a fog.

Martha. Never seen such a fog, eh? (*Comes nearer and speaks mysteriously.*)

Did you happen to notice how long that fog has been hangin' over this house?

BEELER. How long? Why, since Thursday.

MARTHA. No, sir, since Wednesday night.

BEELER. (*Looking at her, astonished.*) Martha Beeler! You don't mean to say —he *brought* the fog? (*She flounces out without answering. He lights lantern, with dubious head-shaking, and holds it up before the print portraits.*) Mornin', Mr. Darwin. Same to you, Mr. Spencer. Still keepin' things straight? (*Grunts as he turns down his lantern, which is smoking.*) I guess not very.

(*The hall door again opens, and* RHODA WILLIAMS, *a girl of twenty, enters, with* ANNIE BEELER, *a child of ten.* RHODA *is running, with* ANNIE *in laughing pursuit.*)

RHODA. (*Taking refuge behind the table.*) King's X!

ANNIE. (*Catching her.*) You did n't have your fingers crossed.

RHODA. (*Turning* ANNIE *about, and beginning to button the child's long slip.*) And you did n't have your dress buttoned.

ANNIE. That does n't count.

RHODA. Yes, it does, before breakfast!

BEELER. (*At the outer door.*) How does your aunt strike you this morning?

RHODA. (*Sobered.*) She seems wonderfully better.

BEELER. Better!

RHODA. I don't mean her poor body. She 's got past caring for that.

BEELER. (*With sarcasm.*) You mean in her mind, eh?

RHODA. Yes, I mean better in her mind.

BEELER. Because of what this fellow has been sayin' to her, I suppose.

RHODA. Yes, because of that.

BEELER. (*As he puts on an old fur cap.*) An out-and-out fakir!

RHODA. You don't know him.

BEELER. I suppose you do, after forty-eight hours. What in the name of nonsense is he, anyway? And this deaf and dumb Indian boy he drags around with him. What 's his part in the show?

RHODA. I know very little about either of them. But I know Mr. Michaelis is not —what you say.

BEELER. Well, he 's a crank at the best of it. He 's worked your aunt up now so 's she can't sleep. You brought him here, and you 've got to get rid of him. (*Exit by outer door, with inarticulate grumblings, among which can be distinguished.*) Hump! Ulrich Michaelis! There 's a name for you.

ANNIE. What 's a fakir? (RHODA *does not answer.*) Cousin Rho, what 's a fakir?

RHODA. (*Humoring her.*) A man, way off on the other side of the world, in India, who does strange things.

ANNIE. What kind of things?

RHODA. Well, for instance, he throws a rope up in the air, right up in the empty air, with nothing for it to catch on, and then—he—climbs—up—the—rope!

ANNIE. Don't he fall?

(RHODA *shakes her head in portentous negation. Steps are heard descending the stairs. The child fidgets nervously.*)

ANNIE. Listen! He 's coming down!

RHODA. Yes, he 's coming down, right out of the blue sky.

ANNIE. (*In a panic.*) Let me go.

(*She breaks away and retreats to the hall door, watching the stair door open, and* ULRICH MICHAELIS *enter. Thereupon, with a glance of frightened curiosity, she flees.* MICHAELIS *is a man of twenty-eight or thirty, and his dark, emaciated face, wrinkled by sun and wind, looks older. His abundant hair is worn longer than common. His frame, though slight, is powerful, and his way of handling himself has the freedom and largeness which come from much open-air life. There is nevertheless something nervous and restless in his movements. He has a trick of handling things, putting them down only to take them up again immediately, before renouncing them for good. His face shows the effect of sleeplessness, and his gray flannel shirt and dark, coarse clothing are rumpled and neglected.*)

RHODA. (*As he enters.*) Good morning.

MICHAELIS. (*Watching* ANNIE'S *retreat.*) Is—is that child afraid of me?

RHODA. (*As she adds the finishing touches to the breakfast table.*) Oh, Annie 's a queer little body. She has her mother's nerves. And then she sees no one, living here on the back road. If this dreadful fog ever lifts, you 'll see that, though we 're quite near town, it 's almost as if we were in the wilderness. (*The stair door opens, and an Indian boy, about sixteen years old, enters. He is dressed in ordinary clothes; his dark skin, longish hair, and the noiseless tread of his moccasined feet, are the only suggestions of his race. He bows to* RHODA, *who returns his salutation; then, with a glance at* MICHAELIS, *he goes out doors.* RHODA *nods toward the closing door.*) It's really him Annie's afraid of. He's like a creature from another world, to her.

MICHAELIS. (*Looks at her in an odd, startled way.*) Another world?

RHODA. Oh, you're used to his people. Your father was a missionary to the Indians, you told me.

MICHAELIS. Yes.

RHODA. Where?

MICHAELIS. At Acoma.

RHODA. Where is that?

MICHAELIS. (*Standing near the wall map, touches it.*) In New Mexico, by the map.

RHODA. (*Comes nearer.*) What is it like?

MICHAELIS. It's—as you say—another world.

RHODA. Describe it to me.

MICHAELIS. I could n't make you see it. It's—centuries and centuries from our time.—And since I came here, since I entered this house, it has seemed centuries away from my own life.

RHODA. My life has seemed far off, too—my old life—

MICHAELIS. What do you mean by your old life?

RHODA. (*She breaks out impulsively.*) I mean—I mean—. Three days ago I was like one dead! I walked and ate and did my daily tasks, but—I wondered sometimes why people did n't see that I was dead, and scream at me.

MICHAELIS. It was three days ago that I first saw you.

RHODA. Yes.

MICHAELIS. Three nights ago, out there in the moonlit country.

RHODA. Yes.

MICHAELIS. You were unhappy, then?

RHODA. The dead are not unhappy, and I was as one dead.

MICHAELIS. Why was that?

RHODA. I think we die more than once when things are too hard and too bitter.

MICHAELIS. Have things here been hard and bitter?

RHODA. No. All that was before I came here! But it had left me feeling—. The other night, as I walked through the streets of the town, the people seemed like ghosts to me, and I myself like a ghost.

MICHAELIS. I cannot think of you as anything but glad and free.

RHODA. When you met me on the road, and walked home with me, and said those few words, it was as if, all of a sudden, the dead dream was shattered, and I began once more to live. (*Bell rings.*) That is Aunt Mary's bell

(RHODA *goes out by the hall door, wheeling the invalid chair.* MARTHA *enters from the kitchen, carrying a steaming coffee-pot and a platter of smoking meat, which she places on the table.* MICHAELIS *bows to her.*)

MARTHA. (*Snappishly.*) Hope you slept well!

(*She goes to the outer door, rings the breakfast bell loudly, and exits to kitchen.* RHODA *enters, wheeling* MRS. BEELER *in an invalid chair.* MRS. BEELER *is a woman of forty, slight of body, with hair just beginning to silver. Her face has the curious refinement which physical suffering sometimes brings.* ANNIE *lingers at the door, looking timidly at* MICHAELIS, *as he approaches* MRS. BEELER *and takes her hand from the arm of the chair.*)

MICHAELIS. You are better?

MRS. BEELER. (*Speaks with low intensity.*) Much, much better.

(*He puts her hand gently back on the chair arm.* MARTHA *enters with other dishes. She pours out coffee, putting a cup at each plate.* MR. BEELER *has entered from the kitchen, and the boy from outside.* BEELER, *with a glance of annoyance at his wife and* MICHAELIS, *sits down at the head of the table.* RHODA *pushes* MRS. BEELER'S *chair to the foot of the table and stands feeding her, eating her own breakfast meanwhile.*

(MICHAELIS *sits at* MRS. BEELER'S *right,* MARTHA *opposite. At* MR. BEELER'S *right is the Indian boy, at his left* ANNIE'S *vacant chair.* MARTHA *beckons to* ANNIE *to come to the table, but the child, eyeing the strangers, refuses, taking a chair behind her mother by the mantelpiece.* MRS. BEELER *speaks after the meal has progressed for some time in silence.*)

MRS. BEELER. Mat, you have n't said good morning to our guest.

BEELER. (*Gruffly.*) How are you?

(*He helps himself to meat and passes it to the others; the plate goes round the table. There is a constrained silence.* ANNIE *tugs at* RHODA'S *skirt, and asks in dumb show to have her breakfast given her.* RHODA *fills the child's plate, with which she retreats to her place by the mantel.*)

MRS. BEELER. Why does n't Annie come to the table? (*She tries to look around.* RHODA *whispers to* MRS. BEELER, *who looks at her, puzzled.*) *Why* does n't Annie come?

RHODA. She's afraid.

MRS. BEELER. Afraid! What is she afraid of?

RHODA. You know how shy she is, before strangers.

MRS. BEELER. Annie, please come here! Annie!

(*The child refuses, pouting, and gazing at* MICHAELIS.)

RHODA. I would n't urge her. She does n't want to come.

MARTHA. (*Trenchantly.*) Don't blame her!

MRS. BEELER. (*Gently reproving.*) Martha!

MICHAELIS. (*Holding out his hand to* ANNIE.) Won't you come here, my child? (ANNIE *approaches slowly, as if hypnotized.*) You're not afraid of me, are you?

ANNIE. (*Shyly.*) Not if you won't climb up the rope.

MICHAELIS. (*Puzzled.*) Climb up what rope?

RHODA. It's a story I was foolish enough to tell her.—Do eat something, Auntie.

MRS BEELER. I'll drink a little more tea.

(RHODA *raises the cup to* MRS. BEELER'S *lips.*)

BEELER. You can't live on tea, Mary.

MARTHA. I guess she can live on tea better than on some things! (*With a resentful glance at* MICHAELIS.) Some things that some folks seem to live on, and expect other folks to live on.

(MICHAELIS *looks up from* ANNIE, *who has been whispering in his ear.* BEELER *nods at* MARTHA *in covert approval, as she takes up dishes and goes into the kitchen.*)

MRS. BEELER. (*Leans forward across the table to* MICHAELIS.) Don't mind my sister-in-law, Mr. Michaelis. It's her way. She means nothing by it

BEELER. (*Between gulps of coffee, as he finishes his meal.*) Don't know as you've got any call to speak for Martha. She generally means what she says, and I guess she means it now. And what's more, I guess I do, too!

MRS. BEELER. (*Beseechingly.*) Mat!

BEELER. (*Throws down his napkin and rises.*) Very well. It's none of my business, I reckon, as long as it keeps within reason.

(*He puts on his cap and goes out through the kitchen.*)

ANNIE. (*To* MICHAELIS, *continuing the whispered conversation.*) And if you do climb up the rope, do you promise to come down?

MICHAELIS. Yes, I promise to come down.

MRS. BEELER. (*Leans over her plate. The others bow their heads.*) Bless this food to our use, and this day to our strength and our salvation.

RHODA. (*As they lift their heads.*) Perhaps it will be light enough now without the lamp.

(MICHAELIS, *holding* ANNIE'S *hand, rises, goes to the window, and rolls up the shades, while* RHODA *extinguishes the lamp. The fog is still thick, and the light which enters is dull.* RHODA *unpins the napkin from her aunt's breast, and wheels her back from the table. The boy crouches down by the grate, Indian fashion.* ANNIE *looks at him with shy, half-frightened interest.*)

MRS. BEELER. (*Gazing out, from where she sits reclining.*) The blessed sun! I never thought to see it rise again so beautiful.

RHODA. (*Looks at her aunt, puzzled and alarmed.*) But, Auntie, there is n't any sun! It's—

(*She breaks off, seeing* MICHAELIS *place his fingers on his lips as a signal for her to be silent.* MRS. BEELER *turns to* RHODA, *puzzled.*)

MRS. BEELER. There is n't any sun? Why—(RHODA *pretends not to hear.* MRS. BEELER *turns to* MICHAELIS.) What does she mean by saying there is no sun?

MICHAELIS. She means she does n't see it.

MRS. BEELER. (*Still puzzled.*) But—you see it, don't you?

MICHAELIS. I see the same sun that you see.

MRS. BEELER. (*Looks again at* RHODA, *then dismisses her wonderment, and looks out at the window dreamily.*) Another day—and to-morrow the best of all the days of the year.

ANNIE. What day is to-morrow? (*She leaves* MICHAELIS *and comes to her mother's side.*) What day is to-morrow?

MRS. BEELER. (*With exultation in her voice.*) My child, to-morrow is the most wonderful and the most beautiful day of all the year. The day when—all over the whole world—there is singing in the air, and everything rises into new life and happiness.

ANNIE. (*Fretfully.*) Mamma, I don't understand! What day is to-morrow?

MRS. BEELER. To-morrow is Easter.

ANNIE. (*With sudden interest.*) Easter! Can I have some eggs to color?

MRS. BEELER. Ask Aunt Martha.

ANNIE. (*Singsong, as she skips out.*) Eggs to color! Eggs to color!

(RHODA *has meanwhile fetched a large tray from the cupboard and has been piling the dishes noiselessly upon it.*)

RHODA. Shall I wheel you in, Aunt Mary?

MRS. BEELER. Yes, please. (RHODA *wheels the chair toward the hall door, which* MICHAELIS *opens.* MRS. BEELER *gazes at him as she passes.*) Will you come in soon, and sit with me? There is so much that I want to hear.

MICHAELIS. Whenever you are ready.

MRS. BEELER. I will ring my bell.

(*As they go out,* MARTHA *bustles in, gathers up the dish tray and is about to depart, with a vindictive look. At the door she turns, and jerks her head toward the boy.*)

MARTHA. Is it against the law to work where he comes from?

MICHAELIS. (*Abstractedly.*) What?—No.

MARTHA. Then he might as well do me some chores. Not but right, payin' only half board.

MICHAELIS. (*To the boy.*) Do whatever she tells you. (*The boy follows* MARTHA *out.* MICHAELIS *stands by the window in thought. As* RHODA *reënters, he looks up. He speaks significantly, with suppressed excitement.*) She saw the sun!

RHODA. Poor dear Auntie!

MICHAELIS. You pity her?

RHODA. (*After an instant's silence, during which she ponders her reply.*) I think I envy her.

(*She removes the cloth from the table, and begins deftly to put the room in order.* MICHAELIS *watches her with a kind of vague intentness.*)

MICHAELIS. How long did you say she had been sick?

RHODA. More than four years—nearly five.

MICHAELIS. She has never walked in that time?

RHODA. (*Shakes her head.*) Nor used her right hand, either.

MICHAELIS. (*With intensity.*) Are you certain?

RHODA. (*Surprised at his tone.*) Yes—I have n't lived here long, but I am certain.

MICHAELIS. She has tried medicine, doctors?

RHODA. Uncle has spent everything he could earn on them. She has been three times to the mineral baths, once as far as Virginia.

MICHAELIS. But never as far as Bethesda?

RHODA. Bethesda? Where is that?

MICHAELIS. The pool, which is called Bethesda, having five porches.

RHODA. Oh, yes. The pool in the Bible, where once a year an angel troubled the waters, and the sick and the lame and the blind gathered, hoping to be healed.

MICHAELIS. And whoever first, after the troubling of the waters, stepped in, he was made whole of whatsoever disease he had.

RHODA. If anybody could find the way there again, it would be Aunt Mary. (*Pause.*) And if anybody could show her the way it would be—you. (*She goes on in a different tone, as if to escape from the embarrassment of her last speech.*) Her saying just now she saw the sun. She often says things like that. Have you noticed?

MICHAELIS. Yes.

RHODA. (*With hesitation.*) Her brother Seth—the one who died—has she told you about him?

MICHAELIS. Yes.

RHODA. What she thinks happens—since—he died? (MICHAELIS *nods assent.*) And yet in most other ways her mind is perfectly clear.

MICHAELIS. Perhaps in this way it is clearer still.

RHODA. (*Startled.*) You mean—that maybe she really does—*see* her brother?

MICHAELIS. It may be.

RHODA. It would make the world a very

different—a very strange place, if that *were* true.

MICHAELIS. The world *is* a very strange place. (*Pause.*)

RHODA. Tell me a little about your life. That seems to have been very strange.

MICHAELIS. (*Vaguely, as he seats himself by the table.*) I don't know. I can hardly remember what my life was.

RHODA. Why is that?

MICHAELIS. (*Gazing at her.*) Because, since I came into this house, I have seen the vision of another life.

RHODA. (*With hesitation.*) What—other life?

MICHAELIS. Since my boyhood I have been—(*He hesitates.*) I have been a wanderer, almost a fugitive—. And I never knew it, till now—I never knew it till—I looked into your face!

RHODA. (*Avoiding his gaze.*) How should that make you know?

MICHAELIS. (*Leans nearer.*) All my life long I have walked in the light of something to come, some labor, some mission, I have scarcely known what—but I have risen with it and lain down with it, and nothing else has existed for me.—Nothing, until—I lifted my eyes and you stood there. The stars looked down from their places, the earth wheeled on among the stars. Everything was as it had been, and nothing was as it had been; nor ever, ever can it be the same again.

RHODA. (*In a low and agitated voice.*) You must not say these things to me. You are—I am not—. You must not think of me so.

MICHAELIS. I must think of you as I must.

(*Pause.* RHODA *speaks in a lighter tone, as if to relieve the tension of their last words.*)

RHODA. Tell me a little of your boyhood.—What was it like—that place where you lived?

MICHAELIS. (*Becomes absorbed in his own mental pictures as he speaks.*) A great table of stone, rising five hundred feet out of the endless waste of sand. A little adobe house, halfway up the mesa, with the desert far below and the Indian village far above. A few peach trees, and a spring—a sacred spring, which the Indians worshipped in secret. A little chapel, which my father had built with his own hands. He often spent the night there, praying. And there, one night, he died. I found him in the morning, lying as if in quiet prayer before the altar.

RHODA. (*After a moment's hush.*) What did you do after your father died?

MICHAELIS. I went away south, into the mountains, and got work on a sheep range. I was a shepherd for five years.

RHODA. And since then?

MICHAELIS. (*Hesitates.*) Since then I have—wandered about, working here and there to earn enough to live on.

RHODA. I understand well why men take up that life. I should love it myself.

MICHAELIS. I did n't do it because I loved it.

RHODA. Why, then?

MICHAELIS. I was waiting my time.

RHODA. (*In a low tone.*) Your time—for what?

MICHAELIS. To fulfil my life—my real life.

RHODA. Your—real life? (*He sits absorbed in thought without answering.* RHODA *continues, after a long pause.*) There in the mountains, when you were a shepherd—that was not your real life?

MICHAELIS. It was the beginning of it.

RHODA. (*With hesitation.*) Won't you tell me a little about that time?

MICHAELIS. In the fall I would drive the sheep south, through the great basin which sloped down into Mexico, and in the spring back again to the mountains.

RHODA. Were you all alone?

MICHAELIS. There were a few men on the ranges, but they were no more to me than the sheep—not so much.

RHODA. Were n't you dreadfully lonely?

MICHAELIS. No.

RHODA. You had n't even any books to read?

MICHAELIS. (*Takes a book from his coat pocket.*) I had this pocket Bible, that had been my father's. I read that sometimes. But always in a dream, without understanding, without remembering. (*His excitement increases.*) Yet there came a time when whole chapters started up in my mind, as plain as if the printed page were before me, and I understood it all, both the outer meaning and the inner.

RHODA. And you did n't know what made the difference?

MICHAELIS. Yes.

RHODA. What was it?

MICHAELIS. I can't tell you that.

RHODA. Oh, yes!

MICHAELIS. There are no words to tell of it.

RHODA. Yet tell me. I need to know. Believe me, I need to know!

MICHAELIS. (*Slowly, groping for his words.*) It was one morning in the fourth spring. We were back in the mountains again. It was lambing time, and I had been up all night. Just before sunrise, I sat down on a rock to rest. Then—it came.

RHODA. What came? (*He does not answer.*) You saw something? (*He nods for yes.*) What was it?

MICHAELIS. (*Rises, lifting his arms, a prey to uncontrollable excitement.*) The living Christ!—Standing before me on the mountain, amid the grazing sheep.—With these eyes and in this flesh, I saw Him. (*Long pause.*)

RHODA. (*In a low tone.*) You had fallen asleep. It was a dream.

MICHAELIS. (*Shakes his head in negation.*) That was n't all.

(*He turns away. She follows him, and speaks after a silence.*)

RHODA. Tell me the rest. What happened to you, after—after what you saw—that morning in the mountains?

MICHAELIS. (*Begins to talk slowly and reluctantly.*) I lived straight ahead, with the sheep for two years.

RHODA. (*Hesitating.*) Did you ever *see* anything again?

MICHAELIS. No.—But twice—I heard a voice.

RHODA. What kind of a voice?

MICHAELIS. The first time it came at night. I was walking on the top of the mountain, in a stony place. It—it was like a wind among the stones.

RHODA. What did it say?

MICHAELIS. It said, "Prepare! Prepare!"

RHODA. And the second time?

MICHAELIS. In the same place, at dawn. The voice said, "Go forth, it is finished!" I looked round me and saw nothing. Then it came again, like a wind among the stones, "Go forth, it is begun!"

RHODA. And you obeyed?

MICHAELIS. I found a man to take my place, and started north. Three days after, I climbed the mesa toward my old home. Above, in the pueblo, I heard the sound of tom-toms and wailing squaws. They told me that the young son of the chief lay dead in my father's chapel. I sat beside him all day and all night. Just before daylight—

(*He breaks off abruptly.*)

RHODA. Go on!

MICHAELIS. Just before daylight, when the other watchers were asleep, the power of the spirit came strong upon me. I bowed myself upon the boy's body, and prayed. My heart burned within me, for I felt his heart begin to beat! His eyes opened. I told him to arise, and he arose. He that was dead arose and was alive again!

(*Pause.* MRS. BEELER'S *bell rings.* MICHAELIS *starts, looks about him as if awakened from a dream, then slowly goes toward the hall door.* RHODA *follows and detains him.*)

RHODA. (*In a low tone.*) How long had he lain—for dead?

MICHAELIS. Three days.

RHODA. (*With hesitation.*) I have heard that people have lain as long as that in a trance, breathing so lightly that it could not be told, except by holding a glass before the face.

MICHAELIS. (*Startled.*) Is that true?

RHODA. I have read so.

MICHAELIS. I wonder—I wonder. (*He stands in deep thought.*) But I have had other signs.

RHODA. What other signs?

MICHAELIS. Many, many. Up and down the land! (*Pause.*) I wonder.—I—I almost wish it were so!

(*With bent head he goes out.* RHODA *stands looking after him until the inner door closes, then sits before the fire in revery.* BEELER *comes in from the barn. He wears his old fur cap, and holds in one hand a bulky Sunday newspaper, in the other some battered harness, an awl, twine, and wax, which he deposits on the window seat. He lays the paper on the table, and unfolds from it a large colored print, which he holds up and looks at with relish.*)

BEELER. These Sunday papers do get up fine supplements. I would n't take money for that picture.

RHODA. (*Looks at it absently.*) What does it mean?

BEELER. (*Reads.*) "Pan and the Pilgrim." Guess you never heard of Pan, did you?

RHODA. Yes. One of the old heathen gods.

BEELER. Call him heathen if you like! The folks that worshipped him thought he was orthodox, I guess.

(*He pins up the print, which repre-*

sents a palmer of crusading times surprised in the midst of a forest by the god Pan.)

RHODA. What does the picture mean?

BEELER. Well, Pan there, he was a kind of a nature god. The old Romans thought him out, to stand for a lot of things.

RHODA. What kind of things?

BEELER. Natural things, with plenty of sap and mischief in 'em. Growin' plants, and frisky animals, and young folks in love. (*He points to the figure of Pan, then to the Pilgrim, as he talks.*) There he sits playin' Jenny-come-kiss-me on his dod-gasted mouth-organ, when along comes one of them fellows out of a monastery, with religion on the brain. Pikin' for Jerusalem, to get a saint's toe-nail and a splinter of the true cross. (MARTHA *enters from the kitchen and potters about the room "redding up."*) Look at him! Do you think he 'll ever get to Jerusalem? Not this trip! He hears the pipes o' Pan. He hears women callin' and fiddles squeakin' love-tunes in the woods. It 'll take more than a monk's robe on his back and a shaved head on his shoulders to keep him straight, I reckon. He 'll call to mind that young fellows had blood in their veins when Adam was a farmer, and whoop-la! he 'll be off to the county fair, to dance ring-around-a-rosy with Matildy Jane! (*Pause, as he takes off his cap and lights his pipe.*) Like to see our friend Michaelis meet up with Mr. Pan. Don't believe Michaelis ever looked cross-eyed at a girl. (*He examines* RHODA *quizzically.*) You would n't make up bad as Matildy Jane yourself, Rho, but sufferin' Job, he can't tell the difference between crow's feet and dimples!

MARTHA. Don't you be so sure!

BEELER. Hello! Dan'el come to judgment! Never seen an old maid yet that could n't squeeze a love story out of a flat-iron.

MARTHA. I may be an old maid, and you may be an old wind-bag, but I've got eyes in my head. (*To* RHODA.) Where did you meet up with him, anyway?

(RHODA, *plunged in thought, does not answer.*)

BEELER. Wake up, Rhody! Marthy asked you where you met up with our new boarder.

RHODA. On the road, coming home from the village.

BEELER. What made you bring him here?

RHODA. He wanted a quiet place to stay, and this was the best I knew.

MARTHA. Guess it was!—A snap for him. (*She goes out by the hall door.*)

(RHODA *rises, takes the lamp off the mantel, and during the following cleans and refills it.*)

BEELER. (*As he takes off his coat, and hangs it up.*) Rhody, ain't this religious business rather a new thing with you? Up there in St. Louis, did n't go in for it much up there, did you?

RHODA. (*Looks at him quickly.*) Why do you ask that?

BEELER. Oh, I gathered, from things I heard, that you cared more about dancin' than about prayin', up there. (*She turns away.*) That young fellow that was so sweet on you in St. Louis year before last, he wa' n't much in the psalm-singin' line, was he?

RHODA. (*Startled and pale.*) Who told you about him?

BEELER. Oh, Mary's friends, the Higginses, used to write us about your affairs. We thought it would be a hitch-up, sure as shootin'. Studyin' to be a doctor, was n't he?

RHODA. Uncle, please never speak to me about him again!

BEELER. All right, all right, my girl. I've been young myself, and I know youth is touchy as a gum-boil when it comes to love affairs. So it 's all off, is it?

RHODA. Yes.

BEELER. (*Sits down to mend the harness.*) If you 're partial to the pill trade, we 've got a brand new doctor in town now. Took old Doctor Martin's place. He 'll be up here to see Mary in a day or two, and you can look him over.

RHODA. What is his name?

BEELER. (*Tries in vain to recall it.*) Blamed if I can remember. Only seen him once. But I tell you, he 's smart as tacks. Chuck full of Jamaica ginger. The very kind I 'd have swore you 'd take to, a while back, before you lost your fun and your spirit. When I first saw you on your father's farm out in Kansas, you was as wild a little gypsy as I ever set eyes on. I said then to your dad, "There 's a filly that 'll need a good breakin'." I never thought I 'd see you takin' up with these Gospel pedlers.

(MARTHA *comes in from the hall and fusses about, dusting, etc. She points in the direction of* MRS. BEELER'S *room.*)

MARTHA. They 're prayer-meetin' it again. And Mary lyin' there as if she saw the pearly gates openin' before her eyes.

BEELER. (*Half to himself as he works.*) Poor Mary!—Mary 's a strange woman.

MARTHA. (*To* RHODA.) Your mother was the same way, Rhody. The whole Beardsley tribe for that matter. But Mary was the worst. It begun with Mary as soon as her brother Seth got drowned.

BEELER. (*Looks up, angry.*) None of that, Sis!

MARTHA. I guess my tongue 's my own.

BEELER. No, it ain't. I won't have any more of that talk around me, do you hear? I put my foot down a year ago.

MARTHA. (*Points to his foot derisively.*) It 's big enough and ugly enough, Heaven knows, but you can put it down as hard as you like, it won't keep a man's sperrit in his grave—not when he 's a mind to come out!

BEELER. (*Astonished.*) Martha Beeler!

MARTHA. That 's my name.

(*She flounces out into the kitchen, covering her retreat with her last speech.*)

BEELER. (*Looking after her.*) My kingdom! Martha! I thought she had some horse sense left.

RHODA. (*Slowly, as she finishes with the lamp.*) Uncle, it 's hard to live side by side with Aunt Mary and not—

BEELER. (*In angry challenge.*) And not what?

RHODA. And not believe there 's something more in these matters than "horse sense" will account for.

BEELER. (*Hotly, as if a sore point has been touched upon.*) There 's nothing more than science will account for. (*He points to a shelf of books.*) You can read it up any day you like. Read that book yonder, chapter called Hallucinations. Pathological, that 's what it is, pathological.

RHODA. What does that mean? (BEELER *taps his forehead significantly.*) Uncle, you know that 's not true!

BEELER. (*Growls to himself.*) Pathological, up and down.

(RHODA *replaces the lamp on the mantel.* MARTHA *opens the kitchen door and calls in.*)

MARTHA. Here 's Uncle Abe!

BEELER. Uncle Abe? Thought he was a goner.

(UNCLE ABE *enters. He is an old negro, with gray hair and thin, gray beard. He is somewhat bowed, and carries a stick, but he is not decrepit. His clothes are spattered with mud.* MARTHA *enters with him; she is stirring something in a bowl, and during the following continues to do so, though more and more interruptedly and absent-mindedly.*)

BEELER. Hello, Uncle Abe.

UNCLE ABE. Good-mawnin', Mista Beeler.

BEELER. Where 've you been all winter? Thought you 'd gone up Salt River.

UNCLE ABE. (*Shakes his head reassuringly.*) Ain' nevah goin' up no Salt River, yo' Uncle Abe ain't.

BEELER. (*Indicating* RHODA.) Make you acquainted with my wife's niece, Miss Williams.

(UNCLE ABE *bows.*)

RHODA. (*Pushing forward a chair.*) Sit down, Uncle. I don't see how you found your way in this dreadful fog.

UNCLE ABE. Fawg don' matta' nothin' to me, honey. Don' mean nothin' 'tall. (*He speaks with exaltation and restrained excitement.*) Yo' ol' Uncle keeps on tellin' 'em, dis hyah fawg an' darkness don' mean nothin' 'tall!

(RHODA *and* MARTHA *look at him puzzled.* BEELER, *busy over his harness, has not been struck by the old negro's words.*)

BEELER. How 's the ginseng crop this year?

UNCLE ABE. They ain' no mo' gimsing!

BEELER. No more ginseng? What do you mean?

UNCLE ABE. De good Lawd, he ain' goin' fool roun' no mo' wif no gimsing!

BEELER. (*Amused.*) Why, I thought your ginseng bitters was His main holt.

UNCLE ABE. (*With a touch of regret.*) Use to be, Mars' Beeler. It shore use to be.—Yes, sah. Bless de Lawd! (*Shakes his head in reminiscence.*) He sartinly did set sto' by them thah bitters.

BEELER. (*With lazy amusement.*) So the Lord 's gone back on ginseng now, has He?

UNCLE ABE. Yes, sah.

BEELER. What makes you think so?

UNCLE ABE. (*Solemnly.*) Roots all kill by de fros'! (*His manner grows more and more mysterious; he half closes his eyes, as he goes on in a strange, mounting singsong.*) Knowed it more'n a monf ago, fo' dis hyah blin' worl' lef' de plough in de ploughshare an' de ungroun' wheat betwixen de millstones, and went a-follerin' aftah dis hyah new star outen de Eas', like a bride follerin' aftah de bridegroom!

(MARTHA *taps her forehead significantly, and goes back to her batter.*)

BEELER. New star, Uncle? Tell us about it. Sounds interesting.

UNCLE ABE. (*Stares at each of them in turn.*) Ain' you-all heerd?

BEELER. You've got the advantage of us.

UNCLE ABE. Ain' you-all heerd 'bout de Healer?

BEELER. Healer? What kind of a healer?

UNCLE ABE. (*With mounting indignation at* BEELER'S *tone.*) De Bible kin', dat 's what kin'! De kin' what makes de lame fer to walk, and de blin' fer to see, an' de daid fer to riz up outen their daid col' graves. That 's what kin'! Mean to say you-all ain' heerd nothin' 'bout him, you po' chillun o' dawkness?

(MARTHA *and* BEELER *look at each other in amazement.* RHODA *sits looking at the old negro, white and tense with excitement.*)

BEELER. Nope. (*Recollecting.*) Hold on!

MARTHA. (*To* BEELER.) Don't you remember, in the papers, two or three weeks ago? Where was it? Somewheres out West.

BEELER. Believe I did read some such goin's-on. Don't pay much attention to such nonsense.

UNCLE ABE. (*Solemn and threatening.*) Tek keer, Mistah Beeler! Tek keer what you say 'fore dese here cloudy witnesses. Don' you go cuttin' yo'self off from de Kingdom. Nor you, Mis' Martha, nor you, honey. Don' ye do it! It 's a-comin'. Yo' ol' Uncle Abe he 's seen and heerd.

RHODA. Tell us quickly what you mean!

UNCLE ABE. Mean jes' what I says, honey. Night fo' last, de Healer, he come, like 's if he jes' plum' drop from de sky. (*More mysteriously.*) An' whar 's he gone to? You listen to yo' ol' Uncle Abe a-tellin' you. He ain' gone nowhars! He 's jes' meechin' roun' in de fawg, a-waitin' fer de Lawd to call folks. En He 's a-callin' 'em! He 's a-callin' 'em by tens an' by hundreds. Town 's full a'ready, honey. Main Street look jes' lak a fiel' hospital, down Souf durin' de wah!

MARTHA. (*Meeting* BEELER'S *astonished look.*) What did I tell you? Maybe you 'll listen to *me* next time.

RHODA. (*To* UNCLE ABE, *in a low, agitated voice.*) This man you call the Healer—is he alone?

UNCLE ABE. No, honey; folks says he don' nevah go nowheres by hisse'f. Always got that thah young man wif 'im what he raise from de daid.

BEELER. (*Rises, with a shrug.*) Good evening! (*He crosses to the portraits of Darwin and Spencer.*) You made quite a stir in your time, did n't you? Well, it 's all up with you!

MARTHA. (*In a voice strident with nervousness.*) Raised from the dead?

UNCLE ABE. That 's what they says, Mis' Martha. Folks calls 'im Laz'rus in ref'ence to de Bible chil' what riz up jes' same way lak', outen de daid col' tomb.

(*The Indian boy enters from the kitchen, his shoes and trousers spattered with mud.* UNCLE ABE *looks at him, then at the others, and whispers to* RHODA. MARTHA *bustles forward, hiding her agitation in scolding speech.*)

MARTHA. Well, did you get my coffee and my sal-soda?

(LAZARUS *points, without speaking, to the kitchen.*)

BEELER. (*To* MARTHA.) Did you send him to the store?

MARTHA. Yes, I did send him to the store. If I had my way, I 'd send him—further.

(*The boy hesitates, then goes stolidly out by the stair door.* UNCLE ABE *lifts his arm ecstatically.*)

UNCLE ABE. That 's him! I tell ye that 's the chil' what 's said "Howdy" to the daid folks down yonder. I 'se seen 'im in my dreams, an' now I 'se seen 'im wif dese hyah two eyes.—O Lawd, bless dis hyah house o' grace!

BEELER. I guess it 's about time that fellow come out and exploded some of this tomfoolery.

(*He starts towards his wife's room.*)

RHODA. (*Stopping him.*) Please don't.

BEELER. (*Peevishly.*) There 's got to be an end to this hoodoo business in my house.

(ANNIE *enters from the kitchen, dabbled with dye. She holds two colored eggs in her hands.*)

ANNIE. Look! I 've colored two.

MARTHA. Good gracious, child. What a mess!

ANNIE. Pa! Play crack with me! Just once, to see how it goes.

BEELER. Go in and ask your mother if she'll let you.

(ANNIE, *her eggs in her apron, opens the hall door. About to pass out, she stops, drops the eggs with a scream, and runs back, gazing towards the hall as she takes refuge behind* RHODA'S *skirts.*)

ANNIE. Pa! Auntie! Ma's walking!

(MRS. BEELER *enters, walking uncertainly, her face full of intense exaltation.* MICHAELIS *comes just behind her, transfigured by spiritual excitement.*)

BEELER AND MARTHA. (*Starting forward.*) Mary!

RHODA. Aunt Mary!

(MRS. BEELER *advances into the room, reaching out her hand to* ANNIE, *who takes it in speechless fright. She bends over and kisses the child's head, then stretches out her other hand to her husband.*)

MRS. BEELER. Mat, I'm cured! The Lord has heard our prayers, for His saint's sake.

BEELER. Why, Mary, I can't believe this—it's too—it's not possible!

MRS. BEELER. (*Looking at* MICHAELIS.) It is written that he who has faith, even as a grain of mustard seed—. I have had faith.

MARTHA. Law, you've had faith enough any time these five years, Mary. There was something else wanting, 'pears to me.

MRS. BEELER. There was wanting the word of true belief, saying, "Suffer no more! Stoop and drink of the waters of mercy and healing."

(*Outside, the shrill soprano of a woman is heard, taking up a hymn. At the sound* MICHAELIS *goes to the window. He stands rigid, listening to the hymn to the end of the verse, when other voices join in the chorus. The fog has partially cleared.*

MICHAELIS. (*Turning slowly to* RHODA.) Who are they?

RHODA. Sick people.

MICHAELIS. How did they find out I was here?

RHODA. It was known you were somewhere near.—They have been gathering for days.—They saw the boy, just now, in the village.

MRS. BEELER. (*Comes a step or two nearer* MICHAELIS.) Your great hour is at hand!

(*He looks distractedly about. The light has faded from his face, giving place to strong nervous agitation, resembling fear. He speaks as if to himself.*)

MICHAELIS. My hour!—My hour!—And I—and I—!

(*He puts his hand over his eyes, as if to shut out some vision of dread.*)

MRS. BEELER. You will not fail them? You cannot fail them now.

(MICHAELIS *looks at* MRS. BEELER, *then for a long time at* RHODA. *He gathers himself together, and gazes steadfastly before him, as at some unseen presence.*)

MICHAELIS. No.—I have waited so long. I have had such deep assurances.—I must not fail. I must not fail.

ACT SECOND.

It is late afternoon of the same day. MRS. BEELER *sits in a low chair near the window. She has ceased reading the Testament, which lies open in her lap.* UNCLE ABE *sits on the floor with* ANNIE. *They are playing with building blocks, piling up and tearing down various ambitious structures.*

(RHODA *enters from outside, with hat and cloak, carrying a large bunch of Easter lilies.*)

RHODA. (*Kissing her aunt.*) Still sitting up! You're not strong enough yet to do this. See, I've brought you some Easter lilies. (*She hands one to* MRS. BEELER. *As she takes off her things, she sees the old negro gazing at her.*) Well, Uncle Abe?

UNCLE ABE. I's awake an' a-watchin', honey!

(*He turns again to the child, shaking his head as at some unspoken thought, while* RHODA *arranges the flowers in a vase.*)

MRS. BEELER. Rhoda!

RHODA. Yes, Aunt Mary?

MRS. BEELER. Come here. (RHODA *approaches.* MRS. BEELER *speaks low, with suppressed excitement.*) What is the news, outside?

RHODA. You must n't excite yourself. You must keep your strength.

MRS. BEELER. I shall be strong enough.—

Are the people still gathering from the town?

RHODA. Yes, and they keep coming in from other places.

MRS. BEELER. Are there many of them?

RHODA. Many! Many! It 's as if the whole world knew.

MRS. BEELER. The more there are, the greater will be the witness.—(*Pause.*) When do you think he will go out to them?

RHODA. They believe he is waiting for Easter morning.

(MARTHA *enters from kitchen, with bonnet and shawl on, and a large basket in her hand.*)

MARTHA. Mary, you 'd ought to be abed. You're tempting Providence. (*She takes off her bonnet and shawl, and deposits the basket.*) I saw your doctor down in the village, and he allowed he 'd come up to see you this afternoon. He was all on end about your bein' able to walk.

RHODA. I did n't know till to-day you had a doctor.

MRS. BEELER. Yes. He 's a young man who 's just come here to build up a practice.

MARTHA. (*To* RHODA.) You better finish packin' the basket. There 's a lot o' hungry mouths to feed out yonder.

(*Exit by hall door.* RHODA *continues the preparation of the basket, taking articles from the cupboard and packing them.* ANNIE *has climbed on a chair by the picture of Pan and the Pilgrim. She points at the figure of Pan.*)

ANNIE. Uncle Abe, tell me who that is.

UNCLE ABE. (*Glancing at* MRS. BEELER *and* RHODA.) H'sh!

ANNIE. What 's he doing up there in the bushes, blowing on that funny whistle?

UNCLE ABE. Look hyah, chil', you jus' wastin' my time. I got frough wif dis hyah fool pictuh long 'go!

(*He tries to draw her away; she resists.*)

ANNIE. (*Petulantly.*) Uncle Abe! Who is it?

UNCLE ABE. (*Whispers, makes big eyes.*) That thah 's Ole Nick, that 's who that thah is! That thah 's de Black Man!

(ANNIE, *terror-stricken, jumps down and retreats to her mother's chair.* MRS. BEELER *rouses from her revery and strokes her child's head.*)

MRS. BEELER. Oh, my child, how happy you are to see this while you are so young! You will never forget, will you, dear?

ANNIE. (*Fidgeting.*) Forget what?

MRS. BEELER. Tell me that whatever happens to you in the world, you won't forget that once, when you were a little girl, you saw the heavens standing open, and felt that God was very near, and full of pity for His children.

ANNIE. I don't know what you 're talking about! I can't hardly breathe the way people are in this house.

MRS BEELER. You will understand, some day, what wonderful things your childish eyes looked on.

(ANNIE *retreats to* UNCLE ABE, *who bends over the child and whispers in her ear. She grows amused, and begins to sway as to a tune, then chants.*

ANNIE.

"Mary an' a' Martha 's jus' gone along,
Mary an' a' Martha 's jus' gone along,
Mary an' a' Martha 's jus' gone along,
Ring dem charmin' bells."

(*As she finishes the rhyme she runs out into the hall.* MRS. BEELER *begins again to read her Testament. The old negro approaches* MRS. BEELER *and* RHODA, *and speaks mysteriously.*)

UNCLE ABE. That thah chil' she 's talkin' sense. They 's sumpin' ain't right about dis hyah house.

MRS. BEELER. Not right? What do you mean?

UNCLE ABE. (*Shakes his head dubiously.*) Dunno, Mis' Beeler. I 's jes' a ole fool colored pusson, been waitin' fer de great day what de 'Postle done promise. En hyah 's de great day 'bout to dawn, an' de Lawd's Chosen 'bout to show Hisse'f in clouds o' glory 'fore de worl', an' lo 'n' behol'—(*He leans closer and whispers.*) de Lawd's Chosen One, he 's done got a spell on 'im!

MRS. BEELER. (*Shocked and startled.*) Uncle Abe!

UNCLE ABE. (*Pointing at the Pan and the Pilgrim.*) Why do you keep that thah pictuh nail up thah fur?

MRS. BEELER. My husband likes it.

UNCLE ABE. Mighty funny kin' o' man, like to hev de Black Man lookin' pop-eyed at folks all day an' all night, puttin' de spell on folks!

MRS. BEELER. That 's not the Black Man.

UNCLE ABE. That 's him, shore 's yo' born! Jes' what he looks like. I seen 'im, more 'n once.

RHODA. Seen the Black Man, Uncle?

UNCLE ABE. Yais, ma'am. I 's spied 'im, sittin' in de paw-paw bushes in de springtime, when de snakes a-runnin', an' de jays a-hollerin', an de crick a-talkin' sassy to hisse'f. (*He leans nearer, more mysteriously.*) En what you s'pose I heerd him whis'lin', for all de worl' lak dem scan'lous bluejays? (*Chants in a high, trilling voice.*) "Chillun, chillun, they ain' no Gawd, they ain' no sin nor no jedgment, they 's jes' springtime an' happy days, and folks carryin' on. Whar 's yo' lil gal, Abe Johnson? Whar 's yo' lil sweet-heart gal?" An' me on'y got religion wintah befo', peekin' roun' pie-eyed, skeered good. En fo' you could say "De Lawd 's my Shepherd," kerchunk goes de Black Man in de mud-puddle, change' into a big green bull-frog!

MRS. BEELER. You just imagined all that.

UNCLE ABE. (*Indignant.*) Jes' 'magine! Don' I know de Devil when I sees him, near 'nough to say "Howdy"?

MRS. BEELER. There is n't any Devil.

UNCLE ABE. (*Astounded.*) Ain't no Devil?

MRS. BEELER. No.

(UNCLE ABE *goes, with puzzled head-shakings, towards the kitchen door. He stops to smell the Easter lilies, then raises his head and looks at her again, with puzzled scrutiny.*)

UNCLE ABE. Mis' Beelah, did I understan' you to say—they ain'—no Devil?

MRS. BEELER. (*Touching her breast.*) Only here, Uncle Abe. (*The old negro stares at her and* RHODA, *and goes into the kitchen, feeling his own breast and shaking his head dubiously.* MRS. BEELER *looks at the picture.*) Do you think your Uncle Mat would mind if we took that picture down? (RHODA *unpins the picture from the wall, rolls it up, and lays it on the bookshelf. Her aunt goes on, hesitatingly.*) Do you know, Rhoda, I have sometimes thought—You won't be hurt?

RHODA. No.

MRS. BEELER. I—I know what that old negro says is all foolishness, but—there *is* something the matter with Mr. Michaelis. Have you noticed?

RHODA. (*Avoiding her aunt's gaze.*) Yes.

MRS. BEELER. Just when his great work is about to begin!—What do you think it can be?

RHODA. How should I know, Aunt Mary?

MRS. BEELER. I thought maybe—Rhoda, I have seen him look at you so strangely! Like—like the Pilgrim in the picture, when he hears that heathen creature playing on the pipe.—You are such a wild creature, or you used to be.

(RHODA *comes to her aunt and stands a moment in silence.*)

RHODA. Auntie.

MRS. BEELER. Yes?

RHODA. I think I ought to go away.

MRS. BEELER. (*Astonished.*) Go away? Why?

RHODA. So as not to—hinder him.

MRS. BEELER. (*Caressing her.*) There, you have taken what I said too seriously. It was only a sick woman's imagination.

RHODA. No, it was the truth. You see it, though you try not to. Even Uncle Abe sees it. Just when Mr. Michaelis most needs his strength, weakness has come upon him.

MRS. BEELER. You mean—? (*She hesitates.*) You mean—because of you?—Rhoda, look at me. (RHODA *avoids her aunt's gaze;* MRS. BEELER *draws down the girl's face and gazes at it.*) Is there anything—that I don't know—between you and him?

RHODA. I—I must go away.—I ought to have gone before.

MRS. BEELER. My child, this—this troubles me very much. He is different from other men, and you—and you—

RHODA. (*With passion.*) Say it, say it! What am I?

MRS. BEELER. Don't be hurt, Rhoda, but—you have a wild nature. You are like your father. I remember when he used to drive over to see sister Jane, with his keen face and eagle eyes, behind his span of wild colts, I used to tremble for my gentle sister. You are just like him, or you used to be. (RHODA *breaks away from her aunt, and takes her hat and cloak.* MRS. BEELER *rises with perturbation, and crosses to detain her.*) What are you going to do?

RHODA. I am going away—I *must* go away.

(MARTHA *enters from the hall.*)

MRS. BEELER. (*Speaks lower.*) Promise me you won't! Promise me!

MARTHA. To look at that, now! Seein'

you on your feet, Mary, gives me a new start every time.

MRS. BEELER. (*To* RHODA.) You promise?

(RHODA *bows her head as in assent.*)

MARTHA. Doctor's in the parlor. Shall I bring him in here?

MRS. BEELER. No. I think I will rest awhile. He can come to my room. (*She walks unsteadily. The others try to help her, but she motions them back.*) No. It's so good to feel that I can walk alone!

MARTHA. It does beat all!

MRS. BEELER. I'll just lie down on the couch. I want to go out, before dark, and speak to the people.

(MR. BEELER *enters from the kitchen and crosses to help his wife. The others give place to him.*)

Oh, Mat, our good days are coming back! I shall be strong and well for you again.

BEELER. Yes, Mary. There will be nothing to separate us any more.

MRS. BEELER. (*Points at his books.*) Not even—them? (*He goes to the alcove, takes the books from the shelf, raises the lid of the window-seat, and throws them in.* MRS. BEELER *points to the pictures of Darwin and Spencer.*) Nor them? (*He unpins the pictures, lays them upon the heap of books, and returns to her.*) You don't know how happy that makes me!

(*They go out by the hall door.* MARTHA, *as she lowers the lid of the window-seat, points derisively at the heap.*)

MARTHA. That's a good riddance of bad rubbish! (*She comes to the table and continues packing the basket.*) You'd better help me with this basket. Them folks will starve to death, if the neighborhood round don't give 'em a bite to eat. (RHODA *fetches other articles from the cupboard.*) I'd like to know what they think we are made of, with butter at twenty-five cents a pound and flour worth its weight in diamonds!

RHODA. All the neighbors are helping, and none of them with our cause for thankfulness.

MARTHA. That's no sign you should go plasterin' on that butter like you was a bricklayer tryin' to bust the contractor!

(*She takes the bread from* RHODA *and scrapes the butter thin.*)

RHODA. (*As the clock strikes five.*) It's time for Aunt Mary to have her tea. Shall I make it?

MARTHA. You make it! Not unless you want to lay her flat on her back again!

(*As she flounces out,* ANNIE *enters from the hall. She points with one hand at the retreating Martha, with the other toward her mother's room.*)

ANNIE. (*Sings with sly emphasis.*)

"Mary an' a' Martha 's jus' gone along,
Mary an' a' Martha 's jus' gone along,
Mary an' a' Martha 's jus' gone along,
Ring dem charmin' bells."

(*She climbs upon a chair by the table, and fingers the contents of basket as she sings.*)

RHODA. What's got into you, little imp?

ANNIE. (*Brazenly.*) I've been peeping through mamma's keyhole.

RHODA. That's not nice.

ANNIE. I know it, but the minister's in there and Dr. Littlefield.

RHODA. (*Startled.*) Who?

ANNIE. You know, mamma's doctor.—Oh, he's never come since you've been here.

RHODA. (*In a changed voice, as she takes the child by the shoulders.*) What does he look like?

ANNIE. Don't, you're hurting me!—He's too red in the face, and looks kind of—insulting—and he wears the most *beautiful* neckties, and— (*Exhausted by her efforts at description.*) Oh, I don't know! (*She sings as she climbs down, and goes out by the kitchen door.*)

"Free grace, undyin' love,
Free grace, undyin' love,
Free grace, undyin' love,
Ring dem lovely bells."

(DR. LITTLEFIELD *enters from* MRS. BEELER'S *room. He speaks back to* BEELER *on the threshold.*)

LITTLEFIELD. Don't bother! I'll find it. (*Looking for something, he approaches* RHODA, *who has her back turned.*) Beg pardon. Have you seen a pocket thermometer I left here? (*She faces him. He starts back in surprise.*) Bless my soul and body! Rhoda Williams! (*He closes the hall door, returns to her, and stands somewhat disconcerted.*) Here of all places!

RHODA. Mrs. Beeler is my aunt.

LITTLEFIELD. Well, well! The world is small.—Been here long?

RHODA. Only a month.

LITTLEFIELD. And before that?

RHODA. It 's a long story. Besides, you would n't understand.

LITTLEFIELD. You might let me try. What in the world have you been doing all this time?

RHODA. I have been searching for something.

LITTLEFIELD. What was it?

RHODA. My own lost self. My own—lost soul.

LITTLEFIELD. (*Amused at her solemnity.*) You 're a queer bundle of goods. Always were. Head full of solemn notions about life, and at the same time, when it came to a lark,—Oh, I 'm no grandmother, but when you got on your high horse—well!

(*He waves his hands expressively.*)

RHODA. (*Bursts out.*) The great town, the people, the noise, and the lights—after seventeen years of life on a dead prairie, where I 'd hardly heard a laugh or seen a happy face!—All the same, the prairie had me still.

LITTLEFIELD. You don't mean you went back to the farm?

RHODA. I mean that the years I 'd spent out there in that endless stretch of earth and sky—. (*She breaks off, with a weary gesture.*) There 's no use going into that. You would n't understand.

LITTLEFIELD. No, I walk on simple shoe leather and eat mere victuals.—Just the same, it was n't square of you to clear out that way—vanish into air without a word or a sign.

RHODA. (*Looking at him steadily.*) You know very well why I went.

LITTLEFIELD. (*Returning her gaze, unabashed, chants with meaning and relish.*)

"Hey diddle, diddle,
The cat and the fiddle,
The cow jumped over the moon."

(RHODA *takes up the basket and goes toward the outer door. He intercepts her.*)

RHODA. Let me pass.

LITTLEFIELD. You 're not taking part in this camp-meeting enthusiasm, are you?

RHODA. Yes.

(*As he stares at her, his astonishment changes to amusement; he chuckles to himself, then bursts out laughing, as in humorous reminiscence.*)

LITTLEFIELD. Bless my soul! And to think that only a couple of little years ago—Oh, *bless* my soul!

(*The stair door opens.* MICHAELIS *appears. His face is flushed, his hair disordered, and his whole person expresses a feverish and precarious exaltation.*)

MICHAELIS. (*Looks at* LITTLEFIELD *with vague query, then at* RHODA.) Excuse me, I am very thirsty. I came down for a glass of water.

(RHODA *goes to the kitchen door, where she turns. The doctor puts on a pair of nose-glasses and scans* MICHAELIS *with interest. He holds out his hand, which* MICHAELIS *takes.*)

LITTLEFIELD. We ought to know each other. We 're colleagues, in a way.

MICHAELIS. Colleagues?

LITTLEFIELD. In a way, yes. I 'm a practising physician. (*Exit* RHODA.) You seem to have the call on us professionals, to judge by the number of your clients out yonder. (*He points out of the window.*) To say nothing of Exhibit One!

(*He points to the hall door.*)

MICHAELIS. (*Vaguely.*) I—I don't know that I— (RHODA *enters from the kitchen, with water, which he takes.*) Thank you.

(*He drinks thirstily.* MR. BEELER *appears in the hall door; he looks at the group, taken aback.*)

BEELER. Oh—!

LITTLEFIELD. I stopped to chat with your niece. She and I happen to be old acquaintances.

BEELER. You don't say?—Would you mind coming in here for a minute?

LITTLEFIELD. (*Following him out.*) What 's up?

BEELER. My wife 's got it in her head that she 's called upon to—

(*Door closes.* MICHAELIS, *who has followed* LITTLEFIELD *with his eyes, sets down the glass, and turns slowly to* RHODA.)

MICHAELIS. Who is that?

RHODA. My aunt's doctor.

MICHAELIS. You know him well?

RHODA. Yes.—No.

MICHAELIS. What does that mean?

RHODA. I have n't seen him for nearly two years.—I can't remember much about the person I was, two years ago.

MICHAELIS. Yes! Yes! I understand. (*He turns away, lifting his hands, speak-

ing half to himself.) That these lives of ours should be poured like a jelly, from one mould into another, until God Himself cannot remember what they were two years ago, or two hours ago!

RHODA. Why do you say that? (*He does not answer, but walks nervously about.* RHODA, *watching him, speaks, after a silence.*) Last month—out West—were there many people there?

MICHAELIS. No.—Two or three.

RHODA. The papers said—

MICHAELIS. When the crowd began to gather, I—went away.

RHODA. Why?

MICHAELIS. My time had not come.

(*He has stopped before the map and stands gazing at it.*)

RHODA. Has it come now? (*She comes closer.*) —Has your time come now?

MICHAELIS. Yes.

RHODA. How do you know?

MICHAELIS. (*Points at the map.*) It is written there!

RHODA. How do you mean, written there?

MICHAELIS. Can't you see it?

RHODA. I see the map, nothing more.

MICHAELIS. (*Points again, gazing fixedly.*) It seems to me to be written in fire.

RHODA. What seems written?

MICHAELIS. What I have been doing, all these five years.

RHODA. Since your work began?

MICHAELIS. It has never begun. Many times I have thought, "Now," and some man or woman has risen up healed, and looked at me with eyes of prophecy. But a Voice would cry, "On, on!" and I would go forward, driven by a force and a will not my own.—I did n't know what it all meant, but I know now. (*He points at the map, his manner transformed with excitement and exaltation.*) It is written there. It is written in letters of fire. My eyes are opened, and I see!

RHODA. (*Following his gaze, then looking at him again, awed and bewildered.*) What is it that you see?

MICHAELIS. The cross!

RHODA. I—I don't understand.

MICHAELIS. All those places where the hand was lifted for a moment, and the power flowed into me— (*He places his finger at various points on the map; these points lie in two transverse lines, between the Mississippi and the Pacific; one line runs roughly north and south, the other east and west.*) Look! There was such a place, and there another, and there, and there. And there was one, and there, and there.—Do you see?

RHODA. I see.—It makes a kind of cross

MICHAELIS. You see it, too! And do you see what it means—this sign that my feet have marked across the length and breadth of a continent? (*He begins again to pace the room.*) —And that crowd of stricken souls out yonder, raised up as by miracle, their broken bodies crying to be healed,—do you see what they mean?

RHODA. (*In a steady voice.*) They mean what my aunt said this morning. They mean that your great hour has come.

MICHAELIS. My hour! my hour! (*He comes nearer, and speaks in a quieter tone.*) I knew a young Indian once, a Hopi boy, who made songs and sang them to his people. One evening we sat on the roof of the chief's house and asked him to sing. He shook his head, and went away in the starlight. The next morning, I found him among the rocks under the mesa, with an empty bottle by his side.—He never sang again! Drunkenness had taken him. He never sang again, or made another verse.

RHODA. What has that to do with you? It 's not—? You don't mean that you—?

MICHAELIS. No. There is a stronger drink for such as I am!

RHODA. (*Forcing herself to go on.*) What—"stronger drink"?

MICHAELIS. (*Wildly.*) The wine of this world!—The wine-bowl that crowns the feasting table of the children of this world.

RHODA. What do you mean by—the wine of this world?

MICHAELIS. You know that! Every woman knows. (*He points out of the window, at the sky flushed with sunset color.*) Out there, at this moment, in city and country, souls, thousands upon thousands of souls, are dashing in pieces the cup that holds the wine of heaven, the wine of God's shed blood, and lifting the cups of passion and of love, that crown the feasting table of the children of this earth! Look! The very sky is blood-red with the lifted cups. And we two are in the midst of them. Listen what I sing there, on the hills of light in the sunset: "Oh, how beautiful upon the mountains are the feet of my beloved!" (*A song rises outside, loud and near at hand—*MICHAELIS *listens, his ex-*

pression gradually changing from passionate excitement to brooding distress. Vaguely, as the music grows fainter and dies away.) I—we were saying—. (*He grasps her arm in nervous apprehension.*) For God's sake, tell me.—Are there many people—waiting—out there?

RHODA. Hundreds, if not thousands.

MICHAELIS. (*Walks about.*) Thousands. —Thousands of thousands!— (*He stops beside her.*) You won't leave me alone?

RHODA. (*Hesitates, then speaks with decision.*) No.

MICHAELIS. (*Continuing his walk.*) Thousands of thousands!

(*The hall door opens,* DR. LITTLEFIELD *and a Clergyman, the* REV. JOHN CULPEPPER, *enter. The latter stares inquiringly from* MICHAELIS *to the* DOCTOR, *who nods affirmatively, and adjusts his glasses.*)

CULPEPPER. (*Mutters to* LITTLEFIELD.) Nonsense! Sacrilegious nonsense!

LITTLEFIELD. (*Same tone.*) I've done my best.

(*Behind them comes* MRS. BEELER, *supported by her Husband. At the same moment* MARTHA *enters from the kitchen, with tea;* UNCLE ABE *and* ANNIE *follow.*)

BEELER. (*On the threshold.*) Mary, take another minute to consider.

(MRS. BEELER, *as if without hearing this protest, gazes at* MICHAELIS, *and advances into the room with a gesture of the arms which causes her supporter to loosen his hold, though he follows slightly behind, to render aid if necessary.*)

MRS. BEELER. (*To* MICHAELIS.) Tell me that I may go out, and stand before them for a testimony!

LITTLEFIELD. As a physician, I must formally protest.

CULPEPPER. And I as a minister of the Gospel.

MRS. BEELER. (*To* MICHAELIS, *with a nervous, despairing gesture.*) Speak to them! Explain to them! I am too weak.

(*There is a sound of excited voices outside, near at hand, then a sudden trample of footsteps at the entrance door. As* BEELER *goes hurriedly to the door it bursts open and a young woman with a baby in her arms crowds past him, and stands looking wildly about the room.*)

BEELER. (*As he forces the others back.*) You can't come in here, my friends! Stand back!

(*The woman gazes from one to another of the men. The old negro points at* MICHAELIS. *She advances to him, holding out the child.*)

MOTHER. Don't let my baby die! For Christ's sake, don't let him die!

(*He examines the child's face, touches the mother's head tenderly, and signs to* RHODA *to take them into the inner room.*)

MICHAELIS. Take her with you, I will come.

RHODA. (*With gentle urgency, to the woman.*) Come with me.

(*She leads the woman out through the hall door.*)

MICHAELIS. (*To* MRS. BEELER, *as he points outside.*) Tell them to wait until to-morrow at sunrise. (MR. *and* MRS. BEELER *move toward the entrance door; some of the others start after, some linger, curious to know what will happen to the child.* MICHAELIS *turns upon them with a commanding gesture.*) Go, all of you!

(*The room is cleared except for* LITTLEFIELD, *who goes last, stops in the doorway, closes the door, and approaches* MICHAELIS. *He speaks in a friendly and reasonable tone.*)

LITTLEFIELD. You're on the wrong track, my friend.

MICHAELIS. I asked you to go.

LITTLEFIELD. I heard you. I want to say a word or two first. For your own sake and for that woman's sake, you'd better listen. You can't do anything for her baby.

MICHAELIS. Is that for you to say?

LITTLEFIELD. Yes, sir! It is most decidedly for me to say.

MICHAELIS. By what authority?

LITTLEFIELD. By the authority of medical knowledge.—You are a very remarkable man, with a very remarkable gift. In your own field, I take off my hat to you. If you knew yourself as science knows you, you might make the greatest doctor living. Your handling of Mrs. Beeler's case was masterly. But—come right down to it—*you* didn't work the cure.

MICHAELIS. I know that.

LITTLEFIELD. Who do you think did?

MICHAELIS. (*Raising his hands.*) He whom I serve, and whom you blaspheme!

LITTLEFIELD. No, sir! He whom *I* serve,

and whom *you* blaspheme—Nature. Or rather, Mrs. Beeler did it herself.

MICHAELIS. Herself?

LITTLEFIELD. You gave her a jog, so to speak, here, or here, (*Touches his brain and heart.*) and she did the rest. But you can't do the same to everybody. Above all, you can't do it to a baby in arms. There's nothing either here or here, (*Touches brain and heart.*) to get hold of. I'm a modest man, and as I say, in your own field you're a wonder. But in a case like this one— (*He points to the hall door.*) I'm worth a million of you.

MICHAELIS. (*Moves as if to give place to him, with a challenging gesture toward the door.*) Try!

LITTLEFIELD. (*Shrugs.*) Not much! The woman would n't listen to me. And if she did, and I failed—oh, I'm no miracle worker!—they'd make short work of me, out there. (*He points out and adds significantly.*) They're in no mood for failures, out there. (MICHAELIS'S *gaze, as if in spite of himself, goes to the window. He rests his hand on the table, to stop its trembling.* LITTLEFIELD *goes on, watching him with interest.*) Nervously speaking, you are a high power machine. The dynamo that runs you is what is called "faith," "religious inspiration," or what-not. It's a dynamo which nowadays easily gets out of order. Well, my friend, as a doctor, I warn you that your little dynamo is out of order.— In other words, you've lost your grip. You're in a funk.

(RHODA *opens the hall door and looks anxiously at the two.* MICHAELIS *approaches her with averted eyes. As he is about to pass out, she speaks timidly.*)

RHODA. Do you want me?

MICHAELIS. (*In a toneless voice.*) No.

(*She watches him until the inner door shuts. She and* LITTLEFIELD *confront each other in silence for a moment across the width of the room.*)

RHODA. (*Forcing herself to speak calmly.*) Please go.

LITTLEFIELD. (*Drops his professional tone for one of cynical badinage.*) You make up well as one of the Wise Virgins, whose lamps are trimmed and burning for the bridegroom to pass by. I hope that personage won't disappoint you, nor the several hundred others, out yonder, whose lamps are trimmed and burning.

(*The outer door opens.* MRS. BEELER *enters, supported by her husband, and accompanied by* MARTHA *and the* REV. CULPEPPER, *with* UNCLE ABE *following in the rear.* RHODA *hastens to her aunt's side.*)

MRS. BEELER. Ah, Rhoda, I wish you had been out there with me. Such beautiful human faces! Such poor, suffering, believing human faces, lit up by such a wonderful new hope! (*She turns to the minister.*) Was n't it a wonderful thing to see?

CULPEPPER. It is wonderful to see human nature so credulous. And to me, very painful.

MRS. BEELER. To-morrow you will see how right these poor souls are to lift their trust so high.— (*To* RHODA.) Where is he now? (RHODA *points in the direction of her own room.*) How happy that young mother's heart will be to-night!

UNCLE ABE. (*Solemnly.*) Amen!

CULPEPPER. (*In a dry tone.*) We will hope so.

(*They move to the hall door, where* BEELER *resigns his wife to* RHODA. *The two pass out.*

(CULPEPPER, LITTLEFIELD, *and* BEELER *remain. During the following conversation,* MARTHA *lights the lamp, after directing* UNCLE ABE, *by a gesture, to take the provision basket into the kitchen. He does so.*)

LITTLEFIELD. (*Pointing through the window.*) They're just laying siege to you, ain't they? I guess they won't let your man give them the slip, this time—even though you do let him run loose.

BEELER. (*With severity.*) You have seen my wife walk alone to-day, the first time in five years.

LITTLEFIELD. I beg your pardon. I understand how you feel about it. (MARTHA *goes out into the kitchen.*) And even if it proves to be only temporary—

BEELER. Temporary!

LITTLEFIELD. Permanent, let us hope. Anyway, it's a very remarkable case. Astonishing. I've only known one just like it—personally, I mean.

BEELER. (*Astounded.*) Just like it?

LITTLEFIELD. Well, pretty much. Happened in Chicago when I was an interne at St. Luke's.

BEELER. Then it's not—there's nothing—peculiar about it?

LITTLEFIELD. Yes, sir-ree! Mighty peculiar!

BEELER. I mean nothing, as you might say, outside nature?

LITTLEFIELD. O, bless you, you can't get outside nature nowadays! (*Moves his hands in a wide circle.*) Tight as a drum, no air-holes.—Devilish queer, though—pardon me, Mr. Culpepper—really amazing, the power of the mind over the body.

CULPEPPER. Would you be good enough to let us hear some of your professional experiences?

LITTLEFIELD. (*Lights a cigarette, as he leans on the edge of the table.*) Don't have to go to professional medicine for cases. They 're lying around loose. Why, when I was at Ann Arbor—in a fraternity initiation—we bared a chap's shoulders, showed him a white-hot poker, blindfolded him, told him to stand steady, and—touched him with a piece of ice. A piece of ice, I tell you! What happened? Damned if it—pardon me, Mr. Culpepper—blessed if it did n't *burn* him—carries the scars to this day. Then there was that case in Denver. Ever hear about that? A young girl, nervous patient. Nails driven through the palms of her hands,—tenpenny nails,—under the hypnotic suggestion that she was n't being hurt. Did n't leave a cicatrice as big as a bee sting! Fact!

BEELER. You think my wife's case is like these?

LITTLEFIELD. Precisely; with religious excitement to help out. (*He points outside.*) They 're getting ready for Kingdom come over it, out yonder, dear Dr. Culpepper.

BEELER. They 're worked up enough, if that 's all that 's needed.

LITTLEFIELD. Worked up! Elijah in a chariot of fire, distributing cure-alls as he mounts to glory. They 've got their ascension robes on, especially the niggers.

CULPEPPER. (*With severity.*) I take it you are the late Dr. Martin's successor.

LITTLEFIELD. I have the honor.

CULPEPPER. Old Dr. Martin would never have taken a flippant tone in such a crisis.

LITTLEFIELD. Flippant? By no means! A little light-headed. My profession is attacked. At its very roots, sir.—(*With relish.*) As far as that goes, I 'm afraid yours is, too.

CULPEPPER. (*To* BEELER, *ignoring the gibe.*) Am I to understand that you countenance these proceedings?

BEELER. (*Pointing to the invalid chair.*) If your wife had spent five years helpless in that chair, I guess you 'd countenance any proceedings that set her on her feet.

CULPEPPER. (*Towers threateningly.*) If your wife is the woman she was, she would rather sit helpless forever beside the Rock of Ages, than dance and flaunt herself in the house of idols!

BEELER. (*With depreciating humor.*) O, I guess she ain't doin' much flauntin' of herself in any house of idols.—You 've heard Doctor here say it 's all natural enough. Maybe this kind of cure is the coming thing.

LITTLEFIELD. The Brother would drive us doctors into the poorhouse, if he could keep up the pace. And you preachers, too, as far as that goes. If he could keep up the pace! Well—(*Sucks at his cigarette deliberately.*) lucky for us, he *can't* keep it up.

BEELER. Why can't he keep it up?

LITTLEFIELD. Can't stand the strain.—Oh, I have n't seen him operate, but I 'm willing to bet his miracles take it out of him!

CULPEPPER. (*Takes his hat and goes toward the outer door.*) Miracles, indeed!

LITTLEFIELD. (*Following.*) Oh, wait for me, Doctor; we 're both in the same boat!

BEELER. Hope you gentlemen will come back again to-night, and soon, too. Don't know what 'll happen if things go wrong in there.

(*Points towards the hall.*)

LITTLEFIELD. All right—you can count on me—

BEELER. (*To* CULPEPPER.) And you?

CULPEPPER. I seldom shirk my duty.

(BEELER *closes the door after them.*)

(MARTHA *enters from the kitchen, with a pan of dough, which she sets before the fire to raise.*)

BEELER. You keepin' an eye out, Marthy?

MARTHA. Guess your barn 'd 'a' been afire, if I had n't been keepin' an eye out.

BEELER. I warned 'em about fire!

MARTHA. Haymow ketched. If I had n't been there to put it out, we 'd 'a' been without a roof by now.

BEELER. Guess I better go keep an eye out myself.

MARTHA. Guess you had!

(BEELER *goes out by the kitchen.*

MARTHA *takes up mechanically her eternal task of setting things to rights—gathering up* ANNIE'S *toys and arranging the furniture in more precise order. Meanwhile,* RHODA *enters from the hall with the mother of the sick child, a frail young woman of nervous type. She clings to* RHODA *feverishly.*)

MOTHER. Don't leave me!

RHODA. You must n't worry. Your baby will get well. (RHODA *sinks in a low easy chair before the fire, and the woman kneels beside her, her face hidden on the chair arm.*) You must keep up your courage and your trust. That will help more than anything.

MOTHER. I'm afraid!

RHODA. Think of those others out there, who are waiting too, without the glimpse of comfort you 've had.

MOTHER. (*Bursts out.*) I ain't had no comfort! When I heard him pray for my child, I—I don't know—I kept sayin' to myself—"O God, it 's me that 's stretchin' out my hands to you, not him. Don't punish me for his cold words!"

(MARTHA, *who has been listening, shakes her head significantly.*)

RHODA. Cold words!

MOTHER. Yes, I know it 's wrong. I 'll try to feel different. It 's because I ain't had nothin' to do with religion for so long.—If my baby gets well, I 'll make up for it. I 'll make up for everything.

(*The woman rises.* RHODA *kisses her.*)

RHODA. I shall be here if you want me. And I shall—pray for you.

(*The mother goes out. Distant singing is heard.* MARTHA *comes to the mantelpiece with matches, which she arranges in the match tray. She looks at* RHODA, *who sits with closed eyes.*)

MARTHA. Guess you 're about dead beat.

RHODA. I think I never was so tired in my life.

MARTHA. Worry does it, more 'n work. Better try and doze off, Rhody.

(*The hall door opens, and* ANNIE *enters. She comes to* MARTHA, *and clings nervously to her skirts.*)

ANNIE. Aunt Martha! I want to stay with you. You 're the only person in this house that ain't different. What 's the matter with Mamma?

MARTHA. She 's cured, I reckon.

ANNIE. How did she get cured?

MARTHA. You can search me!

ANNIE. Did that man cure her?

MARTHA. That 's what she says, and I don't hear him denyin' it.

ANNIE. (*Whining.*) I don't want her to be cured!

MARTHA. Annie Beeler! Don't want your mother to be cured?

ANNIE. No, I don't. I want her to be like she always has been. She don't seem like my Mamma at all this way. What 's the matter with all those people out there? Why don't we have any supper? (*She bursts out crying and clings feverishly to* MARTHA.) Oh, what 's going to happen to us?

MARTHA. There, Annie, don't cry. (*She looks at* RHODA, *throws a cover over her knees, and draws* ANNIE *away, speaking low.*) Come out in the kitchen, and I 'll give you your supper.

(*Exeunt. The singing grows louder and nearer.* MICHAELIS *enters from the hall. His hair is dishevelled, his collar open, his manner feverish and distraught. He looks closely at* RHODA, *sees she is sleeping, then paces the floor nervously, gazing out of the window in the direction of the singing. At length he comes to* RHODA *again, and bends over her, studying her face. She starts up, confused and terror-stricken, from her doze.*)

RHODA. What—what is the matter? Oh, you frightened me so! (MICHAELIS *turns away without answering.*) What has happened? Why are you here?

MICHAELIS. You had dropped asleep. You are weary.

RHODA. (*Collecting her thoughts with difficulty.*) I was dreaming—such a strange dream.

MICHAELIS. What did you dream?

RHODA. I thought it was morning; the sun had risen, and—and you were out there, in the midst of the crowd.

MICHAELIS. (*Excitedly.*) Go on! What happened?

RHODA. I—I can't remember the rest.

MICHAELIS. (*Grasps her arm, speaks low.*) You must remember! Did I—succeed?

RHODA. (*Helplessly.*) I—it 's all a blur in my mind.

MICHAELIS. (*Darkly.*) You don't want me to know that, in your dream, I failed.

RHODA. No, no. That is not so. (*Pause. She speaks with hesitation.*) Perhaps this is not the time. Perhaps you are not ready.

MICHAELIS. What does that matter? *He* is ready.

(*He points at the map.*)

RHODA. (*Gazing at the map, with mystic conviction.*) You will succeed! You must succeed! (*He paces the room. She stops him, pointing toward the hall door.*) How is the child? (*He hesitates. She repeats the words anxiously.*) How is the child? (*He shakes his head gloomily for answer.*) It will get well, I am sure.

MICHAELIS. If it does not, I am judged.

RHODA. Oh, don't say that or think it!

MICHAELIS. I am weighed in the balance and found wanting!

RHODA. You cannot hang the whole issue and meaning of your life upon so slight a thread.

MICHAELIS. The whole issue and meaning of the world hang on threads as slight. If this one is slight. To the mother it is not slight, nor to the God who put into her eyes, as she looked at me, all the doubt and question of the suffering earth.

RHODA. You must remember that it is only a little child. Its mind is not open. You cannot influence it—can you?

MICHAELIS. Once that little life in my hand would have been as clay in the hands of the potter. If I cannot help now, it is because my ministry has been taken from me and given to another, who will be strong where I am weak, and faithful where I am unfaithful.

(*Another song rises outside, distant.*)

RHODA. (*Comes closer to him.*) Tell me this. Speak plainly to me. Is it because of me that your weakness and unfaith have come upon you? Is it because of me?

MICHAELIS. (*Looking at her steadily.*) Yes.—(*He comes nearer.*) Before creation, beyond time, God not yet risen from His sleep, you stand and call to me, and I listen in a dream that I dreamed before Eden.

RHODA. (*Shrinking from him.*) You must not say such things to me.—You must not think of me so.—You must not!

(*He follows her, his passion mounting.*)

MICHAELIS. All my life long I have known you, and fled from you. I have heard you singing on the hills of sleep and have fled from you into the waking day. I have seen you in the spring forest, dancing and throwing your webs of sunlight to snare me; on moonlit mountains, laughing and calling; in the streets of crowded cities, beckoning and disappearing in the crowd—and everywhere I have fled from you, holding above my head the sign of God's power in me, my gift and my mission.—What use? What use? It has crumbled, and I do not care!

RHODA. Oh, don't speak such words, I beseech you. Let me go. This must not, shall not be!

(*She makes another attempt to escape. He presses upon her until she stands at bay.*)

MICHAELIS. You are all that I have feared and shunned and missed on earth, and now I have you, the rest is as nothing. (*He takes her, feebly resisting, into his arms.*) I know a place out there, high in the great mountains. Heaven-piercing walls of stone, a valley of trees and sweet water in the midst—grass and flowers, such flowers as you have never dreamed could grow.—There we will take our happiness. A year—a month—a day—what matter? We will make a lifetime of each hour!

RHODA. (*Yielding to his embrace, whispers.*) Don't talk. Don't think. Only—love me. A little while. A little while.

(*The deep hush of their embrace is broken by a cry from within. The young mother opens the hall door in a distraction of terror and grief.*)

MOTHER. Come here! Come quick! (MICHAELIS *and* RHODA *draw apart. He stares at the woman, as if not remembering who she is.*) I can't rouse him! My baby 's gone. Oh, my God, he 's dead!

(*She disappears.* RHODA *follows, drawing* MICHAELIS, *dazed and half resisting, with her. The room remains vacant for a short time, the stage held by distant singing.* BEELER *enters from the kitchen. There is a knock at the outer door, which he opens.* LITTLEFIELD, CULPEPPER, *and* UNCLE ABE *enter.*)

LITTLEFIELD. Your man has n't vamoosed, has he? Uncle Abe here says he saw the Indian boy slipping by in the fog.

BEELER. (*Turns to the negro inquiringly.*) Alone?

UNCLE ABE. (*Mumbles half to himself.*) 'Lone. 'Spec' he was alone. Did n't even have his own flesh and bones wif 'im!

BEELER. What's that?

UNCLE ABE. (*Holds up his right hand, which he eyes with superstitious interest.*) Put dis hyar han' right frough him!—Shore's you're bo'n. Right plum' frough 'im whar he lives.

CULPEPPER. Mediæval! Absolutely mediæval!

LITTLEFIELD. Not a bit of it. It's up to date, and a little more, too.

CULPEPPER. I'm astonished that you take this situation flippantly.

LITTLEFIELD. Not for a minute. My bread and butter are at stake. (*Wickedly.*) Yours too, you know.

(MRS. BEELER *enters, alone, from the hall. She is in a state of vague alarm. Her husband hastens to help her.*)

MRS. BEELER. What is it? What is the matter? I thought I heard—

(*She breaks off, as a murmur of voices rises outside. There is a sound of stumbling and crowding on the outer steps, and violent knocking. The outer door is forced open, and a crowa of excited people is about to pour into the room.* BEELER, *the Doctor, and the Preacher are able to force the crowd back only after several have made an entrance.*)

BEELER. Keep back! You can't come in here.

(*As he pushes them roughly back, excited voices speak together.*)

VOICES IN THE CROWD. Where is he?—They say he's gone away. We seen his boy makin' for the woods.—Oh, it's not true! Make him come out.

BEELER. Curse you, keep back, I say!

(RHODA *has entered from the hall, and* MARTHA *from the kitchen. The two women support* MRS. BEELER, *who remains standing, the fear deepening in her face.*)

A VOICE. (*On the outskirts of the crowd.*) Where's he gone to?

BEELER. He's here. In the next room. Keep back! Here he comes now.

(MICHAELIS *appears in the hall door. There is a low murmur of excitement, expectation, and awe among the people crowded in the entrance.* BEELER *crosses to help his wife, and the other men step to one side, leaving* MICHAELIS *to confront the crowd alone. Confused, half-whispered exclamations:*)

VOICES IN THE CROWD. Hallelujah! Emmanuel!

A NEGRO. Praise de Lamb.

A WOMAN. (*Above the murmuring voices.*) "He hath risen, and His enemies are scattered."

MICHAELIS. Who said that?

(*A woman, obscurely seen in the crowd, lifts her hands and cries again, this time in a voice ecstatic and piercing.*)

A WOMAN. "The Lord hath risen, and His enemies are scattered!"

MICHAELIS. His enemies are scattered! Year after year I have heard His voice calling me—and year after year I have said, "Show me the way." And He showed me the way. He brought me to this house, and He raised up the believing multitude around me. But in that hour I failed Him, I failed Him. He has smitten me, as His enemies are smitten.—As a whirlwind He has scattered me and taken my strength from me forever. (*He advances into the room, with a gesture backward through the open door.*) In yonder room a child lies dead on its mother's knees, and the mother's eyes follow me with curses. (*At the news of the child's death,* MRS. BEELER *has sunk with a low moan into a chair, where she lies white and motionless.* MICHAELIS *turns to her.*) And here lies one who rose at my call, and was as one risen; but now—(*He breaks off, raises his hand to her, and speaks in a voice of pleading.*) Arise, my sister! (*She makes a feeble gesture of the left hand.*) Rise up once more, I beseech you!

(*She attempts to rise, but falls back helpless.*)

BEELER. (*Bending over her.*) Can't you get up, Mother?

(*She shakes her head.*)

MICHAELIS. (*Turning to the people.*) Despair not, for another will come, and another and yet another, to show you the way. But as for me—(*He sinks down by the table, and gazes before him, muttering in a tragic whisper.*) Broken! Broken! Broken!

ACT THIRD.

The next morning, just before sunrise. Both door and windows are open, and a light breeze sways the curtains. Outside is a tree-shaded and vine-clad porch, with balustrade, beyond which is a tangle of flowering bushes and fruit trees in bloom. The effect is of a rich warm dawn—a sudden onset of summer weather after a bleak spring.

BEELER, *with* UNCLE ABE *looking on, is busy putting up the pictures which he has taken down in the preceding act.* MARTHA *enters from the hall.*

BEELER. (*To* MARTHA.) Is Mary up?

MARTHA. Yes. Wants to go out on the porch and watch the sun rise, same as she 's done every Easter morning since Seth died.

BEELER. Won't hurt her, I reckon, bad off as she is.—A reg'lar old-fashioned, sunshiny, blossomy spring mornin'—summer here with a jump and fine growin' weather. (*Pause.*) All the same, sun might as well stay in China this Easter!

MARTHA. Is that why you 're tackin' up them fool pictures again?

BEELER. Yes, ma'am. That 's just why. Religion!

MARTHA. You wa' n't so sure yesterday, when you saw your wife stand up on her two dead feet and walk.

BEELER. Well, she ain't walkin' now.

MARTHA. No, she ain't, poor thing.

BEELER. Natural cure, natural relapse. Doctor says the new medical books explain it.

MARTHA. Give it a name, maybe!

BEELER. (*Bursts out petulantly.*) You women don't want things explained, any more 'n Abe here! You prefer hocus-pocus. And nothin' will teach you. Take Rhody! Sees Michaelis flunk his job miserable. Sees Mary go down like a woman shot, hands and legs paralyzed again,—Doctor says, for good, this time. And what does the girl do about it? Spends the night out yonder laborin' with them benighted sick folks, tellin' 'em the healer will make good. Lots of makin' good he 'll do! (*He points at the ceiling.*) A fine picture of a healer he makes.

MARTHA. (*Looking up.*) Still as a stone! I 'd rather have him ragin' round same as yesterday, like a lion with the epizoötic.

BEELER. He 's a dead one. Rhody might as well give up tryin' to make folks think different.

MARTHA. Maybe Rhody holds she 's to blame.

BEELER. To blame? To blame for what?

MARTHA. For him a-peterin' out.

BEELER. What 's she got to do with it?

MARTHA. Maybe she ain't got nothin' to do with it, and maybe she 's got a whole lot.

BEELER. Marthy, I don't want it to get out, but you 're a plum' luny sentimental old maid fool!

(UNCLE ABE *has been hovering, with superstitious interest, near the picture of Pan and the Pilgrim. With side glances at it, he speaks, taking advantage of the lull in conversation which follows* BEELER'S *outburst.*)

UNCLE ABE. Mistah Beelah, 'scuse me troublin' you, but—'scuse me troublin' you.

BEELER. What is it, Abe?

UNCLE ABE. It 's purty brash o' me to be askin', but—Mista Beelah, fur de Lawd's sake give me that thar devil—pictuh!

BEELER. What do *you* want with it?

UNCLE ABE. Want to hang it up in my ole cabin. (*His tone rises to one of eager pleading.*) Mars Beelah, you give it to me! For Gawd's sake, say Ole Uncle Abe kin have it, to hang up in his ole cabin.

BEELER. Well, if you feel as strong as that about it, Abe, take it along.

UNCLE ABE. (*As he unpins it with feverish eagerness.*) Thank ye, Mistah Beelah, thank ye. I 'll wo'k fur ye and I 'll slave fur ye, long as the worl' stan's. Maybe it ain't goin' to stan' much longer aftah all. Maybe de chariot s comin' down in de fiery clouds 'fo' great while. An' what 'll yo' ole Uncle Abe be doin'? He 'll be on his knees 'fo' a big roarin' fire, singing hallelujah, an' a-jammin' red-hot needles right plum' frough dis heah black devil's breas' bone! I 'se got him now! I 'll fix 'm. (*Shakes his fist at the print, as he goes toward the kitchen.*) Put yo' black spell on the Lawd's chosen, would ye? I 'se got ye. I 'll make ye sing, "Jesus, my ransom," right out 'n yo' ugly black mouf!

(*Exit.*)

BEELER. There 's a purty exhibition for this present year o' grace! Thinks our friend Pan there has bewitched the healer.

MARTHA. Maybe he has!

BEELER. Thought you said Rhody done it.

MARTHA. Same thing, I reckon, by all that you tell about that Panjandrum and his goin's on!

BEELER. Nonsense!

MARTHA. If you 're so wise, why do *you* think Michaelis petered out?

BEELER. Could n't stand the strain. Bit off more 'n he could chaw, in the healin' line.—Never looked at Rhody.

MARTHA. Looked at her till he could n't see nothin' else, in heaven or earth or the other place.

BEELER. You 're dead wrong. I tell you he never looked cross-eyed at Rhody, nor Rhody at him. Doctor 's more in her line.—By the way, did you give the Doctor a snack to stay his stomach?

MARTHA. Done nothin' but feed him all night long. Seems to be mighty exhaustin' work to tend a sick baby.

BEELER. Does he think it 'll live?

MARTHA. Not likely. But he thinks he will, if fed reg'lar.—What do you call that trance the baby 's in?

BEELER. Doctor calls it comy. Spelled it out for me: c-o-m-a, comy.

(BEELER *goes out on the porch and disappears.* MARTHA *continues her task of tidying up the room.* MICHAELIS *enters from the stair, carrying his hat and a foot-traveller's knapsack.* MARTHA *regards him with curiosity, tempered now by feminine sympathy with the defeated.*)

MARTHA. Good morning, sir.

MICHAELIS. (*Tonelessly.*) Good morning.

MARTHA. (*Pointing at his hat and knapsack.*) Hope you ain't off. Don't mind sayin' the way you acted was human decent, sendin' for Doctor when you found the baby wa' n't dead, an' you wa' n't no healer any more.

MICHAELIS. Is it any better?

(MARTHA *makes a disconsolate gesture, implying that there is little or no hope.* MICHAELIS *turns away with bent head.* ANNIE *enters from the kitchen.* MICHAELIS *holds out his hand to her, and she takes it with shy hesitation.*)

MARTHA. Guess you 'd like to know where Rhody is, would n't you? She 's where she 's been all night,—out yonder with the sick folks.

MICHAELIS. What is she doing there?

MARTHA. Feedin' 'em, first off, an' then heart'nin' of 'em up. That 's a purty hard job, I reckon; but it 's the way o' women when they feel like she does.

(MICHAELIS *sinks in a chair, drawing* ANNIE *to him.* MRS. BEELER'S *bell rings;* MARTHA *goes out by the hall door.* ANNIE *watches his bent head in silence for a moment.*)

ANNIE. Are you ever going up again, on the rope?

MICHAELIS. (*Not remembering.*) On the rope?

ANNIE. You know . . . the magic rope.—Ain't you ever going to climb up in the sky again?

MICHAELIS. (*Recollecting.*) Never again, Annie. Never again.

ANNIE. Have you got the rope still?

MICHAELIS. No, I have lost it.

ANNIE. Won't you ever find it?

MICHAELIS. It can only be found by some one who will know how to use it better than I did.

ANNIE. How better?

MICHAELIS. By some one who can climb up, toward the sun and the stars, and yet never leave the earth, the cities, and the people.

ANNIE. Then he 'll have to take them up with him. (MICHAELIS *nods for yes.*) Gracious! (*She runs to the porch door to meet* RHODA, *who appears outside.*) Cousin Rhoda! What do you think he says about the magic rope?

RHODA. What, Annie?

ANNIE. He says that first thing you know, everything will be going up in the air, towns and people and everything.

RHODA. Does he?

ANNIE. (*Runs out into the hall, balancing her arms above her head and gazing up laughingly.*) Dear me! That will be very *tippy!*

(RHODA *enters.*)

MICHAELIS. You are here! The fear came over me, just now—

RHODA. I could not go until I had told you the truth—about myself—about us.

MICHAELIS. You will tell me the whole truth, and I will tell you the same. But that will be for later. Come! Come away with me, into the new life.

RHODA. A life rooted in the failure of all that life has meant to you from the beginning!

MICHAELIS. Until yesterday I did not know what my life was.

RHODA. You do not know that, even yet. You know it now less than ever—what your life is, what it means to you, what it means to the world.

MICHAELIS. To the world it can mean nothing. That is ended. But to us it can mean happiness. Let us make haste to gather it. Come!

RHODA. Where do you want me to go?

MICHAELIS. Anywhere—to that place I told you of—high in the great mountains.

RHODA. I was there last night.

MICHAELIS. In your thoughts?

RHODA. I was there, and saw all the beauty of it, all the peace. But one thing was not there, and for lack of it, in a little while the beauty faded and the peace was gone.

MICHAELIS. What was not there?

RHODA. The work you have to do.

MICHAELIS. That was a dream I could not realize. I have striven, and I have failed.

RHODA. Do you know why you have failed?

MICHAELIS. Yes.

RHODA. Tell me why.

MICHAELIS. Because I have loved you more than the visions that came to me in desert places, more than the powers that fell upon me at the bedside of the sick, more than the spirit hands and spirit voices that have guided me on my way.

RHODA. What of the sick and suffering out yonder, who are waiting and hoping against hope? What of them?

MICHAELIS. I cannot help them.

RHODA. Once you dreamed you could.

MICHAELIS. Yes. But that is over.

RHODA. And who is to blame that that great dream is over?

MICHAELIS. No one is to blame. It has happened so.

RHODA. Does n't it seem strange that the love of a woman entering into your heart should take away such a dream as that?

MICHAELIS. I do not question. It is so.

RHODA. But if your love had fallen, by some sad chance, upon a woman who was not worthy of love?

MICHAELIS. What are you saying?

RHODA. You know less than nothing of me. You have not asked me a single question about my life.

MICHAELIS. There was no need.

RHODA. There was need! There was need!

MICHAELIS. Be careful what you say. Go on!

RHODA. In the first hour of our meeting, and all the hours of the next day, you swept me along and lifted me above myself, like a strong wind. I did n't know what you were. I did n't know why I was happy and exalted. It was so long since I had been happy, and I had never been as happy as that, or anything like it. Then, yesterday morning, came the revelation of what you were, like a blinding light out of the sky! And while I stood dazed, trembling, I saw something descend upon you like a shadow. You loved me, and that love was dreadful to you. You thought it was so because I was a woman and stole your spirit's strength away. But it was not that. It was because I was a *wicked* woman.

MICHAELIS. Why do you call yourself a wicked woman?

RHODA. Because I am so.

MICHAELIS. I cannot believe it.

RHODA. It is true.

MICHAELIS. Is that why you wanted to go away?

RHODA. Yes, I tried to go away. You would n't let me go. Then I tried to tell you the truth. I knew why I took your strength away, and I had nerved myself to tell you why. But you began to speak—those wild words. I could not resist you. You took me in your arms; and all the power of your soul went from you, and your life went crashing down in darkness. (*Long pause.*)

MICHAELIS. Wicked? A wicked woman?

RHODA. I was young then, wild-hearted, pitifully ignorant. I thought that love had come to me. Girls are so eager for love. They snatch at the shadow of it.—That is what I did.—I am not trying to plead for myself.—Some things are not to be forgiven.—Somewhere in my nature there was a taint—a plague-spot.—If life is given me, I shall find it and root it out. I only ask for time to do that. But meanwhile I have done what I could. I have told you the truth. I have set you free. I have given you back your mission.

(DR. LITTLEFIELD *enters, carrying his hat and medicine case. He looks sharply at* RHODA, *then turns to* MICHAELIS. *His manner towards him is politely contemptuous, toward* RHODA *it is full of covert passion, modified by his habitual cynicism and satire.*)

LITTLEFIELD. (*To* RHODA.) Good morning. (*To* MICHAELIS.) Good morning, my friend. I understood that you sent for me, last night.

MICHAELIS. I did.

LITTLEFIELD. Glad to accommodate a fellow practitioner, even if he is in a side line. Some folks think your way of business is a little shady, but Lord, if they knew the secrets of *our* charnel-house!

MICHAELIS. How did you leave the child?

LITTLEFIELD. Done for. I said I was worth a million of you in a case like this, but I did n't realize how far things had gone. The next time, call me in a little sooner. (*He writes on his note pad, tears out a leaf, and lays it on the table.*) Mrs. Beeler will continue the old prescription, alternating with this. (*He puts the note pad in his pocket, and turns to* RHODA. *He speaks in a tone which implies command, under the veil of request.*) Will you walk a ways with me, Miss Williams?

RHODA. (*Pale and trembling.*) No.

LITTLEFIELD. Pardon! I must have a short talk. It is important.

RHODA. I cannot go with you.

LITTLEFIELD. I think you had better reconsider.

MICHAELIS. (*Astonished at his tone.*) You have heard that she does not wish to go.

LITTLEFIELD. (*Ignoring* MICHAELIS.) I have no time to waste, and I shall not stop to mince my words. You are coming with me, and you are coming now.

MICHAELIS. (*To* RHODA.) Who is this man?

LITTLEFIELD. (*Wheeling upon him angrily.*) 'Pon my honor! "Who is this man?" "Remove the worm!" Decidedly tart, from a miracle-monger in a state of bankruptcy.

MICHAELIS. (*To* RHODA.) Is this the man you told me of?

RHODA. (*Steadily.*) Yes.

LITTLEFIELD. (*To* RHODA, *as he eyes* MICHAELIS *with dislike.*) So you have called in a father confessor, eh? (*To* MICHAELIS.) Well, since the lady can't keep her secrets to herself, this *is* the man. Very painful, no doubt, but these little things will happen. (*To* RHODA.) I should have chosen a more secluded nook to say this in, but you 're skittish, as I have learned to my cost, and likely to bolt. What I want to say is, *don't* bolt. It won't do you any good.—I 've found you once, and I 'll find you again, no matter what rabbit's hole you dodge into. (*To* MICHAELIS.) This ain't George Littlefield, M.D., talking now. It 's the caveman of Borneo. He 's got arms as long as rakes, and teeth that are a caution.—Look out for him!

MICHAELIS. (*Holding himself in stern restraint.*) Your arms and teeth are long enough, and eager enough to do damage, but they will not avail you here. This girl is in other keeping, and I dare to say, better.

LITTLEFIELD. In other keeping, eh? Yours, I suppose.

MICHAELIS. Yes, mine.

LITTLEFIELD. Bless my soul! (*He turns to* RHODA, *pointedly ignoring* MICHAELIS.) Look here, Rho, be sensible. I 'm tired of this hole of a town already. We 'll go west and renew our youth. Country 's big, and nobody to meddle. You 'll flourish like a green bay tree. (RHODA *turns distractedly, as to escape; he intercepts her.*) Confound it, if you 're set on it, I 'll marry you! Say yes, and let John the Baptist here give us his blessing. Speak up. Is it a go?—Till death us do part.

MICHAELIS. Death has already parted you and her.

LITTLEFIELD. So? I feel like a reasonably healthy corpse.

MICHAELIS. There is no health in you. Every word you speak gives off corruption.

LITTLEFIELD. Indeed! My advice to you is, make tracks for your starvation desert. A parcel of locoed Indians are about right for a busted prophet.

MICHAELIS. What I am is no matter. What this girl is, though you lived a thousand years, you would never have the grace to imagine. She gave you her young love, in childish blindness, not knowing what she did, and you killed it idly, wantonly, as a beast tortures its frail victim, for sport. You find her again, still weak and bleeding from her wounds, and you fling her marriage, in words whose every syllable is an insult. Marriage! When every fibre of her nature must cry out against you, if she is woman. Take your words and your looks from her, and that instantly, or you will curse the day you ever brought your evil presence into her life. (*He advances upon him threateningly.*) Instantly, I say, or by the wrath of God your wretched soul, if you have one, shall go this hour to its account!

LITTLEFIELD. (*Backing toward the door, scared, but keeping his brazen tone.*) All right.—I 'm off.—Caveman for caveman, you 've got the reach! (*To* RHODA.) But remember, my lady, we 're not quits by a jug-full. You 'll hear from me yet.

MICHAELIS. She shall never hear from you, nor of you.

LITTLEFIELD. (*In the door.*) Last call, old girl!—Women!

(*He goes out, slamming the door behind him. Long pause.*)

MICHAELIS. Poor child! Poor child!

RHODA. I am sorry that you have had to suffer this.

MICHAELIS. It is you who have suffered.

(MARTHA *enters from the hall, wheeling* MRS. BEELER *in the invalid chair. She lies lower than in the first act, her manner is weaker and more dejected.* RHODA, *whose back is turned, goes on as the two women enter.*)

RHODA. I deserve to suffer, but it will always be sweet to me that in my need you defended me, and gave me back my courage.

(MICHAELIS *goes to* MRS. BEELER; *she gives him her left hand as at first.*)

MRS. BEELER. My poor friend! (MARTHA, *resigning the chair to* RHODA, *goes out.* MRS. BEELER *looks up at* RHODA *anxiously.*) What were you saying when I came in? (*As* RHODA *does not answer, she turns to* MICHAELIS.) Something about your defending her.—Against what?

MICHAELIS. Nothing. Her nature is its own defence.

MRS. BEELER. (*Caressing her.*) Ah, no! She needs help. She cannot bear it that this disaster has come, through her. It has made her morbid. She says things about herself, that make me tremble. Has she spoken to you—about herself?

MICHAELIS. She has laid her heart bare to me.

MRS. BEELER. That is good. Young people, when they are generous, always lay disaster at their own door. (*She kisses* RHODA. *The girl goes into the porch, where she lingers a moment, then disappears.* MRS. BEELER *sinks back in her chair again, overtaken by despondency.*) Is n't it strange that I should be lying here again, and all those poor people waking up into a new day that is no new day at all, but the old weary day they have known so long? Is n't it strange, and sad?

MICHAELIS. I ask you not to lose hope.

MRS. BEELER. (*Rousing from her dejection into vague excitement.*) You ask me that?—Is there—any hope? Oh, don't deceive me—now! I could n't bear it now!—Is there any hope?

MICHAELIS. A half-hour ago I thought there was none. But now I say, have hope.

MRS. BEELER. (*Eagerly.*) Do you? Do you? Oh, I wonder—I wonder if that could be the meaning—?

MICHAELIS. The meaning—?

MRS. BEELER. Of something I felt, just now, as I sat there in my room by the open window.

MICHAELIS. What was it?

MRS. BEELER. I—I don't know how to describe it.—It was like a new sweetness in the air.

(*She looks out at the open window, where the spring breeze lightly wafts the curtains.*)

MICHAELIS. The lilacs have opened during the night.

MRS. BEELER. It was not the lilacs.—I get it now again, in this room. (*She looks toward the lilies and shakes her head.*) No, it is not the lilies either. If it were anyone else, I should be ashamed to say what I think. (*She draws him down and speaks mysteriously.*) It is not real flowers at all!

(*Song rises outside—faint and distant.*)

MICHAELIS. What is it to you?

MRS. BEELER. It is like—it is like some kindness in the air, some new-born happiness—or a new hope rising. Now you will think I am—not quite right in my mind, as Mat does, and Martha!

MICHAELIS. Mrs. Beeler, there is such a perfume about us this beautiful Easter morning. You perceive it, with senses which suffering and a pure soul have made fine beyond the measure of woman. There is a kindness in the air, new-born happiness, and new-risen hope.

MRS. BEELER. From whose heart does it rise?

MICHAELIS. From mine, from Rhoda's heart, though she knows it not, from yours, and soon, by God's mercy, from the heart of this waiting multitude.

(*The song, though still distant, grows louder.* MRS. BEELER *turns to* MICHAELIS *and gazes intently into his face.*)

MRS. BEELER. The light has come into your face again! You are—you are—Oh, my brother, what has come to you?

MICHAELIS. I have shaken off my burden. Do you shake off yours. What is pain but a kind of selfishness? What is disease but a kind of sin? Lay your suffering and your sickness from you as an out-worn garment. Rise up! It is Easter morning. One comes, needing you. Rise up and welcome her!

(MRS. BEELER *rises and goes to meet* RHODA, *entering from the porch.*)

RHODA. Aunt Mary! You are walking again!

MRS. BEELER. He told me to arise, and once more my dead limbs heard.

RHODA. God in His mercy be thanked!

MRS. BEELER. I rose without knowing what I did. It was as if a wind lifted me.

RHODA. Yes, yes. For good, this time!

MRS. BEELER. So different from yesterday. I was still weak then, and my limbs were heavy. Now I feel as if wings were on my shoulders. (*She looks toward the outer door, and listens to the singing, now risen to a more joyful strain.*) I must go out to them. (*She turns to* MICHAELIS.) Say that I may go out, and give them the good tidings of great joy.

MICHAELIS. May the Lord be with you as you go! (*To* RHODA, *who starts to help her aunt.*) Alone!

MRS. BEELER. Yes, alone. I want to go alone. (*She takes a lily from the vase, and lifting it above her head, goes out through the porch, which is now flooded with sunshine. As she goes out she says:*) The Easter sun has risen, with healing in its wings!

(*She crosses the porch and disappears.*)

RHODA. I felt something dragging me back. It was Aunt Mary's spirit.

MICHAELIS. No, it was mine.

RHODA. Yours?

MICHAELIS. My spirit, crying to you that I was delivered.

RHODA. I delivered you. That is enough happiness for one life.

MICHAELIS. You delivered me, yes. But not as you dream. Yesterday when the multitude began to gather, the thing I had been waiting for all my life was there, and I—because of you—I was not ready. In that blind hour my life sank in ruin.—I had thought love denied to such as had my work to do, and in the darkness of that thought disaster overwhelmed me.—I have come to know that God does not deny love to any of his children, but gives it as a beautiful and simple gift to them all.—Upon each head be the use that is made of it!

RHODA. It is not I—who—harm you?

MICHAELIS. It is you who bless me, and give me back the strength that I had lost.

RHODA. I?

MICHAELIS. A little while ago you told me your life's bitter story. I tasted your struggle, went down with you into the depths of your anguish, and in those depths,—the miracle! Behold, once more the stars looked down upon me from their places, and I stood wondering as a child wonders. Out of those depths arose new-born happiness and new-risen hope. For in those star-lit depths of pain and grief, I had found at last true love. You needed me. You needed all the powers I had thrown away for your sake. You needed what the whole world needs—healing, healing, and as I rose to meet that need, the power that I had lost poured back into my soul.

RHODA. Oh, if I thought that could be!

MICHAELIS. By the mystery that is man, and the mercy that is God, I say it is so.—(*Puts his hand on her head, and gazes into her face.*) I looked into your eyes once, and they were terrible as an army with banners. I look again now, and I see they are only a girl's eyes, very weak, very pitiful. I told you of a place, high in the great mountains. I tell you now of another place higher yet, in more mysterious mountains. Let us go there together, step by step, from faith to faith, and from strength to strength, for I see depths of life open and heights of love come out, which I never dreamed of till now!

(*A song rises outside, nearer and louder than before.*)

RHODA. Against your own words they trust you still.

MICHAELIS. It was you who held them to their trust!

RHODA. You will go out to them now.

MICHAELIS. (*As he kisses her.*) Until the victory!

(*The song rises to a great hymn, of martial and joyous rhythm. They go together to the threshold. They look at each other in silence.* RHODA *speaks, with suppressed meaning.*)

RHODA. Shall it be—on earth?

MICHAELIS. On the good human earth, which I never possessed till now!

RHODA. But now—these waiting souls, prisoned in their pain—

MICHAELIS. By faith all prisoned souls shall be delivered.

RHODA. By faith.

MICHAELIS. By faith which makes all things possible, which brings all things to pass.

(*He disappears.* RHODA *stands looking after him. The young mother hurries in.*)

THE YOUNG MOTHER. (*Ecstatic, breathless.*) Come here—My baby! I believe —I do believe— (*She disappears.*)

RHODA. (*Following her.*) I believe. I do believe!

(*The music rises into a vast chorus of many mingled strains.*)

THE SCARECROW

A TRAGEDY OF THE LUDICROUS

BY

Percy MacKaye

THE SCARECROW

The Scarecrow represents the romance of the fantastic, with its basis in American history. It was suggested by Hawthorne's story of "Feathertop," published originally in 1852 and afterwards included in the *Mosses from an Old Manse.* Mr. MacKaye has modified the nature of the characters decidedly, has added characters, and, as he says in the preface to the published play, has substituted the element of human sympathy for that of irony.

Percy MacKaye was born in New York City, March 16, 1875, the son of Steele MacKaye and Mary Medbery, who herself dramatized *Pride and Prejudice.* He grew up in the atmosphere of the theatre and before entering Harvard College in 1893 he had written a series of choral songs for his father's projected "Spectatorio" at the World's Fair in 1893. He graduated from Harvard College in 1897. During his junior year, he wrote a poetical play *Sappho,* which was acted by Harvard and Wellesley students. After two years of European travel and study he returned to New York and taught in a private school, continuing to write plays. The turning point in his career came when his *Canterbury Pilgrims* was accepted by E. H. Sothern in 1903. Since 1904 he has devoted himself entirely to dramatic work, living at Cornish, New Hampshire.

Mr. MacKaye stands in our drama for high standards of dramatic writing. He represents the movement for a civic and national theatre, untrammelled by commercial considerations, and he has brought into recent prominence the idea of the community masque or pageant, in itself one of the most significant dramatic movements of the time. At the same time he is not simply a theorist, but has proved his ability to write plays that succeed upon the stage.

He has written sixteen plays, ten masques or pageants, and four operas. His plays have been performed except the first, *A Garland to Sylvia,* and *Fenris the Wolf,* a masterly study of the mutual effects of purity and passion, laid in a setting of Northern mythology. The acted plays, arranged in the order of their composition and with their dates of publication indicated in parentheses, are: *The Canterbury Pilgrims* (1903), a dramatization of the relations between Chaucer and his characters, first performed at the Park Extension Theatre, Savannah, Georgia, April 30, 1909; *The Scarecrow* (1908); *Jeanne d'Arc,* an historical play (1906), first produced at the Lyric Theatre, Philadelphia, October 15, 1906; *Sappho and Phaon* (1907), a Greek play with the theme of the contrasted influence of family ties and sexual love, first performed at the Opera House, Providence, Rhode Island, October 14, 1907; *Mater* (1908), a comedy based on American politics, first performed at the Van Ness Theatre, San Francisco, California, August 3, 1908; *Anti-Matrimony* (1910), a clever satire upon the influence of modern continental playwrights upon the ideas of marriage held by two young Americans, first performed in the Theatre at Ann Arbor, Michigan, March 10, 1910; *Tomorrow* (1912), a play dealing seriously with the problem of selection in the matter of marriage, first performed at the Little Theatre, Philadelphia, October 31, 1913; *A Thousand Years Ago* (1914), an Oriental romance, first performed at the Shubert Theatre, New York, December 1, 1913, and *Yankee Fantasies* (1912), five one-act plays, four of which have been performed, and two of which, *Gettysburg* and *Sam Average,* are upon national themes.

The group of Masques and Pageants include the *Saint Gaudens Masque-Prologue* (1909), first produced June 20, 1905, by the Cornish Colony in honor of Augustus St. Gaudens; the *Gloucester Pageant* (1903), produced under the auspices of the city of Gloucester in honor of President Taft, August 3, 1909; *A Masque of Labor* (1912), projected but not yet performed; *Sanctuary, a Bird Masque* (1914), given first, September 12, 1913, in honor of President and Mrs. Wilson, at Meriden, New Hampshire, and repeated many times, 120 performances being given in the Southern and Western States before over 200,000 spectators by the Redpath Chautauqua players; *Saint Louis: A Civic Masque* (1914), given in St. Louis to celebrate the one hundred and fiftieth anniversary of the founding of the city, from May 28 to June 1, 1914; *The New Citizenship, a Civic Ritual* (1915), given February 14, 1916, in New York City, for Lincoln's Birthday and, most significant, *Caliban, A Community Masque* (1916), produced May 25 to June 2, 1916, in New York City as a part of the Shakespeare Tercentenary Celebration. This masque, founded on *The Tempest,* and having as its main theme the regeneration of Caliban through his love for Miranda, was magnificently produced at the Stadium of the College of the City of New York and marks a new epoch in the community drama. Of the operas, *Sinbad the Sailor* (1917) and *The Immigrants* (1915), with music by Mr. F. S. Converse, have not as yet been produced. *The Canterbury Pilgrims* (1916), with music by Mr. Reginald de Koven, was first produced at the Metropolitan Opera House in New York, March 8, 1917.

The Scarecrow was first performed by the Harvard Dramatic Club, on December 7, 1909. Its first professional performance was given at the Middlesex Theatre, Middletown, Connecticut, December 30, 1910. The cast as given remained the same at its first New York performance, at the Garrick Theatre, January 17, 1911, except that the part of "Rachel" was taken by Miss Fola La Follette. The play is dedicated by the author to his mother, for the reason (as he has told the editor) that, but for her sympathetic interest and assistance, it would probably not have been written. The version here printed has been revised by Mr. MacKaye and represents the acting version used by Mr. Frank Reicher during two seasons in the United States, and by Miss Muriel Pratt at the Theatre Royal, Bristol, England. It is also the version translated into

German by Dr. Walther Fischer, of the University of Pennsylvania, for the professional use of Herr Rudolf Schildkraut in Germany, at the "Deutsches Theater," Berlin, under the direction of Professor Max Reinhardt. It has also been translated into French by Professor M. Garnier, of the Sorbonne, Paris.

The individual plays may be found in printed form, as indicated above. Mr. MacKaye's poems, which have appeared in several editions, may be had most conveniently in the complete edition of his *Poems and Plays,* in two volumes, issued by Macmillan Company in 1916. In this edition, *The Canterbury Pilgrims, Jeanne d'Arc, Sappho and Phaon, The Scarecrow,* and *Mater* have been reprinted. His essays on dramatic subjects may be found in *The Playhouse and the Play* (1909), and *The Civic Theatre* (1912). He has also in press: *Steele MacKaye, A Memoir and Two Plays.* For an interesting foreign criticism of his work, especially of *The Scarecrow,* see M. Garnier, *M. Percy MacKaye,* in *La Revue du Mois,* April 10, 1909.

The editor is indebted to the courtesy of Mr. MacKaye for permission to reprint the play and for the biographical details and the information concerning the plays upon which this introduction is based.

Note to Revised Edition

Since the publication of the First Edition, Mr. Mackaye has produced the following dramatic works:

Plays—Washington, the Man Who Made Us (1919), a Ballad Play, was first produced in its entirety (under the title "George Washington") at the Belasco Theatre, Washington, D. C., February 23, 1920, one portion of it (the Valley Forge Action) having been previously produced in French—translated by Pierre de Lanux—at Copeau's Theatre du Vieux Colombier, New York, Feb. 17, 1919. This Action and other Actions of the play have also been translated into fourteen different languages by the Foreign Language Information Service Bureau of the Red Cross for publication and production in foreign language theatres in America.

Masques—Caliban was also presented on a still more splendid scale, by co-operation of nineteen districts of Greater Boston, at the Harvard Stadium, Cambridge, June 28 to July 21 (inclusive), 1917.

The Evergreen Tree (1917), a Christmas Masque, was first produced by North Dakota Agricultural College, at Fargo, N. D., Dec. 15, 1917.

The Roll Call (1918), a Masque of the Red Cross, was first produced during Roll Call Week, December 16–23, 1918, simultaneously in different states throughout America. *The Will of Song* (with Harry Barnhart, 1919), a Dramatic Service of Community Singing, was first produced at Orange, N. J., May 2 and 3, 1919.

Operas—Rip Van Winkle, a Folk Opera (1919), with music by Reginald e Koven, was first produced by the Chicago Opera Association at the Auditorium Theatre, Chicago, Jan. 2, 1920.

Note to Third Edition.

Since 1920, two plays by Mr. Mackaye have been produced:

This Fine-Pretty World, a comedy of the Kentucky mountains (1924), first produced at the Neighborhood Playhouse, New York City, December 26, 1923.

Napoleon Crossing the Rockies, a play of the Kentucky mountains (*Century Magazine,* April, 1924), first produced at the Carnegie Institute, Pittsburgh, May 21, 1924.

Since 1920, Mr. Mackaye has held the Fellowship in Poetry at Miami University, Oxford, Ohio. In recognition of his services, the University conferred upon him, in June 1924, the honorary degree of Doctor of Letters.

Note to Fourth Edition.

An extended treatment of Mr. MacKaye's plays is to be found in T. H. Dickinson's *Playwrights of the New American Theater* (1924), pp. 1-55. See also the present editor's *History of the American Drama from the Civil War to the Present Day,* Vol. 2, pp. 27–49.

Note to Fifth Edition.

Mr. MacKaye's recent dramatic publications consist of *Kentucky Mountain Fantasies,* containing three one-act plays (1928), and a revised version of *Yankee Fantasies.* His biography of his father, *Epoch,* 2 vol., 1927, is a significant contribution to dramatic history.

Note to Seventh Edition.

One of MacKaye's most ambitious efforts is *The Mystery of Hamlet, King of Denmark;* or *What We Will, A Sequence of Four Plays in Prologue* to Shakespeare's *Hamlet,* produced at the Pasadena Playhouse, April 14, 15, 16 and 17, 1949, and published in 1949. The drama deals with Hamlet's father, his love for Gertrude and her betrayal by Claudius, his brother. Scenes from Shakespeare's *Hamlet* are interspersed. The conception is daring but impressive and the poetry is at times of a high order, but the comedy is weak and the organization loose.

TO

MY MOTHER

In Memory of Auspicious
"Counting of the Crows"
By Old New England Cornfields

CAST OF CHARACTERS

At the First Professional Performance

Middlesex Theatre, Middletown, Connecticut, December 30, 1910

Justice Gilead Merton .... Mr. Brigham Royce
Goody Rickby ("Blacksmith Bess") .... Miss Alice Fischer
Lord Ravensbane ("Marquis of Oxford, Baron of Wittenberg, Elector of Worms, and Count of Cordova"), their hypothetical son .... Mr. Frank Reicher
Dickon, a Yankee improvisation of the Prince of Darkness .. Mr. Edmund Breese
Rachel Merton, niece of the Justice .... Miss Beatrice Irwin
Mistress Cynthia Merton, sister of the Justice .... Mrs. Felix Morris
Richard Talbot, Esquire, betrothed to Rachel .... Mr. Earle Browne
Sir Charles Reddington, Lieutenant-Governor .... Mr. H. J. Carvill
Mistress Reddington } his daughters. { .... Miss Zenaidee Williams
Amelia Reddington } his daughters. { .... Miss Georgia Dvorak
Captain Bugby, the Governor's Secretary .... Mr. Regan Hughston
Minister Dodge .... Mr. Clifford Leigh
Mistress Dodge, his wife .... Miss Eleanor Sheldon
Rev. Master Rand, of Harvard College .... Mr. William Lewis
Rev. Master Todd, of Harvard College .... Mr. Harry Lillford
Micah, a servant of the Justice .... Mr. Harold N. Cheshir

Time—Late seventeenth century.
Place—A town in Massachusetts.

THE SCARECROW

ACT FIRST.

The interior of a blacksmith shop. On the right of the stage toward the center there is a forge. On the left stands a loft, from which are hanging dried corn-stalks, hay, and the yellow ears of cattle-corn. Toward the rear is a wide double door, closed when the curtain rises. Through this door—when later it is opened—is visible a New England landscape in the late springtime: a distant wood; stone walls, high elms, a well-sweep; and, in the near foreground, a ploughed field, from which the green shoots of early corn are just appearing. The blackened walls of the shop are covered with a miscellaneous collection of old iron, horseshoes, and cart-wheels, the usual appurtenances of a smithy. In the right-hand corner, however, is an array of things quite out of keeping with the shop proper: musical instruments, puppets, tall clocks, and fantastical junk. Conspicuous amongst these articles is a large standing mirror, framed grotesquely in old gold and curtained by a dull stuff, embroidered with peaked caps and crescent moons.

Just before the scene opens, a hammer is heard ringing briskly upon steel. As the curtain rises there is discovered, standing at the anvil in the flickering light of a bright flame from the forge, a woman—powerful, ruddy, proud with a certain masterful beauty, white-haired (as though prematurely), bare-armed to the elbows, clad in a dark skirt (above her ankles), a loose blouse, open at the throat; a leathern apron and a workman's cap. The woman is GOODY RICKBY. *On the anvil she is shaping a piece of iron. Beside her stands a framework of iron formed like the ribs and backbone of a man. For a few moments she continues to ply her hammer, amid a shower of sparks, till suddenly the flame on the forge dies down.*

GOODY RICKBY. Dickon! More flame.

A VOICE. (*Above her.*) Yea, Goody.

(*The flame in the forge spurts up high and suddenly.*)

GOODY RICKBY. Nay, not so fierce.

THE VOICE. (*At her side.*) *Votre pardon, madame.* (*The flame subsides.*) Is that better?

GOODY RICKBY. That will do. (*With her tongs, she thrusts the iron into the flame; it turns white-hot.*) Quick work; nothing like brimstone for the smithy trade. (*At the anvil, she begins to weld the iron rib onto the framework.*) There, my beauty! We'll make a stout set of ribs for you. I'll see to it this year that I have a scarecrow can outstand all the nor'easters that blow. I've no notion to lose my corn-crop this summer. (*Outside, the faint cawings of crows are heard. Putting down her tongs and hammer,* GOODY RICKBY *strides to the double door, and flinging it wide open, lets in the gray light of dawn. She looks out over the fields and shakes her fist.*) So ye're up before me and the sun, are ye? (*Squinting against the light.*) There's one! Nay, two. Aha!

One for sorrow,
Two for mirth—

Good! This time we'll have the laugh on our side. (*She returns to the forge, where again the fire has died out.*) Dickon! Fire! Come, come, where be thy wits?

THE VOICE. (*Sleepily from the forge.*) 'T is early, dame.

GOODY RICKBY. The more need—

(*Takes up her tongs.*)

THE VOICE. (*Screams.*) Ow!

GOODY RICKBY. Ha! Have I got thee? (*From the blackness of the forge she pulls out with her tongs, by the right ear, the figure of a devil, horned and tailed. In general aspect, though he resembles a mediæval familiar demon, yet the suggestions of a goatish beard, a shrewdly humorous smile, and (when he speaks) the slightest of nasal drawls, remotely simulate a species of Yankee rustic.* GOODY RICKBY *substitutes her fingers for the tongs.*) Now, Dickon!

DICKON. *Deus!* I have n't been nabbed like that since St. Dunstan tweaked my nose. Well, sweet Goody?

GOODY RICKBY. The bellows!

DICKON. (*Going slowly to the forge.*) Why, 't is hardly dawn yet. Honest folks are still abed. It makes a long day.

GOODY RICKBY. (*Working while* DICKON *plies the bellows.*) Aye, for your black pets, the crows, to work in. That 's why we must be at it early. You heard 'em. We must have this scarecrow of ours out in the field at his post before sunrise. Here, I 've made the frame strong, so as to stand the weather; *you* must make the body lifelike so as to fool the crows. This year, we must make 'em think it 's a real human crittur.

DICKON. To fool the philosophers is my specialty, but the crows—hm!

GOODY RICKBY. Pooh! That staggers thee!

DICKON. Madame Rickby, prod not the quick of my genius. I am Phidias, I am Raphael, I am the Lord God!—You shall see—(*Demands with a gesture.*) Yonder broom-stick.

GOODY RICKBY. (*Fetching him a broom from the corner.*) Good boy!

DICKON. (*Straddling the handle.*) Ha, ha! gee up! my Salem mare. (*Then, pseudo-philosophically.*) A broomstick —that 's for imagination! (*He begins to construct the scarecrow, while* GOODY RICKBY, *assisting, brings the constructive parts from various nooks and corners.*) We are all pretty artists, to be sure, Bessie. Phidias, he sculptures the gods; Raphael, he paints the angels; the Lord God, he creates Adam; and Dickon —fetch me the poker—aha! Dickon! What doth Dickon? He nullifies 'em all; he endows the Scarecrow! A poker: here 's his conscience. There 's two fine legs to walk on,—imagination and conscience. Yonder flails now! The ideal —the *beau idéal,* dame—that 's what we artists seek. The apotheosis of scarecrows! And pray, what 's a scarecrow? Why, the antithesis of Adam.—"Let there be candles!" quoth the Lord God, sitting in the dark. "Let there be candle-extinguishers," saith Dickon. "I am made in the image of my maker," quoth Adam. "Look at yourself in the glass," saith Goodman Scarecrow. (*Taking two implements from* GOODY RICKBY.) Fine! fine! here are flails—one for wit, t' other for satire. *Sapristi!* with two such arms, my lad, how thou wilt work thy way in the world!

GOODY RICKBY. You talk as if you were making a real mortal, Dickon.

DICKON. To fool a crow, Goody, I must fashion a crittur that will first deceive a man.

GOODY RICKBY. He 'll scarce do that without a head. (*Pointing to the loft.*) What think ye of yonder Jack-o'-lantern? 'T was made last Hallowe'en.

DICKON. Rare, my Psyche! We shall collaborate. Here! (*Running up the ladder, he tosses down a yellow hollowed pumpkin to* GOODY RICKBY, *who catches it. Then rummaging forth an armful of cornstalks, ears, tassels, dried squashes, gourds, beets, etc., he descends and throws them in a heap on the floor.*) Whist! (*As he drops them.*) Gourd, carrot, turnip, beet:—the anatomy.

GOODY RICKBY. (*Placing the pumpkin on the shoulders.*) Look!

DICKON. *O Johannes Baptista!* What wouldst thou have given for such a head! I helped Salome to cut his off, dame, and it looked not half so appetizing on her charger. Tut! Copernicus wore once such a pumpkin, but it is rotten. Look at his golden smile! Hail, Phœbus Apollo!

GOODY RICKBY. 'T is the finest scarecrow in town.

DICKON. Nay, poor soul, 't is but a skeleton yet. He must have a man's heart in him. (*Picking a big red beet from among the cornstalks, he places it under the left side of the ribs.*) Hush! Dost thou hear it *beat?*

GOODY RICKBY. Thou merry rogue!

DICKON. Now for the lungs of him. (*Snatching a small pair of bellows from a peg on the wall.*) That 's for eloquence! He 'll preach the black knaves a sermon on theft. And now—(*Here, with* GOODY RICKBY'S *help, he stuffs the framework with the gourds, corn, etc., from the loft, weaving the husks about the legs and arms.*) Here goes for digestion and inherited instincts! More corn, Goody. Now he 'll fight for his own flesh and blood!

GOODY RICKBY. (*Laughing.*) Dickon, I am proud of thee.

DICKON. Wait till you see his peruke. (*Seizing a feather duster made of crow's feathers.*) *Voici!* Scalps of the enemy! (*Pulling them apart, he arranges *the feathers on the pumpkin, like a gentleman's wig.)* A rare conqueror!

GOODY RICKBY. Oh, you beauty!

DICKON. And now a bit of comfort for dark days and stormy nights. (*Taking a piece of corn-cob with the kernels on it,* DICKON *makes a pipe, which he puts into the scarecrow's mouth.*) So! There, Goody! I tell thee, with yonder brand-new coat and breeches of mine—those there in my cupboard!—we'll make him a lad to be proud of. (*Taking the clothes, which* GOODY RICKBY *brings—a pair of fine scarlet breeches and a gold-embroidered coat with ruffles of lace—he puts them upon the scarecrow. Then, eying it like a connoisseur, makes a few finishing touches.*) Why, dame, he'll be a son to thee.

GOODY RICKBY. A son? Aye, if I had but a son!

DICKON. Why, here you have him. (*To the scarecrow.*) Thou wilt scare the crows off thy mother's cornfield—won't my pretty? And send 'em all over t' other side the wall to her dear neighbor's, the Justice Gilead Merton's.

GOODY RICKBY. Justice Merton! Nay, if they'd only peck his eyes out, instead of his corn.

DICKON. (*Grinning.*) Yet the Justice was a dear friend of "Blacksmith Bess."

GOODY RICKBY. Aye, "Blacksmith Bess"! If I had n't had a good stout arm when he cast me off with the babe, I might have starved for all his worship cared.

DICKON. True, Bessie; 't was a scurvy trick he played on thee—and on me, that took such pains to bring you together—to steal a young maid's heart—

GOODY RICKBY. And then toss it away like a bad penny to the gutter! And the child—to die! (*Lifting her hammer in rage.*) Ha! If I could get the worshipful Justice Gilead into my power again—(*She drops the hammer sullenly on the anvil.*) But no! I shall beat my life away on this anvil, whilst my justice clinks his gold, and drinks his port to a fat old age. Justice! Ha—justice of God!

DICKON. Whist, dame! Talk of angels and hear the rustle of their relatives.

GOODY RICKBY. (*Turning, watches outside a girl's figure approaching.*) His niece—Rachel Merton! What can she want so early? Nay, I mind me; 't is the mirror. She's a maid after our own hearts, boy,—no Sabbath-go-to-meeting airs about *her!* She hath read the books of the *magi* from cover to cover, and paid me good guineas for 'em, though her uncle knows naught on 't. Besides, she's in love, Dickon.

DICKON. (*Indicating the scarecrow.*) Ah? With *him?* Is it a rendezvous?

GOODY RICKBY. (*With a laugh.*) Pff! Begone!

DICKON. (*Shakes his finger at the scarecrow.*) Thou naughty rogue!

(*Then, still smiling slyly, with his head placed confidentially next to the scarecrow's ear, as if whispering, and with his hand pointing to the maiden outside,* DICKON *fades away into air.* RACHEL *enters, nervous and hesitant.* GOODY RICKBY *makes her a curtsy, which she acknowledges by a nod, half absent-minded.*)

GOODY RICKBY. Mistress Rachel Merton—so early! I hope your uncle, our worshipful Justice, is not ill?

RACHEL. No, my uncle is quite well. The early morning suits me best for a walk. You are—quite alone?

GOODY RICKBY. Quite alone, mistress. (*Bitterly.*) Oh, folks don't call on Goody Rickby—except on business.

RACHEL. (*Absently, looking round in the dim shop.*) Yes—you must be busy. Is it—is it here?

GOODY RICKBY. You mean the—

RACHEL. (*Starting back, with a cry.*) Ah! who's that?

GOODY RICKBY. (*Chuckling.*) Fear not, mistress; 't is nothing but a scarecrow. I'm going to put him in my cornfield yonder. The crows are so pesky this year.

RACHEL. (*Draws her skirts away with a shiver.*) How loathsome!

GOODY RICKBY. (*Vastly pleased.*) He'll do.

RACHEL. Ah, here!—This is *the* mirror?

GOODY RICKBY. Yea, mistress, and a wonderful glass it is, as I told you. I would n't sell it to most comers, but seeing how you and Master Talbot—

RACHEL. Yes; that will do.

GOODY RICKBY. You see, if the town folks guessed what it was, well— You've heard tell of the gibbets on Salem Hill? There's not many in New England like you, Mistress Rachel. You know enough to approve some miracles—outside the Scriptures.

RACHEL. You are quite sure the glass will do all you say? It—never fails?

GOODBY RICKBY. Ah, now, mistress, how could it? 'T is the glass of truth—(*insinuatingly*)—the glass of true lovers. It shows folks just as they are; no shams, no varnish. If a wolf should dress himself in a white sheep's wool, this glass would reflect the black beast inside it.

RACHEL. (*With awe.*) The black beast! But what of the sins of the soul, Goody? Vanity, hypocrisy, and — and inconstancy? Will it surely reveal them?

GOODY RICKBY. I have told you, my young lady. If it doth not as I say, bring it back and get your money again. Oh, trust me, sweeting, an old dame hath eyes in her heart yet. If your lover be false, this glass shall pluck his fine feathers!

RACHEL. (*With aloofness.*) 'T is no question of that. I wish the glass to—to amuse me.

GOODY RICKBY. (*Laughing.*) Why, then, try it on some of your neighbors.

RACHEL. You ask a large price for it.

GOODY RICKBY. (*Shrugs.*) I run risks. Besides, where will you get another?

RACHEL. That is true. Here, I will buy it. That is the sum you mentioned, I believe?

(*She hands a purse to* GOODY RICKBY, *who opens it and counts over some coin.*)

GOODY RICKBY. Let see; let see.

RACHEL. Well?

GOODY RICKBY. Good: 't is good. Folks call me a witch, mistress. Well—harkee —a witch's word is as good as a justice's gold. The glass is yours—with my blessing.

RACHEI. Spare yourself that, dame. But the glass: how am I to get it? How will you send it to me—quietly?

GOODY RICKBY. Trust me for that. I 've a willing lad that helps me with such errands; a neighbor o' mine. (*Calls.*) Ebenezer!

RACHEL. (*Startled.*) What! is he here?

GOODY RICKBY. In the hayloft. The boy 's an orphan; he sleeps there o' times. Ebenezer!

(*A raw, disheveled country boy appears in the loft, slides down the ladder, and shuffles up sleepily.*)

THE BOY. Evenin'.

RACHEL. (*Drawing* GOODY RICKBY *aside.*) You understand; I desire no comment about this purchase.

GOODY RICKBY. Nor I, mistress, be sure.

RACHEL. Is he—?

GOODY RICKBY. (*Tapping her forehead significantly.*) Trust his wits who hath no wit; he 's mum.

RACHEL. Oh!

THE BOY. (*Gaping.*) Job?

GOODY RICKBY. Yea, rumple-head! His job this morning is to bear yonder glass to the house of Justice Merton—the big one on the hill; to the side door. Mind, no gabbing. Doth he catch?

THE BOY. (*Nodding and grinning.*) 'E swallows.

RACHEL. But is the boy strong enough?

GOODY RICKBY. Him? (*Pointing to the anvil.*) Ebenezer!

(*The boy spits on his palms, takes hold of the anvil, lifts it, drops it again, sits on it, and grins at the door, just as* RICHARD TALBOT *appears there, from outside.*)

RACHEL. Gracious!

GOODY RICKBY. Trust him. He'll carry the glass for you.

RACHEL. I will return home at once, then. Let him go quietly to the side door, and wait for me. Good-morning.

(*Turning, she confronts* RICHARD.)

RICHARD. Good-morning.

RACHEL. Richard!—Squire Talbot, you—you are abroad early.

RICHARD. As early as Mistress Rachel. Is it pardonable? I caught sight of you walking in this direction, so I thought it wise to follow, lest—

(*Looks hard at* GOODY RICKBY.)

RACHEL. Very kind. Thanks. We can return together. (*To* GOODY RICKBY.) You will make sure that I receive the—the article.

GOODY RICKBY. Trust me, mistress.

(*She curtsies to* RICHARD.)

RICHARD. (*Bluntly, looking from one to the other.*) What article?

(RACHEL *ignores the question and starts to pass out.* RICHARD *frowns at* GOODY RICKBY, *who stammers.*)

GOODY RICKBY. Begging your pardon, sir?

RICHARD. What article? I said. (*After a short, embarrassed pause, more sternly.*) Well?

GOODY RICKBY. Oh, the article! Yonder old glass, to be sure, sir. A quaint piece, your honor.

RICHARD. Rachel, you have n't come here at sunrise to buy—that thing?

RACHEL. Verily, "that thing," and at sunrise. A pretty time for a pretty purchase. Are you coming?

RICHARD. (*In a low tone.*) More witchcraft nonsense? Do you realize this is serious?

RACHEL. Oh, of course. You know I am desperately mystical, so pray let us not discuss it. Good-bye.

RICHARD. Rachel, just a moment. If you want a mirror, you shall have the prettiest one in New England. Or I will import you one from London. Only—I beg of you—don't buy stolen goods.

GOODY RICKBY. Stolen goods?

RACHEL. (*Aside to* RICHARD.) Don't! don't!

RICHARD. (*To* GOODY RICKBY.) Can you account for this mirror—how you came by it?

GOODY RICKBY. I'll show ye! I'll show ye! Stolen—ha!

RICHARD. Come, old swindler, keep your mirror, and give this lady back her money.

GOODY RICKBY. I'll damn ye both, I will!—Stolen!

RACHEL. (*Imploringly.*) Will you come?

RICHARD. Look you, old Rickby; this is not the first time. Charm all the broomsticks in town, if you like; bewitch all the tables and saucepans and mirrors you please; but gull no more money out of young girls. Mind you! We 're not so enterprising in this town as at Salem; but—*it may come to it!* So look sharp! I 'm not blind to what 's going on here.

GOODY RICKBY. Not blind, Master Puritan? Oho! You can see through all my counterfeits, can ye? So! you would scrape all the wonder out'n the world, as I 've scraped all the meat out'n my punkin-head yonder! Aha! wait and see! Afore sundown, I 'll send ye a nut to crack, shall make your orthodox jaws ache. Your servant, Master Deuteronomy!

RICHARD. (*To* RACHEL, *who has seized his arm.*) We 'll go.

(*Exeunt* RICHARD *and* RACHEL.)

GOODY RICKBY. (*Calls shrilly after them.*) Trot away, pretty team; toss your heads. I 'll unhitch ye and take off your blinders.

THE SLOUCHING BOY. (*Capering and grimacing in front of the mirror, shrieks with laughter.*) Ohoho!

GOODY RICKBY. (*Returning, she mutters savagely.*) "Stolen goods!" (*Screams.*) Dickon! Stop laughing.

THE BOY. O Lord! O Lord!

GOODY RICKBY. What tickles thy mirth now?

THE BOY. For to think that the soul of an orphan innocent, what lives in a hayloft, should wear horns.

(*On looking into the mirror, the spectator perceives therein that the reflection of the slouching boy is the horned demon figure of* DICKON, *who performs the same antics in pantomime within the glass as the boy does without.*)

GOODY RICKBY. Yea; 't is a wise devil that knows his own face in the glass. But hark now! thou must find me a rival for this cock-squire,—dost hear? A rival, that shall steal away the heart of his Mistress Rachel.

DICKON. And take her to church?

GOODY RICKBY. To church or to hell. All 's one.

DICKON. A rival! (*Pointing at the glass.*) How would *he* serve—in there? Dear Ebenezer! Fancy the deacons in the vestry, Goody, and her uncle, the Justice, when they saw him escorting the bride to the altar, with his tail round her waist!

GOODY RICKBY. Tut, tut! Think it over in earnest, and meantime take her the glass. Wait, we 'd best fold it up small, so as not to attract notice on the road. (DICKON, *who has already drawn the curtains over the glass, grasps one side of the large frame,* GOODY RICKBY *the other.*) Now! (*Pushing their shoulders against the two sides, the frame disappears and* DICKON *holds in his hand a mirror about a foot square, of the same design.*) So! Be off! And mind, a rival for Richard!

DICKON.

For Richard a rival,
Dear Goody Rickby
Wants Dickon's connival:
Lord! What can the trick be?

(*To the scarecrow.*) By-by, Sonny; take care of thy mother.

(DICKON *slouches out with the glass, whistling.*)

GOODY RICKBY. Mother! Yea, if only I had a son—the Justice Merton's and mine! If the brat had but lived now to remind him of those merry days, which he has forgotten. Zooks, would n't I put a spoke in his wheel! But no such luck for me! No such luck!

(*As she goes to the forge, the stout figure of a man appears in the doorway behind her. Under one arm he carries a large book, in the other hand a gold-headed cane. He hesitates, embarrassed.*)

THE MAN. Permit me, madam.

GOODY RICKBY. (*Turning.*) Ah, him—Justice Merton!

JUSTICE MERTON. (*Removing his hat, steps over the sill, and lays his great book on the table; then with a supercilious look, he puts his hat firmly on again.*) Permit me, dame.

GOODY RICKBY. You!

(*With confused, affected hauteur, the* JUSTICE *shifts from foot to foot, flourishing his cane. As he speaks,* GOODY RICKBY, *with a shrewd, painful expression, draws slowly backward toward the door, left, which opens into an inner room. Reaching it, she opens it part way, stands facing him, and listens.*)

JUSTICE MERTON. I have had the honor—permit me—to entertain suspicions; to rise early, to follow my niece, to meet just now Squire Talbot; to hear his remarks concerning—hem!—you, dame! to call here—permit me—to express myself and inquire—

GOODY RICKBY. Concerning your waistcoat?

(*Turning quickly, she snatches an article of apparel which hangs on the inner side of the door, and holds it up.*)

JUSTICE MERTON. (*Starting, crimson.*) Woman!

GOODY RICKBY. You left it behind—the last time.

JUSTICE MERTON. I have not the honor to remember—

GOODY RICKBY. The one I embroidered?

JUSTICE MERTON. 'T is a matter of—

GOODY RICKBY. Of some two-and-twenty years. (*Stretching out the narrow width of the waistcoat.*) Will you try it on now, dearie?

JUSTICE MERTON. Unconscionable! Un-un-unconscionable witch!

GOODY RICKBY. Witchling—thou used to say.

JUSTICE MERTON. Pah! pah! I forget myself. Pride, permit me, goeth before a fall. As a magistrate, Rickby, I have already borne with you long! The last straw, however, breaks the camel's back.

GOODY RICKBY. Poor camel!

JUSTICE MERTON. You have soiled, you have smirched, the virgin reputation of my niece. You have inveigled her into notions of witchcraft; already the neighbors are beginning to talk. 'T is a long lane which hath no turning, saith the Lord. Permit me—as a witch, thou art judged. Thou shalt hang.

A VOICE. (*Behind him.*) And me, too?

JUSTICE MERTON. (*Turns about and stares.*) I beg pardon.

THE VOICE. (*In front of him.*) Not at all.

JUSTICE MERTON. Did—did somebody speak?

THE VOICE. Don't you recognize my voice? *Still and small,* you know. If you will kindly let me out, we can chat.

JUSTICE MERTON. (*Turning fiercely on* GOODY RICKBY.) These are thy sorceries. But I fear them not. The righteous man walketh with God. (*Going to the book which lies on the table.*) Satan, I ban thee! I will read from the Holy Scriptures!

(*Unclasping the Bible, he flings open the ponderous covers.*—DICKON *steps forth in smoke.*)

DICKON. Thanks; it was stuffy in there.

JUSTICE MERTON. (*Clasping his hands.*) Dickon!

DICKON. (*Moving a step nearer on the table.*) Hullo, Gilly! Hullo, Bess!

JUSTICE MERTON. Dickon! No! No!

DICKON. Do ye mind Auld Lang Syne—the chorus that night, Gilly? (*Sings.*)

Gil-ead, Gil-ead, Gil-ead Merton,
He was a silly head, silly head, Certain,
When he forgot to steal a bed-Curtain.

Encore, now!

JUSTICE MERTON. No, no, be merciful! I will not harm her; she shall not hang; I swear it, I swear it! (DICKON *disappears.*) I swear—ah! Is he gone? Witchcraft! Witchcraft! I have witnesed it. 'T is proved on thee, slut. I swear it: thou shalt hang.

(*Exit wildly.*)

GOODY RICKBY. Ay, Gilead! I shall hang *on!* Ahaha! Dickon, thou angel! Ah, Satan! Satan! For a son now!

DICKON. (*Reappearing.*) *Videlicet,* in law—a bastard. *N' est ce pas?*

GOODY RICKBY. Yea, in law and in justice, I should 'a' had one now. Worse luck that he died.

DICKON. One-and-twenty years ago? (GOODY RICKBY *nods.*) Good; he should be of age now. One-and-twenty—a pretty age, too, for a rival. Haha!—For arrival?—Marry, he shall arrive, then; arrive and marry and inherit his patrimony—all on his birthday! Come, to work!

GOODY RICKBY. What rant is this?

DICKON. Yet, Dickon, it pains me to perform such an anachronism. All this mediævalism in Massachusetts!—These old-fashioned flames and alchemic accompaniments, when I 've tried so hard to be a native American product; it jars. But *che vuole!* I 'm naturally middle-aged. I have n't been really myself, let me think,—since 1492!

GOODY RICKBY. What art thou mooning about?

DICKON. (*Still impenetrable.*) There was my old friend in Germany, Dr. Johann Faustus; he was nigh such a bag of old rubbish when I made him over. Ain't it trite! No, you can't teach an old dog like me new tricks. Still, a scarecrow! that 's decidedly local color. Come, then; a Yankee masterpiece! (*Seizing* GOODY RICKBY *by the arm, and placing her before the scarecrow, he makes a bow and wave of introduction.*) Behold, madam, your son—illegitimate; the future affianced of Mistress Rachel Merton, the heir-elect, through matrimony, of Merton House,—Gilead Merton second: Lord Ravensbane! Your lordship—your mother.

GOODY RICKBY. Dickon! Can you do it?

DICKON. I can—try.

GOODY RICKBY. You will create him for me?—(*wickedly*)—and for Gilead!

DICKON. I will—for a kiss.

GOODY RICKBY. (*About to embrace him.*) Dickon!

DICKON. (*Dodging her.*) Later. Now, the waistcoat.

GOODY RICKBY. (*Handing it.*) Rare! Rare! He shall go wooing in 't—like his father.

DICKON. (*Shifting the scarecrow's gold-trimmed coat, slips on the embroidered waistcoat and replaces the coat.*) Stand still, Jack! So, my macaroni. *Perfecto!* Stay—a walking-stick!

GOODY RICKBY. (*Wrenching a spoke out of an old rickety wheel.*) Here: the spoke for Gilead. He used to take me to drive in the chaise it came out of.

DICKON. (*Placing the spoke as a cane, in the scarecrow's sleeve, views him with satisfaction.*) *Sic!* There, Jacky! *Filius fit non nascitur.*—Sam Hill! My Latin is stale. "In the beginning, was the—gourd!" Of these thy modest ingredients may thy spirit smack!

(*Making various mystic passes with his hands,* DICKON *intones, now deep and solemn, now with fanciful shrill rapidity, this incantation.*)

Flail, flip;
Broom, sweep;
Sic itur!
Cornstalk
And turnip, talk!
Turn crittur!

Pulse, beet;
Gourd, eat;
Ave Hellas!
Poker and punkin,
Stir the old junk in;
Breathe, bellows!

Corn-cob,
And crow's feather,
End the job;
Jumble the rest o' the rubbish together;
Dovetail and tune 'em.
E pluribus unum!

(*The scarecrow remains stock still.*)
The devil! Have I lost the hang of it? Ah! Hullo! He 's dropped his pipe. What 's a dandy without his 'baccy! (*Picking up the pipe, he shows it to* GOODY RICKBY, *pointing into the pipe-bowl.*) 'T is my own brand, Goody: brimstone. Without it he 'd be naught but a scarecrow. (*Restoring the corn-cob pipe to the scarecrow's mouth.*) 'T is the life and breath of him. So; hand me yon hazel switch, Goody. (*Waving it.*) Presto!

Brighten, coal,
I' the dusk between us!
Whiten, soul!
Propinquat Venus!

(A *whiff of smoke puffs from the scarecrow's pipe.*)
Sic! Sic! Jacobus! (*Another whiff.*) Bravo!

(*The whiffs grow more rapid and the thing trembles.*)

GOODY RICKBY. Puff! puff, manny, for thy life!

DICKON. *Fiat, fœtus!*—Huzza! *Noch einmal!* Go it!

(*Clouds of smoke issue from the pipe, half fill the shop, and envelop the creature, who staggers.*[1])

GOODY RICKBY. See! See his eyes!

DICKON. (*Beckoning with one finger.*) *Veni fili! Veni!* Take 'ee first step, *bambino!*—Toddle!

(*The* SCARECROW *makes a stiff lurch forward and falls sidewise against the anvil, propped half-reclining against which he leans rigid, emitting fainter puffs of smoke in gasps.*)

GOODY RICKBY. (*Screams.*) Have a care! He 's fallen.

DICKON. Well done, Punkin Jack! Thou shalt be knighted for that! (*Striking him on the shoulder with the hazel rod.*) Rise, Lord Ravensbane!

(*The* SCARECROW *totters to his feet, and makes a forlorn rectilinear salutation.*)

GOODY RICKBY. Look! He bows.—He flaps his flails at thee. He smiles like a tik-doo-loo-roo!

DICKON. (*With a profound reverence, backing away.*) Will his lordship deign to follow his tutor?

(*With hitches and jerks, the* SCARECROW *follows* DICKON.)

GOODY RICKBY. O Lord! Lord! the style o' the broomstick!

DICKON. (*Holding ready a high-backed chair.*) Will his lordship be seated and rest himself? (*Awkwardly the* SCARECROW *half falls into the chair; his head sinks sideways, and his pipe falls out.* DICKON *snatches it up instantly and restores it to his mouth.*) Puff! Puff, *puer;* 't is thy life. (*The* SCARECROW *puffs again.*) Is his lordship's tobacco refreshing?

GOODY RICKBY. Look now! The red color in his cheeks. The beet-juice is pumping, oho!

DICKON. (*Offering his arm.*) Your lordship will deign to receive an audience? (*The* SCARECROW *takes his arm and rises.*) The Marchioness of Rickby, your lady mother, entreats leave to present herself.

GOODY RICKBY. (*Curtsying low.*) My son!

[1] At Dickon's words, "Come to work!" on p. 855 the living actor, concealed by the smoke, and disguised, has substituted himself for the elegantly clad effigy. His make-up, of course, approximates to the latter, but the grotesque contours of his expression gradually, throughout the remainder of the act, become refined and sublimated till, at the *finale*, they are of a lordly and distinguished taste.

DICKON. (*Holding the pipe, and waving the hazel rod.*) *Dicite!* Speak! (*The* SCARECROW, *blowing out his last mouthful of smoke, opens his mouth, gasps, gurgles, and is silent.*) *In principio erat verbum!* Accost thy mother!

(*The* SCARECROW, *clutching at his side in a struggle for coherence, fixes a pathetic look of pain on* GOODY RICKBY.)

THE SCARECROW. Mother!

GOODY RICKBY. (*With a scream of hysterical laughter, seizes both* DICKON'S *hands and dances him about the forge.*) O, Beelzebub! I shall die!

DICKON. Thou hast thy son.

(DICKON *whispers in the* SCARECROW'S *ear, shakes his finger, and exit.*)

GOODY RICKBY. He called me "mother." Again, boy, again.

THE SCARECROW. From the bottom of my heart—mother.

GOODY RICKBY. "The bottom of his heart"! —Nay, thou killest me.

THE SCARECROW. Permit me, madam!

GOODY RICKBY. Gilead! Gilead himself! Waistcoat, "permit me," and all: thy father over again, I tell thee.

THE SCARECROW. (*With a slight stammer.*) It gives me—I assure you—lady —the deepest happiness.

GOODY RICKBY. Just so the old hypocrite spoke when I said I'd have him. But thou hast a sweeter deference, my son.

(*Reënter* DICKON; *he is dressed all in black, save for a white stock—a suit of plain elegance.*)

DICKON. Now, my lord, your tutor is ready.

THE SCARECROW. (*To* GOODY RICKBY.) I have the honor—permit me—to wish you—good-morning.

(*Bows and takes a step after* DICKON, *who, taking a three-cornered cocked hat from a peg, goes toward the door.*)

GOODY RICKBY. Whoa! Whoa, Jack! Whither away?

DICKON. (*Presenting the hat.*) Deign to reply, sir.

THE SCARECROW. I go—with my tutor—Master Dickonson—to pay my respects—to his worship—the Justice—Merton—to solicit—the hand—of his daughter—the fair Mistress—Rachel. (*With another bow.*) Permit me.

GOODY RICKBY. Permit ye? God speed

ye! Thou must teach him his tricks, Dickon.

DICKON. Trust me, Goody. Between here and Justice Merton's, I will play the mother-hen, and I promise thee, our bantling shall be as stuffed with compliments as a callow chick with caterpillars. (*As he throws open the big doors, the cawing of crows is heard again.*) Hark! your lordship's retainers acclaim you on your birthday. They bid you welcome to your majority. Listen! "Long live Lord Ravensbane! Caw!"

GOODY RICKBY. Look! Count 'em, Dickon.

One for sorrow,
Two for mirth,
Three for a wedding,
Four for a birth—

Four on 'em! So! Good luck on thy birthday! And see! There's three on 'em flying into the Justice's field.

—Flight o' the crows
Tells how the wind blows!—

A wedding! Get thee gone. Wed the girl, and sting the Justice. Bless ye, my son!

THE SCARECROW. (*With a profound reverence.*) Mother—believe me—to be—your ladyship's—most devoted—and obedient—son.

DICKON. (*Prompting him aloud.*) Ravensbane.

THE SCARECROW. (*Donning his hat, lifts his head in hauteur, shakes his lace ruffle over his hand, turns his shoulder, nods slightly, and speaks for the first time with complete mastery of his voice.*) Hm! Ravensbane!

(*With one hand in the arm of* DICKON, *the other twirling his cane (the converted chaise-spoke), wreathed in halos of smoke from his pipe, the fantastical figure hitches elegantly forth into the daylight, amid louder acclamations of the crows.*)

ACT SECOND.

The same morning. JUSTICE MERTON'S *parlor, furnished and designed in the style of the early colonial period. On the right wall hangs a portrait of the* JUSTICE *as a young man; on the left wall, an old-fashioned looking-glass. At the right of the room stands the Glass of Truth, draped—as in the blacksmith shop—with the strange, embroidered curtain. In front of it are discovered* RACHEL *and* RICHARD; RACHEL *is about to draw the curtain.*

RACHEL. Now! Are you willing?

RICHARD. So you suspect me of dark, villainous practices?

RACHEL. No, no, foolish Dick.

RICHARD. Still, I am to be tested; is that it?

RACHEL. That's it.

RICHARD. As your true lover.

RACHEL. Well, yes.

RICHARD. Why, of course, then, I consent. A true lover always consents to the follies of his lady-love.

RACHEL. Thank you, Dick; I trust the glass will sustain your character. Now; when I draw the curtain—

RICHARD. (*Staying her hand.*) What if I be false?

RACHEL. Then, sir, the glass will reflect you as the subtle fox that you are.

RICHARD. And you—as the goose?

RACHEL. Very likely. Ah! but, Richard, dear, we must n't laugh. It may prove very serious. You do not guess—you do not dream all the mysteries—

RICHARD. (*Shaking his head, with a grave smile.*) You pluck at too many mysteries. Remember our first mother Eve!

RACHEL. But this is the glass of truth; and Goody Rickby told me—

RICHARD. Rickby, forsooth!

RACHEL. Nay, come; let's have it over. (*She draws the curtain, covers her eyes, steps back by* RICHARD'S *side, looks at the glass, and gives a joyous cry.*) Ah! there you are, dear! There we are, both of us—just as we have always seemed to each other, true. 'T is proved. Is n't it wonderful?

RICHARD. Miraculous! That a mirror bought in a blacksmith shop, before sunrise, for twenty pounds, should prove to be actually—a mirror!

RACHEL. Richard, I'm so happy.

(*Enter* JUSTICE MERTON *and* MISTRESS MERTON.)

RICHARD. (*Embracing her.*) Happy, art thou, sweet goose? Why, then, God bless Goody Rickby.

JUSTICE MERTON. Strange words from you, Squire Talbot.

(RACHEL *and* RICHARD *part quickly;* RACHEL *draws the curtain over the mirror;* RICHARD *stands stiffly.*)

RICHARD. Justice Merton! Why, sir, the old witch is more innocent, perhaps, than I represented her.
JUSTICE MERTON. A witch, believe me, is never innocent. (*Taking their hands, he brings them together and kisses* RACHEL *on the forehead.*) Permit me, young lovers. I was once young myself, young and amorous.
MISTRESS MERTON. (*In a low voice.*) Verily!
JUSTICE MERTON. My fair niece, my worthy young man, beware of witchcraft.
MISTRESS MERTON. And Goody Rickby, too, brother?
JUSTICE MERTON. That woman shall answer for her deeds. She is proscribed.
RACHEL. Proscribed? What is that?
MISTRESS MERTON. (*Examining the mirror.*) What is this?
JUSTICE MERTON. She shall hang.
RACHEL. Uncle, no! Not merely because of my purchase this morning?
JUSTICE MERTON. Your purchase?
MISTRESS MERTON. (*Pointing to the mirror.*) That, I suppose.
JUSTICE MERTON. What! you purchased that mirror of her? You brought it here?
RACHEL. No, the boy brought it; I found it here when I returned.
JUSTICE MERTON. What! From her shop? From her infamous den, into my parlor! (*To* MISTRESS MERTON.) Call the servant. (*Himself calling.*) Micah! Away with it! Micah!
RACHEL. Uncle Gilead, I bought—
JUSTICE MERTON. Micah, I say! Where is the man?
RACHEL. Listen, uncle. I bought it with my own money.
JUSTICE MERTON. Thine own money! Wilt have the neighbors gossip? Wilt have me, thyself, my house, suspected of complicity with witches?

(*Enter* MICAH.)

Micah, take this away.
MICAH. Yes, sir; but, sir—
JUSTICE MERTON. Out of my house!
MICAH. There be visitors.
JUSTICE MERTON. Away with—
MISTRESS MERTON. (*Touching his arm.*) Gilead!
MICAH. Visitors, sir; gentry.
JUSTICE MERTON. Ah!
MICAH. Shall I show them in, sir?
JUSTICE MERTON. Visitors! In the morning? Who are they?
MICAH. Strangers, sir. I should judge they be very high gentry; lords, sir.
ALL. Lords!
MICAH. At least, one on 'em, sir. The other—the dark gentleman—told me they left their horses at the inn, sir.
MISTRESS MERTON. Hark! (*The faces of all wear suddenly a startled expression.*) Where is that unearthly sound?
JUSTICE MERTON. (*Listening.*) Is it in the cellar?
MICAH. 'T is just the dog howling, madam. When he spied the gentry he turned tail and run below.
MISTRESS MERTON. Oh, the dog!
JUSTICE MERTON. Show the gentlemen here, Micah. Don't keep them waiting. A lord! (*To* RACHEL.) We shall talk of this matter later.—A lord!

(*Turning to the small glass on the wall, he arranges his peruke and attire.*)

RACHEL. (*To* RICHARD.) What a fortunate interruption! But, dear Dick! I wish we need n't meet these strangers now.
RICHARD. Would you really rather we were alone together?

(*They chat aside, absorbed in each other.*)

JUSTICE MERTON. Think of it, Cynthia, a lord!
MISTRESS MERTON. (*Dusting the furniture hastily with her handkerchief.*) And such dust!
RACHEL. (*To* RICHARD.) You know, dear, we need only be introduced, and then we can steal away together.

(*Reënter* MICAH.)

MICAH. (*Announcing.*) Lord Ravensbane: Marquis of Oxford, Baron of Wittenberg, Elector of Worms, and Count of Cordova; Master Dickonson.

(*Enter* RAVENSBANE *and* DICKON.)

JUSTICE MERTON. Gentlemen, permit me, you are excessively welcome. I am deeply gratified to meet—
DICKON. Lord Ravensbane, of the Rookeries, Somersetshire.
JUSTICE MERTON. Lord Ravensbane—his lordship's most truly honored.
RAVENSBANE. Truly honored.
JUSTICE MERTON. (*Turning to* DICKON.) His lordship's—?
DICKON. Tutor.

JUSTICE MERTON. (*Checking his effusiveness.*) Ah, so!

DICKON. Justice Merton, I believe.

JUSTICE MERTON. Of Merton House.—May I present—permit me, your lordship—my sister, Mistress Merton.

RAVENSBANE. Mistress Merton.

JUSTICE MERTON. And my—and my—(*under his breath*)—Rachel! (RACHEL *remains with a bored expression behind* RICHARD.)—My young neighbor, Squire Talbot, Squire Richard Talbot of—of—

RICHARD. Of nowhere, sir.

RAVENSBANE. (*Nods.*) Nowhere.

JUSTICE MERTON. And permit me, Lord Ravensbane, my niece—Mistress Rachel Merton.

RAVENSBANE. (*Bows low.*) Mistress Rachel Merton.

RACHEL. (*Curtsies.*) Lord Ravensbane.

(*As they raise their heads, their eyes meet and are fascinated.* DICKON *just then takes* RAVENSBANE'S *pipe and fills it.*)

RAVENSBANE. Mistress Rachel!

RACHEL. Your lordship!

(DICKON *returns the pipe.*)

MISTRESS MERTON. A pipe! Gilead!—in the parlor!

(JUSTICE MERTON *frowns silence.*)

JUSTICE MERTON. Your lordship—ahem!—has just arrived in town?

DICKON. From London, via New Amsterdam.

RICHARD. (*Aside.*) Is he staring at *you?* Are you ill, Rachel?

RACHEL. (*Indifferently.*) What?

JUSTICE MERTON. Lord Ravensbane honors my humble roof.

DICKON. (*Touches* RAVENSBANE'S *arm.*) Your lordship—"roof."

RAVENSBANE. (*Starting, turns to* MERTON.) Nay, sir, the roof of my father's oldest friend bestows generous hospitality upon his only son.

JUSTICE MERTON. Only son—ah, yes! Your father—

RAVENSBANE. My father, I trust, sir, has never forgotten the intimate companionship, the touching devotion, the unceasing solicitude for his happiness which you, sir, manifested to him in the days of his youth.

JUSTICE MERTON. Really, your lordship, the—the slight favors which—hem! some years ago, I was privileged to show your illustrious father—

RAVENSBANE. Permit me!—Because, however, of his present infirmities—for I regret to say that my father is suffering a temporary aberration of mind—

JUSTICE MERTON. You distress me!

RAVENSBANE. My lady mother has charged me with a double mission here in New England. On my quitting my home, sir, to explore the wideness and the mystery of this world, my mother bade me be sure to call upon his worship, the Justice Merton; and deliver to him, first, my father's remembrances; and secondly, my mother's epistle.

DICKON. (*Handing to* JUSTICE MERTON *a sealed document.*) Her ladyship's letter, sir.

JUSTICE MERTON. (*Examining the seal with awe, speaks aside to* MISTRESS MERTON.) Cynthia!—a crested seal!

DICKON. His lordship's crest, sir: rooks rampant.

JUSTICE MERTON. (*Embarrassed, breaks the seal.*) Permit me.

RACHEL. (*Looking at* RAVENSBANE.) Have you noticed his bearing, Richard: what personal distinction! what inbred nobility! Every inch a true lord!

RICHARD. He may be a lord, my dear, but he walks like a broomstick.

RACHEL. How dare you!

(*Turns abruptly away; as she does so, a fold of her gown catches in a chair.*)

RAVENSBANE. Mistress Rachel—permit me.

(*Stooping, he extricates the fold of her gown.*)

RACHEL. Oh, thank you.

(*They go aside together.*)

JUSTICE MERTON. (*To* DICKON, *glancing up from the letter.*) I am astonished—overpowered!

RICHARD. (*To* MISTRESS MERTON.) So Lord Ravensbane and his family are old friends of yours?

MISTRESS MERTON. (*Monosyllabically.*) I never heard the name before, Richard.

RAVENSBANE. (*To* RACHEL, *taking her hand after a whisper from* DICKON.) Believe me, sweet lady, it will give me the deepest pleasure.

RACHEL. Can you really tell fortunes?

RAVENSBANE. More than that; I can bestow them.

(RAVENSBANE *leads* RACHEL *off, left, into an adjoining room, the door of which remains open.* RICHARD *follows them.* MISTRESS MERTON *follows him, murmuring, "Richard!"* DICKON *stands where he can watch them in the room off scene, while he speaks to the* JUSTICE.)

JUSTICE MERTON. (*To* DICKON, *glancing up from the letter.*) I am astonished—overpowered! But is her ladyship really serious? An offer of marriage!

DICKON. Pray read it again, sir.

JUSTICE MERTON. (*Reads.*) "To the Worshipful, the Justice Gilead Merton, Merton House.

"My Honorable Friend and Benefactor:

"With these brief lines I commend to you our son"—*our* son!

DICKON. She speaks likewise for his young lordship's father, sir.

JUSTICE MERTON. Ah! of course. (*Reads.*) "In a strange land, I entrust him to you as to a father." Honored, believe me! "I have only to add my earnest hope that the natural gifts, graces, and inherited fortune"—ah—!

DICKON. Twenty thousand pounds—on his father's demise.

JUSTICE MERTON. Ah!—"fortune of this young scion of nobility will so propitiate the heart of your niece, Mistress Rachel Merton, as to cause her to accept his proffered hand in matrimony";—but—but—but Squire Talbot is betrothed to—well, well, we shall see;—"in matrimony, and thus cement the early bonds of interest and affection between your honored self and his lordship's father; not to mention, dear sir, your worship's ever grateful and obedient admirer,

"ELIZABETH,

"Marchioness of R."

Of R.! of R.! Will you believe me, my dear sir, so long is it since my travels in England—I visited at so many—hem! noble estates—permit me, it is so awkward, but—

DICKON. (*With his peculiar intonation of Act First.*) Not at all.

RAVENSBANE. (*Calls from the adjoining room.*) Dickon, my pipe!

(DICKON *glides away.*)

JUSTICE MERTON. (*Starting in perturbation. To* DICKON.) Permit me, one moment; I did not catch your name.

DICKON. My name? Dickonson.

JUSTICE MERTON. (*With a gasp of relief.*) Ah, Dickonson! Thank you, I mistook the word.

DICKON. A compound, your worship. (*With a malignant smile.*) Dickon-(*then, jerking his thumb toward the next room*) son! (*Bowing.*) Both at your service.

JUSTICE MERTON. Is he—he there?

DICKON. Bessie's brat; yes; it did n't die, after all, poor suckling! Dickon weaned it. Saved it for balm of Gilead. Raised it for joyful home-coming. Prodigal's return! Twenty-first birthday! Happy son! Happy father!

JUSTICE MERTON. My—son!

DICKON. Felicitations!

JUSTICE MERTON. (*Faintly.*) What—what do you want?

DICKON. Only the happiness of your dear ones—the union of these young hearts and hands.

JUSTICE MERTON. What! he will dare—an illegitimate—

DICKON. Fie, fie, Gilly! Why, the brat is a lord now.

JUSTICE MERTON. Oh, the disgrace! Spare me that, Dickon. And she is innocent; she is already betrothed.

DICKON. Twiddle-twaddle! 'T is a brilliant match; besides, her ladyship's heart is set upon it.

JUSTICE MERTON. Her ladyship—?

DICKON. The Marchioness of Rickby.

JUSTICE MERTON. (*Glowering.*) Rickby! —I had forgotten.

DICKON. Her ladyship has never forgotten. So, you see, your worship's alternatives are most simple. Alternative one: advance his lordship's suit with your niece as speedily as possible, and save all scandal. Alternative two: impede his lordship's suit, and—

JUSTICE MERTON. Don't, Dickon! don't reveal the truth; not disgrace now!

DICKON. Good; we are agreed, then?

JUSTICE MERTON. I have no choice.

DICKON. (*Cheerfully.*) Why, true; we ignored that, did n't we?

MISTRESS MERTON. (*Reëntering.*) This young lord—Why, Gilead, are you ill?

JUSTICE MERTON. (*With a great effort, commands himself.*) Not in the least.

MISTRESS MERTON. Rachel's deportment, my dear brother—I tell you, they are fortune-telling!

JUSTICE MERTON. Tush! Tush!

MISTRESS MERTON. Tush? "Tush" to me? Tush! (*She goes out right.*)

(RAVENSBANE *and* RACHEL *reënter from the adjoining room, followed shortly by* RICHARD.)

RACHEL. I am really at a loss. Your lordship's hand is so very peculiar.

RAVENSBANE. Ah! Peculiar.

RACHEL. This, now, is the line of life.

RAVENSBANE. Of life, yes?

RACHEL. But it begins so abruptly, and see! it breaks off and ends nowhere. And just so here with this line—the line of—of love.

RAVENSBANE. Of love. So; it breaks?

RACHEL. Yes.

RAVENSBANE. Ah, then, that must be the *heart* line.

RACHEL. Why, Lord Ravensbane, your pulse. Really, if I am cruel, you are quite heartless. I declare I can't feel your heart beat at all.

RAVENSBANE. Ah, mistress, that is because I have just lost it.

RACHEL. (*Archly.*) Where?

RAVENSBANE. (*Faintly.*) Dickon, my pipe!

RACHEL. Alas! my lord, are you ill?

DICKON. (*Restoring the lighted pipe to* RAVENSBANE, *speaks aside.*) Pardon me, sweet young lady, I must confide to you that his lordship's heart is peculiarly responsive to his emotions. When he feels very ardently, it quite stops. Hence the use of his pipe.

RACHEL. Oh! Is smoking, then, necessary for his heart?

DICKON. Absolutely—to equilibrate the valvular palpitations. Without his pipe—should his lordship experience, for instance, the emotion of love—he might die.

RACHEL. You alarm me!

DICKON. But this is for you only, Mistress Rachel. We may confide in you?

RACHEL. Oh, utterly, sir.

DICKON. His lordship, you know, is so sensitive.

RAVENSBANE. (*To* RACHEL.) You have given it back to me. Why did not you keep it?

RACHEL. What, my lord?

RAVENSBANE. My heart.

RICHARD. Intolerable! Do you approve of *this,* sir? Are Lord Ravensbane's credentials satisfactory?

JUSTICE MERTON. Eminently, eminently.

RICHARD. Ah! So her ladyship's letter is—

JUSTICE MERTON. Charming; charming. (*To* RAVENSBANE.) Your lordship will, I trust, make my house your home.

RAVENSBANE. My home, sir.

RACHEL. (*To* DICKON, *who has spoken to her.*) Really? (*To* JUSTICE MERTON.) Why, uncle, what is this Master Dickonson tells us?

JUSTICE MERTON. What! What! he has revealed—

RACHEL. Yes, indeed.

JUSTICE MERTON. Rachel! Rachel!

RACHEL. (*Laughingly to* RAVENSBANE.) My uncle is doubtless astonished to find you so grown.

RAVENSBANE. (*Laughingly to* JUSTICE MERTON.) I am doubtless astonished, sir, to be so grown.

JUSTICE MERTON. (*To* DICKON.) You have—

DICKON. Merely remarked, sir, that your worship had often dandled his lordship—as an infant.

JUSTICE MERTON. (*Smiling lugubriously.*) Quite so—as an infant merely.

RACHEL. How interesting! Then you must have seen his lordship's home in England.

JUSTICE MERTON. As you say.

RACHEL. (*To* RAVENSBANE.) Do describe it to us. We are so isolated here from the grand world. Do you know, I always imagine England to be an enchanted isle, like one of the old Hesperides, teeming with fruits of solid gold.

RAVENSBANE. Ah, yes! my mother raises them.

RACHEL. Fruits of gold?

RAVENSBANE. Round like the rising sun. She calls them—ah! punkins.

MISTRESS MERTON. "Punkins"!

JUSTICE MERTON. (*Aside, grinding his teeth.*) Scoundrel! Scoundrel!

RACHEL. (*Laughing.*) Your lordship pokes fun at us.

DICKON. His lordship is an artist in words, mistress. I have noticed that in whatever country he is traveling, he tinges his vocabulary with the local idiom. His lordship means, of course, not pumpkins, but pomegranates.

RACHEL. We forgive him. But, your lordship, please be serious and describe to us your hall.

RAVENSBANE. Quite serious: the hall. Yes, yes; in the middle burns a great fire—on a black—ah! black altar.

DICKON. A Druidical heirloom. His lordship's mother collects antiques.

RACHEL. How fascinating!

RAVENSBANE. Fascinating! On the walls hang pieces of iron.

DICKON. Trophies of Saxon warfare.

RAVENSBANE. And rusty horseshoes.

GENERAL MURMURS. Horseshoes!

DICKON. Presents from the German Emperor. They were worn by the steeds of Charlemagne.

RAVENSBANE. Quite so; and broken cartwheels.

DICKON. Relics of British chariots.

RACHEL. How mediæval it must be! (*To* JUSTICE MERTON.) And to think you never described it to us!

MISTRESS MERTON. True, brother; you have been singularly reticent.

JUSTICE MERTON. Permit me; it is impossible to report all one sees on one's travels.

MISTRESS MERTON. Evidently.

RACHEL. But surely your lordship's mother has other diversions besides collecting antiques. I have heard that in England ladies followed the hounds; and sometimes—(*looking at her aunt and lowering her voice*)—they even dance.

RAVENSBANE. Dance—ah, yes; my lady mother dances about the—the altar; she swings high a hammer.

DICKON. Your lordship, your lordship! Pray, sir, check this vein of poetry. Lord Ravensbane symbolizes as a hammer and altar a golf-stick and tee—a Scottish game, which her ladyship plays on her Highland estates.

RICHARD. (*To* MISTRESS MERTON.) What do you think of this?

MISTRESS MERTON. (*With a scandalized look toward her brother.*) He said to me "tush."

RICHARD. (*To* JUSTICE MERTON, *indicating* DICKON.) Who is this magpie?

JUSTICE MERTON. (*Hisses in fury.*) Satan!

RICHARD. I beg pardon!

JUSTICE MERTON. Satan, sir,—makes you jealous.

RICHARD. (*Bows stiffly.*) Good-morning. (*Walking up to* RAVENSBANE.) Lord Ravensbane, I have a rustic colonial question to ask. Is it the latest fashion to smoke incessantly in ladies' parlors, or is it—mediæval?

DICKON. His lordship's health, sir, necessitates—

RICHARD. I addressed his lordship.

RAVENSBANE. In the matter of fashions, sir— (*Hands his pipe to be refilled.*) My pipe, Dickon!

(*While* DICKON *holds his pipe—somewhat longer than usual—*RAVENSBANE, *with his mouth open as if about to speak, relapses into a vacant stare.*)

RICHARD. Well?

DICKON. (*As he lights the pipe for* RAVENSBANE, *speaks suavely and low as if not to be overheard by him.*) Pardon me. The fact is, my young pupil is sensitive; the wound from his latest duel is not quite healed; you observe a slight lameness, an occasional—absence of mind.

RACHEL. A wound—in a real duel?

DICKON. (*Aside.*) You, mistress, know the *true* reason—his lordship's heart.

RICHARD. (*To* RAVENSBANE, *who is still staring vacantly into space.*) Well, well, your lordship. (RAVENSBANE *pays no attention.*) You were saying—? (DICKON *returns the pipe*)—in the matter of fashions, sir—?

RAVENSBANE. (*Regaining slowly a look of intelligence, draws himself up with affronted hauteur.*) Permit me! (*Puffs several wreaths of smoke into the air.*) I *am* the fashions.

RICHARD. (*Going.*) Insufferable!

(*He pauses at the door.*)

MISTRESS MERTON. (*To* JUSTICE MERTON.) Well—what do you think of that?

JUSTICE MERTON. Spoken like King Charles himself.

MISTRESS MERTON. Brother! brother! is there nothing wrong here?

(*Going out, she passes* DICKON, *starts at a look which he gives her, and goes out, right, flustered. Following her,* JUSTICE MERTON *is stopped by* DICKON, *and led off left by him.*)

RACHEL. (*To* RAVENSBANE.) I—object to the smoke? Why, I think it is charming.

RICHARD. (*Who has returned from the door, speaks in a low, constrained voice.*) Rachel!

RACHEL. Oh!—you?

RICHARD. You take quickly to European fashions.

RACHEL. Yes? To what one in particular?

RICHARD. Two; smoking and flirtation.

RACHEL. Jealous?

RICHARD. Of an idiot? I hope not. Manners differ, however. Your confidences to his lordship have evidently not included—your relation to me.

RACHEL. Oh, our relations!

RICHARD. Of course, since you wish him to continue in ignorance—

RACHEL. Not at all. He shall know at once. Lord Ravensbane!

RAVENSBANE. Fair mistress!

RICHARD. Rachel, stop! I did not mean—

RACHEL. (*To* RAVENSBANE.) My uncle did not introduce to you with sufficient elaboration this gentleman. Will you allow me to do so now?

RAVENSBANE. I adore Mistress Rachel's elaborations.

RACHEL. Lord Ravensbane, I beg to present Squire Talbot, *my betrothed.*

RAVENSBANE. Betrothed! Is it—(*noticing* RICHARD'S *frown*)—is it pleasant?

RACHEL. (*To* RICHARD.) Are you satisfied?

RICHARD. (*Trembling with feeling.*) *More* than satisfied. (*Exit.*)

RAVENSBANE. (*Looking after him.*) Ah! Betrothed is *not* pleasant.

RACHEL. Not always.

RAVENSBANE. (*Anxiously.*) Mistress Rachel is not pleased?

RACHEL. (*Biting her lip, looks after* RICHARD.) With him.

RAVENSBANE. Mistress Rachel will smile again?

RACHEL. Soon.

RAVENSBANE. (*Ardent.*) Ah! What can Lord Ravensbane do to make her smile? See! will you puff my pipe? It is very pleasant. (*Offering the pipe.*)

RACHEL. (*Smiling.*) Shall I try?

(*Takes hold of it mischievously.*)

(*Enter* JUSTICE MERTON *and* DICKON, left.)

JUSTICE MERTON. (*In a great voice.*) Rachel!

RACHEL. Why, uncle!

JUSTICE MERTON. (*Speaks suavely to* RAVENSBANE.) Permit me, your lordship—Rachel, you will kindly withdraw for a few moments; I desire to confer with Lord Ravensbane concerning his mother's—her ladyship's letter—(*obsequiously to* DICKON)—that is, if you think, sir, that your noble pupil is not too fatigued.

DICKON. Not at all; I think his lordship will listen to you with much pleasure.

RAVENSBANE. (*Bowing to* JUSTICE MERTON, *but looking at* RACHEL.) With much pleasure.

DICKON. And in the mean time, if Mistress Rachel will allow me, I will assist her in writing those invitations which your worship desires to send in her name.

JUSTICE MERTON. Invitations—from my niece?

DICKON. To his Excellency, the Lieutenant-Governor; to your friends, the Reverend Masters at Harvard College, etc., etc.; in brief, to all your worship's select social acquaintance in the vicinity—to meet his lordship. It was so thoughtful in you to suggest it, sir, and believe me, his lordship appreciates your courtesy in arranging the reception in his honor for this afternoon.

RACHEL. (*To* JUSTICE MERTON.) This afternoon! Are we really to give his lordship a reception? And will it be here, uncle?

DICKON. (*Looking at him narrowly.*) Your worship said here, I believe?

JUSTICE MERTON. Quite so, sir; quite so, quite so.

DICKON. Permit me to act as your scribe, Mistress Rachel.

RACHEL. With pleasure. (*With a curtsy to* RAVENSBANE.) Till we meet again!

(*Exit, right.*)

DICKON. (*Aside to* JUSTICE MERTON.) I advise nothing rash, Gilly; the brat has a weak heart. (*Aside, as he passes* RAVENSBANE.) Remember, Jack! Puff! Puff!

RAVENSBANE. (*Staring at the door.*) She is gone.

JUSTICE MERTON. Impostor! You, at least, shall not play the lord and master to my face.

RAVENSBANE. Quite—gone!

JUSTICE MERTON. I know with whom I have to deal. If I be any judge of my own flesh and blood—permit me—you shall quail before me.

RAVENSBANE. (*Dejectedly.*) She did not smile—(*Joyously.*) She smiled!

JUSTICE MERTON. Affected rogue! I know thee. I know thy feigned pauses, thy assumed vagaries. Speak; how much do you want?

RAVENSBANE. (*Ecstatically.*) Ah! Mistress Rachel!

JUSTICE MERTON. Her! Scoundrel, if thou dost name her again, my innocent—my sweet maid! If thou dost—thou godless spawn of temptation—mark you, I will put an end—

(*Reaching for a pistol that rests in a rack on the wall,—the intervening form of* DICKON *suddenly appears, pockets the pistol, and exit.*)

DICKON. I beg pardon; I forgot something.

JUSTICE MERTON. (*Sinking into a chair.*) God, Thou art just!

(*He holds his head in his hands and weeps.*)

RAVENSBANE. (*For the first time, since

RACHEL'S *departure, observing* MERTON.) Permit me, sir, are you ill?

JUSTICE MERTON. (*Recoiling.*) What art thou!

RAVENSBANE. (*Monotonously.*) I am Lord Ravensbane: Marquis of Oxford, Baron of Wittenberg, Elector of Worms, and—(*As* JUSTICE MERTON *covers his face again.*) Shall I call Dickon? (*Walking quickly toward the door, calls.*) Dickon!

JUSTICE MERTON (*Starting up.*) No, do not call him. Tell me: I hate thee not; thou wast innocent. Tell me!—I thought thou hadst died as a babe.—Where has Dickon, our tyrant, kept thee these twenty years?

RAVENSBANE. (*With gentle courtesy.*) Master Dickonson is my tutor.

JUSTICE MERTON. And why has thy mother—Ah, I know well; I deserve all. But yet, it must not be published now! I am a justice now, an honored citizen—and my young niece—Thy mother will not demand so much.

RAVENSBANE. My mother is the Marchioness of Rickby.

JUSTICE MERTON. Yes, yes; 't was well planned, a clever trick. 'T was skillful of her. But surely thy mother gave thee commands to—

RAVENSBANE. My mother gave me her blessing.

JUSTICE MERTON. Ah, 't is well, then. Young man, my son, I too will give thee my blessing, if thou wilt but go—go instantly—go with half my fortune—but leave me my honor—and my Rachel?

RAVENSBANE. Rachel? Rachel is yours? No, no, Mistress Rachel is mine. We are ours.

JUSTICE MERTON. (*Pleadingly.*) Consider the disgrace—you, an illegitimate—and she—oh, think what thou art!

RAVENSBANE. (*Monotonously, puffing smoke at the end.*) I am Lord Ravensbane: Marquis of Oxford, Baron of Wittenberg, Elector of Worms, and Count—

JUSTICE MERTON. (*Wrenching the pipe from* RAVENSBANE'S *hand and lips.*) Devil's child! Boor! Buffoon! (*Flinging the pipe away.*) I will stand thy insults no longer. If thou hast no heart—

RAVENSBANE. (*Putting his hand to his side, staggers.*) Ah! my heart!

JUSTICE MERTON. Hypocrite! Thou canst not fool me. I am thy father.

RAVENSBANE. (*Faintly, stretches out his hand to him for support.*) Father!

JUSTICE MERTON. Stand away. Thou mayst break thy heart and mine and the devil's, but thou shalt not break Rachel's.

RAVENSBANE. (*Faintly.*) Mistress Rachel is mine— (*He staggers again, and falls, half reclining, upon a chair. More faintly he speaks, beginning to change expression.*) Her eyes are mine; her smiles are mine.

(*His eyes close.*)

JUSTICE MERTON. Good God! Can it be —his heart? (*With agitated swiftness, he feels and listens at* RAVENSBANE'S *side.*) Not a motion; not a sound! Yea, God, Thou art good! 'T is his heart. He is—ah! he is my son. Judge Almighty, if he should die now; may I not be still a moment more and make sure? No, no, my son—he is changing. (*Calls.*) Help! Help! Rachel! Master Dickonson! Help! Richard! Cynthia! Come hither!

(*Enter* DICKON *and* RACHEL.)

RACHEL. Uncle!

JUSTICE MERTON. Bring wine. Lord Ravensbane has fainted.

RACHEL. Oh! (*Turning swiftly to go.*) Micah, wine.

DICKON. (*Detaining her.*) Stay! His pipe! Where is his lordship's pipe?

RACHEL. Oh, terrible!

(*Enter, at different doors,* MISTRESS MERTON *and* RICHARD.)

MISTRESS MERTON. What 's the matter?

JUSTICE MERTON. (*To* RACHEL.) He threw it away. He is worse. Bring the wine.

MISTRESS MERTON. Look! How strange he appears!

RACHEL. (*Searching distractedly.*) The pipe! His lordship's pipe! It is lost, Master Dickonson.

DICKON. (*Stooping, as if searching, with his back turned, having picked up the pipe, is filling and lighting it.*) It must be found. This is a heart attack, my friends; his lordship's life depends on the nicotine.

(*Deftly he places the pipe in* RACHEL'S *way.*)

RACHEL. Thank God! Here it is. (*Carrying it to the prostrate form of* RAVENS-

BANE, *she lifts his head and is about to put the pipe in his mouth.*) Shall I—shall I put it in?

RICHARD. No! not you.

RACHEL. Sir!

RICHARD. Let his tutor perform that office.

RACHEL. (*Lifting* LORD RAVENSBANE'S *head again.*) My lord!

RICHARD *and* JUSTICE MERTON. (*Together.*) Rachel!

DICKON. Pardon me, Mistress Rachel; give the pipe at once. Only a token of true affection can revive his lordship now.

RICHARD. (*As* RACHEL *puts the pipe to* RAVENSBANE'S lips.) I forbid it, Rachel.

RACHEL. (*Watching only* RAVENSBANE.) My lord—my lord!

MISTRESS MERTON. Give him air; unbutton his coat. (RACHEL *unbuttons* RAVENSBANE'S *coat, revealing the embroidered waistcoat.*) Ah, Heavens! What do I see?

JUSTICE MERTON. (*Looks, blanches, and signs silence to* MISTRESS MERTON.) Cynthia!

MISTRESS MERTON. (*Aside to* JUSTICE MERTON, *with deep tensity.*) That waistcoat! that waistcoat! Brother, hast thou never seen it before?

JUSTICE MERTON. Never, my sister.

DICKON. See! He puffs—he revives. He is coming to himself.

RACHEL. (*As* RAVENSBANE *rises to his feet.*) At last!

DICKON. Look! he is restored.

RACHEL. God be thanked!

DICKON. My lord, Mistress Rachel has saved your life.

RAVENSBANE. (*Taking* RACHEL'S *hand.*) Mistress Rachel is mine; we are ours.

RICHARD. Dare to repeat that.

RAVENSBANE. (*Looking at* RACHEL.) Her eyes are mine.

RICHARD. (*Flinging his glove in his face.*) And that, sir, is yours.

RACHEL. Richard!

RICHARD. I believe such is the proper fashion in England. If your lordship's last dueling wound is sufficiently healed, perhaps you will deign a reply.

RACHEL. Richard! Your lordship!

RAVENSBANE. (*Stoops, picks up the glove, pockets it, bows to* RACHEL, *and steps close to* RICHARD.) Permit me!

(*He blows a puff of smoke full in* RICHARD'S *face.*)

ACT THIRD.

The same day. Late afternoon. The same scene as in Act Second.

RAVENSBANE *and* DICKON *are seated at the table, on which are lying two flails.* RAVENSBANE *is dressed in a costume which, composed of silk and jewels, subtly approximates in design to that of his original grosser composition. So artfully, however, is this contrived that, to one ignorant of his origin, his dress would appear to be merely an odd personal whimsy; whereas, to one initiated, it would stamp him grotesquely as the apotheosis of scarecrows.*

DICKON *is sitting in a pedagogical attitude;* RAVENSBANE *stands near him, making a profound bow in the opposite direction.*

RAVENSBANE. Believe me, ladies, with the true sincerity of the heart.

DICKON. Inflection a little more lachrymose, please: "The *true* sincerity of the *heart.*"

RAVENSBANE. Believe me, ladies, with the *true* sincerity of the *heart.*

DICKON. Prettily, prettily! Next!

RAVENSBANE. (*Changing his mien, as if addressing another person.*) Verily, sir, as that prince of poets, the immortal Virgil, has remarked:—

"Adeo in teneris consuescere multum est."

DICKON. *Basta!* The next.

RAVENSBANE. (*With another change to courtly manner.*) Trust me, your Excellency, I will inform his Majesty of your courtesy.

DICKON. "His Majesty" more emphatic. Remember! You must impress all of the guests this afternoon. But continue, Cobby, dear; the retort now to the challenge!

RAVENSBANE. (*With a superb air.*) The second, I believe.

DICKON. Quite so, my lord.

RAVENSBANE. Sir! the local person whom you represent has done himself the honor of submitting to me a challenge to mortal combat. Sir! Since the remotest times of my feudal ancestors, in such affairs of honor, choice of weapons has ever been the—

DICKON. Prerogative!

RAVENSBANE. Prerogative of the challenged. Sir! This right of etiquette must be observed. Nevertheless, believe me, I have no selfish desire that my superior—

DICKON. Attainments!

RAVENSBANE. Attainments in this art should assume advantage over my challenger's ignorance. I have, therefore, chosen those combative utensils most appropriate both to his own humble origin and to local tradition. Permit me, sir, to reveal my choice. (*Pointing grandly to the table.*) There are my weapons!

DICKON. Delicious! O thou exquisite flower of love! How thy natal composites have burst in bloom!—The pumpkin in thee to a golden collarette; thy mop of crow's wings to these raven locks; thy broomstick to a lordly limp; thy corn-silk to these pale-tinted tassels. Verily in the gallery of scarecrows, thou art the Apollo Belvedere!

RAVENSBANE. Mistress Rachel—I may see her now?

DICKON. Romeo! Romeo! Was ever such an amorous puppet show!

RAVENSBANE. Mistress Rachel!

DICKON. Wait; let me think! Thou art wound up now, my pretty apparatus, for at least six-and-thirty hours. The wooden angel Gabriel that trumpets the hours on the big clock in Venice is not a more punctual manikin than thou with my speeches. Thou shouldst run, therefore,—

RAVENSBANE. (*Frowning darkly at* DICKON.) Stop talking; permit me! A tutor should know his place.

DICKON. (*Rubbing his hands.*) Nay, your lordship is beyond comparison.

RAVENSBANE. (*In a terrible voice.*) She will come? I shall see her?

(*Enter* MICAH.)

MICAH. Pardon, my lord.

RAVENSBANE. (*Turning joyfully to* MICAH.) Is it she?

MICAH. Captain Bugby, my lord, the Governor's secretary.

DICKON. Good. Squire Talbot's second. Show him in.

RAVENSBANE. (*Flinging despairingly into a chair.*) Ah! ah!

MICAH. (*Lifting the flails from the table.*) Beg pardon, sir; shall I remove—

DICKON. Drop them; go.

MICAH. But, sir—

DICKON. Go, thou slave! (*Exit* MICAH.) (DICKON *hands* RAVENSBANE *a book.*) Here, my lord; read. You must be found reading.

RAVENSBANE. (*In childlike despair.*) She will not come! I shall not see her! (*Throwing the book into the fireplace.*) She does not come!

DICKON. Fie, fie, Jack; thou must not be breaking thy Dickon's apron-strings with a will of thine own. Come!

RAVENSBANE. Mistress Rachel—

DICKON. Be good, boy, and thou shalt see her soon.

(*Enter* CAPTAIN BUGBY.)

Your lordship was saying—Oh! Captain Bugby?

CAPTAIN BUGBY. (*Nervous and awed.*) Captain Bugby, sir, ah! at Lord Ravensbane's service—ah!

DICKON. I am Master Dickonson, his lordship's tutor.

CAPTAIN BUGBY. Happy, sir.

DICKON. (*To* RAVENSBANE.) My lord, this gentleman waits upon you from Squire Talbot. (*To* CAPTAIN BUGBY.) In regard to the challenge this morning, I presume?

CAPTAIN BUGBY. The affair, ah! the affair of this morning, sir.

RAVENSBANE. (*With his former superb air—to* CAPTAIN BUGBY.) The second, I believe?

CAPTAIN BUGBY. Quite so, my lord.

RAVENSBANE. Sir! the local person whom you represent has done himself the honor of submitting to me a challenge to mortal combat. Sir! Since the remotest times of my feudal ancestors, in such affairs of honor, choice of weapons has ever been the pre-pre- (DICKON *looks at him intensely.*) prerogative of the challenged. Sir! this right of etiquette must be observed.

CAPTAIN BUGBY. Indeed, yes, my lord.

DICKON. Pray do not interrupt. (*To* RAVENSBANE.) Your lordship: "observed."

RAVENSBANE. —observed. Nevertheless, believe me, I have no selfish desire that my superior a-a-at-attainments in this art should assume advantage over my challenger's ignorance. I have, therefore, chosen those combative utensils most appropriate both to his own humble origin and to local tradition. Permit me, sir, to reveal my choice. (*Pointing to the table.*) There are my weapons!

CAPTAIN BUGBY. (*Looking bewildered.*) These, my lord?

RAVENSBANE. Those.

CAPTAIN BUGBY. But these are—are flails.

RAVENSBANE. Flails.

CAPTAIN BUGBY. Flails, my lord?—Do I understand that your lordship and Squire Talbot—

RAVENSBANE. Exactly.

CAPTAIN BUGBY. But your lordship—flails!

(DICKON'S *intense glance focusses on* RAVENSBANE'S *face with the faintest of smiles.*)

RAVENSBANE. My adversary should be deft in their use. He has doubtless wielded them frequently on his barn floor.

CAPTAIN BUGBY. Ahaha! I understand now. Your lordship—ah! is a wit. Haha! Flails!

DICKON. His lordship's satire is poignant.

CAPTAIN BUGBY. Indeed, sir, so keen that I must apologize for laughing at my principal's expense. But—(*soberly to* RAVENSBANE)—my lord, if you will deign to speak one moment seriously—

RAVENSBANE. Seriously?

CAPTAIN BUGBY. I will take pleasure in informing Squire Talbot—ah! as to your *real* preference for—

RAVENSBANE. For flails, sir. I have, permit me, nothing further to say. Flails are final. (*Turns away haughtily.*)

CAPTAIN BUGBY. Eh! What! Must I really report—?

DICKON. Lord Ravensbane's will is inflexible.

CAPTAIN BUGBY. And his wit, sir, incomparable. I am sorry for the Squire, but 't will be the greatest joke in years. Ah! will you tell me—is it—(*indicating* RAVENSBANE'S *smoking*)—is it the latest fashion?

DICKON. Lord Ravensbane is always the latest.

CAPTAIN BUGBY. Obliged servant, sir. Aha! Such a joke as—O Lord! flails. (*Exit.*)

DICKON. (*Gayly to* RAVENSBANE.) Bravo, my pumpky dear! That squelches the jealous betrothed. Now nothing remains but for you to continue to dazzle the enamored Rachel, and so present yourself to the Justice as a pseudo-son-nephew-in-law.

RAVENSBANE. I may go to Mistress Rachel?

DICKON. She will come to you. She is reading now a poem from you, which I left on her dressing-table.

RAVENSBANE. She is reading a poem from me?

DICKON. With your pardon, my lord, I penned it for you. I am something of a poetaster. Indeed, I flatter myself that I have dictated some of the finest lines in literature.

RAVENSBANE. Dickon! She will come?

DICKON. She comes!

(*Enter* RACHEL, *reading from a piece of paper.*)

(DICKON *draws* RAVENSBANE *back.*)

RACHEL. (*Reads.*) "To Mistress R——, enchantress:—

"If faith in witchcraft be a sin,
Alas! what peril he is in
Who plights his faith and love in thee,
Sweetest maid of sorcery.

"If witchcraft be a whirling brain,
A roving eye, a heart of pain,
Whose wound no thread of fate can stitch,
How hast thou conjured, cruel witch,—

With the brain, eye, heart, and total mortal residue of thine enamored.
"JACK LANTHORNE,
"[LORD R——.]"

(DICKON *goes out.*)

RACHEL. "To Mistress R——, enchantress:" R! It *must* be. R—— must mean—

RAVENSBANE. (*With passionate deference.*) Rachel!

RACHEL. Ah! How you surprised me, my lord!

RAVENSBANE. You are come again; you are come again.

RACHEL. Has anything happened? Oh, my lord, I have been in such terror. Promise me that there shall be—no—duel!

RAVENSBANE. No duel.

RACHEL. Oh, I am so gratefully happy!

RAVENSBANE. I know I am only a thing to make Mistress Rachel happy. Ah! look at me once more. When you look at me, I live.

RACHEL. It is strange, indeed, my lord, how the familiar world, the daylight, the heavens themselves have changed since your arrival.

RAVENSBANE. This is the world; this is the light; this is the heavens themselves. Mistress Rachel is looking at me.

RACHEL. For me, it is less strange, perhaps. I never saw a real lord before. But you, my lord, must have seen so many, many girls in the great world.

RAVENSBANE. No, no; never.

RACHEL. No other girls before to-day, my lord!

RAVENSBANE. Before to-day? I do not know; I do not care. I was not—here. To-day I was born—in your eyes. Ah! my brain whirls!

RACHEL. (*Smiling.*)

"If witchcraft be a whirling brain,
A roving eye, a heart of pain,—"

(*In a whisper.*) My lord, do you really believe in witchcraft?

RAVENSBANE. With all my heart.

RACHEL. And approve of it?

RAVENSBANE. With all my soul.

RACHEL. So do I—that is, innocent witchcraft; not to harm anybody, you know, but just to feel all the dark mystery and the trembling excitement—the way you feel when you blow out your candle all alone in your bedroom and watch the little smoke fade away in the moonshine.

RAVENSBANE. Fade away in the moonshine!

RACHEL. Oh, but we must n't speak of it. In a town like this, all such mysticism is considered damnable. But your lordship understands and approves? I am so glad! Have you read the *Philosophical Considerations* of Glanville, the *Saducismus Triumphatus,* and the *Presignifications of Dreams?* What kind of witchcraft, my lord, do you believe in?

RAVENSBANE. In all yours.

RACHEL. Nay, your lordship must not take me for a real witch. I can only tell fortunes, you know—like this morning.

RAVENSBANE. I know; you told how my heart would break.

RACHEL. Oh, that 's palmistry, and that is n't always certain. But the surest way to prophesy—do you know what it is?

RAVENSBANE. Tell me.

RACHEL. To count the crows. Do you know how?

One for sorrow—

RAVENSBANE. Ha, yes!—

Two for mirth!

RACHEL.

Three for a wedding—

RAVENSBANE.

Four for a birth—

RACHEL.

And five for the happiest thing on earth!

RAVENSBANE. Mistress Rachel, come! Let us go and count five crows.

RACHEL. (*Delightedly.*) Why, my lord, how did *you* ever learn it? I got it from an old goody here in town—a real witchwife. If you will promise not to tell a secret, I will show you—But you must promise!

RAVENSBANE. I promise.

RACHEL. Come, then. I will show you a real piece of witchcraft that I bought from her this morning—the glass of truth. There! Behind that curtain. If you look in, you will see— But come; I will show you. (*They put their hands on the cords of the curtain.*) Just pull that string, and—ah!

DICKON. (*Stepping out through the curtain.*) My lord, your pipe.

RACHEL. Master Dickonson, how you frightened me!

DICKON. So excessively sorry!

RACHEL. But how did you—?

DICKON. I believe you were showing his lordship—

RACHEL. (*Turning hurriedly away.*) Oh, nothing; nothing at all.

RAVENSBANE. (*Sternly to* DICKON.) Why do you come?

DICKON. (*Handing back* RAVENSBANE'S *pipe, filled.*) Allow me. (*Aside.*) 'T is high time you came to the point, Jack; 't is near your lordship's reception. Woo and win, boy; woo and win.

RAVENSBANE. (*Haughtily.*) Leave me.

DICKON. Your lordship 's humble, very humble. (*Exit.*)

RACHEL. (*Shivering.*) My dear lord, why do you keep this man?

RAVENSBANE. I—keep this man?

RACHEL. Pardon my rudeness—I cannot endure him.

RAVENSBANE. You do not like him? Ah, then, I do not like him also. We will send him away—you and I.

RACHEL. You, my lord, of course; but I—

RAVENSBANE. You will be Dickon! You will be with me always and light my pipe. And I will live for you, and fight for you, and kill your betrothed!

RACHEL. (*Drawing away.*) No, no!

RAVENSBANE. Ah! but your eyes say "yes." Mistress Rachel leaves me; but Rachel in her eyes remains. Is it not so?

RACHEL. What can I say, my lord! It

is true that since my eyes met yours, a new passion has entered into my soul. I have felt—but 't is so impertinent, my lord, so absurd in me, a mere girl, and you a nobleman of power—yet I have felt it irresistibly, my dear lord,—a longing to help you. I am so sorry for you —so sorry for you! I pity you deeply. —Forgive me; forgive me, my lord!

RAVENSBANE. It is enough.

RACHEL. Indeed, indeed, 't is so rude of me,—'t is so unreasonable.

RAVENSBANE. It is enough. I grow—I grow—I grow! I am a plant; you give it rain and sun. I am a flower; you give it light and dew. I am a soul, you give it love and speech. I grow. Toward you—toward you I grow!

RACHEL. My lord, I do not understand it, how so poor and mere a girl as I can have helped you. Yet I do believe it is so; for I feel it so. What can I do for you?

RAVENSBANE. Be mine. Let me be yours.

RACHEL. But, my lord—do I love you?

RAVENSBANE. What is "I love you"? Is it a kiss, a sigh, an embrace? Ah! then, you do not love me.—"I love you": is it to nourish, to nestle, to lift up, to smile upon, to make greater—a worm? Ah! then, you love me.

(*Enter* RICHARD *at left back, unobserved.*)

RACHEL. Do not speak so of yourself, my lord; nor exalt me so falsely.

RAVENSBANE. Be mine.

RACHEL. A great glory has descended upon this day.

RAVENSBANE. Be mine.

RACHEL. Could I but be sure that this glory is love—Oh, *then!*

(*Turns toward* RAVENSBANE.)

RICHARD. (*Stepping between them.*) It is *not* love; it is witchcraft.

RACHEL. Who are you?—Richard?

RICHARD. You have, indeed, forgotten me? Would to God, Rachel, I could forget you.

RAVENSBANE. Ah, permit me, sir—

RICHARD. Silence! (*To* RACHEL.) Against my will, I am a convert to your own mysticism; for nothing less than damnable illusion could so instantly wean your heart from me to—this. I do not pretend to understand it; but that it is witchcraft I am convinced; and I will save you from it.

RACHEL. Go; please go.

RAVENSBANE. Permit me, sir; you have not replied yet to flails!

RICHARD. Permit *me,* sir. (*Taking something from his coat.*) My answer is—bare cob! (*Holding out a shelled corncob.*) Thresh this, sir, for your antagonist. 'T is the only one worthy your lordship.

(*Tosses it contemptuously toward him.*)

RAVENSBANE. Upon my honor, as a man—

RICHARD. As a *man,* forsooth! Were you, indeed, a man, Lord Ravensbane, I would have accepted your weapons, and flailed you out of New England. But it is not my custom to chastise runagates from asylums, or to banter further words with a natural and a ninny.

RACHEL. Squire Talbot! Will you leave my uncle's house?

RAVENSBANE. One moment, mistress:—I did not wholly catch the import of this gentleman's speech, but I fancy I have insulted him by my reply to his challenge. One insult may perhaps be remedied by another. Sir, permit me to call *you* a ninny, and to offer you—(*drawing his sword and offering it*)—swords.

RICHARD. Thanks; I reject the offer.

RAVENSBANE. (*Turning away despondently.*) He rejects it. Well!

RACHEL. (*To* RICHARD.) And *now* will you leave?

RICHARD. At once. But one word more. Rachel—Rachel, have you forgotten this morning and the Glass of Truth?

RACHEL. (*Coldly.*) No.

RICHARD. Call it a fancy now if you will. I scoffed at it; yes. Yet *you* believed it. I loved you truly, you said. Well, have I changed?

RACHEL. Yes.

RICHARD. Will you test me again—in the glass?

RACHEL. No. Go; leave us.

RICHARD. I will go. I have still a word with your aunt.

RAVENSBANE. (*To* RICHARD.) I beg your pardon, sir. You said just now that had I been a man—

RICHARD. I say, Lord Ravensbane, that the straight fiber of a true man never warps the love of a woman. As for yourself, you have my contempt and pity. Pray to God, sir, pray to God to make you a man. (*Exit.*)

RACHEL. Oh! it is intolerable! (*To* RAVENSBANE.) My dear lord, I do believe in my heart that I love you, and if so, I will with gratitude be your wife. But, my lord, strange glamors, strange darknesses reel, and bewilder my mind. I must be alone; I must think and decide. Will you give me this tassel?

RAVENSBANE. (*Unfastening a silk tassel from his coat and giving it to her.*) Oh, take it.

RACHEL. If I decide that I love you, that I will be your wife—I will wear it this afternoon at the reception. Good-bye. (*Exit, right.*)

RAVENSBANE. Mistress Rachel!— (*He is left alone. As he looks about gropingly, and raises his arms in vague prayer,* DICKON *appears from the right and watches him, with a smile.*) God, are you here? Dear God, I pray to you—make me to be a man! (*Exit, left.*)

DICKON. Poor Jacky! Thou shouldst 'a' prayed to t' other one.

(*Enter, right,* JUSTICE MERTON.)

JUSTICE MERTON. (*To* DICKON.) Will you not listen? Will you not listen!

DICKON. Such a delightful room!

JUSTICE MERTON. Are you merciless?

DICKON. And such a living portrait of your worship! The waistcoat is so beautifully executed.

JUSTICE MERTON. If I pay him ten thousand pounds—

(*Enter, right,* MISTRESS MERTON, *who goes toward the table. Enter, left,* MICAH.)

MISTRESS MERTON. Flails! Flails in the parlor!

MICAH. The minister and his wife have turned into the gate, madam.

MISTRESS MERTON. The guests! Is it so late?

MICAH. Four o'clock, madam.

MISTRESS MERTON. Remove these things at once.

MICAH. Yes, madam. (*He lifts them, and starts for the door where he pauses to look back and speak.*) Madam, in all my past years of service at Merton House, I never waited upon a lord till to-day. Madam, in all my future years of service at Merton House, I trust I may never wait upon a lord again.

MISTRESS MERTON. Micah, mind the knocker.

MICAH. Yes, madam.

(*Exit at left back. Sounds of a brass knocker outside.*)

MISTRESS MERTON. Rachel! Rachel! (*Exit, left.*)

JUSTICE MERTON. (*To* DICKON.) So you are contented with nothing less than the sacrifice of my niece!

(*Enter* MICAH.)

MICAH. Minister Dodge, your Worship; and Mistress Dodge. (*Exit.*)

(*Enter the* MINISTER *and his* WIFE.)

JUSTICE MERTON. (*Stepping forward to receive them.*) Believe me, this is a great privilege.—Madam! (*Bowing.*)

MINISTER DODGE. (*Taking his hand.*) The privilege is ours, Justice; to enter a righteous man's house is to stand, as it were, on God's threshold.

JUSTICE MERTON. (*Nervously.*) Amen, amen. Permit me—ah! Lord Ravensbane, my young guest of honor, will be here directly—permit me to present his lordship's tutor, Master Dickonson; the Reverend Master Dodge, Mistress Dodge.

MINISTER DODGE. (*Offering his hand.*) Master Dickonson, sir—

DICKON. (*Barely touching the minister's fingers, bows charmingly to his wife.*) Madam, of all professions in the world, your husband's most allures me.

MISTRESS DODGE. 'T is a worthy one, sir.

DICKON. Ah! Mistress Dodge, and so arduous—especially for a minister's wife. (*He leads her to a chair.*)

MISTRESS DODGE. (*Accepting the chair.*) Thank you.

MINISTER DODGE. Lord Ravensbane comes from abroad?

JUSTICE MERTON. From London.

MINISTER DODGE. An old friend of yours, I understand.

JUSTICE MERTON. From London, yes. Did I say from London? Quite so; from London.

(*Enter* MICAH.)

MICAH. Captain Bugby, the Governor's secretary. (*Exit.*)

(*Enter* CAPTAIN BUGBY. *He walks with a slight lameness, and holds daintily in his hand a pipe, from which he puffs with dandy deliberation.*)

CAPTAIN BUGBY. Justice Merton, your very humble servant.

JUSTICE MERTON. Believe me, Captain Bugby.

CAPTAIN BUGBY. (*Profusely.*) Ah, Master Dickonson! my dear friend Master Dickonson—this is, indeed—ah! How is his lordship since—aha! but discretion! Mistress Dodge—her servant! Ah! yes—(*indicating his pipe with a smile of satisfaction*)—the latest, I assure you; the very latest from London. Ask Master Dickonson.

MINISTER DODGE. (*Looking at* CAPTAIN BUGBY.) These will hatch out in the springtime.

CAPTAIN BUGBY. (*Confidentially to* DICKON.) But really, my good friend, may not I venture to inquire how his lordship—ah! has been in health since the—ah! since—

DICKON. (*Impressively.*) Oh! quite, quite!

(*Enter* MISTRESS MERTON; *she joins* JUSTICE MERTON *and* MINISTER DODGE.)

CAPTAIN BUGBY. You know, I informed Squire Talbot of his lordship's epigrammatic retort—his retort of—shh! ha haha! Oh, that reply was a stiletto; 't was sharper than a sword-thrust, I assure you. To have conceived it—'t was inspiration; but to have expressed it—oh! 't was genius. Hush! "Flails"! Oh! It sticks me now in the ribs. I shall die with concealing it.

MINISTER DODGE. (*To* MISTRESS MERTON.) 'T is true, mistress; but if there were more like your brother in the parish, the conscience of the community would be clearer.

(*Enter* MICAH.)

MICAH. The Reverend Master Rand of Harvard College; the Reverend Master Todd of Harvard College. (*Exit.*)

(*Enter two elderly, straight-backed divines.*)

JUSTICE MERTON. (*Greeting them.*) Permit me, gentlemen; this is fortunate—before your return to Cambridge.

(*He conducts them to* MISTRESS MERTON *and* MINISTER DODGE. DICKON *is ingratiating himself with* MISTRESS DODGE; CAPTAIN BUGBY, *laughed at by both parties, is received by neither.*)

CAPTAIN BUGBY. (*Puffing smoke toward the ceiling.*) Really, I cannot understand what keeps his Excellency, the Lieutenant-Governor, so long. He has two such charming daughters, Master Dickonson—

DICKON. (*To* MISTRESS DODGE.) Yes, yes; such suspicious women with their charms are an insult to the virtuous ladies of the parish.

CAPTAIN BUGBY. How, sir!

MISTRESS DODGE. And to think that she should actually shoe horses herself!

CAPTAIN BUGBY. (*Piqued, walks another way.*) Well!

REV. MASTER RAND. (*To* JUSTICE MERTON.) It would not be countenanced in the college yard, sir.

REV. MASTER TODD. A pipe! Nay, *mores inhibitæ!*

JUSTICE MERTON. 'T is most unfortunate, gentlemen; but I understand 't is the new vogue in London.

(*Enter* MICAH.)

MICAH. His Excellency, Sir Charles Reddington, Lieutenant-Governor; the Mistress Reddingtons.

CAPTAIN BUGBY. At last!

MISTRESS MERTON. (*Aside.*) Micah. (MICAH *goes to her.*)

(*Enter* SIR CHARLES, MISTRESS REDDINGTON, *and* AMELIA REDDINGTON.)

JUSTICE MERTON. Your Excellency, this is, indeed, a distinguished honor.

SIR CHARLES. (*Shaking hands.*) Fine weather, Merton. Where 's your young lord?

THE TWO GIRLS. (*Curtsying.*) Justice Merton, Mistress Merton. (MICAH *goes out.*)

CAPTAIN BUGBY. Oh, my dear Mistress Reddington! Charming Mistress Amelia! You are so very late, but you shall hear —hush!

MISTRESS REDDINGTON. (*Noticing his pipe.*) Why, what is this, Captain?

CAPTAIN BUGBY. Oh, the latest, I assure you, the very latest. Wait till you see his lordship.

AMELIA. What! is n't he here? (*Laughing.*) La, Captain! Do look at the man!

CAPTAIN BUGBY. Oh, he 's coming directly. Quite the mode—what?

(*He talks to them aside, where they titter.*)

SIR CHARLES. (*To* DICKON.) What say? Traveling for his health?

DICKON. Partially, your Excellency; but my young pupil and master is a singularly affectionate nature.

THE TWO GIRLS. (*To* CAPTAIN BUGBY.) What! flails—really!

(*They burst into laughter among themselves.*)

DICKON. He has journeyed here to Massachusetts peculiarly to pay this visit to

Justice Merton—his father's dearest friend.

SIR CHARLES. Ah! knew him abroad, eh?

DICKON. In Rome, your Excellency.

MISTRESS DODGE. (*To* JUSTICE MERTON.) Why, I thought it was in London.

JUSTICE MERTON. London, true, quite so; we made a trip together to Lisbon—ah! Rome.

DICKON. Paris, was it not, sir?

JUSTICE MERTON. (*In great distress.*) Paris, Paris, very true; I am—I am—sometimes I am—

(*Enter* MICAH, *right.*)

MICAH. (*Announces.*) Lord Ravensbane.

(*Enter right,* RAVENSBANE *with* RACHEL.)

JUSTICE MERTON. (*With a gasp of relief.*) Ah! his lordship is arrived.

(*Murmurs of "his lordship" and a flutter among the girls and* CAPTAIN BUGBY.)

CAPTAIN BUGBY. Look!—Now!

JUSTICE MERTON. Welcome, my lord! (*To* SIR CHARLES.) Your Excellency, let me introduce—permit me—

RAVENSBANE. Permit *me;* (*addressing her*) Mistress Rachel!—Mistress Rachel will introduce—

RACHEL. (*Curtsying.*) Sir Charles, allow me to present my friend, Lord Ravensbane.

MISTRESS REDDINGTON. (*Aside to* AMELIA.) Her *friend*—did you hear?

SIR CHARLES. Mistress Rachel, I see you are as pretty as ever. Lord Ravensbane, your hand, sir.

RAVENSBANE. Trust me, your Excellency, I will inform his Majesty of your courtesy.

CAPTAIN BUGBY. (*Watching* RAVENSBANE *with chagrin.*) On my life! he 's lost his limp.

RAVENSBANE. (*Apart to* RACHEL.) You said: "A great glory has descended upon this day."

RACHEL. (*Shyly.*) My lord!

RAVENSBANE. Be sure—O mistress, be sure—that this glory is love.

SIR CHARLES. My daughters, Fanny and Amelia—Lord Ravensbane.

THE TWO GIRLS. (*Curtsying.*) Your lordship!

SIR CHARLES. Good girls, but silly.

THE TWO GIRLS. Papa!

RAVENSBANE. Believe me, ladies, with the *true* sincerity of the *heart.*

MISTRESS REDDINGTON. Is n't he perfection!

CAPTAIN BUGBY. What said I?

AMELIA. (*Giggling.*) I can't help thinking of flails.

SIR CHARLES. (*In a loud whisper aside to* JUSTICE MERTON.) Is it congratulations for your niece?

JUSTICE MERTON. Not—not precisely.

DICKON. (*To* JUSTICE MERTON.) Your worship—a word. (*Leads him aside.*)

RAVENSBANE. (*Whom* RACHEL *continues to introduce to the guests, speaks to* MASTER RAND.) Verily, sir, as that prince of poets, the immortal Virgil, has remarked:

"Adeo in teneris consuescere multum est."

REV. MASTER TODD. His lordship is evidently a university man.

REV. MASTER RAND. Evidently most accomplished.

JUSTICE MERTON. (*Aside to* DICKON.) A song! Why, it is beyond all bounds of custom and decorum.

DICKON. Believe me, there is no such flatterer to win the maiden heart as music.

JUSTICE MERTON. And here; in this presence! Never!

DICKON. Nevertheless, it will amuse me vastly, and you will announce it.

JUSTICE MERTON. (*With hesitant embarrassment, which he seeks to conceal.*) Your Excellency and friends, I have great pleasure in announcing his lordship's condescension in consenting to regale our present company—with a song.

SEVERAL VOICES. (*In various degrees of amazement and curiosity.*) A song!

MISTRESS MERTON. Gilead! What is this?

JUSTICE MERTON. The selection is a German ballad—a particular favorite at the court of Prussia, where his lordship last rendered it. His tutor has made a translation which is entitled—

DICKON. "The Prognostication of the Crows."

ALL. Crows!

JUSTICE MERTON. And I am requested to remind you that in the ancient heathen mythology of Germany, the crow or raven was the fateful bird of the god Woden.

CAPTAIN BUGBY. How prodigiously novel!

MINISTER DODGE. (*Frowning.*) Unparalleled!

SIR CHARLES. A ballad! Come now, that sounds like old England again. Let 's have it. Will his lordship sing without music?

JUSTICE MERTON. Master Dickonson, hem! has been—persuaded—to accompany his lordship on the spinet.

AMELIA. How delightful!

REV. MASTER RAND. (*Aside to* TODD.) Shall we remain?

REV. MASTER TODD. We must.

RAVENSBANE. (*To* RACHEL.) My tassel, dear mistress; you do not wear it?

RACHEL. My heart still wavers, my lord. But whilst you sing, I will decide.

RAVENSBANE. Whilst I sing? My fate, then, is waiting at the end of a song?

RACHEL. At the end of a song.

DICKON. (*Calling to* RAVENSBANE.) Your lordship!

RAVENSBANE. (*Starting, turns to the company.*) Permit me.

(DICKON *sits at the spinet. At first, his fingers in playing give sound only to the soft tinkling notes of that ancient instrument; but gradually, strange notes and harmonies of an aërial orchestra mingle with, and at length drown, the spinet. The final chorus is produced solely by fantastic symphonic cawings, as of countless crows, in harsh but musical accord. During the song* RICHARD *enters.* DICKON'S *music, however, does not cease but fills the intervals between the verses. To his accompaniment, amid the whispered and gradually increasing wonder, resentment, and dismay of the assembled guests,* RAVENSBANE, *with his eyes fixed upon* RACHEL, *sings.*)

"Baron von Rabentod arose;
(The golden sun was rising)
Before him flew a flock of crows:
Sing heigh! Sing heigh! Sing heigh!
Sing—

"Ill speed, ill speed thee, baron-wight;
Ill speed thy palfrey pawing!
Blithe is the morn but black the night
That hears a raven's cawing."

(*Chorus.*)
Caw! Caw! Caw!

MISTRESS DODGE. (*Whispers to her husband.*) Did you hear them?

MINISTER DODGE. Hush!

AMELIA. (*Sotto voce.*) What *can* it be?

CAPTAIN BUGBY. Oh, the latest, be sure.

DICKON. You note, my friends, the accompanying harmonics; they are an intrinsic part of the ballad, and may not be omitted.

RAVENSBANE. (*Sings.*)

"The baron reckèd not a pin;
(For the golden sun was rising)
He rode to woo, he rode to win;
Sing heigh! Sing heigh! Sing heigh!
Sing—

"He rode into his prince's hall
Through knights and damsels flow'ry:
'Thy daughter, prince, I bid thee call;
I claim her hand and dowry.'"

(*Enter* RICHARD. MISTRESS MERTON *seizes his arm nervously*)

SIR CHARLES. (*To* CAPTAIN BUGBY.) This gentleman's playing is rather ventriloquistical.

CAPTAIN BUGBY. Quite, as it were.

REV. MASTER TODD. This smells unholy.

REV. MASTER RAND. (*To* TODD.) Shall we leave?

RAVENSBANE. (*Sings.*)

"What cock is this, with crest so high,
That crows with such a pother?"
"Baron von Rabentod am I;
Methinks we know each other."

"Now welcome, welcome, dear guest of mine,
So long why didst thou tarry?
Now, for the sake of auld lang syne,
My daughter thou shalt marry."

AMELIA. (*To* BUGBY.) And he kept right on smoking!

MINISTER DODGE. (*Who, with* RAND *and* TODD, *has risen uneasily.*) This smacks of witchcraft.

RAVENSBANE. (*Sings.*)

The bride is brought, the priest as well;
(The golden sun was passing)
They stood beside the altar rail;
Sing ah! Sing ah! Sing ah! Sing—
"Woman, with this ring I thee wed."
What makes his voice so awing?
The baron by the bride is dead:
Outside the crows were cawing.

(*Chorus, which grows tumultuous, seeming to fill the room with the invisible birds.*)

Caw! Caw! Caw!

(*The guests rise in confusion.* DICKON *still plays delightedly, and the strange music continues.*)

MINISTER DODGE. This is no longer godly. —Justice Merton! Justice Merton, sir!—

RAVENSBANE. (*To* RACHEL, *who holds his tassel in her hand.*) Ah! and you have my tassel!

RACHEL. See! I will wear it now. You yourself shall fasten it.

RAVENSBANE. Rachel! Mistress!

RACHEL. My dear lord!

(*As* RAVENSBANE *is placing the silken tassel on* RACHEL'S *breast to fasten it there,* RICHARD, *by the mirror, takes hold of the curtain strings.*)

RICHARD. I told you—witchcraft, like murder will out! Lovers! Behold yourselves! (*He pulls the curtain back.*)

RACHEL. (*Looking into the glass, screams and turns her gaze fearfully upon* RAVENSBANE.) Ah! Do not look!

DICKON. (*Who, having turned round from the spinet, has leaped forward, now turns back again, biting his finger.*) Too late!

(*In the glass are reflected the figures of* RACHEL *and* RAVENSBANE—RACHEL *just as she herself appears, but* RAVENSBANE *in his essential form of a scarecrow, in every movement reflecting* RAVENSBANE'S *motions. The thing in the glass is about to pin a wisp of corn-silk on the mirrored breast of the maiden.*)

RAVENSBANE. What is there?

RACHEL. (*Looking again, starts away from* RAVENSBANE.) Leave me! Leave me!—Richard!

(*She faints in* RICHARD'S *arms.*)

RAVENSBANE. Fear not, mistress, I will kill the thing. (*Drawing his sword, he rushes at the glass. Within, the scarecrow, with a drawn wheel-spoke, approaches him at equal speed. They come face to face and recoil.*) Ah! ah! Fear'st thou me? What art thou? Why, 't is a glass. Thou mockest me? Look, look, mistress, it mocks me! O God, no! no! Take it away. Dear God, do not look!—It is I!

ALL. (*Rushing to the doors.*) Witchcraft! Witchcraft!

(*As* RAVENSBANE *stands frantically confronting his abject reflection, struck in a like posture of despair, the curtain falls.*)

ACT FOURTH.

The scene is the same, but it is night. The moon, shining in broadly at the window, discovers RAVENSBANE *alone, prostrate before the mirror. Raised on one arm to a half-sitting posture, he gazes fixedly at the vaguely seen image of the scarecrow prostrate in the glass.*

RAVENSBANE. All have left me—but not thou. Rachel has left me; her eyes have turned away from me; she is gone. All that I loved, all that loved me, have left me. A thousand ages—a thousand ages ago, they went away; and thou and I have gazed upon each other's desertedness. Speak! and be pitiful! If thou art I, inscrutable image, if thou dost feel these pangs thine own, show then self-mercy; speak! What art thou? What am I? Why are we here? How comes it that we feel and guess and suffer? Nay, though thou answer not these doubts, yet mock them, mock them aloud, even as there, monstrous, thou counterfeitest mine actions. Speak, abject enigma!—Speak, poor shadow, thou—(*Recoiling wildly.*) Stand back, inanity! Thrust not thy mawkish face in pity toward me. Ape and idiot! Scarecrow!—to console me! Haha!—A flail and broomstick! a cob, a gourd and pumpkin, to fuse and sublimate themselves into a mage-philosopher, who discourseth metaphysics to itself—itself, God! Dost Thou hear? Itself! For even such am I—I whom Thou madest to love Rachel. Why, God—haha! dost Thou dwell in this thing? Is it Thou that peerest forth *at* me—*from* me? Why, hark then; Thou shalt listen, and answer—if Thou canst. Between the rise and setting of a sun, I have walked in this world of Thine. I have been thrilled with wonder; I have been calmed with knowledge; I have trembled with joy and passion. Power, beauty, love have ravished me. Infinity itself, like a dream, has blazed before me with the certitude of prophecy; and I have cried, "This world, the heavens, time itself, are mine to conquer," and I have thrust forth mine arm to wear Thy shield forever—and lo! for my shield Thou reachest me—a mirror, and whisperest: "Know thyself! Thou art—a scarecrow: a tinkling clod, a rigmarole of dust, a lump of ordure, contemptible, superfluous, inane!" Haha! Hahaha! And with such scarecrows Thou dost people a planet! O ludicrous! Monstrous! Ludicrous! At least, I thank Thee.

God! at least this breathing bathos can laugh at itself. Thou hast vouchsafed to me, Spirit,—hahaha!—to know myself. Mine, mine is the consummation of man—even self-contempt! (*Pointing in the glass with an agony of derision.*) Scarecrow! Scarecrow! Scarecrow!

THE IMAGE IN THE GLASS. (*More and more faintly.*) Scarecrow! Scarecrow! Scarecrow!

(RAVENSBANE *throws himself prone upon the floor, beneath the window, sobbing. There is a pause of silence, and the moon shines brighter. —Slowly then* RAVENSBANE, *getting to his knees, looks out into the night.*)

RAVENSBANE. What face are you, high up through the twinkling leaves? Do you not, like all the rest, turn, aghast, your eyes away from me—me, abject enormity, groveling at your feet? Gracious being, do you not fear—despise me? O white peace of the world, beneath your gaze the clouds glow silver, and the herded cattle, slumbering far afield, crouch—beautiful. The slough shines lustrous as a bridal veil. Beautiful face, you are Rachel's, and you have changed the world. Nothing is mean, but you have made it miraculous; nothing is loathsome, nothing ludicrous, but you have converted it to loveliness, that even this shadow of a mockery myself, cast by your light, gives me the dear assurance I am a man. Rachel, mistress, mother, out of my suffering you have brought forth my soul. I am saved!

THE IMAGE IN THE GLASS. A very pretty sophistry.

(*The moonlight grows dimmer, as at the passing of a cloud.*)

RAVENSBANE. Ah! what voice has snatched you from me?

THE IMAGE. A most poetified pumpkin!

RAVENSBANE. Thing! dost thou speak at last? My soul abhors thee.

THE IMAGE. I *am* thy soul.

RAVENSBANE. Thou liest.

THE IMAGE. Our daddy Dickon and our mother Rickby begot and conceived us at sunrise, in a Jack-o'-lantern.

RAVENSBANE. Thou liest, torturing illusion. Thou art but a phantom in a glass.

THE IMAGE. Why, very true. So art thou. *We* are a pretty phantom in a glass.

RAVENSBANE. It is a lie. I am no longer thou. I feel it; I am a man.

THE IMAGE.

And prithee, what 's a man? Man 's but a mirror,
Wherein the imps and angels play charades,
Make faces, mope, and pull each other's hair—
Till crack! the sly urchin Death shivers the glass,
And the bare coffin boards show underneath.

RAVENSBANE. Yea! if it be so, thou coggery! if both of us be indeed but illusions, why, now let us end together. But if it be not so, then let *me* for evermore be free of thee. Now is the test—the glass! (*Springing to the fireplace, he seizes an iron crosspiece from the andirons.*) I 'll play your urchin Death and shatter it. Let see what shall survive!

(*He rushes to strike the glass with the iron.* DICKON *steps out of the mirror, closing the curtain.*)

DICKON. I would n't, really!

RAVENSBANE. Dickon! dear Dickon! is it you?

DICKON. Yes, Jacky! it 's dear Dickon, and I really would n't.

RAVENSBANE. Would n't what, Dickon?

DICKON. Sweep the cobwebs off the sky with thine aspiring broomstick. When a man questions fate, 't is bad digestion. When a scarecrow does it, 't is bad taste.

RAVENSBANE. At last, *you* will tell me the truth, Dickon! Am I, then—that thing?

DICKON. You must n't be so skeptical. Of course you 're that thing.

RAVENSBANE. Ah me despicable! Rachel, why didst thou ever look upon me?

DICKON. I fear, cobby, thou hast never studied woman's heart and hero-worship. Take thyself now. I remarked to Goody Bess, thy mother, this morning, as I was chucking her thy pate from the hayloft, that thou wouldst make a Mark Antony or an Alexander before night.

RAVENSBANE. Cease! cease! in pity's name. You do not know the agony of being ridiculous.

DICKON. Nay, Jacky, all mortals are ridiculous. Like you, they were rummaged out of the muck; and like you, they shall return to the dunghill. I advise 'em, like you, to enjoy the interim, and smoke.

RAVENSBANE. This pipe, this ludicrous pipe that I forever set to my lips and puff! Why must I, Dickon? Why?

DICKON. To avoid extinction—merely. You see, 't is just as your fellow in there (*pointing to the glass*) explained. You yourself are the subtlest of mirrors, polished out of pumpkin and pipe-smoke. Into this mirror the fair Mistress Rachel has projected her lovely image, and thus provided you with what men call a soul.

RAVENSBANE. Ah! then, I have a soul—the truth of me? Mistress Rachel has indeed made me a man?

DICKON. Don't flatter thyself, cobby. Break thy pipe, and whiff—soul, Mistress Rachel, man, truth, and this pretty world itself, go up in the last smoke.

RAVENSBANE. No, no! not Mistress Rachel.

DICKON. Mistress Rachel exists for your lordship merely in your lordship's pipe-bowl.

RAVENSBANE. Wretched, niggling caricature that I am! All is lost to me—lost!

DICKON. "Paradise Lost" again! Always blaming it on me. There 's that gaunt fellow in England has lately wrote a parody on me when I was in the apple business.

RAVENSBANE. (*Falling on his knees and bowing his head.*) O God! I am so contemptible!

(*Enter, at door back,* GOODY RICKBY; *her blacksmith garb is hidden under a dingy black mantle with a peaked hood.*)

DICKON. Good verse, too, for a parody! (*Ruminating, raises one arm rhetorically above* RAVENSBANE.)

—"Farewell, happy fields
Where joy forever dwells! Hail, horrors; hail,
Infernal world! and thou, profoundest hell,
Receive thy new possessor."

GOODY RICKBY. (*Seizing his arm.*) Dickon!

DICKON. Hullo! You, Bess!

GOODY RICKBY. There 's not a minute to lose. Justice Merton and the neighbors have ended their conference at Minister Dodge's, and are returning here.

DICKON. Well, let 'em come. We 're ready.

GOODY RICKBY. But thou toldst me they had discovered—

DICKON. A scarecrow in a mirror. Well? The glass is bewitched; that 's all.

GOODY RICKBY. All? Witchcraft is hanging—that 's all! And the mirror was bought of me—of me, the witch. Wilt thou be my hangman, Dickon?

DICKON. Wilt thou give me a kiss, Goody? When did ever thy Dickon desert thee?

GOODY RICKBY. But how, boy, wilt thou—

DICKON. Trust me, and thy son. When the Justice's niece is thy daughter-in-law, all will be safe. For the Justice will cherish his niece's family.

GOODY RICKBY. But when he knows—

DICKON. But he shall *not* know. How can he? When the glass is denounced as a fraud, how will he, or any person, ever know that we made this fellow out of rubbish? Who, forsooth, but a poet—or a devil—*would* believe it? You must n't credit men with our imaginations, my dear.

GOODY RICKBY. Then thou wilt pull me through this safe?

DICKON. As I adore thee—and my own reputation.

GOODY RICKBY. (*At the window.*) I see their lanterns down the road.

DICKON. Stay, marchioness—his lordship! My lord—your lady mother.

GOODY RICKBY. (*Curtsying, laughs shrilly.*) Your servant—my son!

(*About to depart.*)

RAVENSBANE. Ye lie! both of you!—I was born of Rachel.

DICKON. Tut, tut, Jacky; you must n't mix up mothers and prospective wives at your age. It 's fatal.

GOODY RICKBY. (*Excitedly.*) They 're coming! (*Exit.*)

DICKON. (*Calling after her.*) Fear not; I 'll overtake thee.

RAVENSBANE. She is coming; Rachel is coming, and I may not look upon her!

DICKON. Eh? Why not?

RAVENSBANE. I am a monster.

DICKON. Fie! fie! Thou shalt have her.

RAVENSBANE. Have her, Dickon?

DICKON. For lover and wife.

RAVENSBANE. For wife?

DICKON. For wife and all. Thou hast but to obey.

RAVENSBANE. Ah! who will do this for me?

DICKON. I!

RAVENSBANE. Dickon! Wilt make me a man—a man and worthy of her?

DICKON. Fiddlededee! I make over no masterpieces. Thy mistress shall be Cinderella, and drive to her palace with her gilded pumpkin.

RAVENSBANE. It is the end.

DICKON. What! You 'll not?
RAVENSBANE. Never.
DICKON. Harkee, manikin. Hast thou learned to suffer?
RAVENSBANE. (*Wringing his hands.*) O God!
DICKON. *I* taught thee. Shall I teach thee further?
RAVENSBANE. Thou canst not.
DICKON. Cannot—ha! What if I should teach Rachel, too?
RAVENSBANE. Rachel!—Ah! now I know thee.
DICKON. (*Bowing.*) Flattered.
RAVENSBANE. Devil! Thou wouldst not torment Rachel?
DICKON. Not if my lord—
RAVENSBANE. Speak! What must I do?
DICKON. *Not* speak. Be silent, my lord, and acquiesce in all I say.
RAVENSBANE. I will be silent.
DICKON. And acquiesce?
RAVENSBANE. I will be silent.

(*Enter* MINISTER DODGE, *accompanied by* SIR CHARLES REDDINGTON, CAPTAIN BUGBY, *the* REVEREND MASTERS RAND *and* TODD, *and followed by* JUSTICE MERTON, RICHARD, MISTRESS MERTON, *and* RACHEL. RICHARD *and* RACHEL *stand somewhat apart,* RACHEL *drawing close to* RICHARD *and hiding her face. All wear their outer wraps, and two or three hold lanterns, which, save the moon, throw the only light upon the scene. All enter solemn and silent.*)

MINISTER DODGE. Lord, be Thou present with us, in this unholy spot!
SEVERAL MEN'S VOICES. Amen.
DICKON. Friends! Have you seized her?
MINISTER DODGE. Stand from us.
DICKON. Sir, the witch! Surely you did not let her escape?
ALL. The witch?
DICKON. A dame in a peaked hood. She has but now fled the house. She called herself—Goody Rickby.
ALL. Goody Rickby!
MISTRESS MERTON. She here!
DICKON. Yea, mistress, and hath confessed all the damnable art, by which all of us have lately been so terrorized.
JUSTICE MERTON. What confessed she?
MINISTER DODGE. What said she?
DICKON. This: It appeareth that, for some time past, she hath cherished revengeful thoughts against our honored host. Justice Merton.
MINISTER DODGE. Yea, he hath often righteously condemned her!
DICKON. Precisely! So, in revenge, she bewitched yonder mirror, and this very morning unlawfully inveigled this sweet young lady into purchasing it.
SIR CHARLES. Mistress Rachel!
MINISTER DODGE. (*To* RACHEL.) Didst thou purchase that glass?
RACHEL. (*In a low voice.*) Yes.
MINISTER DODGE. From Goody Rickby?
RACHEL. Yes. (*Clinging to* RICHARD.) O, Richard!
MINISTER DODGE. But the image; what was the damnable image in the glass?
DICKON. A familiar devil of hers—a sly imp, who wears to mortal eyes the shape of a scarecrow. It seems she commanded this devil to reveal himself in the glass as my lord's own image, that thus she might wreck Justice Merton's family felicity.
MINISTER DODGE. Infamous!
DICKON. Indeed, sir, it was this very devil whom but now she stole here to consult withal, when she encountered me, attendant here upon my poor prostrate lord, and—held by the wrath in my eye—confessed it all.
SIR CHARLES. Thunder and brimstone! Where is this accursed hag?
DICKON. Alas—gone, gone! If you had but stopped her.
MINISTER DODGE. I know her den—the blacksmith shop. Let us seize her there!
SIR CHARLES. (*Starting.*) Which way?
MINISTER DODGE. To the left.
SIR CHARLES. Go on, there.
MINISTER DODGE. My honored friends, come with us. Heaven shield, with her guilt, the innocent!

(*Exeunt all but* RICHARD, RACHEL, DICKON, *and* RAVENSBANE.)

DICKON. So, then, dear friends, this strange incident is happily elucidated. Bygones, therefore, be bygones. The future brightens—with orange-blossoms. Hymen and Felicity stand with us here ready to unite two amorous and bashful lovers. His lordship is reticent; yet to you alone, of all beautiful ladies, Mistress Rachel—
RAVENSBANE. (*In a mighty voice.*) Silence!
DICKON. My lord would—
RAVENSBANE. Silence! Dare not to speak to her!
DICKON. (*Biting his lip.*) My babe is weaned.

(*He steps back, and disappears, left, in the dimness.*)

RACHEL. (*Still at* RICHARD'S *side.*) Oh, my lord, if I have made you suffer—

RICHARD. (*Appealingly.*) Rachel!

RAVENSBANE. (*Approaching her, raises one arm to screen his face.*) Gracious lady! let fall your eyes; look not upon me. If I dare now speak once more to you, 't is because I would have you know—Oh, forgive me!—that I love you.

RICHARD. Sir! This lady has renewed her promise to be my wife.

RAVENSBANE. Your wife, or not, I love her.

RICHARD. Zounds!

RAVENSBANE. Forbear, and hear me! For one wonderful day I have gazed upon this, your world. A million forms—of trees, of stones, of stars, of men, of common things—have swum like motes before my eyes; but one alone was wholly beautiful. That form was Rachel: to her alone I was not ludicrous; to her I also was beautiful. Therefore, I love her.

RICHARD. Sir!

RAVENSBANE. You talk to me of mothers, mistresses, lovers, and wives and sisters, and you say men love these. What is love? The night and day of the world—the *all* of life, the all which must include both you and me and God, of whom you dream. Well, then, I love you, Rachel. What shall prevent me? Mistress, mother, wife—thou art all to me!

RICHARD. My lord, I can only reply for Mistress Rachel, that you speak like one who does not understand this world.

RAVENSBANE. O, God! sir, and do you? If so, tell me—tell me before it be too late—why, in this world, such a thing as *I* can love and talk of love. Why, in this world, a true man and woman, like you and your betrothed, can look upon this counterfeit and be deceived.

RACHEL and RICHARD. Counterfeit?

RAVENSBANE. Me—on me—the ignominy of the earth, the laughing-stock of the angels!

RACHEL. Are you not Lord Ravensbane?

RAVENSBANE. No, I am *not* Lord Ravensbane. I am a nobleman of husks, bewitched from a pumpkin. I am Lord Scarecrow!

RACHEL. Ah me, the image in the glass was true?

RAVENSBANE. Yes, true. It is the glass of truth—Thank God for you, dear.

DICKON. (*His face only reappearing in the mirror, speaks low.*) Remember! if you dare—Rachel shall suffer for it.

RAVENSBANE. You lie. She is above your power.

DICKON. Still, thou darest not—

RAVENSBANE. Fool, I dare. (RAVENSBANE *turns to* RACHEL. *While he speaks,* DICKON'S *face slowly fades and disappears.*) Mistress, this pipe is I. This intermittent smoke holds, in its nebula, Venus, Mars, the world. If I should break it—chaos and the dark! And this of me that now stands up will sink jumbled upon the floor—a scarecrow. See! I break it. (*He breaks the pipe in his hands, and flings the pieces to the ground; then turns, agonized, to* RACHEL.) Oh, Rachel, could I have been a man—!

(*He sways, staggering.*)

RACHEL. Richard! Richard! support him. (*She draws the curtain of the mirror, just opposite which* RAVENSBANE *has sunk upon the floor. At her cry, he starts up faintly and gazes at his reflection, which is seen to be a normal image of himself.*) Look, look: the glass!

RAVENSBANE. Who is it?

RACHEL. Yourself, my lord—'t is the glass of truth.

RAVENSBANE. (*His face lighting with an exalted joy, starts to his feet, erect, before the glass.*) A man! (*He falls back into the arms of the two lovers.*) Rachel!

RICHARD. (*Bending over him.*) Dead!

RACHEL. (*With an exalted look.*) But a man!

THE BOSS

BY

Edward Sheldon

Printed, for the first time, by permission of the author.

THE BOSS

The Boss represents the play dealing with political and business interests. Its author, Edward Brewster Sheldon, was born in Chicago, February 4, 1886, the son of Theodore and Mary Strong Sheldon. He graduated from Harvard College in 1907, and took the degree of A.M. from Harvard University in 1908. He had been interested in the writing of plays while an undergraduate, and had his first professional success in little more than a year after graduation.

On November 12, 1908, at the Opera House, Providence, Rhode Island, Mrs. Fiske produced his play, *Salvation Nell,* which was a stage success. A complete list of his plays since then includes *The Nigger,* produced first at the New Theatre, New York City, December 4, 1909; *The Boss* (1911); *Princess Zim-Zim,* played first at the Harmanus Bleecker Hall, Albany, New York, December 4, 1911; *Egypt,* first played at The Playhouse, Hudson, New York, September 18, 1912; *The High Road,* produced first at His Majesty's Theatre, Montreal, Canada, October 14, 1912; *Romance,* played first at Harmanus Bleecker Hall, Albany, February 6, 1913, and *The Garden of Paradise,* first produced at the Park Theatre, November 28, 1914. Mr. Sheldon also dramatized *Das Hohe Lied* of Hermann Sudermann in 1914, under the title of *The Song of Songs,* adapting the original to American conditions. It was, however, not a success from a dramatic standpoint.

The most important plays of Mr. Sheldon are *Salvation Nell, The Nigger, The Boss, Romance,* and *The Garden of Paradise.* In these plays he has treated five quite different themes, and shown a dramatic craftmanship, at times, of a high order. *Salvation Nell* reproduced with fidelity scenes in the street life of New York City, and placed against a background of drunkenness and vice, the work of the Salvation Army. *The Nigger* showed real power in treating the theme of a young Southerner with political ambitions and great family pride who finds that he is of mixed blood. The ending is somewhat inconclusive, but there are portions of the play, such as the letter of the quadroon to her master, which are remarkable pieces of writing.

The Boss was the third of these realistic studies of American life. Business and politics form the background, but the attention of the audience is centred upon the relations of "Regan" and his wife. They are strongly contrasted types and at first glance their union seems impossible. Yet Mr. Sheldon has indicated unobtrusively enough but surely with sufficient definiteness, the inherent attraction which the strength of "Regan" had for "Emily Griswold" and the way in which her pity and sympathy finally turned to something deeper. The playwright has avoided the temptation to make "The Boss" a hero; he is a very human person, and the acting of Mr. Holbrook Blinn in the part was masterly. For these reasons the play was selected to represent Mr. Sheldon's work, since *Salvation Nell* was hardly available as a play for reading and study, and copyright considerations prevented the inclusion of *Romance*. *Romance* is so far his greatest play, and the remarkable acting of Miss Doris Keane as *Madame Cavallini,* the Italian opera singer whose love story is the theme of the drama, illustrated again the great strength of Mr. Sheldon, his ability as a practical playwright. *Romance* was produced at the Lyric Theatre, London, on September 30, 1915. Miss Keane gave 1128 performances of *Romance* in London and it has been played in Australia, New Zealand, South Africa, British India, Egypt, Christiana, Stockholm, and the Swedish Provinces.

The Garden of Paradise is a dramatization of the story of *The Little Mermaid,* by Hans Andersen, with the love note dominant. While this is pure romance, it is, of all Mr. Sheldon's work, most distinctly a piece of literature, and he has shown his versatility in turning from the realistic study to the poetic interpretation of fairy life.

The Boss was first produced at the Garrick Theatre, Detroit, Michigan, January 9, 1911. It was played first in New York City at the Astor Theatre, January 30, 1911.

The Nigger (1910), *Romance* (1914), and *The Garden of Paradise* (1915) have been published by the Macmillan Company. *The Boss* is now printed for the first time from the manuscript especially prepared by Mr. Sheldon for this collection. The editor is indebted to the courtesy of the author for permission to print the play. For details concerning the play he has to thank Mr. Sheldon and his agent, Miss Alice Kauser.

For criticism of *The Boss,* see J. E. Metcalfe, in *Life,* Vol. 57, pp. 308–9, February 9, 1911, and *The Theatre,* Vol. 13, pp. vi–viii, March, 1911.

NOTE TO THIRD EDITION.

To the great loss of our stage, Mr. Sheldon has been suffering from an illness which has prevented him from making any consistent progress in his dramatic work. *The Lonely Heart* was produced in Baltimore on October 24, 1921. *Bewitched,* written in collaboration with Mr. Sidney Howard, opened in New York on October 1, but although there was general critical approval, it did not meet with the popular success it had experienced on the road.

According to *L'Atlantique,* "one of the most recent dramatic works from America, *Romance,* by M. Edward Sheldon, has now become, thanks to the perfect translation of MM. Robert de Flers and François de Croisset, 'une authentique pièce française.'" The first performance in France took place at Théâtre de l'Athénée, Paris, December 24, 1923.

Note to Fourth Edition.

A melodrama, *Lulu Belle,* announced as by Edward Sheldon and Charles MacArthur, was produced at the Broad Street Theatre, Philadelphia, by David Belasco, January 26, 1926. While there was a certain vividness in the representation of the tenements and the café through which the passion of George Randall pursued the negro harlot, the work was below the standard of Sheldon's other plays.

Note to Fifth Edition.

Jenny, by Margaret Ayer Barnes and Edward Sheldon, was produced at the Booth Theatre, New York, October 8, 1929. It is a romantic play of social life, in which Miss Jane Cowl portrayed with success the character of an actress who helps the head of a modern family to solve his problem. *Dishonored Lady,* in which Mr. Sheldon also collaborated with Mrs. Barnes, and in which Miss Katharine Cornell took the leading rôle, had its first production in New York, on February 4, 1930.

Note to Seventh Edition.

Edward Sheldon died April 2, 1946. An authorized biography by Marion Meigs Woods is in progress.

THE ORIGINAL CAST OF CHARACTERS

In the order of their first appearance

GARRICK THEATRE, DETROIT, MICHIGAN, JANUARY 9, 1911

JAMES D. GRISWOLD, of Griswold and Company, Contractors, Mr. Henry Weaver
DONALD GRISWOLD, his son .... Mr. Howard Estabrook
EMILY GRISWOLD, his daughter .... Miss Emily Stevens
MITCHELL, Mr. Griswold's butler .... Mr. Henry Sargent
LAWRENCE DUNCAN .... Mr. Kenneth Hill
MICHAEL R. REGAN, of Regan and Company, Contractors ... Mr. Holbrook Blinn
DAVIS, his private secretary .... Mr. J. Hammond Dailey
MRS. CUYLER .... Miss Ruth Benson
GATES, Mrs. Regan's butler .... Mr. John M. Troughton
"PORKY" McCOY, Regan's representative in the Fourth Ward .... Mr. H. A. LaMotte
SCANLAN .... Mr. Wilmer Dame
ARCHBISHOP SULLIVAN .... Mr. Frank Sheridan
A COOK .... Miss Bella Paul
A FRENCH MAID .... Miss Rose Wincott
LIEUTENANT OF POLICE .... Mr. Frank Julian
A POLICE OFFICER .... Mr. James MacDonald
ANOTHER POLICE OFFICER .... Mr. H. G. Weir

ACT I

Mr. Griswold's drawing-room, the afternoon of Oct. 28th.

ACT II

Mr. Regan's library. The evening of April 29th.

ACT III

The same. The following morning.

ACT IV

Inspector's room at the Police Station, three days later.

Place—One of the Eastern lake-ports.
Time—Now.

THE BOSS

ACT FIRST.

Griswold's drawing room, the afternoon of Oct. 28th. At the back, double doors leading into the hall, which can be seen when the doors are opened. A newel post and balustrade leading upstairs are also seen in the hall. At right two large windows looking upon the lawn and street beyond. To right—front, near the windows, is a low tea table, at present occupied by cigarette box, ash tray, and flowers. To the right at back is a baby grand piano, facing the windows. Near this is a big grandfather chair. Other chairs, smaller table. In several large vases on tables, piano, and the mantelpiece, are quantities of superb American Beauty roses. They strike the eye at once. At left the fireplace.

As the curtain rises, Griswold is seen walking nervously to and fro. He is a well-bred man of fifty or so, carefully and soberly dressed. He looks very worried, and keeps glancing at his watch. He stops to throw the stump of his cigar into the grate, then lights another and recommences his restless walk. Suddenly he stops at the window, glances out, then goes quickly to the door at back, opens it and listens. The closing of the front door is heard.

GRISWOLD. (*Calling.*) That you, Donald?

DONALD. (*Outside.*) Yes.

GRISWOLD. Come in here.

(DONALD *appears still in his overcoat and gloves, a newspaper under his arm. He is a distinguished-looking, brilliant, eager young man of about thirty. The following scene is to be played at high tension by both men,—sharply, quickly, nervously.*)

Now what did he say?

DONALD. Wait till I shut the door. (*He does so.*)

GRISWOLD. Well?

DONALD. (*Turning.*) It 's all right--he says he 'll come here at five and talk it over. (*Puts hat and paper on piano.*)

GRISWOLD. (*Infinitely relieved.*) Thank God! You 've been just an hour and five minutes. I did n't know what to think!

DONALD. (*Taking off his gloves at piano.*) He kept me waiting. His office is jam full.

GRISWOLD. (*Quickly.*) D 'you think the people know, then?

DONALD. Know what?

GRISWOLD. That he 's pushed us out of business.

DONALD. (*Takes off his coat, puts it on the piano.*) Not yet. Remember—the Western Amalgamated only went over to him to-day. When did they wire us? About two o'clock?

GRISWOLD. (*Turning away.*) All the rest 'll follow suit within a month!

DONALD. (*Takes up newspaper.*) Steady, father!

GRISWOLD. Did you have any chance to talk to him?

DONALD. Not much. He chewed a big cigar and put his feet on the desk, and told me he 'd had his eyes on our grain-contracts ever since he began handling freight in '92.

GRISWOLD. Of course he wanted them—why, they 're the big reason this city has for existing! Half the wheat that goes into the world gets there through this port!

DONALD. (*Half to himself.*) I wish I 'd smashed him in the face—right before his stenographers!

GRISWOLD. (*Walking up and down.*) I 've run the business as well as I could. I felt a public responsibility—you know that!

DONALD. And now this Irish tough of an ex-barkeep has come along and swindled and blackjacked and knifed his way up to the place you 've—

GRISWOLD. (*Stopping him.*) Don't, my boy, don't! He 'll be here in half an hour. We 've got to keep cool and think!

DONALD. (*Continuing his own line of thought.*) Why, we could have managed him if we 'd been willing to stoop a bit and dabble in his own dirt!

GRISWOLD. (*Desperately.*) We must think—that 's it!—think!

DONALD. (*Satirically.*) You could have put him up at the clubs, introduced him to Emily, had him here to the house—I could have clapped him on the back, called him by the first name—(*Angrily.*) That 's what he wanted! He 'd have paid for that!

GRISWOLD. Donald! Drop it! We 've got just an hour to get up something before he comes!

DONALD. But he 's a disgrace to the city! He knows it, and he knows we know it, and that 's why he hates us so! (*Sharply.*) Father, let me ring him up and tell him we 've changed our minds—we 'll get on without any arbitrating!

GRISWOLD. Not let him come?

DONALD. Yes. What 's the use? He 's just doing it to gloat over us. He hopes we 're going to crawl and whine! He 'd enjoy that!

GRISWOLD. I don't care. I've got to see him and find out if there is n't some way out.

DONALD. There is n't.

GRISWOLD. There must be! My boy, d 'you realize what we 're in for?

DONALD. Do I?

GRISWOLD. It is n't as if the money were the only thing!

DONALD. (*Soothingly.*) I know that.

GRISWOLD. It 's the integrity of the firm—it 's my own good name—

DONALD. Please, father!

GRISWOLD. Those notes—those savings-bank notes—what about them? They 're due on December 1st. If we fail I can't meet them—those banks 'll go under like that— (*Snaps fingers.*)

DONALD. Stop, father, don't!

GRISWOLD. And, Donald, d 'you know what those stockholders are going to say? They 're going to say, "He was a director—Griswold was a director, and—" (*Door closes off stage.*)

DONALD. (*Interrupting.*) That sounds like the front door.

GRISWOLD. What—?

DONALD. (*Goes to the door, opens it, listens. Then, reassuringly.*) It 's all right! Just Emily.

(EMILY GRISWOLD *appears. She is a brilliant, beautiful, assured young woman of about 28, dressed very simply for the street, wearing furs.*)

EMILY. (*Stopping on seeing them.*) Hello! Whatever made you two come home so early—(*Suddenly.*) Dad, you 're ill! You 're white as a sheet! Don—(*Frightened.*) Why, what 's the matter? What 's happened?

DONALD. Nothing. Nothing at all.

EMILY. Yes, there is. Oh, tell me, please, quick!

GRISWOLD. It 's all right, dear, Donald and I have to talk business with a man we could n't very well ask to the office, so I suggested his coming here. You are n't expecting anyone to tea, are you?

EMILY. Just Laurie Duncan—he does n't count. (*Still anxiously.*) Oh, dad, you do look dreadfully!

GRISWOLD. Then we can use this room—yes, that would be better than taking him upstairs.

EMILY. Him?

GRISWOLD. You see, it 's "Shindy Mike."

EMILY. (*Surprised.*) You don't mean Regan. (*Slight pause. She looks at* DONALD, *then back to* GRISWOLD.) What have you two got to see Regan about?

DONALD. Oh, a lot of things a woman would n't understand. (*Buries himself in a newspaper.*)

EMILY. Don't be so snappy, Don!

DONALD. (*Over paper.*) You may be all right down in the slums but you 're no good when it comes to business. D 'you hear? No earthly good!

EMILY. You 're evidently in one of your fox-terrier moods to-day.

DONALD. Well, is she, father?

GRISWOLD. (*Nervously,*) Stop squabbling, please.

EMILY. (*Protesting.*) But, dad, I—

GRISWOLD. (*Interrupting.*) How 's my young scientific philanthropist? You 've spent the whole afternoon in your beloved slums, have n't you? Well, where did you go?

EMILY. (*Taking off her furs.*) Oh, down in the Fourth Ward, around the docks.

GRISWOLD. Regan's district. (*He becomes lost in his own thoughts.*)

EMILY. Yes. Oh, it 's too sorrowful! The men spend all their wages on drink, so of course the women can't feed the children and they have n't any shoes or coal—think of it!—with the winter coming on! And the worst of it is they don't really care. They just seem tired and listless and they say they can't help it and that I don't understand. Well, perhaps I don't, but every time I see their faces I feel all of a sudden how much the world is carrying on its back, and it makes me want to cry, because there's so little, so awfully little that I can do to help.

DONALD. That's perfectly true, so why don't you drop it, Emily, and act like other girls? Those people can get on without you. You're not so important as all that.

EMILY. (*Smiling.*) As a matter of fact, I'm awfully important.

DONALD. What?

EMILY. You ought to hear what Mrs. Moriarity said to Mrs. Scanlan about me!

DONALD. Oh!

EMILY. She said if the angels were n't built on my style, not even God could make her go to Heaven!

DONALD. (*Grinning.*) Mrs. Moriarity must be somewhat of a humorist.

EMILY. So don't ask me to stop working —I won't! Not until I have a big club house for the men, and a cooking school for the women—

DONALD. (*Interrupting.*) And an incubator for the children. That it?

EMILY. (*Smiling.*) Yes, that's it.

GRISWOLD. (*To* DONALD.) Are you sure he said five o'clock?

DONALD. Yes, why? It's only twenty-five minutes now.

(*Glances at watch and clock and looks out of window.*)

EMILY. (*Annoyed.*) Dad, you have n't listened to one word I've been saying.

GRISWOLD. (*Rousing himself.*) Have n't I, dear? I'm awfully sorry, but I've got so much on my mind.

EMILY. I know it! Something is the matter! Dad, I feel so guilty. I've spent the whole day down in the ward and you've been in trouble and I have n't been here to help you. I don't think your Emily's much good after all. But please forgive her, dear, for my sake, and tell me all about it.

DONALD. (*Warningly.*) Now, father!

GRISWOLD. Nothing, dear. I said so once.

EMILY. Wait a moment—(*Looking up and speaking positively.*) It's Regan.

DONALD. Now, Emily, we have to talk business, and there is n't much time, so run along, dear, please! D'you mind?

(*He takes her by her arms and pushes her toward the door.*)

EMILY. (*Shaking him off.*) Yes, of course I mind. I'm going to stay and hear what you have to say.

DONALD. No, you're not!

(*Goes to table.*)

EMILY. Don, stop contradicting me! Even though I *am* a girl, I'm one of the family and I intend to be consulted whenever anything important is going on!

DONALD. This is private, though. D'you hear? *Private!*

EMILY. (*Obstinately.*) I don't care if it is or not.

DONALD. (*Fuming.*) Father, make her go away!

GRISWOLD. (*Soothingly.*) Now, dear, please—

EMILY. (*Interrupting suddenly.*) I know what it is! Will you tell me if I'm right?

DONALD. You don't know anything about it.

EMILY. Don't I, though? Regan's trying to steal dad's contracts with the grain companies!

DONALD. Emily, you make me tired!

EMILY. (*Turning to* GRISWOLD.) Is n't that right, dear?

GRISWOLD. No.

DONALD. (*To* EMILY, *approvingly.*) There! What did I tell you!

GRISWOLD. (*In dry emotion.*) He *has* stolen them. He's done us, Emily.

EMILY. (*Gasping.*) What?

DONALD. (*Sharply.*) Father, d'you think this is wise?

GRISWOLD. She's got to hear it sooner or later!

EMILY. (*With parted lips.*) You don't mean—the Western—

GRISWOLD. Yes, the Western went over to him to-day.

EMILY. But the others?

GRISWOLD. They'll follow like sheep. No, we're finished this time—finished!

(*He turns away quickly.*)

EMILY. (*Rushing to him.*) But, Dad, you must n't give up! You must arrange it with him—discuss it, come to an understanding.

GRISWOLD. That's why we've asked him here this afternoon, but—

(*He makes a despairing gesture.*)

EMILY. (*Imploringly.*) Don, can't you manage it somehow?

DONALD. I'll do my best. (*With a smothered exclamation.*) If we could get him to keep those thieving hands off the Western for one month—only one month!—could n't I make him lie down and take the count!

EMILY. (*Eagerly.*) How?

DONALD. The easiest thing in the world.

EMILY. Well, tell us.

GRISWOLD. Go on, my boy.

DONALD. I 'd get his men to strike.

EMILY. Get his men to strike? Could you do it?

DONALD. Could I? Good Lord! Why, they 're just like a powder magazine waiting for the match! All they need is a leader who 's studied law and has a little nerve.

GRISWOLD. How many of them are there?

DONALD. Over eight thousand. And sick to death of being rounded up like Texas steers with a gang of toughs for cowboys! I could get after his liquor system, too—the public now does n't even realize he has one!

EMILY. His liquor system?

GRISWOLD. (*Pointing to* EMILY.) There —you see!

EMILY. What is his liquor system, Don?

DONALD. (*Rather impatiently.*) Why, it 's his money that is back of every saloon in the Fourth Ward and each employee who won't leave half his wages on a Regan bar before he goes home Saturday night gets his quit notice when the whistle blows on Monday morning.

EMILY. (*Shocked.*) Is that true?

DONALD. True? Of course it 's true! And that 's just one of the little tricks that have made him what he is to-day!

EMILY. Then *that 's* why the men come home drunk, and the children have no food, and the women say I don't understand.

DONALD. People say that Shindy 's out for the dollar! It 's a lie—he 's out for the dime. And you can take it from me that every penny he owns he 's ripped out of a human heart!

EMILY. Don! Why did n't you tell me this before?

DONALD. What 's the matter?

EMILY. I 've met him!

GRISWOLD. Regan?

DONALD. Where?

EMILY. At a dinner the Streeters gave. He rides in the park. Why, we cantered around the bridle-path twice only this morning!

DONALD. (*In strong reproof.*) Emily!

GRISWOLD. My child!

EMILY. (*Apologetic.*) He—he was n't at all what I 'd expected. Of course he was tough. But there was something—nice about him. (*A movement from* DONALD *and* GRISWOLD.) Really there was—something—oh, I don't know, dad, but—why, he was just like a little boy!

DONALD. (*Bitterly.*) "Little boy"! Rot! You 're a nice sort of a girl, you are—playing around with the crook who 's stolen your father's business.

EMILY. (*Interrupting resentfully.*) Well, I did n't know it, did I? You and dad never open your mouths to me and then when anything happens it 's all my fault! I suppose I—

(MITCHELL *enters.*)

What do you want, Mitchell?

MITCHELL. (*Announcing.*) Mr. Duncan.

(*He holds open the door and* LAWRENCE DUNCAN *comes in. He is a lazy, attractive young man of about twenty-six.*)

DUNCAN. (*Gaily.*) Well, Emily! I 'm glad you don't spend all your time in the Fourth Ward. How-d' you-do, sir? Hello, Don.

DONALD. (*Constrainedly.*) Hello.

DUNCAN. (*Suspiciously.*) Mr. Griswold, have these two been scrapping again? (*To* EMILY.) What 's the matter?

EMILY. You talk as if this were a Peace Conference. (*Looking at* DONALD.) But it is n't!

(*She sits down at the piano.*)

DONALD. (*Returning the look.*) Not by a long shot!

DUNCAN. (*Gaily.*) I believe you! (EMILY *plays piano.* DUNCAN *goes towards her, leaning over piano.*) Please let 's have tea. I 'm awfully hungry.

(DONALD *looks at watch uneasily.*)

EMILY. Tea?

DUNCAN. Yes, you know you promised. (*Suddenly.*) Oh, if you 've forgotten, don't bother. I 'll come another time.

(*He turns to the door.*)

EMILY. (*Smiling.*) Of course! I remember now! (DONALD *signals across to his father that they leave the room.* EMILY *stops playing.*) Sit down, Laurie, and don't be a goose! (*To* GRISWOLD.) When that man appears, I 'll tell Mitchell to send him up to the library.

GRISWOLD. Very well, dear.

EMILY. (*Stopping him.*) Daddy, listen! (*Wistfully.*) So long as you and Don and I are well and have each other, I don't think we ought to worry much, no matter how badly business goes. Do you?

GRISWOLD. (*Coldly.*) My dear, I'm afraid you don't understand these things. (*To* DUNCAN.) Good-bye, my boy. Remember me to your mother.

DUNCAN. Thanks, Mr. Griswold. Good night. (GRISWOLD *goes out.*)

EMILY. Don, will you forgive me?

DONALD. (*Trying to be stern.*) You don't deserve it.

EMILY. (*Coaxingly.*) Not if I promise never, never, *never* to do it again?

DONALD. (*Relaxing into a smile.*) Don't bother! I'll take care of that! Oh, Laurie, shall we have some squash Saturday?

DUNCAN. All right. Bye-bye, old man!

(DONALD *goes out, closing the door.*)

EMILY. (*Pressing a bell.*) Oh, dear! I do have such trouble keeping my men-folks in order! (DUNCAN *laughs.*) Don't laugh, Laurie. I'm depressed to-day.

DUNCAN. (*Sympathetically.*) What's the matter?

EMILY. (*Her voice trembling.*) Life. That's all. Just life.

(MITCHELL *comes in with tea tray.*)

(EMILY *goes to tea table.*) Here comes your precious tea! Never say again I don't keep my word! (*To* MITCHELL.) Have you put on some of those little biscuits Mr. Duncan's so fond of? Oh yes, I see. Thank you.

(MITCHELL *has taken the flowers from the table and put them on the piano, replacing them with the tea tray. Then he goes out quietly.*)

EMILY. (*Filling the tea pot.*) Now pull up the big chair, and we'll have a nice comfy time! You'd better begin by 'fessing up, don't you think?

DUNCAN. (*Obeying her.*) What about?

EMILY. (*Seated, nodding.*) Those roses.

DUNCAN. (*Promptly.*) Not guilty!

EMILY. Don't be absurd! They came just as usual—four huge boxes of them. You might admit it, Laurie, when you see me wearing one.

DUNCAN. I may be a liar, but I have odd moments of telling the truth—honestly I have! And I feel one coming on now.

EMILY. Well, let it come.

DUNCAN. I'm far too hard up to send you American Beauties—at twenty-five a dozen—oh, yes, I've priced them, all right! (*His tone deepening.*) Although you know, Emily, if I could, I'd have you walk on rose leaves for the rest of your life.

EMILY. (*Quickly.*) Rose leaves! Oh, people irritate me so when they talk like that! If you'd seen what I have this afternoon, you'd—(*Checking herself.*) How do you like your tea? Five lumps and cream?

(*He stops, looking at her curiously.*)

DUNCAN. Oh, I don't want any tea, Emily.

EMILY. No tea? Then what did you come for? You said—

DUNCAN. (*Very nervously and obviously bracing himself.*) I came because I wanted to ask you something. I've been trying to get up courage for weeks, but —but—why, there's something about you that frightens me—it always has! For heaven's sake, stop *thinking* a moment, can't you? Emily, don't look at me like that—it's horrible! (*In an outburst.*) Emily, will you marry me? Yes, that's it—I want you to marry me! Now I've done it! (*He wipes his forehead.*)

EMILY. (*In mild reproof.*) Oh, my dear boy!

DUNCAN. Well? What about it?

EMILY. I'm afraid you mustn't talk to me that way any more.

DUNCAN. Mustn't talk to you that way? Why not?

EMILY. I couldn't, that's all. Now let's talk about something else.

DUNCAN. No, we won't—not till we've finished this! I think I've known you long enough, Emily, to say a few things you ought to hear, so I'm going to light right in. You haven't treated me squarely.

EMILY. Why not?

DUNCAN. Just because you're clever and beautiful and know five times as much as most men that's no reason for leading them on.

EMILY. (*Interrupting indignantly.*) I *don't* lead them on!

DUNCAN. (*Positively.*) Yes, you do! You do lead them on! And then when you've got them all tangled up, poor devils, you take delight in turning them down!

EMILY. Oh, that's not fair!

DUNCAN. What if they weren't up on philanthropy, economics, civic responsibility and all that sort of thing? They were mighty fine fellows, some of them! And that counts a whole lot. No, Emily,

I 'm afraid now I believe what I used to think I never could—that you have n't any heart, after all!

EMILY. (*Impatiently holding out plate.*) Oh, take a biscuit and stop being silly.

DUNCAN. (*Refusing the plate.*) No, thanks. No biscuit. Everybody said you had n't, but I 've been fool enough to think I knew better. Well, I don't—any more! So good-bye.

(*He rises and goes towards door.*)

EMILY. (*Simply and seriously.*) No, wait. Laurie, you must n't go like that. You may be right about me—I don't know. I feel that way myself lots of times! And yet I do believe—way down—deep down—I believe there *is* a man waiting for me somewhere, and that I 'll know him when he comes along!

DUNCAN. (*Wistfully.*) Don't I look the least bit like him? Could n't you manage to mistake us in the dark?

EMILY. (*Smiling.*) I 'm afraid not, Laurie. (*He turns silently away.*) —Oh, please don't be hurt! You 've been my best friend for so long I—I don't think I could get on without you now.

DUNCAN. Emily!

EMILY. You know the way I mean. But I wish—d' you mind if I say it? It 's only because I 'm so fond of you!

DUNCAN. (*Grimly.*) No, go ahead. I can stand anything now.

EMILY. (*Wistfully.*) I wish you 'd wake up, Laurie! You 've been asleep all your life. Oh, I know you 've had a good time, and I like good times so much myself that I feel I ought n't to say a word. But—but there *is* something more. I wish when you walk down the street, everybody would turn and say: "There goes Lawrence Duncan. He 's done a lot to help this city. He 's a fine man and I 'm proud of him!" (*Breaking off.*) I suppose I 'm talking nonsense, Laurie, but you know what I mean.

DUNCAN. Yes, of course, I do. You mean why don't I go down there and start basket-ball teams and boxing classes for those kids in the Fourth Ward. Well, I don't know how.

EMILY. (*Wistfully.*) But you could learn.

DUNCAN. I tell you, Emily, it 's not in my line.

EMILY. People said that to me, but I went right ahead.

DUNCAN. But I 'd just make a fool of myself—everybody I know would be laughing at me.

EMILY. They used to laugh at me—perhaps they still do. The only difference is, I never hear them any more. They seem so far away.

(*She is lost in a sort of dreamy enthusiasm.*)

DUNCAN. (*Uncomfortably.*) Emily, you 've been working too hard down there. You 're a little bit cracked on that subject—you 're morbid, really you are! Now listen, dear. Leave all those dirty people for a little while and come up here where you belong.

EMILY. Do you mean that?

DUNCAN. Of course I mean it.

EMILY. (*After a slight pause.*) Then there 's no use talking any more.

(*Enter* MITCHELL.)

MITCHELL. Mr. Regan, madam. He says Mr. Griswold is expecting him.

EMILY. Mr. Regan? Oh, yes. Put him in the reception-room, Mitchell, until I go upstairs. Then bring him in here. I 'll tell Mr. Griswold. (MITCHELL *bows.*) And Mr. Duncan is going.

(MITCHELL *holds open the door, hesitates. Then, seeing that* DUNCAN *is not going, he disappears.*)

DUNCAN. "Shindy Mike"?

EMILY. (*Nodding.*) Yes, it 's business. That 's why I 'm so worried.

DUNCAN. (*Smiling.*) When *he* walks down the street everybody turns and looks at *him*—

EMILY. (*Interrupting and smiling.*) Ssh! Be quiet! He 's out there in the hall! Good-bye. Come to dinner Thursday. Will you?

DUNCAN. If you want me?

EMILY. I do!

DUNCAN. Then of course I shall. (*He kisses her hands lightly before she can take them away.*) God bless you, dear!

(*He goes out.* EMILY, *with a sigh, goes to the piano, takes up her furs and gloves, and turns to the door. Just as she reaches it there is the sound of voices outside in the hall.*)

REGAN'S VOICE. (*Outside.*) That 's O. K.! Here 's a dollar fer ye—g'wan and take it! Ye won't? All right, I 'm goin' in anyway.

(REGAN *walks in, putting a bill back in his pocket. On seeing* EMILY *he stops in sudden embarrassment, and smiles.*)

REGAN. Pardon me, Miss Griswold. I thought I 'd just step in an' ask ye how ye was feelin' after yer ride.

EMILY. I believe my father 's expecting you, Mr. Regan. If you 'll wait I 'll send him down.

REGAN. (*Shyly stopping her.*) Say, Miss Griswold, would you mind sittin' here while I talk to ye fer a minute? I won't keep ye long.

EMILY. I 'm afraid I can't, Mr. Regan. Good afternoon.

REGAN. Good afternoon, Miss.

(*She goes out at the back of the stage without looking at him or smiling.* REGAN *is left to himself. He is a man of about 38, the Irish-American bull-dog type, talks and looks like the tough who has risen to a great position and is not yet at home in it. He is apt to be too polite and ceremonious, but when he is moved or excited this drops easily away. He is elaborately dressed in a morning coat, with a gardenia in his buttonhole. He wears a diamond scarfpin, and is very conscious of his clothes. After* EMILY *goes he begins looking about the room, notices the flowers with a good deal of satisfaction. He looks at himself in the mirror, straightens his tie, and then glances suddenly at the door to see if he has been detected. He consults his watch, just as the door opens and* GRISWOLD *and* DONALD *come in.*)

GRISWOLD. Mr. Regan.

REGAN. (*Shaking hands effusively.*) Glad t' see ye, sir. An' the young man, too—(*shakes hands with* DONALD) glad t' see ye!

GRISWOLD. (*Coldly.*) Sit down, Mr. Regan. I don't want to take too much of your valuable time.

REGAN. (*Genially.*) Aw, there 's no rush! I got all day! (*There is a silence,* GRISWOLD *and* DONALD *exchange glances.* REGAN *realizes that he is being criticized. He turns ugly in a moment.*) Well, if you two gents is so strong for business, let 's get at it. Ye asked me t' come. Here I am. What d' ye want?

GRISWOLD. All right, Mr. Regan, I 'll go straight to the point. I 've been handling all the grain that 's landed in this city for nearly twenty-five years. Since '95 you 've managed to get hold of the freight contracts. You were on the inside of dock-life. You knew how to manage those men. You could make them work for an impossible wage. Well, you 've succeeded and now you naturally want the grain contracts, too. I 've done my best, but I 'm afraid I 've been too conservative to fight the conditions you 've created.

(*During this speech* REGAN *has lighted a huge cigar, which he puffs arrogantly.*)

REGAN. You mean I 'm a grafter an' a thief, but ye 'll be damned if yer one, too. That it?

GRISWOLD. (*Smiling.*) You have a clear way of putting things, Mr. Regan. Well, I heard to-day from the Western Amalgamated that you've offered them terms I can't possibly meet. All the smaller companies will follow the Western, of course. Mr. Regan, you 've beaten me. You control the grain-handling business of this country.

REGAN. (*Leaning back.*) Well, what are ye goin' t' do about it?

GRISWOLD. Wait just a moment! I want to make the situation perfectly clear. For a good many years I 've been rather prominent in the direction of three very important savings-banks—

REGAN. (*Interrupting.*) The People's Trust, the Union Deposit, and the Farmers' Loan. An' they put up the money you 've been fightin' me with. Ye got in securities that won't be worth the paper they 're wrote on—(GRISWOLD *and* DONALD *exchange a quick look*) if ye lose that fight. An' ye *have* lost it, Griswold! I 've smashed ye an' ye know it! Ye 'll file yer petition within a week—they 'll be a run on those banks an' they 'll go t' hell so quick they 'll never know what 's struck 'em. That it?

GRISWOLD. (*Inarticulately.*) That 's it. How did you find out?

REGAN. How do I find out anythin'? I pound an' pay until they cough it up—see?

GRISWOLD. If you take over my credit now you 'll shake the credit of the whole state.

REGAN. I don't give a Bronx cocktail fer the credit o' the state. The wheat 's got t' be handled an' s' long 's I got that I can hang on through any run that ever happened. An' what 's more, I 'll make good money doin' it!

GRISWOLD. Mr. Regan—

REGAN. (*Leaning forward.*) But you can't. Say, d' ye know where a run would land *you?* In state's prison, with a steady job as laundry-man a-washin' underwear.

GRISWOLD. But my securities—

REGAN. Aw hell! D' ye think a jury o' reformed porch climbers is goin' t' believe them securities was any better when ye gave 'em than they are now? Hear me laugh! Ha! Ha! No, ye was a director an' ye used the bank's funds to float yer own business an' ye got left. That 's how it 'll look on the front page o' the one-cent daily! Remember that Omaha man—what was his name? Kimball—Kendall? He got twenty fer a deal enough like yours t' be its long-lost brother! An' that was before the days o' *Collier's Weekly,* too—Gawd bless its little soul!

GRISWOLD. (*Sternly.*) I was inside the law. If anything happens it was only a set of circumstances—why, I 'd have cut off my hand before I—

DONALD. (*Warningly.*) Father!

(GRISWOLD *subsides.*)

REGAN. (*Contemptuously.*) Aw, go tell that t' the birdies in the park! 'T ain't what ye *do* that counts in this world. It 's what folks *think* ye done!

GRISWOLD. Look here, Regan, give me six months before taking over the Western. I have some loans coming in. I can stick it through by then. Six months!

REGAN. Nixy—too long.

GRISWOLD. (*Quickly.*) Four!

REGAN. (*Briskly.*) Not on yer gay young life!

GRISWOLD. One—only one! It can't hurt you! At the end you 'll get the business just the same!

REGAN. (*Enjoying himself.*) Yeah, but I think I ought t' be makin' a moral example of ye. Guy with swell position, born with a silk hat, looks down on Irish up-starts, turns the whole block into an ice house when he meets 'em on the street—

GRISWOLD. (*Protesting.*) Mr. Regan—

DONALD. Let him go on, father.

REGAN. What d' ye think the depositors in them banks are going t' think about yer principles when they find that all their savin's have gone bla-a-h? Why, th' Fourth Ward alone 's got over two thousand accounts in the People's Trust! Sure, they 're only Irish hooligans that would n't know a cream-de-menth from a grand piano, but what are ye goin' t' tell 'em, Mr. Griswold, when they up and smash yer beak off on yer way to jail?

GRISWOLD. That 'll do!

DONALD. (*To* REGAN.) Yes, Regan, I guess we 've had enough.

REGAN. Aw gee, the trouble with you patent-leather slobs is ye can't tell a joke when ye get it in th' eye! Now I 'm not tryin' t' do ye—I 'm not, s' 'elp me Gawd! Wot d' ye say to a—a compromise?

GRISWOLD. (*Eagerly.*) Compromise?

REGAN. Wot d' ye say t' a bunch-up o' the two firms!

GRISWOLD. Bunch-up?

REGAN. Sure! Take hold good an' hard, spit on 'em, squeeze 'em t'gether, an' out she comes—"Regan, Griswold & Co."! Naw, damn it, yer gettin' t' be an old man an' the drinks is on me. "Griswold, Regan & Co. Contractors"! (DONALD *and* GRISWOLD *exchange glances of amazement.*) There! How does that sound?

GRISWOLD. Amalgamation?

REGAN That 's it, but my mouth 's too full o' teeth t' say it. Gee, could n't we give this town a hunch, you an' me? I wonder! You 'd supply the polish an' the style, talk it up big with the church members an' first families, an' meanwhile I 'd be round in the back yard with my coat off, a-doin' the *work!*

GRISWOLD. You mean the new firm would be run by you according to your present successful standards, while I 'd be in front to keep the people from examining too closely into what we were doing? That it?

REGAN. Straight in the bull's eye. Well?

DONALD. You can't do it, father!

GRISWOLD. I know all about that, but I must think of those small depositors.

DONALD. That 's beyond us, father. We can't help them. But here 's a man asking you to come down from the principles on which you based your life and brought us up—to come down to his own dirty tricks. There 's only one answer to a man like that, father, and that 's the door!

REGAN. (*Angrily.*) Oh, that 's yer line o' talk, is it? (*Controls himself with difficulty.*) No, I won't let ye get a rise out o' me—we got too much t' settle. Griswold, if ye come in with me on this I 'll let ye manage the business any way ye like—I don't care how honest ye make it! Oh, we 'll lose money, o' course, but Gawd above us! Money ain't everythin', 'Specially when ye got a nice bunch o' real estate up-town, a-ripenin' away like bananas in a dago's bed.

GRISWOLD. (*Suspiciously.*) D' you mean you 'll be willing to take the lead from me?

REGAN. Sure! I 'll jump in an' give morality a good fair show. After all, times is changin', an' it may pay now better 'n it used to!

GRISWOLD. In that case, I 'm inclined to say I—

REGAN. (*Quickly.*) Ye 'll take me up? Good! Shake on it! (*Enthusiastically seizing his hand.*) This is a great day for Mike Regan all right, all right!

DONALD. Wait a second, father. What 's he letting us down so easy for? (*Looking at* REGAN.) Why, he 's got us nailed and he knows it!

GRISWOLD. Donald, I don't think you quite appreciate all Mr. Regan is offering—

DONALD. (*Interrupting.*) Yes, I do, and I don't like it—not one little bit! (*Turning to* REGAN.) There 's something else. Why don't you lay it on the table and be done with it? (*A pause.*)

REGAN. (*Ill at ease, throwing away his cigar.*) Yer a smart kid, ain't ye? Wish I had a couple like ye in the office. Well, ye 've called my bluff an' I don't mind showin' my hand.

(*He hesitates.*)

GRISWOLD. Go on.

DONALD. The whole thing—mind!

(*Pause.*)

REGAN. (*Struggling in his embarrassment.*) It 's hard to say somehow—I dunno why it should be. Ye see, Mr. Griswold, I did n't care nothin' about squarin' things this way when I started in t' grab yer business.

DONALD. I believe you. Go on.

REGAN. But I 've been thinkin' now I 'd like t' make up good an' close t' ye, 'cause— (*He stops.*)

DONALD. (*Sharply.*) Well? Because what?

REGAN. 'Cause I want t' ask yer daughter if by any chance she 'd mind bein'—Mrs. R.

GRISWOLD. What?

REGAN. Marry me—that 's wot!

(*There is a moment of stupefaction.*)

DONALD. (*Enraged.*) Well, this is the finishing touch!

REGAN. (*Ugly.*) I tell ye it 's yer only chanst.

GRISWOLD. (*Controlling himself.*) That 's all, Mr. Regan. Don't let us keep you.

REGAN. (*In all the glory of his toughness.*) Aw, ye t'ink youse hell, don't ye?

DONALD. Get out that door!

REGAN. I 'll learn ye, ye bunch o' stuck-up high-brows! I 'll learn ye that I 'm it an' yer nit!

DONALD. Oh, we all know what you can do and we don't care, but if you 're not gone in one minute I 'll call the butler and have him kick you down the front steps!

REGAN. (*Doggedly.*) I came here with a proposition, an' two hundred bloody butlers could n't bounce me before I get an answer.

GRISWOLD. You 've got it, Mr. Regan.

REGAN. Not from her.

DONALD. Don't you dare say her name!

REGAN. (*Whining indignantly.*) Why not? Damn it, ain't I askin' her t' marry me?

DONALD. (*About to attack him.*) You—

(*Enter* EMILY.)

EMILY. Dad, has—(*She stops on seeing Regan.*) Oh, I beg your pardon. I thought you and Don were alone.

GRISWOLD. (*Trying to be polite.*) Mr. Regan is leaving, dear. In just a few moments!

DONALD. Go away, Emily. Please!

(EMILY *starts to obey and is arrested by* REGAN'S *voice.*)

REGAN. Pardon me, Miss Griswold, do ye mind comin' in fer a minute an' shuttin' the door.

GRISWOLD. That 'll do, dear, we 'll excuse you.

DONALD. (*Irritated.*) Go away, Emily!

REGAN. (*Gently.*) Will you come in an' sit down? (*She looks at him, pauses, hesitates.*) I 'm askin' ye t' sit down.

(*She hesitates again, then still looking at him, obeys.*)

DONALD. Well, of all the—Emily, dad and I won't want you here! We 've said so twice and—

REGAN. (*Breaking in.*) I guess I 'm the one t' do the talkin'. Listen to me, Miss Griswold.

EMILY. (*Raising her eyebrows.*) I 'm listening, Mr. Regan.

(*Pause.* DONALD *and* GRISWOLD *are amazed.*)

REGAN. (*Hesitatingly.*) I ain't seen ye more 'n four times, but I 'm no horse-car when it comes t' makin' up my mind. I 'm thirty-eight years old, an' never had a sick day in my life, 'cept when some guy laid me out scrappin' an' mostly I can say it 's been the other way round. I drink now an' then, but havin' been a bar-keep when young, I know t' a finger how much I can carry, so I never throw in no more. I never gamble nor play the races, fer the simple reason they seem kind o' slow 'long side o' my business. An' I never got mixed up with women o' any size or color 'cause I been on the jump, I s'pose, an' they tell me women takes a lot o' time. But now I 'm gettin' along, an' I 've made my pile, an' I feel like settlin' down an' havin' someone pour my coffee in the morning an' put my slippers on the steam-heater at night.

EMILY. (*Leaning forward.*) You mean—

REGAN. I guess yer wise, I want t' marry ye.

DONALD. To get a social position for his dirty politics!

REGAN. (*Sternly.*) Young feller, I can put this through without no buttin' in—understan'? (*To* EMILY.) Ye could help me, Miss Griswold, an' I ain't ashamed t' say it. But that ain't the reason why I want ye.

EMILY. (*Calmly.*) Is n't it, Mr. Regan? Suppose you tell me, then, what is?

REGAN. I love ye—(*Controlling himself.*) Well, that 's why.

(*She shrinks a little and looks at him fixedly until* DONALD *speaks.*)

DONALD. Yes, and he 's offered to buy you. He 's got us right against the wall and he says he 'll let us off. He 's offered father a partnership, promised to back him up in everything.

EMILY. What?

DONALD. And it 's all on the condition that we pass you over like a Van Dyck portrait, for that man to hang in his drawing-room.

EMILY. (*With a little smile.*) Dear old dad! Don! If we 're going to the poorhouse, then at least we 'll make it a family party!

DONALD. (*Triumphantly.*) Ah, I knew you 'd say that! We can't help a smash-up! It 's not our fault if the banks go under!

EMILY. Banks go under?

DONALD. And anyway, Regan, there 's no use your staying here now, so move along there and be quick about it.

EMILY. Banks go under? (*To* DONALD.) What do you mean?

DONALD. Oh, for heaven's sake, don't bother, dear! It 's all right—I mean, you can't do anything!

EMILY. But I don't understand. And I want to, Don. I intend to.

DONALD. Drop it, dear—please.

EMILY. Dad—?

DONALD. (*Warningly.*) Now, father!

GRISWOLD. Wait until later, Emily.

EMILY. Mr. Regan, do *you* know anything about this?

REGAN. (*Briefly.*) I know the whole blamed thing.

EMILY. Then tell me, please.

DONALD. Don't listen to him, dear! He 's got it all wrong, and—

REGAN. (*Grimly.*) Oh, have I? I don't know 'bout that! (*To* EMILY.) Your father 's borrowed money from three big savin's-banks. He just *happens* t' be a d'rector in 'em all! When he goes bankrupt, that 'll start a run. They 'll stop payment—

EMILY. Stop payment?

REGAN. Yeah, an' all them scoopers o' mine that yer so stuck on—they 'll lose ev'ry bit o' dough they 've managed t' scrape t'gether.

EMILY. You don't mean—

REGAN. Sure. They got their cash in the People's Trust—the steady ones, I mean. It 's the only savin's bank the Fourth Ward patronizes. Well, it 's just that very cash yer pa here borrowed, an' if he can't pay it back—why, they get left. See? (*Pause.*)

EMILY. (*Turning to* GRISWOLD.) Dad, is this true?

GRISWOLD. In a measure, yes.

EMILY. And all those men down there are going to lose their money?

GRISWOLD. (*Hesitating.*) There may be —some difficulty. I don't deny that, but—

EMILY. (*Gently interrupting.*) But, daddy, dear, they have so little. It means everything to them. And we—why, we 're responsible, don't you see?

GRISWOLD. (*Defending himself.*) It 's a tremendous misfortune as far as they go, but I acted with the strictest honesty and I don't see—

EMILY. (*Interrupting him and turning to* REGAN.) Is n't there anything else you 'll take? Won't you offer that partnership on any other basis?

REGAN. I guess not. What would I be gettin'?

DONALD. Partnership? D' you think father would consider for a minute any—

EMILY. (*Interrupting, speaking to* REGAN.) He 's right. Father won't do it now. But would you be satisfied with half the grain companies, putting the other half entirely in his hands? Would you promise to go ahead under that arrangement and leave him *absolutely* alone?

REGAN. Yeah, but what about me? Will him and that young feller promise t' leave *me* alone?

EMILY. (*Haughtily.*) Mr. Regan, I think you can rely on my family's doing the honest thing.

REGAN. (*After a moment of hesitation.*) All right. I'll give 'em half, that 's square. Is it a deal now? Take me up?

EMILY. (*A little wildly.*) I've got to! There 's nothing else for me to do!

DONALD. (*Appalled.*) Emily, don't be a fool!

GRISWOLD. D' you know what you 're saying, my child?

REGAN. (*Deeply moved, holding out his hand.*) Put it there, Miss! Put it there, an' shake!

GRISWOLD. (*Strongly.*) My dear!

DONALD. For heaven's sake, Emily, think who you are!

EMILY. I can't! All I can think of are the men who have their hard earned little accounts in those banks! You have n't seen their wives and children. You don't know the misery they 're struggling under. But *I 've* seen it. *I* know! And anything I can do to keep those pitiful little families from giving up and going all to pieces, why I intend to do it! And nothing that you or father or anybody else can say is going to stop me!

DONALD. (*To* REGAN.) You hear that? Tell her you don't want her! Tell her you won't take her! You tell her or I 'll—

REGAN. Aw, g' wan! You smoke too many cigarettes!

DONALD. (*Beside himself.*) You—

GRISWOLD. Donald! Keep quiet! The servants!

DONALD. (*Lowering his voice.*) I can see now! You 've cooked this whole thing up! You 've been meeting on the sly, trying to carry on an affair! You know we 'd never let you marry him, so you make him get a strangle-hold on father's business and then you think you 've got us gagged and bound!

REGAN. (*Flaming.*) You cut that now!

DONALD. You think I 'm afraid of you, Regan, but I 'm not. And I tell you now, right between the eyes, if you go on with this dirty scheme to get hold of my sister, I 'll—

REGAN. (*As he pauses.*) Well, wot 'll ye do?

DONALD. (*Ominously.*) Wait and see.

EMILY. (*Warningly.*) Remember, Don. If Mr. Regan does n't interfere with you, you have no right to interfere with him. That 's settled.

DONALD. (*Desperately.*) You 're crazy! Give it up! Emily! Darling!

EMILY. I can't.

DONALD. D' you realize what you 're doing? You 're choosing between us,—yes, you are! It 's dad and I against this man!

EMILY. (*Passionately.*) I 'm *not* choosing! Oh, Don, dear, can't you *see?*

DONALD. I can see you 're a base, disloyal, little—

REGAN. (*Interrupting.*) Quit pickin' on her now! I 've stood here long enough a-listenin' t' yer gab, and if that 's the line o' talk ye hand out at home, I don't blame her fer wantin' t' beat it! Gee, the only thing that jolts me is she ain't skipped before!

DONALD. (*Turning to* GRISWOLD.) Come along, father. I 've had enough of this.

REGAN. (*Facetiously.*) Don't let me keep ye!

DONALD. (*To* EMILY.) As for you—(*Checking himself.*) We 'll talk about it later.

(*He goes out with a final look at* REGAN.)

GRISWOLD. (*To* EMILY.) Coming, dear?

EMILY. No, I have several things to talk over with Mr. Regan.

GRISWOLD. (*Quietly.*) Then I 'll stay.

EMILY. (*With difficulty.*) Please don't.

GRISWOLD. You mean—(*Looking at* REGAN.) I 'd be in the way?

EMILY. (*Barely able to control herself.*) Yes. (*Pause.*)

GRISWOLD. (*Inarticulately.*) I 'm sorry—I 'm—

(*He waits a moment, straightens himself, and goes without looking back.*)

EMILY. (*As soon as the door shuts, with a despairing sob.*) Daddy! Daddy!

REGAN. (*With rough tenderness.*) I 'm awful sorry fer ye, Miss, but they 'll come round all right, if ye just sit tight. They always do, an'—

EMILY. (*Interrupting him.*) Before we go further I must make you understand one thing. I don't care for you. I feel quite sure I never can. We 've got to face that fact together, you and I.

REGAN. Well?

EMILY. (*Bravely.*) I 'll keep my word. I 'll—I 'll marry you. But if I do, it 's with the understanding that everything stops at the church door. I won't really be your wife. I can't. That 's all there is to it, I—I can't—(*He comes towards her.*) No, wait till I 've finished. You were perfectly right when you called it a deal. I 'll help you with my position. I 'll do the best I can for you that way—

REGAN. (*Pained.*) Aw quit it!

EMILY. (*Closing her eyes and going on.*) And in return you 'll let go my father. I 'm perfectly above-board, perfectly clear. Just an every day bargain. If you want me—on that basis, remember! —you can have me. (*Looking at him.*) Well?

REGAN. (*After a pause.*) That 's a pretty sharp offer yer makin' me, but— I don't care, I 'll close with it now!

EMILY. You don't mean—you 'll take those terms?

REGAN. I take what I can get—see? And then I get a little more.

EMILY. You won't this time—

REGAN. (*Lightly.*) I 'll run the chanst!

EMILY. (*Controlling herself.*) Very well, then, there 's nothing more to be said. My family are going to make trouble, so I think we 'd better finish it up as soon as we conveniently can.

REGAN. I 'll get the license, t'night. We 'll be married the first thing in the mornin'. That suit ye?

EMILY. Could you make it in the afternoon, about three? I have a luncheon engagement.

REGAN. Sure. I 'll have everythin' ready an' O. K. an' meet ye on the steps o' St. Patrick's at five minutes to.

EMILY. (*Suddenly.*) Mr. Regan, change your mind! Don't do it! Let me off! Please! Oh, please!

REGAN. (*Passionately.*) I won't! (*In an outburst.*) I won't let ye off! I won't!

(*He tries to take her in his arms.*)

EMILY. (*Shuddering and turning away.*) Remember—

REGAN. (*Controlling himself with a mighty effort.*) All right. It 's three sharp, then. (*He goes to door.*)

EMILY. Three sharp.

REGAN. (*His hand on the knob.*) Don't keep me waitin'.

EMILY. I 'm always prompt.

REGAN. (*With an irrepressible smile.*) Oh, before I go, there 's one thing I want t' thank ye fer. (*Shyly.*) That rose o' mine yer wearin'—t' was lookin' at that kept my nerve up all the time!

EMILY. So it 's been you—!

REGAN. Sure. I thought you 'd caught on long ago.

EMILY. (*Bitterly, as she unpins the rose.*) No. I had n't "caught on"!

(*As she speaks he goes out, softly closing the door behind him. She throws the rose on tea table.*)

ACT SECOND.

REGAN'S *library, the evening of April 29th. It is a new, elaborate, and obviously expensive room, controlled, however, by good taste. On right three long windows with heavy brocaded curtains. At right, above the windows and facing down-stage, a door leading to* REGAN'S *office. At back a recessed fireplace and seats on both sides of it. At left, a dor leading to the hall and the rest of the house reached by a step and landing. The wall space above and below this door is occupied by bookcases, filled by expensive bindings. At right-centre, half facing the audience, a long library table, with lamps, papers, and writing materials, also a desk telephone and a tray containing whiskey glasses and a syphon. Behind it stands a large chair and in front of it a wide comfortable couch. Near the windows is another smaller table with a lamp. The lighting is soft and restful.*

As the curtain rises, DAVIS, REGAN'S *secretary,—a small, worn, little man,—is discovered hunting about among the papers on the desk.—From the left comes the sound of people laughing and talking. Then the door opens, showing brilliant lights and increased noise of talk and laughter, and* REGAN *enters furtively, closing the door behind him. He is in evening dress.*

REGAN. Say! That guy ain't come in with the ultimatum?

DAVIS. No, sir, not yet. I—I 'm afraid I 'm in the way here.

REGAN. Aw, that 's O. K. I got through

another dinner, Davis. I 'm gettin' better every day. They 'll have me smokin' cigarettes first thing I know. Say, we got a swell bunch there t'night. Gee, it makes me sweat t' talk t' 'em, though! I just sneaked in here a minute t' cool down. Well, I suppose I might as well be gettin' back on me book job.

DAVIS. Book job?

REGAN. Yeah, I 'm gettin' lit'rary, Davis. (*Looking at book shelves.*) I 've read from there to there. Wot are ye after?

DAVIS. I'm hunting for that interview with young Griswold in the *Record-Times.*

REGAN. The one tellin' how he organized his Labor Union an' got our men t' strike?

DAVIS. Yes, sir.

REGAN. G'wan! I used that t' light a cigar.

DAVIS. All right, sir. Then I 've finished for to-night?

REGAN. Go home and get some sleep. Ye need sleep when we got a big scrap on like this.

DAVIS. That 's what my wife says, too.

REGAN. Say, how are the kids?

DAVIS. Fine, sir. The new school 's exactly what they needed. (*Nervously.*) We—we never can thank you as you ought to be thanked for—

REGAN. (*Interrupting.*) Aw, rats! Now don't begin on that again. I did n't do nothin' but write a check, an'—

(*The door opens and* MRS. CUYLER *comes in quickly. She is a fashionable young woman—outspoken, though kindly. She is in evening dress.*)

MRS. CUYLER. I saw you escape, Mr. Regan, and I just made up my mind I would n't let you!

REGAN. Well, ye see, Mrs. Cuyler, I 'm expectin' a visit from one o' them strikers. They 're sendin' me wot they call their Union Ultimatum! (*To* DAVIS.) Good-night, son.

DAVIS. (*Going out.*) Good-night, sir.

MRS. CUYLER. The strike? Oh, how exciting! I 'm just back from Europe, but I hear it 's been the talk of the town for two months!

REGAN. (*Proudly.*) Yeah. We 've kept things going at quite a clip.

MRS. CUYLER. Tell me—how 's it all going to end? Will you up and crush your brother-in-law or will your brother-in-law up and crush you? Oh, I do hope somebody 's crushed!

REGAN. (*Opening humidor.*) Then ye 'd better get out yer handkerchief fer him! They did n't call me "Shindy Mike" for nothin'. I never got licked by a bunch o' scoopers before an' I guess I 'm too old to begin.

(*He takes out a long black cigar and sticks it in his mouth.*)

MRS. CUYLER. (*Clapping her hands impulsively.*) That 's splendid! Keep it up! (*She comes to the sofa.*)

REGAN. Aw, g'wan! Yer kiddin' me!

MRS. CUYLER. No, I 'm not. I don't think I dare. I 've always been so afraid of you, Mr. Regan. I believe you were the original Bogey that my nurse used to frighten me with when I would n't go to sleep—long ago! But now I 've seen you I 'm disappointed, because you 're not a Bogey at all. You're just a—a—

REGAN. Well, cut it loose!

MRS. CUYLER. A man! A rather bad man, I suppose, but oh dear! that only makes me envy Emily the more!

REGAN. Envy her?

MRS. CUYLER. There 's so much she can do to help you, Mr. Regan. And the men we help the most are the men we love the best, after all!

REGAN. Help me? I wish she would! I want t' be helped—an' I would n't mind a little lovin', too.

MRS. CUYLER. (*Cheerfully.*) Give her time, Mr. Regan. Emily 's a wonderful girl, even if she is a snob.

REGAN. A snob?

MRS. CUYLER. Yes. Morally, I mean. And on the whole you 're such a shady character, I don't blame the poor dear if she 's mixed up at the start.

REGAN. No, I don't blame her neither—when I stop t' think.

MRS. CUYLER. (*Reflectively.*) It *is* rather hard on her, you know, having you swear at that wretched butler before all her guests.

REGAN. (*Proudly.*) Why, I only did it twice!

MRS. CUYLER. Twice!

REGAN. Well, I guess that 's somethin'! I used t' cuss him every time he passed me the pertaters!

MRS. CUYLER. Oh, dear! (*She laughs, then more seriously.*) Mr. Regan, will you do something for me?

REGAN. (*Suspiciously.*) Wot d' ye want?

MRS. CUYLER. Be humane! Light that cigar and kill it quickly! Don't torture it any more!

REGAN. (*Laughing.*) Guess ye think I can't even be decent to a piece o' tobacco!

(*He throws his cigar in the grate.*)

MRS. CUYLER. (*Comfortably.*) Well, Mr. Regan, you really are a very black sheep! Do you know I could hardly make my husband come to dine with you to-night? He said he wanted to go to that big mass-meeting. It 's quite true! I had to be unusually firm with him!

REGAN. (*Grimly.*) Poor feller! Tell him he can go t' the meetin' later on and yell "T' hell with Regan!" all the louder fer havin' lapped up my champagne. (*At sofa.*)

MRS. CUYLER. And your old friend, the Archbishop. Emily said he was taken ill at the last moment, so *he* could n't come. But I don't believe it, Mr. Regan, do you? I think he was annoyed because your men broke into that Union saloon this afternoon and sort of accidentally killed the proprietor.

REGAN. Well, it don't seem to bother *you* much.

MRS. CUYLER. Oh, nothing ever bothers me. You see, I 'm just a fan. I never get right down and play. But from the grandstand I see most of the fine points of the game. And that 's why, Mr. Regan, you and Emily are very near my heart this evening.

(*Enter* GATES.)

GATES. Beg pardon, madam, but Mr. Cuyler is leaving. Mrs. Regan asked me to tell you.

MRS. CUYLER. What nonsense! Why, it 's barely nine! Very well, I 'll be there directly. (*Piano is heard in the next room.*) Are n't husbands bores?

REGAN. I s'pose—I s'pose we are.

MRS. CUYLER. No, not you! You 're lots of things, but—I think there 's no danger of your boring any one! You know, Mr. Regan, I must be fearfully immoral! I enjoy so much what I entirely disapprove of. You, for instance. (*He looks at her.*) Now, Emily can't do that —never could! It seems too bad, and yet—and yet I somehow think it 's going to be the making of you both!

REGAN. Mrs. Cuyler, would you mind helpin' me do somethin'?

MRS. CUYLER. What is it?

REGAN. (*Taking two jewelers' boxes from his pocket.*) Tell me which one of these she 'd like the best.

(*He gives the larger one to her.*)

MRS. CUYLER. (*Opening the box.*) What 's this? A frog—a diamond frog, with ruby eyes!

REGAN. (*Proudly.*) I picked out that! Sort o' cute, ain't he? Kind o' natural! Pipe his leg there! O' course live frogs are green with spots all over 'em but that don't make no diff'rence when it comes t' joolry, does it?

MRS. CUYLER. (*Trying not to laugh.*) Not a bit. I think he 's sweet, Mr. Regan. What 's the other?

REGAN. (*Contemptuously.*) Aw—just a pearl ring. (*Showing box to her.*) The guy at the store was nutty over it, but gee! It seems kind o' cheap t' me, 'longside the other!

MRS. CUYLER. It 's beautiful.

REGAN. That so? Well, I 'm strong fer diamonds, speakin' fer myself. They give the wealthy look, an' ain't that wot everybody 's after?

MRS. CUYLER. Mr. Regan.

REGAN. Yeah?

MRS. CUYLER. I 'd give her the one you chose yourself. I 'd give her the frog. (*Hands back boxes.*)

REGAN. (*Pleased.*) All right. I will.

MRS. CUYLER. What is it? Her birthday?

REGAN. Naw. We was married six months ago t'day. I just want her t' know that I remembered, that 's all. Listen! D' you hear her playin' in there? It makes me kind o'—kind o' homesick fer some place I 've never seen. (*A pause.*)

MRS. CUYLER. You will, Mr. Regan, before so very long. Good-bye, God bless you, "Shindy Mike"!

(*She smiles at him swiftly, waves her hand and goes out. He stands for a moment looking after her.*)

(GATES *enters by the other door.*)

GATES. I beg pardon, sir.

REGAN. That striker shown up yet?

GATES. No, sir, it 's Mr. McCoy.

REGAN. McCoy? Where?

GATES. There in the office, sir. He rang the side bell, and I thought as you—

REGAN. What right have you got t' think? I 'll do all the thinkin' that goes on in this house! (*Turning to door.*) Come in here, Porky!

(GATES *has held the door open for* MCCOY, *—a good-looking, reckless young tough, carrying a soft hat in his hand.*)

GATES. (*Timidly.*) May I ask, sir, if—

REGAN. (*Interrupting impatiently.*) Aw, go t' hell!

GATES. Very good, sir. (*He goes out.*)

MCCOY. (*Eagerly.*) Say, Mike—

REGAN. (*Interrupting.*) Wait a second! What about Hurley's bar? Did ye smash it good?

MCCOY. (*Impatiently.*) Yeah, we put it on the blink. But, Mike—

REGAN. (*Interrupting.*) An' Hurley? Wot about him?

MCCOY. (*Again impatiently.*) It 's all right. We laid him out just like ye wanted.

REGAN. (*Relieved.*) So *that 's* O. K. Now tell me why yer not at St. Mary's Hall this minute, a listenin' t' them guys like I told ye to?

MCCOY. (*Embarrassed.*) Say, Mike, somethin' 's doin'.

REGAN. (*Sternly.*) Well?

MCCOY. An' I just thought I 'd drop in an' tell ye 'bout it on my way to the meetin'.

REGAN. G'wan! Spit it out!

MCCOY. My missus—

REGAN. Wot?

MCCOY. (*With a sudden grin.*) It 's a boy!

REGAN. (*Joyfully.*) Naw!

MCCOY. (*Delighted.*) Sure! He weighs nine pounds! The cutest little duck ye ever seen in all yer life!

REGAN. An' yer good woman?

MCCOY. Doin' fine. Everythin' goin on slick!

REGAN. Say, when did it—?

MCCOY. 'Bout five o'clock, when I was out a-smashin' Hurley's bar—*you* know.

REGAN. Porky, shake! (*They do so violently and solemnly.*) We 'll have a drop o' this t' celebrate.

(*Turns to the table and pours out some whiskey.*)

MCCOY. The christenin' 's on Sunday week, an' she said I was t' tell ye ye 'd got t' stand up with the kid an' leave us name him Michael R.

REGAN I 'll be a proud man that day, Porky. (*Giving him a glass.*) Now let her go t' Michael Regan McCoy!

MCCOY. Michael Regan *Ignatius* McCoy.

REGAN. Gawd help him, may he grow up to be as swell a scrapper an' as fine a friend as his old man was before him!

(*They both drink their liquor at a gulp.*)

MCCOY. I thank ye kindly, Mike!

(*Pause. They both look at each other.*)

REGAN. Say, Porky, is it true what they say?

MCCOY. What?

REGAN. (*With solemn curiosity.*) That kids ain't got no hair on 'em when they 're born?

MCCOY. (*In some heat.*) Whoever says that 's a liar, an' I 'll bust him in the mug! Mine 's got a bunch o' hair! An' what 's more—it curls!

REGAN. An' their eyes, now. Ain't they closed like kittens fer a week or two?

MCCOY. A week or two nothin'! Why, he lay there a-blinkin' an' a-winkin' at me like we 'd known each other all our lives!

REGAN. Ain't it queer now—ain't it queer how people come into the world!

MCCOY. That 's right.

REGAN. (*Wistfully.*) I don't s'pose—a man really knows wot life means 'nless he 's got a kid.

(*The music in the next room stops.*)

MCCOY. Sure thing. (*Enthusiastically.*) Say, Mike, we 're just a-waitin' fer *yer* first one t' come t' make a bonfire of the whole blame Ward! We 'll—

REGAN. (*Quickly.*) Quit it!

(*He rises.*)

MCCOY. Wot 's bitin' ye?

REGAN. (*Looking around towards door.*) Can't ye see? Me wife!

(*They rise, as the door opens and* EMILY *comes in, humming the air she has just been playing. She sees the two men and stops short. Then, with distant carelessness*) *:*

EMILY. Oh, I beg your pardon. I thought you were in your office. Is that you, Mr. McCoy? How d' you do?

MCCOY. (*Bowing nervously.*) Fine, ma'am, I thank ye! The same t' you, ma'am. It 's—it 's getting cold this evenin', ain't it?

EMILY. Is it? Well, I won't disturb you. (*She turns to the door.*)

REGAN. (*Eagerly.*) No, don't go. I got somethin' I want t' give ye. (*Speaking aside out of the corner of his mouth.*) Beat it, Porky!

McCoy. Wot 's bitin' you?

Regan. Fade away! Ain't ye got the manners to see when ye ain't wanted?

McCoy. (*Suddenly.*) Pardon me. Good evenin', ma'am. I hope ye sleep well, ma'am. See ye later, Mike.

(*Goes out very embarrassed.*)

Emily. (*As the door closes.*) Good night, Mr. McCoy.

Regan. (*Confidentially.*) He means well, Porky does. But ye see the poor feller ain't had no social advantages. But ye 'd like Porky if ye kind o' got acquainted with him. Aw, I know he 's a mut in a parlor but gee! he 's an ace in a bar! (*Slight pause.*) Say, yer lookin' swell t'night! I kept pipin' ye at dinner an' sayin' t' myself, "Gee!" says I, "She 's got all them other dames lashed t' the mast!"

Emily. I think I 'll go upstairs, Michael. I 'm feeling rather tired.

Regan. No, wait. D' you know what day this is?

Emily. Day?

Regan. Yeah. It 's April 29th.

Emily. Well?

Regan. Well, think back six months.

Emily. (*Suddenly.*) I 'd forgotten!

Regan. I had n't. So I took the liberty o'—

(*He takes the jeweler's box from his pocket.*)

Emily. (*Under her breath.*) Six months! Why, it seems six years!

Regan. It don't t' me. (*Timidly.*) Say, Emily!

Emily. (*Turning to him.*) What? (*Seeing the box.*) Oh, no—

Regan. Aw, g'wan! Take it! It 's just a little keep-sake. (*He presses it into her hand.*) Just somethin' t' show I 'm still on me job—"strivin' t' please"—like they say in the ads.

Emily. (*Trying to give it back to him.*) Take it back, Michael.

Regan. Wot?

Emily. Credit it wherever you got it and send the money to Father Kelly for his strikers' Home Fund.

Regan. Strikers?

Emily. The women and children—you understand—

Regan. (*Eagerly.*) But ye ain't even looked at it—say, it 's a di'mond frog with—

Emily. (*Interrupting.*) Oh, take it!

(*Pause.*)

Regan. (*Taking it.*) I 'm sorry. I did n't know ye minded when I gave ye things. Gee, if I 'd only known I 'd—

(*He stops short with an effort, turning towards the door.*)

Emily. That 's all right. Good night.

Regan. Good night. I won't bother ye no more.

(*He slowly goes out.* Emily *stands for a moment, then turns quickly to other door just as it opens and* Gates *appears.*)

Gates. Madam.

Emily. Well, Gates?

Gates. There 's a gentleman to see you.

Emily. Now? I 'm not at home.

Gates. It 's Mr. Griswold, madam.

Emily. Who?

Gates. Mr. Donald Griswold.

Emily. (*Faintly.*) Why—why—

Gates. And he said I was to tell you it 's most important.

Emily. Then I think you 'd better show him in.

Gates. Very good, madam.

(*He goes out. She crosses to the other door, opens it, listens. Then, satisfied, closes it and returns to the middle of the room as* Gates *shows in* Donald.)

Donald. (*Constrained.*) Hello, Emily.

Emily. (*To* Gates.) That 'll do, Gates. Will you shut the door? (Gates *bows and does so. When they are alone* Emily *throws her arms about* Donald's *neck with a smothered cry.*) Don, my dear! Oh! Oh! I 'm so glad you 've come!

Donald. (*Rather stiffly.*) Are you? I thought—it might be the other way round, after all that 's happened.

Emily. Don't be foolish, dear! I have n't seen you for so long! It 's five months now! Oh, Don! Come along—sit down here and tell me about everything! How 's dad?

Donald. Very well. His rheumatism came back in January, but nothing serious.

Emily. Did he have old Cortlandt?

Donald. Yes.

Emily. I wish he 'd change. They say this new man, Winters, is awfully good.

Donald. Imagine father changing doctors after all these years!

Emily. Don!

Donald. Yes?

Emily. How 's the business?

Donald. All right. Though don't you

think it's rather rough on dad and me to ask?

EMILY. Don, why would n't either of you answer my letters?

DONALD. (*Gravely.*) We both took your marriage pretty hard, you know.

EMILY. And I've been so proud! I would n't give in and try to make up—even though I wanted to so often! But now—my dear, I never realized before how much I love you!

DONALD. (*Uncomfortably.*) I'm chairman of that big strikers' mass-meeting to-night, and I've got to be at St. Mary's Hall by nine-thirty, so you see I have n't got much time. I—Emily, where's Regan?

EMILY. Oh, I don't know. In there, I think. Don, you're looking thin, and awfully tired! Can't you get off for a week and—

DONALD. (*Interrupting her.*) Excuse me, but I'm in an awful rush, and what I want to know is—

EMILY. (*Fiddling with his tie.*) Why, that's the very last tie I knitted for you! How well it's worn!

DONALD. (*Impatiently pulling away from her.*) Do listen, Emily! I want to know what side you take in this anti-Regan movement.

EMILY. What side?

DONALD. Yes. How do you feel about the strike, for instance?

EMILY. (*Vaguely.*) Strike?

DONALD. Yes, strike. The Union strike we're running against him. Where do you stand?

EMILY. I don't know.

DONALD. You don't know?

EMILY. I've never meddled in his business. I've just done all I could to help the wives and children of the men he employs and let it go at that. I've been cowardly about facing things, I know. But to-night—the Archibshop wrote me a note. He would n't dine here. He told me such dreadful things. They killed a saloon-keeper this afternoon.

DONALD. I know—Dave Hurley.

EMILY. (*Breaking down.*) Oh, Don, I've been having a terrible time! It just seems sometimes as if I could n't keep it up a minute longer! Be good to me, dear—please—I need it—I need some one to be good to me!

(*She turns to him, sobbing like a child.*)

DONALD. (*Melting for the first time and petting her tenderly.*) Poor little girl! There now—don't cry! I'm right here! Your big brother's right here and he'll take care of you exactly the way he used to!

EMILY. (*Trying to control herself.*) I—I can't help it! It's just too—splendid to have you back—again—

DONALD. Is it? Then you'll try to help me, won't you?

EMILY. (*Drying her eyes.*) Help you?

DONALD. Yes. It's like this. We—

EMILY. (*Interrupting.*) Don, give me your hand.

DONALD. (*Doing so.*) They're getting Regan's men to strike and join the Union at the rate of a hundred a day. Unless something happens we'll make him shut down business by Monday at the latest. Why, even now the Western companies are getting scared—

EMILY. (*Interrupting.*) Does he know that?

DONALD. No, but he will. They say he can't stand up much longer and he won't! He can't! No matter how many dirty tricks he's carrying up his sleeve!

EMILY. Dirty tricks? (*Looking at him intently.*) What d' you mean?

DONALD. (*Confidentially.*) Why, Gleason—he's our attorney—Gleason thinks that Regan's just lying low until he can get a couple of thousand niggers up from Georgia or Alabama, and start 'em working at the docks at a quarter a white man's wage. He could do it, too. Damn him, he's the only man I know who could!

EMILY. Ssh! Don! Be careful! He'll hear you!

DONALD. (*Lowering his voice.*) But before I get after the railroads and head him off, I've got to be dead sure of the whole proposition, and that's why I've come to you.

EMILY. To me?

DONALD. (*Eagerly.*) Yes. What about it? Is that his little game?

EMILY. (*After a slight pause, withdrawing her hand.*) I don't know. I've told you I never interfere in his business.

DONALD. Well, I want you to do a little interfering now—for me. I want you to find out whether this is true, and I want you to find out what road he's going to bring 'em over. Then we'll wait and nab him in the act. I'm glad he's in. You can get it out of him to-night.

EMILY. Don, dear, it—

DONALD. (*Interrupting.*) I'll ring you up to-morrow about eleven and—

EMILY. (*Interrupting.*) Don, I could n't do that.

DONALD. (*Impatiently.*) Why, of course you could. Just tell him you 're interested! Get him talking, you know how —he 'll take care of the rest.

EMILY. I mean—I would n't do it.

DONALD. What?

EMILY. (*Uncomfortably.*) After all, he 's my husband.

DONALD. But you 're on our side! You 're one of us! I 'm your brother, when it comes to that.

EMILY. I—I could n't, dear. That 's all.

DONALD. You must! It 's your only chance to show dad and me you 're sorry for what you did—that you 're fond of us still!

EMILY. (*Rising.*) I won't, I tell you! I can't!

DONALD. (*Rising.*) You 'd better look out, Emily, or you 'll make me think you approve of everything that man is doing —killing saloon-keepers and all the rest!

EMILY. (*Indignantly turns on him.*) I don't approve of it! You know I don't! You know I hate it from the bottom of my soul!

DONALD. (*Instantly.*) Then why don't you help us stop it? You can. You hold the chance right there in your two hands! Good Lord, don't you realize the importance?

EMILY. Yes, of course I realize—but I just know it 's impossible.

DONALD. It is n't!

EMILY. (*Her temper rising.*) It is! And what 's more you have no right to come and ask me!

DONALD. (*Angrily.*) Oh, very well, then. One thing 's sure—I 'll never come again.

EMILY. If that 's the only sort of reason that brings you, I hope you never do!

DONALD. Emily!

EMILY. What do you mean by stirring up all this trouble anyway? Did n't my husband help you just about as generously as any man could? Did n't he pull you up and get you on your feet and give you half his business exactly as he said he would? He 's kept his word, Michael has. He promised he 'd leave you alone and he 's done it, too! And that, I believe, is more than *you* can say!

DONALD. (*Turning angrily.*) I never gave my word!

EMILY. You 're my brother, so I did n't see the need of asking for it. But now —oh, Don, you 've made me feel ashamed of you! I 'm ashamed of my family for the very first time!

DONALD. (*Amazed.*) Do you mean that?

EMILY. Yes, I do.

DONALD. You 're sure?

EMILY. Quite sure.

DONALD. (*Between his teeth.*) Good night, then.

EMILY. Good—

(*She stops short as the door opens and* REGAN *appears. A pause.*)

REGAN. (*To* DONALD.) Get out o' my house, ye dam', sneakin' little son-of-a-gun, before I—

EMILY. (*Flaming.*) Stop that!

REGAN. (*Turning to her.*) Wot?

EMILY. He 's my brother, and he can come when he pleases and go when he pleases, so long as I choose to let him.

REGAN. (*Sternly.*) See here, Emily, I 've never got my back up before t' night, but now you 're gettin' just a little bit too gay! D 'ye know wot ye are before yer anyone else—I don't care if it 's sister or daughter or life-long friend? Yer Mrs. Regan—got it? Mrs. R.! An' if ye think yer goin' t' sit on *my* parlor sofa, in the middle o' *my* house, an' tell the guy I 'm scrappin' to a finish how t' land me on the jaw—

EMILY. (*Interrupting.*) I did n't say a word! You can ask him if I did! (*Appealing to her brother.*) Don!

REGAN. Then I *did* ring the bell! That *was* the reason why ye come in here t'night! Gee, fer a good boy, yer getting on great—you are! First ye let me help ye when yer down and out. Then, by way o' thankin' me, ye sneak around an' get me men t' strike. An' now I find ye tryin' t' make me own wife welch on me! This may be honest, Griswold, but if it is—give me the other thing!

DONALD. Don't worry, you 've got that already.

REGAN. Now beat it, ye rubber-soled porch-climber ye! Beat it, an' if I ever catch ye in my house again, ye won't get out alive!

DONALD. (*Coolly.*) All right. Keep an eye on St. Mary's Hall to-night, Regan, if you want to know how things are going. There 'll be a few live wires you don't expect. (*Telephone rings.*)

EMILY. (*Impulsively.*) Don!

DONALD. No, I'm through with you.

(*He goes out.* EMILY *stands by door with head bowed.* REGAN *has gone to answer telephone, leaning over desk with one knee on sofa.*)

REGAN. (*At the telephone.*) Hello. That you, Porky? Yeah. Yer at the Hall? Well? Have they got a full house? Speak up, there's such a damn lot o' noise! What about the street outside? Jammed for blocks? Men, women, an'— (*He smothers a furious exclamation.*) Naw, go on. I did n't say nothin'. Has the Mayor come? I can't hear, they got a band playin', ain't they? Waitin' fer young Griswold? Yeah. He's comin' in his auto. I wish 't was in his hearse. Wot?

(GATES *enters.*)

GATES. Is Mr. Regan there?

EMILY. He's telephoning, Gates.

REGAN. (*Hanging up receiver and turning about angrily.*) Well, wot d' ye want? (*Irritably.*) Come on! I won't have no foolin' t'night!

GATES. A man from the Labor Union. He said you—

REGAN. (*Interrupting.*) Bring him in. (GATES *turns to go.* REGAN *suddenly roars.*) Say, get a move on there, ye knock-kneed Britisher, or I'll take the crease out the back o' yer neck with the toe o' my boot!

GATES. (*Outraged.*) Sir—I—

REGAN. Ye fat-headed second-girl! Beat it now an' bring him in!

(GATES *goes out quickly.*)

EMILY. (*Trembling.*) You must not talk to the servants that way while I'm in the room! I can't stand it! I just can't! (*A pause.*)

REGAN. (*Shamefacedly at last.*) Aw, say, I did n't mean all that. I'm sorry.

(GATES *opens the door and shows in the Union delegate, a rather poorly-dressed, defiant-looking, slouchy laborer, wearing his Sunday clothes.*)

You from the Union?

SCANLAN. Yeah.

REGAN. Wot's yer name?

SCANLAN. Scanlan.

REGAN. Sixth Division?

SCANLAN. Yeah.

REGAN. I'm on. I fired ye one day when ye got too flip. Remember that?

EMILY. How d' you do, Mr. Scanlan?

SCANLAN. (*Startled.*) Why, ma'am, I— (*He pauses, embarrassed.*)

EMILY. I hope that Mrs. Scanlan is feeling better than when I saw her yesterday?

SCANLAN. Thanks, ma'am. The doc, he says she's just about the same.

EMILY. (*Brightly.*) Well, we ought to be thankful she's no worse! (*To* REGAN.) Excuse us, Michael, Mrs. Scanlan's an old friend of mine, and she has bronchitis.

REGAN. Oh, is that so? (*To* SCANLAN, *uncomfortably.*) Well, come on! Wot d' ye want? Choke it up! I ain't got much time!

SCANLAN. (*Beginning his speech.*) At the meetin' o' the board last night we passed a resolution—

REGAN. (*Impatiently.*) Aw, damn yer resolution! Wot's the least ye'll take?

SCANLAN. (*Briefly.*) Ten hour day, two shifts, an' a general superintendent elected by the Union.

REGAN. (*Grimly.*) Anythin' more?

SCANLAN. Yeah. Our own saloon an' no one fired fer usin' 'em 'stead of yours.

REGAN. (*Between his teeth.*) Go on!

SCANLAN. Twenty-five per cent raise on wages, an' I guess that's all.

REGAN. All? Say, don't ye want me watch an' chain?

SCANLAN. (*Doggedly.*) We don't want nothin', Mr. Regan, that ain't ours by rights.

REGAN. (*With sudden and ominous calm.*) Who framed up that resolution?

SCANLAN. Wot's the diff, s' long as it was carried?

REGAN. Was it Griswold?

SCANLAN. (*Defiantly.*) I ain't a-sayin'.

REGAN. (*Softly.*) Griswold! I thought so!

SCANLAN. (*More defiantly.*) Well, wot's the answer?

REGAN. Oh! Ye want me answer, do ye?

SCANLAN. (*Insolently.*) Yeah. An' if it ain't the kind we like, we'll soak ye all the harder later on.

REGAN. (*Ominously still.*) Oh, ye'll soak me all the harder later on!

SCANLAN. (*Openly bullying.*) Aw, gee! Ye make me sick! Come off that bum perch, Regan! We done ye, and ye know we done ye, an' there ain't a word more to be said!

REGAN. (*Suddenly springing on him like a wild animal.*) Ain't there?

(*He strikes the man with tremendous

force, EMILY *shrieks, the man falls and lies quivering on the floor.* REGAN *draws back to kick him in the side.*)

EMILY. (*Coming between them, pale and very firm.*) Michael!

REGAN. (*Thickly.*) Wot 's that—?

EMILY. (*Looking at him firmly.*) Michael, it 's I. (*He looks at her as if seeing her for the first time. There is a pause. Her gaze subdues him. At last she speaks quietly.*) Get some whiskey.

(*She turns and kneels by the wounded man, examining him.*)

REGAN. (*Returning with the glass.*) Is he out?

EMILY. (*Pouring whiskey between his lips.*) He 's stunned, that 's all. (*Looking up at* REGAN.) It 's a fine thing to send a man back this way to his dying wife.

REGAN. Dyin'! But I thought ye said—

EMILY. (*Interrupting.*) It is n't bronchitis. It 's pneumonia, and it was brought on from cold and hunger. The doctor says she won't last out the week. She made him promise not to tell her husband until the end.

REGAN. Why?

EMILY. Because she did n't wish to stand between him and his striker's work. (REGAN *gives a muttered exclamation and sits on couch, his face in hands.*) That 's what you 're fighting, Michael, and you 'll never beat that spirit in a thousand years.

REGAN. Has she—got any kids?

EMILY. Four. The youngest boy was born last summer. (REGAN *has taken a roll of bills from his pocket hastily. He comes to where* SCANLAN *lies.*) What are you doing now?

REGAN. (*Bending over and slipping the money in* SCANLAN'S *pocket.*) Just a couple o' bills, that 's all. He 'll find 'em in the mornin'.

EMILY. (*Bitterly.*) You nearly kill him, and when he 's lying here, stunned and helpless, you think you can make up by putting money in his pocket! Oh, what 's the use?

REGAN. (*Instantly.*) Use? Why, ain't ye got no feelin's? Don't ye realize this man 's got a sick wife an' four kids—one of 'em a baby born last summer? Don't ye know he ain't had no wages since this strike was on? His wife needs medicine t' pull her through an' them growin' kids ought t' stoke up three times a day on meat an' pertaters? (*Door bell is heard.*) Say, wot 's the matter with ye anyway? Why—(*He interrupts himself suddenly and turns to listen. A pause. He goes over to the window and looks out.* SCANLAN *moves and groans aloud.* REGAN *turns quickly back.*) It 's His Grace!

EMILY. The Archbishop?

REGAN. Yeah! He 's comin' here to see me. We got t' get this guy out o' the way.

EMILY. (*Busy with* SCANLAN.) Wait! I think he 's coming to. (*To* SCANLAN.) Mr. Scanlan—(SCANLAN *makes another movement and tries to sit up. She helps him.*) There! You 're feeling better, are n't you? (SCANLAN *sees* REGAN *and guards himself.*) It 's all right—all right! Nobody 's going to hurt you, Mr. Scanlan! (*To* REGAN, *quickly.*) Help him up, Michael.

REGAN. (*Doing so.*) Where 'll I stick him?

EMILY. I don't know. In your office, I suppose. (REGAN *half drags, half carries him towards door.*) I hear Gates. Can you manage him alone?

REGAN. Sure.

EMILY. (*Whispering.*) Put him in the big chair.

REGAN. (*As he is dragging* SCANLAN *through the door.*) An' the Bish?

EMILY. I 'll talk to him.

(REGAN *and* SCANLAN *disappear. She closes the door after them and turns just as the other door opens and* GATES *appears.*)

GATES. (*Announcing.*) His Grace, the Archbishop.

(*There is an instant's pause, then the* ARCHBISHOP *enters. He is a big-jowled Irishman, of much the same physical type as* REGAN. *He is dressed in clerical frock coat.*)

EMILY. (*Coming forward cordially, her hand outstretched.*) Your Grace!

ARCHBISHOP. (*In his deep, rich voice, to which the traces of a former accent still cling.*) Mrs. Regan, this is indeed a great pleasure.

EMILY. Michael will be here directly. Won't you sit down? He 's just attending to a little business for a—a friend.

ARCHBISHOP. I hope ye did n't take offense at my refusin' t' come t' yer party t'night, but after what I 'd heard—

EMILY. I understand. Oh, I understand perfectly.

ARCHBISHOP. (*Very winningly.*) Mrs. Regan, can't ye do somethin' t' stop him?

EMILY. Please, your Grace—

ARCHBISHOP. He 'll listen t' a good woman. I remember once his old mother tellin' me how she kept him off the streets for a week just by askin' him t' help her with the dishes after supper. An' he did it!

EMILY. (*Bitterly.*) For a week.

ARCHBISHOP. (*Smiling wisely.*) Well, she was only his mother.

EMILY. I 'm only his wife.

ARCHBISHOP. I know. An' I thought when he came t' me that day an' said, "Father," says he, "I 'm goin' t' get married!"—I thought our Lady from Heaven had dropped a smile right down into his heart. But now—

EMILY. (*Interrupting.*) Please! Please, not any more! (*Trying to control her voice.*) You don't know—

ARCHBISHOP. I know there 's mighty little any man can do if his good woman 's made up her mind the other way round. Ah, try it just once, me daughter, an' remember yer two souls will stand t' gether on the Judgment Day!

EMILY. (*Coldly.*) I feel that I have no right to interfere.

(*The door opens, and* REGAN *appears, a book in his hand.*)

REGAN. (*Pretending not to see the* ARCHBISHOP.) I 've just been readin' the most interestin' book, me dear—(*Starting.*) Well, if there ain't his Grace! Gawd save yer Rev'rence, I did n't see ye at all!

(*He kisses the* ARCHBISHOP'S *ring devoutly.*)

EMILY. Good night, your Grace.

ARCHBISHOP. Oh, don't go, Mrs. Regan, there 's nothing we have to say that you should n't hear.

EMILY. Very well. I 'll be back directly. (*She goes into next room.*)

ARCHBISHOP. (*Gravely.*) I 'm on my way t' the meetin' at St. Mary's Hall.

REGAN. (*Interrupting quickly.*) Ye ain't a-goin' t' speak against me, Father?

ARCHBISHOP. That 's just what I 've got t' do.

REGAN. But why?

ARCHBISHOP. Young Griswold was talkin' t' me three hours this afternoon an' I find I 've kept my mouth shut long enough.

REGAN. Well, if ye open up now, I see my finish.

ARCHBISHOP. (*Earnestly.*) My son, I hope t' God ye do!

REGAN. Aw, Father!

ARCHBISHOP. So I just stopped in on me way down—just for the sake o' old times, Mickey—to ask if ye won't give in before it 's all too late.

REGAN. (*Between his teeth.*) Give in an' take a lickin'!

ARCHBISHOP. (*With a troubled smile.*) A lickin'! Ah, it 's true you never were much good at that from the day yer family moved into Dugan's bar an' my old father—God rest his soul!—came over from the old country to run my uncle's grocery down the block! D' you remember?

REGAN. (*Laughing.*) Say, we used t' guy the life out o' ye back there. When ye first came over, every time ye opened that mouth o' yers, ye 'd let out a begorra green enough to turn the Fourth of July into St. Patrick's day!

ARCHBISHOP. (*Amused.*) Sure, Mickey, an' it 's true ye never would let me be! Only yesterday I was thinkin' o' the time ye got a corner in dead cats an' sold 'em for a dime apiece—a nickel the kitten—t' tie on the end o' strings an' slam us decent boys with when we came out from our Sunday school!

REGAN. Sure, I remember! Gee, I had a swell time that day, an' I made a dollar an' twenty cents, too!

ARCHBISHOP. Yes, ye always were the J. P. Morgan o' the whole Fourth Ward! But remember when ye 'd go too far, I 'd rise up in the name of righteousness an' beat the pants clean off yer legs!

REGAN. Well, ye was older 'n me an' a blame sight bigger, too!

ARCHBISHOP. An' then ye 'd lay fer me in Clancy's alley, with a brick in one hand an' a piece o' lead-pipe in the other—

REGAN. (*Interrupting.*) Waitin' fer hours at a stretch t' put ye t' sleep, like the good kind friend I was!

(ARCHBISHOP *looks at him, somewhat taken aback.*)

ARCHBISHOP (*Reflecting.*) Well, thank God fer one thing, Mickey. Ye never could aim straight when it came t' the plumbin'!

REGAN. 'Member our last scrap behind them packin' boxes on the night before ye sailed away t' Rome? Gee, I can feel that knock-out ye gave me after twenty-five years!

ARCHBISHOP. (*Smiling.*) An' mighty little good it 's done ye, I 'm thinkin'! Ye know, Mickey, ye have n't changed much since those days.

REGAN. Nor you neither, Terry—(*Suddenly embarrassed.*) Savin' yer Reverence's pardon.

ARCHBISHOP. (*Laughing.*) Ah, Mickey, what a priest you 'd have made!

REGAN. An' you, yer Grace,—gee, what a politician!

ARCHBISHOP. (*Affectionately.*) Mickey!

REGAN. Yes, Father?

ARCHBISHOP. Give it up, my son! Get away from Clancy's alley!

(EMILY *enters.*)

Why, ye 've been livin' here all yer life an' ye need a change, so why don't you start in t'night an' square yerself with the whole town by handin' these men over what they want? (*Slight pause. Then putting his hand on* REGAN'S *arm.*) It 's fer you I 'm askin' it, Mickey. Just fer you.

REGAN. Well, an' if I don't?

ARCHBISHOP. Then I 'll go to this meetin' t'night an' tell these men that the Church o' God is right behind 'em, an' I 'll never let up till I 've struck ye t' the ground, my son, an' I can do it! Ye know I can! (*Pause.*)

REGAN. All right. Ye 've got me. I give in.

ARCHBISHOP. D'ye mean it?

REGAN. Sure. There 's nothin' else t' do.

ARCHBISHOP. My son, I—

REGAN. (*Interrupting.*) If ye go straight home from here without showin' yourself or speakin' at the meetin', I 'll send 'em word t'morrer mornin' that I 'm down an' by Sunday we 'll have settled on the terms.

ARCHBISHOP. D' you promise?

REGAN. (*Brazenly.*) Sure I promise.

ARCHBISHOP. (*Doubtfully.*) Are ye sincere? Can I trust ye to play me square?

REGAN. Ye can trust me like ye 'd trust yerself. In fact, I 've sort o' grown t' feel that the Union 's right an' I 'm all wrong. An' feelin' that way I 'd like t' make up fer wot I done t' them poor fellows in the past.

ARCHBISHOP. (*Still doubtfully.*) How long have ye been feelin' this way, Mickey?

REGAN. Aw, I dunno. Two weeks—off an' on.

ARCHBISHOP. How about this afternoon?

REGAN. (*Innocently.*) This afternoon?

ARCHBISHOP. Yes.

REGAN. I dunno nothin' about this afternoon.

ARCHBISHOP. Ye mean ye have n't heard?

REGAN. I swear I ain't heard nothin'! G'wan, wot is it?

ARCHBISHOP. (*Incredulous.*) About yer own gang, McCoy and all the rest a-breakin' into Hurley's saloon an' clubbin' the poor man until—

REGAN. (*Virtuously.*) Now ain't that just too bad! I told the boys again an' again they 'd better look out fer their foolin' or it would get 'em into trouble!

ARCHBISHOP. Foolin'!

REGAN. They 're young, ye know, an' they got t' work hard fer a livin'. So I never feel like blamin' 'em too much when they try t' get a little enjoyment out o' life.

ARCHBISHOP. Enjoyment!

REGAN. (*Shaking his head.*) But ev'ry now an' then they go too far. I 've noticed that. They sometimes go too far! Say, Father, they ain't killed Hurley, have they?

ARCHBISHOP. We don't know yet. But, Mickey— (*He hesitates.*)

REGAN. Yeah, Father?

ARCHBISHOP. (*Significantly.*) Yer quite sure no orders came from you this afternoon t' do this thing?

REGAN. I swear t' Gawd I never heard a word about it up t' now! (*Pause. The telephone on desk rings.*) That 's McCoy now. He 's at the meetin', tellin me how it 's goin'. (*Answering the call.*) Hello, Porky. Yeah. (*Very severely.*) Say, wot d' ye mean by never tellin' me 'bout this Hurley business? Ye ain't had time? Well, you come up here after the meetin' and I 'll have somethin' t' say t' ye—understand? The idea o' such goin's on! Why, folks 'll think I put ye up to it meself! Yeah! Don't apologize now! It don't do no good, an' it makes me all the sorer! Now who 's been speakin' down there? Young Griswold? How 's she goin'? Enthusiasm risin'? (*With a savage laugh.*) Is that so? Well, ain't that nice? Rumor o' what? The last speaker t' be the Archbishop? G'wan, His Grace is standin' right beside me now an' he says he ain't goin' near the hall t'night!

(*He turns and looks up appealingly at the* ARCHBISHOP.)

ARCHBISHOP. God help me, I believe ye, Mickey, an' I'll give ye this one last chance.

REGAN. (*Turning triumphantly to the telephone.*) Yeah, ye can bet on it! It 's O. K. Just take my word. So give 'em all my love, Porky, an' tell 'em I don't care what the hell they say!

(*He rings off with a grin.*)

ARCHBISHOP. In a week, then, everythin' will be settled fer good?

REGAN. (*His eyes gleaming.*) Just one week, an' I 'll have settled 'em fer good an' all!

EMILY. (*Suddenly.*) D' you hear that?

ARCHBISHOP. Mrs. Regan! I—

EMILY. D' you know what he means?

REGAN. Stop that!

EMILY. (*Facing him.*) I won't! I won't stop until I 've told His Grace that not one single word you 've said is true!

ARCHBISHOP. What—?

REGAN. Say, yer crazy! Gee, my wife 's gone off her nut!

EMILY. (*To the* ARCHBISHOP.) He 's lied to you. He 's taken you in from the very beginning. Why, he has n't the least intention of giving up one inch to those strikers!

REGAN. Don't listen to her, Father!

EMILY. He 's just fighting for time. Time! That 's all he wants! A week? Why, in a week he 's going to have two thousand negroes sent up from Alabama to take the place of Union men!

REGAN. (*Forgetting himself.*) Who told ye that!

EMILY. Look at him! He has the truth written all over his face!

REGAN. (*Turning away with clenched hands.*) Gawd—

ARCHBISHOP. (*Sternly.*) Well? What have ye got t' say?

REGAN. (*Pulling himself together.*) My wife 's—all off. She don't know me, that 's all. I say I 've had a change o' heart! I swear I feel as if every one o' them blame strikers was me brother!

EMILY. How dare you say that? Open that door, your Grace, and look into the next room. The man you 'll see there brought the Union Ultimatum to this house to-night. He 'll show you how my husband treats his brothers!

REGAN. Father! Just a second! Now listen to me please—

ARCHBISHOP. (*Pushing* REGAN *out of the way.*) Get out o' me way!

(*He goes across the room, opens the door, and disappears into* REGAN'S *office.* REGAN *drops his mask for a moment and has an animal spasm of rage, keeping perfectly silent the while.* EMILY *stands with her breast heaving. After a moment their looks meet. A pause. Then the* ARCHBISHOP *reappears, a stern, commanding figure.*)

REGAN. (*Attempting to detain him.*) Say, it was an accident! He fell down by himself! I never meant to hurt him! Why, he 's one o' me very best friends! I would n't a-had this happen fer—aw, Father, wait now! Say, where are ye goin?

ARCHBISHOP. (*In righteous heat.*) To St. Mary's Hall, t' talk to the citizens o' this town as a priest has never talked to 'em before! And when I 'm through, Michael Regan, you 'll stand naked an' tremblin' before the whole world, an' not one man will let ye touch his garment as he passes by!

REGAN. (*Seizing his arm and whining.*) Aw, wot 's yer rush? I did n't mean t' get ye sore! Honest t' Gawd, I did n't! Aw, come, Father, yer not a-goin t' leave me this way! That ain't no way t' treat an old friend! Say, Father, I—

ARCHBISHOP. (*Interrupting.*) Let me by!

REGAN. (*Not budging.*) Sure I will, only I just want t' make ye understand how I feel about yer goin' down there an'—

ARCHBISHOP. Let me by, Michael Regan!

REGAN. (*Throwing aside his conciliatory manner.*) All right! When that meetin 's finished, an' not one second before!

EMILY. Michael!

ARCHBISHOP. Do you think you can hold me here against my will?

REGAN. (*Recklessly.*) I don't think. I'm sure! An' if ye don't believe it, why off with yer coat, Terry Sullivan, and we 'll see if all the Saints can save ye from a lickin'!

ARCHBISHOP. Down on your knees, Michael Regan! Fall down on yer knees an' pray fergiveness fer those blasphemies! Rebellious child, have ye forgotten that the armies of the Lord protect His servants? Have ye forgotten the great Church standin' like a mighty rock against the waves o' sin? D' ye think a wretched straw like you can break its power or change its end from what was written in the Angel's Book, a million years ago?

REGAN. (*Muttering.*) Aw g'wan—I did n't mean nothin'—

ARCHBISHOP. D' you think a fool can stand alone and shake the deep foundations o' the world? Out o' my way, presumptuous man!

(REGAN, *cowed, steps back, and the* ARCHBISHOP *sweeps past him with real majesty and strength. As soon as the door shuts on him,* REGAN *turns fiercely and bitterly to* EMILY.)

REGAN. (*In an outburst.*) That 's a swell turn ye just done me, ain't it? Goin' back on yer husband, tryin' t' soak him ev'ry way ye could!

EMILY. Please, Michael—

REGAN. Say, ain't I treated ye well? Ain't I done ev'rythin' I thought ye wanted? Ain't I given up half me business t' yer old man? Ain't I put ye in a swell house an' deposited a cool million to yer credit in the First National?

EMILY. Don't, Michael!

REGAN. Ain't I kept out o' yer way as much as I could—a-sneakin' in the back door, beatin' it to my room whenever I heard ye comin'?

EMILY. Michael—

REGAN. I 've tried t' make livin' here easy fer ye, and wot do I get in return? Ye wait till I 'm scrappin' with both hands an' breathin' hard, an' then ye up and stick a knife in me back, ye—

EMILY. (*Interrupting wildly.*) I did n't!

REGAN. Wot 's that?

EMILY. I just spoke out because I could n't help it! I could n't see you do a thing like that!

REGAN. Aw, it 's too bad about you!

EMILY. But now 's your chance to make it up! Michael, listen! *It 's your chance!*

REGAN. Chance! With him on his way down there t' talk against me? I ain't got no chance! All I got is a finish!

EMILY. Don't let him do it for you! Give in of your own accord, before anyone can make you!

REGAN. Give in?

EMILY. Yes, call up the mass meeting! Tell them you 've heard their ultimatum! Tell them you accept it! Then when the Archbishop comes, he 'll find out what you 've done, and oh! he 'll be so glad!

REGAN. I won't quit while I got the life still in me!

EMILY. You must! Oh, Michael, I don't want you to do this just to help those men or to please the Archbishop or to make me happy! I want you to do it for yourself!

REGAN. Naw!

EMILY. Don't you see what it means? Don't you understand? You 're the only one I 'm thinking of! It 's all for you! Everything 's for you!

REGAN. Naw!

EMILY. Michael! You must!

REGAN. I said I won't!

EMILY. (*Desperately.*) Please!

(*She puts her hand on his arm.*)

REGAN. (*Throwing her off.*) Give in? Accept their ultimatum? Let them scoopers know they got me licked? Say, wot d' ye think I am?

(*Telephone rings.*)

EMILY. (*Hopelessly.*) Oh! I don't know! I don't know!

REGAN. (*At telephone.*) Hello? Who is it? Porky? Wot? He 's speakin'? In the name o' the Holy Catholic Church? Wot? Never t' work fer me again? Wot 's all that noise? Cheerin'? (*Suddenly he dashes the instrument to the desk without ringing off and glares at* EMILY.) Well, ye 've done the trick, d' ye hear? Ye done the trick! Now go on! Tell me yer glad! Spit it out! Get it off your chest, an' laugh! Say, why don't ye laugh? I 'm just waitin' fer that laugh! Ye think I 'm smashed! Ye think I 'm finished! Ye think I 'm knocked t' hell! Well, I ain't! D' ye hear? I ain't! I 'll beat 'em yet! By Gawd, I 'll beat 'em yet!

(*His fist crashes on the desk as the curtain falls.*)

ACT THIRD.

SCENE. *The scene is the same as in Act Second, the next morning about nine o'clock. The room is in slight disorder, the desk is covered with newspapers, memoranda, and clippings. Newspapers with glaring headlines are tumbled all about the floor. Chairs have been moved from their regular positions.* REGAN *is sitting behind the desk, thus half facing the audience. He still wears his dress trousers, silk socks and pumps, with a jersey. He is chewing the end of an unlighted cigar—a pile of ashes and butts lies near the whiskey tray, near at hand. He is pale and unshaven. As the curtain rises he is running through the morning papers, one after the other.* DAVIS, *his secretary, is seated at the other end of the table, his stenographic books before him, awaiting* REGAN'S *next orders.*

REGAN. (*Muttering as he glances at the headlines.*) "Boss Regan falls at last—Repudiated by grain companies—Long fight ends in complete defeat—" (*Throws it aside.*) Gimme the *Tribune.*

DAVIS. Here it is, sir.

REGAN. (*Reading.*) "Mass-meeting at St. Mary's—Interference o' Archbishop—" (*Looking up.*) Gee, *they* got me in the oven, too! How's the *Courier?*

DAVIS. Antagonistic, I'm afraid.

REGAN. G' wan, let's have it! (*Reading.*) "Regan's finish—City's free at last—" (GATES *enters, carrying a breakfast tray with coffee and toast.* REGAN *shakes his head at him in disgusted disapproval.*) Say, you get out o' here! I won't have no dumb-waiter in here this mornin'.

GATES. Mrs. Regan told me to bring you some coffee, sir. She heard you'd been down-town all night and had no breakfast when you came in.

REGAN. (*Almost to himself.*) Well, wot d' you think o' that?

GATES. (*Doubtfully.*) I beg pardon, sir, I—

REGAN. (*Irritably.*) Say, wot's bitin' ye? Can't ye stick it down? Yeah—here on the table! D' ye think I'm goin' t' feed standin' up—like a mule? (GATES *comes around to the desk beside* REGAN *and puts down the tray.*) Got any eggs?

GATES. No, sir, I— (*Starting to go.*)

REGAN. Well, move along and lay a couple—quick! (GATES *looks bewildered.*) Two fried eggs! Grasp it?

GATES. Very well, sir. (*He goes out.*)

REGAN. Read the *Leader* editorial.

DAVIS. Yes, sir.

REGAN. There it is.

(*He kicks it toward* DAVIS, *then half sits down on end of desk.*)

DAVIS. (*Picking it up and reading it rapidly.*) "We take off our hats to the men who have raised the present issue against Mr. Regan's methods." (*He hesitates.*)

REGAN. Well? Got a cramp?

DAVIS. (*Resuming hastily.*) "We congratulate our citizens upon their enthusiastic support of the strike which has just ended. Thanks to Mr. Donald Griswold and his union, 'Shindy Mike' no longer holds this city in his grip. The merciless crook who"—er—is there any use going on, Mr. Regan?

REGAN. (*Calmly.*) Say, that's libel, ain't it? I'll sue Waterman for fifty thousand. File it. The little ink-slingin' mice—I'll show 'em! (*The butler enters.*) Say, can't I sit here two minutes without yer makin' me a present o' your mug?

GATES. More wires, sir, sent up from the office by special messenger.

REGAN. (*Sitting down.*) Read 'em, Davis, quick!

DAVIS. (*Reading them.*) United Transport—Chicago Freight—Erie Navigation—

REGAN. That all?

DAVIS. Yes, sir.

REGAN. (*Sinking back disappointed.*) Well, wot have they got to say? All gone back on me? That it? Speak up, can't ye?

DAVIS. (*Reading the telegrams.*) Yes, they've all cancelled their contracts. They're all negotiating a return to Griswold.

REGAN. I knew they would! Take a wire.

DAVIS. (*Sitting at the end of the table and taking up his stenographic notebook.*) Yes, sir?

REGAN. (*Walking up and down.*) Freight—Navigation—Transport—all the same messages—(*Dictating.*) Fail t' understand yer attitude. My position in this town never better. Will have situation controlled within a week. Urge no action until you see my representative—

DAVIS. (*Timidly.*) But, Mr. Regan—?

REGAN. Well, choke it up!

DAVIS. (*Desperately.*) They can read in any paper in the country that the strike's broken—that we're beaten—

REGAN. (*Interrupting savagely.*) Aw, dry up! (*Noticing the butler, who has all the time been standing at the door.*) Say, come out that trance an' tell us wot yer waitin' fer?

GATES. I beg pardon, sir, there're nine more gentlemen from the papers waiting to see you and—

REGAN. (*Interrupting.*) Tell 'em t' go t' hell!

GATES. (*With dignity.*) I have, sir, several times.

REGAN. (*Amused.*) Well, see they get there, understand?

GATES. Yes, sir, but—

REGAN. (*Suddenly.*) Now you get a move on before I catch ye on the nut with— (*He seizes the whiskey bottle with a threatening gesture, half real, half mocking.* GATES *goes out quickly. The telephone rings on the desk.* REGAN *answers it.*) Hello? Porky? Where are ye? Down in the Ward? Yeah. G'wan—who? Young Griswold? Wot 's he doin' down there? Speakin' t' my own men? Tryin' t' make 'em join the Union? I—wot 's that? (*Exploding.*) Yeah, choke him off, sure, stop him! But say, Porky, none o' that Hurley business now! No, take care o' him. Don't hurt him, just hustle him out quick, see? (*He rings off and turns to* DAVIS.) Griswold down on Lake Street, right in the middle o' the Ward, tryin' t' show my own gang how to bust me! The damn fool, he don't know wot he 's doin'. As sure as me name 's Regan, that guy don't know wot he 's doin'!

(*He rises furiously.*)

DAVIS. (*Alarmed.*) Mr. Regan, don't go on so. Remember, you 've been up all night!

REGAN. (*Controlling himself with an effort.*) An' I got a long, hard day ahead. Yer right, me son. Now sit down an' we 'll get t' work. I 'll tell ye wot I 'm goin' to' do. I 'm—

(*The door opens, and* EMILY *appears, very fresh and charming, carrying a covered plate.*)

EMILY. (*Brightly.*) Good morning.

DAVIS and REGAN. Good morning.

(DAVIS *goes out.*)

EMILY. I 'm sorry I did n't think of the eggs, Michael. Here they are.

REGAN. (*Who has taken off his hat on seeing her.*) Thank ye kindly. (*Gulping.*) I always think it 's a good idea t' begin the day with a couple o' fried eggs!

EMILY. Are they all right?

REGAN. (*Looking at them.*) Yeah, they look slick—(*Glancing shyly at her.*) I mean—I mean they look real nice!

EMILY. I 'm glad.

REGAN. (*Still shy.*) Say, Em'ly—

EMILY. Yes?

REGAN. (*Looking away.*) Thank ye for rememberin' all this. It was just wot I needed. An'—an' ye was awful kind t' think o' me.

EMILY. (*Embarrased.*) Why, that 's all right, Michael. (*Assuming authority.*) Go on! Sit down now! Everything 'll get cold if you wait!

REGAN. (*Timidly.*) Ye don't feel like a fried egg yerself, do ye?

EMILY. (*Smiling.*) Thank you, I had breakfast upstairs. But I 'll pour your coffee, if you like.

REGAN. (*Eagerly.*) I wish ye would.

EMILY. (*Sitting at the desk.*) How many lumps do you take?

REGAN. Four. (EMILY *laughs.*) I like things awful sweet.

EMILY. (*Smiling.*) That 's not very grown-up, is it?

REGAN. (*Looking at her.*) Perhaps I 'm not as grown-up as ye think. (*Slight pause.*) Gee, but this seems natural!

EMILY. (*Busy.*) What seems natural?

REGAN. (*Slowly.*) Aw, I dunno. Just t' have you sittin' in the sunshine, pourin' out me coffee. That 's all.

EMILY. (*Looking up innocently.*) Why, I never did it before to-day.

REGAN. I know, but it seems natural all the same.

(*Their eyes meet. There is a pause.*)

EMILY. (*Rising in an embarrassed way.*) Well, there you are! Now drink it right away while it 's hot.

REGAN. (*Coming around below desk and sitting down.*) Say, it smells fine!

(*He eats and drinks. She watches him anxiously.*)

EMILY. (*At last.*) Gates said you were down at your office all night. Could n't you manage to take a nap?

REGAN. Naw. I 'm afraid I ain't got no time fer sleepin'.

EMILY. That 's too bad.

REGAN. Is it? Well, I guess there 's nothin' t' do about it. (*He drinks.*)

EMILY. (*Suddenly.*) Oh, before I forget it! Everybody who accepted for dinner to-morrow night has sent in a—a more or less polite lie. They won't come, Michael.

REGAN. (*Eating his eggs.*) Well, I guess I can stand that. Gee, I 'd rather beat up three heavyweights any day than talk polite t' one o' yer lady friends!

EMILY. (*Almost to herself.*) Even Lucy Darrow and the Gilmores! I did n't think it of them somehow. (*Remembering where she is.*) So if you want to, you can make another engagement. That 's all. I just thought I 'd tell you.

(*She goes to door.*)

REGAN. (*With a short savage laugh.*) Another engagement? You talk like I was an English dook at Newport! Why, do you know there ain't ten people in this town 'd let me eat out their ash-cans—free o' charge?

EMILY. (*With a sudden impulse of pity.*) Michael, I want to—

REGAN. Well?

EMILY. I want you to know I 'm sorry. That 's all.

REGAN. (*With amused cunning.*) Sorry fer wot? Me? Well, don't you lose no sleep about it! Just lie back an' watch me—see?

EMILY. Watch you?

REGAN. Yeah. It 's goin' t' be a slick show!

EMILY. What do you mean?

REGAN. D' ye think them slobs have got me down? Ha! I 'm just puttin' up a little con game now, but the minute they let go me arms and say, "This trip he 's done fer!" why, then 's the time I 'll up and nail 'em t' the wall!

EMILY. I don't understand!

REGAN. (*Mysteriously.*) Well, sit tight and ye will. (*Drinks coffee.*)

EMILY. (*Faltering.*) Is n't it all over? Are n't you—beaten?

REGAN. (*Amused.*) Beat? *Me?* Say, d 'you know what I 'm going t' do?

EMILY. No.

REGAN. Then I don't mind tellin' ye. Ever been to Montreal?

EMILY. No.

REGAN. Well, I have. It 's a slick place —Montreal. Good climate, theatres, swell people, an' all that. How 'd ye like t' live there, Em'ly?

EMILY. (*Startled.*) *Live* there?

REGAN. Yeah. 'Cause yer goin' to, young woman. If ye hang on t' me, that 's where yer headed fer!

EMILY. (*Staring at him.*) What d' you mean, Michael?

REGAN. (*Emphatically.*) I'm goin' t' turn the ocean grain traffic from this town t' Montreal.

EMILY. What?

REGAN. (*Quickly.*) I said I 'd get back at 'em good an' hard, and that 's how I 'm goin' t' do it.

EMILY. (*Stammering.*) But—but, Michael—

REGAN. (*Interrupting.*) I sent the Western a wire last night, offerin' 'em half rates if they 'd unload at Montreal. As soon as I got time t' build me own elevators, that is. An' here 's their answer—(*Picking it from the desk.*) Come in half an hour ago. (*Tosses it to* EMILY.)

EMILY. (*Sitting on couch, reading.*) "Accept offer. Have notified our Eastern agents. Please expect shipments at Montreal by 15th."

REGAN. (*In triumph.*) I got 'em goin', Em'ly, I got 'em goin'! I knew they 'd take me up when they heard the rates I 'm offerin'! There was n't nothin' else to do. An' I made them Montreal contractors a proposition they don't dare to throw down! I 'm waitin' for their answer now. (*Looking at clock on desk.*)

EMILY. Those Canadian officials are awfully down on American business. I remember once when Dad tried to start a branch at—

REGAN. (*Interrupting.*) Aw, they got their price! Damn 'em, ye can bet on that! An' I guess I 'm big enough to stand it, too!

EMILY. You mean?

REGAN. (*Brazenly.*) Sure. I 'd tip 'em like I would a bunch o' bell-hops!

EMILY. I see. But is n't that—risky?

REGAN. (*Carelessly.*) Naw. If they get found out, they 're done. If *I* get found out, I done right—see?

EMILY. And you think it will pay?

REGAN. (*Exploding.*) Pay? Who wants to make it pay? I don't! All I want is to get back at this town an' that 's wot I 'm goin' t' do!

(*The door left opens and* GATES *appears.*)

GATES. Another telegram, sir.

REGAN. (*Eagerly.*) Give it here! (*He seizes and opens and reads it. Then, with an outburst of triumph.*) It 's O. K.! D' ye hear? They take me up! The job 's done! The whole job 's done!

EMILY. Is it from Montreal?

REGAN. (*Handing it to her.*) Yeah. Oh, gee, but this is swell!

GATES. Any answer, sir? I told the boy to wait.

REGAN. Naw. Yeah, give him this! (*Tossing* GATES *a silver dollar.* GATES *stumbles and drops the coin.*) Aw, go back t' cricket! Go back t' cricket! Tell him to keep the change. He 's brought me the best news I ever had!

(GATES *has picked up coin and goes out.*)

EMILY. (*Crumpling up telegram.*) Now, Michael, listen!

REGAN. Yeah?

EMILY. There's one thing I want to make perfectly clear.

REGAN. (*Lighting a cigar.*) Wot's that?

EMILY. If you go to Montreal, you go alone.

REGAN. Oh, I do, do I?

EMILY. Yes, I won't live anywhere else but here.

REGAN. Ye'll find it sort o' lonesome work, I guess.

EMILY. Lonesome?

REGAN. Yeah. When I quit, d'ye know wot this town'll be?

EMILY. What?

REGAN. A line o' shanties, two saloons, an' a dead dawg in the middle of the street.

EMILY. You're very foolish, Michael.

REGAN. All right, you wait an' see. I tell you I'm goin' to strip this place till it'll have to crawl into a barrel! I won't leave it so much as a toothbrush and a pair o' shoestrings to its name!

EMILY. I don't believe it.

REGAN. All right. But just the same, ye'd better stick it on my tombstone. One o' them big marble crosses with a couple o' first class angels at the bottom, an' underneath—all in them fancy letters—"Gawd help Mike Regan. He turned the wheat t' Montreal."

EMILY. I don't believe a word you're saying.

REGAN. (*Looking up a number in the telephone book.*) All right, then. Don't!

EMILY. Michael.

REGAN. Wot? (*Running his finger down the page.*) People's Gas—Home—Institute—Line—Magazine—Market—

EMILY. Michael, have you absolutely made up your mind about this?

REGAN. Yeah. (*Reading.*) Printing—Theatre—Trust— (*Stopping.*) 2800 Main.

(*He takes up telephone receiver*)

EMILY. Then I suppose you'll be going up to Montreal immediately.

REGAN. (*To operator.*) 2800 Main. (*To her.*) As soon as I've cleaned up things down here. (*To the operator.*) 2800 Main. 2800 I said.

EMILY. Cleaned up things?

REGAN. Yeah. Got hold me cash.

EMILY. What *do* you mean?

REGAN. Why, ye don't think I'll go off an' leave any loose change floatin' round, do ye?

EMILY. I don't understand.

REGAN. (*To operator, suddenly.*) Fer Gawd's sake, get a move on! 2800 Main! (*To* EMILY.) Why, I got over ten millions invested in this place. Nearly eleven, when ye come down to it. An' when I skip, me dough skips with me—see?

EMILY. No, I *don't* see. I don't see at all!

REGAN. (*At telephone.*) Hello! People's Trust? Yeah. Connect me with Mr. Fairbanks. Well, I know he's the president, that's why I want to talk to him. My name's Regan. Yeah, Michael R. Got it? (*Pause. He puffs at his cigar.* EMILY *watches him.*) Hello, that you, Fairbanks? Oh, I'm feelin' fine! Them strikers? Well, I ain't finished with 'em yet, an' that's why I called ye up. Yeah, that's wot I mean. I want ye t' call in all the mortgages. Sure! Foreclosure. I don't care where they are! Them guys ain't paid no interest on 'em fer the last—well, *I* did n't start the strike, did I? 'T was n't *my* fault! (*Angrily.*) I don't give a damn *wot* happens to 'em! They ain't paid me my interest an' I just foreclose—see? Yeah, I'm callin' in all my loans. Sure! Every security I got—all over the town! Wot? Oh, I just feel like it, that's all. Say, you go ahead an' do just like I say! Huh? Naw, cut that. I—say, Fairbanks, that'll do for you, understand?

(*He rings off suddenly, then turns to find* EMILY *close beside him.*)

EMILY. Michael!

REGAN. Gee, I thought ye'd gone!

EMILY. Michael, I want to know what mortgages those are.

REGAN. Aw, just little ones, down round Lake Street.

EMILY. Lake Street!

REGAN. Yeah. That end o' town.

EMILY. Lake Street! Why, that's the Fourth Ward!

REGAN. (*Carelessly.*) Sure. O' course. So it is!

EMILY. You've bought up mortgages in the Fourth Ward?

REGAN. Looks that way.

EMILY. And now you're going to foreclose?

REGAN. Yeah. Why not?

EMILY. What's going to happen to those men?

REGAN. Wot men?

EMILY. The men who live down there.

The men you've employed for years.

REGAN. Ye mean the men that raised this strike an' beat me? They're goin' t' lose their happy homes. That's wot's goin' happen to *them!* Ye go down there next week an' ye'll find every sidewalk in the Ward piled up with bedquilts an' bureaus an' rockin' chairs an' gas stoves.

EMILY. (*Involuntarily.*) Oh, no!

REGAN. (*Continuing.*) Yeah, an' ye'll run across yer friend Mrs. Moriarity, sittin' on the corner o' Lake an' River sellin' matches in the rain. An' Scanlan, ye remember Scanlan? Well, he'll be sweepin' streets. If he's lucky, that is—

EMILY. (*Interrupting.*) No!

REGAN. An' the only grub the Baxter kids'll get will be them little minnies ye fish fer off the docks, an' old lady Hogan'll have t' climb out o' bed an' sling a sack over her shoulder an' start in alley-lickin'!

EMILY. (*Shrilly.*) Stop it! Michael!

REGAN. (*Triumphantly.*) An' all the time *I'll* be leanin' back up there in Montreal, smokin' me cigar an' takin' it all in!

(*He tilts back chair, stretches, and puts his feet on desk.*)

EMILY. But, Michael, those families have suffered enough already. The strike nearly finished them! They have nothing left!

REGAN. Ah, I thought I'd wake ye up. (*Intensely.*) Well, it serves 'em right!

EMILY. And they're the very people that made you! They've given you everything you have—every tiny little thing!

REGAN. Wot of it?

EMILY. Don't you see? You can't turn on them this way.

REGAN. Can't I? Say, watch me!

EMILY. Jump on them from behind like some wild animal they've had to punish—

REGAN. Aw, dry up on that!

EMILY. Get even, get back at them, just to satisfy your own miserable little idea of revenge!

REGAN. (*Bursting out.*) Revenge! That's it! I got 'em all like that! (*Holding out one hand with slowly closing fingers.*) I'm goin' t' squeeze 'em till I hear their bones a-crackin'!

EMILY. No, you can't! It's too cruel! Too hideously cruel!

REGAN. Aw, forget it!

EMILY. I married you to keep these people from being ruined. I gave up a great deal when I did that, Michael, and now I'm not going to see my sacrifice—(REGAN *turns quickly*) that's what it was!—I won't see my sacrifice turned into an absolutely useless thing.

REGAN. Well, how are ye goin' to help it?

EMILY. (*Hysterically.*) I don't know. I don't know anything except that I'm your wife. And so you can't do this. I'm your wife—do you understand?—your wife—

REGAN. (*Turns in an outburst.*) You lie! Yer not my wife an' ye know it! My wife! (*He laughs.*) That's a good one, that is! I guess if ye was my wife I might be feelin' different. I guess I'd have no right t' start a big thing that me missus was so strong against. But you! Ye've built a wall round yerself t' keep me out, an' gee! it done the job! Why, I seen ye crack a smile at the butler there an' talk t' him almost like he was human! But me! Say, have ye ever done any more than that t' me? No, by Gawd, ye let me live here in the same house with ye day after day, ye let me lie alone there in my bed night after night, thinkin' o' the locked door between us an' sufferin' through the black hours like I did n't know a man could suffer, wishin' the day would break an' find me dead—

EMILY. (*Trembling.*) Michael!

REGAN. (*Close to her.*) Ye say ye feel sorry fer them strikers. Well, lemme tell ye right here, there's not one of 'em that ain't got more 'n me! I don't care if he's cold an' his stummick's empty an' the window's busted an' the roof's leakin'! *He's got someone t' love him,* so I guess he'll see it through! But me—! Why, ye kept it all back from me, all wot I want most in the world, me feelin's, me rights—why, the best things Gawd ever gave us men! Wot have ye done with 'em, woman? An' say now, where do ye get the nerve to call yerself my wife?

EMILY. Michael, you have no right to talk to me like this. You may have forgotten the agreement we made before I married you, but I have n't. I've lived up to every word of it. I've done every single thing I said I would. (*He starts to speak.*) No, wait! There's something else. I've been perfectly right, but I—I did n't realize you felt like this. I did n't dream you—but, Michael, so long as you do, I 'm willing now to go on. I 'm willing to go ahead. I 'm willing to make another bargain.

REGAN. (*Quickly.*) Wot 's that?

EMILY. (*With difficulty.*) I 'll change. I 'll be different.

REGAN. Be different—? (*Suddenly and fiercely.*) Say, quit that or some day I 'll—

EMILY. (*Interrupting.*) Why—don't you *want* me to be different?

REGAN. (*Looking at her with almost a sob.*) You know—*oh gee, you know!*

EMILY. All right, then. I will—

REGAN. (*Interrupting.*) Huh?

EMILY. (*Finishing quickly.*) If you give up this dreadful idea of yours! If you stay here and take your beating like a man!

REGAN. (*Panting.*) D' ye mean—say, ye don't mean if—

EMILY. Yes, I do.

REGAN. Naw! Ye can't. (*Gulping.*) Beat it now! I give ye warnin'! Beat it while ye got the chanst!

(*He covers his face with his hands.*)

EMILY. (*Proudly.*) I won't.

REGAN. Don't—

EMILY. Well?

REGAN. (*Agonized.*) Oh, my Gawd!

EMILY. (*With her last vestige of strength.*) Tell me—

REGAN. (*Rushing at her with a cry.*) Em'ly! (*Gathering her to him.*) I 'd go t' hell fer this an' lay there, Em'ly, an' lay a-smilin' there forever an' forever! Stop shakin'! Hold yer head up, sweetie! (*Loudly and triumphantly.*) I love ye! I love ye!

(*For the first time he kisses her.*)

EMILY. (*Trying to tear herself away.*) Stop it! Keep away!

REGAN. (*Triumphantly.*) Ye love me! Gee, ye love me an' I never knew!

EMILY. I don't! I hate you!

REGAN. (*Intoxicated.*) Yer givin' in 'cause ye *want* to—

EMILY. (*With a cry of horror.*) Stop it! *Stop it, I tell you!*

REGAN. (*Through his teeth.*) Yer doin' it of yer own free will!

EMILY. (*Furiously breaking away.*) How dare you say that!

REGAN. Well, ain't it true?

EMILY. (*Violently.*) No! No! I tell you I 'm selling myself for a price! A price!

REGAN. Em'ly!

EMILY. I 'm paying you just as if it were money! I 'm paying you cash down—because it 's the only thing you 'll take!

REGAN. Em'ly, fer the love o' Gawd!

EMILY. (*Beside herself.*) I want you to know—I 've got to make you understand! It 's just another bargain! You 're getting me cheap—d' you hear that?—cheap! I 'm going dirt cheap—

REGAN. (*Strongly.*) Stop it! (*He covers her mouth with his hand.*) I done some rotten things in me time, an' I guess ye know it, too, but gee! I never done nothin' half so rotten as wot yer doin' now!

EMILY. (*Hysterically.*) Oh—! Oh—!

REGAN. (*Scornfully.*) Sellin' yourself! Payin' me cash down! Goin' cheap! (*In a sort of rage.*) Gawd, d' ye think I want ye, if that 's how ye come? D' ye think I 'll take my wife that way? I guess ye don't know much about real men! If ye did, ye 'd never try t' pull off such a deal. Ye 'd never a' made me feel ashamed o' ye—yeah, *ashamed!*—like I 'm feelin' now—

EMILY. (*Laughing and crying.*) Ashamed—? You—?

REGAN. (*Fiercely.*) I tell ye my kids are goin' t' be born 'cause I loved their mother with all me body an' mind an' soul, an' 'cause she loved me back with all o' hers! An' if such things as that can't be, why then, so help me Gawd, I 'll have no kids at all!

MCCOY. (*Bursting in from right.*) Mike! (*He stands leaning against the wall.*) 'Scuse me—(REGAN *releases* EMILY, *who goes out the other door quickly.*) Say, Mike!

REGAN. (*Turning.*) Gee, Porky, ye look all in! Wot 's the game?

MCCOY. (*Panting.*) It 's—young Griswold!

REGAN. Who? Come over here an' tell me.

MCCOY. (*Half falling on the sofa.*) Gimme a drink—I run—all the way from —Lake Street—

REGAN. Sit down. (*At the desk, pouring whiskey.*) Well—g' wan.

MCCOY. He came down t' the ward t' spiel—*you* know. He got up on a barrel a-wearin' one o' them nobby little dips, an' he just sailed into ye, Mike, sayin' how he got ye licked, callin' ye all the dirty names he could think of. An' I sorter went off me nut an' seein' as I happened to have a brick in me hand, I guess I just heaved it—an' it caught him in the head—an'—an' he went down.

REGAN. (*Glancing round.*) You—(*He goes to the door by which* EMILY *left and closes it. Then, in a low voice, turning round.*) Is he dead? (*Pause.*) Is he dead? (*Taking* McCOY *by lapels of coat and pulling him around fiercely.*) G' wan an' tell me! Tell me! Ye got to tell me!

McCOY. (*Not looking at him.*) I dunno. They took him into Dugan's café an' then the ambulance came and got him.

(*Pause.*)

REGAN. (*In an outburst, throwing* McCOY *against the back of sofa.*) Damn ye, Porky! Damn ye—damn ye—

McCOY. (*Terrified.*) Say, Mike, I did n't mean to do it—honest t' God, I did n't! All I wanted was t' knock his lid off! Aw, wot did he come down fer anyways? He might a-knowed he 'd get soaked in yer own ward—

REGAN. An' I 'd a-given me right arm t' have kept him safe!

McCOY. I know ye would. But there 's no use talkin' now—(*Clinging to him.*) Wot 'll I do? Mike, I got a sick wife an' a new kid! Tell me wot 'll I do?

REGAN. Shut up, Porky, or the whole house 'll hear ye! Now listen! Did any one see ye fire that brick?

PORKY. Naw. They was all lookin' at him. I was on the outside.

REGAN. Yer sure nobody piped ye?

PORKY. Sure. Why, I 'm one o' the guys that carried him into the café!

REGAN. Then it 's all right. Go home t' the wife and kid, an' keep yer mouth shut, understand?

McCOY. Not do nothin'?

REGAN. Not a damn thing. An' if there 's any trouble, I 'll look after ye.

McCOY. Aw, thank ye, Mike—(*Grasps* REGAN'S *hand.*) I knew ye 'd fix it up fer me!

REGAN. G'wan now! Beat it! Remember me t' the missus. An' how 's the kid t'day?

McCOY. (*Eagerly.*) Gettin' bigger. An' gee! his wrinkles is all comin' off!

(*Enter* DAVIS.)

DAVIS. Mr. Regan.

REGAN. (*To* DAVIS.) Wait a second.

McCOY. You 're sure that 's all O. K.?

REGAN. I said so once.

McCOY. Thank ye, Mike. S' long.

(*He goes out.*)

REGAN. (*To* DAVIS, *who is at window.*) Well, wot d' *you* want?

(*The low murmur of an approaching crowd is heard in the distance.*)

DAVIS. (*Turning.*) Mr. Regan, d' you hear anything?

REGAN. (*After listening a moment.*) Yeah. Wot is it?

DAVIS. Sounds like a crowd. I think they 're coming up Concord Avenue.

REGAN. (*Looking out window.*) The hell they are!

DAVIS. And there 's a gentleman says he *must* see you.

REGAN. I won't see no one.

DAVIS. Here he is.

(*Enter* DUNCAN, *full of excitement.*)

DUNCAN. Regan!

REGAN. (*Over his shoulder.*) Well, what d' you want?

DUNCAN. Donald Griswold went down to speak in the Fourth Ward and was set on by some of your toughs. He 's hurt —nobody knows how badly. He may be dead. (*The sound outside increases.*)

REGAN. An' that out there?

DUNCAN. The whole town 's up in arms. They 're sure you did it.

REGAN. (*Turns sharply.*) Me?

DUNCAN. Or had it done. They 're sure you gave the orders.

REGAN. O' course they are.

DUNCAN. Regan, I came to tell you the police are on their way. Mr. Griswold 's had a warrant sworn out. You 're going to be arrested.

REGAN. Damnation!

DUNCAN. Come on, the alley 's clear, but it won't be in five minutes. I have a motor waiting on the corner of McDonald Street. We 'll have you ten miles away by the time that patrol gets here.

REGAN. Say, who are you anyway?

DUNCAN. My name 's Duncan.

REGAN. Yer one o' his friends, then?

DUNCAN. Whose?

REGAN. Griswold's.

DUNCAN. What of it? I 'm here to help you now. Don't you believe it?

REGAN. Aw, wot yer givin' me?

DUNCAN. It 's true!

REGAN. Help *Regan?*

DUNCAN. No, damn you, not Regan! Emily Griswold's husband!

REGAN. (*Quickly.*) Cut it now!

DUNCAN. She 's your wife, Regan! You 've got to think about her!

REGAN. That 's all right! I can manage my wife without no buttin' in from anybody—understand?

DUNCAN. You can't! That mob 'll be here in a minute and this house won't be safe. I 'm going to bring my motor to the side door. Tell her to come down this minute. I 'm going to take her home.

(*He goes out quickly. The sound outside has become an angry roar. It is getting nearer.*)

DAVIS. (*At window.*) Why, they don't look like strikers!

REGAN. (*Looking out window.*) Strikers? Ye blame fool, it 's the town!

DAVIS. The town?

REGAN. The whole damn town! (*Half to himself.*) Gee, here 's where we 're up against it!

DAVIS. (*More and more excited.*) Why! They 're a lot of well dressed men! They have n't any hats! They look—why, they must be drunk!

REGAN. Aw, g' wan! They 're about as drunk as a bunch o' tigers! (*The roar increases.*) Hear that? They 're mad —mad clean through!

DAVIS. Look at them! The street 's full! Why, there must be hundreds!

REGAN. Thousands is more like it.

DAVIS. But—but what are they doing up here? Mr. Regan, what are they after?

REGAN. (*Grimly.*) Can't ye see? Why, they come t' make a little friendly call on me, that 's all.

DAVIS. (*Frightened.*) Oh, no, sir, not that! It—it must be a fire!

REGAN. Fire be damned! If ye ever heard a mob a-coughin' that way before, ye 'd never ask again wot it means!

(*The roar becomes louder, confused and angry, as the mob is supposed to climb the fence and trample up the lawn.*)

DAVIS. You don't—?

REGAN. Sure I do. Why, every manjack down there 's out fer blood! Somethin' happened in the ward, an' they 're comin' straight fer me.

DAVIS. (*Looking out again.*) Mr. Regan! Look! That 's Scanlan on the sidewalk—the man with the brown coat! I 'd know him anywhere! And there—d' you see? right beside him?—why, it 's old Archibald Houghton, the vice-president of the First National—

REGAN. Houghton! (*Laughing.*) Ha! Ha!

DAVIS. And the fellow climbing the fence —is n't that Grayson? The senior member of Grayson, Grayson and Company?

REGAN. Yeah. An' that feller behind him, that 's young Harry Huntington! See? The guy with the cigarette.

DAVIS. (*Looking in a new direction.*) They 're a lot of strikers, too! And look there! See those Italians by the gate? Why, they 're all mixed up! gentlemen and toughs, scoopers and big business men!

(*There is a great outburst under the very windows.*)

REGAN. (*Jovially.*) But they all take hold of hands when it comes t' hatin' me!

DAVIS. (*Drawing back.*) Look out, sir, they 're right below there! They 'll see you—(*Crash of glass.*) Good Lord!

REGAN. Go upstairs an' tell me wife to come down. Mr. Duncan 's here to get her.

DAVIS. Yes, sir.

(*He goes out. Outside the door are heard the servants in terrified confusion.*)

GATES. (*Running in.*) Mr. Regan! Mr. Regan! There 's a crowd of very dangerous-looking fellows outside!

(*He is followed by two terrified* MAIDS. *They all stand huddled near the door, very much frightened. Another crash from outside.*)

THE CROWD. (*Individual voices.*) That 's right! Fire another! Gimme that brick! Come out o' there! He don't dare! The damn coward! Smash his winders!

REGAN. (*At telephone.*) Choke it off! I can't hear!

THE MAIDS. Mr. Regan! Mr. Regan!

REGAN. Choke it off! (*Telephoning.*) Hello. Gimme P'lice Headquarters. Yeah. (*Pause, during which another storm of yells and calls is heard outside.*) This headquarters? I 'm Regan. Yeah, Michael R. Say, I got a mob outside here a-smashin' me winders. Can ye hear 'em? Naw? (*He holds the transmitter toward the window. Another crash of glass outside and yell.*) Not now? Well, take me word fer it an' send up Kelly with the reserves! send up all ye got—see? I 'll need 'em, every one! S' long!

THE CROWD. Break into the side! Keep it up! Pull the house down! Aim higher—ye missed it that trip! There! I got her!

(*Another crash followed by a general yell.*)

THE FRENCH MAID. *J'ai peur! J'ai terriblement peur! C'est des assassins—oui, des assassins!*

(*A brick crashes through one of the windows, falling to the floor amid a shower of broken glass. There is a general commotion.* REGAN *goes to the window.*)

THE CROWD. (*Outside.*) He 's in there! Try the next one! Soak him! That 's right! Let her go!

(*Another brick crashes in.* REGAN *runs to the desk and opens one of the drawers.*)

FRENCH MAIDS. *Oh, Mon Dieu! C'est des apaches! Quelle horreur!*

THE OTHER MAID. Mr. Gates! Oh, sir! What 'll we do?

GATES. Be calm, young women, be calm!

(*He gathers them together and pushes them towards the door.*)

THE CROWD. Regan! Where is he? We want Regan! Regan! (*Another stone crashes in. A table is overturned and lamp broken. All the servants shriek and rush out.*) The sneak! The coward! Come out where we can see you! Regan! Regan! We want Regan!

REGAN. (*Taking his automatic revolver from desk-drawer.*) Ye would, would ye? Ye dirty dawgs, a-tryin' t' frighten the women! Ye wait there! *I 'll* show ye! (*He runs to the window, opens it, and stands there. At his appearance a chorus of yells goes up and more missiles are hurled.*) Well, here I am! I 'm the man ye want! Take a good look at me! I 'm right here an' I ain't goin' t' move!

THE CROWD. (*Howling.*) We 'll show ye! We got ye! Look at him! Kill him! Kill him!

REGAN. That 's right! Yell away! Yellin' don't hurt nobody, so keep it up! G' wan! I like t' hear ye! But if ye bust so much as one more pane o' glass, by Gawd, I 'll empty this repeater without stoppin' once to wink!

(*He covers them with his weapon. There is a dead pause, then a chorus of angry moans and jeers.*)

THE CROWD. Ah! 'T ain't loaded! He don't dare! It 's one o' his tricks! *I 'll* show him! Where 's that brick!

REGAN. Say there, ye big slob with the red bandana—yes, you! Drop that brick or ye—wot? All right, I—(*He lifts his pistol and aims quickly. Then, laughing triumphantly.*) Aw, I knew I 'd get ye! What 's the answer? Yer scared! The whole damn crowd o' ye are scared! Ye know I 'm here with nothin' but me wife an' a bunch o' second-girls, but I 've got ye goin', yer hangin' over the ropes—

(*The roar of the enraged crowd surges up again.*)

THE CROWD. (*Enraged.*) We are, hey? We 'll show ye! Stop his gaff! Bust in the door! We ain't scared! He can't kid us! G' wan, that 's right! Don't quit!

REGAN. (*Raising his pistol.*) Say, stop right there—d' ye hear? The first guy that puts his mat on them steps 'll get a bullet through his nut—understand? Now come on! Say, why don't ye come on an' get me? I 'm right here, all ready, just a-waitin' fer ye!

ONE VOICE. (*Then all.*) Lynch him! Get a rope, boys, an' lynch him! *Lynch him.*

(*The gong and hoofs of a police patrol are heard in the distance, gradually growing nearer.*)

REGAN. What 's that? I did n't catch on t'—oh, all right! Fine an' dandy! If ye want t' lynch me, mister, come right up an' start in! That 's it! Aw, don't be bashful! Come along!

(*During the end of this speech the mob raises a sullen roar.*)

THE CROWD. Don't let him kid us! Get in the bunch! We 'll stop his drip! He can't do nothin'! (*The patrol is now close by.*) Cheese it! The cops!

(*The door behind* REGAN *opens and* EMILY *appears. She stands calmly at the top of the stairs, putting on her gloves. She is dressed for the street.*)

POLICE VOICES. Whoa! Whoa! (*Clanging of gong and hoofs very loud, then cease.*) Stand back there! Stand back! Move on! Get out o' here! Get off that fence! Go on home now! Shove 'em back! Kelly! Move on or I 'll cave your head in! No back talk. Move on an' keep movin'. Yes, you! Move on! Move on!

THE CROWD. All right! All right! Wot 's yer hurry! Say, wait a minute!

Let go me arm! All right, I 'm goin', ain't I?

REGAN. (*Howling derisively, laughing, taunting, as police shove back the mob.*) That 's it! Give it to 'em, boys! Beat 'em up, Kelley! Club their nuts off! Soak 'em! Kill 'em! (*Bursting into a roar of triumphant laughter, he closes the window and draws the portières together, turns, and for the first time sees his wife.*) Oh, that 's you!

EMILY. (*Calmly.*) Where 's Mr. Duncan? Mr. Davis said he was here.

REGAN. Is that all Davis told ye?

EMILY. Yes.

REGAN. (*To himself.*) Oh, my Gawd!

EMILY. Is Mr. Duncan downstairs? Mr. Davis *said* the library.

REGAN. He 's out gettin' the auto through the crowd. He 's come t' take ye home.

EMILY. (*Joyfully.*) Home? Is Don here, too? I mean—my brother?

REGAN. Naw, I 'm afraid—I 'm afraid he ain't here.

EMILY. Well, I 'll go downstairs and wait. (*She starts to go.*)

REGAN. No, stay here. (*She stops.*) There 's somethin' I got t' tell ye.

EMILY. What is it? Well, why don't you tell me? (*Pause.*) Michael, d' you know you 're making me—rather nervous?

REGAN. Sit down.

EMILY. (*Obeying.*) Go on. (*Pause.*)

REGAN. (*Beginning in a business-like way.*) Yer brother—

EMILY. (*Quickly.*) Well?

REGAN. (*Continuing.*) Well, he went down t' the Fourth Ward about ten o'clock this mornin' t' talk t' all the men who 'd stuck by me an' had n't joined the Union.

EMILY. Yes. Go on.

REGAN. Porky McCoy 'phoned me he was doin' it an' I got mad an' said t' head him off. Then you came in and we got t' talkin' an' I fergot all about him. An' you ducked out an' the mob collected down there an' I felt sure somethin' had gone wrong—

EMILY. (*Suspecting.*) Michael!

REGAN. But I did n't know a thing—s' elp me Gawd if I did!—until Porky came an' told me all about it.

EMILY. (*Breathing heavily.*) About what?

REGAN. Yer brother. (*Pause.*)

EMILY. (*Finally.*) Tell me—tell me quick! What 's happened to him?

REGAN. Well, he was sayin' some rotten stuff about me an' that made the fellers sore an' they began firin' things. Porky says it was a brick that caught him on the head. They got him t' the hospital as quick as they could—

EMILY. (*Screaming.*) Oh—!

REGAN. (*Breaking out and rushing to her.*) Em'ly, ye don't believe I done it? Ye don't believe I done a thing like that? No, ye don't, ye can't—

EMILY. (*Covering her face with her hands.*) Don!

REGAN. I never knew a thing about it till Porky told me! Ye know that, don't ye, Emily? Ye know I would n't a-had it happen fer anythin' in the world! I—

EMILY. (*Rocking to and fro.*) Don! Don!

REGAN. (*Breaking down.*) Em'ly ye gotter believe me! I 'm on the level this trip! I am! I swear t' Gawd I am!

EMILY. (*Not seeing him.*) Oh, Don!

REGAN. I got the whole town lined up against me. I 'm all alone, but if ye believe me, Em'ly, I don't care! An' I 'll be good from now on. I 'll be as good as I know how. I 'll throw up Montreal. I won't foreclose no mortgages. I 'll do anythin' ye want if ye only believe me now! Oh, yer goin' to! Ye do! I knew ye would! I knew!

(*He throws himself on his knees before her and bursts into tears, his face buried in her lap, like a little boy.*)

EMILY. (*For the first time realizing his presence.*) Don't touch me.

(*She pushes him away with a gesture of horror and rises.*)

REGAN. Em'ly!

EMILY. Don't come near me!

REGAN. (*Seizing her hand.*) Wot d' ye mean?

EMILY. Stop it! Keep away!

REGAN. (*Fiercely.*) So *you* think I done it, too? Tell me! G' wan! I say ye gotter tell me!

EMILY. I don't think! *I know!* (*Pause.*)

REGAN. (*With a wild Irish yell.*) A-aah! (*Throwing her hand away.*) If you believe I done a thing like that, all right! We 'll call it off! Go ahead! Wot are ye waitin' fer? Clear out o' my house! Beat it! Move along! (*She rushes out.*) Em'ly! Em'ly! I did n't mean that! I swear t' Gawd I did n't know nothin' about it! Don't go! Don't leave me, Em'ly! I ain't got no one else! I 'm all alone—

(*Enter three plainclothes police officers by the other door. They are followed by two in uniform.*)

INSPECTOR. I 'm sorry, sir, but you 've got t' come along with us. There 's a cab waitin' an'—

(REGAN *turns, looks at the officers a moment, then slowly puts on his overcoat and hat, pours and drinks a glass of whiskey, lights a cigar, takes a handful from the humidor, puts them in his pocket, picks up a newspaper, puts it under his arm, and goes nonchalantly towards the door.*)

REGAN. (*Casually.*) Come on, boys.

(*He goes up the steps and out, followed by the officers, as the curtain falls.*)

ACT FOURTH.

REGAN'S *rooms in the Police Station, three days later. It is a plain room, with a bed, a bureau at right. At back a large barred window through which the city can be seen. Near window, a big deal table covered with papers, an electric lamp, a big box of cigars, a whiskey bottle and glasses. Near the door is a waiter's stand, holding a tray covered with napkin.*

REGAN *is sitting on the window ledge, smoking, and dictating to* DAVIS. *He wears a sack-suit and looks very tired. He is evidently keeping up with difficulty. His fighting spirit is broken.*

REGAN. (*Dictating.*) "I hope my change o' plans will not put you or your officers t' any inconvenience." Got that?

DAVIS. "Any inconvenience." Yes, sir.

REGAN. (*Continuing.*) "Shiftin' the grain traffic from this town t' Montreal would have been just the sort of a job I most enjoy puttin' through, an' I intended t' go into it fer all I was worth. But circumstances over which I have no control make it impossible fer me t' do so. Wishin' yer business all success an' so forth"—just finish her up, Davis. You know how.

DAVIS. (*Writing.*) So that 's the end of Montreal. (*Pause.*)

REGAN. Davis.

DAVIS. (*Finishing and looking up.*) Yes, sir?

REGAN. There 's somethin' I want t' talk t' ye about. I won't be needin' a secretary much longer.

DAVIS. Please, sir! Don't let 's go into that now.

REGAN. Why not? We got to, sooner or later. I was sort o' goin' t' suggest that you take an int'rest in the business.

DAVIS. The business?

REGAN. Yeah. *My* business. You 've been with me eight years an' ye know it backwards an' I could hand it right over t' ye t'morrer. P'raps you could run it better 'n I did—I dunno. But, gee! I bet no one on God's green earth could make it pay so well!

DAVIS. Mr. Regan.

REGAN. Yeah?

DAVIS. Don't feel so discouraged. It 's going to be all right. You 're going to get out of here within a week and—

REGAN. A week? (*He laughs.*) I wonder!

DAVIS. Mr. Regan, you must n't give up like this. It 's not like you, sir, if you don't mind my saying so.

REGAN. That 's right. I dunno myself these days!

DAVIS. Brace up, sir! Pull yourself together! Look on the bright side of it!

REGAN. Aw, wot 's the good? (*Sitting on bed.*) Hodges was here this mornin'.

DAVIS. (*Eagerly.*) Hodges? What did he say?

REGAN. He says if Griswold dies, I 'll be indicted for murder in the first degree.

DAVIS. Mr. Hodges missed his job. Lawyer—? He ought to have been a wet nurse! Why, Mr. Regan, there 's more nerve in one of your back teeth than in two hundred Hodges!

REGAN. He says the District Attorney 's working night an' day fer a conviction. They 're goin' over me record with a fine tooth comb. They 're gettin' evidence from *ev'rywhere.*

DAVIS. Evidence? Let 'em get it! They can't prove you slung that brick and they can't prove you *had* it slung.

REGAN. He says there 's only one way t' clear meself. We got t' find the guy who done it an' make him swear he was n't carryin' out my orders.

DAVIS. You never gave any orders!

REGAN. I know. But I got t' prove I did n't.

DAVIS. Well, does Hodges think that man

is going to walk in here and say, "Please, mister, I slung that brick and now, if it is n't too much trouble, won't you kindly electrocute me?" Is that what he 's waiting for?

REGAN. Aw, gee, I don't know wot t' do!

DAVIS. Whoever he is, I bet by now he 's half way to Nevada. No, Mr. Regan, if you get out of here, it 'll be without *his* help—

REGAN. *If* I get out!

DAVIS. And you 're going to! D' you hear that, Mr. Regan, you 're *going* to!

REGAN. All right, me son, all right. (*Looking at watch.*) Half past four. Wot time are ye goin' t' call fer Mrs. Regan t' bring her down?

DAVIS. Quarter to five, sir.

REGAN. Ye 'd better be hustlin', then.

DAVIS. (*Getting overcoat.*) Don't worry, sir. I 'll be there. (*Pause.*)

REGAN. Say, Davis.

DAVIS. Yes, sir?

REGAN. (*Not looking at him.*) D' ye happen to remember wot she said last night when ye gave her me message?

DAVIS. Why, she—seemed surprised.

REGAN. (*Eagerly.*) Yeah? And then?

DAVIS. She asked why you had to see her. I said just what you told me to say, that it was important business connected with the Fourth Ward mortgages. She seemed doubtful for a moment and then said she 'd come. That 's all.

REGAN. An' ye asked after her brother? Ye did n't ferget that?

DAVIS. No. She said his condition had n't changed—that it would n't till after the operation.

REGAN. An' Jameson was goin' t' operate t'morrer. (*A knock at door.*) Come in. (*The door opens and an officer enters.*) Well?

OFFICER. Porky McCoy 's downstairs. He wants to see you.

REGAN. (*Eagerly.*) McCoy? Send him along.

OFFICER. All right, sir. (*He goes out.*)

REGAN. (*Turning joyfully to* DAVIS.) It 's Porky, d' ye hear? He 's stuck by me! I knew he would n't welch like all the rest!

DAVIS. I 'll start along, then. (*Looking at a package of papers.*) Oh, Mr. Regan, what d' you want done with these?

REGAN. Wot are they?

DAVIS. All the Montreal contracts and estimates.

REGAN. Just leave 'em on the table. I 'll look after 'em.

DAVIS. Very well, sir. I—

(*There is a knock at the door.*)

REGAN. (*Opening it.*) Come on in, Porky! (*As he enters,* REGAN *pulls him in by the hand.*) Gee, man, but I 'm glad t' see ye!

MCCOY. Hello, Mike.

REGAN. How 's the wife an'—(*Looking at him.*) Say, wot 's the matter?

MCCOY. Nothin'.

(*They stare at one another.*)

DAVIS. (*At the door.*) Good-night, sir. (*He waits a moment for* REGAN *to answer, then goes out quietly.*)

REGAN. Have a cigar?

MCCOY. Naw.

REGAN. A drink?

MCCOY. Naw, thanks.

REGAN. Say, Porky. Ye ain't sore at me, are ye?

MCCOY. Sore at you? Oh, Mike— (*Pause.*)

REGAN. (*Standing looking at him.*) Porky, ye got somethin' on yer mind. Now go ahead an' lay it out to me, son. (*Pause.*)

MCCOY. (*Blurting it out.*) Mike, I never knew they 'd think ye did fer Griswold! Gee, ye could a-knocked me over with a feather when I heard they 'd pulled ye in!

REGAN. I know that, me son, I know that.

MCCOY. I did n't mean t' play ye dirty, Mike—honest, I did n't! I did n't mean t' go back on ye! I would n't do that fer anythin' in the world!

REGAN. O' course ye would n't, Porky!

MCCOY. But I been readin' the papers, an' hearin' folks talk, an' seein' wot a good case they 've made out against ye, Mike, an' when Larry Dugan come in an' showed me wot that damn District Attorney had in this evenin's *Post,* I—I went into the kitchen where my wife was nursin' the kid, an' I begun bawlin'—an', gee, in about three minutes I 'd told her the whole thing!

REGAN. Ye told her?

MCCOY. Yeah, an' when I 'd finished, she said ye 'd been a good friend to me, Mike, an' it was up t' me. An'—an' she brought my overcoat—an' here I am, Mike, an' I guess that 's all.

REGAN. (*Tenderly patting him on shoulder.*) Ye poor feller.

MCCOY. (*In agony.*) Aw, don't! Smash me! Kick me! Beat me t' pieces! I won't say nothin'. But don't be good t' me, Mike! I can't stand it—I can't—I can't—

(*He breaks down and cries, his head on the table.*)

REGAN. (*Putting his hand on his shoulder.*) Say, Porky! (*Standing over him.*) D' ye remember one night in my old bar on Lake Street? Gee, it 's fifteen years ago now! An' ye took my side when Kelley's gang came in t' murder me fer holdin' back his nomination? All the rest had gone back on me, it was us two against eight. But we got behind the bar, an' ye grabbed the bung-starter, an' I broke four bottles o' Canadian rye over Kelley's head before I laid him out. Gee, that was a swell scrap! An' then, when it was all over, ye remember my comin' up t' ye where ye was leanin' over the big round table and a-wipin' the blood off yer chin, an' sayin', "McCoy," I says—fer I did n't know ye as well then, Porky, as I do now—"McCoy," says I, "ye 've done me a good turn t'night, an' p'raps sometime I 'll have a chance t' pay ye back. But anyway," I says, "from this time on, so help me Gawd, there won't nothin' come between us two. They don't make nothin' thin enough fer that!"

MCCOY. (*Looking up.*) Mike!

REGAN. (*Very tenderly.*) Well, that chance I talked about—it 's been fifteen years a-comin', Porky, but I got it now. An' I guess I 'll hang right on.

MCCOY. Wot d' ye mean?

REGAN. (*Clapping his shoulders.*) Go home an' tell the missus an' the kid it 's all right! Mike Regan says it 's all right!

MCCOY. But, Mike, I done it!

REGAN. Ye did not, Porky. The man that done it skipped an' we can't find him—see?

MCCOY. (*Not understanding.*) Mike, I ain't skipped! I 'm right here! I 'm willin' t' pay up!

REGAN. (*Smiling.*) Aw, come off! Ye don't know nothin' about it! Nothin'—nothin' at all!

MCCOY. Mike! I 'm on! Yer tryin' t' let me off!

REGAN. Gee, Porky, but yer wise t'day.

MCCOY. But say, d' ye know wot 'll happen t' *you?*

REGAN. Now don't ye bother yer nut about me. I 'll get out o' here.

MCCOY. Ye won't! If Griswold croaks. this town 'll finish ye fer good, understand? It won't lie back until it 's buried ye in quick-lime—

REGAN. (*Interrupting.*) Gee, perhaps ye think I care! P'raps ye think I got a lot t' live fer! Well, if ye do, yer off! Way off! Miles off!

MCCOY. But yer wife—

REGAN. (*Turning away abruptly.*) Me wife? I ain't got one.

MCCOY. But yer kids? The family that 's comin' t' ye—

REGAN. Fam'ly? (*He laughs aloud.*)

MCCOY. But yer business? *That 's* there! Ye got *that* all right!

REGAN. (*Bursting out.*) Quit it! I 'm sick o' the business! I hate it! I wish t' Gawd I 'd never seen it! Damn the business, that 's wot I say! Damn it! Damn it!

MCCOY. (*Frightened.*) I did n't mean nothin'.

REGAN. (*Controlling himself.*) That 's all right, Porky. I 'm sort o' done up t'day. But now ye see how I ain't got nothin' to live fer. An' remember, you got everythin'—everythin' a man can have! So go home now an' tell the wife. She 'll be a-waitin' an' a-worryin' an' ye ought t' let her know.

MCCOY. But, Mike, I—

REGAN. (*Interrupting.*) Wotever ye did, Porky, ye did it as my man. Ye did it fer me, understand! An' as head o' the firm, I guess I stand responsible fer me employee! (*With a change of manner, taking out his pocket-book.*) Say, Porky, wot day did you say the christenin' was?

MCCOY. Christenin'?

REGAN. Yeah. (*Smiling.*) Michael Regan Ignatius McCoy.

MCCOY. It 's Sunday week, but—

REGAN. (*Taking out a bill and putting it in* MCCOY'S *hand.*) Well, you take this an' get the boy a present. One o' them silver mugs is the reg'lar thing. An' if there 's anythin' left over, just set up drinks fer the crowd, will ye?

MCCOY. No, Mike, I—

REGAN. (*Pressing the bill into his hand.*) Aw, rats! G' wan an' take it! An' tell the good woman I 'm—I 'm awful sorry I can't be at the church meself that day to hold the kid. Ye know I was—kind o' lookin' forward t' that somehow, but—

(*He hesitates, embarrassed.*)

MCCOY. (*Bursting out.*) Mike, I won't let ye do this! I did fer Griswold! It was my fault an' now it 's up t' me t'—

REGAN. Aw, shut yer face!

McCOY. I won't! I'm goin' straight downstairs an' tell 'em how it happened—

REGAN. (*Roaring.*) You dry up or I 'll bust yer jaw! (*Slight pause.*) Ye 'll tell 'em downstairs? Ye 'll tell 'em nothin'! D' ye hear? Ye 'll walk out of this place without openin' yer mug wide enough t' spit, an' ye 'll do it 'cause I tell ye to, by Gawd! there ain't no bigger reason! (*Knock at door.*) Come in. (*The door opens and the officer appears.*) Wot d' ye want?

THE OFFICER. There 's a lady to see you, sir. (*There is a slight pause.*)

REGAN. (*Suspiciously.*) 'T ain't another one o' them female reporters?

THE OFFICER. No, sir, it 's yer wife. She 's down in the Inspector's office.

REGAN. All right. I'm ready. Ask her to come up.

OFFICER. All right, sir.

(*The officer goes out.*)

McCOY. S' long.

REGAN. S' long, Porky.

McCOY. Would ye mind—shakin' hands?

REGAN. Why should I mind, me son? (*He does so.*)

McCOY. Gee, yer the best I—I ever met!

REGAN. Aw g' wan!

(PORKY *goes out quickly.* REGAN, *left alone, looks about, then quickly and awkwardly begins tidying up the room, fixing the napkin to cover the tray. He makes the desk a little more orderly, throwing cigar ends and ashes in waste basket. He picks up the cuspidor and drops it behind the washstand. He pours water in the basin, washes his hands, wipes them on the towel, throws the towel behind the washstand, sets the pitcher back in the bowl in the water. While brushing his coat, he sees his pajamas and throws them under the pillow, thumps the pillow, and is covering the red blanket with the counterpane when* EMILY *softly opens the door and pauses, watching him. He does not see her.*)

EMILY. (*At last.*) Michael.

REGAN. (*Starting suddenly and turning.*) Is that you? I did n't hear ye.

EMILY. (*Entering.*) They said to go right in.

REGAN. (*Very embarrassed.*) Sure. O' course. (*Pause.*) Won't ye—sit down? (*He offers her a chair.*)

EMILY. Thank you.

(*She sits. There is another awkward pause.*)

REGAN. I—hope yer feelin' well?

EMILY. Oh, I 'm well enough—but—rather tired, that 's all.

REGAN. (*Sympathetically.*) I know. (*Pause.*)

REGAN and EMILY. (*Simultaneously.*) Yer lookin'— You look— (*They both stop.*)

REGAN. (*Politely.*) I beg yer pardon. After you!

EMILY. (*Glancing about uneasily.*) You look—fairly comfortable here. Somehow I did n't expect to find things as—as comfortable.

REGAN. (*Embarrassed, looking about too.*) Yeah, they been real good t' me—the boys have. Davis comes here ev'ry day, an' I got a telephone in the hall, an' they send in me grub from that hotel across the street. No, it ain't so bad—when—when ye get used to it. (*Pause.*)

EMILY. (*Nervously.*) Mr. Davis said you wanted to see me about those Fourth Ward mortgages.

REGAN. Yeah. I want to make an assignment. I want to deed 'em over t' you, if ye don't mind.

EMILY. Deed them over to me? How do you mean?

REGAN. Put 'em in yer name. Let ye work 'em the way you want, give 'em t' ye—understand?

EMILY. But—I thought you were going to foreclose?

REGAN. I changed me mind.

EMILY. Why?

REGAN. (*Not looking at her, speaking with difficulty.*) I dunno. (*At window.*) When yer up against it—the way I am now—ye sort o' feel like squarin' ev'rythin' up. An' I thought, seein' ye was so int'rested in them folks down there, ye 'd like t' have an eye on 'em yerself an' keep 'em out o' trouble. They 're just like kids, ye know. They need lookin' after. (*A pause.*)

EMILY. (*Softly.*) Oh, Michael!

REGAN. (*Glancing up at her.*) Will ye do it, then?

EMILY. Yes, I 'll do it—if you want me to.

REGAN. (*Very business-like.*) All right. I had Hodges frame up an acceptance of the assignment. (*Taking it from envelope.*) Will ye look at it? It 's very short, ye see, but it covers the ground.

(*She looks at him, but when he holds out the paper she takes it and bends her head.*) Is there anythin' ye don't understand? I know them legal words is apt t' mix a lady up.

EMILY. (*Turning away to wipe her eyes without letting him see her.*) No, it 's quite clear—quite—

REGAN. Then would ye mind signin' it now? An' I 'll give it to Hodges in the mornin'.

EMILY. Where do I sign?

REGAN. There under my name—(*Gives her a pen.*) Look out, it 's sort of inky.

EMILY. It 's all right.

(*She takes the pen and signs the paper.*)

REGAN. There! *You 're* the boss now. You 're the boss o' the Fourth Ward! P'raps ye 'll be a better one than me!

EMILY. (*Simply.*) Thank you, Michael. (*A pause. He waves the paper to dry it.*) I—I suppose you 'll be going to Montreal very soon?

REGAN. Naw.

EMILY. Why not?

REGAN. (*Thumb towards window.*) Look at them bars. Ain't they a good reason?

EMILY. But, Michael—

REGAN. (*Interrupting.*) I might as well tell ye right now. I don't stand much show o' gettin' out o' here.

EMILY. You mean—on account of Don?

(*Slight pause.*)

REGAN. (*Looking away.*) Yeah.

(*Another pause.*)

EMILY. Then you don't know?

REGAN. Know what?

EMILY. That it 's all right? That he 's going to get well?

REGAN. (*Joyfully.*) Naw!

EMILY. That 's what Dr. Jameson says. He operated at two o'clock.

REGAN. To-day!

EMILY. And Don knew me before I left the hospital.

REGAN. (*Spontaneously.*) Aw gee, I 'm glad! I 'm awful glad!

EMILY. (*Looking away.*) Yes, it means a lot to you, too, does n't it?

REGAN. (*Suddenly shy.*) Well, I—I was n't thinkin' of meself just then.

EMILY. (*Still looking away.*) So you can probably go North, after all.

REGAN. Yeah. I s'pose I can. (*He has the package of papers* DAVIS *left.*) I s'pose I can. But—somehow I guess I won't.

(*He tears up the papers, carefully, methodically, and drops them in the basket.*)

EMILY. Michael, what—what are those papers?

REGAN. (*Looking at the pieces.*) My contracts with Montreal. Or wot 's left of 'em.

EMILY. You 're giving that up, too?

REGAN. It looks that way.

EMILY. But why? You don't have to.

REGAN. (*Bitterly.*) Can't I do a decent thing sometimes just fer the fun of it?

EMILY. You don't mean—you 're doing it for yourself?

REGAN. (*Sourly.*) Well, I ain't doin' it fer anyone else, am I? (*A pause.*)

EMILY. (*With growing emotion.*) Michael, I sided against you yesterday.

REGAN. (*Under his breath.*) I know that.

EMILY. Well, you 'd done so many dreadful things, and I knew how you felt about Don. When you told me, it all seemed to go together. I—I could n't think—

REGAN. Don't begin on that again! Please!

EMILY. But now—Michael, look at me!

(*He does so. A pause.*)

EMILY. (*Putting her hands on his shoulders.*) It 's all right. I 'm sure now. I know you did n't do it.

REGAN. (*Imploring.*) Ye don't mean ye believe me?

EMILY. Yes, and oh, Michael! You 've got to forgive me for not believing you before! (*She takes his hand.*)

REGAN. (*Roughly.*) Quit it! Don't!

EMILY. (*Taking both hands.*) But I 'll make up for it—you see! And now we 're going to turn our backs on everything that 's happened. We 're going to look up! We 're going to look ahead! We 're going to start all over, you and I, together!

REGAN. Aw quit it, don't talk that way! Go home! Go way, d' ye hear? Leave me be, I tell ye! Leave me be!

EMILY. I won't! I can't! I married you, Michael, and when a woman marries a man I believe she promises all sorts of things I 've never lived up to. But now you need me and I can help you—why, I think it 's a good time to begin!

REGAN. Ye don't mean yer willing t' do all that—fer me?

EMILY. Willing? Why, I want to. Don't you see? *I want to!* (*Pause.*)

REGAN. (*Collecting himself.*) Thank ye. Thank ye kindly. I know yer just saying that t' make things easy fer me, but I 'm—I 'm awful obliged to ye.

EMILY. I 'm *not*, Michael! You don't understand, you—

REGAN. (*Interrupting.*) Gee, I 've been sort o' feelin' our finish comin' on fer the last six months, an' now—all of a sudden—it 's right here. An' somehow I can look it in the face an' keep on smilin' just the same.

EMILY. What do you mean?

REGAN. You was right when you said that you an' me have got t' start all over again. Only this time we got t' start alone.

EMILY. But, Michael—

REGAN. Now, wait a second, Em'ly. I guess we need n't bother much. now we 're at the end. If anyone could a-pulled this off, why, we 'd a-been the ones. But we did n't have no show. We was in all wrong, dead wrong, from the very beginnin'.

EMILY. Was it—so wrong?

REGAN. Yeah. I was wrong in thinkin' I could ever make ye happy an' you was wrong—well, in thinkin' ye could ever let me try. I guess 't was my fault, mostly. You was doin' it fer a bunch o' scoopers, an' I was just out fer meself—like I always been. I might a-known there could n't be nothin' between us two—a guy born in a back room over a bar an' a lady like yerself—

EMILY. Don't! Please don't!

REGAN. D' ye know one thing I learned from bein' with ye this way? An' gee! I don't see just wot good it 's ever goin' t' do me! (*Slowly and with difficulty.*) Folks have t' love each other awful hard before they can get married. If you an' me had done that—why, we could a-stood up an' looked the world in the eye an' told it t' go t' hell! But as it is—

(*His voice breaks.*)

EMILY. Michael!

REGAN. It 's all right, the bill 's paid, the account 's closed. An' if there 's any fergivin' t' be done, I 'll do my share. I hope Gawd gives ye everythin' ye never could get from me—an' that ye live happy—an' grow old slow—an' good luck t' ye now, me darlin'! Good luck t' ye an' good-bye!

(*He turns away.*)

(*The door opens and* THE INSPECTOR *comes in.*)

THE INSPECTOR. Mr. Regan?

REGAN. Well?

THE INSPECTOR. That man, McCoy—

REGAN. (*Sharply.*) Huh?

THE INSPECTOR. It 's all right, sir. He let out the whole thing. (REGAN *smothers an exclamation.*) He went downstairs to Judge Swain and made an affidavit. The Judge has ordered your release and you can leave us, Mr. Regan, any time you like.

REGAN. Porky—!

EMILY. (*In a low voice, to* THE INSPECTOR.) *He* did it, then?

THE INSPECTOR. That 's what he 's sworn to, ma'am. (*A pause.*)

EMILY. Would you call my chauffeur? I 'm—I 'm going to take my husband home.

THE INSPECTOR. (*Softly.*) Sure, ma'am—sure. (*He goes out.*)

EMILY. (*Turning to* REGAN.) Michael, there 's something I 've never told you.

REGAN. (*Dully.*) Is there?

EMILY. I 've never told you, because I never knew it until now.

REGAN. Did n't ye?

EMILY. Can't you guess what it is?

REGAN. I 'm no good at guessin' when it comes t' you.

EMILY. All right, then, I 'll tell you. I think—I think—I think it 's going to be all right.

REGAN. *Wot 's* goin' to be all right?

(*She runs over to the clothes rack.*)

EMILY. Is this your overcoat?—(*Taking it from the rack.*) Here now—put it on! (*She holds it for him.*) And your hat—(*He starts to take it.*) Wait! I 'll show you how you 'll have to wear it now. (*She puts it on his head. He pushes it on one side.*) No—straight! (*She straightens it.*) Quite straight! It 's always bothered me before.

REGAN. (*Feeling it gingerly.*) Like that?

EMILY. Like that. Now take it off!

REGAN. Why?

EMILY. (*Half-laughing, half-crying.*) D' you think I 'm going to let you kiss me with it on?

(*He throws his hat across the room and catches her in his arms as the curtain falls.*)

HE AND SHE

BY

Rachel Crothers

Printed for the first time by permission of the author, Miss Rachel Crothers.

HE AND SHE

He and She represents the drama of married life in which the relations of husband and wife are modified by the rival claims of professional jealousy. It is one of the most striking of the plays which deal with the general question of woman's rights and responsibilities, of which its author has stood for some time as a representative in drama.

Rachel Crothers was born in Bloomington, Illinois, and graduated from the State Normal School. Her father, Dr. Eli Kirk Crothers, was a friend and contemporary of Lincoln, while her mother studied medicine after she was forty years of age, and became the first woman physician in that part of Illinois. In a letter to the editor written in response to his request for biographical details, Miss Crothers says:

"My interest in the stage was entirely foreign to the deeply religious conservative traditions of my family but began when I was very small, asserting itself through the writing of plays—the first one to be produced being *Every Cloud Has a Silver Lining, or the Ruined Merchant,* all five of the characters played by myself and a friend at the age of twelve—to an invited audience of amazed and admiring friends."

After her graduation from school, Miss Crothers studied dramatic art in Boston and New York and was for three seasons on the stage. She then began seriously writing plays. Her first play to be professionally produced was a clever one-act sketch, *The Rector,* played at the Madison Square Theatre, New York, April 3, 1902, dealing with the choice of a wife by a young clergyman. Then followed *The Three of Us,* performed at the Madison Square Theatre, October, 1906; *The Coming of Mrs. Patrick,* at the same theatre, October, 1907; *Myself Bettina,* first played by Maxine Elliott at Powers Theatre, Chicago, January, 1908; *A Man's World,* played by Mary Mannering at the Comedy Theatre, New York, Feb. 8, 1910; *The Herfords* (*He and She*) (1912); *Young Wisdom,* played by Mabel and Edith Talliaferro at the Criterion Theatre, New York, January, 1914; *Ourselves,* played by Grace Elliston at the Lyric Theatre, New York, November, 1913; *The Heart of Paddy Whack,* played by Chauncey Olcott at the Grand Opera House, New York, November, 1914. *Old Lady 31,* after a tryout on the road, opened at the Thirty-ninth Street Theatre, New York City, on October 30, 1916, and had a successful run. Her most recent plays were *A Little Journey,* which was first played at the Little Theatre, New York, December 26, 1918, and *39 East,* which opened at the Broadhurst Theatre, March 31, 1919.

He and She was first tried out on the road during the fall of 1911. It was then renamed *The Herfords* and was first played by the cast as here given at the Plymouth Theatre in Boston, February 5, 1912.

After extensive revision, the play was revived and produced at the Little Theatre, New York, February 12, 1920, under the title *He and She.* At this revival Miss Crothers herself played the part of "Ann Herford," Mr. Cyril Keightley that of "Tom Herford" and Miss Faire Binney that of "Millicent."

The most significant of Miss Crothers' plays are those in which she deals with a problem created by some demand of woman's nature. In *The Three of Us* she shows the strong sisterly affection of a woman for her younger brother who is hardly worthy of it but who is saved by the power of her love. In *A Man's World* she attacks the basis of social and moral law which treats the woman unfairly. In *Ourselves* she shows the responsibility of good women for the so-called double standard of morality. In *He and She* she draws in a masterly way the effect which the rivalry of a wife in an artistic profession has upon the relations of her husband and herself and also upon her treatment of her daughter.

A Man's World has been published by Richard Badger; *The Rector, Young Wisdom* and *The Three of Us* by Samuel French. *He and She* is now printed for the first time through the courtesy of the author, from a manuscript prepared especially by her for this collection. In order to reflect the changes made in the revival of 1920, in the Revised Edition, the entire play has been reprinted from a revised manuscript furnished by Miss Crothers.

NOTE TO THIRD EDITION.

In *Nice People,* first played at the Klaw Theatre, New York, March 2, 1921, Miss Crothers drew a strong picture of a certain form of social life which developed in this country after the Great War. It was a popular success. *Everyday,* which was first played in Atlantic City, October 27, 1921, while an interesting study of the revolt of a young girl against the stifling circumstances of her life in a small town, did not succeed. *Mary the Third* began on February 5, 1923, a long run at the Thirty-ninth Street Theatre, New York. It revealed the differences in the points of view of three generations of women toward the question of marriage. *Expressing Willie,* produced by the Equity Players, April 16, 1924, at the Forty-eighth Street Theatre, was a clever satire on the artificial efforts at self expression of certain social types.

Nice People was published in *Contemporary American Plays,* edited by A. H. Quinn, New York, 1923. *Mary the Third, Old Lady 31* and *A Little Journey* were issued together in one volume in 1923. *Expressing Willie, 39 East* and *Nice People* were published in one volume in 1924, also by Brentano.

Note to Fourth Edition.

A Lady's Virtue, first produced in Chicago, October, 1925, dealt with the character of the eternal courtesan, and her struggle with the claims of a wife who is not her mental equal. While not up to Miss Crothers' standard, it was a popular success. *Venus,* produced in December, 1927 in New York, dealt with an improbable situation and was quickly withdrawn.

The Heart of Paddy Whack and *Once Upon A Time* were published in 1925 by Samuel French.

Note to Fifth Edition.

In *Let Us Be Gay,* first produced at the Little Theatre, New York, February 21, 1929, Miss Crothers wrote one of the best plays of her career, and one of the popular successes of the season. It is a social comedy of fine quality, with brilliant dialogue, and marks the continued progress in Miss Crothers' art, since it reveals even a broader sympathy with the man's point of view in the relationship of marriage than was expressed in *He and She.* The play has been published by Samuel French (1929).

Note to Sixth Edition.

As Husbands Go, first produced March 5, 1931, was a striking contrast between the character of an American husband and that of an Englishman who had fallen in love with his wife. The triumph of the husband was skilfully secured through the impression he makes upon the lover, in one of the best comedy scenes in recent years. *When Ladies Meet* (October 6, 1932), drew a corresponding conflict between a wife and a young woman writer who had fallen in love with her husband. Both women act like persons of breeding and their meeting and parting were wrought out with Miss Crothers' usual skill in dialogue. *Susan and God,* first tried out in Philadelphia on April 12, 1937, and opening in New York, much revised, on October 18, was a delicious satire upon a charming but selfish woman, who tries to make a social asset out of the so-called Oxford Movement.

As Husbands Go and *When Ladies Meet* are published by Samuel French. For criticism of Miss Crothers' plays see A. H. Quinn's *A History of the American Drama from the Civil War to the Present Day,* Revised Edition, two volumes in one, published by Appleton-Century-Crofts, Inc., 1936, Vol. 2, pp. 50–61, 250–251, 333–334.

CAST OF CHARACTERS

Plymouth Theatre, Boston, February 5, 1912

TOM HERFORD, a sculptor........................Mr. Charles Waldron

ANN HERFORD, his wife........................Miss Viola Allen

DAISY HERFORD, his sister........................Miss Grace Elliston

MILLICENT, his daughter........................Miss Beatrice Prentice

DR. REMINGTON, his father-in-law........................Mr. George Fawcett

KEITH McKENZIE, his assistant........................Mr. John Westley

RUTH CREEL, his wife's friend........................Miss Jessie Izette

ELLEN, a maid........................Miss Emily Varian

HE AND SHE

ACT FIRST

Scene: The Herford Studio.

The room is in the basement floor of a large old fashioned house in lower New York—and shows that it has been made over and adapted to the needs of a sculptor.

At right center back are double doors opening into the workroom. At right of these doors is a recess showing it has been cut in. The ceiling of the half of the room which is towards the audience is much higher than the other part—showing that the room which is on the floor above has been used to give height to this part of the studio.

The break made in the ceiling is supported by an interesting old carved column—very evidently brought from Italy—and in the overhanging part of the wall is set a very beautiful old Italian frieze in bas relief—a few faded colors showing.

At lower left is a large studio window.

At lower right side a single door leading into hall. At upper left corner, a cupboard is built in, in harmony with the construction of the room, and showing, when opened, drawers and compartments for holding sculptors' tools, etc.

Before the window, at right center, is a scaffold built to hold a section of a frieze. At its base is a revolving table, holding modeling clay, tools, etc. In front of the scaffold is a short pair of steps. At centre, is a long table holding rolls of sketches, a desk set—a book or two, pencils, compasses, several pieces of modeling.

There are a number of chairs about and a piece of rich brocade in vivid coloring thrown over the back of one.

The room is simple, dignified, beautiful, full of taste and strength. Soft afternoon sunshine streams in from the wide window. KEITH MACKENZIE *and* TOM HERFORD *are lifting one section of a bas relief frieze about 3 by 5—and placing it on the scaffolding.*

MCKENZIE *is about 35, tall, good-looking, in a pleasing, common-place way; also wearing a sculptor's working clothes—but of a practical and not artistic sort.*

TOM HEREFORD *is 40, a fine specimen of the vigorous American-artist type. Virile, fresh, alive and generous in nature and viewpoint. He wears the stamp of confidence and success.*

TOM. (*As they lift the frieze.*) Come on! There she is! Put her over—no, this way, about half a foot. That's right. There! Let's have a look. (TOM *goes down to hanging switch and turns on the light. As he does so, he says*:) Wait! (*The lights are turned up.*) (*Turning to* KEITH.) What do you think.

KEITH. It's a great thing, Governor! Going to be a walk-away for you. You'll win it as sure as guns. I *know* it. I bet you land the $100,000.00 as sure as you're standing there, governor.

TOM. Oh, I don't know. The biggest fellows in the country are going in for this competition.

KEITH. Well— you're *one* of the biggest. *I* think you're *the* biggest—and you've turned out the best thing you've ever done in your life. (*Going to stand above table.*)

TOM. That's damned nice of you, McKenzie. It *does* look pretty good out here. Doesn't it? (*He goes up on the steps—to touch the frieze.*)

KEITH. (*After a pause.*) Governor.

TOM. (*Working at his frieze.*) Um?

KEITH. I want to ask you something. Not from curiosity—but because—I'd like to know for my own sake. You needn't answer of course—if you don't want to.

TOM. Go on. Fire away.

KEITH. Have you ever been sorry that Mrs. Herford is a sculptor—instead of just your wife?

TOM. Not for a minute.

KEITH. I've been thinking a lot about it all lately.

TOM. About you and Ruth. you mean?

KEITH. Yes. She'll marry me in the fall if I let her keep on working.

TOM. And?

KEITH. Well—I—Hang it all! I don't *want* her to. I can take care of her now. At first it was different—when I was grubbing along—but since I've been with you, you've put me on my feet. I'll never be *great*—I know that all right—but I can take care of her.

TOM. (*Working at frieze.*) But she *wants* to keep on, doesn't she?

KEITH. Yes, but—

TOM. Good Heavens, boy—you're not bitten with that bug I hope. "I want my girl by my own fireside to live for me alone."

KEITH. Oh—

TOM. Why Ruth Creel's a howling success—the way she's climbed up in that magazine—why in the name of Christopher, do you want her to stop?

KEITH. (*At right end of table, figuring mechanically on some papers on table.*) How can she keep on at that and keep house too?

TOM. Well they *do*, you know—somehow.

KEITH. Oh, Mrs. Herford's different. She's working right here with you—and her time is her own. But Ruth's tied down to office hours and it's slavery—that's what it is.

TOM. *She* doesn't think so. Does she?

KEITH. I want a home. I want children.

TOM. Of course. But that doesn't mean she'll have to give up her profession forever.

KEATH. Oh, I'm strong for women doing anything they want to do—in *general*—But when it's the girl you love and want to marry, it's different.

TOM. It ought not to be.

KEITH. When you come down to brass tacks—

ANN. (*Coming quickly in from the workroom, and stopping as she sees the frieze.*) Oh Tom!

(ANN HERFORD *is 38. Intensely feminine and a strong vibrating personality which radiates warmth and vitality. She wears a long linen working smock—a soft rich red in color. Her sleeves are rolled up and her general appearance shows that she is at work and has stopped only to look at* TOM'S *frieze.*)

KEITH. Looks great out here—doesn't it, Mrs. Herford?

ANN. Um.

KEITH. Aren't you—more sure now than ever it will win?

ANN. Um. — (*Starting to speak and checking herself.*)

TOM. What?

ANN. Nothing Your horses *are* marvelous, Tom. I wish we could see it all together—now. Don't you? The rest of the twenty sections—so we could see how much we—how much we—*feel* the running.

TOM. Don't you feel it in this piece?

ANN. Of course.

KEITH. I do—tremendously. I think it's wonderful. (*He goes into workroom.*)

TOM. Ann—what were you going to say a minute ago about the frieze?

ANN. A—I don't know.

TOM. Don't hedge. Several times lately you've started to say something and haven't got it out. What is it? Any suggestions?

ANN. How do you feel about it yourself, boy? Are you satisfied?

TOM. Does that mean you aren't?

ANN. I asked you.

TOM. Well—it's the best that's in me. Why? What's the matter? You don't like it after all.

ANN. Like it? It's a strong—noble—beautiful thing.

TOM. *But*—

ANN. Dearest—is it—just exactly what your first conception of it was? Has it turned out just as you first felt it?

TOM. Why yes—not absolutely in detail of course. It's improved a lot I think—in the working—but in the main, yes—it's *just* the same. Why do you say that?

ANN. You know of course, but—

TOM. Say it—Say it. What have you got in your mind?

ANN. I don't know that I can—but in the beginning it had a feeling of swiftness, of rushing—swirling—as if your soul were let loose in it, Tom—too big, too free to be held in and confined. But, somehow, now that it's finished—

TOM. Go on.

ANN. That wild thing has gone out of it. It's crystalized into something magnificent but a little conventional.

TOM. Good heavens, Ann, you can't call that *conventional?*

ANN. Well—orthodox then. It's noble of course—but that inexplainable thing which made it great—is *gone*—for me. Perhaps it's just me—my imagination—because I care so much.

TOM. It is imagination. It's much stronger than when I began.

ANN. Is it?

TOM. Of course. You're trying to put something fantastic into it which never was there at all. That's not *me*. What I've done I've got through a certain strong solid boldness. That's why I think this stands a good chance. It's the very best thing I've ever done, Ann, by all—

KIETH. (*Opening the workroom door.*) Governor—will you show Guido and me about something please—Just a minute? (*There is a slight pause.*) (*Tom looks at the frieze.*)

TOM. I don't see what you mean at all, dear girl. Thanks a lot—but I think you're wrong this time. (*He goes into workroom. Ann looks again at the frieze as* RUTH CREEL *comes in from hall.*)

ANN. (*Going quickly to* RUTH.) Oh, Ruth—bless you! (*She kisses her warmly.*)

RUTH. I came straight from the office and I'm dirty as a pig. (ANN *points to* TOM'S *frieze.*) Is that it? (ANN *nods.*) Well?

ANN. Oh, Ruth—I'm sick in the bottom of my soul. I hope—I hope—I'm wrong. I *must* be wrong. Tom knows better than I do; but—I can't help it. I tell myself I'm a fool—and the more I try to persuade myself the more it comes back. Ruth, it isn't the same. It isn't. What ever it was that lifted it above good work and made it a thing of inspiration—is gone. It's gone—*gone*.

RUTH. Have you—told Tom how you feel?

ANN. Just this minute. He says I'm wrong absolutely—that it's the best thing he's ever done.

RUTH. I hope to God you are wrong—but I bet you're not. You *know*. Did you—have you told him the other thing?

ANN. Not yet. But I've finished it.

RUTH. Absolutely?

ANN. I worked down here last night till three o'clock this morning.

RUTH. Well—how is it?

ANN. Oh, I don't dare think. It can't be as good as it seems to me.

RUTH. *Of course* it can. Why shouldn't it be? Aren't you going to offer it to him right away—before it's too late?

ANN. How *can* I? It frightens me to pieces to even think of it—but, oh,—my dear, my dear—it's alive and fresh and *new*. It is. It is. If he only would take it—my idea—and put his wonderful work—his wonderful execution into it.

RUTH. Perhaps he'll be *fired* with it—jump at it.

ANN. I'm afraid, he won't—and I'm afraid of *this* for him. It would nearly kill him to lose. He's counting on winning. Keith and everybody are so dead sure of him.

RUTH. Show him yours for goodness—

ANN. Be careful. He'll be back in a minute.

RUTH. I'll skip upstairs and make myself presentable.

ANN. Go in my room, dear. (RUTH *goes out through hall.* TOM *and* KEITH *come back from workroom.* ANN *goes to* TOM *—they stand a moment—looking at the frieze.* ANN *slaps* TOM *on the back, without speaking, and goes on into workroom.*)

KEITH. (*After a pause.*) I agree with you in general, governor. But when it comes down to the girl you love and want to marry, it's different.

TOM. Why is it?

KEITH. The world has got to have homes to live in and who's going to make 'em if the women don't do it?

TOM. (*Smiling at* KEITH *tolerantly.*) Oh, come—come.

KEITH. Do you mean to say you wouldn't rather your sister Daisy was married and keeping her own house instead of working here as your secretary?

TOM. But she *isn't* married— and she won't live with Ann and me unless it's a business proposition. I respect her *tremendously* for it—tremendously.

KEITH. Well, Daisy's a big, plucky, independent thing anyway—but Ruth's a little delicate fragile—

TOM. With a mind bigger than most of the *men* you know.

KEITH. Oh, mind be damned. I want a wife.

DAISY. (*Coming in from the hall.*) Oh—Tom—it's out here. How corking!

(DAISY HERFORD *is twenty-eight—strong, wholesome, handsome, with the charm of health and freshness. She wears a severe serge gown and carries a pencil and stenographer's pad.*)

TOM. Well—sis, how do you like it?

DAISY. I adore it. I hope you haven't any doubts now about winning.

TOM. I've plenty of 'em—but somehow today it looks as if it stood a pretty good chance.

DAISY. Chance! I never was so sure of anything in my life.

KEITH. Daisy—maybe you know just *what* ought to be *where* with *this stuff*.

DAISY. I've been itching to get at it. Let's put all the tools on that side.

KEITH. I *have* started.

DAISY. And throw the trash in here. (*Pushing the box with her foot.*)

KEITH. Can you help me now?

DAISY. Yes. Tom, do you want me to write to the Ward people about that marble again?

TOM. Yes I do. Shake them up. Tell 'em if it isn't here by the first of the month I won't take it.

DAISY. (*Making a note in her note-book.*) Um—um.

MILLICENT HERFORD *rushes in from hall at left.* MILLICENT *is 16—pretty—eager—full of vitality and will—half child, half woman. She is charmingly dressed in an afternoon frock and picture hat and is at the moment happy and exhilarated.*)

MILLICENT. Father, where's mother?

TOM. In the work-room. But you can't go in. (*As* MILLICENT *starts to work-room.*)

MILLICENT. Why not?

TOM. She's finishing something and said not to let *any* one stop her.

MILLICENT. Oh *dear!* I think I *might*. It's awfully important. Couldn't I just poke my head in the door a minute?

TOM. Not for a second.

MILLICENT. Sakes, I wish Mother wouldn't work in my Christmas vacation. It's an awful bore. Don't you think she might stop the little while I'm at home, Aunt Daisy?

DAISY. None of my business. Don't ask me.

KEITH. If you ask *me*—yes I think she might.

TOM. That's nonsense. Your mother's doing about everything that *can* be done to make your vacation a success, isn't she?

MILLICENT. Yes, of course.

TOM. Then I don't see that there's any reason why she shouldn't be allowed a little time for herself.

MILLICENT. But I want her *now*. Aren't my new pumps stemmy, Aunt Daisy?

DAISY. Aren't they what?

MILLICENT. Stemmy. Wake up, Aunt Daisy. Oh, the luncheon was gorgeous. All the girls were there and the matinee was heavenly.

KEITH. What play?

MILLICENT. "The Flame of Love." You needn't laugh, father. It's the best play in town. The leading man is a peach. Honestly, he's the best looking thing I ever saw in my life. We were all crazy about him. Belle Stevens took off her violets and threw them right *at* him. She makes me tired, though. I don't think seventeen is so terribly much older than sixteen, do you, Aunt Daisy?

DAISY. (*Still at the cupboard.*) It depends on whether you're sixteen or seventeen—how much older it is.

MILLICENT. I don't care—I wouldn't wear a ring as big as hers if I had one. Oh, Aunt Daisy, may I borrow your earrings? (*Going to* DAISY.)

DAISY. Help yourself.

MILLICENT. Thanks, you're a duck. I could combostulate you for that. How much longer do you think mother will be, daddie?

TOM. Couldn't say.

MILLICENT. Well, tell her I *have* to see her the minute she comes out. Don't forget. (*She hurries off through hall.*)

TOM. She's grown up over night somehow. I can't get used to it.

KEITH. And she went away to school a few months ago just a girl. Amazing, isn't it?

DAISY. Not a bit. What do you expect? She's free now—cut loose. Boarding school does that pretty quickly.

TOM. I suppose so—and I suppose it's good for her. (*Looking at the frieze he goes into the work-room.*)

KEITH. The Governor's darned cheerful about the frieze to-day.

DAISY. I should think he *would* be. It's great. (KEITH *and* DAISY *go on clearing out cupboard.*)

KEITH. I'd give a good deal to know what Mrs. Herford actually thinks of it.

DAISY. Why she *loves* it.

KEITH. She looks at it with such a sort of a—I don't know. I can't help wondering if she *is* so dead certain of it as the rest of us are.

DAISY. I hope she doesn't discourage Tom. After all *he* likes it and he knows more about it than anybody else. Ann's criticism is wonderful, of course, but still Tom *is the artist*.

KEITH. You're just as jealous for your brother as you can be, aren't you, Daisy? All right for the missus to be clever, but you want Tom to be supreme in everything, don't you?

DAISY. He *is*. (*Leaning over the box.*)

KEITH. You're a brick. Daisy, have you ever been in love in your life?

DAISY. What do you mean? (*Lifting her head—startled and embarrassed.*)

KEITH. I've been thinking an awful lot lately about this business of married women working. What do *you* think of it—now honestly?

DAISY. What difference does it make—what I think?

KEITH. Of course, there's no reason on earth why you shouldn't be in it. You don't care a hang for men—and—

DAISY. You mean men don't care a hang for me.

KEITH. No I don't. I don't mean that at all. But you're so independent men are sort of afraid of you.

DAISY. Oh, don't apologize. You mean I'm a plain, practical girl meant to take care of myself.

KEITH. Well—that's what you *want* to be, isn't it?

DAISY. Never mind about me. Let's change the subject.

KEITH. You needn't be so touchy. I talk awfully frankly about my affairs and you never say a word about yourself.

DAISY. Why should I? I'm not interesting and you're not interested.

KEITH. I am too. You're the best pal a fellow ever had. I don't know any other girl I could have worked with all his time—day in and day out and not either been dead sick of or sort of—you know sweet on, in a way.

DAISY. You needn't rub it in.

KEITH. Why, Daisy, old girl, what *is* the matter? What in the dickens are you so huffy about?

DAISY. Just let me and my idiosyncrasies alone, please.

KEITH. Heavens! Can't I say what I think?

DAISY. No, you can't. I don't want to hear it. I know just what I seem like to other people—so there's no use explaining me to myself.

KEITH. All I meant was if you *were* in love would you give up your job and—

DAISY. But I'm *not* in love, so stop thinking about it.

KEITH. Gosh! I thought *you* had common sense, but you're just as queer as the rest of them. What I want to know is—if a girl loves a man well enough to marry him why in hell she can't stay at home and—

DAISY. What's the matter? (*As* KEITH *cuts his finger on the tool he is holding.*) Did you cut your finger?

KEITH. Not much.

DAISY. (*With a sudden tenderness.*) Let me see.

KEITH. It's nothing.

DAISY. It is too. Hold still. I'll tie it up for you. (*She ties his finger with her own handkerchief.*) Anything the —hold still. Anything the matter with one of your fingers would put you out of commission.

KEITH. Might be a good idea. I don't think Ruth believes in me much. Doesn't think I'll get much farther.

DAISY. (*Warmly.*) I don't know why. I think you've got plenty for her to believe in. Well—speaking of angels. How are you, Ruth? (*As* RUTH *comes in from the hall.*)

KEITH. Oh—hello, dear.

RUTH. Hello. What's the matter?

KEITH. Nothing.

DAISY. KEITH was waxing emphatic about *you* and over emphasized a finger. (*She turns back to cupboard.*)

RUTH. I'm sorry. (*Touching* KEITH'*s hand as he comes down to her.*)

KEITH. How are you?

RUTH. Dead. This day's been twenty-four hours long. (*Sitting at left end of table.*)

KEITH. (*Coming down to* RUTH.) *Has* anything gone wrong?

RUTH. No—but a young author from the eloquent West has been fighting me since nine o'clock this morning.

KEITH. What about?

RUTH. He's got a perfectly magnificent story—or idea for one, rather—but it's so crudely written that it's impossible to publish it.

DAISY. I suppose you can re-write it for him.

RUTH. No, he won't let me. Wants to do it all himself. Oh, he's so stubborn and so funny and so splendid. So outlandishly conceited and so adorably boyish I wanted to slap him one minute and kiss him the next.

KEITH. Why didn't you do both and you'd have got what you wanted.

RUTH. I was afraid to risk it.

KEITH. (*Nodding towards* TOM'S *frieze.*) Doesn't that hit you in the eye?

RUTH. Awfully like Tom, isn't it? Strong and splendid.

KEITH. What are you thinking—

RUTH. Oh, nothing—only I wish Ann had—I wish Ann had gone in for this competition too.

KEITH. What?

DAISY. Why on earth should she?

RUTH. Why shouldn't she?

DAISY. Ruth, you're daffy about Ann. Always have been.

KEITH. She does beautiful work for a woman—but ye gods—she's not in *this* class.

RUTH. And she never *will* be if she's held back and told she's limited. I think she has genius and the sooner she makes a bold dash and tries for something big the better.

DAISY. Nonsense! Tom's pushed her and believed in her always. You can't say *he's* held her back.

RUTH. (*To* KEITH.) I've heard *you* say she has genius—lots of times.

KEITH. So she has—in a way. She has more imagination than the governor, but, great Peter, when it comes to execution and the real thing she isn't *in* it with him. How could she be? She's a woman.

RUTH. Don't be any more anti-deluvian or prehistoric than you can help, Keith. Don't *you* think Ann's more original and really innately gifted than Tom is, Daisy?

DAISY. *I do not.* She's terribly good. Of course—no doubt about that—but good Lord, Tom's *great*—a really *great* artist. (DAISY *starts to hall door.*)

RUTH. Why do you go, Daisy?

DAISY. Must. I have bushels of letters to get off.

RUTH. You look as fresh and rosy as if you were just beginning the day. How do you do it?

DAISY. Oh, I'm not expressing my soul in my job—merely earning by bread and butter. I suppose that's why I look so husky at twilight. (DAISY *goes out through hall.*)

RUTH. (*Looking after* DAISY.) Do you know—I don't believe Daisy likes me any more.

KEITH. (*Sitting on left end of table near* RUTH.) Kiss me. (RUTH *leans her head towards* KEITH. *He kisses her cheek.*)

RUTH. She's so marvelously good-natured—queer she's getting snappy at me lately.

KEITH. I'm awfully glad you came.

RUTH. Does it hurt? (*Touching his finger.*)

KEITH. Not much.

RUTH. I wonder why she doesn't like me?

KEITH. What are you talking about? I'm asked to stay to dinner, too.

RUTH. That's nice.

KEITH. I can't bear to see you so tired, dear.

RUTH. I'll be all right when I have some tea.

KEITH. This time next year you could be in your own home—away from those damnable office hours and the drudgery —if you only would. If you only *would.*

RUTH. It never seems to occur to you that I might be a little less tired but bored to death without my job.

KEITH. If you really cared for me the way you used to—you wouldn't be bored.

RUTH. Oh let's not begin that.

KEITH. But do you love me, dear. *Do* you?

RUTH. I've been telling you so for a pretty long time, haven't I.

KEITH. Are you tired of it?

RUTH. There isn't any reason on earth why you should *think* I am.

KEITH. Well, I do think it. I worry about it all the time. I know you're brilliant and successful—but you—after all you say you love me—and I don't see— (*He stops with a sigh.*) You're awful pretty today. Your face is like a flower.

RUTH. Oh—

KEITH. Yes, it is. I love you so.

RUTH. Dear old boy! I love you.

KEITH. Do you, Ruth? *Do* you?

RUTH. I've never loved anyone else. You've filled all that side of my life and you've made it beautiful. We must hang together dear— (*Putting both her hands over one of his.*) And understand and give things up for each other. But it must be fifty-fifty, dearest. I can make you happy, Keith—Oh I can. And I'll be so happy and contented with you if you'll only— (KEITH *turns away impatiently.*) I've never had a home for a minute—in my whole life—nor a relative since I was three—of any sort or description—not a soul who belonged to me but you.

KEITH. I want you to have the sweetest little home in the world.

RUTH. Think of having our own little dinners and all the nice people we know at our table—*ours.*

KEITH. Yes—but—*how can you do it if you're away all day?*

RUTH. Oh Keith, dear boy, you—the whole trouble is you think housekeeping is making a home—and the two things aren't the same at all—at all, at all.

KEITH. Well, they can't be separated.

RUTH. Oh, yes, they can. Love—love makes a home—not tables and chairs. We can *afford* more if I work, too. We can *pay* some one to do the stuff you think I ought to do. And you'll go on climbing up in your work and I'll go on in mine and we'll both grow to something and *be* somebody and have something to give each other. It will be fair—we'll be pulling together—pals and lovers like Tom and Ann. That's why they're so ideally happy.

KEITH. Yes, but we're different. We couldn't—

RUTH. You're not fair, Keith.

KEITH. Great guns, Ruth—neither are you.

RUTH. I am. I am perfectly. (*Their voices rise together.*)

TOM. (*Coming back from the workroom.*) What's the row? Hello, Ruthie Creel.

RUTH. (*Giving her hand to* TOM.) Hello, you nice Tommie Herford. I always lose my heart to you in your working clothes.

TOM. You have my heart in any kind of clothes.

RUTH. Keith's cross with me, Tom. You're much nicer to me than he is.

KEITH. You never spring any of your revolutionary speeches on Herford. You save all your really soothing remarks for me.

RUTH. Tom, am I revolutionary? Aren't I just a little cooing dove?

TOM. Absolutely.

DAISY. (*Coming in from hall.*) Dr. Remington's here. Millicent's bringing him down. But he says he wants to sit upstairs on the parlor sofa, not down in the cellar. Tom, will you sign these letters now? (*Daisy puts the letters on the table—*TOM *goes towards the table as* MILLICENT *comes in from the hall bringing* DR. REMINGTON *by the hand.*)

(DR. REMINGTON *is 65. He is inclined to portliness and his keen humor and kindliness are combined with an understanding and wisdom which make him a very strong and a very lovable man. His manner and speech are a little deliberate. He has a twinkling readiness to tease but the weight and dignity of a successful and important physician.*)

TOM. Hello—hello—hello.

REMINGTON. How are you?

KEITH. (*Taking* REMINGTON'S *overcoat.*) How are you, Dr. Remington? (RUTH *comes to the doctor to take his hat and stick.*)

REMINGTON. Hello, McKenzie. And here's that pretty little Ruth thing—knowing so much it makes my head ache.

RUTH. So long as it's your head and not mine I don't mind.

MILLICENT. Oh, thank you for the chocolates, grandfather. They're just the kind I adore. I could absolutely combostulate you— (*Giving him a violent hug.*) Five pounds, daddie.

TOM. You're a fine doctor!

REMINGTON. Chocolate's about the best medicine I know of if you want a girl to love you. Where's your mother?

MILLICENT. In the cave. (*Pointing to workroom.*)

REMINGTON. Can't she be excavated? Go and dig her out.

MILLICENT. They won't let me. You do it.

REMINGTON. Hasn't anybody got the courage to do it? (KEITH *starts towards the door with box.*)

DAISY. Not me.

REMINGTON. Well, McKenzie, go and tell her to let the work go to thunder and come and see her dad. (KEITH *goes into workroom.*) Is that the thing that's going to get the hundred thousand for you?

TOM. If—yes.

REMINGTON. Well, go to it—boy. I hope you hit it. (*Sitting in the large chair at left.*)

TOM. Thanks. I'm doing my durndest. Daisy, you've got some of these dimensions wrong. Keith will have to give them to you again.

DAISY. Oh, I'm sorry.

REMINGTON. It's a good thing you're working for your own brother, Daisy—nobody else would have you.

DAISY. You're the only person in the whole world who isn't impressed with my business ability.

REMINGTON. Stuff! I wager you say in your prayers every night—Oh, Lord, deliver me from this job and get me a good husband.

DAISY. (*Laughing with the others and going to* REMINGTON.) That's a very stemmy tie you're wearing. Do you get me?

REMINGTON. Not exactly. All I know is I'd rather be stemmy than seedy.

KEITH. (*Opening the workroom door.*) Don't you want me to carry that in for you, Mrs. Herford?

ANN. (*From within.*) No, no—I'd rather do it myself.

KEITH. It's too heavy for you.

ANN. No it isn't. (ANN *comes in carrying the figure of a woman in the nude —about a foot high. The figure is in wet clay and stands on a modeling board.*)

TOM. Steady there! Steady! Let me take it.

ANN. Don't touch it!

REMINGTON. Hello there!

ANN. Hello, daddy! I couldn't come out until I finished my lady. Isn't she nice? She's ready to be cast now. Come and look at her, Tom. She isn't so bad?

TOM. She looks pretty good to me.

REMINGTON. She looks a little chilly to me. Why don't you put a full suit of clothes on one of 'em—just for a change, Ann?

ANN. You nice, horrid, sweet, adorable, cross old thing! Why didn't you come yesterday. I don't see why I love you so when you never do anything I want you to.

REMINGTON. If I did I wouldn't be half as irresistible. Aren't you going to stop for the day now and pay a little attention to me?

ANN. I *am.*

MILLICENT. Mother, when can I see you? Alone I mean.

ANN. After awhile. Have you had a nice day, dear?

MILLICENT. Gorgeous! But I have to see you about something.

ANN. You do? (*Holding* MILLICENT.) Look at her—dad. Hasn't she grown?

MILLICENT. Mother, may I stay home from school one more day?

ANN. Gracious! Is that what you want to see me about?

MILLICENT. That's just one thing. Can't I, mother? All the girls are staying over. Mayn't I? Please—please.

ANN. I have to think a little. Let's wait and talk it over. Daisy, aren't we going to have some tea?

DAISY. It will be ready in a minute.

REMINGTON. Thank God! Then we'll go upstairs.

ANN. No, down here—it's much nicer. You'll have to get used to it, dad.

MILLICENT. Well—you be thinking—but you be thinking—*yes*—for I've just *got* to stay over. I've just got to. It would be perfectly ridiculous if I didn't. (*She goes out through hall.*)

REMINGTON. (*Nodding after* MILLICENT.) Getting more like you every day, Ann.

ANN. She's *your* grandchild, you know.

REMINGTON. I like 'em that way. I'd rather she was stubborn as a mule than have a wabbly spine.

ANN. (*Taking off her smock.*) But a little wabbling once in a while is rather a pleasant thing to live with. For instance, it would make me very happy indeed if you wabbled enough to admit that this is a beautiful studio and that having it in the house where we live is the most sensible thing in the world.

REMINGTON. It would be all right if you'd stay upstairs and mind your own business. Tom, if you don't look out you'll be so mixed up you'll be upstairs keeping house and Ann will be downstairs keeping shop.

TOM. I don't know how I'd keep house—but Ann could keep shop all right.

REMINGTON. Is that the way you feel about it, McKenzie? When you're married are you going to stay at home and polish up while Ruth goes on running the magazine?

KEITH. It looks as if that's about the way it'll have to be.

RUTH. (*Bringing the cake down to table.*) That's a splendid suggestion, Dr. Remington. Keith thinks somebody's got to do it for a successful marriage—and *I* won't—so why not you, dear? (*Pointing at* KEITH.) (KEITH *looks at* RUTH *and turns away in hopeless disgust.*)

REMINGTON. (*Winking at* RUTH *and lowering his voice to her.*) Keep at it. He'll come to it. (ANN *laughs as she cuts the cake.*)

KEITH. I don't see that it's so funny.

REMINGTON. (*Going to table to get a piece of cake.*) You bet it's not funny. Daisy, would you like your husband to wash the dishes if you happened to be too much occupied to do it yourself?

DAISY. I'd kill him if he did. (*Bringing the cream and sugar to large table.*)

REMINGTON. Oh—well—with one perfectly normal woman in the room I'm much more comfortable. (*He settles himself elaborately in his chair at left.*)

KEITH. I'm serious. I'd like to know if there's anything queer or preposterous in a fellow wanting a girl to give up hard, slavish work and let him take care of her when she marries him.

RUTH. When she wants to do the work. Don't leave that out.

TOM. I don't see that you, Keith, or any other fellow has got any kick coming so long as the girl makes you happy.

KEITH. I'd like to hear your angle on it if you don't mind, doctor.

RUTH. Yes. Keith loves to hear his mid-Victorian ideas well supported.

REMINGTON. Oh, I'm not so moth-eaten as I may look. In fact, I'm a damned sight more advanced than you women are. You're still yelling about your right to do anything on land or sea you want to do. We gave you that long ago.

ANN. So nice of you!

RUTH. (*Sitting below the table at right.*) Why talk about it all then? What else is there to it?

REMINGTON. Put this in your pipe. The more women make good—the more they come into the vital machinery of running the world, the more they complicate their own lives and the more tragedies they lay up for themselves.

RUTH. The more they escape—you mean.

ANN. (*As she pours the tea.*) There isn't a single hard thing that can happen to a woman that isn't made easier by being able to make her own living. And you know it.

REMINGON. Oh. It's a hopeless subject for conversation. What everybody says is true. There's the rub.

DAISY. Two?

REMINGTON. Three. (KEITH *gives a cup of tea to* REMINGTON.)

TOM. Go on. What were you going to say?

ANN. Yes, go on, dad.

REMINGTON. (*To Ann.*) You hang on to yourself then till I get through. The development of women hasn't changed the laws of creation.

ANN. Oh yes it has. (REMINGTON *looks at her.*) Sorry. Go on.

REMINGTON. Sex is still the strongest force in the world. (*He looks at* ANN *again.*)

ANN. (*Smiling.*) Go on.

REMINGTON. And no matter how far she goes she doesn't change the fundamental laws of her own—

TOM. Individuality?

RUTH. Type?

DAISY. Character?

KEITH. Ego.

RUTH. Psychology.

ANN. Species.

TOM. Breed.

DAISY. Spots.

REMINGTON. *No!*—Mechanism—mechanism. And when the sensitive—involved—complex elements of a woman's nature become entangled in the responsibility of a man's work—and the two things fight for first place in her—she's got a hell of a mess on hand.

ANN. But her psychological mechanism *has* changed.

REMINGTON. No.

ANN. Yes.

TOM. Yes, I think it has.

KEITH. It couldn't.

RUTH. But it *has*. Women who are really doing things nowadays are an absolutely different breed from the one-sided domestic animals they used to be.

ANN. But men don't realize how deeply and fiercely creative women love their work.

REMINGTON. That's just it—Just what I'm getting at. A woman of genius puts in her work the same fierce love she puts into her child or her man. That's where her fight is—for one or the other of 'em has got to be the stronger in her. It isn't a question of her *right* to do things—nor her ability—God knows—plenty of 'em are beating men at their own jobs now. Why, I sometimes think she'll go so far that the great battle of the future will be between the sexes for supremacy. But I tell you—she has tragedies ahead of her—the tragedy of choice between the two sides of her own nature.

RUTH. Well, thank you—I'll take any and all of the hard things that go *with* my job—but none of the ones that come from being a dub and giving it up.

REMINGTON. How about you, Daisy? Could any man on earth make you stop typewriting and live for him alone?

DAISY. Oh, I'm not in this class. Ann and Ruth both have men to depend on if they want them. I'm taking care of myself because I've *got* to—and I must say this soul tragedy of choice stuff makes me a little tired. (*She starts toward hall.*)

REMINGTON. (*Stopping* DAISY *by taking her hand.*) If I were twenty or thirty years younger, I'd go in for you strong.

DAISY. Yes, I know—I'm just the kind that *older* men appreciate very deeply. (*She goes out.*)

REMINGTON. Poor Daisy.

ANN. Poor Daisy. She's the happiest, most independent thing in the world. (*Straightening the things on the table —*KEITH *having taken the tea tray away.*)

RUTH. Much to be envied. No strings to *her* independence.

KEITH. And so cocky and spunky—nobody can even ask her if she's ever been in love.

REMINGTON. Sure sign she has been then.

TOM. But she never has.

REMINGTON. How do you know?

TOM. I've been pretty close to her all my life. No blighted bud about Daisy.

REMINGTON. She's putting up a darned good bluff, I must say.

RUTH. Bluff? What do you mean?

ANN. Father thinks there isn't a girl alive who wouldn't rather have a beau than a job.

REMINGTON. I do. And Daisy *looks* so self-reliant she *has* to be cocky to keep up appearances. Under her skin, she's not half the man that little lady-like looking thing Ruth is.

RUTH. Now, Dr. Remington, you may go upstairs.

REMINGTON. I haven't time now. I've wasted it all down here.

RUTH. Oh, come and look at the living room just a minute. It's too beautiful.

REMINGTON. Has it got a carpet on it yet?

ANN. Yes, absolutely finished.

REMINGTON. Because I don't mind saying my feet are like ice from this confounded brick floor.

RUTH. Oh, the beautiful tiles!

REMINGTON. I'll take a little less Italian beauty and a little more American comfort in mine. (RUTH, REMINGTON *and* KEITH *go out through hall.*)

TOM. (*Stopping* ANN *as she starts with the others.*) Ann—about this thing. Why in the name of heaven didn't you say you were disappointed in it long ago?

ANN. I kept hoping each day I was mistaken; that what I missed would come back. But when I saw it out here—I'm afraid of it, Tom.

TOM. Afraid of what? That I'll fail? Lose it? (ANN *nods.*) Nonsense! You're tired of it. There can't be such a change in it as all that. The idea's absolutely the same and I've *worked* as I never—

ANN. I know. I know! And oh, the beauty—the beauty of the work! That's the pity.

TOM. Pity?

ANN. I mean somebody without *half* your skill as an artist may have an idea—an *idea* that's *new.*

TOM. Oh bosh! Nothing can be done, anyhow. It's too late. Besides, I don't agree with you. I honestly do not, Ann. I know you're saying this because you're trying to boost me and get the best out of me; but the thing's done, you know. Don't confuse me. I must go on now. What's the use of talking about it? It's too late.

ANN. No, it isn't.

TOM. It is. Of course it is. You can't expect me to begin all over again and put into it a subtle intangible something I don't even feel. Damn it? It will have to fail then.

ANN. (*Taking hold of Tom quickly.*) It can't. You've got to win, Tom. You've *got* to. It's the most important thing you've ever done. Think of where it will put you. Think of the money.

TOM. I *have* thought. I've done the best that's *in* me, I tell you. It *is* the best, the very best I've ever—

ANN. But it isn't. It isn't. It isn't as great as your last two things—

TOM. Oh—

ANN. Tom—listen—you don't know how hard it is to say it. I'd rather you won this than anything that could possibly happen. You know that. Don't you?

TOM. Of course. But this isn't getting anywhere. It will have to go in as it stands.

ANN. Wait—I—I've wanted to talk to you about something for a long time—but I wasn't sure—and now I *am.*

TOM. Well—

MILLICENT. (*Coming back through hall.*) Thank goodness, mother. I can't wait any longer.

ANN. (*To* MILLICENT.) Oh, just a minute, dear.

TOM. No, that's all right. There's nothing more to be said.

ANN. I appreciate what you mean—yes I do. But it doesn't get me. And all I can do is to go after it as I see it. (*He goes into workroom.* ANN *stands looking at the frieze.*)

MILLICENT. (*Pulling Ann toward table.*) Mother—come here. Mother, *please.* Why—what I wanted to—sit down. (*Putting* ANN *into a chair above the long table.*) Every *one* of the girls are staying over tomorrow. It looks as if you were having such a slow time that you didn't have anything to do *but* go back to school if you don't stay. And I want—Why Fanny's going to have a party tomorrow night—just a little one, and I want to have eight of them to dinner first. (*Sitting at right end of table.*)

ANN. Oh—

MILLICENT. Only eight. You see, Fanny's brother's home, too, and—you see it's—Everybody has dinners and things you know before they go to the dance, you know, and—will you, Mother? Can't I?

ANN. But dearest you've done so much since you've been home. You can't get back to school too soon. New York is dreadful. It really is! The sensible mothers can't compete with the idiotic ones who let girls do all these silly things.

MILLICENT. Don't be foolish, Mother.

ANN. And school does begin tomorrow. And they expect—

MILLICENT. They don't expect us to be back. All the really smart girls stay over. It's only the deadly slow ones who are there on time. Please, mother—*please.* There'll only be eight of us; and Fanny's done so much for me I think it's as little as I could do to have her brother to dinner. Don't you?

ANN. Is he nice?

MILLICENT. Yes he is. He's older, you know and more fun. He got full dress clothes this Christmas—long tails, you know, and he looks perfectly—Mother, you're not listening. (ANN'*s eyes have gone back to the frieze again.*)

ANN. Yes, I am dear—Yes I am. Full dress clothes.

MILLICENT. Well—May I?

ANN. Dearest—I may be frightfully busy tomorrow. I may have to do the most important thing I've ever done in my life and if I do it would be awfully hard to have—

MILLICENT. Oh, now mother! Fanny's mother's had a party or something for her *every* single night. She took her to the Plaza to dance after the matinee today and I've never been to a hotel or any exciting place in my life. You try to keep me so young mother and, jiminy cricket, I'm sixteen.

ANN. Positively ancient.

MILLICENT. Well—sixteen's old enough for *any* thing. Will you mother—please —*please.* (*Kissing her mother's throat.*)

ANN. But what would I do if I had to do this other thing?

MILLICENT. What other thing? Can't it wait?

ANN. No it can't. That's just it. Your father may—I may be working with him all day tomorrow.

MILLICENT. You needn't have such a terribly *elaborate* dinner,—you know, but I'm crazy to do it. In fact I just have to. I've already asked most of them and they're dying to come.

ANN. You didn't, Kitten—how could you?

MILLICENT. But Mother, it's so *important* —and I don't see how I can get out of it now. You wouldn't want me to be compromised or anything, would you?

ANN. (*Laughing and kissing Millicent.*) You blessed baby—you ought to be spanked.

MILLICENT. You're an angel, mummie. You will—won't you? (*Putting her cheek against* ANN'*s.*)

ANN. What have you got in your ears?

MILLICENT. Earrings of course.

ANN. Heavens! Take them off.

MILLICENT. Oh, *mother!* All the girls wear them.

ANN. Take them off!

MILLICENT. But they have so much style.

ANN. Style your granny! Take them off or I'll bite 'em off. (MILLICENT *squirms and giggles as* ANN *bites her ears.*)

MILLICENT. Wait—wait. I will. I think you're mean to make me. You have such terribly strict ideas.

ANN. Your ears are much prettier than those things. Can't you understand that nothing is so attractive as just being natural? Why cover up with stuff like that?

MILLICENT. You *are* funny! You'll stay at home and meet everybody tomorrow night, won't you? I want them to see you. You are sweet, mummy.

ANN. Do you love me a lot?

MILLICENT. Of course. (*Kissing* ANN.)

ANN. (*Rising suddenly and going to look at the frieze.*) Oh, I'm so unhappy.

MILLICENT. Why? What's the matter? I should think you'd be tickled to death if father's going to get all that money.

TOM. (*Coming in from the workroom quickly.*) You say— (*He stops seeing* MILLICENT.)

MILLICENT. Aren't you coming up, now to plan it all?

ANN. In a few—

TOM. Go on Millicent. (MILLICENT *skips out.*) Why didn't you speak the minute you saw it go wrong—or thought you did?

ANN. I was never *sure,* until today, dear.

TOM. I don't agree with you at all but still it isn't exactly inspiring—knowing you think I'm going to fail.

ANN. Tom—I'm sorry.

TOM. It's all right—but you know I care more what you think than anybody in the world and—I—it's sort of a knockout.

ANN. I had to tell you the truth—when I *was* sure. I *had* to. Tom—listen—since you've been working at this an idea has come to me. At first I thought the idea was too big for me—that I never could carry it out—and then I said I won't *let* myself be afraid—and it's grown and grown night and day. Last night I finished it—down here—

TOM. The—

ANN. The drawings—I want you to look at them—and if—if you like it—if you think the idea is better than yours I want you to take it—use it, instead of yours.

TOM. Why Ann, you're not serious. (*She nods.*) Good heavens, child, you know —you know how tremendous this thing is as well as I do.

ANN. Yes I do! But I tell you my idea is big. Oh, I knew you'd look like that when I told you. You can't believe it of course—but Tom—. It's there—something vital and *alive*—with a strange charm in it. And I offer it to you dear—if you want it.

TOM. (*Taking her in his arms strongly and kissing her passionately.*) You generous darling! It's like you to do this. You dear—I love you for it.

ANN. (*Responding warmly to his love.*) I want you to have it. It's more than I ever dared dream I could do.

TOM. But darling—you couldn't possibly do anything for a scheme as big as this.

ANN. Why do you take that for granted? Why do you say that—before you've even seen my sketches?

TOM. (*After a pause.*) Well—where are they?

ANN. (*Taking a key out of her pocket.*) In the lower drawer in my cupboard.

TOM. (*Taking the key.*) No, don't come with me.

ANN. But I—

TOM. I don't want you to explain anything. I want it to strike me fresh. But I'm going to hit hard—right from the shoulder. If it's good—all right. If it's bad—all right. And I expect you to take it like a man. (ANN *nods.* TOM *hurries into workroom as* RUTH *comes in from hall.*)

RUTH. Have you told him?

ANN. Yes—he's gone to look at my sketches now.

RUTH. Ann—I've been thinking. You're a fool to give away your ideas. Make your models and send them in yourself.

ANN. What?

RUTH. Certainly. Why not?

ANN. Oh, Ruth—I couldn't. Some day I will. Someday.

RUTH. Some day! You've got the biggest idea you've ever had. Do it—send it in—yourself—on your *own feet.*

ANN. Tom would think I was out of my—

RUTH. *You* know it's good—don't you?

ANN. *Yes, I do.*

RUTH. It belongs to *you*—and if you don't take care of it and give it its chance, you kill something which is more important than you are. Don't forget *that.* You're not just the talented woman, you've got *downright genius,* and you ought to make everything give way to that. *Everything.* If you don't, you're weak.

ANN. Wait and see what Tom says. He'll know. He's so dead right about my stuff—always.

RUTH. Oh, you lucky people! Pulling together. If Keith only had a little of it towards me. Ann, what *shall* I do?

ANN. (*With quick sympathy.*) What, dear?

RUTH. He's never, never, never going to know what a sacrifice it will be for me to stop just as I'm getting what I've slaved and struggled for all these years. And I can't bear to hurt him.

ANN. Dear old Keith. He just *can't see.* And he loves you so.

KEITH. (*Coming in from hall.*) Why did you come back down here?

RUTH. Just to run away from—you. No, I didn't. (*Going to him sweetly.*) You know I didn't.

ANN. (*As* DAISY *comes in from hall.*) Daisy, tell me the minute Tom comes out.

KEITH. (*To* RUTH.) I'll be up in a minute. I've got to cover some stuff in there. (*Exit* ANN *and* RUTH.)

KEITH. You're a wonder, Daisy. You don't mind sitting up late to get your letters off, do you?

DAISY. Oh, no—I'm healthy.

KEATH. You're a peach. I'm sorry I made you huffy. All I meant was that no man would ever think he could ask you to marry him unless he had an awfully big bank-roll to offer.

(REMINGTON *comes in from hall to get his hat and stick—just in time to hear Keith's last remark.* DAISY *rises—consciously.* KEITH *goes into workroom.* REMINGTON *goes to end of table.*)

DAISY. I suppose that speech sounded rather queer. He was talking about Ruth, of course.

REMINGTON. Don't apologize or you'll make me suspicious.

DAISY. Now—

REMINGTON. It sounded very much as if he were making love to *you.*

DAISY. Oh—

REMINGTON. I wish to God he would. You'd—be a much better wife for him than the other one.

DAISY. You—

REMINGTON. You know you would. Why don't you go in and get him? Cut the other one out.

DAISY. How *dare* you say such a thing to me?

REMINGTON. Why shouldn't I say it?

DAISY. Because you have no *right* to. I haven't the slightest interest in Keith McKenzie—not the slightest.

REMINGTON. No. I can see that.

DAISY. What do you mean?

REMINGTON. (*Suddenly understanding.*) Why my dear girl, I didn't mean anything. I'm sorry.

DAISY. I don't know why in the world you said such a thing to me.

REMINGTON. Well—well—forget it.

DAISY. You don't think from anything I've ever done or said—

REMINGTON. I don't think anything—I don't know anything. . .

DAISY. I don't see *why* you said it.

ANN. (*Coming from hall.*) What's the matter?

(*As* DAISY *breaks away from* REMINGTON *who is holding her by the wrists.*)

DAISY. Let me go, please. I'm in a hurry. (DAISY *rushes out through hall.*)

ANN. What on earth are you doing to Daisy?

REMINGTON. She's doing things to me.

ANN. What?

REMINGTON. Convincing me of some of my old-fashioned ideas. (TOM *rushes in from the workroom with a large roll of drawings.*)

TOM. Ann—they're wonderful.

ANN. Oh—Tom!

TOM. (*Spreading the roll of sketches on the table*—ANN *helping him.*) Beautiful! Astoundingly beautiful! Well as I know you, I didn't think you had it in you.

ANN. I can't believe it. Are you going to use it.

TOM. Oh, my dear girl. That's different. Now don't be hurt. Why Ann—it isn't possible. You—you're mistaken—way off. I don't know what's got into you. This is imaginative and charming and graceful—full of abandon and fantasy and even vitality—but ye gods, child, it isn't in *this* class.

ANN. But you could strengthen it. It will grow. You'll see more in it. Really you will. Don't make up your mind yet.

REMINGTON. What are you talking about? What has she done?

TOM. Drawings for a frieze—like this. And they're amazing, doctor. Positively amazing.

REMINGTON. You don't say.

TOM. Wait—let's see what McKenzie says. McKenzie—

ANN. (*Pounding on the workroom door.*) Keith—Keith—come here—quickly.

REMINGTON. Looks beautiful to me, daughter. When did you do all this? Do you mean to say you didn't know anything about it, Tom?

TOM. Not a thing. She's been— (KEITH *comes in.*). Here McKenzie. Look at this. Here's a scheme Mrs. Herford's worked out. Begins here—See—see? Get it? What do you think?

KEITH. Mrs. Herford?

TOM. Yes. Do you get it?

MCKENZIE. Of course.

TOM. Well? What do you say?

KEITH. I say it's as beautiful as anything I ever saw.

TOM. Great! And what do you think of it for a big place like mine?

KEITH. For *that?*

TOM. Yes.

KEITH. Oh—I—too fanciful, isn't it? Would the crowd understand it? Needs a big clear striking thing like that. Don't you think?

TOM. Then you don't think it's as good as mine for this competition.

KEITH. As yours? Heavens no!

ANN. (*Standing at right—facing the three men.*) Then do you know what I'm going to do?

KEITH AND TOM. What?

ANN. Make my models and send them in myself.

TOM, KEITH AND REMINGTON. What?

ANN. Why not?

REMINGTON. You don't mean it, daughter.

ANN. I do. I mean it with my whole soul.

REMINGTON. Why do you want to do anything so foolish?

ANN. Because I *made* it. Because it's my work. You all say it's good. Why shouldn't I send it? I don't mind failure. I only want it to stand its little chance with the rest. I love it. It means more to me than I can possibly—why shouldn't I? I *want* to.

TOM. Then do it. Why not? It's your own affair. Go ahead. (*Putting out the hand of a good pal-ship to her.*)

ANN. Oh, Tom—thank you. You're splendid.

(*The curtain falls.*)

ACT II

TIME: *Four months later—about nine in the evening. The living room in the Herford house.*

The room is long and wide, dignified and restful in proportions. At center back a large fireplace with a severe mantel in cream marble. A wide window covers the entire left wall, and wide doors at right lead into the library. A single door at back, left of fireplace, leads into hall. The walls are hung in a soft dull silk which throws out the strong simple lines of the woodwork. A bright wood fire is burning and soft lights throw a warm glow over the gray carpet and the furniture which is distinguished and artistic but distinctly comfortable, giving the room the air of being much lived in and used.

AT CURTAIN: *The room is empty a moment.* DAISY *is singing in the library at right.* ELLEN, *a maid, middle-aged and kindly, comes from hall carrying a silver coffee service.*

DAISY. (*As she comes in from library.*) Here's your coffee, girls. Come in here. Put the flowers over there, Ellen.

(ELLEN *moves the vase of flowers and makes room for the coffee service on table right center.* RUTH *comes in from the library with a book.* ELLEN *goes to fire and pokes it, then straightens the writing things on the desk.*)

DAISY. Ann, here's your coffee.

ANN. (*Calling from library.*) I don't want any, thank you. What time is it, Daisy?

DAISY. About nine. Why?

ANN. Oh, the postman. I'm waiting for the last mail.

DAISY. Well, don't. A watched pot you know. (*To* RUTH.) She's watched every mail for a week. I almost think Ann will be more disappointed than Tom himself if he doesn't get the commission. (*They take their coffee to the fire.*)

RUTH. I hope to goodness he does. Every body's so dead sure of him.

DAISY. Almost too sure. I'm beginning to be frightened myself. The time's about up.

ANN. (*Hurrying in from the library.*) That's the postman—isn't it?

ELLEN. No ma'am. Beggin' your pardon. It ain't—I'm listenin' too.

ANN. Are you, Ellen? Keep on and bring it up the minute it comes.

ELLEN. Faith I will. I've got the habit meself lately of watchin' for the mail.

ANN. Have you?

ELLEN. Every time I hear the whistle I drop whatever I'm doin' like it was hot—and run.

ANN. Do you?

ELLEN. And just before I open the door I say—The Holy Saints be praised, I hope it's come this time—whatever it is they're lookin' fer. (*She goes out through the hall.*)

ANN. Oh, dear! It gets worse as the time grows shorter.

DAISY. Ann, working yourself up like this won't make Tom get the commission. Stop thinking about it.

ANN. But I can't, Daisy Dimple. He ought to hear tonight if he's ever going to.

DAISY. Well, I'll be glad when it's all over and we know one way or the other—and can settle down to ordinary life again. It's almost given me nervous indigestion.

ANN. Listen! There's the postman.

RUTH. (*Jumping so that her cup and saucer almost fall.*) Oh, Ann, you're getting me so excited, I'll listen for the postman all the rest of my life.

ANN. I know I shall. Oh, Tom must get it. He *must*. If he does, I'll wire Millicent. (*Taking up a picture of Millicent which stands in a frame on the table.*) I think I'll run up to school Sunday just to give her a good hug. I get so hungry for her!

RUTH. Isn't it splendid the school is so really what it ought to be?

ANN. Yes. So much that's sweet and right that one can't get in New York for a girl.

DAISY. (*Sewing on a frock which is nearly finished.*) She seems pretty keen about it herself.

ANN. Yes—rather. Easter vacation when I was working day and night to get my models off, she was perfectly contented to stay at school.

RUTH. She's an adorable kiddie but I don't envy you your job.

ANN. Why?

RUTH. I think being a mother is the most gigantic, difficult, important and thankless thing in the world.

DAISY. That's the most sensible remark I ever heard you give vent to, Ruth.

ANN. There's something much more glorious in it than being thanked. You'll miss the most wonderful thing in the world, Ruth, if you don't have children.

RUTH. I know. I know. But work has taken that all out of me. It does, you know. It would bore me stiff to take care of a baby.

DAISY. That's a pleasant prospect for Keith. Do you expect *him* to do it?

RUTH. (*Making herself comfortable on the couch.*) I'm not going to *have* children.

ANN. (*Going to sit at the fire.*) That's perfectly fair if he knows it. No reason why you should if you don't want 'em.

DAISY. Well, I think it's a *rotten* way to live.

RUTH. Wait till you decide to marry somebody yourself, young lady, and see how *you* like giving up everything that interests you most.

DAISY. Well, by Jove, if I ever *do* marry, I'll *marry* and do all the things that belong to my side of the game. No halfway business for me. You might as well be a man's mistress and be done with it.

RUTH. (*Half serious — half joking.*) That's the ideal relationship for a man and woman. Each to keep his independence in absolutely every way—and live together merely because they charm each other. But somehow we don't seem to be able to make it respectable.

DAISY. I suppose that's very clever and modern.

RUTH. Oh, no—it's as old as the everlasting hills. The trouble is children are apt to set in and mess things up. It's hard on *them*.

DAISY. So far as I can see most everything that's modern is hard on children.

ANN. (*Laughing.*) How's the gown getting on, Daisy?

DAISY. Most finished.

RUTH. That's awfully pretty.

ANN. Slip it on so we can see.

DAISY. Oh, I can't.

ANN. (*Rising and walking to* DAISY.) Yes, you can—over that one—just to give us an idea.

DAISY. I'll look a tub and it really makes me quite respectably straight up and down.

ANN. You're a perfectly scrumptious size and shape. Isn't she, Ruth?

RUTH. Magnificent!

DAISY. Yes, Ruth, skinny women always enthuse over their fat friends.

RUTH. (*Rising and goes to* DAISY.) Oh, you aren't fat, Daisy. That is, not too fat. How does this go. It's terribly complicated, isn't it?

DAISY. No—perfectly simple. Wait—this goes over here.

ANN. No, it doesn't, does it?

DAISY. Yes, it does. Right there. Don't you see? The style of the whole gown depends on that.

RUTH. You must have it on wrong side before.

DAISY. Nonsense! Can't you see, Ann? It's as simple as can be.

ANN. Yes, I know dear—but does this go on the shoulder—or down on your hip? (*They all talk at once for a moment on the subject of where the end of the girdle fastens.*) Oh, here! I see, of course! There!

DAISY. Now, does it make me look big?

RUTH. You want to look big, don't you?

DAISY. Well, I want to look life size. Don't you see how much better I am through here than I was last year, Ann? (*Touching her hip.*)

ANN. Much. The female form divine is improving all the time anyway—gradually getting back to what it was in the beginning.

DAISY. I don't expect to look like you in it, Ruth.

RUTH. Oh, don't you, dear? Then why don't you have it stick out this way as much as possible so everybody will know you *mean* to look broad? There's everything in that, you know.

DAISY. I think it would be awfully good on you—to fill out what you haven't got. Then everybody would know you didn't *mean* to look so narrow—even if you *are*.

ANN. You're both delightful. Perfect specimens of your types. When I look at Ruth I think the most alluring charm a woman can have is beautiful bones without a superfluous ounce of flesh on them. And when I look at you, Daisy, I think after all, there's nothing so stunning as a big strong girl with perfectly natural lines—so natural that we know she'd be even better looking with no clothes on at all.

DAISY. Heavens, Ann! Your sculptor's eye is a little embarrassing.

RUTH. Evidently you think my clothes help me out a good deal. But at least I'm free and comfortable, too. Can you touch the floor, Daisy?

DAISY. Of course. (*The two women bend—touching the floor with the tips of their fingers.*)

(TOM, REMINGTON *and* KEITH *come in from the hall.*)

TOM. What's going on?

REMINGTON. What are you trying to do, Ruth—swim or fly?

ANN. We're just saying that the waist measure expands as we *broaden* in our ideas.

KEITH. Is that the fashion now?

RUTH. Yes—broad and free.

REMINGTON. That's *one* thing you women have to acknowledge men have more sense about than you have.

ANN, RUTH, DAISY. What?

REMINGTON. Our figures. We've had the same shape since the Garden of Eden and you've had hundreds of absolutely different kinds.

ANN. Turn around, Daisy, I want to try something. (*She accidentally sticks a pin into* DAISY'S *shoulder.*)

DAISY. Ouch!

ANN. Oh, I'm sorry! You seem to be so close to your clothes.

REMINGTON. What are you doing to her?

DAISY. She's sticking pins into me.

ANN. For her own good. Isn't that pretty?

TOM. What?

ANN. The frock.

TOM. Is that new?

KEITH. Which?

DAISY. Do you mean to say you don't realize I have on something different from what I wore at dinner?

RUTH. No use dressing for Keith. He never sees anything.

DAISY. I'm going to undress now. Perhaps that will interest you more. (ANN *begins to unfasten the gown.*)

REMINGTON. Much more.

ANN. Was *that* the postman?

DAISY. No, it was *not*.

REMINGTON. The postman habit is getting on my nerves. You're all jumping and listening till you'll have St. Vitus dance if you don't stop.

ANN. How can we help it?

REMINGTON. After all, a few other competitions have been lost and won—and people have lived through it. It's not the only thing in life.

TOM. You'd think it was if you had $100,000 at stake. (ELLEN *comes in from hall and takes out the coffee tray.*)

ANN. Aren't we going to have some bridge? Who wants to play? I know you do, daddy.

REMINGTON. I have to get even with you for that last rubber, Tom.

TOM. You can't do it.

DAISY. I want to play, with you, doctor.

REMINGTON. Come on.

RUTH. I'm afraid to play *against* you.

REMINGTON. (*Turning at the library door.*) What's that?

OTHERS. What?

REMINGTON. The postman!

OTHERS. Oh! RUTH *and* DAISY *go into library R. with* REMINGTON.)

ANN. (*To* TOM *and* KEITH.) Coming?

TOM. You go, Keith. I want to look at the paper a minute.

KEITH. Oh, my game's no good. You go.

ANN. Now don't stay out here and listen and wait. If there is any mail Ellen will bring it straight up.

TOM. I won't. I'll be with you—in two minutes.

ANN. Anyway—tonight doesn't necessarily decide it. There may be still two or three more days. Isn't that so, Keith?

KEITH. Yes, I think so.

REMINGTON, RUTH, DAISY. (*Calling from the library.*) Come on. Come on.

ANN. Coming. (*She goes in.*)

KEITH. That's straight. I do think so—(*A pause.* TOM *reads.*) Don't you?

TOM. I'm trying to—but these last few days of waiting have been—

KEITH. Don't lose your nerve, Herford. I'm just as sure as I was the first day. If by any wild chance you *don't* get it—it will be a fluke.

TOM. Oh, no. Oh, no, not by any means. The men judging this *know*. I'd trust them with anything. The fellows who lose will have no kick coming on that score.

KEITH. Well—I don't see how you *can* lose.

TOM. A man's a fool to let himself count on an uncertainty. I don't mean that I've lost sight of the fact that I might lose—not for a second—but I confess—as the time has grown shorter I've realized I *want* it even more than I thought I did.

KEITH. Of course you want it. Aside from the glory—it's an *awful lot of money*—governor, an awful lot of money.

TOM. *It is.* It would put us straight—clear up the house entirely and make it possible to do only the things a fellow wants to do. That's what I'm after. Then—No more competitions for me, thank you. Is that the 'phone? I'm as bad as Ann—jumping and listening. Damn it! I want to *know*—one way or the other.

KEITH. Of course you do. The cursed waiting is enough to make you cut your throat.

ELLEN. (*Opening the hall door.*) The telephone for Mr. Herford.

TOM. Who is it?

ELLEN. I couldn't just get the name, sir.

KEITH. Want me to go?

TOM. If you don't mind, old man. (ELLEN *goes out.*)

KEITH. (*Starting to the door and turning.*) It couldn't be—you wouldn't get word that way—would you?

TOM. Uh?—Oh—nonsense! No—no—nonsense! I'll go—No, I—you go—old man. That's not it—of course. (TOM *listens a moment—showing a tense anxiety.*)

RUTH. (*Coming in from the library.*) They're waiting for you, Tom. The cards are dealt. Where's Keith?

TOM. He'll be back in a minute.

RUTH. Aren't you going in?

TOM. Why don't you take my place? I don't feel a bit—

RUTH. I did offer to but Dr. Remington said he would like to *play* bridge this evening, not *teach* it. Wouldn't it be seventh heaven to speak the truth on all occasions as unconcernedly as Dr. Remington does? Imagine the sheer bliss of letting go and spitting it all out. Have you ever counted the lies you told in just one day, Tom?

TOM. No—I've never had time. (TOM *starts to go into the library and turns to see if* RUTH *is coming.*)

RUTH. No—I'm going to wait for Keith. TOM *goes in—Ruth reads for a moment.*)

KEITH. (*Coming back from the hall.*) That was—

RUTH. What?

KEITH. Millicent or her school or something. Such a bad connection; they're going to call again in a few minutes. Is that dress new, dear?

RUTH. I've had it three years.

KEITH. It's awfully pretty. I wish you'd wear it all the time.

RUTH. I do.

KEITH. Aren't we going in to play?

RUTH. No, I don't feel like it. Come and sit down, dear. Oh, are you going to sit way over there?

KEITH. Not 'specially. (*Drawing chair near the couch*—KEITH *sits facing* RUTH.)

RUTH. Comfortable?

KEITH. Not very.

RUTH. Have you read this?

KEITH. No. Any good.

RUTH. Yes—Good enough. (*She rises, going to the fireplace.*)

KEITH. What's the matter? I thought you wanted to talk. Where are you going?

RUTH. No place.

KEITH. You got the fidgets too?

RUTH. Sort of.

KEITH. Well, stop it. Herford's going to be all right. There'll be news in a day or so now.

RUTH. I wasn't thinking of that. I have something to tell you.

KEITH. Then why don't you come and tell it?

RUTH. And if you aren't fine about it—it will be the greatest disappointment in my whole life.

(*Going to* KEITH *and putting a hand on his shoulder.*)

KEITH. You mean if I don't think just what you want me to about it. Go on. I s'pose I know, anyway.

RUTH. Then if you do—but you don't. It's so wonderful you couldn't guess. And you'll just *have* to see it the right way, because if you don't it would mean you're what I know you're *not*. Down in your real soul, Keith, you're generous and fair and right.

KEITH. Suppose you communicate it to me first and discuss my soul afterwards.

RUTH. (*Sitting on couch facing* KEITH.) Well—Oh you *will* be sweet won't you, Keithie?

KEITH. I can see it's going to be something *very* pleasant for *me*.

RUTH. It is if you . . .

KEITH. It's wonderful if I'm not a fool and a pig. Yes, I know. Go on. Go on.

RUTH. Now don't begin that way—please dear. Don't shut up your mind before I even tell you.

KEITH. Suppose you *do* tell me.

RUTH. Well— last week there was a row in the office over a matter concerning the policy of the magazine and I differed with all the men in my department. At last I was sent for by the Editor in Chief. He was terribly severe at first, and I was frightened to pieces—but I stuck to my guns—and bless your soul he sent for me again today and said they had had a meeting of the directors and that they decided—oh, it's too—

KEITH. What? What?

RUTH. They had decided to make me Editor of the Woman's Magazine. (*Fighting back her tears.*) Isn't it funny?

KEITH. And I suppose all this introduction means you accepted—without even asking me?

RUTH. Why, of course. Oh, Keith, don't you understand what this means to me?

KEITH. I understand that unless it means more to you than I do—you wouldn't hesitate a minute to chuck it.

RUTH. It's hopeless—we'll never—never see it the same way.

KEITH. You've never made the slightest effort to see it *my* way.

RUTH. What you ask of me is to cut off one half of my life and throw it away. What I ask of you is only an experiment—to let me try and see if I can't make things comfortable and smooth and happy for us—and still take this big thing that has come as a result of all my years of hard work and fighting for it.

KEITH. You'll never stop if you don't now. Once you get deeper in it you'll be swamped—eaten up by it.

RUTH. Don't, Keith. I can't bear it. It's too unutterably selfish.

KEITH. (*Rising and pushing his chair away.*) All right—I'm selfish—but I'm human—and I'll bet my hat I'm just like every nine men out of ten. What in the name of heaven does loving a girl amount to if you don't want to take care of her from start to finish? A man's no good if he doesn't feel that way, I tell you. He's a pup—and ought to be shot.

RUTH. (*Rising.*) But what about *me*—and what I want and have to have—in order to be happy?

KEITH. That's it. That is the point. You won't be happy without it. You want the excitement of it—that hustle and bustle outside.

RUTH. I want it just as you want your work—and you haven't any more right to ask me to give up mine than I have to ask you to stop *yours.*

KEITH. You simply don't *love* me.

RUTH. What rot! What nonsense!

KEITH. You don't love me.

RUTH. It's hopeless. You've decided then. You won't compromise—so we'll end it.

KEITH What do you mean?

RUTH. (*Going to the hall door.*) You've made your own choice. We'll end it now.

KEITH. (*Following her.*) No—Ruth—I won't give you up.

RUTH. You have. You have given me up.

KEITH. Ruth—wait.

RUTH. It's best, Keith. Don't hate me. You'll see it's best in a little while. We'll learn to be friends. I want you to be happy, dear boy—I do. And I couldn't make you so. We'll end it now. It's the best for us both.

KEITH. Ruth—

(*She goes out quickly, closing the door.* KEITH *turns to the fire.*)

DAISY. (*Knocking and opening the library door.*) Excuse me. May I come in to get my sewing? Where's Ruth?

KEITH. (*With his back to* DAISY.) Don't know.

DAISY. Well, don't bite my head off. I can always tell when you and Ruth have been discussing the *emancipation* of women.

(*Sitting below table and taking her dress to sew.*)

KEITH. You *all* think you're superior beings.

DAISY. Of course.

KEITH. (*Beginning to walk about.*) Yes, you do. You're just as bad as the rest of them—worse. The minute a woman makes enough to buy the clothes on her back, she thinks she and God Almighty are running the earth and men are just little insects crawling around. (DAISY *laughs.*) Oh, you can laugh. It's so—and you *know* it. Every one of you that have got the bee in your bonnet of doing something — *doing* something, are through with the men. Look at *you. You've* cut men out entirely and you think you're too smart to marry one. Now, don't you? Isn't that the reason?

DAISY. (*Threading her needle.*) Don't bully-rag me. Say it all to Ruth.

KEITH. I tell you it's all rot—business for women. It spoils every one of you. Why aren't *you* in a home of your own instead of hustling for your bread and butter? It's because you're too damned conceited. You think you know more than any man you ever saw and you think you don't need one. You wait—You'll see—some day.

(*Going back to the fire.*)

DAISY. You amuse me.

KEITH. There you *are*—that's about what I'm for.

DAISY. There's a button off your coat. Looks horrid.

KEITH. I know. I've got it.

(*Pulling his finger in waistcoat pocket.*)

DAISY. Have you got it there? (KEITH *shows her the button.*) Come here, I'll do it.

KEITH. Never mind. I'll *nail* it on.

DAISY. Come here. (KEITH *goes slowly to her.*) You'll have to take your coat off. It's bad luck to sew anything *on* you.

KEITH. Oh—

DAISY. Go on—take it off. (KEITH *takes off his coat reluctantly and watches* DAISY *as she examines the coat.*) Good Gracious, the lining's ripped, too.

KEITH. Yes.

DAISY. Poor old fellow! Are these some of your stitches?

KEITH. (*Drawing the chair from C. and sitting L. before* DAISY.) What's the matter with 'em?

DAISY. Looks like carpet thread. (*Snipping some threads.*) See, I'll just draw this together and that'll be all right.

(*She begins to sing an old ditty—Keith gradually hums with her, keeping time with his hands and feet and relaxing into a good humor.*)

KEITH. (*Soothed for a moment.*) How does it happen you're so handy with a needle? I thought you were all for business.

DAISY. Well, I can sew a button on if *you can.*

KEITH. I tell you it changes all women —business. They make a little money themselves and want luxury and won't live without it.

DAISY. Sometimes—yes. But there are lots and lots and lots of women taking care of themselves—putting up the bluff of being independent and happy who would be so glad to live in a little flat and do their own work—just to be the nicest thing in the world to some man.

KEITH. Wouldn't you think that Ruth would like that better than the office?

DAISY. No—not the lamp light and the needle for Ruth. Keith, don't ask her to give up her work—don't you see, she's more clever, in her way than you are in yours. She'll go further, and if you make her stop, she'll hate you some day because she'll think you've kept her back. That's a hard thing to say—but it's the truth.

KEITH. You mean I'm a failure.

DAISY. (*Genuinely.*) No—no—I don't mean that, Keith.

KEITH. I work—Gosh, how I work, but I'll never *do* anything. Why haven't I got what Mrs. Herford's got? She sent models off for this frieze that any *man* would be proud to send. Why couldn't I?

DAISY. Seems kind of mixed up and unfair—doesn't it?

KEITH. You bet it's unfair. I work like a dog and never get anywhere. If Ruth throws me over, I'll never have the home I'm working for. That's what I want —a home. I'll never have it now.

DAISY. Oh, yes you will.

KEITH. I'm done for.

DAISY. No, you're not. There are too many women in the world—who—could —love you.

KEITH. I'm no good.

DAISY. Some woman might think that you—your—the way you work—and your honesty and *loyalty* are the greatest things a man can have.

KEITH. Um!

DAISY. *Some* woman might use all her cleverness and ingenuity to make the little flat beautiful—to show you what your own home—could be—to give you a better dinner than you thought you could afford.

KEITH. (*Sitting with his head in his hands.*) That kind of a woman is a thing of the past.

DAISY. Oh no, they're not. They're lying around *thick.* The trouble is—a *woman* can't *ask.* Even if a man is—just at her hand—and she knows she could make him happy—she can't *tell* him—she can't open his eyes—she has to hide what might make things right for both of them. Because she's a woman.

KEITH. Oh—love doesn't cut much ice with a woman. Women are all *brain* nowadays.

DAISY. (*With sudden warmth.*) That's enough to use all the brains a woman's got—to make a home—to bring up children—and to keep a man's love.

KEITH. (*Raising his head slowly and looking at Daisy.*) I never expected to hear *you* say a thing like that. There's some excuse for *you* being in business.

DAISY. Yes, of course. (*Rising and holding the coat.*) I'm not the marrying kind.

KEITH. (*Getting into the coat.*) Much obliged. Would *you* be willing to give up work and marry a man on a small salary—if you loved him?

DAISY. You make me laugh.

KEITH. What's the matter, Daisy?

DAISY. Nothing.

KEITH. I never saw tears in your eyes before. Women are funny things.

DAISY. Yes, we're funny. There's only one thing on earth funnier.

KEITH. What?

DAISY. Men.

REMINGTON. (*Coming in from the library.*) Did I leave my other glasses in here?

DAISY. (*Beginning to look for them.*) I haven't seen them.

REMINGTON. I've lost one game because I didn't have 'em and I don't propose to give 'em another.

DAISY. What a shame! Help look for them, Keith.

REMINGTON. I'm pretty blind—but thank God not quite as bad as you, Keith.

KEITH. What? There's nothing the matter with my eyes.

REMINGTON. (*Looking insinuatingly at* DAISY.) Don't you think there is, Daisy?

DAISY. (*Trying to look unconscious.*) Are you *sure* you left those glasses in here?

REMINGTON. It's as bad a case of short sightedness as I ever saw.

DAISY. Oh—

(*The doctor holds her and turns her, pushing her toward* KEITH.)

REMINGTON. Daisy, don't you see that queer blind look in his eyes?

DAISY. No—I don't.

KEITH. What do you mean? (REMINGTON *laughs.*) Do you see the joke, Daisy?

REMINGTON. It's no joke—is it Daisy?

DAISY. I don't know what on earth you're talking about. I'm going to get those glasses. (*Going to hall door.*) You probably left them in your hoat in the call. I mean in your hall in the coat —I mean—

REMINGTON. That's all right, Daisy—we know what you mean. At least I do.

DAISY. Oh you— (ELLEN *comes in from hall.*) What is it, Ellen?

ELLEN. The telephone, Miss Herford.

DAISY. For me?

ELLEN. They said any one of the family.

DAISY. I'll go.

(*She goes out followed by* ELLEN.)

REMINGTON. *There's* a woman who knows how to take care of a man.

KEITH. I'm afraid that's not her object in life. They all have something else to do.

REMINGTON. What's the matter with you?

KEITH. I'm done for.

REMINGTON. Ruth, you mean?

KEITH. She won't marry me unless she goes on working.

REMINGTON. She's right, too.

KEITH. What?

REMINGTON. Of course. You haven't any more right to ask that clever little woman to throw away half her life and to be the tail to your kite than you have to ask her to cut her throat. Open your eyes and look around. There are always other women.

KEITH. *Never.* Never in the world for me.

REMINGTON. I give you about three months.

KEITH. Do you think I could ever—

REMINGTON. Certainly I do. Look at Daisy, for instance. A fine, sweet wholesome girl with no kinks and no abnormal ambitions.

KEITH. Daisy?

REMINGTON. Don't blow your brains out for a couple of days. Talk it over with her. She thinks you're about the finest thing going.

KEITH. *What?*

REMINGTON. Fact! Don't try to hold on to the woman who's getting away from you, but take the one who is coming your way.

KEITH. You're crazy. Mad as a hatter. What are you giving me?

REMINGTON. Just a little professional advice—*free.* She's head over heels in love with you, I tell you.

DAISY. (*Coming in from hall in great excitement. She has a case for glasses in her hand.*) Dr. Remington, that was long distance. They telephoned from school that Millicent has gone.

KEITH. Gone?

REMINGTON. Gone where?

DAISY. Left school suddenly tonight without saying a word to anyone.

REMINGTON and KEITH. What?

DAISY. As soon as they knew—they 'phoned the station, and found she had taken the train for New York.

REMINGTON. What train?

DAISY. The one that gets here at nine o'clock.

KEITH. (*Looking at his watch.*) It's 9:15 now.

DAISY. Shall I tell Ann?

REMINGTON. No—no—wait. We'll give her fifteen minutes more to get to the house. No use frightening Ann.

KEITH. Do you think she *is* coming home?

DAISY. Why do you say that, Keith? What put such an idea into your head?

KEITH. Why wouldn't she say so—wire or write or something?

DAISY. Oh, it's too horrible. Doctor, oughtn't we to tell them now?

REMINGTON. No—no—

DAISY. But we're wasting time. What if she *shouldn't* come?

KEITH. I think I'll dash down to the station anyway. The train might be late.

REMINGTON. No—no. They'd ask where you'd gone. Wait fifteen minutes—I think she'll be here. I don't want to frighten—

(ANNE *comes in from the library.*)

ANNE. Well, I never saw people so wildly keen about playing as you are. What's the matter with you?

REMINGTON. I've been waiting all this time—for my glasses. Come on Daisy.

(*Taking the glasses from* DAISY, *he goes into library.*)

ANN. You look worried, Daisy.

DAISY. No—I'm only—

ELLEN. (*Coming in from hall with eight letters on a small tray.*) The mail, Mrs. Herford.

ANN. Oh! (*She snatches the letters, taking off the three top ones.*). It's come! Tom's letter.

KEITH and DAISY. What?

(ELLEN *goes out through hall L. C.*)

ANN. It is! It is—as true as I live.

KEITH. Great Scott!

DAISY. Then he's got it. He's got it.

ANN. Sh! Ask him to come here.

DAISY. It's too good to be true. It's too good!

(DAISY *goes into the library.*)

KEITH. I can't tell you how glad I am, Mrs. Herford. I can't tell you.

ANN. (*Scarcely able to speak.*) Ask him to come here.

KEITH. (*Going into library.*) Mrs. Herford wants you, Governor.

TOM. (*Within.*) Come and play, Ann.

ANN. (*Throwing the other letters on the table.*) Come here just a minute, Tom, please.

TOM. (*Coming to door.*) What is it?

ANN. Shut the door. It's come. (*Showing the letter. Tom opens and reads it. A look of sickening disappointment comes into his face.*) No? Oh, Tom!

TOM. I was their *second* choice!

ANN. Oh, Tom, don't take it like that. What difference does it make after all? You know you did a big thing. It's all luck—anyway.

TOM. I'll pull up in a minute. Well, it means taking hold of something else pretty quick. Going at it again.

ANN. Yes, keeping at it—that's it. What a TERRIBLE lot chance has to do with it.

TOM. Oh no, that isn't it.

ANN. Yes, it is, too.

TOM. No—I failed. I didn't get it, that's all.

ANN. You'll do something greater—next time—because of this.

TOM. (*Taking her hand.*) You're a brick! Now, see here, don't you be cut up about this. It's not the end of everything, you know. Stop that! You're not crying, I hope?

ANN. No, I'm not. Of course, I'm not! (*With passionate tenderness.*) Oh, my boy. I never loved you so much—never believed in you as I do now. This is only a little hard place that will make you all the stronger.

TOM. Dear old girl! What would I do without you? I'll tell the others and get it over. (*Rising, he stops, staring at one of the letters on the table.*) Ann!

ANN. Um?

TOM. (*Taking up a letter.*) Ann—here's one for you, too.

ANN. What? (*She tears open the letter.*) Tom! They've given the commission to me! Look! Read it! Is that what it says? Is it? Now aren't you glad you let me do it? You haven't lost! We've got it. Say you're glad. Say you're proud of me, dear. That's the best part of it all.

TOM. Of course, I am, dear, of course I am.

ANN. Oh, Tom, I wanted you to get it more than I ever wanted anything in my life, but this is SOMETHING to be thankful for. Doesn't this almost make it right?

TOM. Yes, dear, yes. Don't think of me. That's over—that part of it. Tell the others now.

ANN. Wait!

TOM. Aren't you going to?

ANN. I only want to be sure that you're just as happy that *I* won, as I would have been if YOU had.

TOM. Of course, I am. You know that. (*Kissing her.*)

ANN. Tell the others, then, Tom—I can't.

TOM. (*Opening the library doors.*) What do you think has happened?

DAISY. (*Rushing in.*) Tom got it. Didn't you, Tom? You did. You did! Oh, I'm so glad. (*She kisses him.*)

KEITH. (*Following* DAISY *in.*) Well—governor—what did I tell you?

REMINGTON. (*In doorway.*) Pretty fine—isn't it?

ANN. You tell them, Tom.

TOM. Ann got it!

DAISY. What?

TOM. Isn't it great?

ANN. You won't believe it. But you can see the letter. Now, father, don't you think getting that is better than being nursemaid and housekeeper? Now, don't you, honestly?

REMINGTON. I do not.

ANN. What?

REMINGTON. I do not.

ANN. Oh, I can laugh at your theories now. You haven't a leg to stand on. Has he, Tom? Be a dear father and say you're glad.

REMINGTON. I'm not. I'd rather you'd failed a thousand times over—for your own good. What are you going to do with Millicent while you're making this thing?

ANN. How can you be so hard and narrow, Father?

REMINGTON. What if you did win? You've got something far greater than making statues to do.

TOM. Doctor, you're excited.

REMINGTON. Not a bit. I'm only telling the truth. This is your *business* you know—and it would have been far better for *both* of you if *you'd won the thing.*

TOM. I don't see the argument. Ann got it because she sent in a better model than I did. I don't see that anything else has anything to do with the case.

(*Tom goes out through hall.*)

ANN. (*Turning to sit on the couch.*) At least *Tom's* glad I got it.

REMINGTON. He's stung to the quick. You've humiliated him in his own eyes (*He goes to the fireplace.*)

ANN. I *can't* understand why you feel this way about it, father.

DAISY. Oh, its *natural* enough.

ANN. (*Turning to* DAISY *in amazement.*) Aren't *you* glad for me—Daisy?

DAISY. Yes, but—I—I'm awfully sorry for Tom.

(*She goes out through hall.*)

ANN. What's the matter with them all, Keith?

KEITH. Oh—as Daisy says—it's natural, Mrs. Herford.

(*He goes out after* DAISY.)

REMINGTON. (*Coming down to* ANN.) Daughter, I'm afraid I was a little too stiff just now. I didn't mean to be unkind.

ANN. (*Rising and starting to hall door.*) Oh, it doesn't matter.

REMINGTON. (*Stopping her.*) Yes, it does matter. I wouldn't hurt you for the world.

ANN. But you've *always* fought me, Father. You've *never* thought I had any right to work—never believed in my ability, now that I've proved I have some— Why can't you acknowledge it?

REMINGTON. Ann, this is a dangerous moment in your life. Tom's beaten—humiliated—knocked out. You did it —he can't stand it.

ANN. What have I done? Tom has a big nature. He's not little and petty enough to be hurt because I won.

REMINGTON. You're *blind.* He's had a blow tonight that no man on earth could stand.

ANN. Not Tom. I won't believe it.

REMINGTON. Yes, I say. I know what I'm talking about. Ann, be careful how you move now. Use your woman's tact, your love. Make Tom know that he is the greatest thing in the world to you—that you'd even give up all this work idea—if—he wanted—you to.

ANN. *What?* Tom wouldn't let me.

REMINGTON. Ask him. Ask him. See what he'd say.

ANN. Why, I wouldn't insult him. He'd think I thought he was—

(TOM *comes in from the hall*—ANN *checks herself and turns away quickly to fire.*)

TOM. (*After a pause.*) What's the matter?

REMINGTON. Nothing — nothing. Ann and I were just having a little argument as usual. I'll be back in a few minutes.

(*Looking at his watch he goes into hall.*)

TOM. (*Going slowly to* ANN.) I hope you're not still fighting about the—your frieze?

ANN. They're all so funny, Tom—the way they act about it. It hurts. But so long as you're glad, it doesn't matter what anyone else thinks. Say you're glad, dear. I want you to be as happy as I would be if you had won.

TOM. You know I am, dear. You know that.

ANN. (*With a sigh of relief* ANN *sits at left of fire.*) Think how I'll have to work. I can't even go to the country in the summer.

TOM. (*Sitting opposite* ANN *at the fire.*) And what will you do with Millicent this summer?

ANN. Oh, there are lots of nice things for her to do. The money! Think what it will mean to you!

TOM. Let me tell you one thing, Ann, in the beginning. I'll never touch a penny of the money.

ANN. What?

TOM. Not a cent of it.

ANN. What are you talking about?

TOM. That's your money. Put it away for yourself.

ANN. I never heard you say anything so absolutely unreasonable before in my life.

TOM. If you think I'm unreasonable, all right. But that's understood about the money. We won't discuss it.

ANN. Well, we *will* discuss it. Why shouldn't you use my money as well as I yours?

TOM. That's about as different as day and night.

ANN. Why is it?

TOM. Because I'm taking care of *you*. It's all right if you never do another day's work in your life. You're doing it because you want to, I'm doing it because I've got to. If you were alone it would be a different thing. But I'm here, and so long as I am I'll make what keeps us going.

ANN. But I'll help you.

TOM. No, you won't.

ANN. I *will*. I'm going on just as far as I have ability to go, and if you refuse to take any money I may make—if you refuse to use it for our mutual good, you're unjust and taking an unfair advan—— Oh, Tom! what are we saying? We're out of our senses—both of us. You didn't mean what you said. Did you? It would—— I simply couldn't bear it if you did. You didn't—did you?

TOM. I did— of course.

ANN. Tom—after all these years of pulling together, now that I've *done* something, why do you suddenly balk?

TOM. (*Rising.*) Good Heavens! Do you think I'm going to use your money? Don't try to run my end of it. It's the same old story—when you come down to it, a woman can't mix up in a man's business. (*He moves away.*)

ANN. Mix up in it? Isn't it a good thing for you that I got this commission?

TOM. No. I don't know that it's a good thing from any standpoint to have it known that I failed, but my wife succeeded.

ANN. I thought you said you were glad—proud of me.

TOM. It's too — distracting—too — takes you away from more important things.

ANN. What things?

TOM. Millicent and me.

ANN. Oh, Tom—— don't. You know that you and Millicent come before everything on earth to me.

TOM. No.

ANN. You do.

TOM. We don't—now. Your ambition comes first.

ANN. (*She rises, going to him.*) Tom, I worship you. You know that, don't you?

TOM. I'm beginning to hate this work and everything in connection with it.

ANN. But you taught me—helped me—pushed me on. What's changed you?

TOM. I let you do it in the first place because I thought it was right. I wanted you to do the thing you wanted to do.

ANN. Well?

TOM. I was a fool. I didn't see what it would lead to. It's taking you away from everything else—and there'll be no end to it. Your ambition will carry you away till the home and Millicent and I are nothing to you!

ANN. Tom—look at me. Be honest. Are you sorry—— *sorry* I got this commission?

TOM. I'm sorry it's the most important thing in the world to you.

ANN. Oh! Why do you say that to me? How can you?

TOM. Haven't I just seen it? You're getting rid of Millicent now because you don't want her to interfere with your work.

ANN. No!

TOM. You're pushing her out of your life.

ANN. No!

TOM. You said just now you were going to send her away alone in the summer. I don't like that. She's got to be with you—I want you to keep her with you.

ANN. But that's impossible. You know that. If I stop work now I might as well give up the frieze entirely.

TOM. Then give it up.

ANN. What?

TOM. Give up the whole thing—forever. Why shouldn't you?

ANN. Do you mean that?

TOM. Yes.

ANN. Tom—I love you. Don't ask this sacrifice of me to prove my love.

TOM. Could you make it? Could you?

ANN. Don't ask it! Don't ask if for your own sake. I want to keep on loving you. I want to believe you're what I thought you were. Don't make me think you're just like every other man.

TOM. I am a man—and you're my wife and Millicent's our daughter. Unless you come back to the things a woman's always had to do—and always will—we can't go on. We can't go on.

ANN. (*Following him around the table.*) Tom—if you're just a little hurt—just a little jealous because I won——

TOM. Oh——

ANN. That's natural—I can understand that.

TOM. Oh—don't——

ANN. But, oh, Tom, the other—— to ask me to give it all up. I could never forgive that. Take it back, Tom—take it back.

TOM. Good God, Ann, can't you see? You're a woman and I'm a man. You're not free in the same way. If you won't stop because I ask it—I say you *must*.

ANN. You can't say that to me. You can't.

TOM. I do say it.

ANN. No!

TOM. I say it because I know it's *right*.

ANN. It isn't.

TOM. I can't make you see it.

ANN. It isn't.

TOM. I don't know how—but everything in me tells me it's right.

ANN. Tom—listen to me.

TOM. If you won't do it because I ask you—I demand it. I say you've *got* to.

ANN. Tom—you can kill our love by just what you do now.

TOM. Then this work *is* the biggest thing in the world to you?

ANN. What is more important to us both—to our happiness than just that?

MILLICENT. (*Calling outside door L. C.*) Mother! (*A startled pause as* ANN *and* TOM *turn towards hall door.*) Mother! I'm home, where are you?

(MILLICENT *opens the hall door and rushes into the room.*)

ANN. Millicent! What are you doing here?

MILLICENT. I came home, mother.

ANN. Why?

MILLICENT. Because I had to.

ANN. Are you ill, dear?

MILLICENT. No. No.

TOM. Is anything wrong at school?

MILLICENT. No, but I won't go back.

TOM. But why won't you? What's the trouble?

MILLICENT. I won't go back.

TOM. But you can't do a thing like this. I won't allow it.

MILLICENT. You wouldn't let me come home when I wanted to and now I can't go back. I won't—— everything's different now. I won't go back and you can't make me.

(*She turns and rushes out of the room and* TOM *and* ANN *stare at each other as the curtain falls.*)

ACT III

TIME: *Half an hour later.*

SCENE: *Same as Act II. Ruth is writing at the desk.* DAISY *opens the hall door and stops, listening back into the hall.*

RUTH. (*Quickly.*) What's the matter?

DAISY. Nothing. I was looking to see who went up the stairs. It's Dr. Remington.

RUTH. How's Millicent now?

DAISY. Ann's with her—getting her to bed.

RUTH. Do you know yet why she came home?

DIASY. I don't know whether Ann's got it out of her yet or not.

RUTH. What do you think? Why on earth didn't she tell them at school?

DAISY. I haven't the dimmest—but she didn't do it without some good reason. I'll bet anything on that. Millicent's a pretty level-headed youngster.

RUTH. She's a pretty self-willed one. Ann will send her right back of course.

DAISY. I don't know whether she will or not. Millicent's got some rather decided ideas of her own on that.

RUTH. But she'll *have* to go. Why shouldn't she? Ann will make her.

DAISY. Tom will have something to say about it.

RUTH. It's for Ann to decide surely.

DAISY. Not at all. I don't see why. She is Tom's child, too, you know, and this is his house and he pays the bills at school and if he doesn't want her to go back you can bet she jolly well won't go. I only hope Millicent tells the whole business whatever it is. Ann is so excited over the frieze I don't know whether she'll have the patience to handle Millicent right or not. She's not easy.

RUTH. It's awful for Ann to be upset now—of all times—when she has to begin this gigantic work.

DAISY. Oh—I wish the damned frieze were in Guinea and that Ann had nothing to do but take care of Tom and Millicent—like any other woman. I'd give *anything* if she hadn't won the competition.

RUTH. Daisy!

DAISY. Oh, I would. I have a ghastly feeling that something horrible is going to come of it—if it hasn't already come.

RUTH. What do you mean?

DAISY. I tell you it is not possible for a man and woman to love each other and live together and be happy—unless the man is—*it*.

RUTH. Speaking of the dark ages! You ought to live in a harem. How any girl who makes her own bread and butter can be so old fashioned as you are—I can't see.

DAISY. You've got so used to your own ideas your forget that I am the average normal woman the world is full of.

RUTH. Nonsense! You're almost extinct. I'm the average normal woman the world is full of—and it's going to be fuller and fuller.

DAISY. I'll bet on plenty of us—left—(*Indicating herself*) on Judgment day.

RUTH. I want to laugh when I think how mistaken we've been calling you a bachelor girl. Why you'd make the best wife of anybody I know.

DAISY. I s'pose you mean that as an insult.

RUTH. But you *seem* so self reliant men are sort of afraid of you—

REMINGTON. (*Coming in from hall and feeling a certain restraint in the two girls.*) Am I in the wrong camp.

RUTH and DAISY. No, no. Come in.

REMINGTON. I have to stay some place. I'm going to hang around till Millicent quiets down—and then I'll clear out.

DAISY. Is she ill?

REMINGTON. Oh, no. Just a little worked up and excited.

RUTH. Why do you think she came home, Dr. Remington?

REMINGTON. I don't know what to think—unless she has *"boy"* in the head.

DAISY. Goodness no! Not yet!

REMINGTON. She's sixteen. You can't choke it off to save your life.

RUTH. Oh, she's a baby!

REMINGTON. Don't fool yourself. She won't wait as long as you two have to sit by her own fireside with children on her knee.

RUTH. Oh—

REMINGTON. That's the only thing in the game that's worth a cent—anyway. (*As* KEITH *comes in from the hall.*) Isn't that so, Keith?

KEITH. What's that?

REMINGTON. I've just been telling these two that love and children are the greatest things on earth. Ruth doesn't agree with me—but Daisy—

RUTH. I must go.

DAISY. I must go up to Ann. (RUTH *goes out.*)

REMINGTON. Let *me* go. They both seem terribly anxious to get out when you come in, Keith. Or maybe I'm in the way. I'll go.

DAISY. Don't be silly. I really must see if I can do anything for Ann.

REMINGTON. No, you mustn't. She's waiting for me to see Millicent. By the way, Keith—tomorrow's Sunday. I always take a run into the country in the motor on Sunday. Come along and bring either Ruth or Daisy. Take your choice. I know which one I'd take. (*He goes into the hall.*)

DAISY. Isn't he a goose.

KEITH. Would it bore you to go, Daisy?

DAISY. Nonsense! Ruth will.

KEITH. It would be awfully good of you. Tomorrow's going to be a hard day for me to get through. Ruth told me tonight that she—I'm afraid it's all over.

DAISY. Why don't you compromise?

KEITH. There's nothing to compromise about. She's all wrong. Don't you think so?

DAISY. Oh, don't ask me. I don't know anything about it.

KEITH. Wait a minute. I—won't you go tomorrow, Daisy.

DAISY. Ask Ruth. It will be a good chance to make up.

KEITH. You're so *practical* and like such *different* things—maybe you'd think flying along through the country and lunching at some nice little out-of-the-way place was too frivolous—

DAISY. Oh yes, I don't like anything but being shut up in the house all day, pounding at my typewriter and splitting my head to get the bills straight. To actually go off with a man—for a whole day—and have a little fun—like any other woman—would be too unheard of. Of course, I couldn't do anything as silly as that.

KEITH. Oh—

DAISY. I wouldn't be amusing anyway. Dr. Remington—well, he's sixty, and you'd be thinking of Ruth and I'd sit there like a stick—the sensible, practical woman who couldn't possibly be interesting and fascinating because no man would take the trouble to find out how devilish and alluring and altogether exciting I could be if I had the chance. (*She throws open the door and goes out.* KEITH *stares after her.*)

TOM. (*Coming in from library after a moment.*) I thought you'd gone, McKenzie.

KEITH. No, but I'm going.

REMINGTON. (*Coming back from hall.*) Good night, McKenzie. I'll dig you up in the morning, ten o'clock. Sharp, mind. And I'll call for Daisy first.

KEITH. (*At hall door.*) All right. Much obliged, Doctor. (*Turning back.*) How'd you know it was Daisy?

REMINGTON. I didn't—but I do now.

KEITH. Good night. (*He goes out.*)

TOM. Well—how is she? How is Millicent?

REMINGTON. Oh, she's not ill—but the child's nervous as a witch—all strung up. She's worried about something—got something on her mind and naturally her head aches and she has a little fever—but that won't hurt her.

TOM. Got something on her mind? What?

REMINGTON. She didn't confide in me.

TOM. What *could* she have on her mind?

REMINGTON. I don't think she's committed murder—but she's *got* a mind, you know— There's no reason why she shouldn't have something *on* it.

TOM. Well, *I* don't know what to do with her.

REMINGTON. If you think she ought *not* to go back to school, say so. Tell Ann those are your orders.

TOM. I don't give orders to Ann.

REMINGTON. The devil you don't. She'd like it. A woman—a dog and a walnut tree—the more you beat 'em, the better they be.

TOM. The walnut tree business doesn't work with Ann. I made a fool of myself tonight by telling her I wouldn't touch the money she gets out of this thing. She doesn't understand. I've made her think I'm jealous because she won.

REMINGTON. Well, aren't you?

TOM. *No!* I tell you it's something else. Something sort of gave way under my feet when I opened her letter.

REMINGTON. I know. I know.

TOM. Doctor, for the Lord's sake, don't think I'm mean. I don't want to drag her back—but she seems gone somehow—she doesn't *need* me any more. *That's* what hurts.

REMINGTON. Of course, it hurts.

TOM. Much as I've loved to have her with me—working away at my elbow—wonderful as it all was—sometimes I've wished I hadn't seen her all day—that I had her to go home to—fresh and rested—waiting for *me* and that I was running the machine alone for her. She'll never understand. I've acted like a skunk.

REMINGTON. Y-e-s—I guess you have—so have I—unjust—pig-headed. No more right to say the things I've said to her than I have to spank her—except that she's—the most precious thing in the world to me—and I'd rather see her happy—as a woman—than *the greatest artist in the world.*

TOM. That's it. I want her here—*mine.* But I s'pose that's rotten and wrong.

REMINGTON. Yes—I s'pose it is. But you're despising yourself for something that's been in your bones—boy—since the beginning of time. Men and women will go through hell over this before it shakes down into shape. *You're* right and *she's* right and you're tearing each other like mad dogs over it because you love each other.

TOM. That's it. If another *man* had got it I'd take my licking without whining. What's the matter with me? Why can't I be that way to *her?*

REMINGTON. (*Shaking his head with a wistful smile.*) Male and female created He them. I don't take back any of the stuff I said to her before she went into this. She's fighting you now for her rights—but she laid her genius at your feet once and she'd do it again if—

ANN. (*Coming in from the hall and speaking after a pause.*) Well, father—what do you say about Millicent?

REMINGTON. My advice is that you let her stay at home for a while.

ANN. This is only a caprice—and it would be the worst thing in the world to give in to her. Unless you say as a physician—that she's too ill to—

REMINGTON. I don't say she's too ill—physically. You must decide for yourself. I'll go up and see her again and if she isn't asleep then I'll give her a mild sleeping powder. Ann, I put her in your arms first—and the look that came into your eyes then was as near divinity as we ever get. Oh, my daughter—don't let the new restlessness and strife of the world about you blind you to the old things—the real things. (*He goes out.*)

ANN. (*After a pause.*) You agree with me, don't you, that it's better for her to go back.

TOM. Do whatever you think best.

ANN. But what do *you* think?

TOM. It doesn't matter what I think, does it?

MILLICENT. (*Opening the door.*) Mother, aren't you coming back? (*Millicent wears a soft robe over her night gown. Her hair is down her back.*)

ANN. Millicent—why did you get out of bed?

MILLICENT. I couldn't sleep. (*Running and jumping into the middle of the couch.*)

ANN. Run back—quickly.

MILLICENT. In a minute. It's so quiet upstairs I couldn't sleep. I'm used to the girls.

ANN. You'll catch cold.

MILLICENT. Goodness, mother, I'm roasting.

ANN. *Millicent*—what *shall* I do with you.

MILLICENT. Is that what you and dad were talking about? What did Grandfather say? I don't care what he says. I'm not going back to school. You're on my side—aren't you, Dad?

TOM. Whatever your mother thinks is right, of course.

MILLICENT. Is it true—what Daisy told me—that you got the contract for a big frieze and not father? Is it? Is it, father? (*Looking from one to the other.*)

TOM. Yes. It's quite true.

ANN. Millicent, go to bed.

MILLICENT. I think that's perfectly horrid, mother. Why should they give it to you? I think father ought to have it—he's the man. Don't you think people will think it's funny that you didn't get it? I should think it would make them lose confidence in you. (*A pause.* TOM *stalks out—closing the door.*) Is father hurt because you got it? I should think he would be.

ANN. Millicent, I've had quite enough of this. Go up to bed at once.

MILLICENT. Will you come up and sleep with me?

ANN. Of course not. (*Walking about restlessly.*)

MILLICENT. Why not?

ANN. Neither one of us would sleep a wink.

MILLICENT. That wouldn't matter. I don't want to be alone.

ANN. Come now—I won't speak to you again.

MILLICENT. What have you decided about school?

ANN. I'll tell you in the morning.

MILLICENT. I won't go up till you tell me.

ANN. Millicent—you will go at once, I say.

MILLICENT. Oh, Mother, don't be cross. Sit down and talk a minute.

ANN. It's late, dear. You must—

MILLICENT. That's nothing. We girls often talk till twelve.

ANN. Till twelve? Do the teachers know it.

MILLICENT. Oh, mother, you're lovely! Don't you suppose they *know* that they don't know everything that's going on? Come and sit down, Mummie.

ANN. No! You must go to bed.

MILLICENT. But I won't go back to school.

ANN. (*Going to* MILLICENT, *who is still on the couch.*) You make it terribly hard for me, Millicent. You don't know what's good for you, of course. I don't expect you to—but I *do* expect you to be obedient.

MILLICENT. But, Mother, I tell you I—

ANN. Don't be so rebellious. Now come upstairs, please dear, and—

MILLICENT. But I won't go back to school, mother, dear. I won't.

ANN. You say I treat you like a child. You *force* me to. If you don't want me to punish you—go upstairs at once and don't say another word.

MILLICENT. I won't go back.

ANN. Stop, I say!

MILLICENT. I know what I want to do. I'm sixteen.

ANN. (*Their voices rising together.*) You're my child. You will obey me.

MILLICENT. But I won't. You don't understand. I can't mother, I can't—I can't.

ANN. Why? Why can't you?

MILLICENT. Because I—I'm going to be married.

ANN. You silly child!

MILLICENT. It's the truth, Mother. I am.

ANN. Don't say a thing like that, even in fun.

MILLICENT. It's the truth, I tell you. I'm going to be married.

ANN. Some time you are, of course—you mean.

MILLICENT. No—now—soon. That's why I left. That's why I'm not going back.

ANN. (*After drawing a chair to the couch and sitting before* MILLICENT.) What do you mean?

MILLICENT. I—he—we—we're engaged.

ANN. He—who?

MILLICENT. You—You don't know him.

ANN. Who?

MILLICENT. He's—he's perfectly wonderful.

ANN. *Who is he?*

MILLICENT. Now, Mother, wait. He—he isn't rich—

ANN. Well—

MILLICENT. He's poor—but he's perfectly wonderful—he works and he's so noble about it.

ANN. What does he do?

MILLICENT. He—he—Oh, mother, it's hard to explain, because he's so different.

ANN. *What does he do?*

MILLICENT. Well—just now he—he drives the motor at school—because you see he's so proud he—

ANN. Drives the motor—a chauffeur, you mean?

MILLICENT. People call him that, of course—but he isn't— (ANN *rises.*) Mother— (ANN *goes to the door and locks it—going back to* MILLICENT, *who had risen.*) Now, Mother, don't look like that.

ANN. Sit down.

MILLICENT. *Don't* look like that. Let me tell you about it.

ANN. (*Sitting again.*) Yes, tell me about it.

MILLICENT. Oh, I—hardly know how to begin.

ANN. He drives the motor—the school motor, you say?

MILLICENT. Yes—to the trains, you know—and into town and to church.

ANN. Who is his father?

MILLICENT. Why—I—I don't know who he is. I've never met his father.

ANN. What is his name?

MILLICENT. His father's name? I don't know.

ANN. The *boy's* name.

MILLICENT. Willie Kern.

ANN. How does he happen to drive a motor?

MILLICENT. Well, I don't know just *how* it happened—he's so clever you know, and of course he isn't really a chauffeur at all.

ANN. What is he then?

MILLICENT. Oh, Mother! He just happens to run the school motor.

ANN. And what did he do before that?

MILLICENT. Why he—he ran *another* motor. Oh, now, Mother, you don't understand at all. (*She breaks into sobs and throws herself full length on the couch.* ANN *sits rigidly.*) Just because he's poor and clever and drives a motor is no reason why you should act this way. (*Sitting up.*) He's going to do something else. He's going to come to New York to get a different position. And we'll be married as soon as he gets it, and that's why I came home—to tell you. So there—you see I can't go back to school. (*She rises and starts to the door.*)

ANN. Millicent! Come here.

MILLICENT. That's all there is to tell. I'm going to bed now.

ANN. (*Rising.*) You know this is the most wild and impossible thing in the world.

MILLICENT. I don't. It *isn't* impossible. I'm going to marry him. I love him better than you or father or anybody in the world and I'm going to marry him.

ANN. Stop! Do you want to disgrace us? How any child of mine could speak—even speak to such a— Oh, the disappointment! Where's your pride? How *could* you? How could you? Millicent, if you'll promise me to give this up I won't say a word to your father.

MILLICENT. No—no—I'm going.

ANN. Don't unlock that door.

MILLICENT. I want to go now.

ANN. You'll never see this boy again. Never speak to him—never write to him—never hear of him. I shall send you away where he'll never know—

MILLICENT. (*Coming back to couch.*) You won't! He loves me and I love him. He understands me. All that vacation when you wouldn't let me come home and all the other girls had gone he was just as good to me as he could be. He knew how lonely I was and he—we got engaged that vacation. You wouldn't let me come home.

ANN. Millicent—you don't know what you're saying. You don't know what you're doing.

MILLICENT. Oh, yes, I do, Mother. It's you that don't know. You don't understand.

ANN. (*Kneeling before Millicent.*) My darling—why—didn't you tell me this when you said you wanted to come home? Why didn't you tell me then? (*Sobbing,* ANN *buries her face in* MILLICENT'S *lap.*)

MILLICENT. I would have told you—if you'd let me come home—but you wouldn't—and I was so lonely there without the girls and—we—we got engaged. You don't understand, Mother.

ANN. (*Lifting her face to* MILLICENT.) Oh, yes, I do, dear. Yes, I do. Tell me —all about it. When did you first know him? How did you—happen to speak to him—I mean to—to love him.

MILLICENT. Oh, Mother, why I—he—I just did—he's so handsome and so nice. You haven't any idea how nice he is, Mother.

ANN. Haven't I, dear? What is he like? Tell me *everything*—how did it begin?

MILLICENT. He—the first time I really knew he was so different you know—

ANN. Yes, dear.

MILLICENT. Was one Sunday morning I was ready for church before anybody else and I went out to get in the motor and ran down the steps and fell, and he jumped out and picked me up and put me in the motor, and of course I thanked him and we had to wait quite a while for the others, and I found out how different and really wonderful he was. All the girls were crazy about him. Here's his picture. (*Drawing out a locket which is on a chain around her neck.*) It's just a little snapshot which I took myself one morning—and you can't really tell from this how awfully good looking he is. (ANN *seizes the locket and looks closely at the picture.*) His eyes are the most wonderful—and his lashes are the longest I ever saw. You can't see his teeth and they are—well, you'd just love his teeth, Mother.

ANN. Would I, dear? Have you seen very much of him? Hawe you seen him any place besides in the motor, I mean? (MILLICENT *hesitates.*) Tell me, dear—everything. I shall understand.

MILLICENT. Well, of course, Mother—I *had* to see him some place else after school began again and the girls were all back and I wasn't going for the mail any more.

ANN. Of course; and where *did* you see him?

MILLICENT. Why, you see, it—it was awfully hard, Mummie, because I couldn't tell anybody. Nobody would have *understood*—except Fanny. She's such a dear. She's been so sympathetic through the whole thing, and she has helped me a lot. There is a fire escape out of our room and Mondays and Thursdays at nine o'clock at night—

ANN. Oh—

MILLICENT. What, Mother?

ANN. Nothing—go on, dear.

MILLICENT. At exactly nine I'd put on Fanny's long black coat and go down, and he was always there and we always went down in the arbor just a little while.

ANN. The arbor? Where was the arbor?

MILLICENT. Down the path of the other side of the drive—not far from the house; but of course nobody went near it at that time of night—in cold weather and—and we'd talk a while and then I'd run back. You don't mind, do you, Mother. What else could I do?

ANN. And—he's kissed you—of course?

MILLICENT. Of course.

ANN. And you've kissed him?

MILLICENT. (*Lowering her eyes.*) Why yes—Mother—we're engaged.

ANN. And what did he say to you there in the arbor?

MILLICENT. I can't tell you *everything* he said, Mother.

ANN. Why not, Millicent? I'm your mother. No one on earth is so close to you—or loves you so much—or cares so much for your happiness—and understands so well. I remember when I was engaged to your father—I wasn't much older than you—I know, dear. Tell me what he said.

MILLICENT. He thinks I'm pretty, Mother.

ANN. Yes, dear.

MILLICENT. And he thinks I'm wonderful to understand him and to know what he really is in spite of what he happens to be doing.

ANN. Yes—and how long did you usually stay there in the arbor?

MILLICENT. Oh, not very long, only last time it was longer. He teased so and I couldn't help it. He—he—I—

ANN. How long was it that time?

MILLICENT. Oh—it—it was almost two hours last time.

ANN. And what did you do all that time? Wasn't it cold?

MILLICENT. He made me put on his overcoat—He *just made* me.

ANN. (*Holding* MILLICENT *close in her arms.*) And he held you close—and kissed you—and told you how much he loved you?

MILLICENT. Yes, I love him so—Mother—but—I—tonight, was the last night to go again—but I—

ANN. (*Holding* MILLICENT *off as she searches her face.*) Yes, dear?

MILLICENT. I—I was—afraid to go.

ANN. (*Shrieking.*) Why?

MILLICENT. Oh, Mother—Was it wicked to be afraid? I ran away—I wanted to be with you. (ANN *snatches* MILLICENT *in her arms. Her head falls against* MILLICENT *and* MILLICENT'S *arms hold her close as she sobs. Someone tries the door and knocks.*)

TOM. (*In the hall.*) Ann!—Ann!

ANN. Yes?

TOM. Why is the door locked?

ANN. Millicent and I are talking. Wait just a few minutes. And Tom—tell her grandfather not to wait to see Millicent again tonight. She's all right.

TOM. Sure?

ANN. I'm sure.

MILLICENT. (*In a whisper—after listening a moment.*) What are you going to tell father?

ANN. (*Sitting on the floor.*) Well—you see, dear—you're too young to be married now—much too young—and—

MILLICENT. Oh, now, Mother, if you're going to talk *that* way. Wait till you see him.

ANN. That's just what I want to do. I've got such a lovely plan for us—for the summer.

MILLICENT. But I want to be married as soon as he gets his—

ANN. I know, his position—and while he's looking and getting settled you and I will go abroad.

MILLICENT. You're awfully good, Mother, but if you really want to do something for me—I'd rather you'd give me that money to be married.

ANN. But Millicent, my dear child—I *have* to go. I'm so tired. I've been working awfully hard this winter. You're the only one in the world who could really be with me and take care of me. I *need* you.

MILLICENT. Poor Mother! I don't want to be *selfish* and if you *need* me—I'll go.

ANN. (*Catching* MILLICENT *in her arms.*) Thank you, dear.

MILLICENT. *If* you'll promise me that I can be married when I get back.

ANN. (*Getting to her feet.*) If—you—*still—want* to—marry him when you come—back with me—you may. I promise.

MILLICENT. Mother! I didn't know you loved me so much.

ANN. Didn't you, dear? Now go to bed. (*They start to the door together.* ANN *catches* MILLICENT *again, kissing her tenderly as though she were something new and precious.*)

MILLICENT. What's the matter, Mother?

ANN. Nothing, dear— Good night.

MILLICENT. Good night.

TOM. (*Coming into doorway as* MILLICENT *unlocks and opens the door.*) Not in bed yet?

MILLICENT. (*Throwing her arms about her father's neck.*) Oh, dad. I'm so happy. (*She goes out.*)

ANN. (*Sitting at the fire.*) Come, in, Tom. I want to talk to you about Millicent.

TOM. (*Closing the door and going to* ANN.) What's the matter?

ANN. She thinks she's in love.

TOM. What?

ANN. Our baby. She wants to be married.

TOM. What do you mean?

ANN. That's why she came home.

TOM. Good Heavens, Ann! Married? What has she got mixed up in? How did such a thing happen? How *could* it?

ANN. Because I didn't let her come home when she wanted to. Don't say anything, Tom. I can't bear it now.

TOM. (*Putting a hand on her head tenderly.*) Don't dear! Don't! It—might have—happened—anyway.

ANN. Oh, the things that *can* happen!

TOM. Has she told you everything?

ANN. Everything.

TOM. What have you said to her? What are you going to do?

ANN. I'm going to take her away—and win her—till she gives up of her own free will—I shall have to have the wisdom of all the ages. I shall have to be more fascinating than the boy. That's a pretty big undertaking, Tom. I wonder if I'll be equal to it.

TOM. You mean you're going to give up your frieze and go away with her? (ANN *nods her head.*) You can't do it, Ann.

ANN. (*Rising and moving away.*) Oh, yes, I can.

TOM. You cannot. Don't lose your head. You're pledged to finish it and deliver it at a certain time. You can't play fast and lose with a big piece of work like that.

ANN. *You'll* have to make my frieze, Tom.

TOM. I will not! I utterly and absolutely refuse to. You make Millicent behave and break this thing up and you go on with your—

ANN. I can't. I can't. She's been in danger—absolute danger.

TOM. How?

ANN. Oh, I'll tell you. I'll tell you. She ran away to me—to me—and I was pushing her off. My little girl! She's got to be held tight in my arms and carried through.

TOM. Ann, I'm not going to allow this to wipe out what you've done. I'll settle her—

ANN. Tom, you can't speak of it to her—not breathe it—

TOM. Of course I will.

ANN. No you won't . If we cross her she'll get at him some way—somehow.

TOM. I'm not going to let you sacrifice yourself for a wayward—

ANN. It's my job. She is what I've given to life. If I fail her now—my whole life's a failure. Will you make my frieze, dear, will you?

TOM. No. It's *yours.* You've got to have the glory of it. Ann, I haven't been fair—but you're going to have this and all that's coming to you. I'm not going to let anything take it away from you. It's too important. My God, you've not only beaten me—you've won over the biggest men in the field—with your own brain and your own hands—in a fair, fine, hard fight. You're cut up now—but if you should give this thing up—there'll be times when you'd eat your heart out to be at work on it—when the artist in you will *yell* to be let out.

ANN. I know. I know. And I'll hate you because you're doing it—and I'll hate myself because I gave it up—and I'll almost—hate—her. I know. I know. You needn't tell me. Why I've seen my men and women up there—their strong limbs stretched—their hair blown back. I've seen the crowd looking up—I've heard people say—"A woman did that" and my heart has almost burst with pride—not so much that *I* had done it—but for *all* women. And then the door opened—and Millicent came in. There isn't any choice, Tom—she's part of my body—part of my soul. Will you make my frieze, dear, will you? (*Falling against him.*)

TOM. (*Taking her in his arms.*) My darling! I'll do whatever makes it easiest for you. Don't think I don't know *all—all*—it means to you. My God, it's hard.

ANN. (*Releasing herself and going to the hall door.*) Put out the light. I hope she's asleep. (*They go out into the lighted hall. After a moment*

THE CURTAIN FALLS.)

BEYOND THE HORIZON

A PLAY IN THREE ACTS

BY

Eugene O'Neill

Reprinted from the Revised Edition by special arrangement with Mr. Eugene O'Neill and Boni and Liveright.

BEYOND THE HORIZON *

Beyond the Horizon represents the idealism of youth which demands adventure, and even when frustrated by love, is conscious at the end that the very possession of the dreams has been worth while. It presents also the work of the playwright who is generally recognized to be the most significant of those who are now writing for the stage in America.

So much that is incorrect has been published concerning the career of Eugene O'Neill that it is a pleasure to present the facts of his life as given by the playwright himself, in a letter written at the request of the editor.

"As for the autobiography, I'll give it to you in brief herewith: I was born October 16, 1888. My first seven years were spent mainly in the larger towns all over the United States—my mother accompanying my father on his road tours in *Monte Cristo* and repertoire, although she was never an actress and had rather an aversion for the atmosphere and people of the stage in general. After that came boarding school for six years in Catholic schools—then four years at Betts Academy, Stamford, Connecticut and then Princeton University for one year in the Class of 1910. Then I worked for over a year as secretary of a mail order house, a small affair, in New York City. The firm went into bankruptcy. I never took it seriously. Discovering a chance to work off some of my latent romanticism I went to Spanish Honduras with a mining engineer on a prospecting expedition—at the end of eight months or so caught the malarial fever so bad that I had to be sent home. Much hardship, little romance, no gold. On my return to the United States I was made assistant manager of *The White Sister* Company and toured from St. Louis back through the Middle West to Boston with them. Having read Conrad's *Nigger of the Narcissus* some time before—also Jack London—I got the urge for the sea, sailing ships. So I sailed from Boston for Buenos Aires on a Norwegian Barque—sixty-five days out of sight of land. I remained in Buenos Aires for a year or so—worked with Westinghouse Electric Company, Swift Packing Company, Singer Sewing Machine Company, at different times. (This was in years 1910–1911.) I also worked on a cattle boat taking a voyage from Buenos Aires to Durban, South Africa and return. Then I was 'on the beach' for a considerable period in Buenos Aires with no job, eating and place to sleep intermittent. Finally I returned home as an ordinary seaman on a British tramp steamer to New York. After a period in New York loafing I became able seaman on the American Line steamers 'New York' and 'Philadelphia.' This was my last experience as a sailor. I then became an actor in my father's company playing in *Monte Cristo* sketch, touring the Orpheum circuit in the far West. Then I worked as a reporter on a morning paper, New

* This Introduction has been completely revised for the Sixth Edition.

London, Connecticut for six months or so. My health then broke down with a slight touch of pulmonary tuberculosis resulting, so I spent six months in a sanitarium. After I was released I started to write for the first time—this was in 1913, the latter part I think. In that winter, 1913–1914, I wrote eight one-act plays and two long plays. Of these *Bound East for Cardiff* is the only one worth remembering. In 1914–15 I attended Professor Baker's course at Harvard. The winter of 1915–16 was spent in Greenwich Village. In the summer of 1916 I came to Provincetown, joined the Provincetown Players and acted in my own plays, *Bound East for Cardiff* and *Thirst* at the theatre shed on the wharf here. When they opened the first season in New York, *Cardiff* was on the opening bill.''

Since then Mr. O'Neill has devoted himself to the writing and direction of his plays. In 1936 his international eminence was recognized by the award of the Nobel Prize for Literature.

The Provincetown Players have produced nearly all of Mr. O'Neill's one act plays, *In the Zone* being the first to be performed elsewhere, being put on at the Comedy Theatre, October 31, 1917 by the Washington Square Players. After the reorganization of the Provincetown Theatre group in 1923, Mr. O'Neill continued as Associate Director of the Experimental Theatre. His association with the courageous band of producers, playwrights and actors, under the leadership of Mr. Kenneth Macgowan, Mr. Robert Edmond Jones, Mr. James Light, and Miss M. Eleanor Fitzgerald, has been one of the most fruitful in the history of the American theatre.

Beyond the Horizon was Mr. O'Neill's first play to be performed by a strictly professional company, being put on at a special matinee at the Morosco Theatre, February 2, 1920. It had a successful run at the Criterion and the Little Theatres in New York but when taken to Chicago in the fall was not a popular success. It was however acclaimed by competent critics as the most significant play that had appeared on the American stage for many years and was awarded the Pulitzer Prize for the best American play for 1919–20. The cast was adequate, Mr. Richard Bennett as Robert Mayo, Mr. Robert Kelly as Andy and Mrs. Louise Closser Hale as Mrs. Atkins giving especially brilliant performances. While Mr. O'Neill's art has deepened and his inventive quality has progressed, *Beyond the Horizon* still remains in some ways the best of his plays for study. For it is based upon the great truth that there is nothing so precious in our lives as our illusions; its form is compact, the action is unified and progressive and the tragedy is inevitable. It has been played by many Little Theatre organizations throughout the United States, and almost invariably with artistic and financial success.

In the story of the two brothers, Robert and Andy Mayo, he drew a vivid contrast of character and he made that contrast dramatic through their love for the same woman whose shallow passion clutched at both their ambitions and wrecked them. In Robert Mayo we see O'Neill's own passion for adventure ''beyond the horizon.'' where the sea is calling him. Robert is about to realize it when Ruth lets him see she cares for him and he gives up his dreams to marry her and settle down to the farming life for which he is unfit. Andy, unable to stay to watch their happiness, accepts the opportunity Robert has refused and yet, successful as he seems to be, the play leaves him with a realization that all he has won has been the money which is so easily lost. For to him, the farm was in the blood and his happiness was in it. How little he made of the "far foreign places" is seen in Act II, Scene 2, when he describes with powerful realism just how the sailor travels much but sees nothing. For Robert, who had the vision, the adventure would have been far different. It is unfortunate that the play was not first performed as it was written and as it is printed. The second scene of Act III was omitted and the play closed on Andy's words "Damn you, you never told him" transferred to the first scene as Andy entered Robert's room to find him dead. For in the acted version there was lost the great meaning of the play, expressed in Robert's words on the hillside: "You mustn't feel sorry for me. Don't you see I'm happy at last—free—free—freed from the farm—free to wander on and on eternally!—I've won to my trip—beyond the horizon!" With a total misunderstanding of Mr. O'Neill's work, he has often been referred to as a pessimist. But in this fine last scene of *Beyond the Horizon* he revealed the truth that even if unrealized, Robert's dreams had made life worth while to him. On the contrary to Andy has come discontent and to Ruth that "spent calm beyond the further troubling of any hope."

In *The Emperor Jones,* produced first at the Provincetown Theatre on November 1, 1920 and later at the Selwyn and the Princess Theatres, Mr. O'Neill created the character of "Brutus Jones," a negro adventurer who dominates a West Indian island by his courage and unscrupulousness. In this play Mr. O'Neill substituted a unity of impression for the unity of action. *Diff'rent,* a two-act play laid in a seaport village in New England in 1890 and in 1920, was first produced at the Provincetown Theatre on December 27, 1920, and was taken to the Princess Theatre on January 29, 1921. *Gold,* an expansion of a one-act play *Where the Cross is Made,* was produced at the Frazee Theatre, June 1, 1921 but failed. These two plays were less significant than *Anna Christie,* a masterly portrayal of the regeneration of a woman through the influence of the sea and the effect of a great passion for the one kind of man who might save her from the effects of the past. In this play Miss Pauline Lord and Mr. George Marion as Anna Christie and Chris Christopherson, her father, gave two remarkable performances. The play received the Pulitzer Prize for the season of 1921–22. It opened at the Vanderbilt Theatre, November 2, 1921, and after a successful run went on tour.

The Straw, in which Mr. O'Neill showed how love and hope can almost triumph even at the hour of death, had a short run at the Greenwich Village Theatre beginning November 10, 1921. The superb acting of Mr. Otto Kruger and Miss Margalo Gillmore in the last scene of this play was unable to save one of the finest of Mr. O'Neill's plays from the disastrous effects of the worst theatrical season in recent years.

The First Man, a dramatic picture of the struggle which may occur in a man's soul between his love for his child and his profession, was performed at the Neighborhood Playhouse, March 4, 1922, as part of the season's repertoire. *The Hairy Ape,* like *The Emperor Jones* was presented in a series of scenes rather than in acts. It represented the struggle upward of a merely physical type, a stoker on an ocean liner, and the tragedy of misguided power which such a struggle brings about. No place in the scheme of things is found for such a being and he is finally crushed to death by the gorilla in the Zoological Gardens who has had no more sympathy with him than his fellow human beings. *The Hairy Ape* was first produced March 9, 1922 at the Provincetown Theatre and was then taken to the Plymouth Theatre, where it ran until it was taken on tour. *Welded,* a conflict between a man and woman whose capacity to torture each other is measured only in the terms of their great mutual passion, had only a short run at the Thirty Ninth Street Theatre, beginning March 17, 1924. The leading members of the cast were incapable of interpreting the spiritual significance of the drama. Mr. O'Neill's next play, *All God's Chillun Got Wings* provoked much discussion on account of its treatment of the race question. The present editor is probably one of many who did not realize the significance of the play at first reading but who were profoundly impressed by the chief character, "Jim Harris" as interpreted by Mr. Paul Robeson. On November 3, 1924, four of the earlier one act plays of the sea, *The Moon of the Caribbees, The Long Voyage Home, In the Zone,* and *Bound East for Cardiff* were produced together at the Provincetown Theatre as the *S. S. Glencairn.* It was a highly interesting experience to note the way in which the recurrence of the characters brought into the production a unity of impression. *Desire Under the Elms,* which was first produced at the Greenwich Village Theatre on November 11, 1924, is a searching study of the New England nature with a background of the middle of the last century. It reveals in the characters of Ephraim Cabot and Eben, his son, a combination of profound belief in the supernatural; the determination to win in a hard struggle even against God; the recognition of God as an opponent who is to be respected rather than loved; and at the same time a shrewd disposition to maintain one's own property rights. Mr. Walter Huston gave a sympathetic interpretation of Ephraim Cabot, one of the most profoundly studied of Mr. O'Neill's characters.

With *The Fountain,* written during 1921–22, but not produced until 1925, Mr. O'Neill began a period of romantic symbolism. Juan Ponce de Leon became a symbol of the search for the fountain of eternal youth, and even in his failure, there was a note of exaltation. In *The Great God Brown,* produced January 23, 1926, at the Greenwich Village Theatre, Mr. O'Neill represented symbolically the struggle between the creative artist and the modern world. The characters wore masks at times, which concealed their real natures, and the tragedy which overcomes Brown, the business man, when he inherits the mask of Dion Anthony, the artist, and is torn by the duality of his nature, made a profound impression. *Marco Millions,* first performed on January 9, 1928, is a romance of the days of Marco Polo, whose spirit of commercial adventure is contrasted with the longing of the Orient, patient in its wisdom, and hoping for new light from the West, but receiving only the latest financial methods. The Theatre Guild made of it a gorgeous spectacle. The Guild also produced *Strange Interlude* on January 30, 1928, a profound study of a woman's clutch upon the lives of five men, her father, her husband, her son, and her two other lovers, who represent the spiritual and the physical elements in love. In this play, which held audiences spellbound through nine acts, Mr. O'Neill prefaced the words spoken by the characters to each other by thoughts uttered aloud, which the art of the production made natural and impressive. *Lazarus Laughed,* published in 1927, was produced at the Pasadena Community Playhouse, in California, April 9, 1928. It portrays the life of Lazarus, after his return from the grave, bearing the message that there is no death. Through vivid stage pictures in which large groups of characters, masked to typify various aspects of mankind, form a chorus, Lazarus conquers even the Emperor Tiberius by the force of his spirit, but becomes eventually a martyr. *Dynamo,* a symbolic play in which Mr. O'Neill dramatized his conception of the conflict between science and certain forms of religion, was produced at the Martin Beck Theatre, February 11, 1929, and was published, with considerable revision, in the same year. On the stage, the struggle was not as convincing as is usually the case in his plays.

In *Mourning Becomes Electra,* first produced by the Theatre Guild, October 26, 1931, Mr. O'Neill matched his strength with the greatest of the Greek dramatists and came out triumphant. He retold the story of Electra in the setting of New England at the close of the Civil War, and created an impressive tragedy from the lives of the Mannon family, in their loves and hates, and in their unbreakable pride. Those who saw Lavinia Mannon, played superbly by Alice Brady, go into the empty Mannon house, the last of her race, knew that they had been present at one of the great moments in the American theatre. Mr. O'Neill's next play, *Ah! Wilderness,* another Guild production, October 2, 1933, was a tender and compelling domestic comedy in which a father's love for his children was expressed without sentimentality. It gave Mr. George M. Cohan a fine opportunity, of which he took full advantage. *Days Without End* (January 8, 1934) was an artistic rather than a popular success in New York, although warmly praised when it was produced in Dublin at the Abbey Theatre. It is a profound study of the conflict in a man's nature between his good and evil spirit, in which he is saved by a return to his earlier faith.

A complete list of the foreign performances of Mr. O'Neill's plays cannot be given, since many are produced without authorization. Based upon information furnished by Mr. O'Neill and his agent, Mr. Madden, and supplemented by other sources, the following account will indicate at least the wide spread interest in his work abroad. At the Everyman Theatre in London, Mr. Norman

MacDermott produced *In the Zone* (June 15, 1921), *Diff'rent* (October 4, 1921) and *Ile* (April 17, 1922). *Anna Christie* was produced in London at the Strand Theatre, April 10, 1923. It was received with unstinted critical admiration although popular approval was not continuous. When produced at the Deutsches Theatre in Berlin, October 10, 1923, it was translated by the Hungarian dramatist, Lengyel, and Anna Christie shot herself! Notwithstanding this unfortunate introduction to the Continent, it has been played in 1923 in Sweden, Norway and Denmark, in 1924 in Spain, in Vienna and in Moscow and, in Paolo Giordani's translation, in Italy. It has been played in English through many of the coast cities in the Orient. *The Emperor Jones* was produced in Paris on October 30, 1923 at the Odéon, in a translation by Maurice Bourgeois, the title role being taken by Benglia, a noted negro colonial actor. Again great liberties were taken with the play by M. Gémier, the director, who omitted the striking scene in the slave ship, and interpolated meaningless pantomimes. It was also produced in Berlin, Vienna and Prague. *The Hairy Ape* was played in Sydney, Australia, in Prague and at the Kamerny Theatre in Moscow, where Tairoff also produced *Desire Under the Elms* in 1926 and *All God's Chillun Got Wings* in 1929. *Strange Interlude* was played in London in 1931 and *Mourning Becomes Electra* in 1933 at Stockholm. The announcement of the Nobel Prize Award to Mr. O'Neill in 1936 stimulated revivals of *Strange Interlude* and *Mourning Becomes Electra* in Sweden, and productions of the latter play in Budapest, Prague and London, where it was put on November 19, 1937, at the Westminster Theatre.

Beyond the Horizon was performed at the Norske Theater in Oslo, Norway, in June, 1937. It has also had the unusual distinction of being produced in Wales in a Welsh version in February, 1937, and of having been translated into Japanese.

Mr. O'Neill's plays have been published in many forms. Through his courtesy *Beyond the Horizon* is presented here in the revised form which appeared in his first collected Autograph Edition in 1924. Another limited edition, with prefaces by the author, was issued by Scribners in twelve volumes in 1934. Random House has taken over the publication of his works in popular form and issues them in separate volumes, usually containing two or more plays. They also publish the Nobel Prize Edition, containing nine plays. Practically all of Mr. O'Neill's plays have been widely circulated in translation on the continent of Europe.

A Bibliography of the Works of Eugene O'Neill, by Ralph Sanborn and Barrett H. Clark, was published in 1931 by Random House. Mr. Clark has also issued a critical biography, *Eugene O'Neill, the Man and His Plays,* revised in 1936 and published by McBride and Company. See for extended criticism, *Eugene O'Neill,* by Richard D. Skinner (1935), and "Eugene O'Neill,

Poet and Mystic,'' in *A History of the American Drama from the Civil War to the Present Day,* by A. H. Quinn, Revised Edition, two volumes in one, published by Appleton-Century-Crofts, Inc., 1936, Vol. 2, chaps. 21 and 24. A list of Mr. O'Neill's plays, with bibliography, is on pages 384–387.

Note to Seventh Edition.

On October 9, 1946, *The Iceman Cometh* was produced by the Theatre Guild. The main plot centers upon Theodore Hickman, a salesman, who gives a party for a group of derelicts living in a rooming house, drawn from places in which Mr. O'Neill had once lived. Hickman is symbolic of Death, and when at his suggestion they try to regain the positions they have lost, they fail, but they have been freed from the torment of indecision. Hickman kills his wife because he cannot give up the dissipation that is bringing her sorrow. *Lazarus Laughed* was produced at the Fordham University Theatre for several nights beginning April 8, 1948. *A Moon for the Misbegotten* was tried out on the road, opening for the first time at the Hartman Theatre, Columbus, Ohio, on February 20, 1947. It did not go into New York. It is a tragedy laid in Connecticut, in 1923, the central motive being the passion of Josie Hogan, a tall powerful woman, daughter of a tenant farmer, and Jim Tyrone, a man of education, but a weakling and a drunkard. Like so many of Mr. O'Neill's characters, they are in the grip of a fate that is not accidental but springs from their own natures and they part inevitably. Some of Mr. O'Neill's early plays, unprinted and unproduced, on which he had neglected to renew copyright, were published without his consent and against his wishes, in 1950, under the title *The Lost Plays of Eugene O'Neill.*

Among the many recent discussions the most important are: Sophus K. Winther, *Eugene O'Neill, A Critical Study,* 1934; a revised biography by B. H. Clark, 1947; a list of foreign editions of O'Neill's works by Horst Frenz, *Bulletin of Bibliography,* Vol. 18 (1943), pp. 33–34. Maurice Lanoire's ''Eugene O'Neill,'' *Revue de Paris* (Feb. 1, 1937), pp. 595–612 is a sympathetic analysis.

CAST OF CHARACTERS

(in the order of their appearance)

Morosco Theatre, New York, February 2, 1920

ROBERT MAYO	sons of JAMES MAYO	Richard Bennett
ANDREW MAYO		Robert Kelly

RUTH ATKINS...Elsie Rizer
CAPT. DICK SCOTT, MRS. MAYO's brother, of the bark *Sunda*......Sidney Macy
MRS. KATE MAYO, wife of JAMES MAYO..........................Mary Jeffery
JAMES MAYO, a farmer.......................................Erville Alderson
MRS. ATKINS, RUTH's widowed mother....................Louise Closser Hale
MARY..Elfin Finn
BEN, a farm hand...George Hadden
DR. FAWCETT...George Riddell

ACT I

SCENE I: The Road. Sunset of a day in Spring.
SCENE II: The Farm House. The same night.

ACT II

(*Three years later*)

SCENE I: The Farm House. Noon of a Summer day.
SCENE II: The top of a hill on the farm overlooking the sea. The following day.

ACT III

(*Five years later*)

SCENE I: The Farm House. Dawn of a day in late Fall.
SCENE II: The Road. Sunrise.

BEYOND THE HORIZON

ACT ONE

Scene One

Scene. *A section of country highway. The road runs diagonally from the left, forward, to the right, rear, and can be seen in the distance winding toward the horizon like a pale ribbon between the low, rolling hills with their freshly plowed fields clearly divided from each other, checkerboard fashion, by the lines of stone walls and rough snake fences.*

The forward triangle cut off by the road is a section of a field from the dark earth of which myriad bright-green blades of fall-sown rye are sprouting. A straggling line of piled rocks, too low to be called a wall, separates this field from the road.

To the rear of the road is a ditch with a sloping, grassy bank on the far side. From the center of this an old, gnarled apple tree, just budding into leaf, strains its twisted branches heavenwards, black against the pallor of distance: A snake-fence sidles from left to right along the top of the bank, passing beneath the apple tree.

The hushed twilight of the day in May is just beginning. The horizon hills are still rimmed by a faint line of flame, and the sky above them glows with the crimson flush of the sunset. This fades gradually as the action of the scene progresses.

At the rise of the curtain, Robert Mayo *is discovered sitting on the fence. He is a tall, slender young man of twenty-three. There is a touch of the poet about him expressed in his high forehead and wide, dark eyes. His features are delicate and refined, leaning to weakness in the mouth and chin. He is dressed in gray corduroy trousers pushed into high laced boots, and a blue flannel shirt with a bright colored tie. He is reading a book by the fading sunset light. He shuts this, keeping a finger in to mark the place, and turns his head toward the horizon, gazing out over the fields and hills. His lips move as if he were reciting something to himself.*

His brother Andrew *comes along the road from the right, returning from his work in the fields. He is twenty-seven years old, an opposite type to* Robert*—husky, sun-bronzed, handsome in a large-featured, manly fashion—a son of the soil, intelligent in a shrewd way, but with nothing of the intellectual about him. He wears overalls, leather boots, a gray flannel shirt open at the neck, and a soft, mud-stained hat pushed back on his head. He stops to talk to* Robert, *leaning on the hoe he carries.*

Andrew. (*Seeing* Robert *has not noticed his presence—in a loud shout.*) Hey there! (Robert *turns with a start. Seeing who it is, he smiles.*) Gosh, you do take the prize for day-dreaming! And I see you've toted one of the old books along with you. (*He crosses the ditch and sits on the fence near his brother.*) What is it this time—poetry, I'll bet. (*He reaches for the book.*) Let me see.

Robert. (*Handing it to him rather reluctantly.*) Look out you don't get it full of dirt.

Andrew. (*Glancing at his hands.*) That isn't dirt—it's good clean earth. (*He turns over the pages. His eyes read something and he gives an exclamation of disgust.*) Hump! (*With a provoking grin at his brother he reads aloud in a doleful, sing-song voice.*) "I have loved wind and light and the bright sea. But holy and most sacred night, not as I love and have loved thee." (*He hands the book back.*) Here! Take it and bury it. I suppose it's that year in college gave you a liking for that kind of stuff. I'm darn glad I stopped at High School, or maybe I'd been crazy too.

(*He grins and slaps* ROBERT *on the back affectionately.*) Imagine me reading poetry and plowing at the same time! The team'd run away, I'll bet.

ROBERT. (*Laughing.*) Or picture me plowing.

ANDREW. You should have gone back to college last fall, like I know you wanted to. You're fitted for that sort of thing—just as I ain't.

ROBERT. You know why I didn't go back, Andy. Pa didn't like the idea, even if he didn't say so; and I know he wanted the money to use improving the farm. And besides, I'm not keen on being a student, just because you see me reading books all the time. What I want to do now is keep on moving so that I won't take root in any one place.

ANDREW. Well, the trip you're leaving on to-morrow will keep you moving all right. (*At this mention of the trip they both fall silent. There is a pause. Finally* ANDREW *goes on, awkwardly, attempting to speak casually.*) Uncle says you'll be gone three years.

ROBERT. About that, he figures.

ANDREW. (*Moodily.*) That's a long time.

ROBERT. Not so long when you come to consider it. You know the *Sunda* sails around the Horn for Yokohama first, and that's a long voyage on a sailing ship; and if we go to any of the other places Uncle Dick mentions—India, or Australia, or South Africa, or South America—they'll be long voyages, too.

ANDREW. You can have all those foreign parts for all of me. (*After a pause.*) Ma's going to miss you a lot, Rob.

ROBERT. Yes—and I'll miss her.

ANDREW. And Pa ain't feeling none too happy to have you go—though he's been trying not to show it.

ROBERT. I can see how he feels.

ANDREW. And you can bet that I'm not giving any cheers about it. (*He puts one hand on the fence near* ROBERT.)

ROBERT. (*Putting one hand on top of* ANDREW'S *with a gesture almost of shyness.*) I know that, too, Andy.

ANDREW. I'll miss you as much as anybody, I guess. You see, you and I ain't like most brothers—always fighting and separated a lot of the time, while we've always been together—just the two of us. It's different with us. That's why it hits so hard, I guess.

ROBERT. (*With feeling.*) It's just as hard for me. Andy—believe that! I hate to leave you and the old folks—but—I feel I've got to. There's something calling me— (*He points to the horizon.*) Oh, I can't just explain it to you, Andy.

ANDREW. No need to, Rob. (*Angry at himself.*) Hell! You want to go—that's all there is to it; and I wouldn't have you miss this chance for the world.

ROBERT. It's fine of you to feel that way, Andy.

ANDREW. Huh! I'd be a nice son-of-a-gun if I didn't, wouldn't I? When I know how you need this sea trip to make a new man of you—in the body, I mean—and give you your full health back.

ROBERT. (*A trifle impatiently.*) All of you seem to keep harping on my health. You were so used to seeing me lying around the house in the old days that you never will get over the notion that I'm a chronic invalid. You don't realize how I've bucked up in the past few years. If I had no other excuse for going on Uncle Dick's ship but just my health, I'd stay right here and start in plowing.

ANDREW. Can't be done. Farming ain't your nature. There's all the difference shown in just the way us two feel about the farm. You—well, you like the home part of it, I expect; but as a place to work and grow things, you hate it. Ain't that right?

ROBERT. Yes, I suppose it is. For you it's different. You're a Mayo through and through. You're wedded to the soil. You're as much a product of it as an ear of corn is, or a tree. Father is the same. This farm is his life-work, and he's happy in knowing that another Mayo, inspired by the same love, will take up the work where he leaves off. I can understand your attitude, and Pa's; and I think it's wonderful and sincere. But I—well, I'm not made that way.

ANDREW. No, you ain't; but when it comes to understanding, I guess I realize that you've got your own angle of looking at things.

ROBERT. (*Musingly.*) I wonder if you do really.

ANDREW. (*Confidently.*) Sure I do. You've seen a bit of the world, enough to make the farm seem small, and you've got the itch to see it all.

ROBERT. It's more than that, Andy.

ANDREW. Oh, of course. I know you're going to learn navigation, and all about a ship, so's you can be an officer. That's natural, too. There's fair pay in it, I expect, when you consider that you've always got a home and grub thrown in; and if you're set on traveling, you can go anywhere you're a mind to without paying fare.

ROBERT. (*With a smile that is half sad.*) It's more than that, Andy.

ANDREW. Sure it is. There's always a chance of a good thing coming your way in some of those foreign ports or other. I've heard there are great opportunities for a young fellow with his eyes open in some of those new countries that are just being opened up. (*Jovially.*) I'll bet that's what you've been turning over in your mind under all your quietness! (*He slaps his brother on the back, with a laugh.*) Well, if you get to be a millionaire all of a sudden, call 'round once in a while and I'll pass the plate to you. We could use a lot of money right here on the farm without hurting it any.

ROBERT. (*Forced to laugh.*) I've never considered that practical side of it for a minute, Andy.

ANDREW. Well, you ought to.

ROBERT. No, I oughtn't. (*Pointing to the horizon—dreamily.*) Supposing I was to tell you that it's just Beauty that's calling me, the beauty of the far off and unknown, the mystery and spell of the East which lures me in the books I've read, the need of the freedom of great wide spaces, the joy of wandering on and on—in quest of the secret which is hidden over there, beyond the horizon? Suppose I told you that was the one and only reason for my going?

ANDREW. I should say you were nutty.

ROBERT. (*Frowning.*) Don't, Andy. I'm serious.

ANDREW. Then you might as well stay here, because we've got all you're looking for right on this farm. There's wide space enough, Lord knows; and you can have all the sea you want by walking a mile down to the beach; and there's plenty of horizon to look at, and beauty enough for anyone, except in the winter. (*He grins.*) As for the mystery and spell, I haven't met 'em yet, but they're probably lying around somewheres. I'll have you understand this is a first class farm with all the fixings. (*He laughs.*)

ROBERT. (*Joining in the laughter in spite of himself.*) It's no use talking to you, you chump!

ANDREW. You'd better not say anything to Uncle Dick about spells and things when you're on the ship. He'll likely chuck you overboard for a Jonah. (*He jumps down from fence.*) I'd better run along. I've got to wash up some as long as Ruth's Ma is coming over for supper.

ROBERT. (*Pointedly—almost bitterly.*) And Ruth.

ANDREW. (*Confused—looking everywhere except at* ROBERT*—trying to appear unconcerned.*) Yes, Ruth'll be staying too. Well, I better hustle, I guess, and—(*He steps over the ditch to the road while he is talking.*)

ROBERT. (*Who appears to be fighting some strong inward emotion—impulsively.*) Wait a minute, Andy! (*He jumps down from the fence.*) There is something I want to— (*He stops abruptly, biting his lips, his face coloring*).

ANDREW. (*Facing him; half-defiantly.*) Yes?

ROBERT. (*Confusedly.*) No—never mind —it doesn't matter, it was nothing.

ANDREW. (*After a pause, during which he stares fixedly at* ROBERT'S *averted face.*) Maybe I can guess—what you were going to say—but I guess you're right not to talk about it. (*He pulls* ROBERT'S *hand from his side and grips it tensely; the two brothers stand looking into each other's eyes for a minute.*) We can't help those things, Rob. (*He turns away, suddenly releasing* ROBERT'S *hand.*) You'll be coming along shortly, won't you?

ROBERT. (*Dully.*) Yes.

ANDREW. See you later, then. (*He walks off down the road to the left.* ROBERT *stares after him for a moment; then climbs to the fence rail again, and looks out over the hills, an expression of deep grief on his face. After a moment or so,* RUTH *enters hurriedly from the left. She is a healthy, blonde, out-of-door girl of twenty, with a graceful, slender figure. Her face, though inclined to roundness, is undeniably pretty, its large eyes of a deep blue set off strikingly by the sun-bronzed complexion. Her small, regular features are marked by a certain strength—an underlying, stubborn fixity of purpose hidden in the frankly-appealing charm of her fresh youthful-*

ness. She wears a simple white dress but no hat.)

RUTH. (*Seeing him.*) Hello, Rob!

ROBERT. (*Startled.*) Hello, Ruth!

RUTH. (*Jumps the ditch and perches on the fence beside him.*) I was looking for you.

ROBERT. (*Pointedly.*) Andy just left here.

RUTH. I know. I met him on the road a second ago. He told me you were here. (*Tenderly playful.*) I wasn't looking for Andy, Smarty, if that's what you mean. I was looking for *you*.

ROBERT. Because I'm going away tomorrow?

RUTH. Because your mother was anxious to have you come home and asked me to look for you. I just wheeled Ma over to your house.

ROBERT. (*Perfunctorily.*) How is your mother?

RUTH. (*A shadow coming over her face.*) She's about the same. She never seems to get any better or any worse. Oh, Rob, I do wish she'd try to make the best of things that can't be helped.

ROBERT. Has she been nagging at you again?

RUTH. (*Nods her head, and then breaks forth rebelliously.*) She never stops nagging. No matter what I do for her she finds fault. If only Pa were still living— (*She stops as if ashamed of her outburst.*) I suppose I shouldn't complain this way. (*She sighs.*) Poor Ma, Lord knows it's hard enough for her. I suppose it's natural to be cross when you're not able ever to walk a step. Oh, I'd like to be going away some place—like you!

ROBERT. It's hard to stay—and equally hard to go, sometimes.

RUTH. There! If I'm not the stupid body! I swore I wasn't going to speak about your trip—until after you'd gone; and there I go, first thing!

ROBERT. Why didn't you want to speak of it?

RUTH. Because I didn't want to spoil this last night you're here. Oh, Rob, I'm going to—we're all going to miss you so awfully. Your mother is going around looking as if she'd burst out crying any minute. You ought to know how I feel. Andy and you and I—why it seems as if we'd always been together.

ROBERT. (*With a wry attempt at a smile.*) You and Andy will still have each other. It'll be harder for me without anyone.

RUTH. But you'll have new sights and new people to take your mind off; while we'll be here with the old, familiar place to remind us every minute of the day. It's a shame you're going—just at this time, in spring, when everything is getting so nice. (*With a sigh.*) I oughtn't to talk that way when I know going's the best thing for you. You're bound to find all sorts of opportunities to get on, your father says.

ROBERT. (*Heatedly.*) I don't give a damn about that! I wouldn't take a voyage across the road for the best opportunity in the world of the kind Pa thinks of. (*He smiles at his own irritation.*) Excuse me, Ruth, for getting worked up over it; but Andy gave me an overdose of the practical considerations.

RUTH. (*Slowly puzzled.*) Well, then, if it isn't— (*With sudden intensity.*) Oh, Rob, why *do* you want to go?

ROBERT. (*Turning to her quickly, in surprise—slowly.*) Why do you ask that, Ruth?

RUTH. (*Dropping her eyes before his searching glance.*) Because— (*Lamely.*) It seems such a shame.

ROBERT. (*Insistently.*) Why?

RUTH. Oh, because—everything.

ROBERT. I could hardly back out now, even if I wanted to. And I'll be forgotten before you know it.

RUTH. (*Indignantly.*) You won't! I'll never forget— (*She stops and turns away to hide her confusion.*)

ROBERT. (*Softly.*) Will you promise me that?

RUTH. (*Evasively.*) Of course. It's mean of you to think that any of us will forget so easily.

ROBERT. (*Disappointedly.*) Oh!

RUTH. (*With an attempt at lightness.*) But you haven't told me your reason for leaving yet?

ROBERT. (*Moodily.*) I doubt if you'll understand. It's difficult to explain, even to myself. Either you feel it, or you don't. I can remember being conscious of it first when I was only a kid—you haven't forgotten what a sickly specimen I was then, in those days, have you?

RUTH. (*With a shudder.*) Let's not think about them.

ROBERT. You'll have to, to understand. Well, in those days, when Ma was fixing meals, she used to get me out of the way by pushing my chair to the west window and telling me to look out and be quiet. That wasn't hard. I guess I was always quiet.

RUTH. (*Compassionately.*) Yes, you always were—and you suffering so much, too!

ROBERT. (*Musingly.*) So I used to stare out over the fields to the hills, out there — (*He points to the horizon*) and somehow after a time I'd forget any pain I was in, and start dreaming. I knew the sea was over beyond those hills,—the folks had told me—and I used to wonder what the sea was like, and try to form a picture of it in my mind. (*With a smile.*) There was all the mystery in the world to me then about that —far-off-sea—and there still is! It called to me then just as it does now. (*After a slight pause.*) And other times my eyes would follow this road, winding off into the distance, toward the hills, as if it, too, was searching for the sea. And I'd promise myself that when I grew up and was strong, I'd follow that road, and it and I would find the sea together. (*With a smile.*) You see, my making this trip is only keeping that promise of long ago.

RUTH. (*Charmed by his low, musical voice telling the dreams of his childhood.*) Yes, I see.

ROBERT. Those were the only happy moments of my life then, dreaming there at the window. I liked to be all alone —those times. I got to know all the different kinds of sunsets by heart. And all those sunsets took place over there— (*He points*) beyond the horizon. So gradually I came to believe that all the wonders of the world happened on the other side of those hills. There was the home of the good fairies who performed beautiful miracles. I believed in fairies then. (*With a smile.*) Perhaps I still do believe in them. Anyway, in those days they were real enough, and sometimes I could actually hear them calling to me to come out and play with them, dance with them down the road in the dusk in a game of hide-and-seek to find out where the sun was hiding himself. They sang their little songs to me, songs that told of all the wonderful things they had in their home on the other side of the hills; and they promised to show me all of them, if I'd only come, come! But I couldn't come then, and I used to cry sometimes and Ma would think I was in pain. (*He breaks off suddenly with a laugh.*) That's why I'm going now, I suppose. For I can still hear them calling. But the horizon is as far away and as luring as ever. (*He turns to her—softly.*) Do you understand now, Ruth?

RUTH. (*Spellbound, in a whisper.*) Yes.

ROBERT. You feel it then?

RUTH. Yes, yes, I do! (*Unconsciously she snuggles close against his side. His arm steals about her as if he were not aware of the action.*) Oh, Rob, how could I help feeling? You tell things so beautifully!

ROBERT. (*Suddenly realizing that his arm is around her, and that her head is resting on his shoulder, gently takes his arm away.* RUTH, *brought back to herself, is overcome with confusion.*) So now you know why I'm going. It's for that reason—that and one other.

RUTH. You've another? Then you must tell me that, too.

ROBERT. (*Looking at her searchingly. She drops her eyes before his gaze.*) I wonder if I ought to. You'll promise not to be angry—whatever it is?

RUTH. (*Softly, her face still averted.*) Yes, I promise.

ROBERT. (*Simply.*) I love you. That's the other reason.

RUTH. (*Hiding her face in her hands.*) Oh, Rob!

ROBERT. I wasn't going to tell you, but I feel I have to. It can't matter now that I'm going so far away, and for so long—perhaps forever. I've loved you all these years, but the realization never came 'til I agreed to go away with Uncle Dick. Then I thought of leaving you, and the pain of that thought revealed to me in a flash—that I loved you, had loved you as long as I could remember. (*He gently pulls one of* RUTH'S *hands away from her face.*) You mustn't mind my telling you this, Ruth. I realize how impossible it all is—and I understand; for the revelation of my own love seemed to open my eyes to the love of others. I saw Andy's love for you—and I knew that you must love him.

RUTH. (*Breaking out stormily.*) I don't!

I don't love Andy! I don't! (ROBERT *stares at her in stupid astonishment.* RUTH *weeps hysterically.*) Whatever—put such a fool notion into—into your head? (*She suddenly throws her arms about his neck and hides her head on his shoulder.*) Oh, Rob! Don't go away! Please! You mustn't, now! You can't! I won't let you! It'd break my—my heart!

ROBERT. (*The expression of stupid bewilderment giving way to one of overwhelming joy. He presses her close to him—slowly and tenderly.*) Do you mean that—that you love me?

RUTH. (*Sobbing.*) Yes, yes—of course I do—what d'you s'pose? (*She lifts up her head and looks into his eyes with a tremulous smile.*) You stupid thing! (*He kisses her.*) I've loved you right along.

ROBERT. (*Mystified.*) But you and Andy were always together!

RUTH. Because you never seemed to want to go any place with me. You were always reading an old book, and not paying any attention to me. I was too proud to let you see I cared because I thought the year you had away to college had made you stuck-up, and you thought yourself too educated to waste any time on me.

ROBERT. (*Kissing her.*) And I was thinking— (*With a laugh.*) What fools we've both been!

RUTH. (*Overcome by a sudden fear.*) You won't go away on the trip, will you, Rob? You'll tell them you can't go on account of me, won't you? You can't go now! You can't!

ROBERT. (*Bewildered.*) Perhaps—you can come too.

RUTH. Oh, Rob, don't be so foolish. You know I can't. Who'd take care of Ma? Don't you see I couldn't go—on her account? (*She clings to him imploringly.*) Please don't go—not now. Tell them you've decided not to. They won't mind. I know your mother and father'll be glad. They'll all be. They don't want you to go so far away from them. Please, Rob! We'll be so happy here together where it's natural and we know things. Please tell me you won't go!

ROBERT. (*Face to face with a definite, final decision, betrays the conflict going on within him.*) But—Ruth—I—Uncle Dick—

RUTH. He won't mind when he knows it's for your happiness to stay. How could he? (*As* ROBERT *remains silent she bursts into sobs again.*) Oh, Rob! And you said—you loved me!

ROBERT. (*Conquered by this appeal—an irrevocable decision in his voice.*) I won't go, Ruth. I promise you. There! Don't cry! (*He presses her to him, stroking her hair tenderly. After a pause he speaks with happy hopefulness.*) Perhaps after all Andy was right—righter than he knew—when he said I could find all the things I was seeking for here, at home on the farm. I think love must have been the secret—the secret that called to me from over the world's rim—the secret beyond every horizon; and when I did not come, it came to me. (*He clasps* RUTH *to him fiercely.*) Oh, Ruth, our love is sweeter than any distant dream! (*He kisses her passionately and steps to the ground, lifting* RUTH *in his arms and carrying her to the road where he puts her down.*)

RUTH. (*With a happy laugh.*) My, but you're strong!

ROBERT. Come! We'll go and tell them at once.

RUTH. (*Dismayed.*) Oh, no, don't, Rob, not 'til after I've gone. There'd be bound to be such a scene with them all together.

ROBERT. (*Kissing her—gaily.*) As you like—little Miss Common Sense!

RUTH. Let's go, then. (*She takes his hand, and they start to go off left.* ROBERT *suddenly stops and turns as though for a last look at the hills and the dying sunset flush.*)

ROBERT. (*Looking upward and pointing.*) See! The first star. (*He bends down and kisses her tenderly.*) *Our* star!

RUTH. (*In a soft murmur.*) Yes. Our very own star. (*They stand for a moment looking up at it, their arms around each other. Then* RUTH *takes his hand again and starts to lead him away.*) Come, Rob, let's go. (*His eyes are fixed again on the horizon as he half turns to follow her.* RUTH *urges.*) We'll be late for supper, Rob.

ROBERT. (*Shakes his head impatiently, as though he were throwing off some disturbing thought—with a laugh.*) All right. We'll run then. Come on! (*They run off laughing as*

THE CURTAIN FALLS.)

ACT ONE

Scene Two

Scene. *The sitting room of the Mayo farm house about nine o'clock the same night. On the left, two windows looking out on the fields. Against the wall between the windows, an old-fashioned walnut desk. In the left corner, rear, a sideboard with a mirror. In the rear wall to the right of the sideboard, a window looking out on the road. Next to the window a door leading out into the yard. Farther right, a black horsehair sofa, and another door opening on a bedroom. In the corner, a straight-backed chair. In the right wall, near the middle, an open doorway leading to the kitchen. Farther forward a double-heater stove with coal scuttle, etc. In the center of the newly carpeted floor, an oak dining room table with a red cover. In the center of the table, a large oil reading lamp. Four chairs, three rockers with crocheted tidies on their backs, and one straight-backed, are placed about the table. The walls are papered a dark red with a scrolly-figured pattern.*

Everything in the room is clean, well-kept, and in its exact place, yet there is no suggestion of primness about the whole. Rather the atmosphere is one of the orderly comfort of a simple, hard-earned prosperity, enjoyed and maintained by the family as a unit.

James Mayo, *his wife, her brother,* Captain Dick Scott, *and* Andrew *are discovered.* Mayo *is his son* Andrew *over again in body and face—an* Andrew *sixty-five years old with a short, square, white beard.* Mrs. Mayo *is a slight, round-faced, rather prim-looking woman of fifty-five who had once been a school teacher. The labors of a farmer's wife have bent but not broken her, and she retains a certain refinement of movement and expression foreign to the* Mayo *part of the family. Whatever of resemblance* Robert *has to his parents may be traced to her. Her brother, the* Captain, *is short and stocky, with a weather-beaten, jovial face and a white mustache—a typical old salt, loud of voice and given to gesture. He is fifty-eight years old.*

James Mayo *sits in front of the table. He wears spectacles, and a farm journal which he has been reading lies in his lap.* The Captain *leans forward from a chair in the rear, his hands on the table in front of him.* Andrew *is tilted back on the straight-backed chair to the left, his chin sunk forward on his chest, staring at the carpet, preoccupied and frowning.*

As the Curtain rises the Captain *is just finishing the relation of some sea episode. The others are pretending an interest which is belied by the absent-minded expressions on their faces.*

The Captain. (*Chuckling.*) And that mission woman, she hails me on the dock as I was acomin' ashore, and she says—with her silly face all screwed up serious as judgment—"Captain," she says, "would you be so kind as to tell me where the sea-gulls sleeps at night?" Blow me if them warn't her exact words! (*He slaps the table with the palm of his hands and laughs loudly. The others force smiles.*) Ain't that just like a fool woman's question? And I looks at her serious as I could, "Ma'm," says I, "I couldn't rightly answer that question. I ain't never seed a sea-gull in his bunk yet. The next time I hears one snorin'," I says, "I'll make a note of where he's turned in, and write you a letter 'bout it." And then she calls me a fool real spiteful and tacks away from me quick. (*He laughs again uproariously.*) So I got rid of her that way. (*The others smile but immediately relapse into expressions of gloom again.*)

Mrs. Mayo. (*Absent-mindedly—feeling that she has to say something.*) But when it comes to that, where *do* sea-gulls sleep, Dick?

Scott. (*Slapping the table.*) Ho! Ho! Listen to her, James. 'Nother one! Well, if that don't beat all hell—'scuse me for cussin', Kate.

Mayo. (*With a twinkle in his eyes.*) They unhitch their wings, Katey, and spreads 'em out on a wave for a bed.

Scott. And then they tells the fish to whistle to 'em when it's time to turn out. Ho! Ho!

Mrs. Mayo. (*With a forced smile.*) You men folks are too smart to live, aren't you? (*She resumes her knitting.* Mayo *pretends to read his paper;* Andrew *stares at the floor.*)

Scott. (*Looks from one to the other of them with a puzzled air. Finally he is unable to bear the thick silence a minute longer, and blurts out*): You folks look as if you was settin' up with a corpse. (*With exaggerated concern.*) God A'mighty, there ain't anyone dead, be there?

MAYO. (*Sharply.*) Don't play the dunce, Dick! You know as well as we do there ain't no great cause to be feelin' chipper.

SCOTT. (*Argumentatively.*) And there ain't no cause to be wearin' mourning, either, I can make out.

MRS. MAYO. (*Indignantly.*) How can you talk that way, Dick Scott, when you're taking our Robbie away from us, in the middle of the night, you might say, just to get on that old boat of yours on time! I think you might wait until morning when he's had his breakfast.

SCOTT. (*Appealing to the others hopelessly.*) Ain't that a woman's way o' seein' things for you? God A'mighty, Kate, I can't give orders to the tide that it's got to be high just when it suits me to have it. I ain't gettin' no fun out o' missin' sleep and leavin' here at six bells myself. (*Protestingly.*) And the *Sunda* ain't an old ship—leastways, not very old—and she's good's she ever was.

MRS. MAYO. (*Her lips trembling.*) I wish Robbie weren't going.

MAYO. (*Looking at her over his glasses—consolingly.*) There, Katey!

MRS. MAYO. (*Rebelliously.*) Well, I *do* wish he wasn't!

SCOTT. You shouldn't be taking it so hard, 's far as I kin see. This vige'll make a man of him. I'll see to it he learns how to navigate, 'n' study for a mate's c'tificate right off—and it'll give him a trade for the rest of his life, if he wants to travel.

MRS. MAYO. But I don't want him to travel all his life. You've got to see he comes home when this trip is over. Then he'll be all well, and he'll want to—to marry—(ANDREW *sits forward in his chair with an abrupt movement*)—and settle down right here. (*She stares down at the knitting in her lap—after a pause.*) I never realized how hard it was going to be for me to have Robbie go—or I wouldn't have considered it a minute.

SCOTT. It ain't no good goin' on that way, Kate, now it's all settled.

MRS. MAYO. (*On the verge of tears.*) It's all right for *you* to talk. You've never had any children. You don't know what it means to be parted from them—and Robbie's my youngest, too. (ANDREW *frowns and fidgets in his chair.*)

ANDREW. (*Suddenly turning to them.*) There's one thing none of you seem to take into consideration—that Rob wants to go. He's dead set on it. He's been dreaming over this trip ever since it was first talked about. It wouldn't be fair to him not to have him go. (*A sudden uneasiness seems to strike him.*) At least, not if he still feels the same way about it he did when he was talking to me this evening.

MAYO. (*With an air of decision.*) Andy's right, Katey. That ends all argyment, you can see that. (*Looking at his big silver watch.*) Wonder what's happened to Robert? He's been gone long enough to wheel the widder to home, certain. He can't be out dreamin' at the stars his last night.

MRS. MAYO. (*A bit reproachfully.*) Why didn't you wheel Mrs. Atkins back tonight, Andy? You usually do when she and Ruth come over.

ANDREW. (*Avoiding her eyes.*) I thought maybe Robert wanted to tonight. He offered to go right away when they were leaving.

MRS. MAYO. He only wanted to be polite.

ANDREW. (*Gets to his feet.*) Well, he'll be right back, I guess. (*He turns to his father.*) Guess I'll go take a look at the black cow, Pa—see if she's ailing any.

MAYO. Yes—better had, son. (ANDREW *goes into the kitchen on the right.*)

SCOTT. (*As he goes out—in a low tone.*) There's the boy that would make a good, strong sea-farin' man—if he'd a mind to.

MAYO. (*Sharply.*) Don't you put no such fool notions in Andy's head, Dick—or you 'n' me's goin' to fall out. (*Then he smiles.*) You couldn't tempt him, no ways. Andy's a Mayo bred in the bone, and he's a born farmer, and a damn good one, too. He'll live and die right here on this farm, like I expect to. (*With proud confidence.*) And he'll make this one of the slickest, best-payin' farms in the state, too, afore he gits through!

SCOTT. Seems to me it's a pretty slick place right now.

MAYO. (*Shaking his head.*) It's too small. We need more land to make it amount to much, and we ain't got the capital to buy it. (ANDREW *enters from the kitchen. His hat is on, and he carries a lighted lantern in his hand. He goes to the door in the rear leading out.*)

ANDREW. (*Opens the door and pauses.*) Anything else you can think of to be done, Pa?

MAYO. No, nothin' I know of. (ANDREW *goes out, shutting the door.*)

MRS. MAYO. (*After a pause.*) What's come over Andy tonight, I wonder? He acts so strange.

MAYO. He does seem sort o' glum and out of sorts. It's 'count o' Robert leavin', I s'pose. (*To* SCOTT.) Dick, you wouldn't believe how them boys o' mine sticks together. They ain't like most brothers. They've been thick as thieves all their lives, with nary a quarrel I kin remember.

SCOTT. No need to tell me that. I can see how they take to each other.

MRS. MAYO. (*Pursuing her train of thought.*) Did you notice, James, how queer everyone was at supper? Robert seemed stirred up about something; and Ruth was so flustered and giggly; and Andy sat there dumb, looking as if he'd lost his best friend; and all of them only nibbled at their food.

MAYO. Guess they was all thinkin' about tomorrow, same as us.

MRS. MAYO. (*Shaking her head.*) No. I'm afraid somethin's happened—somethin' else.

MAYO. You mean—'bout Ruth?

MRS. MAYO. Yes.

MAYO. (*After a pause—frowning.*) I hope her and Andy ain't had a serious fallin'-out. I always sorter hoped they'd hitch up together sooner or later. What d'you say, Dick? Don't you think them two'd pair up well?

SCOTT. (*Nodding his head approvingly.*) A sweet, wholesome couple they'd make.

MAYO. It'd be a good thing for Andy in more ways than one. I ain't what you'd call calculatin' generally, and I b'lieve in lettin' young folks run their affairs to suit themselves; but there's advantages for both o' them in this match you can't overlook in reason. The Atkins farm is right next to ourn. Jined together they'd make a jim-dandy of a place, with plenty o' room to work in. And bein' a widder with only a daughter, and laid up all the time to boot, Mrs. Atkins can't do nothin' with the place as it ought to be done. She needs a man, a first-class farmer, to take hold o' things; and Andy's just the one.

MRS. MAYO. (*Abruptly.*) I don't think Ruth loves Andy.

MAYO. You don't? Well, maybe a woman's eyes is sharper in such things, but—they're always together. And if she don't love him now, she'll likely come around to it in time. (*As* MRS. MAYO *shakes her head.*) You seem mighty fixed in your opinion, Katey. How d'you know?

MRS. MAYO. It's just—what I feel.

MAYO. (*A light breaking over him.*) You don't mean to say— (MRS. MAYO *nods.* MAYO *chuckles scornfully.*) Shucks! I'm losin' my respect for your eyesight, Katey. Why, Robert ain't got no time for Ruth, 'cept as a friend!

MRS. MAYO. (*Warningly.*) Sss-h-h! (*The door from the yard opens, and* ROBERT *enters. He is smiling happily, and humming a song to himself, but as he comes into the room an undercurrent of nervous uneasiness manifests itself in his bearing.*)

MAYO. So here you be at last! (ROBERT *comes forward and sits on* ANDY'S *chair.* MAYO *smiles slyly at his wife.*) What have you been doin' all this time—countin' the stars to see if they all come out right and proper?

ROBERT. There's only one I'll ever look for any more, Pa.

MAYO. (*Reproachfully.*) You might've even not wasted time lookin' for that one—your last night.

MRS. MAYO. (*As if she were speaking to a child.*) You ought to have worn your coat a sharp night like this, Robbie.

SCOTT. (*Disgustedly.*) God A'mighty, Kate, you treat Robert as if he was one year old!

MRS. MAYO. (*Notices* ROBERT'S *nervous uneasiness.*) You look all worked up over something, Robbie. What is it?

ROBERT. (*Swallowing hard, looks quickly from one to the other of them—then begins determinedly.*) Yes, there *is* something—something I must tell you—all of you. (*As he begins to talk* ANDREW *enters quietly from the rear, closing the door behind him, and setting the lighted lantern on the floor. He remains standing by the door, his arms folded, listening to* ROBERT *with a repressed expression of pain on his face.* ROBERT *is so much taken up with what he is going to say that he does not notice* ANDREW'S *presence.*) Something I discovered only this evening—very beautiful and wonderful—something I did not take into consideration previously because I hadn't dared to hope that such happiness could ever come to me. (*Appealingly.*) You must all remember that fact, won't you?

MAYO. (*Frowning.*) Let's get to the point, son.

ROBERT. (*With a trace of defiance.*) Well, the point is this, Pa: I'm not going—I mean—I can't go tomorrow with Uncle Dick—or at any future time, either.

MRS. MAYO. (*With a sharp sigh of joyful relief.*) Oh, Robbie, I'm so glad!

MAYO. (*Astounded.*) You ain't serious, be you, Robert? (*Severely.*) Seems to me it's a pretty late hour in the day for you to be upsettin' all your plans so sudden!

ROBERT. I asked you to remember that until this evening I didn't know myself. I had never dared to dream—

MAYO. (*Irritably.*) What is this foolishness you're talkin' of?

ROBERT. (*Flushing.*) Ruth told me this evening that—she loved me. It was after I'd confessed I loved her. I told her I hadn't been conscious of my love until after the trip had been arranged, and I realized that it would mean—leaving her. That was the truth. I *didn't* know until then. (*As if justifying himself to the others.*) I hadn't intended telling her anything but—suddenly—I felt I must. I didn't think it would matter, because I was going away. And I thought she loved—someone else. (*Slowly—his eyes shining.*) And then she cried and said it was I she'd loved all the time, but I hadn't seen it.

MRS. MAYO. (*Rushes over and throws her arms about him.*) I knew it! I was just telling your father when you came in—and, oh, Robbie, I'm so happy you're not going!

ROBERT. (*Kissing her.*) I knew you'd be glad, Ma.

MAYO. (*Bewilderedly.*) Well, I'll be damned! You do beat all for gettin' folks' minds all tangled up, Robert. And Ruth too! Whatever got into her of a sudden? Why, I was thinkin'—

MRS. MAYO. (*Hurriedly—in a tone of warning.*) Never mind what you were thinking, James. It wouldn't be any use telling us that now. (*Meaningly.*) And what you were hoping for turns out just the same almost, doesn't it?

MAYO. (*Thoughtfully—beginning to see this side of the argument.*) Yes; I suppose you're right, Katey. (*Scratching his head in puzzlement.*) But how it ever came about! It do beat anything ever I heard. (*Finally he gets up with a sheepish grin and walks over to* ROBERT.) We're glad you ain't goin', your Ma and I, for we'd have missed you terrible, that's certain and sure; and we're glad you've found happiness. Ruth's a fine girl and'll make a good wife to you.

ROBERT. (*Much moved.*) Thank you, Pa. (*He grips his father's hand in his.*)

ANDREW. (*His face tense and drawn comes forward and holds out his hand, forcing a smile.*) I guess it's my turn to offer congratulations, isn't it?

ROBERT. (*With a startled cry when his brother appears before him so suddenly.*) Andy! (*Confused.*) Why—I—I didn't see you. Were you here when—

ANDREW. I heard everything you said; and here's wishing you every happiness, you and Ruth. You both deserve the best there is.

ROBERT. (*Taking his hand.*) Thanks, Andy, it's fine of you to— (*His voice dies away as he sees the pain in* ANDREW'S *eyes.*)

ANDREW. (*Giving his brother's hand a final grip.*) Good luck to you both! (*He turns away and goes back to the rear where he bends over the lantern, fumbling with it to hide his emotion from the others.*)

MRS. MAYO. (*To the* CAPTAIN, *who has been too flabbergasted by* ROBERT'S *decision to say a word.*) What's the matter, Dick? Aren't you going to congratulate Robbie?

SCOTT. (*Embarrassed*). Of course I be! (*He gets to his feet and shakes* ROBERT'S *hand, muttering a vague*) Luck to you, boy. (*He stands beside* ROBERT *as if he wanted to say something more but doesn't know how to go about it.*)

ROBERT. Thanks, Uncle Dick.

SCOTT. So you're not acomin' on the *Sunda* with me? (*His voice indicates disbelief.*)

ROBERT. I can't, Uncle—not now. I wouldn't miss it for anything else in the world under any other circumstances. (*He sighs unconsciously.*) But you see I've found—a bigger dream. (*Then with joyous high spirits.*) I want you all to understand one thing—I'm not going to be a loafer on your hands any longer. This means the beginning of a new life for me in every way. I'm going to settle right down and take a real interest in the farm, and do my share. I'll prove to you, Pa, that I'm as good a Mayo as you are—or Andy, when I want to be.

MAYO. (*Kindly, but skeptically.*) That's the right spirit, Robert. Ain't none of us doubts your willin'ness, but you ain't never learned—

ROBERT. Then I'm going to start learning right away, and you'll teach me, won't you?

MAYO. (*Mollifyingly.*) Of course I will, boy, and be glad to, only you'd best go easy at first.

SCOTT. (*Who has listened to this conversation in mingled consternation and amazement.*) You don't mean to tell me you're goin' to let him stay, do you, James?

MAYO. Why, things bein' as they be, Robert's free to do as he's a mind to.

MRS. MAYO. *Let him!* The very idea!

SCOTT. (*More and more ruffled.*) Then all I got to say is, you're a soft, weak-willed critter to be permittin' a boy —and women, too—to be layin' your course for you wherever they damn pleases.

MAYO. (*Slyly amused.*) It's just the same with me as 'twas with you, Dick. You can't order the tides on the seas to suit you, and I ain't pretendin' I can reg'late love for young folks.

SCOTT. (*Scornfully.*) Love! They ain't old enough to know love when they sight it! Love! I'm ashamed of you, Robert, to go lettin' a little huggin' and kissin' in the dark spile your chances to make a man out o' yourself. It ain't common sense—no siree, it ain't—not by a hell of a sight! (*He pounds the table with his fists in exasperation.*)

MRS. MAYO. (*Laughing provokingly at her brother.*) A fine one you are to be talking about love, Dick—an old cranky bachelor like you. Goodness sakes!

SCOTT. (*Exasperated by their joking.*) I've never been a damn fool like most, if that's what you're steerin' at.

MRS. MAYO. (*Tauntingly.*) Sour grapes, aren't they, Dick? (*She laughs.* ROBERT *and his father chuckle.* SCOTT *sputters with annoyance.*) Good gracious, Dick, you do act silly, flying into a temper over nothing.

SCOTT. (*Indignantly.*) Nothin'! You talk as if I wasn't concerned nohow in this here business. Seems to me I've got a right to have my say. Ain't I made all arrangements with the owners and stocked up some special grub all on Robert's account?

ROBERT. You've been fine, Uncle Dick; and I appreciate it. Truly.

MAYO. 'Course; we all does, Dick.

SCOTT. (*Unplacated.*) I've been countin' sure on havin' Robert for company on this vige—to sorta talk to and show things to, and teach, kinda, and I got my mind so set on havin' him I'm goin' to be double lonesome this vige. (*He pounds on the table, attempting to cover up this confession of weakness.*) Darn all this silly lovin' business, anyway. (*Irritably.*) But all this talk ain't tellin' me what I'm to do with that sta'b'd cabin I fixed up. It's all painted white, an' a bran new mattress on the bunk, 'n' new sheets 'n' blankets 'n' things. And Chips built in a book-case so's Robert could take his books along—with a slidin' bar fixed across't it, mind, so's they couldn't fall out no matter how she rolled. (*With excited consternation.*) What d'you suppose my officers is goin' to think when there's no one comes aboard to occupy that sta'b'd cabin? And the men what did the work on it—what'll *they* think? (*He shakes his finger indignantly.*) They're liable as not to suspicion it was a *woman* I'd planned to ship along, and that she gave me the go-by at the last moment! (*He wipes his perspiring brow in anguish at this thought.*) Gawd A'mighty! They're only lookin' to have the laugh on me for something like that. They're liable to b'lieve anything, those fellers is!

MAYO. (*With a wink.*) Then there's nothing to it but for you to get right out and hunt up a wife somewheres for that spic 'n' span cabin. She'll have to be a pretty one, too, to match it. (*He looks at his watch with exaggerated concern.*) You ain't got much time to find her, Dick.

SCOTT. (*As the others smile—sulkily.*) You kin go to thunder, Jim Mayo!

ANDREW. (*Comes forward from where he has been standing by the door, rear, brooding. His face is set in a look of grim determination.*) You needn't worry about that spare cabin, Uncle Dick, if you've a mind to take me in Robert's place.

ROBERT. (*Turning to him quickly.*) Andy! (*He sees at once the fixed resolve in his brother's eyes, and realizes immediately the reason for it—in consternation.*) Andy, you mustn't!

ANDREW. You've made your decision, Rob, and now I've made mine. You're out of this, remember.

ROBERT. (*Hurt by his brother's tone.*) But Andy—

ANDREW. Don't interfere, Rob—that's all I ask. (*Turning to his uncle.*) You haven't answered my question, Uncle Dick.

SCOTT. (*Clearing his throat, with an uneasy side glance at* JAMES MAYO *who is staring at his elder son as if he thought he had suddenly gone mad.*) O' course, I'd be glad to have you, Andy.

ANDREW. It's settled then. I can pack the little I want to take in a few minutes.

MRS. MAYO. Don't be a fool, Dick. Andy's only joking you.

SCOTT. (*Disgruntedly.*) It's hard to tell who's jokin' and who's not in this house.

ANDREW. (*Firmly.*) I'm not joking, Uncle Dick. (*As* SCOTT *looks at him uncertainly.*) You needn't be afraid I'll go back on my word.

ROBERT. (*Hurt by the insinuation he feels in* ANDREW'S *tone.*) Andy! That isn't fair!

MAYO. (*Frowning.*) Seems to me this ain't no subject to joke over—not for Andy.

ANDREW. (*Facing his father.*) I agree with you, Pa, and I tell you again, once and for all, that I've made up my mind to go.

MAYO. (*Dumbfounded—unable to doubt the determination in* ANDREW'S *voice—helplessly.*) But why, son? Why?

ANDREW. (*Evasively.*) I've always wanted to go.

ROBERT. Andy!

ANDREW. (*Half angrily.*) You shut up, Rob! (*Turning to his father again.*) I didn't ever mention it because as long as Rob was going I knew it was no use; but now Rob's staying on here, there isn't any reason for me not to go.

MAYO. (*Breathing hard.*) No reason? Can you stand there and say that to me, Andrew?

MRS. MAYO. (*Hastily—seeing the gathering storm.*) He doesn't mean a word of it. James.

MAYO. (*Making a gesture to her to keep silence.*) Let me talk, Katey. (*In a more kindly tone.*) What's come over you so sudden, Andy? You know's well as I do that it wouldn't be fair o' you to run off at a moment's notice right now when we're up to our necks in hard work.

ANDREW. (*Avoiding his eyes.*) Rob'll hold his end up as soon as he learns.

MAYO. Robert was never cut out for a farmer, and you was.

ANDREW. You can easily get a man to do my work.

MAYO. (*Restraining his anger with an effort.*) It sounds strange to hear you, Andy, that I always thought had good sense, talkin' crazy like that. (*Scornfully.*) Get a man to take your place! You ain't been workin' here for no hire, Andy, that you kin give me your notice to quit like you've done. The farm is your'n as well as mine. You've always worked on it with that understanding; and what you're sayin' you intend doin' is just skulkin' out o' your rightful responsibility.

ANDREW. (*Looking at the floor—simply.*) I'm sorry, Pa. (*After a slight pause.*) It's no use talking any more about it.

MRS. MAYO. (*In relief.*) There! I knew Andy'd come to his senses!

ANDREW. Don't get the wrong idea, Ma. I'm not backing out.

MAYO. You mean you're goin' in spite of—everythin'?

ANDREW. Yes. I'm going. I've got to. (*He looks at his father defiantly.*) I feel I oughtn't to miss this chance to go out into the world and see things, and—I want to go.

MAYO. (*With bitter scorn.*) So—you want to go out into the world and see thin's! (*His voice raised and quivering with anger.*) I never thought I'd live to see the day when a son o' mine'd look me in the face and tell a bare-faced lie! (*Bursting out.*) You're a liar, Andy Mayo, and a mean one to boot!

MRS. MAYO. James!

ROBERT. Pa!

SCOTT. Steady there, Jim!

MAYO. (*Waving their protests aside.*) He is and he knows it.

ANDREW. (*His face flushed.*) I won't argue with you, Pa. You can think as badly of me as you like.

MAYO. (*Shaking his finger at* ANDY, *in a cold rage.*) You know I'm speakin' truth—that's why you're afraid to argy!

You lie when you say you want to go 'way—and see thin's! You ain't got no likin' in the world to go. I've watched you grow up, and I know your ways, and they're my ways. You're runnin' against your own nature, and you're goin' to be a'mighty sorry for it if you do. 'S if I didn't know your real reason for runnin' away! And runnin' away's the only word to fit it. You're runnin' away 'cause you're put out and riled 'cause your own brother's got Ruth 'stead o' you, and—

ANDREW. (*His face crimson—tensely.*) Stop, Pa! I won't stand hearing that—not even from you!

MRS. MAYO. (*Rushing to* ANDY *and putting her arms about him protectingly.*) Don't mind him, Andy dear. He don't mean a word he's saying! (ROBERT *stands rigid, his hands clenched, his face contracted by pain.* SCOTT *sits dumbfounded and open-mouthed.* ANDREW *soothes his mother who is on the verge of tears.*)

MAYO. (*In angry triumph.*) It's the truth, Andy Mayo! And you ought to be bowed in shame to think of it!

ROBERT. (*Protestingly.*) Pa!

MRS. MAYO. (*Coming from* ANDREW *to his father; puts her hands on his shoulders as though to try and push him back in the chair from which he has risen.*) Won't you be still, James? Please won't you?

MAYO. (*Looking at* ANDREW *over his wife's shoulder—stubbornly.*) The truth—God's truth!

MRS. MAYO. Sh-h-h! (*She tries to put a finger across his lips, but he twists his head away.*)

ANDREW. (*Who has regained control over himself.*) You're wrong, Pa, it isn't truth. (*With defiant assertiveness.*) I don't love Ruth. I never loved her, and the thought of such a thing never entered my head.

MAYO. (*With an angry snort of disbelief.*) Hump! You're pilin' lie on lie!

ANDREW. (*Losing his temper—bitterly.*) I suppose it'd be hard for you to explain anyone's wanting to leave this blessed farm except for some outside reason like that. But I'm sick and tired of it—whether you want to believe me or not—and that's why I'm glad to get a chance to move on.

ROBERT. Andy! Don't! You're only making it worse.

ANDREW. (*Sulkily.*) I don't care. I've done my share of work here. I've earned my right to quit when I want to. (*Suddenly overcome with anger and grief; with rising intensity.*) I'm sick and tired of the whole damn business. I hate the farm and every inch of ground in it. I'm sick of digging in the dirt and sweating in the sun like a slave without getting a word of thanks for it. (*Tears of rage starting to his eyes—hoarsely.*) I'm through, through for good and all; and if Uncle Dick won't take me on his ship, I'll find another. I'll get away somewhere, somehow.

MRS. MAYO. (*In a frightened voice.*) Don't you answer him, James. He doesn't know what he's saying. Don't say a word to him 'til he's in his right senses again. Please James, don't—

MAYO. (*Pushes her away from him; his face is drawn and pale with the violence of his passion. He glares at* ANDREW *as if he hated him.*) You dare to—you dare to speak like that to me? You talk like that about this farm—the Mayo farm—where you was born—you—you — (*He clenches his fist above his head and advances threateningly on* ANDREW.) You damned whelp!

MRS. MAYO. (*With a shriek.*) James! (*She covers her face with her hands and sinks weakly into* MAYO'S *chair.* ANDREW *remains standing motionless, his face pale and set.*)

SCOTT. (*Starting to his feet and stretching his arms across the table toward* MAYO.) Easy there, Jim!

ROBERT. (*Throwing himself between father and brother.*) Stop! Are you mad?

MAYO. (*Grabs* ROBERT'S *arm and pushes him aside—then stands for a moment gasping for breath before* ANDREW. *He points to the door with a shaking finger.*) Yes—go!—go!— You're no son o' mine—no son o' mine! You can go to hell if you want to! Don't let me find you here—in the mornin'—or—or—I'll *throw* you out!

ROBERT. Pa! For God's sake!

(MRS. MAYO *bursts into noisy sobbing.*)

MAYO. (*He gulps convulsively and glares at* ANDREW.) You go—tomorrow mornin'—and by God—don't come back—don't dare come back—by God, not while I'm livin'—or I'll—I'll— (*He shakes over his muttered threat and strides toward the door rear, right.*)

MRS. MAYO. (*Rising and throwing her*

arms around him—hysterically.) James! James! Where are you going?

MAYO. *(Incoherently.)* I'm goin'—to bed, Katey. It's late, Katey—it's late. *(He goes out.)*

MRS. MAYO. *(Following him, pleading hysterically.)* James! Take back what you've said to Andy. James! *(She follows him out.* ROBERT *and the* CAPTAIN *stare after them with horrified eyes.* ANDREW *stands rigid, looking straight in front of him, his fists clenched at his sides.)*

SCOTT. *(The first to find his voice—with an explosive sigh.)* Well, if he ain't the devil himself when he's roused! You oughtn't to have talked to him that way, Andy 'bout the damn farm, knowin' how touchy he is about it. *(With another sigh.)* Well, you won't mind what he's said in anger. He'll be sorry for it when he's calmed down a bit.

ANDREW. *(In a dead voice.)* You don't know him. *(Defiantly.)* What's said is said and can't be unsaid; and I've chosen.

ROBERT. *(With violent protest.)* Andy! You can't go! This is all so stupid—and terrible!

ANDREW. *(Coldly.)* I'll talk to you in a minute, Rob. *(Crushed by his brother's attitude* ROBERT *sinks down into a chair, holding his head in his hands.)*

SCOTT. *(Comes and slaps* ANDREW *on the back.)* I'm damned glad you're shippin' on, Andy. I like your spirit, and the way you spoke up to him. *(Lowering his voice to a cautious whisper.)* The sea's the place for a young feller like you that isn't half dead 'n' alive. *(He gives* ANDY *a final approving slap.)* You 'n' me'll get along like twins, see if we don't. I'm goin' aloft to turn in. Don't forget to pack your dunnage. And git some sleep, if you kin. We'll want to sneak out extra early b'fore they're up. It'll do away with more argyments. Robert can drive us down to the town, and bring back the team. *(He goes to the door in the rear, left.)* Well, good night!

ANDREW. Good night. (SCOTT *goes out. The two brothers remain silent for a moment. Then* ANDREW *comes over to his brother and puts a hand on his back. He speaks in a low voice, full of feeling.)* Buck up, Rob. It ain't any use crying over spilt milk; and it'll all turn out for the best—let's hope. It couldn't be helped—what's happened.

ROBERT. *(Wildly.)* But it's a lie, Andy, a lie!

ANDREW. Of course it's a lie. You know it and I know it,—but that's all ought to know it.

ROBERT. Pa'll never forgive you. Oh, the whole affair is so senseless—and tragic. Why did you think you must go away?

ANDREW. You know better than to ask that. You know why. *(Fiercely.)* I can wish you and Ruth all the good luck in the world, and I do, and I mean it; but you can't expect me to stay around here and watch you two together, day after day—and me alone. I couldn't stand it—not after all the plans I'd made to happen on this place thinking—*(His voice breaks)* thinking she cared for me.

ROBERT. *(Putting a hand on his brother's arm.)* God! It's horrible! I feel so guilty—to think that I should be the cause of your suffering, after we'd been such pals all our lives. If I could have foreseen what'd happen, I swear to you I'd have never said a word to Ruth. I swear I wouldn't have, Andy!

ANDREW. I know you wouldn't; and that would've been worse, for Ruth would've suffered then. *(He pats his brother's shoulder.)* It's best as it is. It had to be, and I've got to stand the gaff, that's all. Pa'll see how I felt—after a time. *(As* ROBERT *shakes his head)*—and if he don't—well, it can't be helped.

ROBERT. But think of Ma! God, Andy, you can't go! You can't!

ANDREW. *(Fiercely.)* I've got to go—to get away! I've got to, I tell you. I'd go crazy here, bein' reminded every second of the day what a fool I'd made of myself. I've got to get away and try and forget, if I can. And I'd hate the farm if I stayed, hate it for bringin' things back. I couldn't take interest in the work any more, work with no purpose in sight. Can't you see what a hell it'd be? You love her too, Rob. Put yourself in my place, and remember I haven't stopped loving her, and couldn't if I was to stay. Would that be fair to you or to her? Put yourself in my place. *(He shakes his brother fiercely by the shoulder.)* What'd you do then? Tell me the truth! You love her. What'd you do?

ROBERT. *(Chokingly.)* I'd—I'd go, Andy! *(He buries his face in his hands with a shuddering sob.)* God!

ANDREW. (*Seeming to relax suddenly all over his body—in a low, steady voice.*) Then you know why I got to go; and there's nothing more to be said.

ROBERT. (*In a frenzy of rebellion.*) Why did this have to happen to us? It's damnable! (*He looks about him wildly, as if his vengeance were seeking the responsible fate.*)

ANDREW. (*Soothingly—again putting his hands on his brother's shoulder.*) It's no use fussing any more, Rob. It's done. (*Forcing a smile.*) I guess Ruth's got a right to have who she likes. She made a good choice—and God bless her for it!

ROBERT. Andy! Oh, I wish I could tell half I feel of how fine you are!

ANDREW. (*Interrupting him quickly.*) Shut up! Let's go to bed. I've got to be up long before sun-up. You, too, if you're going to drive us down.

ROBERT. Yes. Yes.

ANDREW. (*Turning down the lamp.*) And I've got to pack yet. (*He yawns with utter weariness.*) I'm as tired as if I'd been plowing twenty-four hours at a stretch. (*Dully.*) I feel—dead. (ROBERT *covers his face again with his hands.* ANDREW *shakes his head as if to get rid of his thoughts, and continues with a poor attempt at cheery briskness.*) I'm going to douse the light. Come on. (*He slaps his brother on the back.* ROBERT *does not move.* ANDREW *bends over and blows out the lamp. His voice comes from the darkness.*) Don't sit there mourning, Rob. It'll all come out in the wash. Come on and get some sleep. Everything'll turn out all right in the end. (ROBERT *can be heard stumbling to his feet, and the dark figures of the two brothers can be seen groping their way toward the doorway in the rear as*

THE CURTAIN FALLS.)

ACT TWO

SCENE ONE

SCENE. *Same as Act One, Scene Two. Sitting room of the farm house about half past twelve in the afternoon of a hot, sun-baked day in mid-summer, three years later. All the windows are open, but no breeze stirs the soiled white curtains. A patched screen door is in the rear. Through it the yard can be seen, its small stretch of lawn divided by the dirt path leading to the door from the gate in the white picket fence which borders the road.*

The room has changed, not so much in its outward appearance as in its general atmosphere. Little significant details give evidence of carelessness, of inefficiency, of an industry gone to seed. The chairs appear shabby from lack of paint; the table cover is spotted and askew; holes show in the curtains; a child's doll, with one arm gone, lies under the table; a hoe stands in a corner; a man's coat is flung on the couch in the rear; the desk is cluttered up with odds and ends; a number of books are piled carelessly on the sideboard. The noon enervation of the sultry, scorching day seems to have penetrated indoors, causing even inanimate objects to wear an aspect of despondent exhaustion.

A place is set at the end of the table, left for someone's dinner. Through the open door to the kitchen comes the clatter of dishes being washed, interrupted at intervals by a woman's irritated voice and the peevish whining of a child.

At the rise of the curtain MRS. MAYO *and* MRS. ATKINS *are discovered sitting facing each other,* MRS. MAYO *to the rear,* MRS. ATKINS *to the right of the table.* MRS. MAYO'S *face has lost all character, disintegrated, become a weak mask wearing a helpless, doleful expression of being constantly on the verge of comfortless tears. She speaks in an uncertain voice, without assertiveness, as if all power of willing had deserted her.* MRS. ATKINS *is in her wheel chair. She is a thin, pale-faced, unintelligent looking woman of about forty-eight, with hard, bright eyes. A victim of partial paralysis for many years, condemned to be pushed from day to day of her life in a wheel chair, she has developed the selfish, irritable nature of the chronic invalid. Both women are dressed in black.* MRS. ATKINS *knits nervously as she talks. A ball of unused yarn, with needles stuck through it, lies on the table before* MRS. MAYO.

MRS. ATKINS. (*With a disapproving glance at the place set on the table.*) Robert's late for his dinner again, as usual. I don't see why Ruth puts up with it, and I've told her so. Many's the time I've said to her, "It's about time you put a stop to his nonsense. Does he suppose you're runnin' a hotel—with no one to help with things?" But she don't pay no attention. She's as bad as he is, a'most—thinks she knows better than an old, sick body like me.

MRS. MAYO. (*Dully.*) Robbie's always late for things. He can't help it, Sarah.

MRS. ATKINS. (*With a snort.*) Can't help it! How you do go on, Kate, findin' excuses for him! Anybody can help anything they've a mind to—as long as they've got health, and ain't rendered helpless like me— (*She adds as a pious afterthought*)—through the will of God.

MRS. MAYO. Robbie can't.

MRS. ATKINS. Can't! It do make me mad, Kate Mayo, to see folks that God gave all the use of their limbs to, potterin' round and wastin' time doin' everything the wrong way—and me powerless to help and at their mercy, you might say. And it ain't that I haven't pointed the right way to 'em. I've talked to Robert thousands of times and told him how things ought to be done. You know that, Kate Mayo. But d'you s'pose he takes any notice of what I say? Or Ruth, either—my own daughter? No, they think I'm a crazy, cranky old woman, half dead a'ready, and the sooner I'm in the grave and out o' their way the better it'd suit them.

MRS. MAYO. You mustn't talk that way, Sarah. They're not as wicked as that. And you've got years and years before you.

MRS. ATKINS. You're like the rest, Kate. You don't know how near the end I am. Well, at least I can go to my eternal rest with a clear conscience. I've done all a body could do to avert ruin from this house. On their heads be it!

MRS. MAYO. (*With hopeless indifference.*) Things might be worse. Robert never had any experience in farming. You can't expect him to learn in a day.

MRS. ATKINS. (*Snappily.*) He's had three years to learn, and he's gettin' worse 'stead of better. Not on'y your place but mine too is driftin' to rack and ruin, and I can't do nothin' to prevent.

MRS. MAYO. (*With a spark of assertiveness.*) You can't say but Robbie works hard, Sarah.

MRS. ATKINS. What good's workin' hard if it don't accomplish anythin', I'd like to know?

MRS. MAYO. Robbie's had bad luck against him.

MRS. ATKINS. Say what you've a mind to, Kate, the proof of the puddin's in the eatin'; and you can't deny that things have been goin' from bad to worse ever since your husband died two years back.

MRS. MAYO. (*Wiping tears from her eyes with her handkerchief.*) It was God's will that he should be taken.

MRS. ATKINS. (*Triumphantly.*) It was God's punishment on James Mayo for the blasphemin' and denyin' of God he done all his sinful life! (MRS. MAYO *begins to weep softly.*) There, Kate, I shouldn't be remindin' you, I know. He's at peace, poor man, and forgiven, let's pray.

MRS. MAYO. (*Wiping her eyes—simply.*) James was a good man.

MRS. ATKINS. (*Ignoring this remark.*) What I was sayin' was that since Robert's been in charge things've been goin' down hill steady. You don't know *how* bad they are. Robert don't let on to you what's happenin'; and you'd never see it yourself if 'twas under your nose. But, thank the Lord, Ruth still comes to me once in a while for advice when she's worried near out of her senses by his goin's-on. Do you know what she told me last night? But I forgot, she said not to tell you—still I think you've got a right to know, and it's my duty not to let such things go on behind your back.

MRS. MAYO. (*Wearily.*) You can tell me if you want to.

MRS. ATKINS. (*Bending over toward her—in a low voice.*) Ruth was almost crazy about it. Robert told her he'd have to mortgage the farm—said he didn't know how he'd pull through 'til harvest without it, and he can't get money any other way. (*She straightens up—indignantly.*) Now what do you think of your Robert?

MRS. MAYO. (*Resignedly.*) If it has to be—

MRS. ATKINS. You don't mean to say you're goin' to sign away your farm, Kate Mayo—after me warnin' you?

MRS. MAYO. I'll do what Robbie says is needful.

MRS. ATKINS. (*Holding up her hands.*) Well, of all the foolishness!—well, it's your farm, not mine, and I've nothin' more to say.

MRS. MAYO. Maybe Robbie'll manage till Andy gets back and sees to things. It can't be long now.

MRS. ATKINS. (*With keen interest.*) Ruth says Andy ought to turn up any day. When does Robert figger he'll get here?

MRS. MAYO. He says he can't calculate exactly on account o' the *Sunda* being a sail boat. Last letter he got was from England, the day they were sailing for home. That was over a month ago, and Robbie thinks they're overdue now.

MRS. ATKINS. We can give praise to God then that he'll be back in the nick o' time. He ought to be tired of travelin' and anxious to get home and settle down to work again.

MRS. MAYO. Andy *has* been working. He's head officer on Dick's boat, he wrote Robbie. You know that.

MRS. ATKINS. That foolin' on ships is all right for a spell, but he must be right sick of it by this.

MRS. MAYO. (*Musingly.*) I wonder if he's changed much. He used to be so fine-looking and strong. (*With a sigh.*) Three years! It seems more like three hundred. (*Her eyes filling—piteously.*) Oh, if James could only have lived 'til he came back—and forgiven him!

MRS. ATKINS. He never would have—not James Mayo! Didn't he keep his heart hardened against him till the last in spite of all you and Robert did to soften him?

MRS. MAYO. (*With a feeble flash of anger.*) Don't you dare say that! (*Brokenly.*) Oh, I know deep down in his heart he forgave Andy, though he was too stubborn ever to own up to it. It was that brought on his death—breaking his heart just on account of his stubborn pride. (*She wipes her eyes with her handkerchief and sobs.*)

MRS. ATKINS. (*Piously.*) It was the will of God. (*The whining crying of the child sounds from the kitchen.* MRS. ATKINS *frowns irritably.*) Drat that young one! Seems as if she cries all the time on purpose to set a body's nerves on edge.

MRS. MAYO. (*Wiping her eyes.*) It's the heat upsets her. Mary doesn't feel any too well these days, poor little child!

MRS. ATKINS. She gets it right from her Pa—bein' sickly all the time. You can't deny Robert was always ailin' as a child. (*She sighs heavily.*) It was a crazy mistake for them two to get married. I argyed against it at the time, but Ruth was so spelled with Robert's wild poetry notions she wouldn't listen to sense. Andy was the one would have been the match for her.

MRS. MAYO. I've often thought since it might have been better the other way. But Ruth and Robbie seems happy enough together.

MRS. ATKINS. At any rate it was God's work—and His will be done. (*The two women sit in silence for a moment.* RUTH *enters from the kitchen, carrying in her arms her two-year-old daughter,* MARY, *a pretty but sickly and ænemic looking child with a tear-stained face.* RUTH *has aged appreciably. Her face has lost its youth and freshness. There is a trace in her expression of something hard and spiteful. She sits in the rocker in front of the table and sighs wearily. She wears a gingham dress with a soiled apron tied around her waist.*)

RUTH. Land sakes, if this isn't a scorcher! That kitchen's like a furnace. Phew! (*She pushes the damp hair back from her forehead.*)

MRS. MAYO. Why didn't you call me to help with the dishes?

RUTH. (*Shortly.*) No. The heat in there'd kill you.

MARY. (*Sees the doll under the table and struggles on her mother's lap.*) Dolly, Mamma! Dolly!

RUTH. (*Pulling her back.*) It's time for your nap. You can't play with Dolly now.

MARY. (*Commencing to cry whiningly.*) Dolly!

MRS. ATKINS. (*Irritably.*) Can't you keep that child still? Her racket's enough to split a body's ears. Put her down and let her play with the doll if it'll quiet her.

RUTH. (*Lifting* MARY *to the floor.*) There! I hope you'll be satisfied and keep still. (MARY *sits down on the floor before the table and plays with the doll in silence.* RUTH *glances at the place set on the table.*) It's a wonder Rob wouldn't try to get to meals on time once in a while.

MRS. MAYO. (*Dully.*) Something must have gone wrong again.

RUTH. (*Wearily.*) I s'pose so. Something's always going wrong these days, it looks like.

MRS. ATKINS. (*Snappily.*) It wouldn't if you possessed a bit of spunk. The idea of you permittin' him to come in to meals at all hours—and you doin' the work! I never heard of such a thin'. You're too easy goin', that's the trouble.

RUTH. Do stop your nagging at me, Ma! I'm sick of hearing you. I'll do as I please about it; and thank you for not interfering. (*She wipes her moist forehead—wearily.*) Phew! It's too hot to argue. Let's talk of something pleasant. (*Curiously.*) Didn't I hear you speaking about Andy a while ago?

MRS. MAYO. We were wondering when he'd get home.

RUTH. (*Brightening.*) Rob says any day now he's liable to drop in and surprise us—him and the Captain. It'll certainly look natural to see him around the farm again.

MRS. ATKINS. Let's hope the farm'll look more natural, too, when he's had a hand at it. The way thin's are now!

RUTH. (*Irritably.*) Will you stop harping on that, Ma? We all know things aren't as they might be. What's the good of your complaining all the time?

MRS. ATKINS. There, Kate Mayo! Ain't that just what I told you? I can't say a word of advice to my own daughter even, she's that stubborn and self-willed.

RUTH. (*Putting her hands over her ears—in exasperation.*) For goodness' sakes, Ma!

MRS. MAYO. (*Dully.*) Never mind. Andy'll fix everything when he comes.

RUTH. (*Hopefully.*) Oh, yes, I know he will. He always did know just the right thing ought to be done. (*With weary vexation.*) It's a shame for him to come home and have to start in with things in such a topsy-turvy.

MRS. MAYO. Andy'll manage.

RUTH. (*Sighing.*) I s'pose it isn't Rob's fault things go wrong with him.

MRS. ATKINS. (*Scornfully.*) Hump! (*She fans herself nervously.*) Land o' Goshen, but it's bakin' in here! Let's go out in under the trees in back where there's a breath of fresh air. Come, Kate. (MRS. MAYO *gets up obediently and starts to wheel the invalid's chair toward the screen door.*) You better come too, Ruth. It'll do you good. Learn him a lesson and let him get his own dinner. Don't be such a fool.

RUTH. (*Going and holding the screen door open for them—listlessly.*) He wouldn't mind. He doesn't eat much. But I can't go anyway. I've got to put baby to bed.

MRS. ATKINS. Let's go, Kate. I'm boilin' in here. (MRS. MAYO *wheels her out and off left.* RUTH *comes back and sits down in her chair.*)

RUTH. (*Mechanically.*) Come and let me take off your shoes and stockings, Mary, that's a good girl. You've got to take your nap now. (*The child continues to play as if she hadn't heard, absorbed in her doll. An eager expression comes over* RUTH'*s tired face. She glances toward the door furtively—then gets up and goes to the desk. Her movements indicate a guilty fear of discovery. She takes a letter from a pigeonhole and retreats swiftly to her chair with it. She opens the envelope and reads the letter with great interest, a flush of excitement coming to her cheeks.* ROBERT *walks up the path and opens the screen door quietly and comes into the room. He, too, has aged. His shoulders are stooped as if under too great a burden. His eyes are dull and lifeless, his face burned by the sun and unshaven for days. Streaks of sweat have smudged the layer of dust on his cheeks. His lips, drawn down at the corners, give him a hopeless, resigned expression. The three years have accentuated the weakness of his mouth and chin. He is dressed in overalls, laced boots, and a flannel shirt open at the neck.*)

ROBERT. (*Throwing his hat over on the sofa—with a great sigh of exhaustion.*) Phew! The sun's hot today! (RUTH *is startled. At first she makes an instinctive motion as if to hide the letter in her bosom. She immediately thinks better of this and sits with the letter in her hands looking at him with defiant eyes. He bends down and kisses her.*)

RUTH. (*Feeling of her cheek—irritably.*) Why don't you shave? You look awful.

ROBERT. (*Indifferently.*) I forgot—and it's too much trouble this weather.

MARY. (*Throwing aside her doll, runs to him with a happy cry.*) Dada! Dada!

ROBERT. (*Swinging her up above his head—lovingly.*) And how's this little girl of mine this hot day, eh?

MARY. (*Screeching happily.*) Dada! Dada!

RUTH. (*In annoyance.*) Don't do that to her! You know it's time for her nap and you'll get her all waked up; then I'll be the one that'll have to sit beside her till she falls asleep.

ROBERT. (*Sitting down in the chair on the left of table and cuddling* MARY *on his lap.* You needn't bother. I'll put her to bed.

RUTH. (*Shortly.*) You've got to get back to your work, I s'pose.

ROBERT. (*With a sigh.*) Yes, I was forgetting. (*He glances at the open letter on* RUTH'S *lap.*) Reading Andy's letter again? I should think you'd know it by heart by this time.

RUTH. (*Coloring as if she'd been accused of something—defiantly.*) I've got a right to read it, haven't I? He says it's meant for all of us.

ROBERT. (*With a trace of irritation.*) Right? Don't be so silly. There's no question of right, I was only saying that you must know all that's in it after so many readings.

RUTH. Well, I don't. (*She puts the letter on the table and gets wearily to her feet.*) I s'pose you'll be wanting your dinner now.

ROBERT. (*Listlessly.*) I don't care. I'm not hungry.

RUTH. And here I been keeping it hot for you!

ROBERT. (*Irritably.*) Oh, all right then. Bring it in and I'll try to eat.

RUTH. I've got to get her to bed first. (*She goes to lift* MARY *off his lap.*) Come, dear. It's after time and you can hardly keep your eyes open now.

MARY. (*Crying.*) No, no! (*Appealing to her father.*)

RUTH. (*Accusingly to* ROBERT.) There! Now see what you've done! I told you not to—

ROBERT. (*Shortly.*) Let her alone, then. She's all right where she is. She'll fall asleep on my lap in a minute if you'll stop bothering her.

RUTH. (*Hotly.*) She'll not do any such thing! She's got to learn to mind me! (*Shaking her finger at* MARY.) You naughty child! Will you come with Mama when she tells you for your own good?

MARY. (*Clinging to her father.*) No, Dada!

RUTH. (*Losing her temper.*) A good spanking's what you need, my young lady—and you'll get one from me if you don't mind better, d'you hear? (MARY *starts to whimper frightenedly.*)

ROBERT. (*With sudden anger.*) Leave her alone! How often have I told you not to threaten her with whipping? I won't have it. (*Soothing the wailing* MARY.) There! There, little girl! Baby mustn't cry. Dada won't like you if you do. Dada'll hold you and you must promise to go to sleep like a good little girl. Will you when Dada asks you?

MARY. (*Cuddling up to him.*) Yes, Dada.

RUTH. (*Looking at them, her pale face set and drawn.*) A fine one you are to be telling folks how to do things! (*She bites her lips. Husband and wife look into each other's eyes with something akin to hatred in their expressions; then* RUTH *turns away with a shrug of affected indifference.*) All right, take care of her then, if you think it's so easy. (*She walks away into the kitchen.*)

ROBERT. (*Smoothing* MARY'S *hair—tenderly.*) We'll show Mama you're a good little girl, won't we?

MARY. (*Crooning drowsily.*) Dada, Dada.

ROBERT. Let's see: Does your mother take off your shoes and stockings before your nap?

MARY. (*Nodding with half-shut eyes.*) Yes, Dada.

ROBERT. (*Taking off her shoes and stockings.*) We'll show Mama we know how to do those things, won't we? There's one old shoe off—and there's the other old shoe—and here's one old stocking—and there's the other old stocking. There we are, all nice and cool and comfy. (*He bends down and kisses her.*) And now will you promise to go right to sleep if Dada takes you to bed? (MARY *nods sleepily.*) That's the good little girl. (*He gathers her up in his arms carefully and carries her into the bedroom. His voice can be heard faintly as he lulls the child to sleep.* RUTH *comes out of the kitchen and gets the plate from the table. She hears the voice from the room and tiptoes to the door to look in. Then she starts for the kitchen but stands for a moment thinking, a look of ill-concealed jealousy on her face. At a noise from inside she hurriedly disappears into the kitchen. A moment later* ROBERT *re-enters. He comes forward and picks up the shoes and stockings which he shoves carelessly under the table. Then, seeing no one about, he goes to the sideboard and selects a book. Coming back to his chair, he sits down and immediately becomes absorbed in reading.* RUTH *returns from the kitchen bringing his plate heaped with food, and a cup of tea. She sets those before him and sits down in her former place.* ROBERT *continues to read, oblivious to the food on the table.*)

RUTH. (*After watching him irritably for a moment.*) For heaven's sakes, put down that old book! Don't you see your dinner's getting cold?

ROBERT. (*Closing his book.*) Excuse me, Ruth. I didn't notice. (*He picks up his knife and fork and begins to eat gingerly, without appetite.*)

RUTH. I should think you might have some feeling for me, Rob, and not always be late for meals. If you think it's fun sweltering in that oven of a kitchen to keep things warm for you, you're mistaken.

ROBERT. I'm sorry, Ruth, really I am. Something crops up every day to delay me. I mean to be here on time.

RUTH. (*With a sigh.*) Mean-tos don't count.

ROBERT. (*With a conciliating smile.*) Then punish me, Ruth. Let the food get cold and don't bother about me.

RUTH. I'd have to wait just the same to wash up after you.

ROBERT. But I can wash up.

RUTH. A nice mess there'd be then!

ROBERT. (*With an attempt at lightness.*) The food is lucky to be able to get cold this weather. (*As* RUTH *doesn't answer or smile he opens his book and resumes his reading, forcing himself to take a mouthful of food every now and then.* RUTH *stares at him in annoyance.*)

RUTH. And besides, you've got your own work that's got to be done.

ROBERT. (*Absent-mindedly, without taking his eyes from the book.*) Yes, of course.

RUTH. (*Spitefully.*) Work you'll never get done by reading books all the time.

ROBERT. (*Shutting the book with a snap.*) Why do you persist in nagging at me for getting pleasure out of reading? Is it because— (*He checks himself abruptly.*)

RUTH. (*Coloring.*) Because I'm too stupid to understand them, I s'pose you were going to say.

ROBERT. (*Shame-facedly.*) No—no. (*In exasperation.*) Why do you goad me into saying things I don't mean? Haven't I got my share of troubles trying to work this cursed farm without your adding to them? You know how hard I've tried to keep things going in spite of bad luck—

RUTH. (*Scornfully.*) Bad luck!

ROBERT. And my own very apparent unfitness for the job, I was going to add; but you can't deny there's been bad luck to it, too. Why don't you take things into consideration? Why can't we pull together? We used to. I know it's hard on you also. Then why can't we help each other instead of hindering?

RUTH. (*Sullenly.*) I do the best I know how.

ROBERT. (*Gets up and puts his hand on her shoulder.*) I know you do. But let's both of us try to do better. We can both improve. Say a word of encouragement once in a while when things go wrong, even if it is my fault. You know the odds I've been up against since Pa died. I'm not a farmer. I've never claimed to be one. But there's nothing else I can do under the circumstances, and I've got to pull things through somehow. With your help, I can do it. With you against me— (*He shrugs his shoulders. There is a pause. Then he bends down and kisses her hair—with an attempt at cheerfulness.*) So you promise that; and I'll promise to be here when the clock strikes—and anything else you tell me to. Is it a bargain?

RUTH. (*Dully.*) I s'pose so. (*They are interrupted by the sound of a loud knock at the kitchen door.*) There's someone at the kitchen door. (*She hurries out. A moment later she reappears.*) It's Ben.

ROBERT. (*Frowning.*) What's the trouble now, I wonder? (*In a loud voice.*) Come on in here, Ben. (BEN *slouches in from the kitchen. He is a hulking, awkward young fellow with a heavy, stupid face and shifty, cunning eyes. He is dressed in overalls, boots, etc., and wears a broad-brimmed hat of coarse straw pushed back on his head.*) Well, Ben, what's the matter?

BEN. (*Drawlingly.*) The mowin' machine's bust.

ROBERT. Why, that can't be. The man fixed it only last week.

BEN. It's bust just the same.

ROBERT. And can't you fix it?

BEN. No. Don't know what's the matter with the goll-darned thing. 'Twon't work, anyhow.

ROBERT. (*Getting up and going for his hat.*) Wait a minute and I'll go look it over. There can't be much the matter with it.

BEN. (*Impudently.*) Don't make no diff'rence t'me whether there be or not. I'm quittin'.

ROBERT. (*Anxiously.*) You don't mean you're throwing up your job here?

BEN. That's what! My month's up today and I want what's owin' t'me.

ROBERT. But why are you quitting now, Ben, when you know I've so much work on hand? I'll have a hard time getting another man at such short notice.

BEN. That's for you to figger. I'm quittin'.

ROBERT. But what's your reason? You haven't any complaint to make about the way you've been treated, have you?

BEN. No. 'Taint that. (*Shaking his finger.*) Look-a-here. I'm sick o' being made fun at, that's what; an' I got a job up to Timms' place; an' I'm quittin' here.

ROBERT. Being made fun of? I don't understand you. Who's making fun of you?

BEN. They all do. When I drive down with the milk in the mornin' they all laughs and jokes at me—that boy up to Harris' and the new feller up to Slocum's, and Bill Evans down to Meade's, and all the rest on 'em.

ROBERT. That's a queer reason for leaving me flat. Won't they laugh at you just the same when you're working for Timms?

BEN. They wouldn't dare to. Timms is the best farm hereabouts. They was laughin' at me for workin' for *you*, that's what! "How're things up to the Mayo place?" they hollers every mornin'. "What's Robert doin' now—pasturin' the cattle in the cornlot? Is he seasonin' his hay with rain this year, same as last?" they shouts. "Or is he inventin' some 'lectrical milkin' engine to fool them dry cows o' his into givin' hard cider?" (*Very much ruffled.*) That's like they talks; and I ain't goin' to put up with it no longer. Everyone's always knowed me as a first-class hand hereabouts, and I ain't wantin' 'em to get no different notion. So I'm quittin' you. And I wants what's comin' to me.

ROBERT. (*Coldly.*) Oh, if that's the case, you can go to the devil. You'll get your money tomorrow when I get back from town—not before!

BEN. (*Turning to doorway to kitchen.*) That suits me. (*As he goes out he speaks back over his shoulder.*) And see that I do get it, or there'll be trouble. (*He disappears and the slamming of the kitchen door is heard.*)

ROBERT. (*As* RUTH *comes from where she has been standing by the doorway and sits down dejectedly in her old place.*) The stupid damn fool! And now what about the haying? That's an example of what I'm up against. No one can say I'm responsible for that.

RUTH. He wouldn't dare act that way with any one else! (*Spitefully, with a glance at* ANDREW'S *letter on the table.*) It's lucky Andy's coming back.

ROBERT. (*Without resentment.*) Yes, Andy'll see the right thing to do in a jiffy. (*With an affectionate smile.*) I wonder if the old chump's changed much? He doesn't seem to from his letters, does he? (*Shaking his head.*) But just the same I doubt if he'll want to settle down to a hum-drum farm life, after all he's been through.

RUTH. (*Resentfully.*) Andy's not like you. He likes the farm.

ROBERT. (*Immersed in his own thoughts—enthusiastically.*) Gad, the things he's seen and experienced! Think of the places he's been! All the wonderful far places I used to dream about! God, how I envy him! What a trip! (*He springs to his feet and instinctively goes to the window and stares out at the horizon.*)

RUTH. (*Bitterly.*) I s'pose you're sorry now you didn't go?

ROBERT. (*Too occupied with his own thoughts to hear her—vindictively.*) Oh, those cursed hills out there that I used to think promised me so much! How I've grown to hate the sight of them! They're like the walls of a narrow prison yard shutting me in from all the freedom and wonder of life! (*He turns back to the room with a gesture of loathing.*) Sometimes I think if it wasn't for you, Ruth, and—(*his voice softening*)—little Mary, I'd chuck everything up and walk down the road with just one desire in my heart—to put the whole rim of the world between me and those hills, and be able to breathe freely once more! (*He sinks down into his chair and smiles with bitter self-scorn.*) There I go dreaming again—my old fool dreams.

RUTH. (*In a low, repressed voice—her eyes smoldering.*) You're not the only one!

ROBERT. (*Buried in his own thoughts—bitterly.*) And Andy, who's had the chance—what has he got out of it? His letters read like the diary of a—of a farmer! "We're in Singapore now. It's a dirty hole of a place and hotter than hell. Two of the crew are down with fever and we're short-handed on the work. I'll be damn glad when we sail again, although tacking back and forth in these blistering seas is a rotten job too!" (*Scornfully.*) That's about the way he summed up his impressions of the East.

RUTH. (*Her repressed voice trembling.*) You needn't make fun of Andy.

ROBERT. When I think—but what's the use? You know I wasn't making fun of Andy personally, but his attitude toward things is—

RUTH. (*Her eyes flashing—bursting into uncontrollable rage.*) You was too making fun of him! And I ain't going to stand for it! You ought to be ashamed of yourself! (ROBERT *stares at her in amazement. She continues fufuriously.*) A fine one to talk about anyone else—after the way you've ruined everything with your lazy loafing!—and the stupid way you do things.

ROBERT. (*Angrily.*) Stop that kind of talk, do you hear?

RUTH. You findin' fault—with your own brother who's ten times the man you ever was or ever will be! You're jealous, that's what! Jealous because he's made a man of himself, while you're nothing but a—but a— (*She stutters incoherently, overcome by rage.*)

ROBERT. Ruth! Ruth! You'll be sorry for talking like that.

RUTH. I won't! I won't never be sorry! I'm only saying what I've been thinking for years.

ROBERT. (*Aghast.*) Ruth! You can't mean that!

RUTH. What do you think—living with a man like you—having to suffer all the time because you've never been man enough to work and do things like other people. But no! You never own up to that. You think you're so much better than other folks, with your college education, where you never learned a thing, and always reading your stupid books instead of working. I s'pose you think I ought to be *proud* to be your wife—a poor, ignorant thing like me! (*Fiercely.*) But I'm not. I hate it! I hate the sight of you. Oh, if I'd only known! If I hadn't been such a fool to listen to your cheap, silly, poetry talk that you learned out of books! If I could have seen how you were in your true self—like you are now—I'd have killed myself before I'd have married you! I was sorry for it before we'd been together a month. I knew what you were really like—when it was too late.

ROBERT. (*His voice raised loudly.*) And now—I'm finding out what you're really like—what a—a creature I've been living with. (*With a harsh laugh.*) God! It wasn't that I haven't guessed how mean and small you are—but I've kept on telling myself that I must be wrong—like a fool!—like a damned fool!

RUTH. You were saying you'd go out on the road if it wasn't for me. Well, you can go, and the sooner the better! I don't care! I'll be glad to get rid of you! The farm'll be better off too. There's been a curse on it ever since you took hold. So go! Go and be a tramp like you've always wanted. It's all you're good for. I can get along without you, don't you worry. (*Exulting fiercely.*) Andy's coming back, don't forget that! He'll attend to things like they should be. He'll show what a man can do! I don't need you. Andy's coming!

ROBERT. (*They are both standing.* ROBERT *grabs her by the shoulders and glares into her eyes.*) What do you mean? (*He shakes her violently.*) What are you thinking of? What's in your evil mind, you—you— (*His voice is a harsh shout.*)

RUTH. (*In a defiant scream.*) Yes, I do mean it! I'd say it if you was to kill me! I do love Andy. I do! I do! I always loved him. (*Exultantly.*) And he loves me! He loves me! I know he does. He always did! And you know he did, too! So go! Go if you want to!

ROBERT. (*Throwing her away from him. She staggers back against the table—thickly.*) You—you slut! (*He stands glaring at her as she leans back, supporting herself by the table, gasping for breath. A loud frightened whimper sounds from the awakened child in the bedroom. It continues. The man and woman stand looking at one another in horror, the extent of their terrible quarrel suddenly brought home to them. A pause. The noise of a horse and carriage comes from the road before the house. The two, suddenly struck by the same premonition, listen to it breathlessly, as to a sound heard in a dream. It stops. They hear* ANDY'S *voice from the road shouting a long hail—"Ahoy there!"*

RUTH. (*With a strangled cry of joy.*) Andy! Andy! (*She rushes and grabs the knob of the screen door, about to fling it open.*)

ROBERT. (*In a voice of command that forces obedience.*) Stop! (*He goes to the door and gently pushes the trembling* RUTH *away from it. The child's crying rises to a louder pitch.*) I'll meet Andy. You better go in to Mary, Ruth. (*She looks at him defiantly for a moment, but there is something in his eyes that makes her turn and walk slowly into the bedroom.*)

ANDY'S VOICE. (*In a louder shout.*) Ahoy there, Rob!

ROBERT. (*In an answering shout of forced cheeriness.*) Hello, Andy! (*He opens the door and walks out as*

THE CURTAIN FALLS.)

ACT TWO

SCENE TWO

SCENE. *The top of a hill on the farm. It is about eleven o'clock the next morning. The day is hot and cloudless. In the distance the sea can be seen.*

The top of the hill slopes downward slightly toward the left. A big boulder stands in the center toward the rear. Further right, a large oak tree. The faint trace of a path leading upward to it from the left foreground can be detected through the bleached, sun-scorched grass.

ROBERT *is discovered sitting on the boulder, his chin resting on his hands, staring out toward the horizon seaward. His face is pale and haggard, his expression one of utter despondency.* MARY *is sitting on the grass near him in the shade, playing with her doll, singing happily to herself. Presently she casts a curious glance at her father, and, propping her doll up against the tree, comes over and clambers to his side.*

MARY. (*Pulling at his hand—solicitously.*) Dada sick?

ROBERT. (*Looking at her with a forced smile.*) No, dear. Why?

MARY. Play wif Mary.

ROBERT. (*Gently.*) No, dear, not today. Dada doesn't feel like playing today.

MARY. (*Protestingly.*) Yes, Dada!

ROBERT. No, dear. Dada does feel sick—a little. He's got a bad headache.

MARY. Mary see. (*He bends his head. She pats his hair.*) Bad head.

ROBERT. (*Kissing her—with a smile.*) There! It's better now, dear, thank you. (*She cuddles up close against him. There is a pause during which each of them looks out seaward. Finally* ROBERT *turns to her tenderly.*) Would you like Dada to go away?—far, far away?

MARY. (*Tearfully.*) No! No! No, Dada, no!

ROBERT. Don't you like Uncle Andy—the man that came yesterday—not the old man with the white mustache—the other?

MARY. Mary loves Dada.

ROBERT. (*With fierce determination.*) He won't go away, baby. He was only joking. He couldn't leave his little Mary. (*He presses the child in his arms.*)

MARY. (*With an exclamation of pain.*) Oh! Hurt!

ROBERT. I'm sorry, little girl. (*He lifts her down to the grass.*) Go play with Dolly, that's a good girl; and be careful to keep in the shade. (*She reluctantly leaves him and takes up her doll again. A moment later she points down the hill to the left.*)

MARY. Mans, Dada.

ROBERT. (*Looking that way.*) It's your Uncle Andy. (*A moment later* ANDREW *comes up from the left, whistling cheerfully. He has changed but little in appearance, except for the fact that his face has been deeply bronzed by his years in the tropics; but there is a decided change in his manner.*

The old easy-going good-nature seems to have been partly lost in a breezy, business-like briskness of voice and gesture. There is an authoritative note in his speech as though he were accustomed to give orders and have them obeyed as a matter of course. He is dressed in the simple blue uniform and cap of a merchant ship's officer.)

ANDREW. Here you are, eh?

ROBERT. Hello, Andy.

ANDREW. (*Going over to* MARY.) And who's this young lady I find you all alone with, eh? Who's this pretty young lady? (*He tickles the laughing, squirming* MARY, *then lifts her up at arm's length over his head.*) Upsy—daisy! (*He sets her down on the ground again.*) And there you are! (*He walks over and sits down on the boulder beside* ROBERT *who moves to one side to make room for him.*) Ruth told me I'd probably find you up top-side here; but I'd have guessed it, anyway. (*He digs his brother in the ribs affectionately.*) Still up to your old tricks, you old beggar! I can remember how you used to come up here to mope and dream in the old days.

ROBERT. (*With a smile.*) I come up here now because it's the coolest place on the farm. I've given up dreaming.

ANDREW. (*Grinning.*) I don't believe it. You can't have changed that much. (*After a pause—with boyish enthusiasm.*) Say, it sure brings back old times to be up here with you having a chin all by our lonesomes again. I feel great being back home.

ROBERT. It's great for us to have you back.

ANDREW. (*After a pause—meaningly.*) I've been looking over the old place with Ruth. Things don't seem to be—

ROBERT. (*His face flushing—interrupts his brother shortly.*) Never mind the damn farm! Let's talk about something interesting. This is the first chance I've had to have a word with you alone. Tell me about your trip.

ANDREW. Why, I thought I told you everything in my letters.

ROBERT. (*Smiling.*) Your letters were—sketchy, to say the least.

ANDREW. Oh, I know I'm no author. You needn't be afraid of hurting my feelings. I'd rather go through a typhoon again than write a letter.

ROBERT. (*With eager interest.*) Then you were through a typhoon?

ANDREW. Yes—in the China sea. Had to run before it under bare poles for two days. I thought we were bound down for Davy Jones, sure. Never dreamed waves could get so big or the wind blow so hard. If it hadn't been for Uncle Dick being such a good skipper we'd have gone to the sharks, all of us. As it was we came out minus a main topmast and had to beat back to Hong-Kong for repairs. But I must have written you all this.

ROBERT. You never mentioned it.

ANDREW. Well, there was so much dirty work getting things ship-shape again I must have forgotten about it.

ROBERT. (*Looking at* ANDREW—*marveling.*) Forget a typhoon? (*With a trace of scorn.*) You're a strange combination, Andy. And is what you've told me all you remember about it?

ANDREW. Oh, I could give you your bellyful of details if I wanted to turn loose on you. It was all-wool-and-a-yard-wide-Hell, I'll tell you. You ought to have been there. I remember thinking about you at the worst of it, and saying to myself: "This'd cure Rob of them ideas of his about the beautiful sea, if he could see it." And it would have too, you bet! (*He nods emphatically.*)

ROBERT. (*Dryly.*) The sea doesn't seem to have impressed you very favorably.

ANDREW. I should say it didn't! I'll never set foot on a ship again if I can help it—except to carry me some place I can't get to by train.

ROBERT. But you studied to become an officer!

ANDREW. Had to do something or I'd gone mad. The days were like years. (*He laughs.*) And as for the East you used to rave about—well, you ought to see it, and *smell* it! One walk down one of their filthy narrow streets with the tropic sun beating on it would sicken you for life with the "wonder and mystery" you used to dream of.

ROBERT. (*Shrinking from his brother with a glance of aversion.*) So all you found in the East was a stench?

ANDREW. *A* stench! Ten thousand of them!

ROBERT. But you did like some of the places, judging from your letters—Sydney, Buenos Aires—

ANDREW. Yes, Sydney's a good town. (*Enthusiastically.*) But Buenos Aires—there's the place for you. Argentine's a country where a fellow has a chance to make good. You're right I like it. And I'll tell you, Rob, that's right where I'm going just as soon as I've seen you folks a while and can get a ship. I can get a berth as second officer, and I'll jump the ship when I get there. I'll need every cent of the wages Uncle's paid me to get a start at something in B. A.

ROBERT. (*Staring at his brother—slowly.*) So you're not going to stay on the farm?

ANDREW. Why sure not! Did you think I was? There wouldn't be any sense. One of us is enough to run this little place.

ROBERT. I suppose it does seem small to you now.

ANDREW. (*Not noticing the sarcasm in* ROBERT'S *tone.*) You've no idea, Rob, What a splendid place Argentine is. I had a letter from a marine insurance chap that I'd made friends with in Hong-Kong, to his brother, who's in the grain business in Buenos Aires. He took quite a fancy to me, and, what's more important, he offered me a job if I'd come back there. I'd have taken it on the spot, only I couldn't leave Uncle Dick in the lurch, and I'd promised you folks to come home. But I'm going back there, you bet, and then you watch me get on! (*He slaps* ROBERT *on the back.*) But don't you think it's a big chance, Rob?

ROBERT. It's fine—for you, Andy.

ANDREW. We call this a farm—but you ought to hear about the farms down there—ten square miles where we've got an acre. It's a new country where big things are opening up—and I want to get in on something big before I die. I'm no fool when it comes to farming, and I know something about grain. I've been reading up a lot on it, too, lately. (*He notices* ROBERT'S *absent-minded expression and laughs.*) Wake up, you old poetry book worm, you! I know my talking about business makes you want to choke me, doesn't it?

ROBERT. (*With an embarrassed smile.*) No, Andy, I—I just happened to think of something else. (*Frowning.*) There've been lots of times lately that I've wished I had some of your faculty for business.

ANDREW. (*Soberly.*) There's something I want to talk about, Rob,—the farm. You don't mind, do you?

ROBERT. No.

ANDREW. I walked over it this morning with Ruth—and she told me about things— (*Evasively.*) I could see the place had run down; but you mustn't blame yourself. When luck's against anyone—

ROBERT. Don't, Andy! It *is* my fault. You know it as well as I do. The best I've ever done was to make ends meet.

ANDREW. (*After a pause.*) I've got over a thousand saved, and you can have that.

ROBERT. (*Firmly.*) No. You need that for your start in Buenos Aires.

ANDREW. I don't. I can—

ROBERT. (*Determinedly.*) No, Andy! Once and for all, no! I won't hear of it!

ANDREW. (*Protestingly.*) You obstinate old son of a gun!

ROBERT. Oh, everything'll be on a sound footing after harvest. Don't worry about it.

ANDREW. (*Doubtfully.*) Maybe. (*After a pause.*) It's too bad Pa couldn't have lived to see things through. (*With feeling.*) It cut me up a lot—hearing he was dead. He never—softened up, did he—about me, I mean?

ROBERT. He never understood, that's a kinder way of putting it. He does now.

ANDREW. (*After a pause.*) You've forgotten all about what—caused me to go, haven't you, Rob? (ROBERT *nods but keeps his face averted.*) I was a slushier damn fool in those days than you were. But it was an act of Providence I did go. It opened my eyes to how I'd been fooling myself. Why, I'd forgotten all about—that—before I'd been at sea six months.

ROBERT. (*Turns and looks into* ANDREW'S *eyes searchingly.*) You're speaking of —Ruth?

ANDREW. (*Confused.*) Yes. I didn't want you to get false notions in your head, or I wouldn't say anything. (*Looking* ROBERT *squarely in the eyes.*) I'm telling you the truth when I say I'd forgotten long ago. It don't sound well for me, getting over things so easy, but I guess it never really amounted to more than a kid idea I was letting rule me. I'm certain now I never was in love—I was getting fun out of thinking I was—and being a hero to myself. (*He heaves *a great sigh of relief.*) There! Gosh, I'm glad that's off my chest. I've been feeling sort of awkward ever since I've been home, thinking of what you two might think. (*A trace of appeal in his voice.*) You've got it all straight now, haven't you, Rob?

ROBERT. (*In a low voice.*) Yes, Andy.

ANDREW. And I'll tell Ruth, too, if I can get up the nerve. She must feel kind of funny having me round—after what used to be—and not knowing how I feel about it.

ROBERT. (*Slowly.*) Perhaps—for her sake—you'd better not tell her.

ANDREW. For her sake? Oh, you mean she wouldn't want to be reminded of my foolishness? Still, I think it'd be worse if—

ROBERT. (*Breaking out—in an agonized voice.*) Do as you please, Andy; but for God's sake, let's not talk about it! (*There is a pause.* ANDREW *stares at* ROBERT *in hurt stupefaction.* ROBERT *continues after a moment in a voice which he vainly attempts to keep calm.*) Excuse me, Andy. This rotten headache has my nerves shot to pieces.

ANDREW. (*Mumbling.*) It's all right, Rob—long as you're not sore at me.

ROBERT. Where did Uncle Dick disappear to this morning?

ANDREW. He went down to the port to see to things on the *Sunda*. He said he didn't know exactly when he'd be back. I'll have to go down and tend to the ship when he comes. That's why I dressed up in these togs.

MARY. (*Pointing down the hill to the left.*) See! Mama! Mama! (*She struggles to her feet.* RUTH *appears at left. She is dressed in white, shows she has been fixing up. She looks pretty, flushed and full of life.*)

MARY. (*Running to her mother.*) Mama!

RUTH. (*Kissing her.*) Hello, dear! (*She walks toward the rock and addresses* ROBERT *coldly.*) Jake wants to see you about something. He finished working where he was. He's waiting for you at the road.

ROBERT. (*Getting up—wearily.*) I'll go down right away. (*As he looks at* RUTH, *noting her changed appearance, his face darkens with pain.*)

RUTH. And take Mary with you, please. (*To* MARY.) Go with Dada, that's a good girl. Grandma has your dinner most ready for you.

ROBERT. (*Shortly.*) Come, Mary!

MARY. (*Taking his hand and dancing happily beside him.*) Dada! Dada! (*They go down the hill to the left.* RUTH *looks after them for a moment, frowning—then turns to* ANDY *with a smile.*) I'm going to sit down. Come on, Andy. It'll be like old times. (*She jumps lightly to the top of the rock and sits down.*) It's so fine and cool up here after the house.

ANDREW. (*Half-sitting on the side of the boulder.*) Yes. It's great.

RUTH. I've taken a holiday in honor of your arrival. (*Laughing excitedly.*) I feel so free I'd like to have wings and fly over the sea. You're a man. You can't know how awful and stupid it is—cooking and washing dishes all the time.

ANDREW. (*Making a wry face.*) I can guess.

RUTH. Besides, your mother just insisted on getting your first dinner to home, she's that happy at having you back. You'd think I was planning to poison you the flurried way she shooed me out of the kitchen.

ANDREW. That's just like Ma, bless her!

RUTH. She's missed you terrible. We all have. And you can't deny the farm has, after what I showed you and told you when we was looking over the place this morning.

ANDREW. (*With a frown.*) Things are run down, that's a fact! It's too darn hard on poor old Rob.

RUTH. (*Scornfully.*) It's his own fault. He never takes any interest in things.

ANDREW. (*Reprovingly.*) You can't blame him. He wasn't born for it; but I know he's done his best for your sake and the old folks and the little girl.

RUTH. (*Indifferently.*) Yes, I suppose he has. (*Gaily.*) But thank the Lord, all those days are over now. The "hard luck" Rob's always blaming won't last long when you take hold, Andy. All the farm's ever needed was someone with the knack of looking ahead and preparing for what's going to happen.

ANDREW. Yes, Rob hasn't got that. He's frank to own up to that himself. I'm going to try and hire a good man for him—an experienced farmer—to work the place on a salary and percentage. That'll take it off of Rob's hands, and he needn't be worrying himself to death any more. He looks all worn out, Ruth. He ought to be careful.

RUTH. (*Absent-mindedly.*) Yes, I s'pose. (*Her mind is filled with premonitions by the first part of his statement.*) Why do you want to hire a man to oversee things? Seems as if now that you're back it wouldn't be needful.

ANDREW. Oh, of course I'll attend to everything while I'm here. I mean after I'm gone.

RUTH. (*As if she couldn't believe her ears.*) Gone!

ANDREW. Yes. When I leave for the Argentine again.

RUTH. (*Aghast.*) You're going away to sea!

ANDREW. Not to sea, no; I'm through with the sea for good as a job. I'm going down to Buenos Aires to get in the grain business.

RUTH. But—that's far off—isn't it?

ANDREW. (*Easily.*) Six thousand miles more or less. It's quite a trip. (*With enthusiasm.*) I've got a peach of a chance down there, Ruth. Ask Rob if I haven't. I've just been telling him all about it.

RUTH. (*A flush of anger coming over her face.*) And didn't he try to stop you from going?

ANDREW. (*In surprise.*) No, of course not. Why?

RUTH. (*Slowly and vindictively.*) That's just like him—not to.

ANDREW. (*Resentfully.*) Rob's too good a chum to try and stop me when he knows I'm set on a thing. And he could see just as soon's I told him what a good chance it was.

RUTH. (*Dazedly.*) And you're bound on going?

ANDREW. Sure thing. Oh, I don't mean right off. I'll have to wait for a ship sailing there for quite a while, likely. Anyway, I want to stay to home and visit with you folks a spell before I go.

RUTH. (*Dumbly.*) I s'pose. (*With sudden anguish.*) Oh, Andy, you can't go! You can't. Why we've all thought—we've all been hoping and praying you was coming home to stay, to settle down on the farm and see to things. You mustn't go! Think of how your Ma'll take on if you go—and how the farm'll be ruined if you leave it to Rob to look after. You can see that.

ANDREW. (*Frowning.*) Rob hasn't done so bad. When I get a man to direct things the farm'll be safe enough.

RUTH. (*Insistently.*) But your Ma—think of her.

ANDREW. She's used to me being away. She won't object when she knows it's best for her and all of us for me to go. You ask Rob. In a couple of years down there I'll make my pile, see if I don't; and then I'll come back and settle down and turn this farm into the crackiest place in the whole state. In the meantime, I can help you both from down there. (*Earnestly.*) I tell you, Ruth, I'm going to make good right from the minute I land, if working hard and a determination to get on can do it; and I *know* they can! (*Excitedly—in a rather boastful tone.*) I tell you, I feel ripe for bigger things than settling down here. The trip did that for me, anyway. It showed me the world is a larger proposition than ever I thought it was in the old days. I couldn't be content any more stuck here like a fly in molasses. It all seems trifling, somehow. You ought to be able to understand what I feel.

RUTH. (*Dully.*) Yes— I s'pose I ought. (*After a pause—a sudden suspicion forming in her mind.*) What did Rob tell you—about me?

ANDREW. Tell? About you? Why, nothing.

RUTH. (*Staring at him intensely.*) Are you telling me the truth, Andy Mayo? Didn't he say—I— (*She stops confusedly.*)

ANDREW. (*Surprised.*) No, he didn't mention you, I can remember. Why? what made you think he did?

RUTH. (*Wringing her hands.*) Oh, I wish I could tell if you're lying or not!

ANDREW. (*Indignantly.*) What're you talking about? I didn't used to lie to you, did I? And what in the name of God is there to lie for?

RUTH. (*Still unconvinced.*) Are you sure—will you swear—it isn't the reason—(*She lowers her eyes and half turns away from him.*) The same reason that made you go last time that's driving you away again? 'Cause if it is—I was going to say—you mustn't go—on that account. (*Her voice sinks to a tremulous, tender whisper as she finishes.*)

ANDREW. (*Confused—forces a laugh.*) Oh, is *that* what you're driving at? Well, you needn't worry about that no more— (*Soberly.*) I don't blame you, Ruth, feeling embarrassed having me around again, after the way I played the dumb fool about going away last time.

RUTH. (*Her hope crushed—with a gasp of pain.*) Oh Andy!

ANDREW. (*Misunderstanding.*) I know I oughtn't to talk about such foolishness to you. Still I figure it's better to get it out of my system so's we three can be together same's years ago, and not be worried thinking one of us might have the wrong notion.

RUTH. Andy! Please! Don't!

ANDREW. Let me finish now that I've started. It'll help clear things up. I don't want you to think once a fool always a fool, and be upset all the time I'm here on my fool account. I want you to believe I put all that silly nonsense back of me a long time ago—and now—it seems—well—as if you'd always been my sister, that's what, Ruth.

RUTH. (*At the end of her endurance—laughing hysterically.*) For God's sake, Andy—won't you please stop talking! (*She again hides her face in her hands, her bowed shoulders trembling.*)

ANDREW. (*Ruefully.*) Seem's if I put my foot in it whenever I open my mouth today. Rob shut me up with almost the same words when I tried speaking to him about it.

RUTH. (*Fiercely.*) You told him—what you've told me?

ANDREW. (*Astounded.*) Why sure! Why not?

RUTH. (*Shuddering.*) Oh, my God!

ANDREW. (*Alarmed.*) Why? Shouldn't I have?

RUTH. (*Hysterically.*) Oh, I don't care what you do! I don't care! Leave me alone! (ANDREW *gets up and walks down the hill to the left, embarrassed, hurt, and greatly puzzled by her behavior.*)

ANDREW. (*After a pause—pointing down the hill.*) Hello. Here they come back—and the Captain's with them. How'd he come to get back so soon, I wonder? That means I've got to hustle down to the port and get on board. Rob's got the baby with him. (*He comes back to the boulder.* RUTH *keeps her face averted from him.*) Gosh, I never saw a father so tied up in a kid as Rob is! He just watches every move she makes. And I don't blame him. You both got a right to feel proud of her. She's surely a little winner. (*He glances at* RUTH *to see if this very obvious attempt to get back in her good graces is having any effect.*) I can see the likeness to Rob standing out all over her, can't you? But there's no denying she's your young one, either. There's something about her eyes—

RUTH. (*Piteously.*) Oh, Andy, I've a headache! I don't want to talk! Leave me alone, won't you please?

ANDREW. (*Stands staring at her for a moment—then walks away saying in a hurt tone*): Everybody hereabouts seems to be on edge today. I begin to feel as if I'm not wanted around. (*He stands near the path, left, kicking at the grass with the toe of his shoe. A moment later* CAPTAIN DICK SCOTT *enters, followed by* ROBERT *carrying* MARY. *The* CAPTAIN *seems scarcely to have changed at all from the jovial, booming person he was three years before. He wears a uniform similar to* ANDREW'S. *He is puffing and breathless from his climb and mops wildly at his perspiring countenance.* ROBERT *casts a quick glance at* ANDREW, *noticing the latter's discomfited look, and then turns his eyes on* RUTH *who, at their approach, has moved so her back is toward them, her chin resting on her hands as she stares out seaward.*)

MARY. Mama! Mama! (ROBERT *puts her down and she runs to her mother.* RUTH *turns and grabs her up in her arms with a sudden fierce tenderness, quickly turning away again from the others. During the following scene she keeps* MARY *in her arms.*)

SCOTT. (*Wheezily.*) Phew! I got great news for you, Andy. Let me get my wind first. Phew! God A'mighty, mountin' this damned hill is worser'n goin' aloft to the skys'l yard in a blow. I got to lay to a while. (*He sits down on the grass, mopping his face.*)

ANDREW. I didn't look for you this soon, Uncle.

SCOTT. I didn't figger it, neither; but I run across a bit o' news down to the Seamen's Home made me 'bout ship and set all sail back here to find you.

ANDREW. (*Eagerly.*) What is it, Uncle?

SCOTT. Passin' by the Home I thought I'd drop in an' let 'em know I'd be lackin' a mate next trip count o' your leavin'. Their man in charge o' the shippin' asked after you 'special curious. "Do you think he'd consider a berth as Second on a steamer, Captain?" he asks.

I was goin' to say no when I thinks o' you wantin' to get back down south to the Plate agen; so I asks him: "What is she and where's she bound?" "She's the *El Paso,* a brand new tramp," he says, "and she's bound for Buenos Aires."

ANDREW. (*His eyes lighting up—excitedly.*) Gosh, that is luck! When does she sail?

SCOTT. Tomorrow mornin'. I didn't know if you'd want to ship away agen so quick an' I told him so. "Tell him I'll hold the berth open for him until late this afternoon," he says. So there you be, an' you can make your own choice.

ANDREW. I'd like to take it. There may not be another ship for Buenos Aires with a vacancy in months. (*His eyes roving from* ROBERT *to* RUTH *and back again—uncertainly.*) Still—damn it all —tomorrow morning *is* soon. I wish she wasn't leaving for a week or so. That'd give me a chance—it seems hard to go right away again when I've just got home. And yet it's a chance in a thousand— (*Appealing to* ROBERT.) What do you think, Rob? What would you do?

ROBERT. (*Forcing a smile.*) He who hesitates, you know. (*Frowning.*) It's a piece of good luck thrown in your way —and—I think you owe it to yourself to jump at it. But don't ask me to decide for you.

RUTH. (*Turning to look at* ANDREW—*in a tone of fierce resentment.*) Yes, go, Andy! (*She turns quickly away again. There is a moment of embarrassed silence.*)

ANDREW. (*Thoughtfully.*) Yes, I guess I will. It'll be the best thing for all of us in the end, don't you think so, Rob? (ROBERT *nods but remains silent.*)

SCOTT. (*Getting to his feet.*) Then, that's settled.

ANDREW. (*Now that he has definitely made a decision his voice rings with hopeful strength and energy.*) Yes, I'll take the berth. The sooner I go the sooner I'll be back, that's a certainty; and I won't come back with empty hands next time. You bet I won't!

SCOTT. You ain't got so much time, Andy. To make sure you'd best leave here soon's you kin. I got to get right back aboard. You'd best come with me.

ANDREW. I'll go to the house and repack my bag right away.

ROBERT. (*Quietly.*) You'll both be here for dinner, won't you?

ANDREW. I don't know. Will there be time? What time is it now, I wonder?

ROBERT. (*Reproachfully.*) Ma's been getting dinner especially for you, Andy.

ANDREW. (*Flushing — shamefacedly.*) Hell! And I was forgetting! Of course I'll stay for dinner if I missed every damned ship in the world. (*He turns to the* CAPTAIN—*briskly.*) Come on, Uncle. Walk down with me to the house and you can tell me more about this berth on the way. I've got to pack before dinner. (*He and the* CAPTAIN *start down to the left.* ANDREW *calls back over his shoulder.*) You're coming soon, aren't you, Rob?

ROBERT. Yes. I'll be right down. (ANDREW *and the* CAPTAIN *leave.* RUTH *puts* MARY *on the ground and hides her face in her hands. Her shoulders shake as if she were sobbing.* ROBERT *stares at her with a grim, somber expression.* MARY *walks backward toward* ROBERT, *her wondering eyes fixed on her mother.*)

MARY. (*Her voice vaguely frightened, taking her father's hand.*) Dada, Mama's cryin', Dada.

ROBERT. (*Bending down and stroking her hair—in a voice he endeavors to keep from being harsh.*) No, she isn't, little girl. The sun hurts her eyes, that's all. Aren't you beginning to feel hungry, Mary?

MARY. (*Decidedly.*) Yes, Dada.

ROBERT. (*Meaningly.*) It must be your dinner time now.

RUTH. (*In a muffled voice.*) I'm coming, Mary. (*She wipes her eyes quickly and, without looking at* ROBERT, *comes and takes* MARY'S *hand—in a dead voice.*) Come on and I'll get your dinner for you. (*She walks out left, her eyes fixed on the ground, the skipping* MARY *tugging at her hand.* ROBERT *waits a moment for them to get ahead and then slowly follows as*

THE CURTAIN FALLS.)

ACT THREE

SCENE ONE

SCENE. *Same as Act Two, Scene One—The sitting room of the farm house about six o'clock in the morning of a day to-*

ward the end of October five years later. It is not yet dawn, but as the action progresses the darkness outside the windows gradually fades to gray.

The room, seen by the light of the shadeless oil lamp with a smoky chimney which stands on the table, presents an appearance of decay, of dissolution. The curtains at the windows are torn and dirty and one of them is missing. The closed desk is gray with accumulated dust as if it had not been used in years. Blotches of dampness disfigure the wall paper. Threadbare trails, leading to the kitchen and outer doors, show in the faded carpet. The top of the coverless table is stained with the imprints of hot dishes and spilled food. The rung of one rocker has been clumsily mended with a piece of plain board. A brown coating of rust covers the unblacked stove. A pile of wood is stacked up carelessly against the wall by the stove.

The whole atmosphere of the room, contrasted with that of former years, is one of an habitual poverty too hopelessly resigned to be any longer ashamed or even conscious of itself.

At the rise of the curtain RUTH *is discovered sitting by the stove, with hands outstretched to the warmth as if the air in the room were damp and cold. A heavy shawl is wrapped about her shoulders, half-concealing her dress of deep mourning. She has aged horribly. Her pale, deeply lined face has the stony lack of expression of one to whom nothing more can ever happen, whose capacity for emotion has been exhausted. When she speaks her voice is without timbre, low and monotonous. The negligent disorder of her dress, the slovenly arrangement of her hair, now streaked with gray, her muddied shoes run down at the heel, give full evidence of the apathy in which she lives.*

Her mother is asleep in her wheel chair beside the stove toward the rear, wrapped up in a blanket.

There is a sound from the open bedroom door in the rear as if someone were getting out of bed. RUTH *turns in that direction with a look of dull annoyance. A moment later* ROBERT *appears in the doorway, leaning weakly against it for support. His hair is long and unkempt, his face and body emaciated. There are bright patches of crimson over his cheek bones and his eyes are burning with fever. He is dressed in corduroy pants, a flannel shirt, and wears worn carpet slippers on his bare feet.*

RUTH. (*Dully.*) S-s-s-h! Ma's asleep.

ROBERT. (*Speaking with an effort.*) I won't wake her. (*He walks weakly to a rocker by the side of the table and sinks down in it exhausted.*)

RUTH. (*Staring at the stove.*) You better come near the fire where it's warm.

ROBERT. No. I'm burning up now.

RUTH. That's the fever. You know the doctor told you not to get up and move around.

ROBERT. (*Irritably.*) That old fossil! He doesn't know anything. Go to bed and stay there—that's his only prescription.

RUTH. (*Indifferently.*) How are you feeling now?

ROBERT. (*Buoyantly.*) Better! Much better than I've felt in ages. Really I'm fine now—only very weak. It's the turning point, I guess. From now on I'll pick up so quick I'll surprise you—and no thanks to that old fool of a country quack, either.

RUTH. He's always tended to us.

ROBERT. Always helped us to die, you mean! He "tended" to Pa and Ma and —(*his voice breaks*)—and to—Mary.

RUTH. (*Dully.*) He did the best he knew, I s'pose. (*After a pause.*) Well, Andy's bringing a specialist with him when he comes. That ought to suit you.

ROBERT. (*Bitterly.*) Is that why you're waiting up all night?

RUTH. Yes.

ROBERT. For Andy?

RUTH. (*Without a trace of feeling.*) Somebody had got to. It's only right for someone to meet him after he's been gone five years.

ROBERT. (*With bitter mockery.*) Five years! It's a long time.

RUTH. Yes.

ROBERT. (*Meaningly.*) To *wait!*

RUTH. (*Indifferently.*) It's past now.

ROBERT. Yes, it's past. (*After a pause.*) Have you got his two telegrams with you? (*Ruth nods.*) Let me see them, will you? My head was so full of fever when they came I couldn't make head or tail to them. (*Hastily.*) But I'm feeling fine now. Let me read them again. (RUTH *takes them from the bosom of her dress and hands them to him.*)

RUTH. Here. The first one's on top.

ROBERT. (*Opening it.*) New York. "Just landed from steamer. Have important business to wind up here. Will be home as soon as deal is completed." (*He smiles bitterly.*) Business first was always Andy's motto. (*He reads.*) "Hope you are all well. Andy." (*He repeats ironically.*) "Hope you are all well!"

RUTH. (*Dully.*) He couldn't know you'd been took sick till I answered that and told him.

ROBERT. (*Contritely.*) Of course he couldn't. I'm a fool. I'm touchy about nothing lately. Just what did you say in your reply?

RUTH. (*Inconsequentially.*) I had to send it collect.

ROBERT. (*Irritably.*) What did you say was the matter with me?

RUTH. I wrote you had lung trouble.

ROBERT. (*Flying into a petty temper.*) You *are* a fool! How often have I explained to you that it's *pleurisy* is the matter with me. You can't seem to get it in your head that the pleura is outside the lungs, not in them!

RUTH. (*Callously.*) I only wrote what Doctor Smith told me.

ROBERT. (*Angrily.*) He's a damned ignoramus!

RUTH. (*Dully.*) Makes no difference. I had to tell Andy something, didn't I?

ROBERT. (*After a pause, opening the other telegram.*) He sent this last evening. Let's see. (*He reads.*) "Leave for home on midnight train. Just received your wire. Am bringing specialist to see Rob. Will motor to farm from Port." (*He calculates.*) What time is it now?

RUTH. Round six, must be.

ROBERT. He ought to be here soon. I'm glad he's bringing a doctor who knows something. A specialist will tell you in a second that there's nothing the matter with my lungs.

RUTH. (*Stolidly.*) You've been coughing an awful lot lately.

ROBERT. (*Irritably.*) What nonsense! For God's sake, haven't you ever had a bad cold yourself? (RUTH *stares at the stove in silence.* ROBERT *fidgets in his chair. There is a pause. Finally* ROBERT'S *eyes are fixed on the sleeping* MRS. ATKINS.) Your mother is lucky to be able to sleep so soundly.

RUTH. Ma's tired. She's been sitting up with me most of the night.

ROBERT. (*Mockingly.*) Is she waiting for Andy, too? (*There is a pause.* ROBERT *sighs.*) I couldn't get to sleep to save my soul. I counted ten million sheep if I counted one. No use! I gave up trying finally and just laid there in the dark thinking. (*He pauses, then continues in a tone of tender sympathy.*) I was thinking about you, Ruth—of how hard these last years must have been for you. (*Appealingly.*) I'm sorry, Ruth.

RUTH. (*In a dead voice.*) I don't know. They're past now. They were hard on all of us.

ROBERT. Yes; on all of us but Andy. (*With a flash of sick jealousy.*) Andy's made a big success of himself—the kind he wanted. (*Mockingly.*) And now he's coming home to let us admire his greatness. (*Frowning—irritably.*) What am I talking about? My brain must be sick, too. (*After a pause.*) Yes, these years have been terrible for both of us. (*His voice is lowered to a trembling whisper.*) Especially the last eight months since Mary—died. (*He forces back a sob with a convulsive shudder—then breaks out in a passionate agony.*) Our last hope of happiness! I could curse God from the bottom of my soul—if there was a God! (*He is racked by a violent fit of coughing and hurriedly puts his handkerchief to his lips.*)

RUTH. (*Without looking at him.*) Mary's better off—being dead.

ROBERT. (*Gloomily.*) We'd all be better off for that matter. (*With a sudden exasperation.*) You tell that mother of yours she's got to stop saying that Mary's death was due to a weak constitution inherited from me. (*On the verge of tears of weakness.*) It's got to stop, I tell you!

RUTH. (*Sharply.*) S-h-h! You'll wake her; and then she'll nag at me—not you.

ROBERT. (*Coughs and lies back in his chair weakly—a pause.*) It's all because your mother's down on me for not begging Andy for help.

RUTH. (*Resentfully.*) You might have. He's got plenty.

ROBERT. How can *you* of all people think of taking money from *him?*

RUTH. (*Dully.*) I don't see the harm. He's your own brother.

ROBERT. (*Shrugging his shoulders.*) What's the use of talking to you? Well, *I* couldn't. (*Proudly.*) And I've managed to keep things going, thank God.

You can't deny that without help I've succeeded in— (*He breaks off with a bitter laugh.*) My God, what am I boasting of? Debts to this one and that, taxes, interest unpaid! I'm a fool! (*He lies back in his chair closing his eyes for a moment, then speaks in a low voice.*) I'll be frank, Ruth. I've been an utter failure, and I've dragged you with me. I couldn't blame you in all justice—for hating me.

RUTH. (*Without feeling.*) I don't hate you. It's been my fault too, I s'pose.

ROBERT. No. You couldn't help loving —Andy.

RUTH. (*Dully.*) I don't love anyone.

ROBERT. (*Waving her remark aside.*) You needn't deny it. It doesn't matter. (*After a pause—with a tender smile.*) Do you know Ruth, what I've been dreaming back there in the dark? (*With a short laugh.*) I was planning our future when I get well. (*He looks at her with appealing eyes as if afraid she will sneer at him. Her expression does not change. She stares at the stove. His voice takes on a note of eagerness.*) After all, why shouldn't we have a future? We're young yet. If we can only shake off the curse of this farm! It's the farm that's ruined our lives, damn it! And now that Andy's coming back—I'm going to sink my foolish pride, Ruth! I'll borrow the money from him to give us a good start in the city. We'll go where people live instead of stagnating, and start all over again. (*Confidently.*) I won't be the failure there that I've been here, Ruth. You won't need to be ashamed of me there. I'll prove to you the reading I've done can be put to some use. (*Vaguely.*) I'll write, or something of that sort. I've always wanted to write. (*Pleadingly.*) You'll want to do that, won't you, Ruth?

RUTH. (*Dully.*) There's Ma.

ROBERT. She can come with us.

RUTH. She wouldn't.

ROBERT. (*Angrily.*) So that's your answer! (*He trembles with violent passion. His voice is so strange that* RUTH *turns to look at him in alarm.*) You're lying, Ruth! Your mother's just an excuse. You want to stay here. You think that because Andy's coming back that— (*He chokes and has an attack of coughing.*)

RUTH. (*Getting up—in a frightened voice.*) What's the matter? (*She goes to him.*) I'll go with you, Rob. Stop that coughing for goodness' sake! It's awful bad for you. (*She soothes him in dull tones.*) I'll go with you to the city—soon's you're well again. Honest I will, Rob, I promise! (ROB *lies back and closes his eyes. She stands looking down at him anxiously.*) Do you feel better now?

ROBERT. Yes. (RUTH *goes back to her chair. After a pause he opens his eyes and sits up in his chair. His face is flushed and happy.*) Then you *will* go, Ruth?

RUTH. Yes.

ROBERT. (Excitedly.) We'll make a new start, Ruth—just you and I. Life owes us some happiness after what we've been through. (*Vehemently.*) It must! Otherwise our suffering would be meaningless—and that is unthinkable.

RUTH. (*Worried by his excitement.*) Yes, yes, of course, Rob, but you mustn't—

ROBERT. Oh, don't be afraid. I feel completely well, really I do—now that I can hope again. Oh if you knew how glorious it feels to have something to look forward to! Can't you feel the thrill of it, too—the vision of a new life opening up after all the horrible years?

RUTH. Yes, yes, but do be—

ROBERT. Nonsense! I won't be careful. I'm getting back all my strength. (*He gets lightly to his feet.*) See! I feel light as a feather. (*He walks to her chair and bends down to kiss her smilingly.*) One kiss—the first in years, isn't it?—to greet the dawn of a new life together.

RUTH. (*Submitting to his kiss—worriedly.*) Sit down, Rob, for goodness' sake!

ROBERT. (*With tender obstinacy—stroking her hair.*) I won't sit down. You're silly to worry. (*He rests one hand on the back of her chair.*) Listen. All our suffering has been a test through which we had to pass to prove ourselves worthy of a finer realization. (*Exultingly.*) And we did pass through it! It hasn't broken us! And now the dream is to come true! Don't you see?

RUTH. (*Looking at him with frightened eyes as if she thought he had gone mad.*) Yes, Rob, I see; but won't you go back to bed now and rest?

ROBERT. No. I'm going to see the sun

rise. It's an augury of good fortune. (*He goes quickly to the window in the rear left, and pushing the curtains aside, stands looking out.* RUTH *springs to her feet and comes quickly to the table, left, where she remains watching* ROBERT *in a tense, expectant attitude. As he peers out his body seems gradually to sag, to grow limp and tired. His voice is mournful as he speaks.*) No sun yet. It isn't time. All I can see is the black rim of the damned hills outlined against a creeping grayness. (*He turns around; letting the curtains fall back, stretching a hand out to the wall to support himself. His false strength of a moment has evaporated leaving his face drawn and hollow eyed. He makes a pitiful attempt to smile.*) That's not a very happy augury, is it? But the sun'll come—soon. (*He sways weakly.*)

RUTH. (*Hurrying to his side and supporting him.*) Please go to bed, won't you, Rob? You don't want to be all wore out when the specialist comes, do you?

ROBERT. (*Quickly.*) No. That's right. He mustn't think I'm sicker than I am. And I feel as if I could sleep now—(*Cheerfully*)—a good, sound, restful sleep.

RUTH. (*Helping him to the bedroom door.*) That's what you need most. (*They go inside. A moment later she reappears calling back.*) I'll shut this door so's you'll be quiet. (*She closes the door and goes quickly to her mother and shakes her by the shoulder.*) Ma! Ma! Wake up!

MRS. ATKINS. (*Coming out of her sleep with a start.*) Glory be! What's the matter with you?

RUTH. It was Rob. He's just been talking to me out here. I put him back to bed. (*Now that she is sure her mother is awake her fear passes and she relapses into dull indifference. She sits down in her chair and stares at the stove—dully.*) He acted—funny; and his eyes looked so—so wild like.

MRS. ATKINS. (*With asperity.*) And is that all you woke me out of a sound sleep for, and scared me near out of my wits?

RUTH. I was afraid. He talked so crazy. I couldn't quiet him. I didn't want to be alone with him that way. Lord knows what he might do.

MRS. ATKINS. (*Scornfully.*) Humph! A help I'd be to you and me not able to move a step! Why didn't you run and get Jake?

RUTH. (*Dully.*) Jake isn't here. He quit last night. He hasn't been paid in three months.

MRS. ATKINS. (*Indignantly.*) I can't blame him. What decent person'd want to work on a place like this? (*With sudden exasperation.*) Oh, I wish you'd never married that man!

RUTH. (*Wearily.*) You oughtn't to talk about him now when he's sick in his bed.

MRS. ATKINS. (*Working herself into a fit of rage.*) You know very well Ruth Mayo, if it wasn't for me helpin' you on the sly out of my savin's, you'd both been in the poor house—and all 'count of his pigheaded pride in not lettin' Andy know the state thin's were in. A nice thin' for me to have to support him out of what I'd saved for my last days—and me an invalid with no one to look to!

RUTH. Andy'll pay you back, Ma. I can tell him so's Rob'll never know.

MRS. ATKINS. (*With a snort.*) What'd Rob think you and him was livin' on, I'd like to know?

RUTH. (*Dully.*) He didn't think about it, I s'pose. (*After a slight pause.*) He said he'd made up his mind to ask Andy for help when he comes. (*As a clock in the kitchen strikes six.*) Six o'clock. Andy ought to get here directly.

MRS. ATKINS. D'you think this special doctor'll do Rob any good?

RUTH. (*Hopelessly.*) I don't know. (*The two women remain silent for a time staring dejectedly at the stove.*)

MRS. ATKINS. (*Shivering irritably.*) For goodness' sake put some wood on that fire. I'm most freezin'!

RUTH. (*Pointing to the door in the rear.*) Don't talk so loud. Let him sleep if he can. (*She gets wearily from the chair and puts a few pieces of wood in the stove.*) This is the last of the wood. I don't know who'll cut more now that Jake's left. (*She sighs and walks to the window in the rear, left, pulls the curtains aside, and looks out.*) It's getting gray out. (*She comes back to the stove.*) Looks like it'd be a nice day. (*She stretches out her hands to warm them.*) Must've been a heavy frost last night. We're paying for the spell of warm weather we've been having. (*The throbbing whine of a motor sounds from the distance outside.*)

MRS. ATKINS. (*Sharply.*) S-h-h! Listen. Ain't that an auto I hear?

RUTH. (*Without interest.*) Yes. It's Andy, I s'pose.

MRS. ATKINS. (*With nervous irritation.*) Don't sit there like a silly goose. Look at the state of this room! What'll this strange doctor think of us? Look at that lamp chimney all smoke! Gracious sakes, Ruth—

RUTH. (*Indifferently.*) I've got a lamp all cleaned up in the kitchen.

MRS. ATKINS. (*Peremptorily.*) Wheel me in there this minute. I don't want him to see me looking a sight. I'll lay down in the room the other side. You don't need me now and I'm dead for sleep. (RUTH *wheels her mother off right. The noise of the motor grows louder, and finally ceases as the car stops on the road before the farm house.* RUTH *returns from the kitchen with a lighted lamp in her hand which she sets on the table beside the other. The sound of footsteps on the path is heard—then a sharp rap on the door.* RUTH *goes and opens it.* ANDREW *enters, followed by* DOCTOR FAWCETT *carrying a small black bag.* ANDREW *has changed greatly. His face seems to have grown highstrung, hardened by the look of decisiveness which comes from being constantly under a strain where judgments on the spur of the moment are compelled to be accurate. His eyes are keener and more alert. There is even a suggestion of ruthless cunning about them. At present, however, his expression is one of tense anxiety.* DOCTOR FAWCETT *is a short, dark, middle-aged man with a Vandyke beard. He wears glasses.*)

RUTH. Hello, Andy! I've been waiting—

ANDREW. (*Kissing her hastily.*) I got here as soon as I could. (*He throws off his cap and heavy overcoat on the table, introducing* RUTH *and the* DOCTOR *as he does so. He is dressed in an expensive business suit and appears stouter.*) My sister-in-law, Mrs. Mayo—Doctor Fawcett. (*They bow to each other silently.* ANDREW *casts a quick glance about the room.*) Where's Rob?

RUTH. (*Pointing.*) In there.

ANDREW. I'll take your coat and hat, Doctor. (*As he helps the* DOCTOR *with his things.*) Is he very bad, Ruth?

RUTH. (*Dully.*) He's been getting weaker.

ANDREW. Damn! This way, Doctor. Bring the lamp, Ruth. (*He goes into the bedroom, followed by the* DOCTOR *and* RUTH *carrying the clean lamp.* RUTH *reappears almost immediately, closing the door behind her, and goes slowly to the outside door, which she opens, and stands in the doorway looking out. The sound of* ANDREW'S *and* ROBERT'S *voices comes from the bedroom. A moment later* ANDREW *re-enters, closing the door softly. He comes forward and sinks down in the rocker on the right of table, leaning his head on his hand. His face is drawn in a shocked expression of great grief. He sighs heavily, staring mournfully in front of him.* RUTH *turns and stands watching him. Then she shuts the door and returns to her chair by the stove, turning it so she can face him.*)

ANDREW. (*Glancing up quickly—in a harsh voice.*) How long has this been going on?

RUTH. You mean—how long has he been sick?

ANDREW. (*Shortly.*) Of course! What else?

RUTH. It was last summer he had a bad spell first, but he's been ailin' ever since Mary died—eight months ago.

ANDREW. (*Harshly.*) Why didn't you let me know—cable me? Do you want him to die, all of you? I'm damned if it doesn't look that way! (*His voice breaking.*) Poor old chap! To be sick in this out-of-the-way hole without anyone to attend to him but a country quack! It's a damned shame!

RUTH. (*Dully.*) I wanted to send you word once, but he only got mad when I told him. He was too proud to ask anything, he said.

ANDREW. Proud? To ask *me?* (*He jumps to his feet and paces nervously back and forth.*) I can't understand the way you've acted. Didn't you see how sick he was getting? Couldn't you realize—why, I nearly dropped in my tracks when I saw him! He looks—(*He shudders*)—terrible! (*With fierce scorn.*) I suppose you're so used to the idea of his being delicate that you took his sickness as a matter of course. God, if I'd only known!

RUTH. (*Without emotion.*) A letter takes so long to get where you were—and we couldn't afford to telegraph. We owed everyone already, and I couldn't ask Ma.

She'd been giving me money out of her savings till she hadn't much left. Don't say anything to Rob about it. I never told him. He'd only be mad at me if he knew. But I had to, because—God knows how we'd have got on if I hadn't.

ANDREW. You mean to say— (*His eyes seem to take in the poverty-stricken appearance of the room for the first time.*) You sent that telegram to me collect. Was it because— (RUTH *nods silently.* ANDREW *pounds on the table with his fist.*) Good God! And all this time I've been—why I've had everything! (*He sits down in his chair and pulls it close to* RUTH's—*impulsively.*) But—I can't get it through my head. Why? Why? What has happened? How did it ever come about? Tell me!

RUTH. (*Dully.*) There's nothing much to tell. Things kept getting worse, that's all—and Rob didn't seem to care. He never took any interest since way back when your Ma died. After that he got men to take charge, and they nearly all cheated him—he couldn't tell—and left one after another. Then after Mary died he didn't pay no heed to anything any more—just stayed indoors and took to reading books again. So I had to ask Ma if she wouldn't help us some.

ANDREW. (*Surprised and horrified.*) Why, damn it, this is frightful! Rob must be mad not to have let me know. Too proud to ask help of *me!* What's the matter with him in God's name? (*A sudden, horrible suspicion entering his mind.*) Ruth! Tell me the truth. His mind hasn't gone back on him, has it?

RUTH. (*Dully.*) I don't know. Mary's dying broke him up terrible—but he's used to her being gone by this, I s'pose.

ANDREW. (*Looking at her queerly.*) Do you mean to say *you're* used to it?

RUTH. (*In a dead tone.*) There's a time comes—when you don't mind any more—anything.

ANDREW. (*Looks at her fixedly for a moment—with great pity.*) I'm sorry, Ruth—if I seemed to blame you. I didn't realize— The sight of Rob lying in bed there, so gone to pieces—it made me furious at everyone. Forgive me, Ruth.

RUTH. There's nothing to forgive. It doesn't matter.

ANDREW. (*Springing to his feet again and pacing up and down.*) Thank God I came back before it was too late. This doctor will know exactly what to do. That's the first thing to think of. When Rob's on his feet again we can get the farm working on a sound basis once more. I'll see to that—before I leave.

RUTH. You're going away again?

ANDREW. I've got to.

RUTH. You wrote Rob you was coming back to stay this time.

ANDREW. I expected to—until I got to New York. Then I learned certain facts that make it necessary. (*With a short laugh.*) To be candid, Ruth, I'm not the rich man you've probably been led to believe by my letters—not now. I was when I wrote them. I made money hand over fist as long as I stuck to legitimate trading; but I wasn't content with that. I wanted it to come easier, so like all the rest of the idiots, I tried speculation. Oh, I won all right! Several times I've been almost a millionaire—on paper—and then come down to earth again with a bump. Finally the strain was too much. I got disgusted with myself and made up my mind to get out and come home and forget it and really live again. (*He gives a harsh laugh.*) And now comes the funny part. The day before the steamer sailed I saw what I thought was a chance to become a millionaire again. (*He snaps his fingers.*) That easy! I plunged. Then, before things broke, I left—I was so confident I couldn't be wrong. But when I landed in New York—I wired you I had business to wind up, didn't I? Well, it was the business that wound me up! (*He smiles grimly, pacing up and down, his hands in his pockets.*)

RUTH. (*Dully.*) You found—you'd lost everything?

ANDREW. (*Sitting down again.*) Practically. (*He takes a cigar from his pocket, bites the end off, and lights it.*) Oh, I don't mean I'm dead broke. I've saved ten thousand from the wreckage, maybe twenty. But that's a poor showing for five years' hard work. That's why I'll have to go back. (*Confidently.*) I can make it up in a year or so down there—and I don't need but a shoestring to start with. (*A weary expression comes over his face and he sighs heavily.*) I wish I didn't have to. I'm sick of it all.

RUTH. It's too bad—things seem to go wrong so.

ANDREW. (*Shaking off his depression—briskly.*) They might be much worse. There's enough left to fix the farm O. K. before I go. I won't leave 'til Rob's on his feet again. In the meantime I'll make things fly around here. (*With satisfaction.*) I need a rest, and the kind of rest I need is hard work in the open —just like I used to do in the old days. (*Stopping abruptly and lowering his voice cautiously.*) Not a word to Rob about my losing money! Remember that, Ruth! You can see why. If he's grown so touchy he'd never accept a cent if he thought I was hard up; see?

RUTH. Yes, Andy. (*After a pause, during which* ANDREW *puffs at his cigar abstractedly, his mind evidently busy with plans for the future, the bedroom door is opened and* DOCTOR FAWCETT *enters, carrying a bag. He closes the door quietly behind him and comes forward, a grave expression on his face.* ANDREW *springs out of his chair.*)

ANDREW. Ah, Doctor! (*He pushes a chair between his own and* RUTH'S.) Won't you have a chair?

FAWCETT. (*Glancing at his watch.*) I must catch the nine o'clock back to the city. It's imperative. I have only a moment. (*Sitting down and clearing his throat—in a perfunctory, impersonal voice.*) The case of your brother, Mr. Mayo, is— (*He stops and glances at* RUTH *and says meaningly to* ANDREW.) Perhaps it would be better if you and I—

RUTH. (*With dogged resentment.*) I know what you mean, Doctor. (*Dully.*) Don't be afraid I can't stand it. I'm used to bearing trouble by this; and I can guess what you've found out. (*She hesitates for a moment—then continues in a monotonous voice.*) Rob's going to die.

ANDREW. (*Angrily.*) Ruth!

FAWCETT. (*Raising his hand as if to command silence.*) I am afraid my diagnosis of your brother's condition forces me to the same conclusion as Mrs. Mayo's.

ANDREW. (*Groaning.*) But, Doctor, surely—

FAWCETT. (*Calmly.*) Your brother hasn't long to live—perhaps a few days, perhaps only a few hours. It's a marvel that he's alive at this moment. My examination revealed that both of his lungs are terribly affected.

ANDREW. (*Brokenly.*) Good God!

(RUTH *keeps her eyes fixed on her lap in a trance-like stare.*)

FAWCETT. I am sorry to have to tell you this. If there was anything that could be done—

ANDREW. There isn't anything?

FAWCETT. (*Shaking his head.*) It's too late. Six months ago there might have—

ANDREW. (*In anguish.*) But if we were to take him to the mountains—or to Arizona—or—

FAWCETT. That might have prolonged his life six months ago. (ANDREW *groans.*) But now— (*He shrugs his shoulders significantly.*)

ANDREW. (*Appalled by a sudden thought.*) Good heavens, you haven't told him this, have you, Doctor?

FAWCETT. No. I lied to him. I said a change of climate— (*He looks at his watch again nervously.*) I must leave you. (*He gets up.*)

ANDREW. (*Getting to his feet—insistently.*) But there must still be some chance—

FAWCETT. (*As if he were reassuring a child.*) There is always that last chance —the miracle. (*He puts on his hat and coat—bowing to* RUTH.) Good-by, Mrs. Mayo.

RUTH. (*Without raising her eyes—dully.*) Good-by.

ANDREW. (*Mechanically.*) I'll walk to the car with you, Doctor. (*They go out of the door.* RUTH *sits motionless. The motor is heard starting and the noise gradually recedes into the distance.* ANDREW *re-enters and sits down in his chair, holding his head in his hands.*) Ruth! (*She lifts her eyes to his.*) Hadn't we better go in and see him? God! I'm afraid to! I know he'll read it in my face. (*The bedroom door is noiselessly opened and* ROBERT *appears in the doorway. His cheeks are flushed with fever, and his eyes appear unusually large and brilliant.* ANDREW *continues with a groan.*) It can't be, Ruth. It can't be as hopeless as he said. There's always a fighting chance. We'll take Rob to Arizona. He's *got* to get well. There *must* be a chance!

ROBERT. (*In a gentle tone.*) Why must there, Andy? (RUTH *turns and stares at him with terrified eyes.*)

ANDREW. (*Whirling around.*) Rob! (*Scoldingly.*) What are you doing out of bed? (*He gets up and goes to him.*) Get right back now and obey the Doc, or you're going to get a licking from me!

ROBERT. (*Ignoring these remarks.*) Help me over to the chair, please, Andy.

ANDREW. Like hell I will! You're going right back to bed, that's where you're going, and stay there! (*He takes hold of* ROBERT'S *arm.*)

ROBERT. (*Mockingly.*) Stay there 'til I die, eh, Andy? (*Coldly.*) Don't behave like a child. I'm sick of lying down. I'll be more rested sitting up. (*As* ANDREW *hesitates—violently.*) I swear I'll get out of bed every time you put me there. You'll have to sit on my chest, and that wouldn't help my health any. Come on, Andy. Don't play the fool. I want to talk to you, and I'm going to. (*With a grim smile.*) A dying man has some rights, hasn't he?

ANDREW. (*With a shudder.*) Don't talk that way, for God's sake! I'll only let you sit down if you'll promise that. Remember. (*He helps* ROBERT *to the chair between his own and* RUTH'S.) Easy now! There you are! Wait, and I'll get a pillow for you. (*He goes into the bedroom.* ROBERT *looks at* RUTH *who shrinks away from him in terror.* ROBERT *smiles bitterly.* ANDREW *comes back with the pillow which he places behind* ROBERT'S *back.*) How's that?

ROBERT. (*With an affectionate smile.*) Fine! Thank you! (*As* ANDREW *sits down.*) Listen, Andy. You've asked me not to talk—and I won't after I've made my position clear. (*Slowly.*) In the first place I know I'm dying. (RUTH *bows her head and covers her face with her hands. She remains like this all during the scene between the two brothers.*)

ANDREW. Rob! That isn't so!

ROBERT. (*Wearily.*) It *is* so! Don't lie to me. After Ruth put me to bed before you came, I saw it clearly for the first time. (*Bitterly.*) I'd been making plans for our future—Ruth's and mine—so it came hard at first—the realization. Then when the doctor examined me, I knew—although he tried to lie about it. And then to make sure I listened at the door to what he told you. So don't mock me with fairy tales about Arizona, or any such rot as that. Because I'm dying is no reason you should treat me as an imbecile or a coward. Now that I'm sure what's happening I can say Kismet to it with all my heart. It was only the silly uncertainty that hurt. (*There is a pause.* ANDREW *looks around in impotent anguish, not knowing what to say.* ROBERT *regards him with an affectionate smile.*)

ANDREW. (*Finally blurts out.*) It isn't foolish. You *have* got a chance. If you heard all the Doctor said that ought to prove it to you.

ROBERT. Oh, you mean when he spoke of the miracle? (*Dryly.*) I don't believe in miracles—in my case. Besides, I know more than any doctor on earth *could* know—because I *feel* what's coming. (*Dismissing the subject.*) But we've agreed not to talk of it. Tell me about yourself, Andy. That's what I'm interested in. Your letters were too brief and far apart to be illuminating.

ANDREW. I meant to write oftener.

ROBERT. (*With a faint trace of irony.*) I judge from them you've accomplished all you set out to do five years ago?

ANDREW. That isn't much to boast of.

ROBERT. (*Surprised.*) Have you really, honestly reached that conclusion?

ANDREW. Well, it doesn't seem to amount to much now.

ROBERT. But you're rich, aren't you?

ANDREW. (*With a quick glance at* RUTH.) Yes, I s'pose so.

ROBERT. I'm glad. You can do to the farm all I've undone. But what did you do down there? Tell me. You went in the grain business with that friend of yours?

ANDREW. Yes. After two years I had a share in it. I sold out last year. (*He is answering* ROBERT'S *questions with great reluctance.*)

ROBERT. And then?

ANDREW. I went in on my own.

ROBERT. Still in grain?

ANDREW. Yes.

ROBERT. What's the matter? You look as if I were accusing you of something.

ANDREW. I'm proud enough of the first four years. It's after that I'm not boasting of. I took to speculating.

ROBERT. In wheat?

ANDREW. Yes.

ROBERT. And you made money—gambling?

ANDREW. Yes.

ROBERT. (*Thoughtfully.*) I've been wondering what the great change was in you. (*After a pause.*) You—a farmer—to gamble in a wheat pit with scraps of paper. There's a spiritual significance in that picture, Andy. (*He smiles bitterly.*) I'm a failure, and Ruth's another—but we can both justly lay some of the blame for our stumbling on God. But you're the deepest-dyed failure of the three, Andy. You've spent eight years running away from yourself. Do you see what I mean? You used to be a creator when you loved the farm. You and life were in harmonious partnership. And now— (*He stops as if seeking vainly for words.*) My brain is muddled. But part of what I mean is that your gambling with the thing you used to love to create proves how far astray— So you'll be punished. You'll have to suffer to win back— (*His voice grows weaker and he sighs wearily.*) It's no use. I can't say it. (*He lies back and closes his eyes, breathing pantingly.*)

ANDREW. (*Slowly.*) I think I know what you're driving at, Rob—and it's true, I guess. (ROBERT *smiles gratefully and stretches out his hand, which* ANDREW *takes in his.*)

ROBERT. I want you to promise me to do one thing, Andy, after—

ANDREW. I'll promise anything, as God is my Judge!

ROBERT. Remember, Andy, Ruth has suffered double her share. (*His voice faltering with weakness.*) Only through contact with suffering, Andy, will you—awaken. Listen. You must marry Ruth—afterwards.

RUTH. (*With a cry.*) Rob! (ROBERT *lies back, his eyes closed, gasping heavily for breath.*)

ANDREW. (*Making signs to her to humor him—gently.*) You're tired out, Rob. You better lie down and rest a while, don't you think? We can talk later on.

ROBERT. (*With a mocking smile.*) Later on! You always were an optimist, Andy! (*He sighs with exhaustion.*) Yes, I'll go and rest a while. (*As* ANDREW *comes to help him.*) It must be near sunrise, isn't it?

ANDREW. It's after six.

ROBERT. (*As* ANDREW *helps him into the bedroom.*) Shut the door, Andy. I want to be alone. (ANDREW *reappears and shuts the door softly. He comes and sits down on his chair again, supporting his head on his hands. His face is drawn with the intensity of his dry-eyed anguish.*)

RUTH. (*Glancing at him—fearfully.*) He's out of his mind now, isn't he?

ANDREW. He may be a little delirious. The fever would do that. (*With impotent rage.*) God, what a shame! And there's nothing we can do but sit and—wait! (*He springs from his chair and walks to the stove.*)

RUTH. (*Dully.*) He was talking—wild—like he used to—only this time it sounded—unnatural, don't you think?

ANDREW. I don't know. The things he said to me had truth in them—even if he did talk them way up in the air, like he always sees things. Still— (*He glances down at* RUTH *keenly.*) Why do you suppose he wanted us to promise we'd—(*Confusedly.*) You know what he said.

RUTH. (*Dully.*) His mind was wandering, I s'pose.

ANDREW. (*With conviction.*) No—there was something back of it.

RUTH. He wanted to make sure I'd be all right—after he'd gone, I expect.

ANDREW. No, it wasn't that. He knows very well I'd naturally look after you without—anything like that.

RUTH. He might be thinking of—something happened five years back, the time you came home from the trip.

ANDREW. What happened? What do you mean?

RUTH. (*Dully.*) We had a fight.

ANDREW. A fight? What has that to do with me?

RUTH. It was about you—in a way.

ANDREW. (*Amazed.*) About *me?*

RUTH. Yes, mostly. You see I'd found out I'd made a mistake about Rob soon after we were married—when it was too late.

ANDREW. Mistake? (*Slowly.*) You mean—you found out you didn't love Rob?

RUTH. Yes.

ANDREW. Good God!

RUTH. And then I thought that when Mary came it'd be different, and I'd love him; but it didn't happen that way. And I couldn't bear with his blundering and book-reading—and I grew to hate him, almost.

ANDREW. Ruth!

RUTH. I couldn't help it. No woman could. It had to be because I loved someone else, I'd found out. (*She sighs wearily.*) It can't do no harm to tell you now—when it's all past and gone—and dead. *You* were the one I really loved—

only I didn't come to the knowledge of it 'til too late.

ANDREW. (*Stunned.*) Ruth! Do you know what you're saying?

RUTH. It was true—then. (*With sudden fierceness.*) How could I help it? No woman could.

ANDREW. Then—you loved me—that time I came home?

RUTH. (*Doggedly.*) I'd known your real reason for leaving home the first time—everybody knew it—and for three years I'd been thinking—

ANDREW. That I loved you?

RUTH. Yes. Then that day on the hill you laughed about what a fool you'd been for loving me once—and I knew it was all over.

ANDREW. Good God, but I never thought — (*He stops, shuddering at his remembrance.*) And did Rob—

RUTH. That was what I'd started to tell. We'd had a fight just before you came and I got crazy mad—and I told him all I've told you.

ANDREW. (*Gaping at her speechlessly for a moment.*) You told Rob—you loved me?

RUTH. Yes.

ANDREW. (*Shrinking away from her in horror.*) You—you—you mad fool, you! How could you do such a thing?

RUTH. I couldn't help it. I'd got to the end of bearing things—without talking.

ANDREW. Then Rob must have known every moment I stayed here! And yet he never said or showed— God, how he must have suffered! Didn't you know how much he loved you?

RUTH. (*Dully.*) Yes. I knew he liked me.

ANDREW. Liked you! What kind of a woman are you? Couldn't you have kept silent? Did you have to torture him? No wonder he's dying! And you've lived together for five years with this between you?

RUTH. We've lived in the same house.

ANDREW. Does he still think—

RUTH. I don't know. We've never spoke a word about it since that day. Maybe, from the way he went on, he s'poses I care for you yet.

ANDREW. But you don't. It's outrageous. It's stupid! You don't love me!

RUTH. (*Slowly.*) I wouldn't know how to feel love, even if I tried, any more.

ANDREW. (*Brutally.*) And I don't love you, that's sure! (*He sinks into his chair, his head between his hands.*) It's damnable such a thing should be between Rob and me. Why, I love Rob better'n anybody in the world and always did. There isn't a thing on God's green earth I wouldn't have done to keep trouble away from him. And I have to be the very one—it's damnable! How am I going to face him again? What can I say to him now? (*He groans with anguished rage. After a pause.*) He asked me to promise—what am I going to do?

RUTH. You can promise—so's it'll ease his mind—and not mean anything.

ANDREW. What? Lie to him now—when he's dying? (*Determinedly.*) No! It's *you* who'll have to do the lying, since it must be done. You've got a chance now to undo some of all the suffering you've brought on Rob. Go in to him! Tell him you never loved me—it was all a mistake. Tell him you only said so because you were mad and didn't know what you were saying! Tell him something, anything, that'll bring him peace!

RUTH. (*Dully.*) He wouldn't believe me.

ANDREW. (*Furiously.*) You've got to make him believe you, do you hear? You've got to—now—hurry—you never know when it may be too late. (*As she hesitates—imploringly.*) For God's sake, Ruth! Don't you see you owe it to him? You'll never forgive yourself if you don't.

RUTH. (*Dully.*) I'll go. (*She gets wearily to her feet and walks slowly toward the bedroom.*) But it won't do any good. (ANDREW'S *eyes are fixed on her anxiously. She opens the door and steps inside the room. She remains standing there for a minute. Then she calls in a frightened voice.*) Rob! Where are you? (*Then she hurries back, trembling with fright.*) Andy! Andy! He's gone!

ANDREW. (*Misunderstanding her—his face pale with dread.*) He's not—

RUTH. (*Interrupting him—hysterically.*) He's gone! The bed's empty. The window's wide open. He must have crawled out into the yard!

ANDREW. (*Springing to his feet. He rushes into the bedroom and returns immediately with an expression of alarmed amazement on his face.*) Come! He can't have gone far! (*Grabbing his hat he takes* RUTH'S *arm and shoves her toward the door.*) Come on! (*Opening the door.*) Let's hope to God— (*The *door closes behind them, cutting off his words as*

THE CURTAIN FALLS.)

ACT THREE

Scene Two

Scene. *Same as Act One, Scene One—A section of country highway. The sky to the east is already alight with bright color and a thin, quivering line of flame is spreading slowly along the horizon rim of the dark hills. The roadside, however, is still steeped in the grayness of the dawn, shadowy and vague. The field in the foreground has a wild uncultivated appearance as if it had been allowed to remain fallow the preceding summer. Parts of the snake-fence in the rear have been broken down. The apple tree is leafless and seems dead.*

Robert *staggers weakly in from the left. He stumbles into the ditch and lies there for a moment; then crawls with a great effort to the top of the bank where he can see the sun rise, and collapses weakly.* Ruth *and* Andrew *come hurriedly along the road from the left.*

Andrew. (*Stopping and looking about him.*) There he is! I knew it! I knew we'd find him here.

Robert. (*Trying to raise himself to a sitting position as they hasten to his side—with a wan smile.*) I thought I'd given you the slip.

Andrew. (*With kindly bullying.*) Well you didn't you old scoundrel, and we're going to take you right back where you belong—in bed. (*He makes a motion to lift* Robert.)

Robert. Don't, Andy. Don't, I tell you!

Andrew. You're in pain?

Robert. (*Simply.*) No. I'm dying. (*He falls back weakly.* Ruth *sinks down beside him with a sob and pillows his head on her lap.* Andrew *stands looking down at him helplessly.* Robert *moves his head restlessly on* Ruth's *lap.*) I couldn't stand it back there in the room. It seemed as if all my life—I'd been cooped in a room. So I thought I'd try to end as I might have—if I'd had the courage—alone—in a ditch by the open road—watching the sun rise.

Andrew. Rob! Don't talk. You're wasting your strength. Rest a while and then we'll carry you—

Robert. Still hoping, Andy? Don't. I know. (*There is a pause during which he breathes heavily, straining his eyes toward the horizon.*) The sun comes so slowly. (*With an ironical smile.*) The doctor told me to go to the far-off places—and I'd be cured. He was right. That was always the cure for me. It's too late—for this life—but— (*He has a fit of coughing which racks his body.*)

Andrew. (*With a hoarse sob.*) Rob! (*He clenches his fists in an impotent rage against fate.*) God! God! (Ruth *sobs brokenly and wipes* Robert's *lips with her handkerchief.*)

Robert. (*In a voice which is suddenly ringing with the happiness of hope.*) You mustn't feel sorry for me. Don't you see I'm happy at last—free—free!—freed from the farm—free to wander on and on—eternally! (*He raises himself on his elbow, his face radiant, and points to the horizon.*) Look! Isn't it beautiful beyond the hills? I can hear the old voices calling me to come— (*Exultantly.*) And this time I'm going! It isn't the end. It's a free beginning—the start of my voyage! I've won to my trip—the right of release—beyond the horizon! Oh, you ought to be glad—glad—for my sake! (*He collapses weakly.*) Andy! (Andrew *bends down to him.*) Remember Ruth—

Andrew. I'll take care of her, I swear to you, Rob!

Robert. Ruth has suffered—remember, Andy—only through sacrifice—the secret beyond there— (*He suddenly raises himself with his last remaining strength and points to the horizon where the edge of the sun's disc is rising from the rim of the hills.*) The sun! (*He remains with his eyes fixed on it for a moment. A rattling noise throbs from his throat. He mumbles.*) Remember! (*And falls back and is still.* Ruth *gives a cry of horror and springs to her feet, shuddering, her hands over her eyes.* Andrew *bends on one knee beside the body, placing a hand over* Robert's *heart, then he kisses his brother reverentially on the forehead and stands up.*)

Andrew. (*Facing* Ruth, *the body between them—in a dead voice.*) He's dead. (*With a sudden burst of fury.*) God damn you, you never told him!

RUTH. (*Piteously.*) He was so happy without my lying to him.

ANDREW. (*Pointing to the body—trembling with the violence of his rage.*) This is your doing, you damn woman, you coward, you murderess!

RUTH. (*Sobbing.*) Don't, Andy! I couldn't help it—and he knew how I'd suffered, too. He told you—to remember.

ANDREW. (*Stares at her for a moment, his rage ebbing away, an expression of deep pity gradually coming over his face. Then he glances down at his brother and speaks brokenly in a compassionate voice.*) Forgive me, Ruth—for his sake—and I'll remember— (RUTH *lets her hands fall from her face and looks at him uncomprehendingly. He lifts his eyes to hers and forces out falteringly.*) I—you—we've both made a mess of things! We must try to help each other—and—in time—we'll come to know what's right— (*Desperately.*) And perhaps we— (*But* RUTH, *if she is aware of his words, gives no sign. She remains silent gazing at him dully with the sad humility of exhaustion, her mind already sinking back into that spent calm beyond the further troubling of any hope.*)

(*THE CURTAIN FALLS.*)

SUN-UP

BY

Lula Vollmer

SUN-UP

Sun-Up represents the folk-play in America. During the last few years there has been a significant movement in this country which has tried to interpret the life of those natives of America who have retained the primitive culture of their ancestors, and whose emotions have remained in that inarticulate and unsophisticated state which allow them free expression and make them therefore well suited for the drama.

The folk-play has been stimulated greatly by the work of Professor Frederick H. Koch, both in North Dakota and in North Carolina, where plays have been written and performed by students at the universities. On the professional stage, William Gillette and Mrs. Frances Hodgson Burnett as early as 1881 represented the North Carolina farmer in contrast with European civilization in *Esmeralda.* But it remained for the season of 1923-24 to witness four plays dealing with the mountaineers of North Carolina and Kentucky; *Sun-Up* and *The Shame Woman,* by Miss Vollmer, *This Fine-Pretty World,* by Mr. Percy MacKaye, and *Hell-Bent fer Heaven,* by Mr. Hatcher Hughes.

Lula Vollmer was born in Keyser, North Carolina and was educated in Episcopal Church boarding schools. She spent three years also in the Normal and Collegiate Institute at Asheville, and her stay here was rich in contacts with the mountain women who brought their wares to the Institute. As a school girl she wrote plays and directed her fellow pupils in them. She learned to know the mountaineers too, through personal observation on their own ground, for her father, a specialist in lumber, took his family each summer to the hill country. After graduation she became a reporter which led her, through her interviews, into direct contact with actors and actresses and fostered her determination to write plays. For four years she was secretary to the president and later, for about five years, was an accountant in the Piedmont Hotel in Atlanta, Georgia. During this period she wrote four plays and several short stories and conducted a column in the *Atlanta Pilot,* a theatrical paper, studying such plays as it was possible for her to see. One of her plays, *Jule,* was afterwards condensed and produced by Miss Louise Coleman in vaudeville.

Finally she realized that a practical playwright must live in or near New York and when she came to that city the first approach to the theatre that offered was that of treasurer in the box-office of the Garrick Theatre. Before this opportunity came she had written *Sun-Up,* an anecdote which she had heard from a friend who was returning from a southern war camp in May, 1918, crystallizing her long cherished desire to place upon the stage these people of her native State. The story told of a boy, whose exclamation when he arrived at camp: "Air this hyar France?" revealed the limitations of his race. While she began to build the play upon this boy, his mother, "the widow Cagle" became eventually the central figure of the tragedy, and Miss Vollmer provided in her character, as interpreted by Miss LaVerne, one of the unforgettable productions of our stage. But it is not only the widow Cagle and her eternal feud with "the law," which has robbed her of her father and her husband and which reaches out to take her son to fight in a cause remote from her sympathy or understanding, which provide fine dramatic material. The girl who hesitates between Rufe Cagle and Sheriff Weeks until the manhood of Rufe challenges the womanhood in her, the vividly drawn pictures of the Todds, father and son, in whom the decadent quality of the mountain whites is revealed, with all lost in Bud Todd except courage, these form a background against which the greater figures of mother and son stand revealed. These characters are developed by conversation which is remarkably natural and in which every word tells. There is hardly a line in the play which is not definitely a step in the progression of the drama. This close unity springs partly from the very nature of the material, the life of a community in which the people are so closely related in their joys and sorrows that one event affects them all and their tragedies spring often from their very limitation of opportunity. Yet *Sun-Up*, like *Beyond the Horizon,* closes on a note of exaltation in which a mother's love has passed beyond the limits of life to commune for a moment with the spirit of the son she had lost. Again Miss Vollmer's art rings true, for to such a woman as the widow Cagle, a message from the spirit world would not seem unnatural.

It is characteristic of the difficulties under which the American playwright labors that while Miss Vollmer was an officer of the Theatre Guild, which has devoted its powerful energies largely to the production of foreign plays, *Sun-Up* should have been produced first by the Beechwood Players at Scarborough, New York. It was put on by Mr. Henry Stillman, who had been impressed by the play when he had been associated with the Garrick Theatre. After the play had passed through other hands and a production had been made at White Plains, New York, the Players Company produced *Sun-Up,* under the direction of Mr. Stillman and Mr. Benjamin Kauser, at the Provincetown Theatre, May 24, 1923. It attracted at once the attention of the discriminating and ran, after transfers to the Lenox Hill Theatre and the Princess Theatre, until May 3, 1924, when it was taken on tour. It was produced at the Vaudeville Theatre, London, May 4, 1925, and after transfer to the Lyric, ran for 234 performances. After a revival in New York in 1928, Miss LaVerne produced the play at Les Maturins in Paris, June 20, 1929.

Miss Vollmer's next play, *The Shame Woman,* opened at the Greenwich Village Theatre, October 16, 1923 and continued after transfers to the Princess and Comedy Theatres, until June, 1924. In August it began its tour through Chicago, Philadelphia and other cities until it closed in Buffalo in November. *The Shame Woman* is another tragedy laid in the North Carolina Mountains. Lize Burns, a woman who has suffered all her life the shame of her early seduction by Craig Anson, who lives in the nearby town, finds that Lily, her adopted daughter, is meeting Anson, now a middle-aged roué and in order to warn Lily, she tells the story of her own career, which is represented in five scenes placed twenty years earlier. To her horror she finds the warning is too late and Lily dies. To save her memory from the stain that has shadowed her own life, Lize kills Anson and goes to the scaffold without revealing the reason. As the play was put on, it ends in the jail, but as it was written there was a tenth scene outside the jail. A crowd had gathered to witness the hanging, but when Lize appears in the doorway, her spiritual awakening has so lifted her beyond the clutch of years that it is Lize, the young woman, that they see. They bow before her; even the terrible Martha Case, the midwife begins to tremble. Miss Florence Rittenhouse as Lize, Miss Dupree, as her mother, and Miss Florence Gerald, as Martha Case, gave notable performances. The midwife, drawn as a brooding figure of implacable fate, is as fine a creation as anything that the Russian drama has brought to us.

The Dunce Boy, produced at Daly's Theatre, April 3, 1925, while not a popular success, contained two well-drawn characters, "Tude" Huckle, a half-wit, who has his emotional nature attuned to impressions beyond the normal, and his mother, who sees in him the consequences of pre-natal influences of the great saw mill in the North Carolina mountains.

Sun-Up was published by Brentano's, New York in 1924 in the Contemporary Drama Series. The editor is indebted to the courtesy of the author and the publishers for permission to reprint the play. Information concerning the plays has been furnished by Miss Vollmer and her agent, Miss Ingersoll, and Miss Vollmer has extended to the editor the privilege of reading the unacted scene from *The Shame Woman.* An interesting account of the effect of *Sun-Up* in stimulating financial support for schools which are rescuing from illiteracy the mountaineers of the Southern States is given in the *New York Herald* for February 3, 1924.

At first glance, the dialect of *Sun-Up* will present apparent inconsistencies, especially in the use of the pronoun "you." On this point, Miss Vollmer writes: "The play was written, of course, for the use of the actor, and I tried to make the dialect as easy as possible for him. For instance: The mountaineer will say, 'I saw yo' dog down the road.' and in the next breath, 'Whut's yer hurry?' Then he will say 'I'll tell ye 'bout that termorrow.'" Naturally the editor has printed the play as it was written by the author, who has read the original copy for this edition and has furnished certain lines in Act Three, Scene Two, which had been omitted when *Sun-Up* was first published.

Note to Fourth Edition.

In *Trigger,* produced at the Little Theatre, New York, December 6, 1927, Miss Vollmer drew the character of a wayward but spirited girl of the mountains, who elicited sympathy in her struggle against the prejudices of her narrow community. The play, however, was hardly up to her standard.

CAST OF CHARACTERS

Provincetown Theatre, New York, May 24, 1923

Widow Cagle	Lucille LaVerne
Pap Todd	Owen Meech
Emmy	Anne Elstner
Bud	Eugene Lockhart
Sheriff Weeks	Franz Bendsben
Rufe Cagle	Alan Birmingham
Preacher	Burnside Babcock
The Stranger	Elliott Cabot
Bob	Norman Dale

ACT I—The Interior of Widow Cagle's Cabin. Noonday. June 5, 1917.

ACT II—Same as Act I. Late afternoon. September.

ACT III—Same as Act I. Scene I. Midnight. February. Scene II. The same. A few hours later.

The scene of this play is in the mountains of western North Carolina, near the city of Asheville.

THE CHARACTERS

Widow Cagle—A frail, but wiry, type of woman. Past middle age. A very positive character, but the tenderness in her nature shows in spite of her efforts to conceal it.

Rufe Cagle—Widow Cagle's son. A young man. Good looking. A positive character also. Gentle and kind in manner, of a build to suggest great physical strength.

Pap Todd—An old man. Slender, but wiry. Personality, that of the "hound dog" type.

Emmy Todd—Todd's daughter. Very pretty girl. Young.

Bud Todd—Todd's son. Strong young mountaineer. Considered by his family, and others, to be half-witted. However, shows intelligence when there is occasion for speech.

Jim Weeks—Deputy-Sheriff. Typical mountaineer in manner and speech. A little better dressed than the others, he is inclined to put on airs. He feels himself better educated than the others. He tries to show this in his talk, but now and then he forgets, and falls back to the mountain mode of speech.

Preacher—Typical mountaineer.

Stranger—A young man from Civilization.

Bob—Rough Mountaineer

SUN-UP

ACT ONE

SCENE: *The interior of a typical mountain cabin. Noonday, June 5, 1917. Fireplace, with mantelpiece, at right. A door in the flat opens to out of doors. A door to left leads to the back room. In the corner between the outside door and the fireplace is a ladder reaching to an opening in the loft. Right of the outside door is a small window. It has window panes, and also an inside wooden shutter which pushes shut and open. The furniture consists of a bed in the corner between the two doors, a rough table, covered with oil cloth, in the center of the room, a bench beside the table, three small straight-back chairs, and an old cupboard. Cooking utensils are near the fireplace. A gun hangs over the door.*

MRS. CAGLE *is seated before the fireplace smoking a corn-cob pipe. Her thoughts seem far away. The door opens, and* PAP TODD *enters.*

TODD. Thought I'd come and set with yer awhile, Mis' Cagle.

MRS. CAGLE. (*Does not look up to greet her visitor.*) Pull ye up a chair.

TODD. (*Pulling a chair toward fireplace.*) How air yer to-day?

MRS. CAGLE. Jest tolerable. (*As* TODD *seats himself and takes out pipe.*) Bring yo' own terbacker?

TODD. Yer, I brung my own. (TODD *fills his pipe and they sit for a moment without conversation.*) Shore is a fine day.

MRS. CAGLE. Shore is.

TODD. (*As he lights his pipe. Takes straw from a broom near fireplace and gets light from fire.*) 'Pears like thar is goin' to be war.

MRS. CAGLE. (*Without concern.*) Who's a feudin' now?

TODD. Hain't that kind er feudin'. 'Pears like hit's the country.

MRS. CAGLE. Yankees agin?

TODD. Reckon so.

MRS. CAGLE. Ye must be mistaken. Ain't no reason for war. Didn't the Yankees free the niggers more than fifty years ago?

TODD. Maybe they want ter make 'em slaves agin.

MRS. CAGLE. Some yarn 'nother.

TODD. Thar's somethin' up. Bud heared all about it when he wuz over to town.

MRS. CAGLE. Bud never could tell nothin' the way he heared it. 'Tain't so. Thar ain't no reason fer war, unless us poor folks fight the rich uns for the way they air bleedin' us to death with the prices for meat and bread. I tell ye, Pap Todd, we uns ought to rise up and fight the rich leeches, but we won't. Poor folks ain't got guts 'nough. That's whut makes 'em poor.

TODD. Yer got no right ter complain, Mis' Cagle. I reckon Rufe makes a good livin' fer yer. He made a good crap last year, and Bud heared over in town that yer had been offered eight hundred dollars fer yer place.

MRS. CAGLE. Bud heared right once. The sheriff wuz over to see me t'other day. 'Pears like a city man has bought the land next to ourn, and he's afeered our place will spile his view. But I ain't a sellin' out to 'blege no rich man.

TODD. Eight hundred dollars is a lot o' money.

MRS. CAGLE. Yes—till hit's spent.

TODD. Well, as I said, Rufe makes a good crap.

MRS. CAGLE. Yes, Rufe makes a good crap, but if he'd raise more corn, and fear the law less, he'd be more of a man like his pap.

TODD. Moonshining?

MRS. CAGLE. Yes, blockadin'. Why not?

TODD. Reckon Rufe is too young to hanker a'ter a jail term. A'ter spendin' about twenty year o' my life thar I ain't a blamin' him much.

MRS. CAGLE. Rufe's pap wuz a Cagle. I wuz an Owens. Thar's many a Cagle, and an Owens too that laid down out thar on the hills and died, but thar ain't one of 'em yit that's ever gone to jail.

TODD. Yer ain't sayin' nothin' again *me* fer goin', be yer, Mis' Cagle?

MRS. CAGLE. No, ye wuz always kind o' puny. (TODD *turns away.*) And if ye ain't got nerve 'nough to stand behind a gun and shoot, I ain't got nothin' in my heart but pity for ye.

TODD. Well, the last time I wuz caught I didn't have no gun.

MRS. CAGLE. That's worse than goin' ter jail.

TODD. Ain't powerful fond er me, be yer, Mis' Cagle? In case Rufe wants ter marry my Emmy, yer wouldn't let that keep 'em apart, would yer, Mis' Cagle?

MRS. CAGLE. When Rufe gits old 'nough he kin marry who he wants. Emmy's *maw wuz good stock.*

TODD. Well, maybe she wuz.

MRS. CAGLE. I thought Emmy wuz a settin' her cap for Sheriff Weeks.

TODD. Kinder thought so myself. I sorter aigged it on—not that I got anythin' agin Rufe—

MRS. CAGLE. Kinder handy for ye to have a sheriff in the family, I reckon.

TODD. Well, yes, and he's older than Rufe. But seems to me lately she's a hankerin' a'ter Rufe, and I ain't agin him.

MRS. CAGLE. Don't reckon they'd ask ye any odds if they want ter git married.

TODD. Reckon not.

MRS. CAGLE. Be mighty funny young folks if they did.

EMMY. (*Entering door without knocking. She carries a pan covered with a tin plate.* BUD *enters with her.* BUD *has a knife and stick and whittles.*) Howdy, Mis' Cagle.

MRS. CAGLE. Howdy, Emmy. Pull ye up a chair.

EMMY. (*Placing pan on table.* BUD *sits down on bed and gazes into space.*) Mis' Cagle, we had a mess o' fresh meat for dinner. I brung ye and Rufe a bite.

MRS. CAGLE. Hit will taste mighty good, I reckon, Emmy. Rufe's a plum fool about fresh meat.

EMMY. Yes'um, I know he is. Pap, Bud's finished plantin' all the seed corn we got. 'Tain't more than half covered the corn patch. Think ye better send him to town a'ter more?

MRS. CAGLE. Maybe Rufe has got some extra seed.

TODD. Yer, maybe he has.

EMMY. Will he be home soon, Mis' Cagle?

MRS. CAGLE. Any minute, I reckon. He wuz powerful sot on goin' ter town this mornin'. He's done wasted half a day now. He oughter be here. (*There is a knock on the door. All eyes are turned toward door.*) Bud, will ye see who that is that cain't open the door for hisself? (BUD *opens the door.* SHERIFF WEEKS *enters.*)

SHERIFF. Good day, Widow Cagle. How you, Mr. Todd? Good mornin', Miss Emmy. How you all?

MRS. CAGLE. Howdy, Sheriff. Pull ye up a chair.

SHERIFF. No'm, ain't got time. Rufe ain't round?

MRS. CAGLE. Not right now.

SHERIFF. Well, Mis' Cagle, wonder if you could show me just whar your piece of ground ends up this side? (*Points off to the right, through the door.*)

MRS. CAGLE. To be shore.

SHERIFF. Would you mind stepping out here and showing me just whar your boundary line runs? Hate to trouble you.

MRS. CAGLE. (*Rising and putting on fly bonnet which is hanging on back of her chair.*) 'Tain't no trouble, but what ye worrin' 'bout my boundary line fer? (*Goes out the door.*)

SHERIFF. (*Turning and smiling at* EMMY.) See you again, Miss Emmy.

(EMMY *flirts with* SHERIFF. SHERIFF *exits.* TODD *gets up and silently follows* MRS. CAGLE *and* SHERIFF *out.* BUD *follows him.*)

EMMY. Whar ye goin', Bud?

BUD. (*Turning.*) Jest goin' to see.

EMMY. Better come back here.

(BUD *goes out.* EMMY *humming a song, goes to dishpan that hangs on wall over cupboard. Uses it as a mirror to primp.* RUFE *enters rather unexpectedly, and catches her at her toilet.*)

RUFE. Howdy, sweetheart.

EMMY. Howdy, Mr. Cagle.

RUFE. Don't you Mister Cagle me. Say it right, now.

EMMY. Howdy, Rufe.

RUFE. That's better. Whar's Mom goin'?

EMMY. Out yonder somew'eres with the Sheriff.

RUFE. Looked to me like the Sheriff wuz a takin' the whole outfit to jail.

EMMY. Oh, Rufe! Shame on ye.

RUFE. (*Laughing at his own joke.*) I'm glad he left ye here.

EMMY. Why?

RUFE. Save me a trip over to yo' house.

EMMY. Is comin' ter my house all that trouble?

RUFE. No trouble, but 'pears like Pap Todd and Bud air allus a stickin' a round.

EMMY. Uh huh.

RUFE. Yes, Pap and Bud's some stickers. Best thing they kin do. Emmy—I got somethin' mighty particular to say ter ye today.

EMMY. What's that, Rufe?

RUFE. Emmy, I want ye to marry me right off.

EMMY. I think that thar's somebody else whut wants me ter do the same thing fer him. He wants me to answer him today, too.

RUFE. I'll answer him fer ye. I'll beat hell outen him. Who is he?

EMMY. I ain't a sayin' if ye cain't guess.

RUFE. Is it Zeke Sanders?

EMMY. 'Tain't Zeke.

RUFE. Or Hank Small?

EMMY. No.

RUFE. 'Tain't that old Sheriff?

EMMY. (*Nods in the affirmative, coquettishly.*) It's him.

RUFE. (*Laughing.*) Good Lord, I thought he wuz a'ter Mom.

EMMY. Rufe!

RUFE. When did he ask ye?

EMMY. Yisterday.

RUFE. I'd shore like ter hand him one! I asked ye a year ago, didn't I, sweetheart?

EMMY. Uh huh.

RUFE. (*Holding out his arms to her.*) Come here, and whisper yo' answer quick. EMMY *is shy, and* RUFE *comes forward and takes her hand.*) Will you marry me right away, Emmy?

EMMY. Whut ye in sech a hurry fer, Rufe?

RUFE. Because, Emmy, I've got to go away soon. I ain't takin' no chances leavin' ye behind, unless ye belong to me—unless ye air mine. Yer love me, don't ye, Emmy?

EMMY. Going away? When?

RUFE. I'll answer yer when ye answer me. Air ye goin' to marry me?

EMMY. I don't know. Whar air ye goin', Rufe?

RUFE. I don't know.

EMMY. (*In a frightened voice.*) Rufe, it ain't that ye air runnin' away. Ye ain't done nothin' wrong, have ye, Rufe?

RUFE. Why, course not, sweetheart—(*Voices off stage.*) But—here comes Mom. Say yes, quick.

EMMY. Not now, Rufe. Wait till tonight. I'll answer ye.

RUFE. (*Eagerly.*) Then ye will come down to the pasture gate to meet me?

EMMY. Yes, jest a'ter sundown.

RUFE. And ye'll tell me then that yer will marry me?

EMMY. I ain't a promisin'.

SHERIFF. (*Off stage.*) Much obliged ter yer, Mis' Cagle.

MRS. CAGLE (*Off stage.*) Yer ain't needin' ter be. (MRS. CAGLE *enters, followed by the* SHERIFF. EMMY *moves up stage.*)

SHERIFF. Howdy, Rufe.

RUFE. Howdy, Sheriff.

SHERIFF. You going along pretty soon, Miss Emmy?

EMMY. Yes, I'm agoin' soon.

SHERIFF. Then I'll walk a piece with you.

RUFE. (*Coming up to* EMMY. *As he follows* EMMY *to far end of room.*) Reckon I'll go long, too, if ye don't mind.

SHERIFF. I ain't exactly pinin' fer yer company— (TODD *and* BUD *enter. Without comment they sit in their respective places.* MRS. CAGLE relights her *pipe.* EMMY *and* RUFE *sit on the bed by the window. A glance passes between* EMMY *and the* SHERIFF; *another glance between* EMMY *and* RUFE. RUFE *grins.*) Well, Mis' Cagle, I calculate you ain't willin' to sell yo' place even at a better price than I offered you last week.

MRS. CAGLE. No, I ain't goin' ter sell.

SHERIFF. Eight hundred dollars is a pretty good price, considering it's war times. In 'nother year it won't be worth that much.

MRS. CAGLE. Whut ye mean by war times?

SHERIFF. You don't mean to tell me that you don't know 'bout the war?

MRS. CAGLE. No, I ain't heared nothin' 'cept whut Bud said.

SHERIFF. (*Pulling a chair up and sitting down.*) Lord, yes. The whole country is at war with the Huns.

MRS. CAGLE. Huns? Who is Huns?

TODD. I fought in sixty-three.

MRS. CAGLE. Never heared of 'em.

TODD. And I got shot in the leg.

SHERIFF. Well, Huns, that's jest a nickname they call 'em. Yes, they done passed a law that every man between twenty-one and thirty-one has got to register, and to-day is the day.

MRS. CAGLE. Register? Whut ye mean?

SHERIFF. Why, sign his name, and tell the Government whar he lives.

TODD. They didn't do that in sixty-three.

MRS. CAGLE. Whut fer?

SHERIFF. So they can know whar to find 'em when they get ready for them to fight. They've got to do it to-day, too. (*Turning toward* RUFE.) Rufe, you and Bud will both have to register. (RUFE *rises.*)

MRS. CAGLE. (*As* RUFE *leaves* EMMY'S *side and comes forward.*) No, they won't. That's all tommyrot.

SHERIFF. Yes, they will. It's the law, and if they don't register the Government will deal with them. Shoot 'em down, I reckon, like deserters.

BUD. (*Frightened.*) Shoot me? Whut I got to do to keep from gittin' shot?

MRS. CAGLE. Nothin', Bud, nothin'.

SHERIFF. Yes, Bud, you got to go to town to-day, in the hall jest this side the depot, and give 'em your name, your age, and tell 'em whar you live. (BUD *looks from one face to the other.*)

MRS. CAGLE. No, ye don't, Bud. Ye stay right here, and plant yo' corn. Whut's the law got to do with you and Rufe?

RUFE. But, Mom—

MRS. CAGLE. Ye got a gun, ain't ye? That's as much as the law's got.

SHERIFF. But Mis' Cagle, the country is at war. You ferget they owe the Government something.

MRS. CAGLE. (*Springing up.*) Whut does Rufe or Bud owe the Guv'ment? The Guv'ment kept Bud's daddy in jail for twenty years 'cause he tried to make an honest livin' outen the corn he planted and raised. Whut did the Guv'ment do to Rufe's pap? Shot him dead. Shot him in the back while he wuz a protectin' his own property. Fight? Well, I reckon if either one of them boys fights, hit will be their own fight, and agin not fer the Guv'ment.

RUFE. (*Coming forward, a few steps to upper end of table.*) Mom, ye air right as far as ye go. Whut ye say is true, but Pap Todd, and my pap too, wuz a doin' whut the Government told them not to do. They wuz a breakin' the law.

MRS. CAGLE. Whut right has the Guv'ment to tell us mountain folks whut to do or whut not to do. Air we beholdin' to them? Air they doin' anything fer us but runnin' up the prices of bread and meat till hit's all we kin do to keep body and soul together!

RUFE. Well, Mom, that ain't the Government's fault.

TODD. They treated me purty well while I wuz in jail.

MRS. CAGLE. Who kin ye lay the fault to, then?

RUFE. It's because we don't know much. We need larnin'. We air ignorant.

SHERIFF. That's what the mountain folks need—larnin'.

MRS. CAGLE. 'Pears like the little ye both got ain't doin' ye much good, 'cept to make plum fools outen both of ye. (*Sits down.*)

RUFE. (*Laughing good-naturedly.*) Neither one of us is got 'nough to run us crazy, Mom.

TODD. Emmy's eddicated purty well. Cain't tell much 'bout Bud. (BUD *looks up.*) He won't talk. He kin write some. (BUD *goes on whittling.*)

MRS. CAGLE. Well, if larnin' air whut we need, air the Guv'ment givin' us schools?

SHERIFF. Yes'um, now and then, and I reckon we would have more schools if our folks would patronize them. Last school we had in the village, the teacher said she had to quit because the children wouldn't come. I guess them that did come didn't larn nothin'.

MRS. CAGLE. Well, I reckon it wuz because the most of 'em wuz a hungry. Ye kin fill a young un's brain all ye want to, but hit's a goin' to run out if thar's a hole in his stomach.

SHERIFF. You cain't say it's up to the Government to feed 'em all, can you, Mis' Cagle?

MRS. CAGLE. No, but it kin let 'em alone when they try to make money the only way they know how—blockadin'.

SHERIFF. That's why I say they need larnin'. Larn' how to do somethin' else.

MRS. CAGLE. I ain't never bin again larnin.' I didn't have none, and Rufe's pap couldn't read, but I allus wanted Rufe to larn as much as he could.

RUFE. Yes, ye did, Mom. Ye done all ye could. I kin recollect once when school wuz a goin' on five miles down the road, I wuz too little to walk it. (*Turns to the others.*) In the mornings Mom used to tote me most of the way. Then when I started home a'ter it wuz over, Mom would leave her work in the corn field, meet me, and tote me the rest of the way home.

MRS. CAGLE. But I wouldn't a had ye larn nothin' if I'd a knowed it wuz a goin' to turn ye into a law lover, and make yer fergit the laws of yo' own folks.

RUFE. I ain't fergot, Mom. I never will, but that little bit o' larnin' taught me to respect somethin' a little higher than my own way of wantin' ter to do things. I'm agoin' ter larn more, some day.

MRS. CAGLE. I want ye to larn books, then, not foolishness.

RUFE. Well, Mom, ain't whut I knowed made me the best farmer on the mountains? Don't I make ye a good livin'?

MRS. CAGLE. I ain't a complainin'. I don't keer how much larnin' ye git if ye don't turn skeered puppy, and lick the boots of them law mongers, like Jim Weeks.

SHERIFF. Now, Mis' Cagle.

RUFE. I ain't, Mom, but ye would want me to do whut I thought wuz right, even if it wuz to go to war, wouldn't ye?

MRS. CAGLE. In this Guv'ment feud?— No— If ye want to fight, son, git Zeb Turner, the man who killed yo' pap.

(*A commotion is heard outside.* BUD *jumps up excitedly, and looks out of the door.*)

BUD. Rufe, Rufe, the cow's out with the calf—the cow's out with the calf. Hit's suckin' all the milk—

(*The* SHERIFF *rises.*)

RUFE. (*Rushing to the door, and out.*) Who left them bars down?

MRS. CAGLE. Pap Todd, you wuz the last one that come through them bars—

(*Goes out as she puts on her fly bonnet.*)

TODD. (*Rising.*) Never teched them bars. I jumped the fence. (*Follows to the door and goes out.* BUD *follows him.*)

BUD. Why, Pap? (*Goes out.*)

SHERIFF. Now ain't I lucky?

EMMY. (*Coming down a step near fireplace.*) How come?

SHERIFF. Got a chance to talk to you.

EMMY. Whut ye got to talk about?

SHERIFF. Our gittin' married.

EMMY. (*Turning away.*) I think there's somebody else wants me to do the same thing to him.

SHERIFF. Who?

EMMY. If ye don't know, I ain't a sayin'.

SHERIFF. (*Putting his hands in his pockets.*) Well, that ain't hard fer me to guess, but I calculate, Miss Emmy, that you air a woman of sense, and want to do the best thing fer yourself in this here gittin' married. Don't you?

EMMY. (*Turning away.*) I ain't a sayin'.

SHERIFF. (*Taking a step towards her.*) Well, the difference between me and Rufe —Rufe's a good (*gestures with right hand*) boy—but the difference is this. Rufe ain't got nothin' but a farm. I got a little farm, and an office besides. Rufe ain't never made nothin' of hisself, and I'm kinder looked up to, and respected.

EMMY. Yes—

SHERIFF. I calculate I could be worse lookin', couldn't I?

(*Pause.* EMMY *looks him over.*)

EMMY. Yes, a little.

SHERIFF. I've told you that I love yer, and I figure there's a little love in your heart for somebody, ain't there?

EMMY. I reckon so.

SHERIFF. Well, is it fer me?

EMMY. I ain't sayin' jest yit.

SHERIFF. Well, seein' us together, I'm willing to take my chances with Rufe. I'll let you choose between me and him. But I'll say this much in my favor. As conditions air, Rufe has got to go to war. I ain't. You stand more chances of being Widow Cagle than you do of bein' Widow Weeks.

EMMY. (*Rising. With great interest.*) Is that whar Rufe's goin'? To war?

SHERIFF. Yes, he will have to go and fight.

EMMY. How come you don't have to go?

SHERIFF. Well, I'm an officer of the law, and besides, I'm a little over the age limit.

EMMY. Ye too old to go?

SHERIFF. No, not too old. I could go, but it ain't compulsory.

EMMY. Rufe don't have to go neither.

SHERIFF. Yes, he will have to go.

EMMY. When?

SHERIFF. Pretty soon. Now you think it over, Miss Emmy, and you'll say it's better all the way 'round to be Mis' Weeks, wife of Sheriff Weeks—

EMMY. Hit would be wife of Deputy-Sheriff Weeks, wouldn't it?

SHERIFF. Yes, but everybody calls me Sheriff, and in time—

(RUFE *and* MRS. CAGLE *enter, quickly followed by* PAP TODD *and* BUD. TODD *is excited.*)

TODD. I tell yer, I jumped the fence.

MRS. CAGLE. (*Going to her chair.*) When? Twenty years ago? (*Takes tobacco from her pocket and begins to fill her pipe.*)

TODD. I didn't leave no bars down. All the time yarmin' about me.

MRS. CAGLE. Set down, Pap.

EMMY. (*Coming forward to meet* RUFE.) Rufe. I cain't come to the pasture gate to-night.

RUFE. (*His countenance falling.*) How come ye cain't, Emmy?

(SHERIFF *grins, and evidences great expectancy.*)

EMMY. I want to give ye my answer now, Rufe.

SHERIFF. That's right, Emmy.

EMMY. (*Coming close to* RUFE.) Air ye willin', Rufe?

RUFE. As ye say, Emmy.

EMMY. Then, Rufe, I'll marry ye.

RUFE. (*Clasping her in his arms.*) I knowed ye would, Emmy.

SHERIFF. Why, Miss Emmy! (*Sits down meekly.*)

TODD. Air ye proposin' to Rufe, Emmy?

MRS. CAGLE. (*To* TODD.) Set down, Pap Todd. (*To* RUFE.) Well, son, if ye air a goin' ter marry Emmy, I reckon ye'll git over the notion of registerin' to fight in this here Guv'ment feud of Jim Weeks'!

RUFE. No, Mom, 'case I done registered this mornin'.

ACT TWO

SCENE: *Same as Act One.*

MRS. CAGLE *is sweeping the floor with a brush broom.* RUFE *enters and puts the hoe inside the door.*

RUFE. (*Wiping the perspiration from his brow.*) Well, Mom, the corn's all hoed. It won't need no more workin'.

MRS. CAGLE. (*Looking up.*) All right, Rufe. How 'bout the tater patch? Put that hoe outside, son—

RUFE. (*Putting the hoe outside the door and going to the basin to wash his hands.*) That's done, too. (*He washes his hands in the basin.*) 'Tain't nothin' more to be done 'cept gatherin' the crap. Ye don't have to worry 'bout that. I've done fixed it up with Bud. He's goin' ter do it all.

MRS. CAGLE. (*Sweeping hearth.*) How much did ye agree to pay him?

RUFE. I done paid him.

MRS. CAGLE. (*Stops sweeping.*) How?

RUFE. (*Going over and drying his hands on her apron.*) With the money I've bin savin' fer my schoolin'.

MRS. CAGLE. I didn't want ye to spend that, son.

RUFE. Well, I heared the Government wuz a goin' ter pay us wages.

MRS. CAGLE. 'Tain't so.

RUFE. Maybe it is, Mom. If it is, I kin save that all the time I'm gone, 'cose they say we won't need no money in France.

MRS. CAGLE. Whar *is* France?

RUFE. I don't know. I heared it wuz 'bout forty miles 't 'other side o' Asheville.

MRS. CAGLE. Goin' a mighty long ways to fight, seems ter me.

RUFE. Maybe it ain't so far. Think it wuz old man Todd that told me.

MRS. CAGLE. I reckon he thinks he's been thar.

RUFE. (*Sitting down.*) I reckon.

MRS. CAGLE. (*Laying the broom down, she gets a pan of green beans from the cupboard, then sits on her chair and begins to string beans.*) Shore is a dry spell.

RUFE. Yes, 'tis. I hope it will stay dry, though, till I git to France. I allus hate to tramp in the mud. 'Spect them roads over thar air pretty bad.

MRS. CAGLE. Yes, I reckon.

RUFE. Mom, I've already fed the cow and the hogs. Sorter early, but I didn't want ter leave it for ye. Bud said he'd milk fer ye to-night.

MRS. CAGLE. I ain't afeered o' work.

RUFE. I know ye ain't, but it's my place to do it. I've done it ever since Pap was kilt.

MRS. CAGLE. Yo' pap wuz a fine man, Rufe.

RUFE. I know he wuz. That makes me think o' somethin' I wanted to say to ye, Mom. Sometimes I've felt that you thought I wuzn't like my pap—that I wuz one of them skeered kind 'cose I wouldn't make whisky.

MRS. CAGLE. No, I never thought ye wuz askeered, but I thought ye wuz kind o' foolish not to make money the easy way. Heap easier ter make moonshine than hit is to make a crap.

RUFE. Well, Mom, it's like this. I ain't afeered o' nothin'. Ye ought ter know that, but I don't believe in whisky. It's bad stuff. I don't drink it myself, and I don't want to sell it to nobody. Look at old man Todd. He made it, and he drunk it too. Bud told me jest t'other day that he knowed he would have more sense if the ole man hadn't bin seech a drunkard. Jest look whut corn juice has made outen that ole man.

MRS. CAGLE. Well, if whisky hadn't done it, killin', or somethin' else would have. He wuz jest naturally born without any backbone.

RUFE. No, I reckon he ain't got much. Ye ain't a mindin' me marryin' Emmy, air ye, Mom?

MRS. CAGLE. No, Emmy cain't help who her pap wuz. She's a good gal, and so wuz her maw.

RUFE. I've done ask Emmy to live here with ye, Mom, so's ye won't be all by yo'self.

MRS. CAGLE. Well, the gal will be company, and she's welcome, but I calculate we'll have the old man and Bud most of the time.

RUFE. No, I done told Bud to eat at home, and let his pap do the cookin'. I told him plain I wuz a payin' him fer his work without eats. Bud ain't no fool, if he is a little queer.

MRS. CAGLE. No, he ain't no fool.

(*Pause.*)

RUFE. Seems kind o' strange to think o' me gittin' married.

MRS. CAGLE. Ye do seem kinder young, Rufe. Don't seem more than yisterday that ye wuz a playin' 'round with mud pies. Times and children do change.

RUFE. Well, Mom, I want ye to know that if I married a hundred women—somehow—you'd always sorter be first in my mind.

MRS. CAGLE. Hit's only natural. I reckon if ye air old enough to fight, ye air old enough to git married. 'Pears to me like a man jest gittin' married ought ter stay at home with his wife.

RUFE. Mom, I hate to go off and leave ye feelin' like that 'bout my goin'. I wish ye could see it like I do. If ye cain't now, maybe ye will some day.

MRS. CAGLE. Yo' pap wuz a brave man.

RUFE. Mom, it's because I'm Pap's son that I want to go. He died fer whut he thought wuz right. Why, Mom, way back fifty years ago even ole Pap Todd had a chance to fight the Yankees. Now, Mom, it's fer ye, and the ole wimen like ye, that I want to go. They say they air goin' to make us slaves this time. We air almost slaves now, bein' so poor, but it could be worse, Mom. Ye know I kin shoot like hell. Nobody kin handle an old gun any better than I kin. Ain't ye willin' to trust me, Mom? Ain't ye willin' fer me to go?

MRS. CAGLE. Ye air yo' own man, son. I ain't one to hold ye back if ye air sot on goin'. But don't ye let 'em make ye go, or scare ye into goin'.

RUFE. I'm a goin' of my own free will.

MRS. CAGLE. Then it 'tain't fer me to say no more.

RUFE. I'll come back as soon as I kin.

MRS. CAGLE. It jest seems a little queer to me that ye air goin' off to fight the Yankees with Zeb Turner, the man who killed yo' pap, still alive.

RUFE. Mom, ye ain't a forgettin' that I tracked Zeb Turner fer nearly a year, air ye? And I found him, Mom, without a gun. When I went to shoot, he lifted his arms and cried "O God," and, Mom, it jest warn't in me to kill a man with the name of his maker on his lips.

MRS. CAGLE. The feud would a said—go with him till he got a gun.

RUFE. Maybe I ought—but when I wuz little, down to the mission school they larned me somethin' different outen the Bible—

MRS. CAGLE. (*After a thoughtful pause.*) Larnin' air a strange thing, son. But if yo' pap wuz alive, ye wouldn't be goin' off to war.

RUFE. Maybe not, Mom—maybe not.

MRS. CAGLE. Got all yo' things together?

RUFE. Yes, and my ole rifle is all cleaned up.

MRS. CAGLE. I reckon ye better take that old quilt offen yo' bed. Kinder help out if ye don't have no bed to lie on.

RUFE. It's sech hot weather don't reckon I'll need it.

MRS. CAGLE. Hot weather cain't last always.

RUFE. (*Rising and looking up at the sun.*) 'Bout time fer Emmy to be comin'.

MRS. CAGLE. Yes, think I hear 'em comin'.

BUD. (*Appearing at the door, carrying a heavy basket.*) Howdy, Mis' Cagle. Howdy, Rufe.

MRS. CAGLE. Howdy, Bud.

RUFE. Howdy, Bud.

BUD. I brung Emmy's things.

MRS. CAGLE. Put 'em in the back room, Bud.

BUD. (*Starting across the room, but at the door stops and turns.*) Preacher's comin' with Pap and Emmy. (*Putting down basket, he puts his hand in his pocket and draws out a pistol. To* RUFE.) Rufe, I brung ye this. If yer gun kicked up yer'd have somethin' else.

RUFE. (*Rising.*) Bud, ye keep that. Ye

might need it to take keer o' Mom and Emmy.

BUD. Yer don't want it?

RUFE. I'm jest as much obleeged, but I want ye to look out fer my wimen folks. Ye keep it.

BUD. (*Putting pistol back in pocket.*) All right.

(BUD *goes to the other room with the basket.* PAP TODD *enters, followed by the* PREACHER *and* EMMY.)

MRS. CAGLE. Howdy, Pap. Howdy, Preacher.

TODD. Yer see, I brung him.

PREACHER. (*Going forward and shaking hands with* MRS. CAGLE, *who does not rise.*) Howdy, Widow Cagle. (*Turning to* RUFE.) Howdy, Rufe.

RUFE. (*Stepping forward and shaking hands with the* PREACHER.) Howdy, sir.

MRS. CAGLE. (*Putting beans in the pot on the fire. She wipes her hands on her apron, and takes pipe and tobacco from her pocket.*) Pull ye up chairs and set down—

(BUD *enters.*)

PREACHER. (*Sitting down.*) Powerful dry spell we air havin'.

MRS. CAGLE. (*Sitting down.*) Powerful.

TODD. Hit wuz a powerful dry spell like this when me and Emmy's maw wuz married.

MRS. CAGLE. Warn't dry much a'ter, wuz it, Pap? (*As she fills her own pipe.* PAP *puts the basin on the floor.*) Bring yo' own terbacker, Preacher?

PREACHER. (*Feeling in his pockets.*) Well, no, reckon I didn't. I come off in sech a hurry.

MRS. CAGLE. (*Breaking off a pipe full and handing it to him.*) Here's a pipe full.

PREACHER. I ain't got my pipe, so I reckon I'll jest chaw it. (*Puts the tobacco in his mouth.*)

MRS. CAGLE. Ye brung yourn, didn't ye, Pap?

TODD. Yer, I brung my own.

MRS. CAGLE. How's meetin's goin' on in the new church, Preacher?

PREACHER. Pretty fair. Had 'bout twelve brethren out last Sabbath.

MRS. CAGLE. Anybody bin shot in the church yit?

PREACHER. No'm, not yit.

MRS. CAGLE. Well, 'tain't hardly old 'nough yit.

PREACHER. They tell me Rufe's goin' to war, Widow Cagle.

MRS. CAGLE. Yes, he's goin'.

PREACHER. Powerful sinful thing. Powerful wicked.

MRS. CAGLE. Most things is to preachers.

TODD. Powerful hurtin' thing when yer git hit in the leg like I did.

PREACHER. I hate mighty bad to see Rufe go off and git shot.

MRS. CAGLE. Rufe kin shoot.

(*Slight pause.*)

RUFE. I reckon.

PREACHER. Well, Rufe, I reckon ye want ter git this thing over as soon as possible.

RUFE. Yes, sir. I got to go by sundown. Crowd of us is goin' to meet some soldiers that's camped down here 'bout half a mile.

PREACHER. All right. You and the bride come and stand here. (PREACHER *rises.* RUFE *and* EMMY *follow his direction.* MRS. CAGLE *and* TODD *calmly smoke on.* BUD *stands aside and watches every move with great interest.*) I reckon ye both air willin'.

RUFE. I reckon.

PREACHER. You, Miss Emmy?

EMMY. I reckon.

(SHERIFF *appears at door.*)

PREACHER. Reckon none of the rest of you's got any objections?

(MRS. CAGLE *shakes her head, "no," and goes on with her smoking.*)

TODD. Reckon me and Bud ain't got nothin' agin it.

SHERIFF. I got a lot agin it but I reckon it's no use.

MRS. CAGLE. Too late, Jim Weeks.

PREACHER. Howdy, Jim.

SHERIFF. Go on, Preacher. I'm agin it but I gotter hold my peace.

PREACHER. Now join hands. (*They do so awkwardly.*) Rufe Cagle, before God and the law, do you take this woman, Emmy Todd, to be your wedded wife?

RUFE. Yes, sir.

PREACHER. Emmy Todd, do you take this man, Rufe Cagle, before God and the law to be your wedded husband?

EMMY. Yes, sir.

PREACHER. Do you both promise to love, and help each other until death parts you?

RUFE. Yes, sir.

EMMY. Yes, sir.

PREACHER. Then, in the name of God and the law I now call you man and wife.

TODD. Amen.

MRS. CAGLE. Sorry, Preacher that ye cain't marry two folks without pullin' in the law.

SHERIFF. Law's law, Mis' Cagle.

(PREACHER *shakes hands with* RUFE *and then* EMMY. *Then* RUFE *and* EMMY *awkwardly shake hands.*)

RUFE. (*Taking plug of tobacco from his hip pocket and handing it to the* PREACHER.) I'm much obleeged to ye, sir.

PREACHER. (*Taking the tobacco eagerly.*) Ye air welcome.

(EMMY *and* RUFE *sit and talk quietly together.* BUD *stands watching them.*)

TODD. In my day we allus had a little celebratin' when young uns got hitched.

MRS. CAGLE. I wuz calculatin' ter feed ye fer supper tonight.

PREACHER. (*Sitting down.*) Now that's kind of you, Mis' Cagle. I sho' will enjoy a bite 'fore I start across the mountain.

TODD. 'Fore supper, Preacher, come over to my house, and I'll give yer a little spirits to take home with yer in case o' sickness.

PREACHER. I do have a tech o' sickness now and then.

MRS. CAGLE. Remember, I ain't a havin' no supper fer drunkards, now.

PREACHER. Oh, I never tech it, Mis' Cagle, 'cept in case of sickness.

TODD. Law, Mis' Cagle, I ain't got 'nough in my house to make the Preacher drunk. (*Rising. Just then a large bottle falls to the floor from under his coat. He goes after it.*) Now, don't that beat hell!

(*Every one, including* MRS. CAGLE *laughs loudly. In the midst of the laughter there comes from the distance strains of "The Star Spangled Banner." Instantly the laughter ceases. All eyes are turned toward the music, and all listen intently. Slowly* MRS. CAGLE *rises to her feet; awkwardly* RUFE *rises. This is done without any knowledge, or intent, of patriotism. The music strikes to their stoic souls, and they know not why. The sun goes down.*)

EMMY. (*On the verge of tears, is the first to speak.*) Ain't that purty?

MRS. CAGLE. Hit's church music, ain't it, Preacher?

PREACHER. (*Sitting again.*) Yes'm, I reckon so. Reckon it's one of them new hymns I don't know.

TODD. Hit's sure a sign—

RUFE. (*Breaking in.*) Of good luck.

BUD. I wisht they'd do it again.

PREACHER. 'Pears like somebody's furnished us music fer the weddin'.

TODD. I might a brought my old fiddle over. I kin bring it, and play a little a'ter supper, cain't I, Mis' Cagle?

MRS. CAGLE. Yes, if ye be sober.

PREACHER. I'll see to that, Widow Cagle. (*Rising.*) I reckon if we git back in time fer supper, we'd better start a'ter that fiddle now, Brother Todd.

TODD. Yes, Mis' Cagle is mighty spry cook, if she do be gettin' along.

MRS. CAGLE. (*Going to the fireplace and stirring the kettle.*) Spryer than ye wuz at my age ten years ago, Pap Todd. Leavin' that licker behind, Pap?

TODD. No'm. Mebbe Preacher'll hev a tech o' sickness on the way over. Come 'long, Preacher.

PREACHER. You air stayin' fer supper, ain't yer, Rufe?

RUFE. (*Coming forward and shaking hands with the* PREACHER.) No sir, I'm goin' in a few minutes now.

PREACHER. Then I'll say good-by to ye. Good luck. I'll pray fer yer.

RUFE. I'd be much obleeged ter ye if yer would. Good-by, sir.

SHERIFF. (*Going towards door.*) Good-by, Rufe.

RUFE. Good-by, Sheriff.

MRS. CAGLE. Ain't ye stayin' fer supper, Sheriff?

SHERIFF. No'm. Ain't hungry. (*Goes out.*)

TODD. (*Shaking hands with* RUFE.) Good-by, Rufe. I hope yer don't git hit in the leg like me.

RUFE. Good-by, Pap Todd.

TODD. When yer fire, Rufe, always shoot sideways, like this— (*Demonstrates.*) Then the Yank that's a shootin' at yer has got ter hit yer the narrow way.

RUFE. I bin shootin' a long time, Pap.

TODD. Yes, but yer ain't never bin shot at by a Yankee. I hope yer don't come home all shot ter pieces like I wuz, Rufe.

RUFE. I reckon I won't. Good-by, Pap.

TODD. Good-by, Rufe.

TODD. (*Turning to* MRS. CAGLE.) Me and the Preacher will be right back, Mis' Cagle. (*Goes out with* PREACHER.)

MRS. CAGLE. See yer do. (*Knocking the ashes out of her pipe, and putting pipe in her pocket.*) I'll get yo' things ready fer ye, Rufe. Better stay and have somethin' hot to eat, son.

RUFE. Wish I could, but I cain't, Mom.

(MRS. CAGLE *goes into the other room.*)

BUD. (*Coming up to* RUFE.) I got to follow Pap, Rufe. (*Holds out hand to* RUFE.) I wisht I wuz a goin' with yer.

RUFE. (*Shaking his hand.*) I want ye to take good care of Emmy and Mom, Bud. Ye'll allus do that, won't yer?

BUD. I done told yer so.

RUFE. I ain't afeered to leave 'em with ye.

BUD. If the Yankees git too many fer yer, let me know and I'll come and help yer out. Don't git hurt, Rufe.

RUFE. Ye ain't no fool, Bud. They may draft ye, too. If they do, ye leave somebody to look a'ter the wimen folks.

BUD. All right. I won't fergit nothin' yer told me. I got ter hurry and ketch Pap, and take his liquor 'way from him. Good-by.

RUFE. Good-by. (BUD *hurries off, wiping his eyes. Turning to* EMMY.) Come here, little un, and give me a kiss while we air by ourselves.

EMMY. (*Quickly throwing her arms about him. He holds her in a close embrace.*) O, Rufe, cain't yer stay? Why do ye have to go? Why do ye have to leave me?

RUFE. Don't, little woman, ye most break my heart. I don't want ter leave ye.

EMMY. Then why do ye go?

RUFE. I have to go, Emmv. That is, I'd be ashamed not to go.

EMMY. Cain't ye wait a week, Rufe? Maybe the war will be over then.

RUFE. No, Emmy, I cain't. Don't tell Mom, but I'm whut they call drafted. They have called my name, and I've got to be thar tomorrow, sometime.

EMMY. In France?

RUFE. I reckon.

EMMY. (*Passionately.*) Then they air a forcin' ye to go.

RUFE. (*Shaking his head.*) No, I don't have to go. I could stay and hide right here on my place, and they never would find me, but I'd be ashamed to face ye and Mom if I stayed, Emmy.

EMMY. But why, Rufe?

RUFE. I cain't explain it. I don't exactly know. I ain't got no education, yet, and I couldn't understand all the soldiers I talked to told me. But hit's somethin' like this, honey. This here country is ourn, 'cose God let us be born here. (MRS. CAGLE *stands in doorway.* RUFE *and* EMMY *do not see her.*) It's fed us, and kinder brung us up. We love it, don't we, Emmy?

EMMY. Yes, Rufe, but—

RUFE. Yes we do. I do, Emmy. I love every rock, and every tree, and every hill 'round here. (*Points.*) Out thar on that hill my pap died fer whut he thought wuz right. He's at rest down thar in the valley near to your maw. Some day Mom will lie thar, and you, and maybe—me. Hit's ours, Emmy. We don't own all the land, but hit's ours jest the same, to love and enjoy 'cose God A'mighty give it to us. There's a lot o' folks, Emmy, that's got a home somew'eres else that wants ourn too. I got to go help defend my hills, and my home, and my wimen folks, ain't I, honey?

(MRS. CAGLE *goes into other room.*)

EMMY. I didn't know all that. Yes, Rufe, ye air a man, and ye got to fight fer what's right. Ye go, and I'll be awaitin' fer ye, and a lovin' ye. And if ye don't come back—

RUFE. I reckon I will, honey.

EMMY. I reckon ye will, but if ye don't, I'll know ye died like yo' Pap. I'll be proud of ye. Jest seems like I cain't stand it, but I kin, 'cause other women have stood it, and I reckon ye ain't no more to me than other women's husbands air to them.

RUFE. That's whut I bin a thinkin', Emmy. Other men whut's goin' have got as much to leave at home as me. I'll write ye, and ye'll take good care o' Mom, and yo'self, won't ye, Emmy?

EMMY. Ye know I will, Rufe.

RUFE. Hit's gittin' late. I got to go.

EMMY. Rufe, kin I walk a little ways with ye? So I won't have to say good-by to ye here. I want to stay with ye as long as I kin, Rufe.

RUFE. Of course, sweetheart. Ye kin go as far as the pasture gate. Here comes Mom. Ye talk to her while I git my *things.* (MRS. CAGLE *enters, sits down in her chair and begins to smoke her pipe.*) Did ye put my snack with my things, Mom?

MRS. CAGLE. Yes, Rufe. Beside yo' gun. (RUFE *goes to other room.*) Gittin' dark quick, ain't it?

EMMY. Yes'um.

MRS. CAGLE. Reckon this dry spell will let up by tomorrow. Looks like it mought rain.

EMMY. Yes'um.

(*There is a pause.* RUFE *enters, pack over his arm and gun in his hand.*)

RUFE. Bud will be over and milk for ye, Mom.

MRS. CAGLE. All right, son.

RUFE. (*After a painful pause.*) Well, reckon I'll have to be goin'.

MRS. CAGLE. (*Smoking calmly on.*) Take keer o' yo'self.

RUFE. Ye do the same, Mom.

MRS. CAGLE. Ye kin write, Emmy kin read the letters.

RUFE. I'll write. (*There is another pause.*) Well—good-by, Mom.

MRS. CAGLE. Good-by, son.

EMMY. Ain't ye goin' to kiss him, Mom?

MRS. CAGLE. (*Without emotion.*) Whut's the use o' sech foolishness.

RUFE. All right. Just as ye say, Mom. God bless ye. (*Tears himself away.*)

MRS. CAGLE. If ye fight, son, shoot to *kill.*

RUFE. (*Going off, followed by* EMMY.) I will, Mom. Good-by.

MRS. CAGLE. Take keer o' yo'self.

(RUFE *and* EMMY *go out. For a moment or two* MRS. CAGLE *calmly smokes on. Then she rises and follows to where she can watch* RUFE *as he goes down the path. The shadows deepen. She appears to strain her eyes as if to catch a last look at him. Then she goes slowly back to the doorway. The hoe* RUFE *left leaning against the house attracts her attention. She lifts the hoe up tenderly, as if it were a living thing, and moves her hand over the handle as if to caress it. The darkness comes. The pipe drops from her mouth.*)

ACT THREE

SCENE ONE

SCENE: *The interior of* WIDOW CAGLE'S *cabin, at night. A fire burns on the hearth. A lighted lantern is on table.* RUFE'S *hoe leans against the wall near the door. Outside a blizzard is raging. Now and then with the increasing violence of the storm, the door of the cabin shakes. There is a weird howling, or whistling of the wind.*

MRS. CAGLE *sits by the fire smoking. Now and then she looks up, and listens to the storm. A yellow envelope is in her hand. She rises and goes to the table. Holding the envelope near the lantern she looks it over with great interest. She then goes to window and opening the wooden shutter peers out into the darkness. She hangs the lantern on a nail by the pane of glass and leaves the wooden shutter open. Still holding the envelope she returns to her chair by the fireplace, and goes on with her smoking. A man's voice is heard above the raging of the storm.*

VOICE. Hallo—Hallo— (MRS. CAGLE *rises and listens. She goes to the window and looks out.*) Hallo—Hallo—Hallo there!

MRS. CAGLE. (*Unbarring door. Calling.*) That ye, Bud?

VOICE. Let me in. Please let me in. I'm almost frozen.

MRS. CAGLE. (*Opening the door wide.*) Who be ye? Whut ye want?

VOICE. Let me in, for God's sake. (*A man stumbles in the door. He is bareheaded, and without an overcoat. His coat and trousers are much too large for him. His shoes are tan, and well fitted.*) Please let me warm, and give me food. (*Hurries to fire and shakes the snow from his clothes.*)

MRS. CAGLE. (*As she closes the door.*) Did Emmy send ye? Did ye come from Pap Todd's?

STRANGER. No, I came from— I lost my way in the snow.

MRS. CAGLE. Well, set down, stranger, and warm yo'self. I got Emmy's supper a warmin' by the fire. Ye kin have part of that.

STRANGER. Let me warm first. I'm dying with cold.

MRS. CAGLE. Did ye come far?

STRANGER. Yes, a long way.

MRS. CAGLE. Maybe ye come from France?

STRANGER. (*With some uneasiness.*) No, no.

MRS. CAGLE. Didn't ye have no hat or overcoat?

STRANGER. I lost them in the storm. It is terrible out.

MRS. CAGLE. The worst in many a year. (*She places the food that is warming by the fire on the table and takes the lantern from the nail by the window and places it on the table.*)

STRANGER. Does that wooden shutter close?

MRS. CAGLE. Yes, hit s'uts.

STRANGER. Would you mind if I close it? It would make the room seem warmer.

MRS. CAGLE. (*Going to window and clos-*

ing the shutter.) No, I ain't got no reason for keepin' it open. Jest thought Emmy might like to see the light when she started home, but I reckon Bud will come with her part o' the way, anyhow.

STRANGER. Who is Bud—who is Emmy?

MRS. CAGLE. (*Looking closely at him as she answers the question that seems to her impertinent.*) Emmy's my daughter-in-law, and Bud's her brother. Bud's a little queer in the head—

STRANGER. I see. How far is this place from Asheville?

MRS. CAGLE. I don't know. I've heared tell of Asheville, but I ain't never bin thar.

STRANGER. What is the name of that little settlement about three miles down the road?

MRS. CAGLE. I allus heared it called town. That's all I know. Whar mought your home be, stranger?

STRANGER. Why—in Virginia.

MRS. CAGLE. I never heard tell o' that place. Be it far from here?

STRANGER. Yes—a few miles.

MRS. CAGLE. Air ye figurin' on gittin' thar tonight?

STRANGER. No, not tonight. The roads are almost beyond travelling.

MRS. CAGLE. Ye kin move yo' chair up, and eat now.

STRANGER. Thank you. (*Moves his chair up to table and eats ravenously.*) Could you keep me for the night? I have a little money. I can pay you.

MRS. CAGLE. No, I don't keep no boarders, but I reckon ye air welcome to sech as I got. (*Looking at him very carefully.*) I reckon that ye air honest?

STRANGER. Well, yes. I try to be.

MRS. CAGLE. (*Getting coffee.*) Then ye kin stay in Rufe's room, and Emmy can sleep with me.

STRANGER. I see you have a hoe in the house. I've always heard that was bad luck.

MRS. CAGLE. I ain't afeered o' bad luck. Hit's Rufe's—my son's hoe, and he's gone off.

STRANGER. Oh, I see.

MRS. CAGLE. (*Eagerly.*) Kin ye read, stranger?

STRANGER. (*Amused.*) A little.

MRS. CAGLE. (*Showing him the yellow envelope.*) Then maybe ye kin read this letter. Hit's from my son.

STRANGER. (*Reaching out to take it.*) I'll try.

MRS. CAGLE. (*Opening the envelope.*) I kin open it.

STRANGER. (*Looking at the single page of contents. Falters as he hands it back to her and answers.*) No, I'm sorry—I can't read that.

MRS. CAGLE. (*Sitting on bench. She shows disappointment as she encloses the page in the envelope.*) Well, no matter. Emmy, his wife, will be here soon. Her pap is sick and she's gone to see him.

STRANGER. How long has your son been gone?

MRS. CAGLE. Since last September. Hit's kinder lonesome since he left. I'm glad ye come.

STRANGER. Thank you. Was your son drafted?

MRS. CAGLE. He registered—that whut ye mean?

STRANGER. Well, yes, and then afterwards they called him—made him go.

MRS. CAGLE. No, he went of his own free will.

STRANGER. (*With something like bitterness.*) I suppose you're very proud of him?

MRS. CAGLE. He's a good boy, Rufe is.

STRANGER. Yes, of course, but I suppose you're very proud of him because he joined the army of his own free will.

MRS. CAGLE. No, I think he'd a showed more sense if he had a stayed home and gathered his crap.

STRANGER. Then you are opposed to his going? (MRS. CAGLE *looks at him inquiringly.*) I mean you weren't willing for him to go?

MRS. CAGLE. Well, he wuz sot on goin'. Seemed to think he oughter. I didn't say nothin' to keep him from doin' whut he thought was right. In spite of whut the Guv'ment done to his pap, Rufe figured he outer help 'em out agin' the Yankees.

STRANGER. (*With surprise.*) The Yankees—?

MRS. CAGLE. Yes. Who he's a fightin'.

STRANGER. (*Laughing good-naturedly.*) Oh, I see.

MRS. CAGLE. Did ye register?

STRANGER. Yes.

MRS. CAGLE. Air ye figurin' on goin'?

STRANGER. There's no way out of it.

MRS. CAGLE. If ye air a man thar is. If ye stay at home they cain't do no more than shoot ye. That's whut they'll do to ye out thar. I'd ruther die at home than somew'eres out thar in the mud.

STRANGER. You mustn't talk that way. If you were heard saying that, they might —shoot you.

MRS. CAGLE. Let 'em shoot. The law killed my man. Hit's got my boy out thar somew'eres. Shootin' me wouldn't matter. (*There is a slight pause.*) Have ye got a maw livin'?

STRANGER. Yes, and she's getting old too. I'm her only son. I'm on my way to see her now—if nothing happens—

(*There is a lull in the storm, and voices are heard outside. The* STRANGER *looks up frightened.*)

SHERIFF. (*Calling outside.*) Hallo, Widow Cagle. You gone to bed? (*The* STRANGER *springs up with terror in his face.*)

MRS. CAGLE. That sounds like the Sheriff's voice.

STRANGER. (*In a frightened whisper.*) Don't let them in. They're after me. I've got to get—home.

MRS. CAGLE. (*Rising and looking at him closely.*) Whut ye done?

STRANGER. Nothing that's really wrong. I swear it. (*There is a knocking at the door.*)

MRS. CAGLE. Ye air goin' home to see yo' maw?

STRANGER. Yes.

MRS. CAGLE. Then they cain't get ye. Go in the back room. Git in bed and cover up yo' head.

STRANGER. They'll find me in there.

MRS. CAGLE. Hurry. They won't git ye. (STRANGER *hurries into the back room. Heavy knocking is heard.* MRS. CAGLE *takes the gun from the corner and goes to the door.*) Who be ye? That ye, Bud?

SHERIFF. It's me, Widow Cagle, Sheriff Weeks.

MRS. CAGLE. (*Opening the door.*) Whut ye want, Sheriff? Lost in the storm?

(SHERIFF *and a man enter.*)

SHERIFF. Hate to trouble you, Mis' Cagle, but me and this here man air looking for a deserter from one of the Army camps.

MRS. CAGLE. I reckon ye kinder froze up, and want to git warm. Well, if it wuzn't sech a cold night I'd make ye go on. Pull ye up chairs, and thaw out.

SHERIFF. (*Looking around as he goes to the fire. His man follows and stands with his back to the fire.*) The fact is, Mis' Cagle, we've tracked the man to this here cabin.

MRS. CAGLE. I reckon he wuz a puttin' fer the woods back yonder.

SHERIFF. There is fresh foot prints in the snow right up to your door, Mis' Cagle.

MRS. CAGLE. Them must be Bud's big feet tracks. He wuz here. I reckon he's home by now.

SHERIFF. There ain't no foot prints leavin', Mrs. Cagle.

MRS. CAGLE. I reckon not 'cose Bud went out the back door.

SHERIFF. I reckon you don't mind me searchin' the house, Mis' Cagle. It's law, you know.

MRS. CAGLE. If ye had a little more common sense, and less law, I'd respect ye more, Sheriff. 'Tain't nobody in the house but me and Emmy. Emmy is in bed asleep. Ye kin search all ye want to so's ye don't wake Emmy. She's bin a settin' up with old Pap Todd. He's bin mighty low.

SHERIFF. Yes, I heared he wuz sick. Well, if you don't mind, Widow Cagle, we'll jest look in under her bed.

MRS. CAGLE. Go ahead. (*Both men enter the back room. She follows to the door with gun in her hand.*) Don't ye put yo' hands on that bed. Come outen thar before ye wake the gal up.

(*The men come out but the* SHERIFF *casts an eye back to the door.*)

SHERIFF. Well, I reckon there ain't nobody in there. Have to look in the loft, too, Mis' Cagle.

MRS. CAGLE. All right. Go ahead. Maybe the next time ye come snoopin' 'round ye'll take my word.

SHERIFF (*to his assistant.*) Bob, you go up in the loft by yourself. I want to git my feet warm 'fore we start out. (*Goes to the fire.* BOB *goes up the ladder to the loft.*) Mighty sorry, Mis' Cagle. It ain't that I dispute your word. We air simply carryin' out the law. This here feller deserted camp. One of the officers caught sight of him in town a little while ago, but he lost him so he set me out lookin' for him.

MRS. CAGLE. I hope he gits away.

SHERIFF. Pretty dangerous talk, Mis' Cagle.

MRS. CAGLE. I ain't afeerd of none o' ye.

SHERIFF. Well, I know you don't mean no harm.

MRS. CAGLE. Mean whut I say. Put on some more logs, Sheriff. I hate fer ye to be cold if ye do belong to the law.

SHERIFF. (*Laughs as he kneels down on

hearth to replenish the fire. Looking up.) Heared from Rufe lately?

MRS. CAGLE. Today.

SHERIFF. How's he gittin' along?

MRS. CAGLE. Pretty well. (*The* SHERIFF *turns his attention again to the fire. The door opens and* EMMY *enters.* MRS. CAGLE *is somewhat confused, but she holds her own. The* SHERIFF *springs to his feet.*) Well, I declare—

SHERIFF. Well, I'll be doggone! Howdy, Miss Emmy.

EMMY. Howdy, Sheriff. Mis' Cagle, Bud said—

MRS. CAGLE. I don't keer whut Bud said. Whut ye mean by foolin' me like that? Trottin' off in the storm when I thought ye wuz in thar a sleepin'.

EMMY. Why, Mis' Cagle—

MRS. CAGLE. Up to some o' yo' tricks again. Puttin' things in yo' bed to make me believe it's ye.

SHERIFF (*striding toward the back door.*) Yes, Miss Emmy, whut did you put in your bed? Let's pull it out and see.

EMMY. Why Mis' Cagle—

(MRS. CAGLE *shakes her head at* EMMY *who seems to realize that something is expected of her. With her gun in her hand* MRS. CAGLE *follows the* SHERIFF *to the door.*)

EMMY. 'Pears to me like ye air mighty much at home, Jim Weeks.

SHERIFF (*from inside of back room.*) Let's see who else makes hisself at home. (MRS. CAGLE *steps to one side of the door, and is about to lift her gun when the* SHERIFF *appears in the doorway holding up a big feather bolster. He laughs.*) Well, Miss Emmy, that's one on me, unless—

BOB. (*Coming down ladder.*) Nothin' alive up thar but rats.

SHERIFF. Well look whut wuz in bed, Bob. Better come and look under the bed agin.

BOB. (*Taking the bolster and going into the back room.*) All right.

SHERIFF. How's your pap, Miss Emmy?

EMMY. He's gittin' better tonight.

BOB. (*Entering.*) Nothin' under thar except these here pertaters. (*Slips the potatoes he holds into his pocket.*)

SHERIFF. All right. Well that bolster, Miss Emmy, is a pretty good joke on me and Mis' Cagle both.

EMMY. Yes—

SHERIFF. I'm powerful sorry, Mis' Cagle, that I had to 'pear to doubt your word. It wuz one of them things that has to be done now and then.

MRS. CAGLE. Well, I hope ye air satisfied. And now if ye be through searchin', I reckon ye kin go. I ain't got nothin' agin ye, Jim Weeks, but I ain't powerful fond of yo' job. When ye come and ain't representin' the law, ye're welcome. When ye air, ye ain't. (*Moving to fireplace.*)

SHERIFF. (*Going to door.* BOB *follows him.*) All right, Mis' Cagle. If I didn't know you so well, I'd shore think you wuz a moonshin'.

MRS. CAGLE. I would be if it warn't so cold that the mash would freeze.

SHERIFF. (*Laughing as he goes out the door.*) Goodnight, Mis' Cagle. Goodnight, Miss Emmy.

(*The door closes and* MRS. CAGLE *bars it.*)

EMMY. What's up, Mis' Cagle?

MRS. CAGLE. (*Listening at outside door, and then going to the back room door and looking in.*) Thar wuz a furriner come here. He wuz young like Rufe. He was a runnin' from the law. I put him in bed, and told the Sheriff hit wuz ye. I reckon he must a slipped through the winder, but I don't see how he done it.

EMMY. He won't have no chance outside in this storm.

MRS. CAGLE. I cain't see how that feller got outen that room.

EMMY. Maybe he ain't out. Maybe he's hid.

MRS. CAGLE. 'Tain't no place fer him to hide.

EMMY. Under the bed?

MRS. CAGLE. The Sheriff made sure he warn't under thar. I reckon he must a squirmed through that window hole, but he shore didn't look little 'nough fer that. Wharever he is, God help him. (*Going toward fire.* EMMY *follows her.*) Yo' pap sobered up yet, Emmy?

EMMY. Yes'um, he's 'bout over it. Swears he won't never tech 'nother drap.

MRS. CAGLE. No, I reckon he won't tech 'nother drop, but he won't mind techin' a quart or two.

EMMY. Bud said ye had a letter, Mis' Cagle.

MRS. CAGLE. Yes, and I'm powerful anxious to hear it, but ye eat yo' supper first, and then ye kin read Rufe's letter. (*She sits down and lights her pipe.*)

EMMY. Let's read the letter first.

MRS. CAGLE. No, he's well, or he wouldn't

a wrote. Yo' supper is a gittin' plum dried up and ruined, whut the stranger didn't eat of it.

STRANGER. (*Appearing in back room door.*) I hope I left you enough to eat.

EMMY. (*Takes plate and sits on floor before fire at* MRS. CAGLE'S *feet. Looks up frightened.*) Oh—yes—plenty.

MRS. CAGLE. (*Turning towards him. Does not show any surprise.*) Thar's plenty. Emmy ain't a big eater. Whar wuz ye?

STRANGER. Under the potato pile. There was a lull in the storm, and I happened to hear your daughter's footsteps as she came up to the house. I thought that would mean another search, so I put the bolster in the bed, and was about to crawl under it when I spied the potato pile in the corner. So, I got behind it, and pulled the potatoes over me.

MRS. CAGLE. Mighty lucky fer ye. I thought he wuz about to git ye. I wuz already to shoot.

STRANGER. You would have shot to save me from arrest?

MRS. CAGLE. I promised that I'd hide ye, didn't I? Besides, I'd like to shoot at Jim Weeks.

STRANGER. But I didn't expect that much protection. I don't know how to thank you.

MRS. CAGLE. Ye air welcome, Stranger, as long as ye air honest, and I reckon ye air if ye ain't done nothin' worse than run away from war. Pull ye up a chair, and set down.

STRANGER. (*Sitting down on the bench beside the table.*) Perhaps it wasn't an honest thing to do, but there were circumstances—

MRS. CAGLE. I don't understand ye.

STRANGER. I mean it was a bit unusual. I was drafted and—

MRS. CAGLE. They forced ye to go to war?

STRANGER. Yes, I'm ashamed to say.

MRS. CAGLE. Didn't ye try to protect yo'self?

STRANGER. You don't understand. I'm ashamed that I didn't go like your son—of my own free will.

MRS. CAGLE. Wuz yo' maw agin yo' goin'?

STRANGER. She took it very hard. But I suppose it was because I whined around so. If I'd been more of a man she wouldn't have felt so badly about it.

MRS. CAGLE. Does she know ye air a comin' home?

STRANGER. No, I was home on leave last week. Yesterday I got a letter from my sister saying that Mother had been crying ever since I left. I kept thinking about it, and brooding over it, and last night we got word that we were to start for France in two or three days. And when I thought what that message would mean to her, I just couldn't stand it. I ran away. I didn't have much money. I couldn't ride. I bought these clothes to hide my uniform. I intended to walk home, but the storm was so terrible—

EMMY. Ye got a wife?

STRANGER. No. I had a sweetheart, but she threw me over when she learned that—I was afraid.

MRS. CAGLE. Afeered of gittin' shot, Stranger.

STRANGER. Yes, I was—

MRS. CAGLE. Well, thar air many a thing that's worse. Being afeered is worse.

STRANGER. Yes, I am beginning to realize that.

EMMY. Rufe wuzn't afeered.

MRS. CAGLE. No, my boy ain't afeered o' hell. I didn't want him to go, 'cose I couldn't see no use of it. But I warn't sayin' nothin' agin him goin' when he though hit wuz right.

EMMY. He said it wuz to pertect his hills, and his home, and his wimen folks.

MRS. CAGLE. He mought a thought so, but I calculate his hills don't need no pertectin', and I reckon his wimen folks kin pertect themselves.

STRANGER. (*Turning to* EMMY.) Your husband was right. (*To* MRS. CAGLE.) You're wrong, Mrs. Cagle. That's your name, isn't it?

MRS. CAGLE. Yes, that's my name.

STRANGER. I hope you'll pardon me for contradicting you, but you and all other women couldn't do anything against the enemy your son is fighting.

MRS. CAGLE. Men folks is always seein' some terrible thing ahead.

STRANGER. It's not the coward speaking now, Mrs. Cagle. It's the man who knows.

MRS. CAGLE. My maw told me when they fought the other war, they wuz allus a skeerin' 'em, and a tellin' 'em about the Yankees a comin'. They did come to some places, but Maw never seed one. She wuzn't afeered then, and I ain't askeered of no Yankee nohow.

STRANGER. You mean German.

MRS. CAGLE. Call 'em whut you want to. They'll allus be Yankees to me.

STRANGER. But Mrs. Cagle, it's not the Yankees this time. That war's over long ago. In this war the Yank and the Rebel are fighting together.

MRS. CAGLE. Ye mean they air fightin' on the same side, Stranger?

STRANGER. Yes, side by side.

MRS. CAGLE. Who air they fightin', Stranger?

STRANGER. The Germans.

MRS. CAGLE. I reckon they've come 'long since my time. I never heared of 'em. Whut's it over, Stranger?

STRANGER. Well, for one thing to protect our country.

EMMY. That's whut Rufe said, Mis' Cagle. He knowed.

MRS. CAGLE. Yes, I heared him, but I didn't think the boy knowed so much. I heared him say this country belonged to us 'cose God A'mighty let us be born here. He said this land had brung us up, and nursed us—kinder pretty speech for a boy like Rufe, ain't it, Stranger?

STRANGER. Yes. He is right.

MRS. CAGLE. (*Taking the envelope from her bosom and handing it to* EMMY.) Read his letter, Emmy. Rufe could allus write sech nice letters. I reckon ye won't mind hearing it, Stranger?

STRANGER. (*Rising. With some uneasiness.*) No. (*Moves back of table.*)

EMMY. (*Rising. Looking at the letter.*) Why Mis' Cagle your name is printed. (*Goes to the lantern and looks at the envelope closely.* MRS. CAGLE *follows and looks over her shoulder.*)

MRS. CAGLE. Read the inside, Emmy.

EMMY. (*Cries out.*) 'Tain't from Rufe, Mom. 'Tain't from him.

MRS. CAGLE. (*Fiercely.*) Who's it from?

EMMY. I cain't read it. I cain't read it.

MRS. CAGLE. (*Taking the letter from the girl and staring at it.*) Great God, why didn't ye l'arn me how to read? (*Hands letter back to* EMMY.) Spell it out, Emmy. Maybe the stranger kin help ye. He kin read a little.

EMMY. (*Sobbing as she takes the letter. The* STRANGER *starts forward as if to take the letter, but stops.*) I'm so afeered—

STRANGER. I'll help you.

EMMY. (*Spells out a letter or two and then speaks the name.*) M-r-s—L—That's yo' name. Mis' Liza Cagle. We r-e-g-r-e-t—

STRANGER. That means—are sorry.

MRS. CAGLE. (*Repeating.*) We air sorry—

EMMY. To i-n-f-o-r-m—

STRANGER. That means—to tell—

MRS. CAGLE. We air sorry to tell—

EMMY. You—that—your—son, Rufe Cagle, d-i-e-d—

MRS. CAGLE. (*Speaking before the* STRANGER. *She stands erect, and rigid, but does not evidence any great emotion otherwise.*) DIED—

EMMY. (*Sobbing as she sinks to a chair.*) O, Mom, Mom—

STRANGER. (*Taking the telegram from her hand and reading.*) February fifth, in action. That means he died—fighting.

MRS. CAGLE. (*Very calmly, but with deep emotion.*) It means my boy is dead. It means the law's got my boy same as his pap.

ACT THREE

SCENE TWO

SCENE: *The same as Scene One. A few hours later. Early morning.*

The stage is dark except for the glow that comes from the fireplace. A figure sits near the fire. It stirs the fire. A brighter glow comes forth. A frying pan or two and a coffee pot are shifted as if a breakfast already prepared is being kept warm. Outside the crow of a rooster is heard several times. The figure of MRS. CAGLE *arises, and goes to the window. She opens the wooden shutter; the faint glimmer of approaching dawn slips in.*

MRS. CAGLE. (*Going and shaking a figure that is lying on the bed.*) Emmy—Emmy. Wake up, Emmy. (*Going to the back room door.*) Git up, Stranger. (*Knocking on door.*) Air ye awake, Stranger?

STRANGER. (*From the back room.*) Yes, Mrs. Cagle.

(*A sob comes from* EMMY'S *bed.*)

MRS. CAGLE. (*Going to bed and speaking kindly.*) Git up, Emmy. Hit's daybreak—at last. (*Goes slowly back to fireplace and sits down.* EMMY, *fully dressed, gets up and comes to the fire.*)

EMMY. O, Mom, I dreamt hit warn't so. I thought that Rufe had come back. (*She sobs softly.*)

MRS. CAGLE. Dreams is a heap o' comfort, sometimes, Emmy. But hit's the wakin' up—

EMMY. Did ye dream too, Mom?

MRS. CAGLE. No, not exactly.

EMMY. Did ye lay down, Mom?

MRS. CAGLE. No, I jest sot here and kept a thinkin'.

EMMY. Ye oughter let me set up with ye, Mom.

MRS. CAGLE. No, I wuz a thinkin'. Seemed to me like Rufe wuz a little boy agin. Seemed to me like hit couldn't be so that he'd growed up, and gone off, and wuzn't a comin' back. Hit seemed to me that he must be little agin, and a sleepin' thar in the bed, and me a settin' up with him sick. I jest kept awaitin' fer him to cry out so's I could take him up in my lap.

EMMY. O, Mom, maybe thar's some mistake.

MRS. CAGLE. No, thar ain't no mistake. I kin remember when he used to stump his toe, or hurt hisself, I'd feel the pain as much as him. And jest like he wuz little agin, somew'eres in here (*clutches her breast*) I kin feel the hurt of a bullet. Jest like when he wuz little, and had hurt hisself.

EMMY. O, Mom, hit's a killin' me, but I'm proud of him. He done whut he thought wuz right.

MRS. CAGLE. Yes. Better call the stranger agin, Emmy. Breakfast will be all spoilt.

STRANGER. (*Entering.*) I'm up, Mrs. Cagle.

MRS. CAGLE. (*Putting food on the table.*) Set down and eat, Stranger. Come, Emmy. Hit's almost sun-up.

(*All sit down. The* STRANGER *eats.* EMMY *makes an attempt, but fails.* MRS. CAGLE *does not eat.*)

MRS. CAGLE. Try to eat, Emmy. I reckon ye'll need yo' strength to git through the day.

EMMY. Ye must eat, too, Mom.

MRS. CAGLE. I et while I wuz a cookin'. Have ye made your plans, stranger?

STRANGER. Yes, Mrs. Cagle.

MRS. CAGLE. Which way ye travelin'?

STRANGER. I'm going—back to the camp.

MRS. CAGLE. Ye ain't afeered?

STRANGER. No, Mrs. Cagle, I'm not afraid.

MRS. CAGLE. Air ye thinkin' of yo' ma?

STRANGER. Yes. I want my mother to have the same right to this land that you have.

MRS. CAGLE. Hit air a costly right.

STRANGER. Yes.

MRS. CAGLE. Well, if ye air sot on goin', Stranger, when ye shoot, remember Rufe, and all the other mothers' sons like him.

STRANGER. I will, Mrs. Cagle. You've made me ashamed. I'm going back. I hope I get there before I am arrested. I want them to know that I wanted to come back.

MRS. CAGLE. I'll put ye up a snack to eat on the way, and I reckon ye better wear one o' Rufe's old hats and his coat.

STRANGER. You are very kind, but I don't like to take your son's things now. If you can lend me just a hat, or a cap—

MRS. CAGLE. Ye air goin' to shoot the dogs that killed him, ain't ye?

STRANGER. Yes.

MRS. CAGLE. Then ye air welcome to his coat too.

STRANGER. Thank you. (MRS. CAGLE *goes into the back room.*) I can never repay you for all your kindness.

EMMY. I hope ye come back.

STRANGER. I hope so, but I can't help thinking of the injustice of things. Your husband had so much to come back to— He went like a man, while I—

EMMY. I'd a loved him jest the same even if he'd bin afeered.

STRANGER. (*Studying her closely.*) I reckon you would have. Perhaps—after all—it's women like you who keep men from being afraid.

MRS. CAGLE. (*From the back room.*) Emmy—

EMMY. (*Springing up and going toward door.*) Yes'um?

(*The* STRANGER *rises and watches* EMMY *with an admiration that is akin to reverence. His lips move as one who dreams of a thing that might be. He shakes his head slowly, and sits down.*)

MRS. CAGLE. (*From the back room.*) Ain't none o' them paper bags saved?

EMMY. Yes'um, thar's one on the shelf thar.

MRS. CAGLE. Here they air.

EMMY. (*Coming back.*) Kin I give ye some more coffee, Stranger?

STRANGER. (*Rising.*) No thank you.

MRS. CAGLE. (*Entering with paper bag in

hand which she proceeds to fill with food at table.) Eat a plenty, Stranger.

STRANGER. I have, thank you.

MRS. CAGLE. I reckon ye better be goin' by good sun-up.

STRANGER. Yes, as soon as possible.

(*There is a loud knocking at the door. All are startled. The man springs up, frightened.*)

EMMY. I reckon that's Bud a comin'.

MRS. CAGLE. I reckon hit is, but ye better hide, Stranger.

STRANGER. Hadn't I better stay and face it?

MRS. CAGLE. No, ye kin hide in the back room.

(*The* STRANGER *goes into the back room.* EMMY *opens door. The* SHERIFF *enters.*)

SHERIFF. Good morning, Miss Emmy. Good morning, Widow Cagle.

EMMY. Come in, Sheriff.

MRS. CAGLE. Good mornin', Sheriff.

SHERIFF. Kinder cleared off this morning. Storm is over, but it shore is cold. Mind me warmin'?

MRS. CAGLE. No. Pull ye up a chair.

SHERIFF. (*Going to the fire, looking the table over.*) I'm kinder early, but I see you got company for breakfast.

MRS. CAGLE. (*Looking at the third plate.*) Yes, I've got company.

SHERIFF. Reckon he must a come a'ter I left last night.

MRS. CAGLE. (*Ignoring the* SHERIFF.) I reckon ye can clear up the table, Emmy, and I'll bring in a little more wood.

EMMY. Yes, Mom. I'll bring in the wood, too, if ye kin wait.

SHERIFF. I said I reckon your company come last night a'ter I left.

MRS. CAGLE. No, he got here last night jest before ye did.

SHERIFF. Where wuz he?

MRS. CAGLE. Under the tater pile.

SHERIFF. I kinder thought so. Well, I'm mighty sorry to disobleege you, or your company, Mis' Cagle, but law is law.

MRS. CAGLE. Don't ye know no other word but law, Jim Weeks? Why don't ye put yo' law to some use? If ye want to fight, why don't ye go fight like Rufe? Ain't ye fitten to use yo' law again' nothin' but wimen, and men folks whut's without guns?

SHERIFF. Now, Mis' Cagle, all this talk ain't going to soften my heart to let this here deserter go—

MRS. CAGLE. I ain't tryin' to soften yo' heart. Ye air goin' to let the stranger go. He ain't no deserter. He ain't nothin' more than a boy. He wuz homesick, and he is a goin' back to war this mornin'.

SHERIFF. But Mis' Cagle, I'm obleeged to—

MRS. CAGLE. Ye ain't a goin' to tech him, Jim Weeks.

SHERIFF. Well, now, Mis' Cagle, me and your son had some differences, of course, but a'ter all I ain't got nothin' agin Rufe.

MRS. CAGLE. Whut's Rufe got to do with it?

SHERIFF. Well, there ain't no use of you denying that Rufe's run away, and come home.

MRS. CAGLE. (*Looking at him in amazement.* EMMY *bursts into tears.* MRS. CAGLE *speaks very quietly.*) Rufe? No, Sheriff, Rufe ain't come home. (*She throws a shawl over her head and goes out the front door.* SHERIFF *goes toward* EMMY *and makes an effort to comfort her.*)

SHERIFF. Now, Miss Emmy, don't take hit so hard. I'd most rather give up my job than to make you cry. Of course, Rufe took the woman I loved, but I ain't a holdin' that agin him. I calculated he wuz the best man to do it, but this here is a case of where I have to do my duty. If he will come out and give hisself up, and don't make no trouble, why fer yo' sake I'll do whut I can fer him. Whar is he?

EMMY. Whar is he? He is a lyin' dead out thar on the battlefield whar he wuz a fightin'.

SHERIFF. (*With great surprise.*) Rufe ain't dead?

EMMY. Yes, Mom got the letter last night.

SHERIFF. I'm sorry. They didn't tell me the name and I didn't look at the warrant. I thought this here deserter wuz him. Mis' Cagle didn't say nothin' to me— I wisht him better luck than that.

EMMY. (*Angrily.*) I don't believe ye. Ye come here to take him to jail. I know ye did, and if he'd a bin here instead of this poor boy that is—if he'd a come to see me and Mom instead o' dyin', ye would a took him, ye would.

SHERIFF. But Miss Emmy—

EMMY. Ye would a took him to jail jest because ye had the power. Once last summer I thought I'd marry ye instead of Rufe, because I kinder looked up to ye as standin' for whut was right. I thought ye wuz brave, but that day Rufe registered I come to know that Rufe wuz the man that wuzn't askeered. (*Breaks into a sob.*)

(MRS. CAGLE *and* BUD *enter.* BUD *carries an armful of wood, which he places on the floor by the fireplace.*)

MRS. CAGLE. Come in, Bud.

BUD. Howdy, Sheriff.

SHERIFF. Good mornin', Bud.

BUD. (*Noticing* EMMY'S *emotion.*) Whut's the matter, Emmy? Whut's he done to ye?

SHERIFF. Miss Emmy's bin tellin' me 'bout Rufe, Mis' Cagle. I'm mighty sorry.

BUD. Rufe?

MRS. CAGLE. Hush, Bud.

BUD. Whar's Rufe?

SHERIFF. They tell me, Bud, that Rufe's dead.

BUD. Rufe dead? 'Tain't so. 'Tain't so. Yisterday—yisterday—I—I—

EMMY. Yes, Bud, Rufe's dead.

BUD. 'Tain't so, 'tain't so. Why yisterday, yisterday I brung the letter.

MRS. CAGLE. That letter told us, Bud.

BUD. (*To* SHERIFF.) Rufe's dead! I want to go to war. Bin shootin' since I could hold a gun. People think I'm foolish in the head. Don't talk much. Took a'ter Maw. Two years 'fore I wuz born she didn't talk. Didn't have nobody to talk to. Pap wuz allus drunk. I kin do whut I'm told to do. I kin read. Kin I go to war?

MRS. CAGLE. No, Bud.

BUD. Rufe's kilt, Mis' Cagle. I got to go. Sheriff, will ye take keer o' my wimen folks?

MRS. CAGLE. Ye don't know whut ye takin' 'bout, Bud. This ain't no feud whar ye have a chance. Hit air murder, and the law air back of hit.

SHERIFF. Mis' Cagle's got it wrong, Bud, but thar ain't no use o' yo' goin' till they call ye.

MRS. CAGLE. They won't call Bud.

SHERIFF. I'm mighty sorry 'bout Rufe, Mis' Cagle, and I'm powerful sorry to force the law at a time like this, but I'm obleeged to take this here deserter to headquarters.

MRS. CAGLE. Sheriff, the law ain't never took nobody outen my house.

SHERIFF. Then ye admit that this deserter is hid here?

MRS. CAGLE. Yes, he's hid in the back room.

SHERIFF. (*Starting toward the back room door and then stopping. After a moment's pause he turns back.*) All right, Mis' Cagle. Outen respect to you in yo' trouble I'll jest wait outside fer him. My deputies wuz to be here at sun-up. We'll surround the house. Thar ain't no use of him tryin' to git away. If he's a man he'll come out and give hisself up.

MRS. CAGLE. A man ain't givin' hisself up to the law.

SHERIFF. (*Becoming irritated.*) Now, Mis' Cagle, I'm a hatin' to say these things to you, when you're in trouble, but last night you harbored a deserter. That's the same as givin' aid to the enemy. Fer that thing I kin throw ye into jail today. I ain't a wantin' to do hit, but I'll have to if you interfere any further with the law.

MRS. CAGLE. I've bin a breakin' the law fer nigh on to forty year, and I ain't afeered to break it again.

SHERIFF. Well, I warn ye. If you make another move to help this deserter git away I'll arrest ye, Mis' Cagle, and take ye to prison. (*He goes toward door, and then stops.*) I'll wait outside, Mis' Cagle. (*He goes out.*)

BUD. (*Half sobbing.*) Rufe's dead.

MRS. CAGLE. (*Following to door and barring it.*) Call the stranger, Emmy.

EMMY. Whut ye goin' to do, Mom?

MRS. CAGLE. We air goin' to fight, Emmy. (*Gets gun.*)

EMMY. No, no, Mom, no.

MRS. CAGLE. (*Ignoring* EMMY *she goes toward the back room door and calls.*) Stranger! Come out, stranger.

STRANGER. (*Entering.*) Mrs. Cagle, I can't hide behind you all any longer. I'll give myself up.

MRS. CAGLE. No, Stranger, we air goin' to take our stand agin' the law.

EMMY. (*Looking out the window.*) They air comin', Mom, the deputies.

MRS. CAGLE. Come away from that window, Emmy.

EMMY. Thar air three of 'em, Mom, and Jim Weeks is a puttin' 'em around the house.

MRS. CAGLE. Thar air four of us. Stranger, kin ye shoot?

STRANGER. No, no, Mrs. Cagle. I'm not worth that. I'm ashamed that I hid last night. I should have been a man and given myself up then.

MRS. CAGLE. Ye call hit bein' a man givin' yo'self up without a fight?

STRANGER. What chance have we against the law? If we open fire on these officers it will mean that we all will be tried on a more serious charge. I alone am guilty— Let me take the consequences. Please, Mrs. Cagle.

MRS. CAGLE. I told ye I'd hide ye, Stranger.

STRANGER. You did, and I thank you. But to fight like this, Mrs. Cagle, it's all wrong.

MRS. CAGLE. (*Looking at him closely.*) Ye ain't afeered air ye?

STRANGER. (*Hesitating, and showing something of the fear in himself.*) Maybe. I tell you what I'll do. I'll watch my chance, and run for it—

MRS. CAGLE. They'll git ye in the back.

STRANGER. (*Peering out the window.*) No, I can make it. Miss Emmy, you go out for wood and leave the door open. I'll take my chance and make for that clump of trees out there.

MRS. CAGLE. Ye air foolish, Stranger.

EMMY. (*Still watching at window.*) Mom, Jim Weeks is a comin' to the house.

MRS. CAGLE. (*Hurrying toward window, points toward the back room.*) Go back, Stranger.

STRANGER. What's the use? They've got me.

MRS. CAGLE. (*With the determination of a command.*) Go back.

(*The* STRANGER *pauses for a moment. His fear gets the better of him and he turns and goes hurriedly into the back room.*)

SHERIFF. (*Trying door and finding it barred, calls.*) Mis' Cagle, open up. I want to speak to ye.

MRS. CAGLE. Ye kin talk through the door.

SHERIFF. I ain't after botherin' ye, Mis' Cagle. I've got news fer ye.

MRS. CAGLE. I ain't wantin' yo' news.

SHERIFF. I give ye my word, Mis' Cagle, to speak to ye and come right out. You'll be powerful interested in whut I got to say.

EMMY. Maybe the Sheriff ain't going to take him, Mom.

MRS. CAGLE. (*Lifting gun and coming toward center of room.*) Open the door, Emmy!

(EMMY *opens the door and the* SHERIFF *enters.*)

SHERIFF. No use for gun play, Mis' Cagle. I ain't after touchin' ye. (*He comes close to her and speaks in a low voice.*) My deputies have jest come, and they brung me the name of this here deserter. (*He takes a paper from inside pocket.*) Hit mought be interestin' for ye to know who it is ye air riskin' yo' own liberty to hide.

MRS. CAGLE. In my house, Jim Weeks, we ask no man his name.

SHERIFF. In this case it mought have been better if yer had. (*He reads from paper in low voice.*) This is a warrant for the arrest of Zeb Turner, J-r.

MRS. CAGLE. (*Repeats.*) Zeb Turner? (*Pause. She shakes her head.*) No, ye air wrong, Sheriff. Zeb Turner air old. The stranger ain't more than a boy.

SHERIFF. Yes, Mis' Cagle, but this is Zeb Turner, Junior. That means—son of—Zeb Turner.

MRS. CAGLE. (*Rigid with emotion.*) Ye mean this boy air—the son—of my man's murderer?

SHERIFF. Yes—this deserter—the same.

MRS. CAGLE. The son of Zeb Turner—

SHERIFF. Now, I'll leave it to yo' judgment, Mis' Cagle, if ye hadn't better jest turn him out to me.

MRS. CAGLE. (*Looking at the back room door and then studying the* SHERIFF *closely.*) Air ye—lyin' to me, Jim Weeks?

SHERIFF. No, and if ye don't believe me, let Miss Emmy read this— (*He turns toward* EMMY *with paper in hand.*)

MRS. CAGLE. Read it, Emmy.

SHERIFF. (*Pointing.*) Right here, Miss Emmy.

EMMY. (*Spelling the words out.*) Z-e-b. Zeb T-u-r-n-e-r—

SHERIFF. That spells Turner. (*Taking the warrant from her.*) Ain't that right, Miss Emmy?

EMMY. Yes, sir.

SHERIFF. Now, Mis' Cagle, if ye air satisfied, I reckon I can take my prisoner.

MRS. CAGLE. (*After a moment's hesitation.*) No, Sheriff, ye kin wait—outside.

SHERIFF. All right, as ye say. If ye need me, jest call. (*Satisfied with his triumph he goes out—smiling.*)

EMMY. (*Coming forward.*) Who is he, Mom?

MRS. CAGLE. (*Standing erect and making no move except to push* EMMY *aside. She stares straight at the back room door, and when she speaks it is to herself rather than in answer to* EMMY'S *questions.*) I fed him—

EMMY. Whut's happened?

MRS. CAGLE. And I hid him—

EMMY. Tell me whut's up, Mom.

MRS. CAGLE. I wuz about to shoot to save him—

EMMY. Mom, who is he?

MRS. CAGLE. The son of the man who killed Rufe's pap.

EMMY. (*Greatly agitated.*) Son of the—man who—killed—Rufe's pap!

MRS. CAGLE. If his pap had lived Rufe wouldn't a gone to war.

BUD. (*Concerned only with his grief.*) Rufe's dead.

MRS. CAGLE. Yes, Bud, Rufe's dead, and one of his murderers air in thar—

EMMY. Ye goin' to give him to the law, Mom?

MRS. CAGLE. (*With some hesitation.*) No—not to—the law.

EMMY. (*With uneasiness.*) Whut ye goin' to do, Mom?

MRS. CAGLE. (*Suddenly turns and going to the door, bars it. Coming back to the table she takes the gun in her hand. She stands for a few seconds staring at the back room door.* BUD *pays no attention to her.* EMMY *watches, too confounded for words or action.* MRS. CAGLE *finally moves toward the door, slowly, but firm in step. She stops for a second at the door, and then in a quiet but commanding voice speaks.*) Come out, Stranger.

STRANGER. (*Entering he feels the tenseness of the scene.*) Has the—Sheriff gone?

MRS. CAGLE. Ye air safe from the Sheriff.

STRANGER. Thank God.

MRS. CAGLE. Yo' name, Stranger.

STRANGER. My name is Zeb Turner.

MRS. CAGLE. And yo' pap's name? Wuz hit Zeb Turner, too?

STRANGER. Yes, Zeb Turner.

MRS. CAGLE. Wuz he a revenuer?

STRANGER. Yes, one of the bravest that ever crossed the mountains. You don't know him, do you?

MRS. CAGLE. Know him? Well, Stranger, Zeb Turner killed my son's pap.

STRANGER. Great God!

MRS. CAGLE. Shot him in the back while he wuz a protectin' his own property.

STRANGER. God Almighty!

MRS. CAGLE. And I've protected ye—

STRANGER. I didn't know, Mrs. Cagle, I—

MRS. CAGLE. Hid ye in my own house—ye, the son of my man's murderer.

STRANGER. I didn't know. Besides, you've got to remember, it was law.

MRS. CAGLE. Law! Law! Allus that word, law. Well, Stranger, the feud has a law, and it air a life for a life.

STRANGER. I understand how you feel, and I don't blame you. Call the Sheriff and give me up.

MRS. CAGLE. Give ye up? No, Stranger, ye air mine to deal with.

EMMY. Mom!

STRANGER. Mrs. Cagle, for your own sake, turn me over to the Sheriff. I'll get what's coming to me.

MRS. CAGLE. If ye've got a gun, Stranger, use hit. The feud will give ye a chance,—the law won't.

STRANGER. I have no gun.

MRS. CAGLE. Thar's Bud's. I'll give ye time to reach hit.

STRANGER. Why, I can't fight you, Mrs. Cagle.

MRS. CAGLE. I'm givin' ye a chance.

STRANGER. I can't take it.

MRS. CAGLE. Then ye better run—

STRANGER. They will take your life for this. (*Shows his fear of her.*)

MRS. CAGLE My life! Whut does that matter? They've took every life that belonged to me. My pap's—my man's—my son's—my little son's life, they took hit, them that hide behind a thing called law.

STRANGER. But Mrs. Cagle, you don't understand—

MRS. CAGLE. I understand that ye air a son of the law, and that ye air in the power of the feud.

STRANGER. (*Pleadingly.*) Mrs. Cagle—

MRS. CAGLE. I'm offerin' ye a chance fer yo' life, but if ye air too much of a coward to take hit, by God I'll— (*Throws the gun to her shoulder.*)

EMMY. (*Throwing herself between* MRS. CAGLE *and* STRANGER.) Mom, ye shan't kill him, ye shan't.

MRS. CAGLE. Git away, Emmy.

EMMY. Mom, he's goin' out thar to shoot the dogs that killed Rufe—

MRS. CAGLE. I ain't a believin' him.

EMMY. Him and Rufe was a fightin' on the same side—

MRS. CAGLE. Out of the way, Emmy—

EMMY. Mom, he cain't help whut his pap done.

MRS. CAGLE. He's a son of the law. Air ye forgettin' whut the law done to yo' pap?

EMMY. My pap wuz a breakin' the law.

MRS. CAGLE. Air ye fergettin' that the law killed Rufe?

EMMY. No, Mom, I ain't a fergettin' ever. But hit warn't the law, Mom, hit wuz hate—Rufe told me—hate like this thing in yo' heart toward him— (*Pointing to* STRANGER.) Fer somethin' he got nothing to do with. It's hate, Mom. Rufe told me the day he went off— (*She breaks into hysterical sobs.*) Rufe told me—

(*Suddenly* MRS. CAGLE *seems to be listening intently to something the others do not hear.*)

MRS. CAGLE. Hush, did ye hear that?

EMMY. Whut, mom?

MRS. CAGLE. (*Listening.*) Hit's music.

EMMY. Hit's the wind on the snow—

MRS. CAGLE. Hush, I tell ye. Hit's him— (*Pause.*) Cain't ye hear him?

(*The* STRANGER *and* EMMY *exchange glances as much as to say that she has gone mad.*)

EMMY. Who, Mom?

MRS. CAGLE. Wait— (*There is a pause—dead silence.*) Yes, son—

EMMY. Mom, whut is hit?

MRS. CAGLE. Be quiet, I tell ye. Whut is it, son?—yes—yes— (*She turns to the others, listening as she speaks.*) Cain't ye hear him speakin'?

EMMY. No, Mom.

MRS. CAGLE. (*After a pause.*) Say hit again, son, so's I kin tell them. (*There is a moment's pause, and then* MRS. CAGLE *repeats in a measured voice.*) As long as thar air hate—thar will be—feuds. As long as thar air women—thar will be—sons. I ain't no more—to you —than other mothers' sons—air to them. Yes, son—whut else? (*Pause.*) Take keer of—yo'self—yes, son—and Emmy. Whut else, son?— (*She strains to hear more but it does not come. She turns to the others.*) Didn't none of ye hear him speakin'?

EMMY. No, Mom. We didn't hear him.

MRS. CAGLE. I heared him.

EMMY. Ye must a thought ye heared him.

MRS. CAGLE. I heared him jest as plain.

EMMY. The dead cain't come back.

MRS. CAGLE. No, I reckon my love went on—out yonder and reached him (*the gun slips to the floor*) and he's told me whut to do. I reckon ye better go, Stranger.

STRANGER. You mean—

MRS. CAGLE. I mean the hate of the feud air gone out of me— Go home, boy, if ye kin.

STRANGER. No, I'm going back to the camp. I'll come back sometime and thank you.

MRS. CAGLE. I reckon if ye put on Bud's coat and cap and pull hit over your face, Jim Weeks will think hits Bud, and let ye go.

STRANGER. But you—what will he do to you?

MRS. CAGLE. Nothin', Stranger. I ain't afeered and, thar ain't no danger unless ye air afeered.

(EMMY *takes* BUD'S *coat and cap from him and hands them quickly to the* STRANGER. He puts them on.)

STRANGER. I'll go.

MRS. CAGLE. Ye better take my gun. Ye might need it.

STRANGER. (*Taking gun.*) Good-by, Mrs. Cagle. If you don't mind—I'll come back some day and thank you.

MRS. CAGLE. I ain't a mindin', Stranger.

EMMY. (*At the window.*) Now's yo' chance.

STRANGER. Good-by— (*He shakes hands with* EMMY.)

MRS. CAGLE. Hurry. (STRANGER *goes quickly out.*)

EMMY. (*Still watching at window.*) Jim Weeks is a turnin'—

MRS. CAGLE. Maybe not, Emmy.

EMMY. No, no—he's passed him, Mom. (*Still watches.*) He's—passed—Jim Weeks.

MRS. CAGLE. (*As if to herself, unconscious of* EMMY'S *presence.*) As long as thar is hate thar will be feuds—and wars—

EMMY. He's safe, Mom. He air down past the woods, and Jim Weeks air watchin' the house.

MRS. CAGLE. He'll make hit through the woods.

EMMY. Oh, I hope he does.

MRS. CAGLE. I reckon, ye better take Pap Todd a little breakfast.

EMMY. Yes'um, I will. (*She comes away from the window and goes to cupboard. She takes a tin bucket which she fills with food at the table.* MRS. CAGLE *takes the broom and sweeps floor around the hearth. Knocks are heard at the door.*)

MRS. CAGLE. Bud, see who that is cain't open the door fer hisself. (BUD *opens the door and the* SHERIFF *enters. He is dumbfounded when he sees* BUD.)

SHERIFF. Well, I'll be doggoned.

MRS. CAGLE. The stranger's gone, Sheriff.

SHERIFF. You let *him* go?

MRS. CAGLE. He air a mother's son, Sheriff.

SHERIFF. Well, I warned ye, Mis' Cagle.

MRS. CAGLE. I'm ready to go to jail.

SHERIFF. All right, come along.

(*Unseen by the others* BUD *draws his gun and covers the* SHERIFF.—*The* SHERIFF *is unconscious of his danger.*)

EMMY. No, no, Sheriff, please—

MRS. CAGLE. Ye kin stay at yo' pap's, Emmy. Ye kin sell the place. Jim Weeks will buy hit.

EMMY. Sell the place? But, Mom, whut would ye do when ye come back?

MRS. CAGLE. I reckon these here hills that borned me, and nursed me kin take keer of me fer a little while.

EMMY. Sheriff, ain't ye rememberin' yo' own ma? Ain't thar no love in yo' heart that can make ye see why Mom done this?

SHERIFF. Duty, Miss Emmy, is a hard thing but thar must be some of us to carry hit out.

MRS. CAGLE. (*Wrapping herself in a large shawl.*) Emmy, ye kin move my things down to yo' pap's— (*She goes to the door where* RUFE'S *hoe stands and caresses the handle.*) And—don't ye fergit—Rufe's hoe—Emmy. (*She looks about the room as if taking a farewell.*) I'm ready—Sheriff.

SHERIFF. (*Looking at her, he shakes his head, and lowers it as if ashamed. As he goes out he says somewhat brokenly.*) Well, not now—Mis' Cagle, not—now.

(BUD *slowly puts the gun back in his pocket.*)

EMMY. O Mom!

MRS. CAGLE. Ye go ahead, Emmy, with yo' pap's breakfast, and I'll dig the snow outen the yard, before the Sheriff gits back.

EMMY. (*Almost in tears.*) He ain't a comin' back, Mom.

MRS. CAGLE. Maybe not, Emmy. I ain't afeered, nohow.

EMMY. Air ye all right, Mom?

MRS. CAGLE. Yes, Emmy.

EMMY. (*Throwing her shawl over her shoulders and head.*) I'll be back soon.

MRS. CAGLE. I reckon you'd better do the wash to-day, hit's blowed up so fair hit won't take the clothes no time to dry.

EMMY. Yes, Mom. (*Taking the pail from the table and going out.*) I won't be long. Come, Bud. (*They go out.* BUD *takes* RUFE'S *coat and throws it around him as he goes out.*)

MRS. CAGLE. (*Drawing her shawl over her head again, and stopping at the door, fingers* RUFE'S *hoe. Once more she listens, but hearing no voice, speaks.*) I heared ye, Rufe. I never knowed nothin' about lovin' anything but ye—till ye showed me hit's lovin' them all that counts. Hit wuz sundown when ye left me, son—(*the morning sun, just rising, comes in through the window*) but hit's sun-up now, and I'm a knowin' God A'mighty is a takin' keer of ye—Rufe. (*She opens the door and the sun floods in. With the hoe in her hand she goes out quietly, and closes the door behind her.*)

THE SILVER CORD

BY

Sidney Howard

THE SILVER CORD

The Silver Cord represents the age-long struggle of a mother for the direction and control of the lives of the men to whom she has given birth. Its author, Sidney Howard, who is one of the most original of the younger generation of playwrights, was born in Oakland, California, June 26, 1891. He grew up in the West, with two extended visits to Italy and Paris. Being threatened with tuberculosis, he spent about three years at Davos Platz, Switzerland, and on ranches in California until he was cured. He graduated from the University of California in 1915, having already written two plays. One of these, a tragedy in blank verse, laid in Avignon during the Black Death, was subsequently produced by the artists' colony at Carmel-by-the-Sea, California, the setting being changed, however, to Monterey. Mr. Howard spent the year 1915–1916 at Harvard College, studying with Dr. Baker, and becoming interested in the then new stagecraft. In the summer of 1916 he volunteered to drive an ambulance, first in France and later in the Balkans, becoming finally a captain in the aviation service of the United States.

Returning to this country in 1919, he became associated with *Life, Hearst's Magazine,* the *New Republic,* and other journals as literary editor and special writer. His translation of D'Annunzio's *Fedra,* made for Nazimova, fell into the hands of Miss Margaret Anglin, who commissioned him to write a play for her, based upon a story of her own. When *Swords* (1921) was completed, however, it was Miss Clare Eames who played the leading part, and she and Mr. Howard were married in 1922. *Swords* is an heroic play in free blank verse, laid in medieval times. Returning to journalism, Mr. Howard was asked to translate Vildrac's *Paquebot Tenacity* (1922), *Casanova,* from the Spanish of Lorenzo de Azertis (1923), and *Sancho Panza,* from the Hungarian of Melchior Lengyel (1923). Spending three months in Venice, he wrote *They Knew What They Wanted.* After sixteen managers had declined it, the Theatre Guild produced it at the Garrick Theatre, November 24, 1924, and it won the Pulitzer Prize. It is a fine domestic drama laid in California, translating the Paolo and Francesca motive to modern times. But the husband, Tony, instead of killing the wife and the friend who have betrayed him, forgives them, in keeping with his nature as we see it. *Lucky Sam McCarver* (1925), a study of the love of a coarse but physically attractive proprietor of a night-club and of Carlotta Ashe, a woman of fashion, failed, but had some strong moments. Two successes came in 1926. *Ned McCobb's Daughter* portrays the character of a courageous

New England woman, Carrie McCobb, who looks disaster in the face calmly and foils her brother-in-law, a bootlegger from New York, so completely as to win even his admiration.

The Silver Cord is a more profound study than anything which preceded it. It is a contrast of two generations, and when Mrs. Phelps plots to break the engagement of her younger son and to ruin the marriage of the elder, she does so with an air of preserving them from disaster. The art with which Mr. Howard has drawn her careful indirect attack is equaled by the skill with which he portrays the direct method of the young wife who, perhaps more secure in her knowledge of her husband's love, states her position with a vocabulary that conceals nothing and strips the situation of any pretenses. Hester, the fiancée of Robin, the younger son, is less secure, and she leaves the field defeated. As Laura Hope Crews played Mrs. Phelps, she almost won the sympathy of the audience in the last act by the spirited defense of her conduct. *The Silver Cord* opened in New York, on December 20, 1926, and was one of the successes of the season. It went on tour, and was played in London, where it scored an artistic rather than a popular success.

Mr. Howard has collaborated with Mr. Edward Sheldon in *Bewitched* (see p. 848, and with Mr. Charles MacArthur in *Salvation,* a play dealing with a woman revivalist, which was produced at the Empire Theatre, January 31, 1928, but ran only a short time. He has also adapted *Michel Auclair,* from the play of the same name by Vildrac (1925); *The Last Night of Don Juan,* by Rostand (1925); and *Morals,* with Charles Recht, from *Morale,* by Ludwig Thoma (1925). An original play, *Half Gods,* had a brief life, when it was presented at the Plymouth Theatre, New York, on December 21, 1929.

Swords (1921) was published by George H. Doran Company; *Lexington, a Pageant Drama,* by the Lexington Historical Society (1924); *They Knew What They Wanted* (1925), by Doubleday, Page and Company; *Lucky Sam McCarver* (1926), *Ned McCobb's Daughter* (1926), *The Silver Cord* (1926), and *Half Gods* (1930) by Charles Scribner's Sons, to whom, together with Mr. Howard, the editor is indebted for permission to reprint *The Silver Cord.* Mr. Howard has also been good enough to furnish biographical details for this introduction.

NOTE TO SIXTH EDITION.

The Late Christopher Bean (1932), adapted from *Prenez Garde à la Peinture,* by René Fauchois, was a remarkable stage success. Mr. Howard changed the original play dexterously to emphasize the part of Abby, the servant, played by Pauline Lord, who alone had appreciated the dead young painter whose "lost works" everyone is striving to acquire. *Alien Corn* (1933) was a vivid contrast of the artist with the provincial atmosphere of a small college town, in which Miss Katharine Cornell made a personal success. The skill of Mr. Howard was shown in his adaptation of Mr. Sinclair Lewis's novel *Dodsworth* (1931). The play, published by Harcourt, Brace and Company in 1934, is prefaced by an introduction in which Mr. Howard and Mr. Lewis discuss their joint contribution. But a comparison of the play with the novel will show how Mr. Howard has not only omitted much of the tiresome detail of the latter but has also added some fine scenes which are not in the novel. Mr. Howard struck a high plane in his adaptation of one chapter of Paul de Kruif's *Microbe Hunters* under the title *Yellow Jack* (1934). Here he dramatized the heroism of science in its search for the germ of yellow fever. It was a much better play than *Paths of Glory* (1935), adapted from the novel by Humphrey Cobb, for it had unity of action, which the bitter and sincere attack on war did not possess. *The Ghost of Yankee Doodle* (1937) was an artistically successful attempt to dramatize the dilemma in which liberals in America will be placed "eighteen months after the commencement of the next world war." Even after the plutocratic publisher has uprooted the Garrison family and brought tragedy to them and to himself, Mr. Howard closes the play on the note of unfailing loyalty to liberalism and idealism.

The Late Christopher Bean and *Paths of Glory* were published by Samuel French, who have also reissued *Alien Corn,* published first by Scribners. *Yellow Jack* was published by Harcourt, Brace and Company. For criticism see A. H. Quinn's *History of the American Drama from the Civil War to the Present Day,* Revised Edition; two volumes in one, published by Appleton-Century-Crofts, Inc. (1936), Vol. 2, pp. 227–233, 271–275, 363–364.

Note to Seventh Edition.

Sidney Howard died as a result of an accident, August 23, 1939. *Madam, Will You Walk?* was produced in November, 1939 in Baltimore but did not reach New York. *Lute Song,* adapted from the Chinese play "Pi-Pa-Ki" by Sidney Howard and Will Irwin, was produced in Philadelphia, December 24, 1945. It was a brilliant spectacle, with music by Raymond Scott.

Letters from Howard to Barrett Clark were published in *Theatre Arts,* Vol. 25 (April, 1941), pp. 276–286.

CAST OF CHARACTERS

John Golden Theatre, New York, December 20, 1926

Mrs. Phelps . . . . . Laura Hope Crews
David, her son . . . . . Elliot Cabot
Robert, her younger son . . . . . Earle Larimore
Christina, David's wife . . . . . Elisabeth Risdon
Hester, Robert's fiancée . . . . . Margalo Gillmore
Maid . . . . . Barbara Bruce

The action occurs in the present day in Mrs. Phelps' house, which is situated in one of the more mature residential developments of an eastern American city.

ACT I—The Living-room on Sunday afternoon.
ACT II—The Living-room again, early that same evening.
ACT III—David's bedroom, later that same evening.
ACT IV—The Living-room, Monday morning after.

THE SILVER CORD

ACT ONE

A living-room, built and decorated in the best manner of 1905, and cluttered with the souvenirs of maternal love, European travel, and an orthodox enthusiasm for the arts. There is a vast quantity of Braun Clement and Arundel Society reproduction of the Renaissance Italian masters. The piano features Grieg, Sibelius and Macdowell. A door gives on a spacious hallway. Windows look out over a snow-covered garden.

The rise of the curtain discloses HESTER *lost in the rotogravure sections of the Sunday papers. She is a lovely, frail phantom of a girl with a look of recent illness about her. She wears the simplest and most charming of house frocks. The doorbell rings. There is the least sound of commotion in the hall.* HESTER *looks up. In a moment, the doors open and* DAVID *enters. He is a personable young man, well enough dressed, and a gentleman. He belongs to the somewhat stolid or unimaginative type which is generally characterized, in this country, as "steady." His smile is slow and wide, his speech slow and to the point. His principal quality is a rare and most charming amiability, but he is clearly lacking in many of the more sophisticated perceptions and he is clearly of a conventional bent in his attitude toward life. The door, as he leaves it open, shows* CHRISTINA, *in the act of shedding her fur coat with the assistance of the maid. She, as* DAVID'S *wife, presents something of a contrast to her husband. She is tall, slender, grave, honest, shy, intelligent, most trusting and, when need be, courageous. She has a scientist's detachment and curiosity and these serve oddly to emphasize a very individual womanliness which is far removed from the accepted feminine. One suspects that, where* DAVID *is stubborn, she is open-minded, where he is blind, she is amazingly clear-sighted. That is the difference which makes one the complement of the other. The common quality which brought them together in the holy bonds of matrimony is their mutual candor.* DAVID *is incapable of subtlety;* CHRISTINA *will not bother with it. The result is congeniality. So much for* DAVID *and* CHRISTINA. HESTER rises.

HESTER. Hello!

DAVID. Eh? . . . Oh, I beg your pardon! The maid said there wasn't anybody home.

HESTER. You're David, aren't you? [*She advances to meet him.*] I'm Hester.

DAVID. You're not! [*He goes quickly toward her and shakes hands as* CHRISTINA *enters.*] Well! [*He turns; smiling broadly to* CHRISTINA.] Look, Chris! Here's Hester who's going to marry my brother Rob.

CHRISTINA. [*With the most charming warmth.*] Isn't she lovely!

HESTER. Oh, I think you're dears, both of you! [*The two women kiss.*] Aren't you hours ahead of time?

CHRISTINA. We caught the one o'clock instead of whatever the other was.

DAVID. Where are Mother and Rob?

HESTER. Your mother's drinking tea at . . . Aren't there some people named Donohue?

DAVID. Great friends of Mother's. Why aren't you there?

HESTER. Not allowed. I'm having a breakdown.

CHRISTINA. Why don't you telephone her, Dave? She'll want to know that you're here.

DAVID. She'll find out soon enough. Where's Rob?

HESTER. Gone skating.

DAVID. [*Turns to the window.*] On the pond? No. There's no one on the pond.

HESTER. Somewhere else, then.

CHRISTINA. [*Hovering over the fire.*] Dave, do you suppose I could get some tea? I'm half frozen.

DAVID. Of course you can. I'll order it. [*To* HESTER.] What's the maid's name?

HESTER. Delia.

DAVID. Delia. It used to be Hannah and before that it was Stacia who got married to our old coachman, Fred. Well, it's not so bad to be home again!

[ROBERT *enters, very much dressed for skating, and carrying his skates.* ROBERT *only faintly suggests his brother. He is more volatile and stammers slightly.*]

ROBERT. [*A shout.*] Dave!

DAVID. Hello, Robert! [*They shake hands vigorously.*] We were just wondering when you'd come in and Hester said . . .

HESTER. [*Speaking at the same time.*] Wasn't it lucky I was here to receive them?

ROBERT. [*As he shakes* CHRISTINA'S *hand.*] I think this is simply magnificent! [*As he strips off his skating things.*] How did you get here so soon? We weren't expecting you for . . .

DAVID. We caught the one o'clock.

CHRISTINA. Just.

DAVID. We thought it would be fun to surprise you.

ROBERT. Mother'll drop dead in her tracks.

DAVID. How *is* she?

ROBERT. Oh, she's in fine form . . . [*To* CHRISTINA.] You'll adore her.

CHRISTINA. I'm sure I shall.

ROBERT. She *is* marvellous, isn't she, Hester?

HESTER. She is indeed. . . . Perfectly marvellous!

DAVID. Mother's immense. And I'm glad, for Chris's sake, that things worked out this way. First Chris sees the old house. Then she meets Hester. Then Rob comes breezing in, full of health. And, last of all, Mother comes.

ROBERT. It's like a play. I always want things to be like a play. Don't you, Hester?

HESTER. I dunno. Why?

ROBERT. Don't you, Christina? [*But he does not wait for an answer—a habit with him in his better humored moments.*] You have to tell us you like this old house, you know. Mother and I wouldn't change it for the world.

CHRISTINA. [*Smiling as she looks around her.*] How about that tea, Dave?

DAVID. Excuse me, Chris! I forgot. . . .

CHRISTINA. [*To* ROBERT.] I've been here three minutes and I'm ordering food already!

ROBERT. Well, let me "do the honors."

DAVID. Honors, hell! Isn't Julia still in the kitchen?

ROBERT. Sure she is.

DAVID. Well, I *must* see Julia! [*He goes.*]

ROBERT. [*To* CHRISTINA.] Julia'll drop dead, too. I expect half the town'll be dropping dead. Dave's always been the Greek god around this place, you know.

HESTER. He should be.

ROBERT. I can remember the time I didn't think so.

[*A door slams. In the hall,* MRS. PHELPS *is heard talking, excitedly.*]

MRS. PHELPS. Those bags! Have they come, Delia?

HESTER. Here's your mother now.

CHRISTINA. So soon? How nice!

[MRS. PHELPS *enters. She is pretty, distinguished, stoutish, soft, disarming and, in short, has everything one could possibly ask including a real gift for looking years younger than her age, which is well past fifty. She boasts a reasonable amount of conventional culture, no great amount of intellect, a superabundant vitality, perfect health and a prattling spirit. At the moment she is still wearing her hat and furs and she looks wildly about her.*]

MRS. PHELPS. Dave! Dave, boy! Where are you, Dave? Where are you? It's Mother, Dave! [*She does not see him in the room and she is already turning back to the hall without a word or a look for anybody else.*] Where are you, Dave? Come here this minute! Don't you hear me, Dave? It's Mother! [*Then* DAVID *appears in the hall.*] Oh, Dave!

DAVID. [*A little abashed by the vigor of this welcome.*] Hello, Mother.

MRS. PHELPS. Dave, is it really you?

DAVID. Guess it must be, Mother.

MRS. PHELPS. Dave, dear! [*She envelops as much of him as she can possibly reach.*]

DAVID. [*Prying loose.*] Well! Glad to see us, Mother?

MRS. PHELPS. Glad!

DAVID. You certainly seem to be glad. . . . But you haven't spoken to . . .

[CHRISTINA, *at his look, steps forward.*]

MRS. PHELPS. [Still not seeing her.] To think I wasn't here!

DAVID. We're ahead of time, you know. Christina . . .

MRS. PHELPS. I must have known somehow. Something just made me put down my cup and rush home. But you're not looking badly. You *are* well, aren't you? I do believe you've put on weight. You must be careful, though, not to take cold this weather. Was the crossing awfully rough? Were you seasick? You haven't been working too hard, have you, Dave boy?

CHRISTINA. [*Unable to stand on one foot any longer.*] He hasn't been working at all. Not for weeks!

MRS. PHELPS. [*She turns at the sound of the strange voice.*] Eh? Oh!

DAVID. I've been trying to make you take notice of Christina, Mother.

MRS. PHELPS. [*With the utmost warmth.*] Oh, my dear Christina, I *am* sorry! [*She kisses* CHRISTINA *on both cheeks.*] Seeing this big boy again quite took me off my feet. Let me look at *you*, now. Why, Dave, she's splendid. Perfectly splendid! I always knew Dave would choose only the best. Didn't I always say so, Dave, boy? [*Which takes her back to* DAVID.] Dave, you *have* been working too hard. I don't like those circles under your eyes.

DAVID. Nonsense, Mother!

CHRISTINA. I think he looks pretty well.

MRS. PHELPS. But only pretty well. I can't help worrying about these big boys of mine. [*Her emotion stops her. She turns gallantly to* ROBERT.] Did you skate, Rob?

ROBERT. As a matter of fact, I couldn't. They've been cutting ice on the pond and it's full of holes.

MRS. PHELPS. I must have signs put up tomorrow. Remember that, everybody. If any of you do go out in this freezing cold, don't take the short cut across the pond. . . . Dave, boy, this is too good to be true. After two whole years away and five, nearly six months married. [*The maid brings tea.*]

DAVID. Here's tea.

MRS. PHELPS. Sit down here beside me, dear, dear Christina. And, Dave, boy, sit over there where I can see you. Just take my furs, Delia, so I can do my duty in comfort. My boy, my boy, you don't know . . . you don't know how happy I am to have you home again! Just hand me my salts, will you, Robin? This excitement has laid me out. Christina, my, dear, how do you take your tea? [*She sits at the table.* ROBIN *has fetched her bottle of "Crown Lavender" from somewhere. She motions him to put it down and proceeds to pour tea.*]

CHRISTINA. Just tea, please. As it comes and nothing in it.

MRS. PHELPS. A real tea drinker! I hope my tea stands the test. [*She passes* CHRISTINA *her cup and ceases to take any notice of her whatsoever.*] Tea, Dave, boy?

DAVID. Please, Mother.

MRS. PHELPS. The same old way?

DAVID. Yes.

MRS. PHELPS. Tea, Robin? [*She hands* DAVID *his cup.*]

ROBERT. [*Busy passing sandwiches and such.*] As usual, please.

MRS. PHELPS. [*Very absent-minded about the salts.*] Who do you suppose was asking after you yesterday, Dave, boy? Old George, the doorman, down at the bank. You remember old George? He's so thrilled about your coming back! And Mrs. Donohue's so thrilled! Such a sweet woman! You know, I'm afraid he's drinking again. You must run right over early tomorrow morning and let her have a look at you. I must have some people in to meet you. Some very nice new people who've come here since you went away. Named Clay. He used to be a publisher in Boston, but he gave it up because he says nobody really cares about good books any more. Of course, this house has been a real godsend to him. I must give a big dinner for you, Dave, and ask all our old friends. I do need your cool head, too, on my business. Robin does his best, but he isn't really a business man. You remember the American Telephone I bought? Mr. Curtin, at the bank, advises me to sell and take my profit, but I don't think so. What do you think, Dave, boy?

HESTER. May I have a cup, please, Mrs. Phelps?

MRS. PHELPS. Hester, my dear, how forgetful of me! How will you have it?

HESTER. As usual.

MRS. PHELPS. Let me see, that's cream and sugar?

HESTER. Only cream. No sugar.

MRS. PHELPS. Of course. Robin, will you give Hester her tea?

ROBERT. [*As he gives* HESTER *the cup.*] You see, we have to take a back seat now.

MRS. PHELPS. A back seat, Robin?

ROBERT. I'm only warning Hester. She's got to know what to expect in this family when Dave's around.

DAVID. Oh, shut up, Rob!

MRS. PHELPS. [*Smiling.*] My two beaux! My two jealous beaux!

ROBERT. Oh, well! Dave's out in the great world now and I'm still the same old homebody I always was. Look at him, Mother!

MRS. PHELPS. [*Looking.*] Oh, my boy, my boy, if you knew what it means to see all my plans and hopes for you fulfilled. I've dreamed of your being an architect ever since . . . ever since . . .

ROBERT. Ever since he first showed an interest in his blocks.

MRS. PHELPS. I have those blocks still, Dave. Do you remember them?

DAVID. Do I remember those blocks!

MRS. PHELPS. [*Solemnly.*] You must never forget them, because it's quite true what Robin says and, some day, when you have children of your own, I shall show them the foundation stones of their father's great career. If I have one gift it's the ability to see what people have in them and to bring it out. I saw what David had in him, even then. And I brought it out. [*She smiles benignly. There is a brief pause. A quizzical frown contracts* CHRISTINA'S *brow.*]

CHRISTINA. It seems a risky business.

MRS. PHELPS. [*Turning with that same start which* CHRISTINA'S *voice caused before.*] What seems a risky business?

CHRISTINA. The way families have of doing that.

MRS. PHELPS. [*Setting her tea-cup down a little too deliberately.*] What could be more natural?

HESTER. [*Coming to* CHRISTINA'S *rescue from an abyss of boredom.*] I see what Christina means. From blocks to architecture *is* a long guess. You might very easily have guessed wrong, you know. I had some rabbits, once, and I loved 'em. Suppose my family had seen what I had in me, then, and brought me up to be a lion tamer?

MRS. PHELPS. [*Offended.*] Really, Hester!

HESTER. Isn't that just what happens to most of us? Christina's job doesn't sound like the kind parents usually pick out for a girl, though.

ROBERT. I'll say it doesn't.

CHRISTINA. My parents did pick it out, though. I'm just like the rest.

HESTER. Well, it only goes to prove what I was saying. Christina might have been a homebody instead of a scientist. I might have been a lion tamer. If only our parents hadn't had ideas about us!

DAVID. One guess is as good as another. I daresay I wanted to be a fireman. What do little girls want to be?

HESTER. Queens.

CHRISTINA. Wouldn't it be a pleasant world with nothing but queens and firemen in it!

ROBERT. I guess Mother knew. She always does know.

HESTER. What I say about children is this: Have 'em. Love 'em. And then leave 'em be.

CHRISTINA. [*Amused.*] I'm not sure that isn't a very profound remark.

MRS. PHELPS. [*She makes up her mind to investigate this daughter-in-law more closely and, with sudden briskness, takes back the conversation.*] Why don't you two great things take the bags upstairs out of the hall?

DAVID. That's an idea.

MRS. PHELPS. Dear Christina's in the little front room, and Dave, you're in the back in your old room.

DAVID. [*Surprised.*] I say, Mother . . . can't we . . .

HESTER. Don't they want to be together, Mrs. Phelps? Let me move out of the guest room and then . . .

MRS. PHELPS. Indeed, I'll do nothing of the sort. Hester's here for a rest and I won't upset her. Dave can be perfectly comfortable in his old room and so can Christina in front and it won't hurt them a bit.

CHRISTINA. Of course not. . . .

HESTER. But, Mrs. Phelps . . .

MRS. PHELPS. Not another word, my dear. [*To* CHRISTINA.] This child has danced herself into a decline and she's got to be taken care of.

DAVID. Right!

ROBERT. Come along, Dave.

MRS. PHELPS. Go and supervise, Hester, and leave me to . . . to visit with my new daughter.

[DAVE *and* ROB *go.* HESTER *following.*]

HESTER. [*As she goes.*] But really, David, I might just as well move. I didn't think. And if you and Christina . . .

MRS. PHELPS. [*A broad smile to* CHRISTINA.] Now, my dear, let me give you another cup of tea.

CHRISTINA. Thank you.

MRS. PHELPS. And take your hat off so

that I can really see you. I've never seen a lady scientist before.

CHRISTINA. I hope I'm not so very different from other women.

MRS. PHELPS. I've quite got over being afraid of you.

CHRISTINA. Afraid of me, Mrs. Phelps?

MRS. PHELPS. Can't you understand that? My big boy sends me a curt cable to say that he's marrying a charming and talented research geologist.

CHRISTINA. Biologist.

MRS. PHELPS. Biologist. It did sound just the least bit in the world improbable.

CHRISTINA. Yes. . . . I can see that.

MRS. PHELPS. Now that I know you, though, I'm very proud to have you for a daughter. Every woman wants a daughter, you know!

CHRISTINA. You're being very nice to me, Mrs. Phelps.

MRS. PHELPS. It isn't at all hard to be nice to you, my dear. Tell me about your tour. You went to Sicily?

CHRISTINA. We did, indeed.

MRS. PHELPS. Sicily, the home of . . . [*She gives herself up to Sicilian emotion*] . . . of all those great ancient . . . poets and . . . poets. To think of your taking my boy to Sicily where I'd always planned to take him! I've never been, you see. How many opportunities we miss! That's what we're always saying of dead people, isn't it? Though, of of course, I shouldn't think of calling David dead merely because he's got married. I do hope you read "Glorious Apollo" before you went to Venice. When I read it, I felt that I had made a new friend. I always make such close friends of my books and, you know, there's no friend like a really good book. And there's nothing like a good historical novel to make a city vivid and interesting. They do bring things back to one. "Glorious Apollo!" What a despicable character that man Byron was! Though I daresay he couldn't have been as bad as he was painted. People do exaggerate so. Especially writers. Do you know "The Little Flowers of St. Francis"?

CHRISTINA. I'm afraid not. Are they exaggerated?

MRS. PHELPS. Well, of course, they're really fairy tales. Only to one with a profoundly religious point of view . . . and, if there's one thing I pride myself on it *is* my profoundly religious point of view . . . I always keep the "Little Flowers" on the table beside my bed. And read *in* them, you know? I quite brought Robin up on them. Dave never took to them. Though Dave loved his regular fairy tales. His Grimm and his Hans Christian. You read, I hope?

CHRISTIAN. I can. I sometimes have to.

MRS. PHELPS. Oh, my dear, I only meant that I think it's so important, for David's happiness, that you should be what *I* call "a reader." Both my boys learned their classics at their mother's knee. Their Scott and their Thackeray. *And* their Dickens. Lighter things too, of course. "Treasure Island" and "Little Lord Fauntleroy." And you went to Prague, too. Dave wrote me from Prague. Such interesting letters, Dave writes! I wondered why you stayed so long in Prague.

CHRISTINA. It's a charming city, and an architect's paradise. Dave and I thought he ought to look at something besides cathedrals and temples. . . . There *is* domestic architecture, you know.

MRS. PHELPS. Yes. I suppose there is.

CHRISTINA. People *do* want houses. I'm inclined to think houses are more interesting than churches nowadays.

MRS. PHELPS. Oh, nowadays! I'm afraid I've very little use for nowadays. I've always thought it a pity that Dave and Rob couldn't have grown up in Italy in the Renaissance and known such men as . . . well, as Cellini.

CHRISTINA. I'm not sure Cellini would have been the ideal companion for a growing boy.

MRS. PHELPS. No? Well, perhaps not. I must certainly take in Prague my next trip abroad. It's really been very hard for me to stay home these last two years. But I said to myself: Dave must have his fling. I don't like mothers who keep their sons tied to their apron strings. I said: Dave will come home to me a complete man. Though I didn't actually look for his bringing you with him, my dear, and coming home a married man. Still . . . So I stayed home with Robin. And I was glad to. I'm not sure I haven't sometimes neglected Robin for David. Given myself too much to the one, not enough to the other. The first born, you know. We mothers are human, however much we may try not to be. Tell me, Christina, you think David *is* well, don't you?

CHRISTINA. Yes, perfectly.

MRS. PHELPS. He didn't seem quite himself just now.

CHRISTINA. Perhaps he was embarrassed.

MRS. PHELPS. With me? His own mother?

CHRISTINA. Wouldn't I have accounted for it?

MRS. PHELPS. How silly of me not to remember that! Tell me what your plans are—if you have any plans, which I hope you haven't, because I've been making so many for you and such perfect ones.

CHRISTINA. Well, as a matter of fact, we haven't many, but what we have are pretty definite.

MRS. PHELPS. Really! Are they really? What are they?

CHRISTINA. Well, we're going to live in New York, of course.

MRS. PHELPS. Why "New York, of course"? It seems to me that you might choose a pleasanter place to live than New York.

CHRISTINA. No doubt of that, Mrs. Phelps. But it does seem a good place for Dave to work and . . .

MRS. PHELPS. Oh, I can't agree with you!

CHRISTINA. I shouldn't have thought there could be two ways about New York for Dave any more than for me.

MRS. PHELPS. For you?

CHRISTINA. It's where my appointment is.

MRS. PHELPS. Your appointment?

CHRISTINA. At the Rockefeller Institute.

MRS. PHELPS. So that's what takes Dave and you to New York? Your geology.

CHRISTINA. Partly. Only it isn't geology. It's biology.

MRS. PHELPS. Of course. Geology's about rocks, isn't it?

CHRISTINA. Largely.

MRS. PHELPS. And biology?

CHRISTINA. Well—about Life.

MRS. PHELPS. [*Getting it clear.*] So you're a student of Life, my dear. I do wish David had called you that instead of the other.

CHRISTINA. I understand how you felt, Mrs. Phelps. I hope you don't hold my job against me.

MRS. PHELPS. [*With deep feeling.*] My dearest Christina, I don't! Oh, if you thought that, I should be heart-broken. You've made my darling David happy, my dear, and for that I'm prepared to love everything about you. Even your job. Do you smoke?

CHRISTINA. Yes, thank you. May I?

MRS. PHELPS. Please. And I shall, too. . . . [*They light cigarettes.*] Don't you like my lighter?

CHRISTINA. It's sweet. And very handy, I should think.

MRS. PHELPS. A friend sent it me from London. Let me give it to you.

CHRISTINA. Oh, no.

MRS. PHELPS. Please? I've not had a chance yet to give my new daughter anything. My dearest Christina . . . please?

CHRISTINA. Thank you. I shall always keep it and use it.

MRS. PHELPS. I like the little ceremonial gift. . . . Now, about your job . . .

CHRISTINA. My job?

MRS. PHELPS. As you call it. I don't like to say "profession" because that has such a sinister sound for a woman. And then science is hardly a profession, is it? Rather more of a hobby. You're planning to continue?

CHRISTINA. With my job? Oh, yes.

MRS. PHELPS. Just as though you hadn't married, I mean?

CHRISTINA. I have to, don't I? To earn my right to call myself a biologist . . .

MRS. PHELPS. Do people call you that?

CHRISTINA. I guess they call me "doctor."

MRS. PHELPS. You're *not* a doctor?

CHRISTINA. Technically, I am.

MRS. PHELPS. Oh, I can never agree with you that women make good doctors!

CHRISTINA. We shan't have to argue that point. I've no intention of practicing.

MRS. PHELPS. Not at all? Above all, not on David?

CHRISTINA. I shouldn't think of it.

MRS. PHELPS. I remember hearing that doctors never do practice on their own families. I remember that when our doctor here had a baby . . . of course, his wife had the baby . . . he called in quite an outsider to deliver the child. I remember how that struck me at the time. Tell me more about yourself, my dear. When Dave cabled me about meeting you and marrying you so suddenly . . .

CHRISTINA. It wasn't so sudden, Mrs. Phelps. I spent a good six or seven months turning him down flat.

MRS. PHELPS. [*Offended.*] Indeed?

CHRISTINA. Dave and I met in Rome last winter. Then he came to Heidelberg where I was working and I accepted him.

. . . I'd never given him the least encouragement before.

MRS. PHELPS. [*As before.*] Indeed?

CHRISTINA. We were married straight off . . . and went to Sicily.

MRS. PHELPS. I didn't know about the preliminaries. Dave never told me. And now you're taking him off to New York!

CHRISTINA. Please don't put it that way.

MRS. PHELPS. I'm stating a fact, my dear girl. After all, you *have* got your— [*She gets it right this time*]—biology to think of.

CHRISTINA. You can't blame me for that, dear Mrs. Phelps, so long as I think of Dave's work, too.

MRS. PHELPS. No. . . . So long as you do that. . . . How did you come to select your career?

CHRISTINA. My father was a doctor. I grew up in his hospital. Everything followed quite naturally.

MRS. PHELPS. Your father—is he living?

CHRISTINA. He died two years ago. Tragically, but rather splendidly.

MRS. PHELPS. How?

CHRISTINA. He'd been experimenting for years in infantile paralysis and . . .

MRS. PHELPS. And he died of that? [CHRISTINA *nods rather solemnly.*] Is your mother living?

CHRISTINA. Oh, yes; at home.

MRS. PHELPS. At home?

CHRISTINA. In Omaha.

MRS. PHELPS. [*Meditatively.*] Omaha . . .

CHRISTINA. Yes.

MRS. PHELPS. Hm . . . And you'll go on with your father's experiments?

CHRISTINA. Oh, no! That's not at all in my line.

MRS. PHELPS. What *is* your line?

CHRISTINA. It's hard to say. I did some rather hard work this last year at Heidelberg on the embryos of chickens. In the egg, you know.

MRS. PHELPS. For heaven's sake, what for?

CHRISTINA. Trying to find out something about what makes growth stop.

MRS. PHELPS. Why . . . ?

CHRISTINA. Curiosity, I guess. Now I'm admitting what low people we scientists are. I think that curiosity's all we have. And a little training.

MRS. PHELPS. Does David follow your work?

CHRISTINA. No. And I don't expect him to.

MRS. PHELPS. Quite right. David wouldn't be appealed to by rotten eggs. . . . Not that he couldn't understand them if they did appeal to him.

CHRISTINA. Of course.

MRS. PHELPS. Isn't the Rockefeller Institute one of those places where they practice vivisection?

CHRISTINA. One of many. Yes. . . .

MRS. PHELPS. Have you . . .

CHRISTINA. What?

MRS. PHELPS. Experimented on animals?

CHRISTINA. Isn't it a part of my job? Dave understands that. You must try to understand it.

MRS. PHELPS. Very well, I shall try, my dear. Now you must listen to me and try to understand me. . . . Look at me. What do you see? Simply—David's mother. I can't say of you that you're simply David's wife, because, clearly, you're many things beside that. But I am simply his mother. . . . I think, as I talk to you, that I belong to a dead age. I wonder if you think that? In my day, we considered a girl immensely courageous and independent who taught school or gave music lessons. Nowadays, girls sell real estate and become scientists and think nothing of it. Give us our due, Christina. We weren't entirely bustles and smelling salts, we girls who did not go into the world. We made a great profession which I fear may be in some danger of vanishing from the face of the earth. We made a profession of motherhood. That may sound old-fashioned to you. Believe me, it had its value. I was trained to be a wife that I might become a mother. [CHRISTINA *is about to protest.* MRS. PHELPS *stops her.*] Your father died of his investigations of a dangerous disease. You called that splendid of him, didn't you? Would you say less of us who gave our lives to being mothers? Mothers of sons, particularly. Listen to me, Christina. David was five, Rob only a little baby, when my husband died. I'd been married six years, not so very happily. I was pretty, as a girl, too. Very pretty. [*This thought holds her for a second.*] For twenty-four years, since my husband died, I've given all my life, all my strength to Dave and Rob. They've been my life and my job. They've taken the place of husband and friends both, for me. Where do I stand, now? Rob is marrying. Dave is married already. This is the end of my life and my job. . . . Oh, I'm not asking for credit or praise. I'm asking for something more substantial. I'm asking you, my dear, dear Christina, not to take all my boy's heart. Leave me, I beg you, a little, little part of it. I've earned that much. I'm not sure I couldn't say that you owe me that much —as David's mother. I believe I've deserved it. Don't you think I have?

CHRISTINA. [*Deeply moved.*] My dear, dear Mrs. Phelps!

MRS. PHELPS. It's agreed then, isn't it, that I'm not to be shut out?

CHRISTINA. Of course you're not!

MRS. PHELPS. Not by you, Christina. Nor by your work?

CHRISTINA. No! No!

MRS. PHELPS. Nor by anything?

CHRISTINA. You must know that I should never come between a mother and her son. You must know that I appreciate what you've done for Dave and all you've always been and meant to him. You *must* know that!

MRS. PHELPS. Christina, my dear, you're a very disarming person. You are indeed. I've known you ten minutes and unloaded my whole heart to you.

CHRISTINA. I'm proud that you trust me.

MRS. PHELPS. [*Patting her hand.*] Thank you, my dear. And now . . . now that you know how I feel . . . now you won't go to New York, will you? You won't take Dave to New York?

CHRISTINA. [*Drawing back in alarm.*] But, Mrs. Phelps!

MRS. PHELPS. Because that *would* be coming between mother and son as you just now said. That could mean only one thing—crowding me out, setting me aside, robbing me. . . .

CHRISTINA. [*Completely baffled.*] You're quite mistaken, Mrs. Phelps! You've no reason to think any such thing!

MRS. PHELPS. Well, it's nice of you to reassure me, and we don't have to worry about it for some time yet. You'll have plenty of time to see how carefully I've worked everything out for David—and for you, too, my dear. You've a nice, long visit ahead and . . .

CHRISTINA. I only wish we *had* a nice long visit, Mrs. Phelps.

MRS. PHELPS. What do you mean?

CHRISTINA. I start work at the Institute a week from tomorrow.

MRS. PHELPS. [*Staggered.*] What *are* you saying, child?

CHRISTINA. We didn't even bring our trunks up, you know.

MRS. PHELPS. [*Recovering herself.*] I'll not hear of it! A week of David after two years without him? What *are* you thinking of? Don't you realize that David has practically been my sole companion for nearly twenty-five years?

CHRISTINA. You've had Robert, too.

MRS. PHELPS. I'm not thinking so much of Robert, now. He isn't threatened as David is.

CHRISTINA. Threatened, Mrs. Phelps?

MRS. PHELPS. I don't want to see David's career sacrificed.

CHRISTINA. But, I'm not planning to sacrifice it.

MRS. PHELPS. You make the word sound disagreeable. I admire your work, Christina, but I am very clearly of the impression that it may easily obliterate David's work.

CHRISTINA. I don't see any conflict.

MRS. PHELPS. Aren't you taking him to New York, which he simply loathes? To live in a stuffy tenement . . . well, an apartment. . . . They're the same thing. . . . Without proper heat or sunshine or food? I told you I'd made plans. I've arranged everything for David's best interest. I can't believe that a girl of your intelligence won't realize how good my arrangements are. I happen to own a very large tract of land here. A very beautiful tract, most desirable for residences. To the north of the Country Club just beside the links. Hilly and wooded. You can see it, off there to the left of the pond. I've had many offers for it, most advantageous offers. But I've held on to it, ever since Dave chose his profession. Pleasant Valley, it's called. I shall change the name to Phelps Manor and open it. David will have charge. David will lay out the streets, design the gateways, build the houses and make his fortune, his reputation and his place in the world out of it.

CHRISTINA. [*Pause, then.*] Don't you mean his place in this part of the world, Mrs. Phelps?

MRS. PHELPS. [*Positively.*] As well this as any. With me to back him, he's certain of a proper start here, and there can't be any doubt about the outcome. His success is assured here and his happiness and prosperity with it. And yours, too. Don't you see that?

CHRISTINA. It certainly sounds safe enough.

MRS. PHELPS. I knew you'd see. Furthermore, he's never happy in New York.

CHRISTINA. Happiness is very important. Only different people have different ideas of it.

MRS. PHELPS. David's always had my ideas. And they're very sound ones.

CHRISTINA. [*Politely.*] I'm sure of it. But perhaps they aren't sound for David. I mean, from what I know of him. . . .

MRS. PHELPS. I'm David's mother, my dear. I know him better than you do.

CHRISTINA. I wonder!

MRS. PHELPS. Oh, I do! And I know how little New York has to offer. I know the competition there. I know what the struggle would be. Look at the choice. On the one hand obscurity, a desk in some other man's office, years of hack work and discouragement. On the other, immediate prominence, unquestionable success . . .

CHRISTINA. With his mother behind him.

MRS. PHELPS. Who better?

CHRISTINA. Oh, I see the difference!

MRS. PHELPS. Yes, don't you! And as to your work, my dear, I'm sure we can keep you busy and contented.

CHRISTINA. [*Smiling in spite of herself.*] How will you do that?

MRS. PHELPS. Well, it's hard to say, offhand. But if we really set our minds to it. . . . I know! I'm the chairman of our hospital here, and I have a great deal of influence with the doctors. We've a beautiful laboratory. You couldn't ask for anything nicer or cleaner or more comfortable than that laboratory. You do your work in a laboratory, I suppose?

CHRISTINA. Usually.

MRS. PHELPS. I'll take you down in the morning and introduce you to Dr. McClintock, homeopathic, but very agreeable, and he'll show you our laboratory. We've just got in a new microscope, too. Oh, a very fine one! One the High School didn't want any more. You'll simply love our laboratory. Oh, you will! It has a splendid new sink with hot and cold running water and quite a good gas stove because it's also the nurses' washroom and diet kitchen. And you'll be allowed to putter around as much as you like whenever it isn't in use by the nurses or the real doctors. I can arrange everything perfectly, my dear. I'm certain that, when you see our laboratory, you'll sit right down and write to Mr. Rockerfeller, who, I'm told, is a very kind old man at heart, and won't misunderstand in the least, that you've found an opening here that's ever so much more desirable than his old Institute, where you won't be obliged to cut up cats and dogs. You will think it over, won't you? Going to New York, I mean. Taking Dave to New York and ruining all his prospects?

CHRISTINA. [*After a pause, in all sincere kindliness.*] Mrs. Phelps, the third time I refused Dave, he asked me for a reason. I told him I couldn't throw myself away on a big frog in a small puddle.

MRS. PHELPS. You don't mean that you want him to be a small frog, a mere polliwog, in a great ocean like New York?

CHRISTINA. I'm afraid that's just what I do mean. And when he came back at me three months later with some real sketches and a great deal more humility and with a real job in a real architect's office . . .

MRS. PHELPS. Has David a job? In New York?

CHRISTINA. A chance anyway. With Michaels.

MRS. PHELPS. Michaels?

CHRISTINA. He's a big man. And he's interested in Dave.

MRS. PHELPS. I don't approve at all. I think it's madness.

CHRISTINA. You may be right. But, isn't it best left to Dave and me?

MRS. PHELPS. [*Deeply hurt at the implication.*] My dear Christina, if you think I'm trying to interfere, you're quite mistaken. You're very unfair. . . . Only tell me what makes you so sure Dave can succeed in New York.

CHRISTINA. I haven't given a thought to whether he'll succeed or not. That depends on his own talent, doesn't it? As to how much he makes, or how we get on, at first, I don't think that matters either . . . so long as Dave stands really on his own feet.

MRS. PHELPS. Oh, Christina, be honest with yourself. You *are* sacrificing David!

CHRISTINA. How?

MRS. PHELPS. By thinking only of yourself, of course.

CHRISTINA. Won't you believe that I'm thinking of both of us?

MRS. PHELPS. How can I? It's too bad of you, really. It means—[*In despair.*]—It means that it's all been for nothing!

CHRISTINA. What has?

MRS. PHELPS. [*Crescendo, as she walks about.*] All, all that I've done for David and given up for him and meant to him!

CHRISTINA. How can you say that?

MRS. PHELPS. I did so want to be friendly with David's wife. If you knew how I've wished and dreamt and prayed for that!

CHRISTINA. [*Rising herself.*] But can't we be friends?

MRS. PHELPS. Some day you'll have a child of your own and then you may know what I mean, if . . .

CHRISTINA. If what?

MRS. PHILPS. [*The last volley.*] If you don't sacrifice your child, too, to this work of yours.

CHRISTINA. [*Deeply distressed.*] Mrs. Phelps, I wish you wouldn't feel that. It makes me feel that I've got off on a very wrong foot here.

[ROBERT *enters.*]

ROBERT. Christina!

CHRISTINA. Yes?

ROBERT. Dave says, if you want a bath before dinner, you'd better be quick about it.

CHRISTINA. I didn't know it was so late. Thanks. [*She goes to* MRS. PHELPS.] You'll see that I do understand, dear Mrs. Phelps. You'll see that it all comes straight somehow and turns out for the best. Life takes care of such things. All we have to do is to keep out of life's way and make the best of things as *healthily* as possible.

MRS. PHELPS. You think I'm selfish.

CHRISTINA. Oh, no! I don't think anything of the sort!

MRS. PHELPS. Because if there's one thing I pride myself on, I may have many faults, but I am not selfish. I haven't a selfish hair in my head.

CHRISTINA. I tell you, I understand.

[*She kisses her quickly and goes out.*]

ROBERT. [*Looking curiously after* CHRISTINA.] Mother!

MRS. PHELPS. [*Wildly.*] Oh, Robin! I'm so lonely! So lonely!

ROBERT. [*Startled.*] Mother!

MRS. PHELPS. I'm afraid I'm a dreadful coward!

ROBERT. *You,* Mother?

MRS. PHELPS. I ought to have been prepared to lose my two great, splendid sons. I've told myself over and over again that the time would come, and now that it *has* come, I can't face it! She's taking Dave away to New York, away from me, away from all the wonderful plans I've made for him here!

ROBERT. Well, if Dave's fool enough to go!

MRS. PHELPS. I shouldn't do to any woman on earth what she's doing to me!

ROBERT. Of course you wouldn't. But then, Christina isn't your sort, is she?

MRS. PHELPS. You've noticed that, too?

ROBERT. Who *is* your sort, Mother? . . . Oh, it's a wonderful gift you've given us.

MRS. PHELPS. What's that, Robin?

ROBERT. A wonderful ideal of womanhood. You know what I mean.

MRS. PHELPS. No. What?

ROBERT. Your own marvellous self, Mother!

MRS. PHELPS. Dave didn't stop to think of any such ideal, did he?

ROBERT. Oh, Dave!

MRS. PHELPS. Perhaps I shouldn't be hurt. But you can't know what it is to be a mother. I nearly died when Dave was born. Hours and hours I suffered for him, trapped in agony. He was a twelve-pound baby, you know. If I could be sure of his happiness!

ROBERT. You mustn't ask too much.

MRS. PHELPS. You're right. No mother should expect any woman to love her son as she loves him.

ROBERT. Your sons don't expect any woman to love them as you do.

MRS. PHELPS. Oh, Robin! Is that how you feel?

ROBERT. I think it must be. [*She looks at him, watching him think it all out.*] It's a funny business, isn't it? After a woman like you has suffered the tortures of the damned bringing us into the world, and worked like a slave to help us grow up in it, we can't wait to cut loose and give up the one thing we can be sure of! And for what? To run every known risk of disillusion and disappointment.

MRS. PHELPS. [*Struck by this.*] What *is* the one thing you can be sure of, Robin?

ROBERT. You are. Don't you know that? Why can't we leave well enough alone?

MRS. PHELPS. Presently you'll be going too, Rob.

ROBERT. Yes . . . I know I shall. . . . But nothing will ever come between us, Mother.

MRS. PHELPS. Come over here by the fire, Robin, and let's forget all these unpleasant things. [*She goes to sit by the fire.*] Let's have a real old-time talk about nothing at all. Sit down. [*He sits as directed on a stool at her feet.*] Head in my lap! [*He obeys.*] So! This has shown me something I've always suspected. That you are *my* son. David takes after his father.

ROBERT. Mother!

MRS. PHELPS. Tell me, Robin, what you meant just now when you said that about the one thing you can be sure of. Did you mean that you've had dark thoughts about *your* future?

ROBERT. I must have meant something of the sort.

MRS. PHELPS. Hm. . . . It was dear of you, my great Robin, to say what you did about my being your ideal. You know my dream has always been to see my two boys married and settled down. But happily! Happily! Has Hester come to any decision about where she wants to spend her honeymoon?

ROBERT. Abroad.

MRS. PHELPS. Nothing more definite than just "abroad"?

ROBERT. No. She doesn't care where we go.

MRS. PHELPS. That seems very odd to me. I took such an interest in my honeymoon. Why, your father and I had every day of it planned, weeks before we were married. . . . Hester hasn't picked out her flat silver yet, either, has she?

ROBERT. I don't think so.

MRS. PHELPS. I can't understand it!

ROBERT. What?

MRS. PHELPS. Her indifference. It rather shocks me. [*She notices that* ROBERT *is shocked, too.*] But I suppose I'm old-fashioned. Like this room. You must give me a little of your time and taste, Robin, before you're married, and advise me about doing this room over.

ROBERT. [*Eagerly.*] Have you come to that at last?

MRS. PHELPS. I'm afraid so. How's Hester planning to do your new home?

ROBERT. [*His spirits subsiding at once.*] Oh, I don't know.

MRS. PHELPS. You don't mean to say she hasn't made *any* plans?

ROBERT. I've been trying to get her interested in house-hunting.

MRS. PHELPS. And she doesn't care about that either?

ROBERT. She says anything will suit her.

MRS. PHELPS. Does she, indeed! Most girls . . . most *normal* girls, that is, look forward so to having their homes to receive their friends in.

ROBERT. She leaves it all to me. She says I know much more about such things than she does.

MRS. PHELPS. How little she understands my poor Robin who ought never to be bothered!

ROBERT. Oh, well!

MRS. PHELPS. Do you happen to know if Hester *has* many friends? I mean, many men friends? Did she have lots of suitors beside you?

ROBERT. I daresay she had loads.

MRS. PHELPS. Do you *know* that she had?

ROBERT. She never told me so. Why?

MRS. PHELPS. I was wondering. She's been out two years. One does wonder how much a girl has been sought after. But, then, why should she have bothered with others when she thought she could land you? You are rather a catch, you know.

ROBERT. I, Mother?

MRS. PHELPS. Any girl would set her cap for you.

ROBERT. I don't believe Hester did that.

MRS. PHELPS. My dear, I wasn't saying that she did! But why shouldn't she? Only . . .

ROBERT. Only what?

MRS. PHELPS. I can't help wondering if Hester's feeling for you is as strong as you think it is. [ROBERT *wonders, too.*] I've been wondering for some time, Robin. I've hesitated to speak to you about it. But after what you've just told me . . .

ROBERT. Well, it's too late to worry now.

MRS. PHELPS. I can't help worrying, though. Marriage is such an important step and you're such a sensitive, shrinking character. It would be too terrible if you had to go through what you were just speaking of—the disillusionment and disappointment. . . . I'm only trying to find out what it is that's come between you two young people.

ROBERT. Nothing has, Mother. Hester isn't you, that's all!

MRS. PHELPS. Nonsense, Robin! . . . It isn't that awful woman I was so worried about when you were at Harvard?

ROBERT. I'm not raising a second crop of wild oats.

MRS. PHELPS. Then it *must* be that risk you were speaking of! Oh, why do boys run that risk! Why will they break away!

ROBERT. I wish I knew!

MRS. PHELPS. Perhaps your trouble is that—[*A pause. Then, very low*]—that you don't love Hester.

ROBERT. Oh, love! I must love her or I wouldn't have asked her to marry me. I guess she loves me in her way. Is her way enough? I'll find that out in time. A man ought to marry.

MRS. PHELPS. [*A little more positively.*] You *don't* love Hester, and it isn't fair to her!

ROBERT. Yes, I do love her! Only I wonder if I'm the marrying kind. Failing the possibility of marrying you. I mean your double.

MRS. PHELPS. [*Always increasing in intensity.*] You don't love Hester.

ROBERT. I do, I tell you! Who could help loving her? I mean . . . Good God, what do I mean?

MRS. PHELPS. Either you don't love Hester or Hester doesn't love you.

ROBERT. She does love me.

MRS. PHELPS. She may say she does, but I haven't seen her showing it.

ROBERT. Mother!

MRS. PHELPS. You don't love Hester and Hester doesn't love you. It's as simple as that, Robin, and you're making a very grave mistake to go on with this. These things may be painful, but they're better faced before than after. Children come after, Robin, and then it's too late! Think, Robin! Think before it's too late! And remember, the happiness of three people is at stake!

ROBERT. Hester's and mine and . . .

MRS. PHELPS. And mine! And mine! . . . Only, I was wrong to say that! You must put my fate out of your mind just as Dave has done. Let Dave find out for himself what he's done. She won't be able to hold him. She won't have time for a home and children. She won't take any more interest in him than Hester takes in you. But you, Robin, *you* can still be saved. I want to save you from throwing yourself away as Dave has. You will face the facts, won't you?

ROBERT. You mean . . . I'm to . . . to break with Hester?

MRS. PHELPS. You will be a man?

ROBERT. [*Pause, then.*] Well . . . I'll . . . I'll try, Mother.

MRS. PHELPS. [*Pause, then*] When?

ROBERT. Well . . . the . . . the first chance I get.

MRS. PHELPS. [*Trying not to appear eager.*] Tonight? . . . You'll have your chance tonight, Robin. I'll see that you get it. Promise me to take it?

ROBERT. [*Pause.*] All right. . . . If you think I'd better. . . . All right. . . .

MRS. PHELPS. Oh, thank God for this confidence between us! Thank God I've saved my boy one more tumble! You'll see it won't be so bad to put up with your mother a little longer! You'll see I've still plenty to give you and to do for you!

ROBERT. My blessed, blessed mother!

MRS. PHELPS. [*Unable to repress her triumph.*] And I won't have to be lonely now! I won't have to be lonely!

ROBERT. No, Mother! No!

[*He takes her in his arms.*]

MRS. PHELPS. Kiss me.

[*He does; on the lips, fervently.* DAVID *comes in, dressed for dinner.*]

DAVID. Hello! That's a pretty picture! . . . Chris'll be down in a minute.

ROBERT. Where's Hester?

DAVID. In Chris's room. I heard them giggling in there. Isn't it grand they've hit it off so well?

ROBERT. [*Meeting his mother's eyes.*] Isn't it? I'll make a cocktail.

[*He goes.*]

DAVID. You like Christina, don't you, Mother?

MRS. PHELPS. Didn't you know I should?

DAVID. Sure I did! After all, I couldn't have gone far wrong on a wife, could I? I mean, having you for a mother would make most girls look pretty cheesey. I waited a long time. And all the time I was waiting for Chris! You'll see how wonderful Chris is. Why, she gets better every day. I don't know how I ever pulled it off. I swear I don't. I certainly had luck.

MRS. PHELPS. You're happy?

DAVID. You bet I'm happy!

MRS. PHELPS. You're not going to let

your happiness crowd me out entirely, are you, Dave boy?

DAVID. [*Amiably irritated.*] Oh, Mother! Lay off!

[ROBERT *returns with shaker and cocktail glasses.*]

ROBERT. This is just a preliminary, Mother. We both need it, before we dress.

MRS. PHELPS. Perhaps we do.

DAVID. Shan't we call Chris and Hester?

MRS. PHELPS. No! Just we three!

ROBERT. It'll never be we three any more. I heard them coming as I crossed the hall.

[*He pours the cocktail into the glasses and goes about passing them.*]

MRS. PHELPS. My two boys! My big one and my little one!

DAVID. [*Calls out.*] Hurry up, Chris!

MRS. PHELPS. If I can keep the little corner Christina doesn't need, Dave . . . that's all I ask. . . .

DAVID. Don't you worry, Mother. [CHRISTINA *and* HESTER *enter. They are both dressed appropriately for the evening.* CHRISTINA *is particularly lovely.*] Here we are!

CHRISTINA. Thank you, Robert.

[*They sip their cocktails.*]

DAVID. Chris!

CHRISTINA. Yes?

DAVID. Let's tell Mother.

CHRISTINA. Now? In front of everybody?

DAVID. It won't hurt 'em to hear.

CHRISTINA. I don't mind, if they don't.

ROBERT. Mind what?

DAVID. It'll make Mother so happy.

MRS. PHELPS. What will?

DAVID. A surprise Chris and I have got to spring on you!

MRS. PHELPS. How nice! What is it?

CHRISTINA. [*A smiling pause—then.*] In about four months I'm going to have a baby.

HESTER. Oh, Christina, how wonderful!

ROBERT. Are you really!

DAVID. Isn't that a grand surprise, Mother?

MRS. PHELPS. [*Recovering as from a body blow.*] Of course . . . David. I'm very glad, my dear. Very glad. . . . Have you a napkin there, Robin? I've spilled my cocktail all over my dress.

CURTAIN

ACT SECOND

THE FIRST SCENE

The living-room again. It is the same evening, after supper. The lamps are lighted. MRS. PHELPS, HESTER, CHRISTINA, DAVID *and* ROB *are all present.* CHRISTINA, HESTER *and* DAVID *are dressed as we saw them at the end of the first act.* ROB *wears his dinner coat and his mother has changed to a simple evening dress. They have only just finished their coffee and* MRS. PHELPS *is busily showing a collection of photographs which she has in a great Indian basket beside her chair.*

CHRISTINA. What were you doing in the sailor suit, Dave?

DAVID. Dancing the hornpipe, I believe.

MRS. PHELPS. [*Fondly.*] That was at Miss Briggs's dancing school. Do you remember Miss Briggs, David?

DAVID. Do I! The hornpipe must have been something special, Mother.

MRS. PHELPS. I see that I've marked it "Masonic Temple, April 6th, 1904."

DAVID. It must have been special. They don't usually dance hornpipes in Masonic Temples.

CHRISTINA. Did Miss Briggs teach you to be graceful, Dave?

DAVID. She did indeed. As a boy I was a gazelle. But I got over it.

CHRISTINA. I'm just as glad. I've known one or two adult gazelles.

MRS. PHELPS. Both David and Robin danced beautifully.

DAVID. I haven't thought of Miss Briggs for years. I remember her so well. She seemed so old to me. She must have been old, too. A good deal older than God. She looked it, in spite of her red hair and her castanets. Spain, she used to say, is the land of the dance.

MRS. PHELPS. She had all the nicest children.

DAVID. Castanets and Spanish shawls . . . *and* a police whistle. She blew the whistle at the boys for running and sliding. God knows what dances she taught us. Very different from the steps you indulge in, Hester, with your low modern tastes.

HESTER. Running and sliding sounds very pleasant.

DAVID. We thought that up for ourselves.

MRS. PHELPS. How long ago that all seems! [*She shows another photograph*]. This is David when he was ten weeks old.

CHRISTINA. Oh, David!

HESTER. Let me see. [CHRISTINA *shows her.*] What a darling baby! Did they always sit them in shells in those days?

MRS. PHELPS. [*Just a little coldly.*] It was a fashion like any other.

CHRISTINA. David on the half shell!

HESTER. Have you ever noticed how much all babies look like Chief Justice Taft?

MRS. PHELPS. [*She takes the photographs back in ill-concealed irritation.*] David was a beautiful child.

DAVID. I didn't always sit in shells. Mother's got one of me on a white fur rug.

MRS. PHELPS. It hangs over my bed to this day.

CHRISTINA. In the nude?

DAVID. No. In an undershirt.

[HESTER *giggles.*]

MRS. PHELPS. Fashions change.

CHRISTINA. I suppose they must. David wouldn't think of being photographed in his undershirt, now. Let me see the picture again, Mrs. Phelps.

MRS. PHELPS. I think that's enough for this evening.

[*She rises, in great dignity, to put the photographs aside.*]

CHRISTINA. Dear Mrs. Phelps, please don't be angry. We were only teasing David. They're awfully interesting pictures.

MRS. PHELPS. Only interesting to me, I'm afraid.

CHRISTINA. Not at all. I loved them. Do show me some more, Mrs. Phelps. Are there many more?

MRS. PHELPS. [*Still stern about them.*] Dave and Robin were photographed twice every month until they were twelve years old.

HESTER. [*Calculating rapidly.*] Good Lord! That makes over two hundred and fifty of each!

MRS. PHELPS. I never counted. I used to study their photographs, month by month, just as I did their weight. I wasn't satisfied to watch only their bodies grow. I wanted a record of the development of their little minds and souls as well. I could compare the expression of Dave's eyes, for instance, at nine, with their expression at eight and a half, and see the increased depth. And I was never disappointed.

HESTER. I knew a mother once who called her son "her beautiful black swan."

MRS. PHELPS. I should never have called either of my sons by such a name!

ROBERT. I can remember when you used to call us your Arab steeds!

MRS. PHELPS. [*Furious.*] Only in fun. Will you put them away, Robin?

[ROBERT *takes the photographs.*]

ROBERT. Sure you don't want to go through the rest, Mother?

MRS. PHELPS. I'm afraid of boring Christina. Christina has other interests, of course. Higher interests than her husband. Higher even than children, I suspect.

[*There is an abashed, awful pause, at this.* CHRISTINA *looks hurt and baffled.* HESTER *is horrified.* DAVID, *puzzled, rises and goes to the window.* ROBERT *smiles to himself as he stows the photographs away.*]

HESTER. [*Breaking out.*] Well, of all the . . .

[CHRISTINA, *catching her eye, stops her.*]

MRS. PHELPS. [*Polite, but dangerous.*] What was it you were about to say, Hester?

HESTER. [*Recovering herself none too expertly.*] I was just looking at Christina's dress. I was just going to say: "Well, of all the lovely dresses I ever saw, that's the loveliest."

CHRISTINA. It *is* nice, isn't it? I got it in Paris. From Poiret. Dave made me.

MRS. PHELPS. [*As she studies the dress.*] I've a little woman right here in town who does well enough for me. I know who that dress *would* look well on! Dave, you remember Clara Judd? Such an exquisite figure, Clara had, and such distinction! That dress *wants* distinction and a figure. You might wear it, too, Hester.

[*There is another painful pause.* CHRISTINA *is really crushed.*]

DAVID. [*Desperately snatching for a change of subject.*] Look, Chris! The moon's up. You can see the kids coasting down the long hill.

CHRISTINA. [*Joining him at the window gratefully.*] If I weren't all dressed up, I'd join them!

HESTER. Don't you love coasting?

CHRISTINA. [*She nods.*] Once last winter we had a big snowfall at Heidelberg. I'd been all day in the laboratory, I remember, straining my eyes out at a scarlet fever culture for our bacteriology man. Krauss, his name was. They called him "The Demon of the Neckar." The theory was that he used to walk along the river bank, thinking up cruel things to say to his students. I never knew such a terrifying man. . . . Well, this day I'm talking about, I came out of Krauss's laboratory into the snow. Into Grimm's fairy tales, as Dave knows, because Dave's seen Heidelberg. Another bacteriologist, a dear boy from Marburg, came with me. We looked at the snow and we wanted to coast. . . . We found a small boy with a very large sled and we rented it, *with* the boy, who wouldn't trust us not to steal it. We certainly coasted. We got so ardent, we took the funicular up the Schlossberg and coasted down from there. The lights came out along the Neckar and the snow turned the colors and colors snow *can* turn and still we coasted. . . . Presently, we had an accident. A bob turned over in front of us with an old man on it. We couldn't stop and so we just hit the bob and the old man and you know how that is when you're going fast! . . . We picked ourselves up—or, rather, dug ourselves out—and went to see if we'd hurt the old fellow and, God save us, it was Krauss himself! . . . I don't mind telling you our hearts sank. We stood there petrified. But we needn't have worried. Krauss didn't mind. He smiled the sweetest smile—you'd *never* have suspected he had it in him!—and touched his cap like a little boy and apologized for his clumsiness. "My age hasn't improved my skill," he said. . . . I could have kissed him. I wasn't quite sure how he'd have taken that, so, instead, I asked him to join us. He was delighted. We kept it up for another hour, we two students and the great god Krauss. *"Jugend ist Trunkenheit ohne Wein!"* he said. I daresay he was quoting a poem. . . . He couldn't have been a day under seventy. Three months later, he died of an inoperable internal tumor. In his notes, they found an observation he had written on his condition that very day we coasted. Think of a man who could write observations on his approaching death and then go off to coast afterwards! It's what life can be and should be. It's the difference between life and self.

MRS. PHELPS. Hm! . . .

HESTER. I think that's the most marvellous story I've heard!

ROBERT. Isn't it marvellous?

HESTER. I wish I'd known such a man!

CHRISTINA. Do you remember the night *we* coasted in Heidelberg, Dave?

DAVID. Do I? [*To his mother.*] Chris means the night she accepted me!

MRS. PHELPS. Does she really?

DAVID. [*Dashed and giving it up.*] Yeah. . . . Let's go outside and watch the kids, Chris. It'll do us good.

CHRISTINA. [*Seeing his point.*] Right! I'd love to!

[*They go.*]

MRS. PHELPS. I'm beginning to wonder if Christina's studies at Heidelberg haven't made her just the least little bit in the world pro-German.

HESTER. Mrs. Phelps, how *can* you say such a thing! [HESTER *looks from* ROBERT *to his mother in amazement.* MRS. PHELPS *sits down at the piano and begins to play the easier portions of one of Chopin's nocturnes.*] I think that was simply inspiring!

MRS. PHELPS. I can't play Chopin if you interrupt me, Hester.

HESTER. I'm sorry. I simply can't get Christina out of my mind.

MRS. PHELPS. What do you mean?

HESTER. I mean that I think she's the most perfect person I've ever seen.

MRS. PHELPS. Do you really? Which way did they go, Robin?

ROBERT. [*At the window.*] Down the front.

MRS. PHELPS. Can you see them?

ROBERT. They're just standing in the road. Now they're moving down under the trees.

MRS. PHELPS. But they can't even *see* the long hill from the trees.

ROBERT. They're not looking at the long hill.

MRS. PHELPS. What *are* they looking at?

ROBERT. Each other. It's quite a romantic picture. Now she's put her head on his shoulder. His arm is around her waist. . . .

MRS. PHELPS. Faugh! Call them in!

[*Her irritation produces a discord in the nocturne.* ROBERT *moves to go.*]

HESTER. Oh, don't, Rob! It's the first chance they've had to be alone together.

MRS. PHELPS. They can be alone without David's catching pneumonia, can't they? She drags him out of doors at night in freezing weather to spoon in the road like a couple of mill hands! I should think she might have some consideration for her husband's health, let alone for my feelings.

HESTER. [*A little hotly.*] In the first place, it was David who dragged *her* out. In the second, they *are* in love and *do* want to be alone. In the third, I don't see any reason for worrying over the health of any man who looks as husky as David does. And in the fourth, if there *is* any worrying to be done, let me remind you that it's Christina and *not* David who is going to have a baby. [MRS. PHELPS *breaks off her playing in the middle of a phrase.*] I'm sorry if I've shocked you, but the truth is, you've both shocked me.

ROBERT. How have we shocked you?

HESTER. By not being a great deal more thrilled over Christina's baby. When I drank my cocktail to it before dinner, neither of you drank yours. When I wanted to talk about it during dinner, you both changed the subject. You haven't mentioned that baby since dinner, except once, and that was catty! You've known about that baby for over two hours and you aren't excited about it yet! Not what *I* call excited.

MRS. PHELPS. If you'll forgive my saying so, Hester, I'm not sure that an unborn baby is quite the most suitable subject for . . .

HESTER. I'm blessed if I see anything bad form about a baby!

ROBERT. No more does Mother—after it's born.

HESTER. I can't wait for that. I *love* thinking about them. And wondering what they're going to be—I mean, boy or girl. Why, we had bets up on my sister's baby for months before he was born.

MRS. PHELPS. I'm not ashamed to be old-fashioned.

HESTER. You ought to be. This is going to be a very remarkable baby. There aren't many born with such parents. And I intend to go right on talking about it with anyone who'll listen to me. Christina doesn't mind. She's just as interested as I am. I've already made her promise to have my sister's obstetrician.

MRS. PHELPS. Really, Hester!

HESTER. I'd go to the ends of the earth for that man. Christina's baby has put me in a very maternal frame of mind.

MRS. PHELPS. Maternal!

HESTER. What I say is: I'm as good as married. I might as well make the best of my opportunities to get used to the idea. Because I intend to have as many babies as possible.

MRS. PHELPS. [*Glancing at* ROBERT.] Is that why you're marrying Rob, Hester?

HESTER. What better reason could I have? I'm sorry if I've shocked you, but, as I said before, you've shocked me and that's that.

[*Coolly,* MRS. PHELPS *goes for the coffee tray. Her eyes meet* ROBERT'S *and there is no mistaking the intention of the look they give him. Then, without a word, she leaves* ROBERT *and* HESTER *alone together.*]

ROBERT. [*Starting after her.*] Mother! . . . Hester didn't mean. . . . Oh. . . . [*He turns back to* HESTER.] Hester, how could you?

HESTER. I don't know. . . . But I don't care if I did!

ROBERT. It doesn't make things any easier for me.

HESTER. Oh, Rob, dear, I *am* sorry!

ROBERT. You've got Mother all ruffled and upset. Now we'll have to smooth her down and have all kinds of explanations and everything. Really, it was too bad of you.

HESTER. I know. I lost my temper. . . . You understand, don't you?

ROBERT. I understand that you're a guest in Mother's house.

HESTER. Is that *all* you understand? Oh, Rob!

ROBERT. I'm sorry, Hester. But, for the moment, I'm thinking of Mother.

HESTER. I see. . . . I'll apologize.

ROBERT. That's up to you.

HESTER. I suppose she'll never forgive me. It isn't this, though.

ROBERT. This?

HESTER. The scene I made.

ROBERT. What do you mean?

HESTER. I don't know. . . . Some mothers like the girls their sons marry.

ROBERT. Doesn't that depend on the girls?

HESTER. Not entirely.

ROBERT. You mustn't be unjust to Mother.

HESTER. Bob, I'm a little tired of hearing about your mother. . . . [*Suddenly penitent again.*] Oh, I didn't mean to say that! I didn't mean it a bit! I'm sorry, Rob. . . . Now I'm apologizing to you. Don't you hear me?

ROBERT. Yes, I hear you. What then?

HESTER. Oh, what difference does it make? I'm not marrying your mother. I'm marrying you. And I love you, Rob! I love you!

ROBERT. Yes, my dear.

HESTER. I'll never be bad again.

ROBERT. I'm willing to take your word for it.

HESTER. You'd better be. Oh, you *are* angry with me, Rob!

ROBERT. No. I'm not.

HESTER. You're a queer one.

ROBERT. Think so? How?

HESTER. As a lover. I've never seen another like you.

ROBERT. Haven't you? [*A thought strikes him.*] Tell me something, Hester.

HESTER. What?

ROBERT. Have you had many?

HESTER. Many what?

ROBERT. Lovers.

HESTER. Oh, Robert, what a thing to say to a lady!

ROBERT. You know what I mean.

HESTER. I'm not quite sure I want to answer.

ROBERT. I'm not asking for their names.

HESTER. Oh, I shouldn't mind that . . . the truth is . . . I don't know . . .

ROBERT. You must.

HESTER. I don't really. I used to think . . . oh, quite often . . . that one of my beaux was coming to the point . . . but . . .

ROBERT. Yes?

HESTER. But none of them ever did.

ROBERT. That surprises me. Why not?

HESTER. I don't think it was entirely lack of allure, Rob.

ROBERT. Of course it wasn't!

HESTER. *I* think it was because I always laughed.

ROBERT. You didn't laugh at me.

HESTER. You looked foolish enough, now that I think of it.

ROBERT. Yes. I daresay. . . . So I *was* the only one.

HESTER. Say the only one I didn't laugh at, please. You make me sound so undesirable.

ROBERT. I didn't mean to. Tell me, Hester . . .

HESTER. Anything.

ROBERT. Have you thought what it will mean to be my wife?

HESTER. A very pleasant life.

ROBERT. For you?

HESTER. I certainly hope so.

ROBERT. I don't know that I quite share your enthusiasm for children.

HESTER. You will.

ROBERT. They don't exactly help a career, you know.

HESTER. Have you got a career?

ROBERT. I fully intend to have one.

HESTER. I'm glad to hear it.

ROBERT. I've got just as much talent as Dave has.

HESTER. What kind of talent?

ROBERT. I haven't decided. I can draw pretty well. I'm not a bad musician. I might decide to compose. I might even write. I've often thought of it. And children, you see . . .

HESTER. I don't know much about careers, but Lincoln had children and adored 'em, and if you can do half as well as he did . . .

ROBERT. Then my preferences aren't to be considered?

HESTER. You just leave things to me. If we're poor, I'll cook and scrub floors. I'll bring up our children. I'll take care of you whether we live in New York or Kamchatka. This business is up to me, Rob. Don't let it worry you.

ROBERT. [*Crushed.*] I only wanted to make sure you understood my point of view.

HESTER. If I don't, I shall, so let's cut this short. [*She goes a little huffily to the window,* ROBERT *watching her uneasily.*] Hello!

ROBERT. What is it?

HESTER. There goes your mother down the road.

ROBERT. [*He joins her.*] So it is! What can she be doing?

HESTER. She's fetching her darling David in out of the cold. I knew she would.

ROBERT. Hester, would you mind not speaking that way of Mother?

HESTER. Can't she leave them alone for a minute?

ROBERT. She's the worrying kind.

HESTER. Oh, rot!

ROBERT. Evidently you're bent on making things as difficult as possible for me.

HESTER. I'm sorry you feel that.

[*A long irritable pause, then*]

ROBERT. Hester?

HESTER. Yes?

ROBERT. Have you thought any more about our honeymoon?

HESTER. Didn't we decide to go abroad?

ROBERT. Abroad's a pretty general term. You were to think *where* you wanted to be taken.

HESTER. I left that to you.

ROBERT. You said you "didn't care."

HESTER. I don't.

ROBERT. Nor where we live after . . . nor how.

HESTER. I don't . . . I don't . . . I want to live with *you*. [*Suddenly warming.*] What's the use of this, Rob?

ROBERT. We've never talked seriously about our marriage before.

HESTER. What is there to say about it?

ROBERT. A great deal.

HESTER. I don't agree. Marriages are things of feeling. They'd better not be talked about.

ROBERT. Real marriages can stand discussion!

HESTER. Rob!

ROBERT. What?

HESTER. That wasn't nice.

ROBERT. Wasn't it?

HESTER. [*Suddenly frightened.*] What's the matter, Rob? I'll talk as seriously as you please. Do I love you? Yes. Am I going to make you a good wife? I hope so, though I *am* only twenty and may make mistakes. Are you going to be happy with me? I hope that, too, but you'll have to answer it for yourself.

ROBERT. I can't answer it.

HESTER. Why can't you?

ROBERT. Because I'm not sure of it.

HESTER. Aren't you, Rob?

ROBERT. These things are better faced before than after.

HESTER. What is it you're trying to say?

ROBERT. If only we could be sure!

HESTER. [*Stunned.*] So that's it!

ROBERT. Are you so sure you want to marry me?

HESTER. How can I be—now?

ROBERT. Marriage is such a serious thing. You don't realize how serious.

HESTER. Don't I?

ROBERT. No. . . . I hope you won't think harshly of me. . . . And, mind you, I haven't said I wanted to break things off. . . . I only want . . .

HESTER. Please, Rob!

ROBERT. No. You've got to hear me out.

HESTER. I've heard enough, thank you!

ROBERT. I'm only trying to look at this thing . . .

HESTER. Seriously. . . . I know. . . .

ROBERT. Because, after all, the happiness of three people is affected by it.

HESTER. Three?

ROBERT. As Mother said, before dinner.

HESTER. So you talked this over with your mother?

ROBERT. Isn't that natural?

HESTER. Is your mother the third?

ROBERT. Wouldn't she be?

HESTER. Yes, I suppose she would. . . . I think you might tell me what else she had to say.

ROBERT. It was all wise and kind. You may be as hard as you like on me, but you mustn't be hard on poor splendid lonely Mother.

HESTER. [*Savage—under her breath.*] So she's lonely, too!

ROBERT. You *will* twist my meaning!

HESTER. You *said* "lonely."

ROBERT. Perhaps I did. But Mother didn't. You know, she never talks about herself.

HESTER. I see. What else did she say about us?

ROBERT. Well, you haven't been very interested in planning our future. She notices such things.

HESTER. What else?

ROBERT. She sees through people, you know.

HESTER. Through me?

ROBERT. She thought, as I must say I do, that we didn't love each other quite enough to . . . At least, she thought we ought to think very carefully before we . . .

HESTER. [*Gripping his two arms with all her strength, she stops him.*] If you really want to be free . . . if you really want that, Rob, it's all right. It's perfectly all right. . . . I'll set you free. . . . Don't worry. . . . Only you've got to say so. You've got to. . . . Answer me, Rob. *Do* you want to be rid of me? [*There is a pause.* ROBERT *cannot hold her gaze and his eyes fall. She takes the blow.*] I guess that's answer enough. [*She draws a little back from him and pulls the engagement ring from her finger.*] Here's your ring.

ROBERT. Hester! Don't do anything you'll be sorry for afterwards! Don't, please! I can't take it yet!

HESTER. [*Without any sign of emotion, she drops it on a table.*] I shall have an easier time of it, if you keep away from me. I want to save my face . . . if I can.

ROBERT. Hester, please!

HESTER. All right, if you won't go, I will.

ROBERT. I'm sorry. Of course I'll go.

HESTER. And take your ring with you.

[*He goes to the table, picks up the ring, pockets it and has just got to the door when* HESTER *breaks into furious, hysterical sobbing. Her sobs rack her and seem, at the same time, to strike* ROBERT *like the blows of a whip.*]

ROBERT. For God's sake, Hester. . . . [*She drops into a chair and sits, staring straight before her, shaken by her sobs of outraged fury and wretchedness.*] Mother! Christina! Come here! Hester . . . [CHRISTINA *appears in the door.* MRS. PHELPS *follows her.* DAVID *appears.* ROBERT *returns to* HESTER.] Can't you pull yourself together? [*She motions him away.*]

CHRISTINA. What's the matter?

ROBERT. It's Hester. Can't you stop her?

MRS. PHELPS. Good heavens, Robin! What's wrong with the child?

ROBERT. She's . . . upset . . . you see, I was just . . . you know . . .

MRS. PHELPS. I see! . . . She's taking it badly.

[HESTER'S *sobs only increase.*]

CHRISTINA. Hester, stop it!

HESTER. I'm all right. . . . I can't . . . I . . . Christina . . . please . . .

CHRISTINA. Open a window, Dave. . . . Haven't you any smelling salts in the house, Mrs. Phelps?

[MRS. PHELPS *goes for them where she left them at tea-time.*]

HESTER. Tell Rob to go away! Tell Rob to go away!

CHRISTINA. Never mind Rob! . . . Get me some aromatic spirits, one of you! Hurry up!

[ROBERT *goes.*]

MRS. PHELPS. Here are my salts.

CHRISTINA. [*Peremptorily.*] Hester! [*She holds the salts for* HESTER *to smell.*] Now, stop it! Stop it, do you hear me?

HESTER. I'm trying to stop. If you'd only send these awful people out! Take me away, Christina! Take me back to New York! I've got to get away from here. I can't face them! I can't! I can't!

CHRISTINA. Now, *stop* it!

DAVID. [*Comes forward from a window.*] Here's some snow in my handkerchief. Rub it on her wrists and temples.

CHRISTINA. Thanks, Dave.

[*She applies it.* HESTER, *by dint of great effort, gradually overcomes her sobs.* ROBERT *returns with a tumbler partly filled with a milky solution of aromatic spirits.*]

MRS. PHELPS. [*Speaking at the same time, in unfeigned wonderment to* DAVID.] Really, I do wonder at what happens to girls nowadays! When I was Hester's age I danced less and saved a little of my strength for self-control.

ROBERT. [*Speaking through.*] Here, Dave. Take this.

[DAVID *takes it.* ROBERT *goes again.* DAVID *gives the tumbler to* CHRISTINA.]

CHRISTINA. Good! Can you drink this now, Hester?

HESTER. Thank you, Christina. I'm all right now. It was only . . .

CHRISTINA. Never mind what it was. Drink this. [HESTER *drinks it.*] There, now. That's better. Just sit still and relax.

DAVID. What on earth brought it on?

MRS. PHELPS. [*Shrugging her shoulders.*] Rob and she must have had a falling out.

DAVID. No ordinary one. . . . Rob! He's gone. . . . That's funny.

MRS. PHELPS. He'd naturally be distressed.

HESTER. I'm really all right, now, Christina . . . and frightfully ashamed. . . .

MRS. PHELPS. You'd better see how Rob is, Dave. His nerves are none too stout. Such scenes aren't good for him.

HESTER. [*In a high, strained voice.*] No, isn't that so, Mrs. Phelps?

MRS. PHELPS. Did you speak to me, Hester?

HESTER. Take the smelling salts to Rob with my love. . . . Oh, God, Christina!

CHRISTINA. Now, never *mind,* Hester. You'll go to pieces again.

HESTER. But I've got to mind! And I'm all right! It won't hurt me. . . . I wish you'd go, David.

CHRISTINA. Yes, Dave, do. I'll come up in a jiffy.

MRS. PHELPS. When Hester's quieted down. [*To* DAVID.] We'd better both go and see how Rob is.

[*She is just going.*]

HESTER. Mrs. Phelps. There's something I want to ask you before we part.

MRS. PHELPS. To-morrow, my dear girl. . . .

HESTER. There isn't going to be any to-morrow.

MRS. PHELPS. What?

HESTER. Rob has just broken our engagement.

MRS. PHILIP. Not really!

CHRISTINA. [*Staggered.*] Hester, what do you mean?

HESTER. I mean what I say. Rob's just broken our engagement.

[CHRISTINA *motions to* DAVE *to go. He obeys.*]

MRS. PHELPS. I'm immensely distressed, of course.

HESTER. [*Shaking her head doggedly.*] He talked it all over with you before dinner. He told me that much, so it won't do you the least bit of good to pretend to be surprised.

MRS. PHELPS. Aren't you forgetting yourself, Hester?

HESTER. You made him do it. Why did you make him do it, Mrs. Phelps?

[CHRISTINA, *amazed, draws back to observe the pair of them.*]

MRS. PHELPS. [*Perfect dignity.*] I don't intend to stand here, Hester, and allow any hysterical girl to be rude to me.

HESTER. [*Driving on querulously.*] I'm not being rude! All I want to know is why you talked Rob into jilting me. Will you answer me, please?

MRS. PHELPS. Such things may be painful, my dear girl, but they're far less painful before than after.

HESTER. He quoted that much.

CHRISTINA. What's the good of this, Hester?

HESTER. I'm only trying to make her tell me why she did it.

MRS. PHELPS. But, Hester! Really! This is absurd!

HESTER. You've got to! You've got to explain!

MRS. PHELPS. I had nothing to do with Robin's change of heart.

HESTER. You must have had, Mrs. Phelps, and I'm demanding an explanation of why you talked Rob into . . .

MRS. PHELPS. Isn't it enough that he found out in time that you weren't the wife for him?

HESTER. That isn't the truth!

CHRISTINA. Hester, darling!

HESTER. Can you tell me what he meant when he said that the happiness of *three* people was at stake?

MRS. PHELPS. He must have been thinking of your happiness as well as his own and mine.

HESTER. What about your loneliness?

MRS. PHELPS. This *is* contemptible of you!

CHRISTINA. Really, Hester, this *can't* do any good!

HESTER. I'm going to make her admit that she made Rob . . .

MRS. PHELPS. [*Exploding.*] Very well, then, since you insist! I did advise my son to break with you. Do you want to know why?

HESTER. Yes!

MRS. PHELPS. Because of your indifference. . . .

HESTER. Oh!

MRS. PHELPS. Because he came to me to say that you neither love him nor make any pretense of loving him . . .

HESTER. Rob said that?

MRS. PHELPS. He even said that you must have misconstrued his friendship and that he never wanted to marry you . . .

HESTER. No!

MRS. PHELPS. And I told him to risk anything . . . anything, rather than such an appalling marriage . . .

HESTER. I don't believe a word of it!

MRS. PHELPS. You may believe it or not!

CHRISTINA. Mrs. Phelps, you had really better let me handle this.

MRS. PHELPS. Willingly.

HESTER. Do you believe I took advantage of Rob, Christina?

CHRISTINA. Of course not!

MRS. PHELPS. So you take her side, Christina!

CHRISTINA. I don't believe *that,* Mrs. Phelps.

MRS. PHELPS. [*She realizes that she has gone too far.*] No? Well, perhaps . . .

CHRISTINA. Whatever Robert may think, I can't believe that he said . . .

MRS. PHELPS. [*Frightened.*] Perhaps he didn't say quite that, in so many words . . . but he certainly meant . . .

HESTER. I'm going. I'm going now. Right this minute.

MRS. PHELPS. There's a train at nine in the morning. It gets you to New York at twelve. I shall have the car for you at eight-thirty.

HESTER. May I have the car now, please, Mrs. Phelps?

MRS. PHELPS. There's no train to-night.

HESTER. It doesn't matter. I won't stay

here. Not another minute. I'll go to the hotel in town.

MRS. PHELPS. You'll do nothing of the sort!

HESTER. You see if I don't!

MRS. PHELPS. You've got to think of appearances!

HESTER. Appearances are your concern. Yours and Rob's. I'm going to the hotel. I don't care what people say! I don't care about anything. I won't stay here!

MRS. PHELPS. Can't you talk to her, Christina? Surely you see . . . for all our sakes!

HESTER. If you won't let me have the car, I'll call a taxi. . . . [*She plunges towards the telephone.*]

MRS. PHELPS. I forbid you!

HESTER. [*Seizing the instrument.*] I want a taxi . . . a taxi. . . . What *is* the number? . . . Well, give it to me. . . . Locust • 4000? Give me Locust 4000!

[MRS. PHELPS *hesitates an instant, then, with terrible coolness, steps forward and jerks the telephone cord from the wall. Except for a startled exclamation, very low, from* CHRISTINA, *there is not a sound.* HESTER *hangs up the receiver and sets down the dead instrument.*]

MRS. PHELPS. [*After an interminable silence.*] You are the only person in the world who has ever forced me to do an undignified thing. I shall not forget it. [*She goes nobly.*]

HESTER. [*Weakly, turning to* CHRISTINA.] Christina, it isn't true what she said. . . . He did. . . . He did want to marry me! Really, he did! He did!

CHRISTINA. Of course he did, darling!

HESTER. I won't stay! I won't stay under that woman's roof!

CHRISTINA. Hester, darling!

HESTER. I'll walk to town!

CHRISTINA. Don't, Hester!

HESTER. That wasn't true, what she said!

CHRISTINA. Of course not!

HESTER. I still love him. . . . Let me go, Christina, I'll walk . . .

CHRISTINA. You can't, at this time of night! It wouldn't be safe!

HESTER. I don't care! I won't stay!

CHRISTINA. There! There! You'll come to bed now, won't you!

HESTER. No! No! I can't! I'd rather die! I'll walk to town.

CHRISTINA. You'll force me to come with you, Hester. I can't let you go alone.

HESTER. I won't stay another minute!

CHRISTINA. Do you want to make me walk with you? Think, Hester! Think what I told you before dinner! Do you want to make me walk all that way in the cold?

HESTER. [*Awed by this.*] Oh, your baby! I didn't mean to forget your baby! Oh, Christina, you mustn't stay, either! This is a dreadful house! You've got to get your baby away from this house, Christina! Awful things happen here!

CHRISTINA. Hester, darling! Won't you please be sensible and come up to bed?

HESTER. [*Speaking at the same time as her nerves begin to go again.*] Awful things, Christina. . . . You'll see if you don't come away! You'll see! . . . She'll do the same thing to you that she's done to me. You'll see! You'll see!

CURTAIN

ACT TWO

SCENE TWO

The curtain rises again, as soon as possible, upon DAVID'S *little bedroom, untouched since the day when* DAVID *went away to Harvard and scorned to take his prep school trophies and souvenirs with him. The furniture is rather more than simple. The bed is single. There is a dresser. There are only a couple of chairs. The curtains at the single window have been freshly laundered and put back in their old state by* MRS. PHELPS *in a spirit of maternal archeology. Insignificant loving cups, won at tennis, stand about the dresser. No pennants, no banners. There might be some tennis racquets, golf sticks, crossed skis, a pair of snow-shoes, class photographs and framed diplomas. There must also be a fairly important reproduction of Velasquez' Don Balthazar Carlos on horseback, selected by* MRS. PHELPS *as* DAVID'S *favorite Old Master. A final touch is* DAVID'S *baby pillow.*

DAVID *stands in his pajamas and socks, about to enter upon the last stages of his preparations to retire for the night. The room has been strewn with clothing during the preliminary stages. Now he is in the ambulatory state of mind. A series of crosses and circumnavigations produces several empty packs of cigarettes from several pockets, corners of the suitcase, etc. This frustration brings on baffled scratchings of the head and legs. Then he gives up the cigarette problem, turns again to the suitcase, spills out several dirty shirts and finally, apparently from the very bottom, extracts a dressing-gown, a pair of slippers, a tooth-brush and some tooth-paste. He sheds the socks, dons the slippers and dressing-gown and sallies forth with brush and paste to do up his teeth in the bathroom. He goes by the door which gives on the hall at the head of the stairs.*

After he has been gone a few seconds, a tiny scratching sound is heard on the other side of the other door to the room and that is opened from without. We see the scratcher at work conveying the impression that a wee mousie wants to come in. The wee mousie is none other than MRS. PHELPS, *all smiles in her best negligée, the most effective garment she wears in the course of the entire play, carrying the largest eiderdown comfort ever seen on any stage.*

The smile fades a little when she discovers that the room is empty. Then its untidiness catches her eye and she shakes her head reprovingly, as who should say: "What creatures these big boys are!" She goes to work at once, true mother that she is, to pick things up. She loves her work and puts her whole heart into it. The trousers are neatly hung over the back of the chair, the coat and waistcoat hung over them. The shirts, socks and underwear are folded and laid chastely on the seat. One or two of the garments receive devout maternal kisses and hugs. Then she goes to the bed, lifts off the suitcase, pushes it underneath, adjusts the eiderdown, smooths the pillow and kisses that. Last, all smiles again, she sits, carefully disposing her laces and ribbons, to await DAVID'S *return. She yearns for it and she has not long to wait.*

DAVID *returns. His mother's beaming smile, as he opens the door, arouses his usual distaste for filial sentimentality. It is intensified, now—and very ill-concealed—by the hour, his costume and recent events. He hesitates in the doorway.*

MRS. PHELPS. Why do you look so startled? It's only Mother!

DAVID. [*Laconic.*] Hello, Mother!

MRS. PHELPS. I came in to ask if you needed anything and . . .

DAVID. Not a thing, thanks.

MRS. PHELPS. And to warn you against opening the window in this weather. Oh, and I brought you that extra cover. I've been picking up after you, too!

DAVID. [*Looking gloomily about.*] You needn't have troubled.

MRS. PHELPS. It took me back to the old days when I used to tuck you up in that same little bed . . .

DAVID. [*A strong hint.*] Yeah. . . . I'm just turning in, Mother.

MRS. PHELPS. [*Regardless.*] . . . And then sit in this very chair and talk over all my problems with you. I feel that I must talk to my big boy to-night. . . . I must get acquainted with my Dave again.

DAVID. [*An even stronger hint.*] We're not exactly strangers, are we? And besides, it's getting late.

MRS. PHELPS. [*Even more persistent.*] It was always in these late hours that we had our talks in the old days when we were still comrades. Oh, are those gone forever? Don't you remember how we used to play that we had an imaginary kingdom where we were king and queen?

DAVID. [*Moribund.*] Did we? I wish Chris 'ud come up.

MRS. PHELPS. [*A frown and she speaks quickly.*] Have you noticed, Dave boy, that your room is just as you left it? I've made a little shrine of it. The same curtains, the same . . .

DAVID. [*Breaking in.*] I suppose Chris is still trying to get Hester quiet?

MRS. PHELPS. I suppose so. . . . And every day I dusted in here myself and every night I prayed in here for . . .

DAVID. [*A little too dryly for good manners.*] Thanks.

MRS. PHELPS. [*Reproachfully.*] Oh, David, you can't get that horrid scene downstairs out of your mind!

DAVID. No.

MRS. PHELPS. Try! I need my big boy so! Because I'm facing the gravest problem of my life, Dave. And you've got to help me.

DAVID. What is it?

MRS. PHELPS. Is it true that I'm of no more use to my two sons?

DAVID. Whatever put such an idea in your head?

MRS. PHELPS. You did.

DAVID. [*Shocked.*] I?

MRS. PHELPS. [*Nodding.*] You weren't really glad to see me this afternoon.

DAVID. [*In all sincerity.*] I was. . . . I was delighted!

MRS. PHELPS. [*Bravely stopping him.*] Not glad as I was to see you. I noticed, Dave! . . . And that made me wonder whether this scientific age—because it is a scientific age, Dave—isn't making more than one boy forget that the bond between mother and son is the strongest bond on earth. . . .

DAVID. [*Not quite sure of the superlative.*] Well, it's certainly strong.

MRS. PHELPS. Do you realize how sinful any boy would be to want to loosen it?

DAVID. Sure, I realize that!

MRS. PHELPS. I see so many poor mothers, no less deserving of love and loyalty than I, neglected and discarded by their children, set aside for other interests.

DAVID. What interests?

MRS. PHELPS. All kinds of things. . . . Wives. . . .

DAVID. [*Shying.*] Nonsense, Mother!

MRS. PHELPS. The Chinese never set any relations above their filial piety. They'd be the greatest people on earth if only they'd stop smoking opium.

DAVID. You haven't any kick, have you? I mean: Rob and I haven't let you down?

MRS. PHELPS. Not yet, Dave. But, you know the old saying?

DAVID. What old saying?

MRS. PHELPS. That a boy's mother is his best friend.

DAVID. Oh! Bet I do!

MRS. PHELPS. Do you think of *your* mother as *your* best friend?

DAVID. None better, certainly.

MRS. PHELPS. None better! Hm! You *can* say, though, that you haven't entirely outgrown me?

DAVID. Of course I haven't! Why, I'd hate to have you think that just because I'm a grown man, I . . .

MRS. PHELPS. No son is ever a grown man to his mother! [*A knock at the door.*] Who can that be at this hour?

DAVID. I hope it's Chris.

[*He starts for the door.*]

MRS. PHELPS. [*Freezing suddenly as she rises.*] Dave!

DAVID. [*Turning.*] What?

MRS. PHELPS. Wait. . . . I mustn't intrude. . . . Good-night. . . .

DAVID. [*Calling out.*] Just a minute! [*To his mother, politely.*] You wouldn't be intruding!

MRS. PHELPS. Not on you, I know. But . . .

DAVID. Not on Chris either!

MRS. PHELPS. I know best. Kiss me good-night.

DAVID. Good-night, Mother. [*He kisses her cheek.*]

MRS. PHELPS. [*A quick hug.*] God bless my big boy!

[*She goes as she came.* DAVID'S *look, as he watches her door close behind her, is baffled. He goes quickly to the other door.* ROBERT *is standing outside.*

DAVID. For Pete's sake, Rob! I thought it was Chris! . . . Why didn't you walk in?

ROBERT. I thought Mother was in here.

DAVID. She was. She just went to bed.

ROBERT. [*Entering.*] She must have thought it was Chris, too!

DAVID. How do you mean?

ROBERT. I shouldn't rush things if I were you.

DAVID. Maybe you're right. Women are too deep for me.

ROBERT. I came in for a smoke. I had to talk to you. I've been sitting in my room wondering what you think of all this.

DAVID. [*Cigarette business.*] I don't think much and that's the truth!

ROBERT. Good God, Dave, can't you be a little easier on me? Didn't you ever feel any doubts when you were engaged? Were you always so sure of Christina that you . . .

DAVID. The first time I asked Chris to marry me, she made it perfectly clear that, as far as she was concerned, I was to consider myself dripping wet. After that I was too damn scared I wouldn't get her to think whether she loved me or not.

ROBERT. [*Darkly.*] And I never had one comfortable moment from the time Hester accepted me.

DAVID. Oh, being in love's like everything else. You've got to put some guts in it.

ROBERT. [*Bitter anger.*] You think I haven't got any guts. You want to make me look like a callous cad! All right, I'll *be* a cad. I don't care what people think about me! But I'll tell you one thing! I'm damned if I'm going to let you turn Mother against me!

DAVID. Do *what?*

ROBERT. You heard me!

DAVID. My God, haven't you outgrown that old stuff yet?

ROBERT. I know from experience what to expect when you and Mother get together. I used to listen at that door, night after night, night after night, while you and Mother sat in here and talked me over. Then I'd watch for the change in her next morning at breakfast when I hadn't slept a wink all night. The way you used to own the earth at those breakfasts! Well, if you try any of that old stuff to-night, I'll lose the only prop I've got left.

DAVID. Isn't it about time you let go of Mother's apron-strings?

ROBERT. You would say that! You don't realize that I'm desperate.

DAVID. Desperate, hell! You're crazy! Mother's gone to bed and . . . [*The wee mousie scratches at the door again.*] What's that?

MRS. PHELPS. [*Entering.*] It's only Mother. Are my two beaux quarreling? Jealous, jealous Robin! What's the matter?

DAVID. Nothing.

MRS. PHELPS. A fine man is a frank man, David! Do you think I didn't hear every word you said? Surely you must know that Hester wasn't worthy of your brother?

DAVID. Wasn't she? Well, let's not talk any more about it.

MRS. PHELPS. Oh, but we must. For all our sakes, we must clear the air. *I* have always taken the stand that my boys could do absolutely no wrong and that it is the proper stand for a mother to take. Didn't I always side with you in your school scrapes? Even against the masters? Even when you were clearly in the wrong? Of course, I did! And I shall not permit one word of criticism against your brother now. Loyalty, Dave! Loyalty! Come, now! Tell Mother all about it!

DAVID. But if you overheard every word we said!

MRS. PHELPS. "Overheard," David? Am I given to eavesdropping?

DAVID. I didn't say so.

MRS. PHELPS. I simply want to make sure I didn't miss anything while I was in my bath.

DAVID. I don't misunderstand him. I'm sorry for Hester, that's all.

ROBERT. We're all sorry for Hester.

DAVID. I don't think it's your place to be too sorry.

ROBERT. Let's drop it, Mother.

MRS. PHELPS. No. I've got to know what's on Dave's mind. My whole life may hang on it. What is it, Dave? [*Carefully sounding.*] If Robin's not to blame, perhaps I am?

ROBERT. [*Horrified.*] Mother!

DAVID. What's the use of getting so worked up over nothing?

MRS. PHELPS. Nothing! Can you say "nothing" after what *we* were talking about a few minutes ago?

DAVID. [*Cornered.*] I only think . . .

MRS. PHELPS. What?

DAVID. Well, that you've both handed Hester a somewhat dirty deal. And Chris must think so, too!

MRS. PHELPS. [*Wary.*] Indeed! And how, please?

DAVID. Well, it comes of what Chris calls "mythologizing."

MRS. PHELPS. [*Frightened.*] Does Christina discuss our family affairs already?

DAVID. No. It's one of her old ideas about people in general. You mythologize Rob into a little tin god. Rob thinks he is a little tin god. Along comes Hester and falls in love with the real Rob. She never heard of your little tin god Rob. She doesn't deliver the incense and tom-toms. That makes you and Rob sore and the whole works goes to hell. That's mythologizing. Believe me, it can make plenty of trouble.

MRS. PHELPS. [*Relieved that the criticism is so general.*] If that's all I'm to blame for, I don't know that I can object. Expecting the best of everyone is, at least, a worthy fault. Still, if I may venture an older woman's opinion on one of Christina's ideas?

DAVID. I wish to God I hadn't started this.

MRS. PHELPS. So do I. But perhaps you'll tell me what Christina would say to the true reason for Robin's break with Hester?

DAVID. What is the true reason?

MRS. PHELPS. Do you want to tell him, Robin?

ROBERT. [*Inspired.*] I broke with Hester

because of an ideal, the ideal of womankind Mother gave us both by being the the great woman that she is. *I* knew *I* couldn't be happy with any woman who fell short of her.

MRS. PHELPS. What becomes of your "dirty deal" now, David?

DAVID. But I'm not going against that ideal, Mother. That's another thing.

ROBERT. You couldn't have troubled much about it when you married!

MRS. PHELPS. You shouldn't have said that, Robin. I haven't had Christina's advantages. I wasn't given a German education.

DAVID. Now, don't take this out on Chris, Mother.

MRS. PHELPS. I think I know a little of a mother's duty toward her daughter-in-law. Good-night, Robin. I must talk with your brother alone, now. And before you quarrel again, stop to think that you are all I have, you two, and try to consider me. It isn't much to ask and it won't be for long. You both know what the doctors think about my heart! Dr. McClintock tells me I may go at any moment. [*Pause, then*] Good-night, Robin.

ROBERT. [*Frightened.*] Good-night, Mother.

MRS. PHELPS. You may come into my room later, if you like. I may need you to comfort me after . . . [*She waves her hand. He leaves. She has never taken her eyes off* DAVID. *When the door closes behind* ROBERT, *she speaks.*] David, in this moment, when your brother and I most needed your loyalty, you have hurt me more than I have ever been hurt in my life before, even by your father.

DAVID. I never meant to hurt you.

MRS. PHELPS. [*Working it up.*] You have been wicked, David! Wicked! Wicked!

DAVID. How?

MRS. PHELPS. You have shown me too clearly that what I most dreaded has already come to pass!

DAVID. What, Mother?

MRS. PHELPS. You *have* loosened the bond between us. You *have* discarded me.

DAVID. [*Horrified.*] But I haven't done any such thing!

MRS. PHELPS. Don't say any more! Act upon your treachery, if you will, but don't, please, don't say another thing. Remember!

"The brave man does it with a sword,
The coward with a word!"

[*And she sweeps out, slamming her door after her.*]

DAVID. [*Speaking through her door.*] But I didn't mean anything. . . . Won't you let me explain? . . . I didn't know what I was talking about!

[*There is no answer. He rattles the door. It is locked. He comes away, swearing softly under his breath. Then, manfully, he takes refuge in sulks. He kicks off his slippers and throws his dressing-gown aside. He lights a cigarette and flounces into bed, snatching up a book or magazine en route. Just as he is settled, his mother's door opens again very slowly.* MRS. PHELPS *presents a tear-stained face to view and comes in.*]

MRS. PHELPS. Smoking in bed, Dave boy?

DAVID. [*Starting up.*] Eh?

MRS. PHELPS. It's only Mother. . . . No, don't get up. . . . Let me sit here as I used to in the old days.

DAVID. [*Sitting up.*] Mother, I didn't mean . . .

MRS. PHELPS. Never mind. I was wrong to be hurt.

DAVID. But you had me all wrong. I mean . . . You and I . . . We're just the same as we always were. . . . Believe me, we are. . . . Why, if anything came to spoil things between us . . .

MRS. PHELPS. [*The first objective conquered.*] That's what I wanted you to say! Now talk to me about Christina.

DAVID. [*Taken aback without knowing why.*] Huh?

MRS. PHELPS. Give me your hand in mine and tell me all about her.

DAVID. [*Obeying rather reluctantly*]. What is there to tell?

MRS. PHELPS. Well, for one thing, tell me you think she's going to like me!

DAVID. [*Warmly.*] She does already!

MRS. PHELPS. Doesn't think I'm an old-fashioned frump?

DAVID. I should say not! How could she?

MRS. PHELPS. She's such a modern young lady. So lovely, but so very up-to-date. You must tell me everything I can do to win her to me. And I'll do it. Though I'm afraid of her, Dave.

DAVID. [*Amused.*] Afraid of Chris? Why?

MRS. PHELPS. She's so much cleverer than I am. She makes me realize that I'm just a timid old lady of the old school.

DAVID. [*Nice indignation.*] You old!

MRS. PHELPS. [*Archly so brave about it.*] Yes, I am!

DAVID. Well, you and Chris are going to be the best friends ever.

MRS. PHELPS. You *are* happy, aren't you?

DAVID. You bet I am!

MRS. PHELPS. Really happy?

DAVID. Couldn't be happier!

MRS. PHELPS. I'm so glad! And I thank God that when your hour struck it didn't strike falsely as it did for Robin. Because any one can see the difference between Christina and Hester. Of course, that's a little the difference between you and Rob. You know what I've always said. You are *my* son. Robert takes after his father. But you mustn't be impatient with Christina if she seems, at first, a little slow, a little resentful of our family. We've always been so close, we three. She's bound to feel a little out of it, at first. A little jealous . . .

DAVID. Not Chris!

MRS. PHELPS. Oh, come now, Dave! I'm sure she's perfect, but you mustn't try to tell me she isn't human. Young wives are sure to be a little bit possessive and exacting and . . . selfish at first.

DAVID. We needn't worry about that.

MRS. PHELPS. No. . . . At first I thought Christina was going to be hard and cold. I didn't expect her to have our sense of humor and I don't believe she has much of that. But we've more than we need already. If only she will learn to care for me as I care for her, we can be so happy, all four of us together, can't we?

DAVID. You bet we can!

MRS. PHELPS. [*Dreamily.*] Building our houses in Phelps Manor. . . . Deciding to put an Italian Villa here and a little bungalow there. . . . [*As* DAVID *grows restive.*] But the important thing for you, Dave boy, is a sense of proportion about your marriage. I'm going to lecture you, now, for your own good. If, at first, Christina does seem a little exacting or unreasonable, particularly about us, remember that she has to adjust herself to a whole new world here, a very different world from her friends in Omaha. And you must never be impatient with her. Because, if you are, I shall take her side against you.

DAVID. You are a great woman, Mother!

MRS. PHELPS. You're the great one! How many boys of your age let their wives undermine all their old associations and loosen all their old ties!

DAVID. Chris wouldn't try that!

MRS. PHELPS. She might not *want* to. But jealous girls think things that aren't so and say things that aren't true. Morbid things.

DAVID. Morbid things? Chris?

MRS. PHELPS. Only you won't pay too much attention or take her seriously. I know that, because you would no more let any one strike at me than I would let any one strike at you.

DAVID. But Chris wouldn't . . .

MRS. PHELPS. As I said to Christina this afternoon: "Christina," I said, "I cannot allow you to sacrifice David!"

DAVID. Chris sacrifice me! How?

MRS. PHELPS. Why, by taking you away from your magnificent opportunity here.

DAVID. Oh!

MRS. PHELPS. Be master in your own house. Meet her selfishness with firmness, her jealousy with fairness and her . . . her exaggerations with a grain of salt. . . .

DAVID. What exaggerations?

MRS. PHELPS. Well, you know . . . a girl . . . a young wife, like Christina . . . *might* possibly make the mistake of . . . well, of taking sides . . . in what happened downstairs, for instance . . . and without fully understanding. . . . You can see how fatal *that* would be. . . . But, if you face the facts always, Dave boy, and nothing *but* the facts, your marriage will be a happy one. And, when you want advice, come to your mother always.

DAVID. Thanks.

MRS. PHELPS. Now, isn't your mother your best friend?

DAVID. You bet you are, Mummy!

MRS. PHELPS. How long it is since you've called me that! Bless you, my dear, dear boy!

[*She leans over to seal her triumph with a kiss.* CHRISTINA'S *entrance follows so closely upon her knock that the picture is still undisturbed for her to see. She has changed her dress for a very simple negligée. Her mood is dangerous.*]

CHRISTINA. Oh, I beg your pardon!

MRS. PHELPS. [*So sweetly, after the very briefest pause.*] Come in, Christina. I was only saying good-night to Dave. Nothing private! You're one of the family now. You must feel free to come and go as you like in the house.

CHRISTINA. Thank you.

MRS. PHELPS. We can accustom ourselves to it, can't we, Dave?

DAVID. Yeah. . . .

CHRISTINA. Dave and I have got so used to sharing the same room, I came in here quite naturally and . . .

MRS. PHELPS. Here's your dressing-gown, Dave boy. We won't look while you slip it on.

[*Confusedly* DAVE *gets out of bed and robes himself.* CHRISTINA'S *eyes meet his mother's.* CHRISTINA'S *eyes have the least flash of scorn in them,* MRS. PHELPS' *the least quaver of fear. In that glance, the two women agree on undying enmity.*]

DAVID. You can . . . you can look now.

CHRISTINA. Are you quite sure *I* may, Mrs. Phelps?

MRS. PHELPS. Whatever else you may have taken from me, Christina, you can*not* take from me the joy of feeling my son here, once more, in his old room, beside me.

CHRISTINA. [*Marking up the first score.*] I haven't meant to take anything from you, Mrs. Phelps.

MRS. PHELPS. [*So sweetly again.*] You know I was only joking. [*She is routed, though.*] Good-night. [*The two women kiss.*] Don't keep Dave up too late. He's very tired. [*She pats* DAVE, *as she passes him on her way to her door.*] You must be tired, too, Christina. How *is* Hester, now?

CHRISTINA. Quite all right, thank you.

MRS. PHELPS. Thank *you!*

[*She blows a kiss to* DAVID *from the door and goes.* CHRISTINA *stands motionless.* DAVID *reaches for a cigarette.*]

DAVID. You look pretty stern, Chris.

CHRISTINA. Do I?

DAVID. You've been a brick.

CHRISTINA. Thanks.

DAVID. Hester *is* all right, isn't she?

CHRISTINA. Yes, poor youngster! I shouldn't be surprised if she were really in luck, Dave.

DAVID. You may be right. But it isn't exactly up to me to say so, is it? [*He lights his cigarette. Her eyes burn him up.*]

CHRISTINA. Dave. . . .

DAVID. Yes?

CHRISTINA. Whom do you love?

DAVID. You. Why?

CHRISTINA. I wondered, that's all. I want to be kissed.

DAVID. That's easy. [*He takes her in his arms.*]

CHRISTINA. Such a tired girl, Dave. . . . I want to be held on to and made much of. . . . I want to feel all safe and warm. . . . I want you to tell me that you're in love with me and that you enjoy being in love with me. Because just loving isn't enough and it's being in love that really matters. . . . Will you tell me all that, please, Dave?

DAVID. [*Hugging her.*] Darling!

CHRISTINA. You haven't kissed me yet.

DAVID. [*Complying, a trifle absent-mindedly.*] There!

CHRISTINA. [*As she draws back from him.*] That isn't what I call making love in a big way.

DAVID. [*Repeating the kiss with more energy.*] Is that better?

CHRISTINA. There's still something lacking. . . . What's the matter? There's nobody watching us.

DAVID. That's a funny thing to say.

CHRISTINA. You take me right back to my first beau in Germany. He never got very far, either. All the English he knew was "water closet."

DAVID. Chris! Shame on you!

CHRISTINA. Shame on *you,* making me take to low jokes to amuse you. . . . I love you.

DAVID. Darling, darling, Chris!

CHRISTINA. I love you! I love you! [*For a moment she clings to him wildly.*] I hate being so far from you to-night, Dave. 'Way off there at the other end of the hall!

DAVID. I'm none too pleased myself. It's just one of Mother's fool ideas. [*He lowers his voice whenever he mentions his mother.*]

CHRISTINA. She naturally wanted you near *her!*

DAVID. That's it. [*His eyes fall beneath her steady gaze.*] We mustn't talk so loud. We'll keep Mother awake. She can hear every sound we make.

CHRISTINA. Let her hear! It'll do her good!

DAVID. That's no way to talk, Chris!

CHRISTINA. Excuse me. I didn't mean to snap. I've been fearfully shaken up tonight.

DAVID. I know you have.

CHRISTINA. And I'm awfully tired.

DAVID. Poor girl!

CHRISTINA. Poor Hester! . . . I don't feel like going to bed yet. I want to talk. Do you mind?

DAVID. Go to it.

CHRISTINA. I've never come up against anything like this before, I've heard of it, but I've never met it. I don't know what to do about it. And it scares me.

DAVID. What does?

CHRISTINA. I don't know how to tell you. [*Then with sudden force.*] But I've got to tell you, Dave. I've got to tell you. There are no two ways about that.

DAVID. What are you driving at?

CHRISTINA. Well . . . [*But she changes her mind.*] May I ask you a question? Rather an intimate one?

DAVID. If you must!

CHRISTINA. Being your wife, I thought I might.

DAVID. Shoot!

CHRISTINA. Do you look on me as apart from all other women? I mean, do you think of all the women in the world and then think of me quite, quite differently? Do you, Dave?

DAVID. I'll bite. Do I?

CHRISTINA. Please answer me. It's awfully important to me just now.

DAVID. Of course I do. . . . Why is it so important just now?

CHRISTINA. Because that's how I feel about you and all the other men in the world. Because that's what being in love must mean and being properly and happily married. Two people, a man and a woman, together by themselves, miles and miles from everybody, from *everybody* else, glancing around, now and then, at all the rest of mankind, at *all* the rest, Dave, and saying: "Are you still there? And getting along all right? Sure there's nothing we can do to help?"

DAVID. Only we do help, don't we?

CHRISTINA. Only really if we feel that way about one another. Only *by* feeling that way.

DAVID. That's pretty deep! You do go off on the damnedest tacks!

CHRISTINA. Don't you see how that feeling between a man and a woman is what keeps life going?

DAVID. Is it?

CHRISTINA. What else could be strong enough?

DAVID. Perhaps you're right. [*Then, unaccountably, he shies.*] But what's the idea in getting so worked up about it?

CHRISTINA. Because it matters so much, Dave . . . just now . . . that you and I feel that way about each other and that we go on feeling that way and exclude everybody, *everybody* else. Tell me you think so, too?

DAVID. Sure, I think so. . . . [*Then, again, he shies from her inner meaning.*] You're getting the worst habit of working yourself up over nothing!

CHRISTINA. Do you realize, Dave, that the blackest sinner on earth is the man . . . or woman . . . who breaks in on that feeling? Or tampers with it in any way? Or perverts it?

DAVID. If you say so, I'll say he is.

CHRISTINA. He!

DAVID. Huh?

CHRISTINA. Never mind. . . . Your brother didn't feel that way about poor Hester, did he?

DAVID. Rob always was a funny egg.

CHRISTINA. Your mother calls him Robin! "Tweet! Tweet! What does the Birdie say?"

DAVID. From all I can gather, Hester didn't feel much of *any* way about him.

CHRISTINA. I know better than that. . . . I've had that child on my hands for the past hour. I've learned an awful lot, Dave. About her, and *from* her.

DAVID. Look here, Chris. . . . Don't you get mixed up in this business, will you?

CHRISTINA. I wonder if I'm not mixed up in it already.

DAVID. Well, don't "take sides."

CHRISTINA. I wonder if I can help taking sides.

DAVID. It's none of our business.

CHRISTINA. I wish I were sure of that. [*Baffled, she again shifts her approach.*] Poor little Hester goes tomorrow morning. How long are we staying?

DAVID. Oh, I dunno.

CHRISTINA. A week?

DAVID. We can't do less, can we?

CHRISTINA. Can't we?

DAVID. Don't you want to? [*There is another pause before* CHRISTINA *shakes her head.* DAVID *frowns.*] You see what comes of taking things so hard?

I'm just as distressed over what's happened as you are. Maybe more. But I certainly don't want to run away. It wouldn't be right. Mother'd never understand. I'd feel like a bum going off and leaving her in the lurch after this. Think what Rob's put her through to-day and what she'll have to go through with Hester's family and all her friends and everybody else before she's done!

CHRISTINA. She seems to be bearing up.

DAVID. You can't be sure with Mother.

CHRISTINA. Can't you?

DAVID. She's so damned game.

CHRISTINA. Is she?

DAVID. Can't you see that? And, anyway, I've got to look around.

CHRISTINA. What at? The houses in Phelps Manor?

DAVID. I know how you feel, Chris, about Mother's helping hand. But I can't be *throwing* away opportunities, now, can I? With the baby coming?

CHRISTINA. [*Gravely.*] No, Dave. Of course, you can't. Neither can I.

DAVID. How do you mean?

CHRISTINA. Forgotten all about *my* opportunities, haven't you?

DAVID. What opportunities?

CHRISTINA. My appointment.

DAVID. Didn't Mother say she could scare up something for you here?

CHRISTINA. She thought she might "scare up" a place where I could "putter around" and keep myself "happy and contented" when the "real doctors" weren't working.

DAVID. She didn't mean anything unkind, Chris. Just give Mother a chance and . . . What are you crying for?

CHRISTINA. [*Hotly untruthful.*] I'm not crying.

DAVID. You are!

CHRISTINA. I can't help it. . . .

DAVID. But what's the matter?

CHRISTINA. It doesn't look as if I'm to have much of a show for my eight years of hard work, does it?

DAVID. Mother and I'll dope out something. I couldn't leave her now. You know that. And anyway, I've got to stay till I get my shirts washed. I've only got two left.

CHRISTINA. Then we stay, of course.

DAVID. And I must say, Chris, that I don't think you're quite playing ball to judge my home and my family entirely on what you've seen tonight. Besides, the whole purpose of this visit was to bring you and Mother together and to show Mother that a lady scientist mayn't be as bad as she sounds. Because you and Mother have just got to hit it off, you know.

CHRISTINA. Have we?

DAVID. You're apt to be impatient, Chris, and I'm afraid you're intolerant.

CHRISTINA. Those are bad faults in a scientist.

DAVID. They're bad faults in anybody. . . . Now, you just give me time and you'll see how things straighten out.

CHRISTINA. Aren't you satisfied with the way our meeting has come off?

DAVID. There's no use pretending it was ideal. I believe in facing the facts always. But don't you worry. Mother gets on *my* nerves sometimes. You just have to remember what a hard life she's had.

CHRISTINA. How has it been hard?

DAVID. Oh, lots of ways. My father wasn't much, you know.

CHRISTINA. I didn't know. You've never mentioned him.

DAVID. He died when I was five.

CHRISTINA. What was the matter with him? Women or drink?

DAVID. Nothing like that. He just didn't amount to much.

CHRISTINA. Made a lot of money, didn't he?

DAVID. Lots.

CHRISTINA. And left your mother rich. What other troubles has she had?

DAVID. Well, her health.

CHRISTINA. It doesn't seem so bad.

DAVID. It is, though. Heart. And I wish I could tell you half of what she's gone through for Rob and me.

CHRISTINA. Go on and tell me. I'd like to hear.

DAVID. I've heard her say she was born without a selfish hair in her head.

CHRISTINA. No!

DAVID. And that's about true. Why, I've seen her nurse Rob through one thing after another when she'd admit to me that she was twice as sick as he was. I've seen her come in here from taking care of him and she'd be half fainting with her bad heart, but there'd be nothing doing when I'd beg her to get him a nurse. She said we were her job and she just wouldn't give in. And the way she always took interest in everything we did. Why, when she used to come up to school, all the boys went just crazy about her.

CHRISTINA. I'm sure they did. [*But she turns the inquiry into more significant channels.*] How did your girl friends get on with her?

DAVID. Oh, they loved her, too! Mother used to give us dances here.

CHRISTINA. Did she invite the girls you were in love with?

DAVID. I never fell in love! Not really. Not till I met you.

CHRISTINA. Darling! [*She smiles rather absently.*] What was the name of the one your mother thought could wear my dress?

DAVID. Clara Judd?

CHRISTINA. Weren't you sweet on Clara?

DAVID. I dunno. What made you ask that?

CHRISTINA. Just something in the way your mother spoke of her this evening. It came back to me. Weren't you?

DAVID. Mother thought so.

CHRISTINA. Used to pester you about Clara, didn't she?

DAVID. She was afraid I was going to marry Clara.

CHRISTINA. I see. Anything wrong with her?

DAVID. With Clara? No. Damn nice girl. You'll meet her.

CHRISTINA. Then why didn't your mother want you to marry her?

DAVID. Thought I was too young.

CHRISTINA. When was it?

DAVID. Summer after the war.

CHRISTINA. You weren't so young, were you?

DAVID. You know Mother.

CHRISTINA. How about your brother? Did he used to fall in love a great deal?

DAVID. I don't know that I'd call it "in love."

CHRISTINA. Why not?

DAVID. It's the family skeleton. She was a chorus girl, my dear. She cost Mother twelve thousand berries.

CHRISTINA. That must have been jolly! Was she the only one or were there others?

DAVID. There were plenty of others. Only they didn't have lawyers.

CHRISTINA. And then Hester?

DAVID. Right.

CHRISTINA. Well, that's all very interesting.

DAVID. What are you trying to prove?

CHRISTINA. An idea this affair of Hester's put into my head. And I must say, it fits in rather extraordinarily.

DAVID. What does?

CHRISTINA. Your being too young to marry after the war and Robert's taking to wild women. . . . And you had to be three thousand miles from home to fall in love with me! Never mind. . . . That's enough of that! Now let me tell *you* something. Only you must promise not to get mad.

DAVID. I won't get mad.

CHRISTINA. Promise?

DAVID. Promise.

CHRISTINA. [*A deep breath, then*] Shirts or no shirts, we've got to get out of here to-morrow.

DAVID. [*As though she had stuck him with a pin.*] Now, Chris! Haven't you been over all that?

CHRISTINA. Yes. But not to the bottom of it.

DAVID. What more is there to say?

CHRISTINA. [*With sudden violence.*] That a defenseless, trusting, little girl has been cruelly treated! We've got to "take sides" with her, Dave!

DAVID. What's the matter with Hester's own family? This is their business, not ours!

CHRISTINA. We owe it to ourselves to *make* it our business.

DAVID. I don't see it.

CHRISTINA. Why don't you see it? What have you put over your eyes that keeps you from seeing it? Do you dare answer that?

DAVID. Dare? What do you mean?

CHRISTINA. "Face the facts," Dave! "Face the facts!"

DAVID. Rot! You're making a mountain out of a mole-hill!

CHRISTINA. Cruelty to children isn't a mole-hill!

DAVID. You're exaggerating! Hester's engagement isn't the first that was ever broken.

CHRISTINA. Think how it was broken and by whom!

DAVID. You just said she was in luck to be rid of Rob. I'll grant you that. I haven't any more use for Rob than you have.

CHRISTINA. Who stands behind Rob?

DAVID. I don't know what you mean.

CHRISTINA. Don't you?

DAVID. No.

CHRISTINA. All right, I'll tell you.

DAVID. [*Quickly.*] You needn't. . . .

Are you trying to pick a fight with me?

CHRISTINA. On the contrary. I'm asking you to stand by me. [*Her eyes corner him.*]

DAVID. I won't go away and leave Mother in the lurch.

CHRISTINA. You see? You do know what I mean!

DAVID. I don't. I'm just telling you I won't let Mother down.

CHRISTINA. You'd rather stand by your mother than by the right, wouldn't you?

DAVID. Oh, the right?

CHRISTINA. Isn't Hester the right?

DAVID. [*Cornered again.*] I can't help it if she is. I won't let Mother down.

CHRISTINA. You'll let *me* down.

DAVID. Oh, Chris! It's late. Come on. Let's turn in.

CHRISTINA. You'd rather stand by your mother than by me, wouldn't you?

DAVID. No, I wouldn't. I tell you Hester's none of our business.

CHRISTINA. You'll admit *this* is?

DAVID. What is?

CHRISTINA. This! . . . Who comes first with you? Your mother or me?

DAVID. Now what's the good of putting things that way?

CHRISTINA. That's what things come to! If your mother and I ever quarreled about anything, if it ever came up to you to choose between sticking by me and sticking by her, which would you stick by?

DAVID. I'd . . . I'd try to do the right thing. . . .

CHRISTINA. That isn't an answer. That's another evasion.

DAVID. But why ask such a question?

CHRISTINA. Because I love you. Because I've got to find out if you love me. And I'm afraid . . . I'm afraid. . . .

DAVID. Why?

CHRISTINA. Because you won't see the facts behind all this. I'm trying to tell you what they are and you won't listen. You can't even hear me.

DAVID. I *can* hear you. And a worse line of hooey I've never listened to in my life.

CHRISTINA. [*Gravely, but with steadily increasing fervor.*] Have you ever thought what it would be like to be trapped in a submarine in an accident? I've learned to-night what that kind of panic would be like. I'm in that kind of panic now, this minute. I've been through the most awful experience of my life to-night. And I've been through it alone. I'm still going through it alone. It's pretty awful to have to face such things alone. . . . No, don't interrupt me. I've got to get this off my chest. Ever since we've been married I've been coming across queer rifts in your feeling for me, like arid places in your heart. Such vast ones, too! I mean, you'll be my perfect lover one day and the next, I'll find myself floundering in sand, and alone, and you nowhere to be seen. We've never been really married, Dave. Only now and then, for a little while at a time, between your retirements into your arid places. . . . I used to wonder what you did there. At first, I thought you did your work there. But you don't. Your work's in my part of your heart, what there is of my part. Then I decided the other was just No-Man's Land. And I thought: little by little, I'll encroach upon it and pour my love upon it, like water on the western desert, and make it flower here and bear fruit there. I thought: then he'll be all alive, all free and all himself; not partly dead and tied and blind; not partly some one else—or nothing. You see, our marriage and your architecture were suffering from the same thing. They only work a little of the time. I meant them both to work all the time. I meant you to work all the time and to win your way, *all* your way, Dave, to complete manhood. And that's a good deal farther than you've got so far. . . . Then we came here and this happened with Hester and your brother and you just stepped aside and did nothing about it! You went to bed. You did worse than that. You retired into your private wastes and sat tight. . . . I've shown you what you should do and you won't see it. I've called to you to come out to me, and you won't come. So now I've discovered what keeps you. Your mother keeps you. It isn't No-Man's Land at all. It's your mother's land. Arid, sterile, and your mother's! You won't let me get in there. Worse than that, you won't let life get in there! Or she won't! . . . That's what I'm afraid of, Dave: your mother's hold on you. And that's what's kept me from getting anywhere with you, all these months. I've seen what she can do with Robert. And what she's done to Hester. I can't help wondering what she may not do with you and to me and to the baby. That's why I'm asking you to take a stand on this business of Hester's, Dave. You'll never find the right any clearer than it is here. It's a kind of test case for me. Don't you see? What you decide about this is what you may, eventually, be expected to decide about . . . about our marriage.

DAVID. [*A pause, then, with sullen violence.*] No! I'm damned if I see!

CHRISTINA. [*Breaking.*] Then I can't hope for much, can I? . . . I feel awfully like a lost soul, right now. . . . Oh, my God, what am I going to do! What am I going to do!

DAVID. I hope you're going to behave. You ought to be ashamed. Just as I was bringing Mother around to you and . . .

CHRISTINA. [*Violently.*] You'd better think a little about bringing me around to your mother!

DAVID. Chris!

CHRISTINA. Why should your mother and I get on?

DAVID. Because you should, that's why. Because she's an older woman and my mother. And you know, just as well as I do . . .

CHRISTINA. I know a great deal better than you that your mother dislikes me fully as much as I dislike her. You're wasting your time trying to bring your mother and me together, because we won't be brought. You say you believe in facing the facts. Well, let's see you face that one!

DAVID. I've never heard anything so outrageous. When you know what Mother means to me and what . . .

CHRISTINA. [*Desperate.*] Your mother! Your mother! Always your mother! She's got you back! Dave, her big boy, who ran off and got married! She's got you back!

DAVID. I won't stand for any more of this. A man's mother is his mother.

CHRISTINA. [*Crescendo.*] And what's his wife, may I ask? Or doesn't she count?

DAVID. This is morbid rot! She warned me you'd be jealous of her!

CHRISTINA. *Did* she?

DAVID. But I never expected anything like this!

CHRISTINA. What's going to become of me?

DAVID. I won't stand for any more. . . .

CHRISTINA. Hester's escaped, but I'm caught! I can't go back and be the old Christina again. She's done for. And Christina, your wife, doesn't even exist! That's the fact I've got to face! I'm going to have a baby by a man who belongs to another woman!

DAVID. Damn it, Chris! Do you want Mother to hear you?

CHRISTINA. Do I not!

[MRS. PHELPS *stands in her door, white, but steady.*]

DAVID. [*Turning, sees her.*] Oh . . . You *did* hear!

MRS. PHELPS. How could I help hearing every word that Christina said?

DAVID. Oh, this is awful!

MRS. PHELPS. We know, now, where we stand, all three of us.

DAVID. Chris, can't you tell her you didn't mean it?

MRS. PHELPS. [*Heroic sarcasm.*] Christina isn't one to say things she doesn't mean. And I have no intention of defending myself.

DAVID. Mother, please! . . . Chris, you'd better beat it.

MRS. PHELPS. I ask her to stay. She has made me afraid ever to be alone with you again. She must have made you afraid to be alone with me.

DAVID. Nonsense, Mother! She hasn't done anything of the sort. You'd better go, Chris. It's the least you can do after what you've said.

CHRISTINA. The very least. I belong with Hester now.

[*She goes quickly.*]

DAVID. [*Turning wildly to his mother.*] I'll straighten everything out in the morning. I swear I will!

MRS. PHELPS. [*A very different, very noble tone.*] This is an old story, Dave boy, and I'm on Christina's side just as I said I should be.

DAVID. I can't have you talking like that, Mother!

MRS. PHELPS. I accept my fate. You have your own life to live with the woman you have chosen. No boy could have given me back the love I gave you. Go to Christina! Make your life with her! No bond binds you to me any longer.

DAVID. That isn't true!

MRS. PHELPS. I'm not complaining. I'm only sorry for one thing. I'm only sorry to see you throw away your chance here your great chance!

DAVID. But I haven't thrown it away. I'll stay here and work for you, if you want me to.

MRS. PHELPS. Christina won't let you. You know that!

DAVID. She's my wife, isn't she?

MRS. PHELPS. Think what that means, Dave! Think what that means!

DAVID. And you're my mother. I'm thinking what that means, too!

MRS. PHELPS. Then it isn't good-bye? Then I've still got my big boy, after all?

DAVID. You bet you've got him!

MRS. PHELPS. [*Triumph.*] Oh, Dave! Dave! Dave!

DAVID. Now, Mummy! [*But a sound downstairs distracts him.*] Hello! What's that? [*She listens, too.*]

MRS. PHELPS. Heavens, it isn't a fire, is it?

DAVID. Wait . . . I'll see. . . .

[*He opens the door into the hall and stands listening.*]

CHRISTINA. [*Off-stage and below.*] I went into her room and she wasn't there and then I looked for her and I found the dining-room window open.

ROBERT. [*Off-stage and below.*] What do you think has happened?

CHRISTINA. [*Off-stage and below.*] I don't like to imagine things, but . . .

ROBERT. [*Off-stage and below.*] Hester, where are you?

CHRISTINA. [*Off-stage and below.*] She's got away! I tell you, she's got away! I shouldn't have left her. . . .

DAVID. [*Speaking during the above.*] What?

MRS. PHELPS. It's Christina and Robert.

DAVID. Something's happened to Hester.

MRS. PHELPS. No!

DAVID. Chris! What's going on?

ROBERT. [*Off-stage.*] Hester! Where are you, Hester?

CHRISTINA. [*Appearing in the hall.*] Hester's got away, Dave. Out by the dining-room window. You'll have to get dressed and find her. She can't get to town to-night in this cold.

DAVID. All right. We'll have a look.

MRS. PHELPS. The little fool! Let her go, Dave!

CHRISTINA. But, Mrs. Phelps, she isn't properly dressed. She didn't even take her coat. . . .

ROBERT. [*Still calling off-stage and below.*] Hester! Where are you, Hester? Hester! . . . Oh, my God!

[CHRISTINA *has walked to the window to look out. She utters an inarticulate scream.*]

DAVID. What is it, Chris?

MRS. PHELPS. Good heavens!

CHRISTINA. [*Strangled with horror.*] It's the pond! The holes in the pond! Quick, Dave, for heaven's sake!

DAVID. What? . . . Oh! . . .

[*He runs out as* CHRISTINA *opens the window.*]

MRS. PHELPS. Dave! . . . [*To* CHRISTINA.] What is it you say?

ROBERT. [*Off-stage and below.*] Dave! For God's sake! Hold on, Hester! Don't struggle!

[DAVID'S *shouts join his.*]

CHRISTINA. [*As she collapses on the bed.*] The pond! . . . I can't look. . . .

MRS. PHELPS. Oh, I've no patience with people who have hysterics!

CHRISTINA. Mrs. Phelps, the girl's drowning!

MRS. PHELPS. Oh, no! . . . Not that! [*She, too, goes to the window, but recoils in horror from what she sees.*] They'll save her, won't they? They must . . . they must save her. . . . If only . . . [*Then a new fear overwhelms her.*] If only those two boys don't catch pneumonia! [*And she leaps to the window to call after her sons as they race, shouting, across the snow.*] Robin, you're not dressed! Dave, get your coat! Are you crazy? Do you *want* to catch pneumonia?

CURTAIN

ACT THREE

The living-room again, and the next morning. MRS. PHELPS *is wearing a simple house dress and busily fixing a great many flowers which she takes from boxes strewn about the stage. After she has been so occupied for a few seconds,* ROBERT *enters.*

ROBERT. The doctor's gone.

MRS. PHELPS. [*Surprised.*] Without seeing me?

ROBERT. It seems so.

MRS. PHELPS. Doesn't that seem very strange to you, Robin? Of course, I thought it best not to go up to Hester's room with him. In view of the perfectly unreasonable attitude she's taken toward me. But, I should have supposed, naturally, that he'd have made his report to me.

ROBERT. He says she may as well go today. He says traveling won't be as bad for her as staying here.

MRS. PHELPS. Did he say that to you?

ROBERT. I couldn't face him. *They* told him the whole story.

MRS. PHELPS. Christina and Hester? [ROBERT *nods.*] I might have known they would. . . . And he listened to them and never so much as asked for me?

ROBERT. What of it!

MRS. PHELPS. He'll never enter this house again!

ROBERT. So *he* said! He also said there's nothing the matter with your heart and never has been anything the matter with it. He said it would take a stick of dynamite to kill you.

MRS. PHELPS. Damned homeopath!

ROBERT. And that isn't the worst.

MRS. PHELPS. What more?

ROBERT. He said that I'd always been a rotter.

MRS. PHELPS. Oh?

ROBERT. And that I couldn't have been anything else—with such a mother.

[*There is venom in this last.* MRS. PHELPS' *lips stiffen under it.*]

MRS. PHELPS. I think you might have spared me that, Robin.

ROBERT. I didn't mean to be nasty.

MRS. PHELPS. No. Still, there are things one doesn't repeat to sensitive people. [*But a dark foreboding will not be downed.*] Somehow, though, I can't help feeling that . . . [*She does not say what she sees in the future.*]

ROBERT. Neither can I.

[*She looks at him in quick fear. Then she returns to her flowers with a shrug.*]

MRS. PHELPS. Oh, well! There can't have been much wrong with the girl if she's able to go this morning.

ROBERT. Thank God for that. [*Then with level-eyed cruelty.*] It might have been serious, though, after what you did to the telephone. Because we couldn't have reached a soul, you know. And without Christina in the house . . .

MRS. PHELPS. How was I to know the little fool wanted to drown herself?

ROBERT. [*Shuddering.*] For heaven's sake, don't put it that way!

MRS. PHELPS. How do *you* put it?

ROBERT. She tried to get away, that's all. And she got lost in the dark and . . .

MRS. PHELPS. I tell you, she tried to kill herself. I've always suspected there was insanity in her family. She had a brother who was an aviator in the war. Everybody knows that aviators are lunatics. Her own conduct has never been what I should call normal. Everything points to insanity. That's another reason why you shouldn't have married her. Because we've never had any of that in our family. Except your father's Bright's Disease. I shall certainly tell every one that Hester is insane.

ROBERT. Perhaps that *will* make things simpler.

MRS. PHELPS. As to the telephone, it's the only thing I've ever done to be ashamed of, and I said as much when I did it. She made me angry with her wanton attacks on you.

ROBERT. I didn't hear any wanton attacks.

MRS. PHELPS. Where were you?

ROBERT. Out there in the hall.

MRS. PHELPS. You couldn't have heard the things she muttered under her breath.

ROBERT. [*An incredulous sneer.*] No! [*There is a pause, sullen on his part, troubled on hers.*] We're just like Macbeth and Lady Macbeth, aren't we?

MRS. PHELPS. For heaven's sakes, how?

ROBERT. We've got into a mess we can't ever get out of. We'll have to get in deeper and deeper until *we* go mad and . . .

MRS. PHELPS. Don't be ridiculous.

ROBERT. I'm sorry, Mother, but I can't help regretting.

MRS. PHELPS. Regretting what?

ROBERT. [*Low.*] Hester.

MRS. PHELPS. Nonsense, Robin! I tell you . . .

ROBERT. What do you know about it? Do you understand me any better than Hester did?

MRS. PHELPS. How *can* you, Robin? I not understand you? Haven't I always told you that however David may take after his father, you are *my* son?

ROBERT. What's that got to do with it?

MRS. PHELPS. Robin!

ROBERT. If I wasn't sure that I *loved* Hester, how on earth can I be sure that I *didn't* love her? I don't know this minute whether I loved her or not. I only know that I'll regret losing her all my life long. [*A movement of exasperation from his mother stops him. Then he concludes.*] Maybe Dave's right about me. Maybe I *am* too weak to love any one.

MRS. PHELPS. [*Frightened—to herself.*] Dave didn't say *that!*

ROBERT. He said I hadn't any guts.

MRS. PHELPS. Ugh! That horrible word! No, Robin. You must put all such thoughts aside.

ROBERT. I suppose I'll have to take your word for it. [*Then with sudden, cold fury.*] But I won't next time.

MRS. PHELPS. Robin! You're not holding *me* responsible?

ROBERT. Who put the idea in my head? Who persuaded me? Who made me promise?

MRS. PHELPS. Are you implying that *I* came between you?

ROBERT. Well, if you didn't, who did?

MRS. PHELPS. Robin! You ought to be ashamed!

ROBERT. Think so?

MRS. PHELPS. That *you* should turn on me! Some day you'll regret this. It won't be Hester, but *this* that you'll regret. . . . When it's too late.

[*And from force of habit her hand steals to her heart.*]

ROBERT. I daresay I've got a life full of regrets ahead of me.

[*He walks sullenly to the window.*]

MRS. PHELPS. You frighten me, Robin! I don't know you like this.

ROBERT. Don't you?

[*There is a pause.* MRS PHELPS *stares at him in growing horror. He looks out of the window.*]

MRS. PHELPS. No.

ROBERT. [*Looking out, his back to her.*] That's too bad. . . . There's Dave putting up danger signs all around the pond! Isn't that like him! After it's too late. [*She turns away from him and dully goes on with her flowers, carrying a bowl of them over to the piano.* ROBERT *watches her coldly. Then a sudden frown contracts his brow and he moves toward her.*] Mother!

MRS. PHELPS. What?

ROBERT. Don't put those flowers there! They're too low!

MRS. PHELPS. Fix them yourself.

ROBERT. [*Changing them with a jar of something else.*] Isn't that better?

MRS. PHELPS. Much. What an eye you have!

ROBERT. Perhaps I'll develop it some day.

MRS. PHELPS. Would you like to?

ROBERT. I've got to do something.

MRS. PHELPS. [*Darkly.*] I quite agree. Every young man should have some profession.

[*Then, suddenly and involuntarily, the boy reverts and is a child again.*]

ROBERT. What are we going to do, Mother?

MRS. PHELPS. [*Low.*] Do?

ROBERT. What are we going to do, you and I? We're in the same boat, you know.

MRS. PHELPS. [*Lower.*] I don't know what you mean.

ROBERT. Well, what am I going to do, then? I can't stay here and face people after this!

MRS. PHELPS. What will there be to face?

ROBERT. [*Crescendo.*] You know as well as I do. This story'll be all over this damn town. And Hester's people aren't going to keep quiet in New York. Her brothers go everywhere I go. My friends will begin cutting me in the street.

MRS. PHELPS. If we say she's insane?

ROBERT. What difference will that make?

MRS. PHELPS. [*Very low.*] The *Paris* sails on Saturday.

ROBERT. [*Pause, then, tremulously.*] What of it?

MRS. PHELPS. We might go to Washington to hurry our passports.

ROBERT. Could we get passage, though?

MRS. PHELPS. [*Slowly.*] I've already wired for it. This morning.

ROBERT. I see. . . . Then we're to sneak away like two guilty fugitives!

MRS. PHELPS. [*Avoiding his eye.*] Sh! Don't say such things!

[DAVID *enters, his cheeks stung crimson by the cold.*]

DAVID. Phew, it's cold. The pond'll be frozen again by to-morrow if this keeps up. What's the doc say about Hester?

ROBERT. She's leaving us to-day.

DAVID. I'm glad she's well enough.

MRS. PHELPS. There never was anything the matter with her.

DAVID. It's easy to see, Mother, that you don't often bathe in that pond in zero weather.

MRS. PHELPS. I hope I have more self-control. Robin, will you see, please, that the car is ready for Hester?

ROBERT. Yes.

[*He goes.*]

DAVID. Anybody seen Chris?

MRS. PHELPS. Not I.

DAVID. No. I suppose not. . . . What's the idea in the floral display?

MRS. PHELPS. I felt I had to have flowers about me.

DAVID. That sounds pretty Green Hattish. . . . It has a festive look, too. I don't see what there is to celebrate.

MRS. PHELPS. [*Noble tragedienne that she is.*] Last night, at a single blow, beauty was stricken out of my life. I can't live without beauty, Dave. You must know that. So I went to the florist this morning and bought these. They comfort me . . . a little.

DAVID. [*That worried look again.*] I've been thinking, Mother, that maybe, all things considered, after last night, it will be as well for me to take Chris away on Wednesday, say.

MRS. PHELPS. If you like.

DAVID. We can come back later. After things have cooled down.

MRS. PHELPS. Later, I hope, and often.

DAVID. Time does make things easier, doesn't it?

MRS. PHELPS. They say so.

DAVID. When scientists get these wild ideas and fly off the handle, they're just as embarrassed afterwards as any one else would be.

MRS. PHELPS. Naturally.

DAVID. And then Hester's running away and the telephone being busted and all. . . .

MRS. PHELPS. I quite understand.

DAVID. I knew you would.

MRS. PHELPS. [*The boxes and paper all stowed away, she sits down to business.*] What I'm wondering now, though, is what I'm to do with Robin? And I'm afraid you've got to help me with him.

DAVID. I'll do anything I can.

MRS. PHELPS. If I were well and able to stand the things I used to stand before my heart went back on me—because it *has* gone back on me—and before my blood pressure got so high . . . I shouldn't trouble you. But as I am, and with Robin on the verge of a complete breakdown . . .

DAVID. But Rob isn't . . .

MRS. PHELPS. Oh, yes, he is, Dave! He said things to me before you came in that no son of mine would dream of saying unless he had something the matter with him. I've got to get him away.

DAVID. Send him abroad.

MRS. PHELPS. I don't think he ought to go alone. He can't face things alone. He's like his father, in that. You're *my* son, you know. That's why I always turn to you.

DAVID. Why not go with him?

MRS. PHELPS. Because I'm really not well enough in case anything should happen. . . . And I don't know what to do. Oh, Dave, boy, do you think . . .

DAVID. What?

MRS. PHELPS. That Christina could spare you for a little? Just a few weeks? Just long enough to get Rob and me settled in some restful place? Do you think she would?

DAVID. There's no need of that!

MRS. PHELPS. Of course, I'd love to have Christina, too. Only I'm afraid that *would* be asking too much. I mean, making her put off her work when she's so set on it.

DAVID. But Rob isn't going to give you any trouble.

MRS. PHELPS. Do you think I'd ask such a sacrifice of you . . . and Christina, if I weren't sure that it's absolutely necessary? Oh, I'm not thinking of myself. I no longer matter. Except that I shouldn't want to die abroad with only Robin there, in his present condition.

DAVID. Don't talk that way, Mother!

MRS. PHELPS. Why not? I'm not asking you to be sorry for me. It's Robin I'm thinking of. Because we haven't done all that we should for Robin. And now that I'm old . . . and sick . . . dying . . .

[*She breaks down.*]

DAVID. You're not, Mother!

MRS. PHELPS. [*Weeping hysterically.*] I can't cope with him. He'll slip back again to drinking and fast women . . .

DAVID. Get hold of yourself, Mother!

MRS. PHELPS. [*More hysterical.*] And when I think of what I might have done for him and realize that it's too late, that I haven't any more time . . . only a few months . . . or weeks . . . I don't know . . . I . . .

[*She really becomes quite faint.*]

DAVID. [*Snatching her hand in terror.*] Mother, what's the matter? Are you ill?

MRS. PHELPS. [*Recovering by inches as she gasps for breath.*] No! It's nothing . . . I . . . Just give me a minute . . . Don't call any one . . . I'll be all right. . . . There! . . . That's better!

DAVID. You scared me to death.

MRS. PHELPS. I scare myself sometimes. You see I do need *somebody's* help.

DAVID. Yes, I see you do.

MRS. PHELPS. And so I thought: well, since Dave *is* going to build my houses in Phelps Manor. . . . You're not going to disappoint me there, I hope?

DAVID. Oh, no!

MRS. PHELPS. Well, then you won't want to start in that New York office.

DAVID. Why not?

MRS. PHELPS. When you'll be leaving so soon to begin here? They wouldn't want you.

DAVID. I hadn't thought of that.

MRS. PHELPS. And so I thought: Well, he can't begin here until April anyway and that leaves him with two idle months on his hands when he might be drawing plans and getting ideas abroad. Think it over, Dave boy.

DAVID. You certainly are a great planner, Mother.

MRS. PHELPS. I make such good plans!

DAVID. When would you be sailing?

MRS. PHELPS. Well, I . . . I *had* thought . . . vaguely . . . of sailing on the *Paris* . . . Saturday . . .

DAVID. Good Lord! Give a man time to think! I want to do the right thing, but I couldn't leave Chris. . . . Not with the baby coming, you know.

MRS. PHELPS. But you'll be home in plenty of time for that.

DAVID. That may all be, but, just the same, I wouldn't feel right to leave her.

[ROBERT *returns.*]

MRS. PHELPS. I've just been telling Dave about our wonderful plans, Robin, and he's so enthusiastic! I shouldn't wonder if he came along with us.

[*A sign to* DAVID *to play up.*]

ROBERT. What *are* the plans?

MRS. PHELPS. Why, your going abroad to study interior decorating, of course.

[ROBERT *looks surprised.*]

DAVID. Oh, is Rob going to do that?

ROBERT. Any objections?

DAVID. I think it's just the job for you. Painting rosebuds on bath-tubs.

ROBERT. I can make your houses look like something after you've finished with them.

MRS. PHELPS. [*Ecstatically.*] My two boys in partnership! Oh, that's always been my dream! Oh, how simply things come straight when people are willing to coöperate and make little sacrifices! If there's one thing I pride myself on, it's my willingness to make little sacrifices. Here we are, we three, a moment ago all at odds with life and with each other; now united and of a single mind . . .

DAVID. This is all very fine. But don't you forget that I've got to talk to Christina . . .

[*But* CHRISTINA *has opened the door upon his very words. She is dressed as she was when she first came to the house. She wears her hat and her fur coat and carries her bag in her hand.*]

CHRISTINA. [*Speaking as she enters.*] Well, now's your chance, Dave. What have you got to talk to me about?

DAVID. [*Staring at her.*] What's the idea, Chris?

CHRISTINA. [*Setting the bag down by the door.*] I'm going away with Hester. Are you coming, too?

DAVID. [*Staggered.*] Now?

CHRISTINA. In a few minutes. I came down ahead. No, don't go, Mrs. Phelps. And won't you stay, too, Robert? I think it's best that we should thrash this question out together, here and now, for good and all.

MRS. PHELPS. What question, Christina?

CHRISTINA. The David question, Mrs. Phelps. Whether David is going on from this point as your son or as my husband.

ROBERT. What?

CHRISTINA. Isn't that the issue? [*She asks the question less of* DAVID *than of* MRS. PHELPS, *who turns to her sons in terror.*]

MRS. PHELPS. I can't go through this a second time!

DAVID. [*Quieting her with a gesture.*] No one expects you to. . . . [*To* CHRISTINA, *pleading almost pathetically.*] You're not going to begin all that again, Chris?

CHRISTINA. I'm afraid I am.

DAVID. But, just as I was getting everything all straightened out . . .

CHRISTINA. Were you doing that?

DAVID. If only you'll leave things be, they'll be all right. You may believe it or not . . .

CHRISTINA. I can't believe it and I can't leave things be. Oh, I'd walk out without a word, even loving you as I do, if I thought this state of affairs made any one of you happy.

ROBERT. What state of affairs?

CHRISTINA. The state of affairs you've all been living in and suffering from, for so long.

MRS. PHELPS. You might let us judge our own happiness.

CHRISTINA. I might, if you had any. But you haven't.

ROBERT. You're quite sure of that?

CHRISTINA. Quite, Robert. You're all of you perfectly miserable! Am I wrong?

MRS. PHELPS. Christina! Please!

ROBERT. Thank you for being sorry for us!

CHRISTINA. You give me such good reason, Robert. Such awfully good reason! Because you're not really bad people, you know. You're just wrong, all wrong, terribly, pitifully, all of you, and you're trapped . . .

MRS. PHELPS. What we say in anger, we sometimes regret, Christina. . . .

CHRISTINA. Oh, I'm not angry. I was, but I've got over it. I rather fancy myself, now, as a sort of scientific Nemesis. I mean to strip this house and to show it up for what it really is. I mean to show you up, Mrs. Phelps. Then Dave can use his own judgment.

MRS. PHELPS. [*Blank terror at this attack.*] Oh! Dave, I . . .

DAVID. Now, Mother! Chris! Haven't you any consideration for our feelings? Are they nothing to you?

CHRISTINA. I'm trying to save my love, my home, my husband and my baby's father. Are they nothing to you?

DAVID. But surely I can be both a good son and a good husband!

CHRISTINA. Not if your mother knows it, you can't!

MRS. PHELPS. [*A last desperate snatch at dignity.*] If you'll excuse me, I'd rather not stay to be insulted again. [*She is going.*]

CHRISTINA. You'll probably lose him if you don't stay, Mrs. Phelps! [MRS. PHELPS *stays.* CHRISTINA *turns to* DAVID.] No, Dave. Ther 's no good in any more pretending. Your mother won't allow you to divide your affections and I refuse to go on living with you on any basis she will allow.

MRS. PHELPS. I cannot see that this is necessary.

CHRISTINA. It's a question a great many young wives leave unsettled, Mrs. Phelps. I'm not going to make that mistake. [*Back to* DAVE *again.*] You see, Dave, I'm not beating about the bush. I'm not persuading you or wasting any time on tact. Do you want your chance or don't you? Because, if you don't, I'll have to get over being in love with you as best I can and . . .

DAVID. I wish you wouldn't talk this way, Chris!

CHRISTINA. Are you coming with me? On the understanding that, for the present, until your affections are definitely settled on your wife and child, you avoid your mother's society entirely. Well? What do you say?

DAVID. I don't know what to say.

CHRISTINA. You never do, Dave darling.

DAVID. I'm too shocked. I've never been so shocked in my life.

CHRISTINA. [*A glance at her wrist watch.*] Just take your time and think before you speak.

DAVID. I don't mean that I don't know what to say about taking my chance, as you call it. I can answer that by reminding you of your duty to me. I can answer that by calling all this what I called it last night. Morbid rot! But I *am* shocked at your talking this way about my mother and to her face, too!

CHRISTINA. Is that your answer?

DAVID. No, it isn't! But a man's mother *is* his mother.

CHRISTINA. So you said last night. I'm not impressed. An embryological accident is no grounds for honor. Neither is a painful confinement, for I understand, Mrs. Phelps, that you're very proud of the way you bore your children. I know all about the legend of yourself as a great woman that you've built up these thirty years for your sons to worship. It hasn't taken me long to see that you're not fit to be any one's mother.

DAVID. Chris!

ROBERT. [*Speaking at the same time.*] See here, now!

MRS. PHELPS. Let her go on! Let her go on! She will explain that or retract it!

CHRISTINA. I'm only too glad to explain. It's just what I've been leading up to. And I'll begin by saying that if my baby ever feels about me as your sons feel about you, I hope that somebody will take a little enameled pistol and shoot me, because I'll deserve it.

MRS. PHELPS. [*Going again.*] I've been insulted once too often.

CHRISTINA. I don't mean to insult you. I'm being as scientific and impersonal as possible.

ROBERT. Good God!

CHRISTINA. [*Regardless.*] Speaking of

insults, though, what explanation can *you* offer *me* for your rudeness to me as a guest in your house?

MRS. PHELPS. I have not been rude to you.

CHRISTINA. You have been appallingly rude. Second question: Why do you resent the fact that I am going to have a baby?

MRS. PHELPS. I don't resent it.

CHRISTINA. Then why are you so churlish about it?

MRS. PHELPS. Your indelicacy about it would have . . .

CHRISTINA. That's another evasion. You're afraid that baby will give me another and stronger hold on David and you mean to separate David and me if it's humanly possible.

MRS. PHELPS. I do not! I do not!

CHRISTINA. Did you or did you not bend every effort to separate Hester and Robert?

MRS. PHELPS. I most certainly did not!

CHRISTINA. Then how do you account for the deliberate and brutal lies you told Hester about Robert? Because she did lie to Hester about you, Robert. She told Hester that you never wanted to marry her.

ROBERT. [*Aghast.*] Mother, you didn't!

MRS. PHELPS. Of course, I didn't!

CHRISTINA. [*Joan of Arc raising the siege of Orleans.*] I heard her. And I heard her call both of you back, last night, when you ran out to save Hester from drowning. I heard her call you back from saving a drowning girl for fear of your catching cold. I heard her. I heard her.

DAVID. [*Shaken.*] You shouldn't have called us, Mother!

CHRISTINA. Can she deny that her one idea is to keep her sons, dependent on her? Can she deny that she opposes any move that either one of you makes toward independence? Can she deny that she is outraged by your natural impulses toward other women?

MRS. PHELPS. [*Furious.*] I deny all of it!

CHRISTINA. You may deny it until you're black in the face; every accusation I make is true! You belong to a type that's very common in this country, Mrs. Phelps—a type of self-centered, self-pitying, son-devouring tigress, with unmentionable proclivities suppressed on the side.

DAVID. Chris!

CHRISTINA. I'm not at all sure it wouldn't be a good idea, just as an example to the rest of the tribe, to hang one of your kind every now and then!

ROBERT. Really!

CHRISTINA. Oh, there are normal mothers around; mothers who *want* their children to be men and women and take care of themselves; mothers who are people, too, and don't have to be afraid of loneliness after they've outlived their motherhood; mothers who can look on their children as people and enjoy them as people and not be forever holding on to them and pawing them and fussing about their health and singing them lullabies and tucking them up as though they were everlasting babies. But you're *not* one of the normal ones, Mrs. Phelps! Look at your sons, if you don't believe me. You've destroyed Robert. You've swallowed him up until there's nothing left of him but an effete make-believe. Now he's gone melancholy mad and disgraced himself. And Dave! Poor Dave! The best he can do is dodge the more desperate kinds of unhappiness by pretending! How he survived at all is beyond me. If you're choking a bit on David, now, that's my fault because you'd have swallowed him up, too, if I hadn't come along to save him! Talk about cannibals! You and your kind beat any cannibals I've ever heard of! And what makes you doubly deadly and dangerous is that people admire you and your kind. They actually admire you! You professional mothers! . . . You see, I'm taking this differently from that poor child upstairs. She's luckier than I am, too. She isn't married to one of your sons. Do you remember what she said about children yesterday? "Have 'em. Love 'em. And leave 'em be."

MRS. PHELPS. You are entitled to your opinions, Christina, just as I am to mine and David is to his. I only hope that he sees the kind of woman he's married. I hope he sees the sordidness, the hardness, the nastiness she offers him for his life.

CHRISTINA. [*An involuntary cry of pain.*] I'm not nasty! I'm not!

MRS. PHELPS. What have you to offer David?

CHRISTINA. A hard time. A chance to work on his own. A chance to *be* on his own. Very little money on which to share with me the burden of raising his child. The pleasure of my society. The solace of my love. The enjoyment of my body. To which I have reason to believe he is not indifferent.

MRS. PHELPS. [*Revolted.*] Ugh!

CHRISTINA. Can you offer so much?

MRS. PHELPS. I offer a mother's love. Or perhaps you scoff at that?

CHRISTINA. Not if it's kept within bounds. I hope my baby loves me. I'm practically certain I'm going to love my baby. But within bounds.

MRS. PHELPS. And what do you mean by within bounds?

CHRISTINA. To love my baby with as much and as deep respect as I hope my baby will feel for me if I deserve its respect. To love my baby unpossessively; above all, unromantically.

MRS. PHELPS. I suppose that's biology! You don't know the difference between good and evil!

CHRISTINA. As a biologist, though, I do know the difference between life and death. And I know sterility when I see it. I doubt if evil is any more than a fancy name for sterility. And sterility, of course, is what you offer Dave. Sterility for his mind as well as for his body. That's your professional mother's stock in trade. Only we've been over that, haven't we? Well, Dave! How about it?

ROBERT. I think this has gone far enough!

MRS. PHELPS. No! This woman has got to answer me one question.

CHRISTINA. Willingly. What is it?

MRS. PHELPS. How old were you when you married?

CHRISTINA. The same age I am now. Twenty-nine.

MRS. PHELPS. I was twenty.

CHRISTINA. Just Hester's age.

MRS. PHELPS. [*Riding over her.*] I was twenty and my husband was fifteen years older than I. Oh, thirty-five isn't old, but he was a widower, too, and an invalid. Everyone told me I'd made a great match. And I thought I had. But before we'd been married a week, I saw my illusions shattered. I knew at the end of a week how miserable and empty my marriage was. He was good to me. He made very few demands on me. But he never dreamed of bringing the least atom of happiness into my life. Or of romance. . . . Only a woman who has lived without romance knows how to value it. . . . That isn't true of my life either. I didn't live without romance. I found it . . . and I'm proud to have found it where you say it doesn't belong . . . in motherhood. I found it in my two babies. In Dave first and in Robin four years later. I found it in doing for them myself all those things which, nowadays, nurses and governesses are hired to do. To spare mothers! I never asked to be spared. . . . Their father died. The night he died, Robin had croup and I had to make the final choice between my duties. I stayed with Robin. You, with your modern ideas and your science, Christina, would you have chosen differently? I knew the difference between life and death that night. And I've known it for every step of the way I battled for Robin's health, every step as I taught Dave his gentleness and his generosity. . . . If I made my mistakes, and I'm only human . . . I'm sorry for them. But I can point to my two sons and say that my mistakes could not have been serious ones. . . . Think! I was a widow, rich and very pretty, at twenty-five. Think what that means! But I had found my duty and I never swerved from it. . . . There was one man in particular. A fine man. But I resisted. I knew that second marriage was not for me. Not when I had my sons. I put them first, always. . . . I shall not stoop to answer any of the foulness you have charged me with. They are beneath my dignity as a woman and my contempt as a mother. No, there is one I cannot leave unanswered. That word "sterility." Sterility is what I offer David, you say. I wonder, is sterility David's word for all he has had of me these thirty years? Let him answer that for himself. All my life I have saved to launch my two boys on their careers, saved in vision as well as in money. I don't offer my sons a love half dedicated to selfish, personal ambition. I don't offer them careers limited by the demands of other careers. I offer David a clear field ahead and a complete love to sustain him, a mother's love, until a real marriage, a suitable marriage may be possible for him. And I do *not* deny that I would cut off my right hand and burn the sight out of my eyes to rid my son of you! . . . That is how I answer your impersonal science, Christina.

CHRISTINA. [*Before either of the boys can speak.*] I see! . . . Well. . . . It's a very plausible and effective answer. And I'm sure you mean it and I believe it's sincere. But it *is* the answer of a woman whose husband let her down pretty hard and turned for satisfaction to her sons. . . . I'm almost sorry I can't say more for it, but I can't. . . . [*She turns from* MRS. PHELPS *to the two sons.*] It's a pity she didn't marry again. Things would have been so much better for both of you if she had. [*Then, with an increasing force, to* DAVID.] But the fact remains, Dave, that she did separate you and me last night and that she separated us because she couldn't bear the thought of our sleeping together. [*They flinch at this, but she downs them.*] And she couldn't bear that because she refuses to believe that you're a grown man and capable of desiring a woman. And that's because, grown man that you are, down, down in the depths of her, she still wants to suckle you at her breast!

DAVID. [*A cry of horror.*] Chris!

ROBERT. [*At the same time.*] Good God!

MRS. PHELPS. [*At the same time.*] No!

CHRISTINA. You find that picture revolting, do you? Well, so it is. . . . I can't wait any longer for your answer, Dave.

DAVID. I don't think you've any sense of decency left in you. Of all the filthy, vile . . .

CHRISTINA. I'm sorry you feel that way.

DAVID. How else *can* I feel?

CHRISTINA. Is that your answer?

DAVID. I want to do the right thing, but . . .

CHRISTINA. Remember me, won't you, on Mother's Day! [*Then she calls out.*] Are you ready, Hester?

DAVID. You make things mighty hard, Chris, for a man who knows what fair play is and gratitude and all those other things I naturally feel for my mother.

CHRISTINA. Do I?

DAVID. What do you expect me to say?

CHRISTINA. I don't know. I've never known. That's been the thrill of it. [HESTER, *dressed for her journey, appears in the door and stands beside* CHRISTINA. CHRISTINA'S *arm encircles the younger girl's shoulders.*] It's time, Hester.

HESTER. Isn't David coming with us?

CHRISTINA. I'm afraid not.

HESTER. Oh, Christina!

CHRISTINA. Sssh! Never mind. It can't be helped.

ROBERT. [*Breaking out.*] Hester! Hester! Couldn't we try again? Couldn't you . . .

HESTER. What?

ROBERT. I mean . . . what are you going to do . . . now?

HESTER. I don't know. [*Then a smile comes through.*] Yes, I do, too, know. I'm going to marry an orphan.

CHRISTINA. [*A long look at* DAVID.] Good-bye, Dave.

DAVID. [*Desperately pleading.*] Chris, you can't! It isn't fair to me!

CHRISTINA. [*Still looking at him.*] I'm sorry it's come to this. . . . It might easily have been so . . . [*Her voice chokes with crying. She picks up her bag where she put it down beside the door and goes quickly out.* HESTER, *with a reproachful glance at* DAVID, *follows her.* DAVID *stands rigid.* MRS. PHELPS *watches him.* ROBERT *covers his face with his hands. Then the front door slams and* DAVID *comes suddenly to life.*]

DAVID. [*A frantic cry.*] Chris! [*He turns excitedly to his mother.*] I'm sorry, Mother, but I guess I'll have to go.

MRS. PHELPS. [*Reeling.*] No, Dave! No! No!

DAVID. I guess she's right.

MRS. PHELPS. Oh, no!! You mustn't say that! You mustn't say that!

DAVID. [*Holding her off from him.*] I can't help it. She said we were trapped. We *are* trapped. I'm trapped.

MRS. PHELPS. [*Absolutely beyond herself.*] No! No! She isn't right! She can't be right! I won't believe it!

DAVID. [*Breaking loose from her.*] I can't help that!

MRS. PHELPS. [*Speaking at the same time.*] For God's sake, Dave, don't go with her! Not with that awful woman, Dave! That wicked woman! For God's sake don't leave me for her, Dave! [*She turns wildly to* ROBERT.] You know it isn't true, Robin! You know it was vile, what she said! Tell him! Tell him! [*But he is gone.*] Dave! My boy! My boy! My boy! Oh, my God! Dave! She isn't right! She isn't, Dave! Dave! Dave! [*The front door slams a second time. An awful pause, then.*] He's gone.

ROBERT. [*Uncovering his face.*] Who? Dave?

MRS. PHELPS. Can you see them from the window?

ROBERT. [*Looking out.*] Yes. . . . They're talking. . . . Now he's kissed her and taken the suitcase. . . . Now he's helping Hester . . . Hester into the car. . . . Now he's getting in. . . . Now they're starting.

MRS. PHELPS. I loved him too much. I've been too happy. Troubles had to come. I must be brave. I must bear my troubles bravely.

ROBERT. [*Turning to her.*] Poor Mother!

MRS. PHELPS. I must remember that I still have one of my great sons. I must keep my mind on that.

ROBERT. [*A step or two toward her.*] That's right, Mother.

MRS. PHELPS. And we'll go abroad, my great Robin and I, and stay as long as ever we please.

ROBERT. [*As he kneels beside her.*] Yes, Mother.

MRS. PHELPS. [*Her voice growing stronger as that deeply religious point of view of hers comes to her rescue.*] And you must remember that David, in his blindness, has forgotten. That mother love suffereth long and is kind; envieth not, is not puffed up, is not easily provoked; beareth all things; believeth all things; hopeth all things; endureth all things. . . . At least, I think *my* love does?

ROBERT. [*Engulfed forever.*] Yes, Mother.

CURTAIN

PARIS BOUND

BY

Philip Barry

PARIS BOUND

Paris Bound is a defence of the institution of marriage, and a criticism of divorce as a solution of marital infelicity. It is carried through in a spirit of high comedy.

Philip Barry was born in Rochester, New York, June 18, 1896. He graduated from Yale University in 1919, having become connected with the Department of State at Washington in April, 1918, and having been attached to the American Embassy in London from May, 1918, to February, 1919. He had been writing plays since his boyhood, and he joined Professor Baker's classes at Harvard University in 1919, remaining, with intermissions, until 1922. In that year he won a prize offered by Richard Herndon for the best play produced in the courses of Professor Baker with *You and I,* which was first performed at Stamford, Connecticut, February 12, 1923, and in New York on February 19 following. The play was recognized by the discriminating students of the drama as the work of a skilful delineator of the problems which arise in a cultivated American family, where sacrifices are made without display. *The Youngest,* whose first performance in New York was at the Gaiety Theatre, December 22, 1924, was a satire upon the pretentiousness of the leading family of a small town. Then came *In A Garden,* tried out in Washington, D. C., and produced first in New York at the Plymouth Theatre, November 16, 1925. This clever, sophisticated depiction of the revolt of a wife who has had her life too carefully arranged for her, and who is about to leave her husband in search for a lost illusion which she finds to have had no real basis, was too subtle for popular approval. *White Wings* (Booth Theatre, New York, October 15, 1926) was even more baffling to its audiences. It was a social satire in a broader sense than those preceding it. The Inches, a family who have been rich street-cleaning contractors for several generations, are contrasted with the Todds, inventors of the automobile, symbolic of progress. But the dialogue was too allusive for popular understanding. With his next play, *John,* first played at Stamford, Connecticut, on October 31, and then at the Klaw Theatre, New York, November 4, 1927, Mr. Barry made his first attempt at historical drama. The figure of John the Baptist is set against a background of Hebrew ambition which tries to use him for its own purposes. *John* is lofty in conception, but proved too remote for contemporary popular taste.

After three artistic successes, all failures from the financial standpoint, Mr. Barry wrote in *Paris Bound* not only the best drama so far of his career, but one of the most popular plays of its season. Opening at Newark, New Jersey, December

20, 1927, as *The Wedding,* it came into New York on December 27, under its present title. It is a plea for the preservation of that intangible but vital relation between husband and wife which is based on the sacramental nature of true marriage. It is no excuse for adultery, but in the strong scene in the third act, James Hutton shows his daughter-in-law that by her determination to divorce her husband for his one offence, she is placing the physical side of marriage above the other more important elements in it. The children, who represent the stability of the family, are never presented on the stage, but they provide, in the scene in which Jim Hutton telephones to them, an appeal all the more vital because it is carried out through comedy. *Cock Robin,* an amusing murder mystery play, written in collaboration with Mr. Elmer Rice, was first produced in Boston, December 26, 1927, and later at the Forty-eighth Street Theatre, New York, January 12, 1928. It had some of Mr. Barry's whimsical touches, but was not characteristic of his usual manner. One of the delightful minor characters in *Paris Bound* was played by the actress for whom Mr. Barry wrote his next play, *Holiday,* first performed at New Haven, November 18, and then at the Plymouth Theatre, New York, November 26, 1928. The central motive is the protest of a young lawyer who wishes to have some leisure to enjoy life in a normal way after a reasonable independence has been secured. His engagement to the daughter of a typical millionaire, her lack of sympathy with his aspirations, and his rescue by her sister made one of the most delightful and one of the most successful plays of the year. Less profound than *Paris Bound,* it was written with Mr. Barry's individual charm.

Mr. Barry's plays are found most conveniently in the uniform edition published in 1929 by Samuel French. This edition includes *You and I, The Youngest, In a Garden, White Wings, Paris Bound, John,* and *Holiday. You and I* was originally published in 1923 by Brentano's; *In a Garden,* by George H. Doran Company in 1926; and *White Wings,* by Boni and Liveright in 1927. For permission to reprint the play the editor is indebted to Mr. Barry and to Samuel French, and he is under further obligation to Mr. Barry for certain details which he has been good enough to furnish concerning the first performances of the plays.

Note to Sixth Edition.

In one of his finest plays, *Hotel Universe,* produced by the Theatre Guild in 1930, Mr. Barry dramatized the truth that an illusion for good or evil is often the most significant element in our lives. One by one a group of Americans at a house party in France are brought back to mental balance by a remarkable character, Stephen Field, whom the world thinks mad. *Tomorrow and Tomorrow* (1931) was a profound study of the married life of a woman who yields to passion for a man who fills a spiritual need her husband cannot satisfy, but who refuses to sacrifice that husband's belief in his paternity of their child, because of her recognition of an obligation greater than passion. Mr. Barry's next play, *The Animal Kingdom* (1932), seemed, when considered superficially, to contradict his philosophy of the marital state, but in reality only emphasized his position that marriage is a union of spiritual qualities far more important than mere physical relations. These plays were stage successes, but *The Joyous Season* (1934) was a popular failure, since its central motive, the way in which a Mother Superior of an order of nuns cures the spiritual ills of her family as a Christmas gift to them, was apparently beyond the understanding of critics and public. Neither did they comprehend *Bright Star* (1935), the tragedy of an egotist and the woman who loves him, though it contains some of Mr. Barry's most deeply moving scenes. *Spring Dance* (1936) was rewritten by Mr. Barry from another play and while it was amusing, it was hardly important.

Mr. Barry's plays continue to be published by Samuel French, with the exception of *Bright Star,* which has been withdrawn for the present. For detailed analysis of his work, see A. H. Quinn's *History of the American Drama from the Civil War to the Present Day,* Revised Edition, two volumes in one (1936), published by Appleton-Century-Crofts, Inc., Vol. 2, pp. 81–84; 275–282; 320–321.

Note to Seventh Edition.

Philip Barry died December 3, 1949, from a heart attack. *Here Come the Clowns,* a profound study of the relations of good and evil, symbolized by a group of vaudeville actors, was produced in New York, December 7, 1938. Barry had published a novel, *War in Heaven* (1938), upon the same theme. A brilliant and successful social comedy, *The Philadelphia Story,* opened in Philadelphia, February 20, 1939, reuniting two divorced lovers through the trust the patrician feels for one of his own kind. *Liberty Jones,* a symbolic picture of the struggle of Liberty against Nazism and Communism, came too early (January 14, 1941) for popular approval of war. A charming comedy, *Without Love,* began in Washington, early in 1942, and represented the growth of passion in two people who had married for reasons connected with politics, which were not clearly worked in to the drama. There was a confusion of a different kind in *Foolish Notion* (March 13, 1945) between real scenes and imaginary characters. Barry's last play, *Second Threshold,* produced January 2, 1952, after some revision by R. E. Sherwood, was one of his best, for he dramatized the point in a successful man's life when he feels it useless to proceed, but is saved by his daughter's love. A critical biography of Philip Barry, by Gerald Hamm, published in photostat form, appeared (Philadelphia, 1946).

CAST OF CHARACTERS

Music Box Theatre, New York, December 27, 1927

JAMES HUTTON	Gilbert Emery
JIM HUTTON	Donn Cook
MARY HUTTON	Madge Kennedy
HELEN WHITE	Martha Mayo
PETER COPE	Edwin Nicander
NORA COPE	Ellen Southbrook
FANNY SHIPPAN	Hope Williams
NOEL FARLEY	Mary Murray
RICHARD PARISH	Donald MacDonald
JULIE	Marie Bruce

ACT I—The upstairs sitting-room of a house in the country near New York: July, six years ago.

ACT II—The music-room on the top floor of a house in uptown New York, near the East River. May, of this year.

ACT III—The music-room, six weeks later. July, of this year.

PARIS BOUND

ACT ONE

SCENE: *The upstairs sitting-room of a house in the country near New York. July, six years ago.*

The sitting-room is a spacious, comfortable room, of no particular period. There is a table and there is a chaise-longue. There are two or three chairs. The entire back wall is bowed into large windows, shaded by awnings from the bright noon-day sun.

Entrance from the hall is at Right.

Entrance into the bedroom is at Left.

At Rise: JULIE, *about 45, a housemaid of a superior type, is listening attentively at the hall doorway. From downstairs, a dance orchestra is heard playing the concluding strains of a tune. The music stops and for a moment there is a dead silence. It is followed by a sudden rush of shouts, cheers, laughter and the sound of two people running upstairs. The orchestra breaks into one triumphal phrase of the wedding-march, and concludes abruptly. Another silence, interrupted by a shout: "She's going to throw it!" Then impatient cries of "Throw it!" "Throw it!" "Why don't you throw it?" Again a silence, briefer this time, then more cheers and laughter.* JULIE *crosses to the bedroom and goes out, closing the door after her. For a moment the room is empty, then, hand-in-hand in the hall doorway, appear* JIM *and* MARY HUTTON. JIM *is twenty-six and* MARY *twenty-two. They have been married two hours. The wedding-breakfast is over, but the guests still remain to see them off.* MARY *is lovely in her wedding-dress and* JIM *almost handsome in cutaway and white waistcoat. Both are flushed with excitement, and very happy.*

JIM. How long do you think you'll be?

MARY. Twenty minutes. What about you?

JIM. Ten at the outside.

MARY. Good.

JIM. Are your bags ready?

MARY. They will be.

JIM. Peter's to take mine out the back way and stow 'em in the motor. We'll drop yours down through the window.

MARY. That will be nice.

JIM.—Only hurry.

MARY. All right. Will you come back for me here?

JIM. Sure. (*A pause.*) Mary—

MARY. What?

JIM.—Fun.

MARY. I've never enjoyed a wedding so much in my life.

JIM. Me neither.

MARY. And I always enjoy weddings.

JIM. Me too.

[*They gaze at each other for a moment, smiling, fascinated. Finally:*

MARY. Jim—you know something?

JIM. What?

MARY.—I'm a fool about you.

JIM. Dear, you've got nothing on me.

MARY. (*A concession.*)—Say fifteen minutes.

JIM. That's better.

MARY. Good-bye, then—

JIM. Good-bye.

MARY. Mind you hurry!

JIM. (*From the hallway.*) Mind *you* do!

[MARY *comes into the sitting-room. She calls:*

MARY. Julie! Where are you, Julie?

[*She goes to a table and finds three telegrams on a tray. The bedroom door is opened and* JULIE *comes in.*

JULIE. Yes, Mrs. Hutton?

MARY.—"Mrs—"—?—Don't do that, dear. Not yet. You'll throw me all off.—Still more telegrams?

JULIE. There were a few addressed to you personally. Miss Archer said to keep them here for you.

[MARY *opens and reads a telegram.*

MARY. Oh dear—(*She reads another.*) —Dear, oh dear.—Julie, I could cry.

JULIE. You should be very happy, Miss.

MARY. I am. (*She opens the third telegram.*)—Everyone downstairs seemed to think you made a good job of me.

JULIE. You looked beautiful.

MARY. (*Reading the telegram.*) Don't I still?

JULIE. Oh, indeed!

MARY. (*Absently.*) Julie—

JULIE. Yes, Miss?

MARY. This morning Aunt Grace asked me if there was anything in this house I wanted to take with me for my house—and I said you.

JULIE. Ah, that was very kind.

MARY. We'll be back in two months. Would you like to come to me in town, in September?

JULIE. There's no one I'd as soon be with, Miss.

MARY. Then we'll call it settled, shall we? I've got a room on the top floor there, for my music: I'll want you to keep just it, and my room, and me. Is that all right?

JULIE. Oh yes, Miss. Yes—anything—

[MARY *hesitates a moment, then tears up the telegrams and moves toward the bedroom.*

MARY. I must rush into my things now. Are the bags locked?

JULIE. (*Following her.*)—All but the small one. I have the checks for the trunks.

MARY. Don't let me forget them. I'm not remembering very well to-day. [*She goes out into the bedroom.* JULIE *follows her and closes the door after them. A moment, then the hall door is again opened and* NORA COPE *enters. She is a pretty girl of about twenty-three, dressed as a wedding-attendant.*

NORA. Will you come in here, Mrs. White?

[HELEN WHITE *enters from the hall. She is a woman of forty-five, slender and distinguished.*

HELEN. Oh thank you—I can't imagine what came over me.

NORA. It *was* hot in that garden. I feel rather wilted myself.

HELEN. I think it was standing so long in the line.

NORA. Can't I get you some water or whisky or something?

HELEN. Oh no—no thank you. This is all I need—(*She seats herself upon the chaise-longue.*)—just to rest a moment. —let me see, now—you were maid-of-honor, weren't you?

NORA.—Matron. I'm Nora Cope.—That funny-looking usher who went up first—he's my husband.

HELEN. A great friend of my son's, then.

NORA. Oh yes—Peter and Jim are just like *that.*

HELEN. (*Smiling.*) It's—rather trying for a mother to be a stranger at her own son's wedding.

NORA. Jim was so touched at your coming such a long way for it.

HELEN. The dear boy.

NORA.—But you knew Mary, didn't you?

HELEN.—For the first time, two hours ago.

NORA. Oh, I see.—How does she strike you?

HELEN. She seems to be such a sweet, attractive girl.

NORA. She's all of that, Mrs. White.

HELEN. I'm so glad.—And Jim *is* a nice boy, isn't he?

NORA. Heavens, yes. Jim's a first-rater.

HELEN. I'm sure they will be very happy.

NORA. I think they've a good chance at it.

HELEN.—A chance, only?

[NORA *shrugs.*

NORA. What more can you say for anyone? (*She smiles.*)—Any two, that is. (FANNY SHIPPAN *enters from the hall, in bridesmaid's dress. She is about* NORA'S *age, bluff, smart, likable.* NORA *greets her.*) Hello, Fanny.

FANNY. Listen: where the devil's Mary? I've looked everywhere except—(*She sees* MRS. WHITE.) Oh—

NORA. You've met Jim's mother, haven't you? (*To* MRS. WHITE.) This is Miss Shippan—

HELEN. How do you do?

FANNY. How do you do, Mrs. Hutton. Wasn't it the loveliest—? Oh, I beg your pardon—

[HELEN *smiles faintly.*

HELEN. "Mrs. White," it is now.

FANNY. Of course.—Trust me to forget it, though. (*To* NORA.) Where *is* the girl?

NORA. In there. (FANNY *crosses toward the bedroom door.*) Fanny—

FANNY. Yes, chick?

NORA. Is Noel all right?

FANNY. Well, not so very—

NORA. I'm worried sick about her.

FANNY. So am I. She acts as if she'd never seen champagne before.

NORA. What's to be done?

FANNY. Peter's keeping an eye on her.

NORA. Much good that'll do.

FANNY. I'll go down again myself, in a minute.

NORA. Don't let on to Mary.

FANNY. I should say not. (*She knocks at the door.*) Oh Mrs. H.! Mrs. H.!

[MARY'S *voice is heard from inside.*

MARY. Is that you, Fanny?

FANNY. Yes, Mrs. H.

MARY. Come in, idiot. What's the matter?

[FANNY *goes out, into the bedroom.* JAMES HUTTON *enters from the hall. He is 47, of youthful figure, and with a fine face, rather humorous about the eyes and mouth.*

JAMES.—Resting after the battle, Nora?

NORA. Wasn't it superb, Mr. Hutton? Weren't you proud of them?

JAMES.—Good-looking son I've got, eh?

NORA. But why not? Look at the parents.

JAMES. That's the girl.

[NORA *moved toward the bedroom.*

NORA. I'll—uh—I'll just go see if—(*She knocks on the door.*) Mary! It's Nora. —Anything I can do?

MARY. (*From the bedroom.*) Come in, darling! I was just shouting for you.

[NORA *goes out, into the bedroom.* JAMES *lights a cigarette, watching* HELEN. *Finally:*

JAMES. Cigarette?

HELEN. No thank you.

[*A pause.*

JAMES. Do you feel any better?

HELEN. Very much. The—heat bothered me frightfully.

JAMES. Is that all that bothered you, Helen?

HELEN. You mean seeing you again?

JAMES. No, I didn't mean that.

HELEN. Extraordinary, how completely we've escaped each other. How long is it?

JAMES. This is nineteen hundred and—: fifteen years.

HELEN. That's quite a time, in a world of this size.

JAMES. You don't come home very often, do you?

HELEN. Home? America?—Never when I can avoid it.

JAMES. Why did you marry White?

HELEN. Because I wanted to.

JAMES. I met him once. I thought him an exceptionally dull man.

HELEN. That depends on how you look at him.—What is it you think "bothered" me?

JAMES. The whole thing: the sight of your boy being married, quite as lovingly, quite as hopefully, as you married me.

HELEN. Oh. (*She reflects.*) I can only hope they make a better job of it than we did.

JAMES. I'm sure they hope so.

HELEN. I'm told they're very well suited to each other.

JAMES. So were we.

HELEN.—Except in certain particulars.

JAMES. Jim is like me in a great many ways, Helen.

HELEN. Then I suppose I should be sorry for her.

[JAMES *rises and bows slightly.*

JAMES. Madame. (*And seats himself again.*)—I'm very fond of Mary. I was rather afraid he was going to marry Noel —not that there's ever been anything between them, but I've always sensed a kind of—

HELEN.—Noel?

JAMES. Noel Farley—one of the bridesmaids—the prettiest, in fact. Pat Farley's girl—you remember Pat and Alice—

HELEN. I thought she was behaving rather cheaply downstairs.

JAMES. Don't be unkind, Helen. I don't think I've ever seen more tragic eyes in a young girl's head.

[*She smiles.*

HELEN. Trust you to note the tragic eyes, James.

[*He looks at her curiously for a moment. Then:*

JAMES. (*Small talk.*)—Charming wedding, wasn't it? Charming house, charming garden, charming breakfast—

HELEN. Quite. Her aunt must have money.

JAMES. She has.

HELEN. Is Mary well-off, too?

JAMES. I believe her father left her considerable.

HELEN. Did both parents die young?—She looks strong enough.

JAMES. They went within two weeks of each other, with influenza.

HELEN. How sad. Jim told me next to nothing in his letter. (*A moment.*) Between them they'll have plenty, then.

JAMES. Helen, I'm amazed at you.

HELEN. Why so?

JAMES. Your coldness. Your utter worldliness.

HELEN. Don't let it distress you too much. —Does Jim like his business?

JAMES. Enormously—and works very hard at it.

HELEN.—Youth, health, love, money and an occupation—they seem to have the odds on their side, at any rate.

JAMES. So did we.

HELEN.—So "More shame to us"?

JAMES. More shame to you, let us say.
[*A brief pause.*

HELEN. The years haven't put wrinkles in your cheek, have they, James?

JAMES. Cheek?

HELEN. Cheek.

[JAMES *shakes his head over her.*

JAMES.—Still bitter. It's amazing.

HELEN. Poor dear, life is such a constant surprise to you.—As I remember, you were amazed when I divorced you.

JAMES. That was an act of resentment on the part of a raw young girl. You're past forty now, and should know better.

HELEN. You still don't accept the impossibility of my living with you after what you did—

JAMES. I shan't ever accept it.

HELEN. Well, I give up. In fact I gave up, some time ago, didn't I?

JAMES. I know: that's one of your troubles. [*She rises.*

HELEN. I'm afraid I must—

JAMES.—Duck—dodge again—get out from under. All right, my dear. [*She turns on him.*

HELEN. Jim, I—! (*She stops abruptly and sinks down into another chair. Then.*) Which of us was in the wrong—you or me?

JAMES.—You were. I may have committed adultery, Helen, but I never committed divorce.

HELEN. When you had your affair with—with that woman—

JAMES. (*Amused.*) Mrs. Bliss, her name was—Kitty Bliss—pretty name—

HELEN.—And a pretty affair! Just pretty enough to destroy our marriage.

JAMES. I think it was you who did the destroying, Helen.

HELEN. How do you figure that?

JAMES.—Through what you made of it. Because, you know, all that *we* had—you and I—*our* province was never touched by it.

HELEN. That's easy enough to say.

JAMES. It's gospel.

HELEN. I'm afraid I don't understand these separate provinces of yours.

JAMES. Mine?—Everyone's!

HELEN. I don't understand them.

JAMES. Well, here's your son Jim: he is attractive to women. His wife Mary is attractive to men. He's twenty-six, she is twenty-two. Is he never to know another woman, or she another man?

HELEN. Know them? But of course!

JAMES. Well, love them, then.

HELEN. Even love them—in a way.

JAMES.—Provided they "behave"—

HELEN. Naturally.

[*He smiles.*

JAMES.—Provided they behave naturally—

HELEN. (*Indignant.*) I didn't say—

JAMES. Well, I don't think it's very important whether they do or not.

HELEN. Then why any marriage at all?

JAMES. Simply because marriage of one woman to one man for a lifetime is the most civilized and beautiful idea poor humanity has ever conceived of.

HELEN. Imagine your thinking so.

JAMES. I've never thought otherwise.—And any two people, I don't care who they are, who marry for love as we did—as most do—and live before the world as man and wife, create between them something they can never get away from and never hope to duplicate.

HELEN. I wonder if they can't.

JAMES. You know they can't.—It's an entity as real as any child is and it's born without them knowing it, simply of the fact that a man and woman in love have elected to face *all* the facts of life together, from under one roof.

HELEN. So I denied our spiritual child—is that it?

JAMES. That will do, yes.

HELEN. It was for that that I left *you,* Jim.

JAMES. You left me because you found out that I had gone with another woman—*found it out.*

HELEN. Wasn't that almost enough?

JAMES. No. It didn't begin to be.—For following a physical impulse which I share with the rest of the animal kingdom, you destroyed a spiritual relationship which belonged only to us. For an act which in reality was of little or no importance to you, you did me out of my marriage and my home, of the daughter I've always longed for—very nearly out of the son I already had. You did a good, thorough job. And after all, where did it land you?

HELEN. Really, James—

JAMES. Yes really—I should like to know.

HELEN. (*Rising.*) I think I've had about enough of this, if you don't mind.

JAMES. I suppose that's the real trouble with you: you can't stand very much. You've dodged things all your life. So now you're soft where you should be hard, and hard as nails where you should be soft. I think you might have struck a better balance if you'd weathered that one rough stretch, as you should have. You might still be the once wronged wife, but you'd be ten times the person you are now.

HELEN. (*Furious.*)—To-day of all days, from you of all people—you who left a young wife who trusted you utterly for a—for some rotten affair.

JAMES. My God, Helen—what *is* all this stuff about—?

HELEN. I'll tell you what it is! It's— [*She stops abruptly, as the bedroom door opens and* FANNY *re-enters, talking back through the open door, into the bedroom:*

FANNY. My dear, I'm the ninth richest woman under thirty in North America, and if I can't give pianos for wedding-presents, I don't know who can. (*She closes the door, and crosses toward the hall, smiling amiably at* JAMES *and* HELEN.) Hello, Mr. Hutton—are you taking care of Mrs. *White* all right? (*Her hand flies to her mouth.*) Oh my Lord—

[JAMES *laughs.* FANNY *accelerates her pace toward the hall door, which opens to admit* JIM, *now dressed for departure.*

JIM. Hi, Fanny. What's the report?

FANNY. (*Passing him.*) She's almost ready.—Another day or two ought to see you off. [*She goes out.* JIM *enters, stopping in surprise at the sight of his father and mother.*

JIM. Well, hello! (*He looks at them amusedly.*)—Happy reunion?

HELEN. Come here, Jim. (*He goes to her. She kisses him.*)—I think she's lovely.

JIM. I have luck, don't I?

HELEN. I think you both have.

JIM. Lord, I feel good. (*He looks at his watch, then calls in the direction of the bedroom door.*) Oh, *Mary!*

MARY. (*From inside.*) Hello, Angel!

JIM. (*To* JAMES.) You see? She adores me—(*To* MARY.) What about those fifteen minutes?

MARY. I'm coming!

JIM. I guess we wait. [*He slumps down into a chair, clasps his hands over his waist, watches* JAMES *and* HELEN, *and begins to whistle a popular song, off-key.*

MARY. Jim!

JIM. Hello!

MARY. Don't do that!

JIM. What?

MARY. Whistle.

JIM. Why?

MARY. It's horrible.

[JIM *looks at* JAMES *in pretended surprise.*

JIM. What can she mean?

JAMES. Do you still take cold baths in the morning, Jim?

JIM. Yes, why?

JAMES.—And do you sing in them?

JIM. Sure, I suppose so.

JAMES. I think I'd give it up, if I were you.

[JIM *stares for a moment, then laughs.*

JIM. What do you advise, Mother?

HELEN. Well, with a musician for a wife I should imagine that simple gasps are better.

JIM. His voice died in his throat.

JAMES. Anything more I can do for you, Son?

JIM. Nothing possibly. You've been a brick.—I told you what I thought about your coming on for it, Mother.

HELEN. I'd have gone around the world, Jimmy.

JIM. You're a great pair, you two.

JAMES. Do you think so?

JIM. I know it. (*A pause.*)—I'm not sure of the ethics of a situation like this, but I'd like to make an inquiry—

JAMES. Go ahead.

JIM. What's it like to be together again? (*He smiles.*)—Excuse me, but I'm in the publishing business.

JAMES. Well, I find it very agreeable.

[JIM *looks to* HELEN.

HELEN. Your father was always an attractive man.

JIM. (*Suddenly.*) Why'd you leave him, Mother?

HELEN. Why I—that is, I—

JIM. I didn't mean to blurt it out quite like that, but I've always wondered.

JAMES. You mean to say you don't know?

JIM. No.—Of course I suppose you just didn't hit it off. But—

JAMES. We hit it off perfectly—

[JIM *looks to* HELEN.

JIM. Then I don't see—

JAMES.—Except in one respect.

[HELEN *turns away.*

JIM. Oh. Never mind—I'm sorry. (*He looks at his watch again.*) Why doesn't that girl hurry? I hate to wait for people.

JAMES.—It happened that I was once what your mother calls "unfaithful" to her.

JIM. (*Incredulously.*) You mean you wanted to quit Mother, and—?

JAMES. Oh no—no, never for a minute.

[*A brief pause.* JIM *turns to his mother.*

JIM. But you—?

HELEN. (*Coldly.*)—But I.

JAMES. (*After a moment.*) Well, what do you think of it, Jim?

JIM. Would *you* like to know, Mother?

HELEN. If you like.

JIM. Well, it strikes me it was quite short-sighted, and pretty unjust, to boot.

[*A pause. Then:*

HELEN.—I imagine, however, that Mary would not think so.

JIM. I'm certain she'd think the same. (*There is an awkward silence.* JIM *adds.*)—Marriage is a pretty big job, of course. But it seems to me that if both people use their heads, they can manage it.

JAMES. You may be sure they can.

JIM. I'm not worried. I think *we'll* stay put, all right.

HELEN. That, I've no doubt, will be largely up to you.

JIM. Oh no—it'll be up to Mary. Nothing'd ever unmarry me.

HELEN. I think you would do well, however, to learn to profit by your father's mistake.

JIM. Aren't you being a little rough on him, Mother? (*He smiles engagingly.*) —I tell you what: I'll do that, if you'll teach Mary to profit by yours.

[*The bedroom door opens and* MARY *comes in in her "going-away dress."* JIM *springs up and rushes to her.*

JIM. Oh, what a handsome wench! Can this be mine? (*He takes her hand and turns her around to* JAMES *and* HELEN.) —Is my wife making a good impression?

JAMES. We are speechless.

MARY. (*To* JIM.) You *can* whistle, if you like.

[JIM *whistles two notes.*

JIM. Is that enough?

MARY. Plenty.

JIM.—Just now and again, to assert my rights.

[MARY *goes to* HELEN *and* JAMES.

MARY. You've been sweet, both of you.

HELEN. So have you, Mary.

JAMES. Stay that way, will you?

MARY. We'll try, won't we, Jim?

JIM. I will. You don't need to. [*She sinks down into a chair, with a sigh.*

MARY. Ladies and Gentlemen, this is the happiest day of my life.

JIM. Don't you believe it. [*He seats himself on the arm of the chair, and takes her hand.*

JAMES. (*To* HELEN.) I think we'd better go down again, don't you?

MARY. Oh no, not yet! We aren't leaving till—Peter!

[PETER COPE *enters from the hall. He wears a cut-away, with a white flower in the button-hole, and carries a tray with a bottle of champagne and several glasses. He is about twenty-eight, robust and amiable. At present he is also pleasantly exhilarated.*

PETER.—Just the day for a picnic. [*He places the tray and napkin on a table near them.*

MARY. Oh Peter—marvellous—

JIM. (*Simultaneously.*) Good man, Peter.

PETER. They said I couldn't make the stairs with it: I said I could.—Where's my wife, Nora?

MARY.—In there, helping Julie.

PETER. I must speak with my good wife, Nora. (*He moves toward the bedroom, stopping for a moment beside* MARY. *He scowls at* JIM.) Leave go that lady's hand, you naughty navy man. (*He drops his hand gently upon* MARY'S *head.*)—Nice girl. Always remember what Granny says, and don't trust a navy man. (*He calls at the bedroom door.*) Nora?

[NORA *replies from inside:*

NORA. Yes?

PETER. Let down the drawbridge! [*He goes out into the bedroom.* JAMES *has filled the glasses. He gives one to* MARY *and one to* HELEN

JAMES. Well, my dears,—here's to a happy, happy life for you. [*He and* JIM *take glasses.*

JIM. (*Raising his.*) Here's to one for all of us.

MARY. Yes.

JAMES. Yes.

[*They sip the wine. The strain is now gone. They are all friends together. Their talk runs with a new animation.*

HELEN. What *are* your plans, Jim?

JIM.—From now, you mean?

JAMES. Yes.

JIM. Well, we ought to make town in two hours and a half at the outside.

MARY. I'll drive part of the way.

JIM. You *will* not.—We'll go straight to the hotel. Peter's reserved rooms.—Where do you want to dine, Darling?

MARY. Have we got a sitting-room?

JIM. Yes.

MARY. There, then. It's less trouble.

JIM. That's my idea.—I wired the man at the club to see what revues he could get seats for, and then to get two for the one he couldn't.

MARY. That sounds promising.

JIM. The boat sails at midnight.—When are *you* going back, Mother?

HELEN. Early next month.

JIM. Be in London, will you?

HELEN. I expect so.

JIM. With him?

HELEN. With my husband, yes.

JAMES.—"White" is the name—pretty name.

JIM. We might try to join up for a day or two. I'd like to meet him.

HELEN. Let's arrange to, by all means.

JIM. The Company wants me to make a yearly trip over, starting next May. So I'll be seeing you regularly, I hope.

HELEN. I do hope so, Dear.

JAMES. (*To* MARY.) What *I* should like to know is, am I to be called Father, or am I not?

MARY. Yes, Father, you are. (*To* HELEN.)—Did you hear what he's given us for our house in town?

HELEN. Tell me.

MARY. Another floor.

HELEN.—Another f—?

JIM.—Floor. And a top floor, at that. Roofs cost like hell.

MARY. It's to be for my music.

HELEN. But how very nice.—And is Jim to be allowed in it?

MARY. Only on rare occasions. The library's his province.

JAMES. (*To* HELEN.) "Province."

HELEN. Be still, James.

JIM. What's the joke?

HELEN. Never mind. (JULIE *enters from the bedroom with two bags, which she places near the center window.* HELEN *rises, goes to* MARY *and kisses her.*) Good-bye, Mary.

MARY. Good-bye, dear. Thanks for coming and thanks for that whopping cheque and I love you, I really do.

[HELEN *smiles, pats her cheek, turns to* JIM *and kisses him.*

HELEN. Good-bye, Jimmy. Be a good boy.

JIM. Bet your life, Mother. Thanks from me, too.

JAMES. (*Kisses* MARY.) Good-bye, daughter. I shan't fret about you two.

MARY. Don't you do it.

[JULIE *goes out again, into the bedroom.* JAMES *shakes hands with* JIM.

JAMES. Have a good trip, son.

JIM. Yes, sir.—See you in the autumn, eh?

JAMES. That's right! (*He holds out his arm to* HELEN.) Come—we must dance together now, and scandalize the guests. We owe it to them. (HELEN *takes his arm. They move toward the hall.* JIM *and* MARY *stand together watching them. At the door,* JAMES *stops and turns to them once more.*) I've only one thing to say to both of you: if at first you don't succeed, don't try again.—Do you second that, Helen?

HELEN. No, I do not. (*She tightens her arm in his.*)—Are you coming?

[JAMES *smiles back at* JIM *and* MARY.

JAMES.—She does, though.

[*They go out into the hall. Waltz music is heard from downstairs until the door closes again after them.* MARY *stands staring at the door. A silence. Then:*

MARY. Oh Jim—how awful—

JIM. I know, Dear—but don't you worry.

MARY. Oh, let's be careful, let's be *careful!*

JIM. We will, Sweet.

[*She sinks down into a chair and gazes in front of her for a moment.* JIM *lights another cigarette.*

MARY. (*Suddenly.*) You know, it occurs to me I've married you under fairly false pretences.

JIM. (*Amused.*) Oh? Such as—?

MARY. I've got a lot of bum theories about marriage. You've never heard them.

JIM. (*Grinning.*) Let's save 'em up for the long winter evenings, shall we?

MARY. I'm afraid I'll forget them.

JIM.—How do they go?

MARY. Well, for one thing, I don't believe much in monopolies.

JIM. No?

MARY. Not for us, anyhow. We're too fond of—people.

JIM. You and me and the great throbbing heart of America—that'll be all right.

MARY.—Not quite so general as that, maybe.

JIM. I shall like you best, Mary.

MARY. So will I you.—But the point is, I don't expect never to see another man, and I don't expect you never to see another girl. We've simply got to *make* ourselves see them! Then there won't ever be the danger of them getting to be —to be—

JIM.—Novelties to us?

MARY. (*Gratefully.*) Exactly.—And I like to be alone a lot. I may seem sullen, but it won't mean anything, really it won't.

JIM. I'll look the other way.

MARY.—"Respect each other's privacy." Oh, that sounds terrible. Hints to the Lovelorn.

JIM. All theories are terrible.

MARY. Of course they are. But what are you going to do?

JIM. Dunno. (*A brief pause.*)—One thing: we're being nice and sensible and modern, aren't we?

MARY. Oh Jim, we've got to be! (JIM'S *smile fades.*) I mean it. We've simply got to be a success. All my life I've seen nothing but—[*She averts her head.*

JIM.—But how can we help but be?! *You—? Me—?*

MARY. It isn't as easy as that, Jim. There's where people make the mistake. It takes work, and they won't work. *I know it takes work.*

JIM. Mary—

MARY. What?

[*His smile reasserts itself.*

JIM.—Beads of sweat'll be standing out on my forehead.

[*She laughs, and holds her hand out to him in a quick gesture. He takes it and kisses it.*

MARY. I'm a fool.

JIM. Nope. Not a bit.—But I think we'll be all right.

MARY. I know we shall.

[*From the bedroom* NORA *enters, followed by* PETER, *who carries a bag in each hand, and a third under one arm. He goes to the window with them.*

NORA. Listen: Peter says Noel Farley's in a dreadful state downstairs.

PETER. I said—

MARY. How do you mean?

JIM. Noel? What's she doing?

PETER. Well, she keeps laughing all the time, and very loud.

NORA. I was wondering if we oughtn't to do something about her.

[*A pause. Finally:*

MARY. What could we?

JIM. Oh Noel's all right. She's just excitable. (*He goes to the center window.*) How are we to get these bags down, Pete?

PETER. I've got Tom down there under the window. (*He calls.*) Are you ready there, Tom?

[*A voice replies from below:*]

VOICE. Right here, sir.

PETER. Here are the bags! (*He turns to the others.*)—And here's the rope. It's a clothesline. Happy Days, from the laundress.

MARY. Do be kind to my lovely new luggage.

NORA. (*To* PETER.) Will it reach?

PETER. Why, it's reach exceeds its grasp.

NORA. Hurry up, stupid, and quit talking.

[*She continues to look troubled over* NOEL. PETER *is tying one end of the line to two bags.*

PETER. Don't cross me. Never cross a Cope.

[JIM *leans out of the window and calls cautiously.*

JIM. All right, Tom?

VOICE. (*From below.*) All right, sir.

PETER.—Scratch a Cope, and you find a wife-beater.

JIM. Heave, Petey.

PETER. What've you got in here, Mary—sand?

MARY. My grandfather was a puddler in a steel-mill. It's the old family tools.

PETER. (*Lifting the bag to the window-sill.*)—Well, I didn't stroke the Vassar crew for nothing.

JIM. What about our get-away, Pete?

PETER. What about it?

MARY. Jim means, can we get away with it?

PETER. I've arranged it all myself, with these two bare hands. You wait here, with the craven bridegroom. When everything's set, I'll tell the orchestra to crash into something appropriate—

MARY. What?

PETER. Well, say "The Bastard King of England."

NORA. (*Impatiently.*) *What,* Peter?

PETER. "Mary is a Grand Old Name."

NORA. They won't know it.

PETER. (*Defiantly.*). But it *is* a grand old name.

JIM. Have them play something I'll recognize.

MARY. What would you?

JIM. (*After a moment's thought.*) Dardanella, or the wedding-march.

PETER. It's an inspiration: I'll have them play the wedding-march.

NORA. *That's* settled.

PETER.—Then you join hands and scurry

down the stairs through the hall and out the door, amid rice and rose-petals. Then buckety-buckety up the driveway toward the car you're supposed to take. You'll recognize it by its decorations and wall-mottoes, mostly very obscene. I printed them out myself, last night.—Sure you wouldn't rather go in that car?

MARY. No, no, idiot!

PETER. Then cut across the tennis-court to the south drive, where Tom'll be with my high-powered Pope-Toledo.

MARY. It's miles.

PETER. Rome wasn't built in a day.

MARY. Can we trust him, Nora?

NORA. Look here, Peter—(PETER *turns to her. She examines his face searchingly.*) Yes.

PETER.—Thanks for the vote of confidence. (*He calls out the window.*)—The South road, near the tennis-court. Forty paces from the old pine. Have you got that, Tom?

VOICE. Yes, sir.

JIM. I'm going to drive, you know.

PETER. He understands.—Now, my boy, I want *your* bag, and I mean to have it. (*He calls again through the window.*) One more to come, Tom!

VOICE. Right, sir.

PETER. I'll meet you with it in the pantry.—Where is it, Massa Jim?

JIM. I'll show you.

[*They move together toward the hall. The door opens and* FANNY *enters.*

FANNY. Listen: something radical's got to be done about Noel.

JIM. Why? What's the matter?

FANNY. I'm afraid Love has reared its ugly head, Jim.

[JIM *turns away, abruptly.*

JIM. You're talking through your hat. (*To* PETER.) Come on—

MARY. Wait a minute.—What's she doing, Fanny?

FANNY. Oh, laughing and carrying on in a generally outrageous manner.

PETER. I saw her glass filled four times at the breakfast.

FANNY. Now all the younger boys are cutting in on her. It's rotten, really.

NORA. Hasn't anyone spoken to her?

FANNY. Jerry and Cooper did. So did I. I've never had such a stare from anyone in my life. Her mother's in the library, dying of mortification.

JIM. You might go down, Pete, and take her for a walk around the garden.

PETER. I tried to. She wouldn't come.

[*A pause.*

FANNY. I'm afraid it'll end by her making some wretched scene or other, and I like Noel.

NORA. (*Sharply.*) Of course you do. So do we.

[*A pause. Finally:*

FANNY. We're all friends, aren't we? (*She looks at the faces around her.*)—Yes. Well, I saw her maid in the dressing-room. She said Noel hadn't slept a wink in three nights. Why, she didn't know.

[*There is a long silence. Then:*

MARY. You go down, Fanny, and tell her Jim wants to see her up here for a moment before we leave.

JIM. Oh *listen,* Mary—!

MARY. You've got to.

FANNY. I think it's the only thing that'll make her pull up, I really do.

JIM. But I tell you—!

MARY. Jim—

JIM. What?

MARY. I don't want anything unpleasant to happen to-day. It's been too lovely.

JIM. But what on earth can *I* say to her?

FANNY. Just tell her to snap out of it.

JIM. Didn't you?

FANNY. I'm not you, Jimmy.

MARY. (*To* FANNY.) Go on, will you?

JIM. No—wait a minute.

MARY. Please, Jim, I'm asking it. (JIM *shrugs helplessly.*) You hold up the signals a few moments, will you, Peter?

PETER. Sure.—But about that bag—

JIM. Come on—we'll get it.

MARY.—And see if Aunt Grace is in her room as you go by.

[*At the door,* JIM *turns to her.*

JIM.—I'll be right back.

MARY. Thanks, Jim.

[*He goes out, followed by* PETER.

FANNY. You're a good soldier, Mary.

MARY. So is Noel.

FANNY. (*Kissing her.*) Good-bye, if I don't see you again. Lots of luck.

MARY. Thanks, Darling. (FANNY *goes out into the hall.* MARY *begins to pull on her gloves. To* NORA:) Well, apparently it's happened.

NORA. Isn't it the devil? You'd think Noel would have sense enough.

[*The seam of a glove breaks.*

MARY. There goes a glove. (*She goes into the bedroom, continuing from there:*) I was probably wrong to ask her to be bridesmaid.

NORA. I don't think so.

MARY. I thought it would put an end to all that wretched talk.

[NORA *seats herself upon the chaise-longue.*

NORA.—Which it did.

MARY. Poor Jim now, though.

NORA. I know.

MARY. It *is* an assignment.

NORA.—He's the only one can do it. It'd be awful for Noel if she was let make a real scene.

[MARY *re-enters with fresh gloves.*

MARY. You know, I think she loves him terribly.

NORA. She'll get over it.

[MARY *ponders.*

MARY.—I wonder doesn't he love her at all—

NORA. (*Astounded.*) What!?

MARY. (*Calmly.*)—It's quite possible. I could understand that. And I don't think I should mind—much.

[NORA *laughs.*

NORA.—You say that to-day. Wait a bit—in a month you'll be for scratching out the eyes of anyone who looks at him sideways.

[MARY *seats herself beside her.*

MARY. I should hate to feel like that.

NORA. You won't be able to help it. It's what we all come to. You get a sense of ownership, or something. It starts to work before you know it.

MARY. But I believe Jim has the right to know as many women as he wants to.

NORA. Know them? How?

MARY. In every sense.

NORA. Big-hearted Mary.

MARY. I mean it. It certainly needn't interfere with me—with us.

NORA. Where'd you get all this, anyhow?

MARY. Some of it, talking to Mr. Hutton one night. Most of it by myself.

NORA. Oh, what a fine about-face you're in for, Mary.

MARY. I don't think so.

NORA.—How about your right to know a few men?

MARY. But of course!

[NORA *looks at her curiously for a moment. Then:*

NORA. Another once-loving pair bound for Paris.

MARY. It's one way of avoiding it, Nora—one good way.

[JIM *comes in from the hall.* NORA *rises.*

JIM. Mary, your Aunt Grace is in there, about to burst into tears.

[MARY *rises.*

MARY. Did you tell her good-bye?

JIM. Yes.

MARY. I'll go right in.

JIM. Don't be long.

[MARY *goes out into the hall.*

NORA. (*To* JIM.) Good-bye to you, young man. Best of luck.

JIM. Good-bye, Nora. You've been wonderful.

[*He kisses her cheek.*

NORA. You know how we feel about you and Mary, don't you?

JIM.—Just as we do about you and Pete, I should imagine.

NORA. It'll be great fun, the four of us.

JIM. Lord! Won't it, though!

[*There is a sound at the door.* NORA *glances at it.*

NORA. It's Noel. Mind your step, Jimmy.

JIM. Don't you worry.

[NORA *goes swiftly to the door, which opens to admit* NOEL FARLEY. *She is twenty-two, and lovely.*

NORA. (*To* NOEL.) Have you seen Peter anywhere?

NOEL. Not for—not for a few minutes, no.

NORA. I must find the man!

[*She goes out, closing the door after her.* NOEL *stands just within the room, looking directly at* JIM, *without moving.*

JIM. Hello, Noel.

NOEL. Fanny said—

JIM. We—uh—we wanted to see you before we left.

NOEL. That was sweet of you. Where is Mary?

JIM. Farewells to Miss Archer. She'll be here in a minute. (*A brief pause.*) Noel—

NOEL. What?

JIM. Will you do something for us?

NOEL. Why of course, Jim. What is it?

JIM.—After—after you see Mary, quit the party and go on home.

[*There is a silence. Then:*

NOEL. (*In a low voice.*) Would you like me to go out the back way?

JIM. I don't think that's necessary, no.

NOEL.—Perhaps it would be better just to hide somewhere, till the rest go.

JIM. (*Turning away.*) You can do as you like, Noel.

NOEL. That's very kind. Thanks.

JIM. I'm sorry to have disturbed you. Forgive me, will you?

NOEL. I don't know. Does it matter?

JIM. No.

NOEL. That's all right, then. (*They stand looking at each other for a long moment. Finally:*) Do you enjoy it, Jim?

JIM. Do I enjoy what?

NOEL.—Standing there, kissing me.

JIM. My God, Noel.

NOEL.—Mine too, Jim.—It's what you've been doing for a long while now—each time we've been together. What's it matter that you've never been much closer to me than this—so long as you've thought it and wished it?

JIM. You've—had a good deal to drink, haven't you?

NOEL. Yes.—But I've been drunker than this before on no wine at all. And so have you, my dear, dear, dear—

JIM. Oh quit it, quit it, will you?

NOEL. I love you, Jim, and I die hard. There should have been two of you, you know—one for me.

JIM. Listen: have I ever said or done the slightest—

NOEL.—I think there *are* two of you—and one *is.*—No, you haven't. But you want me, and I want you and if it keeps up, someday there'll be hell to pay. I'm telling you.

JIM. Noel—

NOEL. I know. You've always behaved with the most praiseworthy restraint. That's been splendid of you, I suppose, though, I rather wish you hadn't. But you can't fool anyone as Irish as me about love. I couldn't have felt as I do about you, if you didn't feel much the same about me. It doesn't happen that way. It takes two.

JIM. I'm sorry, but I don't agree with you.

NOEL. You don't have to.—Nor need you think for a minute that I'm not aware how terribly you love your Mary, and how utterly different it is to what you feel for me. I envy her, but she need never envy me. Not if she's wise.

JIM. How do you mean, wise?

NOEL. *She* knows.

JIM. Noel, I haven't the remotest idea of what you're driving at, I really haven't.

NOEL. Well, great intelligence never was your long-suit, was it? (*A brief pause. She adds:*)—And, *I've* done a tall lot of thinking, these last few weeks. I've damn well had to.

JIM. I can't see you've got very far.

NOEL. I've gone a tremendous way. I'll tell you where I've arrived, if you like.

JIM. You needn't mind.

NOEL. I'd rather—if *you* don't. (*She waits. He is silent.*) It's my little pleasure to acknowledge, now, that I'm yours, heart and soul—

JIM. Noel—

NOEL.—But you needn't let it upset you: I'm inclined to glory in it. A day like to-day is fairly rough-going, of course, but I imagine I'll survive it. Because you see I'm just as sure as I am of my name, that part of you is mine. I can't make head or tail of it—I'm still frightfully balled-up in every direction, but of what's between us, I'm quite sure. I wish we'd been something—important to each other. I wish something actual, had happened. Our chances for pulling out of it would be better, then. But we weren't—and nothing has. So here we are, and here we'll be—and you'd better shun me as you would the devil.

JIM. When you see me running from someone, you'll know it.

NOEL. That's the boy!—Spoken like a Yale man.

JIM. Oh, shut up.

NOEL. You can't be indifferent to me, Jimmy Hut—so don't try. (*She softens in an instant.*) Oh come here a minute—let me look at you. Never mind—I'll come there. (*She moves toward him. Her voice breaks:*) Jim—Jim—

JIM. Quit it, Noel.

[*But she does not:*

NOEL. What a handsome groom you were, Jim—I was proud of you, truly I was. I could feel my heart swell to see you, really I could—so straight, and so well turned-out, and so cock-sure of yourself, and so much in need of a beating. I didn't kiss you when the others did, did I? Here—I shall—

[*She puts her hands upon his shoulders, and leans up to him. He turns away, speaking in an agonized voice:*

JIM. Noel—Oh *damn* it, Noel—this is my wedding-day!

[*She drops her head upon his breast with a sudden sob, then turns and leaves him, tears bright in her eyes.*

NOEL. Stupid—stupid—we'd have had a much better chance, if you'd let that go— Well—(*A pause. She composes herself.*) Is this someone's wine? (*She lifts a full glass from the tray.*) Here's to your great happiness—and may I share in it. (*She drains the glass. There is a knock at the door and a tentative twist of the knob. With an exclamation,* NOEL *sets the glass down upon the tray, dashes the back of her hand across her mouth, leans back on both arms against the table, facing the door, and calls clearly:*) Come in, won't you?

[MARY *enters.*

MARY. Oh hello.—I didn't know who—

NOEL. What do you think, Mary?—Jim's been having me over the coals for enjoying the party too much.

MARY.—Really?

[*She goes to get her handbag from the table.*

NOEL. Yes—can you believe it? But I've sworn I'll be a good girl now. (*She and* MARY *look at each other.* MARY *wins.* NOEL *drops her bantering tone and speaks lowly, honestly:*)—I love you both, Mary. I do love you very much.

MARY. So do we you, Noel.

NOEL.—You know, you have the wisest eyes I've ever seen.

[*There is a silence. Then* MARY *laughs, preferring to laugh.*

MARY. Run along, child. (*She kisses her, briefly.*) We've got to scoot. Good-bye.

NOEL. Good-bye, Jim. Have a good trip.

JIM. Thanks, Noel.

NOEL. (*Lingering.*) Good-bye, Mary—

MARY. Good-bye, dear.

[NOEL *moves in the direction of the hall.*

NOEL. I—I'll just go—and get my wrap—

[*She goes out. A moment, then* MARY *turns to* JIM.

MARY. I think that was a good thing to do.

JIM. I don't know. Anyway, it's done.

MARY. Thanks. (*She smiles at him.*)—Is it still me, Jim?

JIM. (*Darkly.*) Mary, I'll—

[*She laughs.*

MARY. Never mind! (*She glances at her watch.*)—You know, *I'm* about ready to start.

JIM. Tugging at the leash, that's what I am.

MARY. I do hope Peter doesn't muff the signals.

JIM. We'll give him three minutes: after that we'll duck anyway.

MARY.—In the meantime, let's form a group called "Alone at Last," shall we?

[*With a sigh, she seats herself on the chaise-longue.* JIM *drops down beside her, his arm around her.*

JIM. Lord knows I'm willing.

[MARY *closes her eyes.*

MARY.—I'm just so tired, and so happy.

JIM. So am I.

MARY. It's like a warm bath.

JIM. It's better.

MARY. I don't expect to have another serious thought for months on end, now.

JIM. If you feel one stealing up on you, fight like hell.

[MARY *opens her eyes again.*

MARY.—All that silly talk of mine about theories and stratagems and what-nots generally—don't mind it. It's just that when I think anything awful might happen to you and me, my heart slides right down to my toes in a panic. It's just—wanting desperately to guard the most precious thing I've ever had or shall have.

JIM. I know, Darling. That goes for me, too.

MARY. Then it's on—

JIM. You bet it is.—Let's make just one blanket agreement, shall we?

MARY. What is it?

JIM.—Whatever happens, never quit each other.

[*She presses her cheek against his.*

MARY. Never, never.

JIM.—Never in this world.

MARY. In any world. (*A pause. Then suddenly she starts forward.*) What's that music!?

[JIM *goes to the hall door, opens it a crack, listens, then exclaims disgustedly.*

JIM. Dardanella.

MARY.—It may be by way of warning.—You haven't forgotten anything, have you?

JIM. Not a thing.

MARY. As for me— (*Silently and thoughtfully, she ticks seven items off on her fingers, then exclaims:*) Oh!

JIM. What is it? Anything important?

[MARY *rushes to the bedroom door and opens it.*

MARY. Heavens, yes! (*She calls into the bedroom.*) Julie!

JULIE. (*From within.*) Yes, Miss?

MARY. Please be sure to tell Aunt—Miss Archer—that I'd like my piano in the house by the time we get back. I don't care about the other things, but I would like the piano.

JULIE. I'll tell her, Miss.

MARY. Thanks!—Good-bye, dear! (*She*

closes the door, and returns to JIM.) There. That's— (*Suddenly.*) Shh!

JIM. What?

MARY. It's *it!*

JIM. Is it?

MARY. Yes! Listen!

[*And it is the wedding march.*

JIM. You're right.

MARY. Come on, Sweet!

JIM. Where's my hat?

MARY. Oh never mind your hat.

JIM. All right, the hell with it.

MARY. Give me your hand!

JIM.—Give me yours. I'm the man.

[*Their hands fumble for each other.*

MARY. Quit fooling! Hurry up, or they'll murder us!

JIM. What's the rush? We've got fifty years.

MARY. *Are you coming!?*

[*He leans and kisses her cheek, hastily.*

JIM. To Mary from Jim, with love. Here we go!

[*He takes her hand and rushes for the hall. From downstairs, rising above the wedding march, comes the sound of shouts and cheers and laughter. From outside the house, motors starting, electric horns blowing. Through it all, is heard a call from different voices, men's and women's: "Good Luck!" "Best of Luck!" "Good Luck!"*

Curtain.

ACT TWO

SCENE: *The music-room, on the top floor of the Huttons' house, in uptown New York, near the East River. May, of this year. Eleven o'clock in the morning.*

The music-room is unlike most music-rooms, in that it is comfortable, attractively furnished in the modern style and very sunny. Just off center at back, is a high and broad studio-window. There is a fireplace in the right wall, center, of very simple design, in white plaster. The walls are of smooth gray, without pictures. The floor is dark, and bare except for two or three small rugs of plain color. The furniture is low and comfortable. The curtains at the window are of green, in some lively material. There is a bowl of white flowers on a large piano. There are no wall-brackets, the room being lighted at night entirely by four lamps, two made of silvered globes with plain, low shades of coral paper, two of glass globes filled with water, with shades of the same color as the curtains.

Entrance is from the hall, down left.

At Rise: RICHARD PARISH *is seated at the piano, playing from a handwritten score on the stand before him.* MARY *leans against the piano, listening.* RICHARD *is a few months younger than* MARY, *that is to say between twenty-seven and twenty-eight. He has no manners but natural manners, no graces but a natural grace. This, plus the particular spirit which moves him from within, must be the sum of his charm, for he is not at all handsome, not in the least well-dressed and with no gift whatever for making pretty speeches. He plays for a moment or two without speaking. Then:*

RICHARD. (*As he plays.*) This is for the wood-winds. There's no brass at all in the first part. Do you think I need it?

MARY. Wait a minute. (*He plays on a little further.*) No.

RICHARD. I didn't think so.

[*He goes on playing.*

MARY. (*Suddenly.*) There! *That's* what I don't like.

RICHARD. This?

MARY. Yes.

RICHARD. What's the matter with it?

MARY. It's sloppy.

RICHARD. Sloppy!—The way I play it?

MARY. The way you wrote it.

[*Scowling,* RICHARD *tries several variations of the same theme. Finally he repeats one.*

RICHARD.—Is that "sloppy"?

MARY. No.

RICHARD. Neither was the first. I think the first was better.

MARY. That's a pet idea of yours. It isn't always right.

RICHARD. A musician needs a man with a hammer just the way a painter does.

MARY.—Man with a hammer?

RICHARD.—To hit him over the head when a thing's finished.

MARY. Don't fool yourself that *you* do.

RICHARD. You think I'm lazy—

MARY. Maybe.

RICHARD. Mary—

MARY. What?

RICHARD. Oh hell.

MARY. Richard, *I* know the gift you have— Oh yes, it is a gift!—And I've told you you can have this room and this piano every morning you want and all morning and all alone. I don't ever come hanging around except when I'm expressly asked to. And—

RICHARD. (*Grinning.*) You're invited.

[*He leaves the piano, and seats himself facing her.*

MARY. Thanks— How long do you figure it will take you to finish your wretched ballet?

RICHARD. About two months. Less, if you'll help me.

MARY.—*If* I'll—?—It's a godsend.

RICHARD. How's that?

MARY. Jim's off for his trip abroad pretty soon, and I'd like something to help me stand it. Even the children aren't enough. I want a job.

RICHARD. Why don't you go with him?

MARY. I don't know. I just never do. Once I did, the first year. Then the next year I was about to have a baby, and the next year Aunt Grace was about to have an appendix, and the next year I'd just had another baby, and last year both of them had whooping-cough and this year, when I could go, I won't.

RICHARD. Don't you want to?

MARY. Heavens, yes. But I've got some crazy notion that married people need holidays from each other, so I'm making a firm stand. Six weeks. That's no picnic, you know.

[*She seats herself upon the sofa.*

RICHARD. You're a funny pair.

MARY. We're a nice pair, don't you think?

RICHARD.—Sure, very nice.—Terribly in love, too, aren't you?

MARY. Oh yes, terribly.

RICHARD. How long is it?

MARY. Six years the tenth of July.

RICHARD. Pretty good.

MARY. It keeps getting better.

RICHARD. I suppose you aren't likely ever to crash now unless one of you falls in love with someone else.

MARY. I don't think Jim and I could crash even on that.

RICHARD. No?

MARY. No.

RICHARD. Well, there's not much chance it'll happen, is there?

MARY. It might. To Jim, it might.

RICHARD. And if it did—?

MARY. My one fear in the world is that he wouldn't quite understand how little it meant to me.

[*A silence.*

RICHARD. I guess there's nothing to be said to that.

MARY. There it is.

RICHARD. (*After a moment.*) D'you know, I can't tell you how much I grant you two. And it's a funny thing, because you're the kind of people I've resented all my life. I never expected to believe that you could be so—so damned valuable. I used to curse into my beard whenever I passed a house like this. I used to spit on the pavement whenever a decent-looking motor-car passed me. I don't any more, because I've found two among you whom I know to be of absolutely first importance in all the ways I value. You're hard in the right places, you're wise with a most beautiful wisdom, and for your life as you live it, I've nothing but salutes and cheers. You're a revelation to me, Mary.

MARY. (*Overcome.*) Why Richard—

RICHARD. Why, your grandmother. It's true, and I mean it. (*He rises and goes to the piano.*) What about this bollicking ballet? Do you really want to help me get it down?

MARY. I ask for nothing better. The babies are in the country with Aunt Grace. They're thriving. I'll spend four days a week in town and you can come out for week-ends. She's got a Knabe. It's old, and the lacquer's cracked, but it's sweet as a nut.

RICHARD. When does Jim sail?

MARY. Saturday. He was to have gone on the *Paris* to-day but he couldn't get a cabin. Now it's not until the *France,* May fifteenth. I can go to work on the sixteenth.

RICHARD. Lord, it'd be wonderful. You know you *have* got a pretty good ear.

MARY. I've got a first-rate ear, and I can write the stuff down like a house on fire.

RICHARD. Imagine finishing it!

[*A brief pause. Then:*

MARY. How many things *have* you finished, Richard?

RICHARD. Oh be still. (JULIE *enters with a tray containing a glass of milk and a plate of sandwiches.* RICHARD *frowns at it.*)—Speaking of babies, I think I can live without this milk every morning.

MARY. It builds you up. See what a big girl I am.

[JULIE *places the tray on a low table beside* RICHARD.

JULIE. Miss Shippan just telephoned to—

MARY. Fanny Shippan? Telephoned—!?

JULIE. She arrived last evening, and she wished to know if you were lunching at home, and if so—

MARY. I hope you told her Yes, by all means.

JULIE. I did, Miss.

MARY. Thanks, Julie. Set two extra places, then, will you?

JULIE. She said she would not be able to stay. She just wanted to come in for a moment.

MARY. I'll persuade her.

JULIE. Very well, Miss.

[*She goes out.*

MARY. (*To* RICHARD.) That's terribly exciting. She was one of my bridesmaids. I haven't seen her in two years.

RICHARD. Where's she been?

MARY. Oh all over.

RICHARD. I get a feeling in this house that everyone's either just going up a gang-plank or just coming down one—

MARY. That doesn't go for me. I wish it did.—Richard—tell me the way the story goes—of the ballet, I mean.

RICHARD. I don't want you getting the story mixed up with it. *You're* to listen to *notes.*

MARY. Do you suppose for a minute I can think of anything else when I hear them?

[*He looks at her sharply.*

RICHARD. No. As a matter of fact, I don't believe you can.

MARY. Then tell me.

RICHARD. 'Tisn't all worked out yet. It probably never will be.

MARY. Don't you believe it won't!

RICHARD. Probably never get put on, anyway. Probably cost a fortune to put it on.

MARY. Isn't the Russian Ballet rich?

RICHARD. I'd rather an American did it. —No—not the Metropolitan nor any of the Art Boys, either. I'd like some good, hard-boiled revue-manager. Then they'd dance, by God, not waddle around picking dream-flowers off the ground-cloth. And I'd have an orchestra for whom the world didn't end with Debussy.

MARY. I should think you could find a manager.

RICHARD. My only hope is that it *might* be amusing.

MARY. Do tell me how it runs.

RICHARD. Well, to begin with, it's for children.

MARY. Entirely?

RICHARD. Yes. It's a downright fairy-story. If older people want to like it, that's their look-out.

MARY. I see.

RICHARD. It's called "The Friendly Germ." Of course the whole thing is completely cock-eyed, but I think it adds up to make sense.

MARY. What's in it?

RICHARD. Well, there's a lot of religion in it, and a lot of test-tubes and microscopes and down-town at lunch-hour and Madison Square Garden with a hockey-match and that joint in Harlem where I've got a new job playing the piano from twelve to two—it's a swell place, really—and oh, Lord, there's a lot in it really.

MARY. Is there any form to it?

RICHARD. Of course there's form to it. What do you mean, "Is there any form to it?"?

MARY. How does it *run,* I say!?

RICHARD. Well, the first scene's at the Church Conference in the Middle Ages to decide how many angels could dance on the point of a needle. That's the Gregorian stuff you get in the opening movement. My mother used to wheeze it out on an old harmonium in a frame-church at Single River, in Minnesota, and didn't I soak it up, though. That, and the music my father's saw-mill made, and the water. Well, I see the entire chorus in the same wooden robes you see in primitives, and they move like wood, and oh Lord, it sounds terrible—

MARY. No it doesn't.

RICHARD. Then the second scene's in the top tower of the American Needle Building on lower Broadway. A thin white room, sort of a conical shape, up to a point. They've developed a needle with the finest point in the world. They're going to measure it under a microscope and broadcast the happy news to God's whole great big monkey-house. What you hear is the music from the street below: curb brokers, street-cars, motors, feet, frosted chocolate milk-shakes being sucked through straws—

MARY. Exciting!

RICHARD. 'Think so?—Well, they march up to the microscope, take a peek and fall back in astonishment. For cat's sake what is it? The celestial music begins—curtain—then curtain up again on the field of the microscope—

MARY. What?!

[RICHARD'S *gestures become broader.*

RICHARD.—The field of the microscope—

round—enormous—just as you'd see it—a big ground-glass disc, measured off into square areas, tilted back a little.

MARY. Richard!

RICHARD. It's alive with angels, dancing—no wings, you know,—they just know how to use their arms. The germ's a very peculiar individual, with very dancy feet. The angel named Mike, who's our hero, if there is a hero in the cock-eyed thing—he's trying to ride the germ. Finally, just as he gets on his back, you see an enormous instrument come down like that, and separate 'em from the others and push 'em up on a glass-slide and off the scene. So far so good?

MARY. I love it. But watch out that your angel doesn't go whimsical on you.

RICHARD. Not a chance.

MARY. That's the danger, though.

RICHARD. This angel is a real guy. He's superb, this angel. He's a kind of Lindbergh.

MARY. Poor thing—what do they do with him?

RICHARD. He and the germ are taken home by the president of the Needle Works to his apartment.—There sits his lovely daughter, who has been ailing, poor girl. She's being dosed with thyroid extract, with no results. Here's something new to amuse her. All right: Mike and his funny friend get in among the thyroid and grow up to life size.

MARY. Does it work that way?

RICHARD. Ask a doctor.—You see, the germ—

MARY. You might call him Pat—

RICHARD. I intend to. Pat's the germ of the dance: he infects everyone within reach with it. The two of 'em become a sensation. Talk of the town, talk of the country, talk of the world. Mike can do anything—he's the perfect man. Big promoters try to syndicate him. Flying for profit. Dowagers cut each other's throats to get him to dine. Come and meet our Winged Lion. Drawing-room flying at nine, by the celestial Mike. Come and get bitten by Pat, and feel your old legs stir again. Then the girl begins to want Mike all for her very own —the way you want Jim all for yours—the way everyone in love turns fool and says "No shares! This is all mine!"

MARY. They don't, though.

RICHARD. Oh yes they do!—But Mike can't stand it. She gets desperate. All mine! All mine!—There's a chase across the roof of the apartment. They go over the edge—

[*He stops, as* JIM *enters.*

MARY. Why Jim! Hello!

JIM. Hello, Darling. Hello, Parish. How are you?

RICHARD. Fine, thanks. I've just been boring Mary stiff with a couple of Tales of Hoffman.

MARY. He *has* not.—Jim, who do you think telephoned? Fanny. She got in last night. She's coming for lunch, I hope.

JIM. Good. Only I won't be here.

MARY. Why? Where are you off to?

JIM. London first, then—

MARY. What do you *mean?!*

JIM. The French Line telephoned they had a cancellation just this morning, and could put me on the *Paris.*

MARY. Jim!

JIM. She sails at one. Julie's packing bags. I've got to go on account of Proctor. He's off for some other god-forsaken place on the twentieth. I've cabled him I'm coming with a contract for his next three books. He's too good to miss, really.

MARY. I hate his stuff, I hate it!

JIM. He sells, though. If it was really good stuff, I could put the trip off a year.

MARY. But one o'clock!

JIM. It isn't twelve yet. I've got lots of time. Father'll be up with some papers to be signed in a minute, then we'll tear for the river. Do you want to come to the dock?

MARY. Do I want to come to the dock! Oh, I'll kill you, I'll—

RICHARD. (*Rising.*) Here I go.—Lunch some other day, Mary.

MARY. Do you mind?

RICHARD. Not a bit. (*To* JIM.) Good-bye. Have a good trip.

JIM. Thanks. Anything I can do for you in Paris?

RICHARD. You might tell the Art Boys on the Left Bank not to talk quite so much.

JIM. All right, I will.

MARY. I'll telephone you, Richard.

RICHARD. Will you do that? Fine! Good-bye.

MARY. Good-bye! (RICHARD *goes out,* MARY *rushes into* JIM'S *arms.*) Oh Jim, I hate it! It was bad enough not going last year. Now it's worse.

JIM. Come on with me, darling. It's a big cabin.

MARY. No. I can't.

JIM. We'd have fun.
MARY. Shut up, shut up!
JIM. I think this is all rot, you know—this enforced-holiday business.
MARY. Maybe it is.—When will you be back?
JIM. By July—the tenth surely, now. Where's your party for the anniversary to be—here or in the country?
MARY. Here. I'm going to keep the house open till the fifteenth anyway. Do make it in time, Jim. It's important to me. I'm a fool about Christmas and birthdays and things like that.
JIM. You leave it to me. I'll be here.
[MARY *smiles.*
MARY.—I've always said if we got safely past the sixth—
JIM. It's been a good go, hasn't it, Darling?
MARY. Hasn't it, though?
JIM. I'd do it again, wouldn't you?
MARY. Oh, maybe I wouldn't!
JIM. Kiss me, please. Very small: I've got a boat to catch.—Thanks.
MARY. Are you sure you've everything you'll need?
JIM. No, but I'll manage. I made a list and told Julie most of it. She's—(*The telephone rings.*) That must be the country. I put the call in downstairs—
MARY. Aunt Grace won't be there, you know.
JIM. I wanted to tell Jimmy good-bye.
[*He goes to the telephone.*
MARY. You're sweet, Jim.
JIM. So's Jimmy. (*He takes the telephone.*) Hello. All right. (*A moment.*) Hello—Is that you, Frederic? Yes.—Tell Sabina to bring young Jim to the telephone, will you? Thanks—(*He turns to* MARY.) Come here, Darling. Don't stay so far away. (*She comes to him. He stands with his arm around her, and the receiver to his ear. They talk on at random until* SABINA *comes to the telephone.*) How's your special account? All right?
MARY. Bursting.
JIM. What are you going to do about that garden on the roof here?
MARY. Gravel costs enormously.
JIM. Let's have it, anyway.
MARY. I'll order it then.
JIM. Is Collins behaving himself better?
MARY. Some. He's hauled the manure up, at least.
JIM. Tell him I said we're very fond of him, but this next month decides it.
MARY. I did, yesterday.
JIM. Did it ever occur to you that Sabina might drink?
MARY. No. Of course she doesn't.
JIM. I don't like that nose much.
MARY. It's the weather does that. Once I tried to get her to take some brandy for a stomach-ache, and she nearly left in a pet.
JIM. See if you can't get her to work regularly on Mimsie's legs. Massage or something.
MARY. But my dear, *all* babies' legs are like that!
JIM. I'm scared of her growing up with fat legs. Girls ought to have thin legs.
MARY. She will.
JIM.—If she's any daughter of yours.
MARY.—If she's any daughter of mine.
JIM. Don't have any vaccinations or anything till I get back, will you?
MARY. I wasn't planning any.
JIM. Just keep cool with Coolidge.
MARY. You betcha.
JIM. What'll you be doing all the time?
MARY. Music with Richard, mostly. He's got a grand idea for a ballet.
JIM. Where'd you find him, Mary?
MARY.—Richard? He was at the Rosalskys' that night. Don't you remember?
JIM. Oh yes. (*A moment.*)—He's not the kind that makes passes, is he?
MARY. Richard?—Not in the least.
JIM. If anyone does, haul off and paste him one for me.
MARY. No one will.
JIM. *I* would.
MARY. Most men have more manners.
JIM. Mary.
MARY. What?
JIM. I'm in love with you.
MARY.—But what about my children?
JIM. Forget 'em. Come with me in my death-car.
MARY. When do we leave?
JIM. How would, say, twelve-thirty do? We could— (*He turns to the telephone.*) Sabina? Yes. I'm going off to-day instead of next week, Sabina, and I'd like to say good-bye to Jimmy. Is his face clean enough? Yes. Oh yes indeed. I will, Sabina—and Matthew and Mark and Luke, too. Thanks very much.—Hello, Jimmy! How are you? Good! What have you been doing, riding Punch? Does he go any faster? Well, he's still pretty stiff, you know—it was a hard winter.—What's that? He didn't! You tell him for me he's old enough to know

better than that, and if he doesn't he can't *come* on the front lawn. That's right. Listen, Jimmy: I'm going on the big boat this morning.—No, darling—next time maybe. I'm awfully sorry, but they almost didn't have room for me, even. What shall I bring you? Yes.—Yes— Yes, if I can find one. Yes. Yes. Is that all?—Well, anything else you think of, just tell your Mother, and she'll write me. Good-bye, darling—(*He smacks a resounding kiss.*)—Did you get it? (*A moment.*) Yes, so did I. Good-bye, Jimmy. You be a good boy and I will too. Kiss Mimsie good-bye for me and tell her to keep that thumb out of her mouth or I'll beat the tar out of her.—Of course there's tar in her! There's tar in everyone. Why, I knew a man once, and—

MARY. I want to speak with Sabina a minute.

JIM.—And he was nothing *but* tar!—Call 'Bina, will you Jim? Your Mother wants to tell her something—Good-bye, Angel.—You bet I won't! I'll bring a bagful.

[MARY *takes the telephone.* JIM *begins to consult a list.*

MARY. Good-bye, darling. Yes, to-morrow, sure. No—after your nap. Yes, he understands. Of course, he'll tell the Captain. He'll— Sabina? Yes.—Is everything all right? Mimsie? Where? Oh dear. Have you got some of that boric-powder? That's right. And we'd better cut down on the vegetables to-morrow and Sunday. No—the milk of magnesia—just a little in the formula. I'll be out early to-morrow afternoon. If she starts running a fever telephone me, and I'll motor out to-night. Good-bye. (MARY *puts down the telephone and turns to* JIM.) I'll see that Julie's got everything straight.

JIM. She has, I'm sure. Stay, dear. I'll go down myself when Fanny comes.

MARY. What's that? A list?

JIM. Yes. Checked, mostly. Oh, would you tell Peter I can't play golf with him Wednesday—

MARY. (*A mental note.*)—Peter—golf—Wednesday.

JIM. Let's see, now: (*He reads the list and checks the items.*) "Telephone Father"—check. "Telephone country"—check. "Kiss Mary"—(*He kisses her.*)—check. "Don't forget passport"—(*He feels for it.*) "Tell Julie plenty of underwear"—check. "Tell Mary love her"—(*He turns to her.*)—Love you.

MARY. You are good, and kind.

JIM. Check. "About liquor supply—"—If you need anything, telephone Trotter at the Club.

MARY. Trotter?

JIM. Trotter.

MARY.—Liquor—Trotter—Club.

[JIM *looks at the list silently for a moment. Then as he folds it up:*

JIM. "Keep out of draughts, don't eat starchy foods, pump up bicycle-tires and be at foot of West 14th Street at ten minutes to one."

MARY. Ten minutes to one. Six weeks. Jim, Jim, Jim, Jim.

JIM. Aw Mary—

MARY. I'm going to weep.

JIM. Blink your eyes. Swallow.—That's the girl.

MARY. Write me all the time. Cable me every minute.

JIM. You bet I will.

MARY. Don't have a French doctor even for a cold.

JIM. No.

MARY.—If the ship starts to sink, kick all the women and children out of the way and grab the biggest life-belt and—

JIM. You bet.

MARY.—Say your prayers night and morning—and—(*Suddenly she clings to him.*) Oh Jim—Jim—

JIM. Oh cut it out, will you?

[*He kisses her. A moment, then* JAMES HUTTON'S *voice is heard from the hall.*

JAMES. Jim? Mary? (MARY *leaves* JIM'S *arms. He goes swiftly to the window, and stands there with his back to the room, composing himself. There is a silence. Then again* JAMES'S *voice, nearer:*) Are you up here, Mary?

MARY. Yes. Hello, Father. So's Jim. Come on in! (*Then softly, to* JIM.) Darling—come here—

[JIM *comes to her.* JAMES HUTTON *appears in the doorway.*

JIM. Hello, Father.

JAMES. I—er— There was a young woman on your doorstep. She asked me to announce her: A Miss F—

[FANNY *bursts in from the hall.*

FANNY.—It's Fanny! Whoopee! It's Fanny!

MARY. I don't believe it!

[*They embrace.*

FANNY. My dear girl, what fun!

MARY. But you look simply stunning!

FANNY.—If that means fat, I'll have your heart out and— Hello, James, my boy. (*She goes to* JIM *and shakes his hand.*) How is the book business?

JIM. Hello, Fanny. It's great you're back.

FANNY. I'm staying for years. (*She seats herself.*) This rock shall stir from its firm base as soon as I.

JIM. What's the matter? Didn't you like the life among the British?

FANNY. Listen: if ever we have another war with England, I want it understood right here and now, *I* was the one that fired the first shot.

MARY. But my dear—the papers were full of you!

FANNY. I had a salon. I honestly had a salon. I can't tell you what I've been through. Last night when I saw Fifth Avenue, I cried into my lap for fully twenty minutes. It's a nice little city you've got here, friends. It's going to grow. (*To* JIM.) You're not really sailing for that place to-day?

JIM. At one o'clock.

FANNY. Well you're simply crazy, that's all. How are your babies, Mary?

MARY. Wonderful.

FANNY.—Still, it's nice to be in an uninteresting condition again—wot?

MARY. My dear, I've gone mad: I'm supporting three dressmakers.

FANNY. I'm dying to see the new one. Boy or child? I forget.

MARY. Child. Name of Mary. Her mother was a dancing-girl. Come out with me to-morrow, will you? I'll hold a one-man exhibit.

FANNY. I'd love it.—Isn't she pretty, Mr. Hutton?

JAMES. I've always contended that.

FANNY.—I was afraid I might find just a mother. (*To* JIM.) You poor boy, going off on a boat. Don't let them put you at the Captain's table. I was—and the strain was too much: my wrists gave way. Twice I spilled gruel on my bib. It was a fearful trip. Lord knows I'm no beauty, but I'm young and I'm sound, and yet the only real attention I called forth from the whole big *Aquitania* was from a middle-aged professor at Tulane University, named Regan. I said that I was happy as a lark, and he said, But is a lark really happy? Can you bear it?

MARY. Stop, Fanny! We were just feeling so nice and sad over parting.

FANNY.—New York. My Lord, it's wonderful. You forget how wonderful it is. Who'll put me up for the Chamber of Commerce? For the last three months I've been unfurling American flags from my blouse on every occasion. From now on I'm going to be just a home girl. No more nasty, drafty castles for Fanny.

JIM. You weren't presented at Court, were you? There was a rumor.

[*He rises, and moves toward the hall.*

FANNY. James, I was there with ostrich-plumes in my hair. It was a riot. The queen swooned, and the king was carried out screaming. They say that down in White-Chapel the boys were—oh, good-bye—

JIM. Don't stop. I'm just going downstairs a minute to close a bag or two.

MARY. (*Rising.*) I'll—

JIM. No, Darling—really—I'll be right up. Have you got those letters, Father?

JAMES. Miss Anderson's in the library. She'll take your signature.

[FANNY *is groping in her handbag.*

JIM. Good.

FANNY. Wait a minute, Jim. 'Arf a mo'. Presents—pretty presents. (*She gives a small box to* MARY.) These are for you, Mary.

MARY. (*Opening the box.*) "These?" That means earrings.

FANNY. I got them in Venice, for a certain popular song.

[MARY *holds up the earrings.*

MARY. Fanny!

FANNY. Tush, child. I could give pearls, and never feel it.

MARY. You angel. They're simply gorgeous.

[*She puts them on.* FANNY *offers a larger box to* JIM.

FANNY.—And these, James, are for you, to hold your pants up. (JIM *takes the box.*) —Hand-painted braces, for the unexpected guest. I think the scene is from Manon.

JIM. Fanny, you're a girl after my own heart.

FANNY. No, Darling—I was once, but Mary was too quick for me.

JIM. I'll sail in them.

[JAMES *looks at his watch.*

JAMES. You won't sail at all, if you go on this way.

[JIM *looks at his watch.*

JIM. There's something in what you say.

[*He goes out.*

FANN.—Lovely boy, really lovely.—Honestly, Mary, I never saw two happier looking people in my life.

MARY. We're pretty sunk over this trip, just at present.

FANNY.—Most people I know would be cheering. You're in luck. You don't realize it.

MARY. Oh yes we do!

FANNY. (*To* JAMES.) It isn't just put-on, is it?

JAMES. (*Smiling.*) I don't think so.

FANNY. I've got a little skeptical about marriage: me, who had such faith. Paris is simply alive with people you know, getting divorces.

MARY. Well, *I* think it's sickening.

FANNY.—So do I. What I hate most, is what it does to their what-do-you-call-its—souls—characters. Honestly, just listening to their tales, I felt like Bad Fanny, the wickedest woman in Bridgeport. I claim it shows in their faces. You wouldn't know Susie Price.

MARY. *She* isn't, too!

FANNY. Indeed she is!—Her precious little individuality was being stifled.

MARY. Her what?!—I didn't know she had one.

FANNY. Home-life developed it.—But of course as soon as the decree is handed down, she's going to try again with some fifth-rate Englishman. She's living with him now in the South of France somewhere.

MARY. It *is* vile.

FANNY.—Just thank your stars, Girlie. Because there's something awfully wrong with marriage.

MARY. There's something awfully wrong with the people who *get* married.

FANNY. How are Peter and Nora? Are they all right?

MARY. Now don't go *looking* for trouble, Fanny.

FANNY. Catch me! These days I spread oil wherever I go. You have to.

JAMES. Did *you* get to the South at all, Fanny?

FANNY.—Of France? No, worse luck. (*To* MARY.) Oh but I must tell you. Zoe Evans was at Cannes, and—

MARY. I don't know her.

FANNY. I know you don't. But she knows Jim and she said she saw you and him two or three times at—what's the name of that little place up in the mountains back of Antibes? St. Paul du—something—St. Paul du Var! And she was going to speak to you, only—

MARY. (*Carefully.*) When was that?

FANNY. Last May.

MARY. (*More carefully.*) Oh yes.

FANNY.—Only she couldn't get Jim's eye and you both looked so devoted, she concluded you were there to escape Americans. So she didn't. They thought at the inn you were a run-away couple, living in—well, it isn't sin to the French, is it? They'd whipped up quite a nice illicit romance about you. Clever Mary. It must have been fun. Zoe said the *patrone* told her you'd taken the sweetest little studio-place with actually a bathroom. I didn't even know you were over. Why didn't you look me up?

MARY. Well, it was—

FANNY. You *were* trying to avoid Americans!

[*A moment.*

MARY. It was the shortest kind of a trip.

FANNY. You didn't run into Noel, did you? Someone told me she was down there somewhere on the Riviera—or maybe it was Rome.

MARY. No, we didn't.

FANNY. Apparently she's got an idea that she can write or paint or something—

MARY. And can she?

FANNY. I doubt it. There's a girl I never could make out.

MARY. Couldn't you, Fanny? I don't think Noel's hard.

FANNY. I must admit, I never worked much over her.—Your house is just as sweet as ever, Mary.

MARY. I love it.

FANNY. You've changed this room.

MARY. I'm forever changing it.—We're going to put gravel on the roof and make a garden.

FANNY.—Divine.—What time are you going out to-morrow?

MARY. How's three o'clock?

FANNY. That's fine for me.—Sure you want me?

MARY. I should say I do. It's too marvellous, having you back. Are you at the apartment?

FANNY. Yes.

MARY. I'll stop by for you at three, then.

FANNY. I'll be hanging out the window. What time is it now? Oh good lord!—Good-bye, Mr. Hutton—come and dine some night with Mary, will you?

JAMES. I should be glad to.

FANNY. (*To* MARY.) Don't come down with me, dear—honestly. I'm going on the run.

MARY. All right, I shan't.—Shout to Jim as you go by. His room's just below.

FANNY. I'll do that.—The poor lamb, having to leave his Mary.

MARY. Oh he doesn't mind.

FANNY. His face *looked* it.

MARY. Thanks a thousand times for the earrings.

FANNY. There are no two ears I'd sooner seen 'em hang from, Dearie. (*She kisses her.*) Three o'clock, then.

MARY. Three o'clock.

[FANNY *goes out.* MARY *turns slowly, thoughtfully, and stands looking into space. There is a long silence.* JAMES *is watching her. Finally:*

JAMES. Mary—

MARY. Yes?

JAMES. I don't think I should jump to any silly conclusions, if I were you.

MARY. Wouldn't you, Father?

JAMES. No.

MARY. Jim went abroad alone last year. I wasn't with him.

JAMES. No—nor was anyone else.

MARY. You don't think so.

JAMES. I'm sure of it. (*A pause. Suddenly* MARY *goes to the telephone and takes up a telephone-list. She finds the number and puts the receiver to her ear.* JAMES *rises.*) What are you doing?

[MARY *does not answer. Another pause. Then:*

MARY. Plaza 2476.

JAMES. Whom are you calling, Mary?

[MARY *does not answer. Another pause. Then:*

MARY. Hello, is this Plaza 2476?—May I speak with Mrs. Farley, please.—Mrs. Hutton, Mrs. James Hutton. Oh.—Well perhaps *you* could tell me—I wanted to ask Mrs. Farley for Miss Noel's address. Yes.

JAMES. Mary, this is utterly ridiculous. It wasn't Jim at all. The Evans girl was simply mistaken. And even if she wasn't—

MARY. (*To the telephone.*) Yes? "Villa May." Yes. "St. Paul—St. Paul-du-Var—Alpes Maritimes"—Yes, I have it. Thanks very much. No—that's all I wanted. Thank you.

[*She replaces the receiver and stands looking down at the table.*

JAMES. You know, this isn't fair at all. This is—

MARY. I know Jim, Father, and I know Noel. And if they were there together—

[*She cannot finish.*

JAMES. That's a very hasty conclusion, my dear, and so far as I can see, entirely without foundation.

MARY. It's true, Father.

JAMES. How do you know it's true?

MARY. I feel it in my bones. (*She averts her face. Her breath escapes her in a cry.*) Oh—horrible—

JAMES. I can't for the life of me see how you can assume any such thing on any such evidence.

MARY. It's true, it's true!

[*A pause.*

JAMES.—And suppose it were—then what?

MARY. Then it's not me he wants. He wants her.

JAMES. Good heavens, Mary—

[*She turns on him sharply.*

MARY. What do you think, then? Is it both of us he wants?

JAMES. Jim loves you as few women are loved.

MARY. He could hardly love me—and go with her, could he?

JAMES. Couldn't he, Mary?

MARY. No!

JAMES—It's not conceivable, is it?

MARY. If it were, I shouldn't let it be!

JAMES. Ah—I see.

MARY. I'm not doing any sharing—I'm not going any halves with—with—oh, I can't say her name, now.

JAMES. You'll never be called upon to share what you and Jim have.

MARY. He's taken the whole beautiful thing in his hands and done that with it.

[*With a gesture of breaking it in two.*

JAMES. If what you suppose has happened *has* happened, one good crass fact explains it.

MARY—It might have once. Not now.

[*A moment. He watches her. Then:*

JAMES. But Mary, you must know—

MARY. I know that six years ago Jim and I were married.

JIM. (*From the hall below.*) Oh Mary! (*She does not answer.*) Darling—!

[*She goes to the doorway and calls:*

MARY. Yes?

JIM. Where are those shiny new studs of mine?

MARY. They're on the dressing-table in my room.

JIM. Right!—You're all ready, aren't you?

MARY. Yes, I'm ready.—We ought to

leave in two minutes! [*She presses the button at the door.*

JIM. Oh damn it! Let's make it *three*—

[MARY *comes back into the room.*

JAMES. (*Softly.*)—Don't you see, Mary, that *that's* the real thing—and the other just a—? (*Her gesture cuts him short. A moment, then:*) May I ask what you intend to do?

MARY. I don't know, yet. I'll have a month to myself to think in. When he comes back, I'll know.

JAMES. Surely you'll say nothing now.

MARY. I'll say nothing now. (*She closes her eyes in pain, and averts her head.*) I'll say less than nothing.

JAMES.—If you're wise, my dear, you'll say nothing ever.

[JULIE *comes in from the hall with a hat and the coat to* MARY'S *dress.*

JULIE. Was it these you rang for, Mrs. Hutton?

MARY. Yes. Thanks, dear. (*She puts on the hat before a mirror.* JULIE *holds the coat for her.*) Tell Therèse just Mr. Hutton's father for lunch, will you?

JULIE. Very well, Miss.

JAMES. I can—

MARY. No—it's all right, really. (*To* JULIE.) I'm going right out to the country from the dock. Telephone Miss Shippan before dinner and tell her I had to go out to-day, on account of the children. Tell her I can't have her this week-end after all. I'll see her here in town Monday or Tuesday. It's the same apartment. The number's on the card there.

JULIE. Yes, Miss.

JIM *comes in, with a box of flowers.*

JIM. Is the motor here, Julie?

JULIE. Yes, sir.

JIM. Tell Tom to get the bags down, will you?

JULIE. Very well, sir.

JIM. Good-bye, Julie. [*He shakes her hand.*

JULIE. Good-bye, Mr. Hutton. I hope you'll have a very pleasant trip.

JIM. Thanks.—Look after her well, won't you?

JULIE. As well as ever I can, sir.

JIM. That's the girl. (*To* MARY.) Everything's set, dear. We'd better be on our way. [*He gives her the box of flowers.*

JAMES. (*Looking at his watch.*) I think you had.

MARY. What's this? [*She opens the box,* JULIE *goes out.*

JIM. I sent Therèse to the corner for them.

MARY. That was sweet.

JIM. You can't go to a boat without flowers.—What's the matter, darling?

MARY. Why, nothing. Why?

JIM. You look—are you sure you *want* to come to the dock?

MARY. Yes, I'm quite sure. (*She pins the flowers upon her coat.*) These are sweet. They smell sweet—

JAMES. Don't work too hard, will you, son?

JIM. Not me. It'll probably be pretty tough going in London for a while. I thought I might run over to Cannes or Antibes for a few days before sailing. That is, if I've time.

MARY. (*A breath over the flowers.*)—Awfully sweet. (*A brief pause.*)—I though you hated the Riviera. You did when we were there.

JIM. That was in season.

MARY. I didn't know you'd ever been there out of season.

JIM. They say it's another place after the crowds go.—Father, would you tell the bank to cable a couple of thou' to my credit in London?

JAMES. (*Making a note on an envelope.*) Have you got enough now?

JIM. Plenty, thanks.

MARY. Here you are— [*She sets in* JIM'S *buttonhole a flower from her bouquet.*

JIM. Oh thanks, Darling.

JAMES. If you see your mother, give her my love.

JIM. I'll do that.

JAMES. When is it you're coming back?

JIM. I count on catching the *Mauretania* at Cherbourg. She's due here July ninth.—Good-bye, sir! You're a grand guy. [*They shake hands.*

JAMES. Thanks, so are you! Hurry, will you? It's twelve-thirty!

JIM. (*To* MARY.) Come on, Angel—.

MARY. Here I am.

JIM. Just take Jimmy's hand— (*He holds his hand out to her. She puts her hand in it.*)—and away we go!

MARY.—Away we go.

JIM. Wait a minute.—I must have one good last look. [*He takes her other hand, faces her about and looks at her. She returns his gaze, smiling.*

MARY. Is that all right?

JIM. Father—am I in luck, or am I not?

JAMES. I think you're in great luck, son.

[*Swiftly,* JIM *bends over and kisses each of the hands in his. Then he tucks one of them through his arm.*

JIM.—And don't I know it! (*To* MARY, *as they go out.*) Listen, Sweet, I've got a great idea—

MARY. What is it, dear?

JIM.—This stupid enforced-holiday—why not make it only four weeks? You can take a fast boat, and we'd have ten days in Paris, and then come back together. No, but seriously I don't see any reason why we shouldn't have at least a week there, and a *little* holiday together after this idiotic month of— [*His voice has faded out until it is no longer heard.* JAMES *stands alone, looking after them, shaking his head.*

Curtain.

ACT THREE

SCENE: *The music-room, six weeks later. A little after eleven on an early July night.*

The windows are opened wide and two of the lamps are lighted. On a small table at back, there is a tray containing a whisky-decanter, a bowl of cracked ice, some bottles of soda and a plate of sandwiches.

At Rise: At the piano, sits MARY *in a day dress of some soft, cool material. Some sheets of the ballet-score are before her. Others are strewn on the top of the piano, with pen and ink nearby. She plays a brief passage twice over, then a buzzer above the door sounds twice. She goes to the door, presses a button beside it several times, opens the door part way, listens intently then goes back to the piano. After a few moments* JAMES HUTTON *enters from the hall.*

MARY. Hello, Father. (*She rises, and goes to him.*) Thanks for coming. (*She kisses him.*) How are you, anyway?

JAMES. Fine, thanks— *You* look a little white and wan—

MARY. It's the heat. [*She reseats herself at the piano. He remains standing.*

JAMES. I couldn't get a train till seven.

MARY. I'm terribly glad you didn't wait. (*She plays a few notes. Their talk is somewhat constrained.*) Have you been having fun?

JAMES. I've been lying in the sunshine hours a day, trying to get the neuritis out of my shoulder.

MARY. With results, I hope.—Have a cigarette—

JAMES. Thanks, I've got one.—Superb results.

MARY. I thought when you left we'd soon be reading about a smart suicide on Bailey's Beach.

JAMES. So did I. How are the children?

MARY. Simply thriving. I've concluded I fuss over them too much. The less I'm with them, the better they are. Jimmy was thrilled over those fire-works you sent him for the Fourth. He'd never seen such big ones.

[JAMES *smiles. A pause. Then:*

JAMES. It's quite cool up here.

MARY. The river's a great blessing, and I keep the blinds closed from noon to sundown. It's the only way.

[*There is another and more strained pause.* JAMES *clears his throat.*

JAMES. You've decided you prefer town, then.

MARY. Not exactly—but I've had to be in such a lot. I've been working like mad.

JAMES. Music?

MARY. Yes.

JAMES. Whom have you got here with you —Julie?

MARY. No. She's at Aunt Grace's with Sabina and the babies. She needed a rest. No one's with me.

JAMES. But doesn't the house seem rather large to you?

MARY. I live in this room. It's like an apartment. I've had an electric arrangement put on the front-door, so that when it buzzes up here I can open it without going down.

JAMES. I'm not sure how safe that is.

MARY. Oh I don't press the button unless I hear the right signal—two short ones —buzz-buzz—like that. You happened to get it right.

JAMES. You'll have all the postmen in New York in on you.

MARY. I like postmen.

[*Another silence. Then:*

JAMES. I suppose you've heard from Jim.

MARY. There was a radio this morning: "Giant Liner Battered By Storm. Floating Palace Twelve Hours Late. Much Love."

JAMES. No hope of disembarking passengers before morning, I presume.

MARY. The office said not.—She's not due at Quarantine till midnight.

JAMES. I see.

MARY. I wired back I wouldn't try to meet him, and to come right here.—About breakfast-time, I expect.

JAMES. (*At length.*) Well, Mary—?

MARY. Have a whisky-and-soda, won't you?

JAMES. Shall I need it?

[MARY *laughs shortly.*

MARY. You can't tell!

[JAMES *looks at her closely, but does not move.*

JAMES. I'm sorry I didn't get your message till so late.

MARY. I didn't know about your fishing-trip.

JAMES. Anyhow, I came running back, didn't I?

MARY. You were sweet.

[*A brief pause. Then:*

JAMES. Your note was not. (*Another pause.*) *Well,* Mary—?

[MARY *hesitates. Then:*

MARY. I promised to let you know as soon as I did.

JAMES. Yes.

MARY. After Jim left I hoped for awhile that I'd been mistaken about—about Noel and him. I've found out since that I was not. I've found it out definitely.

JAMES. From Jim?

MARY. Oh no!

JAMES.—But you've written him? What have you said?

MARY. I've said nothing. You know, and I know. No one else. I shall tell him as he comes in, in the morning.

JAMES. To-morrow is the tenth, Mary.

MARY. I'm—aware of that—

JAMES. An anniversary, isn't it?

MARY.—Six years is six years. I suppose, as things go, we've done rather well.

JAMES. Don't talk like that. Talk of that sort doesn't belong to you.

[MARY *shrugs.*

MARY. Average, anyway.—What is the average, do you know? Less than six, or more?

JAMES. Stop it, Mary.

MARY. I'm sorry. I'm only speaking as I feel.

JAMES. You're actually going to leave Jim?

MARY. Yes.

JAMES. But only temporarily—not a real separation—

MARY. I'm going to divorce him, Father.

[JAMES *stares at her for a moment, incredulously. With deliberation, she begins to play a passage from the ballet. He goes to the table and makes himself a drink. He turns to her with it in his hand. She stops playing, rises, and meets his gaze steadily. He shakes his head.*

JAMES. Mary, Mary—

MARY. It's too bad, I know. But you see it's all gone, now.

[*Now she is standing against the piano, facing him.*

JAMES. What is? Your love for him?

MARY. I don't know about that. I can't tell about that, yet awhile. But my life with him—that's gone, all right.

JAMES. Only if you let it go.

MARY. I'm afraid I'm not much good at hanging on to things, once they've begun to slip from me. I'm afraid I don't want them much, after that.

JAMES. What a fine, deep love it must have been, eh? (*She looks at him. He explains:*) To chuck the whole thing overboard so lightly, so easily.

MARY. I haven't had much ease these last weeks, Father. And I don't feel light, precisely. But if I mean no more to him than that—

JAMES.—Than what?

MARY.—If his love for me wasn't strong enough to—

JAMES. Listen to me, Mary: if you're going to quit Jim, quit him. But in heaven's name don't let it do this to you.

MARY.—Do what to me?

JAMES.—Fog your intellect, fog your reason—make an honest, fearless, first-rate woman into a softy.

MARY. I beg your pardon?

JAMES. "If I mean no more to him—"—"If his love for me wasn't strong enough—" Really, for you, of all people, to talk that kind of second-rate trash, is about the limit.

MARY. That's going it pretty stiff, don't you think?

JAMES. Yes, I do. And I'm amazed to think you need it.—What on earth has one misstep of Jim's to do with you?

MARY. It has a great deal to do with me.

JAMES. Nonsense!—If your hatred of the Farley girl, or your jealousy of Jim is stronger than anything else you feel, all right. But this sense of grievance—

personal injury—good heavens, what can Noel Farley do to *you?* If Jim has been anything to her—*he* may lose by it, but what *you* lose, I can't see.

MARY. I neither hate Noel nor am I jealous of Jim nor do I feel that I've been injured. But I've lost about everything I had, I think.

JAMES. How so?

MARY. Jim belonged to me. Jim was all my own.

JAMES. Don't glory in your sense of possession, Mary. It's the lowest instinct you've got.

MARY. I'm glorying in very little, now. It's—rather awful to know you're not loved. You miss it terribly.

JAMES. Jim loves you as he always has. I'm as sure of that as I am of my name.

MARY. In any event, I don't feel called upon to share him.

JAMES. I doubt if you've shared anything. If you have, it's the least important element in your whole relationship.

MARY. It seems not to be.

JAMES. I don't mean to belittle sex. It holds a high and dishonored place among other forms of intoxication. But love is something else again, and marriage is still another thing—

MARY. (*Bitterly.*) Yes, and a great thing, isn't it?—Man's most divine conception—pure poetry—religion—sacrament—

JAMES. By heaven, it ought to be!

MARY. I was rather for it myself, if you'll remember. It was church to me, all right. But now, you see, I'm left with all the candles out, and rosy windows smashed and rotten ragtime playing through my church, where there was nothing but plain chant and Palestrina all the whole day long. I think I *have* lost something—

JAMES. Come here, Mary—

[*She goes to him and stands with her head against his shoulder.*

MARY. It's gone, Father. It's gone, it's gone—

JAMES. Only if you let it. Think, child! —Why, you used to say that nothing—

[MARY *raises her head.*

MARY. Yes, I know: theories are fine, before things happen. But once they have, you find you don't think straight, if you're a woman. You can't—you only feel straight.

JAMES. You've had a bad shock, Mary. You've been jolted back into a state of mind you outgrew years ago. These straight feelings you talk of are twisted every which way by all the rubbish about love and marriage they taught you before you learned to think. They're a lot of old words and phrases, that's all.—"Trust betrayed," "deception," "infidelity."—Watch out for them.

MARY. He went from me to her. He chose her over me.

JAMES. There's no choosing to it. You ought to know that physical attraction isn't limited to one man or one woman. It never has been and never will be.

MARY. It must have been more than that.

JAMES. All right, capacity for love, then.

MARY. This isn't just any case of man—wife—mistress, Father. Mistresses are a different kind of person, as a rule. I can understand that sort of compromise, hateful as it would be. But Noel is a person like myself. I've known her all my life.

JAMES. Noel's no more like you than I'm like Lincoln. Mistresses are *always* a different kind of person, Mary, and so are lovers.—Will you tell me something?

MARY. Anything you like.

JAMES. When Jim came back a year ago, did you sense any change in him?

MARY. (*After a moment.*) No. (*Then suddenly.*)—If only he had told me! If only he had been honest! It's so—insulting—

JAMES. Jim is as honest as the day is long: you know that. The fact that he *didn't* tell you—the fact that you felt nothing in your bones, as you say—isn't that evidence enough for you that in his eyes it encroached in no way upon your province?

MARY.—And what about my eyes!?

JAMES. Oh Mary, I wish you might be twenty years older for one moment.

MARY. I should see it the same.

[*There is a silence. Then:*

JAMES.—So you've convinced yourself there's only one thing to do.

MARY. I've tried to convince myself there wasn't.

JAMES.—Paris, with the rest of the defeated sisterhood—ten thousand dollars in hand for some wretched lawyer to bribe mean little French officials with—*you,* Mary—

MARY.—If that's the way it's done. How else?

JAMES. Are you asking me? (*She gestures, lifelessly.*) Then I say not only put divorce completely out of your head but never by so much as one word let him know what you know. Refuse to admit it, Mary. Refuse, even to yourself, to admit it. Above all, don't speak of it. If there's one destructive thing in this world, it's words—spoken—

MARY. I shall tell him the first moment that I see him.

[*A moment. Then:*

JAMES.—Well, it's quite beyond me. I counted on great things for you and Jim. When I stood there beside that boy in that hot little country church six years ago, and saw you coming up to him, I can't tell you what I felt about you both. It seemed to me that you had everything: strength, beauty, youth and wisdom—minds as open as any ever I've encountered—enormous gaiety—a great joy in each other, and in life. Such a wedding-garment as you two brought to your marriage, I've never known.

MARY. Well, it's in rags now, all right.

JAMES. And why?—If you and Jim had spent the last five years at each other's throats, that would be one thing. Actual, hopeless incompatibility I can understand. Drunkenness—cruelty—insanity—. But this, *this*—

MARY—About the best reason there is, I think.

JAMES. Mary, it wasn't three months ago that all of you came to me for Easter. Jim arrived late. You hadn't seen him in three days—three whole days. I heard your voices from the next room. You chattered on about nothing until morning. You laughed a great deal. It was great music, Mary. There was more love in it than in all the sighs and picked-up roses in this world.

MARY. It's no use, Father.

JAMES. No?—Then all that's left for me to say is that a most uncommon marriage is about to go to smash because a once wise woman has become vain and selfish, because a good, hard mind has nicked its edge off on as rotten and false a conception as ever yet existed. You're going to quit Jim because he had "relations," as they say, with another woman —well, suppose he did, what of it? How big a part does that play in *your* life? Do you describe your marriage in those terms alone? I'm appalled you set so slight a value on yourself. I'm appalled that you accept defeat so easily, and on such a count.

MARY. I hoped you would understand me. Evidently you don't. If ours had been just an ordinary, halfway-happy marriage, perhaps it might survive this. But it was so perfect for so long, it can't. It goes from all to nothing.

JAMES.—Talk. (*She confronts him angrily.*) Yes! Everything you've told me to-night confirms my first suspicion: that it's the physical fact alone that you can't escape. All you've said has been just one repeated statement that to you the most important thing in your whole marriage has been your physical relation to your husband.

MARY.—You think so!

JAMES.—Over and over you've said it. And now, because you insist on a monopoly of that particular thing, and find you haven't it, you take the lowest possible advantage of your ample means to indulge yourself in a luxury the lucky poor cannot afford. Bid up vanity! Bid up revenge! (*The buzzer sounds twice.*)—Well, do it, and you're a failure, Mary—a complete failure—not only in your marriage—but in every last department of your life.

MARY. That's enough, I think.

JAMES. I am ashamed of you. I cannot believe—

MARY.—*Quite* enough.

[*He looks at her intently. There is a silence. Then he bows slightly.*

JAMES. Very well. Good-night, my dear.

MARY. Good-night.

[*A brief pause, then:*

JAMES. (*A last appeal.*) Mary—

MARY.—Good-night.

[*The buzzer sounds again. He turns and goes out, stopping at the doorway long enough to press the electric button in response to the buzzer.* MARY *stands for a moment, rigid, then goes to the piano. Her fingers follow the ballet-score, but soundlessly.* RICHARD *enters.*

RICHARD. H'lo.

MARY. Where are the Copes?

RICHARD. How should I know? (*He goes to the window.*)—Hot. Oh my God, how hot—(*He looks out.*) Look at that river to-night, will you—

MARY. I have been.

RICHARD. If ever I get any money, I'm going to buy a small tug and paint her up and live on her.

MARY. That's a divine idea. Let me make the curtains.

RICHARD. I think I'll go on a boat-trip myself to morrow.

MARY. Oh? Where to?

[*He returns from the window.*

RICHARD. Quite a way. (*He throws himself into a chair and sits with his head back, his eyes closed.*) It's wonderful to be able to breathe again.

MARY. Have you had dinner?

RICHARD. Of course I've had dinner. What do you think I live on? Air?

MARY. You've been known to, at times. —How much have you had to drink?

RICHARD. (*Starting forward.*) I've had nothing to drink!

MARY.—Then make yourself a whisky-and-soda, won't you? There are the things—

[RICHARD *stares at the tray, then slumps back again into his chair.*

RICHARD. Later, maybe.

[MARY *looks at him curiously, then:*

MARY. What's the matter, my dear?

RICHARD. Don't say "my dear" to me. Don't say anything to me. Just let me sit here a minute, and then I'll go.

[*There is a long silence.* MARY *rises, picks up a sheet of the ballet-score and frowns over it.*

MARY.—I wanted to ask you: this bit before the policemen come on in the last scene—it sounds to me like—

RICHARD. Oh don't talk about the ballet! Let the ballet alone.

MARY. But it isn't finished!

RICHARD. Let it stay where it is. It's as far as it'll get.

[*A pause. Then:*

MARY. (*Quietly.*)—And precisely what does that mean, may I ask?

RICHARD. Try thinking it out. That helps sometimes.

MARY. (*Chilling.*) I'm afraid it's a little deep for me.

RICHARD. I'm sorry, if it is. You can console yourself it's deeper still for me.

[*There is an ominous silence. Finally:*

MARY.—After all these weeks, and all the work we've done together—you won't put in one good half-hour more and finish it? You actually mean that?

RICHARD. Actually I do.

MARY.—One half-hour.

RICHARD. Who says it'd be only that?

MARY. It needn't be more. Not if it comes.

RICHARD. Well, it won't come.

MARY. How do you know?

RICHARD. I know. (*Suddenly he bursts out.*) What the devil does it matter, anyway? It hasn't a snowball's chance. It never had.

MARY.—So you quit on it.

RICHARD. Sure.

MARY. What do you suppose it means to me? Nothing?

[*He shrugs.*

RICHARD. Oh—agreeable occupation gone —pleasant diversion—you'll find something else.

[*A silence. Then.*

MARY. (*In a small voice.*)—Would you mind going now, please? (*He turns to her quickly. Her voices rises.*) Will you please go?

[*He makes a quick movement toward her, then stops, and murmurs:*

RICHARD. All right.

MARY. (*With intense feeling.*) Richard, how can you do it!?

RICHARD.—How *can't* I do it, you mean.

MARY. Well?

RICHARD. Mary—listen, dear—

MARY. (*Impatiently.*) What? *What?*

RICHARD.—Jim—his boat's late, isn't it?

MARY. Yes, why?

RICHARD. I've got to talk to you.

MARY. Then go ahead and talk.

RICHARD.—Talk for a long time—to-night—

MARY. I don't see how it's to be arranged, do you?

RICHARD. It can be.

MARY. Peter and Nora are coming. They ought to be here now.

RICHARD. Don't answer when they ring.

MARY. (*Directly.*) But I must.

RICHARD. Why?

MARY. I must.

RICHARD. What is it you're afraid of, Mary?

MARY. (*Frowning.*)—Afraid of?

RICHARD. Yes.

[*She looks at him steadily for a moment. Then:*

MARY. Good-bye, Richard. (*He does not answer. She concludes, contemptuously.*) And sometime, if you can manage it, I wish you'd finish *something.*

RICHARD. (*Softly.*) Oh damn you—

MARY. (*In a burst.*)—And damn you! Go and tune pianos, that's where *you* belong! A fine artist *you* are—lazy, dabbling, worthless—

[*He seizes her by the shoulders. She stops. They gaze at each other, tense, furious. At last he speaks.*

RICHARD. I can't finish that ballet, because that ballet's you and me, and we aren't finished and never shall be. So *it* won't.

MARY. (*After a moment, comprehending.*) You can let go my shoulders now.

RICHARD. I won't, though.

MARY. What's it all about, Richard?

RICHARD. I love you, Mary.

MARY. I think you love music, my dear.

RICHARD. You and it—you're one to me.

MARY. Thanks. That's very sweet.

RICHARD. Oh, don't talk like such a fool.

MARY. I don't know what to say to you. What do you want me to say?

RICHARD. Something I'll— Anything you want to.

MARY.—I like you very much—so much, so much. And I shall miss you horribly.

RICHARD. We've been together all the time for weeks—so will I you.

MARY. I shan't know what to do with myself.

RICHARD. But you'll find something, won't you?

MARY. I'll try awfully hard.

RICHARD. Oh, don't you feel a thing for me—not anything at all?

[*She looks at him, a little startled.*

MARY. I never thought—

[*A moment, then:*

RICHARD. *I* think you do, Mary.

MARY.—Do you suppose?

RICHARD. Yes.—Don't *you?*

[*She moves away from him.*

MARY.—It would be very funny if I did.

RICHARD.—And would you laugh a great deal?

MARY. I think I'd cry my eyes out.

RICHARD. Then never mind.

[*She turns to him again, swiftly.*

MARY. Oh, you dear person, you—

RICHARD. Mary—come here to me a moment—

MARY. I can't.

RICHARD.—You don't want to—

MARY. (*Lowly.*) I—didn't say that—

RICHARD. Then why—?

MARY. I don't know. It just seems to me I can't.

RICHARD. (*After a moment.*) All right. —Good-bye. Thanks ever so much for —ever so many things.

MARY. Oh, *don't* say that! It's I, who—

RICHARD. (*An estimate, without self-pity.*) I expect when you take me all in all, I'm just a bum.

MARY. You're a pretty important bum, I think. To me you are, anyhow.

RICHARD. That'll do nicely. Good-bye—

(*He holds out both his hands to her, smiling. She hesitates one instant, then moves directly into his arms, and kisses him. The breath leaves his body in a gasp. His arms tighten about her. She is rigid for a moment, then something within her gives way and she slumps against his breast, her face averted.*) Look up at me!

MARY. No, no—

RICHARD. Look up!

MARY. No—(*She makes a half-movement to leave him, but cannot. She lifts her face to his. They kiss. Again she averts her head, with a choked cry.*) Richard—!

RICHARD. I love you so terribly.

MARY. You—(*She cannot finish. A moment. Then:*) Oh, this isn't me! It can't be—

RICHARD. It *is* you!

MARY. No, no.

RICHARD. For the first time, it's you.

MARY. It's—just something raging inside me. It isn't me—it isn't—

RICHARD. It's *my* you.—It's the you *I* know.

[*She shakes her head.*

MARY. Go quickly—dear Richard—go quickly—

RICHARD. I'm going to stay here with you.

MARY. You're—? But that's—that's not possible. You must go at once.

RICHARD. Oh Mary—

MARY. Please go, please go:—Peter and Nora—they'll be coming.

RICHARD.—When they ring, let them ring. Don't answer.

MARY. I must.

RICHARD. No.—You were tired waiting, weren't you, Mary?

MARY —Was I?—I don't know.

RICHARD.—Don't say anything for a moment. Just stay close to me. Don't speak. (*A long silence. She remains in his arms. At last he speaks, very slowly.*) I can feel your heart beating. It wouldn't beat like that.

[*With a faint cry she strains against him. Another silence. Then:*

MARY. It isn't mine.

RICHARD. It is—and you want me, too—don't you, don't you, Mary?

MARY.—Impossible—it's not possible—

RICHARD.—*Don't* you, Mary? (*She does not answer, but her arms tighten around him.*)—Then where's the difference? Where is it, dear?

MARY. There *is* one. There's a great one.

RICHARD. I don't see it—

MARY. You've got to go—oh, *go,* will you?

RICHARD.—You think it will be just the beginning of something. It won't. It'll be the end. You're always saying things must be finished. So must this, Mary. It must be finished, Sweet, really it must, or we'll haunt each other our whole lives long. We'd never get away from it then, never, never. Oh, why won't you see that, Mary?

MARY. I can't. All I can see is that I'd hate the thought of you, both of us.

RICHARD. No!

MARY. Yes.—It would—simply blast everything in my whole life. (*She leaves him.*)—Oh, how is it I can love him so, and still feel this for you? I don't understand it.

RICHARD. (*Following her.*)—But we aren't three people—you and he and I. We're four people: you and he, and you and I. *His* you can't ever in this world be mine, any more than my you can be his.

MARY.—I don't understand it—

RICHARD. It has nothing to do with anyone or anything but us and our life. Don't you know that, Mary?

MARY. (*Dully.*) Hasn't it, Richard?

RICHARD. I promise you!

MARY. (*Almost inaudibly.*) Do you, Richard—

RICHARD. It won't be taking anything from anyone. You have enough love in you to give me—you keep making it, making it all the time—love and more love.

MARY.—I don't understand this, I don't understand it.

RICHARD. But it's our life, Mary, it really is—there's no one else in it but you and me—there's no one could come into it. Haven't you always said—?

MARY. I've said a lot of things.

RICHARD. Well, there's no need to say anything anymore. Just stay close to me—

[*Once more she is in his arms.*

MARY. No—keep talking—keep on talking—(*He shakes his head, silently. She cries:*] You must! Talk! Talk! Will you *talk?!*

[*Again he shakes his head. There is a silence, finally broken by two sharp rings from the buzzer. She stirs in his arms.*

RICHARD. Let it ring.

[*She is quiet once more. The buzzer sounds again.*

MARY. Oh—floods are breaking all in and around us, and you won't even help me up out of them.

RICHARD. No.

[*The buzzer sounds again, long, insistent. He holds her closer to him. The buzzer stops. She speaks again, this time with despair in her voice.*

MARY. I shouldn't think you'd want me this way. It won't be me at all—it will be—just *any* woman (*A moment. He raises his head slowly, holds her off from him and looks at her intently. Her face is contorted, her eyes imploring.*)—That's true, you know. It *is* true!

[*There are two short and final signals from the buzzer. He turns his head abruptly away from her and stares at the door. Then, in a swift movement, he leaves her, goes to the door and presses the button beside it. With an exclamation, she covers her face. He goes to the piano and seats himself. Then:*

RICHARD. In a few minutes I'll go, Mary. I'll walk down the stairs and out and up along the river to Eighty-ninth Street. I'll sit there on a bench for one half-hour. That's about what they'll stay. Then I'll come back.

MARY. Don't come back.—If you do love me, don't—

[RICHARD *begins to play the piano aimlessly.*

RICHARD.—I'll come back. By then you'll have had time to think, and you can let me in or not, as you like. Before you do, look in the glass at your face and see that it *is* you—*my* you. Then, if you want me, I'll be here.—Is that fair?

MARY. I—suppose so.

RICHARD. (*Playing.*) All right.—Now go to the top of the stairs and call down to them. They're coming up. (MARY *manages to light a cigarette.*) That's it.

MARY. (*With difficulty.*) Richard—anyhow—I want to tell you: I think you are—

RICHARD. There aren't any anyhows yet, my dear. (*He jerks his head in the direction of the door.*) Go ahead—

[MARY *goes to the door, opens it and calls:*

MARY. Hello there!

RICHARD. Good girl.

[NORA'S *voice is heard in protest from below.*

NORA. Well!

MARY. Oh, I can't stand their chatter now! I simply can't.

RICHARD. You've damn well got to.

MARY. Keep playing, won't you?

RICHARD. Sure.

[MARY *goes to a mirror and hastily brushes back her hair and dabs powder upon her face.* NORA *enters.* RICHARD'S *playing becomes louder.*

MARY. Nora!—How are you?

NORA. We couldn't be worse. We've been ringing ten minutes. What on earth's been the matter?

MARY. You can't hear anything up here, with the piano going.

FANNY. (*Entering.*)—Then throw the piano out. We're important people. (*She throws herself into a chair.*) Whew!—Hello, Parish—

RICHARD. Hello, Shippan.—How was the show?

NORA. (*Fanning herself with a handkerchief.*) Not bad.

RICHARD. Sorry I couldn't—

FANNY. *I* never cracked a smile.

RICHARD.—make it.

[PETER *comes puffing in. He and* FANNY *and* NORA *are in evening clothes.*

PETER. Fanny, why are you so tight with your money? Why don't you give these people an elevator? (*He mops his brow.*)—It's a little bit of heaven, and they call it a top-floor. (*He turns pompously to* MARY.) However do you do, my dear?

MARY. All hot and happy, thanks.

[*He turns to* RICHARD.

PETER. Evenin', Massa Parish.

RICHARD. (*Playing.*) Hello.

[*All the voices are pitched high, against the music.*

MARY. (*To* FANNY.) I nearly gave you up. Where have you been?

FANNY. In a cellar on Forty-ninth Street, drinking white wine and seltzer.

PETER. (*Moving toward the whisky.*)—The seltzer was good.

[*He pours himself a drink.*

NORA. Peter won his case against old man Burke this morning.

MARY. You didn't!

NORA. Isn't he bright?

PETER.—I'm glad I did it. He was a beast.

MARY. But no wonder you're celebrating!

PETER. Celebrating? Me? Don't be silly.

[*He stirs the ice noisily in his glass.*

NORA. Peter, will you kindly stop that eternal clash, clash, clash!

FANNY. Poor lamb, it's her old wound again.

NORA. (*Fanning herself.*) I'll die.

FANNY. Not in the house, darling.

PETER.—In the open air, seeking water. (*He raises his glass.*)—*Whisky* and water.

NORA. Don't speak of it.

MARY. Don't speak of what?—That doesn't make sense.

NORA. What does? Can you tell me?

[RICHARD *rises from the piano, takes off his coat and throws it across the bench beside him.*

PETER.—Now there's a good idea.

NORA. (*Irritably.*) What? What?

PETER.—Of Parish's. He cast his coat aside like an old coat.

[RICHARD *reseats himself and continues playing but at lower pitch.*

NORA. We're moving on in one minute, so don't *you* start undressing. (*To* MARY.) —We thought we'd go and dance somewhere.

[MARY *does not answer.*

FANNY. Are you coming?

[*Still* MARY *hears nothing but* RICHARD'S *music. A moment, then:*

NORA. Whoo-hoo! Mary! (MARY *turns to her.*)—Are you listening, darling?

MARY. Of course I am. (*To* FANNY.) What, darling?

FANNY. Come along with us to hell and Rector's, will you?

MARY. Well I should say not.

NORA. Why not?

MARY. (*Absently; still listening to* RICHARD.) It's too hot, and I want some sleep.

FANNY. (*To* NORA.)—So she'll look her prettiest when the great big steamboat brings Daddy home to-morrow.

MARY. (*Smiling.*) Yes. That's it.

[NORA *and* FANNY *are on the sofa.* MARY *stands near the piano, thinking.* PETER *paces, with his whisky.*

PETER. What news of the lad?—Any news is good news.

MARY. He lands at about nine in the morning.

PETER. I can't stay up that long. It's impossible.

NORA. (*To* FANNY, *watching* MARY.) It'll be good to have Jim back, won't it?

—If only to get Mary out of her doldrums.

FANNY. "Doldrums"—there's a funny word. It sounds quite lewd.

NORA. But have you seen Mary much lately?

FANNY. My dear, she sees no one.

NORA. Is she ill, do you think?

FANNY. It were better if she were.

NORA. Not having an affair with someone!

FANNY. Mary? Oh no!

NORA. What is it, then?

FANNY. They say in Poictesme that she loves her husband.

PETER. Will the gray hordes never cease? God! Are we too late?

FANNY. Six weeks without him is just too much to bear, it's too much to bear.

NORA. Never mind. To-morrow we'll have our old Mary back again.

PETER. She had charm, that girl. Always a smile for everyone.

FANNY. And now it's a curse or a blow.

PETER. Love is like that.

MARY. What is it you're playing, Richard?

RICHARD. Listen—

[FANNY *and* NORA *look at each other.*

FANNY. I—uh—I do hope we're not intruding.

MARY. Don't be silly.

PETER. Watch out, Parish, or the young master will thrash you roundly.

RICHARD. Yes?

NORA. (*Suddenly.*) Mary, if you don't give that party to-morrow, I'm off you for life.

FANNY. So am I.

MARY. What party is that?

FANNY. Listen to it! "What party!"

NORA. You aren't actually going to let an anniversary pass without a celebration?

PETER. Say it ain't so, Mary.

NORA. I suppose they'll just dine alone together. That's what she really wants.

FANNY. Don't. My heart's breaking.

MARY. I want nothing of the sort. It's simply that I haven't any servants in town.

NORA. Why not get them in?

PETER.—The railroad, or steam-demon, as it was then called, was invented by Martin Luther in 1821. Since then—

FANNY. I'll lend you a butler with whiskers, if you like.—Or I tell you what! *I'll* give the party!

MARY. No you won't, darling.

FANNY. (*To* NORA.) What can you do with her?

RICHARD. Listening, Mary?

MARY. Yes.

[FANNY *looks from one to the other.*

FANNY. Would you mind telling me what goes on here?

NORA. (*Bursting out.*)—Well, *I* think it's a crime! You could get every single one that was in the wedding.

PETER. I saw Johnny Scott downtown this very noon. "Hello, Johnny," said I. "How are you, Peter?" said he—

NORA.—All except Noel, anyway.

PETER.—Then we went and had a drink.

FANNY.—Noel, too. She's staying with the Potters. I saw it in the Times.

[*A brief pause. Then:*

MARY. Oh, she's back, then—

FANNY. She must be.

PETER. (*Reflectively.*)—Noel Farley—I can see her now—

NORA. Can you? I never could.

PETER. Where's she been all the time?

FANNY.—Living somewhere in a little house-by-the-sea, with only her pets for companions.

PETER. Noel? Like hell she has. (*An afterthought:*) *What* pets?

NORA. Mary, it does seem such a shame. You and Jim can dine alone together for the rest of your lives.

FANNY.—And probably will.—What *I* always say is, one should share one's happiness with one's friends. It makes for better feeling.

MARY. I'm sorry, but I can't face a party.

PETER. (*Wistfully.*) I've got a dandy new bird-call to do with the soup: it's the yellow-bellied wagtail.

MARY. You're all terribly kind, but I simply can't face it.

[*There is a pause.*

PETER. Well that, I should say, is that.

MARY. I'm sorry, but I'm afraid it is.

NORA. (*Bursting out once more.*) Honestly, if you aren't acting queerer than anyone I've ever known—

MARY. I'm sorry, Nora.

[FANNY *looks significantly from* MARY *to* RICHARD.

FANNY. (*To* PETER *and* NORA.) What do you think?—Perhaps we'd better just tiptoe quietly out.

[*Suddenly* MARY *breaks:*

MARY. Fanny, will you *kindly* stop talking like such a fool!

FANNY. Why, you saucy puss. (*She*

stares at her for a moment, then rises and turns to NORA.) Come on, will you? I can't stand much more of this.

NORA. Wait a minute. (*To* MARY.) Now look here, darling, I—(*The buzzer sounds once.* MARY *starts in surprise.* RICHARD *stops playing and listens.*)—Who is it you're expecting?

MARY. (*Rising.*) Why—no one—

RICHARD. A telegram, most likely.

[MARY *goes to the door.*

FANNY. *I'm* going.

MARY. Please wait. I don't know who it is. (*She presses the button and opens the hall door, then turns to* FANNY.) I'm sorry, Fanny—I didn't mean to be rude.

FANNY. Oh, that's all right.

[MARY *presses her fingers against her temples.*

MARY. It's just so damned hot.

PETER. (*Cheerfully.*) Sure it is!—That's what it is: hot.

[RICHARD *is staring at the hall doorway.*

FANNY.—All I want to know is, can we expect some little change after to-morrow.—In you, I mean.

[MARY *looks at her curiously, then laughs shortly. A brief pause. Then:*

MARY. Fanny, after to-morrow you can expect a big change. I promise you you can.

[NORA *has gone to the hall doorway, where she stands listening.*

FANNY. That's all right, then. Mummy understands.

NORA.—Do you want him to come up, whoever it is? Because he's coming.

MARY.—If it's a tel—

[NORA'S *sudden cry cuts her short:*

NORA. Jim!

[*Steps are heard bounding up the stairs.* MARY *stands frozen against the wall by the door.* RICHARD'S *head bends lower over the piano and his hands drop once more upon the keys, which he fingers without sound.* JIM *enters past* MARY.

JIM. Where's Mary? For the love of—! (*He turns and sees her, catches his breath in joy, and says:*) Hello, Mary.

MARY. Hello, Jim.

[*In an instant he is at her side, and has taken her into his arms.*

NORA. (*After a moment.*) Well, if it isn't little friendly-face home again.

[JIM *looks over* MARY'S *shoulder at them.*

PETER. You low cad. You come here with your fine clothes and your city manner, and—

JIM. Hello, Copes!

NORA. It's nice you're back.

FANNY (*Pushing into view.*)—And this is that attractive Shippan girl.

JIM. Fanny! How are you?

FANNY. (*Archly.*) Need you ask, dear?

[JIM *laughs.*

PETER.—All de Eighty-foist Streets togedder again—ain't it grand?

JIM. Oh Lord, if it's not!—Hello, Parish!

[MARY *leaves his arms.*

RICHARD.—Good trip?

JIM. Terrible. The day before yesterday up came a monsoon or something and nearly blew us out of the water.

FANNY. You just can't tell about ole davvil Sea.

JIM. (*To* MARY.) How are the babies?

MARY. They said you wouldn't land until morning. They're simply blooming.

PETER. How'd you work it, Jim?

JIM.—Bribery and corruption. I came in on the mail-boat.

PETER. Just Hutton grit, that's all.

JIM.—And I wasn't above bringing some champagne with me, either.

PETER.—But that's against the law. It's against every decent—where is it?

JIM. No you don't! It's for to-morrow night, to drink the bride's health in—isn't it, Mary?

[MARY *smiles, but does not answer. There is a brief pause.*

NORA. Oh, is there to be a party?

JIM. Of course there's to be a party!

FANNY. Thank God, the militia.

JIM.—And you're all invited.—How about you, Parish? Can you come, too?

RICHARD. I'm sorry. I won't be here.

JIM. Oh? Are you off somewhere?

RICHARD. Yes. I'm going boating.

FANNY. Where? Central Park?

RICHARD. No. Farther.

MARY. What's all this, Richard?

RICHARD. I know the purser on one of the United Fruit Boats. He says he can get me on board as one of the loading-crew. Six in the morning at the Battery. Sail at seven.

FANNY. Just like that!

PETER. *Jim*—(JIM *looks at him.* PETER'S *gesture includes* MARY *and* RICHARD.)—That's your luck, son.

[JIM *looks incredulous for a moment,*

then lights a cigarette, watching RICHARD.

MARY. When did you decide this, Richard?

[*He shrugs.*

RICHARD. To-night.

NORA. Is it to be a long trip?

RICHARD. Not terribly: four or five months.

PETER. I knew a fellow did that once. It was years afterwards before he could even take orange-juice.

JIM. (*Casually.*)—But how about this ballad you and Mary have been writing—

FANNY.—Ballet, idiot.

JIM. Well, ballet, then.—Is it finished?

RICHARD. I've just been playing the end of it. (*He rises and goes to* MARY.) I'll bat it out on paper to-night and send it to you in the morning, Mary.

MARY. That would be perfect.

RICHARD.—When the police finally follow Mike and the girl across the roof of the apartment and they go over the edge, and they look down after them, do you know what they find below in the courtyard?

MARY. You—hadn't decided.

RICHARD. I have now: two bodies.

MARY. (*Lowly.*) I see.

[*There is a silence. Finally:*

JIM. (*Lightly.*) I should think—

FANNY. (*Simultaneously.*) You know, they've been on a regular musical orgy, these two.

RICHARD. (*To* JIM.) It's a nice practical little ballet. It wouldn't cost more than a hundred thousand or so to put on.

JIM. Well, good luck with it, anyhow.

RICHARD. Thanks. I've had that already. (*To* PETER, FANNY *and* NORA.) Good-bye.

NORA. Good-bye. Come to see us when you get back.

FANNY. Good-bye. I think you're sweet.

PETER. Good-bye. They say the bananas are the worst.

RICHARD. I'll watch out for them.—Good-bye, Hutton.

JIM. Good-bye, Richard. (*They shake hands.*) Have a good trip.

RICHARD. Thanks, Jim. Good-bye, Mary—

[MARY *gives him her hand.*

MARY. Write to me, won't you?

RICHARD. Sure! (*He bends toward her. She lifts her face to his. He kisses her.*) Good-bye—

[*He is gone. There is a silence.*

FANNY. Was that fresh, or wasn't it?

MARY. No, Fanny. It was not.

PETER. I've got no technique for that fellow. He makes me feel about as appropriate as a French soldier sitting at a soda-fountain singing Boola-Boola.

NORA. Mary would say that it's because he's an artist and you're not.

PETER. Well, maybe she'd be right.—Anyone have a sandwich?

[*He takes one.*

JIM. Mary, how long are these confounded people going to hang around here?

MARY. They're hopeless.

PETER. I know a hint when I hear one. Come, Nora—

[NORA *and* FANNY *rise.*

JIM. We'll see you all to-morrow, sure.

NORA. Mary said there wasn't to be any party.

JIM. (*Frowning.*) But I thought it was all—

MARY. I don't want a party, Jim.

FANNY. I know, but we do.

PETER. (*To* MARY.) Who are *you*, anyway? Just a guest in your own house.

JIM. Really don't you, Mary? (MARY *shakes her head.* JIM *turns to the others.*) Then there's no party—

PETER.—Telephone us in the morning—a good night's sleep will do you both good. You're tired, Hutton. You have never learned to spare yourself. Remember, mens sana in corpore sano.

[JIM *laughs uncertainly.*

JIM. Get out!

NORA. Good-night! (*To* MARY.) It's great he's back.

MARY. Isn't it?

[PETER, FANNY *and* NORA *move toward the hall.*

NORA. Don't bother to come down with us.

JIM. We wouldn't think of it.

[NORA *goes out,* FANNY *follows her, calling back:*

FANNY. Thanks for the spinach!

PETER. (*Following* FANNY.) But my dear—it wasn't here you got the spinach.

[*They are gone.* MARY *stands leaning against the piano, fortifying herself against the ordeal to come: she must tell* JIM *that she knows about* NOEL*—but then what, then what?* JIM *re-enters, uncertainty still upon him: what had* PETER *meant when he said of* RICHARD'S *departure "That's your luck, Son?" What had that whole curious situa-*

tion he came in on—what had that meant?

JIM. Well, darling—?

MARY. Jim—

JIM. What is it, dear—

MARY. I've got something I—want to talk to you about.

[JIM *looks at her: But it's not possible! Mary? Richard?*

JIM. I'm not certain I want to hear it.

MARY. But it's—it's—

JIM. I'm certain I don't want to hear it! —Come and sit beside me—(*He takes her hand and leads her to the sofa.*) How's father? Have you see him?

MARY. Yes. He's all right. Jim—

JIM. *You* look a little white—

MARY. (*Slowly.*) I've had to be in town a great deal—(*Then, in sudden determination.*) Listen to me Jim! I—

JIM. (*As suddenly.*)—I'm terribly glad you had that music-thing to work on. I think it's rotten not to be busy, when—. Oh, I saw Mother—I went down for the week-end. She's all right, but how she endures that man White, I don't know.

MARY. Is he awful?

JIM. He's such a damn bore. And he's forever taking care of himself. If she had to quit Father, I'd rather she'd married the black sheep of the Jukes family, I swear I would. (MARY *laughs.*) Did you get the roof fixed?

MARY. Jim, it's too perfect.

JIM. I thought you planned to have the party there.

MARY. I did, originally.

[*A pause.*

JIM. How has Sabina been?

MARY. Angelic.

JIM. Did Collins straighten out all right?

MARY. No. He left and took the grass-cutter with him. But I've got a more reliable one now.

JIM. Grass-cutter?

[MARY *laughs.*

MARY. No, Stupid. Gardener.

JIM. Business went marvellously.

MARY. I don't care.

JIM. (*Smiling.*) I know you don't.

MARY. Did you get down to Cannes at all?

JIM. I hadn't time. Oh listen—all the presents, yours and the children's too—they're in my bag—I'll have to send to the dock for it. I'll—(*Suddenly he catches her hand.*) Oh Mary, *do* you?

MARY. (*Lowly.*)—What, Jim?

JIM.—Love me, Mary—? (*She turns away with a cry, half sob, of pain.*) Why what's the matter, dear?

MARY. I don't know—

JIM. Nothing's—really troubling you?

MARY. Jim, you've got to listen to me. I—

JIM. Stop it! (*Then.*) Look here, darling—I don't ever want to hear any bad news about us, do you understand? (*She nods, dumbly.*)—There's nothing ever can affect *us*, you know—nothing in this world.—Is there?

MARY. (*After a long moment.*) No. I expect there's not.

JIM. Then—there'll never be anything but good news, will there? (*She looks at him and shakes her head.*) That's right! (*He lifts her face to his.*)—Mary from Jim. Much love.

[*He kisses her. She murmurs:*

MARY.—Much love.

JIM. Now about this party—

MARY. I haven't done a thing about it.

JIM. There's lots of time.

MARY. It couldn't be very elaborate.

[*Now they are chattering happily.*

JIM. It needn't be. Let's keep it small. That's more fun. Where's your wedding-dress?

MARY. In the top tray of my old trunk. Why?

JIM. Oh do wear it!

MARY. It's miles too long now.

JIM. You could take a hitch in it.

MARY. (*Doubtfully.*) I—

JIM. What are pins for?

MARY. Well—

JIM.—And all the men in cutaways.

MARY. They'll be in camphor in the country.

JIM. We'll give a camphor ball.

[MARY. *laughs.*

MARY. I'll feel a thousand.

JIM. You'll look six.—I wish we could bring the babies in for it.

MARY.—They might come out of a pie and turn hand-springs.

JIM. Are they really blooming?

MARY. Wait till you see them!

JIM. Mary—

MARY. What?

JIM. Where's the motor?

MARY. In the garage, why? (JIM *goes to the telephone.*)—What are you doing?!

JIM. (*To the telephone.*) Rhinelander 0890.—That's right.

MARY. Jim!

JIM. Yes.

MARY. You're a madman. It's two o'clock.

JIM. What's the difference? (*To the telephone.*) Hello—

MARY. It'd be four by the time we got there.

JIM. Four's early.

MARY. It certainly is.

JIM. (*To the telephone.*) Hello, is this the garage? Is that you Sam? Hello, Sam, this is Mr. Hutton—

MARY. Wait a minute! Wait a *minute!*

JIM. (*To the telephone.*)—Just to-night. Half an hour ago. You bet I'm glad. Look here, Sam, it's hot in this attic and we think we need some air—

MARY. Will you *listen* to me!

JIM. Shhh! How can I talk with all this jabber-jabber? (*To the telephone.*)—That's right. Send the roadster right over, will you? Thanks, Sam. See you soon. Make it quick. That's the boy! Good-bye!

[*He replaces the telephone and smiles at* MARY.

MARY. Jim—really—I'm a woman of thirty.

JIM.—Not quite. Come on—

MARY. But they don't wake up until six.

JIM. While we wait we'll pick flowers and match pennies.

[MARY *laughs. Then:*

MARY. I'm not dressed.

JIM. Where's your wrap?

MARY. It's downstairs.

JIM. I love to see them when they're asleep.

MARY. Honestly, Jim, this is ridiculous.

JIM. Tie something round your head and come on. Here—

MARY. Jim, I tell you, I—!

JIM. (*Severely.*) You will do as I say.

MARY. It would be fun, you know.

JIM. Fun—? My dear girl, it's our duty! (*He ties a chiffon scarf around her head.*) There! All you need is the dress now. Come on, sweet.

MARY. Oh, the lights—

JIM. Never mind the lights.

MARY. All right, I won't.

JIM. You haven't forgotten anything, have you?

MARY. Not a thing. Just my dignity.

JIM. That's not serious.

MARY. Who said it was?—Give me your hand.

JIM. You give me yours. (*Their hands fumble for each other. They laugh and move toward the hall.*) Here we go, then—

MARY. Oh, here we go!

[*They go out. Their laughter is heard from the hall.*

Curtain.

WINTERSET

BY

Maxwell Anderson

WINTERSET

Winterset represents the tragedy of modern life, written largely in verse. It is a daring but successful attempt to defy the popular convention that poetry should be limited on the stage to historical themes.

Maxwell Anderson was born in Atlantic, Pennsylvania, December 15, 1888. He graduated from the University of North Dakota in 1911, and spent seven years teaching English in North Dakota and California. While an instructor at Leland Stanford University, he began to write one-act plays. Leaving the teaching profession for journalism, he spent six years as editorial writer on the *San Francisco Bulletin,* the *New Republic,* the *New York Evening Globe* and the *New York World.* During these years he was writing poetry, published in 1925 under the title of *You Who Have Dreams.*

Mr. Anderson's first play to see the professional stage was *White Desert* (1923). This was a verse tragedy, a powerful but sombre play, wrought out of the loneliness of life on the snowy plains of North Dakota. While on the *World* Mr. Anderson met Captain Laurence Stallings, who had lost a leg at Belleau Wood in 1918. They collaborated in *What Price Glory* (1924), a blistering satire upon the futility of war, saved from being merely a satire by the concluding note of the quiet return to duty of the professional soldier, who has no illusions about war. Mr. Anderson and Mr. Stallings collaborated in two more plays, *First Flight* (1925), in which Andrew Jackson's early career was dramatized, and *The Buccaneer* (1925), a melodrama dealing with Captain Henry Morgan, the privateer. Neither was successful.

Sea Wife, a remarkable poetic play, was written in the spring of 1924, but has so far been produced only on special occasions, the initial production being at the University of Minnesota in 1932. Mr. Anderson has withdrawn it pending revision. It is an imaginative and powerful dramatization of an idea suggested by Matthew Arnold's *Forsaken Merman.* Mr. Anderson has, however, created an entirely new situation, in which the sympathy of the audience is centered not upon the merman but upon the woman who has left her own husband for three years to become the bride of the sea.

In 1925 Mr. Anderson's play of tramp life, based on *Beggars of Life* by Jim Tully, revealed the standards of the "hobo" in an entertaining manner. Still better than this play was his domestic drama, *Saturday's Children* (1927), a sympathetic picture of the wistful search for happiness by two young people, before and after marriage. In 1928 Mr. Anderson with the aid of Mr. Harold

Hickerson, dramatized the Sacco-Vanzetti Case under the title of *Gods of the Lightning.* While the play made a favorable impression upon the most competent critics, it lasted for only twenty-nine performances. It is most important now because it proves that such a topic is better treated in more universal terms, as in *Winterset.* It was played in Russia, however, at the Theatre of the Revolution in 1930, as the *History of a Murder. Gypsy* (1929) was a vivid picture of a girl who passed from one man to another, and who was quite frank with all of them.

It was in *Elizabeth the Queen* (1930) that Mr. Anderson established his right to be considered one of the foremost playwrights in the history of the American theatre. Here he created the stirring conflict in Queen Elizabeth's nature between her love for the Earl of Essex and her determination to rule alone in England. Essex, who deems his own race quite as royal as either the Tudors or the Boleyns, is almost as well drawn. Miss Lynn Fontanne made a deep impression as Queen Elizabeth. *Night Over Taos* (1932) was a romantic tragedy, in verse, laid in New Mexico in 1847. The gallant but futile effort of this Spanish outpost to defy the advance of the United States was well portrayed. The play did not succeed in its first production, in New York, but in the summer of 1937 it was the artistic climax of the season at the Pasadena Play House in California. Although *Both Your Houses* (1933) won the Pulitzer Prize and was an honest and stinging attack upon political corruption in Congress, it did not have the dignity or significance of *Mary of Scotland* (1933). Most truly of all the historical characters Mr. Anderson has yet drawn, Mary is a great dramatic figure. From the moment she comes to the bleak shores of Scotland, she fights a losing battle against the forces of intolerance and oligarchy, made concrete in the persons of John Knox and the Scottish lords who are determined upon her ruin. Soon the machinations of Elizabeth, her rival, begin to undermine the loyalty of her subjects, and alone except for the Earl of Bothwell, she tries with the weapon of womanly charm, and with the innate dignity which never left the Stuarts even in their defeat, to avert her doom. Mr. Anderson took liberties with history; the meeting between Mary and Elizabeth never took place, but no audience cared for accuracy when Miss Helen Hayes and Miss Helen Menken faced each other in that great scene. In *Valley Forge* (1934) Mr. Anderson defied the fates in making Washington the central figure of a drama. No play of this kind has succeeded, although many have been tried, for Washington has become an ideal figure and it is therefore a mistake to treat him realistically. To depict him as an ideal figure against a background of reality is also dangerous. The play had, however, some very fine moments.

Winterset (1935) is, so far, Mr. Anderson's most significant play. In his preface to the drama, he recognized the difficulties faced by any playwright who deals with contemporary themes in verse. To quote his own words: "Whether I have solved the problem in *Winterset* is probably of little moment. But it must be solved if we are to have a great theatre in America.'' Knowing the history of English versification, Mr. Anderson wrote *Winterset* as he had *White Desert, Elizabeth the Queen, Mary of Scotland* and his other poetic plays, in a flexible, fluent measure, free from any rigid counting of syllables, but rather following as a model the actual spoken blank verse as it comes from the lips of a good actor. Some of the lines have five stresses; some have four; some have two; it does not matter. In all cases, the emotion of the character dictates the verse. Thus it flows naturally from them and indeed audiences were unaware at times that verse was being spoken. But the rhythm was always there, enriching the utterance. The central motive of *Winterset* lent itself, also, to poetic expression. With a courage justified by the result, Mr. Anderson challenged comparison with *Hamlet* by building up his play upon the effort of a son to prove his father guiltless of a murder for which he had been condemned and executed. The resemblance in the details to the Sacco-Vanzetti Case were also apparent, but Mr. Anderson had progressed far from the time of writing *Gods of the Lightning* and he made the forces at work against Mio Romagna as universal and yet as concrete as possible. Trock and the other gangsters who were the real criminals are as vivid a set of rascals as the stage has seen. Then with an art that defies analysis, Mr. Anderson painted against the forbidding background of a grim bridge that shadows a New York alley, one of the most tragic love stories of our time. His skill is shown most clearly in the way the accidental meeting of Mio and Miriamne, and their realization of the hopelessness of their pursuit of happiness, take on the unalterable outlines of fate. The climax of the play, in which Mio, under the influence of Judge Gaunt's argument, doubts for a moment whether his father was innocent, and his joy when Trock's confession proves that his devotion is not mistaken, are blended with the love story and are not forced by the author into relation with it. The interpretation of Mr. Burgess Meredith of the character of Mio was memorable. *Winterset* was awarded the first prize given by the Drama Critics' Circle in New York. It has been played successfully abroad, notably at Gothenburg, Sweden, June 20, 1937.

During the season of 1936–1937, Mr. Anderson had three plays produced. *The Wingless Victory* was a fine dramatic presentation of the intolerance of Salem, Massachusetts, in 1800. Miss Katharine Cornell gave one of the most impressive performances of her career as Oparre, the Malay princess who is brought home by Nathaniel McQueston, a sea-captain, with tragic results to both of them. The consequence of the defiance of racial integrity has rarely had such a portrayal on the stage. *High Tor* was a fantasy mingled skilfully with reality. Van Dorn, a young man who owns land on the Hudson River which is coveted by speculators, is strengthened in his refusal to sell his acres to them by meeting among the wraiths from the Dutch ship of long ago, Lise, the girl who longs for her home in Amsterdam. As in *Sea Wife,* Mr. Anderson passed from fantasy to reality with an art that permitted of some delightful comedy. It was awarded the Drama Critics' Prize for that year. In *The Masque of Kings,* he dramatized the tragedy of Prince Rudolph of Austria-Hungary and Baroness Mary Vetsera. In Mr. Anderson's hands, however, it became also the struggle of liberal ideas against those of arbitrary power, represented by Emperor Franz Joseph, admirably played by Mr. Dudley Digges. *The Star-Wagon* which opened in New York, September 20, 1937, showed no falling off in Mr. Anderson's power and was one of his greatest popular successes. It is an imaginative play of domestic life in which an elderly inventor devises a machine which will permit those who know the combination to go back to any time in their lives and begin again. Once more Mr. Anderson took an old theme and made a new thing of it. The inventor chooses 1902 as the period to which he desires to return, and there is some delightful comedy in the church choir rehearsal and the picnic. In the end he returns contented to his present life. Mr. Burgess Meredith and Miss Lillian Gish were remarkably happy in their interpretation of the inventor and his wife. Mr. Anderson's one-act play, *The Feast of Ortolans,* was produced over the radio on September 20, 1937, and was published in *Stage* for January, 1938. It was laid in 1789 at the residence of the Duke of Pompignan, near Paris, and was based on the ceremony observed once a year by his family of serving a special dish of ortolans to distinguished guests of the family.

What Price Glory, First Flight and *The Buccaneer* were published in one volume by Harcourt, Brace and Company (1926). *Saturday's Children* was published separately (1927), *Gods of the Lightning* and *Outside Looking In* (1928) together in one volume, and *Elizabeth the Queen* (1930) by Longmans, Green and Company. *Night Over Taos* (1932) and *Both Your Houses* (1933) were published by Samuel French, who have also republished *Elizabeth the Queen.* The limited edition of *Mary of Scotland* (1934) was published by Anderson House, Washington, D. C., the trade edition by Doubleday, Doran and Company. *Valley Forge* (1934), *Winterset* (1935), *The Wingless Victory* (1936), *High Tor* (1937), *The Masque of Kings* (1937) and *The Star-Wagon* (1937) have been published by Anderson House, to whom and to Mr. Maxwell Anderson the editor is indebted for permission to include the play in this volume. Mr. Anderson has also been good enough to furnish certain biographical details.

Students of Mr. Anderson's work should read his *Preface to Poetry in the Theatre,* published as an Introduction to *Winterset,* and his article "Yes, by the Eternal," *Stage,* June, 1937, in both of which he discusses the place of poetry in the modern theatre.

For criticism see *Maxwell Anderson, the Man and His Plays,* by Barrett H. Clark, Samuel French (1933) and A. H. Quinn, *A History of the American*

Drama from the Civil War to the Present Day, Revised Edition, two volumes in one, Appleton-Century-Crofts, Inc. (1936), Vol. 2, pp. 233–236, 266–271, and 318.

NOTE TO SEVENTH EDITION.

Knickerbocker Holiday (October 19, 1938), with a charming book and lyrics by Anderson and music by Kurt Weil, successfully reproduced the atmosphere of Peter Stuyvesant's time. *Key Largo* (November 27, 1939), partly in verse, was a study of the rehabilitation of a man who left his comrades in the Spanish Civil War and died in defending the family of one of them against racketeers in Florida. A profoundly moving play, *Journey to Jerusalem* (October 5, 1940), dramatized the visit of the boy Christ to Jerusalem; it lasted only seventeen performances however. *Candle in the Wind* (October 22, 1941) pictured the gallant struggle of an American girl to save her French lover from the Hitler regime in Paris. Notwithstanding only mild praise from the critics, it was a success with the public. Even more successful was *The Eve of St. Mark* (October 7, 1942), a country boy's reaction to the war, and to his love story with a girl from his neighborhood, leading up to his determination to hold out until the last on an island in the Philippines against the Japanese. *Storm Operation* (January 11, 1944), which was based upon Mr. Anderson's personal observation of the scenes of the campaign in North Africa, closed on January 29. *Truckline Café* (February 27, 1946), a thoughtful presentation of the confusion in marital life after the war, met with the disapproval of the newspaper critics and closed March 9. In *Joan of Lorraine* (Washington, October 29, 1946) Anderson enclosed the play in a series of rehearsal scenes in which the director and the actors discuss the meaning of the drama. It proved a popular success. Notwithstanding the difficulty of making Anne Boleyn an appealing character, Anderson succeeded in *Anne of the Thousand Days* (Philadelphia, November 9, 1948) in building magnificent scenes of passion and tenderness into a successful play. *Lost in the Stars,* based on Alan Paton's novel of South Africa, *Cry the Beloved Country,* with music by Kurt Weil (October 30, 1949) was an outstanding triumph. *Barefoot in Athens* (London, Ontario, October 4, 1951), a dramatization of the contest of Socrates with the communistic democracy of Athens and the fascist rule of Sparta, and his martyrdom for freedom was an artistic but not a popular success. Up to and including *Joan of Lorraine,* Mr. Anderson's plays were published by Anderson House, since then by William Sloane Associates. In 1942, *The Bases of Artistic Creation,* essays by Mr. Anderson and others, were published by the Rutgers Press. His *Off Broadway, Essays About the Theater,* was published by Sloane Associates (1947).

CAST OF CHARACTERS

Martin Beck Theatre, New York, September 25, 1935.

TROCK	Eduardo Ciannelli
SHADOW	Harold Johnsrud
LUCIA	Morton L. Stevens
PINY	Fernanda Eliscu
MIRIAMNE	Margo
GARTH	Theodore Hecht
ESDRAS	Anatole Winogradoff
1ST GIRL	Eva Langbord
2ND GIRL	Ruth Hammond
THE HOBO	John Philliber
JUDGE GAUNT	Richard Bennett
CARR	Billy Quinn
MIO	Burgess Meredith
SAILOR	St. John Terrell
RADICAL	Abner Biberman
POLICEMAN	Anthony Blair
SERGEANT	Harold Martin
TWO YOUNG MEN	Stanley Gould Walter Holbrook

PEDESTRIANS, URCHINS, ETC.

The action of the play begins early on a December morning and ends before midnight the same day.

ACT I

SCENE 1. Under a bridge. Early morning.
SCENE 2. In a tenement. The same morning.
SCENE 3. Under the bridge. Evening.

ACT II

In the tenement. The same evening.

ACT III

Under the bridge. Immediately following.

WINTERSET

ACT ONE

Scene I

Scene: *The scene is the bank of a river under a bridgehead. A gigantic span starts from the rear of the stage and appears to lift over the heads of the audience and out to the left. At the right rear is a wall of solid supporting masonry. To the left an apartment building abuts against the bridge and forms the left wall of the stage with a dark basement window and a door in the brick wall. To the right, and in the foreground, an outcropping of original rock makes a barricade behind which one may enter through a cleft. To the rear, against the masonry, two sheds have been built by waifs and strays for shelter. The river bank, in the foreground, is black rock worn smooth by years of trampling. There is room for exit and entrance to the left around the apartment house, also around the rock to the right. A single street lamp is seen at the left—and a glimmer of apartment lights in the background beyond. It is an early, dark December morning.*

Two Young Men in Blue Serge *lean against the masonry, matching bills.* Trock Estrella *and* Shadow *come in from the left.*

Trock. Go back and watch the car.

(*The* Two Young Men *go out.* Trock *walks to the corner and looks toward the city.*)

You roost of punks and gulls! Sleep, sleep it off,
whatever you had last night, get down in warm,
one big ham-fat against another—sleep,
cling, sleep and rot! Rot out your pasty guts
with diddling, you had no brain to begin. If you had
there'd be no need for us to sleep on iron
who had too much brains for you.

Shadow. Now look, Trock, look,
what would the warden say to talk like that?

Trock. May they die as I die!
By God, what life they've left me
they shall keep me well! I'll have that out of them—
these pismires that walk like men!

Shadow. Because, look, chief,
it's all against science and penology
for you to get out and begin to cuss that way
before your prison vittles are out of you. Hell,
you're supposed to leave the pen full of high thought,
kind of noble-like, loving toward all mankind,
ready to kiss their feet—or whatever parts
they stick out toward you. Look at me!

Trock. I see you.
And even you may not live as long as you think.
You think too many things are funny. Well, laugh.
But it's not so funny.

Shadow. Come on, Trock, you know me.
Anything you say goes, but give me leave
to kid a little.

Trock. Then laugh at somebody else!
It's a lot safer! They've soaked me once too often
in that vat of poisoned hell they keep up-state
to soak men in, and I'm rotten inside, I'm all
one liquid puke inside where I had lungs
once, like yourself! And now they want to get me
and stir me in again—and that'd kill me—
and that's fine for them. But before that happens to me
a lot of these healthy boys'll know what it's like
when you try to breathe and have no place to put air—
they'll learn it from me!

Shadow. They've got nothing on you, chief.

Trock. I don't know yet. That's what I'm here to find out.
If they've got what they might have
it's not a year this time—

no, nor ten. It's screwed down under a lid.—
I can die quick enough, without help.
SHADOW. You're the skinny kind
that lives forever.
TROCK. He gave me a half a year,
the doc at the gate.
SHADOW. Jesus.
TROCK. Six months I get,
and the rest's dirt, six feet.

(LUCIA, *the street-piano man, comes in right from behind the rock and goes to the shed where he keeps his piano.* PINY, *the apple-woman, follows and stands in the entrance.* LUCIA *speaks to* ESTRELLA, *who still stands facing* SHADOW.)

LUCIA. Morning.
(TROCK *and* SHADOW *go out round the apartment house without speaking.*)
PINY. Now what would you call them?
LUCIA. Maybe someting da river washed up.
PINY. Nothing ever washed him—that black one.
LUCIA. Maybe not, maybe so. More like his pa and ma raise-a heem in da cellar.
(*He wheels out the piano.*)
PINY. He certainly gave me a turn.
(*She lays a hand on the rock.*)
LUCIA. You don' live-a right, ol' gal. Take heem easy. Look on da bright-a side. Never say-a die. Me, every day in every way I getta be da regular heller.
(*He starts out.*)

CURTAIN

ACT ONE

SCENE II

SCENE: *A cellar apartment under the apartment building, floored with cement and roofed with huge boa constrictor pipes that run slantwise from left to right, dwarfing the room. An outside door opens to the left and a door at the right rear leads to the interior of the place. A low squat window to the left. A table at the rear and a few chairs and books make up the furniture.* GARTH, *son of* ESDRAS, *sits alone, holding a violin upside down to inspect a crack at its base. He lays the bow on the floor and runs his fingers over the joint.* MIRIAMNE *enters from the rear, a girl of fifteen.* GARTH *looks up, then down again.*

MIRIAMNE. Garth—
GARTH. The glue lets go. It's the steam, I guess.
It splits the hair on your head.
MIRIAMNE. It can't be mended?
GARTH. I can't mend it.
No doubt there are fellows somewhere
who'd mend it for a dollar—and glad to do it.
That is if I had a dollar.—Got a dollar?
No, I thought not.
MIRIAMNE. Garth, you've sat at home here
three days now. You haven't gone out at all.
Something frightens you.
GARTH. Yes?
MIRIAMNE. And father's frightened.
He reads without knowing where. When a shadow falls
across the page he waits for a blow to follow
after the shadow. Then in a little while
he puts his book down softly and goes out
to see who passed.
GARTH. A bill collector, maybe.
We haven't paid the rent.
MIRIAMNE. No.
GARTH. You're a bright girl, sis.—
You see too much. You run along and cook.
Why don't you go to school?
MIRIAMNE. I don't like school.
They whisper behind my back.
GARTH. Yes? About what?
MIRIAMNE. What did the lawyer mean
that wrote to you?
GARTH.
(*Rising.*)
What lawyer?
MIRIAMNE. I found a letter
on the floor of your room. He said, "Don't get me wrong,
but stay in out of the rain the next few days,
just for instance."
GARTH. I thought I burned that letter.
MIRIAMNE. Afterward you did. And then what was printed
about the Estrella gang—you hid it from me,
you and father. What is it—about this murder—?
GARTH. Will you shut up, you fool!
MIRIAMNE. But if you know
why don't you tell them, Garth?
If it's true—what they say—
you knew all the time Romagna wasn't guilty,
and could have said so—

GARTH. Everybody knew
Romagna wasn't guilty! But they weren't listening
to evidence in his favor. They didn't want it.
They don't want it now.
MIRIAMNE. But was that why
they never called on you?—
GARTH. So far as I know
they never'd heard of me—and I can assure you
I knew nothing about it—
MIRIAMNE. But something's wrong—
and it worries father—
GARTH. What could be wrong?
MIRIAMNE. I don't know.
(*A pause.*)
GARTH. And I don't know. You're a good kid, Miriamne,
but you see too many movies. I wasn't mixed up
in any murder, and I don't mean to be.
If I had a dollar to get my fiddle fixed
and another to hire a hall, by God I'd fiddle
some of the prodigies back into Sunday School
where they belong, but I won't get either, and so
I sit here and bite my nails—but if you hoped
I had some criminal romantic past
you'll have to look again!
MIRIAMNE. Oh, Garth, forgive me—
But I want you to be so far above such things
nothing could frighten you. When you seem to shrink
and be afraid, and you're the brother I love,
I want to run there and cry, if there's any question
they care to ask, you'll be quick and glad to answer,
for there's nothing to conceal!
GARTH. And that's all true—
MIRIAMNE. But then I remember—
how you dim the lights—
and we go early to bed—and speak in whispers—
and I could think there's a death somewhere behind us—
an evil death—
GARTH.
(*Hearing a step.*)
Now for God's sake, be quiet!

(ESDRAS, *an old rabbi with a kindly face, enters from the outside. He is hurried and troubled.*)

ESDRAS. I wish to speak alone with someone here
if I may have this room. Miriamne—
MIRIAMNE.
(*Turning to go.*)
Yes, father.

(*The outer door is suddenly thrown open.* TROCK *appears.*)

TROCK.
(*After a pause.*)
You'll excuse me for not knocking.

(SHADOW *follows* TROCK *in.*)

Sometimes it's best to come in quiet. Sometimes
it's a good way to go out. Garth's home, I see.
He might not have been here if I made a point
of knocking at doors.
GARTH. How are you, Trock?
TROCK. I guess
you can see how I am.
(*To* MIRIAMNE.)
Stay here. Stay where you are.
We'd like to make your acquaintance.
—If you want the facts
I'm no better than usual, thanks. Not enough sun,
my physician tells me. Too much close confinement.
A lack of exercise and an overplus
of beans in the diet. You've done well, no doubt?
GARTH. I don't know what makes you think so.
TROCK. Who's the family?
GARTH. My father and my sister.
TROCK. Happy to meet you.
Step inside a minute. The boy and I
have something to talk about.
ESDRAS. No, no—he's said nothing—
nothing, sir, nothing!
TROCK. When I say go out, you go—
ESDRAS.
(*Pointing to the door.*)
Miriamne—
GARTH. Go on out, both of you!
ESDRAS. Oh, sir—I'm old—
old and unhappy—
GARTH. Go on!
(MIRIAMNE *and* ESDRAS *go inside.*)
TROCK. And if you listen
I'll riddle that door!
(SHADOW *shuts the door behind them and stands against it.*)
I just got out, you see,
and I pay my first call on you.

GARTH. Maybe you think
I'm not in the same jam you are.
TROCK. That's what I do think.
Who started looking this up?
GARTH. I wish I knew,
and I wish he was in hell! Some damned professor
with nothing else to do. If you saw his stuff
you know as much as I do.
TROCK. It wasn't you
turning state's evidence?
GARTH. Hell, Trock, use your brain!
The case was closed. They burned Romagna for it
and that finished it. Why should I look for trouble
and maybe get burned myself?
TROCK. Boy, I don't know,
but I just thought I'd find out.
GARTH. I'm going straight, Trock.
I can play this thing, and I'm trying to make a living.
I haven't talked and nobody's talked to me.
Christ—it's the last thing I'd want!
TROCK. Your old man knows.
GARTH. That's where I got the money that last time
when you needed it. He had a little saved up,
but I had to tell him to get it. He's as safe
as Shadow there.
TROCK.
(*Looking at* SHADOW.)
There could be people safer
than that son-of-a-bitch.
SHADOW. Who?
TROCK. You'd be safer dead
along with some other gorillas.
SHADOW. It's beginning to look
as if you'd feel safer with everybody dead,
the whole god-damn world.
TROCK. I would. These Jesus-bitten
professors! Looking up their half-ass cases!
We've got enough without that.
GARTH. There's no evidence
to reopen the thing.
TROCK. And suppose they called on you
and asked you to testify?
GARTH. Why then I'd tell 'em
that all I know is what I read in the papers.
And I'd stick to that.
TROCK. How much does your sister know?
GARTH. I'm honest with you, Trock. She read my name
in the professor's pamphlet, and she was scared
the way anybody would be. She got nothing
from me, and anyway she'd go to the chair
herself before she'd send me there.
TROCK. Like hell.
GARTH. Besides, who wants to go to trial again
except the radicals?—You and I won't spill
and unless we did there's nothing to take to court
as far as I know. Let the radicals go on howling
about getting a dirty deal. They always howl
and nobody gives a damn. This professor's red—
everybody knows it.
TROCK. You're forgetting the judge.
Where's the damn judge?
GARTH. What judge?
TROCK. Read the morning papers.
It says Judge Gaunt's gone off his nut. He's got
that damn trial on his mind, and been going round
proving to everybody he was right all the time
and the radicals were guilty—stopping people
in the street to prove it—and now he's nuts entirely
and nobody knows where he is.
GARTH. Why don't they know?
TROCK. Because he's on the loose somewhere! They've got
the police of three cities looking for him.
GARTH. Judge Gaunt?
TROCK. Yes. Judge Gaunt.
SHADOW. Why should that worry you?
He's crazy, ain't he? And even if he wasn't
he's arguing on your side. You're jittery, chief.
God, all the judges are looney. You've got the jitters,
and you'll damn well give yourself away some time
peeing yourself in public.
(TROCK *half turns toward* SHADOW *in anger.*)
Don't jump the gun now,
I've got pockets in my clothes, too.
(*His hand is in his coat pocket.*)
TROCK. All right. Take it easy.
(*He takes his hand from his pocket, and* SHADOW *does the same.*)

(*To* GARTH.)
Maybe you're lying to me and maybe you're not.
Stay at home a few days.
GARTH. Sure thing. Why not?
TROCK. And when I say stay home I mean stay home.
If I have to go looking for you you'll stay a long time
wherever I find you.
(*To* SHADOW.)
Come on. We'll get out of here.
(*To* GARTH.)
Be seeing you.
(SHADOW *and* TROCK *go out. After a pause* GARTH *walks over to his chair and picks up the violin. Then he puts it down and goes to the inside door, which he opens.*)
GARTH. He's gone.
(MIRIAMNE *enters,* ESDRAS *behind her.*)
MIRIAMNE.
(*Going up to* GARTH.)
Let's not stay here.
(*She puts her hands on his arms.*)
I thought he'd come for something—horrible.
Is he coming back?
GARTH. I don't know.
MIRIAMNE. Who is he, Garth?
GARTH. He'd kill me if I told you who he is,
that is, if he knew.
MIRIAMNE. Then don't say it—
GARTH. Yes, and I'll say it! I was with a gang one time
that robbed a pay roll. I saw a murder done,
and Trock Estrella did it. If that got out
I'd go to the chair and so would he—that's why
he was here today—
MIRIAMNE. But that's not true—
ESDRAS. He says it
to frighten you, child.
GARTH. Oh, no I don't! I say it
because I've held it in too long! I'm damned
if I sit here forever, and look at the door,
waiting for Trock with his sub-machine gun, waiting
for police with a warrant!—I say I'm damned, and I am,
no matter what I do! These piddling scales
on a violin—first position, third, fifth,
arpeggios in E—and what I'm thinking
is Romagna dead for the murder—dead while I sat here
dying inside—dead for the thing Trock did
while I looked on—and I could have saved him, yes—
but I sat here and let him die instead of me
because I wanted to live! Well, it's no life,
and it doesn't matter who I tell, because
I mean to get it over!
MIRIAMNE. Garth, it's not true!
GARTH. I'd take some scum down with me if I died—
that'd be one good deed—
ESDRAS. Son, son, you're mad—
someone will hear—
GARTH. Then let them hear! I've lived
with ghosts too long, and lied too long. God damn you
if you keep me from the truth!—
(*He turns away.*)
Oh, God damn the world!
I don't want to die!
(*He throws himself down.*)
ESDRAS. I should have known.
I thought you hard and sullen,
Garth, my son. And you were a child, and hurt
with a wound that might be healed.
—All men have crimes,
and most of them are hidden, and many are heavy
as yours must be to you.
(GARTH *sobs.*)
They walk the streets
to buy and sell, but a spreading crimson stain
tinges the inner vestments, touches flesh,
and burns the quick. You're not alone.
GARTH. I'm alone
in this.
ESDRAS. Yes, if you hold with the world that only
those who die suddenly should be revenged.
But those whose hearts are cancered, drop by drop
in small ways, little by little, till they've borne
all they can bear, and die—these deaths will go
unpunished now as always. When we're young
we have faith in what is seen, but when we're old
we know that what is seen is traced in air
and built on water. There's no guilt under heaven,
just as there's no heaven, till men believe it—

no earth, till men have seen it, and have a word
to say this is the earth.

GARTH. Well, I say there's an earth,
and I say I'm guilty on it, guilty as hell.

ESDRAS. Yet till it's known you bear no guilt at all—
unless you wish. The days go by like film,
like a long written scroll, a figured veil
unrolling out of darkness into fire
and utterly consumed. And on this veil,
running in sounds and symbols of men's minds
reflected back, life flickers and is shadow
going toward flame. Only what men can see
exists in that shadow. Why must you rise and cry out:
That was I, there in the ravelled tapestry,
there, in that pistol flash, when the man was killed.
I was there, and was one, and am bloodstained!
Let the wind
and fire take that hour to ashes out of time
and out of mind! This thing that men call justice,
this blind snake that strikes men down in the dark,
mindless with fury, keep your hand back from it,
pass by in silence—let it be forgotten, forgotten!—
Oh, my son, my son—have pity!

MIRIAMNE. But if it was true
and someone died—then it was more than shadow—
and it doesn't blow away—

GARTH. Well, it was true.

ESDRAS. Say it if you must. If you have heart to die,
say it, and let them take what's left—there was little
to keep, even before—

GARTH. Oh, I'm a coward—
I always was. I'll be quiet and live. I'll live
even if I have to crawl. I know.

(*He gets up and goes into the inner room.*)

MIRIAMNE. Is it better
to tell a lie and live?

ESDRAS. Yes, child. It's better.

MIRIAMNE. But if I had to do it—
I think I'd die.

ESDRAS. Yes, child. Because you're young.

MIRIAMNE. Is that the only reason?

ESDRAS. The only reason.

CURTAIN

ACT ONE

SCENE III

SCENE: *Under the bridge, evening of the same day. When the curtain rises* MIRIAMNE *is sitting alone on the ledge at the rear of the apartment house. A spray of light falls on her from a street lamp above. She shivers a little in her thin coat, but sits still as if heedless of the weather. Through the rocks on the other side a* TRAMP *comes down to the river bank, hunting a place to sleep. He goes softly to the apple-woman's hut and looks in, then turns away, evidently not daring to preëmpt it. He looks at* MIRIAMNE *doubtfully. The door of the street-piano man is shut. The vagabond passes it and picks carefully among some rags and shavings to the right.* MIRIAMNE *looks up and sees him but makes no sign. She looks down again, and the man curls himself up in a makeshift bed in the corner, pulling a piece of sacking over his shoulders.* TWO GIRLS *come in from round the apartment house.*

1ST GIRL. Honest, I never heard of anything so romantic. Because you never liked him.

2ND GIRL. I certainly never did.

1ST GIRL. You've got to tell me how it happened. You've got to.

2ND GIRL. I couldn't. As long as I live I couldn't. Honest, it was terrible. It was terrible.

1ST GIRL. What was so terrible?

2ND GIRL. The way it happened.

1ST GIRL. Oh, please—not to a soul, never.

2ND GIRL. Well, you know how I hated him because he had such a big mouth. So he reached over and grabbed me, and I began all falling to pieces inside, the way you do—and I said, "Oh no you don't mister," and started screaming and kicked a hole through the windshield and lost a shoe, and he let go and was cursing and growling because he borrowed the car and didn't have money to pay for the windshield, and he started to cry, and I got so sorry for him I let him, and now he wants to marry me.

1ST GIRL. Honest, I never heard of anything so romantic!
(*She sees the sleeping* TRAMP.)
My God, what you won't see!

(*They give the* TRAMP *a wide berth, and go out right. The* TRAMP *sits up looking about him.* JUDGE GAUNT, *an elderly, quiet man, well dressed but in clothes that have seen some weather, comes in uncertainly from the left. He holds a small clipping in his hand and goes up to the* HOBO.)

GAUNT.
(*Tentatively.*)
Your pardon, sir. Your pardon, but perhaps you can tell me the name of this street.
HOBO. Huh?
GAUNT. The name of this street?
HOBO. This ain't no street.
GAUNT. There, where the street lamps are.
HOBO. That's the alley.
GAUNT. Thank you. It has a name, no doubt?
HOBO. That's the alley.
GAUNT. I see. I won't trouble you. You wonder why I ask, I daresay.—I'm a stranger.—Why do you look at me?
(*He steps back.*)
I—I'm not the man you think. You've mistaken me, sir.
HOBO. Huh?
JUDGE. Perhaps misled by a resemblance. But you're mistaken—I had an errand in this city. It's only by accident that I'm here—
HOBO.
(*Muttering.*)
You go to hell.
JUDGE.
(*Going nearer to him, bending over him.*)
Yet why should I deceive you? Before God, I held the proofs in my hands. I hold them still. I tell you the defense was cunning beyond belief, and unscrupulous in its use of propaganda—they gagged at nothing—not even—
(*He rises.*)
No, no—I'm sorry—this will hardly interest you. I'm sorry. I have an errand.
(*He looks toward the street.* ESDRAS *enters from the basement and goes to* MIRIAMNE. *The* JUDGE *steps back into the shadows.*)
ESDRAS. Come in, my daughter. You'll be cold here.
MIRIAMNE. After a while.
ESDRAS. You'll be cold. There's a storm coming.
MIRIAMNE. I didn't want him to see me crying. That was all.
ESDRAS. I know.
MIRIAMNE. I'll come soon.

(ESDRAS *turns reluctantly and goes out the way he came.* MIRIAMNE *rises to go in, pausing to dry her eyes.* MIO *and* CARR, *road boys of seventeen or so, come round the apartment house. The* JUDGE *has disappeared.*)

CARR. Thought you said you were never coming east again.
MIO. Yeah, but—I heard something changed my mind.
CARR. Same old business?
MIO. Yes. Just as soon not talk about it.
CARR. Where did you go from Portland?
MIO. Fishing—I went fishing. God's truth.
CARR. Right after I left?
MIO. Fell in with a fisherman's family on the coast and went after the beautiful mackerel fish that swim in the beautiful sea. Family of Greeks—Aristides Marinos was his lovely name. He sang while he fished. Made the pea-green Pacific ring with his bastard Greek chanties. Then I went to Hollywood High School for a while.
CARR. I'll bet that's a seat of learning.
MIO. It's the hind end of all wisdom. They kicked me out after a time.
CARR. For cause?
MIO. Because I had no permanent address, you see. That means nobody's paying school taxes for you, so out you go.
(*To* MIRIAMNE.)
What's the matter, kid?
MIRIAMNE. Nothing.
(*She looks up at him, and they pause for a moment.*)
Nothing.
MIO. I'm sorry.
MIRIAMNE. It's all right.
(*She withdraws her eyes from his and goes out past him. He turns and looks after her.*)

CARR. Control your chivalry.
MIO. A pretty kid.
CARR. A baby.
MIO. Wait for me.
CARR. Be a long wait?
(MIO *steps swiftly out after* MIRIAMNE, *then returns.*)
Yeah?
MIO. She's gone.
CARR. Think of that.
MIO. No, but I mean—vanished. Presto—into nothing—prodigioso.
CARR. Damn good thing, if you ask me. The homely ones are bad enough, but the lookers are fatal.
MIO. You exaggerate, Carr.
CARR. I doubt it.
MIO. Well, let her go. This river bank's loaded with typhus rats, too. Might as well die one death as another.
CARR. They say chronic alcoholism is nice but expensive. You can always starve to death.
MIO. Not always. I tried it. After the second day I walked thirty miles to Niagara Falls and made a tour of the plant to get the sample of shredded wheat biscuit on the way out.
CARR. Last time I saw you you couldn't think of anything you wanted to do except curse God and pass out. Still feeling low?
MIO. Not much different.
(*He turns away, then comes back.*)
Talk about the lost generation, I'm the only one fits that title. When the State executes your father, and your mother dies of grief, and you know damn well he was innocent, and the authorities of your home town politely inform you they'd consider it a favor if you lived somewhere else—that cuts you off from the world—with a meat-axe.
CARR. They asked you to move?
MIO. It came to that.
CARR. God, that was white of them.
MIO. It probably gave them a headache just to see me after all that agitation. They knew as well as I did my father never staged a holdup. Anyway, I've got a new interest in life now.
CARR. Yes—I saw her.
MIO. I don't mean the skirt.—No, I got wind of something, out west, some college professor investigating the trial and turning up new evidence. Couldn't find anything he'd written out there, so I beat it east and arrived on this blessed island just in time to find the bums holing up in the public library for the winter. I know now what the unemployed have been doing since the depression started. They've been catching up on their reading in the main reference room. Man, what a stench! Maybe I stank, too, but a hobo has the stench of ten because his shoes are poor.
CARR. Tennyson.
MIO. Right. Jeez, I'm glad we met up again! Never knew anybody else that could track me through the driven snow of Victorian literature.
CARR. Now you're cribbing from some half-forgotten criticism of Ben Jonson's Roman plagiarisms.
MIO. Where did you get your education, sap?
CARR. Not in the public library, sap. My father kept a news-stand.
MIO. Well, you're right again.
(*There is a faint rumble of thunder.*)
What's that? Winter thunder?
CARR. Or Mister God, beating on His little tocsin. Maybe announcing the advent of a new social order.
MIO. Or maybe it's going to rain coffee and doughnuts.
CARR. Or maybe it's going to rain.
MIO. Seems more likely.
(*Lowering his voice.*)
Anyhow, I found Professor Hobhouse's discussion of the Romagna case. I think he has something. It occurred to me I might follow it up by doing a little sleuthing on my own account.
CARR. Yes?
MIO. I have done a little. And it leads me to somewhere in that tenement house that backs up against the bridge. That's how I happen to be here.
CARR. They'll never let you get anywhere with it, Mio. I told you that before.
MIO. I know you did.
CARR. The State can't afford to admit it was wrong, you see. Not when there's been that much of a row kicked up over it. So for all practical purposes the State was right and your father robbed the pay roll.
MIO. There's still such a thing as evidence.
CARR. It's something you can buy. In fact, at the moment I don't think of anything you can't buy, including life, honor, virtue, glory, public office, conjugal affection and all kinds of justice, from the traffic court to the immortal nine. Go out and make yourself a pot

of money and you can buy all the justice you want. Convictions obtained, convictions averted. Lowest rates in years.

MIO. I know all that.

CARR. Sure.

MIO. This thing didn't happen to you.
They've left you your name
and whatever place you can take. For my heritage
they've left me one thing only, and that's to be
my father's voice crying up out of the earth
and quicklime where they stuck him. Electrocution
doesn't kill, you know. They eviscerate them
with a turn of the knife in the dissecting room.
The blood spurts out. The man was alive. Then into
the lime pit, leave no trace. Make it short shrift
and chemical dissolution. That's what they thought
of the man that was my father. Then my mother—
I tell you these county burials are swift
and cheap and run for profit! Out of the house
and into the ground, you wife of a dead dog. Wait,
here's some Romagna spawn left.
Something crawls here—
something they called a son. Why couldn't he die
along with his mother? Well, ease him out of town,
ease him out, boys, and see you're not too gentle.
He might come back. And, by their own living Jesus,
I will go back, and hang the carrion
around their necks that made it!
Maybe I can sleep then.
Or even live.

CARR. You have to try it?

MIO. Yes.
Yes. It won't let me alone. I've tried to live
and forget it—but I was birthmarked with hot iron
into the entrails. I've got to find out who did it
and make them see it till it scalds their eyes
and make them admit it till their tongues are blistered
with saying how black they lied!

(HERMAN, *a gawky shoe salesman, enters from the left.*)

HERMAN. Hello. Did you see a couple of girls go this way?

CARR. Couple of girls? Did we see a couple of girls?

MIO. No.

CARR. No. No girls.

(HERMAN *hesitates, then goes out right.* LUCIA *comes in from the left, trundling his piano.* PINY *follows him, weeping.*)

PINY. They've got no right to do it—

LUCIA. All right, hell what, no matter, I got to put him away, I got to put him away, that's what the hell!

(TWO STREET URCHINS *follow him in.*)

PINY. They want everybody on the relief rolls and nobody making a living?

LUCIA. The cops, they do what the big boss says. The big boss, that's the mayor, he says he heard it once too often, the sextette—

PINY. They want graft, that's all. It's a new way to get graft—

LUCIA. Oh, no, no, no! He's a good man, the mayor. He just don't care for music, that's all.

PINY. Why shouldn't you make a living on the street? The National Biscuit Company ropes off Eighth Avenue—and does the mayor do anything? No, the police hit you over the head if you try to go through!

LUCIA. You got the big dough, you get the pull, fine. No big dough, no pull, what the hell, get off the city property! Tomorrow I start cooking chestnuts . . .

(*He strokes the piano fondly. The* TWO GIRLS *and* HERMAN *come back from the right.*)

She's a good little machine, this baby. Cost plenty and two new records I only played twice. See, this one.

(*He starts turning the crank, talking while he plays.*)

Two weeks since they play this one in a picture house.

(A SAILOR *wanders in from the left. One of the* STREET URCHINS *begins suddenly to dance a wild rumba, the others watch.*)

Good boy—see, it's a lulu—it itches in the feet!

(HERMAN, *standing with his girl, tosses the boy a penny. He bows and goes on dancing; the other* UR-

CHIN *joins him. The* SAILOR *tosses a coin.*)

SAILOR. Go it, Cuba! Go it!

(LUCIA *turns the crank, beaming.*)

2ND GIRL. Oh, Herman!

(*She throws her arms round* HERMAN *and they dance.*)

1ST URCHIN. Hey, pipe the professionals!

1ST GIRL. Do your glide, Shirley! Do your glide!

LUCIA. Maybe we can't play in front, maybe we can play behind!

(*The* HOBO *gets up from his nest and comes over to watch.* A YOUNG RADICAL *wanders in.*)

Maybe you don't know, folks! Tonight we play good-bye to the piano! Good-bye forever! No more piano on the streets! No more music! No more money for the music-man! Last time, folks! Good-bye to the piano—good-bye forever!

(MIRIAMNE *comes out the rear door of the apartment and stands watching. The* SAILOR *goes over to the* 1ST GIRL *and they dance together.*)

Maybe you don't know, folks! Tomorrow will be sad as hell, tonight we dance! Tomorrow no more Verdi, no more rumba, no more good time! Tonight we play good-bye to the piano, good-bye forever!

(*The* RADICAL *edges up to* MIRIAMNE, *and asks her to dance. She shakes her head and he goes to* PINY, *who dances with him. The* HOBO *begins to do a few lonely curvets on the side above.*)

Hoy! Hoy! Pick 'em up and take 'em around! Use the head, use the feet! Last time forever!

(*He begins to sing to the air.*)

MIO. Wait for me, will you?

CARR. Now's your chance.

(MIO *goes over to* MIRIAMNE *and holds out a hand, smiling. She stands for a moment uncertain, then dances with him.* ESDRAS *comes out to watch.* JUDGE GAUNT *comes in from the left. There is a rumble of thunder.*)

LUCIA. Hoy! Hoy! Maybe it rains tonight, maybe it snows tomorrow! Tonight we dance good-bye.

(*He sings the air lustily.* A POLICEMAN *comes in from the left and looks on.* TWO OR THREE PEDESTRIANS *follow him.*)

POLICEMAN. Hey you!

(LUCIA *goes on singing.*)

Hey, you!

LUCIA.

(*Still playing.*)

What you want?

POLICEMAN. Sign off!

LUCIA. What you mean? I get off the street!

POLICEMAN. Sign off!

LUCIA.

(*Still playing.*)

What you mean?

(*The* POLICEMAN *walks over to him.* LUCIA *stops playing and the* DANCERS *pause.*)

POLICEMAN. Cut it.

LUCIA. Is this a street?

POLICEMAN. I say cut it out.

(*The* HOBO *goes back to his nest and sits in it, watching.*)

LUCIA. It's the last time. We dance good-bye to the piano.

POLICEMAN. You'll dance good-bye to something else if I catch you cranking that thing again.

LUCIA. All right.

PINY. I'll bet you don't say that to the National Biscuit Company!

POLICEMAN. Lady, you've been selling apples on my beat for some time now, and I said nothing about it—

PINY. Selling apples is allowed—

POLICEMAN. You watch yourself—

(*He takes a short walk around the place and comes upon the* HOBO.)

What are you doing here?

(*The* HOBO *opens his mouth, points to it, and shakes his head.*)

Oh, you are, are you?

(*He comes back to* LUCIA.)

So you trundle your so-called musical instrument to wherever you keep it, and don't let me hear it again.

(*The* RADICAL *leaps on the base of the rock at right. The* 1ST GIRL *turns away from the* SAILOR *toward the* 2ND GIRL *and* HERMAN.)

SAILOR. Hey, captain, what's the matter with the music?

POLICEMAN. Not a thing, admiral.

SAILOR. Well, we had a little party going here—

POLICEMAN. I'll say you did.

2ND GIRL. Please, officer, we want to dance.

POLICEMAN. Go ahead. Dance.

2ND GIRL. But we want music!

POLICEMAN.

(*Turning to go.*)

Sorry. Can't help you.

RADICAL. And there you see it, the perfect example of capitalistic oppression! In a land where music should be free as air and the arts should be encouraged, a uniformed minion of the rich, a guardian myrmidon of the Park Avenue pleasure hunters, steps in and puts a limit on the innocent enjoyments of the poor! We don't go to theatres! Why not? We can't afford it! We don't go to night clubs, where women dance naked and the music drips from saxophones and leaks out of Rudy Vallee—we can't afford that either!—But we might at least dance on the river bank to the strains of a barrel organ—!

(GARTH *comes out of the apartment and listens.*)

POLICEMAN. It's against the law!

RADICAL. What law? I challenge you to tell me what law of God or man—what ordinance—is violated by this spontaneous diversion? None! I say none! An official whim of the masters who should be our servants!—

POLICEMAN. Get down! Get down and shut up!

RADICAL. By what law, by what ordinance do you order me to be quiet?

POLICEMAN. Speaking without a flag. You know it.

RADICAL.

(*Pulling out a small American flag.*)

There's my flag! There's the flag of this United States which used to guarantee the rights of man—the rights of man now violated by every third statute of the commonweal—

POLICEMAN. Don't try to pull tricks on me! I've seen you before! You're not making any speech, and you're climbing down—

JUDGE GAUNT.

(*Who has come quietly forward.*)

One moment, officer. There is some difference of opinion even on the bench as to the elasticity of police power when applied in minor emergencies to preserve civil order. But the weight of authority would certainly favor the defendant in any equable court, and he would be upheld in his demand to be heard.

POLICEMAN. Who are you?

JUDGE GAUNT. Sir, I am not accustomed to answer that question.

POLICEMAN. I don't know you.

GAUNT. I am a judge of some standing, not in your city but in another with similar statutes. You are aware, of course, that the bill of rights is not to be set aside lightly by the officers of any municipality—

POLICEMAN.

(*Looking over* GAUNT'S *somewhat bedraggled costume.*)

Maybe they understand you better in the town you come from, but I don't get your drift.—

(*To the* RADICAL.)

I don't want any trouble, but if you ask for it you'll get plenty. Get down!

RADICAL. I'm not asking for trouble, but I'm staying right here.

(*The* POLICEMAN *moves toward him.*)

GAUNT.

(*Taking the* POLICEMAN'S *arm, but shaken off roughly.*)

I ask this for yourself, truly, not for the dignity of the law nor the maintenance of precedent. Be gentle with them when their threats are childish—be tolerant while you can—for your least harsh word will return on you in the night—return in a storm of cries!—

(*He takes the* POLICEMAN'S *arm again.*)

Whatever they may have said or done, let them disperse in peace! It is better that they go softly, lest when they are dead you see their eyes pleading, and their outstretched hands touch you, fingering cold on your heart!—I have been harsher than you. I have sent men down that long corridor into blinding light and blind darkness!

(*He suddenly draws himself erect and speaks defiantly.*)

And it was well that I did so! I have been an upright judge! They are all liars! Liars!

POLICEMAN.

(*Shaking* GAUNT *off so that he falls.*)

Why, you fool, you're crazy!

GAUNT. Yes, and there are liars on the force! They came to me with their shifty lies!

(*He catches at the* POLICEMAN, *who pushes him away with his foot.*)

POLICEMAN. You think I've got nothing better to do than listen to a crazy fool?

1ST GIRL. Shame, shame!

POLICEMAN. What have I got to be ashamed of? And what's going on here,

anyway? Where in hell did you all come from?
RADICAL. Tread on him! That's right! Tread down the poor and the innocent!
(*There is a protesting murmur in the crowd.*)
SAILOR.
(*Moving in a little.*)
Say, big boy, you don't have to step on the guy.
POLICEMAN.
(*Facing them, stepping back.*)
What's the matter with you? I haven't stepped on anybody!
MIO.
(*At the right, across from the* POLICEMAN.)
Listen now, fellows, give the badge a chance.
He's doing his job, what he gets paid to do,
the same as any of you. They're all picked men,
these metropolitan police, hand picked
for loyalty and a fine up-standing pair
of shoulders on their legs—it's not so easy
to represent the law. Think what he does
for all of us, stamping out crime!
Do you want to be robbed and murdered in your beds?
SAILOR. What's eating you?
RADICAL. He must be a capitalist.
MIO. They pluck them fresh
from Ireland, and a paucity of head-piece
is a prime prerequisite. You from Ireland, buddy?
POLICEMAN.
(*Surly.*)
Where are you from?
MIO. Buddy, I tell you flat
I wish I was from Ireland, and could boast
some Tammany connections. There's only one drawback
about working on the force. It infects the brain,
it eats the cerebrum. There've been cases known,
fine specimens of manhood, too, where autopsies,
conducted in approved scientific fashion,
revealed conditions quite incredible
in policemen's upper layers. In some, a trace,
in others, when they've swung a stick too long,
there was nothing there!—but nothing!
Oh, my friends,
this fine athletic figure of a man
that stands so grim before us, what will they find
when they saw his skull for the last inspection?
I fear me a little puffball dust will blow away
rejoining earth, our mother—and this same dust,
this smoke, this ash on the wind, will represent
all he had left to think with!
THE HOBO. Hooray!
(*The* POLICEMAN *turns on his heel and looks hard at the* HOBO, *who slinks away.*)
POLICEMAN. Oh, yeah?
MIO. My theme
gives ears to the deaf and voice to the dumb! But now
forgive me if I say you were most unkind
in troubling the officer. He's a simple man
of simple tastes, and easily confused
when faced with complex issues. He may reflect
on returning home, that is, so far as he
is capable of reflection, and conclude
that he was kidded out of his uniform pants,
and in his fury when this dawns on him
may smack his wife down!
POLICEMAN. That'll be about enough from you, too, professor!
MIO. May I say that I think you have managed this whole situation rather badly, from the beginning?—
POLICEMAN. You may not!

(TROCK *slips in from the background. The* TWO YOUNG MEN IN SERGE *come with him.*)

MIO. Oh, but your pardon, sir! It's apparent to the least competent among us that you should have gone about your task more subtly—the glove of velvet, the hand of iron, and all that sort of thing—
POLICEMAN. Shut that hole in your face!
MIO. Sir, for that remark I shall be satisfied with nothing less than an unconditional apology! I have an old score to settle with policemen, brother, because they're fools and fat-heads, and you're one of the most fatuous fat-heads

that ever walked his feet flat collecting graft! Tell that to your sergeant back in the booby-hatch.

POLICEMAN. Oh, you want an apology, do you? You'll get an apology out of the other side of your mouth!

(*He steps toward* MIO. CARR *suddenly stands in his path.*)

Get out of my way!

(*He pauses and looks round him; the crowd looks less and less friendly. He lays a hand on his gun and backs to a position where there is nobody behind him.*)

Get out of here, all of you! Get out! What are you trying to do—start a riot?

MIO. There now, that's better! That's in the best police tradition. Incite a riot yourself and then accuse the crowd.

POLICEMAN. It won't be pleasant if I decide to let somebody have it! Get out!

(*The onlookers begin to melt away. The* SAILOR *goes out left with the* GIRLS *and* HERMAN. CARR *and* MIO *go out right,* CARR *whistling "The Star Spangled Banner." The* HOBO *follows them. The* RADICAL *walks past with his head in the air.* PINY *and* LUCIA *leave the piano where it stands and slip away to the left. At the end the* POLICEMAN *is left standin the center, the* JUDGE *near him.* ESDRAS *stands in the doorway.* MIRIAMNE *is left sitting half in shadow and unseen by* ESDRAS.)

JUDGE GAUNT.

(*To the* POLICEMAN.)

Yes, but should a man die, should it be necessary that one man die for the good of many, make not yourself the instrument of death, lest you sleep to wake sobbing! Nay, it avails nothing that you are the law—this delicate ganglion that is the brain, it will not bear these things—!

(*The* POLICEMAN *gives the* JUDGE *the once-over, shrugs, decides to leave him there and starts out left.* GARTH *goes to his father—a fine sleet begins to fall through the street lights.* TROCK *is still visible.*)

GARTH. Get him in here, quick.

ESDRAS. Who, son?

GARTH. The Judge, damn him!

ESDRAS. Is it Judge Gaunt?

GARTH. Who did you think it was? He's crazy as a bedbug and telling the world. Get him inside!

(*He looks round.*)

ESDRAS.

(*Going up to* GAUNT.)

Will you come in, sir?

GAUNT. You will understand, sir. We old men know how softly we must proceed with these things.

ESDRAS. Yes, surely, sir.

GAUNT. It was always my practice—always. They will tell you that of me where I am known. Yet even I am not free of regret—even I. Would you believe it?

ESDRAS. I believe we are none of us free of regret.

GAUNT. None of us? I would it were true. I would I thought it were true.

ESDRAS. Shall we go in, sir? This is sleet that's falling.

GAUNT. Yes. Let us go in.

(ESDRAS, GAUNT *and* GARTH *enter the basement and shut the door.* TROCK *goes out with his men. After a pause* MIO *comes back from the right, alone. He stands at a little distance from* MIRIAMNE.)

MIO. Looks like rain.

(*She is silent.*)

You live around here?

(*She nods gravely.*)

I guess
you thought I meant it—about waiting here to meet me.

(*She nods again.*)

I'd forgotten about it till I got that winter
across the face. You'd better go inside.
I'm not your kind. I'm nobody's kind but my own.
I'm waiting for this to blow over.

(*She rises.*)

I lied. I meant it—
I meant it when I said it—but there's too much black
whirling inside me—for any girl to know.
So go on in. You're somebody's angel child
and they're waiting for you.

MIRIAMNE. Yes. I'll go.

(*She turns.*)

MIO. And tell them
when you get inside where it's warm,
and you love each other,
and mother comes to kiss her darling, tell them
to hang on to it while they can, believe while they can
it's a warm safe world, and Jesus finds his lambs

and carries them in his bosom.—I've seen some lambs
that Jesus missed. If they ever want the truth
tell them that nothing's guaranteed in this climate
except it gets cold in winter, nor on this earth
except you die sometime.
(*He turns away.*)

MIRIAMNE. I have no mother.
And my people are Jews.

MIO. Then you know something about it.

MIRIAMNE. Yes.

MIO. Do you have enough to eat?

MIRIAMNE. Not always.

MIO. What do you believe in?

MIRIAMNE. Nothing.

MIO. Why?

MIRIAMNE. How can one?

MIO. It's easy if you're a fool. You see the words
in books. Honor, it says there, chivalry, freedom,
heroism, enduring love—and these
are words on paper. It's something to have them there.
You'll get them nowhere else.

MIRIAMNE. What hurts you?

MIO. Just that.
You'll get them nowhere else.

MIRIAMNE. Why should you want them?

MIO. I'm alone, that's why. You see those lights,
along the river, cutting across the rain—?
those are the hearths of Brooklyn, and up this way
the love-nests of Manhattan—they turn their points
like knives against me—outcast of the world,
snake in the streets.—I don't want a hand-out.
I sleep and eat.

MIRIAMNE. Do you want me to go with you?

MIO. Where?

MIRIAMNE. Where you go.
(*A pause. He goes nearer to her.*)

MIO. Why, you god-damned little fool—
what made you say that?

MIRIAMNE. I don't know.

MIO. If you have a home
stay in it. I ask for nothing. I've schooled myself
to ask for nothing, and take what I can get,
and get along. If I fell for you, that's my look-out,
and I'll starve it down.

MIRIAMNE. Wherever you go, I'd go.

MIO. What do you know about loving?
How could you know?
Have you ever had a man?

MIRIAMNE.
(*After a slight pause.*)
No. But I know.
Tell me your name.

MIO. Mio. What's yours?

MIRIAMNE. Miriamne.

MIO. There's no such name.

MIRIAMNE. But there's no such name as Mio!
M-I-O. It's no name.

MIO. It's for Bartolomeo.

MIRIAMNE. My mother's name was Miriam,
so they called me Miriamne.

MIO. Meaning little Miriam?

MIRIAMNE. Yes.

MIO. So now little Miriamne will go in
and take up quietly where she dropped them all
her small housewifely cares.—When I first saw you,
not a half-hour ago, I heard myself saying,
this is the face that launches ships for me—
and if I owned a dream—yes, half a dream—
we'd share it. But I have no dream. This earth
came tumbling down from chaos, fire and rock,
and bred up worms, blind worms that sting each other
here in the dark. These blind worms of the earth
took out my father—and killed him, and set a sign
on me—the heir of the serpent—and he was a man
such as men might be if the gods were men—
but they killed him—
as they'll kill all others like him
till the sun cools down to the stabler molecules,
yes, till men spin their tent-worm webs to the stars
and what they think is done, even in the thinking,
and they are the gods, and immortal, and constellations
turn for them all like mill wheels—still as they are
they will be, worms and blind. Enduring love,

oh gods and worms, what mockery!—And yet
I have blood enough in my veins. It goes like music,
singing, because you're here. My body turns
as if you were the sun, and warm. This men called love
in happier times, before the Freudians taught us
to blame it on the glands. Only go in
before you breathe too much of my atmosphere
and catch death from me.

MIRIAMNE. I will take my hands
and weave them to a little house, and there
you shall keep a dream—

MIO. God knows I could use a dream
and even a house.

MIRIAMNE. You're laughing at me, Mio!

MIO. The worms are laughing.
I tell you there's death about me
and you're a child! And I'm alone and half mad
with hate and longing. I shall let you love me
and love you in return, and then, why then
God knows what happens!

MIRIAMNE. Something most unpleasant?

MIO. Love in a box car—love among the children.
I've seen too much of it. Are we to live
in this same house you make with your two hands
mystically, out of air?

MIRIAMNE. No roof, no mortgage!
Well, I shall marry a baker out in Flatbush,
it gives hot bread in the morning! Oh, Mio, Mio,
in all the unwanted places and waste lands
that roll up into the darkness out of sun
and into sun out of dark, there should be one empty
for you and me.

MIO. No.

MIRIAMNE. Then go now and leave me.
I'm only a girl you saw in the tenements,
and there's been nothing said.

MIO. Miriamne.

(*She takes a step toward him.*)

MIRIAMNE. Yes.

(*He kisses her lips lightly.*)

MIO. Why, girl, the transfiguration on the mount
was nothing to your face. It lights from within—
a white chalice holding fire, a flower in flame,
this is your face.

MIRIAMNE. And you shall drink the flame
and never lessen it. And round your head
the aureole shall burn that burns there now,
forever. This I can give you. And so forever
the Freudians are wrong.

MIO. They're well-forgotten
at any rate.

MIRIAMNE. Why did you speak to me
when you first saw me?

MIO. I knew then.

MIRIAMNE. And I came back
because I must see you again. And we danced together
and my heart hurt me. Never, never, never,
though they should bind me down and tear out my eyes,
would I ever hurt you now. Take me with you, Mio,
let them look for us, whoever there is to look,
but we'll be away.

(MIO *turns away toward the tenement.*)

MIO. When I was four years old
we climbed through an iron gate, my mother and I,
to see my father in prison. He stood in the death-cell
and put his hand through the bars and said, My Mio,
I have only this to leave you, that I love you,
and will love you after I die. Love me then, Mio,
when this hard thing comes on you, that you must live
a man despised for your father. That night the guards,
walking in flood-lights brighter than high noon,
led him between them with his trousers slit
and a shaven head for the cathodes. This sleet and rain
that I feel cold here on my face and hands
will find him under thirteen years of clay
in prison ground. Lie still and rest, my father,
for I have not forgotten. When I forget
may I lie blind as you. No other love,
time passing, nor the spaced light-years of suns
shall blur your voice, or tempt me from the path
that clears your name—
till I have these rats in my grip

or sleep deep where you sleep.
(*To* MIRIAMNE.)
I have no house,
nor home, nor love of life, nor fear of death,
nor care for what I eat, or who I sleep with,
or what color of calcimine the Government
will wash itself this year or next to lure
the sheep and feed the wolves. Love somewhere else,
and get your children in some other image
more acceptable to the State! This face of mine
is stamped for sewage!
(*She steps back, surmising.*)

MIRIAMNE. Mio—

MIO. My road is cut
in rock, and leads to one end. If I hurt you, I'm sorry.
One gets over hurts.

MIRIAMNE. What was his name—
your father's name?

MIO. Bartolomeo Romagna.
I'm not ashamed of it.

MIRIAMNE. Why are you here?

MIO. For the reason
I've never had a home. Because I'm a cry
out of a shallow grave, and all roads are mine
that might revenge him!

MIRIAMNE. But Mio–why here–why here?

MIO. I can't tell you that.

MIRIAMNE. No—but—there's someone
lives here—lives not far—and you mean to see him—
you mean to ask him—
(*She pauses.*)

MIO. Who told you that?

MIRIAMNE. His name
is Garth—Garth Esdras—

MIO.
(*After a pause, coming nearer.*)
Who are you, then? You seem
to know a good deal about me.—Were you sent
to say this?

MIRIAMNE. You said there was death about you! Yes,
but nearer than you think! Let it be as it is—
let it all be as it is, never see this place
nor think of it—forget the streets you came
when you're away and safe! Go before you're seen
or spoken to!

MIO. Will you tell me why?

MIRIAMNE. As I love you
I can't tell you—and I can never see you—

MIO. I walk where I please—

MIRIAMNE. Do you think it's easy for me
to send you away?
(*She steps back as if to go.*)

MIO. Where will I find you then
if I should want to see you?

MIRIAMNE. Never—I tell you
I'd bring you death! Even now. Listen!

(SHADOW *and* TROCK *enter between the bridge and the tenement house.* MIRIAMNE *pulls* MIO *back into the shadow of the rock to avoid being seen.*)

TROCK. Why, fine.

SHADOW. You watch it now—just for the record, Trock—
you're going to thank me for staying away from it
and keeping you out. I've seen men get that way,
thinking they had to plug a couple of guys
and then a few more to cover it up, and then
maybe a dozen more. You can't own all
and territory adjacent, and you can't
slough all the witnesses, because every man
you put away has friends—

TROCK. I said all right.
I said fine.

SHADOW. They're going to find this judge,
and if they find him dead it's just too bad,
and I don't want to know anything about it—
and you don't either.

TROCK. You all through?

SHADOW. Why sure.

TROCK. All right.
We're through, too, you know.

SHADOW. Yeah?
(*He becomes wary.*)

TROCK. Yeah, we're through.

SHADOW. I've heard that said before, and afterwards
somebody died.
(TROCK *is silent.*)
Is that what you mean?

TROCK. You can go.
I don't want to see you.

SHADOW. Sure, I'll go.
Maybe you won't mind if I just find out
what you've got on you. Before I turn my back
I'd like to know.
(*Silently and expertly he touches*

Trock's *pockets, extracting a gun.*)
Not that I'd distrust you,
but you know how it is.
(*He pockets the gun.*)
So long, Trock.

Trock. So long.

Shadow. I won't talk.
You can be sure of that.

Trock. I know you won't.

(Shadow *turns and goes out right, past the rock and along the bank. As he goes the* Two Young Men in Blue Serge *enter from the left and walk slowly after* Shadow. *They look toward* Trock *as they enter and he motions with his thumb in the direction taken by* Shadow. *They follow* Shadow *out without haste.* Trock *watches them disappear, then slips out the way he came.* Mio *comes a step forward, looking after the two men. Two or three shots are heard, then silence.* Mio *starts to run after* Shadow.)

Miriamne. Mio!

Mio. What do you know about this?

Miriamne. The other way,
Mio—quick!

(Carr *slips in from the right, in haste.*)

Carr. Look, somebody's just been shot.
He fell in the river. The guys that did the shooting
ran up the bank.

Mio. Come on.

(Mio *and* Carr *run out right.* Miriamne *watches uncertainly, then slowly turns and walks to the rear door of the tenement. She stands there a moment, looking after* Mio, *then goes in, closing the door.* Carr *and* Mio *return.*)

Carr. There's a rip tide past the point.
You'd never find him.

Mio. No.

Carr. You know a man really ought to carry insurance living around here.—God, it's easy, putting a fellow away. I never saw it done before.

Mio.
(*Looking at the place where* Miriamne *stood.*)
They have it all worked out.

Carr. What are you doing now?

Mio. I have a little business to transact in this neighborhood.

Carr. You'd better forget it.

Mio. No.

Carr. Need any help?

Mio. Well, if I did I'd ask you first. But I don't see how it would do any good. So you keep out of it and take care of yourself.

Carr. So long, then.

Mio. So long, Carr.

Carr.
(*Looking down-stream.*)
He was drifting face up. Must be halfway to the island the way the tide runs.
(*He shivers.*)
God, it's cold here. Well—
(*He goes out to the left.* Mio *sits on the edge of the rock.* Lucia *comes stealthily back from between the bridge and the tenement, goes to the street-piano and wheels it away.* Piny *comes in. They take a look at* Mio, *but say nothing.* Lucia *goes into his shelter and* Piny *into hers.* Mio *rises, looks up at the tenement, and goes out to the left.*)

CURTAIN

ACT TWO

Scene: *The basement as in Scene 2 of Act One. The same evening.* Esdras *sits at the table reading,* Miriamne *is seated at the left, listening and intent. The door of the inner room is half open and* Garth's *violin is heard. He is playing the theme from the third movement of Beethoven's Archduke Trio.* Esdras *looks up.*

Esdras. I remember when I came to the end
of all the Talmud said, and the commentaries,
then I was fifty years old—and it was time
to ask what I had learned. I asked this question
and gave myself the answer. In all the Talmud
there was nothing to find but the names of things,
set down that we might call them by those names
and walk without fear among things known. Since then
I have had twenty years to read on and on
and end with Ecclesiastes. Names of names,

evanid days, evanid nights and days
and words that shift their meaning. Space is time,
that which was is now—the men of tomorrow
live, and this is their yesterday. All things
that were and are and will be, have their being
then and now and to come. If this means little
when you are young, remember it. It will return
to mean more when you are old.

MIRIAMNE. I'm sorry—I
was listening for something.

ESDRAS. It doesn't matter.
It's a useless wisdom. It's all I have,
but useless. It may be there is no time,
but we grow old. Do you know his name?

MIRIAMNE. Whose name?

ESDRAS. Why, when we're young and listen for a step
the step should have a name—

(MIRIAMNE, *not hearing, rises and goes to the window.* GARTH *enters from within, carrying his violin and carefully closing the door.*)

GARTH.
(*As* ESDRAS *looks at him.*)
Asleep.

ESDRAS. He may
sleep on through the whole night—then in the morning
we can let them know.

GARTH. We'd be wiser to say nothing—
let him find his own way back.

ESDRAS. How did he come here?

GARTH. He's not too crazy for that. If he wakes again
we'll keep him quiet and shift him off tomorrow.
Somebody'd pick him up.

ESDRAS. How have I come
to this sunken end of a street, at a life's end—?

GARTH. It was cheaper here—not to be transcendental—
So—we say nothing—?

ESDRAS. Nothing.

MIRIAMNE. Garth, there's no place
in this whole city—not one—
where you wouldn't be safer
than here—tonight—or tomorrow.

GARTH.
(*Bitterly.*)
Well, that may be.
What of it?

MIRIAMNE. If you slipped away and took a place somewhere where Trock couldn't find you—

GARTH. Yes—
using what for money? and why do you think
I've sat here so far—because I love my home
so much? No, but if I stepped round the corner
it'd be my last corner and my last step.

MIRIAMNE. And yet—
if you're here—they'll find you here—
Trock will come again—
and there's worse to follow—

GARTH. Do you want to get me killed?

MIRIAMNE. No.

GARTH. There's no way out of it. We'll wait
and take what they send us.

ESDRAS. Hush! You'll wake him.

GARTH. I've done it.
I hear him stirring now.

(*They wait quietly.* JUDGE GAUNT *opens the door and enters.*)

GAUNT.
(*In the doorway.*)
I beg your pardon—
no, no, be seated—keep your place—I've made
your evening difficult enough, I fear;
and I must thank you doubly for your kindness,
for I've been ill—I know it.

ESDRAS. You're better, sir?

GAUNT. Quite recovered, thank you. Able, I hope,
to manage nicely now. You'll be rewarded
for your hospitality—though at this moment
(*He smiles.*)
I'm low in funds.
(*He inspects his billfold.*)
Sir, my embarrassment
is great indeed—and more than monetary,
for I must own my recollection's vague
of how I came here—how we came together—
and what we may have said. My name is Gaunt,
Judge Gaunt, a name long known in the criminal courts,
and not unhonored there.

ESDRAS. My name is Esdras—
and this is Garth, my son. And Miriamne,
the daughter of my old age.

GAUNT. I'm glad to meet you.
Esdras. Garth Esdras.
(*He passes a hand over his eyes.*)
It's not a usual name.
Of late it's been connected with a case—
a case I knew. But this is hardly the man.
Though it's not a usual name.
(*They are silent.*)
Sir, how I came here,
as I have said, I don't well know. Such things
are sometimes not quite accident.
ESDRAS. We found you
outside our door and brought you in.
GAUNT. The brain
can be overworked, and weary, even when the man
would swear to his good health. Sir, on my word
I don't know why I came here, nor how, nor when,
nor what would explain it. Shall we say the machine
begins to wear? I felt no twinge of it.—
You will imagine how much more than galling
I feel it, to ask my way home—and where I am—
but I do ask you that.
ESDRAS. This is New York City—
or part of it.
GAUNT. Not the best part, I presume?
(*He smiles grimly.*)
No, not the best.
ESDRAS. Not typical, no.
GAUNT. And you—
(*To* GARTH.)
you are Garth Esdras?
GARTH. That's my name.
GAUNT. Well, sir,
(*To* ESDRAS.)
I shall lie under the deepest obligation
if you will set an old man on his path,
for I lack the homing instinct, if the truth
were known. North, east and south mean nothing to me
here in this room.
ESDRAS. I can put you in your way.
GARTH. Only you'd be wiser to wait a while—
if I'm any judge.—
GAUNT. It happens I'm the judge—
(*With stiff humor.*)
in more ways than one. You'll forgive me if I say
I find this place and my predicament
somewhat distasteful.
(*He looks round him.*)

GARTH. I don't doubt you do;
but you're better off here.
GAUNT. Nor will you find it wise
to cross my word as lightly as you seem
inclined to do. You've seen me ill and shaken—
and you presume on that.
GARTH. Have it your way.
GAUNT. Doubtless what information is required
we'll find nearby.
ESDRAS. Yes, sir—the terminal,—
if you could walk so far.
GAUNT. I've done some walking—
to look at my shoes.

(*He looks down, then puts out a hand to steady himself.*)

That—that was why I came—
never mind—it was there—and it's gone.
(*To* GARTH.)
Professor Hobhouse—
that's the name—he wrote some trash about you
and printed it in a broadside.
—Since I'm here I can tell you
it's a pure fabrication—lacking facts
and legal import. Senseless and impudent,
written with bias—with malicious intent
to undermine the public confidence
in justice and the courts. I knew it then—
all he brings out about this testimony
you might have given. It's true I could have called you,
but the case was clear—Romagna was known guilty,
and there was nothing to add. If I've endured
some hours of torture over their attacks
upon my probity—and in this torture
have wandered from my place, wandered perhaps
in mind and body—and found my way to face you—
why, yes, it is so—I know it—I beg of you
say nothing. It's not easy to give up
a fair name after a full half century
of service to a state. It may well rock
the surest reason. Therefore I ask of you
say nothing of this visit.
GARTH. I'll say nothing.
ESDRAS. Nor any of us.
GAUNT. Why, no—for you'd lose, too.
You'd have nothing to gain.
ESDRAS. Indeed we know it.
GAUNT. I'll remember you kindly. When I've returned,

there may be some mystery made of where I was—
we'll leave it a mystery?
GARTH. Anything you say.
GAUNT. Why, now I go with much more peace of mind—
if I can call you friends.
ESDRAS. We shall be grateful
for silence on your part, Your Honor.
GAUNT. Sir—
if there were any just end to be served
by speaking out, I'd speak! There is none. No—
bear that in mind!
ESDRAS. We will, Your Honor.
GAUNT. Then—
I'm in some haste. If you can be my guide,
we'll set out now.
ESDRAS. Yes, surely.
(*There is a knock at the door. The four look at each other with some apprehension.* MIRIAMNE *rises.*)
I'll answer it.
MIRIAMNE. Yes.

(*She goes into the inner room and closes the door.* ESDRAS *goes to the outer door. The knock is repeated. He opens the door.* MIO *is there.*)

ESDRAS. Yes, sir.
MIO. May I come in?
ESDRAS. Will you state your business, sir?
It's late—and I'm not at liberty—
MIO. Why, I might say
that I was trying to earn my tuition fees
by peddling magazines. I could say that,
or collecting old newspapers—paying cash—
highest rates—no questions asked—
(*He looks round sharply.*)
GARTH. We've nothing to sell.
What do you want?
MIO. Your pardon, gentlemen.
My business is not of an ordinary kind,
and I felt the need of this slight introduction
while I might get my bearings. Your name is Esdras,
or they told me so outside.
GARTH. What do you want?
MIO. Is that the name?
GARTH. Yes.
MIO. I'll be quick and brief.
I'm the son of a man who died many years ago
for a pay roll robbery in New England. You
should be Garth Esdras, by what I've heard. You have
some knowledge of the crime, if one can believe
what he reads in the public prints, and it might be
that your testimony, if given, would clear my father
of any share in the murder. You may not care
whether he was guilty or not. You may not know.
But I do care—and care deeply, and I've come
to ask you face to face.
GARTH. To ask me what?
MIO. What do you know of it?
ESDRAS. This man Romagna,
Did he have a son?
MIO. Yes, sir, this man Romagna,
as you choose to call him, had a son, and I
am that son, and proud.
ESDRAS. Forgive me.
MIO. Had you known him,
and heard him speak, you'd know why I'm proud, and why
he was no malefactor.
ESDRAS. I quite believe you.
If my son can help he will. But at this moment,
as I told you—could you, I wonder, come tomorrow,
at your own hour?
MIO. Yes.
ESDRAS. By coincidence
we too of late have had this thing in mind—
there have been comments printed, and much discussion
which we could hardly avoid.
MIO. Could you tell me then
in a word?—What you know—
is it for him or against him?—
that's all I need.
ESDRAS. My son knows nothing.
GARTH. No.
The picture-papers lash themselves to a fury
over any rumor—make them up when they're short
of bedroom slops.—This is what happened. I
had known a few members of a gang one time
up there—and after the murder they picked me up
because I looked like someone that was seen

in what they called the murder car. They held me
a little while, but they couldn't identify me
for the most excellent reason I wasn't there
when the thing occurred. A dozen years later now
a professor comes across this, and sees red
and asks why I wasn't called on as a witness
and yips so loud they syndicate his picture
in all the rotos. That's all I know about it.
I wish I could tell you more.

ESDRAS. Let me say too
that I have read some words your father said,
and you were a son fortunate in your father,
whatever the verdict of the world.

MIO. There are few
who think so, but it's true, and I thank you. Then—
that's the whole story?

GARTH. All I know of it.

MIO. They cover their tracks well, the inner ring
that distributes murder. I came three thousand miles
to this dead end.

ESDRAS. If he was innocent
and you know him so, believe it, and let the others
believe as they like.

MIO. Will you tell me how a man's
to live, and face his life, if he can't believe
that truth's like a fire,
and will burn through and be seen
though it takes all the years there are?
While I stand up and have breath in my lungs
I shall be one flame of that fire;
it's all the life I have.

ESDRAS. Then you must live so.
One must live as he can.

MIO. It's the only way
of life my father left me.

ESDRAS. Yes? Yet it's true
the ground we walk on is impacted down
and hard with blood and bones of those who died
unjustly. There's not one title to land or life,
even your own, but was built on rape and murder,
back a few years. It would take a fire indeed
to burn out all this error.

MIO. Then let it burn down,
all of it!

ESDRAS. We ask a great deal of the world
at first—then less—and then less.
We ask for truth
and justice. But this truth's a thing unknown
in the lightest, smallest matter—and as for justice,
who has once seen it done? You loved your father,
and I could have loved him, for every word he spoke
in his trial was sweet and tolerant, but the weight
of what men are and have, rests heavy on
the graves of those who lost. They'll not rise again,
and their causes lie there with them.

GAUNT. If you mean to say
that Bartolomeo Romagna was innocent,
you are wrong. He was guilty.
There may have been injustice
from time to time, by regrettable chance, in our courts,
but not in that case, I assure you.

MIO. Oh, you assure me!
You lie in your scrag teeth, whoever you are!
My father was murdered!

GAUNT. Romagna was found guilty
by all due process of law, and given his chance
to prove his innocence.

MIO. What chance? When a court
panders to mob hysterics, and the jury
comes in loaded to soak an anarchist
and a foreigner, it may be due process of law
but it's also murder!

GAUNT. He should have thought of that
before he spilled blood.

MIO. He?

GAUNT. Sir, I know too well
that he was guilty.

MIO. Who are you? How do you know?
I've searched the records through, the trial and what
came after, and in all that million words
I found not one unbiased argument
to fix the crime on him.

GAUNT. And you yourself,
were you unprejudiced?

MIO. Who are you?

ESDRAS. Sir,
this gentleman is here, as you are here,

to ask my son, as you have asked, what ground
there might be for this talk of new evidence
in your father's case. We gave him the same answer
we've given you.

MIO. I'm sorry. I'd supposed
his cause forgotten except by myself. There's still
a defense committee then?

GAUNT. There may be. I
am not connected with it.

ESDRAS. He is my guest,
and asks to remain unknown.

MIO.
(*After a pause, looking at* GAUNT.)
The judge at the trial
was younger, but he had your face. Can it be
that you're the man?—Yes—Yes.—The jury charge—
I sat there as a child and heard your voice,
and watched that Brahminical mouth. I knew even then
you meant no good to him. And now you're here
to winnow out truth and justice—the fountain-head
of the lies that slew him! Are you Judge Gaunt?

GAUNT. I am.

MIO. Then tell me what damnation to what inferno
would fit the toad that sat in robes and lied
when he gave the charge, and knew he lied! Judge that,
and then go to your place in that hell!

GAUNT. I know and have known
what bitterness can rise against a court
when it must say, putting aside all weakness,
that a man's to die. I can forgive you that,
for you are your father's son, and you think of him
as a son thinks of his father. Certain laws
seem cruel in their operation; it's necessary
that we be cruel to uphold them. This cruelty
is kindness to those I serve.

MIO. I don't doubt that.
I know who it is you serve.

GAUNT. Would I have chosen
to rack myself with other men's despairs,
stop my ears, harden my heart, and listen only
to the voice of law and light, if I had hoped
some private gain for serving? In all my years
on the bench of a long-established commonwealth
not once has my decision been in question
save in this case. Not once before or since.
For hope of heaven or place on earth, or power
or gold, no man has had my voice, nor will
while I still keep the trust that's laid on me
to sentence and define.

MIO. Then why are you here?

GAUNT. My record's clean. I've kept it so. But suppose
with the best intent, among the myriad tongues
that come to testify, I had missed my way
and followed a perjured tale to a lethal end
till a man was forsworn to death? Could I rest or sleep
while there was doubt of this,
even while there was question in a layman's mind?
For always, night and day,
there lies on my brain like a weight, the admonition:
see truly, let nothing sway you; among all functions
there's but one godlike, to judge. Then see to it
you judge as a god would judge, with clarity,
with truth, with what mercy is found consonant
with order and law. Without law men are beasts,
and it's a judge's task to lift and hold them
above themselves. Let a judge be once mistaken
or step aside for a friend, and a gap is made
in the dykes that hold back anarchy and chaos,
and leave men bond but free.

MIO. Then the gap's been made,
and you made it.

GAUNT. I feared that too. May you be a judge
sometime, and know in what fear,
through what nights long

in fear, I scanned and verified and compared
the transcripts of the trial.

MIO. Without prejudice,
no doubt. It was never in your mind to prove
that you'd been right.

GAUNT. And conscious of that, too—
that that might be my purpose—watchful of that,
and jealous as his own lawyer of the rights
that should hedge the defendant!
And still I found no error,
shook not one staple of the bolts that linked
the doer to the deed! Still following on
from step to step, I watched all modern comment,
and saw it centered finally on one fact—
Garth Esdras was not called. This is Garth Esdras,
and you have heard him. Would his deposition
have justified a new trial?

MIO. No. It would not.

GAUNT. And there I come, myself. If the man were still
in his cell, and waiting, I'd have no faint excuse
for another hearing.

MIO. I've told you that I read
the trial from beginning to end. Every word you spoke
was balanced carefully to keep the letter
of the law and still convict—convict, by Christ,
if it tore the seven veils! You stand here now
running cascades of casuistry, to prove
to yourself and me that no judge of rank and breeding
could burn a man out of hate! But that's what you did
under all your varnish!

GAUNT. I've sought for evidence,
and you have sought. Have you found it? Can you cite
one fresh word in defence?

MIO. The trial itself
was shot full of legerdemain, prearranged to lead
the jury astray—

GAUNT. Could you prove that?

MIO. Yes!

GAUNT. And if
the jury were led astray, remember it's
the jury, by our Anglo-Saxon custom,
that finds for guilt or innocence. The judge
is powerless in that matter.

MIO. Not you! Your charge
misled the jury more than the evidence,
accepted every biased meaning, distilled
the poison for them!

GAUNT. But if that were so
I'd be the first, I swear it, to step down
among all men, and hold out both my hands
for manacles—yes, publish it in the streets,
that all I've held most sacred was defiled
by my own act. A judge's brain becomes
a delicate instrument to weigh men's lives
for good and ill—too delicate to bear
much tampering. If he should push aside
the weights and throw the beam, and say, this once
the man is guilty, and I will have it so
though his mouth cry out from the ground, and all the world
revoke my word, he'd have a short way to go
to madness. I think you'd find him in the squares,
stopping the passers-by with arguments,—
see, I was right, the man was guilty there—
this was brought in against him, this—and this—
and I was left no choice! It's no light thing
when a long life's been dedicate to one end
to wrench the mind awry!

MIO. By your own thesis
you should be mad, and no doubt you are.

GAUNT. But my madness
is only this—that I would fain look back
on a life well spent—without one stain—one breath
of stain to flaw the glass—not in men's minds
nor in my own. I take my God as witness
I meant to earn that clearness, and believe
that I have earned it. Yet my name is clouded
with the blackest, fiercest scandal of our age
that's touched a judge. What I can do to wipe
that smutch from my fame I will. I think you know

how deeply I've been hated, for no cause
that I can find there. Can it not be—
and I ask this
quite honestly—that the great injustice lies
on your side and not mine? Time and time again
men have come before me perfect in their lives,
loved by all who knew them, loved at home,
gentle, not vicious, yet caught so ripe red-handed
in some dark violence there was no denying
where the onus lay.

MIO. That was not so with my father!

GAUNT. And yet it seemed so to me. To other men
who sat in judgment on him. Can you be sure—
I ask this in humility—that you,
who were touched closest by the tragedy,
may not have lost perspective—may have brooded
day and night on one theme—till your eyes are tranced
and show you one side only?

MIO. I see well enough.

GAUNT. And would that not be part of the malady—
to look quite steadily at the drift of things
but see there what you wish—not what is there—
not what another man to whom the story
was fresh would say is there?

MIO. You think I'm crazy.
Is that what you meant to say?

GAUNT. I've seen it happen
with the best and wisest men. I but ask the question.
I can't speak for you. Is it not true wherever
you walk, through the little town where you knew him well,
or flying from it, inland or by the sea,
still walking at your side, and sleeping only
when you too sleep, a shadow not your own
follows, pleading and holding out its hands
to be delivered from shame?

MIO. How you know that
by God I don't know.

GAUNT. Because one spectre haunted you and me—
and haunts you still, but for me it's laid to rest
now that my mind is satisfied. He died
justly and not by error.
(*A pause.*)

MIO.
(*Stepping forward.*)
Do you care to know
you've come so near to death it's miracle
that pulse still beats in your splotchy throat?
Do you know
there's murder in me?

GAUNT. There was murder in your sire,
and it's to be expected! I say he died
justly, and he deserved it!

MIO. Yes, you'd like too well
to have me kill you! That would prove your case
and clear your name, and dip my father's name
in stench forever! You'll not get that from me!
Go home and die in bed, get it under cover,
your lux-et-lex putrefaction of the right thing,
you man that walks like a god!

GAUNT. Have I made you angry
by coming too near the truth?

MIO. This sets him up,
this venomous slug, this sets him up in a gown,
deciding who's to walk above the earth
and who's to lie beneath! And giving reasons!
The cobra giving reasons; I'm a god,
by Buddha, holy and worshipful my fang,
and can I sink it in!
(*He pauses, turns as if to go, then sits.*)
This is no good.
This won't help much.
(*The* JUDGE *and* ESDRAS *look at each other.*)

GAUNT. We should be going.

ESDRAS. Yes.
(*They prepare to go.*)
I'll lend you my coat.

GAUNT.
(*Looking at it with distaste.*)
No, keep it. A little rain
shouldn't matter to me.

ESDRAS. It freezes as it falls,
and you've a long way to go.

GAUNT. I'll manage, thank you.

(GAUNT *and* ESDRAS *go out,* ESDRAS *obsequious, closing the door.*)

GARTH.
(*Looking at* MIO's *back.*)
Well?

MIO.
(*Not moving.*)
Let me sit here a moment.

(GARTH *shrugs his shoulders and goes toward the inner door.* MIRIAMNE *opens it and comes out.* GARTH *looks at her, then at* MIO, *then lays his fingers on his lips. She nods.* GARTH *goes out.* MIRIAMNE *sits and watches* MIO. *After a little he turns and sees her.*)

MIO. How did you come here?
MIRIAMNE. I live here.
MIO. Here?
MIRIAMNE. My name is Esdras. Garth
is my brother. The walls are thin.
I heard what was said.
MIO.
(*Stirring wearily.*)
I'm going. This is no place for me.
MIRIAMNE. What place
would be better?
MIO. None. Only it's better to go.
Just to go.
(*She comes over to him, puts her arm round him and kisses his forehead.*)
MIRIAMNE. Mio.
MIO. What do you want?
Your kisses burn me—and your arms. Don't offer
what I'm never to have! I can have nothing. They say
they'll cross the void sometime to the other planets
and men will breathe in that air.
Well, I could breathe there,
but not here now. Not on this ball of mud.
I don't want it.
MIRIAMNE. They can take away so little
with all their words. For you're a king among them.
I heard you, and loved your voice.
MIO. I thought I'd fallen
so low there was no further, and now a pit
opens beneath. It was bad enough that he
should have died innocent, but if he were guilty—
then what's my life—what have I left to do—?
The son of a felon—and what they spat on me
was earned—and I'm drenched with the stuff.
Here on my hands
and cheeks, their spittle hanging! I liked my hands
because they were like his. I tell you I've lived
by his innocence, lived to see it flash
and blind them all—
MIRIAMNE. Never believe them, Mio,
never.
(*She looks toward the inner door.*)
MIO. But it was truth I wanted, truth—
not the lies you'd tell yourself, or tell a woman,
or a woman tells you! The judge with his cobra mouth
may have spat truth—and I may be mad! For me—
your hands are too clean to touch me. I'm to have
the scraps from hotel kitchens—and instead of love
those mottled bodies that hitch themselves through alleys
to sell for dimes or nickels. Go, keep yourself chaste
for the baker bridegroom—baker and son of a baker,
let him get his baker's dozen on you!
MIRIAMNE. No—
say once you love me—say it once; I'll never
ask to hear it twice, nor for any kindness,
and you shall take all I have!

(GARTH *opens the inner door and comes out.*)

GARTH. I interrupt
a love scene, I believe. We can do without
your adolescent mawkishness.
(*To* MIRIAMNE.)
You're a child.
You'll both remember that.
MIRIAMNE. I've said nothing to harm you—
and will say nothing.
GARTH. You're my sister, though,
and I take a certain interest in you. Where
have you two met?
MIRIAMNE. We danced together.
GARTH. Then
the dance is over, I think.
MIRIAMNE. I've always loved you
and tried to help you, Garth. And you've been kind.
Don't spoil it now.
GARTH. Spoil it now?
MIRIAMNE. Because I love him.
I didn't know it would happen. We danced together.

And the world's all changed. I see you through a mist,
and our father, too. If you brought this to nothing
I'd want to die.

GARTH.
(*To* MIO.)
You'd better go.

MIO. Yes, I know.
(*He rises. There is a trembling knock at the door.* MIRIAMNE *goes to it. The* HOBO *is there shivering.*)

HOBO. Miss, could I sleep under the pipes tonight, miss?
Could I, please?

MIRIAMNE. I think—not tonight.

HOBO. There won't be any more nights—
if I don't get warm, miss.

MIRIAMNE. Come in.

(*The* HOBO *comes in, looks round deprecatingly, then goes to a corner beneath a huge heating pipe, which he crawls under as if he'd been there before.*)

HOBO. Yes, miss, thank you.

GARTH. Must we put up with that?

MIRIAMNE. Father let him sleep there—
last winter.

GARTH. Yes, God, yes.

MIO. Well, good night.

MIRIAMNE. Where will you go?

MIO. Yes, where? As if it mattered.

GARTH. Oh, sleep here, too.
We'll have a row of you under the pipes.

MIO. No, thanks.

MIRIAMNE. Mio, I've saved a little money. It's only
some pennies, but you must take it.
(*She shakes some coins out of a box into her hand.*)

MIO. No, thanks.

MIRIAMNE. And I love you.
You've never said you love me.

MIO. Why wouldn't I love you
when you're clean and sweet,
and I've seen nothing sweet or clean
this last ten years? I love you. I leave you that
for what good it may do you. It's none to me.

MIRIAMNE. Then kiss me.

MIO.
(*Looking at* GARTH.)
With that scowling over us? No.
When it rains, some spring
on the planet Mercury, where the spring comes often,
I'll meet you there, let's say. We'll wait for that.
It may be some time till then.

(*The outside door opens and* ESDRAS *enters with* JUDGE GAUNT, *then, after a slight interval,* TROCK *follows.* TROCK *surveys the interior and its occupants one by one, carefully.*)

TROCK. I wouldn't want to cause you inconvenience,
any of you, and especially the Judge.
I think you know that. You've all got things to do—
trains to catch, and so on. But trains can wait.
Hell, nearly anything can wait, you'll find,
only I can't. I'm the only one that can't
because I've got no time. Who's all this here?
Who's that?
(*He points to the* HOBO.)

ESDRAS. He's a poor half-wit, sir,
that sometimes sleeps there.

TROCK. Come out. I say come out,
whoever you are.
(*The* HOBO *stirs and looks up.*)
Yes, I mean you. Come out.
(*The* HOBO *emerges.*)
What's your name?

HOBO. They mostly call me Oke.

TROCK. What do you know?

HOBO. No, sir.

TROCK. Where are you from?

HOBO. I got a piece of bread.
(*He brings it out, trembling.*)

TROCK. Get back in there!
(*The* HOBO *crawls back into his corner.*)
Maybe you want to know why I'm doing this.
Well, I've been robbed, that's why—
robbed five or six times;
the police can't find a thing—so I'm out for myself—
if you want to know.
(*To* MIO.)
Who are you?

MIO. Oh, I'm a half-wit,
came in here by mistake. The difference is
I've got no piece of bread.

TROCK. What's your name?

MIO. My name?
Theophrastus Such. That's respectable.
You'll find it all the way from here to the coast
on the best police blotters.

Only the truth is we're a little touched in the head,
Oke and me. You'd better ask somebody else.

TROCK. Who is he?

ESDRAS. His name's Romagna. He's the son.

TROCK. Then what's he doing here? You said you were on the level.

GARTH. He just walked in. On account of the stuff in the papers. We didn't ask him.

TROCK. God, we are a gathering. Now if we had Shadow we'd be all here, huh? Only I guess we won't see Shadow. No, that's too much to ask.

MIO. Who's Shadow?

TROCK. Now you're putting questions. Shadow was just nobody, you see. He blew away. It might happen to anyone.
(*He looks at* GARTH.)
Yes, anyone at all.

MIO. Why do you keep your hand in your pocket, friend?

TROCK. Because I'm cold, punk. Because I've been outside and it's cold as the tomb of Christ.
(*To* GARTH.)
Listen, there's a car waiting up at the street to take the Judge home. We'll take him to the car.

GARTH. That's not necessary.

ESDRAS. No.

TROCK. I say it is, see? You wouldn't want to let the Judge walk, would you? The Judge is going to ride where he's going, with a couple of chauffeurs, and everything done in style. Don't you worry about the Judge. He'll be taken care of. For good.

GARTH. I want no hand in it.

TROCK. Anything happens to me happens to you too, musician.

GARTH. I know that.

TROCK. Keep your mouth out of it then. And you'd better keep the punk here tonight, just for luck.
(*He turns toward the door. There is a brilliant lightning flash through the windows, followed slowly by dying thunder.* TROCK *opens the door. The rain begins to pour in sheets.*)
Jesus, somebody tipped it over again!
(*A cough racks him.*)
Wait till it's over. It takes ten days off me every time I step into it.
(*He closes the door.*)
Sit down and wait.
(*Lightning flashes again. The thunder is fainter.* ESDRAS, GARTH *and the* JUDGE *sit down.*)

GAUNT. We were born too early. Even you who are young
are not of the elect. In a hundred years
man will put his finger on life itself, and then
he will live as long as he likes. For you and me
we shall die soon—one day, one year more or less,
when or where, it's no matter. It's what we call
an indeterminate sentence. I'm hungry.
(GARTH *looks at* MIRIAMNE.)

MIRIAMNE. There was nothing left tonight.

HOBO. I've got a piece of bread.
(*He breaks his bread in two and hands half to the* JUDGE.)

GAUNT. I thank you, sir.
(*He eats.*)
This is not good bread.
(*He rises.*)
Sir, I am used
to other company. Not better, perhaps, but their clothes
were different. These are what it's the fashion to call
the underprivileged.

TROCK. Oh, hell!
(*He turns toward the door.*)

MIO.
(*To* TROCK.)
It would seem that you and the Judge know each other.
(TROCK *faces him.*)

TROCK. I've been around.

MIO. Maybe you've met before.

TROCK. Maybe we have.

MIO. Will you tell me where?

TROCK. How long do you want to live?

MIO. How long? Oh, I've got big ideas about that.

TROCK. I thought so. Well, so far I've got nothing against you but your name, see? You keep it that way.

(*He opens the door. The rain still falls in torrents. He closes the door. As he turns from it, it opens again, and* SHADOW, *white, bloodstained and dripping, stands in the doorway* GARTH *rises.* TROCK *turns.*)

GAUNT.
(*To* HOBO.)
Yet if one were careful of his health, ate

sparingly, drank not at all, used himself wisely, it might be that even an old man could live to touch immortality. They may come on the secret sooner than we dare hope. You see? It does no harm to try.

TROCK.

(*Backing away from* SHADOW.)

By God, he's out of his grave!

SHADOW.

(*Leaning against the doorway, holding a gun in his hands.*)

Keep your hands where they belong, Trock.
You know me.

TROCK. Don't! Don't! I had nothing to do with it!

(*He backs to the opposite wall.*)

SHADOW. You said the doctor gave you six months to live—well, I don't give you that much. That's what you had, six months, and so you start bumping off your friends to make sure of your damn six months. I got it from you.
I know where I got it.
Because I wouldn't give it to the Judge.
So he wouldn't talk.

TROCK. Honest to God—

SHADOW. What God?
The one that let you put three holes in me
when I was your friend? Well, He let me get up again
and walk till I could find you. That's as far as I get,
but I got there, by God! And I can hear you
even if I can't see!

(*He takes a staggering step forward.*)

A man needs blood
to keep going.—I got this far.—And now I can't see!
It runs out too fast—too fast—
when you've got three slugs
clean through you.
Show me where he is, you fools! He's here!
I got here!

(*He drops the gun.*)

Help me! Help me! Oh, God! Oh, God!
I'm going to die! Where does a man lie down?
I want to lie down!

(MIRIAMNE *starts toward* SHADOW. GARTH *and* ESDRAS *help him into the next room,* MIRIAMNE *following.* TROCK *squats in his corner, breathing hard, looking at the door.* MIO *stands, watching* TROCK. GARTH *returns, wiping his hand with a handkerchief.* MIO *picks up and pockets the gun.* MIRIAMNE *comes back and leans against the door jamb.*)

GAUNT. You will hear it said that an old man makes a good judge, being calm, clear-eyed, without passion. But this is not true. Only the young love truth and justice. The old are savage, wary, violent, swayed by maniac desires, cynical of friendship or love, open to bribery and the temptations of lust, corrupt and dastardly to the heart. I know these old men. What have they left to believe, what have they left to lose? Whorers of daughters, lickers of girls' shoes, contrivers of nastiness in the night, purveyors of perversion, worshippers of possession! Death is the only radical. He comes late, but he comes at last to put away the old men and give the young their places. It was time.

(*He leers.*)

Here's one I heard yesterday:

Marmaduke behind the barn
got his sister in a fix;
he says damn instead of darn;
ain't he cute? He's only six!

THE HOBO. He, he, he!

GAUNT.

And the hoot-owl hoots all night,
and the cuckoo cooks all day,
and what with a minimum grace of God
we pass the time away.

THE HOBO. He, he, he—I got ya!

(*He makes a sign with his thumb.*)

GAUNT.

(*Sings.*)

And he led her all around
and he laid her on the ground
and he ruffled up the feathers of her cuckoo's nest!

HOBO. Ho, ho, ho!

GAUNT. I am not taken with the way you laugh. You should cultivate restraint.

(ESDRAS *reënters.*)

TROCK. Shut the door.

ESDRAS. He won't come back again.

TROCK. I want the door shut! He was dead, I tell you!

(ESDRAS *closes the door.*)

And Romagna was dead, too, once!
Can't they keep a man under ground?

MIO. No. No more! They don't stay underground any more, and they don't stay under water! Why did you have him killed?

TROCK. Stay away from me! I know you!

MIO. Who am I, then?

TROCK. I know you, damn you! Your name's Romagna!

MIO. Yes! And Romagna was dead, too, and Shadow was dead, but the time's come when you can't keep them down, these dead men! They won't stay down! They come in with their heads shot off and their entrails dragging! Hundreds of them! One by one—all you ever had killed! Watch the door! See!—It moves!

TROCK.
(*Looking, fascinated, at the door.*)
Let me out of here!
(*He tries to rise.*)

MIO.
(*The gun in his hand.*)
Oh, no! You'll sit there and wait for them! One by one they'll come through that door, pulling their heads out of the gunny-sacks where you tied them—glauming over you with their rotten hands! They'll see without eyes and crawl over you—Shadow and the paymaster and all the rest of them—putrescent bones without eyes! Now! Look! Look! For I'm first among them!

TROCK. I've done for better men than you! And I'll do for you!

GAUNT.
(*Rapping on the table.*)
Order, gentlemen, order! The witness will remember that a certain decorum is essential in the court-room!

MIO. By God, he'll answer me!

GAUNT.
(*Thundering.*)
Silence! Silence! Let me remind you of courtesy toward the witness! What case is this you try?

MIO. The case of the state against Bartolomeo Romagna for the murder of the paymaster!

GAUNT. Sir, that was disposed of long ago!

MIO. Never disposed of, never, not while I live!

GAUNT. Then we'll have done with it now! I deny the appeal! I have denied the appeal before and I do so again!

HOBO. He, he!—He thinks he's in the moving pictures!

(*A flash of lightning.*)

GAUNT. Who set that flash! Bailiff, clear the court! This is not Flemington, gentlemen! We are not conducting this case to make a journalistic holiday!

(*The thunder rumbles faintly.* GARTH *opens the outside door and faces a solid wall of rain.*)

Stop that man! He's one of the defendants!

(GARTH *closes the door.*)

MIO. Then put him on the stand!

GARTH. What do you think you're doing?

MIO. Have you any objection?

GAUNT. The objection is not sustained. We will hear the new evidence. Call your witness.

MIO. Garth Esdras!

GAUNT. He will take the stand!

GARTH. If you want me to say what I said before I'll say it!

MIO. Call Trock Estrella then!

GAUNT. Trock Estrella to the stand!

TROCK. No, by God!

MIO. Call Shadow, then! He'll talk! You thought he was dead, but he'll get up again and talk!

TROCK.
(*Screaming.*)
What do you want of me?

MIO. You killed the paymaster! You!

TROCK. You lie! It was Shadow killed him!

MIO. And now I know! Now I know!

GAUNT. Again I remind you of courtesy toward the witness!

MIO. I know them now!
Let me remind you of courtesy toward the dead!
He says that Shadow killed him! If Shadow were here
he'd say it was Trock! There were three men involved
in the new version of the crime for which
my father died! Shadow and Trock Estrella
as principals in the murder—Garth as witness!—
Why are they here together?—and you —the Judge—
why are you here? Why, because you were all afraid
and you drew together out of that fear to arrange
a story you could tell! And Trock killed Shadow
and meant to kill the Judge out of that same fear—

to keep them quiet! This is the thing I've hunted
over the earth to find out, and I'd be blind
indeed if I missed it now!
(*To* GAUNT.)
You heard what he said:
It was Shadow killed him! Now let the night conspire
with the sperm of hell! It's plain beyond denial
even to this fox of justice—and all his words
are curses on the wind! You lied! You lied!
You knew this too!

GAUNT.
(*Low.*)
Let me go. Let me go!

MIO. Then why
did you let my father die?

GAUNT. Suppose it known,
but there are things a judge must not believe
though they should head and fester underneath
and press in on his brain. Justice once rendered
in a clear burst of anger, righteously,
upon a very common laborer,
confessed an anarchist, the verdict found
and the precise machinery of law
invoked to know him guilty—think what furor
would rock the state if the court then flatly said
all this was lies—must be reversed? It's better,
as any judge can tell you, in such cases,
holding the common good to be worth more
than small injustice, to let the record stand,
let one man die. For justice, in the main,
is governed by opinion. Communities
will have what they will have, and it's quite as well,
after all, to be rid of anarchists. Our rights
as citizens can be maintained as rights
only while we are held to be the peers
of those who live about us. A vendor of fish
is not protected as a man might be
who kept a market. I own I've sometimes wished
this was not so, but it is. The man you defend
was unfortunate—and his misfortune bore
almost as heavily on me.—I'm broken—
broken across. You're much too young to know
how bitter it is when a worn connection chars
and you can't remember—can't remember.
(*He steps forward.*)
You
will not repeat this? It will go no further?

MIO. No.
No further than the moon takes the tides—no further
than the news went when he died—
when you found him guilty
and they flashed that round the earth. Wherever men
still breathe and think, and know what's done to them
by the powers above, they'll know. That's all I ask.
That'll be enough.
(TROCK *has risen and looks darkly at* MIO.)

GAUNT. Thank you. For I've said some things
a judge should never say.

TROCK. Go right on talking.
Both of you. It won't get far, I guess.

MIO. Oh, you'll see to that?

TROCK. I'll see to it. Me and some others.
Maybe I lost my grip there just for a minute.
That's all right.

MIO. Then see to it! Let it rain!
What can you do to me now when the night's on fire
with this thing I know? Now I could almost wish
there was a god somewhere—I could almost think
there was a god—and he somehow brought me here
and set you down before me here in the rain
where I could wring this out of you! For it's said,
and I've heard it, and I'm free! He was as I thought him,
true and noble and upright, even when he went
to a death contrived because he was as he was
and not your kind! Let it rain! Let the night speak fire
and the city go out with the tide, for he was a man

and I know you now, and I have my day!

(*There is a heavy knock at the outside door.* MIRIAMNE *opens it, at a glance from* GARTH. *The* POLICEMAN *is there in oilskins.*)

POLICEMAN. Evening.
(*He steps in, followed by a* SERGEANT, *similarly dressed.*)
We're looking for someone
might be here. Seen an old man around
acting a little off?
(*To* ESDRAS.)
You know the one
I mean. You saw him out there. Jeez! You've got
a funny crowd here!
(*He looks round. The* HOBO *shrinks into his corner.*)
That's the one I saw.
What do you think?

SERGEANT. That's him. You mean to say
you didn't know him by his pictures?
(*He goes to* GAUNT.)
Come on, old man.
You're going home.

GAUNT. Yes, sir. I've lost my way.
I think I've lost my way.

SERGEANT. I'll say you have.
About three hundred miles. Now don't you worry.
We'll get you back.

GAUNT. I'm a person of some rank
in my own city.

SERGEANT. We know that. One look at you
and we'd know that.

GAUNT. Yes, sir.

POLICEMAN. If it isn't Trock!
Trock Estrella. How are you, Trock?

TROCK. Pretty good,
Thanks.

POLICEMAN. Got out yesterday again, I hear?

TROCK. That's right.

SERGEANT. Hi'ye, Trock?

TROCK. O.K.

SERGEANT. You know we got orders
to watch you pretty close. Be good now, baby,
or back you go. Don't try to pull anything,
not in my district.

TROCK. No, sir.

SERGEANT. No bumping off.
If you want my advice quit carrying a gun.
Try earning your living for once.

TROCK. Yeah.

SERGEANT. That's an idea.
Because if we find any stiffs on the river bank
we'll know who to look for.

MIO. Then look in the other room!
I accuse that man of murder! Trock Estrella!
He's a murderer!

POLICEMAN. Hello. I remember you.

SERGEANT. Well, what murder?

MIO. It was Trock Estrella
that robbed the pay roll thirteen years ago
and did the killing my father died for! You know
the Romagna case! Romagna was innocent,
and Trock Estrella guilty!

SERGEANT.
(*Disgusted.*)
Oh, what the hell!
That's old stuff—the Romagna case.

POLICEMAN. Hey, Sarge!
(*The* SERGEANT *and* POLICEMAN *come closer together.*)
The boy's a professional kidder. He took me over
about half an hour ago. He kids the police
and then ducks out!

SERGEANT. Oh, yeah?

MIO. I'm not kidding now.
You'll find a dead man there in the next room
and Estrella killed him!

SERGEANT. Thirteen years ago?
And nobody smelled him yet?

MIO.
(*Pointing.*)
I accuse this man
of two murders! He killed the paymaster long ago
and had Shadow killed tonight. Look, look for yourself!
He's there all right!

POLICEMAN. Look, boy. You stood out there
and put the booby sign on the dumb police
because they're fresh out of Ireland. Don't try it twice.

SERGEANT.
(*To* GARTH.)
Any corpses here?

GARTH. Not that I know of.

SERGEANT. I thought so.
(MIO *looks at* MIRIAMNE.)
(*To* MIO.)
Think up a better one.

MIO. Have I got to drag him
out here where you can see him?
(*He goes toward the inner door.*)
Can't you scent a murder
when it's under your nose? Look in!
MIRIAMNE. No, no—there's no one—
there's no one there!
SERGEANT.
(*Looking at* MIRIAMNE.)
Take a look inside.
POLICEMAN. Yes, sir.
(*He goes into the inside room. The* SERGEANT *goes up to the door. The* POLICEMAN *returns.*)
He's kidding, Sarge. If there's a cadaver
in here I don't see it.
MIO. You're blind then!
(*He goes into the room, the* SERGEANT *following him.*)
SERGEANT. What do you mean?
(*He comes out,* MIO *following him.*)
When you make a charge of murder it's better to have
the corpus delicti, son. You're the kind puts in
fire alarms to see the engine!
MIO. By God, he was there!
He went in there to die.
SERGEANT. I'll bet he did.
And I'm Haile Selassie's aunt! What's your name?
MIO. Romagna.
(*To* GARTH.)
What have you done with him?
GARTH. I don't know what you mean.
SERGEANT.
(*To Garth.*)
What's he talking about?
GARTH. I wish I could tell you.
I don't know.
SERGEANT. He must have seen something.
POLICEMAN. He's got
the Romagna case on the brain. You watch yourself,
chump, or you'll get run in.
MIO. Then they're in it together!
All of them!
(*To* MIRIAMNE.)
Yes, and you!
GARTH. He's nuts, I say.
MIRIAMNE.
(*Gently.*)
You have dreamed something—isn't it true?
You've dreamed—
But truly, there was no one—
(MIO *looks at her comprehendingly.*)
MIO. You want me to say it.
(*He pauses.*)
Yes, by God, I was dreaming.
SERGEANT.
(*To* POLICEMAN.)
I guess you're right.
We'd better be going. Haven't you got a coat?
GAUNT. No, sir.
SERGEANT. I guess I'll have to lend you mine.
(*He puts his oilskins on* GAUNT.)
Come on, now. It's getting late.
(GAUNT, *the* POLICEMAN *and the* SERGEANT *go out.*)
TROCK. They're welcome to him.
His fuse is damp. Where is that walking fool
with the three slugs in him?
ESDRAS. He fell in the hall beyond
and we left him there.
TROCK. That's lucky for some of us. Is he out this time
or is he still butting around?
ESDRAS. He's dead.
TROCK. That's perfect.
(*To* MIO.)
Don't try using your firearms, amigo baby,
the Sarge is outside.
(*He turns to go.*)
Better ship that carrion
back in the river! The one that walks when he's dead;
maybe he'll walk the distance for you.
GARTH. Coming back?
TROCK. Well, if I come back,
you'll see me. If I don't, you won't. Let the punk
go far as he likes. Turn him loose and let him go.
And may you all rot in hell.
(*He pulls his coat around him and goes to the left.* MIRIAMNE *climbs up to look out a window.*)
MIRIAMNE. He's climbing up to the street,
along the bridgehead.
(*She turns.*)
Quick, Mio! It's safe now! Quick!
GARTH. Let him do as he likes.
MIRIAMNE. What do you mean? Garth! He means to kill him!
You know that!
GARTH. I've no doubt Master Romagna
can run his own campaign.
MIRIAMNE. But he'll be killed!
MIO. Why did you lie about Shadow?
(*There is a pause.* GARTH *shrugs, walks across the room, and sits.*)
You were one of the gang!

GARTH. I can take a death if I have to!
Go tell your story,
only watch your step, for I warn you,
Trock's out gunning
and you may not walk very far. Oh, I could defend it
but it's hardly worth while.
If they get Trock they get me too.
Go tell them. You owe me nothing.

ESDRAS. This Trock you saw,
no one defends him. He's earned his death so often
there's nobody to regret it. But his crime,
his same crime that has dogged you, dogged us down
from what little we had, to live here among the drains,
where the waterbugs break out like a scrofula
on what we eat—and if there's lower to go
we'll go there when you've told your story. And more
that I haven't heart to speak—

MIO.
(*To* GARTH.)
My father died
in your place. And you could have saved him!
You were one of the gang!

GARTH. Why, there you are.
You certainly owe me nothing.

MIRIAMNE.
(*Moaning.*)
I want to die.
I want to go away.

MIO. Yes, and you lied!
And trapped me into it!

MIRIAMNE. But Mio, he's my brother.
I couldn't give them my brother.

MIO. No. You couldn't.
You were quite right. The gods were damned ironic
tonight, and they've worked it out.

ESDRAS. What will be changed
if it comes to trial again? More blood poured out
to a mythical justice, but your father lying still
where he lies now.

MIO. The bright, ironical gods!
What fun they have in heaven! When a man prays hard
for any gift, they give it, and then one more
to boot that makes it useless.
(*To* MIRIAMNE.)
You might have picked
some other stranger to dance with!

MIRIAMNE. I know.

MIO. Or chosen
some other evening to sit outside in the rain.
But no, it had to be this. All my life long
I've wanted only one thing, to say to the world
and prove it: the man you killed was clean and true
and full of love as the twelve-year-old that stood
and taught in the temple. I can say that now
and give my proofs—and now you stick a girl's face
between me and the rites I've sworn the dead
shall have of me! You ask too much! Your brother
can take his chance! He was ready enough to let
an innocent man take certainty for him
to pay for the years he's had. That parts us, then,
but we're parted anyway, by the same dark wind
that blew us together. I shall say what I have to say.
(*He steps back.*)
And I'm not welcome here.

MIRIAMNE. But don't go now! You've stayed
too long! He'll be waiting!

MIO. Well, is this any safer?
Let the winds blow, the four winds of the world,
and take us to the four winds.
(*The three are silent before him. He turns and goes out.*)

CURTAIN

ACT THREE

SCENE: *The river bank outside the tenement, a little before the close of the previous act. The rain still falls through the street lamps. The* TWO NATTY YOUNG MEN IN BLUE SERGE *are leaning against the masonry in a ray of light, concentrating on a game of chance. Each holds in his hand a packet of ten or fifteen crisp bills. They compare the numbers on the top notes and immediately a bill changes hands. This goes on with varying fortune until the tide begins to run toward the* 1ST GUNMAN, *who has accumulated nearly the whole supply. They play on in complete silence, evidently not wishing to make any noise. Occasionally they raise their heads slightly to look carefully about. Luck begins to favor the* 2ND GUNMAN, *and the notes come his way. Neither evinces the slightest interest in how the game goes. They merely play on, bored, half-absorbed. There is a slight noise at the tenement door. They put the bills away and watch.* TROCK *comes out, pulls the door shut and comes over to them. He says a few words too low to be heard, and without changing expression the* YOUNG MEN *saunter toward the right.* TROCK *goes out to the left, and the* 2ND PLAYER, *catching that out of the corner of his eye, lingers in a glimmer of light to go on with the game. The* 1ST, *with an eye on the tenement door, begins to play without ado, and the bills again shift back and forth, then concentrate in the hands of the* 1ST GUNMAN. *The* 2ND *shrugs his shoulders, searches his pockets, finds one bill, and playing with it begins to win heavily. They hear the door opening, and putting the notes away, slip out in front of the rock.* MIO *emerges, closes the door, looks round him and walks to the left. Near the corner of the tenement he pauses, reaches out his hand to try the rain, looks up toward the street, and stands uncertainly a moment. He returns and leans against the tenement wall.* MIRIAMNE *comes out.* MIO *continues to look off into space as if unaware of her. She looks away.*

MIO. This rather takes one off his high horse.—What I mean, tough weather for a hegira. You see, this is my sleeping suit, and if I get it wet—basta!

MIRIAMNE. If you could only hide here.

MIO. Hide?

MIRIAMNE. Lucia would take you in. The street-piano man.

MIO. At the moment I'm afflicted with claustrophobia. I prefer to die in the open, seeking air.

MIRIAMNE. But you could stay there till daylight.

MIO. You're concerned about me.

MIRIAMNE. Shall I ask him?

MIO. No. On the other hand there's a certain reason in your concern. I looked up the street and our old friend Trock hunches patiently under the warehouse eaves.

MIRIAMNE. I was sure of that.

MIO. And here I am, a young man on a cold night, waiting the end of the rain. Being read my lesson by a boy, a blind boy—you know the one I mean. Knee-deep in the salt-marsh, Miriamne, bitten from within, fought.

MIRIAMNE. Wouldn't it be better if you came back in the house?

MIO. You forget my claustrophobia.

MIRIAMNE. Let me walk with you, then. Please. If I stay beside you he wouldn't dare.

MIO. And then again he might.—We don't speak the same language, Miriamne.

MIRIAMNE. I betrayed you. Forgive me.

MIO. I wish I knew this region. There's probably a path along the bank.

MIRIAMNE. Yes. Shadow went that way.

MIO. That's true, too. So here I am, a young man on a wet night, and blind in my weather eye. Stay and talk to me.

MIRIAMNE. If it happens—it's my fault.

MIO. Not at all, sweet. You warned me to keep away. But I would have it. Now I have to find a way out. It's like a chess game. If you think long enough there's always a way out.—For one or the other.—I wonder why white always wins and black always loses in the problems. White to move and mate in three moves. But what if white were to lose—ah, what then? Why, in that case, obviously black would be white and white would be black.—As it often is.—As we often are.—Might makes white. Losers turn black. Do you think I'd have time to draw a gun?

MIRIAMNE. No.

MIO. I'm a fair shot. Also I'm fair game.

(*The door of the tenement opens and* GARTH *comes out to look about quickly. Seeing only* MIO *and* MIRIAMNE *he goes in and comes out again almost immediately carrying one end of a door on which a body lies covered with a cloth. The* HOBO *carries the other end. They go out to the right with their burden.*)

This is the burial of Shadow, then;
feet first he dips, and leaves the haunts of men.
Let us make mourn for Shadow, wetly lying,
in elegiac stanzas and sweet crying.

Be gentle with him, little cold waves and fishes;
nibble him not, respect his skin and tissues—

MIRIAMNE. Must you say such things?

MIO. My dear, some requiem is fitting over the dead, even for Shadow. But the last rhyme was bad.

Whittle him not, respect his dying wishes.

That's better. And then to conclude:

His aromatic virtues, slowly rising
will circumnamb the isle, beyond disguising.
He clung to life beyond the wont of men.
Time and his silence drink us all. Amen.

How I hate these identicals. The French allow them, but the French have no principles anyway. You know, Miriamne, there's really nothing mysterious about human life. It's purely mechanical, like an electric appliance. Stop the engine that runs the generator and the current's broken. When we think the brain gives off a small electric discharge—quite measurable, and constant within limits. But that's not what makes your hair stand up when frightened.

MIRIAMNE. I think it's a mystery.

MIO. Human life? We'll have to wear veils if we're to keep it a mystery much longer. Now if Shadow and I were made up into sausages we'd probably make very good sausages.

MIRIAMNE. Don't—

MIO. I'm sorry. I speak from a high place, far off, long ago, looking down. The cortège returns.

(GARTH *and the* HOBO *return, carrying the door, the cloth lying loosely over it.*)

I hope you placed an obol in his mouth to pay the ferryman? Even among the Greeks a little money was prerequisite to Elysium.

(GARTH *and the* HOBO *go inside, silent.*)

No? It's grim to think of Shadow lingering among lesser shades on the hither side. For lack of a small gratuity.

(ESDRAS *comes out the open door and closes it behind him.*)

ESDRAS. You must wait here, Mio, or go inside. I know
you don't trust me, and I haven't earned your trust.
You're young enough to seek truth—
and there is no truth;
and I know that—
but I shall call the police and see that you
get safely off.

MIO. It's a little late for that.

ESDRAS. I shall try.

MIO. And your terms? For I daresay you make terms?

ESDRAS. No.

MIO. Then let me remind you what will happen.
The police will ask some questions.
When they're answered
they'll ask more, and before they're done with it
your son will be implicated.

ESDRAS. Must he be?

MIO. I shall not keep quiet.

(*A pause.*)

ESDRAS. Still, I'll go.

MIO. I don't ask help, remember. I make no truce.
He's not on my conscience, and I'm not on yours.

ESDRAS. But you
could make it easier, so easily.
He's my only son. Let him live.

MIO. His chance of survival's
better than mine, I'd say.

ESDRAS. I'll go.

MIO. I don't urge it.

ESDRAS. No. I put my son's life in your hands.
When you're gone,
that may come to your mind.

MIO. Don't count on it.

ESDRAS. Oh,
I count on nothing.

(*He turns to go.* MIRIAMNE *runs over to him and silently kisses his hands.*)

Not mine, not mine, my daughter!
They're guilty hands.

(*He goes out left.* GARTH'S *violin is heard within.*)

MIO. There was a war in heaven
once, all the angels on one side, and all
the devils on the other, and since that time
disputes have raged among the learned, concerning
whether the demons won, or the angels. Maybe
the angels won, after all.

MIRIAMNE. And again, perhaps
there are no demons or angels.

MIO. Oh, there are none.
But I could love your father.

MIRIAMNE. I love him. You see,
he's afraid because he's old. The less one has
to lose the more he's afraid.
MIO. Suppose one had
only a short stub end of life, or held
a flashlight with the batteries run down
till the bulb was dim, and knew that he could live
while the glow lasted. Or suppose one knew
that while he stood in a little shelter of time
under a bridgehead, say, he could live, and then,
from then on, nothing. Then to lie and turn
with the earth and sun, and regard them not in the least
when the bulb was extinguished or he stepped beyond
his circle into the cold? How would he live
that last dim quarter-hour, before he went,
minus all recollection, to grow in grass
between cobblestones?
MIRIAMNE. Let me put my arms round you, Mio.
Then if anything comes, it's for me, too.
(*She puts both arms round him.*)
MIO. Only suppose
this circle's charmed! To be safe until he steps
from this lighted space into dark! Time pauses here
and high eternity grows in one quarter-hour
in which to live.
MIRIAMNE. Let me see if anyone's there—
there in the shadows.
(*She looks toward the right.*)
MIO. It might blast our eternity—
blow it to bits. No, don't go. This is forever,
here where we stand. And I ask you, Miriamne,
how does one spend a forever?
MIRIAMNE. You're frightened?
MIO. Yes.
So much that time stands still.
MIRIAMNE. Why didn't I speak—
tell them—when the officers were here? I failed you
in that one moment!
MIO. His life for mine? Oh, no.
I wouldn't want it, and you couldn't give it.
And if I should go on living we're cut apart
by that brother of yours.
MIRIAMNE. Are we?
MIO. Well, think about it.
A body lies between us, buried in quick-lime.
Your allegiance is on the other side of that grave
and not to me.
MIRIAMNE. No, Mio! Mio, I love you!
MIO. I love you, too, but in case my life went on
beyond that barrier of dark—then Garth
would run his risk of dying.
MIRIAMNE. He's punished, Mio.
His life's been torment to him. Let him go,
for my sake, Mio.
MIO. I wish I could. I wish
I'd never seen him—or you. I've steeped too long
in this thing. It's in my teeth and bones. I can't
let go or forget. And I'll not add my lie
to the lies that cumber his ground. We live our days
in a storm of lies that drifts the truth too deep
for path or shovel; but I've set my foot on a truth
for once, and I'll trail it down!
(*A silence.* MIRIAMNE *looks out to the right.*)
MIRIAMNE. There's someone there—
I heard—

(CARR *comes in from the right.*)

MIO. It's Carr.
CARR. That's right. No doubt about it.
Excuse me.
MIO. Glad to see you. This is Miriamne.
Carr's a friend of mine.
CARR. You're better employed
than when I saw you last.
MIO. Bow to the gentleman,
Miriamne. That's meant for you.
MIRIAMNE. Thank you, I'm sure.
Should I leave you, Mio? You want to talk?
MIO. Oh, no,
we've done our talking.
MIRIAMNE. But—
CARR. I'm the one's out of place—
I wandered back because I got worried about you,
that's the truth.—Oh—those two fellows with the hats
down this way, you know, the ones that ran

after we heard the shooting—they're back again,
lingering or malingering down the bank,
revisiting the crime, I guess. They may mean well.

MIO. I'll try to avoid them.

CARR. I didn't care
for the way they looked at me.—No luck, I suppose,
with that case history? The investigation
you had on hand?

MIO. I can't say. By the way,
the stiff that fell in the water and we saw swirling
down the eddy, he came trudging up, later on,
long enough to tell his name. His name was Shadow,
but he's back in the water now. It's all in an evening.
These things happen here.

CARR. Good God!

MIO. I know.
I wouldn't believe it if you told it.

CARR. But—
the man was alive?

MIO. Oh, not for long! He's dunked
for good this time. That's all that's happened.

CARR. Well,
if you don't need me—

MIRIAMNE. You had a message to send—
have you forgotten—?

MIO. I?—Yes, I had a message—
but I won't send it—not now.

MIRIAMNE. Then I will—!

MIO. No.
Let it go the way it is! It's all arranged
another way. You've been a good scout, Carr,
the best I ever knew on the road.

CARR. That sounds
like making your will.

MIO. Not yet, but when I do
I've thought of something to leave you. It's the view
of Mt. Rainier from the Seattle jail,
snow over cloud. And the rusty chain in my pocket
from a pair of handcuffs my father wore. That's all
the worldly goods I'm seized of.

CARR. Look, Mio—hell—
if you're in trouble—

MIO. I'm not. Not at all. I have
a genius that attends me where I go,
and guards me now. I'm fine.

CARR. Well, that's good news.
He'll have his work cut out.

MIO. Oh, he's a genius.

CARR. I'll see you then.
I'll be at the Grand Street place. I'm lucky tonight,
and I can pay. I could even pay for two.

MIO. Thanks, I may take you up.

CARR. Good night.

MIO. Right, Carr.

CARR.
(*To* MIRIAMNE.)
Good night.

MIRIAMNE.
(*After a pause.*)
Good night.
(CARR *goes out to the left.*)
Why did you do that? He's your genius, Mio,
and you let him go.

MIO. I couldn't help it.

MIRIAMNE. Call him.
Run after him and call him!

MIO. I tried to say it
and it strangled in my throat. I might have known
you'd win in the end.

MIRIAMNE. Is it for me?

MIO. For you?
It stuck in my throat, that's all I know.

MIRIAMNE. Oh, Mio,
I never asked for that! I only hoped
Garth could go clear.

MIO. Well, now he will.

MIRIAMNE. But you—
It was your chance!

MIO. I've lost
my taste for revenge if it falls on you. Oh, God,
deliver me from the body of this death
I've dragged behind me all these years! Miriamne!
Miriamne!

MIRIAMNE. Yes!

MIO. Miriamne, if you love me
teach me a treason to what I am, and have been,
till I learn to live like a man! I think I'm waking
from a long trauma of hate and fear and death
that's hemmed me from my birth—and glimpse a life
to be lived in hope—but it's young in me yet, I can't
get free, or forgive! But teach me how to live
and forget to hate!

MIRIAMNE. He would have forgiven.

MIO. He?

MIRIAMNE. Your father.
(*A pause.*)
MIO. Yes.
(*Another pause.*)
You'll think it strange, but I've never remembered that.
MIRIAMNE. How can I help you?
MIO. You have.
MIRIAMNE. If I were a little older—if I knew
the things to say! I can only put out my hands
and give you back the faith you bring to me
by being what you are. Because to me
you are all hope and beauty and brightness drawn
across what's black and mean!
MIO. He'd have forgiven—
Then there's no more to say—I've groped long enough
through this everglades of old revenges—here
the road ends.—Miriamne, Miriamne,
the iron I wore so long—it's eaten through
and fallen from me. Let me have your arms.
They'll say we're children— Well—the world's made up
of children.
MIRIAMNE. Yes.
MIO. But it's too late for me.
MIRIAMNE. No.
(*She goes into his arms, and they kiss for the first time.*)
Then we'll meet again?
MIO. Yes.
MIRIAMNE. Where?
MIO. I'll write—
or send Carr to you.
MIRIAMNE. You won't forget?
MIO. Forget?
Whatever streets I walk, you'll walk them, too,
from now on, and whatever roof or stars
I have to house me, you shall share my roof
and stars and morning. I shall not forget.
MIRIAMNE. God keep you!
MIO. And keep you. And this to remember!
if I should die, Miriamne, this half-hour
is our eternity. I came here seeking
light in darkness, running from the dawn,
and stumbled on a morning.

(*One of the* YOUNG MEN IN SERGE *strolls in casually from the right, looks up and down without expression, then, seemingly having forgotten something, retraces his steps and goes out.* ESDRAS *comes in slowly from the left. He has lost his hat, and his face is bleeding from a slight cut on the temple. He stands abjectly near the tenement.*)

MIRIAMNE. Father—what is it?
(*She goes towards* ESDRAS.)
ESDRAS. Let me alone.
(*He goes nearer to* MIO.)
He wouldn't let me pass.
The street's so icy up along the bridge
I had to crawl on my knees—he kicked me back
three times—and then he held me there—I swear
what I could do I did! I swear to you
I'd save you if I could.
MIO. What makes you think
that I need saving?
ESDRAS. Child, save yourself if you can!
He's waiting for you.
MIO. Well, we knew that before.
ESDRAS. He won't wait much longer. He'll come here—
he told me so. Those damned six months of his—
he wants them all—and you're to die—you'd spread
his guilt—I had to listen to it—
MIO. Wait—
(*He walks forward and looks casually to the right, then returns.*)
There must be some way up through the
house and out across the roof—
ESDRAS. He's watching that. But come in—
and let me look.—
MIO. I'll stay here, thanks. Once in
and I'm a rat in a deadfall—I'll stay here—
look for me if you don't mind.
ESDRAS. Then watch for me—
I'll be on the roof—
(*He goes in hurriedly.*)
MIO.
(*Looking up.*)
Now all you silent powers
that make the sleet and dark, and never yet
have spoken, give us a sign, let the throw be ours
this once, on this longest night, when the winter sets
his foot on the threshold leading up to spring

and enters with remembered cold—let fall
some mercy with the rain. We are two lovers
here in your night, and we wish to live.

MIRIAMNE. Oh, Mio—
if you pray that way, nothing good will come!
You're bitter, Mio.

MIO. How many floors has this building?

MIRIAMNE. Five or six. It's not as high as the bridge.

MIO. No, I thought not. How many pomegranate seeds
did you eat, Persephone?

MIRIAMNE. Oh, darling, darling,
if you die, don't die alone.

MIO. I'm afraid I'm damned
to hell, and you're not damned at all. Good God,
how long he takes to climb!

MIRIAMNE. The stairs are steep.
(*A slight pause.*)

MIO. I'll follow him.

MIRIAMNE. He's there—at the window—now.
He waves you to go back, not to go in.
Mio, see, that path between the rocks—
they're not watching that—they're out at the river—
I can see them there—they can't watch both—
it leads to a street above.

MIO. I'll try it, then.
Kiss me. You'll hear. But if you never hear—
then I'm the king of hell, Persephone,
and I'll expect you.

MIRIAMNE. Oh, lover, keep safe.

MIO. Good-bye.

(*He slips out quickly between the rocks. There is a quick machine gun rat-tat. The violin stops.* MIRIAMNE *runs toward the path.* MIO *comes back slowly, a hand pressed under his heart.*)

It seems you were mistaken.

MIRIAMNE. Oh, God, forgive me!
(*She puts an arm round him. He sinks to his knees.*)
Where is it, Mio? Let me help you in! Quick, quick,
let me help you!

MIO. I hadn't thought to choose—this—ground—
but it will do.
(*He slips down.*)

MIRIAMNE. Oh, God, forgive me!

MIO. Yes?
The king of hell was not forgiven then,
Dis is his name, and Hades is his home—
and he goes alone—

MIRIAMNE. Why does he bleed so? Mio, if you go
I shall go with you.

MIO. It's better to stay alive.
I wanted to stay alive—because of you—
I leave you that—and what he said to me dying:
I love you, and will love you after I die.
Tomorrow, I shall still love you, as I've loved
the stars I'll never see, and all the mornings
that might have been yours and mine. Oh, Miriamne,
you taught me this.

MIRIAMNE. If only I'd never seen you
then you could live—

MIO. That's blasphemy—Oh, God,
there might have been some easier way of it.
You didn't want me to die, did you, Miriamne—?
You didn't send me away—?

MIRIAMNE. Oh, never, never—

MIO. Forgive me—kiss me—I've got blood on your lips—
I'm sorry—it doesn't matter—I'm sorry—

(ESDRAS *and* GARTH *come out.*)

MIRIAMNE. Mio—
I'd have gone to die myself—you must hear this, Mio,
I'd have died to help you—you must listen, sweet,
you must hear it—
(*She rises.*)
I can die, too, see! You! There!
You in the shadows!—You killed him to silence him!
(*She walks toward the path.*)
But I'm not silenced! All that he knew I know,
and I'll tell it tonight! Tonight—
tell it and scream it
through all the streets—that Trock's a murderer
and he hired you for this murder!
Your work's not done—
and you won't live long! Do you hear?
You're murderers, and I know who you are!
(*The machine gun speaks again. She sinks to her knees.* GARTH *runs to her.*)

GARTH. You little fool!
(*He tries to lift her.*)
MIRIAMNE. Don't touch me!
(*She crawls toward* MIO.)
Look, Mio! They killed me, too. Oh, you can believe me
now, Mio. You can believe I wouldn't hurt you,
because I'm dying! Why doesn't he answer me?
Oh, now he'll never know!
(*She sinks down, her hand over her mouth, choking.* GARTH *kneels beside her, then rises, shuddering. The* HOBO *comes out.* LUCIA *and* PINY *look out.*)
ESDRAS. It lacked only this.
GARTH. Yes.
(ESDRAS *bends over* MIRIAMNE, *then rises slowly.*)
Why was the bastard born? Why did he come here?
ESDRAS. Miriamne—Miriamne—yes, and Mio,
one breath shall call you now—forgive us both—
forgive the ancient evil of the earth
that brought you here—
GARTH. Why must she be a fool?
ESDRAS. Well, they were wiser than you and I. To die
when you are young and untouched, that's beggary
to a miser of years, but the devils locked in synod
shake and are daunted when men set their lives
at hazard for the heart's love, and lose. And these,
who were yet children, will weigh more than all
a city's elders when the experiment
is reckoned up in the end. Oh, Miriamne,
and Mio—Mio, my son—know this where you lie,
this is the glory of earth-born men and women,
not to cringe, never to yield, but standing,
take defeat implacable and defiant,
die unsubmitting. I wish that I'd died so,
long ago; before you're old you'll wish
that you had died as they have. On this star,
in this hard star-adventure, knowing not
what the fires mean to right and left, nor whether
a meaning was intended or presumed,
man can stand up, and look out blind, and say:
in all these turning lights I find no clue,
only a masterless night, and in my blood
no certain answer, yet is my mind my own,
yet is my heart a cry toward something dim
in distance, which is higher than I am
and makes me emperor of the endless dark
even in seeking! What odds and ends of life
men may live otherwise, let them live, and then
go out, as I shall go, and you. Our part
is only to bury them. Come, take her up.
They must not lie here.

(LUCIA *and* PINY *come near to help.* ESDRAS *and* GARTH *stoop to carry* MIRIAMNE.)

CURTAIN

COMMAND DECISION

BY

William Wister Haines

COMMAND DECISION

Command Decision represents the dramatic problems presented by war in the air, during the Second World War. Written by a playwright who had seen active service, it presents an interesting contrast with *André, Shenandoah,* and *Secret Service.* From another point of view, it proves that the language of men at war does not have to be overloaded with profanity or obscenity, which disfigure so much writing of today, that these are really interruptions or mere punctuation in the narrative and have no artistic value.

William Wister Haines was born in Des Moines, Iowa, in 1908, the son of Diedrich Jansen and Ella Wister Haines. His mother has written a large volume of newspaper and magazine fiction and has published three novels. Young Haines attended public and private schools in Des Moines, and the Culver Military Academy. In 1931 he was graduated from the University of Pennsylvania as a Bachelor of Science in Economics.

During College vacations, he had worked as a lineman, and he continued after graduation in the service of several power and light companies, construction companies and finally upon the electrification of the Pennsylvania Railroad.

Mr. Haines' first novel, *Slim,* published by the Atlantic Monthly Press (1934), is a realistic picture of a country boy who becomes a lineman, working for a telegraph company. He is uneducated and Mr. Haines makes no effort to idealize him, either in his fights with his enemy lineman or in his love story with a hospital nurse. There is a realistic picture of the dangerous life and some vivid characters, one of whom meets with a tragic death. His next novel, *High Tension* (1938), continued to be laid among the electrical engineers and linemen on a large project. It is a distinct advance upon *Slim;* the details are better merged in the story, which is dramatic and which has some fine characterizations. The love story is set against a stirring background of danger. Except for his period of military service, Mr. Haines has continued to write short stories for magazines, and motion picture scripts.

In March, 1942, he was commissioned as First Lieutenant in the Army Air Force, in which he served for forty-one months, thirty-three of them overseas. His service lay almost entirely in Intelligence, in various commands, including Headquarters Army Air Forces, 8th Composite Command, 8th Fighter Command, 8th Air Force, and United States Strategic Air Force, serving the last eighteen months of the European War for the latter Command in the office of the Assistant Chief of the Air Staff, Royal Air Force.

In response to the request of the editor for information, Mr. Haines wrote,

"It was during this time that I was struck with the moral responsibilities of command. As a staff officer, specializing in study of our enemy, the German Air Force, I was present, to provide detailed information of my subject, at strategic conferences on all levels of command. I emerged with a deep respect for the trials and in general a profound respect for the men who bore them."

After his application for separation from the Service had been granted, Mr. Haines wrote *Command Decision* as a play. On submitting it to the editor of the *Atlantic Monthly,* the latter requested that it be written in novel form for him and it was printed as a serial in the *Atlantic Monthly* prior to book publication by their Press in 1947. Both this novel and *Slim* were republished in England, and *Command Decision* has also been reprinted in Dutch and in Spanish.

As a play, *Command Decision* was first presented at the Cleveland Playhouse, late in 1946, and at the Fulton Theatre in New York on October 1, 1947. It ran for fifty weeks and then went on tour until January, 1949. It was later made into a moving picture. In 1948 it was published as a play.

Mr. Haines' own words above have given the central motive of the play, the terrific responsibility for the decision by Brigadier General Dennis to continue sending bombing planes to destroy important factories in Germany, even though they go beyond the point where they can be defended by the fliers. The losses have been heavy and there is a silent pressure from the men as well as a voluble pressure from Major General Kane, who has come to visit the Station and who is acutely conscious of public and congressional opinion. He arranges that General Dennis shall be transferred and Brigadier General Garnett shall take over the station. Readers will note the striking close of the play when General Garnett makes his own decision. The personal relationship of the officers, and the death of Colonel Martin are woven into the play without any sentimentality. While the novel gives the author space to describe emotions and motives, the dramatic form is better suited for a topic of this kind, and Mr. Haines' instinct in writing the play first was correct.

The Editor is indebted to Mr. Haines for biographical details. He is also under obligation to Mr. Haines and to his agents, Harold Ober Associates, for permission to reprint the play.

A sympathetic review of *Command Decision* is found in John Mason Brown's *Seeing More Things* (1948), pp. 273–281. See also *Theatre Arts,* Vol. 32 (June–July, 1948), for a foreword to the play, published in that issue, by Mr. Haines.

CAST OF CHARACTERS

First Presented by Kermit Bloomgarden

Fulton Theatre, New York City, October 1, 1947

(in order of appearance)

Tech. Sergeant Harold Evans	James Whitmore
War Correspondent Elmer Brockhurst	Edmon Ryan
Brigadier General K. C. Dennis	Paul Kelly
Colonel Ernest Haley	Edward Binns
Captain Lucius Jenks	Arthur Franz
Enlisted Armed Guard	West Hooker
Major General Roland Goodlow Kane	Jay Fassett
Brigadier General Clifton C. Garnett	Paul McGrath
Major Homer Prescott	William Layton
Colonel Edward Martin	Stephen Elliott
Lt. Jake Goldberg	John Randolph
Major Desmond Lansing	Lewis Martin
Major Belding Davis	Robert Pike
Major Rufus Dayhuff	Walter Black
Mr. Arthur Malcolm	Paul Ford
Mr. Oliver Stone	Frank McNellis
N. C. O. Photographer	Leonard Patrick
Captain G. W. C. Lee	James Holden

The entire action of the play takes place in the office of Brigadier General K. C. Dennis at the Headquarters of the 5th American Bombardment Division, Heavy, in England.

ACT I

About 4 P. M. on a Saturday afternoon.

ACT II

Scene 1. About 10 P. M. the same evening.
Scene 2. Sunday noon, the following day.

ACT III

Sunday, the same day. About 8 P. M.

SETTING

The entire action of the play takes place in the office of Brigadier General K. C. Dennis of the Headquarters of the Fifth American Bombardment Division, Heavy, in England.

This office is the round-roofed end of a large Nissen hut. It is a conventional rectangle with a small alcove running back a few feet upstage R. *Along the* R. *wall, ranged from downstage upward, are a wastebasket labeled "Burn," a low sturdy chest labeled "Division Flag Locker." On wall pegs above "Division Flag Locker" hang General Dennis's helmet, gas mask and service .45 in holster. American, British and Division flags droop from standards on floor. On* R. *of wall of alcove are three filing cabinets, one strap-locked and labeled "Top Secret." On back wall of alcove is a pot-bellied coal stove for heating coffee. In* L. *wall of alcove a door gives on Operations Room; through it as action indicates the teleprinter may be heard clicking.*

The back wall is covered by a curtain over the Status Board and a curtain over the map, both being opened as action indicates. Status Board is a blackboard indicating minute-by-minute operational status of planes and crews in the Division's groups. The map is a G. S. G. S.[1] *1 x 250,000, showing part of England, the Channel and North Sea, and that part of Europe roughly bounded by the 48th Parallel, North, and the 15th Meridian, East. (Note: The scale of this map is approximately one inch to four miles.)*

Over the Status Board is hung a large, ripped-off section of a German fighter plane, its marking cross clearly visible to audience. At L. *of map, by door in back wall, are four light-switches, two for long strip light that illuminates map and one each for lights above General Dennis's desk and the map table. An unmounted souvenir Browning .50 machine gun stands on floor under light switches, erect, barrel wired to wall.*

The door, back wall L., *leads to ante-room of the General's office. Legend, "Commanding General," may be seen in reverse lettering on its opaque glass.* L. *of door in corner are three Tommyguns in a rack. Along* L. *wall, running down, are a fire-extinguisher and A. R. P.*[2] *sand and water buckets and a cot.* L. *wall itself is a large window giving on the perimeter track and landing strips of the Operating Group based on Div. Hq. Airfield. Window is blacked out by curtains in night scenes.*

R. *of* C. *is General Dennis's big flat-topped desk, facing* L., *his name-plate on lower end of it plainly discernible to audience. Arm-chair behind it* (R.) *and one for visitors just before it.* L. *of* C. *is a large (3′ x 6′) map table. There are a chair at its* R., *a draughtsman's stool behind it. A rack under it holds rolls of maps and the "Speed At Altitude, Performance Chart" of the German fighter plane, exhibited as action indicates. A long pointer, for use at map, is kept in this rack. At rise of first act curtain a 1′-½″ step-up is under map table.*

The First Act begins about four o'clock on a Saturday afternoon. The Second is divided; Scene One begins about ten o'clock that Saturday night. Scene Two begins about noon on Sunday, the following day. The Third Act begins about eight o'clock that same Sunday evening.

1 Geographic Survey, General Staff.
2 Air Raid Precaution.

COMMAND DECISION

ACT ONE

Curtain rises on empty room. Coffee bubbles on stove. TECH. SGT. HAROLD EVANS *enters.* EVANS *is a tough, independent graduate gunner of twenty-five who has finished his missions and taken a job as the General's man to improve his food, drink, and amusement.*

He pours himself coffee, goes to desk, selects and lights one of the General's cigars and returns with it to coffee at table.

Settles comfortably to cigar and coffee, then scowls as door opens and War Correspondent ELMER BROCKHURST *enters.* BROCKHURST, *middle-aged, reflects the cocky, contemptuous power of the big magazine he represents.*

BROCKHURST. Is General Dennis in, Sergeant?

EVANS. Does it look like it?

BROCKHURST. Seriously, Joe . . .

EVANS. My name isn't Joe. Who let you in here? (BROCKHURST *goes to mask over wall map; scrutinizes it eagerly.*) Who let you in here?

BROCKHURST. I can't hear you. (EVANS *steps to tommy-gun rack, grabs a gun, ejects shell onto floor, covers* BROCKHURST.) Look out! That thing might go off!

EVANS. *Might,* hell! Who let you in here?

BROCKHURST. I've got a pass.

EVANS. I seen General Dennis tear it up.

BROCKHURST. I've got a new pass, from General Dennis's boss.

EVANS. Walk it over here, slow! (*Scared,* BROCKHURST *does.* EVANS *reads.*) "Elmer Brockhurst, accredited correspondent of *Coverage* . . ." that magazine with all the hatchet murders and naked dames?

BROCKHURST. Yeah.

EVANS. ". . . has my authorization to visit any Army Air Forces installation in my command . . . signed . . ." Who?

BROCKHURST. Major General R. G. Kane . . . that's who.

EVANS. A goddamned old Major General and can't sign his name clear enough to read . . . No . . . this *is* old Percent himself.

(*He racks tommy-gun, returns pass, sits down to coffee. Relieved,* BROCKHURST *turns chummy.*)

BROCKHURST. Percent?

EVANS. Kane . . . cause of that publicity about what percent of Germany his gallant forces destroy every afternoon, weather permitting.

BROCKHURST. He tops your boss, anyway.

EVANS. Keep away from that map. When Dennis sees you, he'll spit a snake.

(BROCKHURST *flinches, pours coffee.*)

BROCKHURST. Where is that Fascist megalomaniac?

EVANS. Who?

BROCKHURST. Dennis, that's what he is, a Fascist megalomaniac.

EVANS. What's that?

BROCKHURST. A man so drunk with power he thinks he can cover anything he does with other people's blood.

EVANS. How long you been around the army?

BROCKHURST. Long enough to know that's what Dennis is.

EVANS. That's what all generals are.

BROCKHURST. Where is he, Serge? Sleeping till the mission comes in?

EVANS. You must love that guardhouse, pumping me about missions.

BROCKHURST. Having Dennis lock me in that guardhouse taught me a lot of angles. What became of that German pilot he had there?

EVANS. That isn't a lot of angles . . . that's one.

BROCKHURST. What about that German fighter plane Dennis has under close guard in Hangar Four . . . the one he's been flying himself lately . . . why did he take the worst losses of the war yesterday and then send his bombers even deeper into Germany today?

EVANS. I thought you knew the angles.

BROCKHURST. I know he's got one of his own squadron Commanders under close arrest in the guardhouse right now. (EVANS *starts,* BROCKHURST *presses his advantage.*) Why?

EVANS. He's a bad boy . . . won't brush his teeth.

BROCKHURST. Don't you guys realize that a free press is your protection?

EVANS. Why don't you write your Congressman?

BROCKHURST. I think he already knows it. Cliff Garnett arrived in England last night by special plane.

EVANS. Who's he?

BROCKHURST. Brigadier General Clifton C. Garnett is Secretary to the United Chiefs of Staff in Washington.

EVANS. Oh, God! Now we'll never get the war over.

BROCKHURST. I'll bet you Dennis's war is over this week.

EVANS. You think they'd fire Dennis for one of them Pentagon bellhops?

BROCKHURST. Serge, ever since General Lucas got killed and Dennis took over here the country's been shuddering at his losses . . . people are whispering . . . calling Dennis the Butcher of Bombardment . . .

EVANS. Oh, my aching back . . .

BROCKHURST. Wait and see! Cliff Garnett should have had this job in the first place . . . he's a smart operator and the United Chiefs trust him.

EVANS. They never fired no general yet till they'd give him the Legion of Merit . . . and Dennis ain't got one.

BROCKHURST. They can give 'em mighty quick. Going to miss your hero?

EVANS. He's no hero to me. I've just taken this job—after my twenty-eight missions—to chisel my way to what I really want.

BROCKHURST. Serge, I know R. G. Kane pretty well . . . what would you like?

EVANS. Bartender . . . in a rest camp . . . for battle-weary WACS.

BROCKHURST. Listen, Serge, Dennis is a ruptured duck. But a couple of angles on this deal would be worth some whiskey to me. What became of that German pilot Dennis had in the guardhouse?

EVANS. Whiskey or Scotch?

BROCKHURST. Bonded bourbon.

EVANS. How much?

BROCKHURST. Four bottles.

EVANS. You gave Peterson in the guardhouse two cases . . . just for making the phone call that got you out of there.

BROCKHURST. I did like hell! I gave Peterson one case . . . (*Stops, realizing he's tricked.*) Okay. Call it a case . . . for the whole story, though.

EVANS. (*Secretively.*) Dennis had him locked in there till last night . . .

BROCKHURST. (*Eagerly.*) Yeah?

EVANS. . . . but yesterday the quartermaster run out of Spam. Dennis said by God he'd promised the men meat for breakfast and if they wasn't no other meat we'd just have to use that Kraut pilot . . .

BROCKHURST. Okay . . . you got your joke . . . I've still got my whiskey.

(BROCKHURST *exits.* EVANS *jumps to phone and speaks into it.*)

EVANS. Guardhouse . . . Corporal Peterson, this is Tech Sergeant Evans in the General's office. Bring six of them twelve marbles you just won . . . you know, them tall glass marbles with labels on 'em, to me personally in the General's ante-room . . . You heard me . . . well, Jesus Christ, I'm giving you half of 'em, ain't I? Okay . . . they better be.

(*Hangs up, listens, puts cigar in ashtray on desk and jumps to attention as* BRIGADIER GENERAL K. C. DENNIS *enters.* DENNIS *is about forty, prepossessing, forceful, usually so preoccupied as to appear slightly absent-minded. Does not notice cigar but hears phone click.*)

DENNIS. Was that for me?

EVANS. No, sir.

DENNIS. Any word since the strike message from the mission?

EVANS. No, sir.

DENNIS. (*Picks up cigar and begins smoking it, his mind on business.*) Ask Colonel Haley to step in and have the guard bring Captain Jenks. (EVANS *exits.* DENNIS *walks to window and studies sky.* COLONEL ERNEST HALEY *enters. He is Regular Army, literal, carries papers.*) Anything more from the mission?

HALEY. Just Colonel Martin's radio I woke you for, sir . . . (*Reads it from paper.*) "Primary target plastered. Warm here. Martin."

DENNIS. "Warm . . ."

HALEY. Intelligence *said* they'd fight today, sir.

DENNIS. What about the weather for tomorrow?

HALEY. No change since last reading, sir.

DENNIS. Good. How many planes can I count on having?

(HALEY *strips curtain mask, revealing Division Status, a welter of chalk columns on a blackboard showing minute-by-minute status of Groups' planes and crews.* EVANS *enters quietly and stands at ease through this.*)

HALEY. Thirteen Minor Repairs promised

by fifteen hundred, eighteen from Major Repair by twenty-three hundred, twenty-two Maidenheads from Modification arriving stations now and thirty of those weatherbound new ones took off from Iceland at eleven hundred this morning, sir.

DENNIS. Are the newcomers from Iceland flying Ferry crews or replacements?

HALEY. Mostly Ferry, sir. But we've got twelve crews back from Flak houses, eighteen from Leave and Sick and twenty-eight new ones from Combat Crew Replacement Center today, sir.

DENNIS. And twelve crews finish their missions today?

HALEY. If they get back, sir.

DENNIS. We lose 'em anyway. How many would graduate tomorrow?

HALEY. Depends on who gets back today, sir.

DENNIS. Well, on averages . . . few enough to hold 'em over for an easy last mission?

HALEY. Fourteen . . . maybe. But they're your lead crews, sir.

DENNIS. How do the boys feel, Haley?

HALEY. They're too tired to feel, sir.

DENNIS. What else?

HALEY. (*Fingering papers unhappily.*) Another rape case, I'm afraid, sir.

DENNIS. Combat crew or base personnel?

HALEY. A navigator, sir.

DENNIS. Nuts. When's a navigator had time to get raped?

HALEY. Complaint was he did the raping, sir. Last night.

DENNIS. Between yesterday's mission, and today's . . . ? Who's complaining, the girl or her mother?

HALEY. Her mother, sir. Mrs. Daphne Magruder, Tranquillity Cottage, The High Street, Undershot-Overhill.

EVANS. I know them people, sir.

DENNIS. No doubt. Did our boy go there alone, Haley?

HALEY. I'm afraid he did, sir.

DENNIS. Haley! I've told you before: when these boys tom-cat, they're to go in pairs. How can you expect one man, flying missions, to keep the whole family happy? Have you told the Judge Advocate?

HALEY. Not yet, sir. We're badly bottlenecked for navigators and this man has ten missions more to go on his twenty-five.

EVANS. Would the General like to square . . . that is, to have this matter attended to by negotiation, sir?

DENNIS. Yes.

EVANS. If I could have two gallons of ice cream from mess supply . . .

DENNIS. Get it and get going.

EVANS. With the General's permission, sir, these matters are better negotiated after dark.

DENNIS. All right. What else, Haley?

HALEY. (*Reading paper unhappily.*) Sir, the Society for the Preservation of Cultural and Artistic Treasurers against Vandalism says it *was* our Division that bombed that cathedral. You remember, sir, the man said he was shot up.

DENNIS. I remember . . . he *was* shot up . . .

HALEY. Yes, sir. But next time out that man got hit himself. He's in the hospital now and says he wants to tell the truth. He says the war's turned him into an Atheist . . . and when he saw he couldn't reach the target with his bombs he threw 'em into that cathedral, just to show God what he thought of His lower echelons.

DENNIS. Could he have got back to base with his bombs?

HALEY. (*Hedging.*) He was deep in France . . . with one motor shot out, sir.

DENNIS. Go to the hospital and chew his ass out. Tell him for me we don't haul bombs through the submarine belt to waste on Atheism or any other religion . . . and it better not happen again. Then write the Society it was an emergency necessary to save life. What else?

HALEY. Nothing official, sir, but . . .

DENNIS. But what?

(HALEY *looks sharply at* EVANS, *who reluctantly exits.*)

HALEY. Grapevine says General Kane's in a huddle with the Hemisphere Commander, sir.

DENNIS. What's that got to do with us?

HALEY. Grapevine says there's a big meeting in Washington next week . . . and neither of them is invited.

DENNIS. That's their worry. (*Then, anxiously.*) What day next week?

HALEY. No one knows, sir.

DENNIS. Well, tomorrow's only Sunday . . . you're sure the weather hasn't changed?

HALEY. No, sir . . . last forecast is still fine.

DENNIS. Well, then we'll finish *before* the meeting.

HALEY. I hope so, sir.

DENNIS. *We* haven't had any squawk from Washington yet . . . ?

HALEY. Not yet, sir.

DENNIS. Send Captain Jenks in here.
HALEY. Want me with you, sir?
DENNIS. No. I'll try him alone again. (*Checks* HALEY *at door.*) Has that cable come for Ted Martin yet?
HALEY. Not yet, sir. I've been checking. Mrs. Martin must be late with that baby.
DENNIS. (*Absently.*) She's ten years late . . . (*Then, noticing* HALEY'S *surprise.*) Keep checking; I'd like to meet Ted with good news when he lands. (HALEY *exits.* DENNIS *takes a troubled look at the sky, seats himself with a dossier of papers at desk. A knock is heard at door.*) Come in!

(CAPTAIN LUCIUS JENKS *enters, followed by an* ARMED GUARD. JENKS *is an ordinary-looking kid in flying coveralls, momentarily sullen.* GUARD *follows him to position facing desk and salutes.*)

GUARD. Guard reporting with prisoner as ordered, sir.
DENNIS. Wait outside. (GUARD *exits.*) Jenks, have you thought this over?
JENKS. (*Stonily.*) I thought it over this morning.
DENNIS. You've had more time.
JENKS. I don't need more time.
DENNIS. Damn it, boy, don't you realize this is serious?
JENKS. I'm not getting killed to make you a record. I'll tell the court so, too, and the whole damned world.
DENNIS. What else will you tell them?
JENKS. That you lost forty bombers, four hundred men, by deliberately sending us beyond fighter cover yesterday. This morning, when we're entitled to a milk run, you order us even further into Germany.
DENNIS. Who told you you were entitled to a milk run?
JENKS. You big boys think flak-fodder like us can't even read a calendar, don't you? Where do the Air Forces get those statistical records for sorties and tonnages that General Kane announces regularly? They get 'em on milk runs, over the Channel Ports, the last three days of every month.
DENNIS. Twelve crews took today's target for their last mission.
JENKS. They didn't have the guts to say what they thought of it. If you big shots are entitled to a record racket, so am I.
DENNIS. You were informed, at briefing, of the purpose of this mission.
JENKS. "A very significant target that can kill a lot of our people unless we knock it out." Nuts to that pep talk! Everything in Germany's made to kill people. Why can't we have targets under fighter cover, like General Kane promised?
DENNIS. He didn't promise that.
JENKS. Anyone who knows the Army knows what Kane's . . .
DENNIS. *General* Kane's . . .
JENKS. . . . General Kane's press interview meant. That day we lost nineteen over Bremfurt and the Air Corps turned itself inside out explaining. How do you think the public will like forty yesterday . . . and worse today?
DENNIS. The public isn't my business.
JENKS. How do you think it will like hearing you ordered both these attacks when Kane . . . General Kane, was absent . . .
DENNIS. And that isn't your business. You were ordered to go. After learning the target you refused.
JENKS. I've been to plenty tough targets.
DENNIS. (*Fingering dossier.*) You aborted from the two toughest prior to yesterday.
JENKS. For mechanical malfunctions in my plane . . .
DENNIS. One engineer's examination said "Possibly justifiable." The other said: "Defect not discernible."
JENKS. It was plenty discernible to me and my co-pilot will tell you the same thing, unless he's prejudiced . . .
DENNIS. He should be; he's flying your seat today, and you're a Squadron Commander . . . The Army had trusted you with Command. (*This bites;* JENKS *has begun to look scared.* DENNIS *resumes patiently.*) Now, if you've got any legitimate reason at all . . .
EVANS. (*Enters, announces with a note of warning.*) Major General R. G. Kane and party, sir.

(DENNIS *jumps to attention as* KANE *and* PARTY *enter.* JENKS *steps into background.* KANE, *a shrewd man of fifty odd, tough but capable of a calculated amiability, which is currently on display, leads. Next comes* BRIGADIER GENERAL CLIFTON C. GARNETT, *a virile man in late thirties, meticulously dressed.* KANE'S *aide,* MAJOR HOMER PRESCOTT, *a genteel stooge, follows.* JENKS *remains in background as* DENNIS *minds his military manners, saluting.* EVANS *exits.*)

DENNIS. I'm very sorry, sir. If I'd known

you were visiting my command I should have been at the gate.

KANE. Don't speak of it, my boy! You remember Cliff Garnett, of course?

DENNIS. (*Offering* GARNETT *hand.*) Sir, I was best man when Ted Martin married Cliff's sister.

GARNETT. Casey, how are you?

DENNIS. Fine.

GARNETT. I want you to know we all felt terribly when Joe Lucas was killed.

(DENNIS *glances at* KANE, *who shakes his head slightly.*)

DENNIS. So did we.

GARNETT. But I don't mind telling you some of us in Washington were mighty glad you were here to take over his job.

KANE. (*Manifestly changing subject.*) Cliff here wanted to see a real operational headquarters, so I brought him straight down without waiting on protocol.

DENNIS. How's the Pentagon, Cliff?

GARNETT. (*Nettled.*) A little worried about you, Casey.

DENNIS. Well, that gives them something to do.

GARNETT. I hope it won't be something we wouldn't like.

DENNIS. Are you over for long?

GARNETT. You never know. My orders just said, "Tour of Observation . . ."

KANE. (*Cutting this off.*) And my new aide, Major Prescott, General Dennis.

PRESCOTT. How *do* you do, sir? I'm very happy to meet the commander of our famous Fifth Division.

BROCKHURST. (*Enters.*) I had a hunch you'd come down here today, R. G.

DENNIS. General Kane, I've forbidden this man the station.

KANE. Now, Casey, that's one of the things I came down about.

DENNIS. He was snooping in a restricted hangar and trying to worm information out of my people. I had him in the guardhouse until your counter-order.

BROCKHURST. Kane, the American people are going to be very interested in Dennis's guardhouse.

KANE. (*Sees* JENKS, *hastens to change subject.*) Why, Captain Jenks! Delighted to see you again, my boy.

JENKS. Thank you, sir.

KANE. (*Throws a paternal arm around* JENKS, *and leads him to* GARNETT.) Cliff, this is one of our real heroes!

GARNETT. Is this the Captain Jenks who named his Fortress the Urgent Virgin?

KANE. The best publicity we've had in this war! Three pages and ten pictures in Brockie's magazine. What brings you to headquarters today, my boy? Helping General Dennis?

DENNIS. A disciplinary matter, sir. We'll attend to it later . . . Jenks!

(DENNIS *indicates door, but* KANE *stops* JENKS.)

KANE. No, no! This is what you wanted to see, Cliff; real field problems. Now, Casey, you and Captain Jenks carry on just as if we weren't here. If there's one thing I pride myself on it's not interfering with the vital work of my Divisions.

DENNIS. This isn't a matter for the press, sir.

KANE. (*Sharply.*) Brockie is my friend, General! (*Then, to* JENKS.) What's the disciplinary trouble, my boy? Some of those high-spirited young pilots of yours getting out of hand?

JENKS. Perhaps General Dennis will explain, sir.

DENNIS. Captain Jenks refused to fly today's mission as ordered, sir.

(BROCKHURST *whistles.* OTHERS *react, shocked.*)

KANE. I can't believe it.

JENKS. Do you know what today's target was, General Kane?

DENNIS. (*Sharply.*) Captain, you're still under Security Regulations. There will be no mention of today's target before the press!

BROCKHURST. Security covers a lot, doesn't it, Dennis?

DENNIS. The life of every man we send across the Channel.

BROCKHURST. What about the life of this boy, under you?

KANE. (*To* BROCKHURST.) Brockie, there *is* a question of Security, if you don't mind.

BROCKHURST. O. K., R. G. I *was* trying to help you. (BROCKHURST *exits.*)

DENNIS. The target was Schweinhafen, sir.

KANE. *Schweinhafen!* You've begun Operation Stitch?

DENNIS. Began yesterday, sir, with Posenleben.

KANE. *Posenleben* . . . yesterday? What happened?

DENNIS. Excellent results, sir. Over three-quarters total destruction.

KANE. I mean . . . what were your losses?

DENNIS. Forty planes, sir.

KANE. *Forty!* Good God! Does the press know it?

DENNIS. I put a security blackout on the whole operation as we agreed.

GARNETT. (*Sharply.*) Would someone mind telling a visitor the details of this Operation Stitch?

DENNIS. Kind of a three-horse parlay, Cliff: Posenleben, Schweinhafen . . . (*Eyes* PRESCOTT *and* JENKS.) And one other.

GARNETT. Well, I thought I'd written your directive myself!

DENNIS. Some things aren't in official directives, Cliff.

GARNETT. Evidently. But the United Chiefs are still running the war, Casey. Have you taken it on yourself to change their orders?

KANE. I was going to send them a provisional plan for Operation Stitch, but . . . (*Lamely.*) I didn't know General Dennis intended implementing it so soon. It takes a very rare weather condition.

PRESCOTT. The whole idea was General Dennis's, sir!

DENNIS. And I'll explain it myself, Major! Do you wish to detain Captain Jenks any further, General Kane?

KANE. (*Wishes he were dead, but he has to deal with this.*) Did you go on the Posenleben mission yesterday, Captain?

JENKS. I did, sir. It was a bloody massacre. Today will be worse.

KANE. Any news from today's mission yet, General?

DENNIS. Colonel Martin radioed: "Primary target plastered," sir.

KANE. I mean news about losses?

DENNIS. Ted indicated fighting, sir, but no details. (GARNETT *reacts perceptibly to mention of Ted.*) I see no further need of Captain Jenks at this conference, sir.

KANE. General, as you know, I pride myself on never interfering with the functioning of my subordinate echelons. But in a case that touches one of our combat personnel, I know you will forgive an older commander's concern. With your permission, I should like to speak to Captain Jenks alone.

DENNIS. (*To* OTHERS, *stonily.*) If you gentlemen will come with me . . .

KANE. No, no. You and Cliff stay right here. We'll step outside.

(KANE, JENKS *and* PRESCOTT *go out.* GARNETT *faces* DENNIS *accusingly.*)

GARNETT. So . . . Ted Martin *is* flying missions!

DENNIS. He led the Division today . . . yesterday, too.

GARNETT. Casey, do you think this is fair to my sister?

DENNIS. Cliff, when Helen married Ted, she married the service.

GARNETT. They've waited ten years for this baby. It's due this week. Ted shouldn't be flying missions at all at his age, let alone just now.

DENNIS. He gets paid to.

GARNETT. (*Starts, checks himself, smiles.*) I went to see your family just before leaving, Casey. I've got some letters for you.

DENNIS. Thanks. How are they?

GARNETT. Fine! And terribly proud of you. That pretty daughter of yours says to tell you she's learned to spell three words.

DENNIS. (*Pleased, covering.*) I hope one of them is "No."

GARNETT. She's a charmer, Casey. And young William Mitchell Dennis sent you special orders. You're to destroy all of Germany except one little piece he wants saved for his first bomb. He asked if I thought you could do it.

DENNIS. What did you tell him?

GARNETT. I told him, with war, you never know.

DENNIS. Let's see . . . he was ten this month. Eight more years would be pretty slow . . . even for the United Chiefs.

GARNETT. (*Nettled.*) Casey, you're too old for this brass-baiting. The United Chiefs have their headaches, too. (*Then, with concern.*) Helen is very worried about Ted.

DENNIS. Is she?

GARNETT. You know that always was the trouble between them.

DENNIS. Was it?

GARNETT. In the old days, when you and he were testing those experimental jobs she got so she couldn't even answer the phone. That's why she wouldn't have kids then: she had no security.

DENNIS. Neither did the other girls, Cliff.

GARNETT. (*Defensively.*) I know she left him. But think of her side of it. Five years in boarding houses on Second Lieutenant's pay. Then the morning he made First he had to call his commanding officer a goddamned fool . . .

DENNIS. That's what he was . . .

GARNETT. . . . maybe. But Ted was a Second Lieutenant again by lunch. That afternoon he turned down twelve thousand a year from the best airline in America. What would you have thought?

DENNIS. That he was a rare guy.

GARNETT. She's realized that, Casey. She did go back to him.
DENNIS. What's all this leading to?
GARNETT. Does Ted think she came back to him and is having that kid just because he *is* pretty secure now?
DENNIS. Ask Ted what he thinks.
GARNETT. He and I were never very close. You know what he thinks of you.
DENNIS. Maybe that's because I don't try to run his life.
GARNETT. You don't have to waste it. Ted is too valuable to be flying missions.
DENNIS. What's more important?
GARNETT. (*Hesitates, evades.*) Casey, the service needs Ted . . . for bigger jobs. And he and Helen deserve a little security now. You don't have to send him at his age.
DENNIS. I don't have to send any of 'em. We could all be secure, under Hitler.

(KANE, JENKS *and* PRESCOTT *enter.* KANE *is grave but more assured.*)

KANE. General Dennis, Captain Jenks is obviously the victim of a shock condition induced by the strain of his nineteen missions. It's a medical problem. All he needs is rest.
DENNIS. Sir, Captain Jenks finished ten days in a rest house on Thursday and has been medically certified fit for the completion of his twenty-five missions.

(KANE *looks apoplectic,* PRESCOTT *scrambles for a new excuse.*)

PRESCOTT. Captain Jenks, did you know of any defect in your plane . . . ?
DENNIS. His co-pilot took the plane. It has not aborted.
KANE. (*Catching the straw.*) We won't know until the plane comes back. We'll continue the investigation later, General.
DENNIS. Guard! (GUARD *enters, takes place behind* JENKS.) Return the prisoner to the guardhouse.

(GUARD *and* JENKS *go out.*)

KANE. General, this is very serious.
DENNIS. Every detail will be checked, sir. It happened at five-twenty this morning. I've got the rest of the twenty-four hours to charge him.
KANE. What charge are you considering?
DENNIS. Unless something new comes up the only possible charge is "Desertion in the face of the enemy."
KANE. Good God, boy! We can't shoot a national hero!
DENNIS. Do you think you'll ever have another tough mission if you don't? At group briefing this morning when the target was uncovered I saw five men cross themselves. One fainted. But they went . . . and they know that Jenks didn't.

(KANE *understands but won't face the implication.* PRESCOTT *tries again.*)

PRESCOTT. Couldn't a quiet transfer be arranged . . . to transport or training?
DENNIS. So he could go yellow there and kill passengers or students?
PRESCOTT. Precautions could be taken. There's such a thing as the end justifying the means, sir. This case would put the honor of the Army Air Forces at stake.
DENNIS. It already has. Every man in the Division knows it.
PRESCOTT. I was thinking of the larger picture.
DENNIS. You can afford to.
KANE. Homer, go talk this over with Elmer Brockhurst . . . everything.
DENNIS. Sir! . . .
KANE. Brockie has a remarkable feel for public reaction, Casey. We've got to consider every angle on this.

(PRESCOTT *exits.* DENNIS *extends* JENKS' *201 file to* KANE.)

DENNIS. Look at the Engineers' reports on his two previous abortions.
KANE. (*Ignoring file.*) Have you talked to his group commander?
DENNIS. Didn't you get yesterday's report, sir?
KANE. No. I've been with the Hemisphere Commander.
DENNIS. Colonel Ledgrave went down yesterday, sir.
KANE. My God! Leddy . . . any parachutes seen?
DENNIS. Two, from the waist. But Leddy was riding with the bombardier and she exploded just as the waist gunners got out.

(KANE *is visibly affected,* GARNETT *shocked.*)

GARNETT. That's Roger Ledgrave, class of '29?
DENNIS. Yeah.
GARNETT. Casey, is it necessary . . . for our own people . . . to go so often?
DENNIS. Yes.
KANE. Casey, had Leddy never mentioned Captain Jenks to you?
DENNIS. Never, sir.
KANE. That's my oversight. I had told him, in confidence, that since that publicity in *Coverage* we've been advised to be very careful of Captain Jenks.
DENNIS. I wish I had been told that, sir.

(*Awkward pause;* GARNETT *breaks it.*)

GARNETT. How soon will today's mission be landing, Casey?

DENNIS. In six or seven minutes.

GARNETT. General Kane, I must insist on being briefed about this Operation Stitch. The United Chiefs will have to know.

DENNIS. (*Shocked.*) Haven't you told him anything about it, sir?

KANE. I thought it would be fairer to let you.

DENNIS. (*Reacts, settles to work.*) Six weeks ago a German fighter plane landed on that Number One strip, right outside the window there.

GARNETT. Shot up?

DENNIS. Not a scratch. The pilot was a Czechoslovakian engineer. He'd been forced to work for them, but when they sent him up to the Baltic to test this job he flew it here to us.

GARNETT. Accommodating of him.

DENNIS. That cross was the plane marking. I hung it there as a reminder.

GARNETT. What kind of fighter was it?

DENNIS. Focke-Schmidt 1.

GARNETT. Focke-Schmidt 1 . . . ?

DENNIS. Remember that spy's report out of Lisbon . . . on a new jet-propelled fighter . . . Messerschmidt wing, the new Serrenbach propulsion unit . . . forty-eight thousand ceiling and six hundred at thirty thousand?

GARNETT. Our people said that was impossible.

DENNIS. I know. These are the tests of it. (DENNIS *strips a curtain mask, revealing performance curves inked on graph paper. Red, blue, green and yellow curves are closely grouped, almost parallel. Above, obviously in a class by itself, is the heavy black curve of the Focke-Schmidt 1.* DENNIS *indicates colors as he talks.*) Lightning, Thunderbolt, Mustang, Spit Twelve and . . . Focke-Schmidt 1!

GARNETT. Jesus Christ! . . . Oh, the German job's in kilometers.

DENNIS. No, it isn't. That's miles . . . same as the others.

GARNETT. Who made these tests?

DENNIS. Ted Martin and I.

GARNETT. Yourselves?

DENNIS. Three turns apiece.

GARNETT. (*Awed, tracing black curve.*) You did that . . . after what the doctors told you?

DENNIS. I wanted to be sure. It gave me a week in the hospital to think things over.

GARNETT. (*Examines curves, impressed, rueful.*) Of course our new Mustangs will be a great improvement.

DENNIS. This isn't an improvement, Cliff. This is a revolution.

GARNETT. Even so, when you get enough of our new Mustangs . . .

DENNIS. Can you arrange an armistice until we get 'em?

GARNETT. Casey, I've battled the United Chiefs for every bomber you've got. I've stuck my neck out to get you Mustangs to protect them. I've fought for this Air Corps just as hard as you have. Now, when will the Germans get these jets?

DENNIS. They have three factories entering line production now . . . or rather, they did have, yesterday morning.

GARNETT. New factories?

DENNIS. No. They're converted old bomber plants. The Czech engineer thinks they've got one operating group on conversion training already.

GARNETT. Have you lost any planes to it?

DENNIS. Lost planes don't report. But last week we wrote off three reconnaissance planes for the first time in months. They were stripped to the ribs and flying at forty thousand, but something got them.

KANE. Of course, we don't *know* it was this new jet.

DENNIS. It wasn't mice. (*Moves to map and opens it.*) I've flown this plane and we've photographed the three factories.

GARNETT. Weren't they camouflaged?

DENNIS. Perfectly. We put an infra-red camera on a night fighter and caught 'em after dark with Focke-Schmidts on every apron. (*Indicates three marked spots on map.*) Posenleben, Schweinhafen and Fendelhorst. That's Operation Stitch, for Stitch in Time . . .

GARNETT. They're deep enough in, aren't they?

DENNIS. Goering is thinking better of us these days.

GARNETT. How far beyond friendly fighter cover is that? (DENNIS *swings the conventional arc; it is woefully short of the marks.*) Casey, it's murder to send bombers that far beyond friendly fighter cover.

KANE. And I don't think it's necessary. This jet fighter may have a superior capability on paper, or even when it's flown by men like Casey and Ted Martin. But when I consider American courage and airmanship . . .

DENNIS. (*Indicating graphed perform-*

ance curves.) Courage and airmanship don't fill gaps like this, sir.

GARNETT. Why hasn't this technical data been reported?

DENNIS. It has. Through channels. You'll hear from it next year.

GARNETT. What's your honest opinion of this, Casey?

DENNIS. This can run us out of Europe in sixty days.

KANE. (*Protestingly.*) That's giving them absolute perfection in production, in testing, in crew conversion, in tactics . . .

DENNIS. That's giving them thirty days to get two groups operating and thirty more to catch one of our missions for just half an hour. I put that in my report.

GARNETT. (*Sharply.*) Why didn't you send this report to us?

(DENNIS *is silent.* KANE *has to answer.*)

KANE. I did report to the United Chiefs that we could not exclude the possibility of encountering an unsuspected enemy capability which might compel retrospective alteration of our present estimate of the situation.

GARNETT. Did you approve this Operation Stitch, sir?

(KANE *glares. But* GARNETT *is secretary to the United Chiefs.*)

KANE. I told General Dennis this constitutes a tactical emergency within the scope of a *Division* Commander's discretion.

DENNIS. It's my rap, Cliff. I consider the operation necessary.

GARNETT. Your losses are the United Chief's rap, Casey. Remember, half of them are Admirals. A very substantial body of opinion doesn't believe we can succeed with daylight precision bombardment over Germany.

DENNIS. A very substantial body of opinion didn't believe the Wright brothers could fly.

GARNETT. Casey, you'll have to know it. The United Chiefs are having a global reallocation meeting next Tuesday.

DENNIS. (*Shocked.*) Global *re*-allocation, next Tuesday?

GARNETT. To review the whole record.

DENNIS. Are they getting cold feet on precision bombardment?

GARNETT. It's making a terrible drain on our best industrial capacity and the very cream of our manpower.

KANE. They were upset about our losses, even before this week.

DENNIS. Cliff, were you sent here to slow us up?

GARNETT. Not specifically; but our people felt I should warn you, because you might even scare the United Chiefs into abandoning our whole B-29 strategy in the Pacific.

KANE. I don't think we're justified in making a third attack tomorrow.

DENNIS. Sir! Concentration is the crux of this! You agreed to that.

GARNETT. Why?

DENNIS. Weather. It may be a month before we can get back to Fendelhorst. That's too long.

(*Overscene comes the faint rising roar of the returning bombers.* ALL *hurry to window.*)

GARNETT. There they come now . . .

DENNIS. Four . . . five . . . eight . . . nine . . .

(*Sound rises and then begins to recede; these planes are passing at a distant tangent.*)

GARNETT. Aren't they going to land here?

DENNIS. Not this group; they're based about ten miles north . . . (*Peers intently as sound of two more planes passes.*) . . . ten . . . eleven . . . I made it eleven.

GARNETT. So did I. What's squadron strength here?

(*Sound fades completely.*)

DENNIS. Twelve . . . if it was a squadron.

KANE. My God! That isn't the remains of a group, is it?

DENNIS. Can't tell yet, sir.

KANE. (*Scared, nervous.*) Find out! (DENNIS *reacts, checks himself, exits.*) Cliff, what will Washington think?

(*Teletype up and off.*)

GARNETT. Sir, they'll think you're running a military bucket shop.

KANE. I was *going* to tell them but I didn't think Casey would be so impetuous. At least we are two-thirds done . . .

(BROCKHURST *and* PRESCOTT *enter.*)

PRESCOTT. Sir, Brockie has some ideas I think you should hear.

(*Muffled ring of phone in Ops room.*)

KANE. What's your reaction, Brockie? Tell us frankly.

BROCKHURST. You want it smooth or rough, R. G.?

KANE. Well, your honest reaction, Elmer.

BROCKHURST. Your neck's out a foot.

KANE. *My* neck . . . ?

BROCKHURST. Unless you can pass the buck

to the Hemisphere Commander. You've got a hero to court martial . . . after record losses yesterday and probably again today. You've let security keep this so dark it stinks like Pearl Harbor . . . (*Faint sound of a single bomber high overhead.*) After all, the public makes these bombers and sends you these kids. It's got a right to know.

(*Teletype up as* DENNIS *enters.*)

KANE. Go on, Elmer. I want General Dennis to hear your reaction.

(*Teletype fades.*)

BROCKHURST. He knows it. I've warned him that the press and public . . .

DENNIS. Press and public be goddamned! Your magazine would crucify us for one headline.

BROCKHURST. When did we *ever* . . . ?

DENNIS. After Bremfurt. We needed a second attack to finish there. But by the time you got done with our losses and Washington got done with your insinuations, we were told it was politically impossible to attack there again. *Politically impossible!* Today boys were killed with cannon made at Bremfurt, since that attack.

BROCKHURST. Dennis, the Air Corps spent twenty years begging us to cry wolf at the public to get you planes. Now you've got 'em all you give us is phony official statements and alibis about security. We were asked to help Washington "prepare the country" for the news about Bremfurt. I'm sorry the plan backfired but it wasn't entirely our fault.

DENNIS. However it happened, the boys are dead.

KANE. Was that a group or a squadron, General?

DENNIS. Next to last group, sir. Some stragglers still coming. (*Overscene comes sound of more approaching bombers.* ALL *hurry to window.*) This must be Ted's group now. (*Sound builds to heavy volume through which closer sounds of individual planes with erratic, missing engines are audible.*) Eighteen . . . twenty-two . . . twenty-three . . . twenty-six . . . (*Group sound fades a little. Individual sound of one plane, engines missing wildly, rises in direct approach to building.*)

KANE. My God! They look ragged today . . .

PRESCOTT. (*To* GARNETT.) They look *much* better in tight formation, sir.

GARNETT. Here's one coming right at us!

PRESCOTT. Look, sir! He's got two feathered props!

BROCKHURST. And half his tail's shot off . . . *Look out!* (*Sound of bomber rises.* BROCKHURST, PRESCOTT *and* GARNETT *throw themselves on floor as plane zooms over with terrific crescendo.* KANE *and* DENNIS *remain erect.* EVANS *enters.*)

EVANS. Colonel Martin's group returning, sir. (*Sound recedes. The three men on floor pick themselves up.*)

PRESCOTT. (*To* GARNETT.) Sorry, sir. They're not *supposed* to buzz the bases.

KANE. I'll have that pilot tried!

DENNIS. He isn't buzzing, sir. He's in trouble. (ALL *hurry back to window as sound rises again in circling approach.*) Good boy, he's lining up to land it!

GARNETT. Why don't they bail out . . . she's only salvage anyway!

DENNIS. (*Furiously.*) Can't you see those red flares? He's got wounded aboard! (*Sound rises again as plane continues circling approach, toward building now.*)

GARNETT. Urgent Virgin! Why, that's Captain Jenks's plane!

PRESCOTT. (*To* KANE, *suggestively.*) You see, sir . . . Captain Jenks's plane *is* in bad condition.

DENNIS. It's come from Germany in that condition. (*Peers tensely. Sound rises as plane roars past window, motors still missing wildly.*) *Jesus!* Look at that wheel . . . (*Shouts desperately through window.*) Pick her up, boy! *Pick her up!!!* (*Sound of plane abates, then comes the grinding, crashing sound of a nose-in. Silence. Then the whole building shakes to a thunderous concussion followed immediately by the sound of siren on meat wagon.*[3] HALEY *enters from Ops room. Teletype up as siren fades.*)

HALEY. Left main gas tank. Total loss, sir.

DENNIS. Can you get the others down here?

HALEY. I've sent them to the other fields, sir. There's plenty of room on most of them now.

DENNIS. What was your count on this gang?

HALEY. Twenty-eight, sir. There may be stragglers.

DENNIS. Did you see Ted's plane?

HALEY. No, sir. It may be landing somewhere else, sir.

DENNIS. Aggregate tomorrow's serviceability as fast as possible. (HALEY *exits. Teletype off as door closes.*)

3 Ambulance.

KANE. (*Horrified.*) *Tomorrow!* This is worse than yesterday.

DENNIS. They got their target, sir.

EVANS. (*Blandly.*) The photographers are waiting outside, General Kane.

(KANE *looks nonplussed.*)

PRESCOTT. (*Takes over; severely.*) What photographers?

EVANS. From Public Relations, sir.

PRESCOTT. Who ordered them and on what authority?

EVANS. I did, sir. All generals have their pictures taken everywhere they go. They say it helps the boys' morale.

KANE. Well, of course, if it helps morale . . . We'll go along, General . . . probably drop in on some of your Group Interrogations.

DENNIS. (*Reaching for cap.*) Very well, sir.

KANE. No, no. I wouldn't think of taking you away from here now.

GARNETT. Casey, I'll have more to say to you about this later.

KANE. Casey, you will not order tomorrow's mission until I get back. (DENNIS *salutes.* EVANS *holds door and then follows as* KANE, PRESCOTT *and* GARNETT *go out.* DENNIS *speaks off to Ops room, voice wracked with fear and nervousness.*)

DENNIS. Haley, haven't you *anything* on Ted yet?

HALEY'S VOICE. (*Off.*) Nothing yet, sir.

DENNIS. (*Walks distractedly about room, gathers himself as* EVANS *enters.*) You're going to wisecrack yourself right into the infantry.

EVANS. Sir, we never would have got rid of 'em without photographers.

DENNIS. They're coming back. Alert the cook.

EVANS. Sir, maybe if I was to speak to the cook . . .

DENNIS. None of that! We'll have to give 'em a good dinner. (EVANS *exits.* DENNIS *circles room distractedly again then slumps wearily against desk as* COLONEL TED MARTIN *enters.* MARTIN *is vigorous, skeptical, in mid-thirties. Looks exhausted but exudes great vitality. Face is smoke-stained and clothes are conspicuously drenched with dried blood.* DENNIS *can hardly speak to him at first.*) Ted . . . you all right?

MARTIN. Not a scratch.

DENNIS. What's that blood?

MARTIN. My radio man.

DENNIS. Bad?

MARTIN. Dead.

DENNIS. Oh. Anyone else?

MARTIN. Not in our plane. Got a drink?

DENNIS. Sure. Aren't they serving combat ration to the crews?

MARTIN. Yeah, but I wanted to see you quick. (DENNIS *extends bottle from desk.* MARTIN *drinks deep, continues drinking through scene.*) Ummm . . . that's better.

DENNIS. What happened?

MARTIN. Twenty-millimeter shell, right on the radio panel. Ummmm, I'm getting old. They should have had this war ten years ago.

DENNIS. How do you think I feel?

MARTIN. (*Contrite, covering.*) Sorry, Grandpa.

DENNIS. Tell me about it. Was it rough all the way?

MARTIN. No. It was a milk run for thirty-four minutes after our fighters had to turn back. Then the whole damned Luftwaffe jumped us . . . (*Grins, drinks.*) Those boys must have a new directive, too. From then back to our fighters we shot our guns hot.

DENNIS. When did you get yours?

MARTIN. Just after I radioed you the strike signal. What about the rest?

DENNIS. Looks like forty-two with two down in the channel, so far.

MARTIN. I was afraid of that, from what I saw.

DENNIS. Did you catch fire?

MARTIN. Yes. We were having it hot and heavy so I stayed on the nose gun and Goldberg went back and put it out. He should get something for that, Casey. One of our waist gunners took one look at that fire and went right out through the bomb bay.

DENNIS. Goldberg can have whatever you recommend.

MARTIN. I'll think it over. Then after things quieted down we tried a tourniquet on the kid, but it was too late. (*Shakes head, drinks.*) Didn't I just see Old Percent and Cliff Garnett in a car?

DENNIS. Yeah. The joint's full of big wheels today.

MARTIN. Did Cliff bring any news from Helen?

DENNIS. Letters. There's no cable. I've been checking.

MARTIN. Casey, did they send Cliff over to stop Operation Stitch?

DENNIS. No. Kane hasn't even told Washington about it.

MARTIN. Then what's Cliff doing here?

DENNIS. Warning us that Washington is nervous.

MARTIN. They didn't have to send him for that.

DENNIS. The big wheels are having a Global Re-allocation meeting Tuesday.

MARTIN. Has Cliff re-allocated himself your job?

DENNIS. I think Cliff's got his eye on one of those B-29 commands in the Pacific. They start with two stars.

EVANS. (*Enters.*) Glad to see you back, Colonel Martin. Sir, where do you want General Garnett's footlocker and bedroll?

MARTIN. General Garnett's footlocker and bedroll . . . so, he is moving in?

EVANS. They just arrived, sir.

DENNIS. Number One guest hut, Sergeant. (EVANS *exits.* MARTIN *rises, massages* DENNIS's *shoulder blades with palm.*)

MARTIN. Well, the handle doesn't stick out anyway, Casey.

DENNIS. Ted, I don't envy you Cliff for a brother-in-law, but he's an able staff officer.

MARTIN. Clifton has flown some of the hottest desks in Washington.

DENNIS. We needed those guys . . . to get planes for hoodlums like you and me.

MARTIN. Casey, no record after this war will be worth a damn without Command in it. Cliff knows this is still the best command in the Air Forces. Any brigadier alive would give his next star for your job.

DENNIS. When I finish Operation Stitch they can have it for Corporal's stripes. Thank God we're two-thirds done.

MARTIN. Casey, that's the hell of it: we aren't.

DENNIS. Ted! Are you sure you're all right?

MARTIN. Yeah. *I'm* all right.

DENNIS. You're tired. You did Posenleben yesterday and Schweinhafen today . . .

MARTIN. (*Forcing the words.*) We didn't touch Schweinhafen today.

DENNIS. (*Strickenly.*) What? You signalled me.

MARTIN. Mistake. Before I could correct it the radio man was dead. We plastered some goddamned place that looked exactly like it, forty miles from Schweinhafen.

DENNIS. Are you sure?

MARTIN. Positive.

DENNIS. How did it happen?

MARTIN. Sighting mistake. It was my fault, Casey. When we came on our bombing run there set a little town that looked more like Schweinhafen than Schweinhafen does; same confluence of rivers, railroad and highways, same cathedral a mile to the left, same phony road on the roof camouflage . . . you'll see it yourself in the strike pictures. I was still on the nose gun but I switched with Goldberg long enough for a look through the bombsight myself. We were both sure of it and Goldberg threw the whole load right down the chimney. The others salvoed into our smoke.

DENNIS. How do you know it wasn't Schweinhafen? Sure you weren't turned around?

MARTIN. I swung east to make sure. There was Schweinhafen with its maidenhead still showing. Did you tell Kane we'd hit it?

DENNIS. Yes. What do you think you did hit?

MARTIN. I don't know. Goldberg's checking maps and photos and target folders now. Whatever it was came apart like a powder mill. Did you get any sleep, Casey?

DENNIS. (*Evasively.*) Of course. Tell me . . .

MARTIN. How much?

DENNIS. About . . . about three hours.

MARTIN. You promised me you'd get five.

DENNIS. I had work to do.

MARTIN. Casey, if you don't take better care of yourself someone else will be doing this work anyway.

DENNIS. Maybe this will give us both a rest.

MARTIN. Forty-four bombers for the wrong target. Why don't you castrate me?

DENNIS. Quit hurting. You've had this coming, Ted. It's averages.

MARTIN. What will this do to Operation Stitch?

DENNIS. Set us back one day. We'll do Schweinhafen again tomorrow and Fendelhorst Monday. I'm pretty sure the weather will hold.

MARTIN. Will Kane . . . with Global Re-allocation coming up Tuesday?

DENNIS. He'll have to.

MARTIN. Casey, he had cold feet before we started.

DENNIS. He's our Chief, Ted.

MARTIN. And a good soldier is loyal to his Chief; it says so in the book. But what kind of loyalty is that . . . to fallible men above him, half the time dopes and cowards? What about loyalty to common sense . . . and to the guys who have to do things that aren't in the book . . . like Stitch?

DENNIS. At least he didn't forbid it, Ted.

MARTIN. Did he authorize it? Did he endorse your report and go on record like a man? Not Kane. You're the goat on this one.

DENNIS. Other guys have been killed. If I get canned . . .

MARTIN. If you get canned, it's the end of honest bombardment here.

DENNIS. We've got to tell him, Ted.

MARTIN. (*With passion.*) You *can't* tell him, Casey! What about the guys we've already lost? If Kane quits now, they're wasted. We either finish now or we might as well take precision bombardment back to Arizona. It's us, or the Germans, this week, boy; and you're the only Commander in this hemisphere with guts enough to see it through.

DENNIS. Which of us is going to tell Kane that?

MARTIN. I'll guarantee Kane won't be able to tell today's strike photos from Schweinhafen. Tomorrow we'll knock off Fendelhorst. Monday, when he orders his usual month-end milk run to the French Channel ports, we'll go back and clean up Schweinhafen.

HALEY. (*Enters.*) Fifty-third Wing reports both of today's reconnaissance planes now *two* hours overdue, sir. (DENNIS *nods.* HALEY *exits.*)

MARTIN. Today it's reconnaissance planes! Six weeks from now it'll be whole divisions of bombers, unless we finish the job.

DENNIS. We'll finish, Ted. We'll make him finish!

MARTIN. (*Aghast.*) Casey, you and I know what Operation Stitch means. How can you tell Kane?

DENNIS. He's our Chief, Ted. He's in command.

CURTAIN

ACT TWO

SCENE I

About ten o'clock, the same evening.

Stage is as before at rise. EVANS *is discovered in a posture of slovenly relaxation in* DENNIS'S *chair.* HALEY *enters to make a change in Status Board.*

HALEY. Where have you been for five hours?

EVANS. Sir, there were two of them women, both unhappy.

HALEY. Only two? That wouldn't have bothered me at your age.

EVANS. Well, sir, I hope it doesn't bother me, at your age.

(HALEY *gapes, then both jump to attention as* DENNIS *enters.*)

DENNIS. Where's the twenty-two hundred weather map for tomorrow?

HALEY. They asked us to hold it, pending further developments, sir.

DENNIS. Bad developments?

HALEY. They didn't say so, sir; they promised them soon.

DENNIS. Bring it as fast as you get it. What about Status?

HALEY. I think I can promise four full groups for tomorrow, sir.

DENNIS. That's including last mission crews?

HALEY. Yes, sir. We're scraping bottom at that.

DENNIS. (*Nods, reluctantly. Sees* EVANS, *covers a grin.*) How did you make out, Sergeant?

EVANS. Mission accomplished, sir.

HALEY. (*With relish.*) Not quite, sir. Mrs. Magruder telephoned again. Now she wants Sergeant Evans billeted in her house . . . for protection.

EVANS. (*Horrified.*) What? . . . Look here, sir . . .

DENNIS. (*Amused, dead pan.*) Sergeant, we've got to get ten more missions out of this navigator.

EVANS. Sir, my oath was to preserve, protect and defend the Constitution of the United States . . .

DENNIS. The United States needs navigators, Sergeant.

EVANS. Sir, I wouldn't do this to an Admiral.

DENNIS. We haven't got an Admiral handy.

HALEY. (*Reluctantly.*) Sir, there's one more point . . . that navigator was killed on the mission today.

DENNIS. (*Wearily, heavily.*) Oh. Have his effects examined, before they're sent home.

HALEY. It's being done, sir.

EVANS. Sir, in the circumstances, may I return to military duty?

DENNIS. Yes.

EVANS. (*Starts out, turns back; solicitously.*) Excuse me, General, but . . . have you had your chow yet?

DENNIS. I'm still expecting General Kane for dinner.

EVANS. He'd be pretty stringy, sir. I'll get you something. (*Exits.*)

HALEY. General, the group commanders are sweating for tomorrow's order.

DENNIS. I can't send it till I find General Kane.

HALEY. They need all the time we can give 'em, sir. Most of our ground crews haven't had their clothes off for three days.

DENNIS. Neither has anyone else . . . except Sergeant Evans. (*Thinks, eyes watch.*) Cut a Field Order Tape using the data for Operation Stitch, Phase Two.

HALEY. Phase *Two* . . . sir?

DENNIS. That's what I said.

HALEY. Yes, sir.

(*Starts for door, smouldering.*)

DENNIS. (*Checks him.*) Ernie—! I'm sorry . . . I'm tired.

HALEY. Roger, sir. You ought to get some sleep, Casey. (*Exits.*)

(DENNIS *slumps on desk, exhausted, face down. Almost sleeps. Then stirs quickly as* MARTIN *enters carrying pictures.*)

MARTIN. Sorry, Casey. Why don't you hit that sack for an hour?

DENNIS. (*Stirring.*) You aren't pretty enough for a nurse.

MARTIN. Have you found Percent yet?

DENNIS. Not a trace . . . I've phoned everywhere.

MARTIN. He must be looking for another photographer.

DENNIS. Are these today's strikes?

MARTIN. All we got. There won't be any reconnaissance, thank God.

(*They eye each other, then scrutinize pictures together.*)

DENNIS. This is the one from your plane?

MARTIN. Yeah. Just as we bombed. And this was from our last plane. Look what Goldberg did to it.

DENNIS. God! It's uncanny; these pictures would fool an expert.

MARTIN. (*Deliberately.*) They'd better.

DENNIS. Why?

MARTIN. If you report this mistake to Kane before that Tuesday meeting, you're just giving your job to Cliff.

DENNIS. I'd like to think so.

MARTIN. (*Indicating cross.*) And you're giving Goering those. Do you like to think that?

DENNIS. No.

MARTIN. These pictures will keep Kane happy for twenty-four hours. He doesn't know a strike photo from a gonorrhoea smear. Why do you have to tell him tonight?

DENNIS. Why did you tell me?

MARTIN. I could trust you.

DENNIS. (*Simply.*) He trusts us.

(*They're deadlocked as* KANE, GARNETT, PRESCOTT *and* BROCKHURST *enter.* MARTIN *conceals pictures.*)

KANE. Forgive us, Casey. We've had dinner.

GARNETT. Ted, old man! I want a good talk with you! How are you?

MARTIN. Still kicking.

KANE. Ted, I'm sorry you had such a rough day today, but when you're leading the Division, I never worry about the target.

DENNIS. Sir, my group commanders have got to have tomorrow's field order.

KANE. That's something we have to discuss, Casey. Cliff, will you explain?

GARNETT. Casey, you may think I've ratted on you but I felt our people had to know what's going on. I persuaded General Kane to let me telephone the Air Board in Washington.

DENNIS. What did they say?

GARNETT. Unfortunately, most of 'em are in Florida . . . at the proving grounds.

DENNIS. Testing a new typewriter?

KANE. Casey, I cannot tolerate this attitude. Our Public Relations Policy has put us where we are today.

DENNIS. It sure has.

BROCKHURST. Dennis, a free democracy cannot ignore public opinion.

DENNIS. Let's take that up when it's free again.

BROCKHURST. What?

DENNIS. The problem now is survival, Mr. Brockhurst. (EVANS *enters with sandwiches.*) They've eaten, Sergeant.

EVANS. Do they know you haven't, sir?

KANE. I'm sorry, Casey. Put them down, Sergeant. We're going soon.

EVANS. That's fine, sir.

(*Unloads tray, dead pan.*)

GARNETT. But I did have a very constructive talk with Lester Blackmer. Lester was shocked, but I think I sold him on persuading the Board to let you finish Operation Stitch . . . after Tuesday.

DENNIS. (*Furiously—to* KANE.) Sir! Did you let that little two-star stooge forbid us . . .

KANE. Certainly not! The Chief prides himself on never letting his personal staff interfere with his field commanders!

GARNETT. Casey, if you'll play ball now, everything will be fine, after Tuesday.

DENNIS. Including the weather . . . in Washington?

GARNETT. You'll get weather again.

DENNIS. When . . . after they've got jets? I've waited five weeks for this weather. Twice we had one good day. This takes three in succession. If we ever got 'em again the big wheels would be after us for headline bombing. Submarine pens! Or covering some State Department fourflush in the Balkans.

GARNETT. Nobody can take the politics out of war. But I made Lester agree that since you *are* two-thirds done . . . (LT. JAKE GOLDBERG *enters with strike photographs.* GOLDBERG *is tough of speech, gentle of manner. Like many good bombardiers he is essentially scholarly. Momentarily he is too preoccupied to notice the visitors.*)

GOLDBERG. I've found the damned thing . . . Oh . . . excuse me, sir. You said when I found it . . .

DENNIS. That's right, come in. General Kane, today's lead bombardier, Lieutenant Goldberg.

KANE. Lieutenant, a member of the big chief's advisory council in Washington just told me on the phone that the chief will be very proud of your mission today. (GOLDBERG *looks bored, but* MARTIN *is sweating bullets; tries to pull him out.*)

MARTIN. Sorry, sir. (*But* KANE *has grabbed pictures.*)

KANE. Look, Cliff! Look! Here's the highway coming in, here's the river . . . here's the factory . . .

GOLDBERG. You've got them upside down, sir.

DENNIS. General Kane, I'd like a minute alone with you, sir.

KANE. Of course, Casey. My God! Look at that destruction, Cliff! These will have to go to Washington by special plane.

PRESCOTT. Sir! I'd like to frame these, dramatically, on good white board, with a title . . . The Doom of Schweinhafen!

KANE. Yes! The very thing, Homer!

GOLDBERG. It isn't Schweinhafen, sir.

KANE. Not Schweinhafen? What are they?

GOLDBERG. The Nautilus Torpedo factory at Gritzenheim, sir.

GARNETT. Torpedo factory! General! This is very opportune! Half the United Chiefs are admirals! If we get these to that meeting . . .

KANE. I'll send my own plane! (*Claps* GOLDBERG *on the shoulder.*) You don't know what you've done for us, boy! Showing them that in the midst of the greatest air campaign in history, we still think enough of the larger picture to knock out a torpedo factory, too . . .

DENNIS. I'm sorry, sir. It wasn't *too.* It was *instead.*

KANE. Instead! You let me tell Washington you'd destroyed Schweinhafen!

DENNIS. It was a mistake. We hit this Nautilus place.

KANE. Whose mistake?

DENNIS. Mine, sir. The briefing . . .

MARTIN. The briefing was perfect. I led the division and I loused it up.

GOLDBERG. These gentlemen are covering for me, sir. I was well briefed and I was on the bombsight. I got mixed up in the fighting.

KANE. (*Is confused, but his chagrin has found a focal point.*) Why did you *get* mixed up . . . were you scared?

GOLDBERG. Yes, sir. I'm always scared. But today . . .

KANE. Casey, what are you thinking of—entrusting a mission of this importance to a man who admits he's . . .

DENNIS. (*Furiously.*) Sir, I should like to explain to you . . .

GOLDBERG. (*To* DENNIS.) It's all right, sir. General Kane doesn't understand.

KANE. Do *you* understand what I'd be justified in doing?

GOLDBERG. You ought to shoot me for wasting four hundred and forty guys this afternoon. I'd be grateful if you did. (*Turns and exits without saluting.*)

DENNIS. Sir! Lieutenant Goldberg is on the fourth mission of a *voluntary second tour of duty over German targets only.*

BROCKHURST. I think I'd take it easy on that one, R. G. (*Too late,* KANE *is stricken with contrition.*)

MARTIN. (*Pours it on him with repressed fury.*) Sir, that boy isn't our Division Bombardier by accident. He knows there's a German order waiting for him by name and serial number. He knew it when he volunteered for a second tour. Today he hit what we both thought was the target . . . perfectly . . . I've just written him up for a cluster on his Silver Star.

KANE. Send the citation to me personally.

MARTIN. (*Sincerely.*) Thank you, sir.

KANE. Ted, how many men in the Division know this mistake?

MARTIN. Most of 'em were too busy fighting to care where we were.

KANE. In any case you might have had a recall or change of target signal en route . . . *mightn't you?*

MARTIN. I might have.

KANE. Cliff, do you think it's fair, to the Service, to report this mistake immediately?

GARNETT. I'd have to think about that, sir.

KANE. We reported the strike in good faith. Now, with two more days on naval targets, under fighter cover, we can average down losses, set sortie and tonnage records, and put the Navy under obligation to us just before that meeting.

DENNIS. And that would be the end of Operation Stitch.

KANE. Casey, let's you and I take these pictures to your light table.

(*They start out.* PRESCOTT *stops them.*)

PRESCOTT. Sir, would you ask Brockie here to help me with the wording of the picture captions? They must be right.

BROCKHURST. I'm not as interested in wordings as I was, R. G.

KANE. We need help, Brockie . . . just as you sometimes need help . . . with the censors.

(BROCKHURST *starts, hesitates, then follows the beaming* PRESCOTT *out through ante-room door.* KANE *and* DENNIS *go out into Ops room.* EVANS *exits.*)

MARTIN. Well, Clifton, do you find travel broadening?

GARNETT. Ted, how long has Casey been like this?

MARTIN. Like what?

GARNETT. So strung up . . . so tense . . . ?

MARTIN. Were you sent here to replace him?

GARNETT. I don't think so.

MARTIN. What does Kane think?

GARNETT. He asked me, confidentially, if I'd been sent to replace him.

MARTIN. Jesus! You haven't done anything bad enough to be a *Major* General, have you?

GARNETT. Same old rebel, aren't you, Ted? Listen, old man, Helen is worried about your flying missions.

MARTIN. My insurance is paid up.

GARNETT. Good God, man! I don't mean that. But you know how she is.

MARTIN. I should. Look, Cliff; neither of us is going to change much. Let's drop it.

GARNETT. But you've got the kid to think of now.

MARTIN. That's the point. This isn't like the old barnstorming and testing. Nobody gets a kick out of this.

GARNETT. Exactly.

MARTIN. But if Goldberg can fly missions for my kid, so can I.

GARNETT. But, Ted, you can do so much more, with your experience.

MARTIN. What?

GARNETT. I've been fighting for bombardment in my own way. Now I think the United Chiefs are going to give me a B-29 command in the Pacific to make me prove what I've been saying.

MARTIN. Aren't those B-29s still a long way off?

GARNETT. No. They're coming faster than anyone realizes. Those jobs will be assigned very soon.

MARTIN. So . . . with a B-29 command you will get two stars?

GARNETT. And a lot of headaches.

MARTIN. Cliff, this is not conference fighting. Can you run an operational command?

GARNETT. Joe Lucas did—until he got killed. Casey's doing it. And I'm going to have something they never had.

MARTIN. What?

GARNETT. Brigadier General Ted Martin —for my Chief of Staff.

MARTIN. Me, a Chief of Staff . . . with all those papers?

GARNETT. Adjutants do that. But I need . . . the Air Corps needs . . . your operating experience out there. Incidentally, I'll be able to make you a brigadier immediately. (MARTIN *ponders deeply while* GARNETT *eyes him tensely.*)

MARTIN. Cliff, did Casey cook this up with you . . . to ground me gently . . . *after today?*

GARNETT. Good Lord, no! He doesn't even know this.

MARTIN. Then he isn't trying to get rid of me?

GARNETT. He'd rather cut his arm off. But he'll understand that the service needs you there . . . and it's your chance to make brigadier. Casey isn't selfish.

MARTIN. If you put it to him that way, he'd make me go.

GARNETT. We'll be a perfect team. I'll fight the Navy and you can fight the Japs . . .

MARTIN. And Helen makes Brigadier's wife. It's very neat, Cliff.

GARNETT. Damn it, Ted, that war's just as much for your kid as this one. Why should you throw yourself away here when by waiting . . . ?

MARTIN. The Germans aren't waiting.

GARNETT. Look, if you'd rather we both ask Casey . . .

MARTIN. No you don't. If you say a word to Casey before I think this over, the deal's off.

GARNETT. All right, but think with your head. Those B-29s can save an invasion against Japan. They can save bloody beach-heads and five years of guerrilla warfare. They've got to have the best we've got, Ted.

MARTIN. What else does Helen want?

GARNETT. She wants you to suggest a godfather for the kid. Naturally we've talked about it, but she wants your views.

MARTIN. Who does she want me to view?

GARNETT. Well, R. G. Kane is going to be a big name . . . (KANE *and* DENNIS *enter.*)

KANE. No man alive could tell these pictures from Schweinhafen . . . (*Pauses —eyes* GARNETT.) Cliff—do the United Chiefs actually study strike photos?

GARNETT. (*Shocked—evasive.*) Well, sir, of course they're not trained photo interpreters themselves, but . . . (PRESCOTT *and* BROCKHURST *enter,* BROCKHURST *is now troubled by what he's seen and heard, but* PRESCOTT *wears the happy flush of creative endeavor.*)

PRESCOTT. Sir. I got some draughtsmen to make three-by-five mountings for the panels . . . before and after pictures . . . on good white board with glossy black lettering . . . the first title will be: "Doom of an Axis Torpedo Factory."

DENNIS. Jesus H. Christ!

KANE. General!

BROCKHURST. (*Respectfully.*) General, I want to get this straight. Isn't a torpedo factory a worthwhile target?

DENNIS. The last one would be. The Germans wouldn't miss the first ten.

BROCKHURST. But you have to make a start, on anything worth while.

DENNIS. Fighting submarines by heavy bombardment is not worth while.

BROCKHURST. The Navy thinks it is. And most people agree.

DENNIS. Most people always think you can get something for nothing, Mr. Brockhurst. We're the only force available to strike the Germans in Germany. To wipe out submarines by bombing would cost us every good weather day for a year.

BROCKHURST. Then why don't the United Chiefs straighten this mess out?

GARNETT. The United Chiefs are half admirals. We have to make some concessions to inter-service coöperation.

DENNIS. Did you get my memorandum to the Anointed Chiefs on that?

KANE. I didn't send it up, Casey. It was too provocative.

DENNIS. I offered the Navy a fair trade. I wrote them I'd bomb any naval target in Germany . . . the day after they took those battleships in and shelled the fighter plane factory at Bremen.

BROCKHURST. Can I use that?

KANE. God, no! Half the United Chiefs are admirals, Brockie.

BROCKHURST. Where did I get the idea this war was against the Axis?

DENNIS. General Kane, *may* I send tomorrow's field order?

KANE. Casey, I can't lose another forty planes over Schweinhafen the day after I've told them I've destroyed it.

DENNIS. Sir, you can release the Division to my discretion.

KANE. Whichever of us got hung, we'd still be sabotaging the Chief.

DENNIS. Would you rather sabotage bombardment, sir?

KANE. Casey, I've spent twenty years working for bombardment. The Chief's spent twenty-five. You kids don't know how we've fought.

MARTIN. No?

KANE. *No!* You're giving your youth. We've already given ours. I was twelve years a *Captain,* the Chief was fourteen. We took Billy Mitchell's side when it meant Siberia. They sent us to a cavalry school. I was the second best pilot in America . . . and they assigned me to keeping records of manure disposal. But we never gave up; we never quit trying. We wrote anything we could get printed, we got down on our knees to Hollywood charlatans for pictures, we did those publicity stunts . . . to educate the public and we kept our own fund for the widows. We tested without parachutes; we flew the mail through solid glue in obsolete training planes. The year Hermann Goering dominated the Munich conference our appropriation wasn't as big as the New York City Public Safety Budget . . . and we bought a lot of congressmen liquor, out of our own pockets, to get it.

BROCKHURST. General, why didn't you tell this story?

KANE. And spell it all out for the Germans? Not that they didn't know and count on it . . . but you don't tell stories in uniform. We were promised fifty thousand planes . . . and our boys were never going to fight in foreign wars . . . so the country went back to sleep and we were called back from stables and rifle ranges to make a modern air force . . . out of promises . . . and what was left over after they gave our planes and instructors to every goddamned ambassador in Washington . . .

BROCKHURST. We were told that was to get experience . . .

KANE. There wasn't any experience of daylight precision bombardment. Both the Germans and British had tried it and said it couldn't be done. The Chief said it could . . . But we'd just begun to get the tools to get started when we were in it ourselves . . . with a double war . . . and a fifty-thousand plane paper air force that didn't add up to fifty serviceable bombers . . . (*Turns to* DENNIS *defensively.*) Casey, if we'd had in Nineteen Forty-one the planes you've lost this week we would have had a Munich with the Japs that would have made Hitler's Munich look like International Rotary!

DENNIS. Sir, we've all fought, all our lives, to get an air force. Now we've got to protect our beginnings.

KANE. From what?

DENNIS. (*Indicating cross.*) Those.

KANE. Those things? They're just our acknowledged enemies. They fight us in the open. Do you remember the fight to get our first experimental Fortress? Do you realize how much the Navy wants our planes for sub-patrol . . . and to protect the repairing of those battleships that air power couldn't hurt? Do you know how much the Army wants our pilots for company commanders? Don't you know the British want us to switch to night area bombardment? Do you know there's a plan to fly infantry supplies into China . . . *with bombers?* Do you know what it means that the United Chiefs are half admirals and the Consolidated Chiefs half British? Don't you realize the fight it's taken for Cliff and the others to get us any planes at all?

GARNETT. He's right, Casey. Washington's at the crossroads on us.

KANE. On Tuesday every one of those factions will be at that meeting with its own pet plan for winning the war by naval blockade, or attrition by defensive, or a good sound saber charge. And you want us to send the Chief in there with three days of prohibitive losses hanging over our theory . . .

DENNIS. Damn it, sir! It's not a theory. Ted demolished Posenleben . . .

KANE. And with time and planes and support we can do the same to every factory in Europe. But the decision is at stake now. It isn't just a few losses this week, or even a lot in six months. The Germans are going to kill more of our people, of course. But they won't be any deader than all the ones who've been killed through the last thirty years to get us air power. You can worry about Germany . . . and you should. But I'm fighting the ground forces and the Navy and the Congress and the White House and the people and the press and our allies. You think I don't know the boys call me Old Percent? You think I've enjoyed spreading this mug of mine around the press like a pregnant heiress? You think I don't know what they could do to me for the statistics I've juggled, the strike photos I've doctored, the reports I've gilded, or suppressed. I know . . . and I'd do it all again! I've spent twenty years watching my friends killed and broken and disgraced and discarded for one single idea . . . to get our goddamned country air power! (*Breaks off, muses, resumes heavily.*) Ted, how did the Germans fight today?

MARTIN. Rough, sir.

KANE. No sign the second day in succession hurts them too?

MARTIN. None we could see, sir.

KANE. What do you think they'll be able to do tomorrow?

MARTIN. They'll fight, sir. They don't stand short on guts over there.

DENNIS. Today's Intelligence Summary's done, sir.

KANE. Is your intelligence officer any good?

DENNIS. He's what we have. He's honest and has sense.

KANE. What is he, a synthetic?

DENNIS. Retread, sir. Artilleryman last time, insurance broker since.

KANE. Probably a good husband and father, too. Well, get him.

DENNIS. (*Into phone.*) Ask Major Lansing to step in at once. (*Goes to door, greets him.* MAJOR DESMOND LANSING *enters. He is gray-haired, self-possessed, wears good last War ribbons.*)

LANSING. Major Lansing reporting as ordered, sir.

DENNIS. General Kane, my Assistant Chief of Staff for Intelligence, Major Lansing.

KANE. What will the Germans do tomorrow, Major?

LANSING. That depends upon where we go, sir.

KANE. If we go back to Schweinhafen?

LANSING. They'll order maximum effort as soon as we cross the tenth Meridian East, sir.

(*Indicates tenth Meridian East on map.*)

KANE. How many will they have serviceable?

LANSING. Enough for a hard fight, sir.

KANE. But we've claimed over a hundred and eighty in the last two days.

LANSING. I'm aware of that, sir.

KANE. You don't believe our claims?

LANSING. No, sir.

KANE. Then why do you report them?

LANSING. Orders from your headquarters, sir.

KANE. Oh. Well, you understand that's necessary for the boys' morale. What do you think of Operation Stitch?

LANSING. It's imperative, sir. We're losing forty-odd bombers to conventional fighters for every worth-while mission now. If they get a hundred jets we'll lose a hundred and forty at a time.

KANE. Do you think the Germans know what we're up to?

LANSING. There's no information on that, sir.

KANE. What would you guess?

LANSING. That they don't, sir.

KANE. Why?

LANSING. The Germans don't like to give their superiors bad news, sir.

BROCKHURST. You shock me, Major.

KANE. How can they help reporting what's happened?

LANSING. Their information has to go up through channels, too, sir.

GARNETT. Is that a sarcasm, Major?

LANSING. It's a fact, sir. *Deutschlandsender* just announced they'd destroyed a hundred and sixty of our bombers today, sir.

BROCKHURST. Doubtless for the German boys' morale.

KANE. Major, do you mean to say that if the Germans guessed the truth about Operation Stitch they wouldn't face it among themselves?

LANSING. That would depend on who did the guessing and who did the facing, sir.

KANE. You evidently don't think much of *their* high Command.

LANSING. That's a personal opinion, sir.

GARNETT. I'd like to know how you form it, Major.

LANSING. My observation, sir, is that most soldiers and particularly air men are afflicted with Narcissism. They don't think about their enemies, they think about themselves because their mechanical problems take up all their time. The consequence is that when they've procured their planes and trained their people and learned their tactics, they have to ask amateurs, like me, what to do with them. When the results are bad they fire the amateurs and make the Commanders Field Marshals.

GARNETT. (*Indignantly.*) We don't have Field Marshals!

LANSING. (*Evenly.*) I happened to be thinking of Goering, sir. The battles of Britain and Malta could have been decisive. But Goering lost his nerve over the early losses and diffused his effort. By the time the truth came out the German Air Force had lost not only its offensive power but its freedom of operation. They will be judging us by their own experience.

KANE. What do you mean by that?

LANSING. The Germans never settled on one decisive target system and paid the price for it. They know that every time we've had bad losses we've switched to easy targets for a while.

KANE. If we hit Schweinhafen tomorrow, will the Germans tumble?

LANSING. You're still asking me to guess, sir. I should guess that after two jet factories in quick succession they would face the truth.

KANE. And concentrate every fighter they have in defense of Fendelhorst on Monday?

LANSING. We'd have to expect it, sir.

KANE. And even so, you think it's worth doing?

LANSING. If you wish to continue precision bombardment, sir.

KANE. Thank you, Major.

(LANSING *salutes and exits.*)

GARNETT. That's a very independent Major you keep, Casey.

KANE. Of course, he's really only a civilian.

HALEY. (*Enters, addresses* DENNIS.) There's a weather report you should hear at once, sir.

(MAJOR BELDING DAVIS, *Division Weather Officer, enters.* HALEY *exits.*)

DENNIS. Come in, Major. General Kane, my Division Weather Officer, Major Davis. Go right ahead, Davis. What is it?

DAVIS. Special Flash from Iceland, sir. Just preliminary, but a very interesting cold mass is forming eccentrically . . .

DENNIS. Never mind the genealogy; what will it do?

DAVIS. Blanket the Continent, if it matures as we expect, sir.

DENNIS. When?

DAVIS. On present indications, late Monday afternoon, sir.

DENNIS. When will it close my bases here?

DAVIS. Best estimate now is about fifteen-hundred Monday, sir.

DENNIS. I always said God must love Willi Messerschmidt!

DAVIS. We'll have more for the midnight weather map, sir.

DENNIS. Bring it as you get it. (DAVIS *exits.* DENNIS *turns to* KANE.) There goes our season's weather, sir. We'll make it these next two days or bite our nails off to the elbow.

GARNETT. Casey, we can't afford two more days of heavy losses now . . . just for a theory.

DENNIS. It's not a theory! Doesn't Washington understand our losses? Do you think the Germans would fight like this if they weren't scared of our bombardment?

KANE. Homer, make a note of that for Washington.

(PRESCOTT *whips out notebook, writes.*)

DENNIS. Cliff, we're doing what no one in this war has been able to do yet. We're making the German Air Force fight, on our *initiative* . . . over Germany, where it doesn't dare to refuse combat in order to rest and rebuild. And we're tearing it up . . . *over Germany!* The German Air Force has been the balance of power in this world, ever since Munich. It took the German army everywhere they've been. It beat the Polish Air Force in three days and the Norwegian in three hours . . . it forced the Maginot Line and beat the French in three weeks . . .

KANE. Homer, get this.

DENNIS. The Royal Air Force did win a brilliant battle from it, over England. It was a defensive battle, the kind we're making *Germany* fight now. Even after that the German Air Force was good enough to knock over Yugoslavia and Greece for practice, to capture Crete and dominate the Mediterranean, to chase the Russians back to Moscow and Stalingrad, to blockade the North Cape and very nearly cut the Atlantic lifeline to England. They would have done it if their High Command had backed them up with a few more planes. Now we've made them switch from bomber production to manufacturing jet fighters. We've made them pull whole Groups off the Russians and away from Rommel and put them over *there* across the Channel, *facing us.* Our own people in the Mediterranean are advancing under aerial supremacy . . .

KANE. Homer, get every word of this . . .

DENNIS. Well, get this too, Homer! The Germans know this better than we do. But they're retreating from their costliest conquests and they've broken the balance of their whole air force for just one thing. They know that Fighters, Hurricanes and Spits saved England from either decisive bombardment or invasion. They're developing these jets to make Europe as impregnable as the British made England. And they're going to do it, just as surely as we sit here with our fingers in our asses and let them!

PRESCOTT. Do you want that in, too, sir?

KANE. Not exactly that. Don't take any more. Casey, I agree with you entirely, but we've got to wait.

DENNIS. Sirs, wars are lost by waiting. The Allies waited at Munich. The French and British waited, behind the Maginot Line. The Germans waited, to invade England. The Russians waited, until they had to fight without an Allied Army in the field. We waited, for a little more strength, to coerce Japan. Now we're forcing the fighting . . . But if we wait for the cycle to swing again, we'll be waiting for the Germans to put a roof on the continent, to neutralize the Russians and then to confront our armies on D-Day at the Channel with an air force that's already whipped us. I'm not trying to tell you that Operation Stitch will win the war. But no battle, anywhere in this war, has been won without aerial supremacy. Operation Stitch is the price of that.

KANE. Will you gentlemen wait in the anteroom?

(OTHERS *go out.* GARNETT *hesitates.*)

GARNETT. Did you mean me, too, sir?

KANE. I should like to be alone with General Dennis. (GARNETT *exits, stiffly.*) Casey, you must think me incapable of decision.

DENNIS. Sir, are there factors—on your level—that I don't know?

KANE. Nothing military.

DENNIS. Well, then, sir . . .

KANE. But if Washington screams for blood—I'd have to throw you to the wolves.

DENNIS. I understand that, sir.

KANE. If I have to jettison you, we lose our best Brigadier.

DENNIS. Thank you, sir. But we're all expendable.

KANE. If they have to jettison me, we probably lose bombardment.

DENNIS. Sir, don't you think—at the top—they expect us to fight?

KANE. I hope so, Casey, because . . . I'm releasing the Division to your discretion, with immediate effect.

DENNIS. Thank you, sir.

KANE. You're fully aware of—what may happen?

DENNIS. Perfectly, sir.

KANE. Well, I hope it doesn't. Good luck, my boy. (*Turns to door.*)

EVANS. (*Enters with paper.*) Top Secret relay from Washington for General Kane, sir.

KANE. (*Takes it, reads it, crumbles visibly. Hands it to* DENNIS.) My God! Read it.

DENNIS. (*Reading.*) "Impossible contact Air Board yet. Urgently implore low losses during critical three days next. Representatives Malcolm and Stone of House Military Affairs Committee arriving England this night. Imperative their impressions our situation favorable at any price." (*Stops reading, eyes* KANE, *pretends to be thinking aloud.*) This is an opportune time to be courtmartialling a hero, isn't it, sir?

KANE. My God! Jenks is from Malcolm's State!

DENNIS. So he is.

KANE. We'll have to fix this at once . . . medically. (*Indicates phone.*)

DENNIS. (*Speaks into it.*) Have Major Dayhuff report here immediately. (*Then to* KANE.) Sir, Jenks is bright. He'll understand his nuisance value.

KANE. We'll make it worth his while to play ball with us.

DENNIS. Are you sure we can, sir?

KANE. Bombardment's at stake. If necessary we can have Jenks declared insane from combat fatigue.

DENNIS. That's pretty strong, General.

KANE. In any case I'll have to take back that discretion I've just given you. Tomorrow you will bomb the safest naval target you can find . . . to keep these Congressmen happy.

DENNIS. Sir! This is impossible!

KANE. Nothing's impossible . . . for the service, Casey.

(MAJOR RUFUS DAYHUFF, *a poised graying medical reserve officer, enters, saluting smartly.*)

DAYHUFF. Major Dayhuff reporting as ordered, sir.

DENNIS. General Kane, my Division Medical Officer, Major Dayhuff.

KANE. Good evening, Major. We have a very serious problem.

DENNIS. Doctor, please tell General Kane exactly what you told me about Captain Jenks.

DAYHUFF. I've been through the case myself, sir. I've talked to the Flight Surgeon in Captain Jenks' group and I've talked to Captain Jenks himself.

KANE. What is your opinion, Doctor?

DAYHUFF. There is no medical excuse for Captain Jenks' conduct, sir. He acknowledges this and expects no medical exoneration.

KANE. Mightn't this defiance, in itself, indicate a neurosis or a psychiatric condition . . . ?

DAYHUFF. Doctors can be wrong, sir. In my opinion Jenks is normal.

KANE. Have you entered this in his record?

DAYHUFF. Not yet, sir. But I shall.

KANE. Do you think this is simple cowardice, Major?

DAYHUFF. No, sir. Cowards welcome medical excuses.

KANE. Have you no idea what's wrong with him?

DAYHUFF. A personal opinion, sir. But it's not a medical matter.

KANE. Tell me your opinion.

DAYHUFF. This boy has been corrupted by our press and publicity policy, sir. Jenks has not done anything exceptional enough for all that attention he got. He knew it and he knew that you knew it. He knew the Air Corps was not rewarding him; it was exploiting him. Most men would have laughed it off; many have. But this boy got the idea that he was too valuable to continue combat; too valuable to himself and too valuable to you.

KANE. And your medical opinion is that he's sane and responsible?

DAYHUFF. Yes, sir.

KANE. Thank you, Major. (DAYHUFF *exits.*) Ummm . . . we've got to think of something, Casey.

DENNIS. (*Thoughtfully.*) Sir, any simple lie will clear Jenks. But we need something that won't look too raw to the other crews; we don't want a mutiny.

KANE. My God, no!

DENNIS. Now, sir, Jenks is from Malcolm's State. Suppose he'd had secret orders from his Commanding General—that is, me—to hold himself in readiness for special escort duty to these distinguished visitors . . . *then* he would have been justified . . .

KANE. Why, Casey . . . *Casey!* That's perfect . . . *perfect,* my boy. When I picked you for this job a lot of people thought you were just another over-age test pilot! (*Starts for door.*) I'll never forget this, my boy . . . never!

DENNIS. I'll fix it, sir . . . *as soon as I've ordered Schweinhafen for tomorrow.*

KANE. (*Turns, faces him, aghast.*) This is blackmail.

DENNIS. Bombardment's at stake, General.

KANE. Ingenious, Casey . . . but I order you to release Captain Jenks to me.

DENNIS. Very well, sir. But I shall file formal charges against him unless you agree to let me finish Operation Stitch immediately.

KANE. Casey, this is preposterous . . . if you'll just consider . . .

DENNIS. I have considered, sir.

KANE. You realize that I might not be able to . . . protect you?

DENNIS. I do, sir.

KANE. Well, I was going to release the Division to your discretion anyway . . . if you insist on taking the personal risk . . .

DENNIS. Thank you, sir. (*Speaks into phone.*) Guardhouse . . . Dennis speaking, Lieutenant. You will release Captain Jenks to the personal custody of General Kane.

KANE. In the circumstances, Casey, I'll have to send Washington a correction on today's strike.

DENNIS. I understand that, sir.

KANE. Well, don't bother to come to the gate. (*Exits.*)

DENNIS. (*Slumps from strain, grabs phone, speaks into it.*) Major Davis . . . what about that Iceland weather . . . nothing further, eh? Ask Colonel Haley to step in. (*Stares at map until* HALEY *enters.*) Haley, put Operation Stitch, Phase Two, Schweinhafen, on the printer at once for all Groups for tomorrow, Bomb and fuel loading as before. Routes and timings to follow as soon as we work 'em out.

HALEY. Phase *Two,* sir? You're certain, sir?

DENNIS. Get it clicking. I'll sign the order in a minute.

(HALEY *exits.* MARTIN *enters, worried.*)

MARTIN. What the hell have you done now? Percent went out of here burning like a fuse.

DENNIS. Malcolm of Home Military Affairs arrives here tomorrow. Jenks is from Malcolm's State. So I agreed not to court-martial Jenks for Kane's promise to let us finish Stitch.

MARTIN. Casey, you know Kane will never keep a tough promise.

DENNIS. I can still remember when Kane had guts.

MARTIN. You know you're cutting your own throat, don't you?

DENNIS. Maybe. We figured Stitch would cost some casualties, Ted.

MARTIN. Yeah . . . we did. I'll bet Kane signals me a recall in the air tomorrow.

DENNIS. Not you; I've alerted Claude Minter to lead them tomorrow.

MARTIN. Why?

DENNIS. He's fresh, he's rested, he's coming along fine. Claude's good . . . he's damned good.

MARTIN. I know he's good. He ought to do Fendelhorst Monday.

DENNIS. You've done two of these. I'm tired of sweating you out.

MARTIN. Are you sure that's the only reason, Casey?

DENNIS. Yes.

MARTIN. You're sure the boys wouldn't have a better chance with someone else up front?

DENNIS. Ted, it's a break for the boys every time you lead them . . . but it's no fun to sit here and think about it.

MARTIN. Well, you get paid the first of every month . . . and so do I.

DENNIS. Now listen, Ted . . .

MARTIN. Schweinhafen's *mine,* Casey.

DENNIS. (*Hesitates, picks up phone, speaks into it, heavily.*) Haley, notify

Claude Minter he's on immediate leave, for twenty-four hours. (*Hangs up, eyes* MARTIN.) Now you go get some sleep.

MARTIN. Keep your temper with those Congressmen tomorrow, will you? I don't want to come back here and find you with a Legion of Merit and a ticket home.

DENNIS. Don't worry. I can still do the office chores around here.

MARTIN. (*Starts for ante-room door, stops.*) Casey, Helen wants me to pick a godfather for the kid. Will you take it?

DENNIS. What are you trying to do . . . queer him for life?

MARTIN. I'm serious.

DENNIS. Well, sure.

MARTIN. And I want you to promise me something.

DENNIS. What?

MARTIN. If he ever wants to join the army, you'll take a club and beat his brains right out through his tail.

CURTAIN

ACT TWO

SCENE II

About noon, Sunday.

Curtain rises on the end of a formal presentation for the visiting Congressmen. DENNIS'S *office has been made into a miniature theater, with* CONGRESSMEN MALCOLM *and* STONE, PRESCOTT, BROCKHURST *and* GARNETT *for audience. They face* KANE, *who has just finished lecturing them from graph and symbol exhibits which* EVANS *has changed for him. Among these, "Doom Of An Axis Torpedo Factory" is conspicuous.* KANE *is smiling warmly,* DENNIS *staring stonily at* MALCOLM, *who has claimed the floor.*

MALCOLM. Gennel Kane, it's mighty inspirin' foh representatives of the American people, like me an' Misteh Stone, heah, to come oveh onto foreign soil an' fin' the American Flag flyin' an' undeh it a Fiel' Commandeh who is woythy of ouah great nation an' the boys he comman's. When we get back to ouah own post of duty in the Congress in Washin'ton I promise you that ouah great leadehs theah, mos' of whom I am fohtunate enough to count among mah closes' frien's, are goin' to heah fum mah own lips how fohtunate this country is in some of its commandehs.

KANE. (*Straightfaced.*) Mr. Malcolm, and Mr. Stone, you must make the country understand that the credit for what we do here belongs to the boys. Command is merely a trusteeship of our sacred blood. Often at night I think on the parable of the talents. It must have been a terrible ordeal for those men who were trying to serve their master as best they could, with what they were given. But I think the greater lesson is in the humility we learn about the wisdom of the Master who knew what he was doing when he tested his subordinates. Sometimes I have to pray that our shortages here are only a test through which a Greater Wisdom is measuring our worthiness for a greater service to our people.

STONE. (*Has borne this bravely, as befits a veteran of the House, but he understands it.*) You mean you want more planes, General?

KANE. (*With force.*) Mr. Stone, if the nation wants aerial supremacy we must have them.

STONE. (*Honestly troubled.*) The nation wants aerial supremacy everywhere, General. They all tell us the same thing . . . you people over here, the people in the Pacific, the Navy . . . you're getting most of our available replacements now. And, frankly, we're appalled at the way you're eating up our boys and bombers here. What did you tell us your loss rate is?

KANE. (*Indicating a discarded chart.*) Overall rate of four point eight nine since the beginning of our operations here, sir.

MALCOLM. What are losses this week, Gennel?

KANE. I'll have to tell you that tomorrow, Mr. Malcolm, when I've heard from the other Divisions . . . (*Trying to break it off.*) And now, gentlemen, if you'd like to inspect the station . . .

MALCOLM. Gennel Kane, the country is pretty upset about the way youah Command oveh heah is losin' planes and crews. I and Misteh Stone have come oveh on puhpose to look into it. Now, suh, what were losses in this Division foh this week?

KANE. Have you the figures at hand, General?

DENNIS. (*Rising.*) Ninety-six, sir.

MALCOLM. Ninety-six . . . out of what ove'all stren'th in youah Division?

DENNIS. It varies with the replacement flow; in average it runs between one-eighty and two hundred.

MALCOLM. So . . . you've lost half youah stren'th in a week?

DENNIS. Eighty-four were lost on two particularly difficult missions.

MALCOLM. (*Sulkily.*) Well . . . ! That means neah about twenty-five percent per mission in this Division as against Gennel Kane's overall average of less than five?

KANE. When these are figured into the general average, Mr. Malcolm . . .

MALCOLM. I undehstan' the gennel average, suh! Perhaps Gennel Dennis will explain the discrepancy between his Division an' that.

DENNIS. My Division has the only extension tanks for specially distant targets. Both of these operations were beyond the gasoline range of friendly fighter cover.

MALCOLM. An' the boys lost were deliberately sent beyon' that range?

DENNIS. Yes.

MALCOLM. May I ask who ohdehed these operations?

DENNIS. I did.

MALCOLM. On youah own authority?

DENNIS. Yes.

KANE. General Dennis was within his technical authority.

MALCOLM. (*Is no longer the cheerful clown. He talks and acts the experienced prosecutor closing for the kill.*) I undehstan' the technicalities, Gennel Kane. No one expec's a man of youah responsibilities to ohdeh every attack foh every Division every night. But the fac's appeah to be that the minute youah back was toined, Gennel Dennis took it on his own self to ohdeh these disastrous attacks.

DENNIS. They were not disastrous. Posenleben was the best bombing of the war to date. You saw the pictures. As for yesterday . . .

KANE. (*Hastily.*) The Navy has been begging us to destroy the Nautilus Torpedo Plant, gentlemen. You saw yourselves Major Prescott's presentation on "The Doom Of An Axis Torpedo Factory." That attack was a great piece of interservice cooperation and a very bright spot in General Dennis's record.

MALCOLM. Gennel, I honoh youah loyalty to youah subohdinate, but it seems to me that ouah boys are payin' a pretty bloody price foh Gennel Dennis's recohd.

DENNIS. They're paying a bloody price for the country's record.

MALCOLM. Oh . . . ! So the *country's* responsible foh youah sendin' 'em beyon' frien'ly fighteh coveh?

DENNIS. Yes.

MALCOLM. May I ask how?

DENNIS. How did you vote on the fortification of Guam?

MALCOLM. What?

DENNIS. How did you vote on the fortification of Guam?

STONE. (*Chuckling.*) By God! He's got you, Arthur.

MALCOLM. We'll see who's got who! Gennel Dennis, I want to know why you, puhsonally, are the only single one oveh heah that sen's his Division beyon' fighte' coveh, every time Gennel Kane got his back turned! Every otheh Division consis'enly increases sohties an' tonnages of bombs dropped every month. The only solitary thing you increase is losses!

DENNIS. Sorties and tonnages are meaningless except on the right targets, Mr. Malcolm. If you want statistics, the training commands in America fly more sorties than we do . . . except the ones in your State.

MALCOLM. What you sayin' about mah State?

DENNIS. That every airfield in it is under a foot of water half the year and twelve thousand feet of fog for nine months. But when we asked permission to move to where we could operate efficiently the recommendation was blocked by your committee.

STONE. General Kane, what are you attacking today?

KANE. General Dennis . . .

(DENNIS *strips map curtain, revealing three tapes leading to Cherbourg, Emden and Schweinhafen.* OTHERS *throng to map.*)

DENNIS. It's a three-pronged operation, gentlemen. One of our Divisions attacks the Cherbourg sub-pens. Another attacks a sub-repair yard at Emden. My Division, here in the center, is attacking the Focke-Schmidt aircraft factory at Schweinhafen.

MALCOLM. Didn't I heah this Division attacked Schweinhafen yestehday?

KANE. The target was cloud-covered, Mr. Malcolm, so Colonel Martin very wisely decided to bomb the torpedo factory, which he could plainly see, instead . . .

PRESCOTT. It was a wonderful piece of air generalship. Colonel Martin is leading the Division again today.

MALCOLM. Is youah Division undeh fighteh coveh today, Gennel?

DENNIS. (*At map.*) To here. Another

relay will pick them up here, coming out.

MALCOLM. But they'll be on theah own fum heah to heah an' back?

DENNIS. Yes.

MALCOLM. An' you sent them again on youah own authority?

DENNIS. Yes.

BROCKHURST. Gentlemen, I'm fed up. I can tell you a hatful about the problems of command!

KANE. (*Quickly.*) Brockie, we all appreciate your interest, but . . .

GARNETT. Mr. Malcolm and Mr. Stone could be severely criticized in Washington for accepting anything but official military information.

(MALCOLM *and* STONE *nod, hooked.* BROCKHURST *subsides, helpless.*)

KANE. General Dennis has worked out a very ingenious plan of attack, gentlemen. You see, these other Divisions will draw some of the German fighter groups out to the wings and so reduce concentration against Colonel Martin here in the center.

STONE. Then these other two attacks are timed to prevent concentration against Colonel Martin?

KANE. Yes.

STONE. Do you expect them to succeed, General Dennis?

DENNIS. Not entirely. They may help Colonel Martin a little.

STONE. When do these diversionary attacks bomb their targets?

DENNIS. (*Eyeing watch.*) Very soon now.

STONE. And when does Colonel Martin bomb Schweinhafen?

DENNIS. In about fourteen minutes.

STONE. Then unless these diversions *do* succeed, he's probably fighting right now.

DENNIS. Probably.

(*Awed silence.* MALCOLM *cannot stand the tension.*)

MALCOLM. Gennel Kane, I'm wahnin' you; if we eveh have anotheh of these muhderous attacks . . .

DENNIS. Our operations are determined by military directive.

HALEY. (*Enters.*) Plotting room reports the other Divisions are just about to bomb their targets, General.

KANE. Does the radar screen show any reaction from German fighters, Colonel?

HALEY. None sighted yet, sir.

(HALEY *exits.*)

MALCOLM. Then Cunnel Mahtin's got to run the gauntlet of the whole German fighter force!

KANE. If you'll come with me, gentlemen . . .

PRESCOTT. This way, gentlemen . . .

KANE. We'll have a look at that screen ourselves, down in the radar and signals room. (OTHERS *start out.* KANE *continues pointedly.*) General Dennis will wish to remain in his office. (*As* OTHERS *go out,* KANE *turns frantically back to* DENNIS.) Casey, for Christ's sake be careful! Malcolm's powerful!

DENNIS. Sir, are you going to let Malcolm break our bargain?

KANE. I'll keep it if I can.

DENNIS. What we're going to do with that Jenks boy would strain a pretty tough stomach.

KANE. It's necessary, Casey, for the service.

DENNIS. I only agreed in exchange for your promise to let me finish Operation Stitch tomorrow in spite of Malcolm.

KANE. By tomorrow Malcolm could have us both in the Quartermaster Corps in Greenland! Is everything arranged as we agreed?

DENNIS. Everything, sir.

KANE. And a good lunch?

DENNIS. Yes, sir.

KANE. And plenty to drink?

DENNIS. Why . . . I hadn't thought of that.

KANE. With *Congressmen* here . . . ? Start thinking in double triples!

(KANE *exits.*)

DENNIS. (*Bursts out, oblivious of* EVANS.) Booze! It's a wonder he doesn't want opium and slave girls.

EVANS. Put 'em on field conditions, sir . . . benzedrine and WACS.

DENNIS. Sergeant, is there plenty in the officers' bar?

EVANS. Not a drop, sir. End of the month. Quota's gone.

DENNIS. How about the medical officer?

EVANS. He's been dry ever since those Cabinet members were here, sir.

DENNIS. Goddamn democracy!

EVANS. Sir, there are the combat crews' ration stocks.

DENNIS. They're running low.

EVANS. There's enough for about six missions left, sir.

DENNIS. What's the dope on replacements?

EVANS. Quartermaster's doubtful, sir. Congress says we're depraving our boys with drink . . . and the stuff's getting short in Washington.

DENNIS. These statesmen can go dry for one day. Maybe it will kill them.

EVANS. Sir, General Kane ordered you . . .

DENNIS. I can't sweat whiskey, can I?

EVANS. Sir, just a few bottles from combat ration stocks . . .

DENNIS. Not a drop! Now get the hell out of here . . .

EVANS. I knew there was a catch to this job.

DENNIS. Sergeant, I told you . . . (DENNIS *watches, speechless, while* EVANS *unlocks Division flag locker and produces two bottles of excellent bourbon.*) Where did you get that?

EVANS. Present from an admirer, sir . . . (*Extends a bottle symbolically.*) It still is, sir.

DENNIS. (*Touched, pulling out wallet.*) Nonsense! You could get a fortune for this.

EVANS. No, sir! I'd like just one thing, sir . . . to shake your hand . . .

(*Extends hand hesitantly.* DENNIS *shakes warmly but with embarrassment.*)

DENNIS. What's this for?

EVANS. Telling that servant of the people what a son of a bitch he is. I didn't think you had it in you, sir.

DENNIS. Oh . . . well . . . you'd better get some glasses and water . . . (*Then, checking* EVANS *at door.*) Sergeant, . . . I appreciate this.

EVANS. Well, sir. I'd hate breaking in a new General. (EVANS *exits.*)

DENNIS. (*Calls off.*) Haley! (HALEY *enters.*) Are they getting any fighting on those diversions?

HALEY. Not a blip, sir. General Kane is pretty scared.

DENNIS. Well, he isn't getting shot at. Get Davis with the weather.

(GARNETT *hurries in, excited.* HALEY *exits.*)

GARNETT. Casey, the old man says for God's sake be more discreet. He's scared.

DENNIS. (*Regretfully, pityingly.*) A man who's broken altitude records . . . scared of congressmen!

GARNETT. Confidentially, he knows he's pretty close to that third star.

DENNIS. I wonder if that's where it sets in. Let me know, will you?

GARNETT. You'll be likelier to let me know.

DENNIS. Don't kid me. Haven't you got one of those B-29 commands sewed up for yourself?

GARNETT. Casey, the Air Corps hasn't got B-29 commands sewed up yet, until the United Chiefs decide whether you've proved precision bombardment over here.

DENNIS. When will it be decided?

GARNETT. Ostensibly on Tuesday. But those deals are always fixed before the meetings. They may be deciding this minute.

DENNIS. (*Drily.*) No wonder you've been jittering, Cliff.

GARNETT. Frankly, I'm not as keen for it as I was, since I've seen what command is like.

DENNIS. Don't worry; the boys do the work.

GARNETT. Casey, it takes more than boys. I hate to ask this, but I need Ted Martin for my Chief of Staff out there in the Pacific.

(DENNIS *considers this slowly, while* GARNETT *watches tensely.*)

DENNIS. What can you do for him?

GARNETT. Make him a Brigadier immediately. That Command will carry two stars at the top.

DENNIS. So . . . it *will be* Major General Garnett. Congratulations.

GARNETT. It isn't final yet. But if it *does* come out that way I will need your help with Ted . . . for the good of the service.

DENNIS. How about the good of Ted?

GARNETT. Well, I pointed out to him that he makes Brigadier . . . (*Stops, confused.*) A word from you will cinch it, Casey.

DENNIS. So, he knew about this last night?

GARNETT. Casey, it isn't proselytizing when a guy's your own brother-in-law.

DENNIS. (*Looks at his watch and at map.*) Cliff! Can't you ever do anything straight?

GARNETT. Casey, if I'd thought for a minute that you would object.

DENNIS. Object! Do you think I'd have let him go today if I had known this? . . . I had Claude Minter alerted to lead this attack. And I let Ted talk me into holding Claude over for Fendelhorst tomorrow. Of course the bastard didn't tell me about this.

GARNETT. I'm very sorry, Casey, but you know yourself you have to handle Ted with kid gloves . . .

DENNIS. (*Heavily.*) Don't try to handle him, Cliff; he does that fine.

GARNETT. You mean . . . I can have him . . . ?

DENNIS. For that job . . . of course.

GARNETT. And you'll persuade him?

DENNIS. Yes.

GARNETT. Casey, I don't know how to thank you . . .

DENNIS. Save it; I'm not doing it for you.

GARNETT. I mean for Ted . . . and the service . . .

DENNIS. Those B-29s will need Ted. (HALEY *and* DAVIS *enter with weather map.*) Well, what have you got?

DAVIS. The mass is denser, but that's slowing it up. It's about eighty miles behind expected drift now, sir.

DENNIS. How much longer will that give us?

DAVIS. The Continent will be open for bombing all day tomorrow, but this will start closing in our bases by fifteen hundred, sir.

DENNIS. How does that fit, Haley?

HALEY. Lacks twenty-two minutes, sir. We'd have to take off before first light.

GARNETT. With that gas and bomb load? You'd be inviting formation collisions.

HALEY. That's been the experience, sir.

(EVANS *enters with glasses. Begins setting up an improvised bar.*)

DENNIS. But even by fifteen hundred tomorrow our returning planes could still see the island from, say, fifteen thousand feet?

DAVIS. They could see where it is, sir. This stuff will stack up over England like froth on a beer until it cools enough to move on.

DENNIS. But it will be right down on the deck?

DAVIS. I'm afraid it will be a crash landing condition, sir.

DENNIS. Bring anything new as fast as you get it. (DAVIS *exits.* DENNIS *detains* HALEY.) Have every spare parachute in the Division repacked this afternoon. Tonight, repack enough from the planes so you can fill out with fresh packs for tomorrow.

HALEY. (*Reacts, controls himself.*) Very well, sir. (*Exits.*)

GARNETT. (*Horrified.*) Casey, what the hell are you thinking of?

DENNIS. Paratroops do it. Our crews will land on a friendly island.

GARNETT. But the planes?

DENNIS. They're expendable. The boys can leave them on automatic pilot so they'll fly out to sea and not crash in the villages.

GARNETT. You'd throw away a whole Division of planes for one target?

DENNIS. If we don't finish Fendelhorst tomorrow we've thrown away precision bombardment. That's all these planes are made for.

GARNETT. Have you thought what they'll say in Washington?

DENNIS. I'm thinking what they'll say in Berlin.

BROCKHURST. (*Enters, chastened.*) Dennis, I owe you an apology. I thought you were a butcher. Compared to Kane you're a starry-eyed Boy Scout.

DENNIS. Take your troubles with General Kane to him.

BROCKHURST. I'd take 'em to the whole country if it weren't for your censors. Kane has just sent Colonel Martin a recall signal.

DENNIS. WHAT?

(*Starts for door, checks himself, looks at watch and map, half smiles.*)

GARNETT. (*Horrified.*) He couldn't. What, exactly, did he signal?

BROCKHURST. *Discretion,* to abandon primary target for a target of opportunity under fighter cover.

GARNETT. Kane let Malcolm make him do that?

BROCKHURST. He'll tell you. He asked me to send you down there. (GARNETT *exits.* BROCKHURST *eyes* DENNIS, *who is now studying map.*) That recall signal only establishes Kane's personal alibi. He *knows* Martin's already beyond fighter cover. Recalling him now means taking the losses without getting the result—just from fear.

DENNIS. American Commanders have to fear losses, Mr. Brockhurst.

BROCKHURST. Because of those goddamned congressmen?

DENNIS. Them and you.

BROCKHURST. By me you mean a free press?

DENNIS. And free speech. There are only two choices. Either the state controls the army or the army controls the state.

BROCKHURST. So these cross purposes and confusions and compromises are the price of democracy?

DENNIS. Payable in boys. Our freedom is not as free as it looks, but it still beats the alternative.

BROCKHURST. The boys don't pay all of it. Kane's got you framed like a picture.

DENNIS. General Kane is doing what he thinks best. You don't understand the army.

BROCKHURST. It's only people. I understand people.

DENNIS. No, it's not. It's a receivership for the failures of people. They give us these boys to wipe the slate clean. It's the last resource. The army *has* to win.

BROCKHURST. Even at the sacrifice of all humanity, honor and reason?

DENNIS. That's what war is, Mr. Brockhurst. If we win, those things may get another chance.

BROCKHURST. Dennis, is there nothing I can do to help?

DENNIS. When these boys get your freedom back for you, you might try taking better care of it. Until then the problem is killing.

(KANE, GARNETT, PRESCOTT, MALCOLM *and* STONE *enter.*)

KANE. (*At door.*) . . . and I don't mind telling you it's a terrible responsibility.

MALCOLM. It was a very courageous order, General . . .

STONE. But I don't understand this.

KANE. (*To* DENNIS.) General, as you know, I pride myself on never interfering with normal operations. But today's diversions were so obviously unsuccessful that I felt it my duty to recall Colonel Martin.

MALCOLM. It was a brilliant command decision, Gennel. It was woyth ouah whole trip oveh heah to fin' we got some Commandehs with humanity enough not to deman' the impossible . . . foh recohds.

DENNIS. Did you get a reply from Colonel Martin, General Kane?

KANE. No. He'll probably preserve radio silence back to our fighters.

STONE. (*Persevering.*) Then Colonel Martin already *had* gone beyond fighter cover?

KANE. Of course we're not *certain* he'd gone that far . . .

MALCOLM. (*Sees whiskey, extricates* KANE.) Well, looky here! Drinkin' whisky fum Gawd's own country! Wheah in the worl' did you get this oveh heah, Sahgent?

EVANS. Present to General Dennis from an admirer, sir. (ALL *throng to bar.*)

BROCKHURST. (*Recognizes whiskey, smiles.*) Yes, Sergeant, it was.

(ALL *except* DENNIS *begin to drink. Overscene sound of teleprinter begins to clatter.* DENNIS *reacts, but* STONE *detains him, persisting with question.*)

STONE. Well—it seems to me that if Colonel Martin had already gone *beyond* fighter cover . . .

MALCOLM. You mean Cunnel Mahtin had *been sent* beyon' fighteh coveh by Gennel Dennis when he knew his own self them diversions most likely wouldn't work . . . am I right, Gennel?

DENNIS. You are.

HALEY. (*Enters with a message.*) Liaison message from a Royal Air Force Reconnaissance plane, sir.

DENNIS. Read it.

HALEY. (*Reading.*) "Twelve thirty-nine sighted large formation USAAF Fortresses approx ten-forty-six East, fifty-forty North . . . Altitude twenty-two thousand, heading ninety-eight . . ."

KANE. NINETY-EIGHT . . . he's still going *into* Germany!

HALEY. (*Continuing reading.*) "Unescorted by friendly fighters, under heavy attack, formations good over."

(HALEY *exits.*)

MALCOLM. (*Drinks deeply.*) " 'Unescohted an' undeh heavy attack . . . !' " Gennel Kane, I'm wahnin' you, if we eveh have anotheh attack like this . . .

STONE. Arthur! It's not our place to criticize. If they think it's necessary.

MALCOLM. Necessary! To slaughteh American youth foh one pig-headed Brigadieh to make hisself a puhsonal recohd . . .

HALEY. (*Enters, hesitantly.*) Message you should see, General Dennis . . .

KANE. (*Nervously.*) Read the message, Colonel!

HALEY. (*Reading.*) "Relay on personal cable from message center London in clear for Colonel Edward Martin: new co-pilot made first landing four-fourteen this morning everything fine, Helen."

DENNIS. Jesus! Ted's got a son! Congratulations, Uncle!

(DENNIS *and* GARNETT *shake.*)

KANE. (*Exploits the distraction.*) Gentlemen! Colonel Martin's son!

(OTHERS *throng to drink.*)

DENNIS. Haley, prepare a copy to relay to Ted, but hold it till we hear.

(HALEY *exits.*)

MALCOLM. Till you heah what?

DENNIS. (*Eyeing watch.*) His strike signal. It will be very soon now.

MALCOLM. You tellin' me this Cunnel out theah leadin' the attack been bohn a daddy an' you ain't even goin' to radio him?

DENNIS. He's busy now.

KANE. (*Intervening.*) Fortunately, gentlemen, war also has its pleasant duties. We'll have just time for one of them, General Dennis.

(DENNIS *looks rebellious, checks himself, speaks off to Ops room.*)

EVANS. (*Speaks off to ante-room.*) Let's go.

(G. I. PHOTOGRAPHER *with camera enters and takes position.*)

MALCOLM. General Kane, you fixin' to have this decoration ceremony you was tellin' me about?

KANE. Right now, Mr. Malcolm. (HALEY *enters with citation and medal box.* JENKS, *in best uniform, enters after him.* MALCOLM *jumps to exploit the hero.*) Mr. Malcolm . . . Mr. Stone . . . Captain Jenks.

MALCOLM. Son, I'm proud to meet you, mighty proud! Now if you'll just stan' oveh heah with me . . . (*Grabs* JENKS, *beckons* PHOTOGRAPHER. STONE *jumps briskly to join them.*) Boy! I want a pictuah that will make all America proud of . . . the Captain, heah. (PHOTOGRAPHER *maneuvers.* MALCOLM *and* STONE *almost crowd* JENKS *out of picture.*) All right, son! *Weah* ready!

EVANS. Excuse me, sir . . .

KANE. (*Outraged.*) WHAT . . . ?

EVANS. Would the gentlemen from Congress like to put their glasses over here before the photographing starts . . . ?

(*He steps to them, takes glasses from their hands as he speaks.*)

STONE. Oh, yes . . . thank you, Sergeant.

MALCOLM. You goin' a long way in life, son!

(PHOTOGRAPHER *snaps them, mugging and beaming.*)

KANE. Now, gentlemen, I think we'd better go ahead.

MALCOLM. Are you gettin' this, Elmeh boy?

BROCKHURST. I'm beginning to get it.

(ALL *re-group rapidly.* JENKS *facing* KANE, HALEY *beside them.* MALCOLM *and* STONE *maneuver into good camera range.*)

HALEY. (*Reads from citation.*) "Captain Lucius Jenks for outstandingly heroic and meritorious conduct in aerial warfare . . ." (*Overscene sound of teleprinter clattering is heard.* EVANS *hurries to Ops room.* DENNIS *watches him anxiously.* HALEY *continues reading.*) "Captain Jenks, first as pilot and later as Commander of the 1993rd Bombardment Squadron, Heavy . . ."

(HALEY *breaks off as* EVANS *enters and hands* DENNIS *strip of paper.*)

DENNIS. (*Reading.*) "No mistake this time. Scratch Schweinhafen for me, Ted." Jesus, Haley! He got it . . . HE GOT IT . . . *HE GOT IT!!!* Signal him about his kid!

(HALEY *exits.*)

GARNETT. (*Raises glass.*) Gentlemen! The greatest combat leader in the Army Air Forces!

KANE. (*To* BROCKHURST.) Brockie, I want a feature story on Colonel Martin for this!

(ALL *throng to drink, leaving* MALCOLM *piqued, beside the forgotten* JENKS.)

MALCOLM. Gennel Kane! Ain't we goin' to be photographed with you decoratin' this hero fum mah home State?

PRESCOTT. Sir! Colonel Martin's message asks you to scratch Schweinhafen for him. Now, while the photographer is still here . . .

(*Proffers crayon.* KANE *takes it to map.* CONGRESSMEN *stampede to get into photo.*)

KANE. (*To* PHOTOGRAPHER.) Are we all right, son?

PHOTOGRAPHER. Pull your blouse down over your hips, General.

(PHOTOGRAPHER *trains on them, then stops as* HALEY *enters quietly, hands* DENNIS *a message.* DENNIS *reads it, puts it down quietly, steps away from it.* OTHERS *watch uneasily.* GARNETT *picks it up.*)

GARNETT. (*Reading.*) "Good luck, Casey, we're on fire and going . . ."

MALCOLM. Goin' . . . ? Finish the message, cain't you?

GARNETT. That's all there is.

MALCOLM. All . . . all . . . ? (*Steps over to* DENNIS.) Listen heah! I want to know . . .

DENNIS. Shut up!

MALCOLM. (*Getting it.*) You mean to tell me he's . . .

DENNIS. SHUT UP!

MALCOLM. You telling me to shut up afteh you've done kilt the bes' . . .

(DENNIS *grabs him by lapels, shakes him savagely.*)

KANE. Casey!

(DENNIS *flings* MALCOLM *into a chair.*)

STONE. General Kane, nobody could blame General Dennis.

BROCKHURST. Let's both remember that, Mr. Stone.

GARNETT. Casey, do you realize what . . . we've done to Ted?

DENNIS. Yes.

GARNETT. But we'll have to . . . one of us will have to tell Helen.
DENNIS. I'll tell Helen . . . and then I'll tell Claude Minter's wife.
GARNETT. Claude Minter's wife? (*Eyeing him nervously.*)
DENNIS. Yes. I'll tell her I sent Claude to Fendelhorst tomorrow.
GARNETT. Fendelhorst! Tomorrow!
KANE. Casey, you leave me no choice. I am relieving you of your command with immediate effect. General Garnett, pending confirmation from Washington you will assume command of the Fifth Division. (*Then, sincerely, to* DENNIS.) I'm sorry, my boy. I'm going to recommend you for the Legion of Merit.

CURTAIN

ACT THREE

Sunday, the same day. About 8 P.M. Curtain rises to discover room bare and serviceable as in Act One.

EVANS *enters, puts name plate with* GARNETT'S *name on desk, tosses* DENNIS'S *nameplate into trash box. From offstage singing and mild carousal noises are audible.* EVANS *shakes head disapprovingly, puts coffee to boil and gets out cigar box.* MAJOR DAYHUFF *enters, catching* EVANS *redhanded with cigar box.*

DAYHUFF. (*Amused, covering it.*) Good evening, Evans. Aren't you expecting the General?
EVANS. Any minute now. And I knew he'd want you to have a cigar.
DAYHUFF. Thanks.
EVANS. (*Extends box. It is empty.*) Congressmen! Sorry, sir. I'll have this attended to.
DAYHUFF. All right. How did that wound in your arm heal, Sergeant?
EVANS. (*With gesture.*) Fine, Doctor. I can lift any girl in England off her feet.
DAYHUFF. So I hear. (*Mild carousal noises heard off.*) Aren't you missing a good evening for . . . recreation?
EVANS. I'll be off duty as soon as we send the order for tomorrow.
DAYHUFF. Sergeant, I had it on good authority there wouldn't be a mission tomorrow.
EVANS. Well, mine is straight from the horse's . . . that is, General Kane. When he left here he told Garnett he'd communicate his instructions as soon as he'd made an appreciation of the situation.
DAYHUFF. Can you put that into English?
EVANS. Yes, sir. Order, counter order, disorder . . . and then five feet of teleprinted hot air meaning a milk run to the nearest Channel port.
DAYHUFF. Oh. I take it you don't approve of the change?
EVANS. I expected it.
DAYHUFF. Because of the way Dennis . . . disagreed with those Congressmen?
EVANS. Hell no! They've all buried worse bodies than that. Kane and Washington have been laying for Dennis a long time.
DAYHUFF. What makes you think that?
EVANS. Dennis was trying to get the war over.
DAYHUFF. That's a harsh judgment, Sergeant.
EVANS. We got the signal from Washington confirming Garnett in two hours, didn't we?
DAYHUFF. While we're violating security, what did it say about Dennis?
EVANS. ". . . return to Washington by special plane, for reassignment."
DAYHUFF. Well, for his sake I hope it's an easier assignment.
EVANS. They'll probably make him Air Force Liaison to the Admiral commanding the Washington Aquarium.
DAYHUFF. I'm not so sure Washington will waste a man like that.
EVANS. Maybe they'll let him burn Top Secret waste paper.
DAYHUFF. When you get older it may occur to you that Command is just as tough in Washington as anywhere else. Could you figure out the difference between Kane and Dennis from official reports?
EVANS. Very fast.
DAYHUFF. How?
EVANS. Dennis always had his neck out a foot. But you have to look close for those two stars to tell Kane from a turtle. This Garnett's another.
DAYHUFF. So you'll guarantee nothing worse than a milk run tomorrow?
EVANS. After what happened to Dennis . . . listen to the boys. Disgusting, isn't it, sir?
GARNETT. (*Enters.*) Good evening, Evans. Anything from General Kane?
EVANS. No, sir.
VOICE. (*Offstage.*) Where's my bottle?
GARNETT. What's that racket outside?
EVANS. Just some of the boys, sir. (*Bottle crash offstage.*)

GARNETT. Well, call the guardhouse.
EVANS. Excuse me, sir. May I attend to this for you, sir?
GARNETT. Yes.
EVANS. (*Goes to window, calls off.*) Hey, you, out there . . . shut up!
VOICE. (*Off, evidently drunk.*) Who's telling me to shut up?
EVANS. I am.
VOICE. Do you know who I am?
EVANS. I don't want to know who you are.
VOICE. I am Captain George Washington Culpepper Lee!
EVANS. Well, I am Tech Sergeant Harold Evans . . .
LEE. Oh . . . a Technical Sergeant, eh . . . ?
EVANS. Speaking for Brigadier General Clifton C. Garnett. (*Noise of swiftly receding feet and then silence.*) Thank you, sir.
GARNETT. Thank *you,* Sergeant. See if there are any messages.
DAYHUFF. (*Grins.*) I'm afraid I'm the real culprit, General Garnett.
GARNETT. How?
DAYHUFF. I authorized a small allotment of whiskey from combat crew ration into the messes tonight.
GARNETT. Is this usual?
DAYHUFF. No, sir. The last three days were not usual either, sir.
GARNETT. Is the whole base in this condition?
DAYHUFF. No, *sir!* It wouldn't run one percent. Most of them are asleep.
GARNETT. I see.
DAYHUFF. This is a very special night, sir. And they're veterans. They know they can fly a milk run tomorrow sound asleep.
GARNETT. Does the Division just assume that I'm going to order a milk run?
DAYHUFF. I'm not assuming, sir. That's what I came in to ask.
GARNETT. There are a great many factors in this decision, Major.
DAYHUFF. I represent one of them, sir.
GARNETT. What is your medical estimate, Major?
DAYHUFF. When General Dennis planned Operation Stitch he requested a medical appreciation. I estimated the men could stand three successive days.
GARNETT. Three?
DAYHUFF. We agreed that anything beyond that would have to be decided by military consideration.
GARNETT. In short, the men could do it, if General Kane ordered it?
DAYHUFF. Men can do what they have to, sir.
GARNETT. At a price, eh?
DAYHUFF. Well, sir; two-thirds of these men will be killed in a normal tour of duty anyway . . .
GARNETT. Thank you, Major. (DAYHUFF *exits.* GARNETT *cogitates, calls off.*) Evans! (EVANS *enters.*) Any word from General Kane?
EVANS. No, sir. Coffee's ready, sir.
GARNETT. I didn't order coffee.
EVANS. You will, sir.
GARNETT. (*Sniffs it, likes it.*) Oh, thank you, Sergeant. What else will I need?
EVANS. Cigars and whiskey, sir.
GARNETT. I almost never use them.
EVANS. Your visitors will, sir.
GARNETT. Oh. I guess you and I will be together some time, Evans. Can you suggest anything else I need?
EVANS. You need a new sergeant, sir.
GARNETT. What . . . ? Oh, you're going home to work for General Dennis?
EVANS. (*Bitterly.*) No, sir; he wouldn't take me. I guess they use Colonels for errand boys in Washington. I've decided to go to Nevada to teach gunnery.
GARNETT. *You've* decided . . . ? What do you think this Army is?
EVANS. I'd rather not answer that, sir. But War Department Circular six-nine-five-eight-seven-dash-three says applications from graduate gunners to teach aerial gunnery will be accepted.
GARNETT. Well, if the circular authorizes it . . . ask Colonel Haley to step in. (EVANS *makes for door.* GARNETT *checks him.*) Evans, you *are* a graduate gunner?
EVANS. Yes, sir. Twenty-eight missions.
GARNETT. Would it be too much to ask these boys for a tough one tomorrow?
EVANS. I don't know, sir.
GARNETT. You must know . . . from your own experience.
EVANS. Never had this experience, sir. Nobody in the Army ever asked me anything. They just told me.
GARNETT. Ask Colonel Haley to step in. (EVANS *exits.* GARNETT *visibly sweats.* HALEY *enters.*) Good evening, Haley. Any messages?
HALEY. Other Division Commanders have sent compliments and will await your decision before planning tomorrow's mission, sir.
GARNETT. Anything from General Kane?
HALEY. No, sir.

GARNETT. Wasn't his weather conference tonight at eighteen hundred?

HALEY. Yes, sir.

GARNETT. I suppose on a tricky reading he might wait for twenty hundred developments?

HALEY. He might, sir.

GARNETT. And we haven't had *our* twenty hundred weather yet.

HALEY. Davis is marking the map now, sir. If you want it at once.

GARNETT. No, no. Have you final figures from today yet?

HALEY. (*Handing him paper.*) Right here, sir.

GARNETT. Thirty-nine lost . . . four in the Channel . . . what's this?

HALEY. Both reconnaissance planes unreported again today, sir.

GARNETT. Haley, what about morale?

HALEY. Very good now, sir. What you've heard tonight is just the normal let-down between tough missions and easy ones.

GARNETT. Haley, what do these boys really think about?

HALEY. Their twenty-fifth mission, sir.

GARNETT. Of course. But what else?

HALEY. The normal things, sir. And promotion and decoration, too.

GARNETT. By the normal things, you mean . . . ?

HALEY. Yes, sir. Fortunately the villages around here are full of it.

GARNETT. I should think it would lead to trouble.

HALEY. It does, sir.

GARNETT. What kind?

HALEY. Just the normal kind, sir. These women have been at war a long time. They know the men have to be up and dressed in time for missions.

GARNETT. Is this immorality very widespread?

HALEY. Very, sir. I believe it's as bad as America.

GARNETT. So that kind of morale really takes care of itself?

HALEY. Yes, sir. Keeps down perversion, too. (*Then, briskly.*) If you're ready to go through Status, sir . . .

GARNETT. (*Still stalling.*) Haley, you really think the change of Command has helped morale?

HALEY. They're pretty cheerful tonight, sir.

GARNETT. Well, that's something. You always wonder if they'll be hostile to a new . . . face.

HALEY. All generals look alike to them, sir. (*Pause.*) They figure a new General's always good for a couple of soft missions.

GARNETT. Haley, are those last pictures developed?

HALEY. I'll find out, sir.

(HALEY *exits.*) GARNETT *stews, then looks up, startled, as* CAPTAIN GEORGE WASHINGTON CULPEPPER LEE *enters.* LEE *is an attractive youngster, somewhat drunk. He salutes with exaggerated formality.*)

LEE. Captain Lee reports his presence, sir.

GARNETT. Who?

LEE. Captain George Washington Culpepper Lee, sir.

GARNETT. Lee, you're drunk.

LEE. Yes, sir. I've come in to report myself for that and to apologize for singing under your window and then running away.

GARNETT. Get out of here and go to bed.

LEE. I'm sorry, sir. This hasn't happened before and won't again.

(*Salutes, turns to go;* GARNETT *checks him.*)

GARNETT. Lee, did you go to Schweinhafen today?

LEE. (*Thoughtfully, rather fuddled.*) Yes, sir. I went to Schweinhafen today and I went to Schweinhafen yesterday and went to Posenleben Friday . . . and I've been to Hamburg . . . and Bremen . . . and Kiel . . . and Schweinfurt and Regensburg . . . (*Stops, horrified at himself.*) Excuse me, sir. I only meant to say I'd been to twenty-four of them without taking a drink and I'm ashamed of myself for singing under your window on Easter Sunday.

GARNETT. You go to bed, Lee. It's all right . . . even if it isn't Easter Sunday.

LEE. Beg your pardon, sir. It's my Easter Sunday.

GARNETT. Yours?

LEE. Yes, sir. Resurrection, sir. Today was my twenty-fourth. All I've got to do now is knock off one more little milk run and then go home and live the rest of my life.

GARNETT. Oh. Well, don't behave like this at home.

LEE. I wouldn't think of it, sir. I'm going to get married.

GARNETT. Well, congratulations!

LEE. Yes, sir. We almost did before I came over, but I thought . . . I thought she'd worry more that way.

GARNETT. I see. Now get to bed; the best of luck.

LEE. Thank you, sir. And Happy Easter to you, sir.

(LEE *exits, leaving* GARNETT *to think that one over.*)

HALEY. (*Enters.*) The pictures will be up in a minute and there's a message, sir.

GARNETT. From General Kane?

HALEY. No, sir. The last Group reports all crews provided with freshly packed parachutes for tomorrow in compliance with today's order.

GARNETT. What order?

HALEY. General Dennis's last order this morning, sir. If you remember it was not rescinded.

GARNETT. But that was for a special weather condition. Where *is* that weather man?

HALEY. Coming, sir. It's a tricky reading.

GARNETT. (*Hopefully.*) You mean, it looks worse?

HALEY. He'll have to tell you that, sir.

GARNETT. And you're sure there's nothing from General Kane?

HALEY. Messages are brought as received, sir.

GARNETT. We'll go through Status, Haley. Just give me totals.

(*They move to Status Board.*)

HALEY. I think I can promise a hundred and thirty planes by bomb loading, sir.

GARNETT. One-thirty . . . that's not really four full groups, is it?

HALEY. Today was our third successive day of intensive operations, sir. I'll bet the Germans would be glad to trade serviceability with me . . . and they only have to repair single engine fighters and find one man to a crew.

GARNETT. I wasn't criticizing . . . but we just haven't the strength that General Dennis had, have we?

HALEY. One-thirty's enough for any target in the book, if they hit it.

GARNETT. Planes, perhaps; how about crews?

HALEY. I've been able to piece out one thirty-two, sir.

GARNETT. How many would be on their last mission?

HALEY. Eighteen, sir.

GARNETT. A hundred and eighty boys . . .

HALEY. It's a break for them, sir, to finish on an easy one, if it is an easy one.

GARNETT. Of course that depends entirely on General Kane's orders.

HALEY. Yes, sir. If he sends orders. Shall I see about your weather, sir?

GARNETT. (*Picks up Directive Folder.*) Haley, when General Dennis handed over to me this afternoon there was so much to take in I missed some of the details. It says here: "In the absence of explicit target designation or other order from higher headquarters, division commanders will exercise their own discretion . . ." When should this designation come down?

HALEY. From General Kane's eighteen hundred weather conference tonight, sir.

GARNETT. And if we hear nothing this just applies automatically?

HALEY. Automatically, sir.

MAJOR LANSING. (*Enters, shirt sleeves rolled up, wet hands filled with wet pictures.*) Last pictures from the camera ships in the last Group on today's mission, sir.

GARNETT. There are no pictures from reconnaissance?

LANSING. No, sir. Both reconnaissance planes are unreported again today. These are all we'll have.

GARNETT. How are they?

LANSING. (*Spreading them for scrutiny.*) Wonderful, sir. The next to last Group *did* get the casting furnaces, you see . . . here. And here where the main spar milling shop was there's nothing left but a compound crater.

GARNETT. Then it's complete?

LANSING. Schweinhafen's complete, sir.

GARNETT. I see. Nothing more on Colonel Martin . . . ? No parachutes showing in any of these strike photos?

LANSING. It was very windy over Schweinhafen today, sir. The last Group photos didn't catch any of the parachutes going down. We have one more sighting from Crew Interrogation that agrees exactly with the others. As the fire worked toward his gas tanks, Colonel Martin's plane swung away from the formation, of course, and then exploded. Four parachutes were seen to open afterwards, but there were no individual identifications.

GARNETT. (*Eyeing pictures.*) I wish he could know what he did.

LANSING. Yes, but I'm glad he doesn't know we're not finishing the job.

GARNETT. That's not in our hands, Major.

LANSING. I understand that, sir.

GARNETT. I want you to brief me now on what targets would be best to give these boys a break tomorrow.

(*They move to map.* HALEY *exits.*)

LANSING. The Germans won't fight for anything in France tomorrow, sir. They need a rest as badly as we do.

GARNETT. You keep records of losses and loss expectancy over the different targets, of course?

LANSING. Of course, sir.

GARNETT. Well, what would loss expectancy be . . . along the coastal fringe here, on some of these naval objectives?

LANSING. I wouldn't trust my memory for the figures, sir. But I can have a list prepared for you very quickly.

GARNETT. What would the targets be, the naval targets . . . along here?

LANSING. Minesweeper and E-boat bases along through there, sir.

GARNETT. We have attacked such objectives before, of course?

LANSING. Yes, sir. For the blooding of new Groups. Would you like a loss expectancy list prepared, sir?

GARNETT. Yes. (LANSING *makes for door.* GARNETT *checks him.*) Major, I'd like to ask you a question.

LANSING. Yes, sir.

GARNETT. If you had to decide tomorrow's mission . . . for General Kane . . . would you attack Fendelhorst?

LANSING. Fendelhorst, sir! I'm thankful I don't have to decide that.

GARNETT. But if you did?

LANSING. Sir, I'm afraid my decision would be influenced by a personal reason.

GARNETT. May I ask what that is?

LANSING. General, I regret intruding this upon your considerations. Since you ask me, I have a son, training now in a combat infantry Division, Assault . . . (*Points to cross.*) When those jets have stopped our bombardment they'll make the deadliest strafing planes ever used against ground troops. I'm sorry, sir, but I'm afraid I couldn't help thinking of my boy going up a beach against them.

GARNETT. Yes . . . but what if your boy were flying a bomber tomorrow?

LANSING. I hope I would send him to Fendelhorst, sir.

GARNETT. Thank you, Major.

(LANSING *exits, leaving* GARNETT *to think that over.*)

(HALEY *and* DAVIS *enter.*)

HALEY. Weather's ready, sir.

GARNETT. Is this the same report that General Kane is getting?

DAVIS. No, sir. This is my reading. General Kane's weather people refuse either concurrence or disagreement.

GARNETT. Isn't that unusual?

DAVIS. Very unscientific, sir.

HALEY. Often happens, sir. In such cases we operate on our own weather reading, subject to other instructions. Directive covers it, sir.

GARNETT. Well, what is it?

DAVIS. (*Spreading map on table.*) That cold mass is still slowing down. The entire Continent will be open for bombing all day and you'll have until seventeen hundred over the bases here for landing, sir.

GARNETT. Seventeen hundred . . . five o'clock in the afternoon . . . why, that's enough for . . . anything . . . isn't it?

HALEY. Yes, sir.

GARNETT. Even without parachutes.

HALEY. Yes, sir.

GARNETT. You're sure of this, Davis?

DAVIS. Never sure with weather, sir. If anything, though, this will improve for us during the night.

GARNETT. Thank you, Major.

DAVIS. All right.

(DAVIS *exits.* GARNETT *stews.* HALEY *gets down to business.*)

HALEY. General Garnett, the Group commanders need gas and bomb-loading orders. Their ground crews are so exhausted it will take them twice as long as normal tonight.

GARNETT. Haley, to be perfectly frank, I understood I was going to receive instructions from General Kane . . .

HALEY. But we haven't, sir. And our Directive says: "In the absence of explicit target designation or other orders . . ."

EVANS. (*Enters with message.*) Message for General Garnett from General Kane, sir.

GARNETT. (*Faintly.*) Read it.

(EVANS *looks perplexed, hands message to* HALEY, *who reads.*)

HALEY. (*Reading.*) "General Kane compelled proceed Hemisphere Commander's dinner for Congressmen London, consequently unable to attend weather conference here. Operating procedure will apply as per directive. General Kane desires express especial confidence General Garnett's discretion based on weather. Signed Saybold for Kane."

(*Deadly silence.* DENNIS *enters in trench-coat, carrying cap.* GARNETT *gathers himself.*)

GARNETT. Come in, old man; I'll speak to you in a minute, Haley. (HALEY *and* EVANS *go out.*) Sit down, Casey.

DENNIS. They've just reported my plane's landed and is taking gas. The boys are loading my stuff.

GARNETT. Damn it, man! You don't have to rush off like this.

DENNIS. The order said: "With immediate effect" . . . Cliff, I'm taking Ted's personal stuff to Helen.

GARNETT. Good. You'll go to see her at once?

DENNIS. Of course. No more news, I suppose?

GARNETT. One more crew sighting, exactly like the others, four parachutes.

DENNIS. Yeah.

GARNETT. What will you tell her?

DENNIS. The truth. She won't talk.

GARNETT. How long do we keep it quiet?

DENNIS. For Ted, I'd like eight weeks. They'd dig out every cave in Germany if they thought he was hiding in one of them.

GARNETT. Do you think he is?

DENNIS. No. Not with an explosion where he was riding.

GARNETT. Casey, if he did get down alive . . . and they caught him . . . what then?

DENNIS. If the army gets him it's probably all right. But no one can be responsible for what civilians who've been bombed will do.

GARNETT. But if the army gets him first . . . it's all right?

DENNIS. Probably.

GARNETT. I've been thinking all day about those six boys the Japanese captured . . . alive . . .

DENNIS. I won't go into that side of it with Helen.

GARNETT. She'll be thinking of it. She must have seen those pictures the Japanese released after they got through with them.

DENNIS. Cliff! Will you stop talking about it?

GARNETT. I've been thinking about it all afternoon. I was the guy who *wanted* a B-29 command. God! When I think of ordering boys out over the Japanese . . .

DENNIS. You don't have to think about it. You've got a good job here. Good luck, Cliff . . .

GARNETT. Good, is it? Read that?

(*Hands* DENNIS *the message.*)

DENNIS. (*Reads it, speaks casually.*) Hemisphere Commander's, eh? Well, they'll get real Martinis. That old son of a bitch has the best mess in London.

GARNETT. *Real Martinis* . . . while *I* have to decide about tomorrow.

DENNIS. You don't have to decide anything. You're socked in with bad weather at fifteen hundred tomorrow afternoon.

GARNETT. The weather's changed, Casey; it's good for anything.

DENNIS. The hell you say! Isn't that just like the weather for you?

GARNETT. And Kane is passing the buck to me.

DENNIS. Well, somebody's probably got a heel on his neck, too. Good luck, Cliff . . .

GARNETT. Casey! You can't run out on me like this. What am I going to do?

DENNIS. You're going to command, Clifton . . . and you will be paid the first of every month.

(*Fumbles with coat as if preparing to go.*)

GARNETT. Casey, there's one more thing . . .

DENNIS. (*Eyeing watch.*) Well . . . !

GARNETT. I had a boy in here tonight . . . a pilot . . .

DENNIS. Bitching and screaming like a wounded eagle, I suppose?

GARNETT. (*Indignantly.*) Hell no! He was a nice attractive kid with a lot of guts.

DENNIS. They're all nice attractive kids with a lot of guts.

GARNETT. I know, but this one was a little drunk.

DENNIS. (*Shocked.*) Drunk in *here* . . . (*Then, reflectively.*) Oh. I suppose his co-pilot was killed on the mission today . . . I've had those . . .

GARNETT. No, no . . . that wasn't it . . .

DENNIS. Oh, just nerves? Well, the best thing with those, Cliff, is just to have the M. P.'s throw 'em into bed . . .

GARNETT. Oh, he wasn't that drunk . . .

DENNIS. They need it sometimes. Their crews will sober them up with oxygen in five minutes in the morning and then hop them up with enough benzedrine to get them through the mission. This isn't Washington, Cliff; you can't be too strict with them.

GARNETT. That's not it, Casey. This boy gave me a personal slant . . .

DENNIS. The War Department has provided you with a chaplain for that, Cliff. Tell them to do their crying to him.

GARNETT. Casey, he wasn't crying, he was happy. He told me he's going to get married.

DENNIS. And the only thing you can tell him is that you hope you won't have to kill him before he does . . . It's your baby, Cliff, but I learned long ago to let the chaplain handle those. He's our liaison with the headquarters that decides that . . . if there is one.

GARNETT. Casey! What's happened to you?

DENNIS. Just what's going to happen to you . . . and the sooner I get out of here, the sooner you can get to work.

(*Starts for door.*)

GARNETT. (*Checks him.*) Casey! If you'll help me just this once . . .

DENNIS. It isn't just this once. It's from now on.

GARNETT. When *you* first came over here you had Ted and Joe Lucas to talk to . . .

DENNIS. Joe never talked. He was commanding this Division then, and I was running a Group for him. That's worse. You see them at meals every day and you know a lot of them personally.

GARNETT. But at least you had Joe for a boss until he got killed in that air raid in London.

DENNIS. Did you believe that story?

GARNETT. Why . . . of course . . .

DENNIS. Well, you're old enough to know better. Joe didn't get killed in any air raid in London. It was the night after we first sent them to Mangelburg. Joe didn't want to send them. He knew they weren't ready. Kane knew it, too. But they were crowding Joe and Kane from higher up. Joe counted them in at landing that night and then he went down to London and took a hotel room and shot himself. Then I got the job. Now it's yours. Good luck, Cliff.

GARNETT. *Joe Lucas* . . . did *that* . . . how *could* he?

DENNIS. You'll see how he could. Wait till you've counted in a really bad one that you've ordered yourself. Wait till you start noticing the faces of those kids on the trucks from the replacement centers . . . the new ones coming in. Wait till you start waking up in the afternoon . . . and wondering what it is that makes *those* faces look so much like the faces of the ones you're already killing, that same afternoon. Then go out and puke up your powdered eggs and then take veronal to get back to sleep . . . and then have them wake you up and give you benzedrine to keep you awake while you count in your stragglers and plan your next mission . . . and then you'll see how Joe Lucas could have done it . . .

GARNETT. Joe Lucas! Of all the men in the service . . .

DENNIS. Yes . . . and I've wanted to do the same thing, five or six times when I've signed those field orders . . . and so will you! But that was one thing Joe did for me. He made me think that through. That only helps *one* guy.

GARNETT. But even after that . . . you had Ted . . .

DENNIS. Yes. I had Ted. That's one thing I've done for you, Cliff. I've killed Ted. You won't have to do that.

GARNETT. Casey, you've hated this, every minute of it, haven't you?

DENNIS. I got paid for it.

GARNETT. What will you do now, Casey?

DENNIS. Oh, I guess I still rate a Training Command. I'm going to get one out West somewhere, where I can have Cathy and the kids with me and get a day off now and then to take the boy fishing.

HALEY. (*Enters with list.*) Here's the list Major Lansing prepared for you, sir.

GARNETT. (*Dazedly.*) List?

HALEY. Yes, sir. You ordered it, sir.

GARNETT. Read it.

HALEY. (*Reading.*) "Expectancy of losses from flak against French Channel port targets based on previous experience . . . Brest, 4.9 . . . Cherbourg, 3.4 . . . Calais, 2.2 . . . Dunkirk, 1.6 . . . Dieppe, 1.4 . . ."

GARNETT. That's enough . . .

(HALEY *puts list on desk, starts out.*)

DENNIS. (*Checks him.*) Ernie . . . how did *my* goodbye presents to the boys finally average out?

HALEY. Twenty-four percent Friday, twenty-six percent yesterday and twenty-nine percent today, sir.

DENNIS. Some difference between those and the Channel ports.

HALEY. Many differences, sir.

GARNETT. (*Low-voiced.*) Haley, notify the other Divisions and all our Groups that tomorrow the Fifth Division will attack Fendelhorst.

HALEY. Yes, sir. (*Exits.*)

DENNIS. (*Half-laughs, awkwardly.*) Well . . . Cliff! Good luck . . . *General.*

GARNETT. Save me a job in that training command, will you?

(DENNIS *starts out.* EVANS *enters.*)

EVANS. Change of orders for General Dennis . . . sir . . .

DENNIS. No, you don't . . .

EVANS. From Washington, sir.

DENNIS. I've got my orders. I've gone . . . home.

EVANS. We're instructed to relay the message to your plane, sir. (*Hesitates.*)

GARNETT. (*Takes message, read aloud slowly.*) "With immediate effect, General Dennis will proceed via Gibraltar, Cairo, Karachi, Calcutta and Chungking to . . ." (*Stops, horrified.*) My God, Casey . . . this means a B-29 command . . .

DENNIS. No, by God! They can't! . . . I *WON'T!* (*Then, slowly.*) Cliff, does that say: "With immediate effect"?

GARNETT. I'm afraid it does, Casey.

DENNIS. Yeah . . . Evans! Get your things.

CURTAIN

SOUTH PACIFIC

A MUSICAL PLAY

BY

Richard Rodgers and Oscar Hammerstein, II

LYRICS BY

Oscar Hammerstein, II

BOOK BY

Oscar Hammerstein, II and Joshua Logan

ADAPTED FROM

James A. Michener's

TALES OF THE SOUTH PACIFIC

Published in New York by Random House, Inc., and simultaneously in Toronto, Canada, by Random House of Canada, Limited.

Reprinted by special arrangement with Oscar Hammerstein, II, and by permission of Random House, Inc.

SOUTH PACIFIC

South Pacific represents the musical play, in which the book and lyrics are no longer merely the accompaniment of the music but are themselves literature and are worthy of separate publication.

The foremost exponent of this school of drama, Oscar Hammerstein, II, was born in New York City, July 12, 1895, and graduated from Columbia University in 1916. Even while studying law he had begun to write songs, and he has become one of the foremost exponents of an art in which the oral expression is emphasized. In his preface to *Carmen Jones* (1945), an interesting adaptation of the opera *Carmen* to a situation in which the characters are negroes, Mr. Hammerstein wrote a witty argument for the right of an audience to understand the words of an opera.

In his career, from the beginning in the early twenties, he has followed the tradition of the Gilbert and Sullivan light opera in which the words were written first rather than the custom at that time in the United States of borrowing the music from foreign sources and fitting words to the score. In his preface to the volume of his *Lyrics* (1949), he has written an important contribution to the principles of composition of the musical play and his success has given him an authority which justifies his theory.

Oscar Hammerstein began his career in the organization of his uncle, Arthur Hammerstein, by collaborating with another librettist, Otto Harbach, in *Wildflower* (1923), *Rose Marie* (1924), and *Desert Song* (1926). Among the composers with whom Mr. Hammerstein collaborated were Jerome Kern, Herbert Stodhart, Sigmund Romberg, Rudolph Friml, and Vincent Youmans. He speaks of the invitation from Jerome Kern in 1927 to collaborate with him in dramatizing *Show Boat,* by Edna Ferber, as an important point in his career. Certainly those who hear that musical remember most distinctly the songs like "Ol' Man River" in which the marked word stresses and the strong musical beats represented a primitive feeling sprung from human labor and sorrow. Beginning December 27, 1927, it ran 572 performances in New York before going on the road. Meanwhile Richard Rodgers, born in New York in 1903, who graduated from Columbia in 1931, had been collaborating as composer with Lorenz Hart in several successful musical plays.

The fortunate collaboration of Oscar Hammerstein, II and Richard Rodgers has resulted in some of the outstanding musical plays of our time. *Oklahoma!* was produced by the Theatre Guild at the St. James Theatre, New York, March 31, 1943. It was based on a play by Lynn Riggs, *Green Grow the Lilacs,* also produced by the Theatre Guild, beginning December 29, 1930 in Philadelphia. This had a poetic charm, and although it did not have a long run in New York, it was selected by Burns Mantle as one of the best ten plays of the year. *Oklahoma!* became one of the longest running plays of the period, totalling 2,248 performances when it finally closed its New York run, May 29, 1948, the world's champion musical. It received a Special Pulitzer Award in 1944 for a musical play in English. *Oklahoma!* went on tour with success and played in London, Melbourne, and many other places abroad. The dances of Agnes de Mille contributed their share to this great success, but it was the magical atmosphere of "Oh, What a Beautiful Morning" a song prompted by the opening stage direction of *Green Grow the Lilacs,* which started the play on its remarkable career. The way in which the attitude of the lovers brings out the duet, "People Will Say We're in Love" illustrated the principle that the dramatic situation creates the songs and therefore they are organic. This remained a constant principle in the plays of Hammerstein and Rodgers.

Carousel was produced by the Theatre Guild at the Majestic Theatre, New York, April 19, 1945. Adapted by Benjamin F. Glazer from Ferenc Molnar's *Liliom,* the book and lyrics were by Hammerstein and the music by Rodgers. Although it was popular, *Carousel* did not have the great success of *Oklahoma!* It ran, however, until May 24, 1947, with 690 performances and it received a special award from the Drama Critics Circle. It was laid in the period 1873–1888 in New England. The authors changed the cynical tone of Molnar to one of faith and hope, manifested in the song, "You'll Never Walk Alone."

Allegro was original with Hammerstein and Rodgers. It was produced by the Theatre Guild at the Majestic Theatre, New York, October 10, 1947, ran through the season (268 performances), and continued on the road. The play traces the life of Joseph Taylor from his birth to his middle years. It presents contrasts between love and ambition, and between his opportunity to become a physician in a great city and his desire for service in his small native town. Again there were very attractive songs like "A Fellow Needs a Girl."

South Pacific is a combination of several talents. From the *Tales of the South Pacific* (1946–47), by James A. Michener, which won a Pulitzer Prize for fiction, a book was framed by Hammerstein and Joshua Logan, with lyrics by Hammerstein and music by Richard Rodgers. It opened at the Majestic, April 7, 1949, and is still running. Mr. Michener was born in New York in 1907, took degrees from Swarthmore College and Colorado State College, pursued graduate studies in American Drama at the University of Pennsylvania and travelled extensively, seeing the South Pacific as a reserve officer in the Navy on active duty in 1944–45. Joshua Logan was born in Texas and graduated from Princeton University in 1931. He had been a Captain in the A. A. F. in 1942–46, and was co-author and director of *Mr. Roberts,* a successful comedy about the Navy.

This adaptation of the *Tales of the South Pacific* skillfully emphasizes the love story between the French planter, Emile de Becque, and Nellie Forbush, the nurse, from Little Rock. Her discovery of his children naturally interrupts this story, but the result is in keeping with romance. The subplot dealing with the love of Lieutenant Joseph Cable and Liat, Bloody Mary's daughter, is kept down, but is used effectively. Cable's sacrifice for the sake of the information he gets from radar about the number of the Japanese is very well done. The scenes in the receiving station are very natural. As usual, one remembers best the songs. "Some Enchanted Evening" runs through the play like a motif. "Bali Ha'i" has the magic of the unfamiliar and Oriental. "Younger than Springtime Are You" has the tragic undertone of coming separation. The authors were awarded the Pulitzer Prize for 1949–50, also the Critics' Award for the best musical play in 1948–49; *South Pacific* opened in London, November 7, 1951; in Melbourne, Australia, September 15, 1952, and in Stockholm, September 17, 1952.

The King and I opened at the St. James Theatre, New York, March 20, 1951. It was based upon *Anna and the King of Siam,* a novel by Margaret Landon. Anna Leonowens, an English widow, goes over to Siam in 1866 to teach the children of the King of Siam. She is the only woman who dares to differ with the King and her instructions dealing with the international situation are delightful. The note of sentimentality is kept down and when he dies, she remains to teach the Prince. The songs, as usual, were noteworthy, among them "Hello, Young Lovers."

In making the collaborations with Rodgers, Hammerstein usually writes the words first but he makes clear that the words and music were integrated into a single expression. The best musical plays are written with everything in mind from the first, the book, lyrics, music, and dance. Two important elements in songwriting are first, the singer must be given time to breathe, but even more important is the quality of sincerity.

Carmen Jones (1945), *Oklahoma!* (1943), *Carousel* (1946), and *Allegro* (1947) were published by A. A. Knopf. *South Pacific* (1949), and *The King and I* (1951) were published by Random House.

The editor is indebted to the courtesy of Mr. Hammerstein, Mr. Rodgers, Mr. Logan, and Mr. Michener for their willingness to have the play reproduced, and his appreciation is due especially to Mr. Saxe Commins of Random House for his interest in the arrangements which made it possible to include the drama in this edition.

To our patient Dorothy and Nedda, who liked it even when all the parts were sung and acted by us.

CAST OF CHARACTERS

First Produced by Richard Rodgers and Oscar Hammerstein, II
in association with
Leland Hayward and Joshua Logan

Majestic Theatre, New York City, April 7, 1949

(in order of appearance)

Ngana	Barbara Luna
Jerome	Michael De Leon or Noel De Leon
Henry	Richard Silvera
Ensign Nellie Forbush	Mary Martin
Emile de Becque	Ezio Pinza
Bloody Mary	Juanita Hall
Bloody Mary's Assistant	Musa Williams
Abner	Archie Savage
Stewpot	Henry Slate
Luther Billis	Myron McCormick
Professor	Fred Sadoff
Lt. Joseph Cable, U. S. M. C.	William Tabbert
Capt. George Brackett, U. S. N.	Martin Wolfson
Cmdr. William Harbison, U. S. N.	Harvey Stephens
Yeoman Herbert Quale	Alan Gilbert
Sgt. Kenneth Johnson	Thomas Gleason
Seabee Richard West	Dickinson Eastham
Seabee Morton Wise	Henry Michel
Seaman Tom O'Brien	Bill Dwyer
Radio Operator Bob Mc Caffrey	Biff McGuire
Marine Cpl. Hamilton Steeves	Jim Hawthorne
Staff Sgt. Thomas Hassinger	Jack Fontan
Seaman James Hayes	Beau Tilden
Lt. Genevieve Marshall	Jacqueline Fisher
Ensign Dinah Murphy	Roslyn Lowe
Ensign Janet Mac Gregor	Sandra Deel
Ensign Cora Mac Rae	Bernice Saunders
Ensign Sue Yaeger	Pat Northrop

Ensign Lisa Minelli..Gloria Meli
Ensign Connie Walewska...Mardi Bayne
Ensign Pamela Whitmore...Evelyn Colby
Ensign Bessie Noonan...Helena Schurgot
Liat...Betta St. John
Marcel, Henry's Assistant..Richard Loo
Lt. Bus Adams..Don Fellows
Islanders, Sailors, Marines, Officers: Mary Ann Reeve, Chin Yu, Alex Nicol, Eugene Smith, Richard Loo, William Ferguson

The action of the play takes place on two islands in the South Pacific during the recent war. There is a week's lapse of time between the two acts.

MUSICAL NUMBERS

ACT I

Dites-Moi Pourquoi	NGANA and JEROME
A Cockeyed Optimist	NELLIE
Some Enchanted Evening	EMILE
Bloody Mary Is the Girl I Love	SAILORS, SEABEES, MARINES
There Is Nothing Like a Dame	BILLIS, SAILORS, SEABEES, MARINES
Bali Ha'i	BLOODY MARY
I'm Gonna Wash That Man Right Outa My Hair	NELLIE and NURSES
I'm in Love with a Wonderful Guy	NELLIE and NURSES
Younger Than Springtime	CABLE
Finale	NELLIE and EMILE

ACT II

Soft Shoe Dance	NURSES and SEABEES
Happy Talk	BLOODY MARY, LIAT and CABLE
Honey Bun	NELLIE and BILLIS
You've Got to Be Taught	CABLE
This Nearly Was Mine	EMILE
Reprise: Some Enchanted Evening	Nellie
Finale	

SOUTH PACIFIC

ACT ONE

Scene I

Scene: Emile de Becque's *plantation home on an island in the South Pacific.*

On your right as you look at the stage is a one-storied residence. On your left is a teakwood pagoda at the edge of the cacao grove. House and pagoda are bordered and decked in the bright tropical colors of the flaming hibiscus, the purple bougainvillaea, and the more pale and delicate frangipani. Between the house and the pagoda you can see the bay below and an island on the open sea beyond the bay. Twin volcanoes rise from the island.

At rise: *As the curtain rises, two Eurasian children,* Ngana, *a girl about eleven, and* Jerome, *a boy about eight, are, with humorous dignity, dancing an impromptu minuet. A bird call is heard in the tree above.* Jerome *looks up and imitates the sound. The eyes of both children follow the flight of the bird.* Ngana *runs over to the pagoda and climbs up on a table and poses on it as if it were a stage.* Jerome *lifts his hands and solemnly conducts her as she sings.*

Ngana.

Dites-moi
Pourquoi
La vie est belle,
Dites-moi
Pourquoi
La vie est gai!
Dites-moi
Pourquoi,
Chère mad'moiselle,
Est-ce que
Parce que
Vous m'aimez?

(Henry, *a servant, enters and scolds them.*)

Henry. Allez-vous! Vite! Dans la maison!

Ngana. Non, Henri!

Jerome. (*Mischievously delivering an ultimatum.*) Moi, je reste ici!

Henry. Oh, oui? Nous verrons bien . . . (*He chases* Jerome *around the giggling* Ngana.) Viens, petit moustique!

(Henry *catches* Jerome. *He is not as angry as he pretends to be, but he grabs* Jerome *by the ear and leads him off squealing, followed by* Ngana, *who protests violently.*)

Ngana. Non, Henri . . . non . . . non!

(*As she runs off,* Nellie *and* Emile *are heard offstage from around the corner of the house.*)

Nellie's Voice. What's this one?

Emile's Voice. That is frangipani.

Nellie's Voice. But what a color!

Emile's Voice. You will find many more flowers out here.

(Nellie *enters, looking around her, entranced by the beauty of the scene. She turns upstage to gaze out over the bay.* Henry *comes on from downstage with a tray which he takes over to the coffee table.* Emile, *entering a few paces behind* Nellie, *comes down briskly and addresses* Henry.)

Emile. Je servirai le café.

Henry. Oui, Monsieur.

Emile. C'est tout.

Henry. Oui, Monsieur de Becque.

(Henry *exits.* Nellie *comes down, still under the spell of the surrounding wonder.*)

Nellie. Well, I'm just speechless! . . . And that lunch! Wild chicken— I didn't know it was ever wild. Gosh! I had no idea people lived like this right out in the middle of the Pacific Ocean.

Emile. (*Pouring coffee.*) Sugar?

Nellie. Thanks.

Emile. One?

Nellie. Three. (Emile *smiles.*) I know it's a big load for a demitasse to carry. All right, I'm a hick. You know so many American words, do you know what a hick is?

Emile. A hick is one who lives in a stick.

Nellie. Sticks. Plural. The sticks.

Emile. Pardon. The sticks. I remember now.

Nellie. How long did it take you to build up a plantation like this?

Emile. I came to the Pacific when I was a young man.

(Nellie *studies him for a moment.*)

Nellie. Emile, is it true that all the planters on these islands—are they all running away from something?

EMILE. (*Pausing cautiously before he answers.*) Who is not running away from something? There are fugitives everywhere—Paris, New York, even in Small Rock— (NELLIE *looks puzzled.*) Where you come from . . .

(NELLIE *suddenly understands what he means and bursts out laughing.*)

NELLIE. Oh, Little Rock!

EMILE. (EMILE, *laughing with her and shouting the correction.*) Little Rock! . . . You know fugitives there?

(NELLIE *runs over to where she has left her bag.*)

NELLIE. I'll show you a picture of a Little Rock fugitive. (*Taking a clipping from an envelope in the bag.*) I got this clipping from my mother today.

(*She hands it to* EMILE *who reads:*)

EMILE. "Ensign Nellie Forbush, Arkansas' own Florence Nightingale . . ."

NELLIE. (*Apologetically.*) That was written by Mrs. Leeming, the Social Editor. She went to school with my mother. To read her, you would think that I'm practically the most important nurse in the entire Navy and that I run the fleet hospital all by myself, and it's only a matter of time before I'll be a Lady Admiral.

EMILE. In this picture you do not look much like an Admiral.

NELLIE. Oh, that was taken before I knew what rain and heat and mud could do to your disposition. But it isn't rainy today. Gosh, it's beautiful here. Just look at that yellow sun! You know, I don't think it's the end of the world like everyone else thinks. I can't work myself up to getting that low. (*He smiles.*) Do you think I'm crazy too? They all do over at the fleet hospital. You know what they call me? Knucklehead Nellie. I suppose I am, but I can't help it.

(*She sings.*)

When the sky is a bright canary yellow
I forget every cloud I've ever seen—
So they call me a cockeyed optimist,
Immature and incurably green!

I have heard people rant and rave and bellow
That we're done and we might as well be dead—
But I'm only a cockeyed optimist
And I can't get it into my head.

I hear the human race
Is falling on its face
And hasn't very far to go,
But every whippoorwill
Is selling me a bill
And telling me it just ain't so!

I could say life is just a bowl of jello
And appear more intelligent and smart
But I'm stuck
(Like a dope!)
With a thing called hope,
And I can't get it out of my heart . . . Not this heart!

(*She walks over to him, speaking the next line.*)

Want to know anything else about me?

EMILE. Yes. You say you are a fugitive. When you joined the Navy, what were you running away from?

(*He returns the clipping to her.*)

NELLIE. Gosh, I don't know. It was more like running *to* something. I wanted to see what the world was like—outside Little Rock, I mean. And I wanted to meet different kinds of people and find out if I like them better. And I'm finding out.

(*She suddenly becomes self-conscious.*)

EMILE. (*Tactful.*) Would you like some cognac?

NELLIE. (*Relieved.*) I'd love some.

(EMILE *goes to the table and pours the brandy. In the following verses,* EMILE *and* NELLIE *are not singing to each other. Each is soliloquizing:*)

NELLIE. (*Thoughtfully watching* EMILE.)
Wonder how I'd feel,
Living on a hillside,
Looking on an ocean,
Beautiful and still.

EMILE. (*Pouring the cognac.*)
This is what I need,
This is what I've longed for,
Someone young and smiling
Climbing up my hill!

NELLIE.
We are not alike;
Probably I'd bore him.
He's a cultured Frenchman—
I'm a little hick.

EMILE. (*Pausing as he starts to pour the second glass.*)
Younger men than I,
Officers and doctors,
Probably pursue her—
She could have her pick.

NELLIE. (*She catches his eye. Each averts his eyes from the other.*)
Wonder why I feel
Jittery and jumpy!
I am like a schoolgirl,

Waiting for a dance.

EMILE. (*Carrying the two filled brandy glasses, he approaches* NELLIE.)

Can I ask her now?
I am like a schoolboy!
What will be her answer?
Do I have a chance?

(*He passes* NELLIE *her brandy glass. It is a large snifter type of glass. She has apparently never drunk from one before. She watches him carefully as he lifts his to his lips, and does the same. As they drink, the music rises to great ecstatic heights. One is made aware that in this simple act of two people who are falling in love, each drinking brandy, there are turbulent thoughts and feelings going on in their hearts and brains. They lower their glasses. The music dies down.* EMILE *struggles to say something. He plunges into the middle of his subject as if continuing a thought which he assumes she has sensed.*)

EMILE. In peacetime, the boat from America comes once a month. The ladies—the wives of the planters—often go to Australia during the hot months. It can get very hot here.

NELLIE. It can get hot in Arkansas, too. (*She takes another quick swallow after this one.*)

EMILE. Ah, yes?

NELLIE. (*Nodding her head.*) Uh-huh.

EMILE. (*He puts his glass down on the table.*) I have many books here . . . Marcel Proust? (*She looks blank.*) Anatole France? (*This evokes a faint smile of half-recognition from her.*) Did you study French in school?

NELLIE. Oh, yes.

EMILE. Ah, then you can read French?

NELLIE. (*As though saying, "Of course not."*) No! (*Fearful of having disappointed him, she makes a feeble attempt to add a note of hope.*) I can conjugate a few verbs. (*Realizing how silly this must sound to him, she changes the subject.*) I bet you read a lot.

EMILE. Out here, one becomes hungry to learn everything. (*He rises and paces nervously.*) Not to miss anything, not to let anything good pass by.

(*He pauses and looks down at her, unable to go on. She, feeling he is coming closer to his point, looks up with a sudden encouraging smile.*)

NELLIE. Yes?

EMILE. One waits so long for what is good . . . and when at last it comes, one cannot risk to lose. (*He turns away, searching for more words.*) So . . . so one must speak and act quickly even—even if it seems almost foolish to be so quick. (*He looks at her, worried . . . has he gone too far . . . how will she accept any advance at all he may make to her? She can only smile helplessly back at him. He goes on, speaking quickly.*) I know it is only two weeks. A dinner given at your Officers' Club. Do you remember?

NELLIE. Yes.

EMILE. That is the way things happen sometimes. . . . Isn't it, Nellie?

NELLIE. (*Swallowing hard.*) Yes, it is . . . Emile.

EMILE. (*Singing.*)

Some enchanted evening
You may see a stranger,
You may see a stranger
Across a crowded room—
And somehow you know
(You know even then)
That somewhere you'll see her again and again.

Some enchanted evening
Someone may be laughing,
You may hear her laughing
Across a crowded room—
And night after night
(As strange as it seems)
The sound of her laughter will sing in your dreams.

Who can explain it?
Who can tell you why?
Fools give you reasons—
Wise men never try.

Some enchanted evening
When you find your true love,
When you feel her call you
Across a crowded room—
Then fly to her side,
And make her your own,
Or all through your life you may dream all alone. . . .

Once you have found her
Never let her go,
Once you have found her
Never let her go!

(*There follow several seconds of silence. Neither moves.* EMILE *speaks.*)

EMILE. I am older than you. If we have children, when I die they will be growing up. You could afford to take them back to America—if you like. Think about it.

(*Henry enters.*)

HENRY. Monsieur de Becque, la jeep de Mademoiselle est ici. (NELLIE *and* EMILE *turn as if awakened from a dream.*) La jeep de Mademoiselle. (HENRY *smiles, a wide toothy smile, at* NELLIE.) Votre jeep!

NELLIE. Oh, my jeep! (*She looks at her watch.*) Gosh! Thank you, Henry. I'm on duty in ten minutes!

(HENRY *exits.* NELLIE *holds out her hand to* EMILE.)

EMILE. Before you leave, Nellie, I want to tell you something. A while ago, you asked me a question—why did I leave France?

NELLIE. Oh, Emile, that was none of my business.

EMILE. But I want to tell you. I had to leave France. I killed a man. (*Pause.*)

NELLIE. Why did you kill him?

EMILE. He was a wicked man, a bully. Everyone in our village was glad to see him die, and it was not to my discredit. Do you believe me, Nellie?

(*Another pause—unbearable to him.*)

NELLIE. You have just told me that you killed a man and that it's all right. I hardly know you, and yet I know it's all right.

EMILE. (*Deeply moved.*) Thank you, Nellie. (*His voice suddenly gay and exultant.*) And you like my place?

NELLIE. Yes.

EMILE. You will think?

NELLIE. (*Smiling up at him.*) I will think.

(*They are silent and motionless for a moment. Then she turns suddenly and walks off very quickly. He looks after her and starts to hum softly. He picks up the coffee cup she has left on the fountain and smiles down at it. He holds the cup up so he can examine its rim.*)

EMILE. Lipstick! . . . Three lumps of sugar in this little cup! (*He laughs aloud, then resumes his humming and walks, almost dances, across the stage in time to his own music.* NGANA *and* JEROME *enter and walk behind him across the stage, imitating his happy stride. As* EMILE *puts down the cup, the children join him, humming the same melody. He turns quickly and frowns down on them with mock sternness. They giggle.*) Eh bien!

JEROME. Bravo, Papa!

(*The children both applaud.*)

EMILE. Merci, Monsieur!

NGANA. Nous chantons bien, aussi.

EMILE. Ah, oui?

NGANA. Attends, Papa!

JEROME. (*Parroting* NGANA.) Attends, Papa!

(*He looks at* NGANA *for the signal to start the song. They sing . . .* EMILE *conducting them.*)

NGANA AND JEROME.

Dites moi
Pourquoi
La vie est belle—

(EMILE *joins them.*)

Dites moi
Pourquoi
La vie est gai!
Dites moi
Pourquoi,

(EMILE *and* JEROME *make a deep bow to* NGANA.)

Chère Mad'moiselle,

(EMILE *picks them up, one under each arm, and starts to carry them off as they finish singing the refrain together.*)

Est-ce que
Parce que
Vous m'aimez?

(*The lights fade out and a transparent curtain closes in on them. Before they are out of sight, the characters of the next scene have entered downstage in front of the curtain. All transitions from one scene to another in the play are achieved in this manner so that the effect is of one picture dissolving into the next.*)

ACT ONE

SCENE II

The curtain depicts no specific place but represents the abstract pattern of a large tapa-cloth. In front of this, lounge a group of Seabees, Sailors and Marines. As the lights come up on them and go out on the previous scene, they are singing.

MEN.

Bloody Mary is the girl I love,
Bloody Mary is the girl I love,
Bloody Mary is the girl I love—
Now ain't that too damn bad!

Her skin is as tender as DiMaggio's glove,
Her skin is as tender as DiMaggio's glove,
Her skin is as tender as DiMaggio's glove
Now ain't that too damn bad!

(*The object of this serenade who has been hidden during the song, by two sailors, is now revealed as they move away. This is* BLOODY MARY. *She is small, yellow, with Oriental eyes. She wears black sateen trousers, and a white blouse over which is an old Marine's tunic. On her head is a peach-basket hat. Around her neck is a G. I. identification chain from which hangs a silver Marine emblem. At the end of the singing, she gives out a shrill cackle of laughter with which we shall soon learn to identify her.*)

MARY. (*Looking straight out at the audience.*) Hallo, G. I.! (*She holds up a grass skirt.*) Grass skirt? Very saxy! Fo' dolla'? Saxy grass skirt. Fo' dolla'! Send home Chicago. You like? You buy? (*Her eyes scan the audience as if following a passer-by. Her crafty smile fades to a quick scowl as he apparently passes without buying. She calls after him.*) Where you go? Come back! Chipskate! Crummy G. I.! Sadsack. Droopy-drawers!

MARINE. Tell 'em good, Mary!

MARY. What is good?

MARINE. Tell him he's a stingy bastard!

MARY. (*Delighted at the sound of these new words.*) Stingy bastard! (*She turns back toward the* MARINE *for approval.*) That good?

MARINE. That's great, Mary! You're learning fast.

MARY. (*Calling off again.*) Stingy bastard! (*She cackles gaily and turns back to the* MARINE.) I learn fast. . . . Pretty soon I talk English good as any crummy Marine. (*Calling off once more.*) Stingy bastard!

(*She laughs very loud but the Marines, Seabees and Sailors laugh louder and cheer her. They then resume their serenade.*)

MEN.

Bloody Mary's chewing betel nuts,
She is always chewing betel nuts,
Bloody Mary's chewing betel nuts—
And she don't use Pepsodent.

(*She grins and shows her betel-stained teeth.*)

Now ain't that too damn bad!

(*While this is being sung, the lights come up behind the tapa-cloth transparent curtain revealing:*)

ACT ONE

SCENE III

SCENE: *The edge of a palm grove near the beach. Beyond the beach in the bay can be seen the same twin-peaked island that was evident from* EMILE'S *hillside. On your left, as you look at the stage, is* BLOODY MARY'S *kiosk. This is made of bamboo and canvas. Her merchandise, laid out in front, comprises shells, native hats, local dress material, outrigger canoes and hookahs. Several grass skirts are hanging up around the kiosk. On the right, at first making a puzzling silhouette, then as the lights come up, resolving itself into a contraption of weird detail, is a G. I. homemade washing machine. It looks partly like a giant ice-cream freezer, partly like a windmill. In front of it there is a sign which reads:*

TWISTED AIR HAND LAUNDRY
LUTHER BILLIS ENTERPRISES
SPECIAL RATES FOR SEABEES

As the lights come up, the washing machine is being operated by Carpenter's Mate, Second Class, George Watts, better known as "STEWPOT." *Seabees, Sailors, Marines and some Army men lounge around the scene waiting for whatever diversion* BLOODY MARY *may provide. During the singing which covers this change,* BLOODY MARY *takes a strange-looking object out of her pocket and dangles it in front of a* MARINE.

MARINE. What is that thing?

MARY. (*Holding the small object in her hand.*) Is head. Fifty dolla'.

MARINE. (*Revolted.*) What's it *made* of?

MARY. Made outa head! Is real human.

MARINE. (*Fascinated.*) What makes it so small?

MARY. Shlunk! Only way to keep human head is shlink 'em.

MARINE. No, thanks.

(*He leaves quickly.*)

MARY. (*To a new customer as she holds a grass skirt up to her waist and starts to dance.*) Fo' dolla'. Send home Chicago to saxy sweetheart! She make wave like this.

(*She starts to dance. One of the sailors grabs her and goes into an impromptu jitterbug dance with her. Others join, and soon the beach is alive with gyrating gentlemen of the United States Armed Services. As this spontaneous festivity is at its height,* LUTHER BILLIS *enters, followed by the* PROFESSOR, *both loaded with grass skirts. They come down in front of* BLOODY MARY *and throw the grass skirts at her feet.*)

BILLIS. Here you are, Sweaty Pie! Put them down, Professor. These beautiful skirts were made by myself, the Professor here, and three other Seabees in half the time it takes your native workers to make 'em. (*He picks up a skirt and demonstrates.*) See? No stretch! (Throwing *the skirt back on the ground.*) Look 'em over, Sweaty Pie, and give me your price.

(*At this point, an altercation starts upstage near the washing machine.*)

SAILOR. Look at that shirt!

STEWPOT. Take it up with the manager.

(*He points down to* BILLIS.)

SAILOR. (*Coming down to him.*) Hey, Big Dealer! Hey, Luther Billis!

BILLIS. (*Smoothly.*) What can I do for you, my boy? What's the trouble?

SAILOR. (*Holding up his shirt which has been laundered and is in tatters.*) Look at that shirt!

BILLIS. The Billis Laundry is not responsible for minor burns and tears. (*He turns back laconically to* MARY.) What do you say, Sweatso? What am I offered?

(*The* SAILOR *storms off. The* PROFESSOR, *meanwhile, is showing the beautiful work they do to some other Sailors and Seabees.*)

PROFESSOR. (*Holding up a skirt.*) All hand sewn!

SAILOR. Gee, that's mighty nice work!

BILLIS. (*To* BLOODY MARY.) Do you hear that, Sweaty Pie? You can probably sell these to the chumps for five or six dollars apiece. Now, I'll let you have the whole bunch for . . . say . . . eighty bucks.

MARY. Give you ten dolla'.

BILLIS. What?

MARY. Not enough?

BILLIS. You're damn well right, not enough!

MARY. (*Dropping the skirt at his feet.*) Den you damn well keep.

(*She goes down to another sailor and takes from her pocket a boar's tooth bracelet which she holds up to tempt him.*)

BILLIS. (*Following* BLOODY MARY.) Now look here, Dragon Lady— (*Whatever he was about to say is knocked out of his head by the sight of the bracelet.* BILLIS *is an inveterate and passionate souvenir hunter.*) What's that you got there, a boar's tooth bracelet? Where'd you get that? (*He points to the twin-peaked island.*) Over there on Bali Ha'i?

MARY. (*Smiling craftily.*) You like?

BILLIS. (*Taking bracelet and showing to G.I.'s who have huddled around him.*) You know what that is? A bracelet made out of a single boar's tooth. They cut the tooth from the boar's mouth in a big ceremonial over there on Bali Ha'i. There ain't a souvenir you can pick up in the South Pacific as valuable as this . . . What do you want for it, Mary?

MARY. Hundred dolla'!

BILLIS. Hundred dollars! (*Shocked, but realizing he will pay it, turns to the boys and justifies himself in advance.*) That's cheap. I thought it would be more.

(*He takes the money from his pocket.*)

PROFESSOR. I don't see how she can do it.

MARY. Make you special offer Big Deala'. I trade you boar's tooth bracelet for all grass skirts.

BILLIS. It's a deal.

MARY. Wait a minute. Is no deal till you throw in something for good luck.

BILLIS. Okay. What do you want me to throw in?

MARY. (*Taking money from his hand.*) Hundred dolla'.

BILLIS. Well, for the love of . . .

MARY. (*Shaking his hand, grinning a big Oriental grin.*) Good luck.

(*She exits with grass skirts. The men all crowd around* BILLIS, *shaking his hand in ironic "congratulation."*)

BILLIS. You don't run into these things every day. They're scarce as hens' teeth.

PROFESSOR. They're bigger, too.

BILLIS. That damned Bali Ha'i! (*Turning and looking toward the twin-peaked island.*) Why does it have to be off limits? You can get everything over there. Shrunken heads, bracelets, old ivory—

SAILOR. Young French women!

BILLIS. Knock off! I'm talking about souvenirs.

PROFESSOR. So's he.

BILLIS. (*Pacing restlessly.*) We got to get a boat and get over there. I'm feeling held down again. I need to take a trip.

STEWPOT. Only officers can sign out boats.

BILLIS. I'll get a boat all right. I'll latch onto some officer who's got some imagination . . . that would like to see that Boar's Tooth ceremonial as much as I would . . . It's a hell of a ceremonial! Dancin', drinkin' . . . everything!

SAILOR. Why, you big phony. We all know why you want to go to Bali Ha'i.

BILLIS. Why?

SAILOR. Because the French planters put all their young women over there when they heard the G.I.'s were coming. That's why! It ain't boar's teeth . . . it's women!

BILLIS. It is boar's teeth . . . *and* women!

(*A long pause. All the men are still and thoughtful, each dreaming a similar dream—but his own. Music starts. A* SEABEE *breaks the silence.*)

SEABEE. (*Singing.*)

We got sunlight on the sand,
We got moonlight on the sea.

SAILOR.

We got mangoes and bananas
You can pick right off a tree.

MARINE.

We got volley ball and ping pong
And a lot of dandy games—

BILLIS.

What ain't we got?

ALL.

We ain't got dames!

MARINE.

We get packages from home,

SAILOR.

We get movies, we get shows,

STEWPOT.

We get speeches from our skipper

SOLDIER.

And advice from Tokyo Rose

SEABEE.

We get letters doused wit' poifume,

SAILOR.

We get dizzy from the smell—

BILLIS.

What don't we get?

ALL.

You know damn well!

BILLIS.

We have nothin' to put on a clean, white suit for.
What we need is what there ain't no substitute for!

ALL.

There is nothin' like a dame
Nothin' in the world.
There is nothin' you can name
That is anythin' like a dame.

MARINE.

We feel restless,
We feel blue.

SEABEE.

We feel lonely and, in brief,
We feel every kind of feelin'

PROFESSOR.

But the feelin' of relief.

SAILOR.

We feel hungry as the wolf felt
When he met Red Riding Hood—

ALL.

What don't we feel?

STEWPOT.

We don't feel good!

SAILOR.

Lots of things in life are beautiful, but brother—
There is one particular thing that is nothin' whatsoever in any way shape or form like any other!

ALL.

There is nothin' like a dame—
Nothin' in the world.
There is nothin' you can name
That is anythin' like a dame.

Nothin' else is built the same,
Nothin' in the world
Has a soft and wavy frame
Like the silhouette of a dame.

MARINE. (*With a deep bass voice.*)
There is absolutely nothin' like the frame of a dame!

(*The music continues throughout the following dialogue and action.*)

GIRL'S VOICE. Hut, two, three, four! Get —your—exercise!

(*A husky* NURSE *enters, leading several other* NURSES, *all dressed in bathing suits, playsuits, or fatigues.* NELLIE *is among them. They jog across the stage, their* LEADER *continuing the military count. The men's eyes follow them.*)

A TIRED NURSE. Can't we rest a while?

HUSKY LEADER. Come on you nurses, pick it up!

(NELLIE *drops out of line as the others run off.*)

NELLIE. (*Beckoning to* BILLIS.) Hey, Luther!

STEWPOT. (*Nudging* BILLIS.) Luther!

(BILLIS *turns and goes shyly to* NELLIE, *terribly embarrassed that the men are watching him. He is a different* BILLIS *in front of* NELLIE. *He is unassured and has lost all of his brashness. For him* NELLIE FORBUSH *has "class."*)

BILLIS. Yes, Miss Forbush.

(*All eyes follow him.*)

NELLIE. Have you done what you promised?

BILLIS. Yes, Miss Forbush. (*He pulls out a newspaper package from a hiding place in the roots of a tree and hands it to her.*) I did it all last night. (*With an alarmed look at his comrades, as she starts to unwrap it.*) You don't have to open it now!

(*But* NELLIE *opens the package, much to* BILLIS' *embarrassment. It is her laundry, neatly folded.*)

NELLIE. Oh. You do beautiful work, Luther! (*Two men painfully cling to each other and turn their heads away.* BILLIS *tries to outglare the others in defensive defiance.*) You've even done the pleats in my shorts!

BILLIS. Aw, pleats aren't hard. You better run along now and catch up to your gang.

NELLIE. Pleats are *very* hard. How do you do such delicate work at night, in the dark?

BILLIS. There was a moon!

STEWPOT. (*In a syrupy voice.*) There was a moon!

BILLIS. (*He turns to the men, realizing that they have heard this, and shouts defiantly.*) A full moon!

NELLIE. (*She is wrapping up the package.*) How much, Luther!

BILLIS. (*Earnestly.*) Oh, no, not from you.

NELLIE. Gosh, I guess I'm just about the luckiest nurse on this island to have found you. You're a treasure. (*She turns and runs off.*) Well, good-bye, Luther. Hut, two, three, four!

(*She has gone!* BILLIS *turns and faces the men, trying to bluff it out. He walks belligerently over to* STEWPOT *who with the* PROFESSOR *whistles "There's Nothin' Like a Dame." Then he walks over to another group and they join* STEWPOT *and* PROFESSOR *in whistling. Soon all are whistling.* BILLIS *whistles too. After the refrain is finished,* STEWPOT *looks off reflectively at the departing* NELLIE.)

STEWPOT. *She's* a nice little girl, but some of them nurses—the officers can have them.

PROFESSOR. They got them!

STEWPOT. Well, they can have them!

MARINE. (*Singing.*)

So suppose a dame ain't bright,
Or completely free from flaws,

SAILOR.

Or as faithful as a bird dog,

SEABEE.

Or as kind as Santa Claus,

SOLDIER.

It's a waste of time to worry
Over things that they have not

SAILOR.

Be thankful for

ALL.

The things they got!

HUSKY LEADER. (*Entering.*) Hut, two, three, four. Hut, two, three, four!

(*The exercising nurses enter upstage, jogging in the opposite direction to their previous course.* NELLIE *is again with them. She turns and waves to* BILLIS *and points to the laundry under her arm. The boys all rise and turn upstage, their heads following the girls until they're off. Then the boys continue to turn until they're facing front again.*)

ALL.

There is nothin' you can name
That is anythin' like a dame!
There are no books like a dame,
And nothin' looks like a dame,
There are no drinks like a dame,
And nothin' thinks like a dame,
Nothin' acts like a dame
Or attracts like a dame.
There ain't a thing that's wrong with any man here
That can't be cured by puttin' him near
A girly, womanly, female, feminine dame!

(BLOODY MARY *enters and starts humming the song, as she proceeds to rearrange her new stock of grass skirts.* LT. JOSEPH CABLE *enters. He wears suntans, overseas cap, and carries a musette bag in his hand.* BLOODY MARY *sees him and stops singing. They stand for a moment, looking at each other—she, suspicious and frightened, and he, puzzled and curious.*)

MARY. Hallo.

CABLE. Hello.

(*Music of "Bali Ha'i" is played softly.*)

MARY. You mak' trouble for me?

CABLE. Hunh?

MARY. Are you crummy major?

CABLE. No, I'm even crummier than that. I'm a lieutenant.

MARY. Lootellan?
CABLE. (*Laughing.*) Lootellan.
(*He strolls away from her, toward the men.*)
BILLIS. Hiya, Lootellan. New on the rock?
CABLE. Just came in on that PBY.
BILLIS. Yeah? Where from?
CABLE. A little island south of Marie Louise.
STEWPOT. Then you been up where they use real bullets!
CABLE. Unh-huh.
MARY. (*Who has been looking adoringly at* CABLE.) Hey, Lootellan. You damn saxy man!
CABLE. (*Rocked off his balance for a moment.*) Thanks. You're looking pretty —er—fit yourself.
(*She grins happily at him, showing her betel-stained teeth and crosses, beaming, to her assistant.*)
MARY. (*To assistant.*) Damn saxy!
CABLE. (*To* BILLIS.) Who is she?
BILLIS. She's Tonkinese—used to work for a French planter.
MARY. French planters stingy bastards!
(*She laughs.*)
CABLE. Say, I wonder if any of you know a French planter named de Becque?
BILLIS. Emile de Becque? I think he's the guy lives on top of that hill . . . Do you know him?
CABLE. (*Looking off toward the hill, thoughtfully.*) No, but I'm going to.
(MARY *follows* CABLE, *taking the shrunken head from her pocket.*)
MARY. Hey, Lootellan! Real human head! . . . You got sweetheart? Send home Chicago to saxy sweetheart!
CABLE. No—er—she's a Philadelphia girl.
MARY. Whazzat, Philadelia girl? Whazzat mean? No saxy? (*With a sudden impulse.*) You like I give you free?
BILLIS. Free! You never give *me* anything free.
MARY. You not saxy like Lootellan. (*To* CABLE, *proffering the shrunken head.*) Take!
CABLE. No, thanks. Where'd you get that anyway?
MARY. Bali Ha'i.
STEWPOT. (*Nudging* BILLIS, *pointing to* CABLE, *as he whispers:*) There's your officer! There's your officer!
BILLIS. That's that island over there with the two volcanoes. (*Significantly.*) *Officers* can get launches and go over there.
CABLE. (*Looking out at island.*) Bali Ha'i . . . What does that mean?
MARY. Bali Ha'i mean "I am your special Island" . . . mean . . . "Here I am." Bali Ha'i is *your* special Island, Lootellan. I know! You listen! You hear island call to you. Listen! You no hear something? Listen!
CABLE. (*After listening for a moment.*) I hear the sound of the wind and the waves, that's all.
MARY. You no hear something calling? Listen!
(*Silence.* ALL *listen.*)
STEWPOT. (*Trying to be helpful.*) I think *I* hear something.
BILLIS. (*In a harsh, threatening whisper.*) Shut your big fat mouth!
MARY. Hear voice?
(*She sings to* CABLE, *as he gazes out at the mysterious island.*)

Mos' people live on a lonely island,
Lost in de middle of a foggy sea.
Mos' people long fo' anudder island
One where dey know dey would lak to be . . .

Bali Ha'i
May call you,
Any night, any day.
In your heart
You'll hear it call you
"Come away, come away."

Bali Ha'i
Will whisper
On de wind of de sea,
"Here am I,
Your special island!
Come to me, come to me!"

Your own special hopes,
Your own special dreams
Bloom on de hillside
And shine in de streams.

If you try,
You'll find me
Where de sky meets de sea,
"Here am I,
Your special island!
Come to me, come to me!"

Bali Ha'i!
Bali Ha'i!
Bali Ha'i!

Some day, you'll see me,
Floatin' in de sunshine,
My head stickin' out
F'um a low-flyin' cloud.
You'll hear me call you,

Singin' through de sunshine,
Sweet and clear as can be,
"Come to me,
Here am I,
Come to me!"

If you try,
You'll find me
Where de sky meets de sea,
"Here am I,
Your special island!
Come to me, come to me!"

Bali Ha'i!
Bali Ha'i!
Bali Ha'i!

(BLOODY MARY *exits.* CABLE *seems spellbound by her words.* BILLIS *follows up with a more earthy form of salesmanship.*)

BILLIS. Of course, Lieutenant, right now that island is off limits due to the fact that the French planters have all their young women running around over there. (*He pauses to observe the effect of these significant words.*) Of course, you being an officer, you could get a launch. I'd even be willing to requisition a boat for you. What do you say, Lieutenant? (*Singing throatily.*)

Bali Ha'i may call you
Any night any day.
In your heart you'll
Hear it call you—
Bali Ha'i—Bali Ha'i . . .

Hunh, Lieutenant? (*Pause.*)

CABLE. No.

BILLIS. (*Making a quick shift.*) I see what you mean, being off limits and all. It would take a lot of persuading to get *me* to go over there . . . But, another thing goes on over there—the ceremonial of the boar's tooth. After they kill the boar they pass around some of that coconut liquor and women dance with just skirts on . . . (*His voice becoming evil.*) and everybody gets to know everybody pretty well . . . (*He sings.*)

Bali Ha'i will whisper—

(BILLIS *starts dance as he hums the melody seductively. Then he stops and talks.*)

It's just a little tribal ceremonial and I thought you being up in the shooting war for such a long time without getting any —recreation—I thought you might be interested.

CABLE. I am. But right now I've got to report to the Island Commander.

BILLIS. Oh. (*Shouting officiously.*) Professor! Take the Lieutenant up in the truck.

CABLE. Professor?

BILLIS. That's because he went to college. You go to college?

CABLE. Er—yes.

BILLIS. Where?

CABLE. A place in New Jersey.

BILLIS. Where? Rutgers?

CABLE. No . . . Princeton.

BILLIS. Oh. Folks got money, eh, Lieutenant? (*He leers wisely.*) Don't be ashamed of it. We understand. Say! Maybe you'd like to hear the Professor talk some language. What would you like to hear? Latin? Grecian? (*Grabbing the unwilling* PROFESSOR *by the arm and leading him over to* CABLE.) Aw, give him some Latin!

PROFESSOR. (*The* PROFESSOR *feels pretty silly, but proceeds:*

"Rectius vives Licini—"

BILLIS. Ain't that beautiful!

PROFESSOR.

". . . neque altum
Semper urgendo dum procellas . . ."

(*A crowd gathers around the* PROFESSOR. BILLIS *beams at* CABLE.)

BILLIS. Now, Lieutenant, what did he say?

CABLE. I'm afraid I haven't the slightest idea.

BILLIS. What's the matter, didn't you graduate? (*Disgusted, to the* PROFESSOR.) Take the Lieutenant to the buildings.

(CABLE *and the* PROFESSOR *start to go.*)

PROFESSOR. Aye, aye!

BILLIS. (*To* STEWPOT.) He'll never make Captain.

(*The* PROFESSOR, *suddenly alarmed by something he sees offstage, turns back and starts to make strange signal-noises of warning.*)

PROFESSOR. Whoop-whoop-whoop! (*In a hoarse whisper.*) Iron Belly!

(*The men assume casual and innocent attitudes. Some make bird sounds.* MARY *looks off and walks back to her kiosk to stand defiantly in front of it.* CABLE, *puzzled, stands by to await developments. What develops is that "Iron Belly,"* CAPTAIN BRACKETT, *enters, followed by his executive officer,* COMMANDER HARBISON.)

HARBISON. (*A brusque man.*) Here she is, sir.

(*He points to* BLOODY MARY, *who is standing her ground doggedly in front of her kiosk.* BRACKETT *walks slowly over to her.* HARBISON *takes a few steps toward the men and they move away.* BRACKETT *glares at* MARY. *Undaunted, she glares right back.*)

BRACKETT. You are causing an economic revolution on this island. These French planters can't find a native to pick a coconut or milk a cow because you're paying them ten times as much to make these ridiculous grass skirts.

MARY. French planters stingy bastards!

(STEWPOT *drops a tin bucket. The men control themselves by great efforts, their faces contorted queerly.* BRACKETT *scowls and for the moment can think of no answer.* BILLIS *approaches him, with a snappy salute.*)

BILLIS. Sir! May I make a suggestion, sir?

BRACKETT. (*Returning salute.*) Who are you?

BILLIS. Billis, sir, Luther Billis. (*Making an impressive announcement.*) The natives can now go back to work on the farms. The demand for grass skirts can now be met by us Seabees!

BRACKETT. Dressmakers! (*Starting to blow up.*) Do you mean to tell me the Seabees of the United States Navy are now a lot of—

BILLIS. If you don't like the idea, sir, we can drop it right here, sir. Just say the word. Just pretend I never brought it up.

HARBISON. (*Reflectively.*) Luther Billis.

BILLIS. Yes, sir?

HARBISON. Nothing. Just making a mental note. I want to be sure not to forget your name.

(*Pause, during which* BILLIS *slowly and dejectedly retires.* BRACKETT *turns to* MARY.)

BRACKETT. I want to see you pick up every scrap of this paraphernalia now! And, for the last time, carry it way down there beyond that fence off Navy property.

(MARY *stands firmly planted and immovable! . . .* CABLE *walks to the kiosk and collapses it.*)

CABLE. (*With decisive authority.*) Come on, everybody. Take all this stuff and throw it over that fence.

(*The men quickly obey,* BILLIS *ostentatiously taking charge in front of the two officers.*)

BILLIS. (*To men.*) All right—take it way down there. Off Navy property!

CABLE. (*Strides over to* MARY *and points off.*) You go too!

MARY. (CABLE *can do no wrong in her eyes.*) All right, Lootellan. Thank you.

(*She exits. By this time, all the men have gone, taking her kiosk with them.* BRACKETT, CABLE *and* HARBISON *are left.* BRACKETT *looks at* HARBISON *as if to ask who* CABLE *is.* HARBISON *shrugs his shoulders.* CABLE *turns and exchanges salutes with* BRACKETT.)

BRACKETT. Lieutenant, who are you, anyway?

CABLE. I'm Lieutenant Joseph Cable, sir. I just flew in on that PBY.

BRACKETT. A joy ride?

CABLE. No, sir. Orders.

BRACKETT. A Marine under orders to me?

CABLE. Yes, sir.

BRACKETT. I'm Captain Brackett.

CABLE. How do you do, sir?

BRACKETT. This is Commander Harbison, my Executive Officer. (CABLE *and* HARBISON *exchange hellos, salutes and handshakes.*) Well, what's it all about?

CABLE. My Colonel feels that all these islands are in danger because none of us has been getting first-hand intelligence, and what we need is a coast watch.

HARBISON. A coast watch?

CABLE. A man with a radio hiding out on one of those Jap-held islands, where he could watch for Jap ships when they start down the bottleneck . . . down this way.

BRACKETT. (*Turning to* HARBISON.) What do you think, Bill?

HARBISON. Well, sir, our pilots could do a hell of a lot to Jap convoys with information like that.

BRACKETT. You'd have to sneak this man ashore at night from a submarine.

CABLE. Yes, sir.

HARBISON. Who's going to do it?

CABLE. Well, sir . . . *I've* been elected. (*Pause.*)

BRACKETT. (*After exchanging a look with* HARBISON.) You've got quite an assignment, son.

HARBISON. How long do you think you could last there, sending out messages, before the Japs found you?

CABLE. I think I'd be okay if I could take a man with me who really knew the country. Headquarters has found out there's a French civilian here who used to have a plantation on Marie Louise Island.

HARBISON. Marie Louise! That's a good spot. Right on the bottleneck.

BRACKETT. What's this Frenchman's name?

CABLE. Emile de Becque.

BRACKETT. (*Suddenly excited.*) Meet me in my office in about half an hour, Cable.

(*He starts off, followed by* HARBISON.)

CABLE. Yes, sir.

BRACKETT. Come on, Bill! Maybe we'll get in this war yet!

(*They exit.* CABLE *watches them off, then picks up his musette bag and starts off himself. The music of "Bali Ha'i" is played.* CABLE *stops in his tracks and listens. Then he turns and looks across at the island. . . . Softly, he starts to sing:*)

CABLE.

Bali Ha'i may call you
Any night,
Any day,
In your heart you'll hear it call you,
Come away, come away.
Bali Ha'i, Bali Ha'i, Bali Ha'i.

ACT ONE

SCENE IV

As CABLE *sings, the lights fade slowly. A transparent curtain closes across him.*

Downstage, several G.I.'s enter carrying bales and various articles of equipment. The lights dim out on CABLE *behind the curtain and now, illuminating the forestage, reveal the curtain as depicting a company street.*

SAILOR. (*Crossing stage.*) When are you guys going to get that lumber down in our area?

SEABEE. (*Passing him.*) Aw, knock it off!

SAILOR. We'll never get it finished by Thanksgiving.

(*By this time, the lights are higher on the company street. Natives and G.I.'s are constantly crossing, carrying equipment. Natives are seen sometimes wearing G.I. uniforms and sometimes just native cloths. Two nurses in white uniforms cross. Then* BILLIS *enters, in earnest conversation with* STEWPOT *and the* PROFESSOR.)

BILLIS. Did you tell those guys at the shop to stop making those grass skirts?

STEWPOT. Sure, they just turned out one of these. (*He hands him a small, dark object.*) What do you think of it?

BILLIS. (*Studying it a moment.*) That don't look like a dried-up human head. It looks like an old orange painted with shoe-polish.

STEWPOT. That's what it is.

BILLIS. Go back to the shop and tell them to try again. If I order a dried-up human head, I want a human head . . . dried up!

(*He puts the orange in his pocket.*)

STEWPOT. But—

BILLIS. Fade. Here he comes. (STEWPOT *and the* PROFESSOR *move away as* CABLE *enters.* BILLIS *crosses to him and speaks to him in a low voice, right in* CABLE'S *ear, as he walks alongside him.*) Don't change your expression, Lieutenant. Just act like we're talking casual. I got the boat.

CABLE. (*Stops.*) What boat?

BILLIS. Keep walking down the company street. Keep your voice down. (CABLE *walks slowly and uncertainly.*) I signed out a boat in your name. We're shoving off for Bali Ha'i in forty-five minutes.

CABLE. (*Stopping.*) No, we're not. I've got to see Captain Brackett.

BILLIS. (*An injured man.*) Lieutenant! What are you doing to me? I signed this boat out in your name.

CABLE. Then you're just the man to go back and cancel it. (*Very firmly.*) Forget the whole thing. Okay?

(CABLE *walks off.* BILLIS *looks after him with narrowing eyes and jaw thrust forward.*)

BILLIS. Lieutenant, you and me are going on a boat trip whether you like it or not.

(*He pulls the orange, covered with shoe polish, out of his pocket, and wishing to vent his rage somehow, he turns and hurls it off in the direction opposite that taken by* CABLE.)

A FURIOUS VOICE. (*Offstage.*) Hey! Who the hell threw that?

BILLIS. (*Spoiling for a fight with anyone at all.*) I threw it! What are you gonna do about it?

(*He strides off pugnaciously in the direction of the voice. Before he is off, the curtains have parted on the succeeding scene.*)

ACT ONE

SCENE V

Inside the Island Commander's office. BRACKETT *is sitting at his desk, reading some papers.* HARBISON *stands above him.* CABLE *sits on a chair facing the desk.*

BRACKETT. (*As curtains part.*) Cable . . . we've got some dope on your Frenchman. (*He reads a paper before him.*) Marie Louise Island . . . moved down here sixteen years ago . . . lived with a Polynesian woman for about five years . . . two children by her. She died . . . Here's one thing we've got to clear up. Seems he left France in a hurry. Killed a guy. What do you think of that?

CABLE. Might be a handy man to have around.

(*The phone rings.*)

HARBISON. (*Beckoning to* CABLE.) Cable.

(CABLE *joins him and they inspect a map on the wall.*)

BRACKETT. (*In phone.*) Good . . . send her in. No, we haven't got time for her to change into her uniform. Tell her to come in. (*The men exchange looks and face the doorway where presently* NELLIE *appears.*) Come in, Miss Forbush.

NELLIE. Captain Brackett, please excuse the way . . .

BRACKETT. You look fine. May I present Commander Harbison?

HARBISON. I have the pleasure of meeting Miss Forbush twice a week. (BRACKETT *looks at him, surprised and curious.*) We serve together on the G. I. Entertainment Committee.

BRACKETT. Oh. May I also present Lt. Joseph Cable . . . Miss Forbush. Sit down, Miss Forbush. (*The three men rush to help her sit.* CABLE *gets there first.* NELLIE *sits.* BRACKETT *sits on his desk facing her.* CABLE *drops upstage.* BRACKETT *starts off with light conversation.*) How's the Thanksgiving Entertainment coming along?

NELLIE. Very well, thank you, sir. We practice whenever we get a chance.

(*She wonders why she has been sent for.*)

BRACKETT. About a week ago, you had lunch with a French planter . . . Emile de Becque.

NELLIE. Yes, sir.

BRACKETT. What do you know about him?

NELLIE. (*Thrown off balance.*) Well, I er . . . what do I know about him?

BRACKETT. That's right.

NELLIE. I . . . we . . . met at the Officers' Club dance. He was there and I . . . met him. (*She stops, hoping they will help her along, but they say nothing, so she has to continue.*) Then I had lunch with him that day. . . .

BRACKETT. (*Quickly.*) Yes! Now, what kind of a man is he?

NELLIE. He's very nice . . . He's kind . . . He's attractive. I—er—I just don't know what you want to know, sir.

HARBISON. Miss Forbush, Captain Brackett wants to know, did you discuss politics?

NELLIE. No, sir.

BRACKETT. (*After a long, pitying look at* HARBISON.) Would you have discussed politics, Commander? (*Turning back to* NELLIE.) Now, what we are specifically interested in is—er—when these fellows come out from France, it's generally because they've had some trouble. (NELLIE *looks worried.*) Now . . . has he ever told you anything about that? (NELLIE *hesitates a moment, deliberating just how far to go in her answer.* BRACKETT *tries to help her out, sensing her embarrassment.*) What do you know about his family?

NELLIE. (*Glad to be able to answer a simple specific question without incriminating* EMILE.) He has no family—no wife, nobody.

HARBISON. He hasn't any children?

(CABLE *and* HARBISON *exchange looks.*)

NELLIE. No, sir!

BRACKETT. And you say he's never told you why he left France?

(*Pause. Then* NELLIE *answers as a Navy Ensign should.*)

NELLIE. Yes, sir. He left France because he killed a man.

(*A sigh of relief from* BRACKETT.)

HARBISON. Did he tell you why?

NELLIE. No. But he will if I ask him.

HARBISON. Well, Miss Forbush, that's exactly what we'd like to have you do. Find out as much as you can about him, his background, his opinions, and why he killed this man in France.

NELLIE. In other words, you want me to spy on him.

BRACKETT. Well, I'm afraid it *is* something like that.

NELLIE. Why? (*Alarmed, she rises and faces* BRACKETT *across his desk.*) Do you suspect him of anything?

BRACKETT. (*Lies do not come easy to him.*) No, it's just that we don't know very much about him and he's—er . . . Will you help us, Miss Forbush? (*Pause.*)

NELLIE. I'll try.

BRACKETT. Thank you. You may go now if you wish.

(*She starts toward the door, then turns, thoughtfully, as if asking the question of herself.*)

NELLIE. I don't know very much about him really—do I?

(*Slowly, she goes out. For a moment, the men are silent.*)

CABLE. He's kept a few secrets from her, hasn't he?

BRACKETT. Well, you don't spring a couple of Polynesian kids on a woman right off the bat!

HARBISON. I'm afraid we aren't going to get much out of her. She's obviously in love with him.

CABLE. (*To* HARBISON.) That's hard to believe, sir. They tell me he's a middle-aged man.

BRACKETT. (*Rising from his desk chair. Smoldering.*) Cable! It is a common mistake for boys of your age and athletic ability to underestimate men who have reached their maturity.

CABLE. I didn't mean, sir . . .

BRACKETT. Young women frequently find a grown man attractive, strange as it may seem to you. I myself am over fifty. I am a bachelor and, Cable, I do not, by any means, consider myself—through. (*To* HARBISON *who is suppressing laughter.*) What's the matter, Bill?

HARBISON. Nothing, evidently!

BRACKETT. O. K., Cable. See you at chow. Do you play bridge?

CABLE. Yes, sir.

BRACKETT. Got any money?

CABLE. Yes, sir.

BRACKETT. I'll take it away from you.

CABLE. Yes, sir.

(*He goes out.* BRACKETT *darts a penetrating look at* HARBISON.)

BRACKETT. What makes you so *damn sure* this mission won't work out?

HARBISON. (*Looking at the map.*) Marie Louise Island is twenty-four miles long and three miles wide. Let's say that every time they send out a message they move to another hill. It seems to me, looking at this thing—

BRACKETT. Realistically.

HARBISON. . . . realistically (*Measuring his words.*) they could last about a week.

(*Pause.* BRACKETT *considers this.*)

BRACKETT. Of course, it would be worth it, if it were the right week. With decent information, our side might get moving. Operation Alligator might get off its can.

YEOMAN. (*Entering with large cardboard box.*) Here it is sir, I got it.

BRACKETT. (*To* HARBISON.) Okay, Bill. See you at chow. (HARBISON *looks at the package curiously.*) See you at chow, Bill.

HARBISON. (*Snapping out of it.*) Oh, see you at chow. (*He goes out.*)

BRACKETT. Got the address right?

YEOMAN. I think so, sir. (*Reading the box lid.*) Mrs. Amelia Fortuna. Three twenty-five Euclid Avenue, Shaker Heights, Cleveland, Ohio.

BRACKETT. That's right. I want to pack it myself.

YEOMAN. Yes, sir.

(YEOMAN *exits.* BRACKETT *starts to whistle. He opens the package and takes out a bright yellow grass skirt and shakes it out.* HARBISON *re-enters, stands in doorway, unseen by* BRACKETT, *nods as if his suspicions were confirmed and exits as the lights fade.*)

ACT ONE

SCENE VI

As the lights are fading on the Captain's hut, the company street curtain closes in and the activity seen here before is resumed.

G. I.'s and natives cross, carrying various items of equipment.

NELLIE *enters, walking slowly as she reads a letter. Another* NURSE *in working uniform has some letters in her hand and is moving off.*

NURSE. Going back to the beach, Nellie?

(NELLIE *nods.* NURSE *exits.* CABLE *enters and watches* NELLIE *for a moment.* NELLIE *is now standing still, reading a part of her letter that evokes an occasional groan of irritation from her.* CABLE *grins at her.*)

CABLE. Letter from home?

(NELLIE *looks up, startled by his voice, then grins back at him.*)

NELLIE. Yes. Do you get letters from your mother, telling you that everything you do is wrong?

CABLE. No. My mother thinks everything I do is right. . . . Of course, I don't tell her everything I do.

NELLIE. My mother's so prejudiced.

CABLE. Against Frenchmen?

(*She smiles to acknowledge that she gets the allusion then pursues her anti-maternal tirade.*)

NELLIE. Against anyone outside of Little Rock. She makes a big thing out of two people having different backgrounds.

CABLE. (*Rather hopefully.*) Ages?

NELLIE. Oh, no. Mother says older men are better for girls than younger men.

CABLE. (*Remembering his recent lecture from* BRACKETT *on this subject.*) This has been a discouraging day for me.

NELLIE. Do you agree with Mother about people having things in common? For instance, if the man likes symphony music and the girl likes Dinah Shore—and he reads Marcel Proust and she doesn't read anything . . . Well, what do *you* think? Do you think Mother's right?

CABLE. Well, she might be.

NELLIE. Well, I don't think she is.

CABLE. Well, maybe she's not.

NELLIE. Well, good-bye, Lieutenant. You've helped a lot.

CABLE. Listen, you don't know so much about that guy. You better read that letter over two or three times . . .

NELLIE. I'll show you what I think of that idea.

(*She crumples the letter and throws it on the ground.*)

CABLE. Well, don't say I didn't warn you.

(*He exits.* NELLIE *comes back and picks up the letter and starts reading as she walks off.*)

ACT ONE

SCENE VII

Before NELLIE *is off the lights come up on: The beach. Several nurses are lounging about before taking their swim. More enter. One of them,* DINAH, *is washing an evening dress in a tin tub. Upstage is a home-made shower bath, bearing a sign:*

BILLIS BATH CLUB
SHOWER 15¢
USE OF SOAP 5¢
NO TOWELS SUPPLIED

Two or three SEABEES *stand in attendance, part of* BILLIS' *business empire, no doubt.*

BILLIS. (*Entering.*) Oh, I thought Miss Forbush was here. I brought some hot water for her. (*He goes to shower, climbs a ladder and pours a bucket of water into the tank on top.*) She likes to take a shampoo Fridays.

NELLIE. (*Entering.*) Hello, Luther.

BILLIS. Hello, Miss Forbush. I brought some hot water for you.

NELLIE. Thanks. It'll do me a lot of good to get some of this sand out of my hair.

BILLIS. If you need some extra water for rinsing your hair, my bath-club concession boys will take care of you. When you're ready for the shower, just pull this chain, just like you was . . . Like you was pulling down a window shade. Take care of her, boys.

(*He exits.* NELLIE *enters the shower.*)

NURSE. What'd he want?

NELLIE. Huh?

NURSE. What'd he want?

NELLIE. Who?

NURSE. Iron Belly.

NELLIE. Captain Brackett? Oh, nothing —nothing important. Something about the Thanksgiving show.

SECOND NURSE. Then what's the trouble, Knucklehead?

NELLIE. Huh?

(*She is now soaking her hair and it is difficult for her to hear.*)

SECOND NURSE. I said, what's the trouble?

NELLIE. Oh, nothing. (*The girls look at one another.* NELLIE *comes out of the shower enclosure.*) There's not going to be any trouble any more because I've made up my mind about one thing. (*She takes a deep breath and looks at them dramatically.*) It's all off.

(*She goes back into the shower enclosure.*)

THIRD NURSE. With him?

NELLIE. (*Coming right out again through the swinging doors.*) Unh-hunh. (*She starts back, then stops and turns.*) I'm going to break it off clean before it's too late.

FOURTH NURSE. Knucklehead, what's happened? What'd he do?

NELLIE. *He* didn't do anything. It's just that . . . Well, I guess I don't know anything about him really and before I go any further with this thing—I just better not get started! Don't you think so, too? Diney?

DINAH. Yes, I do.

NELLIE. (*Unprepared for such prompt and unequivocal agreement.*) You do? Well, I guess I do, too. (*She turns to the other girls.*) Well, don't look so dramatic about it. Things like this happen every day. (*She sings:*)

I'm gonna wash that man right outa my hair,
I'm gonna wash that man right outa my hair,
I'm gonna wash that man right outa my hair,
And send him on his way!

(*She struts around splashing soap out of her hair.*)

Get the picture?

I'm gonna wave that man right outa my arms,
I'm gonna wave that man right outa my arms,
I'm gonna wave that man right outa my arms,
And send him on his way!

Don't try to patch it up—

NURSES.
Tear it up, tear it up!

NELLIE.
Wash him out, dry him out—

NURSES.
Push him out, fly him out!

NELLIE.
Cancel him and let him go—

NURSES.
Yea, sister!

I'm gonna wash that man right outa my hair,
I'm gonna wash that man right outa my hair,
I'm gonna wash that man right outa my hair,
And send him on his way!

NELLIE.
If the man don't understand you,
If you fly on separate beams,
Waste no time!
Make a change,
Ride that man right off your range,
Rub him outa the roll call
And drum him outa your dreams!

NURSES.
Oh-ho!

DINAH.
If you laugh at different comics,

ANOTHER NURSE.
If you root for different teams,

NELLIE, DINAH, SECOND NURSE.
Waste no time,
Weep no more,
Show him what the door is for!

NURSES.
Rub him outa the roll call
And drum him outa your dreams!

NELLIE.
You can't light a fire when the wood's all wet,

GIRLS.
No!

NELLIE.
You can't make a butterfly strong,

GIRLS.
Uh-uh!

NELLIE.
You can't fix an egg when it ain't quite good,

NURSES.
And you can't fix a man when he's wrong!

NELLIE.
You can't put back a petal when it falls from a flower,
Or sweeten up a feller when he starts turning sour—

(NELLIE *goes back into the shower, turns on the water and rinses the soap out of her hair.*)

NURSES.
Oh no, Oh no!
If his eyes get dull and fishy
When you look for glints and gleams,
Waste no time,
Make a switch,
Drop him in the nearest ditch!
Rub him outa the roll call
And drum him outa your dreams!
Oh-ho! Oh-ho!

NELLIE. (*Poking her head out from the shower, then dancing down to the nurses, as she sings:*)
I went and washed that man right outa my hair,
I went and washed that man right outa my hair,
I went and washed that man right outa my hair,
And sent him on his way!

NURSES.
She went and washed that man right outa her hair,
She went and washed that man right outa her hair,
She went and washed that man right outa her hair,

(NELLIE *joining them in a triumphant finish.*)

And sent him on his way!

(NELLIE *starts to dry her hair with a towel.* EMILE *enters. She cannot see him because the towel covers her eyes. The other girls quickly slip away to leave them alone, all except* DINAH, *who goes to her tin tub and takes out her evening dress.* NELLIE *is humming and dancing as she dries her hair. Suddenly, she stops. She has seen something on the ground—* EMILE'S *shoe tops! She moves closer to them, holding the towel forward, as a photographer holds his cloth. She patters over to* DINAH *for con-*

firmation, still holding the towel in this manner. DINAH *nods, as if to say: "That's him, all right."* NELLIE *makes a dash for the shower. While* NELLIE *is putting a top-piece on over her bathing bra,* DINAH *stands in front of the shower enclosure, blocking the way, and trying to make conversation with* EMILE. *She looks and feels very silly.*)

DINAH. You'd never think this was an evening dress, would you? We're only allowed to bring two of them—evening dresses . . . only two . . . I brought . . . Yeah, sister!

(*She retreats offstage, with no grace whatever.* NELLIE *comes out of the shower and makes a naive attempt to appear surprised.*)

NELLIE. Hello!

EMILE. Hello. . . . That song . . . is it a new American song?

NELLIE. It's an American type song. We were kind of putting in our own words. (*Looking around.*) Where *is* everybody?

EMILE. It is strange with your American songs. In all of them one is either desirous to get rid of one's lover, or one weeps for a man one cannot have.

NELLIE. That's right.

EMILE. I like a song that says: "I love you and you love me . . . And isn't that fine?"

NELLIE. (*Not very bright at the moment.*) Yes . . . that's fine.

EMILE. I left a note for you at the hospital. It was to ask you to my home for dinner next Friday.

NELLIE. Well, I don't think I'll be able to come, Emile, I—

EMILE. I have asked all my friends. The planters' colony.

NELLIE. (*Determined to wash him out of her hair.*) A big party. Well then, if I can't come, you won't miss me.

EMILE. But it is *for* you. It is for my friends to meet you and—more important —for you to meet them; to give you an idea of what your life would be like here. I want you to know more about me . . . how I live and think—

NELLIE. (*Suddenly remembering her promise to "spy on him."*) More about you?

EMILE. Yes. You know very little about me.

NELLIE. That's right! (*Getting down to business.*) Would you sit down? (EMILE *sits.* NELLIE *paces like a cross-examiner.*) Do you think about politics much . . . And if so what do you think about politics?

EMILE. Do you mean my political philosophy?

NELLIE. I think that's what I mean.

EMILE. Well, to begin with, I believe in the free life—in freedom for everyone.

NELLIE. (*Eagerly.*) Like in the Declaration of Independence?

EMILE. C'est ça. All men are created equal, isn't it?

NELLIE. Emile! You really believe that?

EMILE. Yes.

NELLIE. (*With great relief.*) Well, thank goodness!

EMILE. It is why I am here. . . . Why I killed a man.

NELLIE. (*Brought back to her mission.*) Oh, yes. I meant to ask you about that too . . . I don't want you to think I'm prying into your private life, asking a lot of questions. But . . . I always think it's interesting why a person . . . kills another person.

(EMILE *smiles understandingly.*)

EMILE. Of course, Nellie. That has worried you. (*He turns away to compose his story. Then he begins by stating what he considers the explanation and excuse for the whole thing:*) When I was a boy, I carried my heart in my hand. . . . So . . . when this man came to our town—though my father said he was good—I thought he was bad. (*With a shrug and a smile.*) I was young . . . He attracted all the mean and cruel people to him. Soon he was running our town! He could do anything—take anything . . . I did not like that. I was young. (NELLIE *nods, understanding.*) I stood up in the public square and made a speech. I called upon everyone to stand with me against this man.

NELLIE. What did they do?

EMILE. (*Letting his hands fall helplessly to his side.*) They walked away!

NELLIE. Why?

EMILE. Because they saw him standing behind me. I turned, and he said to me, "I am going to kill you now." We fought. I was never so strong. I knocked him to the ground. And when he fell, his head struck a stone and . . . (*He turns away and lets* NELLIE *imagine the rest.*) I ran to the waterfront and joined a cargo boat. I didn't even know where it was going. I stepped off that boat into another world . . . (*He looks around him, loving all he sees.*) where I am now . . . and where I want to stay. (*He turns to* NELLIE *and impulsively steps toward her, deep sincerity and anxiety in his voice.*) Nellie, will you marry me? . . . There are so few days in our life, Nellie. The time I have with you now is precious to me . . . Have you been thinking?

NELLIE. I have been thinking.

(*Singing, thoughtful, considering.*)

Born on the opposite sides of the sea,
We are as different as people can be,

EMILE.

It's true.

NELLIE.

And yet you want to marry me. . . .

EMILE.

I do.

NELLIE.

I've known you a few short weeks and yet
Somehow you've made my heart forget
All other men I have ever met
But you . . . but you . . .

EMILE.

Some enchanted evening
You may see a stranger,
You may see a stranger
Across a crowded room,
And somehow you know,
You know even then
That somewhere you'll see her
Again and again. . . .

NELLIE.

Who can explain it?
Who can tell you why?

EMILE.

Fools give you reasons,
Wise men never try . . .
Some enchanted evening,
When you find your true love,
When you feel her call you
Across a crowded room,
Then fly to her side
And make her your own,
Or all through your life you may dream all alone!

NELLIE. (*Clinging to him.*)

Once you have found him
Never let him go.

EMILE.

Once you have found her
Never let her go.

(*They kiss.*)

Will you come next Friday?

NELLIE. (*Somewhere, from out of the ether, she hears her voice murmur an inarticulate but automatic assent.*) Uh-huh.

(EMILE *kisses her again and leaves. There is the sound of a girl's laughter offstage and a voice is heard.*)

GIRL'S VOICE. (*Offstage.*) Well, she sure washed him out of her hair!

(*More laughter.* NELLIE *looks defiantly off in the direction of her mocking friends.*)

NELLIE. (*Singing.*)

I expect every one
Of my crowd to make fun
Of my proud protestations of faith in romance,
And they'll say I'm naive
As a babe to believe
Any fable I hear from a person in pants! . . .

Fearlessly I'll face them and argue their doubts away,
Loudly I'll sing about flowers and spring!
Flatly I'll stand on my little flat feet and say,
"Love is a grand and a beautiful thing!"
I'm not ashamed to reveal the world-famous feeling I feel.

I'm as corny as Kansas in August,
I'm as normal as blueberry pie.
No more a smart
Little girl with no heart,
I have found me a wonderful guy.

I am in a conventional dither
With a conventional star in my eye
And, you will note,
There's a lump in my throat
When I speak of that wonderful guy.

I'm as trite and as gay
As a daisy in May
(A cliché coming true!)
I'm bromidic and bright
As a moon-happy night
Pouring light on the dew.

I'm as corny as Kansas in August,
High as a flag on the Fourth of July!
If you'll excuse
An expression I use,
I'm in love
I'm in love
I'm in love
I'm in love
I'm in love with a wonderful guy!

(*The other nurses enter and join in her song; each obviously thinking of her own wonderful guy. The "company street" curtain closes as they sing, and before the light on the girls fades out, the men are seen pursuing the activities which have characterized previous company street scenes. The music of "I'm in Love with a Wonderful Guy" has continued and now the nurses enter and resume singing it.* NELLIE *running on last and finishing in a triumphant coda to the amusement of the G. I.'s. The lights fade on them all as they exit and the next scene is revealed.*)

ACT ONE

SCENE VIII

This is BRACKETT'S *office again.*

BRACKETT, HARBISON *and* CABLE *are all looking intently at* EMILE . . .

BRACKETT. Now, before you give us your answer, I want to impress you with three things. First, you are a civilian and you don't have to go. There's no way of our making you go. Second, this is a very dangerous mission and there's no guarantee that you'll survive—or that it will do any good. Third, that it might do a great good. It might be the means of turning the tide of war in this area.

EMILE. I understand all these things.

BRACKETT. Are you ready to give us your answer?

EMILE. Yes, I am. (*Pause.*) My answer must be no. (CABLE'S *foot comes down from the top of the waste-basket, on which it was resting.* HARBISON *uncrosses his arms.* BRACKETT *and* HARBISON *exchange looks.*) When a man faces death, he must weigh values very carefully. He must weigh the sweetness of his life against the thing he is asked to die for. The probability of death is very great—for both of us. I know that island well, Lieutenant Cable. I am not certain that I believe that what you ask me to do is . . . is—

BRACKETT. We're asking you to help us lick the Japs. It's as simple as that. We're against the Japs.

EMILE. I know what you're against. What are you for? (*He waits for an answer. They have none.*) When I was twenty-two, I thought the world hated bullies as much as I did. I was foolish—I killed one. And I was forced to flee to an island. Since then, I have asked no help from anyone or any country. I have seen these bullies multiply and grow strong. The world sat by and watched.

CABLE. Aw, to hell with this, de Becque, let's be honest! Aren't you just a guy in love with a girl and you're putting her above everything else in the world?

(EMILE *looks at* CABLE *for a moment before answering.*)

EMILE. Yes, I do care about my life with her more than anything else in the world. It is the only thing that is important to me. This I believe in. This I am sure of. This I have. I cannot risk to lose it. Good day, gentlemen.

(*He goes out. There is a pause. All three men have been rocked off their balance.*)

HARBISON. (*Thoughtfully.*) He's an honest man, but he's wrong. Of course, we can't guarantee him a better world if we win. Point is, we can be damned sure it'll be worse if we lose. Can't we? . . . (*Hotly.*) Well, can't we?

BRACKETT. (*Rising.*) Of course. Cable, there's a bottle of Scotch in my bottom drawer. See you tomorrow.

(*He exits quickly.* HARBISON *goes to the desk and takes a bottle from a drawer.*)

HARBISON. This is the one he means.

(*He takes two glasses and starts to pour the Scotch. A* YEOMAN *enters holding a sheaf of papers to be signed.*)

YEOMAN. (*Querulously.*) Commander Harbison! The Old Man walked right out on me with all these orders to be signed! And there's another delegation of French planters here, complaining about that stolen pig—the one the Seabees took and barbecued. And Commander Hutton's here—

HARBISON. (*Grabbing papers from him, irritably.*) Okay, okay! . . . I'll take care of it!

YEOMAN. Well, all right, sir!

CABLE. (*As he takes his glass of Scotch.*) What should I do, Commander Harbison? Go back to my outfit tonight?

HARBISON. (*With his drink in his hand.*) No, take a couple days off and unwind.

CABLE. Unwind?

HARBISON. Sure. Take a boat. Go fishing.

CABLE. (*A light dawning on him, a memory of* BILLIS' *offer and* BLOODY MARY'S *song about Bali Ha'i.*) Boat!

(*He puts his glass down and exits suddenly—as if pulled out of the room!* HARBISON *takes a swallow of Scotch, puts down his glass, looks around for* CABLE, *but* CABLE *has disappeared.*

HARBISON *rubs his face with the gesture of a weary man, and starts to go to work on the papers as the lights fade.*)

ACT ONE

SCENE IX

As BRACKETT'S *office recedes upstage, the tapa-cloth curtain closes and groups of French girls and native girls enter. They sing softly:*

GIRLS.

Bali ha'i t'appele
Dans le jour,
Dans la nuit.
Dans ton coeur,
Toujours resonne,
Par ici,
Me voici.
Si tu veux,
Tu me trouvera
Ou le ciel
Trouve la mer.
Me voici,
Laisse moi te prendre
Par ici,
Me voici,
Bali ha'i,
Bali ha'i,
Bali ha'i!

(*There is a bell ringing offstage. A native* KID *shouts excitedly, "Boat! Boat! Boat!" He runs off left. The girls back away a few steps as* BILLIS, CABLE *and* BLOODY MARY *walk on.*)

CABLE. (*As he enters.*) Look, Billis, I didn't come over here to Bali Ha'i to see anybody cut any boar's teeth out.

BILLIS. It ain't the cutting of the boar's tooth exactly. It's what comes afterwards.

(*During these lines,* MARY *has whispered into a small boy's ear and sent him running off.* CABLE *has crossed the girls and looks back over his shoulder at them.*)

MARY. (*Smiling, understanding perfectly.*) I take you with me. Come, Lootellan. You have good time. (*Calling to a native.*) Marcel! Come here! Billis, Marcel take you to boar ceremony. Lootellan come later. (*Two French girls have caught* CABLE'S *eye, and he has about made up his mind to approach them. He takes a couple of steps toward them, but now two* NUNS *enter and engage them in conversation. Thwarted by this unhappy development,* CABLE *becomes more receptive to* MARY, *who now says:*) Lootellan, come with me. You have good time. Come!

(*She leads him off as the lights fade.*)

ACT ONE

SCENE X

The music swells. A concentration of light in the center of the stage reveals:
The interior of a native hut.
BLOODY MARY *comes in. Even she has to bend low to get through the doorway.* CABLE, *following her, finds himself in the darkness, blinking.*

CABLE. What's this?

MARY. You wait.

CABLE. There's nobody around here.

MARY. You wait, Lootellan.

CABLE. What's going on, Mary? What—

(*He doesn't finish because a small figure has appeared in the doorway. A girl, perhaps seventeen. Her black hair is drawn smooth over her head. Like* BLOODY MARY, *she wears a white blouse and black trousers. Barefooted, she stands, silent, shy and motionless against the wattled wall, looking at* CABLE *with the honest curiosity and admiration of a child.*)

MARY. (*To* CABLE, *with a sly smile.*) You like?

CABLE. (*Never taking his eyes from the girl.*) Who is she?

MARY. Liat.

LIAT. (*Nodding her head and repeating it in a small voice.*) Liat.

MARY. Is French name.

CABLE. (*Still stunned, still gazing at the girl.*) Liat.

MARY. But she no French girl. She Tonkinese like me. We are ver' pretty people— No? . . .

(*She goes closer to* CABLE *and looks at him. She turns to* LIAT *and then back to* CABLE. *The two young people continue to regard each other with silent, longing interest.*)

CABLE. (*Over* MARY'S *head, to* LIAT.) Do you speak English?

MARY. Only a few word. She talk French. (*To* LIAT.) Français!

LIAT. (*Smiling shyly.*) Je parle Français —un peu.

(*She holds her forefinger and thumb close together to show how very little French she speaks.*)

CABLE. (*Grinning, nearly as shy as she.*) Moi, aussi—un peu. (*He holds up his forefinger and thumb, just as she did. They both laugh, and in some strange way,* BLOODY MARY *seems to have been forgotten by both of them. She looks from one to the other. Then, with the air of one who has accomplished a purpose, she waddles to the doorway. As she goes out, she lets the bamboo curtain roll down across the opening, reducing the light inside the hut. There is a long moment of silence.*) Are you afraid of me? (LIAT *looks puzzled. He remembers she knows only a few words of English.*) Oh . . . er . . . avez-vous peur?

LIAT. (*Her young face serious.*) Non. (*He takes a step toward her. She backs closer to the wall.*) Oui! (*He stops and looks at her, worried and hurt. This sign of gentleness wins her. She smiles.*) . . . Non.

(*Now it is she who walks slowly toward him. The music builds in a rapturous upsurge.* CABLE *gathers* LIAT *in his arms. She reaches her small arms up to his neck. He lifts her off her feet. The lights fade slowly as his hand slides her blouse up her back toward her shoulders. The lights dim to complete darkness. Light projections of large and lovely Oriental blossoms are thrown against the drop. Native couples stroll across the stage, only dimly seen. The music mounts ecstatically, then diminishes. The stage is clear. The light comes up on the hut again and moonlight now comes through the opened doorway where* CABLE *stands. He has no shirt on.* LIAT *is seated on the floor, gazing up at him silently; her hair hangs loose down her back.* CABLE *smiles down at her.*)

CABLE. (*Trying to puzzle something out in his mind.*) But you're just a kid . . . How did that Bloody Mary get a kid like you to come here and . . . I don't get it! (*Suddenly realizing that she has not understood.*) Cette vielle femme . . . votre amie?

LIAT. Ma mère.

CABLE. (*Horrified.*) Your mother! Bloody Mary is your mother! But she didn't tell me.

(LIAT, *to divert him from unpleasant thoughts, suddenly throws herself in his lap; they kiss. The sound of a ship's bell is heard in the distance. They sit up.* LIAT *looks panic-striken.*)

LIAT. Non, Non!

(*She covers his ears with her hands.*)

CABLE. (*Looking off.*) It's the boat all right. (*He turns back to her, sees her little face below his, her eyes pleading with him to stay.*) Aw, let them wait.

(*He sings.*)

I touch your hand
And my arms grow strong,
Like a pair of birds
That burst with song.
My eyes look down
At your lovely face
And I hold the world
In my embrace.

Younger than springtime are you,
Softer than starlight are you,
Warmer than winds of June are the gentle lips you gave me.
Gayer than laughter are you,
Sweeter than music are you,
Angel and lover, heaven and earth are you to me,
And when your youth and joy invade my arms
And fill my heart as now they do,
Then,
Younger than springtime am I,
Gayer than laughter am I,
Angel and lover, heaven and earth am I with you . . .

(*He releases her, goes to the door, looks off, then comes back to her. He stoops to pick up his shirt. She tries to get it first. Each has hold of one end of it. He looks down at her and repeats, softly:*)

And when your youth and joy invade my arms
And fill my heart as now they do,
Then, younger than springtime am I,
Gayer than laughter am I
Angel and lover, heaven and earth am I with you.

(*He starts. She clings to her end of his shirt for a moment, then lets it slide through her sad little fingers, and watches him go through the door —out of her life, perhaps. She sinks to her knees. The lights fade.*

Now, again in front of the tapa-cloth curtain, native girls bearing trays of tropical flowers and French girls are gathered in several groups.)

ACT ONE

Scene XI

The girls sing and hum "Bali Ha'i" softly under the scene, as Hawaiians sing "Aloha" to all departing craft. Bloody Mary *and* Billis *are looking off, anxiously awaiting* Cable.

Billis. (*Shouting off.*) Ring the bell again! Ring the bell again! (*Taking a lei from a* Flower-seller.) I'll have another one of those.

(*He drapes the lei around his neck where he already has three others.*)

Mary. He come. He come. He be here soon. Don't worry, Billis.

Billis. Hey, Mary— Please ask those Boar Tooth ceremonial fellows not to be sore at me. I didn't think those girls would do a religious dance with only skirts on. If somebody had told me it was a religious dance, I wouldn't have gotten up and danced with them. (*Looking off.*) Oh! Here he comes! Here he comes.

(Billis *exits toward the boat.* Cable *enters and crosses the stage in a kind of dream.* Mary *smiles, ecstatic, as she sees his face. Several of the French girls try to flirt with* Cable, *but he doesn't know they're alive. He goes right by them.* Mary *then walks past them, her chin in the air, very proudly and triumphantly. The girls' voices rise, singing the final measures of "Bali Ha'i." They throw flowers offstage where* Billis *and* Cable *made their exit. Cries of "Au revoir" and laughter are heard over the singing.*)

Mary. (*Throwing flower garland she has taken from a native girl and shouting to the others.*) Is gonna be my son-in-law. (*Calling off.*) Goo' bye! Come back soon, Lootellan! Bali Ha'i! Come back soon!

The lights fade.

ACT ONE

Scene XII

And other lights come up slowly on Emile's *terrace. The good-byes continue through the darkness and other good-byes from other voices blend in with these . . . all in French.* Henry *enters with another* Servant. *They start to clear glasses, champagne bottles and other left-overs of a gay party which clutter the scene.*

Frenchman. (*Offstage.*) Bali Ha'i . . . Bon soir!

Frenchwoman. (*Offstage.*) Merci, Emile. Merci, mille fois!

(Emile *enters and addresses* Henry.)

Emile. Pas maintenant . . . demain!

Frenchman. (*Offstage.*) A bientot! Bali Ha'i.

(Henry *and the other* Servant *exit.*)

Frenchwoman. (*Offstage.*) Quelle charmante soirée.

Nellie. (*Offstage.*) Good night . . . everybody . . . Good night.

Frenchman. (*Offstage.*) Non, Non . . . Nellie . . . en Français . . . en Français.

Nellie. (*Offstage, laboring with her French.*) Je . . . suis . . . enchantée . . . de faire . . . votre . . . connaissance!

(Emile, *looking off, smiles with amusement and pride. Voices offstage shout "Bravo!" "Formidable!"* Emile *exits.*)

Frenchman. (*Offstage.*) Bon soir, de Becque.

Frenchwoman. (*Offstage.*) Merci mille fois!!!

(*There is the sound of a motor starting loud, then growing fainter.* Emile *and* Nellie *enter and turn back to wave good-bye to the last guests. Then* Nellie *turns to* Emile, *who has been gently urging her farther into the garden. There is high excitement in her voice and she speaks very rapidly.*)

Nellie. Emile, you know I can't stay. And I've got to get that jeep back. I stole it. Or rather, I borrowed it. Or rather a fellow stole it for me. A wonderful man named Billis. I'll have to sneak around behind the hospital as it is.

Emile. In that case, I forbid you to go! If you have to sneak back without anyone seeing you, you might just as well sneak back later.

(Nellie *thinks for an instant, then comes to a quick decision.*)

Nellie. (*Taking off her coat.*) You're absolutely right! (*She looks guiltily at*

EMILE *and screams with laughter. So does he. She puts her coat on the back of a chair.*) I never had such a wonderful time in my whole life. All these lovely people and that cute old man who spoke French with me and made believe he understood me. And that exciting native couple who danced for us. Oh, it's so different from *Little Rock!* (*She screams the last line passionately, as if she hopes Little Rock would hear.* EMILE *laughs uproariously. She suddenly becomes quiet:*) What on earth are you laughing at? Am I drunk?

EMILE. (*Still laughing.*) Oh, no.

NELLIE. Yes, I am. But it isn't the champagne—it's because I'm in love with a wonderful guy!

(*She sings this last line. They waltz to the music of "I'm in Love with a Wonderful Guy!"* NELLIE *resumes singing.*)

If you'll excuse an expression I use,
I'm in love, I'm in love, I'm in love—

EMILE. (*Also singing.*)

I'm in love, I'm in love and the girl that I love—She thinks
I'm a wonderful guy!

(*They stop, exhausted and laughing. She turns and notices a half-filled glass of champagne which has been left by one of the guests. She takes it up and drinks it.*)

NELLIE. Imagine leaving all this wonderful champagne! (*She drinks out of this one, then takes another one. She hands it to* EMILE.) Here, Emile. You have some, too. It's such a waste!

EMILE. Here—here's another bottle.

(*He goes over to a long table which is under the windows on the porch. There are several buckets of champagne there. He takes one and fills two clean glasses and brings them to* NELLIE. *Meanwhile, she leans back, stretching her arms behind her head. Dreamily, she sings:*)

NELLIE.

This is how it feels,
Living on a hillside . . .

(*She speaks as the melody in the orchestra continues.*)

Here we are just like two old married people. Our guests have gone home and we're alone.

EMILE. (*Handing her the glass of champagne, singing:*)

This is what I need,
This is what I've longed for—
Someone young and smiling,
Here upon my hill—

(*The orchestra starts the music of "A Cockeyed Optimist."* NELLIE *has been thinking.*)

NELLIE. Emile, you know, my mother says we have nothing in common. But she's wrong. We have something very important in common—very much in common.

EMILE. Yes, we're both in love.

NELLIE. Yes, but more than that. We're—we're the same kind of people fundamentally—you and me. We appreciate things! We get enthusiastic about things. It's really quite exciting when two people are like that. We're not blasé. You know what I mean?

EMILE. We're both knuckleheads, cockeyed optimists.

(*They both laugh and start to sing:*)

NELLIE.

I hear the human race
Is falling on its face . . .

EMILE.

And hasn't very far to go!

NELLIE.

But every whippoorwill
Is selling me a bill
And telling me it just ain't so.

BOTH. (*Harmonizing—"Sweet Adeline" fashion.*)

I could say life is just a bowl of jello
And appear more intelligent and smart,
But I'm stuck,
Like a dope,
With a thing called hope,
And I can't get it out of my heart . . .

(*Dwelling on the fancy ending:*)

Not this heart!

(*They smile in each other's eyes.* EMILE *suddenly gets an idea and rises.*)

EMILE. Nellie, I have a surprise for you. You sit over there—something that I have been preparing for two days. Close your eyes. No peeking.

(EMILE *looks around first for a prop, sees her coat, then makes her go over and sit by the fountain.* NELLIE *is mystified, but excited, like a child waiting for a surprise.* EMILE *takes her coat and throwing it over his head, using it to simulate a towel, he imitates her as he found her on the beach the other day.*)

I'm going to wash that man right out of my hair,
I'm going to wash that man right out of my hair,

NELLIE. Oh, no! No!

(*She writhes with embarrassment and laughter as he continues:*)

EMILE.

I'm going to wash that man right out of my hair
And send him on his way! . . .

(*She covers her eyes.*)

Don't try to patch it up,
Tear it up, tear it up,
Wash him out, dry him out,
Push him out, fly him out,
Cancel him, and let him go—
Yea, Sister!

(*He finishes, waving his arms wildly.*)

NELLIE. (*Applauding.*) That's wonderful, Emile.

(EMILE *lifts the coat and, looking off, sees* NGANA *and* JEROME *as they enter in their nightgowns, followed by* HENRY.)

EMILE. Bon soir!

(NELLIE *turns, looks at the children and is immediately enchanted. She kneels before the two of them, holding them at arm's length.*)

NELLIE. You're the cutest things I ever saw in my whole life! What are your names? You probably can't understand a word I'm saying, but, oh, my goodness, you're cute.

EMILE. Nellie, I want you to meet Ngana and Jerome. Ngana and Jerome, Nellie.

NGANA AND JEROME. Nellie . . .

EMILE. (*To the children.*) Maintenant au lit . . . vite!

HENRY. Venez, Petits!

NGANA. Bon soir, Nellie.

JEROME. Bon soir, Nellie.

(*They wave to* NELLIE, *as* HENRY *leads them out.*)

NELLIE. Bon soir! (*Turning to* EMILE.) Oh, aren't they adorable! Those big black eyes staring at you out of those sweet little faces! Are they Henry's?

EMILE. They're mine.

NELLIE. (*Carrying out what she thinks is a joke.*) Oh, of course, they look exactly like you, don't they? Where did you hide their mother?

EMILE. She's dead, Nellie.

NELLIE. She's— (*She turns.*) Emile, they *are* yours!

EMILE. Yes, Nellie. I'm their father.

NELLIE. And—their mother . . . was a . . . was . . . a . . .

EMILE. Polynesian. (NELLIE *is stunned. She turns away, trying to collect herself.*) And she was beautiful, Nellie, and charming, too.

NELLIE. But you and she . . .

EMILE. I want you to know I have no apologies. I came here as a young man. I lived as I could.

NELLIE. Of course.

EMILE. But I have not been selfish. No woman ever hated me or tried to hurt me.

NELLIE. No woman could ever want to hurt you, Emile. (*Suddenly, feeling she must get away as quickly as she can.*) Oh, what time is it? I promised to get that jeep back! (*She looks at her wrist watch.*) Oh, this is awful. Look at the time!

(*She grabs her coat.* EMILE *tries to stop her.*)

EMILE. Nellie, wait, please. I'll drive you home.

NELLIE. You will do no such thing. Anyway, I couldn't leave the jeep here. I've got to get it back by—

EMILE. Don't go now, Nellie. Don't go yet, please.

NELLIE. (*Rattling on very fast.*) Yes, I must go now. This is terrible! I won't be able to face the girls at the hospital. You can't imagine the way they look at you when you come in late . . . I'll call you, Emile. I'll come by tomorrow. (*Suddenly remembering.*) Oh, no! Oh, dear! There are those awful rehearsals for Thanksgiving Day—I'm teaching them a dance and they want to rehearse night and day—but after that— (*Shifting quickly.*) Oh, thank you for tonight, Emile. I had a wonderful time. It was the nicest party and you're a perfect host. Good-bye. Please stay here, Emile. Don't go out to the jeep, please.

EMILE. (*Grabbing her arms, feeling her slipping away from him.*) Nellie, I love you. Do you hear me, Nellie? I love you!

NELLIE. And I love you, too. Honestly I do— Please let me go! Please let me go!

(NELLIE *goes off. She runs as fast as she can.* EMILE *watches for a second. The motor of the jeep starts and fades away quickly, as though the jeep were driven away very, very fast. The music of "Some Enchanted Evening" swells as* EMILE *looks down and picks up a coffee cup that has been left on the fountain.*)

EMILE. (*Singing, as he looks down at the cup.*)

Once you have found her,
Never let her go.

Once you have found her,
Never let her go!
CURTAIN

ACT TWO

Scene I

The stage during a performance of "The Thanksgiving Follies."

A dance is in progress, four girls and four boys. NELLIE *is one of the girls. They meticulously perform the steps and evolutions of a dance routine no more distinguished or original than any that might be produced by a Navy nurse who had been the moving spirit in the amateur theatre of Little Rock. Not one of the dancers makes a single mistake. Nobody smiles. Tense concentration is evident in this laboriously perfect performance. During the course of the dance, there are solo "step-outs" after which each soloist soberly steps back into place. The most complicated unison step is saved for the exit, which they execute with vigorous precision.*

On either side, in the downstage corners of the stage, G. I.'s are sitting as if there had not been enough seats and the audience overflowed up onto the stage. There are no chairs. They are seated and sprawled on the floor of the stage.

NELLIE *returns to the stage, a sheaf of notes in her hand and talks into the microphone.*

NELLIE. It has been called to our attention that owing to some trouble with the mimeograph, the last part of the program is kind of blurry, so I will read off who did the last number. (*Reading.*) The handstand was by Marine Sergeant Johnson. (*Applause.*) The Barrel Roll was done by Lieutenant J. G. Bessie May Sue Ellie Jaeger. (*Applause.*) The solo featuring the hitch-kick and scissors . . . those are the names of the steps . . . was by Ensign Cora McRae. (*Applause.*) The Pin Wheel . . . you know— (*She demonstrates by waving her leg in imitation of* STEWPOT.) was by Stewpot . . . I mean George Watts, Carpenter's Mate, Third Class.

(*Applause.* STEWPOT'S *head protrudes from the wings.*)

STEWPOT. Second class.

(*Applause.*)

NELLIE. The multiple revolutions and— (NELLIE *becomes self-consciously modest.*) incidentally the dance steps were by Ensign Nellie Forbush. (*She bows. Applause.*) Now the next is a most unusual treat. An exhibition of weight lifting by Marine Staff Sergeant Thomas Hassinger.

(HASSINGER *enters from right. He flexes muscles. Applause and shouts from "audience" on the corner of the stage.*)

SAILOR. Atta boy, Muscles!

(*The lights start fading.*)

NELLIE. . . . and Sergeant Johnson . . . (JOHNSON *enters.*) Marine Corporal . . .

(*The lights are out.*)

VOICE IN DARK. Hey, lights . . . the lights are out . . . Billis!

NELLIE. Bill-is . . . what the heck happened to the lights?

OTHER VOICES. "It's the generator." "Generator ran out of gas." "Switch over to the other one." "Mike . . . turn on the truck lights."

NELLIE. Keep your seats, everybody! There's nothing wrong except that the lights went out.

VOICES. "Look where you're going." "How the hell can I look when I can't see?"

(*The lights come up. The set has been changed in the darkness. We are now in:*)

ACT TWO

Scene II

In back of the stage.

SEABEE. We'll have that other generator on in a minute.

BILLIS. They got the truck lights on. That's something.

(*Applause offstage, right.*)

STEWPOT. (*Looking off toward "stage."*) The weight-lifting act got started.

BILLIS. Good . . . (*He notices two Seabees who are pushing a large roll of cable.*) What I can't understand is how some guys ain't got the artistic imagination to put gas in a generator so a show can be a success . . . especially when they're on the committee.

FIRST SEABEE. You're on the committee, too. Why didn't you tell us it wasn't gassed up?

BILLIS. I'm acting in the show and I'm stage manager and producer. I can't figure out everything, can I?

SECOND SEABEE. Sure you can. Just put your two heads together.

(He and his companion exit, pushing the roll of cable before them.)

BILLIS. *(Calling off.)* Look, jerk! I got a production on my hands. *(Turning to* STEWPOT.) How's the weight-lifting act going?

STEWPOT. I can't tell. Nobody's clapping.

BILLIS. If nobody's clapping, they ain't going good. You ought to be able to figure that out. Put your two heads together.

STEWPOT. You was the one with two heads.

(EMILE *enters. He carries a bunch of flowers in his hand. He has a serious "set" expression in his eyes.)*

EMILE. Pardon, can you tell me where I can find Miss Forbush?

BILLIS. *(Shrewdly sensing trouble and determined to protect* NELLIE.) She's on stage now. She's the Emcee. She can't talk to nobody right now. Do you want me to take the flowers in to her?

EMILE. No. I would prefer to give them to her myself.

BILLIS. Are you Mister de Becque?

EMILE. Yes.

BILLIS. Look, Mister de Becque. Do me a favor, will you? Don't try and see her tonight.

EMILE. Why?

BILLIS. We got her in a great mood tonight and I don't want anything to upset her again.

EMILE. She has been upset?

BILLIS. Upset! She's asked for a transfer to another island. And day before yesterday, she busted out crying right in the middle of rehearsal. Said she couldn't go on with the show. And she wouldn't have either unless Captain Brackett talked to her and told her how important it was to the Base. So do us all a favor—don't try to see her now.

EMILE. She's asked for a transfer?

BILLIS. Don't tell her I told you. Nobody's supposed to know.

EMILE. I must see her. Tonight!

BILLIS. Then stay out of sight till after the show. I'll take the flowers to her.

(EMILE *gives him the flowers.* BILLIS *and* STEWPOT *exit.* CABLE *enters. He doesn't see* EMILE *at first.)*

CABLE. Hey, Billis— Billis!

EMILE. *(Peering through the semi-darkness.)* Lieutenant Cable?

CABLE. *(Putting his fingers to his lips in a mocking gesture.)* Ssh! Lieutenant Cable is supposed to be in his little bed over at the hospital.

EMILE. You have not been well?

CABLE. I'm okay now. Fever gone. They can't hold me in that damned place any longer. I'm looking for a guy named Billis, a great guy for getting boats. *(His voice rising, tense and shrill.)* And I need a boat right now. I've got to get to my island.

EMILE. *(Worried by* CABLE'S *strangeness.)* What?

CABLE. That damned island with the two volcanoes on it. You ever been over there?

EMILE. Why, yes, I—

CABLE. I went over there every day till this damned malaria stopped me. Have you sailed over early in the morning? With warm rain playing across your face? (LIAT *enters. He sees her, but doesn't believe his eyes.)* Beginning to see her again like last night.

LIAT. *(Calling offstage.)* Ma mère! C'est lui!

(She turns and, like a young deer, glides over to the amazed CABLE *and embraces him before the equally amazed* EMILE. MARY *waddles on.)*

CABLE. *(Holding* LIAT *tight.)* I thought I was dreaming.

LIAT. *(Laughing.)* Non.

(She holds him tighter.)

CABLE. *(He holds her away from him and looks at her.)* What are you doing over here?

MARY. *(Grimly.)* She come in big white boat—bigger than your boat. Belong Jacques Barrere. He want to marry Liat. *(To* EMILE.) You know him. (EMILE *nods. She turns back to* CABLE.) Is white man, too. And very rich!

CABLE. *(To* LIAT.) Is that the old planter you told me about? The one who drinks? *(His eye catches* EMILE'S. EMILE *nods.* CABLE *cries out as if hurt.)* Oh, my God! *(He turns angrily to* MARY.) You can't let her marry a man like that.

MARY. Hokay! Then *you* marry her.

EMILE. *(Angrily, to* MARY.) Tais-toi! Il est malade! . . . Tu comprends? (MARY *is temporarily silenced.* EMILE *turns to* CABLE *and his voice becomes gentle and sympathetic.)* Lieutenant, I am worried about you. You are ill.

Will you allow me to see you back to the hospital?

CABLE. You're worried about me! That's funny. The fellow who says he lives on an island all by himself and doesn't worry about anybody—Japs, Americans, Germans—anybody. Why pick out *me* to worry about?

EMILE. (*Stiffly.*) Forgive me. I'm sorry, Lieutenant.

(*He leaves.* MARY *goes to* CABLE *to make one last plea for her daughter's dream.*)

MARY. Lootellan, you like Liat. . . . Marry Liat! You have good life here. Look, Lootellan, I am rich. I save six hundred dolla' before war. Since war I make two thousand dolla' . . . war go on I make maybe more. Sell grass skirts, boar's teeth, real human heads. Give all de money to you an' Liat. You no have to work. I work for you. . . . (*Soft music is played.*) All day long, you and Liat be together! Walk through woods, swim in sea, sing, dance, talk happy. No think about Philadelia. Is no good. Talk about beautiful things and make love all day long. You like? You buy?

(*She sings. Throughout the song,* LIAT *performs what seem to be traditional gestures.*)

Happy Talk,
Keep talkin' Happy Talk!
Talk about tings you'd like to do.
You got to have a dream—
If you don' have a dream
How you gonna have a dream come true?

Talk about a moon
Floatin' in de sky,
Lookin' like a lily on a lake:
Talk about a bird
Learnin' how to fly,
Makin' all de music he can make.

Happy Talk,
Keep talkin' Happy Talk!
Talk about tings you'd like to do.
You got to have a dream—
If you don' have a dream
How you gonna have a dream come true?

Talk about a star
Lookin' like a toy,
Peekin' through de branches of a tree.
Talk about a girl,
Talk about a boy
Countin' all de ripples on de sea.

Happy Talk,
Keep talkin' Happy Talk!
Talk about tings you'd like to do.
You got to have a dream—
If you don' have a dream
How you gonna have a dream come true?

(LIAT *now performs a gentle, childish dance. At the end of it, she returns to* CABLE'S *side and* MARY *resumes her song:*)

Talk about a boy
Sayin' to de girl,
"Golly, baby, I'm a lucky cuss!"
Talk about a girl
Saying to de boy,
"You an' me is lucky to be us."

(LIAT *and* CABLE *kiss.* MARY'S *voice becomes triumphant.*)

Happy Talk,
Keep talkin' Happy Talk!
Talk about tings you'd like to do.
You got to have a dream—
If you don' have a dream
How you gonna have a dream come true?

If you don' talk happy
An' you never have a dream
Den you'll never have a dream come true.

(*Speaking eagerly.*)

Is good idea . . . you like?

(*She laughs gaily and looks in* CABLE'S *eyes, anxious to see the answer.* CABLE *is deeply disturbed. He takes a gold watch from his pocket and puts it in* LIAT'S *hand.*)

CABLE. Liat, I want you to have this. It's a man's watch but it's a good one—belonged to my grandfather. It's kind of a lucky piece, too. My dad carried it all through the last war. Beautiful, isn't it?

(LIAT *has taken the watch, her eyes gleaming with pride.*)

MARY. When I see you firs' time. I know you good man for Liat. And she good girl for you. You have special good babies.

(*Pause.* CABLE *looks tortured.*)

CABLE. (*Forcing the words out.*) Mary, I can't . . . marry . . . Liat.

MARY. (*Letting out her rage and disappointment in a shout, as she grabs* LIAT'S *arm.*) Was your las' chance! Now she marry Jacques Barrere. Come, Liat! (LIAT *runs to* CABLE. MARY *pulls her away.*) Give me watch. (LIAT *clasps it tight in her hands.* MARY *wrests it from her and yells at* CABLE.) Stingy bastard!

(*She throws it on the ground and it smashes.* CABLE *looks on, dazed, stunned.* MARY *pulls* LIAT *off.* CABLE *kneels down, gathers up the pieces and puts them in his pocket. Meanwhile, several of the men come on, dressed for the finale of the show. They are looking back over their shoulders at* LIAT *and* MARY *whom they must have just passed.*)

PROFESSOR. Hey! Did you get a load of that little Tonkinese girl?

(*They continue up to the stage door as they speak.*)

MARINE. Yeah.

(*Applause off.* NELLIE'S *voice is heard through the loudspeaker.*)

NELLIE. (*Offstage.*) Now, boys, before we come to the last act of our show, it is my great pleasure to bring you our skipper, Captain George Brackett.

(*Applause.* CABLE *looks off at* LIAT *as she passes out of his life.*)

CABLE. (*Singing.*)

Younger than springtime were you,
Softer than starlight were you,
Angel and lover, heaven and earth
Were you to me. . . .

ACT TWO

SCENE III

The lights fade to complete darkness. BRACKETT'S *voice is heard in the loudspeaker. During his speech, the lights come up, revealing:*

The G.I. Stage, as before. BRACKETT *is speaking into a microphone.*

BRACKETT. Up to now, our side has been having the hell beat out of it in two hemispheres and we're not going to get to go home until that situation is reversed. It may take a long time before we can get any big operation under way, so it's things like this, like this show tonight, that keep us going. Now I understand that I am not generally considered a sentimental type. (*Laughter and cries of "Oh, boy!" "Check," "You can say that again," etc., from the boys on the corners of the stage.*) Once or twice I understand I have been referred to as "Old Iron Belly."

VOICES. "Once or twice." "Just about a million times." (*Loud laughter.*)

BRACKETT. I resent that very much because I had already chosen that as my private name for our Executive Officer, Commander Harbison. (*Big laugh. Applause.* BRACKETT *calls into the wings.*) Take a bow, Commander.

(*Two of the girls pull* COMMANDER HARBISON *out.*)

SAILOR. I wish I was a commander!

(HARBISON, *flanked by the two girls, stands beside* BRACKETT *as he continues:*)

BRACKETT. I want you to know that both "Old Iron Bellies" sat here tonight and had a hell of a good time. And we want to thank that hard working committee of Nurses and Seabees who made the costumes out of rope and mosquito nets, comic books and newspapers . . .

(*He fingers the comic-paper skirt of one of the girls.*)

SAILOR. Ah, ah—captain!

(BRACKETT *frowns, but pulls himself together.*)

BRACKETT. . . . and thought up these jokes and these grand songs. And I just want to say on this Thanksgiving Day, to all of them from all of us, thank you. (*Applause from the boys, but it is comically feeble. Obviously, they'd like to get on with the show.*) And now I'm going to ask Commander Harbison to announce the next act which is the Finale of our Thanksgiving entertainment.

(*He hands* HARBISON *a paper.* HARBISON *reads from a small card.*)

HARBISON. The next and last will be a song sung by Bosun Butch Forbush . . . (*He looks kind of puzzled.*) . . . and that Siren of the Coral Sea . . . gorgeous, voluptuous and petite Mademoiselle Lutheria . . . (*Ending in a high, surprised voice, as he reads the name of his pet abomination.*) . . . Billis!

BRACKETT. (*Laughing.*) Come on, Bill.

(*He leads off* HARBISON, *who is looking at the paper, puzzled. The music of "Honey-Bun" starts and* NELLIE *enters, dressed as a sailor, in a borrowed white sailor suit, three times too big for her.*)

NELLIE. (*Singing.*)

My doll is as dainty as a sparrow,
Her figure is something to applaud.
Where she's narrow, she's as narrow as an arrow
And she's broad where a broad should be broad!

A hundred and one
Pounds of fun—

That's my little Honey-Bun!
Get a load of Honey-Bun tonight!

I'm speakin' of my
Sweetie Pie,
Only sixty inches high—
Ev'ry inch is packed with dynamite!

Her hair is blonde and curly,
Her curls are hurly-burly.
Her lips are pips!
I call her hips:
"Twirly"
And "Whirly."
She's my baby,
I'm her Pap!
I'm her booby,
She's my trap!
I am caught and I don't wanta run
'Cause I'm havin' so much fun with Honey-Bun!

(NELLIE *starts a second refrain, meanwhile having considerable difficulty with her sagging trousers. Now* BILLIS *enters, dressed as a South Sea siren in a straw-colored wig, long lashes fantastically painted on his eyelids, lips painted in bright carmine, two cocoanut shells on his chest to simulate "femininity" and a battleship tatooed on his bare midriff. He and* NELLIE *dance. For an exit, she leads him off, singing a special ending.*)

NELLIE.
She's my baby,
I'm her Pap!
I'm her booby,
She's my trap!
I am caught and I don't wanta run
'Cause I'm havin' so much fun with Honey-Bun!
(Believe me, sonny)
She's a cookie who can cook you till you're done,
(Ain't bein' funny)
Sonny,
Put your money
On my Honey-Bun!

(*After they exit,* NELLIE *returns for a bow. Then* BILLIS *enters with* EMILE'S *flowers and presents them to her. Thinking they are from* BILLIS, *she kisses him. He exits in a delirious daze. She exits as the girls enter, singing.*)

GIRLS.
A hundred and one
Pounds of fun—
That's my little Honey-Bun
Get a load of Honey-Bun tonight.

I'm speakin' of my
Sweetie Pie,
Only sixty inches high—
Every inch is packed with dynamite.

(*The girls are dressed in home-made costumes representing island natives. The materials are fish-net, parachute cloth, large tropical leaves and flowers —anything they could find and sew together. At the end of their line is* BILLIS *still dressed as a girl. As the song proceeds, he is the butt of many a slur from his comrades. While passing one of them, he is shocked and infuriated to feel a hand thrust up his skirt. He turns to swing on him, but he can't get out of line and spoil the number; "On with the show!" He is grim and stoic—even when another boy lifts one of the cocoanuts in his "brassiere" and steals a package of cigarettes therefrom. The girls and* BILLIS *continue singing through these impromptu shenanigans.*)

GIRLS.
Her hair is blonde and curly,
Her curls are hurly-burly.
Her lips are pips!
I call her hips:
"Twirly" and "Whirly."

She's my baby,
I'm her Pap!
I'm her booby,
She's my trap!
I am caught and I don't wanta run
'Cause I'm havin' so much fun with Honey-Bun!

(*All lining up for finale.*)

And that's the finish,
And it's time to go for now the show is done.

(*Balance of* "COMPANY" *comes on.*)

We hope you liked us,
And we hope that when you leave your seat and run
Down to the Mess Hall
You'll enjoy your dinner each and every one.

(NELLIE *makes a special entrance, now wearing a new costume.*)

NELLIE. (*Very brightly.*) Enjoy your turkey.

ALL. (*Pointing to* BILLIS.) And put some chestnut dressing on our Honey-Bun!

(*The curtain is slow.* NELLIE *signals for it and jumps up to help pull it down. The lights are off. Boys on the stage wave their flashlights out at the audience, addressing them as if they were all G. I.'s. "See you down at the mess hall," etc. When the clamor dies down, two lines are distinguishable.*)

SAILOR. How d'ye like the show?

MARINE. It stunk!

ACT TWO

SCENE IV

Now the lights come up on the scene behind the stage.

The girls come off the stage and file into their dressing shack. BILLIS *follows them in. After a few moments, he comes hurtling out, minus his wig. A few seconds later, the wig is thrown out by one of the girls in the dressing room.*

BILLIS. Oh, I beg your pardon.

(*At this moment, he turns and faces* NELLIE, *who has just come down the steps from the stage with another girl.*)

NELLIE. (*Seeing* BILLIS.) Oh, Luther, you really are a honey-bun! These beautiful flowers! I needed someone to think of me tonight. I appreciate it, Luther—you don't know how much.

BILLIS. (*Very emotionally.*) Miss Forbush, I would like you to know I consider you the most wonderful woman in the entire world—officer and all. And I just can't go on being such a heel as to let you think I thought of giving you those flowers.

NELLIE. But you did give them to me and I—

BILLIS. (*Shoving a card at* NELLIE.) Here's the card that came with them. (*She reads the card, then turns away—deeply affected.*) Are you all right, Miss Forbush? (*She nods her head.*) I'll be waiting around the area here in case you need me. Just—just sing out.

(*He exits.* NELLIE *is on the point of tears.* CABLE, *who has been sitting on a bench below the ladies' dressing shack, now rises and approaches* NELLIE.)

CABLE. (*Sympathetically, but taking a light tone.*) What's the matter, Nellie the nurse? Having diplomatic difficulties with France?

(NELLIE *turns, startled.*)

NELLIE. (*Immediately becoming the professional nurse.*) Joe Cable! Who let you out of the hospital?

CABLE. Me. I'm okay.

(*She leads him to the bench and feels his forehead and pulse.*)

NELLIE. (*Accusingly.*) Joe! You're trying to get over to Bali Ha'i. That little girl you told me about!

CABLE. (*Nodding thoughtfully.*) Liat. I've just seen her for the last time, I guess. I love her and yet I just heard myself saying I can't marry her. What's the matter with me, Nellie? What kind of a guy am I, anyway?

NELLIE. You're all right. You're just far away from home. We're both so far away from home.

(*She looks at the card. He takes her hand.* EMILE *enters. He is earnest and importunate.*)

EMILE. Nellie! I must see you.

NELLIE. Emile! I—

EMILE. Will you excuse us, Lieutenant Cable?

(CABLE *starts to leave.*)

NELLIE. No, wait a minute, Joe. Stay. Please! (*To* EMILE.) I've been meaning to call you but—

EMILE. You have asked for a transfer, why? What does it mean?

NELLIE. I'll explain it to you tomorrow, Emile. I'm—

EMILE. No. Now. What does it mean, Nellie?

NELLIE. It means that I can't marry you. Do you understand? I can't marry you.

EMILE. Nellie— Because of my children?

NELLIE. Not because of your children. They're sweet.

EMILE. It is their Polynesian mother then—their mother and I.

NELLIE. . . . Yes. I can't help it. It isn't as if I could give you a good reason. There is no reason. This is emotional. This is something that is born in me.

EMILE. (*Shouting the words in bitter protest.*) It is not. I do not believe this is born in you.

NELLIE. Then why do I feel the way I do? All I know is that I can't help it. I can't help it! Explain how we feel, Joe—

(JOE *gives her no help. She runs up to the door of the dressing shack.*)

EMILE. Nellie!

NELLIE. (*Calling in.*) Dinah, are you ready?

NURSE. Yes, Nellie.

NELLIE. I'll go with you.

(*The other nurse comes out and they exit quickly.* EMILE *turns angrily to* CABLE.)

EMILE. What makes her talk like that? Why do you have this feeling, you and she? I do not believe it is born in you. I do not believe it.

CABLE. It's not born in you! It happens *after* you're born . . .

(CABLE *sings the following words, as if figuring this whole question out for the first time.*)

You've got to be taught to hate and fear,
You've got to be taught from year to year,
It's got to be drummed in your dear little ear—
You've got to be carefully taught!

You've got to be taught to be afraid
Of people whose eyes are oddly made,
And people whose skin is a different shade—
You've got to be carefully taught.

You've got to be taught before it's too late,
Before you are six or seven or eight,
To hate all the people your relatives hate—
You've got to be carefully taught!
You've got to be carefully taught!

(*Speaking, going close to* EMILE, *his voice filled with the emotion of discovery and firm in a new determination.*)

You've got the right idea, de Becque—live on an island. Yes, sir, if I get out of this thing alive, I'm not going back there! I'm coming here. All I care about is right here. To hell with the rest.

EMILE. (*Thoughtfully.*) When all you care about is here . . . this is a good place to be. When all you care about is taken away from you, there is no place . . . (*Walking away from* CABLE, *now talking to himself.*) I came so close to it . . . so close. (*Singing:*)

One dream in my heart,
One love to be living for,
One love to be living for—
This nearly was mine.

One girl for my dreams,
One partner in Paradise,
This promise of Paradise—
This nearly was mine.

Close to my heart she came,
Only to fly away,
Only to fly as day
Flies from moonlight!

Now, now I'm alone,
Still dreaming of Paradise.
Still saying that Paradise
Once nearly was mine.

So clear and deep are my fancies
Of things I wish were true,
I'll keep remembering evenings
I wish I'd spent with you.
I'll keep remembering kisses
From lips I'll never own
And all the lovely adventures
That we have never known.

One dream in my heart
One love to be living for
One love to be living for—
This nearly was mine.

One girl for my dreams,
One partner in Paradise.
This promise of Paradise—
This nearly was mine.

Close to my heart she came,
Only to fly away,
Only to fly as day
Flies from moonlight!

Now . . . now I'm alone,
Still dreaming of Paradise,
Still saying that Paradise
Once nearly was mine.

(*He drops to the bench, a lonely and disconsolate figure.*)

CABLE. (*Going to him.*) De Becque, would you reconsider going up there with me to Marie Louise Island? I mean, now that you haven't got so much to lose? We could do a good job, I think—you and I. (EMILE *doesn't answer.*) You know, back home when *I* used to get in a jam, I used to go hunting. That's what I think I'll do now. Good hunting up there around Marie Louise. Jap carriers . . . cargo boats . . . troopships . . . big game. (*He looks at* EMILE, *craftily considering how much headway he has made.* EMILE *smiles a little.*) When I go up, what side of the island should I land on?

EMILE. The south side.

CABLE. Why?

EMILE. There's a cove there . . . and rocks. I have sailed in behind these rocks many times.

CABLE. Could a submarine get in between those rocks without being observed?

EMILE. Yes. If you know the channel.

CABLE. And after I land, what will I do?

EMILE. You will get in touch with my friends, Basile and Inato—two black men—wonderful hunters. They will hide us in the hills.

CABLE. (*His eyes lighting up.*) Us? Are you going with me?

EMILE. (*A new strength in his voice.*) Of course. You are too young to be out alone. Let's go and find Captain Brackett.

CABLE. (*Delirious.*) Wait till that old bastard Brackett hears this. He'll jump out of his skin!

EMILE. I would like to see this kind of a jump. Come on!

(*They go off quickly together.* BILLIS *rushes on and looks after them. Obviously, he's been listening. He thinks it over for a moment, "dopes it out." Then, with sudden decision, he takes one last puff on a cigarette butt, flings it away, and follows after them.*)

ACT TWO

SCENE V

The lights go out and almost immediately the sound of an airplane motor is heard, revving up, ready for the take-off. The lights come up between the tapa-cloth and the dark-green drop.

Several Naval Aircraft mechanics are standing with their backs to the audience—They look off, watching tensely. As the plane is heard taking off, they raise their hands and shout in an exultant, defiant manner.

The music reaches a climax and the lights fade out on them, as they exit.

Lights in center come on simultaneously, revealing:

ACT TWO

SCENE VI

This is the communications office or radio room. The back wall is covered with communications equipment of all sorts: boards, lights, switches. There is a speaker, a small table with a receiving set, various telephones and sending equipment. A COMMUNICATIONS ENLISTED MAN *is sitting at the table with earphones. He is working the dials in front of him.* CAPTAIN BRACKETT *is seated on an upturned waste basket. On the floor, are several empty Coca-Cola bottles and several full ones. He is eating a sandwich and alternately guzzling from a bottle of Coca-Cola. There are a couple of empty Coca-Cola bottles on the* ENLISTED MAN'S *desk, too.* BRACKETT *is listening avidly for any possible sound that might come from the loudspeaker. After a moment, there is a crackle.*

BRACKETT. (*Excitedly.*) What's that? What's that? (*The* ENLISTED MAN *cannot hear him, because he has earphones.* BRACKETT *suddenly becomes conscious of this. He pokes the* ENLISTED MAN *in the back. The* ENLISTED MAN, *controlling himself, turns and looks at* BRACKETT, *as a nurse would at an anxious, complaining patient. He pulls the earphones away from his ear.*) What was that?

ENLISTED MAN. (*Quietly.*) That was . . . nothing, sir.

(*He readjusts his earphones and turns to his dials again.* BRACKETT, *unsatisfied by this, pokes the* ENLISTED MAN *again. The* ENLISTED MAN *winces, then patiently takes the earphones from his ears.*)

BRACKETT. Sounded to me like someone trying to send a message . . . sounded like code.

ENLISTED MAN. That was not code, sir. That sound you just heard was the contraction of the tin roof. It's the metal, cooling off at night.

BRACKETT. Oh.

ENLISTED MAN. Sir, if you'd like to go back to your office, I'll let you know as soon as . . .

BRACKETT. No, no, I'll stay right here. I don't want to add to your problems.

ENLISTED MAN. (*He turns back to his dials.*) Yes, sir.

(BRACKETT *impatiently looks at his watch and compares it with the watch on the* ENLISTED MAN'S *desk. He talks to the* ENLISTED MAN *who cannot hear him.*)

BRACKETT. We ought to be getting a message now. We ought to be getting a message, that's all. They'd have time to land and establish some sort of an observation post by now, don't you think so? (*He realizes that the* ENLISTED MAN *cannot hear.*) Oh.

(*He sits back in a position of listening.* HARBISON *enters. He is very stern, more upset than we have ever seen him.)*

HARBISON. Captain Brackett?

BRACKETT. Yeah, what is it? What is it? Don't interrupt me now, Bill. I'm very busy.

HARBISON. It's about this Seabee out here, sir, Billis! Commander Perkins over at Operations estimates that Billis' act this morning cost the Navy over six hundred thousand dollars!

BRACKETT. Six hundred— By God, I'm going to chew that guy's—send him in here!

HARBISON. Yes, sir.

(*He exits.* BRACKETT *goes over and taps the* ENLISTED MAN *on the shoulder. The* ENLISTED MAN *removes earphones.*)

BRACKETT. Let me know the moment you get any word. No matter what I'm doing, you just break right in.

ENLISTED MAN. Yes, sir.

(*He goes back to his work.* BRACKETT *paces another second and then* BILLIS *enters, wary, on guard; his face is flaming red, his nose is a white triangle, covered with zinc-oxide. He wears an undershirt. His arms are red, except for two patches of zinc-oxide on his shoulders. He is followed by* LIEUTENANT BUS ADAMS *and* COMMANDER HARBISON, *who closes the door.*)

HARBISON. (*Pushing* BILLIS *in.*) Get in there! Captain Brackett, this is Lieutenant Bus Adams, who flew the mission.

BRACKETT. H'y'a, Adams.

ADAMS. Captain.

(BRACKETT *beckons* BILLIS *to him.* BILLIS *walks over to him slowly, not knowing what may hit him.*)

BRACKETT. One man like you in an outfit is like a rotten apple in a barrel. Just what did you feel like—sitting down there all day long in that rubber boat in the middle of Empress Augusta Bay with the whole damn Navy Air Force trying to rescue you? And how the hell can you fall out of a PBY anyway?

BILLIS. Well, sir, the Jap anti-aircraft busted a hole in the side of the plane and —I fell through . . . the wind just sucked me out.

BRACKETT. So I'm to understand that you deliberately hid in the baggage compartment of a plane that you knew was taking off on a very dangerous mission. You had sand enough to do that all right. And then the moment an anti-aircraft gun hit the plane you fell out. The wind just sucked you out . . . you and your little parachute! I don't think you fell out, Billis, I think you jumped out. Which did you do?

BILLIS. Well, sir . . . er . . . it was sort of half and half . . . if you get the picture.

BRACKETT. This is one of the most humiliating things that ever happened to me. Adams, when did you discover he was on the plane?

ADAMS. Well, sir, we'd been out about an hour—it was still dark, I know. Well, we were flying across Marie Louise. The Jap anti-aircraft spotted us and made that hit. That's when Luther . . . er . . . this fellow here . . . that's when he . . . left the ship. I just circled once . . . time enough to drop him a rubber boat. Some New Zealanders in P-40s spotted him though and kept circling around him while I flew across the island and landed alongside the sub, let Joe and the Frenchman off. By the time I got back to the other side of the island, our Navy planes were flying around in the air above this guy like a thick swarm of bees. (*He turns to grin at* HARBISON, *who gives him no returning grin. He clears his throat and turns back to* BRACKETT.) They kept the Jap guns occupied while I slipped down and scooped him off the rubber boat. You'd have thought this guy was a ninety-million-dollar cruiser they were out to protect. There must have been fifty-five or sixty planes.

BILLIS. Sixty-two.

BRACKETT. You're not far off, Adams. Harbison tells me this thing cost the Navy about six hundred thousand dollars.

BILLIS. (*His face lighting up.*) Six hundred thous . . . !

BRACKETT. What the hell are you so happy about?

BILLIS. I was just thinking about my uncle. (*To* ADAMS.) Remember my uncle I was telling you about? He used to tell my old man I'd never be worth a dime! Him and his lousy slot machines. . . . Can you imagine a guy . . .

(*He catches sight of* HARBISON'S *scowl and shuts up quickly.*)

BRACKETT. Why the hell did you do this anyway, Billis? What would make a man do a thing like this?

BILLIS. Well, sir, a fellow has to keep

moving. You know . . . you get kind of held down. If you're itching to take a trip to pick up a few souvenirs, you got to kind of horn in . . . if you get the picture.

BRACKETT. How did you know about it?

BILLIS. I didn't know about it, exactly. It's just when I heard Lieutenant Cable talking to that fellow de Becque, right away I know something's in the air. A project. That's what I like, Captain. Projects. Don't you?

HARBISON. Billis, you've broken every regulation in the book. And, by God, Captain Brackett and I are going to throw it at you.

ADAMS. Sir. May I barge in? My co-pilot watched this whole thing, you know, and he thinks that this fellow Billis down there in the rubber boat with all those planes over him caused a kind of diversionary action. While all those Japs were busy shooting at the planes and at Billis on the other side of the island, that sub was sliding into that little cove and depositing the Frenchman and Joe Cable in behind those rocks.

BRACKETT. What the hell do you want me to do? Give this guy a Bronze Star?

BILLIS. I don't want any Bronze Star, Captain. But I could use a little freedom. A little room to swing around in . . . if you know what I mean. If you get the picture.

BRACKETT. Get out of here. Get the hell out of here!

(*Moving up after* BILLIS. BILLIS *flees through the door.*)

HARBISON. I'd have thrown him in the brig. And I will too, if I get the ghost of a chance.

(*Suddenly, the* RADIO OPERATOR *becomes very excited and waves his arm at* CAPTAIN BRACKETT. *We begin to hear squeaks and static from the loudspeaker and through it we hear* EMILE DE BECQUE'S *voice. Everyone on the stage turns. All eyes and ears are focused on the loudspeaker.*)

EMILE'S VOICE. —And so we are here. This is our first chance to send news to you. We have made contact with former friends of mine. We have set up quarters in a mango tree—no room but a lovely view. . . . First the weather: rain clouds over Bougainville, The Treasuries, Choiseul and New Georgia. We expect rain in this region from nine o'clock to two o'clock. Pardon? Oh—my friend Joe corrects me. Oh—nine hundred to fourteen hundred. And now, our military expert, Joe.

CABLE'S VOICE. All you Navy, Marine and Army Pilots write this down. (ADAMS *whips out his notebook and writes it as* CABLE *speaks.*) Surface craft—nineteen troop barges headed down the bottle neck; speed about eleven knots. Ought to pass Banika at about twenty hundred tonight, escorted by heavy warships. (BRACKETT *and* HARBISON *smile triumphantly.*) There ought to be some way to knock off a few of these.

(CABLE'S *voice continues under the following speeches.*)

ADAMS. Oh, boy! (*He goes to door.*)

HARBISON. Where you going?

ADAMS. Don't want to miss that take off. We'll be going out in waves tonight—waves—

(*He exits quickly.* BRACKETT *sits down on waste basket and opens another Coke.*)

BRACKETT. Sit down, Bill. (HARBISON *sits, listening intently.* BRACKETT *hands him a Coca-Cola.* HARBISON *takes it.*) Here.

HARBISON. Thanks.

BRACKETT. You know what I like, Bill? Projects—don't you?

(*Lights start to fade.*)

CABLE'S VOICE. (*Which has been continuing over above dialogue.*) As for aircraft, there is little indication of activity at the moment. But twenty-two bombers—Bettys—went by at 0600, headed southwest. There was fighter escort, not heavy . . . They should reach—

(*The lights are now off the scene, but another part of the stage is lighted, revealing a group of pilots around a radio set, being briefed by an* OPERATIONS OFFICER.)

ACT TWO

SCENE VII

OPERATIONS OFFICER. Listen carefully.

EMILE'S VOICE. Ceiling today unlimited. Thirty-three fighters—Zeros—have moved in from Bougainville. Their course is approximately 23 degrees— Undoubtedly, heavy bombers will follow.

OFFICER. (*To pilots who are writing.*) Got that?

(*Lights out. Light hits another group.*)

NAVY PILOT. (*To a group of officers.*) Well, gentlemen, here's the hot tip for today. Joe and the Frenchman have sighted twenty surface craft heading southeast from Vella Lavella. Christmas is just two weeks away. Let's give those two characters a present—a beautiful view of no ships coming back.

AN OFFICER. Okay, that's all right with me.

(*They exit. Lights fade off and return to center of stage, revealing:*)

ACT TWO

SCENE VIII

The Radio Shack again.

BRACKETT *is pacing up and down.* HARBISON *is standing near the door, a pleading expression on his face.*

HARBISON. Sir, you just have to tell her something some time. She hasn't seen him for two weeks. She might as well know it now.

BRACKETT. Okay. Send her in. Send her in. I always have to do the tough jobs.

(HARBISON *exits. A second later,* NELLIE *enters, followed by* HARBISON. *She goes to* BRACKETT *and immediately plunges into the subject closest to her heart. Her speech is unplanned. She knows she has no right to ask her question, but she must have an answer.*)

NELLIE. Captain Brackett, I know this isn't regular. . . . It's about Emile de Becque. I went to his house a week ago to . . . You know how people have arguments and then days later you think of a good answer. . . . Well, I went to his house, and he wasn't there. I even asked the children . . . he has two little children . . . and they didn't seem to know where he'd gone. At least, I think that's what they said—they only speak French. And then tonight while I was on duty in the ward—we have a lot of fighter pilots over there, the boys who knocked out that convoy yesterday—you know how fighter pilots talk—about "Immelmanns" and "wingovers" and things. I never listen usually but they kept talking about a Frenchman—the Frenchman said this, and the Frenchman said that . . . and I was wondering if this Frenchman they were talking about could be—*my* Frenchman. (*Pause.*)

BRACKETT. Yes, Miss Forbush, it is. I couldn't tell you before but . . . As a matter of fact, if you wait here a few minutes, you can hear his voice.

NELLIE. His voice? Where is he?

BRACKETT. With Lieutenant Cable behind enemy lines.

NELLIE. Behind . . . !

(*The* RADIO OPERATOR *snaps his fingers. All heads turn up toward the loudspeaker. They listen to* EMILE'S *voice on the radio.*)

EMILE'S VOICE. Hello. Hello, my friends and allies. My message today must be brief . . . and sad. Lieutenant Cable, my friend, Joe, died last night. He died from wounds he received three days ago. I will never know a finer man. I wish he could have told you the good news. The Japanese are pulling out and there is great confusion. Our guess is that the Japs will try to evacuate troops from Cape Esperance tonight. You may not hear from us for several days. We must move again. Two planes are overhead. They are looking for us, we think. We believe that . . . (*His speech is interrupted. There is the sound of a plane motor.* EMILE'S *voice is heard shouting excitedly "off mike."*) What? . . . What? (*"In mike."*) Good-bye!

(*There is a moment's silence. The* RADIO OPERATOR *works the dials.*)

BRACKETT. Is that all? Is that all? Can't you get them back?

RADIO OPERATOR. No, sir. They're cut off.

NELLIE. (*Tears in her eyes.*) Poor Joe. Poor little Joe Cable. (*She grabs* BRACKETT *and holds tightly to his arms.*) Captain Brackett . . . Do you think there's a chance I'll ever see Emile de Becque again? If you don't think so, will you tell me?

BRACKETT. There's a chance . . . of course there's a chance.

NELLIE. (*Turning to* HARBISON.) I didn't know he was going.

BRACKETT. Of course not. How could he tell you he was going? Now don't blame Emile de Becque. He's okay . . . he's a wonderful guy!

(NELLIE *tries to answer, swallows hard, and can make only an inarticulate sound of assent.*)

NELLIE. Uh-huh! (*She exits quickly.*)

BRACKETT. He has got a chance, hasn't he, Bill?

HARBISON. (*Hoarsely.*) Of course. There's always a chance!

BRACKETT. Come on! Let's get out of here!

(*Both exit, as the shack recedes upstage and a group of officers and nurses enter downstage to walk across the company street.*)

ACT TWO

SCENE IX

The officers and nurses are singing the refrain of "I'm in Love with a Wonderful Guy."

NELLIE *walks on from the opposite side, looking straight ahead of her, a set expression on her face.*

NURSE. (*As they pass her.*) Coming to the dance, Nellie?

(NELLIE *just shakes her head and passes them.*)

A LIEUTENANT. What's the matter with her?

(*Three girls in a trio and in a spirit of kidding* NELLIE, *sing back over their shoulders at her, "She's in love, she's in love, she's in love, she's in love with a wonderful guy." Even before they have reached the end of this, the lights have started to dim. Now the lights come up in back, revealing:*)

ACT TWO

SCENE X

The Beach.

NELLIE *walks on. The strain of "I'm in love, I'm in love, I'm in love" ringing in her ears and cutting deeply into her heart.* NELLIE *walks up and looks over the sea.*

Pause. Then she speaks softly.

NELLIE. Come back so I can tell you something. I know what counts now. You. All those other things—the woman you had before—her color . . . (*She laughs bitterly.*) What piffle! What a pinhead I was! Come back so I can tell you. Oh, my God, don't die until I can tell you! All that matters is you and I being together. That's all! Just together—The way we wanted it to be the first night we met! Remember? . . . Remember?

(*She sings.*)

Some enchanted evening
When you find your true love,
When you feel him call you
Across a crowded room—
Then fly to his side,
And make him your own,
Or all through your life you may dream all alone . . .

(*Music continues. She speaks.*)

Don't die, Emile.

(*As the last line of the refrain is played,* BLOODY MARY *walks on and addresses* NELLIE, *timidly.*)

MARY. Miss Nurse! (NELLIE, *shocked by the sudden sound of an intruding voice, turns and emits a startled scream.*) Please, please, Miss Nurse?

NELLIE. Who are you? What do you want?

MARY. Where is Lootellan Cable?

NELLIE. Who *are* you?

MARY. I am mother of Liat.

NELLIE. Who?

MARY. Liat. She won't marry no one but Lootellan Cable.

(LIAT *walks on slowly.* MARY *moves her forward and shows her to* NELLIE. NELLIE *looks at this girl and realizes who she is.*)

NELLIE. Oh. (NELLIE *rushes to her impulsively and embraces her.*) Oh, my darling!

(*As she clasps* LIAT *in her arms, the noises of the company street burst harshly as the curtains close and we are plunged abruptly into:*)

ACT TWO

SCENE XI

The company street is crowded with members of all Forces, ready to embark. There are sounds of truck convoys passing. Over the loudspeaker the following is heard:

VOICE ON LOUDSPEAKER. All right, hear this. All those outfits that are waiting for loading, please keep in position. We'll get to you as soon as your boat is ready for you.

(BILLIS, STEWPOT *and the* PROFESSOR *enter.*)

STEWPOT. Hey, Billis, let's head back, huh? Our gang's about a mile back down the beach. Suppose they call our names?

PROFESSOR. Yeah! They may be ready for us to go aboard.

BILLIS. They won't be ready for hours yet . . . this is the Navy. (*He turns and regards the scene offstage.*) Eager Beavers! Look at that beach . . . swarmin' with 10,000 guys—all jerks! (*Picking out a likely "jerk."*) Hey, are you a Marine?

MARINE. (*Turning.*) Yeah!

BILLIS. Are you booked on one of those LCT's?

MARINE. I guess so, why?

BILLIS. They'll shake the belly off you, you know. (*He takes out a small package.*) Five bucks and you can have it.

MARINE. What is it?

BILLIS. Seasick remedy. You'll be needing it.

MARINE. Aw, knock off! (*Pulls out a handful of packages from his pocket.*) That stuff's issued. We all got it. Who are you tryin' to fool?

BILLIS. (*Turning to* STEWPOT.) These Marines are getting smarter every day.

OFFICER. (*Passing through.*) All right, all right. Stay with your own unit. (*To a nurse in combat uniform.*) Ensign, you too. For Heaven's sake, don't get spread out over here. We're trying to get this thing organized as quickly as possible, so for God's sake, stay with your outfit! (*To* BILLIS.) Say, Seabee . . . you belong down the beach.

BILLIS. (*Saluting officer.*) Excuse me, sir, could you tell me where we could find Captain Brackett?

OFFICER. He's up at the head of the company street. He'll be along any minute now.

BILLIS. (*Saluting.*) Thank you, sir. That's all, sir.

(*The* OFFICER, *having started off, stops in his tracks, stunned and rocked off his balance by being thus "dismissed" by* BILLIS. *Oh, well—too many important things to be done right now! He goes on his way, shouting:*)

OFFICER. All right! Stay in line! How many times have I told you . . .

(*He is off. A* NURSE *comes by.*)

BILLIS. Hello, Miss McGregor. You nurses going too?

NURSE. Only a few of us. We're going to fly back some wounded.

BILLIS. Is Miss Forbush going with you?

NURSE. I don't know. She may be staying here with the hospital.

(*She starts to leave.*)

BILLIS. Oh, Miss McGregor . . . you don't get airsick, do you? I was thinking maybe if you got three bucks handy, you might be able to use this little package I got here.

NURSE. (*Looking down at it.*) Oh, that stuff's no good . . . we gave that up last month.

BILLIS. (*Turning to* STEWPOT.) That's a female jerk! (BRACKETT *and* HARBISON *enter.*) I beg pardon, sir . . . could I speak to you a minute?

BRACKETT. (*Peering through the semi-darkness.*) Who's that?

BILLIS. Billis, sir . . . Luther Billis.

BRACKETT. Oh. What do you want, Billis? We're moving out pretty soon.

BILLIS. Yes, sir, I know. I'd like to do something for Miss Forbush, sir. Stewpot and the Professor and me was wondering if anything is being done about rescuing the Frenchman off that island. We hereby volunteer for such a project . . . a triple diversionary activity, like I done to get 'em on there. You could drop us in three rubber boats on three different sides of the island . . . confuse the hell out of the Japs. . . . Get the picture?

BRACKETT. It's very fine of you, Billis . . . but you're too late for diversionary activity. That started this morning before the sun came up. Operation Alligator got under way. Landings were made on fourteen Japanese-held islands.

BILLIS. I think that's very unfair, sir. The first thing they should have done was try to rescue that Frenchman.

HARBISON. The Admiral agrees with you, Billis. Marie Louise was the first island they hit.

BILLIS. Did they get him? Is he alive?

BRACKETT. We don't know. Lieutenant Bus Adams flew up there to find out. He hasn't come back. But if the Frenchman's dead, it *is* unfair. It's too damned bad if a part of this huge operation couldn't have saved one of the two guys who made it all possible.

HARBISON. (*Gazing off.*) Look at the beach . . . far as you can see . . . men waiting to board ships. The whole picture of the South Pacific has changed. We're going the other way.

OFFICER. Captain Brackett, sir . . . the launch is ready to take you to your ship.

BILLIS. You got a ship, sir?

BRACKETT. Yes, Harbison and I've got a ship. I'm no longer a lousy Island Commander. Come on, Bill.

BILLIS. Good-bye, Commander Harbison.

HARBISON. Good-bye, Billis. Oh, by the way, I never did get you in the brig . . . did I?

BILLIS. (*Laughing almost too heartily at his triumph.*) No! Ha-ha.

HARBISON. Oh, I forgot!

BILLIS. (*Still laughing.*) Forgot what, sir?

HARBISON. Your unit'll be on our ship. I'll be seeing all of you.

(*Dismay from* BILLIS, STEWPOT *and the* PROFESSOR.)

BRACKETT. Come on, Bill.

(BRACKETT *and* HARBISON *exit.*)

OFFICER. (*Entering.*) All right . . . let's start those trucks moving out—all units on the company street. We're ready to load you. All Nurses will board assigned planes—Seabees to embark on Carrier 6. All Marines to board LCT's. Any questions? MOVE OUT!

(*The sound trucks roar. The music which has been playing under the scene mounts in volume. The men march off. Nurses in hospital uniform stand waving to the men and the nurses in combat uniform who leave with them. Soon the groups are all dispersed and lights come up in back, revealing:*)

ACT TWO

SCENE XII

EMILE'*s terrace.*

It is late afternoon. Sunset—reddish light. The drone of planes can be heard. JEROME *stands on a table.* NELLIE *holds him.* NGANA *is beside her. All look off.*

NELLIE. (*Pointing off.*) The big ones are battleships and the little ones are destroyers—or cruisers—I never can tell the difference. (*She looks up in the air.*) And what on earth are those?

JEROME. P-40s.

NELLIE. Oh, that's right. They're all moving out, you see, because, well . . . there's been a big change. They won't be around here much any more, just off and on, a few of us. Did you understand anything I said? Vous ne comprenez pas?

NGANA. Oui, oui, nous comprenons.

(JEROME *nods his head.*)

JEROME. Oui.

NELLIE. Now, while I'm down at the hospital, you've got to promise me to mangez everything—everything that's put before you on the table—sur le tobler. Sur la tobler?

NGANA. (*Smiling patiently.*) Sur la table.

NELLIE. (*She smiles, congratulating herself.*) Now come back here, Jerome, and sit down. (*She starts to place the children at the table, on which a bowl of soup and some plates have been set. At this point,* BUS ADAMS *appears upstage—a weary figure. Behind him comes* EMILE *in dirt-stained uniform, helmet, paratroop boots and musette bag.* BUS *calls his attention to the planes droning above. Neither sees* NELLIE *or the children.* NELLIE *pushes the kids down, on the bench, as they playfully balk at being seated.*) Ass—say—yay—voo. (*They sit.* EMILE *turns sharply at the sound of her voice.*) Now you have to learn to mind me when I talk to you and be nice to me too. Because I love you very much. Now, *mangez.*

(EMILE'*s face lights up with grateful happiness.* BUS *knows it's time for him to shove off, and he does.* NELLIE *proceeds to ladle soup from the large bowl into three small bowls.*)

JEROME. (*His eyes twinkling mischievously.*) Chantez, Nellie.

NELLIE. I will not sing that song. You just want to laugh at my French accent. (*The kids put their spoons down—on strike.*) All right, but you've got to help me.

NELLIE, NGANA, AND JEROME.

Dites moi
Pourquoi

(NELLIE *is stuck. The children sing the next line without her.*)

La vie est belle.

NELLIE. (*Repeating, quickly, to catch up to them.*)

La vie est belle.

(*Meanwhile* EMILE *has crossed behind them.* NELLIE *is looking out front, not seeing him, trying to remember the lyrics, continues to sing with the children.*)

Dites moi
Pourquoi . . .

(*She turns to the children.*)

Pourquoi what?

(*She sees* EMILE.)

EMILE. (*Answering her, singing.*)

La vie est gai!

(NELLIE *gazes at him, hypnotized—her voice gone. The children rush to embrace him.*)

EMILE, NGANA, AND JEROME.

Dites moi
Pourquoi,
Chère mad'moiselle—

(EMILE *leans forward and sings straight at* NELLIE.)

EMILE.

Est-ce que
Parce que
Vous m'aimez—

(*The music continues. The children drink their soup.* NELLIE *comes back to consciousness enough to realize that* EMILE *must be hungry. She leans over and hands him the large bowl of soup with an air of "nothing's-too-good-for-the-boss!" Then she passes him the soup ladle! But he doesn't use it. Instead, he thrusts his hand forward.* NELLIE *clasps it. Looking into each other's eyes, they hold this position as the curtain falls.*)

GENERAL BIBLIOGRAPHY OF THE AMERICAN DRAMA

Bibliographies concerning the individual playwrights are given in the introductions, and except in cases of books of a general nature, the items are not repeated here.

HISTORY AND CRITICISM OF THE DRAMA AND STAGE

Adams, Agatha B., *Paul Green of Chapel Hill* (Chapel Hill, N. C., 1951).

American Playwrights on the American Drama, Articles by Augustin Daly, Edward Harrigan, William Gillette, John Grosvenor, Steele MacKaye and William Winter, Supplement to *Harper's Weekly* (Feb. 2, 1889).

Anderson, Maxwell, *The Essence of Tragedy* (Washington, D. C., 1939).

The Art of Playwrighting, Lectures delivered at the University of Pennsylvania, by Jesse Lynch Williams, Langdon Mitchell, Lord Dunsany, Gilbert Emery, and Rachel Crothers (Philadelphia, 1928).

Atkinson, Brooks, *Broadway Scrapbook, Theatre Arts* (1947).

Austin, Mary, "Spanish Manuscripts in the Southwest," *Southwest Review,* Vol. 19 (July, 1934), pp. 401–409.

———, "Folk Plays of the Southwest," *Theatre Arts Monthly,* Vol. 18 (Aug., 1933), pp. 599–650.

Block, Anita, *The Changing World in Play and Theatre* (Boston, 1939).

Blum, Daniel A., *A Pictorial History of the American Theatre* (New York, 1950).

Boyd, Alice Katherine, *The Interchange of Plays between London and New York, 1910–1939* (New York, 1948).

Bradley, Sculley, "The Emergence of the Modern Drama," *Literary History of the United States,* Vol. 2 (New York, 1948), pp. 1000–1015.

Brown, John Mason, *Broadway in Review* (New York, 1940).

———, *Still Seeing Things* (New York, 1950).

Brown, T. A., *A History of the New York Stage: From the First Performance in 1732 to 1901,* 3 Vols. (New York, 1903).

Castaneda, C. E., "The First American Play," *Catholic World* (Jan., 1932), reprinted as Vol. III, No. 1, of *Preliminary Studies,* Texas Catholic Historical Society (Jan., 1936).

Carolina Playbook, Twenty-fifth Anniversary Commemorative Issue, Archibald Henderson, Ed. (Chapel Hill, March–June, 1943).

Carson, Wm. G. B., *The Theatre on the Frontier* (Chicago, 1932).

Cheney, Sheldon, *The Art Theater* (New York, 1917; Revised, 1925).

———, *The Theatre,* Revised Ed. (New York, 1952).

Clapp, W. W., *A Record of the Boston Stage* (Boston and Cambridge, 1853).

Clark, Barrett H., *The British and American Drama of Today* (New York, 1915).

———, *A Study of the Modern Drama* (New York, 1925; Revised, 1928; 1934).

———, and George Freedley, Eds., *A History of Modern Drama* (New York, 1947).

Clark, Barrett H., *Intimate Portraits* (New York, 1951). [Biographical Sketches of Playwrights]

Coad, Oral S., and Mims, Edwin, Jr., *The American Stage,* Vol. 14 of *The Pageant of America* (New Haven, 1929).

Coad, Oral S., "The First Century of the New Brunswick Stage," *Rutgers Univ. Libr.,* Part I, Vol. 5 (Dec., 1941), pp. 15–36; Part II, Vol. 5 (June, 1942), pp. 78–89; Part III, VI (June, 1943), pp. 52–57.

Cooke, John Esten, *The Virginia Comedians or Old Days in the Old Dominion* (New York, 1854). [A novel, in which an interesting description of Hallam's company is given.]

Crawford, M. C., *The Romance of the American Theatre* (Boston, 1913; Revised, 1925).

Daly, C. P., *First Theater in America,* Dunlap Society Publications, Ser. 2, Vol. 1 (New York, 1896).

Daly, Joseph Francis, *The Life of Augustin Daly* (New York, 1917).

Dickinson, Thomas H., *Playwrights of the New American Theater* (New York, 1924).

Dolman, John, Jr., *The Art of Play Production* (New York, 1928).

———, *The Art of Acting* (New York, 1949).

Dunlap, William, *History of the American Theatre* (New York, 1832; London, 2 Vols., 1833).

Dunlap, William, Diary of (1766–1839): The Memoirs of a Dramatist, Theatrical Manager, Painter, Critic, Novelist, and Historian, 3 Vols. Dorothy C. Barck, Ed. (New York Historical Society, 1930).

Durang, Charles, *The Philadelphia Stage. From the year 1749 to the year 1855. Partly compiled from the papers of his father, the late John Durang; with notes by the editors* [of the Philadelphia *Sunday Dispatch*]. Published serially in the Philadelphia *Dispatch* as follows: First series, 1749–1821, beginning in the issue of May 7, 1854; Second series, 1822–1830, beginning June 29, 1856; Third series, 1830/1–1855, beginning July 8, 1860.

Eaton, W. P., *The Actor's Heritage* (Boston, 1924).

———, *The American Stage of Today* (Boston, 1910).

Flanagan, Hallie, *Arena* (New York, 1940).

———, *Dynamo* (New York, 1943).

Ford, P. L., *Some Notes towards an Essay on The Beginnings of American Dramatic Literature, 1606–1789* (Privately printed, Brooklyn, 1893). Also "The Beginnings of American Dramatic Literature," *New England Mag.*, New Series, Vol. 11 (February, 1894), pp. 673–687.

———, *Washington and the Theater,* Dunlap Society Publications, Ser. 2, Vol. 8 (New York, 1899).

Frenz, Horst, "American Drama and World Drama," *Coll. Eng.*, Vol. 6 (March, 1945), pp. 319–325.

Free, Joseph M., "The Ante-Bellum Theatre of the Old Natchez Region," *Jour. Miss. Hist.*, Vol. 5 (1943), pp. 14–27.

Freedley, George, and John B. Reeves, *A History of the Theatre* (New York, 1941).

Gergely, Emro Joseph, *Hungarian Drama in New York* (Philadelphia, 1947).

Gohdes, Clarence, "Amusements on the Stage," *The Literature of the American People* (New York, 1951), pp. 790–809.

Hamar, C. E., "Scenery on the Early American Stage," *Theatre Annual,* Vol. 7 (1848–1849), pp. 84–103.

Hoole, W. Stanley, "Charleston Theatricals during the Tragic Decade, 1860–1869," *Jour. of So. Hist.*, Vol. 11 (Nov., 1945), pp. 538–547.

———, *The Ante Bellum Charleston Theatre* (University of Alabama Press, 1946).

Hornblow, Arthur, *History of the Theatre in America from its Beginnings to the Present Time,* 2 Vols. (Philadelphia, 1919).

Howells, William Dean, "The Recent Dramatic Season," *North American Review,* Vol. 132 (1901), pp. 468–480.

Howells, Mildred, *Life in Letters of William Dean Howells,* 2 Vols. (New York, 1928).

Hughes, Glenn, *The Penthouse Theatre, History and Technique* (New York, 1942).

———, *A History of the American Theatre* (New York, 1951).

Hutton, Laurence, *Curiosities of the American Stage* (New York, 1891).

Ireland, J. N., *Records of the New York Stage, from 1750 to 1860,* 2 Vols. (New York, 1866–1867).

Isaacs, Edith, "The Negro in the American Theatre," *Theatre Arts,* Vol. 26, pp. 494–526; 527–532; 533–538; 538–543. Published as volume, 1947.
———, and Gilder, Rosamund, "American Musical Comedy," *Theatre Arts,* Vol. 29 (August, 1945), pp. 452–493.
James, Reese D., *Old Drury of Philadelphia: A History of the Philadelphia Stage, 1800–1835* (Philadelphia, 1932).
Koster, Donald A., *The Theme of Divorce in the American Drama* (Philadelphia, 1942).
Krutch, Joseph W., *The American Drama Since 1918* (New York, 1940).
Leary, Lewis, "First Theatrical Performance in North America," *Amer. Notes & Queries,* Vol. 2 (Sept., 1942), p. 84.
Mammen, Edward W., "The Old Stock Company: The Boston Museum and other 19th Century Theatres," *More Books* (Jan., Feb., March, April, May, 1944).
Mason, Hamilton, *The French Theatre in New York* (New York, 1940).
McCullough, Bruce W., *The Life and Writings of Richard Penn Smith, with a Reprint of His Play, "The Deformed,"* 1830 (Menasha, Wisconsin, 1917).
Macgowan, Kenneth, and Jones, Robert Edmond, *The Theatre of Tomorrow* (New York, 1921).
Macgowan, Kenneth, *Footlights Across America* (New York, 1929).
Matthews, Brander, *Playwrights on Playmaking* (New York, 1923).
———, *Rip Van Winkle Goes to the Play, and Other Essays on Plays and Players* (New York, 1926).
Moses, Montrose J., *The American Dramatist* (Boston, 1911; Revised, 1925).
———, "The Drama, 1860–1918," *The Cambridge History of American Literature,* Vol. 3 (New York, 1921), pp. 266–298; Bibliography, Vol. 4, pp. 760–774.
———, and Brown, John Mason, *The American Theatre as Seen by its Critics, 1752–1934* (New York, 1934).
Murdock, Kenneth P., "The Expanding Literary Horizon," *The Literature of the American People* (New York, 1951), pp. 156–171.
Odell, George C. D., *Annals of the New York Stage,* Vols. 1–15 (New York, 1927–1949).
Pollock, Thomas Clark, *The Philadelphia Theatre in the Eighteenth Century* (Philadelphia, 1933).
Quinn, Arthur Hobson, *A History of the American Drama from the Beginning to the Civil War* (New York, 1923; Revised, 1943). [Contains a list of plays, from 1665 to 1860, with dates of publication and first performance.]
———, *A History of the American Drama from the Civil War to the Present Day,* 2 Vols. (New York, 1927; Revised, two volumes in one, with an additional chapter, New York, 1936). [Contains a list of all significant plays from 1860 to 1936, as above.]
———, "The Early Drama, 1756–1860," *The Cambridge History of American Literature,* Vol. 1 (New York, 1917), pp. 215–232; Bibliography, pp. 490–507.
———, "Herne and Ibsen. Theory and Facts," *Am. Lit.,* Vol. 19 (May, 1947), pp. 171–177.
———, "Revolt and Celebration in the Drama," *The Literature of the American People* (New York, 1951), pp. 466–518.
Rosenbach, A. S. W., *The First Theatrical Company in America* (Worcester, Mass., 1939).
Schoenberger, Harold W., *American Adaptations of French Plays on the New York and Philadelphia Stages, 1790–1833* (Philadelphia, 1924).
Seilhamer, G. O., *History of the American Theatre,* 3 Vols. (Philadelphia, 1888–1891).
Simonson, Lee, *The Art of Scenic Design* (New York, 1950).
Skinner, Richard Dana, *Our Changing Theatre* (New York, 1931).
Smither, Nelle, "A History of the English Theater, at New Orleans, 1806–1842," *Louisiana Hist. Quarterly,* Vol. 28 (Jan.–April, 1945), pp. 1–406. Rep. as volume, 1947.
Sonneck, O. G., *Early Opera in America* (New York, London, and Boston, 1915).
Stevens, Thomas Wood, *The Theatre from Athens to Broadway* (New York, 1932).
Stewart, G. R., Jr., "The Drama in a Frontier Theater" (Princeton, 1935), pp. 183–204.

Selden, Samuel, *First Steps in Acting* (New York, 1947).
Strang, L. C., *Players and Plays of the Last Quarter Century,* 2 Vols. (Boston, 1902).
Stuart, Donald Clive, *The Development of Dramatic Art* (New York, 1928).
Thomas, Augustus, *The Print of My Remembrance* (New York, 1922).
Tompkins, E., and Kilby, Q., *The History of the Boston Theatre, 1854–1901* (Boston and New York, 1908).
Towse, John R., *Sixty Years of the Theater* (New York, 1916).
Villard, Léonie, *Le Théatre Américain* (Paris, 1929).
Waldo, L. P., *The French Drama in America in the Eighteenth Century and its Influence on the American Drama of that Period* (Baltimore, 1942).
Ware, Ralph H., *American Adaptations of French Plays on the New York and Philadelphia Stages from 1834 to the Civil War* (Philadelphia, 1930).
Wemyss, F. C., *Chronology of the American Stage from 1752 to 1852* (New York, n. d. [1852]).
Whicher, George F., "Vitalizers of the Drama," *The Literature of the American People* (New York, 1951), pp. 927–941.
Willis, Eola, *The Charleston Stage in the XVIII Century* (Columbia, S. C., 1924).
Wilson, Arthur Herman, *A History of the Philadelphia Theatre, 1835 to 1855* (Philadelphia, 1935).
Winter, William, *The Life of David Belasco,* 2 Vols. (New York, 1918).
Young, Stark, *Immortal Shadows, A Book of Dramatic Criticism* (New York, 1948).

BIBLIOGRAPHIES AND LISTS OF PLAYS

Baker, Blanch M., *Dramatic Bibliography; An Annotated List of Books on the History and Criticism of the Drama and Stage and on the Allied Arts of the Theatre* (New York, 1933).
A continuation of the above, with title *Theatre and Allied Arts; A Guide to Books Dealing with the History, Criticism and Technic of the Drama and Theatre and Related Arts and Crafts* (New York, 1952).
Clapp, J. B., and Edgett, E. F., *Plays of the Present,* Dunlap Society Publications, Ser. 2, extra Vol. (New York, 1902).
Dramatic Compositions Copyrighted in the United States, 1870–1916, 2 Vols. and Index Vol. Issued by the Library of Congress.
Dramas and Works for Oral Delivery (Issued biannually since 1947 as pts. 3 and 4 of the *Catalogue of Copyright Entries,* 3rd series by the Copyright Office, Library of Congress, Washington, D. C. From 1891 to 1946, title and pt. of *Catalogue* vary).
Faxon, Frederick W., Ed., *The Bulletin of Bibliography and Dramatic Index* (Published quarterly, Boston).
———, Ed., *The Dramatic Index,* Part 2 of *The Annual Magazine Subject Index* (Annually since 1909).
Firkins, Ira Ten Eyck, *Index to Plays, 1800–1926* (New York, 1927; Supplement, 1935).
Gilder, Rosamund, *A Theatre Library: A Bibliography of One Hundred Books Relating to the Theatre* (New York, 1932).
———, and Freedley, George, *Theatre Collections in Libraries and Museums* (New York, 1936).
Hill, Frank P., *American Plays—Printed 1714–1830—A Bibliographical Record* (Stanford, 1934).
Logassa, Hannah, and Winifred der Nooy, *An Index to One Act Plays* (Boston, 1924; Supplements, 1932, 1940, 1948).
Ottemiller, John H., *Index to Plays in Collections,* Second Ed., Revised (Washington, 1951).

Roden, R. F., *Later American Plays, 1831–1900,* Dunlap Society Publications, Ser. 2, Vol. 12 (New York, 1900).
Sobel, Bernard, *The Theatre Handbook and Digests of Plays* (Boston and New York, 1943).
Wegelin, Oscar, *Early American Plays, 1714–1830,* Dunlap Society Publications, Ser. 2, Vol. 10 (New York, 1900; Revised ed., 1905).

COLLECTIONS

(In the Order of Publication)

Quinn, Arthur H., *Representative American Plays* (New York, 1917; Seventh Edition, 1953).
Moses, Montrose J., *Representative Plays by American Dramatists,* 3 Vols. (New York, 1918–1925).
Mantle, Burns, *The Best Plays of 1919–1920* and of succeeding years. Continued by John Chapman.
Baker, George Pierce, *Modern American Plays* (New York, 1920).
Shay, Frank, *Twenty Contemporary One-Act Plays* [American] (New York, 1921; Revised edition, 1922).
Koch, Frederick H., *Carolina Folk Plays,* vols. beginning in 1922 and culminating in *Carolina Folk Plays* (1941).
Quinn, Arthur Hobson, *Contemporary American Plays* (New York, 1923).
One Act Plays for Stage and Study. [Ten volumes have appeared, 1924–1949, issued by Samuel French, containing one-act plays, chiefly American.]
Shay, Frank, *One Thousand and one Plays for the Little Theatre* (New York, 1923).
Moses, Montrose J., *Representative American Dramas, National and Local* (Boston, 1925; Revised by J. W. Krupt, New York, 1941).
Locke, Alain, and Gregory, Montgomery, *Plays of Negro Life* (New York, 1927).
Leverton, Garrett H., *Plays for the College Theatre* (New York, 1933).
Mantle, Burns, and Sherwood, Garrison P., *The Best Plays of 1909–1919* (New York, 1933).
Cordell, Richard A., and Chandler, Frank, *Twentieth Century Plays, American* (New York, 1934).
Halline, Allan G., *American Plays* (New York, 1935).
Cordell, Kathryn C., *Pulitzer Prize Plays* (New York, 1935).
The Theatre Guild Anthology, With an Introduction by the Board of Directors of the Theatre Guild (New York, 1936).
In 1940 and 1941 a series of twenty volumes, entitled *America's Lost Plays,* under the general editorship of Barrett H. Clark, made available for the first time a large number of unprinted plays. For the complete lists see the *History of the American Drama from the Beginning to the Civil War,* pp. 397–398, and the *History of the American Drama from the Civil War to the Present Day,* pp. 403–404, by A. H. Quinn. In 1943 Clark issued a selection, entitled *Favorite American Plays of the 19th Century* (Princeton, 1943). In 1951 with W. H. Davenport, he edited *Nine Modern American Plays* (New York).
Koch, Frederick H., *American Folk Plays* (New York, 1939).
Mantle, Burns, and Sherwood, G. P., *The Best Plays of 1899–1909* (New York, 1944).
Warnock, Robert, *Representative Modern Plays, American* (Chicago, 1952).

BIOGRAPHIES OF ACTORS AND MANAGERS, AND SIMILAR WORKS GIVING INFORMATION CONCERNING THE DRAMA

Alger, William R., *Life of Edwin Forrest.* 2 Vols. (Philadelphia, 1877).
Barrett, Lawrence, *Edwin Forrest* (Boston, 1882).

Belasco, David, *The Theatre through its Stage Door,* L. V. De Foe, Ed. (New York, 1919).
Butler, Frances Anne Kemble, *Records of a Girlhood* (New York, 1879).
Clapp, J. B., and E. F. Edgett, *Players of the Present,* Dunlap Society Publications, Ser. 2, Vols. 9, 11, 13 (New York, 1899–1901).
Cornell, Katharine, *I Wanted to be an Actress* (New York, 1939).
Davis, Owen, *My First Fifty Years in the Theatre* (Boston, 1950).
Drew, John, *My Years on the Stage* (New York, 1922).
Drew, Mrs. John, Autobiographical Sketch of (New York, 1899).
Eaton, Walter Prichard, *The Theatre Guild* (New York, 1929).
Edgett, E. F., *Edward Loomis Davenport,* Dunlap Society Publications, Ser. 2, Vol. 14 (New York, 1901).
Frohman, Daniel, and Marcosson, Isaac F., *Charles Frohman* (New York, 1916).
Frohman, Daniel, *Daniel Frohman Presents* (New York, 1935).
Hanau, Stella, and Deutsch, Helen, *The Provincetown* (New York, 1931).
Hutton, Laurence, *Edwin Booth* (New York, 1893).
The Autobiography of Joseph Jefferson (New York, 1890).
Langner, Lawrence, *The Magic Curtain* (New York, 1951).
Leavitt, M. B., *Fifty Years of Theatrical Management* (New York, 1912).
Le Gallienne, Eva, *At 33* (New York, 1933).
Matthews, Brander, and Hutton, Laurence, *Actors and Actresses of Great Britain and the United States from the Days of David Garrick to the Present Time* (New York, 1886).
Middleton, George, These Things are Mine (New York, 1949).
Mowatt, Anna Cora (Mrs. Ritchie), *The Autobiography of an Actress, or Eight Years on the Stage* (Boston, 1854).
Murdoch, James E., *The Stage, or Recollections of Actors and Acting from an Experience of Fifty Years* (Philadelphia, 1880).
Reed, Joseph V., *The Curtain Falls* (New York, 1935).
Rees, James, *The Life of Edwin Forrest* (Philadelphia, n. d. [1874]).
Russell, Charles E., *Julia Marlowe, Her Life and Art* (New York, 1926).
Simonson, Lee, *The Stage Is Set* (New York, 1932).
Skinner, Cornelia Otis, *Family Circle* (New York, 1948).
Skinner, Otis, *Footlights and Spotlights* (Indianapolis, 1924).
Sothern, Edward H., *The Melancholy Tale of Me: My Remembrances* (New York, 1916).
Wemyss, Francis C., *Twenty-Six Years of the Life of an Actor and Manager,* 2 Vols. (New York, 1847).
Wallack, Lester, *Memories of Fifty Years* (New York, 1889).
Winter, William, *The Jeffersons* (Boston, 1881).
———, *Life and Art of Richard Mansfield,* 2 Vols. (New York, 1891).
———, *Other Days; Being Chronicles and Memories of the Stage* (New York, 1908).
———, *The Wallet of Time, Containing Personal, Biographical, and Critical Reminiscences of the American Theatre,* 2 Vols. (New York, 1913).
Wood, W. B., *Personal Recollections of the Stage. . . . During a Period of Forty Years* (Philadelphia, 1855).